Twentieth Anniversary Edition

Blue Book
of Gun Values™
by S.P. Fjestad

Twentieth Anniversary Edition
Blue Book of Gun Values™

Publisher's Note:

This book is the result of nonstop and continual firearms research obtained by attending gun shows, and communicating with gun dealers, collectors, company historians, contributing editors, and other knowledgeable industry professionals worldwide each year. This book represents an analysis of prices for which collectible firearms have actually been selling during that period at an average retail level. Although every reasonable effort has been made to compile an accurate and reliable guide, gun prices may vary significantly depending on such factors as the locality of the sale, the number of sales we were able to consider, and economic conditions. Accordingly, no representation can be made that the guns listed may be bought or sold at prices indicated, nor shall the author or publisher be responsible for any error made in compiling and recording such prices and related information.

CONTENTS

Title Page 1
Publisher's Note/Copyright 2
Table of Contents 3
Cover Description 4
Blue Book Publications, Inc. general information 5
Acknowledgements 6-7
Foreword 8-9
How to Use This Book 10-13
Correspondence/Appraisals/PCS information 14-15
Buying or Selling? - a Unique Concept 16
GunTracker ad 17
Blue Book of Guitars & Pool Cues ads 18
Colt Black Powder Reproductions & Replicas ad 19
Blasts from the Past - 1-20 Ed. pictorial/information 20-21
Publisher's Overview of the Firearms Marketplace 22-23
Buying Tomorrow's Collectables Today by Jim Carmichel 24-25
Gun Collecting by R.L. Wilson 26-27
NSSF Editorial from Bob Delfay 28-29
Manufacturer's Editorial from Magnum Research 30-31
Distributor's Editorial from Davidson's 32-33
Rep Groups Editorial from Owen Brown 34-35
Sporting Goods Dealer Editorial from Jeff Poet 36-37
Collectible Dealer Editorial from Jim Supica, Jr. 38-41
Working Mom's Perspective Editorial from Trudy Weise 42
Teenage Impressions Editorial from Jed Weise 43
Legal editorial from Evan Nappen 44-45
Legislative/Conservationist Editorial from Jim Klatt 46-47
Press Editorial from Steve Comas 48-49
Press Editorial from JB Wood 50-51
Gun Show Groupie Gastronomic Highlights from John Risdahl 52-53
Perverted Pixelations from the Past 54
The Blue Book Bunch 55
Anatomy of a Handgun 56
Anatomy of a Rifle 57
Anatomy of a Shotgun 58
Glossary 59-63
Abbreviations 64
NRA Membership Form/Bequests 65-67
Hunting and Shooting Sports Heritage Fund 68
Buffalo Bill Historical Center 69
Grading Criteria 70
NRA Condition Standards 71
PPGS Explanation by S.P. Fjestad™ 72
Photo Percentage Grading System 73-120
20th Edition Calendar 98
20th edition/GunTracker Order card ......(unnumbered, between pages 120-121)
Colt Blackpowder Insert Order Card ......(unnumbered, between pages 696-697)
Modern/Antique Firearms Text 121-1,368
Modern Airguns Text 1,369-1,413
Trademark Index 1,414-1,451
Trademark Matchup by Importer/Company 1,452-1,453
Serialization 1,454-1,478
Store Brand Cross-Over List 1,479-1,484
Proofmarks 1,485-1,490
Firearms Associations 1,491-1,493
References/Periodicals listings 1,494-1,497
Older PPGS Cross-referencing 1,498-1,499
BATF Guide 1,500
Show Time! - 1999-2000 1,501
Index 1,502-1,511
P.S. 1,512

ABOUT THE COVER

Despite its retro looking simplistic appearance, this 20th Anniversary Edition's deceptively complicated cover design and printability certainly put men, machines, foil, and ink to the task before getting into your hands. The goal was a clean, keep it simple design, but using as much high tech printing horsepower as possible to "pop" the 20th Edition cover medallion. In that behalf, Phoenix Color, one of the world's leading component printing specialists, was contracted to do the work because of the overall complexity of this job. The various elements/stages (sometimes these can be mutually incompatible) included initial medallion design and support artwork, hand sculpting the precise dies for embossing the medallion and lettering, and a sequence of separate printing operations including stamping the flat gold foil areas on blank cover press sheets first, followed by printing the 4 color process (including printing on the top of foil).

Once these critical operations had been completed (already 2 separate machine passes), the cover press sheets went through another stage, where a one mil thick matte film laminate was adhered to the entire cover, giving it the bulletproof durability and tough, scuff resistant exterior finish. After completion, the spot UV (ultra violet) finish was sprayed on the masked out areas, giving the highlighted images, medallion, and cover lettering a glossy, wet look - note the back cover pistol and accessories. Only then were these high mileage press sheets ready for their last roller ride through the always critical embossing stage. These 5 separate processes successfully completed are somewhere between art, science, and advanced witchcraft in the printing world.

Once precisely trimmed in another plant 1,000 miles away, these finished covers were hotglued to the interior 1,512 pages while going through the bindery. After months of planning, preparation, and thwarting off the various technical uprisings, the completed 20th Editions left the bindery for packaging at the rate of approx. 8,000 per hour. Scary!

Many long time Blue Book subscribers are aware of how the cover artwork has evolved over the years. Since the covers are one of the easiest ways of identifying the older editions, all 20 book covers are pictured on pages 20-21. If you are trying to fill in an edition or complete a set (not easy), use these pages as a visual guide and order form.

> Here are a few offhand comments about our previous 4-color cover achievements.

● **5th Edition** - during a jewelry photo shoot while managing the IRI gift division, the author brought with the gold Colt SAA, took off one of his boa cowboy boots, set it on top of some Bacote wood, sprinkled in a few leftover props, and viola, a cover was born (and on another division's budget!). Sweet!

● **12th Edition** - first Blue Book to incorporate a composite image. The exquisite Astra Broomhandle image was electronically overlaid on an Image Bank rented pyramid transparency, complete with drop shadow. While easily achieved today, complex electronic compositing in 1991 was in the rocket science stage.

● **13th Edition** - yes, that's the author on the cover. B&W photo was taken in IGH back yard, then blown up to 16 x 24 in. on Ilford paper, and sent to Thomas Crane, award winning wildlife artist, who painted in the blue sky and background, colored the Pigeon Grade Model 12, and added the dog and flushing grouse. A brand new hat used on the shoot was aged a couple of decades by overpainting. Anyone ever see that empty 16 ga. Super-X halfway to the ground?

● **15th Edition** - compliment winner to date, and technically the most challenging. Background is polarized picture of ice melting off the home office skylight, Walther PPK/S had $21,000 worth of computer imaging, after which it was elaborately foil stamped and embossed. While at IWA during 1994, a completed press sheet was shown to the commercial director of Walther. He smiled, pushed on the magazine release button, and tried to pull the mag. out of the bottom!

● **17th Edition** - first winter setting. 3-D foiled snowflakes - expensive, but worth it. A different concept, combined with a yesteryear setting, resulted in a lot of kudos.

● **19th Edition** - great artwork, embossing, and printing. Matte lam batch must have previously been used to accelerate the curling of barrel staves.

Last, but not least, you're probably wondering why this edition's medallion states 20th Anniversary Edition, with a 1981 date. While the 1st Edition was published in 1981, two editions were published during 1982, explaining the twenty editions during the past 19 years.

> Cover design and layout - Thomas D. Heller & S.P. Fjestad
> Production Manager - Thomas D. Heller
> Cover printing, foil stamping, and embossing - Phoenix Color, located in Hagerstown, MD.
> Text printing - Custom Printing, located in Owensville, MO.
> Embossing die work - Bill Johns & crew at Midwest Engraving, located in Paola, KS.

While many of you have probably dealt with our company for years, it may be helpful for you to know a little bit more about our operation and what we are currently publishing. **As this edition goes to press, the following titles/products are currently available, unless otherwise specified:**

Blue Book of Gun Values, 20th Anniversary Edition
by S.P. Fjestad
GunTracker, new firearms inventory computer software program
utilizing the 20th Edition Blue Book of Gun Values database
Blue Book of Electric Guitars, 5th Edition
by Steven Cherne, edited by S.P. Fjestad
Blue Book of Acoustic Guitars, 5th Edition
by Steven Cherne, edited by S.P. Fjestad
Blue Book of Pool Cues, 2nd Edition (summer 1999 release)
by Brad Simpson, edited by Victor Stein and Paul Rubino
Billiard Encyclopedia, 2nd Edition
by Victor Stein and Paul Rubino
The Book of Colt Firearms 2nd Edition
by R.L. Wilson
Colt Black Powder Reproductions & Replicas
by Dennis Adler
Mossberg - More Gun For The Money
by Victor and Cheryl Havlin
Classic Sporting Collectables Auction Service Catalogs
Volumes 2-3
Classic Sporting Collectables Pocket Guide

Tear-out order forms are provided between pages 120-121 and 696-697 for the *Blue Book of Gun Values*, *GunTracker*, **and** *Colt Blackpowder Reproductions & Replicas*. **If you would like to get more information about any of the above publications/products, simply contact us with your needs.**

Corporate Headquarters are:
Blue Book Publications, Inc.
8009 - 34th Avenue South, Suite 175
Minneapolis, MN 55425   U.S.A.

Since our phone system is equipped with voice mail, you may also wish to know extension numbers which have been provided below:

Ext. No.: 11 - Tom Stock	Ext. No.: 17 - Honored Guest
Ext. No.: 12 - Production Room	Ext. No.: 18 - Angela Singletary
Ext. No.: 13 - S.P. Fjestad	Ext. No.: 19 - Cassandra Faulkner
Ext. No.: 15 - Thomas D. Heller	Ext. No.: 22 - DJ Pallum
Ext. No.: 16 - John Allen	Ext. No.: 25 - Beth Marthaler

Phone No. 612-854-5229 • Orders Only: 800-877-4867
Additionally, an after hours answering service is available for both ordering and leaving messages.
FAX No. 612-853-1486 (available 24 hours a day)
E-Mail: bluebook@bluebookinc.com • Website: http://www.bluebookinc.com
Office hours are: 8:30am - 5:00pm CST, Monday - Friday.

We would like to thank all of you for your business in the past - you are the reason(s) we are successful. Our goal remains the same to give you the best products, the most accurate and up-to-date information for the money, and the highest level of customer service available in today's marketplace. If somethings right, tell the world over time. If somethings wrong, please tell us immediately.

ACKNOWLEDGEMENTS

Undoubtedly, one of the most frequently asked questions received over the years is, "How do you come up with the prices for the book?". The standard reply has evolved into, "Simple, there's a big price wheel in the office (dubbed the Wheel of Misfortune) - you simply spin it, wait for the motion to stop, look at the number, and there's your price!" Seriously, almost all the currently manufactured firearms values and information are done by yours truly. On many of the older sections, the professionals listed below typically specialize within a certain company/trademark/configuration, and their expertise and knowledge obtained and shared within these specific areas has helped this publication tremendously over the years. These people are truly experts within their field(s) and deserve much of the credit. Despite using a PC since 1982 in writing each new manuscript, this scribe is proud to say that not once has a computer set a price in this text. Each new *Blue Book of Gun Values*™ is pretty much a fresh batch of cookies. While the publishing recipe stays the same, each year the ingredients get better. Very few other resources are used, since there seems to be nothing else that's as up-to-date or useful. Every new entry/revision is put in knowing that the courtroom could be the final stop if it's wrong. Once again, the people listed below are to be thanked for their contributions, and more importantly, sharing their knowledge. Without them, this new 20th Edition might have been under 1,000 pages!

Leonardo M. Antaris, M.D.

J.L. Spinks

Steve Engleson

Lowell Pauli

Bob Ball

Dave Kosowski

James W. Whitcomb

Robert Rayburn

James A. Buelow

Evan Whildin

Lynn Oliver

Richard Bauter & Chip Hewlett of
   Browning

R.L. Wilson

Kevin Cherry

John Gyde

Dr. Robert & Toshika Beeman

Dennis Adler

John Kopec

Jeff Faintich

Charles E. Carder

Charles Layson

Fred Sweeney

Thomas Koessl

Stefan Freiherr von Rink

J.B. Wood

John Lacy

LeRoy Merz

William Drollinger

Randy Shuman

William R. Mook

Richard Machniak

Jim Supica

Kathleen Hoyt - Colt historian

Jack Heath - Remington historian

Roy Jinks - S&W historian

Dwight Van Brunt from Kimber

Ing. Marek Brazda from Cesk`a
   Zbrojovka

Robert (Doc) Adelman a.k.a.,
   the "mad" rocket scientist

Daniel Sheil, Jr.

F.R. "Rudy" Etchen of
   Remington Arms Co.
Bill Allen
Don & Carol Wilkerson
Charles Semmer
Thomas Mintner
Jim Jasken
Mike Weatherby
Earl Sheehan, Jr.
Major Mark Rendina
Roger Morris
Syd & David M. Rachwal
Brad Simpson
Rick Crosier
Roy Marcot
W.H. Fluitt
Lewis Yearout
Joe Prather from Griffin & Howe
Eric M. Larson
Robert Greenleaf
David Avery, D.D.S.
Patrick McKune
Hal Hamilton
W. R. Powell
Richard Rohal
Don Anderson
Dean Rinehart
Edmund Goldshinsky of
   Marlin Firearms
Karl Lippard
T. Rees Day
James Goergen
Les Hovenkamp
F.E. "Pete" Wall
David Noll

Bob Jones
Harrison Carroll
Buck Dickinson
A.O. Salvo
Alvin Olson
Sal Raimondi
Larry Baer
John Dougan
Jim Lutes
Morris Hallowell IV
Gary Goodpaster
David Buehn
John Picchietti
Ray Saign
Jim Ellis
Richard Skeuse of Parker
   Reproductions
Bruce Canfield
Larry Orr
Charlie Price
Don Criswell
Norm Carroso
Robert White
Thad Scott
Pat Redmond
Byron Price, Howard Madaus, Paul
   Fees, Dena Hollowell, Jane Sanders,
   & crew at the Buffalo Bill Historical
   Center in Cody, WY
Mims Reed
Ruger Collectors Association (RCA)
Colt Collectors Association (CCA)
Remington Society of America
Marlin Firearms Collectors
   Association, Ltd.

FOREWORD

Twenty Editions - can you believe it? Neither can I - what a ride! Since the book has been expanded to over 1,500 pages, this scribe decided to call in a few markers and have some of the industry's most recognizable people write their take on what's happened to the firearms industry over the past several decades, in addition to crystal balling the future. Don't miss these important articles, there's something there for everyone.

One of the many things I don't do a very good job at is looking back and remembering. Getting the transmission in reverse has always been tough for me. So in this Foreword (in as fine print as possible) you'll get the real story on how the *Blue Book of Gun Values*™ came to be.

The phone rang in the barn - it was July, 1980. It's Inga Schermerhorn, the personnel director from Investment Rarities, Inc., wanting to know if I wanted to come down to Minneapolis and interview for a "gun broker" job. Holstein calves were bellowing in the background - no kidding. The reply was "How soon can I start?" followed by, "Why don't you come down to Minneapolis on Thursday, and I'll set up an interview with Jim Cook, he's the owner". After driving down to Minneapolis, it was logical to stay with Patrick Lucking, a friend of mine who was living on the west side.

Getting up the next morning, and throwing on my best Frostbite Falls threads, this unemployed person drove to One Appletree Square in an attempt to make a good impression on one of the country's most successful precious metals companies. Upon arriving, Pam gave me an aptitude test - it was pretty simple to figure out that the place was a total madhouse. It seemed like every phone was ringing, and reminded me of an ant pile that someone had just stepped on. Keep in mind, this was when the gold and silver markets were going through their seismic gyrations. While hard to imagine, the company was in the process of going from $40 million in sales during 1979, to over a $½ billion the following year! After waiting nearly 3 hours, a secretary came out and said, "Jim will see you now". Walking into his spacious 15th floor corner office, while pushing a cheeseburger into his mouth, he looks at me and says, "You're a lousy speller". I humbly agreed, after which he added, "Your math was perfect, can you work hard?" After assuring him that growing up on a dairy farm was no picnic, he laughed, and asked me how soon I could start.

After working in the Firearms and Gift divisions for several years, the phone rang one afternoon - it was Jim Cook again. "Barry Fain just got seriously injured in a shooting accident. Do you think you could take over the *Blue Book of Gun Values*™? "Yeah, right, Jim. I'm currently manager of 2 divisions, sell gold & silver on the side, and now you want me to do a book." We all know how that conversation ended. The rest, like they say, is history. Even though he fired me 3 times, he was a pretty good boss, and the opportunities were endless, if you wanted the work. During 1989, the *Blue Book of Gun Values*™ was sold to a newly formed company, Blue Book Publications, Inc. Believe it or not I haven't left One Appletree Square since 1980.

My first Blue Book was the 3rd Edition - it went awful. While most of the drudgery and double end candle burning have since been flushed down the toilet a long time ago, I'll never forget hand writing the revisions and updates on multiple Wilson-Jones columnar notebooks after work, sending them to California, where they were typeset, followed by at least 2 months of proofing and correcting. The following year (1983), I informed Tom Stock, IRI's CFO, that if he didn't buy me one of those new personal computers (PC), some one else could do the book.

FOREWORD

My first computer was an NEC APC 186 with optional 10 Meg hard drive - it cost $6,200. 5 books were written on that machine, and it's probably the reason this project started gaining acceptance, because it saved so much typesetting time. Believe it or not, it's still cranking, and besides, those 8-inch floppy disks are so cool.

During this technical exploratory period, I was lucky enough to hook up with Tom Lundin, who managed to convert the type-setting punch-tape "data base" into a manageable PC format that allowed direct word processing revisions and editions. To this day, Tom (The Wizard) continues to earn his Numero Uno status for his technical wizardry and being a pro's pro.

So here's the way this project works. Starting right after November, the annual ritual begins - sending out letters to the firearms manufacturers and contributing editors in an attempt to get next year's information and pricing updates/revisions sent to us. The book is written at the home office (i.e., the Ranch), in Inver Grove Heights. Every possible publishing technical innovation and 5 separate U.S. West phone lines assure that telecommunications won't be a problem or get overloaded during "combat" situations. This high tech setup enables us to revise a section(s), publish it within minutes, and fax it out for approval. During this stage, time becomes very compressed. Towards the end, every tick counts.

Over the editions, the amount of time racked up by myself and other production personnel has been staggering. A conservative estimate of man-hours accumulated in front of a computer monitor is somewhere over 17,000. The worst it ever got was the week I put in 120 hours, 38 of them in a row! At the end, time is always the biggest enemy. To get the information into your hands as expeditiously as possible requires a lot of self-sacrifice. I call it the 3-D concept - decisiveness, discipline, and dedication, with discipline being the operative word. On a good day, if all the stars are aligned properly (i.e., computers working, Ventura Publishing not cranky, phones not ringing, an extra toner cartridge for the printer, etc.), we can crank out 1,000 pages! For those of you still reading, please don't try this at home.

So thanks for the memories and your continued support. It's been a lot of hard work, but it's been worth it. Thomas Edison said it best, "Genius is 99% perspiration, and 1% inspiration". The best part of this job is getting to meet the people, obtaining the additional knowledge, turning various hobbies into a good job, the intoxicating smell of freshly detonated gun powder, making regular and sizable bank deposits, and don't forget the frequent flier mileage!

As stated last year, making sure that we keep our guns is not someone else's job any more - it is up to all of us. Remember, if you don't consistently pull the trigger on your gun(s) now, you may be helping someone else pull the trigger on our gun rights later.

Sincerely,

S.P. Fjestad
Author & Publisher
Blue Book of Gun Values™

HOW TO USE THIS BOOK

The prices listed in the 20th Anniversary Edition of the *Blue Book of Gun Values* are based on national average retail prices for both antique and modern firearms. **This is not a firearms wholesale pricing guide** (I doubt if there could be such a thing). More importantly, do not expect to walk into a gun/pawn shop or gun show and think that the proprietor/dealer should pay you the retail price listed within this text for your gun(s). Resale offers on most models could be anywhere from near retail to 20%-50% less than the values listed, depending upon locality, desirability, dealer inventory, and profitability. In other words, if you want to receive 100% of the price (retail value), then you have to do 100% of the work (become the retailer, which also includes assuming 100% of the risk).

Percentages of original condition (with corresponding prices) are listed between 10%-100% for most antiques (unless configuration, rarity, and age preclude upper conditions), and 60%-100% on modern firearms since condition below 60% is seldom encountered (or purchased). Please consult our revised, 48-page, Photo Percentage Grading System™ located on pages 73-120 to learn more about the condition of your firearm(s).

Since condition is the overriding factor in price evaluation, study these photos and captions carefully to learn more about the condition of your specimen(s). Please refer to the Abbreviations Section (page 64) for a complete listing of abbreviations used within this text. Also, the Glossary is now located on pages 59-63. Updated ATF regional information also is provided in this edition - see page 1,500. You may also want to check out the Store Brand Cross-Over List on pages 1,479-1,484, hundreds of models are referenced. Additionally, a PPGS Cross-Referencing Index is provided on pages 1,498-1,499, linking up all the older makes/models previously pictured in the editions 11-18.

Since this 20th Edition is over 1,500 pages, **it may be easier to zero in on a particular model by referring to the updated Index on pages 1,502-1,511.** On trademarks/companies with more than one configuration of firearms, individual category names are now listed alphabetically. Hopefully, the alphabetical tabs on page sides will also assist you in finding your section(s) faster. As in previous editions, the NRA condition standards and grading criteria have been included to make the conversion to percentages easier (see pages 70 and 71). This will especially be helpful when evaluating antiques.

To find a model in this text, first look under the name of the manufacturer, importer, or brand name (please consult the Index if necessary). Next, find the correct category name(s) (Pistols, Rifles, Shotguns, etc.). When applicable, antiques will appear before modern guns and are subdivided like modern firearms.

Once you find the correct model or sub-model under its respective subheading, determine the specimen's percentage of original condition (see the Photo Percentage Grading System™ on pages 73-120) and find the corresponding percentage column showing the price. Commemoratives or special/limited editions will generally appear last under a manufacturer's heading. For those of you who would like to make notes within this publication, there may be a Notes Page at the end of each alphabetical section allowing you room for notes and miscellaneous observations.

For the sake of simplicity, the following organizational framework has been adopted throughout this publication.

1. Alphabetical names are located on the top of right-facing, odd-numbered pages and appear as follows:

M section

2. Trademark, manufacturer, brand name, importer, or organization is listed in bold face type alphabetically, i.e.,

BRNO, COOPER ARMS, FABARM, HIGH STANDARD

3. Manufacturer information is listed directly beneath the trademark heading, i.e.,

   Current manufacturer located in London, England. Purdey has been making top quality firearms since 1814 - annual production is approximately 55 guns.

4. Manufacturer notes may appear next under individual heading descriptions and can be differentiated by the following typeface,

> Orvis imports various shotguns under subcontract with various international manufacturers. Typical custom order delivery time is 2-8 months. Most of these private label models with approximate the values of the equivalent model manufactured by the subcontractor.

5. Next classification is the category name (in alphabetical sequence) in upper case (inside a screened gray box) referring mostly to a firearm's configuration, i.e.,

COMMEMORATIVES, PISTOLS, REVOLVERS, RIFLES, SHOTGUNS

6. A further sub-classification may appear under a category name in both upper and lower case, as depicted below. These are sub-categories of a major category name.

Lugers: KDF, Interarms, Stoeger, & Recent Import

7. Following a category or sub-category name, a category note may follow to help explain the category, and appears as follows:

> Note: Post-WWII Lugers have been manufactured by Mauser Werke in Oberndorf, W. Germany during the 1970s, and by both Stoeger Industries and Mitchell Arms (see separate listings) in recent years. Currently, the Stoeger Luger is the only Luger available for sale domestically.

8. Model names appear flush left, are bold faced, and capitalized either in chronological order (normally) or alphabetical order (sometimes, the previous model name and/or close subvariation will appear at the end in parenthesis) and are listed under the individual category names, examples include:

1929 SWISS BERN, DAKOTA MODEL 10, M1 SUPER 90 FIELD

9. Model descriptions are denoted by the following typeface and usually include information, i.e.,

> — calibers, gauges, action type, barrel lengths, finishes, weight, and other descriptive data are further categorized adjacent to model names in this typeface. This is where most of the information is listed for each specific model including identifiable features and possibly some production data (including quantity, circa of manufacture, discontinuance date, if known).

10. Variations within a model appear as sub-models - they are differentiated from model names by an artistic icon (✳) prefix, are indented, and are in upper and lower case type, i.e.,

✳ *Pacific Edition DU, Grade III, Model 92F Deluxe, Target Model, Linder mfg.*

and are usually followed by a short description of that sub-model. These sub-model descriptions have the same typeface as the model descriptions, i.e.,

> — additional sub-model information that could include finishes, calibers, barrel lengths, special order features, and other production data specific for that sub-model.

11. Now included is yet another layer of model/information nomenclature differentiating sub-models from variations of sub-models or a lower hierarchy of sub-model information. These items are indented in from the sub-models, have the icon graphic (➤) and are in upper/lower case, i.e.,

> ➤ **Earlier Mfg. Without Invector Choking, Nickel Finish, Lady Elite, Stainless Steel A description for this level of model information may appear next to the sub-entry, and uses the same typeface as model and submodel descriptions shown above.**

12. Manufacturer and other notes/information appear in smaller type, and should be read since they contain both important and other critical, up-to-date information, i.e.,

> The Signature Painted Model includes special paint treatment on stock and forearm, featuring Browning logos and trademark - mfg. 1993-94.

13. Extra cost features/special value orders and other value added/subtracted features are placed directly under individual price lines or in some cases, category names. These individual lines appear bolder than other descriptive typeface, i.e.,

> **Add 100% for the first 114 pistols with oversize "United States Property" marking.**
> **Subtract $1,845 for heavy barrel variation, which does not include sub-gauge tubes.**

14. On many discontinued models/variations after 1985, a line may appear under the price line, indicating the last manufacturer's suggested retail price flush right on the page, i.e.,

> Last Mfg.'s Sug. Retail was $8,875.

15. Grading lines normally appear at the top of each page and in the middle if pricing lines change. If you are uncertain as to how to properly grade a particular firearm, please refer to the Photo Percentage Grading System™ on pages 73-120 for more assistance. The most commonly encountered grading line (shown with typical price line) in this text is from 100%-60%, i.e.,

Grading	100%	98%	95%	90%	80%	70%	60%
Mfg.'s Sug. Retail $700	$625	$550	$500	$450	$400	$360	$330

Antique grading lines have additional values listed for 100%-10%, 80%-10%, 100%-Grey finish grading lines, as older weapons are normally encountered in condition factors of 60% or less. N/A indicates this particular model is not encountered enough in either 98% or 100% original condition to warrant pricing. Examples (with pricing lines) are as follows:

100%	98%	95%	90%	80%	70%	60%	50%	40%	30%	20%	10%
$650	$575	$475	$425	$375	$335	$305	$275	$250	$220	$195	$165
N/A	N/A	$475	$425	$375	$340	$300	$275	$250	$220	$195	$165

An additional antique grading line (with price line) is listed below, starting at 80% as original specimens are seldomly seen or encountered above 80%. Values also start at 80%.

Grading	80%	70%	60%	50%	40%	30%	20%	10%
	$2,650	$2,365	$1,925	$1,650	$1,425	$1,275	$1,125	$995

The grading line below (with price line) in lower condition factors includes Traces, which stands for traces of blue, and grey, which translates into a gun whose overall finish has a greyish color.

Grading	100%	95%	80%	50%	20%	Traces	Grey
	$350	$315	$260	$210	$175	$140	$120

Commemorative/limited edition grading and pricing lines will appear as follows:

Grading	100%	issue price	qty made
	$2,500	$550	100

In some cases, an organization's or company's listing (i.e. Ducks Unlimited, the National Wild Turkey Federation, etc.) of guns will appear as follows:

MANUFACTURER	MODEL	QUANTITY	YEAR	ISSUE PRICE
Browning	Model A5 12 ga. NWTF	500	1990	$925

16. Price line format is as follows - when the price line shown below (with proper grading line) is encountered,

Grading	100%	98%	95%	90%	80%	70%	60%
Mfg.'s Sug. Retail $1,350	$1,150	$950	$750	$675	$600	$525	$450

it automatically indicates the gun is currently manufactured and the manufacturer's retail price is shown left of the 100% column. Following are the 100%-60% values. **This 100% price is the national average price a consumer will typically expect to pay for that model in NIB unfired condition.** 100% specimens without boxes, warranties, etc., that are currently manufactured must be discounted slightly (5%-20%, depending on the desirability of make and model). This 100% price also assumes not previously sold at retail.

17. A currently manufactured gun without a retail price published by the manufacturer/importer will appear as follows:

No Mfg.'s Retail	$425	$375	$295	$260	$230	$200	$185
Grading	**100%**	**98%**	**95%**	**90%**	**80%**	**70%**	**60%**

Obviously, the 100% price is the national average price a consumer will pay for a gun in new condition. Again, this assumes NIB condition, and not previously sold at retail.

18. When a currently manufactured stainless steel or limited mfg./special edition firearm with or without retail pricing is encountered, it will not have prices listed from 90%-60%, as these lower condition factors are priced approximately the same as the 90% price. The price lines will appear as follows:

Mfg.'s Sug. Retail	$1,000	$825	$725	$600
No Mfg. Sug. Retail		$350	$300	$250

19. A price line with 7 values listed and represented below indicates a discontinued, out of production model with values shown for 100%-60% conditions. Values are normally not listed for 50%-10% condition factors, since these lower conditions are seldom encountered on recently discontinued models. Examples include:

$10,500	$9,250	$8,000	$7,250	$6,500	$5,750	$4,900
N/A	$450	$400	$350	$315	$260	$210

50%-10% values however, will in many cases approximate the 60% price since any gun's shooting value will usually keep the price close to the 60% value, unless the gun has been shot to a point where the action may be loose or questionable. Obviously, no "Mfg.'s Sug. Retail" will appear in the left margin, but a last manufacturer's suggested retail price may appear flush right below the price line, automatically indicating a discontinued gun, i.e.,

Last Mfg.'s Sug. Retail was $1,650.

20. Early Winchester lever action grading and price lines incorporate price ranges on certain Winchester models which are most frequently encountered in 50% or less condition. These grading and price range lines appear as follows:

Above Average	Average	Below Average
$3,750 - $2,600	$2,450 - $1,450	$1,250 - $600

An explanation of what to look for in these three condition ranges will precede this information in that section. The 20th Edition also includes a grading/price line that represents percentages and respective values for guns above 50% condition. This grading/value line appears as follows:

95% = $895	90% = $775	80% = $600	70% = $495	60% = $395	50% = $295

   Since this publication is over 1,500 pages, you may want to take advantage of our new expanded Index (pages 1,502-1,511) as a speedy alternative to going through the pages.
   Enlarged in the 20th Edition are sections on Trademark Index (pages 1,414-1,451), Modern Airguns (1,369-1,413), Model Serialization breakdown of major trademarks (pages 1,454-1,478), and a Store Brand Cross-Over List (pages 1,479-1,484). When using the Model Serialization section, make sure your model is listed and find the serial number within the yearly range listings.

GUN QUESTIONS/APPRAISALS POLICY & PREFERRED CUSTOMER SERVICE (PCS)

We certainly never asked for this - it just happened. Whether we wanted it or not, Blue Book Publications, Inc. has ended up in the driver's seat as the clearing-house for gun information. While somewhat manageable for the past 15 years, a new change of policy has been implemented to better serve our customers. **Unfortunately, we can no longer answer gun-related questions, including pricing, or perform appraisals at no charge.** Because the volume of gun questions now requires full-time attention, we have developed a Preferred Customer Service (PCS) program that will enable us to provide you with the service you have come to expect from Blue Book Publications, Inc.

We hope that you can appreciate this policy change. To ensure that the research dept. can answer every gun question with an equal degree of seriousness and thoroughness, a $100,000 firearms library is maintained and constantly updated. Additionally, hundreds of both new and old factory brochures, price sheets, and dealer inventory listings are kept on file to help assist in answering the thousands of gun-related questions that are received annually. For those questions that require further "digging", we are fortunate enough to have many leading experts in their various fields only a phone call/fax/email away. It's a huge job, takes a lot of time, and we answer every question like we could go to court on it.

Our new Preferred Customer Service (PCS) program is explained later in this text, and may be ordered by calling (800) 877-4867.

POLICY FOR GUN QUESTIONS

Our policy for answering gun questions by phone, fax, or email is as follows:

Gun question telephone hours are 9 a.m. to 4:00 p.m., M-F, CST, no exceptions please. **Unless you are a current PCS member, the charge is $10 per gun question, payable by a major credit card. If you haven't already taken advantage of our new Preferred Customer Service program, please call (800) 877-4867 and join.** Telephone pricing requests will be given within a value range only, since in many cases, a condition factor cannot be accurately represented through a telecommunications device. **Whenever possible, we will answer your questions(s) during the initial phone call.** However, in an effort to reduce phone and research time, we may take the information requested over the telephone, and call you back once the necessary answer(s) has been sufficiently researched.

Faxed questions will be treated similarly to phone questions, and answered in the order in which they are received. You **must** provide us with the necessary gun information, however, if you want an accurate answer. Please enclose your phone and fax numbers, and all pertinent information, including major credit card number and expiration date. **Again, unless you are a current PCS member, the charge is $10 per gun question.** Without providing us with all the information, your request(s) may go unanswered, and will certainly be delayed.

Emailed questions will also be put in a FIFO system (first in, first out), along with letters, telephone messages, and faxes. We have noticed a sense of urgency in some email requests. Placing all gun questions in this FIFO system guarantees that everyone will be treated equally. When you email, please supply us all the necessary gun information, if you want an accurate answer. Also include your major credit card number & expiration date. **Again, unless you are a current PCS member, the charge is $10 per gun question.** Without providing us with all the information, your request(s) may be delayed or go unanswered entirely. Remember - poor planning on your part does not constitute an emergency on ours.

Letter questions (preferred, with photos) will also be answered in the order of arrival. Good quality photos would certainly help, especially if a written appraisal is required. Make sure you include

GUN QUESTIONS/APPRAISALS POLICY & PREFERRED CUSTOMER SERVICE (PCS)

the proper return address and phone number. Again, unless you are a current PCS member, the charge is $10 per gun question.

APPRAISAL INFORMATION

Written appraisals will be performed only if the following criteria are met:
If you wish to have a gun(s) appraised accurately based on the correct condition factor(s), we must have either good quality photos with a complete description including manufacturers name, model, gauge/caliber, barrel length or be able to inspect the specimen(s) personally. Our charge for a written appraisal is $20 per gun, up to 5 guns. At 6 guns, the charge is normally $15 per gun. If you are a current PCS member, you are entitled to one free appraisal per edition. Larger collections may be discounted somewhat, depending on the complexity and the size of the collection. Unfortunately, we cannot appraise emailed requests with images, as the condition factor cannot be accurately ascertained. Please allow 2-3 weeks response time per appraisal request.

ADDITIONAL SERVICES

Individuals requesting a photocopy of a particular page or section from any edition for insurance or reference purposes will be billed at $5 per page, up to 5 pages, and $3.50 per page thereafter. Simply let us know what you would like copied, including which edition (will assume 20th, unless specified), and how you would like it sent to you (mail or fax only).

GUNTRACKER 2.0: A NEW COMPUTER ALTERNATIVE FOR USING THE 20TH EDITION

Many of you may have already seen the ad for GunTracker 2.0, a new software program utilizing the database of the 20th edition. This new program allows you keep an accurate record of your firearms inventory, including pricing by individual condition factor. For those of you who have a newer computer system and like to do your own inventory analysis, this is the only software program currently available with enough horsepower to make this a fairly simple operation. Later this year, we also plan on putting GunTracker 2.0 on our web site, enabling instant electronic access to the 20th edition! Payment will be made through a secured credit card transfer. For more information on GunTracker 2.0, please refer to page 17.

JOIN OUR NEW PREFERRED CUSTOMER SERVICE PROGRAM (PCS) for GUN QUESTION & APPRAISALS answered by industry professionals

This is a great deal and a valuable service, and the price is only $25 per edition. As a PCS member you are automatically entitled to $60 worth of toll-free gun questions and one written appraisal! When Preferred Customers telecommunicate gun questions, it will enable us to know who you are immediately, and deal with your question(s) expeditiously.

TURNAROUND TIME

Utilizing this new PCS policy will hopefully enable us to answer most gun questions as expeditiously as possible. Our goal is to answer most telephone, mail, email, or faxed gun questions in no longer than 7 days. This also assumes that all information needed to process the question(s) is initially provided, otherwise delays may occur. In instances where additional time is required to properly

GUN QUESTIONS/APPRAISALS POLICY
& PREFERRED CUSTOMER SERVICE (PCS)

research your request, you will be notified within the first two weeks.

We hope that you can appreciate this new policy regarding gun questions and/or appraisals. Just as millions of computer users are now paying for reliable and speedy hardware/software support, it is time to take a similar service approach ensuring that the most accurate and up-to-date gun information is provided to you on a professional and reliable basis.

> **Please direct all gun questions and appraisals to the following:**
>
> **Blue Book Publications, Inc.**
> **Attn: Research Dept.**
> **8009 34th Ave. S., Suite 175**
> **Minneapolis, MN 55425 USA**
>
> **Phone: 800-877-4867**
> **(toll-free in U.S. & Canada)**
> **Fax: 612-853-1486**
> **Email: guns@bluebookinc.com**

BUYING OR SELLING?

Interested in buying or selling a particular firearm(s)? Or maybe hesitating because you are unsure of what a fair market price should be? Depending on what you are interested in, a referral will be made that will enable you to be sure that you are getting what you paid for (or getting paid a fair price). This service is designed to help all those people who are worried or scared about purchasing a potentially "bad gun" or getting "ripped off" when selling. Remember, Blue Book Publications is a publisher, not a gun dealer, so we have no vested interest in trying to buy/sell your firearms. Our established international network of reliable dealers and collectors allows your particular sell request to be referred to the right company/individual, based on both your region and area of collectibility. There is no charge for this referral service (a thank you would be nice) - we are simply connecting you with the best person(s)/company possible within your field of collecting ensuring that you get a fair deal. This hybrid matchmaking can make 25%- 50% worth of difference on potentially buying or selling a gun. All replies are treated strictly confidentially. Written correspondence/replies should be directed to:

> Blue Book of Gun Values
> Attn: S.P. Fjestad
> 8009 34th Ave. So.,
> Minneapolis, MN 55425 USA
> Phone No.: 612-854-5229, ext. 14
> FAX NO.: 612-853-1486

GUNTRACKER™

All new version incorporates the Twentieth Edition Blue Book of Gun Values prices, data, and more!

20th EDITION UPGRADE
$29.95
FULL VERSION $49.95

"At last! A sensible reason for owning a computer. It's *GunTracker™!* If you own a computer and more than one firearm, your next purchase should be *GunTracker™.*"
Jim Carmichel - Shooting Editor, *Outdoor Life Magazine*

GunTracker 2.0 contains all the features that made it famous in its first year on the market. Plus, **WE LISTENED!**
The new 2.0 release is full of new features and improvements:

- **Faster!** More user friendly! Loading and model search times are now much faster.

- **New!** Custom Reports. *GunTracker* now lets you select the specific firearms you would like to print on your reports. This feature is useful for dealers or anyone attending a gun show for focusing the list of items printed on *GunTracker's* reports.

- **Improved!** *GunTracker's* key screens and reports have all been completely rewritten with an emphasis on SPEED.

- **New!** Merge Collections. *GunTracker* users who purchase entire gun collections can merge all the new pieces directly into their own collection without reentering any data.

- **Improved!** The new 'Add Items from Book' interface displays gun information just like the actual *Blue Book of Gun Values.* Makes it easier for old dogs to avoid having to learn too many new tricks!

- **New!** Enter items into your Wish List which aren't listed in the *Blue Book of Gun Values.*

- **New!** Access the *GunTracker* World Wide Web page directly from the *GunTracker* program. Makes it easier to go to the web to download program upgrades and other *GunTracker*-related information.

- **New!** All screens in *GunTracker* can be resized by the user.

- **New!** Computer savvy readers will be pleased to know that plans are underway to get this 20th Edition PPGS incorporated into *GunTracker 2.0*, due for release in mid-June. This will help you to get a firearms grading fix on your computer monitor while using *GunTracker.*

- **Plus . . .** all the original features which made GunTracker the program that experts and casual users alike are raving about.

SEE OUR INSERT ORDER CARD BETWEEN PAGES 120 - 121

800-877-4867

5th Edition
Blue Book of Electric Guitars™

The largest, most comprehensive book ever published on electric guitars, containing almost 800 pages, 1,000+ trademarks, nearly 1,200 photos, and over 35,000 prices!

"A great reference resource for the guitar enthusiasts. I can only guess at the work involved in gathering so much information."
Paul Reed Smith - PRS Guitars

$29.95 + S/H

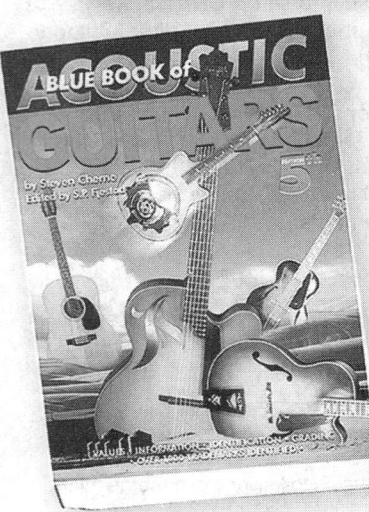

5th Edition
Blue Book of Acoustic Guitars™

The largest, most comprehensive book ever published on acoustic guitars, with almost 500 pages, 500+ trademarks, 400+ photos, and over 20,000 prices!

"This 5th Edition Blue Book of Acoustic Guitars™ will provide dealers, collectors, and serious guitar enthusiasts with an invaluable resource, incredibly thorough and packed with detail."
C.F. Martin IV - Chairman & CEO, C.F. Martin & Co.

$24.95 + S/H

2nd Edition
Blue Book of Pool Cues™

The largest, most comprehensive book ever published on pool cues, with 512 pages, 500+ trademarks, 400+ photos, and over 20,000 prices! Includes all new 48 page color section featuring top quality cues from many of the world's premier cue makers. Most of this information is not available anywhere else, at any price!
Due for release, summer - 1999

$29.95 + S/H

A Blast from the Past.

Colt Blackpowder Reproductions & Replicas
A Collector's & Shooter's Guide
by Dennis Adler

An industry first, illustrated volume on black powder firearms and recently manufactured reproductions/replicas of such famous makes as Colt, Remington, etc. Included is a history of the Colt percussion revolver and similar makes, with photos. Reproductions are covered in detail, with many limited and/or special editions, and also guns manufactured by major Italian manufacturers, with an in-depth look at these factories and guns they have made for American companies and organizations. Chapters include practical percussion shooting and detailed loading information by gun and caliber, cowboy action shooting, and Civil War re-enactments. Additionally, this publication has information on shooting and maintaining black powder pistols, as well as a complete black powder pricing guide with model descriptions providing the most up-to-date information on most recently manufactured makes and models. Dennis Adler is well-known in the automotive community for his photographic and literary achievements. This book is a visual masterpiece!

Two years, 3000 photographs, and thousands of frequent flyer miles later, this landmark publication featuring the history and manufacturing of today's fine replica black powder arms can now be yours!

$33.95
(includes 4th class shipping)

Also available in hard cover with dust jacket
limited quantities available for $53.95 (includes 4th class shipping.)

ORDER TODAY!

SEE OUR INSERT ORDER CARD BETWEEN PAGES 696 - 697

To Order Call:
800-877-4867

Published by
Blue Book Publications, Inc.
8009 34th Ave. So. Suite 175
Minneapolis, MN 55425
www.bluebookinc.com
email: bluebook@bluebookinc.com
International: 612-854-5229 • Fax: 612-853-1486

LOOKING BACK

Now that we've got 20 Editions under the belt, we've noticed that more and more people are interested in purchasing older editions - maybe even trying to complete a set.

Pictured below are the first 20 Editions, complete with publishing dates, original list prices, publisher's current retail values, and other pertinent information.

If you are interested in buying one or more of these older editions, please contact us and be specific about which edition(s) you are looking for. Editions 1-10 are very hard to get a hold of, and are usually in very limited supply. Many times, we can put you on a waiting list for those editions you're interested in. Earlier hardcovers are ultra-rare, were not marketed or sold commercially, and typically were given away to contributing editors and industry VIPs.

If you'd like to sell an older edition(s) - we are interested in excellent condition books only if possible - please send in (UPS shipment preferable) your copy(s) to our address on the back cover, Attn: Buy/Sell. Please allow 7-10 days for a reply, including a price quotation. Older edition availability is not possible using our web site - please contact us by letter, telephone, fax, or email.

1st Edition (Vol. I, No. I) - published in Mar., 1981, MSR - $12.95, current value range, 80%=$55, 98%=$80, 352 pages, softcover only.

2nd Edition (Vol. II, No. I) - published in Feb., 1982, MSR - $12.95, current value range 80%=$50, 98%=$75.

3rd Edition (Vol. II, No.II) - published in Aug. 1982, MSR - $12.95, current value range, 80%=$50, 98%=$75, first time the database was published from a PC platform

4th Edition - published in July, 1983, MSR - $12.95, current value range, 80%=$45, 98%=$65, Modern Black Powder & Modern Airguns sections introduced.

5th Edition - published in June, 1984, MSR - $13.95, current value range, 80%=$40, 98%=$60, 1st hardcover.

6th Edition - published in June, 1985, MSR - $13.95, current value range, 80%=$35, 98%=$55.

7th Edition - published in June, 1986, MSR - $14.95, current value range, 80%=$40, 98%=$50.

8th Edition - published in June, 1987, MSR - $14.95, current value range, 80%=$40, 98%=$50.

9th Edition - published in June, 1988, MSR - $14.95, current value range, 80%=$35, 98%=$45.

10th Edition - published in June, 1989, MSR - $17.95, current value range, 80%=$30, 98%=$40, hardcover also.

11th Edition - published in June, 1990, MSR - $17.95, current value range, 80%=$30, 98%=$40, hardcover also, 1st year for PPGS.

12th Edition - published in June, 1991, MSR - $19.95, current value range, 80%=$30, 98%=$40, hardcover also.

13th Edition - published in June, 1992, MSR - $19.95, current value range, 80%=$25, 98%=$35, hardcover also.

14th Edition - published in May, 1993, MSR - $24.95, current value range, 80%=$25, 98%=$35, hardcover also.

15th Edition - published in May, 1994, MSR - $24.95, current value range, 80%=$20, 98%=$30, hardcover also.

16th Edition - published in April, 1995, MSR - $24.95, current value range, 80%=$20, 98%=$30, hardcover also.

17th Edition - published in April, 1996, MSR - $27.95, current value, 98%=$25, hardcover also.

18th Edition - published in April, 1997, MSR - $27.95, current value, 98%=$25, hardcover also, last year for Modern Black Powder Section.

19th Edition - published in May, 1998, MSR - $29.95, current value, 98%=$25, hardcover also, GunTracker 1.0 software program released 9/98.

20th Edition - published in April, 1999, MSR - $29.95, 1,512 pages, hardcover also, GunTracker 2.0 software program and upgrade released 6/99.

GunTracker Software Program - 1st Release, June, 1998, GunTracker 2.0, release - June, 1999, MSR - $49.95, annual upgrade, MSR - $29.95.

PUBLISHERS OVERVIEW OF THE FIREARMS MARKETPLACE

by S.P. Fjestad

Here's the arithmetic - my best guesstimate is that there are at least 300 million guns in the U.S., probably over 85% that still operate. If you banned all the guns in America tomorrow, it would take over 13 years to melt them down at a rate of 60,000 per day! Read that 10 semi-trucks full each and every day. It's really too bad the antis don't get this simple fact - making 300 million guns disappear isn't going to happen, or is it logical to think that it could be done. Even if you got rid of 80% of them, there would still be over 60 million guns remaining. 300 mil is 300 mil. We're going to have to deal with them - elimination is not an option.

With violence, particularly gun related violence, being a concern for everyone these days, it's important to remember our nation's history. Ours has always been a nation of violence, and nothing has changed. It just gets reported better now. We were armed, dangerous, and violent in 1776, and we are even more bristling with every type of outrageous armament today. Truly, the melting pot concept in America may soon reach a meltdown temperature - you can feel it - is going up every hour. Our pot has been too hot for too long, and is definitely showing some signs of cracking.

Do you really think that if we took all the various minority and ethnic groups out of Los Angeles, spread out each cultural/ethnic faction 150 miles apart in Montana with one road going in/out, there would still be the same amount of firearms crime and violence within these same people? Of course not. But when you put dozens of different nationalities and cultures within a tight urban environment, cook them for a couple of months in an asphalt paved 100+ degree oven extending over 600 square miles, you can expect violence, crime, and gunfire 24 hours a day.

The moral is simple. You can't make or govern cultures to get along. Never could, never will. Freedom has always carried a stiff price. It's not a gift - it requires constant vigilance. One of the prices we pay for our freedom is the thousands of people that are butchered annually because of our inherent cultural/ethnic differences. While it's easy to rationalize American blood spilled overseas to preserve our freedom, it seems like a big price to pay when the bloodletting occurs within our shores.

Independence and freedom have always carried a stiff price tag. Our best defense has always been a strong offense. Are we overpaying for freedom these days? Is all the violence, crime and destruction (some of it firearms related) worth it? Can we afford this anymore? And more importantly, if you didn't have our freedom and independence, what would it be worth to you? No one seems to mind or complain about America winning WWI or WWII. And we didn't do it with gun control or major press badmouthing and second guessing. I've always said that without guns in America, the 4th of July would be another country's holiday.

Domestic firearms politics will continue to be an open volcano spewing lava in all 50 states during the remainder of this presidential term. One thing you can count on - it's already happening - the general idea here is that the more gun laws you can layer throughout cities and states, crime (and violence?) will decrease.

What worries me about the gun issue is that there will always be yet another model, configuration, caliber, high capacity magazine, bullet type, or even sighting system that the anti-gun movement will put at the end of their domino chain. When will the Beretta Model 92-F be reclassified as a military style assault pistol and made unfit to own? My point is that once you have allowed these "peace and anti-crime crusaders" into the foyer of your house, sooner or later they will make routine appearances in your dining room, living room, bedrooms, attic, basement, and maybe even crawl down your well.

And, although you will not remember agreeing with them on the banning of one or two "non-sporting" weapons, you will be surprised when you go to your gun cabinet one day and find one remaining .177 caliber air rifle with which to do your sport shooting. I sometimes wonder what Thomas Jefferson, George Washington, or Andrew Jackson would say today if they could comment on some of the recent anti-gun legislation. Andy especially would not be pleased.

Of immediate importance is the recent rash of cities suing the firearms manufacturers for knowingly distributing guns close to the areas where crime is rampant. While it is unfortunate that the mayors of these cities have not been able to control crime through their political, legal, and enforcement agencies, this is not the fault of the gun industry - how can the ultimate failure on their end be transferred and used as an excuse to further legislate today's firearms manufacturers and distributors? Following in the footsteps of the recent tobacco litigation, this is a very dangerous situation for law abiding gun owners. Isn't the American citizen ultimately responsible for what he/she does, both good and bad? Taking responsibility for one's actions has always been the central nervous system for our democracy. Nothing is anybody's fault anymore - especially if you have a good attorney (just ask O.J.!). If we're not careful, it's going to be harder to find a gun shop in a big city than to find a virgin stogie in Slick Willie's Oral office.

Once we all accept the fact that both guns and gun related violence are not going to go away in this country, no matter how many laws and increased legislation we pour on top of this issue, maybe we should concentrate on how guns can be more safely integrated into our society, with the law abiding citizen becoming a crucial part of the solution - fighting crime.

Nothing hurts crime more than an armed and dangerous, intelligent, law abiding citizen defending him/her self. Obviously, the police aren't going to save your ass when things get tough, especially in a high crime, large urban environment. Because of our inherent freedoms, we have the choice and the chance to protect ourselves.

We're going to see a lot of changes a lot faster than you think during the next 3-4 years. As e-commerce becomes a way of life and embedded into our society, the entire firearms industry marketing will shift away from a print media form of advertising (especially at the distributor level) to mostly digital. Firearms dealers who specialize in out-of-production guns and antiques will either be on this new digital fast track, or be doomed to slowly but surely fade away after a last-ditch B&W ad campaign that generated little revenue. New gun dealers, to survive, will be driven by the consumer information available on the World Wide Web. It's going to be exciting, but there will be major changes.

Please take the time to read the editorial on the following pages. It represents a lot of different viewpoints from within the industry, including some very recognizable names and industry leaders, as well as my neighbors and their dogs. Once again, my pen has runneth over. Thanks for your continued help and support over the years - very much appreciated. ■

Buying Tomorrow's Collectibles Today

by Jim Carmichel

Jim Carmichel is the shooting editor for *Outdoor Life* magazine, and the author of *The Book of the Rifle*, soon to be reprinted by the *Varmint Hunter Magazine*, located in Pierre, SD.

When Steve Fjestad, the Publisher of this and other successful books, asked me to do a short article for these pages, I had to let him know that I make no claims to being an authority on firearms values and I'm not even what you'd call a gun collector. But on the other hand, I've accumulated a few guns over the years that are now considered collectors' items, even though that was not my intent.

For example, back when I first got into the business of testing ammunition and developing handloads, the most accurate rifles commonly available were the Target Grade Model-70 Winchesters. Their heavy barrels and wide, target-style forends made them steady on the sandbags, which made ammo testing at the benchrest easy and reliable. Also, they were relatively inexpensive and came in a wide range of calibers, so over the years I accumulated quite a few Target M-70's, along with several more of the standard grade M-70's. In time, however, rifles more

accurate than the old M-70's became available and as the sophistication of my work increased, the Winchesters that had served me so well were banished to my gun room's back rack.

Then, sometime during the 1970's, I began to notice something interesting! At gun shows where I had paid, say, $200 for a pristine Target Grade M-70 a decade before, traders were now asking - and getting - upwards of $1,000 and even more for the same rifle! What's more, dealers were advertising for old M-70's and some of the prices they offered for rifles in uncommon calibers were as much as ten or even more times what I had originally paid. Wow! The temptation was to sell the lot (I didn't call it a collection then – and still don't), but like a favored heir who comes into possession of some prime blue chip stocks, it was more fascinating to hold on to the rifles and watch their values escalate. When the price was right I bought even more M-70's. After all, a stock certificate isn't much fun, but a fine gun, like good art, is a joy forever.

As I watched the collectors' market for old M-70's develop I began to note that, like a stock market, there were periodic fluctuations in prices. For example, the prices would rise for a while, then reach a plateau and sometimes even decline a bit before beginning to climb again. The usual explanation for these fluctuations is "supply and demand", but as I watched the market rise, stabilize, and then rise again, it became apparent that it was more predictable than generally thought, and that there is a smart time to buy M-70's. The index I watch is the spread between prices for the old M-70's being asked by dealers (which, by the way, is closely linked to values in the Blue Book), and the price of currently manufactured M-70's. No one seriously questions that an M-70 of Pre-1964 vintage is more desirable than those currently made —even if you only want it for hunting – but sometimes we tend to go to sleep and the retail prices of the new models climb close to what old models are bringing. Then dealers and collectors wake up and prices for the old guns take a jump. For example, the gun show prices of a pretty good Pre- '64 M-70 in standard calibers (.30/06-.270, etc.) has ranged in the $500 to $700 bracket for a while now, while retail prices for new manufacture M-70's has climbed to nearly $650! The average Joe Hunter, who has always hankered for an old M-70, sees what's happening and says to himself, " Why should I buy a new M-70, when I can get the model I've always wanted for about the same money?" Boom! Demand for the old models increase and prices take a jump. So you don't have to be a rocket scientist to figure out when to buy old M-70's and predict when prices are going to leap. It's the stock market all over again (and again, and again…).

Of course, old M-70's in rare calibers fetch a lot more dough than the popular calibers, and there's no shortage of folks who bemoan their fate for not having bought M-70's in .35 Rem. or .300 Savage back when they cost the same as other calibers. But that's the exact point of what you should be looking for NOW! Those "rare" calibers became rare because no one wanted them at the time. So why not thumb through some of today's gun catalogs and ask yourself which models and calibers aren't likely to be popular.

Recent history teaches us a lot, with one example being the pathetic Models- 600 and 660 rifles that Remington made a few years ago. Though they were light and nicely accurate, they had all the appeal of a road-killed possum, and after a few years of production they were dropped because no one seemed to want them. But now, shooters and collectors have decided they are pretty nice after all and prices are beginning to soar. One version,

the 600 Magnum, came in 6.5 and .350 Rem. Magnum calibers. These two woebe-gotten calibers received such a cold reception that the Magnum 600 was dropped after three years of scant production. Nowadays, put one of the 600 Mags. on your table at a gun show and collectors will cluster like buzzards on a dead horse.

And what about S&W's sweet-shooting K-22's and K-38's? These are among the most popular revolvers ever made, and no pistol shooter can long be without a matched brace of the two calibers. But do you remember there was once a K-32 also? No one seemed to want this middlin' caliber so S&W quietly removed it from their line. Have you priced one recently? WOW!

One of the most beautifully made autoloading shotguns of all time was Winchester's Super-X. They were a bit pricey when introduced and a bit heavy, so sales never took off the way folks at Winchester had hoped. Because of sagging sales, plus the fact that the Super-X's were expensive to make, they were made only for six or seven years and discontinued in 1981, to be replaced with a shotgun that was cheaper to make. Just after the Super-X was discontinued, dealers dumped remaining stocks for $200 or even less! Smart investors who realized that a gun that good, of which so few were made, could only go up in value. This year Winchester introduced a new auto-loader called the Super-X2, which, despite the name, is an entirely different gun and comparing it to the slick finished original Super-X is like comparing a muddy shoe string to a silk ribbon. Which means that prices of the old Super-X's are going to be out of sight.

There are dozens of similar examples of ugly ducklings that became Prince Charmings, but the smart collector only uses such examples from the past to predict the future. Remember, tomorrow's collectables are being made today! No matter which corner of the gun world you look into, there's always a hidden treasure waiting to be discovered, the trick is to find it first. ■

> …" Why should I buy a new M-70, when I can get the model I've always wanted for about the same money?"…

Gun Collecting

by R.L. Wilson

R.L. Wilson

The world's leading authority on Colt firearms and firearms engraving, R.L. Wilson has written over 30 books on pistols and longarms, including *Colt - An American Legend*, and *The Book of Colt Firearms*.

Approximately twenty years ago, when the *Blue Book of Gun Values* was about to join the ranks of firearms publications, this writer was toiling on the creation of the Colt/Christie's Auction of Rare and Historic Firearms - no doubt Steve Fjestad will agree that both were landmark events in the history of arms collecting. From the marked success of that sale, held on Park Avenue in New York City and done with the full support of the Colt Firearms Division of Colt Industries, there came, slowly but surely, an avalanche of firearms auctions.

There is no question that the most striking change in the arms collecting world in those twenty editions has been the increase of these auctions, and as a part of the process, the explosion of interest in arms collecting, and in values of many collectible firearms. Big companies like Christie's, Sotheby's, and Butterfield & Butterfield are promoting gun collecting, as they promote their auctions.

Although my experience in the firearms field has been largely as an antiquarian, my book projects have led into such diverse spheres as the guns of Colt and Winchester, the art of engraving, arms of the West, hunting and conservation, museums, and in effect - the whole exciting, dynamic and fascinating world of guns. To celebrate the Millennium, my first title for the new century will be *The World of Beretta, An International Legend* (the official company history, simultaneously published in five languages).

The campaign of deceit from the rabid anti-gun activists has dampened our enjoyment of guns - all too often we are on the defensive, and portrayed unpleasantly in the mainstream press (whatever happened to holding criminals responsible for their actions?). One can sense from the Clinton/Lewinsky scandal that the politics of demonization and spite have been part of our burden of being in the firearms business: it would have been much better for our field if frontal attacks had not been made on Clinton, his wife, and others. Name-calling and the targeting of powerful politicians have been instrumental in creating a backlash against gun people, making us targets of derision and antagonism from all too many in the mainstream media - a powerful force who want to destroy the "gun culture".

The magical world of collectors' firearms is a domain to which the entire firearms field owes a considerable vote of appreciation. The reason is quite simple: collectors - whether antique or modern - generally have much more money at their disposal than those from nearly all of the several other firearms specialties. As a consequence, although our numbers are usually less, we have access, we have the connections, and we can reach people in power, including the press, publishers, elected officials, and others of influence.

Collectors are also inclined to be particularly introspective, studied, and dedicated to passing on to others what we have learned, experienced and observed.

Much of the acceleration of activity in the world of arms collecting has occurred over the past several decades. Although my career goes back some 45 years, beginning in the field first as a collector and then as a museum curator (in the 1950s and 1960s), much of the striking growth in collecting has occurred in the period since the *Blue Book of Gun Values* was first published: the escalating values, the proliferation of gun books, magazines and even newspapers and the overall expansion of the collecting world. In all of these, the explosion of activity and interest has been nothing less than sensational.

The fact that some collectables have achieved $1,000,000+ prices has drawn new interest, and more enthusiasts. These sales figures were largely reached in a public way - by auction - and in the process, these sales proved that collectors' guns can be extremely valuable. When prices are big, the press is big too. This is one of the reasons antique arms rate among the collectables on the "Antiques Road Show" television program, syndicated to PBS stations around the country.

Further, television has discovered the world of collectors guns in the series "The Story of the Gun" and "Tales of the "Gun" - the first on the A & E network, and the second, its 39-hour sequel on the History Channel.

When attending antique arms shows, like the Las Vegas extravaganza of Wallace Beinfeld, I now hear more comments made about the television programs - in some of which I've appeared - than on my own books! An executive with the producers of the series for the History and A & E networks, Greystone Productions, has said the ratings for these programs are much higher than had been expected. The series started at four hours, then went to an extra 13, then yet another 13, and most recently - yet another 13!

The Royal Armouries Museum's loan exhibition, based on the recently published Buffalo Bill's Wild West book, will spread the word to a vast international mainstream audience about the wonders of historic guns, and the sharpshooters - like Annie Oakley - of the Wild West shows. This is all positive, and reflects a deep interest throughout our culture in firearms. Following its opening this May, in Leeds, the exhibition travels over a two-year period to the Autry Museum of Western Heritage, the National Cowboy Hall of Fame, and the Tennessee State Museum.

The future of firearms will not be easy. Those who want to take away our firearms rights are powerful, and have no qualms about being dishonest to get their way. We must be more sophisticated, and present the best possible image. The key will be in one word: education.

Gun companies will be a major factor in all of this, and - the misguided major city mayors' suits notwithstanding - are in a much more powerful position than the average private citizen. One of the things that impresses me about Beretta, as an example, is its unique stature as the world's oldest industrial company. The Beretta elegance and Italian style, beautiful guns, and continental flavor - all show-cased in strikingly beautiful New York and Dallas galleries - have been instrumental in bringing more influential people into the shooting sports. Make guns fashionable, the way they were in Annie Oakley's day, and we have won back much of our lost territory.

One of the positive things to come out of all the strife over guns is that the field of firearms is far better organized than ever before in history. More and more people are realizing that we are right, and the other side is wrong. Groups like the National Rifle Association, the National Shooting Sports Foundation, The American Shooting Sports Council, Ducks Unlimited and Safari Club International (including its "Sportsmen Against Hunger" program) are all effective instruments in the battle to protect our right to firearms ownership.

Vital to gaining support in this battle is reaching a largely overlooked audience - namely women, many of whom vote, but few of whom have been properly introduced to the world of firearms. Here again, the world of collecting has a strong appeal, because women are attracted to the beauty of collectors' firearms, and to the history.

The *Blue Book of Gun Values* is part of this vital campaign toward understanding and victory, and features yet another appeal of firearms - these wonderful objects tend to escalate in values, i.e., the profit motive.

Finally, the world of re-enactors, including organized competitions like Cowboy Action Shooting, has a position in the front line of the great gun battle. More shooting ranges are needed, more places for expanding our audience, and our base of gun-owners.

Firearms are our most treasured heritage as Americans. We can take pride in entering battle to preserve that legacy for future generations. That battleground will be the most important many of us will ever experience. Thank goodness for the art and craftsmanship, history, mechanics and romance of collectors guns - all powerful ingredients to help educate the media and the public in our noble cause. ∎

Robert Delfay
President & CEO
National Shooting Sports Foundation

Perhaps never before in our nation's history has the value of firearms been so debated as in this last decade of the 20th century. "Value," in this context, is not about the worth of individual firearms as found in this fascinating and useful 20th Anniversary Edition *Blue Book of Gun Values*, but about the value we attach to responsible firearms ownership.

Needless to say, at the National Shooting Sports Foundation (NSSF) we value the right to own and use firearms highly, and we are working diligently to see that our shooting sports heritage is preserved for the next generation and beyond.

NSSF's chartered mission is *to promote a better understanding of and more active participation in the shooting sports.* As an industry trade organization, we have been fulfilling that mission since 1961 through many different programs. Because of the current climate surrounding firearms, however, I believe NSSF and its programs have never been needed more.

While the shooting sports continue to grow in popularity, particularly in the target shooting and women's shooting segments, the image of the firearm, largely defined by the media and our urban-based society, has taken a beating. So, ironically, this is at once a time of great potential for the shooting sports, as well as a time for great concern about them.

NSSF has identified two critical points for maintaining our shooting sports heritage in the United States – attracting new participants to our sports and regaining our rightful, responsible image. We're working on the former by continuing tried-and-true programs such as our award-winning education videos for schools and by developing new initiatives like our exciting STEP OUTSIDE™ program. We're attacking the image problem with the most aggressive public education effort in history – an effort we've called "Taking Charge of Tomorrow."

Let's talk about the public education campaign first.

This year marks the beginning of a new outreach program NSSF has undertaken in partnership with the Porter Novelli communications agency. A highlight of this multi-million dollar public relations campaign is a series of advertisements that will reach opinion-makers in our society. It is hoped that in the long run, these "intellectual elite" - university professors, authors, columnists, lecturers - will take a fresh look (or first look) at the shooting sports, understand them better, and become more accepting of them. Gradually, their opinions will trickle down to students, readers and voters.

This communications effort, approved by the NSSF Board of Governors last year, was prompted because for too long our industry has allowed its adversaries to frame the discussion and the debate. However, with comments like " . . . I don't have any knowledge on it to really make a good opinion," influential Americans tell us that the debate is not closed and there is still an opportunity to tell our side. We intend to seize this opportunity and tell our story widely.

Meanwhile, the backbone of NSSF's work is its programs promoting the shooting sports at the grassroots level.

The program with the most potential for attracting newcomers to our sports is STEP OUTSIDE, which encourages sportsmen and sportswomen to introduce first-timers to the traditional outdoor sports of target shooting, hunting, archery and fishing. Any sportsman can participate in STEP OUTSIDE – simply ask a friend, daughter, business associate or neighbor to "step outside" with you to try a favorite outdoor sport. A Roper-Starch survey has showed that over 100 million Americans would accept an invitation to participate in one of these traditional outdoor sports – the compelling statistic that led to the formation of STEP OUTSIDE. The program's concept has been referred to as "brilliant in its simplicity and its flexibility," since it can be one person introducing one person, one employer hosting 100 employees, or one state agency hosting an open house for thousands.

NSSF's many programs range from the high-profile Chevy Truck "Shooting Sports . . . America" series on ESPN, which brings the shooting sports into the homes of millions of viewers, to our understated shooting range development services, which ensure there will be inviting, comfortable facilities for all shooters to enjoy in the future.

Before highlighting some of these programs, I'd like to mention that NSSF is the creator and owner of the SHOT SHOW, the largest trade show of its kind in the world. Begun in 1979, the Shooting, Hunting and Outdoor Trade (SHOT) Show now welcomes 1,400 exhibiting companies and an average of 30,000 industry professionals to this annual four-day event.

There is such diversity among NSSF's many programs that we find it helpful to refer to them as *communication* initiatives and *participation* initiatives – both essential to the future viability of the shooting sports.

Examples of our *communication* programs include our promotional and safety literature publications. "Welcome to the Shooting Sports" and "Firearms Safety Depends On You" are just two of more than 45 titles available free, or at modest cost, to individuals and organizations. Our "Un-endangered Species" and "Wildlife for Tomorrow" educational videos have been distributed to some 100,000 schools across the country. A new magazine, *The Range Report*, supplies useful information to managers and operators of shooting ranges/clubs. And for the last several years, NSSF has brought together leaders of the industry and state agencies to discuss mutual concerns and plan for the future at the Shooting Sports Summit.

On the *participation* side, in addition to STEP OUTSIDE, is the Chevy Truck SPORTSMAN'S TEAM CHALLENGE®, a made-for-TV shooting competition; a 4-H Shooting Sports program and International Hunter Education Association program, both supported by NSSF to provide youth and safety instruction; target inserts in *Boys' Life* and *Scouting* magazines that promote participation through an awards system; the Women's Shooting Sports Foundation, which introduces thousands of women each year to the shooting sports; and Summer Biathlon, a warm-weather version of biathlon created by NSSF that introduces running enthusiasts to target shooting and which has the potential to become an official Olympic sport by the 2004 Games.

Recently, challenges to our industry have led the NSSF Board of Governors to establish the Hunting and Shooting Sports Heritage Fund. The fund is based on 1% of hunting- and shooting-related sales and will support the public education effort and a response to politically motivated lawsuits filed against the industry.

While such large efforts as the Heritage Fund are sometimes needed to help us safeguard our 200-year-old traditions, the best way to insure the continuation of our shooting sports heritage is by introducing someone to the fun and enjoyment of shooting and having that person become a lifelong advocate of the shooting sports. Teaching responsible and safe gun ownership goes hand and hand with that partnership.

With your help, NSSF believes it will overcome the challenges of today and that the shooting sports industry will be not only a viable recreation, but also an extremely popular one, in the 21st century.

(If you would like to know more about NSSF's programs, check out our Web site at www.nssf.org, or call 203-426-1320.) ∎

A Manufacturer's Perspective

right, **James Z. Skildum** - Executive Vice President, Magnum Research Inc.

left, **Douglas A. Evans** - President/COO, Magnum Research Inc.

middle, **Dinner!**

Magnum Research, Inc. is not a manufacturer in the absolute; we do not own factories and machinery. We do own patents, concepts, and proprietary intellectual property for unique firearms and firearms accessories that are manufactured for us by the best sub-contractors worldwide. We are in the truest sense a marketing company, which strives to bring new concepts to firearms that meet the changing demands of the shooting/hunting public.

The past twenty years has seen significant changes in market demands and available technology. The late 1970's saw "make my day" and the Model 29 S&W - "the world's most powerful handgun" - it was a time of increased demand and supply shortages. The Model 66 S&W was the most coveted law enforcement product of the time. The early 1980's were a period of growth for the semi-auto handguns. The new Desert Eagle pistol from Magnum Research, Inc., was introduced in 1984 and still remains a revolutionary product. This semi-auto is a gas-operated pistol that reliably feeds and extracts standard .357 Mag. & .44 Mag. rimmed cartridges (including the new, powerful .50AE Mag.).

In the late 1980's, 9mm semi-autos began to be looked at as an alternative to revolvers, and then our government, in its infinite wisdom, decided to switch to a NATO compatible sidearm. Out with the Colt 1911, and in with the high-capacity Beretta Model 92 - the rush was on. Firearms power was substituted for stopping power and both consumers and law enforcement embraced the concept. Millions of high capacity 9mms entered the market, but guess what? Again, our government determined in 1994, that we had to stop shooting after 11 rounds. Bill Clinton, our "firearms salesman of the year", created a consumer frenzy to purchase products, many soon to be banned. The U.S. firearms industry sold virtually everything that could be produced - we were all marketing geniuses.

The inevitable market collapse of 1995 & 1996 saw manufacturers scrambling to understand what the consumer might want to buy. Stopping power (read .45 ACP semi-autos and .357 Mag. & .44 Mag. Revolvers) was back on top. The increase in the number of states with "shall issue" concealed carry laws has created a growing market for compact, lightweight, and concealable 9mms and .40 S&Ws. Consumers are now buying a variety of handguns to suit different requirements.

A rather quiet, but significant trend, is the growing popularity of handgun hunting, a market segment that Magnum Research, Inc. has paid special attention to. The Desert Eagle pistol in .44 Mag. & .50 AE Mag., and the Lone Eagle pistol (chambered in 15 calibers from .223 to .30-06) are exceptional hunting handguns. Other companies such as Thompson Center and Freedom Arms have also been producing fine products for handgun hunting, and have now been joined by Weatherby, Savage and Taurus in producing powerful and accurate hunting handguns for all big game.

Firearms manufacturing today is like every other industry; competitive pressure to hold and reduce costs has meant millions of dollars invested in state of the art machinery, processes and materials. Magnum Research's patented Magnum Lite graphite barrels for both centerfire and rimfire rifles are a good example. Six times stiffer than steel, better heat dissipation, and reduced weight brings rifle performance to a new height of accuracy and performance. Polymers and exotic metals like titanium are now common in state of the art firearms - and there is a lot more to come in the 21st century.

The future of the shooting sports is all of our responsibility. We must continue to support the many conservation organizations with our time and money. The anti-gun, anti-hunting crowd is well organized and well financed, and they are not going to give up. To succeed and prosper, we must be politically active. We may not be able to change the antis, but we must educate the majority of increasing urban Americans that hunting and shooting sports are legitimate activities for responsible citizens, that the social contract (living law-abiding lives) we've embraced for over 200 years is as valid today as when the founders wrote the Bill of Rights.

It is not our fault that failed liberal social policies have created an underclass of poor, uneducated urban citizens with no social contract at all - the rule of law is that crooks don't care about social responsibility. Personal responsibility means obeying and respecting the law, and working intelligently with our legislators to change law when appropriate. In November 1998, Minnesota voters overwhelmingly passed a constitutional amendment "to forever preserve the right to hunt and fish - in accordance to the law" with a full 77% yes vote. Responsible citizens can effect change.

The greatest danger to our future is apathy; the anti-attacks continue to escalate. Mayor Daley of Chicago is suing the gun industry for damages to his underclass of dysfunctional people. As ludicrous as it sounds, he is blaming the gun industry for his failure to enforce federal, state, and local law. But more than that, he's ignoring the people who don't share the same social contract as we do. In my own opinion, that is unconscionable. The freedoms we enjoy come at a price, we must continue to pay that price, subscribe to the same social contact, so that all Americans can be free to exercise their freedom responsibly.

Firearms manufacturers continue to research and develop the most efficient and user friendly products possible. It is in the manufacturer's best interest to produce products that perform reliably and safely, it is in the industry's best interest to comply with all standards of performance, both those established by the industry and government regulators. And it is in the industry's best interest to provide the firearms consumer with the best information on how to properly and responsibly use a firearm. The industry whole-heartedly supports firearm education and training - emphasizing the responsible use, in accordance with law, of products, which by their design, is the potential of lethal use. Firearms consumers must personally accept the awesome responsibility of firearm ownership, to act at all times in a manner that is safe to them and to society, and to act in accordance with the laws by which we are governed.

The threat to the firearms industry can only be strengthened by responsible firearms owners. Today's manufacturers, distributors, and dealers are doing an excellent job educating firearms consumers on understanding firearms and how to use them safely. Magnum Research provides a cable lock, free with all its firearms purchases (this is also available to any customer who currently owns a Magnum Research firearm product). It is, however, only the firearm owner who can make the necessary decisions to safely store and use a firearm responsibly. We are the final ultimate safety device, and every individual firearms owner is ultimately responsible for a gun's lawful or unlawful use. The acceptance of this personal responsibility is the essence of our social contract as enumerated in our constitution.

A Wholesaler's Perspective

Bryan Tucker

Davidson's is one of the oldest wholesalers in the gun business, founded during the Great Depression in 1932. From humble beginnings as wholesaler of used auto parts, Davidson's has continued to evolve and fine tune it's operations to become known as the industry's firearms specialist and for offering unique and perhaps, evolutionary services.

President of Davidson's since 1991, Bryan Tucker is very active in the firearms industry and is currently serving a two-year term as the President of the National Association of Sporting Goods Wholesalers and as a Governor on the Board of of the National Shooting Sports Foundation.

The firearms business has undergone many changes during the last 20 years, increasingly profound as the product moves from the manufacturer to the end consumer. This period saw its most dramatic change in the retail environment. The long gun market saw the emergence of discount mass-merchants such as Wal-Mart and K-mart play increasingly dominant roles, while the hand gun market was left largely to specialty gun shops and sporting good retailers.

Prior to this period, the local hardware, general merchandise, and department/catalog stores such as Sears and JCPenney were major "players" in the retail firearms market. Many factors led to the abandonment of the firearms category by these enterprises. Perhaps the most notable were profit margin erosion due to the increased "discounters" market share, new competition from the emergence of "specialty" stores, and an increasingly negative perception of firearms. This profound change in the firearms retail "landscape" led additionally to dramatic changes in the wholesale distribution segment of the firearms market.

One very significant change that occurred in wholesale firearms distribution during the late 1970's and early 1980's was a large exodus by hardware wholesalers. These wholesalers saw their customers increasingly "de-emphasizing" the firearms category and could not afford to divert and dilute their sales and marketing efforts to include the service of the emerging specialty shops. At the same time these emerging firearms "specialists" were giving rise to large, "shooting sports wholesalers" whose focus and expertise additionally contributed to the exodus by the hardware wholesalers.

Many of the competitive advantages enjoyed by this new breed of wholesaler could also be attributed to changes in the sales and distribution methods. With cost savings created from the wide implementation of 800 and Watts long distance services, coupled with the increasing use of low cost "parcel delivery", this "new breed" could simply out service many of the hardware wholesalers.

Many of the firearms wholesalers who employed wide spread use of these relatively new sales and distribution methods emerged from being defined as a "regional" wholesaler into the new category of being a "national" distributor. In fact, these very services would largely determine a wholesaler's future. These older "regional" wholesalers would generally have a large majority of their sales done by "road warriors" or traveling salesmen calling on accounts throughout his assigned geographic territory. This established system was opposed to the new breed of "national" wholesalers, who would typically have a great portion of their sales done through "inside" sales professionals who could call on the accounts more often and more cost effectively, without geographic limitations. Additionally, the "regional" category would very often utilize its own trucks with scheduled deliveries to customers, while the "national" category would largely ship immediately upon request via the parcel delivery services, often at a lower cost - depending on product mix, shipment volume, and customer proximity. Over the last 10 -15 years, the wholesale firearms marketplace, with a few notable exceptions, has experienced a large consolidation toward this "national" breed of large wholesalers.

The past twenty years has seen many changes in the wholesale firearms market. However, the next 20 years will undoubtedly see more changes in the industry than ever before. The astounding pace of technological advancement is one of the significant factors that will shape the wholesale firearm market. Wholesalers that are most effectively able to harness and assimilate emerging technologies may be able to carve out a real competitive advantage in the years to come. The proliferation of Internet use and the instantaneous availability of information will put more power into the consumer's hand. While being able to electronically shop, consumers can not purchase firearms directly over the internet, and are restricted to purchasing from licensed retail dealers in accordance with all federal, state and local regulations. A potential firearms owner no longer has to scan and read through piles of magazines or drive hundreds of miles looking for information on the firearms they're interested in. They will simply "log on" to the net, and within moments conduct specific product research, market availability, and determine the preferred retailer from which to purchase - and without aggravation or leaving the comforts of home.

Davidson's, the only wholesaler to offer a Guaranteed Lifetime Replacement Warranty, is the first distributor to utilize the power of the Internet in support of our customers, the firearms dealer. In early November 1998, Davidson's launched a new, state-of-the-art website, check out our "Gallery of Guns," (www.galleryofguns.com). This on-line service provides the consumer with the best resource to learn more about the wide range and availability of makes and models offered today, not last month. This site offers detailed specifications, full-color pictures, industry news, market availability and a quick search on thousands of various models. Combine these features with the only Gun E-card feature in the industry, up-to-date special offers, and rebate opportunities from the industry's premier manufacturers, and the site is destined to become a haven for our customer's customer.

Technological advancement is sure to change the firearms industry - but attacks in the regulatory, legislative, and most recently, the litigation arena are sure to impact the legitimate individual gun owner as never before. At the time of this writing, the firearms industry is undergoing an unprecedented onslaught of legal threats. The mayors of New Orleans, Chicago, Bridgeport (CT), Atlanta, and Miami have recently sued the industry's handgun manufacturers. Their allegations accuse handgun manufacturers of knowingly over supplying the firearms market in addition to being negligent in their lack of development of "smart gun" technology. These cases, while somewhat dissimilar in some of their accusations, have one thing in common - the dismissal of the concept of "personal responsibility". They seem determined to set a new legal precedent - that the manufacturers can somehow be held liable for the criminal misuse of their products. Criminals should be swiftly and harshly punished for their crimes, whether it is the illegal use or transfer of firearms, larceny or any offense.

As an individual gun owner, get involved by joining organizations that aim to protect your gun rights, promote the positive aspects of the shooting sports within your community, and be sure to make your voice heard in upcoming elections. Additionally, I would like to ask all of you to support the industry's manufacturers that are working to support you. Recently the National Shooting Sports Foundation formed the "Hunting and Shooting Sports Heritage Fund" where manufacturers are asked to voluntarily contribute 1% of their gross sales to the protection of the nation's great firearms heritage. The participant's products will proudly display a logo pronouncing their involvement. Please support these manufacturers via your purchases!

While destined for great change, the future of the wholesale distribution, as well as all facets of the firearms industry , holds a very promising future. To ensure this future, we must adapt quickly, defend our heritage, and most of all, unite in our constitutionally guaranteed firearms rights and freedoms. ∎

A Rep Group Perspective

Owen J. Brown
President, Owen J. Brown & Associates
Began his firearms industry career in
1959 working in retail stores until 1964.
Spent seven years with a leading west
coast wholesaler of firearms and formed
his own sales rep group in 1971.

An old adage says, "The only thing constant is change". This has certainly been true for the firearms industry over the past 20 years. In an attempt to document these many changes from the standpoint of the manufacturer's sales representative, author and longtime friend Steve Fjestad asked us to give an overview of the last 2 decades in the gun business for this, the 20th Anniversary edition of the *Blue Book of Gun Values.*

Owen Brown & Associates was established in 1971, and has been dedicated to selling and servicing firearms retailers and distributors throughout the western United States. Our rep group represents some of the most prestigious firearms and accessory related companies in our industry. We were fortunate enough to have started our group at a time when the industry was healthy and thriving. This was a time when the NRA was primarily in the business of promoting the shooting sports. Anti-gun and animal rights groups were a vocal minority, considered by many to be a bunch of misguided housefraus with no power to enact policy. Guns had yet to become taboo, and the NRA was not the evil empire in the eyes of the media.

In the 1970's, the western United States boasted a large network of distributors, numerous discount chain stores, automotive & hardware stores, independent retailers, and a few mass merchants who all carried firearms and ammunition. In fact, it seemed as if every town was able to support its own successful firearms retailer. This was a time when the gun business was very healthy. Gun shows flourished. Hunting and shooting sports alike were popular and were supported by many communities. There were a greater number of public lands open to both hunters and shooters alike. The local gun range was often like a social club for the outdoorsman, and the celluloid gun violence was still in check.

As the 1970's progressed however, a gradual change started to take place. Numerous hardware wholesale companies dropped guns and ammunition from their product mix, resulting in automotive and hardware retailers doing the same. A few large retailers such as Gemco and Yellow Front stores disappeared from the marketplace. Independents still thrived, but change was coming.

The urbanization increased in the west, and some shooting areas became private land, or were incorporated into city bounds. Firearms legislation was starting to become more restrictive. Plastic guns, cop killer bullets, assault weapons, and Saturday night specials all became favorite buzzwords of the firearms ignorant media. Hollywood's portrayal of gun violence was starting to spiral out of control, and a growing anti-gun movement was quietly building steam.

The early 1980s witnessed the growth of the big box retailers. Commonly known as "Marts", these retailers presented a new challenge for the independent dealer. Buying groups such as NBS, Sports Inc., and Worldwide formed to enhance the independent retailers buying power, and make them more competitive. In a time of shrinking margins, wholesale companies started to shift their emphasis away from road salesmen and telemarketing became the best way for dealers to purchase inventory at reduced prices.

This period also saw dramatic changes in the firearms distribution in the west. Small to mid-sized firearms wholesale companies were purchased by larger firms as the acquisition fever took hold in the gun industry. Other companies tried to expand westward, only to find themselves closing shop a few years later due to financial difficulties. The remaining West Coast wholesalers shifted their emphasis towards servicing an increasing number of mass marketers and chain accounts while the independent retailer was left to purchase inventory from midwestern wholesalers with strong telemarketing sales forces.

The 1980's brought other changes as well. The 1981 attempted assassination on President Reagan provided the catalyst the anti-gun movement needed to advance their agenda. From this point on, every senseless act of gun violence was proclaimed to be a mandate for more gun laws and further firearms restrictions. The media, always eager for a sound bite, gladly jumped on board with the antis, and further demonized firearms and their owners. Hollywood was continually glorifying gun violence and criminal culture on film. Waiting periods for gun purchases were increasing, and the noose on gun rights was ever tightening. In response, the NRA formed the Institute for Legislative Action (ILA) to combat an increasing stream of gun legislation.

Increasing urbanization and public land closures further limited the number of venues available to the hunter/shooter in the west. Skyrocketing insurance costs and a proliferation of mass merchants created barriers to entering the market for many independent retailers. Those who did enter experienced stagnated sales and many closed down after just a few years of operation.

More and more anti-gun groups began to form during the 1980's. The antis gained their first victories in California by eliminating mountain lion hunting. The non-endangered cougars showed their gratitude with an increasing number of attacks on humans. A proposition to halt all handgun sales in California made it to the state ballot, and was soundly defeated. California's waiting period on gun sales increased to 15 days, as registration fees continued to increase.

Imported guns started to hit the market en mass as the iron curtain fell. SKS rifles, Tokarev pistols, Lee-Enfields, Mausers, and the semi-auto AK-47 were showing up at distributors and retailers in good quantities. The fact that these firearms and their ammunition were readily available at a low retail price fueled sales of these guns in the west.

In the west, the Roberti-Roos assault weapons bill of 1989 passed in California, requiring registration of dozens of military style semi-automatic rifles and pistols. This of course drove price and demand through the roof. Manufacturers responded to this bill by manufacturing rifles and pistols that did not fall within the criteria of an "assault weapon" as designated by Roberti-Roos. In the end, firearms owners protested this bill by mass non-compliance. It is estimated that only 10% of the owners of such firearms ever registered their weapons with the state.

The 1990s ushered in a new presidential administration, and the greatest threat firearms owners have faced to date. It has been said that President Clinton has done more to further the gun business than anyone in the industry could have, and to a degree this certainly was the case in the west. FFL holders increased to an all time high of nearly 330,000. NRA membership hit 3 million. Firearms and magazine sales hit all time highs, as the L.A. riots, the Night Stalker, and pending crime bill had everyone scrambling for guns. The distribution channels were strained during this time as everything anyone could produce was being bought up in record quantities. Firearms and high capacity magazine prices increased in response to this demand.

The crime bill ultimately passed, as did a number of other anti-gun measures in response to incidents like the Stockton schoolyard shooting, Luby's Cafeteria shooting, New York subway shooting, and a number of isolated incidents which impacted America's 20 million responsible gun owners. The importation of surplus military arms from overseas was halted. New magazine production was limited to 10 rounds, and those evil "assault weapons" were now federally regulated. New restrictions on FFL holders have cut their numbers in half over the past 5 years.

The firearms industry is currently under siege from a new threat - the class action lawsuit. Recently, New York City sued every handgun manufacturer for deaths attributed to firearms misuse. Guess what happened in the liberal courts of New York? The antis won. Other major cities in the U.S. are certain to follow New York's lead. Firearms manufacturers, distributors, and retailers may not be legislated out of business, but we could be forced out of business via bankruptcy from a wave of frivolous lawsuits. For this reason, anyone who makes their living from the firearms industry, whether they are a sales rep, salesman, or shop owner, should become a member of the NSSF (National Shooting Sports Foundation). This organization acts as the point man for the industry in legislative circles, bringing together many voices as one. Membership is expensive, but so is a career change.

Additionally, it is extremely important that all gun owners also stand united against all attempts at further anti-gun legislation. It is a must to spend $30 a year to join the NRA. For the cost of 2 boxes of ammunition, you can do your part to help protect the sport you love. After all, once our firearms freedoms are lost, the costs of getting them back will most likely be measured in lives, not dollars.

The past 2 decades have seen a tremendous amount of change in our business. While our industry is still a healthy one, we find that we must now operate by checking behind us often, looking for whatever attack on our gun rights that will be sneaking up on us next. What the future will bring to our industry is unknown. One thing is certain however; change will be a part of the gun business of the 20th century.

■

A Dealer Perspective

JAY'S SPORTING GOODS, INC.
Jeff Poet, President

Jay's has to be one of the best mom-and-pop success stories in sporting goods retailing. Jay's Sporting Goods began humbly in 1968, when Jay Poet converted his one car garage into a gun store. By 1974, the business had been incorporated and moved to a 10,000 square foot building in downtown Clare, which has a population of around 5,000 people in central Michigan. By 1988 Jay's moved to a 36,000 square foot building and added another 50,000 in 1994. Although Jay passed away in 1989, the business is still run by the family, son Jeff, wife Kathy, brother John, mom Arlene, children Stephanie and Derrick. An emphasis on quality staff and products, along with promoting shooting sports to youth and other important groups, has earned Jay's the 1999 Sporting Goods Retailer of the Year award.

What an honor it is to be able to write something that will be put in the *Blue Book of Gun Values*. My mother, Arlene Poet Yost, brother John Poet, and myself Jeff Poet have been the gun and sporting goods business now for nearly 30 years. Of course that put my brother and I in diapers in the early years, but it is all we have ever known. My father Jay Poet started the business out of a one car garage in the late 1960's. In 1989 he succumbed to cancer leaving the three of us and my wife Kathy to run the business. We have seen changes over the years and what a better time than going into the new millennium to reflect on those and also look to the year 2000 and beyond.

The gun business is an exciting and always changing world and in rural northern Michigan it is always closely related to hunting. Guns are always the most fascinating to look back at and see all the changes that have taken place, along with which ones have withstood the test of time to become modern day classics, 10/22's, 700's, M77's, 1100 & 870's, A-Bolt's, 1300's, 500's, 110's and the list goes on. Even with these current production guns, most all of them have incorporated new improved safety mechanisms. Other enhancements over the years to these classics, and new introductions, have been the selection to include synthetic stocks, stainless barrels and actions, muzzle breaks, and totally camouflaged guns. These types of options are rivaling the sales of the traditional wood stocked, blue finished guns. Even though these are not new inventions, they have in the past 10 years increased in popularity with the shooting public to meet the need to improve performance and maintenance. But the most profound changes have taken place in the muzzleloader category. Just thinking back prior to 1985 it is mind boggling the differences in looks and proficiency that have taken place. Formerly selling exclusively sidelock Hawkin style muzzleloaders, today in upwards of 70% of sales are in modern inline, enhanced ignition, muzzleloaders.

The handgun business has changed greatly over the past 20 years. From a time when the .357 and .44 magnum revolvers were king to the semi-auto pistol being today's favorite in popularity. The wheel guns haven't seemed to change as dramatically as the semi. From the standard .22 LR to the .50 cal. Desert Eagle auto there is more selection today than ever before with new caliber's like 40S&W and 10mm. Law enforcement surely lead the way in popularity with the semi-auto. With law enforcement using semi's, this proved to the average citizen the reliability of a semi-auto. Also the advantage of the higher magazine capacity and speed has shown up in more units sold at retail.

Even with all the changes in the guns themselves the greatest change has been in gun regulations and the increasing negative attitude towards firearms in this country. From the initiation of the 4473 form, the Yellow, in 1968 to handgun permits and registration in Michigan, to five day wait, to the FBI NICS background check of today, gun regulations have gotten tougher and tougher for the legitimate retailer to administer. Politicians keep chipping away at the availability of legitimate firearms purchases. It is much harder for gun dealers and gunsmiths to stay in business with the administrative overhead of meeting new and continuously changing regulations.

The national problem, lack of personal responsibility, has cost everyone in their firearms purchases with the cost of product liability passed on in the purchase price. On the other side of that issue are those who are taking responsible gun ownership seriously and purchasing items that weren't readily available or affordable years ago, such as trigger locking devices and lockable storage cabinets or safes. And probably the most impacting measure over the years has been the increased education of the youth in gun safety and operation.

Today things are different than they were twenty years ago and it didn't all come overnight. I have already touched on many of the popular preferences of today. There are always new and changing products on the shelves. Each year we look forward to seeing what the new products are and that's what makes this business fun.

Interactive computer games are extremely popular now and reaches a generally young consumer. Most of these games are quite sophisticated and include everything a real hunting trip would include. Games aren't the only thing popular in the firearms computer world. Developing ballistic charts, coefficients and experimenting with handloads electronically before actually loading them are very popular and have been introduced from the reloading companies. And if you're not aware, the most unique software I have been using recently is the electronic version of *Blue Book of Gun Values* "GunTracker". We have used the *Blue Book* as a bible for trade-ins and informational references in the store for years. I was really impressed with the electronic version and have also logged all my personal guns on the computer I have at home. It truly is the best software for keeping track of not only your guns but their values also, and the reports are fantastic.

Things are not only different in the world of products but also in our hunting patterns. The single biggest issue in this area seems to be the lack of access of land to hunt. Leasing seems to be a very popular method to obtain an area to hunt, but can be very costly. For the survival of hunting we need to make sure that there is accessible land to all that want the opportunity to hunt. There are many great conservation clubs out there to help us hold on to and grow our opportunities to pursue game such as Ducks Unlimited, National Wild Turkey Federation, Rocky Mountain Elk Foundation, Pheasants Forever, Whitetails Unlimited, Quail Unlimited and many more. Women are afield in larger numbers than ever before and we all need to make sure we make them feel welcome. They are becoming the only influence in many homes over the youth of today, and unfortunately up until recently the shooting industry hasn't given them much reason to feel good about shooting sports. At the retail level the selection of products has been limited but growing all the time to better meet a woman's needs.

I don't believe there will be the same amount of new products introduced over the next couple of years as we have been accustomed to seeing, because most of the gun manufactures will be putting their resources into defending themselves legally and politically. Also, many believe that new products are not the answer to long term survival, but introducing the shooting sports to markets outside the traditional. More money will be spent on introducing women, children and minorities to the shooting sports. You will see more cooperation on the part of retailers, manufactures, ranges, and government wildlife agencies to work together to sponsor events and raise the awareness to the general public about how much fun the shooting sports can be.

The most troubling trend started in 1998, when large cities began to sue the firearms manufactures in similar style to that of the tobacco industry. There is such a difference in the two and in the outcome of the proper use of the products. We all could face a very serious loss if the lawsuits continue, with no firearms to shoot, collect, hunt with, defend ourselves, or anything else. The anti-gunners are attacking everyone that engages in the commerce of firearms, including manufacturers, distributors, and retailers. This group of business channels don't have the deep pockets of the Tobacco industry and things will be over much sooner if quick, united, and decisive action isn't taken.

So if you don't belong to the NRA, join now. Understanding that not everyone agrees on all methods all the time, we need not be fragmented at this time and throw the baby out with the bath water. The NRA has just begun to assist the industry in the defense of these unreasonable law suits brought by the large cities. We have as retailer two organizations that represent us from an economic viewpoint and they are National Shooting Sports Foundation (NSSF) and the American Shooting Sports Council (ASSC). Write or call your congress men and women to let them know your opinion on each gun issue that comes up in the future to insure our privilege to our shooting sports. ∎

A Dealer Perspective

Old Town Station, Ltd.

Antique Arms
by Appointment - 492-3000
9300 Renner, Ste. B, North Entrance

Jim Supica, Old Town Station, Lenexa KS
913-492-3000

Ok, I have finally tumbled to the fact that I am to Blue Book Publications, Inc. what Stuttering John is to the Howard Stern Show — a freelance correspondent given assignments more for the entertainment value of watching him thrash about rather than for any anticipated enlightenment. Why else would Steve Fjestad tell me to write a treatise on the last two decades of Gun Collecting?

Trying to describe the trends and futures of gun collecting is like the blind men trying to describe the elephant. To the one handling the trunk, an elephant is like a snake. To the one with the leg, an elephant is like a tree, and so forth. As far as gun collecting goes, I'm fairly sure I've had firm hold of the tail for the last twenty years, so I consulted with some dealers, collectors and enthusiasts who are hanging on to more savory portions of elephantine anatomy to help with this synopsis.

EVOLUTION OF GUN SHOWS. The last twenty years has seen the evolution of two distinct types of guns shows. In "the good old days", gun shows tended to be shows for collectors and part time dealers who were buying and trading amongst themselves to enhance their collections. From these roots, shows have split into "Collector Shows" and "Commercial Shows".

Collector shows still have a predominance of collector guns offered for sale. Their hallmarks include some or all of the following — sponsorship by an NRA affiliated collector club, display competition, and restriction on what type of items can be sold (usually at a minimum restricting table material to guns & gun related material, and sometimes limiting the types of guns that can be offered). There seem to be more full time professional dealers traveling the show circuit than in the past, and often many of the transactions at these collector shows are between dealers, who may be buying or selling for a collector client.

Commercial shows have sprung up all over the country in the past two decades. They tend to be run by commercial promoters, often offer a wide range of modern current production firearms, and often allow a wide range of non-gun related "flea market" material. In part, it is probably the increasing popularity of general "flea market" type forums that explains the rise of commercial shows. Modern folklore is that you get the bargains at the weekend bazaars. Some store front gun dealers have taken to setting up at gun shows on the weekends, selling the same merchandise there that they offer at their stores, due to the public's perception that if it's sold off a folding table, it must be a good buy.

The future of shows - Watch for increasing assaults on shows by socially liberal administrations. Commercial gun shows may be vulnerable to a revised interpretation of the administrative definition of "gun shows" by the BATF that would eliminate dealer sales at commercially promoted shows.

AUCTIONS — One of the most dramatic changes in gun collecting over the last twenty years has been the emergence of cataloged auctions as possibly the leading method for sale and purchase of high end collectible arms. Some dealers have turned into auctioneers as this market expands. The Future - An argument could be made that there are more "live" auction formats available than the market can support. This could result in both opportunities and risks for collectors. The risk is that a few unethical auctioneers faced with increased competition may stretch the credibility of their descriptions (remembering that the fine print in the Terms and Conditions usually disclaims any guarantee that the descriptions are accurate).   The opportunity is that it is often possible to pick up bargains at auctions where the number of guns significantly exceeds the buying power of the audience. Look for mail auctions & internet auctions to expand (see below).

NEW SALES FORUMS — The well-indexed *Gun List* classified ads paper came to be a major force in peddling used & collectible guns over the past two decades. It provides a handy forum for buyers and sellers, especially for discontinued or used modern guns selling in the $150 to $700 range. The venerable *Shotgun News* has recently switched to the indexed format. There has also been something of a resurgence of mail order catalogs published by individual dealers. The Future — The single biggest trend in the future of Gun Collecting is the emergence of the internet as a viable medium for buying and selling. In addition to individual dealer/collector web sites, forums such as Guns America and other on-line sales & auction sites promise to soon dominate the collecting market.

CONDITION OVER RARITY — The recent decades have seen more emphasis on high condition guns rather than the older interest in rare specimens regardless of condition. The Future - Some knowledgeable dealers and collectors predict a pendulum swing back to an interest in rarity.

THE COWBOYS ARE COMING! Especially in the past 5 years, the fun and emerging sport of Cowboy Action Shooting through organizations such as SASS and NCOWS has increased the interest in guns from the 1860's to 1890's era, along with a demand for "shooters" from these eras, driving the market values for these guns up. The Future - Some would say that this sport has peaked. This, combined with increased availability and variety of reproductions which may safely and reliably be fired with modern smokeless ammunition may lead to a softening of demand for these guns.

COLLECTING PRIVATE RYAN — As "the Last Great Generation" ages, there is an increased interest in the history and firearms of World War II. These guns also represent an affordable collecting field for younger collectors who may not be able to afford Henrys and Pattersons. The Future — Look for this trend to continue.

WIDE OPEN FIELDS - In the olden days, "collector guns" tended to mean percussion & Single Action Army Colts, brass frame Winchesters, Kentucky Rifles, and, for the "young & wild" crowd, Lugers.   Over the last twenty years, there has been a greater appreciation for a much wider range of firearms.   The Future - some prominent dealers report the following as hot fields for the immediate future — American swords, percussion revolvers, Rugers, and frontier S&W's (and no, it wasn't me who made that prediction). Mentioned as slowing down — auto pistols.

ALL THAT GLITTERS . . .   The last twenty years saw the collapse of the commemorative firearms market.   These "instant collectables" were popular in the 1960's and 70's with a generation of collectors who wanted affordable decorated guns.   The collectors of the 80's and 90's have generally shunned them, resulting in a stagnant market.   Some see a similar trend with modern custom engraved guns, suggesting that decorated guns are a waning trend (although antique and classic engraved guns seem to continue to enjoy popularity.   The Future - a comeback? If commemoratives appeal to you, they still represent an affordable collecting field.   It's even more possible that modern custom engraved guns done by good engravers in recent years may represent a buying opportunity.

CONVERTS, RECONVERTS, DECONVERTS - This has been a long term psychological disorder among collectors, and it continues.... Flintlocks which were converted to percussion muskets are converted back to flintlocks .... "Cavalry" SAA's which the Army converted to short barrel mixed number "Artilleries" are converted back to "Cavalry" models ..... Percussion revolvers converted to cartridge are converted back while reproduction percussion revolvers are converted to cartridge for Cowboy Action shooters ... Barrels that were bobbed to clear a holster easier or carry better on horseback are "stretched" to their original length .... U.S. WWII arms that were refurbished by the military in the Cold War are reconverted to WWII configuration ... The Future — KNOCK IT OFF! Enough is enough. Leave those fine old guns with period of use modifications AS YOU FIND THEM. Honestly!

SCANDALOUS FAKERY BECOMES RESPECTABLE RESTORATION - I guess this was predictable along with the increased emphasis on condition of the past few years. As the demand for "as new" guns outstripped the supply, a cottage industry of restoring old guns sprang up, and continues to become more and more sophisticated and capable of recreating the original appearance of a firearm. The Future — Expertly restored guns are redefining the condition grading systems. The values for professionally restored guns are finding their own price level somewhere between high condition original finish, and low condition or inexpertly refinished guns. Professional restorations, along with "old" refinishes and factory or arsenal refinishes are establishing a set of market values above what the traditional NRA condition definitions say a refinished gun should bring. Also look for the availability of expert restoration to shake confidence in the high premium assigned to old "mint" guns, unless they come with a long pedigree showing they have not been tampered with.

THE IMPACT OF LEGISLATION — No question that gun collecting has been repeatedly whipsawed by the ravages of the latest political fashion. The past two decades have seen such legislation-driven phenomena as the reintroduction of affordable military arms with the lifting of the import ban, the handgun buying frenzy preceding "Brady I" (and the sales slump following it), and the skyrocketing values of "assault rifles" and hi-cap magazines as soon as their manufacture was prohibited. The Future — Here are the two Prime, and conflicting, trends —

1. Tell someone he can't have something, he'll want to have it.
2. Make someone think the government is going to outlaw his stuff, he'll want to dump it.

There is little question that gun owners' rights continue to be assaulted by legislation and administrative intervention. There are some pessimistic dealers and collectors who believe that ownership of "modern" firearms will come under greater and greater restriction, and who are quietly shifting their inventory or collection to pre-1899 "antiques". Others would argue that an attack on modern gun ownership will inevitably be accompanied or closely followed by similar restrictions on the currently unregulated antiques.

BREAKING UP THE BIG COLLECTIONS - For much of this recent period, the complaint has been that "all the good stuff has been squirreled away". Some see this trend reversing itself in the last few years. One prominent dealer notes that the truly great collections have been broken up, and that there are many more collections with 2 or 3 great pieces in them rather than a limited number of great collections corralling the major pieces in a given field. There may be several reasons for this. The continuing increasing values provide a strong incentive to sell. A generation of collectors is aging and liquidating their collections or having them liquidated by their estates. The Future - Look for this trend to continue as more collections compiled during the 60's and 70's are liquidated, usually at auction.

THE INFORMATION EXPLOSION — You are holding in your hand one of the artifacts that has most shaped gun collecting over the past two decades. The publishing and continuing refinement of authoritative price guides, with perhaps *Blue Book* as the industry standard, has given new and experienced collectors access to general information that once was the province of only the most sophisticated collectors and dealers. It has also given a level of comfort with the enduring and quantifiable value of collectible guns. The body of information continues to expand as more collectors and researchers publish more detailed books on their respective fields. The Future - There's a dark cloud on the horizon, as some newer collectors overlook the traditional advice of "Before you buy a gun, buy a book". One prominent collector noted that today, all you need to do to be a collector is show up at an auction with a bunch of money. Educate yourself first.

THE GREYING OF THE GUN SHOW - "Where are the young collectors?" is the most common lament of the collecting community. This problem goes far beyond wondering who's going to be around to buy your collection when it's time to sell. The failure to instill an appreciation of guns and their unique role in our history jeopardizes our children's and grandchildren's future freedoms.

This may be partially alarmist, as few young collectors can afford the high prices the "classic" collectible arms are bringing these days. There are lots of future collectors buying their first SKS or military surplus rifle or police trade-in revolver. However, it is a legitimate concern that so-called "mainstream" media demonizes gun owners and collectors while glamorizing irresponsible gun handling and irrational gun violence, potentially having a tremendous negative impact on what should be the "next generation" of collectors. Further, shooting opportunities for young people are fewer and fewer.

The Future — Is entirely up to you. My best "gun experience" this year was when I hired my son's scout patrol to help inventory a big collection of military guns. These 11 to 13 year old boys were instinctively fascinated by the guns, as boys have always been, and were quick to learn and practice safe firearms handling for their chore. They asked about the history and function of the guns, and spent as much time admiring them as they did putting them in storage. Each went home happy, with a few dollars in their pocket, a new appreciation of guns, AND a gen-you-wine bayonet with which to start their OWN collection.

Do yourself and the future a favor — Teach a daughter to shoot. Take a nephew and his friend to a gun show. Ask your grandson to help you wipe down your collection. Don't push, guide. Let them ask, and teach as they are ready to learn. Reward responsible gun habits with gun handling privileges. And always always teach safety and respect for firearms. You'll feel good. And you'll be doing good.

Anyway, that's how I see it, reporting here from the tail of the elephant.

Acknowledgements — Thanks to the following individuals for sharing their expertise — Wally Beinfield, Jeff Faintich, John Gangel, Kurt House, C.R. Suydam, Fred Sweeney, and Joe Wanenmacher. ◼

Carnac the Mag.-nificent.

Consumers

A Working Mom's Perspective, by Trudy Weise

Trudy Weise

Trudy Weise is an elementary school teacher that loves to be in the great outdoors. She enjoys spending time with her family hunting, and fishing.

Growing up in the city, in a non-hunting family, didn't stifle my love of the great outdoors. I was the type of child that was always catching, collecting, and chasing my sister with nature's treasures. So it wasn't unusual that I married an outdoorsman. I remember buying my first gun, a 20 ga., single shot Winchester, to go on a trap shooting date. That led to other guns, my favorite being my 30-30 Winchester. This love of hunting and shooting began as a teenager, and has continued for over 2 decades.

My love of hunting is two-fold. I immensely enjoy the solitude of spending time in nature. Each year deer hunting, I delight in watching all of the creatures that frequent the area of my tree stand, as much as I relish waiting for the unexpecting deer to appear in my sights. But foremost, I must admit, that my true reason for hunting is the bounty. I prefer to eat wild game, so each year I'm pleased if anyone shoots game, for I know there will be wonderful meals ahead.

As a woman and mother, I fancy seeing the excitement on my family's faces when they have a successful hunt. The pride in their eyes and their delightful stories are heartwarming. I was unable to hunt this year, due to extensive knee surgery, and truly missed it more than I expected. I was with them on the hunts, but was unable to accompany them into the woods. As the guns sounded, I could hardly wait for the results. Our family spends much time in pursuit of the cunning grouse. Then the other family members, our two hunting dogs, join us. It is invigorating to see the whole family working together for a cause - dinner - and enjoying themselves immensely.

During any shooting or hunting event, the handling of firearms requires a healthy respect, and I have comfort in knowing that my family is well educated in gun safety. Unfortunately, I've been on the firing range with children who have had little or no gun safety education, so I know its relevance. I believe that education is the key to keeping guns safely in the public's hands. As an educator, I strongly urge parents and fellow teachers to include gun safety in their children's education. There are numerous gun safety classes, Internet resources, and videos available from local police departments. I've used these resources in my classroom, with children as young as Kindergarten, and they are excellent. Even non-hunting parents should enroll their children in gun safety classes. My parents did, and I never regretted it.

I realize that all educators may not possess my opinions of firearms, and have witnessed comments from co-workers such as "Deer hunters should be strung up along with their deer", but I think that both hunting and shooting are excellent sports to be involved in. Each allows for personal challenge and growth, which can be experienced by both genders of all ages.

More shooting and hunting events like "take your kid hunting day" should be offered by area gun clubs, the DNR, or other associations. More shooting classes for all ages should be considered by organizations such as Community Education. These classes could also be offered after school, or in physical education classes. They should definitely be advertised as duo-gender sports. If the male only stereotype is broken, we'll see more female hunters and shooters in the next generation. Good hunting to you! ■

Viewpoints
Teenage Impressions, by Jed Weise

Jed Weise

Jed Weise is a 16 year old who loves hunting and shooting as much as baseball. Grouse and deer are his all-time favorite hunts.

When I was eight years old, I began to shoot and hunt. I started out with a Crosman BB gun that my dad bought for my brother and me. Whether it was shooting at tin cans, hand drawn targets, or squirrels, I was hooked. Hunting became a major part of my life, and it has stuck with me ever since. I now hunt deer every year with my family and friends, and I hunt grouse in northern Minnesota with my family and two dogs, Hawk & Moose.

When I compare shooting and hunting, I would have to say that they are both great sports. They can both be competitive sports, and they can both be sports in which you relax and enjoy times with your hunting and shooting friends. If I would have to choose between the two, I would choose hunting because I enjoy the greater element of surprise involved, and when you get home you can have a delicious meal, that is, if you don't get skunked.

If for some reason I could no longer hunt, I would still be interested in guns and shooting. I would definitely join a shooting league, because my interests wouldn't change. I don't think that very many people would give up their guns just because they couldn't hunt. I know I wouldn't, and I know my friends wouldn't give up their guns either.

Many of my friends think that hunting is a great thing to do. Those are the ones that I know wouldn't give up their guns for anything. Not all of my friends use firearms, though. Some bow hunt and they still feel that hunting is a great sport. It's always fun to share hunting stories with friends who are hunters. My other friends don't disagree with hunting; they just weren't introduced to it when they were younger. It's hard to make someone a hunter when they didn't shoot or hunt as a kid. They just don't know how much fun it really is.

To get more kids interested in shooting, there should be more support for youth shooting leagues and more programs geared towards youth. One of the best programs is "take your kid hunting day". There should be more days like this that are designated for hunting with kids. This would greatly increase the number of youth getting involved with shooting and hunting.

I enjoy owning and caring for my guns, and hope that no one will ever take them away from me. I also think that guns are great collectables. I think that everyone should own a gun, so he/she can get involved in shooting and hunting.

I recently bought a Benelli Sport 12 ga. I would have to say that by far this is my favorite gun. Not only is the Benelli Sport the coolest, but it is the most comfortable and smoothest gun I've ever shot. When shooting machine thrown clay pigeons in the woods last fall, I hit 62 in a row, and it was the first time I ever shot the gun. For these reasons, the Benelli Sport is my favorite.

I enjoy having guns, and I also have fun shooting and hunting. Hopefully, the privilege of hunting is never taken away from people, and youth will always have a chance to hunt, too. ∎

Moose, a Golden Retriever, and Hawkins, a Springer Spaniel are Jed's favorite hunting buddies. They can hardly wait to hit the woods together.

A Legal Perspective

Evan F. Nappen, esq.

Face it. The anti-gunners have made significant progress in diminishing our gun rights. So what's a collector to do? Easy. If you can't beat 'em - at least make money and build your collection. Savvy gun investors already profited on items like High Capacity magazines, Russian and Chinese "military imports", "assault weapons" and even machine guns (1986 ban). All firearms are going to increase in value simply because of the civil litigation against the industry. Consider the following:

THE TOP 12 REASONS WE ARE LOSING OUR GUN RIGHTS & INVESTMENT OPPORTUNITIES HAVE NEVER BEEN BETTER

1. Gun owners are apathetic. Of the estimated 60 million plus gun owners in the United States, only about 5% even belong to the NRA.
2. The Federal Law is the minimum gun control law for the U.S. and the states are encouraged to add on as many more as they want. No anti-gun law is too extreme. There is no cap or maximum other than ineffective and unenforced "Right to Bear Arms". (P.S. This right isn't even supposed to be infringed.)
3. Since 1934, all we have done is lose ground. Anti-gun salami tactics have effectively worked by taking our rights away piece by piece (assault weapons bans, waiting periods, school zones, registration, trigger locks, licensing, handgun bans, large-capacity magazine bans, etc.).
4. We already have over 20,000 "infringements" (anti-gun laws) discouraging new would-be gun owners from joining our ranks.
5. Back door gun confiscation has begun utilizing "domestic violence" laws and other types of forfeiture without any organized opposition from gun owners.
6. Anti-gun bias, slurs, and slander permeate our culture. Gun owners are called and/or associated with being: Gun Nuts, Rambos, Survivalists, Right Wing Militias, Paranoid Wackos, Rednecks, and of course, worst of all, Postal Workers.
7. Political correctness has stunted acceptance and even discussion of hunting, target shooting, personal protection or gun collecting.
8. The media is overwhelmingly committed to the anti-gun cause. When was the last time you saw a pro-gun newscast, television show, movie or newspaper article? Yet, there is no end to the misuse of guns portrayed in the media.
9. Lying, gutless, elitist, authoritarian politicians claiming to be our friends, and then stabbing us in the back by taking action against Gun Rights.
10. Systematically discouraging our youth from recreational shooting, such as hunting or target shooting.
11. Disappearing hunting lands and the closing down of target ranges for noise, pollution, and liability has caused a decline in licensed hunters and new firearm owners.
12. Abuse of process through the civil court system forcing gun manufacturers, dealers, distributors, and even owners to defend themselves in civil actions and face potentially extreme liability.

These concerns are slightly reduced when one considers the following:

TOP 12 REASONS WHY WE ARE NOT GOING TO LOSE OUR GUN RIGHTS...QUICKLY

1. The United States has a hell of a lot of guns in it. Virtually one gun for every man, woman, and child. It would be physically difficult to seize all the guns at once.
2. Americans have a spirit of resistance to government action.
3. Americans love freedom and individualism.
4. A lot of guns are hidden, buried, and/or stashed away in anticipation of further anti-gun success.
5. 3 million plus NRA members can still screw with politicians.
6. The industry is finally waking up (in large part to the anti-gunners efforts).
7. We still have a Republican control in Congress, which although they'll abuse us, they are not as "gung

ho" to do so.

8. Scientific/academic studies like Professor Lott & Professor Kleck have won the academic battle.
9. Our side is a "gun culture", and a culture is not that easy (though not impossible) to extinguish.
10. Wildlife conservation depends on hunter's dollars.
11. Diminishing the shooting, hunting, and outdoors industry means less tax dollars for the government.
12. Truth is on our side.

When analyzing the political situation regarding firearms, it is undeniable that the momentum is on the anti-gun side. Discounting a major event that wakes up Americans and particularly gun owners to opposing this trend, here are my hot picks for the new millennium.

1. Combat handguns without so-called "smart-gun" technology.

Reason: Traditionally, our gun control laws have grandfathered pre-existing guns. Grandfathered guns always have a premium. People who rely on guns to protect themselves will never trust a so-called "smart-gun". (You know it's going to fail the moment you really need it.) The first law abiding defender who dies because his "smart-gun" flunks the test is going to send prices soaring even higher.

2. Semi-automatic rifles.

Reason: The push is still on to ban these types of rifles. The anti-gunners are claiming that the manufacturers simply made cosmetic changes to get around the current ban (which is true, because the ban is simply based on cosmetics). Remember the original 1934 National Firearms Act proposal included a ban on all semi-automatic rifles, all magazines over 12 rounds, and all handguns. The goals haven't changed for 65 years.

3. .50 BAR Caliber Rifles (Barretts, L.A.R., Grizzly 50, semi-auto M-2s, etc.

Reason: The anti-gunners know they can do a real "dog & pony" show with these guns. They can shoot accurately for enormous distances, and they have tremendous power. Be ready for the classic question, "Why does anyone "need" one of these?

4. Reproduction black powder revolvers.

Reason: These guns are legally acquired "without paper". They have the power of a .357 Magnum, and come in all configurations from hideout to LeMat. Squawking has already begun about this loophole.

5. Combat shotguns.

Reason: Look for more "sporting purpose" ATF rulings. (These are of course politically inspired just like the Striker and Street Sweeper magically changed from a sporting shotgun to a destructive device in order to help pass the 1994 Crime Bill.)

An anti-gun investor should be vigilant about gun politics and gun prices. Some key information sources for anti-gun investing are as follows:

1. **The New Gun Week.**

What the Wall Street Journal if for stock investing, The New Gun Week is for anti-gun investing. This newsletter publishes every scrap of gun/political information that comes its way. The New Gun Week is published three times a month by the Second Amendment Foundation, P.O. Box 488, Buffalo, NY 14209 (Tel. 716-885-6408).

2. **The NRA web site, at WWW.NRA.ORG**

Click the word "News" for current news on "Gun Politics". This is a must "bookmark" or "favorite" for anti-gun investors.

3. *Blue Book of Gun Values*

Treasure your old editions. These are great for tracking and spotting market trends and identifying important variations of guns and their values. Now with *GunTracker*, it's like having a computerized "stock portfolio" for your firearms.

Gun laws can and do affect gun prices. Identifying the law's impact can prove quite profitable. As "they" say, knowledge is the power. You won't be as upset next time you hear some jerk proposing a new anti-gun law. Just sit back, smile, and watch your guns grow in value. At least for awhile, anyway! ■

Jim Klatt

Jim Klatt is vice president of TradeMark Communications in Eden Prairie, MN. Many of the agency's clients manufacture and sell outdoor equipment, so volunteering to help the MOHA mission was an easy decision. Jim was president of MOHA from 1994-1998.

In the November general election in 1998, Minnesota voters overwhelmingly passed a constitutional amendment that dealt a blow to animal rights and anti-hunter groups, who have been pushing for trapping, hunting (and even fishing) bans across the U.S. in recent years.

Here's what the new amendment says:

"Hunting and fishing and the taking of game and fish are a valued part of our heritage that shall be forever preserved for the people and shall be managed by law and regulation for the public good."

This amendment, known as Amendment 2 on the 1998 ballot, passed by 77% statewide. It even passed by 65% in the core urban area of Minneapolis and St. Paul, where many urban legislators and political activists have been vocal in opposition to guns and to trapping and hunting for several years.

How did Amendment 2 come to be? In 1994, State Senator Bob Lessard and Minnesota Congressman Collin Peterson called a series of meetings with sportsmen/women to discuss how to head off the growing animal rights/anti-hunting movement before it started to target Minnesota.

As a result of the Lessard/Peterson meetings, the Minnesota Outdoor Heritage Alliance was formed in August of 1994. MOHA set up a Governing Board of up to 50 members, who represent almost all of the hunting, fishing, and trapping groups in the state.

MOHA set a mission statement geared to directly attacking the anti-hunting problem. It reads:

"Our mission is to protect and guarantee the right to pursue the time-honored traditions of hunting and fishing, and related activities, for every Minnesota citizen, in perpetuity, through legislative action, public awareness and education."

At MOHA's initial meetings in 1994, the decision was to go after the constitutional amendment. Reasoning was that state laws can be changed at any time by a few determined individuals, who have a good publicity budget and strong support from key House and Senate Committee chairs. A constitutional amendment can not be changed unless a clear majority of State voters go back to the polls to rescind the amendment. This is a much more difficult and costly task, which explains why amendments are seldom reversed.

Getting the Bills Through the Legislature

So the stage was set in 1994. The next step was to help set up a bi-partisan Outdoor Caucus in the legislature. Leaders of the Caucus became the chief authors of the House and Senate bills for the Amendment. The Caucus, which started slowly, reached 122 members out of a total Legislative body of 201 by 1998. Shortly after winning the Amendment vote, the Caucus membership climbed to 145. Success gets attention.

During the 1995-1996 legislative session, MOHA worked with the Caucus to refine the language and work the bills through the House and Senate. Opposition at the beginning came not only from anti-gun legislators, but also from the Department of Natural Resources, the State Attorney General, and even from some outdoor groups who took the approach that we were better off not rocking the boat with animal rights groups.

A very active public awareness campaign from MOHA and constituent groups gradually turned the DNR in our favor. It took nearly four years to overcome objections from the Attorney General. The AG's office saw the amendment as a problem, causing hundreds of unnecessary legal battles for the State.

The Senate version of the bill passed in 1996, but the House version was blocked. MOHA repeated the legislative process again in 1997-98. By 1997, the Amendment campaign was gaining more public comment and support. MOHA and constituent groups attended dozens of outdoor banquets and many sports and gun shows, spoke to groups, sent mailings and picked up more media coverage.

The Senate bill again sailed through both the 1997/1998 sessions, passing 55-12. The House version was again being held up by the leadership, but by the start of the 1998, the DNR was firmly supporting the bill and the Attorney General's office had dropped opposition. In fact, on the day of the most critical House sub-

State Hunting Amendments Foil Anti-Hunters, by Jim Klatt

committee hearing, with the bill facing several constitutional legal experts brought in by opponents, the Attorney General sent a personal letter to the full committee supporting the amendment.

In addition to that letter of support, MOHA had found its own constitutional expert, Fred Morrison from the University of Minnesota. Morrison is recognized by most of the Minnesota legal community as the expert on the state constitution. Morrison wrote letters of support to each committee, helped refine the language again to make it acceptable to both the Senate and the House, and was the key factor in finally forcing the bill through the House, where it passed unanimously in May, 1998.

The Campaign for Passage

MOHA immediately began the planning to make sure Amendment 2 passed in November. It was not a sure thing. There was no way of knowing how much opposition the animal rights groups would mount. In some states, like Ohio, they had already committed $2 million or more to kill the dove-hunting season.

A fundraising goal of $750,000 was set and a team of top lobbyists with great connection throughout the state volunteered to help. The fundraising program actually generated about $185,000.

This meant that some of the strategic media publicity couldn't be done in the closing days of the campaign. However, wide-spread grass roots support, thousands of mailed pieces, 2,000 yard signs, 75,000 bumper stickers, thousands of volunteer man hours, and more than 75 radio, television and newspaper interviews from August through October, made up for the lack of paid media coverage.

It helped that the anti-hunting and animal rights groups did not choose to fight this battle in a big way. They probably spent about what MOHA did, but they were ineffective in their messages.

Voter Turnout Extraordinary

For a non-presidential election year, the voter turnout in Minnesota, and the support for this amendment, were unusual. A combination of factors probably made this happen. The MOHA grassroots campaign reached every corner of the state, mostly through intense personal contact. The animal rights groups picked on parts of the amendment that could be easily defended, especially with the constitutional expert and the Attorney General supporting it. All three gubernatorial candidates - including Jesse Ventura - publicly supported the amendment in several debates. Nearly all of the House of Representatives incumbents running for re-election also stumped for the amendment, and the amendment got placed on the front page of the ballot, instead of the back - the usual location.

Take the Ball and Run

This was a major victory from a national perspective. More than 20 states had been watching the Minnesota effort closely to see if the amendment route could be successful. Many of those same states are now in the process of pushing similar amendments through their legislature. Even referendum states, like California, are hoping to duplicate this effort.

While a constitutional amendment isn't "absolute" protection for hunting, fishing and trapping, it does set the legal bar much higher for the antis to jump over. In Minnesota's case, the amendment itself, combined with the tapes and transcripts from all of the House and Senate hearings where the purpose of bills was debated and passed, provides any future court with ample legal documentation to support the amendment.

The Amendment's Overall Impact

There is no doubt that the Minnesota amendment has major impact here. In the process of building support, MOHA worked with every group and agency involved with the outdoor community. Coalitions were built that will have a lasting effect. MOHA is now in the unique position of having many legislators coming to the group for advice on all manners of bills affecting hunting, fishing, trapping, and many other related issues.

Most importantly, the amendment's passage puts the state government on notice that one of the largest constituencies in Minnesota can not be taken for granted. ■

Jim Klatt's favorite gun was a Winchester single-shot .22 that his mother bought him for his 10th Christmas. He says it was probably a Model 47. The rifle arrived Christmas Eve, and five boxes of .22 Shorts were in the Christmas stocking. Ten minutes later, he admits, he was in the pasture shooting at tin cans. He remembers the day exactly - sunny, very cold, lots of snow, and the smell of gunpowder, which he says has never left him.

A Press Perspective

Steve Comus

Steve Comus has been a firearms fanatic for decades. Here, he is shown with a London flintlock smoothbore c. 1805.

For the past two years, Steve has been editor of *GUN WORLD*. Starting March 1,1999 of this year, Steve will move to Tucson, Arizona where he will be working for *Safari Club International* in the publications effort there.

Quantum changes and advancements have characterized the firearms industry during the past two decades of this century/millennium. Never before have gun owners had such a breadth and depth of choices. Yet never before have gun owners' rights been so seriously challenged. It is this paradox that must be understood if the right to arms is to be passed on to future generations. Skimming the surface of what has happened in just a couple of decades explains the story. High capacity magazines and the arms to use them have come into full bloom, only to suffer the ravages of government intervention. Synthetic materials and non-ferrous metals have become major items in a host of models and designs. Shotgun slug shooting has evolved to its apex via the development of guns with rifled barrels, as well as high tech, saboted projectile ammo to use in them. In-line muzzleloaders have gone from their infancy to a dominate position among black powder hunters. Action shooting has exploded upon the scene, bringing with it seemingly endless demands for better and more highly evolved arms -- in arenas as far reaching as practical pistol shooting at one end, or cowboy action shooting on the other. Technological advancements in manufacturing equipment and processes have resulted in arms that are generally more accurate, function more smoothly and flawlessly and that are, relatively speaking, more affordable. With the more widespread availability of more perfect arms has come the introduction of high tech ammunition that takes shooters places they never could have gone before.

Overall, gun owners as a demographic group have aged over the past twenty years. This reflects a failure to recruit from among the younger generation(s). Credit the expansion of single-parent families in which the mother is the hands-on parent for much of this situation. However, expanding population also has taken its toll on places to hunt and shoot, which in turn discourages some from ever entering the ranks. Concurrently, gun owners have become more sophisticated. They no longer are as quick to settle for less than equipment that is better. While the various games like action shooting have seen new players join the ranks, twenty years have seen the demise of legions of recreational shooters. This is because it takes more commitment now than it did in the past. Judging from the scenes at public shooting areas around the country, however, it looks like Generation X is destined to come to the rescue. Pierced body parts, brightly colored hair and baggy garb aside, these young folks are appearing more and more frequently at shooting facilities with a seemingly insatiable appetite to pull triggers and make things go bang. Frankly, they represent the hope for the future, and if so, the future doesn't look too bad. After all, they see through the chicanery extant in the land.

Despite overall optimism, it must be noted that all of the achievements and advancements in firearms and the ammo they shoot have occurred despite the most far-reaching and ominous threat to private ownership of arms in the history of Gundom. Local, regional, national and global attacks on arms ownership have been unprecedented and continue to evolve. In one sense, these anti-gun activities have triggered heightened demand from time to time for certain kinds of arms and ammo. And, during these peak demand periods, it has been difficult for the industry to keep up. No one could ignore the wholesale loss of licensed firearms dealers following orchestrated government efforts to rid the land of "kitchen table" dealers and "garage" stores. Short-sighted arms retailers became willing accomplices in this theater of the absurd. By limiting the number of outlets, the government and the several arms retailer lackeys have changed much of the dynamic of ultimate distribution and have concentrated the trade in arms to a more concentrated and controllable network. This, in turn, has chilled much of the traditional activity and now is in the process of edging the prices of arms upward. This trend promises to continue.

All of this has occurred during an unprecedented media attack on arms and those who own them. Gun owners are vilified in an agenda-driven campaign to characterize them as less than fully deserving citizens. This is coupled with a campaign to present firearms as a scourge upon the land that must be eliminated. This media elitism has evolved into full-blown racism as the media focuses upon misuse of arms by criminals in minority communities where they call for draconian laws to address the "gun problem" which could not have existed had it not been for the abject failures of the many social/welfare programs that have stripped the people involved of anything that hints at self worth. It is this anti-gun media blitz which must be brought under control if the future is to be anything but bleak. The media attacks firearms because it is easy to do so. The results of firearm misuse make dramatic images and the human reaction to them makes for gut-wrenching dialogue. Mind-numb, robotic reporters and assignment editors know they can boost their circulation/viewership at will by showing grotesque images of the aftermath of firearms misuse and then wrap their coverage into a tidy package by having some anti-gun talking head regurgitate a simplistic "solution" to the problem. As a counter-part, it is elementary for these media types to focus upon some gun owner who is attempting to address a complex concept, but must try to do it in less air time or printed space than it takes to empty a magazine -- making the gun owner look like an idiot. By coupling all of this with a flood of disinformation and misinformation about arms, and the media have a slam-dunk formula for coverage that furthers their financial position while demagoguing the concept of fairness.

All of this cries out for a heightened awareness of the importance of the right to arms. The antis have time on their side. They have the luxury of being able to chip away at rights, knowing that over time this chipping will reduce rights to a critical point where they can be crushed and eliminated. The game plan is known. We can see it in other countries. It can happen here. To win, gun owners must become active.

First, buy more guns. The healthier the industry, the better for gun owners. But there is more. Embark upon a mission of truth and spread the word. Bring others into the fold. When in doubt, DO something. Certainly, it is assumed that gun owners will become more active politically. But there is more. Set the example. Show others the way. Live the life and do so openly. Most importantly, stay the course. Attrition is our fiercest enemy. Social inclusion is our brightest hope. It all starts and ends in the home. What happens there dictates local realities which, in turn, affect regional, national and global realities.

Ultimately and logically, our future need not be in THEIR hands. What we do and how we do it will determine not just our fate, but the fate of firearms ownership and all other freedoms. Do the right thing. Do it often. Do it well. But by all means, do it. Hope rules. ■

A Writer's Perspective

J.B. Wood
With a regular Model 1930 Commercial Broomhandle & attached shoulder stock.

Marking my fiftieth year in firearms, looking back is no problem. The problem is where to stop. Fortunately, Steve Fjestad has solved that one for me - this being the 20th anniversary of the *Blue Book of Gun Values*. So, what was happening 20 years ago, and how have things changed?

In 1979, the excellent SIG/Sauer pistols began to be available, with the P220 initially marketed by Browning. Hawes also offered it, and the P230. The Heckler & Koch VP70Z could be bought for around $250, and its magazine capacity was 18 rounds, available, pre-Feinstein, to everyone.

High Standard was alive and well, and Sterling Arms announced (but never produced in quantity) a double action .45 auto pistol. Charter Arms had an array of really good revolvers with an average retail price of around $150. The Semmerling LM-4 and the Thomas .45 pistols were briefly available, and both now bring substantial prices.

Moving along to the mid-80s, we must note the arrival of the Glock. It was not the first polymer-frame pistol - George Kellgren knows more about polymer construction than Gaston Glock ever will - but it was the first to be sold in large quantity.

Remember when the news people were squawking about "the plastic pistol that can pass airport detectors", and calling it the "weapon of terrorists"? All of this was untrue, of course - but by the time these lies had been exposed, Glock had received a lot of marvelous, if negative, publicity. Their good agents followed this up with great deals for law enforcement, New York and Miami adopted it, and the rest, as they say, is history.

In about the same time period, Bill Ruger unveiled his P-85. Cosmetically, it was almost as ugly as the Glock. But, like all Ruger guns, it worked infallibly, no matter what was fed to it. It was followed by a succession of models, and the most recent ones are not ugly at all.

There were many other important guns that made their first appearance in these 2 decades, but in this space we can't make a comprehensive list - that would take a book. And there is one - you're holding it.

In the 1979-1999 time period, and even before, there was a definite trend in gunsmithing - the Age of the Specialist. There are now masters of the art who work only on pistols of the Government model 1911 type, or competition guns, or benchrest rifles, or ....well, you get the idea.

To use a medical analogy, the old-time "general practitioner" seems to be going the way of the dinosaur. Specialization does have its good points.

The problem is when a specialist is the sole gunsmith in your area, and you have an old Iver Johnson Champion with a broken barrel latch spring... One bright note: The Gunsmithing Schools are still teaching "general" courses, so maybe there will always be a few "GP" gunsmiths.

For the collector, the price and value trends in our 20 year period could often be described as "crazy". Keeping up with them for the *Blue Book of Gun Values* might have reminded Steve Fjestad of the ancient Chinese saying, "May you live in eventful times".

An example: the Spanish Astra Model 400. 20 years ago, at a gun show, you could pick up a really decent one for around $100. Then, some were offered on the surplus market for about half that. Soon after this, Dr. Leonardo Antaris wrote that excellent book (1988), and the collectors began to realize that they were dealing with some finite numbers. Today, a nice Model 400 will cost you around $400.

An interesting trend is a price increase in the ordinary old top-break revolvers. The Smith & Wesson of this type has always been at a respectable level, because of the many S&W collectors. But now, we're seeing some real money spent on Iver Johnson, H&R, Forehand & Wadsworth, Hopkins & Allen, and so on. Even the little sheath trigger revolvers with the fanciful names have begun to appreciate.

From an investment standpoint, any firearm that will shoot a currently made and easily obtainable cartridge has 2 values. The gun may have only moderate collector value, but in the worst case scenario of general chaos and mobs in the streets, its value will be as good as gold - literally. Apocalypse, anyone?

Speaking of such things reminds me that in the real world of today, in the place they refer to as the "inner city", having a small, inexpensive handgun can be the difference between life and death. Many writers frequently denigrate such guns as the Raven, the Davis, the Lorcin, and so on.

This is elitist bullshit. The guns work, every time. They cost very little. If they are banned, a large group of honest people, the ones who might need them the most, will be left without protection from the predators in their neighborhoods. These people can't afford Smith & Wesson, or SIG/Sauer.

But then, the gun banners know this. They may bleat about "controlling crime", but the real reason for their attacks is that the idea of large numbers of "lower class" people out there armed to the teeth, scares the hell out of them. Maybe it should.

Actually, the main basis for the entire anti-gun movement is also unconnected with crime control. For people - and I use the term loosely - like Schumer, Feinstein, Clinton, etc., there is one thing more important than prestige, money, sex, or anything else: Power.

They will tell you what you can and can't do, and they will love doing it. However, they have a problem. As long as there are large numbers of us out here who are armed, and who are serious about our rights under the 1st, 2nd, and 4th Amendments, there are definite limits to the extent of their orders. Unlike the poor religious wackos in Waco, we are not amateurs.

Am I beginning to sound like a militia recruiter? Nah. This is just basic Constitutional stuff, and often, it's good to remind everyone that we have it. No need to imagine unmarked black helicopters. (If they show up though, aim for the tail rotor.)

Seriously, what can you do? Quite a lot, actually. Join the NRA - in spite of internal squabbles, it's still our main "spokesman". Support GOA, SAF, and the other pro-gun organizations. Write letters to the editorial page of your local newspaper.

When I receive a solicitation letter from any group, I reply with an attached note that I have photocopied in quantity: "Sorry, but regardless of the nobility of the cause, all of my donations now go to GOA, NRA, and other organizations working to protect our 2nd Amendment rights. Please remove my name from your mailing list."

Let's wind it up with a bottom line: When the "jack-booted storm troopers" have come and taken your guns, you are no longer a citizen, you are a serf. Am I suggesting that, in the ultimate extremity, you should resort to violence? Well, at least you'd be in good company: "...our lives, our fortunes, and our sacred honor..." ∎

A final note:

I took over the Gunsmith column, twice, from P.O. Ackley, a tough act to follow. I wrote it for Guns & Ammo, then for Shooting Times from 1974 to April, 1998. At that point, an executive decision by the new owners cancelled the column. Ah well, 23 years is long enough, wouldn't you say?

During most of that time, I used the *Blue Book of Gun Values* as a reference for many answers to questions about gunmakers, dates, and quantities of production. There are several "gun value" books. There is only one *Blue Book of Gun Values*. Happy 20th Anniversary, Steve. Long may you wave.

Gun Groupie Gastronomical Guidebook

by John Risdall
Chairman/CEO, Magnum Research Inc.

Yiihah cowboys! It s great to be able to travel around the world and meet 10 s of thousands of Desert Eagle Pistol owners and fans every year. We get to see more than 100,000 gun aficionados each year at just the five major conventions – NRA, SHOT show, the NASGW wholesalers show, FTE and IWA in Europe – plus hundreds of other stops everywhere. It s great fun to build a product people love.

After 20 plus years in the gun business, my reputation for tracking down great restaurants and eating several desserts before the meal now precedes me. Here are a few of my favorites to try if you like tasty grub.

DENVER – In downtown Denver at Tabor Center the one staple on the tour every year was to hit Bennett s Pit Bar-B-Que with Andy Molchan from *American Firearms Industry Magazine*. The beef brisket sandwich is fantastic at less than $3.00 and the Magnum/AFI staffs would always chow down after a tough day at the show. Whenever you re a mile high – don t miss it.

MINNEAPOLIS/ST. PAUL – D Amico Cucina and Ristorante Luci both have magnifico Italiano – you can t miss at either. Goodfellows has great variations on local game and fish – the Walnut Crusted Walleye is internationally famous. The newcomer Aquavit has its mother restaurant in New York City and the duck is exquisite! The best singular dessert in town is the Raspberry Lace Cookie Cup at Goodfellow s.

SAN FRANCISCO AND NAPA VALLEY – The French Laundry is perhaps the best in the U.S.A. After the appetizer of some truffle, brioche, caviar concoction – I can t remember anything else. The duck at Postrio is superb! The desserts at newcomer Farallon are the best in the city – I went back three times. Get the Brown Berry Buckle!

NEW ORLEANS – The Grill Room at the Windsor Court has the best desserts and the best duck in the world. Emeril s is not only great for dinner but also maybe the best bargain gourmet lunch in the States. NOLA S and Arnaud s are great French Quarter highlights but the Rib Room was in the James Bond movie *Live and Let Die*.

PHILLY – The best chunk of anything I put in my piehole in 1998 was the signature recipe at the Striped Bass Restaurant in Philadelphia. If you re in Philly it s worth the trip to both Le Bec-Fin and Striped Bass – a few storefronts apart on Walnut Street. Le Bec-Fin has the best dessert trolley in the U.S.A. The Baba Au Rhum is the best in the world and the other 40 or so are all world class. Eat as many as you can – I topped out at 22.

PHOENIX – Vincent Guerithault on Camel Back has the 3 best appetizers in the world – seared pepper crusted ahi, salmon quesadillas and sautéed foie gras in peppercorn sauce – plus a selection of entrees that excel and the second best dessert cart in the country.

LA – When you go to visit *Guns & Ammo*, right down the street is Spago, where you can see all the Hollywood stars. The smoked salmon pizza is sublime but bring your wallet. More Italiano chow at Valentino in Santa Monica.

LAS VEGAS – The local version of Spago is great but the best in town in Andre s – not because he s packin Desert Eagles but the chow is wow! Call ahead, get there early, and ask for the tableside salad – 17 aromatic herbs chopped tableside ruins you for other salads for life. Appetizers, entrees, desserts – a gourmet spectacular – can t be beat anywhere!

The World s 12 Best Duck Dinners

My two trusty sidekicks from Magnum, Doug Evans, President, and Jim Skildum, EVP Sales, share my affinity for duck. We ve searched the world for the best crispy duck dinners.

1. **Grill Room** – Windsor Court Hotel – New Orleans
   Simply the best meal of my life – the Varnished Duck with a Ginger Plum Sauce – as soon as we tasted it we asked the waiter for a bucket of the sauce and he brought it. It was preceded by an incredible Garlic Brie Soup. Yow! And all 5 desserts in the menu that night were terrific.
2. **Tour d Argent** – Paris
3. **Vincent s** – Phoenix
4. **Andre s** – Las Vegas
5. **Casbah** – Tel Aviv
6. **Postrio** – San Francisco
7. **Le Bec-Fin** – Philly
8. **Aquavit** – New York & Minneapolis
9. **Goodfellow s** – Minneapolis
10. **Guy Savoy** – Paris
11. **French Laundry** – San Francisco
12. **Spago** – LA & Las Vegas

Thanks for the Memories!

THE BLUE BOOK BUNCH

1. **S.P. Fjestad** - Author/Publisher
2. **Tom Stock** - Managing Director/CFO
3. **Tom Heller** - Art Director/Production Mgr.
4. **John Allen** - Associate Editor
5. **Beth Marthaler** - Operations Manager
6. **Cassandra Faulkner** - Publishing Assistant
7. **D.J. Pallum** - Switchboard/Customer Service
8. **Angela Singletary** - Switchboard/Goddess

ANATOMY OF A HANDGUN

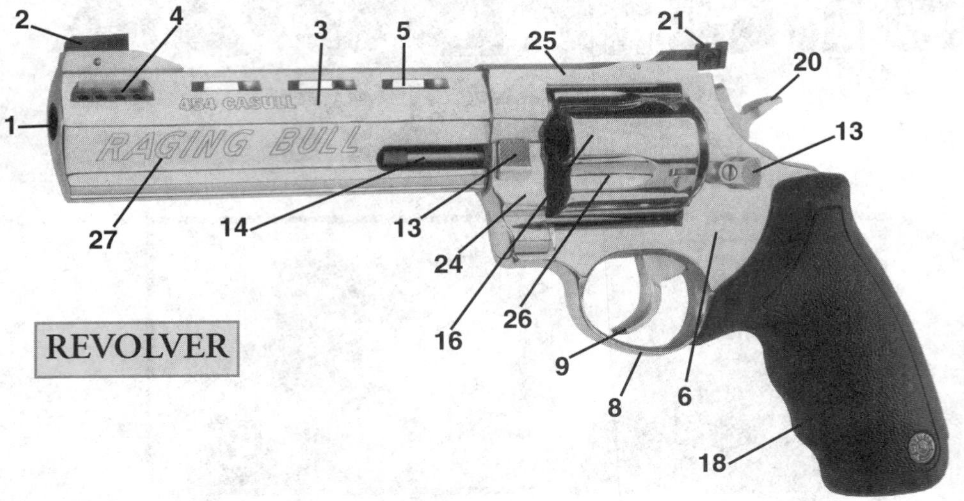

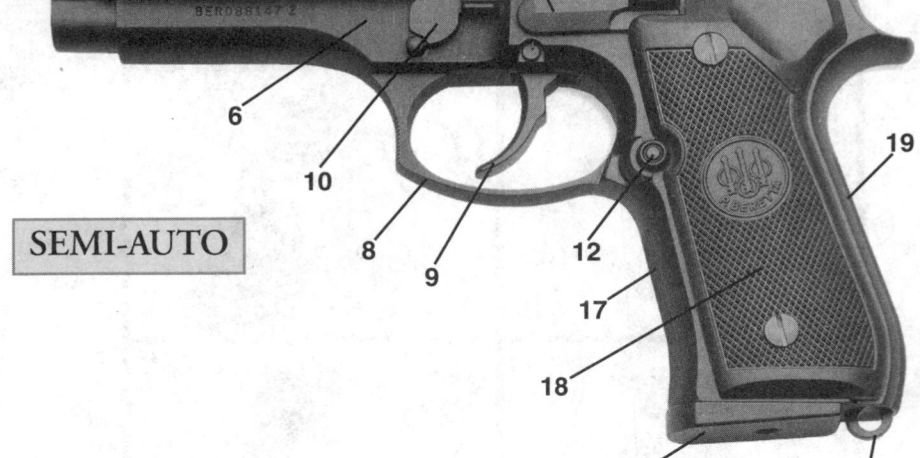

REVOLVER

SEMI-AUTO

1. Muzzle	10. Disassembly Latch	19. Rear Grip Strap
2. Front Sight	11. Slide Release Lever	20. Hammer
3. Barrel	12. Magazine Release Button	21. Rear Sight
4. Gas Ports	13. Cylinder Release Latch	22. Safety Lever
5. Ventilated Rib	14. Extractor Rod	23. Lanyard Loop
6. Frame	15. Magazine	24. Crane
7. Slide	16. Cylinder	25. Top Strap
8. Trigger Guard	17. Front Grip Strap	26. Cylinder Flute
9. Trigger	18. Grip	27. Full Length Barrel Shroud

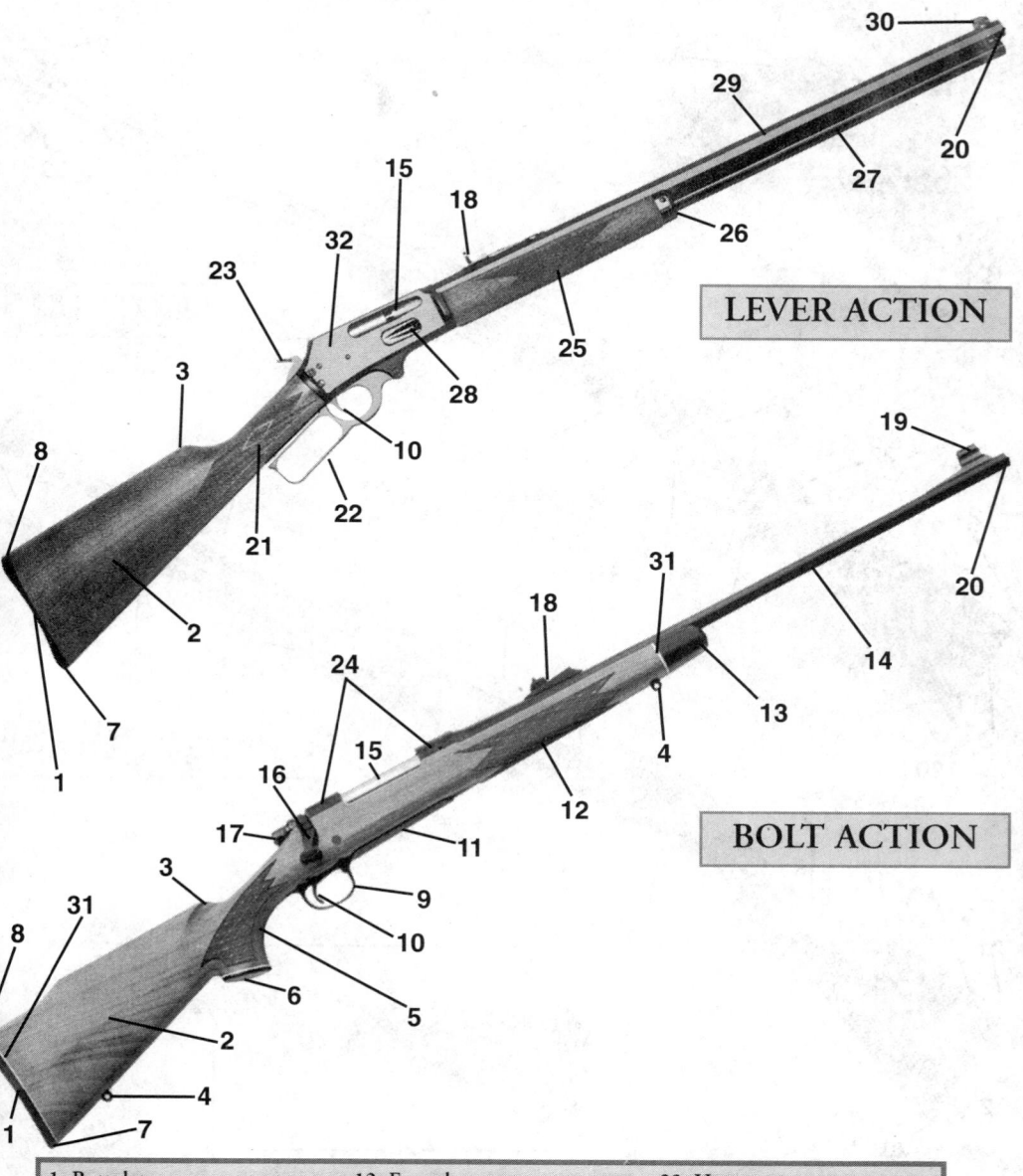

LEVER ACTION

BOLT ACTION

1. Buttplate	12. Forend	23. Hammer
2. Buttstock	13. Forend Cap	24. Receiver
3. Comb	14. Barrel	25. Forearm
4. Sling Swivel Stud	15. Bolt	26. Forearm Cap
5. Semi-Pistol Grip	16. Bolt Handle	27. Magazine Tube
6. Pistol Grip Cap	17. Safety Button	28. Loading Port
7. Toe	18. Rear Sight	29. Octagon Barrel
8. Heel	19. Hooded-Ramp Front Sight	30. Blade Front Sight
9. Trigger Guard	20. Muzzle	31. Spacer
10. Trigger	21. Straight Grip	32. Frame
11. Floor Plate	22. Lever	

ANATOMY OF A SHOTGUN

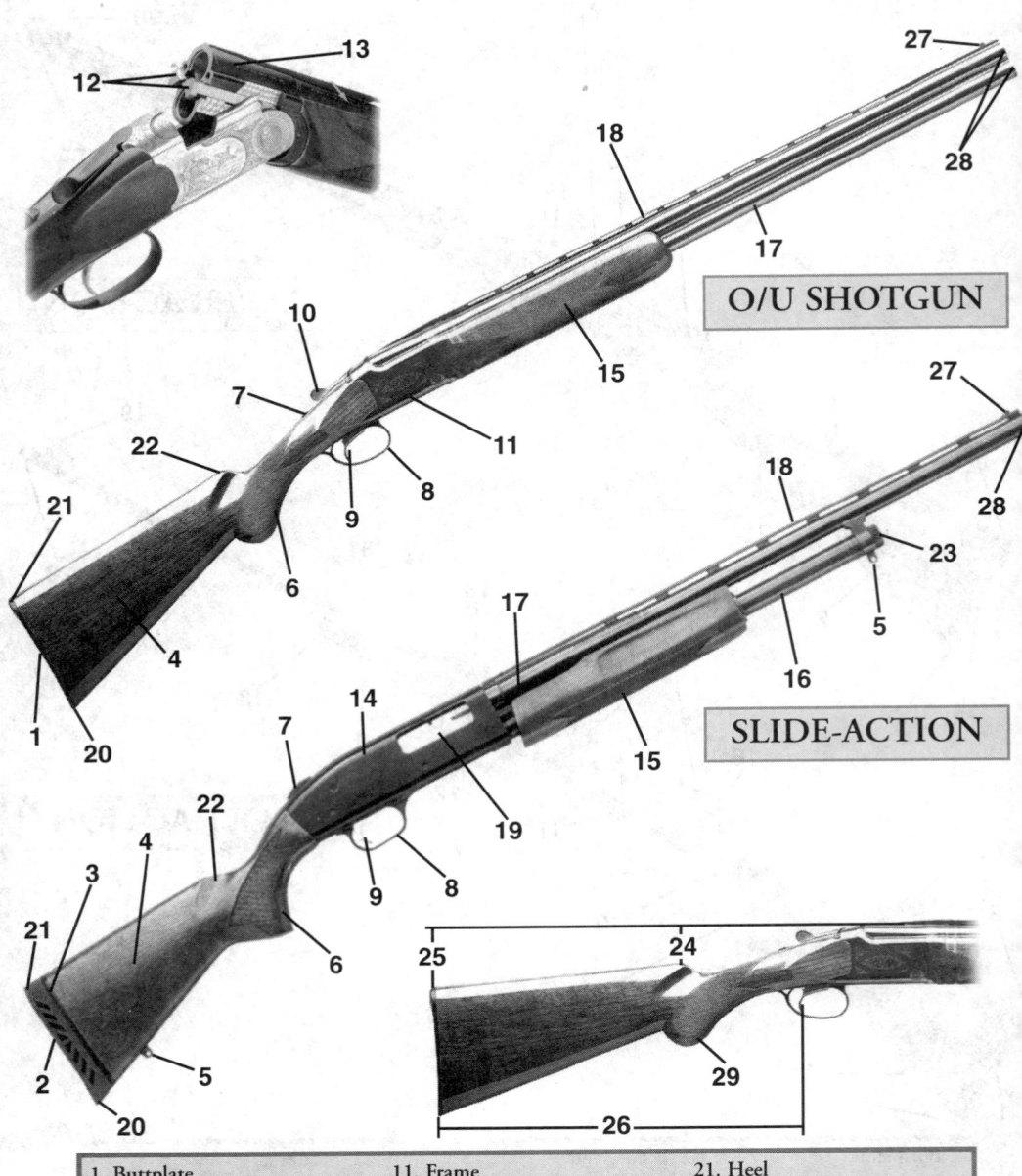

O/U SHOTGUN

SLIDE-ACTION

1. Buttplate	11. Frame	21. Heel
2. Ventilated Recoil Pad	12. Ejectors	22. Comb
3. Spacer	13. Breech	23. Magazine Tube Cap
4. Buttstock	14. Receiver	24. Drop at Comb
5. Sling Swivel Stud	15. Forearm	25. Drop at Heel
6. Semi-Pistol Grip	16. Magazine Tube	26. Length of Pull
7. Safety Button	17. Barrel(s)	27. Front Sight Bead
8. Trigger Guard	18. Ventilated Rib	28. Muzzle
9. Trigger	19. Breech Block	29. Rounded Pistol Grip
10. Top Lever	20. Toe	(Browning Style)

ACCOUTERMENT
All equipment carried by a soldier on outside of uniform, such as buckles, belts, or canteens, but not including weapons.

ACTION
The heart of the gun, receiver, bolt or breechblock feeding and firearm mechanism - see Box-lock, Rolling Block, or Side-lock.

ADJUSTABLE CHOKE
A device built into the muzzle of a shotgun enabling changes from one choke to another.

AIR GUN
A gun that utilizes compressed air or gas to launch the projectile.

APERTURE SIGHT
A rear sight assembly consisting of a hole or aperture located in an adj. rear sight through which the front sight and target are aligned.

AUTO LOADING
See semi-automatic.

BACKSTRAP
That parts of the revolver or pistol frame that are exposed at the rear of the grip.

BARREL
The steel tube (may be a sleeve wrapped in a synthetic material) that a projectile travels through.

BARREL BAND
A metal band, either fixed or adjustable, around the forend of a gun that holds the barrel to the stock.

BARREL THROAT
The breech end of a barrel that is chambered and somewhat funneled for passage of bullet from cartridge case mouth into barrel, also known as forcing cone.

BEAVERTAIL FOREND
A wider than normal forend.

BLUING
The chemical process of artificial oxidation (rusting) applied to gun parts so that the metal attains a dark blue or nearly black appearance.

BORE
Internal dimensions of a barrel (smooth or rifled) that can be measured using the Metric system (ie. Millimeters), English system (ie. Inches), or by the Gauge system (see Gauge). On a rifled barrel the bore is measured across the lands. Also, traditional English term used when referring to diameter of a shotgun muzzle (ga. in U.S. measure).

BOXLOCK ACTION
Typified by Parker shotgun in U.S. and Westley Richards in England. Generally considered not being as strong as the side lock. Developed by Anson & Deeley, the box-lock is hammerless. It has two disadvantages: Hammer pin must be placed directly below knee of action, which is its weakest spot, and action walls must be thinned out to receive locks. These are inserted from below into large slots in action body, which is then closed with a plate. Greener cross-bolt, when made correctly, overcomes many of the box lock weaknesses.

BREECH
That portion of a gun which contains the action, the trigger or firing mechanism, the magazine, and the chamber portion of the barrel(s).

BUCKHORN SIGHT
Open metallic rear sight with sides that curl upward and inward.

BULL BARREL
A heavier, thicker than normal barrel with little or no taper.

BUTT PLATE
A protective plate (usually steel) attached to the butt.

CALIBER
The diameter of the bore.

CHAMBER
Rear part of the barrel that has been reamed out so that it will contain a cartridge. When the breech is closed, the cartridge is supported in the chamber, and the chamber must align the primer with the firing pin, the bullet with the bore.

CHAMBER THROAT
Also called THROAT, is that area in the barrel that is directly forward of the chamber and that tapers to bore diameter.

CHARCOAL COLOR CASE HARDENING
A method of hardening steel and iron while imparting colorful swirls as well as surfaces figure. Normally, the desired metal parts are put in a crucible packed with a mixture of charcoal and finely ground animal bone to temperatures in the 800 degree C - 900 degree C range, after which they are slowly cooled, and then submerged into cold water.

GLOSSARY

CHECKERING
A functional decoration consisting of pointed pyramids cut into the wood generally applied to the pistol grip and forend/forearm areas affording better handling and control.

CHOKE
The muzzle constriction on a shotgun to control spread of the shot.

COCKING INDICATOR
Any device, which the act of cocking a gun moves into a position where it may be seen or felt in, orders to notify the shooter that the gun is cocked. Typical examples are the pins found on some high-grade hammerless shotguns, which protrude slightly when they are cocked, and also the exposed cocking knobs on bolt-action rifles. Exposed hammers found on some rifles and pistols are also considered cocking indicators.

COMB
The portion of the stock on which the shooter's cheek rests.

COMBINATION GUN
Generally a break-open shotgun type configuration fitted with at least one shotgun barrel and one rifle barrel. Such guns may be encountered with either two or three barrels, and less frequently with as many as four or five, and have been known to chamber for as many as four different calibers.

COMPENSATOR
A recoil-reducing device that mounts on the muzzle of a gun to deflect part of the powder gases up and rearward. Also called a "muzzle brake"

CRANE
In a modern solid-frame, swing-out cylinder revolver, the U-shaped yoke on which the cylinder rotates, and which holds the cylinder in the frame.

CROWNING
The rounding or chambering normally done to a barrel muzzle to insure that the mouth of the bore is square with the bore axis and that the edge is countersunk below the surface to protect it from impact damage. Traditionally, crowning was accomplished by spinning an abrasive-coated brass ball against the muzzle while moving it in a figure-eight pattern, until the abrasive had cut away any irregularities and produced a uniform and square mouth.

CRYOGENIC TEMPERING
Computer controlled cooling process that relieves barrel stress by subjecting the barrel to a temperature of -310 degree F for 22 hours.

CYLINDER
A rotating cartridge holder in a revolver. The cartridges are held in chambers and the cylinder turns, either to the left or the right, depending on the gun maker's design, as the hammer is cocked.

CYLINDER ARM
See Crane.

DAMASCENE
The decorating of metal with another metal, either by inlaying or attaching in some fashion.

DAMASCUS BARREL
A barrel made by twisting, forming and welding thin strips of steel around a mandrel.

DERRINGER
Usually refers to a small, cancelable pistol with one or two short barrels.

DOUBLE ACTION
The principle in a revolver or auto-loading pistol wherein the hammer can be cocked and dropped by a single pull of the trigger. Most of these actions also provide capability for single action fire. In auto-loading pistols, double action normally applies only to the first shot of any series, the hammer being cocked by the slide for subsequent shots.

DOUBLE ACTION ONLY
Hammer no longer cocks in single action stage (many new DAO models are hammerless).

DOUBLE-BARRELED
A gun consisting of two barrels joined either side-by-side or one over the other.

DOUBLE-SET TRIGGER
A device that consists of two triggers one to cock the mechanism that spring-assists the other trigger, substantially lightening trigger pull.

DOVETAIL
A flaring machined or hand-cut slot that is also slightly tapered toward one end. Cut into the upper surface of barrels and sometimes actions, the dovetail accepts a corresponding part on which a sight is mounted. Dovetail slot blanks are used to cover the dovetail when the original sight has been removed or lost; this gives the barrel a more pleasing appearance and configuration.

DRILLING
German for "triple", which is their designation for a three-barrel gun.

EJECTOR
Mechanical device used to eject empty cartridges from chamber(s).

GLOSSARY

ENGINE TURNING
Overlapped spots of circular polishing.

ENGLISH STOCK
A very straight, slender-gripped stock.

ENGRAVING
The art of engraving metal in decorative patterns. Scroll engraving is the most common type of hand engraving encountered. Much of today's factory engraving is rolled on which is done mechanically. Hand engraving requires artistry and knowledge of metals and related materials.

ETCHING
A method of decorating metal gun parts, usually done by acid etching or photo engraving.

EXTRACTOR
A device which partially lifts the spent casing(s) from the breech area, allowing the empty shell(s) to be removed manually.

FALLING BLOCK
A single-shot action where the breechblock drops straight down when the lever is actuated.

FIT AND FINISH
Terms used to describe over-all firearm workmanship.

FLOATING BARREL
A barrel bedded to avoid contact with any point on the stock.

FLOOR PLATE
Usually, a removable/hinged plate at the bottom of the receiver covering the magazine well.

FORCING CONE
Forward part of the chamber in a shotgun where the chamber diameter is reduced to bore diameter. The forcing cone aids the passage of shot into the barrel.

FOREARM
Usually a separate piece of wood in front of the receiver and under the barrel used for hand placement when shooting.

FOREND
Usually the forward portion of a one-piece rifle or shotgun stock, but can also refer to a separate piece of wood.

FRAME
The part of a firearm that the action (lock work), barrel, and stock/grip are connected to. Most of the time used when referring to a handgun or hinged frame long gun.

FREE RIFLE
A rifle designed for international-type target shooting. The only restriction on design is weight maximum 8 kilograms (17.6 lbs.).

FRONT STRAP
That part of the revolver or pistol grip frame that faces forward and often joins with the trigger guard. In target guns, notably the .45 ACP, the front strap is often stippled to give shooter's hand a slip-proof surface.

GAUGE/GA.
A unit of measure used to determine a shotgun's bore. Determined by the amount of pure lead balls equaling the bore diameter needed to equal one pound (i.e., a 12 ga. means that 12 lead balls exactly the diameter of the bore weigh one pound). In this text, .410 is referenced as a bore (if it was a gauge, it would be a 68 ga.).

GAUGE VS. BORE DIAMETER
10-Gauge = Bore Diameter of .775 inches or 19.3mm
12-Gauge = Bore Diameter of .729 inches or 18.2mm
16-Gauge = Bore Diameter of .662 inches or 16.8mm
20-Gauge = Bore Diameter of .615 inches or 15.7mm
28-Gauge = Bore Diameter of .550 inches or 13.8mm
68-Gauge = Bore Diameter of .410 inches or 12.6mm

GRIP
The handle used to hold a handgun, or the area of a stock directly behind and attached to the frame/receiver of a long gun.

GRIPS
Can be part of the frame or components attached to the frame used to assist in accuracy, handling, control, and safety of a handgun. Many currently manufactured semi-auto handguns have grips that are molded w/checkering as part of the synthetic frame.

GROOVES
The spiral cuts in the bore of a rifle or handgun barrel that give the bullet its spin or rotation as it moves down the barrel.

HAMMERLESS
Some "hammerless" firearms do in fact have hidden hammers, which are located in the action housing. Truly hammerless guns, such as the Savage M99, have a firing mechanism that is based on a spring-activated firing pin.

GLOSSARY

HEEL
Back end of the upper edge of the butt-stock at the upper edge of the butt-plate or recoil pad.

LAMINATED STOCK
A gunstock made of many layers of wood glued together under pressure. Together, the laminations become very strong, preventing damages from moisture, heat, and warping.

LANDS
Portions of the bore left between the grooves of the rifling in the bore of a firearm. In rifling, the grooves are usually twice the width of the land. Land diameter is measured across the bore, from land to land.

MAGAZINE (mag.)
The container which holds cartridges under spring pressure to be fed into the gun's chamber.

MAGNUM (Mag.)
A modern cartridge with a higher-velocity load or heavier projectile than standard.

MAINSPRING
The spring that delivers energy to the hammer or striker.

MANNLICHER STOCK
A full-length slender stock with slender forend extending to the muzzle (full stock) affording better barrel protection.

MICROMETER SIGHT
A finely adjustable target sight.

MONTE CARLO STOCK
A stock with an elevated comb used primarily for scoped rifles.

MUZZLE
The forward end of the barrel where the projectile exits.

MUZZLE BRAKE
A recoil-reducing device attached to the muzzle.

OVER-UNDER (Superposed)
A two-barrel gun in which the barrels are stacked one on top of the other.

PARALLAX
Occurs in telescopic sights when the primary image of the objective lens does not coincide with the reticle. In practice, parallax is detected in the scope when, as the viewing eye is moved laterally, the image and the reticle appear to move in relation to each other.

PARKERIZING
Matted rust-resistant oxides finish, usually matte or dull gray, or black in color, found on military guns.

PEEP SIGHT
Rear sights consisting of a hole or aperture through which the front sight and target are aligned.

PEPPERBOX
An early form of revolving repeating pistol, in which a number of barrels were bored in a circle in a single piece of metal resembling the cylinder of a modern revolver. Functioning was the same as a revolver, the entire cylinder being revolved to bring successive barrels under the hammer for firing. Though occurring as far back as the 16th century, the pepperbox did not become practical until the advent of the percussion cap in the early 1800s. Pepperboxes were made in a wide variety of sizes and styles, and reached their popularity peak during the percussion period. Few were made after the advent of practical metallic cartridges. Both single- and double-action pepperboxes were made. Single-barreled revolvers after the 1840s were more accurate and easier to handle and soon displaced the rather clumsy and muzzle-heavy pepperbox.

POPE RIB
A rib integral with the barrel. Designed by Harry M. Pope, famed barrel maker and shooter, the rib made it possible to mount a target scope low over the barrel.

PROOFMARK
Proofmarks are usually applied to all parts actually tested, but normally appear on the barrel (and possibly frame), usually indicating the country of origin and circa of proof (especially on European firearms). In the U.S., there is no federalized or government proof house, only the manufacturer's in-house proofmark indicating that a firearm has passed its internal quality control standards per government specifications.

RECEIVER
That part of a rifle or shotgun (excluding hinged frame guns) that houses the bolt, firing pin, mainspring, trigger group, and magazine or ammunition feed system. The barrel is threaded into the somewhat enlarged forward part of the receiver, called the receiver ring. At the rear of the receiver, the butt or stock is fastened. In semi-automatic pistols, the frame or housing is sometimes referred to as the receiver.

RELEASE TRIGGER
A trap shooting trigger that fires the gun when the trigger is released.

RIB
A raised sighting plane affixed to the top of a barrel.

RIFLING
The spirally cut grooves in the bore of a rifle or handgun. The rifling stabilizes the bullet in flight. Rifling

GLOSSARY

may rotate to the left or the right, the higher parts of the bore being called lands, the cuts or lower parts being called the grooves. Many types exist, such as oval, polygonal, button, Newton, Newton-Pope, parabolic, Haddan, Enfield, segmental rifling, etc. Most U.S.-made barrels have a right-hand twist, while British gun makers prefer a left-hand twist. In practice, there seems to be little difference in accuracy or barrel longevity.

ROLLING BLOCK ACTION
Single shot action, designed in the U.S. and widely used in early Remington arms. Also known as the REMINGTON-RIDER action, the breechblock, actuated by a lever, rotates down and back from the chamber. Firing pin is contained in block and is activated by hammer fall.

SCHNABEL FOREND
The curved/carved flared end of the forend that resembles the beak of a bird (Schnabel in German). This type of forend is common on Austrian and German guns; was popular in the U.S., but the popularity of the Schnabel forend/forearm comes and goes with the seasons. A schnozzle forend is often seen on custom stocks and rifles.

SHORT ACTION
A rifle action designed for shorter cartridges.

SIDE-BY-SIDE (JUXTAPOSED)
A two-barrel shotgun where the barrels are arranged side-by-side.

SIDELOCK
A type of action, usually long gun, where the moving parts are located on side of the lock plates, which in turn are inlet in the stock. Usually found only on better quality shotguns and rifles.

SIDE PLATES
Ornamental steel panels normally attached to a box-lock action to simulate a side-lock.

SINGLE ACTION
A firearms design which requires the hammer to be manually cocked for each shot. Also an auto-loading pistol design which requires manual cocking of the hammer for the first shot only.

SINGLE TRIGGER
One trigger on a double-barrel gun. It fires both barrels singly by successive pulls.

SLING SWIVELS
Metal loops affixed to the gun on which a carrying strap is attached.

SPUR TRIGGER
A trigger mounting system that housed the trigger in an extension of the frame in some old guns. The trigger projected only slightly from the front of the extension or spur, and no trigger guard was used on these guns.

STOCKS
See grips.

SUICIDE SPECIAL
A mass-produced variety of inexpensive single action revolvers and derringers, usually with a spur trigger. These guns carried many fancy names; those in good condition have become true collector's items.

TAKE DOWN
A gun which can be easily taken apart in two sections for carrying or shipping.

TANG (S)
The extension straps of the receiver from which the stock is attached.

TOP STRAP
The upper part of a revolver frame, which often is either slightly grooved - the groove serving as rear sight - or which carries at its rearward end a sight that may be adjustable.

TRAP STOCK
A shotgun stock with greater length and less comb drop used for trap shooting.

TWIST BARRELS
A process in which a steel rod (called a mandrel) was wrapped with "skelps" - ribbons of iron. The skelps were then welded in a charcoal fire to form one piece of metal, after which the rod was driven out to be used again. The interior of the resulting tube then had to be laboriously bored out by hand to remove the roughness. Once polished, the outside was smoothed on big grinding wheels, usually turned by waterpower.

VENTILATED RIB
A sighting plane affixed along the length of a shotgun barrel with gaps or slots milled for cooling and light-weight handling.

VIERLING
A German word designating a four barrel gun.

YOUTH DIMENSIONS
Usually refers to shorter stock dimensions and/or lighter weight enabling youth/women to shoot and carry a lighter, shorter firearm.

ABBREVIATIONS

★	Banned due to 1994 Crime Bill
A	Standard Grade Walnut
AA	Extra Grade Walnut
AAA	Best Quality Walnut
ACP	Automatic Colt Pistol
adj.	Adjustable
AE	Automatic Ejectors
appts.	appointments
B	Blue
BAC	Browning Arms Company
BBL	Barrel
BH	Butt Head, pal, not Beavis
BOSS	Ballistic Optimizing Shooting System
BP	Butt Plate or Black Powder
BPE	Black Power Express
BR	Bench Rest
BT	Beavertail
C/B 1994	Introduced because of 1994 Crime Bill
cal.	Caliber
CB	Crescent Buttplate
CC	Case Colors
CCA	Colt Collectors Association
CF	Centerfire
CH	Cross Hair
COMP	Compensated/Competition
CYL	Cylinder
DA	Double Action
DAO	Double Action Only
DB	Double Barrel
DISC	Discontinued
DSL	Detachable Side Locks
DST	Double Set Triggers
DT	Double Triggers
DWM	DeutscheWaffen and Munitions Fabrik
EXC	Excellent
EXT	Extractors
F	Full Choke
F&M	Full & Modified
FA	Forearm
FBT	Full Beavertail Forearm
FE	Fore End
FFL	Federal Firearms License
FK	Flat Knob
FKLT	Flat Knob Long Tang
FM	Full Mag
FN	Fabrique Nationale
FPS	Feet Per Second
ga.	gauge
GCA	Gun Control Act
GOVT	Government
H&H	Holland & Holland
HB	Heavy Barrel
HC	Hard Case
HP	Hollow Point

IC	Improved Cylinder
IM	Improved Modified
intro.	introduced
IPSC	International Practical Shooting Confederation
L	Long
LC	Long Colt
LOP	Length of Pull
LPI	Lines Per Inch
LR	Long Rifle
LT	Long Tang or Light
LTRK	Long Tang Round Knob
M	Modified Choke
M&P	Military & Police
Mag.	Magnum Caliber
mag.	Magazine or Clip
MC	Monte Carlo
MFG	Manufactured/manufacture
MIL SPEC	Mfg. to Military Specifications
MK	Mark
MNJVFC	MN Jesse Ventura Fan Club
MR	Matted Rib
MSR	Manufacturer's Suggested Retail
N	Nickel
N/A	Not Available
NIB	New in Box
NM	National Match
no.	number
NSST	Non Selective Single Trigger
O/U	Over and Under
OA	Overall
OAL	Overall Length
OB	Octagon Barrel
OBFM	Octagon Barrel w/full mag.
OBO	Or Best Offer
OCT	Octagon
ODB	Or Don't Bother
PG	Pistol Grip
POR/P.O.R.	- Price on Request
POST-'89	Paramilitary mfg. after Federal legislation in Nov. 1989
POST-BAN	- Mfg. after September 13, 1994 per **C/B**
PPD	Post Paid
PRE-'89	Paramilitary mfg. before Federal legislation in Nov. 1989
PRE-BAN	Mfg. before September 13, 1994 per C/B
QD	Quick Detachable
RB	Round Barrel/Round Butt
REC	Receiver
REM	Remington
RF	Rimfire

RFM	Rim Fire Magnum
RK	Round Knob
RKLT	Round Knob Long Tang
RR	Red Ramp
S	Short
S&W	Smith & Wesson
S/N	Serial Number
SA	Single Action
SAA	Single Action Army
SAE	Selective Automatic Ejectors
SB	Shotgun Butt
ser.	serial
SG	Straight Grip
SK	Skeet
SMG	Sub Machine Gun
SML	Short Magazine Lee Enfield Rifle
SNT	Single Non-Selective Trigger
SPEC	Special
SPG	Semi-Pistol Grip
SPL	Special
SR	Solid Rib
SRC	Saddle Ring Carbine
SS	Single Shot or Stainless Steel
SST	Single Selective Trigger
ST	Single Trigger
SxS	Side by Side
TD	Take Down
TGT	Target
TH	Target Hammer
TT	Target Trigger
UMC	Union Metallic Cartridge Co.
VG	Very Good
VR	Ventilated Rib
w/o	Without
WBY	Weatherby
WC	Wad Cutter
WCF	Winchester Center Fire
WD	Wood
WFF	Watch For Fakes
WIN	Winchester
WO	White Outline
WRA	Winchester Repeating Arms Co.
WRF	Winchester Rim Fire
WRM	Winchester Rimfire Magnum
WW	World War
WYTL	Would You Take less?
X (1X)	1X Wood Upgrade or Extra Full Choke Tube
XX (2X)	2X Wood Upgrade or Extra Extra Full Choke Tube
XXX (3x)	3X Wood Upgrade - or Movie

DEFENDING YOUR SECOND AMENDMENT RIGHT TO OWN GUNS, HUNT,

For over 125 years the National Rifle Association has been the leader in defending our Second Amendment right to keep and bear arms as well as protecting our hunting rights and traditions. We're fighting the gun banners and animal rights fanatics on all fronts. By joining the NRA, or renewing your existing membership, you will help to keep our unique American traditions alive.

When you join NRA you will receive these great benefits:

NRA Black and Gold Shooters Cap
A no-annual-fee NRA Visa card (for qualified individuals)
Your choice of NRA monthly publications, *American Guardian, American Hunter* or *American Rifleman*

- $10,000 Personal Accident Insurance
- $1,000 in ArmsCare Firearm Insurance
- Hotel, Car Rental, Airfare and Interstate Moving Discounts
- Discounts at local Gun Stores and other Retail Outlets

And much, much, more...

NATIONAL RIFLE ASSOCIATION

☐ 1 Year Regular.........$35   ☐ 3 Year Regular.........$85
☐ 5 Year Regular.........$125   Date_____

NRA Recruiter #R012415A
EK 200016

If renewal, give ID# ☐☐☐☐☐☐☐☐

Payment Information:

Mr./Mrs./Ms. _____

☐ Check/Money Order

Street: _____ Apt.#: _____

Charge to: ☐ MC   ☐ VISA   ☐ Amex

City: _____ State: _____ Zip _____

☐ Discover   Expiration Date ☐☐☐☐

Daytime Phone: (_____)_____

Credit Card#

Choose ONE Magazine: ☐ American Guardian

☐☐☐☐☐☐☐☐☐☐☐☐☐☐☐☐☐

☐ American Rifleman   ☐ American Hunter

Member Signature _____

Contributions gifts or membership dues made or paid to the National Rifle Association of America are not refundable or transferable and are not deductible as charitable contributions for Federal Income Tax purposes.
Mail with payment to: NRA, 11250 Waples Mill Rd., Fairfax, VA 22030

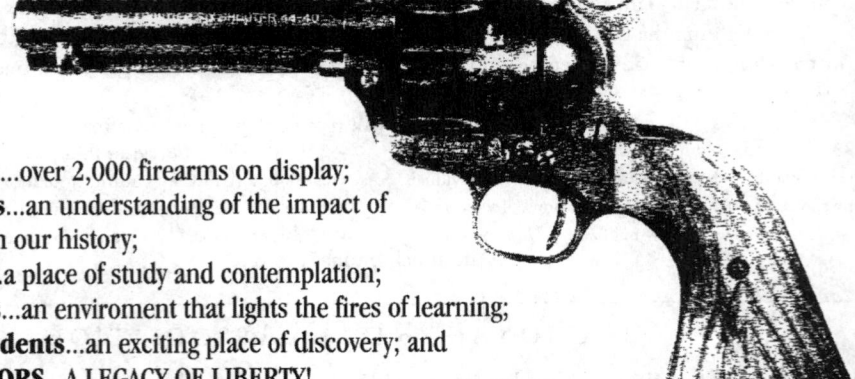

Help Take Charge of Tomorrow

Become a Century Club Member Today!

On November 21, 1998, leaders in the firearms and ammunition industry created The Hunting & Shooting Sports Heritage Fund to reclaim our rightful image in the media and to counter politically-motivated lawsuits against manufacturers, distributors and retailers.

Corporations throughout our industry are committing 1% of their gross sales to fund this multi-million dollar effort.

All segments of the industry are being asked to show their support for this historic program by wearing the Heritage Fund "Century Club" pin. An individual $100 contribution to the Heritage Fund shows your support for efforts to preserve our uniquely American tradition of sporting firearms usage. Each contributor will receive a Century Club lapel pin as a symbol of their personal commitment.

Please send your contribution to the Hunting and Shooting Sports Heritage Fund, c/o Robert Delfay, President and CEO, 11 Mile Hill Road, Newton, CT 06470-2359

Cody, Wyoming

Just 52 miles from the East Entrance to Yellowstone National Park, is home to the world-renowned Buffalo Bill Historical Center. For firearms enthusiasts, the Cody Firearms Museum, located within the Center, is the mecca, where thousands of examples of rare, historically significant arms form the largest collection of American firearms on earth, as well as European firearms dating back to the 16th century. Each year, thousands of visitors make an annual pilgrimage to the Buffalo Bill Historical Center to trace the evolution of firearms technology and learn how firearms helped to shape our American heritage.

The *Blue Book of Gun Values* supports the good works of the Buffalo Bill Historical Center and invites you to do the same by joining its Patrons Association.

In joining, you'll receive a subscription to *Points West*, a quarterly journal of the Center, a free copy of *Treasures of Our West*, featuring highlights of the museum's collection, free admission to the Center and a 15 percent discount in the museum's gift shop.

(cut or tear here and return with payment to: BBHC, 720 Sheridan Avenue, Cody, WY 82414)

Yes! I'm interested in joining the Patrons Association of the Buffalo Bill Historical Center and supporting its work to preserve the history and art of the American West. I understand I am entitled to all benefits listed above, and I am enclosing my gift in the amount of:

- ❏ $25 Individual Member
- ❏ $40 Family/Household Member
- ❏ $100 Centennial Member
- ❏ Other _____
- ❏ Please accept my donation of $_____

❏ My check is enclosed (payable to the Buffalo Bill Historical Center)
❏ Charge my ❏ American Express ❏ Mastercard ❏ VISA ❏ Discover

Acct.# _____ Exp._____ Signature_____
Name (as you would like it to appear on your account)_____
Address _____
City _____ State _____ Zip _____ Phone (____)_____

GRADING CRITERIA

The old, NRA method of firearms grading - relying upon adjectives such as "Excellent" or "Fair" - has served the firearms community for a long time. Today's collectors, however, are turning away from such a subjective system. One person's "Fair" is another person's "Good!"

Most dealers and collectors are now utilizing what is essentially an objective method for deciding the condition of a gun: THE PERCENTAGE OF ORIGINAL FACTORY FINISH(ES) REMAINING ON THE GUN. After looking critically at a variety of firearms and carefully studying the Photo Percentage Grading System™ (pages 73-120), it will soon become evident whether a piece has 100%, 98%, 95%, or less finish remaining. Remember, sometimes an older gun described as NIB can actually be 98% or less condition, simply because of the wear which accumulated by taking it in and out of the box and being handled too many times (commemoratives are especially prone to this problem).Of course, factors such as quality of finish(es), engraving (and other embellishments), special orders/features, historical significance and/or provenance, etc. can and do affect prices immensely. Someone called me a while back, and asked me what his original 1st Generation SAA was worth. I calmly replied, "Somewhere between 600 bucks and a 1/4 million!"

Every gun's unique condition factor - and therefore the price - is best determined by the percentage of original finish remaining, with the key consideration being the overall frame/receiver finish. The key word here is "original," for if anyone other than the factory has refinished the gun, its value as a collector's item has been diminished, with the exception of rare and historical pieces that have been properly restored. Every year, top quality restorations have become more accepted, and prices have gone up proportionally with the quality of the workmanship.

Carefully study the photographs and read the captions on pages 73-120. Note where the finishes of a firearm typically wear off first. These are usually places where the gun accumulates wear from holster/case rubbing, and contact with the hands or body over an extended period of time. A variety of firearms have been shown in four-color to guarantee that your "sampling rate" for observing finishes is as diversified as possible.

It should be noted that the older a collectible firearm is, the smaller the percentage of original finish one can expect to find. Some very old and/or very rare firearms are acceptable to collectors in almost any condition!

For your convenience, NRA Condition Standards are listed next door on page 71. Converting from this grading system to percentages can now be done accurately. **Remember, the price is wrong if the condition factor isn't right!**

CONVERTING TO NRA MODERN STANDARDS

When converting from NRA Modern Standards, the following rules generally apply:

New/Perfect – 100% with or without box. Not mint - new (i.e., no excuses). 100% on currently manufactured firearms assumes NIB condition and not sold previously at retail.

Excellent – 95%+ - 99% (typically).

Very Good – 80% - 95% (should be all original).

Good – 60% - 80% (should be all original).

Fair – 20% - 60% (may or may not be original, but must function properly and shoot).

Poor – under 20% (shooting not a factor).

The NRA conditions listed below have been provided as guidelines to assist the reader in converting and comparing condition factors to the Photo Percentage Grading System(tm) (see pages 73-120). In order to use this book correctly, the reader is urged to consult these condition standards when converting to percentages of condition. Once the gun's condition has been accurately assessed, only then can the correct values be ascertained.

NRA MODERN CONDITION DESCRIPTIONS

New – not previously sold at retail, in same condition as current factory production.

Perfect – in new condition in every respect.

Excellent – new condition, used but little, no noticeable marring of wood or metal, bluing near perfect (except at muzzle or sharp edges).

Very Good – in perfect working condition, no appreciable wear on working surfaces, no corrosion or pitting, only minor surface dents or scratches.

Good – in safe working condition, minor wear on working surfaces, no broken parts, no corrosion or pitting that will interfere with proper functioning.

Fair – in safe working condition, but well worn, perhaps requiring replacement of minor parts or adjustments which should be indicated in advertisement, no rust, but may have corrosion pits which do not render article unsafe or inoperable.

NRA ANTIQUE CONDITION DESCRIPTIONS

Factory New – all original parts; 100% original finish; in perfect condition in every respect, inside and out.

Excellent – all original parts; over 80% original finish; sharp lettering, numerals and design on metal and wood; unmarred wood; fine bore.

Fine – all original parts; over 30% original finish; sharp lettering, numerals and design on metal and wood; minor marks in wood; good bore.

Very Good – all original parts; none to 30% original finish; original metal surfaces smooth with all edges sharp; clear lettering, numerals and design on metal; wood slightly scratched or bruised; bore disregarded for collectors firearms.

Good – some minor replacement parts; metal smoothly rusted or lightly pitted in places, cleaned or reblued; principal lettering, numerals and design on metal legible; wood refinished, scratched, bruised or minor cracks repaired; in good working order.

Fair – some major parts replaced; minor replacement parts may be required; metal rusted, may be lightly pitted all over, vigorously cleaned or reblued; rounded edges of metal and wood; principal lettering, numerals and design on metal partly obliterated; wood scratched, bruised, cracked or repaired where broken; in fair working order or can be easily repaired and placed in working order.

Poor – major and minor parts replaced; major replacement parts required and extensive restoration needed; metal deeply pitted; principal lettering, numerals and design obliterated; wood badly scratched, bruised, cracked or broken; mechanically inoperative, generally undesirable as a collectors firearm.

GETTING THE RIGHT GRADE

This edition's color Photo Percentage Grading System™ (PPGS) marks its 10th Anniversary as a pictorial solution for accurately grading firearms. As in the past, 3 primary categories of firearms have been visually provided: Handguns, Rifles, and Shotguns. Please study the photos and captions to better understand the various condition percentages. The 20th Edition also has "PPGS-o-meters" whenever possible, so you can get a quick fix on condition factors, in addition to a anti-Handgun Control/Dianne Feinstein "paramilitary" calendar on page 98. Enjoy it while you can, it may be banned next year!

Computer savvy readers will be pleased to know that plans are underway to get this 20th Edition PPGS incorporated into GunTracker 2.0, due for release in mid-June. This will help you to get a firearms grading fix on your computer monitor while using GunTracker.

Condition factors pictured (indicated by PPGS-o-meters), unless otherwise noted, are for a gun's approximate percentage of original frame/receiver blue, case colors, nickel, or other type of original finish remaining. On older guns, describing the receiver/frame finish accurately is absolutely critical for providing a gun with a reliable numerical grading "fingerprint".

Additional percentages will refer to other specific parts of a gun (i.e. barrel, wood finish, mag. tube, etc.). Percentages of patina/brown or other finish discoloration factors must also be explained when necessary, and likewise be interpolated accurately. Since we've had quite a few requests for showing older damascus side-by-side shotguns in various condition factors, please check out pages 114-115, to personally inspect the good, the bad, and the ugly! Remember, the price is wrong if the condition factor isn't right.

One of the questions that has evolved over the years is how bore condition affects guns in less than average condition. Dealers have indicated that a good strong bore on an average condition Colt SAA or Winchester lever action will make quite a bit of difference on how and when a gun sells. No surprise here, since shooters are always looking for the best shooting condition they can afford. This is especially true with the rapid growth of cowboy action shooting and related events. Ironically, today's urban cowboys are so concerned about their getup, that they want a retro looking gun to complete their cool garb. This is an interesting, "don't want fresh paint" theory, where some manufacturers are now taking a new gun, aging it, and charging more because of this new demand factor. Go figure!

While this latest PPGS certainly isn't meant to be the Last Testament on firearms grading, it hopefully goes further than anything else published on the subject. As always, the final chapter on intelligence can't be written until you accumulate the additional knowledge learned after you think you know it all.

S.P. Fjestad
Author & Publisher - *Blue Book of Gun Values*™

P.S. Special thankx go out to the Great White LeRoy of the North, Lynn Oliver, Keith Rolf of The Outdoorsman, located in Hopkins, MN, Jeff Sundvall of J&S Custom Guns located in Lakeville, MN, and Vern Berning. All PPGS photography by ASAP studios, S.P. Fjestad, and Cable Photo Systems.

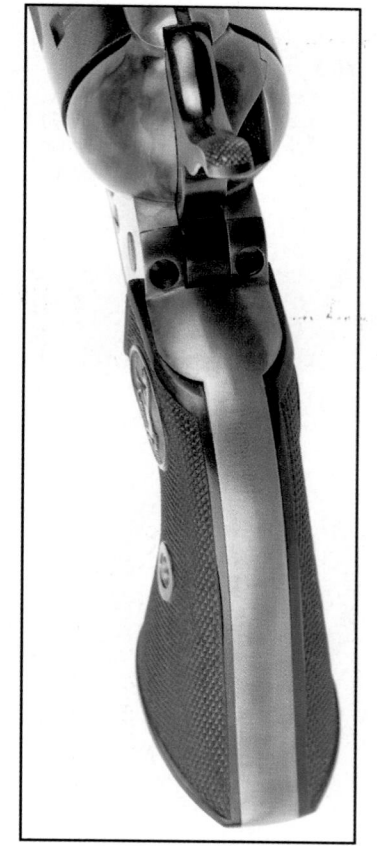

Photos 1 & 2 = Colt SAA, .357 Mag. cal., 5 ½ in. barrel, ser. no. 30,301SA, mint except for rear grip strap polishing, (see photo at right). Fittingly, this all-new **Photo Percentage Grading System** section starts out with the world's most famous and enduring revolver, the Colt Single Action Army. Having been collectible for over a century, Colt SAAs, at today's prices, can literally range from $450-$300,000! Before he died, Keith Cochran, author of *The Colt Peacemaker Encyclopedia, Vol. II,* guesstimated ½ of all pre-WW II revolvers were no longer factory original. So on 1st generation SAAs through ser. no. 343,000, know what you're doing, get a factory letter (if possible), and always be in close proximity to a high output ATM machine. This 2nd generation specimen was manufactured approximately the same time John F. Kennedy was elected during 1960. Note the shininess of the rear grip strap, indicative of after factory polishing. Could be the result of a perfectionist SAA collector, when upon discovering some light freckling (i.e. rust) due to improper storage, decided to make it "perfect" again by polishing the problem areas first, then realizing he had to do the whole grip strap to make it look it consistent. This "perfectionist" mistake cost someone $400-$500. More importantly, he/she had to get rid of it, because with the owner's 100% or nothing attitude, it could never be good enough again.

Photo 3 = Colt SAA, .357 Mag. cal., 5 ½ in. barrel, ser. no. 356,593, approx. 75%-80% frame case colors and 95% overall bluing. Note the slight wear at the end of the barrel and around cylinder flutes on this revolver as compared to Photo 1. Manufactured around Christmas, 1939, 525 SAAs were built in .357 Mag. cal. pre-WWII, making this gun relatively rare.

Photo 4 = Colt SAA, .45 LC, 4 ¾ in. barrel, ser. no. 356,169, approx. 80% frame case colors with light perimeter frame freckling and 85%-90% overall bluing. While this specimen has slightly more case colors than the gun pictured above, note the additional wear at the end of the barrel and between the cylinder lock-up notches. Light pitting must be evaluated per individual gun when determining value.

Photo 5 = Colt SAA, .38 Colt cal., 5 ½ in. barrel, ser. no. 348,684, approx. 30%-40% frame case colors and 70% overall bluing. Another post-WW I – pre-WW II SAA, this example was made in 1926. Close observation will reveal checkering wear on the bottom of the grips. Nice strong patent legend and "non-boogered" frame screws are always a plus on any Colt SAA.

Photo 6 = Colt SAA, .44-40 cal., 4 ¾ in. barrel, ser. no. 336,296, approx. 15%-20% case colors, frame mostly shiny, and approx. 50% overall bluing. Manufactured late during WWI, any condition on a Colt Frontier Six Shooter .44-40 is still collectible. Front frame screw has probably been replaced. Overall wear is consistent, with no one major part being noticeably different than another.

Photo 7 = Colt SAA, .41 Colt, 4 ¾ in. barrel, ser. no. 303,805, finish mostly turned a greyish/brown patina – approx. 15% overall. Again, all wear on this gun seems to "add up" for its overall condition factor. In some areas, the grip checkering is almost gone, and note smooth prancing stallion. In this condition factor, barrel bore wear adversely affects the price tag more than a 90%+ SAA, since the shooting performance is of greater importance to this type of buyer.

Photo 8 = Colt SAA, .45 Colt, 4 ¾ in. barrel, ser. no. 172,433, original finish mostly turned to brown patina, with discolored, badly worn, hard rubber grips. This revolver would fall under the 10%-15% condition factors in this text. While appearing very worn, the original condition factor of this SAA is actually close to average when comparing it with other specimens from this era. This smokeless powder model celebrated its 100th anniversary last year.

Photo 9 = Colt SAA Frontier Six Shooter, .44-40 cal., 4 ¾ in. barrel, ser. no. 161,423, most of the finish has been worn off, and now has a shiny appearance – approx. 5%-10% overall. A black powder frame specimen (note front of frame does not have the horizontal cylinder pin latch as compared to Photos 3-8). This gun was manufactured during the first year of Browning's new Winchester Model 1895. Grips are not original and 7½ in. barrel has been cut down to 4 ¾ in – sight placement on barrel is also wrong.

Photo 10 = Colt SAA, .45 cal, 4 ¾ in. barrel, ser. no. 60,935, condition isn't really a factor on this multiple "organ transplant" example. If you can't see anything wrong with this Colt Revolver, you'd better put a one-year moratorium on your SAA purchases until you bone up on what to look for. This is living proof that gun collecting became more difficult after Eli Whitney came up with interchangeable parts. Believe it or not, if you add up the parts total, this SAA is still worth $1000!

Photo 11 = Hawes Western Marshal Model SAA manufactured by J.P. Sauer & Sohn, .357 Mag., 6 in. barrel, ser. no. 192,413. 95%+ overall – would be near mint without hammer wear and major scratching on frame shoulder. Typical fine German quality with all-steel construction, no hammer-block safety indicates older mfg. While not very collectible, these guns make great shooters, especially since they are usually seen priced between $130-$250.

Photo 12 = Ruger Super Single Six Revolver, .22 LR, 6 ½ in. barrel, ser. no. 535,367, approx. 90% overall. Typical example of a meat & potatos Ruger Single Six Revolver – note the plum-colored bluing on the anodized aluminum ejector rod housing, indicating the metallurgy change between the rest of the gun and this component. 1/8 inch sized serial number indicates post-1962-pre-GCA of 1968 manufacture. This era of production had a "XR3 RED" indicating a redesign cast into the grip frame.

Photo 13 = Ruger Single Six Revolver, .22 LR, 5 ½ in. barrel, ser. no. 146,035, approx. 80% overall condition. Smaller sized serial numbers (1/16 in.) such as this one were produced 1953-1961. Note XR3 frame, steel ejector housing, and black paint missing from inside of Ruger grip medallion (compared to Photos 12 & 14). Another "Old Model", this variation can be denoted by 3 frame screws as opposed to 2 pins found on "New Models" mfg. beginning 1973.

Photo 14 = Ruger Single Six Revolver, .22 LR, 5 ½ in. barrel, ser. no. 107,263, approx. 70%+ overall condition. Ruger Single Six collectors will immediately note this "Heinz 57" has the wrong ejector rod housing (should be steel, not aluminum) and the grip frame has been replaced with XR3 RED type – should be XR3 type. Despite this revolver's non-originality and condition factors, it still makes a good shooter in the $125-$150 price range. Additional wear will not decrease its shooting value any more.

Photo 15 = Colt New Service, .45 LC, ser. no. 342,839, NIB condition. Colt double action collectors can't get enough of these. This specimen was manufactured during 1937, and was never used or fired. Carefully observe the box wear, especially by the end of the barrel and hammer. Due to its age, it's common to see box wear in these areas. Also note quality of metal polishing and finish, in addition to the sharp prancing stallion logo on rear of frame.

Photo 16 = Colt Officer's Model, .38 LC cal., ser. no. 248,197, 95% overall, checkered grips. Nice original specimen, showing minor freckling on barrel end and cylinder. Fire bluing on trigger and grip screw was standard. Observe upper portion of frame Colt logo as compared to Photo 15 – while appearing to have been partially polished away, "weak" logo die hits, barrel address information, and other markings did occur at the factory, are original and not a tell-tale sign of rebluing.

Photo 17 = Colt Police Positive Target, .22 LR, ser. no. 41,601, approx. 90%+ overall. Compare this gun to Photo 16, and observe the cylinder wear on flutes and between lock-up notches. Bottoms of grips also show slight wear and adjustable sights are indicative of a target model. Colt started with wood grip circa 1924 (this gun was mfg. 1936), and DA collectors will note the wider butt of this specimen compared to the earlier round butt variation.

Photo 18 = Colt Model 1878 DA "Colt Frontier Six Shooter" Revolver, .44-40 cal., ser. no. 39,189, nice original early gun with approx. 85%-90% condition. Currently celebrating its 100th anniversary, the fit and finish on these early double action Colts were perfect. This model's barrel and ejector rod housing interchanges with the SAA. The owner spotted this revolver from across the room at a local gun show after a potential buyer held it up in good light, suspecting refinishing.

Photo 19 = Colt Model 1917, .45 ACP, ser. no. 95,419, approx. 80% original thinning brushed blue finish. As with many military wartime handguns, polishing and commercial finishing tend to be overlooked in favor of increased production. Note the rough circular polishing marks on the back of frame and where they meet the horizontal frame polishing below the cylinder. While exterior finish is rough, the inner mechanism is equivalent to any similar commercial model.

Photo 20 = Colt Model 1917, .45 LC, ser. no. 95,419 (left side of Photo 19), 80%-85% original thinning brushed blue finish. The left side of this gun appears to be in slightly better condition than the right side pictured above, and rear frame polishing is more vertical. Interestingly, don't be surprised to see one of these with a crooked front sight, since this military model was sighted in horizontally by using a wooden mallet to bend the front sight!

Photo 21 = Colt New Service, .45 LC, ser. no. 145,386, approx. 80% overall, hard rubber grips. Examine this commercial finish compared to Photo 20. Observe the bolstered barrel where it meets the frame (compare to Photo 24). This revolver is crudely stamped "RCMP 2212", so condition and holster wear is appropriate for use in the Royal Canadian Mounted Police. While its ser. no. indicates 1917 mfg., it was not shipped until Oct. 24th, 1919, due to wartime military considerations.

Photo 22 = Colt New Service, .45 LC, ser. no. 353,244, approx. 75%-80% overall. While the barrel and grips on this gun are near mint, frame and cylinder pitting lower this gun's overall condition factor. Many collectors would rather own a clean, 80%-90% gun than a 95%-98% similar model with this kind of pitting. This type of metal finish condition usually indicates improper storage, where moisture was allowed to oxidize the bluing over a period of time.

Photo 23 = Colt Marshal, .38 Spl., ser. no. 838,365, approx. 70% overall. Typical major wear patterns are exhibited on this specimen, including barrel, cylinder and grips. This variation was basically an Official Police with a rounded butt. Less than 2,500 were manufactured between 1954-1956. While a mint gun might command $800 today, this condition factor is usually priced in the $300-$350 range.

Photo 24 = Colt New Service, .455 Eley cal., ser. no. 61,867, approx. 50%-60% original finish, hard rubber grips. Unless a revolver is ultra-rare due to its configuration (barrel length, caliber, finish, features, etc.), most guns in this condition are shooters, with no collector premiums. Note brownish metal discoloration on straight, untapered barrel and frame. This New Service is poorly stamped R.N.W.M.P.9.3.5 on rear grip strap, another Canadian contract variation of the gun pictured in Photo 21.

Photo 25 = Iver Johnson Top-break Revolver, .38 cal., ser. no. 3,690, approx. 60%-70% overall, shooter status only. If condition is worse than this, it still doesn't make much difference on the price tag. On this type of bottom shelf price point, don't be surprised if an unknown gun shop owner asks you for 4 or 5 forms of I.D. Typically seen priced between $25-$75, and don't bring your American Express card. To maintain respect, leave in safe when having friends over.

Photo 26 = Colt Police Positive, .38 New Police cal., ser. no. 20,553, approx. 40%-50% overall, with pitting. Close observation reveals this is a transition gun, with the New Police frame marking and older Police Positive stamped barrel. Manufactured during 1908, this revolver still maintains a $100-$125 price as a reliable shooter. When purchasing a shooter in a lower price range, always concentrate on how good it is mechanically, rather than quality of exterior finish and other potentially rare features.

Photo 27 = Colt Official Police, .38 Spl., ser. no. 615,076, approx. 80%-85% original nickel finish. This is a good example of what nickel finish looks like once it has flaked off or started to corrode. Nickel finishes are rapidly becoming a thing of the past, as many current manufacturers cannot afford today's hazardous waste costs incurred by the production of such a finish. Butt is marked "P&W No. 24" (perhaps Pratt & Whitney security revolver).

Photo 28 = H&R Top-break, .22 LR, ser. no. 8,908, approx. 70%+ overall. On nickel finished guns, once the nickel has worn or flaked off, only the dark metal remains visible, giving it the appearance of being in worse condition than it is. Indeed, in many cases, an 80% gun with bluing will appear in better condition than a 95% nickel finished variation. Since nickel plating produces a soft finish, surface scratching is more prevalent than on blue finish.

Photo 29 = Colt Detective Special, .38 Spl., ser. no. 395,581, 90%+ overall nickel finish, note slight wear around cylinder notches, barrel end, and bottom of grips. Built during the beginning of the Depression, this revolver retailed for $28.50 in 1930. The grip design was changed to a round butt beginning 1934. Standard finish at the time was blue. It is estimated that approx. 5% of all Colt revolver production was nickel finished. While rarer, most collectors still prefer blue.

Photo 30 = Colt Aircrewman, .38 Spl., ser. no. 3,478LW, 80%-85% overall (cylinder oxidation lowers the condition factor 10%). Originally designed as a lightweight, survival throwaway revolver for the Air Force, this model featured a unique aluminum frame and cylinder. Tests, however, revealed the cylinder could not withstand some .38 Special loads, and the Pentagon, circa 1961, ordered the entire run destroyed — approx. only 2 dozen survived. Cylinder wear is due to intense heat generated when fired (not recommended!).

Photo 31 = Colt Cobra, .38 Spl., ser. no. 75,990, 90%+ overall. Note slight wear on perimeter of lower frame. This is another good example of different metals being used for construction, as the alloy frame bluing retains a different color from the barrel, cylinder and trigger, although a similar bluing process was used. Grip bottoms are just beginning to show slight wear. Compared to the 21 oz. Detective Special, Colt's original "Pocket Rocket", the Cobra weighed only 15 oz.

Photo 32 = Colt Banker's Special Model, .22 LR, ser. no. 369,179, 60% overall. Note bluing discoloration and splotching on receiver and cylinder, while grips are mint. These short-barreled revolvers were mfg. in both .22 LR and .38 New Police calibers, and were primarily used by railway mail clerks of the U.S. Post Office. During the bank robbery era of the Depression, more than a few also found their way into the top desk drawers of worried bankers.

Photo 33 = Colt Gold Cup National Match, .38 Special Mid Range, ser. no. 8591-MR, NIB condition. Slide legend indicates that this is a pre-Series 70 National Match. First offered in 1957 in .45 ACP only, the .38 mid-range or wad-cutter cal. was introduced during 1961. Redesigned in 1962, the result was the so-called Mark III Gold Cup 38 Special. This Colt semi-auto has the Elliason adj. rear sight, mfg. 1972 (parts cleanup). Note top of slide and front frame non-glare matte finish.

Photo 34 = Remington Rand Model 1911A1, .45 ACP, ser. no. 1,322,815, 95% overall, original parkerized military finish. Without frame edge wear, this gun would jump up to 98% in a hurry. Brown plastic grips are mint, and magazine bottom is very clean. Color of parkerized frame and slide is typical for this period of military manufacture. Some enthusiasts seem to think this model is rare – not so, Remington made almost 900,000 of these between 1941-1945, using mostly Colt parts.

95%
0%   100%
Photo Percentage
Grading System™

Photo 35 = Colt Model 1911A1 U.S. Military, .45 ACP, ser. no. 2,302,708, 75%-80% overall. Nice original military model with mostly holster edge wear. Rear of frame next to grip safety shows some abuse – hopefully, a wartime story could justify this. Grips are near perfect, but screws show holster wear. Observe lack of wear on front grip strap, another indication this gun probably went in and out of the holster more often than it was shot.

Photo 36 = Colt Model 1911A1 Commercial, .45 ACP, ser. no. C177,027, approx. 70% overall. Again, note the holster wear on the frame and slide edges – front grip strap shows more wear than Photo 35. The fit and finish on these commercial models were far superior to military production. While this condition factor today isn't worth the big bucks, the shootability is excellent, because of the crisp trigger pull and overall production tolerances are not as sloppy as most military 1911A1s.

Photo 37= Colt Model 1908 Pocket, .380 ACP, ser. no. 64,984, 80%-85% overall. Typical freckling and bluing discoloration are evident on this semi-auto. Also observe nice, strong rampant Colt logo on rear of slide and slight wear on grips. A John Browning design, over 138,000 of this model were made during its 37 years of production – including this 1923 specimen. Outselling its .32 ACP counterpart by over 400%, this model gained rapid consumer acceptance – John Dillinger even preferred it!

Photo 38 = Browning Model 1905-FN (Vest Pocket), second variation, .25 ACP, ser. no. 388,888, 75%-80% overall. Compare the wear on this gun to Photo 37, observe how the front of slide and butt has suffered serious abuse. Not rare, over one million (both variations) were manufactured by Browning between 1906-1959. This Browning model and its configuration became a yardstick for other manufacturers - over 200 different companies manufactured copies of this model! Typically priced in the $120-$150 range in today's shooter marketplace.

Photo 39 = Ruger Standard Model Semi-Auto, .22 LR, ser. no. 410,587, 98%+ overall. Slight frame wear in front of ser. no. knocks this gun out of mint condition. 1/8 in. high ser. no. indicates 1962-1968 mfg. After the GCA of 1968, Sturm Ruger started putting a prefix in front of the serial number. Certainly nothing rare here, simply a nice, original gun with box and papers. Every year, there are a few less specimens in this condition factor, due to normal use and abuse.

Photo 40 = Luger 1920 Commercial Model with grip safety, 7.65 Luger cal., ser. no. 4,089N, 97%-98% overall. One of the more collectible German handguns, there is a Luger for almost everyone's particular preference and budget. Prices can range from $175 to $1,000,000! Original condition is polar north for Luger collectors, and sometimes, the price difference between even 98% and mint can be over double. Observe slight wear at end of barrel, side plate, safety pivot, and grip safety.

Photo 41 = Walther Model PP, .380 ACP (9mm kurz) ser. no. 32,807A, 98% overall, includes cardboard "alligator" box and 15 meter test target. Note very light frame pitting next to finger extension magazine. This pistol is marked "Interarms" on right side. Quantities of used West German Police PPs (mostly in .32 ACP) have been recently imported into the U.S., affecting the normal supply/demand economics for this model. For this reason, earlier guns without recent import markings are currently more desirable.

Photo 42 = Walther Model PPK (Eagle N proofed), .32 ACP (7.65 mm), ser. no. 280,446 K, 95% overall. Standard WW II German commercial pistol - wear on front of slide is indicative of holster use. Note slight wear on magazine release button, it appears that the fire-blued safety lever on this specimen has had the color "touched up". Slight mill marks on frame are typical for this period of manufacture (after April, 1940). Finger extension mag is original.

Photo 43 = WW II P.38, byf-44 (code for Mauser production during 1944), 9mm Para., ser. no. 6,431R, 95% overall. WW II P.38s were made by Mauser, Walther, and Spreewerke, resulting in a variety of manufacturing quality. Early wartime production retained the quality of pre-war commercial models, while late-war guns were inconsistent in finish quality. Condition below 95% on common wartime P.38s loses collectibility in a hurry, as many premium condition pistols survived the war.

Photo 44 = Walther Model PPK (Eagle C Nazi proofed), .32 ACP (7.65 mm), ser. no. 409,844 K, 65%-70% overall. An original wartime Nazi Police issue, this gun has accumulated some serious pitting and rust. Examine circular rough milling on frame (indicative during this period of late war mfg.), in addition to serious pitting on slide grips, and trigger guard. Pin protruding in front of hammer is loaded chamber indicator – obviously, this pistol is ready to fire.

Photo 45 = Walther Olympia Sport Model, .22 LR, ser. no. 53,640, 80%+ overall. Even though this commercial model (mfg. 1936-1940) shows considerable exterior finish wear, its capabilities as a shooter have certainly not been diminished. Equipped with a glass-like mechanism while combining a hot, butter-like trigger pull, this 60 year old gun, in the right hands, will shoot as well or better than anything manufactured today. Seldom seen in today's marketplace, don't underestimate this model's quality and shooting value.

Photo 46 = Magnum Research Stainless Desert Eagle .44 Mag. Pistol? Notta! Becoming ever more popular, this Japanese "air-soft" replica utilizes a working, blowback action supplied by compressed air stored in the magazine to fire plastic pellets. The warning tag attached to the trigger guard lets you know that pointing this type of realistic toy at somebody without their suspecting it originally sent David Horowitz into a tailspin on national television. While a conversation piece, treat it like a real gun!

Photos 47 & 48 = Gastinne Renette (Paris) Parlour Pistol, 6mm rimfire, w/o ser. no., engraved, 95%+ overall. Probably made for a well-to-do pre WW I European who wanted a top-quality rimfire pistol to shoot inside during the winter. If you're looking for Old World quality and craftsmanship, this type of gun offers both at minimal cost. Elaborate wood carving & checkering, platinum & gold inlays on the staggered fluted barrel, extensive engraving, and ultra-smooth rolling block action would cost thousands to replace today. Most of these pistols are in this condition or better, since they were never misused and probably treated as well as the owner's children.

Photo 49 = Olympic Arms OA-93 Semi-Auto Pistol, .223 cal., ser. no. 0P185, mint condition. Bad boy looks - if you're going to go Postal (or need the right piece for Arnold Schwarzenegger's next movie), accept no substitutes! This short-lived pre-Crime Bill model had very limited manufacture, less than 500 were produced before the Feds shut the door on this type of configuration. Of all the guns pictured in the 20th Anniversary Edition **Photo Percentage Grading System**, this pistol got everyone's attention in a hurry during the photo shoot. Hollywood and Willem Dafoe made this model look evil in the Harrison Ford movie, *Clear and Present Danger,* sans scope – go figure!

Twentieth 1999 • Anniversary • 2000 Edition

Blue Book of Gun Values™

		APRIL				S		S		MAY				S

APRIL: 1 2 3 | 4 5 6 7 8 9 10 | 11 12 13 14 15 16 17 | 18 19 20 21 22 23 24 | 25 26 27 28 29 30

MAY: 1 | 2 3 4 5 6 7 8 | 9 10 11 12 13 14 15 | 16 17 18 19 20 21 22 | 23 24 25 26 27 28 29 | 30 31

JUNE: 1 2 3 4 5 | 6 7 8 9 10 11 12 | 13 14 15 16 17 18 19 | 20 21 22 23 24 25 26 | 27 28 29 30

JULY: 1 2 3 | 4 5 6 7 8 9 10 | 11 12 13 14 15 16 17 | 18 19 20 21 22 23 24 | 25 26 27 28 29 30 31

AUGUST: 1 2 3 4 5 6 7 | 8 9 10 11 12 13 14 | 15 16 17 18 19 20 21 | 22 23 24 25 26 27 28 | 29 30 31

SEPTEMBER: 1 2 3 4 | 5 6 7 8 9 10 11 | 12 13 14 15 16 17 18 | 19 20 21 22 23 24 25 | 26 27 28 29 30

OCTOBER: 1 2 | 3 4 5 6 7 8 9 | 10 11 12 13 14 15 16 | 17 18 19 20 21 22 23 | 24 25 26 27 28 29 30 | 31

NOVEMBER: 1 2 3 4 5 6 | 7 8 9 10 11 12 13 | 14 15 16 17 18 19 20 | 21 22 23 24 25 26 27 | 28 29 30

DECEMBER: 1 2 3 4 | 5 6 7 8 9 10 11 | 12 13 14 15 16 17 18 | 19 20 21 22 23 24 25 | 26 27 28 29 30 31

JANUARY: 1 | 2 3 4 5 6 7 8 | 9 10 11 12 13 14 15 | 16 17 18 19 20 21 22 | 23 24 25 26 27 28 29 | 30 31

FEBRUARY: 1 2 3 4 5 | 6 7 8 9 10 11 12 | 13 14 15 16 17 18 19 | 20 21 22 23 24 25 26 | 27 28 29

MARCH: 1 2 3 4 | 5 6 7 8 9 10 11 | 12 13 14 15 16 17 18 | 19 20 21 22 23 24 25 | 26 27 28 29 30 31

Photo 51 = Left side of Marlin Model 94 in Photo 50 – probably 95%+ case colors. If you like strong original case colors, it doesn't get much better than this! This side of the rifle has more vivid case colors than shown above. Colors, mottling, and swirl patterns are indicative of typical Marlin case colors. A Marlin lever action with this amount of original case colors, bluing, and stock/forearm finish is encountered in approximately only 1 out of 500 rifles.

95%

0%   100%

Photo Percentage
Grading System

Photo 50 = Marlin Model 94, .25-20 cal., ser. no. 447,669, 95% overall case colors on frame and lever, 98% bluing on barrel and magazine tube. Marlin & Winchester collectors will always reach a little deeper into their wallets when encountering case colors and overall condition like this. Careful observation will reveal light flaking on sliding breech bolt, minimal hammer wear, and slightly oversized stock and forearm wood (normal for this serial range).

Photo 52 = Marlin Model 1893, .32-40 cal., ser. no. 329,262, 98% vivid case colors. Observe the original case colors on the sliding breech block of this gun compared to the flaked bluing depicted in Photo 50. Also, the stock and forearm condition (note the light dings, nicks and scratches) are not as pristine as pictured above. When this type of superior receiver condition is encountered, barrel and magazine tube bluing should always be 90% or greater.

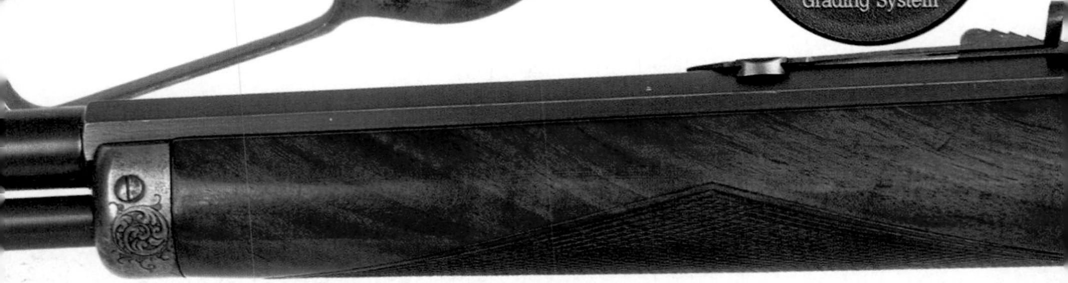

Photo 54 = Left side of engraved Marlin Model 97 pictured below. Engraved No. 2 oval panel scene with perimeter scrollwork depicts a good-sized buck making tracks in a hurry. Marlin's factory engraving patterns included Nos. 1, 2, 3, 5, (four different styles), 10, and 15. This gun has seen very little use as evident by the lack of handling nicks, scratches, and normal dings. Also, almost all the original stock and forearm varnish remains in addition to checkering being sharp.

Photo 53 = Marlin Model 1893, .30-30 cal., ser. no. 235,827, approx. 60% case colors, 95% barrel bluing. This standard rifle features a full octagon barrel and buckhorn rear sight. Overall excellent wood, retaining most of the original stock and forearm varnish. The condition factor of this Marlin Model 1893 is still considerably above the average specimen collectors may encounter at a typical gun show.

Photo 55 = Marlin engraved Model 97, .22 LR cal., ser. no. 417,509, 20%-30% receiver case colors with 95%+ barrel (½ round, ½ octagon) and mag tube bluing. This Deluxe Model 97 features a standard No. 2 Marlin engraving pattern, including forearm cap. Case colors on engraved guns are usually less prominent than a similar model without engraving. Examine the figure in the checkered walnut forearm, always a sign of top-quality American crotch walnut.

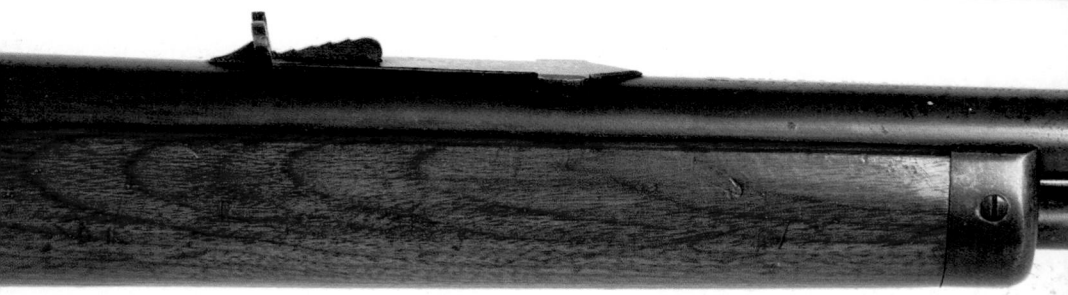

Photo 56 = Marlin Model 94, .32-20 cal., ser. no. 377,920, approx. 20% fading receiver case colors with minor freckling and 90% barrel and mag tube bluing. Note condition of stock as compared to Photo 57. This round barreled rifle is still in better condition than an average gun. Most collectors would consider this Marlin a nice, "no problem" gun – how much would you take for it?

Photo 57 = Marlin Model 1889, .32-20 cal., ser. no. 95,404, plum colored receiver with traces of bluing left in protected areas only, approx. 75% browning barrel blue. Compare the color of this gun's receiver to Photo 56. Notice normal oil soaking in stock and forearm where they meet frame. Careful observation also shows that bolt and frame use different metals, as color of bluing is different.

Photo 58 = Marlin Model 1893, .32-20 cal., ser. no. 336,107, overall receiver finish has turned to a smooth plum-brown patina, devoid of any bluing, but note that frame metal surface is fairly clean with minor surface oxidation. Marlin lever action aficionados have probably already spotted that the front end of this rifle (i.e. barrel, mag. tube, and forearm) is not original and has been replaced by similar parts from a later Model 336 with beavertail forearm.

95%
Photo Percentage
Grading System™
0%   100%

20%
Photo Percentage
Grading System™
0%   100%

50%
Photo Percentage
Grading System™
0%   100%

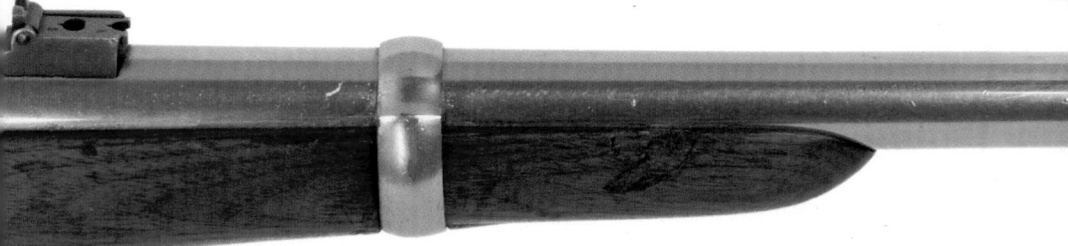

Photo 59 = Remington Rolling Block Baby Carbine, .44-40 cal., no ser. no., approx. 95% overall original nickel finish. Original early Remington nickel finish sometimes looks questionable to the untrained eye, but everything on this Carbine is original. Nicely figured walnut stock and forearm are in excellent condition, except for the gouge on right side of upper tang. Nickel finish in this model is rare, and this specimen's condition factor makes it even more scarce.

Photo 60 = Colt Lightning Saddle Ring Baby Carbine, .44-40 cal., ser. no. 28,454, approx. 20% nickel finish, with receiver mostly dark. This photo proves that a badly worn nickel finish in most cases will look worse than an equally worn blue finish. Yet this specimen rates about average condition when sampling nickel-finished Colt Lightnings. Observe traces of barrel finish around the perimeter of forearm and lack of wood varnish.

Photo 61 = Marlin Model 1894, Saddle Ring Carbine, .44-40 cal., ser. no. 185,126, approx. 50% overall, with factory nickel finish. While this gun's condition does not appear too pleasing, it is an average example of a worn nickel finish from this bygone era. Observe light crack in stock. Very few nickel Marlin Model 1894s are known to exist, so this gun's condition factor takes a back seat due to rarity.

Photo 62 = **Marlin Model 27-S**, .32-20 cal., ser. no. 2,134, 98% bright blue overall - a very crisp specimen with no problems, observe slight wear on back of hammer and overall sharpness of frame edges and octagon barrel. Whenever condition looks this good, be somewhat cautious, as refinishing could explain the superior condition factor. Overpolishing when refinishing sometimes makes these crisp edges look soft, even round. Examine the light wood color, free of oil soaking.

Photo 63 = **Marlin Model 27-S**, .25 cal. (changeable firing pin allows converting from rimfire to centerfire), ser. no. 150, approx. 80%+ bright blue overall. Compare this gun's overall condition factor to the one pictured in Photo 62. The additional wear explains metal and wood coloration differences. The takedown lever is also down on this photo, revealing a thin, circular line of frame wear created when pivoting. Still, a much better than average condition specimen.

Photo 64 = **Marlin Model 20-A**, .22 cal., no ser. no., approx. 50% receiver and barrel bluing, starting to turn a brownish patina. This rifle has good-looking original wood with some wear to varnish. Close scrutiny will reveal the middle screw on top of frame is missing – a minor problem. Since most guns like this were used rather heavily, the condition factor is appropriate for this gun's utilitarian nature.

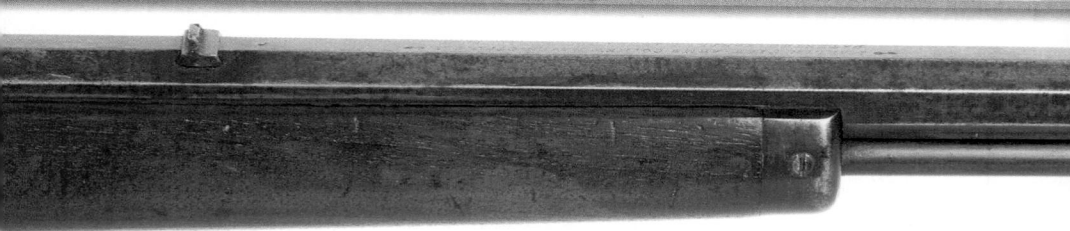

Photo 65 = **Marlin Model 1891 (rare side-loader variation)**, .22 cal., ser. no. 47,791, Plum brown-dark patina finish on receiver and octagon barrel. Typical nicely worn and smooth wood to metal fit, with normal oil soaking evident on average wood - this is an average condition factor for this model. It is important to remember that when this gun was first purchased, it could have literally been used everyday for years, something that happens very rarely in today's firearms marketplace.

Photo 66 = **Winchester Model 1906 slide action**, .22 LR, no ser. no. Traces of bluing left in protected areas with balance of metal finish turning a plum brown patina. Originally priced in 1906 with gumwood stock at $10.50, this model's price appeared inexpensive to the older Model 1890 priced at $16. This type of bread and butter shooter is almost impossible to find today in better than 80% original condition, despite Winchester having made almost 850,000 of this model alone.

Photo 67 = **Winchester Model 1892 Short Rifle**, .44-40 cal., ser. no. 414,816. Mostly greyish patina overall, and apparent nickel finish are explained by the metal becoming shiny with age and wear. Special order 14 in. octagon barrel (very rare), was probably sold to South America originally, as this barrel length was banned due to the 1928 Machine Gun Act, making anything less than 16 in. barrels illegal. Would you believe $2,250 for this rusty dug-up? Moral – Winchester + rarity = BUCK$.

Photo 68 = Army & Navy Sidelock Model, 12 ga., ser. no. 21,488, approx. 10% receiver case colors, mostly in protected areas, 95% barrel bluing, Purdey-style tight scroll and rose engraving, note engraved scalloped shoulders, probably manufactured by W.J. Jeffery for London's Army & Navy store pre-WW I. Many quality English side-by-sides have had their barrels refinished (including this one) – value is not affected that much, however.

Photo 69 = Winchester Model 21, 16 ga., ser. no. 28,721, 95%+ overall, boxlock action, Winchester's best quality, relatively low production side-by-side has always been collectible, especially in the smaller gauges. On this model, always inspect the receiver bottom carefully, as this area is usually the first to accumulate wear, especially flaking. Checkering is still in excellent condition, with only slight point wear in front of forearm.

Photo 70 = Browning Superposed Skeet Model, .410 bore, ser. no. 669J3, 99% overall. A rounded pistol grip indicates pre-1966 mfg., in addition to the light-colored walnut. A good way to tell if a Superposed has been shot a lot, is to notice if the barrel assembly opens almost automatically when the opening lever has been engaged. Another tell-tale sign is when the opening lever has worn its way left of center on the upper tang.

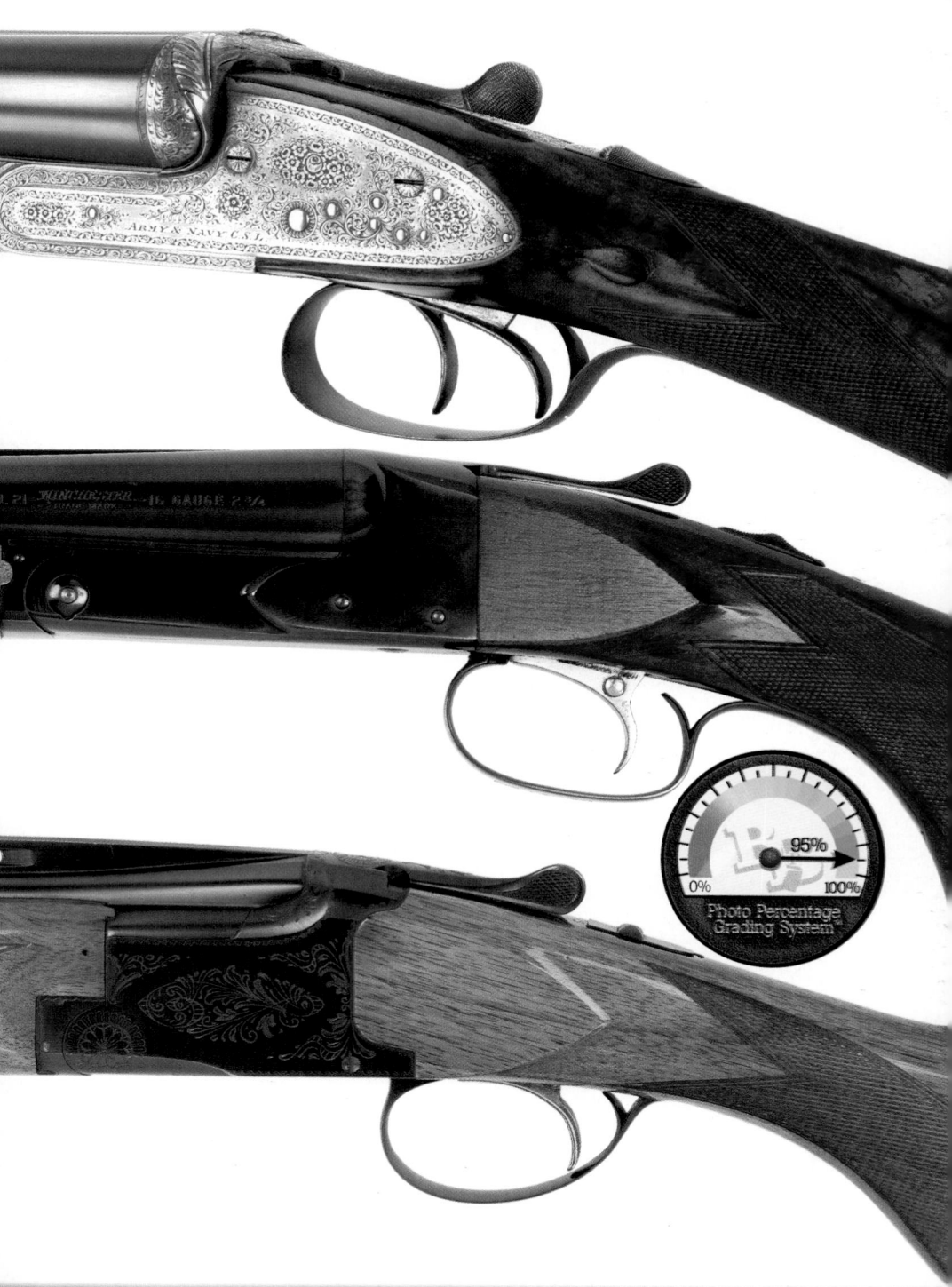

ARMY & NAVY C.S.L.

1 21 WINCHESTER - 16 GAUGE 2 3/4

95%

0%   100%

Photo Percentage
Grading System™

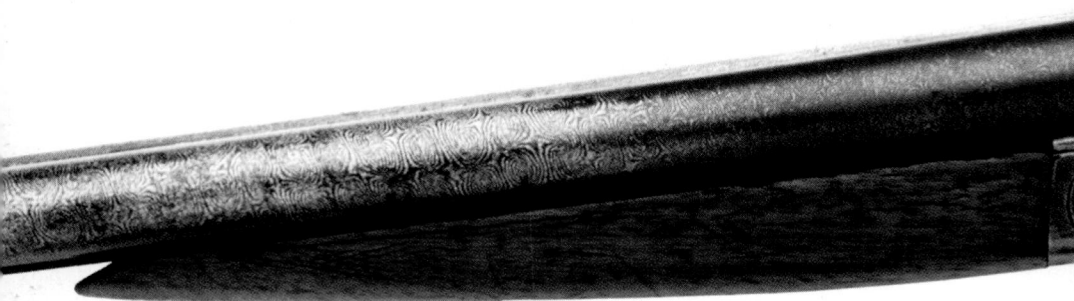

Photo 71 = Remington Damascus Model 1900, 12 ga., ser. no. 316,534, NRA Poor Condition, note poorly installed screw in the chipped stock by frame. Barrels have been cleaned starting halfway up the forearm - observe how the damascus patterning is much more vivid after the layers of surface oxidation, dirt/grime, and dried gun oil have been removed. Thousands of similar condition, under $125 shotguns could also be dramatically improved with a little oil & elbow grease!

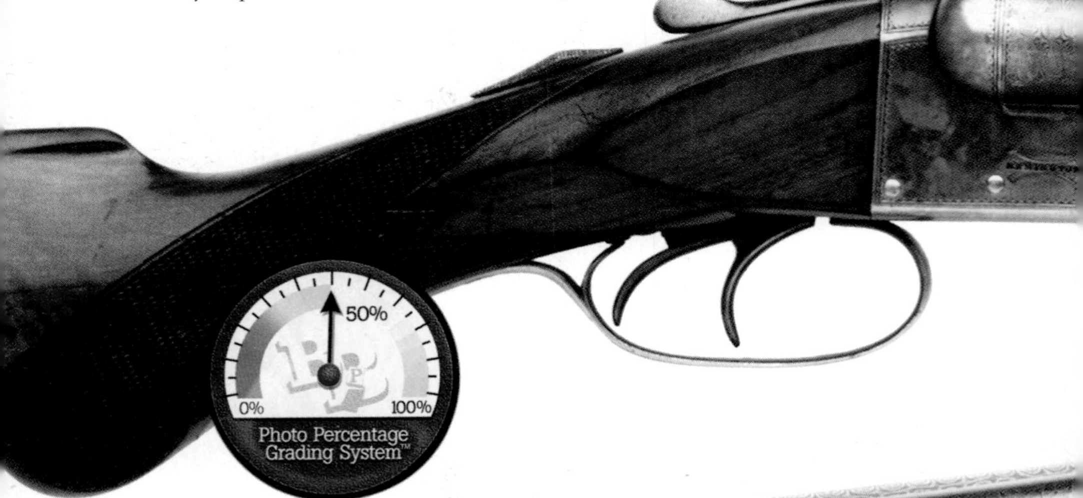

50%

0%   100%

Photo Percentage
Grading System™

Photo 73 = Parker Damascus GH Model, 12 ga., ser. no. 113,550, 100% professional-ly refurbished, a good example of what kind of results you can get from the right gun refur-bished by the right people. Owner originally paid $350 for this shiny, no problem damas-cus Parker. After another $450, it looked like this! Professional restorations can actually enhance a worn-out gun's value, but you **must** have the **right combination** of gun and refurbishing expertise.

Photo 72 = Remington Damascus Model 1894, 12 ga., ser. no. 126, 715, approx. 50% case colors with 80% damascus barrel patterns and wood finish, compare condition to Photo 71. The wide range of damascus steel barrel patterns is also evident looking at the shotguns on these pages. Note how tight these patterns are compared to the Model 1900 pictured above. Older SxSs in this original condition factor or better are becoming more popular every year.

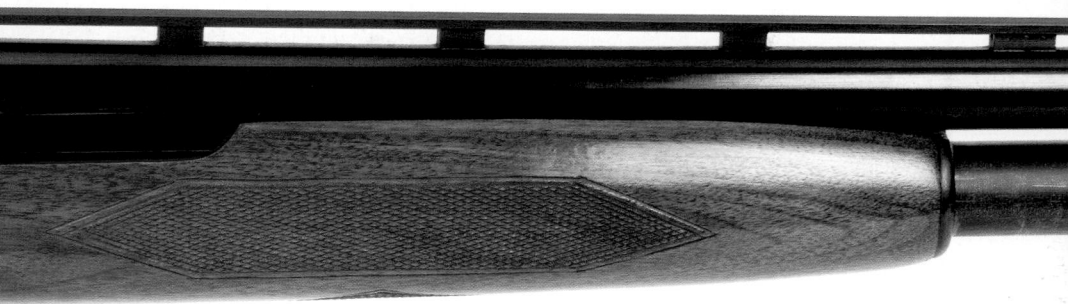

Photo 74 = Winchester Model 12 Trap Model, 12 ga., ser. no. 1,921,515, 98% overall. A nice straight Model 12 that has been shot very little. Notice the lack of wear on magazine tube compared to Photos 76 & 78. No visible wear on checkering and the breech block is still shiny with no horizontal striations, which would indicate frequent use (see Photo 78). Also examine sharp edges and lines on this shotgun's frame.

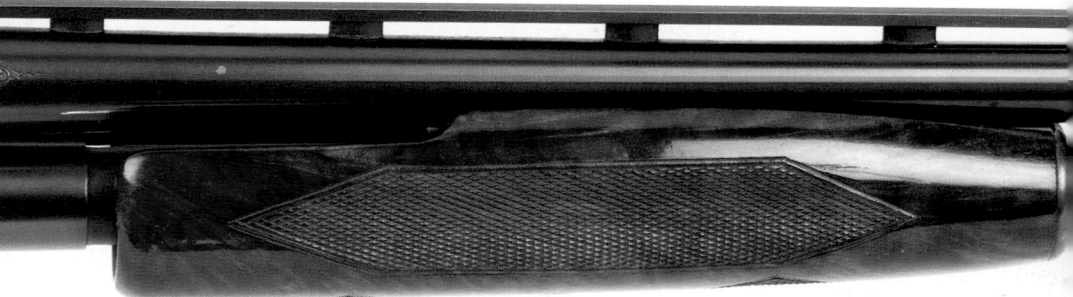

Photo 75 = Winchester Model 12 Pigeon Grade with No. 5 factory engraving, 16 ga., ser. no. 1,844,108, 95%+ overall. Manufactured early in 1960, the engine-turned breech block is tell-tale sign of a Pigeon Grade. The No. 5 engraving pattern was Winchester's most elaborate engraving option at the time, and included light scroll-work on barrel assembly as well. While a plain Jane Model 12 retailed for $109.15, this Pigeon Grade with engraving tipped the scales at almost $450!

Photo 76 = Winchester Model 1912, 20 ga., ser. no. 2,011, 90% overall, full choke. This Model 1912 was built during the first year of manufacture – always a plus for Winchester collectors. Note the original thin-grip stock configuration, mag. tube wear (important on any Model 12), and perfect wood to metal fit. While open choke (cylinder & improved cylinder) Model 12s are currently more desirable than full choke, this first year gun will still command a front row position in a Model 12 collection.

Photo 77 = **Winchester Model 25,** 12 ga., ser. no. 47,808, approx. 85% overall. The Model 12's red-headed cousin, the Model 25 was manufactured 1949-1954 as a non-takedown version of the Model 12. Close inspection reveals major pitting on barrel and magazine hanger bracket. Receiver and slide edge wear are typical for this condition factor. The shooting value of this specimen largely determines its value.

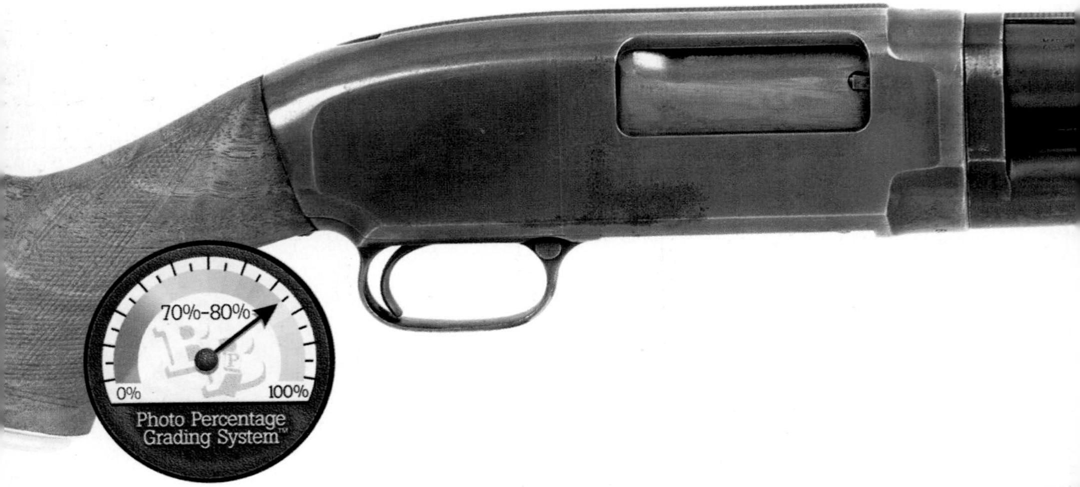

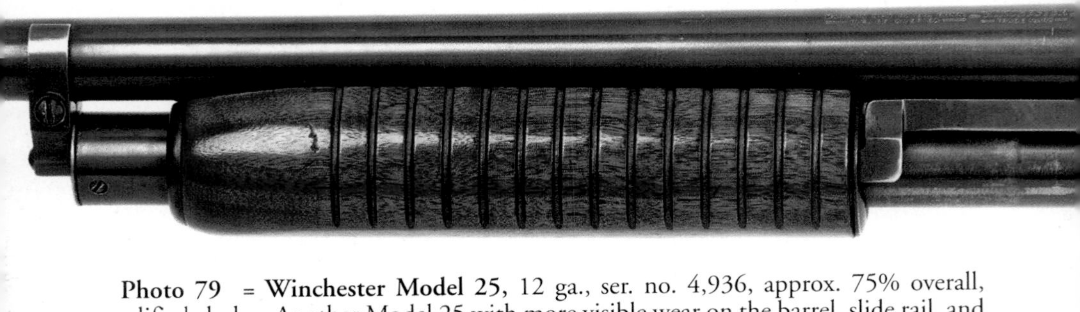

Photo 79 = **Winchester Model 25,** 12 ga., ser. no. 4,936, approx. 75% overall, modified choke. Another Model 25 with more visible wear on the barrel, slide rail, and bottom of magazine tube. Even though this specimen does not have the condition of gun pictured in Photo 77, it also doesn't have any pitting. As a result, many potential buyers would rather own this gun than the one in Photo 77.

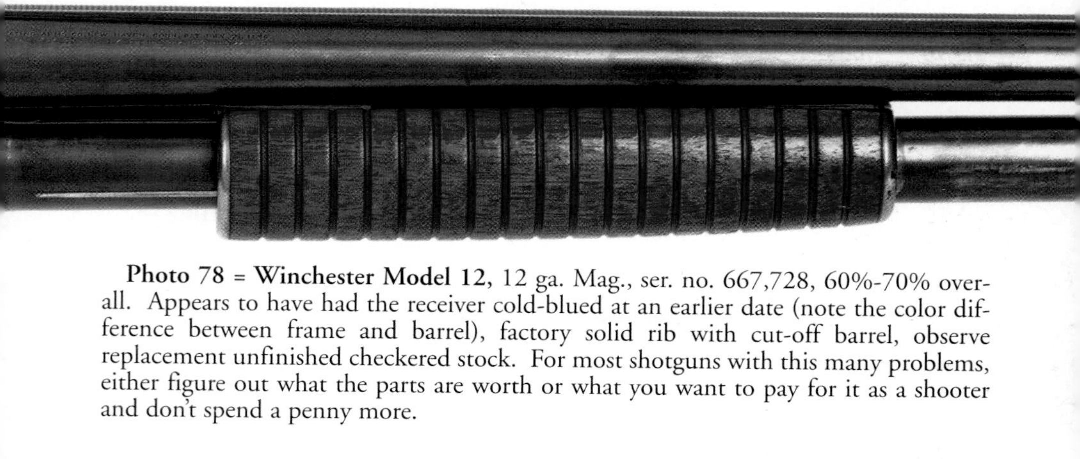

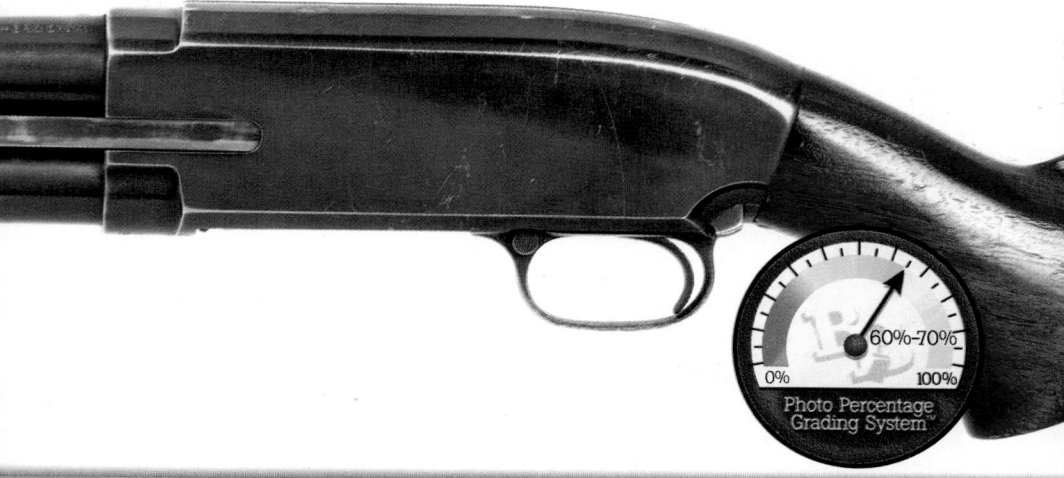

Photo 78 = Winchester Model 12, 12 ga. Mag., ser. no. 667,728, 60%-70% over-all. Appears to have had the receiver cold-blued at an earlier date (note the color difference between frame and barrel), factory solid rib with cut-off barrel, observe replacement unfinished checkered stock. For most shotguns with this many problems, either figure out what the parts are worth or what you want to pay for it as a shooter and don't spend a penny more.

Photos 80 & 81 = F.W. Kessler Drilling manufactured in Suhl, formerly in East Germany, (16 ga. x 16 ga. x 8 x 57mm). As a nice way to end the **Photo Percentage Grading System** in the 20th Anniversary Edition, a best quality German deep relief engraving pattern has been included. Observe Drilling-type safety on back of left side plate. Elaborate sidelock action with 8 pins is typical of German craftsmanship and engineering. Carefully inspect the minute details that were created by this engraver's imagination, hammer and chisel. In the Deutsche tradition, all receiver surfaces have been engraved — observe oak leaves on side plate perimeter and frame shoulders. It's entirely possible to wear out several pair of tennis shoes while walking many gun shows and still never find a gun this good!

A section

A.A.

Previously manufactured by Azanza & Arrizabalaga located in Eibar, Spain.

Grading	100%	98%	95%	90%	80%	70%	60%

PISTOLS: SEMI-AUTO

A.A. — 7.65mm cal., semi-auto pistol, slide marked Azanza & Arrizabalaga Model 1916, A.A. in oval on frame.

	100%	98%	95%	90%	80%	70%	60%
	$130	$105	$85	$65	$55	$50	$45

REIMS — 6.35mm or 7.65mm cal., semi-auto pistol, copies of M1906 Browning, marked 1914 Model.

	100%	98%	95%	90%	80%	70%	60%
	$120	$100	$75	$65	$55	$50	$45

A.A.A.

Previously manufactured by Aldazabal located in Spain.

PISTOLS: SEMI-AUTO

M1919 — 7.65mm cal., semi-auto pistol.

	100%	98%	95%	90%	80%	70%	60%
	$110	$100	$85	$70	$65	$60	$55

A.A. ARMS INC.

Current manufacturer located in Monroe, NC. Distributor, dealer, and direct consumer sales.

AP9 MINI-SERIES PISTOL — 9mm Para. cal., semi-auto blowback paramilitary design, phosphate/blue or nickel finish, 2 barrel lengths, 10 (C/B 1994) or 20★ shot mag.

	100%	98%	95%	90%	80%	70%	60%
No Mfg.'s Retail	$245	$210	$185	$165	$150	$135	$125

    Add $20 for nickel finish.
    Add $200 for AP9 long barrel Target Model (banned 1994).

AR9 CARBINE — similar action to AP9, except has carbine length barrel and side-folding metal stock. Banned 1994.

	100%	98%	95%	90%	80%	70%	60%
	$750	$625	$550	$475	$400	$350	$300

A & B HIGH PERFORMANCE FIREARMS

Current competition pistol manufacturer located in Arvin, CA. Direct consumer sales.

PISTOLS: SEMI-AUTO

LIMITED CLASS — 9mm Para. or .38 Super cal., single action, competition M1911-styled action, STI frame, Ultimatch bull barrel, Caspian slide, Bomar adj. rear sight, blue or chrome finish.

	100%	98%	95%	90%	80%	70%	60%
Mfg.'s Sug. Retail $1,875	$1,875	$1,600	$1,375	$1,150	$925	$700	$550

OPEN CLASS — 9mm Para. or .38 Super cal., single action, competition M1911-styled action, STI frame, Ultimatch or Hybrid compensated barrel, Caspian slide, C-More scope, blue or chrome finish.

	100%	98%	95%	90%	80%	70%	60%
Mfg.'s Sug. Retail $2,800	$2,800	$2,300	$1,875	$1,600	$1,375	$1,000	$750

Grading	100%	98%	95%	90%	80%	70%	60%

A A & R SALES

Previous manufacturer located in South El Monte, CA.

PISTOLS: SEMI-AUTO

HANDGUN — .45 ACP cal., semi-auto patterned after Colt Model 1911 Govt., less weight than normal Colt .45.

	100%	98%	95%	90%	80%	70%	60%
	$225	$205	$175	$155	$145	$135	$125

RIFLES: SEMI-AUTO

RIFLE: MARK IV SPORTER — .308 Win. cal., semi-auto, M-14 style action, clip fed, adj. sights.

	100%	98%	95%	90%	80%	70%	60%
	$295	$260	$225	$200	$175	$155	$140

A F C

Previously manufactured by Auguste Francotte located in Liege, Belgium, 1912-1914.

PISTOLS: SEMI-AUTO

SEMI-AUTO PISTOL — 6.35mm cal., 6 shot mag., frame marked "Francotte Liege".

	100%	98%	95%	90%	80%	70%	60%
	$275	$250	$220	$165	$140	$110	$85

A. J. ORDNANCE

Previous manufacturer located in Covina, CA.

THOMAS — .45 ACP cal., semi-auto, double action only, 6 shot, 3½ in. barrel, fixed sights, checkered plastic grips, delayed blowback action, stainless steel barrel. Disc. mid-1970s.

	100%	98%	95%	90%	80%	70%	60%
	$600	$525	$450	$400	$350	$300	$250

Add 50% for chrome or stainless steel.

A K S (AK-47 & AKM Copies)

Select fire paramilitary design rifle originally designed in Russia (initials refer to Avtomat Kalashnikova, 1947). Russian mfg. select fire AK-47s have not been mfg. since the mid-50's. Semi-auto AK-47 and AKM clones are currently manufactured by several arsenals in China including Norinco and Poly Technologies, Inc., in addition to other countries including the Czech Republic, Bulgaria, Russia, Egypt and Hungary. On April 6th, 1998, recent "sporterized" variations (imported 1994-1998) with thumbhole stocks were banned by presidential order, with further legal action planned.

AK-47s are not rare - over 700 million have been manufactured in China alone since WW II.

AK/AK-47/AKM HISTORY & RECENT IMPORTATION

Since the early 1950s, the AK/AK-47/AKM series of select fire rifles has been the standard issue military rifle of the former Soviet Union and its satellites. It continues to fulfill that role reliably today. The AK series of rifles, from the early variants of the AK-47 through the AKM and AK-74, is undoubtedly the most widely used military small arms design in the world. Developed by Mikhail Kalashnikov (the AK stands for Avtomat Kalashnikova) in 1946, the AK went into full production in 1947 in Izhevsk, Russia. Since then, variants of the original AK-47 have been manufactured by almost every former Soviet bloc country and some free world nations, including Egypt. Even the Israeli Galil borrows design characteristics from the Kalashnikov. The AK action is the basis for numerous other weapons, including the RPK (Ruchnoy Pulemyot Kalashnikova). The basic AK design was changed in the mid-1950s to the AKM and incorporates more efficient production methods, using stamped rather than milled receivers. The AKM's

Grading	100%	98%	95%	90%	80%	70%	60%

modifications also incorporated numerous internal design changes to improve reliability and ease of maintenance.

A

The AK was designed to be, and always has been, a "peasant-proof" military weapon. It is a robust firearm, both in design and function. Its record on the battlefields around the world is impressive, rivaled only by the great M1 Garand of the U.S. or bolt rifles such as the English Mark III Enfield. The original AK-47 prototypes are on display in the Red Army Museum in Moscow.

All of the current semi-auto AK "clones" are copies of the AKM's basic receiver design and internal components minus the full-auto parts. The Saiga rifle, manufactured by the Izhevsk Machining Plant, in Izhevsk, Russia, is the sole Russian entry in this market. It is available in the standard 7.62X39MM, 5.45X39MM and in .410 bore. Other European manufacturers include companies in the Czech Republic, Bulgaria, as well as the former Yugoslavia. The Egyptian-made Maahdi AK clones were also available in the U.S. market.

Value for almost all of the imported AK clones is based solely on their use as sporting or target rifles. Fit and finish varies by country and importer. Most fall on the "low" side. Interest peaked prior to the passage of the 1994 Crime Bill and both AK clones and their "high capacity" magazines were bringing a premium for a short period of time in 1993 and 1994. However, interest waned during 1995-97, and the reduced demand lowered prices. In November of 1997, the Clinton Administration instituted an "administrative suspension" on all import licenses for these types of firearms in order to do a study on their use as "sporting firearms".

On April 6th, 1998, the Clinton Administration, in the political wake of the Jonesboro tragedy, banned the further import of 58 "assault-type" rifles, claiming that these semi-autos could not be classified as sporting weapons - the AK-47 and most related configurations were included. During 1997, firearms importers obtained permits to import almost 600,000 reconfigured rifles - approximately only 20,000 had entered the country when this bill took effect. When the ban occurred, applications were pending to import an additional 1,000,000 guns. Previously, thumbhole-stocked AK Sporters were still legal for import, and recent exporters included the Czech Republic, Russia, and Egypt. No doubt, this para-military rifle design will once again become an active commodity, and pricing could fluctuate considerably depending on how consumers interpret upcoming supply and demand economics (i.e. "Banned! - While They Last - $499!").

RIFLES: SEMI-AUTO, AK-47 & AKM MODELS

Also refer to separate listings under Poly Technologies, Inc., Norinco, Federal Ordnance, B-West, K.B.I., Sentinel Arms, American Arms, Inc., and others who have imported this configuration up until now.

AK-47 (AKM) RECENT IMPORTS — 7.62x39mm (most common cal., former Russian M43 military), 5.45x39mm (Romanian mfg. or Saiga/MAK - recent mfg. only), or .223 Rem. cal., semi-auto Kalashnikov action, stamped (most common) or milled receiver, typically 16½ in. barrel, 5, 10, or 30★ (C/B 1994) shot mag., wood or synthetic stock and forearm except on folding stock model, recent importation (1994-early 1998) mostly had newer "sporterized" fixed stocks with thumbholes, may be supplied with bayonet, sling, cleaning kit, patterned after former military production rifle of China and Russia. Values listed below are for generic mfg.

	100%	98%	95%	90%	80%	70%	60%
	$360	$315	$275	$240	$220	$200	$175

Add 10-15% for 5.45x39mm cal.

Add 10-15% for older folding stock variations.

Chinese & recent Egyptian mfg.	$225	$195	$175	$150	$125	$100	$90

AK-47 technically designates the original select fire (semi or full-auto), Russian made military rifle with milled receiver. Recent semi-auto "clones" normally have stamped

Grading	100%	98%	95%	90%	80%	70%	60%

receivers and are technically designated AKMs. Recent mfg. AK-47 clones refer to rifles with milled receivers. Chinese importation stopped during late 1990.

Yugoslavian, Czechoslovakian, or Hungarian manufactured AK-47s will command premiums over standard Chinese arsenal mfg.

A M A C

See Iver Johnson section in this text. AMAC stands for American Military Arms Corporation manufactured in Jacksonville, AR. AMAC ceased operations early 1993.

A M T

Current trademark manufactured by Galena Industries Inc. located in Irwindale, CA. All new AMTs (Arcadia Machine & Tool) manufactured by Galena Industries Inc. beginning in 1998 have a lifetime warranty. Also see Irwindale Arms, Inc. and Auto-Mag for older discontinued models. Distributor and dealer sales.

PISTOLS: SEMI-AUTO

During late 1993, AMT changed from white outline Millett adj. sights to an adj. 3 dot (white) system mfg. by LPA in Italy.

LIGHTNING — .22 LR cal., semi-auto, stainless steel only, 5 (bull only), 6½, 8½, 10½, or 12½ (disc. 1987) in. bull or tapered barrels, adj. sights and trigger, pistol based on semi-auto Ruger action, tapered barrels. 23,903 were mfg. 1984-87.

$350 $200 $150

Last Mfg.'s Sug. Retail was $289.

This model features a frame grooved for scope mounts, Clark trigger, Millett sights, and either Pachmayr rubber or Wayland wood grips as standard equipment.

* ***Bull's Eye Regulation Target*** — similar to 6½ in. Lightning with bull barrel, except has vent. rib, wooden grips, extended rear sight. Mfg. 1986 only.

$425 $350 $285

Last Mfg.'s Sug. Retail was $436.

BABY AUTOMAG — .22 LR cal., semi-auto, stainless steel only, 8½ in. vent. rib barrel, Millett adj. sights, smooth walnut grips, 1,001 mfg.

$750 $650 $550

AUTOMAG II — .22 Mag. cal., stainless steel only, 3⅜ (Compact Model), 4½, or 6 in. barrel, gas assisted action, white outline Millett adj. sights, grooved Lexan grips, 7 (Compact) or 9 shot mag., 24-32 oz. New 1987.

Mfg.'s Sug. Retail $399 $305 $235 $195

AUTOMAG III — .30 Carbine or 9mm Win. Mag. (mfg. 1993 only) cal., stainless steel, 6⅜ in. barrel, patterned after Colt Govt. Model, white outline Millett adj. sights, grooved Lexan grips, 8 shot mag., 43 oz. New 1992.

Mfg.'s Sug. Retail $499 $410 $310 $250

AUTOMAG IV — 10mm (disc. 1993) or .45 Win. Mag. cal., 6½ (.45 Win. Mag. only) or 8⅝ (disc. 1993) in. barrel, 7/8 shot mag., Millett adj. sights, stainless steel, 46 oz. New 1992.

Mfg.'s Sug. Retail $599 $495 $425 $325

AUTOMAG V — .50 AE cal., stainless steel, 6½ in. barrel, gas venting system reduces recoil, 5 shot mag., 46 oz. Mfg. 1993-95.

$815 $700 $625

Last Mfg.'s Sug. Retail was $900.

AUTOMAG 440 — .440 Cor-Bon cal., special order only. New 1999.

Mfg.'s Sug. Retail $899 $775 $650 $550

Grading	100%	98%	95%	90%	80%	70%	60%

JAVELINA — 10mm cal., semi-auto, 7 in. barrel, 8 shot mag., Millett adj. sights, wraparound Neoprene grips, wide adj. trigger, long grip safety, 48 oz. Mfg. 1992 only.

$560 $460 $360

Last Mfg.'s Sug. Retail was $676.

BACKUP PISTOL — .22 LR (disc. 1987), .357 Sig. (new 1996), .380 ACP, .38 Super (new 1995), 9mm Para. (new 1995), .40 S&W (new 1995), .400 Cor-Bon (new 1997), or .45 ACP (new 1995) cal., semi-auto, choice of traditional double action (disc. 1992) or double action only (new 1992), 2½ (.22 LR or .380 ACP) or 3 in. barrel, stainless steel, Lexan grips, 5 (.380 ACP or .40 S&W), 6, or 8 (.22 LR) shot mag., 18 (.380 ACP only) or 23 oz. Older disc. walnut grip models are worth a slight premium.

* *.22 LR cal.* — .22 LR was in production briefly.

$300 $185 $140

* *.380 ACP cal.*
  Mfg.'s Sug. Retail $319 $225 $175 $135

* *9mm Para., .40 S&W, or .45 ACP cal.*
  Mfg.'s Sug. Retail $319 $225 $175 $135

* *.357 Sig., .38 Super, or .400 Cor-Bon cal.*
  Mfg.'s Sug. Retail $369 $260 $190 $150

In 1992, AMT re-engineered this model and removed all external levers.

BACKUP PISTOL II — .380 ACP cal., single action semi-auto, stainless steel, 2½ in. barrel, 5 shot finger extension mag., black carbon fiber grips, 18 oz. Mfg. 1993-1998.

$260 $190 $150

Last Mfg.'s Sug. Retail was $369.

.45 ACP STANDARD GOVERNMENT MODEL — .45 ACP cal., similar to Colt semi-auto Govt. model, stainless steel, 5 in. barrel, fixed rear sight, loaded chamber indicator, adj. trigger, wraparound neoprene grips, 38 oz.
Mfg.'s Sug. Retail $399 $325 $275 $225

HARDBALLER II — .45 ACP cal., similar to Colt Gold Cup Model, stainless steel, 5 in. barrel, adj. Millett rear sight, serrated rib, loaded chamber indicator, adj. trigger, wraparound neoprene grips, 38 oz.
Mfg.'s Sug. Retail $425 $340 $285 $230

Add $280 for 7 in. Hardballer conversion kit (disc. 1997).

* *Hardballer Longslide* — similar to Hardballer, except 7 in. barrel, longer slide assembly, and also available in .400 Cor-Bon (named .400 Accelerator, new 1998), 46 oz.
  Mfg.'s Sug. Retail $499 $385 $300 $240

  Add $50 for .400 Cor-Bon cal.
  Add $300 for 5 in. Longslide conversion kit (disc. 1997).

COMMANDO — .40 S&W cal., 4 in. barrel, new 1998.
Mfg.'s Sug. Retail $425 $340 $285 $230

SKIPPER — similar to Hardballer, except approx. 1 in. shorter slide on pre-'84 mfg, re-released in 1991 with choice of .40 S&W or .45 ACP cal., 4¼ in. barrel, checkered walnut grips, matte finish stainless steel, Millett adj. rear sight, 7 shot mag., 33 oz. Disc. 1991.

$350 $285 $250

Last Mfg.'s Sug. Retail was $450.

COMBAT SKIPPER — similar to Skipper, only with fixed sights. Disc. 1984.

$375 $330 $295

BULL'S EYE TARGET MODEL — .40 S&W cal., similar to Hardballer with 5 in. barrel, 8 shot mag., adj. Millett sights, wraparound neoprene grips, 38 oz. Mfg. 1991 only.

$400 $340 $295

Last Mfg.'s Sug. Retail was $500.

Grading	100%	98%	95%	90%	80%	70%	60%

A

"ON DUTY" DOUBLE ACTION — 9mm Para., .40 S&W, or .45 ACP (new late 1994) cal., stainless steel slide and barrel, 4½ in. barrel, 10 (C/B 1994), 15★ (9mm Para.), 11★ (.40 S&W), or 9 (.45 ACP) shot mag., 3-dot sighting system, anodized aluminum frame, trigger disconnect safety with inertia firing pin, carbon fiber grips, 32 oz. Mfg. 1991-94.

$385 $295 $250

Last Mfg.'s Sug. Retail was $470.

Add $60 for .45 ACP cal.

In 1992, this model became available with either traditional double action with decocking lever or double action only with safety.

RIFLES:SEMI-AUTO

All AMT rifles were discontinued in 1998.

LIGHTNING (25/22) — .22 LR cal., semi-auto based on Ruger 10-22 action, stainless steel, 30 shot mag., 17½ in. bull or tapered barrel, nylon pistol grip handle and forearm, folding stock with recoil pad or youth stock, fixed sights, 6 lbs. Mfg. 1986-1993.

$220 $175 $150

Last Mfg.'s Sug. Retail was $296.

SMALL GAME HUNTER (SGH) — .22 LR cal., same mechanical action as Lightning, except has matte black nylon stock with checkered forearm and grip, 22 in. barrel, 10 shot mag., no sights, removable recoil pad allows storage in stock, 6 lbs. Mfg. 1986-1993.

$230 $190 $160

Last Mfg.'s Sug. Retail was $300.

SMALL GAME HUNTER II — similar to Small Game Hunter, except has match grade 22 in. heavyweight full-floating barrel, 10 shot rotary mag., black fiberglass nylon stock, no sights, 6 lbs. Mfg. 1993 only.

$230 $190 $160

Last Mfg.'s Sug. Retail was $300.

Add $70 for 17½ in. stainless steel barrel.
Add $150 for 22½ in. stainless steel match grade barrel.

CHALLENGE EDITION (I, II, III) — .22 LR cal., semi-auto target variation featuring McMillan fiberglass stock, 16¼ (choice of 6 in. barrel weight extension or 3 in. muzzle brake, new 1997), 18, 20 (mfg. 1994-96), or 22 (mfg. 1994-96) in. floating stainless steel bull barrel, custom designed or Jewell (new 1997) trigger, custom order through AMT's Custom Shop. Mfg. 1994-98.

$1,075 $750 $650

Last Mfg.'s Sug. Retail was $1,296.

Subtract $200 without Jewell trigger.
Add $144 for 16¼ barrel with 3 in. muzzle brake (Challenge Edition II, new 1997).
Add $85 for 16¼ barrel with 6 in. barrel extension (Challenge Edition III).

★ *Challenge Edition Elite With Bloop Tube* — features 16¼ in. barrel with a 6 in. bloop tube extension enabling increased bullet velocity with muzzle heavy characteristics, McMillan fiberglass STC stock. Mfg. 1996-98.

$1,250 $995 $750

Last Mfg.'s Sug. Retail was $1,498.

Subtract $255 if without compensator.

SPORTER EDITION — .22 LR cal., 16½, 18, 20, or 22 in. tapered sporter barrel, McMillan fiberglass sporter stock. Mfg. 1996 only.

$800 $700 $625

Last Mfg.'s Sug. Retail was $900.

HUNTER EDITION I — .22 LR cal., 18, 20, or 22 in. regular barrel with injection molded sporter stock. Mfg. 1996 only (replaced with Hunter Edition II).

$725 $650 $575

Last Mfg.'s Sug. Retail was $800.

Grading	100%	98%	95%	90%	80%	70%	60%

A

* ***Hunter Edition II*** — .22 LR cal., 22 in. tapered sporter barrel with 2 lb. Jewell trigger, McMillan synthetic sporter stock. Mfg. 1997-98.

$1,175 $925 $725

Last Mfg.'s Sug. Retail was $1,354.

FLY SWATTER I — .22 LR cal., 16½ in. regular barrel with injection molded (1996 only) or Hogue over-molded (new 1997) sporter stock. Mfg. 1996-97.

$700 $595 $495

Last Mfg.'s Sug. Retail was $822.

* ***Fly Swatter II*** — similar to Fly Swatter I, except has 3 in. muzzle brake. Mfg. 1997 only.

$795 $650 $525

Last Mfg.'s Sug. Retail was $936.

BR-50 ACCELERATOR EDITION — .22 LR cal., features 16¼ (new 1998) or 16½ (disc. 1997) in. bull barrel with 3 in. muzzle brake (new 1998), McMillan bench rest stock, Hoehn barrel tuner (disc. 1997), and Jewell trigger. Mfg. 1997-98.

$1,200 $1,025 $795

Last Mfg.'s Sug. Retail was $1,440.

ACCULITE EDITION RIFLE — .22 LR cal., features 18 in. Magnum Research graphite barrel with muzzle brake, thumbhole sporter stock, adj. Jewell trigger, 4 ¾ lbs. Mfg. 1998 only.

$1,095 $765 $650

Last Mfg.'s Sug. Retail was $1,321.

INTIMIDATOR EDITION RIFLE — .22 LR cal., 16¼ Shilen select match grade barrel with 6 in. bloop tube, adj. Jewell trigger, 6¼ lbs. Mfg. 1998 only.

$1,300 $1,000 $765

Last Mfg.'s Sug. Retail was $1,581.

MAGNUM HUNTER — .22 Mag. cal., semi-auto, 20 in. free-floating barrel, drilled and tapped, stainless steel, 10 shot straight stacked mag., w/o sights, drilled and tapped for Weaver 87-A scope base, black synthetic stock, 6 lbs. Mfg. 1995-98.

$410 $325 $280

Last Mfg.'s Sug. Retail was $459.

TARGET RIFLE SEMI-AUTO — .22 LR cal., button rifled Cryogenic treated barrel with target crown, choice of Fajen laminate or Hogue composite stock, 10 shot mag., 1-piece receiver with integral Weaver mount, 7½ lbs. Mfg. 1997-98.

$495 $440 $385

Last Mfg.'s Sug. Retail was $549.

Add $50 for Fajen laminate stock.

RIFLES: BOLT ACTION

BOLT ACTION STANDARD SINGLE SHOT — 11 various cals., post-64 push-feed action, pre-64 3-position side safety, cone breech, composite stock, cryogenic treated stainless steel barrel w/o sights, 8½ lbs. Mfg. 1996-97.

$1,350 $1,025 $800

Last Mfg.'s Sug. Retail was $1,500.

* ***Bolt Action Deluxe Single Shot*** — 11 various cals., Mauser type controlled feeding, short, medium, or long right or left-hand action, pre-64 3-position side safety and claw type extractor, cryogenic treated stainless steel barrel w/o sights, custom Kevlar stock, approx. 8½ lbs. Mfg. 1996 only.

$2,250 $1,750 $1,450

Last Mfg.'s Sug. Retail was $2,400.

BOLT ACTION STANDARD REPEATER — 21 various cals., post-64 push-feed action, Mauser type mag., pre-64 3-position side safety, Model 70 type trigger, composite stock, cryogenic treated stainless steel barrel w/o sights. 8½ lbs. Mfg. 1996 only.

$975 $825 $650

Last Mfg.'s Sug. Retail was $1,110.

Grading	100%	98%	95%	90%	80%	70%	60%

A

* **Bolt Action Deluxe Repeater** — similar features to Bolt Action Deluxe Single Shot, except has Mauser type mag. Mfg. 1996 only.

         $1,425 $1,195 $895

         Last Mfg.'s Sug. Retail was $1,596.

AR-7 INDUSTRIES, LLC

Current manufacturer established 1998, and located in Meriden, CT. Dealer and distributor sales.

RIFLES: SEMI-AUTO

AR-7 EXPLORER RIFLE — .22 LR cal., takedown barreled action stores in synthetic stock which floats, 8 shot mag., adj. sights, 16 in. barrel, black matte finish on AR-7, silvertone on AR-7S, camouflage finish on AR-7C, two-tone (silver receiver with black stock and barrel) on AR-7T, 2½ lbs. New late 1998.

Mfg.'s Sug. Retail	$150	$125	$100	$85	$75	$65	$55	$50

This model was also previously manufactured by Survival Arms, Inc. and Charter Arms - see individual listings for information.

AR-20 SPORTER — similar to AR-22, except has shrouded barrel, tubular stock with pistol grip, 8 shot mag. New late 1998.

Mfg.'s Sug. Retail	$200	$170	$145	$120	$105	$95	$80	$70

This model was also previously manufactured by Survival Arms, Inc. - see individual listing for information.

ASAI AG (ADVANCED SMALL ARMS INDUSTRIES)

Current manufacturer located in Solothurn, Switzerland since 1994. Currently imported by Magnum Research, Inc. located in Minneapolis, MN. Dealer and distributor sales.

PISTOLS:SEMI-AUTO

ONE PRO.45 — 9mm Para, .40 S&W, .400 Cor-Bon (conversion only), or .45 ACP cal., SA or DA, 3 or 3¾ (disc. 1998) in. barrel with polygonal rifling, steel or alloy (new mid-1998) frame, black contoured synthetic grips, black or two-tone finish, 10 shot mag., includes plastic case, extra 10 shot mag., and cleaning kit, 25 or 31 oz. Importation began mid-1997.

Mfg.'s Sug. Retail	$699	$595	$485	$410	$360	$330	$300	$275

Add $209 for .400 Cor-Bon conversion kit without compensator.
Add $249 for .45 ACP or .400 Cor-Bon conversion kit with extended barrel, compensator, and recoil spring guide.

A-SQUARE CO., INC.

Current manufacturer with offices located in Louisville, KY. Previously manufactured until 1991 in Madison, IN. Dealer and consumer direct sales.

A-SQUARE

A-Square also offers at extra cost different grades of walnut, different metal finishes, and various sights/scope rings. Custom calibers are also available upon special order. Values of these special order options can be obtained by contacting A-Square directly.

Grading	100%	98%	95%	90%	80%	70%	60%

RIFLES: BOLT ACTION

Add $250 for A-Grade walnut.
Add $500 for AAA-Grade fancy walnut.
Add $500 for English walnut.
Add $100 for accent package.
Add $200 for stainless steel barrel.
Add $450 for black synthetic stock.
Add $600 for weather impervious package.
Add $240 for 3-leaf steel express sights.
Add $300 for royal high gloss blue finish (disc. 1995).
Add $150 for high gloss polymer wood finish (disc. 1993).

HANNIBAL MODEL — most cals. available, bolt action built on a P-17 Enfield receiver, 22-26 in. barrel, 9 - 11¼ lbs., select walnut with pistol grip and recoil pad. New 1986.

Mfg.'s Sug. Retail	**$3,295**		$3,295	$2,750	$2,400	$2,100	$1,875	$1,725	$1,575

HAMILCAR MODEL — various cals. available, smaller variation of the Hannibal model featuring slimmer design gained by not needing the reinforcement for heavy Mag. cals., 4-7 shot mag., cocks on opening, 8 - 8½ lbs. Introduced 1994.

Mfg.'s Sug. Retail	**$3,295**		$3,295	$2,750	$2,400	$2,100	$1,875	$1,725	$1,575

CAESAR MODEL — most cals. available, bolt action built on a Remington M-700 receiver until 1993, Sako L-V actions were utilized beginning 1993, 22-26 in. barrel, select walnut with pistol grip and recoil pad, primarily a left-handed action with right-hand a special order, 9 - 10¾ lbs. New 1986.

Mfg.'s Sug. Retail	**$3,295**		$3,295	$2,750	$2,400	$2,100	$1,875	$1,725	$1,575

GENGHIS KHAN MODEL — .22-250 Rem., .243 Win., .25-06, or 6mm Rem. cal., features Winchester pre-64 Model 70 action, heavy taper barrel, Coil-Chek stock helps reduce recoil, designed for varmint hunting. New 1995.

Mfg.'s Sug. Retail	**$3,295**		$3,295	$2,750	$2,400	$2,100	$1,875	$1,725	$1,575

A T C S A

Previously manufactured by Armas De Tiro Y Casa located in Spain.

REVOLVERS

COLT POCKET PISTOL COPY — revolver, .38 cal., 6 shot.

	$155	$140	$110	$100	$90	$75	$65

SINGLE SHOT REVOLVER — target pistol.

	$195	$165	$145	$110	$100	$90	$75

AYA (AGUIRRE Y ARANZABAL)

Current manufacturer located in Eibar, Spain since 1917. Currently imported by Armes De Chasse (starting 1992) located in Hertford, NC. Currently distributed by Armes De Chasse, located in Hertford, NC, John F. Rowe, located in Enid, OK, Fieldsport, located in Traverse City, MI, British Game Gun, located in Kent, WA, and New England Custom Gun Service, Ltd., located in West Lebanon, NH. Previous manufacture was by Diarm (circa 1986-88) located in Eibar, Spain. Previously imported by William Larkin Moore 1969-78 (with Agoura, CA import marking) and 1978-1986 (with West Lake, CA import marking). Most AYAs imported by W. L. Moore have ejectors. Retail and dealer sales by importer and AYA select distributors.

AYA manufactured shotguns can be denoted by serialization. Serial numbers over 600,001 with barrel flats marked Arms de Chasse or Scotia Group are post-1988

Grading	100%	98%	95%	90%	80%	70%	60%

A

AYA manufactured while specimens under 600,000 may have been manufactured by Diarm - Diarm manufacture is not covered by the AYA warranty, nor is the resale the same as values listed below.

SHOTGUNS: O/U

Add 10% on current models listed below if other than 12 ga.

AUGUSTA — 12 ga. only, deluxe O/U sidelock, arabesque engraving in deep relief, select walnut. This model has been imported off and on during the past decade and Arms de Chasse should be contacted directly for current pricing information.

		100%	98%	95%	90%	80%	60%
Mfg.'s Sug. Retail	$26,411	$23,500	$5,850	$4,950	$4,250	$3,500	$2,875	$2,350

CORAL "A" — 12 or 16 ga., boxlock action with Kersten cross bolt, vent. rib, ejectors, double triggers. Disc. 1985.

$1,275	$1,050	$875	$775	$695	$625	$560

Last Mfg.'s Sug. Retail was $2,195.

CORAL "B" — similar to Coral A, except for coin-wash engraved receiver. Disc. 1985.

$1,395	$1,100	$925	$820	$720	$650	$595

Last Mfg.'s Sug. Retail was $2,450.

MODEL 37 SUPER — 12, 16, or 20 ga., various barrel lengths and chokes, vent. rib, sidelock, auto ejector, elaborate engraving, high grade wood. Merkel style action. Prices below reflect older models. Disc.

12 ga.	$2,600	$2,350	$2,100	$1,900	$1,700	$1,500	$1,250
16 ga.	$2,550	$2,200	$2,000	$1,700	$1,500	$1,350	$1,150
20 ga.	$3,000	$2,500	$2,200	$1,900	$1,700	$1,600	$1,475

* **New Model 37 Super A** — game scene engraved, detachable sidelock action, nickel steel receiver. This model has been imported off and on during the past decade.

Mfg.'s Sug. Retail	$13,318	$12,250	$5,250	$4,300	$3,750	$3,250	$2,650	$2,175

* **New Model 37 Super B** — fine scroll engraved, detachable sidelock action, nickel steel receiver. Disc. 1985.

$5,250	$4,750	$4,300	$3,720	$3,350	$2,650	$2,175

Last Mfg.'s Sug. Retail was $7,795.

MODEL 77 — 12 ga. only, Merkel style O/U sidelock with Greener crossbolt, deluxe engraving checkering. Disc. 1985.

$3,100	$2,750	$2,500	$2,255	$2,030	$1,805	$1,600

Last Mfg.'s Sug. Retail was $4,100.

MODEL 79 "A" — 12 ga. only, boxlock with double locking lugs, sel. trigger, ejectors. Disc. 1985.

$1,275	$1,075	$965	$880	$790	$705	$640

Last Mfg.'s Sug. Retail was $1,595.

MODEL 79 "B" — similar to Model 79 "A", only more elaborate engraving. Disc. 1985.

$1,395	$1,200	$1,085	$990	$890	$790	$695

Last Mfg.'s Sug. Retail was $1,795.

MODEL 79 "C" — similar to Model 79 "B", only more elaborate engraving, double triggers on request. Disc. 1985.

$2,050	$1,825	$1,605	$1,460	$1,315	$1,165	$1,000

Last Mfg.'s Sug. Retail was $2,650.

SHOTGUNS: SxS

Current retail values on the AYA shotguns listed below could vary somewhat from importer to importer.

On current models listed below, add 10% to values if other than 12 ga.

BOLERO — similar to Matador, with non-selective single trigger and extractors. Disc. 1984.

$440	$360	$330	$305	$275	$250	$220

Grading	100%	98%	95%	90%	80%	70%	60%

COUNTRYMAN GAME GUN — 12 or 20 ga., this model is available from Armes De Chasse only. New 1998.

Mfg.'s Sug. Retail $2,295		$2,050	$1,650	$675	$525	$450	$410	$365

IBERIA — 12 or 20 ga., 3 in., boxlock, double triggers, plain walnut. Disc. 1984.

	$566	$440	$370	$315	$285	$255	$230

IBERIA II — 12 or 16 ga., 28 in. barrels, 2¾ in. chamber only, double triggers, plain walnut. Mfg. 1984-1985 only.

	$515	$430	$370	$315	$285	$255	$230

Last Mfg.'s Sug. Retail was $570.

MATADOR — 10, 12, 16, 20, 28 ga., or .410 bore, 26, 28, or 30 in. barrel, various chokes, Anson & Deeley boxlock, auto ejectors, beavertail forearm, SST, checkered pistol grip stock. Mfg. 1955-1963.

	$475	$375	$325	$275	$225	$200	$180

Add 20% for .410 bore or 28 ga.

MATADOR NO. 2 —similar to Matador, with vent. rib, 12 or 20 ga. only. Disc.

	$525	$425	$360	$315	$265	$225	$200

MATADOR NO. 3A — 12 or 20 ga., 3 in. chamber in 20 ga. only, boxlock, vent. rib, ejectors, SST. Disc. 1985.

	$750	$650	$550	$495	$440	$385	$335

Last Mfg.'s Sug. Retail was $1,235.

SENIOR — 12 ga. only, self-opener, engraved sidelock action, select walnut. Top-of-the-line quality, made to special order only. Lighter up-land version also available. Disc. 1987.

	$15,500	$12,000	$10,000	$8,000	$6,500	$5,500	$4,500

Last Mfg.'s Sug. Retail was $21,000.

NO. 1 — 12 or 20 ga., full sidelock action with third lever fastener, straight grip, ejectors, DTs, elaborate fine scroll engraving. Importation disc. 1987, resumed in 1991.

Mfg.'s Sug. Retail $7,240		$6,325	$2,925	$2,250	$1,800	$1,500	$1,200	$950

Add approx. $100 for rounded action.
Add approx. $2,640 for extra set of barrels.

✷ No. 1 DeLuxe — features premium wood.

Mfg.'s Sug. Retail $7,870		$7,150	$3,350	$2,500	$2,000	$1,750	$1,400	$1,150

Add $200 for rounded action.
Add approx. $2,640 for extra set of barrels.

NO. 2 — 12, 16, 20, 28 ga., or .410 bore, 3 in. chambers, English-style sidelock, ejector, cocking indicators, DTs, third lever fastener. Importation disc. 1987, resumed 1991.

Mfg.'s Sug. Retail $3,395		$2,975	$1,350	$950	$750	$600	$500	$425

Add $100 for rounded action.
Add approx. $1,454 for extra set of barrels.

NO. 3-A — 12, 16, 20, 28 ga., or .410 bore, boxlock, extractors, double triggers. Disc. 1985.

	$640	$540	$495	$450	$400	$375	$350

Last Mfg.'s Sug. Retail was $850.

Add 25%-35% for 28 ga. or .410 bore.

NO. 4 & NO. 4/53 — 12, 16 (disc. 1985), 20, 28 ga., or .410 bore, 3 in. chambers, English-style straight stock, boxlock action, ejectors, double trigger, straight grip stock, No. 4 has standard wood, No. 4/53 has No. 53 wood upgrade. Importation disc. 1987, resumed 1991.

Mfg.'s Sug. Retail $1,850		$1,650	$675	$525	$450	$410	$365	$325

Add $877 for extra set of barrels.
Add approx. $200 for No. 4/53S (includes wood upgrade, NSST, and round knob pistol grip).

Grading	100%	98%	95%	90%	80%	70%	60%

A

NO. 4 DELUXE — English-style, boxlock ejector. Stock, forearm, trigger to order. Importation disc. 1985, resumed 1991.

Mfg.'s Sug. Retail	$3,145		$2,800	$1,175	$900	$800	$740	$680	$625

Add $962 for extra set of barrels.

XXV BOXLOCK (BL) — 12 or 20 ga. only, similar to No. 4 Deluxe, except 25 in. barrels, Churchill rib. Importation disc. 1986, resumed 1991.

Mfg.'s Sug. Retail	$2,980		$2,725	$1,250	$975	$875	$800	$740	$680

Add approx. $1,509 for extra set of barrels.

XXV SIDELOCK (SL) — 12, 16, 20 (disc. 1997), 28 (disc. 1997) ga., or .410 bore (disc. 1997), sidelock ejector, 25 in. barrels, Churchill rib. Stock, forearm, trigger to order. Importation disc. 1986, resumed 1991.

* **12, 16, or 20 ga.**

Mfg.'s Sug. Retail	$4,090		$3,600	$1,750	$1,350	$975	$850	$750	$650

Add approx. $1,720 for extra set of barrels.

NO. 53 — 12, 16 (disc. 1997), or 20 ga., engraved sidelock ejector, sideclips, third lock. Stock, forearm, trigger to order. Importation disc. 1986, resumed 1991.

Mfg.'s Sug. Retail	$4,832		$4,475	$2,050	$1,525	$1,100	$950	$850	$750

Add $1,733 for extra set of barrels.

NO. 56 — 12, 16 (disc. 1997), or 20 ga., sidelock action-engraved, ejectors, sel. trigger. Importation disc. 1985, resumed 1991.

Mfg.'s Sug. Retail	$7,975		$7,250	$3,425	$2,725	$2,300	$1,950	$1,650	$1,400

Add $2,640 for extra set of barrels.

NO. 106 — 12, 16, or 20 ga., English-style boxlock, double trigger, pistol grip, 28 in. barrels. Disc. 1985.

$530	$440	$400	$360	$320	$300	$275

Last Mfg.'s Sug. Retail was $585.

107-LI — 12 or 16 ga., English-style boxlock, double trigger, straight grip, light English scroll engraving. Disc. 1985.

$675	$560	$520	$480	$425	$400	$360

Last Mfg.'s Sug. Retail was $745.

MODEL 116 — 12, 16, or 20 ga., 27-30 in. barrels, any choke, hand detachable H&H sidelocks, double triggers, engraved, select checkered walnut pistol grip stock. Disc. 1985.

$1,000	$845	$795	$750	$675	$600	$500

Last Mfg.'s Sug. Retail was $1,125.

MODEL 117 — 10, 12, 16 or 20 ga., 3 in. chambers, 26-30 in. barrels, any choke, hand detachable H&H sidelocks, ejectors, SST, engraved, select checkered walnut pistol grip stock. Disc. 1986.

$835	$715	$660	$620	$585	$545	$500

Last Mfg.'s Sug. Retail was $1,075.

QUAIL UNLIMITED MODEL 117 — 12 ga. only, 26 in. barrels choked IC/M with 3 in. chambers, upgraded wood and checkering, high gloss bluing, gold colored ST, engraved by Baron Technologies in PA, only 42 mfg. for Quail Unlimited of North America.

$1,650	$1,400	$1,150	$975	$875	$800	$725

This model had a retail price of $1,700 but was made available to Quail Unlimited members for approx. $1,200.

MODEL 210 — 12 or 16 ga., boxlock, exposed hammers, double triggers, plain walnut, light engraving. Disc. 1985.

$795	$675	$550	$475	$435	$395	$350

Last Mfg.'s Sug. Retail was $900.

711 BOXLOCK — 12 ga. only, boxlock, selective trigger, ejectors, vent. rib. Disc. 1984.

$880	$680	$575	$490	$445	$395	$350

Grading	100%	98%	95%	90%	80%	70%	60%

* 711 Sidelock — sidelock action. Mfg. 1985 only.

	100%	98%	95%	90%	80%	70%	60%
	$995	$850	$775	$695	$625	$550	$475

Last Mfg.'s Sug. Retail was $1,250.

ABADIE

Previous trademark of Portuguese military revolvers manufactured by several Belgian makers.

REVOLVERS

MODEL 1878 (OFFICER'S MODEL) — 9.1mm cal., solid frame revolver, 6 shot, ejector rod, officer's issue A.

100%	98%	95%	90%	80%	70%	60%
$220	$195	$165	$130	$120	$110	$100

MODEL 1886 (TROOPER'S MODEL) — similar to 1878, but larger, trooper issue A.

100%	98%	95%	90%	80%	70%	60%
$195	$175	$160	$120	$110	$100	$90

100%	98%	95%	90%	80%	70%	60%	50%	40%	30%	20%	10%

ABBEY, GEORGE T.

Previous manufacturer located in Utica, NY from 1845-1852. Chicago, IL from 1852-1874. Percussion and breechloading firearms.

RIFLES: PERCUSSION

PERCUSSION RIFLE

* .44 cal. — 32 in. octagon barrel.

100%	98%	95%	90%	80%	70%	60%	50%	40%	30%	20%	10%
$605	$550	$470	$415	$370	$340	$305	$275	$250	$220	$195	$165

* .44 cal. — octagon barrel, brass trimmed.

100%	98%	95%	90%	80%	70%	60%	50%	40%	30%	20%	10%
$770	$735	$695	$605	$550	$485	$450	$405	$365	$330	$275	$220

* .44 cal. — 31 in. side-by-side barrels.

100%	98%	95%	90%	80%	70%	60%	50%	40%	30%	20%	10%
$1,210	$1,100	$880	$770	$715	$650	$595	$550	$515	$475	$430	$360

* .44 cal. — O/U, brass trimmed.

100%	98%	95%	90%	80%	70%	60%	50%	40%	30%	20%	10%
$1,485	$1,295	$1,130	$990	$910	$855	$770	$715	$660	$605	$495	$330

ABBEY, F.J. & COMPANY

Previous manufacturer located in Chicago, IL, 1858-1878. Muzzle and breechloading shotguns and rifles.

RIFLES: PERCUSSION

PERCUSSION RIFLE — several variations.

100%	98%	95%	90%	80%	70%	60%	50%	40%	30%	20%	10%
$605	$550	$470	$415	$360	$305	$275	$250	$210	$175	$145	$110

SHOTGUNS: PERCUSSION

PERCUSSION SHOTGUN — several variations.

100%	98%	95%	90%	80%	70%	60%	50%	40%	30%	20%	10%
$800	$715	$635	$550	$470	$415	$360	$320	$285	$250	$210	$155

ABBIATICO & SALVINELLI (FAMARS)

Please refer to the Famars di Abbiatico & Salvinelli srl listing.

ACCU-MATCH INTERNATIONAL INC.

Previous handgun and pistol parts manufacturer located in Mesa, AZ circa 1996.

Grading	100%	98%	95%	90%	80%	70%	60%

A

PISTOLS: SEMI-AUTO

ACCU-MATCH PISTOL — .45 ACP cal., patterned after the Colt Govt. 1911, competition pistol features stainless steel construction with 5½ in. match grade barrel with 3 ports, recoil reduction system, 8 shot mag., 3 dot sight system. Approx. 160 mfg. 1996 only.

		$795	$700	$625	$550	$450	$375	$325

Last Mfg.'s Sug. Retail was $840.

ACCU-TEK

Currently manufactured by Excel Industries, Inc., located in Chino, CA. Dealer direct and distributor sales.

PISTOLS: SEMI-AUTO

MODEL AT-25 — .25 ACP cal., single action, 2½ in. barrel, 7 shot mag. with finger extension, similar design to AT-32, stainless steel, aluminum, or alloy construction with choice of stainless, satin aluminum, or black finish, 11 (Model AT-25AL) or 18 (Model AT-25B, disc.) oz. Mfg. 1992-95.

		$150	$125	$105	$90	$80	$70	$60

Last Mfg.'s Sug. Retail was $182.

Add $5 for satin aluminum (Model AT-25AL) or black (Model AT-25SSB, disc.) finish.

MODEL AT-32SS — .32 ACP cal., single action design, 2½ in. barrel, 5 shot mag. with finger extension, alloy (disc. 1991) or stainless steel (new 1992) construction, manual safety with firing pin block and trigger disconnect, side mag. release, exposed hammer, satin aluminum finish (disc. 1991), 16 oz. Mfg. in U.S. New 1990.

Mfg.'s Sug. Retail	$176	$150	$125	$110	$95	$80	$70	$60

Add $5 for black finish (Model AT-32SSB).

MODEL AT-380SS — .380 ACP cal., similar to Model AT-32, except has 2¾ in. barrel, alloy (disc. 1991) or stainless steel construction, 20 oz. New 1990.

Mfg.'s Sug. Retail	$182	$155	$135	$115	$100	$90	$80	$70

Add $5 for black finish (Model AT-380SSB).

BL-380 — .380 ACP cal., double action only, carbon steel, black finish, compact size, two 5 shot mags., lockable case. New 1997.

Mfg.'s Sug. Retail	$199	$165	$140	$120	$100	$90	$80	$70

MODEL HC-380SS — .380 ACP cal., single action semi-auto, 2½ in. barrel, 10 (C/B 1994) or 13★ shot mag., manual safety with firing pin block and trigger disconnect, exposed hammer, 26 oz. New 1993.

Mfg.'s Sug. Retail	$230	$195	$150	$115

Add $5 for black finish (Model HC-380B, new 1995).

MODEL AT-9SS — 9mm Para. cal., double action only, 3.2 in. barrel, 8 shot mag., firing pin block with no external safeties, black or brushed stainless finish, 3 dot sights adj. for windage, 28 oz. Mfg. 1995-96 only.

		$260	$205	$165

Last Mfg.'s Sug. Retail was $317.

BL-9 — 9mm Para. cal., double action only, carbon steel, black finish, ultra compact size, includes two 5 shot mags., and lockable case. New 1997.

Mfg.'s Sug. Retail	$199	$165	$140	$120	$100	$90	$80	$70

CP-9SS — 9mm Para. cal., double action only, stainless steel, black finish, compact size, 8 shot mag. New 1997.

Mfg.'s Sug. Retail	$265	$220	$165	$125

MODEL XL-9SS — 9mm Para., double action only, stainless steel, 3 in. barrel, 5 shot mag., black pebble finished grips, 3 dot adj. sights, 24 oz. New 1999.

Mfg.'s Sug. Retail	$215	$180	$145	$105

Grading	100%	98%	95%	90%	80%	70%	60%

MODEL AT-40SS — .40 S&W cal., double action only, 3.2 in. barrel, 7 shot mag., firing pin block with no external safeties, black or brushed stainless finish, 3 dot sights adj. for windage, 28 oz. Mfg. 1995-96 only.

			$260	**$205**	**$165**	

Last Mfg.'s Sug. Retail was $317.

CP-40SS — .40 S&W cal., 7 shot mag., otherwise similar to CP-9SS. New 1997.

Mfg.'s Sug. Retail	**$265**		**$220**	**$165**	**$125**

MODEL AT-45SS — .45 ACP cal., similar to Model AT-40SS, except has 6 shot mag., stainless only, 28 oz. Mfg. 1996 only.

			$265	**$210**	**$165**

Last Mfg.'s Sug. Retail was $327.

CP-45SS — .45 ACP cal., 6 shot mag., otherwise similar to CP-40SS. New 1997.

Mfg.'s Sug. Retail	**$265**		**$220**	**$165**	**$125**

ACCURACY INTERNATIONAL LTD.

Current rifle manufacturer located in Hampshire, England since 1982. Currently imported and distributed by Accuracy International North America Inc., located in Oak Ridge, TN. Previously imported until 1998 by Gunsite Training Center, located in Paulden, AZ.

RIFLES: BOLT ACTION

AW MODEL — .308 Win. cal., precision bolt action featuring 26 in. 1:12 twist stainless steel barrel with muzzle brake, 3 lug bolt, 10 shot detachable mag., synthetic thumbhole adj. stock, Parker-Hale bipod, 14 lbs. Importation began 1995.

Mfg.'s Sug. Retail	**$4,351**	**$4,150**	**$3,200**	**$2,550**	**$2,100**	**$1,725**	**$1,500**	**$1,300**

AWP MODEL — similar to AW Model, except has 24 in. barrel w/o muzzle brake, 15 lbs. Importation began 1995.

Mfg.'s Sug. Retail	**$4,214**	**$4,025**	**$3,100**	**$2,450**	**$2,100**	**$1,725**	**$1,500**	**$1,300**

AWM MODEL (SUPER MAGNUM) — .300 Win. Mag. or .338 Lapua cal., 6 lug bolt, 26 or 27 in. 1:9/1:10 twist stainless steel barrel with muzzle brake, Parker-Hale bipod, 5 shot mag., 15½ lbs. Importation began 1995.

Mfg.'s Sug. Retail	**$5,284**	**$4,950**	**$3,750**	**$2,900**	**$2,450**	**$2,000**	**$1,750**	**$1,500**

VARMINT RIFLE — .22 Middlested, .22 BR, .22-250 Rem., .223 Rem., 6mm BR, .243 Win., .308 Win., or 7mm-08 Rem. cal., features 26 in. fluted stainless steel barrel. New 1997.

Mfg.'s Sug. Retail	**$3,290**	**$2,950**	**$2,600**	**$2,250**	**$1,900**	**$1,650**	**$1,475**	**$1,300**

AW50 — .50 BMG, advanced ergonomic design, features built-in anti-recoil system, adj. third supporting leg, folding stock, 35 lbs. New 1998.

Mfg.'s Sug. Retail	**$11,190**	**$10,350**	**$8,750**	**$7,500**	**$6,250**	**$4,950**	**$3,750**	**$2,900**

ACHA

Previous manufacturer located in Domingo Acha, Spain.

PISTOLS: SEMI-AUTO

MODEL 1916 — 6.35mm cal., semi-auto pistol, 7 shot mag., 1903 Browning copy.

	$220	**$165**	**$100**	**$85**	**$65**	**$55**	**$45**

ATLAS — 6.35mm cal., semi-auto pistol, 6 shot mag., slide marked ATLAS, 1906 Browning copy.

	$165	**$140**	**$125**	**$95**	**$75**	**$65**	**$50**

LOOKING GLASS — 6.35mm cal., semi-auto pistol, 6 shot mag., blued or nickel, 1906 Browning copy, slide marked "Looking Glass", many variations.

	$220	**$165**	**$130**	**$100**	**$85**	**$70**	**$55**

Grading			100%	98%	95%	90%	80%	70%	60%

A

LOOKING GLASS — 7.65mm cal., semi-auto pistol, exposed hammer.

			$220	$165	$140	$105	$90	$75	$65

ACME

Previous trade name of Davenport Arms Company Shotguns, Maltby Henley & Co. Revolvers, and Merwin Hulbert & Co. Owl Head Revolvers.

100%	98%	95%	90%	80%	70%	60%	50%	40%	30%	20%	10%

REVOLVERS

SEVEN SHOT REVOLVER — .22 Short rimfire cal., single action.

100%	98%	95%	90%	80%	70%	60%	50%	40%	30%	20%	10%
$360	$310	$240	$185	$165	$150	$120	$110	$100	$90	$65	$55

FIVE SHOT REVOLVER — .32 Short rimfire cal., single action.

100%	98%	95%	90%	80%	70%	60%	50%	40%	30%	20%	10%
$360	$320	$255	$200	$175	$160	$120	$110	$100	$90	$65	$55

ACME ARMS

Previous trade name for Cornwall Hardware Co., NY.

REVOLVERS

SEVEN SHOT — .22 Short rimfire cal., single action.

100%	98%	95%	90%	80%	70%	60%	50%	40%	30%	20%	10%
$275	$250	$210	$185	$165	$155	$140	$125	$110	$90	$85	$75

FIVE SHOT — .32 Short Rimfire cal., single action.

100%	98%	95%	90%	80%	70%	60%	50%	40%	30%	20%	10%
$285	$255	$215	$195	$175	$165	$145	$120	$100	$90	$85	$75

SHOTGUNS: SxS

SIDE-BY-SIDE — 12 ga., damascus barrel.

100%	98%	95%	90%	80%	70%	60%	50%	40%	30%	20%	10%
$275	$240	$195	$165	$145	$125	$110	$95	$65	$60	$50	$45

ACME HAMMERLESS

Previously manufactured by Hopkins & Allen, for Hulbert Brothers, 1893.

REVOLVERS

FIVE SHOT — .32 centerfire cal., double action, top break, non-ejecting.

100%	98%	95%	90%	80%	70%	60%	50%	40%	30%	20%	10%
$145	$125	$100	$90	$80	$70	$60	$50	$40	$30	$20	$15

Also known as Forehand Model 1891, can be hammer or hammerless.

FIVE SHOT — .38 centerfire cal., double action, top break, non-ejecting.

100%	98%	95%	90%	80%	70%	60%	50%	40%	30%	20%	10%
$145	$125	$100	$90	$80	$70	$60	$50	$40	$30	$20	$15

Also known as Forehand Model 1891, can be hammer or hammerless.

ACTION (M.S.)

Previously manufactured by Modesto Santos, located in Eibar, Spain.

Grading			100%	98%	95%	90%	80%	70%	60%

PISTOLS: SEMI-AUTO

MODEL 1915 — 7.65mm cal., semi-auto pistol (French Military).

			100%	98%	95%	90%	80%	70%	60%
			$175	$145	$120	$85	$70	$60	$45

MODEL 1920 — 6.35mm cal., semi-auto pistol, slide marked "Action".

			100%	98%	95%	90%	80%	70%	60%
			$195	$150	$110	$85	$65	$45	$40

Grading	100%	98%	95%	90%	80%	70%	60%

ACTION ARMS LTD.

Previous firearms importer and distributor until 1994, located in Philadelphia, PA. Only Action Arms Models AT84S, AT88S, and the Model B Sporter will be listed under this heading. Galil, Timberwolf, and Uzi trademarks can be located in their respective sections.

PISTOLS: SEMI-AUTO

AT-84S — 9mm Para. cal., selective double action design, patterned after the CZ-75, 4.8 in. barrel, 15 shot mag., originally introduced in 1985.

	100%	98%	95%	90%	80%	70%	60%
	$470	$415	$385	$360	$330	$275	$220

> The AT-84S Series was mfg. in Switzerland by Industrial Technology & Machines A.G. and was sold by Action Arms between June of 1987 and 1989. Serial number range is 01201-06000. No P or H models were ever mfg. in this series (2 or 3 prototypes only).

AT-88S — 9mm or .41 Action Express (available early 1990) cal., selective double action design patterned after CZ-75, 4.8 in. barrel, 15 shot (9mm) or 10 shot (.41 AE) mag., can be "cocked and locked", fixed sights, blued metal, walnut grips, 35.3 oz. Introduced in 1987 with limited production samples being imported in 1989.

	100%	98%	95%	90%	80%	70%	60%
	$500	$450	$395	$360	$330	$275	$220

> A very small quantity of AT-88Ss (various configurations) was made by I.T.M. of Switzerland and finishes included all blue, all chrome, or 2-tone. These pistols may exhibit both I.T.M. and A.A.L. markings. More recent manufacture was performed by Sphinx-Muller of Switzerland. These pistols are still mfg. by Sphinx-Muller, renamed the AT-2000 Series and imported by Sile Distributors.

RIFLES: CARBINES

MODEL B SPORTER — 9mm Para. cal., patterned after the original Uzi Model B Sporter, 16.1 in. barrel, closed breech, thumbhole stock with recoil pad, 10 shot mag., adj. rear sight, 8.8 lbs. Limited importation from China 1994 only.

	100%	98%	95%	90%	80%	70%	60%
	$545	$475	$435	$385	$335	$295	$275

Last Mfg.'s Sug. Retail was $595.

TIMBERWOLF — see separate listing in T section.

ADAMS

Previously manufactured by Deane, Adams, & Deane, located in London, England.

100%	98%	95%	90%	80%	70%	60%	50%	40%	30%	20%	10%

REVOLVERS: PERCUSSION

MODEL 1851 — .38 cal., double action, 4½ in. barrel.

100%	98%	95%	90%	80%	70%	60%	50%	40%	30%	20%	10%
$1,375	$1,265	$1,100	$990	$855	$745	$690	$605	$550	$440	$385	$330

MODEL 1851 — .44 cal., double action, 6 in. barrel.

100%	98%	95%	90%	80%	70%	60%	50%	40%	30%	20%	10%
$935	$880	$800	$690	$550	$495	$440	$395	$340	$305	$275	$255

MODEL 1851 — .50 cal., Dragoon, double action, 8 in. barrel.

100%	98%	95%	90%	80%	70%	60%	50%	40%	30%	20%	10%
$1,375	$1,265	$1,100	$990	$855	$715	$690	$605	$550	$385	$360	$340

MODEL 1851 — .38 cal., cased with accessories.

100%	98%	95%	90%	80%	70%	60%	50%	40%	30%	20%	10%
$1,760	$1,595	$1,375	$1,100	$990	$910	$825	$745	$660	$605	$550	$525

MODEL 1851 — .44 cal., cased with accessories.

100%	98%	95%	90%	80%	70%	60%	50%	40%	30%	20%	10%
$1,295	$1,155	$990	$880	$770	$690	$635	$550	$440	$385	$360	$330

MODEL 1851 — .50 cal., Dragoon, cased with accessories.

100%	98%	95%	90%	80%	70%	60%	50%	40%	30%	20%	10%
$1,680	$1,485	$1,210	$1,185	$990	$880	$800	$715	$635	$550	$495	$470

100%	98%	95%	90%	80%	70%	60%	50%	40%	30%	20%	10%

A ADAMS, JOSEPH

Previous manufacturer located in Birmingham, England.

PISTOLS: FLINTLOCK

OFFICER MODEL — .65 cal., flintlock pistol, Brown Bess.

| $2,850 | $2,500 | $2,250 | $2,000 | $1,800 | $1,600 | $1,400 | $1,100 | $900 | $825 | $725 | $600 |

ADAMY, GEBRÜDER

Previous manufacturer located in Suhl, Germany, circa 1920 - 1930s.

Grading					100%	98%	95%	90%	80%	70%	60%

SHOTGUNS: O/U

SHOTGUN — O/U, double trigger, engraved, cased.

| | | | | | $1,815 | $1,650 | $1,375 | $1,155 | $990 | $880 | $770 |

ADIRONDACK ARMS COMPANY

Previous manufacturer located in Plattsburgh, NY, 1870-1874.

Magazine loaded repeating rifle, .44 cal., brass or iron frame, later model, may also be marked A.S. Babbitt, Plattsburgh, N.Y., absorbed by Winchester in 1874, then disc.

This rifle was designed in 1870 and patented by Orvill M. Robinson in Upper Jay, NY. It was available in .38 and .44 cal. rimfire rifles without a wooden forend and had a high cyclic rate of fire. Original models were made in Plattsburgh, NY, at which time A.S. Babbitt became one of several additional partners. In 1872, Robinson was granted a patent for a second model rifle. It was similar to the 1870, except a wooden forend was added and the operating mechanism was changed considerably. Following these improvements, Mr. Oliver Winchester contacted Mr. Robinson and purchased the entire Robinson company, discontinuing manufacture.

100%	98%	95%	90%	80%	70%	60%	50%	40%	30%	20%	10%

RIFLES

EARLY MODEL — finger holds on hammer.

| $2,400 | $2,100 | $1,750 | $1,450 | $1,325 | $1,200 | $1,075 | $975 | $875 | $775 | $675 | $600 |

LATE MODEL — action worked by buttons top of receiver mid-section.

| $2,200 | $1,950 | $1,675 | $1,300 | $1,200 | $1,100 | $975 | $875 | $775 | $675 | $550 | $495 |

ADLER

Previously manufactured by Engelbrecht & Wolff located in Blasii, Germany, 1905-1907.

Grading					100%	98%	95%	90%	80%	70%	60%

PISTOLS: SEMI-AUTO

SEMI-AUTO PISTOL — 7mm Adler cal., 8 shot mag., cocking lever on top of frame, not competitive in its price range.

| | | | | | $4,000 | $3,250 | $2,500 | $1,950 | $1,750 | $1,495 | $1,100 |

Grading	100%	98%	95%	90%	80%	70%	60%

ADVANTAGE ARMS USA, INC.

Previous manufacturer located in St. Paul, MN. Advantage Arms USA, Inc. was distributed by Wildfire Sports, Inc. also located in St. Paul, MN.

DERRINGERS

MODEL 422 — .22 LR or 22 Mag. cal., 4 barrel double action derringer, rotating firing pin, this model is patterned after the Mossberg "Brownie", 2½ in. barrel, high grade alloy frame and barrel, 4 shot, available in blue, nickel, or QPQ (heat treated but appears blued) finish, 15 oz. Mfg. 1986-87 only.

$150	$135	$115	$105	$95	$85	$75

Last Mfg.'s Sug. Retail was $166.

Add $10 for .22 Mag. cal.
Add $6 for nickel finish.
Add $11 for QPQ finish.

AETNA

Previously manufactured by Harrington & Richardson located in Worchester, MA. Type: single action revolvers, all of the same general size and configuration, solid frame, spur trigger, so called "Suicide Specials" during their day.

100%	98%	95%	90%	80%	70%	60%	50%	40%	30%	20%	10%

REVOLVERS

AETNA NO. 2 — .32 rimfire cal., 5 shot.

100%	98%	95%	90%	80%	70%	60%	50%	40%	30%	20%	10%
$330	$275	$215	$185	$170	$155	$145	$120	$100	$85	$75	$55

AETNA NO. 2½ — .32 rimfire cal., 5 shot.

$330	$275	$215	$185	$170	$155	$145	$120	$100	$85	$75	$55

MODEL 1876 — .22 rimfire cal., 7 shot.

$330	$275	$210	$195	$175	$165	$155	$130	$110	$95	$90	$65

MODEL 1876 — .32 rimfire cal., 5 shot.

$330	$275	$210	$175	$165	$155	$145	$120	$105	$90	$75	$55

MODEL 1876 — .38 rimfire cal., 5 shot.

$330	$275	$220	$205	$195	$175	$165	$145	$120	$105	$95	$85

AETNA ARMS COMPANY

Previous manufacturer located in New York, 1869-1883.

Single action pocket revolver, blued or nickel, birdshead grip, copy of S&W models 1-3, models marked ALLING are worth a slight premium.

REVOLVERS

SEVEN SHOT — .22 rimfire cal.

$250	$235	$210	$195	$175	$165	$155	$130	$110	$95	$90	$65

FIVE SHOT — .32 rimfire cal.

$230	$220	$205	$175	$165	$155	$145	$120	$105	$90	$75	$55

Grading	100%	98%	95%	90%	80%	70%	60%

A

AGNER

Previously manufactured by Saxhoj Products Inc. in Denmark. Imported until 1986 by Beeman Arms, Inc. located in Santa Rosa, CA.

PISTOL: SEMI-AUTO

MODEL M 80 — .22 LR cal. only, stainless steel, semi-auto target pistol, new design features unique security key safety feature, adj. French walnut grips, dry fire mechanism, 5.9 in. barrel, 5 shot mag., limited production, 2.4 lbs. Imported 1981-1986.

$1,125 $1,040 $950

Last Mfg.'s Sug. Retail was $1,295.

Add $100 for left-hand action.

AIR MATCH

Previously imported by Kendall International, located in Paris, KY.

PISTOLS: SINGLE SHOT

AIR MATCH 500 — .22 LR cal. match single shot pistol, target grips, adj. front counterweight, 10½ in. barrel. Imported 1984-86.

$550 $495 $450 $425 $395 $360 $330

Last Mfg.'s Sug. Retail was $788.

AJAX ARMY

Previously distributed by E.C. Meacham Co., maker unknown, circa 1880s.

100%	98%	95%	90%	80%	70%	60%	50%	40%	30%	20%	10%

REVOLVERS

SINGLE ACTION — .44 rimfire cal., spur trigger, solid frame.

$550	$440	$360	$315	$275	$255	$230	$210	$185	$170	$155	$140

AKRILL, E.

Previously manufactured in France, c. mid-1800s.

RIFLES: FLINTLOCK

FLINTLOCK RIFLE — .69 cal., breech loaded, damascus octagon barrel.

$3,300	$2,750	$2,200	$1,980	$1,460	$1,320	$1,240	$1,075	$935	$800	$745	$660

ALAMO RANGER

Previous manufacturer located in Spain.

Grading	100%	98%	95%	90%	80%	70%	60%

REVOLVERS

REVOLVER — .38 cal., Spanish copy of Colt Model 1929.

$140 $120 $110 $100 $90 $85 $75

100%	98%	95%	90%	80%	70%	60%	50%	40%	30%	20%	10%

ALASKA

Previously manufactured by Hood Firearms Company, Norwich, CT, 1873-1884. Dubbed "Suicide Specials" in their day.

REVOLVERS

SINGLE ACTION — .22 rimfire cal, 7 shot, spur trigger, solid frame.

$275	$220	$195	$145	$140	$125	$110	$100	$90	$75	$70	$65

FIVE SHOT — .32 Short rimfire cal.

$220	$195	$160	$155	$150	$140	$125	$105	$95	$85	$75	$70

ALASKAN COMMEMORATIVES

The following is a complete chronological listing of Alaskan special and limited editions.

Grading	100%	Issue Price	Qty. Made

COMMEMORATIVES, SPECIAL EDITIONS, & LIMITED MFG.

1967 ALASKAN PURCHASE CENTENNIAL WINCHESTER 94 CARBINE — see listing under Winchester Commemoratives.

1967 ALASKA PURCHASE CENTENNIAL CONTENDER — .22 Hornet and .357 Mag. cal., Thompson Contender with 2 barrels, Ser. no. range beginning with C0001.

Issue price is unknown and rarity precludes accurate secondary market pricing.

1976 ALASKA PIPELINE COMMEMORATIVE — .45 LC cal., Colt SAA, cased with Kershaw knife.

	100%	Issue Price	Qty. Made
	$1,495	$800	801

1981 ALASKA STATE TROOPER 40TH ANNIVERSARY — .357 Mag. cal., Smith & Wesson Model 19-5, 4 in. barrel, cased with belt buckle and patch.

	100%	Issue Price	Qty. Made
	$850	$500	250

1984 STATE OF ALASKA SILVER ANNIVERSARY EDITION — .44 Mag. cal., Smith & Wesson Model 29-3, 6 in. barrel, cased with bronze brown bear and ivory grips with scrimshaw AK state seal and silver engraving.

	100%	Issue Price	Qty. Made
	$12,250	$10,000	10

1984 ALASKA SILVER ANNIVERSARY — .44 Mag. cal., Smith & Wesson Model 29-3, 6 in. barrel, cased with gold engraving.

	100%	Issue Price	Qty. Made
	$1,500	$1,195	300

1984 ALASKA STATEHOOD 25TH ANNIVERSARY — .338 Win. Mag. cal., Winchester Model 70XTR, sterling silver engraving.

	100%	Issue Price	Qty. Made
	$1,100	$1,080	500

1984 ALASKA 25TH ANNIVERSARY — .357 Mag. cal., Colt Python, 6 in. barrel, engraved brown bear with gold lettering and numbers, cased.

	100%	Issue Price	Qty. Made
	$1,000	$500	200

1988 IDITAROD "1 OF 1,000" — .44 Mag. cal., Smith & Wesson Model 629-1, 6 in. barrel, cased with laser-etched box, while a thousand were planned, only 500 were mfg.

	100%	Issue Price	Qty. Made
	$995	$775	500

1988 ALASKA SERIES "TOKLAT" SPECIAL — .45 Win. Mag. cal., LAR mfg. Grizzly Mag., mfg. for Great Northern Guns in Anchorage, AK, cased with plaque.

	100%	Issue Price	Qty. Made
	$1,800	$1,195	20

A

Grading	100%	Issue Price	Qty. Made

1990 ALASKA "GUIDE" SERIES — .454 Casull cal., Freedom Arms mfg. for Great Northern Guns in Anchorage, AK, 5½ in. barrel, Custom Field Grade, engraved handle.

	$1,900	$1,300	25

1991 ALASKA "MASTER GUIDE" SERIES — .454 Casull cal., Freedom Arms mfg. for Great Northern Guns in Anchorage, AK, 5½ in. barrel, Custom Premier Grade, engraved handle.

	$2,200	$1,600	26

1998 ALASKA "KLONDIKE" COMMEMORATIVE GRADE I — .30-30 Win. cal., Winchester Model 94, 24 in. round barrel, roll engraved with Klondike scene on receiver, sponsored by the Alaskan Gun Collectors Association.

	$550	$550	450

* *1998 Alaska "Klondike" Commemorative Hi-Grade* — similar to Grade I, except has gold plated receiver.

	$1,000	$1,000	100

ALDAZABAL

Previously manufactured by Aldazabal, Leturiondo & Cia., located in Spain.

Grading	100%	98%	95%	90%	80%	70%	60%

PISTOLS: SEMI-AUTO

SEMI-AUTOMATIC PISTOL — 7.65mm cal., 7 shot, Eibar style.

	$195	$165	$110	$100	$90	$75	$65

ALERT

Previously manufactured by Hood Firearms Company, Norwich, CT, 1873-1881. These revolvers were dubbed "Suicide Specials" in their day.

100%	98%	95%	90%	80%	70%	60%	50%	40%	30%	20%	10%

REVOLVERS

SINGLE ACTION — .22 rimfire cal., 7 shot, spur trigger, solid frame.

$220	$195	$165	$145	$130	$125	$110	$100	$90	$75	$70	$65

FIVE SHOT — .32 Short rimfire cal..

$170	$165	$160	$155	$150	$140	$125	$105	$95	$85	$75	$70

ALESSANDRI, LOU, AND SON

Current custom rifle manufacturer located in Rehoboth, MA since 1975.

Lou Alessandri and Son are noted for their top-quality custom rifles (bolt action and side-by-side). Double rifles start at $18,500, while Express bolt actions start at $5,600. All guns are custom built per individual specifications and a wide variety of special order options are available. In addition to building custom rifles, Lou Alessandri and Son also offer a complete line of high-quality cleaning kits and related accessories. For more information regarding both the custom firearms and accessories, please contact this company directly (see Trademark Index).

ALEXIA

Previously manufactured by Hopkins & Allen, located in Norwich, CT, 1867-1915. Also known as: Blue Jacket, Captain Jack, Chichester, Defender, Dictator, Monarch, Mountain Eagle, Hopkins & Allen, Towers Police Safety, and Universal.

100%	98%	95%	90%	80%	70%	60%	50%	40%	30%	20%	10%

REVOLVERS

The revolvers listed below are single action design, solid frame, spur trigger - they were an inexpensive vest pocket pistol issued under numerous names for private companies, octagon barrel.

.22 RIMFIRE — 7 shot.

$165	$160	$155	$145	$130	$125	$110	$100	$90	$75	$70	$65

.32 SHORT RIMFIRE — 5 shot.

$170	$165	$160	$155	$150	$140	$125	$105	$95	$85	$75	$70

SINGLE ACTION .38 SHORT RIMFIRE — 5 shot.

$195	$180	$170	$165	$160	$145	$140	$120	$110	$100	$90	$85

.41 SHORT RIMFIRE — 5 shot.

$220	$210	$205	$195	$180	$170	$160	$145	$125	$110	$100	$90

ALFA

Previously manufactured by Armero Especialistas Reunidas, located in Eibar, Spain, circa 1920.

All revolvers are marked Alfa on grips.

Grading	100%	98%	95%	90%	80%	70%	60%

REVOLVERS

EARLY MODEL — .32, .38, or .44 cal., copies of S&W No. 2 by O. Hermanos.

		$145	$130	$120	$110	$105	$95	$75

Add 50% for .44 cal.

LATE MODEL — .22 LR, .32 S&W, or .38 S&W cal., copies of Colt Police Positive and S&W Military and Police.

		$160	$150	$130	$120	$110	$100	$90

ALKARTASUNA FABRICA DE ARMAS, S.A.

Previous manufacturer located in Guernica, Spain.

PISTOLS: SEMI-AUTO

ALKARTASUNA CARTRIDGE COUNTER — 6.35mm cal., 7 shot, left grip panel cartridge counter, loaded indicator, grip safety.

		$425	$350	$275	$225	$175	$150	$125

ALKARTASUNA RUBY AUTOMATIC — 7.65mm cal., 2 variations - more common is the "Ruby" type, 9 shot, 3⅝ in. barrel, blue, fixed sights, checkered wood or hard rubber grips, used by French Army in WWI and WWII. Mfg. 1917-1922.

		$265	$195	$165	$110	$65	$55	$45

Add 10% for extended barrel.

ALLEN & THURBER

Previous manufacturer/trademark originally located in Grafton, Mass. Ethan Allen started many plants to keep up with expanding business after 1832. Listed below is a chronological order of the firms constituting the family dynasty founded by Ethan Allen.

Grading	100%	98%	95%	90%	80%	70%	60%

E. Allen — Grafton, Mass. 1832-1837

Allen & Thurber — Grafton, Mass. 1837-1842

Allen & Thurber — Norwich, Conn. 1842-1847

Allen & Thurber — Worcester, Mass. 1847-1854

Allen, Thurber, & Co. — Worcester, Mass. 1854-1856

Allen & Wheelock — Worcester, Mass. 1856-1865

E. Allen & Co. — Worcester, Mass. 1865-1871

Forehand & Wadsworth — Worcester, Mass. 1871-1890

Forehand Arms Co. — Worcester, Mass. 1890-1902

No other 19th century American firm produced a wider variety of firearms than did Ethan Allen & subsidiaries.

ALLEN FIREARMS

Previous importer located in Santa Fe, NM importing A. Uberti Firearms until early in 1987. After Allen Firearms closed, Cimarron F.A. Mfg. Co. located in Houston, TX purchased the remaining inventory (in addition to ordering new products under their name).

Allen Firearms was formerly called Western Arms and manufactured both modern and black powder reproduction firearms and accessories patterned after famous older models. Only modern cartridge guns will be shown in this section.

Rather than provide a complete listing of Allen Firearms models, the following rules usually apply. Since Allen Firearms imported A. Uberti firearms, the Uberti section in this text should be referenced for current values regarding models with similar configurations. Collectibility to date has been limited on most Allen Firearms models, and as a rule, up-to-date values on this trademark are established by current importation prices of Uberti firearms. A complete listing of older Allen Firearms models can be found in Blue Book editions Eleven and Twelve. The models listed below are provided since Uberti is not currently manufacturing them.

RIFLES: REPRODUCTIONS

SHARPS/GEMMER SPORTING RIFLE — .45-70 Govt. cal. only, copy of the famous Sharps rifle. Introduced 1985.

$575	$515	$430	$375	$320	$295	$270

Last Mfg.'s Sug. Retail was $599.

1979 JUSTIN CENTENNIAL COMMEMORATIVE — includes specially engraved 1866 sporting rifle and 1873 single action revolver (7½ in. barrel) with gold plated parts and inlay. Both guns are chambered for .44-40 cal. Also includes special hand signed pair of Justin boots, serial numbered belt buckle and presentation oak case. All serial numbers are matching.

Grading	100%	Issue Price	Qty. Made

MODEL 1873 1 of 1,000 — .44-40 cal, special wood, only 1,000 manufactured. Disc. 1985.

	100%	Issue Price	Qty. Made
	$1,350	$1,500	1,000

Grading	100%	98%	95%	90%	80%	70%	60%

ALPHA ARMS INC.

Previous manufacturer located in Flower Mound, TX from 1983-87.
Retail price included custom hard case.

RIFLES: BOLT ACTION

Many special order options including an octagonal barrel, various finishes, and special sights were available at extra cost on the models listed below. These options, while not listed separately by price, will add value to the prices shown below.

ALPHA JAGUAR — available in most calibers from .222 Rem. through .338 Win., Mauser-type barreled action, Alphawood laminate stock, 20 to 24 in. barrel lengths, approx. 6 lbs. Disc. 1987.

* *Grade I Jaguar* — slide safety, supplied with luggage case.

$900	$800	$700	$625	$560	$500	$425

Last Mfg.'s Sug. Retail was $995.

* *Grade II Jaguar* — similar to Grade I Jaguar, except has Douglas premium barrel.

$995	$900	$800	$700	$625	$560	$500

Last Mfg.'s Sug. Retail was $1,095.

* *Grade III Jaguar* — similar to Grade II Jaguar, except has Model 70-type 3-position safety, honed trigger and action.

$1,125	$995	$900	$800	$700	$625	$560

Last Mfg.'s Sug. Retail was $1,395.

* *Grade IV Jaguar* — similar to Grade III Jaguar, except has fully lightened action and installed swivel studs.

$1,250	$1,050	$930	$825	$725	$640	$560

Last Mfg.'s Sug. Retail was $1,595.

ALPHA CUSTOM — available in most calibers from .222 Rem. through .338 Win., many other calibers available on special order, 20 to 24 in. barrel lengths, limited production, right or left-hand, approx. 6 lbs. Mfg. 1984-1987.

$1,525	$1,200	$975	$850	$725	$640	$560

Last Mfg.'s Sug. Retail was $1,735.

ALPHA GRAND SLAM — same general specifications as the Alpha Custom, except comes standard with laminated wood stock, fluted bolt and non-glare matte finished metal parts, right or left-hand, approx., 6½ lbs. Mfg. 1985-1987.

$1,200	$950	$875	$750	$650	$600	$525

Last Mfg.'s Sug. Retail was $1,465.

ALPHA ALASKAN — .308 Win., .350 Rem. Mag., .358 Win., or .458 Win. cal. Action is similar to Alpha Grand Slam, except barrel, receiver, bolt and safety are stainless steel, right or left-hand, approx. 6¾ - 7½ lbs. Mfg. 1985-1987.

$1,525	$1,200	$975	$850	$725	$640	$560

Last Mfg.'s Sug. Retail was $1,735.

ALPHA BIG-FIVE — .300 H&H thru .375 H&H or .458 Win. cal., action is similar to Alpha Jaguar Grade IV, except has reinforced stock and decelerator recoil pad. Mfg. 1987 only.

$1,575	$1,250	$1,050	$895	$750	$640	$560

Last Mfg.'s Sug. Retail was $1,795.

AMERICA REMEMBERS

An organization that privately commissions historical, limited/special editions in conjunction with various manufacturers.

America Remembers is a private non-governmental organization dedicated to the remembrance of notable Americans and important historical American events. Along with its affiliates, the Armed Forces Commemorative Society®, American Heroes and Legends®, and the United States Society of Arms and Armour™, the company produces special issue limited edition firearms. America Remembers

MANUFACTURER	MODEL	EDITION LIMIT	OFFICIAL ISSUE PRICE

purchased the antique arms division of the U.S. Historical Society on April 1, 1994. Older U.S.H.S. firearms can be located in the U section of this text.

LIMITED/SPECIAL EDITIONS

Values listed below reflect America Remembers most recent official issue prices. These do not necessarily represent secondary marketplace prices. No other values are listed since America Remembers limited edition firearms do not appear that frequently in the secondary marketplace. This is because America Remembers typically sells to consumers directly, without involving normal gun dealers and distributors. Because of this consumer direct sales program, many gun dealers do not have a working knowledge about what America Remembers firearms are currently selling for. The publisher suggests that those people owning America Remembers Limited/Special Editions contact America Remembers (See Trademark Index) for current information, including secondary marketplace liquidity.

HANDGUNS

While not specifically mentioned, the handguns listed below all have various degrees of ornamentation and other embellishments (including some inscriptions).

REVOLVERS: BLACK POWDER

Uberti	American Eagle 1860 Army .44 cal.	500	$1,795
Uberti	Johnny Cash Texas Paterson .36 cal.	1,000	$1,500
Uberti	Gettysburg 1863 Revolver .44 cal.	1,863	$1,350
Uberti	Historic U.S. Navy Tribute 1851 Navy .36 cal.	500	$1,595
Uberti	Lone Star Tribute Walker .44 cal.	150	$1,795
Uberti	Texas Ranger Dragoon	1,000	$1,695
Uberti	Walker Sesquicentennial Tribute Revolver .44 cal.	150	$1,995
Colt BP	Whitneyville Hartford Sesquicentennial Dragoon	100	$1,695

REVOLVERS: SINGLE ACTION

Uberti	American Indian Tribute SAA.45 LC	300	$1,795
Uberti	Buffalo Bill Sesquicentennial SAA .45 LC	500	$1,500
Uberti	Doc Holliday SAA .45 LC	200	$1,795
Colt	Interpol SAA .45 LC	154	$4,500
Uberti	Gene Autry Cowboy Edition SAA	1,000	$1,520
Colt	Gene Autry Premier Colt SAA	100	$5,250
Uberti	George Jones SA .45 LC	950	$1,675
Uberti	Herb Jeffries Tribute .45 LC	500	$1,695
Uberti	Hopalong Cassidy Cowboy SAA	950	$1,550
Colt	Hopalong Cassidy Premier Colt SAA	100	$4,500
Colt	Roy Rogers & Dale Evans SAA	250	$2,995
Uberti	Seventh Cavalry SAA Tribute	500	$1,650
Uberti	Tom Mix Tribute SAA .45 LC	200	$1,395
Colt	Tom Mix Premier Edition .45 LC	50	$2,595
Uberti	Travis Tritt SAA .45 LC	500	$1,650
Ruger	Ruger and His Guns Classic .44 Magnum	400	$1,995
Ruger	Ruger and His Guns Classic .44 Magnum	100	$3,595
Uberti	Clayton Moore SAA .45 LC	500	$1,595

SEMI-AUTOS: VJ-DAY TRIBUTE

Colt	American Eagle M-1911A1	2,500	$1,950
Colt	American Patriot M-1911A1	N/A	$1,695
Colt	Army Air Forces Tribute M-1911A1	500	$1,500
Colt	Audie Murphy M-1911A1	1,000	$1,795
Colt	Chuck Yeager Tribute M-1911A1	1,000	$1,750
Colt	Ernie Irvan Tribute M-1911A1	250	$1,895
Colt	Navajo Code Talkers M-1911A1	300 (w/knife)	$3,000
Auto-Ordnance	Pacific Naval Tribute M-1911A1	500	$1,500
Colt	Purple Heart Tribute M-1911A1	250	$1,485
Colt	VJ-Day Tribute M-1911A1	250	$1,495
Colt	Wings of Freedom-USAF 50th Anniversary Tribute M-1911A1	250	$1,485
Colt	Special Operations Associations Tribute M-1991A1	250	$1,595

MANUFACTURER	MODEL	EDITION LIMIT	OFFICIAL ISSUE PRICE
Colt	Berlin Airlift Golden Anniversary Tribute M-1991A1	250	$1,595

RIFLES

MANUFACTURER	MODEL	EDITION LIMIT	OFFICIAL ISSUE PRICE
Winchester	Model 94 (.22 LR) King Richard Tribute	200	$1,495
Winchester	Model 94 (.30-30) American Eagle	500	$1,795
Winchester	Model 94 (.30-30) American Wildlife	300	$1,895
Winchester	Model 94 (.30-30)B. Bill Sesqui. Tribute	300	$2,100
Winchester	Model 94 (.30-30) Babe Ruth Tribute	300	$2,100
Winchester	Model 94 (.30-30) California Sesquicentennial	150	$1,795
Winchester	Model 94 (.30-30) Davey Allison Tribute	500	$1,995
Winchester	Model 94 (.30-30) Deer Hunter Tribute	300	$1,795
Winchester	Model 94 (.30-30) Elvis and Graceland Tribute	1,000	$2,100
Winchester	Model 94 (.30-30) Gene Autry Tribute	300	$2,100
Winchester	Model 94 (.30-30) George Jones Tribute	300	$1,800
Winchester	Model 94 (.30-30) Great North American Rodeo	500	$1,395
Winchester	Model 94 (.30-30) Heroic Indian Leaders	300	$1,650
Winchester	Model 94 (.30-30) Hopalong Cassidy Tribute	500	$1,850
Winchester	Model 94 (.30-30) Leatherneck Sportsman	300	$2,195
Winchester	Model 94 (.30-30) Roy Rogers Tribute	300	$2,100
Winchester	Model 94 (.30-30) Roy Rogers & Gabby Hayes	300	$1,995
Winchester	Model 94 (.30-30) Rusty Wallace Tribute	1,000	$2,100
Winchester	Model 94 (.30-30) Terry Labonte Tribute	1,000	$2,100
Winchester	Model 94 (.30-30) Texas Motor Speedway	500	$2,100
Winchester	Model 94 (.30-30) Ty Murray Tribute	500	$1,695
Winchester	Model 94 (.30-30) Tribute to Yellowstone National Park	150	$1,795
Marlin	Model 336CS (.30-30) Whitetail Trophy	500	$1,495
Marlin	Model 336CS (.30-30) Whitetail Hunter Tribute	300	$1,395
Marlin	Model 336CS (.30-30) Whitetail Deer Trophy	300	$1,495
Marlin	Model 1894 (.45 LC) White Buffalo Spirit Tribute	300	$2,100
Winchester	Model 94 (.45 LC) American Cowboy Tribute	200	$3,195
Winchester	Model 94 (.45 LC) American Indian Tribute	300	$1,250
Winchester	Model 94 (.45 LC) Citation Bass Tribute	300	$1,695
Winchester	Model 94 (.45 LC) Darrell Waltrip 25th Anniversary	1,000	$2,100
Winchester	Model 94 (.45 LC) Monte Hale Tribute	300	$2,100
Winchester	Model 94 (.45 LC) Rex Allen Tribute	500	$1,595
Uberti	Model 1873 (.44-40) Scouts of the Western Frontier	300	$1,995
Thompson Center	Historic Whitetail Muzzleloader (.50 cal.)	300	$1,495
Armi-Sport	Model 1853 (.58 cal.) Confederate Enfield	500	$1,900
Winchester	Model 94 (.30-30) Field & Stream Tribute	300	$1,595
Winchester	Model 94 (.30-30) Wrangler Ft. Worth Tribute	300	$1,895
Winchester	Model 94 (.30-30) Wrangler Gene Autrey, Smiley Burnette, & Pat Buttram Tribute	300	$1,895
Winchester	Model 94 (.30-30) Iron Eyes Cody Tribute	300	$1,850
Winchester	Model 94 (.30-30) NRA Tribute	300	$1,850
Winchester	Model 94 (.30-30) Tribute to the Rough Riders	300	$1,595
Winchester	Model 94 (.30-30) Texas Ranger 175th Anniversary Tribute	300	$1,950
Uberti	Henry (.44-40) A Nation Reunited: Civil War Tribute	300	$1,895
Uberti	Model 1873 (.45 LC) Wyatt Earp Sesquicentennial Tribute	300	$1,895
Marlin	Model 1894 (.45 LC) Cowboy Limited Roy Rogers/Dale Evans Tribute	300	$1,850

SHOTGUNS

MANUFACTURER	MODEL	EDITION LIMIT	OFFICIAL ISSUE PRICE
Remington	Model 870 Wingmaster (12 ga.) Ned & Dale Jarrett	750	$1,895
SIACE	Law & Order (12 ga.) double-hammered shotgun	100	$3,000
Remington	Model 870 (12 ga.) Deer Hunter Tribute	300	$1,495

Grading	100%	98%	95%	90%	80%	70%	60%

AMERICAN ARMS

Previous manufacturer located in Garden Grove, CA.

PISTOLS: SEMI-AUTO

EAGLE 380 — .380 ACP cal. only, stainless steel semi-auto, copy of Walther PPK/S, 6 shot mag., 3¼ in. barrel, limited production, 20 oz.

	$400	$250	$215

Last Mfg.'s Sug. Retail was $289.

Add $25 for case.
Add $50 for case and belt buckle.
Add $25 for black teflon finish (disc. 1985).

AMERICAN ARMS CO.

Previous manufacturer located in Boston, MA from 1870-1901 and Milwaukee, WI. from 1893-1904. American Arms Co. was acquired by Marlin in 1901.

100%	98%	95%	90%	80%	70%	60%	50%	40%	30%	20%	10%

DERRINGERS

O/U DESIGN — .22 Short R.F., .32 Short R.F., or .41 Short R.F. cal., Wheeler Pat. Action, brass frame, spur trigger.

$800	$750	$700	$650	$575	$500	$420	$360	$300	$225	$160	$110

SHOTGUNS: SxS

HAMMERLESS MODEL — 12 ga., semi-hammerless.

$600	$550	$500	$450	$350	$275	$225	$175	$150	$125	$100	$75

WHITMORE PATENT — 10 or 12 ga., hammerless, checkering, SxS. Add 10% for 10 ga. (2⅞ in. chambers).

$685	$625	$575	$520	$460	$400	$340	$270	$200	$150	$125	$100

SINGLESHOT — 12 ga., semi-hammerless, damascus barrel.

$260	$225	$200	$175	$150	$125	$90	$70	$50	$40	$30	$20

AMERICAN ARMS, INC.

Current importer and manufacturer located in North Kansas City, MO. American Arms imports various Spanish shotguns (Grulla, Indesal, Lanber, Norica, and Zabala Hermanos), Italian shotguns including F. Stefano, several European pistols and rifles, and exclusively imports Sites handguns (new 1990) mfg. in Torino, Italy. This company also manufactures several pistols in North Kansas City, MO. American Arms previously imported (1988-89 only) Norica Airguns that may be found under the Norica heading in the Modern Airguns section in the back of this publication.

Grading	100%	98%	95%	90%	80%	70%	60%

PISTOLS: SEMI-AUTO

MODEL TT-9MM TOKAREV — 9mm Para. cal., semi-auto single action, 4½ in. barrel, 9 shot mag., hammer block external safety, 31 oz. Imported 1988-89 only.

	$250	$230	$210	$195	$180	$170	$160

Last Mfg.'s Sug. Retail was $289.

This model is patterned after the Tokarev action and is made from machined steel parts in Yugoslavia.

Grading	100%	98%	95%	90%	80%	70%	60%

MODEL EP-380 — .380 ACP cal., semi-auto double action, stainless steel, 3½ in. barrel, 7 shot mag., wood checkered grips, adj. rear sight, 25 oz. Imported 1988-90 only.

	$375	$325	$250				

Last Mfg.'s Sug. Retail was $449.

This model was made in West Germany.

MODEL PK-22 CLASSIC — .22 LR cal., semi-auto double action, styled after Govt. .45 ACP, 3⅓ in. barrel, 8 shot finger extension mag., black polymer grips, 22 oz. Mfg. 1988-96.

	$165	$140	$115	$100	$90	$80	$70

Last Mfg.'s Sug. Retail was $199.

This model was made in North Kansas City, MO. It has patented safety features such as external hammer block and internal blocking of the firing pin until the trigger is pulled.

MODEL CX-22 CLASSIC — .22 LR cal., style patterned after Walther PPK, 3⅓ in. barrel, 8 shot finger extension mag., 22 oz. Mfg. 1990-95.

	$175	$145	$125	$110	$100	$90	$80

Last Mfg.'s Sug. Retail was $213.

This model was made in North Kansas City, MO. It has patented safety features such as external hammer block and internal blocking of the firing pin until the trigger is pulled.

* **CXC-22** — similar to CX-22 Classic, except has chrome slide. Mfg. in 1990 only.

	$170	$150	$125	$110	$100	$90	$80

Last Mfg.'s Sug. Retail was $189.

MODEL PX-22/25 CLASSIC — .22 LR or .25 ACP (mfg. 1991 only) cal., compact variation of the Model CX-22, 2¾ in. barrel, 7 shot finger extension mag., 15 oz. New 1989, PX-25 was mfg. 1991 only, PX-22 was disc. 1995.

	$175	$145	$125	$110	$100	$90	$80

Last Mfg.'s Sug. Retail was $206.

This model was made in North Kansas City, MO. It has patented safety features such as external hammer block and internal blocking of the firing pin until the trigger is pulled.

MODEL P-98 CLASSIC — .22 LR cal., semi-auto double action patterned after Walther P.38, 5 in. barrel, 8 shot mag., blue/black finish, grooved wraparound grips, 26 oz. Mfg. 1990-96.

	$170	$145	$125	$110	$100	$90	$80

Last Mfg.'s Sug. Retail was $209.

ESCORT — .380 ACP cal., double action only, 3⅜ in. barrel, 7 shot mag., unique thin profile, matte stainless steel, soft polymer grips, polygonal rifling, 19 oz. Mfg. 1995-97.

	$285	$230	$200	$185	$170	$160	$150

Last Mfg.'s Sug. Retail was $349.

SABRE — while this model was advertised, it was never mfg.

SPECTRE — 9mm Para., .40 S&W (mfg. 1991 only), or .45 ACP (new 1993) cal., semi-auto double action, 6 in. barrel with polygonal rifling, 30 shot mag., ambidextrous safety, decocking lever, adj. sights, 4½ lbs., mfg. in Italy by Sites. Imported 1990-1993.

	$500	$325	$275	$240	$200	$185	$170

Last Mfg.'s Sug. Retail was $429.

Add $28 for .45 ACP cal.

This model was previously imported by F.I.E. located in Hialeah, FL (1989-1990).

AUSSIE SEMI-AUTO — 9mm Para. or .40 S&W cal., semi-auto double action, polymer frame with nickeled steel slide and 4¾ in. barrel, 10 shot mag., features 5 safeties, open slide after last shot, 23 oz. Limited importation from Spain 1996 only.

	$350	$250	$225	$200	$185	$170	$160

Last Mfg.'s Sug. Retail was $425.

Grading	100%	98%	95%	90%	80%	70%	60%

A

REVOLVERS: SAA

REGULATOR MODEL — .357 Mag., .44-40, or .45 LC cal., 4¾, 5½ (new 1993), or 7½ in. barrel, reproduction of the Colt Peacemaker, featuring brass trigger guard and back strap, fixed sights, half-cock and hammer block safeties, blade front, grooved rear sights, color case hardened frame and blued barrel/cylinder or nickel finish (new 1999, .45 LC cal. only), walnut grips, 35 oz. Mfg. by Uberti. Importation began 1992.

Mfg.'s Sug. Retail	$320	$270	$230	$200	$185	$170	$160	$150

   Add $55 for nickel finish.
   Add $40 for dual cylinder set (.44-40/.44 Spl. or .45 LC/.45 ACP). Disc. 1998.

* ***Regulator Deluxe*** — similar to Regulator Model, except .45 LC cal. only, all blue charcoal finish (mfg. 1996-97) or color case hardened frame (new 1998), case hardened (pre-1993) or blued (post-1993) steel trigger guard and back strap. Importation disc. 1992, resumed 1994.

Mfg.'s Sug. Retail	$365	$315	$260	$215	$190	$170	$160	$150

   Add $70 for dual cylinder set (.44-40/.44 Spl. or .45 LC/.45 ACP). Disc. 1992.

* ***Buckhorn*** — .44 Mag cal., 4¾, 6, or 7½ in. barrel, otherwise similar to Regulator Model, 44 oz. Imported 1993-96.

		$305	$255	$205	$185	$170	$160	$150

   Last Mfg.'s Sug. Retail was $379.

   Add $10 for Target variation (flat top and adj. rear sight). Imported 1994 only.

* ***Storekeeper*** — .44-40 WCF or .45 LC cal., 4 in. barrel, smooth walnut curved grips, nickel or B/H nickel finish, 31 oz. New 1999.

Mfg.'s Sug. Retail	$375	$320	$265	$215	$190	$170	$160	$150

   Add $44 for B/H nickel finish.

UBERTI BISLEY — .45 LC cal., patterned after the Colt Bisley, case hardened steel frame, 4¾, 5½, or 7½ in. barrel with fixed sights, hammer block safety. Imported 1997-98 only.

		$425	$340	$275	$215	$190	$170	$160

   Last Mfg.'s Sug. Retail was $475.

UBERTI .454 SAA — .454 cal., 6 SR or 7½ in. top-ported barrel, hammer block safety, satin nickel finish, custom hardwood grips, wide trigger, adj. rear sight. Imported 1996-97 only.

		$750	$625	$550	$495	$465	$435	$375

   Last Mfg.'s Sug. Retail was $869.

SILVERADO — .357 Mag., .44 Mag., or .45 LC cal., 4¾, 5½, or 7½ barrel, brushed nickel finish, unfluted cylinder, laminated charcoal grips. Mfg. by Uberti, importation began 1999.

Mfg.'s Sug. Retail	$409	$345	$285	$220	$195	$170	$160	$150

MATEBA AUTO REVOLVER — .357 Mag. cal., combination semi-auto pistol and revolver, unique action allows cylinder and slide assembly to move back when fired, causing the cylinder to rotate, single or double action, 6 shot, 4 or 6 (new 1998) in. barrel, steel/alloy frame, blue finish, flared ergonomic walnut grips, 2¾ lbs. Importation from Italy began 1997.

Mfg.'s Sug. Retail	$1,295	$1,150	$875	$775	$625	$500	$425	$350

   Add $54 for 6 in. barrel.

COMBINATION GUNS

RS COMBO — choice of .222 Rem. or .308 Win. rifle barrel under 12 ga. barrel, engraved boxlock frame with antique silver finish, DTs, 24 in. VR barrels with shotgun choke tubes, rifle sights, grooved for scope mounting, Monte Carlo stock, 7 lbs. 14 oz. Imported 1989 only.

		$675	$595	$550	$495	$450	$420	$385

   Last Mfg.'s Sug. Retail was $749.

Grading	100%	98%	95%	90%	80%	70%	60%

A

RIFLES: O/U

SILVER EXPRESS — 8x57JRS or 9.3x74R cal., O/U boxlock design, gold SNT, monoblock 28 in. separated barrels, manual safety, silver finished receiver with light engraving, skipline checkered walnut stock and forearm, approx. 7¾ lbs. Importation began 1999.

Mfg.'s Sug. Retail	**$1,949**	**$1,800**	**$1,625**	**$1,500**	**$1,375**	**$1,250**	**$1,125**	**$1,000**

RIFLES: SEMI-AUTO

MODEL ZCY 308 — .308 Win. cal., gas operated semi-auto AK-47 type action, Yugoslavian mfg. Imported 1988 only.

	$775	**$650**	**$550**	**$450**	**$400**	**$375**	**$350**

Last Mfg.'s Sug. Retail was $825.

MODEL AKY 39 — 7.62x39mm cal., gas operated semi-auto AK-47 type action, teakwood fixed stock and grip, flip up Tritium night front sight and rear, Yugoslavian mfg. Imported 1988-89 only.

	$550	**$495**	**$440**	**$395**	**$350**	**$300**	**$270**

Last Mfg.'s Sug. Retail was $559.

This model was supplied with sling and cleaning kit.

* *Model AKF 39 Folding Stock* — 7.62x39mm cal., folding stock variation of the Model AKY-39. Imported 1988-89 only.

	$575	**$500**	**$450**	**$400**	**$350**	**$300**	**$270**

Last Mfg.'s Sug. Retail was $589.

EXP-64 SURVIVAL RIFLE — .22 LR cal., semi-auto, takedown rifle stores in oversize synthetic stock compartment, 21 in. barrel, 10 shot mag., open sights, receiver grooved for scope mounting, cross bolt safety, 40 in. overall length, 7 lbs. Imported 1989-90 only.

	$150	**$135**	**$125**	**$115**	**$105**	**$95**	**$85**

Last Mfg.'s Sug. Retail was $169.

MINI-MAX — .22 LR cal., semi-auto, 18¾ in. barrel, wood or black synthetic stock, 10 shot mag., adj. rear sight, 4⅓ lbs. Imported in 1990 only.

	$85	**$75**	**$65**	**$55**	**$45**	**$40**	**$35**

Last Mfg.'s Sug. Retail was $99.

Add $6 for wood stock.

SM 64 TD SPORTER — .22 LR cal., semi-auto, takedown barrel, 21 in. barrel, checkered walnut finished hardwood stock and forend, hooded front sight and adj. rear sight, 7 lbs. Imported 1989-90 only.

	$130	**$115**	**$105**	**$95**	**$85**	**$75**	**$65**

Last Mfg.'s Sug. Retail was $149.

RIFLES: REPRODUCTIONS

MODEL 1860 HENRY REPLICA — .44-40 WCF or .45 LC cal., 24¼ in. blued or white finish (new 1999) barrel, 9 1/4 lbs., mfg. by Uberti.

Mfg.'s Sug. Retail	**$940**	**$835**	**$625**	**$525**	**$425**	**$360**	**$320**	**$260**

Add $50 for white barrel finish.

* *Henry Trapper* — similar to the Henry Replica, except has 18½ in. barrel, 8 lbs. Importation began 1999.

Mfg.'s Sug. Retail	**$940**	**$835**	**$625**	**$525**	**$425**	**$360**	**$320**	**$260**

Add $50 for white barrel finish.

MODEL 1866 WINCHESTER REPLICA — .44-40 WCF or .45 LC cal., 19 (Carbine) or 24¼ (Rifle) in. barrel, approx. 8 lbs., mfg. by Uberti.

Mfg.'s Sug. Retail	**$730**	**$650**	**$550**	**$460**	**$375**	**$300**	**$250**	**$200**

Subtract $20 for Carbine variation (Yellowboy).

Grading	100%	98%	95%	90%	80%	70%	60%

MODEL 1873 WINCHESTER REPLICA — .44-40 WCF or .45 LC cal., 24¼ or 30 (new 1999) in. octagon barrel, case colored receiver, approx. 8¼ lbs., mfg. by Uberti.

Mfg.'s Sug. Retail	$860	$775	$625	$525	$425	$360	$320	$260

Add $80 for 30 in. barrel.

* *Model 1873 Deluxe Winchester Replica* — similar to Model 1873 Winchester Replica, except has better quality checkered pistol grip stock and forearm. Disc. 1997.

	$1,100	$775	$625	$500	$425	$350	$275

Last Mfg.'s Sug. Retail was $1,299.

MODEL 1883 SINGLE SHOT HIGH WALL — .45-70 Govt. cal., 28 in. round barrel, color case hardened frame, 8.82 lbs., mfg. by Uberti. Importation began 1998.

Mfg.'s Sug. Retail	$810	$700	$575	$495	$395	$350	$300	$260

SHARPS CAVALRY CARBINE — .45-70 Govt. cal., 22 in. heavy round barrel, case colored action, blued barrel with adj. rear ladder sight, DST, uncheckered walnut stock and forearm, 8 lbs. 3 oz. Importation began 1999.

Mfg.'s Sug. Retail	$660	$625	$525	$450	$400	$360	$330	$300

SHARPS FRONTIER CARBINE — similar to Cavalry Carbine, except has regular barrel with barrel band and single trigger, 7 lbs. 13 oz. Importation began 1999.

Mfg.'s Sug. Retail	$685	$635	$535	$450	$400	$360	$330	$300

SHARPS 1874 SPORTING RIFLE — .45-70 Govt. cal., 28 in. octagon barrel, checkered walnut stock and forearm, DST, 9 lbs. 3 oz. Importation began 1999.

Mfg.'s Sug. Retail	$685	$635	$535	$450	$400	$360	$330	$300

* *Sharps 1874 Deluxe Sporting Rifle* — similar to Sharps 1874 Sporting Rifle, except has brown barrel finish. Importation began 1999.

Mfg.'s Sug. Retail	$705	$650	$545	$460	$410	$360	$330	$300

SHOTGUNS: O/U

American Arms is currently importing Spanish shotguns manufactured by Zabala Hermanos, Lanber, and Indesal. Italian shotguns are also imported and mfg. by Stefano Fausti (Models Silver, Waterfowl, and Turkey Special). American Arms also imported Franchi Black Magic semi-auto and O/U shotguns until 1998. These shotguns will appear under the Franchi section in this text. Older Diarm models have been listed below.

LINCE — 12 or 20 ga., 3 in. chambers, boxlock with Greener crossbolt, various barrel lengths and chokings, available in either blue or shiny chrome finish, SST, VR, ejectors. Imported 1986 only.

	$510	$400	$380	$360	$340	$320	$300

Last Mfg.'s Sug. Retail was $610.

Add $70 for choke tubes.

SILVER MODEL — 12 or 20 ga. only, similar to Lince Model, except has brushed aluminum finished receiver, no engraving. Imported 1986-87 only.

	$495	$450	$390	$360	$330	$300	$285

Last Mfg.'s Sug. Retail was $545.

Add $50 for multi-chokes.

SILVER I — similar to Silver Model, except also available in 28 ga. or .410 bore (both new 1988), single selective trigger became standard in 1988, extractors, engraved frame, fixed chokes, recoil pad. New 1986.

Mfg.'s Sug. Retail	$649	$535	$430	$350	$300	$285	$270	$255

Add $30 for 28 ga. or .410 bore.

Engraved frame became standard in 1987.

SILVER II — similar to Silver I, except is supplied with choke tubes, deluxe walnut, and ejectors, 16 ga. new 1999. New 1987.

Mfg.'s Sug. Retail	$769	$660	$560	$475	$400	$360	$330	$300

Add $46 for 28 ga. or .410 bore (fixed chokes only).

Grading	100%	98%	95%	90%	80%	70%	60%

* **Silver II Lite (Silver Upland Lite)** — 12, 20, or 28 ga. (disc. 1995), 3 in. chambers (except for 28 ga.), 26 in. VR barrels, with Franchoke tubes (except for 28 ga.), SST, ejectors, engraved frame with antique silver finish, checkered walnut stock and forearm, 5¾-6¼ lbs. Imported 1994-98.

	$800	$660	$550	$485	$440	$400	$360

Last Mfg.'s Sug. Retail was $925.

* **Small Gauge Combo** — includes either 20/28 ga. (new 1997) or 28 ga./.410 bore barrels. Importation began 1989.

Mfg.'s Sug. Retail	$1,239	$1,080	$925	$750	$625	$550	$495	$450

SILVER LITE — 12 or 20 ga., 2¾ in. chambers, boxlock action, 26 in. vent. barrels with VR and choke tubes, blued alloy receiver, SST, ejectors, gold trigger, checkered walnut stock and forearm, 5 lbs. 14 oz. or 6 (12 ga.) lbs., mfg. by Lanber. Imported 1990-92.

	$625	$535	$460	$400	$360	$330	$300

Last Mfg.'s Sug. Retail was $749.

SILVER HUNTER — 12 or 20 ga., steel boxlock action, SST, extractors, monoblock VR 26 or 28 (12 ga. only) in. barrels with 2 choke tubes, checkered walnut stock and forearm. Importation began 1999.

Mfg.'s Sug. Retail	$629	$550	$450	$375	$315	$285	$270	$255

SILVER SPORTING — 12 ga. or 20 ga. (new 1996), Sporting Clay model, boxlock action, 28, 29 (new 1999), or 30 (new 1993) in. ported vent. barrels with channelled broadway VR, choke tubes, and elongated forcing cones, nickel finished engraved receiver, SST, ejectors, figured walnut stock and forearm with handcut checkering, 7 lbs. 6 oz., mfg. by Lanber. Importation began 1990. 1993 manufacture by Pedersoli.

Mfg.'s Sug. Retail	$965	$835	$680	$550	$485	$440	$400	$360

SILVER SKEET — 12 ga. only, similar appearance to Silver Sporting, 26 or 28 (new 1993) in. ported vent. barrels with raised VR, 4 choke tubes, recoil pad, 7 lbs. 6 oz. Imported 1992-1993 only.

	$790	$685	$575	$495	$450	$400	$360

Last Mfg.'s Sug. Retail was $899.

SILVER TRAP — similar appearance to Silver Sporting, 30 in. ported barrels with raised VR, 4 choke tubes, recoil pad, trap stock dimensions, 7¾ lbs. Imported 1992-1993 only.

	$790	$685	$575	$495	$450	$400	$360

Last Mfg.'s Sug. Retail was $899.

STERLING/BRISTOL — 12 or 20 ga., 3 in. chambers, boxlock with Greener crossbolt and false side plates, various barrel lengths and choke tubes, chrome finished receiver with moderate game scene engraving, SST, VR, ejectors. Imported 1986-89.

	$695	$550	$495	$450	$400	$375	$350

Last Mfg.'s Sug. Retail was $825.

Until 1989, this model was designated the Bristol. In 1988, the engraving pattern was changed from game scene to elaborate scroll type.

SIR — 12 or 20 ga., 3 in. chambers, sidelock with Greener crossbolt, various barrel lengths and chokings, chrome finished receiver with game scene engraving, ST, VR, ejectors, deluxe checkered pistol grip stock and forearm. Imported 1986 only.

	$900	$725	$660	$610	$565	$520	$485

Last Mfg.'s Sug. Retail was $1,090.

Add $75 for choke tubes.

ROYAL — 12 or 20 ga., 3 in. chambers, sidelock with Greener crossbolt, various barrel lengths and chokings, chrome finished receiver with elaborate scroll engraving, ST, VR, ejectors, oil finished deluxe checkered pistol grip and forearm. Imported 1986-87 only.

	$1,595	$1,310	$1,080	$960	$850	$750	$675

Last Mfg.'s Sug. Retail was $1,730

Add $65 for choke tubes.

Grading	100%	98%	95%	90%	80%	70%	60%

A

EXCELSIOR — 12 or 20 ga., 3 in. chambers, sidelock with Greener crossbolt, various barrel lengths and chokings, chrome finished receiver with elaborate deep relief engraving and multiple gold inlays, ST, VR, ejectors, oil finished deluxe checkered pistol grip and forearm. Imported 1986-87 only.

	$1,775	$1,510	$1,250	$1,100	$975	$885	$780

Last Mfg.'s Sug. Retail was $1,925.

   Add $70 for choke tubes.

WS/WT - O/U (SILVER) 12 WATERFOWL/TURKEY SPECIAL — 12 ga. only, Mag. chambers (3½ in. was added in 1989), 24 (Turkey - disc. 1996), 26 (Turkey) or 28 (Waterfowl) in. barrels with choke tubes, SST, ejectors, parkerized metal finish, matte finished stock and forearm, Mossy Oak Breakout camo pattern began 1997 for Turkey Special, sling swivels, recoil pad, approx. 7 lbs. New 1987.

Mfg.'s Sug. Retail	$799		$650	$550	$460	$395	$360	$330	$300

   Add $86 for Camo Turkey Model (WT/OU Camo 12, Breakup camo pattern, new 1997).

* **10 ga. Waterfowl** — 10 ga. Mag., double triggers, extractors, matte finishes similar to 12 ga. Waterfowl, beavertail forearm. Imported 1988-89 only.

	$750	$625	$550	$495	$450	$390	$360

Last Mfg.'s Sug. Retail was $829.

WT-O/U10 TURKEY SPECIAL — 10 ga., 3½ in. Mag., 26 in. barrels with choke tubes, SST (became standard in 1990), extractors, recoil pad, non-glare metal finish, 9 lbs. 10 oz. New 1988.

Mfg.'s Sug. Retail	$995		$865	$695	$550	$500	$450	$390	$360

F.S. 200 — 12 ga., trap or skeet model, 26 or 32 in. separated barrels only, SST, ejectors, boxlock with Greener crossbolt, black or chromed receiver, checkered walnut stock and forearm. Imported 1986-87 only.

	$690	$560	$500	$450	$410	$375	$350

Last Mfg.'s Sug. Retail was $835.

F.S. 300 — 12 ga., trap or skeet model, 26, 30, or 32 in. separated barrels only, SST, ejectors, boxlock with Greener crossbolt and false side plates lightly engraved, chromed receiver, checkered walnut stock and forearm. Imported 1986 only.

	$825	$675	$610	$555	$510	$470	$440

Last Mfg.'s Sug. Retail was $995.

F.S. 400 — 12 ga., trap or skeet model, 26, 30, or 32 in. separated barrels only, ST, ejectors, sidelock with Greener crossbolt, lightly engraved chromed receiver, checkered walnut stock and forearm. Imported 1986 only.

	$1,145	$945	$860	$800	$740	$680	$620

Last Mfg.'s Sug. Retail was $1,360.

F.S. 500 — same specifications as F.S. 400. Importation disc. 1985.

	$1,175	$950	$860	$795	$730	$660	$595

Last Mfg.'s Sug. Retail was $1,360.

SHOTGUNS: SxS

American Arms is currently importing Spanish shotguns manufactured by Zabala Hermanos and Grulla. Older discontinued Diarm models will also be shown in this section.

GENTRY/YORK — 12, 16 (disc. 1990), 20, 28 ga., or .410 bore, 3 in. chambers, boxlock, ejectors (extractors after 1986), double or SST (became standard in 1992), chromed receiver features fine scroll engraving, fixed chokes, pistol grip stock with recoil pad and beavertail forearm. New 1986.

Mfg.'s Sug. Retail	$750		$625	$475	$375	$300	$280	$260	$240

   Add $45 for 28 ga. or .410 bore.

   Before 1988 this model was designated York (case coloring began 1988, silver finish began 1993). DTs have been supplied with 28 ga. or .410 bore since 1990.

Grading	100%	98%	95%	90%	80%	70%	60%

BRITTANY — 12 or 20 ga., boxlock action, 25 (20 ga. only, disc. 1996), 26, or 27 (12 ga. only, disc. 1996) in. barrels, SST, ejectors, matted solid rib, choke tubes, engraved case colored frame, checkered walnut straight grip stock with recoil pad and semi-beavertail forearm, 6½ or 7 lbs. New 1989.

Mfg.'s Sug. Retail	$885	$725	$575	$485	$435	$400	$375	$350

    The wood finish was changed in this model from oil to semi-gloss in 1991.

SHOGUN — 10 ga., 3½ in. chambers, boxlock, ejectors, double triggers, chromed receiver features fine scroll engraving. Imported 1986 only.

	$440	$350	$325	$300	$280	$260	$240

    Last Mfg.'s Sug. Retail was $525.

DERBY — 12, 20, 28 (disc. 1991) ga., or .410 bore (disc. 1991) ga., 3 in. chambers, sidelock, ejectors, double (disc. 1989) or SNT, chromed receiver features fine scroll engraving, fixed chokes, straight grip walnut stock and forearm. Imported 1986-94.

	$880	$750	$625	$500	$425	$385	$350

    Last Mfg.'s Sug. Retail was $1,039.

    Add 10% for 28 ga. or .410 bore (disc. 1991).
    Subtract 10% for DT.
    Add approx. 50%-60% for 2-barrel set (20 and 28 ga. - approx. 300 sets mfg.) - disc. 1990.

    This model featured a case-colored receiver between 1988-90 and was changed to coin finish in late 1991. At the same time, the wood finish was changed from oil to semi-gloss.

GRULLA NO. 2 — 12, 20, 28 ga., or .410 bore, hand fitted sidelock action, 26 or 28 in. barrels, DTs, ejectors, fixed chokes, concave rib, case colored receiver with elaborate engraving, deluxe English style straight stock and splinter forearm (checkered and hand rubbed), between 5¾ - 6¼ lbs. New 1989.

    This model is individually handcrafted with less than 800 mfg. each year. Since each gun is built per special order, American Arms should be contacted directly for a price quotation or more information (See Trademark Index). Before going to a special order basis, this model retailed for $3,099 (1994).

    ✳ Small Gauge Set — includes choice of 20/28 ga. or 28 ga./.410 bore barrel combination (26 in. fixed choke barrels). Imported 1989-95.

	$3,600	$3,000	$2,375	$2,000	$1,650	$1,325	$1,150

    Before going to a special order basis, this combination last retailed for $4,219 (1994/5).

WS/SS 10 WATERFOWL SPECIAL — 10 ga. only, 3½ in. chambers, 32 in. barrels, DTs, parkerized finish, sling swivels and camouflaged sling, extractors, fixed chokes, recoil pad, 11 lbs. 3 oz. Imported 1987-1993.

	$560	$500	$440	$400	$375	$350	$325

    Last Mfg.'s Sug. Retail was $639.

WT/SS 10 — 10 ga. only, 3½ in. chambers, similar to TS/SS 12, except as 28 in. barrels with multi-chokes. Importation began 1998.

Mfg.'s Sug. Retail	$860	$775	$650	$550	$450	$400	$375	$350

TS/SS 10/12 TURKEY SPECIAL — 10 (disc. 1995) or 12 ga., Mag. chambers (3½ in. 12 ga. introduced in 1989), 26 in. barrels only, double triggers, parkerized finish, dull finish stock and forearm, sling swivels, recoil pad, choke tubes, 7 lbs. 6 oz. or 10 lbs. 13 oz. (10 ga.). New 1987.

Mfg.'s Sug. Retail	$799	$665	$550	$450	$400	$375	$350	$325

    This model in 12 ga. is supplied with a SST.

SHOTGUNS: SEMI-AUTO

PHANTOM — 12 ga. only, 3 in. chamber, gas operated, 24, 26, or 28 in. VR barrel with 3 choke tubes, black synthetic or checkered walnut stock and forearm, blue finish. Importation began 1999.

Mfg.'s Sug. Retail	$439	$395	$360	$330	$275	$250	$225	$200

A

Grading	100%	98%	95%	90%	80%	70%	60%

* **Phantom HP** — similar to Phantom synthetic, except has 19 in. threaded barrels for external choke tubes, swivel studs, and extended mag. Importation began 1999.

Mfg.'s Sug. Retail $449	$400	$365	$330	$275	$250	$225	$200

SHOTGUNS: SINGLE SHOT

SINGLE SHOT MODEL — 12, 20 ga., or .410 bore, 3 in. Mag., non-exposed hammer, pistol grip stock, non-reflective finish. Imported 1988-89 only.

$90	$80	$70	$60	$55	$50	$45

Last Mfg.'s Sug. Retail was $99.

* **Camper Special** — 12, 20 ga., or .410 bore, 3 in. Mag., folding design, 21 in. barrel, pistol grip. Imported 1988-89 only.

$95	$80	$70	$60	$55	$50	$45

Last Mfg.'s Sug. Retail was $107.

* **Slugger** — 12 or 20 ga., 24 in. Slug shotgun barrel with adj. rear sight and blade front, recoil pad. Imported 1989 only.

$100	$85	$75	$65	$55	$50	$45

Last Mfg.'s Sug. Retail was $115.

* **Youth** — 20 ga. or .410 bore, 26 in. barrel, 12½ in. stock dimensions, recoil pad. Imported 1989 only.

$100	$85	$75	$65	$55	$50	$45

Last Mfg.'s Sug. Retail was $115.

* **Combo** — interchangeable rifle and shotgun barrels, choice of .22 Hornet/12 ga. with 28 in. barrel or .22 LR/20 ga. with 26 in. barrel, includes fitted hard case. Imported 1989 only.

$195	$165	$130	$115	$100	$90	$80

Last Mfg.'s Sug. Retail was $235.

* **10 Ga. Model** — 10 ga. only, 3½ in. chambers, 26 in. multi-choke or 32 in. full fixed choke barrel, non-exposed hammer, non-reflective finish. Imported 1988-89 only.

$135	$115	$95	$80	$70	$60	$55

Last Mfg.'s Sug. Retail was $149.

> Add $30 for multi-chokes (26 in. barrel).

AMERICAN BARLOCK WONDER

Previously manufactured by Crescent Arms for Sears Roebuck & Co.

SHOTGUNS: SxS

SIDE-BY-SIDE — various gauges, hammerless or outside hammer, damascus or steel barrels. Add 15% for steel barrels, smaller gauges.

$240	$225	$200	$175	$140	$100	$75

SINGLE SHOT — various gauges, hammer, steel barrel. Add 35% for smaller gauges.

$125	$115	$100	$90	$75	$60	$50

AMERICAN DERRINGER CORPORATION

Current manufacturer located in Waco, TX 1980-present. Distributor and dealer sales.

DERRINGERS: STAINLESS STEEL

MODEL 1 — available in over 55 cals. including .22 LR through .45-70 Govt., also 2½ in. .410 shot shell, O/U stainless steel derringer, satin or high polish finish, 3 in. barrels, automatic barrel selection, hammer block type safety, 15 oz., spur trigger, rosewood grips. New 1980.

Grading	100%	98%	95%	90%	80%	70%	60%

* Regular Cals. — most cals. between .22 LR and .40 S&W.

Mfg.'s Sug. Retail	$270	$210	$170	$130

    Add $25 for high polish finish.
    Add approx. $130 for .22 Hornet (disc. 1989), .223 Rem., or .30-30 cal.

* Larger Cals. — typically .357 Mag.-.45 Mag. cal.

Mfg.'s Sug. Retail	$335	$280	$220	$180

    Add $25 for high polish finish.
    Subtract approx. $60 for .357 Mag. or .45 ACP cal.
    Add approx. $65 for .41 - .45 Mag. cals.

This model can be ordered with special ser. #s and other custom features at additional cost(s).

* Model 1 Engraved — limited mfg., mostly special ordered.

Mfg.'s Sug. Retail	$1,317	$995	$855	$725

* Model 1 Gambler Millennium 2000 Series — .45 LC/.410 shotshell only, 3 in. barrel, 5,000 mfg. beginning 1998.

Mfg.'s Sug. Retail	$380	$295	$250	$215

LADY DERRINGER — .32 Mag. or .38 Spl. standard cals., also available in .22 LR (disc.), .22 Mag. (disc.), .357 Mag., .380 ACP (disc.), 9mm Para. (disc.), .45 LC, or .45 LC/.410 shotshell cal., O/U top break action, high polish stainless steel, spur trigger, synthetic ivory grips, handfitted action allowing easy cocking, cased in French styled jewelry box, 15½ oz. New 1990.

* Standard Grade — standard model as described above, 1990 mfg. only.

	$215	$185	$160

    Last Mfg.'s Sug. Retail was $250.

LADY DERRINGER II — .38 Spl. only, O/U double action, aluminum frame, trigger guard stops at trigger bottom, 8 oz. New 1999.

Mfg.'s Sug. Retail	$315	$265	$205	$170

* Deluxe Grade — similar to Standard Grade, except synthetic grips are scrimshawed in a cameo or rose design, choice of walnut case or French jewelry box.

Mfg.'s Sug. Retail	$290	$245	$195	$165

    Add $15 for .32 Mag., $45 for .357 Mag., and $75 for .45 LC or .45 LC/.410 shotshell.

* Deluxe Engraved — similar to Deluxe Grade, except hand engraved with circa 1880 patterns. Disc. 1994.

	$650	$515	$400

    Last Mfg.'s Sug. Retail was $750.

Mother-of-pearl grips and personalized engraving were available as extra cost options on this model.

* 14 KT. Gold Engraved — entire Derringer manufactured out of a 14 KT. gold bar (contains approx. 20 oz. of 14 KT. gold and 3 oz. of stainless steel), custom engraved with diamond sights, special order only until late 1993.

	N/A	N/A	N/A

    Last Mfg.'s Sug. Retail was $100,000.

MODEL 1 TEXAS COMMEMORATIVE — .38 Spl., .44-40, or .45 LC cal., similar to Model 1 except has brass frame, stainless steel barrel, and stag grips. 500 mfg. in each cal. starting in 1986.

Grading	100%	Issue Price	Qty. Made
.44-40 cal. (current mfg.)	$315	$350	500
.45 cal. (current mfg.)	$325	$380	500
Add $25 for special serial number.			
.32 Mag.	$205	$255	500+

A

Grading	100%	Issue Price	Qty. Made
.38 Spl. (current mfg.)	$245	$295	500
.22 LR (mfg. 1991-92)	$200	$238	500
.41 Rimfire (not shootable)	$235	$295	500
Fully engraved model	$695	$750	limited

125TH ANNIVERSARY — special edition 125th anniversary variation with pistol case. Disc. 1993.

	100%	Issue Price	Qty. Made
.44-40 or .45 cal.	$285	$320	500
.38 Spl.	$185	$225	500
Deluxe engraved model	$650	$750	limited

Grading	100%	98%	95%	90%	80%	70%	60%

MODEL 3 — .32 Mag. (new 1990 - limited availability) or .38 Spl. cal., single shot, 2½ in. barrel, 8½ oz., spur trigger, rosewood grips. Disc. 1994.

	100%	98%	95%
	$95	$70	$55

Last Mfg.'s Sug. Retail was $120.

MODEL 4 — .357 Mag., .357 Max., .44 Mag., .45 ACP, .45-70 Govt., or .45 LC cal. on upper barrel, 3 in. .410 shotshell lower barrel, O/U derringer combination pistol, 4¹/₁₀ in. barrel, rosewood grips, 16½ oz. New 1985.

		100%	98%	95%	90%
Mfg.'s Sug. Retail	$355	$315	$250	$210	

Add $50 for oversized grips.
Add $90 for .44 Mag. cal. (oversized grips became standard 1997).
Add $145 for .45-70 Govt. cal. in both barrels.

This model was also available on special order in either .50-70 or .50 Saunders cal. (new 1989 - single shot only). Retail was $395.

* **Model 4 Engraved** — .45 LC/.410 shotshell cal., allow 12 weeks for delivery. New 1997.

Mfg.'s Sug. Retail	$1,517	$1,375	$1,100	$900

* **Alaskan Survival Model** — similar to Model 4, except choice of .45-70 Govt. or .44 Mag. cal. upper or lower barrel.

Mfg.'s Sug. Retail	$400	$350	$295	$260

Add $25 for high polish finish.

MODEL 6 — .22 Mag., .357 Mag., .45 LC, .45 ACP, or .45 LC/.410 shotshell cal., O/U, 6 in. barrel, 21 oz. Available in high polish, satin, or gray matte finish (standard). New 1986.

Mfg.'s Sug. Retail	$365	$275	$210	$180

Add $10 for either .45 LC or .45 LC/.410 shotshell.
Add $13 for satin finish (disc. 1994).
Add $25 for high polish finish.
Add $50 for oversized grips (disc. 1994, reinstated 1998).
Add $1,412 for engraving option (new 1997).

* **Model 6 Engraved** — .45 LC/.410 shotshell cal., allow 12 weeks for delivery. New 1997.

Mfg.'s Sug. Retail	$1,717	$1,525	$1,200	$950

MODEL 7 — .22 LR, .22 Mag. (new 1992), .32 Mag., .38 Spl., .38 S&W (disc. 1989), .380 ACP, or .44 Spl. cal., O/U, same basic specifications as Model 1, except ultra lightweight (7½ oz.).

Mfg.'s Sug. Retail	$265	$210	$145	$120

* **.44 Special Cal.** — .44 Spl. cal. only.

Mfg.'s Sug. Retail	$505	$450	$410	$350

MODEL 8 — .45 LC/.410 shotshell cal., O/U, 8 in. barrel, nickel finish, grooved grips, 24 oz. New 1997.

Mfg.'s Sug. Retail	$425	$365	$295	$255

* **Model 8 Engraved** — .45 LC/.410 shotshell cal.. Limited mfg. 1997-98 only.

$1,675	$1,300	$975

Last Mfg.'s Sug. Retail was $1,917.

Grading	100%	98%	95%	90%	80%	70%	60%

MODEL 10 — .38 Spl. (new 1995), .45 ACP, .45 LC, or .45 LC/.410 shotshell (disc. 1997), O/U, 3 in. stainless barrels, aluminum frame and barrel, matte gray finish, 7.5 oz. New 1988.

Mfg.'s Sug. Retail   **$245**   **$210** **$170** **$140**

   Add $80 for .45 LC cal.

   Add $25 for .45 ACP cal.

MODEL 11 — .22 LR (new 1995), .22 Mag. (new 1995), .32 Mag. (new 1995), .380 ACP (new 1995), or .38 Spl. cal., same basic specifications as Model 1, matte gray finish, only 11 oz.

Mfg.'s Sug. Retail   **$250**   **$200** **$155** **$125**

RIMFIRE DOUBLE ACTION — .22 LR or .22 Mag. cal., 3½ in. O/U barrels, double action trigger, dual extraction, hammerless, blue finish with black synthetic grips, 11 oz. Mfg. 1990-95.

   $145 **$115**   **$95**

Last Mfg.'s Sug. Retail was $170.

This O/U Derringer was patterned after the original High Standard design.

DS .22 MAG. — .22 Mag. cal., 3 in. barrel, stainless steel with blue finish, 11 oz. Special order beginning 1998.

Mfg.'s Sug. Retail   **$300**   **$260** **$200** **$165**

DA 38 DOUBLE ACTION — .22 LR (new 1996), .357 Mag. (new 1991), .38 Spl., 9mm Para., or .40 S&W (new 1993) cal., 3 in. O/U barrels, satin stainless steel with aluminum grip frame, double action trigger design, hammerblock thumb safety, choice of checkered rosewood, walnut, or other hardwood grips, 14.5 oz. New 1990.

Mfg.'s Sug. Retail   **$325**   **$265** **$195** **$155**

   Add $10 for 9mm Para. cal.

   Add $40 for .357 Mag. or .40 S&W cal.

   Add $15 for Lady Derringer Model (scrimshawed synthetic ivory grips, .38 Spl. only. Mfg. 1992-94.)

MINI-COP — .22 Mag. cal., 4 shot double action design, stainless steel construction, patterned after the original Mini-Cop mfg. in Torrance, CA. Mfg. 1990-94.

   $250 **$220** **$185**

Last Mfg.'s Sug. Retail was $313.

4-BARREL DERRINGER — .22 LR, .38 Spl., or .357 Mag. cal., double action, similar design to Mini-Cop, semi-matte finish, 28 oz. While advertised beginning 1991 at $425, only a few prototypes were manufactured during 1997.

CUSTOM TARGET MODELS — .38 Spl. Wadcutter or 9mm Federal (disc.) cal., mfg. for End of Trail Derringer Match, limited production. Mfg. 1990-92.

   $695 **$575** **$475**

Last Mfg.'s Sug. Retail was $750.

4 BARREL DERRINGER — while advertised, this model never went into production.

PISTOLS: PEN DESIGN

MODEL 2 PEN PISTOL — .22 LR, .25 ACP, or .32 ACP cal., unique hinged action allows pen to be converted into a legal pistol within two seconds, folding design, 2 in. barrel, cocks on opening action, firing pin block grip safety, brushed stainless finish, 5 oz. Mfg. 1993-1994.

   $145 **$120** **$100**

Last Mfg.'s Sug. Retail was $203.

   Add $24 for .32 ACP cal.

Grading	100%	98%	95%	90%	80%	70%	60%

PISTOLS: SEMI-AUTO

STANDARD MODEL

* .25 Mag. Cal. — .25 Mag., semi-auto single action, less than 100 manufactured in stainless steel only.

	$500	$400	$300				

* .25 ACP Cal. — .25 ACP, semi-auto single action, less than 400 manufactured in stainless steel, less than 50 in blued steel.

	100%	98%	95%
Stainless	$400	$300	$250
Blue	$550	$400	$325

LM-5 — .25 ACP, .32 Mag. (disc. 1997), or .380 ACP (new 1998) cal., compact stainless semi-auto, single action, 2¼ in. barrel, hammerless, wood grips, 4 (.32 Mag. or .380 ACP) or 5 (.25 ACP) shot mag., 15 oz. Limited mfg. beginning 1997.

Mfg.'s Sug. Retail $278 $230 $185 $150

    Add $27 for .32 Mag. cal. (disc. 1997).

* LM-5 .380 ACP

Mfg.'s Sug. Retail $425 $365 $295 $215

PISTOLS: SLIDE-ACTION

LM-4 (SEMMERLING) — .45 ACP cal., 2 in. barrel, super compact, thumb activated slide mechanism, blue finish, 4 shot mag., 24 oz., limited manufacture beginning 1998.

Mfg.'s Sug. Retail $2,500 $2,275 $1,975 $1,850 $1,700 $1,550 $1,450 $1,375

AMERICAN FIREARMS MANUFACTURING CO., INC.

Previous manufacturer located in San Antonio, TX between 1972-1974.

PISTOLS: SEMI-AUTO

AMERICAN .25 AUTOMATIC — .25 ACP cal., 8 shot, 2¹/₁₀ in. barrel, smooth walnut grips, mfg. 1966-74.

	100%	98%	95%	90%	80%	70%	60%
Stainless	$195	$180	$165				
Blue	$165	$150	$140	$120	$100	$90	$85

DERRINGERS

AMERICAN .38 SPL. — .38 Spl. cal., O/U configuration, approx. 3,000-4,000 mfg. between 1972-74.

	$200	$165	$135				

AMERICAN .380 AUTOMATIC — .380 ACP cal., 8 shot, 3½ in. barrel, stainless steel, smooth walnut grips, approx. 10 mfg. 1972-1974.

	$700	$500	$300				

AMERICAN GUN CO.

Previously manufactured by Crescent Firearms Co. and distributed by H. & D. Folsom Co.

REVOLVERS

REVOLVER — .32 S&W cal., 5 shot, double action, top break-open action.

	100%	98%	95%	90%	80%	70%	60%
	$175	$160	$140	$120	$95	$65	$50

Grading	100%	98%	95%	90%	80%	70%	60%

A

SHOTGUNS: SxS

SxS — various gauges, hammer or hammerless, damascus or steel barrels.

	100%	98%	95%	90%	80%	70%	60%
	$240	$225	$200	$175	$140	$100	$75

Add 15% for small gauges or steel barrels.

AMERICAN FRONTIER FIREARMS MFG., INC.

Current manufacturer located in Aguanga, CA since 1995. Direct sales only.

American Frontier Firearms Mfg., Inc. manufactures a line of older replica metallic cartridge firing revolvers (black powder or smokeless). These revolvers are manufactured, fit, and finished in the U.S. Modern smokeless cals. include .22 LR, .32 Spl., .38 Spl., .44 Russian, or .45 LC.

REVOLVERS: REPRODUCTIONS

Production on the models listed below began mid-1997. These revolvers are supplied with standard finish high polish blued steel parts, color case hardened hammer and/or trigger, silver-plated or blued backstrap and trigger guard, and varnished walnut grips. Special orders are also available featuring simulated ivory grips, special finishes, and engraving options.

RICHARDS 1851 NAVY CONVERSION STANDARD MODEL — .38 or .44 cal., non-rebated cyl., 4¾, 5½ or 7½ in. barrel, w/o ejector rod assembly.

Mfg.'s Sug. Retail	$695	$625	$495	$350	$325	$295	$265	$235

RICHARDS & MASON CONVERSION 1851 NAVY STANDARD MODEL — .38 or .44 cal., features Mason ejector rod assembly and non-rebated cyl., otherwise similar to Richards 1851 Navy Conversion.

Mfg.'s Sug. Retail	$695	$625	$495	$350	$325	$295	$265	$235

* *Pocket Richards & Mason Navy Conversion* — .32 cal., non-rebated cyl., 5 shot.

Mfg.'s Sug. Retail	$495	$445	$375	$275	$250	$225	$200	$185

RICHARDS 1860 ARMY CONVERSION STANDARD MODEL — .38 or .44 cal., rebated cyl., with or w/o ejector assembly, 4¾, 5½ or 7½ in. barrel.

Mfg.'s Sug. Retail	$695	$625	$495	$350	$325	$295	$265	$235

* *Pocket Richards Conversion Model* — .32 cal., 5 shot, rebated cyl., 4¾ or 5½ in. round barrel.

Mfg.'s Sug. Retail	$495	$445	$375	$275	$250	$225	$200	$185

RICHARDS 1861 NAVY CONVERSION — same as 1860 Army, except has non-rebated cylinder and Navy sized grips.

Mfg.'s Sug. Retail	$695	$625	$495	$350	$325	$295	$265	$235

1871-72 OPEN-TOP STANDARD MODEL — .38 or .44 cal., 7½ or 8 in. round barrel, non-rebated cyl.

Mfg.'s Sug. Retail	$795	$715	$550	$425	$400	$350	$300	$250

* *1871-72 Open-Top Tiffany Model* — similar to 1871-72 Standard Model, except has engraved gold/silver finished Tiffany grips and also available with 4¾ in. barrel.

Mfg.'s Sug. Retail	$995	$895	$700	$525	$450	$395	$350	$315

* *1871-72 Pocket Model* — .32 cal., 5 shot, 4¾ or 5½ in. round barrel.

Mfg.'s Sug. Retail	$495	$445	$375	$275	$250	$225	$200	$185

REMINGTON NEW MODEL STANDARD — .38, .44, or .45 cal., 5½ or 7½ in. barrel, includes loading lever but w/o ejector rod and gate.

Mfg.'s Sug. Retail	$695	$625	$495	$350	$325	$295	$265	$235

Grading	100%	98%	95%	90%	80%	70%	60%

REMINGTON NEW MODEL ARMY (ARTILLERY OR CALVALRY) — .38, .44, or .45 cal., 5½ (Artillery Model) or 7½ (Calvary Model) in. barrel, supplied with ejector assembly and loading gate, includes government inspector's cartouche on left grip and sub-inspector's initialed small parts.

Mfg.'s Sug. Retail	$795	$715	$550	$425	$400	$350	$300	$250

POCKET REMINGTON — .22, .32, or .38 cal., 3½ in. barrel, with or w/o ejector rod and gate.

Mfg.'s Sug. Retail	$495	$445	$375	$275	$250	$225	$200	$185

AMERICAN HISTORICAL FOUNDATION, THE

A current private organization which privately commissions historical commemoratives in conjunction with leading manufacturers and craftsmen around the world. The Foundation is located in Richmond, VA. Direct to collector sales only, via phone, correspondence or personal visit.

The Foundation's limited edition models are not all manufactured at one time. Rather, guns are fabricated as demand dictates, to always keep availability below demand.

LIMITED/SPECIAL EDITIONS

Values listed below reflect the Foundation's original or most recent issue prices. These do not necessarily represent secondary marketplace prices. No other values are listed since the Foundation's limited edition firearms do not appear that frequently in the secondary marketplace. This is because the Foundation has always sold to consumers directly, without involving normal gun dealers and distributors. Foundation collectors include museums, veterans, and other interested parties who normally keep these items for a considerable time period. Because of this consumer direct sales program, many gun dealers do not have a working knowledge about what AHF firearms are currently selling for. The publisher suggests that those people owning the Foundation's Commemorative Issue firearms contact the Foundation (See Trademark Index) for current information, including secondary marketplace liquidity.

MANUFACTURER	MODEL	QUANTITY	YEAR	MOST RECENT ISSUE PRICE

PISTOLS

Values listed below do not include original display cases (typically priced between $85 and $180).

MANUFACTURER	MODEL	QUANTITY	YEAR	MOST RECENT ISSUE PRICE
Colt	U.S. Marine Mustang .380 ACP	500	1994	$695
Colt	Armed Forces Navy .380 ACP Series	1,911	1994	$995
Colt	Armed Forces Marines .380 ACP Series	1,911	1994	$995
Colt	Armed Forces Army .380 ACP Series	1,911	1994	$995
Colt	Armed Forces Air Force .380 ACP Series	1,911	1994	$995
Auto-Ordnance	Armed Forces Navy M1911A1 Series	1,911	1994	$1,295
Auto-Ordnance	Armed Forces Marines M1911A1 Series	1,911	1994	$1,295
Auto-Ordnance	Armed Forces Army M1911A1 Series	1,911	1994	$1,295
Auto-Ordnance	Armed Forces Air Force M1911A1 Series	1,911	1994	$1,295
Auto-Ordnance	Airborne Jubilee M1911A1	500	-	$1,295
Auto-Ordnance	D-Day Commem. M1911A1	1,000	1994	$1,095
Auto-Ordnance	5-Star General Eisenhower M1911A1	500	-	$1,295
Auto-Ordnance	5-Star General MacArthur M1911A1	500	-	$1,295
Auto-Ordnance	Vietnam War M1911A1	2,500	1990	$1,295
Colt	WWII Series M1911A1 (12 variations)	250/variation	-	$1,495
Colt	WWII 50th Anniversary M1911A1	500 (standard)	1995	$1,495
Colt	WWII 50th Anniversary M1911A1	50 (deluxe)	1995	$2,995
Colt	Gold Cup M1911A1	1,000	1995	$2,195
Auto-Ordnance	Medals of Valor M1911A1 (6 variations)	1,000/variation	1995	$1,295
Beretta	Armed Forces M9 Navy	1,985	1995	$1,795

A

MANUFACTURER	MODEL	QUANTITY	YEAR	MOST RECENT ISSUE PRIC
Beretta	Armed Forces M9 Marines	1,985	1995	$1,795
Beretta	Armed Forces M9 Army	1,985	1995	$1,795
Beretta	Armed Forces M9 Air Force	1,985	1995	$1,795
Beretta	Armed Forces M9 Coast Guard	1,985	1995	$1,795
Beretta	Golden Centurion .40 S&W	200	1994	$2,195
Ruger	40th Anniversary Mark II	950	1990	$1,095
Ruger	Armed Forces Ruger Navy	250	-	$1,095
Ruger	Armed Forces Ruger Marines	250	-	$1,095
Ruger	Armed Forces Ruger Army	250	-	$1,095
Ruger	Armed Forces Ruger Air Force	250	-	$1,095
Baikal	Soviet Makarov	1,000	1994	$895
N/A	Rommel P.38 Collector's Ed.	300	1994	$1,995
N/A	Rommel P.38 Deluxe Ed.	100	1994	$2,995
N/A	WWII Allied Victory P.38	250	1995	$1,695
Browning	2nd Amendment Hi-Power .40 S&W	500	1994	$1,995
Browning	Allied Victory Hi-Power 9mm Para.	500	-	$1,795
Browning	WWII Victory Hi-Power 9mm Para.	500	1995	$1,795
Inglis	Crusade in Europe Hi-Power 9mm	500	1994	$1,495
Inglis	Showcase Edition 9mm	250	1995	$1,295
Inglis	Golden Hi Power 9mm	50	1995	$2,495
N/A	ETO Luger Collector's Edition 9mm	750	-	$1,795
N/A	ETO Luger Deluxe Edition 9mm	50	-	$3,995
N/A	Broomhandle Gen. Officer Ed.	300	1994	$1,995
N/A	Broomhandle Field Marshal Ed.	100	1994	$2,995
S&W	Tactical Competition Collector's Ed..40 S&W	40	-	$2,795
S&W	Tactical Competition Deluxe Ed..40 S&W	10	-	$3,795
S&W	Tactical PC9 9mm	50	1994	$2,595
S&W	Second Amendment Sigma .40 S&W	250	1995	$1,995
IMI	Uzi Pistol 9mm	100	-	$2,495
Luger	Older German Mfg. 9mm	500	1997	$2,495

REVOLVERS

Values listed below do not include original display cases (typically priced between $179 and $395).

Pedersoli	Texas Patterson .36 cal.	950	-	$2,195
Uberti	Model 1847 Walker	950	-	$2,195
Colt	Civil War 2nd Model Dragoon (Union)	125	-	$2,495
Colt	Civil War 2nd Model Dragoon (Confed.)	125	-	$2,495
Uberti	Model 1849 Wells Fargo .31 cal.	950	1995	$1,995
Uberti	J. Davis Model 1851 Navy .36 cal.	250	-	$2,995
Uberti	Gen. Robert E. Lee Model 1851 Navy	1,000	1994	$2,195
Uberti	Wild Bill Hickock Model 1851 Navy	500	-	$1,995
Colt	Colt Golden Tribute Model 1860 Army	950	1994	$1,995
Colt	Col. J. S. Mosby Model 1860 Army	150	-	$2,495
Uberti	1862 Police Revolver .36 cal.	950	1993	$1,895
Navy Arms	J.E.B. Stuart LeMat	500	1987	$2,895
Dan Wesson	200th Constitution .44 Mag. (Coll.)	950	1987	$1,295
Dan Wesson	200th Constitution .44 Mag. (Deluxe)	500	1987	$1,595
Dan Wesson	2nd Amendment .44 Mag. (Collector)	1,500	1989	$1,695
Dan Wesson	2nd Amendment .44 Mag. (Deluxe)	750	1989	$1,895
Dan Wesson	Deer Hunter .44 Mag. (Sportsman)	750	1990	$1,095

This variation is also available in a bear, moose, elk, or sheep edition.

Dan Wesson	Deer Hunter .44 Mag. (Deluxe Trophy)	250	1990	$1,995

This variation is also available in a bear, moose, elk, or sheep edition.

Colt	Legacy Edition Anaconda	1,000	1994	$1,795
Colt	20th Century Python 8 in.	1,000	1995	$2,795
Colt	Legacy King Cobra 6 in.	1,000	1996	$1,795
Uberti	General Patton SAA .45 LC	2,500	1988	$1,995
Uberti	Teddy Roosevelt SAA .44-40	750	-	$1,995
Colt	Heritage Ed. SAA .45 LC 4¾ in.	250	1995	$2,995
Ruger	Cowboy Ltd. Ed. .44 Mag. or .45 LC	500 each	1996	$1,895

MANUFACTURER	MODEL	QUANTITY	YEAR	MOST RECENT ISSUE PRICE
Colt	Old West Sheriff's SAA .45 LC	10	-	$10,995
Enfield	WWII British Commando No. 2 Mk. I	250	-	$995

This price includes display case and Commando Knife mfg. by H.G. Long & Co.

MANUFACTURER	MODEL	QUANTITY	YEAR	MOST RECENT ISSUE PRICE
S&W	Tactical Edition F-Comp	50	1994	$2,795
S&W	Model 625 Bank Note .45 ACP	100	1995	$2,195
S&W	Model 640 Special Edition	250	1993	$2,195
S&W	50 States Ltd. Ed. Model 29	100	1996	$1,895
S&W	Hunter Edition	50	1994	$3,795

RIFLES AND CARBINES

Values listed below do not include original display cases (typically priced between $249 and $299).

MANUFACTURER	MODEL	QUANTITY	YEAR	MOST RECENT ISSUE PRICE
Uberti	50 States Henry (2 per state)	100	-	$11,995
Uberti	Henry Civil War Commem. A. Lincoln	250	-	$3,995
Uberti	Henry Civil War Commem. J. Davis	250	-	$3,995
Browning	Model 1885 Elk Hunter .45-70 Govt.	100	1995	$2,975
Browning	Model 1885 Deer Hunter (Collector)	100	-	$2,975
Browning	Model 1885 Deer Hunter (Deluxe)	10	-	$5,995
Browning	Model 81 No. Amer. Big Game Five	250	1995	$2,495
Ezech & R. Chiappa	Model 1861 Springfield Musket	125	1986	$3,495
Uberti	Constitution Comm. Henry .44-40	200	-	$2,395
Browning	BAR Trophy Edition .30-06	500	1993	$2,195
Winchester	Model 94 Amer. West (Collector)	750	-	$1,895
Winchester	Model 94 Amer. West (Deluxe)	250	-	$2,895
Winchester	Model 94 Centennial 1 of 100 .30-30	100	1995	$2,495
N/A	WWII M1 Garand .30-06	2,500	-	$1,895
N/A	WWII 50th Anniversary Garand (Collector)	500	1995	$1,895
N/A	WWII 50th Anniversary Garand (Deluxe)	50	1995	$3,495
N/A	Armed Forces Basic Training M1 Garand	500	1994	$1,895
N/A	Airborne Golden Jubilee M1A1 Carbine	500	-	$1,495
N/A	WWII 50th Anniv. M1 Carbine (Collector)	550	1995	$1,495
N/A	WWII 50th Anniv. M1 Carbine (Deluxe)	50	1995	$2,495
N/A	Vietnam War M1 Carbine	1,500	1995	$1,495
Auto-Ordnance	Roaring Twenties Thompson	500	1996	$2,195
Auto-Ordnance	Airbone Golden Jubilee Thompson	500	-	$2,195
Auto-Ordnance	Armed Forces Thompson Navy	750	-	$2,195
Auto-Ordnance	Armed Forces Thompson Marines	750	-	$2,195
Auto-Ordnance	Armed Forces Thompson Army	750	-	$2,195
Auto-Ordnance	Armed Forces Thompson Air Force	750	-	$2,195
Auto-Ordnance	Law Enforcement Thompson	1,500	-	$2,195
Auto-Ordnance	ETO/PTO Thompson	500 each	-	$2,195
Auto-Ordnance	Showcase Edition	100	1994	$2,195
Auto-Ordnance	D-Day 50th Anniv. Thompson	500	1994	$2,195
Auto-Ordnance	WWII 50th Anniv. Thompson (Standard)	500	1995	$2,495
Auto-Ordnance	WWII 50th Anniv. Thompson (Deluxe)	50	1995	$4,495
Auto-Ordnance	Korean War Thompson (Standard)	2,000	1984	$2,195
Auto-Ordnance	Korean War Thompson (Engraved)	25	1984	$4,995
Springfield	Vietnam M14 (Collector)	500	1987	$2,495
Springfield	Vietnam M14 (Deluxe)	500	1987	$3,295
Colt	M16 Vietnam War	1,500	-	$2,495
Colt	M16 Vietnam Tribute	1,500	-	$2,495
Colt	Armed Forces M16 Navy	100	-	$2,995
Colt	Armed Forces M16 Marines	100	-	$2,995
Colt	Armed Forces M16 Army	100	-	$2,995
Colt	Armed Forces M16 Air Force	100	-	$2,995
B.F.I.	M16 Airborne	950	-	$2,795
Russian Arsenal	Vietnam War Trophy SKS	1,500	1994	$995
FEG/Hungary	Vietnam War AK-47	1,500	1993	$1,895
I.M.I.	American Armed Forces UZI	400	1988	$2,195
M.A.C.	Special Forces MAC-10 .45 ACP	1,500	-	$1,595
Springfield	WWII '03 Springfield	500	-	$1,695

MANUFACTURER	MODEL	QUANTITY	YEAR	MOST RECENT ISSUE PRICE

SHOTGUNS

Values listed below include original display cases.

Browning	Citori O/U 12 ga.	100	-	$5,795
Browning	A5 Mag. 12 ga.	250	-	$2,595
Browning	B-125 (12 or 20 ga.)	100	-	$10,495
Browning	B-25 (12 or 20 ga.)	50	-	$15,995

Original issue prices were (Citori) $4,995, (B-125) $9,995, and (B-25) $14,500.

Ugartechea	Waterfowl Classic SxS 12 ga.	100	1995	$1,995
H & H	Upland Bird Spl. Ed. 12 or 20 ga.	10	-	$19,995
R. Gamba	French Revolution SxS	200	-	$10,995
Savage	Vietnam War Combat 12 ga.	750	1988	$1,595

AMERICAN HUNTING RIFLES, INC. (AHR)

Current manufacturer established in 1998 and located in Hamilton, MT.

Grading	100%	98%	95%	90%	80%	70%	60%

RIFLES: BOLT ACTION

AMERICAN BIG GAME RIFLE — .270 Win., .30-06, and various Howell proprietary cals., features new pre-64 Winchester Model 70 action, 24 in. chrome-moly sporter barrel, black fiberglass stock with Decelerator recoil pad. New 1999.

Mfg.'s Sug. Retail	$1,495	$1,250	$975	$850	$725	$600	$550	$495

AMERICAN INDUSTRIES

Please refer to the Calico section in this text.

AMERICAN INTERNATIONAL

Previous manufacturer located in Austria.

RIFLES: CARBINES

AMERICAN 180 AUTO CARBINE — .22 LR cal., a specialized design for paramilitary use, 177 round drum mag., 16½ in. barrel, aperture sight, high impact plastic stock.

	$660	$550	$440	$360	$330	$305	$275

Add $550 for Laser Lok System.
Add $125 for Extra Drum Mag. and Winder.

Note: This gun was available in a selective fire version for law enforcement only. The gun also was available with a laser assisted sighting system which, when affixed to the weapon, projected a beam to point of impact.

AMTEC 2000, INC.

Current trademark incorporating Erma Werke (German) and H & R 1871 (U.S.) companies located in Gardner, MA. Amtec 2000, Inc. currently imports the Erma SR 100 rifle (see listing in Erma Suhl section).

REVOLVERS

5 SHOT REVOLVER — .38 S&W cal., 5 shot double action, swing-out cylinder, 2 or 3 in. barrel, transfer bar safety, Pachmayr composition grips, high polish blue, matte electroless nickel, or stainless steel construction, fixed sights, approx. 25 oz., 200 mfg. 1996-98, all were distributed and sold in Europe only (no U.S. pricing).

Grading	100%	98%	95%	90%	80%	70%	60%

A ANCIENS ETABLISSEMENTS PIEPER

Please refer to the Bayard section in this text for Bayard Models 1908, 1923, and 1930. In addition, Bergmann-Bayard Models 1908 and 1910 mfg. in Gaggenau, Germany will appear under the Bergman heading.

ANGEL ARMS INC.

Current manufacturer located in Hayward, CA, beginning 1998.

PISTOLS: SEMI-AUTO

The pistols listed below shoot a unique integrated case projectile (ICP). These projectiles are hollow, contain the powder charge, and since the case is the projectile, there's no ejection.

MODEL 1000 SE GUN ONE — .45 ICP (Integrated Case Projectile) cal., unique semi-auto design, mag tube is located on top of 6 in. fixed barrel, scheduled for production during 1999.

Mfg.'s Sug. Retail	$1,900		$1,900	$1,550	$1,200

MODEL QT 427 ZMR — .427 ICP (Integrated Case Projectile) cal., break open action, 5 shot tube or 10 shot staggered mag, 3½ in. barrel, located underneath clear mag tube, 5 oz., compact size, scheduled for production during 1999.

Mfg.'s Sug. Retail	$900		$900	$775	$600

ANSCHÜTZ

Current manufacturer established in 1856 and currently located in Ulm, Germany. Sporting and certain models of target rifles are currently distributed by AcuSport since 1996, headquartered in Bellefontaine, OH, Go Sportsmen's Supply (1997) located in Billings, MT, and Zanders Sporting Goods (1997) located in Baldwin, IL. Target rifles are imported by various distributors (please see Trademark Index for current listing). Sporting rifles are currently imported exclusively beginning in 1996 by Tristar Sporting Arms. Ltd., located in N. Kansas City, MO. Previously imported and distributed through 1995 in the U.S. by Precision Sales International Inc., located in Westfield, MA.

PISTOLS: BOLT ACTION

Anschütz also manufactures a new MSP Pistol Series with a new ergonomic stock for the silhouette shooters. These variations are designed for target shooting - please contact the distributors for more information on these models, as most are special order.

MODEL 1416P/1451P (EXEMPLAR) — .22 LR cal., bolt action, Match 64 left-hand action (for right-hand shooters), approx. 7 (original Silhouette Model, mfg. 1994-95) or 10 in. barrel, single shot (Model 1451P, new 1997) or repeater with 5 shot mag. (Model 1416P), two-stage trigger, adj. rear sight, receiver grooved for scope, contoured grip and forestock are stippled, 3⅓ lbs., also available for left-hand shooters. Mfg. 1987-1997.

$395	$345	$295	$250	$225	$200	$180

Last Mfg.'s Sug. Retail was $470.

Add $17 for single shot (Model 1451P).

Add $110 for right-hand action (for left-hand shooters).

This model was previously designated the Exemplar until 1996.

* *Exemplar Magnum* — while advertised in 1987, only one .22 Mag. was manufactured.

Grading	100%	98%	95%	90%	80%	70%	60%

* Exemplar XIV — .22 LR cal., similar to Exemplar, except has 14 in. barrel, 4.15 lbs. Imported 1988-95.

	$450	$370	$300	$250	$225	$200	$180

Last Mfg.'s Sug. Retail was $562.

* Exemplar Hornet — .22 Hornet cal., 5 shot mag., Match 54 left-hand action, 10 in. barrel, no sights - tapped and grooved, 4.35 lbs. Imported 1988-95.

	$835	$685	$575	$525	$475	$415	$365

Last Mfg.'s Sug. Retail was $995.

* Model 1416 MSPR/MSPE — .22 LR cal., silhouette variation of the Exemplar pistol, MSPR designates repeater, MSPE designates single shot. Mfg.1997 only.

	$1,100	$875	$750	$625	$525	$450	$375

Last Mfg.'s Sug. Retail was $1,260.

MODEL 64P — .22 LR or .22 Mag. cal., right-hand bolt action, 10 in. barrel drilled and tapped (sights not included), weather proof "Choate" Rynite stock with stippling, 2 stage trigger, 4 shot mag., 3½ lbs. New 1998.

Mfg.'s Sug. Retail	$456		$400	$350	$295	$250	$225	$200	$180

Add $22 for .22 Mag. cal. (Model 64P Mag.).
Add $73 for accessory sight set.

RIFLES: BOLT ACTION, DISC.

Sile Distributors located in NY acted as an import agent during the early 1960s which can be identified by Sile barrel markings. Savage imported Anschütz rifles were available from 1963-1981 and also have Savage/Anschütz barrel markings. While some of those models might not be listed below, refer to models of similar caliber and quality that are listed to ascertain values.

During the period when Savage was importing Anschütz rifles, certain models in the Anschütz line were designated "Savage-Anschütz" for sales by Savage in the U.S. Conversely, certain models manufactured by Savage were designated "Anschütz-Savage" for sale by Anschütz in Europe. Some of these models did not have any modifications but others were restocked, supplied with different sights, and had other different features from their original counterparts. In most cases, the original model numbers were used.

Some "Anschütz-Savage" rifles have made their way into the U.S. While somewhat rare, these rifles are typically based on the Savage Model 110 action. They are not as desirable as those "Savage-Anschütz" marked rifles utilizing the superior Anschütz action. Anschütz also manufactured between 1,000-2,000 rifles utilizing SAKO actions in .222 Rem. cal. in the late 50s-early 60s. These guns will approximate values shown on the discontinued centerfire models listed below.

The models below have been listed in numerical sequence.

MARK 10 TARGET RIFLE — .22 LR cal., single shot, 26 in. heavy barrel, adj. sights, globe front, target stock with full pistol grip, adj. palm stop, mfg. 1963-1981.

	$350	$320	$290	$260	$230	$210	$195

MODEL 54 SPORTER — .22 LR cal., 5 shot mag., 24 in. round tapered barrel, Monte Carlo roll-over cheekpiece, folding leaf sight, checkered pistol grip. Mfg. 1963-1981.

	$675	$595	$525	$450	$400	$360	$330

MODEL 54M — similar to Model 54 Sporter, except .22 Mag. cal.

	$725	$625	$550	$475	$425	$395	$350

MODEL 141 — .22 LR cal., 5 shot clip, 23 in. round tapered barrel, Monte Carlo stock, folding leaf sight. Disc.

	$345	$280	$240	$200	$180	$160	$140

* Model 141M (Mag.) — similar to Model 141, except .22 Mag. cal.

	$400	$365	$300	$265	$225	$200	$180

A

Grading	100%	98%	95%	90%	80%	70%	60%

A

MODEL 153 — .222 Rem. cal., 24 in. barrel, folding leaf rear sight, French walnut stock, rosewood forend tip and pistol grip cap. Mfg. 1963-1981.

| | $550 | $475 | $400 | $375 | $350 | $300 | $280 |

MODEL 153-S — similar to Model 153, 24 in. barrel, double set triggers.

| | $600 | $525 | $450 | $425 | $385 | $330 | $305 |

MODEL 164 — .22 LR cal., 5 shot clip, 23 in. round tapered barrel, Monte Carlo stock, folding leaf sight. Mfg. 1963-1981.

| | $380 | $345 | $280 | $240 | $200 | $180 | $160 |

MODEL 164M — similar to 164, except .22 Mag. cal.

| | $400 | $365 | $300 | $265 | $225 | $200 | $180 |

MODEL 184 — .22 LR cal., 21½ in. barrel, Monte Carlo combination, checkered pistol grip, Schnabel forend, folding leaf sight. Mfg. 1963-1981.

| | $350 | $320 | $290 | $260 | $230 | $210 | $195 |

MODEL 1400 — .22 LR cal., regular barrel, with sights. Disc.

| | $350 | $320 | $290 | $260 | $230 | $210 | $195 |

MODEL 1407 — .22 LR cal. "I.S.U." model, heavy barrel, no sights. Disc.

| | $375 | $340 | $300 | $260 | $230 | $210 | $195 |

MODEL 1408 — .22 LR cal., heavy barrel, no sights. Disc.

| | $375 | $340 | $300 | $260 | $230 | $210 | $195 |

Add $150 for 1408 ED Model.

MODEL 1411 — .22 LR cal., prone position target model, heavy barrel, no sights. Disc.

| | $360 | $320 | $290 | $260 | $230 | $210 | $195 |

MODEL 1413 MATCH — .22 LR cal., adj. cheekpiece, heavy target barrel with no sights, competition model. Disc.

| | $550 | $475 | $420 | $375 | $325 | $285 | $240 |

MODEL 1418 — .22 LR cal., sporter variation, previous importation by Savage Arms.

| | $300 | $260 | $225 | $200 | $175 | $150 | $125 |

MODEL 1418 MANNLICHER — .22 LR cal., hunting model, fine checkering, 5 shot mag.

| | $650 | $575 | $500 | $450 | $365 | $315 | $275 |

MODEL 1450 — .22 LR cal., Sporter, 5 shot mag.

| | $275 | $225 | $200 | $175 | $150 | $125 | $110 |

MODEL 1518 MANNLICHER — deluxe model of Model 1418.

| | $700 | $595 | $540 | $485 | $430 | $375 | $325 |

MODEL 1574 SPORTER — .22 Mag., .222 Rem., .22-250 Rem., .223 Rem., .243 Win., or .308 Win. cal., mfg. by Krico (Kriegeskorte) located at Stuttgart and distributed by Anschütz, approx. 1,000 imported during 1970-73.

| | $795 | $695 | $595 | $540 | $485 | $430 | $375 |

RIFLES: BOLT ACTION SPORTER, .22 LR - RECENT MFG.

KADETT — .22 LR cal., bolt action, youth dimensions, 22 in. barrel, 5 shot clip mag., folding leaf rear sight, single stage trigger, grooved receiver, checkered hard-wood stock, 5½ lbs. Mfg. 1987 only.

| | $235 | $200 | $180 | $165 | $150 | $135 | $120 |

Last Mfg.'s Sug. Retail was $265.

Grading	100%	98%	95%	90%	80%	70%	60%

ACHIEVER — .22 LR cal., bolt action, 19½ in. barrel, single shot, folding leaf rear sight, two stage trigger, grooved receiver, stippled hard-wood stock with vented forearm and adj. length of pull, 5¼ lbs. Mfg. 1987-95.

	$340	$280	$230	$205	$185	$165	$150

Last Mfg.'s Sug. Retail was $399.

* ***Achiever ST*** — .22 LR cal., 2000 MK single shot action, slide safety, two stage trigger, adj. length of pull stock, target sights, approx. 6½ lbs. Mfg. 1994-95.

	$415	$360	$315	$260	$230	$205	$185

Last Mfg.'s Sug. Retail was $485.

* ***Model Woodchucker*** — .22 LR cal., similar to Model 1449D Youth, sold exclusively by R.S.R. Wholesale.

	$210	$185	$165	$150	$135	$120	$110

MODEL 1416D LUXUS/CUSTOM — .22 LR cal., bolt action, 22½ in. barrel, 5 or 10 shot mag., cam cocking system on recent mfg., checkered Monte Carlo walnut stock, folding leaf sight, 6 lbs. 2 oz.

Mfg.'s Sug. Retail	$756	$650	$515	$425	$360	$295	$240	$225

This model utilizes the Match 64 action, similar to the Anschütz Model 1403 Target. Until 1996, this model was designated Model 1416D Custom.

* ***Model 1416D Fiberglass*** — similar to Model 1416D Custom, except has McMillan fiberglass stock in hunter brown color and includes roll-over cheekpiece and checkered Wundhammer swell pistol grip, 5¼ lbs. Imported 1991 only.

	$755	$650	$575	$525	$475	$415	$365

Last Mfg.'s Sug. Retail was $842.

* ***1416D Classic*** — same specifications as 1416D Custom, except straight hardwood stock.

Mfg.'s Sug. Retail	$680	$585	$495	$425	$360	$295	$240	$225

Add $34 for left-hand action (Model 1416LD).

MODEL 1418D — .22 LR cal., Mannlicher full stock, skipline checkering, 19¾ in. barrel, same action as Model 1416D, 5 lbs. 5 oz. Importation disc. 1995, resumed 1998.

Mfg.'s Sug. Retail	$1,164	$975	$800	$665	$550	$495	$425	$360

Add $40 for set trigger (mfg. 1985-89).

MODEL 1448D — .22 Clay Bird, 22½ in. smooth bore barrel w/o sights, repeater, 5 shot mag., checkered walnut stained stock and forend. Importation began 1999.

Mfg.'s Sug. Retail	$416	$365	$330	$310	$280	$260	$240	$220

MODEL 1449D YOUTH — .22 LR cal., bolt action design, youth dimensions, 16¼ in. tapered barrel with adj. rear sight, receiver is grooved for scope mounting, 5 shot mag. with single shot adapter available, European hardwood stock, 12¼ in. trigger pull, 3½ lbs. Imported 1990-91 only.

	$210	$185	$165	$150	$135	$120	$110

Last Mfg.'s Sug. Retail was $249.

MODEL 1451 E/R SPORTER/TARGET — .22 LR cal., single shot (Model 1451E, disc. 1997) or 5 shot repeater (Model 1451R), sporter target model w/o front sight, 22 (new 1998) or 22¾ (disc. 1997) in. barrel w/o sights, stippled pistol grip wood stock and vent. forend, 6½ lbs. New 1996.

Mfg.'s Sug. Retail	$550	$485	$435	$385	$335	$300	$265	$230

Subtract $100 for Model 1451E (single shot).

* ***Model 1451ST-R*** — .22 LR cal., repeater, 5 shot mag., drilled and tapped 22 in. barrel w/o sights, cam cocking system, 2 stage trigger, uncheckered walnut stained hardwood stock. Importation began 1999.

Mfg.'s Sug. Retail	$536	$465	$425	$375	$335	$300	$265	$230

Grading	100%	98%	95%	90%	80%	70%	60%

A

* **Model 1451D Custom** — similar to Model 1451D Classic, except has walnut stock with Monte Carlo cheekpiece, Schnabel forend, and sling swivels, 5 lbs. New 1998.

Mfg.'s Sug. Retail	$430	$375	$340	$320	$295	$285	$265	$230

* **Model 1451D Classic (Super)** — .22 LR cal., 5 shot, 22¾ in. barrel with front sights, grooved receiver, walnut finished straight hardwood stock, 5 lbs. New 1996.

Mfg.'s Sug. Retail	$250	$235	$210	$190	$175	$160	$150	$140

  This model was designated the 1451 Super during 1996-97.

MODEL 1466D REPEATER — .22 LR cal., 24 in. conically tapered barrel with open sights, grooved receiver, checkered Monte Carlo walnut stock and forend. Imported 1996 only.

	$660	$525	$435	$375	$315	$260	$235

Last Mfg.'s Sug. Retail was $766.

MODEL 1700D/1710D CUSTOM - .22 LR — .22 LR cal., bolt action, 54 Sporter action, 5 shot mag., 23¾ (new 1998) or 24 (disc. 1997) in. regular (new 1998) or heavy (disc. 1997) barrel, iron sights, Monte Carlo stock with roll-over cheekpiece and skipline checkering, 6½-7¼ lbs.

Mfg.'s Sug. Retail	$1,290	$1,125	$825	$675	$575	$475	$375	$325

Add $190 for Meistergrade (select walnut and gold etched trigger guard - disc. 1996, resumed 1998 w/o gold trigger guard).

This model was designated 1422D until 1989 when it was changed to the Model 1700D with some modifications. In 1996, model nomenclature changed from Model 1700D Custom to the Model 1710D Custom. The Model 1400D Meistergrade was disc. 1987 - the last advertised retail price was $930.

The Model 1700D Custom employs the Anschütz Match 54 action.

* **1700D Graphite** — similar to Model 1700D Custom, except has McMillan black graphite reinforced stock with Monte Carlo roll-over cheekpiece, includes sling and swivels, 22 in. barrel, 7¼ lbs. Imported 1991-95.

	$1,130	$885	$760	$650	$550	$450	$375

  Last Mfg.'s Sug. Retail was $1,299.

* **1700D/1710D Classic** — same general specifications as 1700D/1710D Custom, regular straight stock, choice of regular or heavy (new 1999) barrel, open sights disc. 1994. Disc. 1994, importation resumed 1998.

Mfg.'s Sug. Retail	$1,224	$1,075	$850	$725	$650	$550	$450	$375

  Add $189 for Meistergrade (select walnut and gold etched trigger guard, disc. 1994).

  This model was designated 1422DCL Classic until 1989 when it was changed to the Model 1700D Classic with some modifications. The Model 1422DCL Classic Meistergrade was disc. 1987 - the last advertised retail price was $875. In 1998, this model was reintroduced as the Model 1710D Classic.

1700D FEATHERWEIGHT (FWT) — similar to Model 1700D Custom, except has matte black McMillan fiberglass stock configured like the Custom Model, 22 in. barrel, no sights, 6¼ lbs. Imported 1989-95.

	$1,075	$895	$775	$650	$550	$450	$375

Last Mfg.'s Sug. Retail was $1,230.

While discontinued, some distributors still have remaining inventories left of this model.

* **1700D Featherweight Deluxe** — similar specification to the 1700D Featherweight, except has skip-line checkered Fibergrain synthetic stock with realistic wood grain. Imported 1990-95.

	$1,235	$1,050	$875	$775	$650	$550	$450

  Last Mfg.'s Sug. Retail was $1,460.

MODEL 1700D BAVARIAN — .22 LR cal., 24 in. barrel, 5 shot mag., checkered European style stock with European Monte Carlo cheekpiece and schnabel forend, 7½ lbs. Mfg. 1988-95.

	$1,165	$935	$775	$650	$550	$450	$375

Last Mfg.'s Sug. Retail was $1,364.

Add $199 for Meistergrade variation (select walnut).

Grading	100%	98%	95%	90%	80%	70%	60%

MODEL 1712D — .22 LR cal., current top-of-the-line sporter rifle with deluxe walnut. Imported 1997-98 only.

	$1,300	$1,100	$895	$775	$650	$550	$450

Last Mfg.'s Sug. Retail was $1,495.

DIE MEISTERMACHER — .22 LR cal., similar action and specifications as Model 1422D Custom, limited edition of 25 guns, select wood, extra polish on metal parts, hand-lapped barrel, with numerous gold inlays including Olympic wreath. Mfg. 1985.

$2,500	$2,000	$1,600

Last Mfg.'s Sug. Retail was $2,475. This variation sold out in late 1988.

RIFLES: BOLT ACTION SPORTER, .22 MAG. - RECENT MFG.

MODEL 1516D LUXUS/CUSTOM — similar to Model 1416D, except .22 Mag. cal., 4 shot mag., 6 lbs. 2 oz.

Mfg.'s Sug. Retail	$780		$675	$525	$450	$375	$325	$265	$230

This model utilizes the Match 64 action, similar to the Anschütz Model 1403 Target. In 1996, model nomenclature changed from the Model 1516D Custom to 1516D Luxus and during 1998, it changed back to 1516D Custom.

* 1516D/DCL Classic — same specifications as 1516D Custom, except regular hardwood stained stock.

Mfg.'s Sug. Retail	$714		$625	$500	$400	$350	$295	$240	$225

MODEL 1518D (LUXUS) — .22 Mag. cal., otherwise similar to Model 1418D (Mannlicher stock), 4 shot mag., 5½ lbs. Importation disc. 1995, reintroduced 1997, nomenclature was changed to Model 1518D in 1997.

Mfg.'s Sug. Retail	$1,187		$1,025	$825	$675	$550	$440	$375	$325

Add $50 for set trigger (disc. 1995).

MODEL 1700D/1720D CUSTOM - .22 MAG. — .22 Mag. cal., bolt action, 5 shot mag., 23¾ (new 1998) or 24 (disc. 1991) in. regular (new 1998) or heavy (disc. 1991) barrel, iron sights, Monte Carlo stock with skipline checkering, 6 lbs. 10 oz - 7¼ lbs. Importation disc. 1991, resumed 1998.

Mfg.'s Sug. Retail	$1,314		$1,125	$900	$750	$650	$550	$450	$375

Last Mfg.'s Sug. Retail was $1,229 for Model 1700D.

Add $192 for Meistergrade variation (select walnut).

This model was designated 1522D until 1989 and then reintroduced as the Model 1700D with some modifications. The Model 1522D Custom Meistergrade was disc. 1985 - last advertised retail price was $678. In 1998, this model was reintroduced as the 1720D Custom.

* 1700D/1720D Classic — same general specifications as 1700D Custom, straight regular stock, choice of heavy (new 1999), or regular diameter barrel. Importation disc. 1991, resumed 1998.

Mfg.'s Sug. Retail	$1,247		$1,095	$875	$725	$625	$525	$425	$350

Last Mfg.'s Sug. Retail was $1,199 for Model 1700D Classic.

Add $192 for Meistergrade variation (select walnut).

This model was designated 1522DCL until 1989 and then reintroduced as the Model 1700D with some modifications. In 1998, this model was reintroduced as the 1720D Classic. The Model 1522DCL Classic Meistergrade was disc. 1985 - the last advertised retail price was $660.

MODEL 1700D BAVARIAN — .22 Mag. cal., 24 in. barrel, clip mag., checkered European style stock with European Monte Carlo cheekpiece and schnabel forend, 7½ lbs. Mfg. 1988-95.

	$1,165	$935	$775	$650	$550	$450	$375

Last Mfg.'s Sug. Retail was $1,364.

Add $199 for Meistergrade variation (select walnut).

Grading	100%	98%	95%	90%	80%	70%	60%

A

RIFLES: BOLT ACTION SPORTER, CENTERFIRE - RECENT MFG.

MODEL 1433D — .22 Hornet cal., special order only, Match 54 target action, Mannlicher full stock, 4 shot mag. Set trigger new 1985 — add $15. Disc. 1986.

	$995	$840	$740	$640	$525	$425	$350

Last Mfg.'s Sug. Retail was $826.

MODEL 1700D/1730D CUSTOM - .22 HORNET — .22 Hornet cal., 24 in. barrel, folding leaf sight, Monte Carlo stock with skipline checkering and rosewood grip cap, 4 shot mag., 7¾ lbs. Model 1432D was disc. 1987, and the Model 1700D was introduced 1989.

Mfg.'s Sug. Retail	$1,440	$1,250	$995	$825	$700	$600	$500	$400

Add $192 for Meistergrade variation (select walnut).

This model was designated 1432D until 1987 and then reintroduced 1989 as the Model 1700D with some modifications. In 1996, model nomenclature changed from the Model 1700D Custom to the Model 1730D Custom. The Model 1432D Custom Meistergrade was disc. 1986 - the last advertised retail price was $770.

The 1700D Custom comes standard with the Anschütz Match 54 action.

* **1700D Graphite** — similar to Model 1700D Custom, except has McMillan black graphite reinforced stock with Monte Carlo roll-over cheekpiece, includes sling and swivels, 22 in. barrel, 7¼ lbs. Imported 1995 only.

		$1,235	$1,025	$840	$725	$625	$525	$425

Last Mfg.'s Sug. Retail was $1,478.

* **Model 1700D/1730D Classic** — same general specifications as 1700D Custom, except regular stock and 23½ (1432DCL), 23¾ regular or heavy (new 1999) - 1730D, or 24 (1700D) in. barrel. Disc. 1994, reintroduced 1998.

Mfg.'s Sug. Retail	$1,375		$1,200	$975	$825	$735	$615	$500	$400

Last Mfg.'s Sug. Retail was $1,395 on the Model 1700D Classic.

Add $192 for Meistergrade variation (select walnut).

This model was designated 1432D until 1987 and then reintroduced 1989 as the Model 1700D with some modifications. In 1998, this model was reintroduced as the Model 1730D Classic. This model comes standard with the Anschütz Match 54 action.

MODEL 1700D BAVARIAN — .22 Hornet or .222 Rem. cal., 24 in. barrel, 5 shot mag., checkered European style stock with European Monte Carlo cheekpiece and schnabel forend, 7½ lbs. Mfg. 1988-95.

	$1,325	$1,050	$900	$775	$650	$550	$425

Last Mfg.'s Sug. Retail was $1,364.

Add $199 for Meistergrade variation (select walnut).

MODEL 1733D — .22 Hornet cal., Mannlicher full stock featuring skipline checkering, European walnut, and rosewood Schnabel tip, 19¾ in. barrel with hooded front sight, 6 lbs. 6 oz. Imported 1993-95, reintroduced 1998.

Mfg.'s Sug. Retail	$1,589		$1,365	$1,050	$875	$750	$625	$500	$400

MODEL 1700D/1740D CUSTOM - .222 REM. — .222 Rem. cal., otherwise similar to Model 1700D Custom, except is also available with 23¾ in. barrel.

Mfg.'s Sug. Retail	$1,440		$1,250	$995	$835	$735	$615	$500	$400

Last Mfg.'s Sug. Retail was $909 on the Model 1532D.

Add $192 for Meistergrade variation (select walnut).

This model was designated 1532D until 1987 and then reintroduced 1989 as the Model 1700D with some modifications. In 1996, model nomenclature changed from the Model 1700D Custom to the Model 1740D Custom. The Model 1532D MG Custom Meistergrade was disc. 1986 - the last advertised retail price was $770.

Grading	100%	98%	95%	90%	80%	70%	60%

* 1700D/1740D Classic — similar to Model 1700D Custom, except regular stock. Disc. 1994, reintroduced 1998.

Mfg.'s Sug. Retail	$1,375	$1,200	$995	$835	$735	$615	$500	$400

Last Mfg.'s Sug. Retail was $849 on Model 1532DCL.
Last Mfg.'s Sug. Retail was $1,395 on Model 1700D Classic.

Add $192 for Meistergrade variation (select walnut).

This model was designated 1532DCL until 1987 and then reintroduced 1989 as the Model 1700D with some modifications. In 1998, this model was reintroduced as the 1740D Classic.

MODEL 1743D — .222 Rem. cal., Mannlicher full stock variation of the Model 1740D. New 1997.

Mfg.'s Sug. Retail	$1,589		$1,365	$1,050	$875	$750	$625	$500	$400

MODEL 1533 — .222 Rem. cal., open sights, checkered walnut stock. Disc. 1994.

			$795	$725	$660	$600	$550	$475	$400

RIFLES: BOLT ACTION, SINGLE SHOT SILHOUETTE

Currently imported Anschütz silhouette rifles can vary somewhat in price, depending on the distributor and inventory.

MODEL 2013 SUPER-MATCH FREE RIFLE (BR-50) — .22 LR cal., single shot, 20 in. heavy barrel, no sights, black synthetic stock with adj. cheekpiece and widened forend ("ANSCHÜTZ BR-50" is stenciled on sides), 15.4 lbs. Limited imported 1994-98.

			$2,225	$1,750	$1,375	$1,050	$900	$725	$625

Last Mfg.'s Sug. Retail was $2,880.

Add $300 for color laminate stock (mfg. 1997-98 only).

Model nomenclature changed from the BR-50 to the Model 2013 in 1997.

MODEL 64S RIFLE — .22 LR cal., single shot, 26 in. round barrel, beavertail forearm, adj. single stage trigger, aperture sights, target stock with Wundhammer grip and adj. butt plate, checkered pistol grip, mfg. 1963-1981.

			$475	$425	$375	$325	$285	$240	$220

Subtract 15% if without sights (Model 64).

This model was available in left or right hand action.

MODEL 64MS R — .22 LR cal., single shot (Model 64MS, disc. 1996) or 5 shot repeater (Model 64MS R), silhouette target model, 21¼ in. barrel, no sights, Wundhammer swell stippled pistol grip stock, adj. trigger, 8 lbs.

Mfg.'s Sug. Retail	$1,130		$725	$675	$550	$450	$375	$350	$325

Add $50 for left-hand action (disc.).

This variation employs a Match 64 action. R suffix nomenclature started 1997.

MODEL 64MP — .22 LR cal., repeater, 5 shot mag., 21.2 in. drilled and tapped heavy barrel, 2 stage trigger, unchecked walnut stained stock and beavertail forend, adj. rubber buttplate. Importation began 1999.

Mfg.'s Sug. Retail	$745		$650	$525	$425	$350	$295	$240	$225

Add $21 for swivel rail.

* Model 64MS - FWT — similar to Model 64MS, except single stage trigger, 6¼ lbs. Disc. 1988.

			$550	$475	$425	$350	$325	$260	$230

Last Mfg.'s Sug. Retail was $596.

MODEL 54.18MS — .22 LR cal., silhouette target model, 22 in. barrel, match 54 single shot action, walnut Wundhammer stock is stippled on pistol grip and entire forearm, no sights, 8 lbs. 6 oz. Disc. 1997.

		$1,295	$1,075	$895	$760	$650	$550	$475

Last Mfg.'s Sug. Retail was $1,579.

Add $96 for left-hand action.

This model employs the Super Match 54 action.

Grading	100%	98%	95%	90%	80%	70%	60%

✴ *Model 54.18MS ED* — same action as Model 54.18MS, except has 19¼ in. barrel (⅞ in. diameter) with 14¼ in. extension tube, 3 removable muzzle weights. Disc. 1988.

	$1,075	$900	$775	$675	$575	$485	$410

Last Mfg.'s Sug. Retail was $1,215.

Add $100 for left-hand action.

MODEL 54.18MS REP — similar to Model 54.18MS, except has repeating action, 5 shot mag., thumbhole wood stock with vented forestock, 7¾ lbs. This model was introduced in 1989 with a wood stock and a retail price of $1,650. In 1990, the stock was changed to a synthetic McMillan fiberglass finished in gray.

Mfg.'s Sug. Retail	$1,840		$1,200	$1,075	$950	$800	$695	$595	$525

Add 10% for wood stock (1989 mfg. only).

This model features a 54 Super Match action with clip mag.

✴ *Model 54.18MS REP Deluxe* — Deluxe version of the Model 54.18MS REP featuring Fibergrain McMillan stock with advanced thumbhole design and stippled checkering. Imported 1990-97.

	$2,035	$1,600	$1,275	$1,025	$915	$785	$695

Last Mfg.'s Sug. Retail was $2,450.

RIFLES: BOLT ACTION MATCH, RECENT MFG.

Currently imported Anschütz match rifles can vary somewhat in price, depending on the distributor and inventory.

MODEL 2000 MK — .22 LR cal., single shot match, 26 in. barrel, aperture sights, 7½ lbs. Disc. 1988.

	$340	$290	$250	$210	$180	$160	$145

Last Mfg.'s Sug. Retail was $400.

MODEL 1403D — .22 LR cal., improved Model 64S match rifle, single shot, no sights, adj. trigger, 8 lbs. 6 oz. Importation disc. in 1990.

	$600	$525	$450	$360	$300	$260	$225

Last Mfg.'s Sug. Retail was $700.

Add $50 for left-hand action (disc. 1988).

MODEL 1803D — .22 LR cal., Match 64 action, 25½ in. target barrel, single stage adj. trigger, blond finished wood with dark stippling on pistol grip and forearm, adj. cheekpiece and butt plate, 8.6 lbs. Imported 1987-1993.

	$850	$725	$625	$525	$430	$365	$310

Last Mfg.'s Sug. Retail was $1,012.

Add $70 for left-hand action (disc. 1989).

MODEL 1808D RT/1808MS R (RUNNING TARGET) — .22 LR cal., single shot running target model, 32½ in. barrel, adj. stock, cheekpiece, trigger, heavy beavertail forend, no sights, muzzle barrel weights, 9¼ lbs. Importation disc. 1998.

	$1,850	$1,400	$1,075	$950	$800	$695	$595

Last Mfg.'s Sug. Retail was $2,220.

Add $50 for left-hand action (disc. 1991).

This model was previously designated Model 1808D RT from 1991-96, and also the Model 1808 ED Super during 1990 and earlier mfg.

MODEL 1808MS R — .22 LR cal., 5 shot repeater designed for metallic silhouette shooting, 19.2 in. barrel w/o sights, thumbhole Monte Carlo stock with grooved forearm featuring "ANSCHÜTZ" in panel scene, approx. 8 lbs. Importation began 1998.

Mfg.'s Sug. Retail	$2,220		$1,475	$1,325	$1,075	$950	$800	$695	$595

Grading	100%	98%	95%	90%	80%	70%	60%

MODEL 1903D — .22 LR cal., similar specifications to the Model 1803D, except has new improved target stock and adj. cheekpiece made from walnut finished European hardwood, color laminated stock mfg. 1995-98, full length stippled checkering on forend and contoured pistol grip, fully adj. new style buttplate, 9.9 lbs. New 1990.

Mfg.'s Sug. Retail	N/A	$695	$640	$550	$495	$430	$400	$365

Add $40 for left-hand action.
Add $130 for color laminated stock (disc. 1998).

MODEL 1907 ISU — .22 LR cal., single shot match "I.S.U." model, 26 in. button-rifled barrel, prone and position shooting, removable cheekpiece, adj. buttplate, hand stippled stock with ventilated forearm and choice of beechwood (new 1997) walnut, blond laminated (disc.), or color laminated (mfg. 1995-96) wood stock, 10½ lbs.

Mfg.'s Sug. Retail	N/A	$1,255	$1,125	$995	$840	$700	$580	$500

Add $20 for left-hand action.
Add $130 for stainless steel barrel.
Add $125 for quick adj. cheekpiece.
Add $125 for color laminated stock (disc.).

This model is also available with an Anschütz stock no. 2213 blue laminate (Alu Color), featuring the most recent technology in stock innovation - POR.

This variation was designated Model 1807 before 1989.

MODEL 1909 — target variation, limited importation 1997-98 only.

			$2,050	$1,550	$1,225	$1,025	$895	$785	$695

Last Mfg.'s Sug. Retail was $2,480.

MODEL 1910 SUPER MATCH II — .22 LR cal., single shot, 27¼ in. barrel, diopter sights, thumbhole stock is fully adj., 12 lbs., model down from 1813 (or 1913), special order only - limited quantities imported until 1998.

			$2,415	$1,925	$1,475	$1,100	$900	$725	$625

Last Mfg.'s Sug. Retail was $2,967.

Add $149 for left-hand action.

This variation was designated as Model 1810 before 1988.

MODEL 1911 PRONE MATCH — .22 LR cal., single shot match prone rifle, 27¼ in. barrel, adj. cheekpiece, buttplate, no sights, 11.9 lbs.

			$1,600	$1,375	$1,175	$995	$925	$785	$695

Last Mfg.'s Sug. Retail was $2,095.

Add $135 for stainless steel barrel.
Add $100 for left-hand action (disc. 1993).

This variation was designated Model 1811 before 1988.

MODEL 1912 LADIES SPORT RIFLE — .22 LR cal., designed for new ladies U.I.T standards, features 1907 barreled action w/o sights, walnut stock with shorter dimensions, 11.4 lbs. Importation began 1999.

Mfg.'s Sug. Retail	N/A	$1,665	$1,500	$1,275	$1,075	$950	$800	$695

MODEL 1913 SUPER MATCH FREE RIFLE — .22 LR cal., single shot, top-of-the-line match rifle, every possible refinement, international diopter sights, 27¼ in. button rifled barrel, hand and palm rest, 14.3 lbs.

Mfg.'s Sug. Retail	N/A	$2,070	$1,775	$1,475	$1,175	$995	$925	$785

Add $130 for left-hand action.
Add $125 for color laminate stock.
Add $135 for stainless steel barrel.

This model is also available with an Anschütz stock no. 2213 blue laminate (Alu Color), featuring the most recent technology in stock innovation - POR.

This variation was designated Model 1813 before 1988.

Grading	100%	98%	95%	90%	80%	70%	60%

MODEL 2007 ISU STANDARD — .22 LR cal., ISU model, choice of 26 in. regular or 19¾ in. barrel with 8 in. detachable tube in front of barrel providing for different sights and counter-weights, adj. cheekpiece and rubber butt plate, grooved and vented forearm, choice of blond or walnut stock, Match 54 action, 10.8 lbs. New 1992.

Mfg.'s Sug. Retail	N/A	$1,645	$1,495	$1,275	$1,075	$950	$800	$695

Add $80 for left-hand action (new 1993).

Add $135 for stainless steel barrel.

This model underwent significant engineering changes during 1994, including a heavier receiver.

MODEL 2012 LADIES SPORT RIFLE — .22 LR cal., utilizes 2007 rectangular receiver barreled action designed for new ladies UIT rules, smaller dimensions, walnut stock, 11.4 lbs. Importation began 1999.

Mfg.'s Sug. Retail	N/A	$2,070	$1,775	$1,475	$1,175	$995	$925	$785

MODEL 2013 SUPER MATCH FREE RIFLE — .22 LR cal., top-of-the-line international target rifle featuring choice of 27 in. standard or 19¾ in. barrel with detachable front tube allowing for different sights and counter-weights, top grain walnut or color laminate stock with adj. hand rest, palm rest, cheekpiece, and elaborate metal butt plate, Match 54 action, 15.4 lbs. New 1992.

Mfg.'s Sug. Retail	N/A	$2,325	$2,000	$1,550	$1,225	$1,025	$895	$785

Add $115 for left-hand action.

Add $175 for color laminate stock.

This model underwent significant engineering changes during 1994.

* *Model 2013 Benchrest* — .22 LR cal., developed especially for benchrest competition, trigger can be adjusted for either light single or two-stage action, 19.6 in. barrel, uncheckered walnut stock with wide forend, 10.3 lbs. Importation began 1999.

Mfg.'s Sug. Retail	N/A	$1,645	$1,495	$1,275	$1,075	$950	$800	$695

RIFLES: BOLT ACTION, BIATHLON

Currently imported Anschütz biathlon rifles can vary somewhat in price, depending on the distributor and inventory.

MODEL 1450B — .22 LR cal., 2000 MK action, 19½ in. barrel, European hardwood with vent. forearm and adj. butt plate, aperture sights, 5 lbs. Mfg. 1993 only.

		$650	$550	$450	$375	$300	$260	$230

Last Mfg.'s Sug. Retail was $765.

MODEL 1403B — .22 LR cal., Match 64 action, 21½ in. barrel, blonde finished European hardwood with stippled pistol grip, Biathlon design allows 4 mags. to be stored in a housing attached to the forend on right side, entry level Biathlon gun, 8½ lbs. Mfg. 1990-92.

		$850	$730	$660	$525	$450	$375	$335

Last Mfg.'s Sug. Retail was $998.

MODEL 1827B — .22 LR cal., biathlon rifle, carries four 5 shot mags. in stock, special biathlon features, 21½ in. barrel, limited mfg.

	$1,875	$1,550	$1,225	$1,025	$895	$785	$695

Last Mfg.'s Sug. Retail was $2,457.

Add $120 for left-hand action (disc. 1989).

In 1990, the stock design was changed permitting 8 mags. to be stored in two housings attached to both the stock and forend on right side.

Grading	100%	98%	95%	90%	80%	70%	60%

* **Model 1827BT Fortner** — same general specifications as Model 1827B, except has Fortner straight pull-through bolt action, color laminated stock became available 1995, blued or stainless barrel, 8.8 lbs. New 1986.

Mfg.'s Sug. Retail	N/A	$2,060	$1,775	$1,475	$1,175	$995	$925	$785

Add $185 for left-hand action.
Add $115 for stainless steel barrel.

In 1990, the stock design was changed permitting 8 mags. to be stored in two housings attached to both the stock and forend on right side.

RIFLES: SEMI-AUTO

MODEL 520/61 — .22 LR cal., semi-auto, 24 in. barrel, 10 shot mag., Monte Carlo stock, 6½ lbs. Disc. 1983.

	$260	$205	$185	$155	$145	$130	$120

MARK 525 SPORTER RIFLE — .22 LR cal., semi-auto, 24 in. barrel, 10 shot mag., adj. rear sight, Monte Carlo stock, 6½ lbs. Imported 1984-95.

	$460	$395	$350	$295	$250	$215	$175

Last Mfg.'s Sug. Retail was $547.

* **Mark 525 Carbine** — similar to Mark 525 Rifle, except has 20 in. barrel. Disc. 1986.

	$400	$315	$265	$225	$200	$180	$160

SHOTGUNS: O/U

Anschütz marked O/U shotguns were manufactured by Miroku of Japan and distributed in Germany only. Several grades of these shotguns were manufactured and while rarely seen in the U.S., values approximate other Miroku O/Us of similar quality and features ($650-$1,000 assuming 95% or better condition).

APACHE

Previous trademark manufactured by Ojanguren Y Vidosa located in Eibar, Spain.

PISTOLS: SEMI-AUTO

SEMI-AUTO — 6.35mm cal., clip fed.

	$190	$175	$160	$140	$120	$95	$75

ARCUS CO.

Current trademark of handguns manufactured in Bulgaria and imported by Miltex, Inc., located in Waldorf, MD. Dealer sales.

PISTOLS: SEMI-AUTO

ARCUS-94 — 9 mm Para. cal., semi-auto, SA or DA, 5¼ in. barrel, 10 shot mag., choice of blue, two-tone, or silver matte metal finish, molded synthetic grips, 32 oz. Importation began 1998.

No Mfg.'s Retail	$385	$335	$295	$250	$200	$180	$160

ARLINGTON ORDNANCE

Previous importer located in Westport, CT until 1996. Formerly located in Weston, CT.

RIFLES: SEMI-AUTO

M1 GARAND RIFLE — .30-06 cal., these Garands were imported from Korea in used condition, various manufacturers, with import stamp. Imported 1991-96.

	$325	$285	$250	$200	$180	$160	$140

Add $40 for stock upgrade (better wood).

Grading	100%	98%	95%	90%	80%	70%	60%

* **Arsenal Restored M1 Garand Rifle** — .30-06 or .308 Win. cal., featured new barrel, rebuilt gas system, and reinspected components. Mfg. 1994-96.

	$475	$385	$325	$285	$250	$200	$180

Add 5% for .308 Win. cal.

TROPHY GARAND — .308 Win. cal. only, action was original mil-spec., included new barrel and checkered walnut stock and forend, recoil pad. Mfg. 1994-96.

	$625	$525	$375	$325	$275	$225	$200

Last Mfg.'s Sug. Retail was $695.

T26 TANKER — .30-06 or .308 Win. cal., included new barrel and other key components, updated stock finish. Mfg. 1994-96.

	$550	$415	$340	$295	$265	$200	$180

.30 CAL. CARBINE — .30 Carbine cal., 18 in. barrel, imported from Korea in used condition, various manufacturers, with import stamp. Imported 1991-1996.

	$225	$185	$160	$140	$125	$115	$100

Add approximately $55 for stock upgrade (better wood).

MODEL FIVE CARBINE — while advertised, this model was never produced.

ARMALITE

Previous manufacturer located in Costa Mesa, CA, approx. 1959-1973.

RIFLES: SEMI-AUTO

AR-7 EXPLORER — .22 LR cal., 16 in. aluminum barrel with steel liner, aperture sight, gun takes down and can be stored in hollow plastic stock, gun will float, mfg. 1959-1973 by Armalite, 1974-1990 by Charter Arms, 1990-1997 by Survival Arms located in Cocoa, FL and currently mfg. beginning 1997 by Henry Repeating Arms Co. located in Brooklyn, NY., and AR-7 Industries, LLC located in Meriden, CT, starting 1998.

	$135	$110	$90	$80	$65	$55	$50

Some unusual early Costa Mesa AR-7 variations have been observed with ported barrels, extendable wire stock, hooded front sight, and hollow pistol grip containing cleaning kit, perhaps indicating a special military contract survival weapon.

AR-7 CUSTOM — similar to AR-7 Explorer, only with custom walnut stock including cheekpiece, pistol grip. Mfg. 1964-1970.

	$185	$150	$125	$100	$90	$80	$70

AR-180 — .223 Rem. cal., semi-auto, gas operated, 18¼ in. barrel, folding stock. Manufactured by Armalite in Costa Mesa, CA, 1969-1972, Howa Machinery Ltd., Nagoya, Japan 1972 and 1973. Since 1976 the AR-180 has been made by Sterling Armament Co. Ltd., Dagenham, Essex, England.

	100%	98%	95%	90%	80%	70%	60%
Sterling Mfg.	$850	$775	$695	$625	$550	$495	$450
Costa Mesa Mfg.	$995	$875	$750	$675	$600	$550	$500
Howa Mfg.	$1,350	$1,110	$995	$875	$795	$725	$650

SHOTGUNS: SEMI-AUTO

AR-17 — 12 ga., semi-auto, 24 in. barrel, interchangeable choke tubes, gas operated, high strength aluminum barrel and receiver, plastic stock and forearm, either gold anodized or black finish. Only 2,000 mfg. 1964-1965.

	$575	$460	$420	$360	$310	$260	$220

Grading	100%	98%	95%	90%	80%	70%	60%

ARMALITE, INC.

New manufacture began in 1995 in Geneseo, IL, after Eagle Arms, Inc. purchased the Armalite trademarks. The Armalite trademark was originally used by Armalite (no relation to Armalite, Inc.) during mfg. in Costa Mesa, CA, approx. 1959-1973 (see Armalite listing above). Dealer direct sales.

RIFLES: BOLT ACTION

AR-50 — .50 BMG cal., single shot bolt action with octagonal receiver embedded into an adj. aluminum stock, 31 in. barrel w/o sights with muzzle brake, removable buttstock, single stage trigger, 29 lbs. New 1999.

Mfg.'s Sug. Retail	$2,250	$1,925	$1,700	$1,550	$1,375	$1,225	$1,100	$1,000

RIFLES: SEMI-AUTO

All Armalite semi-auto rifles have a limited lifetime warranty.

AR-10 SERIES — .243 Win. (new 1998) or .308 Win. cal., semi-auto paramilitary design, various configurations, with or w/o sights and carry handle, choice of green or black (new 1999) finish, supplied with two 10 shot mags. New late 1995.

* ***AR-10B Rifle*** — .308 Win. cal., patterned after the early Armalite AR-10 rifle, featuring tapered M16 handguards, pistol grip, shortened buttstock, distinctive charging bolt on top inside of carry handle, and original brown color, 20 in. barrel, 9½ lbs. New 1999.

Mfg.'s Sug. Retail	$1,630	$1,450	$1,225	$1,075	$975	$850	$750	$675

* ***AR-10T Rifle*** — .243 Win. or .308 Win. cal., features 24 in. chrome-moly 1:11.25 twist heavy barrel, two-stage NM trigger, smooth fiberglass handguard tube, Picatinny rail, w/o sights or carry handle, 10.4 lbs.

Mfg.'s Sug. Retail	$2,075	$1,850	$1,550	$1,275	$1,125	$995	$875	$750

Add $15 for black finish.

* ***AR-10T Carbine*** — .308 Win. cal., similar to AR-10T Rifle, except has 16 in. barrel and standard trigger, 8½ lbs.

Mfg.'s Sug. Retail	$1,970	$1,750	$1,475	$1,225	$1,100	$975	$850	$750

Add $15 for black finish.

* ***AR-10A4 Special Purpose Rifle*** — .243 Win. or .308 Win. cal., features 20 in. chrome-lined 1:12 twist H-Bar barrel, removable front sight, Picatinny rail, w/o carry handle, 9.6 lbs.

Mfg.'s Sug. Retail	$1,378	$1,225	$985	$850	$750	$675	$595	$525

Add $15 for black finish.
Add $104 for stainless steel barrel.

* ***AR-10A4 Carbine*** — .308 Win. cal., similar to AR-10A4 Rifle, except has 16 in. barrel. 9 lbs.

Mfg.'s Sug. Retail	$1,378	$1,225	$985	$850	$750	$675	$595	$525

Add $15 for black finish.
Add $104 for stainless steel barrel.

* ***AR-10A2 Infantry Model Rifle*** — .243 Win. or .308 Win. cal., features 20 in. chrome-lined 1:12 twist H-Bar barrel, includes fixed sights and carry handle, 9¾ lbs.

Mfg.'s Sug. Retail	$1,430	$1,175	$1,000	$850	$750	$675	$595	$525

Add $15 for black finish.
Add $104 for stainless steel barrel.

Grading	100%	98%	95%	90%	80%	70%	60%

A

* **AR-10A2 Carbine** — .308 Win. cal., similar to AR-10A2 Rifle, except has 16 in. barrel, 9 lbs.
  Mfg.'s Sug. Retail $1,430 $1,175 $1,000 $850 $750 $675 $595 $525
  Add $15 for black finish.
  Add $104 for stainless steel barrel.

M15 RIFLE/CARBINE VARIATIONS — .223 Rem. cal., various configurations, barrel lengths, sights, and other features.

* **M15A2 National Match Rifle** — features 20 in. stainless steel NM sleeved 1:8 twist barrel with National Match sights and NM two-stage trigger, grooved barrel shroud, 9 lbs.
  Mfg.'s Sug. Retail $1,430 $1,235 $1,000 $875 $775 $675 $595 $525
  Add $15 for black finish.

* **M15A2 Golden Eagle** — similiar to M15A2 National Match Rifle, except has 20 in. heavy barrel, 9.4 lbs. Limited mfg. 1998 only.
  $1,200 $975 $850 $750 $675 $595 $525
  Last Mfg.'s Sug. Retail was $1,350.

* **M15A2 Service Rifle** — includes 20 in. chrome-lined 1:9 twist barrel, fixed sights and carrying handle, grooved barrel shroud, 8.2 lbs.
  Mfg.'s Sug. Retail $930 $830 $715 $625 $550 $500 $450 $415
  Add $15 for black finish.

* **M15A2 Carbine** — similar to M15A2 Service Rifle, except has 16 in. barrel.
  Mfg.'s Sug. Retail $930 $830 $715 $625 $550 $500 $450 $415
  Add $15 for black finish.

* **M15A4 Special Purpose Rifle** — includes 20 in. chrome-lined H-Bar 1:9 twist barrel with National Match sights, Picatinny rail, detachable carry handle, grooved barrel shroud, 7.8 lbs.
  Mfg.'s Sug. Retail $895 $815 $700 $625 $550 $500 $450 $415
  Add $15 for black finish.

* **M15A4 Carbine** — similar to M15A4 Special Purpose Rifle, except has 16 in. barrel, 7 lbs.
  Mfg.'s Sug. Retail $895 $815 $700 $625 $550 $500 $450 $415
  Add $15 for black finish.

* **M4A1C Carbine** — features 16 in. chrome-lined 1:9 twist heavy barrel with National Match sights and detachable carrying handle, grooved barrel shroud, 7 lbs. Disc. 1997.
  $840 $725 $640 $560 $500 $450 $415
  Last Mfg.'s Sug. Retail was $935.

* **M4C Carbine** — similar to M4A1C Carbine, except has non-removable carrying handle and fixed sights, 7 lbs. Disc. 1997.
  $785 $675 $600 $550 $500 $450 $415
  Last Mfg.'s Sug. Retail was $870.

* **M15A4T Eagle Eye Rifle** — 24 in. stainless steel 1:8 twist heavy barrel, two-stage trigger, smooth fiberglass hand guard, Picatinny front sight rail but w/o sights and carrying handle, 9.2 lbs.
  Mfg.'s Sug. Retail $1,378 $1,225 $985 $850 $750 $675 $595 $525
  Add $15 for black finish.

* **M15A4T Eagle Eye Carbine** — features 16 in. stainless steel 1:9 twist heavy barrel, Picatinny rail, smooth fiberglass handguard tube, 2-stage trigger, 7.6 lbs. New 1997.
  Mfg.'s Sug. Retail $1,222 $1,075 $915 $800 $700 $625 $565 $500
  Add $15 for black finish.

* **M15A4 Predator** — similar to M15A4T Eagle Eye, except has 1:12 twist barrel. Disc. 1996.
  $1,215 $985 $850 $750 $675 $595 $525
  Last Mfg.'s Sug. Retail was $1,350.

Grading	100%	98%	95%	90%	80%	70%	60%

✳ **M15A4 Action Master** — includes 20 in. stainless steel 1:9 twist barrel, two-stage trigger, muzzle brake, Picatinny flat top design w/o sights or carrying handle, 9 lbs. Disc. 1997.

	100%	98%	95%	90%	80%	70%	60%
	$1,050	$900	$800	$700	$625	$565	$500

Last Mfg.'s Sug. Retail was $1,175.

ARMAMENT TECHNOLOGY

Current manufacturer located in Halifax, Nova Scotia, Canada since 1988. Direct consumer sales.

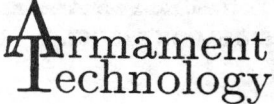

RIFLES: BOLT-ACTION

AT1-C24 TACTICAL RIFLE — .308 Win. or .300 Win. Mag. cal., similar to AT1-M24, except has detachable mag., adj. cheekpiece and buttstock for LOP, includes 3.5x10X 30mm tactical scope and Mil-Spec shipping case, ½" MOA guaranteed, 14.9 lbs. New 1998.

Mfg.'s Sug. Retail	$3,845		$3,845	$3,250	$2,675	$2,200	$1,800	$1,500	$1,275

AT1-M24 TACTICAL RIFLE — .223 Rem. (new 1998), .308 Win., or .300 Win. Mag. cal., bolt action, tactical rifle with competition tuned right or left hand Rem. 700 action, stainless steel barrel, Kevlar reinforced fiberglass stock, Harris bipod, matte black finish, competition trigger, ½" MOA guaranteed, 12.3 lbs.

Mfg.'s Sug. Retail	$3,278		$3,278	$2,700	$2,425	$2,100	$1,875	$1,600	$1,400

ARMAMENT TECHNOLOGY CORP.

Previous manufacturer located in Las Vegas, NV between 1972-1978.

RIFLES: SEMI-AUTO

In addition to the models listed below, ATC also manufactured a select fire pistol named "Firefly II".

MODEL 4 POCKET RIFLE — .22 LR cal., semi-auto action (supplied by Mossberg), 5 in. barrel, shortened rifle (18½ in. overall length) with cut stock, 7 shot mag., approx. 450 mfg., approx. 3 lbs.

		$350	$295	$260	$230	$195	$175	$150

MODEL 6 — full length variation of the Model 4, Mossberg Model 453-T with ATC trademarks, approx. 12 mfg., approx. 5½ lbs.

		$125	$100	$85	$75	$65	$55	$45

M-2 FIREFLY — 9mm Para. cal., featured a unique gas delayed blowback action, paramilitary configuration, collapsible stock, very limited mfg., 4¾ lbs.

		$475	$395	$350	$295	$250	$225	$195

ARMAS AZOR, S.A.

Current manufacturer of double rifles located in Eibar, Spain. No current U.S. importation. Previously imported 1994-97 by Armes De Chasse located in Hertford, NC.

RIFLES: SxS, SIDELOCK

The models listed below are English styled sidelock double rifles. Gold inlay and custom engraving prices are quoted per individual request.

AFRICA MARK I — available in most cals. between 9.3 X 74R and .375 H&H, nominal engraving and select grade wood.

Previous retail prices ranged between $8,000-$10,000.

AFRICA MARK II — available in most cals. between 9.3 X 74R and .375 H&H, African game scene engraving and superior grade wood.

Previous retail prices ranged between $10,000-$12,000.

Grading	100%	98%	95%	90%	80%	70%	60%

A

AFRICA MARK III — available in most cals. between 9.3 X 74R and .470 NE Mag., intricate scroll engraving, cartridge trap, top tang, and superior quality grade wood.

Previous retail prices ranged between $13,000-$18,000.

SHOTGUNS: SxS, SIDELOCK

SIDELOCK MODEL — 12 ga.-.410 bore, English style sidelock game gun.

	$3,275	$2,700	$2,200	$1,750	$1,500	$1,250	$995

Last Mfg.'s Sug. Retail was $3,500.

ARMINEX LTD.

Previous manufacturer located in Scottsdale, AZ.

PISTOLS: SEMI-AUTO

TRI-FIRE — .45 ACP cal., single action auto, interchangeable barrels allow caliber conversion. Available in 5, 6, or 7 (disc. 1984) in. stainless barrel lengths, no grip safety, steel frame construction, ambidextrous thumb safety (on Target and Presentation only), smooth walnut grips, 38 oz. Approx. 400 mfg. between 1981-85.

	$750	$650	$475	$400	$375	$350	$325

Last Mfg.'s Sug. Retail was $396.

Add $50 if presentation cased.
Add approx. $130/conversion unit.

* *Target Model* — same specifications as Tri-Fire, except has 6 or 7 (disc. 1984) in. barrel, very limited mfg.

	$850	$725	$550	$450	$400	$360	$330

Last Mfg.'s Sug. Retail was $448.

ARMINIUS

Previous manufacturer located in Zella-Mehlis, Germany beginning c. 1922-mid 1970s.

PISTOLS: SINGLE SHOT

MODEL 1 — .22 LR cal., target model, adj. sights.

	$275	$210	$195	$165	$155	$140	$110

MODEL 2 — similar to Model 1, except has set trigger.

	$340	$255	$225	$190	$170	$155	$140

REVOLVERS

MODEL 3 — .25 ACP cal., folding trigger, hammerless.

	$175	$135	$125	$105	$100	$90	$80

MODEL 8 — .320 Revolver cal., folding trigger, hammerless.

	$175	$135	$125	$105	$100	$90	$80

MODEL 9 — .32 ACP cal.

	$185	$140	$130	$115	$105	$95	$85

Grading	100%	98%	95%	90%	80%	70%	60%

MODEL 10 — .32 ACP cal., hammerless.

	100%	98%	95%	90%	80%	70%	60%
	$165	$125	$120	$100	$95	$85	$75

TARGET — .22 LR cal.

	100%	98%	95%	90%	80%	70%	60%
	$90	$70	$65	$55	$50	$45	$45

ARMITAGE INTERNATIONAL, LTD.

Previous manufacturer until 1990 located in Seneca, SC.

PISTOLS: SEMI-AUTO

SCARAB SKORPION — 9mm Para. cal, paramilitary design patterned after the Czech Model 61, direct blow back action, 4.63 in. barrel, matte black finish, 12 shot (standard) or 32 shot (optional) mag., 3.5 lbs. Mfg. in U.S. 1989-90 only.

	100%	98%	95%	90%	80%	70%	60%
	$375	$330	$295	$260	$240	$220	$200

Last Mfg.'s Sug. Retail was $400.

Add $45 for threaded flash hider or imitation suppressor.

Only 602 Scarab Skorpions were manufactured during 1989-90.

ARMSCOR

Current trademark of firearms manufactured by Arms Corporation of the Philippines (manufacturing began 1952) starting 1995. Currently imported by K.B.I., Inc. located in Harrisburg, PA beginning 1995. Previously imported by Ruko located in Buffalo, NY until 1995 and by Armscorp Precision Inc. located in San Mateo, CA until 1991.

In 1991, the importation of Arms Corporation of the Philippines firearms was changed to Ruko Products, Inc. located in Buffalo, NY. Barrel markings on firearms imported by Ruko Products, Inc. state "Ruko-Armscor" instead of the older "Armscorp Precision" barrel markings. All Armscorp Precision, Inc. models were discontinued in 1991.

The models listed below also provide cross-referencing for older Armscorp Precision and Ruko imported models.

HANDGUNS

M-200DC REVOLVER — .38 Spl. cal., 6 shot, double action, 2½, 4 (new 1998) or 6 (new 1998) in. barrel, combat style rubber grips, blue only, fixed rear sight, 22 oz. New 1996.

	100%	98%	95%	90%	80%	70%	60%
Mfg.'s Sug. Retail $199	$160	$125	$105	$90	$75	$65	$60

Add $6 for 4 in. barrel or $16 for 6 in. barrel.

M-1911-A1P — .45 ACP cal., patterned after the Colt Govt. Model, 7 shot mag. (2 provided), 5 in. barrel, parkerized finish, skeletonized combat hammer and trigger, 38 oz. Imported 1996-97.

	100%	98%	95%	90%	80%	70%	60%
	$395	$315	$285	$260	$240	$220	$200

Last Mfg.'s Sug. Retail was $479.

RIFLES: BOLT ACTION

M-12Y — .22 LR cal., bolt action, single shot, youth model with 17½ in. barrel. Imported 1997 only.

	100%	98%	95%	90%	80%	70%	60%
	$95	$75	$60	$50	$45	$40	$35

Last Mfg.'s Sug. Retail was $122.

M-14P — .22 LR cal., bolt action, 10 shot mag., 23 in. barrel, open sights, 6 lbs. Disc. 1997.

	100%	98%	95%	90%	80%	70%	60%
	$95	$75	$60	$50	$45	$40	$35

Last Mfg.'s Sug. Retail was $129.

A youth model was also available with shorter dimensions at no extra charge (M-14Y).

Grading	100%	98%	95%	90%	80%	70%	60%

* **M14-D** — .22 LR cal., bolt action, similar to M-14P, except has adj. rear sight and checkered mahogany stock. Importation disc. 1995.

	$105	$85	$70	$60	$50	$45	$40

Last Mfg.'s Sug. Retail was $139.

M-1400LW — .22 LR cal., similar action to M-14P, except has checkered stock and Schnabel forend, 10 shot mag., hard rubber pad, 6 lbs. Imported 1990-92.

	$185	$165	$150	$135	$120	$105	$95

Last Mfg.'s Sug. Retail was $219.

* **M-1400S** — .22 LR cal., similar to M-1500(S), except has 10 shot mag., 6.7 lbs. Imported 1996-97.

	$175	$125	$100	$75	$65	$55	$50

Last Mfg.'s Sug. Retail was $224.

* **M-1400SC (Super Classic)** — .22 LR cal., otherwise similar to M-1500SC, except has 10 shot mag. and 23 in. barrel, 6 lbs. Imported 1990-97.

	$280	$215	$170	$140	$110	$95	$85

Last Mfg.'s Sug. Retail was $355.

M-1500(S) — .22 Mag. cal., deluxe bolt action, 5 shot mag., 21½ in. barrel, checkered mahogany stock, open sights, 6½ lbs. Disc. 1997.

	$180	$135	$95	$75	$65	$55	$50

Last Mfg.'s Sug. Retail was $236.

* **Model 1500LW (Lightweight)** — similar to Model M-1500, except has lightweight classic European styled stock made of checkered American Walnut, with butt pad. Imported 1990-92.

	$190	$170	$150	$135	$120	$105	$95

Last Mfg.'s Sug. Retail was $229.

* **M-1500SC (Super Classic)** — checkered American Walnut stock with hard rubber pad and Monte Carlo cheekpiece, hardwood forend tip, engine turned bolt, 6½ lbs. Imported 1990-97.

	$300	$225	$175	$140	$110	$95	$85

Last Mfg.'s Sug. Retail was $379.

M-1800S (CLASSIC) — .22 Hornet cal., bolt action, 5 shot mag., checkered hardwood stock, adj. rear sight, 6.6 lbs. Imported 1996-97.

	$280	$215	$170	$140	$110	$95	$85

Last Mfg.'s Sug. Retail was $358.

* **M-1800SC (Super Classic)** — similar to M-1800S, except has checkered walnut stock with forend tip, and high polish bluing. Imported 1996-97.

	$400	$330	$265	$215	$170	$140	$110

Last Mfg.'s Sug. Retail was $486.

RIFLES: SEMI-AUTO

M-1600 — .22 LR cal., semi-auto, 15 shot mag., 18 in. barrel, copy of the Armalite M16, ebony stock, 5¼ lbs.

Mfg.'s Sug. Retail	$189		$155	$125	$95	$75	$65	$55	$50

* **M-1600R** — similar to M-1600, except has stainless steel retractable buttstock and vent. barrel hood, 7¼ lbs. Importation disc. 1995.

	$155	$115	$95	$75	$65	$55	$50

Last Mfg.'s Sug. Retail was $199.

M-20P — .22 LR cal., semi-auto, 15 shot mag., 20¾ in. barrel, open sights, 5½ lbs. Disc. 1997.

	$100	$75	$60	$50	$45	$40	$35

Last Mfg.'s Sug. Retail was $129.

* **M-20C** — similar to Model M-20P, except has carbine style stock, barrel band, and curved steel buttplate, 16½ in. barrel, 5¼ lbs.

Mfg.'s Sug. Retail	$149		$120	$95	$75	$60	$50	$45	$40

Grading	100%	98%	95%	90%	80%	70%	60%

M-2000(S) — same specifications as M-20P, except has checkered mahogany stock and adj. rear sight. Disc. 1997.

| | $140 | $120 | $95 | $75 | $60 | $55 | $50 |

Last Mfg.'s Sug. Retail was $213.

* M-2000SC (Super Classic) — similar to M-2000, except has checkered American Walnut stock with cheekpiece and hardwood forend tip, engine turned bolt, 6 lbs. Imported 1990-97.

| | $270 | $215 | $175 | $140 | $110 | $95 | $85 |

Last Mfg.'s Sug. Retail was $340.

MODEL M-50S — .22 LR cal., semi-auto design, 16½ in. shrouded barrel, 25 or 30 shot mag., unchecked mahogany stock, 6½ lbs. Disc. 1995.

| | $155 | $115 | $95 | $75 | $65 | $50 | $45 |

Last Mfg.'s Sug. Retail was $209.

M-AK22(S) — .22 LR cal., semi-auto, copy of the famous Russian Kalashnikov AK-47 rifle, 18½ in. barrel, 10 or 15 (disc.) shot mag., mahogany stock and forearm, 7 lbs.

| Mfg.'s Sug. Retail | $209 | $175 | $150 | $130 | $110 | $90 | $80 | $75 |

* M-AK22(F) — similar to M-AK22, except has metal folding stock, and 30 shot mag. Disc. 1995.

| | $250 | $210 | $185 | $150 | $115 | $95 | $80 |

Last Mfg.'s Sug. Retail was $299.

SHOTGUNS: SLIDE ACTION

MODEL M30 F (INTERCHANGEABLE CHOKES) — 12 ga. only, 28 in. plain barrel with 3 choke tubes, 5 shot mag., unchecked stock and forearm.

| Mfg.'s Sug. Retail | $269 | $225 | $190 | $160 | $140 | $120 | $95 | $85 |

* Model M30 D/IC (Deluxe) — similar to Model M30 IC, except has checkered walnut stock. Importation disc.

| | $235 | $195 | $160 | $130 | $110 | $95 | $85 |

Last Mfg.'s Sug. Retail was $289.

M-30 DG (DEER GUN) — 12 ga. only, law enforcement version of Model M30, 20 in. plain barrel, iron sights, 7 shot mag., about 7 lbs.

| Mfg.'s Sug. Retail | $249 | $195 | $165 | $140 | $120 | $95 | $85 | $75 |

M-30SAS — 12 ga. only, riot configuration with vent. barrel shroud, and Speed feed 4 shot synthetic buttstock and forearm, matte finish. New 1996.

| Mfg.'s Sug. Retail | $289 | $235 | $200 | $170 | $145 | $120 | $95 | $85 |

M-30F — 12 ga. only, 28 in. barrel, fixed mod. choke.

| Mfg.'s Sug. Retail | $239 | $190 | $145 | $110 | $85 | $75 | $65 | $55 |

M-30 R6/R8 (RIOT) — 12 ga. only, similar to Model M30DG, except has front bead sight only, 5 or 7 shot mag., cyl. bore.

| Mfg.'s Sug. Retail | $209 | $175 | $145 | $120 | $105 | $90 | $80 | $75 |

Add $15 for 7 shot mag.

MODEL M30 C (COMBO) — 12 ga., 20 in. barrel, 5 shot mag., unique detachable black synthetic buttstock that separates allowing pistol grip only operation. Disc. 1995.

| | $210 | $175 | $145 | $120 | $100 | $90 | $80 |

Last Mfg.'s Sug. Retail was $289.

MODEL M30 RP (COMBO) — 12 ga. only, same action as M-30 DG, interchangeable black pistol grip, 18¼ in. plain barrel w/front bead sight, 6¼ lbs. Disc. 1995.

| | $210 | $175 | $145 | $120 | $100 | $90 | $80 |

Last Mfg.'s Sug. Retail was $289.

ARMS CORPORATION OF THE PHILIPPINES

Please refer to the Armscor listing in this section.

Grading	100%	98%	95%	90%	80%	70%	60%

A ARMS RESEARCH ASSOCIATES

Previous manufacturer until 1991, located in Stone Park, IL.

RIFLES: SEMI-AUTO

KF SYSTEM — 9mm Para. cal., paramilitary design carbine, 18½ in. barrel, vent. barrel shroud, 20 or 36 shot mag., matte black finish, 7½ lbs., select fire-class III transferable only.

	$395	$350	$300	$275	$250	$230	$210

Last Mfg.'s Sug. Retail was $379.

ARMS TECH LTD.

Previous manufacturer located in Phoenix, AZ 1987-1998.

RIFLES: SEMI-AUTO

SEMI-AUTO RIFLE SUPER MATCH INTERDICTION POLICE MODEL — .243 Win., .300 Win. Mag., or .308 Win. (standard) cal., features 22 in. free floating Schnieder or Douglas air gauged stainless steel barrel, gas operation, McMillan stock, and updated trigger group, detachable box mag., 13¼ lbs. Limited mfg. 1996-98.

$4,550	$4,050	$3,675	$3,300	$3,000	$2,500	$2,000

Last Mfg.'s Sug. Retail was $4,800.

ARMSCORP USA, INC.

Current manufacturer and importer located in Baltimore, MD. Dealer direct sales only.

PISTOLS: SEMI-AUTO

HI POWER — 9mm Para. cal., patterned after Browning design, 4⅔ in. barrel, military finish, 13 shot mag., synthetic checkered grips, spur hammer, 2 lbs. Imported 1989-90 only, mfg. in Argentina.

	$300	$250	$230	$215	$200	$185	$170

Last Mfg.'s Sug. Retail was $450.

Add $15 for round hammer.
Add $50 for hard chrome finish w/combat grips (disc. 1989).

* ***Compact Detective HP*** — similar to Hi Power, except has 3½ in. barrel, 1.9 lbs. Mfg. 1989 only.

	$325	$275	$240	$220	$200	$185	$170

Last Mfg.'s Sug. Retail was $475.

SD-9 — 9mm Para. cal., double action only, blowback mechanism, 3.07 in. barrel, 6 shot mag., frame is fabricated mostly of heavy gauge sheet metal stampings, chamber indicator, limited Israeli mfg., 1½ lbs. Imported 1989-90 only.

	$350	$250	$230	$210	$195	$180	$170

Last Mfg.'s Sug. Retail was $350.

This pistol has also been manufactured by Sirkis Industries - refer to their section in this text.

P22 — .22 LR cal., patterned after the Colt Woodsman, 4 or 6 in. barrel, 10 shot mag., checkered wooden grips, mfg. in Argentina. Imported 1989-90 only.

	$190	$150	$130	$115	$100	$95	$85

Last Mfg.'s Sug. Retail was $225.

RIFLES: SEMI-AUTO

M-14 RIFLE (NORINCO PARTS) — .308 Win. cal., 20 shot mag., newly mfg. M-14 using Norinco parts, wood stock. Mfg. 1991-92 only.

	$600	$525	$475	$425	$375	$325	$275

Last Mfg.'s Sug. Retail was $688.

Grading	100%	98%	95%	90%	80%	70%	60%

M-14R RIFLE (USGI PARTS) — .308 Win. cal., 10 (C/B 1994) or 20★ shot mag., newly manufactured M-14 using original excellent condition forged G.I. parts including USGI fiberglass stock with rubber recoil pad. New 1986.

Mfg.'s Sug. Retail	$1,425	$1,150	$950	$795	$675	$550	$500	$450

Add $25 for G.I. buttplate (disc.)
Add $45 for USGI birch stock (Model M-14RNSB, disc.).
Add $225 for new walnut stock (Model M-14RNS, disc.).

M-14 BEGINNING NATIONAL MATCH — .308 Win. cal., mfg. from hand selected older USGI parts, except for new receiver and new USGI air gauged premium barrel, guaranteed to shoot 1¼ in. group at 100 yards. Mfg. 1993-96.

	$1,625	$1,250	$1,000	$875	$795	$695	$600

Last Mfg.'s Sug. Retail was $1,950.

M-14 NATIONAL MATCH — .308 Win. cal., built in accordance with A.M.T.U. mil. specs., 3 different barrel weights to choose from, NM rear sight system, calibrated mag., leather sling, guaranteed 1" MOA. New 1987.

* **AMTU Competition Model**

Mfg.'s Sug. Retail	$2,295	$1,950	$1,395	$1,100	$950	$875	$795	$700

M21 MATCH RIFLE — .308 Win. cal., NM rear lugged receiver, choice of McMillan fiberglass or laminated wood stock, guaranteed 1" MOA.

Mfg.'s Sug. Retail	$2,995	$2,750	$2,250	$1,650	$1,200	$1,000	$900	$825

T-48 FAL ISRAELI PATTERN RIFLE — .308 Win. cal., mfg. in the U.S. to precise original metric dimensions (parts are interchangeable with original Belgium FAL), forged receiver, hammer forged chrome lined mil.spec. 21 in. barrel (standard or heavy) with flash suppressor, adj. front sight, aperture rear sight, 10 lbs. Imported 1990-92.

	$1,075	$900	$775	$625	$525	$465	$425

Last Mfg.'s Sug. Retail was $1,244.

This model was guaranteed to shoot within 2.5 MOA with match ammunition.

* **T-48 FAL L1A1 Pattern** — .308 Win. cal., fully enclosed forend with vents, 10 lbs. Imported 1992 only.

	$995	$875	$775	$625	$525	$465	$425

Last Mfg.'s Sug. Retail was $1,181.

Add $122 for wooden handguard sporter model (limited supply).

T-48 BUSH MODEL — similar to T-48 FAL, except has 18 in. barrel, 9¾ lbs. Mfg. 1990 only.

	$1,100	$925	$800	$650	$525	$465	$425

Last Mfg.'s Sug. Retail was $1,250.

FRHB — .308 Win. cal., Israeli mfg. with heavy barrel and bipod. Imported 1990 only.

	$1,725	$1,450	$1,150	$975	$875	$795	$725

Last Mfg.'s Sug. Retail was $1,895.

FAL — .308 Win. cal., Armscorp forged receiver, 21 in. Argentinian rebuilt barrel, manufactured to military specs., supplied with one military 20 shot mag., aperture rear sight, 10 lbs. Mfg. 1987-89.

	$850	$750	$600	$540	$465	$420	$375

Last Mfg.'s Sug. Retail was $875.

Subtract $55 if without flash hider.
Add $75 for heavy barrel with bipod (14 lbs.).
Add $400 (last retail) for .22 LR conversion kit.

This model is guaranteed to shoot within 2.5 MOA with match ammunition.

* **FAL Bush Model** — similar to FAL, except has 18 in. barrel with flash suppressor, 9¾ lbs. Mfg. 1989 only.

	$875	$760	$625	$550	$465	$420	$375

Last Mfg.'s Sug. Retail was $900.

Grading	100%	98%	95%	90%	80%	70%	60%

A

* **FAL Para Model** — similar to FAL Bush Model, except has metal folding stock, leaf rear sight. Mfg. 1989 only.

| | $900 | $775 | $635 | $550 | $465 | $420 | $375 |

Last Mfg.'s Sug. Retail was $930.

* **FAL Factory Rebuilt** — factory (Argentine) rebuilt FAL without flash suppressor in excellent condition with Armscorp forged receiver, 9 lbs. 10 oz. Disc. 1989.

| | $695 | $625 | $560 | $520 | $450 | $400 | $360 |

Last Mfg.'s Sug. Retail was $675.

M36 ISRAELI SNIPER RIFLE — .308 Win. cal., gas operated semi-auto, Bullpup configuration, 22 in. free floating barrel, Armscorp M14 receiver, 20 shot mag., includes flash suppressor and bipod, 10 lbs. Civilian offering 1989 only.

| | $2,900 | $2,500 | $2,275 | $2,050 | $1,900 | $1,775 | $1,600 |

Last Mfg.'s Sug. Retail was $3,000.

EXPERT MODEL — .22 LR cal., semi-auto, 20.9 in. barrel, 10 shot mag., wood stock with one-screw takedown, iron sights with grooved receiver, 5.1 lbs. New 1989.

| | $195 | $150 | $125 | $115 | $105 | $95 | $85 |

Last Mfg.'s Sug. Retail was $225.

ARMSPORT, INC.

Current importer and distributor located in Miami, FL specializing in European manufacture and domestic produced accessories. Armsport currently imports shotguns (various configurations, currently made by Sarsilmaz of Turkey), a revolver, and a complete line of accessories (snap caps, scope rings, and cleaning kits). Distributor preferred but dealer direct sales also.

COMBINATION GUNS

2781 AND 2782 — 12 ga./.222 Rem. cal., O/U turkey gun, blued receiver. Model 2782 has chrome receiver. Model 2782 was imported 1985 only. Model 2782 new 1985. Disc. 1989.

| | $650 | $550 | $495 | $440 | $395 | $350 | $300 |

Last Mfg.'s Sug. Retail on Model 2781 was $650.
Last Mfg.'s Sug. Retail on Model 2782 was $750 (disc. 1989).

2783 — similar to Model 2782, except is deluxe model with lateral rib. Imported 1986-1988.

| | $1,350 | $1,075 | $925 | $820 | $750 | $680 | $600 |

Last Mfg.'s Sug. Retail was $1,600.

2784 — same action as Model 2783, except is chambered for .243 Win. Imported 1986-1988.

| | $1,350 | $1,075 | $925 | $820 | $750 | $680 | $600 |

Last Mfg.'s Sug. Retail was $1,600.

2785 — same action as Model 2783, except is chambered for .270 Win. Imported 1986-1988.

| | $1,350 | $1,075 | $925 | $820 | $750 | $680 | $600 |

Last Mfg.'s Sug. Retail was $1,600.

2786 — 20 ga./.222 Rem. cal., O/U turkey gun, otherwise same specifications as Model 2783. Mfg. 1986 only.

| | $1,350 | $1,075 | $925 | $820 | $750 | $680 | $600 |

Last Mfg.'s Sug. Retail was $1,350.

2787 — similar to Model 2786, except is chambered for .243 Win. Mfg. 1986 only.

| | $1,350 | $1,075 | $925 | $820 | $750 | $680 | $600 |

Last Mfg.'s Sug. Retail was $1,350.

2788 — similar to Model 2786, except is chambered for .270 Win. Mfg. 1986 only.

| | $1,350 | $1,075 | $925 | $820 | $750 | $680 | $600 |

Last Mfg.'s Sug. Retail was $1,350.

Grading	100%	98%	95%	90%	80%	70%	60%

4043 — 12, 16, or 20 ga./rifle O/U combination gun, choice of caliber, select walnut, 23½ in. barrels, relief engraved. Disc. 1983.

	$1,675	$1,260	$1,090	$925	$840	$755	$670

4651 — Tikka deluxe O/U shotgun/rifle, exposed hammers, combo. 12 ga./.222. 12 ga. is chambered for 3 in. shells. Disc. 1984.

	$750	$565	$490	$415	$375	$340	$300

4690 — Tikka deluxe O/U shotgun/rifle, hammerless, combo 12 ga./.222. 12 ga. is chambered for 3 in. shells. Disc. 1984.

	$1,095	$820	$750	$700	$650	$575	$500

REVOLVERS

4540 — .38 Spl. cal., single or double action, 6 shot, 4 in. VR barrel with fixed sight, blued finish, checkered grips, approx. 32 oz. Importation began 1999.

Mfg.'s Sug. Retail	$140	$125	$95	$85	$75	$70	$65	$60

RIFLES: REPRODUCTIONS

Armsport is also importing a complete line of Sharps reproduction sporting rifles. Please contact Armsport directly regarding model availability and pricing.

RIFLES: BOLT-ACTION

2801 — .30-06 cal., 24 in. barrel, iron sights, checkered walnut stock and forearm. Imported 1986 only.

	$725	$600	$495	$430	$380	$335	$285

Last Mfg.'s Sug. Retail was $895.

* **2802** — similar to Model 2801, except chambered for .308 Win. cal.

	$725	$600	$495	$430	$380	$335	$285

Last Mfg.'s Sug. Retail was $895.

* **2803** — similar to Model 2801, except chambered for .270 Win. cal.

	$725	$600	$495	$430	$380	$335	$285

Last Mfg.'s Sug. Retail was $895.

* **2804** — similar to Model 2801, except chambered for .243 Win. cal.

	$725	$600	$495	$430	$380	$335	$285

Last Mfg.'s Sug. Retail was $895.

* **2805** — similar to Model 2801, except chambered for 7mm Rem. Mag. cal.

	$725	$600	$495	$430	$380	$335	$285

Last Mfg.'s Sug. Retail was $895.

* **2806** — similar to Model 2801, except chambered for .300 Win. Mag. cal.

	$725	$600	$495	$430	$380	$335	$285

4601, 4603, 4605, & 4606 — Tikka deluxe, .30-06 cal., bolt action. Model 4603 is .270 Win. Model 4605 is 7mm Rem. Model 4606 is 300 Win. Mag. Disc. 1984.

	$725	$545	$450	$380	$340	$295	$260

4602, 4604, & 4607 — Tikka deluxe .308 Win. bolt action. Model 4604 is .243 Win. Model 4607 .222 Rem. Disc. 1983.

	$675	$510	$450	$420	$390	$350	$310

RIFLES: DOUBLE & COMBINATION

4020 — Express set O/U double rifle with ejectors plus an extra set of O/U shotgun barrels. Disc. 1986.

	$3,850	$3,300	$2,860	$2,420	$2,200	$1,980	$1,760

Last Mfg.'s Sug. Retail was $4,400.

Grading	100%	98%	95%	90%	80%	70%	60%

A

4021 — same combination as Model 4020, except rifle has extractors. Disc. 1986.

	$3,400	$2,910	$2,520	$2,135	$1,940	$1,745	$1,550

Last Mfg.'s Sug. Retail was $3,875.

4022 — Express O/U rifle only with ejectors, choice of calibers. Disc. 1986.

	$3,450	$2,945	$2,555	$2,160	$1,965	$1,770	$1,570

Last Mfg.'s Sug. Retail was $3,925.

4023 — similar to Model 4022, except has extractors. Disc. 1986.

	$2,925	$2,515	$2,180	$1,845	$1,675	$1,510	$1,340

Last Mfg.'s Sug. Retail was $3,350.

4010 — Emperor SxS, double rifle with extra set of 20 ga. barrels and forearm. Completely hand made and finished using the best materials and craftsmen, choice of caliber, leather fitted case. Disc. 1983.

	$16,300	$12,225	$10,595	$8,965	$8,150	$7,335	$6,520

4011 — similar to Model 4010, except rifle only, 9.3x74R cal. Disc. 1984.

	$12,750	$9,565	$8,290	$7,015	$6,375	$5,740	$5,100

4012 — Emperor "One-of-a-Kind" SxS rifle/shotgun set. Special engraving finishing per individual customer order, choice of gauges, calibers. Leather fitted case. Rare. Disc. 1983.

	$26,000	$19,500	$16,900	$14,300	$13,000	$11,700	$10,400

4013 — similar to Model 4012, but SxS double rifle only. Disc. 1983.

	$22,850	$17,140	$14,855	$12,570	$11,425	$10,285	$9,140

RIFLES: LEVER-ACTION

4500 & 4501 — .44-40 cal., deluxe copy of Winchester Model 1873 Rifle, engraved. Model 4501 is .357 Mag. Model 4500 (.44-40) disc. in 1984. Model 4501 (.357 Mag.) disc. 1986.

	$1,135	$975	$845	$715	$650	$585	$520

Last Mfg.'s Sug. Retail was $1,296.

4502 & 4503 — .44-40 cal., deluxe copy of Winchester Model 1873 Carbine, engraved. Model 4503 is .357 Mag. Model 4502 (.44-40 WCF) disc. in 1984. Model 4503 (.357 Mag.) disc. 1986.

	$960	$825	$715	$605	$550	$495	$440

Last Mfg.'s Sug. Retail was $1,095.

4504 — .357 Mag. cal., standard copy of Winchester Model 1873 carbine. Disc. 1986.

	$555	$470	$410	$345	$315	$285	$250

Last Mfg.'s Sug. Retail was $625.

RIFLES: SEMI-AUTO

2785 & 2786 — .22 LR cal., semi-auto, 10 shot mag. Model 2786 is military type with 15 shot mag. Imported 1985 only.

	$150	$125	$100	$90	$80	$70	$60

Last Mfg.'s Sug. Retail was $170.

SHOTGUNS: O/U

Armsport choking codes (on rear left of barrels) designate the following: * indicates full choke, ** identifies improved modified choking, *** refers to modified, **** is improved cylinder, ***** indicates cylinder bore.

The models listed below that have -3 suffixes indicate 1988 importation. All models listed below were discontinued in 1993, unless otherwise indicated.

2528 — 12 ga., 3 in. Mag., 28 in. barrels, single trigger with auto ejectors. Disc. 1983.

	$595	$450	$390	$330	$300	$270	$240

2626 — 20 ga., 3 in. Mag., 26 in. barrels, single trigger with auto ejectors. Disc. 1983.

	$595	$450	$390	$330	$300	$270	$240

Grading	100%	98%	95%	90%	80%	70%	60%

2697 & 2698 — 10 ga., 3½ in. Mag., similar to Models 2699 & 2700 except have 3 screw-in choke tubes, Model 2698 has 32 in. barrels. New 1989.

	$1,100	$850	$675	$575	$520	$495	$475

Last Mfg.'s Sug. Retail was $1,299.

2699/2700C & 2700 — 10 ga., 3½ in. Mag., 27 (2699 - new 1989), 28 (2700C), or 32 (2700) in. barrels with 12mm vent. rib, extractors, DTs. New 1986.

	$995	$775	$625	$550	$475	$430	$395

Last Mfg.'s Sug. Retail was $1,190.

* 2700B — similar to Model 2700, except has deluxe walnut (32 in. barrels only). Mfg. 1987 only.

	$660	$575	$480	$430	$395	$370	$350

Last Mfg.'s Sug. Retail was $795.

2701/2702 & 2703/2704 — 12 and 20 ga., 3 in. Mag., 26 and 28 in. barrels, double triggers, extractors. Disc. 1985, and reintroduced 1989. Current models are 2702 and 2704.

	$570	$450	$375	$295	$265	$230	$200

Last Mfg.'s Sug. Retail was $685.

2705 — .410 bore, double triggers, 26 in. barrels, various chokes, extractors, mfg. in Italy. Importation began 1986-disc.

	$670	$525	$425	$350	$300	$275	$235

Last Mfg.'s Sug. Retail was $785.

2706 — 12 ga. only, law enforcement model, 20 in. barrels, double triggers, extractors. Imported 1986 only.

	$330	$280	$260	$240	$220	$200	$185

Last Mfg.'s Sug. Retail was $375.

2707 — 28 ga., otherwise similar to Model 2705. New 1990.

	$670	$525	$425	$350	$300	$275	$235

Last Mfg.'s Sug. Retail was $785.

2708 — 12 ga. only, slug gun, 23 in. barrels, single trigger, ejectors. Importation began 1986.

	$685	$550	$450	$385	$325	$300	$280

Last Mfg.'s Sug. Retail was $840.

A Model 2708-3 was mfg. 1986-1989. This variation had 20 in. barrels, double triggers, and extractors. Values of this earlier variation will be approx. 30-40% less than listed above.

2711, 2713-3, 2721, & 2723 — 12 or 20 ga., 3 in. Mag., 26 or 28 in. barrels, extractors. Models 2721 and 2723 have ejectors and were disc. 1985. Models 2711 and 2713-3 were disc. 1989.

	$445	$385	$340	$310	$275	$250	$230

Last Mfg.'s Sug. Retail was $375 on Models 2721/2723.
Last Mfg.'s Sug. Retail was $535 on Models 2711/2713-3.

Add 25% with ejectors.

2717, 2719, 2720, & 2725 — 12 (Model 2717), 20 (Model 2719), 28 (Model 2725 - new 1990) ga., or .410 (Model 2720) bore, 3 in. Mag. (except Model 2725), 26 or 28 in. barrels, SST.

	$645	$525	$450	$385	$325	$300	$280

Last Mfg.'s Sug. Retail was $765.

Add $70 for 28 ga. or .410 bore.

2712, 2714-3, 2722, & 2724 — 12 or 20 ga., 3 in. Mag., 26 or 28 in. barrels. Models 2712 and 2722 are 12 ga., engraved with 12mm vent. rib. Models 2722 and 2724 have ejectors. Importation of Models 2712, 2722, and 2724 was disc. 1986. Model 2714-3 was disc. 1988.

	$500	$395	$350	$300	$275	$235	$200

Last Mfg.'s Sug. Retail was $615 on Model 2714-3.
Last Mfg.'s Sug. Retail was $395 on Models 2712/2722/2724.

Grading	100%	98%	95%	90%	80%	70%	60%

A

2715-3 & 2716-3 — 12 ga. only, 28 in. barrels with 3 choke tubes, auto ejectors, single trigger. Imported 1988 only.

	$575	$465	$400	$350	$295	$265	$245

Last Mfg.'s Sug. Retail was $680.

2718, 2733, & 2735 — 12 and 20 ga., 3 in. Mag., 26 and 28 in. barrels, SST, extractors. Models 2733/2735 have deluxe Boss actions. Model 2718 was disc. 1985.

	$650	$540	$450	$385	$325	$300	$280

Last Mfg.'s Sug. Retail was $390 on Model 2718.
Last Mfg.'s Sug. Retail was $790 on Model 2733 and 2735.

✱ 2734 & 2736 Sporting Clays — 12 (2734) or 20 (2736) ga., similar to Models 2733 and 2735, except has 3 choke tubes.

	$695	$560	$450	$385	$325	$300	$280

Last Mfg.'s Sug. Retail was $840.

2745, 2746 & 2747 — 12 ga., 3½ in. chambers, 24 (2745), 27/28 (2746) or 31/32 (2747) in. barrels with wide rib and 3 choke tubes, auto extractors, Boss type action. New 1989.

	$715	$575	$450	$385	$325	$300	$280

Last Mfg.'s Sug. Retail was $880.

These models were mfg. by Armi Techniche of Emilio Rizzini located in Italy.

2726, 2728, 2742, & 2744 — 12 and 20 ga., 3 in. Mag., 26 and 28 in. barrels, SST, ejectors. Models 2726 & 2728 were disc. 1985.

	$740	$595	$475	$400	$350	$315	$290

Last Mfg.'s Sug. Retail on Models 2726 & 2728 was $440.
Last Mfg.'s Sug. Retail on Models 2742 & 2744 was $930.

2727-3 & 2729-3 — 1986 designations for Models 2726 & 2728 respectively. -3 suffixes indicate 1988 designations. Importation disc. 1988.

	$550	$450	$385	$330	$295	$265	$245

Last Mfg.'s Sug. Retail was $615.

2727 & 2729 — 12 (Model 2727) or 20 (Model 2729) ga., field model, boxlock action, 26 or 28 in. barrels with wide rib and fixed chokes. New 1990.

	$660	$550	$450	$385	$325	$300	$280

Last Mfg.'s Sug. Retail was $800.

These models have evolved from Models 2726/2728 and Models 2727-3 and 2729-3.

2730 — 12 ga., skeet gun, 27 in. barrel, has six interchangeable chokes, Boss-type action.

	$775	$650	$550	$495	$450	$425	$395

Last Mfg.'s Sug. Retail was $975.

These models were mfg. by Armi Techniche of Emilio Rizzini located in Italy.

✱ 2731 — similar to Model 2730, except is 20 ga. and has 26 in. barrels.

	$795	$675	$565	$525	$465	$435	$400

Last Mfg.'s Sug. Retail was $975.

2732 & 2732/3 — 12 ga. only, competition trap model, 30 in. barrel. New 1990.

	$930	$700	$600	$525	$470	$440	$415

Last Mfg.'s Sug. Retail was $1,165.

Add $110 for Model 2732/3 (includes choke tubes).

These two models were mfg. by Armi Techniche of Emilio Rizzini located in Italy.

2741 & 2743 — 12 (Model 2741) or 20 (Model 2743) ga., field model, 26 or 28 in. barrels with wide rib and fixed chokes, Boss type action. New 1990.

	$665	$550	$450	$385	$325	$300	$280

Last Mfg.'s Sug. Retail was $825.

These models were mfg. by Armi Techniche of Emilio Rizzini located in Italy.

2750 & 2751 — 12 (Model 2750) or 20 (Model 2751) ga., Sporting Clays configuration, 26 or 28 in. barrels with 5 choke tubes, includes engraved sideplates. New 1990.

	$830	$675	$575	$525	$475	$445	$400

Last Mfg.'s Sug. Retail was $1,050.

Grading	100%	98%	95%	90%	80%	70%	60%

2760 — 12 ga., tournament trap model with choke tubes. Mfg. by Ferlib beginning 1991.

	$1,475	$1,200	$995	$800	$675	$600	$540

Last Mfg.'s Sug. Retail was $1,700.

2763 — 12 ga., sporting clays configuration, includes 5 choke tubes, mfg. by Ferlib in Italy - importation began in 1991.

	$1,525	$1,225	$1,000	$800	$675	$600	$540

Last Mfg.'s Sug. Retail was $1,775.

2765 — similar to Model 2763, except is 20 ga. with 26 in. barrels. Imported 1991 only.

	$1,700	$1,350	$1,100	$850	$700	$625	$550

Last Mfg.'s Sug. Retail was $2,000.

2791/2792 (FIELD) — 12 (2791) or 20 (2792) ga., single trigger, 26 (20 ga. only) or 28 in. VR barrels (fixed chokes). Imported 1995-98.

		$650	$565	$500	$450	$400	$350	$295

Last Mfg.'s Sug. Retail was $775.

2795/2796/2797 (SPORTING CLAYS/SKEET) — 12 (2795/2797) or 20 (2796) ga., SST, ejectors, 26 (2796/2797) or 28 (2795) in. VR barrels (includes 5 choke tubes). Imported 1995-98.

		$950	$775	$650	$500	$425	$375	$300

Last Mfg.'s Sug. Retail was $1,150.

2801/2802 — 12 ga., 3 in. chambers, boxlock action, single (2802) or double (2801) triggers, 28 in. VR barrels. Mfg. by Sarsilmaz (in Turkey), importation began 1996.

Mfg.'s Sug. Retail	$500		$415	$360	$300	$275	$250	$225	$200

Add approximately $75 for SST (2802).

2803/2804/2805 — similar to 2801/2802, except 2803 has SST and 2804 has DTs, 26 or 28 (2805) in. VR barrels. Mfg. by Sarsilmaz (in Turkey), importation began 1997.

Mfg.'s Sug. Retail	$500		$415	$360	$300	$275	$250	$225	$200

Add approximately $75 for SST (2803 & 2805).

2807/2808 — 12 ga., 3 in. Mag., SST, 26 or 28 in. VR barrels with 5choke tubes. Importation began 1998.

Mfg.'s Sug. Retail	$695		$615	$475	$400	$350	$300	$275	$250

2820 SPORTING CLAYS — 12 ga., boxlock action, SST, ejectors, deluxe model with checkered walnut stock and forearm, includes 5 choke tubes. Mfg. by E. Rizzini. Imported 1995-98.

	$1,050	$850	$750	$650	$550	$450	$395

Last Mfg.'s Sug. Retail was $1,200.

2831/2832/2833 SPECIAL PERSONAL PICTURED ACTIONS — 12 ga., available in either Trap, Skeet, or Sporting Clays configuration, unique metal photo finishing process allows personalized pictures to be applied to receiver sides. Mfg. by Sarsilmaz (in Turkey), limited importation 1997-98 only.

Style B	$1,075	$875	$750	$650	$550	$450	$395

Last Mfg.'s Sug. Retail was $1,195.

Style C	$1,225	$1,050	$850	$750	$650	$550	$450

Last Mfg.'s Sug. Retail was $1,395.

Add $185 for Sporting Clays (includes five choke tubes).

2843 — 12 ga., hunting configuration, 28 in. VR barrels bored M&F, SST. Mfg. by Rizzini, limited importation 1997-98 only.

	$1,050	$850	$750	$650	$550	$450	$395

Last Mfg.'s Sug. Retail was $1,200.

4014 — Emperor Grade SxS. Individually fitted per customer H&H type action, engraved, fitted leather case, choice of gauge, barrel lengths, etc. Completely hand finished.

	$9,175	$6,885	$5,965	$5,050	$4,590	$4,130	$3,670

Emperor Grade models are disc. Limited availability.

Grading	100%	98%	95%	90%	80%	70%	60%

A

4015 — Emperor "One-of-a-Kind" SxS. Similar to Model 4014, except that every part of the gun is made per customer order. Specifications including style of engraving, dimensions, wood configuration, special requests, etc. No expense spared. Disc. 1984.

	$18,000	$13,500	$11,700	$9,900	$9,000	$8,100	$7,200

4016 — Emperor SxS with outside hammers, fitted leather case, extensively engraved, any gauge. Disc. 1983.

	$4,550	$3,415	$2,960	$2,505	$2,275	$2,050	$1,820

4017 — Emperor "One-of-a-Kind" SxS with outside hammers. Flexibility of options is similar to Model 4015. Disc. 1984.

	$12,750	$9,565	$8,290	$7,015	$6,375	$5,740	$5,100

4030 & 4031 — 12 ga. SxS, Holland-style detachable locks, English walnut, ejectors, engraved. Model 4031 is 20 ga. Disc. 1983.

	$3,950	$2,965	$2,570	$2,175	$1,975	$1,780	$1,580

4032 & 4033 — 12 ga. Premier Mono Trap Gun, 32 in. barrel, ejector. Model 4033 is same, except for 34 in. barrel. Disc. 1986.

	$1,810	$1,560	$1,350	$1,145	$1,040	$935	$830

Last Mfg.'s Sug. Retail was $2,075.

4034 & 4035 — 12 ga. Premier Mono Trap Set, 32 in. single, 30 in. O/U. Model 4035 is same, except has 34 in. single, 32 in. O/U. Disc. 1986.

	$2,565	$2,215	$1,920	$1,625	$1,475	$1,330	$1,180

Last Mfg.'s Sug. Retail was $2,950.

4040 — 12 ga. Slug Special SxS, 23 in. barrels. Disc. 1984.

	$1,325	$995	$865	$730	$665	$600	$530

4046 & 4047 — 12 ga. trap gun, 34 in. barrel, extra trigger mechanism. Model 4047 is 32 in. Disc. 1986.

	$2,860	$2,460	$2,100	$1,850	$1,700	$1,500	$1,300

Last Mfg.'s Sug. Retail was $3,275.

4050 — 12 ga., Pigeon Grade O/U, engraved. Disc. 1986.

	$2,375	$2,025	$1,755	$1,485	$1,350	$1,215	$1,080

Last Mfg.'s Sug. Retail was $2,700.

4055 & 4056 — 12 ga., Premier Skeet, selective trigger, ejectors, engraved, select wood. Model 4056 is 20 ga. Disc. 1983.

	$2,000	$1,500	$1,300	$1,100	$1,000	$900	$800

4061 & 4062 — .410 bore, SxS, single trigger, selective ejectors. Model 4062 is 28 ga. Disc. 1983.

	$995	$750	$650	$550	$500	$450	$400

4063 & 4064 — .410 bore, O/U, single trigger, selective ejectors. Model 4064 is 28 ga. Disc. 1983.

	$995	$750	$650	$550	$500	$450	$400

SHOTGUNS: SEMI-AUTO

2751 — 12 ga., 3 in. Mag., semi-auto, Atis mfg., black anodized receiver, 28 in. barrel. Mfg. 1985-87 only.

	$430	$340	$310	$285	$255	$230	$200

Last Mfg.'s Sug. Retail was $575.

 * **2751A** — similar to Model 2751, except has 30 in. full choke barrel. Mfg. 1986-87 only.

	$430	$340	$310	$285	$255	$230	$200

Last Mfg.'s Sug. Retail was $575.

2752 — same action as Model 2751, except chrome receiver and engraving. Mfg. 1986-87 only.

	$440	$345	$310	$285	$255	$230	$200

Last Mfg.'s Sug. Retail was $600.

Grading	100%	98%	95%	90%	80%	70%	60%

* 2752A — similar to Model 2752, except has 30 in. barrel. Mfg. 1986-87 only.

	$440	$345	$310	$285	$255	$230	$200

Last Mfg.'s Sug. Retail was $600.

2753 — same action as Model 2751, except has 28 in. barrel with 3 interchangeable chokes. Mfg. 1986-87 only.

	$460	$355	$315	$285	$255	$230	$200

Last Mfg.'s Sug. Retail was $650.

* 2753A — similar to Model 2753, except has chrome receiver and engraving. Mfg. 1986-87 only.

	$470	$365	$320	$285	$255	$230	$200

Last Mfg.'s Sug. Retail was $675.

2761 & 2762 — 12 ga., black or chrome receiver, Fabarms made, engraved action, 27 in. barrel. Add $75 for interchangeable choke tubes. Imported during 1985 only.

	$410	$360	$315	$295	$270	$245	$215

Last Mfg.'s Sug. Retail was $475.

2830/2834 — 12 ga., 3 in. Mag., synthetic (2834) or walnut (2830) stock, 26 or 28 in. VR barrel. Mfg. by Sarsilmaz, importation began 1998.

Mfg.'s Sug. Retail	$970	$840	$730	$600	$500	$400	$350	$295

Subtract $50 for black synthetic stock.

SHOTGUNS: SxS AND SINGLE

1033 — 10 ga. SxS, 3½ in. Mag., 32 in. full and full chokes. Disc. 1985.

	$395	$340	$315	$275	$250	$225	$200

Last Mfg.'s Sug. Retail was $450.

1050-1 — 1986 designation for the Model 1051. -1 suffix designates 1988 and later importation.

	$650	$540	$450	$385	$325	$300	$280

Last Mfg.'s Sug. Retail was $785.

1051 & 1052 — 12 ga. SxS, 3 in. Mag., 28 in. mod. & full chokes. Model 1052 is 20 ga., 3 in. Mag., 26 in. Imp. & Mod. Disc. 1985.

	$330	$280	$260	$240	$225	$205	$180

Last Mfg.'s Sug. Retail was $375.

1053-1 — 1986 designation for the Model 1052. -1 suffix designates 1988 and later importation.

	$650	$540	$450	$385	$325	$300	$280

Last Mfg.'s Sug. Retail was $785.

1054-1 & 1055-1 — .410 bore (1054) or 28 (1055) ga. -1 suffix designates 1988 and later importation.

	$700	$600	$500	$450	$400	$365	$330

Last Mfg.'s Sug. Retail was $860.

1055 & 1057 — 28 ga. and .410 bore, SxS, 3 in. Mag., 26 in. barrel, Imp. and Mod. chokes. Model 1057 is 28 ga., 3 in. Mag., 26 in. Imp. & Mod. Disc. 1985.

	$330	$280	$260	$240	$225	$205	$180

Last Mfg.'s Sug. Retail was $375.

Model 1057 was redesignated 1055 in 1985 and Model 1055 was changed to 1054.

1101, 1102, 1103, & 1104 — 12 ga., folding single barrel w/vent. rib. Model 1102 is 20 ga. Model 1103 is .410 bore. Model 1104 is 28 ga. Disc. 1985.

	$125	$105	$90	$75	$70	$65	$60

Last Mfg.'s Sug. Retail was $140.

1107 & 1108 — 12 ga., folding single barrel 19 in., pistol grip. Model 1108 is 20 ga. Disc. 1983.

	$135	$105	$95	$85	$75	$70	$65

Grading	100%	98%	95%	90%	80%	70%	60%

1125, 1126, & 1127 — 12 or 20 ga., single barrel, 3 in. chamber, bottom lever opening, Model 1127 is 20 ga. Imported 1987-95.

	$75	$55	$50	$45	$40	$35	$30

Last Mfg.'s Sug. Retail was $90.

The Model 1125 was disc. 1989, Models 1126/1127 were disc. 1995.

* *1128* — .410 bore, otherwise similar to Models 1125/1126/1127. Importation disc. 1990.

	$75	$55	$50	$45	$40	$35	$30

Last Mfg.'s Sug. Retail was $90.

1212 & 1213 — 12 ga., SxS, outside hammers, engraved action, 20 in. barrels. Model 1213 is 20 ga. Disc. 1983.

	$450	$340	$295	$250	$225	$205	$180

1225 — 12 ga. only, O/U configuration, folding action, top lever break. Mfg. 1986-87 only.

	$275	$235	$200	$185	$170	$165	$150

Last Mfg.'s Sug. Retail was $345.

1226 — 20 ga. only, O/U configuration, folding action, top lever break. Mfg. 1986-87 only.

	$275	$235	$200	$185	$170	$165	$150

Last Mfg.'s Sug. Retail was $345.

SHOTGUNS: SLIDE ACTION

2755 — 12 ga., 7 shot, Atis mfg., black anodized receiver, 24 or 28 in. barrel with VR. Mfg. 1985-87 only.

	$335	$260	$225	$195	$180	$160	$145

Last Mfg.'s Sug. Retail was $395.

* *2755A* — similar to Model 2755, except has 30 in. barrel. Mfg. 1986-87 only.

	$335	$260	$225	$195	$180	$160	$145

2756 — 12 ga., 28 in. VR barrel, 3 interchangeable chokes. Mfg. 1986-87 only.

	$390	$335	$280	$230	$205	$190	$175

Last Mfg.'s Sug. Retail was $465.

* *2756A* — similar to Model 2756, except has 30 in. vent. rib barrel. Mfg. 1986-87 only.

	$390	$335	$280	$230	$205	$190	$175

Last Mfg.'s Sug. Retail was $465.

2757 — 12 ga. only, law enforcement model, 20 in. barrel, black receiver. Mfg. 1986-87 only.

	$310	$250	$205	$190	$175	$155	$140

Last Mfg.'s Sug. Retail was $375.

2766, 2767, & 2768 — 12 ga., Fabarms mfg., 25 in. barrel. Model 2768 has 20 in. barrel. Imported 1985 only.

	$260	$220	$200	$180	$160	$140	$120

Last Mfg.'s Sug. Retail was $300.

2810/2811 — 12 ga., 3 in. chamber, 16 (disc.), 25 (disc.), 26, or 28 in. barrel, black synthetic stock, includes extra pistol grip stock. Sarsilmaz mfg., importation began 1997.

Mfg.'s Sug. Retail	$300	$260	$225	$200	$175	$160	$140	$120

2812 — similar to Models 2810/2811, except has metal stock. Sarsilmaz mfg., importation began 1999.

Mfg.'s Sug. Retail	$350	$300	$265	$230	$200	$175	$160	$140

SHOTGUNS: TRI-BARREL

MODEL 2900 TRILLING — 12 ga., 3 barrel shotgun with 28 in. barrels bored F & M or choke tubes over IC/choke tubes. Importation began 1986-87 and was resumed in 1990.

	$2,900	$2,375	$2,000	$1,650	$1,400	$1,200	$995

Last Mfg.'s Sug. Retail was $3,400.

Subtract 25% for fixed chokes (1986-87 mfg.).

This model was re-introduced in 1990 and includes choke tubes on all 3 barrels.

Grading	100%	98%	95%	90%	80%	70%	60%

ARNOLD ARMS CO., INC.

Current rifle manufacturer located in Arlington, WA since 1994. Dealer (master or associate) and consumer direct sales.

In addition to making a series of accurate rifles built on their own Apollo action, Arnold Arms Co. also builds rifles on Remington, Ruger, Sako (disc.), or Winchester actions. All Arnold Arms rifles have a written guarantee on accuracy, and a 5 year limited warranty. The company also makes proprietary cartridges in 6mm Arnold, .257 Arnold, .270 Arnold, .300 Arnold, .338 Arnold, or .458 Arnold. A wide range of gunsmithing services (including Accu-Pro services) is also available - please contact the factory directly to learn more about these gunsmithing services and custom pricing.

RIFLES: BOLT ACTION

ARNOLD PRO SERIES — .17 Rem. - .416 Rem. Mag. cals., utilizes the standard centerfire bolt action rifles built by Remington, Ruger & Winchester, wide range of stock options, guaranteed to shoot a 1 in. 5 shot group.

Mfg.'s Sug. Retail	$1,295	$1,175	$1,050	$900	$800	$700	$650	$595

Subtract $146 for Ruger M77 MKII CM action.
Above pricing assumes Rem. 700 BDL CM action with walnut stock. A wide range of stock options and rifle configurations are available for this model. Please contact the factory directly for option availability and pricing.

ARNOLD PRECISION SERIES — .17 Rem. - .416 Rem. Mag. cals., rifles are production Remington, Ruger, & Winchester models with a match grade barrel, guaranteed to shoot a ½ in. 5 shot group.

Mfg.'s Sug. Retail	$1,849	$1,695	$1,450	$1,275	$1,175	$1,050	$900	$800

Subtract $154 for Ruger M77 MKII CM action.
Above pricing assumes Rem. 700 BDL CM action with walnut stock. A wide range of stock options and rifle configurations are available for this model. Please contact the factory directly for option availability and pricing.

ARNOLD CUSTOM SERIES — custom rifles built on Remington, Ruger, Sako (disc.) or Winchester actions, made per individual customer specifications, most accurate non-Apollo model, can be ordered in African, Alaskan, Neutralizer, or Varminter configuration.

* *African Series* — available in most cals. between .243 Win. and .458 Win. Mag., Safari, African Trophy, or Grand African grade feature walnut stocks and African or Serengeti grade features synthetic stocks, 22-26 in. barrel, chrome-moly matte finish standard on most models. African Series introduced 1996.

➤ *Safari Rifle* — various cals. between .243 Win. - .458 Win. Mag., No. 5 wraparound checkering pattern, 22 - 26 in. barrel w/o sights, choice of A or AA English walnut stock.

		$5,050	$3,895	$3,475	$3,150	$2,700	$2,350	$2,100

Last Mfg.'s Sug. Retail was $5,528.

Subtract $1,187 for Remington action.
Subtract $1,486 for Sako action.
Subtract $1,490 for Winchester action.
Add $100 for standard polish.
Add $200 for high luster polish/finish.
Add $60 for AA grade English walnut stock.
Add $50 for matte stainless steel construction.

Grading	100%	98%	95%	90%	80%	70%	60%

➤**Trophy Rifle** — .223 Rem. - .338 Win. Mag. and additional wildcat cals., features choice of Remington, Ruger, or Win. trued and accurized chrome-moly matte blued steel action, match grade barrel, black or camo finished synthetic McMillan stock.

Mfg.'s Sug. Retail	$2,595	$2,450	$2,100	$1,875	$1,650	$1,475	$1,275	$1,050

Subtract $166 for Ruger M77 MKII action.
Add $299 for McMillan fibergrain stock.

➤**Grand African Rifle** — various cals. between .338 Win. Mag. - .458 Win. Mag., features choice of Remington, Ruger, or Win. trued and accurized chrome-moly matte blued steel action, 24 or 26 in. barrel with express sights and band, wide range of stock options - standard are McMillan fibergrain synthetic or walnut Hunter Classic, C-M high luster polish/finish or stainless steel.

Mfg.'s Sug. Retail	$3,995	$3,775	$3,250	$2,875	$2,500	$2,225	$2,000	$1,750

Subtract $300 for Winchester action.
Subtract $500 for Ruger M77 MKII action.
Subtract $100 for walnut Hunter Classic stock.
Prices for A grade English walnut stock with ebony forend and steel grip cap start at $6,495 (Rem. M700 action).

✱ **Alaskan Series** — various cals., including wildcats, choice of Remington M700, Ruger M77 MKII, Sako (disc.) or Winchester M70 stainless steel action, various stock options, stainless steel barrel, scope mount only.

➤**Alaskan Trophy** — .300 Win. Mag - .458 Win. Mag. cals., camo or McMillan black synthetic stock, 22-26 in. stainless steel barrel.

Mfg.'s Sug. Retail	$2,695	$2,525	$2,150	$1,900	$1,650	$1,475	$1,275	$1,050

Subtract $266 for Ruger M77 MKII action.

➤**Alaskan Guide Rifle** — .338 Win. Mag. - .458 Win. mag. cals., same components as Alaska Trophy, except has express sights and front barrel band as standard equipment. New 1998.

Mfg.'s Sug. Retail	$3,749	$3,500	$3,000	$2,650	$2,325	$2,200	$1,800	$1,500

Subtract $500 for Winchester M70 SS action.
Subtract $870 for Ruger M77 MKII SS action.

➤**Grand Alaskan Rifle** — various cals. between .300 Win. Mag. - .458 Win. Mag., features AAA or exhibition grade English walnut, includes scope mount and iron sights.

	$6,900	$5,600	$5,000	$4,250	$3,850	$3,400	$2,000

Last Mfg.'s Sug. Retail was $7,750.

Add $1,051 for exhibition grade walnut.
Subtract $1,187 for Remington action.
Subtract $1,436 for Sako action.
Subtract $1,490 for Winchester action.
Add $100 for standard polish.
Add $50 for matte stainless steel construction.

Prices above do not include the cost of the wood blank.

➤**High Country Synthetic Mountain Rifle** — various cals. between .257 Roberts - .338 Win. Mag., fibergrain or black synthetic stock, scope mounts only. Disc. 1997.

	$2,800	$2,425	$2,075	$1,850	$1,650	$1,500	$1,350

Last Mfg.'s Sug. Retail was $3,115.

Add $175 for matte stainless steel construction.

➤**High Country Walnut Rifle** — similar to High Country Synthetic Mountain Rifle, except has AA English walnut stock with No. 5 checkering pattern, scope mounts only. Disc. 1997.

	$4,300	$3,625	$3,275	$2,975	$2,650	$2,350	$2,100

Last Mfg.'s Sug. Retail was $4,670.

Add $350 for stainless steel construction.

Grading	100%	98%	95%	90%	80%	70%	60%

* *Neutralizer Series* — .223 Rem., .308 Win., or .300 Win. Mag. cal., features Remington chrome-moly blued or stainless steel action, match grade barrel, with or w/o detachable box mag, many configurations, finishes, and options.

Mfg.'s Sug. Retail	$2,959		$2,750	$2,250	$1,900	$1,600	$1,350	$1,150	$975

Add $490 for Remington action with box mag.
Add $1,640 for Apollo action with Jewell trigger.

* *Varminter Series* — various cals., including some wildcats, choice of Remington, Ruger, or Winchester action, choice of Varminter I (varmint stock and heavy barrel), or Varminter II (sporter stock and barrel), many configurations, finishes, and options.

Mfg.'s Sug. Retail	$2,595		$2,275	$2,000	$1,750	$1,600	$1,350	$1,150	$975

Add approx. $89 for Varminter I configuration.
Subtract approx. $265 for Ruger M77 action.

* *Competition/Match Series* — .223 Rem., .243 Win., 6mm Rem., .308 Win., or 7mm-08 cal., custom built to customer's specifications, choice of stocks, actions, barrels, accessories, and finishes.

Since each gun is made per special individual order, please contact the company directly for information, including current pricing.

ARNOLD APOLLO SERIES — top-of-the-line Apollo action with 20,000 PSI strength, made per individual customer specifications, generally regarded as the best bolt action design available today.

Since each Apollo acton rifle is made per special individual order, please contact the company directly for information, including current pricing.

REMINGTON SERIES — various cals. between .222 Rem. - .458 Win. Mag., features Remington 700 Series action with Sako extractor, choice of walnut, McMillan, or Pacific Research stock, stainless, standard blue, or bead blasted metal finish. Mfg. 1994-1997.

		$1,650	$1,400	$1,150	$1,025	$875	$750	$625

Last Mfg.'s Sug. Retail was $1,845.

Add $105 for stainless steel construction.
Add $190 for McMillan synthetic stock.
Add $210 for Pacific Research stock.

WINCHESTER SERIES — various cals., features Winchester pre-64 Model 70 action with claw extractor, positive feed, and integral recoil lug, choice of walnut, McMillan, or Pacific Research stock, stainless, standard blue, or bead blasted metal finish. Mfg. 1994-97.

		$1,395	$1,100	$950	$850	$750	$650	$550

Last Mfg.'s Sug. Retail was $1,550.

Add approx. $205 for stainless steel construction.
Add $162 for McMillan synthetic stock.
Add $259 for Pacific Research stock.

ARRIETA, S.L.

Current manufacturer located in Elgoibar, Spain. Currently imported by several importers including New England Arms Corp., Griffin & Howe, Orvis (see separate listing), Quality Arms, and Wingshooting Adventures.

More information can be obtained on Arrieta by contacting the above listed importers.

RIFLES: SxS

R-1 — 7x65R, 8x57JRS, or 9.3x74R cal., boxlock action with engraved sideplates, ejectors, quarter rib barrel with express rear sight.

Mfg.'s Sug. Retail	$8,950		$8,450	$7,000	$5,950	$5,100	$4,600	$4,000	$3,450

Grading	100%	98%	95%	90%	80%	70%	60%

A

R-2 — similar to R-1, except has more elaborate H&H style engraving, elongated tangs, and choice of English or reinforced pistol grip with metal cap, ejectors.

Mfg.'s Sug. Retail	$12,950	$11,700	$9,950	$8,950	$7,850	$6,850	$5,900	$4,950

R-3 — similar to R-1, except includes .375 H&H or .470 NE cal.

Mfg.'s Sug. Retail	$16,500	$14,750	$12,500	$9,950	$8,950	$7,850	$6,850	$5,900

SHOTGUNS: SxS

The models listed below are essentially custom ordered per individual specifications - delivery time is approx. 7-8 months.

All Arrieta shotguns have frames scaled to individual gauges. Standard gauges are 12 & 16. Various special options are available by custom order, and a few are listed below. On the models listed below, there are 4 qualities of action. Fourth quality is used on the Model 550. Third quality is used on Models 557, 578, and 871. Second quality is used on Models 590 and 595 (designed for heavy use). First quality is used on Models 600-903, except for Model 900 (557 action). All Arrieta actions are self-opening except the Models 557, 570, 578, and 871.

ADD THE FOLLOWING AMOUNTS FOR CURRENTLY MANUFACTURED SHOTGUNS.
Add 10% for small gauges (20, 24, 28, 32 ga., or .410 bore).
Add approx. $550 for single trigger depending on action.
Add 10% for matched pair.
Add 10% for rounded action on standard models.
Extra barrels are priced from $1,250-$1,750/set depending on model.

557 STANDARD — 12, 16, or 20 ga., Demi-Bloc steel barrels, detachable engraved sidelocks, double triggers, ejectors.

Mfg.'s Sug. Retail	$2,995	$2,675	$1,900	$1,450s	$1,100	$900	$750	$640

570 LIEJA — 12, 16, or 20 ga., similar to 560 (non-standard model), except has non-detachable sidelocks.

Mfg.'s Sug. Retail	$3,400	$3,075	$2,250	$1,725	$1,325	$1,075	$850	$750

578 VICTORIA — 12, 16, or 20 ga., similar to 570, except is fine English scrollwork engraved.

Mfg.'s Sug. Retail	$3,800	$3,550	$2,450	$1,775	$1,375	$1,100	$925	$850

LIGERA — all gauges, 12 ga. lightweight has 2 in. chambers, lightweight or standard action, includes frame engraving and $750 wood upgrade, 6 lbs., imported exclusively by New England Arms.

Mfg.'s Sug. Retail	$4,950	$4,500	$3,700	$3,000	$2,500	$2,100	$1,775	$1,350

600 IMPERIAL — 12, 16, or 20 ga., top-of-the-line self-opening action, very ornate engraving throughout.

Mfg.'s Sug. Retail	$5,100	$4,600	$3,750	$3,050	$2,500	$2,100	$1,775	$1,350

601 IMPERIAL TIRO — all gauges, sidelock action with nickel plating, ejectors, SST, self-opening action, border engraving.

Mfg.'s Sug. Retail	$5,850	$5,400	$4,900	$4,050	$3,400	$2,950	$2,500	$2,000

801 — all gauges, Holland-style detachable sidelocks, self-opening action, ejectors, coin-wash finish, finest Churchill style engraving.

Mfg.'s Sug. Retail	$8,100	$7,275	$6,600	$5,900	$5,100	$4,600	$4,000	$3,450

Models 801 through 875 are also available with self-opening actions as an option — add $800.

802 — 12, 16, or 20 ga., similar to 801 only non-detachable sidelocks, finest Holland-style engraving.

Mfg.'s Sug. Retail	$8,100	$7,275	$6,600	$5,900	$5,100	$4,600	$4,000	$3,450

"BOSS" ROUND BODY — all gauges, Boss pattern best quality engraving, includes $1,500 wood upgrade, imported exclusively by New England Arms.

Mfg.'s Sug. Retail	$9,750	$9,375	$8,250	$7,150	$5,950	$5,200	$4,400	$3,600

Grading	100%	98%	95%	90%	80%	70%	60%

A

803 — all gauges, similar to 801, finest Purdey-style engraving.
Mfg.'s Sug. Retail $5,950 $5,475 $4,925 $4,050 $3,400 $2,950 $2,500 $2,000

871 — all gauges, rounded frame sidelock action with Demi-Bloc barrels, scroll engraved, ejectors, DTs.
Mfg.'s Sug. Retail $4,750 $4,175 $3,300 $2,700 $2,175 $1,750 $1,450 $1,275

* 871 Extra Finish — includes standard game scene engraving with woodcock and ruffed grouse, this model is exclusively imported by New England Arms.
Mfg.'s Sug. Retail $5,950 $5,475 $4,925 $4,050 $3,400 $2,950 $2,500 $2,000

RENAISSANCE MODEL — all gauges, best quality sidelock, custom engraving, includes $1,500 wood upgrade, manufactured in Spain and engraved in Italy, imported exclusively by New England Arms.

> Prices for this model range from $7,950-$14,500, depending on engraving and wood options.

872 — all gauges, rounded frame sidelock action with Demi-Bloc barrels, elaborate scroll engraving with third lever fastener.
Mfg.'s Sug. Retail $9,850 $9,475 $8,300 $7,200 $5,950 $5,200 $4,400 $3,600

873 — all gauges, sidelock action with Demi-Bloc barrels, game scene engraving, ejectors, SST.
Mfg.'s Sug. Retail $6,950 $6,500 $4,875 $4,000 $3,400 $2,950 $2,500 $2,000

874 — all gauges, sidelock action with Demi-Bloc barrels, action is gold line engraved.
Mfg.'s Sug. Retail $8,000 $7,275 $6,600 $5,900 $5,100 $4,600 $4,000 $3,450

875 — all gauges, top-of-the-line quality, built to individual customer specs. only, elaborate engraving with gold inlays.
Mfg.'s Sug. Retail $13,100 $12,000 $9,950 $8,950 $7,850 $6,850 $5,900 $4,950

931 — all gauges, self-opening action, elaborate engraving, H&H selective ejectors.
Mfg.'s Sug. Retail $13,750 $12,350 $9,975 $9,000 $7,900 $6,950 $5,950 $4,950

ARRIZABALAGA, PEDRO

Current manufacturer located in Eibar, Spain since 1940. Currently imported and distributed by Hi-Grade Imports located in Gilroy, CA and New England Arms Corp. located in Kittery Point, ME.

Arrizabalaga manufactures best quality guns only, carefully made to individual customer specifications. Shotguns listed below have demi-bloc barrels and self-opening hand-detachable locks as standard features. The models listed below are essentially custom ordered per individual specifications - delivery time is approx. 12 months.

ADD THE FOLLOWING AMOUNTS ON ARRIZABALAGA SHOTGUNS:
Add 10% for matched pair.
Add $2,750 (retail) for extra barrels.
Add $500 for 28 ga.
Add $1,000 for .410 bore.
Add $1,000 for single trigger.
Add $250 for pistol grip stock.

SHOTGUNS: SxS

HEAVY SCROLL MODEL — all gauges, sidelock action, elaborate engraving, deluxe oil finished stock and forearm.
Mfg.'s Sug. Retail $10,500 $9,750 $6,700 $5,400 $4,750 $4,300 $3,850 $3,325

ENGLISH SCROLL MODEL — all gauges, sidelock action, English scroll engraving, deluxe oil finished walnut stock and forearm.
Mfg.'s Sug. Retail $11,650 $10,950 $7,300 $5,750 $4,950 $4,500 $4,000 $3,450

A

Grading		100%	98%	95%	90%	80%	70%	60%

MODEL DELUXE — all gauges, limited importation.

   Mfg.'s Sug. Retail $11,500 $10,600 $8,300 $7,000 $5,650 $4,950 $4,500 $4,000

BOSS STYLE ROUND ACTION MODEL — all gauges, features English scroll engraving.

   Mfg.'s Sug. Retail $11,000 $10,250 $8,150 $6,950 $5,650 $4,950 $4,500 $4,000

SPECIAL MODEL — all gauges, sidelock top of the line model, best quality wood and engraving.

   Mfg.'s Sug. Retail $14,666 $13,750 $9,250 $8,500 $7,600 $6,600 $5,900 $4,950

ARSENAL, BULGARIA

Current manufacturer located in Bulgaria. Please refer to Arcus Co. listing for current importation. Previously imported exclusively 1994-96 by Sentinel Arms located in Detroit, MI.

PISTOLS: SEMI-AUTO

MAKAROV MODEL — 9mm Makarov cal., 3⅔ in. barrel, 8 shot mag., black synthetic grips, blued finish. Disc. 1996.

   $185 $165 $125 $115 $105 $95 $85

RIFLES: SEMI-AUTO

BULGARIAN SA-93 — 7.62x39mm cal., Kalashnikov milled action with hardwood thumbhole stock, 16.3 in. barrel, 5 shot detachable mag., 9 lbs. Disc. 1996.

   $335 $295 $250 $215 $190 $180 $170

* **Bulgarian SA-93L** — 7.62x39mm cal., similar to Bulgarian SA-93 except has 20 in. barrel, with or without optics, 9 lbs. Disc. 1996.

   $595 $525 $450 $395 $350 $295 $250

   Add $145 with optics.

BULGARIAN SS-94 — 7.62x39mm cal., Kalashnikov action featuring single shot operation, thumbhole hardwood stock, 5 shot detachable mag., 9 lbs. Disc. 1996.

   $425 $360 $315 $260 $215 $190 $180

ASP

Previously manufactured customized variation of a S&W Model 39-2 semi-auto pistol (or related variations) mfg. by Armament Systems and Procedures located in Appleton, WI.

PISTOLS: SEMI-AUTO

ASP — 9mm Para. cal., compact double action semi-auto, features see-through grips with cut-away mag. making cartridges visible, Teflon coated, re-contoured lightened slide, combat trigger guard, spurless hammer, and mostly painted Guttersnipe rear sight (no front sight), supplied with 3 mags., 24 oz. loaded, approx. 3,000 mfg. until 1981.

   $1,500 $1,275 $1,050 $875 $775 $695 $625

   Add $200 for Tritium filled Guttersnipe.

   This pistol is marked ASP on the magazine extension.

* **ASP Quest For Excellence** — special edition, marked "Quest for Excellence", included buffalo horn grips, presentation book case and letter opener, approx. 100 mfg.

   $3,150 $2,700 $2,400 $2,050 $1,775 $1,525 $1,275

REVOLVERS

ASP REVOLVER — .44 Spl. cal., conversion from a Ruger Speed or Security Six, 5 shot, less than 100 mfg., unmarked.

   $1,275 $1,075 $950 $875 $775 $700 $650

Grading	100%	98%	95%	90%	80%	70%	60%

ASPREY & GARRARD

Asprey & Garrard

A

Current manufacturer located in London, England. While established in 1781, Asprey has been manufacturing high quality shotguns and rifles since 1990. During 1998, the name was changed to Asprey & Garrard. Consumer direct sales only.

Prices indicated below for manufacturer's suggested retail and 100% condition factors are listed in English pounds. All new prices include VAT. Values for used guns in 98%-60% condition factors are priced in U.S. dollars.

RIFLES: BOLT ACTION

BOLT ACTION MAGAZINE RIFLE — various cals., Mauser or Mannlicher action, ¾ rib with standard and two-folding leaf rear sight, best quality pistol grip walnut stock with traditional cheekpiece, custom order only - prices below reflect base model, with leather case and accessories. Magnum or Kurtz action and scopes are priced upon individual quotation only.

		100%	98%	95%	90%	80%	70%	60%
Mfg.'s Sug. Retail	£13,000	£13,000	$14,250	$11,350	$9,300	$7,900	$7,200	$6,500

RIFLES: SxS, SIDELOCK

SxS DOUBLE RIFLE — various cals. up to .700, sidelock ejector with engraved reinforced action, pinless lockplates, best quality walnut, folding leaf rear sight on ¾ rib, custom order only - prices below reflect base models, and include leather case with accessories.

Add £2,250 for detachable scope mounts.

* **Cals. up to .300**

		100%	98%	95%	90%	80%	70%	60%
Mfg.'s Sug. Retail	£45,000	£45,000	$57,500	$47,500	$42,500	$36,500	$29,500	$25,000

* **Cals. up to .470**

		100%	98%	95%	90%	80%	70%	60%
Mfg.'s Sug. Retail	£50,000	£50,000	$62,500	$50,000	$45,000	$38,500	$32,000	$26,500

* **Cals. up to .577**

		100%	98%	95%	90%	80%	70%	60%
Mfg.'s Sug. Retail	£55,000	£55,000	$67,000	$52,500	$47,500	$40,000	$33,500	$27,500

* **.600 and .700 Bore** — prices start at £60,000 and £70,000, respectively.

SHOTGUNS: SxS, SIDELOCK

SIDELOCK MODEL — available in 12 ga. - .410 bore, best quality sidelock ejector model, features pinless lockplates, DTs, best quality checkered walnut, custom order only - prices below reflect base model, and include leather case with accessories.

		100%	98%	95%	90%	80%	70%	60%
Mfg.'s Sug. Retail	£31,000	£31,000	$39,750	$34,250	$30,000	$26,500	$21,050	$17,000

Add £1,750 for ST.

Game scene engraving is available by individual quotation.

ASTRA

Previous manufacturer located in Guernica, Spain. Astra is one of the oldest and most widely recognized trademarks in Spain, with a history dating back to 1908. Though arms were manufactured for many years by UNCETA y COMPANIA., S.A., located in Guernica, Spain, corporate reorganization resulted in renaming the same firm ASTRA SPORT, S.A. (1995-1997), and most recently ASTRA SPORT GUERNIQUESA de MECANIZADO TRATAMIENTO y MONTAJE de ARMAS, S.A. (1997-1998).

Grading	100%	98%	95%	90%	80%	70%	60%

Although the new entity had hoped to acquire STAR patents and relocate to a smaller facility, these efforts were not successful. Foreclosure sealed the factory doors in July, 1998, and all inventory is now held in receivership. A limited number of models may still be available through prior distributors.

PISTOLS: SEMI-AUTO, RECENT MFG.

CONSTABLE — .22 LR (10 shot, disc. in 1990.), .32 ACP (8 shot, disc. 1984), or .380 ACP (7 shot) cal., double action, exposed hammer, 3½ in. barrel, fixed sight, blue or chrome (disc.) finish, plastic grips. Imported 1965-91.

$295	$250	$210	$180	$165	$150	$135

Last Mfg.'s Sug. Retail was $380.

Add $10 for chrome finish or wood grips (disc. in 1990).

* **Constable Stainless** — .380 ACP cal. only, stainless version of the Constable. Mfg. 1986 only.

$350	$300	$240	$220	$200	$175	$150

Last Mfg.'s Sug. Retail was $345.

* **Constable Sport** — similar to Constable, except has 6 in. barrel, blue finish only, 35 oz. Mfg. 1986-87 only.

$325	$245	$210	$180	$165	$150	$135

Last Mfg.'s Sug. Retail was $330.

* **Blue Engraved Constable** — blue engraved. Importation disc. 1987.

$395	$295	$250

Last Mfg.'s Sug. Retail was $375.

Add $20 for .22 LR or checkered wood grips.

* **Chrome Engraved Constable** — chrome engraved. Importation disc. 1987.

$350	$295	$250

Last Mfg.'s Sug. Retail was $390.

Add $20 for .22 LR or checkered wood grips.

CONSTABLE A-60 — .380 ACP cal., double action, 3½ in. barrel, 13 shot mag., ambidextrous safety, adj. rear sight, blue finish only. Imported 1986-91.

$395	$325	$280	$245	$220	$185	$160

Last Mfg.'s Sug. Retail was $475.

MODEL A-70 — 9mm Para. or .40 S&W cal., single action, 3½ in. barrel, steel frame and slide, 7 (.40 S&W) or 8 (9mm Para.) shot mag., compact design, dual safeties, 3-dot sights, matte blue or nickel (new 1993) finish, 25¾ oz. Imported 1991 - 1996.

$275	$250	$225	$200	$185	$170	$160

Last Mfg.'s Sug. Retail was $358.

Add $29 for nickel finish.

* **Model A-70 Stainless** — stainless steel variation of the A-70. Mfg. 1994 only.

$365	$325	$275

Last Mfg.'s Sug. Retail was $435.

MODEL A-75 — 9mm Para., .40 S&W, or .45 ACP (new 1994) cal., action similar to Model A-70, except has selective double action with a decocking lever, steel or aluminum (9mm Para. only) frame. Importation began 1993.

* **9mm Para.** — choice of blue or nickel steel frame or lightweight aluminum frame (23½ oz.), 8 shot mag. Disc. 1997.

$260	$225	$200	$175	$160	$150	$140

Last Mfg.'s Sug. Retail was $303.

Add $17 for nickel finish.
Add $20 for lightweight model (aluminum frame).

* **.40 S&W** — blue or nickel finish, 7 shot mag. Disc. 1997.

$265	$225	$200	$175	$160	$150	$140

Last Mfg.'s Sug. Retail was $310.

Add $19 for nickel finish.

Grading	100%	98%	95%	90%	80%	70%	60%

* .45 ACP — blue or nickel finish, 7 shot mag. Disc. 1997.

$310 **$250** **$225** **$200** **$175** **$160** **$150**

Last Mfg.'s Sug. Retail was $358.

    Add $23 for nickel finish.

* Model A-75 Stainless — stainless steel variation of the A-75. Mfg. 1994 only.

$375 **$325** **$295**

Last Mfg.'s Sug. Retail was $485.

MODEL A-80 — 9mm Para., .38 Super (disc.) or .45 ACP cal., double action, semi-auto, 15 shot mag. (9 for .45 ACP), 3¾ in. barrel. Imported 1982-89.

$370 **$320** **$285** **$265** **$240** **$210** **$185**

Last Mfg.'s Sug. Retail was $425.

    Add $35 for chrome finish (disc.).
    .38 Super cal. in chrome finish will command a premium (10%-20%).

MODEL A-90 — 9mm Para. or .45 ACP cal., 1986 designation for Model A-80 with updated slide mounted safety and pushbutton mag. release, 3¾ in. barrel, 14 shot mag. (9mm), or 8 shot (.45 ACP), blue only, approx. 48 oz. Imported 1986-90, replaced by Model A-100.

$375 **$325** **$295** **$275** **$245** **$225** **$200**

Last Mfg.'s Sug. Retail was $500.

MODEL A-100 — 9mm Para., .40 S&W, or .45 ACP cal., replaced the Model A-90 in 1990, with similar specifications, blue or nickel finish, re-engineered 1993 incorporating increased mag. capacity, 10 (C/B 1994), 17★/9mm, 12★/.40 S&W, or 9 shot/.45 ACP, approx. 29 oz. Imported 1990-97.

$375 **$325** **$295** **$275** **$245** **$225** **$175**

Last Mfg.'s Sug. Retail was $351.

    Add $22 for nickel finish.

MODEL 4000 FALCON — .22 LR, .32 ACP, or .380 ACP cal., 4 in. barrel, fixed sights, blue, plastic grips, exposed hammer. Mfg. 1956-1986.

$450 **$400** **$330** **$260** **$235** **$200** **$150**

Last Mfg.'s Sug. Retail was $340.

    Add 50% for .22 cal.
    Add 10% for .380 ACP.
    Add 100% for engraved M-4000.

* Model 4000 Tri-cal. Kit — includes frame and 3 barrels (.22 LR, .32 ACP, and .380 ACP cals.), may have rust blued, salt blued, or chromed (rare) finish, less than 200 mfg.

$1,250 **$950** **$750**

    Subtract 15% if not in factory box.

PISTOLS: SEMI-AUTO, DISC.

MODEL 1911 — .25 ACP or .32 ACP cal., semi-auto, may have external or internal hammer.

$365 **$265** **$175** **$135** **$115** **$100** **$85**

    Add 50% if with external hammer.

MODEL 1915/1916 — .32 ACP cal., semi-auto.

$350 **$265** **$175** **$135** **$115** **$100** **$85**

    Note: Models 1915/1916 were later referred to as Model 100 Special.

CAMPO GIRO 1913 — mfg. 1913-1914. Ser. No. range 1-1,300.

$3,250 **$2,650** **$1,850** **$1,350** **$925** **$700** **$500**

    Add 10% for matching magazine.

CAMPO GIRO 1913-1916 — mfg. 1915-1919. Ser. No. range 1-13,625.

$1,995 **$1,500** **$950** **$750** **$600** **$500** **$400**

    Add 10% if fit with horn logo grips.
    Add 10% for matching magazine.

Grading	100%	98%	95%	90%	80%	70%	60%

MODEL 200 FIRECAT AUTOMATIC PISTOL — .25 ACP cal., 2¼ in. barrel, 6 shot, blue, plastic grips, mfg. 1920-1968.

| | $240 | $190 | $165 | $145 | $125 | $110 | $100 |

> 100% prices assume N.I.B. condition.
> Add 50% for engraved M-200.

MODEL 300 — .32 ACP or .380 ACP cal., semi-auto.

| | $550 | $400 | $300 | $240 | $210 | $180 | $150 |

> Add 20% if Nazi-proofed.
> Add 200% for engraved M-300.

MODEL 400 AUTOMATIC PISTOL — 9mm Bayard long cal., 9 shot, 6 in. barrel, blue, fixed sights, plastic grips, mfg. 1921-1945.

| | $400 | $325 | $230 | $200 | $170 | $135 | $100 |

> Add 200% for Navy variation.
> Add 100% for Nazi accepted specimens.
>
> Approx. serial range of Nazi accepted specimens (no markings) is S/N 92,851 - 98,850.
>
> This particular model in "reworked" configuration has recently been imported in large quantities.

* **"F. Ascaso" Marked Model 400 Copies** — close copy of the Astra Model 400, produced by the Spanish Republican forces during the later part of the Spanish Civil War, F. Ascaso marked (un-numbered) mags., salt blued, estimated production is approx. 8,000, has identifying logo on slide and grip panels.

| | $600 | $475 | $325 | $250 | $200 | $175 | $150 |

* **R.E. (Republica Espagnola) Marked Model 400 Copies** — ser. range to approx. 15,000, has identifying logo on forward slide and grip panels.

| | $475 | $400 | $295 | $240 | $210 | $170 | $125 |

MODEL 600 MOD. AUTOMATIC — 9mm Para. cal., 8 shot, 5¼ in. barrel, blue, fixed sights, wood or plastic grips, mfg. 1944-1945.

| | $395 | $325 | $250 | $175 | $155 | $140 | $130 |

> Add 100% for Nazi Waffenamt proofing (serial range 1 - 10,500).

MODEL 700 SPECIAL — .32 ACP cal., semi-auto.

| | $600 | $500 | $425 | $350 | $275 | $215 | $170 |

MODEL 800 CONDOR AUTOMATIC — 9mm Para. cal., similar to 600, except has exposed hammer, mfg. 1958-1965.

| | $1,250 | $1,100 | $950 | $800 | $700 | $550 | $500 |

> Add 20% if NIB with accessories.

MODEL 900 — 7.63 Mauser cal., Broomhandle copy, parts non-interchangeable with Mauser. Mfg. from 1928-1936.

| | $2,650 | $1,850 | $1,350 | $850 | $700 | $525 | $425 |

> Add $500 for non-matching shoulder stock.
> Add $750 for matching stock.
> Add 50% for early Bolo grip variation.
> Add 20% for specimens with Japanese characters.

MODEL 902 — 7.63 Mauser cal., semi-auto, similar to 900 except 20 shot mag. Beware of fakes - usually created by welding up selective fire pistols.

| | $13,500 | $10,000 | $7,500 | $3,750 | $2,500 | $2,100 | $1,700 |

> Add $1,250 for original "booted" stock.
> Subtract 60% for selective fire version.

MACHINE PISTOLS — class III, transferrable only, 10 or 20 shot detachable mag., several variations.

| | $3,500 | $2,750 | $1,900 | $1,600 | $1,250 | $900 | $600 |

Grading	100%	98%	95%	90%	80%	70%	60%

MODEL 3000 POCKET AUTOMATIC — .32 ACP or .380 ACP cal., 4 in. barrel, fixed sights, blue, plastic grips, mfg. 1947-1956.

	$550	$395	$305	$250	$205	$175	$145

Add 100% for engraved M3000.

MODEL 1000 OR 1000 SPECIAL — .32 ACP cal., semi-auto, extended frame to hold 12 shot mag.

	$695	$550	$400	$310	$280	$255	$225

MODEL 2000 CUB — .22 Short or .25 ACP cal., 2¼ in. barrel, fixed sights, blue, plastic grips, also chrome finish, mfg. 1954-present, U.S. importation stopped by GCA 68. Astra also made 2000 Cubs for Colt called Jr. Model {see Colt section}.

	$225	$180	$140	$115	$95	$85	$75

Add 25% for chrome finish.
Add 50% for engraved M-2000.

MODEL 2000 CAMPER — .22 Short cal. only, similar to Cub, with 4 in. barrel, mfg. 1955-1960.

	$350	$275	$200	$160	$125	$90	$70

Add 10% if in original box.

REVOLVERS

ASTRA CADIX DOUBLE ACTION REVOLVER — .22 LR cal., 9 shot, .38 Spl., 5 shot, 4 or 6 in. barrel, adj. sights, blue, plastic grips, mfg. 1960-1968.

	$165	$155	$140	$120	$110	$85	$55

.357 D/A REVOLVER — .357 Mag. cal., 6 shot, 3, 4, 6 or 8½ in. barrel (add $10), adj. sights, blue, checkered wood grips, mfg. 1972-1988.

	$250	$215	$185	$170	$155	$140	$125

Last Mfg.'s Sug. Retail was $295.

* *Stainless Steel* — 4 in. barrel only. Disc. 1987.

	$285	$245	$205				

Last Mfg.'s Sug. Retail was $330.

.44/.45 CAL. D/A REVOLVER — .41 Mag. (disc. 1985), .44 Mag. or .45 ACP (disc. 1987) cal., 6 shot, 6 or 8½ in. (.44 Mag. only) barrels. Mfg. 1980-87.

	$280	$235	$210	$190	$180	$170	$160

Last Mfg.'s Sug. Retail was $315.

* *Stainless Steel* — .44 Mag. cal. only, 6 in. barrel only, 2½ lbs. Importation disc. 1993.

	$370	$300	$265				

Last Mfg.'s Sug. Retail was $450.

CONVERTIBLE REVOLVER — 9mm Para. cal. with extra .357 Mag. cal. cylinder, 6 shot, 3 in. barrel, blue only, checkered walnut grips, 2¼ lbs. Imported 1986-1993.

	$335	$275	$250	$225	$200	$180	$160

Last Mfg.'s Sug. Retail was $395.

TERMINATOR — .44 Mag. or .44 Spl. (disc.) cal., 6 shot, adj. rear sight, Roberts rubber grips, 2¾ in. shrouded barrel only. Inventories were depleted in 1989.

Blue finish	$250	$225	$190	$175	$160	$150	$140

Last Mfg.'s Sug. Retail was $250.

Stainless steel	$275	$235	$190				

Last Mfg.'s Sug. Retail was $275.

These models were distributed by Sile Distributors, Inc. located in New York, NY.

ATKIN, HENRY

Current trademark manufactured by Atkin, Grant & Lang, established in 1821 and located in Hertfordshire, England. No current importer.

Grading	100%	98%	95%	90%	80%	70%	60%

A

SHOTGUNS: SxS

Prices below do not include VAT or importation costs.
Add 10% for matched pairs.

BOXLOCK MODEL — 28 (2 mfg.) or 20 (3 mfg.) ga., very limited Millenium Edition.

Mfg.'s Sug. Retail	£14,000	£14,000	$16,170	$14,000	$12,000	$9,950	$8,500	$7,250

SIDELOCK MODEL — 12, 20 ga., or .410 bore, best quality sidelock ejector model with opening assist.

Mfg.'s Sug. Retail	£28,000	£28,000	$32,300	$26,000	$22,500	$19,000	$16,000	$13,750

Add 10% for 20 ga. or .410 bore.

AUSTRALIAN AUTOMATIC ARMS PTY. LTD.

Previous manufacturer located in Tasmania, Australia. Previously imported and distributed by California Armory, Inc. located in San Bruno, CA.

PISTOLS: SEMI-AUTO

SAP — .223 Rem. cal., semi-auto paramilitary design pistol, 10½ in. barrel, 20 shot mag., fiberglass stock and forearm, 5.9 lbs. Imported 1986-1993.

	$725	$650	$575	$525	$495	$475	$450

Last Mfg.'s Sug. Retail was $799.

RIFLES: SEMI-AUTO

SAR — .223 Rem. cal., semi-auto paramilitary design rifle, 16¼ or 20 in. (new 1989) barrel, 5 or 20 shot M-16 style mag., fiberglass stock and forearm, 7½ lbs. Imported 1986-89.

	$725	$625	$550	$510	$465	$410	$370

Last Mfg.'s Sug. Retail was $663.

Add $25 for 20 in. barrel.

Also available in fully auto version (AR).

SAC — .223 Rem. cal., semi-auto paramilitary design carbine, 10½ in. barrel, 20 shot mag., fiberglass stock and forearm, 6.9 lbs. New 1986.

This model is available to class III dealers and law enforcement agencies only.

SP — .223 Rem. cal., semi-auto, sporting configuration, 16¼ or 20 in. barrel, wood stock and forearm, 5 or 20 shot M-16 style mag., 7.5 lbs. Imported late 1991-1993.

	$795	$675	$575	$525	$495	$475	$450

Last Mfg.'s Sug. Retail was $879.

Add $40 for wood stock.

AUTAUGA ARMS, INC.

Current manufacturer located in Prattville, AL, since 1996. Dealer sales.

PISTOLS: SEMI-AUTO

AUTAUGA MKII 32 — .32 ACP cal., double action only, 2 in. barrel, hammerless, blow-back type action, 6 shot mag., stainless steel, black polymer grips, 12 oz. New 1996.

Mfg.'s Sug. Retail	$399		$325	$225	$185

Early guns did not have the MKII designation.

RIFLES: BOLT ACTION

Autauga Arms manufactures a complete line of bolt action rifles for high power rifle competitors, professional hunters, and law enforcement agencies. These guns are custom order per individual specifications, and most delivery times are within 90 days

Grading	100%	98%	95%	90%	80%	70%	60%

of order. Please contact the factory directly to find out more information and pricing on these rifles.

AUTO MAG

Currently manufactured by Automag, Inc., located in Irwindale, CA, beginning 1999. Previously manufactured (circa 1971-1982) by Auto Mag. Corp. and TDE Corp.

Short recoil rotary bolt system made entirely of stainless steel. Most pistols were sold in .44 AMP cal. although .357 AMP was also a popular factory option. Several other calibers and variations were marketed through Lee Jurras including exotics like the .44 Condor (16 in. barrel and scoped - one of a kind). Also, a .30 cal. Cougar with 12 in. barrel and highly polished metal was a one of a kind item. Other limited Jurras variations include The Custom 100 Series (.44 cal., custom tuned, magna ported, special serialization), The Grizzly (.41 cal.), The Backpacker (.357 cal.), in addition to the Metallic Silhouette.

A unique handgun, the Auto Mag was never a commercial success due to high manufacturing costs and initial functioning problems (mostly attributed to hand loading all the ammo - once factory ammo became available, reliability improved significantly). Initial reaction to Dirty Harry's use of this weapon in the movie "Sudden Impact" (1983) made prices escalate considerably, but most values appear to have stablized since 1986. Be aware of fakes - especially of the XP variety (re-serialized, re-stamped, location of markings, etc.). Also, the ease of barrel swapping should be considered when deciding on a potential purchase. Auto Mags were never magna ported from the factory (only The Custom 100 Series). Non-original magna porting actually detracts from the values listed below, since it is a non-factory alteration.

Serial number ranges for the various models are as follows: Pasadena mfg. - A0000 through A03700. TDE North Hollywood - mostly A02500 through A05015 although some were marked with very low ser. no.'s. TDE El Monte mfg. - A05016 through A08300. High Standard guns were originally marked with "H" prefix serial numbers (only 132 made), after which they carried standard "A0" prefix serial numbers. The "H" prefix guns remain a collectors item and command a 25% premium over values listed below. TDE/OMC marked pistols - B00001 through B00370 are known as the "B" series or solid bolt models (only 370 manufactured). This "B" series also commands collector premiums.

AMT manufactured the last two lots of Auto Mags; the first was the "C" series and was basically the same as the "B" except that only 50 guns were fabricated. The last Auto Mags made by AMT were appropriately serial numbered LAST 1 through LAST 50. These guns had the reputation of being the poorest quality but do carry collector premiums. One interesting variation is the North Hollywood "two-line" model. Also, the first .357 cal. pistols manufactured did not have the words AUTO MAG appearing on the gun. These are also collectors items.

In addition to the above calibers, a very few non-factory .22 and .25 cal. prototypes were fabricated by Kent Lomont. These specimens will usually demand a premium over the values listed below. Also, some barrels and pistols were made in Covina, CA.

Less than 10,000 Auto Mags were produced by all manufacturers. All pistols originally had all stainless steel mags.

PISTOLS: SEMI-AUTO

ORIGINAL PASADENA — .44 AMP cal. only, 6½ in. VR barrel.

$2,500 $2,300 $1,995

This model is generally regarded as having the most quality, as all components were milled from Carpenter 455 stainless steel stock.

Grading	100%	98%	95%	90%	80%	70%	60%

A

TDE NORTH HOLLYWOOD

* **.44 AMP** — 6½ in. VR barrel, initial guns were mfg. from existing Pasadena parts, later mfg. required new components made by TDE.

  $2,275 $1,975 $1,850

  Quality on this model goes down in later mfg. (some small parts are not stainless). Because of this, higher serial numbered guns in this model are less desirable.

* **.357 AMP** — two line address.

  $2,500 $2,300 $1,995

  There are no factory records verifying this caliber.

TDE EL MONTE

* **.44 AMP** — 6½ VR, 8, or 10 in. tapered barrel.

  $2,100 $1,800 $1,600

* **.357 AMP** — 6½ VR, 8, or 10 in. tapered barrel.

  $1,800 $1,600 $1,500

HIGH STANDARD — "H" prefixed serial numbers, mfg. by TDE with High Standard markings.

  $2,500 $2,300 $1,995

TDE/OMC "B" SERIES — 6½ VR or 10 in. barrel.

  $2,500 $2,300 $1,995

AMT "C" SERIES — 6½ VR or 10 in. barrel.

  $2,500 $2,300 $1,995

Add 50%+ for L.E. Jurras Custom 100 Series.
Add 10% for Jurras Lion marked models.

Lee Jurras added his Lion's head logo (from 1977 on) on TDE manufactured guns.

There were also a very limited quantity of original shoulder stocks (perhaps less than 5) - extreme rarity precludes accurate price evaluation.

Note: guns were cased (plastic attache style) with accessories. Original Auto-Mag ammo (only original mfg. by CDM in Mexico and Norma in Sweden) is currently selling for approx. $75-$95 a box.

HARRY SANFORD COMMEMORATIVE AUTO MAG — .44 AMP cal., AMT (Galena Industries, Inc.) commemorative reissue, "PASADENA, CALIFORNIA" barrel address with Harry Sanford signature on left rear of slide, cased, limited mfg. of 1,000 pistols beginning 1999.

Mfg.'s Sug. Retail $2,750 $2,750 $2,300 $1,995

AUTO-ORDNANCE CORP.

Current manufacturer located in West Hurley, NY. Consumer, dealer and distributor sales.

Auto-Ordnance Corp. manufactures an exact reproduction of the original 1927 Thompson machine gun. They are currently available in semi-auto only since production ceased on fully automatic variations (Model 1928 and M1) in 1986 (mfg. 1975-1986 including 609 M1s).

PISTOLS: SEMI-AUTO

Beginning 1997, Auto Ordnance discontinued all calibers on the pistols listed below, except for .45 ACP cal. However, .38 Super or 9mm Para. slide kits are currently available for $179. Also, conversion units (converting .45 ACP to .38 Super or 9mm Para.) are available at $195.

Grading	100%	98%	95%	90%	80%	70%	60%

1911 A1 — .38 Super (disc. 1996), 9mm Para. (disc. 1996), .40 S&W (mfg. 1991-93), 10mm (mfg. 1991-96), or .45 ACP cal., 4½ (.40 S&W cal. only) or 5 in. barrel, 7 shot mag., single action, parts interchange with the original Colt Govt. Model, blue or nickel finish, checkered plastic grips, 39 oz.

Mfg.'s Sug. Retail	$425		$345	$285	$250	$235	$225	$215	$200

Add $28 for satin nickel (mfg. 1990-96) or $37 for duo-tone (mfg. 1992-96) finish (.45 ACP only).

* **1911 A1 Deluxe** — .38 Super (disc. 1996), 9mm Para. (disc. 1996), or .45 ACP cal., 5 in. barrel, 3 dot sights, wraparound grips, 39 oz. New 1991.

Mfg.'s Sug. Retail	$439		$365	$315	$260	$235	$225	$215	$200

* **1911 A1 General** — .38 Super (mfg. 1996 only) or .45 ACP cal., 4½ in. barrel with full length recoil guide system, 7 shot mag., blued finish, 3 dot fixed Millett sights, black rubber wraparound grips, Commander styling, 37 oz. Mfg. 1992-98.

			$385	$315	$255	$235	$225	$215	$200

Last Mfg.'s Sug. Retail was $465.

* **1911 A1 Custom High Polish** — .45 ACP cal., 8 shot mag., 5 in. barrel, custom combat hammer, beavertail grip safety, rosewood grips with medallions, 3-dot sights, flat mainspring housing, Videcki speed trigger, 39 oz. New 1997.

Mfg.'s Sug. Retail	$585		$485	$395	$325	$265	$235	$225	$215

* **Parkerized 1911 A1** — .45 ACP cal., no frills variation of the Model 1911 A1, military parkerizing, checkered walnut grips. New 1992.

Mfg.'s Sug. Retail	$400		$330	$275	$250	$235	$225	$215	$200

* **Competition 1911** — .38 Super (1996 only) or .45 ACP cal., competition features include compensated barrel, commander hammer, flat mainspring housing, white 3-dot sighting system, beavertail grip safety, black textured wraparound grips. Mfg. 1993-96.

			$530	$415	$375	$330	$300	$285	$270

Last Mfg.'s Sug. Retail was $636.

Add $10 for .38 Super cal.

MODEL ZG-51 "PIT BULL" — .45 ACP cal. only, compact variation of the 1911 A1, 3⅝ in. standard (disc. 1996) or 4⅜ in. compensated (new 1997) barrel, 7 shot mag., 36 oz. New 1988.

Mfg.'s Sug. Retail	$470		$385	$310	$255	$235	$225	$215	$200

RIFLES: SEMI-AUTO

Until the Crime Bill was passed in 1994, the Auto-Ordnance Thompson replicas listed below were supplied with either 15, 20, or 30 shot mags. Beginning late 1994, Auto-Ordnance began manufacturing 10 round X-drum mags. that resemble the older 50 round L-type drums - retail is approx. $100.

1927 A1 STANDARD — .45 ACP cal., 16 in. plain barrel, solid steel construction, standard military sight, walnut stock and horizontal forearm. Disc. 1986.

			$570	$490	$430	$360	$315	$290	$270

Last Mfg.'s Sug. Retail was $575.

1927 A1 DELUXE — 10mm (mfg. 1991-93) or .45 ACP cal., 16 in. finned barrel, 30 shot original surplus mag., solid steel construction, adj. rear sight, walnut stock and hand grips.

Mfg.'s Sug. Retail	$860		$700	$565	$450	$375	$325	$295	$275

Add $190 for 50* shot drum mag. or $350 for 100 shot drum mag. (mfg. 1990-93) on this model and other 1927 variations. Also add $113 (retail) for Thompson hard case (violin type).

THOMPSON M1 CARBINE — .45 ACP cal., combat model, 16½ in. smooth barrel, 30 shot original surplus mag., side-cocking lever, flat black finish, walnut stock, pistol grip, and grooved forearm, 11½ lbs. New 1986.

Mfg.'s Sug. Retail	$850		$690	$550	$430	$365	$310	$285	$265

Grading	100%	98%	95%	90%	80%	70%	60%

A

1927 A1C LIGHTWEIGHT — .45 ACP cal., similar to 1927 A-1 Deluxe, except receiver made of a lightweight alloy. 20% weight reduction. New 1984.

Mfg.'s Sug. Retail	$855	$695	$560	$450	$370	$320	$295	$275

1927 A1 COMMANDO — .45 ACP cal., 16½ in. finned barrel, black finished stock and forearm, parkerized metal, black nylon sling, 13 lbs. New 1997.

Mfg.'s Sug. Retail	$850	$690	$560	$450	$365	$310	$285	$265

1927 A5 PISTOL/CARBINE — .45 ACP cal., 13 in. finned barrel, alloy construction, overall length 26 in., 10 (C/B 1994) shot mag., 7 lbs. Mfg. disc. 1994.

		$625	$515	$440	$360	$305	$280	$260

Last Mfg.'s Sug. Retail was $765.

1927 A3 - .22 CAL. — .22 LR cal., 16 in. finned barrel, alloy frame and receiver, walnut stock, pistol grip, and forearm pistol grip, 7 lbs. Mfg. disc. 1994.

		$440	$375	$325	$285	$260	$230	$200

Last Mfg.'s Sug. Retail was $510.

AUTO-POINTER

Previous trademark manufactured by Yamamoto Co. Formerly imported by Sloans.

SHOTGUNS: SEMI-AUTO

SEMI-AUTO SHOTGUN — 12 or 20 ga., gas operated. Disc.

	$275	$240	$220	$195	$180	$160	$145

AXTELL RIFLE CO.

Current rifle manufacturer located in Sheridan, MT. Distributed by The Riflesmith Inc., located in Sheridan, MT. Consumer direct sales.

RIFLES: REPRODUCTIONS

Model 1877 Sharps reproductions are available for both long-range and sporting rifles listed below in the following black powder calibers: .40-50, .40-70, .40-90, .45-70 Govt., .45-90, and .45-100 cal. The Riflesmith Inc. should be contacted directly for accessories and/or engraving options.

Add $275 for bull hide rifle case.

NUMBER ONE CREEDMOOR — features 34 in. Rigby style barrel, choice of high-grade black or English checkered walnut stock and forearm with ebony inlays. Long range sights. 10 lbs.

Mfg.'s Sug. Retail	$4,700	$4,700	$3,950	$3,500	$3,025	$2,500	$2,000	$1,500

NUMBER TWO LONG RANGE — choice of 30-34 in. Rigby style barrel, select black or English checkered walnut stock and forearm. Long range sights.

Mfg.'s Sug. Retail	$3,900	$3,900	$3,150	$3,000	$2,525	$2,000	$1,650	$1,300

OVERBAUGH SCHUETZEN — features 26-30 in. octagon barrel, double-set triggers, Schuetzen buttplate with cheekpiece, palm rest, short-range sights, 11-14 lbs.

Mfg.'s Sug. Retail	$4,100	$4,100	$3,300	$3,100	$2,575	$2,025	$1,650	$1,300

LOWER SPORTER — 28 or 30 in. octagon barrel, double-set triggers, steel buttplate with straight grip, standard rifle weight of 9 lbs.

Mfg.'s Sug. Retail	$2,600	$2,600	$2,000	$1,625	$1,300	$995	$825	$700

LOWER BUSINESS — 28 in. contoured round barrel, double-set triggers, black walnut stock has steel shotgun buttplate with straight grip, hunter tang, blade front sights, approx. 8½ lbs. New 1999.

B section

BSA GUNS LIMITED

Current manufacturer established in 1861 and located in Birmingham, England. BSA (Birmingham Small Arms) currently manufactures airguns only. Firearms were imported until 1985 by Precision Sports, from Ithaca, NY and 1986 by BSA Guns Ltd., located in Grand Prairie, TX. Imported and distributed until 1989 by Samco Global Arms, Inc., located in Miami, FL. BSA airguns may be found under the Airgun section of this text.

Grading	100%	98%	95%	90%	80%	70%	60%

RIFLES: RECENT IMPORTATION

Importation of all BSA rimfire and centerfire rifles was disc. 1987.

CF-2 ACTION — .222 Rem., .22-250 Rem., .243 Win., 6.5x55mm, 7x57mm, 7x64mm, 7mm Rem. Mag., .270 Win., .308 Win., .30-06, or .300 Win. Mag. cal., bolt action, barrel length 23-26 in., 7½-8 lbs. CF-2 nomenclature designates an action rather than a model. CF-2 actioned models are listed below. Add $70 for double set trigger option on the below listed models. Limited quantities of English mfg. models remain.

* *Sporter/Classic* — same cals. as above, checkered oil finished walnut stock. Imported 1986-87.

	$325	$275	$250	$225	$210	$195	$180

Last Mfg.'s Sug. Retail was $360.

Sporter Model features Monte Carlo stock, rosewood capped forearm and pistol grip stock, and swivels.

* *Classic Varminter* — .222 Rem. - .243 Win. cals. only, heavy barrel, matte finish, with swivels. Imported 1986 only.

	$325	$275	$250	$225	$210	$190	$175

Last Mfg.'s Sug. Retail was $345.

* *Heavy Barrel Model* — .222 Rem., .22-250 Rem., or .243 Win. cal., approx. 9 lbs., no sights.

	$375	$300	$260	$240	$225	$210	$180

Last Mfg.'s Sug. Retail was $410.

* *Carbine Model* — 20 in. barrel. Disc. 1985.

	$495	$375	$300	$270	$250	$225	$200

Last Mfg.'s Sug. Retail was $480.

* *Stutzen Rifle* — Mannlicher style full length stock, same general specifications as Sporter/Classic, 20½ in. barrel. Not available in 7mm Rem. Mag. or .300 Win. Mag. cal.

	$595	$400	$325	$300	$275	$250	$225

Last Mfg.'s Sug. Retail was $385.

* *Regal Custom* — similar to Sporter Model, except has slim classic European style stock with Schnabel forend, deluxe walnut with extra checkering, ebony forend cap, engraved action and floorplate. Limited importation (1986 only).

	$875	$795	$685	$590	$550	$500	$450

Last Mfg.'s Sug. Retail was $950.

This model was custom made by special order only.

CFT TARGET RIFLE — 7.62mm cal., single shot, bolt action, globe front and aperture rear sights, 26½ in. barrel, 11 lbs. Disc. 1987.

	$675	$590	$550	$500	$450	$400	$360

Last Mfg.'s Sug. Retail was $780.

RIFLES: SINGLE SHOT

NO. 12 MARTINI — .22 LR cal., 29 in. barrel, target sights, straight stock, pre-WWII.

	$450	$400	$300	$275	$250	$200	$175

Grading	100%	98%	95%	90%	80%	70%	60%

MILITARY MARTINI HENRY — various cals., pre-WWII mfg. many configurations and barrel lengths. Pricing takes into consideration most commonly encountered types with no engraving or special orders.

	$650	$575	$500	$460	$430	$375	$350

MARTINI CADET — various cals., mostly military issue, many thousands previously imported into the U.S. from England, many have been sporterized or modified.

	$600	$450	$400	$350	$300	$275	$250

MODEL 15 — similar to 12, except pistol grip stock, better grade target sights, pre-WWII.

	$450	$400	$350	$300	$275	$250	$200

CENTURION MATCH RIFLE — similar to 15, except Centurion guarantee — 1½ in. grouping at 100 yards, 24 in. barrel, pre-WWII.

	$440	$385	$330	$275	$240	$220	$175

MATCH 12/15 — similar to Model 15, except made after WWII.

	$450	$400	$350	$300	$275	$250	$200

MODEL 12/15 — heavy barrel.

	$495	$450	$400	$350	$300	$275	$250

MODEL 13 — lighter version of 12.

	$450	$400	$350	$300	$275	$250	$200

MODEL 13 SPORTER — similar to 13, except has sport sights.

	$450	$400	$350	$300	$275	$250	$200
.22 Hornet	$595	$550	$500	$400	$375	$360	$330

MARTINI INTERNATIONAL MATCH — .22 LR cal., 29 in. heavy barrel, international sights, mfg. 1950-1953.

	$600	$500	$450	$400	$350	$325	$300

INTERNATIONAL LIGHT — 26 in. lightweight barrel.

	$600	$500	$450	$400	$350	$325	$300

INTERNATIONAL MKII — improved trigger, ejectors and stock design, mfg. 1953-1959.

	$700	$600	$550	$500	$450	$400	$350

INTERNATIONAL MKIII — longer action, floating barrel, mfg. 1959-1967.

	$800	$700	$650	$600	$550	$500	$450

INTERNATIONAL ISU — modeled to meet ISU standards, 28 in. barrel, mfg. 1968-disc.

	$800	$700	$650	$600	$550	$500	$450

INTERNATIONAL MARK V — similar to ISU, but heavier barrel, mfg. 1976-disc.

	$800	$700	$650	$600	$550	$500	$450

RIFLES: BOLT ACTION

MAJESTIC FEATHERWEIGHT DELUXE — .243 Win., .270 Win., .308 Win., or .30-06 cal., bolt action, 22 in. barrel, folding sight, checkered European style stock, mfg. 1959-1965.

	$330	$250	$220	$195	$180	$165	$145
.458 Mag.	$445	$375	$305	$275	$220	$210	$200

MAJESTIC DELUXE — .222 Rem., .22 Hornet, .243 Win., 7x57mm, .308 Win., or .30-06 cal., heavier barrel.

	$330	$250	$220	$195	$180	$165	$145

MONARCH DELUXE — similar to Majestic Deluxe, but American design stock, mfg. 1965-1974.

	$350	$275	$250	$220	$195	$180	$165

Grading	100%	98%	95%	90%	80%	70%	60%

MONARCH DELUXE VARMINT — similar to Monarch Deluxe, except .222 Rem. or .243 Win. cal., 24 in. heavy barrel. Disc.

	$370	$305	$275	$250	$210	$195	$180

B

MARTINI ISU MATCH .22 — single shot, bolt action, .22 LR cal. only, similar to CFT Model. Add $100 for Mk. V.H.B. Model. Disc. 1985.

	$825	$700	$600	$530	$475	$435	$400

Last Mfg.'s Sug. Retail was $1,000.

SHOTGUNS: SxS

BSA also manufactured SxS boxlock shotguns in various grades. Normally encountered in 12 ga. with DT's and extractors, these shotguns are of good quality and are typically encountered in the secondary market in the $250-$500 range, assuming standard grade.

B-WEST

Previous importer/distributor located in Tucson, AZ, until 1997.

B-West previously imported rifles (including AK-47 clones, the Saiga, Dragunov, etc.) in addition to an IJ series .380 ACP Makarov pistol.

LES BAER CUSTOM, INC.

Please refer to the L section of this text.

BAFORD ARMS, INC.

Previous manufacturer located in Bristol, TN. Previously distributed by C.L. Reedy & Associates, Inc. located in Melbourne, FL.

PISTOLS: SEMI-AUTO

MODEL 35 FIRE POWER — 9mm Para. cal., semi-auto single action, patterned after the Browning Hi-Power, total stainless steel construction, 4¾ in. barrel, combat hammer and safety, Pachmayr grips, removable barrel bushing, Millett Mk. II sights, 14 shot mag., 32 oz. Introduced late 1988 with limited mfg. until 1993.

	$500	$425	$350

Last Mfg.'s Sug. Retail was $550.

DERRINGERS

THUNDER DERRINGER — .44 Spl. cal./.410 shotshell, single shot, tip-up action, 3 in. barrel, blued steel finish, spur trigger, wood grips. Introduced late 1988 with limited mfg. until 1991, when production permanently ceased.

	$130	$110	$95	$90	$85	$80	$75

Last Mfg.'s Sug. Retail was $130.

Add $90 for interchangeable barrel kit.

Interchangeable pistol barrels are chambered in various calibers between .22 Short and 9mm Para. There are two types: one fits flush while the other facilitates a scope mounting.

BAIKAL

Current trademark manufactured in Izhevsk and Tula, Russia since approx. WWII. Many Baikal SxS and O/U shotguns (airguns also) are currently being imported starting late 1998 by European American Armory Corp., located in Sharpes, FL. Previously imported 1993-96 by Big Bear located in Dallas, TX. Please refer to the European American Armory Corp. listing for more information on current Baikal models.

Baikal (Bajkal is Russian for the lake of the same name) is the first state-run holdover from the former Soviet Union to market firearms, ammunition, and other

B

sporting goods/optics from a variety of plants within Russia. Baikal is the trademark of Izhevsky Mekhanichesky Zavod, a government owned plant in Izhevsk, Russia.

The company was founded in 1942 as part of the Russian National Defense Industry. Upon conclusion of WWII, the company expanded its operation to include non-military weapons (O/U, SxS, and single barrel shotguns). Today, Izhevsky Mekhanichesky Zavod is one of the world's largest manufacturers of military and non-military small arms. The products range from the internationally famous Makarov pistol, sporting shotguns, air pistols and air rifles, to a full array of military weapons.

Izhevsky Mekhanichesky Zavod is also undertaking the task of reintroducing the world to the "Russian Custom Gunsmith". A section of the factory has been set aside for custom one-of-a-kind hand engraved shotguns and rifles. The guns produced by the custom shop are top quality by any standards, and rival many of the custom guns elsewhere. The custom shop also serves as the birthplace for many of the new innovations being introduced by Izhevsky Mekhanichesky Zavod.

The following is a listing of various firearms configurations linked up with the respective manufacturing facility. The Izhevsk Machining Plant is responsible for both centerfire bolt and semi-auto rifles, rimfire bolt and semi-auto rifles (including the SVD/Tiger), the Izhevsk Mechanical Plant is responsible for shotguns and handguns, including the IJ70 and RF target pistols, while the Tula Arms Works is responsible for the TOZ series of rifles, pistols, revolvers and shotguns. Tula is also responsible for refurbishing the Russian SKSs for the American market. Currently, Baikal is producing a complete line of shotguns (O/U, SxS, single shot, and slide-action), in addition to semi-auto pistols, revolvers, and airguns.

In the past, Baikal shotguns have had limited importation into the U.S. 1993 marked the first year that Baikals were officially (and legally) imported into the U.S. because of Russia's previous export restrictions domestically. In prior years, however, a few O/Us have been seen for sale and have no doubt been "imported" into this country one at a time. Earlier manufacture has intermediate level quality, and collector interest is not particularly great. Most older O/U shotguns fall into the $400 - $1,000 range if quality is at par with other more famous trademarks.

COMBINATION GUNS: RECENT IMPORTATION

IZH-94 O/U — 12 ga. over various cals. (domestic and metric), boxlock action, 24 in. separated barrels with rifle sights, gold DT, extractors, choke tube (shotgun barrel), checkered walnut stock and forearm, approx. 7¼ lbs.

Mfg.'s Sug. Retail	$445	$395	$340	$320	$300	$280	$260	$240

Add $31 for 7x57R, 7x65R, or 7.62x53R cal.

PISTOLS: SEMI-AUTO

IJ-70 — .380 ACP or 9x18 Makarov cal., double action semi-auto, all steel blued construction, 4 in. barrel, slide mounted safety with decocking, fully adj. target sights, choice of two 8 shot (IJ-70), two 10 (C/B 1994, Model IJ-70-HC), or two 12★ shot, holster and cleaning rod, checkered plastic grips, 25 oz. Disc. 1996.

		$175	$150	$135	$120	$105	$95	$85

Last Mfg.'s Sug. Retail was $199.

Add $40 for IJ-70-HC (High Capacity).
Add $50 for .380 ACP cal.
Add $10 for nickel finish (disc.).

Grading		100%	98%	95%	90%	80%	70%	60%

SHOTGUNS: O/U, RECENT IMPORTATION

B

IJ-27 FIELD MODEL — 12 or 20 (new 1992) ga., double triggers, extractors, 26 or 28 in. barrels. Disc. 1996.

		100%	98%	95%	90%	80%	70%	60%
		$330	$275	$250	$225	$195	$180	$165

Last Mfg.'s Sug. Retail was $399.

Add $40 for single trigger and automatic ejectors (Model IJ-27EIC).

IZH-27 — 12, 20, 28 ga., or .410 bore, boxlock action, monobloc receiver, walnut checkered stock (with or w/o Monte Carlo) and forearm, extractors, SST, 26 or 28 in. VR barrels with or w/o chokes. Importation began 1999.

Mfg.'s Sug. Retail	$351	$300	$270	$250	$230	$210	$190	$170

Add $37 for multi-chokes (12 or 20 ga. only).
Add $84 for 28 ga. or .410 bore.

IZHMP-233 — 12 ga. only, 3 in. chambers, 26, 28, or 30 in. barrels with multi-chokes, removable trigger group, ejectors, checkered walnut stock and forearm, 7¼ lbs. Importation began 1999.

Mfg.'s Sug. Retail	$702	$625	$550	$500	$450	$400	$360	$330

SHOTGUNS: SEMI-AUTO, RECENT IMPORTATION

MP-151 — 12 ga., 3 in. chamber, 26 or 28 in. plain barrel with 2 choke tubes, black synthetic or checkered walnut Monte Carlo stock, tube or detachable box (available late 1999) mag., approx. 7.8 lbs. Importation began 1999.

Mfg.'s Sug. Retail	$310	$275	$235	$215	$195	$180	$165	$150

SHOTGUNS: SxS, RECENT IMPORTATION

IJ-43 FIELD MODEL — 12 or 20 ga., double triggers, extractors, 20, 26 (disc.), or 28 in. barrels. Disc. 1996.

		100%	98%	95%	90%	80%	70%	60%
		$235	$200	$160	$130	$105	$95	$75

Last Mfg.'s Sug. Retail was $299.

Add $20 for 20 in. barrels bored C/C.

IZH-43 HUNTING MODEL — 12, 20, 28 ga., or .410 bore, 3 in. chamber only on .410 bore, boxlock action with monobloc, SST, 24, 26, or 28 in. barrels with or w/o (28 ga. and .410 bore) choke tubes, checkered walnut stock and forearm. Importation began 1999.

Mfg.'s Sug. Retail	$281	$250	$225	$200	$180	$165	$150	$135

Add $78 for 20, 28 ga., or .410 bore.

IZHMP-213 — 12 ga. only, 3 in. chambers, SST or DT, ejectors, removable trigger assembly, 20, 24, 26, or 28 in. monobloc barrels with choke tubes, checkered walnut stock and forearm, 7¼ lbs. Importation began 1999.

Mfg.'s Sug. Retail	$702	$625	$550	$500	$450	$400	$360	$330

IZH-43 BOUNTY HUNTER II — 12 or 20 ga., 3 in. chambers, designed for cowboy action shooting, choice of hammers or hammerless, SST or DT, 20 in. barrels with or w/o choke tubes, hardwood or walnut stock and forearm, engraved receiver, extractors, 7 lbs. Importation began 1999.

Mfg.'s Sug. Retail	$234	$210	$175	$165	$155	$145	$135	$125

Add approx. $111 for external hammers.
Add $39 for walnut stock and forearm.
Add $46 for SST and walnut stock and forearm.

SHOTGUNS: SINGLE SHOT, RECENT IMPORTATION

IJ-18M — 12, 16, 20 ga., or .410 bore, 26 or 28 in. barrel. Disc. 1996.

		100%	98%	95%	90%	80%	70%	60%
		$60	$50	$40	$35	$30	$30	$25

Last Mfg.'s Sug. Retail was $74.

Grading	100%	98%	95%	90%	80%	70%	60%

IZH-18 — 12, 20 ga., or .410 bore, only .410 bore has 3 in. chamber, 26 or 28 in. barrel, hardwood stock and forearm, ejector, decocking/cocking lever, cocking indicator. Importation began 1998.

Mfg.'s Sug. Retail	$86	$75	$60	$50	$40	$35	$30

Add $3 for Youth Model (20 ga. or .410 bore only).

SHOTGUNS: SLIDE ACTION, RECENT IMPORTATION

IZH-81 — 12 ga. only, 3 in. chamber, 5 shot box mag., 20, 26, or 28 in. plain or VR barrel with (26 or 28 in. barrel only) or w/o choke tubes, hardwood or walnut stock and corncob style forearm, blue finish. Importation began 1999.

Mfg.'s Sug. Retail	$241	$215	$180	$165	$155	$145	$135	$125

Add $17 for walnut stock.
Add $68 for VR barrel (walnut stock only).

BAILONS GUNMAKERS LIMITED

Previous manufacturer located in Birmingham, England until 1993, when operations ceased. Inquiries regarding this trademark (including repairs) should be directed to Guthrie Consulting (see Trademark Index for listing).

RIFLES: BOLT ACTION

HUNTING RIFLE — various cals., modified Mauser bolt action, barrel length to suit from 18 to 30 in., set triggers or match, Habicht Telescope sight (magnification and reticle to suit), engraving, and types of finishes are at optional cost, prices below reflect standard rifle with no options. Imported 1986-1993.

$2,495 $2,250 $1,995 $1,775 $1,625 $1,450 $1,300

Last Mfg.'s Sug. Retail was $2,750.

BAKER, W.H. & CO.

Previous manufacturer located in Syracuse, NY circa 1878-1883.

Originally started by William H. and Ellis L. Baker circa 1878. During this time, Leroy H. and Lyman C. Smith financed the new company, W.H. Baker & Co. circa 1880, L.C. Smith bought the interest from the two Baker partners and continued production with markings reading "L. C. Smith and Co., Maker of the Baker Gun" on the rib, "Baker Pat." on the locks. Smith decided to drop the Baker name in 1883, but continued to manufacture this gun and a shotgun/rifle combination gun in Syracuse, NY until 1888. At this point, the company was sold to the Hunter Brothers and this new company, Baker Gun & Forging Co., began making both the New Baker shotguns (see separate listing below) in addition to the Ithaca gun. The company was sold to the Hunter Brothers circa 1888, and the Hunter Arms Company made L.C. Smith shotguns for approximately 60 years at which point the Marlin Firearms Company bought the business during the early 1940s.

Baker guns were originally 10 or 12 ga., and unusual in that the opening mechanism was operated by pressing forward on the front trigger. While relatively rare, most original Baker guns (including the shotgun/rifle) do not have a lot of original finish remaining. Most specimens are priced in the $400-$850 range, assuming finish is less than 10%. If condition is better than 40%, guns have to be evaluated individually for accurate pricing.

Grading	100%	98%	95%	90%	80%	70%	60%

BAKER GUN & FORGING CO.
Previous manufacturer located in Batavia, NY circa 1889-1933.

B

SHOTGUNS: SxS

Note: Original damascus guns in 80% or better condition with bright case colors will approach the values of steel barrel counterparts. Check for short chambers and make sure barrels haven't been shortened.

THE NEW BAKER — 10 or 12 ga., exposed hammers, damascus barrels, extractors.

	100%	98%	95%	90%	80%	70%	60%
	$350	$300	$260	$225	$195	$175	$150

BATAVIA SPECIAL — 12, 16, or 20 ga., 26, 28, 30, or 32 in. barrels, any standard choke, checkered pistol grip stock, sidelock, extractors.

	$385	$305	$275	$260	$250	$220	$200

BATAVIA LEADER — similar to Special, except has deluxe finish.

	$440	$360	$335	$305	$285	$265	$220
Auto ejectors	$525	$440	$415	$385	$370	$330	$305

BLACK BEAUTY — similar to Batavia Special with light engraving.

	$500	$440	$360	$335	$305	$285	$265

BLACK BEAUTY SPECIAL — similar to Leader, except has engraved, select wood.

	$745	$650	$615	$590	$550	$525	$495
Auto ejectors	$855	$760	$725	$700	$660	$635	$605

BATAVIA EJECTOR — similar to Leader, but finer finish.

	$880	$770	$745	$715	$690	$660	$635
Damascus barrels	$440	$330	$305	$275	$250	$220	$165

BAKER S GRADE — similar to Leader, but finer finish, better grade wood.

	$880	$775	$745	$715	$690	$650	$635
Auto ejectors	$1,100	$990	$965	$935	$910	$880	$745

BAKER R GRADE — similar to Leader, except scroll and game scene engraved, Krupp barrels, fancy wood.

	$1,100	$990	$965	$935	$910	$880	$745
Auto ejectors	$1,320	$1,210	$1,155	$1,100	$1,075	$1,045	$965
Damascus barrel	$550	$415	$385	$360	$330	$275	$230

PARAGON GRADE — custom order only to customer specifications.

	$1,650	$1,430	$1,320	$1,210	$1,155	$1,045	$770
Auto ejectors	$1,815	$1,595	$1,485	$1,375	$1,210	$1,100	$990

EXPERT GRADE — auto ejectors standard, overall finer grade wood and engraving.

	$2,500	$2,100	$1,850	$1,500	$1,250	$1,000	$750

DELUXE GRADE — best quality.

	$3,750	$3,250	$2,950	$2,650	$2,300	$2,000	$1,600

Add $200 for single trigger.

* *Damascus barrels* — also known as Early Paragon Grade. If condition is 50% or less subtract 50% or more. If 90% original condition or better, prices will be the same as for damascus L.C. Smith guns.

SHOTGUNS: SINGLE BARREL TRAP

Baker single barrel trap guns, although more rare than their side-by-side counterparts, are not as desirable as those models listed above. Typically, values will be 50%-75% of a side-by-side model of equal grade.

B

BALLARD RIFLE & CARTRIDGE COMPANY LLC

Current rifle manufacturer located in Cody, WY, since 1996. Dealer and consumer direct sales.

RIFLES: SINGLE SHOT

All Ballard rifles feature receivers milled from solid stock, hand polished barrels, and authentic "packed" case hardening. Many custom features are also available - contact the factory directly for availability and pricing. In addition to the standard models listed below (12 months delivery time), special order models include No. 2 Sporting, No. 4 Perfection, No. 5½ Montana, No. 6 Offhand, No. 8 Union Hill, No. 3F Gallery, and No. 3F Fine Gallery. Prices range from $1,750-$2,750, and allow 12 months for delivery.

1½ HUNTER'S RIFLE — available in 7 cals. between .22 LR - .50-70, single trigger, uncheckered stock and forearm, S style lever action, approx. 10½ lbs. 9¾ - 10½ lbs.

Mfg.'s Sug. Retail	$1,750		$1,650	$1,425	$1,250	$1,050	$925	$850	$725

1¾ FAR WEST RIFLE — available in 8 cals. between .32-40 WCF-.50-90 SS, patterned after the original Ballard Far West Model, 30 or 32 in. standard or heavyweight octagon barrel, double set triggers, ring style lever, 9¾ - 10½ lbs.

Mfg.'s Sug. Retail	$1,950		$1,850	$1,600	$1,325	$1,100	$950	$875	$750

BALLARD NO. 5 PACIFIC — available in 9 cals. between .32-40 WCF-.50-90 SS, includes under-barrel wiping rod, otherwise similar to No. 1¾ Far West Rifle.

Mfg.'s Sug. Retail	$2,475		$2,250	$1,950	$1,600	$1,325	$1,050	$925	$795

BALLARD NO. 4½ MID RANGE — available in 5 cals. between .32-40 WCF-.45-110, configured for black powder cartridge silhouette, half-round, half-octagon 30 or 32 in. standard or heavyweight barrel, single or double set triggers, pistol grip stock, full loop lever, hard rubber Ballard buttplate, Vernier tang sight. 10¾-11½ lbs.

Mfg.'s Sug. Retail	$2,750		$2,500	$2,125	$1,925	$1,575	$1,300	$1,050	$925

BALLARD NO. 7 LONG RANGE RIFLE — available in 5 cals. between .40-65 Win.-.45-110, designed for long range shooting, half-round, half-octagon 32 or 34 in. standard or heavyweight barrel, other features similar to Ballard No. 4½ Mid Range.

Mfg.'s Sug. Retail	$2,750		$2,500	$2,125	$1,925	$1,575	$1,300	$1,050	$925

BALTIMORE ARMS COMPANY

Previous manufacturer of SxS shotguns located in Baltimore, MD circa 1895-1902.

SHOTGUNS: SxS

STYLE 1 — mfg. 1895-1900, this variation does not have the improved Hollenbeck barrel locking mechanism characterizd by the eye-shaped hole in the top rib extension.

> There are 4 grades of Baltimore Arms Company shotguns: Field, Grade A, Grade B, and Grade C. Prices generally range from $295-$1,500 depending on condition and grade.

STYLE 2 — mfg. 1900-1902, this variation has the improved barrel locking mechanism and is patent date marked "FEB. 13, 1900" on the water table.

> There are 4 grades of Baltimore Arms Company shotguns: Field, Grade A, Grade B, and Grade C. Prices generally range from $295-$2,000 depending on condition and grade.

BANSNER'S GUNSMITHING SPECIALTIES (BGS)

Current custom rifle/shotgun and related components manufacturer located in Adamstown, PA since 1995. Consumer direct sales.

BANSNER'S

Grading	100%	98%	95%	90%	80%	70%	60%

RIFLES: BOLT ACTION

All Bansner's UR rifles up to approx. June 1, 1999 have either Remington 700 or Winchester post-64 claw extractor actions. After this approx. date, Bansner's started using their own proprietary actions.

UR SERIES (ULTIMATE RIFLE) — various cals. and configurations including different metal finishes and special orders, Douglas Premium Air Gauged Barrel, custom tuned trigger, Pachmayr decelerator recoil pad, various weights.

> Rather than list each model of the UR Series (11 total), the current price range is between $2,095-$2,895.
> Add $150-$190 for muzzle brake, depending on configuration.

HIGH TECH SERIES — various cals., Howa 1500 action with factory barrel and fiberglass stock. New 1997.

Mfg.'s Sug. Retail	$725		$625	$550	$500	$450	$400	$360	$330

BARRETT FIREARMS MANUFACTURING, INC.

Current manufacturer located in Murfreesboro, TN. Dealer direct sales.

RIFLES: SEMI-AUTO

MODEL 82 RIFLE — .50 BMG cal., semi-auto recoil operation, 33-37 in. barrel, 11 shot mag., 2,850 FPS muzzle velocity, scope sight only, parkerized finish, 35 lbs. Mfg. 1985-87.

		$4,350	$3,950	$3,450	$2,700	$2,150	$1,800	$1,500

Last Mfg.'s Sug. Retail for consumers was $3,180 in 1985.

This model underwent design changes since initial production. Only 115 were mfg. starting with ser. no. 100.

MODEL 82A1 — .50 BMG cal., current military configuration, variant of the original Model 82, available to civilians, back-up iron sights provided, 2 mags., and fitted hard case, 29 (new late 1989) or 33 (disc. 1989) in. barrel, 10 shot mag., 32½ lbs. for 1989 and older mfg., 28½ lbs. for 1990 mfg.

Mfg.'s Sug. Retail	$6,800		$6,375	$4,950	$4,250	$3,650	$3,150	$2,650	$2,200

Add $300 for pack-mat backpack case (new 1999).
Add $275 for camo backpack carrying case (disc.)
Add $1,150 for Swarovski 10X scope and rings.

This model boasts official U.S. rifle status following government procurement during Operation Desert Storm. In 1992, a new "arrowhead" shaped muzzle brake was introduced to reduce recoil.

MODEL 98 — .338 Lapua Mag. cal., 10 shot box mag., 24 in. match grade barrel with muzzle brake, bi-pod, 15½ lbs. Scheduled for production mid-1999.

As this edition went to press, prices had yet to be established on this model.

RIFLES: BOLT ACTION

MODEL 90 — .50 BMG cal., bolt action design, 29 in. match grade barrel with muzzle brake, 5 shot detachable box mag., includes extendible bi-pod legs, scope optional, 22 lbs. Mfg. 1990-95.

		$3,450	$2,950	$2,400	$2,150	$1,875	$1,600	$1,500

Last Mfg.'s Sug. Retail was $3,650.

Add $1,150 for Swarovski 10X scope and rings.

MODEL 95 — .50 BMG cal., bolt action design, 29 in. match grade barrel with high efficiency muzzle brake, 5 shot detachable box mag., includes extendible bi-pod legs, scope optional, 22 lbs. New 1995.

Mfg.'s Sug. Retail	$4,700		$4,175	$3,250	$2,600	$2,300	$1,875	$1,600	$1,500

Grading	100%	98%	95%	90%	80%	70%	60%

MODEL 99 — .50 BMG cal., single shot bolt action, 33 in. barrel with muzzle brake, straight through design with pistol grip and bi-pod, 25 lbs. New 1999.

Mfg.'s Sug. Retail	$2,800		$2,500	$2,150	$1,750	$1,600	$1,475	$1,350	$1,225

BAR-STO

Previous manufacturer located in 29 Palms, CA. Bar-Sto still manufactures barrels and firearms related accessories.

PISTOLS: SEMI-AUTO

BAR-STO .25 ACP PISTOL — .25 ACP cal., patterned after the Baby Browning, brushed stainless steel finish, walnut grips, approx. 250 manufactured in circa 1974.

$195 $165 $125

BAUER FIREARMS CORPORATION

Previous manufacturer located in Fraser, MI circa 1971-1984.

PISTOLS: SEMI-AUTO

BAUER .25 ACP — .25 ACP cal., 2½ in. barrel, 6 shot, fixed sights, checkered walnut or pearlite grips, mfg. 1972-1984.

$150 $130 $110 $100 $90 $80 $70

Note: These guns are identical to the Baby Browning, except stainless steel.

* **Bicentennial Model** — .25 ACP cal., engraved with buckle in display case.

$300 $200 $150

DERRINGERS

THE RABBIT — .22 LR cal. and .410 bore, combination gun, all metal construction, O/U configuration. Mfg. 1982-1984.

$125 $100 $90 $80 $70 $60 $50

BAYARD

Previously manufactured by Anciens Etablissements Pieper located in Herstal, Belgium.

Even though Bayard Models 1908, both 1923s, and 1930 were manufactured only by Anciens Etablissements Pieper of Herstal, Belgium, these pistols are listed under this heading as they are most commonly referred to by this trademark designation.

PISTOLS: SEMI-AUTO

.25 and .380 cals. are more rare than the .32s and will command a 20%+ premium above values listed below unless indicated differently.

MODEL 1908 POCKET AUTOMATIC — .25 ACP, .32 ACP, or .380 ACP cal., 6 shot, 2¼ in. barrel, fixed sights, blue, hard rubber grips.

$325 $235 $165 $100 $85 $70 $55

Add 10% for .25 ACP cal.

MODEL 1923 POCKET AUTOMATIC — .25 ACP cal., 2½ in. barrel, blue, fixed sights, checkered hard rubber grips.

$335 $295 $225 $170 $140 $125 $95

BAYARD 1923 POCKET AUTOMATIC — .32 ACP or .380 ACP cal., 6 shot, 3⁵⁄₁₆ in. barrel, fixed sights, blue, checkered hard rubber grips.

$335 $295 $225 $170 $140 $125 $95

Add 100% for .380 ACP cal.

Grading	100%	98%	95%	90%	80%	70%	60%

BAYARD 1930 POCKET AUTOMATIC — slight modification of 1923.

	$335	$250	$200	$170	$145	$120	$95

BEEMAN OUTDOOR SPORTS

Previous importer and distributor located in Santa Rosa, CA.

On April 1, 1993, Beeman Precision Arms, Inc. was split into two independent companies: Beeman Precision Airguns, division of S/R Industries (Maryland Corp.), located in Huntington Beach, CA retains worldwide distribution of Beeman airguns and accessories. Beeman Outdoor Sports, a Division of Robert's Precision Arms, Inc., located in Santa Rosa, CA distributed Feinwerkbau firearms until 1995.

Beeman Precision Arms, Inc. was a large importer, primarily specializing in high quality European air rifles and pistols. Firearms trademarks previously distributed in the U.S. include the following trademarks: Agner (disc. 1986), Erma (disc. 1985), FAS (disc. 1987), Fabarm (disc. 1985), Feinwerkbau, Korth (disc. 1990), Krico (disc. 1988), Unique (disc. 1991), and Weihrauch (disc.). These trademarks appear under their respective alphabetical headings. Air rifles and pistols will appear under those headings in the back of the book.

The firearms listed below were manufactured to Beeman specifications, and are therefore listed under the Beeman firearms heading.

PISTOLS: SEMI-AUTO

BEEMAN MP-08 — .380 ACP cal., Luger type toggle action, 3½ in. barrel, 6 shot mag., blue, 1.4 lbs. Mfg. 1968-1990.

	$395	$335	$275	$240	$185	$145	$115

Last Mfg.'s Sug. Retail was $390.

In 1988, Beeman took over importation of these two models (MP-08 and P-08). These revised models have new Luger style checkered walnut grips and 3½ in. barrel. Previous variations had plastic grips.

BEEMAN P-08 — .22 LR cal., Luger type toggle action, 8 shot mag., 3.8 in. barrel, blue, checkered walnut grips, 1.9 lbs. Mfg. 1969-1990.

	$395	$335	$275	$240	$185	$145	$115

Last Mfg.'s Sug. Retail was $390.

PISTOLS: SINGLE SHOT

MODEL SP/SPX — .22 LR cal., designed for silhouette shooting, 10 in. heavy bull barrel, blued metal parts, birchwood stocks and forearm, aperture sights, 3.9 lbs. Disc. 1994.

	$625	$550	$475	$425	$375	$330	$295

Last Mfg.'s Sug. Retail was $700.

Only a few of these models were actually delivered.

* *Model SPX Deluxe* — similar to Model SPX, except has matte chrome metal finish, hand stippled walnut grips, and Anschütz rear sight. Limited mfg. 1993-94.

	$800	$725	$650	$575	$500	$425	$350

Last Mfg.'s Sug. Retail was $900.

SP STANDARD — .22 LR cal., sidelever action, 8, 10, 12, or 15 in. barrel, adj. sights and walnut grips, single shot. Made in W. Germany. Imported 1985-86 only.

	$250	$220	$180	$170	$160	$150	$140

Last Mfg.'s Sug. Retail was $250.

Add $10 or $30 for 12 or 15 in. barrel respectively.

SP DELUXE — similar to SP Standard, except has forearm, about 3½ lbs. Made in W. Germany. Imported 1985-86 only.

	$275	$240	$200	$185	$170	$155	$145

Last Mfg.'s Sug. Retail was $300.

Add $10 or $30 for 12 or 15 in. barrel respectively.

Grading	100%	98%	95%	90%	80%	70%	60%

BEHOLLA PISTOL

Previously manufactured by Becker & Hollander located in Suhl, Germany.

B

PISTOLS: SEMI-AUTO

BEHOLLA POCKET AUTOMATIC — .32 ACP cal., 7 shot, 2.9 in. barrel, blue, serrated wood or rubber grips, mfg. 1915-1920, from 1920-1925 the same gun was mfg. by Stenda-Werke.

$225	$170	$150	$135	$120	$100	$90

BENELLI

Current manufacturer located in Urbino, Italy. Benelli USA, formed during late 1997, is currently importing all Benelli shotguns and pistols. Company headquarters are located in Accokeek, MD. Shotguns were previously imported 1983-1997 by Heckler & Koch, Inc., located in Sterling, VA. Handguns were previously imported until 1997 by European American Armory, located in Sharpes, FL, in addition to Sile Distributors, Inc., until 1995, located in New York, NY, and Saco, located in Arlington, VA.

PISTOLS: SEMI-AUTO

Models B-77, B-80, and MP3S were previously imported by Sile Distributors. Models MP90S and MP95 are currently imported by Benelli USA.

MODEL B-76 — 9mm Para. cal., selective double action, all steel, 4¼ in. barrel, 8 shot mag., 34 oz. Importation disc. in 1990.

$450	$395	$340	$295	$245	$225	$210

Last Mfg.'s Sug. Retail was $428.

MODEL B-76S TARGET — 9mm Para. cal., similar to B-76, except has 5½ in. barrel, target grips, and adj. rear sights. Importation disc. 1990.

$550	$475	$425	$395	$350	$325	$300

Last Mfg.'s Sug. Retail was $595.

MODEL B-77 — .32 ACP cal., selective double action, all steel, 4¼ in. barrel, 8 shot mag. Importation disc. 1995.

$395	$350	$295	$255	$225	$200	$180

Last Mfg.'s Sug. Retail was $385.

MODEL B-80 — .30 Luger cal., selective double action, all steel, 4¼ in. barrel, 8 shot mag., 34 oz. Importation disc. 1995.

$395	$350	$295	$255	$225	$200	$180

Last Mfg.'s Sug. Retail was $385.

MODEL B-80S TARGET — similar to B-80, except has 5½ in. barrel, target grips, and adj. rear sights. Importation disc. 1995.

$500	$450	$375	$325	$295	$275	$250

Last Mfg.'s Sug. Retail was $572.

MODEL MP3S — .32 S&W Long Wadcutter cal., target variation with 5½ in. barrel, high gloss bluing, target grips, and adj. rear sights. Importation disc. 1995.

$550	$450	$375	$325	$295	$275	$250

Last Mfg.'s Sug. Retail was $785.

MODEL MP90S WORLD CUP — .22 S (disc.), .22 LR, or .32 S&W Wadcutter cal., 4⅓ in. barrel, target pistol featuring forward assisted breech bolt mechanism, anatomic grips, and adj. weight, 5 shot mag., 2.4 lbs. Importation began 1992.

Mfg.'s Sug. Retail	$1,170	$1,025	$925	$775	$675	$600	$525	$475

Add $130 for .32 S&W Wadcutter cal.

Conversion kits were previously available for this model at an extra charge.

Grading	100%	98%	95%	90%	80%	70%	60%

MODEL 95E ATLANTA — .22 LR or .32 S&W Wadcutter cal., 4.4 in. barrel, features inertial recoiling mass system, integral Weaver style base mount, 5 or 9 shot mag., adj. trigger assembly, fully adj. sight, modular firing system, blue or matte chrome finish, smooth laminate or choice of checkered adj. (disc.) or non-adj. walnut grips, 2.5 lbs. New late 1994.

Mfg.'s Sug. Retail	$730	$635	$525	$450	$430	$380	$345	$325

Add $65 for chrome finish.

Add $130 for .32 S&W Wadcutter cal.

This model was originally designated the Model MP95.

SHOTGUNS: SEMI-AUTO, 1985-OLDER

Benelli semi-auto 3rd generation (inertia recoil) shotguns were imported starting in the late 1960s. The receivers were mfg. of light aluminum alloy - the SL-80 Model 121 had a semi-gloss, anodized black finish, the Model 123 had an ornate photo-engraved receiver, and the Model Special 80 had a brushed, white nickel-plated receiver, and the Model 121 M1 had a matte finish receiver, barrel, and stock. All SL-80 shotguns will accept 2¾ or 3 in. shells, and all SL-80 Series 12 ga. Models have interchangeable barrels (except the 121 M1) with 4 different model receivers (121, 121 M1, 123, or Special 80).

The SL-80 Series shotguns were disc. during 1985, and H&K and Benelli USA do not have parts for these guns. Approx. 50,000 SL-80 series shotguns were mfg. before discontinuance - choke markings (located on side or underneath barrel) are as follows: * full choke, ** imp. mod., *** mod., **** imp. cyl. SL-80 series guns used the same action (much different than current mfg.) and all had the split receiver design. Be aware of possible wood cracking where the barrel rests on the thin area of the forend and also on the underside of the buttstock behind trigger guard. When buying or selling a SL-Series shotgun, be aware that when comparing the SL-80 Series with the newer action Benellis (post 1985), there is a big difference between the action, design changes, and actual selling prices in today's marketplace.

100% values within this section assume NIB condition.

Subtract 5% for "SACO" marked Benelli shotguns previously imported by SACO located in Arlington, VA.

SL-80 SERIES MODEL SL-121V — 12 ga., field grade, 26, or 28 in. fixed choke VR barrel, anodized and black semi-gloss finish on lower receiver. Disc. 1985.

	$400	$340	$300	$250	$220	$195	$180

Last Mfg.'s Sug. Retail was $397.

SL-80 SERIES MODEL SL-121/SL-122 SLUG — 12 ga., features Monte Carlo stock and flat bottom Trap Grade beavertail forearm, 21¹⁄₁₆ cyl. bore barrel, fixed open ring rear iron sights and fixed front ramp, 5 shot mag., recoil pad, 7 lbs. 3 oz. Disc. 1985.

	$465	$415	$345	$290	$240	$195	$175

Last Mfg.'s Sug. Retail was $434.

SL-80 SERIES MODEL SL-123V — 12 ga., stylish field grade, receiver Ergal special aluminum alloy with photo engraving, 26 or 28 in. VR barrel with various chokes, approx. 6 lbs. 13 oz. Disc. 1985.

	$465	$415	$345	$290	$240	$195	$175

Last Mfg.'s Sug. Retail was $464.

Add $20 for trap stock, $10 for beavertail forearm and $25 for skeet barrel.

The only difference between the SL-123V and SL-121V is the photo engraved receiver. The SL-123V was at times referred to as the deluxe model when comparing it with the SL-121V. Both models were field grade shotguns.

EX-L — 12 ga., similar in appearance to the Model SL123V, except has hand-engraved receiver, very limited mfg. with unpredictable premiums over Model SL123V.

SL-80 SERIES MODEL 121 M1 POLICE/MILITARY — 12 ga. only, similar in appearance to the Super 90 M1, hardwood stock, 7 shot mag., matte metal and wood finish, most stocks had adj. lateral sling attachment inside of buttstock, 18¾ in. barrel. Disc. 1985.

	$485	$410	$375	$340	$275	$250	$185

B

Grading	100%	98%	95%	90%	80%	70%	60%

MODEL 80 SPECIAL SKEET/TRAP — 12 ga. only, 28 in. VR with mod. choke and phosphorescent bead sight, has trap/skeet Monte Carlo grade/style wood stock with recoil pad, lower receiver is nickel plated, 7 lbs. 10 oz. Disc. 1986.

	100%	98%	95%	90%	80%	70%	60%
	$500	$425	$375	$325	$275	$250	$185

Last Mfg.'s Sug. Retail was $531.

Trap guns should have high comb trap stock and trap grade forearm (not field grade/style wood). Trap guns should also be inspected carefully for internal wear before buying/selling.

SL-80 SERIES MODEL SL201 — 20 ga., 26 in. VR barrel bored mod., black anodized lower receiver, approx. 5 lbs. 10 oz. Disc. 1985.

	100%	98%	95%	90%	80%	70%	60%
	$400	$350	$295	$260	$235	$210	$180

Last Mfg.'s Sug. Retail was $399.

BRI-BENELLI SL-80 123 SLUG GUN — 12 ga. only, premium slug gun featuring SL-80 Series action and drilled and tapped rifle bored barrel by E. R. Shaw Barrel Co., assembled by BRI in the U.S., Monte Carlo stock with beavertail forend, approx. 25 guns total mfg. 1986-1987.

	100%	98%	95%	90%	80%	70%	60%
	$1,895	$1,275	$1,025	$875	$750	$625	$525

Original issue price on this model was $750-$850. These specimens are marked "BRI-Benelli" on barrel. No warranties exist on this model.

SHOTGUNS: SEMI-AUTO, 1986-NEWER

Extra barrels for the currently manufactured models listed below are typically priced in the $300-$480 range.

M1 FIELD (SUPER 90) — 12 ga., 3 in. chamber, inertia recoil operating system, alloy receiver, 21 (new 1990), 24 (new 1990), 26, or 28 in. vent. rib barrel and 3-shot mag., includes 3 screw in choke tubes, satin wood (new 1994), black polymer, or 100% Realtree Xtra brown camo. coverage (new 1997) on receiver, stock, and forearm, approx. 7.3 lbs.

Mfg.'s Sug. Retail	$900		$730	$545	$400	$350	$300	$270	$240

Add $15 for satin wood stock (26 or 28 in. barrel only).
Add $90 for Realtree Xtra brown camo. finish.

This model is available with either a short or extended magazine tube. The short tube is available on all barrel lengths - an extended mag. tube is available on 26 or 28 in. barrel only.

M1 SLUG (SUPER 90) — 12 ga. only, 3 in. Mag., semi-auto, incorporates improvements on the Benelli action, including rotating Montefeltro bolt system, 19¾ cyl. bore (disc. 1997) or 24 (new 1998) in. rifled barrel with iron sights (disc. 1997) or drilled and tapped only (new 1998), 3 (new 1998) or 7 (disc. 1997) shot mag., black fiberglass stock and forearm, 6.7 or 7.6 lbs. New 1986.

Mfg.'s Sug. Retail	$980		$800	$625	$525	$450	$375	$325	$285

Subtract 15% for 19¾ cyl. bore barrel with iron sights.

M1 DEFENSE (SUPER 90) — similar to Super 90 Slug, except has pistol grip stock, 7.1 lbs. Disc. 1998.

	100%	98%	95%	90%	80%	70%	60%
	$685	$525	$395	$325	$300	$270	$250

Last Mfg.'s Sug. Retail was $851.

Add $41 for ghost-ring sighting system.

M1 PRACTICAL (SUPER 90) — 12 ga. only, 26 in. barrel with muzzle brake, designed for IPSC events, oversized safety, speed loader, larger bolt handle, Milspec adj. ghost-ring sight and optics rail, matte metal finish, extended 9 shot mag. tube, 7.6 lbs. New 1998.

Mfg.'s Sug. Retail	$1,175		$975	$825	$695	$550	$400	$340	$300

Grading	100%	98%	95%	90%	80%	70%	60%

M1 TACTICAL (SUPER 90) — 12 ga. only, 18½ in. barrel, fixed rifle or ghost ring sighting system, available with synthetic pistol grip or standard buttstock, includes 3 choke tubes, 7 shot mag., 6½ lbs. New 1993.

Mfg.'s Sug. Retail	$875	$725	$545	$400	$350	$300	$270	$250

Add $65 for ghost-ring sighting system.
Add $10 for pistol grip stock.

* *M1 Tactical M* — similar to M1 Tactical, except has military ghost-ring sights, 7.1 lbs. New 1999.

Mfg.'s Sug. Retail	$935	$775	$575	$425	$375	$315	$275	$250

Add $10 for pistol grip stock.

M1 ENTRY (SUPER 90) — 12 ga. only, includes 14 in. barrel, choice of synthetic pistol grip or standard stock, choice of rifle or ghost-ring sights, 5 shot mag. (2 shot extension), 6.7 lbs. New 1992.

Mfg.'s Sug. Retail	$895	$735	$550	$400	$350	$300	$270	$240

Add $10 for synthetic pistol grip stock.
Add $75 for ghost-ring sighting system.

This model requires special licensing (Class III transfer).

M1 SPORTING SPECIAL (SUPER 90) — 12 ga., 18½ in. barrel, black matte finish, includes ghost ring sighting system, 6½ lbs. Mfg. 1993-97.

		$750	$555	$400	$350	$300	$270	$240

Last Mfg.'s Sug. Retail was $924.

MONTEFELTRO STANDARD HUNTER (SUPER 90) — 12 or 20 (new 1993) ga., 3 in. chamber, 21 (disc. 1997), 24, 26, or 28 in. VR barrel with 3 choke tubes, matte black metal or 100% Realtree camo (20 ga. only, new 1998) finish, checkered walnut stock and forearm with choice of high gloss (disc. 1997) or satin finish, 5 shot mag., approx. 7 lbs. New 1988.

Mfg.'s Sug. Retail	$925	$775	$575	$450	$375	$325	$295	$275

Add $85 for 100% Realtree camo finish on 20 ga. only.
Add $20 for left-hand action (12 ga., 26 or 28 in. barrel only).

A Youth/Ladies model with 12½ in. LOP was released during 1999. Values are the same as above.

* *Montefeltro Limited Edition (Super 90)* — 20 ga. only, nickel plated lower receiver with etched gold highlights, 26 in. VR barrel. Limited mfg. 1995-96.

	$1,825	$1,525	$1,225	$995	$875	$750	$625

Last Mfg.'s Sug. Retail was $2,080.

* *Montefeltro Turkey Gun* — similar to Montefeltro Standard Hunter except has 24 in. VR barrel with 3 choke tubes, satin finish wood only, 7 lbs. Imported 1989 only.

		$575	$440	$370	$330	$295	$275	$260

Last Mfg.'s Sug. Retail was $675.

* *Montefeltro Uplander* — similar to Montefeltro Turkey Gun except has 21 or 24 in. VR barrel with 3 choke tubes, satin finish wood only, 7 lbs. Mfg. 1989-92.

		$650	$550	$450	$375	$330	$295	$275

Last Mfg.'s Sug. Retail was $799.

* *Montefeltro Slug Gun* — deer gun configuration with 19¾ in. slug barrel. Disc. 1992.

		$650	$450	$375	$330	$295	$275	$260

Last Mfg.'s Sug. Retail was $799.

SPORT MODEL — 12 ga., 3 in. chamber, one piece alloy receiver, 26 or 28 in. barrel with 2 removable and interchangable carbon fiber vent. ribs, adj. butt pad and butt stock, oil finished select checkered walnut stock and forearm, "Benelli" outlined in red on matte finished receiver side, approx. 7 lbs. New 1997.

Mfg.'s Sug. Retail	$1,315	$1,075	$875	$725	$575	$475	$395	$350

B

Grading	100%	98%	95%	90%	80%	70%	60%

LEGACY MODEL — 12 or 20 (new 1999) ga., 3 in. chamber, 26 or 28 in. VR barrel, engraved nickel finished alloy lower or all alloy (20 ga. only) receiver, cartridge drop lever, select checkered walnut stock with vent. recoil pad and forearm, mfg. to commemorate the 30th Anniversary of Benelli shotgun manufacturing, 5.8 lbs. - 7.5 lbs. New 1998.

Mfg.'s Sug. Retail	$1,320	$1,075	$875	$725	$575	$475	$395	$350

BLACK EAGLE — 12 ga., 3 in. chamber, Montefeltro action, similar to Montefeltro Super 90 Standard Hunter except has black synthetic stock and forearm, 21 (disc. 1990), 24 (disc. 1990), 26, or 28 (new 1990) in. VR barrel with 3 choke tubes, right hand only. Originally imported 1989-90, resumed 1997 only.

	$825	$675	$550	$450	$375	$315	$285

Last Mfg.'s Sug. Retail was $992.

This configuration changed to competition in 1991 (see Black Eagle Competition Model).

* **Black Eagle Competition Model** — 12 ga. only, designed for competition shooting with action adj. for lighter loads, silver finished etched lower receiver, 26 or 28 in. VR barrel with 5 choke tubes and wrench provided, includes buttstock drop adjustment kit. Mfg. 1991-97.

	$1,025	$795	$675	$550	$475	$375	$300

Last Mfg.'s Sug. Retail was $1,229.

* **Black Eagle 1994 Limited Edition** — 12 ga. only, features 26 in. VR barrel with extra fancy grade checkered walnut and gold inlays on receiver sides, 1,000 mfg. 1994-95 only with special serialization.

	$1,775	$1,500	$1,225	$995	$875	$750	$625

Last Mfg.'s Sug. Retail was $2,000.

* **Black Eagle Slug Gun** — 12 ga., 24 in. rifled barrel with receiver scope mount. Imported 1990-91 only.

	$735	$625	$500	$425	$365	$315	$285

Last Mfg.'s Sug. Retail was $859.

EXECUTIVE SERIES BLACK EAGLE — 12 ga. only, features engraved all-steel lower receiver by Giovanelli, mid-rib barrel bead, extra select grade walnut, 5 choke tubes, and other accessories, choice of 21 (disc.), 24 (disc.), 26, or 28 in. VR barrel. Special order only beginning 1996.

* **Type I**

Mfg.'s Sug. Retail	$4,950		$4,450	$3,600	$2,500

* **Type II**

Mfg.'s Sug. Retail	$5,600		$4,995	$3,950	$2,950

* **Type III**

Mfg.'s Sug. Retail	$6,550		$5,850	$4,400	$3,350

SUPER BLACK EAGLE — 12 ga. only, 3½ in. chamber, updated Montefeltro action accepts all 12 ga. loads, right or left hand (new 1999) action, upper steel/lower alloy receiver, 24, 26, or 28 in. VR barrel with 5 choke tubes and wrench provided, choice of matte finish and satin wood stock, blued finish and high gloss wood finish (26 in. barrel only), or 100% coverage Realtree Xtra brown camo. finish (new 1997) on polymer stock and forearm, black synthetic stock and forearm with matte metal finish became optional 1993, vent. recoil pad, includes buttstock drop adjustment kit, approx. 7.4 lbs. New 1991.

Mfg.'s Sug. Retail	$1,200	$1,000	$850	$725	$595	$475	$425	$375

Add $100 for Realtree camo. wood/metal finish.
Add $15 for satin wood stock and forearm (26 or 28 in. barrel only).
Add $10 for left hand action for either black synthetic stock/forearm or full coverage camo finish.

* **Super Black Eagle Limited Edition** — 12 ga. only, features 26 in. VR barrel with extra fancy grade checkered walnut and gold inlays on nickel plated receiver sides, 1,000 mfg. beginning 1997 with special serialization, 7.4 lbs.

Mfg.'s Sug. Retail	$2,095		$1,825	$1,500	$1,225	$995	$875	$750	$625

Grading	100%	98%	95%	90%	80%	70%	60%

B

* **Super Black Eagle Slug Gun** — 3 in. chamber, includes 24 in. E.R. Shaw rifled barrel with adj. rifle sights, drilled and tapped receiver, matte metal finish, choice of black polymer (new 1993) or satin finished wood, 7.6 lbs. New 1992.

Mfg.'s Sug. Retail	$1,245	$1,025	$850	$675	$525	$400	$340	$300

Add $10 for wood stock.

M3 SUPER 90 — 12 ga. only, defense configuration incorporating convertible (fingertip activated) pump or semi-auto action, 19¾ in. cyl. bore barrel with rifle sights, choice of standard black polymer stock or integral pistol grip (disc. 1996, reintroduced 1999), approx. 7.3 lbs. New 1989.

Mfg.'s Sug. Retail	$1,040		$875	$675	$495	$395	$340	$300	$275

Add $10 for pistol grip stock.
Add $40 for ghost-ring sighting system.
Add $110 for folding stock (mfg. 1990-disc.) - only available as a complete gun.
Add $340 for Model 200 Laser Sight System with bracket (disc.).

SHOTGUNS: SLIDE-ACTION

NOVA — 12 ga., 3½ in. chamber, unique design allows stock and internal metal receiver "shell" to be molded in one polymer shell, Montefeltro rotating bolt, double action bars, 24, 26, or 28 in. VR barrel with choke tubes, matte metal finish, choice of black synthetic or full coverage Realtree Xtra brown camo stock and forearm with grooved hand ribs, mag. stop button in forearm, 7.8 lbs. - 8 lbs. New 1999.

Mfg.'s Sug. Retail	$357		$299	$275	$260	$245	$230	$220	$215

Add $68 for camo finish.

* **Nova Slug** — similar action to Nova, feature 18½ in. smooth bore barrel with rifle sights, black synthetic stock and forearm only, 7.2 lbs. New 1999.

Mfg.'s Sug. Retail	$285		$250	$230	$220	$210	$200	$190	$180

BENSON FIREARMS LTD.

Previous importer for guns manufactured by Aldo Uberti in Italy. Previously imported and distributed from 1987-1989 by Benson Firearms Ltd. located in Seattle, WA. Benson Firearms Ltd. combined with A. Uberti USA Inc. in early 1989 and discontinued importation.

Benson Firearms can be differentiated from other A. Uberti imports by the "Benson Firearms Seattle, WA" barrel marking.

Rather than provide a complete listing of Benson Firearms models, the following rules usually apply. Since Benson Firearms imported A. Uberti firearms, the Uberti section in this text should be referenced for current values regarding models with similar configurations. Collectibility to date has been limited on most Benson Fireams models, and as a rule, up-to-date values on this trademark are established by current importation prices of Uberti firearms. A complete listing of older Benson Firearms models can be found in Blue Book editions Eleven and Twelve.

BENTON & BROWN FIREARMS, INC.

Previous manufacturer located in Fort Worth, TX and Delhi, LA circa 1993-1996.

RIFLES: BOLT ACTION

MODEL 93 — available in 15 cals. between .243 Win. and .375 H&H Mag., patterned after the Model R-84 Blaser, takedown, free floating 22 or 24 in. barrels, right or left-hand action, checkered walnut stock and forearm, 7-8½ lbs. New 1993.

	1,875	$1,550	$1,225	$1,100	$995	$875	$750

Last Mfg.'s Sug. Retail was $2,075.

Subtract $200 for fiberglass stock.
Add $450 per interchangeable barrel.

Grading	100%	98%	95%	90%	80%	70%	60%

BERETTA, DR. FRANCO

Previous manufacturer located in Concesio (Brescia), Italy until 1994.

SHOTGUNS: O/U, BLACK DIAMOND SERIES

Black Diamond target guns were imported exclusively by Double M Shooting Sports until 1988.

FIELD MODEL — 12, 16, 20, 28 ga., or .410 bore, variety of chokes, coin finish receiver.

$595	$550	$495	$450	$395	$365	$335

Last Mfg.'s Sug. Retail was $960.

GRADE ONE — 12, 16, 20, 28 ga., or .410 bore, variety of chokes, coin finish receiver with acid etched engraving, French walnut. Trap or skeet model also available, except in 16 ga.

$1,020	$900	$810	$720	$630	$570	$525

Last Mfg.'s Sug. Retail was $1,440.

GRADE TWO — 12, 16, 20, 28 ga., or .410 bore, variety of chokes, coin finish receiver with moderate engraving, French walnut. Trap or skeet model also available, except in 16 ga.

$1,475	$1,320	$1,200	$1,080	$930	$815	$750

Last Mfg.'s Sug. Retail was $2,040.

GRADE THREE — 12, 16, 20, 28 ga., or .410 bore, variety of chokes, coin finish receiver with scrollwork engraving, French walnut. Trap or skeet model also available, except in 16 ga.

$2,100	$1,920	$1,775	$1,560	$1,410	$1,200	$1,035

Last Mfg.'s Sug. Retail was $3,000.

GRADE FOUR — 12, 16, 20, 28 ga., or .410 bore, variety of chokes, coin finish receiver with elaborate engraving, French walnut. Trap or skeet model also available, except in 16 ga.

$2,500	$2,250	$1,950	$1,650	$1,375	$1,125	$995

Last Mfg.'s Sug. Retail was $3,960.

SKEET SET — includes 12, 20, 28 ga., and .410 bore barrels, available in Grades One through Four.

Multiply values on Grades One - Four by 275% for 4 ga. Skeet sets.

SHOTGUNS: O/U, SxS, & SINGLE BARREL, RECENT MFG.

GAMMA STANDARD O & U — 12, 16, or 20 ga., 26 or 28 in. barrels, coin finish receiver with extensive engraving, Italian walnut. Add $83 with single trigger and ejectors. Imported 1984-1988.

$400	$360	$330	$300	$275	$260	$240

Last Mfg.'s Sug. Retail was $445.

* *Gamma Standard* — with interchangeable choke tubes. Importation disc. 1993.

$825	$695	$525	$425	$325	$250	$195

Last Mfg.'s Sug. Retail was $1,000.

Add 20% for auto ejectors.
Add $100 for single trigger.
Add 36% for Gamma Trap or Skeet variation (ST).

GAMMA DELUXE O & U — 12, 16, or 20 ga., 26 or 28 in. barrels, coin finish receiver with extensive engraving, Italian walnut. Add $84 with single trigger and ejectors. Imported 1984-1988.

$445	$405	$370	$350	$325	$300	$275

Last Mfg.'s Sug. Retail was $480.

* *Gamma Deluxe* — with interchangeable choke tubes. Importation disc. 1988.

$635	$570	$530	$490	$450	$420	$390

Last Mfg.'s Sug. Retail was $685.

Grading	100%	98%	95%	90%	80%	70%	60%

GAMMA TARGET O & U — 12 ga. only, SST, ejectors, Wundhammer swell pistol grip, English walnut stock and beavertail forearm. Imported 1986-1988.

	$550	$505	$455	$410	$370	$350	$325

Last Mfg.'s Sug. Retail was $595.

B

ALPHA STANDARD O & U — 12, 16, or 20 ga., 26 or 28 in. barrels, coin finish receiver with extensive engraving, Italian walnut. Imported 1984-1988, resumed 1993.

	$720	$650	$525	$450	$375	$300	$250

Last Mfg.'s Sug. Retail was $780.

Add 18% for auto ejectors.
Add $100 for single trigger.

ALPHA DELUXE O & U — 12, 16, or 20 ga., 26 or 28 in. barrels, coin finish receiver with extensive engraving, sling swivels, Italian walnut. Add $75 with single trigger and ejectors, $80 for interchangeable choke tubes (disc. 1985). Imported 1984-1988.

	$395	$355	$330	$300	$275	$250	$230

Last Mfg.'s Sug. Retail was $435.

AMERICA STANDARD O & U — .410 bore only, 26 or 28 in. barrels, coin finish receiver with extensive engraving, Italian walnut. Add $85 for Deluxe model. Imported 1984-1988.

	$305	$280	$265	$240	$215	$205	$190

Last Mfg.'s Sug. Retail was $335.

EUROPA O & U — .410 bore only, 26 in. barrels, coin finish receiver with some engraving, Italian walnut. Add $95 for Deluxe model (disc. 1985). Imported 1984-1988.

	$275	$250	$235	$220	$210	$200	$185

Last Mfg.'s Sug. Retail was $295.

FRANCIA STANDARD SxS — .410 bore only, double triggers, extractors, checkered walnut. Imported 1986-1988. Add $19 for Deluxe Model.

	$235	$220	$210	$200	$185	$175	$160

Last Mfg.'s Sug. Retail was $255.

OMEGA STANDARD SxS — 12, 16, or 20 ga., 26 or 28 in. barrels, coin finish receiver with extensive engraving, Italian walnut. Imported 1984-93.

	$780	$695	$550	$450	$375	$300	$250

Last Mfg.'s Sug. Retail was $880.

Add 32% for auto ejectors.
Add 10% for single trigger (disc. 1985).

MILANO O/U — 9mm Flobert, folding design. Imported 1993 only.

	$380	$330	$295	$250	$210	$180	$150

Last Mfg.'s Sug. Retail was $420.

VERONA/BERGAMO SxS — 9mm Flobert, folding design, Bergamo model has hammers, Verona model is hammerless. Imported 1993 only.

	$270	$225	$180	$140	$115	$95	$75

Last Mfg.'s Sug. Retail was $300.

BRESCIA SINGLE BARREL — 9mm Flobert, folding design. Imported 1993 only.

	$175	$150	$130	$110	$90	$70	$55

Last Mfg.'s Sug. Retail was $200.

BETA SINGLE BARREL — 12, 16, 20, 24, 28, 32 ga., or .410 bore, single barrel field gun, VR, chrome finish receiver, folding design. Imported 1985-93.

	$215	$185	$160	$145	$135	$125	$115

Last Mfg.'s Sug. Retail was $240.

Add 10% for VR.

Grading	100%	98%	95%	90%	80%	70%	60%

SHOTGUNS: SEMI-AUTO

ARIETE STANDARD — 12 ga. only, gas operated, 2¾ or 3 in. chamber, various barrel lengths, with or without choke tubes, aluminum receiver, checkered stock and forearm, approx. 6.9 lbs. Imported 1993 only.

	$995	$795	$525	$425	$325	$250	$195

Last Mfg.'s Sug. Retail was $1,180.

Add $20 for 3 in. mag. variation.

SHOTGUNS: SLIDE ACTION

ARIETE — 12 ga. only, 3 in. chamber, various barrel lengths without VR, twin action bars, matte finish, recoil pad. Imported 1993 only.

	$780	$695	$550	$450	$375	$300	$250

Last Mfg.'s Sug. Retail was $880.

BERETTA, PIETRO

Current manufacturer located in Brescia, Italy, 1526-present and Accokeek, MD, 1978 to date. Beretta U.S.A. Corp. was formed in 1977 and is located in Accokeek, MD. Beretta U.S.A. Corp. has been importing Beretta Firearms exclusively since 1980. 1970-1977 manufacture was imported exclusively by Garcia. Distributor sales only.

PISTOLS: SEMI-AUTO, DISC.

MODEL 1910 — .25 ACP cal., single action, 7 shot, fixed sights, wood grips, mfg. 1910-1919.

	$300	$275	$250	$195	$165	$145	$110

MODEL 1915 — 9mm Glisenti cal., Beretta's first military pistol, exaggerated slide stop, safety on rear of tang, checkered wood grips, 7 shot mag., serial range 1-16,000.

	$750	$600	$500	$400	$325	$275	$225

9mm Para. cal. is not interchangeable and potentially dangerous if interchanged with 9mm Glisenti cal.

MODEL 1915-1917 — later 7.65mm cal. variation, 8 shot mag., exaggerated slide stops, wood grips, sold commercially and to the military. A few marked "RM" were issued to the Italian Navy, ser. no. range 16,000-72,000. Mfg. 1917-1921.

	$550	$475	$400	$300	$250	$200	$165

Add 20% if Navy issue.

MODEL 1922 — successor to the Model 1915-1917, mfg. with more open slide and modern slide stop, wood or pressed metal grips, ser. no. range 200,000-243,000. Mfg. 1922-1932.

	$500	$425	$375	$275	$235	$195	$160

MODEL 1923 — 9mm Glisenti cal., 8 shot, 4 in. barrel, fixed sights, usually with pressed steel grips, less frequently smooth wood with PB emblem, occasionally slotted for shoulder stock. Most were purchased by the Italian Army and marked "RE", ser. no. range 300,000-310,400. Mfg. 1923-1926.

	$925	$800	$550	$400	$325	$275	$250

Add 25% if slotted for shoulder stock.

MODEL 1919 — .25 ACP cal., SA, 8 shot mag., offered in several variations. First type in serial range 100,000-156,000, subsequent improvement involved changing the disconnector and left panel in the range 156,000-185,000.

	$375	$325	$275	$225	$195	$165	$135

Grading	100%	98%	95%	90%	80%	70%	60%

MODEL 1926 — similar to Model 1919, except fit with wood panels bearing an encircled PB. Approx. 11,000 pistols were mfg. in ser. no. range 187,000-198,000.

	$350	$315	$270	$220	$190	$160	$130

MODEL 1926-31 — similar to Model 1926, except has small modifications in the slide, grips are no longer impressed with the PB monogram, interrupted serial range from 198,000-200,000 and 600,000-601,000.

	$325	$310	$265	$215	$190	$160	$125

MODEL 318 — .25 ACP cal., 2½ in. barrel, fixed sights, blue, modifications in the slide legend, grip configuration, and magazine floor plate. Limited production during 1936-37, in ser. no. range 609,000-615,000.

	$275	$240	$215	$180	$160	$140	$120

Add 50%-100% for engraved and plated variations if in 98%+ original condition.

Embellished variations of the Model 318 included the Model 319 (engraved/blue), Model 320 (engraved/nickel plated) and Model 321 (engraved/gold plated).

MODEL 418 — .25 ACP cal., fixed sights, similar to Model 318, but with loaded indicator and grip safety (early type is semi-circular, late type is curved), occasionally was made with an alloy frame, popular pistol mfg. 1937-1961 with minor modifications. Later guns are suffixed with the letters A, B, and C, 178,000 mfg.

	$250	$225	$200	$175	$155	$135	$120

Add 50%-100% for engraved and plated variations if in 98%+ original condition.

Embellished variations of the Model 418 included the Model 419 (engraved blue), Model 420 (engraved nickel), and Model 421 (engraved gold plated).

MODEL 1932 — 7.65mm cal., two variations including straight and curved rear grip strap, smooth wood grips bearing PB monogram (commercial) or RM monogram (Italian Navy). 8,000 mfg. in ser. no. range 400,000-408,000.

	$1,150	$900	$700	$550	$400	$350	$300

MODEL 1934 — .380 ACP cal., (9mm Kurz cal.), 3⅜ in. barrel, fixed sights, blue, plastic grips, Italy's service weapon in WWII, one of the most common Beretta pistols - over one million manufactured between 1934-1980, many of the military pistols have a parkerized finish, usually fit with metal-backed grips, later guns have an alphabetical prefix. Post war production (1946) serial numbers start with C00001.

	$375	$325	$275	$225	$195	$165	$135

Add 10% for high polish, unless post-war production.

Add 300% for post-war commercial deluxe pistols which were engraved, gold plated, and cased with a spare mag. and cleaning brush.

MODEL 1935 — similar to the Model 1934, except 7.65mm cal., 3½ in. barrel, fixed sights, blue, plastic grips, the wartime model had poor finish, a small number were fit with an experimental slide safety in the ser. no. range 500,xxx, military issue was often parkerized. 525,000 mfg. 1935-1967.

	$350	$315	$270	$220	$190	$160	$130

Add 10% for high polish, unless post-war production.

Add 300% for post-war commercial deluxe pistols which were engraved, gold plated, and cased with a spare mag. and cleaning brush.

PISTOLS: SEMI-AUTO, POST WWII MFG.

100% values on below listed models assume NIB condition.

MODEL 948 — .22 LR cal., 3½ or 6 in. barrel, fixed sights, hammer.

	$175	$150	$125	$100	$75	$60	$50

MODEL 949 OLYMPIC TARGET — .22 S or LR cal., 8¾ in. barrel, target sights, adj. barrel weights, blue, muzzle brake, checkered wood grips with thumbrest, limited mfg. 1959-1964.

	$660	$550	$495	$385	$305	$250	$195

Grading	100%	98%	95%	90%	80%	70%	60%

MODEL 950CC MINX M2 — .22 Short cal., hinged 2⅜ in. barrel, fixed sights, blue, plastic grips. Mfg. 1955-disc.

	$135	$115	$105	$95	$85	$75	$70

MODEL 950CC SPECIAL MINX M4 — similar to M2, with 4 in. barrel.

	$135	$115	$105	$95	$85	$75	$70

MODEL 950B JETFIRE — similar to M2, in .25 ACP cal..

	$135	$115	$105	$95	$85	$75	$70

MODEL 951 BRIGADIER — 9mm Para. cal., 4½ in. barrel, fixed sights, blue, plastic grips, current Italian service pistol and immediate predecessor to the M92 Series. Mfg. 1952-present.

	$285	$235	$195	$175	$150	$130	$115

Add $350 for "Egyptian" (denoted by EC prefix) or "Israeli" Model.

MODEL 20 — .25 ACP cal., double action, alloy frame, 9 shot, 2½ in. barrel, plastic or walnut grips, 10.9 oz. Disc. 1985.

	$160	$140	$125	$115	$95	$85	$75

Last Mfg.'s Sug. Retail was $214.

MODEL 70 PUMA OR COUGAR — .32 ACP or .380 ACP cal., 3½ in. barrel, fixed or adj. sights, blue, plastic grips, .32 Puma alloy frame, .380 Cougar steel frame. Disc.

	$200	$180	$165	$150	$130	$110	$90

This model is more desirable in .380 ACP cal.

MODEL 70T — .32 ACP cal., similar to Model 70, target sights. Disc.

	$275	$250	$220	$195	$165	$150	$140

MODEL 70S — .22 LR or .380 ACP cal., single action, 3½ in. barrel, 9 shot, blued finish, plastic grips, weight .22 cal. — 18 oz., .380 ACP — 23 oz., steel frame, .22 LR has adj. rear sight. Disc. 1985.

	$240	$210	$185	$170	$155	$140	$125

Last Mfg.'s Sug. Retail was $295.

MODEL 71 JAGUAR — .22 LR cal., version of Model 70, alloy frame. Disc.

	$220	$195	$180	$160	$150	$140	$110

MODEL 72 JAGUAR — similar to 71, with 6 in. barrel. Disc.

	$220	$195	$180	$160	$150	$140	$110

MODEL 76P-76W TARGET PISTOL — .22 LR cal., single action, 11 shot, steel frame, 6 in. barrel, adj. sights, blued finish, thumbrest plastic grips (76-P). Disc. 1985.

	$345	$300	$275	$245	$220	$195	$170

Last Mfg.'s Sug. Retail was $395.

Add $40 for thumbrest wood grips (Model 76-W).

MODEL 80 — .22 Short cal., target pistol with limited importation into the U.S.

	$750	$675	$595	$550	$495	$450	$395

MODEL 81P-81W — .32 ACP cal., double action, 13 shot, 3.8 in. barrel, fixed sights, blue. Imported 1976-1984.

	$300	$250	$225	$195	$175	$155	$135

Add $90 for nickel finish.
Add $20 for wood grips (W Suffix).

MODEL 82W — .32 ACP cal., double action, more compact than Model 81, 10 shot, walnut grips, 17 oz. Importation disc. 1984.

	$295	$250	$225	$195	$175	$155	$135

Add $75 for nickel finish.

Grading	100%	98%	95%	90%	80%	70%	60%

MODEL 84B — .380 ACP cal., double action, brown plastic grips, 13 shot mag., blue finish, fixed sights. Disc.

	$295	$250	$225	$195	$175	$155	$135

B

MODEL 84W-EL — similar to Model 84 only specially engraved, select walnut grips. Presentation case. Disc. 1984.

	$1,025	$770	$720	$615	$565	$520	$460

MODEL 86P-86W — .380 ACP cal. only, double action, tip-up 4⅓ in. barrel, 8 shot mag., plastic or walnut grips, 23 oz. Add $80 for walnut grips (86-W). This model was advertised, but never released.

Mfg.'s Sug. Retail was $480 in 1986.

MODEL 90 DOUBLE ACTION AUTOMATIC — .32 ACP cal., 3⅝ in. barrel, fixed sights, blue, plastic grips. Mfg. 1969-1983.

	$275	$195	$175	$155	$130	$110	$95

Add 25% if without external slide latch.

MODEL 100 — .32 ACP cal., fixed sights. Disc.

	$250	$220	$195	$165	$150	$140	$130

MODEL 101 — similar to Model 70T in .22 LR. Disc.

	$250	$220	$195	$165	$150	$140	$130

MODEL 102 — .22 LR cal., target pistol, single action, steel/alloy construction, plastic grips, 10 shot mag. with finger extension, adj. rear sight. Disc.

	$325	$250	$220	$195	$165	$150	$140

PISTOLS: SEMI-AUTO, RECENT MFG.

On Beretta's large frame pistols, alphabetical suffixes refer to the following: F Model - double/single action system with external safety decocking lever, G Model - double/single action system with external decocking only lever, D Model - double action only without safety lever, DS Model - double action only with external safety lever.

MODEL 21(A)-W BOBCAT — .22 LR or .25 ACP cal., double action, alloy frame, 7 (.22 LR) or 8 (.25 ACP) shot mag., 2.4 in. barrel, plastic or walnut (EL Model) grips, 11½ oz.

* *Blue Finish*

Mfg.'s Sug. Retail	$273		$215	$170	$140	$130	$115	$95	$85

Add $76 for engraving and wood grips (EL Model).

* *Nickel Finish*

Mfg.'s Sug. Retail	$316		$250	$210	$160	$140	$130	$115	$95

* *Matte Finish* — matte finished metal, plastic grips. Introduced 1992.

Mfg.'s Sug. Retail	$242		$195	$160	$135	$115	$95	$85	$80

This model is manufactured by Beretta U.S.A. Corp. in Accokeek, MD.

* *Lady Beretta* — .22 LR cal. only, similar to Model 21-W, except is specially serial numbered and has gold etching on top of frame and slide sides. Supplied with a blue velvet drawstring bag. 1990 issue.

	$245	$185	$160	$140	$130	$115	$100

Last Mfg.'s Sug. Retail was $285.

This model was sold exclusively by Lew Horton Distributing Co.

MODEL 71 — .22 LR cal., single action, 8 shot, 6 in. barrel, plastic grips with thumbrest, finger extension mag. Imported 1987 only.

	$190	$160	$140	$130	$115	$95	$85

Last Mfg.'s Sug. Retail was $215.

Grading	100%	98%	95%	90%	80%	70%	60%

MODEL 84P-84W CHEETAH — .380 ACP cal., single/double action semi-auto, 3.82 in. barrel, alloy frame, steel slide, 10 (C/B 1994) or 13* shot staggered mag., firing pin block, ambidextrous manual safety (also used as a decocking lever), low dot profile sights, curved trigger guard, plastic or wood grips, blue (disc.), Bruniton, or nickel finish, 23 oz.

Mfg.'s Sug. Retail	$543	$425	$340	$300	$270	$240	$210	$190

    Add $29 for wood grips (Model 84W).
    Add $72 for nickel finish (includes checkered wood grips).

* ***Model 84F*** — similar specifications to the Model 84P-84W, except patterned after the Model 92F Govt. Model, matte black Bruniton finish, squared off trigger guard, plastic or wood grips, 23 oz. Mfg. 1990 only.

		$395	$330	$300	$270	$240	$210	$190

    Last Mfg.'s Sug. Retail was $479.

MODEL 85P-85W CHEETAH — .380 ACP cal., same general specifications as the Model 84, except slimmer profile because of 8 shot straight line mag., Model 85P has plastic grips, 22 oz.

Mfg.'s Sug. Retail	$513	$400	$320	$275	$240	$210	$190	$175

    Add $60 for nickel finish (includes wood grips).
    Add $32 for wood grips with blue finish (Model 85W).

* ***Model 85F*** — similar specifications to the Model 85P-85W, except patterned after the Model 92F Govt. Model, matte black Bruniton finish, squared off trigger guard, plastic or wood grips, 21.8 oz. Mfg. in 1990 only.

		$375	$300	$270	$240	$210	$190	$175

    Last Mfg.'s Sug. Retail was $440.

    Add $25 for wood grips.

MODEL 86 CHEETAH — .380 ACP cal., double action semi-auto with 4.4 in. tip-up barrel, 8 shot mag., checkered walnut grips, matte finish, fixed sights, gold trigger, 23.3 oz. Importation began 1991.

Mfg.'s Sug. Retail	$545	$450	$360	$295	$250	$225	$190	$175

MODEL 87 CHEETAH — .22 LR cal., double action semi-auto, 7 shot mag., 3.82 or 6 in. target barrel with counterweight (disc. 1994), wood grips, 20 oz. (3.82 in. barrel). Importation began 1986.

Mfg.'s Sug. Retail	$543	$435	$345	$285	$245	$210	$190	$175

* ***Model 87 Target*** — single action only target variation of the Model 87 with 6 in. barrel, 23.3 oz. Disc. 1994.

		$415	$350	$285	$245	$210	$190	$175

    Last Mfg.'s Sug. Retail was $510.

MODEL 89 GOLD STANDARD — .22 LR cal., single action target semi-auto, matte Bruniton black finish on metal parts, 6 in. barrel, 10 shot mag., anatomical wood grips, adj. sights, 41 oz. Importation began 1988.

Mfg.'s Sug. Retail	$771	$610	$495	$400	$350	$300	$275	$250

MODEL 92 (FIRST SERIES) — Early production Model 92s had a flat slide, frame mounted safety, and mag. release button at base of pistol grip. Production of the M92 was approx. 5,000 pistols. Originally mfg. 1976. Disc.

		$550	$500	$400	$300	$255	$240	$220

MODEL 92S (SECOND SERIES) — similar to Model 92, except has an ambidextrous slide mounted firing pin safety. Disc.

		$500	$435	$360	$300	$250	$240	$220

MODEL 92SB-P (THIRD SERIES) — 9mm Luger cal., double action, 16 shot, 4.92 in. barrel, fixed sights, alloy frame, high-polish blued finish, plastic grips (Model 92SB-P), conventionally located push button magazine release, 34½ oz. Mfg. 1980-1985.

		$475	$425	$385	$345	$310	$285	$260

    Last Mfg.'s Sug. Retail was $600.

Grading	100%	98%	95%	90%	80%	70%	60%

* **Model 92SB-W** — similar to above, only with wood grips. Disc. 1985.

	$495	$430	$390	$355	$330	$290	$260

Last Mfg.'s Sug. Retail was $620.

MODEL 92SB-P COMPACT — similar to Model 92SB, except has 4.3 in. barrel, 14 shot, plastic grips (Model 92SB-P), rarer when frontstrap has curved lip, 31 oz. Disc. 1985.

	$500	$440	$385	$345	$310	$285	$260

Last Mfg.'s Sug. Retail was $620.

Add $60 for nickel finish.

* **Model 92SB-W Compact** — similar to above only with wood grips. Disc. 1985.

	$525	$465	$395	$355	$335	$300	$280

Last Mfg.'s Sug. Retail was $635.

MODEL 92D — 9mm Para. cal., double action only, otherwise similar to Model 92F, except does not have a manual safety lever, includes black plastic grips, 3 dot sights, 33.8 oz. Introduced 1992 - disc. 1998.

	$460	$360	$300	$250	$210	$190	$175

Last Mfg.'s Sug. Retail was $586.

Add $90 for Tritium (new 1994) sight system.
Add 10% for Trijicon (disc.) sights.

* **Model 92D Centurion** — 9mm Para. cal., compact variation with 4.3 in. barrel, plastic grips only, without safety, choice of 3 dot or Tritium sights. Mfg. 1994-98.

	$460	$360	$300	$250	$210	$190	$175

Last Mfg.'s Sug. Retail was $586.

Add $90 for Tritium sights.

MODEL 92F & 92FS — 9mm Para. cal., official U.S. military variation of 92 Series, 4.9 in. barrel, alloy frame, steel slide, 10 (C/B 1994) or 15★ shot mag., chamber loaded indicator, matte black Bruniton finish, squared off trigger guard to facilitate two-hand shooting, extended mag. base, choice of regular or 3 dot sights (new 1991). Model 92F-P has plastic grips. Model 92F-W has wood grips. New 1984.

Mfg.'s Sug. Retail	$629		$540	$440	$395	$360	$330	$300	$275

Add approx. $20 for checkered wood grips (Model 92F-W, disc. 1998).
Add approx. $80 for Tritium sight system (mfg. 1994-98).
Add 10% for Trijicon (disc.) sights.
Add approx. $175 for gold engraving/accenting (Model EL-3, 92F-W only, disc. 1998).
Add $395 for 9mm Competition Conversion Kit (mfg. 1992-98).

The Model 92FS incorporates a slide retaining pin engineering change not included in the Model 92F.

The U.S. military on January 15, 1985 announced that the Model 92F (M9) would replace the Colt Govt. Model .45 ACP as the standard government issue sidearm. Because of domestic political pressures, Congress requested that a new sidearm competition be conducted again in 1988. The result of this second trial was that the Department of the Army announced on May 22, 1989 that Beretta had won again. This military contract with Beretta U.S.A. Corp. involves over 320,000 Model M9 (military designation for the commercial Model 92F) being manufactured for U.S. military consumption in the 1990s. Actual delivery of commercial Model 92s began in January of 1986. Actual M9 delivery to U.S. Armed Forces has exceeded 430,000 units to date.

* **Model 92F & 92FS Stainless** — similar to Model 92F/92FS, except is mfg. from stainless steel, satin finish with plastic grips, 3 dot sights, initially released to law enforcement agencies only, this model is now commercially manufactured in quantity.

Mfg.'s Sug. Retail	$691		$575	$465	$380

Add approx. $20 for wood grips (disc. 1998).
Add approx. $90 for Trijicon (1993 only) or Tritium (mfg. 1994-98) sight system.

B

* ***Model 92F & 92FS Centurion*** — similar to Model 92F, except has compact barrel slide unit with full size frame, 4.3 in. barrel, choice of plastic or wood grips, 3 dot sight system, same length as Model 92F Compact, 10 (C/B 1994) or 15★ shot mag., 33.2 oz. Introduced 1992 - disc. 1998.

	$525	$435	$395	$365	$335	$300	$275

Last Mfg.'s Sug. Retail was $613.

Add approx. $20 for checkered walnut grips (Model 92F Wood).
Add $90 for Tritium sight system (mfg. 1994-98).
Add 10% for Trijicon sights (disc).

* ***Model 92FS Brigadier*** — similar to the Model 92FS, except has heavier slide to reduce felt recoil, wraparound rubber grips, and 3 dot sights, 35.3 oz. New 1999.

Mfg.'s Sug. Retail	$675		$580	$465	$410	$375	$335	$300	$275

* ***Model 92F-ELS*** — deluxe variation of the Model 92F featuring high polish stainless steel finish with gold highlights on trim, frame etchings, and small parts, plastic grips. Mfg. 1992-94.

$685	$550	$425	

Last Mfg.'s Sug. Retail was $790.

* ***Model 92FS 470th Anniversary Limited Edition*** — features stainless steel construction with mirror polished finish, smooth select walnut grips with inlaid gold plated medallions, gold filled engraving with Mr. Ugo Gussalli-Beretta's signature, 470th Anniversary logos, only 470 mfg. (with "1 of 470" gold filled on each gun) beginning 1999, lockable walnut case.

Mfg.'s Sug. Retail	$2,002		$1,775	$1,450	$1,050

* ***Model 92F Deluxe*** — deluxe model featuring gold or silver plating and elaborate engraving. Imported 1993-98.

$4,950	$3,750	$2,500

Last Mfg.'s Sug. Retail was $5,434.

MODEL 92F WITH U.S. M9 MARKED SLIDE/FRAME — 9mm Para. cal., approx. 2,000 mfg. with special serial no. range and "BERO" prefix.

$1,550	$1,325	$1,100	$900	$775	$675	$550

M9 LIMITED STANDARD EDITION — commercial limited edition of the U.S. Govt. M9 military pistol, features gold inscribed slide legend "The First Decade 1985-1995", Air Force or Marine Corps emblems on right slide side, 10,000 mfg. during 1995-97.

$575	$475	$425

Last Mfg.'s Sug. Retail was $643.

* ***M9 Limited Deluxe Edition*** — features checkered walnut grips, gold-plated hammer, grip screws, and mag. release button. Disc. 1997.

$650	$525	$475

Last Mfg.'s Sug. Retail was $750.

M9 SPECIAL EDITION — patterned after the U.S. Armed Forces M9, special M9-XXXX ser. no. range, one 15 shot mag., dot and post sight system, M9 military packaging including Army operator's manual, Bianchi M12 holster, mag. pouch, and web pistol belt. New 1998.

Mfg.'s Sug. Retail	$828		$715	$560	$475

MODEL 92 COMPACT L TYPE M — same features as the Model 92FS, except has 4.3 in. barrel, overall height is 5.3 in., Bruniton matte finish, choice of single/double or double action only (disc. 1998), plastic grips, single column 8 shot mag., 30.9 oz. New 1998.

Mfg.'s Sug. Retail	$629		$535	$440	$395	$365	$335	$300	$275

Add approx. $90 for Tritium sight system (disc. 1998).
Subtract approx. $25 for double action only (disc. 1998).

Grading	100%	98%	95%	90%	80%	70%	60%

MODEL 92F COMPACT — similar to Model 92F, except has 4.3 in. barrel and 13 shot mag., plastic or wood grips, 31½ oz. While temporarily suspended in 1986, production was resumed 1989-1993.

	$550	$450	$415	$375	$335	$300	$275

Last Mfg.'s Sug. Retail was $625.

> Add $20 for checkered walnut grips (Model 92F Wood).
> Add $65 for Trijicon sight system.

* Model 92F Compact "M" — similar to Model 92F Compact, except has 8 shot straight line mag., plastic grips only. Imported 1990-93.

	$550	$450	$415	$375	$335	$300	$275

Last Mfg.'s Sug. Retail was $625.

> Add $65 for Trijicon sight system.
> Approx. 1,200 92SBM Models were imported in the 1980s.

MODEL 92FS COMPACT — 9mm Para. cal., similar to Model 92 Compact L Type M, except has 10 shot staggered mag., 32 oz. New 1999.

Mfg.'s Sug. Retail	$629	$535	$440	$395	$365	$335	$300	$275

MODEL 92G — 9mm Para. cal., identical to the Model 92F, except features a spring loaded decocking lever that safely lowers the hammer allowing fire-ready when unholstering the pistol. New 1990.

> The Model 92G is sold to law enforcement agencies only and prices are slightly higher than the standard Model 92FS. This pistol has been used by French Gendarmes since 1987.

MODEL 96D — .40 S&W cal., double action only variation of the Model 96F, no safety, 3 dot sight system, 33.8 oz. Introduced 1992 - disc. 1998.

	$460	$360	$300	$250	$210	$190	$175

Last Mfg.'s Sug. Retail was $586.

> Add $90 for Tritium sight system (new 1994).
> Add $65 for Trijicon sights (disc.).

* Model 96D Centurion — similar to Model 96D, except is compact variation with 4.3 in. barrel, 3 dot sights. Mfg. 1994-98.

	$460	$360	$300	$250	$210	$190	$175

Last Mfg.'s Sug. Retail was $586.

> Add $90 for Tritium sight system.

MODEL 96F & 96FS — .40 S&W cal., similar to Model 92F, 4.9 in. barrel, plastic grips only, flared grip with grip strap serrations, Bruniton matte black finish, 3 dot sight system, 10 shot mag., 33.4 oz. Introduced 1992.

Mfg.'s Sug. Retail	$613	$525	$435	$395	$365	$335	$300	$275

> Add $91 for Tritium sight system (new 1994).
> Add 10% for Trijicon sights (disc.).

* Model 96F Compact — while advertised, this model was never mfg. (suggested retail was $640).

* Model 96F Centurion — similar to Model 96F, except has 4.3 in. barrel, 33.2 oz. New 1992.

Mfg.'s Sug. Retail	$613	$525	$435	$395	$365	$335	$300	$275

> Add $91 for Tritium sight system (new 1994).

* Model 96 Brigadier — similar to Model 96FS, except has heavier slide to reduce felt recoil, wraparound rubber grips, and 3 dot sights, 35.3 oz. New 1999.

Mfg.'s Sug. Retail	$675	$580	$465	$410	$375	$335	$300	$275

* Model 96FS Stainless — stainless variation of the Model 96FS, rubber grips, 34.4 oz. Importation began 1999.

Mfg.'s Sug. Retail	$691	$595	$465	$410

Grading	100%	98%	95%	90%	80%	70%	60%

* **Model 96 Stock** — .40 S&W cal., designed for practical shooting competition, includes accurized barrel bushing, 4.9 in. barrel, competition frame mounted ambidextrous safety, 3 interchangeable front sights, checkered front and back grip straps, aluminum grips, beveled mag. well, cased with two mags. and tool kit, 35 oz. New 1997.

Mfg.'s Sug. Retail	$1,407	$1,200	$995	$865	$725	$600	$550	$495

* **Model 96 Combat** — .40 S&W cal., single action only, similar to Model 96 Stock, except has factory tuned trigger, 4.9 (new 1998) or 5.9 in. barrel with weight and fully adj. rear target sight, aluminum or plastic grips. New 1997.

Mfg.'s Sug. Retail	$1,341	$1,150	$965	$850	$725	$600	$550	$495

   Add $293 for 5.9 in. barrel or $258 for both barrels (Combat combo).

MODEL 950 BS (JETFIRE) — .22 Short (disc. 1992) or .25 ACP cal., single action, alloy frame, 8 shot (.25 cal. only) or 6 shot mag., tip-up 2½ and 4 in. (.22 only) barrel, plastic grips, thumb safety, matte (new 1992, plastic grips only), blue, or nickel finish, 8 or 10 oz.

Mfg.'s Sug. Retail	$220	$175	$135	$115	$100	$90	$80	$70

   Add $22 for blue finish.
   Add $80 for nickel finish.

   This model is manufactured by Beretta U.S.A. Corp. in Accokeek, MD.

* **Model 950 EL** — same general specifications as Model 950 BS, only with wood grips and gold plated parts.

Mfg.'s Sug. Retail	$337	$275	$230	$200	$180	$165	$150	$135

MODEL 3032 TOMCAT — .32 ACP cal., similar to Model 21 Bobcat, except has 2.45 in. barrel, 7 shot mag., choice of matte or blue finish, plastic grips. New 1996.

Mfg.'s Sug. Retail	$326	$255	$190	$160	$135	$115	$95	$85

   Add $29 for blue finish.

MODEL 8000 COUGAR — 9mm Para. cal., single/double or DA only, short recoil system with 3.6 in. rotating barrel, 10 shot mag., fixed sights, anodized aluminum alloy frame, Bruniton matte black finish, 33.5 oz. New 1995.

Mfg.'s Sug. Retail	$646	$560	$455	$400	$365	$330	$300	$275

   Add $22 for single/double action operation.

* **Model 8000 Mini Cougar** — similar to Model 8000 Cougar, except overall height has been reduced to 4½ in. and weight is 27.6 oz. New 1998.

Mfg.'s Sug. Retail	$646	$560	$455	$400	$365	$330	$300	$275

   Add $22 for single/double action operation.

MODEL 8040 COUGAR — .40 S&W cal., single/double or DA only, short recoil system with 3.6 in. rotating barrel, 10 shot mag., fixed sights, anodized aluminum alloy frame, Bruniton matte black finish, 33.5 oz. New 1995.

Mfg.'s Sug. Retail	$646	$560	$455	$400	$365	$330	$300	$275

   Add $22 for single/double action.

* **Model 8040 Mini Cougar** — similar to Model 8040 Cougar, except overall height has been reduced to 4½ in. and weight is 27.6 oz, supplied with 8 and extended 10 shot mag. New 1998.

Mfg.'s Sug. Retail	$646	$560	$455	$400	$365	$330	$300	$275

   Add $22 for single/double action operation.

MODEL 8045 COUGAR — .45 ACP cal., 8 shot mag., otherwise similar to Models 8000 and 8040. New 1998.

Mfg.'s Sug. Retail	$696	$590	$475	$415	$375	$335	$300	$275

   Add $23 for single/double action.

Grading	100%	98%	95%	90%	80%	70%	60%

B

* ***Model 8045 Mini Cougar*** — similar to Model 8045 Cougar, except overall height has been reduced to 4½ in. and weight is 27.6 oz, supplied with 6 shot mag. Importation began 1999.

Mfg.'s Sug. Retail	**$696**	**$590**	**$475**	**$415**	**$375**	**$335**	**$300**	**$275**

   Add $23 for single/double action operation.

RIFLES: BOLT ACTION, RECENT MFG.

MODEL 500 CUSTOM — .222 Rem., .223 Rem., .243 Win., .270 Win., .30-06, or .308 Win. cal., 3 action lengths, 24 in. barrel, iron sights, checkered walnut stock with recoil pad. Importation was resumed 1988 only.

		$595	**$530**	**$450**	**$395**	**$350**	**$315**	**$275**

Last Mfg.'s Sug. Retail was $725.

* ***Model 500 S*** — similar to Model 500, except is equipped with iron sights. Imported 1986 only.

		$615	**$560**	**$460**	**$400**	**$350**	**$315**	**$275**

Last Mfg.'s Sug. Retail was $700.

* ***Model 500 DL*** — same specifications as Model 500, only better walnut and light engraving. Disc. 1986.

	$1,395	**$1,260**	**$1,000**	**$875**	**$795**	**$725**	**$650**

Last Mfg.'s Sug. Retail was $1,595.

* ***Model 500 DLS*** — similar to Model 500 DL, except is equipped with iron sights. Imported 1986 only.

	$1,420	**$1,285**	**$1,020**	**$875**	**$795**	**$725**	**$650**

Last Mfg.'s Sug. Retail was $1,625.

* ***Model 500 EELL*** — same specifications as Model 500 DL, only select walnut and more engraving. Disc. 1986.

	$1,550	**$1,260**	**$1,150**	**$1,000**	**$875**	**$800**	**$725**

Last Mfg.'s Sug. Retail was $1,745.

* ***Model 500 EELLS*** — similar to Model 500 EELL, except is equipped with iron sights. Imported 1986 only.

	$1,575	**$1,425**	**$1,200**	**$1,120**	**$875**	**$800**	**$725**

Last Mfg.'s Sug. Retail was $1,785.

MODEL 501 — .243 Win. or .308 Win. cal., medium bolt action, 6 shot, 23 in. barrel, no sights, checkered walnut stock. Disc. 1986.

		$595	**$530**	**$465**	**$395**	**$350**	**$315**	**$275**

Last Mfg.'s Sug. Retail was $665.

* ***Model 501 S*** — similar to Model 501, except is equipped with iron sights. Imported 1986 only.

		$615	**$560**	**$460**	**$400**	**$350**	**$315**	**$275**

Last Mfg.'s Sug. Retail was $700.

* ***Model 501 DL*** — same specifications as Model 501, only better walnut and light engraving. Disc. 1986.

	$1,395	**$1,260**	**$1,000**	**$875**	**$795**	**$725**	**$650**

Last Mfg.'s Sug. Retail was $1,575.

* ***Model 501 DLS*** — similar to Model 501 DL, except is equipped with iron sights. Imported 1986 only.

	$1,420	**$1,285**	**$1,020**	**$875**	**$795**	**$725**	**$650**

Last Mfg.'s Sug. Retail was $1,625.

* ***Model 501 EELL*** — same specifications as Model 501 DL, only select walnut and more engraving. Disc. 1986.

	$1,550	**$1,260**	**$1,150**	**$1,000**	**$875**	**$800**	**$725**

Last Mfg.'s Sug. Retail was $1,745.

* ***Model 501 EELLS*** — similar to Model 501 EELL, except is equipped with iron sights. Imported 1986 only.

	$1,575	**$1,425**	**$1,200**	**$1,120**	**$875**	**$800**	**$725**

Last Mfg.'s Sug. Retail was $1,785.

Grading	100%	98%	95%	90%	80%	70%	60%

MODEL 502 — .30-06, .270 or 7mm Rem. Mag. cal., long bolt action, 5 or 6 shot, 24 in. barrel, no sights, checkered walnut stock. Disc. 1986.

| | $625 | $565 | $490 | $440 | $395 | $360 | $330 |

Last Mfg.'s Sug. Retail was $710.

* *Model 502 S* — similar to Model 502, except is equipped with iron sights. Imported 1986 only.

| | $650 | $595 | $525 | $460 | $395 | $360 | $330 |

Last Mfg.'s Sug. Retail was $745.

* *Model 502 DL* — same specifications as Model 502, only better walnut and light engraving. Also available in .375 H&H Mag. Disc. 1986.

| | $1,495 | $1,310 | $1,175 | $1,025 | $900 | $775 | $695 |

Last Mfg.'s Sug. Retail was $1,640.

* *Model 502 DLS* — similar to Model 502, except is equipped with iron sights. Imported 1986 only.

| | $1,410 | $1,325 | $1,175 | $1,025 | $900 | $775 | $695 |

Last Mfg.'s Sug. Retail was $1,660.

* *Model 502 EELL* — same specifications as Model 502 DL, only select walnut and more engraving. Also available in .375 H&H Mag. Disc. 1986.

| | $1,575 | $1,425 | $1,200 | $1,120 | $875 | $800 | $725 |

Last Mfg.'s Sug. Retail was $1,785.

* *Model 502 EELLS* — similar to Model 502 EELL, except is equipped with iron sights. Imported 1986 only.

| | $1,575 | $1,425 | $1,200 | $1,120 | $875 | $800 | $725 |

Last Mfg.'s Sug. Retail was $1,785.

MATO MODEL — .270 Win., .280 Rem., .30-06, .300 Win. Mag., .338 Win. Mag., .375 H&H, or 7mm Rem. Mag. cal., 23.6 in. barrel, composite black synthetic stock, Mauser style action with controlled round feeding, 3 position safety, 3 or 4 shot detachable box mag., adj. trigger, black satin metal finish, mfg. in the U.S., 8 lbs. New 1997.

| Mfg.'s Sug. Retail | $1,560 | | $1,375 | $1,100 | $975 | $825 | $675 | $550 | $495 |

Add $355 for .375 H&H cal. (includes muzzle brake and iron sights).

* *Mato Model Deluxe* — same cals. as the standard model, features deluxe checkered walnut with ebony forend tip, 7.9 lbs. New 1997.

| Mfg.'s Sug. Retail | $2,080 | | $1,725 | $1,375 | $1,100 | $975 | $800 | $650 | $575 |

Add $390 for .375 H&H cal. (includes muzzle brake and iron sights).

RIFLES: SEMI-AUTO, RECENT MFG.

BM-59 M-1 GARAND — with original Beretta M1 receiver, only 200 imported into the U.S.

| | $1,850 | $1,475 | $1,250 | $1,000 | $895 | $850 | $800 |

Last Mfg.'s Sug. Retail was $2,080.

BM-62 — similar to BM-59, except has flash suppressor and is Italian marked.

| | $1,850 | $1,475 | $1,250 | $1,000 | $895 | $850 | $800 |

AR-70 — .222 Rem. or .223 Rem. cal., semi-auto paramilitary design rifle, 5, 8 or 30 shot mag., diopter sights, epoxy finish, 17.72 in. barrel, 8.3 lbs.

| | $1,650 | $1,500 | $1,275 | $1,050 | $875 | $725 | $600 |

Last Mfg.'s Sug. Retail was $1,065.

1989 Federal legislation banned the importation of this model into U.S.

RIFLES: CUSTOM, RECENT MFG.

Current high grade Beretta O/U and SxS rifles are sold only by premium grade franchised Beretta dealers. For a listing of these dealers, contact a Beretta Gallery (see Trademark Index).

Add $630 for Cookleigh scope mounts or $1,400 for Zeiss 4x32mm scope on Models SS06 and 455.

Grading	100%	98%	95%	90%	80%	70%	60%

B

MODEL S686/S689 SILVER SABLE O/U — .30-06, 9.3x74R, or .444 cal. (disc. 1995), boxlock action, double triggers. Importation began 1995.

Mfg.'s Sug. Retail	$4,200	$3,650	$2,950	$2,275	$1,850	$1,550	$1,275	$1,050

MODEL S689 GOLD SABLE O/U — 9.3x74R or 30-06 cal., boxlock action, nickel (disc. 1985) or case hardened (new 1986) receiver, double triggers, 23 in. barrels, auto ejectors, sling swivels, 7.7 lbs.

Mfg.'s Sug. Retail	$6,300	$5,350	$4,650	$3,900	$3,000	$2,350	$1,900	$1,600

Add $1,000 for scope and claw mounts (disc.).

MODEL S686/S689 EELL DIAMOND SABLE O/U — .30-06, 9.3x74R, or .444 Marlin cal., moderate engraving. New 1995.

Mfg.'s Sug. Retail	$13,125	$11,750	$9,100	$7,900	$6,750	$5,975	$5,325	$4,700

Add $1,000 for an extra set of 20 ga. barrels with fitting.

SSO EXPRESS O/U — .375 H&H or .458 Win. Mag. cal., sidelock action, case hardened receiver, double triggers, 23 in. barrels, auto ejectors, 11 lbs., cased. Importation disc. 1989.

	$12,500	$9,500	$8,250	$6,950	$6,100	$5,600	$4,875

Last Mfg.'s Sug. Retail was $17,533.

Add $425 for claw mounts.

* *SSO5 EXPRESS O/U* — similar to SSO Express except has more elaborate engraving and better walnut.

	$14,250	$11,750	$8,750	$7,500	$6,750	$6,100	$5,600

Last Mfg.'s Sug. Retail was $19,600.

SSO6 EXPRESS CUSTOM SIDELOCK O/U — 9.3x74R, .375 H&H, or .458 Win. Mag. cal., next to top-of-the-line sidelock double rifle, individually built to the customer's specifications, cased. New 1990.

Mfg.'s Sug. Retail	$41,225	$33,950	$19,750	$16,000	$12,250	$9,750	$8,750	$7,000

Add $5,500 for extra set of barrels.

* *SS06 EELL Gold Custom* — same cals. as SS06 Express, features multiple gold inlays and best quality wood.

Mfg.'s Sug. Retail	$48,300	$39,750	$25,000	$18,500	$14,000	$11,500	$9,000	$7,500

Add $5,900 for extra set of barrels.

MODEL 455 SIDE-BY-SIDE — .375 H&H, .416 Rigby, .458 Win. Mag., .470 NE, or .500 3 in. NE cal., top of the line sidelock double rifle, individually built to the customer's specifications, cased. New 1990.

Mfg.'s Sug. Retail	$55,650	$46,250	$36,500	$28,500	$24,000	$19,250	$16,000	$13,000

* *Model 455 EELL* — similar cals. as Model 455 SxS, top-of-the-line custom sidelock double rifle featuring every refinement of the gunmaker's art, cased.

Mfg.'s Sug. Retail	$72,450	$61,000	$44,000	$38,000	$31,000	$25,000	$21,750	$18,000

SHOTGUNS: O/U, DISC.

BL-1 — 12 ga., 26, 28, or 30 in. barrels, various chokes, boxlock, extractors, double triggers, checkered pistol grip stock. Mfg. 1968-1973.

	$385	$330	$275	$220	$190	$175	$160

BL-2 — similar to BL-1, with single selective trigger, more engraving.

	$420	$385	$360	$305	$265	$225	$185

BL-2 STAKE-OUT — riot configuration with 18 in. barrels, DT, blue finish, approx. 6,000 mfg.

	$400	$340	$275	$220	$190	$175	$160

BL-2/S — similar to BL-2, with vent. rib and speed trigger. Mfg. 1974-1976.

	$440	$385	$330	$305	$265	$225	$185

Grading	100%	98%	95%	90%	80%	70%	60%

BL-3 — O/U, similar to BL-2, with more engraving, vent. rib and ejectors, also available in 20 ga. Mfg. 1968-1976.

	$595	$550	$525	$470	$440	$385	$350

BL-3 SKEET

	$660	$605	$580	$525	$470	$415	$370

BL-3 TRAP

	$580	$520	$495	$450	$415	$375	$335

BL-4 — deluxe version of BL-3, more engraving, better wood.

	$795	$715	$625	$595	$550	$495	$450

BL-4 SKEET

	$850	$745	$675	$635	$550	$495	$450

BL-4 TRAP

	$695	$625	$575	$525	$475	$425	$360

BL-5 — higher grade version of BL-4.

	$1,050	$925	$855	$775	$700	$625	$575

BL-5 SKEET

	$1,100	$960	$875	$795	$725	$650	$595

BL-5 TRAP

	$925	$850	$775	$695	$595	$525	$465

BL-6 — boxlock with scroll engraved sideplates, ejectors, SST.

	$1,450	$1,250	$1,025	$935	$850	$765	$680

BL-6 SKEET

	$1,525	$1,300	$1,075	$975	$915	$825	$715

BL-6 TRAP

	$1,295	$1,100	$950	$885	$810	$715	$650

MODEL S55 B — 12 or 20 ga., O/U, 26, 28, or 30 in. barrels, various chokes, boxlock, extractors, selective trigger, checkered pistol grip stock. Disc.

	$550	$495	$440	$385	$330	$300	$280

MODEL S56 E — similar to S55B, with engraved receiver and auto ejectors. Disc.

	$605	$555	$515	$460	$415	$365	$330

MODEL S58 SKEET — similar to S56E, with 26 in. Bohler steel barrels, skeet bore, wide vent. rib, skeet.

	$770	$695	$630	$550	$495	$445	$395

MODEL S58 TRAP — similar to S58 Skeet, with 30 in. barrels, imp. mod. and full choke, Monte Carlo stock with pad.

	$700	$625	$550	$495	$450	$410	$365

SILVER SNIPE — 12 or 20 ga., 26, 28, or 30 in. barrels, boxlock, extractors, trigger optional, checkered pistol grip stock. Mfg. 1955-1967.

	$450	$415	$370	$330	$295	$265	$230

   ✱ *Silver Snipe SST* — with vent. rib and SST.

	$550	$495	$440	$415	$360	$330	$295

      Add 25% for ejectors.

GOLDEN SNIPE — similar to Silver Snipe, with auto ejectors and vent. rib standard.

	$660	$605	$550	$525	$470	$430	$385

   ✱ *Golden Snipe SST* — with SST.

	$715	$660	$605	$580	$525	$465	$410

Grading	100%	98%	95%	90%	80%	70%	60%

MODEL (S)57 E — higher quality version of Golden Snipe. Mfg. 1955-1967.

	100%	98%	95%	90%	80%	70%	60%
	$825	$770	$660	$635	$550	$495	$450

* *Model (S)57 E SST* — with single selective trigger.

	100%	98%	95%	90%	80%	70%	60%
	$880	$825	$715	$690	$605	$540	$495

ASE MODEL — 12 or 20 ga., light border scroll engraving, mfg. approx. 1947-1964.

	100%	98%	95%	90%	80%	70%	60%
12 ga.	$1,975	$1,600	$1,375	$1,050	$895	$750	$625
20 ga.	$3,475	$3,050	$2,675	$2,275	$1,875	$1,500	$1,175

ASEL MODEL — 12 or 20 ga., 26, 28, or 30 in. barrels, various chokes, single trigger, receiver moderately engraved, checkered pistol grip stock, auto ejectors. Mfg. 1947-1964.

	100%	98%	95%	90%	80%	70%	60%
12 ga.	$2,750	$2,375	$1,975	$1,600	$1,375	$1,050	$895
20 ga.	$4,250	$3,750	$3,300	$2,850	$2,475	$2,050	$1,650

ASEELL MODEL — 12 or 20 ga., full coverage engraving, very limited mfg.

	100%	98%	95%	90%	80%	70%	60%
12 ga.	$3,250	$2,775	$2,350	$1,925	$1,575	$1,300	$1,150
20 ga.	$7,500	$6,950	$6,150	$5,400	$4,875	$4,250	$3,500

GRADE 100 — 12 ga., 26, 28, or 30 in. barrels, any choke, sidelock, double trigger, auto ejectors, checkered pistol grip or straight stock.

	100%	98%	95%	90%	80%	70%	60%
	$1,820	$1,550	$1,300	$1,100	$900	$775	$695

MODEL 200 — similar to 100, with chrome lined bores and action parts, higher quality engraving.

	100%	98%	95%	90%	80%	70%	60%
	$2,310	$2,000	$1,870	$1,650	$1,375	$1,100	$875

MODEL 680 — 12 ga. only, competition trap and skeet model, boxlock, various chokes. Mono-trap model available. Silver finish receiver, hand engraved, premium walnut. Disc.

	100%	98%	95%	90%	80%	70%	60%
	$1,215	$1,030	$870	$790	$715	$635	$550

Add approx. $300 for 2 barrel combo. package.

SHOTGUNS: O/U, FIELD - RECENT MFG.

All models listed in this category are field grade configuration regardless of model nomenclature.

BERETTA CHOKES AND THEIR CODES (ON REAR LEFT-SIDE OF BARREL)

* designates full choke (F).

** designates improved modified choke (IM).

*** designates modified choke (M).

**** designates improved cylinder choke (IC).

FK designates skeet (SK).

***** designates cylinder bore (CYL).

MODEL 685 — 12 or 20 ga. 2¾ or 3 in. chambers, matte chromed receiver, extractors, single trigger. Disc. 1986.

	100%	98%	95%	90%	80%	70%	60%
	$595	$525	$460	$420	$360	$320	$295

Last Mfg.'s Sug. Retail was $875.

MODEL S686 ONYX — 12 or 20 ga., 3 in. chambers, boxlock action, 26 or 28 in. barrels with multi-chokes, matte finish on metal parts, choice of standard pistol grip or English straight (disc. 1999) stock with gloss (new 1999) or matte wood finish, single trigger, ejectors. New 1988.

		100%	98%	95%	90%	80%	70%	60%
Mfg.'s Sug. Retail	$1,520	$1,225	$925	$750	$600	$550	$480	$425

* *Model S686 (Onyx) Magnum* — 12 ga. only, similar to Model S686 Onyx, except has 3½ in. chambers. Mfg. 1993, reintroduced 1996.

		100%	98%	95%	90%	80%	70%	60%
Mfg.'s Sug. Retail	$1,520	$1,225	$925	$750	$600	$550	$480	$425

Grading	100%	98%	95%	90%	80%	70%	60%

* **Model 686 (Onyx) Ultralight** — 12 ga. only, 2¾ in. chambers, Ergal alloy receiver reinforced with titanium plate, electroless nickel finish receiver with game scene engraving (new 1998) or matte black finish on receiver (disc. 1997) and 26 or 28 in. VR barrels, checkered walnut stock and forearm, choke tubes, gilded lettering and logo (disc. 1997), gold SST, ejectors, very light weight, 5 lbs. 11 oz. Importation began 1992.

Mfg.'s Sug. Retail	$1,795	$1,475	$1,075	$825	$650	$575	$525	$475

* **Model 686 (Onyx) Ultralight Deluxe** — 12 ga. only, 2¾ in. chambers, similiar to 1998 Model 686 Ultralight, except has gold game scene engraving and select walnut stock and forearm. New 1998.

Mfg.'s Sug. Retail	$1,985	$1,650	$1,375	$1,175	$950	$875	$800	$695

* **Model 686 Essential** — 12 ga. only, 3 in. chambers, 26 or 28 in. VR separated barrels with choke tubes, checkered high-gloss walnut stock and forearm, matte finished metal, 6.7 lbs. Mfg. 1994-96.

	$965	$775	$600	$550	$500	$450	$415

Last Mfg.'s Sug. Retail was $1,186.

* **Model S686 Silver Essential** — 12 ga. only, 3 in. chambers, 26 or 28 in. VR separated barrels with choke tubes, checkered matte finished walnut stock and forearm, matte chrome finished receiver, 6.7 lbs. Imported 1997-98 only.

	$940	$795	$625	$550	$500	$450	$415

Last Mfg.'s Sug. Retail was $1,070.

* **Model S686 Whitewing** — 12 or 20 ga., 3 in. chambers, 26 or 28 in. VR barrels, similar to Model 686 Silver Essential, except has checkered gloss finish walnut stock and silver polished receiver with game scene engraving. New 1999.

Mfg.'s Sug. Retail	$1,255	$1,100	$975	$850	$750	$650	$525	$400

* **Model 686 (Onyx) Silver Perdiz/Silver Pigeon** — 12, 20, or 28 (new 1995) ga., 3 in. chambers (except for 28 ga.), 26 or 28 in. VR barrels with choke tubes, choice of polished (new 1999) or regular nickel finished receiver with scroll engraving, gold trigger, gloss finish checkered pistol grip or straight grip walnut stock and forearm. New 1992.

Mfg.'s Sug. Retail	$1,795	$1,475	$1,075	$895	$750	$650	$575	$525

Subtract $55 for English straight grip stock (20 ga. only).

During 1996, the model nomenclature was changed from the Silver Perdiz to the Silver Pigeon.

* **Model 686 (Onyx) Silver Perdiz/Silver Pigeon Combo** — similar to Model 686 Onyx, except is supplied with 1 set each of 20 ga. (28 in.) and 28 ga. (26 in.) barrels, polished receiver became standard 1999. Introduced 1986.

Mfg.'s Sug. Retail	$2,485	$1,975	$1,475	$1,250	$975	$875	$820	$775

MODEL 686(L) SILVER PERDIZ — 12 (disc. 1990), 20 (disc. 1990), or 28 ga., field model, boxlock action, various barrels/chokes, ejectors, single trigger, engraved silver finished receiver, special walnut, pistol or straight grip stock, fixed chokes disc. 1987. Importation disc. 1994.

	$1,100	$850	$650	$575	$525	$460	$415

Last Mfg.'s Sug. Retail was $1,355.

Subtract 10% with fixed chokes (disc.).

MODEL S686 EL GOLD PERDIZ — 12 or 20 ga., 3 in. chambers, boxlock action with floral scroll engraved sideplates, silver receiver finish, 26 or 28 (20 ga. only beginning 1997) VR in. barrels with choke tubes, gold SST, checkered walnut stock and forearm, cased, approx. 6.8 lbs. Mfg. 1992-97.

	$1,600	$1,350	$1,150	$950	$875	$800	$695

Last Mfg.'s Sug. Retail was $1,930.

MODEL S687(L) SILVER PIGEON — 12 or 20 ga., 3 in. chambers, boxlock, various barrels/chokes, ejectors, game scene engraved nickel finished receiver, gloss finished select walnut stock and forearm, approx. 6.8 lbs., fitted case is optional.

Mfg.'s Sug. Retail $2,185 $1,775 $1,425 $1,200 $975 $875 $800 $695

Subtract 10% without multi-chokes (disc.).

The "L" suffix model nomenclature was disc. 1996.

B

MODEL S687 SILVER PIGEON II — 12 ga. only, similar to Model S687 Silver Pigeon, except has deep relief engraved game scenes on receiver sides and oil finished (matte) walnut stock and forearm. New 1999.

Mfg.'s Sug. Retail $2,050 $1,675 $1,350 $1,150 $950 $850 $750 $650

MODEL 687 DU — 12 (1990 release), 20, 28 ga. (1992 release), or .410 bore, mfg. for DU dinner gun auctions and membership, prices may vary significantly from region to region.

   $1,950 $1,700 $1,450 $1,175 $895 $725 $575

MODEL 687 L ONYX — 12 or 20 ga., 3 in. chambers, same game scene engraving as standard Model 687 L, except has Onyx blackened receiver, multi-chokes standard. Mfg. 1990 only.

   $1,250 $995 $825 $700 $635 $575 $525

Last Mfg.'s Sug. Retail was $1,590.

MODEL 687 GOLDEN ONYX — 12 or 20 ga., 3 in. chambers, similar to Model 686 Onyx, except has more engraving, better walnut, and several gold inlays. Imported 1988-89 only.

   $1,375 $1,075 $875 $775 $685 $635 $575

Last Mfg.'s Sug. Retail was $1,800.

MODEL S687 EL GOLD PIGEON — same general specifications as Model 687L, except also available in 28 ga. (new 1990) or .410 (new 1990) bore, 2¾ or 3 in. chambers, boxlock with gold inlaid game scene on sideplates, highly figured walnut, and more engraving, oval nameplate, approx. 6.8 lbs, cased.

Mfg.'s Sug. Retail $3,935 $3,225 $2,400 $1,925 $1,575 $1,350 $1,150 $1,000

Add $170 for 28 ga. or .410 bore.

∗ *Model 687 EL DU* — small frame 28 ga., released 1992 for DU auctions and membership.

   $2,850 $2,200 $1,800 $1,550 $1,400 $1,200 $1,050

MODEL 687 EL ONYX — 12 or 20 ga., 3 in. chambers, simulated sidelock plates with classic scroll engraving. Mfg. 1990 only.

   $2,295 $2,000 $1,725 $1,500 $1,350 $1,150 $1,000

Last Mfg.'s Sug. Retail was $2,660.

MODEL S687 EELL DIAMOND PIGEON — 12, 20, or 28 ga., boxlock action, silver receiver with full sideplates and hand engraved game scenes, 26 or 28 (not available in 28 ga.) in. VR barrels, 3 (except 28 ga.) in. chambers and gold plated trigger, cased, multi-chokes introduced 1988, 6.8 lbs.

Mfg.'s Sug. Retail $5,375 $4,225 $3,250 $2,600 $2,050 $1,725 $1,500 $1,250

Subtract 10% if without multi-chokes.

This model is also available with a straight grip English stock at no extra charge (20 ga. only).

∗ *Model S687 EELL Combo* — includes one set of 28 ga. (26 in. barrels with multi-chokes) and one set of 20 ga. (choice of 26 or 28 multi-choke) barrels, cased.

Mfg.'s Sug. Retail $5,995 $4,950 $3,675 $2,800 $2,150 $1,750 $1,500 $1,250

Subtract 10% for fixed chokes.

Multi-chokes became standard in 1991.

Grading	100%	98%	95%	90%	80%	70%	60%

MODEL ASE 90 PIGEON — 12 ga. only, 28 in. fixed choke (IM/F) vent. barrels with VR, new design features nickel-chromium-molybdenum receiver with special hardening and cross bolt engaging 2 monobloc lugs, detachable trigger grouping, V-shaped main springs, cold hammered barrels, choice of silver or blued receiver with gold etching and no engraving, top quality checkered walnut stock and forearm with vent. recoil pad, choke tubes, 7 lbs. 13 oz., cased. Imported 1992-94.

$7,100 $5,950 $4,850 $3,950 $3,300 $2,850 $2,500
Last Mfg.'s Sug. Retail was $8,070.

SHOTGUNS: O/U, SKEET - RECENT MFG.

Full descriptions for the models listed below may be found under the corresponding model numbers in the Field Shotguns category.

MODEL S682 GOLD SKEET — 12, 20 (disc. 1991), 28 ga. (disc. 1988), or .410 bore (disc. 1988), competition skeet model, 26 (disc.) or 28 in. barrels, boxlock, skeet chokes, silver finish (disc.) or Greystone (titanium nitrate) receiver, hand engraved, premium walnut, cased. New 1984.

Mfg.'s Sug. Retail $2,850 $2,325 $1,775 $1,350 $1,075 $950 $895 $800

* *Model S682 Gold Skeet With Adj. Stock* — similar to Model S682 Gold Skeet, except has fully adj. stock, allowing the comb, drop, and cast to be adjusted per shooter. Importation began 1999.
Mfg.'s Sug. Retail $3,410 $2,975 $2,575 $2,200 $1,775 $1,350 $1,075 $950

* *Model 682 Super Skeet* — 12 ga. only, 28 in. VR barrels bored SK/SK featuring factory porting, stock has separate adj. comb cheekpiece. Mfg. 1991-95.

$2,560 $1,925 $1,650 $1,475 $1,275 $1,050 $950
Last Mfg.'s Sug. Retail was $3,006.

* *Model 682 Skeet Deluxe* — similar to Model 682, except deluxe walnut and elaborate engraving. Disc. 1986.

$2,650 $2,300 $2,100 $1,850 $1,600 $1,400 $1,200
Last Mfg.'s Sug. Retail was $3,000.

* *Model 682 2-Barrel Skeet Set* — 12 ga. only, two barrel set bored for skeet and sporting clays competition. Imported 1988 only.

$4,950 $4,200 $3,675 $3,175 $2,850 $2,500 $2,175
Last Mfg.'s Sug. Retail was $6,650.

* *Model 682 4-Ga. Skeet Set* — four barrel skeet set comes with interchangeable barrels (28 in.) in 12, 20, 28 ga.'s, and .410 bore. Imported 1985-95.

$5,000 $3,995 $3,300 $2,850 $2,500 $2,175 $1,900
Last Mfg.'s Sug. Retail was $6,037.

MODEL S686 SKEET SILVER PERDIZ/SILVER PIGEON — 12 ga. only, 28 in. VR barrels bored SK/SK, checkered walnut stock and forearm, Silver Perdiz was disc. 1996 and featured silver finish, while Silver Pigeon nomenclature began 1997 and features nickel finish, 7.6 lbs. Imported 1994-98.

$1,425 $1,295 $900 $675 $595 $550 $480
Last Mfg.'s Sug. Retail was $1,795.

MODEL S687 EELL SKEET DIAMOND PIGEON — 12 ga. only, fixed chokes, 28 in. barrels, cased.
Mfg.'s Sug. Retail $4,790 $4,025 $2,975 $2,500 $2,000 $1,800 $1,500 $1,250

* *Model S687 EELL Skeet Diamond Pigeon With Adj. Stock* — similar to Model S687 EELL Skeet Diamond Pigeon, except has fully adj. stock, allowing the comb, drop, and cast to be adjusted per shooter. Importation began 1999.
Mfg.'s Sug. Retail $5,810 $5,100 $4,550 $4,025 $3,300 $2,500 $2,000 $1,600

* *Model S687 EELL 4-Ga. Skeet Set* — four ga. skeet set, cased. Imported 1988-1998.

$7,200 $6,150 $4,750 $3,900 $3,400 $3,000 $2,700
Last Mfg.'s Sug. Retail was $8,405.

Grading	100%	98%	95%	90%	80%	70%	60%

MODEL ASE 90 GOLD SKEET — 12 ga. only, 28 in. fixed choke vent. barrels with VR, similar action and specifications as the Model ASE 90 Pigeon, except has more elaborate hand scroll engraving and extra fine wood, 7.6 lbs., cased. New 1992.

Mfg.'s Sug. Retail	$12,060	$10,500	$6,650	$5,250	$4,150	$3,300	$2,850	$2,500

B

SHOTGUNS: O/U, SPORTING CLAYS - RECENT MFG.

These variations have been specifically designed for sporting clay target shooting. All models listed below have 3 in. chambers, unless specified otherwise. Full descriptions for the models listed below may be found under the corresponding model numbers in the Field Shotguns category.

MODEL S682 CONTINENTAL COURSE — 12 ga. only, 2¾ in. chambers, 28 or 30 (disc. 1995) in. VR barrels with multi-chokes, designed for English Sporting Clays courses, previously was Model Super Sport with tapered rib, cased. Mfg. 1993-97.

	$1,950	$1,575	$1,275	$1,000	$895	$795	$725

Last Mfg.'s Sug. Retail was $2,345.

MODEL S682 GOLD SPORTING — 12 or 20 (mfg. 1992-94) ga., similar specifications to Model 682 Skeet, 2¾ in. chambers, 28, 30 (new 1989), or 31 (new 1997) in. unported or ported (new 1995) VR barrels, except over-field stock dimensions and hand engraved silver (disc.) or Greystone (titanium nitrate) finished receiver, cased, 7.6 lbs. Multi-chokes are standard.

Mfg.'s Sug. Retail	$3,000	$2,500	$1,875	$1,375	$1,075	$950	$895	$800

Add $135 for ported barrels (28 or 30 in. only).
Add $865 for extra set of 12 ga. barrels (combo. package - mfg. 1990-94).

MODEL 682 SUPER SPORTING — 12 ga. only, 2¾ in. chambers, 28 or 30 in. VR ported (new 1993) barrels with multi-chokes and tapered rib, otherwise similar to Model 682 Sporting, cased, 7.6 lbs. Imported 1989-95.

	$2,515	$1,975	$1,425	$1,050	$950	$895	$800

Last Mfg.'s Sug. Retail was $3,017.

Beginning 1993, this model featured a special fully adj. stock and LOP.

MODEL 686 SPORTING/SPECIAL SPORTING — 12 ga. only, 3 in. chambers, deluxe checkered walnut stock and forearm with over-field dimensions, 28 or 30 (new 1991) in. barrels only, multi-chokes standard. Mfg. 1987-92.

	$1,600	$1,300	$1,050	$925	$875	$775	$695

Last Mfg.'s Sug. Retail was $1,940.

The Model 686 Special Sporting is marked "Model S686 Special", and the barrels are marked "Sporting".

* *Model S686 Silver Perdiz/Silver Pigeon Sporting* — 12 or 20 ga., 28 or 30 in. VR barrels with multi-chokes, 7.7 lbs. New 1993.

Mfg.'s Sug. Retail	$1,850	$1,475	$1,025	$750	$600	$525	$460	$415

Until 1994, this model was named the Model 686 Hunter Sport. Between 1994-95, this model was named the S686 Silver Perdiz, and beginning 1996, this model was again renamed to the 686 Silver Pigeon Sporting.

* *Model 686 Silver Perdiz/S686 Silver Pigeon Sporting Combo* — 12 ga., includes extra set of 30 in. barrels. Model 686 Silver Perdiz was manufactured 1991-95, Model S686 Silver Pigeon introduced 1997.

Mfg.'s Sug. Retail	$2,210	$1,925	$1,700	$1,475	$1,250	$1,025	$900	$800

Last Mfg.'s Sug. Retail was $2,687 for the 686 Silver Perdiz Combo.

MODEL 686 COLLECTION SPORT — 12 ga. only, features multi-colored checkered wood stock and forearm, 28 in. VR barrels, 7.7 lbs. Mfg. 1996 only.

	$1,225	$900	$695	$575	$525	$460	$415

Last Mfg.'s Sug. Retail was $1,499.

Grading	100%	98%	95%	90%	80%	70%	60%

MODEL 686 ONYX SPORTING — 12 ga. only, 28 or 30 in. vent. fixed choke barrels with VR, high luster blue finish with gold lettering on receiver sides. Mfg. 1992 only.

			$1,600	$1,300	$1,050	$925	$875	$775	$695

Last Mfg.'s Sug. Retail was $1,940.

* *Model 686 Onyx Sporting w/Multi-chokes* — 12 ga. only, 28 or 30 in. VR barrels with multi-chokes, matte wood finish, choice of semi-matte black (disc. 1998) or polished black receiver with "P. Beretta" engraved in gold, 7.7 lbs. New 1993.

Mfg.'s Sug. Retail $1,575 $1,275 $950 $750 $595 $525 $460 $415

* *Model 686 English Course* — 12 ga. only, features 28 in. VR barrels and special reverse tapered VR with special sighting plane designed for English courses. Mfg. 1991-92.

$1,675 $1,350 $1,050 $925 $875 $775 $695

Last Mfg.'s Sug. Retail was $2,015.

MODEL S687(L) SILVER PERDIZ/SILVER PIGEON SPORTING — 12 or 20 ga. only, deluxe checkered walnut stock and forearm with over-field dimensions, 28 or 30 (12 ga. only) in. barrels, multi-chokes standard. New 1987.

Mfg.'s Sug. Retail $2,270 $1,925 $1,500 $1,200 $975 $875 $775 $675

Add $750 for extra set of 12 ga. barrels (combo. package - new 1991).

* *Model 687 English Course* — 12 ga. only, features 28 in. VR barrels and special reverse tapered VR with special sighting plane designed for English courses. Mfg. 1991-92.

$2,225 $1,750 $1,325 $1,050 $950 $895 $800

Last Mfg.'s Sug. Retail was $2,630.

* *Model S687 Silver Pigeon II Sporting* — 12 ga. only, features deep relief game scene engraving on receiver sides, matte oil finished select walnut stock and forearm, 28 or 30 in. barrels with choke tube, 7.7 lbs. Importation began 1999.

Mfg.'s Sug. Retail $2,105 $1,800 $1,400 $1,150 $950 $850 $775 $675

MODEL S687 EL GOLD PIGEON SPORTING — 12 ga. only, 28 or 30 in. VR barrels with multi-chokes, 7.7 lbs. New 1993.

Mfg.'s Sug. Retail $4,015 $3,600 $3,050 $2,600 $2,200 $1,850 $1,500 $1,250

MODEL S687 EELL DIAMOND PIGEON SPORTING — 12 or 20 (disc. 1992) ga. only, deluxe checkered walnut stock and forearm with over-field dimensions, 28 or 30 (new 1995) in. barrels only, multi-chokes standard, cased, 7.6 lbs. New 1987.

Mfg.'s Sug. Retail $5,515 $4,575 $3,425 $2,600 $2,050 $1,725 $1,500 $1,250

Subtract $735 for 2¾ in. chambers (28 in. barrels only).
Add $875 for extra set of barrels (combo. package - 1990 mfg. only).

MODEL ASE 90 GOLD SPORTING CLAYS — 12 ga. only, 28, 30, or 31 (new 1997) in. vent. barrels with VR, similar action and specifications to Model ASE 90 Pigeon, 7.5 lbs., cased. New 1992.

Mfg.'s Sug. Retail $12,145 $8,750 $6,675 $5,250 $4,150 $3,300 $2,850 $2,500

SHOTGUNS: O/U, TRAP - RECENT MFG.

Full descriptions for the models listed below may be found under the corresponding model numbers in the Field Shotguns category.

MODEL S682 GOLD TRAP (GOLD X) — 12 ga. only, competition trap model, Greystone (titanium nitrate) or Bruniton finish (matte black, disc.), 30 or 32 in. barrels with or w/o choke tubes (became standard 1996), adj. trigger, supplied with case, 8.8 lbs. New 1985.

Mfg.'s Sug. Retail $3,000 $2,325 $1,750 $1,350 $1,175 $950 $895 $800

Subtract 10% without choke tubes.
Subtract 5% if without multi-chokes.

Grading	100%	98%	95%	90%	80%	70%	60%

* **Model S682 Mono/Top Combo (Gold X)** — 12 ga. only, supplied with mono under or upper single barrel and O/U barrel sets, multi-chokes became standard 1996. Otherwise same specifications as Model S682 Gold Trap. Cased.

  Mfg.'s Sug. Retail   **$3,845**   **$3,075** **$2,325** **$1,875** **$1,575** **$1,375** **$1,200** **$1,000**
  Add $115 for combo package (includes extra set of 34 in. barrels).
  Subtract 5% if without multi-chokes.

* **Model S682 Gold Trap Adjustable Stock** — 12 ga. only, features Monte Carlo style stock with adj. comb, stock drop and cast may also be adjusted, 30 or 32 in. barrels, 8.8 lbs. New 1998.

  Mfg.'s Sug. Retail   **$3,510**   **$2,950** **$2,300** **$1,875** **$1,575** **$1,375** **$1,200** **$1,000**
  Add $960 for combo package (includes extra set of 34 in. barrels).

* **Model 682 Mono** — single under-barrel trap model, high post vent. rib, 32 or 34 in. barrel. Imported 1985-1988.

  $1,530 **$1,400** **$1,200** **$1,025** **$925** **$875** **$775**
  Last Mfg.'s Sug. Retail was $1,890.

* **Model S682 Gold Live Bird (Pigeon Trap)** — 12 ga. only, includes features for international style pigeon and competition shooters including international style stock, standard or flat (new 1995) VR, and mid-rib sights, Greystone (new 1991) or matte black (disc.) metal finish, semi-gloss American walnut stock, light scroll engraving, sliding trigger, includes multi-chokes, cased, 8.8 lbs. Imported 1990-98.

  $2,250 **$1,700** **$1,325** **$1,175** **$950** **$895** **$800**
  Last Mfg.'s Sug. Retail was $2,910.
  Add $71 for tapered flat rib (disc. 1995).

* **Model 682 Gold X Trap Mono (Top Single)** — 12 ga. only, single over-barrel trap model, 32 or 34 in. barrel. Imported 1986-95.

  $2,275 **$1,775** **$1,325** **$1,050** **$950** **$895** **$800**
  Last Mfg.'s Sug. Retail was $2,734.
  Subtract 5% if without multi-chokes.
  Multi-chokes became standard in 1989.

* **Model 682 Unsingle** — 12 ga. only, single under barrel trap model with 32 in. high post VR, choke tubes. Imported 1992-94.

  $2,225 **$1,750** **$1,325** **$1,050** **$950** **$895** **$800**
  Last Mfg.'s Sug. Retail was $2,650.

MODEL S682 (GOLD X) SUPER TRAP — 12 ga. only, competition trap model, 30 in. barrels, step tapered rib, factory porting, LOP, and separate stock cheekpiece are adjustable, cased. Imported 1991-95.

  $2,300 **$1,800** **$1,400** **$1,075** **$950** **$895** **$800**
  Last Mfg.'s Sug. Retail was $2,907.
  Add $69 for multi-chokes.

* **Model S682 Top Mono Super Trap (Gold X)** — 12 ga. only, single over-barrel trap model, 32 or 34 in. barrel with choice of fixed or multi-chokes. Imported 1991-95.

  $2,485 **$1,850** **$1,400** **$1,095** **$975** **$900** **$800**
  Last Mfg.'s Sug. Retail was $3,083.
  Add $73 for multi-chokes (32 in. barrels only) or 34 in. barrels.

* **Model S682 Gold Super Trap Top Combo (Gold X)** — 12 ga. only, supplied with upper single barrel and O/U barrel sets. Otherwise same specifications as Model 682 Super Trap, multi-chokes became standard 1996, cased. Imported 1991-97.

  $3,300 **$2,400** **$1,925** **$1,650** **$1,375** **$1,200** **$1,000**
  Last Mfg.'s Sug. Retail was $4,040.

MODEL S686 SILVER PIGEON TRAP — 12 ga. only, low-profile action, 30 in. VR barrels with ³⁄₈ in. flat rib, matte wood finish, nickel finished receiver with scroll engraving, 7.7 lbs. New 1997.

  Mfg.'s Sug. Retail   **$1,795**   **$1,425** **$1,000** **$725** **$600** **$525** **$460** **$415**

Grading	100%	98%	95%	90%	80%	70%	60%

✱ **Model S686 Trap Top Mono** — 12 ga. only, single over-barrel trap model, 32 or 34 in. barrel with multi-chokes, gloss wood finish. 8.14 lbs. New 1998.

Mfg.'s Sug. Retail $1,795 $1,425 $1,000 $725 $600 $525 $460 $415

MODEL 686 INTERNATIONAL — 12 ga. only, 30 in. VR barrels bored IM/F, checkered walnut stock and forearm. Imported 1994 only.

$1,075 $800 $625 $550 $500 $460 $415
Last Mfg.'s Sug. Retail was $1,300.

MODEL S687 EELL DIAMOND PIGEON (X TRAP) — 12 ga. only, boxlock action with engraved black (new 1992) or silver (disc. 1991) finished side plates, Monte Carlo stock with recoil pad, 30 in. barrels with choke tubes, cased, 8.8 lbs.

Mfg.'s Sug. Retail $4,815 $4,050 $3,175 $2,475 $2,050 $1,725 $1,500 $1,250

✱ **Model S687 EELL Diamond Pigeon Trap Top Mono** — 12 ga. only, single over-barrel trap model, 32 or 34 in. barrel, fixed chokes standard. Imported 1988-92, resumed 1996.

Mfg.'s Sug. Retail $5,060 $4,250 $3,300 $2,575 $2,050 $1,725 $1,500 $1,250
Add $45 for multi-chokes.

✱ **Model S687 EELL Diamond Pigeon X Bottom Mono Trap Combo** — 12 ga. only, supplied with 30 or 32 in. O/U barrels and a mono trap bottom barrel. Imported 1986-1988, resumed 1994-95.

$4,250 $3,300 $3,400 $3,000 $2,775 $2,550 $2,250
Last Mfg.'s Sug. Retail was $4,984.

Add $53 for multi-chokes.

✱ **Model S687 EELL Diamond Pigeon X Top Mono Trap Combo** — 12 ga. only, supplied with 30 or 32 in. O/U barrels and a mono trap upper barrel, multi-chokes became standard 1995. Mfg. 1988-1997.

$5,075 $4,025 $3,300 $2,875 $2,500 $2,175 $1,900
Last Mfg.'s Sug. Retail was $6,070.

Subtract 5% if without multi-chokes.

MODEL ASE 90 GOLD TRAP — 12 ga. only, 30 in. vent. barrels with VR, similar action and specifications to Model ASE 90 Pigeon, 8.2 lbs., cased with extra trigger group, multi-chokes became standard 1995. New 1992.

Mfg.'s Sug. Retail $12,145 $10,550 $6,675 $5,250 $4,150 $3,300 $2,850 $2,500
Subtract 5% if without multi-chokes.
Add $3,910 for Trap Combo package.

SHOTGUNS: O/U, CUSTOM GRADE - RECENT MFG.

Current high grade Beretta O/U and SxS shotguns are sold only by premium grade franchised Beretta dealers. For a listing of these dealers, contact a Beretta Gallery (see Trademark Index).

Where applicable, Beretta's new SST, with selector switch built into safety, is more desirable than older manufacture utilizing the disc. single, non-selective trigger.

JUBILEE — 12, 20, 28 ga., or .410 bore, choice of Field or Sporting Clays configuration, supplied with case. New 1998.

Mfg.'s Sug. Retail $12,750 $10,950 $7,300 $5,650 $4,500 $3,100 $2,780 $2,500
Add $1,000 for small gauges (20, 28 ga., or .410 bore)

SO-2 — 12 ga., 26-30 in. barrels, sidelock, any chokes, vent. rib, auto ejectors, SST, checkered stock in various configurations (field, skeet, or trap), grades differ in wood, engraving, and finish, cased. SO series mfg. 1948-disc.

$3,750 $3,000 $2,600 $2,200 $1,900 $1,675 $1,475

SO-3 — 2nd grade of the SO series. Disc. 1987.

$4,650 $4,000 $3,600 $3,200 $2,800 $2,400 $2,000
Last Mfg.'s Sug. Retail was $8,250.

SO-3 EL — grade-up from SO-3 with better wood and engraving. Disc. 1985.

$5,750 $5,000 $4,500 $4,000 $3,600 $3,200 $2,800
Last Mfg.'s Sug. Retail was $8,100.

Grading	100%	98%	95%	90%	80%	70%	60%

SO-3 EELL — best quality model, custom specifications, choice of engraving motifs. Disc. 1987.

| | **$8,995** | **$7,975** | **$6,700** | **$5,750** | **$5,000** | **$4,500** | **$3,950** |

Last Mfg.'s Sug. Retail was $11,625.

Add $1,000/set of O/U barrels.

SO-4 — 12 ga., sidelock, available in field, skeet, or trap configurations, custom specs., fluorescent sights, wide rib, cased. Disc. 1987.

| | **$5,750** | **$5,000** | **$4,500** | **$4,000** | **$3,600** | **$3,200** | **$2,800** |

Last Mfg.'s Sug. Retail was $8,700.

Add $1,000 for extra set of O/U barrels.

ASE GOLD — see individual models with descriptions under Skeet, Sporting Clays, and Trap category names.

ASE 90 DE LUXE — 12 ga. only, specifications furnished by customer, Sporting or Field Model, cased. New 1996.

| Mfg.'s Sug. Retail | **$20,500** | | **$18,750** | **$15,250** | **$12,750** | **$10,000** | **$8,750** | **$7,250** | **$6,000** |

SO-5 COMPETITION — best quality O/U, extensively engraved, top quality checkered walnut stock (semi-pistol grip) and forearm, available in either Trap, Skeet, or Sporting configurations, limited importation, leather cased.

| Mfg.'s Sug. Retail | **$19,500** | | **$16,200** | **$10,000** | **$8,250** | **$6,850** | **$5,950** | **$5,200** | **$4,500** |

Add $5,900 for extra set of barrels.
Add $3,500 for Trap Combo set (disc.).

SO-5 EELL — next to top-of-the-line model, available in either Trap, Skeet, or Sporting Clays configuration, custom built to customer dimensions. Importation disc. 1988.

| | **$12,750** | **$10,000** | **$8,500** | **$7,500** | **$6,500** | **$5,500** | **$4,500** |

Last Mfg.'s Sug. Retail was $21,750.

SO-6 COMPETITION — 12 ga. only high quality O/U, extensively scroll engraved, top quality checkered walnut stock (semi-pistol grip) and forearm, choice of Field (reintroduced during 1998), Trap, Skeet, or Sporting Clays configuration, built to customer specifications, limited importation, leather cased.

| Mfg.'s Sug. Retail | **$26,775** | | **$22,500** | **$15,000** | **$11,000** | **$8,500** | **$7,450** | **$6,350** | **$5,100** |

Add $5,900 for extra set of barrels.

SO-6 EELL — 12 ga., current next to top-of-the-line model, field dimensions, custom built to customer specifications, leather cased.

| Mfg.'s Sug. Retail | **$42,800** | | **$36,000** | **$24,500** | **$20,000** | **$15,250** | **$12,000** | **$9,000** | **$7,250** |

Add $5,950 for extra set of barrels.

SO-6 EESS — 12 ga., features green enamel sideplates with diamond inlays. New 1998.

Please contact the Beretta Gallery directly for current pricing information on this model.

* **SO-6 EESS w/o Diamonds** — features red or blue enamel sideplates, w/o diamonds. New 1998.

| Mfg.'s Sug. Retail | **$42,800** | | **$36,000** | **$24,500** | **$20,000** | **$15,250** | **$12,000** | **$9,000** | **$7,250** |

SO-9 — 12, 20, 28 ga., or .410 bore, top-of-the-line sidelock model, 1990 was the first time the SO series was offered in smaller gauges, 28 ga. or .410 bore models have smaller proportionate frames. New 1990.

| Mfg.'s Sug. Retail | **$46,725** | | **$38,250** | **$27,500** | **$20,500** | **$16,000** | **$12,000** | **$9,200** | **$7,000** |

Add $5,900 for extra set of barrels.

SHOTGUNS: SxS, RECENT MFG.

MODEL 409 PB — 12, 16, 20, or 28 ga., 27, 28, and 30 in. barrels, various chokes, double triggers, plain extractors, checkered pistol grip stock. Mfg. 1934-1964.

| | **$770** | **$660** | **$605** | **$550** | **$495** | **$440** | **$385** |

Add 20% for 20 ga.
Add 100% for 28 ga.

Grading	100%	98%	95%	90%	80%	70%	60%

MODEL 410 E — higher quality, auto ejector version of 409 PB.

	100%	98%	95%	90%	80%	70%	60%
12 ga.	$1,275	$1,000	$895	$775	$675	$575	$475
20 ga.	$1,750	$1,550	$1,275	$1,000	$895	$775	$675
28 ga.	$4,250	$3,775	$3,300	$2,800	$2,275	$1,800	$1,450

MODEL 410 — similar to 410 E, except 10 ga. Mag., 32 in. barrel, full choke, heavier construction, mfg. 1934-1981.

	100%	98%	95%	90%	80%	70%	60%
	$1,200	$995	$880	$795	$700	$625	$550

MODEL 411 E — similar to 409 PB, with false sideplates and finer finishing. Mfg. 1934-1964.

	100%	98%	95%	90%	80%	70%	60%
12 ga.	$1,950	$1,600	$1,325	$1,050	$895	$775	$675
20 ga.	$2,500	$2,200	$1,650	$1,275	$1,000	$895	$775
28 ga.	$4,250	$3,775	$3,300	$2,800	$2,275	$1,800	$1,450

MODEL 424-426 — 12 and 20 ga. (Model 426 only), 26 and 28 in. barrels, various chokes, boxlock, extractors, double triggers, light engraving, checkered straight stock. Add $115 for Model 426.

	100%	98%	95%	90%	80%	70%	60%
	$1,395	$1,125	$950	$800	$675	$600	$550

MODEL 426 E — similar to 424, with auto ejectors, SST, select wood and more intricate engraving, silver pigeon inlay. Disc. 1983.

	100%	98%	95%	90%	80%	70%	60%
	$1,850	$1,575	$1,250	$1,025	$875	$700	$625

MODEL 625 — 12 or 20 ga., 26-30 in. barrels, various chokes, boxlock, extractors, DTs or SST, light engraving, checkered straight stock. Imported 1984-1986.

	100%	98%	95%	90%	80%	70%	60%
	$795	$745	$660	$580	$530	$485	$440

Last Mfg.'s Sug. Retail was $835.

Add 20% for 20 ga.
Add 15% for SST.

MODEL GR-2 — 12 and 20 ga.'s, 26 and 28 in. barrels, various chokes, boxlock, extractors, double triggers, checkered pistol grip stock. Mfg. 1968-1976.

	100%	98%	95%	90%	80%	70%	60%
	$660	$605	$550	$495	$385	$330	$275

MODEL GR-3 — similar to GR-2, with select wood and more engraving. Mfg. 1968-1976.

	100%	98%	95%	90%	80%	70%	60%
	$770	$715	$640	$560	$475	$425	$375

MODEL GR-4 — similar to GR-3, with auto ejectors. Mfg. 1968-1976.

	100%	98%	95%	90%	80%	70%	60%
	$1,250	$1,075	$900	$775	$675	$600	$500

SILVER HAWK — 12 ga. Mag. & 10 ga. Mag. with double triggers and extractors. Disc. 1967.

	100%	98%	95%	90%	80%	70%	60%
	$495	$380	$325	$275	$250	$225	$200

Add $100 for 10 ga.

SILVER HAWK FEATHERWEIGHT — 12, 16, 20, or 28 ga., 26-32 in. barrels, high solid rib, various chokes, single or double triggers, checkered pistol grip stock, beavertail forearm. Disc. 1967.

	100%	98%	95%	90%	80%	70%	60%
	$495	$440	$415	$385	$360	$330	$275
Single trigger	$550	$495	$440	$415	$385	$360	$330

* *Model 470 Silver Hawk* — 12 or 20 ga., 3 in. chambers, 26 or 28 in. barrels with choice of fixed or multi-chokes (new 1999), satin chrome receiver finish, selector lever on forearm allows either automatic ejection or mechanical extraction, straight grip stock with matte finish, 5.9 - 6.5 lbs. New 1998.

		100%	98%	95%	90%	80%	70%	60%
Mfg.'s Sug. Retail	$3,630	$2,775	$2,025	$1,575	$1,250	$1,000	$925	$850

Add $125 for multi-chokes (new 1999).

MODEL 626 FIELD — 12 or 20 (disc. 1987) ga., 2¾ in. chambers, 26 and 28 in. barrels, various chokes, boxlock, ejectors, single trigger, moderate engraving, pistol grip or straight checkered stock. Imported 1984-1988.

	100%	98%	95%	90%	80%	70%	60%
	$995	$895	$795	$685	$595	$540	$490

Last Mfg.'s Sug. Retail was $995.

Add 20% for 20 ga.

Grading	100%	98%	95%	90%	80%	70%	60%

MODEL 626 ONYX — 12 or 20 ga., 3 in. chambers, 26 or 28 (new 1990) in. VR barrels with multi-chokes, matte finished metal parts, select checkered walnut stock and forearm. Imported 1988-1993.

	100%	98%	95%	90%	80%	70%	60%
	$1,425	$1,125	$850	$750	$685	$595	$540

Last Mfg.'s Sug. Retail was $1,870.

* ***Model 626 Onyx Magnum*** — 12 ga. only, 3½ in. chambers. Mfg. 1990-92.

	100%	98%	95%	90%	80%	70%	60%
	$1,425	$1,175	$900	$800	$700	$600	$550

Last Mfg.'s Sug. Retail was $1,870.

Add 20% for 20 ga.

MODEL 627 EL FIELD — 12 and 20 (disc. 1987) ga., 2¾ (disc. 1990) or 3 in. (became standard in 1991) chambers, 26 and 28 in. barrels, various chokes, boxlock, ejectors, single trigger, extensive engraving, pistol grip or straight checkered stock, cased. Imported 1985-1993.

	100%	98%	95%	90%	80%	70%	60%
	$2,725	$2,150	$1,775	$1,500	$1,350	$1,150	$1,000

Last Mfg.'s Sug. Retail was $3,270.

Subtract 5% for fixed chokes and 2¾ in. chambers.

* ***Model 627 EL Sport*** — similar to Model 627 EL Field, except 12 ga. only, knurled rib, sporting clays dimensions. Importation disc. 1988.

	100%	98%	95%	90%	80%	70%	60%
	$2,725	$2,150	$1,775	$1,500	$1,350	$1,150	$1,000

Last Mfg.'s Sug. Retail was $1,995.

MODEL 627 EELL — 12 or 20 (disc. 1987) ga., 2¾ (disc.) or 3 (12 ga. only) in. chambers, 26 or 28 in. barrels, various chokes, boxlock, ejectors, single trigger, elaborate engraving, pistol grip or straight English checkered stock, cased. Imported 1985-1993.

	100%	98%	95%	90%	80%	70%	60%
	$4,600	$3,850	$3,300	$2,850	$2,500	$2,175	$1,900

Last Mfg.'s Sug. Retail was $5,405.

Subtract 5% if fixed chokes only.

Multi-chokes became standard in 1991.

SHOTGUNS: SxS, CUSTOM GRADE

Current high grade Beretta O/U and SxS shotguns are sold only by premium grade franchised Beretta dealers. For a listing of these dealers, contact a Beretta Gallery (see Trademark Index).

Where applicable, Beretta's new SST, with selector switch built into safety, is more desirable than older manufacture utilizing the disc. single, non-selective trigger.

MODEL 450 SERIES — 12 ga. only, built to individual customer order, various levels of engraving. Disc.

* ***Model 450 EL*** — incorporates H&H type sidelocks.

	100%	98%	95%	90%	80%	70%	60%
	$7,500	$6,950	$5,750	$5,250	$4,700	$4,200	$3,600

* ***Model 450 EELL*** — features third fastener with H&H type sidelocks.

	100%	98%	95%	90%	80%	70%	60%
	$8,000	$7,350	$6,000	$5,500	$4,850	$4,300	$3,750

SO-6 — same general specifications and embellishments as the SO series O/U guns, but SxS. Mfg. 1948-1982.

	100%	98%	95%	90%	80%	70%	60%
	$5,900	$5,500	$5,280	$5,060	$4,840	$4,400	$3,850

SO-7 — top of the line SxS, finest quality wood, more elaborate engraving. Disc.

	100%	98%	95%	90%	80%	70%	60%
	$8,250	$7,700	$7,150	$6,600	$6,050	$5,500	$4,620

MODEL 451 SERIES — 12 ga., totally hand-made, sidelock action, ejectors, scroll engraving. Custom made to order with fitted luggage case, various grades have increasing embellishments in EL Models.

* ***Model 451*** — disc. 1987.

	100%	98%	95%	90%	80%	70%	60%
	$6,000	$5,200	$4,875	$4,600	$4,300	$3,995	$3,600

Last Mfg.'s Sug. Retail was $12,375.

Grading	100%	98%	95%	90%	80%	70%	60%

B

* **Model 451 E** — 12 ga. only, double triggers, specifications furnished by individual customer. Imported 1989 only.

  $14,650 $10,950 $9,750 $8,500 $7,800 $6,750 $5,800
  Last Mfg.'s Sug. Retail was $20,467.

  Add $4,000 for extra set of barrels.
  Add $750 for SST.

* **Model 451 EL** — disc. 1984.

  $6,450 $5,400 $4,875 $4,600 $4,300 $4,000 $3,600

* **Model 451 EELL** — previous top-of-the-line model, choice of engraving motifs per customer specifications. Disc. 1987, reintroduced 1989 only.

  $17,500 $12,950 $11,000 $8,500 $7,800 $6,750 $5,950
  Last Mfg.'s Sug. Retail in 1989 was $24,367.
  Last Mfg.'s Sug. Retail in 1987 was $14,925.

MODEL 452 CUSTOM — 12 ga. only, next to top-of-the-line side-by side shotgun featuring H&H style detachable locks, built to customer's specifications, leather cased. New 1990.

  Mfg.'s Sug. Retail $33,500 $27,750 $19,750 $15,500 $11,500 $8,750 $6,650 $5,500
  Add $5,900 for extra set of barrels.

* **Model 452 EELL Custom** — 12 ga. only, top-of-the-line custom sidelock model featuring every refinement, built to customer's specifications, leather cased. Importation began 1992.

  Mfg.'s Sug. Retail $43,500 $36,750 $26,250 $20,000 $15,250 $11,500 $8,950 $6,750
  Add $5,900 for extra set of barrels.

MODEL 470 EL CUSTOM — 12 or 20 ga., mfg. by Beretta's custom shop per individual order. New 1999.

  Mfg.'s Sug. Retail $6,150 $5,000 $3,625 $2,750 $2,150 $1,725 $1,500 $1,200
  Add $125 for 20 ga.

* **Model 470 EELL** — similar to Model 470 EL Custom, except has select walnut and more engraving. New 1999.

  Mfg.'s Sug. Retail $12,800 $10,975 $7,325 $5,650 $4,500 $3,100 $2,780 $2,500
  Add $125 for 20 ga.

SHOTGUNS: SINGLE BARREL, DISC.

MARK II TRAP — 12 ga., 32 or 34 in. wide vent. rib, full choke, boxlock with auto ejector, Monte Carlo stock, recoil pad. Mfg. 1972-1976.

  $550 $450 $400 $360 $330 $295 $260

MODEL FS-1 SINGLE BARREL — 12, 16, 20, 28 ga., or .410 bore, 26 or 28 in. barrels, full choke, checkered semi-pistol grip, under lever break open, folds to length of barrel (also known as Companion).

  $175 $150 $125 $110 $100 $90 $80

TR-1 TRAP — 12 ga., 32 in. full choke barrel, under lever break open, Monte Carlo pistol grip stock with pad, engraved. Mfg. 1968-1971.

  $275 $250 $220 $195 $140 $110 $100

TR-2 TRAP — similar to TR-1, with high rib, mfg. 1969-1973.

  $290 $260 $230 $205 $150 $120 $110

MODEL 412 — 12, 20, 28 ga., or .410 bore, monobloc construction, folding action, sling swivels, checkered walnut stock and forearm, 5 lbs. Importation disc. 1988.

  $190 $170 $125 $100 $85 $70 $60
  Last Mfg.'s Sug. Retail was $215.

Grading	100%	98%	95%	90%	80%	70%	60%

SHOTGUNS: SLIDE ACTION, DISC.

MODEL SL-2 — 12 ga., 26, 28, or 30 in. barrels, various chokes, vent. rib, checkered pistol grip stock. Mfg. 1968-1971.

	$300	$275	$250	$220	$195	$165	$140

SILVER PIGEON — 12 ga., various chokes, light engraving.

	$250	$200	$175	$160	$150	$140	$130

GOLD PIGEON — 12 ga., various chokes, vent. rib, engraved. Add $200 for deluxe models.

	$475	$375	$310	$275	$240	$215	$195

RUBY PIGEON — 12 ga., various chokes, vent. rib, elaborately engraved, special deluxe walnut.

	$600	$475	$395	$350	$295	$260	$230

SHOTGUNS: SEMI-AUTO, DISC.

SILVER LARK — 12 ga., various chokes.

	$295	$260	$240	$220	$200	$185	$170

GOLD LARK — 12 ga., vent. rib, light scroll engraving, select walnut.

	$480	$400	$325	$260	$230	$210	$195

RUBY LARK — 12 ga., vent. rib, heavy engraving, deluxe walnut.

	$675	$550	$475	$395	$350	$295	$260

MODEL AL-1 — 12 and 20 ga., semi-auto gas operated, 26, 28, and 30 in. plain barrel, various chokes, checkered pistol grip stock. Mfg. 1971-1973.

	$385	$360	$330	$305	$250	$195	$165

MODEL AL-2 — 12 or 20 ga., 26, 28, or 30 in. barrels, vent. rib, various chokes, gas operated, checkered pistol grip stock. Mfg. 1973-1975.

	$330	$305	$275	$250	$220	$195	$165

MODEL AL-2 SKEET — similar to AL-2, with 26 in. wide rib skeet bored barrel, mfg. 1973-1975.

	$395	$360	$320	$275	$220	$200	$185

MODEL AL-2 TRAP — similar to AL-2, with 30 in. full choke barrel, wide rib, Monte Carlo stock, with recoil pad. Mfg. 1973-1975.

	$375	$345	$315	$285	$250	$195	$165

MODEL AL-2 MAGNUM — 12 or 20 ga., 3 in. chamber, heavier action bar, 28 and 30 in. mod. or full choke. Mfg. 1973-1975.

	$415	$385	$330	$275	$250	$230	$210

MODEL AL-3 — continuation of the AL-2 series. Mfg. 1975-1976.

	100%	98%	95%	90%	80%	70%	60%
Field grade	$395	$360	$330	$260	$240	$220	$190
Magnum grade	$425	$385	$330	$275	$250	$230	$210
Skeet grade	$400	$360	$330	$260	$240	$220	$190
Trap grade	$385	$350	$295	$250	$225	$210	$185

MODEL AL-3 DELUXE TRAP — similar to AL-3, with fully engraved receiver, premium grade wood. Mfg. 1975-1976.

	$770	$715	$660	$605	$550	$495	$440

SHOTGUNS: SEMI-AUTO, RECENT MFG.

It is possible on some of the models listed below to have production variances occur, including different engraving motifs, stock configurations and specifications, finishes, etc. These have occurred when Beretta changed from production of one model to another.

Grading	100%	98%	95%	90%	80%	70%	60%

Also, some European and English distributors have sold their excess inventory through Beretta U.S.A., creating additional variations/configurations that are not normally imported domestically. While sometimes rare, these specimens typically do not command premiums over Beretta's domestic models.

BERETTA CHOKES AND THEIR CODES (ON REAR LEFT-SIDE OF BARREL)

* designates full choke (F).

** designates improved modified choke (IM).

*** designates modified choke (M).

**** designates improved cylinder choke (IC).

FK designates skeet (SK).

***** designates cylinder bore (CYL).

MODEL 1200 FIELD — 12 ga., inertia recoil system, 28 in. VR barrels with multi-chokes, checkered European walnut stock and forearm (pre-1989), matte black polymer stock and forearm (starting 1989), recoil pad, 4 shot mag., approx. 8 lbs. Imported 1984-1989.

	100%	98%	95%	90%	80%	70%	60%
	$475	$415	$350	$295	$250	$225	$200

Last Mfg.'s Sug. Retail was $580.

* **Model 1200 Riot** — 12 ga. only, 2¾ or 3 in. chamber, 20 in. cyl. bore barrel with iron sights, extended mag. Imported 1989-90 only.

	100%	98%	95%	90%	80%	70%	60%
	$525	$425	$350	$295	$250	$225	$200

Last Mfg.'s Sug. Retail was $660.

MODEL 1201 FIELD MAGNUM — 12 ga., 3 in. chamber, 24, 26, or 28 in. VR barrel with multi-chokes (2), matte black polymer stock and forearm. Imported 1989-94.

	100%	98%	95%	90%	80%	70%	60%
	$500	$395	$340	$285	$250	$225	$200

Last Mfg.'s Sug. Retail was $625.

The Model 1201 can be differentiated from the Model 1200 by stock spacers to adjust length.

* **Model 1201 FP Riot** — 12 ga., riot configuration featuring 18 (new 1997) or 20 (disc. 1996) in. cylinder bore barrel, 5 shot mag, choice of adj. rifle sights (disc.), Tritium sights (disc. 1998), or ghost ring (new 1999) sights, matte wood and metal finish, 6.3 lbs. New 1991.

Mfg.'s Sug. Retail	$860	$675	$500	$375	$325	$265	$225	$200

Add $80 for Tritium sights (mfg. 1997-98).
Add $45 for pistol grip configuration (Model 1201 FPG3 - mfg. 1994 only).

MODEL 300/301 — continuation of the AL-3 series, scroll engraved receiver. Mfg. 1977-1982.

	100%	98%	95%	90%	80%	70%	60%
Field grade	$395	$360	$330	$260	$240	$220	$190
Magnum grade	$425	$385	$330	$275	$250	$230	$210
Skeet grade	$400	$360	$330	$260	$240	$220	$190
Trap grade	$385	$350	$295	$250	$225	$210	$185

Beretta changed model nomenclature rapidly during the Model 300 Series. In approx. 10 months, the evolution of this model had progressed from the 300 to 303 Series. Beginning with the Model 303, all receivers were milled with a 3 in. ejection port window.

MODEL 301 SLUG GUN — 22 in. barrel, with sights. Disc.

	100%	98%	95%	90%	80%	70%	60%
	$395	$360	$330	$305	$265	$230	$190

MODEL 302 — 12 or 20 ga., self-compensating gas operation semi-auto, designed for both 2¾ and 3 in. shells, available with interchangeable chokes, slug barrel, trap and skeet models (disc.), VR, mag. cut-off. Mfg. 1982-1987. This model was superceded by the Model 303.

	100%	98%	95%	90%	80%	70%	60%
	$395	$365	$340	$310	$280	$255	$225

Last Mfg.'s Sug. Retail was $480.

Add $30 for multi-choke set.

Grading	100%	98%	95%	90%	80%	70%	60%

* **Model 302 Super Lusso** — same specifications as Model A302, but includes hand engraved receiver, many gold plated parts, and stock and forearm made from presentation grade walnut. Disc. 1986.

	$2,150	$1,950	$1,750	$1,550	$1,300	$1,050	$895

Last Mfg.'s Sug. Retail was $2,500.

MODEL A-303 FIELD — 12 (disc. 1993) or 20 ga., 2¾ or 3 in. chambers, same gas operation as the Model 302, 26 or 28 in. VR barrel, high-strength alloy receiver, select wood with choice pistol grip or straight English stock, beavertail forearm, multi-chokes became standard 1987. Disc. 1996.

		$655	$465	$380	$335	$300	$270	$240

Last Mfg.'s Sug. Retail was $799.

Subtract 10% without multi-chokes.
Subtract $20 for straight grip English stock.

* **A-303 Upland** — 12 (disc. 1993) or 20 ga., 2¾ or 3 in. chamber, 24 in. VR barrel with multi-chokes, English style straight stock, approx. 7 lbs. Importation began 1989. Disc. 1996.

$640	$465	$380	$335	$300	$270	$240

Last Mfg.'s Sug. Retail was $772.

* **A-303 Waterfowl/Turkey** — 12 ga. only, 3 in. chamber, choice of 24, 26, 28, or 30 in. VR barrel, matte finished wood and metal, multi-chokes are standard. Imported 1991 only.

$540	$450	$395	$350	$300	$270	$240

Last Mfg.'s Sug. Retail was $665.

* **A-303 Sporting** — 12 (disc. 1994) or 20 (new 1991) ga. only, 2¾ in. chambers, sporting clay dimensions, 28 or 30 (12 ga. only) in. VR barrel with multi-chokes. Mfg. 1988-96.

$685	$510	$445	$375	$325	$300	$275

Last Mfg.'s Sug. Retail was $822.

* **A-303 Skeet** — 12 (disc. 1994) or 20 ga., 26 in. VR barrel with fixed skeet choking. Importation disc. 1995.

$615	$440	$375	$335	$300	$270	$240

Last Mfg.'s Sug. Retail was $736.

* **A-303 Super Skeet** — 12 ga. only, 28 in. VR fixed choke barrel, features factory porting, adj. LOP, and adj. separate cheekpiece on stock. Mfg. 1991-92.

$975	$750	$625	$500	$425	$365	$300

Last Mfg.'s Sug. Retail was $1,160.

* **A-303 Trap** — 12 ga. only, 30 or 32 in. VR barrel with fixed choking or multi-chokes. Importation disc. 1994.

$615	$425	$360	$325	$280	$250	$220

Last Mfg.'s Sug. Retail was $735.

Add $40 for multi-chokes (with Monte Carlo stock).

* **A-303 Super Trap** — 12 ga. only, 30 or 32 in. VR multi-choke barrel with step tapered rib, features factory porting, adj. LOP, and adj. separate cheekpiece on stock. Mfg. 1991-92.

$1,025	$775	$625	$500	$425	$365	$300

Last Mfg.'s Sug. Retail was $1,210.

* **A-303 Slug** — 12 or 20 ga., 3 in. chamber (12 ga. only), 22 in. cylinder bore barrel, iron sights. Importation disc. 1991.

$540	$425	$360	$325	$295	$265	$240

Last Mfg.'s Sug. Retail was $665.

* **A-303 Youth** — 20 ga. only, 2¾ or 3 (disc.) in. chamber, 24 in. VR barrel with multi-chokes, shortened stock, approx. 6 lbs. Mfg. 1988-96.

$640	$450	$375	$330	$300	$270	$240

Last Mfg.'s Sug. Retail was $772.

Grading	100%	98%	95%	90%	80%	70%	60%

MODEL AL390 FIELD SILVER MALLARD — 12 or 20 (new 1997) ga. only, 3 in. chamber, features new gas system that will accept all 2¾ and 3 in. shotshells, single stainless steel piston with self regulating valve, mag. cut-off on left side of receiver, 22 slug (12 ga. only, new 1994), 24, 26, 28, or 30 (12 ga. only) in. VR barrel with Mobilchoke system, choice of gloss or matte (includes sling swivels) wood finish on lightly engraved receiver, adj. checkered walnut stock, gold trigger, 6.4 (20 ga.) or 7.2 (12 ga.) lbs. New 1992.

Mfg.'s Sug. Retail	$860	$700	$525	$415	$350	$300	$270	$240

  Add $25 for 20 ga.
  Add $25 for 26, 28, or 30 in. barrel (12 ga. only).

  Beginning 1997, Beretta introduced the "AL" Series of the 390, which is the lightweight variation of the 390. Prior to 1997, this model was designated the A390 Series.

* **Model AL390 Field Deluxe Gold Mallard** — similar to Model 390 Field, except has gold accents on receiver frame, including a gold inlaid snipe, setter, and P. Beretta signature, deluxe walnut, 7.2 lbs. New 1993.

Mfg.'s Sug. Retail	$1,025	$850	$575	$460	$400	$360	$320	$285

  Add $30 for 20 ga.
  Add $30 for 26, 28, or 30 in. barrel (12 ga. only).

* **Model AL390 Silver Mallard Synthetic** — 12 ga. only, 3 in. chamber, 24, 26, 28, or 30 in. barrel with multi-choke, black synthetic stock and forearm with sling swivels, matte finish, approx. 7.2 lbs. New 1996.

Mfg.'s Sug. Retail	$885	$715	$535	$425	$350	$300	$270	$240

* **Model AL390 Silver Mallard Camouflage** — 12 ga. only, 3 in. chamber, Advantage camo finish on entire gun, 24 or 28 in. VR barrel with choke tubes, synthetic stock and forearm, 7.2 lbs. New 1997.

Mfg.'s Sug. Retail	$1,020	$825	$600	$450	$375	$300	$270	$240

* **Model AL390 Silver Mallard Slug** — 12 ga. only, 3 in. chamber, 22 in. barrel with slug choke, gloss wood finish, adj. rear sight, approx. 6.8 or 7.4 (Model A390) lbs. Mfg. 1995-97.

			$700	$525	$415	$350	$300	$270	$240

                                  Last Mfg.'s Sug. Retail was $860.

* **Model AL390 Silver Mallard Youth** — 20 ga. only, 3 in. chamber, gloss wood finish, 24 in. VR barrel only with choke tubes, features youth stock dimensions, 6.4 lbs. New 1997.

Mfg.'s Sug. Retail	$885	$715	$550	$425	$350	$300	$270	$240

MODEL AL390 SPORT SPORTING — 12 or 20 (new 1997) ga., 3 in. chamber, designed for sporting clays competition, similar to Model 390 Sport Skeet, 28 or 30 (12 ga. only) in. VR ported or unported barrel with choke tube, 6.8 (20 ga.) or 7.6 (12 ga.) lbs. Importation began 1995.

Mfg.'s Sug. Retail	$925	$775	$540	$425	$350	$300	$270	$240

  Add $70 for ported barrel.

* **Model AL390 Sport Sporting Collection** — 12 or 20 (Youth Model) ga., 3 in. chamber, 26 (20 ga. only), 28 in. VR barrel with multi-choke, features multi-colored, gloss finished stock and forearm, 6.7 (20 ga.) or 7.6 (12 ga.) lbs. New 1998.

Mfg.'s Sug. Retail	$965	$795	$575	$450	$365	$315	$275	$240

  The 20 ga. in this model is a youth model with 13½ LOP.

* **Model AL390 Sport Gold Sporting** — 12 ga. only, 28 or 30 in. VR barrel with multi-chokes, gloss finished wood, gold engraved receiver, 7.6 lbs. New 1997.

Mfg.'s Sug. Retail	$1,145	$925	$725	$575	$525	$495	$460	$425

* **Model AL390 Sport Diamond Sporting** — 12 ga. only, 3 in. chamber, silver sided receiver with multiple gold inlays, EELL quality stock and forearm with oil finish, matte 28 or 30 in. barrel with multi-chokes, oval nameplate on stock, 7.6 lbs. New 1998.

Mfg.'s Sug. Retail	$3,075	$2,750	$2,400	$2,050	$1,800	$1,600	$1,400	$1,175

Grading	100%	98%	95%	90%	80%	70%	60%

* *Model AL390 Sport Sporting Youth* — 20 ga. only, 3 in. chamber, matte finished checkered stock and forearm, 26 in. VR barrel only with choke tubes, features youth stock dimensions (13½ LOP), 6.7 lbs. Imported 1997-98 only.

	$755	$525	$400	$350	$300	$270	$240

Last Mfg.'s Sug. Retail was $900.

MODEL AL390 SPORT SKEET — 12 ga. only, 3 in. chamber, 26 (disc.) or 28 in. SK bored VR barrel, matte finish on wood and metal, black rubber recoil pad, 7.6 lbs. Importation began 1995.

Mfg.'s Sug. Retail	$890	$745	$525	$415	$350	$300	$270	$240

Add $105 for ported barrel (28 in. only).

* *Model AL390 Sport Super Skeet* — 12 ga. only, 28 in. skeet choke VR ported barrels, includes adj. stock comb and LOP (using 3 different recoil pads) approx. 8.1 lbs. New 1993.

Mfg.'s Sug. Retail	$1,160	$965	$750	$565	$525	$475	$440	$400

MODEL AL390 SPORT TRAP — 12 ga. only, 3 in. chamber, 30 or 32 in. VR barrel, matte finish on wood and metal, black rubber recoil pad, 7.8 or 8¼ (A390) lbs. Importation began 1995.

Mfg.'s Sug. Retail	$890	$740	$525	$415	$360	$300	$270	$240

Add $35 for multi-choke barrel (30 in. only).

Add approx. $105 for ported barrel (fixed 30 in. or multi-choke).

* *Model AL390 Sport Super Trap* — 12 ga. only, 30 or 32 in. VR multi-choke ported barrels, adj. stock comb and LOP, approx. 8 lbs. Mfg. 1993-97.

	$995	$775	$600	$550	$495	$460	$425

Last Mfg.'s Sug. Retail was $1,215.

MODEL ES100 PINTAIL (VICTORIA) — 12 ga., 3 in. chamber, uses Montefeltro short action, 24, 26, or 28 (new 1999) in. VR barrel, choice of matte finished wood (disc. 1998) or black synthetic stock and forearm (new 1999), includes sling swivels, 7.3 lbs. New 1993.

Mfg.'s Sug. Retail	$815	$675	$465	$385	$330	$280	$250	$230

In 1999, this model was renamed the ES 100 Pintail (with synthetic stock).

* *ES100 Rifled Slug (Pintail Rifled Slug)* — 12 ga., 3 in. chamber, 24 in. rifled barrel with drilled and tapped upper receiver, barrel and upper receiver are permanently joined, anti-glare matte black metal finish, choice of matte finished wood (disc. 1998) or black synthetic (new 1999) stock and forearm, includes swivels, 7 lbs. New 1998.

Mfg.'s Sug. Retail	$985	$825	$700	$500	$400	$325	$280	$250

In 1999, the model nomenclature changed from Pintail Rifled Slug to ES100 Rifled Slug.

* *Pintail Slug (Victoria)* — 12 ga. only, 24 in. slug barrel, includes rifle sights and rifle choke tubes, 7 lbs. Imported 1993-95.

	$595	$425	$360	$325	$280	$250	$230

Last Mfg.'s Sug. Retail was $700.

COMMEMORATIVES

MODEL A-303 DUCKS UNLIMITED — 12 or 20 ga., D.U. serialization, 5,500 mfg. in 12 ga. 1986-87, 3,500 mfg. in 20 ga. 1987-88.

12 ga.	$575	$450	$350
20 ga.	$675	$475	$375

These D.U. Models had no retail pricing from Beretta. Rather, they were auctioned off at D.U. dinners, and as a result, prices could vary substantially from region to region.

MODEL 687 O/U SHOTGUN TERCENTENNIAL — 12 ga., comes with S.S.T. and ejectors. Limited production, only 300 manufactured.

	$2,500	$1,950	$1,400

MODEL 84 PISTOL TERCENTENNIAL — commemorative, only 300 manufactured. Fully engraved with gold inlays. Presentation case. Only 100 imported to U.S.

	$1,450	$1,100	$850

100%	98%	95%	90%	80%	70%	60%	50%	40%	30%	20%	10%

BERGMANN

Previous manufacturer located in Gaggenau, Germany circa 1892-1944. Re-established in 1931 under Bergmann Erben.

PISTOLS: SEMI-AUTO

Prices established are for original guns with matching parts.

MODEL 1894 (ANTIQUE) — 8mm "Bergmann Schmeisser" cal. Extremely rare.

100%	98%	95%	90%	80%	70%	60%	50%	40%	30%	20%	10%
N/A	N/A	$18,500	$16,000	$12,000	$8,000	$7,500	$7,000	$6,500	$6,000	$5,500	$5,000

MODEL 1896-NO. 2 — 5mm cal., smaller type frame.

| $2,250 | $1,850 | $1,600 | $1,300 | $1,100 | $895 | $715 | $660 | $610 | $565 | $515 | $450 |

Add 50% for "folding trigger" version.

MODEL 1896-NO. 3 — 6.5mm - 80mm cal. barrel.

| $3,250 | $2,750 | $2,250 | $1,800 | $1,450 | $925 | $750 | $700 | $665 | $630 | $600 | $565 |

Add 10% for early pistols without extractors and narrow grips.
Add 20% if hexagonal chamber.
Add 100% for target variation.

MODEL 1896-NO. 4 — 8mm cal., military contract. Rarely seen.

| $4,950 | $4,250 | $3,500 | $3,000 | $2,200 | $1,500 | $900 | $725 | $665 | $630 | $600 | $565 |

MODEL 1897-NO. 5 — 7.8mm cal., commercial manufacture. May be fit with shoulder stock.

| $6,000 | $4,750 | $3,500 | $3,000 | $2,200 | $1,500 | $925 | $750 | $700 | $665 | $630 | $600 |

Add 200% for long barrel carbine version.
Add 100% if fit with shoulder stock, add another 20% to total if matching stock.

BERGMANN MARS MODEL 1903 — .30 or 9mm Bergmann cal.

| $4,000 | $3,500 | $3,000 | $2,500 | $2,000 | $1,750 | $1,500 | $1,250 | $1,000 | $750 | $600 | $500 |

Add 100% if fit with shoulder stock.
Add 25% if .30 caliber (first 100 pistols).

MODEL 2 — .25 cal., small frame. Add $100 for Model 2A.

| $350 | $295 | $260 | $240 | $215 | $180 | $160 | $135 | $115 | $95 | $80 | $65 |

MODEL 3 — .25 cal., small frame. Add $100 for Model 3A.

| $350 | $295 | $260 | $240 | $215 | $180 | $160 | $135 | $115 | $95 | $80 | $65 |

ERBEN — .25 cal., Models I, II, and Special (.32 cal.).

| $335 | $300 | $285 | $260 | $240 | $215 | $180 | $160 | $135 | $115 | $95 | $80 |

PISTOLS: SEMI-AUTO · BERGMANN-BAYARD

Even though the below listed Bergmann-Bayard models were manufactured only by Anciens Etablissements Pieper of Herstal, Belgium, these pistols are listed under this heading as they are most commonly referred to by this trademark designation.

MODEL 1908 STANDARD COMMERCIAL — 9mm Bergmann/Bayard cal., identified by a mounted knight on the left magazine housing and is without finger cuts at base of magazine housing.

| $1,850 | $1,350 | $1,000 | $750 | $600 | $500 | $400 | $360 | $335 | $310 | $285 | $260 |

Add 25% if backstrap is slotted for shoulder stock.
Add $3,000 for excellent original leather/wood shoulder stock.

MODEL 1908 SPANISH CONTRACT — 9mm Bergmann/Bayard cal., total contract was for 3,000 pistols, can be identified from standard commercial pistols by the Spanish military acceptance stamp struck on the receiver.

| $1,450 | $1,100 | $900 | $750 | $600 | $450 | $400 | $360 | $335 | $310 | $285 | $260 |

100%	98%	95%	90%	80%	70%	60%	50%	40%	30%	20%	10%

B

MODEL 1910 STANDARD COMMERCIAL — 9mm Bergmann/Bayard cal., mechanically similar to Model 1908 Standard Commercial except has finger cuts in bottom of magazine housing, circular grooves are present on each side of magazine base.

| $1,250 | $1,000 | $700 | $600 | $500 | $400 | $350 | $315 | $280 | $265 | $245 | $225 |

MODEL 1910 DANISH GOVERNMENT CONTRACT — 9mm Bergmann/Bayard cal., Trolit grips were used for the original conversion, followed later by wood replacements, total contract was for 4,840 pistols with delivery mfg. 1911-1914. This variation can be identified from the usual commercial pistols by the Danish proof mark on the left receiver side and Danish inventory number on right side of receiver.

| $1,450 | $1,150 | $900 | $750 | $600 | $450 | $400 | $360 | $335 | $310 | $285 | $260 |

Subtract 20% if converted and overstamped M.1910/21.

MODEL 1910/21 TOJHUS — 9mm Bergmann/Bayard cal., these pistols are marked "Haerens Tojhus" and are numbered from 1-900, original grips were black Trolit, replacement grips are either all smooth or with checkered circles above and below grip screw.

| $1,750 | $1,400 | $1,000 | $750 | $600 | $500 | $400 | $360 | $335 | $310 | $285 | $260 |

This contract was manufactured by the Danish Royal Arsenal located in Copenhagen.

MODEL 1910/21 RUSTKAMMER — 9mm Bergmann/Bayard cal., pistols are marked "Haerens Rustkammer", and numbered 901-2204, grip replacements are the same as noted for Haerens Tojhus.

| $1,600 | $1,250 | $995 | $750 | $600 | $450 | $400 | $360 | $335 | $310 | $285 | $260 |

This contract was manufactured by the Danish Royal Arsenal located in Copenhagen.

WAYNE BERGQUIST CUSTOM PISTOLS

Current custom pistolsmith located in Naples, FL. The company should be contacted directly (see Trademark Index for current information) regarding their Bullseye, IPSC/Tactical, Defense/Carry, or IPSC models.

BERNARDELLI, VINCENZO

Previous manufacturer located in Brescia, Italy from 1721- August, 1997. Previously imported and distributed until 1997 by Armsport, Inc. located in Miami, FL. Previously imported and distributed by Magnum Research, Inc. located in Minneapolis, MN (1989-92), Quality Arms, Inc. located in Houston, TX, Armes De Chasse located in Chadds Ford, PA, Stoeger located in New York, NY, and Action Arms, Ltd. located in Philadelphia, PA.

There is some confusion on the Bernardelli trademark as there have been three different companies (Pietro Bernardelli, Vincenzo Bernardelli, and Santini Bernardelli) that have produced firearms. During the late 1980s, there were quite a lot of Pietro Bernardellis that were "dumped" in the American marketplace - these guns do not have the quality of Vincenzo Bernardelli and are not covered within the scope of this text.

Grading			100%	98%	95%	90%	80%	70%	60%

COMBINATION GUNS

MODEL 190 — 12, 16, or 20 ga. under .243 Win., .30-06, or .308 Win. cal., combination rifle/shotgun, boxlock action, DTs, extractors. Imported 1989 only.

| $1,295 | $1,025 | $895 | $800 | $700 | $600 | $525 |

Last Mfg.'s Sug. Retail was $1,393.

Add $700 for extra set of 12 ga. O/U barrels.

Grading	100%	98%	95%	90%	80%	70%	60%

MODEL COMB 2000 — 12, 16, or 20 ga. under choice of rifle cals., ejectors, set trigger. Imported 1990-97.

		$2,300	$1,550	$1,075	$875	$750	$675	$575

Last Mfg.'s Sug. Retail was $2,920.

Add $621 for extra set of O/U shotgun barrels (Model COMB 2000S - disc.).

MODEL 120 — 12 ga. over choice of 12 cals., deluxe checkered walnut stock and forearm, iron sights, double triggers, vent. recoil pad, coin washed receiver with light engraving.

	$1,950	$1,585	$1,300	$1,050	$850	$760	$650

Last Mfg.'s Sug. Retail was $2,411.

Add $130 for extra set of shotgun barrels.

PISTOLS: SEMI-AUTO, DISC.

VEST POCKET MODEL — .25 ACP cal., 2⅛ in. barrel, fixed sights, blue, bakelite grips. Mfg. 1945-1948.

	$250	$195	$165	$140	$110	$90	$65

BABY SEMI-AUTO — .22 S or L cal., 2⅛ in. barrel, fixed sights, blue, bakelite grips. Mfg. 1949-1968.

	$250	$175	$150	$130	$100	$90	$80

SPORTER MODEL — .22 LR cal., 6, 8, or 10 in. barrels, target sights, blue, wood grips. Mfg. 1949-1968.

	$305	$275	$220	$165	$140	$110	$85

MODEL 60 — .22 LR cal., .32 ACP, or .380 ACP cal., 3½ in. barrel, fixed sights, blue, bakelite grips. Mfg. 1959-present.

	$220	$195	$180	$165	$155	$135	$120

This model is not imported domestically.

MODEL 68 — .22 Short or .22 LR cal., vest pocket model, 6 shot, bakelite grips, 8½ oz. Disc.

	$140	$120	$110	$100	$90	$80	$70

This model is not imported domestically.

PISTOLS: SEMI-AUTO

MODEL 80 — .22 LR or .380 ACP cal., 3½ in. barrel, adj. sights, blue, thumbrest plastic grips. Imported 1968-1988.

	$185	$160	$150	$140	$130	$115	$100

Add $5 for .380 ACP.

Note: This model was produced to conform to import regulations of GCA 1968. Importation of this model was disc. 1988.

MODEL USA — .22 LR, .32 ACP (disc.), or .380 ACP. cal., semi-auto, single action, steel frame, loaded chamber indicator, adj. sights, target bakelite grips, 7 shot (.380 ACP) or 10 shot (.22 LR) mag. Disc. 1997.

	$380	$295	$250	$215	$185	$165	$145

Last Mfg.'s Sug. Retail was $425.

Add $60 for chrome finish.

This model has the same technical specifications as the Model 60.

MODEL AMR — .22 LR, .32 ACP (disc.), or .380 ACP cal., similar action to USA Model except has 6 in. barrel and adj. rear sight. Disc. 1994.

	$395	$325	$275	$225	$185	$165	$145

Last Mfg.'s Sug. Retail was $445.

MODEL 90 SPORT TARGET — .32 ACP or .22 LR cal., similar to Model 80, with 6 in. barrel. Imported 1968-1988.

	$210	$185	$170	$155	$140	$120	$110

Last Mfg.'s Sug. Retail was $245.

Grading	100%	98%	95%	90%	80%	70%	60%

MODEL 69 TARGET — .22 LR cal., target semi-auto, single action, 5.9 in. heavy barrel, 10 shot mag., wraparound checkered wood grips, 38 oz.

	$575	$475	$400	$350	$275	$225	$185

Last Mfg.'s Sug. Retail was $660.

B

This model was previously designated Model 100.

MODEL 100 TARGET — .22 LR cal., 5.9 in. barrel, adj. sight, blue, checkered wood, thumbrest grips, cased. Imported 1968-1988.

	$395	$325	$295	$260	$225	$190	$175

Last Mfg.'s Sug. Retail was $360.

P-ONE — 9mm Para. or .40 S&W cal., double action, 10 shot mag., choice of matte black or chrome finish. Imported 1993-97.

	$580	$495	$400	$360	$330	$295	$265

Last Mfg.'s Sug. Retail was $684.

Add $36 for chrome finish.
Add $36 for wood grips.

* P-One Compact — compact variation of the P-One. Disc. 1997.

	$595	$500	$400	$360	$330	$295	$265

Last Mfg.'s Sug. Retail was $702.

Add $48 for chrome finish.
Add $48 for wood grips.

MODEL P010 TARGET — .22 LR cal., single action, 5.9 in. barrel, adj. sights and trigger, matte black finish, large anatomic walnut stippled grips with thumbrest, 10 shot mag., 40.5 oz. Imported 1989-92, re-introduced 1995-97.

	$675	$575	$495	$425	$375	$325	$275

Last Mfg.'s Sug. Retail was $768.

Add $132 for wood case and two sets of weights.

MODEL P018 — 7.65mm (disc. 1988), .380 ACP (mfg. 1993-94), or 9mm Para. cal., double action, semi-auto, steel construction, 4⅞ in. barrel, 10 (C/B 1994) or 16★ shot mag., black plastic (standard) or walnut checkered (disc. 1992) grips, blue (disc.), black (new 1994), or chrome finish, 36 oz. Imported 1985-96.

	$485	$400	$350	$300	$275	$250	$230

Last Mfg.'s Sug. Retail was $560.

Add $40 for walnut grips (disc. 1992).
Add $60 for chrome finish.
Add $30 for carrying case w/combination lock (disc. 1989).

This model was extensively redesigned in 1989 and included a "cocked and locked" feature, thumb mag. release, loaded chamber indicator, as well as other improvements.

* P018 Compact — .380 ACP or 9mm Para. cal., similar to Model P018 except has 4 in. barrel and 10 (C/B 1994) or 14★ shot mag., approx. 2 lbs. Imported 1989-96.

	$545	$430	$375	$310	$275	$250	$230

Last Mfg.'s Sug. Retail was $610.

Add $55 for chrome finish.

This model was also redesigned in 1989 to incorporate the same features as the Model P018.

PRACTICAL VB — 9x21mm cal., comp. gun built for IPSC competition, various configurations, black or matte chrome finish, 2, 4, or 6 port compensating system. Mfg. 1993-97.

	$1,100	$925	$775	$675	$575	$475	$400

Last Mfg.'s Sug. Retail was $1,260.

Add $60 for 4 port compensator.
Add $60 for chrome finish.

Grading	100%	98%	95%	90%	80%	70%	60%

B

* **Practical VB Customized** — state-of-the-art competition pistol featuring 4+2 port compensating system. Mfg. 1993-97.

	$1,775	$1,325	$1,100	$975	$850	$725	$600

Last Mfg.'s Sug. Retail was $1,920.

> Add $60 for chrome finish.

RIFLES: DOUBLE

EXPRESS VB — various cals., side-by-side sidelock action, ejectors, single or double triggers. Imported 1990-97.

	$5,475	$4,100	$3,400	$2,725	$2,275	$1,900	$1,600

Last Mfg.'s Sug. Retail was $6,000.

> Add $1,000 for Deluxe Model (double triggers).

EXPRESS 2000 — .30-06, 7x65R, 8x57JRS, or 9.3x74R cal., O/U boxlock design, single or double trigger, extractors, checkered walnut stock and forearm. Imported 1994-97.

	$2,600	$1,995	$1,600	$1,275	$1,100	$975	$875

Last Mfg.'s Sug. Retail was $3,192.

> Add $130 for single trigger.

MINERVA EXPRESS — various cals., exposed hammers, extractors, double triggers, moderate engraving. Imported 1995-97.

	$4,975	$3,850	$3,250	$2,725	$2,275	$1,900	$1,600

Last Mfg.'s Sug. Retail was $5,850.

RIFLES: SEMI-AUTO

CARBINA .22 — .22 LR cal., blow back action. Imported 1990-97.

			$575	$375	$295	$210	$170	$150	$135

Last Mfg.'s Sug. Retail was $720.

SHOTGUNS: SxS, DISC.

Bernardelli side-by-side shotguns were manufactured with straight grip, English-style stocks with pistol grip available as a special order. Importation of Bernardelli shotguns was inconsistent over the years.

A wide variety of special order options was available on these shotguns.

Barrel choke markings for V. Bernardelli shotguns are as follows; Full: *, Impr. Mod: **, Mod: ***, Impr. Cyl: ****, Cylinder: CL.

MODEL 110 — 12 ga., trap or skeet model, separated barrels, high post rib.

	$2,000	$1,500	$1,300	$1,100	$1,000	$900	$800

MODEL 110 EXTRA — similar to Model 110, except engraved.

	$3,021	$2,265	$1,970	$1,665	$1,510	$1,360	$1,210

S. UBERTO 1 GAMECOCK — 12, 16, 20, or 28 ga., 25¾ in. imp. cyl. and mod., 27½ in. full and mod., hammerless, boxlock, extractors, two triggers, English style stock, checkered.

	$853	$635	$605	$550	$495	$440	$415

> Add 20% for ejectors.

BRESCIA HAMMER DOUBLE BARREL — 12, 16, or 20 ga., 25¾, 27½ and 29½ in. mod. and full, 12 ga., 25½ in. imp. cyl. and mod., sidelock, extractors, two triggers, straight English stock, splinter forearm, checkered. Importation disc.

	$2,050	$795	$600	$450	$425	$395	$350

Last Mfg.'s Sug. Retail was $2,482.

Sudden drop in values reflects desirability factor in today's marketplace.

ITALIA HAMMER DOUBLE BARREL — similar to Brescia, except higher grade engraving and wood. Importation disc.

	$2,275	$1,200	$900	$735	$650	$600	$550

Last Mfg.'s Sug. Retail was $2,844.

Sudden drop in values reflects desirability factor in today's marketplace.

Grading	100%	98%	95%	90%	80%	70%	60%

ITALIA EXTRA HAMMER — 12, 16, or 20 ga., hammer double. Top-of-the-line hammer model. Importation disc.

	$6,400	$3,150	$2,200	$1,650	$1,375	$1,050	$800

Last Mfg.'s Sug. Retail was $7,861.

B

Sudden drop in values reflects desirability factor in today's marketplace.

MODEL 112 — 12 ga., entry-level model with extractors and DTs. Imported 1989 only.

	$850	$750	$675	$625	$550	$495	$450

Last Mfg.'s Sug. Retail was $998.

Add $65 for single trigger (Model 112 M - disc.).

MODEL 112 E — 12 ga., Anson & Deeley action, light engraving. Importation disc. 1989.

	$995	$850	$775	$695	$625	$550	$495

Last Mfg.'s Sug. Retail was $1,108.

MODEL 112 SI/S (EM) — similar to Model 112E, except has single or double triggers. Disc. 1997.

	$1,795	$1,000	$825	$725	$650	$550	$450

Last Mfg.'s Sug. Retail was $2,100.

Add $174 for ejectors.
Add $138 for ST.
Add $420 for choke tubes.

* *Model 112 EM - MC* — similar to Model 112 EM, except has 3 in. chambers and 5 choke tubes. Imported 1990-1992.

	$1,600	$1,000	$850	$775	$675	$575	$495

Last Mfg.'s Sug. Retail was $1,971.

* *Model 112 EM-MC-WF* — includes 3½ in. chambers, waterfowl model with matte finish, single trigger and 3 choke tubes. Importation disc. 1990.

	$1,275	$975	$850	$775	$675	$575	$495

Last Mfg.'s Sug. Retail was $1,444.

S. UBERTO 1 — 12, 16, 20, or 28 ga., Anson & Deeley action, Purdey locks, light engraving, case hardened receiver, double triggers, extractors.

	$1,050	$900	$800	$700	$625	$550	$495

Last Mfg.'s Sug. Retail was $1,164.

Add $65 for single trigger (Model S. Uberto 1M).

* *S. Uberto 1E* — similar to S. Uberto 1, except with ejectors. Importation disc. 1990.

	$1,175	$950	$850	$740	$650	$565	$495

Last Mfg.'s Sug. Retail was $1,357.

Add $65 for single trigger (Model S. Uberto 1EM).

S. UBERTO 2 — 12, 16, 20, and 28 ga.'s, Anson & Deeley action, Purdey locks, light scroll engraving, silver finished receiver, double triggers, extractors. Importation disc. 1989, resumed 1993 -97.

	$1,375	$1,150	$875	$725	$650	$550	$450

Last Mfg.'s Sug. Retail was $1,580.

Add $35 for single trigger (Model S. Uberto 2M - disc.).

* *S. Uberto 2E* — similar to S. Uberto 2, except with ejectors. Disc. 1997.

	$1,525	$1,300	$1,050	$875	$725	$650	$550

Last Mfg.'s Sug. Retail was $1,710.

Add $80 for single trigger (Model S. Uberto 2EM - disc.).

S. UBERTO FS — 12, 16, 20, or 28 ga., Purdey locks, relief engraved with hunting scenes on silver finished receiver, double triggers, extractors. Importation disc. 1989, resumed 1993-97.

	$1,695	$1,450	$1,125	$895	$750	$675	$575

Last Mfg.'s Sug. Retail was $1,915.

Add $65 for single trigger (Model S. Uberto FSM - disc. 1989).

Grading	100%	98%	95%	90%	80%	70%	60%

* **S. Uberto FSE** — similar to S. Uberto FS, except with ejectors. Importation disc. 1989.

	$1,375	$1,100	$975	$850	$750	$625	$550

Last Mfg.'s Sug. Retail was $1,537.

Add $65 for single trigger (Model S. Uberto FSEM).

ROMA 3 — similar to S. Uberto, double triggers, extractors, false sideplates, case hardened receiver. Importation disc. 1989, resumed 1993-97.

	$1,425	$1,200	$895	$775	$675	$575	$475

Last Mfg.'s Sug. Retail was $1,625.

Add $65 for single trigger (Model Roma 3M - disc.).

* **Roma 3E** — similar to Roma 3, except with ejectors. Disc. 1997.

	$1,550	$1,325	$1,050	$875	$725	$650	$550

Last Mfg.'s Sug. Retail was $1,770.

Add $80 for single trigger (Model Roma 3EM - disc.).

ROMA 4 — more deluxe model than Roma 3, false sideplates, scroll engraved, silver finished receiver. Importation disc. 1989.

	$1,250	$1,025	$900	$800	$700	$625	$550

Last Mfg.'s Sug. Retail was $1,439.

Add $65 for single trigger (Model Roma 4M).

* **Roma 4E** — similar to Roma 4, except with ejectors. Disc. 1997.

	$1,775	$1,475	$1,150	$925	$775	$675	$575

Last Mfg.'s Sug. Retail was $2,000.

Add $80 for single trigger (Model Roma 4EM - disc.).

ROMA 6 — 12, 16, 20, or 28 ga., fully engraved sideplates with hunting scenes, Purdey locks, silver finish receiver, single trigger, finely figured English walnut. Importation disc. 1989.

	$1,395	$1,150	$975	$875	$775	$675	$600

Last Mfg.'s Sug. Retail was $1,619.

Add $175 for single trigger (Model Roma 6M).

* **Roma 6E** — similar to Roma 6, except with ejectors, 16 ga. was disc. 1989. Disc. 1997.

	$2,400	$1,825	$1,475	$1,150	$925	$775	$675

Last Mfg.'s Sug. Retail was $2,880.

Add $180 for single trigger (Model Roma 6EM).

ROMA 7 — 12 ga., ejectors, grade up from the Roma 6. Imported 1994-97.

	$3,200	$2,200	$1,675	$1,375	$995	$875	$750

Last Mfg.'s Sug. Retail was $3,840.

ROMA 8 — 12 ga., ejectors, grade up from the Roma 7. Imported 1994-97.

	$3,700	$2,700	$1,950	$1,675	$1,375	$995	$875

Last Mfg.'s Sug. Retail was $4,740.

ROMA 9 — 12 ga., ejectors, grade up from the Roma 8. Imported 1994-97.

	$4,550	$3,200	$2,500	$1,950	$1,675	$1,375	$995

Last Mfg.'s Sug. Retail was $5,520.

ELIO — 12 ga. only, lightweight, extractors, fine English style scroll engraving on silver finish receiver. Importation disc. 1989.

	$1,125	$925	$850	$740	$650	$565	$475

Last Mfg.'s Sug. Retail was $1,238.

Add $65 for single trigger (Model Elio M).

* **Elio E** — similar to Elio, except with ejectors. Importation disc. 1989.

	$1,200	$1,000	$895	$795	$695	$595	$500

Last Mfg.'s Sug. Retail was $1,353.

Add $65 for single trigger (Model Elio EM).

Grading		100%	98%	95%	90%	80%	70%	60%

SLUG GUN — 12 ga. only, 23¾ in. slug bored barrels, extractors, Anson & Deeley action, Purdey locks, lightly engraved, silver finish receiver. Importation disc. 1990.

$1,325 **$1,000** **$895** **$795** **$695** **$595** **$500**
Last Mfg.'s Sug. Retail was $1,575.

Add $65 for single trigger (Model Slug M).

SLUG LUSSO — 12 ga. only, 23¾ in. slug bored barrels, sideplates, with extensive engraving featuring hunting scenes, cheekpiece, ejectors, silver finished receiver. Importation disc. 1992.

$2,325 **$1,550** **$1,200** **$995** **$875** **$750** **$650**
Last Mfg.'s Sug. Retail was $2,793.

Add $80 for single trigger (Model Slug Lusso M).

This model was previously designated Slug Deluxe (1988 or earlier).

HEMINGWAY — 12, 20, or 28 (new 1992) ga., boxlock action, coin finished receiver with game scene engraving, 23½ in. barrels, DTs, deluxe checkered walnut stock and forearm, 6¼ lbs. Disc. 1997.

$2,050 **$1,500** **$1,050** **$875** **$750** **$675** **$575**
Last Mfg.'s Sug. Retail was $2,520.

Add $70 for single trigger.
Add $120 for single selective trigger.

HEMINGWAY DE LUXE — similar to Hemingway, except is also available in 16 ga. and has sideplates, better wood, and more engraving. Disc. 1997.

$2,350 **$1,750** **$1,150** **$925** **$775** **$675** **$575**
Last Mfg.'s Sug. Retail was $2,874.

Add $126 for single trigger (Model Hemingway De Luxe M).

LAS PALOMAS PIGEON — 12 ga. live pigeon gun, single trigger, special dimensions for live pigeon shooting. Disc. 1997.

$3,125 **$2,550** **$2,000** **$1,700** **$1,375** **$995** **$875**
Last Mfg.'s Sug. Retail was $3,700.

Add $750 for Pigeon Model (includes single trigger).

HOLLAND V.B. LISCIO — 12 ga. only, Holland type sidelocks, light engraving, silver finish receiver, single trigger, ejectors, select walnut. Disc. 1997.

$10,350 **$5,300** **$4,450** **$3,900** **$3,350** **$2,850** **$2,400**
Last Mfg.'s Sug. Retail was $12,600.

HOLLAND V.B. INCISO — 12 ga. only, H&H sidelock action, Purdey locks, various barrel lengths, single trigger, ejectors, straight or pistol grip stock, 100% engraved on coin finished receiver. Importation disc. 1992.

$10,700 **$7,000** **$5,500** **$4,700** **$4,200** **$3,500** **$3,000**
Last Mfg.'s Sug. Retail was $12,929.

HOLLAND V.B. LUSSO — 12 ga. only, H&H sidelock action, Purdey locks, various barrel lengths, single trigger, ejectors, straight or pistol grip stock, same features as Holland V.B. Inciso, only extra select wood and game scene engraving. Importation disc. 1992.

$8,900 **$7,900** **$6,500** **$5,200** **$4,750** **$4,000** **$3,450**
Last Mfg.'s Sug. Retail was $14,377.

HOLLAND V.B. EXTRA — 12 ga. only, H&H style action, any barrel length and choke, double triggers, auto ejectors, straight or pistol grip stock, 100% engraved on coin finished receiver. Prices are completely dependent upon individual customer specifications. Values listed below are for engraving pattern No. 3. Importation disc. 1992.

$13,250 **$9,700** **$7,450** **$6,150** **$5,200** **$4,600** **$3,950**
Last Mfg.'s Sug. Retail was $16,549.

Add $1,034 for engraving pattern No. 4.
Add $4,551 for engraving pattern No. 12.
Add $8,895 for engraving pattern No. 20.
Add $621 for single trigger.

Older specimens ordered before 1992 could have values considerably lower than those listed above.

Grading	100%	98%	95%	90%	80%	70%	60%

HOLLAND V.B. GOLD — top-of-the-line model, made to individual order. Very limited production and ultra-rare. Importation disc. 1992.

	$47,500	$32,500	$24,000	$18,500	$13,000	$11,500	$9,950

Last Mfg.'s Sug. Retail was $57,922.

Older specimens ordered before 1992 could have values considerably lower than those listed above.

SHOTGUNS: O/U

MODEL 115 HUNTING — 12 ga. only, boxlock action, monobloc frame, inclined plane lockings, blued receiver, single trigger, ejectors. Importation disc. 1989.

	$1,770	$1,425	$1,225	$1,000	$895	$750	$650

Last Mfg.'s Sug. Retail was $1,915.

* *Model 115S* — similar to 115, except moderate engraving.

	$2,150	$1,925	$1,745	$1,500	$1,250	$1,025	$950

Last Mfg.'s Sug. Retail was $2,500.

* *Model 115L* — similar to 115S, except extensive scroll engraving on silver finish receiver.

	$2,600	$2,375	$2,050	$1,750	$1,450	$1,100	$850

Last Mfg.'s Sug. Retail was $3,170.

* *Model 115E* — sideplate, boxlock action, ejector, bulino game scene engraving.

	$4,650	$4,125	$3,600	$3,100	$2,650	$2,200	$1,800

Last Mfg.'s Sug. Retail was $5,200.

MODEL 115 TARGET — 12 ga. only, same specifications as Model 115, except trap dimensions. Importation disc. 1989.

	$1,800	$1,595	$1,375	$1,175	$1,000	$895	$750

Last Mfg.'s Sug. Retail was $2,160.

* *Model 115S* — same specifications as 115 Target, except light engraving. Importation disc. 1992.

	$3,275	$2,425	$1,825	$1,500	$1,250	$1,025	$895

Last Mfg.'s Sug. Retail was $3,920.

This model is available in either Pigeon, Skeet, Sporting Clays, or Trap configuration.

* *Model 115L* — similar to 115S, except extensive scroll engraving on silver finish receiver. Importation disc. 1990.

	$3,700	$2,995	$2,600	$2,375	$2,050	$1,750	$1,450

Last Mfg.'s Sug. Retail was $4,201.

* *Model 115E* — same specifications as 115S, except with extensively engraved sideplates. Importation disc. 1990.

	$5,950	$4,800	$4,125	$3,600	$3,100	$2,650	$2,200

Last Mfg.'s Sug. Retail was $6,827.

* *Model 115S Trap/Skeet* — 12 ga. only, available in Trap or Skeet configuration, ejectors, single trigger. Disc. 1997.

	$3,250	$2,450	$1,825	$1,425	$995	$875	$725

Last Mfg.'s Sug. Retail was $3,780.

* *Model 115S Sporting Clays* — 12 ga. only, SST, ejectors, choke tubes. Imported 1995-97.

	$3,875	$3,350	$2,775	$2,100	$1,750	$1,500	$1,350

Last Mfg.'s Sug. Retail was $4,200.

MODEL 190 TARGET — 12 ga, SST, ejectors, engraved silver receiver, select checkered walnut stock and forearm. Imported 1986-1989.

	$1,425	$1,095	$925	$800	$700	$600	$525

Last Mfg.'s Sug. Retail was $1,572.

* *Model 190 MC* — similar to Model 190 Target except has Monte Carlo stock. Imported 1989 only.

	$1,000	$825	$700	$600	$525	$475	$450

Last Mfg.'s Sug. Retail was $1,155.

Grading	100%	98%	95%	90%	80%	70%	60%

* *Model 190 Special* — 12 ga. only, similar to Model 190 Target, except has better walnut and engraving. Imported 1988-1989.

	$1,335	**$1,000**	**$895**	**$800**	**$700**	**$600**	**$525**

Last Mfg.'s Sug. Retail was $1,456.

B

Add $75 for single trigger (Model 190 Special MS).

These variations are hunting models.

MODEL 192 FIELD — 12 ga. only, single or double triggers, ejectors, choke tubes optional. Imported 1995-97.

	$1,175	**$895**	**$750**	**$650**	**$550**	**$450**	**$375**

Last Mfg.'s Sug. Retail was $1,425.

Add $65 for single trigger.
Add $200 for choke tubes.
Add $350 for 192 Special (includes double triggers, ejectors).

MODEL 192 MS COMPETITION — 12 ga. only, ejectors, selective or non-selective triggers, multi-chokes standard on Sporting Clays Model. Mfg. 1990-97.

	$1,725	**$1,475**	**$1,150**	**$925**	**$775**	**$675**	**$575**

Last Mfg.'s Sug. Retail was $1,930.

Add $120 for SST.
Add $200 for choke tubes.
Add $485 for Special Sport.

This model was available in either Pigeon, Skeet, Sporting Clays, Special Sport, or Trap configuration.

MODEL 192 MS-MC HUNTING — 12 ga. only, boxlock action with engraved coin finished receiver, 3 in. chambers, ejectors, SST, 26¾ or 28 in. VR barrels with choke tubes, steel shot compatible. Imported 1990-1992.

	$1,400	**$995**	**$825**	**$700**	**$600**	**$525**	**$475**

Last Mfg.'s Sug. Retail was $1,833.

* *Model 192 MS-MC-WF* — waterfowler variation which includes 3½ in. chambers, 3 choke tubes, and SST. Imported 1990 only.

	$1,275	**$950**	**$875**	**$775**	**$675**	**$575**	**$500**

Last Mfg.'s Sug. Retail was $1,444.

MODEL 200 LIGHTWEIGHT MS — 12 ga. only, silver grey finished receiver with game scene engraving, ejectors, DTs. Imported 1988-1989, resumed 1993-97.

	$1,325	**$975**	**$850**	**$725**	**$650**	**$550**	**$450**

Last Mfg.'s Sug. Retail was $1,525.

MODEL 220 MS HUNTING — 12 or 20 ga., silver grey finished receiver with engraving. Mfg. 1988-1997.

	$1,350	**$995**	**$850**	**$725**	**$650**	**$550**	**$450**

Last Mfg.'s Sug. Retail was $1,560.

Add $75 for SST.
Add $180 for 12 ga. slug variation with DTs (new 1994).
Add $700 for extra set of 12 ga. barrels (disc. 1990).

This model was available with either a pistol grip or English grip (straight) stock.

MODEL LUCK — 12 ga., ejectors, boxlock action, choice of double or single trigger. Imported 1994-97.

	$1,450	**$995**	**$725**	**$650**	**$550**	**$450**	**$375**

Last Mfg.'s Sug. Retail was $1,795.

Add $275 for single trigger.

SATURNO MS-MC COMPETITION — 12 ga. only, sporter configuration, boxlock action with lightly engraved side plates, ejectors, DTs. Imported 1991-97.

	$2,325	**$1,725**	**$1,150**	**$925**	**$775**	**$675**	**$575**

Last Mfg.'s Sug. Retail was $2,760.

This model was available in either Pigeon, Skeet, Sporting Clays, or Trap configuration.

Grading	100%	98%	95%	90%	80%	70%	60%

SATURNO MS-MC HUNTING — 12 ga. only, boxlock action with lightly engraved side plates, ejectors, SST, includes multi-chokes. Imported 1991-1992.

	$2,275	$1,525	$1,050	$875	$750	$695	$600

Last Mfg.'s Sug. Retail was $2,609.

ORIONE S — 12 ga., double Purdey lock, VR, ejectors, engraved nickel finish receiver. Importation disc. 1989.

	$1,175	$1,025	$860	$760	$650	$560	$510

Last Mfg.'s Sug. Retail was $1,425.

ORIONE L — similar to Orione S, single trigger, finer engraving, English or pistol type select walnut stock. Importation disc. 1989.

	$1,285	$1,125	$950	$840	$750	$650	$550

Last Mfg.'s Sug. Retail was $1,550.

ORIONE E — top-of-the-line, deep relief engraving. Importation disc. 1989.

	$1,375	$1,200	$1,020	$900	$820	$710	$650

Last Mfg.'s Sug. Retail was $1,660.

SHOTGUNS: SEMI-AUTO

MODEL 9MM FLOBERT — 9mm Flobert cal. (rimfire shot cartridge), 24.4 in. smooth bore barrel, 3 shot mag., steel receiver, walnut stock and forearm with sling and swivels, 5 lbs. 3 oz. Disc. 1997.

	$385	$265	$175	$150	$125	$105	$95

Last Mfg.'s Sug. Retail was $474.

SHOTGUNS: FOLDING MODELS

SINGLE BARREL — 12, 16, 20, 24, 28, 32 ga., or .410 bore, gun folds in half. Importation disc. 1990.

	$230	$185	$150	$135	$125	$115	$100

Last Mfg.'s Sug. Retail was $265.

DOUBLE BARREL — 12 and 16 ga., gun folds in half, double triggers. Previously available in Europe only.

	$570	$430	$370	$315	$285	$260	$230

BERSA

Current manufacturer located in Argentina. Currently imported and distributed exclusively by Eagle Imports, Inc. located in Wanamassa, NJ. Previously imported and distributed before 1988 by Rock Island Armory located in Geneseo, IL, Outdoor Sports Headquarters, Inc. located in Dayton, OH, and R.S.A. Enterprises, Inc. located in Ocean, NJ. Dealer and distributor sales only.

PISTOLS: SEMI-AUTO

THUNDER 9 — 9mm Para. cal., double action semi-auto, 3½ in. barrel, 10 (C/B 1994) or 14★ shot mag., ambidextrous manual safety and decocking lever, automatic firing pin safety, 3-dot sights, aluminum frame, wraparound matte black polymer grips, link-free locked breech design, non-glare matte blue, satin nickel (new 1995), or duo-tone (new 1995) finish. Imported 1993-95.

	$400	$335	$295	$265	$235	$210	$190

Last Mfg.'s Sug. Retail was $475.

Add $17 for duo-tone finish.
Add $50 for satin nickel finish.

Grading	100%	98%	95%	90%	80%	70%	60%

THUNDER 22 (MODEL 23) — .22 LR cal., double action semi-auto, 9 shot mag., 3½ in. barrel, black polymer (new 1997) or walnut (disc. 1996) grips, 24½ oz. Imported 1988-1998.

	$230	$195	$155	$125	$115	$105	$95

Last Mfg.'s Sug. Retail was $265.

Add $17 for satin nickel finish.

THUNDER 380 — .380 ACP cal., double action, 3½ in. barrel, fixed sights, 7 shot mag., deep blue, satin nickel, or duo-tone (disc. 1995) finish, rubber grips, 25¾ oz. Imported 1995-98.

	$235	$195	$155	$125	$115	$105	$95

Last Mfg.'s Sug. Retail was $275.

Add $16 for satin nickel finish.
Add $16 for duo-tone finish.

❋ *Thunder 380 DLX* — .380 ACP cal., 9 shot mag., black polymer grips, extended slide release and mag. bottom, polished blue, 3 dot sights. New 1997.

Mfg.'s Sug. Retail	$275		$235	$195	$160	$125	$115	$105	$95

❋ *Thunder 380 Plus* — similar to Thunder 380, except has 10 shot mag. Mfg. 1995-97.

	$265	$210	$165	$130	$115	$105	$95

Last Mfg.'s Sug. Retail was $316.

Add $32 for satin nickel finish.
Add $17 for duo-tone finish.

MODEL 83 — .380 ACP cal., double action semi-auto, 3½ in. barrel, blued or satin nickel finish, custom walnut grips, 6 shot mag., 24½ oz. Imported 1988-94.

	$235	$180	$150	$125	$115	$105	$95

Last Mfg.'s Sug. Retail was $288.

Add $34 for satin nickel finish.

MODEL 85 — .380 ACP cal., similar specifications to Model 83 except has 12 or 13 shot mag., 30½ oz. Imported 1988-94.

	$285	$245	$220	$195	$170	$150	$130

Last Mfg.'s Sug. Retail was $340.

Add $47 for satin nickel finish.

MODEL 86 — .380 ACP cal., blue matte or nickel finish, undercover model, wraparound rubber grips, 12 shot mag. Imported 1991-94.

	$315	$265	$225	$200	$170	$150	$130

Last Mfg.'s Sug. Retail was $375.

Add $29 for nickel finish.

MODEL 90 — 9mm Para. cal., single action, semi-auto, steel frame, checkered walnut grips, 13 shot mag., deep blue finish. Imported 1990-91 only.

	$325	$280	$250	$220	$195	$170	$150

Last Mfg.'s Sug. Retail was $384.

SERIES 95 — .380 ACP cal., double action, 3½ in. barrel, fixed sights, 7 shot mag., matte blue or satin nickel finish, black polymer grips, 23 oz. New 1995.

Mfg.'s Sug. Retail	$249		$210	$175	$145	$125	$115	$105	$95

Add $16 for satin nickel finish.

MODEL 223 — .22 LR cal., single action semi-auto, 10 shot mag., 3½ in. barrel, squared-off trigger guard, nylon grips, blued action. Importation disc. 1987.

	$200	$170	$150	$125	$115	$105	$95

Last Mfg.'s Sug. Retail was $239.

MODEL 224 — similar to Model 223, except has 4 in. barrel. Imported 1987 only.

	$200	$170	$150	$125	$115	$105	$95

Last Mfg.'s Sug. Retail was $239.

MODEL 225 — similar to Model 223, except has 5 in. barrel and 10 shot mag. Disc. 1987.

	$155	$135	$125	$115	$105	$95	$85

Last Mfg.'s Sug. Retail was $170.

Grading	100%	98%	95%	90%	80%	70%	60%

MODEL 226 — similar to Model 225, except has 6 in. barrel. Importation disc. 1987.

	$200	$170	$150	$125	$115	$105	$95

Last Mfg.'s Sug. Retail was $239.

B

MODEL 323 — .32 ACP cal., single action semi-auto, 8 shot mag., thumbrest plastic grips, 25 oz. Disc. 1987.

	$105	$95	$85	$75	$65	$55	$45

Last Mfg.'s Sug. Retail was $125.

MODEL 383 — .380 ACP cal., single or double action semi-auto, 3½ in. barrel, blued finish, nylon grips, 7 shot mag. Importation disc. 1988.

	$120	$95	$90	$80	$70	$60	$50

Last Mfg.'s Sug. Retail was $188 for single action.
Last Mfg.'s Sug. Retail was $239 for double action.

Add $15 for double action.

BERTUZZI

Current manufacturer located in Brescia, Italy since 1886. Imported and distributed exclusively by New England Arms Co. located in Kittery Point, ME.

Bertuzzi makes only best quality sidelock O/U and SxS shotguns - only 40-50 guns are mfg. annually and all are custom ordered per individual specifications.

SHOTGUNS: SxS

MODEL ORIONE — 12 ga., scalloped Anson & Deeley boxlock action, beavertail forearm, single trigger, auto ejector. This model is available on special order only — contact the distributor listed above for availability, prices, and options. Importation disc. 1994. Retail prices started at $4,500.

BEST QUALITY SIDELOCK — various gauges, best quality sidelock model with extensive engraving. Prices start at $18,500.

HAMMER GUN — all gauges, upper tang safety, double triggers, fine quality engraving. Prices start at $12,500 with ejectors and single trigger. The self-cocking, auto-ejector mechanism is popular in this model and prices can vary between $15,000-$25,000.

SHOTGUNS: O/U

ZEUS — 12 ga., sidelock, auto ejector, deluxe engraving, deluxe wood checkering, SST. This model is available on special order only — contact the distributor listed above for availability, prices, and options. Importation disc. 1994. Retail prices generally ranged from $18,500-$27,500.

ZEUS EXTRA LUSSO — 12 ga., sidelock, auto ejector, deluxe wood, deluxe checkering and engraving, SST. This model is available on special order only — contact the distributor listed above for availability, prices, and options. Prices generally range $25,000+.

BOSS SYSTEM — 12 or 20 ga., features Boss locking system. Importation began 1995. Prices start at $45,000.

BESCHI, MARIO

Previous manufacturer until circa 1995 located in Italy.

SHOTGUNS: SxS

EXTRA LUSSO SIDELOCK — 12 or 20 ga., elaborate game scene engraving.

	100%	98%	95%	90%	80%	70%	60%
12 ga.	$12,000	$10,750	$9,250	$8,000	$6,750	$5,500	$4,250
20 ga.	$12,000	$10,750	$9,250	$8,000	$6,750	$5,500	$4,250

Grading	100%	98%	95%	90%	80%	70%	60%

BOXLOCK MODEL — prices assume moderate engraving.

	$1,650	$1,475	$1,300	$1,050	$850	$650	$500

SHOTGUNS: O/U

BOXLOCK MODEL — 12 or 20 ga., standard model with light engraving.

	$3,000	$2,600	$2,300	$1,950	$1,600	$1,300	$995

BIG BEAR ARMS & SPORTING GOODS INC.

Current importer located in Carrollton, TX beginning 1992, specializing in the importation of both Russian military surplus and new firearms. Distributor and dealer direct sales.

PISTOLS: SEMI-AUTO

IZH-70 MAKAROV — .380 ACP or 9mm Makarov cal., 8 shot mag., current mfg. from Russia. Importation began 1994.

Mfg.'s Sug. Retail	$325	$265	$185	$155	$135	$115	$100	$90

RIFLES: SEMI-AUTO

SAIGA SPORTER RIFLE — 7.62x39mm, semi-auto with improved Kalashnikov design, checkered hardwood (disc.) or synthetic stock and forearm, 5 or 10 (disc.) shot mag. Importation began 1996.

Mfg.'s Sug. Retail	$750	$575	$400	$325	$250	$225	$200	$175

Add $169 for 3.5X scope and mount.

SHOTGUNS

SAIGA SEMI-AUTO — .410 bore, 3 in. chamber, paramilitary configuration. Importation began 1996.

Mfg.'s Sug. Retail	$499	$425	$350	$295	$250	$200	$180	$165

IJ-27 O/U — 12 ga., 2¾ in. chambers. Importation began 1995.

Mfg.'s Sug. Retail	$499	$425	$350	$295	$250	$200	$180	$165

IJ-39E O/U — 12 ga., 2¾ in. chambers. Importation began 1995.

Mfg.'s Sug. Retail	$895	$760	$600	$495	$400	$360	$330	$295

IJ-43 SxS — 12 ga., 2¾ in. chambers. Importation began 1995.

Mfg.'s Sug. Retail	$399	$325	$250	$200	$175	$155	$145	$135

BIG HORN ARMS CORP.

Previous manufacturer located in Watertown, SD.

PISTOLS: SINGLE SHOT

TARGET PISTOL — .22 Short cal. only, unique action permitting auto. ejection, ambidextrous stock made of molded Tufflex with carvings, 26 oz. Approx. 1,200 mfg. Disc. in the late '60s.

	$175	$150	$135	$125	$115	$105	$95

SHOTGUNS: SINGLE SHOT

LIL' MAGNUM SHOTGUN — .410 diameter reloadable shot cartridge, single shot open bolt operation, included reloading equipment, approx. 2,000 mfg. in the late '60s.

	$125	$100	$75	$65	$55	$50	$45

Grading	100%	98%	95%	90%	80%	70%	60%

BIGHORN RIFLE CO.

Previous manufacturer located in Orem, UT.

PISTOLS: BOLT ACTION

BIGHORN PISTOL — .22 LR cal., bolt action design, research is underway to gather more information concerning this model.

RIFLES: BOLT ACTION

BIGHORN RIFLE — Mauser action, choice of calibers, custom made bolt action of high quality, interchangeable barrels (gun is supplied with 2 barrels), adj. trigger, deluxe walnut stock, many custom options. Mfg. 1984 only.

	100%	98%	95%	90%	80%	70%	60%
	$2,100	$1,800	$1,600	$1,400	$1,200	$1,000	$850

BILL HANUS BIRDGUNS

Current importer/dealer located in Newport, OR. Bill Hanus previously imported Armas Ugartechea located in Eibar, Spain until 1997. Previously imported by Galaxy Imports located in Victoria, TX.

BINGHAM, LTD.

Previous manufacturer located in Norcross, GA circa 1976-1985.

RIFLES: BOLT ACTION

BANTAM — .22 LR or 22 Mag. cal., bolt action single shot, 18½ in. barrel. Disc. 1985.

	100%	98%	95%	90%	80%	70%	60%
	$110	$90	$75	$65	$55	$45	$40

Last Mfg.'s Sug. Retail was $120.

RIFLES: SEMI-AUTO

PPS 50 — .22 LR cal. only, blowback action, 50 round drum mag., standard model has Beechwood stock. Add $20 for deluxe model with walnut stock. Duramil model has chrome finish and walnut stock — add $30. Disc. 1985.

	100%	98%	95%	90%	80%	70%	60%
	$195	$160	$145	$135	$125	$110	$100

Last Mfg.'s Sug. Retail was $230.

This model was styled after the Soviet WWII Model PPSh Sub Machine Gun.

AK-22 — .22 LR cal. only, blowback action, styled after AK-47, 15 shot mag. standard, 29 shot mag. available. Standard model has Beechwood stock. Deluxe model has walnut stock — add $20. Disc. 1985.

	100%	98%	95%	90%	80%	70%	60%
	$225	$195	$160	$145	$135	$125	$110

Last Mfg.'s Sug. Retail was $230.

GALIL-22 — .22 LR cal. only, patterned after Galil semi-auto paramilitary design rifle. Disc.

	100%	98%	95%	90%	80%	70%	60%
	$225	$195	$160	$145	$135	$125	$110

FG-9 — 9mm Para. cal., blowback action, semi-auto paramilitary design carbine, 20½ in. barrel. New design for 1984. While advertised this model was never manufactured.

BITTNER

Previously manufactured by Gustav Bittner located in Vieprty, Bohemia (Austria, Hungary), circa 1893.

PISTOLS

BITTNER MODEL 1893 — 7.7mm Bittner cal., pistol with hand activated repeater mechanism, box magazine, checkered grips, limited manufacture in circa 1893.

	100%	98%	95%	90%	80%	70%	60%
	$5,500	$4,500	$3,500	$2,700	$2,300	$1,900	$1,500

Grading	100%	98%	95%	90%	80%	70%	60%

BLAND, THOMAS & SONS GUNMAKERS LTD.

Current English manufacturer located in England since 1840. This firm was purchased in 1990 by Woodcock Hill located in Benton, PA. Manufacturer direct sales only.

B

Woodcock Hill should be contacted directly (address listed in Trademark Index) for more information (including current models and prices) regarding Thomas Bland & Sons firearms. Prices will vary depending on the exchange rate between the pound/dollar.

RIFLES: CUSTOM

Double rifles are available in almost all calibers and specifications. Prices vary between $14,000 - $45,000 depending upon configuration, finish, and accessories. Bolt action rifles are available in any type of action, most popular calibers, and other special options. The bolt action models are not manufactured in England. Prices begin at $1,500.

SHOTGUNS: CUSTOM

Both boxlock and sidelock best quality shotguns are available in all gauges with prices ranging between $9,000 - $40,000 depending upon configuration, finish, and accessories.

BLASER

Currently manufactured by Blaser Jagdwaffen GmbH **Blaser**
in Isny im Allgäu, Germany. Currently imported and
distributed by SIG Arms located in Exeter, NH. Previously distributed until 1998 by Autumn Sales Inc. located in Fort Worth, TX. Dealer sales.

Blaser Jagdwaffen manufactures a large variety of rifles, drillings, and combination guns for the European market that are not imported domestically.

RIFLES: BOLT ACTION

MODEL R-84 BOLT ACTION — .22-250 Rem. (disc. 1993), .243 Win., 6mm Rem., .25-06 Rem., .270 Win., .280 Rem., or .30-06 standard cals., .257 Wby. Mag., .264 Win. Mag., 7mm Rem. Mag., .300 Win. Mag., .300 Wby. Mag., .338 Win. Mag., or .375 H&H cal., 23 or 24 (Mag. cals. only) in. interchangeable barrel, scroll engraving on receiver, short bolt action with 60 degree rotation, checkered Turkish walnut stock and forearm, approx. 7 lbs. Mfg. 1988-94.

$2,100	$1,575	$1,275	$1,050	$950	$850	$775

Last Mfg.'s Sug. Retail was $2,300.

    Add $50 for left-hand action.
    Add $600 per interchangeable barrel (w/scope mounts).

This model features the scope being mounted directly to the barrel (and not the receiver). Since the scope mounts are on the barrel extension, this takedown rifle is unique in that it does not require re-zeroing when the rifle is reassembled, regardless of caliber change.

* ***Model R84 Deluxe*** — features a better grade of Turkish walnut with a North American game scene engraved on receiver, silver pistol grip cap with animal scene engraving.

$2,375	$2,025	$1,650	$1,200	$1,000	$925	$825

Last Mfg.'s Sug. Retail was $2,600.

    Add $50 for left hand action.

* ***Model R84 Super Deluxe*** — best grade Turkish walnut with receiver featuring African game scene engraving (animals are in gold and silver), and silver pistol grip cap with gold animal engraving.

$2,675	$2,225	$1,775	$1,300	$1,100	$975	$895

Last Mfg.'s Sug. Retail was $2,950.

    Add $50 for left hand action.

B

Grading	100%	98%	95%	90%	80%	70%	60%

MODEL R-93 CLASSIC — available in 14 domestic (.22-250 Rem. - .416 Rem. Mag.) and 8 European (6x62 Freres - 9.3x62mm) calibers, 22, 24 (Mag. cals.), or 27½ (disc.) in. barrel, unique patented rifle features straight pull bolt action (0 degree bolt lift), 360 degree radial locking system eliminates bolt rotation, unique safety offering cartridge in chamber capability, 3 shot mag, features interchangeable barrel system and newly designed bolt, searfree trigger mechanism, matte finished nickel receiver with engraving, non-glare "black velvet" barrel finish, integrated low scope mounts standard (1994-97 only), custom gun case with combination lock became standard 1998, 6½ - 7 lbs. Importation began 1994, R-93 Classic introduced 1998.

Mfg.'s Sug. Retail   **$3,495**   **$3,125 $2,850 $2,475 $2,175 $1,775 $1,300 $1,100**
   Add $525 per interchangeable barrel (w/o mounts).
   Add $210 for left-hand action.

   During 1998, this model's nomenclature changed to the R-93 Classic. Scope mounts are no longer included.

   Between 1994-97, this model retailed for approx. $2,800 and a Deluxe Grade was available for $3,100, while the Super Deluxe Grade retailed for $3,500.

* *Model R-93 Safari (Classic)* — .416 Rem. cal., features 24 in. heavy barrel, open sights, large forearm, 9½ lbs. Importation began 1994, this model was renamed the R-93 Classic in 1998.
Mfg.'s Sug. Retail   **$4,285**   **$3,725 $3,275 $2,600 $2,250 $1,825 $1,350 $1,150**

* *Model R-93 Attache* — same cals. as R-93 Classic, except not available in .416 Rem. Mag, features premium walnut stock and forearm with receiver wood panel inserts, wood bolt knob, ebony forearm tip, fluted barrel, includes case, approx. 6½ lbs. New 1998.
Mfg.'s Sug. Retail   **$5,125**   **$4,650 $4,125 $3,600 $3,150 $2,600 $2,150 $1,725**
   Add $625 per interchangeable barrel (w/o mounts).

* *Model R-93 Grand Luxe* — same cals. as R-93 Attache, deluxe model with high grade checkered walnut stock and forearm, fully hand engraved receiver, 3 shot mag, 6½ - 7 lbs. New 1999.
Mfg.'s Sug. Retail   **$4,675**   **$4,025 $3,475 $2,700 $2,300 $1,850 $1,350 $1,150**

* *Model R-93 Long Range Sporter* — .308 Win. cal. only, competition styled long range sporter with adj. trigger and stock, 10 shot removable box mag, free floating fluted barrel, many competition features, 10.4 lbs. New 1999.
Mfg.'s Sug. Retail   **$2,130**   **$1,825 $1,595 $1,350 $1,150 $1,000 $875 $795**

* *Model R-93 Synthetic* — available in 15 cals. between .22-250 Rem. - .416 Rem. Mag., also available by special order in the same European cals. as the Model R-93 Repeater, features one-piece conventional black synthetic stock, 22 or 26 in. barrel, without scope mounts and rings, 6½ - 7 lbs. New 1998.
Mfg.'s Sug. Retail   **$1,495**   **$1,325 $1,100 $975 $875 $775 $695 $625**
   Add $790 for Safari Model in .416 Rem. Mag.
   Add $525 per interchangeable barrel (w/o mounts).

* *Model R-93 LX* — similar cals. as Model R-93 Synthetic, except includes .416 Rem. Mag., features checkered walnut stock and forearm, coin finished stippled receiver sides, without scope mounts and rings, 6½ - 7 lbs. New 1998.
Mfg.'s Sug. Retail   **$1,795**   **$1,595 $1,350 $1,150 $1,000 $875 $795 $695**
   Add $790 for Safari LX Model in .416 Rem. Mag.
   Add $525 per interchangeable barrel (w/o mounts).

Grading	100%	98%	95%	90%	80%	70%	60%

ULTIMATE BOLT ACTION — .22-250 Rem., .243 Win., .25-06 Rem., .270 Win., .308 Win., .30-06, 7x57mm, 7x64mm, .264 Win. Mag., 7mm Rem. Mag., .300 Win. Mag., .338 Win. Mag., or .375 H&H cal., unique bolt action design with 60 degree bolt throw, interchangeable barrel capability, 3 locking lugs, safety lever cocks and uncocks the firing pin spring, exposed hammer, aluminum receiver, 22 or 24 in. barrel, single set trigger, silver finished receiver has light engraving, select checkered walnut stock and forearm, 6¾ lbs. Extra interchangeable barrels are $545 each, extra bolt heads are $175 each. Mfg. 1985-1989.

$1,350	**$1,100**	**$975**	**$925**	**$825**	**$750**	**$675**	

Last Mfg.'s Sug. Retail was $1,495.

All models were available in left-hand version at no extra charge.

MODEL K77 A SINGLE SHOT — .22-250 Rem., .243 Win., 6.5x55mm, .270 Win., 7x57R, 7x65R, or .30-06 standard cals., 7mm Rem. Mag., .300 Win. Mag. or .300 Wby. Mag. cal., break open action, 23 or 24 in. barrel, 3 piece take down, upper tang safety, checkered walnut stock and forearm, engraved silver finished receiver, sling swivels, 5½ lbs. Imported 1988-90.

$2,000	**$1,675**	**$1,475**	**$1,300**	**$1,100**	**$925**	**$800**

Last Mfg.'s Sug. Retail was $2,280.

Add $50 for Mag. calibers.
Add $730-$778 per interchangeable barrel.

ULTIMATE BOLT ACTION - SPECIAL ORDER — all of the models listed below may have been ordered with a buttstock cartridge trap — add $250-$500 depending on model. Mfg. was disc. 1989 on all models. Please contact SIG Arms for more information regarding Blaser's current extensive listing of special order rifles.

* *Ultimate Deluxe* — similar to Ultimate, except better wood and game scene engraving.

$1,425	**$1,175**	**$1,000**	**$950**	**$850**	**$775**	**$700**

Last Mfg.'s Sug. Retail was $1,595.

* *Ultimate Deluxe Carbine* — .243 Win. or .308 Win. cal. only, 19½ in. barrel with full length forearm. New 1986.

$1,600	**$1,375**	**$1,150**	**$1,000**	**$900**	**$825**	**$750**

Last Mfg.'s Sug. Retail was $1,800.

* *Ultimate Super Deluxe* — similar to Ultimate Deluxe, except features better wood and game scene engraving. New 1986.

$3,750	**$3,250**	**$2,900**	**$2,600**	**$2,300**	**$2,100**	**$1,850**

Last Mfg.'s Sug. Retail was $4,030.

* *Ultimate Exclusive* — similar to Ultimate Super Deluxe, except features better wood and game scene engraving. New 1986.

$4,850	**$4,300**	**$3,500**	**$2,975**	**$2,600**	**$2,275**	**$1,975**

Last Mfg.'s Sug. Retail was $5,655.

Add $700 per interchangeable barrel.

* *Ultimate Super Exclusive* — similar to Ultimate Exclusive, except features better wood and game scene engraving. New 1986.

$7,700	**$6,800**	**$5,750**	**$4,700**	**$3,950**	**$3,450**	**$2,950**

Last Mfg.'s Sug. Retail was $8,905.

Add $950 per interchangeable barrel.

* *Ultimate Royal* — best quality Ultimate, featuring Bavarian cheekpiece and checkering/carving on stock and forearm, elaborate game scene engraving, gold plated hammer. New 1986.

$9,000	**$7,500**	**$6,750**	**$6,000**	**$5,375**	**$4,600**	**$4,000**

Last Mfg.'s Sug. Retail was $11,500.

Add $1,200 per interchangeable barrel.

Grading	100%	98%	95%	90%	80%	70%	60%

BOHICA

Previous manufacturer and customizer located in Sedalia, CO circa 1993-94.

RIFLES: SEMI-AUTO

M16-SA — .223 Rem., .50 AE, or various custom cals., AR-15 style, 16 or 20 in. barrel, A-2 sights, standard handguard, approx. 950 were mfg. through September, 1994.

$1,375	$1,225	$1,000	$850	$725	$600	$525

Add $100 for flat-top receiver with scope rail.
Add $65 for two-piece, free floating handguard.

In addition to the rifles listed above, Bohica also manufactured a M16-SA Match variation (retail was $2,295, approx. 10 mfg.), a pistol version of the M16-SA in both 7 and 10 in. barrel (retail was $1,995, approx. 50 mfg.), and a limited run of M16-SA in .50 AE cal. (retail was $1,695, approx. 25 mfg.).

BOITO

Previous manufacturer located in Brazil. Previously imported by F.I.E. Corp. located in Hialeah, FL.

Boito shotguns were inexpensive, utilitarian shotguns that are shootable, but not collectible. Because of this, prices typically range between $100 - $225, depending on the gauge and condition.

BOND ARMS, INC.

Current manufacturer located in Granbury, Texas beginning 1998.

DERRINGERS: O/U

TEXAS DEFENDER — 9mm Para., .32 H&R Mag., .357 Mag., .357 Max, .40 S&W, .44 Mag., .45 ACP, or .45 LC/.410 shot shell cals., O/U design, 3 in. barrels with spring loaded extractors, stainless steel, removable trigger guard, rebounding hammer, crossbolt safety, spring loaded cammed locking lever, 21 oz. New 1998.

Mfg.'s Sug. Retail	$339		$285	$235	$195	

Add $109 per extra set of barrels.

CENTURY 2000 DEFENDER (C2K) — .410 bore/.45 LC cal. with 2½ in. chambers and 3 in. barrels, or .410 bore with 3 in. chambers and 3½ in. barrels. New 1999.

Mfg.'s Sug. Retail	$359		$300	$245	$195	

BORCHARDT

Previous pistol design originating in Germany circa 1894-1897.

PISTOLS: SEMI-AUTO

Prices below assume matching parts and original condition.

MODEL 1893 — 7.65mm cal., original Luger design, 6½ in. barrel, blue finish with fire-blued small parts, checkered walnut grips, 8 shot mag., distinguished by elongated spring mechanism housing located behind the toggle assembly, may include accessories (mags., holster, stock) and/or case.

* *Ludwig Loewe Mfg.* — serial numbered 1-1104.

> Gun Only

$12,000	$10,500	$9,000	$7,500	$6,250	$4,950	$3,750

Original stocks (with attached leather holster) are priced starting at $3,500.

> **Cased With Accessories** — original cased gun was supplied with matching shoulder stock, detachable cheekpiece, leather holster, 3 regular mags. and a hold-open mag.

$23,500	$18,000	$12,500	$10,000	$8,000	$6,500	$5,000

Grading	100%	98%	95%	90%	80%	70%	60%

✳ DWM Mfg. — starting approx. 1895, serial numbered 1105-3000.

➤ **Gun Only**

	$11,250	$9,995	$8,500	$7,000	$5,750	$4,350	$3,250

Original stocks (with attached leather holster) are priced starting at $3,500.

➤ **Cased With Accessories** — original cased gun was supplied with unnumbered shoulder stock, detachable cheekpiece, leather holster, 3 regular mags. and a hold-open mag.

	$22,500	$18,000	$12,500	$10,000	$8,000	$6,500	$5,000

BOSS & CO., LTD.

Current manufacturer located in London, England 1812 to date. Direct sales from the manufacturer only.

Boss manufactures some of the world's finest shotguns and rifles (best quality guns only). Their shotguns and rifles have always been custom built per individual order. Approximately 10,000 have been manufactured to date. Listed below are the basic models (does not include special orders, optional engraving patterns, and other possible options) with current retail values computed at 1 pound (£1.00 = $1.65) and are for standard models only.

RIFLES: BOLT ACTION

BOSS BOLT ACTION — .270 Win. or .275 Rigby cal., Mauser action with Walther premium sporter barrel, Win. Model 70 three position side safety, box mag, includes mounts and Zeiss scope.

Mfg.'s Sug. Retail	$17,325	$17,325	$12,500	$10,000	$7,500	$6,500	$5,500	$4,500

RIFLES: O/U, CUSTOM

Boss Express O/U double rifles are quoted per individual request only. Current pricing for the .470 NE or .500 NE cal. starts at $156,000 (w/o VAT). Approx. 12½ lbs. Older double rifles must be appraised individually.

SHOTGUNS: CUSTOM

Prices below DO NOT include English VAT.

BOSS SxS — all gauges (16 ga. is currently POR), barrel lengths and chokes to specifications, bar-action sidelock, easy open/close action (not self-opening), square or rounded action, checkered stock, pistol grip (optional) or straight grip stock, single (patented 3 pull system) or double triggers, splinter or beavertail (optional) forearm, traditional English rose & scroll engraving.

Mfg.'s Sug. Retail	$54,450	$54,450	$47,100	$33,250	$22,500	$18,750	$15,000	$13,000

Add $3,300 for 20 ga.
Add $9,075 for 28 ga. or .410 bore.
Add $1,650 surcharge for ordering a pair of matched guns.

Note: above values represent base gun only. Any additional engraving (tight rose and scroll is the traditional standard) and/or special orders will add considerably to the above prices.

BOSS O/U — 12, 20, 28 ga., or .410 bore standard, barrel lengths and chokes to specifications, shell-framed sidelock, auto ejectors, double triggers or single non-selective, English straight stock standard to specifications, VR or pistol grip stock optional, traditional English rose & scroll fine engraving, limited availability.

Mfg.'s Sug. Retail	$82,500	$82,500	$70,650	$52,100	$37,500	$32,500	$27,500	$22,500

Add $4,125 for 20 ga.
Add $8,250 for 28 ga. or .410 bore.
Add $3,300 surcharge for ordering a pair of matched guns.

Note: above values represent base gun only. Any additional engraving (tight rose and scroll is the traditional standard) and/or special orders will add considerably to the above prices.

Grading	100%	98%	95%	90%	80%	70%	60%

BOSWELL, CHARLES

Previous trademark manufactured in London, England and Charlotte, NC.

In 1988, Charles Boswell was purchased by U.S. interests and Cape Horn International (previously Cape Horn Outfitters) located in Charlotte, NC and was retained to sell and manufacture the Boswell Guns in the U.S. In addition to acquiring their entire inventory of English manufactured firearms, Charles Boswell fabricated new shotguns and double rifles in the U.S. using the best materials including English lock mechanisms and retained the Charles Boswell Co. trademark. Every gun was custom ordered to an individual client's requirements/specifications. Previously imported by Saxon Arms, Ltd., located in Clearwater, FL.

RIFLES: SxS

BOXLOCK SxS RIFLE — .300 Express, .375 H&H, .458 Win. Mag., or .500 NE cal., made to individual order, choice of game scene engraving, Anson & Deeley boxlock actions, select European hybrid walnut, double triggers, leather cased. Disc. 1996.

$31,000 $27,000 $23,000 $19,000 $16,500 $15,000 $13,250
Last Mfg.'s Sug. Retail was $35,000.

* **.600 Nitro Express**

   This model was priced by quotation only. A .600 NE sold for $123,000 in 1991. Disc. 1996.

SIDELOCK SxS RIFLE — .300 Express, .375 H&H, or .458 Win. Mag. cal., made to individual order, choice of game scene engraving, H&H sidelock action, select European hybrid walnut, double triggers, leather cased. Disc. 1996.

$55,000 $47,500 $40,000 $35,000 $31,000 $25,000 $21,500
Last Mfg.'s Sug. Retail was $65,000.

* **.600 Nitro Express**

$95,000 $70,000 $54,500 $43,500 $37,500 $31,000 $26,000
Last Mfg.'s Sug. Retail was $125,000.

SHOTGUNS: SxS

BOXLOCK SxS — previously made to individual order, choice of engraving - including game scenes with gold, Anson & Deeley boxlock actions, select European hybrid walnut, double triggers, leather cased. While each shotgun was priced per individual special order, the below listed prices represented standard features and embellishments. Disc. 1996.

* **Best Quality**

$8,650 $7,650 $6,500 $5,650 $4,800 $4,200 $3,750
Last Mfg.'s Sug. Retail was $9,500.

* **Deluxe Grade** — game scene engraved.

$9,175 $8,500 $7,250 $6,000 $5,000 $4,400 $3,750
Last Mfg.'s Sug. Retail was $10,500.

   Add $900 for single trigger.
   Add $2,800 for extra set of barrels.
   Add $2,200 for smaller gauges.

FEATHERWEIGHT MONARCH GRADE — lavishly engraved with gold game scenes, lightweight model, specifications per individual customer special order. Mfg. 1989-1996.

* **Boxlock Model**

$11,250 $9,750 $7,350 $6,000 $5,000 $4,400 $3,750
Last Mfg.'s Sug. Retail was $12,500.

* **Sidelock Model**

$21,250 $18,750 $15,000 $12,750 $10,000 $7,950 $6,250
Last Mfg.'s Sug. Retail was $25,000.

Grading	100%	98%	95%	90%	80%	70%	60%

SIDELOCK SxS — previously made to individual order, choice of game scene engraving, H&H sidelock action, select European hybrid walnut, double triggers, leather cased, currently mfg. While each shotgun was priced per individual special order, the below listed values represented standard features and embellishments.

$16,000	$14,000	$12,750	$10,000	$9,000	$8,500	$7,750

Last Mfg.'s Sug. Retail was $17,500.

Add $4,000 for smaller gauges except .410 bore — add $5,000.
Add $2,800 for extra set of barrels.
Add $2,800 for extra set of .410 bore barrels.

BREDA MECCANICA BRESCIANA

Current manufacturer located in Brescia, Italy. Previous company name was Ernesto Breda. No current domestic importer - please refer to the Trademark Index for current factory information. Older importation was by Diana Imports Co., located in San Francisco, CA.

SHOTGUNS: SEMI-AUTO

GOLD SERIES SEMI-AUTO — 12 or 20 (lightweight) ga., semi-auto, 2¾ in., 25 or 27 in. barrels, gas operated. Current model has interchangeable choke tubes, vent. rib is standard. Add $26 for choke tubes (each).

* *Antares Standard* — all steel construction. Importation disc. 1988.

$440	$375	$340	$310	$285	$260	$240

Last Mfg.'s Sug. Retail was $495.

* *Argus* — lightweight standard, weighs only 6.6 lbs. Importation disc. 1988.

$450	$380	$340	$310	$285	$260	$240

Last Mfg.'s Sug. Retail was $510.

* *Aries* — Magnum, 3 in. chambers, 7.9 lbs. Importation disc. 1988.

$460	$395	$350	$320	$295	$270	$250

Last Mfg.'s Sug. Retail was $525.

STANDARD — 12 ga., semi-auto, 2¾ in., 25 or 27 in. barrels, recoil operated, lightly engraved. Current model has interchangeable choke tubes. Add $35 for vent. rib, $20 for choke tubes (each). Disc.

$300	$275	$255	$230	$215	$200	$180

GRADE 1 — 12 ga., similar to standard, except with fancier wood and engraving.

$575	$530	$485	$440	$410	$380	$350

GRADE 2 — 12 ga., exceeds Grade 1 on embellishments.

$685	$620	$560	$500	$460	$420	$375

GRADE 3 — 12 ga., top-of-the-line semi-auto.

$850	$790	$700	$640	$590	$540	$480

MAGNUM MODEL — 12 ga. only, chambered for 3 in. shells. Add $20 for vent. rib.

$470	$415	$380	$350	$315	$290	$265

ALTAIR SPECIAL — 12 ga. semi-auto, 2¾ in., 25 or 27 in. barrels, gas operated, alloy construction. Current model has interchangeable choke tubes, vent. rib is standard. Add $25 for choke tubes (each). Choice of blued or chromed receiver.

$440	$375	$340	$310	$285	$260	$240

Last Mfg.'s Sug. Retail was $495.

Grading	100%	98%	95%	90%	80%	70%	60%

SHOTGUNS: O/U

VEGA SPECIAL — 12 or 20 ga., boxlock action, 26 or 28 in. barrels, single trigger, ejectors, blue only.

	$575	$495	$460	$440	$400	$375	$350

Last Mfg.'s Sug. Retail was $650.

VEGA SPECIAL TRAP — 12 ga. only, boxlock action, triggers and locks designed for competition shooting, 30 or 32 in. barrels, single trigger, ejectors, blue only.

	$885	$820	$760	$720	$675	$635	$575

Last Mfg.'s Sug. Retail was $1,114.

SIRIO STANDARD — 12 or 20 ga., boxlock action, 26 or 28 in. barrels, single trigger, ejectors, blue only, action extensively engraved. Also available in skeet model (28 in. barrels).

	$2,000	$1,850	$1,630	$1,480	$1,320	$1,200	$1,050

Last Mfg.'s Sug. Retail was $2,225.

SHOTGUNS: SxS

ANDROMEDA SPECIAL — 12 ga. only, single trigger, ejectors, select checkered walnut, satin finish receiver with elaborate engraving.

	$640	$550	$480	$420	$365	$300	$250

Last Mfg.'s Sug. Retail was $685.

BREN 10

Previous trademark manufactured 1983-86 by Dornaus & Dixon Ent., Inc., located in Huntington Beach, CA.

Bren 10 magazines played an important part in the failure of these pistols to be accepted by consumers. Originally, Bren magazines were not shipped in some cases until a year after the customer received his gun. The complications arising around manufacturing a reliable magazine domestically lead to the downfall of this company. For this reason, original Bren 10 magazines are currently selling for $125-$150 if new (watch for fakes).

PISTOLS: SEMI-AUTO

Note: the Bren 10 shoots a Norma factory loaded 10mm auto. cartridge. Ballistically, it is very close to a .41 Mag. Bren pistols also have unique power seal rifling, with five lands and grooves. While in production, Bren pistols underwent (4) engineering changes, the most important probably being re-designing the floorplate of the magazine, thus preventing mag. shifting while undergoing recoil.

100% values in this section assume NIB condition. Subtract 10% without box/manual.

BREN 10 STANDARD MODEL — 10mm cal. only, semi-auto selective double action design, blue slide/silver frame finish, 5 in. barrel, 11 shot, stainless steel frame, usually supplied with two mags. although early mfg. did not include a mag. because of design problems, "83SM" ser. no. prefix. Mfg. 1984-86.

	$1,550	$1,250	$975

Last Mfg.'s Sug. Retail was $500.

Add $600 for .45 conversion unit.

BREN 10 MILITARY/POLICE MODEL — 10mm cal. only, identical to standard model, except has all black finish, "83MP" ser. no. prefix. Mfg. 1984–86.

	$1,495	$1,195	$950

Last Mfg.'s Sug. Retail was $550.

BREN 10 SPECIAL FORCES MODEL — 10mm cal. only, commercial version of the military pistol submitted to the U.S. gov't. Model D has dark finish. Model L has light finish, "SFD" ser. no. prefix on Model D, "SFL" ser. no. prefix on Model L. Disc. 1986.

Dark finish - Model D	$1,595	$1,275	$975
Light finish - Model L	$1,895	$1,575	$1,275

Last Mfg.'s Sug. Retail was $600.

Grading	100%	98%	95%	90%	80%	70%	60%

BREN 10 DUAL-MASTER PRESENTATION MODEL — 10mm and .45 ACP cal., supplied with extra slide and barrel (numbered to gun) to accommodate the .45 ACP, same mags. (two) for both cals., extra fine finish, light scroll engraving, with wood presentation case, "83DM" ser. no. prefix, less than 50 mfg. Disc. 1986.

B

$3,900 $3,000 $2,500
Last Mfg.'s Sug. Retail was $800.

BREN 10 JEFF COOPER COMMEMORATIVE — 10mm cal. only, while 2,000 were annnounced for mfg., sources believe less than 30 were actually made, 22Kt. gold plated detailing, laser engraved stocks, special presentation chest. Disc. 1986.

$4,800 $4,500 $3,900
Last Mfg.'s Sug. Retail was $2,000.

MARKSMAN MODEL — .45 ACP cal., 250 mfg. (in its own ser. range) for a retail shop in Chicago called "The Marksman", action similar to Bren 10 Standard Model, "MSM" ser. no. prefix.

$1,200 $895 $695

Add $650 for 10mm conversion unit.
Add $100 for original nylon carrying case marked "Marksman".

BRETTON

Current manufacturer located in Saint-Etienne, France. Imported and distributed by Mandall Shooting Supplies, Inc. located in Scottsdale, AZ.

SHOTGUNS: O/U

All Bretton shotguns are extremely lightweight and well balanced because of their unique design (permitting total disassembly including barrels) and use of various composition alloys.

BABY STANDARD (SPRINT MODEL) — 12 or 20 ga. only, sliding breech action allows barrels to move straight forward, 27½ in. separated barrels, double triggers, side opening lever, blued action and barrels, recoil pad, checkered walnut stock and forearm, 4.8 lbs.

Mfg.'s Sug. Retail	$995	$885	$700	$625	$575	$475	$430	$395

Available from Mandall Shooting Supply, Inc. only.

SPRINT DELUXE — 12, 16 (disc.), or 20 ga., action similar to Baby Standard, engraved coin finished receiver, 27½ in. separated barrels, deluxe checkered walnut stock and forearm, extremely lightweight, 4.8 lbs. Importation disc. 1994.

$895 $725 $625 $575 $475 $430 $395
Last Mfg.'s Sug. Retail was $975.

Available from Quality Arms, Inc. and Mandall Shooting Supply, Inc.

FAIR PLAY MODEL — 12 or 20 ga., differs from Sprint Models in that action pivots like normal O/U, 27½ in. separated barrels, lightweight construction, 4.8 lbs.

Mfg.'s Sug. Retail	$966		$850	$675	$625	$575	$475	$430	$395

Add $64 for Fair Play Limited Model.

BRILEY

Current pistol and rifle manufacturer located in Houston, TX since 1976. Briley also manufactures a complete line of top quality shotgun barrel tubes and chokes - please contact the factory directly (see Trademark Index) for more information on these shotgun accessories.

Grading	100%	98%	95%	90%	80%	70%	60%

B

PISTOLS: SEMI-AUTO

FANTOM — 9mm Para., .38 Super, .40 S&W, or .45 ACP cal., features Caspian aluminum wide body frame, Briley match barrel, and many competition features, hot blue slide finish and armor coated frame, 8 or 10 shot mag, black synthetic grips, approx. 24 oz. New 1998.

Mfg.'s Sug. Retail	$1,795	$1,595	$1,250	$1,050	$875	$750	$625	$575

Add $95 for hard chrome finish.
Add $350 for 2 port barrel compensator.

ADVANTAGE — 9mm Para., .40 S&W, or .45 ACP cal., features 5 in. Briley match barrel, checkered walnut grips and front grip strap, hot blue finish. New 1998.

Mfg.'s Sug. Retail	$1,495	$1,375	$1,150	$975	$850	$725	$625	$575

Add $175 for hard chrome finish.

VERSATILITY PLUS — 9mm Para., .40 S&W, or .45 ACP cal., features 1911 Govt. length modular or Caspian frame, 5 in. barrel, checkered black synthetic grips and front grip strap, squared off trigger guard, hot blue finish. New 1998.

Mfg.'s Sug. Retail	$1,695	$1,500	$1,200	$995	$850	$725	$600	$550

Add $175 for hard chrome finish.

SIGNATURE SERIES — .40 S&W cal. only, similar to Versatility Plus. New 1998.

Mfg.'s Sug. Retail	$1,995	$1,795	$1,525	$1,250	$1,050	$875	$750	$625

Add $175 for hard chrome finish.

PLATE MASTER — 9mm Para. or .38 Super cal., features 1911 Govt. length frame, Briley TCII titanium barrel compensator, Briley scope mount, and other competition features, hot blue finish. New 1998.

Mfg.'s Sug. Retail	$1,795	$1,595	$1,250	$1,050	$875	$750	$625	$575

Add $175 for hard chrome finish.

EL PRESIDENTE — 9mm Para. or .38 Super cal., top-of-the-line competition model with Briley quad compensator with side ports, checkered synthetic grips and front grip strap, squared off trigger guard. New 1998.

Mfg.'s Sug. Retail	$2,195	$1,975	$1,775	$1,525	$1,250	$1,050	$875	$750

Add $175 for hard chrome finish.

RIFLES: BOLT ACTION

TRANS PECOS — .22-250 Rem., .243 Win., .260 Rem., .308 Win., or 7mm-08 Rem. cal., solid aluminum frame fits metal to metal with barreled action, bench rest grade Jewell trigger, match grade L. Walther barrel, 3 lug 45 degree one-piece bolt, choice of black synthetic (single shot) or checkered high gloss stock and forearm (repeater). New 1998.

Mfg.'s Sug. Retail	$3,495	$3,200	$2,750	$2,275	$1,950	$1,775	$1,525	$1,250

Subtract $500 for single shot action.

RIFLES: SEMI-AUTO

Briley manufactures a line of accurized semi-auto rifles featuring a Briley 10/22 action. Models include the Briley 10/22 BMG ($950 retail), the Briley 10/22 Classic Sporter ($600 retail), and the Briley 10/22 Hunter ($600 retail). please contact the company directly for more information on these rifles.

BRITARMS

Previous trademark manufactured by Berdan Gunmakers Ltd. located in England. Previously imported and distributed until 1994 by Mandall Shooting Supplies, Inc. located in Scottsdale, AZ. Previously by Action Arms Ltd. (1982-83) located in Philadelphia, PA.

Grading	100%	98%	95%	90%	80%	70%	60%

Britarms Target Pistols had very limited importation into the U.S. While Britarms manufactured other models, only the Model 2000 is listed since it was formally imported through U.S. firms.

PISTOLS: SEMI-AUTO

Model 2000 (MK II) — .22 LR cal., standard fire target semi-auto pistol, adj. trigger and rear sight, anatomical adj. grips, 5.82 in. barrel, 5 shot mag., 3 lbs., limited importation, including approx. 200 through Action Arms Ltd.

$995	$825	$700	$625	$550	$495	$450

Last Mfg.'s Sug. Retail was $1,295.

This model features a bolt hold-open mechanism which serves as a manual safety to allow importation.

BRNO ARMS (ZBROJOVKA BRNO)

Currently manufactured by Zbrojovka Brno located in Brno, Czech Republic (formerly Czechoslovakia) since 1916. Currently imported and distributed by Euro-Imports, located in El Cajon, CA. Previously imported by Bohemia Arms located in Fountain Valley, CA until 1997. Brno rifles, shotguns, and combination guns produced at the Brno factory were previously imported and distributed by Magnum Research Inc. located in Minneapolis, MN (c. 1994-96). In the early '50s, Brno rifles were imported by Continental Arms Corp. located in New York City. Pragotrade located in Ontario, Canada also imports this trademark for Canada currently (and exclusively). Previously imported by T.D. Arms located in New Baltimore, MI.

As more history is becoming available on this important European trademark, the following biographical sketch will provide some information. Circa 1918, some military personnel took over the controlling interest of the Austro-Hungarian armament shop in Brno, Czechoslovakia, renaming it The State Armament and Engineering Works. Approximately a year later, the name was changed to Czechoslovak State Armament Works. The former provinces of Bohemia and Moravia had long been firearms manufacturing centers within their regions. Prior to 1924, this firm was involved mainly with Mauser Model 98 type rifles (both assembly and mfg.).

Pistol manufacture was tranferred from Brno to Ceská Zbrojovka, located in Strakonice, Czechoslovakia, circa 1923. During 1964-1966, the Czech government transferred the production of long guns from Zbrojovka Brno to Ceská Zbrojovka Uhersky Brod. During the 1970s & 1980s, the arms production of Zbrojovka Brno accounted for less than 3% of its total capacity. The activities of this company were deverted into the production of typewriters, diesel motors, and automatic machine tools. While many firearm designs originated in Brno, Zbrojovka Brno was not the manufacturer. Because of this, the long guns manufactured in the mid-1960s, including the ZKK 600 - 602 series and ZKM rimfires, were manufactured in CZ Uhersky Brod. Because of the Czech government's decision to merge manufacture within both companies, the Brno trademark was also used by Ceská Zbrojovka Uhersky Brod.

This relationship was terminated in 1983, when both companies became part of the Agrozet conglomerate. While confusing, the arms utlizing the Brno trademark were not produced in Brno during this time. All firearms exported from Czechoslovakia at the time carried the Brno logo, and most of them were manufactured by Ceska Zbrojovka Uhersky Brod.

CZ PISTOLS & RIFLES

See separate listing under CZ in this text.

Grading	100%	98%	95%	90%	80%	70%	60%

PISTOLS: SEMI-AUTO

MODEL ZBP-99 — 9mm Para. or .40 S&W cal., double action, 4 in. barrel with fixed sights, firing pin safety block and chambered cartridge indicator, plastic frame with steel action guides, decocking, locked action, approx. 28 oz.

While advertised in 1998, this gun has yet to be imported.

REVOLVERS

ZKR 551 — .32 S&W Long or .38 Spl. cal., double action, fixed access 6 shot cylinder, adj. sights, checkered wood grips with thumb rest, 6 in. barrel, approx. 2 lbs. Importation began 1999.

Mfg.'s Sug. Retail	$1,556	$1,375	$1,100	$978	$875	$775	$675	$600

RIFLES: BOLT ACTION

The Brno Lightweight Sporter was introduced in the late 1930s. A small quantity was manufactured during pre-war and WWII. Most production occured between 1946-1955. Total production of this model was approx. 40,000+ units. A design change was implemented at approximately serial number 23,000, at which time the receiver was changed to a double square bridge dovetailed to accept scope mounts.

Earlier mfg. had a rounded receiver and some had claw type scope mounts installed. These guns were referenced as Models 21 and 22 domestically, but no model designation appears on the gun. Available cals. were 6.5x57mm, 7x57mm, 7x64mm, 8x57mm, or 8x60mm. Configuration was small ring Mauser 98 receiver with double set trigger(s), butterknife bolt, checkered walnut pistol grip stock (half or full length), with cheekpiece and sling swivels, late production incorporated four variations and two barrel lengths (20.5 or 23.6 in.).

BRNO RIFLES MAY BE DATED BY THE 2-DIGIT DATE BESIDE THEIR PROOFMARKS.

HORNET SPORTER (MODEL ZKW 465) — .22 Hornet cal., miniature Mauser action, $22\frac{3}{4}$ in. barrel, 5 shot clip mag., 3-leaf express sight, double set trigger(s), checkered pistol grip stock, also called Z-B Mauser, serial range noted is 02,901-37,393, approx. 40,000 mfg. between 1949-1973.

	$875	$700	$600	$470	$385	$305	$220

There are few examples in .218 Bee and .222 Rem. cal. - premiums can be added.

This model was redesigned with a subsequent designation of ZKB 680 Fox in approx. 1975.

MODEL ZG-47 — .270 Win., .30-06, 7x57mm, 7x64mm, 8x64S, 8x57mm, 9.3x62mm, or 10.75x68mm cal., large ring Mauser 98 action with 20mm dovetails on receiver ring and bridge, single trigger, hinged floorplate, rollover type safety and bolt handle designed for low scope mounting, $23\frac{1}{2}$ in. barrel, checkered pistol grip walnut stock with sling swivels and Schnabel forend, approx. serial range is 0-20,000, mfg. and exported world-wide between 1956-1962 (approx.).

	$995	$875	$700	$600	$470	$385	$305

Early specimens of this model are marked "BRNO MADE IN CZECHOSLOVAKIA". This model is generally regarded as being one of the finest rifles that Brno has manufactured.

MODEL G 33-40 — 8mm cal., mfg. between 1940-42, prices below assume sporterized condition.

	$350	$295	$260	$230	$200	$175	$150

Grading	100%	98%	95%	90%	80%	70%	60%

MODEL 21H — 6.5x57mm, 7x57mm, 7x64mm (scarce), or 8x57mm cal., featherweight style design of the small ring Mauser type action, with (post-1949) or without 20mm dovetails on receiver ring and bridge, 20½ or 23 in. barrel, butterknife style bolt handle, double set triggers, 2-leaf rear sight, checkered pistol grip walnut stock with cheekpiece and plastic buttplate/grip cap, small Schnabel forend, sling swivels included, noted serialization is 14,410-40,098, mfg. approx. 1946-1955.

	$850	$675	$575	$470	$385	$305	$220

> This model was available in 4 different variations: short barrel/short stock, short barrel/full length stock, long barrel/short stock, long barrel/full length stock. The left receiver rail on these models is marked "ZBROJOVKA BRNO, NARODNI PODNIK".

MODEL 22F — similar to 21H, with full length stock. Disc.

	$1,050	$900	$700	$525	$440	$360	$275

MODEL 1 — .22 LR cal., 22¾ in. barrel, 3-leaf sight, 5 shot clip mag., checkered pistol, 6 lbs. Mfg. 1946-1957.

	$595	$540	$485	$405	$375	$320	$265

MODEL 2 — similar to Model 1, with checkered deluxe walnut stock.

	$635	$570	$515	$430	$405	$350	$295

MODEL 3 — .22 LR cal., target rifle model with 27½ in. heavy barrel, adj. click target sights, 5 shot clip mag., plain target style stock with large swivels, 9½ lbs. Mfg. 1949-1956.

	$635	$570	$515	$430	$405	$350	$295

MODEL 4 — similar to Model 3, except has improved trigger design and safety. Mfg. 1957-1962.

	$700	$635	$570	$515	$430	$405	$350

MODEL 5 — similar to Model 1, except has improved trigger design and safety. Mfg. 1957-1973.

	$650	$570	$515	$430	$405	$350	$295

BRNO 98 STANDARD — .243 Win., .270 Win., .30-06, .308 Win., .300 Win. Mag., 7x64mm, or 9.3x62mm cal., Mauser 98 style action, 23.6 in. barrel with or without iron sights, checkered walnut stock with Bavarian cheekpiece, single or set trigger, 7¼ lbs. Importation began 1998.

Mfg.'s Sug. Retail	$578	$495	$395	$360	$325	$295	$280	$265

Add $48 for Mag. cals.
Add $117 for single set trigger.

＊ Brno 98 Mannlicher — similar to Brno 98 Standard, except has full length stock. New 1998.

Mfg.'s Sug. Retail	$791	$675	$540	$475	$385	$350	$315	$295

Add $46 for Mag. cals.

MODEL ZKB-110 SINGLE SHOT — .22 Hornet, .222 Rem., 5.6x52R, 5.6x50mm Mag., 6.5x57R, 7x57R, or 8x57JRS cal., single shot break open rifle/shotgun, top lever opening, 23.6 in. barrel, uncheckered (Standard Model) or checkered walnut stock with Bavarian cheekpiece and forearm (Lux Model), includes sling swivels, 6 lbs. Importation began 1998.

Mfg.'s Sug. Retail	$263	$225	$185	$160	$140	$120	$110	$100

Add $77 for ZKB-110 Lux Model.
Add $48 for 7x57R or 8x57JRS cal.
Add approx. $127 for interchangeable 12 ga. shotgun barrel.

MODEL ZOM-451 — .22 LR cal., straight pull bolt action, 7 shot mag., 22 in. barrel with adj. rear sight, adj. trigger, uncheckered beech stock, 5¼ lbs.

> While advertised in 1998, this model has yet to be imported.

MODEL ZKM-451 — .22 LR cal. Importation began 1995.

Mfg.'s Sug. Retail	$261	$220	$200	$185	$170	$155	$140	$125

Add $73 for Lux Model (deluxe checkered wood).

Grading	100%	98%	95%	90%	80%	70%	60%

B

MODEL ZKM-452 — please refer to the CZ listing in this text for current information (current mfg. is by CZ).

MODEL ZKM-456 LUX SPORTER — .22 LR cal., bolt action, 5 or 10 shot mag., 24.4 in. barrel, folding rear sight, blued finish, beechwood stock with pistol grip, 6.8 lbs. Imported 1992-98.

	$315	$260	$215	$175	$155	$135	$120

Last Mfg.'s Sug. Retail was $370.

Add $18 for micrometer rear sight (ZKM-456 MI).

* ***Model 456 L/LK Target*** — .22 LR cal., Target variation of the ZKM-456 Lux featuring 25 or 28 in. barrel with adj. front and rear sights, 10.1 lbs. Imported 1992-98.

	$305	$250	$210	$170	$150	$130	$115

Last Mfg.'s Sug. Retail was $358.

Add $7 for 25 in. barrel.

* ***Model 456 Match Single Shot*** — .22 LR cal., designed for UIT competition at 50 M, features 27½ in. barrel, adj. cheekpiece and buttplate, aperture sights, 9.9 lbs. Imported 1992-98.

	$375	$335	$280	$250	$215	$175	$155

Last Mfg.'s Sug. Retail was $459.

ZKK 600 — please refer to the CZ listing in this text for current information (recent mfg. is by CZ).

ZKK 601 — please refer to the CZ listing in this text for current information (recent mfg. was by CZ).

ZKK 602 — please refer to the CZ listing in this text for current information (current mfg. is by CZ).

ZKB 680 (FOX II) — .22 Hornet or .222 Rem. (disc.) cal., 23½ in. barrel, 5 shot mag., set triggers, 5 lbs. 12 oz. Importation disc. 1991.

	$445	$380	$340	$295	$255	$230	$200

Last Mfg.'s Sug. Retail was $499.

RIFLES: SEMI-AUTO

ZKM-611 — .22 Mag. cal., 20½ in. barrel, 6, 10 (C/B 1994), or 12★ shot mag., black metal finish, beechwood (new 1996) or checkered walnut stock and forend, grooved receiver, 6.2 lbs. Importation began 1992.

Mfg.'s Sug. Retail	$465	$395	$350	$300	$265	$230	$200	$185

Add $70 for walnut stock.

MODEL 581 — .22 LR cal., semi-auto, select walnut stock, adj. sights, 5 shot mag. Disc.

	$600	$540	$495	$440	$395	$350	$295

RIFLES: O/U

ZH-344, 348, & 349 — 7x57R (Model ZH-344), 7x65R (Model ZH-348), or 8x57JRS (Model ZH-349) cal., 23.6 in. VR barrels, double triggers, skip line checkering, sling swivels, approx. 7½ lbs. Importation began 1998.

Mfg.'s Sug. Retail	$1,297	$1,100	$978	$875	$775	$675	$600	$550

Add $324-$829 for interchangeable barrels in various cals/gauges.

SUPER EXPRESS — 7x65R, 9.3x74R, .375 H&H, or .458 Win. Mag. (disc.) cal., sidelock action with Kersten breech crossbolt, hand engraved, skipline checkering, approx. 9 lbs. Importation disc. 1992.

	$3,450	$2,875	$2,300	$1,875	$1,600	$1,375	$1,200

Last Mfg.'s Sug. Retail was $3,900.

This model previously could be ordered with 6 different types of engraving options. They were: Grade I — add $2,060, Grade II — add $1,030, Grade III — add $1,545, Grade IV — add $1,030, Grade V — add $620, Grade VI — add $660.

Grading	100%	98%	95%	90%	80%	70%	60%

SUPER SAFARI — 7x64R, .375 H&H Mag., or 9.3x74R cal., action derived from the Super Express, sidelock, DT with set trigger built in, adj. point of impact, 23.6 in. barrels with open sights, deluxe skipline checkered walnut stock and forearm with vent. recoil pad, approx. 9 lbs. Imported 1992-disc.

	$2,375	$1,975	$1,675	$1,450	$1,225	$1,000	$900

SHOTGUNS/COMBINATIONS GUNS: O/U

The current models listed below are being imported and distributed by Euro-Imports, located in El Cajon, CA.

ZH-300 SHOTGUN — 12 ga. only, double triggers with rear trigger doubling as single trigger, 27½ in. barrels, 7 lbs. Imported 1986-92.

	$530	$430	$395	$360	$330	$300	$275

Last Mfg.'s Sug. Retail was $599.

This model is available in skeet, trap, or field configuration.

ZH-301 FIELD SHOTGUN — 12 or 16 ga. field, 27½ in. barrels, optional Monte Carlo stock (disc.).

Mfg.'s Sug. Retail	$677		$600	$475	$375	$315	$240	$200	$180

Add $20 for Monte Carlo stock.

ZH-302 SKEET SHOTGUN — 12 ga., skeet model, 26 in. barrels, optional Monte Carlo stock (disc.).

Mfg.'s Sug. Retail	$710		$650	$515	$375	$300	$250	$225	$195

Add $20 for Monte Carlo stock.

ZH-303 TRAP SHOTGUN — 12 ga., trap model, 30 in. barrels, optional Monte Carlo stock (disc.).

Mfg.'s Sug. Retail	$710		$650	$515	$375	$300	$250	$225	$195

Add $20 for Monte Carlo stock.

ZH-300 SERIES COMBINATION GUNS — 7x57R x 12 ga. (ZH-304), 6x52R x 12 ga. (ZH-305), 6x50R Mag. x 12 ga. (ZH-306), .22 Hornet x 12 ga. (ZH-307), 7x65R x 12 ga. (ZH-308), 8x57JRS x 12 ga. (ZH-309), 7x57R x 16 ga. (ZH-324), 7x65R x 16 ga. (ZH-328), combination rifle/shotgun, optional adj. trigger and Monte Carlo stock. Importation disc. 1994 - reintroduced 1999.

Mfg.'s Sug. Retail	$821		$695	$575	$425	$350	$300	$250	$195

Add $73 for cheekpiece and set trigger.
Add $35 for adj. trigger (disc.).
Add $20 for Monte Carlo stock (disc.).

ZH 300 Series over and unders are unique in that they permit 8 different interchangeable barrels including rifle and shotgun sets, interrupter on double trigger, blued action, engraved, diamond checkered walnut.

MODEL ZH-300 COMBO SET — Model ZH-300 style engraving and features, equipped with 8 interchangeable barrels that include various O/U configurations including shotgun/shotgun and shotgun/rifle configurations in various ga.'s and cals. Imported 1986-91.

	$2,950	$2,600	$2,250	$2,000	$1,800	$1,600	$1,450

Last Mfg.'s Sug. Retail was $3,500.

MODEL 500/501 SHOTGUN — 12 ga. only, 28 in. VR barrels, double or single trigger.

Mfg.'s Sug. Retail	$975		$845	$725	$625	$525	$425	$350	$295

Add $50 for single trigger.

Grading	100%	98%	95%	90%	80%	70%	60%

* ***Model 500 Combo Set*** — shotgun/rifle set comprised of 4 barrels including 12 ga. over barrels with choice of 5.6x52R (disc.), 7x57R, 7x65R, or 12 ga. under barrels (in either field, skeet, or trap chokings), sling swivels, set trigger on rifle/shotgun combo, chemically engraved, about 7½ lbs. Imported 1987-91.

	$1,925	$1,625	$1,400	$1,200	$1,075	$950	$825

Last Mfg.'s Sug. Retail was $2,169.

This model is available in limited quanitity.

MODEL 502 SERIES COMBINATION GUN — 12 ga. only, ejectors, combination shotgun/rifle available in .222 Rem., .243 Win., .30-06, .308 Win., and 4 metric cals., fixed choke, acid etched engraving, skipline checkering and cheekpiece. New 1986.

Mfg.'s Sug. Retail	$1,174	$1,050	$850	$695	$600	$525	$425	$350

Add $699 for interchangeable 12 ga. shotgun barrels (new 1998).

BS-571/572 SHOTGUN/COMBINATION GUN — 12 ga. only, boxlock action with ejectors, 6x65R (disc.) or 7x65R rifle cal. only. Limited importation 1992-95.

	$825	$700	$600	$550	$475	$425	$375

Last Mfg.'s Sug. Retail was $995.

Add approx. $115 for rifle/shotgun (12 ga. only) combination (Model 572).

MODEL 571 SUPER SERIES — 12 ga. field, skeet, and trap configuration as well as combination shotgun/rifle in 12 ga. x 7x57R or 7x65R cal. Importation disc. 1991.

	$800	$700	$640	$590	$550	$515	$475

Last Mfg.'s Sug. Retail was $899.

Add $70 for single trigger or trap/skeet configuration (disc.).
Add $700 for extra set of 12 ga. field barrels.
Add $1,101 for hand engraving.

* ***Super Combo*** — 3 barrel set including 12 ga., 7x57R, and 7x65R barrels. Imported 1987-90.

	$1,925	$1,640	$1,425	$1,250	$1,100	$1,000	$925

Last Mfg.'s Sug. Retail was $2,169.

SHOTGUNS: SxS

ZP-49 — 12 ga. only, ejectors, double triggers, true sidelock, Purdey-type top bolt, cocking indicators, walnut stock, swivels. Imported 1986-91.

	$535	$460	$420	$385	$350	$320	$290

Last Mfg.'s Sug. Retail was $589.

Add $20 for engraving.

ZP-149 — similar to ZP-49, except has game scene engraving on sideplates, choice of English or pistol grip stock. Imported 1986-1998.

	$575	$495	$425	$350	$300	$250	$225

Last Mfg.'s Sug. Retail was $676.

Add $23 for pistol grip stock.

ZP-349 — 12 ga. only, extractors, double triggers, true sidelock, Purdey-type top bolt, cocking indicators, walnut stock with cheek piece, beavertail forearm, swivels, 7.3 lbs. Imported 1986 only.

	$450	$390	$360	$325	$300	$270	$250

Last Mfg.'s Sug. Retail was $520.

Add $20 for engraving.

SHOTGUNS: SINGLE SHOT

ZBK 100 — 12 or 20 ga., 3 in. chamber, walnut stock and forearm. Importation began 1999.

Mfg.'s Sug. Retail	$203	$180	$160	$140	$120	$105	$95	$85

BROCKMAN'S CUSTOM GUNSMITHING

Current custom rifle manufacturer and gunsmith located in Gooding, Idaho since 1986. Consumer direct sales only.

Grading	100%	98%	95%	90%	80%	70%	60%

Brockman's Custom Gunsmithing manufactures a wide variety of custom bolt action rifles typically based on Win. Model 70, Rem. Model 700, or Dakota actions. Specific models and/or configurations include the Universal Hunter (base price $2,300), Dangerous Game, Ladies rifles (base price $2,100-$2,895), Scout rifles, and handcrafted custom rifles. Additionally, Brockman's makes general purpose lever action rifles based on Marlin actions. Please contact the company directly to learn more about their wide variety of custom rifles and gunsmithing services.

B

BROLIN ARMS, INC.

Current importer of handguns (FEG mfg.), rifles (older Mauser military, see Mauser listing), shotguns (Chinese mfg.), and airguns established in 1995 and currently located in Pomona, CA. Previously located in La Verne, CA until 1997.

PISTOLS: SEMI-AUTO, SINGLE ACTION

LEGEND SERIES MODEL L45 — .45 ACP cal., patterned after the Colt 1911 Government Model, features include throated match 5 in. barrel, polished feed ramp, flared ejection port, beveled mag. well, flat top slide, flat mainspring housing, front strap high relief cut, aluminum lightweight extended trigger, high visibility sights, 7 shot mag., commander style hammer and checkered walnut grips, 38 oz. Mfg. 1995-98.

	$425	$365	$325	$295	$275	$250	$225

Last Mfg.'s Sug. Retail was $500.

* *Legend Series Model L45C (Compact)* — similar to Model L45, except has 4 in. barrel, 35 oz. Mfg. 1995-98.

	$440	$380	$330	$295	$275	$250	$225

Last Mfg.'s Sug. Retail was $520.

* *Legend Series Model L45T* — features standard frame with compact slide, 4 in. barrel, 36 oz. Mfg. 1997-98.

	$440	$380	$330	$295	$275	$250	$225

Last Mfg.'s Sug. Retail was $520.

PATRIOT SERIES MODEL P45 COMP — .45 ACP cal., similar to Legend Series Model L45, except has one-piece match 4 in. barrel with integral dual port compensator, 7 shot mag., Millett or Novak combat sights (new 1997), test target provided, choice of blue or satin (frame only) finish, 38 oz. Mfg. 1996-97 only.

	$585	$475	$415	$365	$325	$285	$250

Last Mfg.'s Sug. Retail was $649.

Add $70 for Novak combat sights (new 1997).
Add $20 for T-tone finish (frame only).

* *Patriot Series Model P45C (Compact)* — .45 ACP cal., similar to Model P45 Comp, except has 3¼ in. barrel with integral conical lock-up system, 34.5 oz. Mfg. 1996-97.

	$610	$495	$425	$375	$325	$285	$250

Last Mfg.'s Sug. Retail was $689.

Add $70 for Novak combat sights.
Add $20 for T-tone finish (frame only).

* *Patriot Series Model P45T* — features standard frame with compact slide, 3.25 in. barrel, 35.5 oz. Mfg. 1997 only.

	$620	$500	$425	$375	$325	$285	$250

Last Mfg.'s Sug. Retail was $699.

Add $60 for Novak combat sights (new 1997).
Add $10 for T-tone finish (frame only).

Grading	100%	98%	95%	90%	80%	70%	60%

PRO STOCK MODEL COMPETITION PISTOL — .45 ACP cal., competition pistol featuring most state-of-the-art competitive improvements, 5 in. barrel, 8 shot mag., blue or satin (frame only) finish, signature wood grips, 40 oz. Mfg. 1996-97.

	$685	$550	$475	$415	$360	$295	$260

Last Mfg.'s Sug. Retail was $779.

Add $20 for T-tone finish (frame only).

* ***Pro Comp Model Competition Pistol*** — similar to Pro Stock Model, except has 4 in. dual port compensated heavy match barrel, blue or satin (frame only) finish, 40 oz. Mfg. 1996-97.

	$800	$650	$525	$435	$375	$325	$295

Last Mfg.'s Sug. Retail was $919.

Add $10 for T-tone finish (frame only).

TAC 11 — .45 ACP cal., 5 in. conical barrel w/o bushing, beavertail grip safety, 8 shot mag., T-tone or blue finish, Novak low profile combat or Tritium sights, black rubber contour grips, 37 oz. Mfg. 1997-98.

	$595	$485	$425	$365	$325	$285	$250

Last Mfg.'s Sug. Retail was $670.

Add $90 for Tritium sights (disc. 1997).

* ***Tac 11 Compact*** — similar to Tac 11, except has shorter barrel. Mfg. 1998 only.

	$610	$495	$435	$365	$325	$285	$250

Last Mfg.'s Sug. Retail was $690.

Add $60 for hard-chrome finish.

GOLD SERIES — .45 ACP cal., 5 in. barrel w/o barrel bushing and supported chamber, IPSC configuration with many features, adj. aluminum trigger, front and rear slide serations, stainless steel construction with choice of natural stainless or blue stainless finish. Limited mfg. 1998 only.

	$715	$625	$525				

Last Mfg.'s Sug. Retail was $800.

PISTOLS: SEMI-AUTO, DOUBLE ACTION

The models listed below had limited manufacture 1998 only.

TAC SERIES SERVICE MODEL — .45 ACP cal., full sized double action service pistol, single/double action, 8 shot single column mag., front and rear slide serations, combat style trigger guard, royal or satin blue finish, low profile 3-dot sights. Mfg. 1998 only.

	$360	$315	$285	$260	$240	$220	$200

Last Mfg.'s Sug. Retail was $400.

Add $20 for royal blue finish.

TAC SERIES FULL SIZE MODEL — 9mm Para., .40 S&W, or .45 ACP cal., similar to Tac Series Service Model, except longer barrel, checkered walnut or plastic grips, 8 (.45 ACP only) or 10 shot mag. Mfg. 1998 only.

	$360	$315	$285	$260	$240	$220	$200

Last Mfg.'s Sug. Retail was $400.

Add $20 for royal blue finish.

TAC SERIES COMPACT MODEL — 9mm Para. or .40 S&W cal., shortened barrel/slide with full size frame, 10 shot mag. Mfg. 1998 only.

	$360	$315	$285	$260	$240	$220	$200

Last Mfg.'s Sug. Retail was $400.

Add $20 for royal blue finish.

TAC SERIES BANTAM MODEL — 9mm Para. or .40 S&W cal., super compact size, single/double action with concealed hammer, all steel construction, 3-dot sights. Mfg. 1998 only.

	$360	$315	$285	$260	$240	$220	$200

Last Mfg.'s Sug. Retail was $399.

Grading	100%	98%	95%	90%	80%	70%	60%

BANTAM MODEL — 9mm Para. or .40 S&W cal., single or double action, super compact size, concealed hammer, all steel construction, 3-dot sights, royal blue or matte finish. Mfg. by FEG beginning 1999.

Mfg.'s Sug. Retail	$399		$360	$315	$285	$260	$240	$220	$200

B

PISTOLS: CUSTOM

Brolin Arms manufactured a small quantity of high performance M1911 based custom combat and competition pistols during 1998 only. The Formula Z Model Custom Combat Model retail price range was $1,300-$1,600, the Formula One RS Limited Class Competition Model was priced at $2,000-$2,300, and the Formula One RZ Competition Race Gun Model topped the line at $2,450-$2,750.

SHOTGUNS: SEMI-AUTO

MODEL BL-12 — 12 ga. only, 3 in. chamber, 18½ (security) or 28 (field) in. VR barrel with 3 choke tubes (Beretta compatible), satin blue finish, choice of wood or synthetic stock and forearm. Mfg. 1998 only.

			$375	$325	$300	$280	$260	$240	$220

Last Mfg.'s Sug. Retail was $430.

MODEL SAS-12 — 12 ga. only, 2¾ in. chamber, 24 in. barrel with IC choke tube, 3 (standard) or 5 shot (disc. late 1998) detachable box mag., synthetic stock and forearm, gas operated. New 1998.

Mfg.'s Sug. Retail	$499		$445	$385	$335	$300	$280	$260	$240

Add $39 for extra 3 or 5 (disc.) shot mag.

SHOTGUNS: SLIDE ACTION

Brolin shotguns are manufactured by Hawk Industries.

FIELD SERIES — 12 ga. only, 3 in. chamber, 24, 26, 28, or 30 in. VR barrel with mod. choke tube, steel receiver and aluminum trigger guard, choice of black synthetic or wood stock, bead sights, 5 shot mag., matte finish, 7.3 lbs. Mfg. 1997-98.

			$195	$170	$155	$140	$130	$120	$110

Last Mfg.'s Sug. Retail was $240.

* **Field Combo** — includes choice of extra 12 ga. 18½ or 22 in. barrel, choice of regular or pistol grip stock. Mfg. 1997-98.

			$230	$195	$175	$155	$140	$130	$120

Last Mfg.'s Sug. Retail was $270.

Add approx. $25 for rifled deer barrel.

LAWMAN MODEL — 12 ga. only, 3 in. chamber, action patterned after the Rem. Model 870 (disc. 1998) or the Ithaca Model 37 (new 1999) 18½ in. barrel, choice of bead, rifle (disc. 1998), or ghost ring (disc. 1998) sights, matte (disc. 1998), nickel (disc. 1997), royal blue (new 1998), satin blue (new 1998) or hard chrome finish, black synthetic or hardwood stock and forearm, 7 lbs. Mfg. in China beginning in 1997.

Mfg.'s Sug. Retail	$189		$165	$155	$145	$135	$125	$115	$105

Add $20 for nickel finish (disc. 1997).
Add $20 for hard chrome finish.
Add $20 for ghost ring sights.

SLUG SPECIAL — 12 ga. only, 3 in. chamber, choice of 18½ or 22 in. barrel with either rifle sights, ghost ring, or cantilevered scope mount, wood or synthetic stock, choice of fixed IC choke, 4 in. extended rifled choke, or fully rifled barrel, 5 shot mag. Mfg. 1998 only.

			$230	$180	$165	$150	$140	$130	$120

Last Mfg.'s Sug. Retail was $270.

Add $10 for rifled barrel.
Add $20 for cantilevered scope mount.

Grading	100%	98%	95%	90%	80%	70%	60%

SLUGMASTER — 12 ga. only, 3 in. chamber, action patterned after the Model 37 Ithaca, bottom ejection, choice of royal blue metal finish with wood stock or satin blue metal with synthetic stock, rifle sights, mfg. in China. New 1999.

Mfg.'s Sug. Retail	$189	$165	$155	$145	$135	$125	$115	$105

TURKEY SPECIAL — 12 ga. only, 3 in. chamber, 22 in. VR barrel with extra-full extended turkey choke, choice of wood or synthetic stock. Mfg. 1998 only.

	$215	$165	$155	$145	$135	$125	$115

Last Mfg.'s Sug. Retail was $250.

BRONCO

Previous trademark manufactured by Echave Y Arizmendi, located in Eibar, Spain.

PISTOLS: SEMI-AUTO

MODEL 1918 POCKET AUTOMATIC — 7.65mm cal., 6 shot, 2½ in. barrel, fixed sights, blue, hard rubber grips. Mfg. 1918-1925.

	$175	$150	$100	$80	$70	$60	$50

VEST POCKET AUTOMATIC — 6.35mm cal., small frame. Disc.

	$160	$125	$110	$95	$80	$60	$40

DAVID MCKAY BROWN (GUNMAKERS) LTD.

Current long gun manufacturer established in 1967 and located in Bothwell, Glasgow, Scotland. Makers of Scottish Round Action Side-by-Side and Over & Under shotguns and rifles (approx. 30 guns mfg. annually). David McKay Brown apprenticed with Alex Martin Ltd. and John Dickson & Son before establishing his own gunmaking company. All guns made to customer order on round actions. Delivery approximately 18 months. Available through U.S. agent, Griffin & Howe, New York City and Bernardsville, NJ or the manufacturer directly.

Prices indicated below for manufacturer's suggested retail and 100% condition factors are listed in English pounds. All new prices include VAT. Values for used guns in 98%-60% condition factors are priced in U.S. dollars.

RIFLES: CUSTOM, SxS

David Mckay Brown should be contacted directly for a firm quotation on a SxS double rifle.

SHOTGUNS: CUSTOM

Add £250 for Pistol/Prince of Wales grip.

SxS SHOTGUN — 12, 16, 20, 28 ga., or .410 bore, features rounded case colored action, double triggers, full scroll engraving, custom order only.

Mfg.'s Sug. Retail	£23,000	£23,000	£26,750	£22,750	£18,750	£15,000	£13,000	£11,000

Add £1,000 for .410 bore.
Add £750 for single trigger.

O/U SHOTGUN — 12, 16, 20, 28 ga., or .410 bore, features rounded case colored action, double triggers, full scroll engraving, custom order only.

Mfg.'s Sug. Retail	£29,000	£29,000	£35,750	£31,000	£26,500	£22,500	£18,500	£14,750

Add £1,000 for .410 bore.
Add £750 for single trigger.

BROWN PRECISION, INC.

Current manufacturer located in Los Molinos, CA since 1967. Consumer direct sales.

Grading	100%	98%	95%	90%	80%	70%	60%

Brown Precision Inc. manufactures primarily rifles using Remington or Winchester actions and restocks them using a combination of Kevlar, Fiberglass and Graphite (wrinkle finish) to save weight. Stock colors are green, brown, grey, black, camo brown, camo green, or camo grey.

B

PISTOLS: BOLT ACTION

CUSTOM XP-100 HIGH COUNTRY — various cals., includes highly tuned XP-100 single shot action with Shilen stainless match grade barrel, electroless nickel or Teflon finish, fiberglass stock. Limited mfg. 1993-96.

	100%	98%	95%	90%	80%	70%	60%
	$1,550	$1,375	$1,150	$950	$775	$650	$525

Last Mfg.'s Sug. Retail was $1,690.

RIFLES: BOLT ACTION

STANDARD HIGH COUNTRY BOLT ACTION RIFLE — various cals. within those factory barreled actions, choice of Rem. 700 ADL/BDL, Model 7, Ruger 77, or Win. Model 70 action, brown fiberglass/Kevlar stock (various colors), sling swivels and pad. Mfg. 1975-present.

Mfg.'s Sug. Retail	$1,275	$1,135	$925	$750	$625	$525	$440	$400

Add $65 for Mag. cals.
Add approx. $120 for Rem. 700 BDL/Model 7, Ruger 77, or standard Win. Model 70 action.
Add $320 for Win. Model 70 Super Grade action with controlled round feeding.
Add approx. $150 for left-hand BDL, Ruger 77, or Win. M-70 action.

✶ *Custom High Country* — similar to High Country, except many custom features can be added. Prices available per individual work order.

Mfg.'s Sug. Retail	$2,220	$2,050	$1,625	$1,425	$1,175	$950	$725	$575

Add $65 for Mag. cals.

HIGH COUNTRY YOUTH RIFLE — various cals., choice of Rem. Model 7 or 700 factory barreled action, fiberglass stock. New 1993.

Mfg.'s Sug. Retail	$1,395	$1,215	$1,000	$795	$675	$550	$495	$440

MODEL 7 SUPER LIGHT — .223 Rem., .243 Win., 6mm Rem., 7mm-08 Rem., or .308 Win. cal., Model 7 action, 18 in. factory barrel, no sights, 5 lbs. 4 oz. Disc. 1992.

	$995	$900	$750	$650	$575	$500	$450

Last Mfg.'s Sug. Retail was $1,059.

This model could have been special ordered with similar options from the Custom High Country Model, with the exception of left-hand action.

LAW ENFORCEMENT SELECTIVE TARGET — .308 Win. cal., Model 700 Varmint action with 20, 22, or 24 in. factory barrel, O.D. green camouflage treatment. Disc. 1992.

	$995	$900	$750	$650	$575	$500	$450

Last Mfg.'s Sug. Retail was $1,086.

This model could have been special ordered with similar options from the Custom High Country Model, with the exception of left-hand action.

TACTICAL ELITE — various cals. and custom features, customized per individual order. New 1997.

Mfg.'s Sug. Retail	$2,595	$2,325	$1,950	$1,600	$1,375	$1,175	$995	$825

PRO VARMINTER — various cals., includes custom tuned Rem. Model 700 ADL action, Shilen match stainless steel barrel. New 1993.

Mfg.'s Sug. Retail	$2,095	$1,875	$1,525	$1,225	$995	$775	$650	$525

Add $150 for left-hand action.
Add $430 for optional Rem. Model 40-XB action.

Grading	100%	98%	95%	90%	80%	70%	60%

PRO HUNTER — available in over 25 cals., Model 700 ADL or Model 70 action, match grade stainless steel barrel, dull electroless nickel, blue, or teflon finish, express sights, synthetic stock (four different colors). New 1988.

Mfg.'s Sug. Retail	$2,855	$2,500	$2,075	$1,675	$1,425	$1,200	$995	$825

Add $150 for left-hand action.

✱ **Pro Hunter Elite** — various cals., includes many custom order features. New 1993.

Mfg.'s Sug. Retail	$3,725	$3,425	$2,850	$2,325	$1,975	$1,700	$1,525	$1,250

In late 1991, improvements were made including decelerator recoil pad, barrel band swivel, and speed lock firing pin spring.

BROWN PRECISION WINCHESTER 70 — .270 Win. or .30-06 cal., 22 in. featherweight barrel, camo stock in four colors with black recoil pad, 6¼ lbs. Mfg. 1989-92.

$650	$575	$475	$425	$385	$325	$300

Last Mfg.'s Sug. Retail was $750.

Add $20 for 7mm Rem. Mag. (24 in. sporter barrel).

BLASER BOLT ACTION RIFLE — standard Camex Blaser cals. and action, fiberglass stock and nickel plated barrel. Disc. 1989.

$1,395	$1,150	$995	$875	$750	$675	$600

Last Mfg.'s Sug. Retail was $1,395.

BROWNING

Current manufacturer with headquarters located in Morgan, UT. Browning guns originally were manufactured in Ogden, UT, circa 1880. Browning firearms are manufactured by Fabrique Nationale in Herstal and Liege, Belgium. Since 1976, Browning has also contracted Miroku of Japan and A.T.I. in Salt Lake City, UT to manufacture both long arms and handguns. In 1992, Browning (including F.N.) was acquired by GIAT of France. During late 1997, the French government received $82 million for the sale of F.N. Herstal from the Walloon business region surrounding Fabrique Nationale in Belgium.

The category names within the Browning section have been arranged in an alphabetical format: — PISTOLS (& variations), RIFLES (& variations), SHOTGUNS (& variations), LIMITED EDITIONS-COMMEMORATIVES.

BROWNING HISTORY

The Browning firm, first known as J.M. Browning & Bro., was established in Ogden, Utah about 1880. Later known as Browning Brothers and Browning Arms Company (BAC), the firm actually manufactured only one gun — the Model 1878 Single Shot which was John M.'s first patent. Winchester bought the production and distribution rights to this gun in 1883, bringing it out as the Winchester M1885. From that time until 1900, Mr. Browning sold Winchester the exclusive rights to 31 rifles and 13 shotguns, of which Winchester produced only 7 rifles (M1885SS: the lever actions M1886, 1892, 1894 and 1895: and the slide action .22s M1890 and 1906) and 3 shotguns (M1887, M1893 and M1897). The other models were bought from Browning simply to keep them out of the hands of other arms makers.

John M. Browning, perhaps the greatest firearms inventor the world has ever known, was directly responsible for an estimated 80 separate firearms that evolved from his 128 patents. During his most prolific period from 1894 to 1910, Browning sold the rights to his rifles, semi-auto pistols, shotguns and machine guns to Winchester, Remington, Colt and Stevens in this country and to Fabrique Nationale for sale outside the U.S. Every Colt and FN semi-auto pistol is based on a Browning patent. In 1902, Browning broke off relations with Winchester when the company refused to negotiate a royalty arrangement for his new semi-auto shotgun(A-5). Browning took the prototype to FN where it became the most commercially successful of all his inventions. FN has produced 6 automatic pistols, 3 rifles and 2 shotguns designed by John M. Browning and is still a major producer of arms sold by Browning in the U.S. and by FN distributors worldwide.

Our American military was armed for many years with Browning designed weaponry, not the least of which is the venerable "Old Slabside" 1911 Govt. Model .45 ACP. Today, the firm that bears the Browning name still stands at the forefront with the other makers of fine sporting firearms.

BROWNING FACTS

Note: Between 1966-1971 Browning used a salt-curing process to speed the drying time needed for their walnut stock blanks. Unfortunately, the salt would be released from the wood and oxidize the metal surface(s) after a period of time. These guns, especially bolt action rifles in all grades, some BARs, Superposed shotguns, and T-bolt models should be examined carefully around the edges of the wood for signs of freckling and rust. Discount values on guns which show tell-tale characteristics of salt corrosion 15%-50%, depending on how bad rusting has occurred. Check screws and wood under butt plate as well. Original long gun owners of salt wood guns who still have their warranty card are still eligible for Browning factory refurbishing without charge. Otherwise, Browning has a standardized charge for each model.

Since the inception and standardization of steel shot for hunting purposes, the desirability factor of shotguns has changed considerably. On newer manufacture, choke tubes have become very desirable, and specimens without choke tubes (especially guns with longer barrels) must be discounted somewhat. Browning does not recommend using steel shot in any Superposed (B-25) or older Belgian Auto-5 barrels.

BROWNING VALUES INFORMATION

Editor's Note: It is important to note the differences in values of Browning firearms manufactured in Belgium by F.N. and those made recently in Japan by Miroku. We feel that these values are somewhat higher because of collector interest in Belgian guns, and not as the result of any inferiority of the quality of Browning guns made anywhere else.

AS A FINAL NOTE: Most post-war Brownings are collectible only if in 95% or better condition as most models have relatively high mfg. and are not that old. Condition under 95% is normally very shootable, but not as collectible and values for 95% or less condition could be lower than shown in some areas.

Most 100% values in this section assume NIB condition. Subtract 10% without box/manual. Also, all add-ons or deductions in this section reflect retail pricing without any discounting. On higher grade Browning firearms that are engraved, signed specimens by FN's master engravers Funken, J. Baerten, Vrancken, and Watrin will command premiums over the values listed below.

BROWNING SERIALIZATION

In addition to the Browning serialization listed in the back of this text, the following codes will determine the year and origin of those guns made from 1975 to date. The 2 letters in the middle of the serial number are the code designations for year of manufacture. They represent the following: RV - 1975, RT - 1976, RR - 1977, RP - 1978, RN - 1979, PM - 1980, PZ - 1981, PY - 1982, PX - 1983, PW - 1984, PV - 1985, PT -1986, PR - 1987, PP - 1988, PN - 1989, NM - 1990, NZ - 1991, NY - 1992, NX - 1993, NW - 1994, NV - 1995, NT - 1996, NR - 1997, NP - 1998, NN - 1999, MM - 2000.

Since most Brownings use a 3-digit model identification code (appearing first on European or U.S. mfg. guns and last on Japanese mfg.), both where and when the specimen was made can easily be determined (i.e. Ser. No. 611RP2785 would be a Model B-2000 made in Belgium, and assembled in Portugal during 1978 with 2785 being the Ser. No.— Ser. No. 01479PX368 indicates a BSS 20 ga. mfg. in Japan in 1983).

BROWNING

Grading	100%	98%	95%	90%	80%	70%	60%

PISTOLS: SEMI-AUTO, F.N. PRODUCTION UNLESS OTHERWISE NOTED

B

MODEL 1900-FN — 7.65mm cal., first Belgian Browning, 4 in. barrel. 724,500 mfg. 1899-1910.

	100%	98%	95%	90%	80%	70%	60%
	$350	$295	$240	$200	$160	$130	$100

Add 30% for early pistols with "pistol logo" grips.
Add $200-$600 for Russian (crossed rifle) markings.

MODEL 1903-FN — 9mm Browning Long cal., 5 in. barrel. 58,400 mfg. 1903-1939.

	$500	$425	$350	$300	$260	$220	$180

Add 100% if slotted to accept shoulder stock - beware of fakes.

This variation was also manufactured with a detachable shoulder stock — this accessory is rare and can add as much as $2,000 to values listed above.

MODEL 1903-SWEDISH CONTRACT — 9mm Browning Long cal., manufactured by Husqvarna and Swedish Arsenal (so marked), many were imported into U.S. and converted to .380 ACP from original Browning 9mm Long.

	$300	$260	$230	$200	$180	$150	$125

Subtract 25% for .380 ACP conversion.

MODEL 1905-FN (VEST POCKET) — 6.35mm cal. (.25 ACP), dubbed "Vest Pocket" model, 2 in. barrel, manufactured by Fabrique Nationale, Herstal, Belgium. 1,086,133, mfg. 1906-1959.

* *First Variation* — no slide lock/safety lever.

	$350	$285	$255	$225	$170	$135	$100

Add 10% for nickel finish.
Add $300-$600 for Russian (crossed rifle) markings.

* *Second Variation* — post 1908, with slide lock/safety lever.

	$325	$285	$255	$210	$170	$135	$100

Add 10% for nickel finish.
Add $300-$600 for Russian (crossed rifle) markings.

MODEL 1910-FN (MODEL 1955) — 7.65mm (.32 ACP) or Browning 9mm short (.380 ACP) cal., 4 in. barrel. FN manufacture. 701,266 mfg. 1912-1980.

	$325	$300	$275	$250	$225	$195	$150

Add 20% if BAC marked and .380 ACP cal.
Add 30% if BAC marked and 7.65mm cal.
Add $100 minimum for special contract markings.

This model is also referred to as the Model 1955. BAC marked pistols were imported 1954-1968.

MODEL 1922 OR 10/22 FN — 7.65mm (.32 ACP) or .380 ACP cal., modified Model 1910 with 4½ in. barrel, longer grip frame and mag., made for commercial sale as well as military contracts. Several hundred thousand made by Nazis during the occupation of Liege, Belgium 1940-1944. Mfg. between 1912-1959.

	$240	$215	$195	$175	$150	$125	$110

Add 10% for Waffenamt proofing.
Add 20% for foreign contracts.
Add 20% if .380 ACP Waffenamt proofed.
Add $100 minimum for special contract markings.

The Model 10/22 and M1922 are the same pistol. The Model 1910 was modified by FN technicians for sale to Serbian armed forces in 1923. Also sold to France, Holland, Yugoslavia, and other countries. Also made by the German military 1940-1944.

Grading	100%	98%	95%	90%	80%	70%	60%

FN "BABY" MODEL — 6.35mm (.25 ACP) cal., lighter, smaller modification of Browning Model 1905 Vest Pocket, w/o grip safety or separate slide lock lever, 2 in. barrel, imported under BAC trademark from 1954-1970 in standard blue finish, lightweight nickel or alumnium frame, and engraved Renaissance models. Over 510,000 mfg. 1931-1983.

* **FN Marked** — slide marked Fabrique Nationale, blued finish standard.

		$395	$350	$310	$280	$245	$225	$200

* **BAC Marked** — slide marked Browning Arms Co., blued finish standard.

		$300	$265	$225	$195	$180	$165	$150

* **Lightweight model** — nickel or aluminum (introduced 1954) frame, with pearl grips.

		$395	$350	$310	$280	$245	$225	$200

* **Renaissance model** — engraved, satin grey finish.

		$875	$725	$550

Add 20% if coin finished.

FN/BROWNING MODEL 10/71 — .380 ACP cal., 4½ in. barrel, modified version of Model 1922 (10/22)in .380 ACP cal., grip safety, includes target sights and grips in addition to incorporating a magazine finger tip extension designed to comply with GCA of 1968. Sold in U.S. by BAC 1970-1974 as the "Standard .380", still mfg. by FN as Model 125.

		$375	$295	$250	$220	$205	$190	$160

* **Renaissance Model**

		$950	$750	$625

MODEL 1935 HI-POWER — 9mm Para. cal., 13 shot mag., 4²¹⁄₃₂ in. barrel, Browning's last pistol design, millions made 1927 to date in variations for commercial, military, and police use in over 68 countries, first imported under BAC trademark in 1954.

Please refer to the Fabrique Nationale section of this book for pre-1954 variations (including pre-WWII, WWII, and earlier commercial models), as well as contemporary production of those variations not imported by BAC.

HI-POWER: POST-1954 MFG. — 9mm Para. or .40 S&W (new 1995) cal., similar to FN model 1935, has BAC slide marking, 10 (C/B 1994) or 13★ shot mag., 4⅝ in. barrel, polished blue finish, checkered walnut grips, fixed sights, molded grips were introduced in 1986, ambidextrous safety was added to all models in 1989, approx. 32 (9mm Para.) or 35 (.40 S&W) oz. Mfg. 1954-present.

* **Polished Blue Finish** — includes fixed sights.

Mfg.'s Sug. Retail	$615		$500	$395	$335	$300	$280	$260	$240

Subtract $30 for molded grips (disc. 1990).
Add 25% for ring hammer and internal extractor.
Add 10% for ring hammer and external (more recent) extractor.

Major identifying factors of the Hi-Power are as follows: the "Thumb-Print" feature was mfg. from the beginning (including FN mfg.) through 1958, old style internal extractor was mfg. from the beginning (including FN mfg.) through 1962, the "T" SN prefix (T-Series start visible extractor) was mfg. 1963-1968, 69C through 77C SN prefixes were mfg. 1969-1977, rounded type Ring Hammers with new external extractor were mfg. from 1962-1969. Spur Hammers are mfg. 1970-present, and the "245" SN prefix has been mfg. 1977-present.

Older specimens in original black, maroon, or red/black plastic boxes were mfg. 1954-1965 and are very scarce - add $100+ in value. Black pouches (circa 1965-1968, especially with gold metal zipper) will also command a $25-$50 premium, depending on condition.

* **Adj. sights**

Mfg.'s Sug. Retail	$668		$535	$410	$365	$330	$300	$280	$255

Grading	100%	98%	95%	90%	80%	70%	60%

✳ Mark III Matte Blue Finish — 9mm Para. or .40 S&W (new 1994) cal., non-glare matte finish, ambidextrous safety, tapered dovetail rear fixed sight, molded grips, Mark III designation became standard in 1994, 35 oz. New 1985.

Mfg.'s Sug. Retail	$579	$495	$370	$315	$280	$260	$240	$225

Recently, Hi-Powers that appear to have a "black" finish have been noticed. These guns are painted rather than blued and some parties have been selling them as original military FNs. Do not confuse these painted specimens for original pistols and remember, original guns will be worth more than refinished pistols. Also, beware of 9mm Para. cal. pistols manufactured in Argentina under F.N. license.

✳ Silver Chrome Finish — 9mm Para. or .40 S&W (new 1995) cal., entire gun finished in silver chrome, includes adj. sights and Pachmayr rubber grips, 36 (9mm Para.) or 39 (.40 S&W) oz. New 1991.

Mfg.'s Sug. Retail	$684	$545	$425	$365	$330	$300	$280	$255

✳ Practical Model — 9mm Para. or .40 S&W (new 1995) cal., features blued slide, silver-chromed frame finish, wraparound Pachmayr rubber grips, round style serrated hammer, and choice of adj. sights (new 1993) or removable front sight, 36 (9mm Para.) or 39 (.40 S&W) oz. New 1990.

Mfg.'s Sug. Retail	$662	$535	$415	$355	$325	$300	$280	$255

Add $55 for adj. sights.

✳ Nickel/Silver Chrome finish — not to be confused with stainless steel (never offered in the Hi-Power). Also, this finish is different from the silver chrome finish released in 1991. Disc. 1985.

			$550	$475	$415	$375	$360	$340	$315

Last Mfg.'s Sug. Retail was $525.

✳ .30 Luger Hi-Power — .30 Luger cal., mfg. for European sales (most are marked BAC on slide), approx. 1,500 imported late 1986-89, similar specifications as 9mm Para. model.

		$595	$495	$415	$375	$360	$340	$315

This model was never cataloged for sale by BAC in the U.S. A few specimens have been noted with F.N. markings.

✳ GP Competition — 9mm Para. cal., competition model with 6 in. barrel, detent adj. rear sight, rubber wraparound grips, front counterweight, improved barrel bushing, decreased trigger pull, approx. 36½ oz.

		$725	$600	$500	$425	$395	$350	$325

The original GP Competition came in a black plastic case w/accesories and is more desirable than later imported specimens which were computer serial numbered and came in a styrofoam box. Above prices are for older models — subtract 10% if newer model (computer serial numbered). This model was never cataloged for sale by BAC in the U.S., and it is not serviced by Browning.

✳ Tangent Rear Sight Model — 9mm Para. cal., manufactured from 1965-1978. Adj. rear sight to 500 meters. A total of approx. 7,000 were imported by Browning Arms Co. Early pistols are designated by "T" prefix and were mfg. 1964-69, later pistols had spur hammers and 69C-76C ser. no. prefixes.

		$725	$600	$525	$440	$400	$370	$340

Add $100 for "T" prefix.
Add $50 for original pouch and instruction manual.

✳ Capitan Polished Blue Finish — 9mm Para. cal., features 50-500 meter tangent rear sight, blued finish with walnut grips, 32 oz. New 1993.

Mfg.'s Sug. Retail	$728	$585	$485	$390	$345	$300	$280	$260

B

* ***Tangent Rear Sight Slotted*** — 9mm Para. cal., variation with grip strap slotted to accommodate shoulder stock. Early pistols had "T" prefixes. Later pistols had spur hammers and are in the serial range 73CXXXX-74CXXXX.

	$1,200	$975	$775	$650	$525	$440	$400

Add $150 if with "T" prefix.

This variation will command a premium; beware of fakes, however (carefully examine slot milling and look for ser. no. in 3 places).

BCA EDITION HI-POWER — 9mm Para. cal., limited edition made specifically for the Browning Collectors Association in 1980.

	$675	$550	$450

GOLD LINE HI-POWER — 9mm Para. cal., blued finish with gold line perimeter engraving.

	$3,000	$2,350	$1,900

Add 10% for Ring Hammer.

RENAISSANCE HI-POWER — 9mm Para. cal., extensive scroll engraving on grey silver receiver, synthetic pearl grips, gold plated trigger. Disc. 1980

Round Hammer/fixed sights	$1,350	$995	$795
Spur Hammer/fixed sights	$1,225	$895	$695

Add 5% for adj. sights.
Add $200 for internal extractor.
Add $100 for "Thumb Print".
Add $75-$100 for orginal pouch and booklet.
Add $500 for older individual blue leatherette case.

CASED GRADE I SET — one each .25 ACP, .380 ACP, and 9mm Para. cal., Hi-Power Grade I Models in walnut or black vinyl case, non-matching serial numbers.

	$1,500	$1,250	$895

CASED RENAISSANCE SET — one each .25 ACP, .380 ACP, and 9mm Para. cal., Hi-Power Renaissance models in walnut or black vinyl case, non-matching serial numbers. Offered 1954-1969.

	$3,650	$3,000	$2,250

Add 15% for coin finish.

All original Renaissance Cased Sets had a Ring Hammer 9mm Para. Hi-Power.

CENTENNIAL MODEL HI-POWER — similar to fixed sight Hi-Power, chrome plated with inscription "Browning Centennial/1878-1978", engraved on side, cased, 3,500 mfg. in 1978. Original issue price was $495.

	$725	$595	$450

CENTENNIAL MODEL HI-POWER 1 OF 100 — 9mm Para. cal., features extensive engraving, checkered walnut grips with border. 100 mfg. during 1989 - 34 were sold in U.S., 66 were sold in Europe.

	$4,250	$3,250	$1,950

LOUIS XVI MODEL — 9mm Para., chemically etched throughout in leaf scroll patterns, satin finish, checkered grips, walnut case. Disc. 1984.

	$950	$825	$600

Add 5% for adj. sights.

9 MM CLASSIC SERIES - PISTOL — 9mm Para. cal., Hi-Power action, less than 2,500 manufactured in Classic model and under 350 manufactured in Gold Classic. Both editions feature multiple engraved scenes, and a special silver grey finish, presentation grips, cased. Mfg. 1984-86.

	$950	$675	$495

Last Mfg.'s Sug. Retail was $1,000.

* *Gold Classic* — 5 gold inlays, select walnut grips are both checkered and carved. 500 mfg. 1984-86.

	100%	98%	95%
	$1,950	**$1,450**	**$1,150**

Last Mfg.'s Sug. Retail was $2,000.

HI-POWER DOUBLE ACTION — this model was first listed in the Browning catalog in 1985 but was never manufactured. The proposed 1985 retail price was $494.

BDM DOUBLE ACTION — 9mm Para. cal., new double mode design featuring slide selector allowing choice between pistol (true double action operation) or revolver mode (full hammer decocking after each shot), available in double mode, single mode (BPM-D decocker, new 1997), or double action only (BRM-DAO, new 1997), dual purpose decocking lever/safety, 4.73 in. barrel, 10 (C/B 1994) or 15★ shot mag., matte blue finish, black molded wraparound grips, unique breech block allows visible cartridge inspection, adj. rear sight, 31 oz, mfg. in U.S. 1991-97.

100%	98%	95%	90%	80%	70%	60%
$465	**$395**	**$365**	**$330**	**$300**	**$280**	**$260**

Last Mfg.'s Sug. Retail was $551.

This model features hammer block and firing pin block safeties.

* *BDM Practical* — similar to Standard BDM, except has matte blue slide and silver chrome frame. Mfg. 1997-98.

100%	98%	95%	90%	80%	70%	60%
$480	**$400**	**$365**	**$330**	**$300**	**$280**	**$260**

Last Mfg.'s Sug. Retail was $571.

* *BDM Silver Chrome* — similar to Standard BDM, except has silver chrome finish. Only 119 mfg. in 1997 only.

100%	98%	95%	90%	80%	70%	60%
$480	**$400**	**$365**	**$330**	**$300**	**$280**	**$260**

Last Mfg.'s Sug. Retail was $571.

FN DA 9 — 9mm Para. cal., choice of double action or double action only, 4⅝ in. barrel, molded rubber grips, 10 shot mag., 31 oz. Mfg. by FN. While advertised in 1996, this model was never produced - the retail price was listed at $613.

BDA-380 — .380 ACP cal., double action, 10 (C/B 1994) or 14★ shot, 3¹³/₁₆ in. barrel, fixed sights, smooth walnut grips, 23 oz., introduced 1982 - recent production was by Beretta. Disc. 1997.

100%	98%	95%	90%	80%	70%	60%
$450	**$345**	**$260**	**$220**	**$175**	**$150**	**$125**

Last Mfg.'s Sug. Retail was $564.

Nickel finish	100%	98%	95%	90%	80%	70%	60%
	$480	**$360**	**$275**	**$230**	**$180**	**$150**	**$125**

Last Mfg.'s Sug. Retail was $607.

BDA MODEL — 9mm Para. (9 shot, 2,740 mfg.), .38 Super (752 mfg.), or .45 ACP (7 shot) cal., mfg. from 1977-1980 by Sig-Sauer of W. Germany (same as Sig-Sauer 220).

	100%	98%	95%	90%	80%	70%	60%
9mm Para.	**$550**	**$450**	**$375**	**$295**	**$250**	**$225**	**$200**
.38 Super	**$650**	**$575**	**$495**	**$450**	**$390**	**$350**	**$320**
.45 ACP	**$550**	**$450**	**$375**	**$295**	**$250**	**$225**	**$200**

NOMAD MODEL — .22 LR cal., 10 shot, 4½ and 6¾ in. barrels, steel or alloy frame, adj. sights, blued finish, black plastic grips. Mfg. 1962-1974 by FN.

100%	98%	95%	90%	80%	70%	60%
$295	**$245**	**$185**	**$140**	**$125**	**$100**	**$85**

Add 10% for alloy frame.

CHALLENGER MODEL — .22 LR cal., 10 shot, 4½ and 6¾ in. barrels, steel frame, adj. sights, checkered walnut or plastic (mfg. 1974 only) wraparound grips, gold plated trigger. Mfg. 1962-1975 by FN.

100%	98%	95%	90%	80%	70%	60%
$375	**$315**	**$265**	**$215**	**$190**	**$170**	**$155**

Add 10% for late production plastic grips.

* *Renaissance* — engraved satin nickel finish.

100%	98%	95%
$1,350	**$1,000**	**$650**

* *Gold Line* — blued finish, gold lining on perimeter of frame surfaces.

100%	98%	95%
$1,350	**$1,000**	**$650**

Grading	100%	98%	95%	90%	80%	70%	60%

CHALLENGER II — .22 LR cal., Salt Lake City mfg., 6¾ in. barrel, steel frame, plastic impregnated hardwood grips, 38 oz. Mfg. 1975-1982.

| | $230 | $180 | $170 | $145 | $135 | $120 | $110 |

* **Challenger II BCA Commemorative** — .22 LR cal., mfg. to commemorate BCA's fourth anniversary.

| | $295 | $240 | $175 | | | | |

CHALLENGER III — .22 LR cal., Salt Lake City mfg., 5½ in. bull barrel, 11 shot, alloy frame, adj. sights, 35 oz. Mfg. 1982-1985.

| | $220 | $190 | $170 | $145 | $135 | $120 | $110 |

Last Mfg.'s Sug. Retail was $240.

CHALLENGER III SPORTER — similar to Challenger III, except 6¾ in. round barrel, wide trigger, 29 oz. Mfg. 1982-85.

| | $220 | $190 | $170 | $145 | $135 | $120 | $110 |

Last Mfg.'s Sug. Retail was $240.

BUCK MARK STANDARD .22 — .22 LR cal., 11 shot, 5½ in. bull barrel, composite grips with skipline checkering (disc. 1990) or molded rubber grips (new 1991), adj. sights, gold trigger, matte blued finish, 36 oz. New 1985.

| Mfg.'s Sug. Retail | $265 | $195 | $160 | $135 | $120 | $110 | $100 | $90 |

Add $47 for nickel finish (new 1991).

Buck Mark models are manufactured in Salt Lake City, UT.

* **Buck Mark Micro Standard** — similar to Buck Mark Standard, except has 4 in. barrel, choice of standard or nickel finish, 32 oz. New 1992.

| Mfg.'s Sug. Retail | $265 | $195 | $160 | $130 | $120 | $110 | $100 | $90 |

Add $47 for nickel finish.

* **Buck Mark Micro Plus** — similar to Micro Buck Mark, except has ambidextrous contoured laminated wood grips, nickel (new 1996) or blue finish.

| Mfg.'s Sug. Retail | $324 | $245 | $195 | $145 | $135 | $120 | $110 | $100 |

Add $30 for nickel finish.

* **Buck Mark Challenge** — features smaller grip circumference for smaller hands, smooth walnut grips with medallions, matte blue finish, 5½ in. lightweight barrel, Pro-Target sights, 25 oz. New 1999.

| Mfg.'s Sug. Retail | $296 | $220 | $175 | $135 | $120 | $110 | $100 | $90 |

* **Buck Mark Micro Challenge** — similar to Buck Mark Challenge, except has 4 in. barrel. 23 oz. New 1999.

| Mfg.'s Sug. Retail | $296 | $220 | $175 | $135 | $120 | $110 | $100 | $90 |

* **Buck Mark Camper** — features 5½ in. heavy barrel, ambidextrous molded black composite grips, matte blue or satin nickel finish, Pro-Target sights, 34 oz. New 1999.

| Mfg.'s Sug. Retail | $234 | $180 | $150 | $125 | $115 | $100 | $95 | $85 |

* **Buck Mark Plus** — similar to Buck Mark, except has uncheckered laminated wood grips and choice of nickel (new 1996) or high polish blue. New 1987.

| Mfg.'s Sug. Retail | $324 | $245 | $195 | $145 | $135 | $120 | $110 | $100 |

Add $30 for nickel finish.

* **Buck Mark Bullseye Standard** — similar to Buck Mark Bullseye Target, except has molded composite grips. New 1996.

| Mfg.'s Sug. Retail | $389 | $305 | $250 | $200 | $170 | $150 | $135 | $120 |

* **Buck Mark Bullseye Target** — Bullseye model featuring 16 click per turn Pro-Target rear sight, 7¼ in. fluted barrel, matte blue finish, adj. trigger pull, contoured rosewood target or wraparound finger groove grips, 10 shot mag., 31 oz. New 1996.

| Mfg.'s Sug. Retail | $500 | $370 | $285 | $225 | $185 | $165 | $140 | $125 |

Grading	100%	98%	95%	90%	80%	70%	60%

* **Buck Mark 5.5 Field** — same action and barrel as the Target 5.5, except sights are designed for field use, anodized blue finish, contoured walnut grips, choice of contoured walnut or walnut wraparound finger groove grips (new 1992), 35½ oz. New 1991.

Mfg.'s Sug. Retail	$425	$320	$260	$215	$180	$160	$140	$125

* **Buck Mark 5.5 Target** — same action as Buck Mark, 5½ in. barrel with serrated top rib allowing adj. sight positioning, target sights, matte blue finish, choice of contoured walnut or walnut wraparound finger groove grips (new 1992), 35 oz. New 1990.

Mfg.'s Sug. Retail	$425	$320	$260	$215	$180	$160	$140	$125

Add $52 for nickel finish (new 1994).

* **Buck Mark 5.5 Gold Target** — similar to 5.5 Target, except has gold anodized frame and top rib. Introduced in 1991.

Mfg.'s Sug. Retail	$477	$355	$275	$220	$180	$160	$140	$125

* **Buck Mark Varmint** — same action as Buck Mark, 9⅞ in. barrel with serrated top rib allowing adj. sight positioning, laminated wood grips, choice of contoured walnut or walnut wraparound finger groove grips (new 1992), optional detachable forearm, matte blue, 48 oz. New 1987.

Mfg.'s Sug. Retail	$403	$315	$255	$200	$175	$155	$135	$120

* **Buck Mark Silhouette** — silhouette variation of the Buck Mark, 9⅞ in. bull barrel with serrated top rib allowing adj. sight positioning, hooded target sights, laminated wood stocks and forearm, choice of contoured walnut or walnut wraparound finger groove grips (new 1992), matte blue, 53 oz. New 1987.

Mfg.'s Sug. Retail	$448	$360	$285	$230	$195	$170	$150	$135

* **Buck Mark Unlimited Silhouette (Match)** — similar to Silhouette Model featuring 14 in. barrel with set back front sight, choice of contoured walnut or walnut wraparound finger groove grips (new 1992), 64 oz. Mfg. 1991-99.

	$425	$330	$270	$230	$195	$170	$150

Last Mfg.'s Sug. Retail was $536.

MEDALIST TARGET MODEL — .22 LR cal., 6¾ in. barrel, vent. rib, adj. target sights and barrel weights (3 supplied), blued finish, target walnut grips with thumbrest, dry-fire mechanism, 46 oz., cased. Mfg. 1964-1975 by FN.

	$795	$650	$575	$495	$425	$375	$325

Subtract 15% if without case and accessories.

Gold Line (407 mfg. 1963)	$1,950	$1,400	$950
Renaissance Model	$2,350	$1,750	$1,250

A total of 337 were mfg. by FN 1964-82.

BAC Edition Engraved (60 mfg.)	$2,450	$1,900	$1,400

INTERNATIONAL MEDALIST — target variation model manufactured 1977-80, 5.9 in. barrel, only 681 made with BAC markings and blued finish. Currently manufactured by FN in the parkerized international configuration.

	$615	$535	$475	$410	$350	$300	$275
Early Model	$795	$625	$550	$425	$360	$330	$280

RIFLES: SINGLE SHOT

	Above Average	Average	Below Average

MODEL 1878 STANDARD — various cals., J.M. Browning's first patent, fewer than 600 made (highest known ser. no. is 542) by Browning Brothers in Ogden, Utah between 1878-1883, octagon barrel marked "Browning Bros. Ogden, Utah USA" plain wood stock and forearm with and without pistol grips, crescent steel buttplate, with or without ramrod, several receiver configurations, a very few were made in the deluxe model, seldom found in better than average used condition.

	$16,000 - $12,000	$12,000 - $8,000	$8,000 - $6,000

Grading	100%	98%	95%	90%	80%	70%	60%

B

Add 50% for Deluxe Rifle (checkered stock and forearm).
Add 10% for Early Rifle with Sharps Borchardt type lever.
Add 40% for Early Rifle stamped "Ogden, U.T.".
Add 20% for any caliber other than .40-70 SS or .45-70 Govt.
Subtract 20% if stock and/or forearm have been replaced.
Subtract 20% if the original sights have been removed or replaced incorrectly.
Add 25% for Late Model with rammer rod under barrel held by two thimbles (known as "Montana Model").

Add 10% minimum for any non-standard feature, such as single or double set trigger asssemblies, removable lower stock tang, round barrel, with Ballard type stock bolts, fore-end caps of silver or pewter or other metal.

Calibers in this model are listed from rarest to most commonly encountered: .50-70 Govt., .45 Sharps, .44 Rem., .40-90 Sharps, .44-77 Sharps, .45-70 Govt., and .40-70 Sharps Straight.

This model is rare since approx. only 550 were mfg. (approx. ser. range 1-550). This patent was sold to Winchester, which became their Model 1885 single shot. To date, less than 100 original Model 1878s have been encountered indicating a high mortality rate (most remaining specimens in poor original condition). An inherent weakness of the original design was the way the stock attached to the action - Winchester later corrected this design flaw. A few remaining examples are not serial numbered. Barter guns are rifles that have Browning stamped actions and barrels of an older gunsmith's identity.

MODEL B-78 — .22-250 Rem., 6mm Rem., .243 Win., .25-06 Rem., 7mm Mag., .30-06, or .45-70 Govt. cal., 24 or 26 in. round or octagon barrel, lever activated falling block, no sights except .45-70 Govt., checkered walnut stock, approx. 24,000 mfg. 1973-1982.

	100%	98%	95%	90%	80%	70%	60%
	$695	$595	$465	$325	$295	$275	$250
.45-70 Govt. cal.	$795	$650	$475	$325	$295	$275	$250

The Model B-78 was reintroduced as the Model 1885 in 1985.

MODEL 1885 HIGH WALL — .22-250 Rem., .223 Rem. (disc. 1994), .270 Win., .30-06, 7mm Rem. Mag., .45-70 Govt., or .454 Casull (new 1998) cal., falling block action, sear safety, 28 in. octagonal barrel, adj. trigger, no sights, checkered walnut stock and Schnabel forearm, exposed hammer, gold trigger, 8¾ lbs. Introduced 1985.

Mfg.'s Sug. Retail	$987	$750	$575	$450	$360	$330	$295	$275

This model in .45-70 Govt. cal. is equipped with open sights.

MODEL 1885 LOW WALL — .22 Hornet, .223 Rem., .243 Win., or .260 Rem. (new 1999) cal., action patterned after the Winchester Low Wall receiver, 24 in. barrel, adj. trigger, features thinner 24 in. barrel, 6¼ lbs. New 1995.

Mfg.'s Sug. Retail	$987	$750	$575	$450	$360	$330	$295	$275

MODEL 1885 HIGH WALL TRADITIONAL HUNTER — .30-30 Win., .38-55 WCF, or .45-70 Govt. cal., High-Wall action, 30 in. octagon barrel with ejector, blued receiver, rear tang aperture sight, crescent buttplate, checkered stock and forearm, approx. 9 lbs. New 1997.

Mfg.'s Sug. Retail	$1,208	$1,065	$775	$585	$450	$360	$330	$295

MODEL 1885 LOW WALL TRADITIONAL HUNTER — .357 Mag., .44 Mag., or .45 LC cal., 24 in. half-round, half-octagon barrel, case colored receiver and buttplate, gold bead front, semi-buckhorn rear, and upper tang aperture sights, 6½ lbs. New 1998.

Mfg.'s Sug. Retail	$1,276	$1,120	$795	$615	$450	$375	$330	$295

MODEL 1885 BPCR (BLACK POWDER CARTRIDGE) — .40-65 Win. (black powder only) or .45-70 Govt. (black powder or smokeless) cal., case colored high wall action, 30 in. half-round, half-octagon barrel, checkered pistol grip stock with shotgun butt, w/o ejector system and shell deflector, vernier tang rear sight and globe front sight with spirit level, approx. 11 lbs. New 1996.

Mfg.'s Sug. Retail	$1,749	$1,585	$1,275	$1,085	$925	$800	$700	$600

Grading	100%	98%	95%	90%	80%	70%	60%

B

* **Model 1885 BPCR Creedmoor** — .45-90 cal., blued receiver, 34 in. half-round, half-octagon barrel with globe front and aperture rear tang sights, 11¾ lbs. New 1998.

   Mfg.'s Sug. Retail   **$1,764**   **$1,595** **$1,285** **$1,090** **$925** **$800** **$700** **$600**

RIFLES: SEMI-AUTO, .22 LR

GRADES I - VI — .22 LR or .22 Short (disc.) cal., takedown design, 11 shot (16 for .22 Short) tube mag. in buttstock, 19¼ in. barrel in LR, 22¼ in. barrel in short (rare), checkered pistol grip stock, semi-beavertail forearm, stock has hole machined halfway to allow partial filling of tube mag., adj. folding rear sight, grades differ in finish, amount of engraving, and grade of wood, 4¾ lbs. Mfg. 1914-1976 by FN, 1976-present by Miroku in Japan.

* **Grade I — FN**

                $525 **$415** **$325** **$250** **$195** **$165** **$150**

    Add 25% for "Shorts only" or thumb wheel rear sight older models if in 95% or better condition.

    FN Grade I's have a lightly engraved blued steel receiver, checkered walnut, blued trigger, and a variety of rear sights.

* **Grade I — Miroku**

    Mfg.'s Sug. Retail   **$415**   **$325** **$255** **$210** **$180** **$160** **$150** **$140**

    Miroku manufactured .22s can be determined by year of manufacture in the following manner: RV suffix - 1975, RT - 1976, RR - 1977, RP - 1978, RN - 1979, PM - 1980, PZ - 1981, PY - 1982, PX - 1983, PW - 1984, PV - 1985, PT - 1986, PR - 1987, PP - 1988, PN - 1989, NM - 1990, NZ - 1991, NY - 1992, NX - 1993, NW - 1994, NV - 1995, NT - 1996, NR - 1997, NP - 1998, NN - 1999, MM - 2000.

* **Grade II — FN**

                $1,095 **$850** **$650** **$400** **$325** **$295** **$260**

    FN Grade II's have grey chromed receiver, deluxe wood with finer checkering, gold plated trigger, and engraving depicting two squirrels and two prairie dogs. Signed or unsigned by engraver.

* **Grade II — Miroku** — disc. 1984.

                $425 **$350** **$295** **$225** **$200** **$180** **$160**

* **Grade III — FN**

                $2,450 **$1,950** **$1,400** **$850** **$770** **$715** **$605**

    FN Grade III's have coin finish or grey chromed receiver, extra deluxe walnut with skipline checkering, gold plated trigger, and more elaborate game scene engraving usually featuring a dog flushing ducks or upland game. Signed or unsigned by engraver (Funken, J. Baerten, Vrancken, and Watrin will command premiums over values listed above). A few were also special ordered with blued finish and special engraving — these command an extra premium.

* **Grade III — Miroku** — disc. 1983.

                $850 **$650** **$540** **$495** **$450** **$400** **$360**

* **Grade VI — Miroku** — game scene engraved with gold plating, choice of blued or greyed receiver, deluxe walnut. New 1987.

    Mfg.'s Sug. Retail   **$860**   **$710** **$540** **$425** **$365** **$325** **$295** **$260**

BAR-22 — .22 LR cal., 20¼ in. barrel, 15 shot tube mag., folding leaf sight, high polish alloy receiver, checkered pistol grip stock, 5 lbs. 13 oz. Mfg. 1977-1985 by Miroku.

                $275 **$225** **$185** **$170** **$155** **$140** **$125**
                                    Last Mfg.'s Sug. Retail was $245.

BAR-22 GRADE II — engraved model of BAR-22 featuring game scenes on silver greyed alloy receiver, select French walnut. Disc. 1985.

                $450 **$325** **$245** **$210** **$195** **$175** **$160**
                                    Last Mfg.'s Sug. Retail was $350.

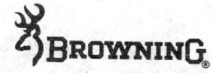

Grading	100%	98%	95%	90%	80%	70%	60%

RIFLES: SEMI-AUTO, BAR SERIES

BROWNING PATENT 1900 — .35 Rem. cal. only, features matted rib barrel and checkered stock and forearm, similar to Remington Model 8 auto-loading rifle, 4,913 mfg. 1910-1931 by FN.

	100%	98%	95%	90%	80%	70%	60%
	$650	$575	$495	$440	$385	$340	$300

BAR SEMI-AUTO — .243 Win., .270 Win., .280 Rem. (new 1990), .308 Win., or .30-06 cal. available in standard model, Mag. cals. include 7mm Rem., .300 Win., and .338 Win. Mag. (reintroduced 1990), gas operated, blued receiver, 22 or 24 (Mag. only) in. barrel, rotary bolt with seven lugs, folding leaf sight, walnut stock. Grades differ in engraving, finish, and grade of wood, in 1993, to celebrate the 25th Anniversary of the BAR, Browning introduced the BAR MK II Safari (see model listed below), approx. 7 lbs. 6 oz. Mfg. 1967-present (includes BAR MK II).

Add 15% for FN mfg. and assembled BARs (marked "Made in Belgium").
Add 10% for .338 Win. Mag. cal. (FN mfg. only).

Note: Original .338s were limited production, mostly seen in the deluxe Grade II only. During the last year of FN .338 production, several were delivered in a Grade I by FN. Although being rarer than the Grade II, it is not as desirable. The following prices are for Portugese assembled guns, manufactured by FN, and are so stamped on the barrel.

* **Grade I** — standard grade without engraving, blued finish. Ordering this model without sights became an option in 1988. Disc. 1992.

	100%	98%	95%	90%	80%	70%	60%
	$540	$450	$395	$350	$325	$300	$280

Last Mfg.'s Sug. Retail was $633.

Subtract $16 without sights.

FN mfg. and assembled Grade Is can be denoted by light scroll engraving on the receiver.

* **Grade I Magnum** — standard grade without engraving, with recoil pad, 8 lbs. 6 oz. Disc. 1992.

	100%	98%	95%	90%	80%	70%	60%
	$575	$495	$425	$375	$350	$330	$310

Last Mfg.'s Sug. Retail was $680.

Subtract $16 without sights.

Ordering this gun without sights became an option in 1988.

* **Grade II** — blued receiver, engraved with big game heads. Mfg. 1967-1974.

	100%	98%	95%	90%	80%	70%	60%
	$695	$595	$550	$525	$470	$440	$415

This model was previously designated Deluxe.

* **Grade II Magnum** — magnum version of Grade II. Mfg. 1967-1974.

	100%	98%	95%	90%	80%	70%	60%
	$750	$650	$595	$550	$510	$460	$430

* **Grade III** — features elk and sheep game scenes etched on greyed steel receiver, select checkered stock and forearm. Disc. 1984.

	100%	98%	95%	90%	80%	70%	60%
	$925	$800	$660	$620	$580	$560	$540

* **Grade III Magnum** — magnum version of Grade III. Disc. 1984.

	100%	98%	95%	90%	80%	70%	60%
	$1,025	$850	$700	$660	$620	$595	$580

* **Grade IV** — engraved satin finish greyed receiver depicts big game animal scenes and trigger guard, carved borders on checkering. Disc. 1989.

	100%	98%	95%	90%	80%	70%	60%
	$1,475	$1,300	$1,150	$1,000	$900	$825	$750

Last Mfg.'s Sug. Retail was $1,670.

* **Grade IV Magnum** — magnum version of Grade IV. Disc. 1984.

	100%	98%	95%	90%	80%	70%	60%
	$1,675	$1,495	$1,225	$1,050	$950	$850	$775

Last Mfg.'s Sug. Retail was $1,720.

* **Grade V** — more elaborate engraving than Grade IV, with gold inlays. Mfg. 1971-1974.

	100%	98%	95%	90%	80%	70%	60%
	$3,000	$2,600	$2,250	$1,850	$1,600	$1,450	$1,250

* **Grade V Magnum** — magnum version of Grade V.

	100%	98%	95%	90%	80%	70%	60%
	$3,650	$2,900	$2,400	$1,950	$1,700	$1,595	$1,400

Grading	100%	98%	95%	90%	80%	70%	60%

BAR NORTH AMERICAN DEER RIFLE ISSUE — .30-06 cal. only, BAR style action with silver grey finish and engraved action, 600 total production, walnut cased with accessories. Disc. 1983 but were sold through 1989.

$2,650 $2,100 $1,700

Last Mfg.'s Sug. Retail was $3,550.

BAR MK II SAFARI — .22-250 Rem. (mfg. 1997 only), .25-06 Rem. (new 1997), .243 Win., .270 Win., .30-06, .308 Win., .270 Wby. Mag. (new 1996), 7mm Rem. Mag., .300 Win. Mag., or .338 Win. Mag. cal., improved BAR action featuring redesigned bolt release, new gas operating system, and reduced recoil, removable trigger assembly, 22 or 24 (Mag. cals. only) in. barrel with (adj. for windage and elevation) or without sights, BOSS became optional 1994, blued finish with engraved receiver, checkered walnut stock and forearm, gold trigger, detachable box mag., approx. 7 lbs. 6 oz. except for Mag. cals. (8 lbs. 6 oz.). Mfg. by F.N. in Belgium. New 1993.

Mfg.'s Sug. Retail	$743	$630	$500	$435	$380	$350	$330	$310

Add $54 for Mag. cals.
Add $17 for open sights (not available in .270 Wby. Mag.).

The new BAR MK II Safari does not have interchangable magazine capability with the older pre-1993 BARs.

* **BAR Classic Mark II Safari** — .270 Win., .30-06, 7mm Rem. Mag. or .300 Win. Mag. cal., similar to BAR Mark II Safari, except has satin finished checkered stock and forearm, 7 lbs. 6 oz. - 8 lbs. 6 oz. New 1999.

Mfg.'s Sug. Retail	$743	$630	$500	$435	$380	$350	$330	$310

Add $54 for Mag. cals.
Add $17 for open sights.

* **BAR Mark II Safari with BOSS** — similar to BAR MK II Safari, except with BOSS (ballistic optimizing shooting system) accurizing adj. assembly on barrel end, not available in .270 Wby. Mag., no sights. New 1994.

Mfg.'s Sug. Retail	$803	$705	$570	$485	$410	$370	$335	$310

Add $54 for Mag. cals.

* **BAR Mark II Lightweight** — .243 Win., .270 Win., .30-06, .308 Win., 7mm Rem. Mag. (new 1999), .300 Win. Mag. (new 1999), or .338 Win. Mag. (new 1999) cal., features alloy receiver and 20 or 24 (Mag. cals. only) in. barrel, matte wood and barrel finish, open sights, 7 lbs. 2 oz. New 1997.

Mfg.'s Sug. Retail	$760	$640	$500	$430	$380	$350	$330	$310

Add $54 for Mag. cals. (new 1999).

* **BAR MK II Lightweight with BOSS** — similar to BAR Mark II Lightweight, except has 24 in. barrel with BOSS, 8 lbs., 6 oz. New 1999.

Mfg.'s Sug. Retail	$857	$740	$585	$495	$415	$370	$335	$310

* **BAR MK II Grade III** — features Grade III engraving pattern. Mfg. by the FN custom shop beginning 1996.

Mfg.'s Sug. Retail	$3,754	$3,100	$1,875	$1,375	$1,000	$775	$675	$575

* **BAR MK II Grade IV** — features Grade IV engraving pattern. Mfg. by the FN custom shop beginning 1996.

Mfg.'s Sug. Retail	$3,833	$3,165	$1,925	$1,400	$1,025	$795	$675	$575

RIFLES: SEMI-AUTO, FAL SERIES

The following semi-auto FALs were imported by BAC in limited numbers. Current production FALs can be found under the Fabrique Nationale heading.

FAL G SERIES STANDARD — 7.62mm cal., paramilitary design rifle, wood buttstock, wood or nylon forearm, milled receiver.

$3,200 $2,850 $2,300 $1,950 $1,650 $1,350 $1,040

B

* **G Series Heavy Barrel** — wood furniture, milled receiver with special bipod.

	100%	98%	95%	90%	80%	70%	60%
	$6,000	$5,250	$4,700	$4,160	$3,600	$3,100	$2,650

* **G Series Lightweight** — lightweight variation of the FAL.

	100%	98%	95%	90%	80%	70%	60%
	$4,000	$3,500	$3,000	$2,500	$2,100	$1,875	$1,600

The Lightweight Model had the trigger frame, magazine, and return spring tube made out of aluminum.

* **Browning Arms Co. Import** — milled receiver, wood or nylon furniture.

	100%	98%	95%	90%	80%	70%	60%
	$2,400	$2,000	$1,700	$1,550	$1,400	$1,275	$1,150

* **CAL Prototype** — originally imported in 1980, prototype to the current FN FNC, at first declared illegal but later given amnesty, only 20 imported.

	100%	98%	95%	90%	80%	70%	60%
	$6,000	$5,250	$4,700	$4,160	$3,600	$3,100	$2,650

G series FALs were imported between 1959-1962 by Browning Arms Co. This rifle was declared illegal by the GCA of 1968 and was exempted 5 years later. Total numbers exempted are: Standard model-1822, Heavy Barrel model-21, Paratrooper model-5.

RIFLES: LEVER ACTION

BL-22 GRADE I — .22 S, L, and LR cal., 20 in. barrel, short throw (33 degree) lever, folding leaf sight, 15 shot (LR) mag., exposed hammer, Western style gloss finished uncheckered stock and forearm, 5 lbs. Mfg. 1970-present by Miroku.

Mfg.'s Sug. Retail	$360		$285	$220	$180	$150	$125	$110	$100

* **BL-22 Classic** — similar to BL-22 Grade I, except has satin finished stock and forearm. New 1999, mfg. by Miroku.

Mfg.'s Sug. Retail	$360		$285	$220	$180	$150	$125	$110	$100

BL-22 GRADE II — same general specifications as BL-22, except scroll engraved blue receiver and deluxe high gloss checkered walnut stock and forearm.

Mfg.'s Sug. Retail	$412		$330	$260	$200	$170	$140	$125	$115

* **BL-22 Grade II Classic** — similar to BL-22 Grade II, except has satin finished stock and forearm. New 1999, mfg. by Miroku.

Mfg.'s Sug. Retail	$412		$330	$260	$200	$170	$140	$125	$115

MODEL 53 DELUXE LIMITED EDITION — .32-20 WCF cal. (round nose or hollow point bullets only), patterned after the original Winchester Model 53 (redesigned Model 1892), 7 shot tube mag., high polished blued metal, open sights, 22 in. tapered barrel, high grade checkered walnut stock featuring full pistol grip cap and shotgun style metal butt plate, 6½ lbs. Only 5,000 mfg. in 1990.

	$525	$425	$395

Last Mfg.'s Sug. Retail was $675.

MODEL 65 GRADE I LIMITED EDITION — .218 Bee cal., patterned after the Winchester Model 65, round tapered 24 in. barrel, open sights (hooded front), blued metal finish, 7 shot tube mag., uncheckered pistol grip stock and semi-beavertail forearm, metal butt plate, 6¾ lbs. 3,500 total mfg. for Grade I in 1989 only, inventory depleted in 1990.

	$475	$400	$375

Last Mfg.'s Sug. Retail was $550.

* **Model 65 High Grade** — greyed receiver (and lever) with scroll engraving and gold plated animals, gold plated trigger, deluxe checkered walnut stock and semi-beavertail forearm. 1,500 total mfg. in 1989, inventory depleted in 1990.

	$850	$775	$700

Last Mfg.'s Sug. Retail was $850.

MODEL 71 LIMITED EDITION CARBINE — .348 Win. cal., reproduction of the Winchester Model 71 Carbine, 20 in. barrel, open sights, 4 shot mag., 8 lbs. New 1987 with inventory depleted in 1990.

Grading	100%	98%	95%	90%	80%	70%	60%

* **Grade I** — uncheckered satin finished walnut stock and forearm. 4,000 mfg. 1986-87 only.

  $450 $400 $365 $340 $320 $300 $275

  Last Mfg.'s Sug. Retail was $600.

* **High Grade** — deluxe checkered walnut stock and forearm with high gloss finish, scroll engraved-grey receiver with gold inlays and trigger. 3,000 mfg. 1986-87 only.

  $795 $600 $500

  Last Mfg.'s Sug. Retail was $980.

MODEL 71 LIMITED EDITION RIFLE — .348 Win. cal., reproduction of the Winchester Model 71 Rifle, 24 in. barrel, open sights, 4 shot mag., 8 lbs. 2 oz. Mfg. 1986-87 only with inventory depleted in 1990.

* **Grade I** — uncheckered satin finished walnut stock and forearm. 3,000 mfg. 1986-87 only.

  $495 $425 $375 $350 $325 $300 $275

  Last Mfg.'s Sug. Retail was $600.

* **High Grade** — deluxe checkered walnut stock and forearm with high gloss finish, scroll engraved-grey receiver with gold inlays and trigger. 3,000 mfg. 1986-87 only.

  $850 $625 $525

  Last Mfg.'s Sug. Retail was $980.

MODEL 81/BLR SHORT ACTION — .22-250 Rem., .222 Rem. (disc. 1989), .223 Rem., .243 Win., .257 Roberts (disc. 1992), 7mm-08 Rem., .284 Win. (disc. 1994), .308 Win., or .358 Win. (disc. 1992) cal., steel receiver, rotary bolt locking lugs, 20 in. barrel with band, 3 (.284 Win. only) or 4 shot detachable mag., adj. rear sight, checkered straight grip stock, recoil pad, approx. 7 lbs, no sights optional 1988-89.

.243 Win., .308 Win. and 7mm-08 Rem. cals. are the most popular in this model.

* **Model BLR USA** — .243 Win. or .308 Win. cal., this model was originally scheduled to be manufactured by TRW in Cleveland, OH for Browning. Originally assembled in 1966, these rifles are considered prototypes as they were never sold through regular channels and at one time were scheduled to be destroyed. Approx. 50-250 of these rifles exist, some still NIB.

  $995 $895 $750 $600 $550 $500 $450

  This variation has a 2-line legend on the right side marked "MADE IN USA" and "PATENT PENDING".

* **Model BLR Belgium** — .243 Win. or .308 Win. cal., mfg. was moved to F.N. in Belgium with original assembly beginning 1969 and concluding in 1973. This F.N. model included a number of small dimensioning and engraving changes.

  $525 $450 $400 $370 $345 $315 $275

* **Model BLR Japan** — cals. as noted above, mfg. was moved to Miroku in Japan 1974-1980. Early guns during 1974 had stocks with impressed checkering. By 1975, cut checkering and gloss wood finish was used on stocks and forearms.

  $450 $365 $300 $265 $225 $195 $165

  Last Mfg.'s Sug. Retail was $550.

  Add $40 without sights (scarce).

* **Model BLR 81 Short Action** — cals. as noted above, mfg. 1981-1995 by Miroku in Japan.

  $450 $365 $300 $265 $225 $195 $165

  Last Mfg.'s Sug. Retail was $550.

* **Model BLR 81 Long Action** — .270 Win., .30-06, or 7mm Rem Mag. cal., incorporates distinct design changes, 22 or 24 in. barrel, approx. 8½ lbs. Mfg. 1991-95 by Miroku.

  $450 $365 $300 $265 $230 $200 $170

  Last Mfg.'s Sug. Retail was $580.

Grading	100%	98%	95%	90%	80%	70%	60%

NEW MODEL LIGHTNING BLR (SHORT ACTION) — .22-250 Rem., .223 Rem. (disc. 1998), .243 Win., 7mm-08 Rem., or .308 Win. cal., rotary bolt locking lugs, 20 in. barrel w/o barrel band, similar action as the BLR 81, but features aluminum alloy receiver, checkered pistol grip stock and forearm, rack and pinion geared slide, fold down hammer, trigger travels with lever, 3-5 shot detachable mag., adj. rear sight, approx. 6½ - 7¾ lbs. Mfg. by Miroku beginning late 1995.

Mfg.'s Sug. Retail	$600	$460	$360	$295	$255	$220	$195	$165

* *New Model Lightning BLR (Long Action)* — .270 Win., .30-06, .300 Win. Mag. (new 1997), or 7mm Rem. Mag. cal., 22 or 24 (Mag. cals.) in. barrel, approx. 7½ lbs. Mfg. by Miroku beginning 1995.

Mfg.'s Sug. Retail	$634	$485	$380	$315	$275	$230	$200	$170

MODEL 1886 LIMITED EDITION GRADE I RIFLE — .45-70 Govt. cal. only, patterned after the Winchester Model 1886, blued receiver, 26 in. octagon barrel, full mag., crescent butt plate, open sights. 7,000 mfg. 1986 only.

	$1,150	$950	$750

Last Mfg.'s Sug. Retail was $578.

* *Model 1886 Limited Edition High Grade Rifle* — same general specifications as Model 1886, except has checkered high grade walnut stock and forearm, greyed steel receiver, with game scene engraving including elk and American Bison, gold accenting with "1 of 3,000" engraved on top of barrel. 3,000 mfg. 1986 only.

	$1,795	$1,350	$995

Last Mfg.'s Sug. Retail was $935.

* *Model 1886 Montana Centennial Rifle* — similar to Model 1886 High Grade. 2,000 mfg. 1986 only to commemorate Montana Centennial.

	$1,795	$1,350	$995

Last Mfg.'s Sug. Retail was $935.

MODEL 1886 LIMITED EDITION GRADE I CARBINE — .45-70 Govt. cal. only, saddle ring carbine, patterned after the Winchester Model 1886 Carbine, blued receiver, 22 in. round barrel, 8 shot full mag., crescent butt plate, open sights. 7,000 total mfg. 1992-1993.

	$750	$575	$450

Last Mfg.'s Sug. Retail was $750.

* *Model 1886 Limited Edition High Grade Carbine* — same general specifications as Model 1886, except has checkered high grade walnut stock and forearm, greyed steel receiver, with game scene engraving including bear and elk, gold accenting, 3,000 total mfg. 1992-1993.

	$1,095	$850	$675

Last Mfg.'s Sug. Retail was $1,175.

B-92 CARBINE — .357 Mag. or .44 Rem. Mag. cal., 20 in. barrel, patterned after the Winchester Model 92, 11 shot mag. (tubular), blued finish. Disc. 1986.

	$475	$375	$295	$200	$175	$160	$150

Last Mfg.'s Sug. Retail was $342.

* *B-92 Centennial* — .44 Mag. cal., 6,000 mfg. in 1978.

	$495	$395	$350

Last Mfg.'s Sug. Retail was $220.

* *B-92 BCA Commemorative* — mfg. to commemorate BCA's third anniversary.

	$495	$395	$350

MODEL 1895 LIMITED EDITION GRADE I — .30/40 Krag or .30-06 cal. only, patterned after the Winchester Model 1895, blued receiver, 24 in. barrel, 4 shot mag.(box type), select walnut, rear buckhorn sight, 8 lbs. Mfg. 1984 only.

	100%	98%	95%	90%	80%	70%	60%
.30/40 Krag	$550	$475	$375	$325	$300	$280	$260
.30-06	$650	$525	$400	$350	$325	$300	$280

Production totaled 6,000 in the .30-06 cal. and 2,000 in .30/40 Krag for this model.

Grading	100%	98%	95%	90%	80%	70%	60%

B

* **Model 1895 Limited Edition High Grade** — same general specifications as Model 1895, except gold plated game scenes on satin finish receiver, gold trigger, and finely checkered select French walnut.

| | $1,095 | $950 | $850 | | | | |

Production totaled 1,000 in the .30-06 cal. and 1,000 in .30/40 Krag for this model.

RIFLES: BOLT ACTION, RIMFIRE A-BOLT SERIES

A-BOLT GRADE I RIMFIRE — .22 LR or .22 Mag. (new 1989) cal., 60 degree bolt throw, 22 in. barrel, checkered walnut stock and forearm or laminated stock (scarce - approx. 1,500 mfg., 390 had no sights), 5 or 15 (optional) shot mag., adj. trigger, available with or without open sights, 5 lbs. 9 oz. Mfg. 1986-96.

* **.22 LR cal.**

| | $320 | $255 | $195 | $175 | $160 | $145 | $130 |

Last Mfg.'s Sug. Retail was $425.

Add $14 for open sights.

A 15 shot mag. is also available for this model at $45 retail.

* **.22 Win. Mag. cal.**

| | $375 | $295 | $225 | $195 | $175 | $160 | $150 |

Last Mfg.'s Sug. Retail was 493.

Add $21 for open sights.

A-BOLT GOLD MEDALLION RIMFIRE — .22 LR cal. only, similar to A-Bolt, except has high grade select walnut stock checkered 22 lines per inch, rosewood pistol and forend cap, high gloss finish, gold filled lettering and moderate engraving, solid recoil pad. Mfg. 1988-96.

| | $455 | $365 | $310 | $270 | $240 | $225 | $210 |

Last Mfg.'s Sug. Retail was $567.

RIFLES: BOLT ACTION, CENTERFIRE A-BOLT SERIES

A-BOLT HUNTER MODEL — available in .25-06 Rem., .270 Win., .280 Rem. (new 1988), .30-06, 7mm Rem. Mag., .300 Win. Mag., or .338 Win. Mag. cal. in long action, short action available in .223 Rem. (new 1988), .22-250 Rem., .243 Win., .257 Roberts, .284 Win. (new 1989), 7mm-08 Rem., or .308 Win. cal., 3 or 4 shot mag., matte blue finish, 3 lug rotary bolt locking, 22 (short action only), 24 in. (disc. 1987), or 26 in. barrel (new 1988 - long action Mag. cals. only), 60 degree bolt throw, adj. trigger, hidden detachable mag., with or without sights, top tang thumb safety, checkered pistol grip stock, 6 lbs. 3 oz. - 7 lbs. 11oz. Mfg. 1985-1993 by Miroku. Replaced by A-Bolt Model II in 1994.

| | $415 | $340 | $295 | $265 | $240 | $225 | $210 |

Last Mfg.'s Sug. Retail was $510.

Add $65 for open sights.

* **Medallion Model** — same A-Bolt specifications, except also available in .375 H&H cal., features better grade walnut stock with rosewood pistol grip and forend cap, synthetic floor plate, high lustre bluing, no sights. Disc. 1993. Replaced by A-Bolt Medallion Model II in 1994.

| | $475 | $385 | $330 | $290 | $265 | $250 | $235 |

Last Mfg.'s Sug. Retail was $597.

Add $25 for left-hand action (avail. in long action cals. only).
Add $100 for .375 H&H cal. (open sights only).

Left hand action available in .25-06 Rem., .270 Win., .280 Rem., .30-06, 7mm Rem. Mag., .300 Win. Mag., .338 Win. Mag., or .375 H&H cal.

* **Micro Medallion Model** — .223 Rem. (new 1988), .22-250 Rem., .243 Win., .257 Roberts, .284 Win., .308 Win., or 7mm-08 Rem. cal., scaled down variation of the A-Bolt Hunter Model, 20 in. barrel, short action only, 13⁵⁄₁₆ in. LOP, 3 shot mag., no sights, 6 lbs. 3 oz. for short action. Mfg. 1988-1993. Replaced by A-Bolt Micro Medallion Model II in 1994.

| | $475 | $385 | $330 | $290 | $265 | $250 | $235 |

Last Mfg.'s Sug. Retail was $597.

Grading	100%	98%	95%	90%	80%	70%	60%

⁕ Gold Medallion Model — .270 Win., .30-06, .300 Win. Mag. (new 1993), or 7mm Rem. Mag. cal., similar to Medallion Model, except has extra select walnut stock with continental style cheekpiece, gold lettering and light engraving, no sights. Mfg. 1988-1993. Replaced by A-Bolt Gold Medallion Model II in 1994.

	$670	$535	$430	$360	$330	$300	$265

Last Mfg.'s Sug. Retail was $810.

⁕ Euro-Bolt — .22-250 Rem., .243 Win., .270 Win., .30-06, .308 Win., or 7mm Rem. Mag. cal., features European styling including Schnabel style forearm, rounded rear receiver, Mannlicher style bolt, European cheekpiece on satin finished checkered stock, low-luster bluing, hinged floor plate with removable mag., cocking indicator, upper tang thumb activated safety, 6 lbs. 14 oz. - 7 lbs. 6 oz. (Mag.). Mfg. 1993-96.

	$600	$475	$395	$350	$300	$265	$250

Last Mfg.'s Sug. Retail was $700.

⁕ Stainless Stalker — .22-250 Rem. (left-hand only, new 1993), .25-06 Rem., .270 Win., .280 Rem., .30-06, 7mm Rem. Mag., .300 Win. Mag., .338 Win. Mag. or .375 H&H (new 1990) cal., action and barrel are stainless steel, matte black graphite fiberglass composite stock, dull stainless finish, no sights, 6 lbs. 11 oz. - 7 lbs. 3 oz. Mfg. 1987-1993. Replaced by Stainless Stalker II in 1994.

	$575	$430	$350

Last Mfg.'s Sug. Retail was $665.

Add $100 for .375 H&H cal.
Add $20 for left hand action.

Originally, this model was offered in .270 Win., .30-06, or 7mm Rem. Mag. cal. only.

⁕ Camo Stalker — .270 Win., .30-06, or 7mm Rem. Mag. cal., laminated black and green wood stock, matte finish on metal parts, no sights. Mfg. 1987-1989.

	$400	$340	$310	$285	$250	$230	$215

Last Mfg.'s Sug. Retail was $483.

⁕ Composite Stalker — .25-06 Rem., .270 Win., .280 Rem., .30-06, 7mm Rem. Mag., .300 Win. Mag., or .338 Win. Mag. cal., black graphite fiberglass composite stock, matte non–glare metal finish, 6 lbs. 11 oz. - 7 lbs. 3 oz. Mfg. 1988-1993. Replaced by Composite Stalker II in 1994.

	$410	$340	$295	$265	$240	$225	$210

Last Mfg.'s Sug. Retail was $525.

A-BOLT BIGHORN SHEEP ISSUE — .270 Win. cal. only, 22 in. barrel, high grade walnut stock with gloss finish and skipline checkering, deep relief engraving on receiver barrel, floorplate, and trigger guard, two 24Kt. inlays depicting bighorn sheep. 600 mfg. 1986-87 only.

	$895	$750	$625

Last Mfg.'s Sug. Retail was $1,365.

A-BOLT PRONGHORN ISSUE — .243 Win. cal., presentation grade walnut with skipline checkering and pearl borders, receiver and barrel engraving, multiple gold inlays on receiver top and floor plate. 500 mfg. 1987 only.

	$850	$725	$600

Last Mfg.'s Sug. Retail was $1,302.

RIFLES: BOLT ACTION, CENTERFIRE A-BOLT II SERIES

The A-Bolt II Series differs from the original A-Bolt variations (disc. 1993) in that a new anti-bind bolt featuring a non-rotating bolt sleeve has been incorporated in addition to an improved trigger system. Consumers also may have their name/inscription engraved on the flat bolt-face on any A-Bolt II Series variation for an additional $25. Browning introduced the BOSS (ballistic optimizing shooting system) in 1994 as an option on A-Bolt rifles, except Micro-Medallion models and the .375 H&H caliber.

A-BOLT HUNTER II — cals. similar to A-Bolt series, except not available in .257 Roberts or .284 Win. cal., .260 Rem. cal. new 1999, 22 or 26 in. barrel, available without sights, open sights, or with BOSS, 6 lbs. 7 oz. - 7 lbs. 3 oz. New 1994.

Grading	100%	98%	95%	90%	80%	70%	60%

* **Hunter Model II** — available in 12 cals. between .22-250 Rem. - .338 Win. Mag., 22 or 26 in. barrel with or w/o open sights.

Mfg.'s Sug. Retail	$557	$435	$370	$310	$270	$240	$225	$210

Add $69 for open sights (available in 8 cals., disc. 1998).

➤ **Hunter Model II with BOSS** — same cals. as Hunter Model II until 1999, available only in .22-250 Rem., .243 Win., .270 Win., .280 Rem., .30-06, or .308 Win. cal. beginning 1999, features 22 or 26 (Mag. cals. only, disc. 1998) in. barrel with BOSS. New 1994.

Mfg.'s Sug. Retail	$617	$510	$455	$400	$350	$300	$275	$250

* **Micro Hunter** — .22 Hornet, .22-250 Rem., .243 Win., .260 Rem., .308 Win., or 7mm-08 Rem. cal., features shorter LOP and 20 in. barrel (22 in. for .22 Hornet) w/o sights, checkered walnut stock and forend, approx. 6 lbs. New 1999.

Mfg.'s Sug. Retail	$557	$435	$370	$310	$270	$240	$225	$210

* **Medallion Model II** — available in 13 cals. between .22-250 Rem. - .375 H&H, .260 Rem. new 1999, similar to Medallion Model with A-Bolt II improvements, without sights. New 1994.

Mfg.'s Sug. Retail	$662	$540	$475	$410	$350	$300	$275	$250

Add $105 for .375 H&H cal. (open sights only).
Add $26 for left-hand action.

Left hand action available in .25-06 Rem. (disc. 1998), .270 Win., .280 Rem. (disc. 1997), .30-06, 7mm Rem. Mag., .300 Win. Mag., .338 Win. Mag. (disc. 1998), or .375 H&H (disc. 1997) cal.

➤ **Medallion Model II with BOSS** — similar to Medallion Model II, except has 22 or 26 in. BOSS barrel. New 1994.

Mfg.'s Sug. Retail	$722	$610	$510	$430	$385	$325	$295	$265

Add $105 for .375 H&H cal. (open sights only).
Add $26 for left-hand action.

Left hand action available in .270 Win., .280 Rem. (disc. 1998), .30-06, 7mm Rem. Mag., .300 Win. Mag., or .375 H&H (disc. 1998) cal.

* **Micro Medallion Model II** — .22 Hornet, .22-250 Rem., .223 Rem., .243 Win., 7mm-08 Rem., .284 Win. (disc. 1997), or .308 Win. cal., similar to Micro Medallion Model with A-Bolt II improvements, 20 or 22 (.22 Hornet only) in. barrel without sights, 6 lbs. Mfg. 1994-98.

		$525	$465	$400	$350	$300	$275	$250

Last Mfg.'s Sug. Retail was $636.

* **Custom Trophy** — .270 Win., .30-06, .300 Win. Mag., or 7mm Rem. Mag. cal., features 24 or 26 (Mag. cals. only) in. octagon barrel with gold band at muzzle, no sights, gold outlines on barrel and receiver, checkered select American walnut stock with shadowline cheekpiece and skeleton pistol grip, approx. 7½ lbs. New 1998.

Mfg.'s Sug. Retail	$1,360	$1,095	$895	$785	$650	$525	$450	$375

* **Gold Medallion Model II** — .270 Win., .30-06, .300 Win. Mag. or 7mm Rem. Mag. cal., similar to Gold Medallion Model, except has A-Bolt II improvements, 22 or 26 in. barrel, approx. 7½ lbs. Mfg. 1994-98.

		$695	$595	$450	$375	$335	$300	$265

Last Mfg.'s Sug. Retail was $855.

➤ **Gold Medallion Model II with BOSS** — mfg. 1994-97.

		$750	$625	$525	$450	$375	$325	$285

Last Mfg.'s Sug. Retail was $916.

* **White Gold Medallion** — .270 Win., .30-06, .300 Win. Mag., or 7mm Rem. Mag. cal., stainless steel receiver and barrel, gold engraving, checkered high gloss walnut stock with cheekpiece and rosewood forend cap, 7 lbs. 3 oz. - 7 lbs. 11 oz. New 1999.

Mfg.'s Sug. Retail	$949	$780	$645	$530	$450	$375	$325	$285

➤ **White Gold Medallion with BOSS** — similar to White Gold Medallion, except has barrel with BOSS.

Mfg.'s Sug. Retail	$1,009	$825	$675	$550	$465	$385	$330	$295

Grading	100%	98%	95%	90%	80%	70%	60%

B

* ***Eclipse with BOSS*** — .22-250 Rem., .243 Win. (disc. 1997), .270 Win., .30-06, .308 Win., or 7mm Rem. Mag. cal., features laminated thumbhole wood stock with cheekpiece, long action, 22 or 26 (7mm Rem. Mag. only) in. barrel with BOSS, 7½ - 8 lbs. New 1996.

Mfg.'s Sug. Retail	$941	$765	$640	$535	$455	$375	$325	$285

➤ **Eclipse Varmint with BOSS** — .22-250 Rem., .223 Rem., or .308 Win. cal., 24 in. heavy barrel with BOSS, 4 shot mag., otherwise similar to Eclipse Model, approx. 9 lbs. New 1996.

Mfg.'s Sug. Retail	$969	$810	$655	$535	$455	$375	$325	$285

➤ **Eclipse M-1000 with BOSS** — .300 Win. Mag. cal., features special 26 in. heavy target barrel, refined trigger system, 9 lbs. 13 oz.

Mfg.'s Sug. Retail	$969	$810	$655	$535	$455	$375	$325	$285

* ***Varmint II with BOSS*** — .22-250 Rem., .223 Rem., or .308 Win. (new 1995) cal., features A-Bolt II improvements, 22 in. heavy barrel with BOSS, blued/gloss or satin/matte (new 1995) finish, black laminated wood stock with checkering, palm swell, and solid recoil pad, without sights, 9 lbs. New 1994.

Mfg.'s Sug. Retail	$853	$700	$590	$460	$380	$335	$300	$265

* ***Euro-Bolt II*** — .243 Win., .30-06, .308 Win., or 7mm Rem. Mag. cal., similar to Euro-Bolt with A-Bolt II improvements, 22 or 26 (7mm Rem. Mag. only) in. barrel w/o sights, 6 lbs. 7 oz. - 7 lbs. 3 oz. (Mag.). Mfg. 1994-96.

	$625	$510	$410	$355	$300	$265	$250

Last Mfg.'s Sug. Retail was $824.

➤ **Euro-Bolt II with BOSS** — .243 Win. or .308 Win. cal., 22 in. barrel with BOSS, 6 lbs. 7 oz.

	$725	$600	$500	$425	$350	$325	$295

Last Mfg.'s Sug. Retail was $922.

* ***Stainless Stalker II*** — similar to Stainless Stalker with A-Bolt improvements, also available in .22-250 Rem. (new 1995), .223 Rem. (new 1995), .243 Win. (new 1994), or 7mm-08 Rem. (new 1995), .308 Win. (new 1995), or .260 Rem. (new 1999) cal., without sights, 6 lbs. 4 oz. - 7 lbs. 3 oz. New 1994.

Mfg.'s Sug. Retail	$737	$620	$460	$355

Add $102 for .375 H&H cal. (open sights only).
Add $23 for left-hand action.

Left-hand action cals. include .270 Win., .280 Rem. (disc. 1998), .30-06, .300 Win. Mag., .338 Win. Mag., .375 H&H, or 7mm Rem. Mag.

➤ **Stainless Stalker II with BOSS** — available in 14 cals. between .22-250 Rem. and .375 H&H, 22 or 26 (Mag. cals. only) in. barrel with BOSS.

Mfg.'s Sug. Retail	$797	$680	$510	$420

Add $102 for .375 H&H cal. (open sights only).
Add $23 for left-hand action.

Left-hand action cals. include .25-06 Rem. (disc. 1998), .270 Win., .280 Rem. (disc. 1998), .30-06, .300 Win. Mag., .338 Win. Mag., .375 H&H, or 7mm Rem. Mag.

* ***Composite Stalker II*** — similar to Composite Stalker with A-Bolt II improvements, also available in .223 Rem., .22-250 Rem., .243 Win., .260 Rem. (new 1999), 7mm-08 Rem., or .308 Win. cal., 22 or 26 (Mag. cals. only) in. barrel without sights, 6 lbs. 4 oz. - 7 lbs. 3 oz. New 1994.

Mfg.'s Sug. Retail	$580	$440	$360	$305	$270	$240	$225	$210

➤ **Composite Stalker II with BOSS** — available in 12 cals. between .22-250 Rem. - .338 Win. Mag. (.22-250 Rem. disc. 1997), 22 or 26 (Mag. cals. only) in. barrel with BOSS.

Mfg.'s Sug. Retail	$640	$535	$460	$380	$325	$285	$250	$225

* ***Greywolf*** — .25-06 Rem., .270 Win., .280 Rem., .30-06, .300 Win. Mag., .338 Win. Mag., or 7mm Rem. Mag. cal., stainless steel, classic sporter with select walnut stock. Limited mfg. during 1994 only.

	$850	$675	$595

Last Mfg.'s Sug. Retail was $935.

Grading	100%	98%	95%	90%	80%	70%	60%

B

RIFLES: BOLT ACTION

MODEL 52 LIMITED EDITION — .22 LR cal., virtually identical to the original Winchester Model 52C Sporter, except for minor safety enhancements, bolt action, 24 in. drilled and tapped barrel, 5 shot detachable mag., pistol grip walnut stock with oil style finish, deep blue finish, adj. trigger, two position safety, 7 lbs. 5,000 mfg. 1991-92.

$495   **$425**   **$395**

Last Mfg.'s Sug. Retail was $500.

MODEL BBR — .25-06 Rem., .270 Win., .30-06, 7mm Mag., .300 Win. Mag. or .338 Win. Mag. cal., short action available in .22-250 Rem., 243 Win., 257 Roberts, 7mm-08 Rem., or 308 Win. cal., 24 in. standard or heavy barrel, 60 degree throw, fluted bolt, adj. trigger, hidden detachable mag., no sights, checkered pistol grip, Monte Carlo stock. Mfg. 1978-1984 by Miroku.

$470   **$360**   **$330**   **$305**   **$250**   **$220**   **$200**

Some rare production calibers will add premiums to the values listed above (i.e., add 50% for .243 Win. cal.).

BBR RIFLE ELK ISSUE — 7mm Rem. Mag. cal., bolt action rifle, 1,000 manufactured, deeply blued receiver which has multiple animals gold inlaid, high grade walnut stock and forearm feature skipline checkering. Disc. 1986.

$1,195   **$950**   **$795**

Last Mfg.'s Sug. Retail was $1,395.

T-BOLT T-1 — .22 LR cal., straight pull bolt action, 5 shot mag., 22 in. barrel, adj. rear sight, 5½ lbs., plain pistol grip stock. Mfg. 1965-1974 by FN.

$395   **$350**   **$295**   **$255**   **$210**   **$180**   **$160**

Add 10%-15% for left-hand model (mfg. 1967-74 only).

An aperture rear sight was standard for the first nine years of production.

T-BOLT T-2 — similar to T-1, only with select checkered walnut stock (lacquer finished), pinned front sight blade, 24 in. barrel, 6 lbs.

$550   **$415**   **$340**   **$295**   **$240**   **$200**   **$180**

Add 10%-15% for left-hand model (mfg. 1969-74 only).

* ***Late production T-2*** — features oil finished stock, press fit plastic front sight, and Browning computerized serialization.

$395   **$315**   **$260**   **$210**   **$180**   **$160**   **$140**

FN HIGH-POWER BOLT ACTION MODEL — .222 Rem. (Sako action), .222 Rem. Mag. (Sako action), .22-250 Rem. (Sako action), .243 Win., .257 Roberts, .264 Win. Mag., .270 Win., .284 Win. (Sako action), .30-06, .308 Win., 7mm Mag., .300 Win. Mag., .308 Norma Mag., .300 H&H, .338 Win. Mag., .375 H&H, or .458 Win. Mag. cal., standard Mauser type action with either short or long (more desirable) extractor, 22 or 24 in. (heavy available) barrel, folding leaf sight, checkered pistol grip stock. Mfg. 1959-1974 by FN.

The .243 Win. and .308 Win. cals. were built on the small ring Mauser action prior to using the Sako medium action.

Note: Grades differ in engraving, finish, checkering, and grade of wood. It should be noted that the salt wood problem is more common in these high powered models. Guns should be checked carefully for rust below wood surfaces.

* ***Safari Grade*** — basic model with blued finish.

	100%	98%	95%	90%	80%	70%	60%
Standard cals.	$795	$675	$550	$450	$400	$350	$325
Mag. cals.	$900	$750	$650	$595	$525	$450	$400
.257 Roberts	$1,295	$1,050	$825	$700	$600	$525	$450
.284 Win.	$1,550	$1,200	$950	$800	$700	$600	$500
.308 Norma Mag.	$1,050	$850	$700	$600	$525	$450	$400
.338 Win. Mag.	$1,150	$950	$850	$735	$650	$595	$525
.375 H&H	$1,300	$1,000	$800	$700	$600	$525	$450
.458 Win. Mag.	$1,095	$995	$895	$750	$625	$525	$450

Grading	100%	98%	95%	90%	80%	70%	60%

Add 15% for Magnum long extractor models.

Between 1963 and 1974, Browning also offered short and medium barrelled actions in the Safari, Medallion and Olympian Grades. These models have Sako barrelled actions and were stocked by FN. Medium weight barrels could also be ordered.

* *Safari Grade - Short Sako Action* — short action, .222 Rem. or .222 Rem. Mag. cal.

	$800	$675	$550	$450	$400	$350	$325

* *Safari Grade - Medium Sako Action* — medium action, .22-250 Rem., .243 Win., .284 Win. or .308 Win. cal.

	$800	$675	$550	$450	$400	$350	$325

Add 50% for .284 Win. cal. (mfg. 1965-1976).

In .284 Win. cal., only 162 rifles were mfg. in Safari Grade, 20 in Medallion Grade, and 10 in Olympian Grade.

* *Medallion Grade* — features select figured walnut with skipline checkering, rosewood grip and forearm caps, blue/black lustre bluing, receiver and barrel portion scroll engraved, ram's head engraved on floor plate.

	$1,250	$995	$895	$795	$700	$600	$500

Add 10%-50% for rare calibers.
Add 15% for Mag. cals. with long extractor.

Caliber rarity is as follows: .264 Win. Mag. (least rare), .300 H&H, .375 H&H long extractor, .222 Rem./.222 Rem. Mag., .284 Win. (rarest).

This model was also available with a Sako short or medium action - cals. are the same as listed for the Sako Safari.

* *Olympian Grade* — top-of-the-line model featuring highly figured walnut stock that is both checkered and carved. Receiver, floor plate, and trigger guard are chrome plated in a satin finish that has deep relief animal scenes engraved, as well as deep scroll work on other metal parts.

	$2,750	$2,350	$1,925	$1,700	$1,550	$1,350	$1,175

Add 10%-50% for rare calibers.
Add 15% for Mag. cals. with long extractor.

Caliber rarity is as follows: .264 Win. Mag. (least rare), .300 H&H, .375 H&H long extractor, .222 Rem./.222 Rem. Mag., .284 Win. (rarest).

This model was also available with a Sako short or medium action - cals. are the same as listed for the Sako Safari.

RIFLES: SLIDE ACTION

BPR — .243 Win., .270 Win., .30-06, .308 Win., .300 Win. Mag., or 7mm Rem. Mag. cal., 7 lug rotary bolt, blued alloy receiver, 22 or 24 (Mag. cals. only) in. barrel with open sights, features downward camming slide action assembly, checkered walnut stock and forend, cross-bolt safety, 3 or 4 shot mag., approx. 7 lbs. 3 oz. New 1997.

Mfg.'s Sug. Retail	$718	$630	$560	$510	$455	$400	$360	$330

Add $54 for Mag. cals.

BPR-22 — .22 LR or .22 Mag. cal., short-stroke action, 20¼ in. barrel, 11 shot tube mag., mfg. 1977-1982.

	$275	$195	$170	$160	$140	$130	$100

* *BPR-22 Grade II* — similar to BPR-22, only engraved action, select walnut.

	$450	$350	$295	$260	$230	$200	$175

Add 10% for .22 Mag. cal.

TROMBONE MODEL — .22 LR cal. only, slide action with tube mag., fixed sights, takedown, 24 in. barrel, hammerless, similar to Win. Model 61, with either F.N. or U.S. (rare) barrel address.

BROWNING

Grading	100%	98%	95%	90%	80%	70%	60%
* **FN Barrel Address**	$695	$550	$400	$350	$295	$260	$225
* **BAC Barrel Markings**	$850	$695	$495	$425	$350	$295	$250

Over 150,000 "Trombones" were mfg. by FN from 1922-1974. About 3,200 were imported by BAC in late 1960s. Very rare with factory engraving.

BCA GRADE III FN TROMBONE — only 60 manufactured for the Browning Collectors Association 1985-86, silver engraved frame with deluxe walnut.

$2,350 $1,995 $1,600

RIFLES: O/U

EXPRESS RIFLE — .270 Win., .30-06 cal., or 9.3x74R cal., Superposed style action. 24 in. barrels, auto ejectors, Fleur-de-lis engraving, single trigger, folding leaf rear sight, 6 lbs. 14 oz., cased. Disc. 1986.

$2,500 $2,150 $1,750 $1,475 $1,300 $1,100 $900
Last Mfg.'s Sug. Retail was $3,125.

GRADE I CONTINENTAL SET — includes .30-06 O/U rifle barrels with extra set of 20 ga. O/U shotgun barrels (26½ in.), rifle barrels are 24 in., SST, ejectors, blued receiver with scroll engraving, supplied with 2 barrel takedown case. Disc.

$3,495 $2,995 $2,495 $1,795 $1,495 $1,295 $1,050

SHOTGUNS: SEMI-AUTO, DISC.

BROWNING CHOKES AND THEIR CODES (ON REAR LEFT-SIDE OF BARREL)

* designates full choke (F).

*- designates improved modified choke (IM).

** designates modified choke (M).

**- designates improved cylinder choke (IC).

**$ designates skeet (SK).

*** designates cylinder bore (CYL).

INV. designates barrel is threaded for Browning Invector choke tube system.

INV. PLUS designates back-bored barrels.

AUTO-5 STANDARD - 1903-1939 MFG. — 12 or 16 ga.(introduced in U.S. in 1923), 26-32 in. barrel, recoil operated, various chokes, checkered pistol grip stock, mfg. 1903-1939 and limited post-war mfg. by FN, grades differ in engraving, inlays, and grade of wood. Approx. ser. range 1-229,000 (12ga.), 1-128,000 (16 ga.).

	100%	98%	95%	90%	80%	70%	60%
Grade 1	$425	$375	$325	$285	$250	$200	$175
Solid matte rib	$495	$425	$375	$325	$275	$250	$215
With vent. rib	$550	$475	$400	$350	$300	$250	$215
Grade 2.(disc.1940)	$1,250	$1,000	$875	$750	$625	$550	$495
Solid matte rib	$1,450	$1,150	$1,000	$875	$750	$625	$575
With vent. rib	$1,625	$1,300	$1,200	$1,000	$850	$750	$650
Grade 3.(disc. 1940)	$2,500	$2,200	$1,975	$1,775	$1,500	$1,250	$995
Solid matte rib	$2,700	$2,400	$2,100	$1,850	$1,650	$1,375	$1,100
With vent. rib	$2,950	$2,550	$2,250	$2,000	$1,775	$1,500	$1,225
Grade 4.(disc. 1940)	$3,995	$3,655	$3,300	$2,995	$2,550	$2,050	$1,600
Solid matte rib	$4,150	$3,885	$3,450	$3,175	$2,700	$2,200	$1,800

Early models with safety mounted in front of trigger guard are not as desirable as there are potential safety problems inherent in the design.

Pre-WWII 16 ga. A-5s could be chambered for 2⁹⁄₁₆ in. shells. These shotguns are considerably less desirable than 16 ga. A-5s chambered for 2¾ in. modern shotshells. Since some guns have been modified to 2¾ in., careful inspection is advised before

B

purchasing or shooting. The $2\%_{16}$ chambered guns can be modified by the Browning Service Dept. to accept $2\frac{3}{4}$ in. shells if so desired.

Recently, a small quantity of extended mag., 5 or 8 shot, pre-1939 FN Military/Police A-5s were imported with POL markings below the ser. no. and 24 in. barrels. Prices range from $295-$450, depending on condition (mostly good to very good condition).

"AMERICAN BROWNING" AUTO-5 — 12, 16, or 20 ga., Remington-produced model of the Auto-5, very similar to the Remington Model 11, except with Browning logo, mag. cut-off, and different engraving, over 38,000 mfg. in 12 ga., over 14,000 in 16 ga., and 11,000 in 20 ga., stocks have Remington style round knob pistol grips with black plastic caps. Mfg. 1940-1949 and ser. numbered approx. 229,000-346,000, 12 ga. has "B" prefix on left side of receiver, "A" denotes 16 ga., and "C" denotes 20 ga.

	100%	98%	95%	90%	80%	70%	60%
	$325	$275	$250	$225	$200	$180	$160

Add 10% for vent. rib and/or 20 ga.

An easy way to identify this configuration is to look for the "A", "B", or "C" prefix on the left side of receiver.

AUTO-5 STANDARDWEIGHT — 12, 20, or 16 ga., recoil operation, 26-32 in. barrels, standard production gun between 1952-1969, various chokes, checkered walnut stock and forearm, synthetic Browning marked butt plate, lacquer (until approx. 1966) or polyurethane finish, buttstock has either round knob pistol grip (1952-1976) or flat knob (introduced 1967), watch for cracked forearms on all A-5s (due to barrel recoil), between $7\frac{1}{3}$-8 lbs.

	100%	98%	95%	90%	80%	70%	60%
Plain barrel	$425	$375	$325	$295	$270	$240	$210
Matted rib	$525	$450	$400	$350	$300	$275	$245
Vent rib	$550	$460	$410	$370	$325	$300	$265

Add 10% for NIB condition.

Barrel addresses appeared as follows: 1952-1958 "St. Louis, Missouri", 1959-1968 "St. Louis, Missouri and Montreal P.Q.", 1969-1975 "Morgan, Utah and Montreal, P.Q.". Make sure barrel address date matches year of mfg. (see listings in the back of this text). Standardweight models had H or M prefixes.

SHOTGUNS: SEMI-AUTO, RECENT MFG.

Miroku manufactured A-5s can be determined by year of manufacture in the following manner: RV suffix - 1975, RT - 1976, RR - 1977, RP - 1978, RN - 1979, PM - 1980, PZ - 1981, PY - 1982, PX - 1983, PW - 1984, PV - 1985, PT - 1986, PR - 1987, PP - 1988, PN - 1989, NM - 1990, NZ - 1991, NY - 1992, NX - 1993, NW - 1994, NV - 1995, NT - 1996, NR - 1997, NP - 1998, NN - 1999, MM - 2000.

On November 26, 1997, Browning announced that the venerable Auto-5 would finally be discontinued. Final shipments were made in February, 1998.

NOTE: Barrels are interchangeable between older Belgium A-5 models and recent Japanese A-5s mfg. by Miroku. A different barrel ring design might necessitate some minor sanding of the inner forearm on the older model, but otherwise, these barrels are fully interchangeable.

NOTE: The use of steel shot is recommended ONLY in those recent models manufactured in Japan incorporating the Invector choke system - NOT in the older Belgium variations.

Add 10-15% for the round knob (rounded pistol grip knob on stock) variation on FN models only.

AUTO-5 LIGHTWEIGHT (LIGHT 12) — 12 or 20 ga., recoil operated, 26, 28, and 30 in. barrels, various chokes, scroll engraved receiver, checkered pistol grip stock, approx. 10 oz. lighter than Standardweight, mfg. 1952-1976 by FN, mfg. 1976-present by Miroku in Japan. Over 2,750,000 A-5s were mfg. by FN in all configurations between 1902-1976.

	100%	98%	95%	90%	80%	70%	60%
FN model	$400	$375	$325	$295	$270	$240	$215
FN-vent. rib	$650	$500	$400	$350	$325	$295	$260

Add 10% for NIB condition.
Add 10% for 20 ga. with VR.

Grading	100%	98%	95%	90%	80%	70%	60%

❋ Light 12 Miroku — 12 ga. only, 22, 26, 28, or 30 in. VR (became standard 1986) barrel with Invector choke system, approx. 8-8½ lbs. Mfg. 1976-Feb., 1998.

| | $650 | $485 | $400 | $350 | $300 | $280 | $260 |

Last Mfg.'s Sug. Retail was $840.

Subtract 10% without Invector chokes.

❋ Light 20 Miroku — 20 ga. only, 2¾ in. chamber, similar to original Belgium Light 20, VR, 22 (new 1995), 26, or 28 in. barrel, Invector chokes standard until 1993, Invector Plus choking became standard 1994, 6 lbs. 12 oz - 7 lbs. 2 oz. Mfg. 1987-1997.

| | $650 | $495 | $410 | $365 | $325 | $295 | $270 |

Last Mfg.'s Sug. Retail was $840.

AUTO-5 MAGNUM — 12 or 20 ga., 3 in. chamber, 26, 28, 30, or 32 in. barrels, various chokes, VR, similar to Standard, 8½ - 9 lbs. Mfg. 1958-1976 by FN, 1976-Feb., 1998 by Miroku.

| **FN model.** | $550 | $450 | $400 | $350 | $320 | $260 | $240 |
| **FN-vent. rib.** | $675 | $575 | $525 | $480 | $430 | $340 | $315 |

Add 10% for NIB condition.
Add 15% for 20 ga. with VR if NIB.

Between 1976-1985 approx. 2,000 Belgian 12 ga. A-5 Mags. were imported into the U.S. These late models can be differentiated by serialization — also, slight premiums may be asked. The 20 ga. Mag. was not introduced until 1967.

❋ A-5 Mag. Miroku — 12 or 20 ga., VR barrel with Invector choke system until 1993, Invector Plus choking became standard 1994, 8½ - 9 lbs. Disc. 1997.

| | $695 | $540 | $445 | $385 | $350 | $325 | $290 |

Last Mfg.'s Sug. Retail was $866.

Subtract $87 for 20 ga. Mag.
Subtract 10% without Invector chokes.

AUTO-5 STALKER — 12 ga. only, 2¾ (Light-12) or 3 (Mag. Stalker) in. chamber, 22 (Light-12 only), 26, 28, or 30, or 32 (Mag. only) in. VR barrel with Invector chokes, black matte finish graphite-fiberglass stock and forearm, matte finished metal, recoil pad, 8 lbs. 1 oz. - 8 lbs. 13 oz. Mfg. 1992-97.

| | $650 | $485 | $410 | $350 | $300 | $280 | $260 |

Last Mfg.'s Sug. Retail was $840.

Add $26 for Mag. Stalker.

AUTO-5 LIGHT 12 BUCK SPECIAL — similar to Standard only with 24 in. barrel, slug bore, adj. sight, mfg. 1958-1976 by FN, mfg. 1976-1984 and 1989 again by Miroku, 8 lbs. 6 oz. Between 1985-1988, Buck Special barrels were available at extra cost.

❋ FN Mfg.

| | $675 | $475 | $410 | $370 | $330 | $295 | $240 |

❋ Miroku model — mfg. 1989-1997.

| | $645 | $500 | $425 | $360 | $320 | $290 | $260 |

Last Mfg.'s Sug. Retail was $829.

Add $35 for Buck Special on 3 in. Mag. receiver.

AUTO-5 SKEET — similar to Standard Light, only with 26 or 28 in. skeet bored, vent. rib barrel. Pre-1976 mfg. by FN, 1976-1983 mfg. by Miroku.

❋ FN Mfg.

| | $550 | $425 | $375 | $325 | $295 | $270 | $240 |

Add 20% for vent. rib.

❋ Standard Miroku

| | $460 | $420 | $380 | $340 | $300 | $270 | $250 |

AUTO-5 TRAP MODEL — 12 ga. only, similar to Standard, 30 in. full vent. rib barrel, 8½ lbs., mfg. by FN until 1971.

| | $595 | $525 | $465 | $410 | $335 | $320 | $295 |

Grading	100%	98%	95%	90%	80%	70%	60%

AUTO-5 SWEET 16 — 16 ga. ($2\frac{3}{4}$ in. chamber) only and approx. 10 oz. lighter, similar to Standardweight Model, gold plated trigger. Mfg. 1950-1976 by Fabrique Nationale.

	100%	98%	95%	90%	80%	70%	60%
Plain Barrel	$525	$415	$350	$295	$250	$220	$195
Solid Matte Rib	$695	$575	$465	$375	$295	$250	$225
Vent. Rib	$950	$750	$575	$425	$375	$325	$275

* **Sweet 16 Miroku** — 16 ga. only, similar to original Belgium Sweet 16, VR, invector choke standard. Mfg. 1987-92.

$580	$475	$420	$380	$340	$300	$270

Last Mfg.'s Sug. Retail was $720.

AUTO-5 2-MILLIONTH COMMEMORATIVE — 12 ga., 2,500 mfg., 1971-74 mfg., special walnut, engraving, high-luster bluing, cased with Browning book. Issue price — $550-$700.

$1,195	$900	$750

A-5 CLASSIC SERIES SHOTGUN — 12 ga., 5,000 mfg. in Classic model, 500 mfg. in Gold Classic. Both editions feature game scenes, John M. Browning's profile, and other inscriptions, special silver grey finished receiver. Introduced 1984.

* **Classic Model** — no inlays. Factory inventories were depleted in 1987.

$950	$750	$600

Last Mfg.'s Sug. Retail was $1,260.

* **Gold Classic Model** — features 5 inlays depicting duck hunting scenes. Mfg. 1986 with inventory depleted 1989.

$3,500	$2,750	$1,950

Last Mfg.'s Sug. Retail was $6,500.

A-5 BCA COMMEMORATIVE — 12 ga., 3 in. Mag., round knob, Belgian mfg., issue price was $595.

$650	$575	$450

A-5 DU 50TH ANNIVERSARY

* **A-5 DU Light 12** — 12 ga. only, 5,500 mfg. in 1987 only for Ducks Unlimited chapters throughout North America. Prices will fluctuate greatly from chapter to chapter as these guns were auctioned to the highest bidder. Receiver is specially engraved and has "Fiftieth year" depicted on right side of receiver, deluxe checkered stock and forearm, high gloss blue.

$950	$750	$600

* **A-5 DU Sweet Sixteen** — 16 ga. only, companion 1988-89 DU auction gun, 4500 mfg. 1988 only.

$950	$750	$600

* **A-5 DU Light 20** — 20 ga. only, companion 1990 DU auction gun, 4500 mfg. 1990 only.

$950	$750	$600

DOUBLE AUTOMATIC SHOTGUN — 12 ga. only, short recoil action, 2 shot, 26, 28, or 30 in. barrel, various chokes, checkered pistol grip stock, blued steel receiver. Mfg. 1952-1971.

	100%	98%	95%	90%	80%	70%	60%
	$475	$400	$350	$300	$260	$220	$195
w/vent. rib	$650	$495	$420	$375	$325	$295	$245

TWELVETTE DOUBLE AUTO — similar to Double Auto, except hiduminum (aircraft alloy) frame and color anodized in blue, silver, brown, green, and black, approx. 7 lbs. without rib. Approx. 67,000 (all variations) mfg. 1952-1971.

	100%	98%	95%	90%	80%	70%	60%
	$475	$400	$350	$295	$250	$220	$200
w/vent. rib	$650	$495	$425	$395	$340	$280	$250

Add 20-25% for dark red, royal blue, brown, or gold colored receivers (rare).

Grading	100%	98%	95%	90%	80%	70%	60%

TWENTYWEIGHT DOUBLE AUTO — similar to Twelvette, but ¾ pound lighter, 26½ in. barrel only. Mfg. 1952-1971.

	$575	$450	$375	$295	$235	$220	$200
w/vent. rib	$725	$625	$525	$450	$400	$350	$295

B/2000 STANDARD — 12 or 20 ga., 26, 28, or 30 in. barrel, various chokes, vent. rib, gas operated, checkered pistol grip stock, Belgium manufactured but assembled in Portugal, approx. 115,000 imported into the U.S. between 1974-1983.

$360	$325	$295	$275	$250	$225	$195

B/2000 MAGNUM — similar to B/2000 Auto Shotgun, except with 3 in. chambered barrel (all receivers were the same), recoil pad, vent. rib.

$385	$340	$310	$280	$260	$230	$200

B/2000 SKEET — similar to Standard, with 26 in. skeet bored barrel, floating vent. rib, skeet stock, pad.

$375	$325	$295	$275	$250	$225	$195

B/2000 TRAP — similar to Standard, with 30 or 32 in. barrel bored F or IM, floating rib, Monte Carlo trap stock.

$375	$325	$295	$275	$250	$225	$195

B/2000 BUCK SPECIAL — 12 or 20 ga., barrel sights on 24 in. barrel.

$375	$325	$295	$275	$250	$225	$195

1976 CANADIAN OLYMPICS B2000 — 12 ga., 100 manufactured in 1976 for Canadian sales only, high polish blue with multiple gold inlays including Olympic crest, 30 in. barrel, cased. Issue price was $1,295.

$1,395	$995	$695

MODEL B-80 — 12 or 20 ga., 3 in. capability by changing barrel, gas operation, 4 shot, hunting models use choice of steel or aluminum receiver, anodized aluminum was used in the Superlight (12 ga. mfg. 1984 only), 6 to 8 lbs. 1 oz. Buck special disc. 1984. Components manufactured by Beretta of Italy and finished and assembled FN's plant in Portugal. Mfg. 1981-late 1988, final inventory was sold in 1991. Invector chokes became standard in 1985.

$450	$375	$325	$295	$275	$250	$230

Last Mfg.'s Sug. Retail was $562.

Steel frames were reintroduced into production again in 1988.

* ***Model B-80 Upland Special*** — 12 or 20 ga., 2¾ in. chamber, 22 in. vent. rib barrel, straight grip stock, invector chokes. Mfg. 1986-1988.

$475	$390	$340	$305	$280	$260	$240

Last Mfg.'s Sug. Retail was $562.

MODEL B 80 DU COMMEMORATIVE — mfg. for American DU Chapters (The Plains and others), price fluctuates greatly as collector support is sometimes limited. Unless new, this model's values approximate those of the regular Model B-80. If NIB, values recently have been in the $700-$995 range.

A-500R — 12 ga. only, 3 in. chamber, new design utilizing short recoil system with a four-lug rotary bolt design, capable of shooting all 12 gauge loads interchangeably, magazine cut-off, 26, 28, or 30 in. VR barrel with Invector chokes standard, 24 in. barrel on Buck Special (fixed choke), high polished blued finish with red accents on receiver sides, gold trigger, checkered semi-pistol grip walnut stock with vent. recoil pad, 7 lbs. 11 oz. - 8 lbs. 1 oz. Mfg. 1987-1993.

$475	$425	$375	$325	$295	$275	$250

Last Mfg.'s Sug. Retail was $560.

Add $33 for Buck Special variation (Invector chokes).

This model features fewer moving parts than many other semi-auto shotguns due to the short recoil operating system.

Grading	100%	98%	95%	90%	80%	70%	60%

A-500G HUNTING — similar to A-500, except is gas operated, distinguishable by "A-500G" in gold accents on receiver, capable of shooting all 2¾ or 3 in. shells interchangeably, approx. 8 lbs. Mfg. 1990-1993.

	$555	$425	$375	$325	$295	$275	$250

Last Mfg.'s Sug. Retail was $653.

A Buck Special variation was mfg. until 1992. No premiums currently exist.

* **A-500G Sporting Clays** — 12 ga. only, Sporting Clays variation with 30 in. VR barrel, 8 lbs. 2 oz. Mfg. 1992-1993.

	$555	$425	$375	$325	$295	$275	$250

Last Mfg.'s Sug. Retail was $653.

GOLD HUNTER — 12 or 20 ga., 3 in. chamber, self-cleaning piston rod gas action with self-regulation, alloy receiver with non-glare black finish and "Gold Hunter" on receiver side, 26, 28, or 30 (12 ga. only) in. VR Invector Plus (12 ga. only) or Invector (20 ga. only) choked barrel, cross-bolt safety, checkered walnut stock and forearm with recoil pad (vent on 12 ga.), 6 lbs. 12 oz. - 7 lbs. 9 oz. Parts mfg. in Belgium and final assembly in Portugal. New 1994.

Mfg.'s Sug. Retail	$772	$640	$465	$390	$330	$295	$275	$250

* **Gold Hunter Classic** — similar to Gold Hunter, except has semi-hump back receiver design, magazine cutoff, adj. comb, and satin finished wood, 26 or 28 in. VR barrel. New 1999.

Mfg.'s Sug. Retail	$772	$640	$465	$390	$330	$295	$275	$250

* **Gold Hunter High Grade Classic** — 12 ga. only, similar to Gold Hunter Classic, except has nickel finished receiver featuring multiple gold inlays (ducks and dogs) and light scroll engraving, deluxe checkered walnut stock and forearm, 28 in. barrel only, 6 lbs. 14 oz. New 1999.

Mfg.'s Sug. Retail	$1,427	$1,275	$1,025	$925	$800	$700	$625	$550

* **Gold Turkey/Waterfowl Hunter Camo** — similar to Gold Hunter, full coverage (including barrel) Mossy Oak Breakup camo finish, 24 in. VR barrel with Hi-Viz sights and extra full choke tube, 7 lbs. New 1999.

Mfg.'s Sug. Retail	$772	$640	$465	$390	$330	$295	$275	$250

* **Gold Waterfowl Mossy Oak Breakup/Shadow Grass** — similar to Gold Hunter, choice of full coverage (including barrel) Mossy Oak Breakup or Shadow Grass camo finish, 24 (Mossy Oak Breakup only), 26 (Mossy Oak Shadow Grass only), or 28 (Mossy Oak Shadow Grass only) in. VR back-bored barrel with Invector Plus choke tubes, approx. 7¼ lbs. New 1999.

Mfg.'s Sug. Retail	$842	$700	$510	$415	$345	$300	$275	$250

Add $10 for Mossy Oak Breakup pattern.

* **Gold 3½ in. Hunter** — 12 ga., 3½ in. chamber, 26, 28, or 30 in. VR barrel with Invector Plus choking, otherwise similar to Gold Hunter, 3-4 shot mag., approx. 7 lbs. 10 oz. New 1998.

Mfg.'s Sug. Retail	$929	$795	$640	$560	$480	$400	$365	$335

* **Gold 3½ in. Turkey/Waterfowl Hunter** — similar to Gold 3½ in. Hunter, full coverage (including barrel) Mossy Oak Breakup camo finish, 24 in. VR barrel with extra full choke tube, 7¼ lbs. New 1999.

Mfg.'s Sug. Retail	$929	$795	$640	$560	$480	$400	$365	$335

* **Gold 3½ in. Waterfowl Mossy Oak Breakup/Shadow Grass** — similar to Gold 3½ in. Hunter, choice of full coverage (including barrel) Mossy Oak Breakup or Shadow Grass camo finish, 24 (Mossy Oak Breakup only), 26 (Mossy Oak Shadow Grass only), or 28 (Mossy Oak Shadow Grass only) in. VR back-bored barrel with Invector Plus choke tubes, approx. 7½ lbs. New 1999.

Mfg.'s Sug. Retail	$999	$850	$675	$585	$490	$410	$365	$335

Add $10 for Mossy Oak Breakup pattern.

Grading	100%	98%	95%	90%	80%	70%	60%

✱ *Gold Deer Hunter* — 12 ga. only, 22 in. barrel with choice of 5 in. rifled invector choke or rifled barrel, cantilevered scope mount, sling swivels, 7¾ lbs. New 1997.

Mfg.'s Sug. Retail	$839	$710	$500	$415	$350	$300	$275	$250

   Subtract $42 for rifled choke tube.

   ▶ **Gold Deer Hunter with Mossy Oak Breakup camo** — similar to Gold Deer Hunter, except has full Mossy Oak Breakup camo coverage. New 1999.

Mfg.'s Sug. Retail	$909	$780	$630	$550	$475	$400	$365	$335

GOLD STALKER — similar to Gold Hunter, except has checkered black composite stock and forearm, approx. 7½ lbs. New 1998.

Mfg.'s Sug. Retail	$772	$640	$465	$390	$330	$295	$275	$250

✱ *Gold Stalker Classic* — similar to Gold Stalker, except has semi-hump back receiver design, magazine cutoff and adj. comb, 26 or 28 in. VR barrel. New 1999.

Mfg.'s Sug. Retail	$772	$640	$465	$390	$330	$295	$275	$250

✱ *Gold Turkey/Waterfowl Stalker* — similar to Gold Stalker, except has 24 in. VR barrel with extra full choke tube, Hi-Viz sights, matte non-glare wood and finish, 7 lbs. New 1999.

Mfg.'s Sug. Retail	$792	$655	$475	$395	$335	$295	$275	$250

✱ *Gold 3½ in. Stalker* — 12 ga., 3½ in. chamber, 26, 28, or 30 in. VR barrel with Invector Plus choking, otherwise similar to Gold Stalker, 3-4 shot mag., approx. 7 lbs. 10 oz. New 1998.

Mfg.'s Sug. Retail	$929	$795	$640	$560	$480	$400	$365	$335

✱ *Gold 3½ Turkey/Waterfowl Stalker* — similar to Gold 3½ Stalker, except has 24 in. VR barrel with extra full choke tube, matte non-glare wood and finish, 7¼ lbs. New 1999.

Mfg.'s Sug. Retail	$949	$810	$650	$565	$480	$400	$365	$335

✱ *Gold Deer Stalker* — 12 ga. only, 22 in. rifled barrel, cantilevered scope mount, sling swivels, 7¾ lbs. New 1997.

Mfg.'s Sug. Retail	$839	$710	$500	$415	$350	$300	$275	$250

GOLD SPORTING CLAYS — similar to Gold Hunter, except has 2¾ in. chamber, 28 or 30 in. ported barrel with Invector Plus choking, approx. 7½ lbs. New 1996.

Mfg.'s Sug. Retail	$798	$665	$485	$410	$345	$305	$275	$250

✱ *Gold Sporting Ladies/Youth* — similar to Gold Sporting Clays, except has shorter 14¼ LOP stock, 28 in. barrel only, 7 lbs. 6 oz. New 1999.

Mfg.'s Sug. Retail	$798	$665	$485	$410	$345	$305	$275	$250

✱ *Golden Clays* — 12 ga. only, 2¾ in. chamber, nickel finished engraved receiver with gold accents and game birds, deluxe checkered walnut stock and forearm, 28 or 30 in. VR ported barrel, approx. 7¼ lbs. New 1999.

Mfg.'s Sug. Retail	$1,267	$1,025	$850	$750	$650	$525	$450	$375

BSA 10 — while advertised, this gun had its model nomenclature changed to the Gold 10 Ga. before mfg. started.

GOLD 10 GA. — 10 ga. Mag., 3½ in. chamber, short stroke self-cleaning gas action, 4 shot mag., steel receiver with choice of high polish (Hunting Model) or dull finish (Stalker Model, disc. 1998) bluing, 26 (disc. 1998), 28, or 30 in. VR standard Invector choke barrel, available with either high-gloss checkered walnut (Hunting) or matte black fiberglass (Stalker, disc. 1998) stock and forearm, vent recoil pad, beginning 1999, this model includes a 24 in. matte finish Turkey barrel, approx. 10 lbs. 10 oz., mfg. by Miroku, Japan. New 1994.

Mfg.'s Sug. Retail	$1,059	$910	$740	$635	$525	$450	$400	$350

   Subtract $75 if w/o extra 24 in. Turkey barrel.

Grading	100%	98%	95%	90%	80%	70%	60%

SHOTGUNS: O/U, SUPERPOSED

SUPERPOSED SHOTGUN: 1931-1976 MANUFACTURE — 12, 20, 28 ga., or .410 bore, 26½, 28, 30, or 32 in. barrels, various chokes, boxlock, auto ejectors, SST, DT, or twin single triggers (early mfg.), checkered pistol grip stock, mfg. 1931-1940 and 1949-1976 by FN, grades differ in amount of engraving, inlay, general quality of workmanship and wood. Currently, shorter barreled (26½ in.) Superposed models with field open chokes are bringing a premium over a F & M model. Prices below assume vent. rib barrels.

NOTE: The use of steel shot is NOT recommended in any Superposed Series manufactured in Belgium (B-25 variations).

BROWNING CHOKES AND THEIR CODES (ON BARREL)

* designates full choke (F).

*- designates improved modified choke (IM).

** designates modified choke (M).

**- designates improved cylinder choke (IC).

**$ designates skeet (SK).

*** designates cylinder bore (CYL).

SKEET MODELS were available in every ga. and grade.

TRAP MODELS were available in every grade in 12 ga. only.

BROADWAY TRAP MODELS (mfg. 1961-1975) featured a ⅝in. wide vent. rib and were also available in every grade.
Subtract 5%-10% for guns with matted ribs.

* *Grade I Lightning or Standardweight* — the Grade I has a blued steel frame with hand engraved scroll and rosette patterns, checkered walnut stock and forearm. Grade I Standard was disc. 1973, Grade I Lightning (6 oz. lighter than Standardweight) was disc. 1976.

12 ga.	$1,650	$1,175	$975	$875	$825	$750	$700
20 ga.	$2,250	$1,850	$1,650	$1,350	$1,150	$1,000	$925
28 ga.	$3,500	$3,250	$2,950	$2,750	$2,500	$2,250	$2,100
.410 bore	$2,400	$2,250	$1,950	$1,750	$1,500	$1,350	$1,225

Subtract 10%-15% for Grade I Standardweight (12 ga. only).
Add 10%-25% for Superlight Models (12 ga. mfg. 1967-1976, 20 ga. mfg. 1969-1976, 28 ga. and .410 bore mfg. 1970-76).
Add 15%-20% for round knob, long tang stock variations (pre-1966), unless Skeet choked.
Subtract 10%-15% for Trap Models (including Broadway Trap).
Subtract 10%-15% for newer Skeet style model with beavertail forearm and recoil pad.

* *Grade I Magnum* — 12 ga. only, 3 in. chambers with standard Browning recoil pad. Disc. 1976.

12 ga.	$1,495	$1,175	$950	$875	$825	$775	$725

This model with 30 in. barrels is now popular again as Sporting Clays shooters like this desirable configuration.

* *Pigeon Grade* — designated Grade II after WWII and renamed Pigeon in October, 1959. This grade featured a silver grey receiver with 2 flying pigeons surrounded by fine scroll engraving on each side of the frame. The receiver bottom and tangs also exhibit fine scroll work. The Pigeon Grade was disc. 1974.

12 ga.	$3,250	$2,500	$1,950	$1,825	$1,650	$1,570	$1,485
20 ga.	$3,500	$3,250	$2,750	$2,350	$2,150	$1,995	$1,850
28 ga.	$4,500	$4,150	$3,500	$3,150	$2,850	$2,500	$2,250
.410 bore	$3,750	$3,450	$3,100	$2,750	$2,450	$2,150	$1,900

Add 10%-25% for Superlight Models (12 ga. mfg. 1967-1976, 20 ga. mfg. 1969-1976, 28 ga. and .410 bore mfg. 1970-76).

Grading	100%	98%	95%	90%	80%	70%	60%

B

Add 15%-20% for round knob, long tang stock variations (pre-1966), unless Skeet choked.
Subtract 10%-15% for Trap Models (including Broadway Trap).
Subtract 10%-15% for newer Skeet style model with beavertail forearm and recoil pad.

* **Grade III** — satin finished receiver with game scene engraving featuring pheasants and fighting cocks on receiver, receiver bottom has a retriever and pheasant. Disc. October, 1959.

	100%	98%	95%	90%	80%	70%	60%
12 ga.	$3,250	$2,500	$1,950	$1,825	$1,650	$1,570	$1,485
20 ga.	$3,950	$3,600	$3,250	$2,750	$2,400	$2,150	$1,875
28 ga.	$4,950	$4,500	$3,950	$3,500	$3,150	$2,850	$2,575
.410 bore	$4,150	$3,750	$3,400	$2,950	$2,600	$2,350	$2,100

Subtract 10%-15% for Trap Model.

* **Pointer Grade** — also designated Grade III, manufactured post-war only until renamed Pointer in early October, 1959. Features engraved silver grey receiver with a Pointer on one side, and a Setter on the other, select walnut. Disc. 1966, except for special orders.

	100%	98%	95%	90%	80%	70%	60%
12 ga.	$4,250	$3,250	$2,450	$2,050	$1,850	$1,700	$1,625
20 ga.	$4,950	$4,500	$3,950	$3,500	$3,150	$2,950	$2,700
28 ga.	$6,500	$5,750	$5,000	$4,500	$3,950	$3,500	$3,150
.410 bore	$5,250	$4,725	$4,300	$3,800	$3,450	$3,100	$2,850

Add 10%-25% for Superlight Models (12 ga. mfg. 1967-1976, 20 ga. mfg. 1969-1976, 28 ga. and .410 bore mfg. 1970-76).
Add 15%-20% for round knob, long tang stock variations (pre-1966), unless Skeet choked.
Subtract 10%-15% for Trap Models (including Broadway Trap).
Subtract 10%-15% for newer Skeet style model with beavertail forearm and recoil pad.

* **Grade IV** — limited manufacture between 1950-1959, engraving usually featured a dog and bird scene in deep relief.

	100%	98%	95%	90%	80%	70%	60%
12 ga.	$4,250	$3,250	$2,450	$2,050	$1,850	$1,700	$1,625
20 ga.	$5,500	$4,950	$4,500	$3,950	$3,500	$3,150	$2,800
28 ga.	$7,500	$6,500	$5,950	$5,000	$4,500	$4,000	$3,650
.410 bore	$6,000	$5,500	$5,000	$4,500	$4,000	$3,500	$3,150

Subtract 10%-15% for Trap Model.

* **Diana Grade** — also designated Grade V in post-war manufacture until renamed Diana in October, 1959. Pre-WWII Grade Vs featured more delicate scroll engraving with deer adorning the right side and wild boar shown on the left. Post-WWII guns exhibit deep relief engraving with duck and pheasant game scenes on each frame side, select checkered walnut stock and forearm. Disc. 1976.

	100%	98%	95%	90%	80%	70%	60%
12 ga.	$4,950	$4,000	$2,850	$2,150	$1,900	$1,800	$1,700
20 ga.	$5,500	$5,000	$4,500	$3,750	$3,500	$3,150	$2,800
28 ga.	$7,500	$6,500	$5,950	$5,000	$4,500	$4,000	$3,650
.410 bore	$5,500	$5,000	$4,500	$4,000	$3,500	$3,150	$2,800

Add 10%-25% for Superlight Models (12 ga. mfg. 1967-1976, 20 ga. mfg. 1969-1976, 28 ga. and .410 bore mfg. 1970-76).
Add 15%-20% for round knob, long tang stock variations (pre-1966), unless Skeet choked.
Subtract 10%-15% for Trap Models (including Broadway Trap).
Subtract 10%-15% for newer Skeet style model with beavertail forearm and recoil pad.

* **Midas Grade** — also designated Grade VI during post-war manufacture until renamed Midas in October, 1959. Pre-WWII Midas Grades featured an inlaid pigeon with outstretched wings on blued frame sides and bottom plus trigger guard. This earlier Midas also exhibited multiple gold escutcheons and gold lining. Post-war models feature deep relief scroll engraving with gold inlaid ducks and pheasants on frame sides and a quail on the bottom. Ejector trip rods, ejector hammers and firing pins are also 18Kt. gold plated. Finest checkered walnut. Disc. 1976.

	100%	98%	95%	90%	80%	70%	60%
12 ga.	$6,250	$5,400	$3,650	$2,950	$2,600	$2,250	$1,900
20 ga.	$7,500	$6,500	$5,500	$5,000	$4,500	$4,000	$3,650

Grading	100%	98%	95%	90%	80%	70%	60%
28 ga.	$10,000	$8,500	$7,500	$6,500	$5,500	$5,000	$4,650
.410 bore	$7,000	$6,000	$5,000	$4,500	$4,000	$3,500	$3,150

Add 10%-25% for Superlight Models (12 ga. mfg. 1967-1976, 20 ga. mfg. 1969-1976, 28 ga. and .410 bore mfg. 1970-76).
Add 15%-20% for round knob, long tang stock variations (pre-1966), unless Skeet choked.
Subtract 10%-15% for Trap Models (including Broadway Trap).
Subtract 10%-15% for newer Skeet style model with beavertail forearm and recoil pad.

* *Grade VI* — 12 or 20 ga. only, offered from 1955 to October, 1959 only. Elaborate deep relief scroll engraved with multiple gold inlays.

	100%	98%	95%	90%	80%	70%	60%
12 ga.	$6,000	$5,000	$4,600	$4,200	$3,850	$3,500	$3,250
20 ga.	$8,500	$7,500	$6,500	$5,750	$5,000	$4,500	$4,100

Subtract 10%-15% for Trap Model.

SUPERPOSED SUPERLIGHT — please refer to the previous Superposed listings for Superlight values.

There is also a Quail Unlimited limited edition in the Superlight series. Values tend to be 10%-20% higher, but are difficult to ascertain because so few are bought and sold each year.

EXPOSITION/EXHIBITION MODEL

This specially manufactured Superposed saw limited production from the mid '60s through 1976. Later models had their own serial range (usually 3 digit) with a "C" prefix. Grades A through G ranged from fairly simple scroll designs without gold inlays up to extremely ornate designs featuring multi-colored gold inlaid game figures. Most of these guns were produced by FN for display purposes, potential production models, or potential engraving standardization. Many of these Exhibition/Exposition Superposed models were consigned to Browning Arms Co. during the 1970s because of the depressed market conditions of that time. Prices are determined by the embellishments and engraving per individual gun (A Grade being the lowest, F Grade with gold being the highest). Prices usually start at around $5,000, while a F Grade with extensive gold inlays could reach 5 digits.

SUPERPOSED WITH EXTRA BARREL(S) OR SUPER-TUBES

Could be ordered from the factory in the following combinations: 12 or 20 ga. with one extra set of barrels in same ga. 12 ga. with one extra set in 20 ga. 12 or 20 ga. with two extra barrel sets of same ga. 20 ga. with one extra set in either 28 ga. or .410 bore. 20 ga. with both 28 ga. and .410 bore barrel sets. 28 ga. with extra set of .410 bore barrels. Super-Tubes were adaptable on 12 ga. guns only; came from the factory cased with accessories, 16½ in. long, factory installation.
Grade I extra barrel set(s) — add 40-50% of the gun's value for each extra set. Add approx. $1,500 per barrel set in higher grades.
Super-Tubes — available for 12 ga. only, single ga. — add $250.
Super-Tube Set — 3 ga. set (20, 28 ga., and .410 bore) — add $400.

BICENTENNIAL SUPERPOSED SUPERLIGHT SHOTGUN — specially engraved limited edition Model, 51 mfg. — one for each state and Washington, D.C. Left side has U.S. Flag, bald eagle and state emblem inlaid in gold. Right side has gold inlaid hunter and turkey. Blued receiver, fancy checkered English stock, Schnabel forend, velvet lined wood case. Made 1976 by FN.

$8,500　$7,500　$6,000

WATERFOWL SUPERPOSED SHOTGUN SERIES — 12 ga., 500 made of each issue. Gold inlays with extensive engraving, lightning action, 28 in. barrels, full-length walnut case, factory inventories were depleted on Mallard, Pintail, and Black Duck Issues in 1989.

* *1981 Mallard Issue*

$4,750　$3,750　$2,500

Last Mfg.'s Sug. Retail was $7,000.

This issue was sold out in 1988.

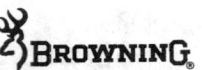

Grading	100%	98%	95%	90%	80%	70%	60%

* 1982 Pintail Issue

$4,750　$3,750　$2,500

Last Mfg.'s Sug. Retail was $7,000.

* 1983 Black Duck Issue

$4,750　$3,750　$2,500

Last Mfg.'s Sug. Retail was $8,800.

OVER/UNDER CLASSIC SERIES SHOTGUN — 20 ga. only, 26 in. barrels, less than 2,500 manufactured in Classic model and under 350 manufactured in Gold Classic. Both editions feature multiple engraved scenes and a special silver grey finish. Select American walnut featuring oil finish. Available 1986 only.

$1,850　$1,500　$1,200

Last Mfg.'s Sug. Retail was $2,000.

* Gold Classic — 8 gold inlays, select walnut forearm and stock are both checkered and carved, many were shipped back to Belgium due to poor sales domestically. Available 1986 only.

$5,995　$4,150　$3,150

Last Mfg.'s Sug. Retail was $6,000.

SUPERPOSED SHOTGUN: 1983-86 MANUFACTURE — 12 or 20 ga. In 1983, Browning announced renewed production of the famous Belgium "Superposed" O/U in Grade I only. Available in Lightning or Superlight models, 3 in. chambers in Lightning 20 ga., 26½ or 28 in. barrels. Belgium manufactured from 1983-86.

* Grade I — limited mfg., not compatible with steel shot.

	100%	98%	95%	90%	80%	70%	60%
Lightning	$1,995	$1,795	$1,395	$1,000	$800	$675	$550
Superlight	$2,495	$2,195	$1,695	$1,295	$1,000	$850	$675

Last Mfg.'s Sug. Retail was $1,995.

SUPERPOSED PRESENTATION MODELS (P1-P4) — custom made versions of the Lightning Field, Super Light, Trap, and Skeet guns, specifications the same as Standard models, with differences in finish, engraving and inlay(s), and grade of wood and checkering. These guns were introduced by FN in 1977 and were disc. after 1984. Add $1,775 for extra set of barrels, add $3,600 for 2 sets of extra barrels.

>   Add 20% for 20 ga.
>   Add 30% for 28 ga.
>   Add 20% for .410 bore.
>   Subtract 10% for P Series Trap Models.
>   Subtract 10%-15% for P Series Broadway Trap Models.
>   Subtract 10%-15% for P Series Skeet 12 and 20 ga. guns.

Since P Series Superposed were disc. 1985, collector interest has increased slightly. Interestingly, the P series models are rarer than most of the pre-1976 high grade Superposed models.

* Presentation 1 — silver grey or blued receiver, oak leaf and fine scroll engraved, choice of 6 different animal scenes.

$2,850　$2,350　$1,995　$1,750　$1,500　$1,250　$1,000

* Presentation 1 w/gold inlays — similar to Presentation 1, only with gold inlays.

$3,450　$2,800　$2,350　$2,050　$1,825　$1,700　$1,500

* Presentation 2 — silver grey or blued receiver, high relief engraving, choice of 3 different sets of game scenes.

$3,400　$2,750　$2,300　$2,050　$1,825　$1,700　$1,500

* Presentation 2 w/gold inlays — similar to Presentation 2, only with gold inlays.

$3,950　$3,250　$2,550　$2,150　$1,925　$1,750　$1,550

* Presentation 3 — silver grey or blued receiver, more elaborate high relief engraving with choice of partridges, mallards or geese depicted on frame sides in 18Kt. gold.

$5,450　$4,700　$4,100　$3,600　$3,200　$2,875　$2,300

Grading	100%	98%	95%	90%	80%	70%	60%

B

* **Presentation 4** — features engraved side plates in either silver grey or blued finish, engraved game scenes include waterfowl on right frame side, 5 pheasants on left frame side, 2 quail on receiver bottom, and a retriever's head on trigger guard. Extra figure walnut stock and forearm.

	$6,000	$4,950	$4,350	$3,825	$3,350	$2,950	$2,375

* **Presentation 4 w/gold inlays** — similar to Presentation 4, only with game scenes inlaid in 18Kt. gold.

	$7,500	$6,500	$5,265	$4,750	$4,250	$3,650	$2,950

P SERIES SUPERLIGHT — available in various configurations including multi-barrel sets. Typically, add 20-25% onto the values listed for the regular P series as shown above. Also add 20-40% for the 28 ga.

LIEGE O/U — 12 ga., 26½, 28 or 30 in. barrels, various chokes, boxlock, auto ejectors, non-selective single trigger, vent. rib, checkered pistol grip stock. Approx. 10,000 mfg. 1973-1975 by FN.

	$750	$625	$575	$500	$425	$400	$375

This model is also known as the B-26.

B-26 — with BAC markings. Mfg. 1973-75.

	$750	$625	$575	$500	$425	$400	$375

B-27 — F.N. manufactured modified B-26, imported into the U.S. in 1984, same action as Liege (B 26), blued or satin finished receiver with light engraving, no BAC markings and never cataloged.

* **Standard Game** — 28 in. barrels, ⁹/₃₂ in. vent. rib, pistol grip stock, Schnabel forearm, SST, blued receiver, choking M/F only.

	$650	$575	$525	$475	$425	$400	$375

Also available in Skeet model with gold "Browning" logo on blued receiver. Prices are the same.

* **Deluxe Game (Grade II)** — similar to Standard Grade, except has 30 in. barrels, better wood and English scroll engraved satin finished receiver, choking M/F only.

	$875	$725	$625	$575	$510	$475	$445

* **Grand Deluxe Game** — 28 in. IC/IM & M/F choked barrels, game scene engraved, signed by the engraver, 90% receiver coverage.

	$1,100	$850	$775	$700	$640	$580	$520

This model was also available in a Trap configuration — values are about the same as above.

* **Deluxe Skeet** — similar to Deluxe, except is designed for skeet shooting.

	$850	$725	$625	$575	$510	$475	$445

International Skeet is also available at same price; hand fit pistol grip with stippling and International Type recoil pad.

* **Deluxe Trap** — similar to Deluxe, except is configured for trap shooting.

	$750	$650	$560	$530	$500	$475	$445

* **City of Liege Commemorative** — limited edition of 250 units manufactured to commemorate the 1,000th anniversary of the city of Liege, cased. Only 29 imported into the U.S.

	$1,125	$975	$910	$850	$775	$700	$600

ST-100 — 12 ga., Belgian mfg., O/U trap configuration with separated barrels and adj. point of impact, manufactured 1979-1981 for European sale mostly, floating VR, ST, deluxe checkered walnut stock and forearm, non-BAC model.

	$2,375	$1,950	$1,700	$1,400	$1,200	$975	$825

Grading	100%	98%	95%	90%	80%	70%	60%

SHOTGUNS: O/U, SUPERPOSED HIGH GRADES: 1985-PRESENT

Browning, in 1985, resumed production of the Superposed in Pigeon, Pointer, Diana, and Midas grades. They are available in 12 and 20 ga. only, in either a Lightning or Superlight configuration. These higher grades are custom ordered from the factory with delivery ranging from 8 to more than 12 months. Custom options can be special ordered on each grade with corresponding prices being higher than shown below. B-25 engraving patterns on these various grades will nearly duplicate those styles manufactured before 1976. Skeet models are not available.

B-25 — 12 or 20 ga. only, original Superposed Model manufactured entirely from parts fabricated in Herstal, Belgium. Also available in Superlight configuration.

* **Grade I Traditional**

	100%	98%	95%	90%	80%	70%	60%
Mfg.'s Sug. Retail $7,192	$6,200	$1,350	$1,100	$900	$775	$650	$575

* **Pigeon Grade**

	100%	98%	95%	90%	80%	70%	60%
Mfg.'s Sug. Retail $9,056	$8,000	$2,750	$1,950	$1,825	$1,650	$1,570	$1,485

Add $2,900 for an extra set of barrels.

* **Pointer Grade**

	100%	98%	95%	90%	80%	70%	60%
Mfg.'s Sug. Retail $10,448	$9,350	$3,450	$2,500	$2,050	$1,850	$1,700	$1,625

Add $3,100 for an extra set of barrels.

* **Diana Grade**

	100%	98%	95%	90%	80%	70%	60%
Mfg.'s Sug. Retail $10,868	$9,650	$4,300	$2,850	$2,200	$1,900	$1,800	$1,700

Add $4,400 for an extra set of barrels.

* **Midas Grade**

	100%	98%	95%	90%	80%	70%	60%
Mfg.'s Sug. Retail $15,225	$13,250	$6,500	$4,500	$3,000	$2,600	$2,250	$1,900

Add $5,000 for an extra set of barrels.

B-125 — 12 or 20 ga. only, retains all the features of the original Superposed, except parts are subcontracted worldwide to decrease production costs and are assembled "in the white" at Herstal's Custom Gun Shop in Belgium, choice of three different engraving styles and two receiver finishes. Introduced 1988.

* **Hunting Model** — available in either Hunting Lightning or Superlight configuration.

➤ **"A" Style Engraving** — blued receiver with border engraving featuring Browning logo engraved on each side.

	100%	98%	95%	90%	80%	70%	60%
Mfg.'s Sug. Retail $4,699	$4,000	$3,000	$2,150	$1,700	$1,450	$1,275	$1,050

➤ **"B" Style Engraving** — coin finished receiver with smaller game scene engravings.

	100%	98%	95%	90%	80%	70%	60%
Mfg.'s Sug. Retail $5,040	$4,225	$3,250	$2,250	$1,800	$1,500	$1,300	$1,100

➤ **"C" Style Engraving** — coin finished receiver with elaborate scroll work and game scene engraving.

	100%	98%	95%	90%	80%	70%	60%
Mfg.'s Sug. Retail $5,539	$4,625	$3,475	$2,450	$1,900	$1,600	$1,400	$1,200

* **Sporting Clays Model** — 12 ga. only, designed for sporting clays competition and includes Invector plus choke tube system.

➤ **"A" Style Engraving** — blued receiver with border engraving featuring Browning logo engraved on each side.

	100%	98%	95%	90%	80%	70%	60%
Mfg.'s Sug. Retail $4,699	$4,000	$3,000	$2,150	$1,700	$1,450	$1,275	$1,050

➤ **"B" Style Engraving** — coin finished receiver with smaller game scene engravings.

	100%	98%	95%	90%	80%	70%	60%
Mfg.'s Sug. Retail $5,040	$4,225	$3,250	$2,250	$1,800	$1,500	$1,300	$1,100

➤ **"C" Style Engraving** — coin finished receiver with elaborate scroll work and game scene engraving.

	100%	98%	95%	90%	80%	70%	60%
Mfg.'s Sug. Retail $5,539	$4,625	$3,475	$2,450	$1,900	$1,600	$1,400	$1,200

* **Trap Model** — standard F-1 style engraving.

	100%	98%	95%	90%	80%	70%	60%
Mfg.'s Sug. Retail $8,531	$7,250	$3,550	$2,325	$1,750	$1,450	$1,275	$1,050

 **BROWNING, *cont.* 333**

B

Grading	100%	98%	95%	90%	80%	70%	60%

SHOTGUNS: O/U, CITORI HUNTING SERIES

All Citori shotguns which incorporate the Invector choke tube system may be used with steel shot.

Invector Plus choke tubes are designed for backbored barrels. DO NOT USE Standard Invector choke tubes in barrels marked for the Invector Plus choking system.

CITORI HUNTING MODELS — 12, 16 (mfg. 1986-89), 20, 28 ga. (disc. 1994) or .410 bore (disc. 1994), 26, 28, or 30 in. barrels, various chokes, boxlock, auto ejectors, SST, vent. rib, features checkered semi-pistol grip stock with grooved semi-beavertail forearm, grades differ in amount of engraving, finish, and wood. Invector chokes became standard in 1988, Invector Plus chokes became standard 1995 on 12 or 20 ga., 6 lbs. 9 oz. - 8 lbs. 5 oz. Mfg. 1973-present by Miroku.

* *Grade I 12 or 20 ga.*
  ➤ Earlier Mfg. without Invector Choking

	100%	98%	95%	90%	80%	70%	60%
	$750	$675	$575	$525	$475	$425	$395

Add 15% for 16 ga. if in 90%+ original condition.

➤ Current Mfg. with Invector Choking — 12 or 20 ga., 3 in. chambers, 20 ga. available with Standard Invector or Invector Plus (new 1994) choking system, Invector Plus choking standard on recently mfg. 12 ga., 6 lbs. 9 oz. - 8 lbs. 5 oz.

Mfg.'s Sug. Retail	$1,334		$995	$725	$595	$500	$450	$395	$350

* *Grade I Smaller Gauges*
  ➤ 28 ga. or .410 bore — without Invector choking. Disc. 1994.

	$850	$700	$575	$495	$450	$395	$350

Last Mfg.'s Sug. Retail was $1,097.

* *Grade II* — 12, 20, 28 ga., or .410 bore. Disc. 1983.

	$995	$810	$740	$685	$610	$570	$540

* *Grade III* — 12, 16 (mfg. 1986-89), 20, 28 ga. (disc. 1994), or .410 bore (disc. 1994), greyed steel receiver with engraved game scenes featuring grouse (20 ga.) and ducks (12 ga.), Invector chokes standard, Invector Plus became standard in 12 ga. in 1994. Mfg. 1985-95.

	$1,425	$1,025	$835	$725	$625	$585	$550

Last Mfg.'s Sug. Retail was $1,875.

Add 15% for 16 ga. if in 90%+ original condition.
Add 15%-25% for 28 ga. or .410 bore (both disc. 1989).

* *Grade V* — 12, 20, 28 ga., or .410 bore, extensive deep relief engraving with game scenes on satin grey receiver. Disc. 1984.

	$1,550	$1,265	$1,100	$990	$880	$795	$695

* *Grade VI* — 12, 16 (mfg. 1986-89), 20, 28 ga. (disc. 1992), or .410 bore (disc. 1989), blued or greyed receiver with extensive engraving including multiple gold inlays, Standard Invector (12 ga. disc. 1993) or Invector Plus chokes. Mfg. 1985-95.

	$2,100	$1,500	$1,225	$1,000	$895	$795	$695

Last Mfg.'s Sug. Retail was $2,715.

Add 15% for 16 ga. if in 90%+ original condition.
Add 15%-25% for 28 ga.

* *3½ in. Magnum Model* — 12 ga., 3½ in. chambers, 28 or 30 in. VR barrels with back-bored Invector plus choke tubes, with recoil pad, approx. 8½ lbs. 9 oz. New 1989.

Mfg.'s Sug. Retail	$1,418		$1,150	$850	$775	$650	$575	$525	$475

* *Sporting Hunter* — 12 or 20 ga., 3 or 3½ (12 ga. only) in. chambers, 26, 28, or 30 (12 ga. only) in. barrels with Invector Plus choking, configured for both hunting and sporting clays shooting, Superposed style forearm, contoured recoil pad, front and center bead sights, gloss or satin (3½ in. only) wood finish, 6 lbs. 9 oz. - 8 lbs. 9 oz. New 1998.

Mfg.'s Sug. Retail	$1,500		$1,175	$850	$700	$565	$475	$425	$375

Add $95 for 3½ in. Mag. (wood satin finish only).

Grading	100%	98%	95%	90%	80%	70%	60%

* **Satin Hunter** — 12 ga. only, 3 or 3½ in. chambers, 26, 28, or 30 (3½ in. Mag. only, disc. 1998) in. VR backbored barrels with Invector Plus choking, features satin wood finish, 7 lbs. 13 oz. - 8 lbs. 5 oz. New 1998.

Mfg.'s Sug. Retail	$1,318		$960	$745	$600	$500	$450	$395	$350

    Add $102 for 3½ in. Mag.

* **Upland Special** — 12, 16 (mfg. 1989 only), or 20 ga., shortened checkered straight grip stock (14 LOP), 24 in. barrels, Invector (12 ga. disc. 1993) or Invector Plus choking, 6-6¾ lbs. New 1984.

Mfg.'s Sug. Retail	$1,442		$1,065	$800	$625	$525	$450	$425	$395

    Add 15% for 16 ga. if in 90%+ original condition.
    Subtract $125 for Invector choking.

CITORI SUPERLIGHT MODELS — 12, 20, 28 ga., or .410 bore, 2¾ in. chambers except for .410 bore, English stock, oil finish, Invector chokes became standard in 1988, Invector Plus became standard 1995 for 12 or 20 ga., approx. 6 lbs.-6¾ lbs. Mfg. 1983-present.

* **Grade I 12 or 20 ga.**
    ➤ **Earlier Mfg. without Invector Choking**

		$795	$700	$600	$550	$495	$445	$395

    ➤ **Current Mfg. with Invector Choking** — 12 or 20 ga., 20 ga. available with Standard Invector or Invector Plus (new 1994, became standard 1995) choking system, Invector Plus choking standard on recently mfg. 12 ga.

Mfg.'s Sug. Retail	$1,442		$1,065	$800	$625	$525	$450	$425	$395

    Subtract $125 for Standard Invector choking in 20 ga.

* **Grade I Smaller Gauges**
    ➤ **28 ga. or .410 bore** — without Invector choking until 1993, Invector choking became an option in 1994 and standard in 1995.

Mfg.'s Sug. Retail	$1,511		$1,175	$850	$695	$575	$495	$450	$425

    Subtract 10% if without Invector choke tubes.

* **Superlight Feather** — 12 ga. only, greyed alloy receiver, 26 in. Invector choked VR barrels, straight grip English stock and scaled down Schnabel forearm, 6¼ lbs. New 1999.

Mfg.'s Sug. Retail	$1,592		$1,235	$900	$725	$595	$495	$450	$425

* **Grade III** — same gauges as Grade I, Standard Invector on 12 or 20 (disc.) ga. or Invector Plus (standard in 12 ga. beginning 1994) chokes. New 1986.

Mfg.'s Sug. Retail	$2,127		$1,625	$1,200	$925	$795	$650	$585	$550

    Add $240 for 28 ga. or .410 bore (disc. 1997).
    Subtract 10% if without Invector choke tubes.

* **Grade V** — sideplate available. Disc. 1984.

		$1,550	$1,265	$1,100	$990	$880	$795	$695

* **Grade VI** — older mfg. has Invector chokes standard (option on 28 ga. or .410 bore beginning 1994) or Invector Plus (standard and available in 12 or 20 ga. only) chokes, choice of blue or grey (new 1996) receiver finish.

Mfg.'s Sug. Retail	$3,095		$2,325	$1,725	$1,325	$1,175	$975	$800	$700

    Subtract 10% for 28 ga. or .410 bore without choke tubes.
    Add $239 for 28 ga. or .410 bore with Standard Invector choking.

CITORI SPORTER MODELS — similar to Citori Superlight, except with 3 in. chambers, 26 in. barrels, various chokes, straight grip stock, Schnabel forearm. Disc. 1983.

		$875	$740	$600	$550	$495	$440	$385

    Add $50 for 28 ga. or .410 bore.

* **Sporter Grade II** — 12, 20, 28 ga., or .410 bore.

		$1,250	$1,075	$1,020	$965	$880	$770	$715

Grading	100%	98%	95%	90%	80%	70%	60%

B

* *Sporter Grade V* — 12, 20, 28 ga., or .410 bore.

	100%	98%	95%	90%	80%	70%	60%
	$1,575	$1,395	$1,225	$1,100	$990	$880	$825

CITORI LIGHTNING MODELS — 12, 16 (disc. 1989), 20, 28 ga., or .410 bore, (3½ in. 12 ga. was introduced 1989), 26, 28, or 30 in. barrels, Invector chokes standard on newer mfg. smaller ga.'s, Invector Plus became standard 1995 for 12 or 20 ga., boxlock, auto ejectors, SST, vent. rib, features checkered round knob pistol grip stock and slimmer forearm, grades differ in amount of engraving, finish, and quality of wood, approx. 6¼-8 lbs. Introduced 1988.

* *Grade I 12, 16 or 20 ga.*
  ➤ **Earlier Mfg. without Invector Choking**

	$795	$700	$600	$550	$495	$445	$395

Add 15% for 16 ga.

  ➤ **Current Mfg. with Invector Choking** — 12 or 20 ga., Invector (disc. 1994) or Invector Plus choking (became standard on 12 ga. in 1994, 20 ga. in 1995).

Mfg.'s Sug. Retail	**$1,432**	$1,065	$800	$635	$560	$450	$395	$350

Subtract 10% for Standard Invector choking.

* *Grade I Smaller Gauges*
  ➤ **28 ga. or .410 bore** — without Invector choking until 1993, Invector choking became an option in 1994, standard in 1995.

Mfg.'s Sug. Retail	**$1,489**	$1,150	$850	$700	$600	$500	$435	$385

Subtract 10% if without Standard Invector choking.

* *Grade III* — 12, 16 (disc. 1989), 20, 28 ga., or .410 bore, greyed steel receiver with engraved game scenes, older mfg. may or may not have Invector choking, Invector Plus choking is now standard on 12 or 20 ga. New 1988.

Mfg.'s Sug. Retail	**$2,127**	$1,625	$1,200	$925	$795	$665	$595	$550

Subtract 10% if without Invector choking.
Add 15% for 16 ga. (disc. 1989).

  ➤ **Grade III Smaller Gauges** — 28 ga. or .410 bore, 26 in. VR barrels with or without Standard Invector choking.

Mfg.'s Sug. Retail	**$2,377**	$1,840	$1,350	$1,025	$875	$700	$625	$575

Subtract 10% if without Invector choking.

* *Grade VI* — 12, 16 (disc. 1989), 20, 28 ga., or .410 bore, blued or greyed receiver with extensive engraving including 8 gold inlays.

Mfg.'s Sug. Retail	**$3,095**	$2,325	$1,725	$1,325	$1,175	$975	$800	$700

Add 15% for 16 ga. (disc. 1989).

  ➤ **Grade VI Smaller Gauges** — 28 ga. or .410 bore, 26 in. VR barrels with or without Standard Invector choking.

Mfg.'s Sug. Retail	**$3,334**	$2,625	$1,900	$1,425	$1,250	$1,025	$875	$775

Subtract 10% if without Invector choke tubes.

LIGHTNING FEATHER — 12 ga. only, 3 in. chambers, greyed alloy receiver, 26 or 28 in. Invector choked VR barrels, select checkered walnut stock and forearm, approx. 7 lbs. 10 oz. New 1999.

Mfg.'s Sug. Retail	**$1,582**	$1,225	$900	$725	$595	$495	$450	$425

GRAN LIGHTNING (GL) MODEL — 12, 20, 28 ga. (new 1994), or .410 bore (new 1994) only, 3 in. chambers, similar to Lightning Model, except has higher grade walnut stock and forearm with satin/oil finish, includes recoil pad, 26 or 28 in. barrels, Invector chokes standard on newer mfg. smaller ga.'s, Invector Plus became standard 1995 for 12 or 20 ga., 6¾ - 8 lbs. New 1990.

Mfg.'s Sug. Retail	**$1,963**	$1,565	$1,095	$950	$800	$675	$595	$550

  ➤ **Gran Lightning Smaller Gauges** — 28 ga. or .410 bore, 26 in. VR barrels with Standard Invector choking.

Mfg.'s Sug. Retail	**$2,068**	$1,675	$1,200	$1,025	$850	$695	$625	$575

ΒROWNING.

Grading	100%	98%	95%	90%	80%	70%	60%

WHITE LIGHTNING — 12 or 20 ga., 3 in. chambers, silver nitride receiver with scroll and rosette engraving, satin wood finish with round pistol grip stock and vent recoil pad, 26 or 28 in. VR barrels with Invector Plus choking, 6 lbs. 9 oz - 8 lbs. 1 oz. New 1998.

Mfg.'s Sug. Retail	$1,478	$1,165	$875	$725	$595	$475	$425	$395

MICRO LIGHTNING — 20 ga. only, 2¾ in. chambers, 24 in. VR barrels, Invector or Invector Plus (new 1994) choking, 13¾ LOP (½ in. shorter), 6 lbs. 3 oz. New 1991.

✳ *Grade I*

Mfg.'s Sug. Retail	$1,486	$1,170	$875	$725	$595	$475	$425	$395

    Subtract 10% for standard Invector choking.

✳ *Grade III* — Invector (disc. 1993) or Invector Plus choking. Mfg. 1993-94.

	$1,415	$1,050	$850	$750	$625	$585	$550

    Last Mfg.'s Sug. Retail was $1,850.

✳ *Grade VI* — Mfg. 1993-94.

	$2,025	$1,575	$1,225	$1,025	$895	$795	$695

    Last Mfg.'s Sug. Retail was $2,680.

    Subtract $267 for standard Invector choking.

SHOTGUNS: O/U, CITORI SPORTING CLAYS

All sporting clays models mfg. after 1994 have the Triple Trigger System which includes 3 interchangeable trigger shoes.

MODEL 325 — 12 or 20 ga., 28, 30, or 32 (12 ga. only) in. 10mm VR barrels with Invector Plus choking, 12 ga. has ported barrels, European styling featuring checkered walnut stock and Schnabel forearm, greyed nitrous finished receiver, top tang safety, SST, ejectors, 6 lbs. 12 oz. - 7 lbs. 15 oz. Mfg. 1993-94.

	$1,395	$975	$850	$715	$575	$495	$450

    Last Mfg.'s Sug. Retail was $1,625.

✳ *Model 325 Golden Clays* — 12 or 20 ga., 28, 30, or 32 in. ported (12 ga. only) or unported (20 ga. only) VR barrels, Invector Plus choking, Model 325 Grade II features, satin grey receiver with engraving and gold inlays depicting a transitional hunting to clay pigeon scene. Mfg. 1994 only.

	$2,425	$1,850	$1,450	$1,150	$975	$875	$825

    Last Mfg.'s Sug. Retail was $3,030.

MODEL 425 SPORTING CLAYS GRADE I — 12 or 20 ga., 28, 30, or 32 (12 ga. only) in. 10mm VR barrels with Invector Plus choking, 12 ga. has ported barrels, with or without adj. comb, European styling featuring checkered walnut stock and Schnabel forearm, mono-bloc action with greyed nitrous finished receiver, top tang safety, SST, ejectors, solid pad, approx. 6¾ - 8 lbs. New 1995.

Mfg.'s Sug. Retail	$1,855		$1,550	$1,075	$895	$725	$575	$495	$450

    Add $220 for adj. comb.

✳ *Model 425 Golden Clays (GC)* — 12 or 20 ga., 28, 30, or 32 in. ported (12 ga. only) or unported (20 ga. only) VR barrels, with (disc. 1998) or without adj. comb, Invector Plus choking, Model 325 Grade II features, satin grey receiver with engraving and gold inlays depicting a transitional hunting to clay pigeon scene. New 1995.

Mfg.'s Sug. Retail	$3,507		$2,800	$2,050	$1,550	$1,200	$995	$875	$825

    Add $210 for adj. comb (disc. 1998).

✳ *Model 425 WSSF* — 12 ga. only, special dimensions for Women's Shooting Sports Foundation, features painted turquoise finish with WSSF logo on stock or natural walnut finish (new 1997), 7¼ lbs. New 1995.

Mfg.'s Sug. Retail	$1,855		$1,550	$1,075	$895	$725	$575	$495	$450

Grading	100%	98%	95%	90%	80%	70%	60%

MODEL 802 EXTENDED SWING (ES) SPORTER — 12 ga. only, 2¾ in. chambers, features 28 in. ventilated ported VR barrels (low post, 6.2mm wide) which accept either Invector Plus 2 or 4 stainless steel extension tubes (extends barrels to 30 or 32 in.), adj. pull trigger, slimmer checkered and Schnabel forearm, 7 lbs. 5 oz. New 1996.

Mfg.'s Sug. Retail	$1,965	$1,660	$1,145	$950	$765	$615	$525	$475

GTI GRADE I — 12 ga. only, 28 or 30 in. barrel with 13mm vent. rib and barrels, red lettering on receiver during 1989 only - changed to gold lettering and borders with Browning logo in 1990, checkered stock and semi-beavertail forearm, ported barrels were introduced 1990 and became standard 1992, Invector chokes standard, back-bored Invector plus chokes became standard in 1990, approx. 8 lbs. Mfg. 1989-94.

	$1,225	$885	$700	$600	$525	$495	$450

Last Mfg.'s Sug. Retail was $1,450.

Subtract $75 without ported barrels (disc. 1992).
Add $35 for Signature Painted Model.

The Signature Painted Model includes special paint treatment on stock and forearm featuring Browning logos and trademark - new 1993.

* *GTI Golden Clays* — 12 ga. only, 28, 30, or 32 in. ported VR barrels, Invector Plus choking, GTI features, satin grey receiver with Grade VI level of engraving and gold inlays depicting a transitional hunting to clay pigeon scene. Mfg. 1993-94.

	$2,350	$1,800	$1,450	$1,150	$975	$875	$825

Last Mfg.'s Sug. Retail was $2,930.

GRADE I SPECIAL SPORTING — 12 ga. only, 2¾ in. chambers, target dimensions, high-post tapered rib, 28, 30, or 32 in. barrels, full pistol grip with palm swell, adj. comb became optional in 1994, approx. 8 lbs. 3 oz. New 1989.

Mfg.'s Sug. Retail	$1,636	$1,295	$925	$775	$635	$525	$495	$450

Add $220 for adj. comb.
Add $35 for Signature Painted Model (disc. 1994).
Subtract $75 without ported barrels (disc. 1992).
Add $800 for 2 barrel set (28 and 30 in. barrels), disc. 1990.

The Signature Painted Model includes special paint treatment on stock and forearm featuring Browning logos and trademark - mfg. 1993-94.

Ported barrels were new in 1990 and became standard in 1992.

In 1990, the Grade I designation was added to this model. Changes include back-bored barrels with Invector plus choke tubes.

* *Special Sporting Golden Clays (GC)* — 12 ga. only, 28, 30, or 32 in. ported barrels with high-post VR, Invector Plus choking, Special Sporting features, satin grey receiver with Grade VI level of engraving and gold inlays depicting a transitional hunting to clay pigeon scene. Mfg. 1993-98.

	$2,575	$1,925	$1,500	$1,175	$995	$875	$825

Last Mfg.'s Sug. Retail was $3,203.

Add $210 for adj. comb.

GRADE I SPECIAL SPORTING PIGEON GRADE — 12 ga. only, Vector Plus choking and ported barrels, higher grade of Special Sporting model featuring higher grade walnut and gold line receiver accents. Mfg. 1993-94.

	$1,400	$975	$850	$700	$575	$495	$450

Last Mfg.'s Sug. Retail was $1,630.

ULTRA SPORTER — 12 ga. only, 28, 30, or 32 in. barrels with vent rib separating barrels, low tapered 13-10mm VR, blue or grey (new 1996) receiver with gold accents, satin finished checkered pistol grip stock and forearm, Invector Plus choking, 7 lbs. 10 oz. - 8 lbs. 4 oz. New 1995.

Mfg.'s Sug. Retail	$1,800	$1,525	$1,050	$875	$750	$575	$495	$450

Add $210 for adj. comb (disc. 1998).
This model was designated GTI until 1995.

Grading	100%	98%	95%	90%	80%	70%	60%

B

* ***Ultra Sporter Golden Clays (GC)*** — 12 ga. only, features better wood and satin finished engraved receiver with gold inlays clay target scene. New 1995.

Mfg.'s Sug. Retail	$3,396		$2,750	$2,025	$1,575	$1,200	$1,000	$875	$825

   Add $210 for adj. comb (disc. 1997).

XS — 12, 20, 28 ga. or .410 bore, greyed receiver with 24 Kt. gold accents and light engraving, 28 or 30 in. ported vent. barrels with VR and Invector Plus choking, select checkered walnut stock and and Schnabel forearm, 6 lbs. 7 oz. - 8 lbs. 2 oz. New 1999.

Mfg.'s Sug. Retail	$2,011		$1,600	$1,175	$925	$775	$650	$585	$550

   Add $66 for 28 ga. or .410 bore.

GRADE I LIGHTNING SPORTING — features 3 in. chambers, rounded pistol grip, Lightning style forearm, choice of high or low post VR, standard or adj. (new 1995) comb stock, "Lightning Sporting Clays Edition" inscribed and gold-filled on receiver, 28 in. ported or 30 in. ported or unported (disc.) barrels, approx. 8½ lbs. New 1989.

Mfg.'s Sug. Retail	$1,564		$1,295	$925	$775	$625	$525	$495	$450

   Add $210 for adj. comb (disc. 1998).
   Add $72 for high-post rib.
   Subtract 10% if with unported barrels.

   The Signature Painted Model includes special paint treatment on stock and forearm featuring Browning logos and trademark - mfg. 1993-94.

   Ported barrels were new in 1990 and became standard in 1992.

   In 1990, the Grade I designation was added to this model. Changes include back-bored barrels with Invector plus choke tubes.

* ***Lightning Sporting Golden Clays (GC)*** — 12 ga. only, 28, 30, or 32 (disc.) in. ported barrels with choice of low or high-post VR, standard or adj. (new 1995) comb stock, Invector Plus choking, Lightning Sporting features, satin grey receiver with Grade VI level of engraving and gold inlays depicting a transitional hunting to clay birds scene, approx. 8½ lbs. Mfg. 1993-98.

			$2,495	$1,850	$1,475	$1,150	$995	$875	$825

   Last Mfg.'s Sug. Retail was $3,092.

   Add $210 for adj. comb.
   Add $111 for high-post VR.

GRADE I LIGHTNING SPORTING PIGEON GRADE — 12 ga. only, higher grade model featuring higher grade walnut and gold line receiver accents. Mfg. 1993-94.

			$1,350	$950	$850	$700	$575	$495	$450

   Last Mfg.'s Sug. Retail was $1,566.

   Add $64 for high-post VR.

SPORTING HUNTER — please refer to description and pricing under Shotguns: O/U Citori Hunting Series category.

SHOTGUNS: O/U, CITORI SKEET

CITORI SKEET/SPECIAL SKEET MODELS — 12, 20, 28 ga., or .410 bore, same action as Citori Field, only with high post target rib (standard 1985), 26 and 28 in. skeet barrels, recoil pad, Invector chokes became standard in 1990 in 12 and 20 ga., Invector Plus chokes with ported barrels were an option during 1992 and became standard on the 12 ga. in 1994, new Special Skeet models were introduced during 1995 with decreased weight (¼ lb. lighter) and better swing/balance characteristics.

* ***Grade I***

   ➤ **12 or 20 Ga.** — Invector Plus choking, high-post target rib, and ported barrels became standard in 1994, 7¼ - 8 lbs.

Mfg.'s Sug. Retail	$1,658		$1,325	$950	$765	$625	$525	$495	$450

Grading	100%	98%	95%	90%	80%	70%	60%

B

Add $210 for adj. comb (mfg. 1995-98).
Subtract 10% if without Invector chokes.

Earlier mfg. skeet guns had a low profile, wide VR.

➤ **Smaller Gauges** — 28 ga. or .410 bore, 6 lbs. 15 oz.

Mfg.'s Sug. Retail	$1,627	$1,300	$950	$775	$650	$550	$500	$450

Subtract 10% if without Invector chokes.

* *Grade II* — 12, 20, 28 ga., or .410 bore, high rib. Disc. 1983.

	$1,000	$850	$800	$740	$690	$650	$600

* *Grade III* — 12, 20, 28 ga., or .410 bore, Invector chokes originally in 12 and 20. and became an option on 28 ga. and .410 bore in 1994. New 1986.

➤ **12 or 20 Ga.** — Invector Plus choking, high-post target rib, and ported barrels became standard in 1994.

Mfg.'s Sug. Retail	$2,310	$1,775	$1,300	$975	$795	$650	$550	$495

Add $210 for adj. comb (mfg. 1995-98).

➤ **Smaller Gauges** — 28 ga. or .410 bore.

Mfg.'s Sug. Retail	$2,316	$1,795	$1,325	$975	$825	$675	$595	$550

Subtract 10% if without standard Invector choking (new 1994).

* *Grade V* — 12, 20, 28 ga., or .410 bore, high rib. Disc. 1984.

	$1,495	$1,265	$1,100	$990	$880	$795	$650

* *Grade VI* — Skeet gauges, choice of blue or grey finished receiver with multi gold inlays, deluxe walnut. Disc. 1995.

➤ **12 Ga.** — Invector Plus choking, high-post target rib, and ported barrels became standard in 1994.

	$2,025	$1,600	$1,325	$1,100	$960	$875	$825

Last Mfg.'s Sug. Retail was $2,555.

➤ **Smaller Gauges** — 20, 28 ga., or .410 bore, 20 ga. available with standard Invector choking, 28 ga. and .410 bore are choked SK/SK.

	$2,000	$1,600	$1,325	$1,100	$960	$875	$825

Last Mfg.'s Sug. Retail was $2,518.

* *Skeet Golden Clays (GC)* — 12, 20, 28 ga., or .410 bore, 26 or 28 in. ported VR barrels, Invector Plus choking, Skeet features, satin grey receiver with Grade VI level of engraving and gold inlays depicting a transitional hunting to clay pigeon scene. New 1993.

➤ **12 or 20 Ga.** — Invector (disc. 1995) or Invector Plus choking, high-post target rib, and ported barrels (12 ga. only).

Mfg.'s Sug. Retail	$3,434	$2,800	$2,025	$1,625	$1,250	$1,050	$900	$825

Add $210 for adj. comb (mfg. 1995-98).
Subtract approx. 10% if without Invector Plus choking.

➤ **Smaller Gauges** — 28 ga. or .410 bore, standard Invector or fixed SK/SK choking.

Mfg.'s Sug. Retail	$3,356	$2,725	$2,050	$1,675	$1,300	$1,075	$950	$850

Subtract approx. 10% with fixed choking.

CITORI 3 GAUGE SKEET SETS — supplied with one 20 ga. frame, 1 removable forearm, and 3 barrels consisting of 20, 28 ga. and .410 bore, cased. Mfg. 1987-96.

* *Grade I* — with high post target rib, standard Invector choking became standard 1994.

	$2,525	$2,075	$1,675	$1,450	$1,275	$1,050	$975

Last Mfg.'s Sug. Retail was $3,100.

* *Grade III* — with high post target rib, available with standard Invector choking (new 1994) or fixed SK/SK chokes.

	$3,100	$2,350	$1,875	$1,550	$1,395	$1,250	$1,125

Last Mfg.'s Sug. Retail was $3,900.

Subtract 10% for fixed SK/SK chokes.

Grading	100%	98%	95%	90%	80%	70%	60%

B

* *Grade VI* — with high post target rib, fixed SK/SK chokes only. Disc. 1994.

  $3,250 $2,500 $2,000 $1,775 $1,600 $1,400 $1,275
  Last Mfg.'s Sug. Retail was $3,990.

* *Golden Clays* — features Golden Clays accents and engraving, standard Invector choking. Mfg. 1994-95 only.

  $4,250 $3,075 $2,600 $2,100 $1,900 $1,750 $1,600
  Last Mfg.'s Sug. Retail was $5,100.

CITORI 4 GAUGE SKEET SETS — supplied with one 12 ga. frame, 1 removable forearm, and 4 barrels consisting of 12, 20, 28 ga., and .410 bore, cased. Imported 1985 only.

* *Grade I* — with high post target rib, choice of standard Invector (new 1994) or fixed SK/SK choking.

  $3,750 $2,850 $2,400 $1,975 $1,800 $1,775 $1,600
  Last Mfg.'s Sug. Retail was $4,450.

  Subtract 10% for fixed SK/SK choking.

* *Grade III* — with high post target rib, choice of standard Invector (new 1994) or fixed SK/SK choking.

  $4,575 $3,250 $2,700 $2,250 $1,950 $1,800 $1,700
  Last Mfg.'s Sug. Retail was $5,450.

  Subtract 10% for fixed SK/SK choking.

* *Grade VI* — with high post target rib, fixed SK/SK choking only. Disc. 1994.

  $4,600 $3,350 $2,775 $2,300 $2,100 $2,000 $1,900
  Last Mfg.'s Sug. Retail was $5,225.

* *Golden Clays* — features Golden Clays accents and engraving, standard Invector choking. Mfg. 1994 only.

  $5,650 $4,100 $3,300 $2,600 $2,350 $2,100 $1,975
  Last Mfg.'s Sug. Retail was $6,750.

SHOTGUNS: O/U, CITORI TRAP

CITORI TRAP MODELS — 12 ga., similar to Standard Citori, 30 or 32 in. barrels, trap chokes, Monte Carlo stock, recoil pad. Invector chokes became standard in 1988, Invector Plus chokes with ported barrels became an option in 1992, and were made standard in 1993, new Special Trap models were introduced during 1995 with decreased weight (¼ lb. lighter) and better swing/balance characteristics.

* *Grade I Special Trap* — new 1995, approx. 8½ lbs.

  Mfg.'s Sug. Retail   **$1,658 $1,340 $975 $795 $650 $525 $495 $450**
  Add $220 for adj. comb (new 1995).
  Subtract 10% without Invector chokes or high rib.

* *Trap Combination Set* — Grade I only, 32 in. O/U and 34 in. single barrel, cased. Disc.

  $1,395 $1,100 $975 $900 $825 $775 $725

* *Grade I Plus Trap* — features adj. rib and stock, back-bored barrels, Invector Plus choke system. Mfg. 1990-94.

  $1,560 $1,200 $940 $800 $700 $600 $500
  Last Mfg.'s Sug. Retail was $2,005.

  Add 5% for ported barrels.

  In 1991 this model included a travel vault gun case at no extra charge. Subtract $50 for older mfg. without travel case.

* *Grade I Plus Trap Combo* — includes ported barrels with Invector Plus choking and extra standard single ported barrel, luggage case. Mfg. 1992-94.

  $2,850 $2,425 $2,100 $1,900 $1,700 $1,500 $1,250
  Last Mfg.'s Sug. Retail was $3,435.

Grading	100%	98%	95%	90%	80%	70%	60%

B

* **Plus Trap Golden Clays** — 12 ga. only, 30 or 32 in. ported VR barrels, Invector Plus choking, Trap features, satin grey receiver with Grade VI level of engraving and gold inlays depicting a transitional hunting to clay birds scene. Mfg. 1993-94.

  $2,850 $2,275 $1,900 $1,600 $1,400 $1,200 $995
  Last Mfg.'s Sug. Retail was $3,435.

* **Plus Trap Golden Clays Combo** — includes O/U ported barrels with Invector Plus choking and extra standard single ported barrel, luggage case. Mfg. 1993-94.

  $4,425 $3,300 $2,775 $2,250 $1,925 $1,800 $1,700
  Last Mfg.'s Sug. Retail was $5,200.

* **XT Monte Carlo** — 12 ga. only, features greyed receiver with 24 Kt. gold accents and light engraving, 30 or 32 in. vent. backbored barrels with high-post VR, checkered high gloss Monte Carlo walnut stock and forearm, waffle-style recoil pad, approx. 8½ lbs. New 1999.

  Mfg.'s Sug. Retail $1,834 $1,450 $1,050 $825 $675 $575 $500 $450
  Add $220 for adj. comb.

* **Pigeon Grade** — 12 ga. only, features extra deluxe walnut, Invector Plus ported barrels, and receiver gold accents. Mfg. 1993-94.

  $1,715 $1,250 $950 $800 $700 $600 $500
  Last Mfg.'s Sug. Retail was $2,225.

* **Signature Painted** — 12 ga. only, features painted red/black stock with Browning logos on stock and forearm, Invector Plus ported barrels. Mfg. 1993-94.

  $1,595 $1,200 $940 $800 $700 $600 $500
  Last Mfg.'s Sug. Retail was $2,065.

* **Grade II** — high post rib. Disc. 1983.

  $1,000 $850 $800 $740 $690 $650 $600

* **Grade III** — 12 ga. only, high post rib, Invector Plus choking and ported barrels became standard in 1994. New 1986.

  Mfg.'s Sug. Retail $2,310 $1,795 $1,250 $950 $795 $625 $550 $495
  Add $220 for adj. comb. (new 1996).
  Subtract 10% if without Invector Plus chokes or ported barrels.

* **Grade V** — high post rib. Disc. 1984.

  $1,475 $1,150 $990 $880 $795 $710 $620

* **Grade VI** — 12 ga. only, Invector chokes became standard in 1985, Invector Plus chokes became standard in 1994. Disc. 1994.

  $1,925 $1,525 $1,225 $1,100 $960 $875 $825
  Last Mfg.'s Sug. Retail was $2,555.

  Subtract $150 if without Invector Plus chokes or ported barrels.

* **Trap Golden Clays (GC)** — 12 ga. only, 30 or 32 in. ported VR barrels, Invector Plus choking, Trap features, Monte Carlo or regular stock, satin grey receiver with Grade VI level of engraving and gold inlays depicting a transitional hunting to clay pigeon scene. New 1993.

  Mfg.'s Sug. Retail $3,434 $2,800 $2,025 $1,625 $1,250 $1,050 $900 $825
  Add $220 for adj. comb (new 1995).

SHOTGUNS: SINGLE BARREL, BT-99 & BT-100

BT-99 STANDARD TRAP GUN — 12 ga., 32 or 34 in. vent. rib barrel, mod., imp. mod., or full choke, boxlock, auto ejector, checkered pistol grip with Monte Carlo or conventional style stock, beavertail forearm. Invector chokes became standard in 1986 and ported barrel with Invector Plus chokes became standard in 1992, back boring became standard in 1993. Values below assume Invector Plus choking with ported barrel. Mfg. 1968-94 by Miroku.

  $895 $700 $550 $460 $400 $360 $330
  Last Mfg.'s Sug. Retail was $1,288.

  Subtract $125 without Invector chokes or ported barrels.

Grading	100%	98%	95%	90%	80%	70%	60%

B

* ***BT-99 2 Barrel Set*** — without Invector choking or barrel porting. Disc. 1983.

| | $1,050 | $850 | $750 | $700 | $650 | $600 | $550 |

* ***BT-99 Stainless*** — features all stainless construction with Invector Plus ported 32 or 34 in. black VR barrel. Mfg. 1993-94.

| | $1,325 | $995 | $850 | $700 | $575 | $495 | $450 |

Last Mfg.'s Sug. Retail was $1,738.

* ***Pigeon Grade*** — features higher grade walnut and gold receiver accents, Invector chokes and ported barrels. Mfg. 1993-94.

| | $1,225 | $895 | $715 | $600 | $525 | $495 | $450 |

Last Mfg.'s Sug. Retail was $1,505.

Older pre-1985 mfg.

| | $1,275 | $950 | $775 | $650 | $575 | $525 | $475 |

Older Pigeon Grade guns featured a satin grey receiver with deep relief, engraved pigeons in a fleur-de-lis background.

* ***Signature Painted*** — features painted red/black stock with Browning logos on stock and forearm, Invector Plus ported barrels. Mfg. 1993-94.

| | $1,015 | $715 | $550 | $460 | $400 | $360 | $330 |

Last Mfg.'s Sug. Retail was $1,323.

* ***BT-99 Golden Clays*** — features high-grade wood and gold outline receiver and inlays depicting a transitional hunting to clay pigeon scene. Mfg. 1994 only.

| | $2,300 | $1,750 | $1,450 | $1,125 | $975 | $875 | $795 |

Last Mfg.'s Sug. Retail was $2,800.

GRADE I BT-99 PLUS — similar to BT-99, except has adj. rib to control point of impact and new recoil reduction system that reduces felt recoil by 50%, stock has adj. comb and butt plate (recoil pad), back-bored barrel, Invector chokes, 8¾ lbs. Mfg. 1989-94.

| | $1,200 | $1,000 | $875 | $775 | $675 | $595 | $550 |

Last Mfg.'s Sug. Retail was $1,835.

Add 5% for ported barrel.

In 1990, the Grade I designation was added to this model. Changes include back-bored barrels with Invector plus choke tubes. In 1991, this model was supplied with a travel vault gun case as standard equipment. Older mfg. will not have these cases as an original accessory.

Beginning 1991, a Micro Plus Model was introduced that incorporates smaller dimensions (shorter stock and choice of shorter barrel). Values are the same as listed above.

* ***BT-99 Plus Stainless*** — features all stainless construction with Invector Plus ported 32 or 34 in. black VR barrel. Mfg. 1993-94.

Beginning 1991, a Micro Plus Model was introduced that incorporates smaller dimensions (shorter stock and choice of shorter barrel). Values are the same as listed above.

| | $1,710 | $1,245 | $975 | $800 | $700 | $600 | $500 |

Last Mfg.'s Sug. Retail was $2,240.

* ***BT-99 Plus Pigeon Grade*** — features higher grade walnut and gold receiver accents, Invector chokes and ported barrels. Mfg. 1993-disc.

| | $1,595 | $1,200 | $925 | $800 | $700 | $600 | $500 |

Last Mfg.'s Sug. Retail was $2,065.

Beginning 1991, a Micro Plus Model was introduced that incorporates smaller dimensions (shorter stock and choice of shorter barrel). Values are the same as listed above.

* ***BT-99 Plus Signature Painted*** — features painted red/black stock with Browning logos on stock and forearm, Invector Plus ported barrels. Mfg. 1993-94.

| | $1,500 | $1,150 | $915 | $800 | $700 | $600 | $500 |

Last Mfg.'s Sug. Retail was $1,890.

Beginning 1991, a Micro Plus Model was introduced that incorporates smaller dimensions (shorter stock and choice of shorter barrel). Values are the same as listed above.

Grading	100%	98%	95%	90%	80%	70%	60%

B

* **BT-99 Plus Golden Clays** — features high-grade wood and gold outline receiver and inlays depicting a transitional hunting to clay pigeon scene. Mfg. 1994 only.

	$2,700	$2,350	$2,050	$1,850	$1,700	$1,550	$1,395

Last Mfg.'s Sug. Retail was $3,205.

Beginning 1991, a Micro Plus Model was introduced that incorporates smaller dimensions (shorter stock and choice of shorter barrel). Values are the same as listed above.

BT-99 MAX — 12 ga. only, choice of blued steel with engraving or stainless steel barrel, receiver, and trigger guard, 32 or 34 in. high post VR ported barrel, thin forearm with finger grooves, select walnut pistol grip stock (regular or Monte Carlo) with high gloss finish, ejector/extractor selector, no safety, approx. 8 lbs. 10 oz. Mfg. 1995-96.

	$1,250	$925	$725	$600	$525	$495	$450

Last Mfg.'s Sug. Retail was $1,496.

Add $400 for stainless steel.

BT-100 STANDARD TRAP GUN — 12 ga. only, 32 or 34 in. steel high-post ported Invector Plus or fixed choked (F) barrel, without safety, choice of blue or stainless steel receiver, removable trigger assembly, ejector selector (either ejects or extracts) adj. comb and thumbhole stock are optional, approx. 8 lbs. 10 oz. New 1995.

Mfg.'s Sug. Retail	$2,095		$1,725	$1,150	$950	$750	$575	$495	$450

Subtract $49 for fixed choke.
Add $220 for adj. comb.
Add $289 for thumbhole stock (new 1995).
Add $552 for replacement trigger assembly (blue or stainless).

* **Stainless BT-100** — features stainless steel barrel, receiver, trigger guard and top lever.

Mfg.'s Sug. Retail	$2,536		$2,150	$1,400	$1,075

Subtract $49 for fixed choke.
Add $220 for adj. comb.
Add $289 for thumbhole stock (new 1995).
Add $552 for replacement trigger assembly (blue or stainless).

BT-100 LOW LUSTER — features 32 or 34 in. Invector Plus barrel, low luster metal/wood finish, conventional type stock without Monte Carlo, quick removable trigger with adj. trigger pull, 8 lbs. 10 oz. New 1998.

Mfg.'s Sug. Retail	$1,667		$1,360	$1,100	$935	$750	$650	$575	$495

SHOTGUNS: SINGLE BARREL, RECOILLESS TRAP

RECOILLESS SINGLE BARREL TRAP — 12 ga., special bolt action design that eliminates 72% of felt recoil, 27 (also available in Micro Model) or 30 in. high-post vent. rib Invector Plus choked back-bored barrel, rib adjusts for 3 points of impact (3, 6 or 9 in.), stock has adj. pull (2 sizes) and comb height, anodized receiver, no safety, approx. 8½ lbs. Mfg. 1994-96.

	$825	$725	$650	$575	$500	$450	$400

Last Mfg.'s Sug. Retail was $1,995.

The Micro Model features a 27 in. barrel and shorter length of pull.

* **Signature Painted** — features painted red/black stock with Browning logos on stock and forearm, Invector Plus ported barrels. Mfg. 1994 only.

	$1,580	$1,050	$895	$725	$575	$495	$450

Last Mfg.'s Sug. Retail was $1,900.

SHOTGUNS: BOLT ACTION, A-BOLT SERIES

A-BOLT MODEL — 12 ga. only, 3 in. chamber, 2 shot mag., same bolt system as A-Bolt II Rifle, 22 or 23 in. barrel (rifled or Invector with rifled tube), available in Stalker Model with graphite fiberglass composite stock or Hunter Model with select satin finished walnut stock, dull matte finished barrel and receiver, top tang safety, choice of no sights (new 1996) or adj. rear sight, drilled and tapped receiver, approx. 7 lbs. Mfg. by Miroku 1995-98.

Grading	100%	98%	95%	90%	80%	70%	60%

B

* ***Stalker Model***

	$435	$335	$300	$275	$260	$240	$220

Last Mfg.'s Sug. Retail was $720.

Add $25 for open sights.
Add $100 for rifled barrel.

* ***Hunter Model***

	$425	$325	$295	$275	$260	$240	$220

Last Mfg.'s Sug. Retail was $805.

Add $24 for open sights.
Add $100 for rifled barrel.

SHOTGUNS: SxS, DISC.

BSS MODEL — 12 or 20 ga., 26, 28, or 30 in. barrels, various chokes, boxlock, auto ejectors, checkered pistol grip stock, beavertail forearm, selective single trigger. Mfg. 1971-1988 by Miroku.

	$795	$650	$450	$400	$365	$330	$300

Last Mfg.'s Sug. Retail was $775.

Add 10%-15% for 20 ga.

Early guns had a single non-selective trigger (silver plated) — subtract 10%.

* ***Grade II*** — satin greyed steel receiver featuring an engraved pheasant, duck, quail and dogs. Disc. 1983.

	$1,100	$950	$800	$700	$600	$525	$450

SPORTER MODEL — has straight grip stock and slim forearm, oil finish, 26 or 28 in. barrels. Disc. 1988.

	$895	$750	$550	$500	$445	$410	$370

Last Mfg.'s Sug. Retail was $775.

Add 10%-15% for 20 ga.

* ***Sporter Model Grade II*** — satin greyed steel receiver featuring an engraved pheasant, duck, quail and dogs. Disc. 1983.

	$1,100	$995	$895	$675	$575	$475	$425

Add 10%-15% for 20 ga.

BSS SIDELOCK — 12 or 20 ga., engraved sidelock action in satin grey finish, ST, 26 or 28 in. barrels, English select walnut stock, splinter forend. Mfg. 1983-1988 in Miroku in Japan.

12 ga.	$1,995	$1,450	$1,125	$975	$825	$750	$675
20 ga.	$2,400	$1,750	$1,375	$1,100	$900	$800	$700

Last Mfg.'s Sug. Retail was $2,000.

SHOTGUNS: SLIDE ACTION

BPS MODELS — 12, 20, or 28 (new 1994) ga., gauges are chambered for Mag. ammunition. Invector option (standard for 1985) allows 6 screw-in choke tubes to be interchanged, Invector Plus chokes became standard in 1993 (except 28 ga.), bottom ejection, double action bars, top tang safety, 5 shot capacity, vent. rib, all steel receiver with variety of finishes, receiver engraving became standard 1991 and was disc. during 1998, 20 and 28 ga. are approx. 1/2 lb. lighter than 12 ga. Field Models. Mfg. by Miroku 1977-to-date.

* ***Field/Hunting Model*** — 12, 20, or 28 (new 1994) ga., 2¾ (28 ga. only) or 3 in. chamber, Invector or Invector Plus (new 1994 in 20 ga.) choking, various barrel lengths, Invector Plus choking became standard 1995 (except 28 ga.), 7 lbs. - 8 lbs. 3 oz.

Mfg.'s Sug. Retail	$444		$360	$285	$250	$225	$200	$185	$170

Subtract 10% if without Invector Plus choke tubes.

* ***Stalker Model*** — 12 ga. only, 3 in. chamber, all metal parts have a dull matte finish, non-glare black synthetic composite stock and forearm, 24 (new 1999), 26, 28, or 30 in. VR barrel, approx. 7 lbs. 9 oz. New 1987.

Mfg.'s Sug. Retail	$444		$360	$285	$250	$225	$200	$185	$170

Grading	100%	98%	95%	90%	80%	70%	60%

B

* **Waterfowl Camo** — 12 ga. only, 3 in. chamber, features Mossy Oak Shadow Grass full camo treatment, 24, 26, or 28 in. barrel, approx. 7 lbs. 10 oz. New 1999.

Mfg.'s Sug. Retail	$514	$415	$365	$325	$300	$275	$245	$215

* **Magnum Hunting or Stalker 3½ in.** — 10 or 12 ga., 3½ in. chamber, 12 ga. 3½ in. chamber was new 1989, 24 (disc. 1997, reintroduced 1999), 26, 28, or 30 (disc. 1997) in. barrel with Invector chokes and vent. rib, 4 shot mag., 8 lbs. 2 oz. - 8 lbs. 12 oz. (12 ga.) or 8 lbs. 15 oz. - 9 lbs. 8 oz. (10 ga.).

Mfg.'s Sug. Retail	$532	$430	$375	$330	$315	$275	$245	$215

In 1990, the back-bored Invector plus choke tube system became standard in 12 ga. 3½ in. chamber only.

➤ **Camo Magnum Hunting 3½ in.** — similar to Magnum Hunting or Stalker, features Mossy Oak Shadow Grass full camo treatment, 24, 26, or 28 in. barrel, approx. 9¼ lbs. New 1999.

Mfg.'s Sug. Retail	$602	$500	$465	$395	$350	$310	$290	$275

* **Magnum Hunting Waterfowl** — 10 ga., 3½ in. Mag. with choice of 28 or 30 in. matte finished VR barrel with standard Invector choking, features higher grade walnut and gold trimmed receiver with Waterfowl outlined, approx. 9 lbs. 6 oz. Mfg. 1993-98.

	$615	$525	$450	$400	$350	$315	$285

Last Mfg.'s Sug. Retail was $750.

* **Pigeon Grade** — 12 ga. only, 3 in. chamber, features high grade walnut and gold trimmed receiver, 26 or 28 in. VR barrel with Invector chokes, 7 lbs. 10 oz. Mfg. 1992-98.

	$500	$465	$395	$350	$310	$290	$275

Last Mfg.'s Sug. Retail was $603.

* **Upland Special** — 12 or 20 ga., 22 in. barrel, straight grip stock with Schnabel forearm, Invector (pre-1994) or Invector Plus (new 1994, standard 1995) choking, 6½ - 7½ lbs. Mfg. 1985-current.

Mfg.'s Sug. Retail	$444	$360	$285	$250	$225	$200	$185	$170

Subtract 10% if without Invector Plus choke tubes.

* **Turkey Special** — 12 ga. only, 3 in. chamber, 20½ in. lightened barrel, non-glare walnut stock, matte finished barrel and receiver, receiver is drilled and tapped for scope base, rifle-style stock dimensions, sling swivels, new extra-full Invector choke tube, 7 lbs. 7 oz. New 1992.

Mfg.'s Sug. Retail	$482	$390	$335	$270	$240	$215	$190	$175

* **Micro - Youth and Ladies Model** — 20 ga. only, 22 in. vent. rib barrel, straight grip shortened stock, Invector (pre-1994) or Invector Plus (new 1994, standard 1995) choking, 6¾ lbs. Mfg. beginning 1986.

Mfg.'s Sug. Retail	$444	$360	$285	$250	$225	$200	$185	$170

Subtract 10% if without Invector Plus choke tubes.

* **Deer Special (DG, DS or DH)** — 12 ga. only, 3 in. chamber, 20½ in. barrel with 5 in. rifled choke tube or rifled barrel (DH, cantilever scope mount with satin finish only, new 1997), iron sights, scope mount base, choice of gloss (DG, disc. 1997) or satin (DS) finish checkered stock with recoil pad and forearm, sling swivels, polished or matte finished metal, 7 lbs. 7 oz. New 1992.

Mfg.'s Sug. Retail	$516	$410	$350	$285	$250	$220	$195	$175

Add $32 for 22 in. rifled barrel (Model DH).

* **Buck Special** — 12 or 20 (disc. 1984) ga., 3 in. chamber, 24 in. cyl. bore barrel, iron sights, 7 lbs. 10 oz. Reintroduced 1988-disc. 1998.

	$335	$275	$230	$200	$185	$175	$160

Last Mfg.'s Sug. Retail was $409.

* **3½ in. Buck Special** — 10 or 12 (disc. 1994) ga., 3½ in. chambers, 24 in. cyl. bore barrel, 7 lbs. 10 oz. Mfg. 1990-97.

	$570	$460	$410	$370	$335	$310	$290

Last Mfg.'s Sug. Retail was $677.

Grading	100%	98%	95%	90%	80%	70%	60%

* **Trap Model** — 12 ga., 30 in. barrel. Disc. 1984 but trap barrels were available separately for several years.

	$360	$300	$270	$230	$210	$190	$170

* **Wild Turkey Federation Commemorative** — only 500 manufactured. Disc. 1991.

	$495	$395	$325

* **Pacific Edition DU** — limited mfg., DU serialization, cased.

	$595	$475	$350

* **The Coastal DU** — limited mfg., DU serialization, cased.

	$595	$475	$350

* **Waterfowl Deluxe** — 12 ga. Mag., gold trigger and etching, invector chokes, limited mfg.

	$625	$525	$450

MODEL 12 LIMITED EDITION SERIES

* **Grade I 20 Ga.** — 20 ga. only, 2¾ in. chamber only, reproduction of the famous Winchester Model 12 with slight design improvements, 26 in. VR barrel bored modified, 5 shot mag., high post floating rib, walnut stock and forearm with semi-gloss finish, take down, serialization format similar to 28 ga., 7 lbs. 1 oz. 8,000 mfg. in 1988 with inventory depleted 1990.

	$450	$400	$300

Last Mfg.'s Sug. Retail was $735.

Browning limited manufacture to 8,000 Grade I 20 Ga.'s.

* **Grade V 20 Ga.** — similar specifications to Grade I, except has select walnut checkered 22 lines per inch with high gloss finish, extensive game scene engraving including multiple gold inlays serialization format similar to 28 ga. Mfg. 1988 only.

	$795	$695	$575

Last Mfg.'s Sug. Retail was $1,187.

Browning Arms Company limited manufacture to 4,000 Grade V 20 Ga.'s.

* **Grade I 28 Ga.** — 28 ga. only, similar to Grade I 20 Ga., except in 28 ga., 26 in. VR modified choke barrel, 5 digit ser. no. with NM872 suffix. 7,000 mfg. 1991-92.

	$450	$400	$300

Last Mfg.'s Sug. Retail was $772.

* **Grade V 28 ga.** — 28 ga. only, similar to Grade V 20 ga., except in 28 ga., 26 in. VR modified choke barrel, 5 digit ser. no. with NM972 suffix. 5,000 mfg. 1991-92.

	$795	$695	$575

Last Mfg.'s Sug. Retail was $1,246.

MODEL 42 LIMITED EDITION

* **Model 42 Grade I** — .410 bore, 3 in. chamber, reproduction of the Winchester Model 42 with slight design improvements, 26 in. VR full choke barrel, select walnut stock, 5 digit ser. no. with NZ882 suffix, 6 lbs. 12 oz. 6,000 mfg. late 1991-1993.

	$495	$400	$300

Last Mfg.'s Sug. Retail was $800.

* **Model 42 Grade V** — .410 bore, engraving and embellishments similar to the Model 12 Grade V, 5 digit ser. no. with NZ982 suffix, 6,000 mfg. late 1991-1993.

	$795	$695	$575

Last Mfg.'s Sug. Retail was $1,360.

COMMEMORATIVES, SPECIAL EDITIONS, & LIMITED MFG.

BICENTENNIAL 1876-1976 SET — .45-70 Govt. cal., Model 78 rifle with specially engraved receiver, silver finish, fancy wood, cased, with engraved knife and medallion, 1,000 sets mfg. in 1976. Issue price — $1,500.

	$1,750	$1,300	$850

Grading	100%	98%	95%	90%	80%	70%	60%

B

JONATHAN BROWNING MOUNTAIN RIFLE — 50 cal., percussion, 30 in. octagon barrel, single set trigger, engraved lock plate, select walnut stock, cased with medallion and powder horn, 1,000 mfg. in 1978. Issue price — $650.

	$750	$595	$400				

MOUNTAIN RIFLE — similar to Jonathan Browning Mountain Rifle, without Centennial embellishments, not cased. Also in .45 or .54 cal.

	$595	$525	$475	$400	$350	$300	$250

CENTENNIAL O/U RIFLE/SHOTGUN — 20 ga. O/U shotgun w/extra set of .30-06 O/U rifle barrels. Shotgun barrels are 26½ in., rifle barrels are 24 in., SST, ejectors, elaborate scroll engraved receiver with 2 gold inlays, special oil finish walnut, deluxe walnut full-length case. 500 mfg. 1978 only.

	$4,450	$3,900	$3,150	$2,550	$2,100	$1,850	$1,650

Last Mfg.'s Sug. Retail was $7,000.

CENTENNIAL SET — complete Browning set mfg. in 1978, includes the Centennial O/U Rifle/Shotgun, 9mm Hi-Power, B92 .44 Mag., Mountain Rifle, and a set of three knives.

	$6,250	$5,000	$3,950				

1 OF 50 BICENTENNIAL RIFLE — .30-06 cal., Model 78 single shot with 26 in. octagon barrel, includes special engraving by Neil Hartliep (non-factory), extra fine walnut, 4X wide angle scope, special luggage case. 50 mfg. (one for each state) during 1976 only and sold by silent mail order bidding (minimum bid was $3,100 in 1976).

As very few specimens are bought or sold each year, pricing is rather unpredictable. A few specimens have been sold in the $5,000 range recently. Remember, the work on this gun was subcontracted by Centennial Guns (division of Frigon Guns located in Clay Center, KS).

BRUCHET

Current manufacturer located in Saint Etienne, France. Distributed exclusively from 1982-1989 by Wes Gilpin located in Dallas, TX. In 1989, Bruchet was able to get permission to use the older Darne trademark and all new manufacture will be entered under the Darne listing.

Paul Bruchet has been manufacturing his shotguns patterned after the Darne action since 1981, following his tenure at Darne as line foreman until 1979 (at which time the Darne plant closed). These new Bruchet Models were designated "A" or "B". All shotguns were totally hand made with approx. 50 guns being mfg. each year.

Since Paul Bruchet was able to retain the Darne trademark in 1989, please refer to the Darne section in this text for current manufacture.

SHOTGUNS: SxS

MODEL A — 12, 16, 20, 28 ga., or .410 bore, small key opening, ejectors, double triggers only, basically 4 variations (1, 1A, 2, and 2A), wide assortment of customer specified special orders.

Retail values were as follows: Model 1A started at under $2,000, the Model 2 started at $3,000, and the Model 2A started at $3,500. Each additional grade represented more embellishments and better grade of walnut. Magnum chambers could be ordered at a small surcharge. Importation began 1982, values represent the last published retail prices from 1989.

MODEL B — 12, 16, 20, 28 ga., or .410 bore, large key opening, self-opening (assisted) action, ejectors, double triggers only, basically special ordered to individual customer specifications.

Retail values were as follows: Model B starts at $5,800 and included deluxe carrying case. Each additional upgrade represented more embellishments and a better grade of walnut.

Grading			100%	98%	95%	90%	80%	70%	60%

Magnum chambers could be ordered at a small surcharge. Importation began 1982, values represent the last published retail prices from 1989.

B BRYCO ARMS

Current manufacturer located in Irvine, CA. Distributed by Jennings Firearms, Inc. located in Carson City, NV. Distributor sales only.

PISTOLS: SEMI-AUTO, SINGLE ACTION

MODEL T-22 — .22 LR cal., target pistol featuring adj. rear sight, loaded chamber indicator, mag. safety, and last shot, slide hold open. New 1997.

	Mfg.'s Sug. Retail	$179		$130	$100	$85	$75	$65	$60	$55

MODEL J-25 — .25 ACP cal., aluminum alloy frame, 2.5 in. barrel, single action, synthetic ivory, walnut, or black combat grips, positive safety, 11 oz. Mfg. 1988-95.

			$60	$50	$45	$40	$35	$30	$30

Last Mfg.'s Sug. Retail was $70.

This model was available in either satin nickel, bright chrome, or black teflon finish.

MODEL M-32/M-38 — .22 LR (disc.), .32 ACP, or .380 ACP cal., semi-auto single action, 2.8 in. barrel, pressure cast fabrication using non-ferrous alloy, chrome or blue finish, black combat grips, 16 oz. New 1991.

	Mfg.'s Sug. Retail	$79		$65	$50	$40	$35	$30	$30	$30

Add $20 for .380 ACP cal.

MODEL M-48 — .22 LR, .32 ACP, or .380 ACP cal., semi-auto single action, 4 in. barrel, larger frame variation of the M-38, chrome or blue finish, black combat grips, 24 oz. Mfg. 1991-95.

		$85	$75	$65	$55	$50	$45	$40

Last Mfg.'s Sug. Retail was $96.

MODEL M-58 — .380 ACP or 9mm Para. cal., 3¼ in. barrel, 10 or 12 shot mag., blue or nickel finish, black synthetic grips, 36 oz. Disc. 1995.

		$85	$75	$65	$55	$50	$45	$40

Last Mfg.'s Sug. Retail was $100 for the .380 ACP, $119 for 9mm Para.

Add $15 for 9mm Para. cal.

MODEL M-59 — .380 ACP or 9mm Para. cal., 4 in. barrel, 10 shot mag., blue or nickel finish, black synthetic grips, 36 oz. Disc. 1995.

		$95	$85	$75	$70	$65	$60	$55

Last Mfg.'s Sug. Retail was $119.

Add $15 for 9mm Para. cal.

JENNINGS NINE — 9mm Para. cal., single action, redesigned model 59, frame mounted ejector, contour grips, loaded chamber indicator, 30 oz. New 1997.

	Mfg.'s Sug. Retail	$145		$120	$100	$85	$75	$65	$55	$50

BUDISCHOWSKY

Previous manufacturer located in Mt. Clemens, MI.

PISTOLS: SEMI-AUTO

TP-70 — .22 LR cal., double action, 2½ in. barrel, stainless steel, fixed sights, plastic grips. Mfg. 1973-1977.

		$440	$385	$330

TP-70 — similar to TP-70, except .25 ACP cal. Mfg. 1973-1977.

		$330	$275	$220

Note: In 1977, Norton Arms marketed this pistol. Quality of workmanship is not on par with the early Budischowsky and values are approx. 35% less.

Grading	100%	98%	95%	90%	80%	70%	60%

SEMI-AUTO PISTOL — .223 Rem. cal., 11⅝ in. barrel, 20 or 30 shot mag., fixed sights, a novel paramilitary designed type pistol.

	100%	98%	95%	90%	80%	70%	60%
	$470	$415	$385	$360	$305	$250	$220

B

RIFLES: SEMI-AUTO

PARAMILITARY DESIGN RIFLE — .223 Rem. cal., semi-auto, 18 in. barrel, wood paramilitary stock.

	$505	$440	$415	$385	$330	$275	$250

PARAMILITARY DESIGN RIFLE W/FOLDING STOCK

	$575	$500	$450	$425	$395	$360	$330

BULLARD ARMS

Previous manufacturer located in Springfield, MA, circa 1880s. Designed by prolific inventor James Bullard, the design, quality, and workmanship of Bullard rifles rivaled those of any competitor during the 1880s. Bullard made two basic rifles: a lever action repeater and a single shot. The repeater was made in two frame styles: large and small. The single shot was also made in two basic styles; solid frame and detachable-interchangeable barrel model.

100%	98%	95%	90%	80%	70%	60%	50%	40%	30%	20%	10%

RIFLES: LEVER ACTION

LEVER ACTION REPEATER — rack and pinion style lever activated mechanism, mag. mounted under barrel, loaded through underside of action while lever was opened, blued finish with various parts (including receiver) sometimes case hardened.

* **Large Frame** — .40-60, .45-60, .45-70 Govt., .45-75, .50-95 and .40-70 Bullard, .40-90 Bullard, .45-85 Bullard or .50-115 Bullard cal., 26 or 28 in. round, octagon, or part round barrel, crescent steel or hard rubber buttplates with elk motif, ser. no. range 1-1,500 and 2,000-3,000.

N/A	N/A	$2,800	$2,450	$1,950	$1,750	$1,625	$1,450	$1,275	$1,150	$975	$850

Add 25% for .40-90 Bullard, .50-95, or .50-115 Bullard cal.
Add 25% for deluxe checkered wood with pistol grip.

Various military and experimental models are found in this frame size and will command significant premiums.

* **Small Frame** — .32-40 Bullard or .38-45 Bullard cal., (other calibers cataloged, but essentially unknown), 24, 26, or 28 in. round, octagon or part round barrel, crescent steel or hard rubber buttplates with turkey motif, ser. no. range 1,500-2,000.

N/A	N/A	$2,400	$2,000	$1,750	$1,550	$1,375	$1,175	$1,025	$900	$825	$750

Add 25% for deluxe checkered wood with pistol grip.
Add 40% for any caliber other than .32-40 and .38-45.

Although the small frame saw less production and is scarcer than the large frame repeater, it was not as popular, and is typically priced less than a large frame model.

RIFLES: SINGLE SHOT

SINGLE SHOT MODEL — thin receiver with full lever, similar in appearance to small frame repeater action, except shorter (several parts including lever will interchange), 26, 28, or 30 in. round, octagon, or part round barrel, blued finish with various parts sometimes case hardened (including receiver), crescent steel or hard rubber buttplates, ser. no. range 3,500-4,100.

100%	98%	95%	90%	80%	70%	60%	50%	40%	30%	20%	10%

B

* **Solid Frame** — wide variety of cals. from .22 rimfire to .50 cal., (.22 and .32-40 are most common), essentially one frame size, except the .22 was somewhat smaller.

N/A	N/A	$2,500	$2,200	$1,850	$1,575	$1,450	$1,375	$1,250	$1,125	$995	$900

* **Detachable-Interchangeable Barrel Model** — same cals. as small frame model with two frame sizes - small (.38 cal. and smaller) and large (.40 cal. and larger), interchangeable barrels could not be switched between the two frame sizes, barrel and breech detach from action.

N/A	N/A	$2,500	$2,200	$1,850	$1,575	$1,450	$1,375	$1,250	$1,125	$995	$900

Add 20% for large frame.
Add 30% for .50 cals.
Add 30% for extra barrel with forend (numbers matching).
Add 30% for Schuetzen model.
Add 25% for deluxe checkered wood with pistol grip.

BUL TRANSMARK LTD.

Current manufacturer located in Tel Aviv, Israel. Currently imported and distributed in North America by International Security Academy (ISA) located in Los Angeles, CA, beginning 1997. Previously imported until 1996 by All America Sales, Inc. located in Memphis, TN.

Grading	100%	98%	95%	90%	80%	70%	60%

PISTOLS: SEMI-AUTO

M-5 frame kits only are also available at $399 retail.

BUL IMPACT — 9mm Para., .40 S&W or. 45 ACP cal., double action, choice of 3.85 (compact) or 4.75 (full size) in. barrel, matte black polymer frame, choice of blue or hard chrome slide finish, fixed sights, 10 shot mag, approx. 26 oz. New 1999.

As this edition went to press, this model has yet to be imported. The Bul Impact has an optional locking system built into the thumb safety mechanism.

BUL STORM — same cals. as the Bul Impact, double action, all steel construction, 4¾ in. barrel, black polymer grips, choice of blue, chrome, or two-tone finish, 3 dot sights, 36 oz. New 1999.

As this edition went to press, this model has yet to be imported.

* **Bul Storm Compact** — similar to Bul Storm, except has 3.85 in. barrel, 33 oz. New 1999.

As this edition went to press, this model has yet to be imported.

BUL M-5 STANDARD GOVERNMENT — .38 Super, 9mm Para., .40 S&W, or .45 ACP cal., single action, 5 in. barrel, polymer double column frame, steel slide, aluminum speed trigger, checkered front and rear grip straps, blue finish, 10 shot mag., 31 oz. Importation began 1995.

Mfg.'s Sug. Retail	$670		$565	$500	$450	$400	$360	$330	$300

Add $28 for .38 Super or .40 S&W cal.

* **Bul M-5 Standard Commander** — similar to M-5, except has 4¼ in. barrel, 29 oz. New 1998.

Mfg.'s Sug. Retail	$670		$565	$500	$450	$400	$360	$330	$300

Add $28 for .38 Super or .40 S&W cal.

* **Bul M-5 Standard Street Comp.** — similar to M-5 Standard Commander, except has single port compensated 4¼ in. barrel, 32 oz. New 1998.

Mfg.'s Sug. Retail	$1,060		$960	$825	$700	$600	$500	$450	$375

Add $28 for .38 Super or .40 S&W cal.

Grading	100%	98%	95%	90%	80%	70%	60%

B

* **Bul M-5 Multi Caliber** — similar cals. as the M-5 Standard Government, includes 3 upper-ends including Commander length, another with adj. sights, and a third with a single port compensator, cased. New 1999.

  Mfg.'s Sug. Retail **$1,768** **$1,575** **$1,275** **$1,050** **$850** **$725** **$625** **$525**

BUL M-5 STANDARD IPSC — .38 Super, 9mm Para., .40 S&W, or .45 ACP cal., configured for IPSC competition, with custom slide to frame fit and match grade barrel bushing. New 1998.

  Mfg.'s Sug. Retail **$1,100** **$985** **$850** **$725** **$625** **$525** **$475** **$400**
  Add $111 for .38 Super or .40 S&W cal.

BUL M-5 STANDARD MATCH — IPSC custom race gun, includes multi-port compensator system. New 1998.

  Mfg.'s Sug. Retail **$1,655** **$1,500** **$1,200** **$1,000** **$825** **$700** **$600** **$500**
  Add $24 for .38 Super or .40 S&W cal.

BUL M-5 JET — same cals. as the M-5 Standard IPSC, features Commander length with 4¼ in. barrel and 4 port top compensation, 31 oz. New 1999.

  Mfg.'s Sug. Retail **$1,158** **$1,025** **$875** **$725** **$625** **$525** **$475** **$400**
  Add $51 for .38 Super or .40 S&W cal.

BUL M-5 MODIFIED — 9mm Para., .38 Super, .40 S&W or .45 ACP cal., designed for Modified class competition, features new Optima 2000 optic sight fitted to slide, 5 port top compensation. New 1999. carrying case, 38 oz. New 1998.

  Mfg.'s Sug. Retail **$2,116** **$1,850** **$1,650** **$1,425** **$1,200** **$1,000** **$825** **$700**

BUL M-5 TARGET — same cals. as the M-5 Modified, features 6 in. slide and barrel, choice of sights, and match grade oversize barrel bushing, includes 3 mags and carrying case, 38 oz. New 1999.

  Mfg.'s Sug. Retail **$1,584** **$1,425** **$1,150** **$950** **$800** **$675** **$575** **$475**
  Add $315 for Aristocrat Tri-state sights.

BUL M-5 STANDARD ULTIMATE RACER — top-level IPSC competition gun, includes 3 mags. and carrying case, 38 oz. New 1998.

  Mfg.'s Sug. Retail **$1,813** **$1,600** **$1,275** **$1,050** **$850** **$725** **$625** **$525**
  Add $65 for scope mount.
  Add $453 for fitted C-more optical sight.

BUSHMASTER FIREARMS

Currently manufactured by Bushmaster Firearms/Quality Parts Company located in Windham, ME. Older mfg. was by Gwinn Arms Co. located in Winston-Salem, NC 1972-1974. The Quality Parts Co. gained control in 1986. Distributor, dealer, or consumer direct sales.

PISTOLS: SEMI-AUTO

BUSHMASTER PISTOL — .223 Rem. cal., top bolt (older models with aluminum receivers) or side bolt (most recent mfg.) operation, steel frame (current mfg.), 11½ in. barrel, parkerized finish, adj. sights, wood stock, 5¼ lbs.

  $500 **$425** **$350** **$280** **$250** **$225** **$180**
  Last Mfg.'s Sug. Retail was $375.
  Add $40 for electroless nickel finish (disc. 1988).
  This model uses a 30 shot M-16 mag. and the AK-47 gas system.

Grading	100%	98%	95%	90%	80%	70%	60%

RIFLES: SEMI-AUTO, RECENT MFG.

B

BUSHMASTER RIFLE — .223 Rem. cal., semi-auto., top bolt (older models with aluminum receivers) or side bolt (current mfg.) operation, steel frame (current mfg.), 18½ in. barrel, parkerized finish, adj. sights, wood stock, 6¼ lbs., base values are for folding stock model.

	$425	$325	$280	$250	$225	$180	$140

Last Mfg.'s Sug. Retail was $350.

> Add $40 for electroless nickel finish (disc. 1988).
> Add $65 for fixed rock maple wood stock.
> This model uses a 30 shot M-16 mag. and the AK-47 gas system.

* **Rifle Combination System** — includes rifle with both metal folding stock and wood stock with pistol grip.

	$400	$360	$330	$300	$275	$250	$230

Last Mfg.'s Sug. Retail was $450.

XM15-E2S TARGET RIFLE — .223 Rem. cal., semi-auto patterned after the Colt AR-15, 20, 24, or 26 in. Govt. spec. match grade chrome lined barrel, manganese phosphate barrel finish, rear sight adj. for windage and elevation, Cage flash suppressor (disc. 1994), approx. 8.6 lbs. Mfg. began 1989 in U.S.

No Mfg.'s Retail	$895	$795	$700	$650	$575	$525	$475

> Add $70 for fluted barrel.
> Add $15 for 24 in. or $25 for 26 in. barrel.

* **XM15-E2S Carbine** — similar to above, except with telescoping buttstock and 11½ (disc. 1995), 14 (disc. 1994), or 16 in. barrel with (disc. 1994) or w/o suppressor, approx. 7 lbs. Mfg. began 1989.

No Mfg.'s Retail	$875	$775	$675	$625	$550	$495	$450

> Add $70 for fluted barrel.
> Add approx. $20 for dissipator model (features lengthened handguard).
> This model does not have the target rear sight system of the XM15-E2S rifle.

* **E2 Carbine** — .223 Rem. cal., features 16 in. match chrome barrel with new M16A2 handguard and short suppressor, choice of A1 or E2 sights. Mfg. 1994-95.

	$895	$825	$725	$650	$600	$550	$500

> Add approx. $50 for E2 sighting system.

V-MATCH COMPETITION RIFLE — .223 Rem. cal., top-of-the line match/competition rifle, flat-top receiver with extended aluminum barrel shroud, choice of 20, 24, or 26 in. barrel, 8.3 lbs. New 1994.

No Mfg.'s Retail	$975	$850	$725	$650	$575	$515	$465

> Add $70 for fluted barrel.
> Add $15 for 24 in. or $25 for 26 in. barrel.

* **V-Match Commando Carbine** — similar to V-Match Competition Rifle, except has 16 in. barrel. New 1997.

No Mfg.'s Retail	$960	$840	$715	$650	$575	$515	$465

> Add $70 for fluted barrel.

DCM COMPETITION RIFLE — .223 Rem. cal., includes DCM competition features such as modified A2 rear sight, 20 in. extra heavy 1 in. diameter competition barrel, custom trigger job, and free-floating hand guard. New 1998.

No Mfg.'s Retail	$1,375	$1,100	$975	$875	$800	$725	$650

M17S BULLPUP — .223 Rem. cal., semi-auto bullpup configuration featuring gas operated rotating bolt, 10 (C/B 1994) or 30★ shot mag., 21½ plain or 22 (disc.) in. barrel with flash-hider (disc.), glass composites and aluminum materials, phosphate coating, 8.2 lbs. New 1992.

C section

CETME

Previous manufacturer located in Madrid, Spain. CETME is an abbreviation for Centro Estudios Technicos de Materiales Especiales.

Grading			100%	98%	95%	90%	80%	70%	60%	

RIFLES: SEMI-AUTO

AUTOLOADING RIFLE — .308 Win. cal., 17¾ in. barrel, gas operated, roller cam action, similar to HK-91 in appearance, wood military style stock, aperture rear sight.

$715	$660	$605	$550	$440	$385	$330

C Z (CESKÁ ZBROJOVKA)

Current manufacturer located in Uhersky Brod, Czech Republic, 1936-current. Previous manufacture was in Strakonice, Czechoslovakia circa 1923-late 1950s. Newly manufactured CZ firearms are currently imported exclusively by CZ USA located in Kansas City, KS. Previously imported by Magnum Research, Inc. located in Minneapolis, MN until mid-1994. Previously imported before 1994 by Action Arms Ltd. located in Philadelphia, PA.

Ceská Zbrojovka simply means Czech weapons factory. CZ's full name is Ceská Zbrojovka a.s. Uhersky Brod, often abbreviated to CZUB a.s., meaning joint stock company. Uhersky Brod is the town the factory is located in. Zbrojovka Brno means weapons or arms factory located in Brno.

Zbrojovka Brno was built in 1916-1918, as a subsidiary of the Vienna Arsenal. After WWI, this factory was given the responsibility of providing the newly formed Czechoslavakian military with infantry weapons - specifically rifles and light machine guns. Circa 1923, pistol manufacture was transferred from Brno to Ceská Zbrojovka, located in the town of Strakonice, southwest of Bohemia. Since the location change, Zbrojovka Brno has never produced pistols on any great scale (please refer to the Brno section in this text for more information).

Ceská Zbrojovka Strakonice began developing many innovative and revolutionary pistol designs. These models, including the CZ-24, CZ-27, and CZ-52 are certainly well-known throughout the world. During the mid-1950s, CZ's facilities were converted to making motorcycles and precision engineering products. Trying to re-establish themselves in the commercial firearms industry, their U.S. partner currently is Springfield Armory.

Ceská Zbrojovka, located in the town of Uhersky Brod, was founded in 1936, as a subsidiary of Ceská Zbrojovka Strakonice, in a government decision designed to move firearms production further away from the German border, and out of the reach of German bombers. Uhersky Brod is located approx. 60 miles east of Brno. Before WWII, the factory produced aircraft machine guns (LK-30), the military pistol (CZ-38 in 9mm Para.), in addition to rifle Models Z242-Z247. During WWII, the factory was taken over by the Germans, and the facilities were used for the production of aircraft machine guns (German designed MG 17s) and related components for other models of military weapons.

Shortly after WWII, Ceská Zbrojovka Uhersky Brod resumed production of firearms for the civilian marketplace, including the CZ 241 semi-auto shotgun, and some O/U shotguns. The production of pistols commenced during the mid-1950s, with the introduction of the Model CZ-50 and other small pistol models named DUO in 6.35mm cal. Up to this point, the main pistol producer in Czechoslovakia was CZ

Stakonice as stated above. The CZ-52 pistol was the last model they produced. Since the end of the 1950s, Ceská Zbrojovka Uhersky Brod has become the sole producer of pistols.

After WWII, the Ceská Zbrojovka Uhersky Brod became massively involved in other types of production besides sporting and hunting firearms. Production reached a high during the 1980s, when hunting/sporting firearms manufacture resulted in approx. 30% of total production. The balance of manufacture was devoted to the production of power hydraulics for tractors, while gears and accessory drive boxes for speed reduction in turbo prop airplane engines made up the rest.

During 1964-1966, the Czech government transferred the production of long guns from Zbrojovka Brno to Ceská Zbrojovka Uhersky Brod. During the 1970s & 1980s, the arms production of Zbrojovka Brno accounted for less than 3% of its total capacity. The activities of this company were diverted into the production of typewriters, diesel motors, and automatic machine tools. While many firearm designs originated in Brno, Zbrojovka Brno was not the manufacturer. Because of this, the long guns manufactured in the mid-1960s, including the ZKK 600 - 602 series and ZKM rimfires, were manufactured in CZ Uhersky Brod. Because of the Czech government's decision to merge manufacture within both companies, the Brno trademark was also used by Ceská Zbrojovka Uhersky Brod.

This relationship was terminated in 1983, when both companies became part of the Agrozet conglomerate. While confusing, the arms utilizing the Brno trademark were not produced in Brno during this time. All firearms exported from Czechoslovakia at the time carried the Brno logo, and most of them were manufactured by Ceská Zbrojovka Uhersky Brod.

During 1975, Ceská Zbrojovka Uhersky Brod designed and began manufacture of the famous CZ-75 pistol. Production in quantity began in 1977. To date, over 700,000 CZ-75s have been produced. This semi-auto has been made in many variations and/or modifications to suit the many military and commercial contracts. During the mid-1980s, the CZ factory released the CZ-85, basically a CZ-75 with ambidextrous safety and slide stop. In the mid-1990s, production of the CZ-100 began - this new model featured a polymer frame. The CZ 550 line of rifles was also introduced at this same time.

With the Iron Curtain descending on Europe after WWII, communist bloc countries including Czechoslovakia had little exportation to the U.S. With the decline in communism during the past decade, more and more products (including firearms from the Czech Republic) will see their way into the U.S. without the 65% importation tax previously levied on goods from older communist bloc countries.

COMBINATION GUNS

CZ 584 SOLO — 12 ga. and 7x57mm Mauser rifle/shotgun combination , .222 Rem., .223 Rem. (new 1994), .243 Win. (new 1994), .30-06 (new 1994), 7mm Mauser (new 1994), and .308 Win. cals. also available, 24½ in. barrels, similar action to CZ 581 O/U shotgun, extractors or ejectors, rifle sights, approx. 7.4 lbs. Importation disc. 1986, resumed 1994 - disc. 1995, importation resumed 1999.

Mfg.'s Sug. Retail	$799	$695	$600	$550	$475	$425	$385	$350

Add 20% for ejectors.

PISTOLS: SEMI-AUTO, DISC.

The models listed below were made in Ceská Zbrojovka Strakonice, with the exception of some models manufactured in Ceská Zbrojovka Prague during the Nazi occupation of Czechoslovakia. The VZ38 was also produced in Uhersky Brod.

Grading	100%	98%	95%	90%	80%	70%	60%

"DUO" POCKET AUTOMATIC — .25 ACP cal., 6 shot, 2⅛ in. barrel, fixed sights, blue or nickel, plastic grips. Mfg. 1926-present (current Z pistol by Brno).

	$200	$185	$170	$150	$125	$100	$75

> Add 40% for WWII years.
>
> This model was manufactured by Dushek and is similar to the Z pistol equivalent by Brno.

CZ 22 — .380 ACP cal., derived from Mauser variation and manufactured under license from Mauser. Mfg. 1923 only.

	$400	$350	$320	$300	$275	$235	$200

CZ 24 — .380 ACP cal.

* **Standard Frame** — 8 shot mag. Over 175,000 mfg. 1924-38. Over half issued to Czech Army. Same general design as CZ 22 except no gap between trigger and frame. Production continued to 1941.

	$350	$320	$290	$260	$230	$195	$150

> Add $50 if Nazi proofed.
> Add 200% if Kriegsmarine proofed (scarce, be wary of counterfeit markings).

* **Long Frame** — 9 shot mag.

	$1,000	$850	$700	$550	$400	$350	$300

> Add $750 if fit with stock slot (either standard frame or long frame).

CZ 27 — .32 ACP cal.

* **"CESKA" Slide Legend Variation** — slanted slide grooves, high polish, available as Prewar Commercial, DR proofed, or Nazi proofed. Ser. range 16,000-21,500.

	$550	$450	$350	$300	$250	$200	$150

* **"BÖHEIMISCHE" Slide Legend Variation** — vertical slide grooves, high or medium polish, Nazi Police pistols dated 1941, 1942, or 1943 marked with Eagle/K on left trigger guard web, ser. no. range 21,500-261,000.

	$265	$225	$185	$150	$135	$120	$110

> Add 125% if 1941 dated.
> Add 100% if 1942 or 1943 dated.
> Add 200% if Kriegsmarine proofed (beware of counterfeit markings).

* **"fnh" Slide Legend Variation** — Medium polish or phosphate. Ser. range 261,000-476,000.

	$225	$185	$150	$125	$100	$85	$70

> Add 50% for late phosphate war finish.

* **"Silencer Barrel" Variation** — a small number of phosphate pistols were fitted with an extended barrel for silencer attachment. Usually in 450,000-460,000 ser. range.

	$950	$800	$600	$500	$400	$375	$350

* **Post WWII mfg.** — dated 1945, 1946, 1947, 1948, 1949, 1950, 1951. These models will have the "NARODNI PODNIK" inscription on slide.

> Currently, these variations average $250 in 95%+ condition while reworks (very common) average under $200.

VZ 38 DOUBLE ACTION AUTOMATIC — .380 ACP cal., 9 shot, double action only, 4⅝ in. barrel, fixed sights, blue, plastic grips. Mfg. 1938-1939.

	$400	$335	$275	$225	$170	$140	$125

> For Waffenampt proofed (E/WaA76 on barrel and left frame), usually phosphate finished and either unnumbered or in B291,000-B293,000 ser. range — add $1,000.
>
> Changed to Model 39T after 1939.

VZ 38 "BULGARIAN CONTRACT" — .380 ACP cal., 9 shot, single or double action, prominent safety on left frame. Usually in 420,000-423,000 ser. range.

	$1,350	$1,100	$900	$750	$600	$500	$400

Grading	100%	98%	95%	90%	80%	70%	60%

MODEL 1945 DOUBLE ACTION AUTOMATIC — .25 ACP cal., 8 shot, 2½ in. barrel, fixed sights, blue, plastic grips. Double action only. Mfg. between 1945-1952.

	$250	$200	$165	$150	$140	$130	$120

PISTOLS: SEMI-AUTO, RECENT MFG.

The CZ-52 was manufactured in Strakonice.

CZ-50/70 — .32 ACP cal., double action, blowback action, 3¾ in. barrel, loaded chamber indicator, 8 shot mag.

	$150	$125	$110	$100	$90	$80	$70

Used models are currently imported by Century International Arms, Inc. located in St. Albans, VT.

CZ-52 — 7.62 Tokarev or 9mm Para. cal., single action semi-auto, roller locking breech system, 4.9 in. barrel, 8 shot mag.

	$180	$150	$135	$125	$95	$85	$75

Add $40 for extra 9mm Para. barrel.

Used models are currently imported by Century International Arms, Inc. located in St. Albans, VT.

CZ-70 — 7.65mm/.32 ACP cal., double action, similar to Walther PP, 8 shot mag., 1 lb. 9 oz. Disc.

	$400	$350	$300	$275	$250	$225	$200

A very limited quantity of this model was imported.

CZ-75 (B) — 9mm Para. or .40 S&W (disc. 1997, reintroduced 1999) cal., Poldi steel, selective double action or double action only (.40 S&W only), thumb safety, 4¾ in. barrel, 10 (C/B 1994) or 15★ shot mag., currently available in black polymer (standard), matte blue (disc. 1994), high polish (disc. 1994), glossy blue (new 1999), dual tone (new 1998), or nickel (new 1994) finish, black plastic grips, early guns were shipped with two mags., B suffix model nomenclature was added 1998, 34.3 oz.

Mfg.'s Sug. Retail	$459	$390	$325	$280	$255	$225	$210	$195

Add $279 for CZ Kadet .22 LR adapter (includes .22 LR upper slide assembly and mag., new 1998).

"First Model" variations, mostly imported by Pragotrade of Canada, are identifiable by short slide rails, no half-cock feature, and were mostly available in high polish blue only. These early pistols sell for $1,000 if NIB condition, chrome engraved $1,500 (NIB), factory competition $1,350 (NIB).

★ **CZ-75 Semi-Compact** — 9mm Para. cal. only, 13 shot mag., choice of black polymer, matte, or high polish blue finish. Imported 1994 only.

	$350	$300	$275	$250	$230	$250	$200

Last Mfg.'s Sug. Retail was $519.

Add $20 for matte blue finish.
Add $40 for high polish blue finish.

★ **CZ-75 Compact** — similar to CZ-75, full-size frame, except has 3.9 in. barrel, 10 (C/B 1994) or 13★ shot mag., checkered walnut grips, 32 oz. New 1993.

Mfg.'s Sug. Retail	$499	$415	$350	$315	$285	$255	$230	$210

Add $279 for CZ Kadet .22 LR adapter (includes .22 LR upper slide assembly and mag., new 1998).

★ **CZ-75 Kadet** — .22 LR cal., black polymer finish, 10 shot mag, 4.88 in. barrel. New 1999.

Mfg.'s Sug. Retail	$486	$400	$335	$300	$285	$255	$230	$210

★ **CZ-75 Champion** — .40 S&W cal., dual tone finish, IPSC competition features including 2 port compensator, finger grooved synthetic grips, target trigger and sights, 4½ in. barrel, approx. 2.2 lbs. Importation began 1999.

Mfg.'s Sug. Retail	$1,484	$1,325	$1,100	$975	$850	$725	$600	$500

Grading	100%	98%	95%	90%	80%	70%	60%

* **CZ-75 ST** — .40 S&W cal., dual tone finish. New 1999.
  Mfg.'s Sug. Retail $1,038 $925 $850 $725 $600 $525 $450 $350

* **Model CZ-75 Special Editions** — 9mm Para. cal., similar to CZ-75, except has optional special edition finishes including all matte nickel, bright nickel frame, matte chrome, all brushed chrome, bright chrome, or gold frame, choice of matching finish slide, master blue slide, gold appointments, or master blue slide with gold appointments, price line refers to all matte nickel finish. Imported 1993-94 by Action Arms only.

  $525 $465 $415 $375 $335 $310 $285
  Last Mfg.'s Sug. Retail was $699.

  Add approx. $120 for matte nickel frame with master blue appts.
  Add approx. $180 for matte nickel with gold appts, matte nickel frame with master blue slide and gold appts, master blue with gold appts., or gold frame with master blue slide.

CZ-82 — 9x18mm Makarov cal., current Czech military sidearm, recent exportation to W. Germany in Makarov chambering.

This model is similar to the CZ-83 except for cal. Prices are similar to the model CZ-83.

CZ-83 — .32 ACP (disc. 1994, reintroduced 1999) or .380 ACP (new 1986), or 9mm Makarov (new 1999) cal., modern design, 3 dot sights, 3.8 in. barrel, choice of carry modes, blue (disc. 1994), glossy blue (new 1998), satin nickel (new 1999), or black polymer (disc. 1997) finish, black synthetic grips, 10 (C/B 1994), 12★ (.380 ACP) or 15★ (.32 ACP) shot mag., 26.2 oz. Mfg. began 1985, but U.S. importation started in 1992.
  Mfg.'s Sug. Retail $378 $315 $250 $220 $195 $180 $170 $160

* **CZ-83 Special Editions** — .380 ACP cal. only, similar to CZ-83, has optional special edition finishes including all matte nickel, master high polish blue, bright nickel frame, matte chrome, all brushed chrome, bright chrome, or gold frame, choice of matching finish slide, master blue slide, gold appointments, or master blue slide with gold appointments, price line refers to all matte nickel or high polish blue finish. Importation disc. 1994.

  $425 $375 $335 $295 $250 $225 $200
  Last Mfg.'s Sug. Retail was $569.

  Add approx. $90 for matte nickel frame with master blue appts.
  Add approx. $175 for matte nickel with gold appts, matte nickel frame with master blue slide and gold appts, master blue with gold appts, or gold frame with master blue slide.

CZ-85 (B) — 9mm Para. or 9x21mm (imported 1993-94 only) cal., variation of the CZ-75 with ambidextrous controls, new plastic grip design, sight rib, available in black polymer, matte blue (disc. 1994), or high-gloss blue (9mm Para. only, disc. 1994) finish, includes firing pin block and finger rest trigger, plastic grips, B suffix model nomenclature was added during 1998.
  Mfg.'s Sug. Retail $483 $410 $345 $310 $285 $255 $230 $210
  Add $225 for CZ Kadet .22 LR adapter (includes .22 LR upper slide assembly and mag., mfg. 1998 only).

* **CZ-85 Combat** — similar to CZ-85, except has fully adj. rear sight, walnut (disc. 1994) or black plastic (new 1994) grips, extended mag. release, and free dropping mag. Importation began 1992.
  Mfg.'s Sug. Retail $540 $440 $385 $350 $325 $295 $265 $240
  Add $19 for glossy blue, satin nickel, or duo-tone finish.
  Add $225 for CZ Kadet .22 LR adapter (includes .22 LR upper slide assembly and mag., mfg. 1998 only).

* **CZ-85 Champion** — .40 S&W or 9x21mm cal., similar to CZ-75 Champion, except has 3 port compensator. New 1999.
  Mfg.'s Sug. Retail $1,484 $1,325 $1,100 $975 $850 $725 $600 $500

Grading	100%	98%	95%	90%	80%	70%	60%

* **Model CZ-85 Special Editions** — 9mm Para. cal., similar to CZ-85, has optional special edition finishes including all matte nickel, bright nickel frame, matte chrome, all brushed chrome, bright chrome, or gold frame, choice of matching finish slide, master blue slide, gold appointments, or master blue slide with gold appointments, price line refers to all matte nickel finish. Imported 1993-94 only.

	$575	$495	$450	$395	$350	$325	$285

Last Mfg.'s Sug. Retail was $749.

Subtract $60 for matte nickel frame with master blue slide.
Add $130 for matte nickel frame with master blue appts, matte nickel with gold appts, matte nickel frame with master blue slide and gold appts, master blue with gold appts. or gold frame with master blue slide.

* **Model CZ-85 Combat Special Editions** — 9mm Para. cal., similar finishes to Model CZ-85 Special Editions, price line refers to all matte nickel finish. Limited importation 1994-95.

	$775	$725	$650	$595	$525	$450	$375

Last Mfg.'s Sug. Retail was $1,049.

Subtract $125 for matte nickel frame with master blue appts.
Add $245 for matte nickel with gold appts, matte nickel frame with master blue slide and gold appts, master blue with gold appts., or gold frame with master blue slide.

CZ-97 (B) — .45 ACP cal., single or double action, manual safety with firing pin block safety, 4.84 in. barrel with short recoil system, black polymer or glossy blue finish, checkered wood grips, double column 10 shot mag., last shot hold open slide, 40 oz. New 1998.

Mfg.'s Sug. Retail	$599	$515	$455	$385	$330	$295	$260	$240

Add $20 for glossy blue finish.

CZ-100 — 9mm Para. or .40 S&W cal., double action only with firing pin block and locked breech, w/o external manual safety, black polymer finish, 3 dot sights, high impact plastic frame, 10 shot mag., 3¾ in. barrel, approx. 24 oz. New 1996.

Mfg.'s Sug. Retail	$432	$370	$310	$280	$255	$225	$210	$195

CZ-122 B SPORT — .22 LR cal., semi-auto, single action only, 6 in. solid ribbed barrel with adj. rear sight, manual and firing pin block safety, last shot hold open slide, steel frame and slide with two-tone finish, ribbed black polymer grips, 10 shot mag., 30 oz. Limited mfg. 1998 only.

	$225	$190	$175	$160	$150	$140	$135

Last Mfg.'s Sug. Retail was $259.

RIFLES: BOLT ACTION, COMMERCIAL MFG.

Ceská Zbrojovka began manufacturing rifles circa 1936. Long gun production was discontinued between 1948-1964, with the exception of the massive military contracts during that time period.

CZ 513 HUNTER — .22 LR cal., entry level bolt action, 5 shot detachable mag., beechwood stock. Imported 1994 only.

	$195	$175	$150	$125	$95	$80	$65

Last Mfg.'s Sug. Retail was $225.

Add $30 for Farmer Model.
This model was imported exclusively by Action Arms.

CZ 527 (LUX) — .22 Hornet, .222 Rem., or .223 Rem. cal., Mauser style bolt action with silent safety, open sights, 5 shot detachable mag., hardwood or checkered walnut stock and forearm (CZ-527 FS), 6.2 lbs. Importation began 1995.

Mfg.'s Sug. Retail	$540		$465	$400	$365	$335	$300	$275	$250

Add $67 for Model CZ-527 FS with checkered walnut stock and forearm.

* **CZ 527 American Classic** — similar to CZ 527 Lux, scope rings included. New 1999.

Mfg.'s Sug. Retail	$540		$465	$400	$365	$335	$300	$275	$250

* **CZ 527 Carbine** — 7.62x39mm cal., carbine configuration with shorter barrel. New 1999.

Mfg.'s Sug. Retail	$540		$465	$400	$365	$335	$300	$275	$250

Grading	100%	98%	95%	90%	80%	70%	60%

CZ 537 — .243 Win., .270 Win., .30-06, .308 Win., or 7x57mm cal., detachable 4 shot (.243 Win. and .308 Win. cals. only) or 5 shot fixed mag., choice of regular or Mannlicher (.30-06 or .308 Win. cal. only) stock, hooded ramp front sight, 7¼ lbs. Importation 1995 only.

	$495	$425	$370	$330	$300	$275	$250

Last Mfg.'s Sug. Retail was $649.

Add $100 for Mannlicher style stock.

✳ CZ 537 Mountain Carbine — .243 Win. only, 19 in. barrel, 5 shot detachable mag., includes ring mounts, 7.1 lbs. Imported 1994 only.

	$525	$450	$375	$330	$300	$275	$250

Last Mfg.'s Sug. Retail was $669.

C

CZ 550 STANDARD — .243 Win., .270 Win. (disc. 1998), .30-06 (disc. 1998), .308 Win., 7x57mm (disc. 1995), 7x64mm (mfg. 1998 only), 6.5x55mm (mfg. 1998 only), or 9.3x62mm (mfg. 1998 only) cal., 4 shot detachable mag. (.243 Win. or .308 Win. only) or internal 5 shot, 23.6 in. barrel, receiver drilled and tapped for Remington 700 style scope base, no sights, checkered walnut stock and forearm, 7¼ lbs. Importation began 1995.

Mfg.'s Sug. Retail	$559	$475	$395	$340	$310	$285	$260	$240

Add $23 for .243 Win. or .308 Win. cal. with removable mag.

✳ CZ 550 Lux — various cals., similar to CZ 550 Standard, except has deluxe checkered walnut stock with Bavarian style cheekpiece and vent. recoil pad. New 1998.

Mfg.'s Sug. Retail	$559	$475	$395	$340	$310	$285	$260	$240

Add $50 for 9.3x62mm cal.

Add $23 for removable mag. (.22-250 Rem., .243 Win., or .308 Win. cal.)

➤ **CZ 550 Battue Lux** — similar to CZ 550 Lux, except has 20½ in. barrel with integral barrel fixed rear sight. Limited mfg. 1998 only.

	$450	$375	$330	$300	$280	$260	$240

Last Mfg.'s Sug. Retail was $519.

Add $30 for .243 Win. or .308 Win. cal. with removable mag.

✳ CZ 550 Magnum Standard — .300 Win. Mag., .375 H&H, .416 Rem. Mag. (disc. 1998), .416 Rigby, .458 Win. Mag., or 7mm Rem. Mag. (importation disc. 1997) cal., 4 or 5 shot fixed mag., 25 in. barrel with express rear sight, checkered hardwood stock, 9¼ lbs. Limited mfg. 1998 only.

	$525	$475	$440	$400	$375	$350	$335

Last Mfg.'s Sug. Retail was $595.

Add $40 for .416 Rem. Mag., .416 Rigby, or .458 Win. Mag. cal.

➤ **CZ 550 Magnum Standard Lux** — similar to CZ 550 Magnum, except has select checkered walnut. New 1998.

Mfg.'s Sug. Retail	$699	$600	$550	$475	$425	$385	$350	$335

Add $40 for .416 Rem. Mag., .416 Rigby, or .458 Win. Mag. cal.

✳ CZ 550 American Classic — .22-250 Rem., .243 Win., .270 Win., .30-06, .308 Win., 7x57mm, or 9.3x62mm cal., features American style walnut stock, fixed or detachable mag, scope rings included. New mid-1999.

Mfg.'s Sug. Retail	$567	$480	$400	$350	$310	$285	$260	$240

Add $15 for detachable mag.

Add $42 for 9.3x62mm cal. (fixed mag only).

✳ CZ 550 FS Mannlicher — similar to CZ 550 Standard, except has Mannlicher full-stock and 20½ in. barrel, 7¼ lbs. Mfg. 1996-98.

	$500	$450	$415	$380	$350	$325	$295

Last Mfg.'s Sug. Retail was $589.

Add $30 for .243 Win. or .308 Win. cal. with removable mag.

✳ CZ 550 Battue FS Mannlicher — similar to CZ 550 FS Mannlicher, except has integral barrel fixed rear sight. Limited mfg. 1998 only.

	$525	$465	$425	$395	$360	$330	$300

Last Mfg.'s Sug. Retail was $609.

Add $30 for .243 Win. or .308 Win. cal. with removable mag.

Grading	100%	98%	95%	90%	80%	70%	60%

* **CZ 550 Minnesota** — similar to CZ 550 Lux, except has select walnut stock w/o cheekpiece, and barrel has no sights. Limited mfg. 1998 only.

	$445	$375	$330	$300	$280	$260	$240

Last Mfg.'s Sug. Retail was $505.

Add $30 for .243 Win. or .308 Win. cal. with removable mag.

MODEL ZKM-452 — .22 LR or .22 Win. Mag. (disc. 1998) cal., bolt action, 5, 6 (.22 Mag. only), or 10 shot mag., 24.8 in. barrel, choice of black synthetic stock and matte nickel metal finish (new 1999) or uncheckered hardwood stock with Schnabel forend and blue metal finish (disc. 1998), adj. rear sight, 6.6 lbs. Importation began 1995 from CZ, earlier mfg. was by Brno.

Mfg.'s Sug. Retail	$344	$285	$225	$195	$170	$150	$135	$120

Add $50 for .22 Win. Mag. cal. (disc. 1998).

* **Model ZKM-452D (Deluxe/Lux)** — similar to ZKM-452 only with checkered walnut stock. Importation began 1995.

Mfg.'s Sug. Retail	$337	$390	$250	$215	$185	$165	$150	$125

Add $41 for .22 Win. Mag. cal.

* **Model ZKM-452 American Classic** — .22 LR or .22 Win. Mag. cal., 5 shot mag, American style walnut stock. New 1999.

Mfg.'s Sug. Retail	$337	$390	$250	$215	$185	$165	$150	$125

Add $41 for .22 Win. Mag. cal.

* **Model ZKM-452 Varmint** — .22 LR cal. only, similar to Model ZKM-452D, except has longer barrel and no sights. New 1998.

Mfg.'s Sug. Retail	$369	$310	$260	$220	$190	$170	$150	$140

ZKK 600 — .270 Win., .30-06, or 7x57mm cal., improved Mauser type action, 23½ in. barrel, checkered walnut stock, 5 shot internal mag., thumb safety, 7.2 lbs. Importation disc. 1995.

	$500	$425	$370	$330	$300	$275	$250

Last Mfg.'s Sug. Retail was $589.

ZKK 601 — .243 Win. or .308 Win. cal., otherwise similar to ZKK 600. Importation disc. 1995.

	$500	$425	$370	$330	$300	$275	$250

Last Mfg.'s Sug. Retail was $589.

ZKK 602 — .300 Win. Mag. (disc.), .375 H&H, .416 Rigby (new 1996), .416 Rem. (new 1996), 8x68mm (disc.), or .458 Win. Mag. cal., similar to ZKK 600, except has 25.2 in. barrel and 3 leaf express rear sight, 9.3 lbs. Disc. 1997.

	$675	$575	$495	$450	$395	$350	$310

Last Mfg.'s Sug. Retail was $799.

RIFLES: SEMI-AUTO

CZ-M52 (1952) — 7.62x45mm Czech cal., semi-auto, 20⅔ in. barrel, 10 shot detachable mag., tangent rear sight, this model was also imported again by Samco Global Arms, Inc. located in Miami, FL.

	$350	$295	$260	$230	$200	$175	$150

CZ-M52/57 (1957) — 7.62x39mm cal., later variation of the CZ-M52.

	$250	$215	$185	$160	$140	$125	$110

CZ-511 — .22 LR cal., semi-auto, blowback action, 22.2 in. barrel, uncheckered beechwood stock, flip-up rear sight, receiver top slotted for scope mounts, 8 shot mag., approx. 5½ lbs. Previously disc. 1986, importation resumed in 1998.

Mfg.'s Sug. Retail	$349	$295	$245	$210	$190	$175	$160	$150

Grading	100%	98%	95%	90%	80%	70%	60%

SHOTGUNS: O/U

CZ 581 SOLO — 12 ga., 2¾ in. chambers, boxlock action with Kersten upper locking mechanism, ejectors, checkered walnut stock and forearm, approx. 7.4 lbs. Importation disc. 1995, resummed during 1999.

Mfg.'s Sug. Retail	$799	$695	$600	$550	$475	$425	$385	$350

Add $30 for single trigger (disc.).

CABANAS

Currently trademark manufactured by Industrias Cabanas, S.A. in Aguilas, Mexico since 1949. Imported and retailed by Mandall Shooting Supplies, Inc. located in Scottsdale, AZ.

Please contact Mandall Shooting Supplies, Inc. for current information regarding this trademark, since to date, it has had limited importation.

CABELA'S INC.

Current sporting goods dealer and catalog company headquartered in Sidney, NE. Consumer direct (store or mail order catalog) sales only.

In addition to the models that are listed below, Cabela's also has a wide variety of black powder muzzleloading rifles and pistols in addition to replicas of popular older Colt and Winchester firearms. Cabela's should be contacted directly (see Trademark Index) to receive the most recent catalog on their complete firearms line-up and related accessories.

SHOTGUNS: SxS

HEMINGWAY MODEL — mfg. for Cabela's by V. Bernardelli located in Italy, ST, ejectors. Disc. 1994.

		$925	$775	$700	$640	$575	$525	$465

Last Mfg.'s Sug. Retail was $975.

AYA GRADE II CUSTOM — mfg. for Cabela's by AYA located in Eibar, Spain, ST, ejectors, similar to AYA Model II with Model 53 engraving and trim. Disc. and sold out.

		$1,295	$,1,150	$895	$775	$700	$640	$575

CALICO LIGHT WEAPONS SYSTEMS

Current manufacturer located in Sparks, NV since 1998. Previously located in Bakersfield, CA. Dealer and distributor sales.

Calico also makes select-fire machine gun pistols and carbines that are mfg. for military or law enforcement use only. These models do not appear in this publication.

A complete line of accessories is available for all Calico carbines and pistols.

RIFLES: CARBINES

LIBERTY 50-100 — 9mm Para. cal., 16.1 in. barrel, downward ejection, aluminum alloy receiver, synthetic stock with pistol grip (some early post-ban specimens had full wood stocks with thumbhole cutouts), 50 or 100 shot helical feed mag., ambidextrous safety, 7 lbs. New 1995.

Mfg.'s Sug. Retail	$765	$675	$575	$495	$425	$385	$350	$300

Add $90 for 100 shot helical feed mag.

Grading	100%	98%	95%	90%	80%	70%	60%

M-100 — .22 LR cal., semi-auto carbine, paramilitary design with folding buttstock, 100 shot helical feed mag., alloy frame, ambidextrous safety, 16.1 in. shrouded barrel with flash suppressor/muzzle brake, 4.2 lbs. empty. Mfg. 1986-94.

	$265	$225	$195	$175	$160	$150	$140

Last Mfg.'s Sug. Retail was $308.

C

* *M-100 FS* — similar to M-100, except has solid stock and barrel does not have flash suppressor. New 1996.

Mfg.'s Sug. Retail	$585	$510	$425	$385	$350	$315	$275	$250

M-101 — while advertised, this model was never mfg.

M-105 SPORTER — similar to M-100, except has walnut distinctively styled buttstock and forend, 4¾ lbs. empty. Mfg. 1989-94.

	$280	$235	$200	$175	$160	$150	$140

Last Mfg.'s Sug. Retail was $335.

M-106 — while advertised, this model was never mfg.

M-900 — 9mm Para. cal., retarded blowback action, paramilitary design with collapsible buttstock, cast aluminum receiver with stainless steel bolt, static cocking handle, 16 in. barrel, fixed rear sight with adj. post front, 50 (standard) or 100 shot helical feed mag., ambidextrous safety, black polymer pistol grip and forend, 3.7 lbs. empty. Mfg. 1989- 1990, reintroduced 1992-1993.

	$560	$475	$350	$300	$285	$270	$255

Last Mfg.'s Sug. Retail was $618.

* *M-900S* — similar to M-900, except has non-collapsible shoulder stock. Disc. 1993.

	$575	$485	$360	$300	$285	$270	$255

Last Mfg.'s Sug. Retail was $632.

* *M-901 Canada Carbine* — 9mm Para. cal., similar to M-900, except has 18½ in. barrel and sliding stock. Disc. 1992.

	$575	$475	$350	$300	$285	$270	$255

Last Mfg.'s Sug. Retail was $643.

This model is also available with solid fixed stock (Model 901S).

M-951 TACTICAL CARBINE — 9mm Para. cal., 16.1 in. barrel, similar appearance to M-900 Carbine, except has muzzle brake and extra pistol grip on front of forearm, 4¾ lbs. Mfg. 1990-94.

	$475	$395	$350	$300	$275	$250	$225

Last Mfg.'s Sug. Retail was $556.

* *M-951S* — similar to M-951, except has synthetic buttstock. Mfg. 1991-94.

	$485	$400	$350	$300	$275	$250	$225

Last Mfg.'s Sug. Retail was $567.

PISTOLS: SEMI-AUTO

M-110 — .22 LR cal., same action as M-100 Carbine, 6 in. barrel with muzzle brake, 100 round helical feed mag., includes notched rear sight and adj. windage front sight, 10½ in. sight radius, ambidextrous safety, pistol grip storage compartment, 2.21 lbs. empty. New 1989.

Mfg.'s Sug. Retail	$515	$435	$365	$295	$250	$225	$200	$180

M-950 — 9mm Para. cal., same operating mechanism as the M-900 Carbine, 6 in. barrel, 50 (standard) or 100 shot helical feed mag., 2¼ lbs. empty. Mfg. 1989-94.

	$450	$375	$325	$285	$260	$240	$225

Last Mfg.'s Sug. Retail was $518.

Many accessories were also available for this model.

CAMEX-BLASER USA, INC.

Previous importer/distributor of Blaser Jagdwaffen Gmbh rifles.

Previously imported Camex-Blaser rifles can be located in the Blaser section in this text.

CAPRINUS

Previous shotgun manufacturer located in Varberg, Sweden.

SHOTGUNS: O/U

CAPRINUS SWEDEN — 12 ga., boxlock action, ejectors, ST, stainless steel receiver, unique design incorporates breaking down without forearm disassembly, 29½ in. barrels with choke tubes, limited mfg. during early 1980s.

$3,750	$3,250	$2,850	$2,400	$2,000	$1,600	$1,200

Last Mfg.'s Sug. Retail was approx. $5,955.

CARL GUSTAF

Current manufacturer located in Eskilstuna, Sweden. No current importer. Previously imported by Hansen & Co. located in Southport, CT during 1994-95, and by Precision Sales International located in Westfield, MA during 1991-93.

RIFLES: BOLT ACTION

MODEL CG 2000 STANDARD GRADE — 6.5x55mm, 7x64mm, 9.3x62mm, .243 Win., .270 Win., .30-06, .308 Win., 7mm Rem. Mag., or .300 Win. Mag. cal., bolt action, Monte Carlo walnut stock with checkering and Wundhammer grip, 24 in. barrel, detachable 3 or 4 shot mag., with or without sights, cold-swaged barrel and receiver, 60 degree bolt, 3-way slide safety, 7½ lbs. Imported began 1991-95.

$1,325	$1,050	$875	$725	$575	$475	$375

Add $540 for Mag. cals.

Last Mfg.'s Sug. Retail was $1,535.

This model is supplied with individual 80 meter signed test targets. This model has also been imported as the Fairfax 2000 series.

* **Model 2000 Luxe Grade** — .270 Win., .30-06, .308 Win., or 6.5x55mm cal., features choice of regular or Mannlicher deluxe walnut stock. Imported 1995 only.

$1,695	$1,400	$1,200	$975	$825	$650	$475

Last Mfg.'s Sug. Retail was $1,935.

A Model 2000 Super-Luxe was also available in 6.5x55mm or .30-06 cal. - retail was $4,250.

MODEL 3000 — various cals., features Sauer action with non-rotating bolt. Previously imported by Aimpoint.

$675	$575	$475	$400	$375	$350	$325

STANDARD BOLT ACTION RIFLE — 6.5x55mm, 7x64mm, .270 Win., 7mm Rem. Mag., .308 Win., .30-06, or 9.3x62mm cal., 24 in. barrel, folding rear sight, checkered classic style stock. Mfg. 1970-1977.

$375	$325	$300	$275	$250	$225	$200

* **Monte Carlo stock**

$450	$395	$350	$300	$275	$250	$225

GRADE II — similar to Monte Carlo Standard, in .22-250 Rem., .25-06 Rem., 6.5x55mm, .270 Win., 7mm Rem. Mag., .308 Win., .30-06, or .300 Win. Mag. cal., select stock and rosewood pistol grip cap, and forearm tip.

$500	$425	$375	$325	$295	$275	$250

GRADE III — similar to Grade II, except fancy wood, deluxe high gloss finish.

$575	$475	$425	$350	$325	$300	$275

Grading	100%	98%	95%	90%	80%	70%	60%

DELUXE — similar to Grade III, except engraved floorplate and trigger guard, Deluxe French walnut, and jeweled bolt.

	$675	$575	$475	$400	$375	$350	$325

VARMINT TARGET MODEL — .222 Rem., .22-250 Rem., .243 Win., bolt action, fast lock time, or 6.5x55mm cal., 27 in. barrel, no sights, large bakelite bolt knob, target type stock. Mfg. 1970. Disc.

	$550	$495	$440	$385	$360	$320	$290

GRAND PRIX SINGLE SHOT TARGET — .22 LR cal., fastest lock time bolt action, 27 in. heavy barrel with adj. weight, no sights, target stock, adj. butt plate. Mfg. 1970. Disc.

	$550	$495	$440	$385	$360	$320	$290

CASARTELLI, CARLO

Current manufacturer located in Brescia, Italy. Imported and distributed by New England Arms Co. located in Kittery Point, ME.

Casartelli rifles and shotguns are available through special order only. Virtually any custom gun can be constructed to the customer's exact specifications and requirements. More information can be obtained by writing the above importer/distributor.

RIFLES

AFRICA MODEL - BOLT ACTION — various heavy and Mag. cals., action is square bridge type Mauser, full coverage game scene engraving appropriate to caliber, takedown, limited production.

Mfg.'s Sug. Retail	$12,000	$12,000	$10,200	$7,500	$5,900	$5,300	$4,700	$4,100

SAFARI MODEL - BOLT ACTION — standard cals., regular Mauser action, full coverage game scene engraving, limited production.

Mfg.'s Sug. Retail	$8,250	$8,250	$6,250	$5,900	$5,250	$4,950	$4,150	$3,650

KENYA - DOUBLE RIFLE — most standard and Mag. cals., sidelock action, elaborate game scene and/or scroll engraving, limited production.

Mfg.'s Sug. Retail	$35,000	$35,000	$24,250	$21,500	$17,750	$14,750	$12,000	$9,950

SHOTGUNS: SxS

SIDELOCK MODEL — various ga.'s, elaborate game scene and/or scroll engraving, limited production.

Mfg.'s Sug. Retail	$17,000	$17,000	$11,500	$9,200	$7,900	$6,500	$5,200	$4,250

CASPIAN ARMS, LTD.

Current parts manufacturer located in Hardwick, VT. Dealer direct sales only.

Caspian Arms currently fabricates both steel and alloy high quality, high capacity frames (standard and compact) and related small parts for the Colt Government Model 1911/A1, including a new damascus slide. Please contact them directly for current information on their extensive line of pistol-related components.

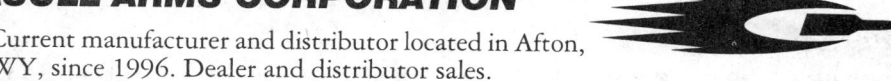

Grading	100%	98%	95%	90%	80%	70%	60%

PISTOLS: SEMI-AUTO

VIETNAM COMMEMORATIVE — .45 ACP, total production was 1,000, hand engraved by J.J. Adams, nickel plated, branch service medallion installed in grips. Limited mfg. 1986-93.

      $1,450   **$995**   **$795**

Last Mfg.'s Sug. Retail was $1,500.

Add $350 for gold plating.
Add $200 for serial numbers below RVN100.

This Vietnam Commemorative was also available in 24Kt. gold hand inlay edition for $14,000 — very limited production.

C

CASULL ARMS CORPORATION

Current manufacturer and distributor located in Afton, WY, since 1996. Dealer and distributor sales.

REVOLVERS

CA2000 MINI-FRAME REVOLVER — .22 LR or .32 ACP cal., double-action, fold up trigger, hammerless, manual safety, hardwood grips. New 1997.

Mfg.'s Sug. Retail   **$395**   **$350** **$295** **$250**

   As this edition went to press, prices had yet to be determined for the .32 ACP cal. CA2000.

CA3000 SMALL FRAME REVOLVER — .22 LR, .22 Mag., .32 Casull (disc. 1998), or .32 H&R Mag. cal., scaled-down frame is 80% the size of the large frame revolver. New 1997.

Mfg.'s Sug. Retail   **$1,495**   **$1,375** **$1,075** **$795**

   Add $225 per extra cylinder.

CA4000 LARGE FRAME REVOLVER — .357 Mag. (disc. 1998), .41 Mag. (disc. 1998), .44 Mag., .45 LC (new 1999), .45 Win. Mag. (new 1999), or .454 Casull cal., single action, various barrel lengths, stainless steel, hardwood grips. New 1997.

Mfg.'s Sug. Retail   **$1,995**   **$1,825** **$1,500** **$1,175**

   Add $245 per extra cylinder (.45 ACP, .45 Win. Mag., or .45 LC cal.).

RIFLES: BOLT ACTION

CAC5000 CONVENTIONAL — standard cals. include .270 Win., .300 Win. Mag., .375 H&H, .458 Win. Mag., or 7mm Rem. Mag. cal., features improved bolt action with conventional extraction, box mag. New 1997.

Mfg.'s Sug. Retail   **$2,495**   **$2,275** **$1,950** **$1,600**

CRS7000 CASULL RIFLE SYSTEM — .30 Casull or 6.5 Casull cal., patented bolt and extraction system, features new, all-metal bedding system allowing take-down and reassembly without affecting accuracy, box mag., stainless barrel without sights, uncheckered walnut stock, sporter or benchrest configuration. New 1997.

Mfg.'s Sug. Retail   **$2,995**   **$2,700** **$2,350** **$2,000**

   As this edition went to press, prices had yet to be established for the benchrest model.

CENTURY INTERNATIONAL ARMS, INC.

Current importer and distributor with offices located in Boca Raton, FL, beginning 1997. Century International Arms, Inc. was previously headquartered in St. Albans, VT until 1997.

CENTURY INTERNATIONAL ARMS INC.

Century International Arms, Inc. has imported a wide variety of used military rifles and pistols, including various Mauser rifle contract models, French Lebels and MAS models, Mannlichers, F.N. Model 49s, Lee Enfields, Hakims, Mosin-Nagants, Egyptian Rashids, Swedish Ljungman Model 42Bs, Chinese and Russian SKSs, and M-1 Carbines/Garands. Imported pistols include various WWI and WWII used military pistols including Mauser Broomhandles, Lugers, P.38s, Argentine mfg. M1911s, and French PA 35s. Additionally, some shotguns have also been imported, in addition to a wide range of accessories, including bayonettes, holsters, stocks, grips, mounts, scopes, etc. Because most of these items range in the $125-$550 price range, individual listings are not listed in this text. Most of these models are in good to new condition overall. In addition, surplus and currently manufactured ammunition is available at very competitive prices. Generally, these models offer good values to the shooter and some may be collectible. Because importation of Eastern Bloc military rifles has changed so dramatically over the past several years, Century International Arms, Inc. should be contacted directly (see Trademark Index) for a copy of their most recent catalog. For a more complete listing of earlier imported models, please refer to the 19th Edition.

RIFLES: SEMI-AUTO

CENTURION 99 SPORTER — .308 Win. cal., mfg. from genuine G3 parts, and American made receiver with integrated scope rail, pistol grip stock, matte black finish, refinished condition only. New 1999.

No Mfg.'s Retail	$750	$600	$550	$525	$500	$475	$450

CENTURY MFG., INC.

Current manufacturer located in Greenfield, IN. Distributed by Century Gun Distributing Inc., located in Greenfield, IN. Dealer or consumer direct sales.

This revolver design was originally manufactured in 1972 by Russell Wilson, who sandcasted the bronze frame (cloned from the Colt SAA configuration) in Evansville, IN. Gene Phelps purchased the manufacturing rights for this gun and formed a partnership with Earl Keller to produce a redesigned frame, also using sandcast bronze.

The original Century revolver was made in Evansville, IN beginning in 1973 (1973 was the 100th anniversary of the .45-70 Govt. cartridge - hence the term Century) and production was halted in 1976 at ser. no. 524. In late 1976, Phelps and Keller (the 2 original partners on the venture) dissolved their partnership and each began manufacturing their own version of the .45-70 revolver. Gene Phelps completely redesigned the gun's interior and began manufacturing the Heritage I, with an investment-cast steel frame, and without the Century's novel cross-bolt safety. Keller's Century Manufacturing, Inc. continued to produce the original Century, with some design refinements, and in 1985 the company was purchased by Dr. Paul Majors.

The current Century revolver features a manganese bronze frame and other components in addition to having a cross-bolt safety. They are produced in .45-70 and various other cals., in Greenfield, IN. Earl Keller died in 1986. The second series is being made in Greenfield, IN with limited production resuming in 1986. Earlier handmade "Evansville" Model 100s (disc.) are currently selling for between $2,500-$3,500, depending on the region.

REVOLVERS

Less than 1,300 Model 100s have been manufactured since 1976. Values below are for .45-70 cal. Other calibers are priced from $2,000 on up.

Grading	100%	98%	95%	90%	80%	70%	60%

MODEL 100 — .30-30 Win. (new 1987), .375 Win. (new 1986), .444 Marlin (new 1986), .45-70 Govt., .50-70 Govt. (new 1987), or .50-110 cal., single action 6 shot, manganese bronze frame, steel cylinder, 6½, 8, 10, or 12 (disc.) in. round or octagon barrel, unique crossbolt safety that locks the hammer, adj. sights, walnut grips, 5 lbs. 14 oz.

Mfg.'s Sug. Retail	$1,500	$1,350	$995	$850	$750	$625	$550	$495

    Add $750 for .50-70 Govt. cal.
    Add $110 for normal octagon barrel.
    Add $200 for stainless steel fabrication.

    Other options are available upon request for this model.

CHAMPLIN FIREARMS, INC.

Current custom manufacturer, gunsmith, and importer located in Enid, OK. Champlin Firearms was established in 1966. Direct sales only.

Champlin Firearms, Inc. manufactures handcrafted rifles built around a patented bolt action of their own design and manufacture. Most guns are built per individual customer order and specifications. Values will vary greatly depending on the configuration, desirability, and special order specifications. All Champlin rifles are built along classic lines with best quality wood and exemplary workmanship. They have been used successfully on safaris and have shot dangerous game throughout the world.

Champlin Firearms, Inc. also inventories a wide selection of high grade, top quality shotguns and rifles (especially top trademark doubles and bolt actions). Contact George Caswell (owner) directly for a current listing (please refer to Trademark Index). Additional services include a complete gunsmithing service for all grades of English double rifles and shotguns. Custom stocks are also built to individual customer specifications. All double rifles are test fired and checked thoroughly upon completion of manufacture or repair. Again, Champlin Firearms should be contacted for consultation and quotation regarding this additional work.

RIFLES: BOLT ACTION

BOLT ACTION RIFLE — various cals., round or octagon barrel, adj. trigger, each rifle is built to customer specifications. Values below represent base gun with standard wood, no options, and no engraving.

Mfg.'s Sug. Retail	$8,500	$8,500	$8,000	$7,000	$6,750	$6,000	$5,250	$4,500

    Many additional special order options are available on this model and Champlin Firearms should be contacted directly for price quotations.

CHAPUIS ARMES

Current manufacturer located in St. Bonnet Le Chateau, France. Currently, Chapuis Armes is exclusively imported by Chadick's, Ltd. located in Terrell, TX. Previously imported by GSI, Inc. located in Trussville, AL until 1995 and Armes De Chasse located in Chadds Ford, PA until 1993.

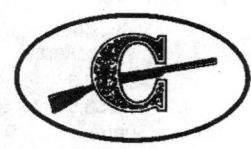

Chapuis rifles and shotguns are manufactured on a limited basis. Most of their emphasis is on high quality double rifles and shotguns. For further information regarding this respected French trademark, please contact the importer listed above.

Grading	100%	98%	95%	90%	80%	70%	60%

RIFLES: O/U

SUPER ORION C15 MODEL — .300 Win. Mag. or .375 H&H cal., notched boxlock action with ejectors, coin finish only, 23.6 in. barrels with quarter rib, engraved action, approx. 8 lbs. Imported 1995-96.

$8,250 $7,150 $6,250 $5,400 $4,200 $3,500 $3,150

Last Mfg.'s Sug. Retail was $9,195.

Add $2,900 for .375 H&H cal.

RIFLES: SxS

RGEX EXPRESS MODEL — .30-06, .300 Win. Mag., 7x65R, 8x57JRS, or 9.3x74R cal., double rifle, ejectors, boxlock action, 23.6 in. barrels, deluxe checkered walnut stock with cheekpiece, full line of options are available, 7 lbs. 6 oz. Imported 1989-1998.

Values below assume metric or .30-06 cal.

$7,675 $5,850 $4,925 $4,250 $3,650 $2,995 $2,450

Last Mfg.'s Sug. Retail was $8,500.

Add approx. $700 for .300 Win. Mag. cal.
Add approx. 60% for HGEX Express Supreme Model (engraved, not avail. in .300 Win. Mag. cal.).
Add 110% for HGEX Express Imperial Model (scroll engraved, not avail. in .300 Win. Mag. cal.).

UGEX UTILITY GRADE EXPRESS — similar to RGEX, except has select walnut. New 1998.

Mfg.'s Sug. Retail $4,950 $4,450 $3,950 $3,500 $2,950 $2,550 $2,100 $1,700
Add $500 for .300 Win. Mag. cal.

AFRICAN P.H. (PROFESSIONAL HUNTER) GRADE I — .30-06, .300 Win. Mag., .375 H&H, .416 Rigby, 9.3x74R, or .470 NE cal., notched boxlock action with English scroll border engraving, case colored receiver, selective ejectors, deluxe walnut stock with English cheekpiece.

Values below are for .375 H&H cal.

Mfg.'s Sug. Retail $7,950 $7,500 $6,250 $5,500 $4,500 $4,000 $3,500 $2,950
Add $2,550 for .470 NE cal.
Add $3,000 for .416 Rigby cal.
Subtract $1,500 for .30-06 or 9.3x74R.
Subtract $1,000 for .300 Win. Mag. cal.

This model was previously designated Express Agex Brousse.

* African PH Grade II — similar to Grade I, except has master signed scroll engraving with game scene on bottom of coin finished receiver.

Values below are for .375 H&H cal.

Mfg.'s Sug. Retail $9,950 $9,375 $8,500 $7,500 $6,250 $5,500 $4,750 $3,900
Add $2,550 for .470 NE cal.
Add $3,550 for .416 Rigby cal.
Subtract $1,500 for .30-06 or 9.3x74R.
Subtract $1,000 for .300 Win. Mag. cal.

BROUSSE MODEL — .375 H&H, .416 Rigby, or .470 NE cal., similar to Grade I Professional Hunter, except has full rose and scroll engraving coverage on coin finished receiver. New 1998.

Mfg.'s Sug. Retail $6,950 $6,400 $5,500 $4,700 $4,100 $3,500 $2,900 $2,450
Add $2,550 for .416 Rigby cal.
Add $2,000 for .470 NE cal.

Grading	100%	98%	95%	90%	80%	70%	60%

SAVANA MODEL — .30-06, .300 Win. Mag., .375 H&H, .416 R Chapuis (disc.), .416 Rigby, .470 NE, or 9.3x74R cal., deluxe version of the Agex Jungle, except has hand-engraved game scenes on action sides and Cape Buffalo head on floorplate of action, case colored (disc.) or coin finish.

Values below are for .375 H&H cal.

Mfg.'s Sug. Retail	$22,500	$19,950	$17,250	$15,250	$13,000	$10,500	$8,750	$7,500

Add $2,000 for .470 NE cal.
Add $3,000 for .416 Rigby cal.
Subtract $2,550 for .30-06 or 9.3x74R.
Subtract $2,000 for .300 Win. Mag. cal.

JUNGLE MODEL — .30-06, .300 Win. Mag., .375 H&H, .416 R Chapuis (mfg. 1993-96), .470 NE (new 1992), or 9.3x74R cal., boxlock action, case colored (disc.) or coin finish, special reinforced receiver with double underbites, 25⅝ in. barrels, fine English scroll engraving with 3 African animals, ejectors, select French walnut with compartment in pistol grip cap.

Values below are for .375 H&H cal.

Mfg.'s Sug. Retail	$12,950	$11,450	$9,750	$8,000	$7,150	$6,250	$5,400	$4,350

Add $2,000 for .470 NE cal.
Add $3,000 for .416 Rigby cal.
Subtract $2,000 for .30-06 or 9.3x74R.
Subtract $1,000 for .300 Win. Mag. cal.

* **Jungle Second Grade** — features elaborate engraving and best quality wood. Disc. 1996.

$26,000	$22,500	$19,000	$16,000	$13,000	$10,000	$8,750

Last Mfg.'s Sug. Retail was $29,395.

Add $3,900 for .470 NE cal.

EXPRESS AGEX AFRICA — same cals. as AGEX Jungle, notched boxlock action, master signed scroll engraving and African game scenes, selective ejectors, cased. Importation disc. 1994.

$19,250	$17,750	$15,250	$13,500	$11,250	$10,000	$9,000

Last Mfg.'s Sug. Retail was $20,954.

Add $2,896 for .470 NE cal.
Add $5,626 for .416 R Chapuis cal.

EXPRESS AGEX SAFARI — similar to AGEX Africa, except has top-of-the-line engraving and wood. Importation disc. 1994.

$29,000	$26,550	$22,350	$19,150	$16,950	$14,000	$12,000

Last Mfg.'s Sug. Retail was $30,375.

Add $2,040 for .470 NE cal.
Add $5,134 for .416 R Chapuis cal.

RIFLES: SINGLE SHOT

OURAL EXEL MODEL — .270 Win., .300 Win. Mag., 7mm Rem. Mag. cal., notched boxlock action, English scroll engraving, extractors, 23⅝ in. barrel, fitted and engraved scope mounts. Importation disc. 1994, reintroduced 1999.

Mfg.'s Sug. Retail	$5,250	$4,875	$4,200	$3,775	$3,250	$2,800	$2,400	$1,775

Add approx. 20% for Oural Luxe Model (features better engraving and wood).
Add approx. 58% for Oural Elite Model (features game scene engraving and presentation walnut).

SHOTGUNS

SPORTING CLAYS MODEL O/U — 12 or 20 (3 in. Mag.) ga., scalloped boxlock action, 27½ or 30 in. VR barrels, ST, case colored receiver with English scroll engraving. Limited importation 1997-98.

$3,675	$3,300	$2,900	$2,500	$2,100	$1,675	$1,300

Last Mfg.'s Sug. Retail was $3,995.

Grading	100%	98%	95%	90%	80%	70%	60%

ST. BONETT MODEL SxS — 12, 16, or 20 (3 in. Mag.) ga., boxlock with case colored (disc.) or coin finished sideplates featuring fine English scroll (disc.) or game scene engraving, 27½ in. monobloc barrels, DT's, ejectors, checkered straight grip walnut stock and forearm, hardshell case. Importation began 1997.

Mfg.'s Sug. Retail	$2,950	$2,675	$2,300	$2,000	$1,675	$1,300	$1,000	$850

CHAPUIS, P. ETS

Current manufacturer located in Saint-Bonnet le Chateau, France.

P. Chapuis specializes in custom order rifles and shotguns. Recently, this company has developed a process to color the receiver sideplates while using traditional engraving techniques - this results in a unique 3-D scene. Currently, this manufacturer has no U.S. importer and should be contacted directly (see Trademark Index) for more model information and current pricing. This is a different company than Chapuis Armes.

CHARLES DALY

See Daly, Charles.

CHARLIN ARMS

Previous manufacturer located in St. Etienne, France.

Charlin Arms previously made shotguns which were patterned after Darne firearms. Typically, they are very high quality and values seem to approximate the Darne guns. Once you have determined the comparable model in Darne, please refer to the Darne section in this book.

CHARTER 2000, INC.

Current manufacturer established during 1998 and located in Shelton, CT.

Charter 2000, Inc. acquired the rights to reproduce the original Charter Arms Undercover Model. Otherwise, it is not affiliated with Charter Arms in any way, nor is it responsible for repair or service on older Charter Arms handguns.

REVOLVERS

UNDERCOVER — .38 Spl. cal., double action, 5 shot, 2 in. barrel, steel or stainless steel construction, checkered synthetic grips with finger grooves, 18 oz. New late 1998.

Mfg.'s Sug. Retail	$225	$200	$180	$160	$145	$130	$120	$110

Add $30 for stainless steel.

CHARTER ARMS

Previously manufactured by Charco, Inc. located in Ansonia, CT 1992-96. Previously manufactured by Charter Arms located in Stratford, CT 1991-earlier.

PISTOLS: SEMI-AUTO

MODEL 40 — .22 LR cal. only, double action semi-auto., 3.3 in. barrel, 8 shot mag., 21½ oz., fixed sights, stainless steel. Mfg. 1984-86.

$265	$240	$220

Last Mfg.'s Sug. Retail was $319.

MODEL 79K — .32 or .380 ACP cal., double action semi-auto., 3.6 in. barrel, 7 shot mag., 24½ oz., fixed sights, stainless steel. Mfg. 1984-86.

$325	$300	$280

Last Mfg.'s Sug. Retail was $390.

Grading	100%	98%	95%	90%	80%	70%	60%

EXPLORER II & S II PISTOL — .22 LR cal., semi-auto survival pistol, barrel unscrews, 8 shot mag., black, gold (disc.), silvertone, or camouflage finish, 6, 8, or 10 in. barrels, simulated walnut grips. Disc. 1986.

	$90	$80	$70	$60	$55	$50	$45

Last Mfg.'s Sug. Retail was $109.

This model uses a modified AR-7 action.

Manufacture of this model was by Survival Arms located in Cocoa, FL.

MODEL 42T (COMPETITION II TARGET) — .22 LR cal. only, single action, 5.9 in. barrel, target model with checkered walnut grips, adj. sights, blue finish only. Mfg. 1984-1985 only.

$490	$450	$395	$350	$300	$260	$220

Last Mfg.'s Sug. Retail was $599.

REVOLVERS: DOUBLE ACTION

All Charter Arms revolvers have a hammer block safety system, 8 groove rifling, unbreakable beryllium copper firing pin, triple safety features, no sideplate, steel frames, and lifetime warranty to the original owner.

BONNIE & CLYDE SET — .32 H&R Mag. (Bonnie) and .38 Spl. (Clyde) cal., matched pair, 6 shot, 2½ in. fully shrouded barrel, wood laminate grips (color coordinated), blued finish, pistols individually marked Bonnie or Clyde on barrels, supplied with gun rugs. Mfg. 1989-91.

$425	$365	$335	$295	$260	$240	$220

LADY ON DUTY — .32 S&W or .38 Spl. cal., 5 (.38 Spl.) or 6 shot, 2 in. shrouded barrel, fixed sights, rose neoprene grips, cased. Mfg. 1995-96.

$195	$165	$145	$130	$115	$100	$85

Last Mfg.'s Sug. Retail was $219.

PATHFINDER — .22 LR or .22 Mag. (disc. 1989) cal., 6 shot, 2, 3, or 6 (disc. 1985) in. barrels, round butt, adj. sights, walnut grips, wide trigger and spur hammer. Disc. 1990.

$185	$150	$125	$110	$90	$70	$50

* *Pathfinder — Square Butt* — .22 LR or .22 Mag. (disc. 1989) cal., 6 in. barrel, square butt, otherwise similar to Pathfinder. Disc. 1990.

$190	$155	$125	$110	$90	$70	$50

* *Pathfinder Stainless* — .22 LR or .22 Mag. (disc. 1989) cal., stainless variation, 3½ in. shrouded barrel. Disc. 1990.

$185	$150	$130

UNDERCOVER — .32 S&W (disc. 1989) or .38 Spl. cal., 5 shot in .38 Spl., 6 shot in .32 S&W, 2 (.38 Spl.) or 3 in. barrel, wide trigger and spur hammer, fixed sights, .38 Spl. can also be ordered with pocket hammer. Disc. 1991.

$175	$145	$115	$100	$90	$85	$80

* *Undercover Stainless* — 2 in. shrouded barrel only. Disc. 1994.

$260	$195	$140

Last Mfg.'s Sug. Retail was $304.

UNDERCOVERETTE — .32 S&W L cal., similar to Undercover, 6 shot, 2 in. barrel, blue. Disc.

$155	$140	$110	$100	$90	$70	$55

BULLDOG — .44 Spl. cal., 5 shot, 2½ or 3 (disc. 1988) in. barrels, wide trigger and spur or pocket hammer, checkered bulldog grips (walnut or neoprene), blue or electroless nickel finish. Disc. 1991, reinstated 1994-disc.1996.

$225	$195	$155	$125	$110	$90	$70

Last Mfg.'s Sug. Retail was $268.

Add $22 for electroless nickel finish.

* *Bulldog Stainless* — 2½ in. bull or 3 (disc. 1989) in. regular barrel. Disc. 1991.

$195	$155	$125

Grading	100%	98%	95%	90%	80%	70%	60%

C

* **Target Bulldog** — .357 Mag. or .44 Spl. cal., 5 shot, 4 in. shrouded barrel, adj. sights, square butt only, blued finish. Mfg. 1980-1988.

| | $225 | $150 | $125 | $110 | $100 | $90 | $80 |

Last Mfg.'s Sug. Retail was $255.

   Subtract $10 for .357 Mag. cal.

* **Target Bulldog Stainless** — 9mm Federal, .357 Mag. or .44 Spl. cal., 5 shot, 5½ in. shrouded VR barrel, adj. sights, square butt target grips only, matte finished, 28 oz. Mfg. 1989-91.

| | $250 | $175 | $125 |

BULLDOG PUG — .44 Spl. cal., 5 shot, 2½ in. shrouded barrel, fixed sights, walnut or neoprene grips. Mfg. 1986-1993.

| | $240 | $195 | $160 | $130 | $110 | $100 | $90 |

Last Mfg.'s Sug. Retail was $279.

* **Bulldog Pug Stainless** — 2½ in. shrouded barrel. Mfg. 1987-1993.

| | $300 | $235 | $175 |

Last Mfg.'s Sug. Retail was $334.

BULLDOG TRACKER — .357 Mag. (.38 Spl.) cal., 5 shot, 2½, 4 (disc. 1989), and 6 (disc. 1989) in. bull barrels, adj. sights, blue only, checkered bulldog grips, square butt on 4 or 6 in. barrel only. Disc. 1986, - reintroduced 1989-91.

| | $185 | $150 | $125 | $110 | $100 | $90 | $80 |

MAGNUM PUG — .357 Mag. cal., 5 shot, fixed sights, 2.2 in. shrouded barrel, blue finish. Mfg. 1995-96.

| | $225 | $195 | $155 | $125 | $110 | $90 | $70 |

Last Mfg.'s Sug. Retail was $268.

POLICE BULLDOG — .32 H&R Mag., .38 Spl. or .44 Spl. cal., 5 (.44 Spl. only) or 6 shot, fixed sights, blue only, 3½ or 4 in. barrel, Neoprene grips or square butt (.44 Spl. only). Disc. 1991.

| | $175 | $140 | $120 | $105 | $95 | $85 | $75 |

   Add $20 for either .44 Spl. cal or 3½ in. shrouded barrel.

* **Stainless Police Bulldog** — .32 Mag., .357 Mag. (new 1989), .38 Spl. (disc. 1988 - reintroduced 1990) or .44 Spl. (new 1989) cal., 5 (.357 Mag. or .44 Spl.) or 6 (.32 Mag. or .38 Spl.) shot, square butt, 3½ or 4 in. shrouded barrel. Mfg. 1987-91.

| | $195 | $160 | $150 | $140 |

   Add $20 for .357 Mag. or .44 Special cal.

   Neoprene grips are standard on these models except for the .357 Mag. (square butt).

POLICE UNDERCOVER — .32 H&R Mag. or .38 Spl. cal., 6 shot, spur or pocket hammer, 2.2 in. shrouded barrel, checkered walnut grips, fixed sights, blue or electroless nickel (new 1994) finish. Disc. 1996.

| | $205 | $175 | $145 | $120 | $100 | $85 | $75 |

Last Mfg.'s Sug. Retail was $238.

   Add $14 for electroless nickel finish.

* **Stainless Police Undercover** — similar to Police Undercover. Disc. 1993.

| | $240 | $185 | $150 |

Last Mfg.'s Sug. Retail was $276.

OFF DUTY — .22 LR (new 1993), .22 Mag. (new 1994), or .38 Spl. cal., 5 (.38 Spl.) or 6 (.22 LR) shot, 2 in. barrel, fixed sights, conventional or DA only, blue, matte black (disc.), or electroless nickel (new 1994) finish. Disc. 1996.

| | $170 | $145 | $120 | $105 | $90 | $85 | $80 |

Last Mfg.'s Sug. Retail was $200.

   Add $39 for electroless nickel finish.
   Add $7 for double action only.

Grading	100%	98%	95%	90%	80%	70%	60%

* ***Stainless Off Duty*** — similar to Off Duty. Disc. 1993.

| | **$235** | **$180** | **$145** | | | | |

Last Mfg.'s Sug. Retail was $268.

PIT BULL — 9mm Federal (rare), .357 Mag. (disc. 1989), or .38 Spl. (disc. 1989) cal., 5 shot, 2½, 3½, or 4 (disc. 1989) in. full shrouded barrel, Neoprene grips, approx. 26 oz. Mfg. 1989-91.

| | **$230** | **$180** | **$150** | **$125** | **$115** | **$100** | **$90** |

* ***Stainless Pit Bull*** — 2½ or 3½ in. shrouded barrel. Disc. 1991.

| | **$240** | **$190** | **$155** | | | | |

RIFLES: SEMI-AUTO

AR-7 EXPLORER RIFLE — .22 LR cal., takedown, barreled action stores in Cycolac synthetic stock, 8 shot mag., adj. sights, 16 in. barrel, black finish on AR-7, silvertone on AR-7S. Camouflage finish new 1986 (AR-7C). Mfg. until 1990.

| | **$125** | **$100** | **$85** | **$75** | **$65** | **$55** | **$50** |

Last Mfg.'s Sug. Retail was $146.

In 1990, the manufacturing of this model was taken over by Survival Arms located in Cocoa, FL. Current mfg. AR-7 rifles will be found under the Henry Repeating Arms Company and Survival Arms headings.

CHIPMUNK RIFLES

Current trademark manufactured by Rogue Rifle Co., Inc., located in Prospect Oregon, since 1997. Previously manufactured by Oregon Arms, Inc. located in Prospect,OR 1988-1996. Previously manufactured by Chipmunk Manufacturing located in Medford, OR until 1988.

PISTOLS: SINGLE SHOT

SILHOUETTE PISTOL — .22 LR cal., bolt action design with 14⅞ in. barrel, iron sights, rear grip walnut stock. Mfg. 1984-88.

| | **$135** | **$115** | **$95** | **$80** | **$70** | **$60** | **$50** |

Last Mfg.'s Sug. Retail was $150.

RIFLES: BOLT ACTION, SINGLE SHOT

CHIPMUNK SINGLE SHOT RIFLE — .22 LR or .22 Win. Mag. (disc. 1987, reintroduced 1999) cal., manually cocked single shot, 16⅛ in. barrel, choice of black coated (new 1999), laminate (new 1999), or uncheckered Monte Carlo walnut stock, iron sights (adj. aperture rear), 30 in. overall length, 2½ lbs.

| Mfg.'s Sug. Retail | **$195** | **$160** | **$125** | **$100** | **$90** | **$80** | **$70** | **$60** |

    Add $16 for .22 Win. Mag.
    Add $15 for laminate stock.
    Subtract $10 for black coated wood stock.

* ***Bull Barrel Model*** — similar to Chipmunk Single Shot rifle, features 18⅛ in. bull barrel, 4 lbs. New 1999.

| Mfg.'s Sug. Retail | **$205** | **$170** | **$130** | **$100** | **$90** | **$80** | **$70** | **$60** |

    Add $16 for .22 Win. Mag.

* ***Deluxe Rifle*** — similar to standard rifle, except has deluxe hand checkered Monte Carlo walnut stock. New 1987.

| Mfg.'s Sug. Retail | **$247** | **$200** | **$170** | **$145** | **$110** | **$90** | **$75** | **$65** |

    Add $16 for .22 Win. Mag. cal.

* ***Chipmunk Special Edition*** — similar to Deluxe Model, except has hand engraving. Please contact the company directly for prices on this model.

Grading		100%	98%	95%	90%	80%	70%	60%

CHRISTENSEN ARMS

Current rifle manufacturer located in Fayette (custom shop) and St. George (factory), UT since 1995. Direct sales only.

Christensen Arms

PISTOLS: SINGLE SHOT

CARBON ONE PISTOL — various cals., graphite barrel lengths up to 14 in., less than 1 in. grouping for 3 shots at 100 yards, satin nickel receiver, approx. 2½-3 lbs. New 1999.

This model is basically a special order, and prices range from $749-$849.

RIFLES: BOLT ACTION

CARBON ONE — most popular cals., features Remington 700 BDL short action, barrel (up to 28 in. long) features a match grade Shilen/Christensen precision stainless steel barrel liner inside a larger diameter graphite/epoxy barrel casing, black synthetic stock, Shilen trigger, 5½-6½ lbs. New 1996.

Mfg.'s Sug. Retail	$2,750		$2,500	$2,200	$1,900	$1,600	$1,400	$1,225	$1,000

Variations include the Carbon Lite (5 lbs.), Carbon King (6-7 lbs., .25-.308 cal.), Carbon Cannon (includes muzzle brake, 6½-7½ lbs., Magnum series), or Carbon Tactical (includes muzzle brake, 6½ lbs., new 1997), or Carbon Conquest (new 1998).

CARBON ONE HUNTER — various popular cals., features Remington M700 (regular or stainless) or Winchester Model 70 stainless action, available with HS Precision or synthetic stock, large diameter graphite barrel with stainless steel barrel liner, 6½-71/4 lbs. New 1999.

Mfg.'s Sug. Retail	$1,499		$1,325	$1,150	$925	$800	$700	$600	$500

CARBONRANGER — .50 BMG and other popular long distance cals., large diameter graphite barrel casing (up to 36 in. long), no stock or forearm, twin rails extending from frame sides are attached to recoil pad, Omni Wind Runner action, bipod and choice of scope are included, 25-32 lbs. New 1998.

Mfg.'s Sug. Retail	$10,625		$9,950	$8,900	$8,000	$7,100	$6,200	$5,300	$4,400

RIFLES: SEMI-AUTO

CARBON ONE CHALLENGE (CUSTOM) — .22 LR cal., features Ruger 10/22 Model 1103 action with modified bolt release, synthetic bull barrel with precision stainless steel liner, 2 lb. Volquartsen trigger, Fajen brown laminated wood stock with thumbhole, approx. 3½ lbs. New 1996.

Mfg.'s Sug. Retail	$999		$895	$750	$600	$525	$475	$400	$350

* **Carbon One Challenge** — .22 LR cal., non custom shop variation, 4 lbs. New 1999.

Mfg.'s Sug. Retail	$599		$550	$495	$440	$400	$365	$330	$295

CARBON CHALLENGE II — similar to Carbon Challenge I, except has AMT stainless receiver and trigger, black synthetic stock, approx. 4½ lbs. Limited 1997-98 only.

			$1,150	$975	$875	$800	$725	$650	$525

Last Mfg.'s Sug. Retail was $1,299.

CHURCHILL GUNMAKERS

Current manufacturer established in 1891, and located in High Wycombe, England since 1996. Previously manufactured in London, England. This company underwent various trading forms until Churchill, Atkin, Grant & Lang Ltd. closed in 1981. Currently, Churchill Gunmakers' rifles and shotguns are manufactured in High Wycombe, England and while they are not imported into the U.S., these models are shown with U.S. prices if purchased in England (less VAT). Prices have been computed at 1 pound (£1.00)= $1.65.

Grading	100%	98%	95%	90%	80%	70%	60%

Churchill Guns are very fine quality, and could be ordered with many custom features. We will list both discontinued and current models and approximate values, but strongly urge competent appraisal if purchase or sale is contemplated.

RIFLES: BOLT ACTION

"ONE OF ONE THOUSAND RIFLE" — .270 Win., 7mm Rem. Mag., .308 Win., .30-06, .300 Win. Mag., .375 H&H, or .458 Win. Mag. cal., Mauser type bolt action, 5 shot standard, 3 shot mag. Magnum, 24 in. barrel, classic French walnut stock, swivel recoil pad with trap, trap pistol grip cap. Mfg. 1973 for Interarms 20th Anniversary, only 100 mfg.

	100%	98%	95%	90%	80%	70%	60%
	$1,400	$1,250	$1,000	$900	$750	$700	$600

RIFLES: SxS

PREMIERE MODEL — .30-06, .300 flanged Mag., .375 flanged Mag., .375 H&H Mag., .470 NE, .500 NE (3 in.) or 9.3x74R standard cal., larger calibers available upon request, 24 or 26 in. chopper lump barrels, double triggers, extended top tang, square or rounded body, color case hardened action, 9½-12½ lbs. Mfg. resumed 1998.

Mfg.'s Sug. Retail	$48,450	$44,000	$36,000	$30,000	$25,000	$20,000	$16,000	$13,750

Prices for current mfg. do not include VAT.

SHOTGUNS: O/U

PREMIERE MODEL — 12, 16, or 20 ga., similar barrels and bores as Premiere SxS Model engraved, sidelock, choice of monobloc or chopper lump barrels, auto ejectors, checkered pistol grip or straight stock, 6 (20 ga.) or 7¼ (12 ga.) lbs.

Mfg.'s Sug. Retail	$36,550	$33,915	$18,000	$14,000	$12,000	$10,000	$9,000	$7,500

Subtract $5,610 for monobloc barrels.
Add $2,210 for 20 ga. (current mfg.).
Add POR for 16 or 28 ga. and .410 bore.
Add $3,060 for SST (current mfg.).
Add 10% for ordering pair of matched guns.
Prices for current mfg. do not include VAT.

SHOTGUNS: SxS

All models below were built or finished to customer specifications pertaining to choking, chambers, barrel lengths, stock measurements, weight, engraving patterns. Standardized patterns did exist, however, for each model. The "XXV" designation referred to the 25 in. barrel length, which was a Churchill specialty and was also a registered trademark.

PREMIERE MODEL — most ga.'s, best quality, easy opening or standard opening, 25 (XXV), 28, 30, or 32 (disc.) in. barrels, any choke, sidelock, auto ejectors, double triggers standard, engraved, color case hardened action, checkered, straight or pistol grip stock, 5 lbs. 14 oz. (20 ga.) or 6 lbs. 6 oz. (12 ga.).

Mfg.'s Sug. Retail	$33,915	$30,000	$14,000	$12,000	$10,000	$9,000	$7,500	$6,500

Add $3,485 for 20 ga. (current mfg.).
Add POR for 16 or 28 ga. and .410 bore.
Add $3,060 for SST (current mfg.).
Add 10% for ordering pair of matched guns.
Prices for current mfg. do not include VAT.

IMPERIAL MODEL — most ga.'s, most barrel lengths, second quality sidelock model, ejectors, mostly standard opening, a few made as easy opening. Also mfg. in some double rifles. Disc.

	$13,500	$11,500	$9,500	$7,500	$6,500	$5,250	$4,000

Add 20% for 20 ga., 40% for 28 ga., and $1,000 for SST, or 35% for double rifle.
Subtract 10% for 16 ga.

Grading	100%	98%	95%	90%	80%	70%	60%

FIELD MODEL — 12 ga. only, most barrel lengths, third quality sidelock model. Disc.

	$9,000	$8,000	$7,000	$6,000	$5,000	$4,500	$3,500

HERCULES MODEL — most ga.'s, 25-30 in. barrels, best quality boxlock model, ejectors, easy opening or standard opening. Also made in some double rifles in .22 Hornet and similar cals.

	$9,000	$8,000	$7,000	$6,000	$5,000	$4,500	$3,500

Add 20% for 20 ga., 40% for 28 ga., $1,000 for SST, and 35% double rifle.
Subtract 10% for 16 ga.

UTILITY MODEL — all ga.'s (mostly encountered in 12 ga.), 25-30 in. barrels, second quality boxlock model, ejectors, checkered straight or pistol grip stock. Disc.

	$6,250	$4,500	$3,500	$3,000	$2,500	$2,000	$1,800

Add 20% for 20 ga., 40% for 28 ga., 60% for .410 bore, and $500 for SST.
Subtract 10% for 16 ga.

CROWN MODEL — 12, 16, 20 ga., or .410 (rare) bore, third quality boxlock model, various barrel lengths. Disc.

	$4,500	$3,500	$3,000	$2,500	$2,000	$1,600	$1,200

Add 20% for 20 ga., 40% for 28 ga., 60% for .410 bore, and $500 for SST.
Subtract 10% for 16 ga.

REGAL MODEL — 12, 16, 20, 28 ga., or .410 bore, second quality boxlock model introduced after WWII, released after Utility Model was disc. Premium for 28 ga. or .410 bore.

	$6,000	$4,300	$3,750	$3,100	$2,500	$2,000	$1,800

Add 20% for 20 ga., 40% for 28 ga., 60% for .410 bore, and $500 for SST.
Subtract 10% for 16 ga.

* **Regal Grade** — 12, 20, 28 ga., or .410 bore, best quality boxlock model, ejectors, standard opening, limited current production.

Mfg.'s Sug. Retail	$5,625		$4,800	$4,000	$3,500	$3,000	$2,500	$2,000	$1,800

CHURCHILL

Previous trademark imported and distributed by Ellett Brothers located in Chapin, SC until 1993. Previously imported (until 1988) by Kassnar Imports, Inc. located in Harrisburg, PA. Not affiliated with E.J. Churchill Gunmakers, Ltd.

In late 1988, the Churchill trademark was sold to Ellett Brothers located in Chapin, SC.

RIFLES: BOLT ACTION

HIGHLANDER — .25-06 Rem., .243 Win., .270 Win., .308 Win., .30-06, 7mm Rem. Mag., or .300 Win. Mag. cal., bolt action, 22 in. barrel, thumb safety, no sights, 3 or 4 shot mag., checkered walnut stock, 7½ lbs. Importation disc. 1991.

	$395	$350	$330	$300	$270	$240	$215

Last Mfg.'s Sug. Retail was $460.

Add $30 for iron sights (disc).

REGENT — same cals. as Highlander, deluxe checkered walnut with Monte Carlo comb and cheekpiece. Last imported by Kassnar in 1988.

	$555	$455	$385	$340	$300	$280	$260

Last Mfg.'s Sug. Retail was $610.

Add $30 for iron sights.

RIFLES: SEMI-AUTO

ROTARY 22 — .22 LR cal, beginners rifle, bolt hold-open device, adj. rear sight, 10 shot rotary mag. Imported 1989 only.

	$120	$105	$95	$85	$75	$65	$55

Last Mfg.'s Sug. Retail was $130.

Grading	100%	98%	95%	90%	80%	70%	60%

SHOTGUNS: O/U

MONARCH — 12, 20, 28 (disc.) ga., or .410 (disc.) bore, 25 (disc.), 26, or 28 in. vent. rib barrels, SST, extractors, boxlock action, DT, silver finish receiver with fine scroll engraving, checkered European walnut stock and forearm, 6½-7½ lbs.

$460	**$370**	**$340**	**$300**	**$250**	**$230**	**$210**

Last Mfg.'s Sug. Retail was $520.

> Add $67 for .410 bore with 26 in. barrels (disc.).
> Subtract $40 without SST.

* ***Monarch Turkey Gun*** — 12 ga. only, 24 in. barrels with matte finish. Imported 1990-1991 only.

$460	**$370**	**$340**	**$300**	**$250**	**$230**	**$210**

Last Mfg.'s Sug. Retail was $529.

SPORTING CLAYS MODEL — 12 ga. only, designed for sporting clays competition with 28 in. VR ported barrels with choke tubes, ejectors, raised target style VR, checkered high gloss finish stock and forearm, 7 lbs. 6 oz. Imported 1992 only.

$800	**$725**	**$650**	**$575**	**$500**	**$450**	**$395**

Last Mfg.'s Sug. Retail was $900.

WINDSOR III — 12, 20 ga., or .410 bore (disc.), 27 or 30 in. barrels, double bottom lock, antique silver finish receiver with fine scroll engraving, extractors, SST, vent. rib, checkered pistol grip and forend. Importation disc. 1991.

$550	**$495**	**$450**	**$380**	**$340**	**$300**	**$280**

Last Mfg.'s Sug. Retail was $625.

> Add $140 for Flyweight Model or choke tubes (disc.).
> Add $75 for .410 bore.

NEW WINDSOR IV — 12 or 20 ga., 3 in. chambers, boxlock action, silver receiver with full scroll engraving, 26 or 28 (12 ga. only) VR barrels with choke tubes, ejectors, SST, checkered walnut pistol grip stock with black rubber vent. recoil pad, finger grooved forearm, gloss finish, gold trigger, 5 year warranty. Mfg. 1992 only.

$625	**$525**	**$450**	**$375**	**$325**	**$295**	**$275**

Last Mfg.'s Sug. Retail was $690.

WINDSOR IV - DISC. — 12, 20, 28 ga., or .410 bore, 26-30 in. barrels, double bottom lock, antique silver finish receiver with fine scroll engraving, ejectors, SST, vent. rib, checkered pistol grip and forend. Interchangeable chokes became standard in 1989. Importation disc. 1991.

$725	**$640**	**$530**	**$470**	**$430**	**$395**	**$360**

Last Mfg.'s Sug. Retail was $852.

> Subtract $52 for 28 ga. or .410 bore.
> Subtract $100 if without choke tubes.

REGENT V — 12 or 20 ga., 27 in. barrels, double bottom lock, antique silver finish receiver with extra fine scroll engraving, ejectors, single trigger, vent. rib, checkered pistol grip and forend. Interchangeable choke tubes standard. Disc. 1986, reintroduced 1990-disc. 1993.

$895	**$795**	**$700**	**$620**	**$560**	**$510**	**$470**

Last Mfg.'s Sug. Retail was $1,100.

> This model was previously designated Regent VII until 1989 when it changed to the Regent V.

REGENT TRAP AND SKEET — 12 or 20 ga., 26 or 30 in. barrels, double bottom lock, antique silver finish receiver with sideplates engraved in fine scroll, ejectors, SST, vent. rib, checkered pistol grip and forend. Importation disc. 1991.

$795	**$650**	**$575**	**$540**	**$485**	**$440**	**$390**

Last Mfg.'s Sug. Retail was $963.

> Add $40 for trap variation.

Grading	100%	98%	95%	90%	80%	70%	60%

REGENT GRADE SHOTGUN/RIFLE COMBINATION — 12 ga. over either .222 Rem., .223 Rem., .243 Win. (disc.), .270 Win., .30-06, or .308 Win. cal., 25 in. barrels, double bottom lock, antique silver finish receiver with extra fine scroll engraving, ejectors, single trigger, vent. rib, checkered pistol grip and forend. Importation disc. 1991.

	$800	**$700**	**$635**	**$560**	**$510**	**$475**	**$440**

Last Mfg.'s Sug. Retail was $927.

C

SHOTGUNS: SxS

WINDSOR I — 10 (disc. 1988), 12, 16, 20, 28 ga., or .410 bore, double barrel, 23-32 in. barrels, Anson and Deeley boxlock, antique silver finish receiver with fine scroll engraving, extractors, double triggers, checkered pistol grip and forend. Importation disc. 1991.

	$550	**$465**	**$450**	**$385**	**$300**	**$250**	**$230**

Last Mfg.'s Sug. Retail was $653.

> Add $150 for 10 ga.
> Add $55 for 28 ga. or .410 bore.
> Add $30 for Flyweight Models (25 in. barrels - disc. 1988).

WINDSOR II — 12 or 20 ga., 26-30 in. barrels, Anson and Deeley boxlock, antique silver finish receiver with fine scroll engraving, ejectors, double triggers, checkered pistol grip and forend. Add $100 for 10 ga. (disc.). Importation disc. 1987.

	$595	**$485**	**$415**	**$350**	**$315**	**$270**	**$240**

Last Mfg.'s Sug. Retail was $638.

WINDSOR VI — 12 or 20 (disc.) ga., 25 or 28 in. barrels, sidelock, antique silver finish receiver with fine scroll engraving, ejectors, double triggers, checkered pistol grip and forend. Disc. 1987.

	$840	**$700**	**$600**	**$550**	**$510**	**$460**	**$420**

Last Mfg.'s Sug. Retail was $900.

ROYAL — 10, 12, 20, 28 ga., or .410 bore, DTs, extractors, checkered walnut stock and forearm, case hardened receiver. Imported late 1988-1991.

	$485	**$405**	**$370**	**$310**	**$275**	**$250**	**$230**

Last Mfg.'s Sug. Retail was $540.

> Add $20 for 28 ga.
> Add $74 for .410 bore.

SHOTGUNS: SEMI-AUTO

STANDARD MODEL — 12 ga. only, gas operated and shoots different loads interchangeably without alterations, 24, 26, 28 in. VR barrel, magazine cut-off, hand checkered walnut with satin finish, matte metal finish, includes ICT choke tubes. New 1990.

	$495	**$415**	**$375**	**$310**	**$275**	**$250**	**$230**

Last Mfg.'s Sug. Retail was $550.

＊ *Turkey Model* — similar to Standard Model, except has 24 in. barrel only. New 1990.

	$510	**$425**	**$380**	**$315**	**$275**	**$250**	**$230**

Last Mfg.'s Sug. Retail was $570.

WINDSOR GRADE — 12 ga. only, 26, 28, or 30 in. barrels, gas operation, anodized alloy receiver, vent. rib, checkered pistol grip and forend, 7½ lbs. Deluxe model includes polished receiver with etching.

	$380	**$320**	**$300**	**$275**	**$250**	**$225**	**$200**

Last Mfg.'s Sug. Retail was $420.

> Add $35 for choke tubes.
> Add $55 for Deluxe model.

Grading	100%	98%	95%	90%	80%	70%	60%

REGENT GRADE — 12 ga. only, 26, 28, or 30 in. barrels, gas operation, anodized alloy receiver, vent. rib, checkered pistol grip and forend, 7½ lbs. Deluxe model includes polished receiver with etching. Disc. 1986.

	$440	$365	$340	$320	$300	$285	$270

Last Mfg.'s Sug. Retail was $495.

Add $35 for choke tubes.
Add $55 for Deluxe model.

SHOTGUNS: SLIDE ACTION

WINDSOR GRADE — 12 ga. only, 26, 27, 28, or 30 in. barrels, double slides, anodized alloy receiver, vent. rib, checkered pistol grip and forend, 7½ lbs. Disc. 1986.

	$385	$330	$310	$275	$250	$225	$200

Last Mfg.'s Sug. Retail was $430.

CIMARRON F.A. CO.

Current importer/distributor/retailer located in Fredricksburg, TX. Currently importing Aldo Uberti, Armi San Marco, and D. Pedersoli firearms and black powder reproductions/replicas. Previously named Old-West Guns Co. Dealer sales only.

REVOLVERS: REPRODUCTIONS

The Cimarron Arms reproductions of the 1873 Colt Peacemaker, mostly mfg. by Uberti, with the exception of limited production by Armi San Marco, are available in two configurations listed below. These pistols are extremely accurate reproductions of the original Colt pre-war Peacemaker and are marked (and machined) the same as the originals, including serial numbers on frames, backstrap, trigger guard, and cylinder. Barrels are radiused and cylinders are beveled. Frames are color case hardened, stocks are walnut - choice of 4¾, 5½, or 7½ in. barrel. All Cimarron SAAs are currently barrel marked "- CIMARRON F.A. MFG. Co. FREDERICKSBURG, TX. U.S.A. -".

The "Old Model" configuration has the older style black powder frame, screw in cylinder pin retainer, and circular "bullseye" ejector head. The Standard Model includes the post-1890 style frame with spring loaded cross-pin cylinder retainer and "half-moon" ejector head. Only the Old Model is available in the authentic old style "charcoal blue" finish (sometimes referred to as fire-bluing).

During 1998, Cimarron introduced an antique finish that resembles the older, worn finish seen on many of the well-used, original Colt SAAs. This finish is a greyish-brown patina color, and certain areas of these guns (end of barrel, grip straps, frame/cylinder edges, and grips) have been artifically aged to give them an authentic "been carried and used for 100 years" appearance.

Add $40 for charcoal blue finish.
Add approx. $50 for antique finish.
Add $120 for custom nickel finish.
Add $45 for hand checkered walnut grips.
Add $600 for "A" style engraving (30% coverage) on SAAs listed below.
Add $700 for "B" style engraving (50% coverage) on SAAs listed below.
Add $1,000 for "C" style engraving (100% coverage) on SAAs listed below.
Add $1,125 for "Texas Cattle Brands" engraving pattern.

FRONTIER SIX SHOOTER — .22 LR (disc. 1995), .22 Mag. (disc.), .357 Mag., .38 Spl.(disc.), .38-40 WCF, .44 Spl. (new 1998), .44-40 WCF, or .45 LC cal., 4¾, 5½, and 7½ in. barrel lengths, steel backstraps and trigger guard.

* *Standard or Old Model*

Mfg.'s Sug. Retail	$469		$395	$300	$250	$220	$195	$175	$160

Add $30 for convertible .45 ACP cylinder.

✴ Sheriff's Model — .44-40 WCF or .45 LC cal., w/o ejector, 3 or 4 (disc. 1992) in. barrel, steel backstraps and trigger guard. Disc. 1998.

	$395	$300	$250	$220	$195	$175	$160

Last Mfg.'s Sug. Retail was $469.

✴ New Sheriff Model — .357 Mag., .44-40 WCF, .44 Spl., or .45 LC cal., 3½ in. barrel, with ejector, Old Model frame only. Importation began 1995.

Mfg.'s Sug. Retail	$469	$395	$300	$250	$220	$195	$175	$160

Add $30 for charcoal blue finish.
Add $35 for checkered walnut grips.

✴ Target Model — similar to Standard Model, except has fully adj. target rear sight, brass or steel backstrap. Importation disc. 1991.

	$355	$280	$255	$220	$195	$175	$160

Last Mfg.'s Sug. Retail was $400.

Add $40 for .357 Mag. cal.

This variation is available in the Standard Model configuration only and with standard finish.

MODEL P SAA — .32-20 WCF, .38-40 WCF, .357 Mag., .44-40 WCF, .44 Spl., or .45 LC cal., features either pinched frame or pre-war configuration, standard finish only, 4¾, 5½, or 7½ in. barrel. Importation began 1996.

Mfg.'s Sug. Retail	$469	$395	$295	$250	$220	$195	$175	$160

Add $30 for convertible .45 ACP cylinder.

EL PISTOLERO — .357 Mag. or .45 LC cal., similar to the Model P, except has brass backstrap and trigger guard, 4¾, 5½, or 7½ in. barrel, case hardened frame with blued barrel and cylinder. Mfg. 1997 only.

	$320	$275	$250	$225	$210	$195	$180

Last Mfg.'s Sug. Retail was $359.

BUNTLINE MODEL — .357 Mag., .44-40 WCF, or .45 LC cal., 18 in. barrel, brass or steel backstrap cut for shoulder stock. Disc. 1989.

	$355	$280	$255	$220	$195	$175	$160

Last Mfg.'s Sug. Retail was $400.

Add $10 for target sights.

BUNTLINE CARBINE — similar cals. to Buntline Model, except also includes .22 LR/.22 Mag. (convertible cylinders), 18 in. barrel, includes non-detachable shoulder stock with brass hardware and finger extension trigger guard. Importation disc. 1991.

	$380	$295	$260	$225	$195	$175	$160

Last Mfg.'s Sug. Retail was $440.

Add $20 for target sights.
Add $20 for .22 LR/.22 Mag. combo.

BUCKHORN — .44 Spl. or .44 Mag. cal., reinforced variation of the Cimarron SAA designed for more powerful cartridges, 4¾, 6 or 7½ in. barrel, brass or steel backstrap. Disc. 1993.

	$355	$285	$260	$220	$195	$175	$160

Last Mfg.'s Sug. Retail was $400.

✴ Buckhorn Convertible Model — .44 Mag./.44-40 WCF cylinders are included, 4¾, 6 or 7½ in. barrel. Disc. 1989.

	$375	$295	$265	$220	$195	$175	$160

Last Mfg.'s Sug. Retail was $427.

Add $12 for target sights.

✴ Buckhorn Target Model — .44 Spl. or .44 Mag. cal., 4¾, 6 or 7½ in. barrel, adj. rear sight. Importation disc. 1991.

	$370	$290	$265	$225	$195	$175	$160

Last Mfg.'s Sug. Retail was $420.

C

Grading	100%	98%	95%	90%	80%	70%	60%

* ***Buckhorn Buntline*** — .44-40 WCF, .44 Spl., or .44 Mag. cal., 18 in. barrel, fixed or target sights. Disc. 1989.

		$370	$285	$265	$220	$195	$175	$160

Last Mfg.'s Sug. Retail was $419.

Add $30 for target sights.

* ***Buckhorn Carbine*** — .44-40 WCF, .44 Spl., or .44 Mag. cal., 18 in. barrel, includes non-detachable shoulder stock with brass hardware and lanyard ring. Disc. 1990.

		$375	$290	$265	$220	$195	$175	$160

Last Mfg.'s Sug. Retail was $429.

Add $30 for target sights.

THUNDERER — .357 Mag., .44 Spl., .44-40 WCF or .45 LC cal., patterned after Colt's Thunderer Model, 3½ or 4¾ in. barrel with full ejector rod housing, birdshead grips, choice of case colored or nickel finish. Importation began 1994.

Mfg.'s Sug. Retail	$489	$410	$310	$260	$220	$195	$175	$160

Add $35 for checkered walnut grips.
Add $40 for convertible .45 ACP cylinder (4¾ in. only).

* ***Thunderer Long Tom*** — .357 Mag., .44-40 WCF or .45 LC cal., 7½ in. barrel. New 1997.

Mfg.'s Sug. Retail	$529	$440	$325	$275	$225	$200	$175	$160

Add $35 for checkered walnut grips.

U.S. 7TH CAVALRY CUSTER MODEL — authentic reproduction of original Colt military cavalry contract, 7½ in. barrel, marked U.S. on lower left frame, one piece walnut grips with military cartouche.

Mfg.'s Sug. Retail	$499	$430	$365	$315	$280	$260	$240	$220

Add $30 for charcoal blue finish.

U.S. CAVALRY MODEL P (A.P. CASEY) — .45 LC cal. only, 7½ in. barrel, Old Model frame. Mfg. 1996-97.

		$430	$365	$315	$280	$260	$240	$220

Last Mfg.'s Sug. Retail was $499.

U.S. ARTILLERY MODEL — Renaldo A. Carr 1895 U.S. Artillery Model Commemorative, 5½ in. barrel, limited mfg.

Mfg.'s Sug. Retail	$499	$430	$365	$315	$280	$260	$240	$220

U.S. ARTILLERY ROUGH RIDER — .45 LC cal. only, 5½ in. barrel, Old Model frame. New 1996.

Mfg.'s Sug. Retail	$499	$430	$365	$315	$280	$260	$240	$220

Add $30 for charcoal blue finish.

7TH CAVALRY CASED SET — U.S. Cavalry Model in case with accessories. Disc. 1990.

		$695	$625	$550	$500	$460	$420	$385

Last Mfg.'s Sug. Retail was $780.

WILD BILL ELLIOT TEXAS CATTLEBRAND — .45 LC cal. Mfg. 1994-96.

		$1,225	$1,025	$875	$750	$625	$550	$475

Last Mfg.'s Sug. Retail was $1,395.

JUDGE ROY BEAN COMMEMORATIVE — mfg. to commemorate Judge Roy Bean's Texas cattlebrand. Disc. 1996

		$1,500	$1,175	$995	$875	$750	$625	$550

Last Mfg.'s Sug. Retail was $1,695.

Grading	100%	98%	95%	90%	80%	70%	60%

SCHOFIELD MODEL NUMBER THREE — .38 Spl. (disc. 1997), .38-40 WCF (disc. 1997), .44 Russian/Spl., .44-40 WCF, .45 Schofield, .45 ACP (disc.), or .45 LC cal., available in 7 (Civilian or Military) or 5 (Wells Fargo only) in. barrel. Mfg. by Armi San Marco beginning 1996.

Mfg.'s Sug. Retail $849	$730	$640	$570	$515	$450	$400	$360

Add $100 for nickel finish.
Add $150 for custom nickel finish.

This model is also available as a "Little Big Horn" variation with sub-inspector markings and "SBL" cartouche.

REVOLVERS: REPRODUCTIONS, REMINGTON

These guns are reproductions of the Models 1875 and 1890.
Add $90 for nickel plating, $10 for charcoal blue finish on models listed below.

MODEL 1875 — .357 Mag., .44-40 WCF, or .45 LC cal., 7½ barrel. Disc. 1993.

	$340	$250	$200	$170	$155	$140	$120

Last Mfg.'s Sug. Retail was $390.

* *Model 1875 Carbine* — same cals. as Model 1875, 18 in. barrel, includes non-detachable shoulder stock with brass hardware and lanyard ring. Importation disc. 1990.

	$410	$340	$300	$265	$230	$200	$180

Last Mfg.'s Sug. Retail was $460.

MODEL 1890 — .357 Mag., .44-40 WCF, or .45 LC cal., 5½ or 7½ in. barrel. Disc. 1993.

	$340	$250	$210	$175	$160	$145	$125

Last Mfg.'s Sug. Retail was $390.

1871 ROLLING BLOCK TARGET PISTOL — .22 LR, .22 Hornet (new 1990), .22 Mag., or .357 Mag. cal., 9½ in. barrel. Importation disc. 1990.

	$250	$200	$180	$160	$140	$125	$110

Last Mfg.'s Sug. Retail was $280.

* *1871 Rolling Block Baby Carbine* — same cals. as Target Pistol, has 22 in. barrel and walnut stock and forearm, brass trigger guard and butt plate. Importation disc. 1990.

	$310	$245	$205	$170	$155	$140	$120

Last Mfg.'s Sug. Retail was $340.

RIFLES: REPRODUCTIONS, REMINGTON ROLLING BLOCK

ROLLING BLOCK SPORTING RIFLE — .45-70 cal., 30 in. barrel, walnut stock and forearm. Imported 1989-1990 only.

	$625	$565	$430	$395	$350	$320	$300

Last Mfg.'s Sug. Retail was $620.

* *Deluxe Rolling Block Sporting Rifle* — similar to standard model, except has select wood. Importation disc. 1990.

	$725	$640	$485	$450	$375	$340	$320

Last Mfg.'s Sug. Retail was $720.

REMINGTON ROLLING BLOCK LONG RANGE CREEDMOOR — .45-70 cal., 30 in. tapered octagon barrel, deluxe checkered walnut stock. Importation began 1997.

Mfg.'s Sug. Retail $1,295	$1,125	$825	$700	$625	$550	$500	$450

RIFLES: REPRODUCTIONS, SHARPS

MODEL 1874 SHARPS SPORTING RIFLE — .45-70 cal., 32 in. barrel, nickel silver front blade and forearm cap, checkered deluxe walnut stock, double set triggers. Importation began 1997.

Mfg.'s Sug. Retail $1,495	$1,295	$1,050	$850	$700	$625	$550	$500

Grading	100%	98%	95%	90%	80%	70%	60%

RIFLES: REPRODUCTIONS, WINCHESTER

HENRY RIFLE/CARBINE — .44-40 WCF, .44 Spl. (mfg. 1993-95), or .45 LC (new 1993) cal., brass frame, 24¼ in. barrel on rifle, 22 (disc. 1995, .44-40 WCF cal. only) in. barrel on carbine.

Mfg.'s Sug. Retail	$1,029	$875	$650	$550	$475	$400	$325	$295

Add $40 for charcoal blue or in-the-white finish.
Add $700 for standard engraving.
Add $875 for Lincoln Presentation engraving.
Previous to 1997, this model could also be special ordered with Grade A engraving ($450 extra), Grade B engraving ($550 extra), and Grade C engraving ($725 extra).

CIVIL WAR HENRY RIFLE — .44-40 WCF or .45 LC (new 1998) cal., 24 in. barrel, patterned after the U.S. issue original inspected by Chas. G. Chapman (C.G.C.) with military inspector's marks and cartouche, military sling swivels became standard in 1996. Importation began 1993.

Mfg.'s Sug. Retail	$1,049	$895	$675	$565	$495	$425	$350	$315

Add $80 for charcoal blue or in-the-white finish.

1866 SPORTING RIFLE (YELLOWBOY) — .22 LR (disc. 1993), .22 Mag. (disc. 1993), .38 Spl. (new 1995), .44-40 WCF, or .45 LC (new 1993) cal., brass receiver, 24 in. octagon barrel.

Mfg.'s Sug. Retail	$839	$725	$550	$440	$375	$285	$240	$200

Add $50 for charcoal blue finish (new 1997).
Add $700 for standard engraving (new 1997).
Add $1,125 for Mexican Eagle engraving (new 1997).
Add $500 (retail) for A engraving, $650 for B engraving, $1,175 for C engraving. Disc. 1996.

1866 YELLOWBOY CARBINE — similar to Model 1866 Sporting Rifle, except has 19 in. round barrel with 2 bands, saddle ring, uncheckered walnut stock and forearm.

Mfg.'s Sug. Retail	$829	$715	$550	$440	$375	$285	$240	$200

Add $40 for charcoal blue finish (new 1997).

* *1866 Trapper Carbine* — .44-40 WCF cal., 16 in. round barrel. Importation disc. 1990.

	$465	$385	$340	$320	$275	$240	$200

Last Mfg.'s Sug. Retail was $538.

* *1866 Yellowboy Indian Carbine* — .22 LR, .22 Mag., .38 Spl., or .44-40 WCF cal., 19 in. round barrel. Disc. 1989.

	$575	$475	$400	$350	$300	$260	$220

Last Mfg.'s Sug. Retail was $649.

This model has a photo engraved brass frame and has brass tacks in stock and forearm.

* *Red Cloud Commemorative Carbine* — same cals. as Yellowboy Indian Carbine, includes special engraving representing Oglalla Indian tribe symbols, brass tacks in forearm and stock. Disc. 1989.

	$575	$475	$400	$350	$300	$260	$220

Last Mfg.'s Sug. Retail was $649.

1873 SPORTING RIFLE — .22 LR (disc. 1993), .22 Mag. (disc. 1993), .357 Mag., .44-40 WCF, or .45 LC cal., 24¼ in. octagon barrel, case hardened receiver, full mag., iron sights.

Mfg.'s Sug. Retail	$949	$815	$625	$525	$450	$375	$325	$295

Add $40 for charcoal blue finish (new 1997).
Add $140 for Deluxe Model with pistol grip.
Add $500 (retail) for A engraving, $650 for B engraving, $1,075 for C engraving, or $1,250 for "1 of 1000" engraving.

* *1873 Short Rifle* — .44-40 WCF or .45 LC cal., features 20 in. octagon barrel, case hardened receiver, iron sights. Importation began 1990.

Mfg.'s Sug. Retail	$949	$815	$625	$525	$450	$375	$325	$295

Add $50 for charcoal blue finish.

Grading	100%	98%	95%	90%	80%	70%	60%

* *1873 Long Range Rifle* — .44-40 WCF or .45 LC cal., includes 30 in. octagon barrel with full mag., case hardened receiver, iron sights. New 1990.

Mfg.'s Sug. Retail	$999		$850	$650	$550	$475	$385	$330	$295

Add $50 for charcoal blue finish (new 1997).
Add $150 for Deluxe Model with pistol grip.

➤ *1873 Long Range Rifle 1 of 1,000* — .45 LC only, extensive engraving. Importation began 1995.

Mfg.'s Sug. Retail	$2,249		$1,875	$1,600	$1,400	$1,150	$925	$800	$700

* *1873 Saddle Ring Carbine* — .22 LR (disc. 1993), .22 Mag. (disc. 1993), .357 Mag., .44-40 WCF, or .45 LC cal., blued steel receiver, with or w/o saddle ring, 19 in. round barrel.

Mfg.'s Sug. Retail	$949		$815	$625	$525	$450	$375	$325	$295

Add $25 for saddle ring.
Add $50 for charcoal blue finish (new 1997).
Add $90 for nickel plating (disc.).

* *1873 Trapper Carbine* — .357 Mag. (new 1990), .44-40 WCF, or .45 LC (new 1990) cal., 16 in. barrel, blue finish only. Importation disc. 1990.

			$575	$475	$400	$350	$300	$260	$220

Last Mfg.'s Sug. Retail was $650.

1885 HI-WALL RIFLE — .40-65 WCF or .45-70 Govt. cal., 28 in. octagon barrel, case hardened finish on frame, iron sights. New 1998.

Mfg.'s Sug. Retail	$995		$850	$675	$575	$475	$375	$325	$295

CLARIDGE HI-TEC INC.

Previous manufacturer located in Northridge, CA 1990-1993. In 1990, Claridge Hi-Tec, Inc. was created and took over Goncz Armament, Inc.

All Claridge Hi-Tec firearms utilized match barrels mfg. in-house that were button-rifled. The Claridge action is an original design and does not copy other actions. Claridge Hi-Tec models can be altered (Law Enforcement Companion Series) to accept Beretta 92F or Sig Model 226 magazines.

PISTOLS

Add $40 for polished stainless steel frame construction.

L-9 PISTOL — 9mm Para., .40 S&W, or .45 ACP cal., semi-auto paramilitary design, 7½ (new 1992) or 9½ (disc. 1991) in. shrouded barrel, aluminum receiver, choice of black matte, matte silver, or polished silver finish, one piece grip, safety locks firing pin in place, 10 (disc.), 17, or 30 shot double row mag., adj. sights, 3¾ lbs. Mfg. 1991-1993.

			$525	$375	$300	$265	$225	$200	$175

Last Mfg.'s Sug. Retail was $598.

A trigger activated laser sighting scope was available in Models M, L, C, and T - add $395 for new mfg.

S-9 PISTOL — similar to L-9, except has 5 in. non-shrouded threaded barrel, 3 lbs. 9 oz. Disc. 1993.

			$475	$350	$280	$250	$225	$200	$175

Last Mfg.'s Sug. Retail was $535.

T-9 PISTOL — similar to L-9, except has 9½ in. barrel. Mfg. 1992-1993.

			$525	$375	$300	$265	$225	$200	$175

Last Mfg.'s Sug. Retail was $598.

M PISTOL — similar to L Model, except has 7½ in. barrel, 3 lbs. Disc. 1991.

			$500	$375	$300	$265	$225	$200	$175

Last Mfg.'s Sug. Retail was $720.

Grading	100%	98%	95%	90%	80%	70%	60%

RIFLES: CARBINES

C-9 CARBINE — same cals. as L and S Model pistols, 16.1 in. shrouded barrel, choice of composite or uncheckered walnut stock and forearm, 5 lbs. 12 oz. Mfg. 1991-1993.

$595	$525	$450	$395	$350	$300	$275

Last Mfg.'s Sug. Retail was $675.

Add $74 for black graphite composite stock.

Add $474 for integral laser model (with graphite stock).

This model was available with either gloss walnut, dull walnut, or black graphite composite stock.

LAW ENFORCEMENT COMPANION (LEC) — 9mm Para., .40 S&W, or .45 ACP cal., 16¼ button rifled barrel, black graphite composition buttstock and foregrip, buttstock also provides space for an extra mag., available in either aluminum or stainless steel frame, matte black finish, available with full integral laser sighting system. Limited mfg. 1992-93.

$650	$575	$495	$425	$375	$325	$295

Last Mfg.'s Sug. Retail was $749.

Add $400 for integral laser sighting system.

CLARK CUSTOM GUNS, INC.

Current custom gun maker and gunsmith located in Princeton, LA. Clark Custom Guns, Inc. has been customizing various configurations of both handguns, rifles, and shotguns, since 1950. It would be impossible to list within the confines of this text the many conversions this company has performed. It is recommended to contact this company directly (see Trademark Index) for an up-to-date price sheet and catalog on their extensive line-up of high quality competition pistols and related components. Custom rifles are also available in addition to various competition parts, related gunsmithing services, and a firearms training facility called The Shootout.

CLASSIC DOUBLES

Previous trademark manufactured in Tochigi City, Japan until 1987. Previously imported and distributed by Classic Doubles International, Inc. located in St. Louis, MO.

The factory closed in 1987, and all Classic Doubles remaining in inventory were sold to GU Wholesalers located in Omaha, NE in 1990. While a few models are still available through GU Wholesalers (call for availability), all values listed below reflect discontinuance of mfg. To date, there has been little collectibility in the Classic Doubles trademark. As a result, values are determined by the shooting value each model has to offer against other competing models in the same configuration. Also, in some regions of the country, 98% condition or less specimens may be priced lower than values shown in this section.

In late 1987, Winchester/Olin discontinued importation of their Japanese shotgun models (Models 101 and 23). At that point, Classic Doubles International, Inc. became the sole importer of these shotguns. There were very few changes made during this changeover of importation. The late manufacture Classic Double shotguns (Models 101 and 201) do not have the Winchester trademark or definitive Winchester proofmark stamped on the barrels. The Model 201 was a new model designation.

SHOTGUNS: O/U, MODEL 101 - FIELD MODELS

The late manufacture Classic Doubles have an interchangeable choke tube system compatible with the older Winchester manufactured models. Prices listed include a luggage style carrying case.

Values listed below for the Classic Doubles Shotguns assume NIB condition - subtract 10%-15% if without box, warranty card, and original shipping container (with packing materials).

Grading	100%	98%	95%	90%	80%	70%	60%

CLASSIC FIELD GRADE I — 12 or 20 ga., 3 in. chambers, vent. rib, 25½ or 28 in. vent. barrels with choke tubes, blued receiver with moderate scroll engraving, ejectors, checkered pistol grip or English stock and forearm, 6¼ - 7 lbs.

	$1,400	$1,250	$1,100	$1,000	$900	$825	$750

Last Mfg.'s Sug. Retail was $1,905.

WATERFOWL MODEL — 12 ga. only, 3 in. chambers, 30 in. barrels with vent. rib and choke tubes, matte blued receiver with moderate engraving, low gloss walnut stock with vent. recoil pad, 7 ¾ lbs.

	$1,150	$995	$895	$800	$700	$600	$500

Last Mfg.'s Sug. Retail was $1,520.

CLASSIC SPORTER — 12 ga. only, made for Sporting Clays competition, 28 or 30 in. vent. barrels and rib with choke tubes, quick detachable stock system, border engraved coin finished receiver with non-reflective matte surface on top frame and lever, checkered walnut stock and forearm, 7¾ lbs.

	$1,995	$1,500	$1,295	$1,150	$1,000	$900	$775

Last Mfg.'s Sug. Retail was $1,980.

> Add $965 for extra barrel.

CLASSIC FIELD GRADE II — 12, 20, 28 ga., or .410 bore, 28 in. VR barrels with choke tubes, deluxe walnut with round knob pistol grip stock and forearm with fine fleur-de-lis checkering, coin finished receiver (different sizes) with game scene engraving featuring hunting motifs on receiver sides and bottom, .410 bore bored M/F only, 6¼ - 7 lbs.

	$1,795	$1,475	$1,275	$1,100	$1,000	$900	$795

Last Mfg.'s Sug. Retail was $2,190.

> Add 15% for .410 bore (baby frame).
> Add 50% for 28 ga. (baby frame).
>
> The lack of supply of the Winchester/Olin Model 101 28 ga. small frame has caused a significant in demand for the .410 bore or 28 ga. The Grade II .410 bore is the only round knob pistol grip produced in both Winchester and Classic Doubles manufacture.

CLASSIC FIELD GRADE II TWO BARREL SET — 12 and 20 ga. barrels, both with Winchokes, 26 in. barrels - 20 ga., 28 in. barrels - 12 ga., coin finished receiver with game scene engraving and borders, 6½ (20 ga.) or 7 (12 ga.) lbs.

	$2,695	$2,175	$1,825	$1,550	$1,375	$1,200	$1,075

Last Mfg.'s Sug. Retail was $3,420.

SHOTGUNS: O/U, MODEL 101 - TARGET MODELS

CLASSIC TRAP SINGLE — 12 ga. only, over single 32 or 34 in. VR barrel with choke tubes, blued receiver with light engraving, choice of Monte Carlo or regular stock, recoil pad, 8½ lbs.

	$1,425	$1,250	$1,100	$1,000	$900	$825	$750

Last Mfg.'s Sug. Retail was $2,070.

CLASSIC TRAP — 12 ga. only, 30 or 32 in. vent. barrels and rib with choke tubes, finish and engraving similar to Classic Trap Single, choice of Monte Carlo or standard stock with recoil pad, 8¾ or 9 lbs.

	$1,300	$1,125	$1,000	$900	$825	$750	$675

Last Mfg.'s Sug. Retail was $1,905.

CLASSIC TRAP COMBO — includes one set of O/U barrels (30 or 32 in.) and one over single barrel (32 or 34 in.), choke tubes, choice of Monte Carlo or standard stock, 8¾ or 9 lbs.

	$2,125	$1,875	$1,600	$1,475	$1,300	$1,175	$995

Last Mfg.'s Sug. Retail was $2,825.

CLASSIC SKEET — 12 or 20 ga., 27½ in. vent. barrels and rib, choke tubes on 12 ga. only, smaller ga.'s are bored SK/SK, similar metal finish to Classic Trap models, 7¼ or 7¾ lbs.

	$1,695	$1,375	$1,175	$1,025	$900	$825	$750

Last Mfg.'s Sug. Retail was $1,905.

Grading	100%	98%	95%	90%	80%	70%	60%

* *Classic Skeet 4 ga. Set* — similar to Classic Skeet except has 4 barrels (12, 20, 28 ga., or .410 bore), 12 ga. has choke tubes, smaller ga.'s are bored SK/SK.

	$3,900	$3,500	$3,100	$2,875	$2,600	$2,300	$1,995

Last Mfg.'s Sug. Retail was $4,765.

SHOTGUNS: SxS

MODEL 201 CLASSIC — 12 or 20 ga., 3 in. chambers, forged steel monobloc with improved lug design, 26 in. choke tube barrels with vent. rib, high lustre bluing, no engraving, SST, ejectors, premium walnut stock and beavertail forearm with fancy checkering pattern, solid red rubber recoil pad, 6¾ - 7 lbs.

	$1,400	$1,200	$995	$775	$650	$575	$495

Last Mfg.'s Sug. Retail was $2,190.

Add $120 for 20 ga.

The 12 ga. could be ordered with choke tubes at no extra charge. Only 63 were mfg. with choke tubes and slight premiums are being asked.

* *Model 201 Classic Small Bore Set* — 28 ga. and .410 bore two barrel set, similar to Model 201 Classic except has smaller frame and overall dimensions, 28 in. VR barrels only bored IC/M on 28 ga. and M/F on .410 bore, very limited importation, 6 or 6½ lbs.

	$4,250	$3,650	$3,250	$2,800	$2,400	$1,950	$1,475

Last Mfg.'s Sug. Retail was $3,675.

CLERKE ARMS, LTD.

Current manufacturer located in Raton, New Mexico since 1997. Previously distributed by Competitor Corp. Inc., located in New Ipswich, NH. Dealer and consumer sales.

PISTOLS: SINGLE SHOT

COMPETITOR PISTOL — available in 16 centerfire and 2 rimfire cals., standard 14 in. barrel, features new uplifting C Breech gun system, extendor slide can be fitted to all Colt .45 ACPs and replicas with no frame modification, matte finish, checkered wood grips. New 1998.

Mfg.'s Sug. Retail	$389	$360	$300	$265	$240	$220	$200	$185

CLERKE PRODUCTS

Previous manufacturer located in Santa Monica, CA.

REVOLVERS: DOUBLE ACTION

DOUBLE ACTION REVOLVER — .22 S, L, LR, or .32 S&W Long cal., inexpensive double action revolvers that sold to dealers for $15 in 1971.

RIFLES: SINGLE SHOT

HI-WALL — single shot rifle, falling block replica of Winchester 1885 High Wall, lever operated, case hardened receiver, 26 in. barrel, available in most modern calibers, no sights, checkered walnut pistol grip stock, Schnabel forearm. Mfg. 1972-1974.

	$250	$225	$185	$175	$150	$140	$125

DELUXE HI-WALL — similar to Hi-Wall, except half octagon barrel, select wood and recoil pad.

	$300	$275	$235	$210	$180	$160	$145

CLIFTON ARMS

Previous manufacturer of custom rifles from 1992-1997 located in Medina, TX. Clifton Arms specialized in composite stocks (with or without integral, retractable bipod).

Grading	100%	98%	95%	90%	80%	70%	60%

Clifton Arms manufactured composite, hand laminated stocks that were patterned after the Dakota 76 stock configuration.

RIFLES: BOLT ACTION

CLIFTON SCOUT RIFLE — .243 Win. (disc. 1993), .30-06, .308 Win., .350 Rem. Mag., .35 Whelen, 7mm-08 Rem. (disc. 1993), or .416 Rem. Mag. cal., choice of Dakota 76, pre-64 Winchester Model 70, or Ruger 77 MK II (standard) stainless action with bolt face altered to controlled round feeding, Shilen stainless premium match grade barrel, Clifton synthetic stock with bipod, many other special orders were available, mfg. 1992-97.
$3,000 $2,350 $1,650

This model was available as a Standard Scout (.308 Win. cal. with 19 in. barrel), Pseudo Scout (.30-06 cal. with 19½ in. barrel), Super Scout (.35 Whelen or .350 Rem. Mag. with 20 in. barrel), or African Scout (.416 Rem. Mag. with 22 in. barrel).

COBRAY INDUSTRIES

See listing under S.W.D. in the S section of this text.

COGSWELL & HARRISON (GUNMAKERS), LTD.

Current manufacturer established in London, England during 1770.

In 1993, Cogswell & Harrison came under new management and have concentrated on building best quality guns utilizing Beesley or Purdey type sidelocks, Woodward styled O/Us, and a round action boxlock.

RIFLES: SxS

Prices indicated below are for manufacturer's suggested retail and 100% condition factors are listed in English pounds. All new prices do not include VAT. Values for used guns in 98%-60% condition factors are priced in U.S. dollars. Allow 12-14 months for delivery on boxlocks, 18-24 months on sidelocks.

BOXLOCK MODEL — various cals., boxlock action, custom order only. New 1999.

Currently, a standard boxlock double rifle in cals. .300 H&H - .470 NE is retailing for approx. £20,800, with standard fine engraving, and w/o case.

SIDELOCK MODEL — standard cals. include .300 H&H, .375 H&H, .465, .470 NE, .577, and .600 NE, Beesley or Purdey type action standard, also available with H&H type system, individually made per customer specifications, 8 lbs. 10 oz. - 14 lbs. 6 oz., depending on caliber. New 1999.

Mfg.'s Sug. Retail	£40,800	£40,800	$50,000	$42,000	$36,000	$30,000	$24,000	$18,000

Add £1,100 for .375 H&H cal.
Add £3,100 for .465 or .470 NE cal.

* Cals. .577 & .600 NE

Mfg.'s Sug. Retail	£50,500	£50,500	$60,000	$50,000	$42,000	$36,000	$30,000	$24,000

SHOTGUNS: O/U, SIDELOCK

WOODWARD TYPE — Woodward style action, finest materials, each gun custom built for individual specifications, delivery time approx. 18-23 months.

Mfg.'s Sug. Retail	£31,770	£31,770	$47,250	$41,000	$36,000	$29,500	$22,350	$16,750

Add £1,250 for 20 ga.
Add £3,500 for 28 ga.

Grading	100%	98%	95%	90%	80%	70%	60%

SHOTGUNS: SxS, OLDER MFG.

REGENCY — 12, 16, or 20 ga., 26, 28, or 30 in. barrels, any choke combination, hammerless Anson & Deeley system, boxlock, double triggers, auto ejectors, straight English stock.

	$2,750	$2,500	$2,250	$2,000	$1,800	$1,600	$1,375

Last Mfg.'s Sug. Retail was $3,200.

AMBASSADOR MODEL — same gauges and barrels as Regency, boxlock with false sideplates, auto ejectors, double triggers, engraved game scene or scroll rose motif, English stock.

	$3,650	$3,100	$2,850	$2,700	$2,500	$2,250	$1,995

Last Mfg.'s Sug. Retail was $4,000.

MARKOR — 12, 16, or 20 ga., 27½ or 30 in. barrel and choke, boxlock, double trigger, English stock. Disc.

	$1,500	$1,350	$1,200	$1,000	$950	$825	$700
Auto ejectors	$1,750	$1,500	$1,350	$1,200	$1,100	$900	$700

HUNTIC MODEL — 12, 16, or 20 ga., 25, 27, or 30 in. barrels, any choke, sidelock, auto ejectors, English style stock. Disc.

	$3,500	$3,200	$3,000	$2,800	$2,500	$2,175	$1,850

SST — add $400.

AVANT TOUT SERIES — 12, 16, or 20 ga., 25, 27½, or 30 in. barrels, boxlock, false sideplates, straight English stock, auto ejectors, series disc.

	$2,250	$1,925	$1,700	$1,495	$1,350	$1,200	$1,075

REX OR AVANT TOUT III — no sideplates.

	$1,800	$1,650	$1,500	$1,350	$1,200	$1,075	$895

SANDHURST OR AVANT TOUT II

	$2,500	$2,300	$2,150	$2,000	$1,750	$1,500	$1,225

KONOR OR AVANT TOUT I

	$2,850	$2,700	$2,500	$2,250	$2,000	$1,775	$1,500

Add $400 for SST.
Add 20% for 20 ga.
Subtract 10% for 16 ga.

BEST QUALITY — 12, 16, or 20 ga.'s, 25, 26, 28, or 30 in. barrels, any choke, hand detachable sidelock, auto ejectors, double triggers standard, English stock.

* *Primic Model* — disc.

	$5,750	$4,650	$4,150	$3,650	$3,050	$2,500	$1,950

* *Victor Model*

	$8,600	$6,250	$5,000	$4,350	$3,740	$3,000	$2,375

Add $400 for SST.
Add 20% for 20 ga.
Subtract 10% for 16 ga.

Note: Degree of engraving and grade of wood are the basic differences among models.

SHOTGUNS: SxS, BOXLOCK & SIDELOCK - CURRENT MFG.

Prices indicated below are for manufacturer's suggested retail and 100% condition factors are listed in English pounds. All new prices do not include VAT. Values for used guns in 98%-60% condition factors are priced in U.S. dollars. Allow 9-12 months for delivery on boxlocks, 18-23 months on sidelocks.

All models below are available in 12, 20, or 28 ga.

Grading	100%	98%	95%	90%	80%	70%	60%

REGENCY — scalloped boxlock action, DT's, 100% large scroll engraving coverage on receiver and tangs, light barrel engraving, checkered straight grip stock with teardrop. Introduced 1970 to commemmorate C&H's bicentennial.

Mfg.'s Sug. Retail £9,760 | £9,760 | $14,750 | $12,250 | $10,000 | $8,000 | $6,500 | $4,950

   Add £310 for 20 ga.
   Add £510 for 28 ga.

VICTORIA — features scalloped round body boxlock action with 100% medium scroll engraving coverage on receiver and tangs, moderate barrel engraving, select checkered stock and forearm.

Mfg.'s Sug. Retail £11,170 | £11,170 | $16,950 | $14,500 | $12,250 | $10,000 | $7,800 | $6,100

   Add £360 for 20 ga.
   Add £585 for 28 ga.

EXTRA QUALITY VICTORIA — similar to Victoria Model, except has better quality wood and more engraving.

Mfg.'s Sug. Retail £13,180 | £13,180 | $18,750 | $16,250 | $14,000 | $11,750 | $8,900 | $7,350

   Add £440 for 20 ga.
   Add £890 for 28 ga.

EXTRA QUALITY (SPECIAL) VICTORIA — top-of-the-line round boxlock action with best quality walnut and chopperlump barrels, removable crosspin, and other refinements.

Mfg.'s Sug. Retail £15,180 | £15,180 | $22,350 | $19,450 | $16,350 | $13,150 | $10,250 | $8,400

   Add £440 for 20 ga.
   Add £810 for 28 ga.

SELF-OPENING SLE SxS — sidelock action, best quality Beesley action and engraving, each gun custom built per individual specifications, delivery time approx. 18-23 months.

Mfg.'s Sug. Retail £27,170 | £27,170 | $41,000 | $36,000 | $29,500 | $22,350 | $16,750 | $12,500

   Add £1,250 for 20 ga.
   Add £3,500 for 28 ga.

COLT'S MANUFACTURING COMPANY, INC.

Current manufacturer with headquarters located in Hartford, CT.

Manufactured from 1836-1841 in Paterson, NJ; 1847 to 1848 in Whitneyville, CT; 1854 to 1864 in London, England; and from 1848 to date in Hartford, CT. Colt Firearms became a division of Colt Industries in 1964. In March, 1990, the Colt Firearms Division was sold to C.F. Holding Corp. located in Hartford, CT, and the new company is called Colt's Manufacturing Company, Inc. The original Hartford plant was closed during 1994, the same year the company was sold again to a new investor group headed by Zilkha Co., located in New York, NY. As this edition went to press, the company has taken the lead in conducting research into "smart gun" technology, and is considering the possibility of manufacturing handguns using personalized coded signals to unlock a gun for firing.

REVOLVERS: PERCUSSION

Prices shown for percussion Colts are for guns only. Original cased guns with accessories will bring a healthy premium over non-cased models (200-350% over a gun only is common). Be very careful when buying an "original" cased gun, as many fake cases have shown up in recent years.

If possible, it is advisable to procure a factory letter (available only within the following ser. no. ranges) before buying, selling, or trading Models 1851 Navy (ser. range 98,000-132,000), 1860 Army (ser. range 2,000-130,000), or 1861 Navy (ser. range 1-10,000). These watermarked letters are available by writing Colt Firearms in Hartford, CT, with a charge of $300 per serial number (if they can research it). Include your name

100%	98%	95%	90%	80%	70%	60%	50%	40%	30%	20%	10%

·and address, Colt model name, serial number, and check to: COLT HISTORIAN, P.O. Box 1868, Hartford, CT 06144. Please allow 4-6 weeks for a response.

Prices shown on the following pages for extremely rare Colt's firearms might not include values in the 90%, 95%, 98%, and 100% condition columns. Prices are very hard to establish since these excellent to mint specimens are seldomly seen or sold.

Revolvers: Percussion, Paterson Variations

POCKET MODEL PATERSON NO. 1 — also known as "Baby Paterson", .28 cal., 5 shot, 2½ in. to 4¾ in. octagon barrels, blued metal, varnished walnut grips. Serial range 1 to approx. 500. Standard bbl. marking "Patent Arms M'g Co. Paterson N.J.-Colt's Pt.". Centaur scene with four horse head trademark and "COLT" on 1¹¹⁄₁₆ in. cylinder of round or square type. Mfg. 1837-1838.

> This and all other Paterson models have 5 shot cylinders and serial numbers are not commonly in evidence externally. Disassembly of the arm is usually necessary to determine the serial number.
>
> The Pocket Model Paterson No. 1 (Baby Paterson) is the first production made handgun in Colt's Paterson, N.J. facility. It is very small in size, almost appearing as a toy or miniature.

* **Standard Production Model** — without attached loading lever.

N/A	N/A	$34,000	$27,000	$21,000	$18,500	$15,000	$13,250	$11,750	$10,250	$9,000	$8,000

* **Late Production Ehlers Model** — with attached loading lever, ³¹⁄₃₂ round back cylinder and recoil shield milled for ease of capping. Barrel marked "Patent Arms Paterson N.J.-Colt's Pt.". Approx. 500 mfg. including the Ehlers Model under Belt Model No. 2 Mfg. 1840-1843.

N/A	N/A	$37,750	$30,000	$23,000	$19,000	$15,500	$13,750	$12,250	$10,750	$9,500	$8,500

BELT MODEL PATERSON NO. 2 — .31 or .34 cal., 5 shot, 2½ in. to 5½ in. octagon barrels, blued metal, varnished walnut grips. Serial range 1- approx. 850 which includes the Belt Model No. 3. All standard production Belt Models No. 2 have straight bottom style grips. Standard bbl. markings "Patent Arms M'g Co. Paterson N-J. Colt's Pt.". Centaur scene with four horse head trademark and "COLT" on cylinder of round or square backed type. Mfg 1837-1840. Somewhat heavier than the Pocket No. 1 revolver.

* **Standard Production Model** — without attached loading lever.

N/A	N/A	$34,000	$27,000	$21,000	$18,500	$15,000	$13,250	$11,750	$10,250	$9,000	$8,000

* **Ehlers Model** — with attached loading lever, 1¹⁄₁₆ in. round back cylinder, recoil shield milled for ease of capping. Barrel marked "Patent Arms Paterson N-J. Colt's Pt.". Approx. 500 mfg. including the Ehlers Model under Pocket Model No. 1. Mfg. 1840-1843.

N/A	N/A	$41,500	$33,000	$26,000	$22,500	$19,000	$15,500	$13,500	$12,000	$10,600	$9,500

BELT MODEL PATERSON NO. 3 — .31 or .34 cal., 5 shot, 3½ in. to 5½ in. octagon barrels, blued metal, a few having case hardened hammers. Varnished walnut grips. Serial range 1- approx. 850 which includes the Belt Model No. 2. All standard production Belt Models No. 3 have the flared bottom style grips. Standard barrel markings "Patent Arms M'g Co. Paterson N-J. Colt's Pt." The square backed cylinder is seen less often than the more common round back, both bearing the Centaur scene with four horse head trademark and "COLT". With both Belt Models, revolvers exhibiting attached loading levers are less common than those without a lever. Mfg. 1837-1840.

* **Standard Model w/o Lever** — without attached loading lever.

N/A	N/A	$34,000	$28,750	$23,000	$19,500	$17,000	$15,000	$13,500	$11,750	$10,500	$9,250

* **Standard Model With Lever** — with attached loading lever and recoil shield milled for ease of capping (scarce).

N/A	N/A	$37,400	$31,000	$25,500	$22,500	$19,750	$17,500	$15,250	$13,500	$12,000	$10,750

100%	98%	95%	90%	80%	70%	60%	50%	40%	30%	20%	10%

HOLSTER MODEL NO. 5 — also known as "Texas Paterson" - .36 cal., 5 shot, 4 in. to 12 in. octagon barrels, blued metal with case hardened frame and hammer. All cylinders bear the stage coach hold-up scene. Varnished walnut grips of flared bottom style. Serial range 1 to approx. 1,000. As with all models of Patersons, the serial number usually cannot be seen without disassembly of the revolver. Very large and heavy compared to the other Paterson models. Enjoys more popularity with collectors because of its military and frontier use. Mfg. 1838-1840.

> Many specimens encountered in this variation show extreme use. Consequently, fine to mint specimens are quite rare and highly prized by collectors. Values are given for non-military marked specimens. Any specimen bearing an authenticated martial marking is truly a rarity and should be appraised individually. NOTE: Watch for fakes here. There are now many times more faked martial markings, often times on non-original Patersons, than there are originals.

* ***Standard Production Model W/O Lever*** — without attached loading lever, round or square backed cylinder.

N/A	N/A	$140,000	$105,000	$82,500	$66,500	$57,000	$49,000	$42,000	$37,000	$32,500	$28,000

* ***Standard Production Model With Lever*** — with attached loading lever, round backed cylinder and recoil shield milled for ease of capping.

N/A	N/A	$152,000	$110,500	$87,500	$73,500	$63,500	$55,000	$47,500	$41,500	$37,000	$32,500

Revolvers: Percussion, Walker Model

WALKER MODEL REVOLVER — .44 cal., 6 shot, 9 in. part round, part octagon barrel, blued metal with case hardened frame, lever and hammer. Cylinder left without finish, brass trigger guard. One piece walnut grips. Mfg. 1847; total production approx. 1,100. Ser. numbers beginning with no. 1 were applied for each of five different military companies (A,B,C,D, & E). The total for the military issue Walkers was approx. 1,000 revolvers; the remaining approx. 100 revolvers were produced for civilian distribution. Barrels marked "Address SamL Colt New-York City". Found on right side of barrel lug is "US" over "1847". Cylinder bears Texas Ranger/Indian fight scene. Various metal parts and walnut grips stamped with Govt. Inspectors' marks.

> Because of these arms being subjected to great extremes of use, they will exhibit high degrees of wear, often to the extent that most or all markings will be worn off. Replaced parts are common and many badly worn and damaged specimens have been extensively rebuilt and restored. NOTE: Use great caution when contemplating the purchase of a Walker. A multitude of out-and-out fakes and "antiqued" reproduction Walkers have been fed into the market over the past few decades. Some of these are old enough (and have aged enough naturally) to almost resemble an authentic specimen. Enlist the services of a qualified expert before your dollars are spent. Only 10-12% of the original production of approx. 1,100 specimens have been accounted for. The acquisition of an authenticated Walker revolver is the ultimate goal of serious Colt collectors.

* ***Standard Military Issue Model***

N/A	N/A	N/A	$250,000	$180,000	$150,000	$130,000	$87,500	$77,500	$67,500	$57,500	$52,500

* ***Limited Civilian Issue Model*** — serial range 1001 to approx. 1100. Similar to military model except Govt. inspectors' marks were not applied. Pricing is difficult on the civilian issue arms. They tend to be in considerably better condition than the much more common military specimens. The factors of scarcity and condition will often bring higher prices from the advanced collector of means, especially in the finer grades of condition. On the other hand, the collector appreciating military usage will pay more for military marked examples. This publication tries to reflect the latest trends on purchase of civilian models.

N/A	N/A	N/A	$245,000	$180,000	$145,000	$125,000	$90,000	$75,000	$65,000	$55,000	$50,000

100%	98%	95%	90%	80%	70%	60%	50%	40%	30%	20%	10%

Revolvers: Percussion, Dragoon Series

WHITNEYVILLE HARTFORD DRAGOON — .44 cal., 6 shot, 7½ in. part octagon, part round barrel, some of the left-over Walker parts were used in Dragoons, blued metal with casehardened frame, lever, hammer, brass trigger guard and steel cylinder bears Texas Ranger and Indian battle scene. Mfg. 1847. Total production approx. 240. Serial range approx. 1,100 to 1,340 in sequence following civilian Walkers.

* *Rear frame cut out for grips*

N/A	N/A	$135,000	$107,000	$86,500	$72,500	$60,000	$53,000	$47,000	$42,000	$38,000	$35,000

* *Straight rear frame*

N/A	N/A	$99,500	$74,000	$53,500	$46,500	$36,500	$30,000	$25,000	$22,000	$20,000	$18,500

FIRST MODEL DRAGOON — .44 cal., 6 shot, 7½ in. round and octagon barrel, blued metal with case hardened frame, lever, hammer, brass grip straps, silvered straps for civilian market, serial range numbered after Hartford Dragoon, 1341 to around 8000. Mfg. 1848-1850. Total production approx. 7,000. Oval cyl. slots, square back trigger guard, Texas Ranger and Indian fight scene on cylinder.

* *Military Model*

N/A	N/A	$48,000	$38,500	$27,500	$21,000	$16,750	$14,250	$11,000	$9,000	$8,000	$7,000

* *Civilian Model*

N/A	N/A	$40,000	$26,000	$22,000	$17,000	$13,000	$10,500	$8,000	$6,500	$6,000	$5,500

FLUCK MODEL DRAGOON — basically a First Model Dragoon, with 7½ in. altered Walker barrels and fully martially marked, should be extensively checked over, used to replace defective Walkers. Mfg. 1848. Total production 300. Serial range approx. 2,216 to 2,515.

N/A	N/A	$45,000	$35,000	$30,000	$23,000	$19,000	$17,000	$15,000	$11,000	$10,000	$9,500

SECOND MODEL DRAGOON — .44 cal., 6 shot, 7½ in. round and octagon barrel, serial range following the First Model Dragoon 8000-10,700. Mfg. 1850-1851. Texas Ranger and Indian fight scene on cylinder.

* *Military Model*

N/A	N/A	$39,000	$30,500	$23,500	$18,000	$14,750	$12,000	$10,000	$8,500	$7,500	$6,500

* *Civilian Model*

N/A	N/A	$34,500	$25,750	$20,000	$16,750	$13,250	$11,500	$9,500	$7,750	$6,500	$5,500

* *New Hampshire or Massachusetts* — notice state markings on front portion of trigger guard.

N/A	N/A	$42,500	$31,750	$24,750	$19,500	$15,750	$13,250	$11,250	$9,500	$8,500	$7,750

THIRD MODEL DRAGOON — .44 cal., 6 shot, 7½ in. round or octagon barrel, same basic features as earlier models, but with round trigger guard and rectangular cylinder slots, serial range approx. 10,200-19,600, some overlapping of numbers, with approx. 10,500 mfg. from 1851-1861. Texas Ranger and Indian fight scene on cylinder.

* *Third Model Dragoon*

N/A	N/A	$32,500	$22,000	$14,500	$12,000	$10,250	$8,900	$7,800	$6,900	$6,250	$5,750

* *Martially marked U.S.*

N/A	N/A	$35,000	$25,000	$19,500	$14,750	$12,750	$11,000	$9,500	$8,250	$7,250	$6,500

* *Third Model* — 8 in. barrel.

N/A	N/A	$37,000	$30,000	$27,000	$23,000	$19,500	$16,500	$14,000	$11,500	$9,500	$8,000

* *First and Second Variation* — shoulder stock model.

N/A	N/A	$37,500	$29,000	$23,000	$19,000	$16,350	$14,000	$11,750	$9,750	$8,250	$7,250

* *Third Variation*

N/A	N/A	$36,000	$28,500	$21,750	$18,500	$15,750	$13,250	$11,000	$9,000	$7,500	$6,500

* *C.L. Dragoon*

N/A	N/A	$48,500	$36,750	$28,000	$23,700	$20,250	$17,250	$14,750	$12,500	$10,500	$8,500

100%	98%	95%	90%	80%	70%	60%	50%	40%	30%	20%	10%

ENGLISH HARTFORD DRAGOON — basically a Third Model Dragoon, assembled at Colt's London factory, with unique serial range 1-700, some were assembled from earlier parts inventories, easy to spot with British proofs of crown over V and crown over GP, the blue was of the English type, many were engraved.

| N/A | N/A | $31,500 | $22,000 | $16,000 | $13,000 | $10,750 | $9,300 | $8,200 | $7,300 | $6,600 | $6,000 |

Recently, several 10-20% condition factory engraved English Dragoons have auctioned off at between $6,000-$8,500, depending on the amount of engraving.

1848 BABY DRAGOONS — .31 cal., 5 shot, 3, 4, 5, or 6 in. octagon barrels, most without loading lever, serial range 1-15,500, a scaled down version of the .44 caliber Dragoons, early ones with Texas Ranger scene and later ones with the holdup scene.

* *Type I* — left hand barrel stamping, Texas Ranger and Indian scene, approx. serial range 1-150.

| N/A | N/A | $15,000 | $11,750 | $9,850 | $8,650 | $7,500 | $6,500 | $5,750 | $5,250 | $4,850 | $4,350 |

* *Type II* — with Texas Ranger and Indian scene, 11,600 serial range, without loading lever.

| N/A | N/A | $11,500 | $8,250 | $7,100 | $5,750 | $4,750 | $3,950 | $3,300 | $3,000 | $2,800 | $2,600 |

* *Type III* — with Stagecoach scene and oval cylinder slots, serial range 10,400-12,000.

| N/A | N/A | $11,500 | $8,450 | $6,800 | $5,450 | $4,500 | $3,800 | $3,200 | $2,800 | $2,500 | $2,200 |

* *Type IV* — with Stagecoach holdup scene, rectangle cylinder slots, serial range 11,000-12,500.

| N/A | N/A | $12,000 | $9,000 | $7,250 | $5,900 | $5,000 | $4,250 | $3,600 | $3,250 | $3,000 | $2,750 |

* *Type V* — with Stagecoach holdup scene, rectangle cylinder slots and loading lever, serial range 11,600-15,500.

| N/A | N/A | $11,000 | $8,450 | $6,800 | $5,450 | $4,500 | $3,800 | $3,200 | $2,850 | $2,550 | $2,250 |

Revolvers: Percussion, Models 1849, 1851, 1855, 1860, 1861, & 1862

1849 POCKET MODEL — .31 cal., 5 or 6 shot, 3, 4, 5, and 6 in. octagon barrels, most with loading levers, blued metal with case hardened frame, lever and hammer, grip straps of brass (silver plated), or steel (silver plated or blued), stagecoach hold-up scene on cylinder, serial range 12,000 to 340,000. Mfg. 1850-1873.

* *First Type* — 4, 5, or 6 in. barrel, loading lever and small or large brass trigger guard.

| N/A | N/A | $3,375 | $2,625 | $2,050 | $1,650 | $1,350 | $1,000 | $750 | $600 | $550 | $475 |

* *Second Type* — 4, 5, or 6 in. barrel, loading lever and steel grip straps.

| N/A | N/A | $4,075 | $3,175 | $2,450 | $1,950 | $1,650 | $1,150 | $850 | $700 | $650 | $575 |

* *Wells Fargo Model* — 3 in. barrel, without loading lever and with small round trigger guard.

| N/A | N/A | $10,750 | $7,650 | $5,350 | $3,750 | $2,650 | $2,000 | $1,700 | $1,525 | $1,375 | $1,150 |

1849 LONDON POCKET MODEL — London pistols were of the same general configuration, but of better finish, serial range 1-11,000. Mfg. 1853-1857.

* *Early Type* — serial numbered under 1500, with small trigger guard and brass grip straps.

| N/A | N/A | $5,450 | $4,450 | $3,650 | $2,950 | $2,350 | $1,850 | $1,450 | $1,150 | $1,000 | $875 |

* *Late Type* — oval trigger guard and steel grip straps.

| N/A | N/A | $3,500 | $2,750 | $2,250 | $1,850 | $1,475 | $1,175 | $950 | $825 | $725 | $625 |

1851 NAVY — .36 cal., 6 shot, 7½ in. octagon barrel and loading lever, blued metal with casehardened frame, lever and hammer, one piece walnut finished grips, cylinder scene of Texas Navy battle with Mexico, serial range 1-highest recorded number was 215,348, three barrel addresses 1-74,000 (ADDRESS SAM COLT, NEW YORK CITY), 74,000-101,000 (ADDRESS SAM COLT, HARTFORD, CT.) 101,000-215,348 (ADDRESS COL. SAM COLT, NEW YORK, U.S. AMERICA). Mfg. 1850-1873.

* *First Model* — square back trigger guard, bottom wedge screw, serial range 1-1,250.

| N/A | N/A | $21,500 | $17,600 | $14,300 | $12,000 | $9,200 | $7,700 | $6,300 | $5,200 | $4,400 | $3,400 |

100%	98%	95%	90%	80%	70%	60%	50%	40%	30%	20%	10%

* **Second Model** — square back trigger guard, top wedge screw, serial range 1,250-4,000.

| N/A | N/A | $14,000 | $9,750 | $7,700 | $6,450 | $5,450 | $4,600 | $3,900 | $3,300 | $2,800 | $2,300 |

* **Third Model** — small round brass trigger guard, serial range 4,200-85,000.

| N/A | N/A | $6,600 | $5,250 | $4,100 | $3,400 | $2,800 | $2,300 | $1,900 | $1,550 | $1,250 | $995 |

* **Fourth Model** — large round brass trigger guard, serial range 85,000-215,348.

| N/A | N/A | $5,875 | $4,775 | $3,975 | $3,175 | $2,600 | $2,125 | $1,750 | $1,425 | $1,175 | $900 |

C

* **Iron Gripstrap Model** — most often seen in fourth model.

| N/A | N/A | $7,400 | $6,000 | $4,925 | $4,175 | $3,425 | $2,750 | $2,200 | $1,750 | $1,425 | $1,125 |

* **Martially Marked U.S. Navies** — brass or iron gripstrap.

| N/A | N/A | $10,750 | $7,500 | $6,000 | $4,750 | $3,750 | $2,900 | $2,325 | $1,875 | $1,500 | $1,200 |

* **Cut for shoulder stock** — first and second type (like third model Dragoon).

| N/A | N/A | $13,500 | $9,000 | $7,000 | $5,500 | $4,500 | $3,750 | $3,000 | $2,450 | $1,950 | $1,475 |

* **Third Type** — four screw frame.

| N/A | N/A | $8,650 | $7,250 | $6,000 | $4,850 | $3,850 | $3,100 | $2,500 | $2,000 | $1,650 | $1,325 |

51 NAVY LONDON MODEL — basically the same gun as the Hartford piece with London barrel address, with British proof marks in serial range 1-42,000. Mfg. 1853-1857.

* **Early First Model** — serial range below 2000, brass grip straps and small trigger guard.

| N/A | N/A | $7,500 | $6,000 | $5,025 | $4,225 | $3,475 | $2,800 | $2,250 | $1,800 | $1,475 | $1,175 |

* **Late Second Model** — balance of production, large round trigger guard, steel grip straps, all London parts.

| N/A | N/A | $6,925 | $5,625 | $4,725 | $3,975 | $3,275 | $2,575 | $2,000 | $1,650 | $1,375 | $1,100 |

1855 SIDEHAMMER POCKET MODEL (ROOT MODEL) — .28 cal., had 3½ in. octagon barrel, .31 cal. usually had 3½ in. or 4½ in. round barrel. Blued with case hardened lever and hammer, one piece wraparound style walnut grips.

> Commonly called the "Root" Model by collectors, manufactured 1855 through 1870. The .28 cal. model serial numbered 1 through approx. 30,000. The .31 cal. round barrel model serial numbered 1 through approx. 14,000. Total production approx. 44,000.

> Easily recognizable by its side mounted hammer and cylinder rotation ratchet at rear of frame.

* **Model 1 and 1A** — .28 cal., 3⁷⁄₁₆ in. octagonal bbl., oct. load lever, Indian/cabin cyl. scene, Hartford barrel address. Serial range 1 to 384.

| N/A | N/A | $5,750 | $3,700 | $3,100 | $2,700 | $2,300 | $2,000 | $1,825 | $1,650 | $1,400 | $1,100 |

* **Model 2** — .28 cal., 3½ in. oct. bbl., Indian/cabin cyl. scene, Hartford barrel address with pointed hand. Serial range 476 to 25,000.

| N/A | N/A | $2,150 | $1,290 | $1,040 | $890 | $765 | $665 | $595 | $535 | $485 | $425 |

* **Model 3** — .28 cal., 3½ in. oct. bbl., full fluted cylinder, Hartford barrel address with pointed hand. Serial range 25,001 to 30,000.

| N/A | N/A | $2,175 | $1,355 | $1,105 | $955 | $830 | $730 | $650 | $585 | $535 | $485 |

* **Model 3A** — .31 cal., 3½ in. oct. bbl., full fluted cylinder, Hartford barrel address. Serial range 1 to 1,350.

| N/A | N/A | $2,200 | $1,250 | $1,100 | $975 | $875 | $775 | $675 | $595 | $535 | $485 |

* **Model 4** — .31 cal., 3½ in. oct. bbl., full fluted cylinder, Hartford barrel address. Serial range 1,351 to 2,400.

| N/A | N/A | $2,200 | $1,250 | $1,100 | $975 | $875 | $775 | $675 | $595 | $535 | $485 |

* **Model 5** — .31 cal., 3½ in. round bbl., full fluted cylinder, "COL. COLT NEW-YORK" barrel address. Serial range 2,401 to 8,000.

| N/A | N/A | $2,200 | $1,250 | $1,100 | $975 | $875 | $775 | $675 | $595 | $535 | $485 |

100%	98%	95%	90%	80%	70%	60%	50%	40%	30%	20%	10%

C

* **Model 5A** — .31 cal., 4½ in. round bbl., included in same serial range as Model 5.

| N/A | N/A | $3,500 | $2,100 | $1,750 | $1,350 | $1,200 | $1,075 | $975 | $875 | $775 | $695 |

* **Model 6** — .31 cal., 3½ in. round bbl., stage coach hold-up cylinder scene, "COL. COLT NEW-YORK" barrel address. Serial range 8,001 through 11,074.

| N/A | N/A | $2,200 | $1,250 | $1,100 | $975 | $875 | $775 | $675 | $595 | $535 | $485 |

* **Model 6A** — .31 cal., 4½ in. round bbl., included in same serial range as Model 6.

| N/A | N/A | $2,200 | $1,250 | $1,100 | $975 | $875 | $775 | $675 | $595 | $535 | $485 |

* **Model 7** — .31 cal., 3½ in. round bbl., stage coach hold-up cylinder scene, "COL. COLT NEW-YORK" barrel address. Cylinder pin retained by screw-in cylinder. Serial range 11,075 through 14,000.

| N/A | N/A | $3,200 | $1,750 | $1,350 | $1,200 | $1,100 | $995 | $900 | $800 | $725 | $650 |

* **Model 7A** — .31 cal., 4½ in. round bbl., including same cylinder scene, barrel address and serial range as Model 7.

| N/A | N/A | $4,025 | $2,400 | $1,750 | $1,375 | $1,250 | $1,150 | $1,025 | $925 | $825 | $750 |

1860 MODEL ARMY — .44 cal., 6 shot, 7½ and 8 in. round barrels with loading lever, blued metal with case hardened frame, lever and hammer, one piece walnut grips, normally blued steel back strap and brass trigger guard, barrel markings were (ADDRESS SAM COLT, HARTFORD, CT.) on early productions and (ADDRESS COL. SAM COLT, NEW YORK, U.S. AMERICA) on balance, serial range 1-about 200,500, Texas Navy scene on round cylinder model. Mfg. 1860-1873.

* **Fluted Cylinder Model** — Fluted Cylinder Model, full length cylinder flutes and no cylinder scene, 7½ or 8 in. barrel, grips of Navy (very rare) or Army size, usually 4 screw frames.

| N/A | N/A | $13,000 | $9,900 | $7,750 | $6,450 | $5,400 | $4,550 | $3,850 | $3,250 | $2,750 | $2,350 |

* **Round Cylinder Model** — roll engraved Texas Navy scene, some with early Hartford address, Army grips, four screw frame to about 50,000 range, most were sold to the U.S. Government and will be martially marked.

| N/A | N/A | $9,700 | $7,250 | $6,000 | $4,850 | $3,850 | $3,100 | $2,500 | $2,000 | $1,650 | $1,375 |

* **Civilian Model** — same general configurations as Round Cylinder Model, but with 3 screw frame, no shoulder stock cuts and better blue finish than military pieces, late New York barrel address.

| N/A | N/A | $9,500 | $6,625 | $5,375 | $4,375 | $3,525 | $2,825 | $2,275 | $1,850 | $1,500 | $1,225 |

1861 MODEL NAVY — .36 cal., 6 shot, 7½ in. round barrel with loading lever, blued metal with case hardened frame, lever and hammer, silver plated brass grip straps, the barrel address was (ADDRESS COL. SAM COLT, NEW YORK, U.S. AMERICA), serial range 1 - 38,843, cylinder scene of Texas Navy and Mexico Battle, mfg. 1861-1873.

* **Fluted Cylinder Navy** — in serial range 1-100, with fluted cylinder and without rolled cylinder scene.

| N/A | N/A | $26,750 | $19,750 | $16,250 | $13,250 | $10,750 | $8,750 | $7,250 | $6,250 | $5,550 | $4,875 |

* **Regular production model**

| N/A | N/A | $11,000 | $8,300 | $6,100 | $4,950 | $3,925 | $3,275 | $2,600 | $2,150 | $1,725 | $1,475 |

* **Martially Marked Navies** — will bear the U.S. stamp and inspector's marks, those marked U.S.N. on butt were of a 650 piece order for the Navy.

| N/A | N/A | $12,500 | $8,600 | $6,600 | $4,950 | $4,050 | $3,350 | $2,775 | $2,300 | $1,900 | $1,550 |

* **London Marked Navy** — with (ADDRESS COL. COLT, LONDON), for barrel address.

| N/A | N/A | $9,450 | $7,525 | $5,925 | $4,775 | $3,900 | $3,225 | $2,675 | $2,225 | $1,850 | $1,475 |

* **Shoulder Stock Cut Navy** — 4 screw frames in serial range 11,000-14,000, made for third style stock (see Dragoon stocks).

| N/A | N/A | $16,500 | $10,500 | $8,000 | $6,500 | $5,500 | $4,650 | $3,950 | $3,350 | $2,850 | $2,375 |

100%	98%	95%	90%	80%	70%	60%	50%	40%	30%	20%	10%

1862 POLICE MODEL — .36 cal., 5 shot half fluted and rebated cylinder, 4½, 5½, and 6½ in. round barrels (also 3½ in. bbl. but quite rare) and loading lever. Mfg. 1861 to 1873. Serial numbered with Model 1862 Pocket Navy, approx. 28,000 1862 Police Models were produced. Blued with case hardened frame, lever and hammer, grip straps silver plated, one piece walnut grips. Serial range 1 through approx. 47,000. Standard barrel marking "AD-DRESS COL. SAML COLT NEW-YORK U.S. AMERICA". "COLTS/PATENT" on left side of frame, "PAT SEPT. 10TH 1850" stamped in cyl. flute.

> Many Model 1862 Police and 1862 Pocket Navy revolvers were converted to cartridge with the advent of the metallic cartridge. Consequently these models in their original cap and ball chambering are quite desirable to collectors.

* **Early Model** — "ADDRESS SAM COLT/HARTFORD CT" barrel address, silvered iron grip straps.

N/A	N/A	$9,700	$6,500	$5,100	$4,250	$3,450	$2,750	$2,200	$1,750	$1,375	$1,075

* **Early Model** — same but silvered brass grip straps.

N/A	N/A	$9,000	$6,150	$4,750	$3,850	$3,000	$2,300	$1,875	$1,535	$1,235	$1,000

* **Standard Production Model** — with New York barrel address.

N/A	N/A	$8,000	$4,200	$3,100	$2,400	$1,975	$1,675	$1,400	$1,175	$925	$775

* **Export Production Model** — with "L" below serial numbers (for export to England), steel grip straps. Most often but not always bearing British proofs.

N/A	N/A	$8,500	$4,470	$3,320	$2,585	$2,135	$1,810	$1,525	$1,275	$1,050	$875

* **London Marked Model** — similar to above, except with "ADDRESS, COL. COLT/LON-DON" address on barrel.

N/A	N/A	$11,500	$8,500	$6,500	$5,100	$4,050	$3,250	$2,750	$2,400	$2,150	$1,800

1862 POCKET MODEL NAVY — .36 cal., 5 shot rebated cylinder, 4½ in., 5½ in., and 6½ in. octagonal barrels with loading lever. Mfg. 1861 to 1873. Serial numbered with Model 1862 Police Model, approx. 19,000 Model 1862 Pocket Navy Revolvers produced. Blued with case hardened frame, lever and hammer, grip straps silver plated brass, one piece walnut grips. Serial range 1 through approx. 47,000. Standard barrel markings "ADDRESS COL. SAML COLT NEW-YORK U.S. AMERICA". "COLTS/PATENT" on left side of frame, stage coach hold-up scene on cylinder.

> Known to collectors for many years as the Model 1853, this model has finally been correctly identified through diligent combing of factory ledgers.

> Because of being produced during the advent of the metallic cartridge, the number remaining in the original cap and ball configuration is rather few; scarce with any serial number, but particularly so in numbers over approx. 19,800.

* **Standard Model** — 4½, 5½ and 6½ barrel lengths.

N/A	N/A	$8,500	$6,175	$4,775	$3,850	$3,000	$2,300	$1,875	$1,535	$1,235	$1,000

* **Export Production Model** — with "L" below serial numbers (for export to England), steel grip straps. Often found with British proofs.

N/A	N/A	$9,000	$7,500	$6,000	$4,750	$3,775	$3,025	$2,475	$2,000	$1,650	$1,375

* **London Marked Model** — similar to above but "ADDRESS COL. COLT/LONDON" address on barrel.

N/A	N/A	$14,175	$10,650	$8,250	$6,550	$5,500	$4,650	$3,950	$3,350	$2,850	$2,375

REVOLVERS: PERCUSSION, 2ND & 3RD GENERATION BLACK POWDER

To learn more about the 2nd & 3rd Generation Percussion Black Powder Series, it is recommended to purchase *Colt Black Powder Reproductions & Replicas - A Collector's & Shooter's Guide* by Dennis A. Adler. This new definitive book is available from Blue Book Publications, Inc. To order, please call, fax, email, or use convenient order form between pages 696-697.

100%	98%	95%	90%	80%	70%	60%	50%	40%	30%	20%	10%

DERRINGERS

FIRST MODEL DERRINGER — .41 rimfire cal., single shot, 2½ in. barrel, scroll engraving standard, blued, nickel, or silver plated barrel, downward pivoting barrel, no grips, serial numbered 1-6,500. Mfg. approx. 1870-1890.

$3,100	$2,350	$2,050	$1,825	$1,625	$1,425	$1,250	$1,075	$875	$750	$675	$650

C

SECOND MODEL DERRINGER — .41 rimfire or centerfire cal., single shot, 2½ in. barrel, scroll engraving standard, blued, nickel, or silver plated barrel, downward pivoting barrel, checkered and varnished walnut grips, "No 2" marked on top of barrel, serial numbered 1-9,000. Mfg. approx. 1870-1890.

$1,650	$1,400	$1,200	$1,060	$935	$835	$730	$630	$585	$535	$500	$475

.41 Centerfire — add 100%.

THIRD MODEL DERRINGER (THUER MODEL) — .41 rimfire or centerfire (rare) cal., single shot, side pivoting 2½ in. barrel, varnished walnut grips, blued barrels, bronze frames were either nickel or silver plated, engraving optional, Colt-barrel address, spur trigger, serial numbered approx. 1-45,000. Mfg. approx. 1875-1910.

$1,400	$1,200	$890	$790	$700	$620	$550	$495	$450	$415	$385	$360

.41 centerfire is worth an additional 30-50% and early models are worth considerably more.

Grading	100%	98%	95%

FOURTH MODEL DERRINGER (FIRING) — .22 Short cal., single shot similar in appearance to the 3rd Model, 2½ in. barrel, approx. 112,000 mfg. between 1959-1963 with either D or N suffix. A few were put in books (sometimes as pairs), picture frames, penholders, bookends, etc. (these will command premiums).

	100%	98%	95%
Gun only	$100	$85	$65
Gun w/accessories	$375	$275	$175

* *Fourth Model Derringer (non-firing)* — this variation was normally used for decoration and is normally encountered in books, picture frames, penholders, bookends, etc. Values below assume all factory materials intact - if not, prices are reduced to $50-$75 for gun only.

$375	$250	$150

Non-firing guns usually do not have the barrel notch, thus preventing the hammer from striking the cartridge.

LORD DERRINGER — .22 Short cal. only, side pivoting Thuer action, gold plated with black chrome barrel and walnut grips. Mfg. approx. 1959-1963 by Colt, cased.

$175	$140	$100

LADY DERRINGER — .22 Short cal. only, side pivoting Thuer action, full gold plated finish with pearlite grips. Mfg. approx. 1959-1963 by Colt, cased.

$175	$140	$100

LORD & LADY CASED SET — one each of the Lord & Lady derringers or combinations, consecutive serial numbers.

$350	$275	$200

LADY CASED SET — cased pair of Lady Derringers.

$350	$275	$200

LORD CASED SET — cased pair of Lord Derringers.

$350	$275	$200

BOOKCASE DERRINGER PAIR — .22 Short cal., consecutively numbered derringers with synthetic ivory grips and nickel finish, cased inside unique hard cover "Colt Derringers" labeled book with red velvet lining, limited mfg. in early '60s.

$350	$275	$200

100%	98%	95%	90%	80%	70%	60%	50%	40%	30%	20%	10%

REVOLVERS: POCKET MODELS

If possible, it is advisable to procure a factory letter before buying/selling this variation (open top only). These water marked letters are available by writing Colt Firearms in Hartford, CT, with a charge of $100 per serial number (if they can research it). Include your name and address, Colt model name, serial number, and check to: COLT HISTORIAN, P.O. Box 1868, Hartford, CT 06101. Please allow 4-6 weeks for a response.

CLOVERLEAF HOUSE PISTOL — .41 Short or L rimfire cal., cloverleaf configured 4 shot cylinder, spur trigger, 1½ or 3 in. barrel, blued or nickel plated, approx. 7,500 mfg. in ser. no. range 1-8,300 during 1871-1876.

| $2,375 | $2,150 | $1,750 | $1,510 | $1,310 | $1,160 | $1,030 | $915 | $815 | $730 | $660 | $610 |

Add 30% for blue finish.
Add 80% for 1½ in. barrel.

This model is sometimes referred to as the Jim Fisk model, as he was murdered by Edward Stokes with a Cloverleaf.

* 5-shot Cloverleaf — similar to 4-shot model, except has round 5-shot cylinder and 2⅝ in. barrel only, approx. 2,500 mfg. in ser. no. range 6,160-9,950 during 1871-1876.

| $2,025 | $1,795 | $1,500 | $1,260 | $1,085 | $940 | $820 | $720 | $640 | $580 | $535 | $500 |

OPEN TOP REVOLVER (OLD LINE) — .22 Short or L rimfire cal., 2⅜ or 2⅞ in. barrel, without topstrap on frame, with or without integral ejector, blued or nickel plated, varnished walnut grips, approx. 114,200 mfg. 1871-1877.

| $1,350 | $1,175 | $1,000 | $900 | $825 | $750 | $700 | $600 | $550 | $450 | $375 | $325 |

Add 30% for blue finish.
Add 120% for Early Model with ejector and high hammer spur.

REVOLVERS: NEW LINE SERIES & VARIATIONS

If possible, it is advisable to procure a factory letter before buying/selling New Line Revolvers. These water marked letters are available by writing Colt Firearms in Hartford, CT, with a charge of $100 per serial number (if they can research it). Include your name and address, Colt model name, serial number, and check to: COLT HISTORIAN, P.O. Box 1868, Hartford, CT 06101. Please allow 4-6 weeks for a response.
Add 30% for blue finish on models listed below.

1ST MODEL — .22, .30, .32, .38, or .41 cal. rim and centerfire, mfg. 1873-1876, 7 (.22 cal. only) or 5 shot, short cylinder flutes, cylinder stop slots cut on exterior of cylinder, 1¾, 2¼, or 4 in. barrel, full nickel or blue/case hardened finish, spur trigger, many thousands mfg. 1873-1884.

| $1,150 | $990 | $875 | $810 | $740 | $685 | $580 | $540 | $425 | $355 | $300 | $250 |

2ND MODEL — similar to 1st Model, except has longer cylinder flutes and cylinder stop slots are on the back of cylinder, may or may not have loading gate. Mfg. 1876-1884.

| $1,050 | $935 | $845 | $775 | $705 | $645 | $540 | $500 | $390 | $320 | $270 | $235 |

Caliber rarity on both models from highest mfg. to lowest is: .22, .32, .30, .41, and .38.

NEW HOUSE MODEL — .38 or .41 cal. centerfire, 5 shot, 2¼ in. barrel, spur trigger, checkered hard rubber grips. Approx. 4,000 mfg. 1880-1886 starting at ser. no. 10,300.

| $1,375 | $1,075 | $950 | $850 | $760 | $675 | $600 | $485 | $425 | $360 | $325 | $310 |

NEW POLICE MODEL — .32, .38, or .41 cal. centerfire, 5 shot, 2¼, 4½, 5, or 6 in. barrel, spur trigger, with or without ejector, stamped or etched "NEW POLICE" on barrel. Approx. 4,000 mfg. 1882-1886.

| $1,675 | $1,425 | $1,225 | $1,050 | $900 | $785 | $700 | $635 | $585 | $550 | $520 | $495 |

REVOLVERS: PERCUSSION CONVERSIONS

The author wishes to once again express thanks to Fred Sweeney for updating the following information in the 20th Edition.

100%	98%	95%	90%	80%	70%	60%	50%	40%	30%	20%	10%

Colt Thuer Conversions

COLT THUER CONVERSIONS (c. 1868-1872) — less than 5,000 produced in all models. This was Colt's first commercial attempt at converting percussion revolvers to fire fixed ammo. Standard features: usually threaded inside rammer for a Thuer loading tool, a hardened flat face on hammer, deepened loading cutout on right side of lug, Thuer ring and back of cylinder have matching assembly numbers. Beware of fakes! Only non-experimental Colt models are listed. Rarity by barrel length will not be considered here. Serial numbers are often missing on cylinder. .31, .36 and .44 CF cal.

Prices for Colt Conversions reflect values for blue and case hardened examples. Nickel plated specimens are rarely seen, but typically sell for 20%-40% less than blue finish.

Any defects, excessive wear, or dulled blue will affect value. Nickeled conversions that have lost their translucence (become cloudy) should be discounted more than usual 20%-40% from blue and case hardened examples - especially on near mint to mint specimens.

* **1849 Pocket**

$25,000	$22,500	$17,500	$15,000	$13,000	$11,000	$9,500	$8,500	$7,500	$6,750	$6,000	$5,000

* **1851 Navy**

$23,000	$21,000	$16,000	$14,000	$12,000	$10,000	$8,500	$7,750	$7,000	$6,500	$5,750	$4,750

* **1860 Army** — the most common Thuer, but popular because it's a large frame model.

$27,000	$24,000	$19,000	$16,000	$14,000	$12,000	$11,000	$10,000	$9,500	$8,500	$7,500	$6,500

* **1861 Navy**

$25,000	$22,500	$19,000	$16,000	$14,000	$11,000	$9,500	$8,500	$7,500	$6,700	$6,000	$5,000

* **1862 Police**

$20,000	$18,000	$15,000	$13,000	$11,000	$8,500	$7,500	$6,750	$6,000	$5,500	$5,000	$4,500

* **1862 Pocket Navy**

$20,000	$18,000	$15,000	$13,000	$11,000	$8,500	$7,500	$6,750	$6,000	$5,500	$5,000	$4,500

Richards Conversions: All Variations

RICHARDS CONVERSION, COLT 1860 ARMY REVOLVER — .44 CF cal., produced C. 1870s, special machining to barrel and breech of cylinder for conversion to a cartridge weapon. Produced in two serial ranges: one numbered under 10,000 and a separate group generally in the 190,000 to 200,000 range.

* **1860 Army First Model Richards** — quick ID: integral rear sight on breech plate. Floating firing pin in breechplate. Front edge of barrel lug is same as 1860 percussion Army. Breechplate extends over rear edge of cylinder.

$24,000	$20,000	$16,000	$13,000	$9,000	$7,000	$6,000	$5,250	$4,500	$4,000	$3,500	$3,000

* **1860 Army Second Model Richards** — quick ID: standard Richards type barrel. A space between face of conversion ring and rear of cylinder when viewed from the side. No integral sight on breechplate, cut away at top allowing hammer to directly strike the cartridge.

$24,000	$22,000	$17,000	$14,500	$9,500	$7,500	$6,500	$6,000	$5,250	$4,500	$4,000	$3,500

* **1860 Army Twelve Stop Cylinder Variation Richards** — quick ID: generally the same as standard model Richards except cylinder has extra "safety" notches between the locking notches. This variation was usually produced in the 100-300, 1000-1700 and 200,000 serial ranges. Cylinder locking notches over chambers often broken through. Watch for alterations.

$27,500	$24,000	$19,000	$15,000	$12,500	$8,500	$7,000	$6,500	$6,000	$5,500	$5,000	$4,500

* **1860 Army U.S. Marked Richards** — quick ID: generally the same as 1st Model Richards (many minor differences). Has "U.S." stamped on left barrel lug and "A" (Ainsworth) inspectors marked in several places. They are converted 1860 percussion Armys, so original numbers are typically in 23,000-144,000 range plus a second set of assembly numbers. Oiled grips, military soft blue finish.

$30,000	$27,000	$22,500	$17,500	$13,000	$9,500	$7,750	$7,000	$6,500	$6,000	$5,500	$4,500

100%	98%	95%	90%	80%	70%	60%	50%	40%	30%	20%	10%

Richards-Mason Conversions: All Variations

1860 ARMY RICHARDS-MASON — .44 CF cal., overall, much rarer than Richards Army Conversions. C. 1870s, approximately 2100 produced. A rare variation has an 1860 Army rebated cylinder and a barrel with a lug shaped similar to 1861 Navy Conversion.

* *1860 Army Richards-Mason* — quick ID: breechplate without integral rear sight, cutout at top so hammer can strike primer directly. A space can be seen between breechplate and rear of cylinder. Rear of lug is a vertical line instead of the bullet shape cutout seen on Richards models.

$25,000	$20,000	$15,000	$12,500	$9,000	$8,000	$7,500	$7,000	$6,250	$5,500	$4,500	$3,750

1851 NAVY RICHARDS-MASON — .38 CF and RF cal., c. 1870s. Produced in two different serial ranges. Has improved Richards-Mason breechplate that is flush with diameter of recoil shield. Difficult to locate in prime condition.

* *1851 Navy Civilian Model Richards-Mason* — quick ID: Richards-Mason breechplate which is same diameter as recoil shield, octagon barrel, mirrored civilian blue. Nickel finish commonly seen.

$11,000	$10,000	$7,500	$6,500	$5,500	$4,500	$4,000	$3,500	$3,000	$2,500	$2,000	$1,500

* *1851 U.S. Navy Richards-Mason* — quick ID: Richards-Mason breechplate, oiled grips, soft blue military finish, produced in US. percussion range of 40,000-90,000 ranges. Inconsistent "U.S.N." and other inspector markings. Iron straps, "U.S." on frame.

$15,000	$13,000	$10,000	$7,500	$6,000	$5,000	$4,500	$4,000	$3,500	$3,000	$2,250	$1,750

1861 NAVY RICHARDS-MASON — produced in civilian and military versions. C. 1870s, made in RF and CF cal. in two serial ranges. Round 7½ in. barrel.

* *1861 Navy Civilian Model Richards-Mason* — quick ID: Richards-Mason breechplate, round 7½ in. barrel with attached ejector housing, unrebated cylinder. When blued, has a commercial high gloss finish.

$13,000	$11,000	$8,500	$6,500	$4,750	$4,250	$3,750	$3,400	$3,000	$2,400	$2,000	$1,500

* *1861 Navy U.S. Navy Richards-Mason* — soft military blue finish, oiled grips, converted from percussion U.S. Navy revolvers, inconsistent military markings, centerfire, set of extra serial numbers often seen on cylinder.

$17,500	$15,000	$11,000	$8,500	$5,500	$5,000	$4,500	$4,000	$3,500	$3,000	$2,500	$2,000

COLT 1862 POLICE & POCKET NAVY RICHARDS-MASON CONVERSIONS (c. 1870s) — .38 RF and CF cal., parts for 1862 Police, 1862 Pocket Navy, as well as 1849 Pockets are often intermixed. As parts bins were depleted, Colt used whatever components that would fit, resulting in a tremendous amount of minor variations. Some barrels were converted from percussion models while others were newly made as cartridge barrels without rammer plugs and loading slots in the lug. There are three different serial ranges (1849, 1862 Police/Pocket Navy, Conversion). 3½ to 6½ in. barrels, again not all features available on all models.

> Nickel plated conversions will bring 20% - 40% less than blue and case hardened specimens.

* *4½ in. Octagon Barrel Model* — quick ID: 4½ in. octagon barrel without ejector. Rebated Pocket Navy Cylinder.

$7,000	$6,000	$5,000	$4,000	$3,000	$2,500	$1,750	$1,350	$1,150	$950	$750	$650

* *Round (Percussion) Barrel Pocket Navy with Ejector* — quick ID: plug in rammer slot; ejector housing, loading cutout in right side of lug, barrel remachined from Pocket Navy percussion barrel, Pocket Navy rebated cylinder. Similar appearance to cartridge barrel variation.

$7,250	$6,250	$5,250	$4,250	$3,000	$2,500	$2,000	$1,750	$1,500	$1,200	$1,000	$850

100%	98%	95%	90%	80%	70%	60%	50%	40%	30%	20%	10%

1862 POLICE AND POCKET NAVY CONVERSION — 4½, 5½, or 6½ in. barrels with 1862 Police percussion profile and added ejector housing. Has rebated Pocket Navy cylinder or rarer half fluted 1862 Police cylinder. 6½ in. barrel will bring a premium.

* *1862 Police/Pocket Navy with Rebated Pocket Navy Cylinder* — quick ID: 1862 Police profile barrel with ejector housing and rebated 1862 Pocket Navy cylinder.

$7,500	$6,500	$4,500	$4,000	$2,750	$2,250	$1,750	$1,400	$1,100	$900	$650	$550

* *1862 Police/Pocket Navy with Half Fluted Cylinder* — quick ID: 1862 Police profile barrel with ejector housing and ½ fluted Police cylinder.

$9,000	$7,500	$5,000	$4,500	$3,250	$2,750	$2,000	$1,600	$1,300	$1,100	$850	$700

Conversions with Round Cartridge Barrel

ROUND CARTRIDGE BARREL WITH EJECTOR — .38 RF and CF cal. 4½, 5½, or 6½ in. barrels produced as a cartridge component without rammer slots and lug cutouts inherent to a percussion barrel.

* *1862 Pocket Navy Round Cartridge Barrel* — quick ID: much shorter lug area than similar model converted from percussion barrel. No slots or loading cutouts on barrel. With ejector housing and Pocket Navy rebated cylinder. Often called the "Baby Open Top". Very scarce.

$9,500	$7,250	$5,750	$5,000	$4,250	$3,250	$2,800	$2,500	$2,000	$1,750	$1,450	$1,250

3½ IN. ROUND CARTRIDGE BARREL CONVERSION — .38 RF or CF cal., sometimes seen with serial numbers that are from 1849 Pocket Model (300,000 range). Barrel newly made for cartridges, not converted from a percussion barrel.

* *3½ in. Round Cartridge Barrel* — quick ID: only type conversion with 3½ in. barrel. No ejector, no loading lever slot or loading cutout in lug area. Pocket Navy rebated cylinder.

$5,000	$4,000	$2,400	$1,800	$1,400	$1,100	$975	$875	$800	$700	$600	$500

REVOLVERS: "OPEN TOP" MODELS

If possible, it is advisable to procure a factory letter before buying/selling this Open Top Revolver. These watermarked letters are available by writing Colt Firearms in Hartford, CT, with a charge of $200 per serial number (if they can research it). Include your name and address, Colt model name, serial number, and check to: COLT HISTO-RIAN, P.O. Box 1868, Hartford, CT 06101. Please allow 4-6 weeks for a response.

1871-72 OPEN TOP MODEL RIMFIRE — .44 cal. rimfire, 6 shot, 7½ in. barrel, without frame topstrap, blued metal with casehardened hammer, serial range 1-approx. 7000, barrel address (ADDRESS COL. SAM COLT, NEW YORK, U.S. AMERICA), forerunner of the single action Army, quite desirable. Mfg. 1871-1872.

Add 20% for blue finish on models listed below.

* *Regular Production Model* — 7½ in. barrel, New York address, Navy grips.

N/A	N/A	$27,500	$22,750	$18,500	$15,000	$12,750	$8,750	$6,750	$6,000	$5,300	$4,850

* *Regular Production* — with Army grips.

N/A	N/A	$24,000	$18,750	$15,000	$12,500	$10,250	$7,000	$5,750	$5,000	$4,450	$4,250

* *Late Production* — with address (COLT PT. F. A. MANUFACTURING CO., HART-FORD, CT., U.S.A.).

N/A	N/A	$21,000	$16,000	$13,000	$10,750	$7,500	$6,000	$5,200	$4,650	$4,150	$3,700

Add 40% for models with 8 in. barrel or COLTS/PATENT frame markings.

REVOLVERS: SAA, 1873-1940 MFG. (SER. NOS. 1 - 357,000)

The author wishes to express thanks to Charles Layson for making the following information available and reformatting the Colt 1st Generation SAA section.

The Colt SAA was produced in 36 calibers with many special order features or combinations available directly from the Colt factory. These factory special order features

100%	98%	95%	90%	80%	70%	60%	50%	40%	30%	20%	10%

can greatly enhance the value of the revolver. The Single Action Colt, or "Peacemaker", as it is often called, is undoubtedly the most collectible handgun in the world, and as such, can command very high prices.

It is prudent to secure several professional opinions as to originality when contemplating an expensive purchase, since many SAAs have been altered or "improved" over the decades. Before he died, Keith Cochran, author of the "Colt Peacemaker Encyclopedia, Vol. II", guesstimated that over ½ of all pre-WWII revolvers were no longer factory original. Because of this, it is advisable to procure a factory letter when buying or selling older or recently manufactured Colt Single Actions (hence guaranteeing original configuration and value credibility). These watermarked letters are based on the original factory handwritten shipping ledgers and are available by writing Colt Firearms in Hartford, CT, with a charge of $100 per serial number. While not totally infallible, these letters are normally very accurate. If Colt cannot provide you with proper documentation after conducting research, they will issue a $50 refund. The charge is $200+ per custom engraved gun - see the Trademark Index for the address. Include your name and address, Colt model name, serial number, and check to: COLT HISTORIAN, P.O. BOX 1868, HARTFORD, CT 06144-1868. Please allow 12-15 weeks for proper response. In addition, phone service SAA configuration validation is also provided on a premium basis on first generation SAAs ONLY (ser. no. range 354,000 - 357,859 cannot be researched) to assist in possible purchases of a critical nature. Fees for this phone service are $150 per gun for 1st Generation SAA pistols, payable by Visa or MasterCard - letter is included for this price. The phone number is 860-244-1343 and ask for the Historical Dept. between the hours of 1-4 P.M. EST.

Values shown below are for guns without special order features. Factory engraving, ivory grips, very rare special order barrel lengths, and special finishes would add considerably to the values shown below. One final word on single action Colts: Black Powder Colts (pre 165,000 serial range) should be scrutinized carefully for potential problems, including refinishing (including aging), replacement parts, restamped serial numbers, and added, non-factory special order features. This makes a major difference in pricing the SAA, as a genuine, original SAA's price tag will vary immensely from a non-original, made-up "parts gun".

SAA - 1ST GENERATION CIVILIAN/COMMERCIAL (MFG. 1873-1940)

SINGLE ACTION ARMY - STANDARD MFG. — over 30 cals., six shot single action revolver, 4¾, 5½, or 7½ in. standard barrel lengths, blue with color case hardened frame or full nickel finish standard, one-piece, varnished walnut grips standard until 1882, when black, gutta percha (hard rubber) grips were introduced with eagle motif. Eagle-less grips became standard after 1892. One-piece wood available upon request until approx. 1903. Rarely seen, two-piece, oil finished, walnut available thereafter. Mfg. 1873-1940.

* *Pinch Frame SAA* — .45 LC cal., 7½ in. barrel, frame pinched to form rear sight, ser. no. range 1-160. Mfg. 1873.

N/A	N/A	N/A	$65,000	$60,000	$55,000	$47,500	$42,000	$37,000	$32,000	$26,000	$20,000

Be aware! There are many counterfeits in this variation.

* *Early Black Powder SAA* — .45 LC cal., 7½ in. barrel standard, blue or nickel finish, distinctive italic script style lettering used in barrel address, 5½ in. barrels introduced in 1875, ser. nos. shared with early martial production, ser. no. range 160-22,000. Mfg. 1873-1876.

N/A	$35,000	$32,000	$28,000	$22,000	$16,000	$14,000	$12,000	$10,000	$8,000	$6,000	$4,000

Subtract 40% for nickel finish.

* *Intermediate Black Powder SAA* — .44-40 WCF (.44 WCF) cal. introduced in ser. no. range 41,000 (1878) as a companion to the Winchester 1873 rifle, other calibers follow, 4¾ or 5½ in. barrel became popular during this era, at appox. 60,000 ser. no. range, round ejector head was changed to oval shape, ser. no. range 22,000-130,000. Mfg. 1876-1890.

N/A	$30,000	$25,000	$22,000	$18,000	$16,000	$12,000	$10,000	$8,000	$6,000	$4,000	$2,800

100%	98%	95%	90%	80%	70%	60%	50%	40%	30%	20%	10%

Subtract 30% for nickel finish.
Add 25% for original box.
Add 10% for 4¾ in. barrel.

✷ Late Black Powder SAA — three line patent date format changes to two line, circled rampant colt stamped on frame, ser. no. range 130,000-165,000. Mfg. 1890-1896.

| $25,000 | $22,000 | $19,000 | $15,000 | $11,000 | $9,000 | $7,500 | $6,700 | $6,000 | $4,500 | $3,500 | $2,200 |

Subtract 20% for nickel finish.
Add 25% for original box.
Add 10% for 4¾ in. barrel.
Add 20% for one-piece wood or eagle grips.

✷ Early Smokeless Powder SAA — several important physical characteristics were changed during this transition period. Most notably, in 1896 when the vertical screw retaining the cylinder pin was eliminated in favor of the horizontal latch. This was similar to what had already been used on the double action models since 1877. The knurling pattern on the hammer spur began a two step revision in 1906. Although Colt advertised their improved smokeless powder single action as early as 1897, they did not add the "VP" proofmark (verified proof, Colt's guarantee for smokeless powder use) to the trigger guard until 1904. Also, the company continued to use black powder rifling (wide grooves and narrow lands) and black powder front sights (small and low) until approx. 1911, when inventories were depleted. While the highest production figures were reached during this period, quality did not suffer. Many collectors feel that the polish, fit, and finish work performed during this 12 year span was at least as good, if not better, than before or since this period. Ser. no. range 165,000-300,000. Mfg. 1896-1908.

| $16,000 | $12,000 | $9,000 | $7,000 | $5,700 | $4,900 | $4,200 | $3,700 | $3,200 | $2,500 | $2,000 | $1,600 |

Subtract 10% for nickel finish.
Add 20% for original box.
Add 25% for checkered walnut grips w/o medallions.
Add 20% for pre-1900 period mfg.

✷ Intermediate Smokeless Powder SAA — transitional changes to front sight and rifling were completed by 1914, the Bisley model was discontinued, the first Colt medallions were found in pearl and ivory grips starting in 1909, the new .44 Special caliber was introduced, the method of bluing was changed, WWI comes and goes, and SAA sales began to decline. 1920 is significant to Colt SAA collectors since this was the year the company completed the relocation of the serial numbers. Those on the trigger guard and backstrap were moved under the grips beginning in the late 338,000 ser. no. range (1919), leaving only the ser. no. on the frame visible. This brought to a close the original ser. no. stamping location which began with the percussion revolvers. Many collectors regard this as the end of the "cowboy" period, ser. no. range 300,000-339,000. Mfg. 1908-1920.

| $12,000 | $9,000 | $7,500 | $5,700 | $4,500 | $3,800 | $3,200 | $2,700 | $2,200 | $1,900 | $1,600 | $1,400 |

Add 15% for original box.
Add 15% for smooth, two-piece walnut grips.
Add 25% for checkered, varnished walnut grips with deep set medallions.

✷ Late Smokeless Powder SAA — complete ser. no. visible only on frame, many cylinders are stamped at rear with the last two digits of ser. no., caliber marking on side of barrel was changed in 1928 to "Colt Single Action Army", followed by caliber, finish on hammer was changed from case hardening to blue with polished sides in 1935, and "V" notch rear sight was replaced with square groove to match wider front sight configuration during 1930, ser. no. range 339,000-358,000. Mfg. 1920-1940.

| $7,800 | $6,700 | $5,500 | $4,200 | $3,700 | $3,200 | $2,700 | $2,200 | $1,800 | $1,600 | $1,400 | $1,200 |

Add 15% for original box.
Add 20% for checkered, oil finished grips with flush medallions, post-1923.
Add 25% for checkered, varnished grips, pre-1924.

100%	98%	95%	90%	80%	70%	60%	50%	40%	30%	20%	10%

SAA - 1ST GENERATION COMMERCIAL, NON-STANDARD MFG.

SINGLE ACTION ARMY, NON-STANDARD MFG. — throughout the 1873-1940 period of production, Colt manufactured several distinct types or configurations of SAAs that varied from the standard and therefore, have special significance to the collector.

* *.22 Rimfire SAA* — 5½ or 7½ in. barrel, both blue and nickel finishes, mfg. in two distinct runs, slightly less than 100 converted from unsold .44 rimfire revolvers on hand in the late 1880's, and in 1891, approx. 20 were mfg. as new guns.

N/A	$30,000	$25,000	$18,000	$16,000	$14,500	$12,500	$11,000	$10,000	$8,500	$7,500	$6,500

Subtract 10% for those converted from .44 rimfire.

* *.44 Rimfire SAA* — .44 Henry rimfire cal., 7½ in. barrel, most were shipped to Mexico and saw hard use, rare with any condition remaining, serial numbered in their own range, 1-1,863. Mfg. 1875-1880.

N/A	N/A	N/A	$30,000	$25,000	$18,000	$15,000	$13,500	$12,500	$11,000	$9,500	$8,000

Beware! Many have been found with cut and/or stretched barrels.

* *Buntline Special Model SAA* — .45 LC cal., 12 or 16 in. non-standard barrel, rear adj. sight, long hammer screw for attachment of shoulder stock, very rare.

N/A	$150,000	$135,000	$120,000	$100,000	$85,000	$75,000	$60,000	$50,000	$42,000	$35,000	$28,000

It is believed only 28 were produced in the 28,800 ser. no. range. Although other standard frame SAAs were mfg. with barrels over 7½ in. long, and these will command higher than normal prices.

* *Etched Panel .44-40 SAA* — during 1878, soon after Colt began offering the .44 WCF cal., the new model nomenclature was changed to "Frontier Model". This may have been changed due to some persuasion from one of Colt's largest wholesalers, B. Kittredge & Co., of Cincinatti, OH. Kittredge had already begun advertising the .45 as the "Peacemaker" in 1876. Starting in the 41,000 ser. no. range, an acid etching process was used to mark the barrels "COLT FRONTIER SIX SHOOTER". Barrels so marked were continued until approx. the 129,000 ser. no. range (circa 1890).

N/A	$35,000	$28,000	$21,000	$16,000	$13,500	$11,000	$9,000	$7,500	$6,200	$5,000	$4,000

Subtract 40% for nickel finish.

This variation continues to be very sought after amongst Colt SAA collectors.

* *Sheriff's Model SAA* — .44-40 WCF or .45 LC cal., 2½, 3, 4, 4¾ (rare) or 7½ (rare) in. barrel, configuration denotes barrel w/o ejector rod housing. Mfg. throughout production until 1927.

N/A	$40,000	$35,000	$28,000	$23,000	$18,000	$16,000	$14,000	$12,000	$10,000	$8,000	$7,000

* *Flat-top Target Model SAA* — various cals. from .22 to .476 Eley, 7½ in. barrel, all blue finish, two-piece smooth walnut or rubber grips standard, occasionally with checkered walnut. Approx. 925 mfg. 1888-1896.

$24,000	$20,000	$18,000	$15,000	$12,000	$10,000	$8,000	$7,000	$6,000	$5,000	$4,000	$3,000

While rare, this model has limited collector appeal.

* *Long Flute Series SAA* — .32 WCF, .38 WCF, .41 LC, .44 S&W Spl., or .45 LC cal., during 1913, Colt decided to make use of approx. 1,500 DA model cylinders remaining in inventory. Since it was necessary to add a bolt lock notch and lead-in on these longer flute cylinders, they looked ahead of current production and blocked off ser. nos. 330,000-331,480 for this special treatment. Shipped 1913-1915.

According to Hull & Radcliffe, whose survey includes 114 long flutes, no .44 WCF long flutes have been found. Quite possibly, the true number of long flutes mfg. slightly exceeds 1,500, and while rare, sell for only 5%-10% more than other SAAs of this period.

100%	98%	95%	90%	80%	70%	60%	50%	40%	30%	20%	10%

C

* **Pre-war parts/Post-war Mfg. SAAs** — .38 WCF or .45 LC cal., 5½ in. blue barrel with case colors, many given as gifts to dignitaries and retiring Colt employees, shipping cartons were both brown and black, approx. 860 SAAs assembled from pre-war parts and shipped after 1945.

   Subtract 10%-20% over late pre-war mfg.

   These SAAs shipped post-war are usually encountered in 95%+ condition.

* **Factory Engraved SAAs** — slightly less than 1% (approx. 3,200) SAAs are thought to have been engraved at the factory or elsewhere by authority from Colt 1873-1940. Colt offered 3 basic grades of engraving and since many of these guns carried special inscriptions, initials, grips, etc., the value ranges are very wide. Factory engraved black powder SAAs typically sell in the $2,500 - $50,000 range, while factory engraved smokeless powder models usually peak in the $25,000 range. Very special or one-of-a-kind pieces, such as the 5 known "panel" engraved guns may bring upward of $300,000, depending on conditions and particulars. The Colt Historical Dept. can document most factory work.

* **Non-factory Engraved SAAs** — value depends upon when and where the engraving was done. Early "New York" or "dealer" engraved guns done outside the factory were usually shipped from Colt in the "soft" or w/o finish. The majority of these were done in the early 1880s, and condition being equal, are generally priced at 50%-75% of factory original specimens. Later guns, well done by a known contemporary artist, are usually priced by adding the values of the gun and the cost of engraving. Poor execution may actually lower the value of a plain, but original gun, as much as refinishing would. Here again, a factory letter can make a big difference. The notation of "soft" in the finish column is almost as desirable as the word "engraved", since the large wholesalers in the northeast used many of the same engravers as Colt.

* **Bisley Model SAA** — features more curved and longer grip strap, smaller hammer raked backward, this model was designed with the target shooter in mind, and named after Bisley, England, location of the international shooting matches during the late 19th and early 20th century. Approx. 45,000 were mfg. 1894-1913.

$9,000	$7,500	$6,000	$4,500	$3,200	$2,800	$2,300	$2,000	$1,800	$1,500	$1,200	$1,000

* **Flat-top Target Bisley SAA** — all standard SAA cals., similar to the Flat-top SAA, usually found with 7½ in. barrel with all blue finish, two-piece walnut or rubber grips. 976 mfg. 1894-1913.

$13,500	$11,250	$9,000	$6,750	$4,800	$4,200	$3,450	$3,000	$2,700	$2,250	$1,800	$1,500

SAA - U.S. MILITARY

SINGLE ACTION ARMY (CAVALRY) - U.S. MILITARY CONTRACT — the Colt SAA was the primary sidearm of the U.S. military forces between 1873 and 1892, carried by all commissioned officers and mounted troops. While sometimes identified as the "Cavalry" model, this revolver was issued to all branches of service and state militia units. A total of 37,063 were purchased by the U.S government at an average cost of $12.50. Specifications called for 7½ in. barrel, .45 LC cal., blue & color case hardened finish, one-piece, oil finished walnut grips. Each gun was stamped with the intitial(s) of a U.S. ordnance principal sub-inspector and finally, with the letters "U.S." on the frame after being approved for delivery to the National Armory at Springfield, MA.

* **Early U.S. Model SAA** — principal sub-inspectors of this early period of military mfg. were O.W. Ainsworth (A), S.B. Lewis (L), A.P. Casey (C), and W.W. Johnson (J), examples with ser. nos. below 20,000 are most desirable and command premium prices, these guns are marked with only the single letter of the last name and were mfg. before 1876.

N/A	N/A	$42,000	$35,000	$25,000	$18,000	$16,000	$14,000	$13,000	$12,000	$10,000	$8,000

   Of this group, early Ainsworth inspected guns are the most valuable.

* **Mid-Range U.S. Model SAA** — the primary ordnance sub-inspectors of this group were John T. Cleveland (J.T.C.), Henry Nettleton (H.N.), and David F. Clark (D.F.C.), these guns fall between ser. nos. 30,693-121,147. Mfg. 1876-1887.

N/A	$40,000	$32,000	$25,000	$18,000	$15,000	$14,000	$13,000	$12,000	$10,000	$8,000	$6,000

100%	98%	95%	90%	80%	70%	60%	50%	40%	30%	20%	10%

* **Late U.S. Model SAA** — all inspected by Rinaldo A. Carr (R.A.C.) from 1890-1891, ser. no range 131,208-140,361. The last SAA purchased by the U.S. government was shipped from the factory on April 29, 1891.

N/A	$25,000	$20,000	$18,000	$15,000	$13,000	$12,000	$10,000	$9,000	$8,000	$6,000	$4,000

Beware of restorations! Many have been done in the last 25 years in all inspector serial ranges. Some have now been skillfully "aged" to look more original. When making a substantial purchase, a letter of authentication from a reliable source is suggested in addition to a factory historical letter. Also ask for a guarantee of originality in writing from the seller. No factory information is available on U.S. Cavalry revolvers below ser. no. 30,600.

* **Artillery Model SAAs** — refers to U.S. government model SAA revolvers with 5½ in. barrels and mis-matched numbered parts. In 1896, it was decided that the barrels of all 15,000+ SAAs in storage should be shortened by 2 inches and re-issued into service at the outbreak of the Spanish-American War. At the same time, Colt replaced worn parts and refurbished all guns back to new condition. Between 1900-1903, these guns were returned to Colt a second time for refurbishing, and were reassembled without regard to matching component serial numbers. This shortcut minimized time and cost for the refurbishing process. Only rarely will one be found with all the matching serial numbers, indicating that it escaped the last refinish - these guns will bring a premium price.

$10,000	$8,700	$7,500	$6,500	$5,400	$4,500	$4,000	$3,500	$3,000	$2,500	$1,800	$1,500

* **New York State Militia SAA** — in 1895, before work began on the artillery models, Colt refurbished 800 SA revolvers supplied by Springfield Armory to honor a request from the state of New York. These guns retained their 7½ in. barrels and all original parts wherever possible (replacement parts were serial numbered to match). All were stamped on the bottom of the grips with the initials of Rinaldo A. Carr (R.A.C.). They were given a high polish blue and case hardened civilian finish with blued hammers. Since all other cavalry models in the government's possession were cut to 5½ in. shortly thereafter, these 800 are quite possibly the only quantity of original 7½ in. guns remaining that could actually have seen service on the frontier. All other 7½ in. cavalry models that are seen today were most likely originally issued to state militias rather than to U.S. government miltary forces. These 800 revolvers therefore occupy a very significant position in the history of Colt firearms.

$18,000	$16,000	$14,000	$10,000	$9,000	$8,000	$7,200	$6,500	$5,000	$4,500	$4,000	$3,000

REVOLVERS: SAA, 2ND GENERATION: 1956-1975 MFG.

The author wishes to express his thanks to Charles Layson for his generous contributions and helping to reformat the 2nd & 3rd Generation Colt SAA information.

Popular demand brought back the Single Action Army in 1956 with minor modifications, most not detectable except to experts. Serial numbers began at 0001SA, and continued to 73,000SA before the "New Model" was introduced in 1976 (ser. no. 80,000SA). Premiums are paid for rare production variances in NIB condition. It should be noted "premium niches" exist in this model as collectors are establishing premiums paid for rarer production variances (the interrelation of barrel length, caliber, frame type, finish quality, year of manufacture, and other special features).

The order of desirability on standard 2nd Generation SAAs is as follows: 4¾ in. barrels are the most desirable, followed by 7½ in., and then 5½ in. Caliber desirability is as follows: .45 LC has the most demand, followed by .44 Spl., .38 Spl., and then .357 Mag. It follows that desirable calibers found with desirable barrel lengths will command healthy premiums - especially if production was unusually low for a particular combination. Reference books specifically on the post-war SAA are a must when determining the rarity factors on these multiple production combinations. Buntlines, Sheriff's Models, and special orders through the Custom Gun Shop are in a class by themselves, and have to be evaluated one at a time.

It is advisable to procure a factory letter when buying or selling older or recently manufactured Colt single actions (hence, guaranteeing authenticity and value credibility). The watermarked letters are available to: Colt's Manufacturing Company, Inc., located in Hartford, CT. The charge is $100 per serial number - if Colt cannot provide

Grading	100%	98%	95%	90%	80%	70%	60%

you with proper documentation after conducting research, they will refund you $50. Please include your name, address, Colt model name, serial number, and payment to: COLT HISTORIAN, P.O. 1868, Hartford, CT, 06144. Please allow adequate time for proper response.

SINGLE ACTION ARMY (2ND GENERATION) — .357 Mag., .38 Spl., .44 Spl., or .45 LC cal., denoted by SA suffix, 3 (Sheriff's Model), 4¾, 5½, 7½, or 12 (Buntline) in. barrel length, all blue, blue/case hardened, or nickel finish. 2nd Generation SAAs have been grouped into the following 3 categories.

* *Early 2nd Generation* — ser. no. range 0001SA to approx. 39,000SA, shipped in one-piece black box similar to pre-war box. Mfg. from 1956-1965.

	100%	98%	95%	90%	80%	70%	60%
.45 LC cal.	$2,000	$1,800	$1,500	$1,200	$1,000	$900	$800
.44 Spl. cal.	$1,850	$1,650	$1,350	$1,050	$900	$800	$700
.38 Spl. cal.	$1,700	$1,500	$1,200	$900	$800	$700	$600
.357 Mag. cal.	$1,500	$1,300	$1,000	$800	$700	$600	$500

    Add 30% for original black box in good condition.
    Add 20% for original nickel finish.
    Add 15% for original 4¾ in. barrel.

* *Mid-range 2nd Generation* — ser. no. range 39,000SA to 70,055SA, shipped in a red and white, two-piece, stagecoach box. Mfg. from 1965-1973.

	100%	98%	95%	90%	80%	70%	60%
.45 LC cal.	$1,400	$1,250	$1,100	$1,000	$900	$800	$700
.44 Spl. cal.	$1,300	$1,150	$1,000	$900	$800	$700	$600
.357 Mag. cal.	$1,000	$900	$800	$700	$600	$550	$450

    Add 15% for original stagecoach box.
    Add 10% for original nickel finish.
    Add 10% for original 4¾ in. barrel.

* *Late 2nd Generation* — ser. no. range 70,055SA to 73,205SA, shipped in a brown, wood grain cardboard shell with 2 styrofoam inserts. Mfg. from 1973-1976.

	100%	98%	95%	90%	80%	70%	60%
.45 LC cal.	$1,200	$1,100	$1,000	$900	$800	$700	$600
.357 Mag. cal.	$1,000	$900	$800	$750	$700	$650	$600

    Add 10% for original brown/styrofoam box.
    Add 10% for original nickel finish.
    Add 10% for original 4¾ in. barrel.

    2nd Generation SAAs w/o eagle black grips (ser. numbered under approx. 52,000SA) are more desirable than those with eagle. Also, flat-top hammers are more desirable than round top hammers found between ser. no. range 27,012SA-61,575SA (mfg. mid-1959-1972).

SHERIFF'S MODEL (1961 MODEL) — .45 LC cal., distinctive configuration with 3 in. barrel and no ejector rod housing, ser. no. followed by SM suffix, 500 were mfg. for Centennial Arms Corp. - 475 had a blue/case hardened finish and 25 were done in nickel.

	$1,800	$1,600	$1,400	$1,200	$1,000	$800	$700

    Add 25% for original two-piece box.
    Add 100% for original nickel finish.

BUNTLINE SPECIAL — .45 LC cal. only, 12 in. barrel, blue/case hardened finish, rubber (early mfg.) or walnut grips. Over 3,900 mfg. between 1957-1975.

	$1,300	$1,200	$1,000	$900	$850	$800	$750

    Add 100% for original nickel finish (rare, watch for refinishing).
    Add 30% for original black box in good condition.

Grading	100%	98%	95%	90%	80%	70%	60%

NEW FRONTIER — .357 Mag., .38 Spl. (rare), .44 Spl., or .45 LC cal., denoted by flat-top frame, adj. rear sight, and "NF" after the serial number, 4¾ (scarce), 5½ (scarce), or 7½ (most common) in. barrel, case hardened frame/blue finish and smooth walnut grips were standard. Aproxx. 4,200 mfg. 1961-1975.

	$1,000	**$950**	**$900**	**$850**	**$800**	**$750**	**$700**

Add 15% for later brown/styrofoam box.
Add 35% for early black and gold box.
Add 25% for 4¾ or 5½ in. barrel.
Add 100% for .38 Spl. cal.

NEW FRONTIER BUNTLINE — .45 LC cal. only, 12 in. barrel, flat-top frame and adj. rear sight. Approx. 72 mfg. 1962-1967.

	$2,000	**$1,800**	**$1,600**	**$1,400**	**$1,200**	**$1,100**	**$1,000**

Add 50% for original black box with gold lettering.

FACTORY ENGRAVED 2ND GENERATION SAAs — approx. 350 revolvers were factory engraved with 90% being in .45 LC cal. Values range from 75%-100% higher than non-engraved specimens, with additional premiums paid for rare styles and configurations and/or for the notoriety of the engraver. Those SAAs done by Albert Herbert and A.A. White are probably the highest priced examples. Always check authenticity when buying, selling, or trading engraved 2nd Generation SAAs with the Colt Historical Dept. The charge for a factory letter per engraved gun is $150, $50 will be refunded if Colt cannot provide historical documentation.

Factory engraved 2nd Generation SAAs are at least 10 times rarer than engraved 3rd Generation pistols.

REVOLVERS: SAA, 3RD GENERATION: 1976-CURRENT MFG.

After a short break in production, Colt Firearms announced the resumption of full scale production of the Single Action on Feb. 4th, 1976, at the N.S.G.A. (National Sporting Goods Association) Bi-Centennial show in Chicago.

The "New Model Colt Single Action Army" or the "Colt Post-War Single Action Army - New Model", as it was commonly referred to at the time, is known today to collectors as the "3rd Generation Colt Single Action Army". Minor changes include a modified, thin front sight contour, and the elimination of the cylinder pin bushing, plus a few other "minor, modern manufacturing techniques that have not change the appearance, feel, action, or performance of this historic handgun...", according to Colt's press release at the time.

Production began with ser. no. 80,000SA, and reached 99,999SA in 1978. At this point, the SA suffix changed to a prefix beginning with SA01001. Serialization reached SA99,999 during 1993, and began over, this time separating the letters SA, and starting with SO2001SA. As this edition went to press, serial numbers had reached S22,000A. For whatever reasons, a few writers have erroneously referred to this current production run as "4th Generation Single Actions". This is an incorrect description, as these revolvers are mechanically identical to those produced since 1976, and should still be considered 3rd Generation guns.

For a listing of Colt's "P-Codes" (referring to the factory's model number designations specifing frame type, caliber, finish, and barrel length), please refer to the Colt Single Action Model Numbers section in the back of this book (located in Colt Serialization).

As with 1st and 2nd Generation Single Actions, a factory letter authenticating configuration and shipping destination can be obtained for $100 by writing to: COLT HISTORIAN, P.O. Box 1868, Hartford, CT, 06144. If Colt cannot provide proper documentation after conducting research, they will issue a refund of $50. Please allow 60-90 days for proper response.

Grading	100%	98%	95%	90%	80%	70%	60%

STANDARD SINGLE ACTION ARMY (3RD GENERATION) — .38-40 WCF (disc.), .44-40 WCF, or .45 LC cal., 4 (disc. 1988), 4¾, 5 (disc. 1987), 5½, or 7½ in. barrel, standard finishes include color case hardened/blue or nickel, plastic black eagle or walnut grips standard, most recent mfg. has blue shipping box with white slip cover.

Mfg.'s Sug. Retail	$1,590	$1,375	$925	$800	$700	$650	$600	$550

Subtract 5% for .44 Spl. cal.
Subtract 10% for .357 Mag. cal.
Add 10% for original .38-40 WCF cal.
Add 25% for original .38 Spl. cal.
Add 50% for original two-piece ivory grips with screw.
Add 70% for original one-piece ivory grips w/o screw.
Add 5% for original brown box with styrofoam inserts (mfg. 1976-1993).

Various custom order barrel lengths have been available on this model for some time.

❋ *Popular SAA Custom Shop Special Order Options:*
Add $175 for special barrel length or cal., add $180 for custom-tuned action, add $155-$175 for extra fluted or $195 for extra unfluted cylinder, add $200 for mirror brite finish (disc.), add $425 for gold or silver plating, add $155 for smooth walnut grips, add $345 for stag grips, add $225 for buffalo horn grips, add $425 for mother of pearl grips, add $760 for plain ivory grips or $1,143 with checkering, add $155 for scrimshaw engraving (3 initials only), add $115 for consecutive serial numbers (pair), add $310 for individual unique serial number, add $105 to modify and shorten ejector housing, add $129 for beveled cylinder, add $155 (per set) for heat blued small parts, add 10% for birdshead and extended butt frames. While a very few screwless frame SAAs have been mfg. to date, the Custom Shop now lists this option as a standard custom order feature.

Please contact the Colt Custom Gun Shop for a written quotation ($25) regarding a custom built SAA with special options/features. Their address is: Colt Manufacturing Company, Inc. P.O. Box 1868, Hartford, CT 06101, ATTN: Custom Shop.

COLT COWBOY SINGLE ACTION ARMY — .45 LC cal., 4¾, 5½, or 7½ in. barrel marked "COLT COWBOY .45 COLT" on left side, transfer bar safety, all steel construction, frame assembly done in the U.S., charcoal case colors on frame with blued metal parts, rampant Colt black competition grips similar in design to those used on 1st generation SAAs, 40 oz. While advertised beginning 1998, this model was not manufactured until 1999.

Mfg.'s Sug. Retail	$599	$525	$450	$425	$395	$375	$350	$335

SHERIFF'S MODEL (3RD GENERATION) — .44-40 WCF or .45 LC cal., 3 in. barrel w/o ejector rod, blue/case colored, nickel, or royal blue finish. Approx. 4,560 guns mfg. 1980-85.

.45 LC cal. (blue/CH)	$1,050	$950	$900	$850	$800	$750	$700

Add 20% for extra convertible cylinder.
Add 10% for original nickel finish.
Add 40% for original ivory grips.
Subtract 10% for .44-40 WCF cal. or all blue finish.

BUNTLINE MODEL (3RD GENERATION) — .44-40 WCF or .45 LC cal. only, 12 in. barrel, blue/case hardened finish, walnut grips.

	$950	$850	$800	$750	$700	$650	$600

Add 10% for original nickel finish.
Add 40% for original ivory grips.

NEW FRONTIER (3RD GENERATION) — .44-40 WCF (rare), .44 Spl., or .45 LC cal., denoted by "NF" serial suffix, 43/4, 5½, or 7½ in. barrel, blue/case hardened finish, flat-top frame, adj. rear sight, plain two-piece walnut grips. Mfg. 1978-1981.

	$900	$850	$800	$750	$700	$650	$600

Add 10% for .44-40 WCF cal.
Add 5% for .44 Spl. cal.
Add 30% for original 4¾ in. barrel.
Add 15% for original 5½ in. barrel.
Add 5% for original brown box with styrofoam inserts.

Serial numbers on the New Frontier started at 01001NF, but during 1980, a few New Frontiers with 5½ in. barrels were produced in the 7,000NF serial range, where 2nd Generation New Frontiers left off. Therefore, a 3rd Generation New Frontier will either have a ser. no. starting with "O" or will have a higher number than 7288NF with no "O" prefix.

NEW FRONTIER BUNTLINE SPECIAL (3RD GENERATION) — .45 LC cal. only, 12 in. barrel, flat-top frame, adj. rear sight, limited mfg. as the New Buntline Commemorative during 1979. Please refer to the Colt Commemorative section for value information.

STOREKEEPER'S MODEL (3RD GENERATION) — .45 LC cal. only, black powder frame, 4 in. barrel w/o ejector rod, full nickel or royal blue/case hardened finish, ivory grips. Approx. 280 mfg. 1984-1985.

		$1,600	$1,450	$1,300	$1,100	$900	$800	$750

Add 10% for original nickel finish.

FACTORY ENGRAVED SAAs (3RD GENERATION) — the rarity of the SAA configuration in addition to the notability of the engraver will make the difference on the premiums commanded. 3rd Generation factory engraved SAAs were produced in much greater numbers than were 2nd Generation SAAs. Over 80% of engraved 3rd Generation SAAs are .45 LC caliber, the majority have 7½ in. barrels, and some variation of blue finish. Grade "C" (41% of engraved mfg.) and Grade "D" (24% of engraved mfg.) dominate production.

* *Class "A" Engraved (25% coverage)*

		$1,550	$1,200	$1,050	$900	$800	$700	$600

* *Class "B" Engraved (50% coverage)*

		$1,850	$1,400	$1,250	$1,100	$1,000	$900	$800

* *Class "C" Engraved (75% coverage)*

		$2,300	$1,750	$1,400	$1,300	$1,200	$1,100	$1,000

* *Class "D" Engraved (100% coverage)*

		$2,800	$2,200	$1,800	$1,400	$1,300	$1,200	

Add 10% for original nickel finish.
Add 25% for 4¾ in. barrel.
Add 15% for 5½ in. barrel.
Add 10% for calibers other than .45 LC.
Add 30% for factory ivory grips.

CUSTOM & SPECIAL ENGRAVED EDITIONS (3RD GENERATION) — beginning in 1976, with the introduction of the "New Model" SAA (3rd Generation), the Colt Custom Shop produced many custom and special edition engraved Single Army Action revolvers. According to Mr. Don Wilkerson, author of The Post-War Single Action Revolver 1976-1986, "the term custom edition is defined as a group of identical revolvers assembled under the direction of the Custom Gun Shop at Colt's and sold through the normal distribution system. A custom edition differs from a special edition in that special editions are a group of revolvers made up to a customer's unique specifications, and sold as a group to one purchaser...". While the exact number is not known, it is thought that approx. 3,500 SAAs have been engraved since 1976. Since each edition is unique, values vary widely, depending upon the notability of the engraver, the amount and type of coverage, and the number produced. Models listed below are recent Colt Custom Editions.

Grading	100%	98%	95%	90%	80%	70%	60%

C

* *Engraved European Model* — 9mm Para. cal., nickel finish only, 4¾, 5½, or 7½ in. barrel, rosewood grips with silver medallions, 40-43 oz. Mfg. 1991-92 only.

  $1,395 $1,195 $995

  Last Mfg.'s Sug. Retail was $1,990.

* *Engraved U.S. Model* — .45 ACP cal., royal blue finish only, 4¾, 5½, or 7½ in. barrel, walnut grips, 40-43 oz. Mfg. 1991-92 only.

  $1,295 $1,095 $875

  Last Mfg.'s Sug. Retail was $1,960.

* *Old World Engravers Sampler* — .45 LC cal., 5½ in. barrel, nickel finish, buffalo horn grips, includes four unique styles of engraving. Mfg. 1997-98.

  $2,750 $2,400 $2,000

  Last Mfg.'s Sug. Retail was $3,100.

* *Legend Rodeo II SAA* — disc. 1998.

  $1,950 $1,500 $1,250

  Last Mfg.'s Sug. Retail was $2,450.

* *125th Anniversary Edition* — 2 line frame address, "45 COLT" barrel address marked barrel, beveled cylinder, oven blue finish, 1,000 mfg. beginning 1997.

  Mfg.'s Sug. Retail $1,615 $1,300 $995 $750

SAA CUSTOM SHOP ENGRAVING PRICES - PRE-1997 — values below represent 1995 published SAA Custom Shop A-D engraving options, before the company started separate Standard, Expert, and Master level pricing during 1997. For current Colt Custom Shop engraving prices, please refer to the "Colt Custom Shop Engraving - Current Mfg." listed below.

> Add $1,163 for Class "A" engraving (25% metal coverage).
> Add $2,324 for Class "B" engraving (50% metal coverage).
> Add $3,487 for Class "C" engraving (75% metal coverage).
> Add $4,647 for Class "D" engraving (100% metal coverage).
> Add an additional 13% (approx.) for buntline engraving.

Standard Engraving was performed mostly by standard level factory engravers and engraving options generally include A-D style coverage. Typically, gold work was not performed by these engravers and specimens are mostly unsigned. Expert Engravers executed classic American style scroll, no gold, and may be signed.

COLT CUSTOM SHOP ENGRAVING - CURRENT MFG.

The chart below indicates current Custom Shop engraving prices for the various frame sizes, amount of engraving coverage, and the three levels of engraving execution (i.e., Standard, Expert, and Master levels). SAAs are considered large frame, revolvers and full-size Government Models are considered medium frame, and Government Model 380s are considered small frame.

LARGE FRAME SIZE

ENGRAVING COVERAGE	STANDARD LEVEL	EXPERT LEVEL	MASTER LEVEL
A	$800	$900 (disc.)	$1,200 (disc.)
B	$900	$1,700	$2,500
C	$1,200	$2,500	$3,600
D	$1,600	$3,600	$4,800

MEDIUM FRAME SIZE

A	$900	N/A	N/A
B	$1,000	$1,200	$1,600
C	$1,200	$1,600	$2,400
D	$1,600	$2,400	$3,200

SMALL FRAME SIZE

ENGRAVING COVERAGE	STANDARD LEVEL	EXPERT LEVEL	MASTER LEVEL
Factory small frame engraving was disc. 1998.			
A	$400	$600	$800
B	$600	$800	$1,000
C	$800	$1,100	$1,500
D	$1,100	$1,300	$1,900

Add 20% to large frame pricing for Buntline Models.
Subtract 20% from small frame pricing for Mustang Models.
Other Custom Shop options are priced on request.

C

Grading	100%	98%	95%	90%	80%	70%	60%

REVOLVERS: SAA, SCOUT MODEL

100% values below assume NIB condition. Subtract 10% without box.

FRONTIER SCOUT (Q or F SUFFIX) — .22 LR or .22 Mag. (introduced after 1960) cal., "Q" or "F" suffix, blue with bright alloy frame, all blue, or duotone ("Q" models only) finish (rare), 4¾ or 9½ (Buntline) barrel, available with interchangeable cylinders after 1964, black composition or walnut grips, approx. 246,000 mfg. 1957-1970.

| | $450 | $375 | $275 | $225 | $175 | $150 | $140 |

Add 10% for extra cylinder.
Add 20% for Buntline model.
Add 25% for "Q" suffix - mfg. 1957-58 only.

FRONTIER SCOUT (K SUFFIX) — Zamac alloy frame version of "Q" Model with "K" suffix, blue or nickel finish with walnut stocks, approx. 44,000 mfg. 1960-1970.

| | $500 | $395 | $275 | $225 | $175 | $150 | $140 |

This model used the alloy Zamac for manufacture (as opposed to aluminum in the "Q" and "F" suffix models), and specimens are 6 oz. heavier as a result.

FRONTIER SCOUT '62 (P SUFFIX) — blue finish version of "K" Model, except has "P" suffix, staglite grips, approx. 68,000 mfg. 1962-1970.

| | $500 | $395 | $275 | $225 | $175 | $150 | $140 |

PEACEMAKER — .22 LR/.22 Mag. cal., color casehardened steel frame, 4¾, 6, or 7½ (nicknamed Buntline Model but may be marked Peacemaker or Buntline) in. barrel, black composition grips, furnished with interchangeable .22 LR/.22 Mag. cylinders, approx. 190,000 mfg. 1970-1977.

| | $500 | $350 | $275 | $225 | $175 | $150 | $140 |

Add 20% for 4¾ in. barrel.
Subtract 10% if without extra cylinder.
This model can be denoted by a "G" or "L" prefix.

NEW FRONTIER — similar features as Peacemaker Model, except with flat top frame, ramp front and adj. rear sight, mfg. 1970-1977. Reintroduced in 1982 without convertible .22 Mag. cylinder and added cross bolt safety, available in Coltguard finish, all blue finish became standard in 1985, mfg. disc. 1986.

| | $325 | $275 | $215 | $185 | $155 | $140 | $130 |

Last Mfg.'s Sug. Retail was $181.

Add 15% for Buntline model or 4¾ in. barrel.
This model can be denoted by a "G" or "L" prefix.

PISTOLS: SEMI-AUTO, DISC.

Until several years ago, the Single Action Army revolver commanded the most attention among Colt handgun collectors. Since 1987, Colt Semi-Autos have been in tremendous demand and have out-accelerated many other areas of Colt collecting. Because condition and originality play such a key role in determining Colt Semi-Auto prices, many variations have had their values pushed upward to the point where it is

Grading	100%	98%	95%	90%	80%	70%	60%

difficult to accurately determine a realistic price - especially on those models in 98% original condition or better. As a result, some of the rarer models seldomly encountered in true 100% original condition have had their values deleted since extreme rarity precludes accurate price evaluation in this 100% condition category. As always, the hardest prices to ascertain when firearms market conditions are bullish are the 98-100% values.

C

MODEL 1900 — .38 ACP cal., 6 in. barrel, blue, plain walnut grips - checkered hard rubber grips after S/N 2,450, high spur hammer, sight safety. Mfg. 1900-1903.

	N/A	$6,500	$4,650	$3,150	$2,000	$1,700	$1,350

Add 60%+ for USN marked.
Add 50% for US marked with inspector initials.
Subtract 30%-50% for sight safety altered (factory refinished).
This model is serial numbered approx. between 1-4,274.

MODEL 1902 SPORTING — .38 ACP, 6 in. barrel, blue, fixed sights, checkered hard rubber grips, no safety, high spur hammer and round hammer. Mfg. 1902-1908.

	N/A	$2,750	$1,850	$1,250	$850	$725	$650

This model is serial numbered approx. 4,275-11,000 and 30,000-30,190.

MODEL 1902 MILITARY — .38 ACP cal., 6 in. barrel, blue, similar to 1902 Sporting, hammer changed to spur type in 1908, checkered black hard rubber grips, lanyard swivel on bottom rear of left grip. Mfg. 1902-1929.

	N/A	$2,300	$1,550	$950	$750	$625	$500

Add 30% for front slide checkering.
Add 20% with original box and instructions.
This model is serial numbered approx. 11,000-16,000 and 30,200-43,266.

MODEL 1902 MILITARY-U.S. ARMY MARKED — similar specifications to 1902 Military, only serial number range 15,001-15,200.

	N/A	$7,500	$5,750	$4,750	$3,700	$2,900	$2,250

MODEL 1903 POCKET (38 ACP) — .38 ACP cal., 4½ in. barrel, blue finish standard, checkered black hard rubber grips, similar to 1902 Sporting, but 4½ in. barrel, 7½ in. overall. Mfg. 1903-1929.

$1,450	$1,150	$850	$700	$525	$475	$425

Add 30% for early round hammer.
Add 20% with original box and instructions.
This model is serial numbered approx. 16,000-47,226.

MODEL 1903 POCKET (MODEL M 32 ACP) — .32 ACP cal., 4 in. barrel, charcoal blue, checkered hard rubber grips, hammerless, slide lock and grip safety, barrel lock bushing. Mfg. 1903-1946.

$575	$425	$350	$300	$275	$250	$200

Add 20% for nickel finish (mostly w/pearl grips).
Add 60% for first model (Type I) mfg. 1903-1911 if in 100%-98% condition. If lower than 98%, add 20%.
Add 30% for Type II if in 100%-98% condition.
Add 10% with original box and instructions.

Type I - 32 ACPs have a 4 in. barrel, barrel bushing, no magazine safety, and are serial numbered 1-71,999.

Type II - 32 ACPs still retain their barrel bushing but have a 3¾ in. barrel and were mfg. from 1908-1910. They are serial numbered 72,000-105,050.

Type III - 32 ACPs do not have a barrel bushing and were mfg. from 1910-1926. They are serial numbered 105,051-468,096.

Type IV - 32 ACPs have the added magazine safety (of which there are both the commercial and "U.S. Property" variations). They are serial numbered 468,097-554,446.

Grading	100%	98%	95%	90%	80%	70%	60%

* **Model 1903 Parkerized** — U.S. property, 3¼ in. barrel, no barrel bushing, magazine safety, serial numbered 554,447-572,214.

	100%	98%	95%	90%	80%	70%	60%
	$950	$775	$625	$475	$375	$320	$275

Add 50% for blue U.S. Property S/N 554,447 - approx. 562,000.
Add 20% with original box and instructions.

The 100% value on this model assumes NIB condition.

* **Model 1903 General Officer's Pistol** — .32 ACP cal., blue (mfg. until 1942) or parkerized (mfg. started 1942) finish.

	100%	98%	95%	90%	80%	70%	60%
Parkerized	$1,800	$1,550	$1,275	$1,100	$975	$875	$775
Blue Finish	$2,500	$2,250	$1,975	$1,725	$1,500	$1,300	$1,100

Values above assume issue to a General, and there must be paperwork to link up the gun to the recipient.

MODEL 1905 — .45 ACP cal., 5 in. barrel, blue, fixed sights, checkered walnut stocks, similar to 1902 .38 ACP. Mfg. 1905-1911.

	100%	98%	95%	90%	80%	70%	60%
	N/A	$4,475	$2,750	$1,650	$1,250	$950	$775

Add 50% for factory slotted specimens (500 manufactured).
Add 250% for 1907 U.S. Military Contract variation (205 manufactured).

The shoulder stock option for this pistol is exceedingly rare. Depending on the condition, this accessory can add $7,500-$10,000 to the price of the gun.

MODEL 1908 POCKET (MODEL M 380 ACP) — .380 ACP cal., first issue, 3¾ in. barrel only, similar to Pocket Model .32 ACP (32 ACP), except chambered for .380 ACP. Mfg. 1908-1940.

	100%	98%	95%	90%	80%	70%	60%
	$850	$650	$450	$350	$300	$250	$225

Add 15% for Type II (see explanation below).
Add $100 for nickel finish.
Add 15% for pearl grips.

100% values assume NIB condition. Subtract 15% if without cardboard box. Pearl grips are normally encountered with nickel finish on this model.

Type II - 380 ACPs with barrel bushing and were mfg. 1908-1910 (6,251 mfg.). They are serial numbered 1-6,251.

Type III - 380 ACPs do not have a barrel bushing and were mfg. 1910-1926. They are serial numbered 6,252-92,893.

Type IV - 380 ACPs have the added magazine safety (of which there are both the commercial and "U.S. Property" variations). They are serial numbered 92,894-134,499.

* **Model 1908 "U.S. Property"** — blue finish only, U.S. property. Serial numbered 134,500-138,000.

	100%	98%	95%	90%	80%	70%	60%
	$2,000	$1,400	$925	$750	$650	$500	$350

* **Model 1908 General Officer's Pistol** — .380 ACP cal., blue finish only.

	100%	98%	95%	90%	80%	70%	60%
	$2,700	$2,400	$2,100	$1,850	$1,600	$1,400	$1,200

Values above assume issue to a General, and there must be paperwork to link up the gun to the recipient.

VEST POCKET MODEL 1908-HAMMERLESS — .25 ACP cal., 2 in. barrel, fixed sights, checkered hard rubber grips on early models, walnut on later, magazine disconnect added on guns made after 1916. Mfg. 1908-1946.

	100%	98%	95%	90%	80%	70%	60%
Blue finish	$575	$425	$325	$275	$225	$200	$155
Nickel finish	$695	$475	$335	$285	$240	$215	$175

Add 15% for pearl grips.

100% values assume NIB condition. Subtract 15% if without cardboard box in 95% or better condition only. This model was also supplied with a suede purse - add $25-$50, depending on condition.
Add 100% if "U.S. Property" marked.

Grading	100%	98%	95%	90%	80%	70%	60%

MODEL 1909 — .45 ACP cal., straight handle design, 5 in. barrel, checkered walnut grips, approx. 22 mfg., ultra rare.

> Extreme rarity factor precludes accurate price evaluation by individual condition factors. Specimens that are original and over 90% have sold for over $35,000 recently.

MODEL 1910 — .45 ACP cal., while not a production model, this gun is probably the most desirable semi-auto Colt pistol. A nice specimen at a recent auction was gavelled down at $195,000.

GENERAL OFFICER'S PISTOL — issued not only to Generals, but many were also issued to the OSS, U.S. Navy, and other government agencies, .32 ACP cal. U.S. Properties were blued until 1942, after which the parkerized finish became standard (most went to England and exhibit British proofmarks), .380 cal. U.S. Properties were always blued, 1911A1 WWII specimens have standard military finish, and the Rock Island Arsenal .45s were all issued to Generals - see listing below.

M15 (RIA mfg.)   **$4,750**   **$4,250**   **$3,250**   **$2,900**   **$2,500**   **$1,850**   **$1,500**

> Please refer to separate Model 1903, Model 1908, and Model 1911A1 Military General Officer's Model listings.

PISTOLS: SEMI-AUTO, GOVT. MODEL 1911 COMMERCIAL VARIATIONS

MODEL 1911 — .45 ACP cal., 5 in. barrel, fixed sights, 7 shot mag., flat main spring housing, polished blue finish only (commercial and original military), checkered walnut grips. Colt licensed other companies to manufacture under government contracts, 39 oz. Mfg. 1912-1925.

> Most M1911 variations listed below are not as collectible if under 60% original condition. However, they are still very desirable as shooters and values (if in original condition) will approximate the 60% prices if in good mechanical condition.
>
> Colt Model 1911s continue to enjoy high demand as of this writing and prices continue to be strong in the 95%-100% condition factors. Be careful on the 98%+ condition specimens, especially the rarer variations. Some collectors are now requiring a potential high-dollar Model 1911 to pass a metallurgical X-ray examination before purchasing.

* ***Model 1911 Commercial*** — denoted by "C" preceding serial number, approx. ser. number range C1-C138,532. Watch for fakes.

    ➤ **Model 1911 High Polish Blue** — mfg. 1912 through ser. no. 4,500.

          $4,500   **$3,500**   **$2,750**   **$1,800**   **$1,200**   **$800**   **$600**

    ➤ **Model 1911 Regular Finish** — pistols mfg. after ser. no. 4,500.

          $2,750   **$1,750**   **$1,200**   **$900**   **$700**   **$575**   **$450**

Subtract 15% if without cardboard box in 100% condition only.

Approx. 138,532 were mfg. between 1912-1925.

100% values assume NIB condition.

PISTOLS: SEMI-AUTO, GOVT. MODEL 1911 MILITARY VARIATIONS

All pistols in this section are .45 ACP (11.25mm) cal., unless so noted.

COLT MFG. MODEL 1911 MILITARY — right side of slide marked "MODEL OF 1911 U.S. ARMY", blue finish only (NOT parkerized unless reworked).

1912-1913 mfg.   **$2,900**   **$1,995**   **$1,325**   **$925**   **$550**   **$475**   **$400**

Add 100% for the first 114 pistols with oversize "United States Property" marking.
Add 75% for pistols in the ser. no. range 115-2,400.

1914-1925 mfg.   **$2,300**   **$1,600**   **$975**   **$625**   **$525**   **$425**   **$375**

> Over 2,550,000 M1911 pistols were ordered for WWI and WWII by U.S. Government but approx. 650,000 were mfg. between 1911-1925. Those pistols with a parkerized finish will indicate post-WWI reworking, usually marked with an arsenal code (ie. AA-AUGUSTA ARSENAL, SA-SPRINGFIELD ARSENAL, etc.). These reworks do not have the same values as original, unaltered specimens and prices generally are in the $325-$550 range.

Grading	100%	98%	95%	90%	80%	70%	60%

NORTH AMERICAN ARMS COMPANY — less than 100 mfg. in Quebec, Ontario during 1918 only, blued finish. Be very wary of fakes, as this variation is perhaps the most desirable Colt WWI Govt. semi-auto.

	N/A	$20,000	$16,500	$13,250	$10,000	$8,500	$7,000

Most mint/100% specimens encountered in this model have been refinished - be careful.

REMINGTON - UMC — over 21,500 mfg. (ser. numbered 1-21,676) in 1918-1919 only, blued finish.

	N/A	$2,500	$1,675	$950	$700	$575	$525

Most mint/100% specimens encountered in this model have been refinished - be careful.

SPRINGFIELD ARMORY — approx. 30,000 mfg. between 1914–1915, blued finish.

	N/A	$2,575	$1,525	$975	$725	$600	$550

Serialization is 72,751-83,855, 102,597-107,596, 113,497-120,566, and 125,567-133,186.

Most mint/100% specimens encountered in this model have been refinished - be careful.

U.S. NAVY — over 31,000 mfg. for U.S. Navy contract between 1911-1914 in defined serial ranges, blued finish. Marked "MODEL OF 1911 U.S. NAVY" on right slide side.

$4,450	$2,800	$1,950	$1,700	$1,375	$995	$750

Add 100% for specimens under serial no. 3,500.

U.S. Navy specimens are seldomly found in over 80% original condition because of the corrosive factor encountered while at sea.

U.S. MARINE CORPS. — approx. 13,500 mfg. between 1911-1913 and 1916-1918 in defined serial ranges, blued finish, right side of slide marked "MODEL OF 1911 U.S. ARMY".

$3,200	$2,675	$2,025	$1,725	$1,275	$1,050	$750

WWI BRITISH SERIES — .455 cal., serialized W19,000-W110,695, marked "CALIBRE 455", blued finish, proofed with broad arrow British Ordnance punch. Mfg. 1915-1919.

$2,750	$2,150	$1,400	$975	$775	$650	$550

Many WWI British-series M1911s were exported back to the U.S. following WWI and were converted to .45 ACP. Usually, a "5" has been crossed-out of the original cal. designation.

BRITISH RAF REWORK — this variation is the WWI British series re-issued to RAF officers in the early 1920s, blued finish, differentiated by hand-stamped "RAF" or "R.A.F." on left side of frame.

$1,250	$1,050	$825	$675	$575	$495	$460

A.J. SAVAGE MUNITIONS CO. — mfg. slides only, blued finish, marked in middle on left side of slide with flaming ordnance bomb with "S" in center.

$1,425	$1,125	$875	$725	$625	$550	$495

NORWEGIAN TRIAL MODEL 1911 COLT — 11.25mm cal., approx. 300 mfg. with "C" prefix in 1913-14 only, usually encountered in 90% or less condition.

$1,875	$1,325	$995	$875	$775	$625	$525

These guns were ordered for Norwegian service evaluation and were mfg. by Colt in Hartford, CT.

NORWEGIAN MODEL 1912 11.25MM — 11.25mm cal., mfg. under license from Colt's during 1917, "M1912" slide designation, approx. 95 mfg.

$3,950	$3,500	$3,000	$2,500	$2,100	$1,825	$1,475

NORWEGIAN 1914 11.25MM — This model has a distinctive extended slide release, all parts should be serial numbered and have matching numbers, approx. 20,000 mfg. between 1919-1932.

$1,000	$825	$695	$525	$475	$425	$375

Add 150% for Waffenamt Nazi mfg. (mfg. 1945 only).

Nazi production of the M1914 began in 1941, with serialization beginning where 1932 mfg. left off (approx. 21,000 range). Between 1941-42, approx. 7,000 pistols were mfg.

Grading	100%	98%	95%	90%	80%	70%	60%

without Waffenamt stampings. Nazi stamped guns (all 1945 dated) began in the mid-29,000 serial range and existing specimens indicate that more than 32,000 were mfg. with the Nazi Eagle.

ARGENTINE CONTRACT MODEL 1916 — identified by the Argentine seal on top of slide, 1,000 mfg. in ser. range C20,001-C21,000, mfg. 1916.

	$1,400	$1,000	$725	$575	$450	$410	$350

Most specimens of this model have been refinished.

RUSSIAN CONTRACT — approx. 50,000 mfg. with frame marked "ANGLO ZAKAZIVAT", blued finish. Mfg. 1915-1917.

	$3,500	$2,900	$2,500	$1,800	$1,250	$1,100	$1,000

Several years ago, a European distributor imported a quantity of this Russian contract variation with a C prefix, but marked "ANGLO ZAKAZIVAT". This contract is seldolmly encountered - beware of fakes.

PISTOLS: SEMI-AUTO, GOVT. MODEL 1911A1 COMMERCIAL VARIATIONS

All pistols in this section are .45 ACP cal., unless so noted.

MODEL 1911A1 — blue or parkerized, checkered walnut grips, plastic on later military guns, checkered arched mainspring housing and longer grip safety spur. As in the Model 1911, Colt licensed other companies to produce under govt. contract during WWII. Mfg. 1925-1970.

Inspect carefully for arsenal reworks (so marked by proofing, normally on left side of frame above or behind trigger), and reparkerizing.

Most M1911A1 variations listed below are not as collectible if under 60% original condition. However, they are still very desirable as shooters and values (if in original condition) will approximate the 60% prices if in good mechanical condition.

PRE-WWII COLT COMMERCIAL — "C" preceding serial number, mfg. 1925-1942. Approx. ser. no. range C138,533-C215,000.

	$2,500	$1,950	$1,225	$850	$695	$550	$425

Add 50% for nickel finish.
Add 20% with original box and instructions.

1946-1969 COLT COMMERCIAL — 5 in. barrel, fixed sights, "C" prefix until 1950 when changed to "C" suffix, approx. 196,000 mfg. 1946-1970.

* *1946-1950 Mfg.* — C-Prefix with serial numbers C221,000 - C240,227.

	$1,450	$1,175	$900	$750	$675	$550	$475

* *1950-1970 Mfg.* — C-Suffix with serial numbers 240,228C - 336,169C.

	$850	$745	$675	$550	$475	$425	$400

Add 10% for nickel finish.

SUPER .38 AUTOMATIC PISTOL — identical to Govt. Model .45, except chambered for .38 Super automatic, blue or nickel finish. Mfg. 1928-1970.

	100%	98%	95%	90%	80%	70%	60%
Pre-War	$2,900	$2,375	$1,750	$1,250	$1,000	$875	$750
2nd Model	$1,350	$1,100	$875	$725	$660	$550	$475
3rd Model	$1,100	$875	$725	$660	$575	$500	$435
4th Model	$895	$775	$675	$575	$500	$435	$385
CS Prefix	$850	$745	$675	$550	$475	$415	$375

Add approx. 50% for nickel finish.

Pre-war variations are serialized below approx. 37,000.

The 2nd Model may be differentiated by noticing the heavier barrel and Rampant Colt on right side. The 3rd Model has a fat barrel with Rampant Colt on left side. The 4th Model has a thin barrel and Rampant Colt on left side.

Grading	100%	98%	95%	90%	80%	70%	60%

SUPER MATCH .38 — similar to Super .38, but hand honed action, match grade barrel. Mfg. 1935-1946. Examine carefully for fakes.

Fixed sights	$4,950	$4,150	$3,450	$2,350	$1,575	$1,275	$1,050

Add 35% for adj. sights (be cautious of fixed sight Super Matches converted to adj. sights).

A Colt historical letter is available for this model at $100 each.

MATCH .38 AMU — .38 rimless Spl. cal. (cartridges were mfg. by Win.), this variation was mfg. by Colt from a .38 Super frame (and has .38 Super serialization) with a .38 AMU conversion kit slide, the Army took .45 frames and assembled their guns using .38 AMU kits, blued finish.

	100%	98%	95%	90%	80%	70%	60%
Colt mfg. (unmodified)	$2,500	$2,200	$1,900	$1,675	$1,400	$1,175	$975
Army modified	$1,400	$1,200	$995	$800	$650	$550	$495
AMU kit only	$550	$475	$425	$385	$350	$325	$295

On this configuration, the barrel, slide, and mag. were marked ".38 AMU".

SUPER MATCH .38 MS — .38 Super cal., 1961 mfg., serial numbered 101MS - 855MS, 754 total manufactured, same configuration as the .38 Midrange.

	$2,800	$2,500	$1,750	$1,495	$1,375	$1,175	$1,000

1968-1969 BB TRANSITIONAL — denoted by BB prefix on serial number.

	$995	$850	$625	$550	$495	$425	$375

.45 ACP TO .22 LR CONVERSION UNIT — consists of slide assembly, barrel, bushing, floating chamber, ejector, recoil spring and guide, fitted with Stevens adj. rear sight, mfg. 1938 to 1947. Colt Master adj. sight 1947-54.

	$395	$350	$285	$195	$175	$150	$125

Add 100% for prewar mfg. (U-prefix S/N on top of slide).
Add 200% for pre-war documented Marine Corp units.

.22 LR TO .45 ACP CONVERSION UNIT — converted service Ace .22 to .45 ACP cal. Mfg. 1938-1942. Very rare — 112 mfg.

	$3,500	$2,500	$1,750	$1,000	$800	$700	$600

These units have "U" prefixed serial numbers on top of slide.

PISTOLS: SEMI-AUTO, GOVT. MODEL 1911A1 MILITARY VARIATIONS

All pistols in this section are .45 ACP (11.25mm) cal., unless so noted.

COLT MFG. MODEL 1911A1 MILITARY — approx. 1,643,068 mfg. between 1924-1945, ser. nos. 700,000 - on up, right side of frame marked "M1911A1 U.S. ARMY".

	$1,150	$895	$625	$485	$385	$350	$325

Add 50% for 1937-38 mfg.
Add 50% for 1939 Navy variation (S/N 713,646 - 717,281).
Add 20% for 1942 Navy ser. no. range.

On early 1911A1 military models with bright blue finish — add 150% if condition is 98% or better.

A large grouping of over 7,000 Commercial 1911A1s was transferred to the U.S. government - these pistols had their commercial serial numbers crudely removed (in ser. range 860,000 - 866,000) and renumbered with a new military serial number. Some of these guns are unusual as the frames and slides have been cut for the Schwartz safety. This variation is rare, and a 20%-30% premium exists depending on the condition.

✶ *Model 1911A1 General Officer's Pistol* — standard military finish.

(WWII mfg.)	$1,500	$1,250	$1,050	$875	$775	$675	$595

Values above assume issue to a General, and there must be paperwork to link up the gun to the recipient.

DRAKE NATIONAL MATCH — Drake made slides only for use by U.S. Army Marksmanship Unit to allow assembly of match guns.

	$1,275	$1,075	$850	$700	$585	$510	$450

Grading	100%	98%	95%	90%	80%	70%	60%

GOVERNMENT NATIONAL MATCH REWORKS — assembled by government armorers, all parts marked "NM", parkerized finish. Most will be S.A. marked.

	$1,275	$1,075	$850	$675	$585	$510	$450

Add 25% for Air Force pistols marked "AFPG" on slide.

These pistols were made specifically for the U.S. shooting team at Camp Perry.

ITHACA — approx. 369,129 mfg. 1943-1945 in Ithaca, NY, ser. no. ranges 856,405 - 916,404, 1,208,674 - 1,279,673, 1,441,431 - 1,471,430, 1,743,847 - 1,890,503, 2,075,104 - 2,134,403, and 2,619,014 - 2,693,613. Parkerized finish.

	$800	$600	$500	$450	$375	$350	$325

Add 20% with original shipping carton.

UNION SWITCH AND SIGNAL — approx. 55,000 mfg. 1943 only in Swissvale, PA, ser. no. range 1,041,405 - 1,096,404. Sandblast and blue finish.

	$1,495	$1,150	$900	$600	$500	$450	$425

REMINGTON RAND — approx. 1,086,624 mfg. 1943-1945 in Syracuse, NY, ser. no. ranges 916,405 - 1,041,404, 1,279,649 - 1,441,430, 1,471,431 - 1,609,528, 1,743,847 - 1,816,641, 1,890,504 - 2,075,103, 2,134,404 - 2,244,803, and 2,380,014 - 2,619,013. Parkerized finish.

	$795	$625	$525	$425	$375	$350	$325

Add 20% with original shipping carton.

SINGER MFG. CO. — 500 mfg. 1942 in Elizabeth, NJ, ser. no. range S800,001 - S800,500. Blued finish with plastic grips.

	N/A	$20,000	$16,500	$13,250	$10,000	$8,500	$7,000

The Singer 1911A1 variation is one of the most sought after Colt models. In recent years, values have increased significantly and as a result, many fakes have emerged. Most specimens are now recognized by ser. no. and be very cautious when contemplating a purchase. Some collectors unsure of authenticity are now requiring X-ray testing to determine originality (slide restampings, ser. no. changes, etc.).

MEXICAN CONTRACT — mfg. approx. 1921-1927 with "C" prefix ser. nos., frames marked "EJERCITO MEXICANO", most surviving examples show much use.

	$2,650	$1,975	$1,525	$1,250	$975	$775	$575

BRAZILIAN CONTRACT

	$2,600	$1,950	$1,500	$1,250	$975	$775	$575

ARGENTINE CONTRACT MODEL 1927 — serial numbered 1-10,000 under the mainspring housing and on the top of slide (should be matching), must have Argentine crest and "Model 1927" on right side of slide, external serial number applied to the outside of frame by the Argentine Arsenal, most have been Arsenal refinished.

	$1,150	$950	$795	$675	$595	$525	$475

ARGENTINE MFG. — in 1927, the Argentina Arsenal "DGFM-FMAP" began manufacturing the Model 1911A1. The slide marking is two lines and reads "EJERCITO ARGENTINO SIST.COLT.CAL. 11.25mm MOD.1927".

	$750	$650	$500	$450	$400	$350	$325

Add 20% for Argentine Navy "ARMADA NACIONAL" (small shipments between 1912-1948). Markings vary on different types.

This variation is not to be confused with the Ballester Molina/Rigaud Models (sold by Hispano Argentino Fabrica de Automoviles SA, Buenos Aires, Argentina - also known as the HAFDASA). Please refer to the Hispano Argentino Fabrica de Automovilas SA section of this text.

ARGENTINE SERVICE MODEL ACE — .22 LR cal., conversion of the 1927 Argentine Contract Model, bottom right side of slide is marked "TRANSE A CAL .22 POR EST. VENTUR-INI S.A.". Originally imported during 1996, this model was arsenal refinished and most pistols were in the 70%-95% condition range.

	$575	$525	$475	$425	$400	$375	$350

Grading	100%	98%	95%	90%	80%	70%	60%

PISTOLS: SEMI-AUTO, ACE MODELS - PRE-WWII

COMMERCIAL ACE — .22 LR cal., similar to Government .45 ACP, but in .22LR cal., 4¾ in. barrel, blue, adj. sights, checkered walnut grips, almost 11,000 mfg. (ser. no. range 1-10,935) 1931-1941 and 1947.

	$2,600	$1,900	$1,300	$975	$775	$600	$500

Add 20% with original box and instructions.

SERVICE MODEL ACE — .22 LR cal., 5 in. barrel, blue or parkerized finish, similar to .45 ACP National Match except for caliber, has floating chamber to simulate .45 ACP recoil, limited mfg. 1935-1945.

	$2,600	$2,100	$1,800	$1,225	$875	$675	$575

Add 20% with original box and instructions.

This variation is marked "SERVICE MODEL" on left frame, serial numbers have "SM" prefix and have ranges to approx. 13,800. Parkerized finish is less desirable - subtract 10%.

PISTOLS: SEMI-AUTO, NATIONAL MATCH MODELS - PRE-WWII

NATIONAL MATCH — .45 ACP cal., similar to Government Model, except has hand honed action, match grade barrel, blue. Mfg. 1933-1941 within ser. no. range C164,800 - C215,000.

Add 10% with original box and instructions.

* **Fixed sights**

	$2,750	$2,150	$1,350	$925	$625	$550	$500

* **Adj. sights**

	$3,650	$2,950	$1,975	$1,625	$1,275	$1,075	$850

PISTOLS: SEMI-AUTO, NATIONAL MATCH MODELS - POST-WWII

GOLD CUP NATIONAL MATCH — .45 ACP cal., match grade barrel, new design bushing, flat mainspring housing, long adj. stop trigger, hand fitted slide with enlarged ejection port, adj. target sights, gold medallions in grips, "NM" suffix. Mfg. 1957-1970.

	$1,095	$900	$650	$500	$450	$425	$400

Add 10% with original box and instructions.

Note: This model was the first National Match Model manufactured following WW II.

GOLD CUP MKIII NATIONAL MATCH — .38 Spl. cal., similar to Gold Cup National Match, except chambered for .38 Spl., mid-range wadcutter, NMR or MR suffix. Mfg. 1961-1974.

	$1,100	$895	$775	$675	$625	$525	$475

Add 10% with original box and instructions.

MKIV/SERIES 70 GOLD CUP NATIONAL MATCH — .45 ACP cal., flat mainspring housing, accurizer barrel and bushing, adj. trigger, target hammer, solid rib, Colt-Elliason sight. Mfg. 1970-1983.

	$850	$750	$595	$495	$450	$395	$375

MKIV/SERIES 70 GOLD CUP 75TH ANNIVERSARY NATIONAL MATCH — similar to Gold Cup, except was mfg. for commemorative aspect of Camp Perry, 1978, 200 mfg. 1978 only.

	$1,160	$995	$850	$750	$675	$595	$525

GOLD CUP MKIV SERIES 80 NATIONAL MATCH — .45 ACP cal., 5 in. barrel, 7 or 8 (new 1992) shot mag., 39 oz., Colt-Elliason adj. rear sight, wide grooved adj. target trigger, under cut front sight, flat mainspring housing, critical internal parts are hand honed. Mfg. 1983-1996.

	$735	$575	$460	$400	$380	$350	$325

Last Mfg.'s Sug. Retail was $937.

In 1992, this model was updated to accept an 8 shot mag.

Grading	100%	98%	95%	90%	80%	70%	60%

C

* **Stainless Gold Cup National Match** — similar to Gold Cup, only manufactured from stainless steel, matte finish, mfg. late 1986-1996.

$800	$600	$495

Last Mfg.'s Sug. Retail was $1,003.

> **Add $70 for "Ultimate" bright stainless steel finish.**

* **.38 Super Elite National Match** — two-tone gun (stainless slide and blued frame), special edition by Accu-Sports.

$1,100	$925	$825

* **Bullseye National Match** — .45 ACP cal., hand built, tuned, and adjusted by Colt's custom gunsmiths for precise match accuracy, includes factory installed Bomar sights, equipped with carrying case and 2 extra mags. Mfg. 1991-92.

$1,325	$1,075	$895	$800	$725	$650	$600

Last Mfg.'s Sug. Retail was $1,500.

* **Presentation Gold Cup** — .45 ACP cal., similar to regular Gold Cup Series 80 National Match, except has a deep blue-mirror bright finish accented by custom jeweled hammer, trigger, and barrel hood. Supplied with oak and velvet custom case. Mfg. 1991-92.

$1,075	$895	$800	$725	$650	$600	$550

Last Mfg.'s Sug. Retail was $1,195.

GOLD CUP TROPHY — .45 ACP cal., flat mainspring housing, 7 or 8 shot mag., accurizer barrel and bushing, adj. trigger, target hammer, Colt-Elliason sight, checkered wrap-around rubber grips, shipped with test target, 39 oz. New 1997.

Mfg.'s Sug. Retail	$1,050		$875	$625	$500	$450	$395	$350	$325

> This model replaced the MKIV/Series 80 Gold Cup National Match in 1997, and is only available from the Colt Custom Gun Shop.

* **Stainless Gold Cup Trophy** — similar to Gold Cup Trophy, only manufactured from stainless steel, matte finish, 39 oz. New 1997.

Mfg.'s Sug. Retail	$1,116		$895	$650	$525

PISTOLS: SEMI-AUTO, SINGLE ACTION - RECENT MFG.

SEMI-AUTO CUSTOM SHOP ENGRAVING PRICING - PRE-1991

Values below represent pre-1991 factory semi-auto Custom Shop A-D engraving options, before they started separate Standard, Expert, and Master level pricing (1997). It should also be understood that, in most cases, the quality of the engraving and notoriety of the engraver can be as important as the amount of coverage.

SMALL FRAME ENGRAVING OPTIONS (INCLUDES MUSTANG, .380 ACP GOVERNMENT, DETECTIVE SPECIAL, AND DIAMONDBACK)

> CLASS "A" ENGRAVING (1/4 METAL COVERAGE) — ADD $776.
> CLASS "B" ENGRAVING (1/2 METAL COVERAGE) — ADD $959.
> CLASS "C" ENGRAVING (3/4 METAL COVERAGE) — ADD $1,426.
> CLASS "D" ENGRAVING (FULL METAL COVERAGE) — ADD $1,814.

MEDIUM FRAME ENGRAVING OPTIONS (INCLUDES .45 ACP GOLD CUP, GOVERNMENT MODEL, OFFICER'S ACP, PYTHON, COMBAT COMMANDER, KING COBRA, TROOPER MKV, LAWMAN MKV, AND DELTA ELITE)

> CLASS "A" ENGRAVING (1/4 METAL COVERAGE) — ADD $969.
> CLASS "B" ENGRAVING (1/2 METAL COVERAGE) — ADD $1,199.
> CLASS "C" ENGRAVING (3/4 METAL COVERAGE) — ADD $1,783.
> CLASS "D" ENGRAVING (FULL METAL COVERAGE) — ADD $2,289.
> Add 7% for 6 in. barrel, 14% for 8 in. barrel, or 25% for stainless steel construction.

Grading	100%	98%	95%	90%	80%	70%	60%

Special engraving/options include inlays, seals, custom grips, lettering, prices were quoted upon request. Smooth ivory grips were $215 extra (1990 retail).

Beginning in 1991, Colt began shipping all models in a distinctive blue plastic carrying case/shipping container.

SEMI-AUTO CURRENT CUSTOM SHOP ENGRAVING PRICING

Please refer to the "Colt Custom Shop Engraving - Current Mfg." listing earlier in this section for current semi-auto engraving options and pricing. Semi-auto custom order quotations from Colt are available at $25 each (deductible from work order).

JUNIOR POCKET MODEL — .22 S or .25 ACP cal., 2¼ in. barrel, blue, checkered walnut grips, made by Astra in Spain from 1958-1968.

	100%	98%	95%	90%	80%	70%	60%
.22 Short	$320	$280	$240	$210	$180	$160	$140
.25 ACP	$260	$235	$195	$180	$150	$140	$130

Add 10% for nickel finish.

A very few conversion kits were offered for this model. They are rare and asking prices are $250-$325 if in mint condition.

COLT AUTOMATIC CALIBER .25 — .25 ACP cal., mfg. by Firearms International for Colt between 1970-1973.

100%	98%	95%	90%	80%	70%	60%
$300	$275	$225	$185	$150	$140	$130

COMMANDER (PRE-70 SERIES) — 9mm Para, .38 Super, or .45 ACP cal., 4¼ in. barrel, full size grips, steel or alloy (Lightweight Model) variations. Mfg. 1950-1976.

	100%	98%	95%	90%	80%	70%	60%
9mm Para.	$650	$550	$475	$395	$365	$325	$295
.38 Super/.45 ACP	$750	$650	$550	$450	$395	$350	$300

Add 50% for Springfield Armory test pistols.

This model has a "LW" suffix.

GOVERNMENT MODEL MKIV/SERIES 70 — .45 ACP, .38 Super, 9mm Para., or 9mm Steyr cal., 5 in. barrel, checkered walnut grips/medallion. A slight premium might be asked for the Series 70 models if NIB. Series 70 models were mfg. 1970-1983 and serial numbered with "SM" prefixes (approx. 3,000 mfg.), "70G" prefixes 1970-1976, "70L" and "70S" prefixes also (see Serialization section for more information), "G70" suffixes 1976-1980, "B70" suffixes 1979-1981, and "70B" prefixes 1981-1983.

	100%	98%	95%	90%	80%	70%	60%
Blue finish	$725	$575	$475	$400	$350	$315	$285
Nickel finish	$800	$595	$495	$415	$365	$320	$290

9mm Steyr was made for European exportation only. However, a few specimens have found their way into the United States. Prices for NIB specimens are in the $750 range.

* *Series 70 Combat Govt.* —.45 ACP cal., bluish-black metal finish, features modifications for combat shooting, forerunner to the Combat Elite.

100%	98%	95%	90%	80%	70%	60%
$750	$650	$550	$550	$365	$325	$285

* *Series 70 Lightweight Commander* — 7.65mm (.30 Luger), 9mm Para, .38 Super, or .45 ACP cal., 4¼ in. barrel, full size grips, this model is denoted by a "CLW" prefix. Mfg. 1970-1983.

	100%	98%	95%	90%	80%	70%	60%
9mm Para.	$525	$465	$415	$350	$325	$300	$275
.38 Super/.45 ACP	$600	$525	$465	$425	$375	$325	$295
7.65mm	$2,500	$2,000	$1,575	$1,250	$995	$875	$750

500 Lightweight Commanders were mfg. in 7.65mm cal. during 1971. While most of these were mfg. for export trade, 5 were sold in the U.S.

* *Series 70 Combat Commander*

100%	98%	95%	90%	80%	70%	60%
$575	$500	$425	$395	$365	$325	$285

This model was also available in satin nickel finish (scarce).

Grading	100%	98%	95%	90%	80%	70%	60%

* ***Conversion Unit*** — converts .45 ACP to .22 LR, mfg. 1954-84 with either Accro adj. rear sight or fixed sight.

Adj. Sight	$395	$325	$275	$220	$195	$165	$140
Fixed Sight	$450	$350	$275	$225	$190	$165	$140

    Add 20% for conversion units in satin nickel finish (very scarce).

POST-WAR ACE SERVICE MODEL — .22 LR cal., similar specifications to previous Pre-WWII manufacture, blue (most common) or electroless nickel from Custom Shop finish, "SM" prefix (most common) or "B 70" suffix, approx. 30,000 mfg. between 1978-1982.

        $825 $675 $575 $525 $450 $425 $395

    This model is serial numbered approx. SM14,001-SM43,830.

GOVERNMENT MODEL MKIV/SERIES 80 — .38 Super, 9mm Para. (disc. 1992), or .45 ACP (disc. 1996) cal., single action, 5 in. barrel, 7 or 8 (new 1992) shot mag. in .45 ACP, approx. 38 oz., action has firing pin safety, checkered walnut (pre-1991 mfg.) or rubber combat style grips with medallion (new 1991). Production started in 1983 with ser. no. FG01000.

* ***Blue Finish*** — this finish was disc. in 1997.

        $525 $465 $380 $350 $315 $285 $260
                                    Last Mfg.'s Sug. Retail was $600.

    Add $20 for 9mm Para. (disc. 1992) cal.

* ***Nickel Finish*** — .45 ACP (disc. 1986) or .38 Super (disc. in 1987) cal.

        $575 $475 $385 $340 $315 $295 $275
                                      Last Mfg.'s Sug. Retail was $735.

* ***Satin Nickel/Blue*** — is supplied with Colt-Pachmayr grips. Disc. 1986.

        $510 $445 $370 $345 $310 $280 $255
                                      Last Mfg.'s Sug. Retail was $557.

* ***Stainless Steel*** — 9mm Para. (mfg. 1991-92), .38 Super (new 1990), .40 S&W (new 1992) or .45 ACP cal. Disc. 1998.

        $640 $520 $430
                                      Last Mfg.'s Sug. Retail was $813.

    Add $20 for 9mm Para. (disc. 1992) cal.

* ***"Ultimate" Bright Stainless Steel*** — .38 Super (new 1991) or .45 ACP cal., high polish stainless finish. Mfg. 1986-96.

        $675 $520 $455
                                      Last Mfg.'s Sug. Retail was $863.

* ***Limited Class Model .45 ACP*** — .45 ACP cal., designed for tactical competition, includes parkerized matte finish, lightweight composite trigger, ambidextrous safety, upswept grip safety, beveled mag. well, accurized, includes signed target. Mfg. 1994-97.

        $725 $575 $450 $400 $350 $325 $300
                                      Last Mfg.'s Sug. Retail was $936.

* ***Custom Compensated Model .45 ACP*** — .45 ACP cal., designed for serious competitive shooting, blue slide with full profile BAT Compensator, Bomar rear sight, flared funnel mag. well. Mfg. by Custom Shop 1994-98.

    $1,900 $1,500 $1,250 $1,000 $875 $750 $625
                                      Last Mfg.'s Sug. Retail was $2,428.

* ***Custom Tactical Model - Level I*** — .45 ACP cal., designed for tactical competition, Commander style hammer, beveled/contoured mag. well, nylon flat mainspring housing, ambidextrous safety, long nylon trigger with over-travel stop, available in Officer's or Commmander's length. Introduced 1998.

Mfg.'s Sug. Retail	**$730**	$640	$560	$495	$450	$400	$360	$330

    ➤ **Custom Tactical Model - Level II** — similar to Level I, except has Videcki long aluminum trigger with over-travel stop, Heine fixed combat sights, Colt match grade barrel bushing, high-ride grip safety with palm swell, double diamond stocks. Introduced 1998.

Mfg.'s Sug. Retail	**$935**	$825	$750	$650	$575	$495	$400	$300

Grading	100%	98%	95%	90%	80%	70%	60%

➤ **Custom Tactical Model - Level III** — similar to Level II, except has Bo-Mar adj. rear sight, super match hammer. Introduced 1998.

Mfg.'s Sug. Retail	$1,350	$1,150	$1,025	$875	$750	$650	$575	$495

COMBAT GOVERNMENT SERIES 80 — .45 ACP cal., dark matte metal finish, features modifications for combat shooting, successor to the Series 70 Combat Govt. Disc.

	$575	$495	$400	$345	$310	$280	$255

* *Special Combat Government Competition Model* — .45 ACP cal., competition model featuring skeletized trigger, custom tuning, polished ramp, throated barrel, flared ejection port, and cut-out hammer. Supplied with two 8 shot mags., hard chrome slide and receiver, Bomar rear and Clark dovetail front sight, flared mag. well, shipped with certified target. New 1992.

Mfg.'s Sug. Retail	$1,532	$1,275	$995	$895	$775	$650	$575	$495

* *Special Combat Government (Carry Model)* — similar to Special Combat Government, except has royal blue finish, bar-dot night sights, and ambidextrous safety. New 1992.

Mfg.'s Sug. Retail	$1,365	$1,125	$925	$750	$650	$575	$495	$400

* *Combat Elite* — .38 Super or .45 ACP cal., similar to Gold Cup, only with wraparound rubber grips, beveled magazine well, stainless steel receiver with carbon steel slide, and Accro adj. sighting system. Disc. 1996.

	$730	$620	$455	$400	$360	$330	$300

Last Mfg.'s Sug. Retail was $895.

* *Conversion Unit - Series 80* — converts Series 80 Govt. Model only to .22 LR or 9mm Para., mfg. 1984-86, 1995, and 1998, with Accro adj. rear sight.

9mm Para.	$525	$450	$375	$325	$250	$200	$175
.22 LR (mfg. 1984-86)	$525	$450	$375	$325	$250	$200	$175

Last Mfg.'s Sug. Retail was $305.

.22 LR (mfg. 1995 only, rare)	$675	$550	$450	$375	$325	$250	$200

➤ **Colt Ace II Conversion Unit** — similar to above, except features an aluminum slide and barrel w/o floating chamber, does not have hold open feature. Mfg. 1998.

	$350	$295	$275	$225	$190	$175	$150

COMBAT TARGET MODEL SERIES 80 — .45 ACP cal. only, 5 in. barrel, adj. sights, matte finish. Mfg. 1997 only.

	$615	$495	$400	$350	$320	$300	$280

Last Mfg.'s Sug. Retail was $768.

* *Combat Target Model Stainless* — similar to Combat Target Model, except stainless steel finish. Mfg. 1997 only.

	$745	$625	$500

Last Mfg.'s Sug. Retail was $820.

COMMANDER LIGHTWEIGHT SERIES 80 — .45 ACP cal., 4¼ in. barrel, similar to Government Model, except shorter and lighter alloy frame, fixed sights, round spur hammer, 27½ oz. Mfg. 1983-1997.

	$595	$485	$395	$345	$320	$300	$280

Last Mfg.'s Sug. Retail was $735.

Add 10% for .38 Super or 9mm Para. (disc.) cals.

COMBAT COMMANDER SERIES 80 — .38 Super (disc.), 9mm Para. (disc. 1992), or .45 ACP cal., similar to Lightweight, except has steel frame.

* *Blued Finish* — disc. 1996.

	$575	$475	$385	$340	$315	$295	$275

Last Mfg.'s Sug. Retail was $735.

Add $20 for 9mm Para. (disc.) or .38 Super (disc.) cal.

* *Blued Slide/Stainless Steel Receiver* — .45 ACP cal., two-tone matte finish, upswept grip safety, lightweight perforated trigger, black Hogue grips, 8 shot mag., 35 oz. Mfg. 1998 only.

	$650	$525	$450	$410	$380	$350	$325

Last Mfg.'s Sug. Retail was $813.

Grading	100%	98%	95%	90%	80%	70%	60%

C

* **Stainless Steel** — .38 Super (mfg. 1992-97) or .45 ACP cal. Mfg. 1990-98.

	$640	$520	$430				

Last Mfg.'s Sug. Retail was $813.

* **Satin Nickel** — disc. 1986.

	$575	$475	$410	$365	$310	$275	$250

Last Mfg.'s Sug. Retail was $550.

* **Gold Cup Commander** — .45 ACP cal., features custom shop alterations including heavy duty adj. target sights, beveled mag. well, serrated front strap, checkered mainspring housing, wide grip safety, and Palo Alto wood grips. Mfg. 1991-1993.

	$865	$715	$595	$550	$495	$440	$395

Last Mfg.'s Sug. Retail was $936.

* **Gold Cup Commander Stainless** — stainless variation of the Gold Cup Commander. Mfg. 1992 - disc.

	$870	$715	$595				

Last Mfg.'s Sug. Retail was $949

OFFICER'S MODEL SERIES 80 — .45 ACP cal. only, 3½ in. barrel, 34 oz., 6 shot mag., short version of the Government Model. Mfg. 1985 - disc.

* **Blued Finish** — disc. 1996.

	$575	$475	$385	$340	$315	$295	$275

Last Mfg.'s Sug. Retail was $735.

* **Matte Blued Finish**

	$525	$440	$370	$330	$280	$250	$225

Last Mfg.'s Sug. Retail was $625 (disc. 1991).

* **Officer's Stainless Steel** — matte stainless steel finish. Mfg. 1986-1997.

	$640	$520	$430				

Last Mfg.'s Sug. Retail was $813.

Add $74 for "Ultimate" bright stainless steel finish (mfg. 1987-96).

* **Officer's Lightweight** — similar to Officer's ACP, except has alloy frame and weighs 24 oz. Mfg. 1986-1997.

	$575	$475	$385	$340	$315	$295	$275

Last Mfg.'s Sug. Retail was $735.

* **Concealed Carry Officer** — .45 ACP cal., features matte stainless steel slide with matte blue aluminum alloy receiver, 7 shot mag., black contoured Hogue grips, upswept grip safety, lightweight perforated trigger, 26 oz. Mfg. 1998 only.

	$650	$525	$450	$410	$380	$350	$325

Last Mfg.'s Sug. Retail was $813.

* **Officer's Satin Nickel** — disc. 1985.

	$575	$475	$450	$375	$295	$260	$235

Last Mfg.'s Sug. Retail was $513.

* **General Officer's Model** — bright stainless steel with rosewood grips, special edition. Disc. 1996.

	$650	$550	$450				

Last Mfg.'s Sug. Retail was $750.

COLT DEFENDER — .40 S&W (new 1999) or .45 ACP cal., 3 in. barrel with 3 dot sights, 7 shot mag., rubber wrap-around grips with finger grooves, lightweight perforated trigger, steel slide with aluminum frame finished in matte stainless, firing pin safety, 22½ oz. New 1998.

Mfg.'s Sug. Retail	$750	$625	$525	$450			

GOLD CUP NATIONAL MATCH MKIV/SERIES 80 — .45 ACP cal., flat mainspring housing, 8 shot mag., accurizer barrel and bushing, adj. trigger, target hammer, solid rib, Colt-Elliason sight. Mfg. 1983-1996.

	$735	$575	$460	$400	$380	$350	$325

Last Mfg.'s Sug. Retail was $937.

In 1992, this model was updated to accept an 8 shot mag. During 1997, this updated model was designated the Colt Gold Cup Trophy.

Grading	100%	98%	95%	90%	80%	70%	60%

* Stainless Gold Cup National Match — similar to Gold Cup, only manufactured from stainless steel, matte finish. Mfg. late 1986-1996.

	$800	**$600**	**$495**				

Last Mfg.'s Sug. Retail was $1,003.

Add $70 for "Ultimate" brite stainless steel finish.

GOLD CUP TROPHY — .45 ACP cal., flat mainspring housing, 7 or 8 shot mag., accurizer barrel and bushing, adj. trigger, target hammer, Colt-Elliason sight, checkered wrap-around rubber grips, shipped with test target, 39 oz. New 1997.

Mfg.'s Sug. Retail	**$1,050**	**$875**	**$625**	**$495**	**$425**	**$395**	**$350**	**$325**

This model replaced the MKIV/Series 80 Gold Cup National Match in 1997, and is only available from the Colt Custom Gun Shop.

* Stainless Gold Cup Trophy — similar to Gold Cup Trophy, only manufactured from stainless steel, matte finish, 39 oz. New 1997.

Mfg.'s Sug. Retail	**$1,116**	**$895**	**$650**	**$525**			

MODEL M1991 A1 MKIV SERIES 80 — 9mm Para. or .45 ACP cal., similar to original WWII issue pistols with government issue parkerized finish, fixed sights, and black composite grips, 5 in. barrel, 7 shot mag., 38 oz., includes brown molded case. New 1991.

Mfg.'s Sug. Retail	**$556**	**$460**	**$375**	**$335**	**$295**	**$275**	**$250**	**$225**

This model is serialized consecutively with the last batch of Govt. models manufactured during 1945.

* Model M1991 Stainless Steel — features matte stainless steel finish. New 1996.

Mfg.'s Sug. Retail	**$610**	**$510**	**$440**	**$355**			

* Model M1991 A1 Officer's Compact — similar to Model M1991 A1, except has 3½ in. barrel, 6 shot mag., 34 oz. New 1992.

Mfg.'s Sug. Retail	**$556**	**$460**	**$375**	**$335**	**$295**	**$275**	**$250**	**$225**

➤ **Model M1991 A1 Officer's Stainless Compact** — similar to Model M1991 A1 Officer's Compact, except is stainless steel. New 1999.

Mfg.'s Sug. Retail	**$610**	**$510**	**$440**	**$355**			

* Model M1991 A1 Commander — .45 ACP cal., 4¼ in. barrel, full size grip, 7 shot mag., parkerized finish, 36 oz. New 1993.

Mfg.'s Sug. Retail	**$556**	**$460**	**$375**	**$335**	**$295**	**$275**	**$250**	**$225**

➤ **Model M1991 A1 Stainless Commander** — similar to Model M1991 A1 Commander, except is stainless steel. New 1999.

Mfg.'s Sug. Retail	**$610**	**$510**	**$440**	**$355**			

DELTA ELITE — 10mm cal., 5 in. barrel, black neoprene grips, high profile 3 dot sights, blue finish, 8 shot mag., 38 oz. Mfg. 1987-96.

	$700	**$515**	**$450**	**$375**	**$335**	**$300**	**$275**

Last Mfg.'s Sug. Retail was $807.

The first 500 guns of this model (mfg. 1985) were called the Delta Elite First Edition, and featured laser engraving with gold-fill, smooth wood grips, and were furnished with presentation cases. Current pricing is in the $795-$995 range.

* Stainless Steel — matte stainless steel finish. Mfg. 1989-96.

	$750	**$550**	**$455**				

Last Mfg.'s Sug. Retail was $860.

Add $78 for "Ultimate" brite stainless steel finish (disc. 1993).

The first 1,000 guns of this model (mfg. 1988) were called the Delta Elite First Edition, and featured stamp lettering on slide, black rubber grips, and did not have display cases. Current pricing is in the $795-$850 range.

DELTA GOLD CUP STAINLESS — 10mm cal., target variation, includes Accro adj. rear sight and trigger (serrated also), wraparound combat grips. Mfg. 1989-1993, re-released 1995-96.

	$900	**$650**	**$525**				

Last Mfg.'s Sug. Retail was $1,027.

Grading	100%	98%	95%	90%	80%	70%	60%

C

* ***Delta Gold Cup Blue*** — similar to Delta Gold Cup Stainless, except has blue finish. Mfg. 1991 only.

	$775	$600	$500	$450	$400	$360	$330

Last Mfg.'s Sug. Retail was $870.

.380 GOVERNMENT MODEL SERIES 80 — .380 ACP cal. only, single action, 3¼ in. barrel, 7 shot mag., fixed sights, composition stocks, 21¾ oz. New 1985.

* ***Blue Finish*** — finish disc. in 1997.

	$360	$300	$235	$215	$200	$190	$180

Last Mfg.'s Sug. Retail was $474.

* ***Nickel Finish*** — bright polish nickel finish with white composite grips. Disc. 1994.

	$405	$330	$270	$240	$220	$210	$200

Last Mfg.'s Sug. Retail was $504.

* ***Coltguard Finish*** — employs a high strength electroless matte nickel finish. Mfg. 1986-1989.

	$375	$325	$260	$235	$210	$200	$185

Last Mfg.'s Sug. Retail was $406.

* ***Stainless Steel*** — mfg. 1989-1997.

	$395	$335	$270

Last Mfg.'s Sug. Retail was $508.

GOVT. POCKETLITE L.W. — similar to .380 Series 80 Govt. Model, except frame is mfg. with alloy, blue or nickel/stainless (mfg. 1992-1993) finish only, black composition grips, 14 ¾ oz. Mfg. 1991-97.

	$360	$295	$250	$215	$200	$190	$180

Last Mfg.'s Sug. Retail was $462.

Add $30 for nickel/stainless finish (disc. 1993).

* ***Govt. Pocketlite Teflon Nickel/Stainless*** — similar to Govt. Pocketlite L.W., except has combination of Teflon nickel, stainless steel finish. Mfg. 1997-98.

	$395	$335	$270

Last Mfg.'s Sug. Retail was $508.

MUSTANG — similar to .380 Series Govt., except has 2¾ in. barrel, single action, 5 or 6 (new 1992) shot mag., blue finish only, 18½ oz. Mfg. 1986-1997.

	$370	$300	$250	$215	$200	$190	$180

Last Mfg.'s Sug. Retail was $462.

* ***Nickel finish*** — bright polish nickel finish with white composite grips. Mfg. 1987-94.

	$405	$330	$270	$240	$220	$210	$200

Last Mfg.'s Sug. Retail was $504.

* ***Stainless Steel*** — stainless steel variation of the Mustang. Mfg. 1990-97.

	$395	$335	$270

Last Mfg.'s Sug. Retail was $508.

* ***Coltguard finish*** — employs a high strength electroless matte nickel finish. Mfg. 1987.

	$330	$300	$260	$235	$210	$200	$185

Last Mfg.'s Sug. Retail was $406.

MUSTANG PLUS II — .380 ACP cal. only, 2¾ in. barrel, blued finish, black composition grips, 7 shot mag., 20 oz. Mfg. 1988-96.

	$370	$300	$250	$215	$200	$190	$180

Last Mfg.'s Sug. Retail was $462.

This model has the full grip length of the .380 Government Model.

* ***Stainless Steel*** — stainless steel variation of the Mustang Plus II. Mfg. 1990-97.

	$395	$335	$270

Last Mfg.'s Sug. Retail was $508.

Grading	100%	98%	95%	90%	80%	70%	60%

MUSTANG POCKETLITE L.W. — similar to Mustang, except has aluminum alloy receiver and stainless slide, blue (disc. 1997) or nickel/stainless finish, black composite grips, 12½ oz. Introduced 1987.

	$370	$300	$250	$215	$200	$190	$180

Last Mfg.'s Sug. Retail was $462.

* *Nickel/Stainless Steel Finish* — similar to Mustang Pocketlite, except has nickel finish frame and stainless steel slide. Mfg. 1991-96.

	$385	$330	$270	$230	$200	$190	$180

Last Mfg.'s Sug. Retail was $493.

* *Mustang Pocketlite Teflon Nickel/Stainless* — similar to Mustang Pocketlite L.W., except has combination of Teflon nickel, stainless steel finish. New 1997.

Mfg.'s Sug. Retail $508 $395 $335 $270

* *Lady Elite* — features hard chrome receiver, blue slide with silver painted rollmark, finger extension mag., soft carrying case, limited mfg. 1995-96.

$525 $450 $325 $250 $225 $200 $185

Last Mfg.'s Sug. Retail was $612.

* *Nite Lite .380* — .380 ACP cal., features bar-dot glowing night sight, Teflon coated alloy receiver with stainless slide, finger extension mag., includes carrying case. Mfg. 1994 only.

$495 $425 $325 $250 $225 $200 $185

Last Mfg.'s Sug. Retail was $577.

PISTOLS: SEMI-AUTO, DOUBLE ACTION - RECENT MFG.

DOUBLE EAGLE SERIES 90 I & II — 9mm Para. (mfg. 1991 only), .38 Super (mfg. 1991 only), .45 ACP, or 10mm (disc. 1993) cal., double action semi-auto that operates on the Browning/Colt short recoil, link pivot locking system used by the Govt. Model, 5 in. barrel, matte stainless steel only, 3 dot sighting system or Accro adj. rear sight (disc. 1994), checkered synthetic Xenoy grips, 8 shot mag. (9 shot in 9mm Para. or .38 Super cal.), decocking lever, squared off combat trigger guard, 39 oz. Mfg. 1990-96.

$610 $500 $425

Last Mfg.'s Sug. Retail was $727.

Add $50 for 9mm Para. or .38 Super cal.
Add $20 for 10mm cal.

The first edition (1,000 mfg. in 1989) on this model did not have a decocking lever - retail was $916.

* *Double Eagle Combat Commander* — .40 S&W (new 1992) or .45 ACP cal., 4¼ in. barrel, 8 shot mag., white dot sights, 36 oz. Mfg. 1991-96.

$610 $500 $425

Last Mfg.'s Sug. Retail was $727.

* *Officer's Model* — .45 ACP cal., 3½ in. barrel, 8 shot mag., 35 oz. Mfg. 1991-disc.

$610 $500 $425

Last Mfg.'s Sug. Retail was $727.

* *Officer's Lightweight Model* — .45 ACP cal. only, 3½ in. barrel, alloy frame with blue finish only, white dot sights, 25 oz. Mfg. 1991-1993.

$650 $525 $450 $400 $360 $330 $295

Last Mfg.'s Sug. Retail was $696.

ALL AMERICAN MODEL 2000 — 9mm Para. cal. only, double action semi-auto, new design features roller-bearing mounted trigger allowing double action only trigger pull every shot, utilizes a recoil operated rotary action featuring integral locking lugs similar to the military M-16 rifle, hammerless, 4½ in. barrel, matte finished steel slide and polymer receiver, 15 shot mag., 3-dot sighting system, ambidextrous mag. release, black synthetic checkered grips, internal striker block safety, checkered trigger guard and front grip strap, 29 oz. Manufacturing difficulty forced discontinuance and design and tooling were returned to Reed Knight. Mfg. 1991-1993.

Grading	100%	98%	95%	90%	80%	70%	60%

* Model 2000 - Polymer Frame

| | $725 | $650 | $525 | $450 | $375 | $325 | $275 |

Last Mfg.'s Sug. Retail was $575.

This model could also be converted to a shorter version using a 3¾ in. barrel/bushing kit (no tools or other components were needed - $75 retail during 1993 only).

* Model 2000 - Aluminum Frame — similar to polymer Model 2000, except frame is aluminum, serial numbered RK00001-RK03000 to commemorate the designer (Reed Knight), mfg. 1993.

| | $750 | $650 | $525 | $450 | $375 | $325 | $275 |

Last Mfg.'s Sug. Retail was $575.

PONY SERIES 90 — .380 ACP cal., double action only, 2¾ in. barrel, bobbed hammer, 6 shot mag., stainless construction, brushed finish, fixed sights, black composition grips, 19 oz. Mfg. 1997 only.

| | $425 | $350 | $295 |

Last Mfg.'s Sug. Retail was $529.

* Pony Pocketlite Lightweight — .380 ACP cal., similar to Pony Series 90, except utilizes aluminum and stainless steel construction, brushed finish, 13 oz. New 1997.

| Mfg.'s Sug. Retail | $529 | $425 | $350 | $295 |

POCKET NINE — 9mm Para. cal., double action only, 2¼ in. barrel, aluminum frame, ultra slim profile, 6 shot mag, matte/brushed stainless steel, wraparound rubber grips, 3-dot sights, 17 oz. New 1999.

| Mfg.'s Sug. Retail | $615 | $500 | $425 | $350 |

PISTOLS: SEMI-AUTO, .22 CAL. - WOODSMAN SERIES

The publisher wishes to once again express his thanks to Major Robert J. Rayburn for his continued generous contributions of information regarding the Colt Woodsman Series.

The Colt Woodsman was made for 62 years, and included a multitude of variations/options in models, sights, barrels, grips, markings, etc. Many of the variations are quite scarce and desirable, but generally known only to specialized collectors. The following price guidelines are for standard production models, and only for those specimens in unmodified, factory original condition.

Over 690,000 Woodsmans with variations were mfg. between 1915-1977.

Factory engraved and special order Woodsmans are relatively rare and very desirable. Prices can fluctuate greatly, and auctions can sometimes be the only source of supply for these seldomly encountered pistols.

Note: All 100% condition Woodsmans with the original serial numbered box, test target, instruction folder, hang tag, and screw driver typically command a 10-25% premium, depending on the model's age and rarity.

PRE-WOODSMAN — .22 LR cal., 6⅝ in. barrel. 10 shot mag., blue only, bottom mag. release, checkered wood grips, adj. front and rear sights. Mfg. 1915-1927, production totaled about 54,000, this model was officially named "Colt Automatic Pistol, Caliber .22 Target Model", magazine base has 2-line legend "CAL .22" "COLT". Standard velocity ammo. only.

| | $1,195 | $900 | $575 | $475 | $375 | $300 | $275 |

This model was manufactured to use standard velocity ammunition only (not high speed). Colt did offer a conversion kit for high velocity ammo. after the transition to high velocity in 1931.

Woodsmans mfg. between 1915-1922 had a lightweight pencil barrel (approx. serial range 1-31,000). The medium barrel was introduced in 1922 and was retained until the 90,000 serial range (approx. mfg. 1922-1934).

Grading	100%	98%	95%	90%	80%	70%	60%

WOODSMAN 1ST SERIES — .22 LR cal., 10 shot mag., blue only, bottom mag. release, checkered wood grips, marked "The Woodsman" on receiver, adj. sights, mfg. from 1927-1947, total production was approx. 112,000.

Note: Guns made prior to 1931 were designed for standard velocity .22 LR ammunition only. The new style main spring housing, designed for high velocity ammunition, began appearing at approx. ser. no. 80,000 and was completely phased in by approx. ser. no. 85,000. Later guns, INCLUDING ALL PISTOLS MADE AFTER WWII, were designed for high velocity ammunition.

Between 1934 and 1947 a tapered barrel was standard production (approx. ser. range 90,000-187,423).

* **Sport Model** — 4½ in. barrel, this model was introduced in 1933.

	$1,095	$895	$595	$495	$450	$395	$350

Add 10% for "half-moon" front sight.

Approx. serial range on this variation is 86,105 - 187,423 from 1933 to 1947.

* **Target Model** — 6⅝ in. barrel.

	$975	$700	$475	$400	$325	$275	$250

Note: Colt discontinued the 1st series in 1947. These guns are quite different from the 2nd series started later in 1947.

WOODSMAN 1ST SERIES MATCH TARGET — .22 LR cal. only, 6⅝ in. heavy barrel, commonly called "Bullseye" Match Target, mfg. 1938-1944, production totaled around 16,000. Difficult to find in mint condition. Values listed assume original one-piece extended walnut grips.

	$2,200	$1,500	$995	$750	$575	$475	$400

The correct magazine on this model has a 3-line legend "COLT WOODSMAN", "CAL. 22 L.R.", and "MATCH TARGET MOD.".

* **"U.S. Property" Marked** — approx. 4,000 Match Target Woodsmans were sold to the U.S. Army and U.S. Navy during WWII. Most have serial numbers above MT12500, although some were shipped out of sequence with lower numbers. The wartime guns had elongated plastic stocks and standard blue finish, although some of them are now parkerized as the result of arsenal refinishing or other non-factory modifications. They are marked with either "US PROPERTY" or the ordnance wheel with crossed cannon, as well as the initials of the govt. inspector. Some also have additional markings.

	$2,295	$1,895	$1,425	$1,150	$925	$750	$575

Check parkerized finish carefully for originality on this variation, as some "recent parkerizing" has been observed.

WOODSMAN 2ND SERIES — .22 LR cal. only, slide stop and hold open, push button mag. release on this model is located on the left side of frame, Coltwood plastic grips (mfg. 1947-1950) or brown plastic grips (mfg. 1950-1955), total production on all 2nd Series was (not including the Challenger) approx. 146,000. Mfg. 1947-1955.

* **Sport Model** — 4½ in. barrel.

	$795	$595	$495	$395	$350	$295	$250

* **Target Model** — 6 in. barrel.

	$695	$550	$450	$350	$325	$275	$225

* **Match Target Model** — 4½ in. heavy barrel. This variation will command a premium over the 6 in. barrel.

	$995	$795	$595	$450	$425	$400	$375

* **Match Target Model** — 6 in. heavy barrel.

	$795	$695	$500	$400	$350	$325	$300

C

Grading	100%	98%	95%	90%	80%	70%	60%

WOODSMAN 3RD SERIES — .22 LR cal. only, slide stop and hold open, mfg. between 1955-1977, black plastic grips (mfg. 1955-1960) or walnut grips (1960-1977), 3rd Models can be differentiated from 2nd Models by their bottom mag. release. Total production of all 3rd series Woodsman models (not including the Huntsman or Targetsman) exceeded 100,000.

* ***Sport Model*** — 4½ in. barrel.

$595	$495	$395	$325	$300	$275	$250

* ***Target Model*** — 6 in. barrel.

$550	$450	$350	$275	$250	$235	$225

* ***Match Target Model*** — 4½ or 6 in. heavy barrel.

$695	$595	$495	$400	$350	$325	$295

Add $100 4½ in. barrel if condition is 95% or better.

CHALLENGER MODEL — similar to Woodsman 2rd Series, only with fixed sights, without hold open, and bottom mag. release, 4½ and 6 in. barrels, mfg. between 1950-1955 with total production reaching approx. 77,000. Plastic grips.

$450	$350	$275	$250	$225	$210	$180

HUNTSMAN MODEL — .22 LR cal. only, fixed sights and no hold open, 4½ and 6 in. barrels, black plastic grips to serial number 141094-C - walnut grips after that cutoff, mfg. between 1955-1977 with total production reaching over 100,000.

$395	$295	$250	$225	$200	$180	$160

The Huntsman is very similar to the Challenger Model, except is built on a 3rd series frame.

* ***Huntsman Model S Master Series*** — approx. 400 Model S Masters were sold in 1983. This was a parts clean up by Colt, using Huntsman frames left over from the last days of production. They were equipped with automatic slide stop and Elliason rear sight, gold etching on the slide, and a French fitted walnut case marked "1 of 400". Approx. 285 had straight, non-tapered Huntsman barrel, while the remainder had the tapered Woodsman Sport barrel with pinned front sight.

Huntsman barrel	$995	$600	$500	$425	$350	$325	$295
Woodsman barrel	$1,095	$700	$600	$500	$425	$350	$325

Above values assume original walnut case included. Values for this model in 98%-60% original condition are hard to compute, as most are mint or new.

TARGETSMAN MODEL — similar to the Huntsman, except has adj. rear sight and thumbrest on left grip, 6 in. barrel only, approx. 65,000 mfg. 1959-1977.

$495	$395	$295	$260	$240	$220	$200

CADET — .22 LR cal., 4½ in. barrel, stainless steel, 10 shot mag., predecessor to the Colt 22 Model, originally introduced in 1994, fixed sights, this model was disc. by 1995 because of litigation involving the trademarked model name, 33½ oz.

$235	$195	$170

COLT 22 — .22 LR cal., 4½ in. VR barrel, stainless steel, fixed sights, 10 shot mag., one-piece black Pachmayr rubber grips, 33½ oz. Mfg. 1994-98.

$225	$190	$170

Last Mfg.'s Sug. Retail was $248.

* ***Colt 22 Target*** — .22 LR cal., 6 in. VR barrel with full length grooved sight rib, adj. rear sight, 40½ oz. New 1995.

Mfg.'s Sug. Retail	$377		$290	$225	$190

100%	98%	95%	90%	80%	70%	60%	50%	40%	30%	20%	10%

REVOLVERS: DOUBLE ACTION

MODEL 1877 LIGHTNING — .38 Colt or .32 Colt (very rare) cal., 2, 2½, 3½, 4½, or 6 in. barrels without ejector, 4½, 5, 6, 7, or 7½ in. barrels with ejector, 6 shot double action, long cylinder fluting, blued finish with case hardened frame and hammer, full nickel plating also available. Over 166,000 mfg. from 1877-1910.

$1,775	$1,500	$1,200	$950	$875	$775	$700	$650	$575	$475	$350	$295

MODEL 1877 THUNDERER — .41 Colt cal. only, otherwise same general specifications as Model 1877 Lightning.

$1,800	$1,600	$1,150	$975	$875	$775	$675	$600	$525	$450	$325	$285

MODEL 1878 DA — .22 LR (very rare), .32-20 WCF (scarce), .38-40 WCF (scarce, approx. 1,600 mfg.), .41 LC (scarce), .44-40 WCF (Colt Frontier Six Shooter), .45 LC, .450 Eley, .455 Eley, or .476 Eley cal., 2½ (scarce), 3½, or 4 in. barrels without ejector, 4¾, 5½, or 7½ in. with ejector, 6 in. is 1902 U.S. Revolver (Alaskan/Phillipines Models), 6 shot cylinder with long flutes, pinched frame, removable trigger guard, early guns have checkered walnut stocks, later guns have hard black rubber. Mfg. 1878-1905. Over 51,000 made.

$5,250	$4,750	$3,750	$3,000	$2,500	$1,750	$1,500	$950	$850	$750	$625	$500

This model in .44-40 WCF was called the Colt Frontier Six Shooter, and this inscription is either etched or roll marked on the barrel.

This model is commonly encountered with a broken mechanism. Since original parts are scarce, at least $500 must be deducted for a non-working action.

Many original 1878 barrels have "found their way" on the front end of a SAA frame, since the barrels are interchangable. Because of this, many "original" Model 1878 DAs may have an incorrect and/or later SAA Colt barrel attached. Watch yourself here!

MODEL 1889 "NAVY" (NEW NAVY DA, MODEL OF 1889) — .38 Short and Long Colt, and .41 Short and Long Colt cal., 3, 4½, and 6 in. barrel, wood or rubber grips, blue or nickel finish, the first solid frame, swing out cylinder with no visible locking latches (rotates counter-clockwise), sideplate is also on the right-hand side of frame, Colt produced approx. 28,000 mfg. 1889-1894, 1st 5,000 were ordered by U.S. Navy, with some additional orders later in production - hence name.

* *Blue finish*

$1,750	$1,550	$1,350	$1,150	$950	$750	$650	$575	$500	$425	$350	$300

Add 40% for 3 in. barrel.
Add 35% for .38 Short or Long Colt cal.
Add 65%-100% for U.S. Navy Contract (S.N. 1-5,000), U.S.N. on butt (.38 LC cal. only), depending on condition.

MODEL 1892 "NEW ARMY & NAVY" (2ND ISSUE) — similar to 1889 Navy, but double cylinder notches, double locking bolt, and shorter flutes, square cyl. release thumb catch, .32-20 WCF cal. (uncommon) added in 1905, mfg. 1892-1907.

$1,350	$1,100	$900	$700	$500	$400	$300	$250	$225	$210	$195	$180

Add $100-$500 for U.S.N. markings, depending on condition.
Add 25% for 3 in. barrel.

* *Models 1892, 1894, 1895, 1896, 1901, 1903* — these were variations of the Model 1892, military model values will approximate those shown above, while civilian models wil be approx. 10%-25% less, depending on condition.

OFFICER'S MODEL TARGET (FIRST ISSUE) — .38 Spl. (most common) or .38 Long Colt cal., 6 in. barrel, cylinder rotates counter-clockwise and sideplate is on right-hand side of frame, adj. front - adj. rear type sights, high luster blue, flat-top. Mfg. 1904-1908.

$1,250	$1,000	$850	$695	$595	$550	$495	$395	$295	$275	$250	$225

100%	98%	95%	90%	80%	70%	60%	50%	40%	30%	20%	10%

OFFICER'S MODEL TARGET (SECOND ISSUE) — .32 Colt or .38 Spl. cal., 4, 4½, 5, 6, or 7½ in. barrel, cylinder rotates clockwise, high luster blue through 1916, adj. front - adj. rear type sights, checkered walnut grips, deep set medallions in grips were standard from 1913-1923. Mfg. 1908-1926.

$825	$795	$600	$515	$450	$395	$330	$290	$250	$225	$210	$195

Add 60% for .32 Colt cal.
Add 50% for 4, 4½, or 5 in. barrel.

OFFICER'S MODEL TARGET (THIRD ISSUE) — similar design to the Second Issue, .22 cal. was added beginning 1930. Mfg. 1927-1949.

$725	$675	$600	$500	$450	$375	$325	$295	$265	$245	$225	$205

Add 10% for .22 LR cal. (mfg. started 1930).

MODEL 1905 MARINE CORPS — .38 Short or Long, similar to New Navy Second Issue, except has a round butt, and 6 in. barrel only. Mfg. 1905-1909 in approx. ser. no. range 10,001-10,926, about 926 mfg.

$2,650	$2,350	$2,050	$1,750	$1,625	$1,425	$1,250	$1,000	$895	$795	$695	$595

Add 30% for Military issue marked "USMC" on butt.

ARMY SPECIAL MODEL — .32-20 WCF, .38 (various), and .41 Colt cals., 4, 4½, 5, and 6 in. barrels, hard rubber grips standard through 1923 - checkered wood with medallions beginning 1924, fixed sights, rounded checkered cylinder release thumb catch, smooth trigger, has heavier frame than New Navy, approx. ser. no. range 291,000-540,000. Mfg. 1908-1927.

* Blue finish

$600	$550	$450	$350	$295	$265	$245	$230	$215	$200	$185	$175

Add 15% for nickel finish.

NEW SERVICE MODEL — .38 Spl., .357 Mag., .38-40 WCF, .44-40 WCF, .44 Russian, .44 Spl., .45 ACP, .45 LC, .450 Eley, .455 Eley, or .476 Eley cals., 4, 5, or 6 in. barrels in .357 Mag. and .38 Spl., 4½, 5½, and 7½ in. barrel in all others, blue or nickel finish, originally hard rubber (until approx. late '20s), with later guns having walnut grips. Mfg. 1898-1942. Rare cals. (.450 and .476 Eley cals.) will command premiums over values listed below.

New Service Models marked "NEW SERVICE 45 COLT" in .45 ACP cal. with shorter cylinder for rimmed cartridge are rare.

* Commercial

$1,500	$1,375	$1,175	$1,000	$925	$850	$775	$650	$500	$425	$375	$295

* 1909 Army Model

$1,550	$1,275	$1,125	$1,000	$925	$850	$775	$680	$590	$510	$435	$375

* 1909 Navy Model — shortest production run of the Model 1909 variations.

$2,450	$2,100	$1,825	$1,450	$1,150	$1,000	$895	$775	$600	$500	$450	$395

* 1909 - USMC

$2,850	$2,400	$2,100	$1,775	$1,500	$1,250	$975	$825	$700	$600	$500	$450

* 1917 Army

$995	$850	$750	$670	$610	$525	$455	$390	$335	$295	$250	$200

* 1917 Civilian/Commercial (1917 C/CM) — .45 ACP cal., 5½ in. barrel only, last patent date is OCT 5, 1926, checkered walnut grips with medallions, left side of barrel marked "Colt Model 1917 Auto Ctge." approx. 1,000 mfg. during 1932, serialized 335,000-336,000.

$1,500	$1,275	$1,050	$850	$650	$525	$450	$415	$385	$350	$325	$295

* 1917 Civilian/Commercial (Piece Parts Model) — .38-40 WCF, .44-40 WCF, or .45 LC cal., 4½ or 5½ in. barrel, hard rubber grips, or checkered walnut with medallions, last patent date is July 4, 1905, approx. 1,000 mfg. serialized 336,450-337,500.

$1,200	$995	$900	$800	$625	$495	$415	$380	$360	$330	$300	$275

100%	98%	95%	90%	80%	70%	60%	50%	40%	30%	20%	10%

* **New Service Target** — similar to New Service Model, flat-top frame, hand-honed action and adj. front - adj. rear type sights, 6 (scarce) or 7½ in. barrel, square butt, round butt available after 1930, checkered grip straps, checkered walnut grips with medallion after 1913, blue or nickel (scarce) finish. Mfg. 1900-1940.

$2,650	$2,100	$1,750	$1,500	$1,250	$900	$750	$635	$550	$460	$400	$350

Add 40% for 6 in. barrel.

* **Shooting Master** — various cals. from 38 Spl. through .45 LC, 6 in. barrel, checkered walnut grips with Colt Medallion, machined grip straps, trigger, hammer, and ejector rod head, round or square butt, approx. ser. no. range 333,000 - 350,000.

$1,250	$1,100	$975	$900	$825	$755	$665	$575	$500	$435	$395	$375

Add 35% for .357 Mag.

Add 200% for .44 Spl., .45 ACP, or .45 LC cal.

The Shooting Master could be ordered with a square butt after 1933.

OFFICIAL POLICE PRE-WAR — .32-20 WCF (disc. 1942), .38-200 (British), .41 long (disc. 1930), .38 Spl., or .22 LR (introduced 1930 - 4 or 6 in. barrel only, 4 in. scarce) cal., 6 shot, round (very scarce) or square butt, 4, 5, or 6 in. barrels, 2 in. barrel (scarce) in .38 Spl., checkered walnut grips, fixed sights. Mfg. 1927-1946.

* **Blue finish**

$525	$475	$395	$325	$295	$265	$235	$210	$185	$165	$145	$135

Add 15% for nickel finish.

Add 15% for .22 LR cal.

OFFICIAL POLICE POST-WAR — .22 LR or .38 Spl. cal., 2, 4, 5, or 6 in. barrel, Coltwood plastic grips 1947-1954 - checkered walnut thereafter, fixed sights, mfg. 1947-1969.

$425	$375	$325	$295	$265	$235	$210	$185	$165	$145	$135	$125

Add 15% for nickel finish.

Add 15% for .22 cal.

On this model, the 2 in. barrel in .38 Spl. cal. is scarce. .22 cal. was available with 4 or 6 in. barrel only.

MARSHAL MODEL — .38 Spl. cal., 2 (less common) or 4 in. barrel, round butt, differentiated by "M" suffix and "COLT MARSHAL" on barrel, about 2,500 mfg. 1954-1956 in approx. ser. no. range 833350-M through 845320-M.

$800	$700	$600	$475	$395	$335	$305	$275	$245	$215	$180	$160

Add 60% for 2 in. barrel.

COMMANDO MODEL — .38 Spl. cal., 2 in. (less common), 4 in. (common), or 6 in. (rare) barrel, parkerized finish, about 50,000 mfg. between 1942-1945, 32 oz., marked "COLT COMMANDO" on barrel.

$595	$495	$400	$350	$300	$275	$250	$200	$175	$150	$135	$120

Add 15% for 2 in. barrel.

OFFICIAL POLICE MKIII — .38 Spl. cal., 4, 5, or 6 in. barrels. Mfg. 1969-1975.

* **Blue finish**

$325	$235	$180	$150	$135	$125	$115	$105	$100	$95	$90	$85

* **Nickel finish**

$350	$250	$195	$175	$165	$155	$145	$135	$125	$115	$105	$100

METROPOLITAN MK III — .38 Spl. cal., similar to Official Police, except heavier and 4 in. heavy barrel only, blue finish. Mfg. 1969-1972.

$495	$395	$300	$250	$200	$180	$160	$140	$120	$110	$100	$90

100%	98%	95%	90%	80%	70%	60%	50%	40%	30%	20%	10%

OFFICER'S MODEL SPECIAL (FOURTH ISSUE) — .22 LR or .38 Spl. cal., 6 in. barrel, blue, similar to Third Issue, only heavier non-tapered barrel, new style hammer and "Coltmaster Sight", checkered plastic grips. Mfg. 1949-1952.

| $575 | $500 | $450 | $375 | $325 | $295 | $265 | $245 | $225 | $205 | $190 | $175 |

    Add $75 for .22 LR cal.

OFFICER'S MODEL MATCH (FIFTH ISSUE) — .22 LR, .22 Mag, or .38 Spl. cal., 6 in. barrel, single (rare) or double action, tapered heavy barrel, wide spur hammer, Accro sight, large target grips (walnut). Mfg. 1953-1969.

| $475 | $425 | $375 | $325 | $300 | $275 | $250 | $225 | $200 | $185 | $170 | $155 |

    Add $75 for .22 LR cal.
    Add 100% for .22 Mag. cal. (approx. 850 mfg.).

   Officer's Model Match Single Action only — limited mfg.

| $1,325 | $1,200 | $995 | $925 | $850 | $775 | $700 | $650 | $600 | $550 | $475 | $425 |

OFFICER'S MODEL MATCH MK III (SIXTH ISSUE) — .38 Spl. cal. only, 6 in. shrouded VR barrel, wide spur hammer, Accro sights, target grips, 496 mfg. 1969-70 only.

| $1,325 | $1,200 | $995 | $925 | $850 | $775 | $700 | $650 | $600 | $550 | $475 | $425 |

NEW POCKET — .32 Short and LC, or .32 Colt New Police cal., 2½, 3½, 5, or 6 in. barrel, rubber grips, blue or nickel finish. Mfg. 1895-1905.

| $650 | $550 | $440 | $350 | $300 | $275 | $250 | $215 | $190 | $170 | $150 | $140 |

POCKET POSITIVE — similar to New Pocket, except has positive lock feature, also chambered for .32 Colt, .32 S&W, and .32 Colt New Police cals. Mfg. 1905-1940.

   Blue finish

| $525 | $465 | $385 | $350 | $325 | $295 | $265 | $235 | $210 | $185 | $165 | $145 |

    Add 15%-20% for nickel finish.

NEW POLICE — .32 Colt and .32 Colt New Police cal., 2½, 4, and 6 in. barrels, fixed sights, same frame as New Pocket, except larger grips, rubber grips. Mfg. 1896-1907.

   Blue finish

| $650 | $550 | $475 | $375 | $325 | $275 | $215 | $185 | $170 | $160 | $150 | $145 |

    Add 25% for nickel finish.

NEW POLICE TARGET — .32 Colt cal., 6 in. barrel, blue, approx. 5,000 mfg. 1897-1907.

| $1,050 | $900 | $775 | $650 | $475 | $395 | $350 | $300 | $275 | $250 | $225 | $200 |

POLICE POSITIVE (FIRST ISSUE) — .32 Colt, .32 New Police, .38 New Police, or .38 S&W cals., 2½ in. (.32 only), 4, 5, or 6 in. barrels, improved "positive lock" version of the New Police, hard rubber grips standard through 1923, checkered walnut grips became standard 1924, denoted by 1905 last patent date and smooth top strap. Mfg. 1907-1927.

   Blue finish

| $435 | $385 | $335 | $295 | $275 | $250 | $225 | $205 | $185 | $170 | $160 | $150 |

    Add 15% for nickel finish.

POLICE POSITIVE (SECOND ISSUE) — similar to Police Positive First Issue, except has 1926 last patent date, serrated top strap, and walnut grips were standard. Mfg. 1928-1947.

| $435 | $385 | $335 | $295 | $275 | $250 | $225 | $205 | $185 | $170 | $160 | $150 |

    Add 15% for nickel finish.

POLICE POSITIVE TARGET MODEL (FIRST ISSUE, MODEL "G") — .22 LR, .22 WRF, .32 Colt, or .32 New Police cals., 6 in. barrel, blue, adj. sight, hard rubber grips standard through 1923, checkered walnut grips thereafter, 22 oz. Mfg. 1907-1925.

| $750 | $625 | $575 | $525 | $475 | $425 | $390 | $360 | $325 | $285 | $250 | $210 |

    Add 40% for .32 cal.

    The last barrel patent date on this model was July 4, 1905.

100%	98%	95%	90%	80%	70%	60%	50%	40%	30%	20%	10%

POLICE POSITIVE TARGET MODEL (SECOND ISSUE, MODEL "C") — similar to First Issue, except has slightly heavier frame and a last patent date of Oct. 5, 1926, 26 oz. Mfg. 1926-1941.

| $750 | $625 | $575 | $525 | $475 | $425 | $390 | $360 | $325 | $285 | $250 | $210 |

Add 40% for .32 cal.

POLICE POSITIVE SPECIAL (FIRST ISSUE) — .32-20 WCF, .32 New Police, .38 New Police, or .38 Spl. cals., 4, 5, or 6 in. barrels, fixed sights, frame longer to permit longer cylinder, denoted by 1905 last patent date on top of barrel, longer frame and smooth top strap, rubber grips. Mfg. 1907-1927.

| $495 | $450 | $395 | $325 | $300 | $275 | $250 | $225 | $200 | $185 | $170 | $155 |

POLICE POSITIVE SPECIAL (SECOND ISSUE) — similar to Police Postitive Special (First Issue), except has 1926 last patent date on top of barrel, wood grips only, smooth (early mfg.) or checkered (later mfg.) trigger, and serrated top strap. Mfg. 1928-1946.

| $495 | $450 | $395 | $325 | $300 | $275 | $250 | $225 | $200 | $185 | $170 | $155 |

CAMP PERRY MODEL — .22 LR cal., 8 in. (less common) or 10 in., Officer's Model frame modified to accept a flat single shot chamber. The model name was stamped on the left side of the chamber, the only single shot Colt on a revolver frame. 2,488 mfg. between 1926-1941.

| $1,695 | $1,375 | $1,150 | $950 | $875 | $775 | $715 | $645 | $575 | $495 | $425 | $365 |

Add 25% for 8 in. barrel.

BANKER'S SPECIAL — 2 in. barrel, blue, square butt standard through 1933, round butt standard 1934-1940. Mfg. 1926-1940.

* **.38 cal.** — available in .38 Colt Police Positive (New Police) or .38 S&W cal.

| $1,150 | $975 | $750 | $595 | $495 | $395 | $325 | $275 | $235 | $205 | $185 | $165 |

Add 45% for nickel finish.

* **.22 LR cal.**

| $2,000 | $1,750 | $1,450 | $1,100 | $750 | $650 | $550 | $475 | $425 | $385 | $355 | $325 |

Add 30% for nickel finish.

COURIER — .22 S, L, & LR cals., .32 New Police, double action, 6 shot, 3 in. barrel, approx. 3,053 mfg. 1953-1956.

| $775 | $700 | $640 | $550 | $475 | $425 | $395 | $350 | $325 | $295 | $260 | $230 |

Add 10% for .22 cal.

Even though fewer .22 cal. Couriers were mfg. than Banker's Specials, the Banker's Specials are still more desirable, as they are less frequently encountered in 95-100% condition.

AIRCREWMAN SPECIAL — .38 Spl. cal., double action, aluminum frame, 2 in. barrel, 11 oz., fixed sights, checkered walnut grips overlapping at top of frame, inset with silver Air Force buttons, mfg. 1951 mostly.

| $4,000 | $3,500 | $2,750 | $2,100 | $1,700 | $1,350 | $1,075 | $950 | $850 | $750 | $675 | $595 |

Approx. 1,200 mfg. within ser. no. range 2,900LW - 7,775LW. Perhaps less than 25 have survived.

BORDER PATROL — .38 Spl. cal., double action, 6 shot, 4 in. heavy barrel, 400 mfg. during 1952 only in 823,000 ser. no. range.

| $2,850 | $2,400 | $1,875 | $1,400 | $1,125 | $995 | $875 | $775 | $675 | $595 | $525 | $475 |

This model is built on the Official Police Model frame.

DETECTIVE SPECIAL PRE-WAR (FIRST ISSUE) — .38 Spl. cal., 2 in. barrel, blue, wood grips, square butt standard through 1933, round butt standard 1934-1936. Mfg. 1927-1946.

| $750 | $650 | $525 | $425 | $375 | $325 | $275 | $250 | $225 | $205 | $190 | $175 |

Add 15% for nickel finish.
Add 20% for square butt.

100%	98%	95%	90%	80%	70%	60%	50%	40%	30%	20%	10%

DETECTIVE SPECIAL POST-WAR (SECOND ISSUE) — .32 New Police, .38 New Police, or .38 Spl. cal., 2 or 3 (scarce) in. barrel, plastic grips 1947-1954 - wood grips thereafter, wrap-under wood grips started in 1966. Mfg. 1947-1972.

| $445 | $385 | $325 | $250 | $225 | $200 | $185 | $170 | $160 | $150 | $140 | $120 |

  Add 15% for nickel finish.
  Add 15% for 3 in. barrel.

C

COBRA (FIRST ISSUE) — .22 LR, .32 Colt NP, .38 Colt NP, or .38 Spl. cal., first issue, 2, 3, or 4 (square butt only) in. barrel, blue or nickel finish, similar to Detective Special, only alloy frame and available in .22 LR, very early guns had plastic grips with silver medallions, changed to plastic w/o medallions, and finally changed to wood grips. Mfg. 1950-1972.

| $445 | $385 | $325 | $250 | $225 | $200 | $185 | $170 | $160 | $150 | $140 | $120 |

  Add 20% for .22 LR cal.
  Add 15% for nickel finish.
  Add 15% for .38 cal. with 3 in. barrel.
  The .22 LR cal. is available in 3 in. barrel only.

AGENT (FIRST ISSUE) — .38 Spl. cal., similar to Cobra first issue, except shorter grip frame. Mfg. 1955-1972.

| $425 | $375 | $295 | $235 | $200 | $180 | $160 | $145 | $130 | $120 | $110 | $100 |

AGENT L.W. — .38 Spl. cal., similar to First Issue, except shrouded ejector rod, alloy frame, matte finish since 1982. Mfg. 1973-86.

| $375 | $325 | $275 | $215 | $175 | $160 | $145 | $135 | $125 | $115 | $105 | $100 |

  Last Mfg.'s Sug. Retail was $260.

COBRA (SECOND ISSUE) — .38 Spl. cal., similar to Cobra first issue, except shrouded ejector rod, many were shipped with factory installed hammer shroud. Mfg. 1973-1981.

| $395 | $365 | $275 | $250 | $225 | $200 | $190 | $175 | $160 | $150 | $140 | $120 |

DETECTIVE SPECIAL (THIRD ISSUE) — .38 Spl. cal., similar to Second Issue, shrouded ejector rod, 2 or 3 (scarce) in. barrel, fixed sights, wraparound wood grips. Mfg. 1973-86.

| $395 | $365 | $275 | $250 | $225 | $200 | $190 | $175 | $160 | $150 | $140 | $120 |

  Last Mfg.'s Sug. Retail was $429.

  Add $50 for nickel.
  Add 15% for 3 in. barrel.
  Also available with class A engraving - add $590 if in 98% condition or better.

COMMANDO SPECIAL — .38 Spl. cal., similar to Detective Special with steel frame, shrouded ejector rod, 2 in. barrel, matte parkerized finish, rubber grips. Mfg. 1984-86.

| $425 | $325 | $265 | $225 | $195 | $170 | $155 | $140 | $125 | $115 | $105 | $100 |

  Last Mfg.'s Sug. Retail was $260.

POLICE POSITIVE SPECIAL (THIRD ISSUE) — .38 Spl. cal., similar to Detective Special Second Issue, except 4, 5 or 6 in. barrel. Mfg. 1947-76.

| $395 | $350 | $300 | $225 | $195 | $170 | $155 | $140 | $125 | $115 | $105 | $100 |

POLICE POSITIVE SPECIAL (FOURTH ISSUE) — .38 Spl. cal., shrouded ejector rod housing only, steel frame, blue or nickel finish. Mfg. 1977-78 only.

| $395 | $350 | $300 | $220 | $185 | $170 | $150 | $135 | $125 | $115 | $105 | $100 |

  Add 10% for nickel finish.

VIPER MODEL — .38 Spl. cal., similar to Police Positive Special (Fourth Issue), alloy frame, 4 in. ejector rod housing only. Mfg. 1977 only.

| $425 | $375 | $325 | $250 | $225 | $200 | $190 | $175 | $160 | $150 | $140 | $120 |

  Add 30% for nickel finish.

100%	98%	95%	90%	80%	70%	60%	50%	40%	30%	20%	10%

DIAMONDBACK — .22 LR, .22 Mag. (limited mfg.), or .38 Spl. cal., 2½ (scarce in .22 LR), 4, or 6 in. VR barrel, adj. sights, steel frame, checkered walnut grips. Mfg. 1966-86.

100%	98%	95%	90%	80%	70%	60%	50%	40%	30%	20%	10%
$450	$400	$350	$265	$245	$225	$205	$190	$175	$160	$150	$140

Last Mfg.'s Sug. Retail was $461.

Add $55 for nickel finish.
Add 20% for .22 LR cal.
Add 30% for .22 LR cal. with 2½ in. barrel or .22 Mag. cal.

Note: Approx. 2,200 Diamondbacks were made with 6 in. barrels and nickel finish in .22 cal. - made 1979. Add additional $150 for 100% specimens.

COLT .357 MAG — 4 in. or 6 in. barrel, heavy frame, Accro sight, blue or nickel finish, checkered walnut grips. Later guns marked Trooper. Mfg. 1953-1961.

* *Standard hammer*

100%	98%	95%	90%	80%	70%	60%	50%	40%	30%	20%	10%
$525	$475	$425	$295	$275	$265	$255	$245	$230	$220	$210	$200

* *Wide hammer w/target grips*

100%	98%	95%	90%	80%	70%	60%	50%	40%	30%	20%	10%
$550	$500	$450	$300	$285	$265	$255	$245	$235	$225	$215	$205

TROOPER — .22 LR (4 in. only, scarce), .357 Mag., or .38 Spl. cal., 4 or 6 in. barrel, blue or nickel finish, quick draw ramp front sight, adj. rear sight, checkered walnut grips. Mfg. 1953-1969.

* *Standard hammer*

100%	98%	95%	90%	80%	70%	60%	50%	40%	30%	20%	10%
$425	$375	$300	$210	$200	$190	$180	$170	$165	$160	$155	$150

* *Wide hammer and target grips*

100%	98%	95%	90%	80%	70%	60%	50%	40%	30%	20%	10%
$450	$400	$350	$225	$210	$200	$190	$180	$170	$165	$160	$155

Add $75-$125 for .22 LR cal. (4 in. barrel only), depending on condition.
Add 15% for nickel finish.

Grading	100%	98%	95%	90%	80%	70%	60%

TROOPER MK III — .22 LR, .22 Mag., .357 Mag., or .38 Spl. cal., 4, 6, or 8 in. solid rib barrel, adj. sights, walnut target grips, redesigned lock work to reduce amount of hand fitting needed on earlier predecessors. Mfg. 1969-1983.

	100%	98%	95%	90%	80%	70%	60%
Blue finish	$325	$275	$190	$180	$170	$160	$150
Nickel finish	$345	$275	$200	$190	$180	$170	$160

TROOPER MK V — .357 Mag. cal. only, 4 or 6 in. barrel, adj. sights, walnut target grips, improved version of Mark III action, vent. rib barrel, redesigned 1982. Disc. 1986.

* *Blue finish*

	100%	98%	95%	90%	80%	70%	60%
	$375	$315	$275	$215	$185	$170	$160

Last Mfg.'s Sug. Retail was $362.

* *Nickel finish*

	100%	98%	95%	90%	80%	70%	60%
	$400	$350	$300	$235	$200	$185	$170

Last Mfg.'s Sug. Retail was $396.

LAWMAN MK III — .357 Mag. cal., 2 in. and 4 in. barrel, unshrouded or shrouded ejector rod for 2 in. barrel, fixed sights, checkered walnut grips. Mfg. 1969-1983.

	100%	98%	95%	90%	80%	70%	60%
Blue finish	$295	$240	$190	$180	$170	$160	$150
Nickel finish	$315	$250	$200	$190	$180	$170	$160

LAWMAN MK V — .357 Mag. cal., 2 or 4 in. barrel, shrouded ejector rod for 2 in. barrel, fixed sights, checkered walnut grips, improved version of MK III action. Mfg. 1984 and 1985 only.

* *Blue finish*

	100%	98%	95%	90%	80%	70%	60%
	$295	$250	$200	$175	$160	$150	$140

Last Mfg.'s Sug. Retail was $309.

* *Nickel finish*

	100%	98%	95%	90%	80%	70%	60%
	$325	$280	$225	$200	$180	$170	$160

Last Mfg.'s Sug. Retail was $328.

C

Grading	100%	98%	95%	90%	80%	70%	60%

BORDER PATROL (SECOND ISSUE) — .357 Mag. cal., 4 in. heavy barrel, Trooper Mark III frame, limited mfg. in 1970-75.

* **Blue Finish** — 5,356 mfg.

	$525	$450	$375	$275	$235	$200	$180

* **Nickel Finish** — 1,152 mfg.

	$625	$550	$475	$375	$325	$275	$235

PEACEKEEPER — .357 Mag. cal. only, similar to Trooper MK V, 4 or 6 in. barrel, matte blue finish, rubber combat grips, adj. rear sight, about 42 oz. Mfg. 1985-1987.

	$320	$275	$245	$205	$195	$180	$165

Last Mfg.'s Sug. Retail was $330.

BOA — .357 Mag. cal., deep blue polish, full length ejector shroud with Mark V action, 600 each mfg. in 4 and 6 in. barrel lengths. Entire production run was purchased by Lew Horton Distributing Co., Inc. located in Southboro, MA. 1985 retail was $525.

	$595	$525	$450	$415	$375	$350	$325

* **Boa Set** — 100 sets mfg. including 4 and 6 in. barrels with fully shrouded ejector rod housing, consecutive serial numbers, cases were supplied by Lew Horton. 1985 retail was $1,200.

	$1,450	$1,100	$875

POLICE POSITIVE (FOURTH ISSUE) — .38 Spl. cal., 6 shot, 4 in. barrel, blue finish, fixed sights, black composition grips, 25 oz. Mfg. 1994-95.

	$345	$290	$250	$225	$195	$180	$165

Last Mfg.'s Sug. Retail was $400.

POLICE POSITIVE MARK MK V (FIFTH ISSUE) — .38 Spl. cal., full shrouded 4 in. barrel, steel frame, blue or nickel finish, rubber grips. Mfg. 1994-95.

	$345	$290	$250	$225	$195	$180	$165

Add 10% for nickel finish.

DETECTIVE SPECIAL (FOURTH ISSUE) — .38 Spl. cal., 6 shot, 2 in. barrel, alloy frame, blue finish, black composition grips with gold medallions, 21 oz. Reintroduced 1993, disc. 1995.

	$345	$290	$250	$225	$195	$180	$165

Last Mfg.'s Sug. Retail was $400.

* **Bobbed Detective Special** — .38 Spl. cal., double action only with bobbed hammer, night front sight, honed action, choice of hard chrome or standard blue finish. Mfg. 1994-95.

	$525	$450	$350	$275	$225	$195	$175

Last Mfg.'s Sug. Retail was $599.

Add $30 for hard chrome finish.

COLT .38 SF-VI — .38 Spl. cal., 6 shot, 2 or 4 in. barrel, transfer bar safety, choice of matte (2 in.), bright polished (4 in.), or black (4 in.) finish, stainless steel, regular or bobbed (4 in. barrel only) hammer, fixed sights, black composition combat grips, 21 oz. Mfg. 1995-96.

	$350	$290	$250	$225	$195	$180	$165

Last Mfg.'s Sug. Retail was $408.

* **Colt Special Lady** — while advertised during 1996, this model had very limited mfg.

COLT .38 DSII — .357 Mag. (new 1998) or .38 Spl. cal., 6 shot, 2 in. barrel, stainless steel, service hammer, rubber combat style checkered grips, 21 oz. Mfg. 1997-98.

	$365	$295	$250

Last Mfg.'s Sug. Retail was $435.

This model features a redesigned trigger grouping and is capable of shooting .38+P ammo.

COLT MAGNUM CARRY — .357 Mag. cal., 6 shot, 2 in. barrel, transfer bar safety, satin stainless steel, wraparound rubber grips with finger grooves, ramp front sight, 21 oz. New 1999.

Mfg.'s Sug. Retail	$460		$380	$300	$255

Grading	100%	98%	95%	90%	80%	70%	60%

COMBAT COBRA — .357 Mag. cal., 2½ in. barrel, special edition for Lew Horton with CC prefix and stainless steel construction.

	100%	98%	95%	90%	80%	70%	60%
	$495	$450	$395	$350	$315	$280	$250

KING COBRA — .357 Mag. cal., blued metal, black neoprene round butt grips, 2 ½ (new 1990), 4 or 6 in. solid rib barrel only, outline sights, approx. 42 oz. (4 in. barrel). Mfg. 1988-92.

	100%	98%	95%	90%	80%	70%	60%
	$335	$295	$260	$235	$210	$200	$185

Last Mfg.'s Sug. Retail was $410.

KING COBRA STAINLESS — .357 Mag. cal., stainless steel construction, black neoprene round butt grips, 2½ (mfg. 1988-94), 4, 6, or 8 (mfg. 1990-94) in. solid rib barrel, outline sights, approx. 36 oz. (2½ in. barrel). Mfg. late 1987-92, production resumed 1994, disc. 1998.

	100%	98%	95%
	$400	$340	$265

Last Mfg.'s Sug. Retail was $485.

* **King Cobra "Ultimate" Bright Stainless** — similar to King Cobra, except for bright stainless steel, 2 ½ (new 1990), 4, 6, or 8 (new 1991) in. barrel. Mfg. 1988-92.

	100%	98%	95%
	$400	$340	$280

Last Mfg.'s Sug. Retail was $470.

PYTHON — .357 Mag. cal., 2½ (disc. 1994), 3 (disc., very scarce), 4, 6, or 8 in. barrel with vent rib, royal blue finish, full shrouded ejector rod, adj. rear sight, checkered walnut grips (prior to 1991), rubber Hogue monogrips (2½ or 4 in. barrel), or rubber target (6 or 8 in. barrel) grips, 38-48 oz. Mfg. 1955-1996.

* **Blue or royal blue finish**

	100%	98%	95%	90%	80%	70%	60%
	$575	$450	$375	$325	$300	$275	$250

Last Mfg.'s Sug. Retail was $815.

The standard Python was disc. during 1996. Current mfg. is through the Colt Custom Shop (see listings below), and must be special ordered.

Early 2½, 4 or 6 in. Pythons without letter prefix before ser. no. will bring a small premium if in 100% condition or NIB, as well as the disc. 3 in. barrel. There were also a few Pythons mfg. in .256, .38 Spl., .41 Mag., and .44 Spl. cals. While the .22 LR and the .22 WMR (.22 Mag.) were advertised in earlier factory catalogs, they were never manufactured - only a few prototypes exist. The amount of premium on these cals. depends on how serious (and deep-pocketed) the Python collector is.

A California distributor special ordered a quantity of 3 in. barreled Pythons, which at the time were not available. Colt probably utilized made-up 8 in. guns and either had them modified or re-barreled, with the distributors name part of the barrel marking. These guns are an unusual variant (sometimes referred to as a Combat Python), and are priced similarly to factory 3 in. barrel Pythons.

* **Nickel finish** — available in polished or satin nickel, disc. 1985.

	100%	98%	95%	90%	80%	70%	60%
	$550	$460	$415	$365	$325	$300	$275

Last Mfg.'s Sug. Retail was $693.

* **Stainless Steel Python** — stainless steel construction, matte finish, neoprene target or combat stocks, 2½ (disc. 1994), 4, 6 or 8 (new 1989) in. barrel. Mfg. 1983-1996.

	100%	98%	95%
	$680	$575	$450

Last Mfg.'s Sug. Retail was $904.

The 6 in. barrel includes neoprene target stocks.

* **"Ultimate" Bright Stainless Steel** — deluxe, highly polished stainless model, 2½ (disc.), 4, 6, or 8 in. VR barrel. Mfg. 1985-disc.

	100%	98%	95%
	$700	$585	$455

Last Mfg.'s Sug. Retail was $935.

PYTHON ELITE — .357 Mag. cal., 4 or 6 in. VR barrel, choice of royal blue (mfg. 1997 only) or stainless steel, Colt-Elliason adj. rear sight, rubber service style grips, 38 or 43½ oz. New 1997, disc. 1998, reintroduced 1999.

	100%	98%	95%	90%	80%	70%	60%
Mfg.'s Sug. Retail	$929	$775	$550	$475	$400	$350	$300	$275

This model was available by custom order only through the Colt Custom Shop.

Grading	100%	98%	95%	90%	80%	70%	60%

* **Python Elite Stainless** — similar to Python Elite, except is stainless steel. New 1997.

  Mfg.'s Sug. Retail   **$1,018**   **$875**   **$650**   **$550**

  This model is available by custom order only through the Colt Custom Shop.

ULTIMATE PYTHON — .357 Mag. cal., specially tuned by the custom gun shop, supplied with both Colt-Elliason target and Accro white outline sighting systems, walnut and rubber grips also included, choice of Colt Royal Blue or Ultimate Stainless finish, 6 in. barrel only. Mfg. 1991-1993.

     $1,025   **$850**   **$775**   **$695**   **$625**   **$550**   **$475**

Last Mfg.'s Sug. Retail was $1,140.

   Add $120 for Ultimate Stainless Model.

PYTHON HUNTER — .357 Mag. cal., 8 in. barrel, includes Leupold 2X scope, Halliburton aluminum case and accessories. Mfg. 1981 only.

     $1,195   **$1,000**   **$750**   **$650**   **$595**   **$540**   **$495**

Last Mfg.'s Sug. Retail was $995.

PYTHON SILHOUETTE — .357 Mag. cal., 8 in. barrel, includes Leupold 2X scope, similar to Python Hunter, except barrel is roll marked with Silhouette name and scope position has been moved rearward, black luggage type case. Mfg. circa 1983.

     $1,195   **$1,000**   **$750**   **$650**   **$595**   **$540**   **$495**

PYTHON .38 SPECIAL — 8 in. barrel, blue or nickel finish. Disc.

     $595   **$500**   **$425**   **$375**   **$350**   **$325**   **$300**

GRIZZLY — .357 Mag. cal., 6 in. barrel, matte stainless finish, approx. 500 mfg.

     $575   **$475**   **$425**   **$375**   **$350**   **$325**   **$295**

   This model was mfg. by the Colt Custom Shop.

WHITETAILER — .357 Mag. cal., 8 in. barrel, matte stainless finish, aluminum hard shell cased with 2X scope.

     $1,095   **$950**   **$750**   **$650**   **$595**   **$540**   **$495**

* **Whitetailer II** — similar to Whitetailer, except has high polish finish.

     $1,050   **$875**   **$750**   **$650**   **$595**   **$540**   **$495**

ANACONDA — .44 Mag. or .45 LC (6 in. only, new 1992) cal., double action, 4 (.44 Mag. only, new 1991), 6, or 8 (new 1991, .44 Mag. only) in. VR barrel, transfer bar safety system, 6 shot, choice of matte or Realtree Grey camo (.44 Mag. with 8 in. barrel only, mfg. 1996 only) metal finish, stainless steel only, black neoprene combat grips with Colt medallion, red ramp front sight, full length ejector rod housing, white outline rear adj. sight, approx. 47-59 oz. New 1990.

   Mfg.'s Sug. Retail   **$629**   **$510**   **$415**   **$355**

   Add $128 for Realtree Grey camo finish (disc. 1996).

* **Anaconda with scope** — .44 Mag. cal. only, 8 in. barrel, Realtree Grey camo finish on gun and scope. Mfg. 1996 only.

     $795   **$625**   **$475**

Last Mfg.'s Sug. Retail was $999.

* **Anaconda Hunter** — .44 Mag. cal., supplied with Leupold 2X scope, carrying case, cleaning accessories, and both walnut and rubber grips, 8 in. barrel only. Mfg. 1991-1993.

     $1,095   **$895**   **$725**

Last Mfg.'s Sug. Retail was $1,200.

* **Custom Anaconda** — .44 Mag. cal., features 6 or 8 in. Magna-ported barrel and Colt-Elliason rear sight, contoured trigger, and Pachmayr rubber grips, brushed stainless steel. Mfg. 1992-1993, re-released 1995-96.

     $595   **$525**   **$450**   **$365**

Last Mfg.'s Sug. Retail was $870.

Grading	100%	98%	95%	90%	80%	70%	60%

* **Anaconda 1st Edition** — .44 Mag. cal., ultimate stainless finish, special rollmark on left side of barrel reads "Colt Anaconda First Edition", with aluminum carrying case, ser. no. range MM00001-MM01000, 1,000 mfg. 1990 only.

			$895	$750	$625	

100%	98%	95%	90%	80%	70%	60%	50%	40%	30%	20%	10%

RIFLES: PRE-1904

A Colt letter of provenance for the Lightning models listed below is $100/each for the large frame and $75/each for the small/medium frames. Colt-Burgess model factory letters are also available at $100/each.

FIRST MODEL RING LEVER — .34, .36, .38, .40, or .44 cal., 8 or 10 shot revolving cylinder, 32 in. octagon barrel, walnut stock, no forend, 200 mfg., Percussion. Mfg. 1837-1838.

* **Standard Model**

100%	98%	95%	90%	80%	70%	60%	50%	40%	30%	20%	10%
N/A	N/A	N/A	$37,500	$28,000	$21,500	$16,500	$13,500	$11,000	$9,000	$7,500	$6,500

* **Improved Model** — attached loading lever.

N/A	N/A	N/A	$41,000	$29,650	$22,750	$17,500	$14,500	$12,000	$10,000	$8,500	$7,500

SECOND MODEL RING LEVER — similar to First Model, without top strap over cylinder, .44 caliber only, Percussion, 5000 mfg., 1838-1841.

* **Standard Model**

N/A	N/A	N/A	$33,500	$24,500	$17,000	$13,000	$11,000	$8,780	$7,200	$6,300	$5,650

* **Improved Model**

N/A	N/A	N/A	$34,750	$26,000	$17,750	$13,300	$11,200	$8,900	$7,325	$6,390	$5,725

MODEL 1839 CARBINE — .52 smooth bore cal., 6 shot cylinder, 24 in. barrel, exposed hammer for cocking, blued, walnut stock, percussion, approx. 950 mfg., 1838-1841.

* **Early Model**

N/A	N/A	N/A	$38,500	$29,000	$22,000	$17,500	$14,750	$11,500	$9,350	$7,750	$6,750

* **Standard Model** — no loading lever.

N/A	N/A	N/A	$31,000	$22,500	$17,000	$13,500	$11,250	$9,000	$7,500	$6,600	$6,000

MODEL 1855 REVOLVING — .36, .44, or .56 cal., various barrel lengths and stock styles, 5 or 6 shot cylinder, blued with walnut buttstock, no forend, percussion. Mfg. 1856-1864.

* **½ Stock Sporter** — 24, 27, or 30 in. barrel, approx. 1500 mfg.

N/A	N/A	N/A	$11,500	$9,000	$7,850	$7,000	$6,500	$6,000	$5,500	$5,100	$4,750

* **Full Stock Sporter** — 21, 24, 27, 30, or 31 in. barrel, approx. 2000 mfg.

N/A	N/A	N/A	$13,500	$11,275	$9,150	$8,250	$7,500	$6,950	$6,500	$6,100	$5,750

* **Military Model, U.S.** — marked, 21-37 in. barrel, 9310 mfg.

N/A	N/A	N/A	$17,500	$14,650	$11,900	$10,500	$9,800	$9,050	$8,450	$7,900	$7,475

* **.36 Caliber Carbine Model** — 15, 18, or 21 in. barrel, 4400 mfg.

N/A	N/A	N/A	$17,150	$14,350	$11,660	$10,525	$9,600	$8,875	$8,275	$7,750	$7,300

* **.56 Caliber Artillery Carbine** — 5 shot, 21 in. barrel with bayonet lug and forestock, approx. 64 mfg.

N/A	N/A	N/A	$19,000	$16,500	$13,500	$10,875	$10,125	$3,300	$9,450	$9,000	$8,400

* **Shotgun Model** — .60 or .75 cal., smooth bore, 27, 30, 33, or 36 in. barrels, 1100 mfg.

N/A	N/A	N/A	$12,750	$11,000	$9,000	$8,000	$7,250	$6,750	$6,300	$6,000	$5,600

BERDAN — .42 bottle-necked CF cal., approx. 30,000 mfg. 1866-circa 1870. Scarce since most were sent to Russia and have Russian barrel markings, approx. 50-100 are Hartford marked.

100%	98%	95%	90%	80%	70%	60%	50%	40%	30%	20%	10%

* *Berdan Rifle* — .32½ in. barrel, approx. 10 lbs.

| $6,250 | $4,750 | $3,850 | $3,250 | $2,750 | $2,250 | $1,850 | $1,650 | $1,450 | $1,325 | $1,250 | $1,175 |

* *Berdan Carbine* — half stock, 18¼ in. barrel, approx. 50 mfg., both Russian and Hartford marked.

| $12,500 | $10,750 | $9,350 | $8,300 | $7,600 | $6,725 | $6,100 | $5,500 | $4,750 | $3,950 | $3,275 | $2,750 |

MODEL 1861 MUSKET — .58 cal., percussion, muzzle loader, 40 in. barrel, with 3 bands, metal parts, white walnut stock, 75,000 mfg., 1861-1865.

| $2,750 | $2,500 | $2,350 | $1,895 | $1,750 | $1,650 | $1,500 | $1,350 | $1,250 | $1,150 | $1,000 | $850 |

COLT-BURGESS LEVER ACTION — .44-40 WCF cal., 25½ in. barrel, 15 shot tube mag., blue with case hardened lever and hammer, walnut stock, 6400 mfg., 1883-1885.

| $8,750 | $7,450 | $6,350 | $5,500 | $4,900 | $4,465 | $4,170 | $3,930 | $3,700 | $3,525 | $3,350 | $3,100 |

COLT-BURGESS CARBINE — similar to Rifle, with 20 in. barrel.

| $11,500 | $9,950 | $8,750 | $7,900 | $7,300 | $6,725 | $6,250 | $5,850 | $5,500 | $5,200 | $4,950 | $4,750 |

COLT-BURGESS BABY CARBINE — similar to Carbine, with lightened frame.

| $14,000 | $12,250 | $10,750 | $9,720 | $8,975 | $8,275 | $7,695 | $7,200 | $6,765 | $6,395 | $6,100 | $5,850 |

LIGHTNING SLIDE ACTION - SMALL FRAME — .22 cal., 24 in. barrel, open sights, walnut straight stock, round or octagon barrel, 90,000 mfg. Mfg. 1887-1904.

| $2,300 | $1,650 | $1,250 | $1,000 | $795 | $650 | $575 | $535 | $495 | $450 | $400 | $375 |

LIGHTNING SLIDE ACTION - MEDIUM FRAME — in .32-20 WCF, .38-40 WCF, or .44-40 WCF cal., similar to small frame, except with 26 in. barrel and larger frame.

| $3,250 | $2,550 | $2,150 | $1,775 | $1,475 | $1,175 | $950 | $775 | $650 | $550 | $495 | $450 |

LIGHTNING CARBINE MEDIUM FRAME — similar to Rifle, with 20 in. barrel.

| $5,250 | $3,850 | $3,250 | $2,850 | $2,450 | $2,150 | $1,950 | $1,750 | $1,450 | $1,175 | $1,050 | $950 |

LIGHTNING BABY CARBINE MEDIUM FRAME — lightened version of Carbine.

| $7,000 | $5,500 | $4,750 | $4,000 | $3,450 | $2,950 | $2,450 | $2,100 | $1,850 | $1,650 | $1,425 | $1,350 |

LIGHTNING SLIDE ACTION - LARGE FRAME — .38-56 WCF, .40-60 WCF, .45-60 WCF, .45-65 WCF, .45-85 WCF, or .50-95 Express cal., large version of previously described Lightnings, 6,500 mfg. 1887-1894.

| $6,250 | $4,750 | $3,850 | $3,250 | $2,750 | $2,250 | $1,850 | $1,650 | $1,450 | $1,325 | $1,250 | $1,175 |

Add 25% for .50-95 Express cal.

LIGHTNING CARBINE LARGE FRAME — 22 in. barrel.

| $11,500 | $9,000 | $7,500 | $6,250 | $5,350 | $4,850 | $4,375 | $3,925 | $3,625 | $3,375 | $3,150 | $2,975 |

BABY CARBINE LARGE FRAME — lightened version.

| $13,500 | $10,750 | $9,700 | $8,500 | $7,750 | $6,850 | $6,300 | $5,825 | $5,425 | $5,075 | $4,775 | $4,350 |

Add 50% for .50-95 Express cal.

DOUBLE RIFLE SxS — various cals. in the .45 range, hammers, very limited production between 1878-1880. Most guns were owned by friends of Caldwell Colt — Sam Colt's son, the original designer. Colt Double Rifles are extremely rare and desirable, and should be examined carefully. Prices typically range between $15,000-$25,000, if all original.

Grading					100%	98%	95%	90%	80%	70%	60%

RIFLES: RIMFIRE, DISC.

COLTEER 1-22 — .22 LR or .22 Mag. cal., single shot bolt action, 20, 22, or 24 (.22 Mag. only, w/o sights) in. round barrel, adj. rear sight (20 or 22 in. barrel), plain walnut stock. Approx. 50,000 mfg. 1957-1966.

| | | | | | $275 | $215 | $175 | $140 | $110 | $95 | $80 |

Add 10% for .22 Mag. cal.

Grading	100%	98%	95%	90%	80%	70%	60%

STAGECOACH — .22 LR cal., semi-auto, 16½ in. barrel, 13 shot mag., deluxe walnut, saddle ring w/leather thong, roll-engraved hold-up scene. Over 25,000 mfg. 1965-mid '70s.

	$325	$275	$215	$175	$140	$110	$90

COLTEER — .22 LR cal., similar to Stagecoach, except 19 3/8 in. barrel, 15 shot mag., no engraving and plain walnut. Over 25,000 mfg. 1965-mid '70s.

	$275	$215	$175	$140	$110	$95	$80

COURIER — similar to Colteer semi-auto, except pistol-grip stock and enlarged forearm. Mfg. 1970-mid '70s.

	$275	$215	$175	$140	$110	$95	$80

RIFLES: BOLT ACTION, CENTERFIRE

COLT "57" — .243 Win. or .30-06 cal., FN Mauser action, mfg. by Jefferson Mfg. Co. in N. Haven, CT during 1957, approx. 5,000 mfg. starting at ser. no. 1, checkered American Monte Carlo walnut stock, wraparound front sight.

	$595	$550	$500	$450	$400	$350	$325

This model was also available in a deluxe version with deluxe hand checkered walnut stock — add 15%.

COLTSMAN STANDARD RIFLE — .223 Rem., .243 Win., .264 Win. Mag., .30-06, .300 Win. Mag., .308 Win. cal., mfg. by Kodiak, Mauser or Sako-action, 22 in. or 24 in.(.300 Win. Mag.), 5 or 6 shot mag. Approx. 10,000 (both models) mfg. 1958-1966.

	$495	$450	$425	$400	$350	$325	$300

COLTSMAN CUSTOM RIFLE — deluxe variation including deluxe walnut with skipline checkering and rosewood forearm cap.

	$695	$650	$600	$550	$500	$450	$400

COLT SAUER RIFLE (STANDARD ACTION) — non-rotating bolt action, manufactured in Germany by J. P. Sauer & Sohn, .25-06 Rem., .270 Win. or .30-06 cal., 24 in. barrel, 4 round mag., no sights, checkered walnut stock with rosewood forend tip and pistol grip cap, recoil pad. Disc. 1985.

	$1,150	$975	$800	$700	$660	$620	$575

Last Mfg.'s Sug. Retail was $1,257.

This model was also available in a Grade IV with silver receiver. Each caliber featured a different engraved animal. Add 50%-70%, depending on condition and caliber desirabilty.

COLT SAUER SHORT ACTION — similar to the standard except in .22-250 Rem., .243 Win. cal. or .308 Win. Disc. 1985.

	$1,200	$975	$800	$700	$660	$620	$575

Last Mfg.'s Sug. Retail was $1,257.

COLT SAUER MAGNUM — similar to the standard except in 7mm Rem. Mag., 300 Win. Mag., or 300 Weatherby Mag. cal. Disc. 1985.

	$1,250	$1,000	$800	$700	$660	$620	$575

Last Mfg.'s Sug. Retail was $1,300.

COLT SAUER GRAND ALASKAN — heavier version in .375 H&H cal., adj. sights.

	$1,375	$1,125	$995	$900	$820	$740	$690

COLT SAUER GRAND AFRICAN — .458 Win. Mag. cal., 4 round capacity, 9 lb. 12 oz. Disc. 1985.

	$1,450	$1,150	$995	$900	$820	$740	$690

Last Mfg.'s Sug. Retail was $1,400.

COLT LIGHT RIFLE — .243 Win., .270 Win., .280 Rem., .25-06 Rem., .30-06, .308 Win., .300 Win. Mag., or 7mm Rem. Mag. cal., short or long action, matte black synthetic stock, matte metal finish, adj. trigger, 3 position side safety, approx. 5.4 lbs. in short action. New 1999.

As this edition went to press, prices had yet to be established on this model.

Grading	100%	98%	95%	90%	80%	70%	60%

RIFLES: SINGLE SHOT, CENTERFIRE

COLT-SHARPS RIFLE — .17 Bee, .22-250 Rem., .243 Win., .25-06 Rem., 7mm Rem. Mag., .30-06, or .375 H&H cal., Sharps falling block action, high-gloss bluing, deluxe checkered walnut stock and forearm. Approx. 500 mfg. 1970-1977.

	100%	98%	95%	90%	80%	70%	60%
	$2,295	$1,950	$1,650	$1,200	$1,000	$800	$650

C | DRILLINGS

COLT SAUER DRILLING — 12 ga./.30-06 or .243 Win. cal. combo gun, 25 in. barrels, engraved, 8 lbs. Disc. 1985.

	100%	98%	95%	90%	80%	70%	60%
	$2,950	$2,500	$2,100	$1,800	$1,500	$1,250	$1,000

Last Mfg.'s Sug. Retail was $4,228.

RIFLES: SEMI-AUTO, AR-15 & VARIATIONS

Prices of currently manufactured models listed below automatically refer to post-ban (if any) configurations.

Rifling twists on the Colt AR-15 have changed throughout the years. They started with a 1:12 in. twist, changed to a 1:7 in. twist (to match with the new, longer .223 Rem./5.56mm SS109-type bullet), and finally changed to a 1:9 in. twist in combination with 1:7 in. twist models as a compromise for bullets in the 50-68 grain range. Current mfg. AR-15s/Match Targets have rifling twists/turns incorporated into the model descriptions.

Add $368 for Colt Scout Sight C-More on current mfg.
Add $444 for Colt Tactical Sight C-More on current mfg.
Older mfg. with green boxes will command a premium.

SP-1 — .223 Rem. cal., original Colt paramilitary configuration without forward bolt assist, finishes included parkerizing and electroless nickel. Mfg. 1963-84.

	$995	$850	$750	$650	$600	$550	$495

SPORTER II (R6500) — .223 Rem. cal., various configurations, disc.

	$1,150	$995	$875	$750	$675	$595	$525

MATCH TARGET LIGHTWEIGHT (R/MT6430, R/MT6530, or R/MT6830) — .223 Rem. (6530, 1 turn in 7 in.), 7.62x39mm (6830, new 1992, disc. 1996, 1 turn in 12 in.), or 9mm Para. (6430, new 1992, disc. 1996, 1 turn in 10 in.) cal., features 16 in. barrel (non-threaded per C/B 1994) cals., initially shorter stock and handguard, adj. rear sight for windage and elevation, includes 2 detachable 5, 8, or 9 (new 1999) shot mags., approx. 7 lbs. New 1991.

Mfg.'s Sug. Retail	$1,010	$850	$750	$700	$650	$600	$550	$495
Pre-ban		$975	$875	$775	$650	$600	$550	$500

Add $154 for .22 LR conversion kit (disc. 1994).

TARGET GOVT. MODEL RIFLE (R6550/R or MT6551) — .223 Rem. cal., semi-auto version of the M-16 rifle with forward bolt assist, gas operated, 20 in. barrel (1 turn in 7 in.), straight line black nylon stock, aperture rear, post front sight, 5, 8, 9 (new 1999), 20 (disc.), or 30 (disc.) shot detachable box mag., Model 6550 was disc. 1990, 7½ lbs.

Mfg.'s Sug. Retail	$1,040	$895	$795	$725	$660	$600	$550	$495
Pre-ban		$895	$825	$725	$625	$575	$525	$475

Add $154 for .22 LR conversion kit (mfg. 1990-94).
Subtract $70 for older field-style rear sight assembly (pre-1987).

In 1987, Colt replaced the AR-15A2 Sporter II Rifle with the AR-15A2 Govt. Model. This new model has the 800 meter rear sighting system housed in the receiver's carrying handle (similar to the M-16 A2).

Grading	100%	98%	95%	90%	80%	70%	60%

MATCH TARGET COMPETITION H-BAR RIFLE (R or MT6700) — .223 Rem. cal., features
flat top upper receiver for scope mounting, 20 in. barrel (1 turn in 9 in.), quick detachable
carry handle which incorporates a 600-meter rear sighting system, counterbored muzzle,
dovetailed upper receiver is grooved to accept Weaver style scope rings, supplied with two
5, 8, or 9 (new 1999) shot mags., cleaning kit, and sling, matte black finish, 8½ lbs. New
1992.

		100%	98%	95%	90%	80%	70%	60%
Mfg.'s Sug. Retail	$1,090	$925	$825	$775	$700	$625	$575	$525
Pre-ban		$995	$875	$750	$675	$595	$550	$495

Add $60 for compensator (MT6700C, new 1999).

COMPETITION H-BAR RIFLE RANGE SELECTED (R6700CH) — similar to Sporter Competition I, except has been range selected for optimal accuracy, includes Cordura nylon case, 3-9X rubber armored variable scope, and cleaning kit, 10½ lbs. Limited mfg. 1992 only.

	100%	98%	95%	90%	80%	70%	60%
Pre-ban	$1,575	$1,350	$1,200	$995	$875	$750	$675

Last Mfg.'s Sug. Retail was $1,527.

MATCH TARGET H-BAR (R6600/R or MT6601) — similar to AR-15A2 Govt. Model Rifle,
except has heavy 20 in. barrel (1 turn in 7 in.), Model 6600 was disc. 1993, 8 lbs. New 1986.

		100%	98%	95%	90%	80%	70%	60%
Mfg.'s Sug. Retail	$1,085	$925	$825	$775	$700	$625	$575	$525
Pre-ban		$1,050	$895	$775	$675	$625	$575	$525

Add $60 for compensator (MT6601C, new 1999).
Add $154 for .22 LR conversion kit (mfg. 1990-94).

* *Match Delta H-Bar (M6600DH/6601DH)* — similar to AR-15A2 H-Bar, except has 3-9X rubber
armored variable scope, removable cheekpiece, adj. scope mount, and leather sling, range
selected. Aluminum cased. Mfg. 1987-1991.

	100%	98%	95%	90%	80%	70%	60%
	$1,150	$995	$850	$775	$700	$625	$550

Last Mfg.'s Sug. Retail was $1,460.

Add $160 for .22 LR conversion kit (mfg. 1990-91).

COLT ACCURIZED RIFLE (CR6724) — .223 Rem. cal., 24 in. barrel, matte finish, accurized
AR-15, 8 (disc. 1998) or 9 (new 1999) shot mag., 9.41 lbs. New 1997.

		100%	98%	95%	90%	80%	70%
Mfg.'s Sug. Retail	$1,295	$1,050	$925	$825	$775	$700	$625	$575

MATCH TARGET COMPETITION H-BAR II (MT6731) — .223 Rem. cal., 16.1 in. barrel (1 turn
in 9 in.), matte finish, 7.1 lbs. New 1995.

		100%	98%	95%	90%	80%	70%	60%
Mfg.'s Sug. Retail	$1,065	$900	$835	$775	$700	$625	$575	$525

AR-15A2 SPORTER II — .223 Rem., standard 20 in. barrel, rear sight adj. for windage only,
7½ lbs. Disc. 1989.

	100%	98%	95%	90%	80%	70%	60%
	$995	$900	$800	$700	$600	$525	$470

Last Mfg.'s Sug. Retail was $740.

AR-15A2 CARBINE — similar to older AR-15A2 Sporter II Rifle, except has collapsible
buttstock, field sights, 16 in. barrel, shortened forearm, 5 lbs. 13 oz. Disc. 1988.

	100%	98%	95%	90%	80%	70%	60%
	$1,095	$950	$850	$750	$650	$575	$500

Last Mfg.'s Sug. Retail was $770.

AR-15A2 GOVT. MODEL CARBINE (R6520) — similar to AR-15A2 Govt. Model Rifle,
except has collapsible buttstock, 800 meter adj. rear sight, 16 in. barrel, 5 lbs. 13 oz.,
shortened forearm. Mfg. 1988-1990 (civilian sales disc. because of Federal/State regulations).

	100%	98%	95%	90%	80%	70%	60%
	$1,250	$1,050	$925	$825	$675	$600	$575

Last Mfg.'s Sug. Retail was $880.

* *AR-15 9mm Para. Carbine (R6450)* — similar to AR-15A2 Carbine, except 9mm Para. cal. with
20 shot mag., 6 lbs. 5 oz. Mfg. 1985-86 only.

	100%	98%	95%	90%	80%	70%	60%
	$1,295	$1,100	$925	$850	$775	$700	$650

Last Mfg.'s Sug. Retail was $696.

AR-15 SCOPE (3X/4X) AND MOUNT — initially offered with 3X scope, then switched to 4X.
Disc.

	100%	98%	95%
	$250	$200	$165

Last Mfg.'s Sug. Retail was $344.

100%	98%	95%	90%	80%	70%	60%	50%	40%	30%	20%	10%

SHOTGUNS: O/U

ARMSMEAR — 12 ga. only, 2¾ in. chambers, mfg. by Worshipful Co. Gunmakers of London, boxlock action with engraved sideplates, checkered high-grade European walnut stock and forearm, 28 (HE) or 30 (LE) in. VR barrels with screw-in chokes, choice of light (Armsmear 12 LE) or heavy (Armsmear 12 HE) engraving, 7½ lbs. This model was originally advertised in 1995.

    While advertised, this model was never manufactured.

SHOTGUNS: SxS, DISC.

    Strong, original case colors and vivid damascus barrel patterning will make the difference when determining values on the Models 1878 and 1883. Remember, these are black powder shotguns.

MODEL 1878 HAMMER SHOTGUN — 10 or 12 ga., 28-32 in. blued or browned damascus barrels, double triggers, sideplates, case hardened breech, non-automatic ejectors, semi-pistol grip stock, 22,683 mfg. between 1878-1889. Many of these guns were ordered with special features - these original guns command premiums above the prices listed below.

  $3,750 $3,250 $2,950 $2,675 $2,200 $1,925 $1,650 $1,485 $1,100 $990 $880 $725

MODEL 1883 HAMMERLESS — 8, 10 or 12 ga., 28-32 in. damascus barrels, many deluxe custom orders occur in this model. Mfg. from 1883-1895. Approx. serial range is No. 1-3,050 and 4,055-8,365. Seldom encountered in mint condition.

  $4,250 $3,750 $3,350 $2,995 $2,675 $2,200 $1,925 $1,650 $1,485 $1,100 $990 $875

    This model was generally a custom order gun with no standard grades being designated. Quality was extremely high, and the high cost of manufacture is a large reason why the gun never sold in large numbers commercially. The Model 1883 was discontinued after only 12 years of manufacture (it was one of the most expensive shotguns during its day). Values above assume moderate engraving and above average walnut.

Grading	100%	98%	95%	90%	80%	70%	60%

SxS SHOTGUN MFG. 1961-62 — 12 ga. or 16 ga., various barrel lengths, DTs, checkered stock and forearm, mfg. in France 1961-62 by Fabrication Mechanique, estimated total between 25-50 guns in serial range 467,000-469,000.

                      $675 $595 $525 $450 $400 $360 $320

SHOTGUNS: SEMI-AUTO

STANDARD AUTO SHOTGUN — 12 or 20 ga. (also available in Mags.), mfg. by Franchi of Italy, aluminum frame, 26, 28, 30, or 32 in. plain or VR barrel, almost 5,300 mfg. (both models) 1962-1966.

                      $375 $350 $325 $295 $260 $230 $200

    Add $50 for VR barrel.

CUSTOM AUTO SHOTGUN — similar to Standard Model, except deluxe walnut, hand engraved receiver. Mfg. 1962-1966.

                      $475 $425 $375 $350 $325 $295 $260

SHOTGUNS: SLIDE ACTION

COLTSMAN PUMP SHOTGUN — 12, 16, or 20 ga., Franchi frame assembled by both Kodiak and Montgomery Wards, 26 or 28 in. plain barrel, aluminum frame. Approx. 2,000 mfg. 1961-1965.

                      $325 $295 $260 $230 $200 $180 $165

COMMEMORATIVES, SPECIAL EDITIONS, & LIMITED MFG.

    During the course of a year, we receive many phone calls and letters on Colt special editions and limited editions that do not appear in this section. It should be noted that a factory commemorative issue is a gun that has been manufactured, marketed, and sold through the auspices of the specific trademark (in this case Colt). There have literally been hundreds of special and limited editions which, although mostly made by Colt (some were subcontracted), were not marketed or retailed by Colt. These guns are NOT Colt commemoratives and, for the most part, do not have the desirability factor that the factory commemoratives have. Your best alternative to find out more information about the multitude of these special/limited editions is to write: COLT HISTORIAN, P.O. Box 1868, Hartford, CT, 06144. If anyone could have any information, it will be the factory. Their research fee starts at $75 per gun, and if they cannot obtain additional information on the variation you request, they will refund $50. Unfortunately, in some cases, a special/limited edition may not be researchable. In situations like this, do not confuse rarity with desirability.

Typically, special and limited editions are made for distributors. These sub-contracts seem to be mostly made to signify/commemorate an organization, state, special event or occasion, personality, etc. These are typically marketed and sold through a distributor to dealers, or a company/individual to those people who want to purchase them. These special editions may or may not have a retail price and often times, since demand is regional, values decrease rapidly in other areas of the country. In some cases, if the distributor/wholesaler who ordered the initial special/limited edition is known (and still in business), you may be able to find more information by contacting them directly. Desirability is the key to determining values on these editions.

Until recently, the over-production of many factory commemoratives had created a "softness" in the commemorative marketplace. Approximately a decade ago, Colt decided to cut down on commemorative manufacture after perhaps too many years of over-production. Many commemorative consumers were starting to think that the "limited manufacture" guns had become more of a company marketing tool and sales gimmick rather than a legitimate vehicle for investment potential and collector support. During the end of this period of commemorative "over-production", both distributors and retailers finally saw their commemorative inventory levels gradually reach zero - perhaps the first time in over two decades that they were sold out of factory commemoratives. In other words, the commemorative "blow-out" sales were over. As this transition from distributor/dealer inventory to consumer purchases occurred, the commemorative marketplace became stronger and prices began to rise.

Because the commemorative consumer is now more in charge (consumers now own most of the guns since distributor/dealer inventories are depleted) than during the 1980s, commemorative firearms are possibly as strong as they have ever been. When the supply side of commemorative economics has to be purchased from knowledgable collectors or savvy dealers and demand stays the same or increases slightly, prices have no choice but to go up. If and when the manufacturers crank up the commemorative production runs again (and it won't be like the good old days), the old marketplace characteristics may reappear. Until then, however, the commemorative marketplace remains strong, with values becoming more predictable.

As a reminder on commemoratives, I would like to repeat a few facts, especially for the beginning collector, but applicable to all manufacturers of commemoratives. Commemoratives are current production guns designed as a reproduction of an historically famous gun model, or as a tie-in with historically famous persons or events. They are generally of very excellent quality and often embellished with select woods and finishes such as silver, nickel, or gold plating. Obviously, they are manufactured to be instant collectibles and to be pleasing to the eye. As with firearms in general, not all commemorative models have achieved collector status, although most enjoy an active market - especially recently. Consecutive-numbered pairs as well as collections based on the same serial number will bring a premium. Remember that handguns usually are in some type of wood presentation case, and that rifles may be cased or in packaging with graphics styled to the particular theme of the collectible. The original factory packaging and papers should always accompany the firearm, as they are necessary to realize full value at the time of sale.

All commemorative firearms should be absolutely new, unfired, and as issued, since any obvious use or wear removes it from collector status and lowers its value significantly. Many owners have allowed their commemoratives to sit in their boxes while encased in plastic wrappers for years without inspecting them for corrosion or oxidation damage. This is risky, especially if stored inside a plastic wrapper for long periods of time, since any accumulated moisture cannot escape. Periodic inspection should be implemented to ensure no damage occurs - this is important, since even light "freckling" created from touching the metal surfaces can reduce values significantly. A fired gun with obvious wear or without its original packaging can lose as much as 50% of its normal value - many used commemoratives get sold as "fancy shooters" with little, if any, premiums being asked.

A final note on commemoratives: One of the characteristics of commemoratives/special editions is that over the years of ownership, most of the original amount manufactured stays in the same NIB condition. Thus, if supply always is constant and in one condition, demand has to increase before price appreciation can occur. After 38 years of commemorative/special edition production, many models' performance records can be accurately analyzed and the appreciation (or depreciation) can be compared against other purchases of equal vintage. You be the judge.

Grading	100%	Issue Price	Qty. Made
1961 GENESEO, ILLINOIS 125TH ANNIVERSARY DERRINGER	$650	$28	104
1961 SHERIFF'S MODEL — blue and case hardened, 3 in. barrel, SM suffix.	$1,995	$130	478
1961 SHERIFF'S MODEL — nickel, 3 in. barrel, SM suffix.	$5,000	$140	25
1961 125TH ANNIVERSARY MODEL SAA	$1,195	$150	7,390
1961 KANSAS STATEHOOD SCOUT	$395	$75	6,201
1961 PONY EXPRESS CENTENNIAL SCOUT	$450	$80	1,007
1961 CIVIL WAR CENTENNIAL PISTOL .22 SHORT	$175	$33	24,114
1962 ROCK ISLAND ARSENAL CENTENNIAL SCOUT	$250	$39	550
1962 COLUMBUS, OHIO SESQUICENTENNIAL SCOUT	$550	$100	200
1962 FORT FINDLAY, OHIO SESQUICENTENNIAL SCOUT	$650	$90	110
1962 FORT FINDLAY CASE PAIR — .22 LR and .22 Mag. cals.	$2,500	$185	20
1962 NEW MEXICO GOLDEN ANNIVERSARY SCOUT	$395	$80	1,000
1962 FORT MCPHERSON, NEBRASKA CENTENNIAL DERRINGER	$395	$29	300
1962 WEST VIRGINIA STATEHOOD CENTENNIAL SCOUT	$395	$75	3,452
1963 WEST VIRGINIA STATEHOOD CENTENNIAL SAA .45	$1,195	$150	600
1963 ARIZONA TERRITORIAL CENTENNIAL SCOUT	$395	$75	5,355
1963 ARIZONA TERRITORIAL CENTENNIAL SAA .45	$1,195	$150	1,280

C

Grading	100%	Issue Price	Qty. Made
1963 CAROLINA CHARTER TERCENTENARY SCOUT			
	$395	$75	300
1963 CAROLINA CHARTER TERCENTENARY 22/45 COMBO			
	$1,595	$240	251
1963 H. COOK "1 TO 100" 22/45 COMBO			
	$1,795	$275	100
1963 FORT STEPHENSON, OHIO SESQUICENTENNIAL SCOUT			
	$550	$75	200
1963 BATTLE OF GETTYSBURG CENTENNIAL SCOUT			
	$395	$90	1,019
1963 IDAHO TERRITORIAL CENTENNIAL SCOUT			
	$395	$75	902
1963 GEN. JOHN HUNT MORGAN INDIANA RAID SCOUT			
	$650	$75	100
1964 CHERRY'S SPORTING GOODS 35TH ANNIVERSARY 22/45 COMBO			
	$1,695	$275	100
1964 NEVADA STATEHOOD CENTENNIAL SCOUT			
	$395	$75	3,984
1964 NEVADA STATEHOOD CENTENNIAL SAA .45			
	$1,195	$150	1,688
1964 NEVADA STATEHOOD CENTENNIAL 22/45 COMBO			
	$1,595	$240	189
1964 NEVADA ST. CENT. 22/45 COMBO W/EXTRA ENGR. CYLS.			
	$1,695	$350	577
1964 NEVADA "BATTLE BORN" SCOUT			
	$395	$85	981
1964 NEVADA "BATTLE BORN" SAA .45			
	$1,395	$175	80
1964 NEVADA "BATTLE BORN" 22/45 COMBO			
	$2,595	$265	20
1964 MONTANA TERRITORIAL CENTENNIAL SCOUT			
	$395	$75	2,300
1964 MONTANA TERRITORIAL CENTENNIAL SAA .45			
	$1,195	$150	851
1964 WYOMING DIAMOND JUBILEE SCOUT			
	$395	$75	2,357
1964 GENERAL HOOD CENTENNIAL SCOUT			
	$395	$75	1,503
1964 NEW JERSEY TERCENTENARY SCOUT			
	$395	$75	1,001
1964 NEW JERSEY TERCENTENARY SAA .45			
	$1,195	$150	250
1964 ST. LOUIS BICENTENNIAL SCOUT			
	$395	$75	802
1964 ST. LOUIS BICENTENNIAL SAA .45			
	$1,195	$150	200
1964 ST. LOUIS BICENTENNIAL 22/45 COMBO			
	$1,595	$240	250

Grading	100%	Issue Price	Qty. Made
1964 CALIFORNIA GOLD RUSH SCOUT			
	$395	$80	500
1964 PONY EXPRESS PRESENTATION SAA .45			
	$1,395	$250	1,004
1964 CHAMIZAL TREATY SCOUT			
	$395	$85	450
1964 CHAMIZAL TREATY SAA .45			
	$1,295	$170	50
1964 CHAMIZAL TREATY 22/45 COMBO			
	$1,995	$280	50
1964 COL. SAM COLT SESQUI. PRESENTATION SAA .45			
	$1,195	$225	4,750
1964 COL. SAM COLT SESQUI. DELUXE PRES. SAA .45			
	$2,500	$500	200
1964 COL. SAM COLT SESQUI. SPEC. DELUXE PRES. SAA .45			
	$4,000	$1,000	50
1964 WYATT EARP BUNTLINE SAA .45			
	$2,250	$250	150
1965 OREGON TRAIL SCOUT			
	$395	$75	1,995
1965 JOAQUIN MURIETTA 22/45 COMBO			
	$1,695	$350	100
1965 FORTY-NINER MINER SCOUT			
	$395	$85	500
1965 OLD FT. DES MOINES RECONSTRUCTION SCOUT			
	$395	$90	700
1965 OLD FT. DES MOINES RECONSTRUCTION SAA .45			
	$1,295	$170	100
1965 OLD FT. DES MOINES RECONSTRUCTION 22/45 COMBO			
	$1,695	$290	100
1965 APPOMATTOX CENTENNIAL SCOUT			
	$395	$75	1,001
1965 APPOMATTOX CENTENNIAL SAA .45			
	$1,195	$150	250
1965 APPOMATTOX CENTENNIAL 22/45 COMBO			
	$1,595	$240	250
1965 GENERAL MEADE CAMPAIGN SCOUT			
	$395	$75	1,197
1965 ST. AUGUSTINE QUADRACENTENNIAL SCOUT			
	$395	$85	500
1965 KANSAS COWTOWN SERIES — Wichita Scout.			
	$395	$85	500
1966 KANSAS COWTOWN SERIES — Dodge City Scout.			
	$395	$85	500
1966 COLORADO GOLD RUSH SCOUT			
	$395	$85	1,350
1966 OKLAHOMA DIAMOND JUBILEE			
	$395	$85	1,343

Grading	100%	Issue Price	Qty. Made
1966 DAKOTA TERRITORY SCOUT			
	$395	$85	1,000
1966 GENERAL MEADE SAA .45			
	$1,195	$165	200
1966 ABERCROMBIE & FITCH "TRAILBLAZER" — New York.			
	$1,095	$275	200
1966 KANSAS COWTOWN SERIES — Abilene Scout.			
	$395	$95	500
1966 INDIANA SESQUICENTENNIAL SCOUT			
	$395	$85	1,500
1966 PONY EXPRESS .45 SAA 4-SQUARE SET (4 GUNS)			
	$5,995	$1,400	unknown
1966 CALIFORNIA GOLD RUSH SAA .45			
	$1,395	$175	130
1966 ABERCROMBIE & FITCH "TRAILBLAZER" — Chicago.			
	$1,095	$275	100
1966 ABERCROMBIE & FITCH "TRAILBLAZER" — San Francisco.			
	$1,095	$275	100
1967 LAWMAN SERIES — Bat Masterson Scout.			
	$395	$90	3,000
1967 LAWMAN SERIES — Bat Masterson SAA .45.			
	$1,295	$180	500
1967 ALAMO SCOUT			
	$395	$85	4,250
1967 ALAMO SAA .45			
	$1,195	$165	750
1967 ALAMO 22/45 COMBO			
	$1,595	$265	250
1967 KANSAS COWTOWN SERIES — Coffeyville Scout.			
	$395	$95	500
1967 KANSAS TRAIL SERIES — Chisolm Trail Scout.			
	$395	$100	500
1967 WWI SERIES — .45 ACP cal., Chateau Thierry.			
	$695	$200	7,400
1967 WWI SERIES — Chateau Thierry Deluxe.			
	$1,350	$500	75
1967 WWI SERIES — Chateau Thierry Spec. Deluxe.			
	$2,750	$1,000	25
1968 NEBRASKA CENTENNIAL SCOUT			
	$395	$100	7,001
1968 KANSAS TRAIL SERIES — Pawnee Trail Scout.			
	$395	$110	501
1968 WWI SERIES — .45 ACP cal., Belleau Wood.			
	$695	$200	7,400
1968 WWI SERIES — Belleau Wood Deluxe.			
	$1,350	$500	75

C

Grading	100%	Issue Price	Qty. Made
1968 WWI SERIES — Belleau Wood Special Deluxe.			
	$2,750	$1,000	25
1968 LAWMAN SERIES — Pat Garrett Scout.			
	$425	$110	3,000
1968 LAWMAN SERIES — Pat Garrett .45 SAA.			
	$1,195	$220	500
1969 GEN. NATHAN BEDFORD FORREST SCOUT			
	$395	$110	3,000
1969 KANSAS TRAIL SERIES — Santa Fe Trail Scout.			
	$395	$120	501
1969 WWI SERIES — .45 ACP cal., Battle of 2nd Marne.			
	$695	$220	7,400
1969 WWI SERIES — Battle of 2nd Marne Deluxe.			
	$1,350	$500	75
1969 WWI SERIES — Battle of 2nd Marne Spec. Deluxe.			
	$2,750	$1,000	25
1969 ALABAMA SESQUICENTENNIAL SCOUT			
	$395	$110	3,001
1969 ALABAMA SESQUICENTENNIAL .45 SAA			
	$15,000	unknown	1
1969 GOLDEN SPIKE SCOUT			
	$395	$135	11,000
1969 KANSAS TRAIL SERIES — Shawnee Trail Scout.			
	$395	$120	501
1969 WWI SERIES — .45 ACP cal., Meuse-Argonne			
	$695	$220	7,400
1969 WWI SERIES — Meuse-Argonne Deluxe.			
	$1,350	$500	75
1969 WWI SERIES — Meuse-Argonne Spec. Deluxe.			
	$2,750	$1,000	25
1969 ARKANSAS TERRITORIAL SESQUICENTENNIAL SCOUT			
	$395	$110	3,500
1969 LAWMAN SERIES — .45 SAA Wild Bill Hickok.			
	$1,195	$220	500
1969 LAWMAN SERIES — Wild Bill Hickok Scout.			
	$395	$117	3,000
1969 CALIFORNIA BICENTENNIAL SCOUT			
	$395	$135	5,000
1970 KANSAS FORT SERIES — Ft. Larned Scout.			
	$395	$120	500
1970 WWII SERIES — European Theatre.			
	$695	$250	11,500
1970 WWII SERIES — Pacific Theatre.			
	$695	$250	11,500

Note: A complete set of the WWI and WWII Series standard grade models (6 guns) with matching serial numbers in NIB condition is currently selling in the $4,500 range.

Grading	100%	Issue Price	Qty. Made
1970 TEXAS RANGER SAA .45			
	$2,250	$650	1,000
1970 TEXAS RANGER GRADE I (95% ENGRAVING COVERAGE)			
	$6,000	N/A	90
1970 TEXAS RANGER GRADE II (75% ENGRAVING COVERAGE)			
	$5,500	$2,250	80
1970 TEXAS RANGER GRADE III (50% ENGRAVING COVERAGE)			
	$5,000	$2,950	90
1970 KANSAS FORTS — Ft. Hays Scout.			
	$395	$130	500
1970 MAINE SESQUICENTENNIAL SCOUT			
	$395	$120	3,000
1970 MISSOURI SESQUICENTENNIAL SCOUT			
	$395	$125	3,000
1970 MISSOURI SESQUICENTENNIAL .45 SAA			
	$1,095	$220	900
1970 KANSAS FORTS — Ft. Riley Scout.			
	$395	$130	500
1970 LAWMAN SERIES — Wyatt Earp Scout.			
	$450	$125	3,000
1970 LAWMAN SERIES — Wyatt Earp .45 SAA.			
	$2,250	$395	500
1971 NRA CENTENNIAL .45 SAA			
	$1,195	$250	5,000
1971 NRA CENTENNIAL .357 SAA			
	$850	$250	5,000
1971 NRA CENTENNIAL GOLD CUP .45 ACP			
	$850	$250	2,500
1971 1851 NAVY — U.S. Grant.			
	$595	$250	4,750
1971 1851 NAVY — Robert E. Lee.			
	$595	$250	4,750
1971 1851 NAVY — Lee-Grant Set.			
	$1,350	$500	250
1971 KANSAS SERIES — Ft. Scott Scout.			
	$395	$130	500
1972 FLORIDA TERRITORY SESQUICENTENNIAL SCOUT			
	$395	$125	2,001
1972 ARIZONA RANGER SCOUT			
	$395	$135	3,001
1975 PEACEMAKER CENTENNIAL .45			
	$1,395	$300	1,500
1975 PEACEMAKER CENTENNIAL 44.40			
	$1,395	$300	1,500
1975 PEACEMAKER CENT. CASED PAIR			
	$2,895	$625	500

C

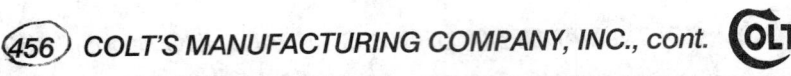
Grading	100%	Issue Price	Qty. Made

USS TEXAS BATTLESHIP SPECIAL EDITION (1975) — .45 ACP cal., Model 1911A1 with special embellishments, nickel finish, this model is not a factory commemorative.

	$895	unknown	500

USS ARIZONA BATTLESHIP SPECIAL EDITION (1975) — .45 ACP cal., Model 1911A1 with special embellishments, nickel finish, this model is not a factory commemorative.

	$895	unknown	500

1976 U.S. BICENTENNIAL SET — includes SAA .45, Python .357 Mag. cals., and black powder Dragoon in walnut display case with drawers.

	$1,995	$1,695	1,776

1976 BICENTENNIAL SAA FREEDOM COLTS — consisted of A, B, and C sets, set As were engraved, Bs had gold work and accessories, Cs were similar to Bs, but had shoulder stock. Set A prices averaged $1,500-$3,000 in 1976, set B prices varied between $3,500-$20,000, and set C prices started at $5,000. Total mfg. was 4 set As, 6 set Bs, and 1 set C. These sets in today's marketplace are too rare to accurately evaluate and pricing is literally "what the market will bear".

These guns were all engraved by Dwain Wright located in Applegate, OR.

1977 2ND AMENDMENT .22

	$395	$195	3,020

1977 U.S. CAVALRY 200TH ANNIVERSARY SET

	$1,250	$995	3,000

1978 STATEHOOD 3RD MODEL DRAGOON

	$6,995	$12,500	52

1979 NED BUNTLINE .45 SAA

	$895	$895	3,000

OHIO PRESIDENT'S SPECIAL EDITION (1979) — .45 ACP cal., Model 1911A1 with special Ohio embellishments, this is not a factory commemorative.

	$850	unknown	250

1979 TOMBSTONE CENTENNIAL .45 SAA — .45 LC cal., 7½ in. barrel, nickel finish, two-piece walnut stocks, P-1876 Model, etched with scroll engraving and Western scenes. 300 mfg. (200 singles and 50 pairs).

	$1,295	$995	300

This model was not sold retail through the auspices of Colt.

1980 DRUG ENFORCEMENT AGENCY (DEA) .45 AUTO

	$1,100	$550	910

This model was not sold retail through the auspices of Colt.

1980 OLYMPICS ACE MODEL SPECIAL EDITION

	$1,150	$1,000	200

This model was not sold retail through the auspices of Colt.

1980 HERITAGE-WALKER .44 PERCUSSION

	$950	$1,475	1,847

1981 "JOHN M. BROWNING" .45 ACP SEMI-AUTO

	$895	$1,100	3,000

1980-81 .45 ACP GOVT. SIGNATURE SERIES — .45 ACP cal., blue finished Govt. slide with gold auroplated slide or nickel finish. 250 mfg. in both finishes.

	$895	$833	250

Add $50 for blue finish.

1980-81 ACE SIGNATURE SERIES — .22 LR cal., featured Cocobolo grips with medallions, blued finish with photo engraving, cased. 1,000 mfg.

	$900	$955	1,000

Grading	100%	Issue Price	Qty. Made

1981 BUFFALO BILL SPECIAL EDITION — .44-40 WCF cal., 7½ in. barrel, gold and silver plating, Class C engraved, ivory grips, leather cased, 250 mfg. serialized 1BB-250BB.

	$4,975	unknown	250

This model was a special edition (not commemorative) that was made specifically for the Buffalo Bill Historical Center.

1982 JOHN WAYNE SAA STANDARD

	$1,995	$2,995	3,100

While advertising literature indicated 3,100 were mfg., 3,041 were sold.

1982 JOHN WAYNE SAA DELUXE

	$7,500	$10,000	500

While advertising literature indicated 500 were mfg., only 90 were sold.

1982 JOHN WAYNE SAA PRESENTATION

	$12,000	$20,000	100

While advertising literature indicated 100 were mfg., only 47 were sold.

Note: Each grade of the above John Wayne commemoratives has its own serial number range.

1983 BUFFALO BILL WILD WEST SHOW CENTENNIAL SAA .45

	$1,350	$1,350	500

1983 CCA LIMITED EDITION SAA — .44-40 WCF cal., 4¾ in. barrel, nickel finish, fleur-de-lis checkered wood grips, 250 mfg. in 1983 to commemorate Colt Collector's Assn.

	$1,295	$825	250

This model was not sold retail through the auspices of Colt.

1983 "ARMORY MODEL" SAA .45 ACP — this model had limited production, and should not be confused as being a commemorative. So called because was shipped with extra .45 long Colt cylinder and the "Colt Armory Edition" book by E. Grant, presentation cased.

	$1,495	$1,125	500

Armory model commemoratives available with class A engraving — $2,062, B engraving — $2,395, C engraving — $2,995, D engraving — $3,500. 20 total available.

1983 PYTHON SILVER SNAKE SPECIAL EDITION — .357 Mag. cal., 6 in. barrel, black chrome stainless steel, Pachmayr grips with custom shop pewter medallions, etched engraving, includes custom gun pouch.

	$1,225	$1,150	250

1984 1ST EDITION GOVT. MODEL .380 ACP

	$425	$425	1,000

Serial range RC00000-01000.

1984 JOHN WAYNE "DUKE" FRONTIER .22

	$495	$475	5,000

1984 COLT/WINCHESTER SET — 1 ea. of the Model 1894 Winchester carbine and Colt Peacemaker, serial numbered 1WC-4440WC, .44-40 WCF cal., elaborate gold etching, cased. Pistol became available for sale individually in 1986 - see individual listing below for values.

Please refer to 1984 Winchester/Colt Set in the Winchester Commemorative section in this text.

WINCHESTER/COLT SAA — .44-40 WCF cal., 7½ in. barrel, gold etching, this commemorative was originally made as part of the 1984 Winchester/Colt rifle-pistol set, but was later able to be purchased individually. Originally mfg. 1984.

	$895	N/A	4,000

Grading	100%	Issue Price	Qty. Made

1984 USA EDITION SAA — .44-40 WCF cal., 7½ in. barrel, old style black powder frame, bullseye ejector rod head, 3 line patent date, high polished blue with gold line engraving. 100 guns total mfg. — 1 for each state and its capitol.

	$3,500	$4,995	100

1984 KIT CARSON .22 NEW FRONTIER — 6 in. barrel, color case hardened frame, gold artwork, serial numbered KCC0001-KCC1000, cased.

	$395	$550	1,000

1984 SECOND EDITION GOVT. MODEL .380 ACP — serial numbered 00000-01000RC.

	$495	$525	1,000

1984 OFFICER'S COMMENCEMENT ISSUE — Officer's ACP with Marine Corps emblem, rosewood grips, silver plated oak leaf scroll, cased.

	$650	$700	1,000

This model was not sold retail through the auspices of Colt.

1984 THEODORE ROOSEVELT COMMEMORATIVE SAA — .44-40 WCF cal., 7½ in. barrel, black powder frame, case colored receiver, factory "B" hand engraving, ivory stocks, cased.

	$1,695	$1,695	500

1984 NORTH AMERICAN OILMEN SAA BUNTLINE — .45 Long Colt cal., 12 in. barrel, non-fluted cylinder, elaborate gold etching, ebony grips with ivory inlays, stand-up glass case, ser. nos. 1-100 mfg. for Canada, 101-200 for the U.S.

	$3,250	$3,900	200

This model was not sold retail through the auspices of Colt.

1985 TEXAS 150th SESQUICENTENNIAL SAA — .45 cal., Sheriff's model, 4¾ in. barrel, mirror bright blue, gold etching, 24 Kt. gold plated backstrap and trigger guard, smooth ivory grips, French fit oak presentation case. Mfg. 1985 only.

* *Standard Model* — 1,000 mfg.

	$1,295	$1,836	1,000

* *Premier Model* — elaborate engraving, 75 mfg.

	$4,995	$7,995	75

1986 150th ANNIVERSARY SAA — .45 Long Colt cal., 10 in. barrel, 50% engraved, royal blue finish, Goncalo Alves smooth grips, 150th anniversary logo in stocks, cherrywood case. 490 mfg. 1986 only.

	$1,595	$1,595	490

1986 150th ANNIVERSARY ENGRAVING SAMPLER SAA — various cals., 4 different engraving styles on metal surfaces, 75% coverage, ivory grips, signed by the engraver, available with either blue or nickel finish. New 1986.

	$2,500	$1,613	unknown

1986 150th ANNIVERSARY ENGRAVING SAMPLER .45 M1911A1 — .45 ACP cal., 4 different engraving styles on metal surfaces, 75% coverage, ivory grips, signed by the engraver, available with either blue or nickel finish. New 1986.

	$1,095	$1,155	unknown

Add $60 for nickel.

1986 MUSTANG FIRST EDITION — .380 ACP cal., 1,000 manufactured serialized MU00001-MU01000 (the first thousand of production), rosewood stocks, walnut presentation case. Mfg. 1986 only.

	$450	$475	1,000

OFFICER'S ACP HEIRLOOM EDITION — .45 ACP cal., personalized with individual's choice for serial number (ie. John Smith 1), mirror brite bluing, jeweled barrel, hammer, and trigger, ivory grips, with historical letter and mahogany case. New 1986.

	$1,550	$1,643	open

Grading	100%	Issue Price	Qty. Made

1986 DOUBLE DIAMOND SET — set is comprised of a Python Ultimate .357 Mag. revolver and Officer's Model .45 ACP, both guns in stainless steel, smooth rosewood grips, presentation cased. 1,000 sets mfg. 1986 only, serial numbered 1-1,000 (matched).

$1,595 $1,575   1,000

DELTA MATCH H-BAR RIFLE — AR-15 A2 H-Bar rifle selectively chosen and equipped with 3x9 variable power rubber armored scope, leather sling, shoulder stock cheekpiece, cased. Mfg. 1987.

$1,500 $1,425   open

12TH MAN-'SPIRIT OF AGGIELAND' — .45 ACP cal., mfg. to commemorate Texas A & M University, serial numbered TAM001-TAM999, 24Kt gold plating including wreaths on left frame and inscription on right, cherrywood glass top presentation case, includes personalized class graduation inscription. Available 1987 only.

$950 $950   999

This model was not sold retail through the auspices of Colt.

KLAY-COLT 1851 NAVY — .36 cal., cased reproduction of the 3rd Model 1851 Navy, special fabrication insuring old world quality, charcoal bluing, heat treated screws and accessories, cased. Introduced 1986.

* **Standard Edition** — no engraving.

$1,850 $1,850   150

* **Engraved Edition** — choice of engraving.

$3,150 $3,150   50

Optional engraving patterns with or without gold inlays available at extra cost.

COMBAT ELITE CUSTOM EDITION — .45 ACP cal., with ambidextrous thumb safety, wide grip safety, hand honed action, and carrying case, ser. numbered CG00001 - CG00500. Mfg. 1987.

$900 $900   500

1987 SHERIFF'S EDITION — set of 5 SAA Sheriff's configuration pistols in .45 LC cal., barrel lengths include 2, 2½, 3, 4, and 5½ in., royal blue finish, smooth rosewood grips with medallions, supplied with glass top display case which displays the revolvers in a circle around a brass sheriff's badge. Serialization has 3 numeral prefix (which is the same in each set), followed by the letters "SE", followed by 1 or 2 numerals (indicating barrel length) - i.e. serial number 002SE25 indicates the second set built, Sheriff's Edition (SE), and a barrel length of 2½ inches.

$4,250 $7,500   100 sets

1989 SNAKE EYES LIMITED EDITION — includes two Python revolvers (2½ in. barrels), one finished in brite stainless steel and the other in royal blue finish, grips are ivory-like with scrimshaw "snake eyes" dice on left side and royal flush poker hand on right, includes chips and playing cards, 500 sets only of consecutive serial numbers. New 1989.

$1,950 $2,950   500

1990 SAA HEIRLOOM II EDITION — .45 LC cal., 7½ in. barrel, color case hardened frame and hammer, balance of metal finished in Colt Royal Blue, one piece American Walnut grips with cartouche on lower left side, personalized inscription on backstrap, walnut cased. Available 1990 only.

$1,395 $1,600   open

1990 JOE FOSS LIMITED EDITION .45 ACP GOVT. MODEL — .45 ACP cal., first limited edition in Colt's All American Hero Series, commemorates Joe Foss, famous American WWII Marine Fighter Pilot, gun features gold etched scenes on slide sides, smooth walnut grips, while 2,500 were advertised, only 300+ were mfg. serial numbered beginning with JF 0001. French fitted walnut presentation case, 38 oz. Mfg. 1990 only.

$1,225 $1,375   300+

Grading	100%	Issue Price	Qty. Made

1911A1 50th ANNIVERSARY BATTLE OF THE BULGE — .45 ACP cal., special edition commemorating the Battle of the Bulge, silver plated with gold inlays, 300 mfg. serialized BB001-BB300.

| | $1,250 | $1,250 | 300 |

> Add $150 for deluxe presentation case.

> This special edition is sold exclusively by Cherry's located in Greensboro, NC.

C COMMANDO ARMS

Previous manufacturer located in Knoxville, TN.

Commando Arms became the new name for Volunteer Enterprises in the late 1970s.

Grading	100%	98%	95%	90%	80%	70%	60%

RIFLES: CARBINES

MARK 45 — .45 ACP cal., carbine styled after the Thompson sub-machine gun, 16½ in. barrel.

| | $495 | $425 | $350 | $315 | $280 | $225 | $195 |

COMPETITOR CORPORATION

Current manufacturer established in 1988 and located in New Ipswich, NH. Previously located until 1995 in West Groton, MA. Dealer direct or distributor sales.

PISTOLS: SINGLE SHOT

COMPETITOR — available in over 260 cals. from .17 LR - .50 AE, ranging from small rimfire to large belted Magnums, 14 in. barrel, rotary cannon action, cocks on opening, dual sliding thumb and trigger safety, rotary style ejector, click adj. sights, matte blue or optional electroless nickel finish, choice of synthetic, laminated, or natural wood grips (ambidextrous), extractor or ejector, approx. 59-70 oz. New 1988.

| Mfg.'s Sug. Retail | $415 | | $355 | $310 | $275 | $250 | $225 | $200 | $185 |

> Add $25 for laminated wood stock.
> Add $50 for walnut grips.
> Add $55 for electroless nickel finish (barreled action only).
> Add $160 for extra 14 in. standard cal. barrel with sights.
> Add $195 for 10½ - 16 in. standard cal. barrel with sights.
> Add $225 for 17-23 in. barrel.
> Add $60 for factory installed muzzle brake.

CONNECTICUT SHOTGUN MANUFACTURING CO.

Current shotgun manufacturer located in New Britain, CT since 1995.

SHOTGUNS: O/U, SIDELOCK

A. GALAZAN MODEL — 12, 16, 20, 28 ga., or .410 bore, features strong, low profile sidelock action with Boss-style metal reinforced forearm, top-of-the-line model utilizing best quality materials and U.S. workmanship.

> Each gun is custom-built to the customer's exact specifications and prices start at $38,000 without engraving.

CONNECTICUT VALLEY CLASSICS, INC.

Previously manufactured by Cooper Arms, located in Stevensville, MT 1996-1998. CVC, Inc. was a division of CVC Sports, Inc. Previous sales and marketing offices were located in Holyoke, MA until 1996 and in Westport, CT 1993-95.

Grading	100%	98%	95%	90%	80%	70%	60%

SHOTGUNS: O/U

The models listed below have receiver dimensions built to the exact specifications of the original Classic Doubles Model 101. The only difference is that the tang spacer has been made an integral part of the frame.

Add $1,350 for each additional barrel set.

CLASSIC 101 SPORTER — 12 ga. only, boxlock action, monoblock, 28, 30, or 32 in. VR barrels with multi-chokes, SST, ejectors, nickel finished receiver with light engraving, checkered American black walnut stock and forearm with low luster finish, approx. 7¾ lbs.

	$1,875	$1,550	$1,225	$1,000	$825	$700	$600

Last Mfg.'s Sug. Retail was $2,195.

CLASSIC SPORTER SB — 12 ga. only, boxlock action, entry level sporter model. Mfg. 1997-98.

	$2,250	$1,875	$1,575	$1,175	$950	$775	$650

Last Mfg.'s Sug. Retail was $2,495.

GRADE I CLASSIC SPORTER — 12 ga. only, boxlock action, monoblock, 28, 30, or 32 in. vented barrels with VR, lengthened forcing cones, and 2⅜ in. multi-chokes, SST, ejectors, stainless steel receiver with light engraving, checkered 20 LPI AA American black walnut stock and forearm with low luster finish, approx. 7¾ lbs. Disc. 1998.

	$2,695	$2,100	$1,675	$1,250	$1,000	$825	$700

Last Mfg.'s Sug. Retail was $2,995.

* **Women's Classic Sporter** — similar to Grade I Classic Sporter, except has smaller stock dimensions and 28 in. barrels only, 7½ lbs. Mfg. 1996-98.

	$2,695	$2,100	$1,675	$1,250	$1,000	$825	$700

Last Mfg.'s Sug. Retail was $2,995.

This model was also available in Grade II or Grade III Woman's Classic Sporter.

* **Grade II Classic Sporter** — similar to Grade I Classic Sporter, except has AAA American or Claro walnut with 22 LPI hand-checkering, 30 in. barrels only.

	$3,100	$2,350	$1,800	$1,325	$1,050	$850	$725

Last Mfg.'s Sug. Retail was $3,595.

* **Grade III Classic Sporter** — similar to Grade II Classic Sporter, except has Fleur-de-lis checkering patterns and gold accents. Disc. 1998.

	$3,600	$2,750	$1,975	$1,450	$1,175	$925	$750

Last Mfg.'s Sug. Retail was $4,195.

GRADE I CLASSIC FIELD — 12 ga. only, similar to Grade I Classic Sporter, except has solid rib and standard flush-mounted choke-tubes, 27½ in. barrels, 7½ lbs. Mfg. 1996-98.

	$2,695	$2,100	$1,675	$1,250	$1,000	$825	$700

Last Mfg.'s Sug. Retail was $2,995.

* **Classic Waterfowler** — 12 ga. only, 30 or 32 (disc. 1995) in. VR barrels, non-reflective surfaces, bird scene engraving, overbored barrels with lengthened forcing cones and four standard CVC chokes, 8 lbs. Mfg. 1993-98.

	$2,495	$2,000	$1,575	$1,175	$950	$775	$650

Last Mfg.'s Sug. Retail was $2,795.

* **Grade II Classic Field** — similar to Grade I Classic Field, except has AAA American or Claro walnut with 22 LPI hand-checkering.

	$3,025	$2,250	$1,750	$1,300	$1,050	$850	$725

Last Mfg.'s Sug. Retail was $3,495.

* **Grade III Classic/English Field** — similar to Grade II Classic Field, except has Fleur-de-lis checkering patterns and gold accents, choice of straight English (25½ in. VR barrels only) or pistol grip stock. Disc. 1998.

	$3,575	$2,850	$2,025	$1,500	$1,200	$925	$750

Last Mfg.'s Sug. Retail was $4,195.

Add $100 for straight English stock.

Grading	100%	98%	95%	90%	80%	70%	60%

CLASSIC SKEET — 12 ga. only, 29 in. vented barrels with 9mm VR, otherwise similar to Grade I Classic Sporter, 7½ lbs. Mfg. 1996-98.

	$2,695	$2,100	$1,675	$1,250	$1,000	$825	$700

Last Mfg.'s Sug. Retail was $2,995.

CLASSIC FLYER — 12 ga. only, live bird gun featuring AAA walnut and 22 LPI checkering, oil finish, 30 in. vented overbored barrels with 11mm tapered top rib and lengthened forcing cones, scroll engraving with pigeon scene on bottom, 8 lbs. Mfg. 1996-98.

	$3,100	$2,350	$1,800	$1,325	$1,050	$850	$725

Last Mfg.'s Sug. Retail was $3,595.

CONTENTO/VENTURA

Previously imported by Ventura Imports in Seal Beach, CA. Ventura also imported Bertuzzi and Piotti.

SHOTGUNS: O/U

CONTENTO O/U — 12 ga., 32 in. barrels, boxlock, optional screw in choke tubes, high vent. rib, SST, auto ejectors, hand checkered Monte Carlo trap stock.

	$1,045	$990	$935	$880	$770	$690	$635

MK 2 — includes O/U barrels, with extra single barrel.

	$1,375	$1,320	$1,265	$1,210	$1,100	$1,020	$965

MK 2 — leather cased, combination set.

	$1,705	$1,650	$1,595	$1,540	$1,430	$1,350	$1,295

MK 3 — engraved, O/U.

	$1,650	$1,570	$1,485	$1,375	$1,295	$1,185	$1,100

MK 3 — includes O/U barrels, with extra single barrel.

	$2,200	$2,035	$1,925	$1,815	$1,650	$1,595	$1,515

MK 3 — leather cased, combination set.

	$2,750	$2,420	$2,200	$2,090	$1,955	$1,815	$1,760

SHOTGUNS: SxS

MODEL 51 — 12, 16, 20, 28 ga., or .410 bore, 26-32 in. barrels, various chokes, extractors, boxlock, double triggers, checkered straight stock.

	$385	$360	$330	$305	$250	$220	$165
Auto ejectors	$495	$440	$385	$360	$305	$275	$220

MODEL 52 — 10 ga., double triggers only, otherwise similar to Model 51.

	$525	$495	$470	$415	$360	$305	$250

MODEL 53 — deluxe version of Model 51, scalloped frame, auto ejectors.

	$470	$440	$415	$385	$330	$275	$220
SST	$605	$550	$525	$495	$440	$385	$330

MODEL 61 — 12 or 20 ga., 26, 27, 28, or 30 in. barrels, H&H sidelocks, various chokes, floral engraved, hand detachable locks, cocking indicators, select walnut pistol grip stock, auto ejectors.

	$880	$825	$770	$745	$690	$605	$550
SST	$1,020	$965	$910	$855	$800	$715	$660

MODEL 65 — similar to Model 61, with elaborate engraving and quality hand finishing.

	$1,100	$1,045	$990	$965	$880	$825	$770

CONTINENTAL ARMS CORPORATION

Previous importer that imported high quality shotguns and rifles (usually Belgian), circa mid '50s - mid '70s.

Grading	100%	98%	95%	90%	80%	70%	60%

RIFLES

BOLT ACTION — mostly large cals., typically custom Mauser action, makers include Defourney and Dumoulin.

Specimens should be evaluated individually due to the many configurations and embellishments encountered.

DOUBLE RIFLE — .270 Win., .303 British, .30-40 Krag, .348 Win., .30-06, .375 H&H, .400 Jeffreys, .470, .475, .500, or .600, Nitro Express cal., 24 or 26 in. barrels, Anson & Deeley boxlock system, although some sidelocks were mfg., double triggers, checkered stock.

$5,500	$4,620	$3,850	$3,300	$2,970	$2,750	$2,420

Add 10% for boxlock with sideplates.
Add 15% for ejectors.
Add 25% for .375 H&H and larger cals.

SHOTGUNS: O/U

Add 10% for .410 bore.
Add 20% for 28 ga.
Add 10% for Defourney mfg.

CENTAURE BOXLOCK — 12, 20, 28 ga., or .410 bore, ejectors, light engraving, chopper lump barrels with cross-bolt double underlocks, SST, 3-piece forearm.

$1,750	$1,500	$1,350	$1,200	$1,025	$875	$750

CENTAURE LIEGE ROYAL CROWN GRADE — similar to Centaure Boxlock, except has game scene engraving, better figured wood and silver crown inlay.

$2,650	$2,400	$2,150	$1,825	$1,600	$1,400	$1,200

CENTAURE IMPERIAL CROWN GRADE — similar to Royal Crown Grade, except has higher grade wood, extensive game scene engraving, oak leaf engraving on barrels, and gold inlay on top lever.

$3,950	$3,600	$3,350	$3,150	$2,900	$2,700	$2,500

SHOTGUNS: SxS

Add 10% for .410 bore.
Add 20% for 28 ga.
Add 10% for Defourney mfg.

CENTAURE — all gauges, basic boxlock action with double triggers and extractors.

$950	$895	$850	$700	$500	$400	$300

Add 35% for ejectors.

CENTAURE ROYAL CROWN GRADE — all gauges, single trigger, ejectors, checkered stock and forearm, game scene engraving, can be identified by silver crown inlaid on top lever.

$2,950	$2,700	$2,500	$2,300	$2,100	$1,950	$1,750

CENTAURE IMPERIAL CROWN GRADE — similar to Royal Crown, except gold inlay on top lever, extensive game scene engraving on receiver and barrels.

$3,600	$3,300	$3,000	$2,750	$2,500	$2,250	$2,000

COOEY MACHINE & ARMS CO. LTD.

Previous manufacturer located in Cobourg, Ontario - Canada 1903-1961. During 1961, Cooey was sold to the Olin Corporation and placed under the supervision of the Winchester Western Division. At that point, the manufacture of Winchesters (primarily for Winchester Canada) began and continued through the mid-'70s.

Models manufactured by Cooey pre-1961 include various repeating .22 rifles, single shot shotguns (Models 84 and 840), and maybe a few others. There is limited information available on the variety of shotguns and rifles manufactured by this company (most distribution occurred in Canada). To date, there is limited collector

Grading	100%	98%	95%	90%	80%	70%	60%

demand for most models in this trademark and values should be based on the shooting utility rather than collector premiums due to rarity. Most values will range between $75-$150.

RIFLES: BOLT ACTION

COOEY .22 RIFLE — .22 LR cal., post-WWI mfg., bolt action, open sights.

	100%	98%	95%	90%	80%	70%	60%
	$150	$130	$110	$95	$80	$70	$60

COONAN ARMS

Currently manufactured by K & B Custom, and distributed by JS Worldwide Distribution Co. located in Maplewood, MN since late 1996. Previously located in St. Paul, MN, until 1996. Dealer and distributor sales.

PISTOLS: SEMI-AUTO

COONAN .357 MAG. MODEL B — .357 Mag. cal. only, stainless steel and alloy construction, single action, semi-auto, design based on the Colt Model 1911, 7 shot mag., 5 or 6 (new 1989) in. barrel, smooth or checkered (new 1996) walnut grips, Teflon finish options new 1996, 42 oz. New 1983.

Mfg.'s Sug. Retail $735 $685 $535 $425

> Add $40 for checkered walnut grips.
> Add $33 for 6 in. barrel (new 1989).
> Add $140 for Millett adj. rear sight.
> Add $165 for BoMar sight.
> Add $45 for .38 Spl. conversion kit (new 1986).

This model can be differentiated from the Model A in that it has an extended grip safety lever, linkless barrel system, trigger bar slot is enclosed, and recontoured rear grip strap. This model became standard in 1985.

* ***Coonan .357 Cadet Model*** — similar to .357 Mag. Model B, except is compact variation with 3.9 in. barrel and 6 shot mag., 39 oz. New 1993.

  Mfg.'s Sug. Retail $855 $785 $630 $500
  Options are similar to those listed above for the Model B.

* ***Coonan .357 Cadet II*** — features standard grip with 7/8 shot mag. New 1996.

  Mfg.'s Sug. Retail $855 $785 $630 $500
  Options are similar to those listed above for the Model B.

* ***Model B Compensated*** — 6 in. barrel with compensator, new 1990.

  Mfg.'s Sug. Retail $1,015 $900 $795 $650
  Options are similar to those listed above for the Model B.

* ***Model Classic Compensated*** — features 5 in. barrel with integral compensator, Millett white/orange outline sights, checkered black walnut grips, Teflon black and matte stainless two-tone finish, 42 oz. New 1996.

  Mfg.'s Sug. Retail $1,400 $1,275 $1,025 $825 $675 $595 $525 $450

COONAN .357 MAG. MODEL A — original model without above listed improvements, special order only, inventory depleted in 1991. Serialization is under 2,000 for this model (less than 1,200 were mfg.). While discontinued, the factory has a few guns remaining in inventory.

                    $1,150 $775 $550
                              Last Mfg.'s Sug. Retail was $625.

> Add approx. $350 for early variations with engraved slide.

This variation will also shoot .38+P loads. The first 25 Model A's were engraved on both sides of slide.

Grading	100%	98%	95%	90%	80%	70%	60%

COONAN .41 MAGNUM — .41 Mag. cal., 5 in. barrel, smooth or checkered walnut grips. New 1997.

Mfg.'s Sug. Retail	$825	$760	$625	$500			

Options are similar to those listed above for the .357 Mag.

COOPER ARMS

Currently manufactured by Cooper Firearms of Montana, Inc. since 1999, and located in Stevensville, MT since 1991. Cooper Firearms of Montana, Inc. is no longer associated with Connecticut Valley Classic or CVC Sports, Inc. Dealer direct sales only.

C

RIFLES: BOLT ACTION

Approx. 6,200 Cooper rifles have been manufactured in over 50 calibers to date.

MODEL 21 SINGLE SHOT — various medium size cals., 3 front locking lugs. New 1998.

* **Model 21 Classic** — various cals., single shot, 20 in. chrome moly match grade barrel, stock is AA Claro walnut with 20 LPI hand checkering and hand rubbed oil finish, machined aluminum trigger guard, matte metal finish, approx. 7-7¼ lbs. New 1999.

Mfg.'s Sug. Retail	$995	$875	$750	$625	$550	$495	$450	$400

* **Model 21 Custom Classic** — includes Brownell No. 1 checkering pattern, ebony forend tip, and steel grip cap.

Mfg.'s Sug. Retail	$1,950	$1,675	$1,275	$950	$750	$650	$550	$475

* **Model 21 Western Classic** — various cals., features octagon barrel and case hardened action and bolt. New 1997.

Mfg.'s Sug. Retail	$2,195	$1,900	$1,400	$1,000	$750	$650	$550	$475

* **Model 21 Varminter** — various cals., 24 in. stainless steel match grade barrel, stock is AA Claro walnut with 20 LPI hand checkering and hand rubbed oil finish, machined aluminum trigger guard, approx. 7-7¼ lbs. New 1999.

Mfg.'s Sug. Retail	$995	$875	$750	$625	$550	$495	$450	$400

* **Model 21 Varmint Extreme** — various cals. between .17 Rem.-.223 Rem. (including metric cals.), features heavy Varmint stainless barrel, checkered stock. New 1994.

Mfg.'s Sug. Retail	$1,750	$1,525	$1,175	$875	$700	$600	$525	$450

Add $465 for Benchrest Model with Jewell trigger (mfg. 1995-96).

MODEL 22 — various mid-action cals., larger scale action of the Model 21.

* **Model 22 Classic** — various mid-action cals., 20 in. chrome moly match grade barrel, stock is AA Claro walnut with 20 LPI hand checkering and hand rubbed oil finish, machined aluminum trigger guard, matte metal finish, approx. 7-7¼ lbs. New 1999.

Mfg.'s Sug. Retail	$995	$875	$750	$625	$550	$495	$450	$400

* **Model 22 Custom Classic** — includes Brownell No. 1 checkering pattern, ebony forend tip, and steel grip cap.

Mfg.'s Sug. Retail	$1,995	$1,750	$1,300	$975	$750	$650	$550	$475

* **Model 22 Western Classic** — various cals., features octagon barrel and case hardened action and bolt, only 2 have been mfg. to date. New 1997.

Mfg.'s Sug. Retail	$2,195	$1,900	$1,450	$1,050	$850	$750	$650	$550

* **Model 22 Pro-Varmint Extreme** — .220 Swift, .22 BR (new 1996), .22-250 Rem., .243 Win., .25-06 Rem., .308 Win., 6mm PPC, 6.5x55mm (new 1996) or 7.62x39mm (new 1996) cal., available in either Pro-Varmint, Bench rest, or Black Jack (black synthetic stock) configuration. New 1995.

Mfg.'s Sug. Retail	$1,795	$1,525	$1,175	$900	$725	$625	$550	$475

Add $400 for Benchrest Model.

Grading	100%	98%	95%	90%	80%	70%	60%

MODEL 22 CLASSIC REPEATER — .22-250 Rem., .243 Win., .308 Win., or 7mm-08 Rem. cal., 3 shot mag. While advertised during 1996 only at $2,400 retail, this model was never mfg.

MODEL CUSTOM CLASSIC — .22 LR, .22 Mag., .22 Hornet or .222 Rem. cal., features Anschutz Match 54 action with deluxe walnut stock with American features and smaller trigger guard. New 1996.

Mfg.'s Sug. Retail	$1,995	$1,750	$1,375	$1,075	$900	$725	$600	$500

MODEL CUSTOM MANNLICHER — .22 LR, .22 Mag., .22 Hornet, .222 Rem. cal., features newest Anschutz Match 54 action with deluxe Mannlicher walnut stock and other special features. New 1996.

Mfg.'s Sug. Retail	$2,195	$1,975	$1,625	$1,425	$1,225	$975	$850	$700

MODEL 36 SPORTSMAN — .22 LR, .17 CCM, or .22 Hornet cal., without Shilen barrel, standard wood with rubber recoil pad. Mfg. 1994 only.

	$675	$575	$495	$450	$400	$350	$295

Last Mfg.'s Sug. Retail was $750.

MODEL 36 MARKSMAN — .22 LR, .17 CCM, or .22 Hornet cal., 4 shot mag., 23 in. chrome moly barrel, AA Claro walnut with 22 LPI checkering, 45 degree bolt, sling swivels, hand rubbed oil finish, 7 lbs. Mfg. 1992-94.

	$975	$750	$625	$550	$495	$450	$400

Last Mfg.'s Sug. Retail was $1,125.

* *Model 36 Montana Trail Blazer* — .22 LR cal. only, lightweight field gun with sporter barrel. Mfg. 1996 only.

	$1,300	$1,025	$775	$650	$575	$475	$425

Last Mfg.'s Sug. Retail was $1,475.

* *Model 36 Classic* — .22 LR cal. only, features choice of AAA Claro or AA French walnut with Monte Carlo cheekpiece. Disc. 1996.

	$1,500	$1,175	$875	$700	$625	$525	$450

Last Mfg.'s Sug. Retail was $1,695.

* *Model 36 Varmint Extreme* — various cals., heavy Varmint stainless barrel, checkered stock. Mfg. 1997 only.

	$1,525	$1,175	$875	$700	$625	$525	$450

Last Mfg.'s Sug. Retail was $1,695.

* *Model 36 Western Classic* — various cals., features octagon barrel and case hardened action and bolt. New 1997.

Mfg.'s Sug. Retail	$2,195	$1,900	$1,400	$1,000	$775	$650	$550	$475

* *Model 36 Custom Classic* — includes Brownell No. 1 checkering pattern, ebony forend tip, and steel grip cap.

Mfg.'s Sug. Retail	$1,850	$1,625	$1,325	$1,050	$825	$700	$600	$500

* *Model 36 TRP-1* — target variation of the Model 36 with ISU synthetic stock and adj. cheekpiece, 23 in. Wiseman/McMillan stainless steel or chrome moly barrel, single shot, fully adj. single stage trigger, vent. forearm. Mfg. 1992-1993.

	$950	$795	$625	$525	$475	$425	$375

Last Mfg.'s Sug. Retail was $1,095.

* *Model MS-36 (TRP-1S)* — silhouette variation of the Model 36 TRP-1, clear epoxy finish, silhouette style stock, Pachmayr buttpad. Mfg. 1992-1993.

	$895	$725	$625	$550	$495	$450	$400

Last Mfg.'s Sug. Retail was $995.

* *Model 36 BR-50* — .22 LR cal., benchrest variation featuring black synthetic stock and heavy stainless barrel, Jewell trigger. New 1993.

Mfg.'s Sug. Retail	$1,950	$1,675	$1,250	$950	$750	$650	$550	$475

Grading	100%	98%	95%	90%	80%	70%	60%

* **Model 36 IR-50/50** — .22 LR cal. only, lightweight sporter style competition rifle with heavy 20 in. barrel. New 1996.

Mfg.'s Sug. Retail	$1,950		$1,675	$1,250	$950	$750	$650	$550	$475

* **Model 36 Featherweight** — .17 CCM, .22 LR, or .22 Hornet cal., features matte black synthetic stock and metal, Jewell trigger. New 1994.

Mfg.'s Sug. Retail	$1,795		$1,600	$1,225	$900	$700	$625	$525	$450

MODEL 38 SPORTER — .17 CCM, or .22 CCM cal., 3 shot mag., 24 in. chrome moly barrel, AA Claro walnut with 22 LPI checkering, 45 degree bolt, sling swivels, hand rubbed oil finish, 8 lbs. Mfg. 1992-1993.

		$965	$750	$625	$550	$495	$450	$400

Last Mfg.'s Sug. Retail was $1,095.

Add $100 for Standard Grade (AA Claro walnut).
Add $200 for Custom Grade.
Add $300 for Custom Classic Grade.

The custom grade includes choice of AAA Claro or AA French walnut with Monte Carlo cheekpiece.

The .17 CCM and .22 CCM cartridges designate Cooper Centerfire Magnum. Basically, the .22 CCM is a centerfire derivative of the .22 Mag. cal., and the .17 CCM is simply a necked down variation.

* **Model 38 Repeater (Deluxe)** — deluxe variation of the Model 38 Sporter, 650 mfg. 1992-1994.

	$1,750	$1,400	$1,000	$775	$650	$550	$475

MODEL 38 SINGLE SHOT — small, mostly rimmed cals., 3 front locking lugs. New 1998.

* **Model 38 Classic** — various cals., single shot, 20 in. chrome moly match grade barrel, stock is AA Claro walnut with 20 LPI hand checkering and hand rubbed oil finish, machined aluminum trigger guard, matte metal finish, approx. 7-7¼ lbs. New 1999.

Mfg.'s Sug. Retail	$995		$875	$750	$625	$550	$495	$450	$400

* **Model 38 Custom Classic** — includes Brownell No. 1 checkering pattern, ebony forend tip, and steel grip cap.

Mfg.'s Sug. Retail	$1,950		$1,700	$1,300	$975	$750	$650	$550	$475

* **Model 38 Western Classic** — various cals., features octagon barrel and case hardened action and bolt. New 1997.

Mfg.'s Sug. Retail	$2,195		$1,900	$1,400	$1,000	$775	$650	$550	$475

* **Model 38 Varminter** — various cals., single shot, 24 in. stainless steel match grade barrel, stock is AA Claro walnut with 20 LPI hand checkering and hand rubbed oil finish, machined aluminum trigger guard, approx. 7-7¼ lbs. New 1999.

Mfg.'s Sug. Retail	$995		$875	$750	$625	$550	$495	$450	$400

* **Model 38 Varmint Extreme** — various cals. including the new .19-223, heavy stainless steel barrel w/o sights, checkered stock. New 1997.

Mfg.'s Sug. Retail	$1,750		$1,550	$1,195	$875	$700	$625	$525	$450

MODEL 40 — .17 CCM (disc. 1995), .17 Ackley Hornet, .22 CCM (disc. 1995), .22 Hornet, or .22 K Hornet cal., 3 lug action, incorporates Anschütz mag., choice of Classic, Custom Classic, or Classic Varminter configuration. Mfg. 1995-96.

	$1,600	$1,200	$950	$750	$650	$550	$475

Last Mfg.'s Sug. Retail was $1,825.

Add $200 for Custom Classic or Classic Varminter (disc.) Model.

MODEL 72 MONTANA PLAINSMAN — various cals., single shot featuring case colored Win. Model 1885 action with heavy octagon barrel, double set triggers, deluxe checkered straight grip stock and forearm, no sights. While advertising during 1997 at a retail price of $2,195, this model was never mfg.

Grading	100%	98%	95%	90%	80%	70%	60%

COP

Previous Derringer manufacturer located in Torrance, CA.

DERRINGERS

COP DERRINGER — .357 Mag. cal., 4 shot, 3 in. barrel, stainless steel mfg., single action, wood grips, 28 oz. COP stands for Compact Off-Duty Police. Disc.

	100%	98%	95%	90%	80%	70%	60%
	$350	$325	$285	$260	$240	$220	$200

COSMI, AMERICO & FIGLIO

Current semi-auto shotgun manufacturer located in Tor-rette, Italy since 1930. Please contact either the factory directly or New England Arms Co. for pricing and model availability (see Trademark Index).

Approximately 7,000 Cosmi shotguns have been manufactured since 1930. They are known for their unique mechanism and high-quality fabrication techniques.

SHOTGUNS: SEMI-AUTO

STANDARD MODEL — 12 or 20 ga., 2¾ or 3 in. chamber, semi-auto, unique pivoting break open action loads cartridges into stock chamber from inside of receiver, 8 shot mag. with 3 shot option reducer, steel, alloy, or titanium frame, Boehler Antinit steel barrel (moves when shooting) available with or without choke tubes, all internal parts are mfg. from special chrome-nickel steel or titanium (new 1990), custom order gun only with dimensions specified by individual customer (approx. 6 month delivery time).

* **Standard Grade** — barrel and attached receiver assembly are blued, frame is chromed-nickel steel or aluminum, no engraving.

	Mfg.'s Sug. Retail	$9,800		$9,400	$8,250	$7,300	$6,400	$5,500	$4,600	$3,800

* **Model De Luxe** — features 3 different levels of engraving and select walnut.

➤ No. 1 or No. 2 Engraving Pattern

	Mfg.'s Sug. Retail	$14,000		$13,000	$10,750	$9,400	$8,250	$7,300	$6,400	$5,500

➤ No. 3 Engraving Pattern

	Mfg.'s Sug. Retail	$11,200		$10,000	$9,300	$8,250	$7,300	$6,400	$5,500	$4,600

Cosmi also manufactures an Extra Deluxe Series with more elaborate engraving and upgraded wood. Series C specimens start at $29,400, Series B start at $25,200, and Series A (top-of-the-line) start at $37,800.

* **Titanium Model** — 12 or 20 ga., receiver made out of machined titanium, approx. 6.8 lbs. in 12 ga., approx. 5.7 lbs. in 20 ga. New 1990.

	Mfg.'s Sug. Retail	$14,000		$13,000	$10,750	$9,400	$8,250	$7,300	$6,400	$5,500

This model is also available with optional engraving styles 1-5. Engraving prices vary between $1,400-$11,200.

COUNTY, S.A.L.

Current shotgun manufacturer located in Eibar, Spain. No current importation.

SHOTGUNS: O/U

County manufactures a wide variety of both boxlock and sidelock O/Us. Please contact the factory directly to obtain current model and pricing information (see Trademark Index).

Grading	100%	98%	95%	90%	80%	70%	60%

CRESCENT FIRE ARMS CO. & CRESCENT-DAVIS ARMS CO.

Previously manufactured 1888-1893 in Norwich, CT. Merged with N.R. Davis in the 1900s by H&D Folsom to form Crescent-Davis. In early 1930, Savage Arms Corp. bought Davis-Warner from Folsom. In late 1930, Savage bought Crescent Firearms Co., Norwich, CT, and formed a new company, "Crescent-Davis Arms Corp., Norwich, CT". C-D operated independently of J. Stevens Arms Co. Later, circa 1933, the company moved C-D assets to Chicopee Falls, MA and let Connecticut take buildings in Norwich in lieu of taxes.

Crescent Firearms Company remains best known as a manufacturer of "house brand" shotguns (i.e., Crescent private labeled guns for retailers, distributors, mail-order houses, etc.). Over 100 different trademarks have been observed to date, manufactured by Crescent - almost all the remaining specimens today are priced as shooters, and have no collector value.

SHOTGUNS

SxS SHOTGUN — values below assume standard models with double triggers, extractors, original finish, and 100% working order. Sidelock actions were also available and will command premiums from prices listed below. Shotguns with exposed hammers can equal their hammerless counterparts if condition is 80% or better.

	100%	98%	95%	90%	80%	70%	60%
12 ga.	$195	$175	$150	$125	$100	$85	$65
16 ga.	$195	$175	$150	$125	$100	$85	$65
20 ga.	$295	$265	$230	$200	$170	$150	$125
28 ga.	$375	$325	$280	$250	$200	$150	$100
.410 bore	$400	$350	$300	$250	$200	$150	$100

KNICKERBOCKER — 20 ga., 14 in. nickel-plated barrels, case-hardened receiver, pistol grip, mfg. circa 1900's.

Extreme rarity factor precludes accurate pricing information.

NEW EMPIRE — 20 ga. or .410 bore, 12¼ in. blued barrels, case-hardened receiver.

$900	$850	$700	$750	$500	$450	$400

VICTOR EJECTOR — .410 bore, 12 in. single barrel, total production unknown, possibly prototype for Crescent Certified Shotgun.

Extreme rarity factor precludes accurate pricing information.

AUTO & BURGLAR GUN (NFA) — hammerless .410 smooth bore or 20 ga., 12¼ in. barrels, extremely rare firearm whose total production and years of manufacture are unknown at this time (only known documentation is its mention in an advertisement by "Saul Ruben, The Gun Store, 68 E. Long St., Columbus, OH" of the October 1932 issue of **Hunter-Trapper-Trapper**, which lists a $14.75 retail price. One known specimen, a .410 bore, bears ser. no. 9, and its receiver is marked **New Empire**. Establishing a reliable value may be difficult, but it could be logically expected to approximate those for a nonstandard or special-order Ithaca Auto & Burglar Gun. The Crescent Auto & Burglar Gun may have been distributed by the H.&D. Folsom Arms Co. of New York City through its manufacturing division, the Crescent Firearms Co., Norwich, CT. Crescent's sellers included the Belknap Hardware Co., Louisville, KY and Hibbard-Spencer-Bartlett Co., Chicago, IL.

Grading	100%	98%	95%	90%	80%	70%	60%

CRESCENT CERTIFIED SHOTGUN — .410 smooth bore, 12½ in. barrel, approx. 4,000 mfg. from approx. 1930-32 by the Crescent-Davis Arms Corp., and possibly thereafter until 1934 by the J. Stevens Arms Co., left receiver side is stamped "Crescent Certified Shotgun/Crescent-Davis Arms Corp./Norwich, Conn. U.S.A.", also termed the "Ever-Ready" Model 200 and advertised with a blued frame, but specimens with "tiger stripe" and regular case coloring have been observed, guns not currently registered with ATF cannot be legally owned and are subject to seizure.

		$1,200	$1,000	$900	$800	$700	$600	$500

Add $100-$300 for original cardboard box.

CRICKET RIFLE

Please refer to the Keystone Sporting Arms, Inc. section in this text.

CROSSFIRE LLC

Current manufacturer located in La Grange, GA beginning 1998. Dealer and consumer sales.

COMBINATION GUNS

CROSSFIRE MK-I — 12 ga. (2¾ in. chamber) over .223 Rem. cal., unique slide action O/U design allows stacked shotgun/rifle configuration, 20 in. shotgun barrel with invector chokes over 18 in. rifle barrel, detachable 4 (shotgun) and 5 (rifle) shot mags., open sights, Weaver style rail scope mount, synthetic stock and forearm, choice of black (MK-I) or all-camo (MK-IC) finish, single trigger with ambidextrous fire control lever, 8.6 lbs. Introduced mid-1998.

Mfg.'s Sug. Retail	$1,895		$1,750	$1,550	$1,350	$1,175	$995	$895	$825

Add $100 for camo finish.

CUMBERLAND MOUNTAIN ARMS, INC.

Current manufacturer located in Winchester, TN since early 1993. Consumer direct sales.

RIFLES: SINGLE SHOT

PLATEAU RIFLE — .40-65 or .45-70 Govt. cal., patterned after the Browning Hi-wall single shot, various barrel lengths up to 32 in., manual safety, blued receiver and barrel, Marble's style buckhorn rear sight, receiver drilled for scope mounts. New 1993.

Mfg.'s Sug. Retail	$1,295		$1,075	$825	$675	$575	$500	$450	$400

Add approx. $200-$350 for deluxe wood.

CUSTOM GUN GUILD

Previous manufacturer located in Doraville, GA.

WOOD'S MODEL IV SINGLE SHOT — various cals., custom manufactured, falling block type single shot, lightweight, only 5½ lbs. Mfg. 1984 only.

D section

DGS, INC.

Current rifle custom gunsmith located in Casper, WY. Custom gunsmith Dale A. Storey manufactures a variety of rifles built per individual customer order only. They include the Storey Custom, Storey Lightweight, as well as other variations. Please contact the company directly for more information and current prices on these quality custom rifles.

CUSTOM GUNSMITHING

D

DPMS, INC.

Current manufacturer located in Becker, MN since 1986. DPMS (Defense Procurement Manufacturing Services, Inc.) has been manufacturing AR-15 style rifles since 1993. Distributor, dealer, and consumer direct sales.

Grading	100%	98%	95%	90%	80%	70%	60%

PISTOLS: SLIDE ACTION

PANTHER PUMP PISTOL — .223 Rem. cal., slide action paramilitary design, 10½ in. threaded heavy barrel, aluminum handguard incorporates slide action mechanism, pistol grip only (no stock), carrying handle with sights, 5 lbs.

Mfg.'s Sug. Retail	$1,595		$1,475	$1,200	$1,025	$925	$825	$700	$575

RIFLES: BOLT ACTION

BOLT ACTION SNIPER/VARMINT SERIES — various cals., 3 different configurations including Sniper, Informal Target Varmint, and Field Grade Varmint, features match barrel, action, and tuned trigger. Prices for the Sniper rifle start at approx. $2,400 while the Varmint guns start at approx. $1,800.

RIFLES: SEMI-AUTO

PANTHER AR-15 SERIES — .223 Rem. cal., semi-auto or slide action, paramilitary design, various barrel lengths and configurations, 10 shot mag., black synthetic stock and forearm, various weights. Introduced 1993.

* ***Panther Classic*** — 20 in. heavy barrel, ribbed barrel shroud, includes carrying handle with sights, 8 lbs.

Mfg.'s Sug. Retail	$799		$725	$625	$550	$475	$425	$375	$335

Add approx. $76 for left-hand variation (Southpaw Panther).

* ***Panther Bulldog*** — 20 in. stainless fluted bull barrel, flat-top, adj. buttstock, vented free float handguard, 11 lbs.

Mfg.'s Sug. Retail	$1,219		$1,150	$835	$725	$625	$550	$475	$425

* ***Panther DCM*** — 20 in. stainless steel heavy barrel, adj. sights, black Zytel composition buttstock, 9 lbs. New 1998.

Mfg.'s Sug. Retail	$1,099		$995	$795	$675	$595	$525	$460	$415

* ***Panther Sixteen*** — 16 in. steel heavy barrel, adj. sights, black Zytel composition buttstock, 6½ lbs. New 1998.

Mfg.'s Sug. Retail	$789		$715	$625	$550	$475	$425	$375	$335

Add $55 for free floating barrel and vent. handguard.

Grading	100%	98%	95%	90%	80%	70%	60%

* ***Panther Carbine*** — 16 in. heavy barrel, collapsible stock, includes carrying handle, 6½ lbs.

Mfg.'s Sug. Retail $629	$560	$500	$460	$430	$400	$385	$370

This model is available for law enforcement only.

* ***Prairie Panther*** — 20 in. heavy fluted barrel, flat-top, vented free float handguard, 8¾ lbs.

Mfg.'s Sug. Retail $959	$875	$750	$635	$550	$475	$425	$375

* ***Arctic Panther*** — similar to Panther Bull, except has white powder coat finish on receiver and handguard, 10 lbs. New 1997.

Mfg.'s Sug. Retail $1,099	$995	$795	$675	$595	$525	$460	$415

* ***Panther Bull*** — features 16, 20 (standard), or 24 in. stainless free floating bull barrel, flat-top, aluminum forearm, 10 lbs.

Mfg.'s Sug. Retail $915	$835	$725	$600	$525	$450	$400	$360

Subtract $30 for 16 in. barrel (Panther Bull Sixteen).
Add $130 for Panther Bull SST Sixteen with stainless lower receiver.
Add $30 for 24 in. barrel (Panther Bull Twenty-Four).

➤ **Panther Bull Classic** — features 20 in. steel 1 in. bull barrel, adj. sights, 10 lbs. New 1998.

Mfg.'s Sug. Retail $905	$825	$725	$600	$525	$450	$400	$360

➤ **Panther Bull Twenty-Four Special** — features 24 in. stainless fluted barrel, adj. A2 buttstock with sniper pistol grip. New 1998.

Mfg.'s Sug. Retail $1,189	$1,075	$825	$700	$600	$525	$460	$415

* ***Panther Super Bull*** — 16, 20, or 24 in. extra heavy bull barrel, flat top receiver, free float handguard, approx. 11 lbs. Mfg. 1997-98.

	$925	$835	$725	$600	$525	$450	$400

Last Mfg.'s Sug. Retail was $1005.

* ***Panther Extreme Super Bull*** — features 24 in. extra heavy stainless steel bull barrel (1⅛ in. diameter barrel), flat top, hi-rider upper receiver, skeletonized A2 buttstock, 11¾ lbs. New 1999.

Mfg.'s Sug. Retail $1,219	$1,100	$835	$715	$600	$525	$460	$415

RIFLES: SLIDE ACTION

* ***Panther Pump*** — .223 Rem. cal., paramilitary design, 20 in. threaded heavy barrel, aluminum handguard incorporates slide action mechanism, carrying handle with sights, 8½ lbs.

Mfg.'s Sug. Retail $1,695	$1,500	$1,350	$1,150	$995	$875	$750	$625

DSA INC.

Current manufacturer, importer, and distributor located in Round Lake, IL.

DSA Inc. is a manufacturer that sells FAL/SA58 .308 Win. cal. rifles for both civilian and law enforcement purposes (L.E. certificates must be filled out for L.E. purchases). Until recently, DSA, Inc. also imported a sporterized Sig 550 rifle.

RIFLES: SEMI-AUTO

SA58 STANDARD RIFLE — .308 Win. cal., FAL design using high precision CNC machinery, 21 (standard or bull) or 24 in. (bull only) steel or stainless steel barrel, black synthetic stock, pistol grip attached to frame, 9-11½ lbs.

Mfg.'s Sug. Retail $1,495	$1,325	$1,150	$995	$875	$750	$625	$550

Add $300 for stainless steel bull barrel.
Add $200 for medium contour stainless steel barrel.

Grading	100%	98%	95%	90%	80%	70%	60%

✱ **SA58 Standard Carbine** — similar to SA58 Standard Rifle, except has 16¼ in. barrel, 9.2 lbs. New 1999.

Mfg.'s Sug. Retail **$1,795** $1,575 $1,375 $1,175 $995 $875 $750 $625

> Add $200 for stainless steel mini-carbine (includes scope mount).

DWM

Previous manufacturer located in Berlin, Germany circa 1900-1930. DWM (Deutsche Waffen und Munitions Fabriken) manufactured Lugers are listed in the Luger section.

PISTOLS: SEMI-AUTO

POCKET AUTOMATIC — 7.65mm cal., 3½ in. barrel, blue, hard rubber grips. Mfg. 1921-1931.

$700 $630 $580 $500 $420 $380 $330

DAEWOO

Current manufacturer located in Korea. No current importation. Previous importation included Kimber of America, Inc. until 1997, Daewoo Precision Industries, Ltd., until mid-1996, located in Southampton, PA, and previously distributed by Nationwide Sports Distributors 1993-96. Previously imported by KBI, Inc. and Firstshot, Inc., both located in Harrisburg, PA.

Daewoo makes a variety of firearms, most of which are not imported into the U.S.

PISTOLS: SEMI-AUTO

DH380 — .380 ACP cal., double action design. Imported 1995-96.

$330 $285 $260 $235 $210 $185 $165
Last Mfg.'s Sug. Retail was $375.

DH40 — .40 S&W cal., otherwise similar to DP51. Imported 1995-96.

$385 $325 $295 $250 $225 $200 $180
Last Mfg.'s Sug. Retail was $450.

DP51 STANDARD (S), COMPACT (C), OR (B) — 9mm Para. cal., double action enabling lowering hammer w/o depressing trigger, 3½ (DP51 C or S) or 4 (DP51 B) in. barrel, 10 (C/B 1994), 12★ (.40 S&W), or 13★ (9mm Para.) shot mag., 3-dot sighting, tri-action mechanism, ambidextrous controls, alloy receiver, polished or sand-blasted black finish, 28 or 32 oz., includes lockable carrying case with accessories. Imported 1991-96.

$350 $295 $270 $250 $225 $200 $180
Last Mfg.'s Sug. Retail was $400.

> Add $45 for DP51 Compact.

DP52 — .22 LR cal., double action, 3.8 in. barrel, alloy receiver, 10 shot mag., blue finish, 23 oz. Imported 1994-96.

$320 $275 $225 $200 $180 $165 $150
Last Mfg.'s Sug. Retail was $380.

RIFLES: SEMI-AUTO

MAX II (K2) — .223 Rem. cal., paramilitary design rifle, 18 in. barrel, gas operated rotating bolt, folding fiberglass stock, interchangeable mags. with the Colt M16, 7 lbs. Importation disc. 1986.

$725 $650 $575 $500 $450 $415 $375
Last Mfg.'s Sug. Retail was $609.

Grading	100%	98%	95%	90%	80%	70%	60%

* **MAX I (K1A1)** — similar to above, except has retractable stock. Importation disc. 1986.

| | **$725** | **$650** | **$575** | **$500** | **$450** | **$415** | **$375** |

Last Mfg.'s Sug. Retail was $592.

DR200 — .223 Rem. cal., paramilitary configuration with sporterized stock, 10 shot mag. Imported 1995-96.

| | **$475** | **$425** | **$395** | **$375** | **$350** | **$325** | **$300** |

Last Mfg.'s Sug. Retail was $535.

DR300 — 7.62x39mm cal., paramilitary configuration with or w/o thumbhole stock. Importation disc.

| | **$475** | **$425** | **$395** | **$375** | **$350** | **$325** | **$300** |

DAISY

Current airgun manufacturer located in Rogers, AR. Also see Daisy section under Modern Airguns.

RIFLES: SINGLE SHOT, DISC.

V/L STANDARD RIFLE — .22 V/L cal. (caseless air ignited cartridge), 1,100 FPS, 18 in. barrel, plastic stock, approx. 19,000 mfg. 1968-1969.

| | **$200** | **$175** | **$150** | **$125** | **$95** | **$80** | **$65** |

V/L PRESENTATION — similar to Collector's Kit, except does not have owner's name inscribed on butt plate, walnut stock, 4,000 mfg. for dealers.

| | **$235** | **$195** | **$160** | **$130** | **$100** | **$85** | **$70** |

Last Mfg.'s Sug. Retail was $125.

V/L COLLECTOR'S KIT — comes with case, gun cradles, 300 rounds of ammo, and a gold plated brass butt plate with owner's name and serial number of gun, approx. 4,000 mfg., available only by direct factory order.

| | **$350** | **$250** | **$200** | **$165** | **$125** | **$100** | **$85** |

Last Mfg.'s Sug. Retail was $125.

Note: The Daisy .22 V/L was discontinued because the BATF ruled that the gun constituted a firearm, and since Daisy was federally licensed to manufacture air weapons only, the factory decided to discontinue manufacture.

RIFLES: BOLT ACTION, DISC.

All Legacy models have a removable trigger, slings and swivels, takedown barrel, dovetail receiver for scope mounting, rifled inner steel barrel with 12 lands and grooves, and an adj. rear sight. Weight is between 6½-7 lbs.

MODEL 8 — .22 S or LR cal., single shot, 16 in. barrel, black synthetic stock, 30,000 mfg. for Walmart only 1987-88.

| | **$175** | **$150** | **$125** | **$95** | **$80** | **$70** | **$55** |

During 1987, Daisy assembled this model using left-over Iver Johnson parts.

LEGACY MODELS 2201/2211 — .22 LR cal., single shot, bolt action, plastic (2201) or walnut finished hardwood (2211) stock, models vary in features, prices range from $150-$175. Mfg. 1988-91.

LEGACY MODELS 2202/2212 — .22 LR cal., bolt action repeater, 10 shot rotary mag., plastic (2202) or walnut finished hardwood (2212) stock, models vary in features, prices range from $150-$175. Mfg. 1988-91.

Model 2202 has copolymer stock with adj. butt plate.

Grading	100%	98%	95%	90%	80%	70%	60%

RIFLES: SEMI-AUTO

LEGACY MODELS 2203/2213 — .22 LR cal., 7 shot box mag., models vary in features, prices range from $165-$190. Mfg. 1988-91.

> Model 2203 has copolymer stock with adj. butt plate. Model 2213 has American hardwood stock.

DAKIN GUN CO.
Previous manufacturer located in San Francisco, CA circa 1960s.

SHOTGUNS: O/U

MODEL 170 — 12, 16, 20 ga., or .410 bore, boxlock, light engraving, double triggers, vent rib.

	100%	98%	95%	90%	80%	70%	60%
	$495	$400	$325	$275	$245	$220	$195

SHOTGUNS: SxS

MODEL 100 — 12 or 20 ga., boxlock, engraved, double trigger.

	100%	98%	95%	90%	80%	70%	60%
	$425	$350	$275	$240	$205	$190	$170

MODEL 147 — 12 or 20 ga., boxlock, engraved, vent. rib, double trigger.

	100%	98%	95%	90%	80%	70%	60%
	$495	$385	$300	$265	$235	$215	$195

MODEL 160 — 12 or 20 ga., boxlock, single trigger, ejectors, vent. rib.

	100%	98%	95%	90%	80%	70%	60%
	$825	$700	$595	$495	$450	$395	$360

MODEL 215 — 12 or 20 ga., sidelock, heavy engraving, special walnut, single trigger, ejectors, vent. rib.

	100%	98%	95%	90%	80%	70%	60%
	$2,250	$1,900	$1,675	$1,300	$1,100	$925	$775

DAKOTA ARMS, INC.
Current manufacturer established in 1987, located in Sturgis, SD. Dealer and direct sales through manufacturer only.

> Dakota Arms models listed below are also available with many custom options - please contact the factory directly for availability and pricing. Left-hand rifles are also available at no extra charge on all models. Actions (barreled or unbarreled) may also be purchased separately - please contact the manufacturer directly for individual quotations.

RIFLES: BOLT ACTION

DAKOTA .22 RIFLE — .22 LR or .22 Hornet (disc.) cal., combines features of the Win. Model 52 Sporter and Dakota 76, full sized receiver, trigger and striker block safety similar to Dakota 76, 5 shot mag., 22 in. chrome moly barrel, checkered walnut stock, no sights, 6½ lbs. Mfg. 1992-98.

	100%	98%	95%	90%	80%	70%	60%
	$1,550	$1,150	$900	$800	$695	$625	$550

Last Mfg.'s Sug. Retail was $1,795.

DAKOTA TRAVELER — various cals. between .25-06 Rem. - .458 Win. Mag., in addition to Dakota proprietary calibers, almost seamless take down rifle based on the Dakota 76 design, threadless disassembly ensuring scope stability and accuracy, in addition to no possibility of increasing the head space during repeated disassembly, wood stock, right or left-hand action. New 1999.

Mfg.'s Sug. Retail	$3,995	95%	90%	80%	70%	60%	
		$3,650	$2,950	$2,450	$1,950	$1,650	$1,350	$1,050

> Add $200 for Safari cals.
> Add $1,500-$1,750 per interchangable barrel, depending on caliber.

Grading		100%	98%	95%	90%	80%	70%	60%

DAKOTA 76 CLASSIC GRADE — available in various cals. (short, standard, or long action), custom frame incorporating many Win. Model 70 features, 21 or 23 in. barrel, Mauser type extractor, checkered X English walnut stock, 7½ lbs. Left-hand action available at no extra charge. New 1987.

Mfg.'s Sug. Retail	$3,195	$2,850	$2,000	$1,550	$1,200	$990	$880	$770

This Model is also available with a composite stock at no extra charge.

DAKOTA 76 VARMINT GRADE — available in 9 cals. between .17 Rem. and 6mm PPC, single shot bolt-action, heavy barrel. Mfg. 1994-97.

		$2,275	$1,775	$1,425	$1,175	$990	$880	$770

Last Mfg.'s Sug. Retail was $2,500.

DAKOTA 76 SAFARI GRADE — available in various cals., 23 in. barrel, one-piece drop trigger guard assembly with hinged floor plate, checkered XXX English walnut stock with ebony forearm tip. Left-hand action available at no extra charge, 8½ lbs. New 1987.

Mfg.'s Sug. Retail	$4,195	$3,700	$2,900	$2,450	$1,950	$1,650	$1,350	$1,050

Subtract $400 (retail) if ordered with composite stock (disc.).

DAKOTA 76 AFRICAN GRADE — .404 Jeffery, .416 Dakota, .416 Rigby, or .450 Dakota cal., 4 shot mag., select wood with cross bolts in the stock, other features similar to Safari Grade Model, 24 in. barrel, "R" prefix on serial number, 9½ lbs. New 1989.

Mfg.'s Sug. Retail	$4,695	$4,250	$3,550	$2,975	$2,450	$2,000	$1,675	$1,400

DAKOTA 76 ALPINE GRADE — .22-250 Rem., .243 Win., 6mm Rem., .250-3000 Savage, 7mm-08 Rem., .308 Win., or .358 Win. cal., short action variation of the Classic Grade, 21 or 23 in. barrel, lighter weight model featuring a blind 4 shot mag., checkered X English walnut slimmer stock and barrel, serial numbered with a "K" prefix, 6½ lbs. Mfg. 1989-92.

		$1,850	$1,495	$1,300	$1,075	$925	$800	$700

Last Mfg.'s Sug. Retail was $1,995.

Other calibers were available on a special order basis.

DAKOTA T-76 LONGBOW — .300 Dakota Mag., .330 Dakota Mag., or .338 Lapua Mag. cal., 28 in. stainless barrel, tactical designed for long range, black synthetic stock with adj. comb, includes Picatinny optical rail, Model 70 style trigger, matte finish metal, controlled round feeding, includes deployment kit, 13.7 lbs. New 1997.

Mfg.'s Sug. Retail	$4,250	$3,750	$3,250	$2,750	$2,350	$1,925	$1,650	$1,350

DAKOTA MODEL 97 LIGHTWEIGHT HUNTER — available in most popular cals. between .22-250 Rem. and .308 Win., features fiberglass stock with black recoil pad, right hand only, 6 lbs. New 1998.

Mfg.'s Sug. Retail	$1,795	$1,600	$1,375	$1,075	$900	$750	$625	$550

Add $400 for Wood Hunter 97 (includes semi-fancy wood and blind mag.).
Add $700 for Deluxe Hunter 97 (includes semi-fancy wood and point panel checkering with floorplate).

DAKOTA MODEL 97 LONG RANGE HUNTER — available in 13 popular cals. between .25-06 Rem. and .375 Dakota Mag., composite black H-S Precision stock, 24 or 26 in. barrel, adj. match trigger, Model 76 ejector system, approx. 7.7 lbs. New 1997.

Mfg.'s Sug. Retail	$1,795	$1,600	$1,375	$1,075	$900	$750	$625	$550

Add $400 for Wood Hunter 97 (includes semi-fancy wood and blind mag.).
Add $700 for Deluxe Hunter 97 (includes semi-fancy wood and point panel checkering with floorplate).

RIFLES: SINGLE SHOT

DAKOTA MODEL 10 — available in most rimmed and rimless commercially loaded standard and Mag. cals., standard or enlarged Magnum (new 1994) action, 23 in. round barrel, top tang safety, deluxe checkered XX English walnut stock and forearm, 6 lbs. New 1990.

Mfg.'s Sug. Retail	$3,195	$2,850	$2,000	$1,550	$1,200	$990	$880	$770

Add $300 for Mag. cals.

Grading	100%	98%	95%	90%	80%	70%	60%

DAKOTA MODEL 97 VARMINT HUNTER — various varmint cals., rounded short action, 24 in. chrome-moly barrel, adj. trigger, X walnut with ½ in. black pad, right hand only, approx. 8 lbs. New 1998.

Mfg.'s Sug. Retail	**$1,795**	**$1,600**	**$1,375**	**$1,075**	**$900**	**$750**	**$625**	**$550**

SHOTGUNS: SxS

CLASSIC GRADE — 20 ga. only, case colored round boxlock action, 27 in. barrels with fixed chokes, DTs, straight grip checkered English walnut stock and splinter forearm, no engraving, 6 lbs. Mfg. 1996-98.

$7,450	**$6,750**	**$6,000**	**$5,400**	**$4,800**	**$4,200**	**$3,450**

Last Mfg.'s Sug. Retail was $7,950.

PREMIER GRADE — similar to Dakota Classic Field Grade, 27 in. barrels, exhibition grade English walnut, French grey metal finish, 50% engraving coverage, straight grip, splinter forend, DT, hand-rubbed oil finish stock, game rib with gold bead, ejectors, choice of chokes.

Mfg.'s Sug. Retail	**$12,000**	**$12,000**	**$8,950**	**$7,500**	**$6,450**	**$5,500**	**$4,750**	**$4,000**

DAKOTA AMERICAN LEGEND — 20 ga. only, fully scroll-engraved coin finish round boxlock action with gold inlays, French grey metal finish, special select English walnut mfg. to customer dimensions, 27 in. barrels with game rib and gold bead, straight grip, DT, round action, ejectors, choice of chokes, oak and leather trunk case, 6 lbs. New 1996.

Mfg.'s Sug. Retail	**$18,000**	**$16,000**	**$13,000**	**$11,000**	**$9,250**	**$7,500**	**$6,250**	**$5,000**

Only 100 guns are scheduled to be mfg. Also offered in a 12 ga. and .410 bore/28 ga. set.

DAKOTA SINGLE ACTION REVOLVERS

Current Dakota Revolvers are manufactured in Italy, and imported and distributed by E.M.F. Co., Inc. located in Santa Ana, CA. Dealer direct sales only.

Other firearms imported by E.M.F. Co., Inc. will be found in the E section of this book.

REVOLVERS: REPRODUCTIONS

Most Dakota SAAs to date have been manufactured by Armi San Marco.

OLD MODEL SAA — .22 LR, .32-20 WCF, .357 Mag., .38-40 WCF, .44 Spl., .44-40 WCF, or .45 LC cal., copy of the Colt SAA, 4⅝, 5½, or 7½ in. barrels, blue finish, case hardened frame, 1-piece walnut grips, solid brass backstrap and trigger guard. Importation disc. 1991.

$325	**$250**	**$200**	**$175**	**$150**	**$135**	**$120**

Last Mfg.'s Sug. Retail was $600.

Add $100 for nickel finish (disc.).
Add $110 for convertible cylinders.

* *Engraved Old Model* — .32-20 WCF, .357 Mag., .38-40 WCF, .44-40 WCF, or .45 cal., 4¾, 5½ or 7½ in. barrel. Disc. 1993, reintroduced 1996, disc. 1998.

$695	**$500**	**$425**	**$350**	**$325**	**$300**	**$275**

Last Mfg.'s Sug. Retail was $840.

Add $160 for nickel finish (disc.).

* *Cattlebrand Engraved* — .44-40 WCF or .45 LC cal., 5½ or 7½ in. barrel, patterned after the famous Colt Cattlebrand variation (features various cattlebrands engraved on the barrel, frame and cylinder). Imported 1992-1993, reintroduced 1996, disc. 1998.

$695	**$500**	**$425**	**$350**	**$325**	**$300**	**$275**

Last Mfg.'s Sug. Retail was $840.

Add $140 for silver-plating.

Grading	100%	98%	95%	90%	80%	70%	60%

PREMIER CUSTOM — various cals, case colored frame, choice of black Colt style or stag grips. Importation began 1999.

Mfg.'s Sug. Retail	$735	$550	$400	$350	$325	$300	$285	$275

Add $150 for stag grips.

NEW MODEL SAA — .357 Mag., .44-40 WCF, or .45 LC cal., features forged steel frame, black nickel backstrap and trigger guard, 4 (.45 LC cal. with standard grips), 4¾, 5½, or 7½ in. barrel, choice of case hardened or nickel frame, one piece walnut grips, original Colt type hammer (without transfer bar safety). Importation began 1991.

Mfg.'s Sug. Retail	$435	$340	$285	$230	$175	$150	$135	$120

Add $100 for combo. cylinder.
Add $160 for nickel finish (bright or satin).

* *Sheriff Model* — cals. similar to New Model, 3½ in. barrel. Importation began 1997.

Mfg.'s Sug. Retail	$435	$340	$285	$230	$175	$150	$135	$120

DAKOTA PREMIER SAA — .45 LC cal., black powder frame, initial mfg. was with 4⅝ or 5½ in. barrel, set screw cylinder pin release, steel backstrap and trigger guard, one-piece grips. This model was the predecessor to the New Hartford Model.

	$375	$295	$250	$190	$170	$160	$150

Last Mfg.'s Sug. Retail was $520.

NEW HARTFORD MODEL SAA — .22 LR (disc. 1992), .32-20 WCF, .357 Mag., .38-40 WCF, .44-40 WCF, .44 Spl., or .45 LC cal., features forged steel frame, backstrap, and trigger guard, exact reproduction of Colt's 1st or 2nd generation SAA, choice of black powder (with base pin frame set screw) or 2nd generation (push button cylinder pin release) frame, case hardened frame, original Colt markings, 4 (.45 LC cal. with standard grips), 4¾, 5½ or 7½ in. barrel. Importation began 1991.

Mfg.'s Sug. Retail	$550	$395	$350	$275	$225	$175	$150	$130

Add $100 for combo. cylinder (.45 ACP/.44 Spl.).
Add $35 for .32-20 WCF, .38-40 WCF, or .44 Spl. cal.
Add $160 for nickel finish (bright or satin).

* *Pinkerton Model* — same cals. as New Hartford Model, except .32-20 WCF, .357 Mag., .44-40 WCF, .44 Spl. are disc., birdshead grips, 4 in. barrel. New 1994.

Mfg.'s Sug. Retail	$570	$425	$345	$280	$220	$185	$160	$150

Add $40 for .32-20 WCF (disc.), .38-40 WCF, or .44 Spl. (disc.) cal.

* *Express Model* — .45 LC cal., features "Lightning" grips, 4 or 4¾ in. barrel, New Model. Importation began 1999.

Mfg.'s Sug. Retail	$570	$425	$345	$280	$220	$185	$160	$150

* *Cavalry Model* — .45 LC cal., 7½ in. barrel, faithful reproduction of the original Colt Cavalry Model, one-piece walnut grips with inspector cartouche, case hardened frame and hammer. Importation began 1991.

Mfg.'s Sug. Retail	$585	$435	$350	$285	$220	$185	$160	$150

* *Artillery Model* — .45 LC cal., similar to Cavalry Model, except has 5½ in. barrel. Importation began 1991.

Mfg.'s Sug. Retail	$585	$435	$350	$285	$220	$185	$160	$150

* *Texas Sesquicentennial* — .45 LC cal., 4¾ in. barrel, 50 mfg. for Texas Sesquicentennial with special engraving, includes numbered belt buckle and presentation case. Disc. 1991.

	$1,200	$925	$725

Original list price was $4,550.

* *Target Model* — .357 Mag., .44-40 WCF, or .45 LC cal., 5½ or 7½ in. barrel, case hardened frame, brass backstrap. Imported 1987-90.

	$325	$240	$185	$150	$140	$130	$120

Last Mfg.'s Sug. Retail was $500.

Grading	100%	98%	95%	90%	80%	70%	60%

* **Buntline Model** — .357 Mag. (disc.), .44-40 WCF (disc.), or .45 LC cal., blue only, 10 (new 1997) or 12 in. barrel. Importation disc. 1990, reintroduced 1997.

Mfg.'s Sug. Retail	$670	$500	$375	$300	$250	$215	$195	$175

* **Buckhorn Model** — 16¼ in. barrel, otherwise similar to Buntline. Importation disc. 1987.

	$295	$250	$180	$170	$160	$150	$140

Last Mfg.'s Sug. Retail was $495.

SHERIFF'S OLD/NEW MODEL SAA — .32-20 WCF (disc.), .357 Mag., .38-40 WCF (disc.), .44 Spl. (disc.), .44-40 WCF, or .45 LC cal., 3½ in. barrel only. Importation disc. 1991, resumed 1994.

Mfg.'s Sug. Retail	$550	$415	$335	$275	$220	$185	$160	$150

U.S. ARMY SAA — variety of cals., premium quality construction. Disc. 1985.

	$300	$205	$180	$165	$155	$145	$135

Last Mfg.'s Sug. Retail was $395.

* **U.S. Army Commemorative** — .45 LC cal., 7½ in. barrel, serial numbered 1-500, blue finish, case hardened frame, steel backstrap and trigger guard, 1-piece walnut grips. Importation disc. 1987.

	$350	$265	$185	$170	$160	$150	$135

Last Mfg.'s Sug. Retail was $495.

CONVERTIBLE MODEL SAA — available with .22 LR/.22 Mag., .32-20 WCF/.32 H&R Mag., .357 Mag./9mm Para., or .44-40 WCF/.44 Spl. cal., .45 LC/.45 ACP double cylinders. Imported 1986-90.

	$380	$310	$260	$220	$195	$170	$150

Last Mfg.'s Sug. Retail was $580.

FAST DRAW MODEL SAA — .22 LR, .22 Mag., .32-20 WCF, .32 H&R Mag., .357 Mag., .38-40 WCF, 9mm Para., .44 Spl., .44-40 WCF, .45 ACP, or .45 LC cal., case hardened frame, 4⅝ in. barrel. Importation disc. 1990.

	$340	$295	$225	$165	$150	$135	$125

Last Mfg.'s Sug. Retail was $480.

BISLEY MODEL SAA — .22 LR (disc.), .22 Mag.(disc.), .32-20 WCF (disc.), .32 H&R Mag. (disc.), .38-40 WCF, .357 Mag., 9mm Para. (disc.), .44 Spl. (disc.), .44-40 WCF, .45 ACP (disc.), or .45 LC (current mfg.) cal., 4¾ (disc. 1994), 5½, or 7½ in. barrel lengths. Imported 1986-91, reintroduced 1993-disc. 1995, reintroduced 1997.

Mfg.'s Sug. Retail	$600	$425	$350	$275	$225	$185	$160	$150

    Add 435 for .38-40 WCF.
    Add $125 for nickel finish (bright or satin - disc.).
    Add $112 for combo. cylinder (.45 ACP - disc.).

* **Engraved Bisley** — .32-20 WCF, .38-40 WCF, .357 Mag., .44-40 WCF, or .45 LC cal. (disc. 1990), 4¾, 5½ or 7½ in. barrel, action engraved throughout. Imported 1987-91.

	$425	$350	$275	$250	$225	$200	$180

Last Mfg.'s Sug. Retail was $570.

    Add $100 for nickel finish.

1873 FRONTIER MODEL SAA — .22 LR cal., 4¾ in. barrel, case colored frame, black nickel backstrap and trigger guard. Mfg. by IAR, importation began 1999.

Mfg.'s Sug. Retail	$450	$350	$295	$235	$175	$150	$135	$120

DALVAR OF USA

Current importer of recently manufactured Radom pistols located in Richardson, TX since 1997. Please refer to the Radom listing in this text.

DALY, CHARLES: PRUSSIAN MFG.

Previously manufactured in Prussia.

Charles Daly was an importer whose goal was to give the U.S. shotgun consumer a European manufactured gun of similar quality to the premier American shotguns

Grading	100%	98%	95%	90%	80%	70%	60%

of the same era. In that behalf, he had various European firms fabricate shotguns with American shooting features and preferences. Many "Prussian" Dalys were built by various firms in Suhl, Germany. Importation ceased prior to WWII. These Prussian Charles Dalys utilized the finest materials and best workmanship of their time.

DRILLINGS

DRILLING MODEL — 12, 16, or 20 ga.'s and .25-20 WCF, .25-35 WCF, or .30-30 WCF cal., 3 barrel combination gun, extractors, double triggers, engraved action, select walnut, mfg. by both Linder and Sauer. Linder mfg. guns are extremely rare - very few specimens are to be found domestically. Sauer guns were not marked for grade, but rather had three levels of engraving which determined the grade. Most Sauer guns had a tang mounted aperture rear sight and a separate rifle cock and were sidelocks. Disc. 1933.

* **Superior Quality** — borderline engraving only.

	100%	98%	95%	90%	80%	70%	60%
Sauer mfg.	$3,000	$2,600	$2,300	$2,000	$1,700	$1,500	$1,200

* **Diamond Quality** — full scroll engraving.

	100%	98%	95%	90%	80%	70%	60%
Sauer mfg.	$5,500	$4,800	$4,400	$4,000	$3,500	$3,000	$2,200

* **Regent Diamond Quality** — top-of-the-line model featuring full game scene coverage.

	100%	98%	95%	90%	80%	70%	60%
Linder mfg.	$12,000	$11,000	$10,000	$9,000	$7,000	$6,000	$5,000
Sauer mfg.	$8,000	$7,000	$6,700	$6,000	$5,000	$4,000	$3,000

RIFLES

BOLT ACTION GRADE I — .22 Hornet cal., mfg. by F. Jaeger & Co. of Suhl, Germany, 5 shot mag., 24 in. barrel, miniature Mauser bolt action, deluxe walnut. Disc.

100%	98%	95%	90%	80%	70%	60%
$820	$615	$535	$455	$410	$370	$330

SHOTGUNS

In the higher grade Prussian Daly variations, there is quite a bit of difference in their manufacture, including engraving options, levels of wood embellishment, and other extra cost features at the time. H. A. Linder produced approx. 2,500 guns (ser. numbered accordingly), and many of the higher grades show a noticeable difference in the amount of engraving (from minimal to considerable game scene engraving), can be either case colored only or have gold inlaid birds and animals (the number of which can also vary), barrels can have various levels of engraving on both the breech and muzzle ends - all of these factors have considerable impact on the overall value of a particular specimen. It is estimated that it took three craftsmen one year to produce a single Diamond Regent gun.

COMMANIDER O&U — 12, 16, 20, 28 ga., or .410 bore, Anson & Deeley boxlock action, single or double triggers, ejectors. Mfg. in Belgium circa 1939.

* **Model 100**

100%	98%	95%	90%	80%	70%	60%
$500	$375	$325	$275	$250	$225	$200

Add $100 for single trigger.

* **Model 200** — similar to Model 100, except has deluxe walnut.

100%	98%	95%	90%	80%	70%	60%
$650	$490	$425	$360	$325	$300	$260

Add 10%-30% for 28 ga. and .410 bore.

EMPIRE O&U — 12, 16, or 20 ga., various barrel lengths, Anson & Deeley boxlock, ejectors and double triggers, fine engraving, deluxe walnut. Disc. 1933.

100%	98%	95%	90%	80%	70%	60%
$4,000	$3,400	$2,750	$2,375	$2,000	$1,825	$1,625

DIAMOND O&U — similar to Empire model, only finer workmanship and materials.

100%	98%	95%	90%	80%	70%	60%
$5,000	$4,300	$3,475	$3,000	$2,600	$2,300	$2,000

Grading	100%	98%	95%	90%	80%	70%	60%

SUPERIOR SxS — 10, 12, 20, 28 ga., or .410 bore, Anson & Deeley boxlock, various barrel lengths, extractors. Disc. 1933.

	100%	98%	95%	90%	80%	70%	60%
	$1,050	$790	$690	$580	$525	$475	$420

EMPIRE SxS — similar to Superior, only more engraving and better wood.

	100%	98%	95%	90%	80%	70%	60%
Linder mfg.	$5,000	$4,400	$3,900	$3,500	$2,800	$2,200	$1,500
Sauer mfg.	$4,200	$3,500	$3,100	$2,800	$2,200	$1,800	$1,400

DIAMOND SxS — similar to Empire model, only more elaborate and with gold inlays.

	100%	98%	95%	90%	80%	70%	60%
Linder mfg.	$10,000	$9,000	$8,500	$8,000	$7,000	$6,000	$4,500
Sauer mfg.	$7,000	$6,200	$5,500	$5,000	$4,000	$3,000	$2,000

Subtract 20%-25% if without gold inlays.

DIAMOND REGENT SxS — top-of-the-line Prussian side-by-side and with gold inlays.

	100%	98%	95%	90%	80%	70%	60%
Linder mfg.	$16,000	$13,500	$12,000	$11,000	$8,500	$7,000	$5,000
Sauer mfg.	$8,500	$7,700	$7,000	$6,500	$5,000	$4,000	$3,000

EMPIRE SINGLE BARREL TRAP — 12 ga., 30-34 in. barrel, Anson & Deeley boxlock, ejector, vent. rib, finely engraved with select walnut, chopper lump extension, top quality. Disc. 1933.

	100%	98%	95%	90%	80%	70%	60%
Linder mfg.	$3,995	$3,500	$3,100	$2,800	$2,200	$1,800	$1,400
Sauer mfg.	$2,150	$1,675	$1,475	$1,100	$960	$850	$750

SEXTUPLE SINGLE BARREL TRAP — 12 ga., 30-34 in. barrel, six locking bolts, ejector, vent. rib, elaborately engraved and checkered. Regent Diamond Model has better engraving and wood.

* *Empire Quality*

	100%	98%	95%	90%	80%	70%	60%
Linder mfg.	$4,600	$4,150	$3,650	$3,100	$2,800	$2,200	$1,800
Sauer mfg.	$2,600	$2,100	$1,700	$1,400	$1,100	$900	$750

* *Regent Diamond Quality*

	100%	98%	95%	90%	80%	70%	60%
Linder mfg.	$5,000	$4,400	$3,900	$3,500	$2,800	$2,200	$1,500
Sauer mfg.	$3,300	$2,850	$2,400	$1,950	$1,650	$1,350	$995

DALY, CHARLES: JAPANESE MFG.

Previously manufactured by B.C. Miroku, located in Kochi, Japan until 1976.

SHOTGUNS: O/U

In the early sixties, C. Daly guns were manufactured by the firm of B.C. Miroku in Kochi, Japan. This Japanese gun manufacturing company has produced guns for many companies, Browning being the biggest current customer. Miroku guns are high quality with excellent fit and finish. Many of them are highly engraved and are fine examples of the gunmaker's art. Charles Daly Miroku Guns are becoming quite collectible in some areas (smaller gauges with open chokes). Their production ceased in 1976.

O/U MODELS — 12, 20, 28 ga., or .410 bore, 26, 28, or 30 in. vent. rib barrels, various chokes, boxlock, auto ejectors, SST, select walnut checkered pistol grip stock, Superior and Diamond Grade Trap have Monte Carlo stocks, the grades differ in amount of engraving and wood. Mfg. 1963-1976 by Miroku.

Approx. 1,000 28 ga. Lightweight guns were manufactured. All 28 ga. Lightweights (approx. ser. range 230,185-230,998) have barrel spacing $3/4$ in. center to center, while the normal 28 ga. has a measurement of $7/8$ in. After the Charles Daly line of O/Us were mechanically redesigned, both the 28 ga. and .410 bore were made on only the new 20 ga. frame. To date, no one has observed a .410 bore Lightweight Charles Daly.
Add 20% for 20 ga. on models listed below.
Add 50% for 28 ga. on models listed below.
Add 60% for .410 bore on models listed below.
Add 100% for original 28 ga. Lightweight models (rare).

Grading	100%	98%	95%	90%	80%	70%	60%

D

* **Field Grade** — 12 or 20 ga., light engraving.

	100%	98%	95%	90%	80%	70%	60%
	$675	$625	$550	$525	$500	$450	$395

* **Venture Grade** — all gauges, moderate engraving.

	$595	$550	$495	$470	$440	$415	$360

* **Venture Skeet** — 26 in. barrels choked skeet and skeet.

	$625	$575	$525	$495	$470	$440	$385

* **Venture Trap** — 30 in. imp. mod. and full.

	$575	$530	$495	$470	$415	$360	$330

* **Superior Grade** — all gauges, select checkered walnut stock with round knob, scroll engraving similar to Grade I Browning Superposed.

	$850	$775	$700	$650	$600	$550	$495

* **Superior Trap**

	$725	$625	$575	$550	$500	$440	$390

   This model had an optional selective ejection system enabling the shooter to deactivate the ejectors.

* **Diamond Grade** — all gauges, extensive engraving with better quality wood.

	$1,125	$990	$935	$880	$770	$715	$660

* **Diamond Grade Skeet**

	$1,150	$1,025	$950	$880	$770	$715	$660

* **Diamond Grade Trap**

	$950	$885	$800	$740	$685	$620	$560

* **Wide Rib Diamond Grade Flat-Top Trap**

	$950	$885	$800	$740	$685	$620	$560

* **Diamond Regent Grade** — mostly 12 ga., extensive frame engraving with gold inlays, rare.

	$2,000	$1,700	$1,425	$1,275	$1,100	$990	$880

SHOTGUNS: SxS

EMPIRE SHOTGUN — 12, 16, or 20 ga., 26, 28, or 30 in. barrels, various chokes, boxlock, extractors, single trigger, checkered pistol grip stock. Mfg. 1968-1971.

	$545	$495	$470	$415	$360	$305	$250
Vent. rib	$595	$535	$500	$450	$400	$350	$300

1974 WILDLIFE COMMEMORATIVE — duck scene engraved, Diamond Grade, Trap, or Skeet, limited to 500 guns. Mfg. 1974 only.

	$1,650	$1,430	$1,320	$1,100	$990	$880	$770

SHOTGUNS: SINGLE BARREL, TRAP

SUPERIOR GRADE SINGLE BARREL TRAP — 12 ga., 32 or 34 in. vent. rib, full choke barrel, auto ejector, Monte Carlo stock with recoil pad. Mfg. 1968-1976.

	$550	$525	$495	$440	$385	$330	$305

DALY, CHARLES: 1976 TO PRESENT

Currently manufactured trademark imported since late 1996 by KBI, Inc. located in Harrisburg, PA. Previously imported by Outdoor Sports Headquarters, Inc. located in Dayton, OH until 1995.

The Charles Daly "Novamatic" shotguns were produced in 1968 by Breda in Italy.

Grading	100%	98%	95%	90%	80%	70%	60%

COMBINATION GUNS

SUPERIOR COMBINATION MODEL — 12 ga. with choice of .22 Hornet, .22-250 Rem. (disc. 1998), .223 Rem., .243 Win. (disc. 1998), .270 Win. (disc. 1998), .30-06, or .308 Win. (disc. 1998) cal., boxlock action, 23½ in. barrels. Importation began 1997.

Mfg.'s Sug. Retail	$1,209	$1,065	$900	$800	$700	$600	$500	$450

EMPIRE COMBINATION MODEL — 12 ga. with choice of .22 Hornet, .22-250 Rem. (disc. 1998), .223 Rem., .243 Win. (disc. 1998) , .270 Win. (disc. 1998), .30-06, or .308 Win. (disc. 1998) cal., boxlock action, 23½ in. barrels, engraved with choice checkered walnut stock and forearm. Importation began 1997.

Mfg.'s Sug. Retail	$1,729	$1,550	$1,325	$1,100	$950	$800	$700	$600

D

PISTOLS: SEMI-AUTO

GOVERNMENT 1911-A1P — .45 ACP cal., steel frame, single action, skeletonized combat hammer and trigger, ambidextrous safety, 8 or 10 shot mag., extended slide release and beavertail grip safety, oversized and lowered ejection port, 5 in. barrel with solid barrel bushing, matte blue (Field FS), stainless slide/blue frame (Superior FS, new 1999), or all stainless (Empire FS, new 1999) finish, includes two 8 or 10 shot mags. and lockable carrying case. New 1998.

Mfg.'s Sug. Retail	$449	$395	$350	$325	$310	$295	$280	$165

    Add $30 for Superior FS Model.
    Add $60 for Empire FS Model.
    Add $199 for .22 LR conversion kit with adj. sight.

COMMANDER 1911-A1P — similar to Government 1911-A1P, except has 4 in. Commander barrel and features. Importation began 1999.

Mfg.'s Sug. Retail	$449	$395	$350	$325	$310	$295	$280	$165

    Add $30 for Superior FS Model (includes stainless steel slide and blue frame).
    Add $60 for Empire FS Model (full stainless steel construction).

OFFICER'S 1911-A1P — similar to Commander, except has 3½ in. barrel and Officer's Model features. Importation began 1999.

Mfg.'s Sug. Retail	$449	$395	$350	$325	$310	$295	$280	$165

    Add $30 for Superior FS Model (includes stainless steel slide and blue frame).
    Add $60 for Empire FS Model (full stainless steel construction).

COMMANDER 1911-A1 POLYMER FRAME — .45 ACP only, features polymer frame, 4 in. barrel, available in matte blue (Field PC) or stainless slide/blue frame (Superior PC). Importation began 1999.

Mfg.'s Sug. Retail	$509	$440	$385	$350	$325	$295	$280	$165

    Add $20 for Superior FS Model (includes stainless steel slide and blue frame).

RIFLES: BOLT ACTION

MAUSER 98 — .243 Win., .270 Win., .30-06, .308 Win., .300 Win. Mag., .375 H&H, .458 Win. Mag., or 7mm Rem. Mag. cal., Mauser 98 action, 23 in. barrel, 3-5 shot, hinged floorplate, fiberglass/graphite composite (Field Grade) or checkered European walnut (Superior grade) stock, open sights, drilled and tapped receiver, side safety. Limited importation 1998 only.

    ✳ **Field Grade** — features fiberglass/graphite composite stock.

	$315	$275	$250	$225	$200	$185	$170

                                  Last Mfg.'s Sug. Retail was $359.

    Add $190 for .375 H&H or .458 Win. Mag. cal.

    ✳ **Superior Grade** — features checkered European walnut stock.

	$360	$315	$275	$250	$225	$200	$185

                                  Last Mfg.'s Sug. Retail was $419.

    Add $200 for .375 H&H or .458 Win. Mag. cal.

Grading	100%	98%	95%	90%	80%	70%	60%

MINI-MAUSER 98 — .22 Hornet, .22-250 Rem., .223 Rem., or 7.62x39mm cal., similar to Mauser 98, except has 19¼ in. barrel, 5 shot. Mfg. 1998 only.

* **Field Grade** — features fiberglass/graphite composite stock.

	$345	$295	$265	$230	$200	$185	$170

Last Mfg.'s Sug. Retail was $399.

* **Superior Grade** — features checkered European walnut stock.

	$380	$325	$280	$250	$225	$200	$185

Last Mfg.'s Sug. Retail was $449.

RIFLES: BOLT ACTION, RIMFIRE

FIELD GRADE — .22 LR cal., 16¼ (True Youth Standard), 17½ (Youth), or 22⅝ (Standard) in. barrel, single shot (True Youth Standard) or 6 shot mag., all steel shrouded action, grooved receiver, walnut finished hardwood stock. New 1998.

Mfg.'s Sug. Retail	$124	$105	$90	$80	$70	$60	$55	$50

Add $19 for single shot True Youth Standard with shortened dimensions.

* **Superior Grade** — .22 LR, .22 Mag., or .22 Hornet cal., 22⅝ in. barrel, 5 or 6 shot mag., features checkered walnut finished stock with adj. rear sight. New 1998.

Mfg.'s Sug. Retail	$179	$150	$120	$100	$90	$80	$70	$60

Add $20 for .22 Mag. cal.
Add $170 for .22 Hornet cal.

* **Empire Grade** — similar to Superior Grade, except has checkered California walnut stock with rosewood grip and forend caps, high polish bluing and damascened bolt. New 1998.

Mfg.'s Sug. Retail	$329	$280	$255	$235	$215	$195	$180	$170

Add $20 for .22 Mag. cal.
Add $120 for .22 Hornet cal.

RIFLES: SEMI-AUTO

SEMI-AUTO RIFLE — .22 LR cal., steel receiver, 20¾ in. barrel with adj. rear sight, 10 shot mag. New 1998.

* **Field Grade** — features uncheckered walnut finished hardwood stock.

Mfg.'s Sug. Retail	$124	$105	$90	$80	$70	$60	$55	$50

* **Superior Grade** — features checkered walnut finished stock.

Mfg.'s Sug. Retail	$199	$165	$130	$100	$90	$80	$70	$60

* **Empire Grade** — features checkered California walnut stock.

Mfg.'s Sug. Retail	$309	$260	$235	$215	$195	$180	$170	$160

SHOTGUNS: O/U

Current O/U production is from Italy.

PRESENTATION MODEL — 12 or 20 ga., with choke tubes, Purdey double underlug locking action with decorative engraved sideplates, French walnut, single trigger, ejectors. Disc. 1986.

	$995	$840	$750	$670	$615	$560	$520

Last Mfg.'s Sug. Retail was $1,165.

FIELD HUNTER MODEL — 12, 20, 28 ga., or .410 bore, similar to DeLuxe Model except has fixed chokes, extractors, machine stock checkering, and blued receiver. New 1989.

Mfg.'s Sug. Retail	$749	$635	$450	$385	$330	$295	$275	$260

Add $60 for 28 ga. or $100 for .410 bore.

Grading	100%	98%	95%	90%	80%	70%	60%

* Field Hunter with Ejectors — similar to Field Hunter, except has ejectors, multi-chokes (not available on 28 ga. or .410 bore) and Monte Carlo stock. Importation began 1997.

Mfg.'s Sug. Retail	$949	$830	$725	$630	$550	$475	$395	$350

Subtract $60 for 28 ga.

* Field Hunter Ultra-Light — 12 or 20 ga., alloy frame, 26 in. VR barrels only with fixed IC/M chokes, thin forearm, approx. 5½ lbs. Importation began 1999.

Mfg.'s Sug. Retail	$859	$715	$500	$425	$375	$325	$295	$275

DELUXE MODEL — 12, 20, 28 ga. (disc. 1995), or .410 bore (disc. 1995), boxlock with self adj. crossbolt, 26 or 28 in. chrome lined VR barrels with internal choke tubes, SST, ejectors, antique silver finish on receiver, deluxe hand checkered walnut stock and forearm. Imported 1989-96.

	$650	$525	$475	$425	$400	$375	$350

Last Mfg.'s Sug. Retail was $770.

SPORTING CLAYS MODEL — 12 ga. only, SST, ejectors, silver engraved receiver, checkered walnut stock and forearm, screw-in chokes, 28 (disc.) or 30 (new 1996) in. VR ported barrels. Imported 1995-96.

	$775	$700	$625	$550	$475	$395	$350

Last Mfg.'s Sug. Retail was $895.

SUPERIOR II — 12 or 20 ga., various chokes, boxlock action, single trigger, ejectors, engraved. Disc. 1988.

	$675	$575	$475	$425	$395	$375	$350

Last Mfg.'s Sug. Retail was $875.

Add $35 for 12 ga. Mag. (disc. 1987).

FIELD III — 12 or 20 ga., various chokes, boxlock action, single trigger. Disc. 1989.

	$395	$370	$340	$315	$285	$260	$230

Last Mfg.'s Sug. Retail was $450.

SUPERIOR HUNTER — 12, 20, 28 ga. (new 1998), or .410 bore, 3 in. chambers (except 28 ga.), boxlock action, ejectors, 26, 28, or 30 in. VR barrels with multi-chokes (except 28 ga. and .410 bore), select Monte Carlo walnut stock and forearm. Importation began 1997.

Mfg.'s Sug. Retail	$1,139	$1,050	$925	$775	$650	$550	$475	$395

Subtract $80 for 28 ga. or $40 for .410 bore.

* Superior Sporting — 12 or 20 ga. (disc. 1998), 26 (disc. 1998), 28, or 30 (12 ga. only) in. VR barrels with multi-chokes. Importation began 1997.

Mfg.'s Sug. Retail	$1,219	$1,075	$925	$775	$650	$550	$475	$395

* Superior Trap — 12 ga. only, 30 in. VR barrels with choice of fixed chokes or multi-chokes, regular or Monte Carlo stock. Importation began 1997.

Mfg.'s Sug. Retail	$1,259	$1,100	$950	$795	$650	$550	$475	$395

Subtract $120 if w/o multi-chokes with Monte Carlo stock.

* Superior Skeet — 12 or 20 ga., 26 in. VR barrels with choice of Skeet fixed chokes or multi-chokes, regular or Monte Carlo stock. Imported 1997-98.

	$935	$800	$700	$600	$500	$450	$375

Last Mfg.'s Sug. Retail was $1,039.

Add $120 for multi-chokes with Monte Carlo stock.

EMPIRE DL HUNTER — 12, 20, 28 ga., or .410 bore, boxlock action, silver receiver with game scene engraving, ejectors, SST, 26 or 28 (12 or 20 ga. only) in. VR barrels with multi-chokes (except 28 ga. and .410 bore). Imported 1997-98.

	$1,025	$875	$750	$650	$550	$475	$395

Last Mfg.'s Sug. Retail was $1,159.

Add $65 for 28 ga. or $110 for .410 bore.

Grading	100%	98%	95%	90%	80%	70%	60%

EMPIRE EDL HUNTER — similar to Empire DL Hunter, except has engraved sideplates featuring game scenes. New 1998.

Mfg.'s Sug. Retail	$1,549	$1,300	$1,025	$850	$725	$625	$500	$450

Subtract $40 for 28 ga. or .410 bore.

✱ Empire Sporting — 12 or 20 ga. (disc. 1999), 26 (disc. 1999), 28, or 30 (12 ga. only) in. VR barrels with multi-chokes. Importation began 1997.

Mfg.'s Sug. Retail	$1,449	$1,250	$995	$850	$725	$625	$500	$450

✱ Empire Trap — 12 ga. only, 30 or 32 in. VR barrels with choice of fixed chokes (32 in. barrel only) or multi-chokes, regular (disc. 1998) or Monte Carlo stock. Importation began 1997.

Mfg.'s Sug. Retail	$1,489	$1,275	$950	$825	$700	$600	$475	$425

Subtract 10% if w/o multi-chokes.

✱ Empire Mono Trap — features single top barrel, standard or adj. Monte Carlo stock. Importation began 1999.

Mfg.'s Sug. Retail	$1,519	$1,300	$950	$825	$700	$600	$475	$425

Add $640 for adj. Monte Carlo stock.

✱ Empire Trap Combo — includes mono 32 in. barrel and extra set of 30 in. O/U barrels, standard or adj. Monte Carlo stock. Importation began 1999.

Mfg.'s Sug. Retail	$2,309	$2,050	$1,725	$1,475	$1,250	$975	$850	$675

Add $640 for adj. Monte Carlo stock.

✱ Empire Skeet — 12 or 20 ga., 26 in. VR barrels with choice of Skeet fixed chokes or multi-chokes, regular or Monte Carlo stock. Imported 1997-98.

$1,050	$875	$750	$650	$550	$475	$395

Last Mfg.'s Sug. Retail was $1,189.

Add $125 for multi-chokes with Monte Carlo stock.

DIAMOND FIELD — 12 or 20 ga. (disc. 1986) Mag., with choke tubes. Same action as Presentation Model without sideplates, engraved, select walnut, single trigger, ejectors. Disc. 1986.

$695	$600	$550	$510	$460	$420	$380

Last Mfg.'s Sug. Retail was $895.

✱ Diamond Trap or Skeet — 12 ga. only, 26 or 30 in. barrels only. Disc. 1986.

$850	$700	$550	$500	$475	$450	$425

Last Mfg.'s Sug. Retail was $1,050.

Subtract $50 for Skeet Model.

DIAMOND GTX DL HUNTER — 12, 20, 28 ga., or .410 bore, sidelock action, ejectors, SST, elaborate engraving with select checkered walnut stock and forearm, 26, 28 (12 or 20 ga. only), or 30 (12 ga. only) in. VR barrels with multi-chokes (except 28 ga. and .410 bore). Imported 1997 only.

$11,250	$9,000	$7,000	$5,700	$4,900	$4,200	$3,750

Last Mfg.'s Sug. Retail was $12,399.

✱ Diamond GTX EDL Hunter — more elaborate variation of the Diamond GTX DL Hunter. Imported 1997 only.

$13,750	$11,250	$9,000	$7,000	$5,700	$4,900	$4,200

Last Mfg.'s Sug. Retail was $15,999.

✱ Diamond GTX Sporting — 12 or 20 (disc. 1998) ga., 28 or 30 (12 ga. only) in. VR barrels with multi-chokes. Importation began 1997.

Mfg.'s Sug. Retail	$5,629	$5,100	$4,650	$4,200	$3,650	$3,150	$2,750	$2,175

✱ Diamond GTX Trap — 12 ga. only, 30 in. VR barrels with choice of fixed or multi-chokes, regular or adj. (new 1999) Monte Carlo stock. Importation began 1997.

Mfg.'s Sug. Retail	$6,429	$5,650	$4,750	$4,300	$3,775	$3,150	$2,750	$2,175

Subtract 5% w/o fixed chokes.

Grading	100%	98%	95%	90%	80%	70%	60%

* **Diamond GTX Mono Trap** — features single top barrel, adj. Monte Carlo stock. Importation began 1999.

  Mfg.'s Sug. Retail $6,349 $5,575 $4,725 $4,300 $3,775 $3,150 $2,750 $2,175

* **Diamond GTX Trap Combo** — includes 32 in. mono barrel and extra set of 30 in. O/U barrels, adj. Monte Carlo stock. Importation began 1999.

  Mfg.'s Sug. Retail $7,129 $6,550 $5,650 $4,750 $4,300 $3,775 $3,150 $2,750

* **Diamond GTX Skeet** — 12 or 20 ga., 26 or 28 (20 ga. only with Monte Carlo stock) in. VR barrels with choice of Skeet fixed chokes or multi-chokes, regular or Monte Carlo stock. Imported 1997-98.

  $4,700 $4,100 $3,800 $3,400 $2,975 $2,700 $2,100

  Last Mfg.'s Sug. Retail was $5,149.

  Add $140 for multi-chokes with Monte Carlo stock.

DIAMOND REGENT GTX DL HUNTER — 12, 20, 28 ga., or .410 bore, sidelock action, ejectors, SST, best quality engraving with premium checkered walnut stock and forearm, 26, 28 (12 or 20 ga. only), or 30 (12 ga. only) in. VR barrels with multi-chokes (except 28 ga. and .410 bore). Imported 1997 only.

  $19,750 $16,250 $13,750 $11,250 $9,000 $7,000 $5,700

  Last Mfg.'s Sug. Retail was $22,299.

* **Diamond Regent GTX EDL Hunter** — top-of-the-line model incorporating best quality engraving and premium walnut. Imported 1997 only.

  $23,000 $19,500 $16,000 $13,750 $10,500 $8,750 $7,700

  Last Mfg.'s Sug. Retail was $26,429.

SHOTGUNS: SEMI-AUTO

The Novamatic series was not imported by Outdoor Sport Headquarters, Inc.

NOVAMATIC LIGHTWEIGHT MODEL — 12 ga., 26 or 28 in. barrel, various chokes, available with quick choke interchangeable tubes, checkered pistol grip stock, similar to the Breda shotgun. Mfg. 1968 only.

  $305 $275 $250 $220 $195 $165 $140

  Add $25 for vent. rib.
  Add $15 for quick choke.

NOVAMATIC SUPER LIGHTWEIGHT — 12 or 20 ga., similar to Lightweight, except approx. ½ lb. lighter.

  $330 $305 $275 $250 $220 $195 $165

  Add $25 for vent. rib.
  Add $15 for quick choke.

NOVAMATIC MAGNUM — 12 or 20 ga. with 3 in. chambers, similar to Lightweight, 28 or 30 in. vent rib barrel, full choke.

  $330 $305 $275 $250 $220 $195 $165

NOVAMATIC TRAP — similar to Lightweight, with 30 in. full vent. rib barrel, Monte Carlo stock.

  $360 $330 $305 $275 $250 $220 $195

CHARLES DALY AUTOMATIC — 12 ga., 2¾ or 3 in. chambers, gas operation, alloy frame, pistol grip (high gloss) or English stock, vent. rib, 5 shot mag. Also available as slug gun with iron sights. Invector chokes became standard in 1986. Disc. 1988.

  $320 $275 $235 $205 $190 $170 $150

  Last Mfg.'s Sug. Retail was $365.

  Add $15 for oil finished English stock.

MULTI-XII — 12 ga. only, 3 in. chamber, 27 in. VR multichoke barrel, self adjusting gas operation, deluxe checkered walnut stock with recoil pad and forearm. Imported 1987-88 only.

  $425 $360 $320 $285 $250 $225 $195

  Last Mfg.'s Sug. Retail was $498.

Grading	100%	98%	95%	90%	80%	70%	60%

FIELD HUNTER — 12 ga. only, gas operated, 24, 26, 28, or 30 in. VR barrel with multi-chokes, choice of standard wood/metal or 100% Advantage Camo coverage, synthetic stock and forearm. Importation began 1999.

Mfg.'s Sug. Retail	$399	$365	$325	$295	$275	$250	$225	$200

Add $100 for 100% Advantage Camo coverage.

* *Field Slug* — 12 ga. only, 22 in. cyl. bore barrel with adj. sights, blue or nickel finish. Importation began 1999.

Mfg.'s Sug. Retail	$399	$365	$325	$295	$275	$250	$225	$200

Add $30 for nickel finish.

SUPERIOR HUNTER — similar to Field Hunter, except has 20 LPI checkered Turkish walnut stock and forearm, gold highlights and trigger, not available with 26 in. barrel. Importation began 1999.

Mfg.'s Sug. Retail	$499	$445	$395	$365	$325	$295	$275	$250

* *Superior Sporting* — 12 ga. only, similar to Superior Hunter, except has 28 or 30 in. ported 10mm VR barrels. Importation began 1999.

Mfg.'s Sug. Retail	$529	$465	$415	$375	$330	$300	$275	$250

* *Superior Trap* — 12 ga. only, 30 or 32 in. ported barrel with front and mid bead sights. Importation began 1999.

Mfg.'s Sug. Retail	$539	$470	$395	$350	$325	$295	$275	$250

SHOTGUNS: SxS

FIELD III — 12 or 20 ga., various chokes, boxlock action, single trigger. Disc.

	$350	$315	$285	$260	$230	$210	$195

FIELD HUNTER MODEL — 10, 12, 20, 28 ga., or .410 bore, boxlock action, 26, 28, 30 (12 ga. only), or 32 (10 ga. only) in. barrels, fixed or multi-chokes. Importation began 1997.

Mfg.'s Sug. Retail	$789	$680	$465	$395	$340	$295	$275	$260

Add $40 for 28 ga. or .410 bore.
Add $160 for 10 ga.
Add $120 for ejectors and multi-chokes (not available in 28 ga. or .410 bore).

SUPERIOR — 12 or 20 ga., boxlock action, various chokes, single trigger. Disc. 1985.

	$550	$470	$405	$345	$315	$280	$250

Last Mfg.'s Sug. Retail was $624.

SUPERIOR HUNTER — 12 ,20, or 28 (new 1999) ga., 26 or 28 in. barrels with fixed chokes. Importation began 1997.

Mfg.'s Sug. Retail	$999	$850	$750	$635	$550	$475	$395	$350

Add $50 for 28 ga.

LUXE MODEL — 12 (disc. 1991) or 20 ga., boxlock action, SST, ejectors, 26 in. barrels with choke tubes, checkered pistol grip walnut stock with semi-beavertail forearm, recoil pad. Imported 1990-94.

	$575	$450	$395	$350	$315	$285	$260

Last Mfg.'s Sug. Retail was $650.

This model was manufactured by Hermanos located in Spain.

EMPIRE HUNTER — 12, 20, or 28 (disc. 1998) ga., 26 or 28 in. barrels with fixed chokes. Importation began 1997.

Mfg.'s Sug. Retail	$1,299	$1,125	$950	$775	$675	$575	$475	$425

DIAMOND DL — 12, 20, 28 ga., or .410 bore, sidelock action with engraving and select checkered walnut stock and forearm, 26 or 28 in. barrels with fixed chokes. Importation began 1997.

Mfg.'s Sug. Retail	$6,749	$5,875	$4,850	$4,300	$3,750	$3,200	$2,750	$2,175

Add $300 for 28 ga. or .410 bore.

Grading	100%	98%	95%	90%	80%	70%	60%

DIAMOND REGENT DL — 12, 20, 28 ga., or .410 bore, sidelock action with best quality engraving and premium checkered walnut stock and forearm, 26 or 28 in. barrels with fixed chokes. Imported 1997 only.

	100%	98%	95%	90%	80%	70%	60%
	$18,950	$15,750	$13,250	$10,750	$8,900	$6,900	$5,600

Last Mfg.'s Sug. Retail was $21,659.

SHOTGUNS: SINGLE SHOT

COUNTRY SQUIRE FOLDING MODEL — .410 bore, choice of SxS or O/U folding action, gold DT, extractors, checkered walnut stock and forearm, 25½ in. F/F barrels. Importation began 1999.

Mfg.'s Sug. Retail	$479		$425	$375	$325	$285	$240	$200	$160

Add $480 for O/U configuration with VR barrels.

D

SHOTGUNS: SLIDE ACTION

FIELD HUNTER — 12 ga. only, 3 in. chamber, 24, 26, 28, or 30 in. VR barrel with multi-choke, synthetic stock and forearm, choice of standard wood/metal or 100% Advantage Camo coverage. Importation began 1999.

Mfg.'s Sug. Retail	$259		$225	$195	$180	$165	$155	$145	$135

Add $120 for Advantage Camo coverage.

* *Field Slug* — 12 ga. only, 18½ in. cyl. bore barrel with adj. sights, blue or nickel finish. Importation began 1999.

Mfg.'s Sug. Retail	$249		$225	$195	$180	$165	$150	$135	$125

Add $20 for nickel finish.

DAN ARMS OF AMERICA

Previous trademark of shotguns manufactured in Italy by Silma. Previously imported by Dan Arms of America located in Allentown, PA and by Dan Arms of North America (previously called Sportsman's Emporium Ltd.) located in Fort Washington, PA.

All shotguns listed below were discontinued in early 1988.

SHOTGUNS: O/U

LUX GRADE I — 12 or 20 ga., 3 in. Mag. chambers, 26, 28, or 30 in. barrels, vent rib, extractors, pistol grip, double trigger, European walnut.

	$280	$220	$210	$200	$190	$180	$170

Last Mfg.'s Sug. Retail was $350.

LUX GRADE II — 12 ga. only, 3 in. Mag. chambers, 26, 28, or 30 in. barrels, vent. rib, extractors, pistol grip, single trigger, European walnut.

	$320	$250	$240	$230	$215	$200	$190

Last Mfg.'s Sug. Retail was $395.

LUX GRADE III — 12 or 20 ga., 3 in. Mag. chambers, 26, 28, or 30 in. barrels, vent rib, ejectors, pistol grip, single trigger, checkered European walnut.

	$375	$300	$285	$270	$255	$240	$220

Last Mfg.'s Sug. Retail was $450.

LUX GRADE IV — 12 ga. only, 3 in. Mag. chambers, 28 in. barrels, vent. rib, ejectors, pistol grip, single trigger, checkered European walnut, multi-choked with 5 tubes.

	$460	$390	$350	$310	$285	$265	$245

Last Mfg.'s Sug. Retail was $550.

SKEET MODEL — 12 ga. only, 26½ in. barrels, 10mm vent. rib, anatomical pistol grip.

	$550	$450	$400	$355	$320	$300	$285

Last Mfg.'s Sug. Retail was $650.

Grading	100%	98%	95%	90%	80%	70%	60%

TRAP MODEL — 12 ga. only, 30 in. barrels, 10mm vent. rib, anatomical pistol grip.

	$550	$450	$400	$355	$320	$300	$285

Last Mfg.'s Sug. Retail was $650.

SILVERSNIPE — 12 or 20 ga., made to customer specifications, sideplates, select high grade walnut, name engraving upon request.

	$1,300	$1,200	$1,050	$900	$800	$700	$600

Last Mfg.'s Sug. Retail was $1,475.

SHOTGUNS: SxS

FIELD MODEL — 12, 16, 20, 28 ga., or .410 bore, double triggers, extractors, 26 or 28 in. barrels.

	$285	$220	$210	$200	$190	$180	$170

Last Mfg.'s Sug. Retail was $350.

DELUXE FIELD MODEL — 12 or 20 ga., single triggers, ejectors, 26 or 28 in. barrels.

	$440	$375	$340	$310	$290	$260	$230

Last Mfg.'s Sug. Retail was $500.

DARDICK

Previous manufacturer located in Hamden, CT.

PISTOLS: SEMI-AUTO

SERIES 1100 — .38 Dardick Tround cal., double action, 10 shot mag.

	$560	$420	$365	$310	$255	$225	$200

Dardick ammunition in itself is collectible - currently, individual rounds are selling in the $5-$10 range.

SERIES 1500 — .22, .30, or .38 Dardick Tround cal., double action.

	$875	$660	$570	$490	$440	$395	$350

Subtract 40% for .30 cal.

Note: carbine conversion units (.22 or .38 cal) add $175 — $400.

DARNE S.A.

Current manufacturer producing shotguns 1881-1979 and 1990 to date in Saint Etienne, France. Darne also began making double rifles circa 1996. Currently imported by The Drumming Stump, Inc. located in Circle Pines, MN beginning 1996. Previously imported by Wes Gilpin located in Dallas, TX until 1992.

CARABINE EXPRESS

DARNE

For F. Darne Fils Ainé please refer to the F Section. Also, please refer to the Bruchet section for 1982-1990 mfg. utilizing the Darne action.

RIFLES: DOUBLE

MODEL R EXPRESS SxS — 8x57 JRS or 9.3x74R cal., double rifle version of the Darne Model R Series shotgun, many options available, including style of rib, sights, stock configuration, etc. Importation began 1996.

Mfg.'s Sug. Retail	$11,995	$10,750	$9,000	$7,725	$6,350	$5,350	$4,300	$3,650

EXPRESS SUPERPOSEÉ — .30-06, 8x57 JRS, or 9.3.74R cal., double rifle version of the Darne O/U shotgun, boxlock with false sideplates, straight grip stock, many options available. Importation began 1996.

Mfg.'s Sug. Retail	$6,400	$5,825	$5,000	$4,250	$3,425	$2,850	$2,300	$1,950

Grading	100%	98%	95%	90%	80%	70%	60%

SHOTGUNS: SxS, PRE-1980 MFG.

DARNE SLIDING BREECH SHOTGUN — 12, 16, 20, or 28 ga., SxS, unique action utilizes sliding breech lock-up, high quality mfg., 27½ in. barrel standard with other lengths available, any choke combination, either straight grip or pistol grip stock, checkered, models differ in amount of engraving and grade of wood.

	100%	98%	95%	90%	80%	70%	60%
* Bird Hunter Model R11	$850	$700	$625	$550	$495	$440	$360
* Pheasant Hunter Model R15	$1,950	$1,750	$1,625	$1,500	$1,425	$1,300	$1,100
* Magnum Model R16	$1,500	$1,350	$1,250	$1,125	$1,000	$900	$800
* Quail Hunter Model V19	$2,950	$2,550	$2,250	$2,000	$1,800	$1,650	$1,500
* Model V22	$3,300	$3,000	$2,600	$2,300	$2,050	$1,850	$1,600
* Hors Series No. 1 Model V	$3,950	$3,575	$3,300	$3,080	$2,750	$2,200	$1,850

SHOTGUNS: 1989-CURRENT MFG.

In 1990, Paul Bruchet (the old Darne plant superintendent) obtained permission to once again use the Darne trademark. Hence, all 1990 and later mfg. has been produced by Paul Bruchet.

All new mfg. Darnes can be choked to the customer's choice. All models listed below have automatic ejectors, are oil finished by hand, and may be barreled to any length (except for Models R 11, 12, and 13). All prices are subject to change without notice.

O/U Models

SB1 — similar to SB3, traditional European O/U, DT, extractors, straight or semi-pistol grip stock. Importation began 1998.

		100%	98%	95%	90%	80%	70%	60%
Mfg.'s Sug. Retail	$2,700	$2,475	$2,000	$1,650	$1,450	$1,100	$950	$825

SB2 — similar to SB3, except has scroll engraving, wood upgrade, and 28 in. barrels. Importation began 1996.

		100%	98%	95%	90%	80%	70%	60%
Mfg.'s Sug. Retail	$3,500	$3,100	$2,400	$1,975	$1,625	$1,250	$1,000	$875

SB3 — 12 or 20 ga., scalloped boxlock action, extractors, 26 in. barrels, DTs, choice of English straight grip stock or semi-pistol grip. Importation began 1996.

		100%	98%	95%	90%	80%	70%	60%
Mfg.'s Sug. Retail	$4,600	$4,175	$2,900	$2,300	$1,925	$1,800	$1,650	$1,375

SxS Sliding Breech Models

R 11 — 12 or 16 ga., half pistol grip stock, light engraving.

		100%	98%	95%	90%	80%	70%	60%
Mfg.'s Sug. Retail	$4,500	$4,000	$2,825	$2,275	$1,925	$1,775	$1,650	$1,375

Add $437 for R 11 Slug (includes duck bill rib).

R 12 — similar to R 11, except with better engraving.

		100%	98%	95%	90%	80%	70%	60%
Mfg.'s Sug. Retail	$5,600	$5,000	$3,425	$2,675	$2,200	$1,900	$1,775	$1,650

R 13 — 12, 16, or 20 ga., straight or pistol grip stock, traditional action with bouquet engraving and obturator discs.

		100%	98%	95%	90%	80%	70%	60%
Mfg.'s Sug. Retail	$6,100	$5,600	$3,975	$3,175	$2,575	$2,200	$1,925	$1,760

R 14 — 12, 16, or 20 ga., slug gun, choice of forearms, light engraving, and optional cheek rest pistol grip stock is also available.

		100%	98%	95%	90%	80%	70%	60%
Mfg.'s Sug. Retail	$6,200	$5,675	$4,000	$3,175	$2,350	$2,000	$1,825	$1,675

Grading	100%	98%	95%	90%	80%	70%	60%

R 15 — 12, 16, 20, 24, 28 ga., or .410 bore, select walnut stock and forearm with fine checkering, large scroll engraving, obturator disks.

Mfg.'s Sug. Retail	$7,400		$6,625	$4,400	$3,500	$2,850	$2,400	$1,975	$1,825

R 16 — same as R 15, except has 3 in. chambers.

Mfg.'s Sug. Retail	$7,500		$6,700	$4,450	$3,525	$2,850	$2,400	$1,975	$1,825

R 17 — 12 (including Mag.), 16, 20, 24, 28 ga., or .410 bore., Magnum model (3 in. chambers), customer's choice engraving patterns, superior quality wood finish.

Mfg.'s Sug. Retail	$8,900		$8,100	$6,900	$5,900	$4,950	$3,625	$2,950	$2,575

V 19 — all gauges, easy opening large key action, top quality walnut and checkering, full coverage rose and scroll engraving with chiseled fences.

Mfg.'s Sug. Retail	$10,995		$9,925	$8,500	$7,300	$6,100	$5,150	$4,200	$3,150

V 20 — similar to V 19, except has deep relief rosace engraving and chiseled fences.

Mfg.'s Sug. Retail	$12,300		$10,975	$8,950	$7,600	$6,275	$5,350	$4,200	$3,150

V 21 — similar to V 19, except has 100% coverage English rose and scroll engraving and chiseled fences.

Mfg.'s Sug. Retail	$14,400		$12,750	$10,250	$8,650	$7,425	$6,150	$5,250	$4,200

V 22 — similar to V 21, except has 100% engraving coverage featuring bouquet patterns and deeply chiseled fences, sculpted shoulders, best quality walnut.

Mfg.'s Sug. Retail	$18,900		$16,750	$13,500	$11,000	$9,775	$8,500	$7,225	$6,000

VHS — all gauges, top-of-the-line model incorporating customers choice of engraving style, type of inlays, and checkering pattern, best quality wood. Due to the unique nature of this model, each specimen must be appraised individually. New guns are priced per individual customer order.

DAVID MILLER CO.

Current custom rifle manufacturer located in Tucson, AZ since 1973.

The David Miller Co. is a custom rifle maker fabricating best quality bolt action rifles only. All guns are essentially built per individual custom order and the company should be contacted directly for more information and price quotations. Currently manufactured D. Miller rifles feature the new Winchester Model 70 Super Grade action. Used rifles have to be appraised one-at-a-time to ascertain up-to-date values. Several of Mr. Miller's rifles have sold for over $100,000, and almost any feature(s) can be special ordered to produce a truly one-of-a-kind firearm.

DAVIDSON FIREARMS

Previously manufactured by Fabrica De Armas, located in Eibar, Spain.

SHOTGUNS: SxS

MODEL 63B — 12, 16, 20, 28 ga., or .410 bore, 25, 26, 28, or 30 in. barrels, Anson & Deeley boxlock, engraved and nickel plated frame, various chokes, walnut checkered stock. Mfg. 1963-disc.

		$275	$260	$220	$200	$175	$165	$155

* *Model 63B Magnum* — similar to 63B, except 10 ga. Mag., 12, or 20 ga. Mag., 32 in. barrel.

12 or 20 ga.		$360	$340	$310	$275	$230	$195	$165
10 ga.		$385	$370	$340	$305	$250	$220	$195

MODEL 69SL — 12 or 20 ga., true detachable sidelock action, engraved nickel plated action, 26 in. and 28 in. barrels, imp. cyl. and mod., mod. and full, checkered walnut stock. Mfg. 1963-1976.

		$415	$395	$375	$340	$320	$290	$260

Grading	100%	98%	95%	90%	80%	70%	60%

MODEL 73 STAGECOACH — 12 or 20 ga., detachable sidelock exposed hammers, 3 in. chambers, 20 in. mod. and full barrels, checkered walnut stock. Mfg. 1976-disc.

	$275	$260	$220	$200	$175	$165	$155

DAVIS INDUSTRIES

Current manufacturer located in Chino, CA since 1995. Previously located in Mira Loma, CA until 1995. Distributor sales only.

Davis Industries provides a lifetime warranty on all products.

DERRINGERS

D-SERIES DERRINGER — .22 LR, .22 Mag., .25 ACP, .32 ACP, .32 H&R Mag. (new 1995), .38 Spl. (new 1992), or 9mm Para. cal., O/U steel construction, 2.4 or 2¾ (.38 Spl. only) in. vent. rib barrel, 9½ or 11½ oz., black Teflon or chrome finish.

Mfg.'s Sug. Retail	$85		$65	$55	$45	$40	$35	$30	$30

Add $23 for Big-Bore series (larger frame) in .22 Mag., .32 H&R Mag., or .38 Spl. cal.
Add $29 for Long-Bore cals. (.22 Mag., .32 H&R Mag. - disc., .38 Spl., or 9mm Para.).

In this series, the .25 ACP cal. is the Model D-25 and the .32 ACP cal. is the Model D-32.

LONG BORE DERRINGER — .22 Mag., .32 H&R Mag. (disc. 1998), .38 Spl., or 9mm Para. cal., similar to D Series, except has 3¾ in. barrel, 13 oz. New 1995.

Mfg.'s Sug. Retail	$110		$95	$70	$60	$55	$45	$40	$35

PISTOLS: SEMI-AUTO

P-32 — .32 ACP cal., single action, 6 shot mag., 2.8 in. barrel, black Teflon or chrome finish, laminated wood grips, 22 oz. New 1987.

Mfg.'s Sug. Retail	$79		$70	$60	$50	$50	$40	$35	$35

P-380 — .380 ACP cal., single action, similar to P-32, 5 shot mag., 2.8 in. barrel, 22 oz., bright chrome or black Teflon finish, internal shock resister for recoil, wood (disc.) or black synthetic grips. New 1989.

Mfg.'s Sug. Retail	$87		$75	$65	$55	$50	$40	$35	$35

DEFOURNEY

Current long gun manufacturer located in Belgium.

Defourney specializes in both quality sidelock and boxlock (with or w/o sideplates) shotguns. Prices range from $750-$3,250 for boxlock shotguns and start in the $2,500 range for sidelock models, assuming 80% or better original condition.

DEMAS, ETS

Current manufacturer located in St. Etienne, France since 1967. No current importation.

Demas manufactures a full line of quality O/U and SxS rifles and shotguns. Prices vary according to configuration, engraving options, and quality of wood. Please contact the factory directly for current information and domestic prices.

DEMRO

Previous manufacturer located in Manchester, CT.

RIFLES: SEMI-AUTO

T.A.C. MODEL 1 RIFLE — .45 ACP or 9mm Luger cal., blow back operation, 16⅞ in. barrel, open bolt fire combination, lock-in receiver must be set to fire, also available in carbine model and fully auto.

	$595	$525	$475	$425	$395	$360	$330

Grading	100%	98%	95%	90%	80%	70%	60%

XF-7 WASP CARBINE — .45 ACP or 9mm Luger cal., blow back operation, 16⅞ in. barrel, also available in fully auto.

	$595	$525	$475	$425	$395	$360	$330

Add $45 for case.

DEPAR

Current manufacturer located in Istanbul, Turkey. No current importation.

Depar manufactures both semi-auto and O/U shotguns. Please contact the factory directly regarding potential importation of the models listed below and current pricing.

SHOTGUNS

ATAK O/U — 12 ga. only, 2¾ in. chambers, ejectors, SST. Available directly from the factory.

Mfg.'s Sug. Retail	$350	$350	$295	$250	$225	$200	$185	$170

Add $100 with scroll engraving and walnut stock and forearm.

ATILGAN SEMI-AUTO — 12 ga. only, 3 in. chamber, gas operated, includes multichokes. Available directly from the factory.

Mfg.'s Sug. Retail	$195	$170	$150	$135	$125	$115	$105	$95

* *Atilgan Semi-Auto De Luxe* — similar to Atilgan Semi-Auto, except has engraved receiver and deluxe walnut stock and forearm.

Mfg.'s Sug. Retail	$350	$350	$295	$250	$225	$200	$185	$170

SAFARI SLIDE ACTION — 12 ga. only, 3 in. chamber, synthetic stock standard. Available directly from the factory.

Mfg.'s Sug. Retail	$170	$170	$150	$135	$125	$115	$105	$95

Add $15 for walnut stock and forearm.
Add $75 for nickel chrome receiver finish and light scroll engraving.

DESERT INDUSTRIES, INC.

Previous manufacturer located in Las Vegas, NV 1991-96. See listing under Steel City Arms, Inc. for older models.

In 1990, Desert Industries, Inc. was created - this new company took over Steel City Arms, Inc. More recently manufactured guns will have the Las Vegas slide address.

PISTOLS: SEMI-AUTO

THE DOUBLE DEUCE — .22 LR cal., double action, 2½ in. barrel, matte stainless steel construction, 6 shot mag., rosewood grips, 15 oz. Mfg. 1991-96.

	$350	$295	$275	$250	$225	$200	$175

Last Mfg.'s Sug. Retail was $400.

TWO BIT SPECIAL — .25 ACP cal., double action, 2½ in. barrel, similar to Double Deuce, except has 5 shot mag., 15 oz. Mfg. 1991-96.

	$350	$295	$275	$250	$225	$200	$175

Last Mfg.'s Sug. Retail was $400.

DETONICS FIREARMS INDUSTRIES

Previous manufacturer located in Bellevue, WA 1976-1988. Detonics was sold in early 1988 to the New Detonics Manufacturing Corporation, a wholly owned subsidiary of "1045 Investors Group Limited".

Please refer to the New Detonics Manufacturing Corporation in the "N" section of this text for complete model listings of both companies.

DIARM S.A.

Previous manufacturing conglomerate (25 companies) located in Deba, Spain 1986-1989. Previously imported and distributed by American Arms, Inc. located in North

Kansas City, MO. Older Diarm models can be found under the American Arms, Inc. heading in this publication.

DOMINGO ACHA

Previous manufacturer located in Spain.

PISTOLS: SEMI-AUTO

LOOKING GLASS — .25 and .32 cal. auto pistol.

	100%	98%	95%	90%	80%	70%	60%
	$150	$125	$105	$85	$75	$60	$50

DOMINO, IGI

Previous Italian company absorbed during 1990 by FAS (see separate listing in F section). Previously imported by Mandall Shooting Supplies located in Scottsdale, AZ.

MODEL OP 601 MATCH PISTOL — .22 Short cal., 5 shot, 5.6 in. barrel, match sights, full target grips, vent barrel and slide to reduce recoil, adj. and removable trigger.

	$1,300	$1,000	$715	$635	$550	$495	$440

Last Mfg.'s Sug. Retail was $1,495.

MODEL SP 602 MATCH PISTOL — .22 LR cal., 5½ in. barrel, similar to 601, but .22 LR and slightly different trigger.

	$1,300	$1,100	$800	$700	$600	$550	$495

Last Mfg.'s Sug. Retail was $1,495.

DOWNSIZER CORPORATION

Current pistol manufacturer established in 1994, and located in Santee, CA. Dealer sales only.

DERRINGERS

MODEL WSP (WORLD'S SMALLEST PISTOL) — 9mm Para., .357 Mag., .357 Sig., .40 S&W, or .45 ACP cal., single shot pistol, tip-up 2.1 in. barrel with push button release, double action only, synthetic grips, stainless steel, overall size is smaller than a playing card, 11 oz. New 1997.

Mfg.'s Sug. Retail	$359		$300	$245	$195		

DREYSE PISTOL

Previously manufactured by Rheinische Metallwaren and Machinenfabrik, located in Sommerda, Germany.

PISTOLS: SEMI-AUTO

MODEL 1907 AUTOMATIC — 7.65mm/.32 ACP cal., 8 shot, 3½ in. barrel, blue, fixed sights, hard rubber grips. Mfg. 1907-1914.

	$250	$185	$150	$120	$95	$75	$50

MODEL 1910 — 9mm Para. cal., mfg. 1912-1915. Production estimated at 1,000 pistols, usually in 12xx or 13xx ser. no. range. Seldomly encountered.

	$6,500	$5,500	$4,500	$3,500	$2,500	$2,000	$1,500

VEST POCKET AUTOMATIC — .25 ACP cal., 6 shot, 2 in. barrel, blue, fixed sights, hard rubber grips. Mfg. 1912-1915.

	$325	$235	$150	$130	$100	$75	$65

D

DRILLINGS

A Drilling is a three-barrel combination gun (two shotgun barrels and a rifle barrel, vice versa, or three shotgun barrels). Normally, two triggers fire the shotgun barrels and one of them activates the rifle barrel when the barrel selector is moved forward (usually located on the upper tang). Most well made Drillings in above average condition are surprisingly accurate when using the rifle barrel(s).

Please refer to illustrations below depicting the most commonly encountered Drilling configurations.

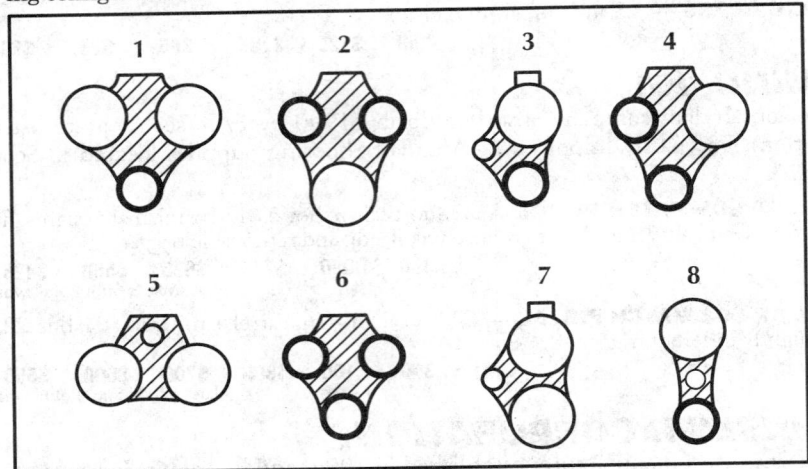

Drilling Illustration Explanations

Illustration No. 1 - Normal Drilling configuration with 2 shotgun barrels over a rimmed, centerfire rifle (most are 16 ga. x 16 ga. by either 9.3x72R or 8x57JR cal.).

Illustration No. 2 - Two rifle barrels over a shotgun. This configuration will normally command twice the price as No. 1. German designation is "Doppelbüchsdrilling".

Illustration No. 3 - Three barrels with no two being the same gauge or caliber. This configuration is very collectible, especially if the smallest caliber is .22 LR. Again, price will be double of No. 1.

Illustration No. 4 - Sometimes called a Bock Drilling with one shotgun and two rifle barrels. This variation brings a good premium over No. 1.

Illustration No. 5 - Rib Drilling with rifle caliber generally small (.22LR or .22 Hornet). German designation is "Schienendrilling".

Illustration No. 6 - Three shotgun barrels with the same gauge. This configuration is quite rare and healthy premiums are charged over No. 1.

Illustration No. 7 - A variation of No. 3, this configuration features shotgun O/U barrels with a rifle barrel on the side. German designation is "Bock-Doppelflinte mit seitlichem Kleinkaliberlauf".

Illustration No. 8 - Very unusual - a 3-barrel drilling in vertical design - 2 rifle barrels under a shotgun barrel. This configuration is seldomly encountered.

The following German nomenclatures apply as follows: single barrel rifle = Büchse; SxS double rifle = Doppelbüchse; O/U double rifle = Bock-Doppelbüchse; SxS double shotgun = Doppelflinte; O/U double shotgun = Bock-Doppelflinte; SxS double shotgun, rifle bbl. under = Drilling; SxS double shotgun, rifle bbl. on top = Schienendrilling; single shotgun, rifle bbl. under = Bock-Büchsflinte; single shotgun, rifle bbl. at side = Büchsflinte; single shotgun, rifle bbl. under and at side = Bock-Drilling; double rifle, shot bbl. under = Doppelbüchsdrilling; O/U double shotgun, rifle bbl. at side = Bock-Doppelflinte mit seitlichem Kleinkaliberlauf; SxS double shotgun, plus two rifle bbls. = Vierling.

Drilling History

For over 140 years Drillings have been the classic hunting gun of many European countries, especially Germany and Austria. Because a single hunting trip may require shooting both wildfowl and animals (often times within several hours), Europeans have long favored a single long-arm that could afford both rifle and shotgun shooting, be reliable, and not wear the hunter out while transporting it in the field. Americans, on the other hand, have not placed as much emphasis on this combination gun principle, and more often than not have chosen to buy both a rifle and shotgun for each specific hunting application. Since Drillings are becoming more popular, collectibility has improved in this country for those collectors who see the utility and functionality of these mostly hand assembled weapons. Very few Drillings manufactured before WWII are alike today in configuration and condition.

Drilling Calibers

Some people may be confused as to how the European metric calibers compare to domestic cartridges in terms of overall performance. This comparison has been added to assist you when contemplating what type of field performance, velocity, and killing power you can expect in these European calibers: 9.3x74 is similar to .375 Win. Mag., 9.3x72R is similar to .44 Mag. or .44-40 WCF, 8x57JRS is similar to .30-06, .30-30 Win. is 7.62x51R, 8x57JR is similar to .30-06, 7x65R is similar to .280 Rem., 7x57R is similar to .257 Roberts, 6.5x57R is similar to .243 Win., 5.6x52R is a .22 Savage Hi-Power, 5.6x34R is similar to .22 Hornet.

Drilling Values and Condition Factors

Rather than list the various manufacturers of Drillings (there are hundreds), it should be noted that guns with major trademarks and established provenances (i.e. Charles Daly, Colt Sauer, Ferlach addressed, Heym, Krieghoff, J.P. Sauer, Suhl addressed, etc.) will usually be more collectible than other lesser known brands - even if the quality of workmanship is similar. Some Drillings were assembled from manufactured parts by skilled and crafted gunsmiths and are sometimes better quality than factory specimens. Pre-war specimens are generally more desirable to collectors (even though less expensive than post-war variations) and to date, have outperformed post-war specimens in price appreciation. Many older pre-war specimens were designed for rimmed cartridges with lower breech pressures and should not be re-bored or reloaded for the "hotter" cartridges/loads available today. It should be noted that since Drillings are more complex than a typical shotgun, most of the manufacture has been done by hand - some guns have taken individual craftsmen over a year to fabricate! Ordering a new Drilling today would be a very expensive proposition, and buying a good used specimen will save you thousands of dollars (and maybe a year wait). For these reasons, many collectors feel Drillings today are under-priced since they can be purchased at a fraction of the cost for a new one (and may well be better quality also).

Condition is another major consideration - a gun that shows much use and is not operationally intact/correct may bring several thousand dollars less than another similar specimen showing little wear and excellent original finish (including the case colors).

Most above average condition boxlock Drillings in the above mentioned trademarks start in the $1,750 range and can go to $8,000 and higher if the configuration, features, and condition are all desirable. Average Drillings usually sell in the $1,500 - $2,000 range assuming worn condition, metric calibers and few features. For these reasons, Drillings have to be evaluated one at a time and a COMPETENT appraisal/evaluation should be procured before buying or selling a specimen.

Drillings with original claw-mounted scopes (rail-mount or swing-off) are worth 30-40% premiums.

Many post-war variations are valued for their hunting use only, and do not have the collectibility of the pre-war guns.

Features That Add Value To Drillings

Drillings with American calibers and smaller gauges will sometimes be more desirable (and expensive) than the European metric calibers (i.e. a gun configured 20 ga. x 20 ga. by .243 Win. will sell for more than a similar gun in 16 ga. x 16 ga. by 9.3 x 72R

Grading	100%	98%	95%	90%	80%	70%	60%

cal.). The most commonly encountered gauges and calibers are 16 ga. (most pre-war guns are chambered for 2⁹⁄₁₆ in.). In addition, a sidelock action will be more desirable than a boxlock, and a lot more expensive if the locks are also detachable.

Drilling aficionados will mention there are four main things to look for when contemplating a drilling purchase - beauty, condition, quality, and features. Features and embellishments become very critical in ascertaining Drilling values also - a gun with deep relief engraving, carved stock, claw mounts w/scope, buffalo horn trigger guard and butt plate, cocking indicators, two position front sight (i.e. night sight), middle set of express sights, adj. trigger, concealed upper tang peep sight, a non-Greener safety system, lightweight (under 6½ lbs.), separate rifle cocking, shotgun barrel inserts in .22LR or .22 Mag. cal. (approx. 8 or 11 in. long), cartridge trap, etc. is going to be A LOT more collectible than a plain-Jane hammer model with a loose action.

Features That Detract Value From Drillings

If it isn't beautiful, it probably won't sell. Beauty sells.

Observations On Drilling Collectibility

Condition determines whether a Nitro-proofed Drilling's value is comparable to its black powder or damascus barrel counterparts.

DRULOV

Previous handgun manufacturer located in north Bohemia.

PISTOLS: SINGLE SHOT

PAV — .22 LR cal., single shot, 9¾ in. barrel, all steel construction. Imported 1986 only.

	$95	$85	$75	$65	$60	$55	$50

Last Mfg.'s Sug. Retail was $105.

DRULOV 70 — .22 LR cal., single shot. Add $30 for set trigger. Disc. 1986.

	$105	$95	$85	$75	$70	$65	$60

Last Mfg.'s Sug. Retail was $115.

DRULOV 75 — .22 LR cal., single shot with set trigger & micrometer sights. Also available in left-hand. Importation disc. 1991.

	$300	$250	$215	$185	$155	$140	$120

Last Mfg.'s Sug. Retail was $349.

DRULOV 78 — .22 LR cal., similar to Drulov 75. Imported 1986 only.

	$275	$240	$200	$175	$150	$130	$110

Last Mfg.'s Sug. Retail was $180.

DUBIEL ARMS COMPANY

Previous manufacturer located in Sherman, TX. Dubiel Arms made custom bolt action rifles from 1973-approx. 1990.

RIFLES: BOLT ACTION

BOLT ACTION RIFLE — .22-250 Rem.-.458 Win. Mag. cals., custom made bolt action, barrel length and weight to order, no sights, Canjar trigger, all steel parts, custom made rifle stocks available in five styles. Disc.

	$2,000	$1,750	$1,500	$1,275	$1,125	$975	$825

Last Mfg.'s Sug. Retail was $2,500.

DUCKS UNLIMITED, INC.

National wildlife organization with headquarters located in Memphis, TN.

SHOTGUNS: DINNER GUNS (GUN-OF-THE-YEAR)

The makes and models listed below reflect "dinner guns" only. Dinner guns (Gun-of-the-Year) refer to those shotguns sold at the various annual banquets held by Ducks Unlimited chapters. Dinner guns do not have a retail price. Rather, banquet auction prices can vary substantially from chapter to chapter, as well as secondary market values.

MANUFACTURER	MODEL	QUANTITY	YEAR
Remington	Model 1100 12 ga.	500	1973
Remington	Model 870 12 ga.	600	1974
Winchester	Model 12 12 ga.	800	1975
Winchester	Model Super X-1 12 ga.	900	1976
Ithaca	Model 37 12 ga. (40th Ann'y)	1,125	1977
Ithaca	Model 51 12 ga.	1,250	1978
Weatherby	Model Patrician 12 ga.	1,600	1979
Weatherby	Model Centurion 12 ga.	2,000	1980
Remington	Model 1100 12 ga. Mag.	2,400	1981
Remington	Model 870 12 ga. Mag.	3,000	1982
Browning	Model B-80 12 ga.	3,400	1983
Browning	Model BPS 12 ga.	3,800	1984
Remington	Model 1100 12 ga.	4,500	1985
Beretta	Model A303 12 ga.	5,500	1986
Beretta	Model A303 20 ga.	3,500	1987
Browning	Model A5 12 ga. (50th Ann'y)	5,000	1987
Browning	Model A5 16 ga.	4,500	1988
Browning	Model A500 12 ga.	4,500	1989
Browning	Model A5 20 ga.	4,500	1990
Beretta	Model A390 12 ga.	4,200	1991
Franchi	Model Semi-Auto 12 ga.	4,200	1992
Winchester	Model 12 20 ga.	3,800	1993
Browning	Model A500R 12 ga.	3,300	1994
Browning	Model 12 Repro. 28 ga.	1,000	1995
Browning	Model BPS 12 ga.	3,500	1996
Browning	Model Gold Hunter	2,500	1997

This model commemorates DU's 60th anniversary.

Remington	Model 11-87 12 ga.	3,500	1998
Browning	Model BPS 20 ga.	3,500	1999

DUMOULIN, ERNEST S.P.R.L.

Current manufacturer located in Herstal, Belgium. Currently imported beginning 1998 by Armes De Chasse LLC, located in Hertford, NC. Previously imported and retailed on a very limited basis by Midwest Gun Sport located in Zebulon, NC until 1990 (formerly from Ellisville, MO.). Older importation was by Abercrombie & Fitch located in New York, NY.

Most Ernest Dumoulin drillings, rifles, and shotguns are essentially custom ordered firearms with a long list of options available which, in some cases, can easily double the values of models shown below. Because of this, these options are not listed individually.

Grading	100%	98%	95%	90%	80%	70%	60%

COMBINATION GUNS

EAGLE MODEL — O/U configuration (shotgun barrel on bottom), 12 or 20 ga., .22 Hornet, .222 Rem., .222 Rem. Mag., 6mm Rem., .243 Win., .25-06 Rem., .30-06, 6.5x57R, 7x57R, 8x57JRS, or 9.3x74R cal., boxlock action. 1989-disc.

$2,700 $2,400 $2,175 $1,850 $1,595 $1,400 $1,195
Last Mfg.'s Sug. Retail was $2,700.

RIFLES: BOLT ACTION

E. Dumoulin has had very limited importation since 1989. Beginning 1998, some bolt action models are once again being imported into the U.S.

BAVARIA DELUXE — .243 Win. through .458 Win. cals., 21½, 24, or 25½ in. octagonal barrel, French walnut stock with rosewood forend tip and pistol grip cap, no sights, custom made essentially with Sako (disc.) or Mauser action. Many engraving options available from $510-$1,900. Disc. 1985.

Series I

$995 $890 $775 $650 $575 $530 $460
Last Mfg.'s Sug. Retail was $1,080.

Add 15% for .375 H&H or .458 Win. Mag. cal.

RIFLE MOUSQUETON — .243 Win. through .338 Win. cals., 20 in. barrel, Mannlicher style, French walnut stock and pistol grip cap, no sights, custom made essentially with Sako or Mauser action. Many engraving options available from $510 - $1,900. Disc.

$720 $620 $560 $510 $470 $420 $360

CENTURION MODEL — .270 Win. through .458 Win. cals., 21½, 24, or 25½ in. barrels, French walnut stock with rosewood forearm tip and pistol grip cap, no sights, custom made essentially with Sako or Mauser action. Many engraving options available from $510 - $1,900. Importation disc. 1986.

$660 $590 $535 $480 $425 $390 $360
Last Mfg.'s Sug. Retail was $740.

CENTURION CLASSIC — standard cals. only, similar to Centurion, Mauser 98 action only and has better wood.

$1,525 $1,375 $1,175 $975 $800 $700 $600
Last Mfg.'s Sug. Retail was $1,525.

These models were also available in Mag. cals. that are divided into 4 groups — 1, 2, 3, and 4 Mag. Series. These options retailed in the $50 - $300 price range.

* *Diane* — grade up from Centurion Classic, 22 in. barrel, Mauser 98 action, M-70 safety, adj. steel trigger.

$1,450 $1,250 $1,000 $825 $700 $600 $500
Last Mfg.'s Sug. Retail was $1,450.

* *Amazone* — grade up from Diane, 20 in. barrel, full stock.

$1,750 $1,525 $1,325 $1,075 $865 $750 $600
Last Mfg.'s Sug. Retail was $1,750.

* *Bavaria Deluxe* — .243 Win. through .458 Win. cals., 21½, 24, or 25½ in. octagonal barrel, French walnut stock with rosewood forend tip and pistol grip cap, no sights, custom made essentially with Sako (disc.) or Mauser action. Many engraving options available from $510 - $1,900.

$1,900 $1,675 $1,450 $1,200 $995 $775 $650
Last Mfg.'s Sug. Retail was $1,900.

* *Safari* — Mag. cals. only.

$2,350 $1,775 $1,475 $1,200 $995 $775 $650
Last Mfg.'s Sug. Retail was $2,350.

MANNLICHER MODEL — various cals., Mauser type bolt action, full stocked. Disc. 1985.

$730 $660 $580 $520 $470 $430 $395
Last Mfg.'s Sug. Retail was $825.

Grading	100%	98%	95%	90%	80%	70%	60%

* ***Mannlicher Classic*** — similar to basic Mannlicher, except has better walnut. Disc. 1985.

| | $995 | $890 | $775 | $650 | $575 | $530 | $460 |

Last Mfg.'s Sug. Retail was $1,065.

MATCH MODEL — match target rifle, adj. sights and stock. Disc. 1985.

| | $1,640 | $1,490 | $1,300 | $1,050 | $900 | $800 | $700 |

Last Mfg.'s Sug. Retail was $1,860.

* ***Match NATO*** — 7.62 cal. match rifle. Disc. 1985.

| | $2,640 | $2,400 | $2,175 | $1,850 | $1,595 | $1,400 | $1,195 |

Last Mfg.'s Sug. Retail was $3,000.

ST. HUBERT MODEL — Sako action, various cals. and barrel lengths. Disc. 1985.

| | $1,900 | $1,700 | $1,495 | $1,300 | $1,150 | $995 | $850 |

Last Mfg.'s Sug. Retail was $2,125.

D

SAFARI SPORTSMAN — .416 Rigby, .375 H&H, .505 Gibbs, or .404 Jeffreys cal., Mauser 98 action, 4 shot mag., limited availability in 1986.

| | $4,000 | $3,550 | $3,250 | $2,800 | $2,400 | $2,000 | $1,750 |

Last Mfg.'s Sug. Retail was $4,000.

Add $300 for .505 Gibbs cal.

SAFARI PROFESSIONAL — various Mag. cals., prices below reflect rifle w/o engraving. Importation began 1999.

| Mfg.'s Sug. Retail | $9,919 | $9,100 | $8,150 | $7,400 | $6,500 | $5,500 | $4,500 | $3,750 |

AFRICAN PRO — similar to Safari Sportsman except has ebony or buffalo horn forend tip, tilting hood for the front sight, multiple folding rear sight.

| | $4,800 | $4,000 | $3,550 | $3,250 | $2,800 | $2,400 | $2,000 |

Last Mfg.'s Sug. Retail was $4,800.

GRAND CLASSIC — various cals., prices below reflect rifle w/o engraving. Importation began 1998.

| Mfg.'s Sug. Retail | $7,840 | $7,300 | $6,500 | $5,500 | $4,500 | $3,750 | $3,000 | $2,500 |

RIFLES: SxS

EUROPA I — .22 Hornet, .222 Rem., .222 Rem. Mag., 6mm Rem., .243 Win., .25-06 Rem., .30-06, 6.5x57R, 7x57R, 8x57JRS, or 9.3x74R cal., Anson & Deeley boxlock action, moderate engraving. 1989-disc.

| | $4,800 | $4,200 | $3,800 | $3,500 | $3,250 | $2,995 | $2,700 |

Last Mfg.'s Sug. Retail was $4,800.

CONTINENTAL I — same calibers as Europa I, sidelock action, 12 engraving options to choose from, many options available on special order. 1989-disc.

| | $8,600 | $7,700 | $6,995 | $6,400 | $5,600 | $4,750 | $4,150 |

Last Mfg.'s Sug. Retail was $8,600.

"PIONNIER" EXPRESS MODEL — assorted cals. from .22 Hornet through .600 Nitro Express, SxS configuration, heavily engraved, select walnut. Limited production, Anson & Deeley triple lock action, sideplates available at extra charge.

* ***P-I and P-II*** — English style scroll or bouquet (P-II) engraving.

| | $7,850 | $6,500 | $5,825 | $5,200 | $4,650 | $4,160 | $3,700 |

Last Mfg.'s Sug. Retail was $7,850.

Add $400 for P-II engraving.

* ***P III*** — English style lace engraving (tapestry style).

| | $8,640 | $7,750 | $7,000 | $6,400 | $5,600 | $4,750 | $4,150 |

Last Mfg.'s Sug. Retail was $8,640.

* ***P-IV through P-VIII*** — various styles of royal engraving with or without hunting scenes.

| | $9,100 | $7,995 | $7,450 | $6,800 | $6,000 | $5,000 | $4,350 |

Last Mfg.'s Sug. Retail was $9,100.

Add $400 for gold inlays.

Grading	100%	98%	95%	90%	80%	70%	60%

* **P-IX through P-XII** — Louis XVI style engraving.

$9,540 $8,600 $7,800 $7,250 $6,400 $5,250 $4,500
Last Mfg.'s Sug. Retail was $9,540.

* **Pionnier Magnum** — .338 Win. Mag., .375 H&H, .416 Rigby, .416 Hoffman, .458 Win. Mag., .577 Nitro Express, or .600 Nitro Express cal.. Boxlock action with Greener crossbolt.

$10,900 $9,400 $8,650 $7,800 $7,000 $6,450 $5,825
Last Mfg.'s Sug. Retail was $10,900.

PIONNIER RECENT IMPORTATION — .300 H&H, .300 Win. Mag., .338 Win. Mag., .375 H&H, .416 Rigby, .458 Win. Mag., or .470 NE cal., similar action as described above, prices below reflect rifle w/o engraving. Importation began 1999.

Mfg.'s Sug. Retail $16,195 $15,000 $12,250 $9,975 $8,200 $7,000 $6,000 $5,000

ARISTOCRATE MODEL — available in all cals. up to .375 H&H (also in 20 ga.), single shot action with low profile, exhibition oil finished walnut stock and forearm. Values below assume standard model (12 engraving options available). Imported 1987-1988 only.

$9,100 $8,450 $7,775 $7,000 $6,450 $5,825 $5,275
Last Mfg.'s Sug. Retail was $10,400.

PRESTIGE SIDELOCK — similar cals. as the Pionnier Model, best quality sidelock, triple locking, 10 different presentation options available, values below reflect standard model without options. Custom order only, 1 year waiting period. Mfg. began 1986.

Mfg.'s Sug. Retail $32,980 $29,000 $25,000 $21,750 $19,250 $16,250 $13,750 $11,000

FLEURON SIDELOCK — 6.5x57R, 7x57R, 7x65R, .30 Blaser, 8x57 JRS, 8x57 RS, or 9.3x74R cal., made per individual customer specifications. Importation began 1999.

Mfg.'s Sug. Retail $29,957 $26,000 $21,750 $19,250 $16,750 $14,000 $11,750 $9,975

SHOTGUNS: O/U

BOSS ROYAL SUPERPOSED — 12, 20 or 28 ga., full sidelock, exhibition grade walnut, double triggers, top-of-the-line quality, built to special order. Values listed assume standard gun (12 engraving options available). 1987-disc.

$18,500 $16,000 $13,750 $11,000 $9,775 $8,000 $6,950
Last Mfg.'s Sug. Retail was $18,500.

Add 6% for 28 ga.

SUPERPOSED EXPRESS "INTERNATIONAL" — O/U shotgun, includes extra set of rifle barrels, 20 ga., 7 choices of rifle cals., deluxe walnut. Elaborate engraving patterns available at extra charge, limited production. Disc. 1985.

$2,400 $2,000 $1,800 $1,575 $1,400 $1,200 $1,050
Last Mfg.'s Sug. Retail was $2,490.

SHOTGUNS: SxS

EUROPA MODEL — 12, 20, 28 ga., or .410 bore, Anson & Deeley boxlock action, single or double trigger, moderately engraved, oil finished stock and forearm, choice of 6 engraving options. 1989-disc.

$3,300 $2,750 $2,350 $2,000 $1,800 $1,575 $1,400
Last Mfg.'s Sug. Retail was $3,300.

LIEGE MODEL — 12, 16 (disc. 1986), 20, or 28 ga., Anson & Deeley locking action, elaborate engraving, deluxe walnut. 1986-disc.

* **Luxe Model**

$5,300 $4,600 $3,900 $3,300 $2,900 $2,600 $2,300
Last Mfg.'s Sug. Retail was $5,900 (disc. 1988).

Grading	100%	98%	95%	90%	80%	70%	60%

* Grand Luxe

$6,900 $6,000 $5,000 $4,300 $3,600 $3,200 $2,875
Last Mfg.'s Sug. Retail was $6,900.

Add 15% for 28 ga.
Add 15% for sideplates.

Many engraving options and other special order features can be added to the above models.

CONTINENTAL MODEL — 12, 20, 28 ga., or .410 bore, sidelock action, double or single trigger, deluxe oil finished walnut stock, choice of 6 engraving options. 1989-disc.

$7,400 $6,250 $5,200 $4,400 $3,700 $3,200 $2,875
Last Mfg.'s Sug. Retail was $7,400.

D

ETENDARD MODEL — 12, 20, 28 ga., or .410 bore, full sidelock, exhibition grade walnut, double triggers, top-of-the-line quality, built to special order. Values listed assume standard gun (many engraving options available). Mfg. began 1987.

Mfg.'s Sug. Retail $29,200 $25,750 $21,750 $19,250 $16,750 $14,000 $11,750 $9,975
Add $890 for 20, 28 ga. or .410 bore.

DUMOULIN, HENRI & FILS

Current manufacturer located in Herstal, Belgium. Imported and distributed by New England Arms, Co. located in Kittery Point, ME.

H. Dumoulin has manufactured quality firearms in Liege/Herstal, Belgium since 1947. They specialize in big-bore, high quality bolt action rifles, generally built on Mauser 98 or commercial Mauser actions, which have been used successfully on countless safaris. The improved Imperial Magnum action was developed and introduced in 1987.

RIFLES: BOLT ACTION

GRAND LUXE BOLT ACTION — .300 Wby. Mag., .338 Win. Mag., .375 H&H, .378 Wby. Mag., .404 Jeffrey, .416 Rigby, .460 Wby. Mag., or .505 Gibbs cal., 24, 25.6, or 26 in. barrel, European walnut stock with ebony forend tip and pistol grip cap, folding leaf sights with hooded front, custom made on the Dumoulin Imperial Magnum double square bridge action. Many engraving options available.

Mfg.'s Sug. Retail $7,000 $6,850 $6,200 $5,500 $4,950 $4,300 $3,600 $3,200
Add $500 for left hand action.
Add $850 for extended top and bottom tang.
Add $800 for claw mounts.
Add $700 for .505 Gibbs cal.

SOVEREIGN — available in same cals. as Grand Luxe Bolt Action, except with a higher quality finish, knurled bolt handles, gold inlayed lettering. Many engraving options available.

Pricing on this model depends on engraving, wood and other options. Imperial Magnum is also available in various stages of completion, barreled actions, actions in the white, etc. Please contact New England Arms, Co. directly for quotation.

RIFLES: CUSTOM

SxS BOXLOCK RIFLE — boxlock action, best quality double rifle, highly figured European walnut, finely hand checkered with standard scroll engraving. Custom ordered to customer's dimensions. Prices start at $12,000.

SxS SIDELOCK RIFLE — sidelock action, best quality hand detachable locks, top quality European walnut, finely hand checkered with standard scroll engraving. Additional engraving or deluxe wood quoted on request. Prices start at $15,000.

SHOTGUNS: CUSTOM

BOXLOCK MODEL — available in most ga.'s, individually built per customer special order. The importer should be contacted directly for more information and a price quotation.

SIDELOCK MODEL — available in most ga.'s, individually built per customer special order. The importer should be contacted directly for more information and a price quotation.

DUMOULIN HERSTAL S.A.

Current manufacturer established in 1997 and located in Herstal, Belgium. This manufacturer's sister company is Ernest Dumoulin S.P.R.L. Currently imported by Arms De Chasse, LLC, located in Hertford, NC.

Dumoulin Herstal manufactures a complete line of quality bolt action rifles in many configurations and calibers. They also produce their own A2000 LM (Long Magnum) action, based on the 1930s Mauser Oberndorf design, which is available separately. Please contact the factory directly regarding current information, including model availability and prices.

RIFLES: BOLT ACTION

The following models employ the A 2000 Dumoulin action featuring forged flat top receiver, 3 locking lugs with claw extractors, and one-piece bolt, handle, and knob.

ADVENTURER SERIES — various cals. from .25-06 Rem. - .458 Win. Mag., configurations include Euro 2000 and Euroforest. Importation began 1999.

Depending on variation and caliber, prices for this series range from $1,510 - $1,936.

GENTLEMAN HUNTER SERIES (LIEGE MODEL) — various cals. from .25-06 Rem. - .458 Win. Mag., including some additional Safari cals., configurations include Liege, Liege Safari, Liege Full Stock (Mannlicher), or Liege Thumbhole. Importation began 1999.

Depending on variation and caliber, prices for this series range from $2,368 - $3,268.

TRADITIONAL LIEGE CRAFTSMAN SERIES (HERSTAL MODEL) — various cals. from .25-06 Rem. - .458 Win. Mag., including many Safari cals., configurations include Herstal, Herstal Full Stock (Mannlicher), or Herstal Safari (5 shot mag.). Importation began 1999.

Depending on variation and caliber, prices for this series range from $3,232 - $5,053.

MODEL WHITE HUNTER SAFARI SPECIAL — .375 H&H, .416 Rigby, .416 Wby. Mag., .500 Jeffery, or .505 Gibbs cal., other cals. available upon request, this model features the proprietary Dumoulin Herstal A. 2000/LM (Long Magnum) action, hinged floorplate, express sights, deluxe checkered walnut stock with ebony forend. Importation began 1999.

Prices for this model start at $7,902.

E section

E.M.F. CO., INC.

Current importer and distributor located in Santa Ana, CA. Distributor and dealer sales.

Grading	100%	98%	95%	90%	80%	70%	60%

DERRINGERS: REPRODUCTIONS

STANDARD MODEL — .22 Short cal., copy of Colt Model Lord or Lady Derringer, blue, gold (disc.), or silver gold finish. Importation disc. 1992, but limited quantities remain.

	$95	$80	$70	$60	$55	$50	$45

Last Mfg.'s Sug. Retail was $125.

PISTOLS: REPRODUCTIONS

REMINGTON ROLLING BLOCK PISTOL — .357 Mag. cal., rolling block design. Disc. 1992.

	$300	$225	$185	$165	$155	$145	$135

Last Mfg.'s Sug. Retail was $395.

1875 REMINGTON OUTLAW — .357 Mag., .44-40 WCF, or .45 LC cal., copy of the Rem. Model 1875 SA, 5½ (disc.) or 7½ in. barrel only, case hardened frame, walnut grips, blue only. Mfg. by A. Uberti.

Mfg.'s Sug. Retail	$575	$395	$295	$200	$165	$155	$145	$135

Add $15 for steel trigger guard.
Add $160 for nickel plating (bright or satin).
Add $250 for engraving (disc.).
Add $85 for convertible cylinder (.45 LC/.45 ACP).

1890 REMINGTON POLICE SINGLE ACTION — .357 Mag., .44-40 WCF, or .45 LC cal., 5½ in. barrel, lanyard ring in buttstock, blue frame, walnut grips, mfg. by A. Uberti. New 1986.

Mfg.'s Sug. Retail	$590	$410	$300	$215	$175	$155	$145	$135

Add $10 for steel trigger guard.
Add $160 for nickel plating (bright or satin).
Add $85 for convertible cylinder (.45 LC/.45 ACP).
Add $260 for engraving.

SCHOFIELD MODEL — .45 LC cal., replica of the original S&W Schofield, choice of 5 (Wells Fargo) or 7 in. (Civilian) barrel, blue finish. Importation began 1999.

Mfg.'s Sug. Retail	$835	$695	$500	$425	$350	$325	$300	$275

RIFLES: SEMI-AUTO, REPRODUCTIONS

These models are authentic shooting reproductions previously mfg. in Italy.

AP 74 — .22 LR or .32 ACP cal., copy of the Colt AR-15, 15 shot mag., 20 in. barrel, 6¾ lbs. Importation disc. 1989.

	$295	$250	$200	$175	$155	$145	$135

Last Mfg.'s Sug. Retail was $295.

Add $25 for .32 cal.

* **Sporter Carbine** — .22 LR cal. only, wood sporter stock. Importation disc. 1989.

	$320	$275	$225	$195	$175	$160	$140

Last Mfg.'s Sug. Retail was $320.

Grading	100%	98%	95%	90%	80%	70%	60%

* **Paramilitary Paratrooper Carbine** — .22 LR cal. only, folding wire stock, black nylon on para-military design model. Importation disc. 1987.

	$260	$190	$175	$165	$155	$145	$135

Last Mfg.'s Sug. Retail was $325.

Add $10 for wood folding stock.

* **"Dressed" Military Model** — with Cyclops scope, Colt bayonet, sling, and bipod. Disc. 1986.

	$330	$265	$240	$220	$200	$185	$170

Last Mfg.'s Sug. Retail was $450.

GALIL — .22 LR cal. only, reproduction of the Israeli Galil. Importation disc. 1989.

	$295	$250	$200	$175	$155	$145	$135

Last Mfg.'s Sug. Retail was $295.

KALASHNIKOV AK-47 — .22 LR cal. only, reproduction of the Russian AK-47, semi-auto. Importation disc. 1989.

	$295	$250	$200	$175	$155	$145	$135

Last Mfg.'s Sug. Retail was $295.

FRENCH M.A.S. — .22 LR cal. only, reproduction of the French Bull-Pup Combat Rifle, with carrying handle, 29 shot mag. Importation disc. 1989.

	$320	$265	$240	$220	$200	$185	$170

Last Mfg.'s Sug. Retail was $320.

M1 CARBINE — .30 cal. only, copy of the U.S. Military M1 Carbine. Disc. 1985.

	$175	$150	$140	$130	$120	$110	$100

Last Mfg.'s Sug. Retail was $205.

Add $43 for Paratrooper variation.

RIFLES: REMINGTON REPRODUCTIONS

ROLLING BLOCK CARBINE — .45-70 Govt. cal., authentic reproduction of the Remington Rolling Block Carbine, 30 in. octagon barrel. Importation began 1991.

Mfg.'s Sug. Retail	$960	$725	$585	$450	$325	$250	$235	$220

BABY ROLLING BLOCK CARBINE — .357 Mag. cal. Mfg. 1992 only.

	$395	$300	$260	$220	$185	$160	$140

Last Mfg.'s Sug. Retail was $490.

REVOLVING CARBINE — .357 Mag. (disc.), .44-40 WCF (disc.), or .45 LC cal., 18 in. barrel, Model 1875 Army Single Action design, 5 lbs. Importation disc. 1995.

	$720	$550	$445	$325	$295	$260	$230

Last Mfg.'s Sug. Retail was $960.

TEXAS CARBINE (1858 REMINGTON) — .22 LR cal., action patterned after Remington revolving carbine, 21 in. octagon barrel, wood stock and forearm, brass frame. Also available with extra .22 Mag. cylinder. Importation disc. 1998.

	$295	$225	$175	$150	$135	$125	$110

Last Mfg.'s Sug. Retail was $400.

RIFLES: SHARPS REPRODUCTIONS

SHARPS SPORTING OR MILITARY RIFLE — .45-70 Govt. cal., copy of the Sharps Single Shot, 28 in. octagonal barrel, case hardened frame, single or double set triggers.

Mfg.'s Sug. Retail	$870	$660	$525	$425	$325	$295	$260	$230

Add $60 for blued Deluxe rifle with double set triggers.
Add $90 for browned Deluxe rifle with double set triggers.

An engraved version of this model is also available for $2,850, in addition to a Pedersoli Deluxe rifle variation for $1,600.

* **Carbine Model** — saddle ring carbine with 22 in. round barrel, single trigger.

Mfg.'s Sug. Retail	$870	$660	$525	$425	$325	$295	$260	$230

Grading	100%	98%	95%	90%	80%	70%	60%

RIFLES: WINCHESTER REPRODUCTIONS

DELUXE 1860 HENRY RIFLE — .44-40 WCF or .45 LC cal. only, deluxe walnut, reproduction of New Haven Arms Co.'s Henry Rifle, blued or white barrel. New 1987.

Mfg.'s Sug. Retail	$1,000	$825	$600	$450	$330	$295	$260	$230

Add $50 for white barrel.

* ***Engraved Henry Rifle*** — similar to deluxe Henry Rifle except has hand engraved receiver. Imported 1987-90.

	$1,350	$975	$700	$525	$400	$340	$295

Last Mfg.'s Sug. Retail was $1,598.

1866 YELLOWBOY CARBINE — .22 LR (disc.), .38 Spl., .44-40 WCF, or .45 LC (new 1993) cal., 19 in. barrel, saddle ring carbine, brass frame.

Mfg.'s Sug. Retail	$800	$600	$425	$335	$250	$235	$220	$200

* ***1866 Rifle*** — same cals. as 1866 Yellowboy Carbine, 20 (short rifle, new 1999) or 24¼ in. barrel.

Mfg.'s Sug. Retail	$800	$600	$425	$335	$250	$235	$220	$200

* ***Engraved Yellowboy Carbine*** — .38 Spl. or .44-40 WCF cal. Importation disc. 1990.

	$875	$575	$440	$330	$295	$260	$230

Last Mfg.'s Sug. Retail was $1,080.

1873 CARBINE — .22 Mag. (disc.), .32-20 WCF (new 1999), .357 Mag., .44-40 WCF, or .45 LC cal., 19 in. barrel, copy of the Winchester Model 1873, blued or case hardened receiver.

Mfg.'s Sug. Retail	$935	$750	$600	$450	$330	$295	$260	$230

* ***1873 Rifle*** — .32-20 WCF (new 1999), .357 Mag., .44-40 WCF, or .45 LC cal., 20 (short rifle, new 1999) or 24¼ in. barrel, case hardened receiver.

Mfg.'s Sug. Retail	$950	$765	$600	$450	$330	$295	$260	$230

* ***1873 "Young Boy" Carbine/Rifle*** — .22 LR cal., blued steel, 19 or or 24¼ in. barrel. Imported 1995-96.

	$800	$600	$450	$330	$295	$260	$230

Last Mfg.'s Sug. Retail was $1,050.

Add $50 for rifle barrel.

* ***Engraved Rifle*** — .357 Mag. or .44-40 WCF cal. only. Importation disc. 1987.

	$895	$635	$500	$450	$400	$360	$325

Last Mfg.'s Sug. Retail was $850.

PREMIER 1873 CARBINE & RIFLE — .45 LC cal., case hardened frame, uncheckered walnut stock and forearm, full mag., rifle has 24¼ in. barrel, carbine has 19 in. barrel. Imported 1988-1989 only.

	$850	$595	$450	$330	$295	$260	$230

Last Mfg.'s Sug. Retail was $1,160.

1885 HIGH WALL RIFLE — .45-70 Govt. cal., action patterned after the Winchester Model 1885 High Wall, 30 in. barrel, checkered walnut stock. Importation began 1998.

Mfg.'s Sug. Retail	$1,170	$895	$675	$550	$450	$375	$325	$295

1892 RIFLE — .44-40 WCF or .45 LC cal., action patterned after the Winchester Model 1892, case hardened receiver, 24 in. octagon barrel with buckhorn sights, standard stock with crescent buttplate and forearm. Importation began 1998.

Mfg.'s Sug. Retail	$835	$695	$595	$495	$395	$350	$325	$295

E

Grading	100%	98%	95%	90%	80%	70%	60%

84 GUN CO.

Previous manufacturer located in Eighty Four, PA. Circa early 1970s.

RIFLES: BOLT ACTION

CLASSIC RIFLE — various calibers. Grades 1-4.

	100%	98%	95%	90%	80%	70%	60%
Grade 1	$420	$315	$275	$235	$210	$190	$170
Grade 2	$780	$585	$512	$430	$390	$355	$315
Grade 3	$860	$645	$560	$475	$430	$390	$345
Grade 4	$1,580	$1,185	$1,030	$870	$790	$715	$640

LOBO RIFLE — various calibers. Grades standard, 1-4.

	100%	98%	95%	90%	80%	70%	60%
Standard	$415	$315	$270	$230	$210	$190	$170
Grade 1	$540	$405	$355	$300	$270	$245	$220
Grade 2	$795	$600	$520	$440	$400	$360	$320
Grade 3	$1,600	$1,200	$1,040	$880	$800	$720	$640
Grade 4	$2,350	$1,765	$1,530	$1,295	$1,175	$1,060	$940

PENNSYLVANIA RIFLE — various calibers. Grades standard, 1-4.

	100%	98%	95%	90%	80%	70%	60%
Standard	$420	$315	$275	$235	$210	$190	$170
Grade 1	$540	$405	$355	$300	$270	$245	$220
Grade 2	$795	$600	$520	$440	$400	$360	$320
Grade 3	$1,600	$1,200	$1,040	$880	$800	$720	$640
Grade 4	$2,350	$1,765	$1,530	$1,295	$1,175	$1,060	$940

EAGLE ARMS, INC.

Current division of ArmaLite, Inc., located in Geneseo, IL. During 1995, Eagle Arms, Inc. became a division of ArmaLite, Inc. Manufacture of pre-1995 Eagle Arms rifles was in Coal Valley, IL.

> During 1995, Eagle Arms, Inc. reintroduced the ArmaLite trademark. The new company was organized under the ArmaLite name and Eagle Arms is now a division of ArmaLite. Currently, all post-ban rifles manufactured after this merger are part of the new ArmaLite series.

RIFLES: SEMI-AUTO, DISC.

On the models listed below, A2 accessories include collapsible carbine type buttstock (disc. per 1994 C/B) and forward bolt assist mechanism, accessories are similar, except also have national match sights. The A2 suffix indicates rifle is supplied with carrying handle, A4 designates a flat-top receiver, some are equipped with a detachable carrying handle.

MODEL EA-15 E-1 RIFLE — .223 Rem. cal., patterned after the Colt AR-15A2, 20 in. barrel, forward bolt assist, 7 lbs. Mfg. 1990-1993.

100%	98%	95%	90%	80%	70%	60%
$750	$650	$575	$475	$400	$365	$325

Last Mfg.'s Sug. Retail was $800.

* **M15 A2 Carbine (EA9025C/EA9027C)** — features collapsible (disc. per C/B 1994) or fixed (new 1994) buttstock and 16 in. barrel, 5 lbs. 14 oz. Mfg. 1990-95.

100%	98%	95%	90%	80%	70%	60%
$795	$725	$600	$525	$450	$400	$375

Last Mfg.'s Sug. Retail was $870.

   1997 retail for the pre-ban models is $1,100 (EA9396).

   Beginning 1993, the A2 accessory kit became standard on this model.

* **M15 A2 H-BAR Rifle (EA9040C)** — features heavy Target barrel, 8 lbs. 14 oz., includes E-2 accessories. Mfg. 1990-95.

100%	98%	95%	90%	80%	70%	60%
$825	$725	$600	$525	$450	$400	$375

Last Mfg.'s Sug. Retail was $895.

   1997 retail for this pre-ban model is $1,100 (EA9200).

Grading	100%	98%	95%	90%	80%	70%	60%

* **M15 A4 Eagle Spirit (EA9055S)** — includes 16 in. premium air gauged national match barrel, fixed stock, full length tubular aluminum hand guard, designed for IPSC shooting, includes match grade accessories, 8 lbs. 6 oz. Mfg. 1993-95.

		$1,075	$875	$725	$600	$525	$450	$400

Last Mfg.'s Sug. Retail was $1,200.

The pre-ban variation of this model is sold out - 1995 retail was $1,475 (EA9603).

* **M15 A2 Golden Eagle (EA9049S)** — similar to M15 A2 H-BAR, except has (N.M.) National Match accessories, 20 in. extra heavy barrel, 12 lbs. 12 oz. Mfg 1991-95.

		$1,075	$875	$725	$600	$525	$450	$400

Last Mfg.'s Sug. Retail was $1,200.

1997 retail for this pre-ban model is $1,300 (EA9500).

* **M15 A4 Eagle Eye (EA9901)** — includes 24 in. free floating 1 in. barrel with tubular aluminum hand guard, weighted buttstock, designed for silhouette matches, 14 lbs. Mfg. 1993-95.

	$1,325	$1,075	$875	$725	$600	$525	$450

Last Mfg.'s Sug. Retail was $1,495.

* **M15 Action Master (EA9052S)** — match rifle, solid aluminum handguard tube that allows for free floating 20 in. barrel with compensator, N.M. accessories, fixed stock, 8 lbs. 5 oz. Mfg. 1992-95.

		$1,075	$875	$725	$600	$525	$450	$400

Last Mfg.'s Sug. Retail was $1,200.

The pre-ban variation of this model is sold out - 1995 retail was $1,475 (EA5600).

* **M15 A4 Special Purpose Rifle (EA9042C)** — 20 in. barrel, flat-top (A4) or detachable handle receiver. Disc. 1995.

	$850	$725	$600	$525	$450	$400	$375

Last Mfg.'s Sug. Retail was $955.

The pre-ban variation of this model is sold out - 1995 retail was $1,165 (EA9204).

* **M15 A4 Predator (EA9902)** — post-ban only, 18 in. barrel, National Match trigger, flat-top (A4) or detachable handle receiver. Mfg. 1995 only.

		$1,125	$895	$725	$600	$525	$450	$400

Last Mfg.'s Sug. Retail was $1,350.

EFFEBI SNC

Current manufacturer located in Concesio, Italy since 1994. Previously named Dr. Franco Beretta until 1994. Also refer to the Dr. Franco Beretta listing.

> To date, Effebi snc di F. Beretta & C. has had limited importation into the U.S. The manufacturer should be contacted directly (see Trademark Index) for more information regarding current pricing and shotgun model availability.

EGO ARMAS, S.A.

Current manufacturer located in Eibar, Spain. No current U.S. importation.

> Ego Armas manufactures high quality sidelock double rifles ranging in price from $4,000-$14,000. Calibers include .375 H&H and .416 Rigby in their high quality deluxe models. Mounted scopes are also available. Boxlock and sidelock shotguns are also available ranging in price from $400-$4,000. More information, including current models and approximate U.S. pricing, can be obtained by contacting this manufacturer directly (see Trademark Index).

Grading	100%	98%	95%	90%	80%	70%	60%

ENFIELD

Previously manufactured by the Royal Small Arms Factory, located in Middlesex, England.

REVOLVERS

NO. 2 MK. I REVOLVER — .380 British Service (based on .38 S&W with a 200 grain bullet) cal., double action, 6 shot, 5 in. barrel, fixed sights, blue, composition grips, top break, issued to British army 1932.

	$235	$195	$175	$140	$130	$120	$110

RIFLES: BOLT ACTION

SMLE stands for Rifle, Short, Magazine, Lee-Enfield. The SMLE rifles served the British Military from 1902-1954.

NO. 1 MK. III SMLE — .303 British cal., bolt action, 10 shot mag., 25.2 in. barrel, open sights, long range volley sights, magazine cut-off, adopted by British Army in 1907.

	$225	$190	$150	$125	$100	$90	$75

NO. 1 MK. III SMLE — a simplified rifle adopted by the British during WWI, volley sights and magazine cut-off deleted, the most common variation of SMLE.

	$225	$190	$150	$125	$100	$90	$75

NO. 2 MK. IV — .22 LR cal., single shot, recently imported from Australia.

	$495	$425	$375	$315	$260	$215	$160

NO. 3 MK. I PATTERN 14 RIFLE — .303 British cal., modified Mauser type bolt action, issued as substitute standard by British Army during WWI, manufactured in U.S. (the later U.S. 1917 Enfield is identical except for caliber and sights).

	$225	$190	$150	$125	$100	$90	$75

NO. 3 MK. I — .22 LR cal., single shot military training model.

	$350	$300	$275	$250	$225	$200	$175

NO. 4 MK. I — an improved SMLE with aperture rear sight, stronger receiver and more easily manufactured parts, adopted in 1939 by the British Army.

	$215	$185	$145	$120	$95	$75	$55

This model was manufactured during WWII in Canada, England, and the U.S. To determine which armory manufactured this model, the following information should be studied. Savage-Stevens mfg. is denoted by "US Property S" with a C in ser. no., Canadian mfg. (Long Branch, Ontario) is indicated by "Long Branch" - no code, British mfg. was by B.S.A., Shirley and marked "M.47C"., Royal Ordnance Factory (near Liverpool) marked "ROF(F)", or Royal Ordnance Factory (near Sheffield) marked "ROFM" or "RM" or "M".

* *No. 4 Mark I T Sniper Model* — with or w/o scope, with or w/o case.

	100%	98%	95%	90%	80%	70%	60%
Gun w/o scope	$575	$495	$450	$385	$315	$285	$260
Gun with scope	$1,425	$1,275	$1,075	$950	$875	$825	$750

Add $175-$225 for case, depending on condition.

NO. 5 MK. I JUNGLE CARBINE — .303 British cal., a shorter, lighter version of the No. 4 MK. I with a 20.5 in. barrel, flash hider, recoil pad and shortened forend and hand guard, 7.2 lbs., developed during WWII.

	$350	$275	$200	$150	$125	$100	$85

ENFIELD AMERICA, INC.

Previous manufacturer located in Atlanta, GA.

Grading	100%	98%	95%	90%	80%	70%	60%

PISTOLS: SEMI-AUTO

MP-9 — 9mm Para. cal., paramilitary design, similar to MP-45. Mfg. 1985.

	$550	$475	$425	$350	$295	$260	$240

Add $150 for carbine kit.

MP-45 — .45 ACP cal., paramilitary design, 4½, 6, 8, 10, or 18½ in. shrouded barrel, parkerized finish, 10, 30, 40, or 50 shot mag., 6 lbs. Mfg. 1985 only.

	$550	$475	$425	$350	$295	$260	$240

Last Mfg.'s Sug. Retail was $350.

ENTRÉPRISE ARMS INC.

Current manufacturer of pistols and related components located in Irwindale, CA, since 1996. Dealer sales only.

PISTOLS: SEMI-AUTO

The models listed below are patterned after the Colt M1911, but have "Widebody" frames.

ELITE SERIES — .45 ACP cal., 3¼ in. barrel, features steel 1911 Widebody frame, flat mainspring housing, flared ejection port, 10 shot mag., bead blasted black oxide finish, tactical sights, 36 oz. New 1997.

* **Elite P325**

Mfg.'s Sug. Retail	$740	$660	$565	$500	$450	$400	$360	$330

* **Elite P425** — similar to Elite P325, except has 4¼ in. barrel, 38 oz. New 1997.

Mfg.'s Sug. Retail	$740	$660	$565	$500	$450	$400	$360	$330

* **Elite P500** — similar to Elite P325, except has 5 in. barrel, 40 oz. New 1997.

Mfg.'s Sug. Retail	$740	$660	$565	$500	$450	$400	$360	$330

TACTICAL SERIES — .45 ACP cal., 3¼ in. barrel, features Tactical Widebody with "De-horned" slide and frame allowing snag-free carry, narrow ambidextrous thumb safety, 10 shot mag., low profile Novak or ghost ring sights, squared trigger guard, flat main spring housing, matte black oxide finish, 36 oz. New 1997.

* **Tactical P325**

Mfg.'s Sug. Retail	$979	$875	$750	$650	$575	$500	$450	$395

➤ **Tactical P325 Plus** — similar to P325, except has short officer's length slide/barrel fitted onto a full government frame, designed as concealed carry pistol. New 1998.

Mfg.'s Sug. Retail	$1,049	$925	$825	$725	$650	$575	$500	$450

* **Tactical P425** — similar to Tactical P325, except has 4¼ in. barrel, 38 oz. New 1997.

Mfg.'s Sug. Retail	$979	$875	$750	$650	$575	$500	$450	$395

* **Tactical P500** — similar to Tactical P325, except has 5 in. barrel, 40 oz. New 1997.

Mfg.'s Sug. Retail	$979	$875	$750	$650	$575	$500	$450	$395

MEDALIST SERIES (TITLEIST, P500 NATIONAL MATCH) — .40 S&W or .45 ACP cal., 5 in. barrel, features tighter tolerances and numerous custom features, 10 shot mag., front and rear slide serrations, blued slide, includes Bo-Mar low mount rear adj. sight, 40 oz. New 1997.

Mfg.'s Sug. Retail	$979	$875	$750	$675	$575	$525	$475	$425

Add $120 for .40 S&W cal.

During 1999, this model's nomenclature changed from the Titleist Series to the Medalist Series.

Grading	100%	98%	95%	90%	80%	70%	60%

BOXER SERIES — similar to Titleist Series, except has fully machined "high mass" and flat-top slide. New 1998.

Mfg.'s Sug. Retail	$1,099	$950	$875	$750	$675	$575	$525	$475

TOURNAMENT SHOOTER MODEL (TSM I-III) — .40 S&W or .45 ACP cal., 5, 5½ (TSM III only), or 6 (.45 ACP only) in. barrel, blued finish, designed for IPSC competition, 10 shot mag., TSM II is standard, 40-44 oz. New 1997.

Mfg.'s Sug. Retail	$2,000	$1,800	$1,550	$1,325	$1,100	$950	$875	$750

Add $300 for TSM I.
Add $700 for TSM III.

ERA

Previous manufacturer located in Brazil.

SHOTGUNS

ERA O/U — 12 or 20 ga., 28 in. vent. rib barrel, full and mod., double triggers, extractors, checkered hardwood stock.

	$275	$250	$225	$200	$170	$150	$125
Trap version	$300	$275	$250	$225	$200	$175	$150
Skeet version	$300	$275	$250	$225	$200	$175	$150

ERA SxS — 12, 20 ga., or .410 bore, 26, 28, or 30 in. barrels, various chokes, double triggers, extractors, checkered pistol grip stock.

	$165	$150	$135	$125	$110	$100	$85

ERA RIOT SxS MODEL — 12 or 20 ga., similar to Double Barrel, 18 in. barrel.

	$185	$175	$150	$140	$125	$110	$95

ERA QUAIL SxS MODEL — 12 or 20 ga., similar to Standard, 20 in. barrel.

	$185	$175	$150	$140	$125	$110	$95

ERMA SUHL, GmbH

Current manufacturer located in Suhl, Germany, since January 1998. During this time, Erma Suhl purchased the remaining assets from Erma-Werke, and production was once again resumed. As this edition went to press, U.S. importation had still not been formalized, but it is likely that U.S. distribution will remain similar to Erma-Werke's previous policy.

RIFLES: BOLT ACTION

SR100 SNIPER RIFLE — .300 Win. Mag., .308 Win., or .338 Lapua Mag. cal., bolt action, tactical rifle featuring brown laminated wood stock with thumbhole, adj. buttplate/cheek-piece, and vent. forend, forged aluminum receiver, 25½ or 29½ in. barrel, muzzle brake, adj. match trigger, approx. 15 lbs. Imported 1997 only.

Mfg.'s Sug. Retail	$8,600	$8,175	$7,250	$6,600	$5,800	$5,000	$4,200	$3,300

This model is imported exclusively by Amtec 2000, Inc., located in Gardner, MA.

ERMA-WERKE

Previous manufacturer located in Dachau, Germany (Erma-Werke production) until bankruptcy occured in October of 1997. Pistols were previously imported and distributed by Precision Sales International, Inc. located in Westfield, MA, Nygord Precision Products located in Prescott, AZ and Mandall's Shooting Supplies, Inc. located in Scottsdale, AZ. Previously distributed by Excam located in Hialeah, FL.

Grading	100%	98%	95%	90%	80%	70%	60%

Erma-Werke also manufactured private label handguns for American Arms Inc. (refer to their section for listings).

PISTOLS: SEMI-AUTO

MODEL LA 22 — .22 LR cal., action patterned after the Luger, mfg. 1964-1967.

	$395	$335	$275	$240	$200	$175	$140

ERMA KGP68A/BEEMAN MP-08 — .32 ACP or .380 ACP cal., Luger type toggle action, 3½ (Beeman) or 4 in. barrel, 6 shot mag., blue, 1.4 lbs. Mfg. 1968-disc.

	$450	$400	$335	$275	$240	$185	$145

Last Mfg.'s Sug. Retail was $500.

This model was imported exclusively by Mandall's Shooting Supplies, Inc. located in Scottsdale, AZ. From 1988-90, Beeman took over importation of this model in .380 ACP cal. only with new Luger style checkered walnut grips and 3½ in. barrel. Previous models had plastic grips.

ERMA KGP69/BEEMAN P-08 — .22 LR cal., Luger type toggle action, 8 shot mag., 3¾ in. barrel, blue, plastic (disc.) or checkered walnut grips. Mfg. 1969-disc.

	$335	$275	$240	$185	$145	$115	$95

Last Mfg.'s Sug. Retail was $390.

Beeman was the sole importer of this model between 1988-90.

MODEL ESP 85A SPORT/MATCH PISTOL — .22 LR or .32 S&W Long Wadcutter cal., blow back semi-auto, 6 in. barrel, 5 or 8 (.32 S&W only) shot mag., choice of sporting or adj. stippled match grips with thumbrest, fully adj. and interchangeable sights, gun is supplied with 1 extra weight, extra mag., sights, disassembly tools, and attache style case ($134 option) with foam rubber cut-outs, 2½ lbs. Imported 1989-1997.

	$1,500	$975	$800	$650	$550	$495	$450

Last Mfg.'s Sug. Retail was $1,785.

Subtract $315 for Junior Model.
Add $215 for .32 S&W cal.
Add $110 for Match Model (with anatomical grips).
Add $980-$1,390 for conversion unit.
Add approx. $215 for chrome finish.
Add $24 for left-hand action (Match Model only - disc. 1994).

ESP 85 refers to Junior Model (new 1995). The ESP 85 series was distributed by Precision Sales International, Inc. and Mandall Shooting Supplies, Inc.

* ***Model ESP 85A Complete Set*** — includes both .22 LR and .32 S&W Long Wadcutter barrels and mags., cased with accessories, complete set was disc. 1991.

	$1,775	$1,525	$1,350	$1,125	$950	$825	$750

Last Mfg.'s Sug. Retail was $1,995.

ET-22 LUGER CARBINE — .22 LR cal., 11¾ in. barrel, blue rear ramp sight, checkered walnut grips and uncheckered forearm, adj. artillery type rear sight, rarely seen.

	$425	$365	$330	$275	$240	$200	$175

Add 20% for leatherette case.

REVOLVERS: DOUBLE ACTION

These models were distributed by Precision Sales International, Inc. only.

ER-772 STANDARD/MATCH — .22 LR cal., standard or match gun with special adj. contoured grips with stippling, 6 in. barrel, action similar to ER-777, fully adj. and extended rear sight, interchangeable front sight, 3 lbs. Imported 1990-94.

	$1,100	$875	$725	$625	$550	$495	$450

Last Mfg.'s Sug. Retail was $1,371.

ER-773 STANDARD/MATCH — .32 S&W Long Wadcutter cal., otherwise similar to ER-772 Match, 2.9 lbs. Imported 1990-95.

	$925	$825	$695	$525	$475	$425	$385

Last Mfg.'s Sug. Retail was $1,068.

Grading	100%	98%	95%	90%	80%	70%	60%

ER-777 STANDARD — .357 Mag. cal., 6 shot, 4 or 5½ in. barrel, solid rib and full barrel shroud, adj. target rear sight, blued steel, checkered sport grips, 2¾ lbs. Imported 1990-95.

| | | $875 | $775 | $650 | $475 | $425 | $385 | $350 |

Last Mfg.'s Sug. Retail was $1,019.

RIFLES

Models listed below were available from Mandall Shooting Supplies, unless otherwise noted.

EM1 .22 CARBINE — .22 LR cal., M1 copy, 10 or 15 shot mag., 18 in. barrel, rear adj. aperature sight, 5.6 lbs. Mfg. 1966-1997.

| $365 | $295 | $250 | $215 | $190 | $175 | $160 |

Last Mfg.'s Sug. Retail was $400.

EGM-1 — similar to EM1 except for unslotted buttstock, 5 shot mag.

| $260 | $230 | $195 | $175 | $150 | $125 | $100 |

Last Mfg.'s Sug. Retail was $295.

EG72 PUMP — .22 LR cal., outside hammer, 15 shot mag., 18½ in. barrel. Mfg. 1970-1976.

| $125 | $95 | $90 | $75 | $70 | $65 | $60 |

EG712 LEVER-ACTION — .22 LR cal., Win. Model 94 copy, tube mag., 18½ in. barrel. Mfg. 1976-1997.

| $260 | $230 | $195 | $175 | $150 | $125 | $100 |

Last Mfg.'s Sug. Retail was $295.

EG-73 — .22 Mag. cal., similar to EG712 12 shot mag. Mfg. 1973-1997.

| $265 | $230 | $195 | $175 | $150 | $125 | $100 |

Last Mfg.'s Sug. Retail was $300.

EUROARMS OF AMERICA

Current black powder manufacturer/importer/distributor located in Winchester, VA.

Euroarms imported a variety of revolvers and rifles mfg. by Armi San Paolo between 1970-1996. Values are currently in the $135-$835 range, depending on configuration and condition.

EUROPEAN AMERICAN ARMORY CORP.

Current importer and distributor located in Sharpes, FL beginning late 1990. Distributor and dealer sales.

EUROPEAN AMERICAN ARMORY

EAA currently imports their handguns from Tanfoglio, located in Italy and from H. Weihrauch, located in Germany. All guns are covered by EAA's lifetime limited warranty.

PISTOLS: SEMI-AUTO, EUROPEAN SERIES

MODEL EA220 — .22 LR cal., 3.88 in. barrel, 10 shot mag., single action, steel frame, 26 oz., blue, chrome or blue/chrome, wood grips. Importation disc. 1992.

| $185 | $150 | $120 | $100 | $95 | · $85 | $75 |

Last Mfg.'s Sug. Retail was $225.

Add approx. $20 for chrome or blue/chrome finish.

MODEL EA22-T — .22 LR cal., 6 in. barrel, 12 shot mag., single action, steel frame, target model, 40 oz. Imported 1991-1993.

| $375 | $295 | $260 | $220 | $185 | $165 | $150 |

Last Mfg.'s Sug. Retail was $450.

Grading	100%	98%	95%	90%	80%	70%	60%

EUROPEAN 32 (320) — .32 ACP cal., 3.88 in. barrel, 7 shot mag., single action, steel frame, 26 oz., blue, chrome or blue/chrome, wood grips. Importation 1991-95.

	$130	$110	$95	$85	$80	$75	$70

Last Mfg.'s Sug. Retail was $161.

Add $14 for chrome finish.

EUROPEAN 380 — .380 ACP cal., single (new 1994) or double (disc. 1994) action, $3\frac{7}{8}$ in. barrel, blue, brushed chrome (disc. 1996), Wonder finish (new 1997), matte blue/chrome (disc. 1993), or blue/gold plated Duo-Tone (European Lady, disc. 1995) finish, 7 shot bottom release mag., steel construction, firing pin safety, external hammer, smooth wood or ivory rose polymer (European Lady) grips, 26 oz. Importation began 1992.

Mfg.'s Sug. Retail	$140	$115	$95	$85	$80	$75	$70	$65

Add $31 for Wonder finish (new 1997).
Add $67 for European Lady model (disc. 1995).
Add $32 for double action design (disc. 1994).
Add $14 for brushed chrome or matte blue/chrome (disc. 1993) finish.

This model employs a unique patented magazine gun lock system.

PISTOLS: SEMI-AUTO, WITNESS SERIES

EA 38 SUPER SERIES — .38 Super cal., action patterned after the CZ-75, selective double action, $4\frac{1}{2}$ in. barrel, steel or polymer frame/steel slide (new 1997), 10 (C/B 1994) or 19★ shot mag., choice of Wonder (heat treated grey satin finish, new 1997), stainless steel (disc. 1996) or blue, blue/chrome (disc. 1994), or brushed chrome (disc. 1996) finish, combat sights, black neoprene grips, 33 oz. Importation began 1994.

Mfg.'s Sug. Retail	$351	$300	$260	$225	$210	$195	$185	$180

Subtract $8 for polymer frame.
Add $17 for Wonder finish.

* *Model EA 38 Stainless* — similar to EA 38, except is stainless steel. Imported 1994-96.

	$525	$435	$350

Last Mfg.'s Sug. Retail was $595.

* *Model EA 38 Compact* — similar to EA 38 Super Series, except has $3\frac{5}{8}$ in. barrel, choice of matte blue or Wonder finish, 30 oz. New 1999.

Mfg.'s Sug. Retail	$351	$300	$260	$225	$210	$195	$185	$180

Subtract $8 for polymer frame.
Add $16 for Wonder finish or ported barrel (polymer frame only).

EA 9 SERIES — 9mm Para. cal., action patterned after the CZ-75, selective double action, $4\frac{1}{2}$ in. barrel, steel or polymer frame/steel slide (new 1997), 10 (C/B 1994) or 16★ shot mag., choice of Wonder (new 1997), stainless steel (disc. 1996) or blue, blue/chrome (disc. 1993), or brushed chrome (disc. 1996) finish, combat sights, black neoprene grips, 33 oz. Importation began late 1990.

Mfg.'s Sug. Retail	$351	$310	$275	$235	$215	$200	$190	$180

Subtract $8 for polymer frame.
Add $16 for Wonder finish.

* *Model EA 9 Stainless* — similar to EA 9, except is stainless steel. Imported 1992-96.

	$420	$350	$295

Last Mfg.'s Sug. Retail was $480.

* *Model EA 9 (L) Compact* — similar to EA 9, except has $3\frac{5}{8}$ in. barrel and 10 (C/B 1994) or 13★ shot mag.

Mfg.'s Sug. Retail	$351	$310	$275	$235	$215	$200	$190	$180

Subtract $8 for polymer frame.
Add $16 for Wonder finish or ported barrel (polymer frame only).

Grading	100%	98%	95%	90%	80%	70%	60%

EA 40 SERIES — .40 S&W cal., action patterned after the CZ-75, selective double action, 4½ in. barrel, steel or polymer frame/steel slide (new 1997), 10 (C/B 1994) or 12★ shot mag., choice of Wonder (new 1997), stainless steel (disc. 1996) or blue, blue/chrome (disc.), or brushed chrome (disc. 1996) finish, combat sights, black neoprene grips, 33 oz. Importation began late 1990.

Mfg.'s Sug. Retail	$351	$310	$275	$235	$215	$200	$190	$180

Subtract $8 for polymer frame.
Add $16 for Wonder finish.

* **Model EA 40 Stainless** — similar to EA 40, except is stainless steel. Imported 1992-96.

	$455	$365	$295

Last Mfg.'s Sug. Retail was $509.

* **Model EA 40 (L) Compact** — similar to EA 40, except has 3⅝ in. barrel and 9 shot mag.

Mfg.'s Sug. Retail	$351	$310	$275	$235	$215	$200	$190	$180

Subtract $8 for polymer frame.
Add $16 for Wonder finish or ported barrel (polymer frame only).

EA 10 SUPER SERIES — 10mm cal., action patterned after the CZ-75, selective double action, 4½ in. barrel, steel frame, 10 or 12★ shot mag., choice of stainless steel (disc.), blue, chrome (disc.), or Wonder (new 1999) finish, combat sights, black neoprene grips, 33 oz. Imported 1994 only, resumed 1999.

Mfg.'s Sug. Retail	$359	$315	$280	$240	$215	$200	$190	$180

Add $16 for Wonder finish.
Add $30 for chrome finish (disc.).
Add $65 for stainless steel (disc.).

* **Model EA 10 Stainless** — similar to EA 10, except is stainless steel.

	$495	$425	$350

Last Mfg.'s Sug. Retail was $566.

* **Model EA 10 Carry Comp** — similar to EA 10, except has 4½ in. compensated barrel, blue finish only. New 1999.

Mfg.'s Sug. Retail	$398	$345	$300	$250	$225	$200	$190	$180

* **Model EA 10 Compact** — similar to EA 10, except has 3⅝ in. barrel and 8 shot mag.

Mfg.'s Sug. Retail	$359	$315	$280	$240	$215	$200	$190	$180

Add $16 for Wonder finish.

EA 41 SERIES — .41 Action Express cal., action patterned after the CZ-75, selective double action, 4½ in. barrel, steel frame, 11 shot mag., blue, blue/chrome, or brushed chrome finish, combat sights, black neoprene grips, 33 oz. Importation disc. 1993.

	$450	$375	$325	$275	$250	$225	$200

Last Mfg.'s Sug. Retail was $595.

Add $40 for blue/chrome or brushed chrome finish.

* **Model EA 41 Compact** — similar to EA 41, except has 3½ in. barrel and 8 shot mag.

	$495	$425	$375	$325	$295	$260	$230

Last Mfg.'s Sug. Retail was $625.

Add $40 for blue/chrome or brushed chrome finish.

EA 45 SERIES — .45 ACP cal., action patterned after the CZ-75, selective double action, 4½ in. standard or compensated (new 1998) barrel, steel frame or polymer frame/steel slide (new 1997), 10 (C/B 1994) or 11★ shot mag., choice of Wonder (new 1997), stainless steel (disc. 1996) or blue, blue/chrome (disc. 1993), or brushed chrome (disc. 1996) finish, combat sights, walnut grips, 35 oz. Importation began late 1990.

Mfg.'s Sug. Retail	$351	$310	$275	$235	$215	$200	$190	$180

Subtract $8 for polymer frame.
Add $16 for Wonder finish.
Add $54 for single port barrel compensator or carry configuration with compensator.

Grading	100%	98%	95%	90%	80%	70%	60%

* **Model EA 45 Stainless** — similar to EA 45, except is stainless steel. Imported 1992-96.

  $510 **$430** **$350**

  Last Mfg.'s Sug. Retail was $595.

* **Model EA 45 (L) Compact** — similar to EA 45, except has 3⅝ in. barrel and 8 shot mag.

Mfg.'s Sug. Retail	$351	$310	$275	$235	$215	$200	$190	$180

  Subtract $8 for polymer frame.
  Add $16 for Wonder finish.
  Add $54 for single port barrel compensator or carry configuration with compensator.

WITNESS SPORT — .38 Super, 9mm Para., .40 S&W, 10mm (disc. 1994), or .45 ACP cal., 4½ in. barrel, full size frame, standard slide length, Duo-Tone finish, extended safety and high capacity mag., target sights. Imported 1994-95.

$535 **$470** **$400** **$375** **$350** **$325** **$295**

Last Mfg.'s Sug. Retail was $616.

Add $86 for .38 Super, 10mm, or .45 ACP cal.

WITNESS SPORT LONG SLIDE — .38 Super, 9mm Para., .40 S&W, 10mm (disc. 1994), or .45 ACP cal., long slide variation of the EA Series, except has 4¾ in. ported or unported barrel and slide, Duo-Tone finish, extended safety and high capacity mag., competition sights, 34½ oz. Importation disc. 1995.

$595 **$500** **$450** **$395** **$350** **$325** **$295**

Last Mfg.'s Sug. Retail was $681.

Add $79 for .38 Super, 10mm, or .45 ACP cal.

WITNESS LIMITED CLASS — .38 Super, 9mm Para., .40 S&W, or .45 ACP cal., match frame, competition grips, high capacity mag., single action trigger, long slide with match barrel and super sight, extended safety, blue finish only. Imported 1994-98.

$855 **$715** **$610** **$500** **$450** **$400** **$375**

Last Mfg.'s Sug. Retail was $967.

WITNESS COMBO PACKAGE — includes one built up frame and 9mm Para./.40 S&W complete conversion kits, blue, chrome, or Duo-Tone (disc. 1994) finish, full size variation with 4½ in. barrel. Imported 1992-97.

$515 **$460** **$400** **$375** **$350** **$325** **$295**

Last Mfg.'s Sug. Retail was $588.

Add $29 for chrome or Duo-Tone finish.

* **Witness Combo Package (L) Compact** — similar to Witness Combo Package, except has 3⅝ in. barrels, blue only. Imported 1994-97.

$515 **$460** **$400** **$375** **$350** **$325** **$295**

Last Mfg.'s Sug. Retail was $588.

WITNESS MULTI-CLASS PISTOL PACKAGE — .38 Super, 9mm Para., 9x21mm, .40 S&W, or .45 ACP cal., consists of one Witness Limited Class Pistol and complete Unlimited Class top half (slide and barrel), dual chamber steel compensator, blue finish only. Imported 1994 only.

$1,450 **$1,200** **$1,025** **$895** **$775** **$650** **$525**

Last Mfg.'s Sug. Retail was $1,638.

WITNESS TRI-CALIBER PACKAGE — includes one built up frame and caliber conversions (9mm Para., .40 S&W, and .41 AE) that include slide, barrel, recoil guide, and spring, matte blue or chrome finish, compact or full size variations, includes carry case. Imported 1992-1993 only.

$975 **$825** **$700** **$575** **$495** **$425** **$375**

Last Mfg.'s Sug. Retail was $1,195.

Add $40 for chrome finish.

E

Grading	100%	98%	95%	90%	80%	70%	60%

WITNESS CARRY COMP GUN — .38 Super (disc. 1997), 9mm Para. (disc. 1997), .40 S&W cal. (disc. 1997), 10mm (disc. 1994, reintroduced 1999), or .45 ACP cal., full size frame with compact slide and 1 in. compensator, 10 (C/B 1994), 12★ (.40 S&W), or 16★ (9mm Para.) shot mag., Wonder (new 1997), blue or Duo-Tone (disc. 1994) finish. Importation began 1992.

Mfg.'s Sug. Retail	$390	$350	$310	$270	$235	$215	$200	$190

Add $16 for Wonder finish.

Add $50 for .38 Super, 10mm, or .45 ACP cal. (blue only).

WITNESS SILVER TEAM — .38 Super, 9mm Para., 9x21mm, 10mm (disc. 1994), .40 S&W, or .45 ACP cal., dual comp. chambers, S/A trigger, super sight and drilled and tapped for scope mount, competition features include hammer, extended safety, paddle mag. release, black rubber grips, double-dip blue finish, high capacity mag. Imported 1992-98.

	$855	$710	$600	$500	$425	$375	$325

Last Mfg.'s Sug. Retail was $967.

WITNESS GOLD TEAM — .38 Super, 9mm Para., 9x21mm, 10mm (disc. 1994), .40 S&W, or .45 ACP cal., triple comp. chambers, S/A trigger, super sight and drilled and tapped for scope mount, top-of-the-line competition model featuring hand-fitted major components and 25 LPI checkering, hard chrome finish. Imported 1992-98.

	$1,875	$1,525	$1,250	$995	$825	$700	$575

Last Mfg.'s Sug. Retail was $2,150.

This model was also available as a frame only - retail was $389.

F.A.B. 92 — 9mm Para. or .40 S&W cal., double action featuring hammer drop safety and decocker (Witness style), 4½ in. barrel, 16★ (9mm Para.) or 12★ (.40 S&W), or 10 (C/B 1994) shot mag., all steel construction, blue, chrome (disc. 1993), or Duo-Tone (disc. 1993) finish, smooth wood grips, 33 oz. Imported 1992-95.

	$335	$280	$235	$210	$190	$170	$155

Last Mfg.'s Sug. Retail was $386.

Add $40 for chrome or Duo-Tone finish.

Add $29 for .40 S&W cal.

F.A.B. designates Foreign American Brands.

★ **F.A.B. 92 Compact** — similar to F.A.B. 92, except has 3⅝ in. barrel, 13★ (9mm Para.), 10 (9mm only, C/B 1994), or 9 (.40 S&W) shot mag., 30 oz. Imported 1992-95.

	$335	$280	$235	$210	$190	$170	$155

Last Mfg.'s Sug. Retail was $386.

Add $40 for chrome or Duo-Tone finish.

Add $29 for .40 S&W cal.

REVOLVERS: DOUBLE ACTION, WINDICATOR SERIES

STANDARD GRADE — .22 LR (disc.), .22LR/.22 Mag. combo. (disc.), .22 Mag. (disc.), .32 H&R (disc. 1993), .357 Mag. (new 1994), or .38 Spl. cal., 2 (.32 H&R, .357 Mag., or .38 Spl. only), 4 (new 1997), or 6 (disc.) in. squared off barrel, blue or chrome (.38 Spl. only, new 1994) finish, 6 (.38 Spl.), 7 (.32 H&R), or 8 (.22 LR/.22 Mag.) shot, finger grooved rubber grips, double or single action. Importation began 1992.

Mfg.'s Sug. Retail	$173		$150	$125	$115	$105	$95	$85	$75

Add $23 for .357 Mag.

Add $14 for .38 Spl. or $38 for .357 Mag. cal. with 4 in. barrel.

Add $78 for .22 LR/.22 Mag. combo. (disc.).

TACTICAL GRADE — .38 Spl. cal. only, fixed sights, 6 shot, 2 in. (bobbed hammer) or 4 in. compensated barrel, blue finish only. Imported 1992-1993.

	$220	$190	$165	$145	$130	$115	$105

Last Mfg.'s Sug. Retail was $295.

Add $80 for 4 in. compensated barrel.

Grading	100%	98%	95%	90%	80%	70%	60%

TARGET GRADE — .22 LR, .357 Mag., or .38 Spl. cal., 6 or 8 (.22 LR) shot, 6 in. squared off barrel, finger grooved hardwood stocks, adj. trigger pull and rear sight, blue finish only, 3.1 lbs. Imported 1992-1993.

	$425	$325	$260	$220	$200	$185	$170

Last Mfg.'s Sug. Retail was $550.

REVOLVERS: SAA, BOUNTY HUNTER SERIES

MODEL EASAB — .22 LR cal., single action revolver, 6 shot, 4¾ in. barrel, blued or chrome (disc. 1991) finish, wood grips. Importation disc. 1995.

	$70	$55	$50	$45	$40	$35	$30

Last Mfg.'s Sug. Retail was $85.

Add $20 for chrome finish.

MODEL EASAMB COMBO — includes .22 LR and .22 Mag. cal. cylinders, 4¾ (standard), 6, or 9 in. barrel, blue finish, wood grips. Importation disc. 1995.

	$85	$75	$65	$55	$50	$45	$40

Last Mfg.'s Sug. Retail was $100.

Add $14 for 9 in. barrel.
Add $40 for gold backstrap and trigger guard (disc.).

BIG BORE BOUNTY HUNTER — .357 Mag., .44 Mag., or .45 LC cal., 4½ (new 1994), 5½ (disc. 1993), or 7½ in. barrel, 6 shot, choice of blue, chrome (mfg. 1994-95), nickel (new 1998), or case colored finish, gold trigger guard/backstrap (disc. 1994), or gold (disc.) finish, 32-41 oz. New 1992.

Mfg.'s Sug. Retail	$289	$250	$215	$180	$160	$150	$135	$125

Add $9 for .44 Mag. or .45 LC cal.
Add $17 for nickel finish.
Add $20 for chrome finish (disc.).
Add $15 for gold-plated grip strap and trigger guard (disc.).
Add approx. $100 for gold plated finish (disc.)

* *Small Bore Bounty Hunter Combo* — includes .22 LR/.22 Mag. cal. cylinders, 4¾ or 6¾ in. barrel, choice of 6 or 8 shot, blue or nickel (new 1998) finish. New 1997.

Mfg.'s Sug. Retail	$197	$170	$145	$125	$115	$105	$95	$85

Add $22 for nickel finish.

RIFLES

EAA rifles were manufactured by Sabatti in Italy (est. 1674), Lu-Mar in Italy, and H. Weihrauch in Germany (see separate listing in the H. Weihrauch section). Imported 1992-96.

SP1822 SPORTER — .22 LR cal., semi-auto, 18½ in. barrel, wood stock and forearm, adj. sights, 10 shot box mag., 5¼-6½ lbs. Imported 1994-96.

	$180	$145	$120	$100	$90	$80	$70

Last Mfg.'s Sug. Retail was $206.

* *SP1822 Thumbhole* — similar to heavy barrel model, except has one-piece Bell & Carlson green synthetic thumbhole stock, without sights. Importation disc. 1995.

	$310	$260	$230	$200	$175	$150	$135

Last Mfg.'s Sug. Retail was $358.

ROVER 870 — .22-250 Rem., .243 Win., .25-06 Rem., .270 Win., .30-06, .308 Win., 7mm Rem. Mag., .300 Win. Mag., or .338 Win. Mag. cal., bolt action rifle featuring all-steel construction with 22 in. hammer-forged rifled barrel, staggered 5 shot internal mag., open sights. Imported 1993 only.

	$795	$695	$600	$550	$495	$450	$395

Last Mfg.'s Sug. Retail was $995.

Grading	100%	98%	95%	90%	80%	70%	60%

SHOTGUNS: O/U

SCIROCCO BASIC — 12 ga. only, single trigger, extractors, 26 or 28 in. fixed choke VR barrels, boxlock action, nickel engraved receiver. Imported 1994-95.

	$425	$350	$315	$285	$260	$240	$220

Last Mfg.'s Sug. Retail was $478.

This model was mfg. by Lu-Mar located in Italy.

SCIROCCO SPORTING CLAYS — 12 ga. only, 28 or 30 in. barrels with 5 choke tubes and wide VR, SST, ejectors, Raybar front sight, nickel engraved receiver. Imported 1994-95.

	$650	$550	$495	$450	$400	$350	$315

Last Mfg.'s Sug. Retail was $734.

This model was mfg. by Lu-Mar located in Italy.

FALCON — 12, 20 ga., or .410 bore, 3 in. chambers, 26, 28, or 30 in. fixed choke VR barrels, boxlock action, single or double trigger, extractors or ejectors, checkered pistol grip and forend. Imported 1993 only.

	$650	$525	$450	$375	$325	$295	$260

Last Mfg.'s Sug. Retail was $795.

Add $80 for .410 bore.
Add $100 for SST and ejectors.

SPORTING CLAYS PRO GOLD — 12 ga. only, 2¾ in. chambers, 28 or 30 in. screw-in choke barrels with wide VR, boxlock action, SST, ejectors, blued receiver with engraving, recoil pad with custom carry case. Imported 1993-1994.

	$850	$725	$650	$575	$525	$475	$425

Last Mfg.'s Sug. Retail was $978.

SHOTGUNS: SEMI-AUTO

BUNDA SERIES — 12 ga. only, 2¾ or 3 in. chamber (depending on barrel) gas operated, 19, 26, 28 or 30 in. barrel with 4 choke tubes, choice of black synthetic or Turkish walnut stock and forearm, aluminum receiver. Limited importation 1998 only.

	$360	$300	$275	$250	$225	$200	$185

Last Mfg.'s Sug. Retail was $406.

Add $9 for Turkish walnut stock and forearm.

SHOTGUNS: SxS

SABA —12, 20, 28 ga., or .410 bore, 3 in. chambers, boxlock action with scrolled nickel finish, DT or SST, 26 or 28 in. fixed choke barrels with raised matted rib, ejectors, checkered stock and forearm with sling swivels. Imported 1993 only.

	$950	$825	$700	$575	$495	$425	$375

Last Mfg.'s Sug. Retail was $1,195.

Add $100 for SST.

SHOTGUNS: SLIDE ACTION

MODEL PM2 — 12 ga. only, slide action, unique 7 shot detachable mag., 20 in. barrel, black wood stock and composite forearm, dual action bars, cross trigger safety, available in matte blue or chrome finish, 6.81 lbs. Imported 1992 only.

	$550	$450	$395	$335	$295	$260	$230

Last Mfg.'s Sug. Retail was $695.

Add $200 for night sights.
Add $75 for matte chrome finish.

EVANS, WILLIAM, GUN & RIFLE MAKERS

Please refer to the W section in this text.

Grading	100%	98%	95%	90%	80%	70%	60%

EVOLUTION USA

Current rifle manufacturer located in White Bird, ID since 1993. Distributor and dealer sales.

RIFLES: BOLT ACTION

COYOTE — .223 Rem., .25-06 Rem., or .308 Win. cal., Rem. 700 action, Grand Master barrel with cryogenic treatment, Kevlar/graphite stock. New 1996.

Mfg.'s Sug. Retail	$1,674	$1,450	$1,250	$1,050	$875	$725	$650	$575

PHANTOM II — various cals., heavy varmint/sniper model, Evolution M1000 stainless steel action, stainless match barrel, Kevlar/graphite stock. New 1999.

Mfg.'s Sug. Retail	$2,353	$2,075	$1,825	$1,575	$1,325	$1,100	$925	$775

YELLOW WOLF — .270 Gibbs, .300 Win. Mag., or 7mm Rem. Mag. cal., designed for big game, Kevlar/graphite stock. New 1996.

Mfg.'s Sug. Retail	$1,639	$1,425	$1,225	$1,025	$875	$725	$650	$575

IMPALA — most popular cals., Rem. Model 700 trued action w/o floor plate, lightweight sporter, Kevlar graphite stock. New 1998.

Mfg.'s Sug. Retail	$1,456	$1,275	$1,050	$950	$750	$650	$575	$500

KUDU — most standard length cals., Winchester Pre-64 Model 70 action, stainless steel match barrel, sporter style Kevlar graphite stock. New 1998.

Mfg.'s Sug. Retail	$2,179	$1,875	$1,650	$1,450	$1,250	$1,050	$875	$725

Add $1,400 for presentation walnut stock.

SHI-AWELA — various cals., medium weight sporter, Evolution M1000 stainless action, stainless match barrel, Kevlar/graphite stock. New 1999.

Mfg.'s Sug. Retail	$2,296	$1,995	$1,750	$1,525	$1,300	$1,075	$900	$750

MBOGO — .375 H&H, .416 Rem., or .458 Win. Mag. cal., choice of Sako (disc.), Dakota (disc.), Rem. Model 700, Win. Pre-64 Model 70, or or stainless steel Evolution M1000 action, stainless steel match barrel, sporter style Kevlar graphite stock. New 1998.

* *Sako (disc.) or Remington Action*

Mfg.'s Sug. Retail	$1,672	$1,450	$1,250	$1,050	$875	$725	$650	$575

* *Win. Pre-64 Model 70 or Evolution Stainless Action*

Mfg.'s Sug. Retail	$2,269	$1,950	$1,700	$1,475	$1,250	$1,050	$875	$725

Add $30 for Evolution stainless action.
Add $1,400 for presentation walnut stock.

* *Dakota Action*

	$2,700	$2,400	$2,000	$1,750	$1,500	$1,250	$1,000

Last Mfg.'s Sug. Retail was $3,142.

MBOGO EXPRESS — .416 Rigby, or .470 NE cal., Dakota Express action, otherwise similar to Mbogo. Mfg. 1998 only.

	$2,850	$2,500	$2,050	$1,775	$1,500	$1,250	$1,000

Last Mfg.'s Sug. Retail was $3,351.

RIFLES: SxS

NYATI — .375 H&H, .416 NE, .470 NE, or .500 NE cal., Anson & Deeley action, engraved receiver, chrome moly barrels, AAA fancy walnust, express sights. New 1999.

Mfg.'s Sug. Retail	$10,800	$9,750	$8,500	$7,400	$6,500	$5,600	$4,700	$3,600

RIFLES: SEMI-AUTO

WOLVERINE — .22 LR cal., Grand Master barrel, Kevlar/graphite stock. New 1996.

Mfg.'s Sug. Retail	$794	$695	$625	$550	$500	$450	$400	$360

Grading	100%	98%	95%	90%	80%	70%	60%

GRENADA — .223 Rem. cal., paramilitary design based on the AR-15 with flat upper receiver, 17 in. stainless steel match barrel with integral muzzle brake, NM trigger.

Mfg.'s Sug. Retail	$1,055	$875	$750	$625	$550	$500	$450	$400

DESERT STORM — similar to Grenada, except has 21 in. match barrel.

Mfg.'s Sug. Retail	$1,159	$950	$800	$650	$550	$500	$450	$400

IWO JIMA — features carrying handle incorporating iron sights, 20 in. stainless steel match barrel, A2 HBAR action, tubular handguard.

		$1,059	$900	$825	$700	$600	$475	$425

EXCAM

Previous importer and distributor located in Hialeah, FL that went out of business late 1990. Excam distributed Dart, Erma, Tanarmi, Targa, & Warrior exclusively for the U.S. These trademarks will appear under Excam only in this book. All importation of Excam firearms ceased in 1990.

All Targa and Tanarmi pistols were manufactured in Gardone V.T., Italy. All Erma and Warrior pistols and rifles were manufactured in W. Germany. Senator O/U shotguns were manufactured by A. Zoli located in Brescia, Italy.

HANDGUNS: TANARMI MFG.

TA 38SB O/U DERRINGER — .38 Spl. cal. only, O/U Derringer-copy of Rem. Model 41, 3 in. barrels, 14 oz., with safety, blue finish only, checkered nylon grips. Importation disc. 1985.

	$90	$75	$65	$55	$50	$45	$40

Last Mfg.'s Sug. Retail was $80.

MODEL TA 22 SAA — .22 LR cal., 6 shot, 4¾ in. barrel, brass trigger guard and grip straps, blued finish, wood grips, 34 oz.

	$85	$70	$60	$55	$50	$45	$40

Last Mfg.'s Sug. Retail was $99.

MODEL TA 76 SAA — .22 LR cal., single action revolver, 4¾ in. barrel, 6 shot, blue finish only, wood grips, 32 oz.

	$85	$65	$55	$50	$45	$40	$35

Last Mfg.'s Sug. Retail was $95.

Add $4 for chrome finish or brass backstrap and trigger guard.

* *Model TA 76M Combo* — includes .22 LR and .22 Mag. cal. cylinders, 4¾ (standard), 6, or 9 in. barrel, blue finish, wood grips.

	$95	$75	$65	$60	$55	$50	$45

Last Mfg.'s Sug. Retail was $105.

Add $6 for chrome plated finish (4¾ in. barrel only).
Add $10 for 6 (Model TA 766) or 9 (Model TA 769) in. barrel.
Add $16 for brass backstrap and trigger guard (N/A in 9 in. barrel).

TA 41 SERIES SEMI-AUTO — .41 Action Express cal., action similar to TA 90 Series, 11 shot mag., matte blue (Model TA 41B) or matte chrome (Model TA 41C) finish, combat sights, black neoprene grips, 38 oz. Imported 1989-90.

	$450	$390	$360	$330	$295	$265	$240

Last Mfg.'s Sug. Retail was $490.

Add $70 for adj. target sights (Model TA 41BT).

* *Model TA 41C* — matte chrome finish.

	$485	$430	$395	$360	$330	$295	$270

Last Mfg.'s Sug. Retail was $550.

Add $50 (retail) for adj. target sights (Model TA 41CT).

* *Model TA 41 SS* — .41 AE cal., compensated variation of the Model TA 41 except has 5 in. ported barrel and slide, blue/chrome finish, competition sights, 40 oz. Import 1989-90.

	$575	$450	$420	$385	$350	$325	$300

Last Mfg.'s Sug. Retail was $650.

Grading	100%	98%	95%	90%	80%	70%	60%

TA 90 SERIES SEMI-AUTO — 9mm Para. cal., double action, copy of the CZ-75, 4¾ in. barrel, steel frame, 15 shot mag., matte blue (Model TA 90B) or matte chrome finish (Model TA 90C), combat sights, wood (disc. 1985) or neoprene grips, 38 oz. New 1985.

	$365	$300	$260	$225	$205	$190	$180

Last Mfg.'s Sug. Retail was $415.

Add $85 for adj. target sights (TA 90BT).

Earlier models featured a polished blue finish and nickel steel alloy frame (35 oz.).

* *Model TA 90C* — matte chrome finish.

	$380	$315	$270	$235	$210	$190	$180

Last Mfg.'s Sug. Retail was $430.

Add $95 for adj. target sights (TA 90CT).

* *Model BTA 90B and C* — 9mm Para. cal., smaller version of TA 90, 3½ in. barrel, 12 shot mag., neoprene grips. Importer 1986-90.

	$380	$315	$270	$235	$210	$190	$180

Last Mfg.'s Sug. Retail was $430.

Add $20 for chrome finish (BTA 90C).

* *Model TA 90 SS* — 9mm Para. cal., compensated variation of the Model TA 90 except has 5 in. ported barrel and slide, blue/chrome finish, competition sights, 40 oz. Imported 1989-90.

	$575	$450	$420	$385	$350	$325	$300

Last Mfg.'s Sug. Retail was $650.

* *TA 90BK* — convertible kit including 2 barrels (9mm and .41 AE) and 2 mags. While advertised, this combination never saw production.

PISTOLS: SEMI-AUTO, ERMA MFG.

RX 22 — .22 LR cal. only, double action-Walther copy, 3¼ in. barrel, 8 shot mag., blue only, plastic grips, 17 oz. Assembled in the U.S. Disc. 1986.

	$140	$125	$105	$95	$90	$85	$80

Last Mfg.'s Sug. Retail was $139.

KGP 22 — .22 LR cal. only, Luger type toggle action, 3.78 in. barrel, 8 shot mag., blue only, plastic grips, 29 oz. Importation disc. 1986.

	$220	$195	$175	$155	$135	$120	$105

Last Mfg.'s Sug. Retail was $220.

KGP 380 — .380 ACP cal. only, Luger type toggle action, 3½ in. barrel, 5 shot mag., blue only, plastic grips, 23 oz. Disc. 1986.

	$250	$215	$185	$160	$145	$135	$125

Last Mfg.'s Sug. Retail was $230.

PISTOLS: SEMI-AUTO, TARGA MFG.

GT 22 SERIES — .22 LR cal., 3.88 in. barrel, 10 shot mag., single action 26 oz., steel frame, either satin chrome (GT 22C) or standard blue (GT 22B) finish, wood grips became standard in 1986. GT 22T is 6 in. barrel target version (12 shot mag.).

	$170	$140	$125	$110	$95	$80	$70

Last Mfg.'s Sug. Retail was $200.

Add $15 for chrome finish (Model GT 22C).

GT 26 and GT 27B OR C — .25 ACP cal., 2½ in. barrel, 6 shot mag., single action, 13 oz., available in standard blue alloy, satin chrome alloy (GT 27B or C), or steel frame (GT 26S), wood grips became standard in 1986.

	$50	$45	$35	$30	$30	$25	$25

Last Mfg.'s Sug. Retail was $56.

Add $59 for steel frame (Model GT 26S).
Add $13 for chrome alloy (Model GT 27C).

Grading	100%	98%	95%	90%	80%	70%	60%

GT 28 SERIES — .25 ACP cal., 2½ in. barrel, 5 shot mag., single action, blue alloy, wood grips. Imported 1990 only.

	$45	$35	$30	$30	$25	$25	$20

Last Mfg.'s Sug. Retail was $51.

Add $18 for chrome finish (Model GT 28C).

GT 32 SERIES — .32 ACP cal., 3.88 in. barrel, 7 shot mag., single action, steel frame, 26 oz., either satin chrome (GT 32C) or standard blue (GT 32B), wood grips became standard in 1986.

	$170	$140	$125	$110	$95	$80	$70

Last Mfg.'s Sug. Retail was $200.

Add $15 for chrome finish (Model GT 32C).

GT 380 ACP SERIES — .380 ACP cal., 3.88 in. barrel, 6 shot mag., single action, steel frame, 26 oz., either satin chrome (GT 380C) or standard blue (GT 380B), wood grips became standard in 1986.

	$175	$145	$135	$125	$115	$105	$95

Last Mfg.'s Sug. Retail was $212.

Add $8 for chrome finish (Model GT 380C).

* **GT 380 LW** — similar to GT 380 Series except has light alloy receiver and 3¼ in. barrel.

	$100	$85	$70	$60	$55	$50	$45

Last Mfg.'s Sug. Retail was $119.

* **GT 380 BE or CE** — engraved models, either blue (BE) or chrome (CE) finish, wood grips. Importation disc. 1989.

	$180	$155	$145	$135	$125	$115	$105

Last Mfg.'s Sug. Retail was $220.

Add $25 for chrome finish (Model GT 380 CE).

GT 380 XE — .380 ACP cal., 3.88 in. barrel, 11 shot mag., blue only, wood grips, 28 oz.

	$190	$165	$155	$145	$135	$125	$115

Last Mfg.'s Sug. Retail was $235.

* **GT 32 XEB** — .32 ACP cal., similar to GT 380 XE, 12 shot mag. Disc. 1985.

	$165	$145	$135	$125	$115	$100	$95

Last Mfg.'s Sug. Retail was $189.

REVOLVERS

RX 38 B — .38 Spl. cal., double action, 6 shot, 2 in. barrel, blue finish only. Imported 1990-disc.

	$85	$65	$55	$50	$45	$40	$35

Last Mfg.'s Sug. Retail was $95.

ALDO UBERTI CATTLEMAN SA REVOLVER — .357 Mag., .44 Mag., or .45 LC cal., 6 shot, single action, 5½, 6, or 7½ in. barrels, target sights, wood grips, blued finish. New 1985. Disc. 1986.

	$295	$250	$195	$165	$150	$140	$130

Last Mfg.'s Sug. Retail was $222.

Add $10 for .44 Mag. cal.

ALDO UBERTI DA INSPECTOR — .38 Spl., double action, 3 or 4 in. barrel, blue finish, wood grips, 6 shot. Disc. 1986.

	$325	$250	$200	$180	$165	$150	$140

Last Mfg.'s Sug. Retail was $240.

Add $17 for adj. sights.

WARRIOR DOUBLE ACTION MODEL W 722 (B) — .22 LR or .22 Mag. cal. only, double action, 6 in. barrel, 8 shot, blue only, plastic grips, 35 oz. Disc. 1986.

	$100	$80	$70	$65	$60	$55	$50

Last Mfg.'s Sug. Retail was $98.

Add $50 for .22 Mag. extra cyl.

Grading	100%	98%	95%	90%	80%	70%	60%

WARRIOR DOUBLE ACTION MODEL W 384 (B) — .38 Spl. cal. only, double action, 4 or 6 in. barrels, 6 shot, blue only, plastic grips, 30 oz. Vent. rib standard. Disc. 1986.

	$135	$110	$100	$90	$80	$70	$65

Last Mfg.'s Sug. Retail was $125.

Add $5 for 6 in. barrel (W 386 B).

WARRIOR DOUBLE ACTION MODEL W 357 — .357 Mag. cal. only, double action, 4 or 6 in. barrels, 6 shot, blue only, plastic grips, 36 oz. Vent. rib standard. 6 in. barrel (W 3576). Disc. 1986.

	$190	$165	$145	$135	$130	$125	$120

Last Mfg.'s Sug. Retail was $185.

RIFLES: ERMA MFG.

EG 712 — .22 LR cal. only, lever action copied after the Win. Model 92, 18½ in. barrel, 15 shot, iron sights. Disc. 1985.

	$180	$160	$140	$125	$115	$100	$90

Last Mfg.'s Sug. Retail was $204.

EG 712L — .22 LR cal. only, lever action copied after the Win. Model 92, 18½ in. octagonal barrel, deluxe walnut silver plated receiver and barrel bands, 15 shot, iron sights. Disc.

	$300	$241	$220	$180	$150	$130	$115

EG 73 — .22 Mag. cal. only, lever action copied after the Win. Model 92, 19¼ in. barrel, 12 shot, iron sights, blue only. Disc. 1985.

	$205	$185	$160	$140	$130	$120	$105

Last Mfg.'s Sug. Retail was $229.

EG 722 — .22 LR cal. only, slide action, 18½ in. barrel, 15 shot, iron sights, blue only. Disc. 1985.

	$180	$160	$140	$125	$115	$100	$90

Last Mfg.'s Sug. Retail was $204.

EM 1 CARBINE — .22 LR or .22 Mag. cal., gas semi-auto, copy of the original M1 carbine, 19½ in. barrel, 15 shot, iron sights, blue only. ESG 22 is .22 Mag. (12 shot). Disc. 1985.

	$175	$155	$140	$125	$115	$100	$90

Last Mfg.'s Sug. Retail was $195.

Add $100 for ESG 22, .22 Mag..

SHOTGUNS: O/U

SENATOR MODEL — 12, 20 ga., or .410 bore, 3 in. chambers, 26 or 28 in. F/M barrels, folding action, double triggers, extractors, vent. barrels and rib, checkered walnut stock and forearm, engraved silver finished receiver. Imported 1986-1987.

	$235	$200	$180	$165	$150	$140	$130

Last Mfg.'s Sug. Retail was $275.

EXEL ARMS OF AMERICA, INC.

Previous importer located in Gardener, MA. Exel Arms previously imported Lanber (Series 100), Ugartechea (Series 200), and Laurona (Series 300) shotguns. Please refer to the appropriate sections for more information on this series.

NOTES

E

F section

F. DARNE FILS AINÉ

Previous manufacturer located in St. Etienne, France.

Francisque Darne was the eldest son of Regis Darne, who developed the sliding breech gun. In the year 1910, Francisque left his father's company to form his own, "F.Darne Fils AinÉ", producing high quality versions of the original 1894 patent "R" model Darne. Regis Darne updated most of his designs in 1909 and allowed the older patents to become public domain.

Francisque Darne died in 1917, but his company remained in production until 1955 under at least four different owners. As is usually the case, the earlier production guns are by far the highest quality. Wide variations in quality exist in this marque, depending on the financial health of the owners at the time of production.

Grading	100%	98%	95%	90%	80%	70%	60%

SHOTGUNS: SxS, PRE-WAR MODELS

F

CLASSIC MODEL — 12 or 16 ga., an exact copy of the first Darne patent of 1894. Available in four grades.

* *Type A* — standard French proof barrels, very light engraving, color case hardened, no quality stamps on barrel flats.

	$1,200	$1,000	$800	$700	$600	$500	$450

* *Type B* — French gray hardened or color case hardened, somewhat more engraving, 1 quality stamp on barrel flats.

	$1,700	$1,400	$1,200	$900	$700	$600	$500

* *Type C* — French gray hardening over modern or old English engraving, double proofed barrels with two quality stamps on barrel flats.

	$2,000	$1,650	$1,350	$1,000	$800	$650	$550

* *Type E* — French gray hardening over elaborate engraving. Better quality wood in either English or semi-pistol grip. Double proof barrels with four quality stamps on barrel flats.

	$2,400	$2,000	$1,600	$1,300	$1,000	$900	$800

MODEL T — 12 or 16 ga., stylistic improvements to the 1894 patent R model. Two-piece stock, barrels removed by holding a button on forend, 4 grades, all were originally color case hardened, never blued.

* *Type T 32* — lightly engraved, 3 quality stamps on barrel flats.

Both the T 32 and T 34 were available in 10 ga. with 70mm or 75mm chambers and 72cm or 76cm barrels on special order. The barrels would carry triple proof in 10 ga.

	$1,950	$1,700	$1,250	$950	$700	$600	$500

Add 30% for 10 ga.

* *Model T 34* — better engraving and wood, 5 quality stamps on barrel flats.

	$2,100	$1,800	$1,500	$1,100	$850	$675	$575

Add 30% for 10 ga.

* *Model T 35* — mono bloc barrels of superior French proof steel, better engraving and wood, 6 quality stamps on barrel flats.

	$2,500	$2,200	$1,800	$1,400	$1,200	$1,000	$800

* *Model T 36* — mono bloc barrels of superior French proof steel, top-of-the-line T model, 7 quality stamps on barrel flats.

	$2,800	$2,500	$2,100	$1,700	$1,400	$1,200	$850

Grading	100%	98%	95%	90%	80%	70%	60%

MODEL FIXED — 12 or 16 ga., further tinkering with the 1894 R model, these located the barrels in a rectangular block cut near the flats. Two grades.

* *Type No. 3* — color case hardened or French gray hardened. Good quality engraved and wood. For pricing, see Type T 34.

* *Type No. 4* — better wood and engraving. For pricing, see Type T 35.

MODEL PLATINUM — 12 or 16 ga., based on the model Fixed, these were top-of-the-line sliding breech guns. Four grades.

* *Type No. 5* — mono bloc barrels, English or art nouveau style engraving, chisled fences.

	$3,100	$2,800	$2,500	$2,200	$1,700	$1,400	$1,100

* *Type No. 6* — mono bloc barrels, English rose and scroll engraving or game scene or art nouveau style, high grade wood.

	$3,400	$2,900	$2,600	$2,350	$1,900	$1,600	$1,200

* *Type No. 7* — mono bloc barrels of top quality French proof steel, engraved in English rose and scroll or deep chisled art nouveau style, superior wood. Pigeon model.

	$3,800	$3,500	$3,000	$2,800	$2,200	$1,900	$1,500

* *Type No. 8* — mono bloc barrels of top quality French proof steel. Top-of-the-line model with all details to customer's wishes. Very rare in any condition. Rarity precludes accurate pricing.

SHOTGUNS: SxS, POST-WAR MODELS

Note: the model name of the following post-war guns is usually engraved on the side of the gun in front of the safety lever.

CLASSIC MODEL — 12 or 16 ga. with modified and full choke on 70 cm barrels, simple case colored gun with no engraving and plain wood in semi-pistol grip or straight stock, 2 quality stamps.

	$1,250	$1,000	$850	$700	$600	$525	$400

BARONNET-BROUSSARD — 12,16, or 20 ga. with 70 cm barrels (two-piece stock on 12 and 16 ga.), lightly engraved with satin chrome receiver finish, Broussard model featured 80 cm barrels but was essentially the same, 3 quality stamps.

	$1,400	$1,200	$1,000	$800	$675	$550	$475

Add 20% for Broussard model.

GOUVERNEUR MODEL — 12, 16, or 20 ga., better engraving and one-piece stock of select walnut, French gray receiver, choice of barrel lengths in 12 ga. (70 cm, 72 cm, or 74 cm.) classic or modern style engraving, 5 quality stamps.

	$1,800	$1,650	$1,200	$1,000	$750	$600	$550

GOUVERNEUR PLUME AND PLUME MAGNUM — same as above, but with plume (swamped rib) on Plume Model, plume rib and 76mm chambers included on Plume Magnum Model. Prices about 10% higher than above models due to these having six quality stamps on flats of barrels in spite of being the same basic gun.

RAMBOUILLET MODEL — 12 or 16 ga., double sears in a large key action somewhat similar to the Darne V models stylistically, one-piece stock of select walnut, in semi-pistol grip or straight style, light engraving on color case hardening, choice of rib, 8 quality stamps.

	$1,500	$1,300	$1,100	$900	$700	$650	$575

AMBASSADEUR MODEL — 12 or 16 ga., large key model with double sears. French gray finish on breech with excellent engraving, one-piece stock of good quality walnut, top-of-the-line production model, 10 quality stamps.

	$2,700	$2,400	$2,200	$1,800	$1,500	$1,100	$850

Grading	100%	98%	95%	90%	80%	70%	60%

PRESTIGE MODEL — top-of-the-line custom gun, mono bloc barrels of Jacob Holtzer steel with plume rib. Large key action with silent operation and double sears, one-piece stock of best quality walnut, in straight style only, 72 cm barrels, excellent full coverage engraving, eight month minimum wait, 12 quality stamps.

	100%	98%	95%	90%	80%	70%	60%
	$3,500	$3,100	$2,900	$2,600	$2,200	$1,700	$1,200

F.A.I.R. TECHNI-MEC (I. RIZZINI)

Current manufacturer established in 1971 and located in Brescia, Italy (owned by Isidoro Rizzini). Currently imported and distributed exclusively by New England Arms Co. located in Kittery Point, ME.

SHOTGUNS: O/U

Techni-Mec manufactures a wide variety of shotguns including O/Us and single shots in assorted models. Some models, however, are not being imported into the U.S. at this time. For more information on the complete Techni-Mec model line-up, please contact New England Arms Co.

MODEL PREMIERE EM — 12, 20, 28 ga., or .410 bore, standard model with ST, ejectors, vent. rib barrels, blued frame. Importation began 1998.

Mfg.'s Sug. Retail	$850		$775	$650	$550	$500	$450	$400	$360

MODEL 500 — 12, 16, 20, 28 ga., or .410 bore, boxlock action with case colored frame and game scene engraving. Importation began 1998.

Mfg.'s Sug. Retail	$2,250		$2,000	$1,750	$1,525	$1,275	$1,075	$950	$825

Add $275 for Model 500 Gold (includes gold inlays on receiver).

Beginning 1999, the 16 ga. has its own frame (approx. 6¼ lbs).

MODEL 600 GOLD — same gauges as Model 500, features case colored receiver with engraved and gold inlaid sideplates. Importation began 1998.

Mfg.'s Sug. Retail	$2,995		$2,650	$2,225	$1,900	$1,675	$1,400	$1,150	$925

MODEL S 610 — 10 ga., 3½ in. Mag., O/U boxlock action, double underlug locking, 32 in. VR barrels, SST, ejectors, checkered walnut stock and forearm. Imported 1991-97.

	$925	$825	$750	$675	$595	$525	$450

Last Mfg.'s Sug. Retail was $1,000.

MODEL SPL 640 — 12, 16, 20, 28 ga., or .410 bore, folding O/U design, DT, 26 in. VR barrels. Importation disc. 1997.

	$465	$390	$325	$260	$215	$180	$160

Last Mfg.'s Sug. Retail was $500.

MODEL 702 — 12, 16, 20, 28 ga., or .410 bore, 2¾ in. chambers, O/U boxlock with sideplates, standard interchangeable chokes available, blued receiver with hand inlaid gold wire outlines on sideplates. Importation began 1995.

Mfg.'s Sug. Retail	$3,995		$3,500	$2,450	$2,000	$1,750	$1,500	$1,350	$1,225

MODEL 900 — similar to Model 702, except has upgraded wood and Bulino/scroll engraving on coin finished receiver. Importation began 1995.

Mfg.'s Sug. Retail	$3,995		$3,500	$2,450	$2,000	$1,750	$1,500	$1,350	$1,225

FAS

Current manufacturer located in Italy. Currently imported and distributed by Nygord Precision Products located in Prescott, AZ, and Mandall Shooting Supplies, located in Scottsdale, AZ. Previously imported by Beeman Precision Arms, Inc. located in Santa Rosa, CA and Osborne's located in Cheboygan, MI.

Grading	100%	98%	95%	90%	80%	70%	60%

PISTOLS: SEMI-AUTO

MODEL 601 — .22 Short cal. only, competition pistol, 5½ in. barrel, 5 shot mag., wraparound match wood grips, 41½ oz.

	Mfg.'s Sug. Retail	$1,250	$1,025	$875	$695	$640	$565	$500	$450

MODEL 602 — .22 LR cal. only, competition pistol, 5.6 in. barrel, 5 shot mag., ergonomically designed match wood grips, 40 oz. Importation disc. 1994.

	$895	$800	$625	$600	$525	$475	$425

Last Mfg.'s Sug. Retail was $1,100.

MODEL 603 — .32 S&W Wadcutter cal. only, competition pistol, 5.6 in. barrel, 5 shot mag., ergonomically designed adj. or non-adj. match wood grips, 40 oz.

	Mfg.'s Sug. Retail	$1,175	$975	$875	$695	$640	$565	$500	$450

MODEL 607 — .22 LR cal. only, semi-auto competition pistol, similar to Model 602, except has removable barrel weights. Importation began 1995.

	Mfg.'s Sug. Retail	$1,175	$975	$875	$695	$640	$565	$500	$450

F FEG

Current manufacturer located in Hungary (FEG stands for Fegyver es Gepyar) since the turn of the century. Currently imported and distributed K.B.I., Inc. located in Harrisburg, PA, and Century International Arms located in St. Albans, VT (see additional information under the Century International Arms in this text). Previously imported and distributed until 1998 by Interarms located in Alexandria, VA.

PISTOLS: SEMI-AUTO, INTERARMS IMPORTED

All FEG pistols were supplied with two mags.

MARK II AP22 — .22 LR cal., double action, 3.4 in. barrel, 8 shot mag., blue finish, black plastic grips, 23 oz. Imported 1997-98.

	$235	$200	$175	$160	$145	$130	$115

Last Mfg.'s Sug. Retail was $269.

MARK II AP — .380 ACP cal., double action, patterned after the Walther PP, 3.9 in. barrel, 7 shot mag., blue finish, black plastic grips, 27 oz. Imported 1997-98.

	$235	$200	$175	$160	$145	$130	$115

Last Mfg.'s Sug. Retail was $269.

MARK II APK — .380 ACP cal., similar to Mark II AP, except is patterned after the Walther PPK/S, 3.4 in. barrel, 7 shot mag., blue finish, black plastic grips, 25 oz. Imported 1997-98.

	$235	$200	$175	$160	$145	$130	$115

Last Mfg.'s Sug. Retail was $269.

PISTOLS: SEMI-AUTO, KBI/CENTURY IMPORTED

MODEL PMK-380 — .380 ACP cal., patterned after Walther PP, alloy frame, double action, 4 in. barrel, plastic grips with thumbrest, blued finish, 21 oz. Importation began 1992.

	Mfg.'s Sug. Retail	$209	$185	$165	$150	$135	$120	$110	$100

MODEL SMC-380 — .380 ACP cal., double action semi-auto, patterned after Walther PPK, alloy frame, 3½ in. barrel, 6 shot mag., plastic grips with thumbrest, blue finish, 18½ oz. Importation began 1993.

	Mfg.'s Sug. Retail	$209	$185	$165	$150	$135	$120	$110	$100

    * *Model SMC-22* — .22 LR cal., 8 shot mag., otherwise similar to Model SMC-380. Importation disc. 1997.

	$210	$195	$180	$165	$150	$135	$115

Last Mfg.'s Sug. Retail was $235.

Grading	100%	98%	95%	90%	80%	70%	60%

MODEL SMC-918 — 9x18 Makarov cal., double action, semi-auto, 7 shot mag. Importation disc. 1997.

	$210	$195	$180	$165	$150	$135	$115

Last Mfg.'s Sug. Retail was $235.

MODEL R-9 — 9mm Para. cal., patterned after Browning Hi-Power, double action, 13 shot mag., blued finish, steel construction, checkered wood grips. Imported 1986-87 only.

	$275	$230	$200	$180	$165	$155	$145

Last Mfg.'s Sug. Retail was $375.

MODEL PPH — .380 ACP cal., patterned after Walther PP, alloy frame, double action, plastic grips with thumbrest, blued finish. Imported 1986-87 only.

	$200	$170	$140	$125	$115	$105	$95

Last Mfg.'s Sug. Retail was $225.

MODEL MBK-9HP — 9mm Para. cal., patterned after Browning Hi-Power, double action, 4⅔ in. barrel, 14 shot mag., blued finish, steel construction, checkered wood grips, 36 oz. Imported 1992 only.

	$315	$270	$250	$225	$200	$185	$170

Last Mfg.'s Sug. Retail was $349.

* *Model MBK-9HPC* — compact variation of the Model MBK-9HP with 4 in. barrel, 34 oz. Imported 1992 only.

	$325	$275	$250	$225	$200	$185	$170

Last Mfg.'s Sug. Retail was $359.

MODEL PJK-9HP — 9mm Para. cal., patterned after Browning Hi-Power, all steel construction, 4¾ in. barrel, thumb safety, 10 (C/B 1994) or 13★ shot mag. and cleaning rod, 32 oz. Importation began 1992.

Mfg.'s Sug. Retail	$249	$215	$195	$180	$165	$145	$130	$120

Add $80 for industrial hard chrome finish (Model PJK-9HPC - includes Uncle Mike's rubber grips).

MODEL GKK-92C — 9mm Para. cal., double action semi-auto, 4 in. barrel, 14 shot mag., improved variation of MBK models, includes same accessories as PJK-9H, 34 oz. Importation disc. 1993.

	$315	$280	$255	$230	$200	$185	$170

Last Mfg.'s Sug. Retail was $369.

MODEL GKK-40C — .40 S&W cal., 9 shot mag., otherwise similar to GKK-45. Imported 1995-96.

	$300	$265	$230	$200	$180	$160	$145

Last Mfg.'s Sug. Retail was $349.

MODEL GKK-45 — .45 ACP cal., double action semi-auto, all steel, 4¼ in. barrel, blue (disc. 1994) or chrome (Model GKK-45C) finish checkered walnut grips, 8 shot mag., approx. 37 oz. Imported 1993-96.

	$300	$265	$230	$200	$180	$160	$145

Last Mfg.'s Sug. Retail was $349.

RIFLES: SEMI-AUTO

MODEL SA-85M — 7.62x39mm cal., sporter rifle utilizing AKM action, 16.3 in. barrel, 6 shot detachable mag., thumbhole stock, 7 lbs. 10 oz. Imported 1991, banned 1998.

	$350	$315	$280	$250	$225	$200	$185

Last Mfg.'s Sug. Retail was $429.

SA-2000M — .223 Rem. or 7.62x39mm cal., sporter rifle with skeletonized Choate synthetic stock, 17¾ in. barrel with muzzle brake, 10 shot detachable mag. Importation began 1999.

Mfg.'s Sug. Retail	$439	$350	$315	$280	$250	$225	$200	$185

Add $20 for .223 Rem. cal.

Grading	100%	98%	95%	90%	80%	70%	60%

FIAS

Current shotgun manufacturer located in Brescia, Italy. Please contact FIAS directly (see listing in Trademark Index) to obtain current information on their models and prices.

F.I.E.

Previous importer (F.I.E. is the acronym for Firearms Import & Export) located in Hialeah, FL until 1990.

F.I.E. filed bankruptcy in November of 1990 and all models are discontinued. Some parts or service for these older firearms may be obtained through Heritage Manufacturing, Inc. located in Opa Locka, FL or Gun Parts Corp. located in (see Trademark Index), even though all warranties on F.I.E. guns are void.

DERRINGERS

MODEL D38 — .38 Spl. cal., O/U, chrome finish only, no transfer bar. Disc. 1985.

	100%	98%	95%	90%	80%	70%	60%
	$70	$60	$55	$45	$40	$35	$30

Last Mfg.'s Sug. Retail was $82.

Add $17 for walnut grips.

MODEL D86 — .38 Spl. cal., single shot, 3 in. barrel, internal transfer bar safety, ammo storage compartment, blue or Dyna-chrome finish, 11 oz. Mfg. 1986 - Disc.

	100%	98%	95%	90%	80%	70%	60%
	$80	$65	$55	$50	$45	$40	$35

Last Mfg.'s Sug. Retail was $95.

Add $9 for Dyna-chrome finish.
Add $25 for deluxe model (walnut stocks).
Add $60 for Misty Gold finish (disc.).

PISTOLS: SEMI-AUTO, TITAN SERIES

TITAN II (E32 SERIES) — .32 ACP (disc. 1988), or .380 ACP, single action, blue (standard) or chrome finish. Mfg. in USA - disc.

	100%	98%	95%	90%	80%	70%	60%
	$195	$160	$135	$120	$105	$95	$85

Last Mfg.'s Sug. Retail was $220.

Add $25 for walnut grips.
Add $10 for chrome finish.

This series was redesigned in 1988 to be shorter and more compact. Older series Titans are worth approx. $50 less than values shown above.

SUPER TITAN II — .32 ACP (disc. 1988), or .380 ACP cal., single action, 12 shot mag. in .32 ACP, 11 for .380 cal., walnut grips, standard blue only. Mfg. U.S. - disc.

	100%	98%	95%	90%	80%	70%	60%
	$215	$185	$155	$135	$120	$105	$95

Last Mfg.'s Sug. Retail was $260.

.22 TITAN II (E22) — .22 LR cal., single action, 10 shot mag., blue finish only. Walnut grips standard. Mfg. 1990 only.

	100%	98%	95%	90%	80%	70%	60%
	$130	$105	$90	$80	$70	$65	$60

Last Mfg.'s Sug. Retail was $161.

* Lady .22 — similar to .22 TITAN II except has combination blue/gold finish with scrimshawed red rose on ivory polymer grips. New 1990.

	100%	98%	95%	90%	80%	70%	60%
	$185	$155	$130	$120	$105	$95	$85

Last Mfg.'s Sug. Retail was $208.

THE BEST (A27) — .25 ACP cal., single action, blue only, deluxe finish, walnut grips, steel frame, 6 shot mag. Mfg. in Spain by Astra. Importation disc. 1988.

	100%	98%	95%	90%	80%	70%	60%
	$125	$105	$90	$80	$70	$65	$60

Last Mfg.'s Sug. Retail was $155.

Grading	100%	98%	95%	90%	80%	70%	60%

.25 TITAN (E27 SERIES) — .25 ACP cal., single action, blue (disc. 1989) or Dyna-chrome finish (standard 1990).

	$60	$50	$45	$40	$35	$30	$30

Last Mfg.'s Sug. Retail was $77.

> Subtract $5 for blued finish.
> Add $26 for gold trim (new 1986).
> Add $62 for Misty Gold finish (1988 only).

* ***Titan Tigress*** — similar to .25 Titan except is entirely gold plated and cased, ladies pistol. Imported 1989-90 only.

	$130	$110	$95

Last Mfg.'s Sug. Retail was $153.

.25 TITAN (E38 SERIES) — .25 ACP cal., similar to E27 series except has standard blue finish. Mfg. 1990 only.

	$50	$45	$40	$35	$30	$30	$25

Last Mfg.'s Sug. Retail was $59.

> Add $9 for Dyna-chrome finish.

SSP SERIES — .32 ACP or .380 ACP cal., single action semi-auto, 3⅛ in. barrel, 5 shot mag., blue or chrome finish, composition grips, 25 oz. Mfg. in U.S. - 1990 only.

	$120	$95	$85	$75	$65	$60	$55

Last Mfg.'s Sug. Retail was $146.

> Add $19 for chrome finish.

* ***Lady SSP*** — similar to SSP except has gold trimmed parts, scrimshawed red rose on ivory polymer grips, and gold case. Mfg. 1990 only.

	$210	$180	$155	$135	$120	$105	$95

Last Mfg.'s Sug. Retail was $250.

TZ-75 — 9mm Para. cal., double action, 4.72 in. barrel, steel frame and slide, 15 shot mag., patterned after the CZ-75 action, 35 oz. Imported 1982-1989. This model was updated in 1988 (Series 88).

	$375	$325	$290	$270	$250	$235	$220

Last Mfg.'s Sug. Retail was $440.

> Add $20 for satin chrome finish (new 1986).
> Add $20 for black rubber grips.

TZ-75 SERIES 88 — 9mm Para. or .41 Action Express cal., improved TZ-75 action, 4.72 in. barrel, steel frame and slide, 11 (.41 AE) or 17 (9mm Para.) shot mag., fixed removable rear sight, choice of matte blue, satin chrome, or blue slide/chrome frame finish, updated CZ-75 action, 35 oz. Mfg. 1988-90.

	$435	$360	$330	$295	$280	$260	$240

Last Mfg.'s Sug. Retail was $519.

> Add $97 for .41 Action Express cal.
> Add $20 for satin chrome on 9mm Para., $29 on .41 AE.
> Add $14 for black rubber grips.
>
> This model was also available with a blue slide/chrome frame (I.P.S.C. configuration) at no extra charge.
>
> The TZ-75 Series 88 was re-engineered in 1988 to include: frame mounted sear locking safety (cocked and locked), Colt style firing pin safety block, improved recessed slide serrations, muzzle barrel swell, bobbed hammer design, elongated combat style slide stop, new mag. release, and removable rear sight.

* ***TZ-75 Combo*** — includes both .41 Action Express and 9mm Para. barrels. Mfg. 1990 only.

	$615	$535	$475	$430	$395	$370	$350

Last Mfg.'s Sug. Retail was $709.

> Add $29 for satin chrome or blue slide/chrome frame finish.

F

Grading	100%	98%	95%	90%	80%	70%	60%

* *TZ-75 Series 88 Govt. Model* — 9mm Para. cal. only, compact variation of the TZ-75 Series 88, 3⅗ in. barrel, 12 shot mag., checkered walnut grips, 33½ oz. Mfg. 1990 only.

		$435	$360	$330	$295	$280	$260	$240

Last Mfg.'s Sug. Retail was $519.

Add $20 for satin chrome or blue slide/chrome frame finish.

* *TZ-75 Series 88 with ported barrel* — similar to the TZ-75 Series 88 except has 5 in. ported barrel and slide. Mfg. 1990 only.

		$615	$535	$475	$430	$395	$370	$350

Last Mfg.'s Sug. Retail was $709.

* *Compensated TZ-75 Series 88* — similar to the TZ-75 Series 88 except has 5¾ in. compensated barrel, 42 oz. Mfg. 1990 only.

		$700	$615	$535	$475	$430	$395	$370

Last Mfg.'s Sug. Retail was $804.

MODEL 722 TP SILHOUETTE PISTOL — .22 LR cal., bolt action target pistol, 10 in. free-floating barrel, 4-way adj. trigger, micro adj. rear sight, 6 or 10 shot mag., stippled pistol grip and forearm, supplied with 2-piece scope mount, 3.4 lbs. Mfg. 1990 only.

		$220	$190	$160	$140	$125	$115	$100

Last Mfg.'s Sug. Retail was $263.

SPECTRE PISTOL — 9mm Para. or .45 ACP cal., double action, unique triple action blowback system with two piece bolt, 6 in. barrel, military style configuration, adj. sights, 30 or 50 (optional with unique 4 column configuation) shot mag., 4.8 lbs. Mfg. 1989-90 only.

		$675	$600	$525	$480	$440	$400	$360

Last Mfg.'s Sug. Retail was $718.

Add $14 for mag. loading tool.

KG-99 — 9mm Para. cal., paramilitary design pistol, 36 shot mag. Mini-99 also available with 20 shot mag. and 3 in. barrel. Disc. 1984.

		$550	$475	$440	$400	$365	$330	$300

This model was not manufactured but sold by F.I.E.

REVOLVERS: DOUBLE ACTION, ARMINIUS SERIES

All pistols under this heading were manufactured in W. Germany under the trademark Arminius. .22 cal. is 8 shot, .32 S&W is 7 shot, all others 6 shot.

MODEL 522TB — .22 LR cal., blue finish, 4 in. barrel, 8 shot.

		$130	$100	$85	$75	$70	$65	$60

Last Mfg.'s Sug. Retail was $174.

Add $23 for walnut grips.

722 SERIES — .22 LR cal., blue (standard) or chrome finish (disc. 1985), 6 in. barrel, 8 shot.

		$125	$100	$90	$80	$70	$65	$60

Last Mfg.'s Sug. Retail was $161.

Add $23 for walnut grips.
Add $49 for .22 LR/.22 Mag. combo.
Add $15 for chrome finish.

STANDARD REVOLVER — .22 LR, .22 Mag., .32 Mag. or .38 Spl. cal., 2 or 4 in. barrel, blued finish, fixed sights, without ejector assembly. U.S. mfg. 1989-90.

		$80	$70	$65	$60	$55	$50	$45

Last Mfg.'s Sug. Retail was $101.

Add $19 for chrome finish (2 in. barrel only).
Add $38 for gold plated finish (2 in. barrel only).
Add $23 for .22 Combo package (2 cylinders - 4 in. barrel only).

Models with 4 in. barrels were available in blued finish only.

Grading	100%	98%	95%	90%	80%	70%	60%

MODEL 532TB — .32 S&W cal., blue (standard) or chrome finish (disc. 1985), adj. sights, 4 in. barrel, 7 shot.

| | $145 | $120 | $100 | $80 | $75 | $70 | $65 |

Last Mfg.'s Sug. Retail was $183.

Add $23 for walnut grips.
Add $15 for chrome finish.

MODEL 732B — similar to Model 532TB, except has 6 in. barrel and fixed sights. Imported 1988 only.

| | $120 | $100 | $90 | $80 | $70 | $65 | $60 |

Last Mfg.'s Sug. Retail was $140.

MODEL N-38 (TITAN TIGER) — .38 Spl. cal., blue (standard) or chrome finish (disc. 1985), 2 or 4 in. barrel, fixed sights. Disc. 1990.

| | $130 | $110 | $95 | $80 | $75 | $65 | $60 |

Last Mfg.'s Sug. Retail was $176.

Add $23 for walnut grips.
Add $15 for chrome finish.

ZEPHYR — .38 Spl. cal., 5 shot, aluminum construction, 2 in. barrel, blue finish, checkered grips, 14 oz. Mfg. 1990 only.

| | $145 | $120 | $100 | $80 | $75 | $70 | $65 |

Last Mfg.'s Sug. Retail was $189.

* *Lady Zephyr* — similar to Zephyr, except has gold trimmed parts, scrimshawed red rose on ivory polymer grips, and gold case. Mfg. 1990 only.

| | $250 | $210 | $180 | $155 | $135 | $115 | $95 |

Last Mfg.'s Sug. Retail was $295.

MODEL 384TB — .38 Spl. cal., blue (standard) or chrome finish (disc. 1985), 6 shot, 4 in. barrel.

| | $150 | $125 | $105 | $85 | $80 | $70 | $65 |

Last Mfg.'s Sug. Retail was $195.

Add $23 for walnut grips.
Add $13 for chrome finish.

MODEL 386TB — .38 Spl. cal., blue (standard) or chrome finish (disc. 1985), 6 shot, 6 in. barrel.

| | $150 | $125 | $105 | $85 | $80 | $70 | $65 |

Last Mfg.'s Sug. Retail was $195.

Add $23 for walnut grips.
Add $13 for chrome finish.

.357 MAG. SERIES — .357 Mag. cal., blue (standard) or chrome finish (disc. 1985), 6 shot, 3 (Model 3573TB), 4 (Model 3574TB), or 6 (Model 3576TB) in. barrels.

| | $200 | $170 | $135 | $120 | $110 | $100 | $90 |

Last Mfg.'s Sug. Retail was $255.

Add $23 for walnut grips.
Add $15 for chrome finish.

Revolvers: Snub-Nose, Disc.

Previously manufactured 2 in. snub-nosed revolvers are listed in the previous category under Standard Revolver, Titan Tiger, and Zephyr.

222 SERIES — .22 LR & .22 Mag. cal., blue (standard) or chrome finish, 2 in. snub-nose barrel. Disc. 1985.

| | $135 | $115 | $90 | $85 | $75 | $65 | $60 |

Last Mfg.'s Sug. Retail was $120.

Add $15 for walnut grips.
Add $45 for .22 LR/.22 Mag. combo.

* *222B SERIES* — .22 LR cal. only 1989, similar to 222 Series, reintroduced 1987-1989.

| | $150 | $120 | $105 | $85 | $80 | $70 | $65 |

Last Mfg.'s Sug. Retail was $185.

Add $45 for .22 LR/.22 Mag. combo (disc. 1988).

Grading	100%	98%	95%	90%	80%	70%	60%

232 SERIES — .32 S&W cal., blue (standard) or chrome finish, 2 in. barrel. Disc.

	100%	98%	95%	90%	80%	70%	60%
	$120	$90	$85	$75	$65	$60	$55

> Add $15 for walnut grips.
> Add $14 for adj. sights.
> Add $28 for chrome finish.

* *232B SERIES* — similar to 232 Series, 2 in. barrel. Reintroduced 1987-1989.

	100%	98%	95%	90%	80%	70%	60%
	$150	$125	$110	$95	$85	$75	$70

Last Mfg.'s Sug. Retail was $185.

> Add $5 for adj. sights.

MODEL 382TB — .38 Spl. cal., blue (standard) or chrome finish, 2 in. barrel. Disc. 1985.

	100%	98%	95%	90%	80%	70%	60%
	$125	$110	$100	$90	$80	$75	$65

Last Mfg.'s Sug. Retail was $145.

> Add $15 for walnut grips.
> Add $16 for chrome finish.

MODEL 3572 — .357 Mag. cal., blue (standard) or chrome finish, 2 in. barrel. Disc. 1984.

	100%	98%	95%	90%	80%	70%	60%
	$223	$170	$160	$135	$125	$115	$100

> Add $15 for walnut grips.
> Add $17 for chrome finish.

F

REVOLVERS: SINGLE ACTION

Combo designations on below listed models indicate 2 cylinders (.22 LR/.22 Mag.).

COWBOY — .22 LR or .22 LR/Mag. cal. combo, 3¼ or 6 in. barrel, blued finish, square butt grip, without ejector tube, fixed sights. U.S. mfg. 1989-90.

	100%	98%	95%	90%	80%	70%	60%
	$75	$65	$50	$45	$40	$35	$30

Last Mfg.'s Sug. Retail was $95.

> Add $23 for combo.

GOLD RUSH — .22 LR or .22 LR/Mag. cal. combo, 3¼, 4¾, or 6½ in. barrel, round (3¼ in. barrel only) or square butt grip, gold band on barrel and cylinder, ivory-tex grips. U.S. mfg. 1989-90.

	100%	98%	95%	90%	80%	70%	60%
	$155	$125	$110	$95	$85	$75	$70

Last Mfg.'s Sug. Retail was $189.

> Add $47 for combo.

TEXAS RANGER (TEX 22 SERIES) — .22 LR or .22 Mag. cal.(combo only), 3¼ (new 1986), 4¾, 6½ (new 1989), 7, or 9 in. barrel, 6 shot, blue only. Mfg. U.S. - disc.

	100%	98%	95%	90%	80%	70%	60%
	$80	$70	$60	$50	$45	$40	$35

Last Mfg.'s Sug. Retail was $108.

> Add $23 for combo.
> Add $6 for 9 in. barrel.

> This model with a 3¼ in. barrel is called the Little Ranger.

BUFFALO SCOUT (E15 SERIES) — .22 LR or .22 Mag. cal., blue (standard) or chrome finish, 4¾ in. barrel. Mfg. in Brescia, Italy - disc.

	100%	98%	95%	90%	80%	70%	60%
	$75	$55	$45	$35	$35	$30	$30

Last Mfg.'s Sug. Retail was $98.

> Add $23 for walnut grips.
> Add $23 for combo.
> Add $9 for chrome or blue/gold finish.

* *The Yellow Rose Combo* — all metal parts 24 Kt. gold plated, smooth walnut grips. Mfg. 1986-90.

	100%	98%	95%
	$130	$110	$95

Last Mfg.'s Sug. Retail was $161.

> Add $151 for scrimshawed ivory polymer grips - walnut cased (new 1989).

Grading	100%	98%	95%	90%	80%	70%	60%

LEGEND SAA (PL-22 SERIES) — .22 LR or .22 Mag. cal., blue only. Mfg. in Brescia, Italy. Disc. 1984.

	$120	$90	$85	$75	$65	$60	$55

> Add $3 for walnut grips.
> Add $17 for combo.

HOMBRE MODEL — .357 Mag., .44 Mag., or .45 LC cal., color case hardened receiver, 5½ (disc. 1985), 6, or 7½ in. barrel, 45 oz., smooth walnut grips. Previously mfg. W. Germany.

	$220	$180	$145	$130	$120	$110	$100

Last Mfg.'s Sug. Retail was $265.

> Add $25 for brass back strap and trigger guard (disc.).

* *Golden Hombre* — same general specifications as Hombre, except all metal surfaces are plated in 24Kt. gold.

	$300	$210	$145

Last Mfg.'s Sug. Retail was $350.

> Add $65 for ivory polymer grips (new 1989).

RIFLES: BOLT-ACTION

MODEL 122 — .22 LR cal., 6 or 10 shot box mag., 21 in. tapered barrel, Monte Carlo walnut stock, adj. sights. Mfg. by Hamilton & Hunter. Mfg. 1986-disc.

	$100	$80	$70	$60	$55	$50	$45

Last Mfg.'s Sug. Retail was $115.

MODEL 322 — .22 LR cal., competition model, 26.2 in. floating barrel, adj. trigger, 6 or 10 shot mag., stippled pistol grip, 7 lbs. Mfg. 1990-disc.

	$580	$425	$380	$340	$295	$260	$230

Last Mfg.'s Sug. Retail was $665.

MODEL 422 — similar to Model 322 except has heavy barrel, 9 lbs. Mfg. 1990-disc.

	$580	$425	$380	$340	$295	$260	$230

Last Mfg.'s Sug. Retail was $665.

RIFLES: SEMI-AUTO

GR-8 BLACK BEAUTY — .22 LR cal., 14 shot, 19½ in. barrel, 64 oz., tubular feed, black nylon stock, patterned after Rem. Nylon 66. Mfg. by C.B.C. of Brazil. F.I.E. Importation disc. 1988, now imported by K.B.I.

	$90	$75	$70	$65	$60	$55	$50

Last Mfg.'s Sug. Retail was $100.

PARA RIFLE — .22 LR cal., paramilitary designed rifle with case, takedown, 11 shot, matte black receiver finish. Mfg. by L. Franchi between 1979-1984. Imported into the U.S. from 1985-88.

	$225	$195	$155	$140	$130	$120	$110

Last Mfg.'s Sug. Retail was $225.

> 8,000 of this model were manufactured by L. Franchi. 5,000 went to the Italian Government and were used as training rifles (with German scopes). The remainder were imported by F.I.E. (without scopes).

SPECTRE CARBINE — 9mm Para. cal., same action as Spectre pistol, paramilitary design carbine, collapsible metal butt stock, 30 or 50 (opt.) shot mag., adj. rear sight, with pistol and forearm grip. Mfg. 1989 - Disc.

	$525	$425	$365	$300	$275	$250	$225

Last Mfg.'s Sug. Retail was $700.

SHOTGUNS

All currently manufactured Franchi shotguns can be located in the Franchi section of this text.

S.O.B. — 12, 20 ga., or .410 bore, 18½ in. single barrel, pistol grip only. Disc. 1984.

	$100	$90	$80	$70	$60	$55	$50

Grading	100%	98%	95%	90%	80%	70%	60%

THE STURDY O/U — 12 or 20 ga., 3 in. chambers, 28 in. barrels, vent. rib and barrels, engraved silver finish receiver, double triggers, extractors, manufactured by Maroccini of Italy. Imported 1985-1988.

	$300	$275	$250	$235	$220	$205	$190

Last Mfg.'s Sug. Retail was $350.

* *Sturdy Deluxe Priti* — similar to The Sturdy model except has deluxe walnut. Importation disc. 1988.

	$325	$290	$260	$240	$225	$205	$195

Last Mfg.'s Sug. Retail was $380.

Add $70 for ejectors, SST, and choke tubes.

* *Model 12 Deluxe* — 12 ga. only, SST, auto ejectors, multi-choked barrels, select walnut. Imported 1988 only.

	$320	$290	$260	$240	$225	$205	$195

Last Mfg.'s Sug. Retail was $380.

THE BRUTE — 12, 20 ga, or .410 bore, 19 in. barrels, 30 in. overall length. Side-by-side action, disc. 1984.

	$195	$150	$140	$120	$110	$100	$90

SPAS-12 — this model appears under the Franchi heading in the F section.

SAS-12 — this model appears under the Franchi heading in the F section.

LAW-12 — this model appears under the Franchi heading in the F section.

FMJ

Current manufacturer located in Copperhill, TN. Dealer sales.

DERRINGERS

SINGLE BARREL DERRINGER — .45 LC/.410 shotshell cal. (2½ in.), spur trigger, black oxide finish, 16 oz. New 1993.

Mfg.'s Sug. Retail	$70	$60	$50	$40	$35	$30	$25	$20

.22 LR/.45 LC O/U — .22 LRx.45 LC/.410 bore. New 1995.

Mfg.'s Sug. Retail	$90	$70	$60	$50	$40	$35	$30	$25

DOUBLE BARREL DERRINGER — .45 LC x .410 shotshell cal. (3 in.), SxS, spur trigger, single hammer, 20 oz. New 1994.

Mfg.'s Sug. Retail	$110	$95	$85	$70	$60	$50	$40	$35

HANDGUNS

MODEL R REVOLVER — .22 LR cal., 6 shot. New 1995.

Mfg.'s Sug. Retail	$90	$70	$60	$50	$40	$35	$30	$25

MODEL MR REVOLVER — .45 LC/.410 shotshell cal., 5 shot, manual rotation. New 1996.

Mfg.'s Sug. Retail	$140	$115	$85	$65	$55	$50	$45	$40

MODEL PP — .22 LR or .380 ACP cal., stainless construction. New 1995.

Mfg.'s Sug. Retail	$150	$120	$90	$70

SHOTGUNS

BEGINNERS SHOTGUN (SH) — .410 bore, 3 in. chamber, spur trigger, fixed skeleton or folding stock, 2 lbs. New 1994.

Mfg.'s Sug. Retail	$100	$85	$70	$60	$50	$40	$35	$30

STANDARD MODEL — .410 bore, fixed or folding stock. New 1996.

Mfg.'s Sug. Retail	$145	$120	$90	$70	$60	$55	$50	$45

Add $5 for folding stock.

Grading	100%	98%	95%	90%	80%	70%	60%

FTL

Previously manufactured by Wilkinson Arms located in Covina, CA for the FTL Marketing Corp. located in N. Hollywood, CA.

PISTOLS: SEMI-AUTO

FTL AUTO NINE — .22 LR cal., single action, hammerless, blowback action, 8 shot mag., checkered plastic grips, fixed sights. Disc.

	$200	$160	$125	$105	$95	$85	$75

FABARM, S.p.A.

Current manufacturer established in 1900 and located in Brescia, Italy. Currently imported and distributed by Heckler & Koch, Inc. beginning 1998. Certain models had limited importation by Ithaca Acquisition Corp. located in King Ferry, NY during 1993-95. Previously imported and distributed (1988-90) by St. Lawrence Sales, Inc. located in Lake Orion, MI. Previously imported until 1986 by Beeman Precision Arms, Inc. located in Santa Rosa, CA.

Fabarm currently manufactures approx. 35,000 shotguns annually.

F

SHOTGUNS: O/U

FIELD MODEL — 12 ga. only, 29⅛ in. VR barrels, single trigger, ejectors, silver finished receiver, also available in Skeet and Trap models. Disc. 1985.

	$695	$595	$550	$500	$460	$420	$390

Last Mfg.'s Sug. Retail was $795.

SKEET/TRAP COMBINATION SET — 12 ga. only, is supplied with both skeet and trap barrel assemblies, cased. Disc. 1986.

	$1,050	$900	$840	$780	$720	$670	$600

Last Mfg.'s Sug. Retail was $1,195.

Add $39 for high gloss wood finish.
Add $30 for auto safety.

Models below have boxlock actions with coin finished receivers and light engraving.

GAMMA FIELD — 12 or 20 (disc.) ga., SST, ejectors, 26, 28, 29, 30, or 32 in. VR barrels, fixed or innerchokes, checkered walnut stock and forearm, 6½ lbs. Imported 1989-95.

	$840	$715	$660	$600	$550	$450	$375

Last Mfg.'s Sug. Retail was $1,044.

Add $28 for 5 innerchokes with wrench (3 in. chambers in 12 ga.).
Add $50 for 20 ga. (3 in. chambers).

* *Gamma AL Superlight* — 12 ga. only, similar to Gamma Field except receiver is made from Ergal light alloy, 6 lbs. Imported 1989-1990.

	$875	$760	$695	$625	$550	$450	$375

Last Mfg.'s Sug. Retail was $970.

Add $41 for 5 innerchokes with wrench.
Add $66 for 20 ga. with 3 in. chambers. New 1990.

This model is chambered for 2¾ in. shells only.

GAMMA SPORTING CLAYS COMPETITION — 12 ga. only, designed for sporting clays competition, SST, 28, 29, or 30 in. VR, (10mm) and barrels supplied with 5 innerchokes, special recoil pad, ejectors, checkered walnut stock and forearm. Imported 1989-95.

	$950	$825	$725	$650	$575	$495	$400

Last Mfg.'s Sug. Retail was $1,175.

Add $17 for trap stock and forearm (disc. - includes 28 in. barrels with 5 choke tubes).

Grading	100%	98%	95%	90%	80%	70%	60%

GAMMA SKEET — 12 ga. only, 27½ or 28 in. VR barrels, SST, ejectors, supplied with 5 innerchokes, special recoil pad, checkered walnut stock and forearm, reversed Skeet chokes new 1994. Imported 1989-95.

	$875	$735	$695	$635	$550	$450	$375

Last Mfg.'s Sug. Retail was $1,107.

GAMMA TRAP — 12 ga. only, 29 or 30 in. VR barrels with special trap chokes and 10mm rib, SST, ejectors, checkered Monte Carlo stock and forearm, 7½ lbs. Imported 1989-95.

	$875	$735	$695	$635	$550	$450	$375

Last Mfg.'s Sug. Retail was $1,107.

GAMMA PARADOX — 12 ga. only, 25 in. VR barrels with top barrel rifled and lower barrel supplied with 3 innerchokes, SST, ejectors, checkered walnut stock and forearm, 6 lbs. 6 oz. Imported 1989-1990.

	$850	$750	$695	$625	$550	$450	$375

Last Mfg.'s Sug. Retail was $945.

* *Gamma Paradox AL Superlight* — similar to Gamma Paradox except receiver is made from Ergal light alloy, 5 lbs. 7 oz. Imported 1989-1990.

	$875	$760	$695	$625	$550	$450	$375

Last Mfg.'s Sug. Retail was $960.

EURALFA — 12 ga., 2¾ in. chambers, 26 or 28 in. VR barrels with fixed chokes, DT or SNT, extractors, blued receiver with photo engraving, 6½ lbs. Imported 1989-1990.

	$495	$460	$420	$390	$350	$310	$275

Last Mfg.'s Sug. Retail was $571.

* *Euralfa AL Superlight* — 12 ga., similar to Euralfa except receiver is made from Ergal light alloy, 6 lbs. Imported 1989-1990.

	$515	$475	$430	$400	$360	$320	$285

Last Mfg.'s Sug. Retail was $603.

* *Euralfa Trap* — 12 ga. only, 3 in. chambers, 30 in. barrels bored IM/F. Imported 1990.

	$550	$495	$460	$430	$400	$360	$320

Last Mfg.'s Sug. Retail was $636.

* *Euralfa Magnum* — 12 ga., 3 in. chambers, 26, 28, or 29 in. VR (10mm wide) barrels with fixed chokes, rubber recoil pad. Imported 1989-1990.

	$515	$475	$430	$400	$360	$320	$285

Last Mfg.'s Sug. Retail was $587.

* *Euralfa Innerchoke* — 12 ga. only, 3 in. chambers, 28 in. barrels. Imported 1990 only.

	$560	$500	$460	$430	$400	$360	$320

Last Mfg.'s Sug. Retail was $652.

* *Euralfa Slug* — 12 ga. only, 24 in. barrels bored cyl./cyl. Imported 1990.

	$500	$475	$430	$400	$360	$320	$285

Last Mfg.'s Sug. Retail was $571.

EURALFA PARADOX — 12 ga. only, similar to Euralfa except 25 in. VR barrels with top barrel rifled and lower barrel supplied with 3 innerchokes, 6 lbs. 6 oz. Imported 1989-1990.

	$550	$495	$460	$430	$400	$360	$320

Last Mfg.'s Sug. Retail was $636.

* *Euralfa Paradox AL Superlight* — similar to Euralfa Paradox except receiver is made from Ergal light alloy, 5 lbs. 7 oz. Imported 1989-1990.

	$550	$495	$460	$430	$400	$360	$320

Last Mfg.'s Sug. Retail was $636.

SILVER LION — 12 or 20 ga., similar to Max Lion, except has standard wood and lockable hard plastic case, ported TriBore barrels became optional during 1999. Importation began 1998.

Mfg.'s Sug. Retail	$1,146	$1,000	$900	$800	$700	$600	$500	$400

Add $118 for ported TriBore barrels.

Grading	100%	98%	95%	90%	80%	70%	60%

* Silver Lion Youth Model — similar to Silver Lion, except has youth dimensions, steel receiver, ported 24 in. TriBore vent. barrels standard, mid rib bead, approx. 6 lbs. New 1999.

Mfg.'s Sug. Retail	$1,331	$1,125	$975	$850	$725	$625	$525	$425

ULTRA MAG LION — 12 ga. only, 3½ in. chambers, 28 in. standard or ported TriBore (new 1999) barrels, choice of non-glare matte metal finish or 100% Advantage Wetlands camo coverage, black colored walnut stock and forearm, non-automatic ejectors, 7.9 lbs., includes lockable plastic case. Importation began 1998.

Mfg.'s Sug. Retail	$1,120	$925	$825	$750	$675	$600	$550	$500

Add $175 for 100% Advantage Wetlands camo coverage.

CAMO TURKEY MODEL — 12 ga. only, 3½ in. chambers, 20 in. separated barrels, unique Picatinny rail on top of receiver allows convenient scop mounting, 100% extra brown camo coverage, includes ultra-full ported choke tubes, locking fitted luggage case, approx. 7½ lbs. New 1999.

Mfg.'s Sug. Retail	$1,295	$1,125	$975	$850	$725	$625	$525	$425

SUPER LIGHT LION — 12 ga. only, 3 in. chambers, lightweight alloy receiver, blue finish, 24 in. vent. standard or ported TriBore (new 1999) barrels with VR, standard checkered walnut stock and forearm, includes lockable hard plastic case, 6½ lbs. Importation began 1998.

Mfg.'s Sug. Retail	$1,053	$895	$800	$750	$675	$600	$550	$500

Add $67 for ported TriBore barrels.

* Super Light Lion Youth Model — similar to Silver Lion Youth Model, except has Ergal 55 aluminum receiver, approx. 5¾ lbs. New 1999.

Mfg.'s Sug. Retail	$1,053	$895	$800	$750	$675	$600	$550	$500

SPORTING CLAY COMPETITION LION — 12 or 20 ga., 3 in. cahmbers, 28 in. vent. ported TriBore barrels with 10mm VR, recoil reducer and buttstock, checkered walnut stock and forearm, adj. SST, includes locking fitted luggage case. New 1999.

Mfg.'s Sug. Retail	$1,365	$1,150	$995	$865	$735	$625	$525	$425

BLACK LION COMPETITION — 12 or 20 ga., competition model featuring blued receiver, 26, 28, or 30 (12 ga. only) in. vent. standard or ported TriBore (new 1999) barrels with VR, deluxe checkered wood, 6.8-7.8 lbs. Importation began 1998.

Mfg.'s Sug. Retail	$1,529	$1,300	$1,025	$875	$775	$675	$600	$550

Add $66 for ported TriBore barrels.

MAX LION — 12 or 20 ga., 3 in. chambers, engraved boxlock action with nickel finish, 26, 28, or 30 in. vent. standard or ported TriBore (new 1999) barrels with VR, rebounding hammers, deluxe checkered stock and forearm, with vent. recoil pad, choke tubes, gold SST, non-automatic safety, includes locking fitted luggage case, 6.8-7.8 lbs. Importation began 1998.

Mfg.'s Sug. Retail	$1,807	$1,625	$1,375	$1,150	$925	$825	$750	$675

Add $67 for ported TriBore barrels.

SHOTGUNS: SEMI-AUTO

The models listed below are gas operated, self compensating, have 4 shot mags., aluminum receivers, twin action bars, blued receiver with photo etched game scene engraving, and checkered walnut stock and forearm.

Add $25 for De Luxe engraving or camouflage wood finish.

DEER GUN — 12 ga. only, 3 in. chamber, 24 in. rifled barrel with front and rear rifle sights, 5 shot mag., 7 lbs. Limited importation 1994-95.

		$695	$475	$425	$375	$325	$300	$285

Last Mfg.'s Sug. Retail was $775.

ELLEGI STANDARD — 12 ga. only, 28 in. VR barrel with fixed choke, blued receiver, gold trigger, 6 lbs. 9 oz. Imported 1989-1990.

		$525	$450	$375	$325	$300	$275	$250

Last Mfg.'s Sug. Retail was $619.

Grading	100%	98%	95%	90%	80%	70%	60%

* *Ellegi Multichoke* — similar to Ellegi Standard except 5 different choke tubes extend length of barrel up to 6 in., average weight is 6 lbs. 9 oz. Imported 1989-1990.

| | $540 | $475 | $395 | $350 | $325 | $300 | $265 |

Last Mfg.'s Sug. Retail was $644.

The standard barrel length on this model is 24½ in. (30½ in. with full extra-long choke tube).

* *Ellegi Innerchoke* — 12 ga. only, 3 in. chamber, 28 in. VR barrel with 5 innerchokes supplied, 7 lbs. Imported 1989-1990.

| | $540 | $475 | $395 | $350 | $325 | $300 | $265 |

Last Mfg.'s Sug. Retail was $644.

* *Ellegi Magnum* — 12 ga. only, 3 in. chamber, 30 in. VR barrel with fixed choke, recoil pad, 7¼ lbs. Imported 1989-1990.

| | $525 | $450 | $375 | $325 | $300 | $275 | $250 |

Last Mfg.'s Sug. Retail was $619.

* *Ellegi Super Goose* — 12 ga. only, 3 in. chamber, 35½ in. VR (12mm wide) barrel with fixed choke, adj. rifle rear sight, supplied with rail for mounting scope rings, rubber recoil pad, designed especially for long range shooting, 7½ lbs. Imported 1989-1990.

| | $625 | $495 | $425 | $375 | $340 | $315 | $280 |

Last Mfg.'s Sug. Retail was $734.

* *Ellegi Slug* — 12 ga. only, 24½ in. barrel, adj. rear sight and bead front, 6 lbs. 9 oz. Imported 1989-1990.

| | $545 | $475 | $395 | $350 | $325 | $300 | $265 |

Last Mfg.'s Sug. Retail was $652.

Add $200 for combo set (includes innerchoked 28 in. barrel).

* *Ellegi Police* — 12 ga. only, 20 in. cylinder bored barrel, matte black receiver, non-glare stock and forearm. Imported 1989-1990.

| | $495 | $425 | $360 | $300 | $275 | $250 | $225 |

Last Mfg.'s Sug. Retail was $587.

RED LION — 12 ga. only, 3 in. chamber, gas operated, alloy receiver, 24, 26, or 28 in. VR barrel, matte finish, reversible safety, checkered walnut stock and forearm, lockable plastic case, approx. 7 lbs. Importation began 1998.

| Mfg.'s Sug. Retail | $804 | $700 | $625 | $550 | $500 | $450 | $400 | $360 |

GOLD LION — similar to Red Lion, except has select walnut. Importation began 1998.

| Mfg.'s Sug. Retail | $914 | $800 | $700 | $625 | $550 | $500 | $450 | $400 |

CAMO LION — 12 ga. only, 3 in. chamber, 20, 24, 26, or 28 in. ported TriBore VR barrel, features 100% Advantage Wetlands camo coverage, approx. 7 lbs. New 1999.

| Mfg.'s Sug. Retail | $978 | $850 | $740 | $640 | $565 | $510 | $450 | $400 |

SPORTING CLAYS LION — 12 ga. only, 28 in. ported TriBore VR barrel, deluxe checkered walnut stock and forearm with olive wood pistol grip cap, matte finish with gold accents on receiver sides, approx. 7.2 lbs. New 1999.

| Mfg.'s Sug. Retail | $959 | $835 | $725 | $635 | $560 | $510 | $450 | $400 |

SHOTGUNS: SxS

The models listed below have boxlock actions with added sideplates.

BETA MODEL — 12 ga. only, 2¾ in. chambers, standard model with checkered walnut stock and forearm, ST, ejectors. Imported 1989 only.

| | $695 | $625 | $550 | $450 | $375 | $300 | $250 |

Last Mfg.'s Sug. Retail was $920.

This model was replaced by the Beta Lux in 1990.

Grading	100%	98%	95%	90%	80%	70%	60%

BETA LUX— 12 ga. only, 3 in. chambers, SST, ejectors, boxlock action, 24, 26, 28, or 30 in. barrels bored F/M, 6.6 lbs. Imported 1990-95.

	$1,100	$875	$725	$625	$550	$475	$400

Last Mfg.'s Sug. Retail was $1,270.

Add $30 for 5 Innerchokes.
Add $114 for competition trap/pigeon model (disc.)

BETA EUROPE — 12 ga. only, deluxe model with coin finished game scene engraved sideplates, 26½ or 27½ in. barrels with fixed chokes, ejectors, DT or SST, checkered English stock and splinter forearm, 6 lbs. 6 oz. Imported 1989-1990.

	$1,400	$1,100	$850	$700	$575	$495	$450

Last Mfg.'s Sug. Retail was $1,711.

Add $33 for semi-beavertail forend.
Add $130 for competition trap/pigeon model.

CLASSIC LION — 12 ga. only, 3 in. chambers, boxlock action, SST, ejectors, 26 in. barrels with 5 choke tubes, approx. 7 lbs. Importation began 1998.

* *Grade I* — features standard grade wood, engraved nickel finished receiver, gold SST, fitted luggage case.

Mfg.'s Sug. Retail	$1,488	$1,250	$995	$775	$675	$600	$550	$500

* *Grade II* — features deluxe wood and removable sideplates with engraving, fitted lugage case.

Mfg.'s Sug. Retail	$2,110	$1,775	$1,425	$1,175	$925	$825	$750	$675

SHOTGUNS: SINGLE BARREL

The models listed below have receivers made out of aluminum alloy, rear trigger guard safety, and matte black finish metal surfaces.

OMEGA STANDARD — 12, 20 ga., or .410 bore, 3 in. chamber, 26 or 28 (12 ga. only) in. barrel, checkered beech stock and forearm, approx. 5 lbs. 5 oz. Imported 1989-1990.

	$120	$95	$80	$70	$60	$55	$50

Last Mfg.'s Sug. Retail was $139.

* *Goose Gun* — 12 ga. only, similar to Omega Standard, except has a 35½ in. barrel, 6 lbs. Imported 1989-1990.

	$135	$115	$90	$80	$70	$60	$55

Last Mfg.'s Sug. Retail was $156.

SHOTGUNS: SLIDE ACTION

The models listed below are variations of the same action based on a twin bar slide system, alloy receiver with anti-glare finish (including barrel), rear trigger guard safety, and 2¾ or 3 in. shell interchangeability.

Add $25 for camouflage wood finish on the models listed below.

MODEL S.D.A.S.S. — 12 ga. only, 3 in. chamber, originally designed for police and self defense use, 8 shot tube mag., 20 or 24½ in. barrel threaded for external choke tubes, approx. 6 lbs. 6 oz. Imported 1989-1990.

	$325	$285	$260	$230	$195	$160	$140

Last Mfg.'s Sug. Retail was $415.

This model with 24½ in. barrel is threaded for external multi-chokes which can add up to 6 in. to the barrel length - available for a $17 extra charge.

* *Special Police* — similar to Model S.D.A.S.S. except has special heavy 20 in. cylinder bored barrel VR, cooling jacket, 6 shot mag., rubber recoil pad. Imported 1989-1990.

	$340	$295	$265	$230	$195	$160	$140

Last Mfg.'s Sug. Retail was $440.

F

Grading	100%	98%	95%	90%	80%	70%	60%

* **Martial** — 12 ga. only, 18, 20, 28, 30, or 35½ (disc. 1989) in. barrel, fixed sights and choke, approx. 6¼ lbs. Imported 1989-1990.

| | $330 | $290 | $260 | $225 | $190 | $160 | $140 |

Last Mfg.'s Sug. Retail was $424.

> Add $41 for VR.
> Add $20 for 35½ (disc. 1989) in. barrel.
> Add $33 for multi-choke (plain rib with 1 choke and wrench).
> Add $65 for innerchoke (includes 1 choke and wrench - VR barrel only).

FP6 — 12 ga. only, 3 in. chamber, 20 in. barrel with vent. heat shield, matte finished metal, black synthetic stock and forearm, various security configurations, includes locking plastic case, 6.6 lbs. Importation began 1998.

| Mfg.'s Sug. Retail | $499 | $430 | $385 | $350 | $315 | $285 | $260 | $240 |

FABBRI s.n.c.

Current manufacturer located in Concesio, Italy (previously located in Brescia). The factory should be contacted directly (see Trademark Index) for more information regarding current information and prices on the models listed below.

Fabbri s.n.c. relocated from Brescia to Concesio during 1969 and underwent a name change from Armi Fabbri to Fabbri s.n.c. during 1989. Currently, Fabbri s.n.c. engravers include Creative Art, Pedersoli, Torcoli, and Francassi. Fabbri manufactures perhaps the highest quality shotguns available in today's marketplace - approx. 20-30 guns are mfg. annually. Delivery times range from 2-4 years.

SHOTGUNS: CUSTOM

SxS SHOTGUN — 12 or 20 ga., one of the world's best current production guns, highest-quality sidelock, ejectors, full engraving, E prefix ser. no. Disc.

> Currently, Fabbri SxS shotguns manufactured within the last decade and in mint condition are priced in the $35,000-$38,000 range. Subtract $15,000 for scroll engraving.

O/U SHOTGUN — 12 or 20 ga., top-of-the-line quality with any combination of engraving, wood, and other options. Current retail starts at approx. $65,000 FOB Italy.

> Mint guns mfg. 1967-1983 are currently priced in the $35,000-$38,500 range, guns mfg. between 1983-1989 are priced in the $45,000 range, and mfg. within the last 10 years are currently priced in the $50,000-$55,000 range. As a final note on Fabbri pricing - hook up the right gauge and engraver, and it's possible to pay $350,000 for one shotgun!

FABRIQUE NATIONALE

Current manufacturer located in Herstal and Liege, Belgium. Current company name is Browning S.A. John M. Browning established a contract with FN in 1900 for exclusive manufacture of various Browning Patent Firearms. In 1992, FN was acquired by GIAT of France. In late 1997, FN was sold to the Walloon business region (area surrounding Liege and Herstal, Belgium).

Also See: Browning Arms under Rifles, Shotguns, and Pistols.

PISTOLS: SEMI-AUTO

For FN models 1900, 1903, 1905, 1910, 1922 (10/22), Baby Model, and the Model 10/71, please refer to the Browning Pistol section in this text.

PISTOLS: SEMI-AUTO, HI-POWER VARIATIONS

The F.N. Hi-Power (also known as P-35) was Browning's last pistol design. A 9mm Para., single action, semi-auto pistol, it was the first to incorporate a staggered high capacity magazine. It has a 4²¹⁄₃₂ in. barrel, 13 shot mag., hammer and mag. safeties, a

Grading	100%	98%	95%	90%	80%	70%	60%

wide variety of finishes and sight options. It's probably the most widely used military pistol in the world.

PRE-WAR COMMERCIAL HP — 9mm Para. cal., single action, blue, wood grips, tangent rear sight, slotted (original) for stock with tangent rear sight, 13 shot mag.

		100%	98%	95%	90%	80%	70%	60%
Tangent sight	& slotted	$1,875	$1,200	$995	$850	$600	$450	$375

> Add $750 for original flat board stock with attached holster in 98%+ condition, $1,250 if with matching ser. no.
> Add $175 for "ODIN" reproduction stock.

PRE-WAR MILITARY CONTRACT — mfg. under military contract for various European countries.

	100%	98%	95%	90%	80%	70%	60%
Lithuanian Crest	N/A	$1,950	$1,500	$995	$700	$600	$500
Estonian Contract ("E.V." or "K.L.")	N/A	$1,950	$1,500	$995	$700	$600	$500

> Since so many better known variations have been manufactured for military contract, the listing above represents the more interesting and collectable models. Pre-war Belgian military HPs are priced similarly to the pre-war Commercial Model.

WWII Production: Waffenamt Proofed

> There is a range of finishes during Nazi production that varies from the excellent pre-war commercial finish on early guns assembled from captured parts to the roughly milled, poorly finished specimens mfg. late in the war. Values below assume all major parts (slide, barrel, and frame) are matching with original magazine.
>
> In recent years, many Nazi production Hi-Powers have had the rear grip strap milled out and slotted to accept a shoulder stock. Careful observation is advised before purchasing a "rare" (and expensive) slotted and tangent sight specimen. Many HPs have been restored, since the restoration is easily accomplished by professionals.

* **Type I: Tangent sights — slotted** — taken from existing pre-war Belgian army pistols, quality is excellent, correct ser. range is quite limited, approx. 40,000-47,000. Ser. range for production under German occupation is 50,001-53,000. All are proofed WaA 613.

100%	98%	95%	90%	80%	70%	60%
$3,750	$2,750	$2,400	$2,000	$1,500	$1,250	$995

> Beware of restorations.

* **Type II** — tangent rear sight only, approx. 90,000 mfg. with generally good quality finish.

100%	98%	95%	90%	80%	70%	60%
$1,600	$1,200	$950	$750	$600	$500	$400

* **Type III Standard Fixed Sights**

100%	98%	95%	90%	80%	70%	60%
$750	$600	$550	$425	$325	$300	$275

POST-OCCUPATION PRODUCTION — commercial mfg. began 1944, first imported with BAC markings in 1954 (see Browning HP section). Military mfg. from 1944-present, early (1944) models are identifiable by an "A" serial number prefix and are not fitted with a magazine safety. In 1947, the rear slide bushing became hardened by a new heat treatment process. Other design modifications were added in 1950. Many thousands manufactured under various government contracts, most will have a T prefix.

> Add $50 if round hammer.
> Add $200-$2,000 for military pistols with crests, depending on condition and variation.

* **Tangent sight only**

100%	98%	95%	90%	80%	70%	60%
$775	$600	$500	$400	$350	$325	$300

> Add $100 for "T" prefix.

* **Tangent sight** — slotted for stock.

100%	98%	95%	90%	80%	70%	60%
$1,200	$1,050	$950	$700	$600	$500	$400

> Add $150 for "T" prefix.
> Add $150 for internal extractor.

Grading	100%	98%	95%	90%	80%	70%	60%

* **Fixed sight** — most common variation.

	100%	98%	95%	90%	80%	70%	60%
	$600	$500	$450	$400	$350	$325	$300

> Add $50 for round hammer.
> Add $50 for internal extractor.

MUSCAT AND OMAN CONTRACT

* **First Model** — 9 guns.

	100%	98%	95%
	$6,000	$5,000	$4,000

* **Second Model** — 27 guns.

	100%	98%	95%
	$4,500	$3,500	$2,000

INGLIS MANUFACTURED HI-POWERS — SEE INGLIS SECTION.

RIFLES: BOLT ACTION

F.N. MAUSER SPORTER DELUXE — available in popular American and European calibers, 24 in. barrel, adj. sight, checkered pistol grip stock. Mfg. 1947-1963.

	100%	98%	95%	90%	80%	70%	60%
	$650	$550	$495	$460	$300	$275	$250

F.N. PRESENTATION GRADE — similar to Deluxe, except engraved and select wood.

	100%	98%	95%	90%	80%	70%	60%
	$1,150	$935	$855	$770	$500	$475	$450

F.N. SUPREME — .243 Win., .270 Win., 7mm Rem. Mag., .308 Win. cal., or .30-06, 24 in. barrel, peep sight, checkered pistol grip stock. Mfg. 1957-1975.

	100%	98%	95%	90%	80%	70%	60%
	$650	$550	$495	$460	$300	$275	$250

F.N. SUPREME MAGNUM — .264 Mag., 7mm Rem. Mag., or .300 Win. Mag. cal., similar to Bolt Action.

	100%	98%	95%	90%	80%	70%	60%
	$675	$575	$540	$495	$325	$275	$250

FN SNIPER RIFLE (MODEL 30) — .308 Win. cal., this model was a Mauser actioned Sniper Rifle equipped with 20 in. extra heavy barrel, flash hider, diopter sights, Hensoldt 4X scope, hard case, bipod, and sling. 51 were imported into the U.S. with the last retail price (1988) being $2,950. When encountered today, values will range from $3,500 and higher (depending on condition).

RIFLES: SEMI-AUTO

MODEL 1949 — 7mm Rem. Mag., 7.65mm, 7.92mm, or .30-06 cal., gas operated 10 shot mag., 23 in. barrel, military rifle, tangent rear sight, military stock. Mfg. 160,000.

	100%	98%	95%	90%	80%	70%	60%
	$450	$365	$275	$250	$225	$185	$155

> Add 10% for .30-06 cal.
> Add 100% for sniper variation.
> Add $650 for correct scope, rings, and mount.

RIFLES: SEMI-AUTO, FAL/LAR/FNC SERIES

After tremendous price increases between 1985-1988, Fabrique Nationale decided in 1988 to discontinue this series completely. Not only are these rifles not exported to the U.S. any longer, but all production has ceased in Belgium as well. The only way FN will produce these models again is if they are given a large military contract - in which case a "side-order" of commercial guns may be built. 1989 Federal legislation regarding this type of paramilitary design also helped push up prices to their current level. FAL rifles were also mfg. in Israel by I.M.I.

F.N. FAL — semi-auto, French designation for the FN L.A.R. (light automatic rifle), otherwise similar to LAR. See values for LAR model listed below.

Grading	100%	98%	95%	90%	80%	70%	60%

F.N. L.A.R. COMPETITION (LIGHT AUTOMATIC RIFLE)

F.N. L.A.R. COMPETITION (LIGHT AUTOMATIC RIFLE) — .308 Win. (7.62x51) cal., semi-auto, competition rifle with match flash hider, 21 in. barrel, adj. 4 position fire selector on automatic models, wood stock, aperture rear sight adj. from 100-600 meters, 9.4 lbs. Mfg. 1981-83.

	$2,000	$1,750	$1,600	$1,450	$1,300	$1,175	$1,000

This model was designated by the factory as the 50.00 Model.

Mid-1987 retail on this model was $1,258. The last Mfg.'s Sug. Retail was $3,179 (this price reflected the last exchange rate and special order status of this model).

* **Heavy barrel rifle** — barrel is twice as heavy as standard L.A.R., includes wood or synthetic stock, short wood forearm, and bi-pod, 12.2 lbs. Importation disc. 1988.

	$2,500	$2,150	$1,850	$1,500	$1,350	$1,200	$1,050

Add $400 for walnut stock.

There were 2 variations of this model. The Model 50.41 had a synthetic butt stock while the Model 50.42 had a wood butt stock with steel butt plate incorporating a top extension used for either shoulder resting or inverted grenade launching.

Mid-1987 retail on this model was $1,497 (Model 50.41) or $1,654 (Model 50.42). The last Mfg.'s Sug. Retail was $3,776 (this price reflected the last exchange rate and special order status of this model).

* **Paratrooper rifle** — similar to L.A.R. model, except has folding stock, 8.3 lbs. Mfg. 1950-1988.

	$2,650	$2,300	$2,150	$1,900	$1,700	$1,500	$1,350

There were 2 variations of the Paratrooper L.A.R. Model. The Model 50.63 had a stationary aperture rear sight and 18 in. barrel. The Model 50.64 was supplied with a 21 in. barrel and had a rear sight calibrated for either 150 or 200 meters. Both models retailed for the same price.

Mid-1987 retail on this model was $1,310 (both the Model 50.63 and 50.64). The last Mfg.'s Sug. Retail was $3,239 (this price reflected the last exchange rate and special order status of this model).

FNC MODEL — .223 Rem. (5.56mm) cal., lightweight combat carbine, 18½ in. barrel, NATO approved, 30 shot mag., 8.4 lbs. Disc. 1987.

	$1,850	$1,650	$1,400	$1,250	$1,050	$950	$825

Add $50 for Paratrooper model (16 or 18½ in. barrel).

While rarer, the 16 in. barrel model incorporated a flash hider that did not perform as well as the flash hider used on the standard 18½ in. barrel.

Mid-1987 retail on this model was $749 (Standard Model) and $782 (Paratrooper Model). The last Mfg.'s Sug. Retail was $2,204 (Standard Model) and $2,322 (Paratrooper Model) - these prices reflected the last exchange rate and special order status of these models.

FALCO, S.R.L.

Current shotgun manufacturer located in Marcheno, Italy. No current importation. Falco manufactures a variety of small gauge shotguns in various configurations, including folding models. Please contact the factory directly for more information on current models and pricing.

FALCON FIREARMS

Previous manufacturer located in Northridge, CA from 1986-1990.

PISTOLS: SEMI-AUTO

PORTSIDER — .45 ACP cal., patterned after Colt M 1911 A-1, stainless steel, fixed sights, 5 in. barrel, 7 shot mag., available in left-hand only. Mfg. 1986-90.

	$500	$425	$375

Last Mfg.'s Sug. Retail was $580.

Grading	100%	98%	95%	90%	80%	70%	60%

* ***Portsider Set*** — features right and left-hand models with matching serial numbers. Only 100 sets mfg. 1986-1987.

$1,300 $1,100 $895

Last Mfg.'s Sug. Retail was $1,400.

GOLD FALCON — .45 ACP cal., machined receiver made from solid 17 Kt. gold alloy, stainless steel slide, diamond sighting system, choice of grips, standard or personalized engraving options. Only 50 mfg.

$25,000 $17,500 $11,500

Last Mfg.'s Sug. Retail was $30,500.

FAMARS, ABBIATICO & SALVINELLI

Current manufacturer located in Gardone, Italy. Currently imported exclusively by A&S of America, located in Jefferson Boro, PA. Exclusively distributed by The First National Gun Banque, located in Colorado Springs, CO.

A&S Famars manufactures some of the world's finest rifles and shotguns - only 50-60 are fabricated annually. All Famars guns include a lifetime warranty. Values listed below are for base models with no extra embellishments or special orders, and are based on an exchange rate of 1,675 lira = $1.00. Because every A&S Famars longarm is an individual custom order, each Famars firearm must have its value ascertained on an individual appraisal basis.

All A&S Famars shotguns are available in Hunting, Trap, Skeet, Sporting Clays, and Pigeon configurations. All models except the Excaliber have demiblock barrels.

RIFLES: SxS, CUSTOM MFG.

Boxlock and sidelock rifles are all best quality and range in calibers between .22 LR and .600 Nitro Express. Each gun is manufactured per individual customer special order, and values below reflect base model pricing with no additional special order features (most models can be ordered with 6 levels of engraving/ornamentation). Further information and price quotations are available by contacting the above listed importer directly.

AFRICAN EXPRESS

Mfg.'s Sug. Retail $25,000 $22,500 $17,250 $12,500 $10,250 $8,750 $7,500 $6,250

VENUS EXPRESS PROFESSIONAL

Mfg.'s Sug. Retail $33,000 $29,000 $26,000 $22,750 $19,000 $15,750 $12,000 $10,750

VENUS EXPRESS EXTRALUSSO — top-of-the-line model.

Prices start at $65,000 on this model.

SHOTGUNS: O/U, CUSTOM MFG.

O/U SIDELOCK MODELS

* ***Jorema*** — 12 or 20 ga.
  Mfg.'s Sug. Retail $25,650 $22,750 $16,750 $12,500 $10,250 $8,750 $7,500 $6,250
  Add 10% for 20 ga.

* ***Jorema Royal***
  Mfg.'s Sug. Retail $32,500 $27,650 $21,250 $16,500 $13,000 $10,000 $8,500 $7,250

* ***Royale SH*** — 12, 20, 28 ga., or .410 bore, bar action.
  Mfg.'s Sug. Retail $34,000 $30,750 $24,250 $19,000 $15,750 $12,250 $10,000 $8,500

O/U COMPETITION MODELS

* ***Excalibur BL*** — detachable locks, monobloc barrels.
  Mfg.'s Sug. Retail $8,400 $8,050 $7,250 $6,500 $5,800 $4,950 $4,250 $3,600

* ***Excalibur BLX*** — detachable locks, with sideplates and monobloc barrels.
  Mfg.'s Sug. Retail $14,500 $13,000 $10,750 $9,000 $7,800 $6,250 $5,250 $4,500

Grading	100%	98%	95%	90%	80%	70%	60%

* **Excaliber SL** — sidelock action, monobloc barrels.
  Mfg.'s Sug. Retail $19,800 $18,250 $13,000 $9,500 $8,250 $6,750 $5,750 $5,000

4-BARREL MODEL

* **Rombo Quattrocanne** — .410 bore only, barrels are arranged in a diamond pattern.
  Mfg.'s Sug. Retail $40,500 $37,750 $33,000 $29,000 $25,500 $21,750 $17,750 $14,750

SHOTGUNS: SxS

CASTORE HAMMER GUN — double barrel, exposed hammers, double triggers, various gauges.
  Mfg.'s Sug. Retail $21,805 $19,650 $12,000 $9,500 $8,800 $6,500 $5,500 $4,500

BOXLOCK MODELS — available with Anson-Deeley boxlock action, scalloped or rounded frame, various engraving patterns available.

* **Zeus** — 12 or 20 ga., features round action.
  Mfg.'s Sug. Retail $18,500 $16,650 $12,000 $9,000 $7,500 $6,250 $5,000 $4,750

* **Tribute** — 12, 20, 28 ga., or .410 bore, scalloped back drop lock action.
  Mfg.'s Sug. Retail $20,000 $18,750 $13,250 $9,750 $8,250 $6,750 $5,750 $5,000

SIDELOCK MODELS

* **Highline (Veneri)** — round body, back action.
  Mfg.'s Sug. Retail $30,000 $27,000 $20,000 $16,000 $12,250 $10,000 $8,500 $7,250

* **Venus** — bar action.
  Mfg.'s Sug. Retail $30,500 $27,300 $20,150 $16,000 $12,250 $10,000 $8,500 $7,250

FANZOJ, JOHANN

Current long gun manufacturer located in Ferlach, Austria. Exclusively distributed since 1998 by Dr. Joseph Cornell, located in Denver, CO.

     Johann Fanzoj manufactures top quality rifles in many configurations. This company is also a member of the Ferlach Guild. Please contact the distributor for current model availability and pricing.

FAUSTI, CAV. STEFANO & FIGLIE SNC.

Current manufacturer located in Marcheno, Italy.

     S. Fausti manufactures shotguns in O/U, SxS, and single shot configurations. American Arms located in N. Kansas City, MO, is currently the exclusive importer for Fausti firearms. Please refer to the American Arms listing for Fausti produced guns.

FEATHER INDUSTRIES, INC.

Previous manufacturer located in Boulder, CO until 1995.

DERRINGERS

GUARDIAN ANGEL 9mm Para./.38 Spl. — 9mm Para. or .38 Spl. cal., O/U design, stainless steel, double action backup derringer. Mfg. 1988-1989 only.
           $130 $95 $75

Last Mfg.'s Sug. Retail was $140.

     This model has interchangeable loading blocks that allow shooting 9mm Para. or .38 Spl. There is no exposed hammer and trigger is totally enclosed.

Grading	100%	98%	95%	90%	80%	70%	60%

GUARDIAN ANGEL .22 LR/.22 MAG. — .22 LR or .22 Mag. cal., design is similar to 9mm Para./.38 Spl. model, loading block breech, 2 in. barrel, fixed sights, 12 oz. Mfg. 1990-95.

	$100	$75	$60				

Last Mfg.'s Sug. Retail was $120.

Add $30 for individual extra loading blocks.

This model has interchangeable loading blocks that allow shooting .22LR or .22 Mag. There is no exposed hammer and the trigger is totally enclosed.

PISTOLS: SEMI-AUTO

MINI-AT — .22 LR cal., pistol variation of the AT-22, 5½ in. shrouded barrel, 20 shot mag., approx. 2 lbs. Mfg. 1986-1989.

$195	$165	$145	$135	$130	$125	$115	

Last Mfg.'s Sug. Retail was $220.

RIFLES: SEMI-AUTO

AT-22 — .22 LR cal., semi-auto blowback action, 17 in. detachable shrouded barrel, collapsible metal stock, adj. rear sight, with sling and swivels, 20 shot mag., 3¼ lbs. Mfg. 1986-95.

$225	$175	$155	$145	$135	$125	$115	

Last Mfg.'s Sug. Retail was $250.

F2 — similar to AT-22, except is equipped with a fixed polymer buttstock. Mfg. 1992-95.

$245	$190	$165	$150	$135	$125	$115	

Last Mfg.'s Sug. Retail was $280.

AT-9 — 9mm Para. cal., semi-auto blowback action, 16 in. barrel, paramilitary design, available with 10 (C/B 1994), 25★, 32 (disc.), or 100 (disc. 1989) mag., 5 lbs. Mfg. 1988-95.

$440	$375	$310	$280	$260	$240	$200	

Last Mfg.'s Sug. Retail was $500.

Add $80 for 100 round drum mag.

F9 — similar to AT-9, except is equipped with a fixed polymer buttstock. Mfg. 1992-95.

$465	$385	$325	$285	$260	$240	$200	

Last Mfg.'s Sug. Retail was $535.

SATURN 30 — 7.62x39mm Kalashnikov cal., semi-auto, gas operated, 19½ in. barrel, composite stock with large thumbhole pistol grip, 5 shot detachable mag., drilled and tapped for scope mounts, adj. rear sight, 8½ lbs. Mfg. in 1990 only.

$695	$575	$475	$425	$375	$325	$280	

Last Mfg.'s Sug. Retail was $695.

KG-9 — 9mm Para. cal., semi-auto blowback action, 25 or 50 shot mag., paramilitary configuration. Mfg. 1989 only.

$550	$475	$425	$375	$325	$275	$240	

Last Mfg.'s Sug. Retail was $560.

SAR-180 — .22 LR cal., semi-auto blowback action, 17½ in. barrel, 165 shot drum mag., fully adj. rear sight, walnut stock with combat style pistol grip and forend, 6¼ lbs. Mfg. 1989 only.

$450	$395	$350	$295	$260	$240	$200	

Last Mfg.'s Sug. Retail was $500.

Add $105 for retractable stock.
Add $395 for laser sight.

This variation was also manufactured for a limited time by ILARCO (Illinois Arms Company), previously located in Itasca, IL.

KG-22 — .22 LR cal., similar to KG-9, 20 shot mag. Mfg. 1989 only.

$295	$250	$200	$175	$155	$145	$135	

Last Mfg.'s Sug. Retail was $300.

Grading	100%	98%	95%	90%	80%	70%	60%

FEDERAL ENGINEERING CORPORATION

Previous manufacturer located in Chicago, IL.

RIFLES: SEMI-AUTO

XC-220 — .22 LR cal., semi-auto paramilitary design rifle, 16⁵/₁₆ in. barrel length, 28 shot mag., machined steel action, 7½ lbs. Mfg. 1984-89.

$395	$350	$300	$275	$250	$230	$210

XC-450 — .45 ACP cal. only, semi-auto paramilitary design carbine, 16½ in. barrel length, 30 shot mag., fires from closed bolt, machined steel action, 8½ lbs. Mfg. 1984-89.

$950	$825	$750	$675	$600	$550	$500

XC-900 — 9mm Para. cal., semi-auto paramilitary design carbine, 16½ in. barrel length, 32 shot mag., fires from closed bolt, machine steel action, 8 lbs. Mfg. 1984-89.

$950	$825	$750	$675	$600	$550	$500

FEDERAL ORDNANCE, INC.

Previous manufacturer/importer/distributor located in South El Monte, CA from 1966-1992. Brickley Trading Co. bought the remaining assets of Federal Ordnance, Inc. in late 1992, and is currently importing various firearms from overseas.

Federal Ordnance imported and distributed both foreign and domestic military handguns and rifles until 1992. In addition, they also fabricated firearms using mostly newer parts. Listed below are those models which were recently manufactured or remanufactured.

PISTOLS: SEMI-AUTO

In addition to the Broomhandle models listed below, Federal Ordnance also manufactured other special editions. These models include the British Model, Cut-Away, Cartridge Counter, Para La Guerra, and others. Prices are in the $800-$950 range (retail).

MODEL 714 BROOMHANDLE — 7.63 Mauser or 9mm Para. cal., 5½ in. barrel, new frame, exterior completely refinished, 10 shot detachable mag., "fair" bore, adj. rear sight. Mfg. 1986-1991.

$550	$500	$450	$400	$350	$325	$300

Last Mfg.'s Sug. Retail was $820.

Add $100 for new barrel.

* **Model 714 Para La Guerra** — 7.63 Mauser or 9mm Para. cal., remanufactured to duplicate Spanish Civil War configuration Broomhandle, includes 10 in. barrel with "Para La Guerra" engraved on side. Mfg. 1990-91 only.

$575	$525	$450	$400	$350	$325	$300

Last Mfg.'s Sug. Retail was $890.

* **Model 714 Bolo** — similar to Model 714 Broomhandle, except has smaller grips, 3.9 in. barrel, 10 shot mag. standard. Mfg. 1988 only.

$550	$500	$450	$400	$350	$325	$300

Last Mfg.'s Sug. Retail was $890.

STANDARD BROOMHANDLE — 7.63 Mauser or 9mm Para. cal., refurbished (new barrels, completely refinished, etc.) C-96 pistols, replaced springs, includes original Chinese shoulder/holster stock. Disc. 1991.

$525	$485	$450	$420	$390	$380	$360

Last Mfg.'s Sug. Retail was $735.

Subtract $150 without shoulder/holster stock.

Grading	100%	98%	95%	90%	80%	70%	60%

* ***Standard Bolo*** — similar to Standard Broomhandle, except Bolo configuration (3.9 in. barrel and smaller grips). Includes original Chinese shoulder/holster stock. Mfg. 1990-91 only.

	$480	$450	$420	$390	$380	$370	$360

Last Mfg.'s Sug. Retail was $530.

RANGER 1911A1 GI — .45 ACP cal., 5 in. barrel, 7 shot mag., steel construction throughout, checkered walnut grips, 40 oz. Mfg. 1988-92.

	$385	$350	$310	$280	$260	$240	$200

Last Mfg.'s Sug. Retail was $440.

> Add $20 for Ranger Extended Model (40 oz. - new 1990).
> Add $40 for Ranger Ambo (ambidextrous safety, 40 oz. - new 1990).
> Add $15 for lightweight Ranger Lite Model (32 oz. - new 1990).
>
> These pistols are patterned after the Colt 1911A1 Govt. Model.

* ***Ranger Ten*** — 10mm cal., otherwise similar to regular Ranger 1911A1. Mfg. 1990-91 only.

	$675	$525	$475	$450	$420	$395	$370

Last Mfg.'s Sug. Retail was $780.

RANGER SUPERCOMP — .45 ACP or 10mm cal., compensated variation of the Ranger 1911A1 with 6 in. compensated barrel, slide, tuned trigger, and other competition features, 42 oz. Mfg. 1990-91 only.

	$1,250	$875	$775	$675	$600	$550	$495

Last Mfg.'s Sug. Retail was $1,390.

> Add $10 for 10mm cal.

THE RANGER ALPHA — .38 Super, 10mm, or .45 ACP cal., 5 or 6 in. barrel, patterned after the Colt Govt. Model. Mfg. 1990-91 only.

	$895	$775	$675	$575	$475	$425	$380

Last Mfg.'s Sug. Retail was $1,000.

> Add $16 for 10mm cal.
> Add $16 for 6 in. barrel.
> Add $9-$25 for ported 5 or 6 in. barrel depending on cal.

PETERS STAHL PS-07 — 10mm or .45 ACP cal., mfg. by Peters Stahl of W. Germany to exacting standards, 6 in. barrel with polygonal rifling, top-of-the-line competition model with compensated barrel and other advanced competition features, 45 oz. Mfg. 1990-91 only.

	$2,350	$1,800	$1,500	$1,200	$995	$825	$700

Last Mfg.'s Sug. Retail was $2,600.

> Add $51 for 10mm cal.
>
> This model was imported in very limited quantities.

RIFLES

ALL AMERICAN SPORTER BOLT ACTION — .30-06 cal., Springfield M1903 receiver, new sporter stock, drilled and tapped for scope base (included), blued finish. Mfg. late 1991-92.

	$165	$145	$120	$100	$90	$80	$75

MODEL 713 DELUXE MAUSER SEMI-AUTO CARBINE — 7.63 Mauser or 9mm Para. cal., 16 in. barrel, detachable stock, one 10 shot and one 20 shot detachable mag., deluxe walnut, leather case with accessories, adj. sights to 1,000 meters, 5 lbs. 1,500 mfg. 1986-92.

	$1,495	$1,250	$1,050				

Last Mfg.'s Sug. Retail was $1,986.

* ***Field Grade Mauser Carbine*** — 7.63 Mauser or 9mm Para. (new 1989) cal., 16 in. barrel, 10 shot fixed mag., nondetachable walnut stock. Mfg. 1987-92.

	$750	$675	$600	$525	$475	$425	$400

Last Mfg.'s Sug. Retail was $1,200.

Grading	100%	98%	95%	90%	80%	70%	60%

M-14 SEMI-AUTO — .308 Win. cal., legal for private ownership (no selector), 20 shot mag., refinished original M-14 parts, available in either filled fiberglass, G.I. fiberglass, refinished wood, or new walnut stock. Mfg. 1986-91.

	$625	$550	$495	$450	$395	$335	$285

Last Mfg.'s Sug. Retail was $700.

Add $50 for filled fiberglass stock.
Add $110 for refinished wood stock.
Add $190 for new walnut stock with handguard.

TANKER GARAND SEMI-AUTO — .30-06 or .308 Win. cal., original U.S. GI parts, 18 in. barrel, new hardwood stock, parkerized finish. Mfg. began late 1991.

	$675	$525	$475	$450	$420	$395	$370

CHINESE RPK 86S-7 SEMI-AUTO — 7.62x39mm cal., semi-auto version of the P.R.C.-RPK light machine gun, 75 shot drum mag., 23¾ in. barrel, with bipod. Imported 1989 only.

	$1,000	$875	$725	$650	$575	$525	$475

Last Mfg.'s Sug. Retail was $500.

FEINWERKBAU

Current manufacturer located in Oberndorf, Germany. Feinwerkbau firearms and airguns (see listings in Airguns section) are imported exclusively by Beeman Precision Airguns, located in Huntington Beach, CA.

Feinwerkbau manufactures some of the world's finest quality target rifles and pistols (.22 LR rimfire and airgun).

PISTOLS: SEMI-AUTO, RIMFIRE

MODEL AW-93 — .22 LR cal., 6 in. barrel, 5 shot mag., ergonomically designed stippled walnut grips with adj. heel, unique damper prevents muzzle jump and recoil, satin nickel finish, top-of-the-line Target pistol, approx. 2½ lbs. New 1993.

Mfg.'s Sug. Retail	$1,695		$1,525	$1,350	$1,150	$950	$850	$750	$625

RIFLES: BOLT ACTION, RIMFIRE

MODEL 2000 — .22 LR cal. only, single shot, match target bolt action rifle, fully adj. trigger, walnut stocks, four variations featuring different specifications. Importation disc. 1988.

* *Universal Model* — 26⅜ in. barrel, aperture sights, stippled pistol grip and forearm, 9¾ lbs.

	$1,150	$925	$850	$735	$650	$595	$550

Last Mfg.'s Sug. Retail was $1,395.

Add $350 for electronic trigger.
Add $160 for left-hand variation.

* *Mini 2000 (Junior)* — 22 in. barrel, aperture sights, stippled pistol grip, 9⅛ lbs.

	$1,025	$875	$825	$700	$625	$575	$525

Last Mfg.'s Sug. Retail was $1,225.

Add $350 for electronic trigger.
Add $150 for left-hand variation.

* *Match Model* — 26¼ in. barrel, adj. cheekpiece on stock, stippled pistol grip and forearm, aperture sights.

	$1,075	$895	$825	$700	$625	$575	$525

Last Mfg.'s Sug. Retail was $1,285.

Add $390 for electronic trigger.
Add $113 for left-hand variation.

Grading	100%	98%	95%	90%	80%	70%	60%

* Running Target — adj. cheekpiece on stock, thumbhole stippled pistol grip, no sights, for running boar competition.

			100%	98%	95%	90%	80%	70%	60%
			$1,150	$925	$850	$735	$650	$595	$550

Last Mfg.'s Sug. Retail was $1,398.

Add $142 for left-hand variation.

MODEL 2600 UNIVERSAL — .22 LR cal. only, similar design to Model 600 air rifle, single shot, 26.3 in. barrel, aperture sights, 10.6 lbs. Imported 1986-94.

	100%	98%	95%	90%	80%	70%	60%
	$1,425	$1,125	$925	$850	$735	$650	$595

Last Mfg.'s Sug. Retail was $1,695.

Add $160 for left-hand variation.

MODEL 2600 ULTRA MATCH FREE RIFLE — .22 LR cal., single shot match gun based on Model 2600 action, 26.1 in. barrel, laminate stock with thumbhole, fully adj. aperture sights, 14 lbs. 1 oz. Mfg. 1986-94.

	100%	98%	95%	90%	80%	70%	60%
	$2,175	$1,750	$1,400	$1,150	$925	$850	$735

Last Mfg.'s Sug. Retail was $2,498.

Add $250 for electronic trigger (disc. 1988).
Add $152 for left-hand variation.

MODEL 2602 UNIVERSAL (UIT) RIFLE — .22 LR cal., designed for Match competition, state-of-the-art Target rifle with different color wood laminations possible. New 1997.

	Mfg.'s Sug. Retail	$1,615	95%	90%	80%	70%	60%
			$1,450	$1,275	$1,125	$975	$850	$725	$600

Add $125 for left-hand action.

MODEL 2602 FREE RIFLE — .22 LR cal., standard Match rifle with state-of-the-art laminated wood stock with thumbhole, adj. cheekpiece, adj. buttplate, and adj. hand rest, features 16¾ in. barrel with unique 13¾ in. squared-off barrel sleeve with sight, diopter sights, top-of-the-line competition rifle, approx. 13.86 lbs. New 1997.

Mfg.'s Sug. Retail $2,365 $2,035 $1,800 $1,575 $1,350 $1,175 $1,000 $850

Add $155 for left-hand action.

MODEL 2602 SUPER MATCH — .22 LR cal., Super Match variation featuring state-of-the-art design, adj. stock, comb, LOP, and trigger pull.

Mfg.'s Sug. Retail $2,370 $2,050 $1,800 $1,575 $1,350 $1,175 $1,000 $850

Add $130 for left-hand action.
Subtract $130 for Model 2602 Sport RT.

FEMARU

Previously manufactured by Femaru-Fegyver-es Gepyar R.T. located in Budapest, Hungary.

PISTOLS: SEMI-AUTO

MODEL 1910 — 7.65mm Roth/Steyr cal., rare and only infrequently encountered. Estimated serial range 1-10,000.

$2,150 $1,750 $1,350 $1,150 $975 $850 $725

MODEL 1929 (29M) — .380 ACP cal., 3.93 in. barrel, 8 shot mag., identifiable by squared-off rear slide with vertical serrations, 2 piece walnut grips, approx. 50,000 mfg.

$400 $340 $275 $215 $185 $165 $145

MODEL 1937 (37M) — .32 ACP or .380 ACP cal., 3.93 in. barrel, 8 shot mag., commercial blue finish, left slide marking "FEMARU FEGYVER ES GEPYAR RT. 37M", vertically grooved 2-piece walnut grips, approx. 200,000 mfg. (.380 ACP cal.) for Hungarian service before Nazi variations began (dubbed "Pistole Modell 37 (ung)", c. 1941), Nazi marked jhv 41 or jhv 44, 27 oz.

$350 $295 $225 $190 $175 $160 $145

Add 50% for Waffenamt proofing (.32 ACP only).
Add another 60% if with holster and 2 matching mags.

Grading	100%	98%	95%	90%	80%	70%	60%

FROMMER STOP POCKET AUTO — .32 ACP or .380 ACP cal., 6 or 7 shot, 3⅞ in. barrel, fixed sights, blue, rubber grips, locked breech, outside hammer. Mfg. 1912-1920.

	100%	98%	95%	90%	80%	70%	60%
	$300	$250	$180	$150	$120	$100	$80

Add 50% for .380 ACP cal.

FROMMER BABY POCKET AUTO — similar to Stop Pocket Auto, except 2 in. barrel, 5 or 6 shot.

	100%	98%	95%	90%	80%	70%	60%
	$250	$215	$180	$150	$115	$90	$70

FROMMER LILIPUT AUTO — .25 ACP cal., blowback action, 6 shot, 2.14 in. barrel, blue, hard rubber grips. Mfg. in early 1920s.

	100%	98%	95%	90%	80%	70%	60%
	$325	$250	$175	$145	$115	$90	$75

FERLACH GUNS

Includes those firearms manufactured in Ferlach, Austria from 1558 to present. Currently, the Ferlach Guild (Genossenschaft) has no exclusive U.S. importer.

Many people are confused that Ferlach is a trademark - it is not. Rather, it is a small village in Austria where a gun guild was started as early as 1558. At that time, it was absolutely necessary that all the people involved in fabricating a firearm were located together in close proximity. This enabled the barrel maker, the stock maker, and the lock mechanism maker to work together closely to ensure that everyone was performing their task(s) correctly, effectively and efficiently. As the individual skills became better and more refined, more and more firearms were manufactured. Eventually, individual gunsmiths began to put their name on the barrel or frame of those guns which they had either manufactured solely or with the help of their fellow Ferlach craftsmen. Since all Ferlach firearms are essentially hand made per individual special order, very few are exactly alike. In the past, the gunsmiths of Ferlach have produced almost every type of shoulder arm imaginable, including such modern weapons as superposed and juxtaposed rifles and shotguns, hammerless drillings, repeating rifles, 3 barrel rifles, combination guns, 4 barrel rifles/shotguns/combination guns (called Vierlings), hammer guns of every type, etc. Some of these specimens represent the highest refinement in the gunmakers trade. Because of the almost unlimited variety of Ferlach variations, it is recommended that a COMPETENT appraisal is procured before buying or selling a specimen.

As is the case with many other European weapons, those models with desirable American features will generally outperform those with European specifications (i.e. a Ferlach sidelock combination gun that is 20 ga. x .243 Win. will be more valuable than a similar specimen chambered for 16 ga. x 5.6 by 50Rmm with sling swivels). Original condition and overall beauty are the primary factors to consider when contemplating buying or selling a Ferlach longarm. Other considerations include: type of action, difficulty of fabrication (Vierlings are very complicated to construct), caliber/gauge desirability, notoriety of gunsmith on barrel legend, elaborateness of embellishments, condition, rarity, accessories, and any provenance a specimen might have.

Today's master gunsmiths of Ferlach carry on the Old World tradition of quality in every respect. Most guns manufactured today are by individual special order with a wide range of calibers/gauges and other special features and options. As of this writing, these gunsmiths in alphabetical order are: LUDWIG BOROVNIK, JOHANN FANZOJ, WILFRIED GLANZNIG, JOSEF HAMBRUSCH, KARL HAUPTMANN, GOTTFRIED JUCH, JOSEF JUST, JAKOB KOSCHAT, JOHANN MICHELITSCH, WALTER OUTSCHAR, HERBERT SCHEIRING, BENEDIKT WINKLER, AND JOSEF WINKLER. Anyone wishing to contact these master gunmakers should either write to the Guild or address them individually at: Ferlach Genossenschaft der Büchsenmachermeister reg.Gen.m.b.H., Waagplatz 6, A-9170 Ferlach, AUSTRIA. Please allow at least 4-6 weeks for a response.

Grading	100%	98%	95%	90%	80%	70%	60%

FERLIB

Current manufacturer located in Gardone V.T., Italy. Currently distributed exclusively by Hi-Grade Imports located in Gilroy, CA.

SHOTGUNS: SxS

Models listed below are available in 10, 12, 16, 20, 24, 28, 32 ga., or .410 bore. Also available for an additional charge are extra quality wood and upgraded engraving.

Add 10% for 24, 28, 32 ga., or .410 bore.
Add $250 for single trigger.
Add $650 for leather case.

HAMMER GUN — boxlock action, exposed hammers, deluxe checkered walnut stock and forearm, blued action. Disc. 1989.

$4,250	$3,500	$3,175	$2,850	$2,350	$2,100	$1,800

Last Mfg.'s Sug. Retail was $4,500.

MODEL F.VI — 12, 16, 20, 28 ga., or .410 bore, Anson & Deeley scalloped boxlock action, ejectors, double triggers, case hardened frame, select checkered stock and forearm. Disc. 1992.

$3,500	$2,950	$2,275	$1,975	$1,600	$1,250	$1,000

Last Mfg.'s Sug. Retail was $3,250.

MODEL F.VII — 12, 16, 20, 28 ga., or .410 bore, Anson & Deeley scalloped boxlock action, ejectors, double triggers, coin finish, full coverage English scroll or game scene engraving, select checkered stock and forearm.

Mfg.'s Sug. Retail	$7,500						
		$6,000	$5,250	$4,950	$4,275	$3,675	$3,000	$2,600

Add 10% for 28 ga. or .410 bore.

MODEL F.VII/SC — 12, 16, 20, 28 ga., or .410 bore, Anson & Deeley scalloped boxlock action, ejectors, double triggers, coin finish, game scene with scroll accent engraving with gold inlays, select checkered stock and forearm.

Mfg.'s Sug. Retail	$7,800						
		$6,200	$5,500	$5,000	$4,500	$3,800	$3,300	$2,750

Add 10% for 28 ga. or .410 bore.

MODEL F.VII SIDEPLATE — 12, 16, 20, 28 ga., or .410 bore, Anson & Deeley boxlock action with sideplates, ejectors, single trigger, coin finish, extensive game scene and scroll accent engraving, select checkered stock and forearm.

Mfg.'s Sug. Retail	$9,600						
		$7,700	$6,800	$6,000	$5,200	$4,450	$3,700	$3,100

Add 10% for 28 ga. or .410 bore.

✳ F.VII/SC Gold — similar to F.VII Sideplate, except with gold inlays.

Mfg.'s Sug. Retail	$13,000						
		$10,400	$9,250	$8,100	$7,275	$6,350	$5,300	$4,350

Add 10% for 28ga. or .410 bore.

F.V. SIDELOCK — various ga.'s, full sidelock action, special order to customer specifications. Values start in the $15,000 range and go up.

FIALA OUTFITTERS INCORPORATED

Previous manufacturer located in New York City, NY.

PISTOLS: SLIDE ACTION

FIALA REPEATING PISTOL — .22 LR cal., 10 shot, 3, 7½, or 20 in. barrel, blue, plain wood grips, resembles an auto loader, but is actually hand operated by moving the slide to eject, load and cock. Mfg. 1920-1923.

$475	$400	$340	$280	$230	$200	$175

Add 50% for 3-barrel set.
Add $150 for original case.
Add $250 for stock.
Add $300 for canvas holster stock.

Grading	100%	98%	95%	90%	80%	70%	60%

FINNISH LION

Previous trademark manufactured by Valmet (now Tikka) located in Sweden. Limited importation into the U.S. by Mandall's Shooting Supplies, Inc. in Scottsdale, AZ.

RIFLES: BOLT ACTION

MATCH RIFLE — .22 LR cal., bolt action, single shot, 29 in. barrel, extended aperture sight, globe front sight, thumbhole stock, adj. hook butt. Mfg. 1937-1972.

	100%	98%	95%	90%	80%	70%	60%
	$495	$415	$360	$305	$250	$210	$195

CHAMPION FREE RIFLE — .22 LR cal., bolt action, single shot, 29 in. barrel, double set trigger, full target stock and accessories. Mfg. 1965-1972.

	100%	98%	95%	90%	80%	70%	60%
	$580	$495	$440	$385	$330	$290	$265

STANDARD ISU TARGET RIFLE — .22 LR cal., bolt action, single shot, 27 in. barrel, full target stock and accessories. Mfg. 1966-1977.

	100%	98%	95%	90%	80%	70%	60%
	$330	$275	$250	$205	$180	$165	$150

TARGET RIFLE — .22 LR cal., target rifle with adj. stock and trigger, bolt action, single shot, aperture sights.

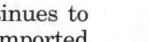

	100%	98%	95%	90%	80%	70%	60%
	$725	$595	$495	$440	$385	$340	$295

Last Mfg.'s Sug. Retail was $795.

FIOCCHI OF AMERICA, INC.

Previous firearms importer and distributor located in Ozark, MO.

Fiocchi of America imported Pardini target pistols until 1990, and continues to manufacture a wide variety of ammunition domestically. Fiocchi also imported Antonio Zoli shotguns until 1988. These trademarks can be found in their respective sections of this text.

FIREARMS INTERNATIONAL (F.I.)

Previous importer/assembler located in Washington, D.C.

F.I. manufactured and imported various shotguns and pistols including the Star D and Iver Johnson Pony handguns. F.I. sold less than 100 .380 ACPs that were marked Colt before the Mustang was introduced - these are rare. While some models are relatively rare, collectability to date has been minimal and most models sell in the $125-$250 range.

FIREARMS INTERNATIONAL, INC.

Current exclusive marketing agent for IAI established in 1997 and located in Houston, TX. Currently mfg. by Israel Arms Ltd., located in Israel.

PISTOLS: SEMI-AUTO

MODEL M5000 COMBAT — .45 ACP cal., patterned after the M1911, features 4¼ stainless barrel, combat style hammer, perforated steel trigger, extended slide stop, 3 dot fixed sights, rubber grips with finger grooves, two-tone finish. New 1998.

Mfg.'s Sug. Retail	$537		$475	$425	$375	$350	$325	$300	$280

FORT WORTH FIREARMS

Current manufacturer located in Fort Worth, TX beginning 1995. Distributor and dealer sales.

Grading	100%	98%	95%	90%	80%	70%	60%

PISTOLS: SEMI-AUTO, RIMFIRE

MATCH MASTER STANDARD — .22 LR cal., $3^7/_8$, $4^1/_2$, $5^1/_2$, $7^1/_2$, or 10 in. bull barrel, double extractors, includes upper push button and standard mag. release, beveled mag. well, angled grip, flared slide, low profile frame. New 1995.

Mfg.'s Sug. Retail	$389	$310	$265	$230	$200	$185	$170	$160

Add $84 for 10 in. bull barrel.

* *Match Master Dovetail* — similar to Match Master Standard, except has $3^7/_8$, $4^1/_2$, or $5^1/_2$ barrel with dovetail rib. New 1995.

Mfg.'s Sug. Retail	$473	$385	$325	$285	$240	$215	$190	$170

* *Match Master Deluxe* — similar to Match Master Standard, except has Weaver rib on barrel. New 1995.

Mfg.'s Sug. Retail	$538	$450	$365	$315	$280	$240	$215	$190

Add $92 for 10 in. barrel.

SPORT KING — .22 LR cal., $4^1/_2$ or $5^1/_2$ in. barrel, blued finish, military grips, drift sight, 10 shot mag. New 1995.

Mfg.'s Sug. Retail	$313	$275	$245	$225	$200	$185	$170	$160

CITATION — .22 LR cal., $5^1/_2$ in. bull or $7^1/_4$ in. fluted barrel, military grips, 10 shot mag. New 1995.

Mfg.'s Sug. Retail	$389	$310	$265	$230	$200	$185	$170	$160

TROPHY — .22 LR cal., $5^1/_2$ or $7^1/_4$ in. bull barrel, blued finish, military grips, 10 shot mag. New 1995.

Mfg.'s Sug. Retail	$411	$330	$285	$240	$200	$185	$170	$160

Add $41 for left-hand action ($5^1/_2$ in. barrel only).

VICTOR — .22 LR cal., $3^7/_8$, $4^1/_2$ (VR or Weaver rib), or $5^1/_2$ (VR or Weaver rib), 8 (Weaver rib), or 10 (Weaver rib) in. barrel, blued finish, military grips, 10 shot mag. New 1995.

Mfg.'s Sug. Retail	$473	$385	$325	$285	$240	$215	$190	$170

Add $65 for $4^1/_2$ or $5^1/_2$ in. Weaver rib barrel.
Add approx. $148 for 8 or 10 in. Weaver rib barrel.

OLYMPIC — .22 LR or Short cal., $6^3/_4$ in. fluted barrel, blued finish, military grips, 10 shot mag. New 1995.

Mfg.'s Sug. Retail	$600	$525	$465	$415	$360	$330	$295	$265

SHARP SHOOTER — .22 LR cal., $5^1/_2$ in. bull barrel, blued finish, military grips, 10 shot mag. New 1995.

Mfg.'s Sug. Retail	$380	$300	$260	$230	$200	$185	$170	$160

RIFLES: BOLT ACTION

YOUTH RIFLE — .22 LR cal., bolt action, single shot, shortened stock dimensions. Mfg. 1995-96.

	$120	$105	$90	$80	$70	$60	$50

Last Mfg.'s Sug. Retail was $138.

SHOTGUNS: SLIDE ACTION

GL 18 — 12 ga. only, security configuration with 18 in. barrel with perforated shroud, thumb operated laser/xenon light built into end of 7 shot mag. tube, ammo storage. Mfg. 1995-96.

	$295	$265	$240	$210	$190	$170	$160

Last Mfg.'s Sug. Retail was $347.

FOX, A.H.

Current manufacturer located in New Britain, CT. The A.H. Fox trademark was brought to life once again during 1993 when the Connecticut Shotgun Manufacturing Company, began producing an A.H. Fox 20 gauge in 5 different grades. Previously manufactured in Philadelphia, PA 1903-1930, and in Utica, NY from 1930-approx. 1946. Manufactured by Savage 1930-1988.

Depending on the remaining A.H. Fox factory data, a factory letter authenticating the configuration of a particular Fox shotgun (not to be confused with the more recent Savage/Stevens designed Fox doubles) may be obtained by contacting John T. Callahan (see Trademark Index for listings and address). If a model number is not known, please include a photo, the ser. no., caliber or ga., barrel length and style, stock and forearm style, markings, patent dates, inspector stamps, etc. The charge for this service is $25.00 for the Sterlingworth Model, and $30.00 for graded models - please allow 2-4 weeks for an adequate response.

Mr. Ansley H. Fox first started manufacturing shotguns in circa 1896. This first company was called the Fox Gun Co. located in Baltimore, MD. Relatively few guns were made and surviving specimens today are very rare. After this venture, he was employed by the Baltimore Gun Co. for several years (circa 1900-1903). Following this period, he formed the Philadelphia Gun Co. where the predecessors to the A.H. Fox Gun Co. models were manufactured. These Philadelphia Gun Co. models (circa 1904) were the same as the newer Fox shotguns except that the hinge pin was removed. Sources indicate that the lowest grade was an "A" with the highest being an "E" (fully engraved and ultra rare). Following this tenure, Mr. Fox went on to form the A.H. Fox Gun Co. that was started approx. 1905. In addition to being an entrepreneur and trend setter, Mr. Fox also had the reputation of being an expert shot in his own right, winning more than a few events on the East Coast around the turn of the century.

The A.H. Fox Gun Company of Philadelphia, Pennsylvania, began production in 1905 and produced high quality double barrel shotguns until 1930. The Savage Arms Company, then of Utica, New York, acquired the Fox Company and produced these guns until 1942, when all but the utilitarian model B series guns were discontinued.

A.H. Fox guns are considered an American classic comparable to L.C. Smith, Parker, and others. Collector interest is high and will undoubtedly grow. The guns do not command quite as high a price as the Smith and Parker guns, but represent a fine investment collectible value.

The Savage made guns from 1930-1942 usually are valued at about 25% less than the early A.H. Fox guns. The recent production B series are just not in the same class and are obviously not intended to be. They are lower priced by today's standards and are designed as a utility grade hunting gun.

FOX COMPANY CHRONOLOGY

1906 - Company formed January 1906, A, B & C Grades introduced in 12 ga. only. D and F Grades introduced in 12 ga. in 1907. Ejector guns introduced in 1908. 1910 saw the introduction of the 12 ga. Sterlingworth - William H. Gough takes over as Chief of Engraving. Ansley Fox resigns in 1911 - first catalog showing Sterlingworth Model (called Model 1911). A-F Grades released in 16 and 20 ga. during 1912, as well as the addition of a 20 ga. Sterlingworth. 16 ga. Sterlingworth introduced in 1913. Fox/Kautsky single trigger introduced in 1914 - engineering transition complete. During 1915, the XE Grade was introduced. The B Grade was dropped in 1918. Single barrel trap guns (J, K, and L Grades) were introduced in 1919. 1920 saw the introduction of the M Grade single barrel trap. In 1922, both the G and HE Grades were released. Beavertail forend and vent. rib were introduced in 1927. 1929 was the Savage buy-out (November), GE Grade dropped. Company moved from Philadelphia, PA to Utica, NY in 1930. Skeeter Grade introduced in 1931 while the 20 ga. HE Grade was disc. 1932 saw the introduction of both the Trap Grade Double and SP Grade. Wildfowl Grade was introduced in 1934. 1935 was the last year of the K and L single barrel trap guns. 1937 was the last year for the J Grade single barrel trap gun. The last 16 and 12 ga. Sterlingworths were built in 1939. The outbreak of the war in 1941 saw the last FE Grade shipped, the Wildfowler Grade dropped, and the introduction of the Model B. 1942 was the last retail catalog. Factory records indicate that the last 12 ga. was shipped in 1945 and the last 20 ga. was shipped during 1946 (SP Grade shipped in December, 1946). However, guns continued to be assembled from left-over parts as late as the 1960s.

FOX SERIAL NUMBER ASSIGNMENTS

The publisher wishes to express his thanks to Mr. Gurney Brown for providing the model serialization and years of mfg. in this section.

Ser. # range 50,000-200,000 — 12 ga. Sterlingworth — 111,556 mfg.
Ser. # range 350,000-400,000 — 16 ga. Sterlingworth — 28,481 mfg.
Ser. # range 250,000-300,000 — 20 ga. Sterlingworth — 21,304 mfg.
Ser. # range 1-50,000 — 12 ga. A-F Grades — 35,280 mfg.
Ser. # range 300,000-350,000 — 16 ga. A-F Grades — 3,875 mfg.
Ser. # range 200,000-250,000 — 20 ga. A-F Grades — 3,974 mfg.
Ser. # range 400,000-400,568 — 12 ga. Single Barrel Traps — 568 mfg.

F

FOX MODELS BY YEARS IN MFG.

Sterlingworth — 1910-1942 mfg. — 32 years.
Wildfowler — 1934-1940 mfg. — 6 years.
Trap Double — 1932-1942 mfg. — 10 years.
Skeeter — 1931-1942 mfg. — 11 years.
SP — 1932-1946 mfg. — 14 years.
A — 1906-1942 mfg. — 36 years.
B — 1906-1919 mfg. — 13 years.
C — 1906-1942 mfg. — 36 years.
D — 1907-1942 mfg. — 35 years.
F — 1907-1940 mfg. — 33 years.
G — 1922-1929 mfg. — 7 years.
H — 1922-1939 mfg. — 17 years.
J — 1919-1937 mfg. — 18 years.
K — 1919-1935 mfg. — 16 years.
L — 1919-1935 mfg. — 16 years.
M — 1920-1937 mfg. — 17 years.
X — 1915-1942 mfg. — 27 years.

SHOTGUNS: SxS, CURRENT MFG.

Delivery time for custom orders is currently 10-14 months, depending on gauge and grade.

The models below are manufactured by the Connecticut Manufacturing Co. located in New Britain, CT. These finely made shotguns have the following standard features: automatic safety, auto ejectors, DTs, Chromox 26, 28, or 30 in. barrels, individual barrel chokings, 2¾ in. chambers, scalloped receiver, Turkish Circassian walnut with hand-rubbed oil finish, choice of straight, semi-pistol or full-pistol grip stock with custom dimensions, splinter forearm, ivory bead sights. Special order options are as follows: Krupp steel barrels ($200), Fox SST ($1,000), walnut upgrades, custom initials ($200-$250), personalized gold inlays on barrel ($500), skeleton steel buttplate ($650), beaver-tail forearm ($650), and traditional leather trunk case with accessories ($750). Multi-barrel sets (same or multi-gauge) are also available with prices ranging from $4,500-$8,200, depending on the grade.

Add $1,000 for 28 ga. and .410 bore guns listed below (except Exhibition Grade).

Grading	100%	98%	95%	90%	80%	70%	60%

CE GRADE — 16 (new 1995), 20, 28 ga. (new 1995), or .410 bore (new 1995), engraved with fine scroll and game scenes, Grade I Turkish Circassian walnut. New 1993.

Mfg.'s Sug. Retail	$9,500	$9,500	$7,500	$5,650	$5,050	$4,300	$3,350	$2,700

XE GRADE — ga.'s similar to CE Grade, scroll work and engraved game scenes, Grade II Turkish Circassian walnut. New 1993.

Mfg.'s Sug. Retail	$11,000	$11,000	$9,000	$7,300	$6,000	$4,850	$3,700	$3,000

DE GRADE — ga.'s similar to CE Grade, intricate and extensive engraving, Grade III highly figured Turkish Circassian walnut. New 1993.

Mfg.'s Sug. Retail	$13,500	$13,500	$10,350	$8,600	$7,300	$6,000	$4,850	$3,500

FE GRADE — ga.'s similar to CE Grade, gold inlays surrounded by different types of scroll work, Grade IV highly figured Turkish Circassian walnut with finest checkering. New 1993.

Mfg.'s Sug. Retail	$18,500	$18,500	$15,000	$11,750	$9,250	$7,750	$6,000	$4,250

EXHIBITION GRADE — ga.'s similar to CE Grade, individually built per customer specifications on a "cost-no-object" basis, includes best-quality leather trunk case with full accessories, Exhibition Grade Turkish Circassian walnut. New 1993.

Mfg.'s Sug. Retail	$26,000	$26,000	$21,000	$16,750	$13,500	$10,250	$8,000	$6,250

100%	98%	95%	90%	80%	70%	60%	50%	40%	30%	20%	10%

F

SHOTGUNS: SxS, DISC.

STERLINGWORTH — 12, 16, or 20 ga., 26, 28, or 30 in. barrels, various chokes, boxlock, extractors, double trigger, checkered pistol grip stock. Mfg. 1905-1930.

N/A	$1,250	$1,050	$875	$750	$650	$500	$450	$400	$365	$325	$275

Add 33% for auto ejectors.
Add 50% for 20 ga.

A single trigger is a very desirable option on this model.

Ser. no. range on 12 ga. Sterlingworths is 50,000-200,000, 16 ga. is 350,000-400,000, and 20 ga. is 250,000-300,000.

STERLINGWORTH DELUXE — similar to Sterlingworth, with recoil pad and ivory bead, 32 in. barrel available.

N/A	$1,500	$1,200	$995	$900	$825	$725	$650	$550	$475	$425	$395

Add $200 for auto ejectors.
Add 50% for 20 ga.

A single trigger was not an option on this model.

STERLINGWORTH SKEET — similar to Sterlingworth, with 26 or 28 in. skeet boring, straight grip stock.

This model is very scarce (only several are known) and the extreme rarity factor precludes accurate price evaluation.

SUPER HE GRADE — 12 ga., 2¾ (very rare) or 3 in. chambered long range gun, 30 and 32 in. full choke, auto ejectors, otherwise similar to Sterlingworth.

N/A	$4,000	$3,500	$3,000	$2,500	$2,100	$1,750	$1,600	$1,500	$1,350	$1,150	$1,000

Add $300 for SST.

Original 3 in. chambered HE grades are marked "not warranteed, see instruction tag" on barrel flats. The HE grade was also manufactured in 20 ga. but is extremely rare. 2¾ in. chambers are rarer than 3 in. guns in this model.

100%	98%	95%	90%	80%	70%	60%	50%	40%	30%	20%	10%

HIGHER GRADE MODELS (A-F) — the following higher grade Fox shotguns are similar to the Sterlingworth in configuration. The grades differ in engraving and inlays, grade of wood and general workmanship. The E designation means auto ejectors.

Early A and B grades have very little engraving and are much less desirable than later models. Values below are for later guns.
VALUES BELOW ARE FOR 12 GA.
Add 50% for 16 ga. (made on same frame as 20 ga.).
Add 75% for 20 ga.
Add $200-$1,000 for vent. rib, depending on grade.
Add $200-$1,000 for SST, depending on grade.
Add $200-$1,000 for beavertail forearm, depending on grade.

Note: These guns were disc. in 1942 by Savage Arms after they mfg. them for 12 years. Pre-1930 guns were made by A.H. Fox Company.

* **A Grade**

100%	98%	95%	90%	80%	70%	60%	50%	40%	30%	20%	10%
N/A	$1,675	$1,375	$1,075	$900	$825	$725	$650	$600	$525	$475	$440

* **AE Grade (ejectors)**

100%	98%	95%	90%	80%	70%	60%	50%	40%	30%	20%	10%
N/A	$2,075	$1,675	$1,400	$1,150	$1,000	$900	$850	$825	$725	$650	$600

* **BE Grade (ejectors)**

100%	98%	95%	90%	80%	70%	60%	50%	40%	30%	20%	10%
N/A	N/A	$3,425	$2,750	$2,300	$2,000	$1,900	$1,800	$1,725	$1,625	$1,525	$1,425

This model is rarely encountered.

* **CE Grade (ejectors)**

100%	98%	95%	90%	80%	70%	60%	50%	40%	30%	20%	10%
N/A	N/A	$4,000	$3,600	$3,300	$3,000	$2,700	$2,500	$2,300	$2,100	$2,000	$1,750

* **XE Grade (ejectors)**

100%	98%	95%	90%	80%	70%	60%	50%	40%	30%	20%	10%
N/A	N/A	$5,650	$5,000	$4,500	$3,800	$3,400	$3,100	$2,875	$2,650	$2,200	$1,975

* **DE Grade (ejectors)**

100%	98%	95%	90%	80%	70%	60%	50%	40%	30%	20%	10%
N/A	N/A	$8,950	$7,500	$6,500	$5,500	$5,100	$4,750	$4,575	$4,350	$4,000	$3,500

* **FE Grade (ejectors)** — top-of-the-line model, only infrequently encountered.

100%	98%	95%	90%	80%	70%	60%	50%	40%	30%	20%	10%
N/A	N/A	$15,000	$12,000	$11,000	$10,000	$9,600	$9,150	$9,000	$8,750	$8,250	$7,700

SINGLE BARREL TRAP — 12 ga., 30 or 32 in. vent. rib barrel, full choke, boxlock, auto ejector, checkered trap style stock and recoil pad. The grades differ in wood, engraving, and overall quality. ME grade is custom built and extremely high quality with gold inlays. These models were disc. 1942. 568 single barrel trap guns were mfg. between 1932-1942 and have a ser. range of 400,000-400,568, with Monte Carlo stock.

Even though trap guns may be rarer than their SxS counterparts, to date their desirability is less since there are simply fewer collectors.

* **JE Grade**

100%	98%	95%	90%	80%	70%	60%	50%	40%	30%	20%	10%
N/A	$3,200	$2,800	$2,500	$2,100	$1,800	$1,600	$1,500	$1,425	$1,325	$1,200	$995

* **KE Grade**

100%	98%	95%	90%	80%	70%	60%	50%	40%	30%	20%	10%
N/A	$4,000	$3,500	$3,200	$2,800	$2,600	$2,400	$2,250	$2,100	$1,975	$1,775	$1,425

* **LE Grade**

100%	98%	95%	90%	80%	70%	60%	50%	40%	30%	20%	10%
N/A	N/A	$5,000	$4,500	$4,100	$3,750	$3,300	$3,000	$2,650	$2,300	$1,975	$1,650

* **ME Grade**

100%	98%	95%	90%	80%	70%	60%	50%	40%	30%	20%	10%
N/A	N/A	$9,150	$8,000	$7,150	$6,250	$5,600	$5,100	$4,850	$4,400	$3,800	$3,200

Grading	100%	98%	95%	90%	80%	70%	60%

MODEL B DOUBLE BARREL — 12, 16, 20 ga., or .410 bore, 24-30 in. barrels, various chokes, vent. rib on newer models, boxlock, extractors, double triggers, checkered pistol grip stock. Mfg. 1940-1986.

100%	98%	95%	90%	80%	70%	60%
$230	$210	$205	$185	$165	$145	$120

Last Mfg.'s Sug. Retail was $250.

Grading	100%	98%	95%	90%	80%	70%	60%

MODEL B-ST — similar to model B, with single trigger. Mfg. 1955-1966.

	$275	$250	$220	$195	$165	$140	$120

MODEL B-DL — similar to model B-ST, with satin chrome receiver, select wood. Mfg. 1962-1965.

	$315	$275	$240	$220	$195	$165	$140

MODEL B-DE — similar to B-DL, with less checkering. Mfg. 1965-1966.

	$295	$255	$230	$210	$180	$155	$125

MODEL B-SE — 12, 20 ga., or .410 bore, single trigger, selective ejectors, vent. rib, beavertail forearm, select walnut. Mfg. 1966-88.

	$415	$370	$325	$280	$240	$210	$180

Last Mfg.'s Sug. Retail was $525.

Add 20% for .410 bore.

Even though there were multiple series designations assigned to this model, there seems to be little difference in desirability. For that reason, other designations will be priced similarly to values shown above.

FRANCHI, LUIGI

Current manufacturer located in Brescia, Italy since mid-1860s. This trademark has been imported for approx. the past 30 years. Currently imported exclusively by Benelli USA, located in Accokeek, MD, since 1998. Previously imported and distributed by American Arms, Inc. located in North Kansas City, MO. Some models were previously imported by FIE firearms located in Hialeah, FL.

Franchi

Also see Sauer/Franchi heading in the S section.

RIFLES: SEMI-AUTO

CENTENNIAL MODEL — .22 LR cal., 21 in. barrel, open sight to commemorate Franchi's 100th anniversary. Mfg. 1968 only.

	$330	$250	$220	$195	$165	$150	$140

* **Engraved deluxe model**

	$415	$330	$305	$275	$240	$200	$165

* **Gallery model**

	$220	$195	$160	$120	$100	$80	$60

SHOTGUNS: SEMI-AUTO

BLACK MAGIC GAME — 12 ga. only, 3 in. chamber with gas metering system, interchangeable shell handling without adjustments, two-tone black alloy receiver with gold accents and trigger, 24, 26, or 28 in. VR barrel with Franchokes, checkered walnut stock and forearm, 7 lbs. Imported 1989-91.

	$550	$450	$395	$330	$300	$270	$240

Last Mfg.'s Sug. Retail was $659.

* **Black Magic Skeet** — skeet variation of the Black Magic Game, 2¾ in. chamber, 26 in. ported VR barrel with fixed Tula skeet choke, skeet dimensioned stock, 7¼ lbs. Imported 1989-91.

	$580	$475	$425	$350	$325	$295	$265

Last Mfg.'s Sug. Retail was $699.

* **Black Magic Trap** — trap variation of the Black Magic Game, 2¾ in. chamber, 30 in. VR barrel with Franchoke system, trap dimensioned stock, 7½ lbs. Imported 1989-91.

	$615	$495	$430	$350	$325	$295	$265

Last Mfg.'s Sug. Retail was $739.

Grading	100%	98%	95%	90%	80%	70%	60%

STANDARD MODEL (48/AL) — 12, 20, or 28 (new 1996) ga., 24, 26, 28, or 30 (disc. in 1990) in. VR barrel, recoil operated, alloy frame, checkered pistol grip stock, VR standard, Franchokes became available in 1989, 12 ga., 6 lbs. 9 oz. and 20 ga., 5 lbs. 6 oz. Mfg. 1950-present.

Mfg.'s Sug. Retail	$560	$435	$365	$300	$270	$250	$230	$210

Add $107 for 28 ga.

Add $30 for 12 ga. 24 in. slug barrel (disc. 1994).

Subtract 10% if without Franchokes.

Starting in 1990, black receiver, gold accents, and Franchokes became standard.

STANDARD MAGNUM (48/AL) — similar to Standard, except has 3 in. chamber with 28 in. (disc. 1988) or 32 in. VR barrel, recoil pad. Mfg. 1954-1990.

			$415	$360	$300	$270	$250	$230	$210

Last Mfg.'s Sug. Retail was $482.

This model was slated to be replaced with the Combo S/T - however, while advertised, the Combo S/T was never mfg.

HUNTER MODEL (48/AL) — similar to Standard, except etched receiver, better wood, VR standard, Franchokes became available in 1989. Mfg. 1950-1990.

			$415	$360	$300	$270	$250	$230	$210

Last Mfg.'s Sug. Retail was $482.

Add $35 for internal Franchokes (3).

This model was imported exclusively by FIE Firearms located in Hialeah, FL.

HUNTER MAGNUM — mfg. 1954-1973.

		$430	$380	$370	$340	$315	$290	$275

PRESTIGE MODEL — 12 ga. only, gas operated, vent. rib, various barrel lengths, alloy receiver, Franchokes became available in 1989. Imported 1985-1989.

		$575	$475	$395	$325	$310	$295	$275

Last Mfg.'s Sug. Retail was $720.

Add $40 for internal Franchokes (3).

This model was imported exclusively by FIE Firearms located in Hialeah, FL.

* *Turkey Model* — similar to Prestige Model except has dull matte black finish, Franchokes standard. Imported 1989 only.

		$615	$515	$425	$350	$320	$300	$280

Last Mfg.'s Sug. Retail was $760.

This model was imported exclusively by FIE Firearms located in Hialeah, FL.

ELITE MODEL — same general specifications as the Prestige Model, only etched receiver, Franchokes became available in 1989. Imported 1985-1989.

		$595	$500	$425	$350	$320	$300	$280

Last Mfg.'s Sug. Retail was $740.

Add $45 for internal Franchokes (3).

This model was imported exclusively by FIE Firearms located in Hialeah, FL.

610 VS — 12 ga., incorporates gas-operated Variopress System, adjusts for both 2¾ and 3 in. shells, 4 lug rotating breech bolt, alloy frame, non-glare finish, 26 or 28 in. VR barrels with Franchokes, checkered walnut stock and forearm. Imported 1997 only.

		$650	$550	$425	$325	$275	$250	$225

Last Mfg.'s Sug. Retail was $750.

Add $45 for engraved receiver and bolt (Model 610 VSL).

F

Grading	100%	98%	95%	90%	80%	70%	60%

612/620 VS — 12 (Model 612) or 20 (Model 620) ga., 3 in. chamber, same Variopress operating system as 610 VS, advanced safety system, black receiver with gold borders, 24, 26, or 28 in. barrel with Franchokes, last shot hold open, choice of checkered walnut (high gloss finish), black synthetic stock and forearm, or 100% Realtree X-tra brown camo coverage. New 1998.

Mfg.'s Sug. Retail	$595	$475	$385	$350	$300	$270	$250	$230

Subtract $16 for synthetic stock and forearm.
Add $62 for Realtree X-tra brown pattern camo coverage (Models 612/620 VS Camo).

* 612 Sporting — 12 ga. only, features silver receiver with black border and gold small parts, 28 in. ported target rib barrel with Franchokes, select checkered walnut stock and forearm. Limited mfg. 1998 only.

		$515	$415	$365	$315	$280	$250	$230

Last Mfg.'s Sug. Retail was $639.

SPAS-12 — 12 ga., 2¾ in. chamber, combat shotgun that offers pump or semi-auto operation, 5 (new 1991) or 8 (disc.) shot tube mag., alloy receiver, synthetic stock with built-in pistol grip (limited quantities were also mfg. with a folding stock or metal fixed stock), one-button switch to change from semi-auto to slide action operation, 21½ in. barrel, 8¾ lbs. Importation disc. 1994.

	$595	$495	$410	$360	$320	$300	$280

Last Mfg.'s Sug. Retail was $769.

This model was imported exclusively by FIE Firearms located in Hialeah, FL until 1990.

SPAS-15 — 12 ga. only, 2¾ in. chamber, operates as either semi-auto or slide action that is convertible with a one-button switch, 6 shot detachable box mag., 21½ in. barrel, lateral folding skeleton stock, carrying handle, 10 lbs. Limited importation 1989 only.

This model had very limited importation (less than 200) as the BATF disallowed further importation almost immediately. Even though the retail was in the $700 range, demand and rarity have pushed prices past the $2,000 level already.

SAS-12 — 12 ga. only, 3 in. chamber, slide action only, synthetic stock with built-in pistol grip, 8 shot tube mag., 21½ in. barrel, 6.8 lbs. Imported 1988-90 only.

	$415	$360	$300	$270	$250	$230	$210

Last Mfg.'s Sug. Retail was $473.

This model was imported exclusively by FIE Firearms located in Hialeah, FL.

LAW-12 — 12 ga. only, 2¾ in. chamber, gas operated semi-auto, synthetic stock with built-in pistol grip, 5 (new 1991) or 8 (disc.) shot tube mag., 21½ in. barrel, 6¾ lbs. Imported 1988-94.

	$570	$485	$400	$360	$320	$300	$280

Last Mfg.'s Sug. Retail was $719.

TURKEY GUN — 12 ga., similar to Standard Mag., 3 in. chamber only, turkey scene engraved. Mfg. 1963-1965.

	$415	$385	$370	$340	$315	$290	$275

SLUG GUN — 22 in. plain barrel, and rifle sights.

	$360	$330	$315	$295	$275	$255	$240

SKEET GUN — 26 in. skeet choke, vent. rib, select wood. Mfg. 1972-1974.

	$385	$370	$350	$330	$310	$285	$265

ELDORADO — fancy wood and gold filled engraved receiver. Mfg. 1954-1975.

	$450	$420	$395	$380	$360	$340	$320

CROWN GRADE — engraved hunting scene. Mfg. 1954-1975.

	$1,540	$1,320	$1,210	$1,045	$965	$910	$855

DIAMOND GRADE SILVER INLAID SCROLL — mfg. 1954-1975.

	$1,980	$1,735	$1,540	$1,430	$1,210	$1,045	$965

Grading	100%	98%	95%	90%	80%	70%	60%

IMPERIAL GRADE — gold inlaid hunting scene.

	$2,420	**$2,090**	**$1,925**	**$1,760**	**$1,595**	**$1,485**	**$1,320**

Note: Standard, Skeet and Slug with steel frame mfg. 1965-1972, designated "Dynamic" 12 ga., values are the same.

MODEL 500 STANDARD — 12 ga., 26 or 28 in. barrel, various chokes, vent. rib, gas operated, checkered pistol grip stock. Mfg. 1976-disc.

	$330	**$310**	**$305**	**$265**	**$230**	**$195**	**$165**

MODEL 520 DELUXE — engraved receiver.

	$385	**$365**	**$330**	**$290**	**$260**	**$220**	**$195**

MODEL 520 ELDORADO GOLD — fine wood, engraved gold, inlaid receiver. Mfg. 1977-disc.

	$990	**$770**	**$715**	**$660**	**$580**	**$525**	**$470**

MODEL 530 AUTO TRAP — similar to 500, except 30 or 32 in. full choke barrels, very high rib, special trap stock, pad.

	$660	**$550**	**$525**	**$440**	**$415**	**$385**	**$330**

SHOTGUNS: O/U

DE LUXE MODEL PRITI — 12 or 20 ga., boxlock action, ST, ejectors, 26 or 28 in. VR barrels with fixed chokes. Imported 1988-1989 only.

	$395	**$350**	**$315**	**$285**	**$240**	**$215**	**$185**

Last Mfg.'s Sug. Retail was $460.

This model was imported exclusively by FIE Firearms located in Hialeah, FL.

ALCIONE MODEL — 12 ga., 28 in. barrels, less engraving than Alcione SL, separated barrels. Importation disc. 1989.

	$675	**$550**	**$495**	**$460**	**$430**	**$380**	**$335**

Last Mfg.'s Sug. Retail was $800.

Previously designated Diamond Model.

This model was imported exclusively by FIE Firearms located in Hialeah, FL.

ALCIONE SL — 12 ga., 27 or 28 in. barrels, 6 lbs. 13 oz., separated barrels, ejectors, single trigger, silver finished receiver engraved with luggage case. Importation disc. 1986.

	$1,150	**$995**	**$875**	**$800**	**$725**	**$640**	**$550**

Last Mfg.'s Sug. Retail was $1,595.

ALCIONE 2000 SX (FIELD MODEL) — 12 ga., 3 in. chambers, 28 in. barrels, SST, separated barrels, ejectors, single trigger, engraved silver finished receiver with gold accents, with case, 7 lbs. 4 oz. Imported 1997 only.

	$1,675	**$1,495**	**$1,275**	**$1,025**	**$875**	**$750**	**$650**

Last Mfg.'s Sug. Retail was $1,895.

ALCIONE FIELD (97-12 IBS) — 12 ga. only, 3 in. chambers, steel alloy receiver with nickel finish, SST, ejectors, 26, or 28 in. barrels with Franchokes, checkered walnut stock and forearm, includes hard case. New 1998.

Mfg.'s Sug. Retail	**$947**	**$825**	**$750**	**$650**	**$550**	**$500**	**$450**	**$400**

Add $5 for left-hand action (includes cast-on stock).
Add $150 for detachable sideplates (Alcione SL IBS Model, disc.).

ALCIONE SPORT (SL IBS) — 12 ga. only, 2¾ in. chambers (can also be fitted for barrels with 3 in. chambers), SST, ejectors, 29 in. target rib ported barrel with Franchokes, detachable sideplates, includes hard case.

Mfg.'s Sug. Retail	**$1,227**	**$1,050**	**$925**	**$800**	**$675**	**$575**	**$500**	**$450**

Add $20 for left-hand action (includes cast-off stock).

Grading	100%	98%	95%	90%	80%	70%	60%

BLACK MAGIC SPORTING HUNTER — 12 ga. only, 3 in. chambers, 28 in. separated barrels with VR and Franchokes, black receiver with gold accents and trigger, SST, ejectors, checkered walnut stock and forearm, 7 lbs. Imported 1989-91.

	$995	$875	$800	$725	$650	$575	$495

Last Mfg.'s Sug. Retail was $1,249.

The Black Magic Model Series was imported exclusively by American Arms, Inc. located in North Kansas City, MO.

* *Black Magic Lightweight Hunter* — similar to Black Magic Sporting Hunter except 2¾ in. chambers only, 26 in. separated barrels with VR and Franchokes, alloy receiver, 6 lbs. Imported 1989-91.

	$975	$850	$775	$700	$625	$550	$475

Last Mfg.'s Sug. Retail was $1,209.

SPORTING 2000 — 12 ga. only, design for sporting clays or hunting, 28 in. vent. ported (disc. 1993) or unported (new 1997) barrels with target VR and choke tubes, SST, ejectors, select walnut with checkering, solid pad, hard case, 7¾ lbs. Imported 1992-1993, resumed 1997, disc. 1998.

	$1,275	$1,025	$875	$750	$650	$575	$500

Last Mfg.'s Sug. Retail was $1,495.

ARISTOCRAT FIELD — 12 ga., 26, 28, or 30 in. barrels, various chokes, vent. rib, auto ejectors, boxlock, selective single trigger, checkered pistol grip stock. Mfg. 1960-1969.

	$660	$470	$440	$395	$375	$340	$310

ARISTOCRAT MAGNUM — similar to Field, except 32 in. barrel, 3 in. chamber, full choke, pad. Mfg. 1962-1965.

	$660	$470	$440	$395	$375	$340	$310

ARISTOCRAT SKEET — similar to Field, but 26 in. vent. rib, bored skeet no. 1 and no. 2. Mfg. 1960-1969.

	$715	$525	$495	$450	$430	$395	$365

ARISTOCRAT TRAP — 30 in. vent. rib barrel, bored mod. and full, trap stock Mfg. 1960-1969.

	$745	$550	$525	$480	$455	$415	$380

ARISTOCRAT SILVER KING — select wood, engraved coin finished receiver. Mfg. 1962-1969.

	$750	$560	$535	$485	$470	$430	$400

ARISTOCRAT DELUXE — finer wood, more engraving. Mfg. 1960-1966.

	$990	$870	$835	$810	$770	$715	$660

ARISTOCRAT SUPREME — gold inlaid game birds. Mfg. 1960-1966.

	$1,430	$1,265	$1,155	$1,075	$990	$935	$880

ARISTOCRAT IMPERIAL — high grade wood, more engraving. Mfg. 1967-1969.

	$2,640	$2,200	$2,090	$1,925	$1,815	$1,650	$1,430

ARISTOCRAT MONTE CARLO — highest grade wood, elaborate engraving and inlay, mfg. 1967-1969.

	$3,520	$3,080	$2,915	$2,640	$2,420	$2,090	$1,870

FALCONET S — 12 ga., lightweight model of the Alcione SL, 27 or 28 in. barrels, 6 lbs. 1 oz., separated barrels, moderate engraving on silver finish receiver. Disc. 1985.

	$895	$765	$660	$560	$510	$460	$410

Last Mfg.'s Sug. Retail was $1,015.

Grading	100%	98%	95%	90%	80%	70%	60%

FALCONET FIELD — 12, 16, 20, 28 ga., or .410 bore, 24-30 in. barrels, various chokes, auto ejectors, select single trigger, engraved alloy receiver, checkered walnut stock. Mfg. 1968-1975.

Buckskin (light)	$550	$495	$470	$440	$415	$385	$360
Ebony (black)	$550	$495	$470	$440	$415	$385	$360
Silver	$605	$550	$525	$495	$470	$415	$385

   Add 25% for 28 ga. or .410 bore.

FALCONET SKEET — 26 in. barrels, bored skeet no. 1 and no. 2, wide vent. rib, case hardened steel receiver. Mfg. 1970-1974.

	$935	$855	$825	$770	$715	$690	$650

FALCONET INTERNATIONAL SKEET — higher grade wood, more engraving. Mfg. 1970-1974.

	$1,045	$935	$865	$825	$770	$745	$700

FALCONET STANDARD TRAP — 12 ga., 30 in. mod. and full, wide vent. rib, trap stock, pad. Mfg. 1970-1974.

	$935	$855	$825	$770	$715	$690	$650

FALCONET INTERNATIONAL TRAP — higher grade wood, more engraving. Mfg. 1970-1974.

	$1,045	$935	$865	$825	$770	$745	$700

FALCONET 2000 — 12 ga. only, boxlock with alloy receiver featuring silver finish with gold plated game scenes, 26 in. separated barrels with VR and choke tubes, SST, ejectors, select checkered walnut stock and forearm, hard case, 6 lbs. Imported 1992-97.

	$1,245	$975	$850	$725	$650	$575	$500

   Last Mfg.'s Sug. Retail was $1,375.

FALCONET 97-12 IBS — 12 ga. only, 2¾ in. chambers, ultra light alloy receiver with gold inlays, scroll engraving, and nickel finish, SST, ejectors, 26 in. barrels with Franchokes, checkered walnut stock and forearm, includes hard case. New 1998.

Mfg.'s Sug. Retail	$965	$875	$750	$625	$550	$500	$450	$400

PEREGRINE MODEL 451 — 12 ga., 26-28 in. barrels, various chokes, vent. rib, auto ejectors, alloy receiver, selective single trigger, checkered pistol grip stock. Mfg. 1975.

	$605	$550	$525	$495	$440	$415	$360

PEREGRINE MODEL 400 — similar to 451, except steel receiver. Mfg. 1975.

	$660	$605	$570	$540	$495	$460	$385

MODEL 2003 TRAP — 12 ga., 30 or 32 in. barrels, imp. mod. and full, or full and full, boxlock, auto ejectors, single selective trigger, high vent. rib, trap style stock, pad, cased. Mfg. 1976. Disc.

	$1,205	$1,090	$1,045	$910	$855	$770	$660

MODEL 2004 TRAP — similar to 2003, except single barrel, cased. Mfg. 1976. Disc.

	$1,205	$1,090	$1,045	$910	$855	$770	$660

MODEL 2005 COMBINATION TRAP — two sets of barrels, one single, one O/U, cased. Mfg. 1976. Disc.

	$1,815	$1,595	$1,515	$1,320	$1,210	$1,075	$935

MODEL 2005/3 COMBINATION TRAP — three sets of barrels, cased. Mfg. 1976. Disc.

	$2,420	$2,090	$1,980	$1,705	$1,515	$1,485	$1,320

UNDERGUN MODEL 3000 — radical competition trap, very high rib separated barrels, single and O/U, set cased. Disc.

	$2,750	$2,530	$2,310	$2,090	$1,980	$1,870	$1,760

Grading	100%	98%	95%	90%	80%	70%	60%

SHOTGUNS: SxS

AIRONE — 12 ga., choice of barrel length and chokes, box lock, Anson & Deeley, auto ejectors, double triggers, checkered English style stock, engraved. Mfg. 1940-1950.

	$1,320	$1,100	$935	$825	$745	$715	$660

ASTORE — similar to Airone, except less engraving, extractors. Mfg. 1937-1960.

	$990	$910	$770	$715	$635	$580	$550

ASTORE 5 — similar to Astore, except higher grade wood, more engraving, auto ejectors. Disc.

	$2,200	$1,925	$1,650	$1,540	$1,460	$1,375	$1,320

ASTORE II — similar to Astore 5, except less elaborate, currently mfg. in Spain for Franchi.

	$1,210	$1,045	$935	$880	$800	$715	$660

SIDELOCK DOUBLE BARREL — 12, 16, or 20 ga., barrels and choke custom order, stock to order, hand detachable side lock, self-opening action, auto ejectors, six grades offered, they differ only in overall quality and ornamentation, and grade of wood used.

	100%	98%	95%	90%	80%	70%	60%
Condor	$7,700	$6,600	$6,050	$5,720	$5,500	$4,620	$3,960
Imperial	$10,450	$9,350	$8,800	$8,250	$7,480	$6,600	$5,720
Imperiales	$10,670	$9,570	$9,020	$8,470	$7,700	$6,820	$5,940

SIDE-LOCK DOUBLE BARREL

* *No. 5 Imperial Monte Carlo*

	$15,400	$13,200	$11,000	$9,900	$9,350	$8,250	$7,150

* *No. 11 Imperial Monte Carlo*

	$16,500	$14,300	$12,100	$11,000	$10,450	$9,350	$8,250

* *Imperial Monte Carlo Extra*

	$19,800	$17,050	$14,300	$13,200	$12,650	$11,000	$9,900

Note: Imperial Monte Carlo Extra is currently being mfg. on special order only; the other models are disc.

FRANCOTTE, AUGUSTE & CIE. S.A.

Current manufacturer located in Leige, Belgium since 1805. Currently imported by Armes De Chasse located in Hertford, NC. Previously imported by VL&O between 1900-1930s, Abercrombie & Fitch until approx. 1962.

It is important to note that original A. Francotte SxS rifles and shotguns should exhibit the definitive "crown over AF" proofmark on water table.

REVOLVERS

Francotte manufactured Pryse-type revolvers at the end of the previous century, and these revolvers bore the name of the well-known British retailer. Encountered only infrequently domestically, these specimens found overseas are usually priced in the $150-$650 range.

RIFLES

All newly mfg. rifles in this section are custom made to the purchaser's individual specifications. Francotte takes advantage of 5 different frame sizes for its double rifles.

BOLT ACTION MODEL — many calibers available between .18 Bee and .505 Gibbs Mag., select checkered walnut stock, engraved mag. floor plate, gold inlays optional, values below assume engraving.

* *Short Bolt Action* — cals. with shorter cartridges.

Mfg.'s Sug. Retail	$10,600		$9,400	$7,350	$6,000	$4,950	$4,100	$3,300	$2,700

Subtract $3,250 if without engraving.

Grading	100%	98%	95%	90%	80%	70%	60%

* ***Standard Model*** — cals. with medium cartridge lengths.
  Mfg.'s Sug. Retail $8,500 $7,825 $6,100 $4,975 $4,100 $3,300 $2,700 $2,000
  Subtract $2,675 if without engraving.

* ***Magnum Action*** — cals. with longer cartridge lengths.
  Mfg.'s Sug. Retail $14,800 $13,750 $10,850 $9,350 $7,750 $6,400 $4,950 $3,950
  Subtract $7,850 if without engraving.

SINGLE SHOT MOUNTAIN RIFLE — available in a variety of cals., boxlock or sidelock action, custom order only.

* ***Boxlock Mountain Rifle*** — 6.5x50R, 7x57R, or 7x65R cal.
  Mfg.'s Sug. Retail $15,250 $13,900 $11,000 $9,450 $7,850 $6,500 $5,000 $4,000
  Subtract $4,800 if without engraving.
  Add 10% for optional sideplates.

* ***Sidelock Mountain Rifle*** — 7x65R or 7mm Rem. Mag. cal.
  Mfg.'s Sug. Retail $28,000 $24,800 $20,350 $16,650 $13,000 $10,500 $9,000 $8,000
  Subtract $5,725 if without engraving.

BOXLOCK SxS RIFLE — .30-06, .375 H&H, .470 NE, .500-3 in. or 9.3x62mm cal., ejectors, case colored receiver with border engraving (including screws), quarter rib on barrel, deluxe checkered pistol grip walnut stock and forearm. New 1997.
  Mfg.'s Sug. Retail $12,700 $11,850 $9,700 $8,500 $7,250 $6,000 $4,950 $4,100

SIDELOCK SxS RIFLE — .30-06, .375 H&H, .470 NE, .500-3 in. or 9.3x62mm cal., ejectors, case colored receiver with border engraving (including screws), quarter rib on barrel, deluxe checkered pistol grip walnut stock and forearm. New 1997.
  Mfg.'s Sug. Retail $17,500 $16,250 $14,250 $12,500 $10,250 $8,750 $7,250 $6,500

STANDARD SxS BOXLOCK RIFLE — available in a variety of cals., custom order only.
  Mfg.'s Sug. Retail $20,100 $18,650 $15,500 $11,350 $8,750 $6,950 $5,750 $5,000
  Subtract $7,600 if without engraving.
  Add $1,449 for optional sideplates.
  Add 15% for .375 H&H, .458 Win. Mag. cal., or other larger calibers upon request.

STANDARD SxS SIDELOCK RIFLE — available in a variety of cals., custom order only.
  Mfg.'s Sug. Retail $32,000 $29,450 $25,000 $20,250 $16,500 $13,000 $10,500 $9,000
  Subtract $7,000 if without engraving.

SHOTGUNS: SxS

All newly manufactured shotguns in this section are custom made to purchaser's individual specifications. Basic types listed below are also available in 24 or 32 ga. upon special order. Francotte takes advantage of 5 different action sizes, one for each gauge. Auguste Francotte does not manufacture guns by model - all guns are custom order.

Original A. Francotte SxS shotguns must have the "Francotte Choke Bore" marking on the water table. Be wary of fake barrel and frame markings, as some guns have recenty surfaced that are not Francotte, but have the Francotte name.

BOXLOCK SxS — 12, 16, 20, 28 ga., or .410 bore, premium grade Belgium side-by-side, double triggers standard, auto ejectors, English scroll engraving, Anson & Deeley boxlock action.
  Mfg.'s Sug. Retail $16,500 $15,450 $11,250 $8,000 $6,250 $5,000 $4,000 $3,250
  Subtract $5,925 if without engraving.
  Add 10% for 28 ga. or .410 bore.
  Add $1,159 for sideplates with engraving.

* ***Deluxe Anson & Deeley*** — gold inlaid game scenes, and engraving is by customer's personal preference.

    Prices and options are quoted per individual request.

Grading	100%	98%	95%	90%	80%	70%	60%

SIDELOCK SxS — 12, 16, 20, 28 ga., or .410 bore, true sidelock action, Arabesque scroll engraving, various chokes and barrel lengths, custom order only.

Mfg.'s Sug. Retail	$29,300	$27,300	$22,000	$18,750	$15,150	$12,000	$9,000	$7,750

Subtract $4,850 if without engraving.
Add 10% for 28ga. or .410 bore.

* **Deluxe sidelock** — gold inlaid game scenes and engraving are by customer's personal preference.

Prices and options are quoted per individual request.

JUBILEE — case colored receiver with hand engraving.

	100%	98%	95%	90%	80%	70%	60%
	$2,250	$1,875	$1,525	$1,325	$1,100	$975	$850
No. 14	$2,750	$2,250	$1,975	$1,775	$1,600	$1,450	$1,150
No. 18	$2,950	$2,550	$2,250	$1,925	$1,700	$1,550	$1,225
No. 20	$3,450	$2,900	$2,575	$2,275	$1,900	$1,725	$1,375
No. 25	$4,000	$3,500	$3,000	$2,500	$2,150	$1,925	$1,575
No. 30	$5,450	$4,975	$4,500	$4,000	$3,500	$2,500	$2,200

KNOCKABOUT — disc. circa 1975.

	100%	98%	95%	90%	80%	70%	60%
	$2,350	$1,850	$1,575	$1,265	$1,100	$935	$825

Add 75% for 20 ga.
Add approx. 200%-250% for 28 ga. or .410 bore.

NO. 45 EAGLE GRADE — this model can be identified by the gold eagle on frame bottom, disc. circa 1977.

	100%	98%	95%	90%	80%	70%	60%
	$7,650	$6,700	$5,850	$4,950	$4,250	$3,800	$3,000

FRASER, DANL. & CO.

Current manufacturer located in the U.K. Currently imported and distributed by Flying G Ranch, located in Carrizo Springs, TX.

Danl. Fraser & Co. has manufactured rifles since 1873 (originally located in Edinburgh, Scotland). Please contact the importer for current information, including prices.

RIFLES: SINGLE SHOT

HIGHLANDER SINGLE SHOT — .22 LR or .22 Hornet cal., underlever falling block action (color case hardened), 24 in. (½ round, ½ octagon) barrel, folding express-style sights, pistol grip walnut stock with fine checkering. Disc.

	100%	98%	95%	90%	80%	70%	60%
	$415	$335	$300	$280	$260	$240	$220

Last Mfg.'s Sug. Retail was $475.

* **Royal Highlander** — .22 LR or .22 Hornet cal., mfg. in Scotland, rose and scroll engraving with 18 Kt. inlays. Special order only.

FRASER FIREARMS CORP.

Previously manufactured by R.B. Industries, Ltd. until 1990. Previously distributed by Fraser Firearms Corp. located in Fraser, MI.

PISTOLS: SEMI-AUTO

FRASER 25 CAL. — .25 cal. only, copy of the Bauer semi-auto pocket model, 6 shot mag., 2¼ in. barrel, stainless steel construction.

	100%	98%	95%
	$120	$100	$90

Last Mfg.'s Sug. Retail was $133.

Add $17 for Model 2 (black nylon grips).
Add $115 for Model 3 (24 Kt. gold plated).

Grading	100%	98%	95%	90%	80%	70%	60%

FREEDOM ARMS

Current manufacturer located in Freedom, WY. Consumer direct and dealer sales.

REVOLVERS: MINI, STAINLESS STEEL

Because Freedom Arms' manufacturing capacity has been maximized due to the success of the .454 Casull revolver, the mini-revolver series was discontinued beginning 1989. As a result, prices have escalated on these models due to no production and normal demand.

FA-S-22LR (PATRIOT) — .22 LR cal., 5 shot, 1, 1¾ (disc. 1988), or 3 (disc. 1988) in. barrel, Hi-Gloss finish.

$245 $200 $150

Last Mfg.'s Sug. Retail was $153.

Add $15 for 3 in. barrel model (FA-BG-22LR, Minute-Man, disc. 1988).

FA-S-22M (IRONSIDES) — .22 Mag. cal., 4 shot, 1, 1¾ (disc. 1988), or 3 in. barrel, Hi Gloss finish.

$295 $225 $185

Last Mfg.'s Sug. Retail was $177.

Add $43 for 3 in. barrel model (Bostonian).

FA-S-22-LR BUCKLE/REVOLVER COMBINATION — .22 LR cal., 1 in. barrel, pistol is housed in belt buckle.

$275 $225 $185

Last Mfg.'s Sug. Retail was $193.

❋ *.22 Mag. cal.*

$325 $265 $215

Last Mfg.'s Sug. Retail was $216.

REVOLVERS: SA, STAINLESS STEEL

Freedom Arms also offers a complete line of accessories and factory installed options. The factory should be contacted directly for an up-to-date listing and prices. Beginning in 1999, all revolvers are equipped with a safety device. The Model 83 uses a sliding bar safety, while the Model 97 has a transfer bar safety.

Subtract $91 (Field Grade) or $121 (Premier Grade) for no sight, centerfire models.
Subtract $124 (Varmint Class) or $157 (Silouhette Class) for no sight, centerfire models.
Add $130 for 4 port Mag-na-ported barrel.
Add $92 for 2 port Mag-na-ported barrel.

MODEL 83 (252 VARMINT, .22 LR) — .22 LR cal., 5 shot, unique two point firing pin, choice of 5⅛ or 7½ in. barrel, includes express sights, black/green laminated hardwood grips, approx. 3¾ lbs. New 1991.

Mfg.'s Sug. Retail $1,527 $1,245 $900 $725

Add $264 for extra .22 Mag. cylinder.

❋ *Model 83 (252 Silhouette)* — silhouette variation featuring 10 in. barrel with competition sights (adj. front sight blade and ISGW silhouette competition rear sight) and black micarta grips.

Mfg.'s Sug. Retail $1,578 $1,345 $975 $865

Add $23 for front sight hood.

MODEL 83 (353 FIELD GRADE, .357 MAG.) — .357 Mag. cal., 5 shot, 4¾, 6, 7½, or 9 in. barrel on non-glare field grade finish, Pachmayr grips, adj. sights, 3¾ lbs. New 1992.

Mfg.'s Sug. Retail $1,340 $1,145 $900 $700

❋ *Model 83 (353 Premier Grade)* — similar to Field Grade, except has premier grade finish and laminated hardwood grips. New 1992.

Mfg.'s Sug. Retail $1,760 $1,470 $1,050 $775

Grading	100%	98%	95%	90%	80%	70%	60%

* *Model 83 (353 Silhouette)* — includes silhouette competition sights, 9 in. barrel, field grade finish, Pachmayr grips and trigger overtravel screw. New 1992.
  Mfg.'s Sug. Retail **$1,448** **$1,215** **$925** **$695**

MODEL 83 (654 FIELD GRADE, .41 REM. MAG.) — .41 Rem. Mag. cal., 5 shot, 4¾, 6, 7½, or 10 in. barrel. New 1998.
  Mfg.'s Sug. Retail **$1,340** **$1,145** **$900** **$700**

* *Model 83 (654 Premier Grade)* — adj. sight, 4¾, 6, 7½, or 10 in. barrel. New 1998.
  Mfg.'s Sug. Retail **$1,760** **$1,470** **$1,050** **$775**

* *Model 83 (654 Silhouette)* — field grade finish with silhouette competition sights, 10 in. barrel only, includes Pachmayr grips.
  Mfg.'s Sug. Retail **$1,448** **$1,215** **$925** **$695**

MODEL 83 (FIELD GRADE, .44 REM. MAG.) — .44 Rem. Mag. cal., 5 shot, 4¾, 6, 7½, or 10 in. barrel.
  Mfg.'s Sug. Retail **$1,340** **$1,145** **$900** **$700**

* *Model 83 (44 Premier Grade)* — adj. sight, 4¾, 6, 7½, or 10 in. barrel.
  Mfg.'s Sug. Retail **$1,760** **$1,470** **$1,050** **$775**
  Subtract $97 for fixed sight.

* *Model 83 (44 Silhouette)* — field grade finish with silhouette competition sights, 10 in. barrel only, includes Pachmayr grips.
  Mfg.'s Sug. Retail **$1,448** **$1,215** **$925** **$695**

MODEL 83 (.45 LC) — .45 LC only. Disc. 1990.
  $1,200 **$900** **$700**

MODEL 83 (CASULL FIELD GRADE, .454 CASULL) — .454 Casull cal., 5 shot, 4¾ (fixed sight only), 6, 7½, or 10 in. barrel, stainless steel matte finish with Pachmayr presentation grips. New 1988.
  Mfg.'s Sug. Retail **$1,400** **$1,180** **$900** **$700**
  Subtract $78 for fixed sight.

* *Model 83 (.454 Casull Silhouette Model)* — .454 Casull cal., includes 10 in. barrel, Pachmayr grips, field grade finish, silhouette competition sights, and trigger overtravel screw. Special order only.

* *Model 83 Silhouette Pak* — .44 Mag. cal., includes 10 in. barrel revolver, silhouette competition sight, honed action with 3 lb. trigger pull, plastic grips, locking aluminum carrying case with cleaning kit and tool. Mfg. 1990 only.
  $1,000 **$850** **$750**
  Last Mfg.'s Sug. Retail was $1,242.

MODEL 83 (CASULL PREMIER GRADE, .454 CASULL) — .454 Casull cal., 5 shot, stainless steel with brushed finish, single action revolver, 4¾, 6, 7½, or 10 in. standard barrel, laminated hardwood grips, adj. sights. Mfg. 1983-present.
  Mfg.'s Sug. Retail **$1,820** **$1,495** **$1,050** **$795**
  Subtract $97 for fixed sight.

* *Model 83 Silhouette Pak* — .454 Casull cal., includes 10 in. barrel revolver, silhouette competition sight, honed action with 3 lb. trigger pull, hardwood grips, locking aluminum carrying case with cleaning kit and tool. Mfg. 1990 only.
  $1,275 **$995** **$850**
  Last Mfg.'s Sug. Retail was $1,522.

MODEL 83 (757 FIELD GRADE, .475 Linebaugh) — .475 Linebaugh cal., 5 shot, stainless steel, matte finish, Pachmayr grips, 4¾, 6, or 7½ barrel. New 1999.
  Mfg.'s Sug. Retail **$1,400** **$1,180** **$900** **$700**

F

Grading	100%	98%	95%	90%	80%	70%	60%

* **Model 83 (757 Premier Grade)** — adj. sights, brushed finish, impregnated hardwood grips. New 1999.

    Mfg.'s Sug. Retail   **$1,820**   **$1,495 $1,050 $795**

MODEL 83 (555 FIELD GRADE, .50 AE) — .50 AE cal., 5 shot, stainless steel, matte finish, Pachmayr grips, 4¾, 6, 7½, or 10 in. barrel. New 1994.

    Mfg.'s Sug. Retail   **$1,400**   **$1,180 $900 $700**

* **Model 83 (555 Premier Grade)** — adj. sights, brushed finish, impregnated hardwood grips. New 1994.

    Mfg.'s Sug. Retail   **$1,820**   **$1,495 $1,050 $795**

MODEL 83 HUNTER PAK FIELD GRADE — .357 Mag., .44 Rem. Mag., or .454 Casull cal., 7½ in. barrel, plastic grips, field grade low profile adj. sight or no front sight base, sling and studs, locking aluminum carrying case with cleaning kit and tool. Mfg. 1990-1993.

    $1,075 $925 $775

Last Mfg.'s Sug. Retail was $1,333.

    Add $76 for low profile adj. sight and Pachmayr grips.

* **Model 83 Hunter Pak Premier Grade** — .357 Mag., .44 Rem. Mag., or .454 Casull cal., 7½ in. barrel, ebony micarta grips, no sights or premier grade adj. sight, sling and studs, locking aluminum carrying case with cleaning kit and tool. Mfg. 1990-1993.

    $1,395 $1,025 $850

Last Mfg.'s Sug. Retail was $1,611.

    Add $100 for adj. sights.

MODEL 97 — .357 Mag. or .45 LC (new 1999) cal., 5 (.45 LC) or 6 (.357 Mag.) shot, mid-size frame, 5½ or 7½ in. barrel, satin stainless finish, smooth wood grips, choice of fixed or adj. rear sight. New 1997.

    Mfg.'s Sug. Retail   **$1,492**   **$1,265 $950 $725**

    Subtract $101 for fixed sights.
    Add $264 for extra .45 ACP or .38 Spl. cylinder (new 1999).

U.S. DEPUTY MARSHAL — 3 in. barrel only with no ejector, fixed or adj. sights, U.S. Marshal medallion in left hardwood grip. Mfg. 1990-1993.

    $1,325 $900 $750

Last Mfg.'s Sug. Retail was $1475 (fixed sights).
Last Mfg.'s Sug. Retail was $1,558 (adj. sights).

    Add approx. $80 for adj. sights.

SIGNATURE EDITION — .454 Casull cal., high polish stainless steel, 7½ in. barrel only, rosewood grips, cased with accessories, only 93 of 100 were actually mfg.

    $2,300 $1,750 $1,300

Last Mfg.'s Sug. Retail was $2,684.

PRIMUS INTER PARES — 1 of every 100 guns is made in this variation, includes octagonal barrel, ivory grips, 7½ in. barrel, and cased. Disc. 1993.

    Rarity factor precludes accurate pricing.

FRENCH MILITARY

Various configurations manufactured in several locations in France.

PISTOLS: SEMI-AUTO

MODEL 1935A AUTO PISTOL — 7.65mm French Long cal., 8 shot, 4.3 in. barrel, fixed sights, blue, checkered wood grips, French service sidearm. Mfg. 1935-1945.

    $195 $175 $150 $125 $110 $100 $90

    Add 50% if Nazi proofed.

MODEL 1935S — 7.65mm French Long cal., 4⅓ in. barrel, enamel finish, Colt Govt. Model locking system, 26 oz.

    $325 $295 $260 $225 $195 $170 $150

Grading	100%	98%	95%	90%	80%	70%	60%

M.A.B. MODEL C — 7.65mm French Long cal., design based on FN Browning Model 1910, 6.1 in. barrel. Introduced 1933.

	$250	$220	$190	$170	$150	$125	$110

M.A.B. MODEL D — 7.65mm French Long cal., 3.96 in. barrel, single action, similar to Model C, mfg. commercially 1933-1940, many thousands mfg. for the German military during WWII (marked "Pistole MAB Kaliber 7.65mm").

	$275	$225	$200	$175	$150	$125	$110

MODEL M.A.B. PA - 15 — 9mm Para. cal., single action, 16 shot, currently used by French military.

	$550	$500	$450

MODEL M.A.B. PA - 15 TARGET — rare target variation of PA-15, adj. sight, 6 in. barrel, cased.

	$1,250	$1,000	$750

RIFLES: BOLT ACTION

MODEL 1886 LEBEL — 8mm Lebel cal., 32 in. barrel, adj. sight, military stock. Mfg. 1886 - WWII.

	$125	$100	$75	$65	$50	$40	$25

1936 MAS MILITARY RIFLE — 7.5mm MAS cal., 22 in. barrel, adj. sight, military stock, bayonet in forearm. Mfg. 1936-1940.

	$125	$100	$75	$65	$50	$40	$25

MODEL 45 — .22 LR cal., may have Mauser parts, aperture rear sight, post war mfg.

	$400	$360	$330	$275	$235	$200	$175

FRIGON GUNS, INC.

Previously manufactured by Marocchi in Italy. Previously imported by Frigon Guns, Inc. located in Clay Center, KS.

SHOTGUNS

FT-I — 12 ga. only, single barrel trap gun, blued finish, 32 or 34 in. VR barrel, quick-change stock. Mfg. 1986-94.

	$925	$675	$525	$435	$375	$350	$295

Last Mfg.'s Sug. Retail was $1,100.

FT-C — 12 ga. only, quick-change stock, trap combination gun includes 1 single barrel and 1 set of O/U barrels, cased. Mfg. 1986-94.

	$1,700	$1,325	$1,050	$875	$775	$685	$620

Last Mfg.'s Sug. Retail was $1,975.

FS-4 — 4-barrel skeet set including 12, 20, 28 ga., or .410 bore, individual forearms, quick-change stock, vent. barrels (except for .410 bore), cased. Mfg. 1986-94.

	$2,575	$1,975	$1,675	$1,475	$1,350	$1,250	$1,150

Last Mfg.'s Sug. Retail was $2,890.

FROMMER PISTOLS

Previously manufactured by Femaru-Fegyver-es Gepgyar R.T., Budapest, Hungary. Please refer to the Femaru listing in this section.

FURR ARMS

Current manufacturer located in Orem, UT.

NOTES

F

G section

GALEF SHOTGUNS

Previous importer of Zabala Hermanos (Spanish) and Antonio Zoli (Italian) shotguns.

Grading	100%	98%	95%	90%	80%	70%	60%

SHOTGUNS

COMPANION FOLDING SINGLE BARREL — 12, 16, 20, 28 ga., or .410 bore, 28 in. barrel, full choke, 30 in. full, 12 ga. only, hammerless, underlever, checkered pistol grip stock.

	100%	98%	95%	90%	80%	70%	60%
	$155	$125	$100	$85	$75	$65	$55

MONTE CARLO TRAP — 12 ga., single barrel, 32 in. full vent. rib, hammerless, underlever, recoil pad, checkered pistol grip Monte Carlo stock. Disc.

	$225	$185	$175	$150	$135	$125	$100

SILVER SNIPE — 12 or 20 ga., O/U, 3 in. chambers, 26, 28, or 30 in. barrels, imp. cyl. and mod. or full and mod. vent. rib, checkered pistol grip stock, boxlock, extractors, single trigger, mfg. by Angelo Zoli, disc.

	$525	$500	$475	$400	$375	$325	$275

GOLDEN SNIPE — O/U, similar to Silver Snipe, except has auto ejectors.

	$595	$525	$500	$475	$375	$350	$300

SILVER HAWK — 12 or 20 ga., SxS, 3 in. chambers, 26, 28, or 30 in. barrels, imp. cyl. and mod. or mod. and full, boxlock, extractors, checkered pistol grip and beavertail forearm. Mfg. by Angelo Zoli, 1968-1972.

	$450	$400	$375	$350	$300	$275	$250

GALEF ZABALA DOUBLE — 10, 12, 16, or 20 ga., SxS, 22, 26, 28, or 30 in. barrels, boxlock, extractors.

	100%	98%	95%	90%	80%	70%	60%
10 gauge	$250	$230	$200	$175	$150	$140	$125
Other gauges	$200	$175	$150	$130	$120	$110	$100

GALENA INDUSTRIES INC.

Please refer to the AMT listing.

GALIL

Current trademark manufactured by Israel Military Industries (IMI). No current consumer importation. Recent Galil semi-auto sporterized rifles and variations with thumbhole stocks were banned during April, 1998. Beginning late 1996, Galil rifles and pistols were available in selective fire mode only (law enforcement, military only) and are currently imported by UZI America, Inc., a subsidiary of O.F. Mossberg & Sons, Inc. Previously imported by Action Arms, Ltd. located in Philadelphia, PA until 1994. Previously imported by Springfield Armory located in Geneseo, IL and Magnum Research, Inc., located in Minneapolis, MN.

Magnum Research importation can be denoted by a serial number prefix "MR", while Action Arms imported rifles have either "AA" or "AAL" prefixes.

RIFLES: SEMI-AUTO

Models 329, 330 (Hadar II), 331, 332, 339 (sniper system with 6x40 mounted Nimrod scope), 361, 372, 386, and 392 all refer to various configurations of the Galil rifle.

MODEL AR — .223 Rem. cal. or .308 Win. cal., semi-auto paramilitary design rifle, gas operated - rotating bolt, 16.1 in. (.223 Rem. cal. only) or 19 in. (.308 Win. cal. only) barrel, parkerized, folding stock. Flip-up Tritium night sights. 8.6 lbs.

$1,795	$1,500	$1,250	$1,100	$900	$775	$650

Last Mfg.'s Sug. Retail was $950.

Grading	100%	98%	95%	90%	80%	70%	60%

MODEL ARM — similar to Model AR, except includes folding bi-pod, vented hardwood handguard, and carrying handle.

	$2,275	$1,975	$1,650	$1,375	$1,100	$975	$825

Last Mfg.'s Sug. Retail was $1,050.

GALIL SPORTER — similar to above, except has one-piece thumbhole stock, 4 (.308 Win.) or 5 (.223 Rem.) shot mag., choice of wood (disc.) or polymer hand guard, 8½ lbs. Imported 1991-1993.

	$995	$900	$800	$725	$600	$525	$475

Last Mfg.'s Sug. Retail was $950.

HADAR II — .308 cal., gas operated, paramilitary type configuration, 1 piece walnut thumbhole stock with pistol grip and forearm, 18½ in. barrel, adj. rear sight, recoil pad, 4 shot (standard) or 25 shot mag., 10.3 lbs. Imported 1989 only.

	$1,195	$975	$825	$700	$600	$500	$450

Last Mfg.'s Sug. Retail was $998.

SNIPER OUTFIT — .308 cal., semi-auto, limited production, sniper model built to exact I.D.F. specifications for improved accuracy, 20 in. heavy barrel, hardwood folding stock (adj. recoil pad and adj. cheekpiece) and forearm, includes Tritium night sights, bi-pod, detachable 6x40mm Nimrod scope, two 25 shot mags., carrying/storage case, 14.1 lbs. Imported 1989 only.

	$4,500	$4,000	$3,650	$3,150	$2,650	$2,150	$1,750

Last Mfg.'s Sug. Retail was $3,995.

G GAMBA, RENATO

RENATO GAMBA

Current manufacturer located in Gardone V.T., Italy. Gamba of America, a subsidiary of Firing Line, located in Aurora, CO, is the exclusive importer and distributor for Renato Gamba long guns beginning late 1996. Pistols were previously imported and distributed (until 1990) by Armscorp of America, Inc. located in Baltimore, MD. Shotguns were previously (until 1992) imported by Heckler & Koch, Inc. located in Sterling, VA.

Filli Gamba (Gamba Brothers) was founded in 1946. G. Gamba sold his tooling to his brother, Renato, in 1967 when Renato Gamba left his brothers and S.A.B. was formed. Filli Gamba closed in 1989 and the Zanotti firm was also purchsed the same year.

Renato Gamba firearms have had limited importation since 1986. In 1989, several smaller European firearms companies were purchased by R. Gamba and are now part of the Renato Gamba Group. The importation of R. Gamba guns changed in 1990 to reflect their long term interest in exporting firearms to America. Earlier imported models may be rare but have not enjoyed much collectability to date.

PISTOLS: SEMI-AUTO

All models listed below were discontinued for importation approx. 1990.

SAB G90 STANDARD — .30 Luger/7.65 Para. (disc.), 9x18mm Ultra (disc.), or 9mm Para. cal., double action, 4.72 in. barrel, 10 (C/B 1994) or 15★ shot side release mag., blue or chrome (disc.) finish, hammer drop safety on frame, smooth walnut grips, 2.2 lbs.

	$625	$375	$325	$295	$275	$250	$225

Last Mfg.'s Sug. Retail was $736.

Add $65 for chrome finish (disc.).

★ *SAB G90 Competition* — 9mm Para. cal., similar to SAB G90 Standard, except has adj. rear sight, "cocked and locked" operation, and checkered walnut grips. Imported 1990 only.

	$1,175	$425	$375	$325	$300	$275	$250

Last Mfg.'s Sug. Retail was $1,364.

Add $205 for stainless steel (SAB G90 Service Competition).

Grading	100%	98%	95%	90%	80%	70%	60%

SAB G91 COMPACT — similar to SAB G90, except has 3.54 in. barrel, 12 shot mag., 1.87 lbs.

	$625	$375	$325	$295	$275	$250	$225

Last Mfg.'s Sug. Retail was $736.

Add $65 for chrome finish (disc.).

* ***SAB G91 Competition*** — 9mm Para. cal., similar to SAB G91 Compact, except has adj. rear sight, "cocked and locked" operation, and checkered walnut grips. Imported 1990 only.

	$450	$395	$330	$300	$275	$250	$225

Last Mfg.'s Sug. Retail was $575.

SAB G2001 — .380 ACP cal., double action, mfg. from forged and milled steel, high polish blue, neoprene grips, slide mounted manual safety with firing pin block, 10 shot mag.

	$615	$395	$325	$295	$275	$250	$225

Last Mfg.'s Sug. Retail was $699.

REVOLVERS

TRIDENT FAST ACTION — .32 S&W or .38 Spl. cal., 2½ or 3 in. barrel, double action, blued receiver with checkered walnut grips, 6 shot, 23 oz.

	$550	$425	$360	$330	$295	$270	$245

Last Mfg.'s Sug. Retail was $630.

TRIDENT SUPER — .32 S&W or .38 Spl. cal., 4 in. vent. rib barrel, 6 shot, double action, checkered walnut grips, 25 oz.

	$585	$450	$375	$340	$310	$280	$250

Last Mfg.'s Sug. Retail was $683.

TRIDENT MATCH 900 — .32 S&W Long W.C. or .38 Spl. cal., match gun featuring 6 in. heavy barrel and anatomically compatible checkered walnut grips, target sights, 2.2 lbs.

	$750	$660	$595	$525	$475	$430	$390

Last Mfg.'s Sug. Retail was $895.

* ***Trident Match 901*** — similar to Trident Match 900.

	$750	$660	$595	$525	$475	$430	$390

Last Mfg.'s Sug. Retail was $895.

RIFLES

SAFARI EXPRESS SxS — 7x65R, 9.3x74R, or .375 H&H cal., 25 in. barrels with open sights, underlug locking with Greener crossbolt, ejectors except on .375 H&H, coin finished receiver with scroll work and game scene engraving, DTs, deluxe checkered walnut stock with cheekpiece and recoil pad, 9.9 lbs.

	$5,685	$4,575	$3,950	$3,575	$3,175	$2,850	$2,500

Last Mfg.'s Sug. Retail was $6,630.

CONCORDE EXPRESS O/U — .30-06, 8x57LS, or 9.3x75R cal., monoblock receiver, Boss type action, ejectors, cased.

Mfg.'s Sug. Retail	$5,995		$5,500	$4,900	$4,500	$4,100	$3,750	$3,350	$2,950

Add $300 for automatic double safety system.

DAYTONA SL EXPRESS O/U — .30-06, .375 H&H, or 9.3x74R cal., monoblock receiver with Boss type improved action, detachable Gamba trigger assembly, hand engraved sideplates with game scenes and English scroll.

Mfg.'s Sug. Retail	$6,995		$6,500	$5,500	$4,900	$4,500	$4,100	$3,750	$3,350

EXPRESS MAXIM SxS — .375 H&H, .458 Win. Mag., .470 N.E., or .458 Lott (new 1995) cal., sidelock action, fine engraving with big game scenes signed by the master engraver, includes leather case.

Mfg.'s Sug. Retail	$52,500		$47,750	$41,000	$34,000	$26,000	$20,500	$17,500	$13,000

Grading	100%	98%	95%	90%	80%	70%	60%

MUSTANG EXTRA SINGLE SHOT — 5.6x50mm (disc.), 5.6x57R, 6.5x57R (disc.), 7x65R, .222 Rem. (disc.), .243 Win., .270 Win., or .30-06 cal., single 25½ in. barrel configuration with highly engraved sidelock action featuring triple-bite double Purdey locking system with Greener crossbolt, extra fine vine leaf Renaissance engraving (game scene upon request), double-set triggers, best quality checkered walnut stock and forearm, 6.17 lbs.

Mfg.'s Sug. Retail	$14,995		$13,500	$11,250	$9,950	$7,900	$6,900	$6,100	$5,500

RGZ 1000 BOLT ACTION — 7x64mm, .270 Win., 7mm Rem. Mag., or .300 Win. Mag. cal., modified Mauser K-98 action, 20½ in. barrel, pistol grip stock with cheekpiece, 7 lbs.

	$1,100	$885	$825	$760	$700	$640	$575

Last Mfg.'s Sug. Retail was $1,310.

* ***RGX 1000 Express*** — similar to RGZ 1000, except has 23¾ in. barrel and double set triggers, 7.7 lbs.

	$1,255	$960	$875	$795	$725	$650	$575

Last Mfg.'s Sug. Retail was $1,475.

SHOTGUNS: O/U

Most O/U models (except for the Daytona Trap and Concorde Model) listed below were discontinued in 1990 when H&K became the exclusive importer for R. Gamba shotguns.

EUROPA 2000 — 12 ga. only, engraved, silver finished boxlock action with sideplates, vent. rib, single trigger, ejectors, deluxe checkered stock and forearm, 6.84 lbs.

	$1,250	$995	$895	$835	$775	$715	$650

Last Mfg.'s Sug. Retail was $1,475.

EDINBURGH SUPER SLUG — 12 ga. only, trap model, SST, ejectors, engraved action, deluxe checkered stock and forearm.

	$1,225	$980	$895	$835	$775	$715	$650

Last Mfg.'s Sug. Retail was $1,425.

GRIFONE SPORTING TRAP — 12 ga. only, trap model, SST, ejectors, moderately engraved action, deluxe checkered stock and forearm.

	$1,225	$980	$895	$835	$775	$715	$650

Last Mfg.'s Sug. Retail was $1,425.

GRINTA TRAP/SKEET — 12 ga. only, trap/skeet model, SST, ejectors, medium engraving coverage.

	$1,250	$995	$895	$835	$775	$715	$650

Last Mfg.'s Sug. Retail was $1,710.

VICTORY TRAP/SKEET — similar to Grinta Model, except has better walnut and more engraving.

	$1,450	$1,275	$1,050	$995	$895	$835	$775

Last Mfg.'s Sug. Retail was $1,905.

EDINBURG MATCH — similar to Victory Model, except has different style of engraving.

	$1,630	$1,300	$1,100	$995	$895	$835	$775

Last Mfg.'s Sug. Retail was $1,930.

MONTREAL MODEL 90/91 — 12 ga. only, boxlock, interchangeable trigger assembly, select walnut, vent. rib. Available in International Trap, American Skeet, Sporting, and Field models.

	$2,250	$1,650	$1,300	$1,100	$1,000	$900	$800

Add $50 for adj. single barrel.
Add $200 for single selective trigger.

The Model 90 has a flat-sided receiver, while the Model 91 has a Daytona sculpted receiver.

MONTREAL 90/91 AMERICAN TRAP COMBO — 12 ga. only, 32 in. barrels and adj. impact, single 34 in. barrel, interchangeable trigger assembly.

	$2,800	$2,100	$1,820	$1,540	$1,400	$1,260	$1,120

G

Grading	100%	98%	95%	90%	80%	70%	60%

SINGLE BARREL TRAP-MODEL 496 — 12 ga. only, boxlock, vent. rib.

	$1,150	$865	$750	$635	$575	$520	$460

CONCORDE GAME MODEL — 12 or 20 ga., Boss type improved locking system, ejectors, 26¾ or 28 in. VR barrels. Importation began 1995.

Mfg.'s Sug. Retail	$4,995	$4,500	$3,850	$3,400	$2,800	$2,350	$1,900	$1,600

> Add $2,000 for Trap combo.
> Add approx. $500 for Sporting Clays Model (disc.).

* *Grade 7* — includes engraving featuring game scenes and English scroll.

Mfg.'s Sug. Retail	$8,495	$7,600	$6,450	$5,400	$4,400	$3,750	$3,250	$2,575

> Add approx. $500 for Sporting Clays Model (disc.).

* *Grade 8* — features top-of-the-line English scroll engraving.

Mfg.'s Sug. Retail	$6,795	$5,975	$5,100	$4,200	$3,600	$2,925	$2,400	$2,100

> Add approx. $500 for Sporting Clays Model (disc.).

DAYTONA VARIATIONS — 12 ga. only, monolithic boxlock action, SST, ejectors, detachable trigger group, blue or chrome finish standard, available in either Hunting, Skeet, Pigeon, Sporting Clays, Olympic Trap, or American Trap configuration, deluxe walnut with fine English scroll engraving with game scenes. Importation began 1990.

Mfg.'s Sug. Retail	$5,995	$5,150	$4,100	$3,450	$2,800	$2,350	$1,900	$1,500

> Add approx. $675 for Sporting Clays Model.
> Add approx. $1,500 for American Trap configuration (disc.).
> Add $2,000 for Daytona combo package.
> Add $2,250 for extra set of O/U barrels.
> Add $300 for gold inlaid nomenclature.

* *Grade Royale* — top-of-the-line Daytona Model.

Mfg.'s Sug. Retail	$16,495	$14,550	$11,750	$9,750	$8,400	$6,700	$5,000	$4,250

* *Grade Purdey* — features Purdey locking system.

Mfg.'s Sug. Retail	$15,995	$14,250	$11,500	$9,700	$8,350	$6,700	$5,000	$4,250

* *Grade 4 Daytona Model* — most elaborately engraved numbered Daytona model, choice of eagle panel scene or fine scroll engraving.

Mfg.'s Sug. Retail	$12,995	$11,225	$8,475	$6,850	$5,000	$4,250	$3,750	$3,250

> Add approx. $500 for Sporting Clays Model (disc.).

* *Grade 5 Daytona Model* — one grade below Grade 4.

Mfg.'s Sug. Retail	$11,995	$10,225	$7,850	$6,500	$4,500	$3,850	$3,250	$2,750

> Add approx. $500 for Sporting Clays Model (disc.).

* *Grade 6 Daytona Model* — one grade below Grade 5, choice of duck game scene or tight scroll engraving.

Mfg.'s Sug. Retail	$10,995	$9,700	$7,500	$6,250	$4,300	$3,750	$3,250	$2,750

> Add approx. $500 for Sporting Clays Model (disc.).

* *Grade 7 Daytona Model* — one grade below Grade 6, game scene engraving.

Mfg.'s Sug. Retail	$9,495	$8,375	$6,700	$5,250	$4,100	$3,650	$3,150	$2,650

* *Grade 8 Daytona Model* — introductory engraved model.

Mfg.'s Sug. Retail	$7,795	$7,000	$6,200	$4,800	$3,700	$3,300	$2,950	$2,350

DAYTONA SL — deluxe variation of the Daytona Model, except has sideplates with extensive engraving, available in the same configurations as the Daytona Model, includes case. Limited importation 1990-94.

	$10,250	$8,750	$7,250	$5,400	$4,450	$3,950	$3,500

Last Mfg.'s Sug. Retail was $11,500.

> Add $400 for American Trap configuration.

G

Grading	100%	98%	95%	90%	80%	70%	60%

GRADE SL BEST — features elaborate scroll and 24 Kt. gold game scene inlays.

	Mfg.'s Sug. Retail	$26,495	$23,650	$19,750	$17,150	$14,000	$10,500	$8,750	$7,300

GRADE SL VENUS — features elaborate scroll and game scene engraving.

	Mfg.'s Sug. Retail	$24,995	$21,250	$18,750	$16,000	$13,500	$10,500	$8,750	$7,500

* *Grade 1 SL* — elaborate engraving with 24 Kt. gold game scene engraving.

	Mfg.'s Sug. Retail	$19,995	$18,000	$15,250	$13,500	$11,000	$9,450	$8,150	$6,600

* *Grade 2 SL* — elaborate scroll and game scene engraving, w/o gold inlays.

	Mfg.'s Sug. Retail	$16,995	$15,000	$12,000	$9,950	$8,400	$6,700	$5,100	$4,250

* *Grade 3 SL* — features hand engraved sideplates with English scroll and game scenes. Importation began 1995.

	Mfg.'s Sug. Retail	$14,995	$13,500	$11,000	$9,450	$8,150	$6,600	$5,000	$4,250

DAYTONA SLHH — 12 or 20 ga., H&H style sidelock action with Boss improved lock-up, top-of-the-line model, game or competition configuration, includes leather case. Importation began in 1990.

* *Grade 1* — similar to Grade 2, except has better engraving.

	Mfg.'s Sug. Retail	$29,995	$27,000	$23,000	$20,000	$17,000	$13,000	$10,000	$8,950

    Add $2,075 for gold engraving.

* *Grade 2* — available in either Hunting (12 ga. only), Skeet, Trap, Pigeon, or Sporting Clays configuration.

	Mfg.'s Sug. Retail	$27,995	$25,000	$21,000	$18,000	$14,750	$11,000	$9,000	$7,500

* *Grade 3* — features elaborate scroll and game scene engraving.

	Mfg.'s Sug. Retail	$26,995	$24,000	$20,000	$17,250	$14,000	$10,500	$8,750	$7,300

VENUS MODEL — boxlock action with engraved sideplates featuring relief scroll and Goddess of the Hunt engraving.

	Mfg.'s Sug. Retail	$34,995	$31,050	$27,000	$23,000	$20,000	$17,000	$13,000	$10,000

THE BEST — sidelock action with elaborate engraving and multiple 24 Kt. gold game scene inlays.

	Mfg.'s Sug. Retail	$39,995	$36,000	$31,050	$27,000	$23,000	$20,000	$17,000	$13,000

* *One of Thousand* — top-of-the-line model with every possible refinement, individually special ordered only.

    This model starts out at $75,000.

BAYERN 88 COMBINATION GUN — 12 ga. over same cals. listed for Mustang Model, coin finished boxlock action with game scene engraving, double DTs, extractors, deluxe checkered walnut stock with recoil pad, 7½ lbs.

			$1,365	$1,050	$950	$860	$775	$715	$665

Last Mfg.'s Sug. Retail was $1,595.

SHOTGUNS: SxS

Previous to 1989, most of the models listed below were available in 28 ga. on a 28 ga. frame by option.

    Add 20%+ for 28 ga. guns listed below.

HUNTER SUPER — 12 ga. only, Anson & Deeley engraved boxlock action with silver finish, DTs, extractors, 6.84 lbs.

			$1,750	$1,275	$895	$760	$630	$575	$525

Last Mfg.'s Sug. Retail was $1,506.

PRINCIPESSA — 12 or 20 ga., similar to Hunter Super except has English straight grip stock and better engraving, 6.62 lbs. Importation disc. 1994.

			$2,750	$1,900	$1,525	$1,250	$995	$800	$625

Last Mfg.'s Sug. Retail was $2,495.

    Add $200 for single trigger.

Grading	100%	98%	95%	90%	80%	70%	60%

S. VINCENT 580 EXTRA DELUXE — 12 ga. only, custom made to individual preferences,very high quality, sidelock action, engraving coverage 100%.

	$4,950	$4,250	$3,500	$2,750	$2,125	$1,775	$1,625

OXFORD 90 — 12 or 20 ga., boxlock action with Purdey locking system, DTs, ejectors, scroll engraving on sideplates, deluxe checkered straight grip walnut stock with recoil pad or checkered butt, 6.84 lbs. Disc. 1998.

	$3,750	$3,300	$2,875	$2,475	$2,100	$1,700	$1,250

Last Mfg.'s Sug. Retail was $4,300.

Add $245 for single trigger.

OXFORD EXTRA — 20 ga. only, includes elegantly engraved sideplates, ejectors, and better quality hand checkered stock and forearm. Importation began 1992.

Mfg.'s Sug. Retail	$3,750		$3,400	$2,875	$2,475	$2,100	$1,750	$1,400	$1,175

Add $245 for single trigger.

MODEL 624 PRINCE — 12 or 20 ga., boxlock action, ejectors, hand checkered walnut stock and forearm. Importation began 1992.

Mfg.'s Sug. Retail	$3,750		$3,400	$2,875	$2,475	$2,100	$1,750	$1,400	$1,175

Add $245 for single trigger.

MODEL 624 PRINCE EXTRA — similar to Model 624 Prince, except has deep floral hand engraving.

Mfg.'s Sug. Retail	$5,995		$5,400	$4,800	$4,300	$3,700	$3,100	$2,650	$2,100

Add $255 for single trigger.

LONDON — 12 or 20 (disc.) ga., H&H side-lock system, ejectors, DT or SST, chopper lump barrels, English scroll engraving, deluxe checkered straight grip stock and forearm, 6.84 lbs.

Mfg.'s Sug. Retail	$8,995		$8,150	$6,900	$5,900	$4,900	$3,900	$3,500	$3,000

LONDON ROYAL — similar to London Model except has less extensive game scene engraving.

	$6,950	$5,750	$4,750	$3,950	$3,475	$3,050	$2,800

Last Mfg.'s Sug. Retail was $6,730.

AMBASSADOR MODEL — 12 or 20 ga., H&H side-lock system, available with either gold-line engraving on barrels and receiver with blued receiver (Gold and Black Model) or English scroll engraving (English Engraved Model), single trigger, ejectors, deluxe checkered walnut stock and forearm, cased, 6.4 lbs.

Mfg.'s Sug. Retail	$17,995		$16,200	$14,000	$11,750	$9,000	$7,850	$6,700	$5,600

This model is also available in either Field or Sporting versions upon special request.

AMBASSADOR EXECUTIVE — 12 or 20 ga. only, top-of-the-line model, made to individual order only, every possible refinement.

Mfg.'s Sug. Retail	$24,995		$21,250	$18,750	$16,000	$13,500	$10,500	$8,750	$7,500

SHOTGUNS: SLIDE ACTION

MODEL 2100 — 12 ga. Mag., 19½ in. barrel, 7 shot mag., law enforcement configuration with matte black metal and wood, 6.62 lbs. Limited importation.

	$610	$480	$390	$330	$275	$220	$195

Last Mfg.'s Sug. Retail was $715.

GARBI, ARMAS

Current manufacturer located in Eibar, Spain. Imported and distributed exclusively by W.L. Moore & Co. located in Scottsdale, AZ. Distributor and dealer sales.

Currently, Garbi is mfg. 400-500 shotguns per year.

Grading	100%	98%	95%	90%	80%	70%	60%

RIFLES: SxS

Garbi also manufactures a deluxe SxS double rifle in 7x65R, 8x57JRS, 9.3x74R, .300 H&H, or .375 H&H cal. Currently, the base retail price for this Express Rifle is $21,800. Please contact the importer or factory directly for more information (including special orders and prices) on this model.

SHOTGUNS: SxS, DISC.

MODEL 51 A — 12 ga. only, extractors, case hardened finish, straight grip.

	$450	$350	$325	$300	$280	$260	$240

MODEL 51 B — 12, 16, or 20 ga., ejectors, case hardened or coin finish receiver, straight grip.

	$850	$650	$590	$540	$500	$460	$420

MODEL 60 A — 12 ga. only, extractors, case hardened finish, true sidelock, large scroll engraving, cocking indicators, hand checkered butt, choice of grip.

	$725	$575	$530	$475	$440	$400	$360

MODEL 60 B — 12, 16, or 20 ga., ejectors, case hardened or coin finish receiver, extensive engraving, straight grip.

	$1,200	$850	$790	$735	$680	$630	$575

MODEL 62 A — 12 ga. only, extractors, case hardened finish, true sidelock, light engraving, cocking indicators, hand checkered butt, choice of grip.

	$725	$575	$530	$475	$440	$400	$360

MODEL 62 B — 12, 16, or 20 ga. only, ejectors, case hardened or coin finish receiver, extensive engraving, straight grip.

	$1,200	$850	$790	$735	$680	$630	$575

SHOTGUNS: SxS, RECENT MFG.

On the models listed below, add 5% for 28 ga., $850 for single trigger, $160-$295 for beavertail forearm, $1,325-$2,700 per extra set of barrels (depending on grade), and $250 for Churchill style level file-cut rib.

MODEL 71 — 12, 16, or 20 ga., Holland-pattern detachable sidelock ejector double, fine English scroll engraving, oil finish, select walnut, articulated trigger. Importation disc. 1988.

	$2,250	$1,825	$1,500	$1,300	$1,075	$980	$900

Last Mfg.'s Sug. Retail was $2,600.

MODEL 100 — 12, 16, or 20 ga., Holland-pattern detachable sidelock ejector double, Purdey style scroll engraving, chopper lump barrels, oil finish, select walnut, articulated trigger.

Mfg.'s Sug. Retail	$4,600	$4,050	$3,200	$2,350	$1,700	$1,450	$1,200	$1,025

MODEL 101 — 12, 16, or 20 ga., Holland-pattern sidelock ejector double with chopper lump barrels, scroll engraving, selected walnut stock.

Mfg.'s Sug. Retail	$5,950	$5,250	$4,050	$3,000	$2,375	$1,900	$1,650	$1,400

MODEL 102 — 12, 16, 20, or 28 ga., Holland-pattern sidelock ejector double with chopper lump barrels, Holland-type large scroll engraving, selected walnut stock. Importation disc. 1993.

	$5,700	$4,500	$3,450	$2,700	$2,350	$2,000	$1,750

Last Mfg.'s Sug. Retail was $7,100.

MODEL 103A — 12, 16, 20, or 28 ga., Holland-pattern sidelock ejector double with chopper lump barrels, Purdey style fine scroll and rosette engraving, selected walnut stock.

Mfg.'s Sug. Retail	$7,400	$6,500	$4,900	$3,575	$2,800	$2,350	$2,000	$1,750

* **Model 103A Royal** — deluxe variation of the Model 103A, features engraving patterned after the H&H "Royal" or Purdey's rose and scroll styles, extra fancy walnut.

Mfg.'s Sug. Retail	$11,000	$10,025	$8,900	$6,800	$5,350	$4,350	$3,500	$2,750

Grading		100%	98%	95%	90%	80%	70%	60%

MODEL 103B — 12, 16, 20, or 28 ga., Holland-pattern sidelock ejector double with chopper lump barrels of nickel-chrome steel, H&H type easy opening mechanism, Purdey style fine scroll and rosette engraving, well figured walnut stock.

Mfg.'s Sug. Retail	$10,400	$9,150	$6,950	$5,450	$4,400	$3,500	$2,750	$2,250

   * *Model 103B Royal* — deluxe variation of the Model 103B, features engraving patterned after the H&H "Royal" or Purdey's rose and scroll styles, extra fancy walnut.

Mfg.'s Sug. Retail	$14,900	$12,750	$11,000	$10,000	$8,850	$6,750	$5,350	$4,350

MODEL 120 — 12, 16, 20, or 28 ga., Holland-pattern sidelock ejector double with chopper lump barrels of nickel-chrome steel, H&H type easy opening mechanism, game scene engraving-3 patterns available. Well figured walnut stock. Importation disc. 1994.

			$7,500	$6,000	$4,875	$4,125	$3,375	$2,600	$2,200

Last Mfg.'s Sug. Retail was $9,400.

MODEL 200 — 12, 16, 20, or 28 ga., Holland-pattern sidelock ejector double with chopper lump barrels of nickel-chrome steel, heavy-duty locks, magnum proofed, very fine Continental style floral and scroll engraving, well figured walnut stock.

Mfg.'s Sug. Retail	$10,000	$8,750	$6,325	$5,000	$4,225	$3,400	$2,600	$2,200

SPECIAL WLM — 12, 16, 20, or 28 ga., top-of-the-line Holland-pattern sidelock ejector double with chopper lump barrels, full coverage large scroll engraving, fancy-figured walnut stock. Importation disc. 1994.

			$7,500	$6,000	$4,875	$4,125	$3,375	$2,600	$2,200

Last Mfg.'s Sug. Retail was $9,400.

SPECIAL AG — 12, 16, 20, or 28 ga., top-of-the-line Holland-pattern sidelock ejector double with chopper lump barrels, large scroll engraving patterned after Lebeau-Courally, fancy figured walnut stock. Disc.

			$8,000	$6,350	$5,200	$4,300	$3,550	$2,750	$2,300

Last Mfg.'s Sug. Retail was $9,200.

GASTINNE RENETTE

Current manufacturer and retailer established 1812, and located in Paris, France.

Currently being manufactured with limited importation and distribution. Gastinne Renette should be contacted directly (see Trademark Index) for an up-to-date quotation or information on their current model line-up.

RIFLES: BOLT ACTION

Values listed below are base prices for each model - since all guns are made to individual order, the customer can choose the wood, level of engraving, and other special features, all at additional cost. Gastinne Renette should be contacted directly (see Trademark Index) for an individual price quotation.

STANDARD MODEL MAUSER ACTION

Mfg.'s Sug. Retail	$6,000	$6,000	$5,150	$4,450	$3,850	$3,150	$2,550	$1,900

DELUXE MAUSER ACTION

Mfg.'s Sug. Retail	$12,000	$12,000	$10,750	$7,850	$6,850	$5,750	$4,750	$3,900

RIFLES: SxS, DOUBLE

BOXLOCK MODEL — variety of cals., features Anson & Deeley boxlock mechanism, color case hardened receiver. New 1993.

Mfg.'s Sug. Retail	$10,000	$10,000	$7,750	$6,950	$5,850	$4,950	$4,100	$3,200

EUROPEAN SIDELOCK

Mfg.'s Sug. Retail	$36,000	$36,000	$31,000	$27,000	$22,500	$18,750	$15,000	$12,500

AFRICAN SIDELOCK — various Mag. cals. New 1993.

Mfg.'s Sug. Retail	$40,000	$40,000	$33,000	$28,750	$23,500	$19,250	$15,500	$12,750

Grading	100%	98%	95%	90%	80%	70%	60%

STANDARD TYPE G — 9.3x74R, 7.65R, .30-06, or .375 H&H cal., double bolt action, ejectors, reinforced stock, 23¾ in. barrels, bouquet style engraving with deluxe walnut stock and forearm, 7 lbs. 6 oz.

	$2,995	$2,500	$2,150	$1,700	$1,560	$1,480	$1,340

DELUXE TYPE R — 9.3x74R, 7.65R, .30-06, or .375 H&H cal., double bolt action, true sideplates, ejectors, reinforced stock, 23¾ in. barrels, animal engraving with deluxe walnut stock and forearm, 7 lbs. 6 oz.

	$3,875	$3,325	$2,700	$2,175	$1,850	$1,700	$1,525

PRESIDENT TYPE PT — 9.3x74R, 7.65R, .30-06, or .375 H&H cal., double bolt action, true sideplates, ejectors, reinforced stock, 23¾ in. barrels, light engraving with gold line inlays, best quality walnut, 7 lbs. 6 oz.

	$4,250	$3,725	$3,200	$2,650	$2,250	$1,825	$1,600

RIFLES: SINGLE SHOT

FALLING BLOCK MODEL
Mfg.'s Sug. Retail $14,000

	$14,000	$12,000	$9,750	$8,250	$6,750	$5,900	$5,000

SIDELOCK MODEL — features breakdown action. New 1993.
Mfg.'s Sug. Retail $34,000

	$34,000	$29,500	$25,750	$21,250	$18,000	$14,750	$11,350

SHOTGUNS: SxS

MODEL 105 — 12 or 20 ga., Anson and Deeley type triple bolt action, ejectors, double triggers, case hardened frame, 6 lbs. 8 oz.

	$2,250	$1,800	$1,400	$1,250	$1,125	$1,000	$900

MODEL 98 — 12 and 20 ga., Purdey type triple bolt action, ejectors, double triggers, case hardened frame, 6 lbs. 8 oz.

	$2,995	$2,500	$2,000	$1,850	$1,580	$1,430	$1,260

MODEL 202 — 12 or 20 ga., Purdey type triple bolt action, sidelocks, fine English engraving, first grade French walnut, ejectors, double triggers, coin finished receiver, 6 lbs. 10 oz.
Mfg.'s Sug. Retail $5,250

	$4,500	$3,950	$3,250	$2,500	$2,175	$1,875	$1,650

MODEL 353 — 12 or 20 ga., Purdey type triple bolt action, hand detachable sidelocks, Chopper lump barrels, fine English engraving, first grade French walnut, ejectors, double triggers, case hardened receiver, best quality, 6 lbs. 10 oz.
Mfg.'s Sug. Retail $19,950

	$17,500	$13,650	$11,000	$8,900	$6,700	$6,250	$5,750

GATLING GUN COMPANY

Currently manufactured and distributed by Furr Arms, established 1961, and located in Orem, UT.

The Furr Arms-Gatling Gun Company manufactures high quality ⅙, ⅓, ½, ¾, and full scale brass reproductions of famous, antique Gatling guns and cannons. Model Gatling guns include various models and scales from 1874 to 1893. Model cannons include the British Naval Cannon and the James Six Pounder. Prices vary according to the complexity of each model and are available by contacting Furr Arms.

Except for Models 1876 Carriage Gatling (½ scale) and 1876 Camel Tripod (½ scale), all the models listed below may be purchased on a special order basis from the factory. 100% values represent the current manufacturer's suggested retail.

Grading	100%	98%	95%	90%	80%	70%	60%
1874 Carriage $\frac{1}{6}$	$5,000	$4,000	$3,500				
1874 Carriage Gatling $\frac{1}{3}$	$6,500	$5,250	$4,250				
1876 Carriage Gatling $\frac{1}{2}$	$12,000	$9,000	$7,500				
1876 Carriage Gatling $\frac{3}{4}$	$19,000	$15,000	$12,000				
1874 Camel Tripod $\frac{1}{6}$	$4,000	$3,000	$2,500				
1874 Camel Tripod $\frac{1}{3}$	$4,500	$3,500	$2,800				
1876 Camel Tripod $\frac{1}{2}$	$8,000	$6,500	$5,250				
1876 Camel Tripod $\frac{3}{4}$	$12,000	$9,000	$7,500				
1876 Camel Tripod (Full)	$18,000	$14,500	$11,500				
1893 Police Gatling $\frac{1}{6}$	$2,500	$2,100	$1,650				
1893 Police Gatling $\frac{1}{3}$	$3,200	$2,550	$2,000				
1883 Carriage Gatling $\frac{1}{6}$	$5,000	$4,000	$3,500				
1883 Carriage Gatling $\frac{1}{3}$	$6,500	$5,250	$4,250				
James Six Lb. Cannon $\frac{1}{6}$	$900	$750	$575				
James Six Lb. Cannon $\frac{1}{5}$	$2,200	$1,850	$1,400				
James Six Lb. Cannon $\frac{1}{3}$	$3,200	$2,550	$2,000				

* **H.M.S. Victory Naval Cannon $\frac{1}{10}$**

        $500 $375 $325

* **H.M.S. Victory Naval Cannon $\frac{1}{10}$** — this cannon is mounted on an oak ship deck section complete with planking, port lid, and working block and tackle.

        $900 $750 $575

* **H.M.S. Victory Naval Cannon $\frac{1}{3}$**

        $3,200 $2,550 $2,000

G

GAUCHER

Current manufacturer located in St. Etienne, France. Currently imported and distributed by Mandall Shooting Supplies located in Scottsdale, AZ.

During 1997, Gaucher released four shooting rifles with unique sound suppression (approx. 71 dBA) in 9mm Para., 12mm cal., or .410 bore - prices are in the $311-$372 range. Additionally, Gaucher manufactures rifles (O/U and SxS double, bolt action rimfire, and semi-auto rimfire), shotguns (SxS, single shot), and 22 LR cal. target pistols. Please contact either Mandall Shooting Supplies or Gaucher directly (see Trademark Index) for more information and current pricing regarding these firearms.

PISTOLS: SINGLE SHOT, TARGET

MODEL GN1 — .22 LR cal., single shot silhouette pistol featuring 10 in. barrel, adj. sights, anatomically shaped grips, monobloc lever cocking, 2.42 lbs. Limited importation.

    $360 $325 $290 $260 $230 $200 $185
                                    Last Mfg.'s Sug. Retail was $380.

MODEL GP — similar to Model GN1, except has forearm integrated into grip. Limited importation.

    $300 $275 $250 $225 $200 $185 $160
                                      Last Mfg.'s Sug. Retail was $323.

GAVAGE

Previous manufacturer located in Liege, Belgium circa 1936-1943.

Grading	100%	98%	95%	90%	80%	70%	60%

GAVAGE PISTOL — .32 ACP/7.65mm cal., patterned after the "Clement", fixed barrel, limited mfg.

	$375	$325	$250	$200	$175	$150	$125

> This pistol is very rare if encountered with Waffenamt proofmarks - healthy premiums are being asked.

GENTRY, DAVID - CUSTOM GUNMAKER

Current custom rifle maker located in Belgrade, MT.

David Gentry is a current custom rifle builder who usually fabricates rifles to individual custom order requests. Current models include Gentry's Black Beauty, Mountain "70", Gray Ghost, and the Outfitter's Rifle. The Rough Rider Model was disc. 1994. David Gentry also manufactures top quality muzzle brakes, stainless steel Featherlight scope rings (1 in. and 30mm), and performs custom metal-work. Mr. Gentry should be contacted directly (see Trademark Index) for more information on options/prices.

G GERMAN P.38 MILITARY & COMMERCIAL PISTOLS

Previously manufactured P.38s from various German companies, circa 1938-1946.
Also See: Fabrique Nationale, Luger, Mauser, and Walther for other military pistols.

P.38 — 9mm Para. cal., double action, 5 in. barrel, 8 shot mag., fixed sights, brown or black composite grips, blued finish. Many variations exhibiting a variety of metal finishes and codings, 34 oz. Over 1,000,000 manufactured during WW II.

> Note: This model was adopted as the standard service pistol of the German Military in 1938. The P.38 was manufactured by Walther - code "ac" (mfg. 1939-1945), Mauser - code "byf" (mfg. Nov. of 1942-1945), and Spreewerke - code "cyq" (mfg. 1943-1945). The finish on most WWII 1942 and later P.38s is not of the same quality as the pre and early war Walther guns with the Spreewerke (cyq) models being the poorest. Pre-war Walther commercial manufactured P.38s (Models AP and Walther Banner HPs) are comparable to Zero Series - 3rd Issue values listed below.

HP "Heeres Pistole" — 9mm Para. cal., early Walther commercial production, high polish, hand-made, approx. 24,000 mfg. from 1938-1944.

> It is recommended that early variations are evaluated and priced by an expert. Watch for fakes.

* **"Swiss" HP** — experimental first production for Swiss trials, ser. range H1,001-H2,065, H prefix, rectangular firing pin and crown/N proofs.

	$3,000	$2,500	$2,000	$1,700	$1,400	$1,100	$900

* **Standard HP Production** — ser. range 2,080-approx. 24,000, high gloss finish until approx. ser. no. 20,000 - then changed to military blue (1944).

	$1,850	$1,450	$1,100	$900	$700	$600	$500

> Add 10% for Nazi "359" military proof (scarce).
> Add 10% for matching mag.

* **Late War HP Production** — marked "MOD P38" on left slide, rough military blue finish, some frames show heavy tool marks, ser. range 24,000-25,990, w/o matching mags.

	$1,500	$1,100	$900	$700	$600	$500	$450

Grading	100%	98%	95%	90%	80%	70%	60%

ZERO-SERIES — 9mm Para. cal., features Walther banner, high polish finish, 5-digit number w/o suffix. Mfg. 1940.

Add 10% for matching mag.

* **Zero Series - 1st Issue** — internal extractor, square firing pin, ser. range 01-01,000.

| | $5,950 | $4,500 | $3,400 | $2,550 | $1,800 | $1,500 | $1,300 |

* **Zero Series - 2nd Issue** — external extractor, square firing pin, ser. range 01,001-03,445, more difficult to find than 1st Issue.

| | $5,000 | $4,400 | $3,400 | $2,500 | $1,900 | $1,300 | $1,000 |

* **Zero Series - 3rd Issue** — external extractor, round firing pin, 03,446-013,725, after ser. no. 10,000, some models had brown military style grips.

| | $2,500 | $1,625 | $1,150 | $850 | $750 | $600 | $500 |

* **480 code** — "480" appears on slide, first military contract P.38, approx. 7,200 mfg. with ser. range 1-7,665, rare in any condition above 90%.

| | $4,500 | $3,250 | $1,650 | $1,150 | $850 | $700 | $575 |

ac-NO DATE (UNDATED) — 9mm Para. cal., ac (Walther code) appears on slide without date, "ac" on triggerguard, 2,800 mfg. with ser. range 7,356-9,691, rarely encountered in 90% or better original condition.

| | $3,400 | $2,750 | $2,200 | $1,900 | $1,500 | $1,200 | $950 |

Add 20% for matching mag.

G

* **ac-40 Surcharge** — hand-stamped "40" before regular ac-40 production, ser. range 9,691-9,978 A, 10,000 mfg., high polish, rare in any condition above 90%.

| | $2,000 | $1,700 | $1,400 | $1,050 | $900 | $750 | $650 |

Add 20% for matching mag.

ac-40 CODE — 9mm Para. cal., indicates 1940 mfg., the 480 code was dropped in October of 1940, and the "ac" code was started, approx. 10,000 mfg. with ser. range 1B-9,900B.

| | $1,775 | $1,200 | $850 | $600 | $500 | $450 | $400 |

Add 20% for matching mag.

* **ac-41 1st and 2nd Variation** — last military high polish guns, only 1st var. (ser. range 1-4,833 B) has "ac" on left triggerguard, 2nd var. continues to ser. no. 4,527 I.

| | $900 | $800 | $550 | $475 | $400 | $370 | $340 |

Add 20% for matching mag.

ac-41 3RD VAR. or ac-42 CODE — 9mm Para. cal., dull military finish, ser. range (approx.) ac-41, 4,500 I to ac-42, 9,200 K. Matching magazines stop at approx. ac-42, 2,000 B.

| | $850 | $725 | $625 | $500 | $425 | $375 | $325 |

Add 20% for matching mag.

"ac" or "byf" CODED 42-45 — 9mm Para. cal., letters are followed by two digit code corresponding to year of mfg. 1943-1945. Two line codes are more desirable than single line models. Highest P.38 production occurred in 1943 and 1944.

| | $550 | $450 | $375 | $325 | $300 | $260 | $225 |

Add 10% for high polish finish (early 1942 mfg.) and single-line ac 43 code.
Add 20% for "dual tone" (phosphate finish — byf-44 date).
Add 20%-25% for Mauser byf 42 code, less than 20,000 were mfg.

"cyq" CODE AND "ac-45" MISMATCH — 9mm Para. cal., cyq variation typically exhibits rough machining with visible circular milling marks, mismatched slide and frame on ac-45 model.

| | $425 | $375 | $300 | $270 | $250 | $230 | $210 |

Add 25% for A or B prefix on serialization.

Grading	100%	98%	95%	90%	80%	70%	60%

LATE WAR (1945) — 9mm Para. cal., Zero Series with rough milled finish, ser. range 025,960–027,659.

	$1,100	$925	$795	$650	$500	$425	$350

1945 "svw" CODE — 9mm Para. cal., Nazi proofed only, most dual tone finish, some all blue or all gray.

	$1,000	$850	$700	$600	$500	$450	$400

Add 20% for all blue or all gray.
Deduct 50% for French production (Star proof).

1946 "svw" CODE — 9mm Para. cal., Mauser mfg. 1946 with French controlling production.

	$425	$365	$285	$250	$210	$190	$165

GEVARM

Previous manufacturer located in Saint Etienne, France.

RIFLES: SEMI-AUTO

E-1 AUTOLOADING RIFLE — .22 LR cal., 19 in. barrel, open sights, walnut pistol grip stock.

	$165	$130	$110	$100	$85	$65	$55

GIB

Previous trademark manufactured in Spain.

SHOTGUNS: SxS

10 GAUGE MAGNUM SHOTGUN — 10 ga., 3½ in. chambers, 32 in. full choke barrel, case hardened receiver, matted rib, rubber pad, checkered pistol grip walnut stock. Disc.

	$275	$250	$235	$220	$200	$175	$150

GIBBS GUNS, INC.

Previously manufactured by Volunteer Enterprises in Knoxville, TN and previously distributed by Gibbs Guns, Inc. located in Greenback, TN.

RIFLES: CARBINES

MARK 45 CARBINE — .45 ACP cal. only, based on M6 Thompson machine gun, 16½ in. barrel, 5, 15, 30, or 90 shot clip, U.S. mfg. Disc. 1988.

	$315	$275	$225	$180	$165	$155	$145

Last Mfg.'s Sug. Retail was $279.

Add $60 minimum for nickel plating.

GIBBS RIFLE COMPANY

Current manufacturer, importer, and distributor located in Martinsburg, WV. Gibbs Rifle Co. is now in production of the Mauser Model 98 Sporter, in addition to limited mfg. of Parker-Hale rifles. Gibbs also manufactured rifles with the Gibbs trademark in Martinsburg, WV 1991-94, in addition to importing Mauser-Werke firearms until 1995.

Gibbs Rifle Co. also imports a variety of older firearms, including British military rifles and handguns (both original and refurbished condition), a wide variety of used military contract pistols and rifles, in addition to other shooting products and accessories, including a bi-pod patterned after the Parker-Hale M-85.

G

Grading	100%	98%	95%	90%	80%	70%	60%

RIFLES: BOLT ACTION

M-98 MAUSER SPORTER — .270 Win. or .30-06 cal., Mauser M-98 type action, blue finish, sporterized checkered hardwood stock and forend, 24 in. Wilson barrel. Mfg. in Martinsburg, WV, beginning 1998.

Mfg.'s Sug. Retail	$330	$295	$265	$245	$225	$210	$195	$180

2A HUNTER RIFLE/CARBINE — .308 Win. cal., sporterized action features black enamel refinish, synthetic stock, 12 shot mag, and choice of 18 (carbine) or 22½ (rifle) in. barrel with Parker-Hale muzzle brake, approx. 10 lbs. New 1999.

Mfg.'s Sug. Retail	$275	$235	$200	$180	$165	$155	$145	$140

GIBBS ECONOMY SPORTER — 8mm Mauser cal., sporterized military action with good barrel and sporting sights, walnut finished checkered hardwood stock. Mfg. 1993-94.

	$185	$150	$135	$120	$100	$85	$70

Last Mfg.'s Sug. Retail was $205.

GIBBS MAUSER SPORTER — .243 Win., .270 Win., .30-06, or .308 Win. cal., features M-98 action, walnut finished checkered hardwood stock, action is drilled and tapped, flip-up rear sight and ramp front. Mfg. 1993-94.

	$250	$220	$195	$175	$150	$135	$120

Last Mfg.'s Sug. Retail was $295.

MODEL 81 CLASSIC — available in 11 cals. between .22-250 Rem. and 7mm Rem. Mag., 24 in. barrel, open sights, 4 shot mag., select checkered walnut with sling swivels, 7¾ lbs.

	$795	$595	$475	$395	$340	$300	$280

Last Mfg.'s Sug. Retail was $900.

G

* ***Model 81 African*** — .375 H&H or 9.3x62mm cal., similar specifications as Model 81 Classic with quarter rib and express sights, engraved action, Pachmayr recoil pad, 9 lbs.

	$925	$725	$600	$500	$425	$360	$330

Last Mfg.'s Sug. Retail was $1,050.

MODEL 85 SNIPER RIFLE — .308 Win. cal., bolt action, 24 in. heavy barrel, 10 shot mag., camo green synthetic McMillan stock with stippling, built in adj. bi-pod and recoil pad, enlarged contoured bolt, adj. sights, 12 lbs. 6 oz.

	$1,825	$1,450	$1,275	$1,050	$875	$750	$625

Last Mfg.'s Sug. Retail was $2,050.

MODEL 87 TARGET — .243 Win., 6.5x55mm, .308 Win., .30-06, or .300 Win. Mag. cal., target stock, aperture sights. Mfg. disc. 1992.

	$1,375	$1,100	$900	$775	$650	$550	$495

Last Mfg.'s Sug. Retail was $1,500.

MODEL 1000 STANDARD — .22-250 Rem., .243 Win., 6mm Rem., 6.5x55mm, 7x57mm, 7x64mm, .270 Win., .30-06, or .308 Win. cal., 22 in. barrel, 4 shot built in mag., checkered walnut stock with cheekpiece, open sights, 7¼ lbs.

	$425	$375	$325	$290	$260	$240	$220

Last Mfg.'s Sug. Retail was $495.

* ***Model 1000 Clip*** — similar to Model 1000 Standard, except has detachable 4 shot mag.

	$460	$395	$350	$300	$270	$240	$220

Last Mfg.'s Sug. Retail was $535.

MODEL 1100 LIGHTWEIGHT — available in 9 cals. between .22-250 Rem. and .308 Win., 22 in. barrel, open sights, 4 shot mag., 6½ lbs.

	$435	$380	$325	$290	$260	$240	$220

Last Mfg.'s Sug. Retail was $510.

* ***Model 1100M African*** — .375 H&H, or .458 Win. Mag. cal., 24 in. barrel, 4 shot mag., 9½ lbs.

	$825	$650	$575	$500	$450	$425	$400

Last Mfg.'s Sug. Retail was $930.

Grading	100%	98%	95%	90%	80%	70%	60%

MODEL 1200 SUPER — .22-250 Rem., .243 Win., 6mm, 6.5x55mm, 7x64mm, .270 Win., .30-06, or .308 Win. cal., bolt action, Mauser type action, 24 in. barrel, folding sight, skip checkered walnut stock, pad swivels, rosewood pistol grip cap and forend tip.

$495 $400 $350 $325 $285 $270 $255
Last Mfg.'s Sug. Retail was $595.

＊ Model 1200 Super Clip — similar to Model 1200 Super, except has detachable 4 shot box mag.

$525 $425 $375 $350 $300 $280 $265
Last Mfg.'s Sug. Retail was $640.

MODEL 1300S SCOUT — .243 Win. or .308 Win. cal., 20 in. barrel with muzzle brake, internal 5 shot or detachable 5/10 shot mag., laminated checkered birchwood stock, sling swivels, 8½ lbs.

$425 $375 $325 $290 $260 $240 $220
Last Mfg.'s Sug. Retail was $495.

Add $30 for detachable mag. (Model 1300C).

MODEL 1500S SURVIVOR — .308 Win. cal., bolt action, matte stainless construction, black composite (Kevlar/fiberglass) stock, 22 in. barrel, 4 shot mag., 7 lbs. Mfg. began 1993. Disc.

$395 $350 $300 $270 $240 $210 $185
Last Mfg.'s Sug. Retail was $450.

Add $30 for detachable clip (Model 1500C).

This model is made for the Gibbs Rifle Co. by Bell & Carlson, Inc.

G

RIFLES: BOLT ACTION, MIDLAND SERIES

MODEL 2100 MIDLAND DELUXE — similar to Model 2600 Midland, except has checkered walnut stock and pistol grip cap.

$335 $280 $235 $210 $190 $180 $170
Last Mfg.'s Sug. Retail was $390.

MODEL 2600 MIDLAND — .22-250 Rem., .243 Win., 6mm Rem. (disc. 1994), 6.5x55mm (disc. 1994), 7x57mm (disc. 1994), 7x64mm (disc. 1994), .270 Win., .30-06, or .308 Win. cal., 22 in. barrel, 4 shot mag., checkered hardwood stock with Monte Carlo cheekpiece, open sights, drilled and tapped action, 7 lbs. Disc. 1997.

$350 $275 $225 $200 $180 $165 $150
Last Mfg.'s Sug. Retail was $400.

This model was re-introduced during late 1996, utilizing a 1903 Springfield action with choice of 5 shot fixed mag. with hinged floorplate or 3 shot detachable mag.

MIDLAND 2700 LIGHTWEIGHT — lightweight variation of the Model 2100 Midland Deluxe featuring tapered barrel, anodized aluminum trigger housing and lightened stock with full pistol grip and recoil pad, Schnabel forend, 6½ lbs.

$350 $285 $245 $225 $200 $190 $180
Last Mfg.'s Sug. Retail was $415.

MIDLAND 2800 — similar to Model 2600 Midland, except has laminate birchwood stock, re-introduced during late 1996, utilizing a 1903 Springfield action, 7 lbs. Disc. 1997.

$360 $295 $250 $215 $195 $185 $175
Last Mfg.'s Sug. Retail was $430.

SHOTGUNS: SINGLE SHOT

MIDLAND STALKER — 12 ga., trigger bar safety, unique squeeze break open action and cocking system, 28½ in. barrel bored F, hardwood stock and forearm, 6 lbs.

$90 $65 $55 $45 $35 $30 $25
Last Mfg.'s Sug. Retail was $110.

Grading	100%	98%	95%	90%	80%	70%	60%

GLOCK

Currently manufactured by Glock GmbH in Austria beginning 1983. Exclusively imported and distributed by Glock, Inc., located in Smyrna, GA. Distributor sales only.

All Glock pistols have a "safe action" safety system (double action only) which includes trigger safety, firing pin safety, and drop safety. Glock pistols have only 35 parts for reliability and simplicity of operation.

PISTOLS: SEMI-AUTO

MODEL 17/17C SPORT/SERVICE — 9mm Para. cal., double action, polymer frame, mag., trigger and other pistol parts, 4.49 in. steel hexagonal rifled barrel with (Model 17C, new 1999) or w/o ports, steel slide and springs, 10 (C/B 1994), 17★, or 19★ shot mag., adj. (Sport Model) or fixed (Service Model) rear sight, hammerless, includes extra mag., case, and spare rear sight, 24 oz. empty. Importation began late 1985.

Mfg.'s Sug. Retail   **$611**   **$475**   **$415**   **$335**

> Add $28 for adj. rear sight.
> Add $72 for fixed Meprolight sight.
> Add $90 for fixed Trijicon sight.

★ *Model 17L Competition Model* — 9mm Para. cal., competition version of the Model 17, includes internally compensated 6.02 in. barrel, recalibrated trigger pull (3½ lb. pull), adj. rear sight, 25.4 oz. New 1988.

Mfg.'s Sug. Retail   **$795**   **$650**   **$545**   **$425**

> Add $28 for adj. sight.

> Early models with matching barrel ports will command a small premium.

★ *Glock 17 Desert Storm Commemorative* — 9mm Para. cal., features coalition forces listing on top of barrel, inscription on side of slide "NEW WORLD ORDER", 1,000 mfg. in 1991 only.

     $995   **$825**   **$600**

        Last Mfg.'s Sug. Retail was $795.

MODEL 19/19C COMPACT SPORT/SERVICE — 9mm Para. cal., similar to Model 17, except has scaled down dimensions with 4.02 in. ported (Model 19C, new 1999) or unported barrel and serrated grip straps, 10 (C/B 1994), 15★, or 17★ shot mag., fixed (Service Model) or adj. (Sport Model) rear sight, 23 oz. New 1988.

Mfg.'s Sug. Retail   **$611**   **$475**   **$415**   **$335**

> Add $28 for adj. rear sight.
> Add $72 for fixed Meprolight sight.
> Add $90 for fixed Trijicon sight.

> During 1996, AcuSport Corp. commissioned Glock to make a special production run of matching 9mm Para. cal. sets. Each set consists of a Model 19 and 26 with serialization as follows: Model 19 (ser. range AAA0000-AAA0499) and Model 26 (ser. range AAB0000-AAB0499).

MODEL 20/20C SPORT/SERVICE — 10mm Norma cal., similar action to Model 17, features 4.6 in. ported (Model 20C, new 1999) or unported barrel, 10 (C/B 1994) or 15★ shot mag., thicker triggerguard, fixed (Service Model) or adj. (Sport Model) rear sight, 28.4 oz. New 1990.

Mfg.'s Sug. Retail   **$663**   **$575**   **$475**   **$415**

> Add $29 for adj. rear sight.
> Add $73 for fixed Meprolight sight.
> Add $90 for fixed Trijicon sight.

Grading	100%	98%	95%	90%	80%	70%	60%

MODEL 21/21C SPORT/SERVICE — .45 ACP cal., similar to Model 20, except has octagon rifling, 10 (C/B 1994) or 13★ shot mag., 27.2 oz. Introduced May 1991.

  Mfg.'s Sug. Retail $663 $575 $475 $415
   Add $29 for adj. rear sight.
   Add $73 for fixed Meprolight sight.
   Add $90 for fixed Trijicon sight.

MODEL 22/22C SPORT/SERVICE — .40 S&W cal., similar to Model 20, except has 4.49 in. barrel, 10 (C/B 1994) or 15★ shot mag., 24 oz. Introduced 1990.

  Mfg.'s Sug. Retail $611 $475 $415 $335
   Add $28 for adj. rear sight.
   Add $72 for fixed Meprolight sight.
   Add $90 for fixed Trijicon sight.

   200 Model 22s were originally shipped with serial numbers beginning with "NY-1". Somehow, they probably were erroneously numbered at the factory (probably thinking that they somehow were part of the New York State Troopers shipment of Model 17s) during 1990. Premiums will occur on this variation.

MODEL 23/23C COMPACT SPORT/SERVICE — .40 S&W cal., compact variation of the Model 22 with 4.02 in. ported (Model 23C, new 1999) or unported barrel and 10 (C/B 1994) or 13★ shot mag., 22.4 oz. New 1990.

  Mfg.'s Sug. Retail $611 $475 $415 $335
   Add $28 for adj. rear sight.
   Add $72 for fixed Meprolight sight.
   Add $90 for fixed Trijicon sight.

   During 1996, AcuSport Corp. commissioned Glock to make a special production run of matching .40 S&W cal. sets. Each set consists of a Model 23 and 27 with serialization as follows: Model 23 (ser. range AAC0000-AAC1499) and Model 27 (ser. range AAD0000-AAD1499).

MODEL 24/24C — .40 S&W cal., similar to Model 17L Competition, choice of standard or ported (Model 24C) barrel and fixed or adj. rear sight. New 1994.

  Mfg.'s Sug. Retail $795 $665 $525 $415
   Add $40 for compensated barrel.
   Add $28 for adj. rear sight.

MODEL 25 — .380 ACP cal., similar to Model 19 with 4.02 in. barrel, 10 shot mag., 22½ oz. New 1999.

   This model is available for law enforcement only.

MODEL 26 — 9mm Para. cal., sub-compact variation of the Model 19, except has shortened grip, 3½ in. barrel, 10 shot mag., approx. 22 oz. New 1995.

  Mfg.'s Sug. Retail $611 $515 $430 $350
   Add $28 for adj. rear sight.
   Add $72 for fixed Meprolight sight.
   Add $90 for fixed Trijicon sight.

MODEL 27 — .40 S&W cal., sub-compact variation of the Model 23, except has shortened grip, 3½ in. barrel, 9 shot mag., approx. 22 oz. New 1995.

  Mfg.'s Sug. Retail $611 $515 $430 $350
   Add $28 for adj. rear sight.
   Add $72 for fixed Meprolight sight.
   Add $90 for fixed Trijicon sight.

MODEL 28 — .380 ACP cal., similar to Model 25, except has scaled down dimensions with 3.46 in. barrel, approx. 21 oz. New 1999.

   This model is available for law enforcement only.

Grading	100%	98%	95%	90%	80%	70%	60%

MODEL 29 — 10mm Norma cal., sub-compact model featuring 3.78 in. barrel, 10 shot mag., 24.7 oz. New 1997.

Mfg.'s Sug. Retail $668 $560 $475 $415
   Add $29 for adj. rear sight.
   Add $73 for fixed Meprolight sight.
   Add $90 for fixed Trijicon sight.

MODEL 30 — .45 ACP cal., compact Model 21, features octagon rifling and extension on mag., 24 oz. New 1997.

Mfg.'s Sug. Retail $668 $560 $475 $415
   Add $29 for adj. rear sight.
   Add $73 for fixed Meprolight sight.
   Add $90 for fixed Trijicon sight.

MODEL 31/31C — .357 Sig cal., similar to Model 17, 4.49 in. ported (Model 31C, new 1999) or unported barrel, fixed sights, 10 shot mag., 26 oz. New 1998.

Mfg.'s Sug. Retail $611 $515 $430 $350

MODEL 32/32C — .357 Sig cal., similar to Model 19, 4.02 in. ported (Model 32C) or unported barrel, 24 oz. New 1998.

Mfg.'s Sug. Retail $611 $515 $430 $350

MODEL 33 — .357 Sig cal., compact variation of Models 31 & 32, features 3½ in. barrel with shortened frame and magazine housing, 10 shot mag., 22 oz. New 1998.

Mfg.'s Sug. Retail $611 $515 $430 $350

MODEL 34 — 9mm Para. cal., similar construction to Model 17, except has 5.32 in. barrel, extended slide stop lever and magazine catch, fixed sights, target grips with finger grooves and thumbrest, 10 shot mag., 26 oz. New 1998.

Mfg.'s Sug. Retail $760 $650 $550 $475

MODEL 35 — .40 S&W cal., otherwise similar to Model 34. New 1998.

Mfg.'s Sug. Retail $760 $650 $550 $475

MODEL 36 — .45 ACP cal., similar to Model 30, except has single column 6 shot mag., 22½ oz. New 1999.

   As this edition went to press, prices had yet to be established on this model.

GOLAN

See KSN Industries Ltd. listing.

GOLDEN EAGLE

Previous trademark of rifles/shotguns produced by Nikko Limited located in Tochigi, Japan, circa 1975-1981.

   Please refer to the Nikko Firearms Limited listing in this text for a complete chronological history of Nikko - Japan's previous long gun manufacturer.

RIFLES: BOLT ACTION

MODEL 7000 GRADE I — bolt action, all popular American calibers, including .270 Win., and .300 Wby. Mag., 24 or 26 in. barrels, select skipline checkered walnut stock, rosewood forend tip, golden eagle head engraved in pistol grip cap, recoil pad. Mfg. 1976-1981.

         $600 $550 $525 $450 $375 $340 $290

MODEL 7000 GRADE I AFRICAN — .375 H&H and .458 Win. Mag. cal., similar to 7000, open sights.

         $650 $590 $555 $480 $400 $365 $315

MODEL 7000 GRADE II — scroll engraving, better grade wood.

         $690 $625 $590 $510 $430 $395 $340

Grading	100%	98%	95%	90%	80%	70%	60%

SHOTGUNS: O/U

MODEL 5000 GRADE I (FIELD) — 12 or 20 ga., 26, 28, or 30 in. barrels, various chokes, vent. rib, engraved receiver, gold eagle head inlay, auto ejectors, SST, checkered pistol grip beavertail stock. Mfg. 1975-1981.

	100%	98%	95%	90%	80%	70%	60%
	$850	$775	$700	$625	$560	$510	$440

MODEL 5000 GRADE I SKEET — similar to 5000, except 26 or 28 in. skeet bored, wide rib.

	100%	98%	95%	90%	80%	70%	60%
	$875	$800	$725	$650	$580	$510	$440

MODEL 5000 GRADE I TRAP — similar to Field, except 30 or 32 in. barrel, mod. and full, imp. mod. and full, or full and full choke, wide rib, trap stock with pad.

	100%	98%	95%	90%	80%	70%	60%
	$875	$800	$725	$650	$580	$510	$440

MODEL 5000 GRADE II — available in Field, Trap, and Skeet, more engraving, better grade wood, with screaming eagle on receiver in gold.

	100%	98%	95%	90%	80%	70%	60%
	$950	$875	$790	$710	$630	$540	$460
Skeet	$975	$895	$810	$725	$640	$540	$460
Trap	$975	$895	$810	$725	$640	$540	$460

GRANDEE GRADE III — similar to 5000 Grade II, except elaborate engraving, inlays, and better grade wood.

	100%	98%	95%	90%	80%	70%	60%
	$2,500	$2,200	$1,900	$1,575	$1,250	$1,000	$850

G GOLDEN STATE ARMS

Previous importer located in Pasadena, CA. Golden State Arms imported and subcontracted various firearms constructed by European and Japanese manufacturers - achieving private label status on some guns. Most firearms previously imported by Golden State Arms (including private labels) are not that collectible. In many cases, the shooting value will determine the price of a specimen. In some models or configurations which are currently desirable, however, premiums may exist.

GONCZ ARMAMENT, INC.

Previous manufacturer located in North Hollywood, CA circa 1984-1990.

While advertised, BATF records indicate very few Goncz pistols or carbines were actually produced. All of these guns were prototypes or individually hand-built and none were ever mass produced through normal fabrication techniques.

In 1990, Claridge Hi-Tec, Inc. purchased Goncz Armament, Inc.

GRANGER, G.

Current manufacturer located in Saint Etienne, France since 1902. Currently imported and distributed by Champlin Firearms, Inc. located in Enid, OK.

G. Granger manufactures high quality, limited production side-by-side boxlock and sidelock shotguns in 12, 16, or 20 ga. All guns are made on a custom order basis with prices ranging between $20,000 - $40,000. Prices will vary per older customer specifications and appointments.

GRANT, STEPHEN

Current trademark manufactured by Atkin, Grant & Lang, established in 1821, and located in Hertfordshire, England.

The Stephen Grant trademark is responsible for mostly custom order SxS rifles and shotguns. Shotguns can be top or side lever and are equipped with sidelocks and a self-opening mechanism.

RIFLES: SxS

Prices indicated below are for manufacturer's suggested retail and 100% condition factors are listed in English pounds. All new prices do not include VAT or importa-

Grading	100%	98%	95%	90%	80%	70%	60%

tion costs. Values for used guns in 98%-60% condition factors are priced in U.S. dollars.

SIDELOCK MODEL — various cals. between .300 H&H - .577 NE, best quality sidelock, individually made per customer specifications.

Mfg.'s Sug. Retail	£34,000	£34,000	$39,250	$35,000	$31,000	$27,000	$24,000	$20,500

SHOTGUNS: O/U

SIDELOCK MODEL — 12, 16, 20, 28 ga., or 410 bore, best quality sidelock ejector, individually made per customer specifications.

Mfg.'s Sug. Retail	£32,000	£32,000	$37,000	$33,000	$28,750	$26,000	$22,500	$18,000

SHOTGUNS: SxS

SIDELOCK MODEL — 12, 16, 20, 28 ga., or .410 bore, best quality sidelock ejector, top or side lever opening, individually made per customer specifications.

Mfg.'s Sug. Retail	£26,000	£26,000	$30,000	$26,000	$22,000	$18,000	$15,000	$13,000

GREAT WESTERN ARMS COMPANY

Previous importer located in Los Angeles, CA. Founded through the efforts of Mr. Hy Hunter, with William R. Wilson as President.

Originated probably in early 1953. When Colt Firearms Company ceased production of what is known today as "First Generation Single Action Army Revolvers", Mr. Hunter could see the public's continued demand for such a revolver. After several trips to the Colt factory to ascertain Colt's intent of reviving their production of the S.A. Army, and being assured it would never be revived, he founded the G.W. Arms Co. The main change between the Colt S.A. and the G.W. Frontier was removing the firing pin from the hammer and the design of a rebounding firing pin inserted in the revolver frame. This firm also redesigned the Remington Double Derringer and produced a derringer in 2 cals., .38 S&W and .38 S&W Special. Approx. 2,000 of these were mfg. Production of the Frontier probably did not exceed 23,000. When the Colt Company resumed production of their 2nd Generation S.A. 1873 Revolver, it rang the death knell of Great Western Arms Co. products, and the G.W. Arms Co. soon disappeared with its last sales of their "Frontier" being sold as unassembled "Kit Guns" to be assembled by the purchaser.

REVOLVERS: SINGLE ACTION

FRONTIER MODEL SAA — .45 LC, .44-40 WCF, .44 Mag., .44 Spl., .357 Atomic, .357 Mag., .38 S&W Spl., .32-20 WCF, .22 Hornet, or .22 Rimfire cal., 3½, 5½, or 7½ in. barrel, blue with case hardened colors on frame, gate and hammer, all blue, satin blue, nickel, black nickel, copper plated black oxide, gold, silver, gold and silver and parkerizing, grips were imitation stag (plastic), wood, pearl, ivory and sterling silver on special order. Unfinished "Kit Guns" were also sold, allowing buyer to assemble and finish.

$475	$435	$395	$350	$300	$265	$235

Add 50% for Special .22 Target Model with micro sights. Add 100% for Fast Draw Model. Add 25% for electroplated barrels. Add 25% for electroplated cylinder. Add minimum 5% for any finish other than parkerized or blue with case hardened frame. Add 20% for consecutive ser. no. sets. Add 50% if with factory original presentation case. Add 60% if with factory original letter. Add 25% for .44 Mag. or .357 Atomic cal. Add 50% for factory original cals. not listed above. Add 60% for Sheriff Model (called Deputy Model). Add 80% for any barrel length above 7½ in. Add minimum 100% for original factory engraving. Add minimum 300% for original factory engraving with silver and gold. Add 75% for factory sterling silver grips. Add 20% for factory pearl or ivory grips. Add 10% for factory wood grips. Add 30% for any gun with a longer than factory standard or shorter than standard barrel. Deduct 25% for assembled kit guns. Values for unassembled kit gun in original box are same as above.

Grading	100%	98%	95%	90%	80%	70%	60%

DERRINGERS

GREAT WESTERN DERRINGER — .38 S&W or .38 S&W Spl. cal. (not interchangeable). Basically an improved version of the Remington Double Derringer frame.

	100%	98%	95%	90%	80%	70%	60%
	$295	$275	$250	$225	$200	$180	$160

Add 10% for consecutive ser. no. sets.

Add 20% for factory pearl or ivory grips.

Add 25% for factory original casing.

Add minimum 200% for factory original engraving.

GREENER, W.W., LIMITED

Current manufacturer located in Birmingham, England since 1829. W.W. Greener does not have current importation into the U.S. Until 1994, Gibbs Rifle Co. located in Martinsburg, WV was the U.S. agent.

RIFLES: SxS, CURRENT MFG.

Boxlock and sidelock rifle quotations may be obtained by writing the company directly (see Trademark Index). A complete choice of calibers, engraving options, and walnut selection are available on a special order basis only.

SHOTGUNS: SINGLE SHOT

GENERAL PURPOSE — 12 ga., improved Martini action, single shot, 26, 30, or 32 in. barrel, full or mod., auto ejectors, straight checkered stock.

	100%	98%	95%	90%	80%	70%	60%
	$330	$305	$275	$220	$195	$165	$160

GP MK II — 12 ga. only, famed general purpose (GP) English shotgun configuration featuring Greener Martini action, 28 or 30 in. barrel, walnut stock and forearm. Mfg. resumed in 1991.

	Mfg.'s Sug. Retail	98%	95%	90%	80%	70%	60%
Mfg.'s Sug. Retail	$522	$522	$450	$400	$350	$300	$250	$195

Older, used military contract variations of this model have been imported recently - typically seen in the $165-$200 range.

SHOTGUNS: SxS, DISC.

FARKILLER GRADE F35 — 12 ga., 28, 30, or 32 in. barrels, hammerless boxlock, checkered straight or semi-pistol grip stock.

	100%	98%	95%	90%	80%	70%	60%
	$2,420	$2,200	$2,090	$1,870	$1,760	$1,650	$1,540
Auto ejectors	$3,300	$3,025	$2,750	$2,475	$2,035	$1,925	$1,650

FARKILLER GRADE F35 LARGE BORE — 8 or 10 ga., similar to F35 above.

	100%	98%	95%	90%	80%	70%	60%
	$2,750	$2,585	$2,310	$2,090	$1,980	$1,815	$1,650
Auto ejectors	$3,575	$3,300	$3,080	$2,860	$2,640	$2,090	$1,925

HAMMERLESS EJECTOR MODELS — 12, 16, 20, 28 ga., or .410 bore, 26, 28, or 30 in. barrels supplied with any choke combination, auto ejectors, single or double triggers, straight or semi-pistol grip stock, grades differ as follows:

* *Jubilee Grade DH35*

	100%	98%	95%	90%	80%	70%	60%
	$2,420	$2,255	$2,090	$1,925	$1,650	$1,540	$1,375

* *Sovereign Grade DH40*

	100%	98%	95%	90%	80%	70%	60%
	$2,860	$2,695	$2,420	$2,200	$1,980	$1,815	$1,595

* *Crown Grade DH55*

	100%	98%	95%	90%	80%	70%	60%
	$3,300	$3,080	$2,915	$2,750	$2,420	$2,035	$1,760

Grading	100%	98%	95%	90%	80%	70%	60%

* Royal Grade DH75

	$4,400	$4,180	$3,850	$3,300	$3,080	$2,915	$2,640

Add $400 for SST.

Note: Degree of engraving and grade of wood are the basic differences between models.

EMPIRE — 12 ga. only, 2¾ or 3 in., any choke, 28, 30, or 32 in. barrel, hammerless, boxlock, straight stock or semi pistol grip.

	$1,760	$1,540	$1,320	$1,100	$935	$825	$770
Auto ejectors	$1,980	$1,760	$1,540	$1,320	$1,155	$1,045	$990

EMPIRE DELUXE — similar to Empire, only better grade wood.

	$1,980	$1,760	$1,540	$1,320	$1,155	$1,045	$990
Auto ejectors	$2,200	$1,980	$1,760	$1,540	$1,375	$1,265	$1,100

SHOTGUNS: SxS, CURRENT MFG.

Various hard and soft cases are available for the models listed below with prices ranging from $500 up to $3,200.

NO. 5 NEEDHAM EJECTOR —12, 16, 20 ga., or .410 bore, scalloped boxlock action, DT, any barrel length.

Mfg.'s Sug. Retail	$4,470	$4,470	$3,750	$3,175	$2,750	$2,250	$1,825	$1,475

This model has been re-introduced to commemorate the takeover of J. V. Needham by W.W. Greener in 1874.

DH 40 —similar to No. 5 Needham Ejector, except has better engraving and deluxe walnut stock and forearm.

Mfg.'s Sug. Retail	$6,705	$6,705	$5,900	$5,000	$4,250	$3,500	$2,850	$2,100

DH 75 —12 ga. only, 2¾ in. chambers, Greener "Facile Princeps" scalloped boxlock action 27, 28, or 30 in. barrels, case hardened receiver, choice of engraving (game scene or fine scroll work).

Mfg.'s Sug. Retail	$11,175	$11,175	$9,950	$8,450	$7,250	$6,000	$4,950	$3,875

DOH 90 —12, 16, 20 ga., or .410 bore, 2½, 2¾ or 3 in. Mag. chambers, best boxlock featuring Anson & Deeley scalloped boxlock action with Greener easy-opening device, French walnut stock, DT.

Mfg.'s Sug. Retail	$14,900	$14,900	$12,500	$9,750	$8,250	$7,000	$5,850	$4,675

L 120 —12, 16, 20 ga., or .410 bore, best sidelock ejector model with dovetail lump barrels, fine scroll engraving with choice of bright or color case hardened frame finish.

Mfg.'s Sug. Retail	$22,350	$22,350	$19,500	$16,000	$13,000	$10,000	$7,850	$6,000

L 150 —12, 16, 20 ga., or .410 bore, 2½ or 3 in. chambers, very best sidelock ejector model with chopper lump barrels and easy-opening device, bright or color case hardened frame finish.

Mfg.'s Sug. Retail	$29,800	$29,800	$24,000	$21,000	$17,000	$14,000	$11,000	$8,500

L 500 —12, 16, 20 ga., or .410 bore, new St. George sidelock ejector model incorporating top-of-the-line carved engraving, walnut, and workmanship.

Because this model is entirely custom ordered per individual choice, a price quotation is necessary on every order.

GREIFELT AND COMPANY

Previous manufacturer located in Suhl, E. Germany.

Grading	100%	98%	95%	90%	80%	70%	60%

COMBINATION GUNS

COMBINATION MODEL — 12, 16, 20, 28 ga., or .410 bore, shotgun barrel, rifle in any rimmed caliber, 24 or 26 in. solid rib barrel, pre-WWII.

	100%	98%	95%	90%	80%	70%	60%
	$5,200	$4,800	$4,400	$4,000	$3,600	$3,150	$2,800

Add $700 for auto ejectors.
Deduct 10% for 16 ga.
Add 20% for 28 ga. or .410 bore.
Deduct 40-50% for obsolete rifle caliber.
Above values for 12 or 20 ga. over obtainable rifle cartridge.

DRILLINGS

DRILLING MODEL — 12, 16, or 20 ga., SxS shotgun over rimmed rifle caliber, 26 in. barrels, boxlock, extractors, double triggers, rifle sight activated by barrel selector, pre-WWII.

	$3,500	$3,000	$2,750	$2,550	$2,300	$2,000	$1,750

Deduct 10% for 16 ga.
Deduct 40-50% for obsolete cals.
Above values for 12 or 20 ga. over obtainable rifle cartridge.

SHOTGUNS: O/U

GRADE NO. 1 — 12, 16, 20, 28 ga., or .410 bore, O/U, any barrel 26-32 in., choke, vent. or solid rib, Anson & Deeley boxlock, auto ejectors, checkered pistol grip or English stock, pre-war.

12 or 20 ga.	$3,600	$3,200	$2,850	$2,500	$2,100	$1,750	$1,500

Deduct 10% for 16 ga.
Add 30% for 28 ga. or .410 bore.
Add $300 for vent. rib.
Add $400 for SST.

GRADE NO. 3 — similar to No. 1, except less elaborate engraving, pre-WWII.

12 or 20 ga.	$2,850	$2,500	$2,200	$2,000	$1,650	$1,350	$1,200

Deduct 10% for 16 ga.
Add 20% for 28 ga. or .410 bore.
Add $300 for vent. rib.
Add $400 for SST.

MODEL 143E — similar to No. 1, except not as high quality as pre-war model, not available in 28 ga. or .410 bore. Mfg. post-WWII.

	$2,400	$2,150	$1,850	$1,550	$1,350	$1,175	$1,000

Add 10% for vent. rib and SST.

SHOTGUNS: SxS

MODEL 22 — 12 or 20 ga., 28 or 30 in. mod. and full, hammerless, boxlock, false sideplates, extractors, checkered pistol grip or English style stock, post-WWII.

	$2,200	$1,760	$1,595	$1,320	$1,100	$990	$825

MODEL 22E — similar to Model 22, except has auto ejectors.

	$2,750	$2,200	$1,980	$1,760	$1,540	$1,430	$1,265

MODEL 103 — 12 or 16 ga., 28 or 30 in. mod. and full, extractors, double triggers, checkered pistol grip or English stock, post-war.

	$1,980	$1,650	$1,485	$1,210	$990	$880	$715

MODEL 103E — similar to Model 103, except has auto ejectors.

	$2,200	$1,760	$1,595	$1,320	$1,100	$990	$825

GRENDEL, INC.

Previous manufacturer located in Rockledge, FL circa 1990-95.

PISTOLS: SEMI-AUTO

MODEL P-10 SERIES — .380 ACP cal., blowback double action, 10 shot mag., small dimensions, hammerless, matte blue finish, 15 oz. Mfg. disc. 1991.

$140	$125	$115	$105	$95	$90	$85

Last Mfg.'s Sug. Retail was $155.

Add $15 for electroless nickel finish.
Add $15 for nickel green finish.

Green finish was available at no extra charge.

MODEL P-12 — .380 ACP cal., double action only, 3 in. barrel, steel construction with polymer grip area, no external safety, 11 shot Zytel mag., blue or electroless nickel finish, 11 lb. trigger pull, 13 oz. Mfg. 1992-95.

$155	$135	$120	$110	$100	$90	$80

Last Mfg.'s Sug. Retail was $175.

Add $20 for nickel finish.
Add $50 for threaded barrel with muzzle brake parts option.

MODEL P-30 — .22 Mag. cal., blowback similar action to P-12, 5 in. barrel, hammerless, matte black finish, 10 (C/B 1994) or 30★ shot mag., 21 oz. Mfg. 1990-95.

$240	$200	$175	$155	$140	$125	$115

Last Mfg.'s Sug. Retail was $225.

Add $25 for electroless nickel finish (disc. 1991).
Add $35 for scope mount (Weaver base).

★ *Model P-30M* — similar to Model P-30, except has 5.6 in. barrel with removable muzzle brake. Mfg. 1990-95.

$250	$210	$180	$160	$140	$125	$115

Last Mfg.'s Sug. Retail was $235.

Add $25 for electroless nickel finish (disc. 1991).

MODEL P-30L — similar to Model P-30, except has 8 in. barrel with removable muzzle brake, 22 oz. Mfg. 1991-92.

$275	$235	$200	$180	$160	$140	$125

Last Mfg.'s Sug. Retail was $280.

Add $15 for Model P-30LM that allows for fitting various accessories.

MODEL P-31 — .22 Mag. cal., same action as P-30, except has 11 in. barrel, enclosed synthetic barrel shroud and flash hider, 48 oz. Mfg. 1990-95.

$350	$315	$275	$240	$215	$185	$160

Last Mfg.'s Sug. Retail was $345.

RIFLES & CARBINES

MODEL R-31 — similar design to Model P-31, except has 16 in. barrel and telescoping stock, 64 oz. Mfg. 1991-95.

$365	$325	$275	$235	$210	$185	$165

Last Mfg.'s Sug. Retail was $385.

SRT-20F COMPACT — .243 Win. or .308 Win. cal., bolt action based on the Sako A-2 action, 20 in. match grade finned barrel with muzzle brake, folding synthetic stock, integrated bi-pod rest, no sights, 9 shot mag., 6.7 lbs. Disc. 1989.

$575	$525	$475	$395	$365	$340	$320

Last Mfg.'s Sug. Retail was $525.

Grendel previously manufactured the SRT-16F, SRT-20L, and SRT-24 - all were disc. 1988. Values are approx. the same as the SRT-20F.

Grading	100%	98%	95%	90%	80%	70%	60%

GRIFFIN & HOWE

Current custom gunsmith/manufacturer established 1923, and located in New York, NY and Bernardsville, NJ.

Griffin & Howe

Founded in 1923 by Seymour Griffin and James Howe, Griffin & Howe continues to build its custom rifles as well as providing the full spectrum of gunsmithing services and importation of fine English guns.

Griffin & Howe has been building custom rifles since 1923. They also perform a variety of custom gunsmithing services. Prices may vary greatly depending on configuration, desirability, condition and special features. Most used Griffin & Howe Custom Rifles in average condition and without special engraving start at $3,150+ and rise according to condition and nature of the individual gun. Since 1923, fewer than 2,800 have been made. In 1930, Griffin & Howe became a subsidiary of Abercrombie & Fitch and remained with them until 1976, when it became a privately held company. Because all Griffin & Howe rifles are essentially special ordered, accurate pricing can be ascertained only by examining each individual gun. Elaborate specimens by this maker trademark will command over $10,000. Engraving by Joseph Fugger, Winston Churchill, Bob Swartley or Kornbrath will add considerably to the value.

Pricing on new custom rifles, with a wide selection of options, is available directly from Griffin & Howe.

RIFLES: BOLT ACTION

Values below represent a base gun with customer supplied action, normal wood and no options.

G&H CLASSIC FRENCH WALNUT STOCK — custom honed action with lapped lugs, Douglas premium barrel, hand engraving, French walnut sporter stock with ebony forend tip, G&H pistol grip cap, "Griffin & Howe, New York" barrel address, custom order.

	100%	98%	95%	90%	80%	70%	60%
Mfg.'s Sug. Retail $5,500	$5,500	$4,350	$3,550	$3,150	$2,750	$2,500	$2,250

G&H PRE-'64 MODEL 70 CLASSIC SYNTHETIC STOCK — features glass bedded synthetic classic sporter stock in black or woodgrain finish, Douglas premium barrel, "Griffin & Howe, New York" barrel address, custom order.

	100%	98%	95%	90%	80%	70%	60%
Mfg.'s Sug. Retail $2,250	$2,250	$1,900	$1,650	$1,400	$1,175	$995	$850

WIN M70 STANDARD ACTION — for .243 Win., .270 Win., .30-06, or .308 Win. cal.

100%	98%	95%	90%	80%	70%	60%
$5,500	$5,000	$4,500	$3,500	$3,200	$2,800	$2,450

WIN M70 MEDIUM — for .300 Win. Mag., 7mm Rem. Mag., or .338 Win. Mag. cal.

100%	98%	95%	90%	80%	70%	60%
$5,950	$5,350	$4,600	$3,750	$3,400	$3,100	$2,750

WIN M70 MAGNUM — for .375 H&H or .416 Rem. cal.

100%	98%	95%	90%	80%	70%	60%
$6,250	$5,650	$4,850	$3,950	$3,500	$3,000	$2,850

WIN M52 — for .22 LR cal.

100%	98%	95%	90%	80%	70%	60%
$2,500	$2,250	$1,750	$1,650	$1,450	$1,300	$1,150

WIN HIGHWALL

100%	98%	95%	90%	80%	70%	60%
$1,850	$1,650	$1,250	$1,150	$1,000	$950	$850

SPRINGFIELD 1903

100%	98%	95%	90%	80%	70%	60%
$2,450	$2,150	$1,750	$1,550	$1,350	$1,250	$1,100

SPRINGFIELD 1922

100%	98%	95%	90%	80%	70%	60%
$2,450	$2,150	$1,750	$1,550	$1,350	$1,250	$1,100

MAUSER STANDARD

100%	98%	95%	90%	80%	70%	60%
$3,600	$3,200	$2,850	$2,250	$2,000	$1,750	$1,600

G

Grading	100%	98%	95%	90%	80%	70%	60%
MAUSER MAGNUM							
	$7,750	$6,800	$5,700	$5,250	$4,750	$4,300	$3,875
SAVAGE 99							
	$1,850	$1,650	$1,250	$1,150	$1,025	$950	$850

SHOTGUNS: O/U

MADISON — 12, 20, 28 ga., or .410 bore, case hardened receiver, 26½, 28, or 30 in. VR barrels, scroll engraved with gold accents. Mfg. by the Belgian Browning custom shop using a B25 action beginning 1999.

Mfg.'s Sug. Retail	$9,750	$9,000	$8,250	$7,750	$7,150	$6,450	$5,500	$4,500

CLAREMONT — 12 ga. only, case hardened receiver, shallow frame BOSS style lock-up, 30 in. VR barrels standard length, scroll engraving with gold accents. Mfg. by Gamba beginning 1999.

Mfg.'s Sug. Retail	$8,750	$8,250	$7,750	$7,150	$6,500	$5,900	$5,400	$4,700

EXTRA FINISH CLAREMONT — similiar to Claremont, except has coin finished receiver with full coverage acanthus scroll engraving and drop out trigger group. Importation began 1999.

Mfg.'s Sug. Retail	$11,500	$10,800	$9,500	$8,250	$7,000	$6,000	$5,500	$4,800

BROADWAY — 12 or 20 ga., case hardened receiver, 26, 28, or 30 in. VR barrels, scroll engraving with gold accents. Mfg. by the Belgian Browning custom shop using a B125 action beginning 1999.

Mfg.'s Sug. Retail	$5,750	$5,400	$4,600	$4,150	$3,550	$2,950	$2,400	$1,900

SHOTGUNS: SxS

ROUND BODY GAME GUN — 12, 16, 20, 28 ga., or .410 bore, features case colored round frame with sidelock action and 3rd fastener, H&H style selective ejectors, 25-30 in. barrels, double triggers, checkered straight grip stock and splinter forearm, G&H name gold inlaid, cased, mfg. by Arrieta.

Mfg.'s Sug. Retail	$5,750	$5,300	$4,600	$4,100	$3,500	$2,900	$2,400	$1,850

    Add $200 for 28 ga. or .410 bore.

EXTRA FINISH ROUND BODY GAME GUN — similar to Round Body Game Gun, except has coin finished reciever and game scene engraving with gold accents. Importation began 1999.

Mfg.'s Sug. Retail	$8,500	$8,150	$7,400	$6,750	$5,950	$5,200	$4,500	$3,900

    Add $350 for 28 ga. or .410 bore.

GRIFFON

Currently manufactured by Continental Weapons (Pty) Ltd. established in 1996, and located in Midrand, Johannesburg, South Africa. Currently imported and distributed by Griffon USA, Inc., a subsidiary of 21st Century Technologies, Inc., located in Ft. Worth, TX. Previously imported and distributed by First Defense International located in San Clemente, CA.

PISTOLS: SEMI-AUTO

GRIFFON 1911 A1 COMBAT — .45 ACP cal., patterned after the Colt M1911A1, single action, 4.13 in. barrel, 7 shot mag., ported barrel/slide, black finish, Commander hammer, Tritium sights. Importation began 1997.

Mfg.'s Sug. Retail	$495	$445	$375	$335	$300	$275	$250	$225

GRIFFON CW 11 — 9mm Para. cal., 8 shot mag., flat main spring housing, 4 in. barrel without porting, combo blue/chrome finish, perforated trigger, 3 dot sighting system. Importation began 1997.

Mfg.'s Sug. Retail	$495	$445	$375	$335	$300	$275	$250	$225

Grading	100%	98%	95%	90%	80%	70%	60%

GRULLA ARMAS

Current manufacturer located in Eibar, Spain since 1932. Currently imported and distributed by Gunsport, Ltd. Inc. located in Odessa, TX since 1994 and Hi-Grade Imports located in Gilroy, CA.

Grulla Armas manufactures a complete line of quality SxS shotguns in addition to both SxS and bolt action rifles.

RIFLES

C-95 BOLT ACTION — .338 Win. Mag. or .375 H&H cal., deluxe bolt action featuring extensively scroll engraved square bridge receiver with elongated upper tang, octagon barrel with quarter rib and express sights, deluxe checkered wood with ebony forend, custom made per individual order. New 1996.

Mfg.'s Sug. Retail	$7,500	$6,950	$6,400	$5,750	$4,950	$4,300	$3,600	$2,750

E-95 SxS DOUBLE RIFLE — 9.3x74R or .375 H&H cal., top-of-the-line double rifle utilizing H&H type sidelocks with scroll engraving, skeleton steel buttplate, regulated barrels, beavertail forend, custom made per individual order. New 1996.

Mfg.'s Sug. Retail	$20,000	$18,000	$15,750	$13,250	$11,750	$9,650	$8,500	$7,250

SHOTGUNS: SxS, SIDELOCK

The models listed below are currently available in 12, 16, 20, 28 ga., or .410 bore. All guns have double triggers with hinged front, selective auto-ejectors, and straight grip stock with splinter forearm. Values represent standard models with no options.

MODEL 209 - HOLLAND — coin finished receiver with scroll engraving.

Mfg.'s Sug. Retail	$3,450	$2,950	$2,525	$2,125	$1,800	$1,500	$1,325	$1,100

MODEL 215 — similar to Model 209, except has rose and scroll engraving with 3rd lever fastener and better wood.

Mfg.'s Sug. Retail	$4,050	$3,600	$3,000	$2,500	$2,100	$1,800	$1,500	$1,325

MODEL 216 — features delicate scroll engraving with border designs.

Mfg.'s Sug. Retail	$4,550	$4,000	$3,550	$2,975	$2,475	$2,100	$1,800	$1,500

MODEL 219 — similar to Model 216, except has more elaborate engraving and better wood.

Mfg.'s Sug. Retail	$6,050	$5,325	$4,650	$4,000	$3,550	$2,950	$2,475	$1,995

CONSORT — features easy-opening H&H style action, scroll engraving with border fences.

Mfg.'s Sug. Retail	$6,475	$5,875	$5,150	$4,575	$3,850	$3,275	$2,650	$2,200

WINDSOR — similar to Consort Model, except has more engraving.

Mfg.'s Sug. Retail	$6,995	$6,225	$5,600	$4,975	$4,350	$3,750	$3,000	$2,400

MODEL 219-P

Mfg.'s Sug. Retail	$7,750	$7,050	$6,225	$5,600	$4,850	$4,100	$3,200	$2,600

SUPER MH — features Boss style fine engraving with rosettes.

Mfg.'s Sug. Retail	$12,395	$11,400	$9,500	$8,475	$7,425	$6,200	$5,000	$4,150

NUMBER 1 — next to the top-of-the-line gun with best quality features.

Mfg.'s Sug. Retail	$15,550	$13,175	$10,625	$8,800	$7,575	$6,350	$5,150	$4,200

ROYAL — top-of-the-line model with H&H style scroll engraving.

Mfg.'s Sug. Retail	$16,950	$15,100	$12,850	$10,500	$8,750	$7,575	$6,350	$5,150

G

Grading	100%	98%	95%	90%	80%	70%	60%

GUN WORKS, LTD.

Previous manufacturer and distributor located in Buffalo, NY. Early guns were made in Tonawanda, NY.

HANDGUNS

X-CALIBER — .44 Mag. cal., single shot, tip up pistol, 8 in. barrel, matte type blue finish, ergonomic hardwood grips, probably used older Sterling Arms parts and restamped the barrel address. Limited mfg.

	100%	98%	95%	90%	80%	70%	60%
	$350	$300	$260	$230	$200	$175	$150

MODEL 9 — .357 Mag., 9mm Para., .38 Super, or .38 Spl. cal., O/U derringer, electroless nickel finish, 2½ in. barrel, wood grips, Millett sights, 15 oz. Disc. 1986.

	100%	98%	95%	90%	80%	70%	60%
	$135	$120	$105	$95	$65	$55	$50

Last Mfg.'s Sug. Retail was $149.

GUSTAF, CARL

See listing under Carl Gustaf.

GYROJET

See MBA Gyrojet listing in the M Section of this text.

G

NOTES

G

H section

HHF

Current manufacturer established in 1922 and located in Huglu, Turkey. No current importation. Previously imported 1993-96 by Turkish Firearms Corp., located in Allentown, PA and Alex Imports (1997 only), located in Chula Vista, CA. HHF designates Huglu Hunting Firearms.

Grading	100%	98%	95%	90%	80%	70%	60%

SHOTGUNS: O/U

All 12 and 20 ga. shotguns listed below were supplied with five choke tubes. All 12, 16, and 20 ga. shotguns were equipped with automatic ejectors - extractors were available for $200 less.

MODEL 101B — 12 ga. only, trap configuration, 30 or 32 in. separated VR barrels, coin finished receiver with moderate engraving. Imported 1993-96.

	$1,535	$1,225	$975	$775	$650	$525	$475

Last Mfg.'s Sug. Retail was $1,720.

Add $545 for extra top-single barrel (Model 101 B AT-DT).

MODEL 103D FIELD — 12, 16, 20, 28 ga., or .410 bore, 26 or 28 in. vented barrels with VR, coin finished receiver with light engraving. Imported 1994-96.

	$1,515	$1,225	$975	$775	$650	$525	$475

Last Mfg.'s Sug. Retail was $1,700.

Add $55 for 28 ga. or .410 bore.

* *Model 103C* — 12 or 20 ga., skeet model, features 27 or 28 in. separated barrels with VR, blued receiver with light engraving and gold inlays. Imported 1996 only.

	$1,515	$1,225	$975	$775	$650	$525	$475

Last Mfg.'s Sug. Retail was $1,700.

* *Model 103F* — 12 or 20 ga., sporting clays configuration, 28 or 30 in. vented barrels with VR, engraved coin finished receiver with engraved blued side plates. Imported 1996 only.

	$1,650	$1,300	$1,025	$795	$650	$525	$475

Last Mfg.'s Sug. Retail was $1,875.

SHOTGUNS: SxS

MODEL 200A FIELD — 12, 16, 20, 28 ga., or .410 bore, engraved coin finished scalloped boxlock action, SST, 26 or 28 in. SR barrels, checkered walnut stock with cheekpiece and beavertail forearm. Imported 1995-96.

	$975	$825	$700	$600	$500	$400	$300

Last Mfg.'s Sug. Retail was $1,150.

MODEL 201A FIELD — 12, 16, or 20 ga., 28 in. SR barrels only, coin finished boxlock receiver with engraving on side plates. Imported 1995-96.

	$1,515	$1,225	$975	$775	$650	$525	$475

Last Mfg.'s Sug. Retail was $1,700.

MODEL 202A FIELD — 12, 16, or 20 ga., features coin finished boxlock with Greener crossbolt, DTs, splinter forearm, 28 in. SR barrels only. Imported 1995-96.

	$1,075	$875	$750	$625	$525	$400	$300

Last Mfg.'s Sug. Retail was $1,285.

H

Grading	100%	98%	95%	90%	80%	70%	60%

HJS ARMS, INC.

Current manufacturer located in Brownsville, TX. Distributor and dealer sales.

DERRINGERS

FRONTIER FOUR MODEL A01 — .22 LR cal., 4 barrels with rotating firing pin, stainless steel, 2 in. barrels, spur trigger, plastic grips, 5½ oz. New 1993.

Mfg.'s Sug. Retail	$170	$145	$125	$115

FRONTIER FOUR MODEL A03 — similar to Model A01, except has brass frame and blue barrel. New 1995.

Mfg.'s Sug. Retail	$185	$165	$135	$120

LONE STAR MODEL A10 — .38 S&W or .380 ACP cal., single shot, stainless steel, 2 in. barrels, spur trigger, rotating firing pin blocker, plastic grips, 6 oz. New 1993.

Mfg.'s Sug. Retail	$190	$165	$135	$120

H.J.S. INDUSTRIES, INC.

Previous manufacturer located in Brownsville, TX.

DERRINGERS

FRONTIER FOUR DERRINGER — .22 LR cal., 4 shot derringer, stainless steel construction, 5½ oz.

	$115	$90	$80

LONE STAR DERRINGER — .38 S&W cal., single shot derringer, stainless steel construction, 6 oz.

	$137	$105	$95

H & R 1871, INC. (Harrington & Richardson)

Current manufacturer and holding company located in Gardner, MA since 1991.

H & R 1871 Inc. utilizes the original H & R trademark and does not accept warranty work for older (pre-1986 mfg.) Harrington & Richardson, Inc. firearms. Distributor sales only.

The use of the original Harrington & Richardson trademark was permitted during 1991. All new manufacture will use this trademark, but older H & Rs manufactured by Harrington & Richardson, Inc. are not the responsibility of H & R 1871, Inc.

REVOLVERS

Additional revolvers using the New England Firearms trademark may be located in the N section of this text. Beginning 1997, all H & R 1871, Inc. revolvers are supplied with a lockable plastic case.

929 SIDEKICK — .22 LR cal., 9 shot, blued metal, swing-out cylinder, 4 in. heavy barrel, square butt with brown laminate grips, fixed sights, 30 oz. New 1996.

Mfg.'s Sug. Retail	$173	$150	$120	$100	$85	$75	$65	$55

    * 929 Sidekick Trapper Edition — similar to 929 Sidekick, except has grey laminate grips and special barrel markings, limited mfg. 1996 only, distributed through 1996.

	$150	$115	$95	$85	$75	$65	$55

Last Mfg.'s Sug. Retail was $175.

939 PREMIER WESTERN TARGET — .22 LR cal., 9 shot, blued metal, swing-out cylinder, target model with ribbed 6 in. heavy barrel and adj. rear sight, hardwood grips, 36 oz. New 1995.

Mfg.'s Sug. Retail	$190	$150	$125	$105	$90	$75	$65	$55

Grading	100%	98%	95%	90%	80%	70%	60%

FOURTY-NINER (WESTERN 949) — .22 LR cal., 9 shot fixed cylinder, case colored receiver, 5½ or 7½ in. barrel, hardwood grips, fixed sights, approx. 37 oz. New 1995.

Mfg.'s Sug. Retail	$190		$150	$125	$105	$90	$75	$65	$55

SPORTSMAN 999 — .22 LR cal., single or double action, top break action with auto shell ejection, 9 shot, 4 or 6 in. barrel with fluted solid rib, smooth hardwood stocks, transfer bar safety, blue finish, adj. sights, 30-34 oz. Mfg. began 1991.

Mfg.'s Sug. Retail	$285		$230	$180	$145	$125	$115	$100	$90

RIFLES: SINGLE SHOT

ULTRA MODEL — .22-250 Rem. (disc. 1994), .223 Rem. (disc. 1997), .25-06 Rem. (new 1995), .308 Win. (new 1995), .357 Rem. Max. (mfg. 1996-98), 7x57mm (mfg. 1997 only), or 7x64mm (mfg. 1997 only) cal., single shot break-open action, side-lever release, heavy 22 (.22-250 Rem. or .223 Rem.), 22 normal (.308 Win.), or 26 (.25-06 Rem.) in. barrel with scope mount rail, checkered curly maple (disc. 1994) or laminated hardwood Monte Carlo stock with black line recoil pad, sling swivel studs, 7-8 lbs. New 1993.

Mfg.'s Sug. Retail	$255		$215	$170	$135	$115	$105	$95	$85

Subtract $30 for metric cals. (disc.).

This model features a scope rail on .25-06 Rem. and .308 Win. cals.

* *Ultra Varmint Model* — .223 Rem. or .243 Win. cal., features heavy 24 in. barrel, blued finish, natural finish laminate Monte Carlo stock, includes scope mount rail. New 1998.

Mfg.'s Sug. Retail	$255		$215	$175	$135	$115	$105	$95	$85

* *Ultra Comp. Model* — .270 Win. or .30-06 cal., features 24 in. barrel with integral compensator, blue finish, multi-color checkered laminate wood stock and forearm. Approx. 7-8 lbs. New 1997.

Mfg.'s Sug. Retail	$290		$250	$210	$170	$135	$115	$105	$95

* *Rocky Mountain Elk Foundation Commemorative 1st Ed.* — .280 Rem. cal., 26 in. blue barrel, features RMEF medallion in stock, high gloss bluing, 7-8 lbs. Mfg. 1995-96.

	$220	$175	$135

Last Mfg.'s Sug. Retail was $270.

* *Rocky Mountain Elk Foundation Commemorative 2nd Ed.* — .35 Whelen cal., 26 in. blue barrel, features RMEF medallion in multi-color laminate stock and forearm, high gloss bluing, 7-8 lbs. Mfg. 1996-97.

	$260	$215	$160

Last Mfg.'s Sug. Retail was $300.

WHITETAILS UNLIMITED COMMEMORATIVE RIFLE — .30-30 (new 1998) or .45-70 Govt. cal., Topper style break-open action, 22 in. barrel, blue frame with special etching, checkered American walnut stock (with medallion) and forearm. 7 lbs. Mfg. 1997-98.

	$250	$210	$170

Last Mfg.'s Sug. Retail was $290.

SHOTGUNS: SINGLE SHOT

TOPPER 098 — 12, 16 (new 1992), 20, 28 (mfg. 1992-95, reintroduced 1998) ga., or .410 bore, 2¾ or 3 in. chamber, 26 or 28 in. barrel, break open side lever release action, transfer bar safety, ejector, satin nickel frame with blue barrel, black finish hardwood stock with full pistol grip and forearm, 5-6 lbs. Mfg. began 1991.

Mfg.'s Sug. Retail	$118		$95	$80	$70	$60	$50	$40	$35

* *Topper Deluxe* — 12 ga. only, 3½ in. chamber, satin nickel frame with blue barrel, 28 in. barrel with 1 choke tube, black finish hardwood stock (with recoil pad) and forearm, 5-6 lbs. New 1991.

Mfg.'s Sug. Retail	$137		$110	$90	$80	$70	$60	$50	$40

Grading	100%	98%	95%	90%	80%	70%	60%

* **Topper Deluxe Rifled Slug Gun** — 12 ga. only, 3 in. chamber, 24 in. compensated barrel, rifle sights, dark American hardwood stock and forearm, satin nickel frame, approx. 5½ lbs. New 1996.

Mfg.'s Sug. Retail	$170	$150	$115	$95	$85	$75	$65	$55

* **Topper Jr.** — 20 ga. or .410 bore, smaller variation of the Topper 098 with youth dimensions including 22 in. barrel and shortened stock with recoil pad, satin nickel frame with blue barrel, 5-6 lbs. Mfg. began 1991.

Mfg.'s Sug. Retail	$124	$105	$85	$70	$60	$50	$40	$35

* **Topper Jr. Classic** — 20, 28 ga., or .410 bore, 22 in. barrel, checkered American black walnut stock and forearm, recoil pad. Mfg. began 1991.

Mfg.'s Sug. Retail	$147	$120	$95	$80	$70	$60	$50	$40

* **NWTF Turkey Mag.** — 10 (mfg. 1996 only) or 12 (mfg. 1991-95) ga., 3½ in. chamber, 24 in. drilled and tapped barrel with 1 choke tube, entire gun is covered in mossy oak camo, includes sling and swivels, 6 lbs. Mfg. 1991-96.

			$145	$120	$100	$85	$75	$65	$55

Last Mfg.'s Sug. Retail was $180.

This model was part of the National Wild Turkey Federation (NWTF) sponsorship program.

* **1994 NWTF Youth Turkey Gun** — 20 ga., 3 in. chamber, 22 in. full choke barrel, features Realtree camo finish and sling, limited mfg. 1994-95.

			$140	$110	$95	$85	$75	$65	$55

Last Mfg.'s Sug. Retail was $160.

THE TAMER — .410 bore, 3 in. chamber, synthetic thumbhole stock is designed to hold 4 shells, transfer bar safety, 20 in. full choke barrel, electroless nickel finish. New 1994.

Mfg.'s Sug. Retail	$125	$100	$90	$80	$70	$60	$50	$40

SB1-920 ULTRA SLUG HUNTER — .20 ga. only, utilizes 12 ga. action and barrel that has been under-bored to 20 ga. and fully rifled, hardwood Monte Carlo stock and forearm, matte black receiver. Mfg. 1996-Disc.

			$190	$155	$125	$100	$85	$75	$65

Last Mfg.'s Sug. Retail was $225.

ULTRA SLUG HUNTER — 12 or 20 ga., 3 in. chamber, 22 (20 ga., Youth Model) or 24 in. fully rifled heavy barrel, side-release lever, black Monte Carlo hardwood stock with recoil pad, matte finished receiver, 9 lbs. New 1995.

Mfg.'s Sug. Retail	$212	$180	$145	$120	$100	$85	$75	$65

* **Ultra Slug Hunter Deluxe** — similar to Ultra Slug Hunter, except has 24 in. fully rifled compensated barrel, adj. rear sight. New 1997.

Mfg.'s Sug. Retail	$242	$210	$180	$145	$120	$100	$85	$75

WHITETAILS UNLIMITED RIFLE SLUG GUN — 12 ga., 3 in. chamber, 24 in. fully rifled heavy barrel, hand checkered Monte Carlo black laminate stock and forend, Whitetails medallion, hammer extension, swivels and sling. New 1998

Mfg.'s Sug. Retail	$255	$220	$185	$145	$120	$100	$85	$75

H-S PRECISION, INC.

Current custom rifle manufacturer established 1990 and located in Rapid City, SD. H-S Precision, Inc. also manufactures synthetic stocks and custom machine barrels as well.

In addition to the models listed below, H-S Precision, Inc. will also build rifles using a customer's action (Remington 700 ADL or 700 BDL, Sako, Weatherby, or Winchester). These models will be approx. 33% less expensive than values listed below (not available in Sniper Model).

Grading	100%	98%	95%	90%	80%	70%	60%

PISTOLS: SINGLE SHOT

PRO-SERIES 2000 P — .17 Rem., .22-250 Rem., .223 Rem., .243 Win., .257 Roberts, .260 Rem., .308 Win., .35 Rem., 6mm PPC, 7mm-08 Rem., or 7mm BR cal., stainless steel receiver, 15 in. fluted stainless steel barrel, 3 position safety, laminated composite Pro-Series stock, Teflon coated receiver and barrel, choice of varmint (no sights) or silhouette (drilled and tapped for sights) configuration, choice of stock colors. New late 1997.

Mfg.'s Sug. Retail	$1,250	$1,175	$1,025	$975	$850	$750	$650	$575

RIFLES: BOLT ACTION, PRO-SERIES 2000

All H-S Precision rifles feature Kevlar/graphite laminate stocks, cut rifle barrels, and other high tech innovations including a molded in aluminum bedding block system.

VARMINT TAKEDOWN(VTD) — .22-250 Rem., .270 Win., .308 Win., or .300 Win. Mag. cal., accurized Remington Model 700 receiver with H-S stainless steel cut rifled and fluted barrel, 5 or 10 shot detachable mag, Teflon coated metal finish. New 1997.

Mfg.'s Sug. Retail	$1,795	$1,650	$1,375	$1,175	$895	$750	$650	$575

Add $1,000-$1,200 for extra barrel, depending on head size.

SPORTER/VARMINT — .223 Rem., .22 PPC, .22-250 Rem., .243 Win., 6mm PPC, 7mm-08 Rem., or .308 Win. cal. are available in short action, .270 Win., .30-06, 7mm Rem. Mag., .300 Win. Mag., or .338 Win. Mag. cal. are available in long action, Remington ADL action only, each rifle is built per individual specifications. New 1990.

Mfg.'s Sug. Retail	$1,645	$1,525	$1,350	$1,150	$850	$750	$650	$575

Add $50 for Varmint variation.
Add $150 for left-hand action.
Add $880 for extra stainless barrel (disc.).

PRO-HUNTER RIFLE (PHR) — available in 10 Safari cals., 24 or 26 in. fluted stainless steel barrel with cut rifling, Teflon finish, Pro-Series sporter stock, long action only.

Mfg.'s Sug. Retail	$1,795	$1,650	$1,375	$1,175	$895	$750	$650	$575

Add $100 for Pro-Hunter takedown rifle (PTD).

LONG RANGE (TACTICAL MARKSMAN) — .223 Rem., .243 Win., .30-06, .308 Win., 7mm Rem. Mag., or .300 Win. Mag. cal., stainless fluted barrel standard, Remington BDL action. New 1990.

Mfg.'s Sug. Retail	$1,895	$1,750	$1,450	$1,225	$925	$775	$675	$575

Add $150 for left-hand action.

TAKEDOWN TACTICAL LONG RANGE — .22-250 Rem., .243 Win., 7mm-08 Rem., or .308 Win. cal. in short action, .25-06 Rem., .270 Win., .30-06, 7mm Rem. Mag., .300 Win. Mag., or .338 Win. Mag. cal. in long action, stainless steel barrel, Remington BDL takedown action, matte blue finish. New 1990.

Mfg.'s Sug. Retail	$2,395	$2,200	$1,850	$1,450	$1,175	$900	$800	$700

Add $1,000-$1,200 for extra barrel, depending on head size.

TAKEDOWN LONG RANGE (TACTICAL MARKSMAN) — .223 Rem., .243 Win., .30-06, .308 Win., 7mm Rem. Mag., .300 Win. Mag., or .338 Win. Mag. cal., includes "kwik klip" and stainless fluted barrel. Mfg. 1990-97.

	$2,895	$2,225	$1,675	$1,350	$995	$850	$750

Last Mfg.'s Sug. Retail was $2,895.

A complete rifle package consisting of 2 calibers (.308 Win. and .300 Win. Mag.), scope and fitted case was available for $5,200 retail.

H

Grading	100%	98%	95%	90%	80%	70%	60%

HWP INDUSTRIES

Previous manufacturer located in Milwaukee, WI circa 1989.

THE SLEDGEHAMMER — .500 HWP Mag. cal., 5 shot revolver, double action, stainless steel, full shrouded 4 in. barrel (quick change), Pachmayr grips. Limited mfg. 1989 only.

$1,150 $895 $750

Last Mfg.'s Sug. Retail was $1,295.

HAENEL, C.G.

Previous manufacturer located in Suhl, Germany. Haenel mfg. many varieties of firearms between 1925-circa 1940. Currently, Haenel continues to manufacture airguns, mostly for Europe. Presently not imported into the U.S.

During 1925-WWII, C.G. Haenel manufactured a variety of sporting longarms, mostly concentrating on bolt action rifles, drillings, and SxS shotguns. Some of these guns are extremely well executed, and must be appraised individually. If quality, condition, and overall desirability are at a level similar to pre-war Sauers, Krieghoffs, etc., Haenel values could be similar to the trademarks just mentioned. However, a standard grade Haenel rifle/shotgun/drilling, in an obscure metric caliber with no engraving in 70% or less original condition, gets priced for its utilitarian shooting value as opposed to adding a collector premium.

PISTOLS: SEMI-AUTO

SCHMEISSER MODEL 1 & 2 — .25 ACP cal., similar to Baby Browning.

$385 $340 $300 $275 $230 $200 $180

MODELS 200-205 — see Hämmerli-Walther.

RIFLES: BOLT ACTION

MAUSER-MANNLICHER SPORTING RIFLE — 7x57mm, 8x57R, or 9x57R cal., M/88 Mauser type action, 22 or 24 in. octagon barrel, Mannlicher box mag., double set triggers, raised rib on barrel, leaf sight, sporter stock.

$440 $360 $330 $275 $250 $220 $165

88 MAUSER SPORTER — similar to Mauser-Mannlicher, with Mauser 5 shot mag.

$525 $450 $375 $325 $275 $240 $200

HAMBRUSCH JAGDWAFFEN GmbH

Current manufacturer located in Ferlach, Austria since 1752. Currently imported and distributed by CONCO Arms, located in Emmaus, PA.

Hambrusch Jagdwaffen is a member of the Ferlach Gun Guild, and manufactures many types of high-grade long arms including SxS shotguns, combination guns, drillings, double rifles, and single shot rifles. The combinations of these above configurations are almost endless - please contact the factory (see Trademark Index) for current model information and price quotations. Please allow 2 weeks for a reply.

Grading	100%	98%	95%	90%	80%	70%	60%

HÄMMERLI

Current manufacturer located in Lenzburg, Switzerland. Currently imported by SIG Arms Inc. located in Exeter, NH. Currently distributed by SIG Arms, Inc. and Mandall's Shooting Supplies, located in Scottsdale, AZ. Previously imported until 1995 by Hämmerli Pistols USA, located in Groveland, CA. Previously imported by Beeman Precision Arms located in Santa Rosa, CA.

PISTOLS: SINGLE SHOT, RIMFIRE

MODEL 33MP — .22 LR cal., similar to the Model 100, except not available in a deluxe model. Mfg. 1933-1949.

$925	$725	$650	$550	$470	$440	$385

MODEL 100 FREE PISTOL — .22 LR cal., 11½ in. octagon barrel, blue, martini action single shot, set trigger, micro rear sight, walnut stock and forearm. Mfg. 1950-1956.

$880	$660	$605	$550	$470	$440	$385

Add 15%-20% for Olympic rings, "London", and "1948" markings (indicative of Swiss shooting team).

* **Deluxe model** — carved stock.

$990	$770	$715	$660	$580	$550	$495

MODEL 101 — similar to Model 100, but heavy round barrel, improved action and sights, matte finish. Mfg. 1956-1960.

$880	$660	$605	$550	$470	$440	$385

MODEL 102 — similar to Model 101, except high polished finish. Mfg. 1956-1960.

$880	$660	$605	$550	$470	$440	$385

Deluxe model.

$990	$770	$715	$660	$580	$550	$495

MODEL 103 FREE PISTOL — similar to Model 101, except lighter octagon polished barrel. Mfg. 1956-1960.

$935	$715	$660	$605	$580	$550	$495

MODEL 104 MATCH PISTOL — similar to Model 103, except lighter round barrel, redesigned stock, mfg. 1961-1965.

$760	$660	$550	$495	$470	$440	$385

MODEL 105 MATCH PISTOL — similar to Model 103, except redesigned action and stock, octagon barrel. Mfg. 1962-1965.

$935	$715	$660	$605	$580	$550	$495

MODEL 106 MATCH PISTOL — similar to Model 105, except improved trigger.

$910	$690	$580	$525	$495	$470	$415

MODEL 107 MATCH PISTOL — similar to Model 105, except improved trigger.

$990	$770	$660	$550	$525	$495	$440

* **Deluxe model** — engraved and carved wood.

$1,320	$990	$880	$660	$635	$605	$550

MODEL 120-1 SINGLE SHOT FREE PISTOL — .22 LR cal., bolt action, 9.9 in. barrel, blue barrel and receiver, side lever operated, anodized aluminum lever and frame, walnut checkered grips.

$600	$540	$475	$425	$375	$325	$295

MODEL 120-2 — similar to 120-1, except stocks hand contoured.

$600	$540	$475	$425	$375	$325	$295

MODEL 120 HEAVY BARREL — similar to 120-1, with 5.7 in. bull barrel.

Grading	100%	98%	95%	90%	80%	70%	60%

MODEL 150 FREE PISTOL — .22 LR cal., 11.3 in. barrel, improved Martini-type action, set trigger, innovative design incorporating many unusual features. Disc. 1989.

	$1,850	$1,495	$1,275	$1,120	$980	$900	$850

Last Mfg.'s Sug. Retail was $1,980.

Add $113 for left-hand variation.

The Model 150 was replaced by the Model 160.

MODEL 151 FREE PISTOL — replacement for the Model 150 Free Pistol. Imported 1990-1993.

	$1,850	$1,495	$1,275	$1,120	$995	$900	$800

Last Mfg.'s Sug. Retail was $1,980.

MODEL 152 FREE PISTOL — .22 LR cal., 11.3 in. barrel. improved Martini-type action, electronic trigger release, innovative design incorporating many unusual features. State of the art target pistol. Disc. 1992.

	$1,995	$1,600	$1,350	$1,195	$1,090	$990	$895

Last Mfg.'s Sug. Retail was $2,105.

Add $57 for left-hand variation.

MODEL 160 FREE PISTOL — .22 LR cal., similar to Model 150, except has poly-carbon fiber forend, includes carrying case. New 1993.

Mfg.'s Sug. Retail	$2,189		$1,975	$1,550	$1,175	$900	$800	$700	$595

Add $290 for smaller adj. grips.

MODEL 162 FREE PISTOL — .22 LR cal., replacement for the Model 152 Free Pistol, includes poly-carbon fiber forend, includes carrying case. New 1993.

Mfg.'s Sug. Retail	$2,410		$2,150	$1,700	$1,375	$1,125	$900	$800	$700

Add $290 for smaller adj. grips.

PISTOLS: SEMI-AUTO

MODELS 200-205 — see Hämmerli-Walther.

INTERNATIONAL MODEL 206 — .22 LR cal., .22 S, semi-auto, $7^1/_{16}$ in. barrel with muzzle brake, adj. sights, walnut grips, blue. Mfg. 1962-1969.

	$690	$605	$495	$470	$385	$360	$330

INTERNATIONAL MODEL 207 — similar to 206, except adj. grip heel.

	$705	$635	$505	$480	$395	$370	$340

INTERNATIONAL MODEL 208 — .22 LR cal., 9 shot, 6 in. barrel, blue, adj. sights, checkered walnut grips with adj. heel. Mfg. 1966-1988.

	$1,600	$1,300	$1,050	$950	$880	$835	$770

Last Mfg.'s Sug. Retail was $1,755.

This model was replaced by the Model 208S.

* *Model 208S* — similar to Model 208, except has redesigned triggerguard and safety with interchangeable rear sight element. Importation started 1988.

Mfg.'s Sug. Retail	$2,021		$1,800	$1,300	$995	$900	$775	$675	$575

Add $125 for factory scope mount.
Add $180 for smaller adj. grips.

* *Model 208 Deluxe* — similar to Model 208, except has carved grips and elaborate engraving. Importation disc. 1988.

	$2,995	$2,500	$1,995

Last Mfg.'s Sug. Retail was $3,250.

* *Model 208C (Commemorative)* — limited edition commemorative. Disc. 1987.

	$2,100	$1,750	$1,400

Last Mfg.'s Sug. Retail was $2,225.

Grading	100%	98%	95%	90%	80%	70%	60%

INTERNATIONAL MODEL 209 — .22 Short cal., semi-auto, 5 shot, 4¾ in. barrel, muzzle brake, adj. sights, blue, walnut stock. Mfg. 1966-1970.

	$800	$690	$635	$550	$525	$485	$440

INTERNATIONAL MODEL 210 — similar to 209, but grips have adj. heel. Mfg. 1966-1970.

	$800	$715	$660	$590	$540	$525	$495

MODEL 211 — .22 LR cal., semi-auto, 9 shot, 6 in. barrel, adj. sights, blue, similar to Model 208 except non-adj. walnut stocks. Importation disc. 1990.

	$1,550	$1,275	$1,050	$950	$880	$835	$770

Last Mfg.'s Sug. Retail was $1,669.

MODEL 212 HUNTER — .22 LR cal., semi-auto, hunter's pistol, 9 shot, 5 in. barrel, adj. sights, blue, walnut stocks. Importation disc. 1993.

	$1,250	$1,000	$875	$775	$675	$575	$475

Last Mfg.'s Sug. Retail was $1,395.

MODEL 215 — .22 LR cal., semi-auto, Model 208 specs on commercial target model, 9 shot, 5 in. barrel, adj. sights, blue, walnut stocks. Importation disc. 1990.

	$1,395	$1,050	$895	$775	$695	$650	$600

Last Mfg.'s Sug. Retail was $1,505.

MODEL 230 RAPID FIRE PISTOL — .22 S cal., semi-auto, 5 shot, 6.3 in. barrel, blue, adj. sights, smooth walnut grips. Mfg. 1970-1983.

	$705	$635	$580	$530	$485	$450	$415

MODEL 230-2 — similar to 230, except checkered grips with adj. heel. Mfg. 1970-1983.

	$735	$655	$605	$570	$515	$485	$470

MODEL 232-1 RAPID FIRE PISTOL — .22 S cal., semi-auto, 6 shot, 5.1 in. barrel, blue, adj. sights, contoured walnut grips. Importation disc. 1993.

	$1,395	$1,125	$950	$850	$750	$700	$650

Last Mfg.'s Sug. Retail was $1,505.

Add $25 for wraparound grips sizes S-M-LG (Model 232-2).

MODEL 280 — .22 LR or .32 S&W Wadcutter cal., new modular pistol design utilizing carbon fiber synthetic material to replace frame and other critical parts, adj. grips, trigger, and rear sight, 4.6 in. barrel, 5 or 6 shot mag., approx. 2.2 lbs. New 1988.

Mfg.'s Sug. Retail	$1,643		$1,450	$1,125	$900	$800	$675	$575	$475

Add $200 for .32 S&W Wadcutter cal.

Add $765 (.22 LR) or $965 (.32 S&W Wadcutter) for conversion kit.

Add $200 for smaller adj. grips.

A package is also available with both calibers, magazines, and hard case for $2,595.

MODEL SP 20 — .22 LR or .32 S&W Wadcutter cal., replacement for Model 280, features low-level sight line, colored alloy receiver (blue, red, gold, violet, or black), adj. "JPS" buffer system that varies recoil characteristics per individual preference, black Hi-Grip anatomical grips. New 1998.

Mfg.'s Sug. Retail	$1,482		$1,325	$1,050	$875	$775	$675	$575	$475

Add $166 for .32 S&W Wadcutter cal.

MODEL P-240 — see SIG-Hämmerli for this model.

RIFLES: BOLT ACTION, TARGET

OLYMPIC 300 METER — .30-06 cal., bolt action, single shot free rifle, U.S.A. import, 7x57mm overseas, 20½ in. heavy barrel, double set trigger, aperture rear sight, globe front, free rifle stock with thumbhole pistol grip, beavertail forearm, Swiss style target butt. Mfg. 1945-1959.

	$880	$745	$605	$550	$470	$440	$415

Grading	100%	98%	95%	90%	80%	70%	60%

HÄMMERLI-TANNER 300 METER FREE RIFLE — similar to Olympic 300 , except 7.5mm standard, also was available in other calibers. Mfg. 1962-disc.

	$895	$825	$770	$715	$660	$580	$520

Last Mfg.'s Sug. Retail was $935.

MODEL 45 SMALLBORE MATCH RIFLE — .22 LR cal., bolt action, single shot, 27½ in. heavy barrel, same sights and stock type as Hämmerli-Tanner. Mfg. 1945-1957.

	$660	$550	$470	$440	$385	$360	$330

MODEL 54 SMALLBORE MATCH RIFLE — similar to 45 Smallbore, except adj. butt. Mfg. 1954-1957.

	$670	$560	$480	$450	$395	$370	$340

MODEL 503 SMALLBORE FREE RIFLE — similar to 54 Smallbore, except free style stock.

	$660	$550	$470	$440	$385	$360	$330

MODEL 505 MATCH RIFLE — match stock with aperture sights.

	$690	$580	$495	$470	$415	$385	$360

MODEL 506 SMALLBORE MATCH RIFLE — similar to 503 Smallbore. Mfg. 1963-1966.

	$690	$580	$495	$470	$415	$385	$360

SPORTING RIFLE — various calibers, set triggers, Mauser repeating action.

	$725	$650	$490	$425	$360	$325	$300

HÄMMERLI-WALTHER

Previously manufactured semi-auto target pistols made under joint effort from Hämmerli and Walther.

PISTOLS: SEMI-AUTO, RIMFIRE

MODEL 200 OLYMPIA — .22 Short or LR cal., 7½ in. barrel, 1952 type, adj. sights, barrel weight, blue, checkered walnut grips. Mfg. 1952-1958.

	$660	$605	$550	$440	$415	$385	$360

MODEL 200 OLYMPIA — 1958 type, similar to 1952 type, except has muzzle brake. Mfg. 1958-1963.

	$715	$605	$550	$495	$470	$415	$385

MODEL 201 — similar to 200, 1952 type, except 9½ in. barrel. Mfg. 1955-1957.

	$660	$605	$550	$440	$415	$385	$360

MODEL 202 — similar to 201, except adj. heel grips. Mfg. 1955-1957.

	$715	$605	$550	$495	$470	$415	$385

MODEL 203 — similar to 200, except has adj. heel grip.

* *1955 Type* — no muzzle brake.

	$715	$605	$550	$495	$470	$415	$385

* *1958 Type* — muzzle brake.

	$770	$660	$605	$550	$525	$470	$440

MODEL 204 — similar to 200, except .22 LR cal. only.

* *1956 Type* — no muzzle brake.

	$745	$635	$580	$525	$495	$470	$440

* *1958 Type* — muzzle brake.

	$800	$690	$635	$550	$525	$495	$470

MODEL 205 — .22 LR cal., similar to 204, except adj. heel grips.

Grading	100%	98%	95%	90%	80%	70%	60%

* **1956 Type** — no muzzle brake.

	$800	$690	$635	$550	$525	$495	$470

* **1958 Type** — muzzle brake.

	$855	$745	$715	$635	$580	$525	$495

HARRINGTON & RICHARDSON, INC.

Previous manufacturer located in Gardner, MA - formerly from Worchester, MA. Successors to Wesson & Harrington, manufactured from 1871 until January 24, 1986. H & R 1871, Inc. was formed during 1991 (see their listing in the front of this section). H & R 1871, Inc. is not responsible for the warranties or safety of older pre-1986 H & R firearms.

A manufacturer of utilitarian firearms for over 115 years, H & R ceased operation on January 24, 1986. Even though new manufacture (under H & R 1871, Inc.) is utilizing the H & R trademark, the discontinuance of older models in either NIB or mint condition may command slight asking premiums, but probably will not affect values on those handguns only recently discontinued. Most H & R firearms are still purchased for their shooting value rather than collecting potential.

Please refer to H & R listing in the Serialization section for alphabetical suffix information on how to determine year of manufacture for most H & R firearms between 1940-82.

COMBINATION GUNS: SINGLE SHOT

MODEL 058 — 20 ga./.30-30, .22 Rem. Jet, .22 Hornet, .44 Mag., or .357 Mag. cal. combination, 2 separate barrels supplied, blue only. Disc. 1985.

	$155	$130	$110	$95	$85	$75	$65

Last Mfg.'s Sug. Retail was $145.

MODEL 258 COMBINATION HANDY GUN II — supplied with 20 ga., 22 in. barrel and 22 in. rifle barrel in .22 Hornet, .30-30 Win., or .357 Mag. cal., electroless, matte nickel finish, side lever action release, cased, 6½ lbs. Disc. 1985.

	$175	$155	$140	$130	$120	$100	$95

Last Mfg.'s Sug. Retail was $195.

COMMEMORATIVES, SPECIAL EDITIONS, & LIMITED MFG.

ABILENE ANNIVERSARY .22 REVOLVER — 300 mfg. 1967.

	$150	$115	$75

Last Mfg.'s Sug. Retail was $83.50 (1967).

H&R 100TH ANNIVERSARY OFFICER'S MODEL — 1871-1971, Commemorative Officer's Model, Springfield 1873 Replica, Trapdoor, .45-70 Govt. cal., engraved metal work, 26 in. barrel, anniversary plaque on stock, 10,000 mfg. in 1971.

	$595	$550	$500

Last Mfg.'s Sug. Retail was $250.

MODEL 171 AND 171 DELUXE — please refer to listings under Rifles section.

MODEL 173 RIFLE — .45-70 Govt. cal., similar to Officer's Model, no plaque on stock. Mfg. 1972-1983.

	$495	$425	$325

MODEL 174 CARBINE (LITTLE BIG HORN) — .45-70 Govt. cal., Little Big Horn Commercial Carbine. Quantity unknown.

	$395	$325	$250

Last Mfg.'s Sug. Retail was $220 (1972).

MODEL 178 — .45-70 Govt. cal., Infantry Musket Replica, 32 in. barrel. Mfg. 1973-1984.

	$375	$325	$250

Grading	100%	98%	95%	90%	80%	70%	60%

1873 SPRINGFIELD TRAPDOOR — .45-70 Govt. cal., unknown quantities mfg. 1973.

	$450	$350	$275

Last Mfg.'s Sug. Retail was $250.

CUSTER MEMORIAL ISSUE — .45-70 Govt. cal., limited production, deluxe walnut stock, highly engraved, gold inlaid, mahogany display case and two volumes on Custer history. Each weapon bears the name of one who fell at Little Big Horn.

* *Officer's Model* — 25 mfg., must be new with original box/accessories.

	$3,995	$3,150	$2,400

Last Mfg.'s Sug. Retail was $3,000 (1973).

* *Enlisted Men's Model* — 243 mfg., must be new with original box/accessories.

	$1,995	$1,400	$900

Last Mfg.'s Sug. Retail was $2,000 (1973).

PISTOLS: PRE-1942

MODEL 4 — .32 S&W Long 6 shot, or .38 S&W Long 5 shot cal., (1904), double action, 2½, 4½, and 6 in. barrels, blued or nickel, hard rubber grips, solid frame, fixed sights.

$95	$85	$70	$55	$45	$35	$30

MODEL 5 — .32 S&W Long cal., 5 shot only, (1905), double action, same as Model 4.

$95	$85	$70	$55	$45	$35	$30

MODEL 6 — .22 LR cal., 7 shot only, (1906), double action, similar to Model 4.

$95	$85	$70	$55	$45	$35	$30

AMERICAN — .32 S&W, 6 shot, or .38 S&W, 5 shot cal., double action, 2½, 4, or 6 in. barrels, fixed sights, blue or nickel.

$95	$85	$70	$55	$45	$35	$30

YOUNG AMERICAN — .22 Long, 7 shot, or .32 S&W, 5 shot cal., double action, 2, 4½, or 6 in. barrel, fixed sights, blue or nickel.

$95	$85	$70	$55	$45	$35	$30

VEST POCKET — double action, 1⅛ in. barrel, blue or nickel, solid frame, spurless hammer.

$95	$85	$70	$55	$45	$35	$30

HUNTER — .22 LR cal., double action, 10 in. octagon barrel, 9 shot, checkered walnut grips.

$140	$110	$100	$85	$65	$55	$45

TRAPPER — .22 LR cal., double action, 7 shot, 6 in. octagon barrel, checkered walnut stocks.

$140	$120	$100	$85	$65	$55	$45

MODEL 922 — .22 LR cal., first issue, 9 shot, 10 in. octagon barrel on early models, 6 in. round barrel on later models, checkered walnut grips.

$140	$120	$100	$85	$65	$55	$45

AUTOMATIC EJECTING — .32 S&W cal., 6 shot, .38 S&W, 5 shot, double action, 3¼, 4, 5, or 6 in. barrels, hinged break open, blue or nickel finish, fixed sights, black rubber grips.

$160	$150	$105	$90	$75	$65	$55

PREMIER — .22 LR, 7 shot, or .32 S&W, 5 shot cal., double action, break open, small frame.

$95	$85	$70	$55	$45	$35	$30

HAMMERLESS — .22 LR, 7 shot, or .32 S&W, 5 shot cal., double action, 2, 3, 4, 5, or 6 in. barrels, small frame, break open, blue or nickel, black rubber grips.

$125	$110	$100	$85	$65	$55	$45

HAMMERLESS — .32 S&W, 6 shot, or .38 S&W, 5 shot cal., double action, 3¼, 4, 5, or 6 in. barrels, large frame, break open.

$125	$110	$100	$85	$65	$55	$45

Grading	100%	98%	95%	90%	80%	70%	60%

TARGET MODEL — .22 LR, or .22 WRF cal., 7 shot, double action, 6 in. barrel, fixed sights, break open, small frame, blue only, walnut grips.

	$140	$120	$100	$85	$70	$60	$50

.22 SPECIAL — .22 LR, or .22 WRF cal., 7 shot, double action, 6 in. barrel, break open, large frame, blue only, gold plated front sight, walnut grips.

	$165	$140	$120	$100	$85	$70	$60

EXPERT — double action, similar to .22 Special, except 10 in. barrel.

	$150	$140	$120	$100	$85	$70	$60

SPORTSMAN NO. 199 — .22 LR cal., 9 shot, single action, 6 in. barrel, adj. target sights, break open, blue only, checkered walnut grips.

	$275	$235	$195	$165	$140	$110	$90

DEFENDER — .38 S&W cal., double action, 4 or 6 in. barrel, fixed sights, blue, break open, black plastic grips, made during WWII for police reserves and major corporation guards.

	$140	$120	$110	$100	$85	$65	$55

ULTRA SPORTSMAN — .22 LR cal., 9 shot, single action, 6 in. barrel, blue, break open, adj. sights, walnut grips, short cylinder action, wide hammer spur.

	$220	$200	$180	$150	$120	$100	$85

NEW DEFENDER — .22 LR cal., 9 shot, double action, 2 in. barrel, break open, adj. sights, blue, round butt, checkered walnut grip.

	$220	$200	$180	$150	$120	$100	$85

USRA SINGLE SHOT TARGET — .22 LR cal., 7, 8, or 10 in. barrel, blue, hinged break open, adj. sights, walnut grips. Mfg. 1928-1941.

	$440	$415	$385	$330	$290	$250	$195

Add 10% for nickel finish.

.25 CAL. SELF LOADING PISTOL — .25 ACP cal., 6 shot, 2 in. barrel, blue, black rubber grips. 16,630 mfg. 1912-1916.

	$375	$330	$305	$250	$195	$165	$140

.32 CAL. SELF LOADING PISTOL — .32 ACP cal., 8 shot, 3½ in. barrel, fixed sights, black rubber grips. Mfg. 1916-1924.

	$330	$305	$250	$195	$165	$140	$110

Add 20% for type I models if in 90%+ original condition.

Type I models with 12 slide pull grooves are serialized 1-3,025. Type II (more common) are serialized 3,026 - 34,500.

HANDY-GUN — smooth bore (mfg. 1921-1934) or rifled-barrel (mfg. 1931-1934) pistol, available in either 8 or 12¼ in. choked or unchoked barrel in either .410 bore or 28 ga., case hardened (Tiger stripe colors resulting from hot cyanide method) or blued frame. Rifled barrel (.22 LR in blued frame or .32-20 WCF cal. in case colored frame, 12¼ in. barrel) is rare. Early smooth bore guns bear only manufacturer's name, later blued and case-colored guns are stamped H. & R. "Handy-Gun" on left side and manufacturer's name on right side, as are all rifled barrel models. Ser. nos. on barrel lug and frame should match. Smooth bore Handy-Guns (more than 50 variations have been documented) not currently registered with ATF cannot be legally owned and are subject to seizure.

* *Smooth bore* — ser. no. range is 1 - approx. 54,000.

	$595	$495	$400	$350	$295	$250	$200

* *.22 Rimfire* — ser. no. range is 1 - approx. 223.

	$900	$750	$650	$550	$500	$450	$350

H

Grading	100%	98%	95%	90%	80%	70%	60%

* **.32-20 WCF** — ser. no. range is approx. 43,851-43,937.

	100%	98%	95%	90%	80%	70%	60%
	$1,200	$1,000	$800	$650	$550	$500	$450

Add $50-$250 for original box, and $75-$200 for original H&R holster.

Values for smooth bore are for the most common variation (.410 with 12¼ in. choked barrel), premiums of 25%-200% or more for rare variations (8 in. barrel, 28 ga., hooked trigger guard, optional detachable shoulder stock), rarest (just a few were made) is a .410 bore with 18 in. choked barrel mfg. in 1934. "Private branded" or "trade-branded" variations command 25%-100% premiums.

An optional detachable wire stock was available, but not commonly ordered. Most smooth bore variations were not drilled for a shoulder stock.

REVOLVERS: RECENT MFG.

MODEL 504 SQUARE BUTT — .32 H&R Mag. cal., 5 shot, 4 or 6 in. bull barrels, adj. rear sight, swing out cylinder, blue, black plastic and walnut grips. Mfg. 1984 and 1985.

	$165	$145	$135	$120	$110	$100	$90

Last Mfg.'s Sug. Retail was $185.

* *Model 504 Round Butt* — compact design available with 3 or 4 in. barrel only. Disc. 1985.

	$165	$145	$135	$120	$110	$100	$90

Last Mfg.'s Sug. Retail was $185.

MODEL 532 — .32 H&R Mag. cal., 5 shot, 2½ and 4 in. barrels, solid frame revolver, blue, pull pin cylinder, black plastic and walnut grips. Mfg. 1984 and 1985.

	$100	$90	$80	$70	$60	$50	$45

Last Mfg.'s Sug. Retail was $115.

MODEL 586 — .32 H&R Mag. cal., 5 shot, Western-style revolver, double action, 4½, 5½, 7½, or 10 in. barrels, adj. rear sight, fixed cylinder, antique finish, black plastic or walnut grips. Made 1984 and 1985.

	$175	$155	$135	$120	$110	$100	$90

Last Mfg.'s Sug. Retail was $195.

MODEL 603 — .22 Mag. cal., 6 in. barrel, double action. Disc.

	$159	$120	$110	$95	$90	$80	$70

MODEL 604 — same specifications as the Model 603, only has 6 in. bull barrel.

	$170	$130	$115	$95	$90	$80	$70

MODEL 622 — .22 Short, Long, or LR cal., solid frame, 6 shot, 2½, 4, or 6 in. barrels, blue, plastic grips. Mfg. 1957-1985.

	$95	$82	$70	$60	$55	$50	$45

Last Mfg.'s Sug. Retail was $104.

MODEL 623 — same basic specifications as the Model 622, nickel finish only. Disc.

	$115	$95	$75	$60	$55	$50	$45

MODEL 632 GUARDSMAN — .32 S&W cal., 6 shot, 2½ or 4 in. barrel, solid frame, checkered tenite grips, blue. Mfg. 1953-1984.

	$104	$82	$70	$60	$55	$50	$45

MODEL 633 — same basic specifications as the Model 632, only nickel finish. Disc.

	$115	$95	$75	$60	$55	$50	$45

MODEL 642 — .22 Mag cal., 2½ or 4 in. barrel. Disc.

	$95	$70	$65	$60	$50	$45	$40

MODEL 649 CONVERTIBLE — .22 LR or .22 Mag. cal., furnished with extra cylinder, Western style, double action, side loading, 5½ or 7½ in. barrel, 6 shot, walnut grips, blued finish. Mfg. 1976-1985.

	$140	$120	$110	$95	$90	$80	$70

Last Mfg.'s Sug. Retail was $160.

Grading	100%	98%	95%	90%	80%	70%	60%

MODEL 650 CONVERTIBLE — similar to Model 649, except with nickel finish and only available with 5½ in. barrel. Disc. 1985.

	$150	$130	$115	$100	$90	$80	$70

Last Mfg.'s Sug. Retail was $175.

MODEL 666 — .22 LR or .22 Win. Mag. cal., 6 shot, 6 in. barrel, blue, plastic grips, convertible. Mfg. 1976-1982.

	$100	$90	$70	$50	$45	$35	$30

MODEL 676 — .22 LR or .22 Win. Mag. cal., 6 shot, 4½, 5½, 7½, or 12 in. barrel, side load and eject, convertible (includes .22 LR/.22 Mag. cylinders), blue, case hardened frame, one piece walnut stock. Mfg. 1976-1982.

	$140	$120	$100	$85	$60	$45	$35

MODEL 686 CONVERTIBLE — .22 LR or .22 Mag. cal., furnished with extra cylinder, Western style, double action, side loading, 5½, 7½, 10 or 12 in. barrel, 6 shot, walnut grips, color case hardened frame, adj. rear sight, 12 in. barrel. Disc. 1984.

	$185	$160	$140	$125	$110	$90	$80

MODEL 732 — .32 S&W or .32 H&R Mag. cal., 6 shot, 2½ and 4 in. barrels, fixed sights, swing out cylinder, blue, black plastic grips. Add $15 for .32 H&R Mag. cal. Mfg. 1958-disc.

	$127	$100	$85	$75	$65	$55	$45

MODEL 733 — same specifications as the Model 732, only nickel finish and available only with 2½ in. barrel. Add $15 for .32 H&R Mag. cal.

	$140	$125	$110	$85	$75	$60	$50

MODEL 900 — .22 S, L, or LR cal., 9 shot, 2½, 4, or 6 in. barrels, snap out cylinder, blue, black plastic grips. Mfg. 1962-1973.

	$90	$85	$70	$55	$50	$40	$30

MODEL 901 — similar to 900, but chrome with white tenite grips. Mfg. 1962-1963.

	$110	$100	$90	$70	$50	$40	$30

MODEL 904 — .22 S, L, LR cal., double action, 4 or 6 in. bull barrel, target grade, 9 shot. Disc. 1985.

	$150	$135	$120	$105	$95	$80	$70

Last Mfg.'s Sug. Retail was $168.

MODEL 905 — similar to Model 904, except with nickel finish and 4 in. barrel only. Disc. 1985.

	$160	$140	$125	$105	$95	$80	$70

Last Mfg.'s Sug. Retail was $185.

MODEL 922 — .22 LR cal., Second Issue, 9 shot, 2½, 4, or 6 in. barrels, solid frame, blue, plastic grips. Mfg. 1950-1982.

	$85	$70	$60	$45	$40	$30	$25

MODEL 923 — similar to 922, only nickel.

	$90	$75	$65	$50	$45	$35	$30

MODEL 925 DEFENDER — .38 S&W cal., 5 shot, 2½ in. barrel, blue, break open, adj. sight, wraparound one piece grip. Mfg. 1964-1984.

	$130	$120	$100	$85	$70	$60	$50

✳ *Model 935* — similar to Model 925, except with nickel finish.

	$145	$135	$115	$100	$70	$60	$50

MODEL 926 — .22 LR or .38 S&W cal., 5,(.38 S&W) or 9 (.22LR)shot, 4 in. barrel, blue, adj. rear sight, break open, walnut grips. Mfg. 1968-1982.

	$130	$120	$100	$85	$70	$60	$50

✳ *Model 926 Abilene Kansas Centennial* — .22 LR cal., barrel is marked "Abilene Kansas" and "1869 Centennial 1969", mfg. 1969 only.

	$175	$155	$125	$105	$90	$80	$70

Grading	100%	98%	95%	90%	80%	70%	60%

MODEL 929 SIDEKICK — .22 LR cal., 9 shot, 2½, 4, or 6 in. barrels, swing out cylinder, plastic grips, blue. Mfg. 1956-1985.

	$115	$100	$70	$55	$45	$35	$30

Last Mfg.'s Sug. Retail was $127.

MODEL 930 SIDEKICK — similar to 929 Sidekick, only nickel finish and not available with 6 in. barrel. Disc. 1985.

	$125	$110	$80	$65	$55	$45	$40

Last Mfg.'s Sug. Retail was $140.

MODEL 939 ULTRA SIDEKICK — .22 S, L, or LR cal., 9 shot, 6 in. barrel, swing out cylinder, vent rib, adj. sights, blue. Mfg. 1958-1982.

	$110	$100	$85	$70	$55	$45	$30

MODEL 940 ULTRA SIDEKICK — similar to 939, only round barrel. Disc.

	$105	$95	$75	$65	$50	$40	$30

MODEL 949 "FORTY NINER" — .22 S, L, or LR cal., 5½ in. barrel, double action, solid frame, 9 shot, side load and Western style ejection, adj. rear sight, walnut grips. Mfg. 1960-1985.

	$115	$100	$85	$70	$55	$50	$45

Last Mfg.'s Sug. Retail was $127.

MODEL 950 — similar to Model 949, except with nickel finish. Disc. 1985.

	$125	$105	$90	$70	$55	$50	$45

Last Mfg.'s Sug. Retail was $145.

MODEL 976 — similar to 949, only color case hardened frame. Disc.

	$100	$90	$85	$70	$60	$50	$35

MODEL 999 SPORTSMAN — 22 LR cal., Second Issue, .9 shot, 4 or 6 in. vent. rib barrel, top-break action, adj. sights, walnut grips. Mfg. 1950-1985.

	$195	$170	$155	$140	$125	$110	$95

This model was also made in a Sportsman Centennial Commemorative. Add 15%-25% if NIB.

MODEL 999 ENGRAVED — similar to 999, only engraved throughout, 6 in. barrel only. Disc. 1985.

	$425	$375	$300	$260	$225	$190	$175

Last Mfg.'s Sug. Retail was $525.

RIFLES

REISING MODEL 60 — .45 ACP cal., semi-auto, 12 or 20 shot, 18¼ in. barrel, detachable mag. Mfg. 1944-1946.

	$360	$340	$310	$275	$220	$200	$175

MODEL 65 MILITARY — .22 LR cal., 10 shot mag., 23 in. barrel, Redfield aperture rear sight. Mfg. 1944-1946 for USMC.

	$250	$230	$200	$165	$145	$130	$110

MODEL 150 — .22 LR cal., semi-auto, 5 shot. Mfg. 1949-1953.

	$95	$85	$70	$55	$40	$35	$30

MODEL 155 — .44 Mag. or .45-70 Govt. cal., single shot, break open. Mfg. 1972-disc.

	$150	$130	$115	$95	$75	$55	$45

MODEL 157 — .22 Mag., .22 Hornet, or .30-30 cal., single shot, break open, Mannlicher stock. . Mfg. 1976-84.

	$165	$150	$135	$100	$80	$65	$45

MODEL 158 — .22 Jet, .22 Hornet, .30-30, .357 Mag or .44 Mag. cal., single shot break open, 22 in. barrel, side or top lever action release, ejector, case hardened frame. Disc. 1985.

	$150	$135	$125	$90	$80	$60	$50

Last Mfg.'s Sug. Retail was $115.

Grading	100%	98%	95%	90%	80%	70%	60%

✶ Model 158 Combination — supplied with rifle barrel and 20 ga., 26 in. barrel. Disc. 1985.

	$195	$175	$150	$135	$115	$100	$90

Last Mfg.'s Sug. Retail was $145.

MODEL 165 — .22 LR cal., 10 shot. Mfg. 1945-1961.

	$120	$110	$95	$85	$70	$55	$50

MODEL 171 — .45-70 Govt. cal., Model 1873 Trapdoor copy, 22 in. barrel, Model 174 is the deluxe model. Disc.

	$350	$300	$270	$250	$230	$210	$195

MODEL 171-DL — .45-70 Govt. cal., single shot, Springfield copy, 22 in. barrel. Mfg. 1984-1985.

	$400	$350	$295	$250	$225	$200	$185

Last Mfg.'s Sug. Retail was $385.

MODEL 174

	$400	$375	$325	$300	$250	$210	$195

MODEL 300 ULTRA — .22-250 Rem., .243 Win., .270 Win., .30-06, .308 Win., 7mm Mag., or .300 Win. Mag. cal., bolt action, 22 or 24 in. barrel. Mfg. 1965-1978.

	$495	$450	$425	$400	$350	$325	$295

MODEL 301 CARBINE — similar to 300, but 18 in. barrel, full length Mannlicher stock, N/A .22-250 Rem. cal.

	$440	$415	$360	$305	$250	$220	$195

MODEL 317 ULTRA WILDCAT — .17 Rem., .17-223, .222 Rem., or .223 Rem. cal., short action Sako, 20 in. barrel, no sights. Mfg. 1968-1976.

	$550	$525	$500	$450	$400	$350	$325

MODEL 317P PRESENTATION — similar to 317, but deluxe wood basketweave checkering. Mfg. 1968-1976.

	$625	$550	$495	$440	$400	$360	$305

MODEL 333 — 7mm Mag. cal., similar to 300, plainer version. Mfg. 1974 only.

	$250	$230	$215	$180	$160	$140	$120

MODEL 340 — .243 Win., .270 Win., .30-06, .308 Win., 7mm Mauser cal., bolt action, 5 shot, 22 in. barrel, checkered walnut. Mfg. 1982-1984.

	$395	$300	$275	$240	$220	$200	$180

MODEL 360 ULTRA AUTOMATIC — .243 Win. or .308 Win. cal., 3 shot, 22 in. barrel. Mfg. 1965-1978.

	$395	$350	$325	$300	$275	$250	$225

MODEL 370 ULTRA MEDALIST TARGET — .22-250 Rem., .243 Win., or 6mm Rem. cal., Varmint Rifle, 24 in. varmint weight barrel, semi-beavertail forearm. Mfg. 1968-1973.

	$495	$450	$400	$375	$350	$325	$295

MODEL 422 — .22 S, L, or LR cal., slide action. Mfg. 1956-1958.

	$110	$100	$85	$65	$45	$40	$30

Model 450 — similar to Model 451 Medalist only no sights.

	$150	$140	$120	$110	$95	$70	$55

MODEL 451 MEDALIST — .22 LR cal., bolt action, 5 shot, 26 in. barrel. Mfg. 1948-1961.

	$165	$150	$140	$110	$100	$85	$55

MODEL 700 — .22 Win. Mag. cal., semi-auto, 5 shot, clip mag., 22 in. barrel. Mfg. 1977-1985.

	$275	$250	$225	$200	$175	$150	$125

Last Mfg.'s Sug. Retail was $210.

H

Grading	100%	98%	95%	90%	80%	70%	60%

MODEL 700DL — similar to Model 700 except deluxe checkered walnut. 4-power scope is standard, recoil pad. Disc. 1985.

| | $395 | $350 | $325 | $300 | $275 | $250 | $200 |

Last Mfg.'s Sug. Retail was $360.

MODEL 750 — .22 LR cal. single shot bolt action, 22 in. barrel, open sights, youth stock dimensions. Disc. 1985.

| | $85 | $75 | $60 | $50 | $45 | $40 | $35 |

Last Mfg.'s Sug. Retail was $95.

MODEL 865 — .22 LR cal. bolt action, 5 shot mag., 22 in. barrel. Disc. 1985.

| | $90 | $80 | $65 | $55 | $50 | $45 | $40 |

Last Mfg.'s Sug. Retail was $105.

MODEL 5200 TARGET — .22 LR cal. target rifle, heavy 28 in. barrel, adj. trigger, no sights, single shot. 11 lbs. Disc. 1985.

| | $475 | $450 | $400 | $350 | $300 | $275 | $250 |

Last Mfg.'s Sug. Retail was $450.

MODEL 5200 SPORTER — .22 LR cal., bolt action, 5 shot, 24 in. barrel, adj. sights, checkered walnut. Disc. 1983.

| | $595 | $550 | $500 | $475 | $450 | $400 | $350 |

SHOTGUNS

HARRICH NO. 1 — 12 ga., single barrel Trap Gun, 32 or 34 in. full choke, high quality, engraved, vent. rib. Mfg. by Ferlach of Austria from 1971-1975.

| | $1,650 | $1,595 | $1,485 | $1,320 | $1,100 | $880 | $770 |

MODEL 3 HAMMERLESS — similar to Model 8, but no visible external hammer. Mfg. 1908-1942.

| | $85 | $75 | $70 | $55 | $45 | $40 | $30 |

MODEL 5 LIGHTWEIGHT — 24, 28 ga., or .410 bore only. Mfg. 1908-1942.

| | $95 | $90 | $75 | $65 | $55 | $40 | $35 |

MODEL 6 HEAVY BREECH — similar to Model 8, only 10 ga. - 20 ga., heavier barrels. Mfg. 1908-1942.

| | $95 | $85 | $75 | $60 | $50 | $45 | $35 |

MODEL 7 OR 9 BAY STATE — similar to Model 8, only 12, 16, 20 ga., or .410 bore, rounded pistol grip. Mfg. 1908-1942.

| | $85 | $75 | $70 | $55 | $45 | $40 | $30 |

MODEL 8 STANDARD — 12, 16, 20, 24, 28 ga., or .410 bore, single shot, 26-32 in. barrels, plain pistol grip stock, auto ejector, break open. Mfg. 1908-1942.

| | $150 | $125 | $95 | $75 | $65 | $60 | $55 |

Add 100% for 28 ga. or .410 bore.

FOLDING GUN — 12, 16, 20, 28 ga., or .410 bore, hinged frame, barrel folds against stock. Mfg. 1908-1942.

| | $195 | $175 | $150 | $125 | $100 | $85 | $60 |

Add 75% for 28 ga. or .410 bore.

TOPPER — 12, 16, 20 ga., or .410 bore, single shot, top or side lever break open action, 10 different variations of this shotgun, all are very similar and values run too close to differentiate, with ejector. Mfg. 1946-disc.

| | $145 | $125 | $100 | $85 | $70 | $55 | $45 |

Add 15% for Topper Deluxe (Model 488, chrome finish).

This model was also designated the Model 48, Model 158 (not in 28 ga.), Model 162 Buck gun with open sights, and Model 198 (28 ga. or .410 bore only).

Grading	100%	98%	95%	90%	80%	70%	60%

MODEL 088 — 12, 16, 20, 28 ga., or .410 bore, single shot, hammer model, ejector, top or side lever break open action, blue barrel finish with case hardened frame. Disc. 1985.

	$85	$75	$55	$50	$45	$40	$35

Last Mfg.'s Sug. Retail was $95.

MODEL 099 — 12, 16, 20 ga., or .410 bore, similar to Model 088, only electroless nickel finish, ejector, top or side lever break open action. Disc. 1984.

	$95	$80	$60	$55	$50	$45	$40

MODEL 162 — 12 or 20 ga., single shot, 24 in. slug barrel with rifle sights, case hardened frame, top or side lever break open action. Disc. 1984.

	$115	$105	$90	$80	$65	$55	$45

MODEL 176 — 10 (3½ in.), 12, or 20 ga., Mag., single shot, 32-36 in. heavy barrel, top or side lever break open action. Mfg. 1977-1985.

	$110	$95	$80	$70	$60	$50	$45

Last Mfg.'s Sug. Retail was $125.

MODELS 348/349 BOLT ACTION — 12 or 16 ga., 3 shot tube mag., 28 in. barrel (Model 349 has adj. vari-choke), walnut stock, 7½ lbs. Disc.

	$115	$90	$75	$60	$50	$45	$40

MODEL 400 PUMP ACTION — 12, 16, or 20 ga., 28 in. full choke. Mfg. 1955-1967.

	$155	$145	$125	$110	$90	$75	$55

MODEL 401 PUMP — similar to 400, but H&R variable choke. Mfg. 1956-1963.

	$165	$155	$140	$120	$100	$90	$65

MODEL 402 PUMP — .410 bore, similar to 400, lightweight. Mfg. 1959-1967.

	$175	$165	$150	$140	$110	$100	$85

MODEL 403 AUTOLOADER — .410 bore, 26 in. full choke, takedown. Mfg. 1964 only.

	$195	$180	$165	$155	$120	$100	$85

MODEL 404 — 12, 20 ga., or .410 bore, double barrel, SxS, 26 or 28 in. barrel, boxlock, extractors, double triggers. Mfg. by Rossi of Brazil 1969-1972.

	$185	$175	$165	$145	$110	$90	$70

MODEL 404C — similar to 404, only checkered stock.

	$200	$185	$175	$155	$120	$100	$85

MODEL 440 — 12, 16, or 20 ga., pump action, 26, 28, or 30 in. barrels, available in various chokes, plain pistol grip and slide. Mfg. 1968-1973.

	$145	$130	$110	$100	$85	$70	$55

MODEL 442 — pump action, similar to 440, only vent. rib, checkered stock. Mfg. 1969-1973.

	$175	$165	$155	$140	$100	$85	$65

MODEL 490 — 20 ga. or .410 bore, made for junior shooters, Greenwing finish — add $10. Disc. 1984.

	$85	$65	$60	$50	$45	$40	$40

MODEL 1212 — 12 ga., O/U, Field, 2¾ in., 28 in. vent. rib barrels, various chokes, checkered walnut stocks. Mfg. by Lanber Arms, Spain, from 1976-disc.

	$310	$295	$275	$250	$200	$175	$155

MODEL 1212 WATERFOWL — 12 ga., 3 in. chamber, similar to Model 1212, 30 in. barrel.

	$320	$310	$285	$260	$210	$185	$165

H

Grading	100%	98%	95%	90%	80%	70%	60%

HARRIS GUNWORKS

Current manufacturer located in Phoenix, AZ since 1995. Previously named Harris-McMillan Gunworks and G. McMillan and Co., Inc. (please refer to the M section for more information on these two Trademarks).

RIFLES: BOLT ACTION

BENCHREST COMPETITOR — .222 Rem. (disc.), .243 Win., 6mm Rem., 6mm PPC, 6mm BR, or .308 Win. cal., benchrest configuration. New 1993.

Mfg.'s Sug. Retail	$3,050	$2,675	$2,425	$1,950	$1,675	$1,425	$1,200	$1,025

NATIONAL MATCH COMPETITOR — .308 Win., or 7mm-08 Rem. cal. New 1993.

Mfg.'s Sug. Retail	$3,500	$3,125	$2,675	$2,300	$1,875	$1,650	$1,325	$1,100

LONG RANGE TARGET MODEL — .300 Win. Mag., .300 Phoenix, .30-378 Wby. Mag., .30-416 Rigby, .338 Lapua, or 7mm Rem. Mag. cal., black synthetic fully adj. stock, w/o sights, grey barrel finish. New 1996.

Mfg.'s Sug. Retail	$3,620	$3,225	$2,700	$2,325	$1,900	$1,650	$1,325	$1,100

TALON SPORTER — available in various cals. between .22-250 Rem. and .416 Rem., receiver available in either 4340 chrome molybdenum or 17-4 stainless steel, drilled and tapped, match grade barrel. New 1992.

Mfg.'s Sug. Retail	$2,900	$2,600	$2,075	$1,725	$1,375	$1,050	$895	$800

The Talon action is patterned after the Winchester pre-64 Model 70. It features a cone breech, controlled feed, claw extractor, and 3 position safety.

SIGNATURE CLASSIC SPORTER — various cals. available between .22-250 Rem. and .416 Rem., premium wood stock, matte metal finish, buttoning used on rifling for 22 or 24 in. stainless steel barrel, McMillan action made from 4340 chrome moly steel (either left or right-handed), 3 or 4 shot mag. supplied with 5 shot test target. New 1988.

Mfg.'s Sug. Retail	$2,700	$2,450	$2,000	$1,675	$1,325	$1,000	$895	$800

SIGNATURE VARMINTER — similar to Signature Model, except is available in 12 cals. between .22-250 Rem. and .350 Rem. Mag., hand bedded fiberglass stock, adj. trigger, 26 in. heavily contoured barrel. New 1988.

Mfg.'s Sug. Retail	$2,700	$2,450	$2,000	$1,675	$1,325	$1,000	$895	$800

SIGNATURE TITANIUM MOUNTAIN RIFLE — .270 Win., .280 Rem., .30-06, .300 Win. Mag., .338 Win. Mag., or 7mm Rem. Mag. cal., lighter weight variation with shorter stainless steel or graphite/steel composite barrel, 5¾ (w/graphite barrel, or 6½ lbs. New 1990.

Mfg.'s Sug. Retail	$3,300	$2,950	$2,575	$2,300	$1,925	$1,650	$1,325	$1,100

Add $400 with graphite barrel.

SIGNATURE ALASKAN — available in many cals. between .270 Win. and .458 Win. Mag. New 1990.

Mfg.'s Sug. Retail	$3,800	$3,425	$2,725	$2,275	$1,650	$1,250	$1,125	$900

TALON SAFARI — available in many cals. between .300 Win. Mag. and .460 Wby. Mag., hand bedded fiberglass stock, 4 shot mag., 24 in. stainless steel barrel, matte black finish, 9½ lbs. New 1988.

Mfg.'s Sug. Retail	$3,900	$3,650	$2,850	$2,500	$2,150	$2,000	$1,850	$1,700

Add $300 for .300 Phoenix, .30-416 Rigby, .30-378 Wby. Mag., .338 Lapua, .335-378, .338-378, .378 Wby. Mag., .416 Wby. Mag. or Rigby, or .460 Wby. Mag. cal.

The Talon action is patterned after the Winchester pre-64 Model 70. It features a cone breech, controlled feed, claw extractor, and 3 position safety. Older Signature action rifles do not have this new Talon action.

Grading	100%	98%	95%	90%	80%	70%	60%

M-40 SNIPER RIFLE — .308 Win. cal., Remington action with McMillan match grade heavy contour barrel, fiberglass stock with recoil pad, 4 shot mag., 9 lbs. New 1990.

Mfg.'s Sug. Retail	$2,000	$1,825	$1,450	$1,125	$925	$800	$700	$600

M-86 SNIPER RIFLE — .300 Phoenix (disc. 1996), .30-06 (new 1989), .300 Win. Mag. or .308 Win. cal., fiberglass stock, variety of optical sights. New 1988.

Mfg.'s Sug. Retail	$2,700	$2,450	$2,000	$1,675	$1,325	$1,000	$895	$800

Add $300 for .300 Phoenix cal. with Harris action (disc. 1996).
Add $200 for takedown feature (mfg. 1993-96).

.300 PHOENIX — available in most popular .30 cals., special fiberglass stock with adj. cheekpiece and buttplate, right- or left-hand action, 12½ lbs. New 1997.

Mfg.'s Sug. Retail	$3,380	$3,025	$2,650	$2,325	$1,925	$1,675	$1,325	$1,100

M-87 LONG RANGE SNIPER RIFLE — .50 BMG cal., stainless steel bolt action, 29 in. barrel with muzzle brake, single shot, camo synthetic stock, accurate to 1500 meters, 21 lbs. New 1988.

Mfg.'s Sug. Retail	$3,885	$3,450	$2,800	$2,375	$2,000	$1,850	$1,700	$1,575

* M-87R — same specs. as Model 87, except has 5 shot fixed box mag. New 1990.

Mfg.'s Sug. Retail	$4,000	$3,725	$2,950	$2,550	$2,200	$2,000	$1,850	$1,700

M-88 U.S. NAVY — .50 BMG cal., reintroduced U.S. Navy Seal Team shell holder single shot action with thumb hole stock (one-piece or breakdown two-piece), 24 lbs. New 1997.

Mfg.'s Sug. Retail	$3,600	$3,250	$2,600	$2,200	$1,625	$1,250	$1,125	$900

Add $300 for two-piece breakdown stock.

M-89 SNIPER RIFLE — .308 Win. cal., 28 in. barrel with suppressor (also available without), fiberglass stock adj. for length and recoil pad, 15¼ lbs. New 1990.

Mfg.'s Sug. Retail	$3,200	$2,875	$2,525	$2,250	$1,875	$1,650	$1,325	$1,100

Add $425 for muzzle suppressor (disc. 1996).

M-92 BULL PUP — .50 BMG cal., bullpup configuration with shorter barrel. New 1993.

Mfg.'s Sug. Retail	$4,770	$4,300	$3,250	$2,750	$2,300	$2,050	$1,850	$1,700

M-93 — .50 BMG cal., similar to M-87, except has folding stock and detachable 5 or 10 shot box mag. New 1993.

Mfg.'s Sug. Retail	$4,150	$3,800	$3,250	$2,750	$2,300	$2,000	$1,850	$1,700

Add $300 for two-piece folding stock or dovetail combo. quick disassembly fixture.

M-95 TITANIUM/GRAPHITE — .50 BMG cal., features titanium alloy M-87 receiver with graphite barrel and steel liner, single shot or repeater, approx. 18 lbs. New 1997.

Mfg.'s Sug. Retail	$5,085	$4,650	$4,175	$3,475	$2,875	$2,300	$2,050	$1,850

Add $165 for fixed mag.
Add $315 for detachable mag.

M-96 SEMI-AUTO — .50 BMG cal., gas-operated with 5 shot detachable mag., carry handle scope mount, steel receiver, 30 lbs. New 1997.

Mfg.'s Sug. Retail	$6,800	$6,200	$5,625	$5,075	$4,650	$4,175	$3,475	$2,875

RIFLES SxS

BOXLOCK MODEL — various cals. from .270 Win. - .500 NE, engraved boxlock action, 3 leaf express rear sights, AAA wood, high polish barrel blue, equipped with aluminum case and chain, custom order. New 1998.

Mfg.'s Sug. Retail	$12,000	$12,000	$10,000	$8,500	$7,000	$6,000	$5,000	$4,000

Add $1,000 for quick detachable claw scope mounts.
Add $6,000 for additional set of rifle barrels.
Add $5,000 for additional set of shotgun barrels.

Grading	100%	98%	95%	90%	80%	70%	60%

SIDELOCK MODEL — various cals. from .375 H&H - .577 NE, engraved sidelock action, 3 leaf express rear sights, AAA wood, high polish barrel blue, equipped with aluminum case and chain, custom order. New 1998.

Mfg.'s Sug. Retail	$18,200	$18,200	$15,750	$12,000	$10,000	$8,500	$7,000	$6,000

> Add $1,000 for quick detachable claw scope mounts.
> Add $6,000 for additional set of rifle barrels.
> Add $5,000 for additional set of shotgun barrels.

HARTFORD ARMS & EQUIPMENT COMPANY

Previous manufacturer located in Harford, CT circa 1929-1932. Hartford Arms was the forerunner of High Standard Arms Co., who acquired them in 1932.

PISTOLS: SEMI-AUTO, RIMFIRE

HARTFORD AUTOMATIC TARGET — .22 LR cal., 10 shot, 6¾ in. barrel, blue, black rubber grips. Mfg. 1929-1930.

			$650	$575	$500	$450	$375	$300	$275

HARTFORD REPEATING PISTOL — .22 LR cal., similar in appearance to Automatic, except a hand operated repeater. Mfg. 1929-1930.

			$495	$425	$360	$310	$260	$250	$225

HARTFORD SINGLE SHOT TARGET — .22 LR cal., similar in appearance to Automatic, 6¾ in. barrel, target sights, case colored frame and slide, blue barrel, rubber or wood grips. Mfg. 1929-1930.

			$475	$390	$350	$310	$260	$250	$225

HARTMANN & WEISS

Current manufacturer established during 1965 and located in Hamburg, Germany.

Hartmann and Weiss manufactures only top quality longarms, including sidelock SxS shotguns and rifles, falling block single shot rifles (including the Heeren action), and bolt action rifles. Please contact the manufacturer directly for more information and/or a price quotation.

HASKELL MANUFACTURING

Previous manufacturer of .45 ACP cal. semi-auto pistols located in Lima, OH. Previously distributed by MKS Supply located in Mansfield, OH.

Refer to listing under Hi-Point Firearms.

HATFIELD GUN CO., INC.

Previous manufacturer located in St. Joseph, MO. The shotguns listed below were previously manufactured until 1996 by the Hatfield Gun Co., Inc. (designated Hatfield Rifle Works until 1986).

SHOTGUNS: O/U

BOXLOCK — 20 ga. only, boxlock action with satin grey finished receiver, maple stock. Mfg. 1995-96.

			$3,350	$2,950	$2,550	$2,175	$1,725	$1,450	$1,100

Last Mfg.'s Sug. Retail was $3,749.

> Add $1,425 for extra 28 ga. barrels.

SHOTGUNS: SxS

In addition to Grades I and II listed below, Hatfield also offered custom order shotguns built per individual special order - prices started at $3,000.

Grading	100%	98%	95%	90%	80%	70%	60%

GRADE I UPLANDER — 20 or 28 ga., 3 in. chambers, 26 in. IC/M, matted rib barrels, case hardened boxlock action, single trigger, ejectors, deluxe checkered straight grip maple stock and forearm, 5¾ lbs, cased. Mfg. 1987-96.

	$1,975	$1,700	$1,500	$1,325	$1,150	$900	$725

Last Mfg.'s Sug. Retail was $2,249.

Add $800 for extra 28 ga. barrels.

* *Collector's Grade I* — mfg. 1990-92.

	$1,475	$1,200	$1,000	$875	$700	$550	$475

Last Mfg.'s Sug. Retail was $1,625.

Add $400 for extra 28 ga. barrels.

GRADE II PIGEON — similar to Grade I, except has scroll engraving on top lever, sides, floor plate, and triggerguard, cased. Mfg. 1987-96.

	$2,650	$2,250	$1,825	$1,475	$1,100	$900	$775

Last Mfg.'s Sug. Retail was $2,995.

Add $995 for extra 28 ga. barrels.

* *Collector's Grade II* — mfg. 1990-92.

	$2,675	$2,000	$1,600	$1,250	$1,050	$875	$775

Last Mfg.'s Sug. Retail was $3,025.

Add $400 for extra 28 ga. barrels.

GRADE III SUPER PIGEON — includes heavy relief scroll engraving (total coverage) on frame, top lever, floor plate, and triggerguard, leather cased. Mfg. 1987-disc.

	$2,350	$1,900	$1,495	$1,200	$1,025	$900	$775

Last Mfg.'s Sug. Retail was $3,500.

Add $900 for extra 28 ga. barrels.

* *Collector's Grade III* — mfg. 1990-disc.

	$3,000	$2,500	$2,000	$1,750	$1,400	$1,175	$995

Last Mfg.'s Sug. Retail was $4,375.

Add $900 for extra 28 ga. barrels.

GRADE IV GOLDEN QUAIL — more extensive engraving including six 24 Kt. gold inlays on frame and floor plate, 2 gold barrel bands, leather cased. Mfg. 1987-disc.

	$3,995	$3,575	$2,900	$2,350	$1,900	$1,600	$1,300

Last Mfg.'s Sug. Retail was $5,500.

Add $900 for extra 28 ga. barrels.

* *Collector's Grade IV* — mfg. 1990-disc.

	$4,475	$3,900	$3,300	$2,650	$2,175	$1,800	$1,500

Last Mfg.'s Sug. Retail was $6,625.

Add $1,350 for extra 28 ga. barrels.

GRADE V WOODCOCK — previous top-of-the-line model with best quality engraving and multiple gold inlays, leather cased. Mfg. 1987-disc.

	$4,600	$4,400	$3,350	$2,700	$2,175	$1,800	$1,500

Last Mfg.'s Sug. Retail was $6,900.

Add $1,500 for extra 28 ga. barrels.

* *Collector's Grade V* — mfg. 1990-disc.

	$6,200	$5,700	$4,475	$3,900	$3,300	$2,650	$2,200

Last Mfg.'s Sug. Retail was $8,500.

Add $2,000 for extra 28 ga. barrels.

GRADE VI BLACK WIDOW — mfg. 1990-disc.

	$5,200	$4,875	$3,700	$3,000	$2,500	$2,100	$1,800

Last Mfg.'s Sug. Retail was $7,900.

GRADE VII ROYALE — mfg. 1990-disc.

	$5,200	$4,875	$3,700	$3,000	$2,500	$2,100	$1,800

Last Mfg.'s Sug. Retail was $7,900.

H

Grading	100%	98%	95%	90%	80%	70%	60%

GRADE VIII TOP HAT — top-of-the-line model with best quality wood and extensive engraving with gold inlays. Built to individual customer specifications. Mfg. 1990-disc.

| | $12,000 | $9,750 | $8,750 | $7,500 | $6,500 | $5,500 | $4,500 |

Last Mfg.'s Sug. Retail was $17,500.

SIDELOCK MODEL — 20 ga. only, satin grey finished receiver, full engraving. Mfg. 1995-96.

| | $10,750 | $8,750 | $7,500 | $6,250 | $5,000 | $4,850 | $3,600 |

Last Mfg.'s Sug. Retail was $12,000.

* *Grade II Sidelock* — features high relief full coverage engraving, color case hardened receiver, multiple gold and silver inlays.

| | $15,000 | $12,000 | $10,750 | $8,750 | $7,000 | $5,750 | $4,650 |

Last Mfg.'s Sug. Retail was $17,500.

HAWES FIREARMS

Previously manufactured by J.P. Sauer & Sohn in Eckernforde, Germany. Previously imported by Hawes Firearms in Van Nuys, CA.

Rather than give an individual listing of the various single action and double action (including Medallion models) revolvers that have been imported, a generalized price range is as follows: centerfire single actions usually are in the $130-$250 range, centerfire double actions are $175-$295, while .22 rimfire models are typically valued between $60-$140.

HECKLER & KOCH

Current manufacturer located in Oberndorf/Neckar, Germany. Currently imported and distributed by Heckler & Koch, Inc. (U.S. headquarters) located in Sterling, VA (previously located in Chantilly, VA). In early 1991, H & K was absorbed by Royal Ordnance, a division of British Aerospace located in England.

PISTOLS: SEMI-AUTO, RECENT MFG.

HK4 — .380 ACP, .32 ACP, .25 ACP, and .22 LR cals., double action auto, available with all caliber conversion units, 3⅓ in. barrel, blue, plastic grips. Disc. 1984.

	100%	98%	95%	90%	80%	70%	60%
.25 ACP or .32 ACP cal.	$295	$260	$230	$215	$180	$150	$130
.22 LR or .380 ACP cal.	$430	$345	$300	$250	$195	$160	$140

This model was also available as a H & R commemorative model with gold tone plaque on slide and came in a plastic presentation box. Add approx. 25% to .22 LR or .380 ACP cal. prices above if mint or NIB only.

* *.380 ACP with .22 LR conversion*

| | $480 | $385 | $350 | $325 | $310 | $290 | $280 |

* *.380 ACP with all conversions*

| | $590 | $475 | $450 | $420 | $390 | $375 | $360 |

This model was also mfg. in a French model in .22 LR and/or .32 ACP (about 500 imported).

P9S — .45 ACP or 9mm Para. cal., double action combat model, 4 in. barrel, phosphate finish, sculptured plastic grips, fixed sights. Although production ceased in 1984, limited quantities were available until 1989.

| | $650 | $525 | $400 | $360 | $320 | $290 | $265 |

Last Mfg.'s Sug. Retail was $1,299.

P9S TARGET — .45 ACP or 9mm Para. cal., 4 in. barrel, phosphate finish, adj. sights and trigger. Although production ceased in 1984, limited quantities were available until 1989.

| | $1,000 | $800 | $600 | $540 | $500 | $465 | $430 |

Last Mfg.'s Sug. Retail was $1,382.

Grading	100%	98%	95%	90%	80%	70%	60%

P9S COMPETITION KIT — 9mm Para. or .45 ACP (rare) cal., similar to P9S Target, except extra 5½ in. barrel and weight, competition walnut grip, 2 slides. Disc. 1984.

	$1,150	$950	$875	$800	$720	$640	$550

Last Mfg.'s Sug. Retail was $2,250.

P7 PSP — 9mm Para. cal., older variation of the P7 M8, without extended trigger guard, ambidextrous mag. release (European style), or heat shield. Standard production ceased 1986. A re-issue of this model was mfg. in 1990, with approx. 150 produced. Limited quantities still exist.

Mfg.'s Sug. Retail	$1,111	$950	$695	$550	$460	$410	$390	$370

P7 M8 — 9mm Para. cal., unique squeeze cocking single action, extended square combat type trigger guard with heat shield, 4.13 in. fixed barrel with polygonal rifling, 8 shot mag., ambidextrous mag. release, fixed 3-dot sighting system, stippled black plastic grips, black phosphate or nickel (new 1992) finish, includes 2 mags., 28 oz.

Mfg.'s Sug. Retail	$1,222	$925	$775	$675	$550	$450	$410	$390

Add $94 for Tritium sights (various colors, new 1993).
Add $566 for .22 LR conversion kit (barrel, slide, and two mags.).

P7 M13 — similar to P7 M8, only with staggered 13 shot mag., 30 oz. Disc. 1994.

	$1,100	$900	$700	$630	$580	$530	$480

Last Mfg.'s Sug. Retail was $1,330.

Add $85 for Tritium sights (various colors, new 1993).

P7 M10 — .40 S&W cal., similar specifications as P7 M13, except has 10 shot mag., 39 oz. Mfg. 1991-94.

	$975	$800	$725	$650	$600	$550	$495

Last Mfg.'s Sug. Retail was $1,315.

Add $85 for Tritium sights (various colors, new 1993).

P7 K3 — .22 LR or .380 ACP cal., uses unique oil-filled buffer to decrease recoil, 3.8 in. barrel, matte black or nickel (less common) finish, 8 shot mag. (includes 2), 26½ oz. Mfg. 1988-94.

	$840	$715	$600	$525	$450	$410	$390

Last Mfg.'s Sug. Retail was $1,100.

Add $525 for .22 LR conversion kit.
Add $228 for .32 ACP conversion kit.
Add $85 for Tritium sights (various colors, new 1993).

USP 9 — 9mm Para. cal., available in regular DA/SA mode or DA only (10 variants), 4.13 in. barrel with polygonal rifling, Browning-type action with H&K recoil reduction system, polymer frame, all metal surfaces specially treated, can be carried cocked and locked, stippled synthetic grips, bobbed hammer, 3-dot sighting system, multiple safetys, 10 (C/B 1994) or 16★ shot polymer mag., 26½ oz. New 1993.

Mfg.'s Sug. Retail	$655	$580	$485	$430	$385	$350	$325	$295

Add $21 for control lever (safety/decocking lever on right side).
Add $94 for Tritium sights (various colors, new 1993).

★ *USP 9 Stainless* — similar to USP 9, except has satin finished stainless steel slide. New 1996.

Mfg.'s Sug. Retail	$701	$610	$495	$435

Add $21 for control lever (safety/decocking lever on right side).

USP 9 COMPACT — 9mm Para. cal., compact variation of the USP 9 featuring 3.58 in. barrel, 25½ oz. New 1997.

Mfg.'s Sug. Retail	$685	$600	$495	$440	$395	$365	$330	$300

Add $21 for control lever (safety/decocking lever on right side).

★ *USP 9 Compact Stainless* — similar to USP 9 Compact, except has satin finished stainless steel slide. New 1997.

Mfg.'s Sug. Retail	$731	$630	$510	$445

Add $21 for control lever (safety/decocking lever on right side).

Grading	100%	98%	95%	90%	80%	70%	60%

USP 40 — .40 S&W cal., similar to USP 9, 9 variants of DA/SA/DAO, 10 (C/B 1994) or 13★ shot mag., 27¾ oz. New 1993.

Mfg.'s Sug. Retail	$655	$580	$485	$430	$385	$350	$325	$295

    Add $21 for control lever (safety/decocking lever on right side).
    Add $94 for Tritium sights (various colors, new 1993).

★ *USP 40 Stainless* — similar to USP 40, except has satin finished stainless steel slide. New 1996.

Mfg.'s Sug. Retail	$701	$610	$495	$435

    Add $21 for control lever (safety/decocking lever on right side).

USP 40 COMPACT — .40 S&W cal., compact variation of the USP 40 featuring 3.58 in. barrel, 27 oz. New 1997.

Mfg.'s Sug. Retail	$685	$600	$500	$440	$395	$365	$330	$300

    Add $21 for control lever (safety/decocking lever on right side).

★ *USP 40 Compact Stainless* — similar to USP 40 Compact, except has satin finished stainless steel slide. New 1997.

Mfg.'s Sug. Retail	$731	$630	$510	$445

    Add $21 for control lever (safety/decocking lever on right side).

USP 45 — .45 ACP cal., similar to USP 9, 9 variants of DA/SA/DAO, 10 (C/B 1994) or 13★ shot mag., 27¾ oz. New 1995.

Mfg.'s Sug. Retail	$717	$630	$510	$445	$385	$350	$325	$295

    Add $20 for control lever (safety/decocking lever on right side).
    Add $94 for Tritium sights (various colors, new 1993).

★ *USP 45 Stainless* — similar to USP 45, except has satin finished stainless steel slide. New 1996.

Mfg.'s Sug. Retail	$763	$675	$545	$480

    Add $21 for control lever (safety/decocking lever on right side).

★ *USP 45 Match Pistol* — .45 ACP cal., features 6.02 in. compensated barrel with polygonal rifling, micrometer adj. rear sight, barrel weight, and ambidextrous safety, choice of matte black or stainless steel slide, 38 oz. Mfg. 1997-98.

	$1,275	$1,025	$825	$750	$675	$550	$500

                                     Last Mfg.'s Sug. Retail was $1,369.

    Add $72 for stainless steel slide model.

USP EXPERT — .45 ACP cal., features new slide design with 5.2 in. barrel, match grade SA or DA trigger pull, recoil reduction system, reinforced polymer frame, adj. rear sight, approx. 30 oz. New 1999.

Mfg.'s Sug. Retail	$1,369	$1,275	$1,025	$825	$750	$675	$550	$500

USP 45 COMPACT — .45 ACP cal., compact variation of the USP 45, featuring 3.8 in. barrel, 28 oz. New 1998.

Mfg.'s Sug. Retail	$705	$620	$510	$445	$385	$350	$325	$295

    Add $21 for control lever (safety/decocking lever on right side).

★ *USP 45 Compact Stainless* — similar to USP 45 Compact, except has satin finished stainless steel slide. New 1998.

Mfg.'s Sug. Retail	$747	$660	$535	$475

    Add $20 for control lever (safety/decocking lever on right side).

USP 45 TACTICAL PISTOL — .45 ACP cal., enhanced variation of the USP 45, similar to Mark 23, except has 4.92 in. threaded barrel with rubber o ring, adj. target type sights and trigger, limited availability, 36 oz. New 1998.

Mfg.'s Sug. Retail	$965	$875	$775	$700	$625	$550	$500	$450

MARK 23 SPECIAL OPERATIONS PISTOL — .45 ACP cal., 5.87 in. barrel, polymer frame and integral grips, 3-dot sighting, 10 shot mag., squared off trigger guard, 2.6 lbs., limited availability. New 1996.

Mfg.'s Sug. Retail	$2,055	$1,825	$1,595	$1,325	$1,075	$900	$775	$650

Grading	100%	98%	95%	90%	80%	70%	60%

SP 89 — 9mm Para. cal., recoil operated delayed roller-locked bolt system, 4.5 in. barrel, 15 shot mag., adj. aperture rear sight (accepts HK claw-lock scope mounts), 4.4 lbs. Mfg. 1990-1993.

	$2,295	$2,000	$1,650	$1,300	$1,100	$975	$875

Last Mfg.'s Sug. Retail was $1,325.

Add $129 for adj. target grip.

VP 70Z — 9mm Para. cal., 18 shot, double action only, 4½ in. barrel, parkerized finish, plastic receiver/grip assembly. Disc. 1984.

	$475	$400	$325	$275	$250	$230	$210

Add 100% if frame cut for shoulder stock (Model VP 70M).

RIFLES: BOLT ACTION

BASR — .22 LR, .22-250 Rem., 6mm PPC, .300 Win. Mag., .30-06, or .308 Win. cal., Kevlar stock, stainless steel barrel, limited production. Special order only. Mfg. 1986 only.

	$5,750	$5,000	$4,500	$4,000	$3,650	$3,300	$2,600

Last Mfg.'s Sug. Retail was $2,199.

Less than 135 of this variation were manufactured and they are extremely rare. Contractual disputes with the U.S. supplier stopped H&K from receiving any BASR models.

RIFLES: SEMI-AUTO

Most of the models listed below, being of a paramilitary design, were disc. in 1989 due to Federal legislation. Sporterized variations mfg. after 1994 with thumbhole stocks were banned in April, 1998.

In 1991, the HK-91, HK-93, and HK-94 were discontinued. Last published retail prices (1991) were $999 for fixed stock models and $1,199 for retractable stock models.

In the early '70s, S.A.C.O. importers located in Virginia sold the Models 41 and 43 which were the predecessors to the Model 91 and 93, respectively. Values for these earlier variations will be higher than values listed below.

SR-9 — .308 Win. cal., semi-auto sporting rifle, 19.7 in. barrel, Kevlar reinforced fiberglass thumbhole stock and forearm, 5 shot mag., diopter adj. rear sight, accepts H&K claw-lock scope mounts. Mfg. 1990-1993.

	$1,775	$1,450	$1,150	$995	$850	$725	$650

Last Mfg.'s Sug. Retail was $1,199.

While advertised again during 1998, this model was finally banned in April, 1998.

SR-9T — .308 Win. cal., precision target rifle with adj. MSG 90 buttstock and PSG-1 trigger group, 5 shot mag. Mfg. 1992-1993.

	$2,495	$2,100	$1,800	$1,550	$1,150	$995	$850

Last Mfg.'s Sug. Retail was $1,725.

While advertised again during 1998, this model was finally banned in April, 1998.

SR-9TC — .308 Win. cal., similar to SR-9T except has PSG-1 adj. buttstock. Mfg. 1993 only.

	$2,995	$2,600	$2,300	$2,000	$1,675	$1,250	$1,050

Last Mfg.'s Sug. Retail was $1,995.

While advertised again during 1998, this model was finally banned in April, 1998.

PSG-1 — .308 Win. cal. only, high precision marksman's rifle, 5 shot mag., adj. buttstock, includes accessories and case (Hensholdt illuminated 6 x 42 power scope), 17.8 lbs. Importation disc. 1998.

	$9,950	$8,675	$7,500	$6,500	$5,500	$4,500	$3,850

Last Mfg.'s Sug. Retail was $10,811.

MODEL 41 — .308 Win. cal., predecessor to the Model 91 A-2, originally imported by Golden State Arms.

	$1,200	$1,050	$950	$850	$750	$650	$550

MODEL 91 A-2 — .308 Win. cal., semi-auto paramilitary design rifle, delayed roller lock bolt system, antennuated recoil, black cycolac stock, 17.7 in. barrel, 20 shot mag., 9.7 lbs. Importation disc. 1989.

Grading	100%	98%	95%	90%	80%	70%	60%

* *Fixed stock model*

      $1,695 $1,375 $1,150 $995 $895 $795 $695
      Last Mfg.'s Sug. Retail was $999.

    Add $200 for desert camo finish.
    Add $275 for NATO black finish.

* *Model 91 A-3* — with retractable metal stock.

      $2,150 $1,825 $1,500 $1,275 $1,075 $950 $850
      Last Mfg.'s Sug. Retail was $1,114.

    Add $775 for .22 LR conversion kit.

* *Model 91 A-2 Package* — includes A.R.M.S. mount, B-Square rings, Leupold 3x9 compact scope with matte finish. Importation disc. 1988.

      $2,450 $2,150 $1,750 $1,395 $1,175 $995 $875
      Last Mfg.'s Sug. Retail was $1,285.

    Add $300 for retractable stock.

MODEL 93 A-2 — .223 Rem. cal., smaller version of the H&K 91, 25 shot mag., 16.14 in. barrel, 8 lbs.

* *Fixed stock model*

      $1,575 $1,425 $1,200 $1,050 $925 $825 $750
      Last Mfg.'s Sug. Retail was $946.

    Add $200 for desert camo finish.
    Add $275 for NATO black finish.

* *Model 93 A-3* — with retractable metal stock.

      $1,850 $1,675 $1,450 $1,250 $1,075 $975 $850
      Last Mfg.'s Sug. Retail was $1,114.

* *Model 93 A-2 Package* — includes A.R.M.S. mount, B-Square rings, Leupold 3x9 compact scope with matte finish. Importation disc. 1988.

      $2,450 $2,150 $1,700 $1,400 $1,200 $1,050 $950
      Last Mfg.'s Sug. Retail was $1,285.

    Add $300 for retractable stock.

MODEL 94 CARBINE A-2 — 9mm Para. cal., semi-auto carbine, 16.54 in. barrel, aperture rear sight, 15 shot mag. New 1983.

* *Fixed stock model*

      $2,450 $2,150 $1,700 $1,400 $1,200 $1,050 $950
      Last Mfg.'s Sug. Retail was $946.

* *Model 94 Carbine A-3* — retractable metal stock.

      $2,750 $2,400 $2,000 $1,700 $1,475 $1,275 $1,000
      Last Mfg.'s Sug. Retail was $1,114.

* *Model 94 A-2 Package* — includes A.R.M.S. mount, B-Square rings, Leupold 3x9 compact scope with matte finish. Importation disc. 1988.

      $3,000 $2,625 $2,150 $1,900 $1,675 $1,350 $1,100
      Last Mfg.'s Sug. Retail was $1,285.

    Add $300 for retractable stock.

* *Model 94 SGI* — 9mm Para. cal., target rifle, aluminum alloy bi-pod, Leupold 6X scope, 15 or 30 shot mag. Imported 1986 only.

      $2,595 $2,250 $1,900 $1,675 $1,475 $1,275 $1,000
      Last Mfg.'s Sug. Retail was $1,340.

MODEL 270 — .22 LR cal., sporting rifle, 19.7 in. barrel with standard or polygonal rifling, 5 or 20 shot mag., high luster blue, plain walnut stock, approx. 5.7 lbs. Disc. 1985.

      $475 $400 $350 $300 $275 $250 $225
      Last Mfg.'s Sug. Retail was $200.

Grading	100%	98%	95%	90%	80%	70%	60%

MODEL 300 — .22 Mag. cal., 5 or 15 shot, polygonal rifling standard, otherwise similar to H&K 270 with checkered walnut stock. Importation disc. 1989.

| | $675 | $575 | $525 | $450 | $400 | $375 | $350 |

Last Mfg.'s Sug. Retail was $608.

Add $250-$300 for factory H&K scope mount system.

* ***Model 300 Package*** — includes A.R.M.S. mount, B-Square rings, Leupold 3x9 compact scope with matte finish. Importation disc. 1988.

| | $895 | $785 | $700 | $650 | $600 | $550 | $500 |

Last Mfg.'s Sug. Retail was $689.

MODEL 630 — .223 Rem. cal., delayed roller lock bolt system, 17.7 in. barrel, reduced recoil, checkered walnut, 4 or 10 shot mag., 7.04 lbs. Importation disc. 1986.

| | $795 | $725 | $650 | $550 | $495 | $460 | $430 |

Last Mfg.'s Sug. Retail was $784.

Add $250-$300 for factory H&K scope mount system.

The .222 Rem. cal. was also available in this model. Most were French contracts.

MODEL 770 — .308 Win. cal., 3 or 10 shot mag., 19.7 in. barrel, 7.92 lbs., otherwise similar to model 630. Importation disc. 1986.

| | $775 | $695 | $625 | $530 | $485 | $450 | $420 |

Last Mfg.'s Sug. Retail was $797.

Add $250-$300 for factory H&K scope mount system.

Significant price increases stopped the importation of this model.

Approx. 6 Model 770s were imported in .243 Win. cal. during 1984. Values for the .243 Win. cal. will be considerably higher than listed above for the .308 Win. cal.

MODEL 911 — .308 Win. cal., earlier importation. Disc.

| | $1,750 | $1,550 | $1,350 | $1,175 | $950 | $850 | $725 |

MODEL 940 — .30-06 cal., 21.6 in. barrel, 8.62 lbs., otherwise same as Model 770. Importation disc. 1986.

| | $950 | $850 | $725 | $625 | $565 | $500 | $465 |

Last Mfg.'s Sug. Retail was $917.

Add $175-$225 for factory H&K scope mount system.

Cals. 7x64mm and 9.3x62mm were also available in this model.

Significant price increases stopped the importation of this model.

* ***Model 940K***– similar to Model 940, except has 16 in. barrel and higher cheekpiece. Two imported 1984 only.

Rarity precludes accurate price evaluation.

MODELS SL6 & SL7 CARBINE — .223 Rem. or .308 Win. cal., 17.71 in. barrel, delayed roller lock bolt system, reduced recoil, vent. wood hand guard, 3 or 4 shot mag., 8.36 lbs., matte black metal finish, HK-SL6 is .223 Rem. cal., HK-SL7 is .308 Win. cal. Importation disc. in 1986.

| | $725 | $650 | $550 | $495 | $460 | $430 | $400 |

Add $250-$300 for factory H&K scope mount system.

These models are the only sporter variations H&K currently manufactures - no U.S. importation since 1986.

SHOTGUNS: SEMI-AUTO

Previously imported H&K Benelli shotguns can be found under their own heading.

MODEL 512 — 12 ga. only, mfg. by Franchi for German military contract, rifle sights, matte finished metal, walnut stock, fixed choke pattern diverter giving rectangular shot pattern. Importation disc. 1991.

| | $1,500 | $1,300 | $1,100 | $925 | $800 | $700 | $600 |

Last Mfg.'s Wholesale was $1,895.

Grading		100%	98%	95%	90%	80%	70%	60%

HELWAN

Previous trademark imported by Navy Arms Co. and Interarms until 1995.

PISTOLS: SEMI-AUTO

BRIGADIER — 9mm Para. cal., single action, 4.5 in. barrel, all steel construction, 8 shot mag. with finger extension, black plastic grips, 32.6 oz. Imported 1988-94.

			$195	$150	$125	$115	$105	$95	$85

Last Mfg.'s Sug. Retail was $260.

This model is patterned after the Beretta Model 1952. They were manufactured at the Helwan arsenal in Egypt.

HENDRY, RAMSAY & WILCOX

Current manufacturer located in Perth, Scotland.

Hendry, Ramsay & Wilcox manufactures top quality shotguns and rifles and are priced per individual quotation. Please contact the factory directly (see Trademark Index) for more information on this trademark.

HENRY REPEATING ARMS COMPANY

Current manufacturer located in Brooklyn, NY. Distributor and dealer sales.

RIFLES

HENRY LEVER ACTION — .22 LR cal., side ejection, blued steel receiver, 18¼ in. barrel, 15 shot mag. (.22 LR), deluxe American walnut stock and forearm, adj. rear sight and hooded front, 5½ lbs. New 1997.

Mfg.'s Sug. Retail	$230	$195	$175	$160	$150	$140	$130	$120

This model is also available as a Youth Model, with 13 LOP and shorter barrel.

* **Henry Carbine** — similar to Henry Lever Action, except has shorter barrel and large loop lever. New 1998.

Mfg.'s Sug. Retail	$240	$200	$180	$165	$150	$140	$130	$120

* **Henry Goldenboy Lever Action** — features brasslite receiver, buttplate, and rear sight, 20 in. octagon barrel, 16 shot mag. New mid-1999.

Mfg.'s Sug. Retail	$330	$295	$250	$210	$185	$165	$155	$140

HENRY PUMP ACTION — .22 LR cal., blued grooved receiver, 18¼ in. barrel, walnut straight grip stock and forearm, 15 shot mag., adj. rear sight, approx. 5½ lbs. New 1999.

Mfg.'s Sug. Retail	$250	$210	$185	$165	$155	$140	$130	$120

HENRY U.S. SURVIVAL .22 SEMI-AUTO — .22 LR cal., patterned after the Armalite AR-7 with improvements, takedown design enables receiver, mag., and barrel to stow in ABS plastic stock, weather resistant silver or black (new 1999) stock/metal finish, 8 shot mag., adj. sights, 16½ in. long when disassembled and stowed in stock, approx. 2½ lbs. New 1997.

Mfg.'s Sug. Retail	$165	$150	$135	$125	$115	$105	$95	$90

HENRY RIFLE

Please refer to the Winchester section in this text.

HERITAGE MANUFACTURING, INC.

Current manufacturer located in Opa Locka, FL since 1992. Dealer and distributor sales.

Heritage Manufacturing, Inc.

Grading	100%	98%	95%	90%	80%	70%	60%

PISTOLS: SEMI-AUTO

H-25S — .25 ACP cal., 6 shot mag. with finger extension, single action, exposed hammer, choice of blue or blue/gold finish, 13½ oz. New 1995.

Mfg.'s Sug. Retail	$150	$125	$95	$80	$65	$55	$50	$45

  Add $10 for nickel steel.
  Add $10 for Model H-25G (blue/gold finish with checkered grips).

STEALTH SHADOW COMPACT — 9mm Para. or .40 S&W cal., striker fire mechanism, stainless steel slide and 3.9 in. barrel, black all polymer frame, manual safety, 10 shot mag. with finger extension, fixed sights, choice of stainless slide, two-tone stainless slide, or all black finish, 20 oz. New 1996.

Mfg.'s Sug. Retail	$290	$250	$215	$185	$165	$150	$135	$110

Add $40 for .40 S&W cal.

REVOLVERS

ROUGH RIDER SAA SERIES — .22 LR or .22 LR/.22 Mag. cal. combo, SAA design with hammer block safety, blue or nickel (available in combo package only) finish, 4¾, 6½, or 9 in. barrel, smooth wood grips, approx. 33½ oz. New 1993.

Mfg.'s Sug. Retail	$120	$100	$75	$60	$50	$45	$40	$35

  Add $20 for combo package.
  Add $40 for nickel finish (combo package only).
  Add $30 for 9 in. barrel.

* ***Rough Rider SAA with Birds Head Grip*** — .22 LR/.22 Mag. cal. combo only, choice of 2¾ (disc. 1997), 3 (disc. 1994), 3¾, or 4¾ in. barrel. New 1993.

Mfg.'s Sug. Retail	$140	$115	$85	$75	$60	$50	$45	$40

  Add $20 for nickel finish.

SENTRY DA SERIES — .22 Mag. (disc. 1996), .32 Mag. (disc. 1996), .38 Spl., or 9mm Para. (disc. 1996) cal., snubnose design, with 2 or 4 (.22 LR or .38 Spl.) in. barrel, 6 (centerfire) or 8 (rimfire) shot, transfer bar safety, blue or nickel finish, black polymer grips, ramp front sight. Mfg. 1993-97.

	$110	$85	$70	$55	$50	$45	$40

Last Mfg.'s Sug. Retail was $130.

  Add $10 for nickel finish.

HEROLD RIFLE

Previously manufactured by Franz Jaeger, located in Suhl, Germany.

RIFLES: BOLT ACTION

SPORTING RIFLE — .22 Hornet cal., miniature Mauser action, 24 in. barrel, leaf sight, double set trigger, select checkered stock, imported by Daly & Stoeger, pre-WWII.

	$990	$880	$825	$770	$660	$550	$495

HERTERS

Previous importer/distributor/retailer headquartered in Waseca, MN from early 1960s - 1979.

Herters subcontracted various manufacturers (mostly European) to fabricate Powermag revolvers, U-9/J-9 rifles, and shotguns which were mostly patterned after more famous original models. Most of these copies were designed to undersell the competition at the time and while quality in most cases was quite good, consumer sales were not strong enough to continue production. While many Herters models are relatively rare, collectibility to date has been minimal. Herters model values are usually under the original trademarks from which they were derived and to date have been based more on the shooting utility than the collector potential.

Grading	100%	98%	95%	90%	80%	70%	60%

HESSE ARMS

Current manufacturer located in Inver Grove Heights, MN. Dealer and consumer sales.

RIFLES: SEMI-AUTO, RIMFIRE

H22 SERIES — .22 LR cal., stainless steel Ruger 10/22 action, various configurations and features. New 1997.

* *H22 Standard Rifle* — conventional laminate stock with cheekpiece, dovetailed heavy barrel, no sights. New 1997.

Mfg.'s Sug. Retail	$479	$450	$395	$360	$330	$300	$275	$260

* *H22 Wildcat* — features screwed in heavy barrel and laminated stock with thumbhole, no sights. New 1997.

Mfg.'s Sug. Retail	$559	$515	$450	$395	$360	$330	$300	$275

* *H22 Competition* — competition ready rifle featuring glossed finished, laminated competition thumbhole stock, threaded stainless steel barrel. New 1997.

Mfg.'s Sug. Retail	$549	$500	$450	$395	$360	$330	$300	$275

* *H22 Tigershark* — top of the line model featuring laminated free floating cutaway forearm and skeleton stock, screwed in fluted heavy barrel, match chamber, premium glass bedding. New 1997.

Mfg.'s Sug. Retail	$799	$725	$650	$575	$500	$450	$395	$360

RIFLES: SEMI-AUTO, CENTERFIRE

H

HAR-15A2 SERIES — .223 Rem. cal., AR-15 type action, various configurations, barrel lengths and options. New 1997.

* *Standard Rifle/Carbine* — features mil-spec parts, 16 (carbine) or 20 (rifle) in. heavy match grade barrel. New 1997.

Mfg.'s Sug. Retail	$729	$660	$575	$500	$450	$395	$360	$330

* *Bull Gun* — features 1 in. stainless steel barrel with special front sight base. New 1997.

Mfg.'s Sug. Retail	$779	$700	$625	$550	$495	$450	$395	$360

* *National Match* — features ½ minute match sights, CMP legal free float hand guards, match bolt carrier, adj. trigger, individually tested. New 1997.

Mfg.'s Sug. Retail	$999	$925	$800	$725	$650	$575	$500	$450

* *Omega Match* — top-of-the-line features including 1 in. stainless steel barrel, hooked style stock with pistol grip, flatop receiver, capable of ¼ in. groups. New 1997.

Mfg.'s Sug. Retail	$999	$925	$800	$725	$650	$575	$500	$450

* *High Grade* — custom built per individual order. New 1997.

Mfg.'s Sug. Retail	$1,399	$1,275	$1,050	$925	$800	$725	$650	$575

FAL/FALO SERIES — .308 Win. cal., action patterned after the F.N. FAL, various barrel lengths and configurations. New 1997.

* *FAL-H/FALO Standard Rifle* — features 24 in. barrel, synthetic stock. New 1997.

Mfg.'s Sug. Retail	$949	$875	$795	$725	$650	$575	$500	$450

* *FAL-H/FALO Congo Carbine* — features 16 in. barrel. New 1997.

Mfg.'s Sug. Retail	$999	$925	$800	$725	$650	$575	$500	$450

* *FALO Tactical* — features free floating handguard assembly, flatop receiver. New 1997.

Mfg.'s Sug. Retail	$1,149	$1,025	$925	$800	$725	$650	$575	$500

* *FAL-H/FALO High Grade* — custom built per individual order. New 1997.

Mfg.'s Sug. Retail	$1,349	$1,245	$1,025	$925	$800	$725	$650	$575

Grading	100%	98%	95%	90%	80%	70%	60%

M14H STANDARD RIFLE — .308 Win. cal., semi-auto version of the M14 rifle, choice of walnut or wrinkle coat synthetic stock, supplied with extra 10 shot mag. and original M14 stock. New 1997.

Mfg.'s Sug. Retail	$999	$925	$800	$725	$650	$575	$500	$450

Add $110 for M14HE2 variation.

* *M14H Brush Rifle* — features black synthetic stock with 18 in. barrel. New 1997.

Mfg.'s Sug. Retail	$1,059	$975	$825	$735	$650	$575	$500	$450

MODEL 47 RIFLE — 7.62x39mm cal., Kalashnikov type action, black synthetic stock, 20 in. barrel. New 1997.

Mfg.'s Sug. Retail	$599	$525	$450	$400	$360	$330	$300	$275

HEYM, GmbH & CO. JAGDWAFFEN KG.

Current manufacturer established in 1865 and located in Gleichamberg, Germany since 1996. No current U.S. importation. Previously manufactured in Muennerstadt, Germany circa 1950-1996 and Suhl, Germany between 1865-1945. Originally founded in 1865 by F.W. Heym. Previously imported by JagerSport, Ltd. located in Cranston, RI 1993-94 only. Previously imported and distributed by Heckler & Koch, Inc. (until 1993) located in Sterling, VA. Previously imported and distributed by Heym America, Inc. (subsidiary of F.W. Heym of W. Germany) located in Fort Wayne, IN.

Pre-war guns will bring a premium over values listed below.

COMBINATION GUNS

MODEL 22 S2 O/U — rifle/shotgun combination, 12, 16, or 20 ga. (3 in.), under rifle (17 cals. available), single set trigger, takedown feature (standard 1990), coin finish with engraving, 5½ lbs.

	$3,675	$3,000	$2,450	$1,875	$1,575	$1,325	$1,100

Last Mfg.'s Sug. Retail was $4,125.

Subtract $380 without engraving.

This model features a dampened rifle barrel which prevents the "climbing" of groups, thereby enhancing accuracy.

MODEL 55 BF O/U — rifle/shotgun combination, popular U.S. and European cals., shotgun barrels interchangeable in 12 (disc.), 16, or 20 ga., 25 or 28 in. barrels, boxlock, auto ejectors, silver finish, fine German engraving, folding leaf sight, checkered pistol grip stock. Extra barrels — add $3,250 for O/U rifle and $2,250 for O/U shotgun or shotgun/rifle combination.

	$6,500	$5,400	$4,950	$4,525	$3,950	$3,615	$3,210

Last Mfg.'s Sug. Retail was $7,485.

MODEL 88 BF SxS — 2 barrel set with 20 ga. barrels and an extra set of rifle barrels available in cals. .375 H&H Mag., .458 Win. Mag., .470 N.E., or .500 N.E.

	$13,100	$10,750	$9,600	$8,150	$6,900	$5,850	$4,850

Last Mfg.'s Sug. Retail was $15,060.

This model is a larger frame variation of the Model 88 B.

* *Model 88B/F Safari* — includes set of rifle and shotgun barrels, choice of .375 H&H, .458 Win. Mag., .470 NE, or .500 NE cal. and extra set of 20 ga. 3 in. chamber barrels.

	$16,150	$14,100	$11,950	$10,250	$8,950	$6,750	$5,250

Last Mfg.'s Sug. Retail was $18,530.

MODEL 88 F SxS — available in various cals. and 20 ga. with 2¾ or 3 in. chambers.

	$13,300	$11,250	$10,100	$9,400	$8,000	$6,950	$5,800

Last Mfg.'s Sug. Retail was $14,650.

Grading	100%	98%	95%	90%	80%	70%	60%

DRILLINGS

MODEL 33 BOXLOCK STANDARD — 16 or 20 ga., boxlock, Arabesque engraving, shotgun barrels over popular European cals., and .222 Rem., .243 Win., .270 Win., .308 Win., and .30-06 cal. rifle barrel, 25 in. full and mod. barrels, set trigger on rifle, checkered pistol grip stock.

$7,400 $5,950 $4,950 $4,525 $3,950 $3,615 $3,210
Last Mfg.'s Sug. Retail was $8,700.

* *Model 33 Deluxe* — same specifications as Standard Model, only hunting scene engraved.

$7,600 $6,000 $5,000 $4,600 $4,025 $3,700 $3,300
Last Mfg.'s Sug. Retail was $9,080.

MODEL 35 STANDARD — 3 barrels, (two rifle and one shotgun), choice of cals. with top barrel either 16 or 20 ga., light border engraving, 8¼ lbs.

$13,650 $11,000 $9,250 $8,000 $6,850 $5,700 $4,600
Last Mfg.'s Sug. Retail was $15,100.

Add $2,430 for hunting scene engraving.

MODEL 37 SIDELOCK STANDARD — shotgun barrels (12, 16, or 20 ga.) over rifle, detachable sidelocks, select French walnut, border engraving, 8 lbs.

$10,400 $8,800 $7,750 $6,650 $5,700 $4,900 $3,950
Last Mfg.'s Sug. Retail was $11,815.

* *Model 37 Deluxe* — similar to Model 37 Standard, except has large engraved hunting scenes.

$12,000 $9,950 $8,200 $7,475 $6,500 $5,650 $4,600
Last Mfg.'s Sug. Retail was $13,750.

MODEL 37 B STANDARD — rifle barrels over shotgun (20 ga.), sidelock, border engraved, about 8.6 lbs.

$13,250 $10,875 $9,500 $8,400 $7,550 $6,500 $5,650
Last Mfg.'s Sug. Retail was $15,065.

* *Model 37 B Deluxe* — similar to Model 37 B Standard, except has large hunting scene engraving.

$15,600 $12,750 $10,700 $9,450 $8,200 $7,050 $5,750
Last Mfg.'s Sug. Retail was $17,620.

RIFLES: BOLT ACTION

On the models listed below, the "N" suffix in the model denotes standard calibers, whereas "G" refers to Mag. cals.

MODEL SR 20N CLASSIC SPORTER — available in 18 cals., Mauser type bolt action, single trigger, French walnut, 24 in. Krupp steel barrel except Mag. (25 in.).

$1,825 $1,425 $1,100 $900 $800 $700 $600
Last Mfg.'s Sug. Retail was $2,120.

Subtract $70 without iron sights.
Add $430 for left-hand variation.
Add $115 for Mag. cals. (G suffix).

* *Model SR 20 Hunter* — similar to Model SR 20N, except has classic style fiberglass stock with either matte blue or parkerized metal finish. Imported 1988-90.

$1,500 $1,225 $1,050 $900 $800 $700 $600
Last Mfg.'s Sug. Retail was $1,750.

* *Model SR 20L* — Mannlicher style stock, European configuration, 18 in. barrel, 7 lbs.

$1,475 $1,225 $985 $895 $785 $720 $650
Last Mfg.'s Sug. Retail was $1,700.

Grading	100%	98%	95%	90%	80%	70%	60%

SR 20 TROPHY — available in all SR 20 cals., bolt action, 22 or 24 (Mag. cals. only) in. octagonal barrel, classic stock configuration with cheekpiece and recoil pad. Importation began 1989.

	$2,550	$2,100	$1,800	$1,500	$1,250	$985	$895

Last Mfg.'s Sug. Retail was $2,815.

Add $120 for Mag. cals.

This model was also available in either right hand or left-hand action.

SR 20G CLASSIC SPORTER — available in various cals., bolt action, 22 or 24 in. round barrel, steel grip cap. Importation began 1989.

	$1,875	$1,600	$1,300	$1,050	$900	$785	$720

Last Mfg.'s Sug. Retail was $2,235.

Subtract $70 without iron sights.

This model was also available in either right hand or left-hand action.

SR 20 ALPINE — available in standard cals. between .243 Win. and 9.3x62mm, mountain style rifle with Mannlicher forend and classic buttstock, supplied with mounted open sights. Importation began 1989.

	$1,900	$1,650	$1,325	$1,075	$925	$800	$750

Last Mfg.'s Sug. Retail was $2,165.

This model was also available in either right hand or left-hand action.

SR 20 MATCH — .308 Win. cal., 24 in. heavy barrel, target stock with accessory rail, large bolt handle, supplied without sights, 9 lbs. Imported 1991-94.

	$1,860	$1,600	$1,300	$1,050	$900	$785	$720

Last Mfg.'s Sug. Retail was $2,200.

SR 20 CLASSIC SAFARI — .375 H&H, .404 Jeffery (disc.), .425 Express, or .458 Win. Mag. cal., 24 in. barrel only, express rear sight and large front post sights, tight grained walnut. Imported 1989-94.

	$2,150	$1,650	$1,250	$1,050	$875	$800	$700

Last Mfg.'s Sug. Retail was $2,530.

This model was also available in either right hand or left-hand action.

EXPRESS SERIES RIFLE — .338 Lapua Mag., .375 H&H, .378 Wby. Mag., .404 rimless Jeffery (disc. 1992), .416 Rigby, .450 Ackley, .460 Wby. Mag., .500 NE (new 1994), or .500 A-Square cal., express sights, Timney single trigger. Imported 1989-94.

	$5,750	$4,500	$3,825	$3,000	$2,350	$2,000	$1,750

Last Mfg.'s Sug. Retail was $6,550.

Add $375 for muzzle brake (includes installation).
Add $555 for left-hand action (disc. 1992).

* ***.600 NE Rifle*** — .600 NE cal., 24 in. barrel, reinforced action, 2 shot mag. Imported 1991-94.

	$9,950	$8,150	$7,150	$6,000	$5,125	$4,650	$3,975

Last Mfg.'s Sug. Retail was $11,350.

RIFLES: O/U

MODEL 55 B — various cals., engraving similar to Model 55 BF. Importation disc. 1994.

	$9,250	$7,800	$7,000	$6,000	$5,150	$4,700	$4,000

Last Mfg.'s Sug. Retail was $10,800.

Add $5,715 for extra set of interchangeable barrels.

MODEL 55 BS — O/U rifle only with different caliber for each barrel, double set triggers, "Bergstutzen" design.

	$9,000	$7,750	$6,950	$5,950	$5,125	$4,650	$3,975

Last Mfg.'s Sug. Retail was $10,435.

Grading	100%	98%	95%	90%	80%	70%	60%

RIFLES: SxS

MODEL 88 B — available in various cals. up to .375 H&H, SxS double rifle, boxlock action, Krupp steel barrels, double underlocking lugs with Greener crossbolt, ejectors, checkered circassian walnut, built to customer specifications, 7½ lbs. Importation disc. 1994.

$10,750 $9,600 $8,575 $7,100 $6,125 $5,420 $4,575
Last Mfg.'s Sug. Retail was $12,500.

Add $1,950 for .375 H&H cal.

* *Model 88 BSS* — sidelock model with interceptor sears. Importation disc. 1994.

$14,350 $11,925 $10,250 $8,750 $7,425 $6,300 $5,175
Last Mfg.'s Sug. Retail was $16,600.

* *Model 88 B Safari* — available in .375 H&H, .458 Win. Mag., .470 Nitro Express, or .500 Nitro Express cal., 24 in. barrels, 9.9 lbs. Importation disc. 1994.

$14,150 $11,825 $10,000 $8,650 $7,400 $6,300 $5,175
Last Mfg.'s Sug. Retail was $16,400.

Add $5,870 for extra pair of interchangeable rifle barrels.
Add $3,150 for extra pair of interchangeable 20 ga. shotgun barrels.

RIFLES: SINGLE SHOT

MODEL HR 30N — available in many cals., Ruger No. 1 falling block action, 24 in. barrel, French walnut with Bavarian cheekpiece, round barrel, Sporter or full length carbine style French walnut stock, engraved coin finished receiver, 6.6 lbs.

$3,500 $2,975 $2,350 $1,950 $1,675 $1,350 $1,175
Last Mfg.'s Sug. Retail was $4,040.

Add $440 for Mag. cals.
Add $1,710 for Mannlicher stocked Carbine Model.
Add $850 for hunting scene engraving (minimum extra charge).

MODEL HR 38 N — available in many cals., Ruger No. 1 falling block action 24 in. barrel, octagon barrel, French walnut with Bavarian cheekpiece, Sporter or full length carbine style French walnut stock, engraved coin finished receiver, 6.6 lbs.

$4,150 $3,450 $2,875 $2,300 $1,950 $1,675 $1,350
Last Mfg.'s Sug. Retail was $4,835.

Add $235 for Mag. cals.
Add $2,400 for sideplates with engraved large game hunting scenes.

SHOTGUNS: O/U

MODEL 55 F — 16 or 20 ga., ejectors, engraved, 6.6 lbs. Importation disc. 1992.

$5,100 $4,525 $3,950 $3,615 $3,200 $2,775 $2,300
Last Mfg.'s Sug. Retail was $5,500.

MODEL 55 SS — sidelock version of Model 55 F, large engraved hunting scenes.

$4,500 $3,825 $3,300 $2,850 $2,400 $2,000 $1,700
Last Mfg.'s Sug. Retail was $4,890.

MODEL 200 — 20 ga., 3 in. chambers, boxlock action, DTs, 28 in. VR barrels, light engraving, previous importation.

$895 $795 $700 $650 $600 $550 $500

HI-POINT FIREARMS

HI-POINT FIREARMS

Current trademark distributed by MKS Supply, Inc. located in Dayton, Ohio. Dealer and distributor sales.

Prior to 1993, trademarks sold by MKS Supply, Inc. (including Beemiller, Inc., Haskell Manufacturing, Inc., Iberia Firearms, Inc., and Stallard Arms, Inc.) had their own separate manufacturers' markings. Beginning in 1993, Hi-Point Firearms eliminated these individualized markings and chose instead to have currently manufactured guns labeled Hi-Point Firearms.

H

Grading	100%	98%	95%	90%	80%	70%	60%

PISTOLS: SEMI-AUTO

MODEL CF-380 POLYMER — .380 ACP cal., single action, 3½ in. barrel, polymer frame, 3-dot adj. sights, 8 shot mag. with thumb activated release, chrome slide or two-tone black satin finish. New 1995.

Mfg.'s Sug. Retail	$100		$85	$75	$65	$55	$50	$45	$40

JS-9 — 9mm Para. cal., single action, 4½ in. barrel, thumb safety, fixed sights, 8 shot mag., non-glare military blue finish (early mfg.) or black satin finish (new 1991), copolymer synthetic grips, 39 oz. New 1990.

Mfg.'s Sug. Retail	$140		$125	$100	$85	$75	$70	$65	$60

Add $10 for nickel finish (disc.).

This model is manufactured by Beemiller, Inc. located in Mansfield, OH.

* JS-9 Compact (Model C-9) — compact variation of the Model JS-9 with 3½ in. barrel and 8 shot mag., choice of alloy or polymer (new 1994, various slide/frame finishes) frame, 3-dot or adj. sights, 32 (polymer) or 29 oz. New 1993.

Mfg.'s Sug. Retail	$125		$100	$85	$75	$70	$65	$60	$55

Add $8 for adj. sights (disc.).

This model is manufactured by Beemiller, Inc. located in Mansfield, OH.

* JS-9 Comp — features 4 in. barrel with compensator, with (new 1999) or w/o laser sight package, adj. sights, 10 shot mag. New 1998.

Mfg.'s Sug. Retail	$150		$130	$105	$85	$75	$70	$65	$60

Add $35 for laser sights.

JS-40/JC-40 — .40 S&W cal., single action, black finish, 4¾ in. barrel, adj. sights, 8 shot mag., 39 oz. New 1992.

Mfg.'s Sug. Retail	$149		$135	$110	$100	$90	$80	$75	$70

Add $7 for nickel finish (disc. 1994).

This model is manufactured by Iberia Firearms, Inc. located in Iberia, OH.

JS-45/JH-45 — .45 ACP cal., single action, similar to JS-9, except has 7 shot mag. and 4½ in. barrel, adj. sights, 39 oz. New 1991.

Mfg.'s Sug. Retail	$149		$135	$110	$100	$90	$80	$75	$70

Add $10 for nickel finish (disc. 1994).

This model is manufactured by Haskell Mfg., Inc. located in Lima, OH.

RIFLES: SEMI-AUTO, CARBINES

MODEL 995 — 9mm Para. or .40 S&W (new 1999) cal., 16½ in. barrel, one-piece black polymer stock features pistol grip, 10 shot mag., aperture rear sight, parkerized or chrome finish. New 1996.

Mfg.'s Sug. Retail	$189		$160	$130	$110	$95	$85	$75	$70

Add $20 for .40 S&W cal.
Add $36 for detachable compensator, laser, and mount (new 1999).

HIGGINS, J.C.

Previous trademark used on Sears & Roebuck rifles and shotguns manufactured between 1946-1962.

The J.C. Higgins trademark has appeared literally on hundreds of various models (shotguns and rifles) sold through the Sears & Roebuck retail network. Most of these models were manufactured through subcontracts with both domestic and international firearms manufacturers. Typically, they were "spec." guns made to sell at a specific price to undersell the competition. Most of these models were derivatives of existing factory models (i.e., Browning, High Standard, Marlin, Mossberg, Savage, Stevens, Winchester, etc.) with less expensive wood and perhaps missing the features found on those models from which they were derived.

Grading	100%	98%	95%	90%	80%	70%	60%

To date, there has been minimal interest in collecting J.C. Higgins guns, regardless of rarity. Rather than list J.C. Higgins models, a general guideline is that values generally are under the models of their "1st generation relatives" (listed above). The Ranger trademark was also used by Sears & Roebuck - it is not any more desirable than those guns marked J.C. Higgins. As a result, prices are ascertained by the shooting value of the gun, rather than its collector value.

For converting J.C. Higgins models to the sub-contracted manufacturers, please refer to the Store Brand Crossover List after the Serialization section.

HIGH STANDARD

Previous manufacturer located in Hamden, Hartford, and East Hartford, CT. High Standard Mfg. Co. was founded in 1926. They purchased Hartford Arms and Equipment Co. in 1932. The original plant was located in New Haven, CT from 1932-1952 until they moved to a larger facility at Hamden, CT from 1951-1976. High Standard also  operated another Hamden, CT plant between 1940-1949. In 1968 the company was sold to the Leisure Group, Inc. A final move was made to East Hartford, CT in 1977 where they remained until the doors were closed in January, 1984.

High Standard values have risen dramatically over the past several years. Many collectors have realized the rarity and quality factors this trademark has earned (Models C, A, D, E, H-D, H-E, H-A, H-B First Model, G-380, GB, GD, GE, GO - 13 different variations had a total production of less than 43,000 pistols). For these reasons, top condition High Standard pistols are getting more difficult to find each year.

Note: catalog numbers were not always consistent with design series, and in 1966-1967 changed with accessories offered, but not design series.

The approx. ser. number cut-off for New Haven, CT marked guns is 43X,XXX.

The approx. ser. number cut-off for Hamden, CT manufacture is 44X,XXX - 2,495,000 and G or ML 010000 - G or ML 25,000.

The approx. ser. number range for E. Hartford, CT manufacture is ML 25,000 - ML 87,000 and SH 10,000 and SH 35,000.

COMMEMORATIVES, SPECIAL EDITIONS, & LIMITED MFG.

GRISWOLD & GUNNISON — copy of Confederate Revolver, 7½ in. barrel, 500 mfg. in 1974.

$250 $195 $150

Last Mfg.'s Sug. Retail was $175.

LEECH & RIGDON — black powder commemorative, 500 mfg. in 1974.

$250 $195 $150

Last Mfg.'s Sug. Retail was $175.

PRESIDENTIAL DERRINGER — limited mfg. in 1974-77. Cased.

$500 $400 $295

Last Mfg.'s Sug. Retail was $150.

SCHNEIDER & GLASSICK — 1,000 mfg. in 1975 only.

$325 $250 $175

Last Mfg.'s Sug. Retail was $325.

CRUSADER 50TH ANNIVERSARY — .44 Mag. or .45 LC cal., approx. 50 mfg. for each cal. in 8⅜ in. barrel with ⅓ coverage engraving (ser. no. 1-50). Also, advertising materials at the time listed 450 revolvers of each cal. in a 6 in. barrel (ser. no. 51-500). Cased. Mfg. in 1977 only.

Standard Model w/o engraving $1,550 $1,250 $975

Limited availability might affect asking prices considerably. Two gun sets with matching serial numbers were also available - current asking prices are over $3,250.

Grading	100%	98%	95%	90%	80%	70%	60%

BICENTENNIAL BLACK POWDER — .36 cal., 1776-1976 bicentennial edition with belt buckle. Cased.

	$525	$395	$300				

DERRINGERS

FIRST MODEL — .22 S, L, or LR, or .22 WMR cal., double action only O/U, 2 shot, 3½ in. barrels, blue or nickel. Black or white grips. D-100, D-101, DM-101 appears on left side of gun. The first derringer was mfg. about 1962 in Hamden, CT.

	$225	$195	$175	$145	$125	$100	$90

Add $30 for nickel finish.

LATE MODELS — .22 S, L, or LR, or .22 WMR cal., double action only O/U, 3½ in. barrels, 2 shot, blue or nickel, plastic grips. Mfg. in E. Hartford 1978-84.

* **Blue Finish** — .22 LR or .22 Mag. cal. This model was designated #9193 and #9194 when in mfg.

	$225	$195	$175	$145	$125	$100	$90

* **Nickel Finish** — .22 Mag.

	$250	$220	$195	$170	$140	$110	$100

* **Electroless Nickel** — included walnut grips. This model was designated #9420-21.

	$300	$250	$200

* **Silver plated** — includes presentation case. 500 mfg. This model was designated #9341. Ser. no. has "SP" prefix.

	$550	$495	$350

* **Gold plated** — introduced in 1965. Includes presentation case. This model was designated #9195 Ser. No. has "GP" prefix. Mfg. 1964-65.

	$500	$450	$350

Add 120% for a cased, matched set with consecutive serial numbers (mfg. 1965 only).

PISTOLS: SEMI-AUTO, RIMFIRE

Pre-war High Standard Semi-Automatic pistols had 3 different takedown types.

TYPE I-A MFG. 1932-38. Takedown lever on left side of frame next to safety. Round retracting rod on rear of slide. This takedown was used on Models B & C.

TYPE I-B MFG. 1938. Similar to I-A Type except has strengthened rectangular rod on rear of slide.

TYPE II MFG. 1939. Takedown lever located on right side of frame. Round pick-up rod on top of slide.

As a final note on High Standard pistols, original factory boxes have become very desirable. Prices can range from $75-$100 for a good condition Model 106 or 107 factory box to over $150 for an older box of a desirable model.

HAMMERLESS FIXED BARREL SERIES

This series consists of the 5 original pistols mfg. in 1932-1942. All serial numbers are located on forestrap of frame. This series is also sometimes referred to as the "Letter Models".

MODEL B — .22 LR cal., original High Standard pistol, basically the same gun as Hartford Arms 1925 Automatic, small frame, 4½ or 6¾ in. light weight barrel, fixed Patridge type front and rear sights, checkered hard rubber grips with or without H.S. monogram, 10 shot mag. Beginning ser. no. 5,000. Approx. 65,000 mfg. 1932-42.

	$675	$575	$450	$325	$250	$200	$150

Add $75 for I-B Type takedown.

Less than 14,000 pistols with this takedown were mfg.

H

Grading	100%	98%	95%	90%	80%	70%	60%

MODEL S — .22 LR cal., chambered for .22 LR shot shell cartridge, essentially a Model B with a 6¾ in. smooth bore barrel only without choke, left side of slide is stamped "HI-STANDARD MODEL S .22 LR SHOT ONLY", this variation was never a production model with approx. 5-10 guns mfg. total, 10 shot mag., a second variation using Model C slides was called the Model C/S - also not a production model with approx. 5 mfg. Mfg. 1939 only.

Because of the extreme rarity factory of this model, a specimen in almost any condition will bring $3,000 - $5,000. This model was used primarily for pest control.

MODEL C — .22 Short cal.only, identical to Model B in appearance, small frame, 4½ or 6¾ in. light weight barrel, fixed rear sight, checkered hard rubber grips with or without H.S. monogram, this action was adapted for the decreased power of the .22 Short cartridge. Beginning ser. no. 500 to 31XX, later beginning ser. no. 42XXX. Approx. 4,700 mfg. 1936-42.

	100%	98%	95%	90%	80%	70%	60%
	$950	$795	$625	$375	$275	$230	$200

Add $100 for I-A takedown.
Add $250 for I-B takedown.

This model was used primarily for plinking and gallery shooting. The Model C was made in all 3 variations of takedowns - I-A, I-B, and Type 2 (but less than 100 were mfg. in I-B).

MODEL A — .22 LR cal., similar to Model B, except enlarged frame, squared-off butt, 4½ or 6¾ in. light weight barrel, adj. rear sight, checkered walnut grips, automatic slide lock, trigger stop, 10 shot mag. Beginning ser. no. 33XXX. Approx. 7,300 mfg. 1938-42.

	100%	98%	95%	90%	80%	70%	60%
	$850	$695	$550	$360	$260	$220	$200

Add $250 for I-B takedown.

MODEL D — .22 LR cal., identical to Model A except 4½ or 6¾ in. medium weight barrel, adj. sights, walnut grips, slide lock trigger stop, 10 shot mag. Beginning ser. no. 33XXX. Approx. 2,500 mfg. 1938-42.

	100%	98%	95%	90%	80%	70%	60%
	$950	$775	$625	$400	$300	$250	$215

Add $250 for I-B takedown.

MODEL E — .22 LR cal., high quality, deluxe model of the hammerless series, adj. sight, 4½ or 6¾ in. heavy bull barrel, checkered walnut target grips with thumbrest, automatic slide lock, 10 shot mag. Beginning ser. no. 34XXX. Approx. 2,600 mfg. 1938-42.

	100%	98%	95%	90%	80%	70%	60%
	$1,275	$1,045	$875	$575	$440	$360	$300

Add $250 for I-B takedown.

EXPOSED HAMMER - FIXED BARREL SERIES

This series consists of 4 pistols that were introduced in 1940. Frame and slide modified to accommodate external hammer. All ser. numbers located on forestrap of frame. Prefix "H" added to standard model designation with the exception of Model C. Mfg. 1940-42. This series has very low production numbers. May also be referred to as the "Hammer Letter Models".

MODEL H-D — .22 LR cal., first exposed hammer model, similar to Model D, 4½ or 6¾ in. medium weight barrel, adj. sight, target or standard walnut grips, no external safety, 10 shot mag. High quality pistol. Beginning ser. no. 45,463. Approx. 2,000 mfg. 1940-42.

	100%	98%	95%	90%	80%	70%	60%
	$1,650	$1,395	$1,295	$900	$695	$565	$475

This variation is infrequently encountered.

MODEL H-E — .22 LR cal., high quality, deluxe model of exposed hammer series, 4½ or 6¾ in. heavy barrel, adj. sight, deluxe hand checkered walnut grips with thumbrests, no external safety, 10 shot mag. Rarest of the H.S. pistols. Beginning ser. no. 51,802. Approx 1,000 mfg. 1941-42.

	100%	98%	95%	90%	80%	70%	60%
	$2,275	$1,875	$1,450	$950	$725	$600	$500

H

Grading	100%	98%	95%	90%	80%	70%	60%

MODEL H-A — .22 LR cal., similar to Model A, 4½ or 6¾ in. light weight barrel, adj. sight, plain checkered walnut grips, no external safety, 10 shot mag. Very rare gun. Beginning ser. no. 53,176. Approx. 1,000 mfg. 1940-42.

	$1,050	$895	$750	$475	$365	$295	$250

MODEL H-B — .22 LR cal., duplicate of Model B with external hammer, 4½ or 6¾ in. light weight barrel, fixed sight, checkered hard rubber grips with or without H.S. monogram, no external safety, 10 shot mag. This first Model H-B had beginning ser. no. 52,405. Approx. 2,200 mfg. 1940-42.

	$850	$695	$525	$355	$275	$235	$200

* *Model H-B Second Model* — H.S. reintroduced a H-B second model similar to first model, except with external safety. Beginning ser. no. 308XXX. Approx. 25,000 mfg. 1949-1954.

	$750	$595	$435	$310	$235	$200	$170

U.S. MILITARY SERIES

These models are earlier H.S. pistols adapted as training guns during WWII. They were the sole suppliers of the .22 cal. pistol for military training. Ser. numbers located on forestrap of frame.

MODEL B-US — .22 LR cal., adapted Model B with minor changes, available in 4½ in. barrel only, checkered hard rubber grips, fixed sight, marked "Property of U.S." on right side of frame and on top of barrel. Ordnance acceptance crossed cannon stamped on right side of frame above trigger guard, 10 shot mag. Beginning ser. no. 95XXX. Approx. 14,000 mfg. 1942-43.

	$875	$725	$575	$350	$275	$235	$195

MODEL USA-HD — .22 LR cal., this model was developed because the government needed a training pistol similar to the Colt Model 1911 .45 ACP, the result was a Model HD with external safety and fixed sight, 4½ in. medium weight barrel, barrel is marked "Property of USA", black checkered hard rubber grips. First models mfg. had high gloss blue finish, changed to a Parkerized finish near ser. no. 130XXX. Beginning ser. no. 109XXX-153XXX. Approx. 44,000 mfg. 1943-46.

	$775	$625	$525	$320	$250	$200	$170

Add 20% for early blue finish.

MODEL USA-HD-MS — .22 LR cal., variation of the Model USA-HD with attached silencer, mfg. for U.S. Government covert operations, original ownership required NFA transfer, approx. 2,000 mfg.

	$3,850	$3,350	$2,900	$2,500	$2,250	$1,995	$1,750

MODEL H-D MILITARY — .22 LR cal., though called H-D Military, this model was not mfg. for the government, essentially a USA-HD with the addition of adj. sights, 4½ or 6¾ in. barrel, checkered walnut grips, external safety, 10 shot mag. Beginning ser. no. 147XXX. Approx. 150,000 mfg. 1946-55.

	$695	$595	$425	$295	$225	$190	$160

Add 20% for all-blue finish.

MODEL G-380 CENTERFIRE — .380 ACP cal., this is H.S.'s only in-house production of a center-fire pistol, transition model to the G-series using a lever takedown, has exposed hammer, fixed sights, checkered black plastic grips, external safety, 5 in. barrel only, 6 shot mag. Beginning ser. no. 100. Approx. 7,400 mfg. 1947-50.

	$650	$550	$525	$325	$245	$210	$180

THE G-SERIES

This series is hammerless with interchangeable target barrel, 6¾ in. and plinking barrel, 4½ in., consists of 4 pistols, all using lever takedown. An adaptation of the G-380 design. Ser. numbers on right side of slide and rear right side of frame. Mfg. 1949-50.

Grading	100%	98%	95%	90%	80%	70%	60%

MODEL GB — .22 LR cal., similar to Model B with light barrel, small frame, external safety, fixed sight, checkered brown plastic grips, interchangeable 4½ or 6¾ in. barrel with lever takedown, 10 shot mag. Beginning ser. no. 311XXX. Approx. 4,900 mfg. 1949-50.

| | $650 | $550 | $450 | $295 | $225 | $185 | $155 |

> Add 15-20% for both barrels.

MODEL GD — .22 LR cal., large frame with medium weight with interchangeable 4½ or 6¾ in. barrel with lever takedown, featured new adj. "Davis" sight, named for designer G.F. Davis. Grips avail. in plain checkered walnut or deluxe with thumbrest grips, 10 shot mag. Beginning ser. no. 311XXX. Approx. 3,300 mfg. 1949-50.

| | $925 | $795 | $625 | $385 | $295 | $245 | $205 |

> Add 15-20% for both barrels.
>
> This sight is adjustable for both windage and elevation.

MODEL GE — .22 LR cal., deluxe top-of-the-line quality .22 LR pistol, large frame with interchangeable 4½ or 6¾ in. heavy "bull" barrel with lever takedown, "Davis" adj. sight, deluxe walnut hand checkered grips with thumbrest, 10 shot mag. Beginning ser. no. 312XXX. Approx. 2,900 mfg. 1949-50.

| | $1,345 | $1,150 | $875 | $555 | $425 | $360 | $300 |

> Add 15-20% for both barrels.

MODEL G-O — .22 Short cal. cal., adaptation of Model GE in .22 Short cal., also known as First Model Olympic. First fired in Olympic competition in 1948. Deluxe top-of-the-line quality, interchangeable 4½ or 6¾ in. heavy "bull" barrel with lever takedown, "Davis" adj. sight, deluxe hand checkered walnut grips with thumbrests. First High Standard large production gun with aluminum slide. Has unique curved magazine, flat milled surface on top of barrel. Rare. Beginning ser. no. 307XXX. Approx. 1,200 mfg. 1949-50.

| | $1,595 | $1,350 | $1,050 | $625 | $475 | $395 | $345 |

> Add 15-20% for both barrels.
>
> This model has a grooved fore and rear strap.

THE SUPERMATIC SERIES

All of this series were mfg. at the New Haven, CT plant from 1951-53. Consisted of 4 guns, featuring the lever takedown introduced in the G-Series. Hammerless, new positive lock safety, use of one screw to attach grips, no production figures available. Approximate serial range of this series is 340,000- 440,000.

SPORT-KING (FIRST MODEL) — .22 LR cal., 10 shot mag., similar to Field-King but has fixed sight and lightweight interchangeable 4½ or 6¾ in. barrel featuring lever takedown.

| | $525 | $450 | $310 | $225 | $175 | $145 | $125 |

> Add 10-15% for extra barrel.
> Add $50 w/o slide lock.
>
> This model was available with or without slide lock.
>
> The High Standard catalog number for this model was 9080-81, while both barrels were numbered 9082.

FIELD-KING (FIRST MODEL) — .22 LR cal., plain version of Supermatic, 10 shot mag., interchangeable 4½ or 6¾ in. barrels with lever takedown, "Davis" adj. sight, 10 shot mag.

| | $775 | $650 | $495 | $340 | $260 | $210 | $175 |

> Add 10-15% for both barrels.
>
> The High Standard catalog number for this model was 9090-91, while both barrels were numbered 9092.

Grading	100%	98%	95%	90%	80%	70%	60%

SUPERMATIC (FIRST MODEL) — .22 LR cal., 10 shot mag., 4½ or 6¾ in. interchangeable barrel with lever takedown, "Davis" adj. sight, slide lock, front and back straps grooved, serrated rib between front and rear sight, adj. 2 oz. and 3 oz. weights which dovetail into and beneath barrel.

	$895	$750	$575	$370	$280	$225	$195

Add 15-20% for both barrels.

The High Standard catalog numbers for this model were 9070-71, while both barrels were numbered 9072.

OLYMPIC (SECOND MODEL) — .22 Short cal., identical in all respects to the Supermatic, except has aluminum slide for rapid recoil, interchangeable 4½ or 6¾ in. barrel with lever takedown, "Davis" adj. sight, adj. 2 oz. and 3 oz. weights, 10 shot mag.

	$1,175	$950	$775	$485	$375	$315	$265

Add 15-20% for both barrels.

The High Standard catalog numbers for this model were 9043-44, while both barrels were numbered 9045.

QUICK CHANGE CONVERSION KIT — avail. in 1951 to let you shoot both .22 LR or .22 Short in the Supermatic, Olympic, or Field-King models. Featured factory fitted barrel, slide, barrel weights and magazine.

	$550	$450	$350

This kit featured all components fitted neatly into a small maroon and yellow box.

Cat.# 9150 Supermatic/Field King to 22 short, 4½ Bbl.

Cat.# 9151 Supermatic/Field King to 22 short, 6¾ Bbl.

Cat.# 9152 Olympic to Supermatic 22 L.R., 4½ Bbl.

Cat.# 9153 Olympic to Supermatic 22 L.R., 6¾ Bbl.

Cat.# 9154 Olympic to Field King 22 L.R., 4½ Bbl.

Cat.# 9155 Olympic to Field King 22 L.R., 6¾ Bbl.

THE M-100 AND M-101 SERIES

All of this series were mfg. at the Hamden, CT plant from 1954-57. Hammerless design consisting of 5 pistols featuring a new push-button type takedown. The beginning ser. no. for .22 LR pistols only in this series was 443,611. This series featured slanted plastic grips as standard issue. The serial range for this series was 443,XXX-770,XXX. Conversion unit factory nomenclature for this series is as follows:

Cat.# 9150 Supermatic/Field King to 22 short, 4½ Bbl.

Cat.# 9151 Supermatic/Field King to 22 short, 6¾ Bbl.

Cat.# 9152 Olympic to Supermatic 22 L.R., 4½ Bbl.

Cat.# 9153 Olympic to Supermatic 22 L.R., 6¾ Bbl.

Cat.# 9154 Olympic to Field King 22 L.R., 4½ Bbl.

Cat.# 9155 Olympic to Field King 22 L.R., 6¾ Bbl.

M-100/M-101 Conversion unit pricing is similar to the M-102, M-103, and M-104 Conversion units (please refer to that section).

H

Grading	100%	98%	95%	90%	80%	70%	60%

DURA-MATIC — .22 LR cal., 4½ or 6¾ in. barrels, fixed sight, oversized plastic grips. M-100 or M-101 stamped on right side of slide. Mfg. 1954-70. The Duramatic was sold by Sears Roebuck & Co. as the J. C. Higgins Model 80. This Sears variation had some minor exterior differences, but mechanically it was the same. Unique thumb screw takedown, push-button mag. release and oversized trigger guard.

| | **$365** | **$295** | **$225** | **$160** | **$125** | **$105** | **$90** |

Add 20% for extra barrel.
Add 10% for M-100 (has push button to release thumb screw).

The High Standard catalog number for this model was 9124-25, while both barrels were numbered 9126.

SPORT-KING (SECOND MODEL) — .22 LR cal., SK 100 or SK 101 (questions remain about this configuration) stamped on right side of slide, similar to Flite-King but with steel slide and frame, front and rear grip straps on this model are smooth. This model was also avail. in nickel. Fixed rear sight.

| | **$450** | **$375** | **$260** | **$185** | **$140** | **$120** | **$100** |

Add 15-20% for both barrels.
Add 20% for nickel finish.

The High Standard catalog number for this model was 9100-01, while both barrels were numbered 9102.

SPORT-KING LIGHTWEIGHT — .22 LR cal., similar to standard Sport-King, except has forged aluminum alloy frame. The word "Lightweight" is inscribed in script on the left side of frame. Also avail. in nickel. Mfg. 1956-64.

| | **$530** | **$450** | **$315** | **$225** | **$175** | **$150** | **$125** |

Add 20% for nickel finish (H.S. number 9166-67, both barrels - 9168).
Add 15 - 20% for both barrels.

The High Standard catalog number for this model was 9156-57, while both barrels were numbered 9158.

FLITE-KING (FIRST MODEL) — .22 Short cal., LW 100 or LW 101 (questions remain about this configuration) stamped on right side of slide, 10 shot mag., 4½ or 6¾ in. interchangeable light weight barrel with push-button takedown, alloy slide, front and rear grip straps on this model are smooth. First commercial use of aluminum alloy for frame. Fixed rear sight. Mfg. until 1960.

| | **$600** | **$495** | **$380** | **$275** | **$210** | **$175** | **$150** |

Add 15-20% for both barrels.

The High Standard catalog number for this model was 9103-04, while both barrels were numbered 9105.

FIELD-KING (SECOND MODEL) — .22 LR cal., FK 100 or FK 101 stamped on right side of slide, 10 shot mag. 4½ or 6¾ in. interchangeable barrel with push-button takedown, front and rear grip straps on this model are smooth. Slotted stabilizer 6¾ in. target barrel was an option. Adj. rear sight.

| | **$750** | **$615** | **$475** | **$345** | **$265** | **$215** | **$180** |

Add $75 for Models marked FK100.

The High Standard catalog number for this model was 9115-16, while both barrels were numbered 9117.

SUPERMATIC (SECOND MODEL) — .22 LR cal., S 100 or S 101 stamped on right side of slide, 10 shot mag., 4½ or 6¾ in. interchangeable barrel with push-button takedown, adj. 2 oz. or 3 oz. weights. Integral slotted stabilizer with 6¾ in. target barrel was an option. Adj. rear sight.

| | **$850** | **$695** | **$475** | **$350** | **$275** | **$230** | **$195** |

The High Standard catalog number for this model was 9118-19, while both barrels were numbered 9120.

Grading	100%	98%	95%	90%	80%	70%	60%

OLYMPIC (THIRD MODEL) — .22 Short cal., 0-100 or 0-101 stamped on right side of alloy slide, 10 shot mag., $4\frac{1}{2}$ or $6\frac{3}{4}$ in. interchangeable barrel with push-button takedown,adj. 2 oz. or 3 oz. weights. Integral slotted stabilizer $6\frac{3}{4}$ in. target barrel was an option. Adj. rear sight.

$1,025 **$825** **$650** **$425** **$325** **$275** **$235**

    The High Standard catalog number for this model was 9121-22, while both barrels were numbered 9123.

MODEL 102 AND 103 SERIES

    This series included the following and were mfg. in Hamden, CT. The words "Model 102" or "Model 103" and the serial number were inscribed on the right side of slide, and the serial number was duplicated on the right side of the new and longer frame. A new and larger push-button takedown enabling easier use was another improvement. A grooved and wider trigger in addition to a new rear sight were also added on the target models. The 102 Series was mfg. from 1957-1960 and the serial range was approx. 770,XXX-1,100,XXX. The 103 Series was mfg. between 1960-1963 and the approximate serial range was 1,100,XXX-1,330,XXX. Plastic grips were standard and checkered walnut grips with thumbrest were optional.

    Original cased 102/103 Series Trophy, Olympic Trophy, Olympic Citation models, and Special Presentation combinations in 98%+ condition are currently bringing premiums with asking prices in the $1,700-$2,000 range.

SPORT-KING — .22 LR cal., similar to the Series 100/101, but stamped Model 102 or Model 103, nickel finish on the Lighweight Sport King only was available (disc. 1960), the Lightweight Sport King was still available but was disc. in 1964, this basic Sport-King was mfg. from 1958-77.

$395 **$325** **$230** **$165** **$125** **$100** **$85**

    Add 50% for nickel finish on Sport King Lightweight only (catalog nos. 9166-9167, both barrels 9168).

    Add 25% for Sport King Lightweight (catalog nos. 9156-9156, both barrels 9158).

    Add 20% for 102 Models.

    The High Standard catalog number for this model was 9200-9201, while both barrels - (102 only) were numbered 9202.

FLITE-KING — .22 LR cal., similar to Series 100/101, this variation of the Flite-King featured an all steel frame with an alloy slide. Mfg. 1958-1965.

$550 **$450** **$345** **$265** **$215** **$175** **$150**

    Add 10% for 102 Models.

    The High Standard catalog number for this model was 9220-21, while both barrels (102 only) were numbered 9222.

SUPERMATIC TOURNAMENT — .22 LR cal., 10 shot, $4\frac{1}{2}$, $5\frac{1}{2}$ bull (avail. 1963), or $6\frac{3}{4}$ in. straight barrel, brown diamond checkered plastic slant grips, adj. sight, push-button takedown, this model featured smooth front and back grip straps. The govt. ordered a quantity of Mod. 102 Tournament for training. These were marked "US" on right side of frame. Mfg. 1958-1965.

$750 **$615** **$475** **$345** **$265** **$220** **$185**

    The High Standard catalog number for this model was 9270-71, while both barrels were numbered 9272.

    103 series pistols were numbered 9271-9275, ($5\frac{1}{2}$).

SHARPSHOOTER — .22 LR cal., 10 shot, $5\frac{1}{2}$ in. bull barrel. Introduced 1969.

$650 **$535** **$415** **$300** **$230** **$190** **$160**

    Add $100 for Sport King frame.

    The High Standard catalog no. was 9205. First Models used a Sport King frame - Model 103 only.

H

Grading	100%	98%	95%	90%	80%	70%	60%

SUPERMATIC CITATION — .22 LR cal., 10 shot, 6¾, 8, and 10 in. tapered barrels, diamond checkered plastic slant grips, adj. sight, push-button takedown, one grade above Tournament, grooved front and back grip straps, adj. sight located on 8 and 10 in. barrel (a 5½ in. target bull barrel became avail. in 1962), detachable stabilizer and 2 or 3 oz. barrel weights available. Mfg. 1958-65.

	$925	$760	$530	$380	$290	$245	$210

Add $125 for 8 in. barrel.
Add $225 for 10 in. barrel.

The High Standard catalog number for this model was 9260-61-62. 8 in. and 10 in. barrel set, 9262-8, 5½ bull barrel, 103 only - 9263. The govt. ordered a quantity of Mod. 102 Citations for training and are marked "U.S." on left side of frame.

SUPERMATIC TROPHY — .22 LR cal., 10 shot, 6¾ in., 8 in. and 10 in. tapered barrels, 5½ bull and 7¼ in. fluted barrels became avail. in 1962, detachable barrel weights and stabilizer were also available, walnut checkered grips. Features gold trigger, gold safety button and gold inlaid lettering, adj. sight and push-button takedown. Mfg. 1958-63.

	$1,150	$950	$725	$525	$400	$325	$275

Add $150 for 8 in. barrel.
Add $250 for 10 in. barrel.

This variation was High Standard's Top-of-the-Line Target pistol.

The High Standard catalog number for this model was 9250-51-52. 8 in. and 10 in. barrel set, 9252-8, 5½ bull barrel (103 only) - 9254, 7¼ fluted barrel (103 only) - 9255.

ISU OLYMPIC — .22 Short cal., this is the model used to win the 33rd Gold Medal in the Rome Olympics in 1960. 10 shot, 6¾ in. barrel with integral stabilizer, checkered walnut grips, high luster finish, alloy slide. Top-of-the-line Olympic model. Complies with all rapid-fire International Shooting Union regulations. Mfg. 1961-66.

	$1,150	$925	$675	$430	$330	$280	$240

Add $1,000 for Model 9289 marked "Olympic Trophy" if in 98% or better condition.

The High Standard catalog number for this model was 9289-9299, 9289 (103 only).

OLYMPIC — .22 Short cal., same basic gun as Citation but is of lesser quality finish. Adj. sight located on 8 in. barrel. Mfg. 1958-65.

	$1,075	$895	$625	$395	$315	$265	$225

Add $350 for Model 9280-81-82 marked "OLYMPIC CITATION".
Add $150 for 8 in. barrel.
Add $250 for 10 in. barrel.

This model has also been observed with markings "OLYMPIC CITATION". Numbering was 9280-81-82, 8 in. and 10 in. barrel set 9282-8, 5½ bull barrel (Model 103, 1963 only) - 9294.

MODEL 104 SERIES

This series was mfg. from 1964-1972. This is the last series to feature the slant grip trophy pistol. Serial No. range is approx. 1,330,000-2,330,000.

SUPERMATIC TOURNAMENT — .22 LR cal., similar to Model 102/103 series. Mfg. 1964-65.

	$895	$725	$525	$375	$290	$245	$210

The High Standard catalog number for this model was 9271-9275.

The 104 Tournament is quite rare.

SHARPSHOOTER — .22 LR cal., 10 shot, 5½ in. bull barrel. Mfg. 1969-72 (numbered 104) and 1973 (unnumbered).

	$895	$725	$525	$375	$290	$245	$210

The High Standard catalog number for this model was 9205. The 104 Sharpshooter is very rare.

Grading	100%	98%	95%	90%	80%	70%	60%

SUPERMATIC CITATION — .22 LR cal., similar to Model 102/103 series, brown plastic grips or walnut checkered grips, grooved front and back straps.

	$975	$825	$575	$375	$295	$245	$210

Add $150 for 8 in. barrel.
Add $250 for 10 in. barrel.

The 5½ in. bull barrel, 9263 - disc. 1966 (supplied with extra mag). The 5½ in. bull barrel, 9244 - available 1966. The 6¾ in. tapered barrel, 9260 - disc. 1965. The 8 in. tapered barrel, 9261 - disc. 1965. The 10 in. tapered barrel, 9262 - disc. 1965.

SUPERMATIC TROPHY — .22 LR cal., similar to Model 102/103 series, Top-of-the-line target, 5½ in. bull, 7¼ in. fluted barrel available, extra mag., muzzle brake and weights were supplied with gun, grooved front and back straps, checkered walnut grips. Mfg. 1964-65.

	$1,095	$895	$595	$425	$325	$275	$235

Add $50 for high blue finish.

The High Standard catalog number for this model was 9254-55.

OLYMPIC — .22 LR cal., similar to Model 102/103, grooved front and back straps, checkered walnut grips were optional.

	$1,095	$895	$650	$425	$330	$280	$240

Add $100 for catalog number 9295.
Add $150 for 8 in. barrel.

The 5½ in. bull barrel, 9294 - disc. 1964. The 5½ in. bull barrel, 9295 - avail. 1964-65, was supplied with muzzle brake and weights. The 8 in. tapered barrel, 9281 - disc. 1964.

ISU OLYMPIC — .22 Short cal., similar to Model 102/103 Olympic series, grooved front and back straps, 6¾ in. barrel with det. muzzle brake & wts. avail., brown plastic grips standard or walnut checkered grips optional.

	$1,150	$950	$695	$430	$330	$280	$240

The High Standard catalog number for this model was 9237-9299.

CONVERSION KITS MODEL 102/103/104 — Cat. # 9263 Olympic to Supermatic Citation, 6¾ Bbl., Cat. # 9264 Olympic to Supermatic Citation, 8 Bbl., Cat. # 9265 Olympic to Supermatic Citation, 10 Bbl., Cat. # 9283 Supermatic Citation to Olympic, 6¾ Bbl., Cat. # 9284 Supermatic Citation to Olympic, 8 Bbl., Cat. # 9285 Supermatic Citation to Olympic, 10 Bbl., Cat. # 9286 Supermatic Trophy to Olympic, 6¾ Bbl., Cat. # 9287 Supermatic Trophy to Olympic, 8 Bbl., Cat. # 9288 Supermatic Trophy to Olympic, 10 Bbl.

	$500	$450	$400	$325	$275	$225	$195

Add $100 for Trophy Conversions.
Add $125 for 8 in. barrel.
Add $225 for 10 in. barrel.

High Standard did not have a Model 105 Series

MILITARY MODEL 106 SERIES

This series was mfg. 1965-1968. This new military model featured a walnut checkered grip and a frame that has the exact heft and feel of the famous Military 45. This military model features a new slide and a new adj. rear bridge or saddle type sight, permanently fixed to the frame. Front and rear grip straps were stippled and a new design magazine had an extension foot. Removable stabilizer and wts. were available on all models. Beginning serial no. for 106 series was approx. 1,436,000 to 2,030,000.

Grading	100%	98%	95%	90%	80%	70%	60%

SUPERMATIC TOURNAMENT MILITARY — .22 LR cal., bottom of the line target pistol, smooth front & back straps, slide mounted rear sight instead of bridge sight, 5½ in. bull or 6¾ in. straight barrel with military grips.

	$595	$490	$375	$275	$215	$180	$155

Add $100 for 9230-31.

The High Standard catalog no. 9230-31 was disc. early 1966 (supplied with extra mag). 9232-33 became available 1966.

SUPERMATIC CITATION MILITARY — .22 LR cal., middle of the line target pistol, stippled front & back straps, 5½ in. bull barrel or 7¼ in. fluted barrel, new rear bridge or saddle type sight.

	$825	$695	$475	$350	$270	$230	$195

Add $150 for 9240-41.

The High Standard catalog no. 9240-41 was disc. early 1966, (supplied with extra mag., muzzle brake, and weights). 9242-43 became available 1966.

SUPERMATIC TROPHY MILITARY — .22 LR cal., top-of-the-line target pistol, stippled front and back straps, 5½ bull or 7¼ in. fluted barrel avail., gold plated trigger, safety and magazine release, gold filled lettering.

	$995	$825	$575	$425	$325	$275	$235

Add $200 for 9245-46.

The High Standard catalog number for this model 9245-46 was disc. early 1966, (supplied with extra mag., muzzle brake, weights, wrench and cleaning tool). 9247-48 became available 1966.

OLYMPIC MILITARY — .22 Short cal., target pistol, 5½ in. bull barrel, back & front straps, stippled alloy slide, bridge rear sight, military grips, supplied with extra mag. and weights. Disc. early 1966.

	$1,095	$895	$675	$425	$325	$275	$235

The High Standard catalog number for this model was 9235.

OLYMPIC ISU MILITARY — .22 Short cal., target pistol, 6¾ in. tapered barrel with integral stabilizer and wts., front and back straps stippled, rear bridge or saddle type sight, military grips, supplied with extra mag. and weights. Disc. 1966.

	$1,150	$950	$675	$425	$325	$275	$235

Add $150 for 9236.

The High Standard catalog number for this model was 9236. The Model 9238 became available 1966.

MODEL 107 SERIES

The Military 107 Series was mfg. 1968-1972. However, 107 unmarked variations were mfg. 1973-75. ML prefix variations were mfg. 1975 - mid-1981 are also covered within this grouping. The 107 series is basically identical to the Military Model 106 Series. Serial no. range is approx. 2,030,000-2,300,000.

SUPERMATIC TOURNAMENT MILITARY — .22 LR cal., similar to Model 106 series, this was the last of the Tournament pistols, adj. sight replaced the bridge sight, 5½ bull or 6¾ in. tapered barrel. Disc. 1971.

	$550	$450	$350	$250	$195	$165	$135

The High Standard catalog number for this model was 9232-33.

SUPERMATIC CITATION MILITARY — .22 LR cal., similar to Model 106 series, middle of the line target pistol, 7¼ fluted and 5½ in. bull barrel available.

	$750	$650	$495	$350	$275	$220	$185

The High Standard catalog number for this model was 9242-43.

Grading	100%	98%	95%	90%	80%	70%	60%

SUPERMATIC TROPHY MILITARY — .22 LR cal., similar to Model 106 series, top-of-the-line target pistol.

		$895	$750	$550	$400	$315	$250	$210

The High Standard catalog number for this model was 9247-48.

OLYMPIC ISU MILITARY — .22 Short cal., target pistol for Olympic Style Rapid Fire Events. 6³⁄₄ in. fluted barrel with integral stabilizer & two detachable weights.

	$1,100	$950	$775	$475	$375	$305	$255

The High Standard catalog number for this model was 9238.

THE VICTOR — .22 LR cal., introduced 1972, newest and most expensive production target pistol, all steel vented rib running length of barrel until 1974 when it changed to an alloy VR/SR, early adj. sight located on rear of barrel on rib., .22 long rifle built on a military frame, walnut grips, available in 4½ or 5½ in. barrel, push-button takedown, stippled front and rear straps, 10 shot mag., barrel slab sided, wts. are rectangular. Mfg. in Hamden, CT. Stamped "THE VICTOR" on left side of barrel.

	$775	$650	$495	$350	$275	$225	$195

Add $100 for 4½ in. barrel.

The High Standard catalog number for the vent. rib model was catalog number 9216-17.

NUMBERED SERIES

In 1973, High Standard stopped marking the series numbers (either 104 or 107) on the guns. These guns just carry the normal seven digit serial number and are sometimes referred to as "NUMBERED SERIES", "UNNUMBERED SERIES", or "SEVEN- NUMBER SERIES". These pistols include the following - the Sport King, Sharpshooter, Supermatic Citation, Supermatic Trophy, The Victor, and the ISU Olympic (in both military and slant grip models). The serial number range for these guns is 2,330,000 to 2,500,000.

PLINKER — .22 LR cal., introduced in 1970-73. Successor to Duramatic and identical in almost all aspects. Thumb screw takedown.

		$365	$295	$225	$160	$115	$100	$85

Early guns were marked M-101, R.H. slide 1970-71.

The High Standard catalog number for this model was 9214-15.

SPORT KING — .22 LR cal., similar to Series 102/103, 4½ or 6³⁄₄ in. barrel.

		$395	$325	$230	$165	$125	$100	$85

The High Standard catalog number for this Model was 9200-01.

SPORT KING (NICKEL PLATED) — .22 LR cal., this was a nickel plated Sport King with black slanted plastic grips with silver medallion insert on grip. Mfg. 1974-77.

		$475	$390	$280	$200	$155	$130	$110

The High Standard catalog number for this Model was 9208-09.

SHARPSHOOTER — .22 LR cal., successor to the Tournament, introduced in 1969 as part of the Model 103 Series, new model using the slant model grip frame, 5½ in. bull barrel only.

		$575	$450	$325	$250	$195	$165	$140

The High Standard catalog number for this Model was 9205.

SUPERMATIC CITATION — .22 LR cal., identical to 104 Series, 5½ in. bull barrel only.

		$875	$725	$525	$375	$290	$245	$210

The High Standard catalog number for this Model was 9244.

SUPERMATIC CITATION MILITARY — .22 LR cal., similar to 107 Series.

		$875	$725	$525	$375	$290	$245	$210

The High Standard catalog number for this Model was 9242-43.

Grading	100%	98%	95%	90%	80%	70%	60%

SUPERMATIC TROPHY MILITARY — .22 LR cal., similar to 107 Series.

	$875	$725	$525	$375	$290	$245	$210

The High Standard catalog number for this Model was 9247-48.

ISU OLYMPIC — .22 LR cal., identical to 104 Series, 6¾ in. barrel.

	$1,150	$950	$650	$395	$325	$265	$225

The High Standard catalog number for this Model was 9237.

ISU OLYMPIC MILITARY — .22 Short cal., otherwise identical to 107 series.

	$1,150	$950	$650	$395	$325	$265	$225

The High Standard catalog number for this Model was 9238.

THE VICTOR (SLANT GRIP) — .22 LR cal., slant grip, mfg. 1973-74.

	$3,150	$2,575	$1,875	$1,350	$1,025	$850	$715

Add $75 for early steel rib.
Add $200 for solid rib.
Add $150 for 4½ in. barrel.

The High Standard catalog numbers for this model were: 4½ vent. rib, 9218 mfg. 1973-74. 5½ vent. rib, 9219 mfg. 1973-74. 4½ solid rib, 9226 mfg. 1974 only. 5½ solid rib, 9229 mfg. 1974 only.

THE VICTOR — .22 LR cal., similar to 107 series, Hamden mfg., military grips, in 1974, an aluminum vent. rib was used to lighten this variation, a solid rib was also available.

	$695	$575	$440	$315	$245	$200	$335

Add $150 for solid rib.
Add $75 for steel rib.
Add $100 for 4½ in. barrel.

The High Standard catalog number for the solid rib with military grips was 9206-11. The vent. rib model was catalog number 9216-17.

G PREFIX SERIES

Identical to 103/104 series (most models retained the same HS catalog no.) Due to the GCA of 1968, High Standard decided to serialize their rifles and shotguns beginning with ser. no. 3,000,000. In 1975, handgun serialization (pistols, revolvers, and derringers) was up to ser. no. 2,500,000 and High Standard felt they needed an alternate serial number system before handgun serialization reached 3,000,000. They decided to use the following prefixes - G for slant grip pistols, ML for military grip pistols, R for revolvers, and D for derringers. These prefixes were followed by the 5 digit ser. no. This is the last of the slant grip pistols.

SPORT KING — .22 LR cal., identical to 102/103 series, 4½ or 6¾ in. barrel. Disc. 1977.

	$395	$325	$230	$165	$125	$100	$85

The High Standard catalog numbers for this model were 9200-01.

SPORT KING (NICKEL PLATED) — .22 LR cal., identical to 102/103 series, nickel plated, 4½ or 6¾ in. barrel. Disc. 1977.

	$475	$395	$275	$200	$155	$130	$110

The High Standard catalog numbers for this model were 9208-09.

SHARPSHOOTER — .22 LR cal., identical to 103 series, 5½ in. bull barrel only. Disc. 1977.

	$575	$450	$325	$250	$195	$165	$140

The High Standard catalog number for this Model was 9205.

SUPERMATIC CITATION — .22 LR cal., identical to numbered series, 5½ in. bull barrel only. Disc. 1976.

	$875	$725	$525	$375	$295	$245	$210

The High Standard catalog number for this model was 9244.

Grading	100%	98%	95%	90%	80%	70%	60%

OLYMPIC ISU — .22 LR cal., identical to numbered series, 6¾ in. tapered barrel. Disc. 1977.

	$1,150	$950	$650	$425	$315	$270	$230

The High Standard catalog no. for this Model was 9237.

ML PREFIX SERIES

As mentioned in the G Prefix section, High Standard revised their serial numbering system in 1975 from a 7 digit serial number to a five digit serial number with an ML prefix. These guns are basically identical to the guns listed in the 107 series category, but are listed here for chronological and value reasons. Mfg. mid-1975 through 1981. Guns with serial numbers between ML1,000 and ML24,999 were manufactured in Hamden, CT. Guns with serial numbers between ML25,000 and ML87,000 were manufactured in East Hartford, CT.

SPORT KING — .22 LR cal., similar to previous Sport Kings, but they now use military grips. Some of these Sport Kings were labeled "SPORT KING-M". Mfg. 1977-1981 in East Hartford only.

	$325	$265	$195	$135	$105	$85	$70

The High Standard catalog number for this model was 9258-59.

SHARPSHOOTER — .22 LR cal., some of the Sharpshooters with military grips were labeled "SHARPSHOOTER-M". Mfg. 1979-1981 in East Hartford only.

	$450	$365	$275	$200	$155	$125	$105

The High Standard catalog number for this model was 9210.

* ***Sharpshooter Survival Pack*** — introduced 1981, includes Sharpshooter-M pistol, electroless nickel, push-button take down, packaged in canvas carrying case with extra nickel magazine, 5½ in. bull barrel.

	$695	$550	$415	$300	$230	$195	$165

The High Standard catalog number for this model was 9424.

SUPERMATIC CITATION MILITARY — .22 LR cal., similar to previous model.

	$595	$495	$375	$275	$215	$165	$140

Subtract 10% for East Hartford model.

The High Standard catalog number for this model was 9242-43.

SUPERMATIC TROPHY MILITARY — .22 LR cal., similar to previous series.

	$750	$625	$475	$340	$265	$215	$180

Subtract 10% for East Hartford model.

The High Standard catalog number for this model was 9247-48.

SUPERMATIC ISU OLYMPIC MILITARY — .22 Short cal., target pistol, similar to previous model. Disc. 1981.

	$925	$750	$575	$425	$325	$260	$220

Subtract 10% for East Hartford model.

The High Standard catalog number for this model was 9238 (disc. 1977).

THE VICTOR — .22 LR cal., similar to previous model, military grip, vent. or solid rib. Last solid rib mfg. in 1977. Later Victors in this series were stamped simply "VICTOR" above trigger guard.

	$635	$525	$450	$275	$220	$180	$150

Add $150 for solid rib models.
Add $100 for 4½ in. barrel length.
Subtract 10% for East Hartford models.

The High Standard catalog number for this model was 9216-17, catalog number for the solid rib model was 9206-9211 (disc. 1977).

Grading	100%	98%	95%	90%	80%	70%	60%

10-X — .22 LR cal., specifically designed for top flight shooting, 5½ in. bull barrel, push-button takedown. This model used hand-picked parts and was precisely assembled by a High Standard Master Gunsmith (with his initials under the left grip of each gun). Black matte finish, black painted walnut grips, stippled front and back straps. Mfg. 1980 in East Hartford.

* **Push Button Barrel Release**

	$2,350	$2,000	$1,625	$1,195	$925	$715	$595

The High Standard catalog number for this model was 9372.

SH SERIES

This was the last series of High Standard pistols and can be differentiated from the 107/Unnumbered/ML series by the mechanical differences within the frame assembly. Mfg. from mid 1981-1984. Serial No. range was approx. 10,000-35,000 and is prefixed "SH". Features a new barrel release in place of the push button takedown. An allenhead screw attached the frame to the barrel. A few guns were mfg. with push-button takedown from parts left over from the previous series. Also, some guns in this series have a "V" suffix.

SPORT KING — .22 LR cal., similar to ML series, except has allen screw take down, 4½ or 6¾ in. barrel.

	$295	$225	$175	$125	$95	$75	$65

The High Standard catalog number for this model was 9258-59 (disc. 1983).

SPORT KING (SH PREFIX) — .22 LR cal., SH prefix serial no. with allen screw takedown, military grips with new electroless nickel model available. Mfg. 1982-84.

	$365	$325	$225	$145	$115	$95	$80

This model was also called the "SPORT KING-M".

The High Standard catalog number for this model was 9450-51.

SHARPSHOOTER — .22 LR cal., SH prefix serial no. with allen screw takedown, military grips. Mfg. 1982.

	$375	$300	$235	$170	$135	$110	$95

This model was also sometimes called "SHARPSHOOTER-M".

The High Standard catalog number for this model was 9210 (disc. 1982).

SUPERMATIC CITATION MILITARY — .22 LR cal., SH prefix, similar to previous Citation model with allen screw takedown, military grips. Disc. May 1982.

	$495	$395	$325	$225	$175	$140	$120

The High Standard catalog number for this model was 9242-43.

CITATION II — .22 LR cal., 10 shot, new variation of the Supermatic Citation, 5½ and 7¼ in. barrels, checkered military-type wood grips, allen screw takedown, SH prefix serial no., slab sided barrel, electroless nickel model also available, this model replaced the Sharpshooter. Mfg. 1983-84.

	$550	$450	$340	$265	$205	$165	$140

The High Standard catalog number for this model was 9348-49.

SUPERMATIC TROPHY MILITARY — .22 LR cal., similar to previous Trophy Model with SH prefix, allen screw takedown, military grips.

	$650	$535	$395	$295	$225	$175	$150

The High Standard catalog number for this model was 9247-48.

VICTOR — .22 LR cal., similar to previous Victor, new allen screw takedown, SH prefix, military grips, 5½ in. vent. barrel only mfg. in this Victor Series, some Victor ser. numbers had a "V" suffix.

	$550	$450	$350	$250	$195	$155	$130

The High Standard catalog number for this model was 9217.

Grading	100%	98%	95%	90%	80%	70%	60%

10X — .22 LR cal., high quality gun similar to previous 10X, but with allen screw takedown, a High Standard 10X Victor was also offered. These had a 5½ in. vented Victor rib; only a few were mfg., limited mfg. also in 7¼ in. fluted barrel.

* *Allen Screw Barrel Release*

	100%	98%	95%	90%	80%	70%	60%
	$2,000	$1,750	$1,425	$995	$795	$675	$575

Add $1,250 for Victor VR model.

Add $1,000 for fluted barrel.

The High Standard catalog number for this model was 9234-9249-9372.

SURVIVAL PACK — .22 LR cal., Sharpshooter "M" or Citation II electroless nickel, allen screw takedown, packaged in canvas carrying case with extra nickel magazine. Disc. 1984.

	$575	$475	$395	$275	$215	$185	$160

The High Standard catalog number for this model was 9424.

COMMEMORATIVE MODELS

1972 OLYMPIC COMMEMORATIVE — .22 LR cal., a highly engraved version of a Supermatic Trophy Military, Model 107, has 5 Olympic gold rings on right side of receiver, Ser. no. has a "T" prefix, high polish blue finish, 5½ in. bull barrel, lined presentation case avail. Limited edition of 1,000 guns, but it is believed only about 175-200 of these pistols were manufactured due to their high price, issue price was $550. Mfg. 1972-1974 only.

	$4,250	$3,250	$1,900

1974 retail on this model was $605. Early models were marked "MODEL 107", and were not hi-polished.

The High Standard catalog number for this model was 9207.

1980 OLYMPIC COMMEMORATIVE — .22 Short, an ISU Olympic Military with 6¾ in. tapered barrel with integral stabilizer and weights. Has 5 Olympic gold rings on right side of receiver. Produced in a limited edition of 1,000 guns. Ser. no. has a "USA" prefix, blue finish, lined presentation case avail. Mfg. 1980 only.

	$1,395	$900	$700

The High Standard catalog number for this model was 9239.

CONVERSION KITS

These kits for conversion of .22 LR to .22 Short contained an alloy slide with vent. rib, barrel weight, and two Short mags., kit comes in "gun size box" set in styrofoam. These kits were designated either #9370 or #9371 when mfg., depending on the pistol to be converted.

VICTOR KIT — this model was designated #9370 when in mfg.

	$550	$450	$350

TROPHY/CITATION KIT — this kit also includes a stabilizer. This model was designated #9371 when in mfg.

	$550	$450	$350

REVOLVERS

Add 20% for extra convertible cylinder (.22 LR/.22 Mag.) on those models listed below that apply.

SENTINEL — .22 LR cal., 9 shot, swing out cylinder, 3, 4, or 6 in. barrel, aluminum frame, made 1955-1956.

	100%	98%	95%	90%	80%	70%	60%
Blue finish	$120	$110	$100	$95	$85	$70	$55
Blue/Green finish	$120	$110	$100	$95	$85	$70	$55
Nickel finish	$130	$120	$110	$105	$95	$85	$65
Pink finish	$295	$265	$230	$200	$180	$160	$140
Gold finish	$295	$265	$230	$200	$180	$160	$140

Grading	100%	98%	95%	90%	80%	70%	60%

SENTINEL IMPERIAL — similar to Sentinel, with adj. sights, walnut grips, made 1962-1965.

Blue finish	$140	$125	$115	$110	$100	$90	$75
Nickel finish	$150	$140	$125	$120	$110	$100	$90

SENTINEL DELUXE — similar to Sentinel, except adj. sights, wide trigger, 4 and 6 in. barrel, square butt, made 1957-1974.

Blue finish	$140	$125	$115	$110	$100	$90	$75
Nickel finish	$150	$140	$115	$120	$110	$100	$90

SENTINEL SNUB — similar to Deluxe, except checkered bird's-head grip, 2⅜ in. barrel.

Blue finish	$145	$140	$130	$120	$110	$90	$85
Nickel finish	$155	$150	$145	$130	$120	$100	$95

DURANGO — .22 LR cal., double action, steel frame, 4½ and 5½ in. barrel, wood grips, made 1971-1973.

Blue finish	$145	$130	$120	$95	$85	$70	$55
Nickel finish	$150	$140	$125	$105	$95	$85	$65

HOMBRE DOUBLE ACTION — similar to Double Nine steel frame, but no ejector rod housing, 4½ in. barrel, made 1971-1973.

Blue finish	$125	$120	$110	$105	$95	$85	$65
Nickel finish	$140	$130	$120	$115	$105	$95	$75

LONGHORN STEEL FRAME — similar to Double Nine, except 9½ in. barrel.

Fixed sights	$210	$170	$150	$120	$110	$105	$85
Adj. sights	$165	$155	$150	$130	$120	$115	$95

HIGH SIERRA — similar to Double Nine steel frame, except 7 in. octagon barrel, gold plated grip frame. Discontinued in 1984. Add $10 for adj. sights.

Fixed sights	$235	$175	$150	$130	$120	$105	$90

KIT GUN — .22 LR cal., swing out cylinder, 9 shot, 4 in. barrel, adj. sights, blue, walnut grips, made 1970-1973.

	$155	$145	$140	$125	$115	$105	$85

DOUBLE NINE — .22 LR cal., Western style double action, 5½ in. barrel, aluminum frame, simulated stag, ebony or ivory grips, made 1959-1984.

Blue finish	$235	$180	$160	$140	$120	$105	$90
Nickel finish (disc. 1982)	$245	$190	$170	$150	$130	$115	$100

POSSE — similar to Double Nine aluminum, except 3½ in. barrel, blue, brass grip frame, walnut grips, made 1961-1966.

	$120	$110	$95	$90	$85	$70	$55

NATCHEZ — similar to Double Nine aluminum, except has bird's-head grip, made 1961-1966.

	$120	$110	$100	$90	$85	$70	$55

LONGHORN ALUMINUM FRAME — similar to Natchez, but 4½, 5½, and 9½ in. barrel, longhorn hammer spur, made 1961-1966.

	$145	$130	$110	$100	$85	$70	$55

* *9½ in. model* — Discontinued in 1984.

	$250	$190	$160	$140	$120	$100	$90

CAMP GUN DOUBLE ACTION — .22 LR or .22 Win. Mag. cal., 6 in. barrel, blue, adj. rear sight, checkered walnut grips, made 1976-1984.

	$250	$185	$165	$145	$125	$110	$100

SENTINEL 1 DOUBLE ACTION — .22 LR cal., 2, 3, and 4 in. barrel, 9 shot, smooth walnut grips, made 1974-1984.

Blue finish	$235	$180	$160	$140	$120	$105	$90
Nickel finish	$250	$195	$175	$150	$130	$110	$95

Blue w/adj. sights — add $15 to above prices.

Grading	100%	98%	95%	90%	80%	70%	60%

SENTINEL MARK IV DOUBLE ACTION — similar to Sentinel 1, except .22 WRM cal.

Blue finish	$145	$140	$125	$120	$115	$95	$90
Nickel finish	$155	$150	$140	$130	$125	$105	$100

* Adj. sights

	$160	$155	$150	$145	$125	$115	$100

SENTINEL MARK II DOUBLE ACTION — .357 Mag. cal., 6 shot, double action, 2½, 4, and 6 in. barrel, blue, fixed sights, wood grips, made 1974-1976.

$225	$190	$165	$155	$150	$140	$130

SENTINEL MARK III DOUBLE ACTION — similar to Mark II, except adj. sights.

$250	$220	$185	$175	$170	$160	$150

CRUSADER — .357 Mag., .44 Mag. or .45 LC cal., double action employing gear assembly, swing-out cylinder, unique action, adj. sights, limited mfg. starting 1976 because of expensive fabrication.

$600	$525	$450	$400	$360	$320	$295

Add 10% for NIB condition.

RIFLES

SPORT KING FIELD MODEL — .22 S (Hi-Speed), .22 L, .22 LR cal., semi-auto, tube mag., 22 in. barrel, open sight, plain pistol grip stock, made 1960-1966.

$100	$90	$85	$75	$65	$55	$45

SPORT KING SPECIAL — similar to Field, except beavertail forearm and Monte Carlo stock.

$140	$120	$95	$90	$75	$65	$55

SPORT KING CARBINE — similar to Field, except 18 in. barrel, straight grip, barrel band and sling, made 1964-1973.

$170	$150	$120	$110	$100	$90	$85

SPORT KING DELUXE — similar to Special, but stock checkered, made 1966-1975.

$185	$160	$140	$115	$90	$75	$65

HI-POWER FIELD BOLT ACTION — .270 Win. or .30-06 cal., Mauser type action, 4 shot mag., 22 in. barrel, folding rear sight, plain stock, made 1962-1966.

$295	$230	$210	$195	$180	$165	$150

HI-POWER DELUXE — similar to Field, except checkered Monte Carlo stock, swivels, made 1962-1966.

$350	$285	$240	$220	$205	$195	$165

FLITE KING SLIDE ACTION — .22 S, L, or LR cal., 24 in. barrel, tube mag., hammerless, Patridge sight, Monte Carlo stock with pistol grip, semi beavertail forearm, made 1962-1975.

$120	$105	$95	$85	$65	$60	$50

SHOTGUNS

SUPERMATIC FIELD GRADE — 12 ga., 28 and 30 in. barrel, mod. or full, gas operated semi-auto, plain pistol grip stock, made 1960-1966.

$205	$185	$175	$160	$145	$140	$120

SUPERMATIC SPECIAL — 12 ga., similar to Field, 27 in. barrel, adj. choke, made 1960-1966.

$210	$195	$180	$165	$150	$145	$125

SUPERMATIC DELUXE — similar to Field, except vent. rib, checkered stock and forearm, made 1961-1966.

$265	$225	$200	$175	$160	$155	$140

H

Grading	100%	98%	95%	90%	80%	70%	60%

SUPERMATIC TROPHY — similar to Deluxe, except 27 in. barrel, adj. choke.

| | $235 | $215 | $205 | $180 | $165 | $160 | $145 |

SUPERMATIC DUCK — similar to Field, except 3 in. Mag., 30 in. full barrel, recoil pad, made 1961-1966.

| | $275 | $235 | $190 | $160 | $145 | $125 | $110 |

SUPERMATIC DUCK VENT RIB — similar to Duck, vent. rib, checkered stock and forearm, made 1961-1966.

| | $295 | $250 | $210 | $175 | $150 | $130 | $115 |

SUPERMATIC DEER GUN — similar to Field, except 22 in. cylinder bore barrel, rifle sights, checkered stock and forearm, recoil pad, made 1965.

| | $230 | $210 | $200 | $185 | $165 | $155 | $140 |

SUPERMATIC SKEET — similar to Deluxe Rib, except 26 in. barrel, skeet bore, made 1962-1966.

| | $300 | $260 | $225 | $195 | $175 | $160 | $150 |

SUPERMATIC TRAP — similar to Skeet, except 30 in. full barrel, trap stock with pad, made 1962-1966.

| | $245 | $230 | $220 | $205 | $185 | $170 | $160 |

Note: All preceding models, except Deer and Trap, are also chambered for 20 ga., 3 in. Mag. Values are approx. $20 higher.

High Standard restyled the Supermatic Autoloader in 1966. The new model Supermatics are recognized by the new checkering pattern and jeweled bolt. All models previously listed were offered, 12 and 20 ga. values are $25 higher per model. All are considered deluxe models. They were discontinued in 1975.

FLITE KING PUMP FIELD GRADE — 12, 20, 28 ga., or .410 bore, slide action, 26, 28, or 30 in. barrel, imp. cyl., mod., or full choke, plain pistol grip stock and slide, made 1960-1966.

| | $165 | $150 | $140 | $130 | $120 | $110 | $100 |

FLITE KING SPECIAL — 12, 20, 28 ga., or .410 bore, similar to Pump Field, except 27 in. barrel, adj. choke, made 1960-1966.

| | $155 | $130 | $120 | $110 | $100 | $90 | $80 |

FLITE KING DELUXE RIB — 12, 20, 28 ga., or .410 bore, similar to Pump Special, except vent. rib, checkered stock, made 1961-1966.

| | $195 | $175 | $170 | $165 | $155 | $140 | $125 |

FLITE KING TROPHY — 12, 20, 28 ga., or .410 bore, similar to Deluxe Rib, except 27 in. vent. rib barrel, adj. choke, made 1960-1966.

| | $200 | $180 | $175 | $170 | $160 | $145 | $130 |

FLITE KING BRUSH — 12 ga. only, similar to Field, except 18 or 20 in. cylinder bore barrel, rifle sights, made 1962-1964.

| | $185 | $170 | $165 | $160 | $150 | $140 | $120 |

FLITE KING BRUSH DELUXE — 12 ga. only, similar to Brush, except adj. aperture rear sight, checkered stock, recoil pad, swivels and sling, 20 in. barrel only, made 1964-1966.

| | $265 | $230 | $195 | $170 | $155 | $145 | $130 |

FLITE KING SKEET — 12, 20, 28 ga., or .410 bore only, similar to Deluxe Rib, except 26 in. vent. rib, skeet bore, made 1962-1966.

| | $265 | $230 | $195 | $170 | $155 | $145 | $130 |

Add 35% for 28 ga. or .410 bore.

FLITE KING TRAP — 12 ga. only, similar to Deluxe Rib, except 30 in. vent. rib, full choke and pad, made 1962-1966.

| | $250 | $220 | $195 | $165 | $150 | $140 | $125 |

Note: Flite King was available in 16 ga. also, except for the Brush, Skeet, and Trap models. Values are about $20 less per model. A .410 bore was offered in all models that were

Grading	100%	98%	95%	90%	80%	70%	60%

offered in 20 ga., except the Special and Trophy models. Values are generally the same per model.

High Standard restyled the Flite King in 1966. The new models have a jeweled bolt and new checkering pattern. These new guns were available as Deluxe, Deluxe Rib, Brush, Brush Deluxe, Skeet Deluxe, and Trap Deluxe. Their values are about $20 higher per model.

The new redesigned Flite King was also offered in Deluxe, Deluxe Rib, and Deluxe Skeet, in 20, 28 ga., and .410 bore.

MODEL 10B — 12 ga. combat shotgun, 18 in. barrel, semi-auto, unique design incorporates raked pistol grip in front of receiver and metal shoulder pad attached directly to rear of receiver, black cycolac plastic shroud and pistol grip, folding carrying handle, provisions made for attaching a small flashlight to receiver top, extended blade front sight, very compact size (28 in. overall). Discontinued.

	$650	$575	$500	$425	$375	$325	$275

The predecessor to this model was the 10A. This variation had the flashlight built in.

RIOT SHOTGUN — 18 or 20 in. barrel, police riot gun was also offered until 1975. This was a reliable weapon available with or without rifle sights, 12 ga. only on the Flite King Action.

	$195	$165	$155	$140	$130	$120	$115

SUPERMATIC INDY O/U — 12 ga., this model was mfg. in Japan by Nikko and imported in 1974 and 1975, boxlock, fully engraved receiver, selective auto ejectors and single trigger, 27½ sk & sk, 29½ imp. mod. and full, or full and full, trap variation allows air flow with aluminum vent. rib, checkered (skipline) pistol grip stock with pad and vent. forearm.

	$925	$830	$760	$700	$645	$590	$530

SUPERMATIC SHADOW SEVEN O/U — similar to Indy O/U, except less elaborate engraving, unvented forearm, standard vent. rib, regular checkering, no recoil pad, imported 1974-1975.

	$760	$685	$615	$540	$490	$440	$400

SUPERMATIC SHADOW AUTO — 12 and 20 ga., 2¾ or 3 in. chambers in 12 ga., air flow rib, 26 in. imp. cyl. or skeet, 28 in. mod., imp. mod. or full and 30 in. full or trap, checkered walnut stock, gas operated, imported 1974-1975.

	$390	$340	$290	$260	$225	$195	$165

HIGH STANDARD MANUFACTURING COMPANY, INC.

Current manufacturer established in 1993 and located in Houston, TX.

This new company was formed during 1993, utilizing many of the same employees and original material vendors that the original High Standard company used during their period of manufacture (1926-1984).

PISTOLS: SEMI-AUTO, RIMFIRE

SPORT KING — .22 LR cal., 4½ or 6¾ in. barrel, blued finish, military grips, 10 shot mag.

While advertised during 1996, this model has not been produced.

SUPERMATIC CITATION — .22 LR cal., 5½ or 7¼ (disc. 1995) in. barrel, matte blue (disc. 1996) or parkerized finish, military grips, 10 shot mag., 44 oz. New 1994.

Mfg.'s Sug. Retail	$491		$415	$325	$260	$225	$200	$185	$170

Subtract $29 for universal mount scope base.
Add $299 for .22 Short conversion kit (includes VR barrel, slide, and 2 mags.).

Grading	100%	98%	95%	90%	80%	70%	60%

SUPERMATIC CITATION MS — .22 LR cal., features 10 in. barrel with mounting bracket designed for the Metallic Silhouette shooter, 54 oz. New 1997.

Mfg.'s Sug. Retail	$776	$675	$550	$465	$400	$340	$290	$230

Subtract $119 if w/o RPM sights (scope base only).

SUPERMATIC CITATION 10X — .22 LR cal., 5½ in. barrel, blued finish, military grips, High Standard's most accurate pistol, choice of either factory or Shea custom tuning, 10 shot mag., approx. 45 oz. New 1994.

* Factory Tuned 10X

Mfg.'s Sug. Retail	$869		$745	$625	$545	$465	$400	$325	$275

* Custom Shea 10X — limited mfg. (approx. 150 pistols annually), hand-built by Bob Shea. New 1995.

Mfg.'s Sug. Retail	$1,095		$975	$875	$775	$675	$550	$495	$450

SUPERMATIC TOURNAMENT — .22 LR cal., choice of 4½ (disc. 1995), 5½, or 6¾ (disc. 1995) in. barrel, matte blue, non-adj. trigger, approx. 44 oz. Mfg. 1995-97.

	$400	$315	$255	$225	$200	$185	$170

Last Mfg.'s Sug. Retail was $468.

SUPERMATIC TROPHY — .22 LR cal., 5½ or 7¼ in. barrel, blued finish, military grips, 10 shot mag., 44 or 46 oz. New 1994.

Mfg.'s Sug. Retail	$569		$495	$380	$310	$250	$200	$185	$170

Add $81 for 7¼ in. barrel.
Add $299 for .22 Short conversion kit (includes VR barrel, slide, and 2 mags.).
Subtract $59 if with scope base only.

VICTOR — .22 LR cal., 4½ or 5½ in. barrel, blue or parkerized (new 1995, 5½ in. barrel only) finish, military grips, with open sight rib or universal mount (HSUM, blue only, new 1996), 10 shot mag., approx. 45 oz. New 1994.

Mfg.'s Sug. Retail	$591		$500	$375	$350	$250	$200	$185	$170

Subtract $59 if with scope base only.
Add $299 for .22 Short conversion kit (includes VR barrel, slide, and 2 mags.).

* Victor 10X — factory tuned and individually tested, includes test target signed by the gunsmith, 46 oz. New 1997.

Mfg.'s Sug. Retail	$969		$875	$700	$600	$500	$425	$375	$325

* Victor 10X Shea — parkerized finish, 5½ in. barrel only, 150 built by Bob Shea annually, 46 oz. New 1996.

Mfg.'s Sug. Retail	$1,195		$1,075	$925	$825	$750	$625	$550	$495

OLYMPIC I.S.U. — .22 Short cal., 6¾ in. fluted barrel with integral muzzle brake, blued finish, military grips, 10 shot mag. Mfg. 1994-95 only.

	$550	$450	$385	$315	$250	$200	$185

Last Mfg.'s Sug. Retail was $625.

OLYMPIC MILITARY — .22 Short cal., 5½ in. fluted bull barrel with removable stabilizer, aluminum alloy slide with steel frame. New 1995.

Mfg.'s Sug. Retail	$590		$500	$385	$315	$265	$200	$185	$170

Subtract $59 if with scope base only.

OLYMPIC RAPID FIRE — .22 Short cal., 4 in. VR barrel with integral muzzle brake and forward mounted compensator, gold-plated small parts, matte finish, special grips with rear support, adj. trigger, 46 oz. New 1996.

Mfg.'s Sug. Retail	$1,995		$1,800	$1,575	$1,300	$1,025	$875	$750	$625

Grading	100%	98%	95%	90%	80%	70%	60%

HISPANO ARGENTINO FABRICA DE AUTOMOVILES SA (HAFDASA)

Previous car manufacturer located in Buenos Aires, Argentina.

This company accepted and sold both commercial and military pistols manufactured by Ballester-Rigaud initially, followed by Ballester-Molina.

BALLESTER-MOLINA/RIGAUD — .45 ACP or .22 LR cal., 5 in. barrel, patterned after the Colt M-1911A1 except has pinned trigger, is without grip safety, has different sear mechanism, and distinctive pattern retracting grooves in slide. Circa 1930-mid 1940s. Probably an unauthorized copy at the time.

$450	$400	$360	$330	$300	$275	$225

Add 100% for .22 LR.

GEORGE HOENIG, INC.

Current custom rifle builder located in Boise, ID.

George Hoenig manufactures a unique rotary round action rifle that can be configured for either O/U, SxS, or even a Vierling. Opening is achieved by rotating barrels quarter turn to the right, then sliding barrel assembly forward. Because of this, there is no top opening lever. For more information, delivery time, and current pricing (O/U or SxS rifles typically start at approx. $20,000), please contact George Hoenig directly (see Trademark Index).

HOFER-JAGDWAFFEN, PETER

Current master gunsmith located in Ferlach, Austria. Custom order only, best quality rifles (most configurations) and shotguns (O/U and SxS) made per individual order — prices usually start in the $20,000 range, and can go up to over $600,000! Information (including an individualized quotation) can be obtained by writing to Mr. Hofer directly (see Trademark Index).

P.L. HOLEHAN, INC.

Current custom rifle manufacturer located in Tucson, AZ. P.L. Holehan, Inc. is a custom rifle maker fabricating best quality bolt action rifles only. All guns are essentially built per individual custom order and the company should be contacted directly for more information, including special order options/features.

RIFLES: BOLT ACTION

SAFARI GRADE HUNTER — various Safari cals., features Win. M-70 controlled feed claw extractor, double square bridge action, premium grade barrel, satin blue metal finish, choice of fiberglass or oil finished English walnut stock with ebony forend tip, Pachmayr decelerator pad, hinged floor plate.

Mfg.'s Sug. Retail	$4,550	$4,550	$3,875	$3,400	$3,000	$2,500	$2,000	$1,600

Subtract $750 for fiberglass stock.

CLASSIC HUNTER — similar to Safari Grade Hunter, except available in most popular non-Safari cals., hinged floor plate.

Mfg.'s Sug. Retail	$4,050	$4,050	$3,500	$3,000	$2,500	$2,000	$1,600	$1,350

Subtract $700 for fiberglass stock.

LONG RANGE HUNTER — various cals., action similar to Classic Hunter, except has 26 in. fluted barrel, satin blue or matte Teflon metal finish.

Mfg.'s Sug. Retail	$3,950	$3,950	$3,400	$2,950	$2,450	$1,950	$1,600	$1,350

Subtract $500 for fiberglass stock.

Grading	100%	98%	95%	90%	80%	70%	60%

LIGHT WEIGHT HUNTER — various cals., features short action, Win. M-70 controlled feed claw extractor, lightweight 22 in. barrel, standard or blind box mag.

Mfg.'s Sug. Retail	$4,050	$4,050	$3,500	$3,000	$2,500	$2,000	$1,600	$1,350

Subtract $700 for fiberglass stock.
Subtract $400 for blind box mag.

HOLLAND & HOLLAND LTD.

Current manufacturer established in 1835 and located in London, England since 1835. All H&H long guns are built per individual special order. Orders may be placed directly with their recently

HOLLAND & HOLLAND
Established 1835

opened office located in New York, NY or directly with the factory in England. Please refer to these listings in the Trademark Index for address, telephone, or FAX information.

Holland & Holland over the years has justly earned the reputation of producing some of the finest firearms ever manufactured. Their double rifles chambered for the black powder express cartridges are still among the most powerful rifles ever made, while exhibiting outstanding quality and superior craftsmanship. Most of these fine arms were made to order for the famous, wealthy, or royalty of their day. Because of the individual nature of each firearm, these early guns, as with any high grade item, must be individually appraised.

The early double rifles were proofed and regulated with the black powder ammunition of their day. These exposed hammer rifles were almost exclusively sold cased with accessories by Holland & Holland. They are seldom found on the market, and then not in the best of condition. Purchase of these as well as any high grade firearm should include trusted appraisal.

RIFLES: MODERN

ROOK RIFLE — .250, .295/.300, .360, .380 black powder cals., single shot, break-open action, various levels of embellishment - Royal Models were made but most Rook rifles were base models with few extra features. Values today range from $295 (average condition, small cal.) to $1,500 (larger cal., engraving, better wood, perhaps cased). Disc.

BEST QUALITY MAGAZINE RIFLE — Mauser 98 (current mfg.) or Enfield (disc.) action, various cals., incl. .300 H&H, .375 H&H, built per individual customer specifications, checkered French walnut stock available in traditional configuration or with Monte Carlo pattern.

Mfg.'s Sug. Retail	$19,000	$19,000	$15,500	$11,150	$7,500	$5,300	$4,250	$3,600

The values above represent the standard model without additional options or engraving (of which there are a wide array).

DE LUXE MAGAZINE RIFLE — similar to Best Quality, except with deluxe grade walnut and various engraving options, very limited mfg.

There is no standard base price on this model - rather, individual options are custom ordered and are individually priced.

NO. 2 MODEL DOUBLE RIFLE SxS — various British and American cals., 24-28 in. barrels, sidelock, folding leaf sight, checkered French walnut stock, auto ejectors.

		$15,000	$13,000	$11,000	$10,000	$9,000	$7,000	$6,500

ROYAL DOUBLE SxS RIFLE - OLDER MFG. — similar to No. 2, except has deluxe finish and more engraving.

.300 H&H cal. or less	$40,000	$35,000	$30,000	$25,000	$22,000	$19,500	$17,500
Up to .375 H&H cal.	$45,000	$40,000	$35,000	$30,000	$25,000	$22,000	$19,500

Grading	100%	98%	95%	90%	80%	70%	60%
Up to .470 NE cal.	$55,000	$50,000	$45,000	$40,000	$35,000	$30,000	$26,000
Up to .600 NE cal.	$60,000	$55,000	$50,000	$45,000	$40,000	$35,000	$30,000

Subtract 15% if w/o ejectors.
Subtract 20% if w/o reinforced action.

ROYAL DE LUXE SxS RIFLE - LATEST PRODUCTION — same cals. as the Royal Double SxS, top-of-the-line model, every refinement, built to individual order only with almost any option possible.

* **.240 H&H, 7mm H&H, or 8mm cal.**
  Mfg.'s Sug. Retail $90,500

	100%	98%	95%	90%	80%	70%	60%
	$90,500	$61,750	$42,500	$36,250	$31,000	$27,000	$21,000

* **.275 H&H, .300 H&H, or 9.3mm cal.**
  Mfg.'s Sug. Retail $95,000

	100%	98%	95%	90%	80%	70%	60%
	$95,000	$64,500	$44,500	$38,500	$33,000	$28,750	$23,750

* **.375 H&H cal.**
  Mfg.'s Sug. Retail $99,000

	100%	98%	95%	90%	80%	70%	60%
	$99,000	$67,500	$48,000	$41,000	$35,000	$30,000	$25,000

* **.465 H&H cal.**
  Mfg.'s Sug. Retail $99,000

	100%	98%	95%	90%	80%	70%	60%
	$99,000	$70,500	$52,000	$44,000	$38,500	$31,000	$26,000

* **.577 NE or .600 NE cal.**
  Mfg.'s Sug. Retail $115,000

	100%	98%	95%	90%	80%	70%	60%
	$115,000	$84,200	$55,000	$45,000	$39,500	$32,500	$27,250

H&H .700 BORE DOUBLE RIFLE — .700 H&H cal., 1,000 grain jacketed bullet, approx. 19 lbs. with 26 in. barrels chambered 3½ in. This is the largest caliber rifle available in the world today.

* *Royal Model* — this model is not currently mfg. 1997 retail was $115,920.

* *Royal De Luxe Model*
  Mfg.'s Sug. Retail $152,000

	100%	98%	95%
	$152,000	$115,000	$93,500

H

SHOTGUNS: O/U

ROYAL OLD MODEL — 12 ga., customer specifications as to barrel length and choke, hand detachable sidelocks, auto ejectors, checkered straight grip stock. Mfg. until 1951. Very rare, very few mfg.

	100%	98%	95%	90%	80%	70%	60%
	$37,500	$32,000	$28,000	$23,500	$20,000	$18,000	$16,500

Add 5% for single trigger.

ROYAL NEW MODEL — similar to Old Model, with improved narrow action. Mfg. until 1960, fewer than 30 mfg.

	100%	98%	95%	90%	80%	70%	60%
	$36,000	$31,000	$27,000	$22,500	$19,000	$17,000	$15,500

ROYAL SIDELOCK GAME GUN — 12, 20, 28 (new 1997) ga., or .410 bore (new 1997), somewhat similar to New Model, with improved cocking, striking and ejection, slimmer action body, DT, 25 to 30 in. game or VR barrels, 2¾ in. chambers, finest checkered walnut straight hand or pistol grip stock, scroll engraved receiver with color case hardened or bright finish, prototype testing has finished and guns are available for demonstration, 5 lbs. 1 oz - 7 lbs. 8 oz. Written quotations on this re-released model are available by contacting H&H directly (see Trademark Index). Values listed below are for base models only and reflect the most recent factory information. Limited availability.

Mfg.'s Sug. Retail $60,375

	100%	98%	95%	90%	80%	70%	60%
	$60,375	$32,750	$26,000	$21,750	$19,500	$18,250	$16,000

Add $4,470 for single trigger.
Add approx. 10% for 28 ga. or .410 bore.

ROYAL DE LUXE MODEL — similar to Royal Sidelock Game Gun, except choice of more elaborate engraving and exhibition wood.

* *12 or 20 ga.*
  Mfg.'s Sug. Retail $75,000

	100%	98%	95%	90%	80%	70%	60%
	$75,000	$49,000	$37,500	$29,250	$23,500	$20,000	$18,000

Add $4,470 for single trigger.

Grading	100%	98%	95%	90%	80%	70%	60%
* 28 ga. or .410 bore							
Mfg.'s Sug. Retail $84,000	$84,000	$55,000	$41,000	$32,000	$25,500	$22,500	$19,500

SPORTING MODEL — 12 ga. only, 2¾ in. chambers, designed with a trigger plate action, Game or Sporting Clays configuration featuring detachable SST mechanism, 28 to 32 in. game or VR barrels. Options on specifications to include screw-in chokes, 12 ga. - 7½-8 lbs., 20 ga. - 6 lbs. 6 oz. New 1993. Values below reflect most recent factory information. Limited availability.

	100%	98%	95%	90%	80%	70%	60%
* 12 or 16 ga.							
Mfg.'s Sug. Retail $29,380	$29,380	$23,750	$19,500	$15,250	$12,750	$10,750	$8,750

SPORTING DE LUXE MODEL — similar to Sporting O/U Model, except with choice of more elaborate engraving and exhibition wood. New 1993.

	100%	98%	95%	90%	80%	70%	60%
Mfg.'s Sug. Retail $37,650	$37,650	$28,250	$22,750	$17,750	$13,950	$11,000	$9,000

Add $850 for 20 or 28 ga.

SHOTGUNS: SxS

Holland & Holland currently manufactures the Royal De Luxe Game Gun and Royal Game Gun models in sidelock configuration (and are listed below). In addition to the sidelock models, H&H also manufactured the boxlock models Cavalier, Cavalier De Luxe, Northwood, and Northwood De Luxe until recently. The values below assume standard model with double triggers, game rib, standard walnut, or casing. Additional special order features will add considerable value to the price of a new custom order.

In 1988, Holland & Holland absorbed W & C Scott and manufactured the Chatsworth, Bowood, and Kinmount boxlock models until they were discontinued in late 1990. H&H has phased this trademark out, and more information can be found in the W & C Scott section of this text.

NORTHWOOD SxS BOXLOCK — 12, 16 (disc. 1992), 20, or 28 (disc. 1992) ga., 28 or 30 in. barrels, scalloped-case colored receiver, boxlock, auto ejectors, double triggers, border engraving, checkered pistol grip or straight stock. The values shown below are for standard model. Disc. 1993.

$5,950	$5,200	$4,450	$3,850	$3,300	$2,800	$2,300

Last Mfg.'s Sug. Retail was $6,705.

Add approx. 10% for 20 ga.
Add approx. 20% for 28 ga.

* Northwood De Luxe — 12, 16, 20, or 28 ga., scalloped-case colored receiver with moderate engraving and select walnut, double triggers. Disc. 1993.

$6,375	$5,450	$4,600	$3,950	$3,350	$2,850	$2,400

Last Mfg.'s Sug. Retail was $7,450.

Add approx. 10% for 20 ga.
Add approx. 20% for 28 ga.

CAVALIER SxS BOXLOCK — 12, 20, or 28 (disc. 1992) ga., best quality model boxlock with scalloped frame, double triggers, ejectors, and case colored receiver. Disc.

$9,500	$7,750	$6,350	$5,500	$4,850	$4,100	$3,500

Last Mfg.'s Sug. Retail was $11,175.

Add approx. 10% for 20 ga.
Add approx. 20% for 28 ga.

* Cavalier De Luxe — similar to Cavalier Model, except has deluxe walnut and better engraving. Disc. 1993.

$9,950	$8,000	$6,500	$5,600	$4,950	$4,200	$3,600

Last Mfg.'s Sug. Retail was $11,920.

Add approx. 10% for 20 ga.
Add approx. 20% for 28 ga.

Grading	100%	98%	95%	90%	80%	70%	60%

DOMINION GAME GUN — 12, 16, or 20 ga., 25-30 in. barrels, any choke, sidelock, auto ejectors, double triggers, checkered straight grip stock. Disc. 1990.

	$5,650	$4,750	$4,150	$3,650	$3,250	$2,850	$2,425

Add 20% for 20 gauge.

ROYAL HAMMERLESS EJECTOR SIDELOCK (NON-SELF OPENING) — 12, 16, 20, 28 ga., or .410 bore, non-self opening, customer specifications as to barrel length and chokes, hand detachable sidelocks, stocked in pistol grip or straight style to specifications. Mfg. 1885-disc.

	$20,000	$17,500	$14,750	$12,500	$10,000	$9,000	$8,000

Add 20% for 20 ga.
Add 40% for 28 ga.
Add 60% for .410 bore.

Above values are for older, previously manufactured specimens.

ROYAL GAME GUN — 12, 16, 20, 28 ga., or .410 bore, best quality sidelock self opening game gun. Mfg. per individual customer specifications. Values below reflect most recent factory information. Mfg. 1922 to date. Limited availability.

Mfg.'s Sug. Retail	$62,500	$62,500	$54,000	$42,500	$31,500	$22,500	$17,500	$12,750

Add $5,070 for 28 ga. or .410 bore.
Add $4,470 for ST.
Add $3,100 for VR (disc.).

ROYAL DE LUXE GAME GUN — 12, 16, 20, 28 ga., or .410 bore, top-of-the-line sidelock self opening shotgun. Mfg. per individual customer specifications. Current production.

* *12, 16, or 20 ga.*

Mfg.'s Sug. Retail	$70,000	$70,000	$55,000	$43,000	$32,000	$23,000	$18,000	$13,000

* *28 ga. or .410 bore*

Mfg.'s Sug. Retail	$75,000	$75,000	$58,500	$46,500	$35,000	$25,000	$20,000	$15,000

Add $5,600 for ST.
Add $3,100 for VR (disc.).

Older mfg. is sometimes referred to as the De Luxe Model.

BADMINTON SIDELOCK — similar to Royal model, without self opening action. Disc.

	$10,500	$9,000	$8,000	$7,000	$6,000	$5,000	$4,000

Add 20% for 20 ga.
Add 40% for 28 ga.
Add 60% for .410 bore.
Add $1,000 for SST.

Above values are for older, previously manufactured specimens.

* *Badminton Game Gun* — 12 or 20 ga., double or single trigger. Disc. 1988.

	$20,000	$17,000	$14,500	$12,250	$10,000	$8,500	$6,750

Last Mfg.'s Sug. Retail was $28,000.

RIVIERA SIDELOCK — similar to Badminton model, with two sets of barrels. Mfg. until 1967.

	$15,000	$11,500	$9,500	$7,950	$7,100	$6,350	$5,600

Add 20% for 20 ga.
Add 40% for 28 ga.
Add 60% for .410 bore.

CENTENARY SIDELOCK — 12 ga., 2 in. chambers, lightened version of Royal, Badminton, and Dominion grades. The values would be the same as for the standard models, mfg. until 1962.

H

Grading	100%	98%	95%	90%	80%	70%	60%

SHOTGUNS: SINGLE SHOT

SINGLE BARREL TRAP GUN — 12 ga., 30 or 32 in. full choke barrel, vent. rib, boxlock, auto ejector, Monte Carlo pistol grip stock, pad. Disc.

$15,000	$12,000	$10,000	$8,500	$7,500	$6,750	$4,850

Last Mfg.'s Sug. Retail was $28,420.

* Trap Guns - Older Mfg.

	100%	98%	95%	90%	80%	70%	60%
Standard Grade	$5,000	$4,500	$4,000	$3,250	$2,500	$2,250	$2,000
De Luxe Grade	$8,250	$7,000	$6,250	$5,000	$4,500	$3,750	$3,000
Exhibition Grade	$10,500	$8,950	$7,500	$6,000	$5,500	$5,000	$4,250

HOLLOWAY & NAUGHTON

Current company trade name of shotguns manufactured since the late 1800s in England. No current importation.

Please contact the factory directly (see Trademark Index) for more information including individual quotations.

SHOTGUNS: O/U, CUSTOM

O/U MODEL — all gauges, various configurations including field and sporting clays, features shallow coin finished sidelock action with reinforced forearm, SST, exhibition grade wood, engraving per customer specifications, special order only.

Currently, the Hollaway & Naughton O/U Model is priced in the $40,000-$50,000 range.

HOLLOWAY ARMS CO.

Previous manufacturer located in Fort Worth, TX.

Holloway firearms did not make many rifles or carbines before operations ceased.

RIFLES: SEMI-AUTO

HAC MODEL 7 RIFLE — .308 Win. cal., gas operated semi-auto paramilitary design rifle, 20 in. barrel, adj. front and rear sights, 20 shot mag., side folding stock. Mfg. 1984-1985 only. Also available in fully auto (class III dealers only) — add $80. Add $50 for left-hand variation.

$995	$895	$795	$695	$595	$525	$465

Last Mfg.'s Sug. Retail was $675.

* Model 7C Carbine — 16 in. carbine, same general specifications as Model 7. Disc. 1985.

$995	$895	$795	$695	$595	$525	$465

Last Mfg.'s Sug. Retail was $675.

Also available from the manufacturer were the models 7S and 7M (Sniper and Match models).

HOLMES FIREARMS

Previous manufacturer located in Wheeler, AR. Previously distributed by D.B. Distributing, Fayetteville, AR.

These pistols were mfg. in very limited numbers, most were in prototype configuration and exhibit changes from gun to gun. These models were open bolt and subject to 1988 federal legislation regulations.

PISTOLS: SEMI-AUTO

MP-83 — 9mm Para. or .45 ACP cal., paramilitary design pistol, 6 in. barrel, walnut stock and forearm, blued finish, 3½ lbs.

$595	$550	$500	$450	$400	$375	$350

Last Mfg.'s Sug. Retail was $450.

Add $75 for deluxe package.
Add $220 for conversion kit (mfg. 1985 only).

Grading	100%	98%	95%	90%	80%	70%	60%

MP-22 — .22 LR cal., 2½ lbs., steel and aluminum construction, 6 in. barrel, similar appearance to MP-83. Mfg. 1985 only.

	$395	$360	$320	$285	$250	$230	$210

Last Mfg.'s Sug. Retail was $400.

SHOTGUNS

COMBAT 12 — 12 ga., riot configuration, cylinder bore barrel. Disc. 1983.

	$795	$720	$650	$595	$550	$500	$450

Last Mfg.'s Sug. Retail was $750.

HOPKINS & ALLEN ARMS COMPANY, 1902-1914

Previous manufacturer located in Norwich, CT. H&A started their firearms business in 1867, manufacturing percussion revolvers. Before 1870, they were producing rimfire cartridge guns and eventually centerfire handguns and long guns. Prior to 1896, H&A guns were marked "HOPKINS & ALLEN MANUFG. CO. NORWICH CONN." or other private tradenames, including Merwin, Hulbert & Company. Hopkins & Allen guns are about equally priced with Stevens, N.R. Davis, Crescent Firearms Co., etc. There are many exceptions due to the numerous limited production guns, examples are the AA GRADE double shotgun and the "PARROT BEAK" Derringer. Hopkins & Allen also manufactured firearms which were not described in their catalogs.

Compiled from Hopkins & Allen catalogs by Charles E. Carder.

HANDGUNS

Most H&A handguns were nickel plated, with blue finish originally costing $.50 extra, grips were hard rubber, wood or pearl. Some had engraving from low to very good quality. Revolver barrel lengths varied from 1¾-6 in. Calibers were .22 rimfire (.22 S, L, or LR) up to .38-40 WCF. Specific calibers have not been listed in this section.

FOREHAND MODEL — .32 cal., breaktop, double action, five shot. Values range from $60-$150.

FOREHAND MODEL — similar to above except hammerless. (This model was offered in large and small frame). Values range from $60-$150.

FOREHAND MODEL — large frame as above in .32 and .38 centerfire cal. with full hammer or "bobbed" hammer. Values range from $60-$150.

FOREHAND MODEL — solid frame and hard rubber grips, otherwise as above in small frame. Values range from $50-$135.

FOREHAND MODEL — similar to above models, with "folding hammer". .22 rimfires were seven shot, while .32 and .38 centerfires were five shot. By 1909, the Forehand logo was dropped from these revolvers. Values range from $50-$135.

H&A NEW MODEL AUTOMATIC HAMMER REVOLVER — similar to breaktop with hammer, produced in small and large frame, in .22 rimfire, .32 and .38 centerfire cal. Values range from $50-$135.

H&A SOLID FRAME — .32 and .38 centerfire cal., five shot, double action, hammer or "bobbed" hammer. Values range from $40-$140.

H&A XL MODEL — similar to above in .22, .32 and .38 cal. Values range from $40-$140.

H&A RANGE MODEL — .22, .32 and .38 cal., solid frame, loading gate on right side, wood target style grips, single or double action. (Two models, large and small frames.) Values range from $50-$165.

Grading	100%	98%	95%	90%	80%	70%	60%

H&A TRIPLE ACTION SAFETY POLICE REVOLVER — .22, .32 and .38 cal.,breaktop with newly design locking mechanism, hard rubber or pearl grips (considered to be one of the best designed breaktops in its time). Other options for this model, include hammerless, engraved, wood target or pearl grips. Values range from $70-$190.

H&A NEW VEST POCKET DERRINGER — .22 Short rimfire cal., single shot, tip up, single action, 3½ in. overall length, folding trigger, blue or nickel finish, wood or pearl grips with golden monograms. This model was first listed about 1910 and known as the "Parrot Beak". An estimate of less than one thousand were produced and they are very rare. Values range from $550-$1,900.

H&A NEW MODEL TARGET PISTOL — .22 rimfire cal., single shot breaktop with the same new locking mechanism as the Safety Police Revolver, wood target grips with golden monograms, blue finish and 6, 8 or 10 in. barrels. Values range from $200-$450.

H&A NEW MODEL SKELETON STOCK TARGET PISTOL — similar to above, with rounded hard rubber grips with logo, detachable "skeleton metal stock", 18 in. barrel and blue finish. Values range from $250-$525.

RIFLES

Hopkins & Allen started building "falling block" rifles circa 1887-1914 with the buy-out of the Baystate Arms Company. Most commonly seen is the "Junior" model, known after 1902 as 922, 925, and 932. These numbers were in reference to the catalog numbers, not model numbers. In the very late 1890s or early 1900s, the Number 722, 822 and 832 rifles were added. In 1906, a "bolt action" repeater was added to their line, followed in 1909 by a "bolt action" single shot "military". Lyman tang sights were an option for many H&A rifles - add $60-$75. Specific calibers have not been listed in this section.

NUMBER 922 — falling block, lever operated, .22 cal. rimfire, with round bbl.

	100%	98%	95%	90%	80%	70%	60%
	$195	$165	$125	$110	$90	$75	$60

NUMBER 925 — similar to above in .25 cal. rimfire.

	$195	$150	$110	$95	$80	$70	$60

NUMBER 932 — similar to above in .32 cal. rimfire.

	$195	$150	$110	$95	$80	$70	$60

NUMBER 938 — similar to above in .38 S&W centerfire.

	$225	$200	$175	$150	$125	$100	$75

NUMBER 1922 — similar to above in .22 cal. rimfire with octagon bbl.

	$200	$180	$165	$150	$125	$100	$75

NUMBER 1932 — similar to above in .32 cal. rimfire.

	$200	$165	$125	$110	$90	$75	$65

NUMBER 2922 — similar to above in .22 cal. rimfire, with checkering.

	$265	$225	$195	$175	$150	$125	$100

NUMBER 2932 — similar to above in .32 cal. rimfire.

	$265	$225	$195	$175	$150	$125	$100

NUMBER 3922 — similar to above in .22 cal. rimfire, "SCHUETZEN RIFLE", nickeled Swiss butt plate, octagon barrel. (Schuetzen rifles in good cond., are somewhat rare.)

	$495	$450	$400	$365	$325	$275	$200

NUMBER 3925 — similar to above in .25-20 WCF. (This caliber rifle is more rare than the .22 cal. rimfire).

	$650	$600	$550	$500	$450	$350	$250

Grading	100%	98%	95%	90%	80%	70%	60%

NUMBER 44XL — chambered for the 44XL shotshell, similar to Number 922, except has smooth bore. (Referred to as, "TAXIDERMIST'S" or "LADIES GUN").

	100%	98%	95%	90%	80%	70%	60%
	$350	$325	$275	$235	$200	$175	$140

NUMBER 722 — .22 cal. rimfire, rolling block, thumb operated.

	100%	98%	95%	90%	80%	70%	60%
	$195	$1655	$125	$110	$90	$75	$60

SCOUT MILITARY RIFLE — similar to above with military style stock and with a "Bonneted Indian" stamped on the left side of frame. (These are somewhat rare).

	100%	98%	95%	90%	80%	70%	60%
	$325	$285	$250	$200	$175	$150	$135

NUMBER 822 — .22 cal. rimfire, rolling block, lever operated,

	100%	98%	95%	90%	80%	70%	60%
	$195	$175	$150	$125	$100	$85	$75

NUMBER 832 — .32 cal. rimfire, otherwise similar to Model 822 (This model was offered first with "pig tail" type levers and later with "loop" type levers. The "loop levers" are somewhat rare.)

	100%	98%	95%	90%	80%	70%	60%
	$225	$200	$175	$150	$125	$100	$75

NUMBER 4922 — .22 rimfire cal., bolt action, repeater.

	100%	98%	95%	90%	80%	70%	60%
	$135	$120	$100	$80	$70	$60	$50

NUMBER 5022 — similar to above with deluxe checkering.

	100%	98%	95%	90%	80%	70%	60%
	$175	$150	$135	$100	$85	$75	$60

MILITARY RIFLE — similar to above, except single shot with military style stock and sling. (In good condition, these are somewhat rare.)

	100%	98%	95%	90%	80%	70%	60%
	$250	$225	$200	$185	$165	$140	$125

NOISELESS — .22 rimfire, similar to the Number 922, except for checkered wood and the addition of a noise suppressor attached to the muzzle, by means of mating threads inside of suppressor and outside of barrel. The job is so well fitted, that it is difficult to recognize the suppressor. The front sight is attached to a dovetail slot in the suppressor. (These rifles are listed under the National Firearms Act of 1934 and must have proper licensing. Very rare.) Values range from $250-$550.

SHOTGUNS: SxS

Hopkins & Allen purchased Forehand Arms Co. and continued to produce their line of firearms, and after a few years dropped the Forehand name. In 1902, they offered the Forehand double boxlocks with or without outside hammers. Most models were offered in 12, 16 & 20 gauge. Sidelocks were added 1906-09. In 1902, the **AA GRADE**, a very high quality boxlock, was offered for $100 to $125. It had fine Damascus barrels, straight grip, plain or automatic ejectors, fine wood and engraving and was competitive with some Remingtons, L.C. Smiths, Bakers and other fine guns of that era. This gun was very short lived and today is rare. One feature found on all H&A double barrel guns is the "rib extension" or "doll's head."

BOXLOCK — Anson & Deeley type frame, damascus, twist, and steel barrels. Values range from $75-$250.

BOXLOCK — similar to above, except with outside hammers. Values range from $75-$250.

SIDELOCK — hammerless, damascus, twist, and steel barrels. Values range from $90-$250.

SIDELOCK — similar to above, except with outside hammers. Values range from $75-$250.

SHOTGUNS: SINGLE SHOT

H&A produced a "falling block" shotgun in most gauges circa 1887 - early 1900s. Falling Blocks (FBs) in 12 ga. were built on heavy frames with the 20 and 16 gauges sharing a medium frame. Prior to 1902, some FBs were chambered for .45-70 shotshells and, today, these are rare if in good condition. From the 1890s through 1914, 38XL, 44XL

Grading	100%	98%	95%	90%	80%	70%	60%

shotshell guns were periodically offered in the Junior frame. After 1902, "tip-over" single shotguns were offered in Forehand designs and, later, the Davenport designs.

FALLING BLOCK — lever operated, outside hammer. Values range from $100-$275.

BOXLOCK — with outside hammer, damascus, twist, and steel barrels. Values range from $65-$150.

BOXLOCK — hammerless, top safety. Values range from $65-$150.

GOOSE GUNS — outside hammer, 8, 10, or 12 ga., were offered with barrels up to 40 inches long. Values range from $90-$200.

"SAFETY SINGLE GUN" — engraved with outside hammer and top safety. (Was offered in 1911 and recommended for trap shooting for $15.00). Values range from $100-$200.

HORTON, LEW, DIST. CO.

See Lew Horton Dist. Co. listing.

HOWA

Current manufacturer located in Tokyo, Japan beginning 1967.

Currently, Howa sporting rifles are being imported by Interarms/Howa, located in Alexandria, VA. Previously, Howa rifles were imported by Weatherby (Vanguard Series), Smith & Wesson (pre-1985), and Mossberg (1986-87).

RIFLES: BOLT ACTION

MODEL 1500 HUNTER — .22-250 Rem., .223 Rem., .243 Win., .270 Win., .308 Win., .30-06, .300 Win. Mag., .338 Win. Mag. (new 1999), or 7mm Rem. Mag. cal., 3 (Mag. cals. only) or 5 shot, 22 or 24 in. barrel, adj. rear sight and trigger, checkered walnut stock, blue metal finish or stainless steel (new 1999) construction, approx. 7.6 lbs. Imported by Interarms 1988 only, reintroduced during 1999.

Mfg.'s Sug. Retail	$455		$375	$300	$265	$225	$195	$175	$160

    Add $20 for Mag. cals.
    Add $50 for stainless steel.

* *Model 1500 Lightning* — .270 Win., .30-06, .300 Win. Mag., or 7mm Rem. Mag. cal., lightweight variation of the Model 1500 Hunter featuring lightweight Carbolite (synthetic) stock, 7 lbs. Imported 1988-91.

	$415	$335	$290	$260	$240	$225	$205

    Last Mfg.'s Sug. Retail was $539.

    Add $20 for Mag. cals.

LIGHTNING RIFLE — .22-250 Rem., .223 Rem., .243 Win., .270 Win., .30-06, .308 Win., 7mm Rem. Mag., .300 Win. Mag., or .338 Win. Mag. cal., 22 or 24 in. barrel, black synthetic Carbolite stock with cheekpiece and pressed checkering, no sights, 3 or 5 shot mag., high luster bluing or stainless steel, approx. 7.6 lbs. Importation began 1993.

Mfg.'s Sug. Retail	$435		$335	$285	$245	$220	$195	$175	$160

    Add $50 for stainless steel.
    Add $20 for Mag. cals.

MODEL 1500 VARMINT — .22-250 Rem., .223 Rem., or .308 Win. (mfg. 1990-92) cal., 24 in. heavy barrel without sights, 5 shot mag., blue steel or stainless steel (new 1999) construction, black polymer (new 1999) or walnut stock, approx. 9.3 lbs. Imported 1988-92, reintroduced 1999.

Mfg.'s Sug. Retail	$465		$385	$315	$265	$225	$195	$175	$160

    Add $20 for wood stock.
    Add $60 for stainless steel.

Grading	100%	98%	95%	90%	80%	70%	60%

MODEL 1500 PCS — .308 Win. cal., police counter sniper rifle featuring 24 in. barrel, choice of blue metal or stainless steel, black synthetic or checkered walnut stock, no sights, approx. 9.3 lbs. Importation began 1999.

Mfg.'s Sug. Retail	$465	$385	$315	$265	$225	$195	$175	$160

    Add $20 for wood stock.
    Add $60 for stainless steel.

MODEL 1500 TROPHY — .22-250 Rem., .223 Rem., .243 Win., .270 Win., .308 Win., .30-06, .300 Win. Mag., .338 Win. Mag. or 7mm Rem. Mag. cal., 3 (Mag. cals. only) or 5 shot, 22 or 24 in. barrel, adj. rear sight and trigger, select Monte Carlo stock with skipline checkering. Imported 1988-92.

			$528	$410	$335	$290	$260	$240	$225

Last Mfg.'s Sug. Retail was $528.

    Add $20 for Mag. cals.

LIGHTNING WOODGRAIN — .243 Win., .270 Win., .30-06, .308 Win., or 7mm Rem. Mag. cal., features lightweight Carbolite synthetic stock with simulated wood grain and checkering, 22 in. barrel, 5 shot mag., no sights, 7.5 lbs. Imported 1994 only.

				$450	$395	$365	$320	$275	$250	$225

Last Mfg.'s Sug. Retail was $537.

    Add $19 for 7mm Rem. Mag. cal.

REALTREE CAMO RIFLE — .270 Win. or .30-06 (disc. 1993) cal., 22 in. barrel, 5 shot mag., monobloc receiver, drilled and tapped, thumb safety, entire rifle is coated with a Realtree brown leaf camo pattern, no sights, 8 lbs. Imported 1993-94.

				$495	$400	$350	$325	$300	$280	$260

Last Mfg.'s Sug. Retail was $620.

HUG-SAN

Current shotgun manufacturer located in Huglu, Turkey. No current importation.

Hug-San manufactures slide action, semi-auto, and O/U shotguns, in various configurations and gauges. Please contact the factory (see Trademark Index) for more information.

HUNTER ARMS COMPANY

Previous manufacturer located in Fulton, NY circa 1891-1945.

The Hunter Arms Company was formed to manufacture L.C. Smith shotguns. Please refer to the L.C. Smith section in this text for further information regarding this manufacturer (including Fulton, Fulton Special, and Hunter Special models.)

HUSQVARNA

Previous manufacturer located in Husqvarna, Sweden.

Also see: Lahti Pistols

RIFLES: BOLT ACTION

HI-POWER — .220 Swift, .270 Win., or .30-06 cal., Mauser type action, open sight, checkered beech wood. Mfg. 1946-1951, early models found in 6.5x55mm, 8x57R, 9.3x57mm cals.

				$395	$365	$330	$295	$265	$235	$200

MODEL 1951 — similar to Hi-Power, except high profile stock.

				$425	$385	$340	$300	$270	$240	$210

SERIES 1100 DELUXE — similar to Model 1951, except has European walnut and jeweled bolt. Mfg. 1952-1956.

				$440	$360	$330	$310	$290	$275	$250

SERIES 1000 SUPER GRADE — similar to Model 1951, has walnut Monte Carlo stock. Mfg. 1952-1956.

				$440	$360	$330	$310	$290	$275	$250

Grading	100%	98%	95%	90%	80%	70%	60%

SERIES 3100 CROWN GRADE — .243 Win., .270 Win., .30-06, 7x57mm, or .308 Win. cal., improved HVA Mauser action, 24 in. barrel, walnut stock, black forend tip and pistol grip cap. Mfg. 1954-1972.

| | $470 | $385 | $360 | $330 | $315 | $305 | $275 |

SERIES 3000 CROWN GRADE — similar to 3100, except has Monte Carlo stock.

| | $470 | $385 | $360 | $330 | $315 | $305 | $275 |

SERIES 4100 LIGHTWEIGHT — HVA Mauser action, calibers same as 3100, 20½ in. barrel, open sights, lightweight walnut stock, pistol grip, Schnabel forend. Mfg. 1954-1972.

| | $470 | $385 | $360 | $330 | $315 | $305 | $275 |

SERIES 4000 LIGHTWEIGHT — similar to 4100, except has Monte Carlo stock, no sights.

| | $470 | $385 | $360 | $330 | $315 | $305 | $275 |

MODEL 456 LIGHTWEIGHT — similar to 4000/4100, except full length stock. Mfg. 1959-1970.

| | $495 | $415 | $385 | $360 | $330 | $310 | $290 |

SERIES 6000 IMPERIAL GRADE — similar to 3100, except has select wood, 3 leaf folding sight. Mfg. 1968-1970.

| | $580 | $495 | $470 | $440 | $395 | $365 | $330 |

SERIES 6000 IMPERIAL LIGHTWEIGHT — similar to 6000 Imperial, except 20½ in. barrel, lightweight stock.

| | $580 | $495 | $470 | $440 | $395 | $365 | $330 |

SERIES P-3000 PRESENTATION — similar to Crown, except engraved action, special wood. Mfg. 1968-1970.

| | $770 | $660 | $635 | $605 | $550 | $510 | $485 |

MODEL 9000 CROWN GRADE — cals. similar to Model 3100 Crown Grade, except also available in .300 Win. Mag. cal., Husqvarna action, 23½ in. barrel, adj. trigger, adj. sight, walnut stock. Mfg. 1971-1972.

| | $470 | $385 | $360 | $330 | $315 | $305 | $275 |

MODEL 8000 IMPERIAL — similar to 9000, but jeweled bolt, engraved floor plate, no sights and deluxe stock. Mfg. 1971-1972.

| | $605 | $525 | $495 | $470 | $415 | $385 | $350 |

HY-HUNTER INC. FIREARMS MANUFACTURING CO.

Previous manufacturer located in W. Germany, imported by Hy-Hunter Inc.

Previous importer of single action revolvers in various calibers. Typically, prices are determined by their shooting value rather than their collector value. Prices generally range from $100-$175 depending on caliber and finish.

HYPER

Previous manufacturer located in Jenks, OK.

RIFLES: SINGLE SHOT

SINGLE SHOT RIFLE — all calibers, all standard lengths and contours, falling block trigger guard lever activated, adj. trigger, no sights, stocked to customer specifications, in AA grade walnut. Disc. 1984.

| | $2,200 | $1,980 | $1,925 | $1,870 | $1,650 | $1,540 | $1,375 |

Add $75 for stainless barrel.
Add $85 for octagon barrel.

I section

I A B SHOTGUNS

Currently manufactured by Industria Armi Bresciane, Italy. No current importation. Previously distributed by Sporting Arms International, Inc. located in Indianola, MS.

I A B manufactures high quality competition (O/U and single barrel trap or skeet) shotguns in various styles and configurations including combo sets. These guns employ a boxlock action, have ejectors, and various amounts of engraving. Prices for 100% condition usually start in the $550-$900 price range. I A B shotguns are not being imported currently - values for older models will be determined by the prices shooters, not collectors, are willing to pay for them.

IAI

Current importer and distributor located in Houston, TX. Firearms are manufactured by Israel Arms, Ltd., located in Israel. IAI designates Israel Arms International, and should not be confused with Irwindale Arms, Inc. (also I A I) listed below. Please refer to the Israel Arms Ltd. listing later in this section.

I A I

Please refer to the Irwindale Arms, Inc. heading in this section.

IAR, Inc.

Current importer and distributor since 1996 located in San Juan Capistrano, CA.

In addition to the IAR, Inc. models listed below, other trademarks are also distributed by IAR, Inc.

Grading	100%	98%	95%	90%	80%	70%	60%

DERRINGERS

1872 COLT DERRINGER — .22 Short cal., choice of gold or nickel frame, blue, nickel, or gold barrel, smooth walnut grips. New 1997.

Mfg.'s Sug. Retail	$99	$85	$70	$55	$50	$45	$40	$35

Add $26 for case.
Add $20 for nickel or gold barrel.
This model is also available as a double-case set - current retail is $215.

REVOLVERS: SINGLE ACTION

1873 FRONTIER MARSHAL — .357 Mag. or .45 LC, 4¾, 5½, or 7½ in. barrel, case colored frame, polished backstrap and trigger guard, walnut grips. Importation began 1998.

Mfg.'s Sug. Retail	$400	$350	$300	$275	$250	$225	$195	$175

1873 COLT FRONTIER — .22 LR cal., 4¾ in. barrel, case colored frame, black nickel backstrap and trigger guard, smooth walnut grips with IAR, Inc. cartouche. Importation began 1997.

Mfg.'s Sug. Retail	$400	$350	$300	$275	$250	$225	$195	$175

Add $50 for .22 LR/.22 Mag. Combo.
Add $85 for nickel finish.
Add $50 for wood case.
Add $100 for steel grip assembly package.

1873 SIX SHOOTER ¾ SCALE COMBO — .22 LR/.22 Mag. cal. combo, ¾ scale reproduction of the Colt SAA with 5½ in. barrel, case colored receiver, blue finish, smooth walnut grips, steel construction. New 1997.

Mfg.'s Sug. Retail	$400	$350	$300	$275	$250	$225	$195	$175

Grading	100%	98%	95%	90%	80%	70%	60%

SHOTGUNS: SxS, EXPOSED HAMMER

OVERLAND COWBOY — 12 ga., 28 in. barrels, choice of Cowboy or Gentry Model. New 1997.

Mfg.'s Sug. Retail	$1,895		$1,625	$1,400	$1,125	$775	$650	$525	$400

STAGECOACH COWBOY — 12 ga., 20 in. barrels, choice of Cowboy or Gentry Model. New 1997.

Mfg.'s Sug. Retail	$1,895		$1,625	$1,400	$1,125	$775	$650	$525	$400

I G A SHOTGUNS

Current manufacturer located in Veranopolis, Brazil. Currently imported by Stoeger Industries, Inc. located in Wayne, NJ.

SHOTGUNS: SxS

UPLANDER MODEL — 12, 16 (new 1996), 20, 28 ga., or .410 bore, 3 in. chambers, underlug lockup, checkered pistol grip or straight English (20 ga. or .410 bore only) stock, Youth Model also available in .410 bore, double triggers, extractors.

Mfg.'s Sug. Retail	$434		$325	$225	$185	$150	$130	$115	$100

Add $40 for choke tubes (12 or 20 ga.).
Add $12 for Youth Model (.410 bore with 24 in. barrels and shortened stock).
Add $51 for Ladies Model (20 ga. with 24 in. barrels and shortened stock).

DELUXE MODEL — 12, 20, 28 ga., or .410 bore, features better quality checkered walnut stock and forearm, gold triggers, 12 and 20 ga. have choke tubes, 28 ga. and .410 bore have fixed chokes. New 1997.

Mfg.'s Sug. Retail	$559		$425	$365	$310	$270	$230	$195	$170

Subtract $40 for 28 ga. or .410 bore (fixed chokes only).

COACH GUN MODEL — 12, 20 ga., or .410 (new 1991) bore, choice of blue or nickel (new 1996) finish, 20 in. barrels only, choice of dark (nickel finish only) or light hardwood stock.

Mfg.'s Sug. Retail	$415		$310	$215	$175	$145	$125	$110	$100

Add $49 for nickel finish.
Add $64 for engraved stagecoach scene on receiver (new 1996).

* *Coach Deluxe* — similar to Coach Gun Model, includes deluxe checkered walnut stock and forearm, fixed (IC/M) or choke tubes (new 1998), gold triggers. New 1997.

Mfg.'s Sug. Retail	$499		$385	$325	$290	$260	$230	$195	$170

TURKEY SERIES MODEL — 12 ga. only, 3 in. chambers, 24 in. barrels, DT, choke tubes. New 1997.

Mfg.'s Sug. Retail	$559		$425	$365	$310	$270	$230	$195	$170

SHOTGUNS: O/U

CONDOR MODEL — 12 ga. only, single trigger, ejectors, presentation walnut, chrome lined bores. Disc. 1985.

			$580	$500	$450	$410	$375	$350	$325

Last Mfg.'s Sug. Retail was $667.

CONDOR I SINGLE TRIGGER — 12 or 20 ga., 3 in. chambers, sliding underlug action, VR, deluxe checkered walnut, separated barrels.

Mfg.'s Sug. Retail	$559		$425	$340	$265	$230	$210	$195	$180

Choke tubes became standard 1992.

CONDOR II DOUBLE TRIGGER — 12 or 20 (disc.) ga., sliding underlug action, VR, checkered walnut, separated barrels. Disc. 1997.

			$350	$295	$260	$230	$195	$170	$150

Last Mfg.'s Sug. Retail was $459.

Grading	100%	98%	95%	90%	80%	70%	60%

CONDOR SUPREME — 12 or 20 ga., boxlock action, single trigger, ejectors, 26 or 28 in. VR barrels with choke tubes, deluxe checkered walnut stock and forearm. Importation began 1995.

Mfg.'s Sug. Retail	$629	$535	$475	$420	$360	$320	$280	$240

HUNTER CLAYS MODEL — 12 ga. only, ST, ejectors, 28 in. barrels with choke tubes, deluxe checkered stock and forearm, gold trigger. New 1997.

Mfg.'s Sug. Retail	$699	$595	$515	$435	$375	$335	$300	$270

TURKEY SERIES — 12 ga. only, 3 in. chambers, 26 in. VR barrels with choke tubes, ST, ejectors, Advantage camo on wood and metal (except receiver). New 1997.

Mfg.'s Sug. Retail	$729	$615	$525	$450	$380	$335	$300	$270

WATERFOWL SERIES — 12 ga. only, 3 in. chambers, similar to Turkey Series, except has 30 in. barrels. New 1998.

Mfg.'s Sug. Retail	$729	$615	$525	$450	$380	$335	$300	$270

TRAP SERIES — 12 ga., features SST, ejectors, 30 in. VR barrels with choke tubes, deluxe checkered Monte Carlo stock and forearm. New 1998.

Mfg.'s Sug. Retail	$699	$595	$515	$435	$375	$335	$300	$270

ERA 2000 MODELS — 12 ga. only, 26 or 28 in. VR barrels with choke tubes, single trigger. Imported 1992-94.

	$585	$375	$315	$250	$215	$195	$180

Last Mfg.'s Sug. Retail was $710.

REUNA SINGLE BARREL — 12, 20 ga., or .410 bore, exposed hammer with half-cock, extractor. Disc. 1998.

	$95	$70	$60	$50	$45	$40	$35

Last Mfg.'s Sug. Retail was $120.

Add $22 for choke tubes (12 ga. new 1992, 20 ga. new 1993).

* **Reuna Single Barrel Youth** — 20 ga. or .410 bore, 22 in. barrel, features rubber recoil pad. Imported 1993-98.

	$100	$75	$60	$50	$45	$40	$35

Last Mfg.'s Sug. Retail was $132.

IBERIA FIREARMS

Current manufacturer of .40 S&W cal. pistols located in Iberia, OH. Distributed by MKS Supply located in Dayton, OH. Distributor sales only.

Please refer to the Hi-Point section in this text.

IMPERIAL GUN CO. LTD

Previous manufacturer located in Surrey, Great Britain circa 1992-95. The Imperial Gun Co. Ltd. had limited importation into the U.S.

Imperial Gun secondary marketplace values must be based realistically on their competitive shooting value, not collectibility.

INDIAN ARMS

Previously manufactured by Indian Arms Corporation located in Detroit, MI.

PISTOLS: SEMI-AUTO

INDIAN ARMS .380 — .380 ACP cal., patterned after Walther PPK, stainless steel, 3¼ in. barrel, 6 shot mag., natural or blue finish, with (early specimens) or without key lock safety, with or without VR barrel, walnut grips, 20 oz. Mfg. 1975-1977.

	$395	$285	$230

This model had limited manufacture with approx. 1,000 guns being made.

Grading	100%	98%	95%	90%	80%	70%	60%

INDUSTRIA ARMI GALESI

Previous manufacturer located in Brescia, Italy.

PISTOLS: SEMI-AUTO

GALESI MODEL 6 POCKET AUTO — .22 LR or .25 ACP cal., 6 shot, 2¼ in. barrel blue, fixed sights, plastic grips. Mfg. 1930–disc.

	100%	98%	95%	90%	80%	70%	60%
	$130	$120	$105	$90	$75	$65	$55

Add 100% if chrome engraved.

GALESI MODEL 9 POCKET AUTO — .22 LR, .32 ACP, or .380 ACP cal., 8 shot, 3¼ in. barrel, blue, fixed sights, plastic grips. Mfg. 1930–disc.

	100%	98%	95%	90%	80%	70%	60%
	$140	$125	$110	$100	$85	$65	$55

Add 100% if chrome engraved.

INFALLIBLE

Previously manufactured by Warner Arms Corp. located in Norwich, CT and Davis-Warner Arms Corp. located in Assonet, MA.

PISTOLS: SEMI-AUTO

INFALLIBLE PISTOL — .32 ACP cal., 3.2 in. barrel, 7 shot mag., 24.7 oz.

* **Type I** — mfg. and marked "Warner Arms Corp., Norwich, Conn.", serial range is 501-2,299.

	100%	98%	95%	90%	80%	70%	60%
	$325	$295	$270	$250	$225	$200	$180

* **Type II** — marked "Davis-Warner Arms Corporation, Assonet, Massachusetts", serial range is 2,300-5,299.

	100%	98%	95%	90%	80%	70%	60%
	$295	$270	$250	$225	$195	$170	$150

* **Type III** — marked "Warner Arms Corporation, Norwich, Connecticut", serial range is 5,300-7,400.

	100%	98%	95%	90%	80%	70%	60%
	$295	$270	$250	$225	$195	$170	$150

INFINITY FIREARMS

Currently manufactured by Strayer-Voight Inc. since 1994 and located in Grand Prairie, TX.

PISTOLS: SEMI-AUTO

STANDARD MODEL — 9mm Para. (new 1997), .38 Super, 10mm (new 1997), .40 S&W, .45 ACP, 9x23mm, or 9x25mm cal., competition pistol featuring lightweight hardened frame, 5 in. barrel, Novak fixed rear sight, 10 shot mag., and other competition features. New 1994.

Mfg.'s Sug. Retail	$1,601		$1,450	$1,325	$1,100	$925	$775	$650	$525

Add $208 for hybrid barrel.

COMPENSATED PISTOL — similar to Standard Model except includes 9x21mm, 9x23mm, and 9x25mm cals., features 6 port compensated barrel, nickel finished slide and upper frame. New 1994.

Mfg.'s Sug. Retail	$2,209		$1,975	$1,775	$1,525	$1,300	$1,100	$925	$775

Add $28 for 8 port barrel.
Add $242 for Hybricomp barrel.
Add $1,273 per alternate top end (includes barrel, Breechface, and extractor).

During 1998, Infinity developed a slide with an interchangeable breechface; this allows the user to change caliber by installing a new caliber breechface, barrel, and extractor within the same slide. It also provides the shooter a simple and inexpensive method of replacing a worn breechface.

Grading	100%	98%	95%	90%	80%	70%	60%

INGLIS HI-POWERS

Previously manufactured by John Inglis Co. Limited of Toronto, Canada. Over 151,000 Inglis Hi-Powers were manufactured between February 1944 and September 1945 under military contractual agreement.

PISTOLS: SEMI-AUTO

CHINESE CONTRACT PATTERN 35

* ***Chinese No. 1*** — 9mm Para. cal., large Chinese characters (6) on left slide, slotted for stock and tangent sights.

$3,500	$3,000	$2,350	$1,500	$1,000	$750	$600

Add $350 for original wood holster stock.

CH SERIES CANADIAN MILITARY

* ***MK 1-No. 1 Inglis*** — 9mm Para. cal., tangent sight, slotted.

$1,250	$1,100	$800	$725	$650	$550	$450

Add $350 for original wood holster stock. Beware of reproductions.

This model has been recently imported again. Most recent imports are priced $350-$550.

T SERIES CANADIAN MILITARY

* ***MK 1-No. 2 Inglis*** — 9mm Para. cal., fixed sight, without slot, numerical prefix references (0-10) the number of guns in increments of 10,000. Scarcer variations include: 0, 1, 9, and 10.

$650	$525	$450	$395	$345	$295	$275

Add 10% for decal on front strap.
Add 10% for O or 1 variation.
Add 15% for 9 variation.
Add 30% for 10 variation.

This model has been recently imported again. Most recent imports are priced $350-$550.

* ***Inglis "diamond logo"*** — refers to Inglis trademark in diamond shaped logo on left side of slide, mfg. 1946-47 for commercial sales.

$2,250	$1,800	$1,500	$1,200	$800	$600	$400

All Inglis diamond variations are in the 5 CH or 9 T ser. no. range.

* ***MK 1-No. 2 Inglis*** — fixed sight, slotted. Inspect slot carefully.

$1,150	$975	$850	$725	$650	$550	$450

INGRAM

Previously manufactured until late 1982 by Military Armament Corp. (MAC) located in Atlanta, GA.

PISTOLS: SEMI-AUTO

MAC 10 — .45 ACP or 9mm Para. cal., open bolt, pistol version of the sub machine gun, 16 and 32 shot mag., compact construction, all metal construction, rear aperture and front blade sight. Disc. 1982.

$850	$775	$700	$650	$600	$550	$495

Add approx. $160 for accessories (barrel extension, case, and extra mag).

MAC 10A1 — similar to MAC 10 except fires from a closed bolt.

$295	$275	$250	$230	$215	$200	$190

MAC 11 — similar to MAC 10 except in .380 ACP cal.

$650	$595	$550	$525	$500	$480	$460

Grading	100%	98%	95%	90%	80%	70%	60%

INTERARMS

Current importer and distributor located in Alexandria, VA.

Interarms has imported a multitude of trademarks and models since the early 1960s. Most of the models shown below are recent imports, and specific information on older, limited import models can be obtained by contacting Interarms directly. The FEG, Howa (currently imported), Rossi, and Walther trademarks will be found in their own sections listed alphabetically in this text.

PISTOLS: SEMI-AUTO, FEG & HELWAN MFG.

Please refer to the FEG & HELWAN sections in this text.

REVOLVERS: SA, VIRGINIAN SERIES

Virginian Revolvers were previously imported from Europe by various manufacturers (including Hämmerli of Switzerland). They were also manufactured in Midland, VA from 1976-1984. Older models with exceptional quality (including Hämmerli guns) are worth a premium over values listed below.

VIRGINIAN DRAGOON STANDARD — .44 Mag. or .45 LC (mfg. 1982-84) cal., improved action patterned after Colt SAA design, 6 shot, 6, 7½, 8⅜, or 12 (Buntline) in. barrel, blue finish, smooth walnut grips, adj. rear sight, 51 oz. with 7½ in. barrel.

$255	$225	$205	$190	$180	$170	$160

Last Mfg.'s Sug. Retail was $315.

    Add 15% for Buntline Model.

* ***Dragoon Standard Stainless*** — .44 Mag. or .45 LC cal., 6 (disc.), 7½ (disc.), or 8⅜ in. barrel, same general specifications as Standard Dragoon.

$265	$230	$210

Last Mfg.'s Sug. Retail was $315.

DRAGOON SILHOUETTE — .357 Mag. or .44 Mag. cal., stainless steel, 7½, 8⅜, or 10½ in. (standard on .357 Mag.) barrel, special sights and grips.

$365	$320	$275

Last Mfg.'s Sug. Retail was $425.

DRAGOON ENGRAVED — .44 Mag. cal. only, choice of stainless steel or blue finish, 6 or 7½ in. barrel.

$545	$470	$430	$395	$360	$320	$285

Last Mfg.'s Sug. Retail was $625.

    Add $75 for presentation case.

DRAGOON "DEPUTY" — .357 Mag. or .44 Mag. cal., blued barrel, case hardened frame, 5 in. barrel only.

$250	$215	$195	$180	$165	$155	$145

Last Mfg.'s Sug. Retail was $295.

* ***Stainless Deputy*** — similar to above, except .44 Mag. available in 6 in. barrel only, stainless steel.

$255	$225	$205

Last Mfg.'s Sug. Retail was $295.

VIRGINIAN .22 CONVERTIBLE — .22 LR/.22 Mag. cal. cylinders, 5½ in. barrel only, adj. rear sight, 38 oz.

$185	$155	$145	$135	$125	$115	$105

Last Mfg.'s Sug. Retail was $219.

* ***Virginian .22 Convertible Stainless*** — stainless steel fabrication, otherwise similar to above.

$200	$170	$155

Last Mfg.'s Sug. Retail was $239.

Grading	100%	98%	95%	90%	80%	70%	60%

RIFLES: BOLT ACTION, DISC.

MODEL JW-15 — .22 LR cal., 5 shot detachable mag., 23.8 in. barrel, open sights, blued finish, Model 70 style safety, patterned after the Brno Model ZKM, 5.5 lbs. Mfg. by Norinco. Imported 1990-96.

	$85	$70	$60	$50	$40	$35	$30

Last Mfg.'s Sug. Retail was $109.

ENFIELD NO. 4 — .303 British cal., genuine British Commonwealth issue, 25¼ in. barrel, 10 shot box mag., 9 lbs. Importation disc. 1996.

	$75	$60	$50	$40	$35	$35	$35

Last Mfg.'s Sug. Retail was $86.

RIFLES: BOLT ACTION, HOWA MFG.

Please refer to the Howa section in this text.

RIFLES: BOLT ACTION, MAUSER ACTIONS

Whitworth rifles were mfg. in England. Mark X rifles were mfg. in Yugoslavia by Zastava Arms until late 1997.

MARK X VISCOUNT — .22-250 Rem. (disc. 1993), .243 Win. (disc. 1993), .25-06 Rem. (disc. 1993), .270 Win. (disc. 1993), 7x57mm (disc. 1993), 7mm Rem. Mag. (disc. 1994), .308 Win. (disc. 1994), .30-06, or .300 Win. Mag. (disc. 1994) cal., 5 shot, 3 shot mag., 24 in. barrel, adj. rear sight and trigger, classic style Monte Carlo stock. Disc. 1983, re-introduced 1985 - disc. 1996.

	$375	$300	$265	$240	$225	$205	$190

Last Mfg.'s Sug. Retail was $471.

Add $15 for 7mm Rem. Mag. or .300 Win. Mag. cal.

This model is often referred to as the Viscount. Early manufacture was done in Manchester, England. Recent manufacture is in Yugoslavia. Earlier Manchester guns (before approx. 1980) will bring a slight premium over the values listed above.

* *Mini Mark X* — .223 Rem. or 7.62x39mm (new in 1990) cal., miniature M98 Mauser System action, 20 in. barrel with iron sights, checkered hardwood stock, 5 shot mag., adj. trigger, 6.35 lbs. Imported 1987-94.

	$360	$295	$265	$240	$225	$205	$190

Last Mfg.'s Sug. Retail was $455.

* *Lightweight Mark X* — .22-250 Rem. (new 1994), .270 Win. (disc.), .30-06 (disc. 1994), or 7mm Rem. Mag. (disc.) cal., similar to Mark X Viscount, except has Carbolite (synthetic) stock and 20 in. barrel, 7 lbs. Imported 1988-90, reintroduced 1994-97.

	$350	$290	$265	$240	$225	$205	$190

Last Mfg.'s Sug. Retail was $438.

CAVALIER — similar to Viscount, except modern style stock, roll-over cheekpiece, rosewood pistol grip cap and forend tip, recoil pad. Disc.

	$365	$330	$305	$290	$265	$230	$195

MANNLICHER STYLE CARBINE — similar to Cavalier, except 20 in. barrel, full length stock, no Magnum or varmint calibers. Disc.

	$365	$330	$305	$290	$265	$230	$195

CONTINENTAL CARBINE — similar to Mannlicher Style, except with double set trigger. Disc.

	$395	$365	$330	$310	$285	$255	$220

THE MARQUIS — .243 Win., .270 Win., .308 Win., 7x57mm, or .30-06 cal., 20 in. barrel, adj. trigger. Mannlicher style carbine. Disc. 1984.

	$430	$325	$300	$275	$250	$230	$215

ALASKAN — similar to Mark X, except .375 H&H or .458 Win. Mag. cal., recoil pad and extra stock crossbolt. Disc. 1984.

	$460	$350	$330	$310	$290	$250	$210

Grading	100%	98%	95%	90%	80%	70%	60%

MARK X REALTREE — .270 Win. or .30-06 cal., features Realtree Camo finish. Imported 1994-96.

	100%	98%	95%	90%	80%	70%	60%
	$460	$390	$365	$320	$275	$250	$225

Last Mfg.'s Sug. Retail was $549.

MARK X WHITWORTH — current cals. include .270 Win., .30-06, and .300 Win. Mag., Mauser action, 24 in. barrel, open sights, 5 shot mag. (.300 Win. Mag. is only 3), checkered deluxe walnut with ebony forearm tip, thumb safety with sling swivels, adj. trigger, rubber recoil butt plate, 7 lbs. Imported 1984-96.

	100%	98%	95%	90%	80%	70%	60%
	$475	$400	$365	$320	$275	$250	$225

Last Mfg.'s Sug. Retail was $565.

Add $19 for 7mm Rem. Mag. (disc.) or .300 Win. Mag. cal.

This model was the Whitworth American Field Series until 1987. Early manufacture was done in Manchester, England. Recent manufacture is by Zastava located in Yugoslavia. Earlier Manchester guns (before approx. 1980) will bring a slight premium over the values listed above.

WHITWORTH MANNLICHER STYLE CARBINE — .243 Win., .270 Win., .308 Win., 7x57mm, or .30-06 cal., bolt action with full length walnut Mannlicher style stock, open sights, sling swivels, thumb safety, 20 in. barrel, 5 shot mag., 7 lbs. Imported 1984-87.

	100%	98%	95%	90%	80%	70%	60%
	$570	$495	$455	$410	$375	$340	$310

Last Mfg.'s Sug. Retail was $675.

WHITWORTH EXPRESS RIFLE — .375 H&H (disc. 1993) or .458 Win. Mag. cal., 3 shot, 24 in. barrel, 3 leaf express sight, English style walnut stock, checkered pistol grip and forend, 8½ lbs. Imported 1974-96.

	100%	98%	95%	90%	80%	70%	60%
	$600	$540	$465	$425	$395	$375	$350

Last Mfg.'s Sug. Retail was $703.

RIFLES: SEMI-AUTO

22-ATD — .22 LR cal. only, patterned after the Browning Semi-Auto, 19.4 in. barrel, 11 shot mag. in stock, blued finish, checkered hardwood stock, take-down design, adj. rear sight, 4.6 lbs. Mfg. by Norinco 1987-96.

	100%	98%	95%	90%	80%	70%	60%
	$110	$95	$90	$80	$75	$70	$65

Last Mfg.'s Sug. Retail was $121.

Add $16 for camo case (disc.).

INTERDYNAMIC OF AMERICA, INC.

Previous distributor located in Miami, FL 1981-84.

PISTOLS: SEMI-AUTO

KG-9 — 9mm Para. cal., 3 in. barrel, open bolt, paramilitary design pistol. Disc. approx. 1982.

	100%	98%	95%	90%	80%	70%	60%
	$750	$700	$650	$600	$575	$550	$525

KG-99 — 9mm Para. cal., 3 in. barrel, semi-auto paramilitary design pistol, closed bolt, 36 shot mag., 5 in. vent. shroud barrel, blue only, a stainless steel version of the KG-9. Mfg. by Interdynamic 1984 only.

	100%	98%	95%	90%	80%	70%	60%
	$325	$275	$230	$200	$180	$160	$145
KG-99M, mini pistol	$350	$285	$235	$200	$180	$160	$145

INTRATEC

Current manufacturer located in Miami, FL. Distributor sales only.

🛡**INTRATEC**

PISTOLS: SEMI-AUTO

PROTEC-25 — .25 ACP. cal., double action, 2½ in. barrel, 8 shot mag.

	Mfg.'s Sug. Retail						
Mfg.'s Sug. Retail	$112	$90	$70	$55	$40	$35	$30	$25

Add $5 for Tec-Kote finish or black slide/frame finish.

Grading	100%	98%	95%	90%	80%	70%	60%

TEC-DC9 — 9mm Para. cal., paramilitary design pistol, 5 in. shrouded barrel, matte black finish, 10 (C/B 1994) or 32★ shot mag. Mfg. 1985-94.

	$245	$175	$155	$140	$130	$120	$110

Last Mfg.'s Sug. Retail was $269.

★ *TEC-9DCK* — similar to TEC-9, except has new durable Tec-Kote finish with better protection than hard chrome. Mfg. 1991-94.

	$250	$185	$160	$140	$130	$120	$110

Last Mfg.'s Sug. Retail was $297.

★ *TEC-DC9S* — matte stainless version of the TEC-9. Disc. 1994.

	$300	$240	$185

Last Mfg.'s Sug. Retail was $362.

Add $203 for above TEC-9 with accessory package (deluxe case, 3-32 shot mags., paramilitary design grip, and recoil compensator).

TEC-DC9M — mini version of the Model TEC-9, including 3 in. barrel and 20 shot mag. Disc. 1994.

	$245	$175	$155	$140	$130	$120	$110

Last Mfg.'s Sug. Retail was $245.

★ *TEC-DC9MK* — similar to TEC-9M, except has Tec-Kote rust resistant finish. Mfg. 1991-1994.

	$255	$185	$155	$140	$130	$120	$110

Last Mfg.'s Sug. Retail was $277.

★ *TEC-DC9MS* — matte stainless version of the TEC-9M. Disc. 1994.

	$275	$225	$180

Last Mfg.'s Sug. Retail was $339.

TEC-22 "SCORPION" — .22 LR cal., paramilitary design, 4 in. barrel, ambidextrous safety, military matte finish, or electroless nickel, 30 shot mag., adj. sights, 30 oz. Mfg. 1988-94.

	$190	$165	$150	$135	$120	$100	$90

Last Mfg.'s Sug. Retail was $202.

Add $20 for TEC-Kote finish.

★ *TEC-22N* — similar to TEC-22, except has nickel finish. Mfg. 1990 only.

	$200	$175	$160	$140	$125	$105	$95

Last Mfg.'s Sug. Retail was $226.

Add $16 for threaded barrel (Model TEC-22TN).

TEC-22T — threaded barrel variation of the TEC-22 "Scorpion". Mfg 1991-94.

	$145	$125	$110	$100	$90	$80	$70

Last Mfg.'s Sug. Retail was $161.

Add $23 for Tec-Kote finish.

SPORT-22 — .22 LR cal., 4 in. non-threaded barrel, 10 shot Ruger styled rotary mag., matte finish, adj. rear sight, 29½ oz. New 1995.

Mfg.'s Sug. Retail	$130		$110	$90	$80	$70	$60	$50	$45

Add $20 for stainless steel barrel.

CAT-9, CAT-45, CAT-380 — .380 ACP (new 1995), 9mm Para., or .45 ACP (new 1995) cal., double action only, black finish, polymer frame with top sight channel, only 27 parts, blowback action on 9mm Para., locked breech on .45 ACP, 6 (.45 ACP cal.) or 7 (.380 ACP or 9mm Para.) shot mag., 3 or 3¼ (.45 ACP only) in. barrel, 18-21 oz. New 1993.

Mfg.'s Sug. Retail	$235		$195	$165	$145	$130	$115	$100	$90

Subtract $15 for .380 ACP cal.
Add $20 for .45 ACP cal.
Add $15 for Fire Sights.

This series is designed by N. Sirkis of Israel.

AB-10 — 9mm Para. cal., paramilitary design, black synthetic frame, black or stainless steel finish. New 1997.

Mfg.'s Sug. Retail	$255		$215	$175	$155	$135	$120	$105	$95

Grading	100%	98%	95%	90%	80%	70%	60%

INTRATEC U.S.A.
Previous manufacturer located in Miami, FL.

DERRINGERS

TEC-38 DERRINGER — .38 Spl. cal., O/U, 3 in. barrel, blue frame, double action, 13 oz. Mfg. 1986-1988.

$110	$95	$85	$75	$65	$60	$55

Last Mfg.'s Sug. Retail was $125.

PISTOLS: SEMI-AUTO

PROTEC-22 — while advertised for $112 MSR during 1993, this model was never mfg.

TEC-9 — 9mm Para. cal., paramilitary design, 5 in. shrouded barrel, 32 shot mag., disc.

$350	$315	$275	$235	$195	$170	$155

TEC-9C — 9mm Para. cal., carbine variation with 16½ in. barrel, 36 shot mag. Only 1 gun mfg. 1987 - extreme rarity precludes pricing.

INVESTARM, s.p.a.
Current manufacturer located in Marcheno, Italy. No current importer. Please contact the factory directly.

Investarm manufactures a variety of shotgun configurations, including folding single shots, folding O/Us, in addition to muzzle loading black powder rifles.

IRWINDALE ARMS, INC. (IAI)
Previous manufacturer located in Irwindale, CA 1988-1991.

PISTOLS: SEMI-AUTO

In June, 1991, AMT reacquired the manufacturing rights to all IAI models. Please refer to the AMT section for current models.

AUTOMAG III — .30 Carbine or 9mm Win. Mag. (mfg. 1990-92) cal., stainless steel only, 6⅜ in. barrel, patterned after Colt Govt. Model, Millett adj. sights with white outline, grooved Lexan grips, 8 shot mag., 43 oz. Mfg. 1989-91.

$550	$475	$395

Last Mfg.'s Sug. Retail was $606.

AUTOMAG IV — .45 Win. Mag., or 10mm cal., semi-auto, 6½ or 8⅝ (mfg. 1991) in. barrel, 7 shot mag., Millett adj. sights, stainless steel only, 46 oz. Mfg. 1990-91.

$565	$485	$500

Last Mfg.'s Sug. Retail was $630.

JAVELINA — 10mm cal., semi-auto, 5 (disc. 1991) or 7 in. barrel, 8 shot mag., Millett adj. sights, wraparound Neoprene grips, stainless steel, wide adj. trigger, long grip safety, 48 oz. Mfg. 1990-91.

$525	$450	$375

Last Mfg.'s Sug. Retail was $570.

BACKUP PISTOL — .380 ACP cal., semi-auto action, 2½ in. barrel, stainless steel, Lexan grips, 5 shot mag., 18 oz. Older disc. walnut grip models are worth a slight premium. Disc. 1989.

$200	$165	$135

Last Mfg.'s Sug. Retail was $243.

ISRAEL ARMS INTERNATIONAL
Current importer (see Israel Arms Ltd. listing) and manufacturer located in Houston, TX, beginning 1997.

Grading	100%	98%	95%	90%	80%	70%	60%

RIFLES: CARBINES

MODEL 888 M1 CARBINE — .30 Carbine cal., 18 in. barrel, mfg. from new original M1 parts and stock, 15 shot mag., parkerized finish, 5½ lbs. Mfg. by IAI in Houston, TX, beginning 1999.

Mfg.'s Sug. Retail	$600	$525	$450	$400	$365	$335	$295	$260

ISRAEL ARMS LTD.

Current manufacturer located in Kfar Saba, Israel. Imported and distributed exclusively by Israel Arms International, Inc. located in Houston, TX beginning 1997.

PISTOLS: SEMI-AUTO

MODEL 1500 HI POWER — 9mm Para. cal., single action, 3.85 (Compact) or 4.64 (Standard, disc. 1998) in. barrel, two-tone finish, rubberized grips, regular or Meprolite sights, 10 shot mag., 33.6 oz. Imported 1997-98 only.

		$360	$305	$255	$225	$200	$185	$170

Last Mfg.'s Sug. Retail was $413.

Add approx. $160 for two-tone finish with Meprolite sights.

* *Model 1500/1501 Hi-Power Compact* — 9mm Para. or .40 S&W cal., compact variation with 3.85 in. barrel, choice of two-tone (Model 1500) or blue (Model 1501) finish, 32.2 oz. Importation began late 1999.

Mfg.'s Sug. Retail	$412	$360	$305	$255	$225	$200	$185	$170

MODEL 2500 — 9mm Para. or .40 S&W cal., single or double action, ambidextrous safety with decocking feature, steel slide with alloy frame, 3⅞ in. barrel, 10 shot mag., matte black finish, 34 oz. Importation began late 1999.

As this edition went to press, prices had yet to be established on this model.

MODEL 5000/5001 COMBAT — .45 ACP cal., single action, 4¼ in barrel, competition trigger, hammer, and slide stop, front and rear slide serrations, blue (Model 5001) or two-tone (Model 5000) finish, wraparound rubber grips, 42 oz. Importation began 1999.

Mfg.'s Sug. Retail	$397	$350	$300	$255	$225	$200	$185	$170

MODEL 6000/6001 STANDARD — .45 ACP cal., single action, 5 in. stainless steel barrel, features beveled feed ramp, extended slide stop, safety and magazine release, beavertail grip safety and combat style hammer, blue (Model 6001) or two-tone (Model 6000) finish, 38 oz. Importation began 1999.

Mfg.'s Sug. Retail	$397	$350	$300	$255	$225	$200	$185	$170

MODEL 7000/7001 WIDE FRAME — .45 ACP cal., single action, similar to Model 6000/6001, except has double stack mag., blue (Model 7001) or two-tone (Model 7000) finish, 40 oz. Importation began 1999.

Mfg.'s Sug. Retail	$490	$445	$395	$350	$300	$255	$225	$200

ISRAELI MILITARY INDUSTRIES (IMI)

Current manufacturer located in Israel. Limited importation currently.

IMI manufactured guns (both new and disc. models) include Galil, Jericho, Magnum Research, Timberwolf, Uzi, and others, and can be located in their respective sections.

Grading	100%	98%	95%	90%	80%	70%	60%

ITALIAN MILITARY ARMS

Previous more popular Italian military models mfg. since 1891.

PISTOLS: SEMI-AUTO

GLISENTI MODEL 1910 — 9mm Glisenti cal., 4 in. barrel, 7 shot mag., checkered wood grips, official Italian service pistol of both WWI and WWII, 32 oz.

$800	$675	$550	$400	$325	$265	$235

> Warning: 9mm Para. ammunition (9x18mm) cannot be used in this pistol - only 9mm Glisenti, as it is approx. 25% less powerful than the 9mm Para.

BRIXIA — similar to Glisenti Model 1910, except utilizes simplified mfg. techniques, mostly sold to civilians.

$925	$750	$575	$425	$350	$325	$300

SOSSO — 9mm Para. cal., large experimental semi-auto, early pistols were double action and marked "Sosso", late guns were single action and built by FNA. All Sosso pistols feature a unique continuous "chain link" 19 or 21 shot mag. Approx. 5 guns mfg.

> Extreme rarity factor precludes accurate price evaluation.

RIFLES: BOLT ACTION

MODEL 1891 MANNLICHER-CARCANO — 6.5x52mm Carcano cal., 6 shot, 31 in. barrel, straight handle, adj. sight, military stock.

$120	$100	$85	$70	$55	$40	$30

MODEL 38 TERNI MILITARY RIFLE — 7.35x52mm Carcano cal., similar to 1891, except turned down bolt handle, 21 in. barrel and folding bayonet.

$120	$100	$85	$70	$55	$40	$30

ITHACA CLASSIC DOUBLES

Current SxS shotgun manufacturer established during late 1998, and located in Mendon, NY. Consumer direct sales.

The Legend Returns

SHOTGUNS: SxS

All Ithaca Classic Doubles shotguns feature state-of-the-art manufacturing techniques, Italian or U.S. hand engraving (using the original William McGraw patterns), Doug Turnbull bone/charcoal case colors and metal finish, and top quality American feather crotch walnut with precise hand checkering. Each gauge has its own frame size, and serial numbers are continued from the last gun Ithaca manufactured in 1948 (ser. no. 469,999). Canvas, canvas and leather, leather, and oak and leather cases are also available, ranging in price from $139-$1,950. Please contact the company directly regarding special orders and options.

SPECIAL FIELD/SKEET GRADE — 20, 28 ga., or .410 bore, designed for field and clay shooting, DT, ejectors, 26, 28, or 30 in. barrels with fixed chokes, light perimeter hand engraving with metal stippling on shoulders and in front of top opening lever, Turnbull bone and charcoal case colors, checkered pistol grip or English feather crotch walnut stock and forearm, 5lbs. 5 oz. - 5 lbs. 14 oz. New late 1998.

Mfg.'s Sug. Retail	$3,150	$2,950	$2,500	$2,100	$1,750	$1,500	$1,250	$1,100

Add 10% for 28 ga. or .410 bore.

GRADE 4E — 20, 28 ga., or .410 bore, features gold plated triggers, jewelled barrel flats, hand tuned locks, hand engraved three game scenes with bank note scroll, deluxe walnut stock and forearm with fleur de lis pattern and 28 LPI checkering, other specifications similar to Special Field/Skeet Grade. New late 1998.

Mfg.'s Sug. Retail	$4,199	$3,750	$3,325	$2,950	$2,500	$2,100	$1,750	$1,500

Add 10% for 28 ga. or .410 bore.

Grading	100%	98%	95%	90%	80%	70%	60%

GRADE 7E — 20, 28 ga., or .410 bore, features hand engraved oak leaf scroll on frame and barrels, and 24 Kt. flat gold game scene inlays, including a bald eagle on floor plate, exhibition grade American walnut with 12 checkered panels in fleur-de-lis pattern, other specifications similar to Special Field/Skeet Grade. New late 1998.

Mfg.'s Sug. Retail	$8,399	$7,775	$6,750	$5,900	$5,100	$4,500	$3,900	$3,350

Add 10% for 28 ga. or .410 bore.

SOUSA GRADE — 20, 28 ga., or .410 bore, top-of-the-line model with every possible refinement, each gun individually hand fitted, jewelled, and polished, includes famous 24 Kt. Sousa mermaid on trigger guard, other specifications similar to Special Field/Skeet Grade. Special order only, new late 1998.

Mfg.'s Sug. Retail	$10,499	$9,650	$8,725	$7,750	$6,750	$5,900	$5,100	$4,500

Add 10% for 28 ga. or .410 bore.

ITHACA GUN COMPANY LLC

Ithaca Gun

Current manufacturer established during 1996 and located in King Ferry, NY. Ithaca Gun Company, LLC has resumed production on the Model 37 slide action shotgun and variations. Previously manufactured in Ithaca, NY, 1883 to Nov. of 1986. In the past, Ithaca also absorbed companies including Syracuse Arms Co., Lefever Arms Co., Union Fire Arms Co., Wilkes-Barre Gun Co., as well as others.

COMBINATION GUNS

LSA-55 TURKEY GUN — O/U shotgun–rifle combo, 12 ga., .222 Rem., 24½ in. ribbed barrel, exposed hammer, folding rear sight, checkered Monte Carlo stock. Mfg. by Tikka, Finland 1970-1981.

	$605	$550	$415	$495	$425	$385	$330

PISTOLS

X-CALIBER SINGLE SHOT — .22 LR or .44 Mag. cal., break open action with contoured wood grip and forearm, 8, 10 or 15 in. barrel, unique dual firing pin detonates both rimfire and centerfire cartridges. While advertised in 1988, Models 20 and 30 were never sold, even though approx. 300 units were mfg. in 22 cal. only. Production was ceased due to unsolvable manufacturing problems.

ITHACA 50TH ANNIVERSARY MODEL — .45 ACP cal., 5 in. match barrel with bushing, blue polished or tactical matte finish, checkered diamond pattern walnut grips, extended beavertail grip safety, includes plastic case and certificate, only 2,500 mfg. with special serialization 1995-97. Disc.

	$695	$625	$550	$500	$450	$400	$360

Last Mfg.'s Sug. Retail was $795.

This model was offered exclusively by All American Sales, Inc. located in Memphis, TN.

RIFLES: BOLT ACTION

LSA-55 STANDARD — .222 Rem., .22-250 Rem., 6mm Rem., .243 Win., or .308 Win. cal., Mauser type action, 22 in. barrel, leaf sight, 3 shot clip mag., checkered Monte Carlo stock. Mfg. in Finland by Tikka from 1969 to 1977.

	$400	$375	$350	$310	$275	$250	$230

The LSA Model designation stands for Light, Strong, Accurate.

LSA-55 DELUXE — similar to Standard, except rollover cheekpiece, rosewood pistol grip cap and forend tip, skipline checkering, no sights, scope mounts furnished.

	$495	$450	$425	$400	$365	$345	$325

Grading	100%	98%	95%	90%	80%	70%	60%

LSA-55 HEAVY BARREL — similar to LSA-55, except .222 Rem. or .22-250 Rem. cal. only, target heavy barrel, special beavertail stock 8½ lbs.

	$450	$425	$400	$375	$350	$325	$300

LSA-65 — similar to LSA-55, except long action for calibers .25-06 Rem., .270 Win., or .30-06. Mfg. 1969 to 1977.

	$400	$375	$350	$310	$275	$250	$230

LSA-65 DELUXE — similar to LSA-55, except has deluxe checkered walnut stock, .25-06 Rem., .270 Win., or .30-06.

	$495	$450	$425	$400	$365	$345	$325

RIFLES: LEVER ACTION

MODEL 49 SADDLEGUN — .22 LR or .22 Mag. cal., lever action, single shot. Mfg. 1961-1978. Martini-style action.

	$125	$110	$100	$75	$65	$50	$40

Add 15% for .22 Mag. cal.
Add 20% for Deluxe Model.

MODEL 49R — similar to Model 49 Saddlegun, except is slide action repeater. Mfg. 1965-1971.

	$265	$250	$235	$200	$175	$150	$125

Add 15% for .22 Mag. cal.

MODEL 49 PRESENTATION — similar to Model 49 Saddlegun, except gold-plated trigger, hammer, engraved receiver, fancy walnut. Mfg. 1962-1974.

	$295	$275	$250	$235	$200	$165	$135

MODEL 49 ST. LOUIS BICENTENNIAL — like Deluxe Model 49, except inscription on receiver, 200 mfg. 1964.

	$300	$255	$215				

Last Mfg.'s Sug. Retail was $35.

MODEL 66 — 12, 20 ga., or .410 bore single shot lever action, field gun only. Mfg. 1963-1978.

	$125	$95	$90	$75	$70	$65	$55

Add 33% to .410 bore.
Add 25% for VRs that were also available on special order.

✳ _Model 66 RS_ — 20 ga. slug gun with 22 in. barrel and rifle type sights, recoil pad.

	$195	$165	$135	$115	$90	$80	$70

Note: Ventilated ribs were also available on special order — add 25%.

MODEL 72 SADDLEGUN — .22 or .22 Mag. cal., lever action, 18½ in. barrel, hooded front sight. Mfg. 1973-1978 by Erma Werke, W. Germany.

	$300	$250	$225	$175	$145	$130	$120

MODEL 72 DELUXE — similar to Model 72, except has silver finished engraved receiver, deluxe walnut, octagon barrel. Mfg. 1974-1976.

	$350	$300	$250	$225	$175	$145	$130

RIFLES: SEMI-AUTO

MODEL X5-C — .22 LR cal., 7 shot mag., grooved forearm, Model X5-T has tube mag. Mfg. 1958-1964.

	$175	$150	$125	$100	$80	$70	$60

MODEL X-15 — .22 LR cal., similar to X5-C, except forearm is not grooved. Mfg. 1964-1967.

	$175	$150	$125	$100	$80	$70	$60

Grading	100%	98%	95%	90%	80%	70%	60%

RIFLES: SINGLE SHOT

MODEL 89 — .243 Win., .30-06, .375 H&H, .416 Rigby, or 7x57mm cal., falling block action, 26 or 28 in. Shilen barrel, full-length uncheckered walnut stock.

> While advertised at $658 MSR during 1994, this model was never mfg.

SHOTGUNS: O/U, PREVIOUS IMPORTATION

> Note: Ithaca was the sole importer for Perazzi in the '70s. All new and used models will be in the P section under Perazzi. Perazzi currently distributes their own firearms.
>
> Note: Please refer to the Fabarm section in this text for those models previously imported by Ithaca (imported 1994-95).
>
> Note: SKB shotguns previously imported by Ithaca can be found under the SKB heading.

SHOTGUNS: SxS, 1922-1948 MFG.

AUTO & BURGLAR SxS — 20 ga. smooth bore with 10 in. double barrels, case hardened finish, pistol grip, Model A (approx. 2,500 mfg.) has grip spur, Model B (approx. 2,000 mfg.) has squared grip; both were mfg. in lots of about 100 according to demand, and serial numbers are mixed with those of regular Ithaca shotguns. Guns not currently registered with BATF cannot be legally owned and are subject to seizure. Mfg. 1922-1934.

* **Model A** — serial no. range is 343,336-398,365.

$1,850	$1,450	$1,200	$975	$775	$675	$575

* **Model B** — serial no. range is 425,000-464,699.

$1,450	$1,200	$975	$775	$675	$575	$465

> Add $300-$500 for original holster (very rare). Prototype or special order guns (in 16, 28 ga., or .410 bore) are extremely rare and command premiums of 100%+.

ITHACA HAMMERLESS — 12, 16, 20, 28 ga., or .410 bore, 26-32 in. fluid steel or damascus barrels, boxlock, extractors, double triggers, any standard choke, checkered pistol grip stock and forearm, grades shown differ in overall quality, ornamentation, grade of wood, and style of checkering. In 1925, the rotary bolt and stronger frame were adapted (ser. numbers after 400,000 - commonly referred to as NID or New Ithaca Double). Values are the same as for pre-400,000 serial range shotguns. Ithaca doubles incorporated a number of design changes made on the action - they are referred to as the Lewis, Crass, Flues, and Minier frame variations.

> Values below are for guns mfg. between 1925-1948.
> Add $200 for SST.
> Add $150 for SNT.
> Add $350 for VR on Grades 4, 5, 7, and $2,000 Grade.
> Add $200 for VR - lower grades.
> Add $175 for beavertail forearm.
> Add 33% for auto ejectors on Grades No. 1, 2, and 3.
> Subtract 33% if without ejectors on Grades 4E-7E.
> Early hammer doubles in average condition are approx. valued between $175-$450. However, if 60% condition remains (including original case colors), values can approximate those listed below.

100%	98%	95%	90%	80%	70%	60%	50%	40%	30%	20%	10%

FIELD GRADE

* *10 ga. Mag.*

100%	98%	95%	90%	80%	70%	60%	50%	40%	30%	20%	10%
$2,000	$1,800	$1,500	$1,400	$1,300	$1,200	$1,100	$950	$825	$775	$675	$630

> 3½ in. chambered 10 ga. Mags. are serial numbered over 500,000. Total mfg. was approx. 850 guns for all grades. 2⅞ in. chambered 10 ga.'s are priced the same as a 12 ga. A 12

100%	98%	95%	90%	80%	70%	60%	50%	40%	30%	20%	10%

ga., 3 in. model was also made on the 10 ga. frame - only 87 were mfg. and specimens are noted in the 500,000 serial range.

* 12 ga.

100%	98%	95%	90%	80%	70%	60%	50%	40%	30%	20%	10%
$1,000	$800	$600	$550	$500	$450	$415	$380	$350	$325	$300	$280

* 16 ga.

100%	98%	95%	90%	80%	70%	60%	50%	40%	30%	20%	10%
$1,100	$900	$800	$750	$700	$650	$600	$550	$500	$425	$375	$340

* 20 ga.

100%	98%	95%	90%	80%	70%	60%	50%	40%	30%	20%	10%
$1,400	$1,200	$1,000	$900	$850	$800	$750	$700	$600	$550	$500	$440

* 28 ga.

100%	98%	95%	90%	80%	70%	60%	50%	40%	30%	20%	10%
$3,800	$3,400	$2,850	$2,500	$2,200	$2,000	$1,800	$1,700	$1,600	$1,500	$1,400	$1,200

* .410 bore

100%	98%	95%	90%	80%	70%	60%	50%	40%	30%	20%	10%
$3,800	$3,400	$2,850	$2,500	$2,200	$2,000	$1,800	$1,700	$1,600	$1,500	$1,400	$1,200

GRADE NO. 1 — manufactured in both Flues and NID models, similar to Field Grade.

* 12 ga.

100%	98%	95%	90%	80%	70%	60%	50%	40%	30%	20%	10%
$1,225	$1,000	$800	$600	$550	$500	$450	$415	$380	$350	$325	$315

* 16 ga.

100%	98%	95%	90%	80%	70%	60%	50%	40%	30%	20%	10%
$1,375	$1,150	$925	$825	$750	$700	$650	$600	$550	$500	$425	$395

* 20 ga.

100%	98%	95%	90%	80%	70%	60%	50%	40%	30%	20%	10%
$1,700	$1,400	$1,200	$1,000	$900	$850	$800	$750	$700	$600	$550	$525

* 28 ga.

100%	98%	95%	90%	80%	70%	60%	50%	40%	30%	20%	10%
$4,000	$3,400	$2,750	$2,200	$2,000	$1,800	$1,700	$1,600	$1,500	$1,400	$1,200	$1,125

* .410 bore

100%	98%	95%	90%	80%	70%	60%	50%	40%	30%	20%	10%
$4,200	$3,500	$2,850	$2,250	$2,000	$1,800	$1,700	$1,600	$1,500	$1,400	$1,200	$1,125

GRADE NO. 2

* 10 ga. Mag.

100%	98%	95%	90%	80%	70%	60%	50%	40%	30%	20%	10%
$2,400	$2,000	$1,800	$1,600	$1,400	$1,300	$1,200	$1,100	$950	$900	$800	$735

3½ in. chambered 10 ga. Mags. are serial numbered over 500,000. Total mfg. was approx. 850 guns for all grades. 2⅞ in. chambered 10 ga.'s are priced the same as a 12 ga.

* 12 ga.

100%	98%	95%	90%	80%	70%	60%	50%	40%	30%	20%	10%
$1,500	$1,200	$1,000	$800	$600	$550	$500	$450	$415	$380	$350	$335

* 16 ga.

100%	98%	95%	90%	80%	70%	60%	50%	40%	30%	20%	10%
$1,500	$1,200	$1,000	$900	$800	$750	$700	$650	$600	$550	$500	$475

* 20 ga.

100%	98%	95%	90%	80%	70%	60%	50%	40%	30%	20%	10%
$1,800	$1,500	$1,200	$1,100	$1,000	$900	$850	$800	$750	$700	$650	$580

* 28 ga.

100%	98%	95%	90%	80%	70%	60%	50%	40%	30%	20%	10%
$4,950	$3,750	$3,250	$2,500	$2,000	$1,950	$1,850	$1,750	$1,650	$1,550	$1,450	$1,350

* .410 bore

100%	98%	95%	90%	80%	70%	60%	50%	40%	30%	20%	10%
$4,950	$3,750	$3,250	$2,500	$2,000	$1,950	$1,850	$1,750	$1,650	$1,550	$1,450	$1,350

GRADE NO. 3

* 10 ga. Mag.

100%	98%	95%	90%	80%	70%	60%	50%	40%	30%	20%	10%
$3,500	$2,900	$2,300	$1,850	$1,600	$1,400	$1,300	$1,200	$1,100	$950	$825	$735

3½ in. chambered 10 ga. Mags. are serial numbered over 500,000. Total mfg. was approx. 850 guns for all grades. 2⅞ in. chambered 10 ga.'s are priced the same as a 12 ga.

* 12 ga.

100%	98%	95%	90%	80%	70%	60%	50%	40%	30%	20%	10%
$1,850	$1,500	$1,200	$1,000	$800	$750	$700	$650	$600	$550	$500	$475

* 16 ga.

100%	98%	95%	90%	80%	70%	60%	50%	40%	30%	20%	10%
$1,850	$1,500	$1,200	$1,000	$900	$850	$800	$750	$700	$650	$600	$575

100%	98%	95%	90%	80%	70%	60%	50%	40%	30%	20%	10%

* 20 ga.

| $2,400 | $1,800 | $1,500 | $1,300 | $1,200 | $1,100 | $1,000 | $900 | $850 | $800 | $750 | $735 |

* 28 ga. — only 5 mfg.

Extreme rarity factor precludes accurate pricing evaluation.

* .410 bore — only 7 mfg.

Extreme rarity factor precludes accurate pricing evaluation.

GRADE NO. 4E — auto ejectors.

* 10 ga. Mag.

| $4,650 | $3,950 | $3,250 | $2,600 | $2,100 | $1,975 | $1,875 | $1,750 | $1,650 | $1,550 | $1,450 | $1,350 |

$3\frac{1}{2}$ in. chambered 10 ga. Mags. are serial numbered over 500,000. Total mfg. was approx. 850 guns for all grades. $2\frac{7}{8}$ in. chambered 10 ga.'s are priced the same as a 12 ga.

* 12 ga.

| $3,500 | $3,000 | $2,500 | $2,100 | $1,700 | $1,550 | $1,325 | $1,200 | $1,100 | $995 | $875 | $800 |

* 16 ga.

| $4,000 | $3,700 | $3,000 | $2,400 | $2,000 | $1,875 | $1,650 | $1,550 | $1,450 | $1,325 | $1,200 | $1,050 |

* 20 ga.

| N/A | $4,000 | $3,700 | $3,500 | $3,300 | $3,100 | $2,950 | $2,700 | $2,300 | $1,975 | $1,650 | $1,400 |

* 28 ga.

Extreme rarity factor precludes accurate pricing evaluation.

* .410 bore

Extreme rarity factor precludes accurate pricing evaluation.

GRADE NO. 5E — auto ejectors.

* 10 ga. — only 9 mfg.

Extreme rarity factor precludes accurate pricing evaluation.

* 12 ga.

| $4,250 | $3,500 | $3,200 | $3,000 | $2,700 | $2,200 | $1,875 | $1,650 | $1,325 | $1,200 | $1,100 | $1,050 |

* 16 ga.

| $4,250 | $3,500 | $2,800 | $2,500 | $2,200 | $1,875 | $1,750 | $1,550 | $1,425 | $1,325 | $1,200 | $1,150 |

* 20 ga.

| N/A | $4,500 | $4,000 | $3,700 | $3,300 | $3,000 | $2,875 | $2,650 | $2,325 | $2,100 | $1,875 | $1,700 |

* 28 ga.

Extreme rarity factor precludes accurate pricing evaluation.

* .410 bore

Extreme rarity factor precludes accurate pricing evaluation.

GRADE NO. 7E — auto ejectors, only 22 mfg. in all gauges.

Extreme rarity factor precludes accurate pricing evaluation on this model.

$2,000 GRADE — 12 ga., top-of-the-line model, auto ejectors, single selective trigger.

| N/A | N/A | $8,450 | $7,400 | $6,500 | $5,650 | $4,750 | $4,000 | $3,250 | $2,600 | $2,100 | $1,700 |

Rarity on 16 or 20 ga. precludes accurate pricing.

PRE-WAR $1,000 GRADE — 12 ga., top-of-the-line models, auto ejectors, single selective trigger.

| N/A | N/A | $9,500 | $8,450 | $7,400 | $6,500 | $5,650 | $4,750 | $4,000 | $3,250 | $2,600 | $2,250 |

Rarity on 16 or 20 ga. precludes accurate pricing.

Grading	100%	98%	95%	90%	80%	70%	60%

SOUSA GRADE — has mermaids on trigger guard in gold, only 11 manufactured (including one .410 bore). This model is very rare and prices are hard to establish. Recently, the price range has been approx. $15,000-$40,000, depending on gauge and original condition.

> The famous band director and composer, John Phillip Sousa, assisted in the development of this model.

SHOTGUNS: SINGLE BARREL TRAP

CENTURY TRAP — 12 ga., 32 or 34 in. VR barrel, engraved, auto ejector, full choke, checkered walnut stock. Mfg. 1973 and 1976 by SKB.

	100%	98%	95%	90%	80%	70%	60%
	$550	$525	$470	$440	$385	$360	$320

CENTURY II TRAP — improved trap stock version of Century, Monte Carlo stock.

	100%	98%	95%	90%	80%	70%	60%
	$600	$550	$495	$470	$415	$385	$350

SINGLE BARREL TRAP — 12 ga., 30, 32, or 34 in. barrels, VR, boxlock, auto ejector, checkered pistol grip and forearm, grades differ in engraving, overall workmanship, and grade or wood and checkering. Values on these models sometimes vary greatly depending on originality of finish, customer alterations, and other variations trap shooters might use to alter dimensions for their particular shooting requirements. Values below represent trap guns in original, unaltered condition.

> Note: Flues model mfg. prior to 1921 with serial numbers under 400,000 generally have better engraving than NID (New Ithaca Double) models over serial number 400,000 (also referred to as Knick models).

> Trap guns under 60% original condition will be within 25% of the value shown in the 60% column.

* *Victory Grade* — disc. 1938.

	100%	98%	95%	90%	80%	70%	60%
	$995	$850	$775	$675	$575	$495	$440

* *No. 4E* — disc. 1976.

	100%	98%	95%	90%	80%	70%	60%
	$2,450	$2,200	$2,000	$1,825	$1,625	$1,475	$1,350

* *No. 5E* — 12 ga., 32 or 34 in. barrel, custom order only, elaborate engraving, quality worksmanship throughout. Originally mfg. 1925-1986, mfg. resumed 1988-91.

	100%	98%	95%	90%	80%	70%	60%
	$2,950	$2,550	$2,175	$1,900	$1,725	$1,495	$1,300

Last Mfg.'s Sug. Retail was $7,500.

* *No. 6E* — this model was available by special order only. Rarity factor precludes accurate pricing.

* *No. 7E* — disc. 1964.

	100%	98%	95%	90%	80%	70%	60%
	$5,500	$4,700	$4,000	$3,500	$3,000	$2,500	$2,200

* *Dollar Grade* — 12 ga., 32 or 34 in. barrel. Top-of-the-line model custom built to customer specifications. Original mfg. was stopped 1986 and resumed 1988-91.

	100%	98%	95%	90%	80%	70%	60%
	$5,950	$5,200	$4,600	$3,850	$3,250	$2,775	$2,250

Last Mfg.'s Sug. Retail was $10,000.

* *$5,000 Grade* — similar to Pre-War $1,000 grade.

	100%	98%	95%	90%	80%	70%	60%
	$9,500	$8,900	$8,175	$7,650	$6,725	$5,825	$4,950

* *Sousa Grade* — extremely rare.

> Extreme rarity factor precludes accurate pricing evaluation. Prices will be higher than the $5,000 Grade.

Grading	100%	98%	95%	90%	80%	70%	60%

SHOTGUNS: SEMI-AUTO

MODEL 51A FEATHERLIGHT STANDARD — 12 or 20 ga., 30 in. full, 28 in. full or mod., 26 in. imp. cyl., gas operated, autoloading, checkered pistol grip stock. Mfg. 1970-1985. Vent. rib became standard during late production.

	100%	98%	95%	90%	80%	70%	60%
Older models (no VR)	$250	$230	$200	$180	$165	$150	$130
Recent production (w/VR)	$285	$265	$235	$210	$190	$175	$165

Last Mfg.'s Sug. Retail with VR was $477.

MODEL 51A MAGNUM — similar to 51 Standard, except 3 in. shells only, blue finish, recoil pad, VR became standard in 1984. Disc. 1985.

	100%	98%	95%	90%	80%	70%	60%
Older models w/o VR	$265	$235	$220	$205	$180	$165	$150
Vent. rib	$295	$275	$250	$225	$200	$185	$170

MODEL 51A MAGNUM WATERFOWLER — similar to 51 Standard, except 3 in. shells only, matte finished metal & flat finished walnut, recoil pad. Vent. rib standard. Mfg. 1984-1986.

100%	98%	95%	90%	80%	70%	60%
$325	$295	$275	$250	$230	$200	$180

Last Mfg.'s Sug. Retail was $625.

Add $40 for camouflaged exterior finish (mfg. 1986 only).

MODEL 51A SUPREME TRAP — similar to 51 Standard, except 12 ga. only, 30 in. barrel, 7 post rib, full choke, select wood, pad, trap style stock. Add $36 for Monte Carlo. Mfg. 1970-1986.

100%	98%	95%	90%	80%	70%	60%
$425	$365	$315	$295	$270	$250	$230

Last Mfg.'s Sug. Retail was $869.

MODEL 51A SUPREME SKEET — similar to 51 Standard, except 26 in. VR barrel, skeet choke, select wood. Mfg. 1970-present. 20 ga. was available 1983. Disc. 1986.

100%	98%	95%	90%	80%	70%	60%
$465	$395	$340	$300	$280	$260	$240

Last Mfg.'s Sug. Retail was $858.

MODEL 51A DEERSLAYER — similar to 51 Standard, with 24 in. slug barrel, rifle sights, recoil pad, no rib. Mfg. 1972-1983.

100%	98%	95%	90%	80%	70%	60%
$350	$300	$260	$230	$195	$180	$165

Last Mfg.'s Sug. Retail was $477.

MODEL 51A TURKEY GUN — 12 ga. Mag. only, 26 in. barrel, matte finish, sling and swivels included. Mfg. 1984-1986.

100%	98%	95%	90%	80%	70%	60%
$360	$305	$275	$265	$250	$230	$210

Last Mfg.'s Sug. Retail was $625.

MODEL 51 DUCKS UNLIMITED — similar to 51 Deluxe, with D/U emblem on receiver.

100%	98%	95%	90%	80%	70%	60%
$425	$375	$335	$300	$280	$260	$230

MODEL 51 PRESENTATION — 12 ga., blued, engraved, gold engraved receiver with deluxe walnut. Mfg. 1984-1986.

100%	98%	95%	90%	80%	70%	60%
$1,250	$1,000	$875	$700	$575	$450	$325

Last Mfg.'s Sug. Retail was $1,658.

MODEL XL 300 — 12 or 20 ga., gas operated, various barrel lengths with or w/o VR, mfg. 1973-76.

100%	98%	95%	90%	80%	70%	60%
$250	$230	$200	$180	$165	$150	$130

Add 15% for VR barrel.

MODEL XL 900 — 12 or 20 ga., gas operated, various barrel lengths with VR, mfg. 1973-78.

100%	98%	95%	90%	80%	70%	60%
$295	$275	$245	$210	$185	$170	$150

Add 10% for skeet, trap, or slug variations.

Shotguns: Semi-Auto, Mag-10 Series

All Ithaca Mag-10s were disc. 1986.

MAG-10 — 10 ga., 3½ in. Mag., various barrel lengths, stainless steel breech block assembly, gas operated, various chokes, plain barrel, 11 lb. Mfg. 1975-1986.

100% values assume NIB condition - if without, subtract 10%.

Grading	100%	98%	95%	90%	80%	70%	60%

* **Standard Grade** — no checkering, ribless barrel, dull finished wood.

		100%	98%	95%	90%	80%	70%	60%
		$600	$550	$500	$460	$430	$395	$375

Last Mfg.'s Sug. Retail was $726.

* **Standard Grade with VR** — available in 22, 26, 28, or 32 in. barrel lengths - otherwise similar to Standard Grade.

		$595	$550	$495	$450	$400	$360	$330

Last Mfg.'s Sug. Retail was $781.

> Add $60 for camouflaged exterior finish.
> Add $60 for interchangeable choke tubes (3) - became available in 1986.

* **Deluxe Vent** — select checkered walnut stock and forearm, 22, 26, 28, or 32 in. barrels, high lustre wood finish.

		$675	$600	$550	$495	$450	$400	$350

Last Mfg.'s Sug. Retail was $924.

* **Supreme Grade** — extra-select checkered walnut stock and forearm, otherwise similar to Deluxe Vent.

		$795	$725	$675	$595	$550	$495	$450

Last Mfg.'s Sug. Retail was $1,124.

* **Mag. 10 Roadblocker** — 22 in. cylinder bored ribless barrel, parkerized finish.

		$750	$625	$575	$500	$460	$430	$400

Last Mfg.'s Sug. Retail was $741.

* **National Wild Turkey Fed. Special Edition** — mfg. in 1985 only.

		$950	$795	$625

MAG-10 PRESENTATION OR CENTENNIAL — 10 ga. Mag., blued, engraved, gold inlaid receiver, extra fancy walnut. Limited production. Approx. 200 mfg. in Presentation Grade 1983-1986.

		$1,875	$1,550	$1,300	$1,050	$915	$830	$745

Last Mfg.'s Sug. Retail was $1,727.

> This configuration was also offered as a 3 gun set - a NIB set is currently selling in the $4,750 range.

SHOTGUNS: SLIDE ACTION

During late 1996, Ithaca Gun Co., LLC resumed manufacture of the Model 37, while discontinuing the Model 87. In 1987, Ithaca Acquisition Corp. reintroduced the Model 37 as the Model 87. Recently manufactured Model 87s are listed below in addition to both new and older Model 37s (produced pre-1986).

MODEL 37 TRENCH AND RIOT GUNS — see separate listing under Trench Guns in the T Section.

MODEL 37 DS POLICE SPECIAL — 12 ga. only, 18½ in. barrel with rifle sights, Parkerized finish on metal, oil finished stock, typically subcontracted by police departments or law enforcement agencies, with or without unit code markings.

		$295	$250	$225	$200	$185	$170	$160

MODEL 37 FEATHERLIGHT STANDARD — 12, 16, or 20 ga., bottom ejection, 4 shot mag., 26, 28, or 30 in. barrel, hammerless, take down, any standard choke. Mfg. 1937-disc.

		$245	$225	$195	$175	$160	$140	$125

MODEL 37V — similar to 37, except VR. Mfg. 1962-disc.

		$315	$260	$240	$195	$180	$170	$165

> All currently manufactured Model 37s have the Featherlight designation. Prices above are for older manufactured Model 37s.

MODEL 37D — similar to 37, except recoil pad, beavertail forearm, checkered. Mfg. 1954-1981.

		$295	$275	$235	$200	$185	$175	$160

Grading	100%	98%	95%	90%	80%	70%	60%

MODEL 37DV — similar to 37D, except VR. Mfg. 1962-1981.

	100%	98%	95%	90%	80%	70%	60%
	$350	$295	$250	$225	$200	$185	$170

MODEL 37 FIELD GRADE MAGNUM — 12 or 20 ga., 3 in. chambers, VR, walnut stock and corncob forearm, supplied with three choke tubes. Mfg. 1984-1986.

	$300	$240	$195	$180	$170	$165	$150

Last Mfg.'s Sug. Retail was $428.

MODEL 37 FIELD GRADE STANDARD — 12 or 20 ga., economy model, corncob forearm, 26, 28, or 30 in. barrel. Mfg. 1983-1985 only.

	$245	$225	$195	$175	$160	$140	$120

Last Mfg.'s Sug. Retail was $298.

MODEL 37 ULTRALITE — 12 or 20 ga., new manufacture features checkered pistol grip (with Sid Bell red grip cap) and forearm. Mfg. 1996-98.

	$550	$475	$400	$350	$300	$250	$225

Last Mfg.'s Sug. Retail was $600.

MODEL 37 ENGLISH ULTRALITE — 12 or 20 ga., 25 or 26 in. barrels, world's lightest pump, 20 ga. weighs 4¾ lb., 12 ga. weighs 5½ lbs., checkered straight stock. Mfg. 1983-1986.

	$395	$350	$300	$265	$225	$200	$180

Last Mfg.'s Sug. Retail was $522.

MODEL 37R — 12, 16, or 20 ga., solid rib. Mfg. 1937-1967.

	100%	98%	95%	90%	80%	70%	60%
Plain stock	$295	$200	$175	$145	$130	$110	$90
Checkered stock	$335	$245	$200	$175	$165	$145	$120

TURKEYSLAYER — 12 ga. only, choice of 100% camo coverage in Realtree or Advantage pattern, 22 in. barrel with extended choke tube, 7 lbs. New late 1996.

Mfg.'s Sug. Retail	$566	$460	$350	$275	$210	$175	$160	$145

Add $16 for ported choke tube.

* *Youth Turkeyslayer* — 20 ga. only, features 22 in. barrel and shortened youth dimension stock. New 1998.

Mfg.'s Sug. Retail	$566	$460	$350	$275	$210	$175	$160	$145

WATERFOWLER — 12 ga. only, features Wetlands camo treatment and 28 in. barrel designed for shooting steel shot. New 1998.

Mfg.'s Sug. Retail	$596	$480	$360	$285	$215	$175	$160	$145

MODEL 37R DELUXE — similar to 37R, except fancy wood. Mfg. 1937-1955.

	$395	$325	$265	$230	$210	$195	$165

MODEL 37 DELUXE — 12, 16 (Featherlight, new 1999), or 20 ga., similar to Model 87 Field Grade except has cut checkering, 26, 28, or 30 in. VR barrel, high gloss lacquer finish, and gold trigger, newer mfg. includes 3 choke tubes. New 1996.

Mfg.'s Sug. Retail	$546	$440	$335	$260	$200	$175	$160	$145

* *Model 37 Deluxe English* — 20 ga. only, features 24, 26, or 28 in. English style vent. rib barrel, approx. 7 lbs. New 1998.

Mfg.'s Sug. Retail	$546	$440	$335	$260	$200	$175	$160	$145

MODEL 37 NEW CLASSIC — 12, 16 (Featherlight, new 1999), or 20 ga., features knuckle cut receiver, corn cob forearm, hand checkering, and sunburst recoil pad, 26 or 28 in. VR barrel with choke tubes. Limited production beginning 1998.

Mfg.'s Sug. Retail	$696	$600	$475	$375	$300	$260	$230	$200

MODEL 37 SUPREME — 12, 16, or 20 ga., deluxe checkered walnut stock and forearm, 28 or 30 in. VR barrel, engraved receiver, approx. 7¾ lbs. Originally mfg. 1967-1986, reintroduced late 1996-disc. 1997.

	$675	$575	$495	$425	$375	$325	$295

Last Mfg.'s Sug. Retail was $750.

Grading	100%	98%	95%	90%	80%	70%	60%

MODEL 37S SKEET GRADE — similar to 37, except Knicker VR, large forearm, fancy wood. Mfg. 1937-1955.

| | $495 | $445 | $375 | $335 | $300 | $275 | $250 |

MODEL 37T TRAP GRADE — similar to 37S, except trap stock, select walnut, recoil pad. Mfg. 1937-1955.

| | $475 | $425 | $375 | $325 | $295 | $275 | $250 |

Add 20% for early models with Fleur-de-lis checkering.

MODEL 37T TARGET GRADE — replaced 37S and 37T. Mfg. from 1955-1961.

| | $475 | $425 | $375 | $325 | $295 | $275 | $250 |

MODEL 37 DEERSLAYER — 12 ga. only, original Deerslayer, smooth bore with fixed choke only, rifle sights, mfg. c. 1962-1986.

| | $300 | $240 | $195 | $180 | $170 | $165 | $150 |

MODEL 37 SUPER DELUXE DEERSLAYER — similar to Model 37 (87) Deerslayer, except fancy wood. Mfg.1962-1985.

| | $375 | $335 | $300 | $270 | $235 | $210 | $185 |

Last Mfg.'s Sug. Retail was $447.

MODEL 37 DEERSLAYER DELUXE — 12, 16 (new 1999, smooth bore only) or 20 ga., smooth bore or rifled barrel, current manufacture has walnut stock and forearm with cut checkering, light receiver engraving. Production resumed late 1996.

| Mfg.'s Sug. Retail | $516 | $435 | $360 | $300 | $270 | $235 | $210 | $185 |

DEERSLAYER II — 12 or 20 ga., 20 or 25 in. barrel with 1:34 rifling (also available with fast twist 1:25 rifling, 12 ga. only), Monte Carlo stock and forearm with cut checkering, receiver is drilled and tapped for scope mounting, 7 lbs. New late 1996.

| Mfg.'s Sug. Retail | $566 | $460 | $350 | $275 | $210 | $175 | $160 | $145 |

MODEL 37 BICENTENNIAL — 12 ga., engraved, fancy wood, cased with pewter buckle, 1,776 mfg. 1976, 100% value assumes NIB condition with case and belt buckle.

| | $575 | $450 | $325 |

MODEL 37 2500 SERIES CENTENNIAL — 12 ga., customized version of the Model 37 commemorating Ithaca's 100th year anniversary, silver plated, etched antique finish receiver, deluxe walnut. Mfg. 1980-1984.

| | $775 | $625 | $450 |

Last Mfg.'s Sug. Retail was $919.

MODEL 37 PRESENTATION — 12 ga., blued, engraved, gold mounted receiver with extra-fancy walnut, cased, limited production. Mfg. 1981-86.

| | $1,475 | $1,245 | $1,080 | $915 | $830 | $745 | $665 |

Last Mfg.'s Sug. Retail was $1,658.

A 3 gun set was also available - an NIB set is currently priced in the $1,750 range.

MODEL 37 DUCKS UNLIMITED — 12 ga., VR.

| | $385 | $305 | $275 |

MODEL 37 $1000 GRADE — all gauges, deluxe engraving and checkering, gold inlaid, select figured walnut, hand-finished parts. Mfg. 1937-1940.

| | $5,750 | $5,200 | $4,750 | $4,250 | $3,750 | $3,250 | $2,650 |

MODEL 37 $5000 GRADE — similar to $1000 Grade, post-war designation. Mfg. 1947-1967.

| | $5,250 | $4,850 | $4,250 | $3,850 | $3,250 | $2,850 | $2,250 |

MODEL 87 FIELD (BASIC) — 12 or 20 ga., 3 in. chamber, economy model, walnut stock and forearm with pressed checkering, 26, 28, or 30 (disc.) in. barrel with 3 choke tubes standard. Reintroduced 1987-1996.

| | $360 | $290 | $240 | $195 | $170 | $160 | $145 |

Last Mfg.'s Sug. Retail was $477.

Grading	100%	98%	95%	90%	80%	70%	60%

* **Model 87 Basic Field Combo** — 12 or 20 ga., includes 20/25 in. deer barrel with special bore and 28 in. VR multi-choke field barrel, uncheckered walnut stock and corncob forearm, 7 lbs. Mfg. 1989-92.

	$400	$315	$275	$235	$210	$190	$170

Last Mfg.'s Sug. Retail was $459.

Add $32 for rifled bore barrel.
Add $104 for laminated wood (includes rifle bored barrel).

* **Model 87 Camo Field** — 12 ga. only, 3 in. chamber, 24, 26, or 28 in. VR barrel, camo-seal rust resistant finish on exterior parts. Available in either green or brown camo finish. Mfg. began 1986, resumed 1988-disc. 1996.

	$425	$315	$260	$200	$175	$160	$145

Last Mfg.'s Sug. Retail was $542.

* **Model 87 Turkey Field** — 12 ga. only, 24 in. VR barrel with choice of fixed full choke or full choke tube, camo or matte blue finish. Mfg. 1989-1996.

	$365	$285	$235	$190	$170	$160	$145

Last Mfg.'s Sug. Retail was $466.

Add $85 for camo finish.
Add $43 for full choke tube.

MODEL 87 ULTRALITE FIELD — 12 or 20 ga., 3 in. chamber, aluminum receiver, 20 (disc. 1988), 24, 25 (disc. 1988), or 26 in. barrel. 20 ga. weighs 5 lbs., 12 ga. weighs 5¾ lbs., multi-chokes (3) became standard in 1989. Originally mfg. 1985-86, reintroduced 1988-90.

	$445	$375	$295	$240	$210	$190	$170

Last Mfg.'s Sug. Retail was $481.

Add $50 for slim grip model (12½ in. stock - disc. 1985).
Subtract $42 if without multiple choke feature.
The 20 and 25 in. barrels were disc. when mfg. was resumed 1988.

* **Model 87 Ultra Deluxe** — similar to Ultralite Field except has cut checkering, high gloss lacquer finish, and gold trigger. Mfg 1989-91.

	$425	$360	$300	$250	$220	$190	$170

Last Mfg.'s Sug. Retail was $514.

MODEL ENGLISH 87 — 20 ga. only, 3 in. chamber, 24 or 26 in. VR barrel with 3 choke tubes, steel receiver, checkered walnut stock and forearm, recoil pad, 6¾ lbs. Mfg. 1991-96.

	$425	$315	$260	$200	$175	$160	$145

Last Mfg.'s Sug. Retail was $545.

MODEL 87 DELUXE — similar to Model 87 Field Grade except has cut checkering, 26, 28, or 30 in. VR barrel, high gloss lacquer finish, and gold trigger, newer mfg. includes 3 choke tubes. Mfg. 1989-1996.

	$415	$310	$255	$200	$175	$160	$145

Last Mfg.'s Sug. Retail was $533.

Add $54 for combo package (includes 20 in. special bore deer barrel, disc. 1992).
Add $87 for combo package with 20 or 25 in. rifled bore deer barrel, disc. 1992.

* **Model 87 Deluxe Magnum** — 12 or 20 ga., 3 in. chambers, VR, deluxe wood with checkered forearm. Mfg. 1981-1986, production resumed 1988 only.

	$320	$270	$230	$210	$200	$185	$165

Last Mfg.'s Sug. Retail was $395.

Add $77 for Combo package (extra 28 in. barrel).
New mfg. 20 ga. shotguns were available with a 25 in. barrel only (with choke tubes).

MODEL 87 SUPREME GRADE — 12 or 20 ga., presentation walnut, high luster blue, limited production, previously available in either trap, skeet, or field models, fixed chokes. Mfg. 1988-1996.

	$640	$475	$395	$325	$295	$270	$250

Last Mfg.'s Sug. Retail was $809.

Grading	100%	98%	95%	90%	80%	70%	60%

BASIC DEERSLAYER — 12 ga. only, 20 or 25 in. special bore or rifled barrel, oil finished stock and corncob forearm with no checkering, iron sights, matte metal finish, 7 lbs. Mfg. 1989-1996.

	$345	$280	$240	$195	$175	$160	$145

Last Mfg.'s Sug. Retail was $425.

Add $40 for rifled barrel.

MODEL 87 FIELD DEERSLAYER — 12 or 20 ga., rifle slug barrel, 20 or 25 in. special smooth bore barrel with open sights. Mfg. 1959-86, reintroduced 1988-1993.

	$300	$250	$210	$180	$160	$150	$140

Last Mfg.'s Sug. Retail was $364.

MODEL 87 DELUXE DEERSLAYER — similar to Field Deerslayer except has cut checkering, high gloss lacquer finish, and gold trigger. Mfg. 1989-1996.

	$365	$285	$235	$190	$170	$160	$145

Last Mfg.'s Sug. Retail was $465.

Add $34 for rifled bore.
Add $120 for combo package (28 in. multi-choke barrel).

✱ *Model 87 Ultra Deerslayer* — similar to Deluxe Deerslayer except has aluminum frame. Mfg. 1989-90 only.

	$350	$285	$245	$200	$175	$160	$145

Last Mfg.'s Sug. Retail was $444.

MONTE CARLO DEERSLAYER II — 12 ga. only, 20 or 25 in. barrel with rifling, Monte Carlo stock and forearm with cut checkering, receiver is drilled and tapped for scope mounting, 7 lbs. Mfg. 1989-1996.

	$445	$335	$270	$210	$175	$160	$145

Last Mfg.'s Sug. Retail was $567.

DEERSLAYER II FAST TWIST — 12 ga. only, 25 in. rifled permanently fixed barrel, Monte Carlo stock with checkering, receiver is drilled and tapped. Mfg. 1992-1993.

	$440	$385	$325	$275	$235	$200	$180

Last Mfg.'s Sug. Retail was $550.

MODEL 87 MILITARY & POLICE — 12 (3 in.) or 20 (new 1989) ga., short barrel Model 37 w/normal stock or pistol grip only, 18½, 20, or 24¾ (scarce) in. barrel, choice of front bead or rifle sights, front blade was usually a flourescent orange plastic, 5, 8, or 10 shot. Originally disc. 1983, reintroduced 1989-1995.

	$265	$230	$200	$180	$170	$160	$150

Last Mfg.'s Sug. Retail was $323.

Add $104 for nickel finish (mfg. 1991-92 only).
Subtract $35 without parkerizing (disc.).

IVER JOHNSON ARMS, INC.

Previously manufactured in Fitchburg, MA, 1883-1984 and Jacksonville, AR 1984-1993. Formerly Johnson Bye & Co. 1871-1883. Renamed Iver Johnson & Co. in 1871 until 1891. Renamed Iver Johnson's Arms & Cycle Works in 1891 with manufacturing moving to Fitchburg, MA. In 1975 the name changed to Iver Johnson's Arms, Inc., and two years later, company facilities were moved to Middlesex, NJ. In 1982, production was moved to Jacksonville, AR under the trade name Iver Johnson Arms, Inc. In 1983, Universal Firearms, Inc. was acquired by Iver Johnson Arms, Inc.

Iver Johnson Arms was sold in March of 1987 and was acquired by American Military Arms Corporation (AMAC). AMAC ceased operations in early 1993.

PISTOLS: SEMI-AUTO

AMAC also manufactured a Super Enforcer .30 Carbine, Delta 786 9mm Para. (disc. 1989), and the M-2 machine gun in .30 Carbine which are not listed in this text.

Grading	100%	98%	95%	90%	80%	70%	60%

TRAILSMEN PISTOL — .22 LR cal. only, all steel construction, 4½ or 6 in. barrel, blue finish, black checkered composition grips, 10 shot mag., approx. 30 oz. Mfg. 1985-86 and reintroduced 1990 only.

	$200	$165	$145	$130	$120	$110	$100

Last Mfg.'s Sug. Retail was $230.

Add $20 for hardwood stocks and high polish blue (disc. 1990).

PONY PISTOL (PO380 SERIES) — .380 ACP cal. only, semi-auto single action, 3 in. barrel, 6 shot mag., all steel construction, blue or matte blue finish, 20 oz. Mfg. 1985-1986 (by Firearms International) and reintroduced 1990 only.

	$290	$245	$210	$185	$170	$155	$140

Last Mfg.'s Sug. Retail was $330.

* *Pony .380 Stainless* — similar to Pony Pistol, except is stainless steel construction. New 1990 only.

	$315	$280	$240				

Last Mfg.'s Sug. Retail was $365.

* *Nickel Pony* — with nickel finish. Mfg. 1985 only.

	$260	$230	$215	$200	$185	$170	$160

Last Mfg.'s Sug. Retail was $290 for nickel finish.

POCKET PISTOL (TP SERIES) — .22 LR or .25 ACP cal., semi-auto, double action, 3 in. barrel, 7 shot finger tip extension mag., black plastic grips, fixed sights, blue or matte finish, 15 oz. Previously mfg. 1985-86, reintroduced 1988-90.

	$145	$125	$110	$100	$90	$80	$70

Last Mfg.'s Sug. Retail was $165.

Add $15 for nickel finish (disc. 1989).

AMAC-22/25 COMPACT — .22 Short (disc.) or .25 ACP cal., semi-auto, single action, 5 shot mag., 2 in. barrel, all steel construction, plastic grips, 9.3 oz. Disc. 1993.

	$165	$135	$115	$100	$90	$80	$70

Last Mfg.'s Sug. Retail was $200.

Add $10 for nickel finish (disc. 1990).

* *Compact Elite Engraved* — similar to .25 ACP Compact, except has extensive engraving. Mfg. 1991-93.

	$850	$600	$475				

Last Mfg.'s Sug. Retail was $1,000.

SILVER HAWK — .22 LR or .25 ACP cal., double action semi-auto, similar to TP-22 Series, except is stainless steel. Mfg. 1990-93.

	$215	$185	$160				

Last Mfg.'s Sug. Retail was $250.

SUPER ENFORCER (MODEL 3000) — .30 Carbine cal. only, pistol version of the Carbine with 11 in. shrouded barrel. Add $40 for stainless steel (disc. for 1986). Mfg. 1985-1986 only.

	$285	$250	$225	$200	$175	$160	$145

Last Mfg.'s Sug. Retail was $255.

* *Enforcer* — similar to Super Enforcer model, except has 10½ in. barrel. Reintroduced 1988-disc. 1993.

	$325	$275	$240	$200	$175	$160	$145

Last Mfg.'s Sug. Retail was $417.

REVOLVERS

CATTLEMAN MAGNUM — .357 Mag., .44 Mag., or .45 LC cal., single action, 6 shot, Colt replica, 4¾, 5½, or 7½ in. barrel, case color frame, blue barrel, and brass grip frame, smooth walnut grips, fixed sights. Disc. 1984.

	100%	98%	95%	90%	80%	70%	60%
	$190	$175	$150	$140	$130	$125	$110
.44 Mag.	$220	$190	$175	$165	$145	$135	$125

Grading	100%	98%	95%	90%	80%	70%	60%

BUCKHORN MAGNUM — similar to Cattleman, except flat top, adj. sights.

	100%	98%	95%	90%	80%	70%	60%
	$210	$190	$175	$165	$145	$140	$125

BUNTLINE BUCKHORN MAGNUM — similar to Buckhorn, only 18 in. barrel, detachable stock.

	100%	98%	95%	90%	80%	70%	60%
	$345	$310	$295	$275	$260	$250	$225
.44 Mag.	$375	$325	$310	$295	$280	$275	$250

TRAIL BLAZER — .22 LR, or .22 Mag. cal., interchangeable cylinder, 5½ or 6½ in. barrel, blue.

	100%	98%	95%	90%	80%	70%	60%
	$175	$145	$130	$120	$110	$100	$80

MODEL 1900 — .22 L, S, LR, .32 S&W, or .38 S&W cal., double action, 2½, 4½, or 6 in. barrel, fixed sights, blue or nickel, rubber grips. Mfg. 1900-1947.

	100%	98%	95%	90%	80%	70%	60%
	$125	$80	$70	$60	$55	$45	$40

MODEL 1900 TARGET — .22 LR cal., 6 shot, 6 or 9½ in. barrel, blue, fixed sights. Mfg. 1925-1942.

	100%	98%	95%	90%	80%	70%	60%
	$140	$90	$80	$70	$65	$55	$50

TARGET SEALED 8 — .22 LR cal., 8 shot, 6 or 10 in. barrel, blue, fixed sights, rubber grips. Mfg. 1931-1957.

	100%	98%	95%	90%	80%	70%	60%
	$150	$100	$95	$80	$75	$65	$60

TARGET 9 SHOT — similar to Target Sealed 8, except 9 shot. Mfg. 1929-1946.

	100%	98%	95%	90%	80%	70%	60%
	$145	$90	$80	$70	$65	$55	$50

SAFETY HAMMER MODEL — .22 LR, .32 S&W, or .38 S&W cal., 2 or 3 in. barrel standard, 4, 5, or 6 in. available at extra cost, fixed sights, blue (standard) or nickel, break open. Mfg. 1892-1950.

	100%	98%	95%	90%	80%	70%	60%
	$125	$80	$70	$60	$55	$45	$40

SAFETY HAMMERLESS — .32 S&W or .38 S&W cal., 2, 3 (.32 only), 3¼, 4, 5, or 6 in. barrel, double action only, break open, fixed sights, rubber grips, blue or nickel. Mfg. 1895-1950.

	100%	98%	95%	90%	80%	70%	60%
	$125	$100	$95	$80	$75	$65	$60

.22 SUPERSHOT — .22 LR cal., 6 in. barrel, blue, fixed sights, checkered wood grips, break open, no counterbore. Mfg. 1929-1949.

	100%	98%	95%	90%	80%	70%	60%
	$150	$80	$70	$60	$55	$45	$40

TRIGGER COCKING SINGLE ACTION — .22 LR cal., 8 shot, 6 in. barrel, break open, counterbored, blue, checkered wood grips, first pull on trigger cocks, second fires. Mfg. 1940-1947. Rare in 100% condition.

	100%	98%	95%	90%	80%	70%	60%
	$175	$120	$110	$95	$80	$75	$65

.22 TARGET SINGLE ACTION — .22 LR cal., 8 shot, 6 in. barrel, break open, counterbored, checkered wood, adj. grips and sights. Mfg. 1938-1948.

	100%	98%	95%	90%	80%	70%	60%
	$160	$120	$110	$95	$80	$75	$65

SUPERSHOT SEALED 8 — .22 LR cal., 8 shot, break open, blue, adj. sights, checkered wood grips. Mfg. 1931-1957.

	100%	98%	95%	90%	80%	70%	60%
	$175	$130	$120	$110	$90	$85	$75

SUPERSHOT 9 — similar to Sealed 8, only 9 shot, not counterbored. Mfg. 1929-1949.

	100%	98%	95%	90%	80%	70%	60%
	$135	$90	$80	$75	$60	$50	$40

PROTECTOR SEALED 8 — .22 LR cal., 8 shot, 2½ in. barrel, break open, fixed sights, blue, wood grips. Mfg. 1933-1949.

	100%	98%	95%	90%	80%	70%	60%
	$175	$135	$125	$110	$90	$80	$75

SUPERSHOT MODEL 844 — .22 LR cal., 8 shot, 4½ or 6 in. barrel, adj. sights, break open, blue, wood grips. Mfg. 1955-1956.

	100%	98%	95%	90%	80%	70%	60%
	$100	$90	$85	$80	$75	$60	$50

Grading	100%	98%	95%	90%	80%	70%	60%

ARMSWORTH MODEL 855 — .22 LR cal., single action, 8 shot, 6 in. barrel, break open, blue, adj. sights, wood grips, adj. finger rest. Mfg. 1955-1957.

	$135	$125	$120	$110	$90	$80	$75

MODEL 55A TARGET — .22 LR cal., 8 shot, 4½ or 6 in. barrel, solid frame, blue, fixed sights, wood grips, loading gate. Mfg. 1955-1984.

	$75	$65	$55	$45	$35	$30	$15

CADET — .22 LR, .22 WRM, .32 S&W, .38 S&W, or .38 Spl. cal., 2½ in. barrel, blue, fixed sights, plastic grips. Mfg. 1955-1984.

	$110	$90	$80	$75	$65	$55	$50

MODEL 57A TARGET — .22 LR cal., 8 shot, 4½ or 6 in. barrel, solid frame, blue, adj. sights, wood grips. Mfg. 1955-1975.

	$100	$80	$75	$65	$55	$45	$40

MODEL 66 TRAILSMAN — .22 LR cal., 6 in. barrel, break open, blue, adj. sights, rebounding hammer, wood grips. Mfg. 1958-1975.

	$110	$90	$85	$75	$65	$55	$50

SIDEWINDER — .22 LR cal., 6 or 8 shot, 4¾ or 6 in. barrel, solid frame, blue, nickel, or case hardened finish, plastic grips, wood on case color model. Mfg. 1961-disc. 8 shot pre-1975.

	$110	$90	$85	$75	$65	$55	$50

SIDEWINDER S — similar to Sidewinder, except .22 WMR, interchangeable cylinder.

	$125	$100	$95	$85	$75	$65	$60

MODEL 67 VIKING — .22 LR cal., 8 shot, 4½ or 6 in. barrel, break open, blue, adj. sights, wood grips with thumbrest. Mfg. 1964-1975.

	$135	$110	$100	$95	$85	$75	$65

MODEL 67S VIKING — .22 LR, .32 S&W, or .38 S&W cal., 8 shot in .22, 5 shot in .32 or .38, 2¾ in. barrel, break open, adj. sights, plastic grips. Mfg. 1964-1975.

	$130	$100	$95	$85	$75	$60	$50

AMERICAN BULLDOG — .22 LR, .22 WRM, or .38 Spl. cal., 6 shot in .22, 5 shot in .38, 2½ or 4 in. barrel, blue or nickel, adj. sights, plastic grips. Mfg. 1974-1976.

	$135	$110	$100	$90	$80	$65	$60

ROOKIE — .38 Spl. cal., 5 shot, 4 in. barrel, solid frame, blue or nickel, plastic grips. Mfg. 1975-1984.

	$100	$80	$75	$65	$55	$45	$35

SPORTSMAN — .22 LR cal., 6 shot, 4¾ or 6 in. barrel, solid frame, blue, fixed sights, plastic grips. Mfg. 1974-1976.

	$100	$80	$75	$65	$55	$45	$35

DELUXE TARGET — similar to Sportsman, adj. sights. Mfg. 1975-1976.

	$110	$90	$85	$75	$65	$55	$40

SWING OUT — .22 LR, .22 WRM, .32 S&W, or .38 S&W cal., 6 shot in .22, 5 shot in .32 or .38, 2, 3, or 4 in. barrel, VR, 4 or 6 in., blue or nickel, fixed or adj. sights. Mfg. 1977-1984.

	$130	$110	$100	$90	$80	$75	$65

   ✳ VR Barrel — 4 or 6 in. VR barrel, adj. sights.

	$170	$150	$140	$130	$125	$120	$100

Grading	100%	98%	95%	90%	80%	70%	60%

RIFLES

MODEL X — .22 Short, Long, or LR cal., bolt action, single shot, 22 in. barrel, open sight, pistol grip with knob forend. Mfg. 1928-1932.

	100%	98%	95%	90%	80%	70%	60%
	$90	$60	$50	$40	$35	$30	$25

This model was mfg. both in the U.S. and Canada (by Cooey). Canadian models generally have birch stocks.

MODEL 2X — improved Model X, 24 in. heavy barrel, larger stock, adj. sights. Mfg. 1932-1955.

	$120	$95	$75	$50	$40	$35	$30

LI'L CHAMP — .22 LR cal. only, single shot bolt action, 16¼ in. barrel, black molded stock, nickel plated bolt, youth dimensions, (32½ in. overall length), 3 lbs. Introduced 1986, reintroduced 1988 only.

	$75	$60	$50	$45	$40	$35	$35

Last Mfg.'s Sug. Retail was $92.

LONG RANGE RIFLE — .308 Win. (new 1991) or .50 BMG cal., bolt action design, single shot, 29 in. stainless steel fluted barrel with muzzle brake, adj. trigger pull, built in bipod, adj. rail stock, includes Leupold M-1 Ultra 20X scope, 36 lbs. Limited mfg. between 1988-1993.

	$4,350	$3,500	$3,150	$2,750	$2,400	$2,100	$1,800

Last Mfg.'s Sug. Retail was $5,000.

9MM PARA. CARBINE (JJ9MM SERIES) — 9mm Para. cal. only, copy of U.S. military M1, 16 in. barrel, blue finish only, 20 shot mag. Mfg. 1985-86 only.

* *Hardwood Stock Model* — disc. 1986.

	$230	$200	$180	$170	$160	$150	$140

Last Mfg.'s Sug. Retail was $255.

* *Standard Model* — with plastic stock. Disc. 1985.

	$225	$200	$180	$170	$160	$150	$140

Last Mfg.'s Sug. Retail was $250.

* *Folding Plastic Stock Model* — disc. 1985.

	$255	$225	$200	$180	$170	$160	$150

Last Mfg.'s Sug. Retail was $281.

DELTA-786 CARBINE — 9mm Para. cal., semi-auto, patterned after the U.S. military M1 Carbine, 16 in. barrel, matte black finish. Mfg. 1989 only.

	$575	$425	$360	$325	$295	$260	$230

Last Mfg.'s Sug. Retail was $665.

.30 CARBINE CAL. — .30 Carbine or 9mm Para. (new 1991) cal., semi-auto, 18 or 20 (new 1991) in. barrel, available in various stock configurations, hardwood stock. Mfg. 1985-1986, reintroduced 1988-disc. 1993.

	$285	$215	$190	$165	$150	$140	$130

Last Mfg.'s Sug. Retail was $350.

Add $16 for 9mm Para. cal.
Add $35 for walnut stock, Parkerized finish (disc. 1990), or 20 in. barrel (new 1991).

* *Paratrooper Model* — similar to standard model, except has folding synthetic stock. Disc. 1993.

	$345	$270	$225	$195	$165	$150	$140

Last Mfg.'s Sug. Retail was $433.

* *Stainless Steel Variation* — disc. 1985.

	$230	$200	$180				

Last Mfg.'s Sug. Retail was $250.

* *5.7mm Johnson (Spitfire) Cal.* — remilled, add $30 for stainless steel.

	$195	$175	$165	$155	$145	$135	$125

Last Mfg.'s Sug. Retail was $219.

Grading	100%	98%	95%	90%	80%	70%	60%

.22 CAL. U.S. CARBINE — .22 LR or .22 Mag. cal., 18½ in. barrel, except for Mag. (19.3 in.), 5.8 lbs., 15 shot mag., sling swivels. Mfg. 1985-1986, reintroduced 1988 only.

	$150	$120	$110	$100	$90	$85	$80

Last Mfg.'s Sug. Retail was $166 for .22 LR cal.
Last Mfg.'s Sug. Retail was $183 for .22 Mag. cal.

Add $120 for .22 Mag. model (gas operated — disc. 1986).

TARGETMASTER SLIDE ACTION — .22 LR or .22 Mag. (disc. 1986) cal., 18½ in. barrel, 12 shot (LR) tube mag., 5¾ lbs. Mfg. 1985 only, reintroduced 1988-90.

	$175	$140	$125	$115	$100	$90	$80

Last Mfg.'s Sug. Retail was $209.

This model was designated EW.22 HBP previously.

MODEL EW.22 HBL LEVER ACTION (WAGONMASTER) — .22 S, L, and LR or .22 Mag. cal., 18½ in. barrel, walnut finish, hardwood stock, blue finish, 5¾ lbs., grooved for scope mounts. Mfg. 1985-1986, reintroduced 1988-90.

	$175	$140	$125	$115	$100	$90	$80

Last Mfg.'s Sug. Retail was $209.

Add $23 for .22 Mag. cal. (19 in. barrel).

This model was also available in a Junior variation with smaller dimensions; values same as listed above.

TRAIL BLAZER SEMI-AUTO (MODEL IJ.22 HB) — .22 LR cal. only, 10 shot clip mag., 18½ in. barrel, 5.8 lbs. Mfg. 1985 only.

	$115	$100	$90	$85	$80	$75	$70

Last Mfg.'s Sug. Retail was $125.

SHOTGUNS

CHAMPION — 10, 12, 16, 20, 24, 28, 32 ga., or .410 bore, also available in .44, .45, 12mm, or 14mm rifle cal., single barrel shotgun or rifle, 26-32 in. full barrel, exposed hammer, auto ejector, plain pistol grip stock. Mfg. 1909-1956.

	$145	$100	$80	$60	$40	$35	$25

Values on both smaller gauge shotguns and rifles would be considerably higher than those listed above. A mint .32 ga. might command 400% more than the above values. Rifles will also bring premiums over values listed above.

MATTED RIB GRADE — similar to Champion, except not available in 10, 24, 28, or 32 ga., solid rib, checkered stock. Mfg. 1909-1948.

	$165	$115	$95	$70	$50	$45	$40

This model has either a semi-octagon (with top matted) or jacketed breech.

TRAP GRADE — similar to Matted Rib, except 32 in. full barrel, super select wood, 12 ga., vent rib. Mfg. 1909-1942.

	$275	$165	$140	$120	$100	$90	$80

HERCULES GRADE — 12, 16, 20, 28 ga., or .410 bore, 26-32 in. barrels, hammerless, boxlock, various chokes, extractors and double triggers standard, checkered pistol grip or straight stock. Mfg. 1918-1943.

	$795	$525	$450	$425	$375	$335	$310

Add $100 for auto ejectors.
Add $100 for SST.
Add 10% for 16 ga.
Add 20% for 20 ga.
Add 200% for 28 ga.
Add 100% for .410 bore.
Add 200%+ for rare factory engraved specimens.

The Hercules Model was mfg. in both USA and Canada. The Hercules name was dropped in 1936 and became known as the "Iver Johnson Hammerless" until the end of production. Case colored frames were standard until 1936, blued frames were standard

Grading	100%	98%	95%	90%	80%	70%	60%

1937-1943. A special run of Hercules Doubles was built in the 1930s for Montgomery Ward under the "Western Field" Model 53 nomenclature. All Western Field guns had a beavertail forearm, twin ivory sights, and recoil pad. Hercules 28 ga. SxS's are extremely rare.

SKEET-ER MODEL — 12, 16, 20, 28 ga., or .410 bore, similar to Hercules Model, except has blued receiver, super select wood and beavertail forearm, many Skeet-ers were special order guns with options including selective or non-selective Miller trigger, custom stock, barrel chokes, chamber lengths, checkering and wood finishes, sling swivels, recoil pad, checkered butt, VR, and various engraving patterns. Approx. 1,200 mfg. 1933-1942.

	100%	98%	95%	90%	80%	70%	60%
	$1,295	$900	$700	$600	$500	$450	$400

Add 20% for auto ejectors.
Add 20% for SST.
Add 50% for factory VR.
Add 20% for 16 or 20 ga.
Add 100% for 28 ga. or .410 bore.
Add 200% for rare factory engraving.

.410 bore is the most commonly encountered gun and was made on a special small frame. This model was probably responsible for more Skeet records than any other American .410 bore SxS shotgun.

SUPER TRAP — 12 ga. only, 32 in. full VR, boxlock, extractors, checkered pistol grip stock, beavertail forend and recoil pad. Mfg. 1928-1942. Scarce.

	100%	98%	95%	90%	80%	70%	60%
	$1,095	$750	$550	$475	$415	$395	$370

Add $100 for auto ejectors.
Add $100 for SST.

SILVER SHADOW — O/U, 12 ga., 26 or 28 in. barrels, various chokes, extractors, vent rib, checkered pistol grip stock, Italian mfg. Disc.

J section

J.O. ARMS

Previous importer of KSN Industries, Ltd. pistols until 1997.

JMC FABRICATION & MACHINE, INC.

Current manufacturer established 1997 and located in Rockledge, FL.

Grading	100%	98%	95%	90%	80%	70%	60%

RIFLES: BOLT ACTION

MODEL 2000 M/P — .50 BMG cal., rapid takedown, 30 in. barrel, matte black finish, cast aluminum stock with Pachmayr pad, fully adj. bipod, 10 shot staggered mag., two-stage trigger, includes 24X U.S. Optics scope, prices assume all options included, 29½ lbs. New 1998.

Mfg.'s Sug. Retail	$8,500		$7,950	$7,400	$6,800	$6,150	$5,500	$4,900	$4,200

Subtract $2,800 if w/o options.

JP ENTERPRISES, INC.

Current manufacturer and customizer located in St. Paul, MN since 1998. Previously located in Shoreview, MN 1995-98. Dealer and consumer sales.

PISTOLS: SEMI-AUTO

LEVEL I CUSTOM — .45 ACP cal., features Springfield 1911A1 in blue or stainless finish, lapped slide and frame. Mfg. 1995-97.

	$550	$495	$450	$400	$360	$330	$300

Last Mfg.'s Sug. Retail was $599.

Add $51 for stainless steel construction.

LEVEL II CUSTOM — similar to Level I Custom, except has JP complete comp kit, reworked trigger, coco bolo (disc.) or Hogue custom grips. Mfg. 1995-97.

	$850	$750	$650	$550	$500	$450	$400

Last Mfg.'s Sug. Retail was $950.

Add $49 for stainless steel construction.

RIFLES: SEMI-AUTO

BARRACUDA 10/22 — .22 LR cal., features customized Ruger 10/22 action with reworked fire control system, choice of stainless bull or carbon fiber superlight barrel, 3 lb. trigger, color laminated "Barracuda" skeletonized stock. New 1997.

Mfg.'s Sug. Retail	$1,095		$995	$875	$750	$625	$550	$475	$400

A-2 MATCH — .223 Rem. cal., AR-15 style configuration, includes JP fire control system, composite ambidextrous thumbhole stock with pistol grip, Mil-Spec A-2 upper assembly with match rear sight. Mfg. 1995-96.

	$995	$875	$750	$625	$550	$475	$415

Last Mfg.'s Sug. Retail was $1,085.

GRADE I (A-2 FLAT TOP) — .223 Rem. cal., features Eagle Arms lower and International Flat Top upper free floating tube, 16 or 20 in. SGW heavy match barrel with JP recoil eliminator, adj. gas system. New 1995.

Mfg.'s Sug. Retail	$1,395		$1,200	$1,025	$900	$750	$625	$550	$475

Add $500 for NRA Hi-Power version with 24 in. bull barrel and sight package.

* **Grade I IPSC LIMITED CLASS** — similar to Grade I, except has quick detachable match grade iron sights, Versa-pod bipod. New 1999.

Mfg.'s Sug. Retail	$1,695		$1,595	$1,350	$1,125	$975	$775	$625	$550

Grading	100%	98%	95%	90%	80%	70%	60%

GRADE II — .223 Rem. cal., features Mil-spec lower receiver with anodized upper assembly, JP fire control and gas system, 16-24 in. cryo treated stainless barrel, composite thumbhole stock, Harris bipod, choice of multi-color or black handguard, includes hard case. New 1998.

Mfg.'s Sug. Retail	$1,695	$1,595	$1,350	$1,125	$975	$775	$625	$550

GRADE III (THE EDGE) — .223 Rem. cal., match upper/lower receiver system, 2-piece free floating forend, standard or laminated thumbhole wood stock, 16 to 24 in. barrel (cryo treated beginning 1998) with recoil eliminator, includes Harris bipod, top of the line model, includes hard case. New 1996.

Mfg.'s Sug. Retail	$2,595	$2,375	$2,025	$1,700	$1,425	$1,150	$875	$750

Add $250 for laminated thumbhole stock (when ordered with gun).

MODEL AR-10T — .243 Win. or .308 Win. cal., features Armalite receiver system with JP fire control, flat-top receiver, vent. free floating tube, 24 in. cryo treated stainless barrel, black finish. New 1998.

Mfg.'s Sug. Retail	$2,500	$2,300	$1,975	$1,675	$1,425	$1,150	$875	$750

Add $150 for upper assembly in custom color.

* *Model AR-10LW* — lightweight variation of the Model AR-10T, includes 16-20 in. cryo treated stainless barrel, composite fiber tube, black finish only, 7-8 lbs. New 1998.

Mfg.'s Sug. Retail	$1,895	$1,750	$1,450	$1,150	$975	$775	$625	$550

Add $200 for detachable sights.

J R DISTRIBUTING

Current manufacturer located in Moorpark, CA. J R Distributing is a division of J R Sports Distribution Corporation. Dealer and consumer sales.

RIFLES: SEMI-AUTO

.22 MAG. CUSTOM RIFLE — .22 Mag. cal., choice of Ruger 10/22 or AMT action, 20 in. bull barrel with laminate or synthetic stock, 9 shot rotary mag., supplied with hard case. New 1998.

Mfg.'s Sug. Retail	$795	$725	$650	$550	$500	$450	$400	$360

JSL (HEREFORD)

Previous manufacturer located in Hereford, England. Imported until 1994 by Specialty Shooters Supply, Inc. located in Fort Lauderdale, FL.

PISTOLS: SEMI-AUTO

SPITFIRE (G1) — 9mm Para. or 9x21mm cal., patterned after the Czech CZ-75/85, 3.7 in. barrel, ambidextrous safety, commander style hammer, black non-slip rubberized grip panels, investment cast stainless steel fabrication, 10 (C/B 1994) or 15★ shot mag., 2.2 lbs. Imported 1992-94.

* *Spitfire Standard* — includes fixed rear sight, 2 mags., presentation case, and allen key.

	$1,332	$1,100	$925

Last Mfg.'s Sug. Retail was $1,332.

Add $81 for adj. rear sight (Sterling Model).

Grading	100%	98%	95%	90%	80%	70%	60%

JACKSON HOLE FIREARMS

Previous manufacturer located in Jackson Hole, WY circa mid-70s.

RIFLES: BOLT ACTION

STANDARD RIFLE — various cals., Mauser 98 action utilizing patented system for interchangeable barrels, checkered walnut stock.

	100%	98%	95%	90%	80%	70%	60%
	$1,050	$875	$800	$725	$650	$575	$495

Jackson Hole Firearms manufactured a limited quantity of their unique interchangeable barrel bolt action rifles. Collectibility to date has been minimal, and values are affected by the J.P. Sauer Models 90 and 200 which also feature the interchangeable barrel design.

JAGD-UND SPORTWAFFEN SUHL GmbH

Current manufacturer located in Suhl, Germany since 1535.

Currently, the famous Merkel trademark (mfg. by Jagd-Und Sportwaffen Suhl GmbH) is imported by Gun South Inc. located in Trussville, AL. Please refer to the Merkel listing in this text for current information regarding this older European trademark. See the Trademark Index in this text for current factory information.

JAPANESE MILITARY RIFLES

Previously manufactured during WWII in Japan.

Japanese Nambu pistols are located in the N section.

RIFLES: MILITARY

Subtract 20% if National Crest (chrysanthemum flower) has been ground off front receiver ring.

Subtract 20% if serial numbers are not matching.

Subtract 10%-40% for training rifles of each type.

MODEL 38 ARISAKA RIFLE — 6.5X51R Arisaka cal., Jap. Mauser type action, 31 in. barrel, adj. sight, adopted 1905.

	100%	98%	95%	90%	80%	70%	60%
	$165	$135	$105	$95	$75	$65	$50

Add 50%+ for short barrel.

Add 50% for sniper variation.

MODEL 38 CAVALRY CARBINE — 6.5x51R Arisaka cal., similar to T38 Rifle, except shorter barrel. Mfg. 1911.

	100%	98%	95%	90%	80%	70%	60%
	$175	$140	$110	$100	$80	$70	$55

Add 300% for paratrooper variation with hinged stock.

MODEL 44 CAVALRY ARISAKA CARBINE — 6.5x51R Arisaka cal., similar to T38 Carbine, features 19 in. barrel and folding bayonet.

	100%	98%	95%	90%	80%	70%	60%
	$275	$235	$210	$190	$170	$155	$135

MODEL 99 SERVICE RIFLE — 7.7x58mm Arisaka cal., WWII version of Model 38, mostly encountered with shorter barrels than the Model 38 Arisaka Rifle.

	100%	98%	95%	90%	80%	70%	60%
	$175	$140	$110	$100	$80	$70	$55

Add 20% for monopod.

Add 50% for sniper variation.

Add 50%+ for long barrel.

PARATROOPER TAKEDOWN VERSION — 7.7x58mm Arisaka cal., adopted 1940, crossbolt barrel lock.

Type 2	100%	98%	95%	90%	80%	70%	60%
	$475	$375	$275	$225	$190	$165	$135

Grading	100%	98%	95%	90%	80%	70%	60%

JARRETT RIFLES, INC.

Current manufacturer located in Jackson, SC since 1979. Direct custom order sales only.

HANDGUNS

CUSTOM XP-1 HUNTER — various cals., re-machined Remington XP-100 action, Jarrett match grade stainless steel barrel, McMillan fiberglass stock, various options.

Mfg.'s Sug. Retail	$2,950	$2,950	$2,350	$1,950	$1,650	$1,300	$1,050	$995

ULTIMATE REDHAWK — .44 Mag. cal., features Hogue grips and muzzle brake. New 1995.

Mfg.'s Sug. Retail	$1,150	$1,150	$1,025	$850	$675	$575	$500	$450

RIFLES: BOLT ACTION

A wide variety of options are available for Jarrett custom rifles (holders of 16 world records in rifle accuracy). The factory should be contacted directly (see Trademark Index for info.) for pricing and availability regarding these special order options. Custom gunsmithing services are also available and again, the manufacturer should be contacted directly for gunsmith quotations. Custom gunsmithing requires individuals to supply receivers.

Values listed below for Jarrett firearms assume the customer supplies the company with an action - Jarrett then blueprints every action for proper dimensioning and rigid tolerances.

JARRETT CUSTOM RIFLE — various cals., Remington Model 700 right-hand or left-hand action, McMillan fiberglass stock, blued receiver, Jarrett satin finish match grade barrel, sling studs and leather sling, rings and base, weights vary.

Mfg.'s Sug. Retail	$3,050	$3,050	$2,450	$1,950	$1,650	$1,325	$1,050	$900

WALKABOUT — various cals. in short action only, features Remington Model 7 action (left-hand utilizes Rem. Model 700 short action), weights vary. New 1995.

Mfg.'s Sug. Retail	$3,050	$3,050	$2,450	$1,950	$1,650	$1,325	$1,050	$900

COUP de GRACE — various cals. New 1996.

Mfg.'s Sug. Retail	$3,495	$3,495	$2,750	$2,300	$1,800	$1,500	$1,250	$995

NOMBRE UNIQUE SERIES — various cals., 100 mfg. beginning 1999.

Mfg.'s Sug. Retail	$3,695	$3,695	$2,900	$2,400	$1,850	$1,550	$1,250	$995

WINDWALKER SERIES — various cals. up to .30 cal., Rem. M-700 ADL action only, lightweight design, Brown Precision stock, muzzlebrake step, 7¼ lbs. New 1999.

Mfg.'s Sug. Retail	$3,895	$3,895	$3,050	$2,500	$1,900	$1,600	$1,250	$995

Add $790 for Swarovski 3X-10X (42mm) scope.

PROFESSIONAL HUNTER — Mag. cals. to customer's specifications, features Winchester controlled round feed Model 70 action with claw extractor and 3 position bolt shroud safety, Jarrett match grade stainless steel barrel, McMillan stock, quarter rib with iron sights, includes 2 sets of detachable rings and two 1.5X-5X Leupold scopes, takedown action.

Mfg.'s Sug. Retail	$6,200	$6,200	$5,150	$4,350	$3,600	$2,900	$2,300	$1,850

CLASSIC SERIES — various cals., 100 mfg. 1989 only.

	$3,195	$2,650	$2,100	$1,650	$1,375	$1,150	$875

INVESTOR SERIES — various cals., 100 mfg. 1989 only.

	$3,195	$2,650	$2,100	$1,650	$1,375	$1,150	$875

ACCURACY LEGEND SERIES — various cals., similar to Jarrett Custom Rifle, except has many accuracy tune-ups incorporated as well as muzzle brake. 100 mfg. 1993 only.

	$3,495	$2,850	$2,300	$1,850	$1,500	$1,250	$995

Last Mfg.'s Sug. Retail was $3,495.

Grading	100%	98%	95%	90%	80%	70%	60%

COUP de MAIM — various cals., similar to the Jarrett Custom Rifle, includes muzzle brake, matte black or olive drab finish, Model 70 style bolt release. 100 mfg. 1995 only.

	100%	98%	95%	90%	80%	70%	60%
	$2,750	$2,300	$1,800	$1,500	$1,250	$995	$775

Last Mfg.'s Sug. Retail was $3,495.

PRIVATE COLLECTION — various cals., similar quality as the Jarrett Custom Rifle, except many extra cost special order options are included, ser. numbered 1-100. Mfg. 1994 only.

	100%	98%	95%	90%	80%	70%	60%
	$3,495	$2,850	$2,300	$1,850	$1,500	$1,250	$995

Last Mfg.'s Sug. Retail was $3,495.

SILENT PARTNER SERIES — various cals., only 10 mfg. 1994 only.

	100%	98%	95%	90%	80%	70%	60%
	$3,495	$2,850	$2,300	$1,850	$1,500	$1,250	$995

ULTIMATE HUNTER SERIES — various cals., 100 mfg. 1989 only.

	100%	98%	95%	90%	80%	70%	60%
	$3,495	$2,850	$2,300	$1,850	$1,500	$1,250	$995

SHOTGUNS: SLIDE ACTION

Value changes below reflect customer supplied action.

JARRETT ULTIMATE SHOTGUN — 12 ga., Remington Model 870 action with 21 in. hand lapped barrel with interchangeable chokes, 8 shot mag. extension, matte black or olive drab green finish.

	100%	98%	95%	90%	80%	70%	60%
Mfg.'s Sug. Retail $1,000	$1,000	$825	$675	$550	$450	$350	$295

JEFFERY, W.J. & CO. LTD

Previous manufacturer located in London, England.

In addition to making a complete line of their own shotguns and rifles, W.J. Jeffery also was subcontracted by many other exporters, distributors, and retailers (including London's famous Army & Navy department store). Many models were produced and rather than list them individually, a generalized format has been adopted for determining values on both rifles and shotguns.

RIFLES

SINGLE SHOT — various cals., falling block action, checkered walnut stock and forearm, usually multiple folding leaves rear sight (also tangent), excellent quality. Prices start in the $600 range for poor condition specimens in obsolete or undesirable cals. and can go up to $5,000 for 100% condition in .600 Nitro Express.

Subtract substantially for the Martini action variation.

BOXLOCK DOUBLE RIFLE — many cals., various engraving patterns, top or under (usually large cals.) lever opening, multiple folding leaves rear sight, checkered walnut stock and forearm. Prices usually start in the $1,500 range for poor condition in undesirable cals. and can exceed $8,000 if encountered with elaborate engraving in .475 Express or larger cals.

Subtract approx. 40% if with hammers, over 50% if with damascus barrels.

SIDELOCK DOUBLE RIFLE — various cals., available in No. 1 or No. 2 grade, top-lever opening, best quality engraving, deluxe checkered walnut stock and forearm, almost any custom order could be filled. Prices start in the $3,250 range for 60% condition in smaller cals. and can easily go to $12,000+ when found in excellent condition in the larger cals.

Subtract approx. 40% if with hammers, over 50% if with damascus barrels.

SHOTGUNS: SxS

BOXLOCK SHOTGUN — most ga.'s, many combinations of options available, top-lever opening, many ranges of engraving, high quality and worksmanship. Values usually start in the $650 range if in poor condition and can go to $4,500+ if in a small ga. in near new condition ($1,750 for 12 ga.).

Subtract approx. 40% if with hammers, over 50% if with damascus barrels.

Grading	100%	98%	95%	90%	80%	70%	60%

SIDELOCK SHOTGUN — most ga.'s, many combinations of options available, top-lever opening, many ranges of engraving, high quality and worksmanship. Values usually start in the $1,250 range if in poor condition and can go to $8,500+ if in a small ga. in near new condition ($3,950 for 12 ga.).

JENNINGS, B.L., INC.

Previous manufacturer until 1985 located in City of Industry, CA. Currently, Jennings is the exclusive distributor for Bryco, Sundance, and Accu-Tek. The Jennings trademark is now owned by Bryco Arms.

PISTOLS: SEMI-AUTO

MODEL J-22 — .22 LR cal., 6 shot, single action, 2½ in. barrel, positive safety locks sear, satin nickel, bright chrome or black teflon finish, 13 oz. Disc. 1985.

	$65	$50	$40	$35	$30	$30	$30

Last Mfg.'s Sug. Retail was $79.

JERICHO

Previous trademark of Israeli Military Industries (I.M.I.). Previously imported by K.B.I., Inc. located in Harrisburg, PA.

PISTOLS: SEMI-AUTO

JERICHO 941 — 9mm Para. or .40 S&W cal.(new 1991), .41 Action Express (by conversion only), semi-auto double action or single action, 4.72 in. barrel with polygonal rifling, all steel fabrication, 3 dot Tritium sights, 11 or 16 (9mm Para.) shot mag., ambidextrous safety, polymer grips, decocking lever, 38½ oz. Imported 1990-92.

	$550	$475	$425	$375	$325	$295	$260

Last Mfg.'s Sug. Retail was $649.

Add $299 for .41 AE conversion kit.

Industrial hard chrome or nickel finishes were also available for all Jericho pistols.

* ***Jericho 941 Pistol Package*** — includes 9mm Para. and .40 S&W barrels, also includes .41 AE conversion kit, cased with accessories. Mfg. 1990-91 only.

	$695	$625	$550	$495	$450	$400	$360

Last Mfg.'s Sug. Retail was $775.

JOHNSON AUTOMATICS, INC.

Previous manufacturer located in Providence, RI. Johnson Automatics, Inc. moved many times during its history, often with slight name changes. M.M. Johnson, Jr. died in 1965, and the company continued production at 104 Audubon Street in New Haven, CT as Johnson Arms, Inc. mostly specializing in sporter semi-auto rifles in .270 Win. or 30-06.

RIFLES: SEMI-AUTO

MODEL 1941 — .30-06 or 7x57mm cal., 22 in. removable air cooled barrel, recoil operated, perforated metal handguard, aperture sight, military stock. Most were made for Dutch military, some used by U.S. Marine Paratroopers, during WWII all .30-06 and 7x57mm were ordered by South American governments.

	$1,850	$1,575	$1,250	$995	$850	$750	$675

Subtract $50 for 7x57mm cal.
Subtract 10% if serial numbers don't match.

JURRAS

Current custom pistolsmith located in Prescott, AZ. Previously distributed by J & G Sales located in Prescott, AZ.

Ammunition for Jurras pistols was manufactured by Robert Davis, Jr. located in Athens, TN.

PISTOLS

Lee E. Jurras manufactures custom pistols in larger calibers. Almost any caliber is available by special order and the listings below represent a few of his more standard items. Special order inquiries may be directed to Mr. Jurras, in Prescott, AZ.

HOWDAH — available in .375, .416, .460, .475, .500, or .577 Jurras cals., action based on Thompson/Center Contender receiver, 12 in. bull barrel, nitex finish, adj. rear sights, limited mfg. (100).

* **Custom Grade**

$1,150	$925	$800	$725	$650	$575	$500

* **Presentation Grade** — .375 Jurras or .460 Jurras, deluxe Claro walnut stock and forearm.

$2,000	$1,750	$1,500	$1,250	$1,050	$950	$825

.416, .475, .500, or .577 Jurras calibers command a premium on this model.

J

NOTES

J

K section

K.B.I., INC.

Current importer and distributor located in Harrisburg, PA. Distributor and dealer sales.

K.B.I., Inc. currently imports Armscor (Arms Corp. of the Philippines), Charles Daly shotguns, FEG pistols, and Liberty revolvers. These may be found within the correct alphabetical sections. K.B.I. previously imported the Jericho pistol manufactured by I.M.I. from Israel. The Jericho pistol may be found under its own heading in this text.

Grading	100%	98%	95%	90%	80%	70%	60%

PISTOLS: SEMI-AUTO, FEG MFG.

Please refer to the FEG section in this text.

RIFLES: BOLT ACTION

KASSNAR GRADE I — available in 9 cals., thumb safety that locks trigger, with or w/o deluxe sights, 22 in. barrel, 3 or 4 shot mag., includes swivel posts and oil finished standard grade European walnut with recoil pad, 7½ lbs. Imported 1989-1993.

	100%	98%	95%	90%	80%	70%	60%
	$445	$385	$325	$275	$225	$195	$175

Last Mfg.'s Sug. Retail was $499.

NYLON 66 — .22 LR cal., patterned after the Remington Nylon 66. Imported until 1990 from C.B.C. in Brazil, South America.

	100%	98%	95%	90%	80%	70%	60%
	$125	$110	$95	$85	$75	$70	$65

Last Mfg.'s Sug. Retail was $134.

MODEL 122 — .22 LR cal., bolt action design with clip mag. Imported from South America until 1990.

	100%	98%	95%	90%	80%	70%	60%
	$125	$110	$95	$85	$75	$70	$65

Last Mfg.'s Sug. Retail was $136.

MODEL 522 — .22 LR cal., bolt action design with tube mag. Imported from South America until 1990.

	100%	98%	95%	90%	80%	70%	60%
	$130	$115	$100	$85	$75	$70	$65

Last Mfg.'s Sug. Retail was $142.

BANTAM SINGLE SHOT — .22 LR cal., youth dimensions. Imported 1989-90 only.

	100%	98%	95%	90%	80%	70%	60%
	$110	$90	$85	$75	$70	$65	$60

Last Mfg.'s Sug. Retail was $120.

SHOTGUNS

GRADE I O/U — 12, 20, 28 ga., or .410 bore, gold plated SST, extractors, vent. rib, checkered walnut stock and forearm. Imported 1989-1993.

	100%	98%	95%	90%	80%	70%	60%
	$525	$425	$350	$295	$265	$240	$220

Last Mfg.'s Sug. Retail was $599.

Add $70 for 28 ga. or .410 bore.
Add $50 for choke tubes (12 and 20 ga. only).
Add $150 for automatic ejectors (with choke tubes only).

GRADE II SxS — 10, 12, 16, 20, 28 ga., or .410 bore, boxlock action, case hardened receiver, English style checkered European walnut stock with splinter forearm, chrome barrels with concave rib, extractors, double hinged triggers. Imported 1989-90 only.

	100%	98%	95%	90%	80%	70%	60%
	$515	$435	$375	$325	$275	$250	$225

Last Mfg.'s Sug. Retail was $575.

Add $95 for 28 ga. or .410 bore.
Add $85 for 10 ga.

K

Grading			100%	98%	95%	90%	80%	70%	60%

KDF, INC.

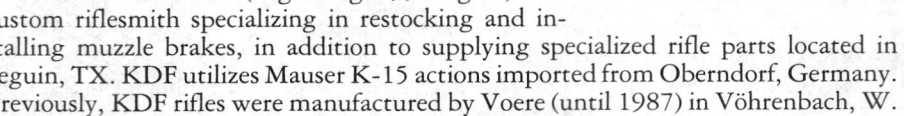

Current manufacturer (beginning 1998 again) and custom riflesmith specializing in restocking and installing muzzle brakes, in addition to supplying specialized rifle parts located in Seguin, TX. KDF utilizes Mauser K-15 actions imported from Oberndorf, Germany. Previously, KDF rifles were manufactured by Voere (until 1987) in Vöhrenbach, W. Germany.

Older KDF rifles were private labeled by Voere and marked KDF. Since Voere was absorbed by Mauser-Werke in 1987, model designations changed. Mauser-Werke does not private label (i.e. newer guns are marked Mauser-Werke), and these rifles can be found under the Mauser-Werke heading in this text. KDF also offers an accurizing service for rifles - the current retail is $249.

RIFLES: BOLT ACTION, U.S. MFG.

In 1989, KDF announced the release of a new American built redesigned Model K15 with many improvements. While advertised, approximately only 25 were manufactured in various cals.

K15 — .22-250 Rem. (disc. 1992), .243 Win., 6mm Rem., .25-06 Rem., .270 Win., .280 Rem., .30-06 cal. or .308 Win. cal., 60 degree short lift bolt action with 3 lugs, Kevlar composite or laminate walnut stock, adj. single stage competition trigger, box magazine, thumb activated slide safety, satin blue finish, 24 in. match grade barrel, deluxe checkered walnut stock with ebony accents and Pachmayr Decelerator recoil pad, approx. 8 lbs. Limited mfg. in U.S. starting 1989.

$1,750 $1,375 $1,150 $950 $750 $650 $575
Last Mfg.'s Sug. Retail was $1,950.

✱ **K15 Magnum** — .270 Wby. Mag., .300 Win. Mag. (disc.), .300 Wby. Mag., 7mm Rem. Mag., .338 Win. Mag., .340 Wby. Mag. (disc.), .375 H&H, .411 KDF, .416 Rem. Mag. (disc.), or .458 Win. Mag. cal., similar to K15, except has 26 in. barrel. Mfg. in U.S. starting 1989. Disc.

$1,795 $1,400 $1,175 $975 $775 $675 $600
Last Mfg.'s Sug. Retail was $2,000.

KDF CLASSIC — cals. similar to K15, custom tuned Remington 700 action, bench rest barrel, Brown Precision stock, KDF accurizing, Arnold jewell custom trigger, matte blue finish, Pachmayr Decelerator pad, includes rings and bases.

$1,750 $1,375 $1,150 $950 $750 $650 $575
Last Mfg.'s Sug. Retail was $1,950.

Add $50 for Mag. cals.

KDF FRONTIER — cals. similar to KDF Classic, custom tuned Winchester Model 70 action, bench rest barrel, Brown Precision stock, KDF accurizing, Arnold jewell custom trigger, matte blue finish, Pachmayr Decelerator pad, includes rings and bases.

$1,750 $1,375 $1,150 $950 $750 $650 $575
Last Mfg.'s Sug. Retail was $1,950.

Add $50 for Mag. cals.
Add $150 for action with positive feeding claw extractor.

KDF VARMINT — varmint cals., custom tuned Remington 700 or XP action, bench rest heavy contour barrel, Brown Precision stock, KDF accurizing, Arnold jewell custom trigger, matte blue finish, Pachmayr Decelerator pad, includes rings and bases.

$2,000 $1,725 $1,425 $1,200 $950 $750 $650
Last Mfg.'s Sug. Retail was $2,250.

Add $250 for Rem. XP action.

KDF MAUSER 98 — .270 Win. or .30-06 cal., sporterized action, Wilson barrel, Butler Creek black synthetic stock, 7.5 lbs. New 1998.

Mfg.'s Sug. Retail	$330	$295	$260	$240	$220	$200	$185	$170

K

Grading	100%	98%	95%	90%	80%	70%	60%

KDF CUSTOM MAUSER PACKAGE — various cals., features custom bolt shroud, adj. trigger, glass bedding, 1 in. rings, and KDF slimline muzzle brake. New 1998.

Mfg.'s Sug. Retail	$750	$675	$550	$500	$450	$400	$360	$330

RIFLES: OLDER VOERE MFG. (PRE-1988)

TITAN SPORTER SERIES — various cals., 24 or 26 in. barrel, select walnut, pistol grip stock.

This series was available with either European Monte Carlo high-luster stock or in classic featherweight configuration with Schnabel forend — add $50-$200.

* *Titan Menor* — .222 Rem. or .223 Rem. cal. Importation disc. 1987.

		$675	$615	$560	$495	$450	$395	$350

Last Mfg.'s Sug. Retail was $765.

Add $100 for Match or Competition model (.223 Rem. cal.).

* *Titan II Standard* — many cals., between .243 Win. and .30-06. Disc. 1988.

		$950	$825	$725	$625	$550	$500	$450

Last Mfg.'s Sug. Retail was $1,075.

Add $100 for Match or Competition model (.308 Win. cal.).

* *Titan II Magnum* — available in cals. between 7mm Rem. Mag. and .375 H&H. Disc. 1988.

		$995	$875	$750	$650	$575	$520	$475

Last Mfg.'s Sug. Retail was $1,125.

* *Titan .411 KDF Mag.* — .411 KDF cal., 26 in. barrel with recoil arrestor, 3 shot mag., blue or electroless nickel finish, 9¼ lbs. Imported 1986-1988.

		$1,175	$965	$810	$725	$650	$575	$520

Last Mfg.'s Sug. Retail was $1,300.

MODEL 2005 — .22 LR cal. only, semi-auto, 19½ in. barrel, Monte Carlo stock, 5 shot clip mag., iron sights, 6 lbs. Imported 1986 only.

		$235	$215	$195	$175	$160	$145	$135

Last Mfg.'s Sug. Retail was $165.

This model was ruled no longer importable by the BATF.

* *Model 2005 Deluxe* — similar to Model 2005, except has deluxe checkered walnut. Mfg. 1986-87 only.

		$260	$230	$210	$185	$165	$145	$135

Last Mfg.'s Sug. Retail was $185.

MODEL 2107 — .22 LR or .22 Mag. cal., bolt action, 19½ in. barrel, 5 shot clip mag., adj. iron sights, 6 lbs. Imported 1986-87 only.

		$175	$150	$125	$105	$95	$85	$80

Last Mfg.'s Sug. Retail was $197.

Add $42 for .22 Mag. cal.

* *Model 2107 Deluxe (Mauser 107)* — similar to Model 2107, except has deluxe checkered walnut. Imported 1986-1988.

		$185	$165	$140	$125	$110	$105	$100

Last Mfg.'s Sug. Retail was $219.

Add $50 for .22 Mag. cal.

This model was redesignated KDF-Mauser Model 107 when Voere distributor/dealer inventories were depleted.

MODEL 2112 — .22 LR or .22 Mag. cal., similar to Model 2107, except has extra select walnut. Imported 1988 only.

		$235	$200	$180	$160	$145	$135	$125

Last Mfg.'s Sug. Retail was $279.

Add $50 for .22 Mag. cal.

K

Grading	100%	98%	95%	90%	80%	70%	60%

K-14 INSTA FIRE RIFLE — .22-250 Rem., .270 Win., .300 Wby. Mag., or .458 Win. Mag. cal., 24 or 26 in. barrel, no sights, ultra fast lock time, hidden detachable mag., checkered Monte Carlo stock, recoil pad. Imported 1971-78.

	100%	98%	95%	90%	80%	70%	60%
	$725	$650	$575	$525	$475	$425	$375
K15 (.22 cal.)	$235	$205	$175	$150	$135	$120	$105

K-15 (MODEL 225) — available in 13 cals. between .243 Win. and .300 Wby. Mag., bolt action, 60 degree bolt lift with 3 locking lugs, ultra fast lock time, adj. trigger, 24 or 26 (Mag. only) in. barrel, 3 or 5 shot mag., no sights, guaranteed ½ in. accuracy at 100 yards, many stock options available at extra cost. Left-handed action available in certain cals. at a $50 charge.

* ***Deluxe Standard Sporter*** — standard model available in 6 regular cals. and 9 Mag. cals. Disc. 1988.

	100%	98%	95%	90%	80%	70%	60%
	$1,075	$950	$810	$700	$625	$550	$495

Last Mfg.'s Sug. Retail was $1,275.

> Add $50 for Magnum action.
> Add $525 for .411 KDF cal.
>
> In addition to the 15 regular cals., it was also possible to order various other factory cals. as a $200 option.
>
> This model was redesignated KDF-Mauser Model 225 when Voere distributor/dealer inventories were depleted.

* ***K-15 Fiberstock Pro-hunter*** — similar to the K-15, except is supplied with fiberglass stock (various colors), choice of parkerized, matte blue, or electroless nickel metal finish, and recoil arrestor installed. Imported 1986-1988.

	100%	98%	95%
	$1,420	$1,200	$950

Last Mfg.'s Sug. Retail was $1,680.

> Add $50 for Magnum action.
>
> This model was redesignated KDF-Mauser Model 225 when Voere distributor/dealer inventories were depleted.

* ***K-15 Dangerous Game*** — .411 KDF Mag. (new cartridge 1985) cal., choice of finishes, oil finished deluxe American walnut stock. Imported 1986-1988.

	100%	98%	95%
	$1,895	$1,500	$1,150

Last Mfg.'s Sug. Retail was $2,100.

> This model was redesignated KDF-Mauser Model 225 when Voere distributor/dealer inventories were depleted.

* ***K-15 Swat Rifle*** — .308 Win. cal. standard, 24 or 26 in. barrel, parkerized metal, oil finished target walnut stock, 3 or 4 shot detachable mag., 10 lbs. Importation disc. 1988.

	100%	98%	95%	90%	80%	70%	60%
	$1,475	$1,250	$1,000	$850	$725	$650	$575

Last Mfg.'s Sug. Retail was $1,725.

K-16 — available in 6 standard cals. between .243 Win. and .300 Win. Mag. in addition to optional cals., modified Remington Model 700 action, standard features include KDF accurizing and Insta Fire ignition, single stage adj. trigger, Dupont Rynite stock (camel or grey), choice of finishes (high-gloss blue standard), recoil pad and quick detachable sling swivels, many options available. Imported 1988 only.

	100%	98%	95%	90%	80%	70%	60%
	$765	$675	$615	$560	$495	$450	$395

Last Mfg.'s Sug. Retail was $876.

> Add $120 for KDF muzzle brake.
> Add $250 for optional cals.
> Add $350 for .411 KDF Mag. cal.

Grading	100%	98%	95%	90%	80%	70%	60%

K-22 (MAUSER 201) — .22 LR or .22 Mag. cal., bolt action, free floating 21 in. barrel, clip 5 shot mag., adj. trigger, scaled down version of the K-15, unusual action incorporates two front-located locking lugs on bolt face that engage Stellite inserts on the front receiver portion, guaranteed 1 in. groupings at 100 yards, blue only, no sights, select walnut stock with cheekpiece, standard model disc. 1987.

	$310	$285	$260	$240	$225	$210	$195

Last Mfg.'s Sug. Retail was $345.

Add $50 for .22 Mag. cal.

* **K-22 Deluxe (Mauser 201)** — better walnut and stock options. Model notation changed in 1988.

	$410	$360	$295	$275	$250	$235	$210

Last Mfg.'s Sug. Retail was $495.

Add $50 for .22 Mag. cal.

This model was redesignated KDF-Mauser Model 201 when Voere distributor/dealer inventories were depleted.

* **K-22 Deluxe Custom** — richly layered walnut and stock options. Importation disc. 1987.

	$655	$595	$550	$495	$450	$395	$350

Last Mfg.'s Sug. Retail was $725.

Add $50 for .22 Mag. cal.

* **K-22 Deluxe Special Select** — top-of-the-line bolt action, double set triggers. Importation disc. 1987.

	$1,060	$950	$850	$750	$695	$650	$595

Last Mfg.'s Sug. Retail was $1,225.

Add $50 for .22 Mag. cal.

SHOTGUNS

CONDOR O/U — 12 ga., 28 in. barrel, various chokes, selective single trigger, auto ejectors, wide VR, boxlock, checkered pistol grip stock, Italian made.

	$660	$635	$605	$580	$525	$470	$415

BRESCIA SxS — 12 ga., 28 in. barrel, full and mod., double triggers, engraved, checkered pistol grip stock.

	$330	$305	$275	$250	$195	$165	$140

K.F.C.

Previously manufactured by Kawaguchiya Firearms Co., Ltd. Previously imported and distributed by La Paloma Marketing, Inc. located in Tucson, AZ.

SHOTGUNS

MODEL 250 SEMI-AUTO — 12 ga. only, semi-auto incorporating a patented, cushioned piston assembly, 26, 28, or 30 in. barrel, matte blue finish, vent. rib standard, checkered premium walnut, 7 lbs. Manufactured 1980-86.

	$360	$290	$270	$250	$235	$220	$205

Last Mfg.'s Sug. Retail was $485.

Add $60 for multi-chokes.

* **Model 250 Deluxe Semi-Auto** — same specifications as Model 250, except has scrolled acid etching panels on both sides of normally black receiver. Disc. 1986.

	$395	$310	$290	$270	$250	$225	$210

Last Mfg.'s Sug. Retail was $520.

FIELD GUN O/U — 12 ga. only, VR, premium grade walnut, semi pistol grip stock, F&IC chokes. Disc. 1986.

	$645	$565	$530	$495	$470	$445	$410

Last Mfg.'s Sug. Retail was $748.

K

Grading		100%	98%	95%	90%	80%	70%	60%

E-1 TRAP OR SKEET O/U — 12 ga. only, VR, oil finished premium grade walnut, semi pistol grip stock, engraved. Disc. 1986.

				$935	$800	$750	$700	$625	$550	$495

Last Mfg.'s Sug. Retail was $1,070.

E-2 TRAP OR SKEET O/U — 12 ga. only, VR, oil finished premium grade walnut, semi pistol grip stock, detailed engraving. Disc. 1986.

	$1,450	$1,250	$1,075	$950	$850	$750	$650

Last Mfg. Sug. Retail was $1,660.

KSN INDUSTRIES LTD.

Previous distributor (1952-1996) located in Houston, TX. Previously imported until 1996 exclusively by J.O. Arms, Inc. located in Houston, TX. Currently mfg. Israel Arms, Ltd. pistols may be found under their individual listing.

PISTOLS: SEMI-AUTO

The pistols listed below were mfg. by Israel Arms, Ltd.

KAREEN MK II — 9mm Para. or .40 S&W (new late 1994) cal., single action, 3.85 (Compact) or 4.64 (Standard) in. barrel, two-tone finish, rubberized grips, regular or Meprolite sights, 10 (C/B 1994), 13★, or 15★ shot mag., 33 oz. Imported 1993-96.

			$360	$305	$255	$225	$200	$185	$170

Last Mfg.'s Sug. Retail was $411.

Add approx. $160 for two-tone finish with Meprolite sights.

★ *Kareen Mk II Compact* — compact variation with 3.85 in. barrel. Imported 1993-96.

		$415	$360	$315	$255	$225	$200	$185

Last Mfg.'s Sug. Retail was $497.

GOLAN MODEL — 9mm Para. or .40 S&W cal., single or double action, ambidextrous safety with decocking feature, steel slide with alloy frame, 3⅞ in. barrel, matte black finish, 29 oz. Imported 1994-96.

		$565	$515	$460	$410	$360	$330	$295

Last Mfg.'s Sug. Retail was $650.

Add $35 for .40 S&W cal.

KAHR ARMS

Current manufacturer located in Blauvelt, NY since 1993. Distributor and dealer sales.

PISTOLS: SEMI-AUTO

All Kahr pistols are supplied with two 7 shot mags., hard polymer case, trigger lock, and lifetime warranty.

KAHR K9 — 9mm Para. cal., trigger cocking, double action only with passive striker block, locked breech with Browning type recoil lug, steel construction, 3½ in. barrel with polygonal rifling, 7 shot mag., wraparound black polymer grips, matte black, black titanium (Black-T, mfg. 1997-98), or electroless nickel (new 1996) finish, 25 oz. New 1993.

Mfg.'s Sug. Retail	$538		$475	$430	$395	$365	$315	$285	$250

Add $74 for electroless nickel finish.
Add $126 for black titanium finish (Black-T).
Add $85 for tritium night sights (new 1996).

★ *Kahr Economy K9* — features black matte finish, shipped with one mag. only. New 1999.

Mfg.'s Sug. Retail	$399		$350	$300	$275	$250	$230	$210	$190

K

Grading	100%	98%	95%	90%	80%	70%	60%

* **Kahr K9 Stainless** — similar to Kahr K9, except is stainless steel. New 1998.

Mfg.'s Sug. Retail	$588	$500	$440	$395			

   Add $85 for tritium night sights.

* **Kahr K9 Elite Stainless** — similar to Kahr K9, except has high polish slide and specially designed combat trigger utilizing shorter trigger stroke. New 1998.

Mfg.'s Sug. Retail	$619	$530	$450	$410			

   Add $85 for tritium night sights.

* **Kahr K9 Wilson Custom Package** — includes Wilson customizing with Metalloy hard chrome frame, black slide, checkered front strap and beveled mag. well. Limited quantities mfg. 1998.

	$1,175	$995	$875	$775	$700	$625	$550

   Last Mfg.'s Sug. Retail was $1,310.

* **Kahr Lady K9** — similar to Kahr K9, except has lightened recoil spring, not available in black titanium finish, 25 oz. New 1997.

Mfg.'s Sug. Retail	$545	$480	$435	$395	$365	$315	$285	$250

   Add $74 for electroless nickel finish.
   Add $85 for tritium night sights (new 1996).

KAHR K9 POLYMER COMPACT — 9mm Para cal., similar to Kahr K9, except has lightweight polymer frame, matte stainless slide, 17.9 oz. New 1999.

Mfg.'s Sug. Retail	$544	$480	$435	$395	$365	$315	$285	$250

* **Kahr K9 Polymer Covert** — similar to Kahr K9 Polymer Compact, except has $\frac{1}{2}$ in. shorter frame, supplied with one 6 and one 7 (with grip extension) shot mag., 16.9 oz. New 1999.

Mfg.'s Sug. Retail	$544	$480	$435	$395	$365	$315	$285	$250

KAHR MK9 — 9mm Para. cal., micro compact variation of the K9 featuring 3 in. barrel, double action only with passive striker block, overall size is 4 in. H x 5½ in. L, duo-tone finish with stainless frame and black titanium slide, includes two 6 shot flush floor plate mags. New 1998.

Mfg.'s Sug. Retail	$749	$650	$575	$515	$465	$425	$395	$375

   Add $85 for tritium night sights.

* **Kahr MK9 Stainless** — similar to MK9, except is stainless steel. New 1998.

Mfg.'s Sug. Retail	$605	$530	$465	$415			

   Add $85 for tritium night sights.

* **Kahr MK9 Elite Stainless** — similar to Kahr MK9, except has high polish slide and specially designed combat trigger utilizing shorter trigger stroke. New 1998.

Mfg.'s Sug. Retail	$648	$550	$475	$415			

   Add $85 for tritium night sights.

KAHR E9 — 9mm Para. cal., economized version of the K9, matte black finish, supplied with one mag. Mfg. 1997 only.

	$395	$365	$335	$300	$280	$265	$250

   Last Mfg.'s Sug. Retail was $433.

KAHR K40 — .40 S&W cal., similar to Kahr K9, except has 6 shot mag., matte black or electroless nickel finish, 26 oz. New 1997.

Mfg.'s Sug. Retail	$552	$485	$440	$395	$365	$315	$285	$250

   Add $74 for electroless nickel finish.
   Add $126 for black titanium finish (Black-T, disc. 1998).
   Add $85 for tritium night sights (new 1996).

* **Kahr K40 Stainless** — similar to Kahr K40, except is stainless steel. New 1997.

Mfg.'s Sug. Retail	$602	$525	$460	$415			

   Add $85 for tritium night sights.

K

Grading	100%	98%	95%	90%	80%	70%	60%

* **Kahr K40 Elite Stainless** — similar to Kahr K40, except has high polish slide and specially designed combat trigger utilizing shorter trigger stroke. New 1998.

  Mfg.'s Sug. Retail   **$646**   **$550**   **$475**   **$415**

  Add $85 for tritium night sights.

* **Kahr K40 Wilson Custom Package** — includes Wilson customizing with Metalloy hard chrome frame, black slide, checkered front strap and beveled mag. well. Limited quantities mfg. 1998.

  $1,175   **$995**   **$875**   **$775**   **$700**   **$625**   **$550**

  Last Mfg.'s Sug. Retail was $1,310.

* **Kahr K40 Covert Stainless (KS40 Small Frame)** — .40 S&W cal., similar to Kahr K40, except grip is ½ in. shorter, supplied with 5 and 6 shot mags., 25 oz. New 1998.

  Mfg.'s Sug. Retail   **$594**   **$515**   **$450**   **$400**

  Add $85 for tritium night sights.

KAHR MK40 — .40 S&W cal., micro compact variation of the Kahr K40, featuring 3 in. barrel, matte stainless frame and slide, supplied with one 5 shot and one 6 shot (with grip extension) mag. New 1999.

  Mfg.'s Sug. Retail   **$605**   **$525**   **$450**   **$400**

  Add $85 for tritium night sights.

KASSNAR IMPORTS, INC.

Previous importer and distributor located in Harrisburg, PA. Kassnar Imports operations ceased April, 1989.

Kassnar also imported Omega shotguns which can be found in their individual section.

PISTOLS: SEMI-AUTO

PJK-9HP — 9mm Para. cal., single action, patterned after the Browning Hi-Power, 4¾ in. barrel, 13 shot mag., cone hammer, checkered walnut grips, 32 oz.

  $225   **$200**   **$185**   **$175**   **$165**   **$155**   **$145**

  Add $15 for VR barrel.

  This pistol was imported from Hungary. Approx. 18,000 (including the MBK-9HP) were imported until importation was disc. because of Federal ramifications.

MBK-9HP — 9mm Para. cal., double action, patterned after the Browning Hi-Power, 4⅔ in. barrel, spur hammer, blued metal, checkered walnut grips, 14 shot mag., 36 oz. Limited importation was stopped in late 1985.

  $295   **$260**   **$230**   **$190**   **$175**   **$165**   **$155**

PMK-380 — .380 ACP cal., double action, patterned after the Walther PP, plastic grips with thumbrest, 4 in. barrel, 7 shot mag., 21 oz. Limited importation.

  $275   **$235**   **$200**   **$185**   **$175**   **$165**   **$155**

  This model was imported in very limited quantities before Interarms began exclusive importation.

KEBERST INTERNATIONAL

Previously manufactured and distributed by Kendall International located in Paris, KY.

RIFLES: BOLT ACTION

KEBERST MODEL 1A — .338 Lapua Mag., .338-416 Rigby, or .338-06 cal., muzzle brake and unique recoil pad, camouflaged synthetic stock, package includes 3-9 power Leupold scope, stainless steel cleaning rod, custom designed case, built to special order only. Mfg. 1987-1988 only.

Grading	100%	98%	95%	90%	80%	70%	60%
	$3,475	$2,850	$2,475	$2,100	$1,750	$1,400	$1,150

Last Mfg.'s Sug. Retail was $3,750.

Add $275 for 10X Ultra scope.

KEL-TEC CNC INDUSTRIES, INC.

Current manufacturer located in Cocoa, FL since 1991. Dealer and distributor sales.

PISTOLS: SEMI-AUTO

P-11 — 9mm Para. cal., double action only, locked breech design, 3.1 in. barrel, composite frame with steel slide, transfer bar safety, matte blue, parkerized (new 1997), hard chrome (new 1999), or electroless nickel (disc. 1995) finish, black, grey, or green (disc. 1998) synthetic grips, 10 shot double column mag., 14.4 oz. New 1995.

Mfg.'s Sug. Retail	$309		$260	$200	$180	$165	$150	$135	$125

 Add $80 for night sights (new 1997).
 Add $41 for parkerized finish (choice of grips).
 Add $54 for hard chrome finish (new 1999).
 Add $30 for electroless nickel finish (disc. 1995).
 Add $175 for 9mm Para. to .40 S&W cal. conversion kit.

* P-11 Stainless — similar to P-11, except is stainless steel, available with black (P-11SB), grey (P-11SGY), or green (P-11SGN) grips. Mfg. 1996-98.

	$350	$275	$230

Last Mfg.'s Sug. Retail was $408.

P-32 — .32 ACP cal., double action only with internal hammer block safety, composite frame with steel slide, 2.68 in. barrel, choice of parkerized, blue, or hard chrome finish, 6.6 oz. New 1999.

Mfg.'s Sug. Retail	$295		$250	$195	$175	$160	$150	$135	$125

 Add $40 for parkerized finish.
 Add $55 for hard chrome finish.

P-40 — .40 S&W cal., double action only with internal hammer block safety, composite frame with steel slide, 3.3 in. barrel, choice of parkerized, blue, or hard chrome finish, 9 or 10 shot mag., 15.8 oz. New 1999.

Mfg.'s Sug. Retail	$325		$270	$210	$185	$165	$155	$135	$125

 Add $41 for parkerized finish.
 Add $58 for hard chrome finish.

RIFLES: SEMI-AUTO, CARBINES

SUB-9 RIFLE — 9mm Para. cal., unique pivoting 16.1 in. barrel rotates upwards and back, allowing overall size reduction and portability (16 in. x 7 in.), interchangable grip assembly will accept most popular, double column, high capacity handgun mags., tube stock with polymer buttplate, matte black finish, 4.6 lbs. New 1997.

Mfg.'s Sug. Retail	$700		$635	$550	$500	$450	$400	$360	$330

SUB-40 RIFLE — .40 S&W cal., otherwise similar to Sub-9 Rifle. New 1999.

Mfg.'s Sug. Retail	$725		$650	$565	$515	$460	$400	$360	$330

KEMEN

Current competition shotgun manufacturer located in El-goibar, Spain since 1990. Imported and exclusively distributed in the U.S. by Armes De Chasse, LLC beginning late 1998. Previously imported and distributed 1996-98 by Hi-Grade Imports, located in Gilroy, CA, and by Puglisi Gun Emporium until 1997 located in Duluth, MN.

K

Grading			100%	98%	95%	90%	80%	70%	60%

SHOTGUNS: O/U

Kemen shotguns are built to individual customer specifications. Their unique metal finish makes them almost impervious to any type of oxidation or rust.

KM-4 STANDARD GRADE — 12 or 20 ga., boxlock action, competition shotgun with 32 in. vent. or separated barrels with VR and Briley choke tubes, detachable trigger group, blued receiver with gold accents, checkered walnut Monte Carlo stock and forearm, cased, 8-8½ lbs.

Mfg.'s Sug. Retail	$6,388		$5,400	$4,400	$3,950	$3,375	$2,850	$2,375	$2,100

Add 7% for 20 ga.

KM-4 LUXE A/B — similar to KM-4 Standard Grade, except has nickel finished receiver with choice of fine scroll or game scene engraving.

Mfg.'s Sug. Retail	$9,972		$8,450	$7,575	$6,900	$6,300	$5,600	$4,950	$4,250

Add 7% for 20 ga.
Add approx. $660 for KM-4 Luxe B.

KM-4 SUPER LUXE A/B/C — similar to KM-4 Luxe A/B, except has nickel finished receiver with more elaborate game scene engraving, A suffix features game scene engraving, B suffix includes gold line engraving, C suffix has high relief scroll work and gold trigger.

Mfg.'s Sug. Retail	$13,270		$11,275	$9,250	$7,650	$6,750	$6,000	$5,000	$4,250

Add 7% for 20 ga.
Add approx. $1,200 for Super Luxe B variation.
Subtract approx. $400 for Super Luxe C variation.

KM-4 EXTRA LUXE A/B/C — similar to KM-4 Super Luxe, except has nickel finished receiver with sideplates and choice of Purdey style fine scroll (Extra Luxe A), extra fine game scene (Extra Luxe B), or gargoyle motif (Extra Luxe C) engraving.

Mfg.'s Sug. Retail	$13,785		$11,700	$9,350	$7,850	$7,000	$6,200	$5,200	$4,500

Add 7% for 20 ga.
Add approx. $2,865 for Extra Luxe B variation.
Add $6,580 for Extra Luxe C variation.

KM-4 EXTRA GOLD A/B — 12 or 20 ga., features engraved sideplate action with multiple gold inlays, select wood.

Mfg.'s Sug. Retail	$20,513		$17,425	$13,500	$10,500	$8,850	$7,650	$6,700	$5,250

Add 7% for 20 ga.
Add approx. $1,420 for Extra Gold B variation.

SUPREMA AX/BX/CX — 12 or 20 ga., top-of-the-line model, sidelock action, Suprema AX features English fine scroll engraving, custom ordered to individual specifications.

Mfg.'s Sug. Retail	$39,045		$33,200	$25,000	$20,500	$16,000	$13,000	$10,250	$8,700

Add 7% for 20 ga.
Subtract approx. $1,360 for Suprema BX variation (game scene engraved).
Subtract approx. $2,725 for Suprema CX variation (100% scroll engraved).

KENDALL INTERNATIONAL

Previous importer/distributor located in Paris, KY. Kendall International also imported Australian Automatic Arms, the Keberst Rifle, and several air rifles that can be found in their respective sections in this text.

KENTUCKY RIFLES

U.S. flintlock/percussion long rifle configuration originating in Pennsylvania. Kentucky rifles are a field unto themselves, and should be evaluated by an experienced and known source for accurate identification and/or price evaluation.

Grading	100%	98%	95%	90%	80%	70%	60%

KENTUCKY RIFLES INDENTIFICATION & PRICING

The author wishes to express his thanks once again to Mr. James Buelow for updating the following information.

The Kentucky rifle was the creation of early settlers from Europe. This new American configuration combined the architectural elements of the English Fowler with the ornamental features of the German Jaeger.

The earliest recorded use of the term "Kentucky rifle" was in a ballad written after the battle of New Orleans. The battle was won by the American Long Rifle, in the hands of 2,000 frontiersmen. During that period, the area west of the 13 colonies was known as Kentucky; hence the name Kentucky rifle.

Kentucky rifles began appearing around the middle of the 18th century and disappeared by the middle of the 19th century. Their origin is credited to eastern Pennsylvania, but soon spread to many other states, including Maryland, Virginia, Tennessee, North Carolina, and areas where the rifle maker found a market for his skills.

The styles vary, but they have two things in common: they are long, and most had curly maple stocks. The bores are found both rifled and smooth. The rifles most prized by the collector are the ones that have relief or incised carving. Carved Kentucky rifles are considered one of America's earliest art forms and are now considered Americana personified. Present values may range from as low as $1,000 all the way up to $50,000+! Non-carved or plain Kentuckys are most often encountered.

The present value of an uncarved, original flintlock Kentucky rifle in average condition is approx. $3,000. An uncarved percussion specimen in average original condition is approx. $2,000. These prices diminish when the Kentucky rifle lacks a maker's name, usually found on the top of the barrel, or if it does not have a patch box. Kentucky rifle values vary greatly, due to maker popularity, quality of carving, condition, rifle style, and a mulititude of other factors.

During the past several decades, many fine contemporary Kentucky rifles have been built by craftsmen who understand the trade. Many of these guns are now available in the secondary marketplace. A large percentage have outstanding craftsmanship, and are highly sought after. These specimens sell in the $2,000-$10,000 range, depending on the notoriety of the builder and the sophistication of the work. Because of this, these guns have to be evaluated one at a time.

The best way to find out the value of a Kentucky rifle is to seek out a knowledgeable Kentucky rifle collector. To find such a person in your area, contact the Kentucky Rifle Association's Administrative Assistant: Ruth Collis, 2319 Sue Ann Dr., Lancaster, PA, 17602.

KEPPELER + FRITZ GmbH

Current rifle manufacturer located in Fichtenberg, Germany. No current importer.

Keppeler manufactures many types of top quality rifles which are typically center-fire and target configured (UIT-CISM, Prone, Free, and Sniper Bullpup). Both metric and domestic calibers are available as well as a variety of special order options. Please contact the factory directly for more information and current pricing (see Trademark Index).

KEPPLINGER, ING. HANNES

Current rifle manufacturer located in Kufstein, Austria. No current importer.

RIFLES

Kepplinger rifles are essentially built per individual order. In addition to his unique bolt action, he also makes other bolt action designs and O/U rifles as well. It is recommended that Mr. Kepplinger of Kufsteiner Waffenstube be contacted for more

Grading	100%	98%	95%	90%	80%	70%	60%

information, including price quotations on his quality, custom order rifles (please refer to the Trademark Index).

3-S SYSTEM RIFLE — various cals., unique short action allows for straight on cartridge loading, high strength alloy main parts, grip safety on lower pistol grip, unique uncocking device allowing manual cocking/decocking of the firing pin spring, 23.6 in. standard barrel, 3 shot detachable mag., iron sights, receiver drilled for scope mounts, best quality wood, available in either Schnabel forearm or Mannlicher configuration, many styles of engraving are optional, 7.14 lbs.

KESSLER ARMS CORPORATION

Previous manufacturer located in Silver Creek, NY.

SHOTGUNS

LEVERMATIC SHOTGUN — 12, 16, or 20 ga., lever action, 26 or 28 in. full choke, takedown, plain pistol grip stock. Disc. 1953.

	$175	$150	$125	$100	$85	$65	$55

BOLT ACTION SHOTGUN — 12, 16, or 20 ga., 26 or 28 in. full, takedown, plain stock. Mfg. 1951-1953.

	$90	$65	$50	$45	$35	$35	$35

KEYSTONE SPORTING ARMS, INC.

Current rifle manufacturer located in Milton, PA since 1996. Distributor and dealer sales.

RIFLES: BOLT ACTION

CRICKETT SPORTER — .22 LR cal., manually cocked single shot, 16⅛ in. barrel with adj. rear aperture sight, steel or stainless steel (new 1999) construction, 11½ in. LOP (youth dimension), choice of walnut, colored laminate, or composite Monte Carlo stock, stainless or blue barrel and receiver, 30 in. overall length, 2½ lbs. New 1997.

Mfg.'s Sug. Retail	$164	$150	$135	$120	$105	$95	$85	$75

Add $23 for laminated stock, in various color schemes, including red, white and blue (add $36 extra).

* *Crickett Custom/Deluxe Sporter* — features deluxe hand checkered stock. New 1998.

Mfg.'s Sug. Retail	$250	$225	$195	$175	$150	$135	$120	$105

Add $10 for deluxe configuration.

J. KIMBALL ARMS CO.

Previous manufacturer located in Detroit, MI circa 1958.

PISTOLS: SEMI-AUTO

AUTOMATIC PISTOL — .30 Carbine or .22 Hornet (very rare) cal., 7 shot, 3 in. (Combat Model) or 5 in. (Target Model) barrel, approx. 32 oz. Less than 300 mfg. in 1958 only.

	$950	$850	$725	$600	$500	$395	$300

Functional weaknesses of this pistol caused discontinuance. Surviving specimens should be checked carefully for slide failures and other potential problems. Values above assume no operational damage to the pistol. .22 Hornet cal. rarity factor precludes accurate price evaluation.

KIMBER

Current trademark manufactured by Kimber Mfg., Inc., established during 1997, with company headquarters and manufacturing located in Yonkers, NY. Previous manufac-

Grading	100%	98%	95%	90%	80%	70%	60%

ture was by Kimber of America, Inc., located in Clackamas, OR circa 1993-97. Distributor and dealer sales.

PISTOLS: SEMI-AUTO, CLASSIC SERIES

All Kimber pistols are shipped with lockable high impact synthetic case. Additionally, a cable lock will be included on all pistols shipped beginning spring, 1999.

CUSTOM MODEL — .45 ACP cal., patterned after the Colt Government Model 1911, 5 in. barrel, various finishes, 7 shot mag., forged steel or synthetic (new 1997) frame, match grade barrel and trigger, dovetail mounted sights, frame, slide, and barrel machined from steel forgings, high beavertail grip safety, choice of checkered walnut or smooth rosewood (new 1999) grips, 38 oz. New 1995.

	100%	98%	95%	90%	80%	70%	60%
Mfg.'s Sug. Retail $657	$550	$485	$415	$360	$330	$300	$275

    Add $13 for walnut or smooth rosewood grips.
    Add $130 for Custom Royal finish.

✳ *Custom Target* — similar to Custom Model, except features Kimber adj. rear sight. New 1998.

	100%	98%	95%	90%	80%	70%	60%
Mfg.'s Sug. Retail $745	$650	$550	$475	$425	$375	$330	$300

✳ *Custom Stainless* — .38 Super (new 1999, special order), 9mm Para (new 1999, special order), .40 S&W (new 1999), or .45 ACP cal., similar to Custom Model, except is stainless steel.

	100%	98%	95%
Mfg.'s Sug. Retail $753	$635	$550	$450

    Add $27 for cals. other than .45 ACP.
    Subtract $27 for stainless limited edition (disc.).

➤ *Custom Stainless Target* — similar to Custom Stainless, except features Kimber adj. rear sight. New 1998.

	100%	98%	95%
Mfg.'s Sug. Retail $843	$710	$595	$495

    Add $27 for cals. other than .45 ACP.
    Subtract $28 for stainless limited edition (disc.).

GOLD MATCH — .45 ACP cal., features Kimber adj. sight, stainless steel match barrel and bushing, match trigger, ambidextrous thumb safety became standard in 1998, 8 or 10 (disc. 1998) shot mag., fancy checkered rosewood grips in double diamond pattern, hand fitted, high polish blue, hand fitted in the Kimber Custom Shop, 38 oz.

	100%	98%	95%	90%	80%	70%	60%
Mfg.'s Sug. Retail $1,019	$925	$800	$675	$600	$500	$450	$400

✳ *Gold Match Stainless* — .38 Super (new 1999, special order), 9mm Para (new 1999, special order), .40 S&W (new 1999), or .45 ACP cal., similar to Gold Match, except is stainless steel, 38 oz.

	100%	98%	95%
Mfg.'s Sug. Retail $1,146	$1,015	$895	$750

    Add $28 for cals. other than .45 ACP.

✳ *Polymer Gold Match* — .45 ACP cal. only, similar to Gold Match, except has polymer frame, 34 oz. New 1999.

	100%	98%	95%	90%	80%	70%	60%
Mfg.'s Sug. Retail $1,085	$965	$825	$700	$625	$525	$450	$400

➤ *Polymer Gold Match Stainless* — similar to Gold Match Stainless, except has polymer frame, 34 oz. New 1999.

	100%	98%	95%
Mfg.'s Sug. Retail $1,235	$1,075	$950	$775

GOLD COMBAT — .45 ACP cal. only, 5 in. barrel, full size carry pistol based on the Gold Match, steel frame and slide, stainless steel match grade barrel and bushing, KimPro finish, tritium night sights, checkered walnut grips, 38 oz. New 1999.

	100%	98%	95%	90%	80%	70%	60%
Mfg.'s Sug. Retail $1,481	$1,275	$995	$875	$750	$650	$575	$400

✳ *Gold Combat Stainless* — similar to Gold Combat, except is all stainless steel. New 1999.

	100%	98%	95%
Mfg.'s Sug. Retail $1,426	$1,225	$975	$850

SUPER MATCH — .45 ACP cal. only, 5 in. barrel, top-of-the-line model, two-tone stainless steel construction, KimPro finish on slide, match grade trigger, custom shop markings, 38 oz. New 1999.

	100%	98%	95%
Mfg.'s Sug. Retail $1,699	$1,425	$1,050	$925

K

Grading	100%	98%	95%	90%	80%	70%	60%

POLYMER MODEL — .45 ACP cal., features widened black polymer frame offering larger mag. capacity, choice of fixed McCormick (Polymer Model) or adj. Kimber target (Polymer Target Model) rear sight, matte black slide, 34 oz. New 1997.

| Mfg.'s Sug. Retail | $814 | $715 | $625 | $535 | $465 | $425 | $375 | $330 |

Add $88 for Polymer Target Model.

* **Polymer Stainless** — .38 Super (new 1999, special order), 9mm Para (new 1999, special order), .40 S&W (new 1999), or .45 ACP cal., similar to Polymer Model, except has satin finish stainless steel slide. New 1998.

| Mfg.'s Sug. Retail | $881 | $795 | $725 | $625 |

Add $28 for cals. other than .45 ACP.
Add $88 for Polymer Stainless Target Model.

* **Polymer Pro Carry** — .45 ACP cal. only, 4 in. bushingless bull barrel, steel slide, 32 oz. New 1999.

| Mfg.'s Sug. Retail | $814 | $715 | $625 | $535 | $465 | $425 | $375 | $330 |

➤ **Polymer Pro Carry Stainless** — similar to Polymer Pro Carry, except has stainless steel slide. New 1999.

| Mfg.'s Sug. Retail | $881 | $795 | $725 | $625 |

COMPACT MODEL — .45 ACP cal., features 4 in. barrel, .4 in. shorter aluminum or steel frame, 7 shot mag., Commander style hammer, single recoil spring, McCormick low profile combat sights, choice of walnut, checkered black synthetic or Cristolbal grips, 28 (aluminum) or 34 (steel) oz. New 1998.

| Mfg.'s Sug. Retail | $677 | $565 | $495 | $425 | $375 | $350 | $325 | $295 |

Add $13 for walnut or Cristobal grips.

* **Compact Stainless** — .40 S&W (new 1999) or .45 ACP cal., similar to Compact Model, except is stainless steel, 34 oz. New 1998.

| Mfg.'s Sug. Retail | $773 | $650 | $550 | $455 |

Add $17 for .40 S&W cal.
Add $13 for Cristolbal grips.

* **Compact Stainless Aluminum** — .40 S&W or .45 ACP cal., features aluminum frame and stainless steel slide, 28 oz. New 1999.

| Mfg.'s Sug. Retail | $745 | $630 | $550 | $450 |

Add $16 for .40 S&W cal.

COMBAT CARRY — .40 S&W or .45 ACP cal., 4 in. barrel, carry model featuring aluminum frame and trigger, stainless steel slide, tritium night sights, and ambidextrous thumb safety, 28 oz. New 1999.

| Mfg.'s Sug. Retail | $1,044 | $940 | $815 | $675 | $600 | $500 | $450 | $400 |

Add $27 for .40 S&W cal.

PRO CARRY — .40 S&W or .45 ACP cal., 4 in. barrel, features full length grip similar to Custom Model, aluminum frame, steel slide, 7 or 8 shot mag., 28 oz. New 1999.

| Mfg.'s Sug. Retail | $676 | $565 | $495 | $425 | $375 | $350 | $325 | $295 |

Add $28 for .40 S&W cal.

* **Pro Carry Stainless** — similar to Pro Carry, except has stainless steel slide. New 1999.

| Mfg.'s Sug. Retail | $745 | $630 | $550 | $450 |

Add $26 for .40 S&W cal.

ULTRA CARRY — .40 S&W or .45 ACP cal., 3 in. barrel, aluminum frame, 7 shot mag., 25 oz. New 1999.

| Mfg.'s Sug. Retail | $676 | $565 | $495 | $425 | $375 | $350 | $325 | $295 |

Add $28 for .40 S&W cal.

Grading	100%	98%	95%	90%	80%	70%	60%

* Ultra Carry Stainless — similar to Ultra Carry, except has stainless steel slide. New 1999.

Mfg.'s Sug. Retail	$745	$630	$550	$450			

Add $26 for .40 S&W cal.

RIFLES: BOLT ACTION

.22 cal. - Repeating and Single Shot

CLASSIC MODEL — .22 LR cal., Mauser claw extractor with 2 position Model 70 type safety, unique eccentric bolt that allows a "centerfire-type" firing pin for faster lock time and greater strength, Claro walnut sporter stock with 18 LPI checkering and satin finish, 22 in. match grade sporter barrel with match chamber, 5 shot mag., steel grip cap, pillar bedding, bead blasted blue finish, adj. trigger, approx. 6½ lbs. New 1999.

Mfg.'s Sug. Retail	$919	$795	$675	$575	$500	$425	$375	$330

SUPERAMERICA MODEL — .22 LR cal., top-of-the-line model with AAA Claro walnut with 22 LPI full wrap checkering, ebony forend tip, and black recoil pad, 5 shot mag., 6½ lbs. New 1999.

Mfg.'s Sug. Retail	$1,493	$1,285	$1,000	$875	$750	$650	$575	$500

SVT (SHORT VARMINT TARGET) MODEL — .22 LR cal., 18 in. fluted stainless steel bull barrel, uncheckered grey laminate wood stock with high comb target design, matte blue action and satin stainless steel barrel, 5 shot mag., no sights, 7½ lbs. New 1999.

Mfg.'s Sug. Retail	$732	$620	$545	$450			

HS (HUNTER SILHOUETTE) MODEL — .22 LR cal., features 24 in. half-fluted medium sporter match grade barrel w/o sights, checkered walnut high comb Monte Carlo stock, adj. trigger, matte blue finish, 7 lbs. New 1999.

Mfg.'s Sug. Retail	$748	$650	$575	$495	$425	$375	$325	$295

MODEL 82C CLASSIC — .22 LR cal., 22 in. drilled and tapped barrel, repeater with 4 shot mag., A Claro checkered walnut stock, polished and blued metal, 6½ lbs. Mfg. 1993-98.

		$775	$625	$550	$475	$400	$360	$330

Last Mfg.'s Sug. Retail was $917.

The C suffix on this model designates manufacture by Kimber of America.

* Stainless Classic — .22 LR cal., features stainless steel barrel with blue action. Approx. 600 mfg. 1997-98.

		$800	$650	$565				

Last Mfg.'s Sug. Retail was $968.

* Varmint Stainless — .22 LR cal., features 25 in. fluted stainless steel barrel, A Claro walnut with 18 LPI side panel checkering. Approx. 1,000 mfg. 1995-98.

		$825	$675	$575				

Last Mfg.'s Sug. Retail was $1,002.

MODEL 82C SVT — .22 LR cal., single shot, features 18 in. fluted heavy stainless barrel with uncheckered high comb target style walnut stock, matte blue action, 7½ lbs. Mfg. 1997 only.

		$675	$550	$495				

Last Mfg.'s Sug. Retail was $825.

SVT designates Short Varmint/Target.

MODEL 82C HS — while advertised during 1997, this model was never manufactured.

MODEL 82C SUPERAMERICA — .22 LR cal., 22 in. drilled and tapped barrel, 4 shot mag., AAA Claro checkered walnut stock with skeletonized pistol grip cap, polished and blued metal, 6½ lbs. New 1993.

Mfg.'s Sug. Retail	$1,488	$1,275	$995	$875	$750	$650	$575	$400

MODEL 82C CUSTOM MATCH — .22 LR cal., features AA French walnut with 22 LPI wraparound checkering, steel Neidner-style buttplate, matte rust blue finish. New 1995.

Mfg.'s Sug. Retail	$2,158	$1,900	$1,525	$1,225	$975	$775	$650	$525

Grading	100%	98%	95%	90%	80%	70%	60%

MODEL 82C SUPER CLASSIC — .22 LR cal., features AAA Claro walnut with 18 LPI side panel checkering, polished and blued metal. Mfg. 1995-96.

	$975	$875	$775	$675	$600	$550	$450

Last Mfg.'s Sug. Retail was $1,090.

Centerfire Models: Single Shot

The models below feature a Mauser style action with controlled round feeding and extraction.

MODEL 84C CLASSIC — while advertised during 1996-97, this model was never manufactured.

MODEL 84C SUPERAMERICA — while advertised during 1996-97, this model was never manufactured.

MODEL 84C VARMINT STAINLESS — while advertised during 1997, this model was never manufactured.

MODEL 84C SINGLE SHOT VARMINT — .17 Rem. or .223 Rem. cal., features 24 (first 200 rifles only), or 25 in. stainless match grade fluted barrel with recess crown, matte blue receiver finish, checkered A Claro walnut stock with beavertail forend, 7½ lbs. New 1997.

Mfg.'s Sug. Retail	**$1,032**		**$895**	**$765**	**$625**

Add $85 for .17 Rem. cal.

MODEL K770 CLASSIC — while advertised during 1997, this model was never manufactured.

MODEL K770 SUPER AMERICA — while advertised during 1997, this model was never manufactured.

Mauser 96 Sporters

MODEL 96 SPORTER — .308 Win. cal., features M-96 action with stainless steel fluted heavy barrel. Mfg. 1995-97.

	$450	$415	$365

Last Mfg.'s Sug. Retail was $520.

During 1995-96, Kimber began sporterizing the Swedish Mauser Model 96 military surplus rifles. They featured stainless steel fluted barrels and a black synthetic Ramline stock, receivers were drilled and tapped to accept Weaver scope mounts, bead blasted bluing, and original reprofiled military bolt. The Sporter configuration included .243 Win., 6.5x55mm, or .308 Win. (only cal. currently mfg., see information above) cal., while the heavy fluted barrel models were available in .22-250 Rem. or .308 Win. (Varmint or Heavy Barrel). Retail prices ranged from $340-$415 for the Standard Sporter, while the Varmint/Heavy barrel variation was priced at approx. $510. Sporter variations were also available as a combo package with scope and hardshell case - add approx. $30.

Mauser 98 Sporters

MODEL 98 SPORTER — .220 Swift (100 mfg.), .257 Roberts (100 mfg.), .270 Win., .280 Rem. (100 mfg.), .30-06, .300 Win. Mag., .338 Win. Mag., or 7mm Rem. Mag. cal., features Mauser M-98 action with stainless match grade fluted barrel, choice of synthetic or Claro walnut stock, and Warne bases, matte black finish receiver. Mfg. 1996-98.

	$465	$425	$375

Last Mfg.'s Sug. Retail was $535.

Add $25 for Mag. cals.
Add $100 for Claro walnut stock.

* *Mauser Model 98 Sporter Matte* — .300 Win. Mag., .338 Win. Mag., or 7mm Rem. Mag. cal., features 25 in. non-fluted sporter barrel, synthetic stock, and Weaver style bases. Disc. 1998.

	$275	$250	$225	$200	$185	$170	$155

Last Mfg.'s Sug. Retail was $339.

K

Grading	100%	98%	95%	90%	80%	70%	60%

KIMBER OF OREGON, INC.

Kimber

Previous manufacturer located in Clackamas, OR circa 1980-1991.

Kimber of Oregon went out of business with its final sale in 1991. Rare models are starting to attract premiums already. In some models, magazines for these fine quality rifles are getting extremely hard to find with healthy premiums being asked. Once "B" suffix models were introduced, older manufacture started being referred to as "A" models.

PISTOLS: BOLT ACTION

PREDATOR MODEL — .221 Fireball, .223 Rem., 6mm TCU (disc. 1987), 7mm TCU, or 6x45mm (disc. 1987) cal., single shot Model 84 action with shortened 14⅞ in. barrel, scope use only, one piece deluxe walnut stock with contoured pistol grip, 5¼ lbs., rare cals. will command a premium. Approx. 200 mfg. 1987-1988 only.

* **Hunter Grade** — AA Claro walnut without checkering. Disc. 1988.

$1,675	$1,450	$1,250	$1,000	$875	$750	$675

Last Mfg.'s Sug. Retail was $995.

* **Super Grade** — similar to Hunter Grade, except has select French walnut with ebony forend tip and 22 lines/in. checkering. Disc. 1988.

$2,275	$1,950	$1,750	$1,500	$1,300	$1,100	$950

Last Mfg.'s Sug. Retail was $1,195.

RIFLES: BOLT ACTION

Note: No suffix in Kimber models denotes pre-1986 action design, "B" suffix models incorporate the new action with improved cocking system, faster lock time, swept-back bolt design, improved recoil lug, and are right-handed.

Add $175 for skeleton grip cap on models listed below.
Add $275 for skeleton buttplate on models listed below.
Add $100 for checkered bolt handle on models listed below.
Add $300 for raised quarter rib.
Add $100 for forend tip.
Extra fancy walnut on any Kimber will always command a premium.

Model 82, .22 cal. Series

STANDARD MODEL 82 — .22 LR, .22 Mag., or .22 Hornet cal., Mauser type rear locking bolt action, 3 (.22 Hornet), 4 (.22 Mag.), or 5 (.22 LR) shot mag., 22 in. (Sporter) or 24 in. (Varmint) barrel, deluxe claro walnut, steel butt plate, rocker style safety, 6½ lbs. Add $100-$200 for .22 Hornet or .22 Mag. cal., depending on the variation.

* **Classic Model** — disc. 1988.

$850	$725	$625	$525	$450	$375	$335

Last Mfg.'s Sug. Retail was $750.

Add $55 for disc. Cascade Model (Monte Carlo cheekpiece).

There were 34 custom Cascades mfg.

* **Custom Classic Model** — higher grade claro walnut, ebony forearm tip, Niedner style steel butt plate. Disc. 1988.

$925	$775	$650	$550	$475	$400	$350

Last Mfg.'s Sug. Retail was $995.

Also previously available in the .218 Bee (approx. 130 standard mfg., 36 Mashburn mfg.) or .25-20 (approx. 200 mfg. single shot only) cals. These cals. may bring a slight premium. Mfg. 1985 only (retail price was $695).

K

Grading	100%	98%	95%	90%	80%	70%	60%

* **Deluxe Grade** — .22 LR cal. only, similar to Custom Classic Model, AA walnut, 5 or 10 (optional) shot mag., 6½ lbs. Mfg. 1989-90 only.

	$995	$895	$700	$595	$525	$450	$395

Last Mfg.'s Sug. Retail was $1,195.

A left-hand variation was also available at no extra charge, but had limited mfg. in 1990.

SPORTER MODEL — .17 Ackley Hornet (approx. 9 mfg.), .17 K. Hornet (approx. 88 mfg.), or .22 LR cal., includes Model 82A action, 22 in. sporter weight barrel, 4 shot mag., round top receiver with bases, checkered stock and forend, 6½ lbs. Mfg. 1991 only.

	$895	$750	$650	$550	$495	$450	$395

Last Mfg.'s Sug. Retail was $995.

RIMFIRE VARMINTER — .22 LR cal. only, Model 82A action, free floating 25 in. medium heavy barrel, laminated stock, 5 or optional 10 shot mag., rubber butt pad, 8¼ lbs. Mfg. 1990-91 only.

	$795	$675	$550	$475	$425	$375	$325

Last Mfg.'s Sug. Retail was $795.

HUNTER GRADE — .22 LR cal. only, similar to Rimfire Varminter with Super America configured barrel and action with low glare metal finish. Mfg. 1990 only.

	$750	$600	$525	$450	$395	$340	$295

Last Mfg.'s Sug. Retail was $895.

MINI CLASSIC — .22 LR cal. only, Model 82 action, 18 in. barrel, steel butt plate, sling swivels. Mfg. 1988 only.

	$550	$475	$415	$375	$340	$300	$275

Last Mfg.'s Sug. Retail was $795.

GOVERNMENT MODEL 82A TARGET — .22 LR cal. only, specifically designed for U.S. Army training, 25 in. heavy target barrel including scope blocks, oversized stock, some rifles are "star" marked indicating an accuracy guarantee, 10¾ lbs. Mfg. 1987-91.

	$695	$575	$500	$450	$400	$350	$325

Last Mfg.'s Sug. Retail was $595.

20,000 rifles were mfg. 1987-1989 to fill the initial U.S. government contract. U.S. property marked guns do exist in private hands - all within a low serial number range (watch markings carefully). Commercial guns were manufactured for the private sector with values listed above.

ALL AMERICAN MATCH — .22 LR cal. only, precision rifled 25 in. free floating target grade barrel, stock is adj. both vertically and for length of pull, fully adj. single stage trigger, approx. 9 lbs. Mfg. 1990-91 only.

	$750	$600	$525	$450	$395	$340	$295

Last Mfg.'s Sug. Retail was $895.

CONTINENTAL — .22 LR, .22 Mag., or .22 Hornet cal., Sporter action only, full length Mannlicher stock, open sights, deluxe walnut. Add $200 for .22 Mag. or .22 Hornet cal. New 1987.

This model was only available as a special order with prices on request from the factory.

* **Super Continental** — similar to Continental, except has AAA claro walnut with 22 lines/in. checkering. Mfg. 1987-1988.

	$1,395	$1,250	$1,000	$875	$795	$700	$625

Last Mfg.'s Sug. Retail was $1,465.

Three laminated stock variations with cheekpieces were mfg.

SUPER AMERICA — top-of-the-line model, includes detachable scope mounts, Niedner checkered steel butt plate and best quality walnut, available in Sporter configuration only. This model was disc. 1988, and reintroduced 1990-91.

	$1,075	$950	$775	$625	$550	$475	$425

Last Mfg.'s Sug. Retail was $1,295.

K

Grading	100%	98%	95%	90%	80%	70%	60%

* **Super Grade** — similar to Super America, AAA walnut, beaded cheekpiece, 5 or 10 (optional) shot mag., 6½ lbs. Mfg. 1989 only.

| | $1,075 | $950 | $775 | $625 | $550 | $475 | $425 |

Last Mfg.'s Sug. Retail was $1,295.

CUSTOM MATCH — .22 LR or .22 Mag. cal., limited edition of 217 rifles, match dimension chamber, French walnut stock with 22 L.P.I. checkering, rust blued finish, other custom rifle features. Introduced 1984.

| | $1,675 | $1,350 | $1,000 | $875 | $795 | $725 | $650 |

Add $200 for .22 Mag. cal.

BROWNELL — .22 LR cal., only 500 mfg. to commemorate the late Leonard Brownell, Mannlicher style extra deluxe claro walnut stock. Mfg. 1986 only.

| | $1,475 | $1,175 | $825 |

Last Mfg.'s Sug. Retail was $1,500.

CENTENNIAL — .22 LR cal. only, limited edition (100 rifles) to commemorate centennial of .22 LR cal., includes hand-picked checkered walnut, moderate engraving, special Wilson Arms match barrel, skeleton butt plate and other refinements, serial numbered C1-C100. Mfg. 1987 only.

| | $2,600 | $2,350 | $1,900 |

Last Mfg.'s Sug. Retail was $2,950.

TENTH ANNIVERSARY ISSUE — .22 LR cal., limited edition, French walnut stock featuring slim forend design with shadowed cheekpiece, Neidner steel buttplate and other refinements. Mfg. 1989 only.

| | $1,495 | $1,200 | $975 |

Add $100 for matte finish.

Model 84 Centerfire Series

Add $75 for forend tip - option A.
Add $300 for iron sights - option B.
Add $100 for checkered bolt handle - option C.
Add $200 for skeleton grip cap - option D.
Add $300 for skeleton buttplate - option G.
Add $250-$300 for 3-position safety in this series.

STANDARD MODEL 84 — .17 Rem., .17 Mach IV (disc. 1987), 6x45 or 47mm (disc. 1987), 5.6x50mm (disc. 1987), .221 Fireball, .222 Rem., .222 Rem. Mag. (disc. 1987), or .223 Rem. cal., "Mini-Mauser" type head locking bolt action, 5 shot mag., 22 (Sporter) or 24 (Varmint) in. barrel, deluxe Claro walnut, steel buttplate, rocker style safety, 6½ lbs.

* **Classic Model** — disc. 1988.

| | $950 | $775 | $625 | $550 | $475 | $425 | $375 |

Last Mfg.'s Sug. Retail was $885.

Add $55 for disc. Cascade Model (Monte Carlo cheekpiece).

Also available in left-hand action in .22 Hornet, .222 Rem., .223 Rem., 6x45mm, 6x47mm, .17 Rem., and .17 Mach IV (very limited mfg.).

CUSTOM CLASSIC MODEL — higher grade Claro walnut, ebony forearm tip, Niedner style steel butt plate. Disc. 1988.

| | $1,150 | $975 | $795 | $650 | $550 | $475 | $425 |

Last Mfg.'s Sug. Retail was $1,130.

* **Deluxe Grade Sporter** — .17 Rem., .221 Rem., or .223 Rem. cal., Mauser action, AA walnut, similar to Custom Classic Model, 6¼ lbs. Mfg. 1989-90.

| | $1,075 | $950 | $775 | $625 | $550 | $475 | $425 |

Last Mfg.'s Sug. Retail was $1,295.

Also available in left-hand action (.223 Rem. cal. only), limited mfg.

K

Grading	100%	98%	95%	90%	80%	70%	60%

CONTINENTAL — .221 Fireball (extremely rare, mfg. 1988 only) .222 Rem. or .223 Rem. cal., Sporter action only, full length Mannlicher stock, open sights, deluxe walnut. New 1987.

This model was only available as a special order with prices on request from the factory.

* **Super Continental** — similar to Continental (same cals.), except has AAA Claro walnut with 22 lines/in. checkering. Mfg. 1987-1988.

| | $1,495 | $1,250 | $950 | $850 | $775 | $695 | $625 |

Last Mfg.'s Sug. Retail was $1,600.

Three laminated stocks were mfg. in .223 Rem. cal.

HUNTER GRADE — .17 Rem., .222 Rem., or .223 Rem. cal., laminated stock, Super America configured action and barrel with low glare metal finish. Mfg. 1990 only.

| | $825 | $650 | $550 | $475 | $425 | $375 | $325 |

Last Mfg.'s Sug. Retail was $995.

SPORTER — .17 Rem., .22 Hornet, .222 Rem., .22-250 Rem., or .223 Rem. cal., 22 in. sporter weight barrel, A grade Claro walnut, round top receiver with bases, 4 shot mag., hand checkering. Mfg. 1991 only.

| | $975 | $800 | $700 | $600 | $550 | $500 | $495 |

Last Mfg.'s Sug. Retail was $1,095.

This model was available in either right or left-hand action.

* **Big Bore Sporter** — .250 Savage or .35 Rem. cal., similar action to Sporter Model, except has ¾ in. red Pachmayr Decelerator recoil pad. Mfg. 1991 only.

Extreme rarity precludes accurate price evaluation - consult an expert when buying/selling this model. This model was available in either right or left-hand action.

Last Mfg.'s Sug. Retail was $1,095.

SUPER AMERICA/SUPER GRADE — .17 Rem., .17 MK IV, .221 Fireball, .22 Hornet, .222 Rem., .222 Rem. Mag., .22-250 Rem., .223 Rem., 5.6x56mm, or 6x47mm cal., 22 in. sporter weight barrel, top-of-the-line, with detachable scope mounts, available in Sporter configuration only, 4 shot mag., right or left-hand action. Disc. 1988, reintroduced 1990-91.

| | $1,425 | $1,195 | $925 | $850 | $775 | $695 | $625 |

Last Mfg.'s Sug. Retail was $1,495.

Be careful when buying rare cals. and/or options on this model.

* **Big Bore Super America** — .250 Savage or .35 Rem. cal., similar action to Super America Model, except has ¾ in. red Pachmayr Decelerator recoil pad. Mfg. 1991 only.

| | $2,100 | $1,775 | $1,425 | $1,125 | $925 | $800 | $700 |

Last Mfg.'s Sug. Retail was $1,495.

CUSTOM MATCH — .222 Rem. or .223 Rem. cal., limited edition of 200 rifles, match dimension chamber, French walnut stock with 22 L.P.I. checkering, rust blued finish, other custom rifle features. Introduced 1986.

| | $2,050 | $1,600 | $1,350 | $995 | $850 | $750 | $650 |

TENTH ANNIVERSARY ISSUE — .223 Rem. cal., limited edition, French walnut stock featuring slim forend design with shadowed cheekpiece, 22 in. barrel, roundtop receiver with mounts, Neidner steel buttplate and other refinements. Mfg. 1989 only.

| | $1,850 | $1,550 | $1,200 |

Add $100 for matte finish.

ULTRA VARMINTER — .17 Rem., .22 Hornet (rare, new 1991), .221 Rem. (disc. 1990), .222 Rem., .22-250 Rem. (rare), or .223 Rem. cal., 24 in. medium weight stainless steel barrel, laminated birch stock, plain buttstock, right or left-hand action, 7¾lbs. Mfg. 1989-91 only.

| | $1,295 | $1,075 | $925 | $775 | $650 | $550 | $475 |

Last Mfg.'s Sug. Retail was $1,295.

Grading	100%	98%	95%	90%	80%	70%	60%

* **Super Varminter** — similar to Ultra Varminter except has steel barrel, AAA walnut stock with beaded cheekpiece, 7¼ lbs. Mfg. 1989-91 only.

	$1,475	$1,250	$975	$850	$725	$600	$500

Last Mfg.'s Sug. Retail was $1,495.

Model 89 Centerfire, Big Game Series

Fewer than 5,000 Model 89 BGRs were mfg.

MODEL 89 BGR — .270 Win., .280 Rem., 7mm Rem. Mag., .30-06, .300 Win. Mag., .338 Win. Mag., or .375 H&H cal., new action incorporates features from both Mauser 98 and Win. pre-64 Model 70, three position safety, 22 or 24 in. barrel, matte blue finish will command a premium. Introduced late 1988.

* **Classic Model** — deluxe Claro walnut checkered 18 lines/in. with steel butt plate. Disc. 1988.

	$790	$675	$550	$475	$395	$340	$295

Last Mfg.'s Sug. Retail was $985.

Add $200 for .375 H&H cal.
Add $100 for matte finish.

* **Custom Classic Model** — higher grade Claro walnut, ebony forearm tip, Niedner style steel butt plate. Disc. 1988.

	$1,025	$865	$750	$625	$500	$440	$365

Last Mfg.'s Sug. Retail was $1,230.

Add $200 for .375 H&H cal.

DELUXE GRADE — similar to Custom Classic Model, round top receiver with Model 70 scope mount hole configuration, AA walnut stock with ebony forend tip and rubber recoil pad (no cheekpiece), 22 or 24 in. barrel, 7½-8½ lbs. New 1989.

* **Featherweight Barrel Model** — .257 Roberts (rare), .25-06 Rem., 7x57mm (rare, disc. 1990), .270 Win., .280 Rem., or .30-06 cal., 5 shot mag., 22 in. Featherweight barrel, right-hand action only, 7½ lbs. Disc. 1990.

	$1,525	$1,175	$975	$825	$700	$600	$525

Last Mfg.'s Sug. Retail was $1,795.

Add $470 for Super America Grade with square bridge, dovetail receiver.
Add $100 for matte finish.

The Super America Grade will accept Kimber double lever scope mounts and has one grade better wood than the Deluxe Grade with beaded cheekpiece.

* **Medium-weight Barrel Model** — .300 Win. Mag., .300 H&H (rare, disc. 1990), .300 Wby. Mag. (very rare, new 1991), .338 Win. Mag., .35 Whelen (rare, disc. 1990), or 7mm Rem. Mag. cal., 3 shot mag., 24 in. medium-weight barrel, right-hand action only, 7¾-8½ lbs. Disc. 1990.

	$1,600	$1,225	$1,000	$850	$725	$625	$550

Last Mfg.'s Sug. Retail was $1,895.

Add $495 for Super America Grade with square bridge, dovetail receiver.
Add $100 for matte finish.

The Super America Grade will accept Kimber double lever scope mounts and has one grade better wood than the Deluxe Grade with beaded cheekpiece.

* **Heavy-weight Barrel Model** — .375 H&H Mag. cal., 3 shot mag., 24 in. heavy-weight barrel, right-hand action only, 9 lbs. Disc. 1990.

	$1,700	$1,275	$1,050	$900	$775	$700	$650

Last Mfg.'s Sug. Retail was $1,995.

Add $495 for Super America Grade with square bridge, dovetail receiver.
Add $100 for matte finish.

The Super America Grade will accept Kimber double lever scope mounts and has one grade better wood than the Deluxe Grade with beaded cheekpiece.

K

Grading	100%	98%	95%	90%	80%	70%	60%

SPORTER MODEL — same cals. as Deluxe/Super America Models, 22 in. featherweight or 24 in. medium or heavy barrel, double square bridge dovetail receiver, A grade Claro walnut stock with ¾ in. red Pachmayr Decelerator recoil pad (Mag. cals. only with 24 in. barrel). Mfg. 1991 only.

$1,325 $1,000 $875 $750 $625 $500 $450

Last Mfg.'s Sug. Retail was $1,595.

> Add $100 for medium Magnum action.
> Add $200 for heavy Magnum action (.375 H&H and .458 Win. Mag. cals.).

HUNTER GRADE — .270 Win., .30-06, .300 Win. Mag., .338 Win. Mag., or 7mm Rem. Mag. cal., laminated stock, Super America configured action and barrel with low glare metal finish. Mfg. 1990-91 only.

$1,250 $975 $850 $725 $600 $500 $450

Last Mfg.'s Sug. Retail was $1,495.

> Add $100 for Mag. cals.

SUPER GRADE — similar to Super America Model, square top frame, AAA walnut, 22 or 24 in. barrel, plain buttstock, 7½-8½ lbs. Mfg. 1989 only.

$1,500 $1,275 $995 $825 $695 $550 $500

Last Mfg.'s Sug. Retail was $1,495.

> Add $100 for .375 H&H cal.
> Add $100 for matte blue metal finish.
> The 24 in. barrel was available in Mag. cals. only.

LIMITED WILDLIFE EDITION SERIES — series of 5 guns, includes .257 Roberts (Whitetail Deer Edition), .270 Win. (Mule Deer Edition), .338 Win. Mag. (Rocky Mt. Elk Edition), 7mm Rem. Mag. (Big Horn Sheep Edition), and .375 H&H (Grizzly Bear Edition) cals. included, hand select walnut, special Shilen Rifle barrel, gold plated trigger, receivers are stamped "Wildlife Edition", special prefix serialization, only 25 sets were to be manufactured in 1991 only, includes rings, swivels, and hard case.

> While advertised, only one .270 Win. Mule Deer model was mfg. Retail price was scheduled to be $3,595.

MODEL 89 AFRICAN — .375 H&H (rare), .416 Rigby (most common) cal., or .505 Gibbs (rare) cal., Magnum action, 24 in. heavy barrel, AA English walnut stock with beaded cheekpiece and rubber recoil pad, includes twin recoil cross bolts, express sights on quarter rib, drop box magazine, 10-10½ lbs. Mfg. 1990-91 only.

$4,250 $3,750 $3,250 $2,575 $2,050 $1,725 $1,525

Last Mfg.'s Sug. Retail was $3,595.

> .375 H&H or .505 Gibbs cal. will command a premium.

K

KIMEL INDUSTRIES, INC.

Previously manufactured until late 1994 by AAArms located in Monroe, NC. Previously distributed by Kimel Industries, Inc. located in Matthews, NC.

PISTOLS: SEMI-AUTO

AP-9 PISTOL — 9mm Para. cal., paramilitary design, blowback action with bolt knob on left side of receiver, 5 in. barrel with vent. shroud, front mounted 10 (C/B 1994) or 20★ shot detachable mag., black matte finish, adj. front sight, 3 lbs. 7 oz. Mfg. 1989-94.

$265 $230 $185 $155 $135 $120 $110

Last Mfg.'s Sug. Retail was $279.

> Add $10 for nickel finish.

★ *Mini AP-9* — compact variation of the AP-9 Model with 3 in. barrel, blue or nickel finish. Mfg. 1991-94.

$265 $230 $185 $155 $135 $120 $110

Last Mfg.'s Sug. Retail was $273.

> Add $10 for nickel finish.

Grading	100%	98%	95%	90%	80%	70%	60%

* **Target AP-9** — target variation of the AP-9 with 12 in. match barrel with shroud, blue finish only. Mfg. 1991-94.

| | $300 | $265 | $235 | $190 | $160 | $140 | $120 |

Last Mfg.'s Sug. Retail was $294.

* **P-95** — similar to AP-9, except without barrel shroud and is supplied with 5 shot mag., parts are interchangeable with AP-9. Mfg. 1990-91 only.

| | $245 | $215 | $175 | $155 | $135 | $120 | $110 |

Last Mfg.'s Sug. Retail was $250.

RIFLES: CARBINES

AR-9 Carbine — 9mm Para. cal., carbine variation of the AP-9 with 16½ in. barrel, 20 shot mag., and steel rod folding stock. Mfg. 1991-94.

| | $350 | $315 | $275 | $220 | $195 | $175 | $155 |

Last Mfg.'s Sug. Retail was $384.

KING'S GUN WORKS INC.

Current custom handgun and accessories manufacturer established during 1949 and currently located in Glendale, CA. Dealer and consumer direct sales.

King's Gun Works manufactures a complete line of custom pistols patterned after Colt M-1911, in addition to many related accessories and/or after-market parts. Please contact the company directly for current information and prices (see Trademark Index listing).

KLEINGUENTHER FIREARMS CO.

Current custom rifle manufacturer located in Seguin, TX. The original KDF Co. was started by Mr. Robert Kleinguenther and sold in the early 1980s. At this juncture, Mr. Kleinguenther started a new company called Kleinguenther Firearms Co. Direct custom order sales only.

RIFLES: BOLT ACTION

Values listed below are for base model only with no additional customer special order options. Mr. Keinguenther will also custom build rifles utilizing customer actions, in addition to performing normal custom gunsmithing.

BOLT ACTION RIFLE — various cals., individual customer special order rifle with a variety of options, guns are guaranteed to shoot ½ M.O.A., choice of actions, various weights. Currently, the manufacturer does not have availability on either the Winchester Model 70 Custom or the Mauser K-15 action.

* **Winchester Model 70 Custom**

| | $975 | $800 | $675 | $575 | $500 | $450 | $400 |

Last Mfg.'s Sug. Retail was $975.

* **Sako Action** — various cals., newer guns feature the ballistic recoil muzzle brake system (60-70% recoil reduction), most newer stocks are mfg. out of high tech laminated wood with 28-32 resin coated panels.

| Mfg.'s Sug. Retail | $1,750 | | $1,750 | $1,450 | $1,200 | $1,025 | $925 | $825 | $750 |

Add $155 for ballistic recoil muzzle brake system.

* **K-15**

| | $1,375 | $1,100 | $950 | $800 | $675 | $575 | $500 |

Last Mfg.'s Sug. Retail was $1,375.

KNIGHT'S MANUFACTURING COMPANY

Current manufacturer located in Vero Beach, FL. Dealer and consumer direct sales.

Grading	100%	98%	95%	90%	80%	70%	60%

RIFLES: SEMI-AUTO

Some of the models listed below were also available in pre-ban configurations.

STONER SR-15 M-5 RIFLE — .223 Rem. cal., 20 in. standard weight barrel, flip-up low profile rear sight, two-stage target trigger, 7.6 lbs. New 1997.

Mfg.'s Sug. Retail	$1,295		$1,175	$1,000	$875	$800	$750	$700	$650

* *Stoner SR-15 M-4 Carbine* — similar to SR-15 rifle, except has 16 in. barrel, choice of fixed synthetic or non-collapsible buttstock. New 1997.

Mfg.'s Sug. Retail	$1,295		$1,175	$1,000	$875	$800	$750	$700	$650

Add $100 for non-collapsible buttstock (SR-15 M-4 K-Carbine).

STONER SR-15 MATCH RIFLE — .223 Rem. cal., features flat-top upper receiver with 20 in. free floating barrel, two-stage match trigger, 7.9 lbs. New 1997.

Mfg.'s Sug. Retail	$1,595		$1,450	$1,275	$1,050	$900	$825	$750	$700

STONER SR-25 SPORTER — .308 Win. cal., 20 in. lightweight barrel, AR-15 configuration with carrying handle, 5, 10, or 20 (disc. per C/B 1994) shot detachable mag., less than 2 MOA guaranteed, non-glare finish, 8.8 lbs. Mfg. 1993-97.

$2,650	$2,250	$1,900	$1,600	$1,300	$1,000	$850

Last Mfg.'s Sug. Retail was $2,995.

* *Stoner SR-25 Carbine* — 16 in. free floating barrel, grooved non-slip handguard, removable carrying handle, 7¾ lbs. New 1995.

Mfg.'s Sug. Retail	$2,995		$2,650	$2,250	$1,900	$1,600	$1,300	$1,000	$850

Add $250 for Rail Adapter System (RAS) forearm - new 1999.

SR-25 MATCH — similar to SR-25 Standard, except has 24 in. free floating match barrel and flattop receiver, less than 1 MOA guaranteed, 10¾ lbs. New 1993.

Mfg.'s Sug. Retail	$2,995		$2,650	$2,250	$1,900	$1,600	$1,300	$1,000	$850

Add $250 for Rail Adapter System (RAS) forearm - new 1999.

* *SR-25 Lightweight Match* — features 20 in. medium contour free floating barrel, 9½ lbs. New 1995.

Mfg.'s Sug. Retail	$2,995		$2,650	$2,250	$1,900	$1,600	$1,300	$1,000	$850

Add $250 for Rail Adapter System (RAS) forearm - new 1999.

"DAVID TUBB" COMPETITION MATCH RIFLE — .260 Rem. or .308 Win. cal., incorporates refinements by David Tubb, top-of-the-line competition match rifle, including adj. and rotating buttstock pad. Mfg. 1998 only.

$5,200	$4,000	$3,600	$3,150	$2,700	$2,300	$1,995

Last Mfg.'s Sug. Retail was $5,995.

STONER SR-50 — .50 BMG cal., features high strength materials and lightweight design, fully locked breech and two lug rotary breech bolt, horizontal 10 shot box mag., tubular receiver supports a removable barrel, approx. 31 lbs. (includes scope and mount). New 1996.

Mfg.'s Sug. Retail	$6,995		$6,300	$5,400	$4,200	$3,600	$3,150	$2,700	$2,300

KODIAK CO.

Previous manufacturer located in North Haven, CT circa 1963-66.

Kodiak Co. was in business for only a short time. They produced the first .22 Mag. semi-auto rifle (Model 260), as well as a centerfire bolt action (Model 158 Deluxe), and a slide action shotgun (Model 458). While Kodiak long guns are rare and extremely well made, collectability to date has been minimal with most specimens selling at a slight premium over similar quality trade name counterparts of that era. Prior to 1963, Kodiak firearms were marketed under the trade name of Jefferson.

Grading	100%	98%	95%	90%	80%	70%	60%

KOLIBRI

Previous trademark manufactured 1914-1925 by H. Grabner located in Krems/Donau, Austria.

PISTOLS: SEMI-AUTO

KOLIBRI PISTOL — 2.7 or 3mm centerfire cal., unrifled barrel, 5 shot box mag., world's smallest semi-auto centerfire pistol.

	100%	98%	95%	90%	80%	70%	60%
	$2,250	$1,950	$1,750	$1,500	$1,350	$1,175	$1,000

Add approx. $300 for original case.
Add approx. 40% for nickel finish (rare).

Individual rounds of 2.7 or 3mm (more rare) ammunition are currently trading in the $75 range as it has the distinction of being the world's smallest centerfire shell (shooting a 3 grain bullet).

KONGSBERG

Previous manufacturer circa 1814-1998 located in Kongsberg, Norway. Previously imported and distributed 1996-98, by Kongsberg America L.L.C. located in Fairfield, CT, and by Lew Horton Distributing Co., Inc. until 1996, located in Westboro, MA.

RIFLES: BOLT ACTION

Add $50 for iron sights on models listed below.

393 SERIES — .22-250 Rem., .243 Win., .270 Win., .30-06, .308 Win., 6.5x55 Swedish, 7mm Rem. Mag., .300 Win. Mag. or .338 Win. Mag. cal., available in either Classic, De Luxe, Thumbhole (.22-250 Rem. or 308 Win. only), or Select (Standard) configuration, checkered pistol grip, forend mounted recoil lug which connects to stock, 3-position rear safety, fixed rotary mag., fully adj. trigger. Imported 1994-98.

* **Classic Model**

	100%	98%	95%	90%	80%	70%	60%
	$875	$750	$675	$575	$495	$440	$385

Last Mfg.'s Sug. Retail was $995.

Add $114 for Mag. cals.
Add $138 for left-hand action.

* **Select Model (Standard Model in Europe)**

	100%	98%	95%	90%	80%	70%	60%
	$860	$735	$660	$560	$495	$440	$385

Last Mfg.'s Sug. Retail was $980.

Add $113 for Mag. cals.
Add $138 for left-hand action.

* **De Luxe Model**

	100%	98%	95%	90%	80%	70%	60%
	$940	$795	$700	$595	$515	$450	$395

Last Mfg.'s Sug. Retail was $1,124.

Add $112 for Mag. cals.
Add $137 for left-hand action.

* **Thumbhole Model** — .22-250 Rem. or .308 Win. cal., features thumbhole stock. Mfg. 1996-98.

	100%	98%	95%	90%	80%	70%	60%
	$1,350	$1,175	$1,000	$875	$750	$625	$500

Last Mfg.'s Sug. Retail was $1,580.

Add $138 for left-hand action.

KORA BRNO

Current revolver trademark manufactured by Kroko a.s., located in Brno, Czech Republic. No current importation.

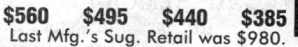

Grading	100%	98%	95%	90%	80%	70%	60%

To date, the Kora Brno revolver line has had little or no importation into the U.S. Models include many configurations of both .22 LR and .38 Spl. cals. Please contact the factory directly for more information (see Trademark Index).

KORRIPHILA

Current trademark manufacturered by Intertex, located in Eislingen, Germany. Currently imported beginning 1999 by Intertex Carousels Corporation, located in Pineville, NC. Previously imported and distributed by Osborne's located in Cheboygan, MI until 1988.

PISTOLS: SEMI-AUTO

Less than 30 Korriphila pistols are made annually.

HSP 701 — 7.65 Luger (disc.), .38 Spl. (disc.), 9mm Para., 9mm Police (disc.), 9mm Steyr (disc.), .45 ACP, or 10mm Norma (disc.) cal., double action, Budischowsky delayed roller block locking system assists in recoil reduction, 40% stainless steel parts, 4 or 5 in. barrel, blue or satin finish, walnut grips, 7 or 9 shot mag., approx. 2.6 lbs, very limited production.

Mfg.'s Sug. Retail	$7,590		$6,500	$5,500	$3,750	$2,950	$2,150	$1,850	$1,675

* *HSP 701 Odin's Eye (Damascus)* — similar to HSP 701, except is completely made from one block of Damascus stainless steel, rosewood grips with Manta skin inlays, custom order only, the world's most expensive currently manufactured semi-auto pistol.

Mfg.'s Sug. Retail	$13,900		$12,250	$10,250	$8,500

KORTH

Current manufacturer established circa 1955, and located in Ratzeburg, Germany. Currently imported by Keng's Firearms Specialty, Inc. beginning 1997, and located in Atlanta, GA. Previously imported by Mandall Shooting Supplies, Inc. located in Scottsdale, AZ, Beeman Precision Arms, located in Santa Rosa, CA and by Osborne's in Cheboygan, MI.

Korth handguns are very high quality and are literally manufactured one-at-a-time, resulting in limited mfg. (less than 100 annually) and importation.

PISTOLS: SEMI-AUTO

KORTH SEMI-AUTO — 9mm Para., .357 Sig, .40 S&W, or 9x21mm IMI cal., double action, 4 in. barrel, all steel construction, 10 shot mag., adj. sights, checkered walnut stocks, top quality manufacture throughout. Introduced 1986 with first guns shipped 1988.

Mfg.'s Sug. Retail	$7,000		$6,300	$4,000	$3,500	$2,950	$2,500	$2,000	$1,750

Add $185 per 9mm Para. or .40 S&W mag.
Add $500 for plasma coated silver matte finish.
Add $1,000 for plasma coated silver polished finish.
Price for interchangeable barrels by request only.

REVOLVERS

The crane of the main cylinder and of the extra cylinder (.22 LR/.22 Mag. or .357 Mag./9mm Para.) are cut from the same billet of steel, and for reasons of smallest tolerance that Korth guarantees, once a gun is made with a single cylinder, the extra convertible cylinder cannot be ordered at a later date. Korth currently produces the world's most expensive revolver.

Grading	100%	98%	95%	90%	80%	70%	60%

SPORT/COMBAT RIMFIRE — .22 LR or .22 Mag. cal., 3, 4 (Combat only), 5¼, or 6 in. barrel (VR available on 4 in. or longer barrel only), 6 shot, micro adj. sights (Sport), Combat sights fully adj., full length shrouded ejector rod, adj. trigger, checkered and oil finished walnut grips, 2.6 lbs. Introduced 1967.

Mfg.'s Sug. Retail	$5,600		$3,750	$2,850	$2,150	$1,850	$1,600	$1,400	$1,250

    Add $300 for Sport Model.
    Add $800 for ISU Match Model.
    Add $800 for special order 8 in. barrel (disc.)
    Subtract $475 if without extra .22 LR cylinder.
    Add $400 for stainless steel (limited mfg.).
    Add $600 for plasma coated silver matte finish.
    Add $1,100 for plasma coated silver polished finish.

SPORT/COMBAT CENTERFIRE — .22 Rem. Jet (disc.), .32 S&W Long, .32 H&R Mag. (disc.), .38 Spl., .357 Mag., or 9mm Para. cal., 2½ (scarce), 3, 4 (Combat only), 5¼ or 6 in. barrel, 5 (1st Model) or 6 shot, otherwise similar specs. as Sport/Combat Rimfire Model, 2.1-2.6 lbs.

Mfg.'s Sug. Retail	$5,600		$5,100	$2,850	$2,150	$1,850	$1,600	$1,400	$1,250

    Add $300 for Sport Model.
    Add $800 for ISU Match Model.
    Add $800 for special order 8 in. barrel (disc.)
    Add $400 for stainless steel (limited mfg.).
    Add $600 for plasma coated silver matte finish.
    Add $1,100 for plasma coated silver polished finish.
    Subtract $475 if without extra 9mm Para. cylinder.

This model is available in additional rimmed and rimless calibers on special order. Most importation has occurred in .357 Mag. cal. only, with or without additional 9mm Para. convertible cylinder.

* *Model Everest, 40 Years Korth, Ltd. Ed.* — .357 Mag., 5¼ in. barrel only, deeply engraved frame and barrel with gold inlays, smooth select walnut grips, cased, only 25 mfg. 1995-96.

	$7,250	$5,950	$4,500

Last Mfg.'s Sug. Retail was $8,500.

PRESENTATION MODEL — deluxe variation of the Sport/Combat Model.

This variation is available with etching, engraving, and other special options that are priced per individual quotation from the importer.

KRAG-JORGENSEN

Previous U.S. magazine fed military rifle. First U.S. (.30-40 Krag) military repeating rifle to shoot smokeless powder ammunition. Manufactured 1894-1904.

There have been many conversions of Krag-Jorgensen rifles - many of which are hard to identify. As a rule, these conversions are not as desirable as the specific models listed below.

RIFLES: BOLT ACTION

M1892-DATED 1894 — .30-40 Krag cal., mfg. by Springfield Armory, with cleaning rod. Note: This model is designated Type I, and has a wide, solid upper barrel band.

	$8,950	$7,500	$6,250	$5,250	$4,250	$3,500	$2,750

* *Receivers dated 1894 or 1895 with 1894, 1895 or 1896 stock cartouche* — .30-40 Krag, designated Type II. Upper band has double strap instead of being solid as in Type I. Model 1892 rifles were dated in two places - receiver dates of 1894 or 1895 and stock cartouche dates of 1894, 1895 or 1896. The final 1892s were completed in 1896, and these rifles retained a number of Model 1892 features such as a stock with a rounded toe, and an early lug leaf Model 1896 rear sight. These late guns are in the 20,000 ser. no. range, and they feature 1894 dated receivers with 1896 stock cartouche date.

	$7,500	$6,500	$5,500	$4,500	$3,750	$3,000	$2,250

Grading	100%	98%	95%	90%	80%	70%	60%

ARSENAL-ALTERED TO M1896 STYLE

	$750	$550	$450	$400	$375	$325	$295

M1896 — .30-40 Krag cal., receivers marked 1896 and Model 1896 with 1896, 1897, 1898 stock cartouche dates. 1,300 rifles were mfg. in this configuration before July 1, 1896 and can be denoted by observing the receiver having the "1896" date w/o the word Model.

	$700	$550	$425	$350	$300	$275	$250

M1896 CARBINE

	$1,000	$900	$800	$600	$550	$500	$475

M1895 CARBINE — .30-40 Krag cal., this is a variant that has receiver dates of 1894, 1895, and 1896 and omits the word "Model". 7,111 carbines were mfg. in a crash program to rearm the regular cavalry. Mfg. mid 1895 to May of 1896. Stock cartouche is dated 1896. Early variation have stocks drilled for two cleaning rods in the butt trap (rare).

	$1,500	$1,250	$1,000	$850	$750	$700	$650

M1896 CADET RIFLE — .30-40 Krag cal., two variations are encountered, the first variation included 400 guns that were issued to the Service Academy, most of which were converted to a standard service rifle configuration. Observed specimens of these converted Cadet rifles are in the 18,000-19,000 ser. no. range. Converted Cadet rifles are easily identified by the filled band spring inletting in the band stock (with 1896 cartouche) - no known unmodified examples. The second variation appears to consist of only 4 guns, only 3 are known to exist.

* **Type I** — ser. no. range 18,000-20,000, arsenal altered to Model 1896 configuration.

	$3,025	$2,750	$2,530	$2,200	$1,815	$1,500	$1,200

* **Type II** — ser. no. range 35,XXX, unaltered Cadet configuration, only 3 known to exist.

  Extreme rarity factor precludes accurate price evaluation. A recent specimen sold for over $40,000.

M1898 RIFLE

	$2,000	$1,100	$850	$650	$550	$400	$350

M1898 CARBINE — .30-40 Krag cal., most legitimate guns fall within the ser. no. range 125,XXX-135,XXX, original guns should have matching cartouche, sights, and ser. no. Most of these guns were converted to the M1899 configuration by replacing the stocks, handguards, and sights.

	$1,800	$1,650	$1,350	$1,100	$875	$800	$750

M1898 NRA CARBINE — features carbine stock and hardware, shortened rifle (22 in.) barreled action, identifiable by full band front sight.

	$850	$725	$600	$525	$450	$375	$325

M1899 CARBINE

	$750	$635	$525	$495	$465	$430	$395

M1899 CARBINE, PHILIPPINE CONSTABULARY — .30-40 Krag cal., 4,980 Model 1899 Krag Carbines were purchased by the Insular government of the Phillipines for use by the constabulary and modified by the U.S. Army at the Manila Ordnance Depot. "JFC" or "CV" were modified by the U.S. Army at Springfield and were school guns, not constabulary carbines. The stateside school variation was named "United States Magazine Carbine, Model of 1899, modified for use with knife bayonet and gun sling."

	$1,500	$1,200	$1,000	$950	$900	$850	$700

Watch yourself - many counterfeits have surfaced in recent years.

KRICO

Current manufacturer located in Vohburg-Irsching, Germany beginning 1996. Previously manufactured in Fürth-Stadeln, Germany by Sportwaffenfabrik Kriegeskorte Gmbh until 1996. Current limited importation by Mandall Shooting Supplies, Inc. located in Scottsdale, AZ.

Grading	100%	98%	95%	90%	80%	70%	60%

Previously imported (until 1988) by Beeman Precision Firearms Inc. located in Santa Rosa, CA.

Between 1983-86, Krico was imported/distributed by over ten U.S. companies/individuals. Beeman Precision Arms imported these rifles 1986-1988 in limited quantities. Krico manufactures a high quality rifle and to date, has had limited domestic distribution.

RIFLES: BOLT ACTION

Values and information below reflect the most current information available to the publisher. Please contact either Mandall Shooting Supplies, Inc. or the factory directly for current pricing and model availability.

SPORTING RIFLE — .22 Hornet or .222 Rem. cal., miniature Mauser action, 4 shot, 22, 24, or 26 in. barrel, single or double set triggers, open sights, checkered walnut stock, pistol grip. Mfg. 1956-1962.

	$605	$550	$495	$440	$400	$360	$305

CARBINE — similar to Sporting Rifle, except 20 or 22 in. barrel, full length stock.

	$635	$580	$415	$470	$420	$375	$320

SPECIAL VARMINT RIFLE — similar to Sporting Rifle, except heavy barrel, no sights.

	$605	$550	$495	$440	$400	$360	$300

MODEL 300 SPORTER — .22 LR, .22 Mag., or .22 Hornet cal., select walnut with straight, checkered stock and fuller forearm, 23½ in. barrel, 5 shot mag., grooved receiver, 6½ lbs.

Mfg.'s Sug. Retail	$595	$550	$495	$450	$410	$380	$350	$320

Add $30 for .22 Mag. cal.
Add $155 for .22 Hornet cal.

This model was designated Model 302 Sporter until 1986.

* *Model 300 Deluxe* — similar to Model 300 Standard, except has deluxe wood and checkering. Importation began 1991.

Mfg.'s Sug. Retail	$695	$625	$550	$480	$430	$385	$350	$320

Add $25 for .22 Mag. cal.
Add $200 for .22 Hornet cal.

MODEL 311 SMALL BORE RIFLE — .22 LR cal. only, bolt action, 5 or 10 shot, 22 in. barrel, single or double set trigger, open sights, checkered stock. Disc.

	$330	$275	$250	$220	$195	$165	$155

Add 30% for Kahles 2½ power scope.

MODEL 320 MANNLICHER SPORTER — .22 LR, .22 Mag., or .22 Hornet cal., full stock sporter, 19½ in. barrel, 5 shot mag., double set triggers, 6 lbs.

Mfg.'s Sug. Retail	$750	$650	$575	$500	$460	$430	$395	$370

Add $25 for .22 Mag. cal.
Add $150 for .22 Hornet cal.

This model was designated Model 304 Mannlicher Sporter until 1986. In 1991 it was redesignated the Model 320 Stutzen.

MODEL 340 S ST — .22 LR cal. only, silhouette model, 21 in. bull barrel, match trigger, no sights, 5 shot mag., stippled pistol grip and forearm, 7½ lbs.

Mfg.'s Sug. Retail	$795	$750	$625	$550	$500	$450	$375	$325

* *Model 340 Kricotronic* — similar to above, except with Krico electronic trigger. Importation disc. 1988.

	$1,295	$995	$900	$800	$690	$600	$550

Last Mfg.'s Sug. Retail was $1,450.

* **Model 340 Mini-Sniper** — non-glare wood and metal finish, military style barrel with muzzle brake, vent. forearm, no sights, match trigger (interchangeable), 5 shot, raised cheekpiece. Importation disc. 1988.

	$1,050	$825	$725	$600	$550	$500	$450

Last Mfg.'s Sug. Retail was $1,200.

BIATHLON MODEL 360 S — .22 LR cal., standard biathlon configuration with conventional straight pull bolt.

Mfg.'s Sug. Retail	$1,695	$1,375	$1,075	$925	$750	$625	$550	$500

BIATHLON MODEL 360 S2 — .22 LR cal., biathlon competition rifle featuring unique pistol grip operated rapid fire action, includes 5 mags., aperture sights, snow guards, and black stock.

Mfg.'s Sug. Retail	$1,595	$1,300	$1,050	$900	$750	$625	$550	$500

MODEL 400 SPORTER — .22 LR or .22 Hornet cal., 23½ in. barrel, select checkered walnut with European style curved cheekpiece, 5 shot mag., open sights, 6.8 lbs.

Mfg.'s Sug. Retail	$895	$840	$750	$625	$550	$500	$450	$375

    Add $55 for .22 Hornet cal.

* **Model 400 Match Single Shot** — .22 LR only, match rifle configuration.

Mfg.'s Sug. Retail	$950	$875	$750	$625	$550	$500	$450	$375

* **Model 400 Silhouette** — .22 LR only, designed for silhouette shooting, no sights.

Mfg.'s Sug. Retail	$775	$725	$615	$550	$500	$450	$375	$325

MODEL 420 L ST MANNLICHER SPORTER — .22 Hornet only, full stock sporter, 19½ in. barrel, double set triggers, 5 shot, 6½ lbs.

	$875	$750	$625	$550	$500	$450	$375

MODEL 440 — .22 Hornet, otherwise similar to Model 340. Importation disc. 1988.

	$900	$725	$575	$525	$450	$400	$360

Last Mfg.'s Sug. Retail was $1,025.

MODEL 600 HUNTING — .222 Rem., .223 Rem., .22-250 Rem., .243 Win., .308 Win., or 5.6x50 Mag. cal., 23½ in. barrel, select checkered walnut with curved European style cheekpiece and vent. forend, 3 or 4 shot mag., open sights, single set trigger, 7 lbs.

Mfg.'s Sug. Retail	$1,295	$1,100	$975	$850	$750	$625	$550	$500

    Add $55 for Model 600 SC.
    Add $300 for Model 600 Benchrest.
    Add $355 for Model 600 in sniper configuration.

    This model is also available in single shot configuration at no extra charge as well as in a Match Model Group I & II - add $100 for Group II.

K

MODEL 620 MANNLICHER SPORTER — same cals. as Model 600, full stock sporter, 20¾ in. barrel, double set triggers, 3 shot mag., 6.8 lbs. Importation disc. 1988.

	$1,165	$965	$875	$760	$695	$650	$590

Last Mfg.'s Sug. Retail was $1,300.

MODEL 640 S ST VARMINT — .22-250 Rem., .222 Rem., or .223 Rem. cal., 23¾ in. heavy barrel, high Monte Carlo comb and full cheekpiece, rosewood forearm tip and grip cap, Wundhammer hand swell, double set triggers, 4 shot mag., 9.6 lbs. Importation disc. 1990.

	$875	$750	$625	$550	$500	$450	$375

Last Mfg.'s Sug. Retail was $950.

* **Model 640 Sniper** — similar to Model 640, except has non-adj. cheekpiece. Importation disc. 1988.

	$1,325	$1,075	$965	$875	$760	$695	$650

Last Mfg.'s Sug. Retail was $1,500.

Grading	100%	98%	95%	90%	80%	70%	60%

MODEL 640 DELUXE/SUPER SNIPER — .223 Rem. or .308 Win. cal., 23 in. barrel, select walnut stock has stippled hand grip, adj. cheekpiece and vent. forearm, engine turned bolt assembly, 3 shot mag., match trigger, 10 lbs. Importation disc. 1988.

$1,495 $1,175 $1,025 $875 $760 $695 $650
Last Mfg.'s Sug. Retail was $1,725.

This model was known as the 650 Sniper/Match until 1986.

MODEL 700A ECONOMY — .222 Rem., .243 Win., or .308 Win. cal. (Group I) or 6.5x55mm, 7x64mm, .270 Win., or .30-06 cal. (Group II), without sights, single trigger. Importation began 1991.

Mfg.'s Sug. Retail	$995		$900	$775	$650	$550	$500	$450	$375

Add $70 for Group II cals.

MODEL 700 SERIES — .17 Rem., .22-250 Rem., .222 Rem., .222 Rem. Mag., .223 Rem., 5.6x50mm Mag., .243 Win., .308 Win., or 5.6x57 RWS cal. (Group I), 6.5x55mm, 7x57mm, .270 Win., 7x64mm, .30-06, or 9.3x72 cal. (Group II), or 6.5x68mm, 7mm Rem. Mag., .300 Win. Mag., 8x68S, 7.5mm Swiss, or 6x62mm Freres (Group III) cal., matte black metal finish, open sights, approx. 7 lbs. Importation began 1991.

* **Model 700 Hunting** — available in Group I or II cals. only, walnut hunting stock with Bavarian cheekpiece, recoil pad, and palm swell grip.

Mfg.'s Sug. Retail	$1,249		$1,075	$950	$850	$750	$625	$550	$500

Add $50 for Group II cals.

* **Model 700 DeLuxe** — similar to Model 700 Hunting, except has better grade walnut and is available in Group III cals. also.

Mfg.'s Sug. Retail	$1,379		$1,150	$1,000	$875	$750	$625	$550	$500

Add $20 for Group II cals.
Add $71 for Group III cals.
Add $150 for left-hand action.
Add $346-$516 for repeating variation in Groups I-III.

* **Model 700 Stutzen** — full stock variation (Mannlicher) of the Model 700 DeLuxe.

Mfg.'s Sug. Retail	$1,450		$1,200	$1,025	$895	$750	$625	$550	$500

Add $39 for Group II cals.
Add $160 for Group III cals.
Add $275 for DeLuxe variation (includes better wood and finish).

MODEL 700 DL R SPORTER — .270 Win. or .30-06 cal., 23½ in. barrel, curved European cheekpiece, select walnut, 3 shot Mag., single set trigger, open sights, 7 lbs. Importation disc. 1990.

$925 $800 $650 $575 $500 $450 $375
Last Mfg.'s Sug. Retail was $1,025.

Subtract $30 for Model 700 DM ST.
Add $470 for Model 700 DLM.

MODEL 720 MANNLICHER SPORTER — similar to Model 700, only has 20¾ in. barrel, double set triggers, 6.8 lbs. Importation disc. 1990.

$1,100 $975 $850 $750 $625 $550 $500
Last Mfg.'s Sug. Retail was $1,295.

* **Model 720 Limited Edition** — .270 Win. cal. only, 24Kt. gold scroll work on bolt handle, receiver, barrel and mounts. Trigger and front side are gold plated. Serial numbered in gold. Disc. 1986.

$2,310 $1,990 $1,700 $1,450 $1,200 $1,050 $950
Last Mfg.'s Sug. Retail was $2,659.

RIFLES: SEMI-AUTO

MODEL 260 SPORTER — .22 LR cal. only, standard features. Importation began 1991.

Mfg.'s Sug. Retail	$595		$550	$495	$450	$410	$380	$350	$320

Grading	100%	98%	95%	90%	80%	70%	60%

H. KRIEGHOFF GUN CO. (SHOTGUNS OF ULM)

Current manufacturer located in Ulm, Germany. Previous manufacture was in Suhl, Germany, circa 1886-1948. Currently imported and distributed by Krieghoff International Inc. located in Ottsville, PA. Dealer direct sales only.

WWII Krieghoff Lugers will appear in the Luger section of this text.

DRILLINGS

H. Krieghoff drillings can be ordered with a variety of cals. (.222 Rem., .243 Win., .270 Win., or .30-06) and special order features. Prices shown below are for standard guns with no options. Better models will have a finer grade walnut and exhibit more elaborate deep relief engraving.

Add $450 for free floating rifle barrels on Trumpf and Neptun Models listed below (both regular steel frame and Dural variations).

Add $1,290 for 3-claw scope mount system.

PLUS MODEL — 12 or 20 ga. over rifle barrel (.222 Rem., .243 Win., .270 Win., or .30-06 cal.), boxlock action, light engraving. New 1988.

Mfg.'s Sug. Retail	$5,975	$4,900	$3,550	$2,750	$2,175	$1,825	$1,525	$1,200

TRUMPF MODEL — 12, 16, or 20 ga. O/U, or rifle shotgun combo., various cals., boxlock, 25 in. barrels, 7½ lbs.

Mfg.'s Sug. Retail	$9,950	$8,300	$6,300	$5,350	$4,250	$3,300	$2,750	$2,200

Add $1,850 for single trigger.

* *Trumpf Dural* — Dural aluminum frame variation of the Trumpf, 6.8 lbs., cased.

Mfg.'s Sug. Retail	$9,950	$8,300	$6,300	$5,350	$4,250	$3,300	$2,750	$2,200

NEPTUN MODEL — 12 or 20 ga., variety of cals., elaborate engraving, sidelocks.

Mfg.'s Sug. Retail	$16,500	$13,250	$10,400	$9,000	$7,550	$6,200	$5,100	$4,150

* *Neptun Dural* — Dural aluminum frame variation of the Neptun, cased.

Mfg.'s Sug. Retail	$16,500	$13,250	$10,400	$9,000	$7,550	$6,200	$5,100	$4,150

NEPTUN PRIMUS MODEL — similar to Neptun Model, only hand detachable sidelocks and elaborate deep relief engraving.

Mfg.'s Sug. Retail	$24,500	$18,500	$13,650	$10,450	$8,400	$7,100	$5,850	$4,950

* *Neptun Primus Dural* — Dural aluminum frame variation available at no extra charge.

Mfg.'s Sug. Retail	$24,500	$18,500	$13,650	$10,450	$8,400	$7,100	$5,850	$4,950

RIFLES: DOUBLE, O/U & SxS

Various grades differ in style and amount of engraving, choice of walnut and various options that can be special ordered.

Add $1,500-$2,500 for 4-claw scope mount (standard or European).

TECK O/U — .30-06, .300 Win. Mag. (disc. 1994), .308 Win., 7x56R (disc. 1994), 7x65R (new 1995), 8x57JRS, 8x75RS (new 1995), 9.3x74R, .375 H&H (disc. 1988), or .458 Win. Mag. cal., 25 in. barrels, boxlock action, cocking indicators, hard case included.

Mfg.'s Sug. Retail	$10,500	$8,725	$6,475	$5,200	$4,300	$3,650	$3,300	$3,000

Add $1,400 for .375 H&H or .458 Win. Mag. cal.

Add $990 for DTs with front set trigger.

* *Teck-Handspanner* — manual cocking, 7x65R, .30-06, or .308 Win. cal. on 16 ga. receiver frame.

Mfg.'s Sug. Retail	$12,495	$10,200	$7,950	$6,675	$5,175	$4,375	$3,950	$3,200

ULTRA O/U — various cals. up to 9.3x74R, features unique manual cocking/self cocking device and interchangeable muzzle wedge for adjustable point of impact. New 1993.

Mfg.'s Sug. Retail	$6,970	$6,300	$5,625	$4,950	$4,250	$3,500	$2,950	$2,250

K

Grading	100%	98%	95%	90%	80%	70%	60%

CLASSIC O/U — same standard cals. as Teck O/U, boxlock action, light engraving. New 1995.

Mfg.'s Sug. Retail $7,850 $6,975 $5,900 $5,150 $4,300 $3,500 $2,950 $2,250

* *Classic O/U Big Bore* — .375 H&H, .416 Rigby, .458 Win. Mag., .470 NE, or .500 NE cal. New 1995.

Mfg.'s Sug. Retail $9,450 $8,250 $6,925 $5,950 $5,000 $4,150 $3,350 $3,150

ULM O/U — similar to Teck Double Rifle, except has any combination of cals., with sidelocks and more elaborate engraving.

Mfg.'s Sug. Retail $17,900 $14,300 $10,350 $8,550 $6,900 $6,100 $5,500 $4,950

     Add $695 for hand detachable sidelocks.
     Add $1,775 with single/double trigger.

* *Ulm Dekor* — sidelock with light scroll engraving. Importation disc. 1991.

                    $10,450 $9,150 $8,000 $6,750 $5,600 $5,000 $4,400
                                Last Mfg.'s Sug. Retail was $12,500.

* *Ulm Primus* — deluxe sidelock.

Mfg.'s Sug. Retail $26,000 $19,750 $13,000 $10,250 $8,100 $6,550 $5,700 $5,300

TRUMPF SxS — boxlock action, similar to Teck model, except in .30-06, 8x57JRS, or 9.3x74R cal. Disc. 1994.

                    $13,200 $9,700 $8,350 $6,900 $6,100 $5,500 $4,950
                                  Last Mfg.'s Sug. Retail was $16,150.

CLASSIC SxS STANDARD — same standard cals. as Teck O/U, boxlock action, 21½ (optional) or 23½ in. regulated barrels, DTs, manual cocking device, removable wedge and integrated front sight in cals. up to .375 H&H, extractors, choice of standard or bavarian style stock, light engraving, with or w/o side plates, various engraving options, 7½-11 lbs. New 1995.

Mfg.'s Sug. Retail $7,850 $6,950 $5,950 $5,150 $4,350 $3,500 $2,950 $2,250

     Add $2,995 for a set of 20 ga./3 in. barrels.
     Add $1,950 for side plates with standard scroll engraving.

* *Classic SxS Big Five (Big Bore)* — .375 H&H, .375 Flanged Mag. NE (new 1996), .416 Rigby, .458 Win. Mag., .470 NE, .500/.416 NE (new 1996) or .500 NE cal. New 1995.

Mfg.'s Sug. Retail $9,450 $8,300 $6,975 $5,975 $5,000 $4,150 $3,350 $3,150

     Add $2,995 for a set of 20 ga./3 in. barrels.
     Add $1,950 for side plates with standard scroll engraving.

NEPTUN SxS — sidelock double rifle, same features as the Ulm model. Importation disc. 1991.

                    $12,750 $10,400 $8,700 $7,350 $6,000 $5,450 $4,995
                                  Last Mfg.'s Sug. Retail was $15,500.

RIFLES: SINGLE SHOT

HUBERTUS RIFLE — available in .222 Rem., .243 Win., .270 Win., .30-06, .308 Win., .270 Wby. Mag., .300 Win. Mag., 7mm Rem. Mag., and in 12 metric cals. between 5.6x50R Mag.-8x57RS, single shot stalking rifle with Kickspanner (unique manual cocking device), engraved boxlock action, 23½ in. quarter ribbed barrel, fast lock time, double underlugs, approx. 6½ lbs. Importation began 1997.

Mfg.'s Sug. Retail $5,850 $5,375 $4,650 $3,975 $3,400 $2,950 $2,575 $1,850

     Add $1,000 for Mag. cals.
     Add $1,950 for sideplates with standard scroll engraving.

SHOTGUNS: O/U

     Subtract 20%-50% for shotguns mfg. before 1960.

Grading	100%	98%	95%	90%	80%	70%	60%

MODEL 32 STANDARD — 12, 20, 28 ga., or .410 bore, O/U, 28-32 in. high rib barrels, ejectors, boxlock, single trigger, select wood. Disc. 1983.

Standard	$3,500	$3,000	$2,700	$2,400	$2,100	$1,800	$1,500
San Remo	$7,000	$6,000	$5,000	$4,000	$3,000	$2,600	$2,200
Monte Carlo	$9,000	$7,500	$6,500	$5,500	$4,000	$3,000	$2,500
Crown	$10,000	$8,000	$7,000	$6,000	$4,500	$3,500	$3,000
Super Crown	$12,000	$10,000	$8,000	$7,000	$5,000	$4,000	$3,500

* *Low Rib* — 28 ga. or .410 bore.

$3,950	$3,575	$2,875	$2,650	$2,200	$1,900	$1,600

Add 50% for two-barrel set.

Allem's Guncraft, Inc. located in Zionsville, PA, still has limited quantities of original Model 32s (both O/U and single barrel) with a choice of 30 or 32 in. barrels (Vandalia or Low Rib). The current retail is $4,495. A limited supply of original Model 32 barrels (O/U and Single) is also available - retail price is $1,895.

MODEL 32 4-BARREL SKEET SET — 12, 20, 28 ga., or .410 bore, O/U, matched barrels in case, grades differ in engraving and wood quality, available as follows:

Standard	$11,250	$9,950	$8,650	$7,450	$6,200	$4,950	$3,700
München Grade	$13,250	$11,250	$9,500	$8,300	$6,600	$5,775	$5,225
San Remo Grade (unmarked)	$16,995	$13,750	$11,000	$9,000	$7,800	$6,600	$6,325
Monte Carlo (Silver Crown, 50 mfg.)	$18,750	$16,000	$13,750	$11,000	$9,000	$7,800	$6,600
Crown Grade (400 mfg.)	$24,995	$21,000	$17,750	$14,750	$12,100	$10,350	$9,650
Super Crown Grade (48 mfg.)	$29,995	$25,750	$20,750	$16,750	$14,775	$12,650	$10,350

K-80 TRAP — 12 ga. only, available in O/U, Unsingle, Top Single (single top barrel), and Combo (O/U with extra trap barrel) configurations, standard model has silver finished receiver, adj. rib allowing variable points of impact (new 1993). In O/U configuration the barrels are separated, about 8½ lbs. A wide variety of custom order options can be ordered on this model.

For the Model K-80 Trap, extra barrels cost $2,900 for O/Us, $2,950 for top single, and $3,575 for unsingle barrel.
$650 for O/U screw-in chokes (5 tubes).
Add $425 for 3 screw-in chokes (single barrel guns only).
Add $425 for single release trigger or $750 for double release trigger.

* *Standard Model* — special order only for Top Single, add 9% for Unsingle, or 40% for Combo Standard K-80 variations.

Mfg.'s Sug. Retail	$7,375	$6,200	$5,025	$4,250	$3,550	$3,000	$2,600	$2,295

* *Bavaria Model* — game scene engraved silver receiver with light scroll perimeter scroll work, select walnut. Special order only for Top Single, add 5% for Unsingle, or 24% for Combo Bavaria variations.

Mfg.'s Sug. Retail	$12,525	$10,575	$7,800	$6,375	$5,000	$4,375	$3,950	$3,300

* *Danube Model* — fine English scrollwork on receiver sides and floor plate. Special order only for Top Single, add 4.5% for Unsingle, or 20% for Combo Danube variations.

Mfg.'s Sug. Retail	$23,625	$19,325	$13,950	$10,750	$9,000	$7,150	$6,570	$5,850

* *Gold Target Model* — deep chiseled scroll engraving with gold line accents, 100% coverage finest quality walnut. Special order only for Top Single, add 3% for Unsingle, and 14% for Combo Gold Target variations.

Mfg.'s Sug. Retail	$27,170	$22,000	$15,500	$12,750	$9,500	$7,750	$7,000	$6,650

* *Centennial Model* — 12 ga. only, available in combo configuration only, 100 only mfg. 1986 to commemorate Krieghoff's centennial year, ser. no. 14501-14600. H. Krieghoff's signature inlaid in gold on frame sides. Add $150 for screw-in interchangeable chokes, $1,755 for 4-barrel set.

$6,000	$5,000	$4,400

Last Mfg.'s Sug. Retail was $5,995.

Grading	100%	98%	95%	90%	80%	70%	60%

K-80 SKEET — 12 ga. only, available in Lightweight (8mm rib), Standardweight (8mm rib), or International (12mm rib) configurations, factory porting on both barrels, 28 in. barrels only, 8.2 lbs.

> For the Model K-80 Skeet, add $925 for International Model (Tula choking/even choking became standard in 1996), $675 for Skeet Special (choke tubes & tapered flat rib).
>
> International Skeet models are supplied with hard case. Standardweight and Lightweight models include soft case.

* ***Standard Model*** — available with either Lightweight (Dural aluminum) or Standardweight frame. Hard case optional.

Mfg.'s Sug. Retail **$6,900**	**$5,850**	**$4,475**	**$3,375**	**$2,850**	**$2,450**	**$2,125**	**$1,900**

* ***Bavaria Model*** — game scene engraved silver receiver with light perimeter scroll work, select walnut. Available in either Standardweight or Lightweight (disc. 1995) configuration.

Mfg.'s Sug. Retail **$12,050**	**$10,050**	**$6,700**	**$5,700**	**$5,000**	**$4,375**	**$3,950**	**$3,300**

* ***Danube Model*** — fine English scrollwork on receiver sides and floor plate. Available in either Standardweight or Lightweight (disc. 1995) configuration.

Mfg.'s Sug. Retail **$23,150**	**$18,475**	**$14,000**	**$10,650**	**$9,000**	**$7,150**	**$6,570**	**$5,850**

* ***Gold Target Model*** — deep chiseled scroll engraving with gold line accents, 100% coverage finest quality walnut. This model is available in Standardweight frame only.

Mfg.'s Sug. Retail **$26,695**	**$21,650**	**$15,350**	**$12,850**	**$9,550**	**$7,750**	**$7,000**	**$6,650**

* ***Centennial Skeet*** — available in skeet configuration — special features as noted above on Centennial Model description listed under K-80 Trap. Mfg. 1986 only.

$3,675	**$3,150**	**$2,700**	

Last Mfg.'s Sug. Retail was $3,980.

K-80 2-BARREL LIGHTWEIGHT SKEET SET — 12 ga., includes one set of 28 in. barrels with Tula chokes and one set of carrier barrels allowing use of sub-gauge tubes (carrier barrels cannot be used for 12 ga.), 8mm rib, hard case standard. New 1988.

* ***Standard Grade***

Mfg.'s Sug. Retail **$11,840**	**$9,400**	**$7,000**	**$5,150**	**$4,300**	**$3,875**	**$3,300**	**$3,000**

> Subtract $1,845 for heavy barrel variation, which does not include sub-gauge tubes.
> Retail price for 2 barrel heavy set with choke tubes is $9,995.

* ***Bavaria Model*** — game scene engraved silver receiver with light perimeter scroll work, select walnut. Importation began 1988.

Mfg.'s Sug. Retail **$16,990**	**$14,975**	**$11,250**	**$8,575**	**$7,200**	**$6,200**	**$5,250**	**$4,800**

> Subtract $1,845 for heavy barrel variation, which does not include sub-gauge tubes.
> Retail price for 2 barrel heavy set with choke tubes is $15,145.

* ***Danube Model*** — fine English scroll work on receiver sides and floor plate. Importation began 1988.

Mfg.'s Sug. Retail **$28,090**	**$22,945**	**$15,250**	**$17,750**	**$9,400**	**$7,750**	**$7,000**	**$6,650**

> Subtract $1,845 for heavy barrel variation, which does not include sub-gauge tubes.
> Retail price for 2 barrel heavy set with choke tubes is $26,245.

* ***Gold Target Model*** — deep chiseled scroll engraving with gold line accents, 100% coverage finest quality walnut.

Mfg.'s Sug. Retail **$31,635**	**$25,975**	**$20,500**	**$15,950**	**$12,375**	**$9,950**	**$8,700**	**$7,500**

> Subtract $1,845 for heavy barrel variation.
> Retail price for 2 barrel heavy set with choke tubes is $29,790.

K-80 4-BARREL SKEET SET — 1 barrel each of 12, 20, 28 ga., and .410 bore, 12 ga. is Tula choked (even patterning), 8mm tapered flat or standard VR, includes hard case. Since most shooters prefer different gauge insert tubes (Briley, etc.) rather than barrel sets, values have gone down considerably recently for these 4 gauge sets.

K

Grading	100%	98%	95%	90%	80%	70%	60%

* ***Standard Grade*** — satin finished receiver with skeet scroll engraving.
  Mfg.'s Sug. Retail $16,950 $13,150 $7,625 $6,275 $5,350 $4,500 $4,000 $3,650

* ***Bavaria Model*** — game scene engraved silver receiver with light perimeter scrollwork, select walnut.
  Mfg.'s Sug. Retail $22,100 $18,200 $12,500 $9,750 $8,250 $6,900 $5,400 $4,350

* ***Danube Model*** — fine English scroll work on receiver sides and floor plate.
  Mfg.'s Sug. Retail $33,200 $26,100 $17,000 $13,000 $10,500 $8,700 $7,500 $6,250

* ***Gold Target Model*** — deep chiseled scroll engraving with gold line accents, 100% coverage finest quality walnut.
  Mfg.'s Sug. Retail $36,745 $29,650 $17,350 $13,000 $10,500 $8,700 $7,500 $6,250

K-80 PIGEON — 12 ga. only, available with 28, 29, or 30 in. barrels, standard tapered step rib, IM/SF choking, available in Lightweight or Standardweight configuration (no extra charge).

> Beginning 1992, the K-80 Pigeon Model is available by special order only. Rather than list the various Pigeon models separately, their current values will be approximately the same as the corresponding K-80 Trap/Skeet Models listed above.

K-80 SPORTING CLAYS O/U — 12 ga. only, 28, 30 (new 1991), or 32 (new 1993) in. barrels with 5 choke tubes, choice of 8mm VR skeet, tapered flat (broadway) or step rib (special order), sporting clay stock dimensions. New 1988.

> Add $3,195 for extra set of O/U barrels with 5 choke tubes.
> Add $2,800 for extra set of O/U barrels with 1 choke tube.

* ***Standard Grade*** — satin finished receiver with sporting scroll engraving.
  Mfg.'s Sug. Retail $8,150 $6,750 $5,425 $4,500 $3,650 $3,000 $2,600 $2,100

* ***Bavaria Model*** — game scene engraved silver receiver with light scroll perimeter scroll work, select walnut.
  Mfg.'s Sug. Retail $13,300 $10,800 $8,200 $6,600 $5,350 $4,450 $3,950 $3,300

* ***Danube Model*** — fine English scroll work on receiver sides and floor plate.
  Mfg.'s Sug. Retail $24,400 $19,000 $13,750 $10,750 $8,350 $7,000 $5,950 $4,950

* ***Gold Target Model*** — deep chiseled scroll engraving with gold line accents, 100% coverage finest quality walnut.
  Mfg.'s Sug. Retail $27,945 $22,350 $16,150 $13,350 $9,700 $7,875 $7,000 $6,650

ULM-P LIVE PIGEON O/U — 12 ga. only, live pigeon gun with hand detachable sidelocks, 28 or 30 in. VR barrels, standard grade has light scrollwork engraving.
  Mfg.'s Sug. Retail $22,500 $17,500 $12,000 $9,175 $7,700 $6,000 $5,450 $4,995

* ***Bavaria Grade*** — similar to Ulm-P, only with elaborate game scene engraving.
  Mfg.'s Sug. Retail $29,500 $22,000 $14,750 $11,450 $8,750 $6,750 $5,700 $5,300

KS-2 O/U SERIES — any ga., full H&H type sidelocks, priced by individual special order. Prices start at $24,000. Custom order only with substantial wait.

SHOTGUNS: O/U OR COMBINATION GUNS

> Add $695 for hand detachable sidelocks (Ulm only).
> Add $1,290 for 4-claw scope mount system.

TECK MODEL — 12 and 16 ga., O/U shotgun or rifle/shotgun combo., various cals. (7x57R, 7x64mm, 7x65R, .30-06, or .308 Win.), boxlock action, Kersten double crossbolt, auto ejectors, 7½ lbs.
  Mfg.'s Sug. Retail $7,750 $6,650 $5,100 $4,400 $3,550 $3,000 $2,600 $2,295

* ***Teck Dural*** — Dural aluminum frame variation of the Teck, 6.8 lbs.
  Mfg.'s Sug. Retail $7,750 $6,625 $5,100 $4,400 $3,550 $3,000 $2,600 $2,295

K

Grading	100%	98%	95%	90%	80%	70%	60%

ULM — similar to Teck, except sidelock and fully engraved with leaf arabesques.

Mfg.'s Sug. Retail **$14,500** **$11,700** **$8,975** **$7,600** **$6,350** **$5,250** **$4,400** **$3,500**

* *Ulm Dural* — Dural aluminum frame variation of the Ulm.

Mfg.'s Sug. Retail **$14,500** **$11,700** **$8,975** **$7,600** **$6,350** **$5,250** **$4,400** **$3,500**

ULM PRIMUS — similar to Ulm, except game scene engraved with English arabesques.

Mfg.'s Sug. Retail **$22,850** **$18,100** **$12,850** **$9,000** **$7,000** **$5,975** **$5,450** **$4,995**

* *Ulm Primus Dural* — Dural aluminum frame variation of the Ulm Primus.

Mfg.'s Sug. Retail **$22,850** **$18,100** **$12,850** **$9,000** **$7,000** **$5,975** **$5,450** **$4,995**

ULTRA — 12 ga. only, combination O/U, various calibers (lower barrel), 25 in. barrels, "Kick-spanner" mechanism allows manual cocking from thumb safety, satin finish receiver, VR, 6 lbs. New 1985.

Mfg.'s Sug. Retail **$4,950** **$3,975** **$2,575** **$1,850** **$1,400** **$1,200** **$1,050** **$900**

* *Ultra-B* — similar to Ultra, except features a selector to switch the front set trigger to the top shotgun barrel. Disc. 1995.

$4,050 **$2,675** **$1,925** **$1,550** **$1,350** **$1,150** **$1,000**

Last Mfg.'s Sug. Retail was $4,990.

SHOTGUNS: SINGLE BARREL TRAP

MODEL 32 — 12 ga., same action as O/U, 32-34 in. barrel, VR, mod., imp. mod., or full choke.

$1,850 **$1,400** **$1,200** **$1,000** **$895** **$795** **$695**

KS-5 — 12 ga. only, 32 or 34 in. barrel, adj. point of impact, innovative trigger configuration, optional choke tubes, redesigned streamlined receiver (new 1993). New 1985.

Mfg.'s Sug. Retail **$3,675** **$3,175** **$2,775** **$2,475** **$2,125** **$1,875** **$1,625** **$1,400**

Add $2,100 per additional barrel.
Add $425 for screw-in choke option.
Add $395 for factory adj. comb stock.
Add $425 for aluminum case.

Adj. point of impact on this model is achieved by means of different, optional front hangers.

* *KS-5 Special* — 12 ga. only, 32 or 34 in. barrel, features adj. rib and comb stock, cased. New 1990.

Mfg.'s Sug. Retail **$4,695** **$4,100** **$3,550** **$2,975** **$2,475** **$2,050** **$1,750** **$1,500**

Add $2,750 per additional barrel.
Add $425 for screw-in choke option.

K

NOTES

K

L section

L.A.R. MANUFACTURING, INC.

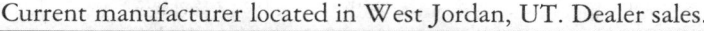

Current manufacturer located in West Jordan, UT. Dealer sales.

Grading	100%	98%	95%	90%	80%	70%	60%

PISTOLS: SEMI-AUTO

GRIZZLY WIN. MAG. MARK I — .357 Mag., .357/.45 Grizzly Win. Mag. (new 1990), .45 ACP, 10mm, or .45 Win. Mag. cal., single action, based on the Colt 1911 design, 5.4 in. (new 1986), 6½ in., 8 in. (new 1987), or 10 in. (new 1987) barrel, parkerized finish, 7 shot mag., ambidextrous safeties, checkered rubber grips, adj. sights, 48 oz. empty. Also can be converted to .45 ACP, 10mm (new 1988), .357 Mag., or .30 Mauser (disc.). New 1984.

* **Short Barrel Lengths** — 5.4 or 6.5 in. barrel.

Mfg.'s Sug. Retail	$1,000		$875	$675	$625	$525	$495	$475	$450

    Add $14 for .357 Mag. cal.
    Add $150 for hard chrome or nickel frame.
    Add $260 for full hard chrome or nickel frame.
    Add $233-$248 for cal. conversion units.

    Conversion units include .357 Mag., 10mm, .40 S&W (1991-1993 only), and .45 ACP cals.

* **Long Barrel Lengths** — .357 Mag., .45 Win. Mag., or .357/.45 Grizzly Win. Mag. (new 1990) cal., 8 or 10 in. barrel, extended slides. Disc. 1995.

		$1,195	$975	$895	$800	$725	$650	$575

    Last Mfg.'s Sug. Retail was $1,313.

    Add $62 for 10 in. barrel.
    Add $24 for .357 Mag.
    Add $143 for scope mounts (disc.).
    Add $110 for muzzle compensator.

* **Grizzly State Special Edition** — .45 Grizzly Win. Mag., 50 mfg. beginning 1998 to commemorate each state (ser. numbers match the order each state was admitted to the union), features gold etchings on frame, gold small parts, faux mother-of-pearl grips, cased. Limited mfg. beginning 1998.

    Please contact the factory regarding prices on this limited production model.

GRIZZLY .44 MAG. MARK 4 — .44 Mag. cal., choice of lusterless blue, parkerized, chrome, or nickel finish, 5⁴/₁₀ or 6½ in. barrel, adj. sights. New 1991.

Mfg.'s Sug. Retail	$1,014		$875	$715	$635	$550	$495	$475	$450

GRIZZLY .50 MARK 5 — .50 Action Express cal., single action semi-auto, 5⁴/₁₀ or 6½ in. barrel, 6 shot mag., checkered walnut grips, 56 oz. New 1993.

Mfg.'s Sug. Retail	$1,152	$1,025	$865	$720	$615	$525	$495	$475

    Add $178-$189 per coversion unit (new 1996).

GRIZZLY WIN. MAG. MARK II — similar to Mark I, except has fixed sights, standard safeties, and different metal finish. Mfg. 1986 only.

		$625	$550	$525	$495	$475	$450	$425

    Last Mfg.'s Sug. Retail was $550.

    Add $25 for .357 Mag.

Grading	100%	98%	95%	90%	80%	70%	60%

RIFLES: BOLT ACTION

BIG BOAR COMPETITOR RIFLE — .50 BMG cal., single shot, bolt action design in bullpup configuration, alloy steel receiver and bolt, 36 in. heavy barrel with compensator, thumb safety, 30.4 lbs, includes bipod, scope mount, leather cheek pad and hard carry case. New 1994.

Mfg.'s Sug. Retail	$2,570	$2,295	$1,925	$1,600	$1,275	$1,100	$995	$895

Add $100 for parkerizing.
Add $250 for nickel frame.
Add $350 for full nickel frame.
Add $329 for tripod and pintel mount.

L E S INCORPORATED

Previous manufacturer located in Morton Grove, IL.

PISTOLS: SEMI-AUTO

P-18 ROGAK — 9mm Para. cal., double action, 18 shot, 5½ in. barrel, stainless steel, black plastic grips with partial thumb rest. Disc.

	$350	$295	$265

* *High polish finish*

	$395	$330	$295

This pistol was patterned after the Steyr Model GB. Approx. 2,300 P-18s were mfg. before being disc.

LABANU INCORPORATED

Labanu, Inc. SKSs were manufactured by Norinco in China, and imported exclusively until 1998 by Labanu Inc., located in Ronkonkoma, NY.

RIFLES: SEMI-AUTO

SKS SPORTER RIFLE — 7.62x39mm cal., sporterized variation of the SKS with thumbhole stock, 16½ in. barrel, includes accessories, 5 lbs. Importation began 1995, banned 1998.

	$150	$135	$120	$100	$90	$85	$80

Last Mfg.'s Sug. Retail was $189.

LAHTI PISTOL

Previous manufacturer located in Husqvarna, Sweden. Also mfg. by Vkt (state rifle factory) in Jyvaskyla, Finland.

PSTOLS: SEMI-AUTO

SWEDISH MODEL 40 — 9mm Para. cal., 4¾ in. barrel, blued finish, fixed sights, plastic grips, mfg. 1940-1944.

	$395	$350	$300	$275	$260	$250	$240

Add 10% for Holster-Rig.

Note: It is important to note that there are diversely marked variations of this pistol, such as RPLT (Danish State Police); such police markings reduce value by about 10%.

FINNISH L-35 — 9mm Para., mfg. 1935-1944.

	$1,050	$900	$825	$760	$680	$620	$575

Add 100% for earlier pistols with shoulder stock lug.

LAKE FIELD ARMS LTD.

Current manufacturer located in Ontario, Canada. Lake Field Arms Ltd. was acquired by Savage Arms, Inc. during late

Grading	100%	98%	95%	90%	80%	70%	60%

1994. Distributor sales only through most major U.S. distributors.

Lake Field rifles manufactured after the Savage acquisition are marked Savage - please refer to the Savage section for current mfg.

RIFLES: .22 RIMFIRE

MARK I — .22 LR cal., single shot bolt action, 20¾ in. rifled or smooth bore barrel, adj. rear sight, thumb rotary safety, walnut finish hardwood stock, 5½ lbs. Disc.

	$110	$75	$65	$55	$50	$40	$30

Last Mfg.'s Sug. Retail was $135.

Add $14 for left-hand variation.

This model is also available in youth dimensions (19 in. barrel) at no extra charge (Model Mark I-Y).

MARK II — .22 LR cal., bolt action, 10 shot clip mag., 20¾ in. barrel, adj. rear sight, thumb rotary safety, walnut finish hardwood stock, 5½ lbs. Disc.

	$120	$80	$70	$60	$50	$40	$30

Last Mfg.'s Sug. Retail was $140.

Add $15 for left-hand variation (mfg. 1993-95).

This model is also available in youth dimensions (19 in. barrel) at no extra charge (Model Mark II-Y).

MODEL 64B — .22 LR cal., semi-auto, side ejection, 10 shot clip mag., 20¼ in. barrel, adj. rear sight, thumb rotary safety, walnut finish hardwood stock, 5½ lbs. Disc.

	$120	$85	$75	$65	$55	$45	$40

Last Mfg.'s Sug. Retail was $143.

MODEL 90B (BIATHLON) — .22 LR cal., biathlon rifle, includes five 5-shot mags., 21 in. barrel, aperture sights, one-piece natural finish hardwood stock, 8¼ lbs. Mfg. 1991-95.

	$430	$300	$225	$195	$170	$150	$130

Last Mfg.'s Sug. Retail was $570.

Add $55 for left-hand variation (new 1993).

MODEL 91T — .22 LR cal., target rifle, single shot, 25 in. barrel with aperture sights, dark hardwood finished stock, 8 lbs. Mfg. 1991-95.

	$340	$255	$215	$175	$150	$135	$115

Last Mfg.'s Sug. Retail was $455.

Add $45 for left-hand variation (mfg. 1993-95).

∗ **Model 91TR** — repeater version of the Model 91T, 5 shot mag. Mfg. 1993-95.

	$360	$265	$215	$175	$150	$135	$115

Last Mfg.'s Sug. Retail was $485.

Add $45 for left-hand variation (mfg. 1993-95).

MODEL 92S — .22 LR cal., 5 shot detachable mag., 21 in. barrel, hardwood stock with Monte Carlo cheekpiece, 8 lbs. Mfg. 1993-95.

	$300	$240	$200	$175	$160	$150	$135

Last Mfg.'s Sug. Retail was $388.

Add $37 for left-hand variation.

MODEL 93M — .22 Mag. cal., 5 shot clip mag., thumb operated rotary safety, 20¾ in. barrel, hardwood stock, 5¾ lbs. Mfg. 1995 only.

	$140	$120	$100	$85	$75	$65	$55

Last Mfg.'s Sug. Retail was $168.

LAKELANDER

Current trademark established during 1976 and currently manufactured by MIPRO AB (c. 1946-present) in Sweden. No current importation. Previously imported and distributed 1996-98 by Lakelander U.S.A., Inc. located in Gulfport, MS.

Grading	100%	98%	95%	90%	80%	70%	60%

RIFLES: BOLT ACTION

LAKELANDER 389 — .270 Win., .30-06, or .308 Win. cal., unique design with many shooter enhancements, 4 shot integrated mag. with rotary swing plate, 3 configurations including Premium (22 in. barrel with skip-line checkering and Monte Carlo stock), Classic (22 in. barrel, standard stock with checkering), Match-Maker (target model with 21.7 in. barrel and competition stock and adj. cheekpiece, .308 Win. only), 7.3-8.4 lbs. Mfg. 1996-98.

	$1,425	$1,225	$995	$850	$700	$600	$500

Last Mfg.'s Sug. Retail was $1,599.

Add $500 for Match-Maker Model.

LAMES

Previous manufacturer located in Italy.

SHOTGUNS: O/U

FIELD MODEL — 12 ga., 26, 28, or 30 in. barrels, various chokes, VR, engraving, SST, auto ejectors, checkered pistol grip stock with pad.

	$400	$380	$365	$350	$325	$300	$275

* *Separated barrels*

	$500	$480	$465	$450	$425	$400	$375

STANDARD TRAP — similar to Field, 30 or 32 in. various trap bore barrels, with wide VR, trap style Monte Carlo stock.

	$600	$575	$550	$525	$425	$400	$450

CALIFORNIA TRAP — similar to Standard Trap, with separated barrels.

	$700	$675	$650	$625	$525	$500	$450

SKEET MODEL — similar to Field, with 26 in. skeet bore barrels, skeet stock and separated barrels.

	$600	$575	$550	$525	$425	$400	$350

LANBER ARMAS S.A.

Current manufacturer located in Zaldibar, Spain. Currently imported by ITC International, Inc. located in Marietta, GA since 1996. Previously imported and distributed until 1994, by Eagle Imports, Inc. located in Wanamassa, NJ. Previously imported by Exel Arms of America, Inc., located in Gardener, MA, and by Lanber Arms of America located in Adrian, MI.

Lanber makes a wide range of quality O/U and semi-auto shotguns.

SHOTGUNS: O/U

The last Mfg.'s Sug. Retail on all models listed below reflects 1987 pricing. Please contact ITC International, Inc. directly (see listing in Trademark Index) for more information on current Lanber model availability and pricing.

EXEL SERIES 100: MODELS 101-104 — 12 ga., boxlock action, vent. rib, extractors, single trigger. Add $16 for 103 Mag., $92 for ejectors (Model 104 only).

	$400	$350	$310	$270	$240	$225	$200

Last Mfg.'s Sug. Retail was $451.

These models were previously designated the 844ST Series.

EXEL MODEL 105 — 12 ga., boxlock action, single trigger, ejectors, Lanber screw-in chokes, deluxe wood, engraved satin finish action.

	$575	$495	$440	$405	$370	$345	$310

Last Mfg.'s Sug. Retail was $644.

This model was previously designated the Model 2004LCH.

Grading	100%	98%	95%	90%	80%	70%	60%

EXEL MODELS 106 & 107 — 12 ga., similar to 105, only more deluxe version with vent. barrels and rib, blued receiver only, interchangeable Lanber screw-in chokes. Trap model is Model 107.

$725	**$625**	**$550**	**$500**	**$475**	**$450**	**$425**

Last Mfg.'s Sug. Retail was $845.

These models were previously designated 2008LCH and 2009LCH respectively.

The following models were imported by Lanber Arms of America, Inc. located in Adrian, MI until business ceased in late 1986.

844 ST — 12 ga. only, boxlock, 26 or 28 in. barrels, choked IC/IM, extractors, SST, automatic safety, VR, European walnut with hand checkering, blued finish with engraved receiver, 7⅛ lbs. Importation disc. 1986.

$395	**$340**	**$320**	**$300**	**$285**	**$270**	**$255**

Last Mfg.'s Sug. Retail was $450.

* *844 MST* — 12 ga. only, 3 in. chambers, 30 in. F & M barrels, otherwise similar to 844 ST. Importation disc. 1986.

$405	**$350**	**$335**	**$320**	**$310**	**$300**	**$295**

Last Mfg.'s Sug. Retail was $470.

2004 LCH — 12 ga. only, boxlock action, 28 in. barrels, SST, ejectors, supplied with 5 screw-in choke tubes, engraved satin finish receiver, checkered European walnut, 7⅜ lbs. Importation disc. 1986.

$575	**$485**	**$460**	**$440**	**$420**	**$395**	**$380**

Last Mfg.'s Sug. Retail was $650.

2004 LCH SKEET — 12 ga. only, 28 in. barrels supplied with 5 choke tubes, blued finish, moderately engraved, select checkered walnut, 7⅜ lbs. Importation disc. 1986.

$740	**$635**	**$585**	**$560**	**$540**	**$520**	**$495**

Last Mfg.'s Sug. Retail was $845.

2004 LCH TRAP — 12 ga. only, 30 in. barrels supplied with 3 choke tubes, European walnut has trap dimensions, blued finish. Importation disc. 1986.

$675	**$625**	**$585**	**$560**	**$540**	**$520**	**$495**

Last Mfg.'s Sug. Retail was $845.

MODEL 82 FIELD GRADE — 12 or 20 ga., 3 in. chambers, boxlock action, SST, ejectors, 26 or 28 in. VR barrels with fixed chokes, checkered walnut stock and forearm. Limited importation 1994 only.

$500	**$425**	**$395**	**$360**	**$330**	**$295**	**$275**

Last Mfg.'s Sug. Retail was $585.

MODEL 87 DELUXE FIELD GRADE — 12 or 20 ga., better quality walnut stock and forearm, 26 (20 ga. only) or 28 in. VR barrels with choke tubes. Limited importation 1994 only.

$800	**$675**	**$575**	**$500**	**$425**	**$350**	**$295**

Last Mfg.'s Sug. Retail was $915.

MODEL 97 SPORTING CLAYS — 12 ga. only, Sporting Clays configuration featuring 28 in. barrels with choke tubes. Limited importation 1994 only.

$835	**$695**	**$585**	**$500**	**$425**	**$350**	**$295**

Last Mfg.'s Sug. Retail was $965.

LANG, JOSEPH

Current trademark manufactured by Atkin, Grant & Lang, located in Hertfordshire, England. No current importer. Please contact the factory directly for more information and model availability.

Prices indicated below are for manufacturer's suggested retail and 100% condition factors are listed in English pounds. All new prices do not include VAT. Values for used guns in 98%-60% condition factors are priced in U.S. dollars.

Grading	100%	98%	95%	90%	80%	70%	60%

RIFLES: SxS

JOSEPH LANG DOUBLE RIFLE — available in cals. between .300 H&H - .577 NE, best quality double rifle, individually made per customer specifications.

Mfg.'s Sug. Retail	£19,000	£19,000	$21,950	$19,000	$16,250	$13,750	$11,750	$10,250

SHOTGUNS: SxS

IMPERIAL SIDELOCK EJECTOR — 12, 16, 20, 28 ga., or .410 bore, best quality sidelock ejector model, individually made per customer specifications.

Mfg.'s Sug. Retail	£25,000	£25,000	$28,875	$24,750	$20,750	$17,250	$15,000	$13,250

LASALLE

Previous manufacturer located in France.

SHOTGUNS

SLIDE ACTION SHOTGUN — 12 or 20 ga., 26, 28, or 30 in. barrels, various chokes, alloy frame, checkered pistol grip stock.

	$250	$225	$200	$175	$150	$125	$100

SEMI-AUTO SHOTGUN — 12 ga., 26, 28, or 30 in. barrels, various chokes, gas operated, checkered pistol grip stock.

	$300	$275	$250	$225	$200	$175	$150

LASERAIM ARMS, INC.

Current distributor located in Little Rock, AR. Currently manufactured in Thermopolis, WY. Laseraim Arms, Inc. is a division of Emerging Technologies, Inc. Direct or limited dealer sales only.

PISTOLS: SEMI-AUTO

SERIES I — .40 S&W, .400 Cor-Bon (new 1998), .45 ACP, or 10mm cal., single action, $3\frac{3}{8}$ (Compact Model), 5, or 6 in. barrel with compensator, ambidextrous safety, all stainless steel metal parts are Teflon coated, beveled mag. well, integral accessory mounts, 7 (.45 ACP) or 8 (10mm or .40 S&W) shot mag., 46 or 52 oz. New 1993.

Mfg.'s Sug. Retail	$349	$325	$295	$265

Add $120 for wireless laser combo (new 1997).

* **Compact Series I** — .40 S&W or .45 ACP cal., features $3\frac{3}{8}$ in. non-ported slide and fixed sights. New 1993.

Mfg.'s Sug. Retail	$349	$325	$295	$265

Series I Illusion and Dream Team variations were made during 1993-94. Retail prices respectively were $650 and $695.

SERIES II — .40 S&W (disc. 1994), .45 ACP, or 10mm cal., similar technical specs. as the Series I, except has non-reflective stainless steel finish, fixed or adj. sights, and $3\frac{3}{8}$ (Compact Model, .45 ACP only), 5, or 7 (.45 ACP only) in. non-compensated barrel, 37 or 43 oz. Mfg. 1993-96.

	$485	$385	$300

Last Mfg.'s Sug. Retail was $550.

Series II Illusion and Dream Team variations were made during 1993-94. Retail prices respectively were $500 and $545.

SERIES III — .45 ACP cal., 5 in. ported barrel, serrated slide, Hogue grips. Mfg. 1994-Disc.

	$595	$465	$415	$375	$345	$310	$275

Last Mfg.'s Sug. Retail was $675.

Grading	100%	98%	95%	90%	80%	70%	60%

SERIES IV — .45 ACP cal., 3⅜ (Compact Model) or 5 in. ported barrel, serrated slide, diamond checkered wood grips. Mfg. 1994-Disc.

	$550	$450	$400	$360	$330	$300	$265

Last Mfg.'s Sug. Retail was $625.

LAURONA

Current trademark manufactured by Armas Eibar, S.A.L., located in Eibar, Spain. Currently imported by Galaxy Imports located in Victoria, TX.

Laurona was founded in Eibar during 1941 by four craftsmen (hence the name Laurona, which in Basque means "of the four"), each a specialist in a discipline of shotgun mfg. Laurona made SxS guns until 1978, at which time they discontinued mfg. to concentrate on the O/U marketplace.

Laurona manufactures high quality O/U shotguns and O/U express rifles/combination guns. Beginning 1992, Laurona switched from a one-piece, demi-block type of fabrication to a monobloc system which has improved strength characteristics while reducing weight in their X-Series line of shotguns and express rifles.

Laurona long guns come standard with a Black Chrome metal finish that is extremely resistant to oxidation. Left hand stocks are available for the 83 MG Super Game, 85 MS Super Game, Trap, and Super Skeet, Silhouette Trap models, and Silhouette Sporting Clays.

Suffix designations on Laurona shotguns refer to the following: G - twin non-selective triggers, S - selective single trigger, M - multi-chokes, T - Tulip, BV - beavertail, U - single non-selected triggers.

All Super Game Models were available with a deluxe package which includes a recoil pad, mid-bead sight, and select wood for an additional $250. Special order dull matte finished barrels (with multi-chokes) were available for an additional $200 - extra barrels were priced between $635 (20 ga.) or $800 (12 ga.) per set.

If more information is required on an older Laurona model not listed in this publication (including ser. no. dating), please contact Galaxy Imports (see Trademark Index). For an accurate appraisal, please send a complete description of your specimen (including Laurona model name, serial number, and other pertinent data - include photos if possible). The charge for this service is $25 per serial number.

RIFLES: O/U CURRENT MFG.

MODEL 2000X EXPRESS RIFLE — .30-06, 8x57 JRS, 8x57 RS, 9.3x74 R, or .375 H&H cal., monobloc construction, 24 in. separated barrels featuring quarter rib sight and convergency adjustment at muzzle, matte black chrome finish, open sights, ejectors or extractors, SST or DT, approx. 8.1 lbs. New 1992.

This model must be custom ordered - please contact Galaxy Imports for more information.

This model accepts Leupold or European styled ring mounts.

✳ *Model 2000X Combo* — includes choice of cals. listed above, except for .375 H&H cal. with 12 ga. under-barrel. New 1992.

This model must be custom ordered - please contact Galaxy Imports for more information.

SHOTGUNS: O/U, RECENT MFG.

While no current Laurona shotguns are listed, Galaxy Imports should be contacted (see listing in Trademark Index) regarding Laurona's current models and domestic pricing.

L

Grading	100%	98%	95%	90%	80%	70%	60%

The author wishes to express his thanks to Thomas E. Barker for making the following information available.

1967 Series (Earliest O/U Model)

MODEL 67 (VERSIONS G & U) — 12 ga., first O/U model mfg. with manual extractors, G designation stands for Gemini for twin select trigger system (triggers will function as single or double), front trigger is non-selective firing in bottom to top sequence, and back trigger in top to bottom sequence, U designation stands for non-selective single triggers, boxlock action and barrel bluing, light walnut stock, skip diamond checkering.

	$500	$400	$350	$300	$250	$200	$150

1971 Series

MODEL 71 (VERSIONS G & U) — similar to Model 67 with minor improvements, bright chrome receiver with rolled engraved game scene, earlier models had traditional solid center ribbed blued barrels, later models had solid ribbed barrels with Black Chrome finish. G & U designations are the same as Model 67.

This model was imported and sold by Sears & Roebuck in 1973-74.

	$500	$400	$350	$300	$250	$200	$150

1982 Series

12 ga. only, similar to Model 71 with auto-ejectors. (Manual extractors were disc.) Firing pins changed to traditional round type, many internal parts were improved for better reliability. Skip diamond and standard checkering. All SUPER Series barrels separated (w/o center rib) with Black Chrome finish and hard chrome bores with long forcing cones in chambers. In most respects, the 82 Models are representative to present day Laurona O/U shotguns and will share most internal parts. G & U designations are the same as Model 67.

MODEL 82 GAME (VERSIONS G & U) — 12 ga, 28 in. black chromed barrels, 2¾ or 3 in. long forcing cones, solid side ribs, hard chrome bores, 5mm vent. rib, chokes ★★★★/★★ or ★★★/★ (IC/IM/M/F), Imperial nickel receiver with Louis XVI style engraving, tulip forend, field stock drop 35/65mm with plastic butt plate, 7 lbs.

	$550	$475	$400	$350	$300	$250	$200

MODEL 82 TRAP COMBO (VERSIONS G & U) — 12 ga., similar to 82 Game, except has 28 (chokes ★★★/★) or 29 (chokes ★★/★) in. barrels, steel rib, 8mm trap buttstock drop 35/55mm with rubber special trap recoil pad, 8 lbs.

	$550	$475	$400	$350	$300	$250	$200

82 TRAP COMPETITION (VERSION U) — 12 ga., similar to 82 Trap Combo, except has 13mm aluminum rib with long white sight, engraved motif on receiver, beavertail fluted forend, Monte Carlo trap stock drop 35/35/55mm with black rubber special trap recoil pad, 8 lbs.

	$600	$550	$475	$400	$350	$300	$250

82 PIGEON COMPETION (VERSION U) — 12 ga., similar to 82 Trap Competition, excpet has 28 in. barrels choked ★★★★/★★ or ★★★/★. Recoil pad special competiton Pachmayr with imitation leather face, 7 lbs, 13 oz.

	$650	$600	$550	$475	$400	$350	$300

Model 82 Super Series

The Super Models listed below have nickel finished receivers with full coverage, delicate scroll engraving with Black Chrome relief and forend iron. All barrels are split (w/o side ribs), and have very durable rust resistance Black Chrome finish.

82 SUPER GAME (VERSIONS G & U) — 12 ga., similar to 82 Game, except has more elaborate fine scroll engraving.

	$575	$475	$400	$350	$300	$250	$200

Grading	100%	98%	95%	90%	80%	70%	60%

82 SUPER TRAP (VERSION U) — 12 ga., similar to 82 Trap Competition, except has special trap Pachmayr recoil pad with imitation leather face and fine scroll engraving.

	$675	$600	$550	$475	$400	$350	$300

82 SUPER SKEET — 12 ga., similar to 82 Super Tap, except has 28 in. barrels choked Skeet/Skeet, buttstock drop 35/65mm with plastic buttplate, 7 lbs.

	$600	$550	$475	$400	$350	$300	$250

82 SUPER PIGEON — 12 ga., similar to 82 Super Trap, except has 28 in. barrels choked ★★★★/★★ or ★★★/★, 7 lbs, 9 oz.

	$675	$600	$550	$475	$400	$350	$300

Model 83 Super Series

83MG SUPER GAME — 12 or 20 ga., 3 in. chambers, 26 (20 ga. only) or 28 in. barrels, 8mm rib, similar to 82 Super Game, except had Laurona's new multi-choke, not compatible with any other brand of screw in chokes because of the Black Chrome plating of the metric threads, 7 lbs.

	$995	$675	$600	$550	$475	$400	$350

Model 84 Super Series

The Super Game Models listed below were available with an extra set of 26 or 28 in. 20 ga. multi-choke barrels and cast-on stocks for left-handed shooters.

Add $400 for multi-choke barrels.
Add $50 for left hand stock.

84S SUPER GAME — 3 in. chambers, similar to 82 Super Game, except for new single selective trigger, ejectors, 28 in. barrels choked IC/IM or M/F, 8mm rib, 7 lbs.

	$675	$600	$550	$475	$400	$350	$300

84S SUPER SKEET — 12 ga. only, 2¾ in. chambers, with elongated forcing cones, 28 in. separated barrels choked Skeet/Skeet, 13mm aluminum rib, extensive fine scroll engraving, rust resistant Black Chrome finish, 7 lbs. Imported 1988-1990.

$1,495	$1,250	$975	$875	$750	$625	$500

84S SUPER TRAP — 12 ga., 29 in. barrels with 2¾ chambers and long forcing cones, chokes IM and full, 13mm aluminum rib, auto ejectors, nickel plated receiver with fine scroll engraving, Black Chrome relief, beavertail forearm, MC or standard trap stock, 7 lbs., 12 oz.

	$1,250	$975	$875	$750	$625	$550	$475

Model 85 Super Series

85MS SUPER GAME — 12 or 20 ga., 3 in. chambers, similar to 83MG Super Game, except for single selective trigger, 7 lbs.

	$995	$675	$600	$550	$475	$400	$350

85MS SUPER TRAP — similar to 84S Super Trap, except for multi-choke in bottom barrel with fixed full on top, 7 lbs., 12 oz.

	$1,250	$975	$875	$750	$625	$550	$475

85MS SUPER PIGEON — similar to 85MS Super Trap, except for 28 in. barrels with fixed IM choke on top with multi-choke on bottom, intended for live bird competition, 7 lbs., 4 oz.

	$1,250	$975	$875	$750	$625	$550	$475

85MS SPECIAL SPORTING — similar to 85MS Super Pigeon, except field butt stock with plastic buttplate, intended for upland game, 7 lbs., 4 oz.

	$1,250	$975	$875	$750	$625	$550	$475

Grading	100%	98%	95%	90%	80%	70%	60%

Excel 300 Series

EXEL 300 SERIES — 12 or 20 ga. The Model 301 is basic field gun, and the Model 310 was the highest grade.

* **Models 301 and 302** — 12 ga., double selective trigger system, ejectors, pistol grip, vent. rib, lightly engraved chrome finish receiver, various chokes and barrel lengths. Importation disc. 1986.

	$485	$415	$380	$340	$300	$275	$250

Last Mfg.'s Sug. Retail was $553.

* **Models 303 and 304** — 12 ga., similar to 301/302, except has better engraving on coin finish receiver, vent. barrels. Importation disc. 1987.

	$545	$470	$430	$385	$340	$315	$270

Last Mfg.'s Sug. Retail was $623.

Previously designated Model 82G Super.

* **Models 305(A) and 306(A)** — 12 or 20 ga., similar to 303/304, except has better engraving on coin finish receiver, screw-in choke tubes. Importation disc. 1987.

	$625	$535	$470	$430	$390	$350	$315

Last Mfg.'s Sug. Retail was $711.

Previously designated Models 83MG and 85MS.

* **Models 307 and 308** — 12 ga., trap model, 29 in. barrels, extensive engraving, Monte Carlo stock. Importation disc. 1987.

	$580	$500	$460	$420	$380	$340	$300

Last Mfg.'s Sug. Retail was $668.

Previously designated Model 82U Trap.

* **Models 309 and 310** — super trap model, 29 in. vent. barrels, more extensive engraving than Models 307/308. Importation disc. 1987.

	$630	$545	$495	$460	$415	$385	$340

Last Mfg.'s Sug. Retail was $726.

Previously designated Model 82 S. Trap.

Silhouette 300 Series

These shotguns are basically the same as the Super Series above, with the following exceptions; this series was readily indentifiable by their white and black chrome striped receiver, with the model engraved on the receiver side. Barrels were multi-choked on both bores and had an 11mm steel rib.

Two types of chokes were used. Some guns came with knurl head type as in the Super Models, and others were made with flush Invector style. A later option for ease of changing chokes was the knurl long choke, which is a flush type with the knurl head added. Both later type chokes (flush and knurl long), can be used in the early multi-choke models with some extension showing.

SILHOUETTE 300 TRAP — 12 ga., 2¾ in. chambers, 29 in. 11mm VR barrels with long forcing cones and hard chrome bores, beavertail forearm and straight comb trap stock with vent. black rubber recoil pad, 8 lbs.

	$1,250	$975	$875	$775	$700	$650	$595

SILHOUETTE 300 SPORTING CLAYS — 12 ga., 3 in. chambers, similar to 300 Trap, except has 28 in. barrels and butt stock is field type with plastic buttplate or hard rubber sporting clays pad, 7½ lbs.

	$1,250	$975	$875	$775	$700	$650	$595

SILHOUETTE 300 ULTRA MAGNUM — 12 ga. 3½ in. chambers, similar to 300 Sporting Clays, Black Chrome finish, 7½ lbs.

	$1,300	$1,025	$875	$775	$700	$650	$595

Grading	100%	98%	95%	90%	80%	70%	60%

SHOTGUNS: SxS, BOXLOCK

Shotguns mfg. after 1975 with "X" after the model number featured Black Chrome barrels and action with hard chrome bores. 28 ga. and .410 bore could be special ordered. SxS shotguns were disc. by Laurona during 1978 in an effort to concentrate on the O/U marketplace.

MODEL 11 — 12, 16, or 20 ga., triple Greener type round crossbolt with independent firing pins bushed into the face of the action, Bellota steel barrels.

	$400	$350	$315	$260	$210	$175	$140

MODEL 13 — 12, 16, or 20 ga., similar to Model 11, except utilizes Purdey type bolt system, extractors are of double radius, sold through Sears & Roebuck.

	$400	$350	$315	$260	$210	$175	$140

* *Model 13 E* — similar to Model 13, except has ejectors.

	$500	$450	$395	$350	$315	$260	$210

* *Model 13 X* — similar to Model 13, except has Black Chrome finished barrels and action with hard chrome bores.

	$500	$450	$395	$350	$315	$260	$210

* *Model 13 XE* — similar to Model 13 E, except has Black Chrome finish and hard chrome bores

	$600	$525	$450	$395	$350	$315	$260

MODEL 15 ECONOMIC PLUMA — 12, 16, or 20 ga., similar to Model 13, except was first model to have hard chrome bores.

	$450	$395	$350	$315	$260	$210	$175

* *Model 15 E Economic Pluma* — similar to Model 15 Economic Pluma, except has ejectors.

	$550	$475	$400	$350	$315	$260	$210

* *Model 15 X* — similar to Model 15 Economic Pluma, except has Black Chrome finish and hard chrome bores.

	$500	$450	$395	$350	$315	$260	$210

* *Model 15 XE* — similar to Model 15 E, except has ejectors.

	$600	$525	$450	$395	$350	$315	$260

MODEL 52 PLUMA — 12, 16, or 20 ga., back of actions scalloped and engraved in fine English scroll, Churchill rib and double radius extractors, hard chrome bores, 6 lbs.

	$750	$675	$600	$525	$450	$395	$350

* *Model 52 E Pluma* — similar to Model 52 pluma, except has ejectors, 6 lbs., 2 oz.

	$850	$750	$675	$600	$525	$450	$395

L

SHOTGUNS: SxS, SIDELOCK

Models listed below were available in 12, 16, or 20 ga. 28 ga. and .410 bore were available by special order.

MODEL 103 — 12, 16, or 20 ga., blued sidelocks with light border engraving, triple Purdey type bolt system, double radius extractors, Bellota steel barrels with hard chrome bores.

	$895	$800	$675	$575	$525	$475	$425

* *Model 103-E* — similar to Model 103 except with ejectors.

	$995	$895	$800	$675	$575	$525	$475

MODEL 104 X — 12, 16, or 20 ga., case colored sidelock with Purdey type bolting system, double radius extractors, fine double safety sidelocks, gas relief vents, articulated trigger, hard chromed bore, demi-block barrels of special Bellota steel, Black Chrome barrels.

	$1,200	$1,075	$925	$825	$700	$600	$525

Grading	100%	98%	95%	90%	80%	70%	60%

* *Model 104 XE* — same as Model 104 X, but with H&H style automatic selective ejectors.

	$1,350	$1,200	$1,075	$925	$825	$700	$575

MODEL 105 X FEATHER — 12, 16, or 20 ga., similar to Model 104 X, except has concave rib, approx. 6 lbs. 2 oz. (12 ga.).

	$1,250	$1,100	$950	$875	$800	$725	$650

* *Model 105 XE Feather* — similar to Model 105 X, except has H&H automatic selective ejectors.

	$1,400	$1,225	$1,075	$925	$850	$775	$700

MODEL 502 FEATHER — 12, 16, or 20 ga., Purdey type bolting system, hand detachable sidelocks, gas relief vents, H&H style automatic selective ejectors, articulated trigger, inside hard chromed demi-block barrels of special Bellota steel, Black Chrome finish, fine English scroll engraving, marble grey or Laurona Imperial finish, Churchill or concave type rib, 6.4 lbs. (12 ga.).

	$2,200	$2,050	$1,875	$1,650	$1,525	$1,400	$1,275

MODEL 801 DELUXE — 12, 16, or 20 ga., similar to Model 502 Feather, except engraving is true deluxe Renaissance style, fully hand made with Laurona Imperial finish, best qulaity checkered walnut stock and forearm.

	$4,400	$4,150	$3,650	$3,250	$2,900	$2,600	$2,250

MODEL 802 EAGLE — 12, 16, or 20 ga., similar to Model 801 Deluxe, except features highly artistic bas-relief engraving of hunting scenes, hand engraved with burin and chisel.

	$5,000	$4,400	$3,900	$3,375	$2,825	$2,375	$1,875

LAW ENFORCEMENT ORDNANCE CORPORATION

Previous manufacturer located in Ridgway, PA until 1990.

SHOTGUNS: SEMI-AUTO

STRIKER-12 — 12 ga. Mag., paramilitary design shotgun featuring 12 shot rotary mag., 18¼ in. barrel, semi-auto, alloy shrouded barrel with PG extension, folding or fixed paramilitary design stock, 9.2 lbs., limited mfg. 1986-1990.

	$595	$550	$500	$450	$425	$395	$375

Last Mfg.'s Sug. Retail was $725.

Add $150 for folding stock.
Add $100 for Marine variation ("Metal Life" finish).

Earlier variations were imported and available to law enforcement agencies only. In 1987, manufacture was started in PA and these firearms could be sold to individuals (18 in. barrel only). This design was originally developed in South Rhodesia.

HARRY LAWSON CO.

Current custom gun manufacturer and customizer established during 1965 and currently located in Tucson, AZ. Consumer direct sales.

Harry Lawson Co. is well known for custom stock work. This company also manufactures their own line of sporting rifles, featuring many innovative stock designs. Please contact the factory directly for more information regarding custom model availability/configuration and current pricing.

RIFLES: BOLT ACTION

LAWSON 650 SERIES — various Wby. Mag. cals., features Wby. Mark V barreled action with choice of Burris scope, mounts, custom stabilizer sling, and Doskocil hardshell case, prices below include new Mark V .340 Wby. Mag. action with black fiberglass "Cochise" stock. Many wood stock options available.

Mfg.'s Sug. Retail	$2,845		$2,600	$2,175	$1,750	$1,500	$1,350	$1,225	$1,100

Grading	100%	98%	95%	90%	80%	70%	60%

LAWSON 650 MOUNTAINEER & ULTRALITE SERIES — various cals., features Rem. 700 barreled action, otherwise similar to Lawson 650 Series, prices below include new Rem. 700 action with black fiberglass "Cochise" stock. Many wood stock options available.

Mfg.'s Sug. Retail	$2,400	$2,150	$1,750	$1,500	$1,350	$1,225	$1,100	$995

LAZZERONI ARMS COMPANY

Current manufacturer located in Tucson, AZ since 1995. Direct/dealer sales.

RIFLES: BOLT ACTION

Lazzeroni ammunition is precision loaded in Lazzeroni's Tucson facility under rigid tolerances. All ammunition is sealed for absolute weatherproofing.

SAKO MODEL TRG-S WARBIRD — .308 Warbird, features Sako TRG action with free floating 26 in. barrel, 3 shot detachable mag., fully adj. trigger, and scope rings. New 1999.

Mfg.'s Sug. Retail	$1,095	$1,000	$900	$825	$750	$675	$600	$525

MODEL 700ST — various Lazzeroni cals., Rem. M-700 action, features remachined bolt face, squared recoil lug and receiver, mag. and follower are replaced with Lazzeroni style units, steel (disc.) or stainless steel (new 1999) action, blue steel or stainless steel 24 in. barrel. New 1998.

Mfg.'s Sug. Retail	$2,395	$2,150	$1,750	$1,425	$1,150	$1,000	$950	$875

MODEL 2000 SERIES — .243 Flash (new 1998), .257 Scramjet, .264 Blackbird (new 1998), .284 Firehawk, .308 Warbird, .338 Titan, .375 Saturn (new 1998), or .416 Meteor (new 1997) features precision machined steel (disc.) or stainless steel (new 1999) receiver, helically fluted bolt with heavy duty extractor, stainless steel match barrel with integral muzzle brake, adj. benchrest trigger, matte finish metal, 3 position firing pin safety on most models (new 1999), 2 or 3 (new 1999) shot internal mag., various stock configurations. New 1996.

* **Model L2000ST-F** — features 27 in. barrel with conventional fiberglass stock.

Mfg.'s Sug. Retail	$4,195	$3,750	$3,350	$2,900	$2,550	$2,250	$1,975	$1,725

* **Model L2000ST-28** — .308 Warbird, shoots 130 grain BarnesX boatail at 4,000 fps, 28 in. stainless steel fluted barrel, includes Schmidt & Bender 4X-16X x 50mm scope, stainless action, black synthetic stock, approx. 8.3 lbs. New 1999.

Mfg.'s Sug. Retail	$6,310	$5,875	$5,250	$4,750	$4,250	$3,750	$3,250	$2,500

    This model is advertised as the flattest shooting hunting rifle currently manufactured, and is zeroed in at 100, 200, and 300 yards.

* **Model L2000ST-W** — features 27 in. barrel with conventional black wood laminate stock. Mfg. 1996 only.

$4,400	$4,050	$3,600	$3,200	$2,800	$2,400	$2,000

Last Mfg.'s Sug. Retail was $4,795.

* **Model L2000ST-WF Package** — features 27 in. barrel with one conventional fiberglass and one black wood laminate stock. Disc. 1997.

$4,875	$4,450	$4,050	$3,600	$3,200	$2,800	$2,400

Last Mfg.'s Sug. Retail was $5,295.

* **Model L2000DG** — 9.53 Saturn or 10.57 Meteor cal. only, features Fibergrain stock finish, removable muzzle brake, 3 shot mag., 24 in. barrel, includes sling swivels, 10.1 lbs. Mfg. 1998 only.

$3,925	$3,500	$3,000	$2,650	$2,300	$1,975	$1,725

Last Mfg.'s Sug. Retail was $4,395.

* **Model L2000SA-F** — .243 Spitfire, .264 Phantom, .284 Tomahawk, .308 Patriot, .338 Galaxy, .358 Eagle, .375 Hellcat, or .416 Maverick cal., short action cals. only, lightweight mountain configuration with 24 in. fluted barrel, 6.8 lbs. New 1998.

Mfg.'s Sug. Retail	$4,195	$3,750	$3,350	$2,900	$2,550	$2,250	$1,975	$1,725

Grading	100%	98%	95%	90%	80%	70%	60%

* **Model L2000SLR** — features 28 in. extra heavy fluted barrel and conventional fiberglass stock, not chambered in .338 Titan. Disc. 1999.

	$3,775	$3,400	$2,975	$2,625	$2,300	$1,975	$1,725

Last Mfg.'s Sug. Retail was $4,195.

* **L2000SP** — 23 in. barrel, thumbhole fiberglass stock.

Mfg.'s Sug. Retail	$4,195	$3,750	$3,350	$2,900	$2,550	$2,250	$1,975	$1,725

* **L2000SP-W** — 23 in. barrel, thumbhole black wood laminate stock.

	$4,400	$4,050	$3,600	$3,200	$2,800	$2,400	$2,000

Last Mfg.'s Sug. Retail was $4,795.

* **L2000SP-FW Package** — features 23 in. barrel with one thumbhole fiberglass and one black wood laminate thumbhole stock. Disc. 1997.

	$4,875	$4,450	$4,050	$3,600	$3,200	$2,800	$2,400

Last Mfg.'s Sug. Retail was $5,295.

LEBEAU-COURALLY

Current manufacturer established during 1865 and located in Liege, Belgium. Currently imported by William Larkin Moore, located in Scottsdale, AZ. Previously imported unitl 1998 by New England Arms Co. located in Kittery Point, ME.

Lebeau-Courally manufactures only best quality rifles and shotguns. Approximately 50 are manufactured annually.

RIFLES: SINGLE SHOT

SINGLE SHOT — 6.5x57 R, 7x65 R, or other metric cals., best quality, boxlock or sidelock action.

The importer should be contacted directly (see Trademark Index) for current information and prices regarding this model.

RIFLES: SxS

BOXLOCK EJECTOR — 8x57 JRS or 9.3x74 R cal., Anson & Deeley boxlock, ejectors, select French walnut stock, quarter rib with ramp front sight, about 8 lbs. Importation disc. 1988, resumed 1993.

Mfg.'s Sug. Retail	$19,100	$17,500	$15,750	$13,250	$11,500	$9,250	$7,500	$6,250

Add $1,400 for standard cals.

SIDELOCK EJECTOR — 7x65 R, 8x57 JRS, 9.3x74 R, .30-06, .375 H&H, .458 Win. Mag., .470 NE (new 1991), or .577 NE (new 1992) cal., chopper lump barrels, reinforced action, select French walnut stock, quarter rib with ramp front sight, approx. 8 lbs.

Mfg.'s Sug. Retail	$48,000	$43,700	$38,000	$31,500	$25,500	$21,250	$18,000	$16,000

SHOTGUNS: O/U

SIDELOCK — 12, 20, or 28 ga., Greener locking system.

Mfg.'s Sug. Retail	$37,600	$33,800	$29,000	$24,500	$20,750	$17,500	$14,500	$11,850

BOSS MODEL — 12 or 20 ga., Boss pattern sidelock with low profile action, top-of-the-line O/U individually made to customer specifications.

Mfg.'s Sug. Retail	$76,000	$69,500	$59,750	$51,750	$41,500	$33,250	$25,000	$21,000

SHOTGUNS: SxS

For currently manufactured shotguns — add $2,950 for single trigger. Older mfg. Lebeau-Courally shotguns have a completely different action and locking system than the newer models.

SOLOGNE — 12, 16, or 20 ga., Anson & Deeley boxlock action, various chokes and barrel lengths, select walnut, no engraving. Add $850 for false sideplates.

Mfg.'s Sug. Retail	$14,650	$13,250	$11,250	$9,350	$7,500	$6,250	$5,150	$4,350

Grading	100%	98%	95%	90%	80%	70%	60%

GRAND RUSSE MODEL — grade up from Sologne Model.

Mfg.'s Sug. Retail	$18,820	$16,480	$13,000	$10,750	$8,475	$7,375	$5,250	$4,450

BOXLOCK EJECTOR — 12, 16, or 20 ga., choice of classic or rounded action, with or without sideplates, select French walnut stock, choice of numerous engraving patterns (optional), 26, 28, or 30 in. barrels, double trigger.

Mfg.'s Sug. Retail	$21,100	$18,800	$16,350	$13,250	$11,000	$9,750	$8,500	$7,250

* *Boxlock with sideplates*

Mfg.'s Sug. Retail	$15,500	$13,850	$11,650	$9,650	$7,700	$6,250	$5,150	$4,350

SIDELOCK EJECTOR — 12, 16, 20, 28 ga., or .410 bore, choice of classic or rounded action, chopper lump barrels, select French walnut stock, choice of numerous engraving patterns (optional), 26, 28, or 30 in. barrels, double triggers.

Mfg.'s Sug. Retail	$43,700	$38,500	$34,250	$29,750	$25,000	$21,750	$18,750	$14,750

Add 10% for 28 ga. or .410 bore.

LEFEVER ARMS COMPANY

Previous shotgun manufacturer located in Syracuse, NY circa 1885-1948.

100%	98%	95%	90%	80%	70%	60%	50%	40%	30%	20%	10%

SHOTGUNS: SxS

The Lefever was the first commercially successful hammerless double barrel shotgun made in America. They were made in Syracuse, NY from 1885-1916, at which time the company was acquired by Ithaca Gun Company. Ithaca made the Lefever after 1916. In 1921, the Box Lock Nitro Special was introduced and in 1934, the Lefever Grade A was introduced. Production of Lefever guns ceased in 1948.

The following is a percentage breakdown of gauges made between 1885-1916 (totaling 100%): 8 ga.—½%, 10 ga.—25%, 12 ga.—60%, 14 ga.—½%, 16 ga.—8%, 20 ga.—6%. Total manufacture was approx. 72,000 during this period. Damascus specimens of this trademark are worth approximately the same if in 60% or better original condition as their fluid steel barrel counterparts because of the rarity and desirability factors. Subtract 10%-30% on values with respective condition factors 50%-10%. Prices shown below for 90% and up condition are very difficult to evaluate and are meant as a guide only - any Lefever shotgun is rare and hard to evaluate if in over 95%.

SIDELOCK MODELS — 10, 12, 16, or 20 ga., 26-32 in. barrels, any choke, boxlock action (even though model nomenclature referred to sidelock model), cocking indicators on all but DS and DSE grades, double triggers standard, checkered straight or pistol grip stock, auto ejectors designated by letter E after grade. Mfg. 1885-1919.

Add 50% for 16 ga.
Add 100% for 20 ga.
Add 10% for SST.

* *I Grade*

100%	98%	95%	90%	80%	70%	60%	50%	40%	30%	20%	10%
$1,375	$1,250	$1,025	$925	$850	$775	$700	$630	$565	$500	$425	$350

* *DS Grade*

100%	98%	95%	90%	80%	70%	60%	50%	40%	30%	20%	10%
$1,375	$1,250	$1,025	$925	$850	$775	$700	$630	$565	$500	$425	$350

* *DSE Grade*

100%	98%	95%	90%	80%	70%	60%	50%	40%	30%	20%	10%
$1,800	$1,525	$1,250	$1,100	$950	$850	$775	$715	$650	$600	$540	$475

* *H Grade*

100%	98%	95%	90%	80%	70%	60%	50%	40%	30%	20%	10%
$1,975	$1,650	$1,300	$1,200	$1,100	$1,000	$950	$900	$800	$750	$650	$550

* *HE Grade*

100%	98%	95%	90%	80%	70%	60%	50%	40%	30%	20%	10%
$2,750	$2,350	$1,800	$1,600	$1,400	$1,250	$1,100	$1,000	$900	$850	$800	$700

L

100%	98%	95%	90%	80%	70%	60%	50%	40%	30%	20%	10%
* G Grade											
$2,200	$1,975	$1,600	$1,500	$1,400	$1,300	$1,200	$1,100	$1,000	$900	$800	$600
* GE Grade											
$2,975	$2,850	$2,200	$1,800	$1,700	$1,500	$1,400	$1,300	$1,200	$1,100	$1,000	$900
* F Grade											
$2,425	$2,150	$1,700	$1,600	$1,500	$1,400	$1,100	$1,000	$900	$800	$700	$650
* FE Grade											
$3,300	$2,950	$2,400	$2,000	$1,800	$1,600	$1,400	$1,300	$1,100	$1,000	$900	$800
* E Grade											
$3,300	$2,700	$2,300	$2,100	$1,900	$1,800	$1,600	$1,400	$1,200	$1,100	$900	$800
* EE Grade											
$4,400	$3,800	$3,200	$3,000	$2,700	$2,500	$2,300	$2,100	$1,900	$1,800	$1,600	$1,500
* D Grade											
$3,850	$3,300	$2,500	$2,200	$2,000	$1,800	$1,600	$1,500	$1,400	$1,200	$1,100	$1,000
* DE Grade											
$5,450	$4,850	$4,000	$3,700	$3,200	$2,700	$2,200	$2,000	$1,800	$1,600	$1,400	$1,200
* C Grade											
$5,450	$4,850	$4,000	$3,200	$2,700	$2,400	$2,200	$2,000	$1,900	$1,800	$1,600	$1,300
* CE Grade											
N/A	N/A	$7,000	$5,500	$4,700	$4,200	$4,000	$3,400	$3,000	$2,500	$2,100	$1,750
* B Grade											
N/A	N/A	$4,850	$4,425	$4,050	$3,675	$3,175	$$2,750	$2,600	$2,400	$2,200	$2,000
* BE Grade											
N/A	N/A	$8,250	$7,500	$6,750	$5,950	$5,100	$4,400	$3,700	$3,500	$3,200	$3,000
* A grade — auto ejectors standard.											
N/A	N/A	$15,500	$13,750	$11,250	$9,250	$8,150	$7,200	$6,300	$5,400	$4,700	$4,200
* AA grade — auto ejectors standard.											
N/A	N/A	$21,750	$18,750	$15,500	$12,750	$10,250	$8,250	$7,150	$6,500	$6,000	$5,500

* Optimus Grade — auto ejectors standard. Extreme rarity precludes accurate percentage pricing.

Grading	100%	98%	95%	90%	80%	70%	60%

* Thousand Dollar Grade — auto ejectors standard. Extreme rarity precludes accurate percentage pricing.

NITRO SPECIAL — 12, 16, 20 ga., or .410 bore, 26-32 in. barrels, various chokes, boxlock, extractors, checkered pistol grip stock. Mfg. 1921-1948.

	100%	98%	95%	90%	80%	70%	60%
	$450	$395	$350	$300	$250	$225	$200

Add $75 for ST.
Add 20% for 16 ga.
Add 50% for 20 ga.
Add 200% for .410 bore.

GRADE A FIELD MODEL — 12, 16, 20 ga., or .410 bore, 26-32 in. barrels, various chokes, boxlock, checkered pistol grip stock. Mfg. 1934-1942.

	100%	98%	95%	90%	80%	70%	60%
	$880	$770	$715	$660	$550	$495	$440

Add 33% for auto ejectors.
Add $75 for ST.
Add $75 for beavertail forearm.

Grading	100%	98%	95%	90%	80%	70%	60%

> Add 20% for 16 ga.
> Add 50% for 20 ga.
> Add 200% for .410 bore.

GRADE A SKEET MODEL — similar to Grade A, with 26 in. skeet bore barrels, auto ejector, single trigger and beavertail forearm standard.

	100%	98%	95%	90%	80%	70%	60%
	$1,155	$1,045	$990	$935	$825	$770	$715

> Add 50% for 16 ga.
> Add 100% for 20 ga.
> Add 200% for .410 bore.

SHOTGUNS: SINGLE BARREL

TRAP GUN — 12 ga. only, 30 or 32 in. VR barrel, full choke, boxlock, auto ejector, checkered pistol grip stock. Disc. 1942.

	100%	98%	95%	90%	80%	70%	60%
	$550	$440	$385	$330	$275	$250	$195

LONG RANGE FIELD — 12, 16, 20 ga., or .410 bore, 26-32 in. barrel, boxlock, extractor, checkered pistol grip stock. Disc. 1942.

	100%	98%	95%	90%	80%	70%	60%
	$330	$275	$250	$220	$165	$140	$120

LEFEVER, D.M. & SON

Previous manufacturer located in Bowling Green, OH circa 1872-1904.

SHOTGUNS

"Uncle Dan" Lefever, founder of Lefever Arms, designed and manufactured the first breech loading double hammerless shotgun made in the U.S. Production started in 1872 and continued in the Syracuse, NY plant until he sold his interest in the Lefever Arms Company during the early 1900s. He then moved to Ohio and started another factory under the name D.M. Lefever & Son. After his death a few years later the Ohio factory was closed, while his old company (Lefever Arms Co.) continued manufacturing Lefevers until being sold to Ithaca Gun Company in the early 1920s. From that point, Lefever Arms Co. was a branch of Ithaca and continued to make shotguns until shortly after WWII.

Total production on D.M. Lefever shotguns between 1901-1904 totaled less than 1,200. Because of their inherent rarity, values listed below show only 10%-80% condition specimens. D.M. Lefever specimens are so rare in 80%+ condition that prices cannot be accurately ascertained.

Grading	80%	70%	60%	50%	40%	30%	20%	10%

SHOTGUNS: SxS

NEW LEFEVER MODEL — 12, 16, or 20 ga., boxlock action, any length barrel and choke on order, auto ejectors standard on all grades except O Excelsior, double triggers standard on all except Uncle Dan grade, optional single triggers available, checkered walnut pistol grip or straight stock, grades differ as to engraving, wood, checkering and overall quality. Mfg. 1904-1906.

> Add 50% for 16 ga.
> Add 10% for SST.

	80%	70%	60%	50%	40%	30%	20%	10%
* **O Excelsior Grade**	$2,365	$1,925	$1,650	$1,475	$1,350	$1,175	$950	$750
* **Excelsior Grade w/ejectors**	$2,640	$2,310	$1,925	$1,595	$1,450	$1,300	$1,045	$825
* **F Grade, No. 9**	$3,000	$2,640	$2,310	$1,925	$1,725	$1,575	$1,300	$1,000

L

Grading	80%	70%	60%	50%	40%	30%	20%	10%
* E Grade, No. 8	$4,000	$3,350	$2,875	$2,300	$2,075	$1,800	$1,575	$1,250
* D Grade, No. 7	$4,400	$4,125	$3,850	$3,375	$2,975	$2,750	$2,500	$1,925
* C Grade, No. 6	$4,950	$4,400	$4,125	$3,850	$3,575	$3,175	$2,750	$2,420
* B Grade, No. 5	$6,600	$5,500	$4,600	$4,275	$3,975	$3,750	$3,450	$3,100
* AA Grade, No. 4	$8,800	$7,700	$6,600	$5,500	$4,850	$4,400	$3,700	$3,350

UNCLE DAN GRADE — extreme rarity factor precludes accurate pricing.

Grading	100%	98%	95%	90%	80%	70%	60%

SHOTGUNS: SINGLE BARREL TRAP

TRAP GUN — 12 ga., 26-32 in. full choke, auto ejector, boxlock, checkered pistol grip stock. Mfg. 1904-1906.

> Extreme rarity factor precludes accurate pricing.

LE FORGERON

Previous manufacturer located in Belgium. Previously imported and distributed by Midwest Gun Sport in Zebulon, NC.

RIFLES: SxS

MODEL 6020 — 9.3x74R cal., boxlock action, beavertail forearm, pistol grip stock.

$4,450	$4,025	$3,750	$3,475	$3,100	$2,800	$2,550

Last Mfg.'s Sug. Retail was $4,900.

Add $700 for sideplates (Model 6040).

MODEL 6030 — sidelock action, engraved action with deluxe French walnut stock and forearm.

$8,475	$7,900	$7,100	$6,300	$5,500	$4,700	$4,000

Last Mfg.'s Sug. Retail was $8,950.

SHOTGUNS: SxS

Prices below represent the last import information available (1989).

BOXLOCK EJECTOR — 20 or 28 ga. only, with or without sideplates, select French walnut stock, choice of engraving patterns (optional), single trigger.

$3,975	$3,650	$3,325	$2,995	$2,600	$2,250	$1,900

Last Mfg.'s Sug. Retail was $4,400.

Add $1,000 for sideplates.

SIDELOCK EJECTOR — 20 or 28 ga. only, select French walnut stock, choice of engraving patterns (optional), rounded action, single trigger.

$10,200	$9,250	$8,500	$7,900	$7,100	$6,300	$5,500

Last Mfg.'s Sug. Retail was $11,600.

LE FRANCAIS PISTOLS

Previously manufactured by Francais d'Armes Et Cycles located in Saint Etienne, France.

PISTOLS: SEMI-AUTO

STAFF OFFICER MODEL AUTOMATIC — .25 ACP cal., 2½ in. barrel, blue, fixed sights, rubber grips, no visible cocking piece. Mfg. 1914-disc.

$275	$230	$200	$165	$140	$115	$80

Grading	100%	98%	95%	90%	80%	70%	60%

POLICEMAN MODEL AUTOMATIC — .32 ACP cal., double action, 7 shot, 3½ in. barrel, hinged finned barrel, blue, fixed sights, rubber grips. Mfg. 1950s.

	100%	98%	95%	90%	80%	70%	60%
	$850	$800	$700	$575	$435	$350	$275

ARMY MODEL AUTOMATIC — 9mm Para. cal., 8 shot, 5 in. barrel, blue, fixed sights, checkered walnut grips. Mfg. 1928-1938. Early model with tapered barrel, later model with finned barrel.

	100%	98%	95%	90%	80%	70%	60%
	$1,400	$1,100	$850	$700	$550	$425	$350

LES BAER CUSTOM, INC.

Current pistol/rifle customizer located in Hillsdale, IL since 1996.

Les Baer has been customizing both 1911 type pistols and select rifles for decades. The company should be contacted directly (see Trademark Index) for an up-to-date price sheet and catalog on their extensive line-up of high quality competition/combat pistols that range in price from $1,390 - $2,990. A wide range of competition parts and related gunsmithing services are also available.

LEW HORTON DIST. CO.

Current firearms distributor located in Westboro, MA. While Lew Horton is not a manufacturer or an importer, this company has been responsible for many special and limited editions that are listed below with quanities, but without prices, since they may vary greatly from region to region. Special/Limited Editions began in 1983.

SPECIAL/LIMITED EDITIONS

Make/Model	Qty. Made	Year Issue	Retail Price
COLT MODELS			
SAA Horse Pistol	100	1983	$1,100
Presidential - Gold SAA & Det. Spec. w/Gold Eye	600	1985	$525
Colt Boa (includes complete production run of 4 & 6 in. barrel)	600	1985	$525
Ultimate Officer's .45 ACP	500	1989	$777
Lt. Commander .45 ACP	800	1985	$590
Combat Cobra 2½ in.	1,000	1987	$500
Lady Colt (MK IV .380 ACP)	1,000	1989	$547
Night Commander .45 ACP	250	1989	$725
El Presidente .38 Super Govt.	350	1990	$800
El Comandante .38 Super Govt.	500	1991	$800
El General .38 Super Govt.	500	1991	$850
El Capitan .38 Super	500	1991	$875
Detective Special	100	1992	$430
Elite Ten/Forty	100	1992	$900
El Patron	500	1992	$850
El Jefe	500	1992	$849
El Dorado	750	1992	$1,099
El Teniente	400	1992	$1,037
El Coronel	750	1993	$900
Classic Gold Cup	300	1993	$1,285
Classic Single Action	180	1993	$680
Night Officer	350	1993	$680
El Presidente Premier Edition	10	1993	$3,000
Classic Government	300	1993	$965

Make/Model	Qty. Made	Year Issue	Retail Price
Night Government	300	1993	$705
El Caballero	500	1994	$986
El Potro	500	1994	$1,025
Frontier Six Shooter	100	1994	$1,849
McCormick Factory Racer	500	1994	$1,149
Springfield Armory Bicentennial Edition	400	1994	$1,000
Springfield Armory Premier Bicentennial	200	1994	$1,213
BERETTA			
Lady Beretta	100	1985	$285
H&R 1871, INC.			
999 Premier Edition	100 pr.	1993	$345
SMITH & WESSON			
Model 25-3 Lew Horton Special	100	1977	$500
Model 29-3 Lew Horton Special	5,000	1984	$425
Model 629-3 Lew Horton Special	5,000	-	$400
Model 24-3 Lew Horton Special	5,000	1983-84	$380
Model 686 Lew Horton Special	-	1984	$450
Model 657-3 Lew Horton Special	5,000	1986	$410
Model 624-2 Lew Horton Special	7,000	1986-87	$395
Model 640 Carry Comp	250	1991	$750
.40 Compensated	150	1992	$1,699
.40 Tactical	200	1992	$1,499
Shorty Forty	-	1992	$950
Model 629 Hunter	200	1992	$1,234
Model 629 Carry Comp	300	1992	$1,000
Model 686 Carry Comp 4 in.	300	1992	$1,000
Model 657 Classic Hunter	350	1993	$545
Shorty 356	-	1993	$999
356 Tactical	-	1993	$1,350
Model 629 Hunter II	200	1993	$1,234
Model 629 Carry Comp II	100	1993	$1,000
Model 686 Carry Comp 3 in.	300	1993	$1,000
686 Competitor	400	1993	$1,100
686 Hunter	200	1993	$1,153
Model 5906 Shorty Nine	200	1993	$999
Model 60 Carry Comp	300	1993	$800
Model 629 Unfluted	300	1993	$1,234
Model 629 Hunter III	300	1994	$1,234
Springfield Armory Bicentennial Edition	500	1994	$775
Paxton Quigley Model 640	250	1994	$800
Model 625 Classic Snub	300	1994	$603
Model 629 Classic Hunter	500	1994	$1,234
Model 629 Quad-magnaported .44 Mag.	150	1994	$900
Shorty Forty Mark II	150	1995	$999
Shorty .40 Mark III	500	1997	$1,025
Shorty .45	225	1997	$1,096
Shorty .45 Mark II	N/A	1997	N/A
Model 625 Hunter .45 LC Fluted	150	1997	$1,234
Model 629 Hunter .44 Mag. Unfluted	500	1997	$1,234
Model 686 Hunter 7 Shot Unfluted	300	1997	$1,234
Model 640 Quadport .357 Mag. 2 in. Barrel	500	1997	$836
Model 681 Quadport .357 Mag. 7 Shot	300	1997	$700
Model 686 7 Shot Night Sight	300	1997	$1,000
F Comp. 3 in. Comp. Barrel	500	1997	$800
Model 629 Classic Carry 3 in. Unfluted	300	1997	$590
MOSSBERG			
Night Persuader Special Edition	300	1990	N/A

Make/Model	Qty. Made	Year	Issue	Retail Price
REMINGTON				
Model 541J Curly Maple	500	1994		$500
SPRINGFIELD				
Night Light Compact 1911 A1 Lightweight	500	1997		$749
Night Light Standard 1911 A1 Lightweight	300	1997		$749
TAURUS				
Model PT-92AF	250	1990		N/A
Model 85 3 in. Ported Blue	500	1995		$229
Model 85 3 in. Ported Stainless	500	1995		$349

In addition to the special/limited editions listed above, Lew Horton also subcontracted special editions that were sold from company flyers and other promotional materials. They include the following Smith & Wesson Models - Classic Hunter M29 (500 mfg. 1989), Model 63 2 in. (500 mfg. 1989), Model 36 2nd Amendment (200 mfg. 1989), Model 60 25th Anniversary (100 mfg. 1989), Model 629 Classic Hunter (mfg. 1986), Model 5967 (500 mfg. 1990), and the Model 3914 (200 mfg. 1990). There are two Remington models - the M1100 Special Field (200 mfg. 1987-88) and the M700 BDL .257 Roberts cal. (500 mfg. 1990). There are three Colt models - the Combat Python (750 mfg. 1987-88), the Pocketlite (350 mfg. 1989), and the Custom Cobra Stainless Sets (2 sizes, mfg. 1989).

LIBERATOR

Previously manufactured by the Guide Lamp Corporation (division of General Motors) circa 1942.

Grading	100%	98%	95%	90%	80%	70%	60%

PISTOLS: SINGLE SHOT

LIBERATOR PISTOL — .45 ACP cal., simplistic design and action utilizing nonstrategic WWII materials, mfg. for European resistance movement during WWII (most were issued or air-dropped in Europe), each gun was individually packaged in a paraffin-coated cardboard box which included the gun, a graphics only (no English) instruction sheet, wood ram rod, and 10 rounds of .45 ACP ammo stored in the gun's butt, 4 in. smooth bore barrel, sheet steel stamping mfg. with welds, 1 million mfg. 1942 only.

$1,000	**$875**	**$750**	**$675**	**$600**	**$525**	**$450**

Add $200 if in original box with instructions.

Even though 1 million of these pistols were mfg., remaining specimens brought into the U.S. with the above listed accessories are rare since all were delivered overseas. While the Liberator's appearance is crude, remember that the entire production run (1 million) was mfg. and ready for overseas shipment in 13 weeks.

LIBERTY

Current trademark imported beginning 1997 by K.B.I., Inc. located in Harrisburg, PA. Distributor and dealer sales.

REVOLVERS: SAA

FRONTIER MODEL — .38-40 Win. (disc. 1998), .357 Mag. (disc. 1998), .44-40 WCF, or .45 LC cal., 4¾, 5½, or 7½ in. barrel, case hardened, bright nickel, or antique silver (new 1999) frame, choice of brass or steel backstrap and trigger guard. Importation began 1997.

Mfg.'s Sug. Retail	$339	$300	$260	$235	$215	$195	$175	$160

Add $120 for antique silver finish (new 1999).
Add $60 for bright nickel finish (.44-40 WCF or .45 LC only).
Add $20 for brass backstrap and trigger guard.

L

Grading	100%	98%	95%	90%	80%	70%	60%

TARGET MODEL — similar to Frontier Model, except is not available in .357 Mag. cal., and has adj. rear sight. Imported 1997-98.

	$300	$265	$240	$220	$200	$180	$165

Last Mfg.'s Sug. Retail was $319.

BISLEY MODEL — .44-40 WCF or .45 LC cal., features Bisley grip configuration, 4¾, 5½, or 7½ in. barrel, case hardened or bright nickel finish, steel backstrap and trigger guard. Importation began 1999.

Mfg.'s Sug. Retail	$459	$415	$365	$325	$295	$260	$230	$200

Add $60 for bright nickel finish.

RIFLES: SxS

LIGHTNING EXPRESS DOUBLE RIFLE — .44-40 WCF, .45 LC, or .45-70 Govt. cal., exposed hammers, 22 in. barrels, choice of case hardened or antique silver finish. Importation began 1999.

Mfg.'s Sug. Retail	$909	$825	$700	$600	$525	$450	$400	$350

Add $20 for antique silver finish.

SHOTGUNS: SxS

LIBERTY COACH GUN — 12 ga. only, exposed hammers, 20 or 24 in. barrels, choice of case hardened or antique silver finish, fixed chokes (cyl./cyl., 20 in. barrels only, or IC/M, 24 in . barrels only). Importation began 1999.

Mfg.'s Sug. Retail	$609	$535	$475	$425	$375	$335	$295	$265

Add $30 for antique silver finish.

* *Liberty Coach Gun/Express Rifle Combination Set* — includes 20 in. 12 ga. barrels, and choice of 22 in. rifle barrels in any Lightning Express cal., blue finish only. Importation began 1999.

Mfg.'s Sug. Retail	$1,159	$1,025	$875	$750	$625	$550	$475	$425

LIBERTY ARMS WORKS, INC.

Previous manufacturer located in West Chester, PA circa 1991-1996.

PISTOLS: SEMI-AUTO

L.A.W. ENFORCER — .22 LR, 9mm Para., 10mm, .40 S&W (new 1994), or .45 ACP cal., patterned after the Ingram MAC 10, single action, 6¼ in. threaded barrel, closed bolt operation, manual safety, 10 (C/B 1994) or 30★ shot mag., 5 lbs. 1 oz. Mfg. 1991-96.

	$495	$450	$415	$385	$335	$295	$275

Last Mfg.'s Sug. Retail was $545.

LIEGEOISE D'ARMES

Previous manufacturer located in Belgium.

> Small manufacturer that specialized in boxlock shotguns, normally engraved and with ejectors. Prices usually range from $600-$1,200, depending on condition and engraving.

LIGNOSE (BERGMAN)

Previous manufacturer located in Suhl, Germany.

PISTOLS: SEMI-AUTO

EINHAND MODEL 2A POCKET AUTOMATIC — 6.35mm/.25 ACP cal., 6 shot, 2 in. barrel, blue, rubber grips, can be cocked by rearward pressure on triggerguard.

	$295	$245	$195	$165	$140	$110	$85

MODEL 3 POCKET AUTOMATIC — similar to 3A, except without one hand cocking trigger guard.

	$250	$220	$195	$165	$140	$110	$85

Grading	100%	98%	95%	90%	80%	70%	60%

MODEL 3A POCKET AUTOMATIC — similar to 2A, except longer grip, 9 shot capacity.

	$395	$325	$250	$200	$140	$110	$85

MODEL 2 POCKET AUTOMATIC — similar to 2A, without one hand cocking triggerguard.

	$325	$265	$215	$165	$90	$75	$55

LILIPUT

Previous trademark mfg. by August Menz, located in Suhl, Germany.

PISTOLS: SEMI-AUTO

4.25mm cal. — 4.25mm centerfire Liliput cal. (shoots 12 grain bullet), blue or nickel finish, limited 1920s mfg.

	$700	$550	$425	$385	$340	$300	$280

6.35mm cal. — .25 ACP cal., mfg. in large quantities pre-WWII.

	$250	$200	$140	$110	$90	$75	$55

LJUNGMAN

Previously manufactured by Carl Gustaf, located in Eskilstuna, Sweden.

RIFLES: SEMI-AUTO

AG 42 — 6.5x55mm Swedish cal., 10 shot mag., wood stock, tangent rear sight, hooded front, bayonet lug, designed in 1941. This was the first mass produced, direct gas operated rifle. This weapon was also used by the Egyptian armed forces and was known as the Hakim, and chambered in 8x57mm Mauser.

	$850	$700	$600	$495	$450	$400	$365

LJUTIC INDUSTRIES, INC.

Current shotgun manufacturer established circa 1955 and located in Yakima, WA. Dealer direct sales only.

Prior to 1960, Ljutic Industries, Inc. was doing business as Ljutic Gun Co.

SHOTGUNS: O/U

LM 6 — 12 ga. only, supplied with one set of O/U barrels, deluxe wood and checkering, separated barrels on O/U.

Mfg.'s Sug. Retail	$14,995	$14,995	$12,000	$9,250	$8,000	$6,950	$6,250	$5,600

Add $5,000 for extra set of O/U barrels.
Add $7,000 for top single barrel (includes 2 pull trigger groups, and 2 forearms).

SHOTGUNS: SINGLE BARREL TRAP

To date approx. 12,500 target shotguns have been manufactured total (all models).

DYNATRAP MODEL — 12 ga., 33 in. barrel, full choke, push button opening, extractor, trap stock.

	$2,500	$2,150	$1,600	$1,475	$1,300	$1,200	$1,100

Add $300 for release trigger.
Add $400 for extra release trigger.
Add $250 for extra pull trigger.

MODEL X-73 MODEL — 12 ga., 33 in. full, push button opening, high rib fancy Monte Carlo stock.

	$2,500	$2,250	$2,000	$1,850	$1,700	$1,600	$1,500

Add $300 for extra pull trigger.
Add $500 for extra release trigger.

Grading	100%	98%	95%	90%	80%	70%	60%

DYNOKIC MODEL — 12 ga., 32 in. choke barrel (includes one choke), checkered walnut stock, many options available. New 1997.

Mfg.'s Sug. Retail	$3,500	$3,500	$3,100	$2,700	$2,300	$1,950	$1,700	$1,450

MONO GUN — 12 ga., 34 in. barrel, custom choked, custom stocked, pull or release trigger, a "built to customers specifications" trap gun. Also known as Standard Rib or Medium Rib.

* ❋ *Standard, Medium, or Olympic Rib Model*

Mfg.'s Sug. Retail	$4,795	$4,795	$3,650	$3,000	$2,775	$2,500	$2,200	$1,900

    Add $300 for screw-in choke tubes.
    Add $1,200 for stainless steel construction.
    Add $3,000 for stainless steel SLE Pro Model.
    Add $1,700 for SLE Pro Package (includes Laib adj. comb, adj. alum. base plate with 2 pads, and Pro barrel with special bore).
    Approximately 3,000 Mono Guns have been manufactured to date.

* ❋ *LTX (Deluxe Mono Trap)* — similar to Mono Gun except has 33 in. medium rib barrel and exhibition wood and checkering.

Mfg.'s Sug. Retail	$5,795	$5,795	$4,350	$3,750	$3,300	$2,950	$2,500	$2,250

    Add $500 for extra pull trigger.
    Add $450 if with release trigger.
    Add $300 for choke tube barrel with 2 chokes.
    Add $850 for extra release trigger.
    Add $2,199 for extra standard rib barrel.
    Add $2,500 for stainless steel LTX SLE Pro Package.
    Add $1,200 for stainless steel LTX or LTX Pro Package.

SPACE GUN — 12 ga. only, single barrel, unusual design permits in-line round stock with recoil pad, circular forearm wraps around barrel, high post rib on muzzle half of barrel.

Mfg.'s Sug. Retail	$5,995	$5,995	$4,150	$3,375	$2,825	$2,300	$2,000	$1,750

SHOTGUNS: SEMI-AUTO

BI MATIC AUTO LOADER — 12 ga., 2 shot, 26-32 in. barrels, low recoil, trap or skeet models available, stock and choking to customer specifications. Limited mfg.

Mfg.'s Sug. Retail	$5,995	$5,995	$4,450	$2,500	$2,100	$1,750	$1,250	$900

    Add $2,000 for extra barrel.
    Add $750 for extra release trigger.

LLAMA - Gabilondo y Cia, S.A.

Current manufacturer located in Vitoria, Spain. Currently imported by Import Sports Inc. located in Wanamassa, NJ. Previously imported and distributed by Stoeger Industries, Inc. located in South Hackensack, NJ until 1993.

PISTOLS: SEMI-AUTO

MODEL IIIA — .380 ACP cal., 7 shot, 3 in. barrel, adj. sights, blue, plastic grips. Mfg. 1951-disc.

	$235	$200	$180	$160	$140	$120	$110

MODEL XA — similar to Model IIIA, except .32 ACP.

	$235	$200	$180	$160	$140	$120	$110

MODEL XV — similar to Model XA, except .22 LR.

	$235	$200	$180	$160	$140	$120	$110

MODELS C-IIIA, C-XA, C-XV — similar to Model C, except engraved chrome.

	$350	$300	$250	$205	$180	$155	$140

Grading	100%	98%	95%	90%	80%	70%	60%

MODELS BE-IIIA, BE-XA, BE-XV — similar to Model CE, except engraved, blue.

	$365	$315	$250	$205	$180	$155	$140

Deluxe Models, all blue or chrome engraved with simulated pearl grips, add $20.

MODEL G-IIIA — similar to IIIA, except gold damascened, simulated pearl grips.

	$1,515	$880	$825	$660	$550	$440	$330

MODEL VIII — .38 Super cal., 9 shot, 5 in. barrel, fixed sights, wood grips. Mfg. 1952-disc.

	$305	$255	$220	$195	$180	$165	$140

MODEL IXA — similar to Model VIII, except .45 ACP.

	$305	$255	$220	$195	$180	$165	$140

MODEL XI — similar to Model IXA, except 9mm Para..

	$305	$255	$220	$195	$180	$165	$140

MODELS C-VIII, C-IXA, C-XI — similar to Model VIII, except satin chrome.

	$360	$315	$285	$260	$220	$195	$165

MODELS CE-VIII, CE-IXA, CE-XI

	$425	$350	$310	$285	$265	$220	$195

MODELS BE-VIII, BE-IXA, BE-XI — similar to Model CE, except blue, engraving.

	$495	$395	$295	$275	$250	$210	$180

Deluxe Models, similar to above, except simulated pearl grips - add $20.

OMNI — .45 ACP or 9mm Para. cal., double action, all steel construction, 2 sear bars, 3 safeties, 4¼ in. barrel, 7 shot mag. in .45 cal., 13 shot mag. in 9mm Para., blue finish. Importation disc. 1986.

9mm Para.	$440	$380	$330	$295	$260	$225	$200

Last Mfg.'s Sug. Retail was $546.

.45 ACP Caliber	$395	$360	$320	$285	$250	$220	$195

Last Mfg.'s Sug. Retail was $500.

SMALL FRAME MODEL — .22 LR (disc. 1994), .32 ACP (disc. 1993), or .380 ACP cal., Colt 1911 A1 design, single action, 3¹¹⁄₁₆ in. barrel, 7 shot mag., 23 oz. Also available in satin chrome, optional engraving patterns. Disc. 1997.

	$220	$180	$155	$135	$120	$110	$100

Last Mfg.'s Sug. Retail was $259.

Add $60 for duo-tone finish (.380 ACP only, mfg. 1991-1993).
Add $33 for satin chrome finish (not avail. in .32 ACP cal.).

COMPACT FRAME MODEL (IX-D) — 9mm Para. (disc.) or .45 ACP cal., scaled down variation of the Large Frame Model, 4¼ in. barrel, 7 or 9 shot mag., 34 or 37 oz. Mfg. 1986-1997.

	$325	$255	$200	$180	$160	$155	$150

Last Mfg.'s Sug. Retail was $409.

Add $16 for satin chrome finish.
Add $90 for duo-tone finish (mfg. 1990-1993).

GOVERNMENT MODEL (IX-C) — 9mm Para. (disc.), .38 Super (mfg. 1988-1996), or .45 ACP cal., similar to Small Frame Model, 5⅛ in. barrel, 36 oz., 9 shot mag. in 9mm Para., 7 shot mag. in .45 ACP. Engraved and deluxe models available also. Disc. 1997.

	$325	$255	$200	$180	$160	$150	$140

Last Mfg.'s Sug. Retail was $409.

Add $16 for satin chrome finish (.45 ACP only).
Add $90 for duo-tone finish (.45 ACP only, mfg. 1991-1993).

L

Grading	100%	98%	95%	90%	80%	70%	60%

MAX-I MODEL — 9mm Para. or .45 ACP cal., patterned after the Colt Govt. Model, single action only, 4¼ (Compact Model) or 5½ in. barrel, 3-dot combat sights, 7 (.45 ACP) or 9 (9mm Para.) shot mag., matte blue, satin chrome, or duo-tone finish, rubber grips, 34 or 36 oz. New 1995.

Mfg.'s Sug. Retail	$299	$265	$225	$200	$180	$160	$150	$140

    Add $10 for duo-tone finish (.45 ACP cal. only).
    Add $16 for satin chrome finish (new 1996).

* ***Max-I Compensated*** — .45 ACP only, 7 or 10 shot mag., features compensated barrel. Disc. 1997.

	$445	$385	$330	$250	$200	$180	$160

                                      Last Mfg.'s Sug. Retail was $492.

    Add $25 for 10 shot model.

MINI-MAX — 9mm Para., .40 S&W, or .45 ACP cal., mini-compact variation featuring 6-8 shot mag., choice of matte, satin chrome, duo-tone (.45 ACP only), or stainless steel finish/construction. New 1996.

Mfg.'s Sug. Retail	$292	$265	$225	$200	$180	$160	$150	$140

    Add $17 for satin chrome finish.
    Add $7 for duo-tone finish (.45 ACP only).
    Add $66 for stainless steel construction (disc.).

* ***Mini-Max Sub Compact*** — 9mm Para., .40 S&W, or .45 ACP cal., 3.14 in. barrel, all steel construction, 3-dot combat sights, 10 shot mag., polymer grips, choice of matte, satin chrome, or duo-tone finish, 31 oz. New 1999.

Mfg.'s Sug. Retail	$308	$275	$230	$200	$180	$160	$150	$140

    Add $16 for satin chrome finish.
    Add $6 for duo-tone finish (.45 ACP cal. only).

MICRO-MAX — .32 ACP (new 1999, matte finish only) or .380 ACP cal., features standard or lightweight steel design, polymer grips, 3 dot combat sights, slimline slide and frame, non-glare matte or satin chrome finish. New 1998.

Mfg.'s Sug. Retail	$265	$245	$210	$190	$170	$160	$150	$140

    Subtract $15 for Ultra Lite Model (disc.).
    Add $17 for satin chrome finish (.380 ACP cal. only, beginning 1999).

MODEL 82 — 9mm Para. cal., double action, 4¼ in. barrel, blue finish, 3-dot sighting system, 15 shot mag., ambidextrous safety, loaded chamber indicator, black polymer grips, 39 oz. Imported 1988-1993.

	$850	$675	$550	$495	$450	$395	$365

                                      Last Mfg.'s Sug. Retail was $975.

MODEL 87 COMPETITION — 9mm Para. cal., competition variation of the Model 82, includes built in ported compensator, oversize magazine and safety release, fixed barrel bushing, beveled rapid load magazine well, 14 shot mag., extended and serrated triggerguard, and adj. trigger. Imported 1989-1993.

	$1,275	$995	$850	$750	$650	$575	$500

                                      Last Mfg.'s Sug. Retail was $1,450.

REVOLVERS: DOUBLE ACTION

MARTIAL MODEL — .22 LR or .38 Spl. cal., 6 shot, 4 and 6 in. barrels, target sights, blue, checkered wood grips. Mfg. 1969-1976.

	$220	$200	$180	$165	$140	$120	$100

DELUXE MARTIAL — similar to Martial, except finish as follows:

		100%	98%	95%	90%	80%	70%	60%
Satin chrome		$275	$250	$220	$195	$165	$140	$120
Chrome, engraved		$305	$275	$250	$220	$195	$165	$140
Blue, engraved		$290	$265	$235	$210	$180	$155	$120
Gold, damascened		$1,430	$880	$770	$660	$550	$495	$415

Grading	100%	98%	95%	90%	80%	70%	60%

COMANCHE I — .22 LR cal., similar to Martial DA, mfg. 1977-1982.

	$255	$220	$195	$165	$155	$140	$110

COMANCHE II — .38 Spl. cal., similar to Martial DA, mfg. 1977-1982 and 1986 in .22 LR and .22 Mag. only.

	$240	$220	$195	$165	$155	$140	$110

Last Mfg.'s Sug. Retail was $272.

COMANCHE III — .22 LR (disc.) or .357 Mag. cal., 6 shot, 4, 6, or 8½ (disc. 1986) in. barrel, blue, adj. sights, checkered walnut grips. Mfg. 1975-95. Before 1977, it was called "Comanche".

	$280	$245	$200	$165	$155	$140	$130

Last Mfg.'s Sug. Retail was $339.

* **Satin Chrome Finish (disc.)**

	$330	$270	$230	$205	$185	$170	$160

Last Mfg.'s Sug. Retail was $395.

* **Gold Finish (disc.)**

	$1,100	$880	$825	$660	$550	$440	$330

SUPER COMANCHE IV — .44 Mag. cal., 6 or 8½ in. VR barrel, adj. sights, blue only. Disc. 1998.

	$350	$285	$235	$220	$205	$185	$175

Last Mfg.'s Sug. Retail was $440.

SUPER COMANCHE V — .357 Mag. cal., 6 shot, 4, 6, or 8½ in. VR barrel, adj. sights, blue only. Importation disc. 1988.

	$335	$275	$230	$210	$200	$190	$180

Last Mfg.'s Sug. Retail was $414.

LONE STAR RIFLE CO., INC.

Current rifle manufacturer established 1992 and located in Conroe, TX, specializing in Remington Rolling Block rifle reproductions. Dealer and consumer direct sales.

RIFLES: REPRODUCTIONS

REMINGTON ROLLING BLOCK SERIES — various black powder cartridge cals., configurations, and options, case colored or nickel plated receiver, rust or nitre blued barrel, extra select checkered walnut, single, single set, and double set triggers.

* **Creedmoor** — features competition long range 34 in. full octagon or half octagon/half round barrel with pistol grip and shotgun butt, single trigger set at 3 lbs., per Creedmor rules, 10 lbs.

Mfg.'s Sug. Retail	$1,850		$1,725	$1,475	$1,200	$975	$850	$725	$600

* **Silhouette** — designed for silhouette competition, with 30, 32, or 34 in. full octagon or half octagon/half round barrel with pistol grip and shotgun butt.

Mfg.'s Sug. Retail	$1,850		$1,725	$1,475	$1,200	$975	$850	$725	$600

* **Silhouette Standard Rifle** — .40-60 or .45-70 Govt. cal., similar to #5 Sporting Standard Rifle, except has 32 in. barrel, steel shotgun butt plate, pistol grip stock, and shortened forearm. New 1999.

Mfg.'s Sug. Retail	$1,495		$1,325	$1,100	$875	$725	$600	$550	$475

* **Cowboy Action Rifle** — .32-40 WCF, .38-55 WCF, .40-65 WCF, .45 LC, or .45-70 Govt. cal., similar to #5 Sporting Standard Rifle, except has heavy 28 in. barrel. New 1999.

Mfg.'s Sug. Retail	$1,495		$1,325	$1,100	$875	$725	$600	$550	$475

* **#5 Sporting Standard Rifle** — .30-40 Krag cal., 26 in. round barrel, single trigger, case colored frame, standard American walnut stock and forearm. New 1999.

Mfg.'s Sug. Retail	$1,495		$1,325	$1,100	$875	$725	$600	$550	$475

L

Grading		100%	98%	95%	90%	80%	70%	60%

* ***Sporting Rifle*** — standard sporting rifle designed for accuracy, 28, 30, or 32 in. barrel, straight grip stock.

Mfg.'s Sug. Retail	$1,850		$1,725	$1,475	$1,200	$975	$850	$725	$600

* ***Deluxe Sporting Rifle*** — deluxe variation of the Sporting Rifle with 28, 30, or 32 in. full octagon or half octagon/half round barrel with pistol grip and shotgun butt, buckhorn rear sight and choice of front sight.

Mfg.'s Sug. Retail	$1,850		$1,725	$1,475	$1,200	$975	$850	$725	$600

* ***Custer Rifle*** — .50-70 cal., an exact reproduction of Gen. G.A. Custer's original Remington Rolling Block, 28 in. octagon barrel with SST, straight grip, crescent buttplate, and rounded forearm tip.

Mfg.'s Sug. Retail	$2,795		$2,500	$2,175	$1,850

* ***Buffalo Rifle*** — .50-90 cal., features relic finish enabling a new gun to appear somewhat worn, double set triggers, exact copy of the original. New 1998.

Mfg.'s Sug. Retail	$2,900		$2,575	$2,225	$1,875

GOVE ROLLING BLOCK — various cals., new rolling block with underlever design by Carlos Gove. New 1998.

Mfg.'s Sug. Retail	$2,250		$2,025	$1,575	$1,350

LORCIN ENGINEERING CO., INC.

Current handgun manufacturer located in Mira Loma, CA. Distributor sales only.

DERRINGERS: O/U

STAINLESS MODEL — .357 Mag. or .45 LC cal., 3½ in. barrel, synthetic grips, tip-up action, rebounding hammer, fixed sights. Mfg. 1996-98.

	$95	$80	$65

Last Mfg.'s Sug. Retail was $110.

PISTOLS: SEMI-AUTO

L-22 MODEL — .22 LR cal., similar to L-25 Model, except 2.55 in. barrel and 9 shot mag., black or chrome finish, 16 oz. New 1992.

Mfg.'s Sug. Retail	$89		$75	$60	$50	$45	$40	$35	$35

L-25 MODEL — .25 ACP cal., single action, 6 shot mag., 2.4 in. barrel, anatomically designed grips to fit hand better, choice of black and gold, chrome and pearl, satin chrome and pearl, Teflon camo finish (new 1992), or black and pearl finish, 13.5 oz. New 1989.

Mfg.'s Sug. Retail	$79		$65	$50	$45	$40	$35	$35	$35

Add $20 for lightweight frame (Model LT 25, new in 1990).

* ***Lady Lorcin*** — same specifications as the L-25 Model, except is available in chrome, satin chrome, or black exterior finish with pink grips. New 1990.

Mfg.'s Sug. Retail	$79		$70	$60	$50	$45	$40	$35	$35

L-32 — .32 ACP cal., single action, 7 shot mag., 3.5 in. barrel, available in black or chrome finish, 23 oz. New 1992.

Mfg.'s Sug. Retail	$89		$80	$70	$60	$50	$45	$40	$35

L-380 — .380 ACP cal., single action, 7 shot mag., 3.5 in. barrel, available in black or chrome finish, 23 oz. New 1992.

Mfg.'s Sug. Retail	$100		$85	$75	$65	$55	$50	$45	$40

LH-380 — .380 ACP cal., similar to L9MM, 36 oz. New 1995.

Mfg.'s Sug. Retail	$149		$125	$115	$100	$90	$85	$80	$75

Grading	100%	98%	95%	90%	80%	70%	60%

L9MM — 9mm Para. cal., single action, 10 (C/B 1994) or 13★ shot mag., 4½ in. barrel, grip safety, black finish, 3-dot sights, 36 oz. New 1994.

Mfg.'s Sug. Retail	$149	$125	$115	$100	$90	$85	$80	$75

Add $20 for disc. 13 shot mag. variation.

LUCCHINI, SANDRO

Current manufacturer located in Sarezzo (Brescia), Italy.

Lucchini manufactures high quality double rifles and shotguns (approx. 8-10 guns annually), many of which have elaborate gold inlay work. Shotguns starting prices are as follows: $6,000 for Anson action without sideplates (add $1,000 for sideplates) and moderate English scroll engraving, $14,000 for standard sidelock with English scroll engraving (add $2,000 for game scene), and $22,000 for best quality sidelock, depending on engraving. Add 10% for 28 ga. or .410 bore, and $500 for single trigger. All shotgun barrels are demi-bloc construction. Double rifles in .375 H&H cal. start at $24,000 - all are constructed with Ferlach barrels. Shotgun barrels are also a custom order for double rifles, or the reverse. Add approx. $8,000 per extra set of rifle barrels and $4,500 per extra set of shotgun barrels. Please contact the North American sales office directly (see Trademark Index) for more current information.

LUCIANO, BOSIS

Current manufacturer located in Travagliato, Italy. Previously imported by William Larkin Moore & Co., located in Scottsdale, AZ.

All Luciano guns are manufactured on a custom order basis only. Annual production is approx. 25 guns. Please contact the factory directly for current availability and pricing. Information listed below represents last published U.S. retail pricing (1998).

SHOTGUNS

Add 10% for 28 ga. or .410 bore, $1,250 for single trigger.

MICHAELANGELO O/U — 12, 20, 28 ga., or .410 bore, Boss style sidelock action, chopper lump barrels. Prices reflect base value w/o engraving options ($3,750-$15,000).

Mfg.'s Sug. Retail	$40,000	$36,000	$31,500	$27,000	$23,500	$20,000	$17,500	$15,500

HAMMER GUN SxS — 12 ga., sidelock action.

Mfg.'s Sug. Retail	$11,500	$10,500	$9,100	$8,100	$7,100	$6,100	$5,100	$4,000

QUEEN SxS — 12, 20, 28 ga. or .410 bore, H&H type sidelock action, chopper lump barrels.

Prices start in the $20,000 range and go up according to special orders.

COUNTRY SxS — 12, 20, 28 ga. or .410 bore, Anson & Deeley type boxlock action, chopper lump barrels.

Prices start in the $12,500 range and go up according to special orders.

LUGERS WITH VARIATIONS

Currently manufactured pistol configuration originated by Georg Luger circa 1899. This trademarked name is currently manufactured by Stoeger Industries, located in Wayne, NJ, and by Mauser-Werke Oberndorf Waffensysteme, located in Oberndorf, Germany. Many previous manufacturers - see main text for more information.

Note: The Luger section in this book is arranged chronologically by year of manufacture (1900 models to Post-War production), under individual manufacturer headings.

Often times, year of production can be hard to nail down, especially on commercial models. An easier way to initially identify your Luger is to categorize by toggle marking first - then by chamber marking within groups (chronologically for dated chambers). Once you know period of manufacture, simply refer to the appropriate subheading in this section. While some rare variations will be excluded in this generalized overview, it will be very helpful to establish correct, basic knowledge about your particular Luger.

While many recently imported Lugers would make workable shooters, they have in no way lowered prices on 90%+ condition specimens due to normal collector activity in top quality only pistols. Recently imported Lugers should have the importer's name visibly stamped on an exterior surface. Most of these imports are in the 9mm Para. - 4 in. barrel configuration.

Every year more and more reblued, restrawed, regripped, reframed, rebarreled Lugers are sold to unknowing military handgun collectors as rare variations. On any expensive contract variation, careful inspection on all parts must be made before potentially purchasing. If in doubt, secure 2 or 3 additional appraisals/observations from qualified individuals. Lugers are a field in themselves and an experienced Winchester dealer would not be qualified to guesstimate the originality of these German handguns.

A final note on Lugers: Original pistols in 95%-100% condition have not been affected by the influx of recent imports as these newly imported guns are usually in 80% and lower condition or have been reblued.

It seems that every year the prices of top quality (98%+ condition) original Lugers get more expensive and less predictable - For this reason, the 100% values on some vintage Lugers have been omitted intentionally, since rarity precludes accurate price evaluation in this condition factor.

Values for all variations of Lugers listed below assume a proper magazine and matching parts.

REFERENCE GUIDE BY TOGGLE MARKING

DWM TOGGLE IDENTIFICATION

* **_DWM MODELS_** — mfg. from 1900 to 1930 in Berlin, Germany.

* **_1900 Models_** — grip safety and "Dished" Toggles, ser. nos. 1-24,999.

* **_1906 Models_** — grip safety, many chamber markings, ser. nos. 25,000-74,000.

* **_1908 Commercial Models_** — no grip safety, 9mm Para., ser. nos. 39,000-74,000.

* **_1908 Military Models_** — no stock lug.

* **_1914 Military Models_** — stock lug, dated 1913-1918.

* **_1920 Commercial Models_** — no grip safety, usually 3⅞ in. barrel. Most common Luger, undated chamber, 7.65mm Para. or 9mm Para.

    Note: Lugers with 4 inch barrels are most frequently encountered in military and commercial models. 6 in. barrels usually denote "Navy" models. 8 in. barrels usually denote "Artillery" models. Guns with barrels over 8 inches are rare and should be checked carefully for originality.

DWM COMMERCIAL LUGERS

DWM MEANS DEUTSCHE WAFFEN & MUNITIONS FABRIKEN
These are models manufactured from 1900-1923 found in the five digit serial range.

MODEL 1900 — ser. range 1-20,000. Configuration: 4¾ in. x .30 Commercial, American Eagle, Swiss.

MODEL 1900 — ser. range 20,001-21,000. Configuration: 4¾ in. x .30 Bulgarian.

MODEL 1902 — ser. range 21,001-25,000. Configuration: 9mm Para. x 4 in. "Fat Barrels" and 11¾ in. x 7.65mm Para. Carbine models, intermixed with 4¾ x 7.65mm Para. American Eagles and Commercials.

MODEL 1906 — ser. range 25,001-39,000. Configuration: Commercial American Eagle, Navy Commercial and Swiss, both 4¾ in. x 7.65mm Para. and 9mm Para. x 4 in. grip safety models.

MODEL 1908 — ser. range 39,001-71,000. Configuration: First 9mm Para. x 4 in. without grip safety, M1908 Commercials were interspersed with 7.65mm Para. and 9mm Para. Eagles, Commercials, Navy Commercials, and a few Carbines and Swiss.

MODEL 1914 — ser. range 71,001-74,000. Configuration: Last pre-WWI Commercial Lugers, made with stock lug, with a few 9mm Para. Commercials mixed in.

MODEL 1920 — ser. range 2,000i-9,999u. Configuration: Post-WWI Commercials, mostly 3⅞ in. x 7.65mm Para. cal.

MODEL 1923 — ser. range 89,001-91,000. Configuration: The last thousand or so made have "safe" on lever and "loaded" on the extractor, 3⅞ in. x 7.65mm Para. barrels.

ERFURT TOGGLE IDENTIFICATION

ERFURT MODELS

Produced from 1911-1914 and 1916-1918 in Erfurt, Germany. Military Model - Chamber dated 1911-1914 and 1916-1918. Erfurt models exhibit the most proof marks and individual parts numbering. Walnut grips.

SIMSON & CO. TOGGLE IDENTIFICATION

SIMSON & CO.

Manufactured 1922 to 1934 in Suhl, Germany. Most Simson Lugers are military models (9mm - 4 in. barrels). During this 12 year period, Simson supplied the German Army Lugers exclusively. Can be dated 1925-1928. Many reworks of WWI DWM Military Lugers were refurbished by Simson, and can be detected by the Simson "Eagle-over-6" proof on repaired parts. A very few Simsons made in 1934 have just an "S" on the toggle (very rare).

L

SWISS TOGGLE IDENTIFICATION

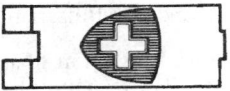 

SWISS BERN MODELS

Manufactured 1924 to 1929 by WAFFENFABRIK Bern, Switzerland. Relatively rare - these Swiss models have "improved" changes (flat and curved front grip strap), 4¾ in. barrels, walnut or plastic grips, grip safety. 1929 model has Geneva Cross in shield on front link.

MAUSER TOGGLE IDENTIFICATION

MAUSER VARIATIONS

Manufactured 1934-1942 in Oberndorf, Germany. Between 1930 and 1934 Mauser Werke was primarily engaged in reworking older Lugers, since transfer of machinery and personnel to the DWM plant in Berlin was completed in 1931. Mauser "Banner" models were made from 1934 to 1942, many are dated from 1939-1942 on the chamber. S/42 models are MOSTLY MILITARY contract guns manufactured between 1934 and 1940, usually chamber marked. "42" toggle marked guns (Mauser code) were mfg. 1939 and 1940 and are dated. "byf" marked toggles indicate guns made for German military use after 1940 and are more common than other military models. The Mauser Werke trademark also appears on those Lugers made in the 1970s.

KRIEGHOFF TOGGLE IDENTIFICATION

KRIEGHOFF MODELS

Manufactured between 1934-1946 in Suhl, Germany. Early Krieghoffs are side frame inscribed. The German Luftwaffe contracted with Krieghoff for military guns in 1935. Early military Krieghoffs have "S" marked chambers, most are chamber dated between 1936 and 1945. Krieghoff Lugers are prized for their quality fit and finish and command higher prices because of their rarity factor.

VICKERS TOGGLE IDENTIFICATION

Grading	100%	98%	95%	90%	80%	70%	60%

VICKERS

Manufactured by Vickers, Ltd., circa 1921, in England from DWM parts for military contract sale to the Netherlands. Added barrel date is a date of arsenal refinish or refurbishing. Distinguishable by Vickers toggle and "rust" marked safety. Serial range is 1-10,100. Grips can be finely checkered with shallow contour or very coarsely checkered. Configuration is 9mm Para., 4 in. barrel, and grip safety.

PISTOLS: SEMI-AUTO, LUGERS & VARIATIONS

Lugers: Pre-1900 & 1900 DWM Mfg.

Values on most 100% Lugers have been omitted intentionally since rarity precludes accurate price evaluation in this condition factor.

1898/99 BORCHARDT LUGER TRANSITIONAL — 7.65mm Para. cal., 5 in. barrel, this is perhaps one of the most desirable Lugers, only few mfg. Examples scarce, no reported sales, an original example would command a price in the 5-figure range.

1899/1900 SWISS TEST MODEL — 7.65mm Para. cal., 4¾ in. barrel, 100 or less mfg., the very first true Luger. Engraved "Swiss Cross" chamber marking.

	N/A	$35,000	$30,000	$22,000	$16,000	$12,000	$8,500

Approx. 50 pistols serial numbered in the 1-50 range.

Buyers should be very cautious when considering a purchase of this rare model, as good fakes do exist.

1900 COMMERCIAL DWM — 7.65mm Para. cal., 4¾ in. barrel, 5,500 mfg.

	N/A	$3,000	$2,500	$2,000	$1,650	$1,325	$950

1900 SWISS COMMERCIAL DWM — 7.65mm Para. cal., 4¾ in. barrel, 2,000 commercially mfg. and 3000 military mfg.

	N/A	$3,750	$3,000	$2,450	$1,750	$1,350	$975

Add 15% for wide trigger (found only in ser. no. range 4,000).

1900 AMERICAN EAGLE DWM — 7.65mm Para. cal., 4¾ in. barrel, approx. 12,000 mfg.

	N/A	$2,950	$1,650	$1,250	$1,000	$850	$650

Add 30% for U.S. Test Model (approx. ser. no. range 6,100-7,100).

1900 BULGARIAN DWM — 7.65mm Para. cal., 4¾ in. barrel, 1,000 mfg., very rare in U.S., most often seen in the 60% and lower condition.

	N/A	$8,750	$5,250	$3,750	$3,150	$2,650	$2,150

Deduct 30% if rebarreled.

Lugers: 1902-DWM Mfg.

1902 COMMERCIAL — 9mm Para. cal., 4 in. barrel, serial number range 22,300-22,400 and 22,900-23,500 (500-600 mfg.). Commonly called "Fat Barrel" model.

	N/A	$7,500	$5,750	$4,650	$3,950	$3,350	$2,750

1902 AMERICAN EAGLE — 9mm Para. cal., 4 in. barrel, 600-700 mfg., commonly called the "Fat Barrel". Same ser. range as 1902 Commercial Model.

	N/A	$8,250	$6,250	$4,850	$4,000	$3,500	$3,000

1902 CARTRIDGE COUNTER AMERICAN EAGLE — 9mm Para. cal., only 50 mfg. with the Powell Indication Device; be extremely wary of fakes. Ser. no. range 22,401-22,450.

	N/A	$26,000	$16,500	$12,250	$9,750	$8,650	$7,500

1902 DANZIG TEST — 7.65mm Para. or 9mm Para. cal., blank toggle, 4 in. barrel, Crown D proofs.

	N/A	$6,500	$5,000	$4,250	$3,400	$2,950	$2,200

Grading	100%	98%	95%	90%	80%	70%	60%

1902 CARBINE — 7.65mm Para. cal., 11¾ in. barrel, approx. 2500 mfg.

Gun w/matching stock	N/A	$11,500	$9,450	$7,250	$5,950	$4,650	$3,500
Gun only	N/A	$7,500	$5,950	$3,500	$2,700	$2,200	$1,800

  Add approx. 40% for American Eagle variation.
  Subtract 20% for non-matching stock.

1902/06 TRANSITIONAL CARBINE — 11¾ in. barrel, 50-100 mfg., may have new model frame. Ser. nos. start at 50,000.

	N/A	$9,000	$6,250	$4,500	$4,200	$4,000	$3,800

  Deduct 30% if without matching stock.

1903 COMMERCIAL — 7.65mm Para. cal., 4 in. barrel, 50 mfg., extractor marked "charge". Ser. range 25,000-25,050, with 90 degree toggle checkering.

	N/A	$6,500	$6,000	$5,500	$5,000	$3,000	$2,500

Lugers: 1904-DWM Mfg.

1904 NAVY DWM — 9mm Para. cal., 6 in. barrel, limited mfg., a Transitional Navy, "Fat Barrel" with 90 degree toggle checkering and toggle lock, should have 2-digit ser. no.

  Extreme rarity precludes accurate price evaluation. Most of these pistols available for sale are fakes - buyer beware.

Lugers: 1906-DWM Mfg.

1906 COMMERCIAL 7.65mm Para. W/"GESICHERT" MARKED SAFETY — 7.65mm Para. cal., 4¾ in. barrel, "GESICHERT" marked safety, long frame. Approx. 750 mfg.

	N/A	$2,750	$1,950	$1,500	$1,125	$900	$750

1906 COMMERCIAL 9mm Para. — 9mm Para. cal., 4 in. barrel, 3,500-4,000 mfg. Scarcer than 7.65mm Para.

	N/A	$1,900	$1,400	$1,050	$900	$775	$650

1906 COMMERCIAL 7.65mm Para. — 7.65mm Para. cal., 4¾ in. barrel, area under safety polished bright, 5000 mfg.

	N/A	$1,825	$1,375	$950	$775	$625	$550

1906 AMERICAN EAGLE - 9mm Para. — 9mm Para. cal., 4 in. barrel, American Eagle stamped in front of breech, 3,000 mfg.

	N/A	$2,495	$1,750	$1,275	$975	$800	$650

1906 AMERICAN EAGLE - 7.65mm Para. — 7.65mm Para. cal., 4¾ in. barrel, 7,500-8,000 mfg. Add 40% for long frame.

	N/A	$2,000	$1,500	$1,050	$850	$725	$600

1906 NAVY COMMERCIAL — 9mm Para. cal., 6 in. barrel, approx. 2,500 mfg.

	N/A	$3,400	$2,600	$1,800	$1,600	$1,200	$950

  Add 50% for 7.65mm Para. cal. with 6 in. barrel.

1906 NAVY MILITARY FIRST ISSUE — 9mm Para. cal., 6 in. barrel, first issue, 19,000 mfg., mostly altered safety marking - "GESICHERT" in upper position. Ser. no. range 1-9,000a.

	N/A	$3,000	$2,250	$1,600	$1,200	$875	$600

  Add 10% for Navy unit markings.
  Add 25% for unaltered safety variation.

1906 NAVY MILITARY SECOND ISSUE — 9mm Para. cal., 6 in. barrel, second issue, 2,000 mfg. Ser. range 9,000a-1,000b.

	N/A	$3,250	$2,500	$1,725	$1,400	$1,100	$900

  Add 10% for Navy unit markings.

Grading	100%	98%	95%	90%	80%	70%	60%

Lugers: 1906-1918 DWM & Erfurt Mfg.

Most common variations in good supply within this section in 50% or less condition will approximate the 60% value. This reflects its value as a representative shooter rather than a higher priced collector's gun.

1906 SWISS COMMERCIAL — 7.65mm Para. or 9mm Para. cal., 4¾ in. barrel, less than 1,000 mfg., Swiss "Cross in Sunburst," short frame.

	N/A	$2,400	$1,750	$1,500	$1,350	$1,200	$1,100

Add 20% for "Cross in Shield".

1906 SWISS MILITARY — 7.65mm Para. cal., 4¾ in. barrel, long frame, Swiss Police has Cross in Shield. Either "Cross in Shield" or "Cross in Sunburst".

	N/A	$2,400	$1,600	$1,200	$900	$800	$700

1906/23 DUTCH — 9mm Para. cal., 4 in. barrel, approx. 4,000 mfg., often seen as arsenal rework.

	N/A	$1,600	$1,400	$900	$750	$600	$525

Add 200% for original finish and barrel.

1906 BRAZILIAN — 7.65mm Para. cal., 4¾ in. barrel, 5,000 mfg., extremely rare in fine condition.

	N/A	$2,500	$1,800	$1,000	$800	$700	$650

1906 BULGARIAN — 7.65mm Para. cal., 4¾ in. barrel, 1,500 mfg., most rebarrelled to 9mm Para. (deduct 60%).

	N/A	$4,200	$3,500	$3,500	$2,000	$1,850	$1,450

This is the rarest Bulgarian - most are fakes or have been restored.

1908 BULGARIAN — 9mm Para. cal., 4 in. barrel, DWM on chamber, 10,000 mfg., extremely rare in mint condition.

	N/A	$2,500	$1,800	$1,000	$825	$750	$675

1906 PORTUGUESE ARMY — 7.65mm Para. cal., 4¾ in. barrel, Manuel II crest on chamber. Approx. 5,000 mfg.

	N/A	$1,675	$1,150	$800	$600	$500	$400

1906 ROYAL PORTUGUESE NAVY — 9mm Para. cal., 4 in. barrel, Anchor & Crown on chamber, very rare. Most are fakes.

	N/A	$9,500	$6,000	$4,000	$2,500	$2,000	$1,500

1906 REPUBLIC OF PORTUGAL NAVY — 7.65mm Para. cal., Anchor R.P. on chamber, very rare. Most are fakes.

	N/A	$9,500	$6,000	$4,000	$2,500	$2,000	$1,500

1906 RUSSIAN — 9mm Para. cal., 4 in. barrel, approx. 1,000 mfg., only 6 reported.

	N/A	$13,750	$9,950	$8,100	$6,400	$5,500	$4,600

1906 VICKERS DUTCH — 9mm Para., 4 in. barrel, approx. 10,000 assembled by Vickers Ltd. from DWM supplied parts.

	N/A	N/A	N/A	N/A	N/A	N/A	$895

1906 FRENCH COMMERCIAL — 7.65mm Para. cal., 4¾ in. barrel.

	N/A	$2,350	$1,800	$1,575	$1,400	$1,200	$995

Add 100% if cased with accessories.

1908 DWM COMMERCIAL AND MILITARY — 9mm Para. cal., 4 in. barrel, Test/Acceptance Model, approx. 500 mfg. Ser. no. range 69,000-71,200.

	N/A	$1,200	$800	$700	$575	$475	$400

1908 NAVY COMMERCIAL — 9mm Para. cal., 6 in. barrel.

	N/A	$3,750	$2,800	$2,200	$1,800	$1,500	$1,300

Add 50% for 7.65mm Para. with 6 in. barrel.

Grading	100%	98%	95%	90%	80%	70%	60%

1908 DWM MILITARY — 9mm Para. cal., 4 in. barrel, approx. 95,000 mfg each year, undated 1st issue or dated 1910-1913, no stock lug, except for a few late 1913 mfg. guns.

	N/A	$875	$675	$525	$450	$400	$350

Add 20%+ for Imperial unit markings (depends on history of unit).
Add 20% for undated or for 1913 date w/stock lug.

Approx. 25,000 1st issue pistols were mfg., 20,000 dated 1910, 15,000 dated 1911, 10,000 dated 1912, 25,000 dated 1913.

1908 DWM COMMERCIAL — 9mm Para. cal., 4 in. barrel, no stock lug or hold open, blank chamber.

	N/A	$800	$600	$450	$400	$350	$300

1910-1914 DATED 1908 ERFURT MILITARY — 9mm Para. cal., 4 in. barrel (dated 1910-1914), 1911, 1912, and most 1913 chamber dates do not have stock lugs.

	N/A	$800	$625	$525	$400	$350	$295

Add 20%+ for Imperial unit markings (depends on history of unit).
Add 20% for 1913 chamber date with stock lug.

WWI ERFURT MILITARY SERIAL RANGES

CHAMBER DATE	OBSERVED LOW SERIAL	OBSERVED HIGH SERIAL	APPROXIMATE QTY. MADE
1911	575	9548	10,000
1912	255	866b	22,000
1913	575	2563b	25,000
1914	2137	539A	25,000
1915	none observed		
1916	13	5764b	80,000
1917	844	2854n	150,000
1918	304	5816s	180,000

Production data appears courtesy of Jan C. Still.

1908 NAVY — 9mm Para. cal., 6 in. barrel, scarce. Ser. No. range 1,000B-10,000B, 9,000 mfg.

	N/A	$3,500	$2,750	$1,950	$1,750	$1,500	$1,350

1908 BOLIVIAN CONTRACT — 9mm Para. cal., 4 in. barrel.

	N/A	$3,000	$2,500	$1,700	$1,300	$1,100	$900

1913 COMMERCIAL DWM — 9mm Para. cal., 4 in. barrel, grip safety and stock lug, horizontal "N" proof mark, 71,000 ser. no. range, rare.

	N/A	$2,250	$1,500	$1,050	$900	$780	$700

1914 COMMERCIAL DWM — 9mm Para. cal., 4 in. barrel, undated, stock lug, horizontal crown-N proofed.

	N/A	$1,600	$1,200	$975	$875	$750	$600

1914 NAVY — 9mm Para. cal., 6 in. barrel, scarce. Dated 1916 and 1917.

	N/A	$3,000	$2,250	$1,600	$1,200	$1,000	$900

Add 20% for 16 date.
Watch for fakes made from 1920 Commercials with new barrels and rear toggles added. Crown M proofs and date will look "fresh" (16 date usually encountered).

Grading	100%	98%	95%	90%	80%	70%	60%

1916-1918 DATED ERFURT MILITARY — 9mm Para. cal., 4 in. barrel, dated 1916-1918 - there are no known 1915 chamber dated Erfurts.

	N/A	$795	$595	$475	$400	$350	$300

Add 20% for 1914 date.
Add $75 for original holster in average+ condition.
Add 10% for matching mag.
Add 50% for 2 matching mags.
Add 20%+ for Imperial unit markings (depends on history of unit).

Note: Date stamped on top frame is date of production; thus dates could be 1914, 1916, 1917, or 1918. All are Military P.08s, however, 99%-100% Erfurts are rare.

1914 ERFURT ARTILLERY — 9mm Para. cal., 1914 date is only one seen, 8 in. barrel.

	N/A	$2,500	$1,750	$1,100	$995	$875	$750

Add 20%+ for Imperial unit markings (depends on history of unit).

1912-1918 DATED WWI DWM MILITARY — 9mm Para. cal., 4 in. barrel. 1912-1918 dated. Most frequently encountered WWI military Luger, stock lug.

	N/A	$850	$595	$475	$400	$350	$295

Add $75 for original holster in average+ condition.
Add 20% for matching mag.
Add 100% for 2 matching mags.
Add 20%+ for Imperial unit markings (depends on history of unit).

Note: Date stamped on top frame is date of production; thus, dates could be 1914, 1915, 1916, 1917, or 1918. All are Military P.08s, however.

WWI DWM MILITARY SERIAL RANGES

CHAMBER DATE	OBSERVED LOW SERIAL	OBSERVED HIGH SERIAL	APPROXIMATE QTY. MADE
1908	(undated) 34	2636b	25,000
1910	5095b	5358d	20,000
1911	1524c	4825e	13,000
1912	599	9974	10,000
1913	2617	3850d	25,000
1914	282	6212c	40,000
1915	1398	2557d	100,000
1916	287	5438q	180,000
1917	587	3521m	60,000
1918	3690	9018n	190,000

Production data appears courtesy of Jan C. Still.

1914-1918 DATED DWM ARTILLERY — 9mm Para. cal., 8 in. barrel. Dated 1914-1918.

	N/A	$1,675	$1,100	$800	$600	$500	$400

Add $350 for matching stock.
Add $200 for proper non-matching stock.
Add $200 for original leather holster with shoulder strap.
Add 100% for rare 1914 chamber date.
Add 20% for 1915 chamber date.
Add 20%+ for Imperial unit markings (depends on history of unit).

Lugers: 1920-1930 DWM

Most common variations in good supply within this section in 50% or less condition will approximate the 60% value. This reflects its value as a representative shooter rather than a higher priced collector's gun.

Grading	100%	98%	95%	90%	80%	70%	60%

1920 DWM OR ERFURT — 9mm Para. cal., 4 in. barrel, military and police, reworked and issued to police units, many thousand reworked, double date also, 1920 and 1921 dated.

| | N/A | $700 | $540 | $450 | $375 | $300 | $250 |

1920 COMMERCIAL — 7.65mm Para. or 9mm Para. cal., 3⅞-4 in. barrel, many thousand produced.

| | N/A | $750 | $475 | $385 | $335 | $285 | $250 |

Add 25% for 9mm Para. cal.

1920 NAVY COMMERCIAL — 9mm Para. cal., 6 in. barrel, very rare rework, Navy rear sight.

| | N/A | $2,000 | $1,400 | $1,000 | $900 | $800 | $700 |

Add 20% for 7.65mm Para. with 6 in. barrel.

1920 COMMERCIAL ARTILLERY — 9mm Para. cal., 8 in. barrel, very rare rework.

| | N/A | $1,350 | $950 | $800 | $600 | $500 | $400 |

While this variation is undoubtedly rarer than the 1914-1918 military Artillery models, it is less desirable.

1920 "LONG BARREL" COMMERCIAL — 7.65mm Para. or 9mm Para. cal., 10-20 in. barrel, extremely rare.

| | N/A | $1,400 | $1,100 | $1,000 | $750 | $655 | $600 |

Watch for fakes - these guns have to be evaluated one at a time. Barrel should have matching nos. and Crown N proof.

1920 NAVY CARBINE — 7.65mm Para. cal., 11¾ in. barrel, long frame (if short frame, be wary of fakes, very few produced). Navy rear sight, no forearm under barrel.

| | N/A | $2,000 | $1,600 | $1,100 | $1,025 | $950 | $850 |

1920 CARBINE — 7.65mm Para. cal., 11¾ in. barrel, very rare.

| Gun only | N/A | $5,450 | $4,750 | $4,000 | $3,000 | $2,500 | $2,000 |
| Gun with stock | N/A | $9,250 | $7,250 | $6,400 | $5,500 | $4,650 | $3,650 |

1920 SWISS REWORK — 7.65mm Para. cal., 3⅝-6 in. barrel, several hundred produced.

| | N/A | $1,400 | $1,100 | $1,000 | $750 | $655 | $600 |

ABERCROMBIE & FITCH COMMERCIAL — 7.65mm Para. or 9mm Para. cal., long frame, 4¾ in. barrel, 100 mfg., total for both cals.

| | N/A | $5,250 | $4,250 | $3,500 | $3,000 | $2,575 | $2,200 |

Add 30% for 6 in. barrels (rare).

Inspect barrel legend very carefully (as in beware of fakes) - must have reinforced frame (look for rib in rear frame well).

1920/21-DWM — 9mm Para. cal., 4 in. barrel.

| | N/A | $700 | $600 | $450 | $400 | $350 | $300 |

Deduct 20% if arsenal reworked.

1920/23 STOEGER AMERICAN EAGLE — 7.65mm Para. or 9mm Para. cal., 3⅝-24 in. barrels, less than 1,000 mfg., made by DWM for Stoeger, sold in USA, longer barrel models have higher value.

| 3⅞ - 6 in. barrels | N/A | $2,500 | $1,450 | $1,200 | $1,050 | $950 | $825 |
| 8 in. barrel | N/A | $4,500 | $2,300 | $2,000 | $1,650 | $1,200 | $995 |

Add 50% for Mauser mfg., safe and loaded extractor, or V ser. no. suffix

Be extremely careful when examining the frame markings on this variation as there are many fakes in the marketplace.

1923 DWM COMMERCIAL — 7.65mm Para. cal., 3⅝ in. barrel, 14,000 mfg. (ser. range 74,000-89,000).

| | N/A | $775 | $500 | $385 | $335 | $285 | $250 |

Grading	100%	98%	95%	90%	80%	70%	60%

1923 DWM "SAFE AND LOADED" COMMERCIAL — 7.65mm Para. cal., "safe and loaded" marked on frame and ejector, 7.65mm Para. cal., 3⅞ in. barrel, safety and extractor marked in English, 2,000 mfg. (ser. range 89,000-91,000).

	N/A	$1,375	$1,000	$850	$600	$500	$420

1923 FINNISH LUGER — 7.65mm Para. cal., approx. 5,000-7,000 units made for Finnish military contract (Army and Navy), marked "SA" surrounded by a rectangle, most have been recently imported into the U.S.

	N/A	$550	$450	$375	$325	$300	$275

Lugers: Krieghoff Mfg.

Add 20% for matching mag. on Krieghoff Models listed below.

1923 DWM/KRIEGHOFF COMMERCIAL — 7.65mm Para. (3⅞ in. barrel only) or 9mm Para. (4 in. barrel only), few mfg., reworked by Krieghoff, chamber dated 1921 or unmarked, most in "i" range, Krieghoff stamped on back-frame. Be wary of fakes.

	N/A	$1,650	$1,300	$1,100	$880	$770	$660

DWM/KRIEGHOFF COMMERCIAL — 7.65mm Para. or 9mm Para. cal., 4 in. barrel, a few hundred made, side frame marked Krieghoff. Most are fake.

	N/A	$2,700	$2,000	$1,650	$1,300	$1,000	$800

KRIEGHOFF COMMERCIAL SIDE FRAME — 7.65mm Para. or 9mm Para. cal., 4 or 6 in. barrel, 1500 mfg., 1,000 with side frame marked, and 500 without. "P" prefix ser. nos.

	N/A	$2,400	$2,000	$1,600	$995	$800	$700

Add 30% for side frame marked 7.65mm Para.

KRIEGHOFF S CODE EARLY — 9mm Para. cal., 4 in. barrel, 1,800 mfg., German Luftwaffe. Has fat walnut grips, "H-K Suhl" toggle.

	N/A	$2,800	$2,200	$1,600	$1,200	$995	$895

KRIEGHOFF S CODE MID SERIES — 9mm Para. cal., 4 in. barrel, 500-700 mfg., Luftwaffe, ser. no. range 1600-2500, fine-checkered plastic grips.

	N/A	$2,650	$1,950	$1,500	$995	$800	$700

KRIEGHOFF S CODE LATE — 9mm Para. cal., 4 in. barrel, 1,800 mfg., Luftwaffe, ser. no. range 2300-4200.

	N/A	$2,500	$1,800	$1,200	$750	$600	$500

KRIEGHOFF GRIP SAFETY — 9mm Para. cal., 4 in. barrel, extremely rare, test trial gun.

	N/A	$3,500	$3,000				

KRIEGHOFF 36 DATE — 9mm Para. cal., 4 in. barrel, 500-700 made, Luftwaffe military, 2 digit date, coarse checkered plastic grips.

	N/A	$2,800	$2,000	$1,650	$1,300	$1,000	$800

KRIEGHOFF 1936-1945 DATED — 9mm Para. cal., 4 in. barrel, approx. 9,000 mfg., 4 digit chamber date, 1936, 1937 and 1940 most common; 1938 and 1941 through 1944 dates command 70-200% premiums. 1945 is extremely rare - add 500%.

	N/A	$2,500	$1,825	$1,550	$1,320	$1,225	$1,100

The 1941 "large date" is very rare - watch for fakes (re-dated frames) on this model in general.

POST-WAR KRIEGHOFF TYPE I — 9mm Para. cal., 4 in. barrel, 150 mfg. for occupation forces, H-K marked toggle link.

	N/A	$2,150	$1,550	$1,350	$1,050	$950	$850

POST-WAR KRIEGHOFF TYPE II — 9mm Para. cal., 4 in. barrel, 150 mfg., unmarked toggle link, many parts proofed "Eagle-over-2".

	N/A	$1,950	$1,350	$1,200	$995	$875	$775

L

Grading	100%	98%	95%	90%	80%	70%	60%

POST-WAR KRIEGHOFF COMMERCIAL — 7.65mm Para. cal., 4 in. barrel, 100-200 mfg., unmarked toggle, many parts proofed "Eagle-over-2".

	N/A	$1,200	$1,100	$1,000	$900	$800	$775

Lugers: Mauser Mfg.

Most common variations in good supply within this section in 50% or less condition will approximate the 60% value. This reflects its value as a representative shooter rather than a higher priced collector's gun.

1935-06 PORTUGUESE GNR — 7.65mm Para. cal., 4¾ in. barrel, 564 mfg., GNR on chamber, Portuguese marked safety and extractor.

	N/A	$2,400	$1,600	$1,300	$1,050	$800	$525

1934/06 MAUSER SWISS COMMERCIAL — 7.65mm Para. cal., 4¾ in. barrel, a few hundred produced, "Cross in Sunburst" or blank chamber, grip safety.

	N/A	$2,800	$2,400	$2,000	$1,500	$1,250	$850

1934 MAUSER BANNER COMMERCIAL — 7.65mm Para. or 9mm Para. cal., 4 in. barrel, hundreds produced, unmarked chamber, "v" suffix to ser. no.

	N/A	$2,000	$1,700	$1,425	$1,150	$950	$725

    Add 15% for "Kal. 7.65" barrel marking.

S/42 K DATE — 9mm Para. cal., 4 in. barrel, approx. 10,000 mfg. during 1934 only for military.

	N/A	$2,750	$2,400	$1,400	$995	$895	$795

    Add 50% for "large eagle over M Navy" proofmark.

S/42 G DATE — 9mm Para. cal., 4 in. barrel, many thousand produced 1935 only.

	N/A	$1,250	$900	$675	$525	$450	$400

    Add 20% for Navy markings.

S/42 DATED CHAMBER — 9mm Para. cal., 4 in. barrel, many thousands produced, "S/42" stamped rear toggle, chamber dated 1936-1940. One of the most frequently encountered WWII military Lugers.

	N/A	$875	$675	$525	$425	$375	$350

    Add $100 for original holster in average+ condition.
    Add 25% for matching mag.
    Add 100% for 2 matching mags.
    Add 75% for Navy markings.
    Add 20% for 1936 date.
    Add 30% for "strawed" 1937 date.

    The last regular production S/42 Models were mfg. approx. April of 1939.

MAUSER PERSIAN (IRANIAN) CONTRACT — 9mm Para. cal., 4 and 8 in. barrels, 1,000 — 8 in. mfg., and 1,000 — 4 in. mfg., Farsi numerals.

		N/A					
4 in. barrel	N/A	$3,750	$3,200	$2,750	$2,250	$2,000	$1,750
Artillery (8 in.)	N/A	$2,400	$2,000	$1,800	$1,650	$1,475	$1,200

    Add 50% for Artillery with matching rig.

    This variation became less desirable after the U.S. hostage situation occurred in Iran.

1936-1942 DATED MAUSER BANNER — 9mm Para. cal., 4 in. barrel, over 1,000 mfg., commercial and contract sales. No sear safety, often have strawed small parts.

	N/A	$1,500	$1,050	$800	$700	$600	$500

MAUSER BANNER DUTCH CONTRACT — 9mm Para. cal., 4 in. barrel, 1,000 mfg., safety marked "Rust". Dated 1936-1940.

	N/A	$2,100	$1,500	$1,000	$600	$500	$400

    Add 25% for 1936, 1937, 1938, or 1939 chamber date.

Grading	100%	98%	95%	90%	80%	70%	60%

MAUSER BANNER SWEDISH CONTRACT — 275 mfg. in 9mm Para. cal., 4¾ in. barrels, dated 1938, 25 mfg. in 9mm Para. cal., dated 1939, 30 mfg. in 7.65mm Para. cal., dated 1939, very rare in 7.65mm Para. dated 1940.

	N/A	$2,700	$1,800	$1,200	$695	$600	$500

Add 15% for 7.65mm Para. cal. (4¾ in. barrel).

CODE "S/42" COMMERCIAL CONTRACT — 9mm Para. cal., 4 in. barrel, a few hundred produced, dated 1938. Commercial proof marks only.

	N/A	$1,200	$975	$750	$650	$550	$500

CODE "42" — 9mm Para. cal., 4 in. barrels, dated 1939-1940, rear toggle marked "42". One of the most frequently encountered WWII military Lugers.

	N/A	$775	$650	$550	$500	$450	$400

Add 40% for Navy markings.
Add $125+ for original holster in average condition.

MAUSER BANNER POLICE — 9mm Para. cal., approx. 30,000 mfg., dated 1939-1942, police contract, have sear safeties, blued small parts. A few observed dated 1938.

	N/A	$1,500	$1,000	$600	$500	$400	$350

Add 30% with 1938 chamber date (rare).

CODE "41-42" — 9mm Para. cal., 4 in. barrel, 2-digit date, approx. 7,000 mfg. in January of 1941, "41" dated chamber, "42" code, most 42 dates are reworks.

	N/A	$1,350	$950	$650	$425	$375	$350

Add $150+ for original holster in average condition.

CODE "byf" — 9mm Para. cal., 4 in. barrel, thousands made, chamber dated 41 and 42. Rear toggle is stamped "byf", standard magazine was "fxo" marked and had an un-numbered plastic bottom. One of the most frequently encountered WWII military Lugers.

	N/A	$925	$775	$575	$450	$375	$350

Add 30% for original black bakelite grips.
Add $150 for original holster in average condition.

Code "byf" Lugers with black bakelite grips are referred to as the "Black Widow" variation.

AUSTRIAN BUNDES HEER — 9mm Para. cal., 4 in. barrel, several hundred produced, Austrian Federal Army, no serial letter suffix-same ser. placement as KU. Rarely encountered in mint condition.

	N/A	$1,400	$1,000	$950	$825	$750	$650

MAUSER 1934 CODE BYF, S/42 AND 42 KU — 9mm Para. cal., 3,500 mfg. Post-1942 Luftwaffe subcontract.

	N/A	$1,700	$1,300	$950	$825	$750	$650

Lugers: Reworks

DEATH'S HEAD REWORK — 9mm Para. cal., 4 in. barrel, very rare, possible early SS unit issue. Most are fakes.

	N/A	$1,800	$995	$850	$700	$600	$450

SIMSON REWORK — 9mm Para. cal., 4 in. barrel, DWM toggles, Simpson Eagle proofs on reworked parts.

	N/A	$750	$550	$450	$375	$325	$295

DOUBLE DATED DWM/ERFURT — 9mm Para. cal., 4 or 8 in. barrel, very scarce. 1920 over 1910-1918 chamber dates. Often with sear safety and mag. safety remnant.

	N/A	$795	$500	$300	$275	$250	$225

Add 75% for intact mag. safety.
Add 40% for 8 in. barrel.

L

Grading	100%	98%	95%	90%	80%	70%	60%

KONZENTRATION LUGER REWORK — 9mm Para. cal., 4 in. barrel, 200-300 marked "KI 1933" and issued to guards working in the first concentration camps - most went to Dachau. Most are fakes.

	N/A	$1,100	$850	$600	$475	$400	$350

Lugers: Simson Mfg.

SIMSON & COMPANY — 7.65mm Para. or 9mm Para. cal., 3⅞ or 4 in. barrel, military and limited commercial sales, many thousands produced, but rarely found.

	N/A	$1,300	$800	$650	$500	$450	$375

SIMSON MILITARY DATED — 9mm Para. cal., 4 in. barrel, 2,000 mfg., dated 1925.

	N/A	$2,250	$1,650	$1,000	$800	$675	$550

> This model is most commonly encountered with a 1925 chamber date.

SIMSON S CODE — 9mm Para. cal., 4 in. barrel, less than 1,000 mfg. Rare.

	N/A	$1,850	$1,300	$975	$675	$550	$475

Lugers: Swiss Bern

1906 BERN — 7.65mm Para. cal., 4¾ in. barrel, "Waffenfabrik Bern" on toggle, Swiss military, bordered checkered walnut grips, exactly 17,874 mfg.

	N/A	$2,375	$1,700	$1,200	$900	$700	$600

1929 SWISS BERN — 7.65mm Para. cal., 4¾ in. barrel, 29,857 mfg., many machining changes to simplify production, straight front grip strap, P prefix designates commercial model, brown or black plastic grips.

	N/A	$1,500	$1,100	$900	$800	$600	$500

Add 20% for ribbed plastic grips and mag. bottom.

Lugers: KDF, Interarms, Stoeger, & Recent Import

Note: Post-WWII Lugers have been manufactured by Mauser Werke in Oberndorf, W. Germany during the 1970s, and by both Stoeger Industries and Mitchell Arms (see separate listing under Mitchell Arms) in recent years. Currently, the Stoeger Luger is the only Luger available for sale domestically. Earlier Mauser importation was by Precision Imports, Inc. located in San Antonio, TX and Interarms of Alexandria, VA (and so marked on these guns).

Prices below for 100% condition Lugers assume NIB status. If without box and accessories, deduct 25%.

INTERARMS MAUSER P.08 — 7.65mm Para. or 9mm Para. cal., 4 or 6 in. barrel, fully-contoured front grip strap.

$1,100	$800	$500	$425	$375	$350	$300

INTERARMS "SWISS-STYLE" MAUSER EAGLE — 7.65mm Para. or 9mm Para. cal., "straight" front grip strap, American eagle logo on top of frame.

$695	$475	$425	$375	$350	$325	$275

Add 10% for 6 in. barrel in 9mm Para..

STOEGER .22 CAL. LUGER — .22 LR cal., toggle action, all steel construction, 4½ in. barrel, 10 shot mag. capacity, previously mfg. in the U.S. until 1985.

$150	$125	$100	$85	$70	$60	$50

Last Mfg.'s Sug. Retail was $200.

* **"1 of 1,000"** — .22 LR cal., 1,000 mfg. in 1984-85, includes wooden box and extra mag.

$295	$225	$175

L

Grading	100%	98%	95%	90%	80%	70%	60%

STOEGER LUGER — 9mm Para. cal., choice of 4 or 6 (Navy) in. barrel, stainless steel construction, choice of polished stainless or matte black (new 1996) upper frame finish, American eagle engraved on top of frame, curved front grip strap, 7 shot mag., plastic mag. bottom, approx. 30 oz. New 1994.

Mfg.'s Sug. Retail	$720	$640	$565	$495

Add $79 for matte black finish.

NEW MODEL CARBINE WITH STOCK — 9mm Para. cal., authentic reproduction of the original Luger Carbine complete with matching stock, accessories, and case. Inventory was depleted during 1998.

$4,995 $3,850 $2,000

Last Mfg.'s Sug. Retail was $7,431.

CARTRIDGE COUNTER — 9mm Para. cal., left grip is slotted and contains a numbered metal strip. Manufacture began 1983, and inventory was depleted during 1998.

$2,650 $1,550 $950

Last Mfg.'s Sug. Retail was $3,865.

COMMEMORATIVE BULGARIAN — 9mm Para. cal., 100 available on U.S. market.

$1,800 $1,200 $800

COMMEMORATIVE RUSSIAN — 9mm Para. cal., 100 available on U.S. market.

$1,800 $1,200 $800

* *Matched pair of each*

$4,000 $2,550 $1,850

MAUSER SPORT PARABELLUM — 7.65mm Para. or 9mm Para. cal., imported target barrel and adj. sights. 10 mfg. of each cal.

$2,500 $2,000 $1,250

MAUSER SPORT PARABELLUM

* *Consecutive pair* — 7.65mm Para. or 9mm Para. cal.

$4,250 $3,175 $1,950

Lugers: Special Interest

SPANDAU LUGER — 9mm Para. cal., 200 mfg. as prototype in 1918, 10 known. Controversial.

Prices vary substantially on this "variation" and are not predictable.

MO4/05 G.L. BABY LUGER — 7.65mm Para. or 9mm Para. cal., 3¼ in. barrel, G.L. proofed, hand-made under Georg Luger's supervision, 2 known to exist. Made with shortened barrel, mag., and grip frame.

BABY LUGER 1925/26 — .380 ACP/.32 ACP cal., prototype, 4 mfg., only 1 known is .380. Only Luger documented by the manufacturer.

VONO REWORK — 7.65mm Para. or 9mm Para. cal., 4 in. barrel, commercial, rework by W.P. Von Nordheim, extremely rare variation.

$1,500 $1,275 $1,050 $900 $800 $700 $600

1900 DWM CARBINE — 7.65mm Para. cal., 11¾ in. barrel, 100 mfg., only one known to exist. Characterized by "Ski slope" sight on rear toggle.

1907 U.S. ARMY TEST TRIAL — .45 ACP cal., at least four mfg., three known to exist. BIG bucks.

CONVERSIONS: JOHN MARTZ — John Martz of Lincoln, CA has converted WWII P.38s and WWI or WWII Lugers into various configurations since 1968. These conversions are known for their quality workmanship and functional accuracy. Below is a generalized listing of variations he has fabricated and their values to date with production totals.

L

Grading	100%	98%	95%	90%	80%	70%	60%

* **.380 ACP Baby Luger** — 6 mfg. (disc.).

  $6,000 $3,200 $2,400

* **7.65mm Para. Baby Luger (Grip Safety)** — 18 mfg. 3 in. barrel.

  $3,000 $2,500 $1,900

* **9mm Para. Baby Luger** — 31 mfg., 2, 2¼, 2½, 2⅝, or 3 in. barrel.

  $2,500 $2,000 $1,500

* **Big-Bore .45 ACP Luger** — 55 mfg., .45 ACP cal., fixed sights, 2¾, 4, 6, or 8 in. barrel.

  $5,000 $3,350 $2,400

* **Navy Model** — .45 ACP cal., 6 or 8 in. barrel, adj. rear Navy sight, estimated mfg. is 25 pistols (Disc.).

  $6,000 $4,450 $3,300

  Add 10% for Navy Model with 100-200 meter rear sight.

* **Navy Model Ltd. Edition** — .38 Super cal., 6 in. barrel, adj. rear Navy sight, 10 mfg. (disc.).

  $5,000 $3,950 $3,100

  Subtract 10% for fixed rear sight (standard model with 4 in. barrel).

* **Standard Model** — .38 Super cal., 4 to 8 in. barrel, fixed sight, 3 mfg.

  $4,500 $3,150 $2,400

* **Target Luger** — .22 Mag. cal., 6 or 9 in. barrel, fixed sight, 11 mfg. (disc.).

  $7,500 $5,400 $3,400

* **Luger Carbines (with shoulder stock)** — 22 Mag. (disc.), 7.65mm Para., 9mm Para., or .38 Super cal., 11-18 in. barrel with adj. rear sights. Disc.

  $7,900 $5,650 $3,600

  Add 20% for .22 Mag. cal. (2 mfg.).

  81 Luger carbines with 16 in. barrels were mfg. with shoulder stocks.

  31 Luger carbines with 12 in. barrels were mfg. w/o shoulder stocks.

* **Experimental Lugers** — experimental pistols have been made in .40 S&W (disc.), .41 AE (disc.), and .357 Mag. Most have 8 in. barrels (except for .40 S&W cal., disc.). Extreme rarity (and not for sale status) precludes accurate price evaluation.

LUGERS: ACCESSORIES

CONVERSION UNITS - .22 cal.

ERMA — (postwar-green cardboard box).

	100%	98%	95%	90%	80%	70%	60%
	$350	$320	$295	$275	$250	$225	$200

ERMA-PREWAR IN WOODEN BOX — Pre-war in wooden box - deduct 20% for mismatched. Add 20% for Nazi Navy property numbered.

	100%	98%	95%	90%	80%	70%	60%
	$825	$750	$650	$550	$550	$430	$400

Detachable Stocks

ARTILLERY TYPE FLAT BOARD

	100%	98%	95%	90%	80%	70%	60%
	$325	$250	$200	$165	$135	$120	$110

NAVAL-TYPE FLAT BOARD

	100%	98%	95%	90%	80%	70%	60%
	$1,250	$995	$750	$600	$450	$410	$350

CARBINE CONTOURED (ORIGINAL)

	100%	98%	95%	90%	80%	70%	60%
	$2,250	$1,775	$1,200	$900	$850	$750	$700

HOLLOW ARTILLERY HOLSTER TYPE — hollow wood broomhandle type-very rare (watch for fakes).

	100%	98%	95%	90%	80%	70%	60%
	$6,750	$6,000	$5,500	$5,000	$4,500	$4,000	$3,500

Grading	100%	98%	95%	90%	80%	70%	60%
IDEAL TELESCOPING WITH GRIPS — mfg. U.S. by Ideal Corp.							
	$1,600	$1,200	$800	$700	$600	$550	$500
"Snail" Drum Magazines							
1ST ISSUE							
	$875	$700	$500				
2ND ISSUE							
	$700	$625	$475				
LOADING TOOL							
	$550	$500	$450				
ARTILLERY HOLSTER RIG, COMPLETE							
	$925	$775	$575				
Subtract 20% if shoulder strap is missing.							
NAVAL HOLSTER RIG, COMPLETE							
	$3,500	$3,000	$2,500	$2,000	$1,500	$1,200	$1,000

LU-MAR s.r.l.

Current shotgun manufacturer located in Gardone, Italy. Limited current importation by EAA, located Sharps, FL.

Lu-Mar makes a wide variety of O/U shotguns. In addition to their fine O/U lineup, Lu-Mar also manufactures SxS, semi-auto, and slide action shotguns. Please contact the factory directly (see Trademark Index) for more information on Lu-Mar's complete line of quality O/U shotguns.

LUNA

Previous manufacturer located in Germany.

PISTOLS: SINGLE SHOT

MODEL 200 FREE PISTOL — .22 LR cal., 11 in. barrel, blue, target sights, checkered target grips, pre-WWII.

	100%	98%	95%	90%	80%	70%	60%
	$1,100	$990	$855	$770	$660	$605	$525

RIFLES: SINGLE SHOT

TARGET RIFLE — falling block action, .22 LR or .22 Hornet cal., 20 in. barrel, adj. sights, target type stocks, pre-WWII.

	100%	98%	95%	90%	80%	70%	60%
	$990	$880	$800	$690	$605	$550	$495

NOTES

M section

MAB

Please refer to listings under the French Military heading.

MAC (MILITARY ARMAMENT CORP.)

Please refer to FMJ and Ingram sections in this text. MAC is located in Ducktown, TN (please refer to the FMJ listing in the Trademark Index for current information).

MAS

Previously manufactured by D'Armes St. Etienne (MAS) located in France.
Please refer to the French Military heading in this text.

MBA GYROJET

Previous manufacturer circa 1966-1969 located in San Ramon, CA.

Grading	100%	98%	95%	90%	80%	70%	60%

PISTOLS: SEMI-AUTO

MARK I GYROJET PISTOL — 12mm or 13mm (no cartridge case) cal., uses spin-stabilized rocket projectiles that accelerate to 1,250 FPS in .12 seconds, 2 in. (rare) or 5 in. barrel, 6 shot semi-auto action drives rocket projectile (primer activated) into fixed firing pin, smooth walnut grips, black, antique nickel, or gold-plated finish, 13 or 16 oz., "A" prefix until ser. no. 49, "B" prefixes followed, there are also other variations and experimental models in addition to the production models listed below. Not particularly accurate.

The rocket ammunition for this model is rare and typically sells in the $20-$25/round range.

* ***Mark I Model A Cased*** — 13mm, black finish, smooth walnut grips, walnut cased with 10 rounds and medal.

	100%	98%	95%	90%	80%	70%	60%
	$1,450	$1,300	$1,100	$950	$875	$795	$700

* ***Mark I Model B Cased*** — 13mm, black, nickel, satin, or green finish, many variations with different grips, casings, and barrel lengths, wood cased.

	100%	98%	95%	90%	80%	70%	60%
	$1,150	$1,000	$900	$800	$700	$600	$500

Add approx. 25% for satin finish.

* ***Mark I Model B Uncased or Cardboard*** — either with cardboard case or no case, black finish.

	98%	95%	90%	80%	70%	60%
	$575	$500	$450	$400	$360	$330	$300

* ***Mark II Model C Uncased or Cardboard*** — 12mm, black finish, walnut grips.

	$575	$500	$450	$400	$360	$330	$300

This variation was manufactured in 12mm to conform with the 1968 GCA, since any caliber over .50 was classified as a destructive device (i.e., 12mm = .49 cal. and 13mm = .51 cal.). In 1982, the 13mm guns were reclassified as curios and relics.

* ***Mark I Presentation Model*** — cased with 10 dummy/live rounds and bronze medal honoring rocket pioneers Robert H. Goddard and Joseph J. Stubbs.

	$2,250	$1,600	$995

RIFLES: SEMI-AUTO, CARBINES

MARK I MODEL A or B CARBINE — 13mm cal., same action as Mark I pistol, black (Model A) or satin (Model B) finish, full stock with pistol grip extension, 18 in. barrel, nickel finish, 4½ lbs. Limited mfg.

	100%	98%	95%	90%	80%	70%	60%
Model A	$1,695	$1,600	$1,475	$1,350	$1,225	$1,100	$1,000
Model B	$1,050	$850	$750	$650	$595	$550	$500

M

Grading	100%	98%	95%	90%	80%	70%	60%

MK ARMS INC.

Previous manufacturer located in Irvine, CA circa 1992.

RIFLES: SEMI-AUTO

MK 760 — 9mm Para. cal., paramilitary design carbine configuration, steel frame, 16 in. shrouded barrel, fires from closed bolt, 14, 24, or 36 shot mag., parkerized finish, folding metal stock, fixed sights. Mfg. 1983-approx. 1992.

$575	$525	$475	$415	$375	$340	$310

Last Mfg.'s Sug. Retail was $575.

MKE

Previous manufacturer located in Ankara, Turkey. Previously distributed by Mandall Shooting Supplies, Inc., located in Scottsdale, AZ.

PISTOLS: SEMI-AUTO

KIRIKKALE AUTOMATIC — 7.65mm Para. (disc.) or .380 ACP cal., double action, 7 shot, blue, fixed sights, checkered plastic grips, this is a close copy of Walther's PP and the Turkish Army's standard service pistol. Disc. 1987.

$365	$295	$240	$215	$185	$170	$155

Last Mfg.'s Sug. Retail was $395.

M.O.A. CORPORATION

Current manufacturer located in Eaton, OH. Dealer direct sales only.

PISTOLS: SINGLE SHOT

Approx. 500-600 maximum pistols are produced annually.

MAXIMUM — available in 30 standard chamberings between .22 Rimfire and .454 Casull cal., additional custom calibers are also available upon special order, single shot lever action pistol, falling block action, Chromoly receiver (disc. 1991), Armoloy coated Chromoly (disc. late 1992), or stainless steel (new 1991, standard 1992) receiver, 8¾ (new 1989), 10½, or 14 in. interchangeable barrel, transfer bar safety, adj. open sights, walnut grips and forearm. New 1986.

Mfg.'s Sug. Retail	$740	$640	$545	$475	$435	$395	$375	$350

Subtract $85 for older steel receiver.
Add $60 for scope mounts.
Add $78 for stainless steel barrel on either receiver.
Add $125 for muzzle brake.
Add $235 per extra steel barrel.
Add $293 per extra stainless steel barrel.

Barrels must be fitted to individual receivers at the factory initially. Afterwards, they can be changed by the customer with the spanner wrench (included with extra barrels).

* **Carbine Model** — cals. up to .250 Sav., stainless receiver, otherwise similar to Maximum, except has 18 in. barrel. Mfg. 1986-87, reintroduced 1994, disc. 1998.

$750	$640	$530	$440	$375	$330	$300

Last Mfg.'s Sug. Retail was $825.

Add $78 for stainless steel barrel.

JAMES MacNAUGHTON & SONS

Current manufacturer located in Moray, Scotland. Currently imported and distributed by James MacNaughton & Sons located in Carrizo Springs, TX.

The firm of James MacNaughton was founded in Edinburgh, Scotland in 1864. During 1947, the company was acquired by John Dickson and during 1996, the ownership of the company changed again, having purchased the manufacturing rights from Dickson. James MacNaughton & Sons is currently planning to introduce

Grading			100%	98%	95%	90%	80%	70%	60%

a traditional, round action shotgun shortly - please contact the importer directly for more information regarding this model and others.

RIFLES: SxS

SIDELOCK RIFLE — .375 H&H or .470 NE cal., specifications per individual customer order.

Prices currently start at approx. $27,125 for this model.

SHOTGUNS

SxS SIDELOCK MODEL — 20 or 28 ga., lightweight construction.

Prices currently start at approx. $36,000 for this model.

MAGNUM RESEARCH, INC.

MAGNUM RESEARCH, INC.

Current trademark of pistols and rifles with company headquarters located in Minneapolis, MN. Centerfire pistols (Desert Eagle Series) are again mfg. by IMI, located in Israel. Previously mfg. by Saco Defense located in Saco, ME during 1995-98, and by TAAS/IMI (Israeli Military Industries) 1986-1995. .22 Rimfire semi-auto pistols (Mountain Eagle) were previously manufactured by Ram-Line. Single shot pistols (Lone Eagle) are manufactured by Magnum Research sub-contractors. Distributed by Magnum Research, Inc., in Minneapolis, MN. Dealer and distributor sales.

In addition to the models listed below, Magnum Research can also provide a variety of special order options through their custom shop including a choice of seven different finishes in addition to various sight systems. Prices can be obtained by contacting Magnum Research directly.

PISTOLS: SEMI-AUTO, .22 CAL.

THE MOUNTAIN EAGLE — .22 LR cal., single action, 6 (new 1995) or 6½ (disc. 1994) in. polymer and steel barrel, features alloy receiver and polymer technology, matte black finish, adj. rear sight, 15 or 20 shot mag. 21 oz. Mfg. 1992-96.

			$185	$155	$135	$115	$100	$85	$75

Last Mfg.'s Sug. Retail was $239.

* ***Mountain Eagle Compact Edition*** — similar to Mountain Eagle, except has 4½ in. barrel with shortened grips, adj. rear sight, 10 or 15 shot mag., plastic case, 19.3 oz. Mfg. 1996 only.

			$165	$135	$120	$105	$95	$80	$70

Last Mfg.'s Sug. Retail was $199.

* ***Mountain Eagle Target Edition*** — .22 LR cal., Target variation of the Mountain Eagle, featuring 8 in. accurized barrel, 2-stage target trigger, jeweled bolt, adj. sights with interchangeable blades, 23 oz. Mfg. 1994-96.

			$235	$185	$150	$135	$120	$105	$95

Last Mfg.'s Sug. Retail was $279.

M

PISTOLS: SEMI-AUTO, DESERT EAGLE SERIES

Magnum Research also offers a Collector's Edition Presentation Series. Special models include a Gold Edition (serial numbered 1-100), a Silver Edition (serial numbered 101-500), and a Bronze Edition (serial numbered 501-1,000). Each pistol from this series is supplied with a walnut presentation case, 2 sided medallion, and certificate of authenticity. Prices are available upon request by contacting Magnum Research directly.

Alloy frames on the Desert Eagle Series of pistols were discontinued in 1992. However, if sufficient demand warrants, these models will once again be available to consumers at the same price as the steel frames.

Beginning late 1995, the Desert Eagle frame assembly for the .357 Mag., .44 Mag., and .50 AE cals. is based on the .50 caliber frame. Externally, all three pistols are now identical in size. This new platform called the Desert Eagle Pistol Mark XIX Component

Grading	100%	98%	95%	90%	80%	70%	60%

System enables .44 Mag. and .50 AE conversions to consist of simply a barrel and a magazine - conversions to or from the .357 Mag. also include a bolt.

Add $195 for custom shop finishes including polished chrome, matte chrome, brushed chrome, bright nickel, satin nickel, polished blue, or polished blue with gold accents. Gold plating is also available for an additional $500.

THE BABY EAGLE — 9mm Para., .40 S&W, or .41 AE cal., double action, all steel construction, 3.62 (9mm Para. only, new 1993) or 4.72 in. barrel, short recoil operation, polygonal rifling, combat styled triggerguard, decocking slide safety or frame mounted safety (Model 9mmF), blued (disc. 1995), standard black (new 1996), or chrome finish, 10 (C/B 1994), 16★ (9mm Para.), 11★ (.41 AE), or 10 (.40 S&W) shot mag., 38½ oz. Model 9mmFS is short barrel with frame mounted safety. Imported 1991-96. Reintroduced mid 1999.

Mfg.'s Sug. Retail	$389	$335	$295	$260	$230	$200	$175	$160

Add $45 for chrome finish (9mm Para. only beginning 1996).

Add $239 for conversion kit (9mm Para. to .41 AE or .41 AE to 9mm Para., includes barrel, spring, and mag.).

MARK XIX .357 MAG. DESERT EAGLE — features .50 cal. frame, standard black finish, 6 or 10 in. barrel, mfg. by Saco 1995-98, and IMI beginning 1998.

Mfg.'s Sug. Retail	$1,099	$935	$800	$675	$550	$475	$400	$350

Add $100 for 10 in. barrel.

MARK VII .357 MAG. DESERT EAGLE — .357 Mag. cal., gas operated, 6 (current standard barrel length), 10, or 14 in. barrel lengths, steel (58.3 oz.) or alloy (47.8 oz.) frame, adaptable to .44 Mag. with optional kit, 9 shot mag. (8 for .44 Mag.). Mfg. 1983-95, limited quantities were made available again during 1998 only.

		$850	$650	$525	$475	$425	$395	$375

Last Mfg.'s Sug. Retail was $929.

Add approx. $150 for 10 or 14 in. barrel (disc. 1995).

Add $495 for .357 Mag. to .41 Mag./.44 Mag. conversion kit (6 in. barrel). Disc. 1995.

Add approx. $685 for .357 Mag. to .44 Mag. conversion kit (10 or 14 in. barrel). Disc. 1995.

 * *Whitetail Special .357 Mag.* — 14 in. barrel, includes scope mount, target walnut grips, and Desert Eagle premiums. Mfg. 1990-1992.

		$925	$750	$650	$550	$450	$400	$375

Last Mfg.'s Sug. Retail was $1,088.

Add $50 for stainless steel frame.

 * *Stainless Steel .357 Mag.* — similar to .357 Mag. Desert Eagle, except has stainless steel frame, 58.3 oz. Mfg. 1987-95.

		$750	$650	$550

Last Mfg.'s Sug. Retail was $839.

Add approx. $150 for 10 or 14 in. barrel.

MARK VII .41 MAG. DESERT EAGLE — .41 Mag. cal., similar to .357 Desert Eagle, 6 in. barrel only, 8 shot mag., steel (62.8 oz.) or alloy (52.3 oz.) frame. Mfg. 1988-95.

		$785	$675	$565	$500	$465	$420	$390

Last Mfg.'s Sug. Retail was $899.

Add $395 for .41 Mag. to .44 Mag. conversion kit (6 in. barrel only).

 * *Stainless Steel .41 Mag.* — similar to .41 Mag. Desert Eagle, except has stainless steel frame, 58.3 oz. Mfg. 1988-95.

		$825	$700	$550

Last Mfg.'s Sug. Retail was $949.

MARK XIX .44 MAG. DESERT EAGLE — features .50 cal. frame, standard black finish, 6 or 10 in. barrel, mfg. by Saco 1995-98, and by IMI beginning 1998.

Mfg.'s Sug. Retail	$1,099	$935	$800	$675	$550	$475	$400	$350

Add $100 for 10 in. barrel.

M

Grading	100%	98%	95%	90%	80%	70%	60%

MARK VII .44 MAG. DESERT EAGLE — .44 Mag. cal., similar to .357 Desert Eagle, 8 shot mag., steel (62.8 oz.) or alloy (52.3 oz.) frame. Originally mfg. 1986-95, rereleased beginning 1998.

Mfg.'s Sug. Retail	$989	$885	$675	$535	$475	$425	$395	$375

Add $80 for alloy frame.
Add approx. $200 for 10 or 14 in. barrel (disc. 1995).
Add $475 for .44 Mag. to .357 Mag. conversion kit (6 in. barrel). Disc. 1995.
Add $675 for .44 Mag. to .357 Mag. conversion kit (10 or 14 in. barrel). Disc. 1995.
Add $395 for .44 Mag. to .41 Mag. conversion kit (6 in. barrel). Disc. 1995.

* ***Stainless Steel .44 Mag.*** — similar to .44 Mag. Desert Eagle, except has stainless steel frame, 58.3 oz. Mfg. 1987-95.

			$825	$700	$550		

Last Mfg.'s Sug. Retail was $949.

Add approx. $210 for 10 or 14 in. barrel.

HUNTER EDITION MARK VII — .357 or .44 Mag. cal., 6 in. barrel with extra 14 in. hunting barrel, includes Leupold 2X EER scope, scope mount. Mfg. late 1987-1993.

			$1,200	$975	$825	$675	$550	$475	$425

Last Mfg.'s Sug. Retail was $1,350.

Add $110 for .44 Mag. cal.

MARK XIX CUSTOM 440 — .440 Cor-Bon cal., similar to Mark XIX .44 Mag. Desert Eagle, 6 or 10 in. barrel, standard black finish. Mfg. by IMI beginning 1999.

Mfg.'s Sug. Retail	$1,299	$1,100	$950	$825	$700	$575	$500	$450	$400

Add $100 for 10 in. barrel.

MARK XIX .50 MAG. DESERT EAGLE — features .50 AE cal., larger frame, standard black finish, 6 or 10 in. barrel, mfg. by Saco 1995-98, and by IMI beginning 1998.

Mfg.'s Sug. Retail	$1,099		$950	$825	$700	$575	$500	$450	$400

Add $100 for 10 in. barrel.

MARK VII .50 MAG. DESERT EAGLE — .50 AE cal., 6 in. barrel, steel only, black standard finish, 7 shot mag., 72.4 oz. Mfg. 1991-95, limited quantities were made available again during 1998 only.

			$950	$825	$700	$575	$500	$450	$400

Last Mfg.'s Sug. Retail was $1,099.

This new cartridge utilized the same rim dimensions as the .44 Mag. and is available with a 300 grain bullet. The .50 Mag. Action Express cal. has 60% more stopping power than the .44 Mag., with a minimal increase in felt recoil.

MARK XIX 3 CAL. COMPONENT SYSTEM — includes Mark XIX .44 Mag. Desert Eagle and 5 barrels including .357 Mag. (6 and 10 in.), .44 Mag., and .50 AE (6 and 10 in.) cals., .357 bolt assembly and ICC aluminum carrying case. New 1998.

Mfg.'s Sug. Retail	$3,500	$3,150	$2,700	$2,250	$1,900	$1,625	$1,300	$1,050

* ***Mark XIX 2 Cal. Component System*** — similar to above, except includes 6 or 10 in. 357 Mag. and .50 AE cal. barrels. New 1998.

Mfg.'s Sug. Retail	$2,300	$2,050	$1,775	$1,625	$1,475	$1,250	$1,000	$850

Add $200 for 10 in. barrels.

M

PISTOLS: SINGLE SHOT

LONE EAGLE (SSP-91) — .22 LR (disc. 1992), .22 Mag. (disc. 1992), .22 Hornet, .22-250 Rem., .223 Rem., .243 Win., .260 Rem. (new 1997), .30-30 Win., .30-06, .300 Win. Mag. (Ltd. ed., new 1997), .308 Win., 6mmBR (disc. 1992), 7mm-08 Rem., 7mmBR, .35 Rem., .357 Max. (disc. 1997), .358 Win., .44 Mag., .440 Cor-Bon (new 1999), .444 Marlin, or 7.62x39mm (new 1996) cal., circular rear breech action, quick change 14 in. barrels (drilled and tapped), black or chrome (new 1997) finish, black synthetic Valox ambidextrous pistol grip, 4 lbs. 3 oz. - 4 lbs. 7 oz. New 1991.

Mfg.'s Sug. Retail	$438		$380	$315	$275	$230	$200	$185	$170

Grading	100%	98%	95%	90%	80%	70%	60%

Add $40 for chrome finish.
Add $35 for adj. hunting sights.
Add $319 for standard black finish barrel, $418 for standard barrel with muzzle brake, $359 for chrome barrel, and $469 for chrome barrel with muzzle brake.

The grip assembly ($119) and barreled actions are available individually on this model.

REVOLVERS

MAXINE BFR MODEL — .444 Marlin, .45 LC/.410 bore, or .45-70 Govt. cal., single or double action, 6 shot, stainless steel, 7½ (.45 LC/.410 bore and .45-70 Govt.) or 10 (.444 Marlin and .45-70 Govt.) in. barrel, checkered rubber grips. New 1999.

Mfg.'s Sug. Retail	$899		$800	$700	$625		

LITTLE MAX BFR MODEL — .22 Hornet, .45 LC+P, .454 Casull, or .50 AE cal., similar to Maxine BFR Model, 6½ (.45 LC+P and .454 Casull cal.), 7½, or 10 (not available in .50 AE or .45 LC+P cal.) barrel. New 1999.

Mfg.'s Sug. Retail	$899		$800	$700	$625		

RIFLES: BOLT-ACTION

MOUNTAIN EAGLE RIFLE — .270 Win., .280 Rem., .30-06, 7mmSTW (new 1998), .300 Win. Mag., .300 Wby. Mag., .338 Win. Mag., .340 Wby. Mag. (disc. 1997), 7mm Rem. Mag., .375 H&H, or .416 Rem. Mag. cal., Sako action, adj. trigger, 4 or 5 shot mag., match grade Krieger barrel with cut rifling, H-S Precision composite stock with aluminum bedding block, includes carrying case. New 1994.

Mfg.'s Sug. Retail	$1,499		$1,325	$1,075	$900	$775	$625	$550	$495

Add $150 for muzzle brake.
Add $60 for left-hand action.
Add $300 for .375 H&H or .416 Rem. Mag. cal.

*   ✳ *Varmint Mountain Eagle* — .222 Rem. or .223 Rem. cal., 26 in. stainless steel heavy fluted barrel, w/o sights, approx. 9¾ lbs. New 1996.

Mfg.'s Sug. Retail	$1,629		$1,425	$1,100	$925			

RIFLES: SEMI-AUTO

Add $130 for Clark custom upgrade (includes Clark deluxe trigger kit, tuned extractor, and bolt release) on the models listed below.

MAGNUM LITE RIFLE — .22 LR cal., features Ruger 10/22 receiver with Acculite barrel utilizing uni-directional graphite carbon fiber. New 1997.

*   ✳ *Magnum Lite Rifle w/Hogue or Fajen Stock* — choice of black Hogue Overmolded or Fajen high stock in either midnight or coffee color. New 1997.

Mfg.'s Sug. Retail	$599		$525	$450	$395	$360	$330	$275	$250

*   ✳ *Magnum Lite Rifle w/Fajen Thumbhole Stock* — features choice of Fajen thumbhole sporter or thumbhole silhouette in midnight or coffee color. New 1997.

Mfg.'s Sug. Retail	$699		$625	$525	$450	$395	$360	$330	$275

Add $100 for thumbhole silhouette stock configuration.

*   ✳ *Magnum Lite Rifle w/Turner Barracuda Stock* — features skeletonized sporter stock in choice of green or coffee laminate. New 1997.

Mfg.'s Sug. Retail	$799		$695	$575	$475	$425	$375	$350	$325

MAGTECH

Current importer and distributor located in Las Vegas, NV. Manufactured by CBC located in Brazil. Distributor sales only.

Grading	100%	98%	95%	90%	80%	70%	60%

RIFLES: BOLT ACTION

MODEL 122 — .22 LR cal., 6 shot detachable clip, safety lever disconnects trigger from firing mechanism, uncheckered hardwood stock, 5.7 lbs. Imported 1992 only.

	$115	$95	$80	$70	$60	$50	$40

Last Mfg.'s Sug. Retail was $131.

SHOTGUNS

MODEL 151 SINGLE SHOT — 12, 16, 20 ga., or .410 bore, 26, 28, or 30 in. barrel, exposed hammer, ejector, front triggerguard opening mechanism, 5 - 6½ lbs. Imported 1992 only.

		$95	$80	$70	$60	$50	$40	$35

Last Mfg.'s Sug. Retail was $109.

MODEL MT-586-2 SLIDE ACTION — 12 ga. only, 3 in. chamber, standard Field model shotgun, 28 in. barrel with fixed chokes, hardwood stock and forearm, double slide bars. Imported 1993-95.

	$190	$175	$160	$140	$130	$120	$110

Last Mfg.'s Sug. Retail was $229.

The Model MT-586 preceded the MT-586-2, the MT-586 was disc. 1994.

* *Model MT-586-2-VR Slide Action* — similar to Model MT-586, except has choice of 26 or 28 in. VR barrel with interchangeable chokes. Imported 1993-95.

	$220	$185	$170	$155	$140	$130	$120

Last Mfg.'s Sug. Retail was $259.

MODEL MT-586 SLIDE ACTION SLUG — 12 ga. only, slug gun featuring 24 in. cylinder bore barrel with rifle sights, matte finished metal parts, and special Monte Carlo stock. Imported 1993-95.

	$195	$180	$165	$145	$130	$120	$110

Last Mfg.'s Sug. Retail was $239.

MODEL MT-586-2P — 12 ga. only, 3 in. chamber, slide action, 19 in. cylinder bore barrel, 7 shot mag., double slide bars, steel construction, hardwood stock, 7.3 lbs. Importation began 1992.

Mfg.'s Sug. Retail	$219	$185	$170	$155	$140	$130	$120	$110

MAKAROV

Pistol design originating from Russia. Russian mfg. Makarovs may be found under "Russian Service Pistol and Rifle" heading in this text. Pistols listed below have recently been imported by various companies, including Century International Arms, Inc. located in St. Albans, VT, and Miltex, Inc., located in La Plata, MD.

PISTOLS: SEMI-AUTO

MAKAROV COPIES — 9mm Makarov cal., patterned after the Soviet PM pistol, mfg. in eastern Germany, Bulgaria, and China, double action, blowback design, all steel, slide mounted safety that doubles as a decocking lever, 3.6 in. barrel, 8 shot mag., 25 oz.

No Mfg.'s Retail		$185	$145	$125	$105	$95	$85	$75

Add approx. $35-$40 for polish blue or silver matte finish (Bulgarian mfg. only).

The importation of this type of pistol increased beginning 1992.

MALIN, F.E.

Previous manufacturer located in England. Previously imported by Saxon Arms, Inc. located in Clearwater, FL. Charles Boswell purchased Malin shortly before manufacture stopped.

M

Grading	100%	98%	95%	90%	80%	70%	60%

SHOTGUNS: SxS, CUSTOM

BOXLOCK — made to individual order, choice of game scene engraving, Anson & Deeley boxlock actions, select European hybrid walnut, double triggers, leather cased. Prices started at $3,750 and each shotgun was priced per individual special order.

SIDELOCK — made to individual order, choice of game scene engraving, H&H sidelock action, select European hybrid walnut, double triggers, leather cased. Prices started at $5,000 and each shotgun were priced per individual special order.

MAMBA

Previously manufactured by Viper Mfg. Co. (a division of Sandock Austral Boksburg) located in South Africa.

PISTOLS: SEMI-AUTO

AUTO PISTOL — 9mm Para. cal., double action, 5 in. barrel, 14 shot mag., designed in Rhodesia, manufacture was not successful due to the non-hardened steel used in the investment cast construction process, poor exterior finish, less than 80 imported into the U.S., and 25 prototypes were built for Navy Arms.

Rarity factor precludes accurate pricing, values vary greatly in different regions.

MANCHESTER ARMS INC.

Previous manufacturer located in Lenoir, TN.

PISTOLS: SEMI-AUTO

COMMANDO MARK 45 — .45 ACP cal., paramilitary type design with detachable mag., wood pistol grip, 5 in. barrel with muzzle brake. Disc.

$450	$395	$350	$300	$265	$235	$200

MANDALL SHOOTING SUPPLIES, INC.

Current importer, distributor, and retailer located in Scottsdale, AZ.

Mandall Shooting Supplies distributes/imports various firearms including pistols, revolvers, rifles, shotguns, as well as other models. Most of these firearms can be located under their individual trademark headings and include FAS, Gaucher, Hämmerli, Krico rifles, and A. Zoli shotguns and rifles.

Due to the fluctuation of the U.S. dollar against the currencies of other countries, the above trademarks can change price during the course of a year. For this reason, Mandall Shooting Supplies, Inc. should be contacted directly for current pricing and special order questions.

MANNLICHER PISTOLS

Previously manufactured in Austria and Switzerland starting circa 1894.

PISTOLS: SEMI-AUTO

MODEL 1894 — 6.5mm or 7.6mm cal., unique blow forward design, fewer than 100 mfg. by Fabrique d' Armes in Neuhausen and OWG, Steyr.

$13,500	$11,000	$9,500	$8,500	$7,500	$6,000	$5,000

MODEL 1897 — 7.63mm Mannlicher cal., first Mannlicher pistol with detachable mag. (matching), unique cocking lever on right frame, approx. 1,000 mfg.

$6,500	$5,500	$4,800	$4,250	$3,750	$3,250	$2,750

Subtract 15% for carbine version.
Add 150% for Model 1896 prototype in similar configuration, but with fixed mag.

Grading	100%	98%	95%	90%	80%	70%	60%
COMMERCIAL MODEL 1901							
	$2,500	$1,800	$1,200	$900	$600	$500	$400
COMMERCIAL MODEL 1905							
	$1,650	$1,200	$800	$500	$400	$350	$300

ARGENTINE MODEL 1905 — 7.65mm cal., Argentine crest on left panel is usually machined off. Values assume matching numbers but removed crest.

	$400	$350	$300	$255	$220	$185	$150

* *Argentine Model 1905 With Original Military Crest*

	$1,650	$1,200	$800	$500	$400	$350	$300

MANNLICHER SCHOENAUER SPORTING RIFLES

Currently manufactured by Steyr, Daimler, Puch, in Austria from 1850s-present. Please refer to Steyr-Mannlicher in this text for currently manufactured rifles.

RIFLES: BOLT ACTIONS, PRE-WWII

Add approx. $175-$200 for all takedown pre-war models listed below.

MODEL 1903 CARBINE — 6.5x54mm Mannlicher Schoenauer cal., 5 shot, 17.7 in. barrel, rotary mag., two leaf rear sight, double set trigger, full length stock.

	$1,050	$875	$775	$675	$575	$525	$475

This caliber may also be referred to as 6.5x53mm.

This model is normally encountered in poor condition.

MODEL 1905 CARBINE — similar to Model 1903, except 9x56mm Mannlicher Schoenauer cal. only, 19.7 in. barrel.

	$900	$775	$695	$650	$550	$495	$450

This model is normally encountered in poor condition. It is perhaps the least desirable of pre-war models because of the wide variation in bore diameters.

MODEL 1908 CARBINE — similar to Model 1905, except in 8x56mm Mannlicher Schoenauer cal. only.

	$900	$775	$695	$650	$550	$495	$450

This model is frequently noticed in better condition factors. Some exceptional takedown variations also exist within this model.

MODEL 1910 CARBINE — similar design to the Model 1905, except originally chambered for 9.5x56mm Mannlicher, .375 Express, or 9.5x57mm Mauser cal., this model was the predecessor of the post-war Model 1924.

	$1,050	$875	$775	$675	$575	$525	$475

MODEL 1924 CARBINE — similar to 1905, except .30-06.

	$995	$825	$725	$625	$525	$475	$425

HIGH VELOCITY SPORTING RIFLE — 7x64 Brenneke, .30-06, 8x60mm Mag., 9.3x62mm, or 10.75x68mm cal., 23.6 in. barrel, 3 leaf sight, half stock.

	$1,050	$875	$775	$675	$575	$525	$475

Add $200 for 10.75x68mm, 7x64 Brenneke, or 8x60mm Mag. cal.

M

RIFLES: BOLT ACTION, POST-WWII

Values below represent standard models with no engraving. Original engraving will add at least $200 to prices listed below with some heavily engraved "Alpine" models selling for large premiums. A variation of the 1950-1952 Series is called the "GK" because of its traditionally styled European stock - which is a variant of the pre-war style and approaches the design of the Model 1961 MCA. Of the calibers listed below for post-WWII models, the 6.5x54mm is considered one of the most desirable, as well as the 9.3x62mm.

In 1951, Steyr (at Stoeger's request) made the following changes to the Model 1950 (named Improved Model 1950). These include: an ebony tip and fuller forend, left-side

Grading	100%	98%	95%	90%	80%	70%	60%

dummy plate cuts for side mount, left-side of receiver was flattened to facilitate side scope mount, and flatter bolt handle requiring slot inside of stock.

In 1952, changes included a carved cheekpiece, change from ¾ in. sling swivels to 1 in., swept back bolt handle, wood on left-side of stock over the dummy sideplate cutout thickened to strengthen the stock with a side mount in place, and removal of loading ears and clip guides, thereby streamlining the receiver and enabling lower scope mounting.

At one time Stoeger listed 18 versions of the M1950-52 family defined as #S-1 through #S-18 with three major differences existing within each block of Model 1950, Improved Model 1950, and Model 1952. The differences were: single and double set triggers (DST), rifle or carbine style, 6.5mm Carbine, single trigger or DST.

MODEL 1950 — various cals. including .244 Rem., .257 Roberts, .270 Win., .280 Rem., .30-06, .358 Win., 6.5x54mm (very desirable), 7x57mm, 8x57mm Mauser, or 9.3x62mm Mauser, bolt action, 5 shot rotary mag., 24 in. barrel, low bolt handle, half length stock, ebony forearm tip. Mfg. 1950-1952.

	100%	98%	95%	90%	80%	70%	60%
	$850	$775	$675	$600	$550	$495	$450

MODEL 1950 CARBINE — similar to Model 1950, except has 20 in. barrel, full length stock. Mfg. 1950-1952.

	$850	$775	$675	$600	$550	$495	$450

MODEL 1950 CARBINE 6.5 — similar to Model 1950 Carbine, except 6.5x54mm cal., 18½ in. barrel. Mfg. 1950-1952.

	$975	$875	$750	$675	$600	$550	$495

Deduct 50% if encountered with oversized bore (over .265 in.).

IMPROVED MODEL 1952 — same specifications as Model 1950, except swept back bolt handle. Mfg. 1952-1956.

	$795	$725	$625	$550	$475	$425	$385

IMPROVED MODEL 1952 CARBINE — .257 Roberts, .270 Win., 7x57mm, or .30-06 cal., swept bolt handle, otherwise similar to Model 1950 Carbine.

	$850	$775	$675	$600	$550	$495	$450

IMPROVED MODEL 1952 6.5 CARBINE — similar to Model 1952 Carbine, except 6.5mm cal., 18½ in. barrel. Mfg. 1952-1956.

	$975	$875	$750	$675	$600	$550	$495

MODEL 1956 RIFLE — similar to Improved Model 1952, except .243 Win. and .30-06 cals., new high comb stock design, 22 in. barrel, half length stock. Mfg. 1956-1960.

	$695	$640	$560	$495	$450	$360	$330

* *Model 1956 Magnum* — includes .257 Wby. Mag., .458 Win. Mag., 6.5x68mm, or 8x68mm cal.

	$950	$850	$725	$650	$575	$525	$475

MODEL 1956 CARBINE — similar to Model 1956 Rifle, except .243 Win., 6.5x53mm, .257 Roberts, .270 Win., 7mm Rem. Mag., .30-06, or .308 Win. cal., 20 in. barrel, full length stock. Mfg. 1956-1960.

	$850	$775	$675	$600	$550	$495	$450

MODEL 1961 MCA RIFLE — similar to Model 1956 Rifle, except Monte Carlo stock. Mfg. 1961-1971.

	$825	$750	$650	$575	$525	$475	$425

MODEL 1961 MCA CARBINE — similar to Model 1956 Carbine, except Monte Carlo stock. Mfg. 1961-1971.

	$850	$775	$675	$600	$550	$495	$450

RIFLES: BOLT ACTION, CURRENT PRODUCTION

Current production guns are now called Steyr-Mannlicher models and can be located under this trademark in the S section.

Grading	100%	98%	95%	90%	80%	70%	60%

MANUFRANCE

Current manufacturer established circa 1887 and located in St. Etienne, France. No current importer.

Manufrance currently manufactures both SxS rifle and shotgun variations (the Robust Models being the most popular) that are not being currently imported in the U.S. Please contact the factory directly for more information, including model availability and domestic prices.

SHOTGUNS

SEMI-AUTO MODEL — 12 ga., 26, 28, or 30 in. imp. cyl., mod. and full, 2¾ or 3 in. chamber, gas operated, walnut stock, black matte receiver, VR.

	$330	$305	$290	$275	$255	$240	$220

FALCOR O/U — 12 ga., VR, 26 in. imp. cyl. and mod., 28 in. mod. and full, SST, auto ejector, chrome lined barrel, walnut checkered stock.

	$715	$665	$635	$605	$550	$495	$470

MANURHIN

Currently manufactured by Chapuis Armes beginning in 1998, and located in Saint Bonnet Le Chateau, France. During 1998, Chapuis Armes purchased Manurhin, and new revolvers are currently being manufactured in a new facility located in Saint Bonnet Le Chateau, France, utilizing the original production machinery. Previously manufactured by Manurhin Equipment 1972-1998, located in Mulhouse, France. Currently available by either contacting the factory directly, or on a special order only basis by ABO Industries located in San Diego, CA (previously Atlantic Business Organization located in New York, NY until 1992). Previously owned by Matra Manurhin Defense. Previously imported and distributed by Sphinx U.S.A. located in Meriden, CT. Previously imported (1984-86) directly by Matra-Manurhin International, Inc., located in Fort Lauderdale, FL.

Manurhin in France has been manufacturing models PP, PPK, and PPK/S since 1952. Previously, they were imported by Interarms out of Alexandria, VA. In 1984, Manurhin imported their new models directly and they were marked Manurhin on the left front slide assembly. This differs from the previous Walther stamped guns. Also, no Interarms logo appears on the right side.

PISTOLS: SEMI-AUTO, DISC.

P-1 — 9mm Para. cal., similar to W. German P-38, double action, 5 in. barrel.

	$350	$325	$300	$275	$230	$215	$200

MODEL P4 — 9mm Para. cal., P.38 variation issued to the French Police when in Berlin during post-WWII.

	$375	$340	$300	$245	$230	$215	$200

MODEL PP — .22 LR, .32 ACP, or .380 ACP cal., 3⅞ in. barrel, 10 shot mag.-.22 LR, 8 shot mag.-.32 ACP, 7 shot mag.-.380 ACP, blue only, all steel construction, double action with positive steel hammer block safety, 24 oz. Add $10 for .22 LR cal., $46 for Durgarde finish. Imported 1984-86.

	$360	$320	$275	$230	$205	$185	$170

Last Mfg.'s Sug. Retail was $419.

* Collector Model — blue finish, special engraving. Imported 1986 only.

	$465	$415	$350

Last Mfg.'s Sug. Retail was $529.

Grading	100%	98%	95%	90%	80%	70%	60%

* **Presentation Model** — blue finish, special ornamentation. Imported 1986 only.

     $720   **$650**   **$500**

     Last Mfg.'s Sug. Retail was $819.

Also available with various engraving options in either blue, nickel, or gold finish - prices range from $222 - $540.

MODEL PPK/S — .22 LR, .32 ACP, or .380 ACP cal., 3¼ in. barrel, 10 shot mag.-.22 LR, 8 shot mag.-.32 ACP, 7 shot mag.-.380 ACP, blue only, all steel construction, double action with positive steel hammer block safety, 23 oz. Add $10 for .22 LR cal. Imported 1984-86.

     $360   **$320**   **$275**   **$230**   **$205**   **$185**   **$170**

     Last Mfg.'s Sug. Retail was $419.

* **PPK/S Durgarde** — similar to above, only with bonded brushed chrome finish. Add $14 for .22 LR cal.

     $410   **$365**   **$325**   **$290**   **$265**   **$250**   **$240**

     Last Mfg.'s Sug. Retail was $465.

* **Collector Model** — blue finish, special engraving. Imported 1986 only.

     $465   **$415**   **$350**

     Last Mfg.'s Sug. Retail was $529.

* **Presentation Model** — blue finish, special ornamentation. Imported 1986 only.

     $720   **$650**   **$500**

     Last Mfg.'s Sug. Retail was $819.

Also available with various engraving options in either blue, nickel, or gold finish - prices range from $222-$540.

PP SPORT — .22 LR cal. only, double action, 6.1 or 8.1 in. barrel, blue finish only, precision adj. sights, contoured plastic grips with thumb rest, 25 oz. New Manurhin design for 1985. Imported 1984-86.

     $675   **$525**   **$430**   **$385**   **$325**   **$290**   **$270**

     Last Mfg.'s Sug. Retail was $635.

Add 10% for 8.1 in. barrel.

* **PP Sport-C** — similar to PP Sport, except has single action with lightened trigger pull.

     $650   **$500**   **$415**   **$370**   **$310**   **$280**   **$260**

     Last Mfg.'s Sug. Retail was $635.

PISTOLS: SEMI-AUTO, CURRENT PRODUCTION

MODEL PP — .380 ACP cal., 3⅞ in. barrel, 7 shot mag., blue only, 24 oz., all steel construction, double action with positive steel hammer block safety. Importation resumed 1988.

Mfg.'s Sug. Retail   **$495**   **$425**   **$360**   **$320**   **$275**   **$230**   **$205**   **$185**

     This model is imported by ABO Industries located in San Diego, CA.

MODEL PPK/S — .380 ACP cal., 3¼ in. barrel, 7 shot mag., blue only, all steel construction, double action with positive steel hammer block safety, 23 oz. Importation resumed 1988.

Mfg.'s Sug. Retail   **$495**   **$425**   **$360**   **$320**   **$275**   **$230**   **$205**   **$185**

     This model is imported by ABO Industries located in San Diego, CA.

REVOLVERS

MODEL 73 DEFENSE — .357 Mag./.38 Spl. cal., 6 shot, 2½, 3, or 4 in. barrel, checkered wood stocks, mfg. to precise tolerances, 31-33½ oz. Importation began 1988.

Mfg.'s Sug. Retail   **$1,340**   **$1,200** **$1,000**   **$850**   **$725**   **$600**   **$500**   **$425**

MODEL 73 GENDARMERIE — .357 Mag./.38 Spl. cal., 6 shot, similar to Model 73 Defense except has adj. sighting components and also is offered in 5¼, 6, or 8 in. barrel lengths. Manufactured for police requirements. Importation began 1988.

Mfg.'s Sug. Retail   **$1,885**   **$1,675** **$1,125**   **$900**   **$750**   **$625**   **$525**   **$450**

Grading	100%	98%	95%	90%	80%	70%	60%

MODEL 73 SPORT — .357 Mag./.38 Spl. cal., 6 shot, sport shooting features include minimized hammer stroke, micrometer rear sight, and free release trigger with fitted adj. sights. Importation began 1988.

Mfg.'s Sug. Retail	**$1,885**		$1,675	$1,125	$900	$750	$625	$525	$450

MODEL 73 CONVERTIBLE — includes choice of .22 LR/.38 Spl. or .22 LR/.32 Long cal. cylinders and barrels (5¾ in. for .38 Spl. and 6 in. for .22 LR/.32 Long). Imported 1988-95.

	$1,925	$1,675	$1,325	$1,125	$950	$800	$700

Last Mfg.'s Sug. Retail was $2,200.

* *3 Cylinder Model 73 Convertible* — similar to Model 73 Convertible except includes 3 calibers (.22 LR, .32 Long, and .38 Spl.). Imported 1988-95.

	$2,375	$1,950	$1,700	$1,375	$1,150	$975	$850

Last Mfg.'s Sug. Retail was $2,690.

MODEL 73 SILHOUETTE — .22 LR or .357 Mag. cal., Silhouette variation with fully adj. rear sight and either 10 (.22 LR) or 10¾ (.357 Mag.) in. heavy barrel with full shroud, contoured wooden target grips, approx. 4 lbs. Importation began 1988.

Mfg.'s Sug. Retail	**$1,975**		$1,750	$1,175	$925	$750	$625	$525	$450

Add $13 for .357 Mag. cal.

MODEL MR 88 — .357 Mag. cal., stainless steel, 4, 5, or 6 in. barrel, fixed sights, rubber grips. Importation began 1996.

Mfg.'s Sug. Retail	**$878**		$775	$625	$450

MODEL MR 96 — .357 Mag. cal., black finish, 3, 4, 5, or 6 in. VR barrel, adj. rear sight, ergonomic rubber grips. Importation began 1996.

Mfg.'s Sug. Retail	**$858**		$750	$615	$425	$375	$350	$325	$295

This model allows the user to unlock, swing the cylinder out, and eject the cases with one movement of the hand.

MARATHON PRODUCTS, INC.

Previously manufactured by Santa Barbara Armaments exclusively for Marathon Products, Inc. Most of the models listed below were also available in kit form, but are not shown in this book.

PISTOLS: SINGLE SHOT

HOT SHOT MODEL — .22 LR cal., single shot, fixed sights, 14¾ in. barrel, hardwood stock with target grip configuration. Mfg. 1986-87.

	$55	$45	$40	$35	$35	$30	$30

Last Mfg.'s Sug. Retail was $60.

RIFLES: BOLT ACTION

.22 FIRST SHOT — .22 LR cal., single shot, 16½ in. barrel, hardwood stock, open sights, 31 in. total length, 3.8 lbs. Mfg. 1985-87.

	$55	$45	$40	$35	$35	$30	$30

Last Mfg.'s Sug. Retail was $60.

* *.22 Super Shot* — similar to First Shot, except with 24 in. barrel and regular dimension stock. Mfg. 1985-87.

	$55	$45	$40	$35	$35	$30	$30

Last Mfg.'s Sug. Retail was $60.

CENTERFIRE MODEL — .243 Win., .270 Win., 7x57mm, 7mm Rem. Mag., .30-06, .300 Win. Mag., or .308 Win. cal., Mauser type action, 5 shot fixed box mag., 24 in. barrel, select walnut with recoil pad, adj. trigger, open sights, 7.9 lbs. Available 1985-86 only.

	$295	$240	$215	$195	$180	$170	$160

Last Mfg.'s Sug. Retail was $320.

M

Grading	100%	98%	95%	90%	80%	70%	60%

MARBLE ARMS & MFG. CO.

Previous firearms manufacturer circa 1907-late 1950s, located in Gladstone, MI. Marble Arms is still in business, manufacturing sights, knives, and compasses.

In addition to axes and compasses, Marble Arms & Mfg. Co. also manufactured their Game Getter O/U combination gun from approx. 1907 to the early 1950s. During this period of production, the gun underwent quite a few changes including sights (an aperture sight mounted on the rear backstrap was optional in 1908), different configuration folding metal stock, and other changes.

GAME GETTER MODELS — .22 S, L, or LR cal., upper rifled barrel over choice of .44-40 Game Getter/.410 bore (2 in.) or .410 (2½ in.) smooth bore lower barrel, choice of 12, 15, or 18 in. separated barrels, folding steel skeleton attached stock, pivoting hammer striker mechanically selects upper or lower barrel, tip-up barrels are opened by pulling trigger guard back, top frame sight standard, gutta percha or walnut stocks, approx. 3½ lbs.

* **Model 1908** — ser. no. range approx. 1-9,981, originally supplied with wood box.

	100%	98%	95%	90%	80%	70%	60%
	$1,650	$1,450	$1,250	$1,000	$875	$750	$625

Add $200-$250 for Model 1908A with original flexible tang sight.

* **Model 1921** — ser. no. range approx. 10,000-20,076, originally supplied with cardboard box.

	100%	98%	95%	90%	80%	70%	60%
	$1,050	$895	$650	$600	$550	$520	$480

Add $125 for original leather holster in good condition.

There were two Marble's models - the Model 1908 and the Model 1921. The Model 1908 also had a 1908A variation which utilized the Marble's flexible tang sight and a 1908B Model which utilized a filler blank in place of the tang sight. A few late Model 1908s were chambered for 2 in. .410 bore. The grip plates on the Model 1908 were hard rubber with fleur-de-lis design and Marble's logo - the last gun was mfg. May of 1914 and sold May 22, 1918.

In 1921, a new model was introduced in similar barrel lengths as the Model 1908. Currently, the 1908 is more desirable since it is a better built gun. The Model 1908 was chambered .22 LR upper barrel and 2 in. .410 bore or .44 shot or .44 ball bottom barrel. The Model 1921 was chambered similarily, had walnut or plastic grips - also, a few were chambered for 2½ in. A few 1908s and 1921s were mfg. with bottom barrels in .25-20 WCF, .32-20 WCF, or .38-40 WCF cal., but specimens are very rare, as is a Game Getter pistol mfg. w/o inlet for shoulder stock.

Above values assume 18 in. barrels or correct registration on 12 or 15 in. models. Those 12 or 15 in. barreled Game Getters not registered during the 1968 BATF amnesty program are not legally transferable today. If not a legal configuration, values will drop considerably since they are basically a black market item and subject to BATF confiscation.

The lower barrel of this model was capable of shooting .410 bore, 2 in. paper or brass shotshells, .410 bore 2½ in. paper shotshell (standard configuration, 2 or 2½ in. marking is located on extractor), and .410 bore or .44 cal. round ball cartridges.

M MARCEL THYS & SONS

Current SxS rifle and shotgun manufacturer established in 1958 and located in Crisnée, Belgium. The U.S. agent is currently Champlin Firearms, located in Enid, OK.

Marcel Thys & Sons manufactures fine quality double rifles and shotguns, with many engraving options and special orders. Since these guns are custom made per individual order, please contact the U.S. agent or the factory directly (see Trademark Index) for current information and domestic prices.

MARGOLIN

Original pistol design by M.V. Margolin developed after WWII as a training firearm for members of the Russian shooting team. The Margolin is currently manufactured

100%	98%	95%	90%	80%	70%	60%	50%	40%	30%	20%	10%

at the Izhevsk mechanical plant located in Izhevsk, Russia as the "MTsN" sporting pistol. Limited importation.

PISTOLS: SEMI-AUTO

TARGET MODEL — .22 LR cal., originally developed from the TT (Tula Tokarev), manufactured to precise tolerances, many specimens are made to individual shooters specifications, seldom encountered in the U.S.A., while rare, desirability to date has been limited, current mfg. - limited importation.

Margolin pistols are typically priced in the $475-$850 range, depending on features and assuming 95%+ original condition. While currently imported Chinese copies are considerably less expensive, they do not have the quality (or accuracy) of the Russian Margolins.

MARLIN FIREARMS COMPANY   *Marlin*®

Current manufacturer located in North Haven, CT. Marlin has been manufacturing firearms since 1870. Recent manufacture (1969-present) is in North Haven, CT. Previously, Marlin was manufactured (1870-1969) in New Haven, CT. Distributor sales only.

PISTOLS: DERRINGERS AND REVOLVERS

Many of these variations in average condition sell in the $150-$250 range, while rarer specimens with 90%+ original condition will be priced considerably higher.

RIFLES: LEVER ACTION, ANTIQUE

Factory information by individual serial number may be available from the Cody Firearms Museum in Cody, WY on the following models: Model 1888, Models 1889 and 1892 (ser. no. range 4,001-355,504 only), Models 1893, 1894, 1895, and 1897 may be researched, since Marlin only had one series of serial numbers for all lever action rifles mfg. 1883-1906.

Values below are for standard models only without special order features.

MODEL 1881 — .32-40 WCF, .38-55 WCF, .40-60 WCF, .45-70 Govt., or .45-85 Marlin cal., tube mag., 28 in. octagonal barrel standard, top ejection, blued finish with case hardened hammer, lever, and butt plate. First models (pre ser. no. 600) are rare, add 200-300% premium. Approx. 20,000 mfg. between 1881-1892.

$1,950	$1,700	$1,450	$1,175	$900	$825	$725	$625	$550	$500	$450	$400

This model came in 3 frame styles for various calibers.
Add approx. 15% for .45-70 cal.

MODEL 1888 — .32-20 WCF, .38-40 WCF, or .44-40 WCF cal., 24 in. octagonal barrel most frequently encountered, top ejection, blued finish with case hardened hammer, lever, and butt plate, short throw lever action principle. Approx. 4,800 mfg. between 1888-1889. Ser. range approx. 19,560 - 27,850.

$2,650	$2,375	$2,075	$1,825	$1,625	$1,400	$1,200	$1,000	$875	$750	$625	$500

MODEL 1889 — .25-20 WCF (very rare), .32-20 WCF, .38-40 WCF, .38-55 WCF, or .44-40 WCF cal., 24 (approx. 39,300 mfg.) or 28 (approx. 2,260 mfg.) in. octagonal barrel most frequently encountered, side ejection with solid top frame, blued finish with case hardened hammer, lever, and butt plate, short throw lever action principle. Approx. 55,000 mfg. between 1889-1899. Ser. range approx. 25,000-100,000.

$1,200	$1,100	$900	$650	$525	$425	$385	$340	$295	$260	$230	$200

Also available as Carbine with either a 15 in. (only 367 mfg.) or 20 in. (approx. 10,000 mfg.) barrel or Musket (30 in. barrel - add 300-500%, very rare).

M

100%	98%	95%	90%	80%	70%	60%	50%	40%	30%	20%	10%

MODEL 1891 — .22 Rimfire and .32 Rimfire/Centerfire cal., 24 in. octagonal barrel most often encountered, choice of side loading (1st variation) or tube loading (2nd variation), blued finish with case hardened hammer, lever, and butt plate, sear safety system on lever action. Approx. 18,650 mfg. between 1891-1897. Ser. No. range is approx. 37,500-118,000.

$1,800	$1,625	$1,450	$1,150	$995	$925	$850	$775	$695	$625	$550	$475

Add 50% for deluxe, pistol grip checkered model.
Subtract 40% for tube loading model (.32 Centerfire).
Add $100 each for special sights (including correct Lyman, Marbles, Beeches combo, etc.).

MODEL 1892 — .22 S, L, or LR, .32 S or L cal., 16, 24, 26, or 28 in. barrel, tubular mag., open sight, plain straight stock. Mfg. 1892-1916.

$1,575	$1,350	$1,175	$875	$725	$675	$600	$525	$475	$425	$385	$340

Add 10% for .22 cal.
Subtract 10% for .32 cal.
Add $100 each for special sights (including correct Lyman, Marbles, Beeches combo, etc.).
.22 cals. will bring a premium in this model.

MODEL 1893 RIFLE — .25-36 Marlin, .30-30 Win., .32 Spl., .32-40 WCF, or .38-55 WCF cal., 20-32 in. round or octagonal barrels, case colored receiver, 10 shot tube mag., straight grip stock. Mfg. 1893-1936. Musket model also mfg. - 30 in. barrel and military style forearm.

$1,895	$1,750	$1,300	$1,100	$950	$800	$600	$450	$400	$375	$350	$325

Subtract 50%-60% for the Model B with blued receiver.
Add approx. 20% for special lightweight model.

Although incorrect, more than a few people refer to all 20 in. barrels as "Lightweight" models. Technically, the Lightweight variation has a 7½ in. forearm rather than the standard 9 in.

Later production guns were marked "Model '93" and have less value. This model had two barrel variations - one was marked "special smokeless steel" while the other was marked "for Black Powder". The latter (also known as Model B) are 1st Models only and have blued receivers rather than case colored.

MODEL 1893 CARBINE — .30-30 Win., .32 Spl., .32-40 WCF cal., or .38-55 WCF cal., 15 (only 61 mfg.) or 20 in. round barrel, case colored receiver, 7 shot tube mag., straight or pistol grip stock. Mfg. 1893-1935.

* **1st Model** — with saddle ring. Mfg. 1893-1915.

$1,675	$1,525	$1,300	$1,100	$950	$825	$700	$600	$500	$400	$375	$350

* **2nd Model** — .30-30 Win. or .32 HPS cal., has "Bulls-eye" in stock, no saddle rings. Mfg. 1922-1935.

$875	$775	$695	$625	$550	$465	$425	$385	$350	$325	$300	$285

MODEL 1894 — .25-20 WCF, .32-20 WCF, .38-40 WCF, or .44-40 WCF cal., case colored receiver, 10 shot tube mag., 24 in. round or octagon barrel, straight or pistol grip stock. Mfg. 1894-1934.

$1,850	$1,550	$1,325	$1,100	$950	$800	$600	$450	$400	$375	$350	$325

Later production guns were marked "Model '94" and have less value. This model was also available in both a Carbine and Musket variation.

MODEL 1895 — .33 WCF, .38-56 WCF, .40-65 WCF, .40-70 WCF, .40-82 WCF, or .45-70 Govt. cal., case colored receiver, 9 shot tube mag., 24 or 26 in. round or octagon barrel standard, other lengths were available, open sights, plain straight or pistol grip stock. Mfg. 1895-1915.

$2,250	$1,800	$1,550	$1,300	$1,000	$850	$750	$700	$650	$600	$550	$525

Premiums exist for .40-70 WCF (approx. 60 mfg.), .45-70 Govt., and .45-90 WCF cal.

In 1912, a lightweight variation was introduced with hard rubber butt plate and half-magazine, cals. were .33 WCF and .45-70 Govt.(commands a premium), and round barrels were either 22 or 24 in. A Carbine variation was also offered with approx. 200 mfg. - premiums may run as high as 150% over rifle values listed above.

Grading		100%	98%	95%	90%	80%	70%	60%

MODEL 1897 — .22 S, L, or LR cal., tube mag., 16, 24, 26, or 28 in. barrel, case colored receiver, takedown, open sights, plain straight or pistol grip stock. Mfg. 1897-1922.

$1,850	$1,550	$1,325	$1,100	$950	$800	$600	$450	$400

Continuing: $375 $350 $325

16 in. barrel "Bicycle Rifles" will bring a premium of 100%.
Add $100 each for special sights (including correct Lyman, Marbles, Beeches combo, etc.).

RIFLES: MODERN PRODUCTION

Year of manufacture can be determined from 1946-1968 by the following letter/numeral prefix: 1946-C, 1947-D, 1948-E, 1949-F, 1950-G, 1951-H, 1952-J, 1953-K, 1954-L, 1955-M, 1956-N, 1957-P, 1958-R, 1959-S, 1960-T, 1961-U, 1962-V, 1963-W, 1964-Y,Z, 1965-AA, 1966-AB, 1967-AC, 1968-AD, 1969-69, 1970-70, 1971-71, 1972-72. Starting in 1973, the year can be determined by subtracting the first 2 numbers of the serial number from 100.

The models below are listed in numerical sequence to assist quick access.

Pressed checkering became standard on many Marlins beginning 1995.

MODEL MR-7 BOLT ACTION — .22-250 Rem. (advertised in 1998, but never mfg.), .243 Win. (advertised in 1998, but never mfg.), .25-06 Rem. (new 1997), .270 Win., .280 Rem. (new 1998) .30-06, or .308 Win. (advertised in 1998, but never mfg.) cal., 4 shot box mag. with removable hinged floorplate, 3 position safety, adj. 3-6 lb. trigger, 22 in. barrel, checkered American walnut stock, cocking indicator, forged receiver, damascened bolt, includes sling swivels, with or without sights, approx. 7½ lbs. New 1996.

Mfg.'s Sug. Retail	$603		$495	$440	$375	$315	$275	$240	$215

Add $40 for open sights (.270 Win., .280 Rem., or .30-06).

* **Model MR-7B** — .270 Win. or .30-06 only, similar to Model MR-7, except has birch stock and forearm with cut checkering. New 1998.

Mfg.'s Sug. Retail	$483		$380	$250	$185	$165	$150	$130	$125

Add $40 for open sights (mfg. 1998 only).

MODEL 9 CAMP CARBINE SEMI-AUTO — 9mm Para. cal. only, 16½ in. barrel, 12 or 20 shot mag. (disc. 1989), 4 shot clip mag. became standard in 1990, sand blasted steel receiver, open sights, last shot automatic hold-open, 6¾ lbs. New 1985.

Mfg.'s Sug. Retail	$443		$340	$230	$170	$150	$140	$130	$125

Add 10% for nickel plating (mfg. 1991-94, Model 9N).

A new high visibility orange front sight post with cutaway hood was added in 1989.

MODEL 18 SLIDE ACTION — .22 S, L, or LR cal., tube mag., 20 in. round or octagon barrel, open sight, exposed hammer, plain straight grip stock. Mfg. 1906-1909.

		$330	$250	$195	$165	$125	$100	$85

MODEL 20 SLIDE ACTION — .22 S, L, or LR cal., 24 in. octagon barrel, open sight, exposed hammer, takedown, plain straight grip stock. Mfg. 1907-1922.

		$300	$250	$195	$165	$125	$100	$85

MODEL 25 SLIDE ACTION — .22 Short cal., tube mag., 23 in. barrel, open sight, exposed hammer, takedown, plain straight grip stock. Mfg. 1909-1910.

		$360	$275	$220	$185	$150	$120	$95

M

MODEL 25MB — .22 Mag. cal., bolt action, 16¼ in. micro-groove barrel, 7 shot clip mag., hardwood stock, takedown action, 6 lbs. Mfg. 1987-88 only.

		$145	$115	$95	$85	$75	$70	$65

Last Mfg.'s Sug. Retail was $173.

This model included both a scope and gun case.

MODEL 25MG GARDEN GUN — .22 Mag. shot shell, features 22 in. smooth bore barrel with front sight only, 7 shot mag., black synthetic stock, thumb safety, 6 lbs. New 1999.

Mfg.'s Sug. Retail	$233		$175	$145	$125	$110	$100	$90	$80

Grading	100%	98%	95%	90%	80%	70%	60%

MODEL 25MN — .22 Mag. cal., bolt action, 7 shot clip mag., 22 in. barrel, walnut finished hardwood stock (pressed checkering became standard 1994), grooved receiver, adj. rear sight (new 1995), 6 lbs. New 1989.

Mfg.'s Sug. Retail	$216	$165	$125	$95	$80	$75	$70	$65

Add $7 for 4X scope.

MODEL 27 SLIDE ACTION — .25RF, .25-20 WCF, or .32-20 WCF cal., ⅔ tube mag., 7 shot, 24 in. octagon barrel, open sight, plain straight grip stock. Mfg. 1910-1916.

	$330	$250	$225	$200	$165	$140	$125

Subtract 15% for .25RF cal.

MODEL 27S — similar to Model 27, with round or octagonal barrel.

	$330	$250	$195	$140	$110	$100	$85

MODEL 29 SLIDE ACTION — similar to Model 20, with 23 in. round barrel, ½ tube mag. Mfg. 1913-1916.

	$330	$250	$195	$140	$110	$100	$85

MODEL 30/30A LEVER ACTION — .30-30 Win. cal., 20 in. barrel, promotional Glenfield model with birch stock and pressed checkering. Mfg. 1964-1983.

	$220	$185	$160	$135	$120	$110	$100

This model was replaced by the Model 30AS in 1983.

MODEL 30AS LEVER ACTION — .30-30 Win. cal. only, 20 in. barrel, walnut finished birch stock (pressed checkering became standard 1995, cut checkering became standard 1998), open sights (adj. rear sight became standard 1995), no frills version of the 336 CS, 7 lbs. New 1983.

Mfg.'s Sug. Retail	$405	$295	$225	$150	$130	$125	$120	$115

Add $44 for 4X scope.

This model was formally part of the Glenfield line.

* *Model 336W (Model 30AW)* — similar to Model 30AS, except has carbine style barrel band and gold trigger.

Mfg.'s Sug. Retail	$411	$300	$230	$150	$130	$125	$120	$115

Add $44 for 4X scope.

This model was previously sold to Wal-Mart only. Model nomenclature was changed during 1998.

MODEL 32 SLIDE ACTION — .22 S, L, or LR cal., ⅔ tube mag., 24 in. octagon barrel, open sight, plain pistol grip stock, hammerless. Mfg. 1914-1915.

	$500	$450	$400	$350	$275	$200	$100

MODEL 1936 — .30-30 Win. or .32 HPS (High Power Special) cal., 6 shot, 20 or 24 in. barrel, tubular mag., open sights, pistol grip stock, barrel band, leaf mainspring, thinner "perch belly" forearm, case colored or blued receiver, upper tang, buttstock has a fluted comb and flat hard rubber buttplate. Mfg. 1936-1937.

	$475	$425	$325	$250	$200	$175	$150

Add 10% for vivid case colors with strong greens, reds, and yellows.
Add 10% for rifles and sporting carbines.

Rifles have "A" suffix, sporting carbine has "SC" suffix, and regular and carbine has "RC" suffix.

The Model 1936 has an upper tang inscription "Model 1936" and a case colored receiver. Also, the Model 1936 did not have a letter prefix in the ser. no.

MODEL 36 - 1ST VARIATION — similar to Model 1936, except has a coil mainspring. Mfg. 1937-1940.

	$475	$425	$375	$300	$225	$175	$150

Add 10% for rifles and sporting carbines.

M

The Model 36 - 1st Variation has an upper tang inscription "Model 1936" and a case colored receiver. Also, the Model 36 - 1st variation did not have a letter prefix in the ser. no.

MODEL 36 - 2ND VARIATION — similar to Model 1936, still has case colored receiver with "Model 1936" on upper tang, buttstock is heavier style and no longer has fluted comb, buttplate is a thicker, slightly curved style - hard rubber, forearm is a heavier beaver-tailed style, "B" prefix in ser. no. Mfg. 1941 only.

	100%	98%	95%	90%	80%	70%	60%
	$450	$395	$325	$275	$250	$200	$165

Add 10% for rifles and sporting carbines.

MODEL 36ADL DELUXE RIFLE — similar to Model 1936, case colored receiver, checkered pistol grip buttstock and forearm, pistol grip cap, Winchester quick detachable swivels with 1 in. sling, "B" prefix in ser. no. Less than 50 mfg. in 1941 only.

	100%	98%	95%	90%	80%	70%	60%
	$800	$725	$600	$450	$325	$275	$250

Both the rear and front swivel bases are attached with two wood screws and are not inletted into the wood.

MODEL 36 - 3RD VARIATION — .30-30 Win. or .32 HPS cal., blued receiver, no upper tang markings, model no. and cal. marked on barrel, rifles have "A" suffix, Deluxe rifle has "ADL" suffix, Sporting Carbine has "SC" suffix, and regular carbine has "RC" suffix. Mfg. 1946-1947.

	100%	98%	95%	90%	80%	70%	60%
	$425	$375	$295	$195	$165	$150	$125

Add 40% for Deluxe model (ADL).
Add 10% for rifles and sporting carbines.

Deluxe rifles (ADL) had a checkered pistol grip stock and forearm with no pistol grip cap. Deluxe rifles also have swivel round studs in buttstock and forearm cap with quick detachable swivels and a 1 in. sling. Also, some standard rifles may have hte "ADL" barrel markings in 1946-47. 1946 mfg. has a lower case "c" prefix and 1947 mfg. has a capital "D" prefix in ser. no.

MODEL 37 SLIDE ACTION — similar to Model 29, with 24 in. barrel, full length tube mag. Mfg. 1913-1916.

	100%	98%	95%	90%	80%	70%	60%
	$330	$250	$195	$165	$125	$100	$85

MODEL 38 SLIDE ACTION — .22 S, L, or LR cal., ⅔ tube mag., 24 in. octagon barrel, open sights, hammerless, takedown, plain pistol grip stock. Mfg. 1920-1930.

	100%	98%	95%	90%	80%	70%	60%
	$330	$250	$195	$165	$125	$100	$85

MODEL 39 LEVER ACTION — .22 S, L, or LR cal., 24 in. octagon barrel with tube mag., open sights, takedown, case hardened receiver and lever, S-shaped pistol grip stock, bluing on barrel, forend tip, mag. tube, bolt, hammer, and screws, various qualities of walnut (X, 2X, or 3X), hard rubber buttplate. Approx. 40-50,000 mfg. 1922-1938.

	100%	98%	95%	90%	80%	70%	60%
	N/A	N/A	$1,495	$1,295	$1,000	$800	$600

Early models with fancy 2X-3X wood will bring a considerable premium.

Excellent original condition in this model is extremely hard to find since most specimens were well used due to the 16/25 shell mag. capacity, reliability, and the fact that the balance point of the gun (the receiver) normally wore first due to carrying wear. Earlier guns without a prefix or with an S prefix are noted for their superior workmanship and fine finish. Later HS prefix (High Speed) are not quite as valuable as these earlier guns.

MODEL 39A — similar to Model 39, with case hardened receiver (mfg. 1939-1945), includes 1st and 2nd Models with round barrel. 3rd Model 1st Variation was introduced in 1946 and has blued receiver, 3rd Model 2nd Variation has flutes in buttstock comb and was introduced in 1951, and 3rd Model 3rd Variation has Micro-Groove rifling, no pistol grip cap, and was introduced in 1954.

M

Grading	100%	98%	95%	90%	80%	70%	60%

✷ 1st Model — case colored frame, no prefix. Mfg. 1939 only.

	$1,000	$900	$775	$650	$500	$400	$300

The first variation of the Model 39A mfg. in 1939 is distinguishable by a buttstock and lever similar to those on earlier Model 39s.

✷ 2nd Model — case colored frame, "B" prefix. Mfg. 1940-45.

	$800	$725	$650	$575	$450	$395	$350

The second variation had a rounded lever like current production and no "S" shape to bottom of pistol grip.

✷ 3rd Model 1st Variation — features blued receiver, new ramp front sight, hard rubber buttplate, and continued Ballard rifling. Mfg. 1946-1950.

	$350	$325	$295	$275	$250	$225	$200

✷ 3rd Model 2nd Variation — similar to 3rd Model 1st Variation, except has flutes in buttstock comb, white plastic spacer next to buttplate, and pistol grip cap with white spacer and brass insert. Mfg. 1951-1953.

	$350	$325	$295	$275	$250	$225	$200

✷ 3rd Model 3rd Variation — similar to 3rd Model 2nd Variation, except has Micro-Groove rifling, and no pistol grip cap. Mfg. 1954-57.

	$300	$275	$250	$225	$150	$125	$100

GOLDEN 39A — similar to Model 39A, with gold-plated trigger, sling swivels. Mfg. 1957-1987.

	$295	$275	$250	$225	$150	$125	$100

Add 30% to pre-1970 (oil finished stock) models.

MODEL 39A "MOUNTIE" — straight grip stock, slim forearm, otherwise similar to 39A. Mfg. 1953-1972.

	$350	$325	$275	$250	$150	$125	$100

✷ Model 39A "MOUNTIE" with K prefix — 24 in. barrel and slender forearm. 4,335 mfg. 1953 only.

	$750	$650	$550	$475	$425	$350	$300

90TH ANNIVERSARY 39A — similar to Model 39A, with chrome barrel and action, select checkered walnut stock, carved squirrel on side of butt stock. 500 mfg. in 1961.

	$1,100	$950	$750	$500	$425	$350	$250

Last Mfg.'s Sug. Retail was $100.

90TH ANNIVERSARY MODEL 39M MOUNTIE CARBINE — similar to 90th Anniversary Model 39A, except 20 in. barrel, straight stock. 500 mfg. in 1960.

	$1,100	$950	$750	$600	$400	$350	$250

Last Mfg.'s Sug. Retail was $100.

MODEL 39A-DL — similar to 90th Anniversary, with blue barrel and action, regular production. Mfg. 1960-1963.

	$795	$695	$575	$450	$350	$250	$175

This model is also known as the "Marlin 39A Squirrel Gun."

MODEL 39A OCTAGON — similar to Golden 39A, with octagon barrel, no pistol grip cap, 2,551 rifles and 2,140 carbines were produced. Mfg. 1973.

	$595	$550	$475	$425	$360	$295	$250

MODEL 39 CARBINE — similar to 39M, with light barrel, 3/4 tube mag. 9,695 mfg. 1963-1967.

	$350	$295	$225	$195	$160	$140	$110

MODEL 39D — similar to 39M, with pistol grip stock. Mfg. 1971-1973.

	$225	$195	$175	$150	$135	$115	$90

M

Grading	100%	98%	95%	90%	80%	70%	60%

MODEL 39AS — .22 LR cal., current production model, lever action, tube mag., 19 shot, 24 in. barrel, walnut stock (cut checkering became standard 1994), open sights, gold trigger, takedown, 6½ lbs.

Mfg.'s Sug. Retail	$481	$370	$250	$170	$145	$130	$110	$100

This model was previously designated the Model 39A. In 1988, the Model 39AS became the standard production model and included a rebounding hammer and hammer block safety.

MODEL 39TDS — .22 LR cal., carbine variation of the Model 39AS, 16½ in. barrel with open sights, 5¼ lbs. Mfg. 1988-95.

	$345	$240	$175	$155	$135	$120	$110

Last Mfg.'s Sug. Retail was $443.

MODEL 39M — carbine version of Model 39A, 20 in. lightweight barrel, 16 shot tube mag., squared finger lever, 6 lbs. Disc. 1987.

	$350	$325	$295	$250	$200	$175	$150

Last Mfg.'s Sug. Retail was $304.

MODEL 39M OCTAGON — similar to Model 39M, with octagon barrel. Mfg. 1973.

	$550	$495	$475	$425	$360	$295	$250

MODEL 39 CENTURY LTD — Marlin Centennial 1870-1970 Commemorative, 20 in. octagon barrel, select walnut straight stock, brass forearm cap and butt plate, name plate in butt. 35,388 mfg. 1970.

	$295	$275	$250	$195	$175	$150	$125

MODEL 39A ARTICLE II — NRA Centennial Commemorative 1871-1971, "Right to Bear Arms" medallion in receiver, 24 in. octagon barrel, fancy pistol grip stock, brass butt plate and forearm cap. 6,244 mfg. 1971.

	$450	$395	$375	$350	$295	$250	$195

MODEL 39M ARTICLE II CARBINE — similar to 39A Article II, with 20 in. barrel, straight grip stock. Mfg. 3,824.

	$450	$395	$375	$350	$295	$250	$195

MODEL 45 CARBINE — .45 ACP cal. only, 7 shot clip mag., sandblasted steel receiver, 16½ in. barrel, last shot hold open device, press checkering, adj. rear sight, 6¾ lbs. New 1986.

Mfg.'s Sug. Retail	$443	$340	$230	$175	$150	$140	$130	$125

A new high visibility orange front sight post with cutaway hood was added in 1989.

MODEL 56 — similar to Model 57 Levermatic, with clip mag. Mfg. 1955-1964.

	$195	$175	$150	$125	$100	$85	$75

MODEL 57 LEVERMATIC — .22 S, L, or LR cal., tube mag., 22 in. barrel, open sight, Monte Carlo pistol grip stock. Mfg. 1959-1965.

	$225	$195	$175	$150	$125	$100	$80

MODEL 57M — Mag. version of Model 57 Levermatic.

	$225	$200	$175	$150	$135	$125	$110

M

MODEL 60SS SEMI-AUTO STAINLESS — .22 LR cal., 14 shot tube mag., stainless steel construction with laminated black/gray birch stock with Monte Carlo cheekpiece, Mar-Shield finish, 22 in. barrel, open sights with adj. rear, 5½ lbs. New 1993.

Mfg.'s Sug. Retail	$265	$205	$170	$145

* *Model 60SB* — similar to Model 60SS, except has uncheckered birch Monte Carlo stock. New 1998.

Mfg.'s Sug. Retail	$212	$160	$150	$130

This model was previously sold to Wal-Mart only.

Grading	100%	98%	95%	90%	80%	70%	60%

* *Model 60SSK* — similar to Model 60SS, except has fiberglass stock with Monte Carlo cheekpiece. New 1998.

Mfg.'s Sug. Retail   **$229**   **$185**   **$160**   **$135**

     Add $14 for 4X scope.

MODEL 62 LEVERMATIC — .256 Mag. or .30 Carbine cal., 4 shot clip mag., 23 in. barrel, open sight, pistol grip Monte Carlo stock. Mfg. 1963-1969.

	100%	98%	95%	90%	80%	70%	60%
.256 Mag.	$350	$325	$300	$250	$200	$175	$150
.30 Carbine	$350	$325	$300	$250	$200	$135	$120

MODEL 70P (PAPOOSE) — .22 LR cal. only, semi-auto, takedown carbine with 16¼ in. barrel, 7 shot clip mag., rustproof receiver, bolt hold open, is supplied with floating nylon carrying case. Mfg. 1986-94.

     $170   **$125**   **$90**   **$75**   **$65**   **$60**   **$55**

           Last Mfg.'s Sug. Retail was $225.

     Subtract $25 if without 4X scope (became standard 1993).

* *Model 70PSS* — similar to Model 70P, except has stainless steel breech bolt and barrel, black checkered synthetic stock with swing swivels, last shot hold-open became standard in 1996, 3¼ lbs. New 1995.

Mfg.'s Sug. Retail   **$272**   **$210**   **$165**   **$135**

* *Model 70HC* — .22 LR cal., semi-auto, carbine with 18 in. barrel. Mfg. 1988-1995.

     $185   **$155**   **$130**   **$120**   **$110**   **$100**   **$90**

MODEL 322 BOLT ACTION VARMINT — .222 Rem. cal., Sako Mauser type action, 3 shot clip mag., 24 in. medium weight barrel, 2 position aperture sight, checkered stock. Mfg. 1954-1957.

     $550   **$500**   **$475**   **$400**   **$325**   **$300**   **$250**

MODEL 336A RIFLE — improved 36A, .30-30 Win., .35 Rem., or .32 Spl. cal., round breech bolt, 24 in. barrel with ⅔ mag. Mfg. 1948-1962, re-introduced 1973-1980.

     $300   **$275**   **$225**   **$200**   **$180**   **$165**   **$145**

     Add 20% for 1st model mfg. 1948-1952.

     Add 10% for 1953-1962 mfg.

     The .35 Rem. cal. was added in 1950, .32 Spl. was disc. in 1962.

* *Model 336ADL Rifle* — similar to Model 336A Rifle, except has deluxe checkered walnut stock and forearm, quick detachable swivels and 1 in. sling. Mfg. 1948-1962.

     $500   **$450**   **$375**   **$325**   **$275**   **$230**   **$200**

     Add 20% for 2nd Model.

     The 336ADL 1st Model (mfg. 1948-1956) did not have a raised comb or cheekpiece. The 2nd Model (mfg. 1957-1962) is identifiable by a Monte Carlo butt stock with raised comb and cheekpiece. Wood was supplied by Bishop.

MODEL 336RC CARBINE — .30-30 Win., .32 Spl., or .35 Rem. cal., standard model carbine. Mfg. 1948-68.

     $300   **$275**   **$200**   **$175**   **$155**   **$140**   **$120**

     Add 10% for 1st Model mfg. 1948-1952.

MODEL 336C CARBINE — .30-30 Win., .32 Spl., or .35 Rem. cal., standard model carbine with 20 in. barrel. Mfg. 1969-1983.

     $250   **$210**   **$185**   **$160**   **$150**   **$135**   **$115**

MODEL 336SC SPORTING CARBINE — similar to Model 336C, with 20 in. barrel and ⅔ length mag. tube, raised comb butt stock (1957-1963). Mfg. 1948-1963.

     $325   **$275**   **$225**   **$190**   **$180**   **$165**   **$145**

     Add 10% for 1st Model mfg. 1948-1952.

Grading	100%	98%	95%	90%	80%	70%	60%

MODEL 336SC .219 ZIPPER — similar to Model 336SC, in .219 Zipper cal., 5 shot mag. Mfg. 1955-1960.

	$495	$450	$375	$330	$275	$250	$220

MODEL 336SD CARBINE — .30-30 Win., .32 Spl., or .35 Rem. cal., deluxe sporting carbine with 20 in. barrel, checkered stock and forearm, raised comb, no cheekpiece, quick detachable swivels and 1 in. sling. Mfg. 1954-1962.

	$595	$525	$400	$275	$200	$185	$165

MODEL 336CS CARBINE LEVER ACTION — .30-30 Win., or .35 Rem. cal., 6 shot tube mag., 20 in. barrel, hammer block safety, American black walnut pistol grip stock (cut checkering became standard 1994), 7 lbs. Introduced 1984.

Mfg.'s Sug. Retail	**$474**	$365	$250	$200	$185	$175	$165	$150

MODEL 336LTS CARBINE — .30-30 Win. cal. only, 16¼ in. barrel, 5 shot tube mag., 6½ lbs. 2,671 mfg. 1988-89 only.

	$375	$295	$225	$185	$175	$165	$150

Last Mfg.'s Sug. Retail was $346.

MODEL 336 COWBOY — .30-30 Win. or .38-55 WCF cal., 6 shot tube mag., squared off finger lever, 24 in. tapered octagon barrel with deep cut Ballard-type rifling (6 grooves), cut checkered straight grip walnut stock and forearm, adj. Marbles semi-buckhorn rear and carbine front sight, ser. no. is on left side of receiver, instead of on tang, 7½ lbs. New 1999.

Mfg.'s Sug. Retail	**$658**	$540	$440	$365	$300	$275	$250	$225

MODEL 336ER (EXTRA RANGE) — .307 (disc. 1984) or .356 Win. cal., 5 shot tube mag., 20 in. barrel, walnut pistol grip stock, open sights, 7 lbs. 2,441 mfg. 1983-86.

	$525	$450	$325	$225	$200	$175	$150

Last Mfg.'s Sug. Retail was $350.

MODEL 336T CARBINE "TEXAN" — .30-30 Win., .35 Rem., or .44 Mag. (1965-1967 only) cal., similar to 336C, with straight stock, 18½ (1983 only) or 20 in. barrel, saddle ring (1965-1971 only). Mfg. 1954-1983.

	$295	$250	$195	$165	$155	$140	$120

MODEL 336DT CARBINE "TEXAN" — select stock version of 336T, longhorn and map of Texas carved on butt stock. Mfg. 1962-1963.

	$595	$525	$425	$300	$200	$150	$135

MODEL 336TS TEXAN — similar to 336 CS, except is .30-30 Win. cal., 18½ in. barrel, straight grip stock and squared finger lever, crossbolt safety. Mfg. 1984-87.

	$240	$185	$160	$150	$140	$130	$120

Last Mfg.'s Sug. Retail was $314.

MODEL 336 OCTAGON RIFLE — .30-30 Win. cal. only, with 22 in. octagon barrel, standard model. 2,414 mfg. 1973 only.

	$500	$425	$300	$250	$200	$175	$150

MODEL 336 MARAUDER CARBINE — .30-30 Win. or .35 Rem. cal., 16¼ in. barrel. 5,856 mfg. 1963-1964.

	$425	$400	$350	$275	$235	$210	$185

M

Add 10% for .35 cal.

Be careful of re-barreled examples of this model.

MODEL 336 MAGNUM CARBINE — .44 Mag. cal., 20 in. standard carbine configuration, w/o saddle ring. 2,823 mfg. 1963-1964 only.

	$350	$295	$245	$225	$195	$170	$160

MODEL 336T — .44 Mag. cal., with saddle ring, 13,895 mfg. 1965-1967.

	$325	$275	$225	$200	$175	$160	$150

Grading	100%	98%	95%	90%	80%	70%	60%

MODEL 336 ZANE GREY CENTURY CARBINE — .30-30 Win. cal., similar to 336 Octagon, 22 in. octagon barrel, Zane Grey medallion inlaid in receiver, select walnut stock, pistol grip, brass butt plate and forearm cap. 7,871 mfg. in 1971.

$395 $325 $250

This model was mfg. to commemorate the 100th anniversary of the birth of Zane Grey.

MODEL 336 PRESENTATION RIFLE — .30-30 Win. cal., 22 in. octagon barrel, engraved action, sold with Model 39 Presentation. Mfg. 1970 only.

$550 $475 $400

MARLIN CENTENNIAL MATCHED PAIR — Model 336 and Model 39 serial numbered the same, .30-30 Win. or .22 LR cal., engraved, deluxe wood, inlaid medallions, cased. 1,000 mfg. sets in 1970.

$1,150 $875 $695

Last Mfg.'s Sug. Retail was $750.

MODEL 375 — similar to Model 336 CS, except is .375 Win. cal. 16,315 mfg. 1980-83.

$350 $295 $225 $200 $175 $160 $150

MODEL 444 LEVER ACTION — .444 Marlin cal., 4 shot tube mag., 24 in. barrel, open sights, straight grip, Monte Carlo stock, recoil pad, swivels, sling. Mfg. 1965-1971.

$325 $300 $245 $225 $200 $185 $160

* *Model 444S* — similar to Model 444, except has pistol grip stock. Mfg. 1972-1983.

$265 $240 $225 $200 $185 $165 $150

MODEL 444P OUTFITTER — .444 Marlin cal., 5 shot tube mag., 18½ in. ported barrel with deep cut Ballard-type rifling (6 grooves), adj. semi-buckhorn folding rear sight with ramp front, checkered straight grip walnut stock and forearm, tapped for scope mount, 6¾ lbs. New 1999.

Mfg.'s Sug. Retail $572 $450 $365 $295 $235 $195 $180 $170

MODEL 444SS SPORTER — .444 Marlin cal., similar to Model 444, with 22 in. barrel and hammer block safety, pistol grip stock without Monte Carlo configuration (cut checkering became standard 1994), 7½ lbs. Mfg. 1984-present.

Mfg.'s Sug. Retail $566 $445 $360 $290 $230 $195 $180 $170

MODEL 455 BOLT ACTION SPORTER — .30-06, or .308 Win. cal., FN Mauser action with Sako trigger, 24 in. barrel, stainless steel barrel, Lyman aperture sight, checkered Monte Carlo pistol grip stock. Mfg. 1957-1959.

$415 $330 $305 $250 $220 $195 $165

MODELS 780, 781, 782, and 783 BOLT ACTION — .22 LR or .22 Mag. (Models 782 and 783) cal., tube or clip mag., 22 in. barrel. Disc. 1988.

$110 $85 $75 $70 $65 $55 $50

Last Mfg.'s Sug. Retail was $162.

Add $17-$25 for Models 782 and 783.

MODELS 880/881 BOLT ACTION — .22 LR or .22 Mag. cal., replacements for Models 780, 781, Model 880 is .22 LR with 7 shot clip mag. and 22 in. barrel, (cut checkering became standard 1994), Model 881 is .22 LR with 17 shot tube mag. and 22 in. barrel, 6 lbs. Mfg. 1989-1997.

$185 $145 $100 $85 $75 $70 $65

Last Mfg.'s Sug. Retail was $251.

Add $10 for Model 881.

* *Model 880SS* — similar to Model 880, except is stainless steel, black fiberglass synthetic stock. New 1994.

Mfg.'s Sug. Retail $280 $220 $160 $110

Grading	100%	98%	95%	90%	80%	70%	60%

✳ **Model 880SQ** — similar to Model 880, except has black fiberglass filled synthetic stock with checkering and heavy 22 in. barrel, without sights and grooved receiver, matte finish, 7 lbs. New 1996.

Mfg.'s Sug. Retail	$294	$225	$165	$115	$95	$80	$70	$65

MODELS 882/883 BOLT ACTION — .22 Win. Mag. cal., 7 shot clip (Model 882) or 12 shot tube mag. (Model 883), checkered (cut checkering became standard 1994), black walnut Monte Carlo stock with Mar-Shield finish, adj. semi-buckhorn rear sight and hooded front, thumb safety, 6 lbs. New 1989.

Mfg.'s Sug. Retail	$286	$220	$165	$110	$95	$85	$75	$70

Add $12 for Model 883.
Add $35 for nickel finish on Model 883N (disc. 1993).

The Models 882 and 883 are the replacements for Models 782 and 783.

✳ **Model 882SS** — .22 Win. Mag. cal., similar to Model 882, except is stainless steel and stock is black synthetic with molded-in checkering, fire sights (red fiber optic inserts with cutaway hood) became standard 1998. New 1995.

Mfg.'s Sug. Retail	$305	$225	$175	$125

✳ **Model 882SSV** — .22 Win. Mag. cal., features 22 in. stainless barrel with black fiberglass reinforced synthetic stock, 7 shot mag., grooved receiver, w/o sights, ring mounts included. New 1997.

Mfg.'s Sug. Retail	$301	$230	$175	$125

✳ **Model 882L** — similar to Model 882, except has laminated hardwood stock. New 1992.

Mfg.'s Sug. Retail	$304	$230	$170	$125	$95	$85	$75	$70

✳ **Model 883SS** — .22 Win. Mag. cal., similar to Model 883, except barrel is stainless steel and stock is laminated two-tone brown birch with Monte Carlo cheekpiece. New 1993.

Mfg.'s Sug. Retail	$317	$245	$180	$125

MODEL 922M SEMI-AUTO — .22 Win. Mag. cal., 7 shot detachable mag., 20½ in. barrel, Garand style safety, alloy receiver, hold-open device, uncheckered or checkered (became standard 1994) walnut stock with solid pad, blued steel (hard coated on receiver), 6½ lbs. New 1993.

Mfg.'s Sug. Retail	$429	$340	$285	$230	$200	$185	$175	$165

MODEL 990 SEMI-AUTO — .22 LR cal. only, 18 shot tube mag., 22 in. barrel, last shot automatic bolt hold-open, Monte Carlo American black walnut stock with pistol grip, 5½ lbs. Disc. 1987.

	$115	$90	$75	$65	$60	$55	$50

Last Mfg.'s Sug. Retail was $159.

MODEL 990L SEMI-AUTO — .22 LR cal., 14 shot tube mag., 22 in. barrel, laminated two-tone brown Monte Carlo stock, gold trigger, adj. rear sight, grooved receiver, 5¾ lbs. Mfg. 1993-94.

	$180	$160	$145	$130	$120	$110	$100

Last Mfg.'s Sug. Retail was $223.

MODEL 995 SEMI-AUTO — .22 LR cal., 7 shot clip mag., 18 in. barrel, Monte Carlo walnut stock, 5 lbs. Disc. 1994.

	$160	$125	$85	$70	$65	$60	$55

Last Mfg.'s Sug. Retail was $206.

✳ **Model 995SS** — .22 LR cal., stainless steel barrel and nickel-plated small parts, black fiberglass stock with molded-in checkering, adj. rear sight, last shot hold-open new 1996, 5 lbs. New 1995.

Mfg.'s Sug. Retail	$255	$195	$145	$110

MODEL 1894 — .44 Spl. or .44 Mag. cal., 20 in. bbl., 10 shot tube mag., adj. sights, straight grip walnut stock and forearm, 6 lbs. Mfg. 1969-1984.

	$400	$300	$250	$195	$165	$145	$130

M

Grading	100%	98%	95%	90%	80%	70%	60%

MODEL 1894C — without hammer block safety, mfg. 1979-1984.

	$375	$275	$225	$180	$160	$145	$130

MODEL 1894 SPORTER — .44 Mag. cal. only, 6 shot half mag. tube, crescent shaped hard rubber buttplate, 1,398 mfg. 1973 only.

	$475	$425	$360	$300	$250	$200	$175

MODEL 1894CS (CARBINE) — copy of original Model 1894, .357 Mag./.38 Spl. cal., 9 shot mag., 18½ in. round barrel, open sights (hooded front became standard 1999), straight grip stock (cut checkering became standard 1994), squared finger lever, 6 lbs. Mfg. 1984-present.

Mfg.'s Sug. Retail	$486	$385	$280	$200	$170	$150	$140	$130

MODEL 1894S — .41 Mag. (disc. 1991), .44 Mag./.44 Spl., or .45 LC (mfg. 1988-91) cal., Model 1894 with addition of cross bolt (S suffix) and hammer block safety, 20 in. barrel, 10 shot tube mag., adj. sights, 6 lbs., straight grip walnut stock and forearm (cut checkering became standard 1994).

Mfg.'s Sug. Retail	$486	$385	$280	$200	$170	$150	$140	$130

* *Model 1894S Limited* — .44 Mag./.44 Spl. cal., features 16¼ in. barrel with "The Marlin Limited" roll stamped on barrel, approx. 1,500 mfg. 1996 only.

	$425	$350	$275

MODEL 1894 COWBOY/COWBOY II — .357 Mag. (new 1997), .44-40 WCF (new 1997), .44 Mag. (new 1997), or .45 LC cal., 10 shot tube mag., incorporates "cowboy shooter" features, straight grip stock with checkering, adj. Marbles-type rear sight, blued finish, 24 in. octagon barrel, 7½ lbs. New 1996.

Mfg.'s Sug. Retail	$723	$570	$455	$365	$300	$250	$225	$195

The Model 1894 Cowboy II refers to the three new cals. introduced 1997.

MODEL 1894M (.22 MAG.) — .22 Mag. cal., with 20 in. barrel, 11 shot tube mag., straight grip walnut stock and forearm, 6¼ lbs. Disc. 1989.

	$275	$210	$180	$150	$135	$125	$115

Last Mfg.'s Sug. Retail was $358.

MODEL 1894CL — .218 Bee (new 1990), .25-20 WCF or .32-20 WCF cal., 6 shot (two-thirds length) tube mag., 22 in. barrel, 6¼ lbs. Mfg. 1988-94.

	$385	$290	$210	$175	$155	$140	$130

Last Mfg.'s Sug. Retail was $502.

MODEL 1894 CENTURY LIMITED — employee special edition featuring gold inlaid Marlin horse and rider logo. 100 mfg. 1994-95 in ser. no. range 1-100.

	$1,150	$825	$525

MODEL 1894 CENTURY LIMITED — .44-40 WCF cal., limited edition commemorative mfg. to celebrate the Model 1894's 100th Anniversary, 24 in. tapered octagon barrel with full 12 shot tube mag., features Giovanelli engraved receiver, bolt, and lever, receiver is case colored using traditional methods, checkered straight grip stock and forearm, crescent butt plate, 6½ lbs. 2,500 mfg. 1994 only.

	$950	$700	$475

Last Mfg.'s Sug. Retail was $1,088.

MODEL 1894 OCTAGON — similar to 1894 Carbine, with octagon barrel. Mfg. 1973.

	$425	$375	$325	$275	$225	$200	$185

MODEL 1895 LEVER ACTION — .45-70 Govt. cal., 4 shot tube mag., 22 in. barrel, open sights, straight grip stock with curved buttplate, forearm cap, sling and swivels. Mfg. 1972-1984.

	$295	$250	$225	$200	$185	$165	$140

Early new Model 1895 Marlins had cut rifling suitable for cast bullets, while later mfg. was switched to Marlins "Micro Groove" shallow rifling. Changes were also made from a straight stock to a pistol grip stock and from a traditional receiver to one with the newer hammer-block, push-button safety. Early guns with a straight grip stock, traditional receiver, and cut rifling command premiums over later mfg. Cut rifling occured during the first year of production only - these guns have a ser. no. prefix of B.O. More

Grading	100%	98%	95%	90%	80%	70%	60%

recently mfg. models have pistol grip, Micro Groove rifling, and hammer-block safety - these newer guns are the least desirable from a collector's standpoint.

* Model 1895S — similar to Model 1895, except has pistol grip stock and straight buttpad.

	100%	98%	95%	90%	80%	70%	60%
	$265	$225	$200	$175	$165	$150	$140

MODEL 1895SS — similar to Model 1895 S only with hammer block safety, cut checkering became standard 1994. New 1983.

Mfg.'s Sug. Retail	$566	$440	$325	$235	$175	$155	$140	$130

* Model 1895SS Cody Stampede 75th Anniversary — .45-70 cal., includes semi-fancy checkered walnut stock with medallion, serial numbered CS-001 - CS-200, 200 mfg. 1994 only.

	$650	$395	$275

Last Mfg.'s Sug. Retail was $695.

MODEL 1895G GUIDE GUN — .45-70 Govt. cal., features 18½ in. ported barrel with Ballard style cut rifling, cut checkered American stock and forearm, 4 shot tube mag., vent. recoil pad, 6¾ lbs. 2,500 to be mfg. beginning 1998.

Mfg.'s Sug. Retail	$572	$450	$335	$235	$175	$155	$140	$130

MODEL 1895 CENTURY LIMITED (CLTD) — .45-70 cal., commemorates Marlin's 125th Anniversary, engraving includes grizzly bear on left side and gold inlaid Marlin horse and rider logo on right, 24 in. half-round half-octagonal barrel, crescent buttplate, satin finished receiver, checkered walnut stock and forearm. Approx. 2,500 mfg. 1995 only.

	$995	$700	$475

Last Mfg.'s Sug. Retail was $1,104.

A Marlin Collector's Association Edition was also mfg. and was the same as the Model 1895 Century Limited.

* Model 1895 Century Limited (CLTD) Employee Edition — features 3 elk on left side and gold inlaid Marlin horse and rider logo on right. 100 mfg. 1995-96 in ser. no. range 1-100.

	$1,200	$800	$575

MODEL 1897 COWBOY — .22 S, L, or LR cal., takedown action, 19 shot (.22 LR cal.), tube mag., rebounding hammer with block safety, 24 in. tapered octagon barrel with Micro-Groove (16 grooves) rifling, cut checkered walnut stock and forearm, adj. Marbles semi-buckhorn rear and carbine front sight with brass bead, high polish blue, 6½ lbs. New 1999.

Mfg.'s Sug. Retail	$648	$530	$435	$360	$300	$275	$250	$225

MODEL 1897 CENTURY LIMITED LEVER ACTION — .22 LR cal., 100th anniversary of the Model 1897, features extensive receiver engraving and gold accenting, 24 in. half round/half octagon barrel with open sights, checkered fancy walnut stock and forearm. Limited mfg. 1997 only, limited quantities still remain.

Mfg.'s Sug. Retail	$1,055	$750	$650	$600

* Model 1897 Century Limited Employee Edition — .22 LR, features gold scroll work on lever, less than 100 mfg. 1997 only in ser. no. range 1-100.

	$1,000	$850	$700

MODEL 1897 ANNIE OAKLEY — .22 LR cal., features 18½ in. tapered octagon barrel with marble sights, blued receiver with rolled scroll engraving featuring gold Annie Oakley etched name on bolt, deluxe checkered walnut stock and forearm. Mfg. 1998 only.

	$925	$800	$675

Last Mfg.'s Sug. Retail was $1,054.

M

An employee variation of this model was made with gold inlays on finger lever, 100 mfg. total.

MODEL 2000 TARGET BOLT ACTION — .22 LR cal., single shot (can be converted), 22 in. heavy barrel with Lyman adj. sights, 2 stage target trigger, molded synthetic stock made from fiberglass and Kevlar with twice baked blue enamel, adj. buttplate, aluminum forearm rail, 8 lbs. Mfg. 1991-95.

	$495	$410	$350	$300	$275	$250	$225

Last Mfg.'s Sug. Retail was $602.

Add $34 for 5-shot clip conversion unit (for summer biathlon competition).

Grading	100%	98%	95%	90%	80%	70%	60%

* **Model 2000A Target** — similar to Model 2000 Target, except has adj. comb, ambidextrous pistol grip, and molded-in logo. Mfg. 1994 only.

| | $525 | $425 | $365 | $315 | $290 | $260 | $230 |

Last Mfg.'s Sug. Retail was $625.

* **Model 2000L** — .22 LR cal., updated version of the Model 2000, featuring grey/black laminated stock, adj. aperature rear and aperature insert front sight, double bedding screws, 8 lbs. New 1996.

| Mfg.'s Sug. Retail | $656 | $535 | $435 | $360 | $300 | $275 | $250 | $225 |

MODEL 7000 SEMI-AUTO — .22 LR cal., 10 shot mag., 18 in. heavy barrel without sights and recessed muzzle, black fiberglass, synthetic stock with molded-in checkering, grooved receiver, scope mounts provided, 6 lbs. New 1997.

| Mfg.'s Sug. Retail | $225 | $190 | $170 | $155 | $140 | $130 | $120 | $110 |

* **Model 7000T** — .22 LR cal., target model with 18 in. heavy barrel, red, white and blue laminated hardwood stock with adj. pad, two stage target trigger with stop, aluminum forend rail with adj. stop, grooved receiver w/o sights, 7½ lbs. New 1999.

| Mfg.'s Sug. Retail | $442 | $350 | $295 | $235 | $200 | $185 | $175 | $165 |

MARLIN PROMOTIONAL MODELS — Models 15 (disc.), 15Y (disc.), 15N (new 1998, 1999 MSR $188), 15YN (Youth Model - new 1989, 1999 MSR $188), 25 (disc.), 25M (disc.), 25N (new 1989, 1999 MSR $189), 60 (1999 MSR $168), 70 (disc.), 70HC (mfg. 1989-95, last 1995 MSR was $167), 75C (disc.), 81TS (new 1998, 1999 MSR $187), 795 Semi-Auto (new 1997, 1999 MSR $159) are inexpensive, utilitarian .22 LR or .22 Mag. cal. (Model 25M only), rifles designed for inexpensive shooting.

Series 15 and 25 Models designate bolt action, Series 60 and 70 designate semi-auto design.

Between 1930 to date, Marlin has made a number of .22 cal. rimfire rifles, bolt action single shots, bolt action repeaters and auto loaders. These have normally been good quality, inexpensive weapons. In 1960, the name Glenfield was also used in connection with these guns. We will list these models for reference purposes with price ranges appearing at the end of each listing.

RIFLES: .22 CAL. BOLT ACTION, SINGLE SHOT

Model 65 — 1932-1938. Price Range $35 - $65.
Model 65E — 1932-1938. Price Range $45 - $75.
Model 100 — 1936-1941. Price Range $45 - $75.
Model 100S Tom Mix Special — disc. Price Range $125 - $250.
Model 100SB — 1936-1941. Price Range $50 - $85.
Model 101 — 1951-disc. Price Range $45 - $75.
Model 101 DL — disc. Price Range $60 - $90.
Model 101 Crown Prince — 1959. Price Range $75 - $150.
Model 101G — 1960-1965, Marlin Glenfield. Price Range $40 - $70.
Model 10 — 1966-disc., Marlin Glenfield. Price Range $40 - $65.
Model 122 — 1966-disc. Price Range $40 - $65.

BOLT ACTION: REPEATING RIFLES

Model 80 — 1934-1939. Price Range $45 - $85.
Model 80E — 1934-1940. Price Range $50 - $90.
Model 80C — 1940-1970. Price Range $50 - $90.
Model 80DL — 1940-1965. Price Range $60 - $95.
Model 80G — 1960-1965, Marlin Glenfield. Price Range $40 - $70.
Model 20 — 1966-disc., Marlin Glenfield. Price Range $40 - $70.
Model 780 — 1971-1988. Price Range $45 - $75.
Model 781 — 1971-1988. Price Range $45 - $75.
Model 782 — 1971-1988, .22 WRM. Price Range $65 - $100.
Model 783 — 1971-1988, .22 WRM. Price Range $65 - $100.
Model 980 — 1962-1970, .22 WRM. Price Range $65 - $100.
Model 81 — 1937-1940. Price Range $25 - $50.

Grading	100%	98%	95%	90%	80%	70%	60%

Model 81E — 1937-1940. Price Range $60 - $85.

Model 81C — 1940-1970. Price Range $60 - $85.

Model 81DL — 1940-1965. Price Range $65 - $90.

Model 81G — 1960-1965 Marlin Glenfield. Price Range $50 - $75.

AUTOLOADING RIFLES

Model 50 — 1931-1935. Price Range $75 - $125.

Model 50E — 1931-1934. Price Range $75 - $135.

Model A-1 — 1936-1940. Price Range $75 - $125.

Model A-1E — 1935-1946. Price Range $75 - $135.

Model A-1C — 1941-1946. Price Range $65 - $125.

Model A-1DL — 1941-1946. Price Range $65 - $135.

Model 88-C — 1948-1956. Price Range $65 - $135.

Model 88-DL — 1953-1956. Price Range $65 - $135.

Model 89-C — 1948-1961. Price Range $65 - $135.

Model 89-DL — 1950-1961. Price Range $65 - $135.

Model 98 — 1957-1959. Price Range $65 - $135.

Model 99 — 1959-1960. Price Range $65 - $135.

Model 99C — 1961-1978. Price Range $65 - $135.

Model 99G — 1960-1965, Marlin Glenfield. Price Range $65 - $135.

Model 60 — 1960-present, Marlin Glenfield (1996 MSR $158).

Model 99DL — 1960-1964. Price Range $65 - $135.

Model 49 — 1968-1970. Price Range $65 - $135.

Model 49DL — 1971-1978. Price Range $65 - $135.

Model 99M1 — 1964-1978. Price Range $65 - $135.

Model 989M2 — 1966-disc. Price Range $65 - $135.

Model 989 — 1962-1965. Price Range $65 - $135.

Model 70 (HC) — 1966-1995, Marlin Glenfield. Price Range $75 - $145.

Model 989G — 1962-1964, Marlin Glenfield. Price Range $65 - $135.

Model 990 — disc. Price Range $65 - $135.

SHOTGUNS: BOLT ACTION

MODEL 50 DL — 12 ga. only, upland game model, 28 in. barrel bored M, black Rynite stock with molded-in checkering, 2 shot mag., 7½ lbs. New 1997.

	100%	98%	95%	90%	80%	70%	60%
Mfg.'s Sug. Retail $330	$255	$195	$150	$125	$115	$100	$90

MODEL 55 — 12, 16, or 20 ga., 2 shot detachable mag., 26 and 28 in. full choke barrel, plain pistol grip stock. Mfg. 1950-1965.

	100%	98%	95%	90%	80%	70%	60%
	$90	$70	$55	$40	$35	$30	$25
With adj. choke	$100	$85	$65	$50	$45	$40	$30

MODEL 55 GOOSE GUN — similar to Model 55, except 12 ga. only, 36 in. full choke barrel, 3 in. chamber, 2 shot clip mag., leather carrying strap and detachable swivels, walnut stock with rubber recoil pad, 8 lbs. Mfg. 1962-96.

	100%	98%	95%	90%	80%	70%	60%
	$235	$185	$145	$125	$115	$100	$90

Last Mfg.'s Sug. Retail was $308.

* ***Model 55 GDL*** — similar to Model 55 Goose Gun, except has black Rynite synthetic stock. New 1997.

	100%	98%	95%	90%	80%	70%	60%
Mfg.'s Sug. Retail $385	$325	$235	$200	$180	$160	$145	$130

MODEL 55 SWAMP GUN — similar to Model 55, 12 ga., 20 in. adj. choke barrel, 3 in. mag. Mfg. 1963-1965.

	100%	98%	95%	90%	80%	70%	60%
	$105	$90	$70	$55	$50	$45	$35

MODEL 55S SLUG GUN — 24 in. barrel, cylinder bore, rifle sights. Mfg. 1974-1983.

	100%	98%	95%	90%	80%	70%	60%
	$140	$120	$110	$95	$85	$55	$40

Grading	100%	98%	95%	90%	80%	70%	60%

MODEL 512 SLUGMASTER — 12 ga., 3 in. chamber, bolt action, 2 shot box mag., 21 in. rifled barrel, adj. rear sight, receiver is drilled and tapped for scope mount (included), walnut finished birch stock with pressed checkering and vent. recoil pad, 8 lbs. New 1994.

Mfg.'s Sug. Retail	$361	$295	$220	$195	$175	$160	$145	$130

✱ *Model 512 DL Slugmaster* — similar to Model 512 Slugmaster, except has black Rynite stock, Fire Sights (with red fiber optic inserts) became standard 1998. Disc. 1998.

	$310	$230	$200	$180	$160	$145	$130

Last Mfg.'s Sug. Retail was $372.

✱ *Model 512 P Slugmaster* — 12 ga., 3 in. chamber, features 21 in. ported fully rifled barrel with front and rear Fire Sights (high visibility red and green fiber optic inserts), 2 shot detachable box mag., black fiberglass synthetic stock with molded-in checkering, receiver is drilled and tapped, 8 lbs. New 1999.

Mfg.'s Sug. Retail	$366	$300	$225	$200	$180	$165	$155	$145

MODEL 5510 — 10 ga., 3½ in. mag., 2 shot clip mag., 34 in. barrel, leather carrying strap and detachable swivels, rubber recoil pad, 10½ lbs. Mfg. 1976-1985.

	$220	$170	$160	$150	$140	$130	$120

Last Mfg.'s Sug. Retail was $282.

SHOTGUNS: LEVER ACTION

MODEL .410 LEVER ACTION — .410 bore, 22 or 26 in. barrel, full choke, lever action, similar to 1893, exposed hammer, plain pistol grip stock. Mfg. 1929-1932 as a stockholders promotional firearm.

	$975	$825	$675	$550	$475	$425	$350

✱ *Model .410 Deluxe* — includes deluxe checkered walnut stock and forearm.

	$1,450	$1,250	$1,000	$875	$750	$625	$525

SHOTGUNS: O/U

MODEL 90 — 12, 16, 20 ga., or .410 bore shotgun or combination gun configuration (12 ga. over .30/30 barrels), 26, 28, or 30 in. barrels, boxlock, extractors, checkered pistol grip stock. Mfg. 1937-1958. Guns made from 1937-1949 had vent. separated barrels, after 1949, solid barrels.

	$450	$385	$360	$330	$290	$265	$230

Add 50% for combination gun configuration.

✱ *With single trigger*

	$550	$495	$470	$440	$400	$375	$340

Add 25% for .410 bore.

SHOTGUNS: SINGLE SHOT

MODEL 60 — 12 ga., 30 or 32 in. barrel, full choke, top lever, break open, exposed hammer, pistol grip stock. Approx. 3,000 mfg.

	$195	$165	$140	$120	$110	$100	$90

M

SHOTGUNS: SLIDE ACTION, 1898-1963 PRODUCTION

During 1998, Marlin issued a service bulletin recommending that slide action exposed hammer Models 1898, 16, 17, 19, 19S, 19G, 19N, 21, 24, 24G, 26, 30, 42, 49, and 49N, in addition to hammerless Models 28, 31, 43, 44, 53, and 63 should not be fired, as many of these guns are 70-100 years old, and system failures can and do happen.

MODEL 1898 — 12 ga., 5 shot tube mag., 26-32 in. barrels, various chokes, exposed hammer, pistol grip stock, grades differ in quality of wood and engraving on C and D. Mfg. 1898-1905.

Grade A	$325	$275	$225	$200	$165	$150	$140
Grade B	$580	$495	$440	$415	$360	$305	$275

Grading	100%	98%	95%	90%	80%	70%	60%
Grade C	$880	$715	$635	$580	$525	$495	$440
Grade D	$1,760	$1,540	$1,320	$1,210	$1,045	$965	$880

Factory information by individual ser. no. from the Cody Firearms Museum may be available for this model in the ser. range 19,601-67,000.

MODEL 16 — 16 ga. only, 26 or 28 in. barrel, various chokes, takedown, pistol grip stock. Mfg. 1904-1910.

Grade A	$325	$275	$225	$200	$165	$150	$140
Grade B	$495	$415	$360	$330	$305	$275	$250
Grade C	$635	$525	$495	$440	$415	$385	$330
Grade D	$1,320	$1,100	$990	$825	$715	$635	$550

MODEL 17 — 12 ga., 30 or 32 in. full choke barrel, solid frame, straight stock. Mfg. 1906-1908.

	$335	$275	$235	$200	$165	$150	$140

MODEL 17 BRUSH GUN — similar to Model 17, with 26 in. cylinder bore barrel. Mfg. 1906-1908.

	$325	$275	$235	$200	$165	$150	$140

MODEL 17 RIOT GUN — similar to Model 17, with 20 in. barrel. Mfg. 1906-1908.

	$325	$275	$235	$200	$165	$150	$140

MODEL 19 — improved lightened version of Model 1898, matte top surface on barrel. Mfg. 1906-1907.

Grade A	$325	$275	$235	$200	$165	$150	$140
Grade B	$495	$415	$360	$330	$305	$275	$250
Grade C	$635	$525	$495	$440	$415	$385	$330
Grade D	$1,320	$1,100	$990	$825	$715	$635	$550

MODEL 21 — straight grip version of Model 19.

Grade A	$325	$275	$235	$200	$165	$150	$140
Grade B	$495	$415	$360	$330	$305	$275	$250
Grade C	$635	$525	$495	$440	$415	$385	$330
Grade D	$1,320	$1,100	$990	$825	$715	$635	$550

MODEL 24 — improved 21, takedown, automatic recoil lock on slide, solid matte rib. Mfg. 1908-1915.

Grade G	$295	$265	$225	$195	$165	$150	$140
Grade A	$325	$275	$235	$200	$165	$150	$140
Grade B	$525	$440	$385	$360	$330	$305	$275
Grade C	$660	$550	$525	$470	$440	$415	$360
Grade D	$1,375	$1,155	$1,045	$880	$770	$660	$580

MODEL 25MG GARDEN GUN — please refer to listing in the Rifles: Bolt Action section.

MODEL 26 — similar to Model 24 Grade A, with solid frame, 30 or 32 in. full choke barrel. Mfg. 1909-1915.

	$275	$230	$210	$195	$165	$150	$140

MODEL 26 BRUSH GUN — 26 in. cylinder bore barrel. Mfg. 1909-1915.

	$275	$230	$210	$195	$165	$150	$140

MODEL 26 RIOT GUN — 20 in. cylinder bore barrel. Mfg. 1909-1915.

	$250	$195	$180	$165	$150	$140	$120

MODEL 28 HAMMERLESS — 12 ga., 26-32 in. barrels, various chokes, takedown, matte top barrel, pistol grip stock. Mfg. 1913-1922.

Grade A	$295	$265	$235	$200	$165	$150	$140
Grade B	$495	$415	$360	$330	$305	$275	$250
Grade C	$635	$525	$495	$440	$415	$385	$330
Grade D	$1,320	$1,100	$990	$825	$715	$635	$550

M

Grading	100%	98%	95%	90%	80%	70%	60%

MODEL 28TS TRAP GUN — similar to Model 28, with 30 in. matte rib barrel, full choke, high comb straight grip stock. Mfg. 1915.

	$415	$330	$275	$250	$220	$195	$165

MODEL 28T — similar to Model 28TS, with fancy wood, checkering, better finish. Mfg. 1915.

	$605	$525	$495	$470	$415	$360	$305

MODEL 30 — similar to Model 16, with automatic recoil lock on slide, also mfg. in 20 ga. 1915-1917 (Model 30-20). Mfg. 1910-1914.

	100%	98%	95%	90%	80%	70%	60%
Grade A	$325	$275	$235	$200	$165	$150	$140
Grade B	$495	$415	$360	$330	$305	$275	$250
Grade C	$635	$525	$495	$440	$415	$385	$330
Grade D	$1,320	$1,100	$990	$825	$715	$635	$550

MODEL 30 FIELD GRADE — similar to Model 30 Grade B, with 25 in. mod. barrel, straight stock. Mfg. 1913-1917.

	$335	$275	$220	$180	$160	$130	$115

MODEL 31 — scaled down small ga. (16 and 20 ga.) version of the Model 28, has 26 and 28 in. barrels, various chokes, Model 31-16 was mfg. 1914-1917, Model 31-20 was mfg. 1911-1923.

	100%	98%	95%	90%	80%	70%	60%
Grade A	$385	$305	$250	$220	$195	$165	$140
Grade B	$495	$415	$360	$330	$305	$275	$250
Grade C	$636	$525	$495	$440	$415	$385	$330
Grade D	$1,320	$1,100	$990	$825	$715	$635	$550

MODEL 31F FIELD GUN — 25 in. mod. barrel. Mfg. 1915-1917.

	$395	$350	$325	$295	$265	$225	$200

MODEL 42A — similar to Model 24, but lesser quality finishing. Mfg. 1922-1934.

	$250	$220	$195	$165	$140	$120	$100

MODEL 43 HAMMERLESS — similar to Model 28, with lesser quality finish. Mfg. 1923-1930.

	$275	$225	$200	$175	$150	$125	$100

MODEL 43TS — similar to Model 28T, lower quality.

	$525	$440	$415	$385	$360	$305	$275

MODEL 44A — similar to Model 31 Grade A, 20 ga. only. Mfg. 1923-1935.

	$360	$275	$250	$220	$195	$165	$140

MODEL 44S — select checkered stock.

	$470	$385	$360	$330	$195	$165	$140

MODEL 49 — lower priced version of Model 42A. They were given to purchasers of 4 shares of Marlin stock. 3,000 mfg. in 1925-1928.

	$440	$360	$305	$275	$220	$195	$165

MODEL 53 — similar to Model 43 Hammerless. Mfg. 1929-1930.

	$330	$275	$250	$220	$195	$165	$140

MODEL 63 — similar to Model 43 Hammerless, later model. Mfg. 1931-1935.

	$330	$250	$220	$195	$165	$140	$110

MODEL 63TS — similar to Model 43TS, with trap style stock.

	$385	$305	$250	$220	$195	$165	$140

MODEL 120 MAGNUM — slide action, 12 ga., 3 in. chamber, 26-38 in. barrel, takedown, various chokes, checkered pistol grip stock. Mfg. 1971-1985.

	$290	$225	$215	$205	$195	$180	$165

Last Mfg.'s Sug. Retail was $370.

Subtract $35 if without VR.

Grading	100%	98%	95%	90%	80%	70%	60%

MODEL 778 — 12 ga. Mag. slide action, 20-38 in. barrels, 7¾ lbs. Disc. 1984.

	$225	$190	$175	$155	$140	$125	$110

PREMIER MARK I — 12 ga. only, aluminum receiver, takedown, manufactured in France for Marlin.

	$200	$180	$160	$150	$140	$120	$95

PREMIER MARK II — similar to Mark I, except with engraved receiver and checkering. Mfg. 1960-1963 in France.

	$275	$235	$200	$175	$150	$125	$100

PREMIER MARK IV — similar to Mark II, only deluxe grade with better wood, more engraving. Mfg. 1960-1963 in France.

	$305	$250	$220	$195	$165	$140	$110
With VR	$330	$275	$250	$220	$195	$165	$140

MAROCCHI

ARMI ⊕ MAROCCHI

Current manufacturer established in 1922 and located in Brescia, Italy. Currently imported and distributed exclusively by Precision Sales International, Inc. located in Westfield, MA.

Marocchi makes a wide variety of quality shotguns and O/U rifles. Many of their models however, are not being imported currently. Discontinued Frigon guns (manufactured by Marocchi) appear under the F section in this text.

COMBINATION GUNS

VALLEY COMBO — 12 ga. over .222 Rem. cal., 23½ in. separated barrels with VR, 3 in. chamber, fold down rear sight and will accept claw scope mounts, fixed cylinder choke, DTs, engraved silver receiver, satin finish walnut Monte Carlo stock with checkering and recoil pad, 8¼ lbs. Disc. 1994.

	$585	$480	$415	$375	$325	$295	$275

Last Mfg.'s Sug. Retail was $700.

SHOTGUNS: O/U, DISC.

The following models were imported exclusively by Sile Distributors, Inc. until 1994. Other Marocchi models were also imported by Sile Distributors on a limited basis.

FIELD MASTER I — 12 ga. only, 26 or 28 in. VR barrels and rib with choke tubes, engraved coin finished receiver, extractors, SNT, checkered walnut stock and forearm. Disc. 1994.

	$455	$395	$325	$275	$240	$215	$200

Last Mfg.'s Sug. Retail was $530.

＊ Field Master II — similar to Field Master I except has SST and choke tubes. Disc. 1994.

	$475	$350	$295	$260	$225	$210	$190

Last Mfg.'s Sug. Retail was $550.

SKEET MODEL — 12 ga. only, 26 in. barrels bored SK/SK. Disc. 1994.

	$445	$395	$325	$275	$240	$215	$200

Last Mfg.'s Sug. Retail was $520.

M

TRAP MODEL — 12 ga. only, 30 in. barrels bored M/F, ejectors. Disc. 1994.

	$560	$485	$415	$360	$300	$260	$230

Last Mfg.'s Sug. Retail was $630.

Grading	100%	98%	95%	90%	80%	70%	60%

AVANZA — 12 or 20 (disc. 1993) ga., 3 in. chambers, monobloc boxlock action, 26 or 28 in. vent. barrels with VR (with or without choke tubes), SST, ejectors, deluxe checkered walnut stock and forearm with vent. recoil pad, high polish bluing with gold accents, all steel lightweight mfg., 6 lbs. 5 oz. - 6 lbs. 13 oz. Imported 1990-95.

| | | | $725 | $595 | $525 | $475 | $425 | $375 | $325 |

Last Mfg.'s Sug. Retail was $829.

> Add $45 for 20 ga. (disc. 1993).
> Subtract 10% if without choke tubes (3).

This model was imported exclusively by Precision Sales International, Inc.

* Avanza Sporting Clays — 12 ga. only, 3 in. chambers, built on 20 ga. frame, 28 in. vent. barrels with VR and choke tubes, select checkered walnut stock with deluxe recoil pad and forearm, gold-plated trigger, 7 lbs. Mfg. 1991-95.

| | | | $780 | $620 | $560 | $500 | $450 | $400 | $350 |

Last Mfg.'s Sug. Retail was $889.

> Add $99 for Premier Grade (disc., included select walnut and gold etched triggerguard).

This model features a trigger that is adjustable for length and pull without special tools.

SHOTGUNS: O/U, CURRENT PRODUCTION

In the U.S., Conquista shotguns are identical in specifications and features to the Marocchi Classic Doubles sold in Europe, with the exception of Classic Doubles U.S.A.

GOLDEN SNIPE III FIELD — 12 ga. only, 3 in. chambers, field configuration with 28 in. VR barrels and choke tubes. New 1998.

| Mfg.'s Sug. Retail | $1,260 | | $1,125 | $925 | $850 | $775 | $700 | $625 | $550 |

CONQUISTA FIELD MAGNUM GRADE I — 12 ga. only, 3 in. chambers, features 28 in. 8mm VR barrels with choke tubes, nickel finished receiver, SST, checkered walnut stock and forearm with smooth rosewood buttplate, approx. 7¼ lbs. New 1999.

| Mfg.'s Sug. Retail | $1,995 | | $1,725 | $1,450 | $1,200 | $1,000 | $850 | $700 | $550 |

GOLDEN SNIPE III SPORTING — 12 ga. only, entry level sporting clays model with 28 or 30 in. VR barrels with choke tubes, checkered walnut stock and forearm. New 1999.

| Mfg.'s Sug. Retail | $1,375 | | $1,200 | $975 | $875 | $800 | $700 | $625 | $550 |

CONQUISTA USA SPORTING — 12 ga. only, 3 in. chambers, features 30 in. vent. barrels with 10mm VR, muzzle porting, back boring, and lengthened forcing cones, blued barrels and receiver with gold accents, checkered standard or adj. walnut stock and forearm, approx. 8 lbs. New 1999.

| Mfg.'s Sug. Retail | $1,995 | | $1,725 | $1,450 | $1,200 | $1,000 | $850 | $700 | $550 |

> Add $151 for adj. stock.

CONQUISTA SPORTING CLAYS — 12 ga. only, boxlock action with brushed coin finish, SST, ejectors, adj. trigger, choice of 28, 30, or 32 in. 10mm VR barrels with choke tubes, right or left-hand (Grade I only) action, checkered walnut stock and forearm with recoil pad, 7⅞ lbs. New 1994.

M

* Grade I — features coin finished receiver with perimeter line engraving.

| Mfg.'s Sug. Retail | $1,995 | | $1,725 | $1,450 | $1,200 | $1,000 | $850 | $700 | $550 |

> Add $125 for left-hand variation.
> Add $151 for adj. stock (new 1999).

* Lady Sport — 12 ga. only, features lighter weight specialized stock designed to fit women, cased, 7½ lbs. New 1995.

| Mfg.'s Sug. Retail | $2,120 | | $1,800 | $1,525 | $1,250 | $1,000 | $850 | $700 | $550 |

> Add $180 for left-hand variation (Sport Spectrum only).
> Add $79 for Lady Sport Spectrum (partially colored receiver).

* Grade II — features better walnut and game scene engraving on receiver.

| Mfg.'s Sug. Retail | $2,330 | | $1,995 | $1,675 | $1,425 | $1,200 | $1,000 | $850 | $700 |

> Add $355 for left-hand variation.

Grading	100%	98%	95%	90%	80%	70%	60%

* **Grade III** — features more elaborate game scene engraving on receiver sides and fine scrollwork throughout rest of action, includes hard gun case and stock wrench.

  Mfg.'s Sug. Retail **$3,599**   **$3,225 $2,650 $2,250 $1,875 $1,650 $1,400 $1,175**

  Add $396 for left-hand variation.

* **Grade IV** — top-of-the-line Sporting Clays model. Importation began 1997. Price available by request only.

CONQUISTA TRAP MODEL — 12 ga. only, Trap configuration, 30 or 32 (disc. 1997) in. 10mm VR barrels with fixed chokes, 8¼ lbs. New 1994.

* **Grade I** — features coin finished receiver with perimeter line engraving.

  Mfg.'s Sug. Retail **$1,995**   **$1,725 $1,475 $1,225 $1,000 $850 $700 $550**

  Add $151 for adj. stock (new 1999).

* **Grade II** — features better walnut and game scene engraving on receiver.

  Mfg.'s Sug. Retail **$2,330**   **$1,995 $1,675 $1,450 $1,200 $1,000 $850 $700**

* **Grade III** — features more elaborate game scene engraving on receiver sides and fine scrollwork throughout rest of action, includes hard gun case and stock wrench.

  Mfg.'s Sug. Retail **$3,599**   **$3,225 $2,650 $2,250 $1,875 $1,650 $1,400 $1,175**

* **Grade IV** — top-of-the-line Trap model. Importation began 1997. Price available by request only.

CONQUISTA SKEET MODEL — 12 ga. only, Skeet configuration, 28 in. 10mm VR barrels with fixed Skeet chokes, 7¾ lbs. New 1994.

* **Grade I** — features coin finished receiver with perimeter line engraving.

  Mfg.'s Sug. Retail **$1,995**   **$1,725 $1,475 $1,225 $1,000 $850 $700 $550**

* **Grade II** — features better walnut and game scene engraving on receiver.

  Mfg.'s Sug. Retail **$2,330**   **$1,995 $1,675 $1,450 $1,200 $1,000 $850 $700**

* **Grade III** — features more elaborate game scene engraving on receiver sides and fine scrollwork throughout rest of action, includes hard gun case and stock wrench.

  Mfg.'s Sug. Retail **$3,599**   **$3,225 $2,650 $2,250 $1,875 $1,650 $1,400 $1,175**

* **Grade IV** — top-of-the-line Skeet model. Importation began 1997. Price available by request only.

CLASSIC DOUBLES MODEL 92 — 12 ga. only, 3 in. chambers, sporting clays configuration featuring 30 in. vented barrels with VR, back-boring, elongated forcing cones, and three screw-in chokes, low profile blued receiver, checkered walnut stock, and Schnabel forearm, adj. trigger, gold receiver accents and trigger. Imported 1996-98.

$1,450 $1,175 $950 $850 $775 $700 $650

Last Mfg.'s Sug. Retail was $1,598.

SHOTGUNS: SINGLE SHOT

MODEL 2000 — 12 ga. only, 3 in. chamber, hammer, 28 in. barrel, ejector, lightly engraved receiver. Importation disc. 1991.

$80 $70 $60 $50 $45 $40 $35

Last Mfg.'s Sug. Retail was $94.

MASQUELIER S.A.

Previous manufacturer located in Belgium. Previously distributed (until 1986) by Ambel Ltd., Inc. located in Sugar Land, TX.

Grading	100%	98%	95%	90%	80%	70%	60%

RIFLES: SxS

CARPATHE — .243 Win., .270 Win., .30-06, 7x57R, or 7x65R cal., single shot, hair trigger, push-down cocking system. Importation disc. 1986.

$3,500 $3,200 $2,900 $2,600 $2,300 $2,100 $1,850
Last Mfg.'s Sug. Retail was $3,850.

EXPRESS — .270 Win., .30-06, 8x57JRS, or 9.3x74R cal., O/U configuration, SST, ejectors. Add $800 for extra set of 20 ga. barrels. Importation disc. 1986.

$3,300 $3,000 $2,800 $2,600 $2,300 $2,100 $1,850
Last Mfg.'s Sug. Retail was $3,600.

ARDENNES MODEL — top-of-the-line model, custom order only. Importation disc. 1986.

$6,600 $6,000 $5,400 $4,800 $4,300 $3,900 $3,450
Last Mfg.'s Sug. Retail was $7,250.

SHOTGUNS:SxS

BOXLOCK — 12 ga. only, 2¾ in. chambers, Anson & Deeley boxlock action, ejectors, fine scroll engraving with French walnut. Importation disc. 1986.

$4,400 $4,000 $3,650 $3,300 $2,995 $2,600 $2,200
Last Mfg.'s Sug. Retail was $4,780.

SIDELOCK — 12 ga. only, 2¾ in. chambers, H&H style sidelocks, auto ejectors, English style fine scroll engraving with French walnut. Importation disc. 1986.

$12,500 $10,000 $8,750 $7,600 $6,700 $5,800 $5,000
Last Mfg.'s Sug. Retail was $15,850.

MATEBA

Current importation is by American Arms, Inc. (see individual listing under American Arms heading). Previously manufactured by Macchine Termo Balistiche located in Italy. Older mfg. had little domestic importation.

REVOLVERS

MATEBA REVOLVER — various cals., 6, 7, or 8 shot, unique design permits barrel to fire lowest shell in cylinder (6 o'clock position), mechanism to rear of cylinder, interchangeable barrels.

Depending on features, older production Matebas usually sell in the $375-$800 range, depending on condition and features.

MATCH GRADE ARMS & AMMUNITION

Current custom rifle manufacturer located in Spring, TX. Consumer direct sales.

RIFLES: BOLT ACTION

ULTRA-LIGHT MODEL — various cals., lightened and skeletonized Wby. Vanguard action, MGA button rifled barrel, Teflon metal finish, camo epoxy stock with Pachmayr decelerator pad, approx. 7 lbs.

Mfg.'s Sug. Retail $1,695 $1,695 $1,450 $1,250 $995 $850 $700 $550

MGA VARMINTER — various cals., squared and lapped Rem. M700 action, stainless steel National Match barrel with Super Eliminator muzzle brake, black Teflon metal finish, camo epoxy stock.

Mfg.'s Sug. Retail $1,995 $1,995 $1,750 $1,500 $1,250 $995 $850 $700

MATHELON ARMES

Current SxS double rifle and drilling manufacturer located in Rumilly, France. No current importation.

Currently, Mathelon Armes manufactures a boxlock drilling, and SxS double rifle in 8x57IRS and 9.374R cal. Please contact the factory directly (see Trademark Index) for more information and current pricing.

Grading	100%	98%	95%	90%	80%	70%	60%

MATRA MANURHIN DEFENSE

Please refer to the Manurhin heading in this section.

MAUSER JAGD-UND SPORTWAFFEN GmbH

Current manufacturer located in Oberndorf, Germany 1871 to date. In January, 1999, SIG Arms purchased the Mauser brand name rights and all associated activities related to small arms production. As this edition went to press, future plans for making Mauser hunting rifles and components were uncertain. Because of this, there is no current importer at this time.

Previously imported exclusively by Brolin Arms, located in Pomona, CA during 1997-98 only. During 1998, the company name was changed from Mauser-Werke Oberndorf Waffensysteme GmbH to the heading name above. During 1994, the name was changed from Mauser-Werke to Mauser-Werke Oberndorf Waffensysteme GmbH. Previously imported by GSI located in Trussville, AL, until 1997, Gibb's Rifle Co., Inc. until 1995, Precision Imports, Inc. located in San Antonio, TX until 1993, and KDF located in Seguin, TX (1987-89). Distributor and dealer sales.

HANDGUNS: EARLY PRODUCTION

MODEL 1877 SINGLE SHOT — 9mm cal., single shot, barrel release in usual hammer position and safety on left side, examples are rare.

	100%	98%	95%	90%	80%	70%	60%
	$10,000	$8,500	$7,000	$6,000	$5,000	$4,000	$3,000

MODEL 1878 "ZIG-ZAG" REVOLVER — 7.6mm, 9mm(most common) or 10.6mm cal., Zig-Zag refers to Z-pattern grooves cut into cylinder, earliest revolvers were solid frame, gate loaded, and chambered in 9mm, most were designed with a hinged frame, third and last version had an "improved" sliding release on the forward frame, most revolvers had a rust blued frame and barrel complementing a fire blued cylinder, grips were checkered or hard rubber with a floral pattern.

	100%	98%	95%	90%	80%	70%	60%
7.6mm	$4,500	$3,750	$2,500	$2,000	$1,850	$1,700	$1,400
9mm	$5,250	$4,250	$3,500	$3,000	$2,250	$1,900	$1,500
10.6mm	$6,500	$5,000	$4,000	$3,200	$2,400	$2,000	$1,600

Add 10% for earliest pistols with "midnight blue" finish. Premiums exist for solid frame, late improved model, and factory cased guns.

PISTOLS: SEMI-AUTO, DISC.

The Models 1906-08, 1912-14, and HSv are very rare and only infrequently encountered. A competent appraisal is advisable before buying or selling these models.

MODEL 1906-08 — 9mm Export (9x25mm) cal., detachable mag., incorporates features of both the pocket pistols and Model 1896 Broomhandle. Ser. range 1-100 (est.).

	100%	98%	95%	90%	80%	70%	60%
	N/A	$35,000	$29,500	$25,000	$19,500	$15,000	$9,950

MODEL 1912-14 — generally chambered for 9mm Para. cal., similar to pocket pistol configuration, but considerably larger, earliest specimens have inscribed slide legend. Those under serial number 100 (approx.) are not slotted for shoulder stock while those over 100 are generally slotted. Ser. range 1-175 (est.).

	100%	98%	95%	90%	80%	70%	60%
	N/A	$20,000	$16,000	$12,000	$10,000	$8,000	$6,000

Add 50% if slotted with matching shoulder stock.

This variation is very rare in .45 ACP cal. or with a tangent rear sight.

M

WTP MODEL I VEST POCKET AUTOMATIC — 6.35mm cal., 6 shot, 2½ in. barrel, blue, rubber grips. Mfg. 1922-1937.

	100%	98%	95%	90%	80%	70%	60%
	$495	$325	$250	$200	$160	$140	$100

Grading	100%	98%	95%	90%	80%	70%	60%

WTP MODEL II — similar to Model I, but 2 in. barrel. Mfg. 1938-1940.

| | $650 | $525 | $450 | $350 | $250 | $200 | $150 |

POCKET MODEL 1910 — 6.35mm or 7.65mm cal., 9 shot, 3 in. barrel, blue fixed sights, checkered walnut or hard rubber grips. Mfg. 1910-1934.

| | $395 | $275 | $180 | $165 | $150 | $140 | $130 |

Add 30% for sidelatch variation.

POCKET MODEL 1914 — similar to Model 1910, but 7.65mm cal., 3.4 in. barrel. Mfg. 1914-1934.

| | $395 | $275 | $175 | $165 | $150 | $145 | $135 |

Add 10% for military acceptance proof by rear sight (Prussian eagle WWI proofs and/or crown D).

Add 500% for the "humpback" model.

POCKET MODEL 1934 — similar to Model 1914, but reshaped grip. Mfg. 1934-1939.

| | $450 | $325 | $210 | $175 | $160 | $150 | $140 |

Add 50% for Waffenamt or Nazi Police.

Add 100% for Nazi Navy marked.

MODEL HSv — 9mm Para. cal., limited mfg., similar features to Model HSc, except has larger dimensions.

| | N/A | $15,000 | $10,000 | $8,500 | $7,000 | $6,500 | $5,500 |

Mauser Pistols: HSc Models

MODEL HSc DOUBLE ACTION — 7.65mm (8 shot) or .380 ACP (7 shot) cal., 3.4 in. barrel, blue or nickel, fixed sights, checkered walnut grips. Mfg. 1938-disc. (most recent mfg. was by R. Gamba in Italy circa 1996).

Mauser Pistols: HSc WWII Military Mfg.

* *Low Grip Screw* — very rare, first variation with ser. numbers starting at 700,000, less than 2,000 mfg.

| | $3,250 | $2,500 | $1,850 | $1,200 | $1,000 | $800 | $650 |

Add 20% if Navy marked.

* *Early Nazi Army* — proofed 655 and 135.

| | $700 | $550 | $425 | $265 | $225 | $200 | $185 |

Add 50% for small 655 additonally test-proofed on left tang.

* *Early Nazi Navy* — marked on front grip strap.

| | $900 | $725 | $540 | $500 | $440 | $395 | $350 |

* *Early Nazi Police* — Eagle L proof only.

| | $600 | $450 | $360 | $320 | $285 | $245 | $200 |

* *Wartime Nazi Army* — proof 135 and WaA 135. Eagle N proofed also.

| | $400 | $325 | $290 | $250 | $200 | $180 | $150 |

* *Wartime Nazi Navy* — proofed on left side of triggerguard.

| | $650 | $525 | $400 | $340 | $295 | $260 | $230 |

* *Wartime Nazi Police* — proofed Eagle L. Add 10% if Eagle F.

| | $500 | $395 | $360 | $320 | $285 | $245 | $200 |

* *Wartime Commercial* — standard WWII Commercial Model.

| | $400 | $325 | $290 | $265 | $200 | $180 | $150 |

* *Swiss Commercial* — ser. range 800,000-900,000. Very rare.

| | $1,400 | $1,250 | $1,125 | $995 | $900 | $850 | $600 |

M

Grading	100%	98%	95%	90%	80%	70%	60%

* **Cutaways** — mfg. to visibly show mechanism. Should not be proofed.

	$1,495	$1,000	$900	$850	$800	$750	$700

Mauser Pistols: HSc Post-WWII Mfg.

* **French Manufacture** — frequently encountered in poor condition — post-WWII production.

	$325	$275	$245	$220	$180	$155	$130

* **Mauser Production** — .32 or .380 cal., 15 shot, mfg. 1968-1981.

	$350	$295	$260	$225	$180	$150	$130

Deduct 20% if not boxed or in .32 cal.

* **Interarms Import** — imported by Interarms from 1983-1985 (Italian mfg. by Gamba).

	$325	$275	$250	$220	$180	$150	$125

Last Mfg.'s Sug. Retail was $415.

* **One of Five Thousand Edition** — American Eagle edition (marked on gun), 5,000 total mfg. (serial numbered 1-5000).

	$400	$325	$275				

* **Armes De Chasse Import** — previously imported by Armes De Chasse located in Chadds Ford, PA on a limited basis. For G15 variation (9 shot) add $58.

	$475	$425	$330	$300	$260	$240	$220

Last Mfg.'s Sug. Retail was $695.

Add $195 for Limited Series.

* **E.A.A. Import** — imported by European American Armory, distributed by RSR Wholesale.

	$265	$225	$195	$175	$150	$125	$110

* **Current Gamba Mfg.** — .32 ACP or .380 ACP cal., steel construction, double action, double safety, stippled walnut grips, recently imported by Gamba, USA until approx. 1996.

	$395	$330	$300	$260	$240	$220	$200

Last Mfg.'s Sug. Retail was $699.

Mauser Pistols: Luger Mfg.

The original Mauser Luger P.08 is still being currently mfg. at the factory, with very limited domestic importation. Both pre-war and post-war Mauser manufactured Lugers will be found in the Luger section of this book.

PISTOLS: SEMI-AUTO, RECENT IMPORTATION

The pistols listed below were manufactured by FEG located in Hungary.

MODEL 80 SA — .380 ACP or 9mm Para. cal., semi-auto single action patterned after the Browning Hi-power, 4⅔ in. barrel, blue finish with checkered walnut grips, round hammer, steel construction, 10 (C/B 1994) or 13★ shot mag., 1.95 lbs. Imported 1992-96.

	$450	$325	$275	$240	$215	$185	$165

Last Mfg.'s Sug. Retail was $520.

MODEL 90 DA — similar to Model 80 SA, except is double action, spur hammer, and has 10 (C/B 1994) or 14★ shot mag., 2.15 lbs. Imported 1992-96.

	$445	$325	$275	$240	$215	$185	$165

Last Mfg.'s Sug. Retail was $516.

M

* **Model 90 DAC** — similar to Model 90 DA, except is compact model with 4⅛ in. barrel, 2.05 lbs. Imported 1992-96.

	$450	$325	$275	$240	$215	$185	$165

Last Mfg.'s Sug. Retail was $520.

PISTOLS: SEMI-AUTO, MODEL 1896 BROOMHANDLES

Note: Manufactured in Oberndorf, Germany between 1897 & 1938.

While many variations of the famous 1896 Broomhandle exist, most common Broomhandles are pre-war Commercials, Model 1930 Commercials, Red 9s, and Bolos. They can be found in chronological order in this section. Holster stocks are a very popular

Grading	100%	98%	95%	90%	80%	70%	60%

accessory in this model. Commercial stocks may be matching or may not be serial numbered to gun (proper stock). Add $300+ for stock depending on overall original condition and if matching/non-matching.

In 1984, Federal legislation once again allowed importation of non-domestic WWI and WWII military handguns. While many of these newer imports would make workable shooters, they have in no way lowered prices on 90%+ condition specimens due to normal collector activity in top quality only pistols. Recently imported Broomhandles should have the importer's name visibly stamped on an exterior surface.

Mauser Broomhandles: Conehammer Variations

STANDARD CONEHAMMER — 7.63 Mauser cal., distinguishable by circular machined upper hammer with concentric rings. 5.5 in. barrel, 23 groove wooden grips, rear adjustable sight available in 1-10, 50-500, 100-300, 50-300, 50-700 meter configurations, 10 shot mag.

	$3,250	$2,500	$1,850	$1,200	$1,050	$925	$700

Add 40% for matching stock.

FIXED SIGHT CONEHAMMER — 7.63 Mauser cal., similar to Standard Conehammer, except has fixed rear sight.

	$4,200	$3,000	$1,800	$1,300	$1,100	$925	$700

6 SHOT CONEHAMMER - FIXED SIGHT — 7.63 Mauser cal., 4¾ in. barrel, 6 shot mag., rare.

	$7,500	$6,000	$4,500	$3,500	$3,000	$2,500	$2,000

* *6 Shot Conehammer w/adjustable sight* — 7.63 Mauser cal., 5.5 in. barrel, very rare.

	$11,000	$8,500	$6,000	$5,000	$4,000	$3,000	$2,500

Sales of this variation are extremely limited.

TURKISH CONEHAMMER — 7.63 Mauser cal., 5.5 in. barrel, 10 shot mag. Approx. 1,000 mfg. for Turkey in 1898, Farsi serial numbers.

	$6,500	$4,500	$3,000	$2,400	$2,100	$1,800	$1,500

"SYSTEM MAUSER" CONEHAMMER — 7.63 Mauser cal., "SYSTEM MAUSER" marked on top of chamber, improved 5.5 in. tapered barrel, 10 shot mag.

	$15,000	$11,000	$6,000	$5,000	$4,000	$3,500	$3,000

* *Stepped barrel variation* — similar to System Mauser variation, except has older 5.5 in. stepped barrel with no taper.

	$22,500	$16,000	$10,000	$8,000	$7,000	$6,000	$5,000

Add 40% for "SYSTEM MAUSER" stock.

20 SHOT CONEHAMMER — 7.63 Mauser cal., 20 shot non-detachable mag., frame can either be flatside or have milled panels, 5.5 in. tapered barrel, extremely rare.

	$30,000	$25,000	$15,000	$12,000	$9,000	$8,000	$7,000

Add 20% for milled panel variation.
Add 40% for matching stock cut for 20 shot mag.

Several restored guns have recently sold in the $10,000 range.

Many fake 20 shot pistols (especially flat side) have surfaced over the last few years. Use extreme caution when considering purchase.

EARLY TRANSITIONAL LARGE RING HAMMER — 7.63 Mauser cal., distinguishable by large, open centered ring, 10 shot mag., 5.5 in. barrel.

	$3,000	$2,250	$1,550	$1,200	$1,050	$925	$700

This variation is normally found in the 12,000-15,000 serial range only.

Mauser Broomhandles: Flatside Variations

Add approximately $500 for a matching shoulder stock on the following models, $350 for non-matching.

Grading	100%	98%	95%	90%	80%	70%	60%

ITALIAN CONTRACT FLATSIDE — 7.63 Mauser cal., distinguishable by flatside frame and DV/AV proofmarks, 10 shot mag., 5.5 in. barrel.

		$3,500	$2,500	$1,600	$1,300	$1,100	$900	$700

This variation is found in the 1-5,000 serial range only.

FLATSIDE COMMERCIAL — 7.63 Mauser cal., 5.5 in. barrel, 23 groove walnut grips, adj. rear sight typically marked 1-10 or 50-1,000.

		$2,700	$2,000	$1,500	$1,000	$800	$600	$400

Early specimens may have pinned rear sights. Found in serial range 20,000-30,000.

Mauser Broomhandles: Post-1900 Variations

Add approximately $400 for a matching shoulder stock on the following models, $325 for non-matching. This assumes excellent condition - exceptions are noted.

PRE-WAR LARGE RING BOLO — 7.63 Mauser cal., 3.9 in. barrel, floral grips, usually found in 29,000 and 40,000 serial range.

		$4,000	$3,000	$2,000	$1,450	$1,000	$700	$450

Add $850 for short pre-war bolo stock, $1,500 if stock matches pistol.

LARGE RING SHALLOW MILLING — 7.63 Mauser cal., 5.5 in. barrel, 23 groove walnut or hard rubber grips, normally found in the 30,000-33,000 ser. range.

		$2,500	$1,600	$1,000	$750	$625	$500	$400

LARGE RING DEEP MILLING — 7.63 Mauser cal., 5.5 in. barrel, 35 groove walnut or hard rubber grips, normally found in the 34,000 ser. range.

		$2,650	$1,650	$1,000	$750	$625	$500	$400

PRE-WAR SMALL RING BOLO — 7.63 Mauser cal., 3.9 in. barrel, floral/checkered rubber or 31-36 groove walnut grips, usually found in 40,000-44,000 serial range.

		$3,250	$2,300	$1,600	$1,200	$800	$575	$400

Add $850 for short pre-war bolo stock, $1,500 if stock matches pistol.

6-SHOT BOLO — 7.63 Mauser cal., distinctive 6 shot mag., 3.9 in. barrel, either fixed rear sight (more common) or adjustable, could have either large ring or small ring hammer.

		$6,500	$5,000	$3,500	$3,000	$2,600	$2,200	$1,500

Add $850 for short pre-war bolo stock, $1,500 if stock matches pistol.

STANDARD PRE-WAR COMMERCIAL — 7.63 Mauser cal., 5.5 in. barrel, 10 shot mag., 34 groove walnut or checkered black rubber grips, typically 50-1,000 meter adj. rear sight.

		$1,600	$1,200	$850	$725	$600	$500	$400

This variation is the most commonly encountered of all M1896 broomhandles. It can be encountered in the 39,000-274,000 serial range. Early guns below serial no. 100,000 are often Von Lengerke and Detmold marked and can be encountered with hard rubber grips. Rifling changed from 4 groove to 6 groove at approx. serial no. 100,000.

Note: This model is once again being imported by domestic distributors/dealers. Condition is somewhat poor, and prices usually start in the $250 range. These specimens usually have been reblued in addition to other reworking because the original condition has generally been very poor.

MAUSER BANNER CHAMBER MARKED — 7.63 Mauser or 9mm Export/9mm Mauser (rare) cal., 5.5 in. barrel, distinguishable by Mauser banner trademark on top of chamber, 32 groove walnut grips. Approx. 10,000 mfg. in serial range 84,000-94,000.

		$2,700	$1,900	$1,250	$850	$725	$600	$500

This model is very similar in appearance to the Pre-War Commercial.

M

Grading	100%	98%	95%	90%	80%	70%	60%

PERSIAN CONTRACT — 7.63 Mauser cal., 5.5 in. barrel, distinguished by Persian lion crest in left rear frame panel, must be in the 154,000 serial range, 50-1,000 meter adj. rear sight.

	$3,750	$2,800	$2,200	$1,600	$1,100	$850	$700

This variation is frequently faked - pay close attention to serial no. and Persian crest.

STANDARD WARTIME COMMERCIAL — 7.63 Mauser cal., 5.5 in. barrel, 10 shot mag., 30 groove walnut grips, adj. 50-1,000 meter rear sight.

	$1,400	$1,000	$750	$650	$550	$450	$350

This variation is encountered almost as frequently as the Standard Pre-War Commercial. It is usually found in the 290,000-440,000 serial range. It was the first model to utilize the "new safety" design, and can be noticed by the "NS" marking on the back of hammer. Similar features as the Pre-War Commercial, except finish and polishing exhibit more machine and tooling marks.

Note: This model is once again being imported by domestic distributors/dealers. Condition is somewhat poor, and prices usually start in the $250 range. These specimens usually have been reblued in addition to other reworking because the original condition has generally been very poor.

RED-9 ADJ. SIGHT — 9mm Para. cal., 5.5 in. barrel, 10 shot mag., 24 groove walnut grips usually marked with large red no. 9, adj. 50-500 meter rear sight, standard WWI military contract model with separate serial range 1-150,000, generally poorly finished. Mfg. 1916-1918.

	$1,850	$1,400	$1,000	$850	$750	$650	$550

Add $600 for matching stock.
Add $350 for non-matching stock.
Add $200 for original leather.
Add 10% if Prussian Eagle proofed on front of magazine well.

Note: Be cautious for originality since metal refinishing is prevalent in this model. The last 10,000 guns of this German military contract are not military proofed, are better polished, and will command a slight premium.

RED-9 FIXED SIGHT — 9mm Para. cal., 3.9 in. barrel, this is a 1920 commercial rework of the Red-9 military, may be dated 1920 and/or have police markings on front grip strap.

	$925	$750	$650	$550	$475	$400	$350

Because of the Treaty of Versailles following WWI, barrels had to be shortened to less than 4 inches and the adj. rear sight removed.

FRENCH GENDARME — 7.63 Mauser cal., 3.9 in. barrel, distinguished by Bolo barrel length on large frame, hard rubber or walnut (rare) grips, found in the serial range 431,000-434,000, adj. 50-500 meter rear sight.

	$2,850	$2,000	$1,250	$850	$700	$550	$400

EARLY POST-WAR BOLO — 7.63 Mauser cal., 3.9 in. barrel, shot extractor, small ring hammer, usually found in the 440,000-500,000 serial range. Fit with full-size stock.

	$2,350	$1,650	$925	$725	$600	$500	$375

Add 50% for long barrel Bolos in approx. the 475,000 serial range.

M

LATE POST-WAR BOLO — 7.63 Mauser cal., 3.9 in. barrel, similar features of Early Post-War Bolo except has Mauser banner trademark on left rear frame panel, usually encountered in the 500,000-700,000+ serial range. Fit with full-size stock.

	$2,600	$1,750	$1,250	$800	$625	$500	$375

Add 10% for late pistols with high polish salt blue finish.

Mauser Broomhandles: Post-1930 Variations

Add approximately $500 for a matching shoulder stock on the following models, $350 for non-matching.

Grading	100%	98%	95%	90%	80%	70%	60%

EARLY MODEL 1930 COMMERCIAL — 7.63 Mauser cal., 5.2 (common) or 5.5 in. stepped barrel, 12 groove walnut grips, adj. 50-1,000 meter rear sight, usually found in the 800,000-890,000 serial range.

	$2,100	$1,500	$950	$750	$625	$500	$375

This broomhandle variation had a high polish, salt blue finish. Small parts are still fire blued and milling grooves were machined in receiver rails.

LATE MODEL 1930 COMMERCIAL — 7.63 Mauser cal., 5.5 in. stepped barrel, similar appearance to early 1930 Commercial except has solid receiver rails and various small parts are salt blued. Ser. range 890,000-921,000 with production ending in late 1930s.

	$2,000	$1,400	$950	$750	$625	$500	$375

This model is serial numbered on rear top of barrel extension assembly.

MODEL 1930 REMOVABLE MAG. — 7.63 Mauser cal., 5.5 in. stepped barrel, 12 groove walnut grips, adj. 50-1,000 meter rear sight, very rare.

	$15,000	$13,000	$9,000	$5,000	$4,000	$3,200	$2,500

Original specimens of this variation have frames without the extra cuts required for the selector switch. Fakes are usually welded up Schnellfeuers made to look original. Only a very few are known in the 84,000-88,000 serial range. They are not slotted for the shoulder stock. Also known as the Model 711.

SCHNELLFEUER (MODEL 712) — 7.63 Mauser cal., 5.5 in. stepped barrel, 12 groove walnut grips, adj. 50-1,000 meter rear sight, switchable full auto variation generally with selector switch, separate serial range 1-100,000, 10 or 20 shot detachable mag. 712 stock is internally grooved for selector switch.

	$4,000	$3,250	$2,600	$2,200	$1,800	$1,500	$1,200

Add $750 for correct stock.

Deduct 60% if Class III transferable only (dealer sample).

The Model 712 is classified as a machine gun and is subject to registration and payment of a $200 transfer tax.

Broomhandle Carbines

FLUTED BARREL MODEL — marked "July 1897".

	$28,000	$16,000	$12,000	$8,000	$6,000	$5,000	$4,000

FLATSIDE CONE HAMMER — 7.63mm cal., 11¾ in. barrel, experimental variation.

	$20,000	$17,500	$12,250	$7,000	$6,000	$5,000	$4,000

FLATSIDE TRANSITIONAL — 7.63mm cal., 11¾ in. barrel.

	$18,500	$14,000	$9,000	$7,000	$6,000	$5,000	$4,000

LARGE RING HAMMER TRANSITIONAL — 7.63mm cal., 11¾ in. barrel.

	$16,000	$12,500	$9,000	$7,000	$6,000	$5,000	$4,000

LARGE RING HAMMER — 7.63mm cal., 14½ in. barrel.

	$16,000	$12,500	$9,000	$8,000	$7,000	$6,000	$5,000

SMALL RING HAMMER — 7.63mm cal., 14½ in. barrel.

	$15,000	$11,500	$8,500	$8,000	$7,000	$6,000	$5,000

M

Broomhandles: Copies from Other Countries

These pistols are Chinese manufactured copies of the original German design.

HAND-MADE MAUSER CHINESE MARKED AND OTHERS — very poorly made Mauser copies, many thousands made.

	$650	$550	$475	$400	$300	$250	$235

HAND-MADE UNMARKED — poor quality.

	$650	$550	$475	$400	$300	$250	$235

Grading	100%	98%	95%	90%	80%	70%	60%

ASIATIC FLATSIDE UNMARKED — better quality, not exceedingly rare.

	$1,200	$950	$740	$680	$600	$500	$400

TAKU-NAVAL DOCKYARD FLATSIDE — machine-made, better quality, not exceedingly rare, approx. 6,000 mfg.

	$1,500	$1,100	$740	$680	$600	$500	$400

Add 30% with correct stock.
Add 5% if with holster.

SHANSEI ARSENAL .45 CAL. — .45 ACP cal., approx. 8,500 mfg., scarce and desirable in excellent condition.

	$6,500	$5,500	$4,250	$3,000	$1,700	$1,600	$1,475

Recently, a small number of currently manufactured pistols have been marketed as "restorations". Buyer beware! These restorations are priced in the $1,500-$2,000 range. Also, fake stocks have recently surfaced.

Broomhandles: Spanish Copies

VERY EARLY ASTRA-900 — Bolo grips, frame has single-line address, approx. 1,200 mfg.

	$3,000	$2,500	$2,200	$2,000	$1,750	$1,600	$1,475

EARLY ASTRA-900 — single-line address, approx. ser. range 1,200-12,000.

	$2,750	$2,000	$1,350	$850	$700	$525	$425

LATE ASTRA-900 — two and three-line address, two-line address ser. range is approx. 12,000-20,000, three-line address ser. range is approx. 20,000-34,400.

	$2,650	$1,850	$1,350	$850	$700	$525	$425

Add 20% for Japanese character variation in the 27,000 serial range or if in Nazi procurement range.

ROYAL SEMI-AUTO — early Royals are mostly seen in semi-auto with round bolts.

	$3,000	$2,450	$1,900	$1,300	$850	$700	$600

There were many variations of the Royals and above values assume standard variation.

ROYAL SELECTIVE FIRE — 7.63mm cal., most of approx. 25,000 Royals manufactured were selective fire, several variations, Class III transferable only. Add 20% if detachable mag., 100% if equipped with pneumatic rate retarder.

Class III	$2,500	$2,200	$2,000	$1,800	$1,700	$1,600	$1,475

This model had either a fixed mag. or detachable mag. May have been fit with pneumatic rate retarder.

RIFLES: BOLT ACTION, MILITARY PRODUCTION

Subtract 30% if bolt is not matching or contract crests have been removed.

ARGENTINA

Model 1891 Rifle Argentine pattern	$350	$300	$250	$200	$150	$110	$90
Model 1891 Carbine	$400	$320	$250	$210	$145	$115	$90
Model 1909 Rifle	$400	$350	$300	$250	$200	$140	$90
Model 1909 Sniper Rifle w/o scope	$1,500	$1,400	$1,350	$1,200	$1,000	$800	$600
Model 1909 Cavalry Carbine	$350	$300	$250	$195	$140	$100	$80
Model 1909 Mountain Carbine	$400	$350	$280	$210	$150	$100	$80
FN Mle 24 Short Rifle	$350	$280	$210	$180	$140	$100	$80
FN Mle 30 Short Rifle	$350	$280	$210	$180	$140	$100	$80

AUSTRIA

Model 1914 Rifle	N/A	N/A	$1,100	$700	$500	$350	$300

Grading	100%	98%	95%	90%	80%	70%	60%
BELGIUM							
Model 1889 Rifle	$400	$325	$275	$200	$140	$95	$75
Model 1889 Carbine	$375	$300	$225	$150	$125	$90	$75
Model 1889 Carbine with "yataghan"	$400	$325	$250	$220	$180	$135	$100
Model 1889 Carbine Lightened	$400	$325	$250	$220	$180	$135	$100
Model 1916 Carbine	$325	$275	$220	$180	$160	$120	$95
Model 1935 Short Rifle	$425	$375	$300	$280	$230	$175	$125
Model 1889/36 Short Rifle	$350	$290	$225	$190	$175	$125	$100
Model 35/46 & 50 SH. Rifles .30-06 cal.	$375	$325	$275	$190	$140	$110	$90
BOLIVIA							
Model 1895 Rifle, (Argentine M1981 Rifle)	$250	$195	$125	$90	$70	$60	$40
Model 1907 Rifle	$350	$295	$250	$210	$180	$140	$110
Model 1907 Short Rifle	$350	$295	$250	$210	$180	$140	$110
Czech marked Model VZ 24 Short Rifle	$300	$275	$200	$175	$120	$90	$75
Standard Modell Mauser Banner Short Rifle	$350	$290	$250	$195	$155	$120	$95
Model 1950 Rifle Series B-50	$300	$270	$250	$200	$170	$140	$110
BRAZIL							
Model 1894 Rifle	$225	$180	$145	$120	$100	$75	$60
Model 1894 Carbine	$250	$190	$145	$120	$100	$75	$60
Model 1904 Mauser Vergueiro Rifle	$295	$200	$160	$110	$90	$80	$60
Model 1904 Rifle	$325	$260	$230	$195	$160	$125	$100
Model 1907 Carbine	$325	$260	$230	$200	$160	$125	$90
Model 1908 Rifle	$350	$250	$200	$150	$100	$80	$60
Model 1908 Short Rifle	$300	$225	$180	$140	$80	$70	$60
Model 1922 Carbine	$325	$280	$220	$150	$90	$80	$70
Model 1924 VZ 24 Carbine	$245	$200	$170	$130	$90	$80	$70
Model 1924/34 Czech Carbine	$325	$280	$240	$150	$110	$90	$80
Model 1908/34 Rifle .30-06 cal.	$325	$280	$220	$150	$100	$80	$70
Model 1935 Mauser Banner Rifle	$550	$375	$280	$220	$170	$130	$100
Model 1935 Mauser Banner Carbine	$550	$375	$280	$220	$170	$130	$100
Model M954 Rifle .30-06 cal.	$275	$225	$180	$150	$120	$100	$80
CHILE							
Model 1893 Rifle - Bent bolt handle	$350	$300	$240	$200	$140	$115	$90
Model 1895 Rifle - Army	$285	$235	$215	$180	$140	$115	$90
Model 1895 Rifle - Anchor crest	$300	$260	$225	$195	$160	$120	$100
Model 1895 Short Rifle	$300	$250	$210	$180	$150	$120	$95
Model 1895 Carbine	$350	$300	$265	$220	$180	$150	$100
Model 1912 Rifle	$295	$250	$225	$200	$160	$120	$100
Model 1912 Short Rifle	$295	$250	$225	$200	$160	$120	$100
Model 1935 Carbine - Mauser Banner	$500	$450	$400	$325	$275	$225	$150
CHINA							
Gew 1871 Rifle - Chinese marked	$550	$450	$380	$325	$290	$275	$250
Kar 1871 Carbine - Chinese marked	$550	$450	$400	$350	$300	$275	$250
Kar 98a Carbine	$550	$475	$400	$350	$300	$275	$250
Model 1907 Rifle - China contract	$600	$550	$450	$375	$300	$275	$250
Model 98/22 Rifle	$400	$350	$325	$300	$260	$225	$195
Model 24/30 FN Short Rifles	$275	$240	$210	$190	$160	$125	$90
Model 21 Chinese-made VZ 24	$400	$350	$325	$300	$250	$195	$160
Std. Modell 1933 Mauser Banner Rifle	$500	$450	$375	$300	$240	$175	$150
Std. Model 1933 Mauser Banner Carbine	$500	$450	$375	$300	$240	$175	$150
Chiang Kai-Shek Rifle - Chinese copy	$350	$300	$250	$190	$160	$125	$100

M

Grading	100%	98%	95%	90%	80%	70%	60%
Chinese VZ 24 P prefix - "1937" SH. Rifle	$400	$350	$300	$225	$175	$140	$110
Chinese copy VZ 24 w/Jap. folding byt.	$600	$550	$495	$400	$350	$300	$275

COLOMBIA

Model 1891 Rifle - Argentine pattern	$250	$195	$125	$90	$70	$60	$40
Model 1912 Rifle - Steyr	$400	$325	$275	$225	$185	$150	$120
Model 1912 Short Rifle - Steyr	$450	$375	$320	$275	$220	$180	$150
Model 24 FN Short Rifle	$300	$280	$230	$160	$125	$90	$65
Model 30 FN Short Rifle	$300	$280	$230	$160	$125	$90	$865
Model VZ 24 Short Rifle	$325	$300	$240	$200	$160	$110	$90
Model 29 Short Rifle - Steyr	$400	$375	$340	$295	$225	$175	$120
Model 1950 Rifle - FN .30-06 cal.	$325	$275	$225	$200	$160	$120	$100

COSTA RICA

Model 1895 Rifle	$300	$275	$225	$180	$140	$110	$90
Model 1910 Rifle	$450	$400	$325	$280	$225	$180	$150
Model 24 FN Short Rifle	$350	$300	$250	$180	$135	$110	$95

CZECHOSLOVAKIA

Model 1919 Mauser - Jelen Rifle	N/A	N/A	$2,500	$2,300	$2,000	$1,800	$1,600
Model 1921 Mauser - Jelen Rifle	N/A	N/A	$2,400	$2,100	$2,000	$1,800	$1,600
Model 98/22 Rifle	$400	$350	$320	$295	$220	$150	$90
Model VZ 23 Short Rifle	$400	$375	$320	$280	$210	$160	$120
Model VZ 23A Short Rifle	$400	$375	$320	$280	$210	$160	$120
Model VZ 24 Short Rifle	$375	$325	$275	$180	$135	$90	$70
Model 98/29 Rifle	$400	$325	$270	$210	$160	$110	$80
Model VZ 08/33 Carbine	$350	$290	$220	$175	$110	$90	$80
Model VZ 12/33 Carbine - light VZ 24	$350	$290	$220	$175	$125	$110	$90
Model VZ 16/33	$500	$450	$390	$340	$275	$195	$145
Model "JC" Short Rifle	$600	$525	$450	$400	$350	$300	$250
Model "L" SH. Rifle cal., .303, Lithuania	N/A	$1,200	$900	$775	$675	$600	$550

DOMINICAN REPUBLIC

M1953 Rifle - Ex-Brazil M1908	$325	$275	$190	$150	$125	$90	$70
M1953 SH. Rifle - Ex-Brazil M1908 SHR.	$325	$275	$190	$150	$125	$90	$70

ECUADOR

Model 1891 Rifle - Argentine pattern	$350	$310	$270	$220	$180	$130	$80
Model 1907 Rifle	$400	$375	$325	$275	$250	$195	$150
Model VZ 23 Short Rifle	$400	$375	$340	$290	$250	$190	$150
Model VZ 24 Short Rifle	$400	$375	$300	$250	$180	$135	$90
Model VZ 12/33 Carbine	$300	$280	$230	$160	$125	$90	$80
Model 24/30 FN Short Rifle	$300	$280	$230	$160	$125	$90	$65

EL SALVADOR

Model 1895 Rifle - Chilean pattern	$300	$275	$225	$180	$140	$110	$90
Model VZ 12/33 Carbine	$300	$280	$230	$160	$125	$90	$80

ESTONIA

Czech Model "L" Short Rifle - .303 cal.	N/A	$1,200	$900	$775	$675	$600	$550

ETHIOPIA

Model 24 FN Short Rifle	$600	$550	$500	$400	$350	$300	$250
Model 24 FN Carbine	$600	$550	$500	$400	$350	$300	$250
Model 1933 Standard Model Rifle	$700	$650	$600	$500	$450	$400	$350

FRANCE

svw MB	⚜ Modified 98K Carbine - Hex. stacking rod	$350	$300	$275	$225	$170	$140	$100

Grading	100%	98%	95%	90%	80%	70%	60%
GERMANY							
Model 1871 Rifle - Gew 71	$750	$650	$575	$495	$425	$350	$295
Model 1871 Carbine - Kar 71	$750	$650	$575	$495	$425	$350	$295
Model 1871 Short Rifle - Jaeger 71	$700	$650	$575	$495	$425	$350	$295
Model 1871/84 Rifle	$650	$550	$400	$350	$300	$225	$150
Model 1888 Commission Rifle	$300	$250	$200	$150	$125	$90	$70
Model 1888/05 Commission Rifle	$300	$250	$200	$150	$125	$90	$70
Model 1888/14 Commission Rifle	$300	$250	$200	$150	$125	$90	$70
Model 1888 Commission Carbine	$400	$350	$300	$225	$200	$175	$140
Model 1891 Comm. Carbine w/stacking hook	$400	$350	$300	$225	$200	$175	$140
Model 1888/97 Rifle	N/A	N/A	N/A	$4,000	$3,500	$3,200	$2,800
Model 1898 Rifle - Gew 98	$500	$425	$315	$265	$190	$110	$90
Model 1898 Carbine - Kar. 98, 16.9 in. bbl.	N/A	N/A	$4,500	$4,000	$3,500	$3,200	$2,800
Model 1898/17 Rifle	N/A	N/A	N/A	$4,200	$3,600	$3,200	$2,800
Model 1898/18 Rifle	N/A	N/A	N/A	$4,200	$3,600	$3,200	$2,800
Model 1909 Self Loading Carbine	N/A	N/A	$5,000	$4,500	$4,200	$3,800	$3,500
Model 1898A Carbine	$500	$425	$350	$290	$250	$190	$150
Model 1898AZ Carbine (also Model 98a)	$500	$425	$350	$290	$250	$190	$150
Model 1898b Carbine	$750	$700	$600	$450	$350	$290	$250
Model Gew. 98 (Transitional)	$400	$375	$350	$310	$275	$240	$210
Model K98k Carbine (1936-45, coded mfg.)	$650	$550	$495	$395	$350	$290	$175
Model K98k, Para-troop model	$2,200	$1,900	$1,500	$1,300	$1,000	$800	$700
Model K98k "Kriegsmodell"	$400	$375	$300	$250	$195	$140	$110
Model 33/40 Carbine ("945" 1940)	$900	$850	$700	$600	$500	$450	$400
Model 33/40 Carbine ("DOT" 1941-43)	$800	$750	$600	$500	$400	$350	$300
Model 24 (T) Rifle	$450	$400	$350	$300	$250	$200	$175
Model 98/40	$450	$400	$350	$300	$250	$200	$175
Model 29 (O) Rifle L/W issue	$800	$700	$650	$600	$550	$500	$460
Model VG-1	N/A	NA/	N/A	$800	$700	$600	$500
G 43 Semi-Automatic Rifle	$1,100	$1,000	$900	$750	$700	$600	$500
G 41M Semi-Automatic Rifle	$3,500	$3,300	$3,000	$2,800	$2,600	$2,300	$2,000
G 41W Semi-Automatic Rifle	$2,800	$2,500	$2,200	$2,000	$1,800	$1,600	$1,400
GREECE							
Model 1930 FN Short Rifle	$400	$325	$300	$275	$200	$150	$90
GUATEMALA							
Czech VZ 24 Short Rifle	$450	$390	$295	$225	$180	$135	$90
HAITI							
ARMEE D'HAITI Model 1930 FN Short Rifle	N/A	N/A	$275	$225	$175	$125	$90
IRAN (PERSIA)							
Model 1895 Rifle	$250	$225	$190	$150	$110	$90	$70
Model 98/29 Rifle	$500	$390	$325	$295	$210	$165	$125
Model 98/29 Short Rifle	$500	$390	$325	$295	$210	$165	$125
Model 49 Carbine	$500	$390	$325	$295	$245	$195	$145
IRAQ							
Model 1948 98k Carbine	$325	$290	$250	$200	$150	$110	$80

M

Grading	100%	98%	95%	90%	80%	70%	60%
ISRAEL							
German 98k with Israeli marks	$290	$250	$215	$175	$145	$100	$80
Czech 98k w/large triggerguard	$290	$250	$195	$160	$140	$100	$80
Model 1954 Short Rifle	$375	$300	$275	$220	$175	$150	$120
LATVIA							
Czech VZ 24 Short Rifle	N/A	N/A	$395	$325	$275	$225	$160
LIBERIA							
Model 24 FN Short Rifle	N/A	N/A	$395	$325	$275	$225	$160
LITHUANIA							
Czech "L" Model Short Rifle (.303)	N/A	N/A	$775	$675	$600	$550	$500
Model VZ 24 Short Rifle	N/A	N/A	$700	$650	$575	$495	$425
Model 30 FN Short Rifle	N/A	N/A	$700	$650	$575	$495	$425
Model 1900 Rifle	$595	$550	$495	$450	$395	$325	$275
MANCHURIA							
Mukden Arsenal Rifle	$1,000	$900	$850	$775	$700	$600	$500
MEXICO							
Model 1895 Rifle	$250	$225	$190	$145	$110	$85	$65
Model 1895 Carbine	$250	$225	$190	$145	$110	$85	$65
Model 1902 Rifle	$350	$295	$250	$200	$140	$110	$85
Model 1907 Rifle	$395	$320	$250	$210	$145	$115	$90
Model 1910 Rifle	$350	$295	$250	$200	$140	$110	$85
Model 1912 Rifle	$350	$295	$250	$200	$140	$110	$85
Model 1924 FN Short Rifle	$295	$275	$215	$185	$125	$100	$80
Model 1924 Carbine	$250	$225	$190	$145	$110	$85	$65
Model 1936 Short Rifle	$295	$275	$215	$185	$125	$100	$80
Model 1954 Short Rifle	$295	$275	$215	$185	$125	$100	$80
MOROCCO							
Model 1950 FN Carbine (.308 Win. or .30-06)	$400	$350	$325	$275	$175	$150	$120
NETHERLANDS							
Model 1950 Carbine "W"or"J" crest	$500	$470	$420	$375	$325	$290	$250
NICARAGUA							
Model VZ 12/33 Short Rifle	N/A	N/A	$275	$195	$140	$120	$100
Model VZ 24 Short Rifle	$450	$400	$350	$295	$225	$190	$150
ORANGE FREE STATE							
Model 1896 Rifle (OVS marked), DWM	N/A	$450	$375	$290	$250	$175	$125
Model 1896 Rifle (OVS marked), Loewe & Sons	N/A	$450	$375	$290	$250	$175	$125
Model 1896 Rifle, Chile overmark	$350	$300	$270	$240	$210	$175	$125
Model 1895 Short Rifle	$350	$290	$270	$240	$210	$175	$125
Model 1895 Carbine	$350	$300	$270	$240	$200	$175	$125

M

Grading	100%	98%	95%	90%	80%	70%	60%
PARAGUAY							
Model 1895 Rifle	$300	$275	$225	$180	$140	$110	$90
Model 1907 Rifle (DWM)	$400	$350	$290	$250	$190	$125	$90
Model 1907 Carbine (Full-stocked)	$450	$395	$325	$280	$195	$150	$120
Model 1927 Rifle (Oviedo)	$300	$260	$230	$195	$150	$90	$75
Model 1927 Short Rifle	$300	$260	$230	$195	$150	$90	$75
Model 1927 Carbine (Full-stocked)	$350	$300	$260	$220	$185	$140	$100
Model 1933 Standard Model Rifle	$395	$350	$290	$225	$175	$120	$95
M24 "Model 1935" FN Short Rifle	$395	$350	$290	$240	$175	$125	$100
PERU							
Model 1891 Rifle (Lange sight)	$300	$250	$200	$150	$100	$75	$60
Model 1891 Carbine (Lange sight)	$300	$250	$200	$150	$100	$75	$60
Model 1909 Rifle	$495	$460	$395	$350	$290	$195	$120
Model VZ 24 Short Rifle (Model 32)	$375	$325	$280	$240	$195	$150	$125
Model VZ 32 Short Rifle (Model 32)	$375	$325	$280	$240	$195	$150	$125
Model 1935 FN Short Rifle (7.65mm/.30-06)	$400	$350	$295	$250	$190	$150	$120
POLAND							
Model 1898 Rifle	$400	$350	$320	$300	$250	$200	$150
Model 1898 Carbine (Kar 98a)	$350	$325	$290	$225	$190	$120	$80
Model 1929 Short Rifle (Wz 29)	$400	$365	$290	$250	$190	$120	$90
PORTUGAL							
Model 1904 Mauser-Verguiero Rifle	$300	$250	$200	$160	$110	$90	$75
Model 1937 Short Rifle	$450	$390	$350	$295	$220	$160	$110
Model 937a Short Rifle	$450	$390	$350	$295	$220	$160	$110
ROMANIA							
Model VZ 24 Short Rifle, "M" or "C" Crest	$400	$350	$320	$260	$220	$180	$120
SAUDI ARABIA							
Model 1930 FN Short Rifle	N/A	N/A	$230	$160	$125	$90	$65
SERBIA							
Model 1878/80 Rifle	N/A	$500	$460	$425	$375	$295	$250
Model 1885 Cavalry Carbine	N/A	$500	$460	$425	$375	$295	$250
Models 1886/6C and 1880/7C	N/A	$500	$450	$400	$350	$280	$225
Model 1899 Rifle	$350	$300	$250	$225	$175	$125	$90
Model 1889/07 Rifle	$350	$300	$250	$225	$175	$125	$90
Model 1899/08 Rifle	$350	$300	$250	$225	$175	$125	$90
Model 1899C Short Rifle	$350	$300	$240	$190	$150	$100	$80
Model 1899/08 Carbine	$500	$450	$395	$325	$250	$195	$150
Model 1910 Rifle	$350	$300	$250	$225	$195	$160	$125
SIAM (THAILAND)							
Model 1902 Rifle (Type 45)	$350	$290	$250	$190	$150	$100	$80
Model 1923 Short Rifle (Type 66)	$350	$290	$250	$190	$150	$100	$90

M

Grading	100%	98%	95%	90%	80%	70%	60%
SLOVAK REPUBLIC							
Model VZ 24 Short Rifle	N/A	$450	$395	$350	$275	$225	$180
SOUTH AFRICAN REPUBLIC							
Model 1896 Rifle "ZAR" marked	N/A	$375	$325	$295	$250	$195	$150
SPAIN							
Model 1891 Rifle	$400	$350	$300	$250	$190	$140	$100
Model 1892 Rifle	$350	$295	$250	$200	$160	$130	$95
Model 1892 Carbine	$350	$275	$240	$220	$180	$150	$120
Model 1893 Rifle	$250	$220	$195	$150	$110	$70	$50
Model 1895 Carbine (Full-stocked)	$300	$275	$250	$195	$150	$110	$80
Model 1916 Short Rifle	$250	$210	$160	$120	$100	$70	$50
Model 1943 Short Rifle	$295	$250	$190	$150	$120	$80	$60
SWEDEN							
Model 1894 Carbine	$450	$380	$340	$260	$200	$160	$120
Model 1896 Rifle	$295	$220	$190	$150	$120	$90	$70
Model 1938 Short Rifle	$275	$220	$190	$130	$100	$80	$65
Model 1940 Short Rifle (8mm)	$600	$550	$500	$450	$375	$325	$275
SYRIA							
Model 1948 Carbine	$325	$275	$210	$175	$120	$85	$60
TURKEY							
Model 1887 Rifle	$600	$550	$450	$325	$275	$225	$195
Model 1887 Carbine	$600	$550	$450	$375	$325	$260	$200
Model 1890 Rifle	$375	$325	$290	$250	$195	$120	$90
Model 1893 Rifle	$300	$250	$200	$150	$100	$80	$70
Model 1903 Rifle	$250	$220	$195	$150	$90	$60	$40
Model 1905 Carbine	$475	$450	$425	$350	$250	$190	$150
Model VZ 98/22 Rifle	$300	$270	$230	$190	$120	$70	$50
Model 1888 Rifle (Turkish marked)	$200	$175	$140	$100	$85	$70	$50
Model 1888/38 Rifle (improved)	$200	$175	$140	$100	$85	$70	$50
Model 1938 Rifle	$200	$175	$150	$110	$95	$75	$60
Model 1938 Short Rifle	$200	$175	$150	$110	$95	$75	$60
URUGUAY							
Model 1895 Rifle	$495	$460	$425	$375	$295	$125	$95
Model 1904 Rifle	$525	$495	$450	$395	$325	$260	$210
Model 1908 Rifle	$500	$475	$425	$380	$325	$290	$250
Model 1980 Short Rifle	$500	$475	$425	$380	$325	$290	$250
Czech VZ 32 Short Rifle (Model 1934)	$375	$350	$320	$280	$225	$175	$120
Czech VZ 24 Short Rifle (Model 1934)	$500	$475	$450	$400	$350	$300	$260
Mle 24 FN Short Rifle	$375	$350	$320	$280	$225	$175	$120
VENEZUELA							
Model 1910 Rifle	$350	$320	$285	$230	$175	$150	$120
Czech VZ 24/26 Short Rifle	$400	$350	$325	$300	$250	$200	$150
Mle 24/30 FN Short Rifle	$450	$425	$380	$350	$295	$225	$195
Mle 24/30 FN Carbine	$450	$425	$380	$350	$295	$225	$195

M

Grading	100%	98%	95%	90%	80%	70%	60%
YEMEN							
Mle 30 Short Rifle (Markings unknown)	N/A	N/A	$285	$260	$210	$175	$150
YUGOSLAVIA							
M90T Short Rifle (ex-Turkish M1890)	N/A	$300	$280	$250	$190	$125	$90
Model M24B Rifle (ex-Mexican M1912)	N/A	N/A	$275	$240	$190	$140	$110
Mle 22 FN Short Rifle	$375	$350	$295	$250	$190	$150	$120
Mle 24 FN Short Rifle	$375	$350	$295	$250	$190	$150	$120
Czech VZ 24 Short Rifle	$395	$350	$300	$250	$185	$160	$135
Model 1924 Short Rifle (Kragujevac)	$325	$295	$270	$225	$185	$160	$135
Model 30 FN Short Rifle	$375	$350	$295	$250	$190	$150	$120
Model 30 FN Carbine	$375	$350	$295	$250	$190	$150	$120

RILFES: BOLT ACTION, OBERNDORF SPORTERS

Approx. 125,000 commercial sporting Mausers were built between 1898 and 1946. Three action lengths; overall measurements: Short (Kurz) 8¼ in., Standard 8¾ in., and Magnum 9¼ in. Optional squarebridge receiver rings for custom sight mounting. Innumerable variations of triggers, barrels, sights and checkering.

Add $350-$550 for conversion unit.
Add 50% for single squarebridge action.
Add 100% for double squarebridge action.
Add 100% for Short (Kurz) action, except on Type K below.
Add 100% for Magnum action, except on African Type below.

SPECIAL RIFLE, TYPE A — expressly made for English market, superior finish, with round tapered barrel, silver-bead front sight on sleeved-on block with matted surface, hinged floorplate, pear shaped bolt knob, horn forend tip and PG cap, sling eyes.

$3,000	$2,400	$2,000	$1,500	$1,000	$750	$575

NORMAL RIFLE, TYPE B — 24 in. barrel, steel-capped PG, Schnabel forend, sling swivels, pear shaped bolt knob, hinged floorplate.

$2,000	$1,500	$1,250	$1,000	$800	$600	$475

LIGHT SHORT RIFLE, TYPE K — 6.5x54 Mauser, 8x51mm, or .250-300 Savage cal., Kurz action, 22 in. barrel, steel PG cap, sling swivels, pear shaped bolt knob, hinged floorplate, hard rubber buttplate.

$4,000	$3,500	$3,000	$2,500	$1,500	$1,250	$1,250

CARBINE, TYPE S — 20 or 24 in. barrel stocked to muzzle, steel PG cap, horn buttplate, sling swivels, pear shaped bolt knob, hinged floorplate.

$2,500	$2,000	$1,750	$1,400	$1,000	$750	$575

CARBINE, TYPE M — 20 in. barrel stocked to muzzle with steel forend cap, steel PG cap, trapdoor steel buttplate holding sectional cleaning rod, butterknife bolt handle, hinged floorplate.

$2,500	$2,000	$1,750	$1,400	$1,000	$750	$575

MILITARY SPORTING RIFLE, TYPE C — stepped round barrel, round bolt knob, half grip, banner Mauser imprint in side of buttstock.

$750	$600	$500	$450	$400	$350	$295

AFRICAN TYPE — 28 in. round barrel, stocked to 4 in. from muzzle, Magnum action, pear shaped bolt knob.

$5,000	$4,000	$3,000	$2,500	$2,250	$2,000	$2,000

RIFLES: BOLT ACTION, RECENT PRODUCTION

As this edition went to press, SIG Arms had completed the purchase of the Mauser brand name and production rights. Because of this, the future of current production Mauser rifles is unknown. As a result, most of the information regarding recently

Grading	100%	98%	95%	90%	80%	70%	60%

manufactured rifles has stayed the same in this section, until when/if importation is once again resumed.

Add $150 for double set triggers on all current models listed below.

MODEL 66A — similar to Model 66S except has American configured laminate stock (wood grain), cals., action, and features are the same as the Model 66S. Imported 1988-89 only.

* **Standard Calibers**

			$1,900	**$1,425**	**$1,150**	**$925**	**$800**	**$700**	**$650**

Last Mfg.'s Sug. Retail was $2,100.

Add $630 per interchangeable barrel.

The A suffix on this model denotes American.

* **Magnum Calibers** — includes Weatherby Mag. cals. also.

$2,050 $1,500 $1,200 $975 $825 $700 $650

Last Mfg.'s Sug. Retail was $2,270.

Add $670 per interchangeable barrel.

* **Big Game Calibers** — includes most popular Mag. cals. up to .458 Win. Mag.

$2,350 $1,900 $1,425 $1,150 $950 $825 $750

Last Mfg.'s Sug. Retail was $2,700.

MODEL 66S STANDARD — telescoping short action, 5.6x57mm, 6.5x57mm, 7x57mm Mauser (disc. 1992), 7x64mm, 9.3x62mm, .243 Win., .270 Win., .30-06, or .308 Win. cal., 24 in. barrel, standard interchangeable barrels, single or double set triggers, adj. and detachable sights, Monte Carlo walnut stock with checkering, swivels, new safety, rosewood tipped forearm and pistol grip, rubber recoil pad, 7½ lbs. Mfg. 1974-1995.

$2,350 $1,275 $995 $875 $775 $695 $625

Last Mfg.'s Sug. Retail was $2,722.

* **Model 66 Magnum** — 28 in. barrel, 6.5x68mm, 8x68S, 9.3x64mm, 7mm Rem. Mag., .300 Win. Mag., or .300 Wby. Mag. cal., 7.9 lbs. Disc. 1995.

$2,500 $1,325 $1,050 $900 $795 $695 $625

Last Mfg.'s Sug. Retail was $2,925.

* **Model 66 Carbine (Stutzen-Mannlicher)** — .243 Win., .270 Win., .30-06, 7x64mm, or 9.3x62mm cal., 21 in. barrel, full-stock (Mannlicher only) and half-stock (disc. in 1989), double or single triggers, 7.5 lbs. Disc. 1995.

$2,500 $1,325 $1,050 $900 $795 $695 $625

Last Mfg.'s Sug. Retail was $2,925.

This model was available in a half-stock "Ultra" variation until 1989. Values are similar to those listed above.

* **Model 66S Diplomat** — similar cals. as the Model 66S Standard, except not available in 5.6x57mm, similar features, except includes selected walnut and special engraving including deer and wild boar game scenes. Disc. 1995.

$4,650 $3,850 $3,350 $2,750 $2,250 $1,850 $1,400

Last Mfg.'s Sug. Retail was $5,317.

Add $390 for Mag. cals. (similar to Model 66S Magnum).

* **Safari/Big Game Model 66** — .375 H&H or .458 Win. Mag. cal., single trigger, 9.3 lbs. Disc. 1995.

$2,950 $1,850 $1,350 $1,025 $875 $775 $650

Last Mfg.'s Sug. Retail was $3,487.

MODEL 66 SM — telescoping short action, .243 Win. (disc.), .270 Win., 7x57mm Mauser (disc.), 7x64mm, .308 Win., .30-06, or 6.5x57mm cal. (disc.), 24 in. barrel, standard interchangeable barrels, set trigger, adj. and detachable sights, Monte Carlo walnut stock with checkering, swivels, new safety, anatomical gripped select walnut stock with Mauser-nose, cocking lever on tang, rubber recoil pad, 7¼ lbs. Importation 1981-95.

$2,875 $1,800 $1,325 $1,025 $875 $775 $650

Last Mfg.'s Sug. Retail was $3,398.

Grading	100%	98%	95%	90%	80%	70%	60%

* **Model 66 SM Ultra** — all standard cals., 21 in. barrel, 7¼ lbs.

	$1,625	$1,325	$1,140	$920	$760	$650	$550

Last Mfg.'s Sug. Retail was $1,903.

* **Model 66SM Magnum** — cals. similar to Model 66 S Magnum, except not available in 9.3x64mm cal., 26 in. barrel, 8.4 lbs. Disc. 1995.

	$3,025	$1,925	$1,375	$1,025	$875	$775	$650

Last Mfg.'s Sug. Retail was $3,578.

* **Model 66SM Diplomat** — similar cals. as the Model 66SM Standard, similar features, except includes selected walnut and special engraving including deer and wild boar game scenes. Disc. 1995.

	$5,075	$3,975	$3,450	$2,775	$2,250	$1,850	$1,400

Last Mfg.'s Sug. Retail was $5,943.

Add $382 for Mag. cals. (similar to Model 66SM Magnum).

* **Model 66SM Carbine (Mannlicher type full stock)** — .30-06 cal. only currently, 21 in. barrel, 7 lbs. Disc. 1995.

	$3,025	$1,925	$1,375	$1,025	$875	$775	$650

Last Mfg.'s Sug. Retail was $3,578.

These models were previously available on a custom order only basis through KDF, Inc. located in Seguin, TX.

MODEL 66 SL — similar to Model 66 SM, except features extra select walnut with special graining, 7¼ lbs. Disc. 1985.

	$1,370	$1,275	$890	$720	$580	$475	$420

Last Mfg.'s Sug. Retail was $1,470.

* **Model 66 SL Ultra** — 7x64mm or .30-06 cal., 21 in. barrel, 7¼ lbs. Disc. 1985.

	$1,475	$1,325	$940	$750	$600	$450	$400

Last Mfg.'s Sug. Retail was $1,520.

* **Magnum Calibers** — similar to Model 66 S, 8.4 lbs. Disc. 1985.

	$1,475	$1,325	$940	$750	$600	$450	$400

Last Mfg.'s Sug. Retail was $1,520.

* **Mannlicher Type Full Stock** — 21 in. barrel, 7 lbs. Disc. 1985.

	$1,475	$1,325	$940	$750	$600	$450	$400

Last Mfg.'s Sug. Retail was $1,520.

MODEL 66SL DIPLOMAT — same specifications as Model 66 SM, except includes selected walnut and special engraving including deer and wild boar game scenes.

Add $93 for Mannlicher full-stock (21 in. barrel).
Add $387 for Mag. cals.

This model was available on an individual custom order basis only. The last published retail price (1988) for a standard model without options was $3,167.

MODEL 660 — U.S. designation of 66S. Imported 1971-1973.

	$925	$820	$720	$600	$500	$450	$400

MODEL 66S DELUXE — special order engraved and inlaid, select wood. Priced per individual customer order. All guns are custom made only.

MODEL 66P — imported 1995 only.

	$4,250	$3,575	$3,075	$2,600	$2,075	$1,700	$1,375

Last Mfg.'s Sug. Retail was $4,888.

MODEL 66SP SUPER MATCH — .300 Win. Mag. or .308 Win. cal., telescoping short action, 27½ in. heavy barrel with muzzle brake, no sights, match trigger, 3 shot mag., select European walnut stock with stippling and thumbhole, adj. cheekpiece and butt plate, includes premium scope, 12 lbs. Never imported domestically.

	$4,150	$3,500	$3,050	$2,600	$2,075	$1,700	$1,375

Last Mfg.'s Sug. Retail was $4,737.

M

Grading	100%	98%	95%	90%	80%	70%	60%

MODEL 77 — .243 Win., .270 Win., 6.5x57mm, 7x64mm, .308 Win., or .30-06 cal., 24 in. barrel, set trigger on tang, adj. and detachable sights, walnut stock with European cheekpiece and hand checkering, swivels, new safety, steel detachable box mag., rubber recoil pad, 7¼ lbs. Disc.

	$1,130	$950	$875	$810	$750	$675	$595

Last Mfg.'s Sug. Retail was $1,331.

* *Model 77 Ultra* — 6.5x57mm, 7x64mm or .30-06 cal., 20 in. barrel, 7.7 lbs. Disc.

	$1,175	$975	$895	$835	$760	$675	$595

Last Mfg.'s Sug. Retail was $1,394.

* *Magnum Calibers* — similar to Model 66S, 8⅛ lbs. Disc.

	$1,175	$975	$895	$835	$760	$675	$595

Last Mfg.'s Sug. Retail was $1,394.

* *Mannlicher type full stock* — 20 in. barrel, Mauser-set trigger, 7.7 lbs. Disc.

	$1,175	$975	$895	$835	$760	$675	$595

Last Mfg.'s Sug. Retail was $1,394.

* *Big Game Model* — .375 H&H cal., 26 in. barrel, 8⅛ lbs. Disc.

	$1,075	$1,000	$900	$795	$675	$575	$475

Last Mfg.'s Sug. Retail was $1,150.

MODEL 77 SPORTSMAN — .243 Win. or .308 Win. cal., sports version of the Model 77, set trigger on tang, no sights, 24 in. barrel, 9 lbs. Disc.

	$1,495	$1,230	$1,075	$985	$895	$820	$740

Last Mfg.'s Sug. Retail was $1,754.

Add $430 for Zeiss 2½-10X scope and mounts.

MODEL 83 MATCH SINGLE SHOT — .308 Win. cal. only, cylinder locking action with 3 locking lugs in rear, match trigger, anatomical match stock with select walnut, adj. comb and butt plate. Disc.

	$2,170	$1,815	$1,660	$1,545	$1,400	$1,195	$925

Last Mfg.'s Sug. Retail was $2,594.

This model is a UIT standard rifle for 300-meter competition.

MODEL 83 MATCH UIT FREE RIFLE — .308 Win. cal. only, cylinder locking action with 3 locking lugs in rear, match trigger, anatomical match stock with select walnut, adj. comb and butt plate. Disc.

	$2,320	$1,940	$1,760	$1,600	$1,430	$1,195	$925

Last Mfg.'s Sug. Retail was $2,771.

MODEL 83 STANDARD RIFLE — similar to Model 83 Match, except has removable 10 shot steel mag., 26 in. barrel. Disc.

	$2,320	$1,950	$1,800	$1,625	$1,460	$1,250	$1,000

Last Mfg.'s Sug. Retail was $2,766.

MODEL 86 LAMINATED/FIBERGLASS (SR) — .308 Win. cal., updated version of the Model 83 action, 25.6 (disc.) or 28¾ (new 1997) in. fluted barrel with muzzle brake, black laminate wood (with thumbhole) or fiberglass (disc.) stock with rail in forearm, adj. trigger, 9 shot detachable mag., cased, 10.8 lbs. Imported 1989-1996, recent mfg. included a 2½x10 power Zeiss tactical scope with detachable mount.

	$10,750	$8,900	$7,700	$6,500	$5,500	$4,500	$3,500

Last Mfg.'s Sug. Retail was $11,795.

MODEL SR 93 — .300 Win. Mag. cal., precision rifle employing skeletonized cast magnesium/aluminum stock, combination right-hand/left-hand bolt, adj. ergonomics, 27 in. fluted barrel with muzzle brake, integrated bi-pod, 4 or 5 shot mag., approx. 13 lbs. without accessories. Disc. 1996.

	$20,000	$17,250	$14,750	$11,950	$8,700	$6,500	$5,000

Last Mfg.'s Sug. Retail was $21,995.

M

Grading	100%	98%	95%	90%	80%	70%	60%

MODEL 94 — .243 Win., .270 Win., .30-06, .308 Win., .300 Win. Mag., 7x64mm, 7mm Rem. Mag., 8x68S (disc. 1996), 9.3x62 Mag. cal., 22 or 24 in. interchangeable barrel, aluminum block in stock bedding system, 60 degree bolt, 6 lug locking system, checkered walnut stock and forearm, 3 or 4 shot mag., lateral slide safety, approx. 7¼ lbs. Mfg. began 1994, U.S. importation was disc. 1995, resumed 1997 only.

| | $1,925 | $1,550 | $1,325 | $1,100 | $925 | $850 | $775 |

Last Mfg.'s Sug. Retail was $2,295.

Add $799 per interchangeable barrel assembly.

MODEL 96 — .25-06 Rem. (new 1997), .270 Win., .30-06, .308 Win. (new 1997), 7x64mm (new 1997), .300 Win. Mag. (new 1997), or 7mm Rem. Mag. (new 1997) cal., 16 lug bolt slides straight back allowing for low scope mounts, 22 or 24 (Mag. cals., new 1997) in. barrel, safety mechanism in bolt in addition to rear 3-position tang safety, checkered walnut stock, 4 (Mag. cals., new 1997) or 5 shot top loading mag., w/o sights, 6¼ lbs. Imported 1996-97.

| | $625 | $550 | $500 | $450 | $400 | $360 | $330 |

Last Mfg.'s Sug. Retail was $699.

MODEL 98 COMMERCIAL — various cals., features original breech mechanisms refurbished to new condition, barrel, trigger system, and stock are new from factory.

This model was mostly distributed in Europe with no domestic MSR.

MODEL 1898 COMMEMORATIVE — 8x57mm Mauser cal., special limited edition model mfg. to commemorate the 100th anniversary of the original M-98, bright royal blue on most major metal parts, bolt and receiver have silver satin finish, checkered select European walnut. 1,998 mfg. 1998 only.

| | $2,175 | $1,775 | $1,500 |

Last Mfg.'s Sug. Retail was $2,300.

MODEL 98 MAGNUM SAFARI — .375 H&H or .416 Rigby cal., original M-98 Magnum action, features custom workmanship, extra select checkered walnut stock, limited mfg. 1998 only.

| | $9,000 | $7,750 | $6,500 | $5,250 | $4,500 | $3,500 | $2,750 |

Last Mfg.'s Sug. Retail was $10,000.

MODEL 99 — 5.6x57mm, 6.5x57mm, 7x57mm, 7x64mm, .243 Win., .25-06 Rem., .270 Win., .30-06 or .308 Win. cal., bolt action with 60 degree throw, 24 in. free-floating barrel, jeweled bolt, available in either hand-rubbed oil or high-luster lacquer finish for stock, mini-claw extractor, adj. single stage trigger, 4 shot detachable mag., no sights, 8 lbs. Imported 1989-disc.

* ***Classic Lacquer Finish*** — high-luster lacquer finish for stock.

| | $1,110 | $925 | $850 | $775 | $700 | $625 | $550 |

Last Mfg.'s Sug. Retail was $1,272.

This model is available with either a Schnabel forearm with regular stock or rosewood capped forearm with American Monte Carlo stock.

* ***Classic Oil Finish*** — hand-rubbed oil finish for stock. Disc.

| | $1,130 | $995 | $875 | $775 | $700 | $625 | $550 |

Last Mfg.'s Sug. Retail was $1,130.

This model is available with either a Schnabel forearm with regular stock or rosewood capped forearm with American Monte Carlo stock.

M

MODEL 99 MAGNUM — 8x68S, 9.3x64mm, 7mm Rem. Mag., .257 Wby. Mag., .270 Wby. Mag., .300 Wby. Mag., .300 Win. Mag., .338 Win. Mag., or .375 H&H cal., similar specifications as Model 99, except has 26 in. barrel and 3 shot mag. Imported 1989-disc.

* ***Classic Lacquer Finish*** — high-luster lacquer finish for stock.

| | $1,135 | $950 | $875 | $775 | $700 | $625 | $550 |

Last Mfg.'s Sug. Retail was $1,322.

This model is available with either a Schnabel forearm with regular stock or rosewood capped forearm with American Monte Carlo stock.

Grading	100%	98%	95%	90%	80%	70%	60%

* **Classic Oil Finish** — hand-rubbed oil finish for stock.

	$1,025	$895	$795	$725	$625	$550	$495

Last Mfg.'s Sug. Retail was $1,180.

This model is available with either a Schnabel forearm with regular stock or rosewood capped forearm with American Monte Carlo stock.

MODEL 225 — available in 13 cals. between .243 Win. and .300 Wby. Mag., bolt action, 60 degree bolt lift with 3 locking lugs, ultra fast lock time, adj. trigger, 24 or 26 (Mag. only) in. barrel, 3 or 5 shot mag., no sights, guaranteed 1/2 in. accuracy at 100 yards, many stock options available at extra cost.

* **Deluxe Standard Sporter** — standard model available in 6 regular cals. and 9 Mag. cals. Importation disc. 1989.

	$1,275	$1,000	$875	$750	$625	$550	$495

Last Mfg.'s Sug. Retail was $1,400.

Add $90 for Mag. cals.

This model was formerly the KDF Model K-15.

MODEL 226 — left-handed variation of the Model 225 with slight changes. Disc. 1989.

	$1,275	$1,000	$875	$750	$625	$550	$495

Last Mfg.'s Sug. Retail was $1,400.

MODEL 2000 (DISC.) — .270 Win., .308 Win., or .30-06 cal., 5 shot mag., 24 in. barrel, leaf rear sight, checkered walnut stock. Mfg. by F.W. Heym for Mauser, 1969-1971.

	$495	$475	$450	$400	$375	$350	$325

MODEL 2000 CLASSIC — .270 Win., .30-06, .308 Win., .300 Win. Mag., or 7mm Rem. Mag. cal., features new design allowing interchangeable calibers from standard to standard and Magnum to Magnum models, bolt locks directly into barrel, detachable mag., deluxe walnut stock with checkering and rosewood forend, double function set trigger, high polish blue, includes studs. New 1998.

Mfg.'s Sug. Retail	$1,800	$1,595	$1,375	$1,125	$950	$825	$700	$575

* **Model 2000 Varmint** — .22-250 Rem. or .243 Win. cal., choice of black synthetic or special varmint wood stock with accessory rail, heavy fluted barrel. New 1998.

Mfg.'s Sug. Retail	$2,200	$1,900	$1,550	$1,350	$1,100	$900	$775	$650

* **Model 2000 Sniper** — .300 Win. Mag. or .308 Win. cal., features heavy fluted barrel, special set trigger system, bi-pod rail, and other special shooting performance features, satin blue metal finish, custom built with individual certificate. New 1998.

Mfg.'s Sug. Retail	$2,200	$1,900	$1,550	$1,350	$1,100	$900	$775	$650

* **Model 2000 Professional** — .300 Win. Mag. or .308 Win. cal., features recoil reduction compensator, camo all-weather special pistol grip stock, satin blue metal finish, custom built with individual certificate. New 1998.

Mfg.'s Sug. Retail	$3,500	$3,175	$2,725	$2,400	$2,100	$1,800	$1,500	$1,250

M

MODEL 3000 — .243 Win., .270 Win., .308 Win., or .30-06 cal., 5 shot mag., 22 in. barrel, no sights, walnut Monte Carlo style stock, rosewood forearm and pistol grip, skipline checkering, recoil pad and swivels. Mfg. 1971-1974.

	$525	$475	$450	$425	$395	$335	$285

MODEL 3000 MAGNUM — similar to 3000, except 7mm Rem. Mag., .300 Win. Mag., or .375 H&H cal., 3 shot mag., 26 in. barrel.

	$575	$525	$475	$450	$415	$350	$295

This model was mfg. by Heym for Mauser.

MODEL 4000 VARMINT RIFLE — similar to 3000, except smaller action, .222 Rem. or .223 Rem. cal., folding leaf rear sight, rubber butt plate.

	$425	$400	$375	$350	$300	$260	$225

This model was mfg. by Heym for Mauser.

Grading	100%	98%	95%	90%	80%	70%	60%

LIGHTNING MODEL — .308 Win. or 7.62x39mm cal., slide-bolt action, locking bolt similar to M-16 enabling locking directly onto free floating short barrel, fixed internal mag., specially bedded receiver, satin blue finish or stainless steel, open sights, synthetic stock available in black, light grey, blue, or NATO green. New 1998.

Mfg.'s Sug. Retail	$550	$495	$425	$375	$325	$295	$275	$250

LIGHTNING HUNTER MODEL — .243 Win., .270 Win., .30-06, .308 Win., .300 Win. Mag., or 7mm Rem. Mag. cal., slide-bolt mechanism, detachable mag., choice of satin blue or bright blue metal finish, checkered satin or high gloss walnut stock, with or w/o sights, free floating barrel, bedded receiver. New 1998.

Mfg.'s Sug. Retail	$730	$650	$575	$500	$450	$400	$360	$330

Add $50 for open sights.
Add $20 for bright blue metal finish with high gloss stock.

* *Lightning Hunter Stainless Steel Model* — similar to Lightning Hunter Model, except has satin finish stainless steel receiver and barrel, checkered satin finished walnut stock. New 1998.

Mfg.'s Sug. Retail	$750	$665	$585	$500

Add $50 for open sights.

LIGHTNING HUNTER ALL-WEATHER MODEL — similar to Lightning Hunter, except has black synthetic stock, satin blue metal finish, scope mounts included, with or w/o sights. New 1998.

Mfg.'s Sug. Retail	$700	$625	$550	$475	$400	$350	$325	$295

Add $50 for open sights.

* *Lightning All-Weather Stainless Steel* — similar to Lightning Hunter All-Weather Model, except is satin stainless steel. New 1998.

Mfg.'s Sug. Retail	$730	$650	$575	$500

Add $50 for open sights.

LIGHTNING VARMINT MODEL — .22-250 Rem., .243 Win., features slide-bolt action, free floating heavy fluted barrel, satin blue metal finish, choice of special varmint wood or synthetic stock. New 1998.

Mfg.'s Sug. Retail	$1,000	$895	$775	$675	$600	$525	$475	$425

* *Lightning Varmint Model Stainless* — similar to Lightning Varmint Model, except is satin stainless steel. New 1998.

Mfg.'s Sug. Retail	$1,000	$895	$775	$675

LIGHTNING SNIPER MODEL — .300 Win. Mag. or .308 Win. cal., slide-bolt action, features free floating heavy fluted barrel w/o sights, special wood or synthetic stock with built in bi-pod rail, detachable mag., satin blue metal finish. New 1998.

Mfg.'s Sug. Retail	$1,000	$895	$775	$675	$600	$525	$475	$425

* *Lightning Sniper Model Stainless* — similar to Lightning Sniper Model, except is satin stainless steel. New 1998.

Mfg.'s Sug. Retail	$1,000	$895	$775	$675

LIGHTNING PROFESSIONAL MODEL — .300 Win. Mag. or .308 Win. cal., slide-bolt action, features special black or camo synthetic adj. stock with pistol grip, special tuned trigger system, free floating heavy fluted barrel, recoil reduction compensator. New 1998.

Mfg.'s Sug. Retail	$1,800	$1,595	$1,375	$1,125	$950	$825	$700	$575

M

RIFLES: BOLT ACTION, .22 CAL.

MODEL 20/22 — .22 LR or .22 Mag. cal., bolt action, features free floating barrel, precision trigger, standard or deluxe checkered walnut stock with stock. New 1998.

Mfg.'s Sug. Retail	$700	$625	$550	$475	$400	$350	$325	$295

Add $100 for Deluxe Model.

Grading	100%	98%	95%	90%	80%	70%	60%

MODEL 107 STANDARD — .22 LR cal. only, bolt action, 19½ in. barrel, 5 shot clip mag., adj. iron sights, 6 lbs. Imported 1988-89, reintroduced 1993 only.

		$300	$260	$215	$185	$170	$155	$140

Last Mfg.'s Sug. Retail was $356.

This model is the same as KDF's previous Model 2107 mfg. by Voere.

* *Model 107 Deluxe* — .22 LR or .22 Mag. cal., similar to Model 107, except has deluxe checkered walnut. Imported 1988-89 only.

		$290	$240	$210	$175	$150	$135	$120

Last Mfg.'s Sug. Retail was $320.

Add $90 for .22 Mag. cal.

This model is the same as KDF's previous Model 2107 Deluxe mfg. by Voere.

MODEL 201 — .22 LR or .22 Mag. cal., bolt action, free-floating 21 in. barrel, clip 5 shot mag., adj. trigger, scaled-down version of the K-15, unusual action incorporates two front-located locking lugs on bolt face that engage Stellite inserts on the front receiver portion, blue only, no sights, beechwood stock with cheekpiece, 6½ lbs. Disc. 1997.

	$635	$515	$465	$415	$365	$315	$260

Last Mfg.'s Sug. Retail was $716.

Add $19 for sights (disc.).
Add $77 for .22 Mag. cal. (Model 201-SM).

This model is the same as KDF's disc. Model K-22 mfg. by Voere. Before 1989, this model came standard with a walnut stock.

* *Model 201 Luxus* — similar to the Model 201 except has walnut stock with rosewood forend. Disc. 1997.

	$710	$650	$550	$475	$425	$375	$295

Last Mfg.'s Sug. Retail was $809.

Add $27 for sights (disc.).
Add $67 for .22 Mag. cal.

This model is the same as KDF's previous Model K-22 Deluxe mfg. by Voere.

MODEL DSM34 — .22 LR cal., bolt action, 25.98 in. barrel. "Deutsches Sportmodell" lightweight trainer, side sling, no bayonet lug.

	$625	$375	$325	$300	$260	$225	$200

MODEL MS 420B — .22 LR Sporter cal., bolt action, pre-war, 5 shot clip mag.

	$1,425	$875	$725	$625	$525	$450	$395

Add 15%-25% for double set triggers (rare).

MODEL ES340 — .22 LR cal., single shot, bolt action, 25½ in. barrel, adj. sights, checkered pistol grip, grooved forearm, pre-1935.

	$725	$425	$350	$325	$295	$260	$230

MODEL ES350 — .22 LR cal., single shot, bolt action, 27½ in. barrel, championship rifle, micrometer rear sight, ramp front sight, checkered full target stock, swivels, pre-1935.

	$925	$550	$500	$460	$430	$400	$375

Add 15%-25% for double set triggers (rare).

MODEL M410 — .22 LR cal., bolt action, repeating, 5 shot detachable mag., 23½ in. barrel, adj. sights, sporter stock, checkered pistol grip, swivels, pre-1935.

		$1,425	$875	$725	$625	$525	$450	$395

Add 15%-25% for double set triggers (rare).

MODEL M420 — .22 LR cal., bolt action, repeating, 5 shot detachable mag., 25½ in. barrel, adj. sights, sporter stock, checkered pistol grip, swivels, pre-1935.

		$1,425	$875	$725	$625	$525	$450	$395

Add 15%-25% for double set triggers (rare).

Grading	100%	98%	95%	90%	80%	70%	60%

MODEL EN310 — .22 LR cal., single shot, bolt action, 19¾ in. barrel, fixed sights, plain pistol grip stock, pre-1935.

	$625	$365	$315	$280	$260	$225	$200

MODEL EL320 — .22 LR cal., single shot, bolt action, 23½ in. barrel, fixed sights, checkered pistol grip stock.

	$695	$395	$330	$295	$275	$250	$225

MODEL KKW — .22 LR cal., single shot, bolt action, target, 26 in. barrel, tangent rear sight, military style stock with bayonet lug. This weapon was also produced by Walther, Gustloff, and Anschütz. It was used as a training rifle in addition to commercial sales. Deduct 15% for 4mm KKW Models.

	$625	$375	$325	$300	$260	$225	$200

MODEL MS350B — .22 LR cal., bolt action, repeating, 5 shot mag., 26¾ in. barrel, grooved receiver for scope or sight, micrometer rear sight, ramp front sight, target stock, checkered pistol grip and forearm, swivels.

	$1,200	$725	$650	$550	$495	$450	$395

MODEL ES350B — .22 LR cal., bolt action, single shot, 5 shot mag., 26¾ in. barrel, grooved receiver for scope or sight, micrometer rear sight, ramp front sight, target stock, checkered pistol grip and forearm, swivels.

	$750	$425	$350	$325	$295	$260	$230

MODEL ES340B — .22 LR cal., bolt action, single shot, 26¾ in. barrel, adj. sight, plain pistol grip stock.

	$650	$375	$325	$300	$260	$225	$200

MODEL MM410BN — .22 LR cal., bolt action sporter, 5 shot mag., 23½ in. barrel, adj. sights, lightweight stock, checkered pistol grip, swivels.

	$1,295	$775	$675	$575	$475	$400	$375

MODEL MS420B — .22 LR cal., bolt action target, 5 shot mag., 26¾ in. barrel, adj. sights, target style stock, checkered pistol grip, swivels.

	$1,100	$650	$575	$500	$450	$400	$365

RIFLES: SEMI-AUTO, .22 LR

MODEL 105 STANDARD — .22 LR cal. only, 10 shot mag., approx. 5 lbs. Imported 1995-97.

	$285	$250	$205	$180	$170	$155	$140

Last Mfg.'s Sug. Retail was $330.

SHOTGUNS

Mauser shotguns were sub-contracted to various European firms and were made in various O/U (including field and target), SxS (both boxlock and sidelock), and single shot configurations. While they are relatively rare (these shotguns had limited importation into the U.S. by Bauer located in Michigan - models included the 496 single shot, 496 SxS, 580 SxS, 610 O/U, 620 O/U, 71E O/U, and others), collectability to date has been minimal. Values will depend on the grade, configuration, features, engraving, and overall desirability. Most of these shotguns have been priced in the $395-$1,350 range, depending on the configuration's desirability.

M

MAVERICK ARMS, INC.

Currently manufactured by Maverick Arms, Inc. located in Eagle Pass, TX. Administrative offices are at O.F. Mossberg & Sons, located in North Haven, CT. Distributor sales only.

SHOTGUNS

Beginning 1992, all Maverick slide action shotguns incorporate twin slide rails in the operating mechanism.

Grading	100%	98%	95%	90%	80%	70%	60%

MODEL 60 SEMI-AUTO — while advertised, this model was never manufactured.

MODEL 88 FIELD MODEL SLIDE ACTION — 12 ga. only, 3 in. chamber, slide-action, 24 (Deer Model with iron sights), 28, or 30 in. plain or VR barrel, wood (disc.) or black synthetic stock and forearm with recoil pad, fixed or Accu-chokes (disc. 1997), aluminum alloy receiver, crossbolt safety, approx. 7¼ lbs. New 1989.

Mfg.'s Sug. Retail	$221	$185	$145	$125	$115	$110	$105	$100

    Add $14 for VR (disc. 1996).
    Add $14 for Deer Model (24 in. cyl. bore barrel).
    Add $18 for choke tube barrel (one choke supplied).

✳ ***Model 88 Deer Combos*** — includes various combinations of extra Deer barrels with rifle sights, 28 in. plain or VR barrel, or extra 18½ in. cyl. bore barrel. Mfg. 1990-95.

		$245	$190	$160	$130	$120	$110	$105

        Last Mfg.'s Sug. Retail was $294.

    Add $10 for VR barrel.
    Add $17 for Accu-choke barrel.
    Add $29 for wood stock and forearm (mfg. 1992 only).

✳ ***Model 88 Security*** — 12 ga., 18½ in. barrel with cyl. bore choke, regular or pistol grip (disc. 1997) synthetic stock, 6 or 8 shot, plain synthetic forearm. New 1993.

Mfg.'s Sug. Retail	$213	$180	$145	$125	$115	$110	$105	$100

    Add $18 for 8 shot model.
    Add $98 for Bullpup configuration (6 or 9 shot) (disc. 1994).
    Add $47-$65 for combo package.

✳ ***Model 88 Combat*** — 12 ga. only, combat design featuring pistol grip stock and forearm, black synthetic stock is extension of receiver, 18½ in. cyl. bore barrel with vented shroud with built-in carrying handle, open sights. Mfg. 1990-92.

		$240	$215	$190	$175	$160	$150	$140

        Last Mfg.'s Sug. Retail was $282.

MODEL 91 SLIDE ACTION — 12 ga. only, 3½ in. chamber, 18½ cyl. bore or 28 in. VR barrel with 1 choke tube, otherwise similar to Model 88. Mfg. 1991-95.

		$230	$190	$170	$160	$150	$140	$130

        Last Mfg.'s Sug. Retail was $269.

    Add $2 for VR barrel.

MODEL 95 BOLT ACTION — 12 ga. only, 3 in. chamber, synthetic stock with recoil pad, 25 in. barrel bored mod., cross-bolt triggerguard safety. New mid-1995.

Mfg.'s Sug. Retail	$184	$155	$135	$115	$100	$90	$80	$70

McMILLAN BROS. RIFLE CO.

Current manufacturer located in Phoenix, AZ since 1993. Dealer and consumer direct sales. During 1998, the company name changed from McBros Rifles to McMillan Bros. Rifle Co.

RIFLES: BOLT ACTION

AMERICAN HUNTER — available in 16 cals. between .22-250 Rem. and .416 Rem. Mag. (disc. 1997), camouflaged fiberglass stock, match grade stainless steel barrel, choice of MCRT (Rem. Model 700 custom type action mfg. to aerospace standards) or MCR (Rem. Model 700 BDL action that has been trued). New 1993.

Mfg.'s Sug. Retail	$2,100	$1,900	$1,650	$1,375	$1,175	$1,000	$850	$750

    Add $500 for MCRT action.

Grading	100%	98%	95%	90%	80%	70%	60%

* ***Yukon Hunter*** — available in 6 Mag. cals. between .300 Wby. Mag. and .416 Rem. Mag., built to aerospace tolerances for any hunting situation, barrel band sling swivel, folding leaf sight, black synthetic stock. New 1993.

Mfg.'s Sug. Retail	$2,400		$2,195	$1,750	$1,475	$1,225	$1,025	$900	$775

   Add $500 for MCRT action.

* ***Outdoorsman*** — .30-378 Wby. Mag. or .338-378 Wby. Mag. (disc. 1997) cal., RT action only. New 1996.

Mfg.'s Sug. Retail	$2,800		$2,325	$1,850	$1,525	$1,250	$1,050	$900	$775

MCR TACTICAL — .308 Win. or .300 Win. Mag. cal. New 1993.

Mfg.'s Sug. Retail	$2,200		$1,975	$1,700	$1,400	$1,200	$1,000	$850	$750

   This model was formerly designated the MCR Sniper Model.

* ***MCRT Tactical*** — similar to MCR Tactical, except is also available in .338 Lapua (new 1998). New 1993.

Mfg.'s Sug. Retail	$2,700		$2,325	$1,850	$1,525	$1,250	$1,050	$900	$775

   This model was formerly designated the MCRT Sniper Model.

BENCHREST COMPETITOR — .222 Rem., 6mm PPC, 6mm BR, 7mm BR, or .308 Win. cal., benchrest configuration. New 1993.

Mfg.'s Sug. Retail	$2,800		$2,400	$1,925	$1,575	$1,275	$1,050	$900	$775

1000 YARD BENCHREST (NATIONAL MATCH COMPETITOR) — .300 Win. Mag. (new 1996), .30-378 Wby. Mag. (new 1996), 7.82 Warbird (new 1996), .308 Win. (disc. 1995) or .338-378 Wby. Mag. (mfg. 1996-97) cal. New 1993.

Mfg.'s Sug. Retail	$2,875		$2,450	$1,950	$1,575	$1,275	$1,050	$900	$775

BOOMER — .50 BMG cal., available as either single shot sporter, repeater sporter, light benchrest, or heavy benchrest variation. New 1993.

Mfg.'s Sug. Retail	$3,700		$3,325	$2,725	$2,275	$1,925	$1,675	$1,375	$1,100

   Add $300 for repeating action.
   Add $400 for Tactical 50 variation.
   Add $50 for light benchrest variation.
   Add $250 for heavy benchrest variation.

McMILLAN, G. & CO. INC.
Previous trademark established circa 1988, located in Phoenix, AZ.

   G. McMillan & Co. Inc. had various barrel markings from 1988-1995 including G. McMillan, Harris - McMillan, and Harris Gunworks (currently manufactured) - please refer to the Harris Gunworks section in this text for current information.

HANDGUNS

WOLVERINE — available in 9mm Para., 10mm, .38 Super, .38 Wad Cutter, .40 S&W, .45 ACP, or .45 Italian cal., interchangeable barrels, competition ready handgun patterned after the Colt 1911. Imported 1992-95.

* ***Combat Wolverine*** — combat features including 5½ in. compensated barrel.

			$1,600	$1,350	$1,025	$875	$750	$625	$550

   Last Mfg.'s Sug. Retail was $1,700.

* ***Competition Match Wolverine*** — competition features including 6 in. non-compensated barrel.

			$1,600	$1,350	$1,025	$875	$750	$625	$550

   Last Mfg.'s Sug. Retail was $1,700.

M

Grading	100%	98%	95%	90%	80%	70%	60%

SIGNATURE JR. BOLT ACTION — available in a variety of cals., utilizes Signature benchrest short action, choice of stainless steel barrel lengths, right or left-hand action, single shot or repeater, McMillan design fiberglass stock, choice of electroless nickel or Teflon finish, 5 lbs. Mfg. 1992-95.

| | $2,175 | $1,775 | $1,350 | $995 | $895 | $800 | $700 |

Last Mfg.'s Sug. Retail was $2,400.

This model was also available in all titanium.

RIFLES: BOLT ACTION

The models listed below were also available with custom wood stocks at varying prices. McMillan also manufactured a custom rifle from a supplied action - features included new barreling, a fiberglass stock, matte black finish, and range testing to guarantee ¾ M.O.A. Prices started at $1,400.

Add $150 for stainless steel receiver on most models listed below.

TALON SPORTER — available in various cals. between .22-250 Rem. and .416 Rem., receiver available in either 4340 chrome molybdenum or 17-4 stainless steel, drilled and tapped, match grade barrel. Mfg. 1992-95.

| | $2,375 | $1,950 | $1,650 | $1,325 | $1,000 | $895 | $800 |

Last Mfg.'s Sug. Retail was $2,600.

The Talon action is patterned after the Winchester pre-64 Model 70. It features a cone breech, controlled feed, claw extractor, and 3 position safety.

SIGNATURE CLASSIC SPORTER — various cals. available between .22-250 Rem. and .416 Rem., premium wood stock, matte metal finish, 22 or 24 in. stainless steel barrel with button rifling, McMillan action made from 4340 chrome moly steel (either left or right-handed), 3 or 4 shot mag. supplied with 5 shot test target. Mfg. 1988-95.

| | $2,250 | $1,850 | $1,350 | $950 | $850 | $750 | $675 |

Last Mfg.'s Sug. Retail was $2,400.

SIGNATURE VARMINTER — similar to Signature Model, except is available in 10 cals. between .22-250 Rem. and .350 Rem. Mag., hand bedded fiberglass stock, adj. trigger, 26 in. heavy contour barrel. Mfg. 1988-95.

| | $2,250 | $1,850 | $1,350 | $995 | $895 | $800 | $700 |

Last Mfg.'s Sug. Retail was $2,400.

SIGNATURE TITANIUM MOUNTAIN RIFLE — .270 Win., .280 Rem., .30-06, .300 Win. Mag., .338 Win. Mag., or 7mm Rem. Mag. cal., lighter weight variation with shorter barrel. Mfg. 1990-95.

| | $2,750 | $2,195 | $1,850 | $1,450 | $1,100 | $925 | $825 |

Last Mfg.'s Sug. Retail was $3,000.

Add $605 for titanium alloy light contour match grade barrel.

SIGNATURE ALASKAN — available in 11 cals. between .270 Win. and .416 Rem. Mfg. 1990-95.

| | $3,050 | $2,475 | $2,100 | $1,575 | $1,200 | $1,000 | $900 |

Last Mfg.'s Sug. Retail was $3,300.

TALON SAFARI — available in 15 cals. between .300 Win. Mag. and .460 Weatherby, hand-bedded fiberglass stock, 4 shot mag., 24 in. stainless steel barrel, matte black finish, 9½ lbs. Mfg. 1988-95.

| | $3,275 | $2,675 | $2,300 | $1,675 | $1,300 | $1,100 | $950 |

Last Mfg.'s Sug. Retail was $3,600.

Add $600 for .300 Phoenix, .338 Lapua, .378 Wby. Mag., .416 Wby. Mag. or Rigby, or .460 Wby. Mag. cal.

The Talon action is patterned after the Winchester pre-64 Model 70. It featured a cone breech, controlled feed, claw extractor, and 3-position safety. Older Signature action rifles did not have this new Talon action.

M-40 SNIPER RIFLE — .308 Win. cal., Remington action with McMillan match grade heavy contour barrel, fiberglass stock with recoil pad, 4 shot mag., 9 lbs. Mfg. 1990-95.

| | $1,675 | $1,375 | $1,050 | $895 | $800 | $700 | $600 |

Last Mfg.'s Sug. Retail was $1,800.

Grading	100%	98%	95%	90%	80%	70%	60%

M-86 SNIPER RIFLE — .300 Phoenix, .30-06 (new 1989), .300 Win. Mag. or .308 Win. cal., fiberglass stock, variety of optical sights. Mfg. 1988-95.

$1,725 $1,400 $1,075 $925 $825 $725 $625
Last Mfg.'s Sug. Retail was $1,900.

Add $550 for .300 Phoenix cal.
Add $200 for takedown feature (new 1993).

* **M-86 Sniper System** — includes Model 86 Sniper Rifle, bipod, Ultra scope, rings, and bases. Cased. Mfg. 1988-92.

$2,460 $2,050 $1,825 $1,600 $1,350 $1,100 $950
Last Mfg.'s Sug. Retail was $2,665.

M-87 LONG RANGE SNIPER RIFLE — .50 BMG cal., stainless steel bolt action, 29 in. barrel with muzzle brake, single shot, camo synthetic stock, accurate to 1500 meters, 21 lbs. Mfg. 1988-95.

$3,350 $2,750 $2,350 $2,000 $1,850 $1,700 $1,575
Last Mfg.'s Sug. Retail was $3,735.

* **M-87 Sniper System** — includes Model 87 Sniper Rifle, bipod, 20X Ultra scope, rings, and bases. Cased. Mfg. 1988-92.

$3,950 $3,400 $3,000 $2,750 $2,450 $2,200 $2,000
Last Mfg.'s Sug. Retail was $4,200.

* **M-87R** — same specs. as Model 87, except has 5 shot fixed box mag. Mfg. 1990-95.

$3,750 $2,950 $2,550 $2,200 $2,000 $1,850 $1,700
Last Mfg.'s Sug. Retail was $4,000.

Add $300 for Combo option.

M-89 SNIPER RIFLE — .308 Win. cal., 28 in. barrel with suppressor (also available without), fiberglass stock adj. for length and recoil pad, 15¼ lbs. Mfg. 1990-95.

$2,075 $1,675 $1,375 $1,050 $895 $800 $700
Last Mfg.'s Sug. Retail was $2,300.

Add $425 for muzzle suppressor.

M-92 BULLPUP — .50 BMG cal., bullpup configuration with shorter barrel. Mfg. 1993-95.

$3,750 $2,950 $2,550 $2,200 $2,000 $1,850 $1,700
Last Mfg.'s Sug. Retail was $4,000.

M-93SN — .50 BMG cal., similar to M-87, except has folding stock and detachable 5 or 10 shot box mag. Mfg. 1993-95.

$3,950 $3,250 $2,750 $2,300 $2,000 $1,850 $1,700
Last Mfg.'s Sug. Retail was $4,300.

.300 PHOENIX LONG RANGE RIFLE — .300 Phoenix cal., special fiberglass stock featuring adj. cheekpieces to accommodate night vision optics, adj. buttplate, 29 in. barrel, conventional box mag., 12½ lbs. Mfg. 1992 only.

$2,700 $2,195 $1,850 $1,450 $1,100 $925 $825
Last Mfg.'s Sug. Retail was $3,000.

.300 Phoenix is a new cartridge developed to function at ranges in excess of 800 yards. It produces muzzle velocities of 3100 ft. per second with a 250 grain bullet.

COMPETITION MODELS — available in Metallic Silhouette (.308 Win. or 7mm-08 Rem. cal. - disc. 1989), National Match (.308 Win. cal. only), Long Range (.300 Win. Mag. only), or Bench Rest (shooter's choice). Each model made specifically for individual competition events. Mfg. 1988-95.

Mfg.'s Sug. Retail $2,600 $2,325 $1,775 $1,450 $1,100 $895 $800 $700
Last Mfg.'s Sug. Retail was $2,600.

Add $200 for Benchrest Model.
Subtract $300 for Metallic Silhouette model (disc. 1989).

MENZ, AUGUST

Previous manufacturer located in Suhl, Germany.
Please refer to listings in the Liliput section of this text.

Grading	100%	98%	95%	90%	80%	70%	60%

MERCURY

Previous importer of Spanish manufactured shotguns.

SHOTGUNS: SxS

MAGNUM MODEL — 10, 12, or 20 ga. Mag., 28 and 32 in. barrels, full and mod., boxlock, extractors, double triggers, engraved frame, checkered pistol grip stock.

	100%	98%	95%	90%	80%	70%	60%
12 or 20 ga.	$300	$275	$250	$225	$200	$180	$150
10 ga.	$400	$375	$325	$300	$275	$225	$200

MERCURY

Previous manufacturer located in Belgium. Previously imported 1962-68 by Tradewinds, Inc. located in Tacoma, WA.

PISTOLS: SEMI-AUTO

MERCURY MODEL — .22 LR cal., 7 shot mag., steel frame, fixed sights.

	100%	98%	95%	90%	80%	70%	60%
	$400	$375	$325	$300	$275	$225	$200

MERKEL

Merkel

Current trademark manufactured by Suhler Jagd-und Sport-waffen GmbH located in Suhl, Germany since circa 1898.
Currently imported exclusively by GSI, Inc. located in Trussville, AL. Previously imported (until 1992) by Armes De Chasse located in Chadds Ford, PA.

For many years Merkel shotguns had a unfair disadvantage in this country because of the politics of importing firearms from communist bloc countries (goods were subject to a 65% non-favored nation tax). With the reunification of Germany in 1991, this trademark has become more competitive domestically. Merkel continues to manufacture high quality guns. Recently manufactured guns beginning 1995 employ an alpha numeric date code for year of manufacture, making it difficult to determine year of manufacture by serial number. Higher grade models (including the 300 Series) continue to be manufactured one at a time by hand, with less than 30 being mfg. annually.

Many Merkel collectors are now categorizing older production guns into 3 different categories. The first is guns made before 1962, when the Berlin Wall was created. The second is the GDR guns (German Democratic Republic). The last is after the Berlin wall came down (post-1991). Premiums are paid on pre-WWII manufacture and some GDR guns. These older production models should be appraised by a knowledgeable person, since there are a lot of things to consider when evaluating these earlier Merkels. Some guns made up for the Nürnberg and Lipsig trade shows have top quality workmanship, especially the engraving.

M | COMBINATION GUNS

O/U MODEL — 12, 16, or 20 ga. (2¾ in. chamber) over 5.6x50R, 5.6x52R, 6.5x55mm, 6.5x57R, 7x57R, 7x65R, 8x57JRS, 9.3x74R, .22 Hornet (disc. 1997), .222 Rem., .243 Win., .30-06, .308 Win., or .375 H&H (disc. 1994) cal., 25.6 in. barrels, various chokes.

	100%	98%	95%	90%	80%	70%	60%
* *Model 210E*							
Mfg.'s Sug. Retail $6,195	$5,700	$4,600	$3,700	$3,150	$2,600	$2,100	$1,800
* *Model 211E*							
Mfg.'s Sug. Retail $7,495	$6,650	$4,750	$3,900	$3,300	$2,775	$2,275	$1,925
* *Model 213E* — disc. 1997.							
	$13,000	$10,750	$8,250	$6,975	$5,825	$4,600	$3,550

Last Mfg.'s Sug. Retail was $14,795.

Grading	100%	98%	95%	90%	80%	70%	60%

✳ Model 313E — disc. 1997.

	100%	98%	95%	90%	80%	70%	60%
	$19,350	$14,950	$12,500	$9,950	$8,350	$7,100	$5,900

Last Mfg.'s Sug. Retail was $22,795.

MODEL 314 — 12 ga. over 8x60mm Mag. cal., detachable H&H sidelock system, elaborate scroll engraving. Disc. pre-WWII.

	100%	98%	95%	90%	80%	70%	60%
	$21,250	$15,750	$13,000	$10,000	$8,500	$7,200	$6,200

SxS MODEL — similar gauges and cals. to O/U Combination Gun, boxlock models included 8EI and 9EI, 10EI is a sidelock, boxlock models ranged in MSRs from $5,500-$7,000 and the Model 10EI MSR was $9,500. Importation disc. 1990.

DRILLINGS

Current Merkel Drillings include a choice of 12, 16, or 20 ga. for the shotgun barrels with the rifle barrel being bored in most popular U.S. and metric cals. between .22 Hornet and 9.3x74R. All current models are boxlocks with extractors. Presently, there are two Drilling models available: Model 96K - MSR $5,995, and the Model 96K engraved - MSR $7,495. Previously, the Model 90 (disc. 1994), 90S (disc. 1997), 90K (disc. 1997), 95 (disc. 1994), 95K (disc. 1998), and 95S (disc. 1997) were also imported. Models differ in the amount of engraving, cocking systems, and quality of wood - please contact the importer for more information on these individual models.

MERKEL ANSON DRILLING — usually 2 shotguns over rifle, although 2 rifles over shotgun have been noted, 12, 16, or 20 ga., calibers 7x57R, 8x57JR, and 9.3x74R cals. most common, others noted, 25.6 in. or 21.6 in. barrels, boxlock, Anson & Deeley system, double triggers, extractors, checkered pistol grip stock, pre-WWII.

MODEL 142 — engraved.

	100%	98%	95%	90%	80%	70%	60%
	$5,000	$4,000	$3,000	$2,750	$2,500	$2,200	$2,000

MODEL 142 — less ornamentation.

	100%	98%	95%	90%	80%	70%	60%
	$4,000	$3,500	$3,000	$2,500	$2,250	$2,100	$2,000

MODEL 145 — least ornamentation.

	100%	98%	95%	90%	80%	70%	60%
	$3,000	$2,800	$2,700	$2,600	$2,500	$2,100	$1,900

RIFLES: BOLT ACTION

MODEL 190 — various cals., Mauser M-98 system, checkered walnut stock and extended forend, values depend on caliber and action size. Disc. pre-WWII.

	100%	98%	95%	90%	80%	70%	60%
	$7,500	$6,500	$5,275	$4,200	$3,200	$2,350	$1,500

Premiums exist for Magnum or Kurtz (short) action.

RIFLES: SINGLE SHOT

MODEL 180 — various cals., with (Model 180E) or w/o ejector, double triggers, checkered walnut stock and extended forend, values depend on caliber and action size. Disc. pre-WWII.

	100%	98%	95%	90%	80%	70%	60%
	$8,500	$7,250	$5,775	$4,600	$3,750	$3,000	$2,500

MODEL 183E — various cals., top of the line rifle with elaborate engraving. Disc. pre-WWII.

	100%	98%	95%	90%	80%	70%	60%
	$12,500	$10,750	$8,250	$6,975	$5,825	$4,600	$3,550

RIFLES: DOUBLE

O/U MODEL — same cals. as the O/U Combination Gun, various actions, engraving options, and other special orders.

✳ Model 220E Boxlock — boxlock Blitz action, scroll engraved case hardened receiver, DTs, pistol grip with cheekpiece. Importation disc. 1994.

	100%	98%	95%	90%	80%	70%	60%
	$9,575	$8,250	$7,150	$6,100	$5,100	$4,250	$3,500

Last Mfg.'s Sug. Retail was $10,795.

M

Grading	100%	98%	95%	90%	80%	70%	60%

* Model 221E Boxlock — similar to 220E, except has silver-grey receiver with hunting scene engraving. Disc. 1998.

	$9,975	$8,450	$7,450	$6,300	$5,100	$4,250	$3,350

Last Mfg.'s Sug. Retail was $10,895.

* Model 223E Sidelock — sidelock action with arabesque engraving featuring large scrolls, side-plates removed without tools. Disc. 1997.

	$16,250	$13,650	$11,000	$9,750	$8,500	$7,400	$6,250

Last Mfg.'s Sug. Retail was $17,895.

* Model 323E Sidelock — similar to 223E Sidelock, except has medium scrollwork engraving, top-of-the-line O/U double rifle. Disc. 1997.

	$23,300	$20,000	$17,500	$13,500	$11,250	$9,750	$8,350

Last Mfg.'s Sug. Retail was $27,195.

MODEL 324 O/U — 8x60mm Mag. cal., premium quality pre-WWII double rifle, elaborate scroll engraving and best quality walnut. Disc. pre-WWII.

	$26,500	$23,000	$20,000	$17,500	$13,500	$11,250	$9,750

SxS MODEL — same cals. as listed for the O/U Combination Gun.

* Model 140-1 — Anson & Deeley boxlock action with cocking indicators, double triggers, engraved case hardened receiver. Importation began 1994.

Mfg.'s Sug. Retail	$5,995	$5,125	$3,850	$3,050	$2,425	$1,975	$1,825	$1,675

Add $385 for H&H ejectors.
Add approx. $200 for set front trigger.
Add $1,000 for engraved hunting scenes on silver/grey receiver (Model 140-1.1).

* Model 150-1 — Anson & Deeley boxlock action with cocking indicators and sideplates, double triggers, silver grayed receiver with Arabesque engraving. Imported 1994-98.

	$6,500	$5,275	$4,375	$3,750	$3,250	$2,675	$2,100

Last Mfg.'s Sug. Retail was $7,495.

Add $385 for H&H ejectors.
Add approx. $200 for set front trigger.

➤ **Model 150-1.1** — similiar to Model 150-1, except has elaborate hunting scene engraving.

Mfg.'s Sug. Retail	$8,995	$7,750	$5,350	$4,250	$3,550	$2,900	$2,400	$2,000

* Model 160S-1 — sidelock action with Greener crossbolt featuring fine Arabesque engraving, H&H ejectors, DTs, pistol grip stock with cheekpiece. Disc. 1998.

	$11,400	$9,350	$7,675	$6,500	$5,300	$4,400	$3,550

Last Mfg.'s Sug. Retail was $13,295.

Add $415 for H&H ejectors.
Add approx. $500 for set front trigger.
Add approx. $1,000 for single non-selective trigger.

➤ **Model 160-1.1** — similiar to Model 150-1, except has elaborate hunting scene engraving on silver-grey receiver.

Mfg.'s Sug. Retail	$14,995	$13,250	$11,000	$9,000	$7,775	$6,600	$5,400	$4,750

MODEL 132 SxS — various cals., boxlock action with triple Greener cross bolt system, barrels, mfg. from Bohler steel, extractors (Model 132) or H&H system ejectors (Model 132E), DT, elaborate engraving and premium checkered walnut stock and forearm, pre-WWII mfg.

	$12,000	$10,500	$8,500	$6,500	$5,750	$4,900	$4,150

Add 20% for ejectors (Model 132E).

SHOTGUNS: O/U, DISC.

MODEL 100 — 12, 16, or 20 ga., various barrel lengths and chokes, boxlock, Greener cross bolt, double triggers, extractors, checkered pistol grip or English style stock, pre-WWII.

	100%	98%	95%	90%	80%	70%	60%
Plain	$1,850	$1,675	$1,450	$1,250	$1,000	$925	$850
Ribbed	$1,950	$1,775	$1,550	$1,300	$1,050	$950	$875

Grading	100%	98%	95%	90%	80%	70%	60%

MODEL 101 — similar to 100, except selective extractors, rib barrel, some English style scroll engraving, pre-WWII.

| | $2,050 | $1,850 | $1,600 | $1,325 | $1,100 | $1,000 | $900 |

MODEL 101E — similar to 100, except auto ejectors, pre-WWII.

| | $2,200 | $2,000 | $1,750 | $1,425 | $1,250 | $1,150 | $1,000 |

MODEL 400 — similar to 101, except arabesque engraving and Kersten double cross bolt, pre-WWII.

| | $2,075 | $1,875 | $1,650 | $1,350 | $1,200 | $1,100 | $975 |

MODEL 400E — similar to 400, except auto ejector, pre-WWII.

| | $2,250 | $2,050 | $1,800 | $1,450 | $1,325 | $1,175 | $1,025 |

MODEL 410 — similar to 400, except more engraving and fancier wood, pre-WWII.

| | $2,200 | $2,000 | $1,750 | $1,425 | $1,250 | $1,150 | $1,000 |

MODEL 410E — similar to 410, except auto ejectors, pre-WWII.

| | $2,325 | $2,175 | $1,900 | $1,600 | $1,450 | $1,225 | $1,100 |

MODEL 200 — 12, 16, 20, 24, 28, or 32 ga., ribbed barrels in various lengths, Kersten double cross bolt, scalloped frame, boxlock, double triggers, extractors, cocking indicators, either pistol grip or English style checkered stock.

| | $2,175 | $1,975 | $1,700 | $1,350 | $1,100 | $990 | $770 |

MODEL 210 — similar to 200, except engraved and better grade wood, pre-WWII.

| | $2,375 | $2,175 | $1,900 | $1,500 | $1,300 | $1,075 | $895 |

MODEL 201 — 12, 16, or 20 ga., Greener crossbolt, hunting engraving or fine arabesque, dark walnut.

| | $2,600 | $2,300 | $2,000 | $1,600 | $1,425 | $1,200 | $995 |

MODEL 201E — similar to 201, except with auto ejectors, pre-WWII.

| | $3,050 | $2,775 | $2,400 | $1,825 | $1,600 | $1,400 | $1,200 |

MODEL 202 — similar to 201, except with false sideplates, higher quality wood, more profuse engraving, pre-WWII.

| | $3,575 | $3,225 | $2,800 | $2,400 | $2,035 | $1,700 | $1,450 |

MODEL 202E — similar to 202, with auto ejectors, pre-WWII.

| | $4,100 | $3,675 | $3,200 | $2,800 | $2,485 | $2,050 | $1,700 |

MODEL 203E — similar to 202E, except better engraving and wood.

| | $5,150 | $4,600 | $4,000 | $3,400 | $2,900 | $2,500 | $2,100 |

MODEL 204E — similar to 203E, but fine English scroll engraving and Merkel sidelocks, ejectors, pre-WWII.

| | $7,150 | $6,500 | $5,650 | $4,900 | $4,300 | $3,850 | $3,300 |

MODEL 300 — 12, 16, 20, 24, 28, or 32 ga., various lengths and choke ribbed barrels, Merkel-Anson boxlock, Kersten double cross bolt, two underlugs, scalloped frame, either English or pistol grip style stock, cocking indicators, pre-WWII.

| | $2,650 | $2,400 | $2,100 | $1,900 | $1,700 | $1,550 | $1,375 |

M

This model is usually encountered without engraving and has standard wood.

MODEL 300E — similar to Model 300, with auto ejectors, pre-WWII.

| | $3,175 | $2,875 | $2,500 | $2,250 | $1,900 | $1,750 | $1,500 |

This model is usually encountered without engraving and has standard wood.

MODEL 301 — similar to Model 300, but more profusely engraved and better grade wood, pre-WWII.

| | $6,600 | $6,000 | $5,250 | $4,250 | $3,995 | $3,500 | $3,000 |

Grading	100%	98%	95%	90%	80%	70%	60%

MODEL 310E — similar to Model 300, with auto ejectors, pre-WWII.

	$7,950	$7,200	$6,250	$5,300	$4,450	$3,900	$3,400

MODEL 302 — similar to Model 301, but has auto ejectors and more elaborate ornamentation, false sideplates and better grade wood.

	$14,000	$12,000	$10,500	$8,500	$6,500	$5,750	$4,900

MODEL 304E — special order version of Model 303E, higher quality and more ornamentation, top of Merkel O/U line.

	$22,500	$18,750	$15,750	$12,000	$10,500	$8,750	$7,500

SHOTGUNS: SxS, PRE-WWII PRODUCTION

Merkel began manufacturing SxS shotguns during 1914.

MODEL 126E — 12, 16, or 20 ga., similar action as the Model 127, except features game scene and other engraving patterns, H&H style system ejectors, pre-WWII mfg.

	$28,250	$24,725	$21,500	$16,500	$12,500	$10,000	$8,800

MODEL 127E — 12, 16, or 20 ga., various barrel lengths and chokes, H&H style hand detachable sidelocks, auto ejectors, double triggers, pistol or English style stock, elaborate scroll engraving only, this is a best grade gun, pre-WWII mfg.

	$28,250	$24,725	$21,500	$16,500	$12,500	$10,000	$8,800

MODEL 128E — 12, 16, or 20 ga., scalloped Anson & Deeley action featuring engine turned removeable locks and hinged floorplate, DT, H&H system ejectors, elaborate scroll and game scene engraving (including scroll work on barrels), deluxe checkered walnut stock and forearm, pre-WWII mfg.

	$14,500	$12,000	$9,500	$7,500	$6,350	$5,400	$4,600

MODEL 130 — 12, 16, or 20 ga., various barrel lengths and chokes, Anson & Deeley action with false side plates, boxlock, auto ejectors, English style or pistol grip stock, elaborate game scenes and arabesque engraving, pre-WWII mfg.

	$16,250	$13,800	$12,000	$9,500	$7,500	$6,350	$5,400

SHOTGUNS: SxS, RECENT PRODUCTION

MODEL 8 — 12, 16 (disc.), or 20 ga., case hardened scalloped boxlock action with light engraving, Greener crossbolt with chopper lump extension, extractors, SST (current) or DT, standard walnut with checkering, pistol grip or English style stock, sling swivels (disc. 1992). Disc. 1994.

	$1,150	$950	$795	$700	$625	$550	$475

Last Mfg.'s Sug. Retail was $1,695.

MODEL 47E — 12, 16, or 20 ga., case hardened scalloped boxlock action with chopper lump extension and Greener crossbolt, 26 (disc.), 26¾, or 28 in. barrels, SST (current) or DT, ejectors, deluxe checkered walnut, pistol grip or English style stock, sling swivels (disc. 1992), 6-7 lbs.

Mfg.'s Sug. Retail	$2,695		$2,195	$1,675	$1,300	$1,025	$875	$750	$650

MODEL 47SL — 12, 16, 20, 28 (disc.) ga., or .410 (disc.) bore, coin finished sidelock action with scroll engraving, Greener crossbolt, ST (current) or DT, deluxe walnut stock (with cheekpiece) and forearm, sling swivels (disc. 1992).

Mfg.'s Sug. Retail	$5,395		$4,750	$4,125	$3,425	$2,800	$2,300	$1,975	$1,625

Add approx. $600 for 28 ga. or .410 bore (mfg. 1992 only).

MODEL 76E — top-of-the-line boxlock shotgun. Importation disc. 1992.

	$2,600	$2,100	$1,850	$1,600	$1,325	$995	$775

Last Mfg.'s Sug. Retail was $3,500.

Grading	100%	98%	95%	90%	80%	70%	60%

MODEL 147 — 12, 16, 20, or 28 (new 1995, 147E only) ga., 26¾ or 28 in. barrels, Anson & Deeley boxlock, any choke, SST (current) or DT, extractors, straight or pistol grip stock, hunting scene engraved. Disc. 1998, some inventory remained until 1999.

$2,400 $1,875 $1,425 $1,100 $875 $750 $650
Last Mfg.'s Sug. Retail was $2,995.

Add $200 for H&H style auto ejectors (Model 147E).

* *Model 147E* — similar to Model 147, except has ejectors.
  Mfg.'s Sug. Retail $3,395 $2,875 $2,450 $2,150 $1,850 $1,525 $1,325 $1,150
  Add $300 for 28 ga.

* *Model 147EL* — similar to Model 147E, except has luxury grade wood upgrade. Importation began 1999.
  Mfg.'s Sug. Retail $4,195 $3,650 $3,200 $2,700 $2,350 $2,000 $1,700 $1,400
  Add $300 for 28 ga.

MODEL 122 — 12, 16, or 20 ga., Anson & Deeley boxlock action with silver greyed false sideplates, H&H ejectors, SST or DT, fine hunting scenes with arabesque engraving, pistol grip or English style stock. Importation began 1993.
Mfg.'s Sug. Retail $4,495 $3,750 $3,375 $3,000 $2,600 $2,300 $2,000 $1,600

MODEL 122E — 12, 16, or 20 ga., coin finished sidelock action with Greener crossbolt and chopper lump extension, cocking indicators, ejectors, DTs, deluxe game scene engraving. Importation disc. 1991.

$4,100 $3,650 $3,200 $2,800 $2,250 $1,950 $1,650
Last Mfg.'s Sug. Retail was $3,500.

MODEL 147SL — 12, 16, 20, 28 ga., or .410 (disc.) bore, coin finished sidelock action with Greener crossbolt and chopper lump extension, 25½ (disc.), 26 (disc.), 26¾, or 28 in. barrels, ejectors, ST (current) or DT, deluxe game scene engraving, 6-7 lbs.
Mfg.'s Sug. Retail $6,995 $6,250 $4,500 $3,675 $3,150 $2,625 $2,175 $1,850
Add $750 for .410 bore (mfg. 1992 only).

* *Model 147SSL* — similar to Model 147SL, except has luxury grade wood upgrade. Importation began 1999.
  Mfg.'s Sug. Retail $7,995 $7,000 $5,000 $3,925 $3,250 $2,650 $2,175 $1,850

MODEL 247SL — 12, 16, or 20 ga., similar to Model 147S, except has deluxe scroll engraving. Importation disc. 1991, resumed 1993.
Mfg.'s Sug. Retail $6,995 $6,250 $4,500 $3,675 $3,150 $2,625 $2,175 $1,850

MODEL 347SL — 12, 16, or 20 ga., similar to Model 247S, except has more elaborate engraving and better walnut. Importation disc. 1991, resumed 1993-97.

$7,000 $4,850 $3,950 $3,350 $2,775 $2,275 $1,925
Last Mfg.'s Sug. Retail was $7,895.

MODEL 447SL — similar to Model 347S, except is also available in 28 ga. and has more delicate scroll engraving. Importation disc. 1991, resumed 1993.
Mfg.'s Sug. Retail $8,995 $7,750 $5,350 $4,250 $3,550 $2,900 $2,400 $2,000

M

SHOTGUNS: O/U, RECENT PRODUCTION

MODEL 200E BOXLOCK — 12, 16, or 20 ga., case hardened scalloped boxlock action with minor scroll engraving, 26 (disc.), 26¾, or 28 in. barrels, checkered European walnut stock and forearm, ejectors, SST or DT, pistol grip or English style stock, solid rib, 6-7 lbs. Importation disc. 1994, quantities remained until 1998.

$3,600 $2,750 $2,150 $1,900 $1,600 $1,300 $1,100
Last Mfg.'s Sug. Retail was $3,995.

* *Model 200ES Skeet* — 12 ga. only, 26¾ in. VR barrels bored skeet/skeet. Imported 1993-94.
  $4,550 $3,950 $3,500 $3,000 $2,500 $2,100 $1,625
  Last Mfg.'s Sug. Retail was $4,995.

Grading	100%	98%	95%	90%	80%	70%	60%

* **Model 200ET Trap** — 12 ga. only, 30 in. VR barrels bored full/full (other choke configurations available upon request). Importation disc. 1994.

	$4,400	$3,750	$3,300	$2,800	$2,300	$2,000	$1,550

Last Mfg.'s Sug. Retail was $5,195.

MODEL 2000EL — 12, 20, or 28 (new 1999) ga., Kersten double cross-bolt lock, scroll engraved, silver receiver, modified Anson & Deeley boxlock action, ejectors, ST or DT, select checkered walnut with pistol grip or English style stock. Importation began 1998.

Mfg.'s Sug. Retail	$5,195	$4,700	$3,800	$3,350	$2,750	$2,250	$1,775	$1,600

* **Model 2000EL Sporter** — similar to Model 2000EL, except chokes are SK/IC only. Importation began 1999.

Mfg.'s Sug. Retail	$5,195	$4,700	$3,800	$3,350	$2,750	$2,250	$1,775	$1,600

MODEL 2001EL (201E) — 12, 16 (disc. 1997), 20, or 28 (new 1995) ga., similar to Model 200E, except has coin finished action with light game scene engraving.

Mfg.'s Sug. Retail	$6,495	$5,625	$4,650	$3,650	$3,225	$2,850	$2,375	$2,125

This model's nomenclature was changed from 201E to 2000EL during 1998.

* **Model 2001EL Sporter** — similar to Model 2001EL, except chokes are SK/IC only. Importation began 1999.

Mfg.'s Sug. Retail	$6,495	$5,625	$4,650	$3,650	$3,225	$2,850	$2,375	$2,125

* **Model 201ES Skeet** — 12 ga. only, 26¾ in. VR barrels bored skeet/skeet. Imported 1993-97.

	$7,850	$6,675	$5,400	$4,300	$3,450	$2,900	$2,250

Last Mfg.'s Sug. Retail was $8,495.

* **Model 201ET Trap** — 12 ga. only, 30 in. VR barrels bored full/full (other choke configurations available upon request). Importation disc. 1997.

	$7,850	$6,675	$5,400	$4,300	$3,450	$2,900	$2,250

Last Mfg.'s Sug. Retail was $8,495.

MODEL 2002EL (202E) — similar to Model 201E, except has fine hunting scenes with arabesque engraving on silver false sideplates, not available in 28 ga. Importation began 1993.

Mfg.'s Sug. Retail	$9,995	$8,575	$7,075	$5,300	$4,500	$3,750	$3,350	$2,850

This model's nomenclature was changed from 202E to 2002EL during 1998.

MODEL 203E SIDELOCK — 12, 16 (disc. 1997), or 20 ga. (24, 28, and 32 ga.'s were once available but are now disc.), 26 (disc.), 26¾, or 28 in. barrels, VR, H&H ejectors, SST (current) or DT, elaborate scroll engraving on coin finished receiver, sidelock screws are H&H style but the removable sidelocks are not, choice of English or pistol grip stock, 6-7 lbs. Disc. 1998.

	$9,750	$6,450	$4,950	$3,900	$3,400	$2,550	$2,150

Last Mfg.'s Sug. Retail was $11,995.

* **Model 203ES Skeet** — 12 ga. only, 26¾ in. VR barrels bored skeet/skeet. Imported 1993-97.

	$12,050	$9,100	$7,300	$5,975	$4,950	$3,950	$3,500

Last Mfg.'s Sug. Retail was $14,595.

* **Model 203ET Trap** — 12 ga. only, 30 in. VR barrels bored full/full (other choke configurations available upon request). Importation disc. 1997.

	$12,050	$9,100	$7,300	$5,975	$4,950	$3,950	$3,500

Last Mfg.'s Sug. Retail was $14,595.

MODEL 303EL (LUXUS) — also available in 28 ga. starting 1998, similar to Model 203EL, except has H&H type sidelock action with hidden thumbnail detachable sidelocks, double under-lugs, more ornamentation and better wood.

Mfg.'s Sug. Retail	$19,995	$17,250	$14,500	$11,750	$9,500	$8,100	$7,000	$5,800

Luxus variations are also encountered in the 201 and 203 series in addition to older pre-war models.

Grading	100%	98%	95%	90%	80%	70%	60%

SHOTGUNS: SPORTING CLAYS

MODEL 47LSC SxS SPORTING CLAYS — 12 ga. only, features Anson & Deeley boxlock action with scroll engraved case hardened receiver, 28 in. barrels with Briley screw-in chokes, H&H style ejectors, SST adj. for length of pull, select grade checkered walnut stock with pistol grip and beavertail forearm, competition recoil pad. Disc. 1994.

$2,725	$2,400	$2,050	$1,725	$1,450	$1,125	$925

Last Mfg.'s Sug. Retail was $2,995.

MODEL 200SC O/U SPORTING CLAYS — 12 ga. only, 3 in. chambers, 30 in. VR fixed choke barrels with lengthened forcing cones, Kersten double cross-bolt lock, color case hardened receiver, Blitz action, SST, fitted luggage case. Imported 1995-96.

$6,750	$4,600	$3,750	$3,200	$2,625	$2,175	$1,850

Last Mfg.'s Sug. Retail was $7,495.

Add $500 for Briley choke tubes (5 total).

MERRILL

Previous manufacturer located in Tucson, AZ. This original pistol design was by Jim Rock, who then joined R.P.M.

A newer variation of the Sportsman, now designated the XL and Hunter Model XL was offered by R.P.M. Please refer to the R.P.M. listing for more information.

PISTOLS: SINGLE SHOT

SPORTSMAN MODEL — .22 S, L, or LR, .22 Mag., .22 Rem. Jet., .22 Hornet, 30 Herrett, .38 Spl., .357 Mag., .256 Win. Mag., .45 LC, .44 Mag., or .30-30 Win. cal., 9 in. barrel, hinged break open available, smooth walnut grips.

$650	$575	$525	$450	$395	$350	$300

Add $70 for interchangeable barrels.
Add $25 for wrist support.

MERWIN HULBERT & CO.

Previous company with headquarters located in New York, NY circa 1874-1891. Previously manufactured at the Hopkins & Allen Manufacturing Co. (not by Hopkins & Allen) factory utilizing their own workforce and equipment which at the time was state-of-the-art.

Merwin Hulbert & Co. were designers and promoters who created a revolver that had such advanced features as an automatic ejection system, streamlined appearance, and ease of shooting.

Grading	100%	95%	80%	50%	20%	Traces	Grey

PISTOLS: POCKET MODELS

Add 25% for blued finish.
Add 25% for extra matching barrel.
Add $300 for pearl, ivory, or mottled grips.

POCKET ARMY S.A. SECOND MODEL

$1,800	$1,400	$1,000	$800	$600	$500	$450

POCKET ARMY S.A. THIRD MODEL

$1,550	$1,175	$900	$725	$575	$475	$425

POCKET ARMY D.A.

$1,500	$1,200	$900	$750	$550	$450	$400

POCKET ARMY FOURTH MODEL

$9,000	$7,500	$5,500	$3,500	$2,500	$1,500	$800

This model is rare and only infrequently encountered.

Grading	100%	95%	80%	50%	20%	Traces	Grey

.38 BIRDSHEAD GRIP

	100%	95%	80%	50%	20%	Traces	Grey
	$1,000	$800	$600	$500	$450	$350	$300

This model is rare and only infrequently encountered.

.38 SAW HANDLE

	100%	95%	80%	50%	20%	Traces	Grey
	$800	$600	$500	$400	$300	$250	$200

.38 SINGLE ACTION

	100%	95%	80%	50%	20%	Traces	Grey
	$2,000	$1,700	$1,400	$1,000	$700	$500	$300

This model is rare and only infrequently encountered.

1ST MODEL .38 CAL. 5 SHOT

* *Spur Trigger, Birdshead Grip*

	100%	95%	80%	50%	20%	Traces	Grey
	$1,000	$800	$600	$500	$450	$350	$300

This model is rare and only infrequently encountered.

* *Spur Trigger, Saw Handle*

	100%	95%	80%	50%	20%	Traces	Grey
	$800	$600	$500	$400	$300	$250	$200

2ND AND 3RD MODELS .38 CAL. 5 SHOT

* *Birdshead Grips*

	100%	95%	80%	50%	20%	Traces	Grey
	$1,000	$800	$600	$500	$450	$350	$300

This model is rare and only infrequently encountered.

* *Saw Handle Double Action*

	100%	95%	80%	50%	20%	Traces	Grey
	$800	$600	$500	$400	$300	$250	$200

.32 CAL. LONG ON .38 CAL. FRAME 7 SHOT

	100%	95%	80%	50%	20%	Traces	Grey
	$1,200	$1,000	$900	$800	$700	$500	$400

This model is rare and only infrequently encountered.

.32 S&W 5 SHOT

	100%	95%	80%	50%	20%	Traces	Grey
	$600	$550	$400	$350	$300	$250	$200

.22 CAL. 7 SHOT

	100%	95%	80%	50%	20%	Traces	Grey
	$500	$450	$350	$250	$200	$150	$100

Add approx. 200% for engraved model.

FOREIGN S.A. .44 CAL.

* *Frontier Army*

	100%	95%	80%	50%	20%	Traces	Grey
	$1,800	$1,400	$1,000	$800	$600	$400	$300

* *Frontier Army D.A.*

	100%	95%	80%	50%	20%	Traces	Grey
	$1,600	$1,200	$900	$700	$500	$400	$300

FOREIGN S.A. .44 CAL. 7 IN.

	100%	95%	80%	50%	20%	Traces	Grey
	$1,500	$1,200	$800	$600	$500	$450	$400

FOREIGN S.A. .44 CAL. 3½ IN.

	100%	95%	80%	50%	20%	Traces	Grey
	$1,100	$700	$500	$400	$300	$250	$200

M

REVOLVERS

FIRST MODEL — .44-40 WCF cal. various barrel lengths.

	100%	95%	80%	50%	20%	Traces	Grey
	$2,000	$1,600	$1,200	$900	$700	$600	$450

ENGRAVED .44-40 WCF CALS.

	100%	95%	80%	50%	20%	Traces	Grey
	$7,000	$6,000	$5,000	$4,000	$3,000	$2,000	$1,000

SECOND MODEL

	100%	95%	80%	50%	20%	Traces	Grey
	$1,800	$1,400	$1,000	$800	$600	$500	$450

ENGRAVED

	100%	95%	80%	50%	20%	Traces	Grey
	$7,000	$6,000	$5,000	$4,000	$3,000	$2,000	$1,000

Grading	100%	95%	80%	50%	20%	Traces	Grey
THIRD MODEL S.A.							
	$1,500	$1,200	$900	$700	$600	$500	$450
THIRD MODEL D.A.							
	$1,400	$1,100	$800	$600	$500	$400	$400
ENGRAVED							
	$6,000	$5,500	$4,500	$3,500	$2,500	$1,500	$1,000

This model is rare and only infrequently encountered.

FOURTH MODEL S.A. — 7 in. barrel.

	100%	95%	80%	50%	20%	Traces	Grey
	$10,000	$8,000	$6,000	$4,000	$3,000	$2,000	$1,000

This model is rare and only infrequently encountered.

FOURTH MODEL S.A. — 5½ in. barrel.

	$4,000	$3,200	$2,500	$2,000	$1,500	$1,100	$800

This model is rare and only infrequently encountered.

FOURTH MODEL D.A. — 5½ in. barrel.

	$3,000	$2,500	$2,000	$1,500	$1,000	$800	$600

This model is rare and only infrequently encountered.

FOURTH MODEL D.A. — 7 in. barrel.

	$9,000	$7,500	$5,500	$3,500	$2,500	$1,000	$800

This model is rare and only infrequently encountered.

FOURTH MODEL S.A. — 3½ in. barrel.

	$10,000	$8,000	$6,000	$4,000	$3,000	$2,000	$1,000

This model is rare and only infrequently encountered.

FOURTH MODEL D.A. — 3½ in. barrel.

	$9,000	$7,500	$5,500	$3,500	$2,500	$1,500	$800

This model is rare and only infrequently encountered.

MICHIGAN ARMS

Previous manufacturer located in Michigan until circa 1981.

Grading	100%	98%	95%	90%	80%	70%	60%

PISTOLS: SEMI-AUTO

GUARDIAN - SS — .380 ACP cal., patterned after the Walther PPK, bears close resemblance to the Indian Arms .380 semi-auto, 3¼ in. barrel, checkered walnut grips with medallion, 6 shot finger extension mag., fixed sights. Limited mfg.

	$375	$295	$225	$210	$190	$170	$150

This model was mfg. by using Indian Arms tooling.

M1911 A1 — .45 ACP cal., patterned after the Colt M1911 A1, fixed sights, 7 shot mag. Disc.

	$450	$395	$350	$275	$225	$210	$190

M

MIDLAND RIFLES

Previous trademark of rifles manufactured by Gibbs Rifle Co. (please refer to the G section for previous models and pricing) and older models mfg. by Parker-Hale, Ltd. (please refer to the P section).

MIIDA

Previous manufactured by Nikko Firearms, Ltd. in Tochigi, Japan. Previously imported by Marubeni America Corp. located in New York, NY circa 1972-1974.

Grading	100%	98%	95%	90%	80%	70%	60%

SHOTGUNS: O/U

MODEL 612 FIELD — 12 ga., 26 or 28 in. barrels, VR, various chokes, boxlock, auto ejectors, single selective trigger, checkered pistol grip stock. Mfg. 1972-1974.

| | $800 | $725 | $650 | $575 | $510 | $440 | $400 |

MODEL 2100 SKEET GUN — similar to Model 612, with 27 in. VR, skeet bore barrels, more elaborate engraving. Mfg. 1972-1974.

| | $875 | $775 | $700 | $615 | $550 | $465 | $425 |

MODEL 2200T TRAP GUN — similar to Model 2100, except with 29¾ in. imp. mod. and full choke barrels, wide VR, 60% engraved coverage and select wood. Mfg. 1972-1974.

| | $925 | $825 | $750 | $665 | $595 | $500 | $450 |

MODEL 2200S SKEET GUN — similar to Model 2200T, except with 27 in. skeet bore barrels.

| | $925 | $825 | $750 | $665 | $595 | $500 | $450 |

MODEL 2300 SERIES TRAP OR SKEET — similar to Model 2200 Trap/Skeet but with more engraving. Mfg. 1972-1974.

| | $975 | $875 | $800 | $715 | $630 | $550 | $500 |

MODEL GRT GRANDEE TRAP GUN — 12 ga., 29¾ in. full choke barrels, single selective trigger, auto ejector, boxlock with side plates, receiver fully engraved as well as breech ends of barrel, triggerguard and locking lever, gold inlaid, extensive silver line inlays, high grade select walnut stock. Mfg. 1972-1974.

| | $2,500 | $2,200 | $1,900 | $1,575 | $1,250 | $1,000 | $850 |

MODEL GRS GRANDEE SKEET GUN — similar to Model GRT, with 27 in. skeet bored barrels.

| | $2,500 | $2,200 | $1,900 | $1,575 | $1,250 | $1,000 | $850 |

MILLER, DAVID CO.

See David Miller Co. listing.

MIL-SPEC INDUSTRIES CORP.

Current pistol manufacturer and related components supplier located in Roslyn Heights, NY since 1996. Dealer sales.

PISTOLS: SEMI-AUTO

MIL-SPEC 1911 A1 — 9mm Para., 9x21mm, 9x22mm, .40 S&W, .45 HP, or .45 ACP cal., high tech polymer and stainless steel frame, beavertail grip safety, aluminum trigger, 10 shot mag., 3¹⁵⁄₁₆ (Compact), 5⁵⁄₁₆ (Combat with compensator), or 5 (Government) in. barrel, choice of wood, plastic, or rubber grips, 39½-46 oz. New late 1996.

| Mfg.'s Sug. Retail | $690 | | $625 | $550 | $500 | $450 | $400 | $360 | $330 |

Add $5 for parkerized finish.
Add $45 for electroless nickel finish.
Add $50 for hard chrome finish.

MILTEX, INC.

Current handgun importer located in La Plata, MD. Please refer to individual listings under Arcus and Makarov.

MIROKU FIREARMS MFG. CO.

Current manufacturer established during 1893 and located in Kochi, Japan. Miroku currently manufactures long arms for Browning and Winchester (please refer to individual sections), in addition to their own line of firearms mostly distributed in Europe.

Grading	100%	98%	95%	90%	80%	70%	60%

Shotguns marked Miroku only without another trademark listing represent that period of manufacture before Miroku began manufacturing shotguns for other companies (i.e. Charles Daly, SKB, Browning, and others). Most guns marked Miroku only were made on a limited basis and although somewhat rare, collector desirability to date has been minimal. Since model notations were not specified in most instances (many shotguns were made to test market demand), a model rundown is virtually impossible. Values can be approx. ascertained by comparing a Miroku shotgun of similar gauge, features, engraving/wood, and condition to an equivalent Japanese Charles Daly model. Miroku also manufactured revolvers up until approx. 1964 which may be designated Liberty Chief - limited importation into the U.S.

MITCHELL ARMS, INC.

Current manufacturer, importer, and distributor located in Fountain Valley, CA. Distributor sales only.

DERRINGERS: O/U

GUARDIAN ANGEL — .22 LR or .22 Mag. cal., double action, hammerless, choice of blue, satin, nickel, or gold finish. Mfg. 1996-97.

	$125	$105	$95	$85	$80	$75	$70

Last Mfg.'s Sug. Retail was $143.

    Add $10 for .22 Mag. cal.
    Add $20 for blue or nickel finish.
    Add $40 for gold finish.
    Add $10 for Deluxe Model with case and angel charm.

PISTOLS: SEMI-AUTO

AMERICAN EAGLE LUGER — 9mm Para. cal., 4 in. barrel, stainless steel with toggle action, checkered American walnut grips, American Eagle version, contoured front grip strap. Disc. 1994.

	$590	$475	$400	$350	$300	$260	$230

Last Mfg.'s Sug. Retail was $695.

ROLLING BLOCK PISTOL — .22 LR, .22 Mag., .223 Rem., .357 Mag., or .45 LC cal., reproduction of the Remington Rolling Block design, 10 in. barrel. Mfg. 1991-92 only.

	$340	$285	$240	$210	$185	$170	$150

Last Mfg.'s Sug. Retail was $395.

Mitchell .22 Cal. Target Pistols

Mitchell Arms manufactured High Standard marked pistols during 1993-94. Due to litigation, the High Standard logo was dropped in 1994, and High Standard model nomenclature was dropped in 1996. These guns feature push button barrel takedown and usually, a choice between stainless steel or royal blue steel construction. Mitchell Arms is not responsible for the older High Standard pistols manufactured in New Haven and East Hartford, CT, even though Mitchell parts are interchangeable with original High Standard pistols.

MONARCH (CITATION II) — .22 LR cal., 5½ bull or 7¼ in. fluted barrel, frame mounted bridge rear sight, checkered walnut grips with thumb rest, push button take down, stippled front and rear grip straps, adj. trigger, travel, and weight, stainless steel or royal blue finish. Mfg. began 1993.

Mfg.'s Sug. Retail	$490	$395	$295	$245	$215	$190	$170	$150

MEDALIST (OLYMPIC I.S.U.) — .22 S or LR (new 1994) cal., military grip style, 6¾ in. special barrel with internal stabilizer, adj. barrel weights, other features similar to Citation II, stainless steel or blue finish. Mfg. began 1993.

Mfg.'s Sug. Retail	$700	$625	$550	$425	$375	$325	$275	$225

M

Grading	100%	98%	95%	90%	80%	70%	60%

BARON (SHARPSHOOTER II) — .22 LR cal., 5½ in. bull barrel, standard trigger, adj. rear sight, smooth grip frame, stainless steel or blue (disc.) finish. Mfg. began 1993.

Mfg.'s Sug. Retail	$400	$320	$280	$240	$210	$185	$160	$135

SPORTSTER (SPORT KING II) — .22 LR cal., 4½ or 6¾ in. tapered barrel, military black checkered plastic grips, stainless steel only, adj. rear sight. Mfg. began 1993.

Mfg.'s Sug. Retail	$330	$270	$220	$185	$160	$135	$120	$110

MEDALLION (TROPHY II) — .22 LR cal., 5½ in. bull or 7¼ in. fluted barrel, military grips with full checkering and thumb rest, bridge rear sight, gold-plated trigger safety and mag. release, stippled front and rear grip straps, stainless steel or royal blue (disc. 1997) finish. New 1993.

Mfg.'s Sug. Retail	$500	$425	$350	$275	$225	$190	$170	$150

SOVEREIGN (VICTOR II) — .22 LR cal., 4½ or 5½ in. full length VR or black rib barrel, checkered walnut grips with thumb rest, stainless steel became standard 1998, gold-plated trigger, safety, mag. release, and side lock, rib mounted sights. New 1993.

Mfg.'s Sug. Retail	$600	$500	$425	$375	$325	$275	$225	$195

Add $80 for Weaver style base built into VR.

HIGH STANDARD COLLECTORS ASSOCIATION SPECIAL EDITIONS

* **HSCA-SE Trophy II** — .22 LR cal., 100 mfg. 1993 only, cased.

  $450 $375 $300

* **HSCA-SE Victor II**

  $495 $400 $325

* **HSCA-SE Citation II**

  $435 $365 $285

* **HSCA-SE Three Gun Set** — includes Trophy II, Olympic II, and Victor II.

  $1,495 $1,295 $1,050

* **HSCA-SE Six Gun Set** — includes 6¾ in. I.S.U. Olympic (.22 Short), 4½ in. Victor, 7¼ in. Citation, 5½ in. Sharpshooter, 4½ in. Sport King, and Trophy Model. Special engraving, cased, HSCA prefix with 2-digit serial number, 19 sets total mfg. 1994 only.

  $2,650 $2,100 $1,675

  Last Mfg.'s Sug. Retail was $2,995.

Mitchell Centerfire Pistols

MODEL 57A (TOKAREV DESIGN) — .30 Mauser cal., single action semi-auto, 9 shot mag., hammer block and mag. safety, all steel construction. Imported from Yugoslavia 1990 only.

$240 $215 $180 $160 $145 $135 $120

Last Mfg.'s Sug. Retail was $280.

MODEL 70A (TOKAREV DESIGN) — 9mm Para. cal., otherwise similar to Model 57A. Imported from Yugoslavia 1990 only.

$240 $215 $180 $160 $145 $135 $120

Last Mfg.'s Sug. Retail was $280.

88A OFFICERS MODEL (TOKAREV DESIGN) — 9mm Para. cal., newer slenderized variation issued to the Officers Corps., short slide and frame, finger extension mag. Imported from Yugoslavia 1990 only.

$255 $225 $190 $165 $145 $135 $120

Last Mfg.'s Sug. Retail was $300.

SKORPION — while advertised during 1987, this model was never mfg.

SPECTRE — while advertised during 1987, this model was never mfg.

M

Grading	100%	98%	95%	90%	80%	70%	60%

1911 GOLD/SIGNATURE SERIES (STANDARD) — .45 ACP cal., features new tapered barrel slide lock-up, wide body accepts staggered mag., full length guide rod recoil buffer assembly, beveled mag. well, blue (disc. 1995) or stainless steel, 8 shot mag., walnut checkered grips, fixed or adj. sights. New 1994-disc.

Blue Finish	$465	$395	$350	$325	$295	$270	$250

Last Mfg.'s Sug. Retail was $535.

* **Stainless Steel** — disc. 1997.

	$675	$585	$525	$475			

Last Mfg.'s Sug. Retail was $675.

* **Tactical Model** — stainless steel, features elongated grip safety and serrated front slide, fixed or adj. rear sight. Mfg. 1996-97.

	$640	$550	$500				

Last Mfg.'s Sug. Retail was $735.

　　　Add $40 for adj. rear sight.

* **Bullseye Model** — similar to Tactical Model, except has fully adj. rear sight. Mfg. 1996-97.

	$850	$700	$575

Last Mfg.'s Sug. Retail was $950.

* **IPSC Limited Model** — choice of ghost ring or adj. rear sight. Mfg. 1996-97.

	$1,075	$875	$675

Last Mfg.'s Sug. Retail was $1,195.

　　　Add $45 for ghost ring sight.

1911 GOLD/SIGNATURE SERIES (WIDE BODY) — .45 ACP cal., features new tapered barrel slide lock-up, full length guide rod recoil buffer assembly, beveled mag. well, blue (disc. 1995) or stainless steel, 10 (C/B 1994) or 13★ shot mag., walnut checkered grips, fixed or adj. sights. Mfg. 1994-97.

Blue Finish	$595	$525	$475	$425	$375	$335	$295

Last Mfg.'s Sug. Retail was $685.

* **Standard Model** — stainless steel, fixed sights, smooth grips. Mfg. 1996-97.

	$765	$650	$550

Last Mfg.'s Sug. Retail was $840.

* **Tactical Model** — stainless steel, features elongated grip safety and serrated front slide, adj. rear sight. Mfg. 1996-97.

	$795	$675	$575

Last Mfg.'s Sug. Retail was $895.

MITCHELL .44 — .44 Mag. cal., 5½ in. barrel, blue finish, 7 shot mag., checkered walnut grips, adj. rear sight. Mfg. 1996-97.

	$1,050	$900	$800	$725	$650	$575	$495

Last Mfg.'s Sug. Retail was $1,190.

JEFF COOPER SIGNATURE/COMMEMORATIVE MODEL — .45 ACP cal., blue finish. Mfg. 1996-97.

Signature Model	$725	$625	$560	$500	$450	$415	$375

Last Mfg.'s Sug. Retail was $795.

* **Commemorative Model** — 1,000 mfg. 1996-97.

	$1,650	$1,400	$1,200	$1,000	$800	$675	$550

Last Mfg.'s Sug. Retail was $1,895.

M

ALPHA SERIES — while advertised in 1995, this model was never mfg.

REVOLVERS: SINGLE ACTION

SINGLE ACTION ARMY — .22 LR (disc.), .357 Mag., .44-40 WCF (new 1998), .44 Mag. (disc.), .45 ACP (disc.), or .45 LC cal., 4¾, 5½, 6 (disc. 1993), or 7½ in. barrel lengths, hammer block safety mechanism, steel construction, case hardened frame, one-piece walnut stock. Imported 1986-94, re-introduced 1997.

Grading	100%	98%	95%	90%	80%	70%	60%

* **Cowboy Model** — .357 Mag., .44-40 WCF, .45 ACP (disc.), or .45 LC cal., 4¾ in. barrel.

  Mfg.'s Sug. Retail $450 $395 $350 $315 $275 $260 $245 $230

  Add $50 for nickel finish.
  Add $50 for adj. rear sight (disc.).
  Add $150 for dual cylinder (.357 Mag./9mm Para., .45 LC/.45 ACP, or .44-40 WCF/.44 Spl.).
  Add $95 for steel back strap and triggerguard (disc.).

  This model is also available in a Bat Masterson variation.

* **U.S. Army Model** — similar to Cowboy Model, except has 5½ in. barrel.

  Mfg.'s Sug. Retail $450 $395 $350 $315 $275 $260 $245 $230

  Add $50 for nickel finish.
  Add $150 for dual cylinder (.357 Mag./9mm Para., .45 LC/.45 ACP, or .44-40 WCF/.44 Spl.).

* **U.S. Cavalry Model** — similar to Cowboy Model, except has 7½ in. barrel.

  Mfg.'s Sug. Retail $450 $395 $350 $315 $275 $260 $245 $230

  Add $150 for dual cylinder (.357 Mag./9mm Para., .45 LC/.45 ACP, or .44-40 WCF/.44 Spl.).
  Add $50 for nickel finish.

* **.44 Mag.** — .44 Mag. cal., fully adj. target sights. Disc. 1992.

  $425 $350 $295 $250 $200 $180 $165
  Last Mfg.'s Sug. Retail was $495.

* **Rimfire Model** — .22 LR cal. Importation disc. 1989.

  $230 $200 $180 $160 $145 $130 $120
  Last Mfg.'s Sug. Retail was $280.

  Add $30 for adj. rear sight.

* **Silhouette Model** — available with 10, 12, or 18 in. barrel in .44 Mag. or .45 LC cal. Importation disc. 1991.

  $395 $325 $260 $220 $195 $170 $155
  Last Mfg.'s Sug. Retail was $450.

  Add $175 for shoulder stock (available with 18 in. barrel only).
  The shoulder stock is available with .44 Mag./.44-40 WCF cals. only.

* **Dual Cylinder** — available in either .22 LR/.22 Mag. (disc.), .22 LR/.22 Mag. stainless (disc. 1988), .357 Mag./9mm Para. (disc. 1993), .44 Mag./.44-40 WCF (disc. 1991), or .45 LC/.45 ACP (new 1990) cal. Imported 1986-94.

  $475 $415 $365 $335 $300 $275 $250
  Last Mfg.'s Sug. Retail was $549.

  Add $50 for adj. rear sight (disc.).
  Add $39 for nickel finish.
  Add $93 for for steel backstrap.

* **Stainless Model** — available in .22 LR or .357 Mag. (disc. 1987) cal. only, adj. sights. Imported 1986-1988 only.

  $260 $225 $195
  Last Mfg.'s Sug. Retail was $301.

  Add $25 for .357 Mag.

BAT MASTERSON MODEL — .45 LC cal., 4¾ , 5½ or 7½ in. barrel with full ejector rod housing, nickel-plated, one-piece walnut stocks, hammer-block safety, rear sight is square notch in frame, two-piece backstrap. Imported 1989-94.

$375 $285 $240 $210 $185 $170 $150
Last Mfg.'s Sug. Retail was $439.

Add $156 for extra .45 ACP cylinder.

MODEL 1875 REMINGTON — .357 Mag. or .45 LC cal., royal blue finish with color case hardened frame, walnut grips. Imported 1990-91.

$345 $285 $245 $210 $185 $170 $150
Last Mfg.'s Sug. Retail was $399.

Add $76 for nickel finish.
Add $51 for extra convertible .45 ACP cylinder.

Grading	100%	98%	95%	90%	80%	70%	60%

REVOLVERS: DOUBLE ACTION

TITAN II — .357 Mag. cal., 6 shot, 2, 4, or 6 in. barrel, blue or stainless, fixed sights, shrouded ejector rod, target hammer. Mfg. 1995 only.

$285	$250	$220	$190	$170	$150	$135

Last Mfg.'s Sug. Retail was $339.

TITAN III — similar to Titan II, except has adj. rear sight. Mfg. 1995 only.

$340	$285	$245	$200	$175	$150	$135

Last Mfg.'s Sug. Retail was $429.

GUARDIAN II — .38 Spl. cal., 6 shot, 3 or 4 in. barrel, fixed sights, blue only, target or combat grips. Mfg. 1995 only.

$240	$215	$185	$165	$145	$130	$120

Last Mfg.'s Sug. Retail was $275.

GUARDIAN III — similar to Guardian II, except has adj. rear sight, and 6 in. barrel. Mfg. 1995 only.

$260	$230	$195	$175	$155	$140	$130

Last Mfg.'s Sug. Retail was $305.

RIFLES: BOLT ACTION, RECENT MAUSER IMPORT

Beginning 1999, Mitchell Arms was able to import a sizeable quantity of WWII Mauser 98Ks manufactured in Yugoslavia during/after WWII. These guns are basically in new condition, having been only test fired over the past 50 years. They are supplied with bayonet and scabbard, military leather sling, original field cleaning kit, and leather ammo pouch. Caliber is 8mm Mauser (7.9x57mm), and all parts numbers match on these rifles. Retail is $250.

RIFLES: DISC.

MODEL 15/22 OR 20/22 SEMI-AUTO CARBINE — .22 LR cal., American walnut stock, high polish blue, detachable 10 shot mag. Mfg. 1994-95.

$155	$125	$105	$95	$85	$75	$65

Last Mfg.'s Sug. Retail was $179.

Subtract $40 for 20/22 Special.
Add $20 for Deluxe model (includes deluxe walnut, rosewood accents, and fine line checkering).

LW22 SEMI-AUTO — .22 LR cal., 10 shot mag., composite or skeleton stock, patterned after Feather Industries semi-auto. Limited mfg. 1996-97.

$240	$220	$195	$175	$160	$145	$130

Last Mfg.'s Sug. Retail was $275.

Add $30 for composite stock.

LW9 SEMI-AUTO — 9mm Para. cal., semi-auto, blowback action, composite or skeleton stock, patterned after Feather Industries 9mm Para. semi-auto. Limited mfg. 1996-97.

$450	$395	$360	$330	$300	$270	$240

Last Mfg.'s Sug. Retail was $500.

Add $35 for composite stock.

MODEL 9303/9304/9305 STANDARD BOLT ACTION — .22 LR (9303) or .22 Mag. (9304, new 1995) cal., standard or deluxe variation, 10 shot mag. Mfg. 1994-95.

$240	$195	$180	$160	$145	$130	$120

Last Mfg.'s Sug. Retail was $275.

Add $14 for .22 Mag. cal.
Subtract $76 for special bolt action (9305).

MODEL 9301/9302 DELUXE BOLT ACTION — similar to 9304/9305, except includes deluxe walnut, rosewood accents, and fine line checkering. Mfg. 1994-95.

$265	$220	$190	$170	$150	$135	$125

Last Mfg.'s Sug. Retail was $313.

Add $12 for .22 Mag. cal.

M

Grading	100%	98%	95%	90%	80%	70%	60%

M-16A3 — .22 LR, .22 Mag. (disc. 1987), or .32 ACP cal., patterned after Colt's AR-15. Mfg. 1987-94.

	$235	$195	$175	$160	$145	$130	$120

Last Mfg.'s Sug. Retail was $266.

Add $100 for .22 Mag. cal. or .32 ACP (disc. 1988).

CAR-15/22 — .22 LR cal., carbine variation of M-16 with shorter barrel and collapsible stock. Mfg. 1990-94.

	$235	$195	$175	$160	$145	$130	$120

Last Mfg.'s Sug. Retail was $266.

GALIL — .22 LR or .22 Mag. cal., patterned after Galil semi-auto paramilitary design rifle, choice of wood stock or folding stock (new 1992). Mfg. 1987-1993.

	$285	$240	$195	$160	$150	$140	$130

Last Mfg.'s Sug. Retail was $359.

MAS — .22 LR or .22 Mag. cal., patterned after French MAS rifle. Mfg. 1987-1993.

	$285	$240	$195	$160	$150	$140	$130

Last Mfg.'s Sug. Retail was $359.

Add $75 for .22 Mag. cal. (disc. 1988).

PPS-30/50 — .22 LR cal., patterned after the Russian WWII PPS military rifle, full length barrel shroud, 20 shot banana clip, adj. rear sight, walnut stock. Mfg. 1989-94.

	$235	$195	$175	$160	$145	$130	$120

Last Mfg.'s Sug. Retail was $266.

Add $100 for 50 shot drum magazine.

SPECTRE CARBINE — while advertised during 1987, this model was never mfg.

AK-22 — .22 LR or .22 Mag. (new 1988) cal., copy of the famous Russian AK-47, fully adj. sights, built in cleaning rod, high quality European walnut or folding stock, 20 shot clip mag. Mfg. 1985-94.

	$235	$195	$175	$160	$145	$130	$120

Last Mfg.'s Sug. Retail was $266.

Add $40 for folding stock.

AK-47 — 7.62x39 cal., copy of the original Kalashnikov AK-47, semi-auto, teak stock and forend, 30 shot steel mag., last shot hold open. Mfg. Yugoslavia. Imported 1986-1989.

	$595	$550	$495	$450	$400	$360	$310

Last Mfg.'s Sug. Retail was $675.

Add $23 for steel folding butt stock.
Add $150 for 75 shot steel drum mag.

* **.308 WIN. NATO AK-47 (M77B1)** — .308 Win. cal., milled receiver, adj. gas port, otherwise similar to AK-47 except has scope rail, day/night Tritium sights, and 20 shot mag. Imported 1989 only.

	$900	$800	$700	$595	$525	$475	$425

Last Mfg.'s Sug. Retail was $775.

Add $600 for military issue sniper scope and rings.

M76 — similar to AK-47, except is 7.92mm cal. and has longer barrel and frame set up for scope mount, counter sniper design, 10 shot mag., mfg. to mil. specs. Imported 1986-1989.

	$1,725	$1,535	$1,350	$1,100	$900	$820	$760

Last Mfg.'s Sug. Retail was $1,995.

SKS-M59 — 7.62x39 cal., copy of the SKS-M59 standard rifle, full walnut stock, fully adj. sights, gas operated. Mfg. in Yugoslavia. Imported 1986-1989.

	$610	$525	$465	$410	$360	$315	$260

Last Mfg.'s Sug. Retail was $699.

R.P.K. — 7.62x39mm or .308 Win. cal., forged heavy barrel with cooling fins, teak stock, detachable bipod, mil. specs. Importation disc. 1992.

	$1,050	$875	$725	$650	$575	$525	$475

Last Mfg.'s Sug. Retail was $1,150.

Add $845 for .308 Win. cal.

Grading	100%	98%	95%	90%	80%	70%	60%

MODEL M-90 — 7.62x39mm or .308 Win. cal., AK-47 type action, in various configurations (heavy barrel, folding or fixed stock, finned barrel, etc.), plastic thumbhole stock, 5 shot mag., limited importation from Yugoslavia 1991-92.

	$750	$650	$550	$495	$450	$395	$350

Last Mfg.'s Sug. Retail was $829.

Add $31 for folding stock.
Add $69 for .308 Win. cal. (wood stock only).

RIFLES: REPRODUCTIONS

HENRY RIFLE — .44-40 WCF cal., polished brass frame, octagonal barrel, original loading system. Imported 1990.

	$840	$650	$585	$520	$465	$415	$375

Last Mfg.'s Sug. Retail was $999.

Iron frame also available at extra charge.

MODEL 1866 — .22 LR (disc.), .38 Spl. (disc.), or .44-40 WCF cal., patterned after the Winchester Model 1866 rifle, solid brass frame, octagon barrel. Imported 1990-1993.

	$715	$535	$465	$415	$375	$335	$295

Last Mfg.'s Sug. Retail was $829.

This model was also available in a carbine variation.

MODEL 1873 — .22 LR (disc.), .38 Spl.(disc), .357 Mag. (disc.), .44-40 WCF (disc.), or .45 LC cal., patterned after the Winchester 1873 rifle, octagon barrel, solid steel frame. Imported 1990-1993.

	$810	$640	$550	$515	$465	$415	$375

Last Mfg.'s Sug. Retail was $950.

This model was also available in a carbine variation until 1992.

SHOTGUNS: SLIDE ACTION

MODEL 9104/9105 — 12 ga. only, features 20 in. barrel with bead sights, 5 shot mag. tube, uncheckered walnut stock and forearm. Mfg. 1994-96.

	$240	$195	$175	$160	$145	$130	$120

Last Mfg.'s Sug. Retail was $279.

Add $20 for adj. rear rifle sight (Model 9105).
Add $20 for interchangeable choke tube (Model 9104 only).

MODEL 9108/9109 — 12 ga. only, all-purpose self-defense model featuring 20 in. barrel with 7 shot mag., choice of military green (special order), brown walnut, or black regular or pistol grip stock and forearm. Mfg. 1994-96.

	$240	$195	$175	$160	$145	$130	$120

Last Mfg.'s Sug. Retail was $279.

Add $20 for adj. rear rifle sight (Model 9109).
Add $20 for interchangeable choke tube (Model 9108 only).

MODEL 9111/9113 — 12 ga. only, 18½ in. barrel with bead sights, 6 shot mag., choice of brown or green synthetic (special order), brown walnut or black regular or pistol grip stock and forearm. Mfg. 1994-96.

	$240	$195	$175	$160	$145	$130	$120

Last Mfg.'s Sug. Retail was $279.

Add $20 for adj. rear rifle sight (Model 9113).
Add $20 for interchangeable choke tube (Model 9111 only).

MODEL 9114 — 12 ga. only, designed for police and riot control, choice of synthetic pistol grip or top folding (disc. 1994) buttstock, 20 in. barrel with iron sights, 6 shot mag. Mfg. 1994-96.

	$295	$255	$210	$180	$160	$145	$130

Last Mfg.'s Sug. Retail was $349.

M

MODEL 9115 — 12 ga. only, design based on Special Air Services riot gun, 18½ in. barrel with vent. heat shield, parkerized finish, 6 shot mag., stealth grey stock featuring 4 shell storage. Mfg. 1994-96.

$295	$255	$210	$180	$160	$145	$130

Last Mfg.'s Sug. Retail was $349.

Add $20 for interchangeable choke tube.

MONTANA ARMORY, INC.

Current distributor of C. Sharps Arms Co. Inc. rifles located in Big Timber, MT. Please refer to the C. Sharps Arms Co. listing in the S section for more information.

MONTGOMERY WARD

Catalog sales/retailer that has subcontracted various domestic and international manufacturers to private label various brand names under the Montgomery Ward conglomerate.

Montgomery Ward shotguns and rifles have appeared under various labels and endorsers, including Western Field and others. There have literally been hundreds of various models (shotguns and rifles) sold through the Montgomery Ward retail network. Most of these models were manufactured through subcontracts with both domestic and international firearms manufacturers. Typically, they were "spec." guns made to sell at a specific price to undersell the competition. Most of these models were derivatives of existing factory models with less expensive wood and perhaps missing the features found on those models from which they were derived. Please refer to the Store Brand Crossover Section in the back of this book for converting Montgomery Ward models to the respective manufacturer.

To date, there has been very little interest in collecting Montgomery Ward guns, regardless of rarity. Rather than list Montgomery Ward models, a general guideline is that values generally are under those of their "1st generation relatives". As a result, prices are ascertained by the shooting value of the gun, rather than its collector value.

MORAVIA l.t.d.

Current manufacturer located in Ostrava, Czech Republic. No current importation. Moravia manufactures both semi-auto pistols (Models P83 Vanad and Mag 95) and rifles. Please contact the factory directly (see Trademark Index) for more information and domestic prices.

MORINI

Current target pistol manufacturer located in Bedano, Switzerland. Currently imported by Nygord Precision Products located in Prescott, AZ. Previously imported and distributed by Osborne's, located in Cheboygan, MI.

M **PISTOLS: .22 CAL. TARGET**

CM-80 STANDARD SINGLE SHOT — .22 LR cal. only, adj. grips, frame, and sights. Importation disc. 1989.

$925	$825	$725	$650	$585	$520	$465

Last Mfg.'s Sug. Retail was $1,015.

Add $50 for left-hand model.

* **CM-80 Super Competition** — similar to CM-80 Standard, except has deluxe finish, and unique plexiglass front sighting system. Importation disc. 1989.

$1,085	$920	$800	$690	$590	$520	$450

Last Mfg.'s Sug. Retail was $1,196.

Add $50 for left-hand model.

Grading	100%	98%	95%	90%	80%	70%	60%

CM-84E FREE PISTOL — .22 LR cal., single shot, anatomical grips, unique electronic trigger features optic beam safety.

Mfg.'s Sug. Retail	**$1,495**	**$1,325**	**$1,100**	**$925**	**$800**	**$675**	**$575**	**$495**

MODEL CM-102E SEMI-AUTO — .22 LR cal., advanced rapid fire competition pistol featuring updated ergonomic grips and flared trigger guard, first target pistol to utilize an electronic trigger. Mfg. 1992-97.

	$1,525	**$1,250**	**$995**	**$895**	**$795**	**$695**	**$595**

Last Mfg.'s Sug. Retail was $1,695.

MOSSBERG, O.F. & SONS, INC.

Current manufacturer located in North Haven, CT, 1964-present and New Haven, CT, 1919-1964. Mossberg acquired Advanced Ordnance Corp. during 1996, a high quality manufacturer utilizing state-of-the-art CNC machinery.

Oscar Mossberg developed an early reputation as a designer and inventor for the Iver Johnson, Marlin-Rockwell, Stevens and Shattuck Arms companies. In 1915, he began producing a 4-shot, .22 palm pistol known as the "Novelty," with revolving firing pin. After producing approx. 600 of these pistols, he sold the patent to C.S. Shattuck, which continued to manufacture under the name "Unique." The first 600 had no markings except serial numbers, and were destined for export to South America. Very few of these original "Novelty" pistols survived in this country, and are extremely rare specimens.

Since 1985, O.F. Mossberg & Sons, Inc. has produced only shotguns and accessories.

DERRINGERS

BROWNIE — .22 LR cal., top break open action, rotating firing pin, 4-bbl. derringer, double action, 4-shot, approx. 32,000 mfg. 1919-1932.

	$350	**$300**	**$275**	**$250**	**$205**	**$175**	**$150**

RIFLES: DISC.

The models listed below appear alphabetically first, followed by numerical models in sequence.

MODEL K — .22 S, L and LR cal., tube mag., hammerless, 22 in. bbl., takedown, open sights, plain straight stock. Mfg. 1922-1931.

	$250	**$225**	**$200**	**$175**	**$150**	**$100**	**$85**

MODEL M — similar to Model K, except has 24 in. octagonal bbl. Mfg. 1928-1931.

	$285	**$250**	**$200**	**$175**	**$150**	**$100**	**$85**

MODEL S — similar to Model K, except has shorter mag. tube and $19\frac{3}{4}$ in. bbl., very rare. Mfg. 1927-1931.

	$350	**$275**	**$225**	**$200**	**$175**	**$150**	**$135**

M

MODEL L — .22 S, L and LR cal., falling block action, single shot, 24 in. takedown bbl., open sights, pistol grip stock. Mfg. 1929-1932.

	$450	**$350**	**$300**	**$275**	**$200**	**$185**	**$165**

MODEL L-1 — rare target version of Model L with Lyman 2A tang sight and factory sling.

Add $50 to Model L values.

MODEL R — .22 S, L and LR cal., bolt action, 24 in. round bbl., first tube feed, ivory bead front sight, open sporting bbl. sight. Mfg. 1930-1932.

	$250	**$225**	**$200**	**$175**	**$150**	**$100**	**$85**

Grading	100%	98%	95%	90%	80%	70%	60%

MODEL B — .22 S, L and LR cal., single shot, bolt action, 22 in. round tapered bbl. Mfg. 1930-1932.

	$165	$125	$100	$75	$60	$50	$35

MODEL C — .22 S, L and LR cal., single shot, 24 in. bbl., ivory bead front sight, open sporting rear sight. Mfg. 1931-1932.

	$165	$125	$100	$75	$60	$50	$35

MODEL C-1 — target version of Model C, Lyman front and rear sights, leather sling and swivels, special walnut stock, rare.

Add $50 to Model C values.

MODELS 10, 14, 20, 21, 25, 25A, 125 — .22 S, L and LR cal., single shot models. Mfg. 1933-1938.

	$165	$125	$100	$75	$60	$50	$35

Add 25% to prices above for models equipped with aperture sights.

MODEL 26B — .22 S, L and LR cal., entirely new design in single shot rifles, easily identified by bolt handle at extreme rear of bolt, 26 in. tapered bbl., hooded ramp front sight, No. 4 rear peep, open bbl. sight, swivels. Mfg. 1938-1941.

	$165	$125	$100	$75	$60	$50	$35

MODEL 26-C — similar to Model 26B with less expensive sights. Mfg. 1938-1941.

	$140	$100	$85	$70	$55	$45	$35

MODEL 26M (OR B26M) — rare version of 26 series model with two-piece Mannlicher-style stock. Mfg. 1938.

	$185	$140	$125	$100	$85	$70	$55

MODEL 30 — .22 S, L and LR cal., single shot, 24 in. bbl., rear peep and ramp front sights, swivels. Mfg. 1933-1935.

	$140	$100	$90	$75	$65	$55	$45

MODEL 34 — similar to Model 30, except with heavy stock, target style. Mfg. 1934-1935.

	$150	$110	$100	$85	$70	$55	$45

MODEL 35 — .22 S, L, LR cal., single shot, first full target model, 26 in. heavy target bbl., walnut stock, hooded front ramp, No. 4 rear peep with adj. aperture, approx. 9½ lbs. Mfg. 1935-1937.

	$275	$225	$200	$175	$150	$125	$90

MODEL 35A — revised version of Model 35, with all-new "master action," approx. 8¼ lbs. Mfg. 1937.

	$275	$235	$210	$185	$160	$135	$110

Add 25% for Model 35A-LS with Lyman sights.

MODEL 40 — .22 S, L, and LR cal., repeater with tube mag., 16 shot, 24 in. bbl., No. 3 Mossberg aperture sight, hooded ramp front sight, swivels, approx. 5 lbs. Mfg. 1933-1935.

	$125	$100	$90	$80	$70	$65	$60

MODEL 44 — similar to Model 40, but with heavier target stock, approx. 6 lbs. Mfg. 1934-1935.

	$150	$125	$100	$90	$80	$70	$65

MODEL 42 — .22 S, L, and LR cal., first model with 7 rd. magazine, 24 in. bbl., front ramp, sporting bbl., rear aperture sights, 42 in. overall length, approx. 5 lbs. Mfg. 1935-1937.

	$125	$100	$90	$80	$70	$65	$60

MODEL 42A — redesign of Model 42, new master action with shorter bolt and receiver. Mfg. 1937-1938.

	$150	$125	$100	$90	$80	$70	$65

MODEL 42B — same basic specs. as Model 42A, approx. 6 lbs. Mfg. 1938-1941.

	$150	$125	$100	$90	$80	$70	$65

M

Grading	100%	98%	95%	90%	80%	70%	60%

MODEL 42C — similar to Model 42B, with open bbl. and bead front sights. Mfg. 1938-1941.

	$110	$100	$90	$80	$65	$55	$45

MODEL 42M — .22 S, L and LR cal., 7-shot magazine, bolt action, two-piece Mannlicher-style stock, 23 in. bbl., 40 in. overall length, 6¾ lb., front ramp, open bbl., receiver aperture sights, trapdoor buttplate for extra mag. in butt stock. Mfg. 1940-1944.

	$175	$150	$135	$110	$100	$75	$50

Add $40 for extra magazine in butt stock.

MODEL 42M(a), 42M(b), 42M(c) — similar to Model 42M with minor changes in extractors and sights. Mfg. 1944-1950.

	$175	$150	$135	$110	$100	$75	$50

MODEL 42MB — military version of the Model 42M, approx. 50,000 mfg. for US and British troops as a training rifle. US Property marked with serial number, usually found w/o bbl. sight. Mfg. 1942-1943.

	$200	$175	$150	$135	$110	$100	$75

Add $50 for Lend-Lease models with British proofs.

MODEL L42A — left-handed version of Model 42A with true left-handed aperture sight, walnut stock, 1¼ in. swivels. Mfg. 1937-1938.

	$225	$200	$175	$150	$135	$125	$100

MODEL 43 — .22 S, L and LR cal., target rifle, 7-round magazine, external trigger adjustment, 13/16 in. diameter barrel, 26 in. long walnut stock with four-position 1¼ in. swivels in front, Lyman 17A front sight, Lyman 57 MS receiver peep sight, rare. Mfg. 1937-1938.

	$250	$225	$200	$185	$175	$150	$135

MODEL L43 — left-handed version of Model 43 target rifle with left-handed Lyman 57 MS rear aperture sight, rare. Mfg. 1937-1938.

	$350	$335	$300	$275	$250	$225	$200

Add $75 for models with true left-handed Mossberg scope.

MODEL 44B — .22 S, L, LR cal. target model, clip fed, 26 in. heavy bbl., 43 in. overall length, approx. 8 lbs., front ramp and No. 4 receiver aperture sights, four-position front swivels, walnut stock. Mfg. 1938-1941.

	$250	$225	$200	$185	$175	$150	$135

MODEL 44US — .22 S, L, LR cal. target model, 7 round magazine, bolt action, 26 in. heavy bbl., overall length 43 in., approx. 8½ lbs., ramp front sight with hood, rear aperture sight, detachable swivels. Mfg. 1943-45.

	$200	$185	$175	$165	$150	$135	$125

MODEL 44US (US PROPERTY MARKED) — used by all branches of military for target training, approx. 53,000 mfg. 1943-1944.

	$320	$295	$260	$230	$215	$190	$170

MODEL 44US(a), 44US(b), 44US(c), 44US(d) — same rifle as 44US with minor changes in sights and extractors. Mfg. 1944-1949.

	$200	$185	$175	$165	$150	$135	$125

M

MODEL 45 — .22 S, L and LR cal., tube fed, bolt action, 24 in. heavy target bbl., overall length 42½ in., approx. 6¾ lbs., hooded front sight, sporting bbl. sight, receiver aperture sight. Mfg. 1935-1937.

	$175	$150	$135	$125	$100	$85	$65

MODEL 45-A — similar to Model 45 with newer, master action. Mfg. 1937-38.

	$175	$150	$135	$125	$100	$85	$65

MODEL L45-A — similar to Model 45-A, true left-handed version. Mfg. 1937-1938.

	$225	$200	$175	$150	$135	$125	$100

Grading	100%	98%	95%	90%	80%	70%	60%

MODEL 46 — .22 S, L and LR cal., tube fed, bolt action, 26 in. heavy bbl., overall 44½ in., beavertail walnut stock, hooded ramp front, rear aperture sight, 7½ lbs. Mfg. 1935-1937.

	$175	$150	$135	$125	$100	$85	$65

MODEL 46T — similar to Model 46 with heavier bbl. and stock. Mfg. 1936-1937.

	$200	$175	$150	$135	$125	$100	$75

MODEL 46A — similar to Model 46 with master action. Mfg. 1937-1938.

	$175	$150	$135	$125	$100	$85	$65

MODEL 46-ALS — similar to Model 46-A with Lyman 17A front sight and 57 MS rear aperture, rare. Mfg. 1937-1938.

	$225	$200	$175	$150	$125	$110	$100

MODEL L46-ALS — similar to Model 46-ALS with true left-handed action and left-handed Lyman rear sight, very rare. Mfg. 1937-1938.

	$325	$300	$275	$250	$225	$200	$175

MODEL 46B — .22 S, L and LR cal., tube fed, new streamlined design, 43⅓ in. overall, walnut stock, 7 lbs. Mfg. 1938-1945.

	$150	$135	$110	$100	$85	$75	$65

MODEL 46B-T — heavy barrel and stock, target version of Model 46-B, rare. Mfg. 1938.

	$200	$175	$150	$135	$110	$95	$85

MODEL 46M — .22 S, L and LR cal., bolt action, tube fed, with two-piece Mannlicher-style walnut stock, 23 in. bbl., overall 40 in., hooded front, sporting bbl., rear aperture sight, 7 lbs. Mfg. 1940-1945.

	$185	$150	$135	$125	$110	$95	$80

MODEL 46M(a), 46M(b) — similar to Model 46M with minor changes in sights. Mfg. 1945-1952.

	$185	$150	$135	$125	$110	$95	$80

MODEL 50 — .22 S, L, LR cal., semi-auto, tube fed through butt stock, 24 in. bbl., overall 43¾ in., hooded front sight, open bbl. sight, no swivels, 6¾ lbs. Mfg. 1939-1942.

	$165	$150	$135	$125	$110	$85	$65

MODEL 51 — similar to Model 50 with receiver aperture sight, heavier, beavertail stock, q.d. swivels, 7¼ lbs. Mfg. 1939.

	$165	$150	$135	$125	$110	$85	$65

MODEL 51M — similar to Model 51 with two-piece Mannlicher style walnut stock, 20 in. bbl, 40 in. overall, front ramp, rear aperture, sporting bbl. sights, 7 lbs. Mfg. 1939-1946.

	$185	$150	$135	$125	$110	$95	$80

MODEL 140B — .22 S, L and LR cal., bolt action, clip fed, 24½ in. bbl., 42 in. overall, walnut stock, front ramp, sporting bbl., rear aperture sight, 5¾ lbs. Mfg. 1957-1958.

	$165	$150	$135	$125	$110	$85	$65

MODEL 140K — similar to Model 140B with post front and no aperture sight. Mfg. 1955-1958.

	$135	$100	$90	$80	$70	$60	$50

MODEL 142A — .22 S, L and LR cal., bolt action, 7 round clip, carbine model with fold down forearm, walnut stock with sling, 18 in. bbl., 27 in. overall length, rear aperture sight and military front sight, no bbl. sight, early models had "T" shaped bolt handles and wood forearms, later models had round knob bolt handle and black plastic forearm, 5 lbs. Mfg. 1949-1957.

	$165	$150	$135	$125	$110	$85	$65

MODEL 142K — similar to Model 142A with less expensive sights, sporting barrel and post front type. No aperture sight. Mfg. 1953-1957.

	$125	$110	$100	$90	$80	$75	$55

Grading	100%	98%	95%	90%	80%	70%	60%

MODEL 144 — .22 S, L, LR cal., full target rifle, heavy 26 in. bbl., 43 in. overall length, 8 lbs., q.d. swivels, four-position front swivels, rear aperture, front ramp sights, "T" shaped bolt handle. Mfg. 1949-1954.

	$200	$185	$165	$150	$135	$125	$110

MODEL 144LS — similar to Model 144, with round knob handle, Lyman 57 MS rear aperture and 17 A front sight. Mfg. 1954-1960.

	$250	$235	$220	$200	$185	$165	$150

MODEL 144LS-A — similar to Model 144LS, with Mossberg S 130 rear aperture in place of Lyman 57 MS. Mfg. 1960-1979.

	$200	$185	$165	$150	$135	$125	$110

MODEL 144LS-B — last generation of 144 series, 27 in. bbl., 15/16 in. diameter, 44 in. overall length, new Mossberg S 331 aperture, Lyman 17 A front sight, 8½ lbs. Mfg. 1979-1985.

	$275	$250	$235	$210	$190	$175	$165

MODEL 146-B — .22 S, L and LR cal., bolt action, tube fed, capacity of 30S, 23L, 20LR, 26 in. bbl., overall length 43¼ in., ramp front sight, leaf bbl. and rear aperture sight, walnut Monte Carlo stock with cheekpiece, QD swivels, adj. trigger, Schnabel forend, 7 lbs. Mfg. 1949-1954.

	$180	$150	$135	$125	$100	$85	$65

MODEL 146B-A — similar to Model 146-B, with different bbl. sight. Mfg. 1954-1958.

	$180	$150	$135	$125	$100	$85	$65

MODEL 151-K — .22 S, L, LR cal., semi-auto, butt fed, 24 in. bbl., overall 44 in., open sights, walnut Monte Carlo stock with cheekpiece and Schnabel forend, 6 lbs. Mfg. 1950-1951.

	$160	$135	$110	$90	$80	$70	$60

MODEL 151(M) — .22 S, L, LR cal., semi-auto butt fed, capacity 15LR, 20 in. bbl., overall 40 in., two-piece Mannlicher-style walnut stock, QD swivels, steel butt plate, hooded ramp front, sporting rear, micro-click aperture sights, 7 lbs. Mfg. 1946-1947.

	$175	$150	$135	$125	$100	$85	$65

MODELS 151M(a), 151M(b), 151M(c) — similar to Model 151M with minor changes in butt plate and sights. Mfg. 1947-1958.

	$175	$150	$135	$125	$100	$85	$65

MODEL 152 — .22 S, L, LR cal., semi-auto, clip fed with 7 round capacity, carbine model with hinged, fold-down forend, Monte Carlo stock with adj. sling, 18 in. bbl., 27 in. overall, receiver aperture and military post front sights, 5 lbs. Mfg. 1948-1952.

	$175	$150	$135	$125	$100	$85	$65

MODEL 152K — similar to Model 152 with open sights. Mfg. 1950-1957.

	$150	$125	$110	$100	$90	$75	$50

MODEL 320B — .22 S, L, LR cal., single shot, junior target model, bolt action, new closed breech design, 24 in. bbl., overall 43½ in., 5¾ lbs., walnut finish Monte Carlo stock with swivels and pistol grip, front ramp, rear aperture and sporting bbl. sights. Mfg. 1960-1971.

	$165	$140	$125	$110	$85	$75	$55

M

MODELS 320K, 320K-A — similar to Model 320B with open sights, no swivels, later models marked 321, 321K. Mfg. 1960-1980.

	$105	$95	$80	$70	$60	$55	$50

MODELS 340B, 340B-A — .22 S, L, LR cal., bolt action, 7 round clip magazine, 24 in. bbl., 43½ in. overall length, walnut, Monte Carlo stock with cheekpiece and pistol grip, front ramp, sporting bbl., rear aperture sights, 6½ lbs. Mfg. 1958-1980.

	$165	$140	$125	$110	$85	$75	$55

Grading	100%	98%	95%	90%	80%	70%	60%

MODELS 340K, 340K-A — similar to Model 340B with open sights, later models marked 341. Mfg. 1958-1980.

	$105	$95	$80	$70	$60	$55	$50

MODEL 340M — .22 S, L, LR cal. bolt action, clip fed, same operating design as other 340 series, with one-piece, walnut Mannlicher-style Monte Carlo stock with pistol grip and swivels, 18½ in. bbl., 38½ in. overall, open rear and bead front sights, rare, 5¼ lbs. Mfg. 1970-1972.

	$250	$235	$210	$200	$185	$175	$165

MODEL 342 — .22 S, L and LR cal., bolt action, clip fed, carbine model with hinged, black plastic, fold-down forend, walnut Monte Carlo stock with swivels and sling, 18 in. bbl., 38 in. overall, military post front and rear aperture sight, 5 lbs. Mfg. 1957-1959.

	$165	$140	$125	$110	$85	$75	$55

MODELS 342K, 342K-A — similar to Model 342 with open sights. Mfg. 1958-1971.

	$105	$95	$80	$70	$60	$55	$50

MODEL 344, 344K — .22 S, L, LR cal., bolt action, clip fed, walnut finish, checkered stock, 344K is carbine length. Mfg. 1985.

	$165	$140	$125	$110	$85	$75	$55

MODEL 346B — .22 S, L, and LR cal., bolt action tube feed, closed-breech design, walnut Monte Carlo stock with cheekpiece, QD swivels, capacity 25S, 20L, 18LR, 24 in. bbl., 42½ in. overall, rear aperture, sporting bbl., hooded front ramp sights, 6½ lbs. Mfg. 1958-1960.

	$165	$140	$125	$110	$85	$75	$55

MODEL 346K, 346K-A — similar to Model 346B w/ open sights. Mfg. 1958-1968.

	$135	$120	$110	$100	$80	$70	$55

MODEL 350K — .22 LR cal., semi-auto, LR only, clip fed, walnut Monte Carlo stock with pistol grip and cheekpiece, 23½ in. bbl., overall 43½ in., open sights, 6 lbs. Mfg. 1958-1960.

	$95	$85	$75	$65	$60	$50	$40

MODEL 350 K-A — similar to Model 350K with dovetail bbl. sight. Mfg. 1960-1968.

	$95	$85	$75	$65	$60	$50	$40

MODEL 351K — .22 LR cal., semi-auto, tube fed through stock, walnut, Monte Carlo stock with pistol grip, 24 in. bbl., 43 in. overall, 6 lbs. Mfg. 1958-1960.

	$95	$85	$75	$65	$60	$50	$40

MODEL 351K-A — similar to Model 351K with dovetail bbl. sight. Mfg. 1960-68.

	$95	$85	$75	$65	$60	$50	$40

MODEL 352 — .22 LR cal., clip fed, carbine model with fold-down black plastic forend, walnut Monte Carlo stock, pistol grip, swivels, web strap, 18 in. bbl., overall 38 in., rear peep, post front sights, 5 lbs. Mfg. 1957-1959.

	$135	$120	$100	$85	$75	$65	$55

MODELS 352K, 352 K-A, 352K-B — similar to Model 352 with open sights. Mfg. 1960-1971.

	$110	$95	$85	$75	$70	$65	$55

MODEL 377, "PLINKSTER" — .22 LR cal., semi-auto, tube fed, synthetic stock with "thumb hole," capacity 15 rds., 20 in. bbl., overall 40 in., 6.25 lbs., equipped with 4X scope. Mfg. 1977-1979.

	$175	$150	$135	$100	$85	$75	$65

MODELS 380, 380S — same basic design as Model 377, only with solid, wood stock, open sights. Model 480 same in 1985. Mfg. 1980-1985.

	$135	$115	$100	$85	$75	$65	$55

M

Grading	100%	98%	95%	90%	80%	70%	60%

MODEL 400 "PALAMINO" — .22 S, L and LR cal., lever action, tube fed, walnut, beavertail stock and forearm, cross bolt safety, 24 in. bbl., overall length, 41 in., bead front, open rear sights, 5½ lbs. Mfg. 1959-1964.

	$225	$195	$170	$150	$135	$100	$85

Model 400-A similar to above in specs and value, dovetail.

MODEL 402 — carbine version of Model 400, bbl. 20 in. Mfg. 1961-1971.

	$225	$195	$170	$150	$135	$100	$85

MODEL 430 — .22 LR cal., semi-auto, tubular mag. under bbl. with capacity of 18 LR, walnut checkered Monte Carlo stock and checkered forend, 24 in. bbl., overall length 43½ in., open sights, 6.25 lbs. Mfg. 1970-1971.

	$135	$115	$100	$85	$75	$65	$55

MODEL 432 — similar to Model 430 above with 20 in. bbl., straight grip, smooth stock and forend, walnut finish. Mfg. 1970-1971.

	$115	$100	$85	$75	$65	$60	$50

MODEL 472 — .30-30 Win. or .35 Rem. cal., lever action carbine, 20 in. barrel, open sights, pistol grip or straight stock, saddle ring on straight model. Mfg. 1972-disc.

	$180	$155	$145	$130	$120	$110	$90

MODEL 472 RIFLE — similar to Carbine, except 24 in. barrel, pistol grip stock. Mfg. 1974-1976.

	$195	$165	$155	$145	$130	$120	$100

MODEL 472 BRUSH GUN — similar to Carbine, except 18 in. barrel, straight stock only. Mfg. 1974-1976.

	$195	$165	$155	$145	$130	$120	$100

MODEL 472 ONE IN FIVE THOUSAND — similar to Brush Gun, except Indian scene etched on receiver, brass butt plate, saddle ring and barrel bands, select stock, only 5,000 mfg., 1974.

	$415	$210	$195	$175	$165	$145	$120

MODEL 479 PCA — .30-30 Win. cal., lever action, 20 in. barrel, 6 shot capacity.

	$195	$135	$120	$110	$95	$85	$75

MODEL 479 RR — limited edition "Roy Rogers" signature model, gold trigger, barrel bands, 5,000 total mfg. New 1983.

	$350	$275	$215				

MODEL 479 — .30-30 Win. cal. only, lever action, 6 shot tube mag., 20 in. barrel with adj. sights, 7 lbs. Mfg. 1985 only.

	$190	$175	$160	$150	$145	$140	$135

Last Mfg.'s Sug. Retail was $232.

Mossberg also has made several .22 bolt action and semi-auto sporters that are in the $115 - $130 price range. While they are good shooting models, they are not covered in this section as they are not collectible.

MODEL 480 — similar to Models 380 and 380S.

	$135	$115	$100	$85	$75	$65	$55

MODEL 620K — .22 Mag. cal., single shot, bolt action, walnut Monte Carlo stock, pistol grip, cheekpiece, sling swivels, 24 in. bbl., overall 44¾ in., open rear, post front sights, 6 lbs. Mfg. 1959-1960.

	$150	$135	$115	$100	$85	$75	$65

MODEL 620K-A — similar to Model 620K with change in bbl. sight. Mfg. 1960-1968.

	$150	$135	$115	$100	$85	$75	$65

MODELS 640K, 640K-S — similar to 620 series, but 5 shot clip repeater. Mfg. 1959-1984.

	$195	$150	$135	$125	$105	$90	$75

Grading	100%	98%	95%	90%	80%	70%	60%

MODEL 640KS — similar to Model 640K with deluxe checkered stock and gold trigger. Mfg. 1960-1968.

	$225	$200	$185	$150	$135	$120	$110

MODEL 640M — full length, Mannlicher-styled stock, version of 640, checkered stock, Monte Carlo, cheekpiece, pistol grip, swivels and leather strap, heavy receiver, jeweled bolt, 20 in. bbl., overall 40¾ in., open rear sights, bead front, 6 lbs. Mfg. 1971.

	$250	$225	$200	$185	$175	$165	$150

MODEL 642K — .22 Mag. cal., carbine style, bolt action, 5 rd. clip, fold-down forend, walnut stock with web sling, 18 in. bbl., overall 38¼ in., open bbl. and bead front sights, 5 lbs. Mfg. 1960-1968.

	$225	$200	$185	$150	$135	$120	$110

MODEL 800 — .222 Rem., .22-250 Rem., .243 Win., or .308 Win. cal., bolt action, 22 in. barrel, folding sight, checkered pistol grip stock. Mfg. 1967-disc.

	$220	$195	$165	$110	$85	$55	$45

MODEL 800VT — similar to 800, except .222 Rem., .22-250 Rem., or .243 Win. cal., 24 in. heavy barrel, no sights. Mfg. 1968-disc.

	$220	$195	$165	$110	$85	$55	$45

MODEL 800M — similar to 800, except 20 in. barrel, full length stock, spoon bolt handle. Mfg. 1969-1972.

	$275	$240	$220	$205	$175	$160	$145

MODEL 800D — similar to 800, with roll-over combination and cheekpiece, checkered stock with rosewood forearm tip and pistol cap, no .222 Rem. available. Mfg. 1970-1973.

	$325	$300	$275	$250	$225	$200	$165

MODEL 810 — .270 Win., .30-06, 6.5mm Rem. Mag., or .338 Win. Mag. cal., bolt action, 22 or 24 in. barrel, rear leaf sight, checkered Monte Carlo stock. Mfg. 1970-disc.

	$300	$275	$250	$225	$200	$175	$150

RIFLES: BOLT ACTION, RECENT PRODUCTION

In 1985, Mossberg purchased the parts inventory and importing rights for those rifles that Smith & Wesson imported from Howa of Japan. These new models were identical to those models which S&W disc.

MODEL 1500 MOUNTAINEER GRADE I — .223 Rem., .243 Win., .270 Win., .30-06, or 7mm Rem. Mag. cal., bolt action, 22 or 24 (7mm Rem. Mag. only) in. barrel, 5 or 6 shot mag., available with or without sights, hardwood stock is satin finished, blued finish, about 7 lbs. 10 oz. Imported 1986-87 only. Add $15 for 7mm Rem. Mag. cal., $25 for iron sights.

	$285	$250	$225	$195	$180	$165	$150

Last Mfg.'s Sug. Retail was $335.

* **Model 1500 Varmint** — .22-250 Rem., .223 Rem., or .308 Win. cal., similar to Model 1500 Grade I, except has 24 in. heavy barrel only, Monte Carlo stock. Imported 1986-87 only. Add $10 for parkerized finish (oil finished stock with swivels — not available in .22-250 Rem. cal.).

	$360	$300	$270	$235	$205	$190	$175

Last Mfg.'s Sug. Retail was $457.

Blued finish and high gloss wood finish available with .22-250 Rem. or .223 Rem. cal. only. Parkerized variation is available in .223 Rem. or .308 Win. cal. only (matte wood finish, includes swivels).

MODEL 1500 MOUNTAINEER GRADE II — similar to Grade I Mountaineer, except has select checkered American walnut stock. Also available in .300 Win. Mag. or .338 Win. Mag. cal. Imported 1986-87 only.

	$315	$270	$235	$205	$190	$175	$160

Last Mfg.'s Sug. Retail was $368.

Add $15 for Mag. cals.
Add $25 for iron sights.

M

Grading	100%	98%	95%	90%	80%	70%	60%

MODEL 1550 — similar to Model 1500, except has detachable mag. and available in standard cals. (.243 Win., .270 Win., or .30-06), with or without sights. Imported 1986-87 only. Add $24 for iron sights.

	$330	$280	$245	$210	$190	$175	$160

Last Mfg.'s Sug. Retail was $391.

MODEL 1700 LS — .243 Win., .270 Win., or .30-06 cal., no sights, jeweled bolt body and knurled bolt handle, detachable mag., Schnabel forend, deluxe checkering, 7 lbs. Imported 1986-87 only.

	$405	$365	$310	$275	$240	$205	$190

Last Mfg.'s Sug. Retail was $492.

Mossberg "Targo" Smoothbore Models

These dual-purpose smoothbore rifles were designed to fire both .22 RF bullets and shotshell ammunition. Targo barrels are threaded either externally (Models 26T, 42TR, 42T, B42T) or internally (Models 320TR, 340TR) at the muzzle for attachment of rifled and smoothbore adapters which enable the shooter to use the gun as a standard rifle, or (with the smoothbore adapter installed) as a miniature shotgun. Mossberg produced a line of Targo accessories including a barrel-mounted miniature clay target launcher, a pistol grip hand trap frame, a hand thrower, a target carrier, clay targets, hard rubber "practice" targets, and a target catching net. The presence of one or more of these accessories augments the value of any model Targo gun. Prices quoted below are for guns with all listed features exclusive of Targo accessories.

MODEL 26-T SINGLE SHOT — .22 RF/shotshell cal., bolt action, thumb lever safety located at rear of bolt, black plastic buttplate and contoured black plastic triggerguard (#R413), rifle-style open rear sight with screw adjustments for windage and elevation, shotgun style elevated front bead sight with removable sight hood, smoothbore and rifled screw-on barrel adapters and spanner wrench for adapter removal and installation, stock generally provided with sling swivels, forend necks down toward muzzle, takedown screw has retaining bail to facilitate removal by hand. Mfg. 1940-42 (only 873 mfg.).

	$600	$450	$375	$335	$280	$245	$220

100% price is estimated since an example would be extremely rare.

MODEL 42T BOLT ACTION REPEATER — .22 RF/shotshell cal., box magazine (7-round) fitted with adapter screw to enable firing of .22 Short cartridges, same safety, buttplate, optional stock swivels, and shotgun style front sight as Model 26T, #R145 contoured black plastic triggerguard, supplied with the smoothbore barrel adapter only (rifled adapter, open rear sight, and front sight hood were not provided), produced 1940-42 (906 guns made), examples in 95% or better condition are uncommon.

	$440	$325	$310	$295	$260	$235	$200

MODEL 42TR BOLT ACTION REPEATER — .22 RF/shotshell cal., produced before and after WWII until roughly 1949. Pre-War (1940-42) guns identical to Model 42T except rifled adapter, open rear sight, and front sight hood were provided, and no stock swivels. The earliest pre-War 42TRs were marked using a 42T barrel stamp and a separate "R" (stamped to the right of the "T"). Post-War (1946-49) guns have slotted takedown screw, magazine plate, shorter unnecked forend, and (frequently) a blued bolt knob. The most common of all Targo guns. A total of 6,577 guns were produced during the period 1940-42 (post-War production figures are not available). Both early and late versions of this model are comparably priced.

	$415	$345	$295	$280	$245	$190	$175

Add $250 for cased gun with clay targets and Targo accessories.

Note: A very small number of 42TRs were supplied with fitted cases and Targo accessories and were used as dealer displays. The pre-War 42TR display guns came in a hard (plywood) luggage case. The post-War guns were supplied in a semi-hard (fiberboard) luggage case. Less than a dozen cased 42TRs are known to exist, though others may surface in the future.

M

Grading	100%	98%	95%	90%	80%	70%	60%

MODEL B42T BOLT ACTION REPEATER — .22 RF/shotshell cal., identical to the Model 42TR, except stock has sling swivels and metal buttplate with trapdoor for magazine storage. Gun was supplied with extended 15-round box magazine in addition to the standard 7-round clip. A comparatively scarce model marketed exclusively through mail order stores (e.g., Spiegel) in the early 1940s. According to factory records, only 250 guns were made, all in 1940.

	$465	$385	$350	$325	$285	$250	$210

MODEL 320TR SINGLE SHOT BOLT ACTION — .22 RF/shotshell, automatic safety with thumb lever located on right side of receiver, black plastic buttplate and contoured black plastic triggerguard. Rifle-style ("U" notch) rear sight adjustable for elevation (via sliding wedge) and windage (by deflecting sight arm laterally by hand). Sporting type vertical blade front sight. Gun supplied with rifled and smoothbore screw-in barrel adapters. A wire target carrier and a hand thrower for launching miniature clay targets were included with each gun. Mfg. 1961-62.

	$320	$240	$225	$190	$150	$135	$115

MODEL 340TR BOLT ACTION REPEATER — .22 RF/shotshell cal., 7-round box magazine featuring adjustable top bar to accommodate feeding of .22 S, L, and LR cartridges. Two known variations of thumb lever safety markings (words "OFF"/"ON" and red dot). Other features identical to Model 320TR. Mfg. 1961-62.

	$345	$265	$240	$215	$165	$145	$125

SHOTGUNS: BOLT ACTION - DISC.

MODELS G-4, 70, 73, 73B — .410 bore, single shot, mfg. 1932-1940.

	$110	$100	$85	$70	$60	$50	$40

MODELS 80, 83, 83B, 83D — .410 bore, 3 or 4 shot, internal top-loading mag., mfg. 1933-1946.

	$135	$110	$95	$75	$60	$50	$40

MODELS 75, 75A, 75B — 20 ga., bolt action, single shot, mfg. 1933-1940.

	$110	$100	$85	$70	$60	$50	$40

MODELS 85, 85A, 85B, 85D — 20 ga., 2 or 3 shot mag., mfg. 1934-1940.

	$110	$100	$85	$70	$60	$50	$40

MODELS 173, 173A, 173Y — .410 bore, single shot, "Y" designates youth model, mfg. 1957-1973.

	$110	$100	$85	$70	$60	$50	$40

MODELS 183, 183D, 283D(a), 183D-B, 183D-C, 183D-D, 183D-E, 183D-F, 183K, 183K-B, 183K-C, 183T, 184T, 184TY, 283T, 284T, 284TY — .410 bore, bolt action shotgun, 2 or 3 shot mag., various screw-on or C-Lect choke on some models, mfg. 1948-1985.

	$125	$110	$95	$75	$60	$55	$50

M

MODELS 185, 185D, 185D-A, 185D-B, 185D-C, 185K, 185K-A, 185K-B — 20 ga., 2 shot 2¾ in. mag., various screw-on or C-Lect chokes, mfg. 1947-1959.

	$125	$110	$95	$75	$60	$55	$50

MODELS 190, 190D, 190D-A, 190K-A, 190K-B — 16 ga., bolt action, 2 shot 2¾ in. mag., various screw-on or C-Lect choke, mfg. 1955-1958.

	$125	$110	$95	$75	$60	$55	$50

MODELS 195, 195A, 195K-A, 195D — same as model 185 Series above, only 12 ga. version, mfg. 1954-1968.

	$125	$110	$95	$75	$60	$55	$50

MODELS 385, 385K, 385KA, 385T, 485A, 485B — 20 ga., bolt action, 3 in. chamber, detachable box mag., mfg. 1960-1986.

	$125	$110	$95	$75	$60	$55	$50

Grading	100%	98%	95%	90%	80%	70%	60%

MODELS 390, 390K-A, 390K-B, 490A — 16 ga., 3 in. chamber, detachable box mag., mfg. 1971-1976.

	$125	$110	$95	$75	$60	$55	$50

MODELS 395, 395K, 395KA, 395S, 395 SPL., 495A, 495B — 12 ga., 3 in. chamber, detachable box mag., mfg. 1963-1983.

	$125	$110	$95	$75	$60	$55	$50

Add $40 for slug barrel ("S" designation) or 38 in. barrel (spl.).

MODELS 595, 595K — 12 ga., bolt action, special police stock, 4 shot mag., mfg. 1983-1985.

	$175	$150	$135	$110	$95	$85	$75

Add $40 for 38 in. barrel (Spl.).

SHOTGUNS: RECENT PRODUCTION

In 1985, Mossberg purchased the parts inventory and manufacturing rights for the shotguns that Smith & Wesson discontinued in 1984. These new models (manufactured in Japan) are identical to those models which S&W discontinued. Parts and warranties are not interchangeable.

During 1994, to celebrate their 75th anniversary, Mossberg released a new Crown Grade variation within most models, including the 500 and 835 Series, which can be differentiated from previous manufacture by cut checkering, redesigned walnut or American hardwood stocks and forearms, screw-in choke tubes, and 4 different camo patterns.

MODEL 200K SLIDE ACTION — slide action shotgun, 12 ga., 28 in., select choke, plain pistol grip stock, black nylon slide handle. Mfg. 1955-1959.

	$130	$110	$100	$90	$65	$55	$40

MODEL 200D — similar to 200K, except interchangeable choke tubes (2). Mfg. 1955-1959.

	$130	$110	$100	$90	$65	$55	$40

MODEL 500 HOME SECURITY SLIDE ACTION — 20 (1996 only) ga. or .410 bore, 18½ in. barrel with spreader choke, Model 500 slide-action, 5 shot mag., blued metal finish, synthetic field stock with pistol grip forearm, 6¼ lbs. New 1990.

Mfg.'s Sug. Retail	$304						
		$255	$215	$190	$165	$145	$125	$110

* *Laser Home Security .410* — includes laser sighting device in right front of forearm. Mfg. 1990-1993.

	$400	$350	$315	$280	$250	$225	$195

Last Mfg.'s Sug. Retail was $451.

MODEL 500 SLIDE ACTION REGAL SERIES — 12 or 20 ga., slide action, 26 or 28 in. barrel, select checkered walnut, VR. Add $19 for Accu-choke. Disc. 1987.

	$240	$195	$175	$165	$155	$145	$135

Last Mfg.'s Sug. Retail was $286.

Add $39 for Combo pack (includes 1 extra 24 in. slugster barrel).

MODEL 500 SLIDE ACTION FIELD — 12, 20 ga., or .410 bore, slide action, 24 in. (with rifle sights) or 20-28 in. barrel (with various chokes), upper receiver slide safety, C Lect (disc.) & Accu-Choke (became standard 1994) choke system, checkered hardwood pistol grip stock after 1973. Mfg. 1962-1998.

	$250	$200	$165	$135	$120	$110	$100

Last Mfg.'s Sug. Retail was $309.

Subtract 10% if without VR (disc.).
Subtract 10% for fixed choke barrel in 12 or 20 ga.

* *Model 500 Slugster* — 12 or 20 (disc. 1997) ga., 24 in. cyl. (disc. 1997) or rifled bore (became standard 1998) barrel, barrel porting became standard in 1998, choice of sights, walnut finished hardwood stock and forearm. Disc. 1998.

	$270	$220	$175	$145	$125	$110	$100

Last Mfg.'s Sug. Retail was $336.

Subtract $75 if w/o barrel porting or rifled bore.

M

Grading	100%	98%	95%	90%	80%	70%	60%

* **Model 500 Bantam** — 20 ga. or .410 bore (new 1991) only, 22 in. (20 ga.), 24 in. fixed choke barrel (.410 bore), or 26 in. VR barrel with Accu-choke(s), blue or blue matte (disc.), Bantam Jake with Realtree Camo finish in 20 ga./22 in. VR barrel only (disc.), 20 ga. has walnut finish stock and .410 bore has synthetic stock (both stocks are tailored for youth dimensions), 6.9 lbs. Mfg. 1990-96, reintroduced 1998 only.

	$240	**$195**	**$165**	**$135**	**$120**	**$110**	**$100**

Last Mfg.'s Sug. Retail was $312.

> Subtract $12 for .410 bore.
> Add $45 for Bantam Jake configuration (disc. 1993).

* **Model 500 Turkey** — 12 or 20 (new 1995) ga., 22 (20 ga. only), or 24 in. barrel, Woodlands metal/wood camo finish. Disc. 1997.

	$265	**$195**	**$150**

Last Mfg.'s Sug. Retail was $324.

> Subtract $15 for 20 ga.
> Add $60 for 24 in. VR barrel with Ghost Ring Sight (12 ga. only).

* **Model 500 Camo** — 12 ga. only, parkerized camo, OFM Camo (standard, mfg. 1991-96), or Woodlands (new 1995) metal and synthetic stock finish, 24 (disc.), 26 (disc.), 28, or 30 (disc.) in. ported (standard 1997) or unported VR barrel (choice of cylinder bore with rifle sights or Accu-II chokes), includes swivels, camo sling, and drilled and tapped receiver, older Speedfeed stock (disc. 1990) holds 4 extra shells. New 1986.

Mfg.'s Sug. Retail	**$348**	**$270**	**$200**	**$150**

> Subtract 10% if without Accu-II choke system.
> Add $30 for Speedfeed in synthetic stock (disc. 1990).

Accu-chokes became standard in 1991. Current models are supplied with 2 choke tubes.

* **Model 500 Bantam Turkey** — 12 ga. only, 24 in. ported barrel with fiber optic sights and XX-full choke tube only, synthetic stock and forearm with Woodlands camo treatment. New 1999.

Mfg.'s Sug. Retail	**$361**	**$285**	**$200**	**$155**	**$135**	**$125**	**$115**	**$100**

> ➤ **Model 500 Turkey Camo Bantam** — 20 ga. only, 22 in. VR barrel with Accu-II X-full choke only. New 1997.

Mfg.'s Sug. Retail	**$361**	**$285**	**$200**	**$155**

* **Model 500 Camo Combo** — 12 or 20 ga., includes a wide variety of extra barrel combinations including slug barrel options, prices vary slightly depending on the configuration (gauge/barrel/choke set-up). Rifled bores, VR barrels, and Accu-chokes became standard in the combo package late 1994. Disc. 1998.

	$375	**$295**	**$250**	**$200**	**$180**	**$160**	**$145**

Last Mfg.'s Sug. Retail was $434.

* **Model 500 Muzzleloader Combo** — 12 ga. only, includes 24 in. (rifled bore only, new 1993) or 28 in. VR Accu-choke barrel and additional 24 in. .50 cal. muzzleloader conversion barrel with rifled bore and iron sights, walnut finished hardwood stock and forearm, 7.2 lbs. Mfg. 1991-96.

	$335	**$280**	**$240**	**$200**	**$180**	**$160**	**$145**

Last Mfg.'s Sug. Retail was $385.

M

* **Model 500 Quail Unlimited** — 20 ga. only, 26 in. VR barrel with Accu-II chokes (3), engraved receiver and hand selected stock and forearm, 3,500 mfg. in 1991 to commemorate the 10th anniversary of Quail Unlimited.

	$295	**$240**	**$195**

Last Mfg.'s Sug. Retail was $359.

* **Model 500 Sporting Steel Shot** — 12 ga. only, 3 in. chamber, 28 in. VR Accu-choke barrel with special Accu-steel tube for shooting steel shot. Mfg. 1987-90.

	$250	**$200**	**$175**	**$165**	**$155**	**$145**	**$135**

> Add $29 for camo stock (disc. 1989).

This model was phased out of production in 1990 since all Mossberg shotguns currently manufactured are capable of shooting steel shot safely. The last mfg.'s sug. retail was $295.

Grading	100%	98%	95%	90%	80%	70%	60%

MODEL 500 SPECIAL HUNTER — 12 or 20 ga., 3 in. chamber, 26 or 28 in. VR barrel with or w/o porting and Accu-Chokes set, parkerized metal finish, black synthetic stock and forearm. New 1999.

Mfg.'s Sug. Retail	$314	$250	$205	$165	$140	$120	$110	$100

MODEL 500 VIKING SLIDE ACTION — 12 or 20 ga., 24 (12 ga. only, with rifled barrel and sights, porting became standard in 1997), 26 (20 ga. only) or 28 (12 ga. only, porting became standard in 1997) in. ported (new 1997, 12 ga. only) or unported VR barrel with one Accu-Choke and twin bead sights, matte finish with green synthetic stock and forearm, approx. 7 lbs. Mfg. 1996-98.

	$230	$190	$155	$135	$120	$110	$100

Last Mfg.'s Sug. Retail was $287.

Add $40 for 12 ga. rifled barrel.
Add $108 for Slug Shooting System with ported barrel.

* *Model 500 Viking Turkey* — 12 ga. only, 24 in. ported VR barrel, green synthetic stock, matte finish, Accu-Choke. Mfg. 1997-98.

	$230	$190	$155	$135	$120	$110	$100

Last Mfg.'s Sug. Retail was $286.

MODEL 500 FIELD CROWN GRADE SLIDE ACTION — 12, 20 (Bantam) ga., or .410 (Bantam) bore, 22 (disc., 20 ga. only), 24, 26, or 28 in. ported (new 1997, 12 ga. only, 26 or 28 in. barrel) or unported VR (unless with rifle sights) barrel, blue finish, walnut finished stock, safety on back of receiver top, Accu-chokes except for .410 bore, supplied with 1 Accu-Choke.

Mfg.'s Sug. Retail	$322	$260	$205	$165	$140	$120	$110	$100

Add approx. $49-$118 for 10 various combo packages.

* *Model 500 Slugster Crown Grade* — 12 or 20 ga., 24 in. ported (standard 1997) or unported (disc. 1996) barrel with choice of cyl. or rifled bore, blue or Marinecote (mfg. 1995-97) finish.

Mfg.'s Sug. Retail	$353	$280	$215	$165	$140	$120	$110	$100

Add $29 for Truglo fiber optic sights (new 1998).
Add $125 for Marinecote finish (with synthetic stock).
Add $29 for rifled bore barrel with trophy scope base and dual-comb stock.

MODEL 500 PERSUADER SLIDE ACTION — 12 or 20 (new 1995) ga., 6 or 8 shot, 18½ in. plain barrel, cyl. bore or Accu-Chokes (new 1995), optional rifle (12 ga./20 in. cyl. bore barrel only) or ghost ring (new 1999) sights, blue or parkerized (12 ga. only) finish, Speedfeed stock was disc. 1990, optional bayonet lug, plain pistol grip wood or synthetic stock.

Mfg.'s Sug. Retail	$293	$240	$185	$160	$145	$130	$115	$100

Add $40 for combo with pistol grip (disc.).
Add $23 for rifle sights (disc., 12 ga. only).
Add $50 for ghost ring sights (new 1999).

* *Night Persuader Special Edition* — 12 ga. only, includes synthetic stock and factory installed Mepro-Light night sight bead sight, only 300 mfg. for Lew Horton Distributing in 1990 only.

	$295	$250	$200	$175	$150	$130	$115

Last Mfg.'s Sug. Retail was $296.

M

MODEL 500 SPECIAL PURPOSE SLIDE ACTION — 12 ga. only, 14 in. barrel bored cyl., choice of blue or parkerized finish, synthetic stock with or without Speedfeed. Disc. 1996.

	$330	$270	$240	$220	$200	$175	$160

Last Mfg.'s Sug. Retail was $378.

Add $21 for Speedfeed stock.
Add $76 for ghost ring sight (parkerized finish only).

Grading	100%	98%	95%	90%	80%	70%	60%

MODEL 500 CRUISER SLIDE ACTION — 12, 20, or .410 (new 1993) ga., 14 (12 ga. only, disc. 1995), 18½, 20, or 21 (20 ga. only - new 1995) in. cylinder bore barrel with shroud, 6 or 8 shot mag., pistol grip forearm only. New 1989.

Mfg.'s Sug. Retail	$293		$240	$190	$165	$150	$145	$135	$120

> Subtract $3 for .410 bore.
> Subtract $10 for 20 ga.
> Add $10 for 8 shot mag.
> Add $96 for 14 in. barrel (disc.).
> Add approx. $34 for camper case (1993-96).

* **Mil-Spec Cruiser** — 12 ga. only, 20 in. barrel bored cyl. with bead sights, built to Mil-Specs., parkerized finish. Mfg. 1997 only.

			$395	$350	$325	$295	$275	$250	$225

Last Mfg.'s Sug. Retail was $478.

MODEL 500 GHOST RING SIGHT SLIDE ACTION — 12 ga. only, 3 in. chamber, 18½ or 20 in. cyl. bore or Accu-Choke (20 in. only - new 1995) barrel, 6 or 9 shot tube mag., blue or parkerized finish, synthetic field stock, includes ghost ring sighting device. Mfg. 1990-97.

			$270	$225	$180	$160	$150	$140	$130

Last Mfg.'s Sug. Retail was $332.

> Add $53 for parkerized finish.
> Add $49 for 9 shot mag. (20 in. barrel only).
> Add $123 for Accu-choke barrel (parkerized finish only).
> Add $134 for Speedfeed stock (new 1994 - 9 shot, 20 in. barrel only).

MODEL 500 MARINER SLIDE ACTION — 12 ga. only, 18½ or 20 in. cyl. bore barrel, 6 or 9 shot, Marinecote finish on all metal parts (more rust-resistant than stainless steel), synthetic stock and forearm, fixed or ghost ring (new 1995) sights.

Mfg.'s Sug. Retail	$425		$360	$275	$210				

> Add $15 for 9 shot model.
> Add $68 for ghost ring sights.
> Add $23 for Speedfeed stock (mini-combo only - disc.).

MODEL 500 CAMPER — 12, 20 ga., or .410 bore only, 18½ in. barrel, synthetic pistol grip (no stock), camo carrying case optional, blued finish. Mfg. 1986-90 only.

			$235	$190	$175	$165	$155	$145	$135

Last Mfg.'s Sug. Retail was $276.

> Add $25 for .410 bore.
> Add $30 for camo case.

MODEL 500 HI-RIB TRAP — 12 ga. only, high post trap rib, 28 or 30 in. barrel. Add $20 for Accu-choke. Disc. 1986.

			$285	$250	$230	$200	$175	$155	$140

Last Mfg.'s Sug. Retail was $334.

MODEL 500 SUPER GRADE — similar to Model 500 Field, except VR and checkered, no 16 ga. Mfg. 1965-1976.

			$250	$215	$180	$170	$160	$140	$130

M

MODEL 500 ATR SUPER GRADE — similar to Model 500 Field, except 12 ga., VR, 30 in. full, checkered Monte Carlo. Mfg. 1968-1971.

			$295	$260	$230	$200	$175	$155	$140

MODEL 500 PIGEON GRADE — similar to 500 Super Grade, except etched and scroll engraving, select wood, floating VR. Mfg. 1971-1975.

			$385	$330	$305	$250	$210	$185	$165

MODEL 500 APTR PIGEON GRADE TRAP — similar to 500 ATR, except trap style stock. Mfg. 1971-1975.

			$440	$415	$330	$250	$220	$200	$175

Grading	100%	98%	95%	90%	80%	70%	60%

MODEL 500 DSPR DUCK STAMP COMMERCIAL — similar to Pigeon Grade, except wood duck etching. 1,000 mfg. 1975.

	100%	98%	95%	90%	80%	70%	60%
	$525	$330	$310	$285	$260	$220	$195

MODEL 500L SERIES — similar to 500 Field Grade, except no 16 ga., etched receiver, new style stock and slide. Mfg. 1977-1983.

	100%	98%	95%	90%	80%	70%	60%
	$250	$220	$210	$200	$175	$165	$140

MODEL 500 BULLPUP — 12 ga. only, 18½ (6 shot) or 20 (9 shot) in. barrel, bullpup configuration, 6 or 9 shot mag., includes shrouded barrel, carrying handle, ejection port in stock, employs high impact materials. Mfg. 1986-1990 by Mossberg, currently mfg. under the Maverick trademark.

	100%	98%	95%
	$350	$300	$255

Last Mfg.'s Sug. Retail was $425.

Add $15 for 8 shot mag. (disc.).

MODEL 500/590 INTIMIDATOR LASER — 12 ga. only, 3 in. chamber, 18½ (Model 500) or 20 (Model 590) in. cyl. bore barrel, 6 (Model 500) or 9 (Model 590) shot tube mag., blue or parkerized finish, synthetic field stock, includes laser sighting device. Mfg. 1990-1993.

* **Model 500 Intimidator**

	100%	98%	95%	90%	80%	70%	60%
	$440	$375	$340	$295	$260	$230	$195

Last Mfg.'s Sug. Retail was $505.

Add $22 for parkerized finish.

* **Model 590 Intimidator**

	100%	98%	95%	90%	80%	70%	60%
	$495	$440	$375	$340	$295	$260	$230

Last Mfg.'s Sug. Retail was $556.

Add $45 for parkerized finish.

SPECIAL PURPOSE 590 SLIDE ACTION — similar to Model 500, except has 9 shot mag., 20 in. cyl. bore barrel with ¾ shroud, and bayonet lug, blued or parkerized finish. New 1987.

Mfg.'s Sug. Retail	$353	98%	95%	90%	80%	70%	60%
		$295	$250	$210	$185	$165	$145	$125

Add $53 for parkerized finish.
Add approx. $105 for ghost ring sights (new 1998) and parkerized finish.
Add $33 for Speedfeed (blue) or $84 for Speedfeed (parkerized) stock.

* **Model 590 Mariner** — similar to Model 500 Mariner except is 9 shot and has 20 in. barrel. Mfg. 1989-1993.

	100%	98%	95%	90%	80%	70%	60%
	$310	$250	$200	$185	$165	$145	$125

Last Mfg.'s Sug. Retail was $353.

Add $17 for Speedfeed stock (disc. 1990).
Add $15 for pistol grip adapter (mini combo - disc.).

* **Model 590 Bullpup** — similar to Model 500 Bullpup except is 9 shot and has 20 in. barrel. Mfg. 1989-90 only.

	100%	98%	95%	90%	80%	70%	60%
	$425	$360	$300	$250	$225	$195	$175

Last Mfg.'s Sug. Retail was $497.

* **Model 590A1** — while advertised during 1997, this model was never mfg.

M

MODEL 695 BOLT ACTION — 12 ga. only, with detachable 2 shot mag., 22 in. barrel with choice of fully rifled and ported or Accu-Choke (disc. 1998) barrel, black synthetic with polished blue (Slug Model with rifle sights) or Woodlands camo finish (Turkey Model with bead sights) on both metal and synthetic stock. New 1996.

Mfg.'s Sug. Retail	$330	98%	95%	90%	80%	70%	60%
		$265	$215	$180	$150	$135	$120	$115

Subtract $50 for Accu-choke barrel.
Add $23 for Truglo fiber optic sights (new 1998).

Grading	100%	98%	95%	90%	80%	70%	60%

MODEL 712 SEMI-AUTO — 12 ga. only, gas operated, shoots 2¾ and 3 in. shells interchangeably, plain barrel or VR, top of receiver safety, checkered hardwood stock, rubber recoil pad, fixed or Accu-Choke II choking. Mfg. 1986-1988 only.

	$285	$250	$220	$200	$190	$175	$160

Last Mfg.'s Sug. Retail was $345.

> Subtract $25 without Accu II choking.
> Add $90 for combo pack (includes 1 extra 24 in. slugster barrel).

* *Model 712 Steel Shot* — similar to Model 712, except has Accu-Steel choking system for steel shot, 28 in. VR barrel. Mfg. 1988 only.

	$290	$250	$220	$200	$190	$175	$160

Last Mfg.'s Sug. Retail was $349.

* *Model 712 Camo/Speedfeed* — 12 ga. only, similar to Model 712, except has camo finished metal parts, stock, and forearm, 24 or 28 in. barrel. Add $20 for Accu II choke. Mfg. 1986-87 only.

	$340	$295	$240

Last Mfg.'s Sug. Retail was $390.

MODEL 712 REGAL SEMI-AUTO — 12 or 20 ga., action same as Model 712, special bright bluing, VR only, deluxe checkered walnut stock and forearm, gold trigger, inlaid medallion on receiver, top of receiver safety. Add $20 for Accu II choke. Mfg. 1986-87 only.

	$310	$280	$250	$225	$200	$185	$170

Last Mfg.'s Sug. Retail was $366.

NEW HAVEN BRAND — similar to previous models, except plainer finish. Disc.

> Values are 20% less per model.

MODEL 835 ULTI-MAG SLIDE ACTION — 12 ga. with 3½ in. chamber (new 1988), slide action, 24 (Turkey Model - new 1990) or 28 in. VR barrel with Accu-Mag choke tubes, 6 shot mag., safety on top rear of receiver, choice of camo synthetic or checkered hardwood stock. Introduced late 1988, disc. 1991.

	$375	$310	$265	$220	$190	$165	$150

Last Mfg.'s Sug. Retail was $430.

Add $30 for synthetic camo field stock.

Various Combo packages were available in this model with prices ranging from $469-$534 depending on barrel chokings and scope base options.

This model was followed by the 835 Regal Series introduced in late 1991.

ULTI-MAG 835 FIELD GRADE SLIDE ACTION — 12 ga. only, 3½ in. chamber, 24 in. cyl. bore (disc.), 24 in. VR (Turkey Special, disc. 1993), or 28 in. ported (new 1997) or unported VR barrel with 1 Accu-Mag choke, walnut finish stock and forearm (pressed checkering became standard 1994), blued finish, approx. 7½ lbs. Disc. 1998.

	$270	$230	$200	$185	$165	$145	$125

Last Mfg.'s Sug. Retail was $331.

Add $40 for combo package (disc. 1993).

ULTI-MAG 835 SPECIAL HUNTER — 12 ga. only, 3½ in. chamber, 26 or 28 in. VR ported barrel with mod. Accu-Mag choke, parkerized finish, black synthetic stock. New 1998.

Mfg.'s Sug. Retail	$347	$280	$240	$200	$185	$165	$145	$125

835 CROWN GRADE SLIDE ACTION — similar to Field Grade, except has gold trigger and cut checkering on walnut finished hardwood stock, blue or OFM Woodland camo (24 in. Turkey only) finish, ported (standard 1997) or unported VR barrel. New 1994.

Mfg.'s Sug. Retail	$346	$290	$240	$205	$185	$165	$145	$125

> Add $15 for parkerized finish with 24 in. Ulti-full choke tube.
> Add $118 for combo package (includes 24 in. deer barrel).

* *Model 835 Turkey Slide Action* — 12 ga. only, 24 in. ported VR barrel, walnut finished stock and forearm. New 1997.

Mfg.'s Sug. Retail	$382	$320	$255	$215	$190	$165	$145	$125

M

Grading	100%	98%	95%	90%	80%	70%	60%

* **Model 835 New Turkey Slide Action** — 12 ga. only, 24 in. ported barrel with Ulti-full choke only, choice of Realtree Xtra brown or Woodlands 100% camo finish, fiber optic sights. New 1999.

Mfg.'s Sug. Retail	$494	$425	$365	$335	$300	$270	$235	$210

* **Ulti-Mag 835 Crown Grade Slide Action** — 12 ga. only, 3½ in. chamber, 28 in. VR ported (standard 1997) or unported barrel, walnut stock and forearm, Accu-Mag choke. Disc. 1998.

	$365	$300	$260	$230	$200	$180	$160

Last Mfg.'s Sug. Retail was $421.

Add $7 for duo-comb stock.

MODEL 835 VIKING SLIDE ACTION — 12 ga. only, 28 in. VR ported (standard 1997) or unported (1996 only) barrel with one Accu-Choke and twin bead sights, matte blue finish with green synthetic stock and forearm, 7.7 lbs. Mfg. 1996-98.

	$260	$225	$200	$185	$165	$145	$125

Last Mfg.'s Sug. Retail was $316.

MODEL 835 CAMO SLIDE ACTION — 12 ga. only, 3½ in. chamber, OFM Woodland Camo (all-purpose camo, combo. only beginning 1997), Realtree (new 1993), Realtree AP (all purpose gray, new 1996), Brown Leaf, or Mossy Oak (new 1994) finish, 24 (Turkey Special) or 28 in. VR ported (standard 1997) or unported barrel with 6 choke tubes, dual comb (disc. 1995) or synthetic stock, 7.7 lbs. New 1991.

Mfg.'s Sug. Retail	$549	$445	$350	$290	$240	$200	$175	$160

Subtract $41 for OFM Marsh finish (disc.).
Add $39 for combo package or $125 for Turkey combo.

OFM Marsh finish on this model includes a dual comb stock.

MODEL 835 WALNUT ULTI-MAG (REGAL) SLIDE ACTION — 12 ga., 3½ in. chamber, 28 in. VR barrel with Accu-Mag chokes (disc. 1996) or 24 in. rifled slug barrel, single (new 1993) or dual comb (2 comb inserts are provided for the stock affording different shooting positions), aluminum receiver, back-bored barrel, double slide bars, high gloss walnut stock with recoil pad, approx. 7½ lbs. Mfg. 1991-96.

	$350	$290	$260	$230	$200	$175	$160

Last Mfg.'s Sug. Retail was $404.

Add $8 for dual comb stock.
Add $30 for 24 in. slug barrel with trophy scope base and dual comb stock.
Add $72-$83 for combo package (includes extra slug barrel with choice of sights).

MODEL 835 WILD TURKEY FED. LIMITED EDITION — 12 ga. with 3½ in. chamber, 24 in. VR barrel with Accu-Mag. chokes, camo finish, includes camo sling, medallion in stock, and 10-pack of Federal Turkey loads. Mfg. 1989 only.

	$425	$360	$295

Last Mfg.'s Sug. Retail was $477.

MODEL 835 NWTF SPECIAL EDITION — 12 ga. only, 24 in. VR barrel with Accu-Mag chokes, features Realtree camo finish, drilled and tapped receiver, 7½ lbs. Mfg. 1991 only to commemorate the National Wild Turkey Federation.

	$380	$300	$225

Last Mfg.'s Sug. Retail was $436.

M

MODEL 835 WATERFOWL LIMITED EDITION — 12 ga. with 3½ in. chamber, 28 in. VR barrel with Accu-Mag. chokes, camo finish, synthetic stock, camo sling. Mfg. 1990 only.

	$425	$360	$295

Last Mfg.'s Sug. Retail was $480.

MODEL 1000 SEMI-AUTO — 12 or 20 ga., gas semi-auto, 2¾ in. chamber, scroll engraved aluminum alloy receiver, plain or VR barrel, also available in trap and skeet configuration, checkered walnut stock and forearm. Imported 1986-87 only. VR became standard in 1987.

	$410	$345	$300	$270	$245	$220	$200

Last Mfg.'s Sug. Retail was $472.

Add $28 for Multi-Choke II.
Deduct $50 if without VR.

Model 1000 barrels are not interchangeable with Model 1000 Super barrels.

Grading	100%	98%	95%	90%	80%	70%	60%

* **Model 1000 Junior** — similar to Model 1000, except 20 ga. only, shortened stock, and 22 in. VR Multi-Choke barrel. Imported 1986-87 only.

| | $425 | $355 | $310 | $275 | $250 | $220 | $200 |

Last Mfg.'s Sug. Retail was $499.

* **Model 1000 Slug** — 12 or 20 ga., 22 in. barrel with rifle sights, recoil pad. Imported 1986-87 only.

| | $405 | $340 | $295 | $270 | $245 | $220 | $200 |

Last Mfg.'s Sug. Retail was $464.

* **Model 1000 Skeet** — 12 or 20 ga., steel receiver, 26 in. VR barrel bored skeet. Mfg. 1986 only.

| | $395 | $335 | $295 | $270 | $245 | $220 | $200 |

Last Mfg.'s Sug. Retail was $439.

MODEL 1000 SUPER SEMI-AUTO — 12 or 20(Super 20) ga., gas semi-auto, 3 in. chambers, shoots 2¾ and 3 in. shells interchangeably, steel receiver, vent. recoil pad, select checkered walnut stock and forearm, Multi-Choke II is standard (except on slug barrel). Slug models are approx. the same price as values listed directly below. Imported 1986-87 only.

| | $495 | $405 | $365 | $330 | $295 | $270 | $245 |

Last Mfg.'s Sug. Retail was $577.

Model 1000 Super barrels are not interchangeable with Model 1000 barrels.

* **Model 1000 Super Waterfowler** — 12 ga. only, matte finished wood and metal, includes swivels and camouflaged sling, 28 in. Multi-Choke barrel. Imported 1986-87 only.

| | $510 | $430 | $370 |

Last Mfg.'s Sug. Retail was $605.

* **Model 1000 Super Skeet** — 12 or 20 ga., 25 in. barrel, jug choking. Imported 1986-87 only.

| | $575 | $495 | $450 | $410 | $375 | $330 | $295 |

Last Mfg.'s Sug. Retail was $658.

* **Model 1000 Super Trap** — 12 ga. only, 30 in. Multi-Choke II barrel with high VR, Monte Carlo stock, recoil pad. Mfg. 1986 only.

| | $470 | $380 | $345 | $320 | $285 | $270 | $250 |

Last Mfg.'s Sug. Retail was $560.

MODEL 3000 SLIDE ACTION — 12 or 20 ga. only, 3 in. chamber, slide action, steel receiver, double action bars, various chokes and VR barrel lengths, checkered walnut stock and forearm, vent. recoil pad. Add $25 for Multi-Choke II. This model was introduced in 1986 and the field version was disc. in 1987.

| | $325 | $275 | $250 | $220 | $200 | $185 | $170 |

Last Mfg.'s Sug. Retail was $360.

* **Model 3000 Waterfowler** — 12 ga. only, similar to Model 3000, except has dull matte finish on wood and metal, includes swivels and camouflaged sling, VR only. Add $30 for Multi-choke II option, $70 for camo/speedfeed stock. Mfg. 1986 only.

| | $340 | $295 | $265 |

Last Mfg.'s Sug. Retail was $386.

* **Model 3000 Law Enforcement** — 12 or 20 ga. only, 18½ or 20 in. cylinder bore only, rifle or bead sights. Mfg. 1986-87 only.

| | $325 | $275 | $250 | $220 | $200 | $185 | $170 |

Last Mfg.'s Sug. Retail was $362.

Add $25 for rifle sights.
Add $33 for black speedfeed stock.

MODEL 5500 SEMI-AUTO — 12 ga., 2¾ or 3 in. mag., gas operated, 18½ - 30 in. barrels. Add $20 for VR. Disc. 1985.

| | $250 | $235 | $205 | $185 | $170 | $155 | $140 |

Last Mfg.'s Sug. Retail was $307.

* **Model 5500 Mag.** — 12 ga. only, 3 in. chamber, 30 in. VR barrel. Disc. 1985.

| | $275 | $250 | $225 | $205 | $190 | $175 | $160 |

Last Mfg.'s Sug. Retail was $325.

M

Grading	100%	98%	95%	90%	80%	70%	60%

MODEL 5500 MKII SEMI-AUTO — 12 ga. only, supplied with 2 VR barrels - 26 in./2¾ in. chamber or 28 in./3 in. chamber VR barrel, includes choice of Accu-II choke tubes (lead shot only) or Accu-Steel choke tubes, blue or camo finish (new 1990), checkered hardwood stock and forearm, top receiver safety, recoil pad, 7½ lbs. Mfg. 1989-92.

	$260	$225	$200	$180	$160	$140	$125

Last Mfg.'s Sug. Retail was $294.

Add $10 for 24 in. rifled bore barrel.

Add $43 for camo metal finish and synthetic stock.

Add $30 for Turkey Model (24 in. barrel, camo finish, and synthetic stock).

This model was also available with different Combo options. Prices varied between $463-$484, depending on configuration of barrel choking.

* *Model 5500 U.S. Shooting Team* — 2¾ in. chamber, 26 in. non-Mag. barrel with VR and Accu-II chokes, blue finish, checkered walnut stock and forearm, 7½ lbs. Mfg. 1991-92.

	$325	$250	$225	$200	$185	$170	$160

Last Mfg.'s Sug. Retail was $376.

* *NWTF Special Edition* — 12 ga. only, 3 in. chamber, 24 in. VR barrel with 1 choke tube, Mossy Oak Camo finish with synthetic stock and forearm, 7.3 lbs. Mfg. 1991-92.

	$365	$300	$265	$235	$200	$175	$160

Last Mfg.'s Sug. Retail was $428.

MODEL 6000 SEMI-AUTO — 12 ga. only, 2¾ or 3 in. chamber 28 in. VR barrel with Accu-choke, economical model with walnut finish stock, blue finish, 7.7 lbs. Mfg. 1993 only.

	$280	$240	$215	$200	$185	$165	$145

Last Mfg.'s Sug. Retail was $321.

MODEL 9200 CROWN SEMI-AUTO — 12 ga. only, 3 in. chamber, gas operated, shoots any shell interchangeably, 18½ (SP only), 22 (Bantam only), 24 in. rifled, 24 (Turkey), 26 (U.S. Shooting Team variation, new 1993), or 28 in. VR barrel with 3 Accu-chokes, engraved aluminum receiver, synthetic (18½ in. barrel only) or walnut stained hard wood stock (1 in. shorter on Bantam Model) and forearm, top tang safety, approx. 7½ lbs. New 1992.

Mfg.'s Sug. Retail	$552	$445	$325	$270	$220	$190	$170	$160

Add approx. $73-$95 for combo package.

Add $33 for Truglo fiber optic sights (mfg. 1998 only).

Add $23 for 24 in. rifled bore barrel with trophy scope base.

Subtract $90 for synthetic stock (Special Purpose with matte blue finish, 18½ in. barrel).

* *Model 9200 Viking* — 12 ga. only, 28 in. VR barrel with one Accu-Choke and twin bead sights, matte finish with green synthetic stock and forearm, 7.7 lbs. Mfg. 1996-98.

	$365	$310	$270	$230	$200	$175	$160

Last Mfg.'s Sug. Retail was $429.

* *Model 9200 Special Hunter* — 12 ga. only, 28 in. VR barrel with Accu-II choke set, parkerized finish, black synthetic stock. New 1998.

Mfg.'s Sug. Retail	$471		$410	$335	$280	$240	$200	$175	$160

* *Model 9200 Camo* — 12 ga. only, similar to Model 9200, except is supplied with OFM (disc. 1996), Mossy Oak, Realtree (mfg. 1994-95), Realtree AP (new 1996) or Woodlands (new 1995) camo finish, 24 (Turkey) or 28 in. VR barrel. New 1992.

Mfg.'s Sug. Retail	$535		$430	$310	$255	$225	$195	$170	$160

Add $79 for Turkey Model with Mossy Oak or Realtree AP camo finish.

Subtract $38 for Turkey Model with Woodlands camo and one choke tube.

➤ Model 9200 New Turkey Camo — 12 ga. only, 24 in. VR barrel with XX-full choke tube only and fiber optic sights, choice of 100% Woodlands or Mossy Oak Shadow Branch camo treatment. New 1999.

Mfg.'s Sug. Retail	$517		$415	$300	$250	$225	$195	$170	$160

Add $95 for Mossy Oak Shadow Branch camo coverage.

M

Grading	100%	98%	95%	90%	80%	70%	60%

✻ Model 9200 Jungle Gun — 12 ga. only, 18½ in. plain barrel with cyl. bore, parkerized metal, synthetic stock. New 1998.

Mfg.'s Sug. Retail	$676	$590	$485	$350	$295	$250	$225	$200

MOUNTAIN RIFLERY

Current custom rifle builder located in Pocatello, ID. Consumer direct sales.

John Bolliger has been producing top quality, custom made bolt action rifles for over 30 years. Currently, Mountain Riflery is concentrating on 3 series of rifles: the Signature Series, the Excalibur Series, and the Crown Series. Since almost all rifles are special ordered per customer specifications (with many options also available), please contact Mountain Riflery directly for more information, including prices.

MOUNTAIN RIFLES INC.

Previous rifle manufacturer located in Palmer, AK 1995-98.

RIFLES: BOLT ACTION

MOUNTAINEER — various cals., choice of M-700 Rem. or M-70 Win. action, Chrome Moly barrel with ultra muzzle brake, Timney trigger, parkerized finish, fiberglass stock with decelerator pad, 5½ lbs. Limited mfg. 1995-98.

$1,825		$1,475	$1,100	$900	$750	$675	$550

Last Mfg.'s Sug. Retail was $1,995.

SUPER MOUNTAINEER — similar to the Mountaineer, except has Kevlar epoxy bedded stock with steel cross-bolts on Mag. cals., 4¼ lbs. Limited 1995-98.

		$2,575	$2,025	$1,475	$1,100	$900	$750	$675

Last Mfg.'s Sug. Retail was $2,895.

PRO MOUNTAINEER K.S. — various cals., Winchester M-70 controlled feed action, choice of fiberglass pillar epoxy bedded, Kevlar, or KSDB (Kevlar Stock Drop Box mag.) stock with decelerator pad, parkerized finish. 6 lbs. Limited mfg. 1995-98.

		$2,395	$1,950	$1,425	$1,050	$875	$725	$650

Last Mfg.'s Sug. Retail was $2,695.

Add $500 for KSDB stock with drop mag.

PRO SAFARI — various cals., Winchester M-70 controlled feed action, high gloss bluing, exhibition grade English walnut with decelerator pad, 4 shot detachable mag. 7-9 lbs. Limited mfg. 1995-98.

		$3,795	$3,350	$2,875	$2,350	$1,775	$1,450	$1,200

Last Mfg.'s Sug. Retail was $3,995.

ULTRA MOUNTAINEER — various cals., features stainless steel match grade barrel with black Kevlar/Graphite thumbhole stock, approx. 5 lbs. New 1997.

		$2,650	$2,075	$1,500	$1,100	$900	$750	$675

Last Mfg.'s Sug. Retail was $2,995.

Add $500 for Rigby length.

M MUSGRAVE

Current manufacturer located in the Republic of South Africa since 1951. No current importation.

Newer models manufactured by Musgrave (imported into Austria and Switzerland) include the Model 90 (features Musgrave action) Standard Rifle, Model 90 Light Rifle, Mini-90, Model 90 Varmint, Model 90 De Luxe Rifle, and Magnum Rifle, in addition to the same series in the Mauser 98 action. More information can be obtained (including prices and availability) by contacting the company directly (see Trademark Index).

Grading	100%	98%	95%	90%	80%	70%	60%

RIFLES: BOLT ACTION

VALIANT BOLT ACTION RIFLE — .243 Win., .270 Win., .30-06, .308 Win., or 7mm Rem. Mag. cal., 24 in. barrel, leaf sight, skip checkered straight stock, pistol grip. Mfg. 1971-1976.

	$375	$325	$275	$250	$220	$195	$175

PREMIER — similar to Valiant, with 26 in. barrel, select Monte Carlo stock, rosewood pistol grip cap and forearm tip.

	$425	$365	$315	$275	$250	$225	$200

RSA SINGLE SHOT TARGET RIFLE — .308 Win. cal. only, 26 in. heavy barrel, target sights and stock. Mfg. 1971-1976.

	$425	$365	$315	$275	$250	$225	$200

MUSKETEER RIFLES

Previous trademark of rifles previously imported by Firearms International Company (FIC), located in Washington, D.C.

RIFLES: BOLT ACTION

SPORTER — .243 Win., .25-06 Rem., .270 Win., .264 Win. Mag., .308 Win., .30-06, 7mm Rem. Mag., or .300 Win. Mag. cal., bolt action, FN Mauser action, 24 in. barrel, no sights, checkered Monte Carlo stock. Mfg. 1963-1972.

	$375	$325	$275	$250	$220	$195	$175

SPORTER DELUXE — adj. trigger, select wood, tear drop pistol grip, skipline checkering.

	$425	$365	$315	$275	$250	$225	$200

CARBINE — similar to Sporter, except 20 in. barrel and full length stock.

	$375	$325	$275	$250	$220	$195	$175

M

NOTES

M

N section

NS FIREARMS CORP.

Current importer located in Atlanta, GA. NS Firearms is a division of KFS, Inc. located in Atlanta, GA. Currently manufactured in China.

Grading	100%	98%	95%	90%	80%	70%	60%

RIFLES: BOLT ACTION

MODEL 522 SPORTER — .22 LR cal., 21 in. cold hammer forged barrel, 5 shot detachable mag., grooved receiver, checkered walnut stock, 7¾ lbs. New 1994.

Mfg.'s Sug. Retail	$299		$250	$215	$185	$165	$145	$125	$110

NAMBU PISTOLS

Previously manufactured in Japan for the Japanese military between 1902-1945.

PISTOLS: SEMI-AUTO

TYPE 14 — 8mm Nambu cal., recoil operated, 4.7 in. barrel, blued, wood grips, 8 shot mag., a simply designed pistol used by Japanese armed forces from 1925-1945.

Type 14 Nambus have a 3 or 4 digit number just forward of the lanyard ring on the right side of frame (on back of grip). Earliest Taisho era pistols are dated 15.11 or 15.12 from the Nagoya arsenal - can be identified by small trigger guard and other early features. Fewer than 100 mfg. To determine year and month of manufacture for most type 14 pistols, add "1925" to the first two digits and the last number will indicate the month (i.e. code 13.3 indicates a gun built in March of 1938).
Add 25% for 3.X date Tokyo.
Add 50% for 2.X date Nagoya.
Add 400% for early Taisho era pistols dated 15.11 or 15.12 from Nagoya arsenal.
Add 10% for matching mag. on models listed below.

* *1925-1930 Mfg.*

		$700	$500	$360	$320	$265	$230	$200

* *1930-1935 Mfg.* — small trigger guard.

		$500	$400	$260	$220	$200	$180	$165

* *1935-1945 Mfg.* — large trigger guard.

		$295	$260	$215	$195	$180	$165	$150

Add 10% for strawed trigger and safety.

TYPE 94 — 8mm Nambu cal., recoil operated, 3.8 in. barrel, blued, and bakelite wood grips, 6 shot mag. Mfg. 1935-1945.

		$275	$225	$185	$160	$150	$135	$120

Add 300% for 10.X date, 200% for 11.X date, 100% for 12.X date, 30% if pre-WWII, and 20% if late square back.

HAMADA NAMBU — .32 ACP or 8mm Nambu (scarce) cal., available with rough (early production, mostly prototypes) or polished (production) finish, very rare.

		$3,250	$2,800	$2,400	$2,000	$1,800	$1,600	$1,475

Add 10% for "in the white" 8mm Nambu.

N

BABY NAMBU — 7mm Nambu cal., 3¼ in. barrel, blued, wood grips, grip safety, one of the most desirable Japanese handguns.

		$2,700	$2,250	$1,800	$1,600	$1,475	$1,300	$1,050

Add 10% for matching mag.
Add 50% for chamber marked "TGE" (Tokyo Gas & Electric).

Grading	100%	98%	95%	90%	80%	70%	60%

PAPA NAMBU (MODEL 1904) — 8mm Nambu cal., 4.7 in. barrel, wood grips, grip safety, 8 shot mag., essentially the same action as the Baby, but a larger version. Mfg. 1904-1925.

	$1,450	$1,250	$1,100	$900	$700	$600	$500

> Add 10% for matching mag.
> Add 50% for chamber marked "TGE" (Tokyo Gas & Electric).

GRANDPA NAMBU — 8mm Nambu cal., similar to Papa Nambu, except has smaller trigger guard and fixed lanyard ring, cherry wood based mag., issued with 2 matching mags. Early Tokyo arsenal or later Thai issue, all Grandpa frames are slotted.

	$5,000	$3,950	$2,950	$2,600	$2,150	$1,850	$1,500

> Add 100% for matching shoulder stock.
> Add $3,500 for spare stock alone.
> Add 10% for second matching mag.
>
> Original stocks are rare and expensive.

1893 REVOLVER (MODEL 26) — 9mm Japanese cal., double action only, 4.7 in. barrel, blued, wood grips. Approx. 59,000 mfg. 1893-1925.

	$450	$350	$250	$200	$150	$135	$120

> Subtract 25% for arsenal rework.
> Add 150% for early mfg. with internal numbers (approx. first 300 revolvers).

NATIONAL WILD TURKEY FEDERATION

Current national organization located in Edgefield, SC.

> Although the National Wild Turkey Federation is not a manufacturer or importer, this organization has been responsible for many special and limited editions that are listed below with quanities but without prices since they may vary greatly from region to region. NWTF suffix after model name indicates National Wild Turkey Federation gun of the year. Some of the models (and current values) may be listed under manufacturer listings in this text.

SHOTGUNS: AUCTION/TRADE EDITIONS

MANUFACTURER	MODEL	QUANTITY	YEAR	ISSUE PRICE
Navy Arms	Black Powder 12 ga. NWTF	500	1983	$350
Winchester	Model 101	300	1985	$1,895
Browning	BPS 12 ga. NWTF	500	1986	$495
American Arms	SxS 10 ga. 3½ in.	150	1985/86	$695
Winchester	Model 1300 Win-Cam 12 ga.	500	1987/88	$449
Winchester	Model 1300 12 ga. Trade Gun	-	-	$458
Beretta	Model A-303 12 ga. NWTF	500	1988/89	$695
Winchester	Model 1300 12 ga. Win-Cam NWTF	500	1989	$479
Winchester	Model 1300 12 ga. Trade Gun	-	-	$458
Browning	Model A5 12 ga. NWTF	500	1990	$925
Mossberg	Model 835 12 ga. Auction	500	1991	$567
Mossberg	Model 835 12 ga. Trade Gun	-	-	$436
Remington	Model 11-87 12 ga. Auction	500	1992	-
Remington	Model 11-87 12 ga. Trade Gun	-	-	$698
Winchester	Model 1300 12 ga. Auction	500	1993	$671
New England Firearms	SxS 20 ga. Auction	-	-	$167
New England Firearms	SxS 12 ga. Trade Gun	-	-	$200
New England Firearms	SxS 10 ga. Trade Gun	-	-	$240
American Arms	Model Turkey 12 ga. Auction	300	1993	-
Mossberg	Model 9200 12 ga. Auction	600	1994	$690
Mossberg	Model 9200 12 ga. Trade	-	1994	-
Luigi Franchi	Model 610 12 ga. Auction	600	1995	-
Fausti	O/U 12 ga. Auction	720	1996	-
New England Firearms	Topper Jr. 20 ga. Auction	-	1996	-

N

MANUFACTURER	MODEL	QUANTITY	YEAR	ISSUE PRICE
Fausti	O/U 12 ga. Auction	900	1997	-
New England Firearms	Jakes Topper Jr. 20 ga. Auction	-	1997	-
Remington	Model 870 12 ga. Auction	1200	1998	-

NAVY ARMS COMPANY

Current importer established during 1958, and located in Ridgefield, NJ. Navy Arms imports are fabricated by various manufacturers including the Italian companies Davide Pedersoli & Co., Pietta & Co., and Uberti & Co. Distributor, dealer, and consumer sales.

Navy Arms also sells a wide variety of original military firearms in used condition. Handguns include the Mauser Broomhandle, Japanese Nambu, Colt 1911 Government Model, Tokarev, Browning Hi-Power, S&W Model 1917, and others. Rifles include Mauser contract models, Japanese Type 38s, Enfields, FNs, Nagants, M1 Carbines, M1 Garands, Chinese SKSs, Egyptian Rashids, French MAS Model 1936s, among others. Most of these firearms are priced in the $75-$500 price range depending on desirability of model and condition. Navy Arms should be contacted directly regarding specific prices for these models.

Grading	100%	98%	95%	90%	80%	70%	60%

PISTOLS

TU-711 MAUSER — 9mm Para. cal., patterned after Mauser 711 (semi-auto version of the Model 712 Schnellfeuer), 5¼ in. barrel, 712 upper receiver that has been converted to 9mm Para. and mounted on new lower receiver, supplied with 10 and 20 shot detachable mag., mfg. in China, 2 lbs. 11 oz. Imported 1992 only.

	$575	$475	$425	$375	$325	$295	$275

Last Mfg.'s Sug. Retail was $650.

TT-OLYMPIA — .22 LR cal., patterned after the Walther Olympia that won 1936 Olympics, 4⅝ in. barrel, checkered walnut grips, mfg. in China, 27 oz. Imported 1992-98.

	$255	$225	$195	$175	$160	$150	$140

Last Mfg.'s Sug. Retail was $290.

TU-90 PISTOL — .30 Tokarev or 9mm Para. cal., patterned after the rare Tokagypt variation (improved TT-33 Tokarev), 4½ in. barrel, single action, wraparound synthetic grips, unique forward motion safety, mfg. in China, 30 oz. Imported 1992-98.

	$115	$100	$90	$80	$70	$60	$50

Last Mfg.'s Sug. Retail was $130.

Add $15 for 9mm Para. cal.
Add $40 for pistol combo (includes both cals.).

LUGER MODEL — .22 LR cal. only, 10 shot mag., Luger toggle type action, available in blued or matte finish, 4, 6, or 8 in. barrel, checkered walnut stocks. Mfg. in U.S. 1986-87 only.

	$140	$120	$95	$85	$75	$70	$65

Last Mfg.'s Sug. Retail was $165.

GRAND PRIX SILHOUETTE — .30-30 Win., 7mm Spl., .44 Mag., or .45-70 Govt. cal., 13¾ in. barrel, non-glare matte blue finish, walnut forearm and grips, adj. heat dispersing aluminum rib, adj. target sights, 4 lbs. Mfg. 1985 only.

	$320	$280	$240	$220	$195	$175	$150

Last Mfg.'s Sug. Retail was $375.

N

Grading	100%	98%	95%	90%	80%	70%	60%

REVOLVERS: REPRODUCTIONS

1873 SINGLE ACTION ARMY — .357 Mag. (new 1998), .44-40 WCF or .45 LC cal., reproduction of the Colt SAA, case hardened frame with blue or nickel (disc. 1998) finish, 3 (Sheriff's Model - mfg. 1992-98), 4¾, 5½, or 7½ in. barrel, approx. 36 oz.

Mfg.'s Sug. Retail	$385	$330	$265	$210	$180	$160	$145	$130

Add $65 for nickel finish.
Add $15 for Pinched Frame Model (7½ in. barrel, .45 LC).
Subtract $20 for brass trigger guard and backstrap (disc.).

* **1873 SAA Economy** — .44-40 WCF or .45 LC cal., 3, 4¾, 5½, or 7½ in. barrel, brass trigger guard and backstrap, 2-piece walnut grips. Imported 1993-96.

	$295	$230	$185	$160	$145	$130	$120

Last Mfg.'s Sug. Retail was $345.

* **Deputy SAA** — .44-40 WCF or .45 LC cal., patterned after the Colt 1877 Thunderer double action, birds head grips, 3, 3½, 4, or 4¾ in. barrel, case colored frame. Imported 1997-98 only.

	$340	$270	$215	$180	$160	$145	$130

Last Mfg.'s Sug. Retail was $405.

* **1873 Flat Top Target Model** — .45 LC cal. only, features flat top frame, 7½ in. barrel only, adj., spring loaded front sight and dovetailed rear sight, 30 oz. Importation began 1999.

Mfg.'s Sug. Retail	$430	$360	$295	$260	$230	$200	$175	$150

* **Bisley Model** — .44-40 WCF or .45 LC cal., patterned after the Colt Bisley, 4¾, 5½, or 7½ in. barrel, case colored frame, spur hammer, walnut grips. Importation began 1997.

Mfg.'s Sug. Retail	$445	$370	$285	$225	$185	$160	$145	$130

➤ **Bisley Flat Top Target Model** — .44-40 WCF or .45 LC cal., features flat top frame, adj. front sight, and dovetailed rear sight, 40 oz. Importation began 1999.

Mfg.'s Sug. Retail	$480	$415	$335	$300	$265	$235	$200	$175

* **1873 SAA Cavalry Model** — .45 LC cal. only, exact replica of the original U.S. Government issue SAA, 7½ in. barrel, arsenal stampings, inspector's cartouche on walnut stocks.

Mfg.'s Sug. Retail	$455	$400	$325	$295	$260	$230	$200	$175

* **1895 SAA Artillery Model** — similar specifications to the Cavalry Model, except has 5½ in barrel.

Mfg.'s Sug. Retail	$455	$400	$325	$295	$260	$230	$200	$175

1875 REMINGTON REVOLVER — .44-40 WCF or .45 LC cal., reproduction of the 1875 Remington revolver, 7½ in. barrel, case colored frame, 41 oz. Importation disc. 1991, resumed 1994.

Mfg.'s Sug. Retail	$435	$360	$295	$260	$230	$200	$175	$150

1890 REMINGTON REVOLVER — .44-40 WCF or .45 LC cal., reproduction of the 1890 Remington revolver, 5½ in. barrel, brass trigger guard and lanyard loop, 39 oz. Importation disc. 1991, resumed 1994.

Mfg.'s Sug. Retail	$445	$370	$295	$260	$230	$200	$175	$150

1875 SCHOFIELD CAVALRY MODEL — .44-40 WCF or .45 LC cal., patterned after the original Schofield Cavalry Model, 7½ in. barrel, 37 oz.. New 1994.

Mfg.'s Sug. Retail	$695	$600	$525	$450	$375	$325	$250	$195

1875 SCHOFIELD WELLS FARGO MODEL — .44-40 WCF or .45 LC cal., 5½ in. barrel, 35 oz.. New 1994.

Mfg.'s Sug. Retail	$695	$600	$525	$450	$375	$325	$250	$195

1875 SCHOFIELD HIDEOUT MODEL — .44-40 WCF or .45 LC cal., similar to Wells Fargo Model, except has 3½ in. barrel, 34 oz. New 1999.

Mfg.'s Sug. Retail	$695	$600	$525	$450	$375	$325	$250	$195

N

Grading	100%	98%	95%	90%	80%	70%	60%

1875 ENGRAVED SCHOFIELD — .44-40 WCF or .45 LC cal., similar to Deluxe Schofield, except does not have gold inlays, extensive B or C coverage scroll engraving on both frame, cylinder, and barrel. Special order only beginning 1999.

Mfg.'s Sug. Retail	**$1,565**	**$1,425**	**$1,225**	**$1,000**	**$875**	**$750**	**$625**	**$525**

Add $215 for C engraving.

1875 DELUXE SCHOFIELD — .44-40 WCF or .45 LC cal., available in Cavalry, Wells Fargo, or Hideout configurations, with light scroll engraving on frame and cylinder with extensive frame, barrel, and cylinder gold line inlays and scroll motifs. Special order only beginning 1999.

Mfg.'s Sug. Retail	**$1,875**	**$1,675**	**$1,450**	**$1,250**	**$995**	**$875**	**$750**	**$625**

NEW MODEL RUSSIAN — .44 Russian cal., patterned after the S&W Model 3 Russian Third Model Single Action, 6½ in. barrel, blued metal with case colored trigger, trigger guard, and hammer, smooth walnut grips, 40 oz. Importation began 1999.

Mfg.'s Sug. Retail	**$745**	**$635**	**$550**	**$465**	**$380**	**$330**	**$250**	**$195**

REVOLVERS: REPRODUCTIONS, COLT CARTRIDGE CONVERSIONS

1851 NAVY CONVERSION — .38 Spl. or .38 Colt cal., patterned after the Colt 1851 Navy Conversion, 5½ or 7½ in. barrel, case colored frame and hammer, blued cylinder and barrel, brass back strap and trigger guard, 40 or 44 oz. Importation began 1999.

Mfg.'s Sug. Retail	**$360**	**$315**	**$250**	**$200**	**$175**	**$160**	**$145**	**$130**

1860 ARMY CONVERSION — .38 Spl. or .38 Colt cal., patterned after the Colt 1860 Army Conversion, other specifications similar to 1851 Navy Conversion. Importation began 1999.

Mfg.'s Sug. Retail	**$360**	**$315**	**$250**	**$200**	**$175**	**$160**	**$145**	**$130**

1861 NAVY CONVERSION — .38 Spl. or .38 Colt cal., patterned after the Colt 1861 Navy Conversion, other specifications similar to 1851 Navy Conversion. Importation began 1999.

Mfg.'s Sug. Retail	**$360**	**$315**	**$250**	**$200**	**$175**	**$160**	**$145**	**$130**

RIFLES: REPRODUCTIONS

REVOLVING CARBINE — .357 Mag., .44-40 WCF, or .45 LC cal., 6 shot cylinder, 20 in. barrel, case hardened frame, straight stock. Mfg. 1968-1984.

	$575	**$475**	**$425**	**$375**	**$325**	**$275**	**$225**

REMINGTON ROLLING BLOCK BUFFALO RIFLE — .444 Marlin (disc.), .45-70 Govt., or .50-70 (disc.) cal., replica of Remington Rolling Block, 26 or 30 in. heavy octagon or ½ round/½ octagon barrel, open sight, straight grip stock. Mfg. 1971-present.

Mfg.'s Sug. Retail	**$745**	**$575**	**$425**	**$325**	**$250**	**$185**	**$160**	**$140**

Brass fittings were disc. during 1998, and replaced with steel fittings.

* *Buffalo Carbine* — similar to Rifle, with 18 in. barrel. Disc. 1985.

	$385	**$325**	**$280**	**$230**	**$180**	**$160**	**$140**

Last Mfg.'s Sug. Retail was $375.

* *Rolling Block Baby Carbine* — .22 LR, .22 Hornet, .357 Mag., or .44-40 WCF cal., replica of small frame Remington, 20 in. octagon or 22 in. round barrel, open sight, straight stock. Mfg. 1968-1984.

	$215	**$175**	**$140**	**$110**	**$90**	**$65**	**$55**

ROLLING BLOCK PLAINS RIFLE — .45-70 Govt. cal., features 30 in. tapered octagon barrel with straight grip stock, bright polished receiver with steel furniture, 9 lbs. Imported 1997-98 only.

	$650	**$500**	**$400**	**$285**	**$195**	**$175**	**$150**

Last Mfg.'s Sug. Retail was $800.

N

Grading	100%	98%	95%	90%	80%	70%	60%

* ***Deluxe Rolling Block Plains Rifle*** — similar to Plains Rifle, except has hand engraved coin finished receiver and trigger guard, rust blued barrel with German silver forearm tip. Imported 1997-98.

	$1,475	$1,250	$1,050	$850	$725	$600	$525

Last Mfg.'s Sug. Retail was $1,625.

ROLLING BLOCK NO. 2 CREEDMOOR TARGET — similar to Buffalo Rifle, in .45-70 Govt. or .50-70 (disc.) cal., with Creedmoor tang sight, color case hardened receiver, checkered walnut.

Mfg.'s Sug. Retail	$900		$715	$540	$400	$285	$195	$175	$150

* ***Deluxe Rolling Block No. 2 Creedmoor Target*** — featured hand engraved coin-finished receiver and trigger guard, rust blued barrel and German silver forearm tip. Imported 1997-98.

	$1,625	$1,400	$1,200	$1,000	$850	$725	$600

Last Mfg.'s Sug. Retail was $1,875.

SHARPS PLAINS RIFLE — .45-70 Govt. cal., 32 in. octagon barrel, case hardened receiver, checkered stock and forearm, double set triggers, 9½ lbs. New 1996.

Mfg.'s Sug. Retail	$1,055		$925	$850	$775	$700	$625	$575	$525

Add $70 for vernier rear tang or $55 for globe sight.

* ***Engraved Sharps Plains Rifle*** — .45-70 Govt. cal., features hand engraved coin finished receiver. Imported 1997-98.

	$2,325	$2,000	$1,800	$1,600	$1,400	$1,200	$995

Last Mfg.'s Sug. Retail was $2,500.

Add $700 for gold inlays (Deluxe Model).

SHARPS BUFFALO RIFLE — .45-70 Govt. or .45-90 cal., 28 in. octagon heavy barrel, case colored receiver, checkered stock, 10 lbs. 10 oz. New 1996.

Mfg.'s Sug. Retail	$1,090		$950	$865	$785	$700	$625	$575	$525

Add $70 for vernier rear tang or $55 for globe sight.

* ***Engraved Sharps Buffalo Rifle*** — .45-70 Govt. or .45-90 cal., features hand engraved coin finished receiver. Imported 1997-98.

	$2,325	$2,000	$1,800	$1,600	$1,400	$1,200	$995

Last Mfg.'s Sug. Retail was $2,515.

Add $700 for gold inlays (Deluxe Model).

SHARPS SPORTING RIFLE — .45-70 Govt. cal., similar to Plains Rifle, except has pistol grip stock. Importation began 1997.

Mfg.'s Sug. Retail	$1,090		$950	$865	$785	$700	$625	$575	$525

1874 SHARPS SNIPER/INFANTRY RIFLE — .45-70 Govt. cal., patterned after the 3-band military sniper rifle, 30 in. barrel, color case hardened frame, hammer, and furniture, ST or DST (Sniper rifle, disc. 1995). New 1994.

Mfg.'s Sug. Retail	$1,060		$895	$780	$650	$475	$395	$350	$325

Add $55 for DST (Sniper).

* ***1874 Sharps Cavalry Carbine*** — .45-70 Govt. cal., patterned after Sharps Cavalry carbine, 22 in. barrel, color case hardened frame, hammer, patchbox, and furniture. New 1994.

Mfg.'s Sug. Retail	$935		$735	$535	$395	$280	$195	$175	$150

1873 SPRINGFIELD INFANTRY RIFLE — .45-70 Govt. cal., 32½ in. barrel, 8 lbs, 4 oz. Importation began 1997.

Mfg.'s Sug. Retail	$995		$840	$750	$650	$475	$395	$350	$325

* ***1873 Springfield Cavalry Carbine*** — similar to the 1873 Springfield Rifle, except has 22 in. barrel, 1 barrel band, 7 lbs. Importation began 1997.

Mfg.'s Sug. Retail	$870		$695	$515	$395	$280	$195	$175	$150

Grading	100%	98%	95%	90%	80%	70%	60%

KODIAK MARK IV DOUBLE RIFLE — .45-70 Govt. cal., patterned after the Colt Double rifle, semi-regulated barrels, hammers, folding leaf rear sight, 24 in. barrels, color cased hardened receiver, 10 lbs. 3 oz. New 1996.

Mfg.'s Sug. Retail	$3,125	$2,800	$2,400	$2,250	$2,000	$1,800	$1,600	$1,400

* *Deluxe Kodiak Mark IV* — similar to Kodiak Mark IV Double rifle, except has brown barrels and hand-engraved satin finished receiver. New 1996.

Mfg.'s Sug. Retail	$4,000	$3,700	$3,150	$2,850	$2,600	$2,375	$2,000	$1,750

HENRY RIFLE — .44-40 WCF, .44 Rimfire (disc. 1989), or .45 LC (new 1998) cal., reproduction of Winchester's famous Henry Rifle, brass or iron frame. New 1985.

Add $370 for "A" pattern engraving (25% coverage) on most variations listed below.
Add $585 for "B" pattern engraving (35% coverage) on most variations listed below.
Add $975 for "C" pattern engraving (50% coverage) on most variations listed below.

The above special order engraving patterns usually require 30-60 days.

* *Military Rifle* — 24 in. barrel, brass frame, blued barrel, walnut stock, original style sling swivels, 9¼ lbs. New 1985.

Mfg.'s Sug. Retail	$895	$700	$550	$450	$350	$275	$225	$195

* *Union Pacific Railroad Commemorative* — .44-40 WCF cal., only 100 mfg.

		$795	$575	$475			

Last Mfg.'s Sug. Retail was $695.

* *Engraved Rifle* — limited mfg., extensive engraving on brass frame. Disc. 1988.

	$1,510	$1,275	$1,100	$900	$750	$650	$550

Last Mfg.'s Sug. Retail was $1,850.

Add $100 for steel frame.

* *Carbine* — 24 in. barrel, limited edition of 1,000 units including 50 engraved specimens, no swivels, 8¼ lbs.

Mfg.'s Sug. Retail	$875	$685	$540	$450	$350	$275	$225	$195

* *Engraved Carbine* — limited production, only 50 mfg. Disc. 1988.

	$1,450	$1,225	$1,075	$900	$750	$650	$550

Last Mfg.'s Sug. Retail was $1,750.

* *Trapper Model* — 16½ in. barrel, 7¼ lbs., 34¼ in. overall length.

Mfg.'s Sug. Retail	$875	$685	$540	$450	$350	$275	$225	$195

* *Iron Frame Model* — with steel frame and butt plate, 24 in. blued barrel, select walnut, 9¼ lbs.

Mfg.'s Sug. Retail	$945	$760	$665	$560	$485	$430	$360	$295

This model is available with either blued or color case hardened receiver.

MODEL 1866 YELLOWBOY CARBINE/RIFLE — .22 LR (disc.), .357 Mag. (disc.), .38 Spl. (new 1998), .44-40 WCF, or .45 LC (new 1998) cal., choice of rifle (24 in. octagon barrel) or carbine (19 in. round barrel), case hardened receiver, replica of the Winchester Model 1866. Mfg. 1972-1984, re-introduced.

Mfg.'s Sug. Retail	$675	$545	$450	$350	$250	$195	$175	$150

Add $10 for rifle variation.

YELLOWBOY TRAPPER — .44-40 WCF cal., 16½ in. barrel.

	$575	$475	$425	$375	$325	$275	$225

N

MODEL 1873 STANDARD CARBINE/RIFLE — .357 Mag. (new 1998), .44-40 WCF or .45 LC cal., choice of rifle (24 in. octagon barrel) or carbine (19 in. round barrel), replica of the Winchester Model 1873.

Mfg.'s Sug. Retail	$800	$695	$600	$515	$425	$350	$295	$250

Add $20 for rifle variation.

* *Model 1873 Trapper* — .44-40 WCF cal., similar to Carbine, with 16½ in. barrel.

	$575	$475	$425	$375	$325	$275	$225

Grading	100%	98%	95%	90%	80%	70%	60%

* **Model 1873 Border Model Rifle** — .357 Mag., .44-40 WCF, or .45 LC cal., features 20 in. short octagon rifle barrel, case hardened receiver with blued barrel, 7 lbs. 6 oz. Importation began 1999.

Mfg.'s Sug. Retail	$820	$715	$610	$520	$425	$350	$295	$250

* **Model 1873 Deluxe Sporting Rifle** — deluxe variation of the Model 1873 featuring case hardened receiver, checkered pistol grip stock, and choice of 24 (carbine) or 30 (rifle, not available in .357 Mag. cal.) in. barrel, 8 lbs. 14 oz. New 1992.

Mfg.'s Sug. Retail	$930	$820	$695	$550	$425	$325	$275	$225

    Add $30 for 30 in. barrel.

* **Model 1873 1 of 1,000** — only 1,000 mfg., deluxe wood, special engraving.

	$1,000	$775	$550

MODEL 1892 STANDARD CARBINE/RIFLE — .357 Mag., .44-40 WCF, or .45 LC cal., features 20 (carbine, w/o forearm cap) or 24 (rifle) in. octagon barrel, choice of brass, blued, or case hardened receiver and crescent butt plate, uncheckered straight grip walnut stock and forearm, 5 lbs. 14 oz. or 7 lbs. Importation began 1999.

Mfg.'s Sug. Retail	$435	$360	$295	$260	$230	$200	$175	$150

    Add $60 for rifle configuration.

* **Model 1892 Short Rifle** — similar to Model 1892 Standard Rifle, except has 20 in. short barrel, not available with brass frame, approx. 6¼ lbs. Importation began 1999.

Mfg.'s Sug. Retail	$495	$400	$325	$275	$245	$210	$185	$155

MODEL 1895 HIGH WALL RIFLE — .45-70 Govt. cal., available with 30 in. medium heavy octagon barrel with crescent butt plate or 28 in. round barrel with shotgun style butt plate, standard open or target sights, case hardened frame and lever, uncheckered European walnut stock and forearm, 9¼ or 10 lbs. Importation began 1999.

Mfg.'s Sug. Retail	$745	$660	$560	$485	$395	$325	$275	$225

    Add $70 for 30 in. octagon barrel.
    Add $100 for target sights (aperture rear tang and globe front).

RIFLES: MODERN PRODUCTION

In addition to the models listed below, Navy Arms in late 1990 purchased the manufacturing rights of the English firm, Parker-Hale. In 1991, Navy Arms built a manufacturing facility located in Martinsburg, WV and produced these rifles domestically 1991-1994. The name of this company is Gibbs Rifle Co., and the current models listed below are made in this location (see Gibbs Rifle Co. listing for more info).

TU-KKW TRAINING RIFLE — .22 LR cal., replica of the German "KKW" Gewehr training rifle, full sized Mauser 98K action with military sights, 26 in. barrel, detachable 5 shot mag., mfg. in China, 8 lbs. Imported 1992-94.

	$210	$180	$150	$135	$120	$105	$90

           Last Mfg.'s Sug. Retail was $310.

    Add $125 for 2¾ power Type 89 quick mount scope (Sniper Trainer).

TU-33/40 CARBINE — .22 LR or 7.62x39mm cal., based on WWII Mauser G33/40 mountain carbine, 20¾ in. barrel, includes sling, adj. rear sight, mfg. in China, 7 lbs. 7 oz. Imported 1992-94.

	$180	$150	$135	$120	$105	$90	$75

           Last Mfg.'s Sug. Retail was $210.

JW-15 RIFLE — .22 LR cal., sporter bolt action based on Brno Model 5 action, 24 in. barrel, detachable 5 shot mag., receiver top is dove-tailed, mfg. in China, 5 lbs. 12 oz. Imported 1992-94.

	$85	$70	$60	$50	$40	$35	$30

           Last Mfg.'s Sug. Retail was $100.

N

Grading	100%	98%	95%	90%	80%	70%	60%

MARTINI TARGET RIFLE — .444 Marlin or .45-70 Govt. cal., single shot, 26 or 30 in. octagon barrel, tang sight, pistol grip stock. Mfg. 1972-1984.

	$480	$420	$350	$250	$195	$175	$150

RPKS-74 — .223 Rem. or 7.62x39mm (new 1989) cal., semi-automatic version of the Chinese RPK Squad Automatic Weapon, Kalashnikov action, 19 in. barrel, integral folding bipod, 9½ lbs. Imported 1988-1989 only.

	$525	$445	$350	$250	$195	$175	$150

Last Mfg.'s Sug. Retail was $649.

MODEL 1 CARBINE/RIFLE — .45-70 Govt. cal., action is sporterized No. 1 MKIII Enfield, choice of 18 (carbine) or 22 (rifle) in. barrel with iron sights, black Zytel Monte Carlo (rifle) or straight grip walnut (carbine) stock, 7 (carbine) or 8½ (rifle) lbs. New 1999.

Mfg.'s Sug. Retail	$375	$325	$255	$200	$175	$160	$145	$130

MODEL 4 CARBINE/RIFLE — .45-70 Govt. cal., action is sporterized No. 4 MKI Enfield, choice of 18 (carbine) or 22 (rifle) in. barrel, blued metal, choice of checkered walnut Monte Carlo (rifle) or uncheckered straight grip (carbine) stock, 7 or 8 lbs. New 1999.

Mfg.'s Sug. Retail	$375	$325	$255	$200	$175	$160	$145	$130

* *Deluxe No. 4 Enfield Sporter* — .303 British cal., synthetic Zytel Monte Carlo stock, 25 in. barrel with original military sights, approx. 8½ lbs. New 1999.

Mfg.'s Sug. Retail	$125	$115	$95	$85	$75	$65	$55	$50

2A HUNTER CARBINE/RIFLE — .308 Win. cal., action is sporterized 2A Enfield, 18 (carbine) or 22 (rifle) in. barrel with Parker-Hale style muzzle brake, includes scope mount, 12 shot mag., black enamel synthetic Zytel stock, 6¾ or 10¼ lbs. New 1999.

Mfg.'s Sug. Retail	$275	$240	$210	$190	$175	$160	$145	$130

Add $50 for rifle variation.

* *Deluxe 2A Enfield Sporter* — .308 Win. cal., 25 in. barrel, black Zytel Monte Carlo stock, original 2A Enfield military sights, approx. 8½ lbs. New 1999.

Mfg.'s Sug. Retail	$150	$130	$110	$95	$85	$75	$65	$55

SHOTGUNS: O/U, RECENT IMPORTATION

Importation of the models listed below was disc. in 1990.

MODEL 83 — 12 or 20 ga., manufactured in Italy by R. Luciano, 3 in. chambers, extractors, double triggers, engraved chrome receiver, vent. barrels (bored M/F or IC/M) and rib. Introduced 1985.

	$280	$240	$215	$195	$170	$160	$150

Last Mfg.'s Sug. Retail was $320.

MODEL 93 — 12 or 20 ga., manufactured in Italy by R. Luciano, 3 in. chambers, ejectors, double triggers, engraved chrome receiver, vent. barrels (bored M/F or IC/M) and rib. Introduced 1985.

	$325	$285	$250	$220	$200	$185	$160

Last Mfg.'s Sug. Retail was $380.

MODEL 95 — similar to Model 93, except with single trigger and multi-chokes (includes 5 tubes), extractors.

	$375	$330	$295	$265	$235	$210	$190

Last Mfg.'s Sug. Retail was $420.

N

MODEL 96 SPORTSMAN — 12 ga. only, 3 in. chambers, vent. barrels and rib, engraved chrome receiver, gold-plated receiver, multi-choked with 5 choke tubes, ejectors. Introduced 1985.

	$470	$425	$375	$330	$295	$260	$230

Last Mfg.'s Sug. Retail was $530.

MODEL 100 — 12, 20, 28 ga., or .410 bore, 3 in. chambers, 26 in. VR barrels, photo-engraved hard chrome receiver, single trigger, extractors, checkered walnut stock and forearm, approx. 6¼ lbs. Introduced 1985.

	$225	$205	$190	$170	$160	$150	$140

Last Mfg.'s Sug. Retail was $250.

Grading	100%	98%	95%	90%	80%	70%	60%

SHOTGUNS: SxS, RECENT IMPORTATION

MODEL 100 — 12 or 20 ga., 3 in. chambers, 27½ in. barrels, checkered European walnut, double triggers, extractors, 6½ or 7 lbs. Imported 1985-1987 only.

			$380	$330	$290	$260	$230	$200	$170

Last Mfg.'s Sug. Retail was $475.

MODEL 150 — similar to Model 100, except with ejectors. Imported 1985-1987 only.

			$455	$395	$350	$310	$280	$250	$220

Last Mfg.'s Sug. Retail was $574.

SHOTGUNS: SINGLE SHOT

MODEL 105 SINGLE BARREL — 12, 20 ga., or .410 bore, 26 or 28 in. full choke barrel only, folding action, engraved chrome receiver, checkered hardwood stock and forearm. New 1985.

			$80	$70	$65	$60	$55	$50	$45

Last Mfg.'s Sug. Retail was $90.

This model was designated the Model 600 before 1988.

* *Model 105 Deluxe* — similar to Model 105, except has European walnut stock and VR.

			$95	$85	$75	$65	$60	$55	$50

Last Mfg.'s Sug. Retail was $105.

This model was designated the Model 600 Deluxe before 1988.

P.V. NELSON, (GUNMAKERS)

Current manufacturer located in Bucks, England (factory is located in London).

P.V. Nelson manufactures best quality shotguns and double rifles per individual customer order. Double rifles feature back action locks, and bolsters for extra strength. Side-by-side and over/under shotguns are available in most gauges, with a choice of rounded or regular action. Please contact the factory directly (see Trademark Index) to find out more information about this quality English manufacturer. P.V. Nelson manufactures 10-20 guns annually.

NESIKA

Current trademark of rifle actions manufactured by Nesika Bay Precision, Inc., located in Poulsbo, WA. Dealer and consumer sales.

Nesika makes some of the most advanced rifle actions available today. As this edition went to press, the company had plans to start manufacturing complete rifles in the near future. Please contact the factory directly for a price list on their actions (7 different types), in addition to more information on their upcoming rifle production.

NEW DETONICS MANUFACTURING CORPORATION

Previous manufacturer located in Phoenix, AZ 1989-1992. Formerly named Detonics Firearms Industries (previous manufacturer located in Bellevue, WA 1976-1988). Detonics was sold in early 1988 to the New Detonics Manufacturing Corporation, a wholly owned subsidiary of "1045 Investors Group Limited".

PISTOLS: SEMI-AUTO, STAINLESS

MARK I — .45 ACP cal., matte blue. Disc. 1981.

			$550	$450	$395				

MARK II — .45 ACP cal., satin nickel finish. Disc. 1979.

			$495	$375	$300				

MARK III — .45 ACP cal., hard chrome finish. Disc. 1979.

			$520	$390	$325				

Grading	100%	98%	95%	90%	80%	70%	60%

MARK IV — .45 ACP cal., polished blue. Disc. 1981.

$539 $410 $360

COMBATMASTER MC1 (FORMERLY MARK I) — .45 ACP, 9mm Para., or .38 Super cal., 3½ in. barrel, two-tone (slide is non-glare blue and frame is matte stainless) finish, 6 shot mag., fixed sights, 28 oz. Disc. 1992.

$775 $575 $450

Last Mfg.'s Sug. Retail was $920.

Add $15 for OM-3 model (polished slide - disc. 1983).
Add $100 for 9mm Para. or .38 Super cal. (disc. 1990).

This model was originally the MC1, then changed to the Mark I, then changed back to the MC1.

COMBATMASTER MARK V — .45 ACP, 9mm Para., or .38 Super cal., matte stainless finish, fixed sights, 6 shot mag. in .45 ACP, 7 shot in 9mm Para. and .38 Super, 3½ in. barrel, 29 oz. empty. This model was disc. 1985.

$620 $550 $495

Last Mfg.'s Sug. Retail was $689.

Add $100 for 9mm Para. or .38 Super cal.

COMBATMASTER MARK VI — .45 ACP, 9mm Para., or .38 Super cal., 3½ in. barrel, 6 shot mag., adj. sights and polished stainless slide sides. Disc. 1989.

$685 $575 $450

Last Mfg.'s Sug. Retail was $795.

Add $100 for 9mm Para. or .38 Super cal.

* **.451 Detonics Mag. Cal.** — limited mfg. 1,000. Disc. 1985.

$1,000 $900 $775

Last Mfg.'s Sug. Retail was $1,165.

COMBATMASTER MARK VII — similar to Mark VI, only no sights, special order only, 25 oz.

$895 $775 $600

Add $100 for 9mm Para. or .38 Super cal.
Add $350 for .451 Detonics Mag., (disc. 1982).

MILITARY COMBAT MC2 — .45 ACP, 9mm Para., or .38 Super cal., dull, non-glare combat finish, fixed sights. Comes with camouflaged pile-lined wallet, and Pachmayr grips. Disc. 1984.

$621 $560 $500

Add $55 for 9mm Para. or .38 Super.

O.S. MODEL — .45 ACP cal. only, emergency backup pistol, similar to Combatmaster, 6 shot mag., choice of satin stainless or all black finish. 2 mfg. 1991 only.

Extreme rarity precludes accurate price evaluation.

SCOREMASTER — .45 ACP or .451 Mag. cal., match gun with closer tolerances, 5 or 6 in. barrel. Millett adj. sights, grip safety, 7 or 8 shot mag., 42 oz. Disc. 1992.

$995 $850 $695

Last Mfg.'s Sug. Retail was $1,178.

Add $40 for 6 in. barrel.

COMPMASTER — .45 ACP cal. only, similar to Scoremaster, except is fully compensated. Mfg. 1988-92.

$1,995 $1,575 $1,250

Last Mfg.'s Sug. Retail was $1,550.

This model was called the Janus Competition Scoremaster in 1988-1989.

COMPETITION MASTER T.F. — .45 ACP cal., competition model with dual port compensator, rotational torque compensating vents, patented coned barrel system, hand tuned trigger, includes all competition modifications. Disc. 1992.

$1,995 $1,575 $1,250

Last Mfg.'s Sug. Retail was $1,550.

N

Grading	100%	98%	95%	90%	80%	70%	60%

SERVICEMASTER — .45 ACP cal. only, shortened version of the Scoremaster, non-glare combat finish, 4¼ in. barrel, coned barrel system, 8 shot mag., interchangeable front and adj. rear sights, 39 oz. Disc. 1986.

$825 $675 $575

Last Mfg.'s Sug. Retail was $686.

* *Servicemaster II* — similar to Servicemaster, except has polished stainless steel finish. Mfg. 1986-92.

$925 $750 $625

Last Mfg.'s Sug. Retail was $998.

New Detonics Ladies Escort Series

This series was designed specifically to suit a woman's shooting requirements.

ROYAL ESCORT — .45 ACP cal., action similar to Combatmaster, 3½ in. barrel, 6 shot mag., black frame, slide and grips are iridescent purple, hammer and trigger are 24 Kt. gold-plated. Mfg. 1990-92.

$860 $675 $525

Last Mfg.'s Sug. Retail was $990.

MIDNIGHT ESCORT — similar to Royal Escort, except is stainless with a black slide and smooth black grips. Mfg. 1990-92.

$965 $725 $580

Last Mfg.'s Sug. Retail was $1,090.

JADE ESCORT — similar to Midnight Escort, except has stainless frame, jade colored slide and grips. Mfg. 1990 only.

$825 $650 $525

Last Mfg.'s Sug. Retail was $918. Less than 25 of this color were mfg.

POCKET 9 — 9mm Para. cal., double action, 3 in. barrel, 6 shot mag., soft matte sheen finish, 26 oz. Limited mfg. 1985-86 only.

$495 $400 $335

Last Mfg.'s Sug. Retail was $458.

The entire Pocket 9 series was disc. 1986.

* *Pocket 9 LS* — similar to Pocket 9, except has 4 in. barrel. Limited mfg. 1986 only.

$575 $450 $375

Last Mfg.'s Sug. Retail was $458.

* *Pocket .380* — similar to Pocket 9, except is .380 ACP cal., 23 oz. Limited mfg. 1986 only.

$575 $450 $375

Last Mfg.'s Sug. Retail was $458.

POWER 9 — 9mm Para. cal., similar to Pocket 9, except has polished slide sides and is supplied with 2 mags. Disc. 1986.

$575 $450 $375

Last Mfg.'s Sug. Retail was $509.

NEW ENGLAND ARMS CORP.

Current importer, distributor, and retailer established during 1975, and located in Kittery Point, ME.

New England Arms Corp. imports, distributes, or retails the following trademarks: Arrieta, P. Arrizabalaga, Bertuzzi, Carlo Casartelli, Americo Cosmi, Henri Dumoulin, Fair Techni-Mec (I. Rizzini), Lebeau-Courally, F.lli Rizzini, B. Rizzini, Luciano Rota, and Fabio Zanotti. These trademarks may be found under their own headings in this text. For further information regarding any one of these manufacturers, please contact the company directly. New England Arms Corp. also offers quality restoration services on best quality shotguns and rifles executed by trained European craftsmen, in addition to performing firearms appraisals and evaluation work.

New England Arms Corp. should not be confused with New England Firearms.

Grading	100%	98%	95%	90%	80%	70%	60%

NEW ENGLAND CUSTOM GUN SERVICE, LTD.

Current company that specializes in custom gun services including checkering, stock fitting/alterations, claw mount scope installation and repair, detachable rifle scope mounts, and other gunsmithing services. Additionally, NECG Ltd. imports Johannsen rifles from Germany. Please contact the company directly regarding more information on their extensive line of products and services, including Johannsen rifles.

NEW ENGLAND FIREARMS

Current manufacturer established 1987, and located in Gardner, MA. Distributor sales only.

All NEF firearms utilize a transfer bar safety and have a $10 service plan which guarantees lifetime warranty.

New England Firearms should not be confused with New England Arms Corp.

REVOLVERS: DOUBLE ACTION

Ultra Models listed below are available in blue finish only. Beginning 1993, all Ultras include lockable storage case.

STANDARD REVOLVER .22 (MODEL R92) — .22 S, L, and LR cal., 9 shot, swing out cylinder, 2½ (disc. 1997), 3 (new 1998) or 4 in. barrel, blue or nickel finish, hardwood stocks, fixed rear sight, 25-28 oz. New 1988.

Mfg.'s Sug. Retail	$144		$125	$95	$85	$70	$60	$55	$40

Add $10 for nickel finish.

* Standard Revolver .32 H&R Mag. (Model R73) — .32 H&R Mag. cal. similar to Standard Revolver .22, except has 5 shot cylinder, 2½ (disc.), 3, or 4 in. barrel, choice of blue or nickel finish (not available with 4 in. barrel), 23-26 oz. New 1988.

Mfg.'s Sug. Retail	$144		$125	$95	$85	$70	$60	$55	$40

Add $10 for nickel finish (2½ or 3 in. barrel only).

ULTRA MODEL — .22 S, L, or LR cal., 9 shot, swing-out cylinder, 4 or 6 in. solid rib target-grade barrel with rebated muzzle and fully adj. rear sight, blue finish, smooth hardwood grips, 36 oz.

Mfg.'s Sug. Retail	$180		$150	$115	$95	$80	$70	$60	$55

ULTRA MAG (MODEL R22) — .22 Mag. cal., 6 shot, 4 (disc. 1997) or 6 in. solid rib barrel, adj. rear sight, swing-out cylinder, blue finish, 36 oz. New 1988.

Mfg.'s Sug. Retail	$180		$150	$115	$95	$80	$70	$60	$55

LADY ULTRA — .32 H&R Mag. cal., swing-out cylinder, 5 shot, blue finish, 3 (disc. 1997, reintroduced 1999) or 4 (mfg. 1998 only) in. barrel with rib, adj. sights, thinner contoured grips, 31 oz. New 1991.

Mfg.'s Sug. Retail	$180		$150	$115	$95	$80	$70	$60	$55

New England Firearms Co. also manufactures blank starter revolvers (.22 or .32 cal.) which are variations of this model - retail is currently $116.

N

Grading	100%	98%	95%	90%	80%	70%	60%

RIFLES: SINGLE SHOT

HANDI-RIFLE — .22 Hornet, .22-250 Rem. (mfg. 1992-94), .223 Rem., .243 Win. (new 1992), .270 Win. (new 1993), .280 Rem. (new 1996), .30-30 Win., .30-06 (new 1992), .308 Win. (new 1998), .357 Mag. (new 1999), .44 Rem. Mag. (new 1996), .45-70 Govt., 7x57mm Mauser (new 1998), or 7x64mm Brenneke (new 1998) cal., break open single shot action, 22 or 26 (.280 Rem. only) in. regular or bull (.223 Rem. or .22-250 Rem.) barrel, blued receiver, walnut stained hardwood stock, scope mount rail or ramp front and adj. folding rear sights, sling swivels, 7 lbs. New 1989.

Mfg.'s Sug. Retail	$212	$175	$140	$115	$95	$80	$70	$60

Add $5 for .280 Rem. cal.

This model in .22-250 Rem., .223 Rem., or .243 Win. cal. is supplied with heavy barrel, scope mount, and no sights.

* ***Handi-Rifle Synthetic*** — .22 Hornet, .223 Rem., .243 Win., .270 Win., .280 Rem., .30-30 Win., .30-06, .44 Rem. Mag., or .45-70 Govt. cal., 22 or 26 (.280 Rem. only) in. barrel, blue finish, features black synthetic stock and forearm, adj. sights on some cals., scope base mount only on others. New 1998.

Mfg.'s Sug. Retail	$220	$185	$145	$115	$100	$85	$80	$75

Add $5 for .280 Rem. cal.

* ***Handi-Rifle Youth*** — .223 Rem. or .243 Win. cal, features 22 in. barrel and shortened stock dimensions, blue finish. New 1998.

Mfg.'s Sug. Retail	$212	$175	$140	$115	$95	$80	$70	$60

* ***10th Anniversary Handi-Rifle*** — same cals. as Handi-Rifle, limited edition features scroll engraving by Ken Hurst, deep bluing on receiver, steel trigger guard and forearm spacer, select hand checkered walnut, less than 100 mfg. 1997 only.

	$695	$475	$350

Last Mfg.'s Sug. Retail was $750.

* ***Handi-Rifle NTA Anniversary Edition*** — .223 Rem. only, 24 in. heavy barrel w/o sights, features checkered black/grey laminate stock and forearm with NTA (National Trapper's Association) medallion in stock. Limited production beginning 1999.

Mfg.'s Sug. Retail	$272	$225	$200	$175	$160	$145	$135	$125

SUPER LIGHT YOUTH — .22 Hornet, .223 Rem., or .243 Win. cal., break open single shot, black synthetic stock and forearm, recoil pad, 20 in. special contour barrel with rebated muzzle, .22 Hornet has sights (Model SB2-SL4), .223 Rem. has scope base and hammer extension (Model SB2-SL3), approx. 5½ lbs. New 1997.

Mfg.'s Sug. Retail	$220	$185	$145	$115	$100	$85	$80	$75

This model is also available as a Youth Model with shorter stock dimensions.

SPORTSTER — .22 LR cal. only, 20 in. mid-weight barrel with Weaver style scope rail, available in either adult or youth dimensions, black polymer stock and forearm. New 1999.

Mfg.'s Sug. Retail	$122	$105	$90	$80	$70	$60	$50	$45

SURVIVOR RIFLE — .223 Rem., .308 Win. (new 1999), .357 Mag. (disc. 1998) cal., similar in design to the Survival Series shotgun, 22 in. barrel, blue or nickel (disc. 1998) finish, .357 Mag. cal. has open sights, .223 Rem. and .308 Win. cal. have integral scope rails, 6 lbs. New 1996.

Mfg.'s Sug. Retail	$220	$185	$150	$120	$95	$80	$70	$60

Add $15 for nickel finish.

N

Grading	100%	98%	95%	90%	80%	70%	60%

SHOTGUNS: SINGLE SHOT

PARDNER — 12, 16 (new 1989), 20, 28 ga.(new 1991), or .410 bore, $2\frac{3}{4}$ or 3 in. chamber (12, 20 ga., and .410 bore), single shot, break open action, safety transfer bar mechanism on hammer, side lever release, color case hardened receiver, 24 (disc.), 26, 28, or 32 in. fixed choke barrel, extractor, walnut stained hardwood stock and forearm, 5-6 lbs. New 1987.

Mfg.'s Sug. Retail	$103	$90	$80	$70	$60	$50	$45	$40

   Add $15 for 32 in. barrel (12 ga. only).

* *Pardner Youth* — 12 (new 1998), 20, 28 ga., or .410 bore, similar to Pardner, except has 22 in. barrel and straight grip stock with recoil pad.

Mfg.'s Sug. Retail	$111	$95	$80	$70	$60	$50	$45	$40

   ➤*Pardner Youth Turkey* — 20 ga. only, features 22 in. full choke barrel and camo wood. New 1999.

Mfg.'s Sug. Retail	$126	$105	$90	$80	$70	$60	$50	$45

* *Pardner Special Purpose 10 ga.* — 10 ga. only, $3\frac{1}{2}$ in. chamber, 24 (Turkey full choke with matte black finish, new 1996), 28, or 32 (new 1996) in. barrel, blue or camo paint finish, recoil pad, $9\frac{1}{2}$ lbs. New 1988.

Mfg.'s Sug. Retail	$169	$140	$115	$95	$75	$65	$55	$45

   Add $15 for camo finish, swivels, and swing.
   Add $30 for 32 in. barrel with camo finish, swivels, and sling.
   Add $29 for 24 in. Turkey full choke variation.

* *Pardner Turkey Gun* — 12 ga. only, 3 or $3\frac{1}{2}$ (camo finish only) in. chamber, 24 in. barrel with fixed or full choke tube, 100% camo or matte black finish. New 1999.

Mfg.'s Sug. Retail	$126	$105	$90	$80	$70	$60	$50	$45

   Add $10 for choke tube.

* *Pardner NRA Foundation Youth* — 20, 28 ga. or .410 bore, 22 in. barrel, high luster bluing, features "NRA Foundation Youth Endowment Edition" laser etched in black on stock, approx. $5\frac{1}{2}$ lbs. New 1999.

Mfg.'s Sug. Retail	$132	$110	$95	$80	$70	$60	$50	$45

* *National Wild Turkey Federation (NWTF)* — 10 or 20 (new 1993) ga., 22 (20 ga. only) or 24 in. barrel with full screw-in choke, full Mossy Oak camo treatment, includes swivels and sling. Mfg. 1992-96.

		$190	$160	$135	$110	$95	$80	$70

                                 Last Mfg.'s Sug. Retail was $230.

   Subtract $80 for 20 ga.

   This model has been drilled and tapped for scope mounts.

SURVIVOR SERIES — 12, 20 ga., or .410/.45 LC (new 1995) bore, 3 in. chamber, 20 (.410/.45 LC) or 22 in. barrel with Mod. choke, blue or electroless nickel finish, synthetic thumbhole designed hollow stock with pistol grip, removable forend holds additional ammo, sling swivels, and black nylon sling, 6 lbs. Mfg. 1992-93, re-instated 1995.

Mfg.'s Sug. Retail	$128	$110	$90	$70	$60	$50	$45	$40

   Add $19 for electroless nickel finish.
   Add $34 for .410/.45 LC bore.

TRACKER SLUG MODEL — 10 ga. x $3\frac{1}{2}$ in. (chamber mfg. 1994 only), 12, or 20 ga., 24 in. cylinder bore barrel, case colored receiver, includes recoil pad and adj. sights, 6 lbs. New 1992.

Mfg.'s Sug. Retail	$139	$115	$90	$75	$60	$50	$45	$40

* *Tracker II* — 12 or 20 ga., 3 in. chamber, similar to Tracker Slug Model except has 24 in. rifled bore barrel. New 1995.

Mfg.'s Sug. Retail	$147	$120	$95	$70	$60	$50	$45	$40

N

Grading	100%	98%	95%	90%	80%	70%	60%

NEWTON ARMS CO.

Previous manufacturer located in Buffalo, NY circa 1913-1932. Also named Charles Newton Rifle Corp. and Buffalo Newton Rifle Co.

RIFLES: BOLT ACTION

NEWTON-MAUSER RIFLE — Oberndorf bolt action, .256 Newton cal., 24 in. barrel, release or double set triggers, checkered pistol grip stock. Pre-WWI mfg.

	100%	98%	95%	90%	80%	70%	60%
	$800	$650	$550	$440	$385	$330	$275

FIRST TYPE STANDARD RIFLE — Newton bolt action, .22 Newton, .256 Newton, .280 Newton, .30 Newton, .33 Newton, .35 Newton, or .30-06 cal., 24 in. barrel, double set triggers, open or aperture sights, checkered pistol grip stock. Mfg. 1916-1918 by Newton Arms.

	100%	98%	95%	90%	80%	70%	60%
	$1,150	$925	$750	$625	$500	$440	$385

SECOND TYPE STANDARD RIFLE — improved Newton action, has Enfield type bolt handle, .256 Newton, .30 Newton, .35 Newton, or .30-06 cal., open sights, checkered pistol grip stock. Mfg. post-WWI by Charles Newton Rifle Corporation.

	100%	98%	95%	90%	80%	70%	60%
	$1,000	$825	$660	$600	$500	$440	$385

BUFFALO NEWTON RIFLE — similar to Second Type. Mfg. 1922-1932 by Buffalo Newton Rifle company.

	100%	98%	95%	90%	80%	70%	60%
	$1,000	$825	$660	$600	$500	$440	$385

SPRINGFIELD NEWTON — kit consisting of a Newton barrel and sporter stock, barrels were chambered for Newton calibers, kits were available to adapt Springfield rifles into Newton calibers in the 1920s when the NRA made the Springfields available to its membership.

	100%	98%	95%	90%	80%	70%	60%
	$595	$540	$495	$450	$410	$375	$330

NIKKO FIREARMS CO. LTD.

Previous manufacturer located in Tochigi, Japan circa 1958-1989.

The publisher wishes to thank the Golden Eagle Collectors Association located at 11144 Slate Creek Road, Grass Valley, CA 95945 for providing this publication with the information listed below. Please refer to the Golden Eagle heading in this text for information on Nikko manufactured Golden Eagle firearms.

Both Nikko Firearms Co., Ltd. and Nikko Arms Co., Ltd. were trade names used by the Kodensha Co., Ltd. of Tochigi, Japan on products they manufactured and distributed worldwide. Nikko is the name of the Prefecture, or district, in which Tochigi City is located, about 50 miles north of Tokyo. The word Nikko translates to English as "sunshine". Kodensha first manufactured or distributed under the Nikko name in April 1955, and exported out of Japan beginning in August 1958. Nothing is known of the origin of the Kodensha Co.

Kodenshá first approached the American shotgun market in about 1958 or '59 using the Japanese export marketing firm of Kyowa-Boeki-Bussan. They contacted various US distributors, and in about 1959 or '60, Continental Arms Co. of New York City began importing the Nikko "Grade 5". Continental imported these Nikko over/unders, in various models and configurations, until about 1972.

In 1962, the Kodensha Co. Ltd. formed a joint venture with Olin/Winchester of New Haven, CT to produce the Winchester Model 101 over/under shotgun. This venture was known as the Olin-Kodensha Co. Ltd. Added a little later was the side-by-side Model 23, and the Model 96 Xpert (a budget priced 101). The "pre-Olin" Kodensha factory was considerably outdated, and the joint venture began a complete modernization process, with the financial and technical assistance of Olin. Millions of dollars of machinery and technology were brought in, and the entire manufacturing process was upgraded to the then current standards.

N

One of the conditions of the joint venture was that Kodensha restrict their own products (made in the same factory, but recorded separately from the joint venture) to sale in Japan only. At the outset of the 25 years that the joint venture existed, Kodensha was probably amenable to this, as they were reaping huge financial and technical benefits from Olin. But, by the mid '60s, when the factory was in place and running smoothly, Kodensha essentially ignored that condition of the agreement, leaving Olin at somewhat of a disadvantage, not wanting to jeopardize their investment or production source. Additionally, Olin/Winchester was allowed only 2 permanent personnel, hardly enough to monitor the activities of a factory which employed up to 400 people. As an example, when walnut stock blanks arrived from France, Kodensha took first pick, and Olin got what was left over.

Kodensha converted an existing building near the manufacturing plant into an assembly area for Nikko, and other brands of guns. This building was probably the "true" Nikko Firearms Co. Ltd. Manufactured components from the Olin-Kodensha factory were carted to the Nikko plant for final assembly and fitting. This "dual-factory" arrangement continued until the mid-1980s. In 1981, for an unknown reason, the Olin-Kodensha name was changed to OK Firearms Co. Ltd. In October 1987, Olin/Winchester sold their interest in OK Firearms to Classic Doubles International, which continued making the 101 style shotgun under their own name. For reasons unknown, Classic Doubles went out of business in December 1988. Shortly thereafter, the entire factory was torn down, and all that remains today is a vacant lot.

During the "dual-factory" days, Nikko produced firearms for the following distributors or retailers: 1) Kanematsu Gosho of Arlington Heights, IL approx. 1974-1982 - distributed Nikko brand shotguns, Golden Eagle brand shotguns and rifles (1975 through March 1977 only); 2) Golden Eagle Firearms, Houston, TX March 1977 through early 1981 - Golden Eagle shotguns and rifles; 3) Tradewinds, Inc. of Tacoma, WA exported from Japan by Caspoll International, Tokyo January 1971 through December 1972 - Shadow Seven; Shadow Indy (Model 707); Gold, Silver, and Black Shadow over/under shotguns; 4) Marubeni America, Inc. of New York City 1972-1974 - Miida brand over/under shotguns; 5) Winchester GMBH of West Germany, manufactured by Olin-Kodensha (dates unknown - early '80s) - Winchester Model 777 rifle (Golden Eagle look-alike); 6) Parker Reproduction shotguns, distributed in the US by Reagent Chemical & Research, Inc. 1984-1988; 7) International Star Commerce Corp. (ISCC) of Salt Lake City, Utah approx. 1982 - distributor of Nikko brand shotguns; 8) Moore Supply Co. of Salt Lake City, UT beginning mid-1981 - distributor of Nikko brand shotguns; 9) USA Nikko, Inc. of Los Angeles, CA (factory reps and distributors of Nikko shotguns), initial date unknown, through December 1981; 10) Weatherby, Inc. of Los Angeles, CA May 1972 to 1981. Centurion semi-auto and Patrician pump shotguns, some Mark 22 rifles. Olympian O/U shotgun and possibly other O/Us from 1978-81. Model 82 semi-auto and Model 92 pump shotguns; 11) Savage Industries of Hamden, CT 1981-1982 - Savage/Fox FA-1 and FP-1 shotguns; 12) Charles Daly. "Automatic" distributed by Sloan's (Japanese made only) mid-1980s; 13) Sears, Roebuck Co. Ted Williams Model 400 and possibly others; 14) Churchill semi-auto, imported by Kassnar mid-1980s; 15) High Standard of Hamden, CT 1974-75 - Supermatic Shadow Indy (Model 707, an O/U), Supermatic Shadow Seven (also O/U), and Supermatic Shadow semi-auto.

NOTE: ALL of the semi-auto shotguns used essentially the same design. Each distributor may have made a few cosmetic or dimensional embellishments to differentiate their gun. Differences exist in barrel/breech fit, magazine caps, pistol grip caps, checkering pattern, piston size, ejector location, fluted bolt. Use caution if interchanging parts. Generally, the same statement can be made about the pump versions also.

N

Grading	100%	98%	95%	90%	80%	70%	60%

NOBLE MFG. CO.

Previous manufacturer located in Haydenville, MA circa 1950-1970.

Nobel manufactured both semi-auto, lever, and slide action rifles in addition to both slide action and SxS shotguns. While most models were relatively inexpensive, good working, utilitarian guns, there has been little collectability to date and most rifles are seen priced in the $35-$85 price range while the shotguns are priced in the $65-$175 range.

NORINCO

Current manufacturer located in China. Currently imported by Norinco Sports U.S.A., located in Diamond Bar, CA. Previous importers have included: Century International Arms, Inc. located in St. Albans, VT; China Sports, Inc. located in Ontario, CA; Interarms located in Alexandria, VA; KBI, Inc. located in Harrisburg, PA; and others. Dealer and distributor sales only.

Norinco pistols, rifles, and shotguns are manufactured in the People's Republic of China by Northern China Industries Corp. (Norinco has over 100 factories). Due to current legislation, Chinese handguns and rifles are not allowed to be imported in the U.S.

PISTOLS: SEMI-AUTO

MODEL 213 — 9mm Para. cal., single action, satin blue finish. Imported 1988 only.

$185	$150	$135	$125	$115	$105	$100

Last Mfg.'s Sug. Retail was $200.

TYPE 54-1 TOKAREV STANDARD — 7.62x25mm Tokarev or .38 Super cal., single action semi-auto, 4.5 in. barrel, 8 shot mag., fixed sights, blue finish, 29 oz. Imported 1989-95.

$125	$100	$80	$70	$65	$60	$55

Last Mfg.'s Sug. Retail was $145.

* **Type 54-1 Double Column** — similar to Standard Model, except is also available in 9mm Para. cal. and has 10 (C/B 1994) or 13★ shot mag., 35 oz. Imported 1991-95.

$155	$135	$120	$110	$100	$90	$80

Last Mfg.'s Sug. Retail was $185.

* **Type 54-1 Compact** — .38 Super, 9mm Para., or 7.62x25mm Tokarev cal., 3.8 in. barrel, 8 shot mag., 27 oz. Imported 1991-95.

$155	$135	$120	$110	$100	$90	$80

Last Mfg.'s Sug. Retail was $185.

TYPE 59 MAKAROV — 9x18mm Makarov or .380 ACP cal., double action semi-auto, 3.5 in. barrel, 8 shot bottom release mag., checkered plastic grips, PPK design with additional features, adj. rear sight, 24 oz. Imported 1989-95.

$150	$135	$125	$115	$95	$85	$75

Last Mfg.'s Sug. Retail was $185.

TYPE 77B — 9mm Para. cal., semi-auto single action, action patterned after the older German Lignose (unique design permits one handed operation utilizing "trigger guard cocking" enabling the slide to be moved backward cocking the hammer), 5 in. barrel, 8 shot mag., adj. rear sight, 34 oz. Limited importation 1991-95.

$350	$295	$250	$225	$195	$165	$135

Last Mfg.'s Sug. Retail was $285.

MODEL 1911 A1 — .45 ACP cal. only, patterned after the Colt 1911 A1, 5 in. barrel, 7 shot mag., fixed sights, blue or parkerized finish, wood grips, 39 oz. Imported 1991-95.

$275	$245	$220	$195	$180	$165	$150

Last Mfg.'s Sug. Retail was $320.

N

Grading	100%	98%	95%	90%	80%	70%	60%

RIFLES: SEMI-AUTO

TYPE 84S AK RIFLE — .223 Rem. cal., semi-auto Kalashnikov action, 16.34 in. barrel, hardwood stock and pistol grip, 30 shot mag., 1,000 meter adj. rear sight, includes bayonet and sheath, 8.87 lbs. Imported 1988-1989 only.

	$575	$450	$400	$360	$330	$300	$285

Last Mfg.'s Sug. Retail was $350.

* **Type 84S-1** — similar to Type 84S AK except has under-folding metal stock. Imported 1989 only.

	$600	$475	$425	$385	$350	$325	$300

Last Mfg.'s Sug. Retail was $350.

* **Type 84S-3** — similar to Type 84S AK except has composite fiber stock (1½ in. longer than wood stock). Imported 1989 only.

	$525	$425	$400	$360	$330	$300	$285

Last Mfg.'s Sug. Retail was $365.

* **Type 84S-5** — similar to Type 84S AK except has side-folding metal stock. Imported 1989 only.

	$700	$575	$425	$385	$350	$325	$300

Last Mfg.'s Sug. Retail was $350.

AK-47 THUMBHOLE — .223 Rem. or 7.62x39mm cal., features new thumbhole stock for legalized import, 5 shot mag. Imported 1991-1993, configuration was restyled and renamed NHM-90/91 in 1994.

	$450	$400	$360	$330	$285	$250	$225

Last Mfg.'s Sug. Retail was $375.

Add $8 for .223 Rem. cal.

NHM-90/91 SPORT — 7.62x39mm cal., choice of 16.34 (NHM-90) or 23.27 (NHM-91) in. barrel, hardwood thumbhole stock, NHM-91 has bipod, 5 shot mag., 9-11 lbs. Imported 1994-95.

	$450	$400	$360	$330	$285	$250	$225

The .223 Rem. cal. was also available for the Model NHM-90. Each Model NHM-90/91 was supplied with three 5 shot mags., sling, and cleaning kit.

MODEL B THUMBHOLE — 9mm Para. cal., patterned after the Uzi, features sporterized thumbhole wood stock, 10 shot mag. Importation 1995 only.

	$550	$485	$440	$400	$360	$330	$295

Last Mfg.'s Sug. Retail was $625.

R.P.K. RIFLE — .308 Win. cal., includes bipod. Importation disc. 1993.

	$600	$550	$495	$425	$395	$375	$325

Last Mfg.'s Sug. Retail was $600.

TYPE SKS — .223 Rem. or 7.62x39mm cal., SKS action, 20.47 in. barrel, 10 (C/B 1994) or 30★ shot clip mag., 1,000 meter adj. rear sight, hardwood stock, new design accepts standard AK mag., with or w/o folding bayonet, 8.8 lbs. Imported 1988-1989, re-introduced 1992-95 with Sporter configuration stock.

	$150	$135	$120	$100	$90	$85	$80

Last Mfg.'s Sug. Retail was $150.

Add $100 for synthetic stock and bayonet.
Subtract 15% if refinished.

N

TYPE 81S AK RIFLE — 7.62x39mm cal., semi-auto Kalashnikov action, 17.5 in. barrel, 5, 30, or 40 shot clip mag., 500 meter adj. rear sight, fixed wood stock, hold open device after last shot, 8 lbs. Imported 1988-1989.

	$495	$450	$400	$360	$330	$300	$285

Last Mfg.'s Sug. Retail was $385.

Grading	100%	98%	95%	90%	80%	70%	60%

* **Type 81S-1** — similar to Type 81S AK except has under-folding metal stock. Imported 1988-1989.

	$525	$475	$425	$385	$350	$325	$300

Last Mfg.'s Sug. Retail was $385.

TYPE 56S-2 — 7.62x39mm cal., older Kalashnikov design with side-folding metal stock. Importation disc. 1989.

	$495	$450	$400	$360	$330	$300	$285

Last Mfg.'s Sug. Retail was $350.

TYPE 86S-7 RPK RIFLE — 7.62x39mm cal., AK action, 23.27 in. heavy barrel with built-in bipod, in-line buttstock, 11.02 lbs. Imported 1988-1989.

	$850	$775	$700	$640	$595	$550	$500

Last Mfg.'s Sug. Retail was $425.

TYPE 86S BULLPUP RIFLE — 7.62x39mm cal., bullpup configuration with AK action, under-folding metal stock, 17¼ in. barrel, ambidextrous cocking design, folding front handle, 7 lbs. Imported 1989 only.

	$725	$650	$575	$525	$460	$410	$350

Last Mfg.'s Sug. Retail was $400.

DRAGUNOV (MODEL 350 NDM-86 OR SVD) — 7.62x54mm Russian, sniper variation of the AK-47, features 24 in. barrel with muzzle brake, special laminated skeletonized wood stock with vent. forearm, detachable 10 shot mag., 8 lbs. 9 oz. Importation disc. 1995.

	$2,775	$2,350	$1,925	$1,575	$1,275	$1,050	$900

Last Mfg.'s Sug. Retail was $3,080.

This model was also imported by Gibbs Rifle Co. located in Martinsburg, WV.

* **Dragunov Carbine** — similar to Dragunov rifle, except shorter barrel, various accessories including a lighted scope were also offered.

	$1,700	$1,500	$1,300	$1,100	$995	$875	$750

OFFICERS NINE — 9mm Para. cal., 16.1 in. barrel, action patterned after the IMI Uzi, 32 shot mag., black military finish, 8.4 lbs. Limited 1988-1989.

	$550	$475	$415	$375	$335	$300	$275

Last Mfg.'s Sug. Retail was $450.

RIFLES: .22 CAL.

MODEL EM-321 — .22 LR cal., slide action, 19.5 in. barrel, 10 shot tube mag., hardwood stock and forearm, fixed sights, 6 lbs. Importation began 1989-90, resumed 1994 - disc.

	$135	$115	$95	$85	$75	$65	$55

TYPE EM-332 — .22 LR cal., bolt action, 18½ in. barrel with adj. rear sight, mag. holder on stock holds two extra 5 shot mags., Monte Carlo stock with cheekpiece and recoil pad, 4½ lbs. Imported 1991-1993.

	$225	$195	$165	$140	$120	$95	$80

SHOTGUNS: O/U

TYPE HL12-203 — 12 ga. only, 2¾ in. chambers, boxlock action, ejectors, 30 in. vent. barrels and rib, single trigger, multi-chokes, checkered stock and forearm, 7½ lbs. Imported 1989-1993.

	$400	$350	$300	$265	$225	$200	$185

SHOTGUNS: SEMI-AUTO

MODEL 2000 FIELD — 12 ga. only, 2¾ in. chamber, steel receiver and aluminum alloy trigger guard, 26 or 28 in. VR barrel with M choke tube, choice of black synthetic or checkered hardwood stock and forearm, approx. 7½ lbs. Importation began late 1999.

Mfg.'s Sug. Retail	$299		$260	$230	$200	$185	$170	$160	$150

Add $8 for wood stock and forearm.

Choke tubes are interchangable with the WinChoke system.

N

Grading	100%	98%	95%	90%	80%	70%	60%

* **Model 2000 Defense** — 12 ga. only, 2¾ in. chamber, 18½ in. barrel with cyl. choke tube and choice of bead, rifle, or ghost ring sights, matte black metal finish, black synthetic stock and forearm with recoil pad. Importation began late 1999.

Mfg.'s Sug. Retail	$282	$245	$225	$190	$175	$160	$155	$145

    Add $5 for rifle sights.
    Add $17 for ghost ring sights.

SHOTGUNS: SxS

MODEL 99 COACH GUN — 12 ga. only, 2¾ in. chambers, exposed hammers, 20 in. barrels with full F/M fixed chokes, blue finish with checkered stock and forearm, 7.2 lbs. Importation began 1999.

Mfg.'s Sug. Retail	$251	$215	$200	$185	$170	$155	$145	$135

SHOTGUNS: SLIDE ACTION

TYPE HL12-102 PUMP — 12 ga. only, 2¾ in. chamber, 28.4 in. barrel, 3 shot mag., crossbolt safety on rear trigger guard, fixed chokes, 9.3 lbs. Imported 1989-1993.

	$230	$200	$175	$165	$150	$135	$120

MODEL 98 FIELD — 12 ga. only, 3 in. chamber, 26 or 28 in. VR barrel with M choke tube, choice of black synthetic or uncheckered hardwood stock and forearm with recoil pad, approx. 7 lbs. Importation began 1999.

Mfg.'s Sug. Retail	$205	$185	$160	$140	$125	$110	$100	$90

    Add $8 for wood stock and forearm.
    Add $55 for Field Combo (includes extra 18½ in. barrel) or $82 for Field Combo with 22 in. slug or turkey barrel.

* **Model 98 Turkey** — similar to Model 98 Field, except has 22 in. VR barrel with extra full choke tube, black synthetic stock and forearm only. Importation began 1999.

Mfg.'s Sug. Retail	$216	$190	$165	$140	$125	$110	$100	$90

* **Model 98 Defense** — 12 ga. only, 3 in. chamber, 18½ in. barrel with cyl. choke tube and choice of bead, rifle, or ghost ring sights, matte black metal finish, black synthetic stock and forearm with recoil pad. Importation began 1999.

Mfg.'s Sug. Retail	$190	$170	$150	$130	$115	$100	$90	$80

    Add $15 for ghost ring sights.

NORSMAN SPORTING ARMS

Current rifle manufacturer/customizer located in Bismarck, ND. Consumer direct sales.

    Norsman specializes in take-down rifles and multiple barrel/caliber configurations. Please contact the factory directly (see Trademark Index) for additional information and prices.

RIFLES: BOLT ACTION

VIKING GRADE — most standard cals., unique NSA takedown action, many options and custom orders available.

Mfg.'s Sug. Retail	$6,000	$5,750	$5,250	$4,500	$3,750	$3,000	$2,500	$2,000

    Add $1,500 per interchangable barrel.

VIKING GRADE MAGNUM — most standard Mag. cals., unique NSA takedown action, many options and custom orders available.

Mfg.'s Sug. Retail	$9,000	$8,600	$8,000	$7,000	$6,000	$5,000	$4,000	$3,000

    Add $2,000 per interchangable barrel.

Grading	100%	98%	95%	90%	80%	70%	60%

NORTH AMERICAN ARMS, INC.

Current manufacturer located in Provo, UT. Distributor and dealer sales.

PISTOLS: SEMI-AUTO

NAA .32 GUARDIAN — .32 ACP cal., double action only, hammerless, stainless steel construction, 6 shot mag., 2.185 in. barrel, fixed low profile sights, smooth black synthetic grips, 13½ oz. New 1999.

Mfg.'s Sug. Retail	$425		$375	$325	$275

REVOLVERS: MINI SERIES

All mini revolvers are manufactured to highest quality control standards and have half-way notches cut on the front cylinder face allowing the hammer to lock up the cylinder between cartridges. This allows the gun to be carried fully loaded without the danger of accidental discharge.

NAA .22 LR — .22 Short (new 1994) or .22 LR cal., 5 shot, single action, spur trigger, 1⅛, 1⅝, or 2½ (disc.) in. barrel, stainless steel, plastic (disc.) or laminated rosewood grips, approx. 4½ oz. Mfg. 1975-present.

Mfg.'s Sug. Retail	$176		$145	$110	$90

> Add $15 for 2½ in. barrel (disc.).
> Add $33 for holster grip accessory.
> Add $39 for quick-release belt buckle option.
>
> The optional holster grip allows the pistol to fold forward allowing concealability, safety, and a clip which allows it to be attached to a belt.

NAA .22 MAGNUM — similar to .22 LR, except in .22 Mag. cal.

Mfg.'s Sug. Retail	$194		$160	$125	$100

> Add $18 for 2½ in. barrel (disc.).
> Add $34 for quick-release belt buckle option.

NAA .22 MAGNUM CONVERTIBLE — similar to NAA .22 Mag., except has extra LR cylinder in pouch.

Mfg.'s Sug. Retail	$231		$195	$160	$115

> Add $18 for 2½ in. barrel (disc.).

MINI-MASTER TARGET REVOLVER — .22 LR or .22 Mag. cal., 5 shot, 4 in. heavy vent. barrel, unfluted bull cylinder, spur trigger, fixed or adj. white outline rear sight, oversize black rubber Mini-master grip, 10.7 oz. New 1990.

Mfg.'s Sug. Retail	$281		$240	$195	$170

> Add $37 for extra combo cylinder.
> Add $18 for adj. rear sight (elevation only).
>
> This model was also available in hot fuschia colored oversized grips.

MINI-MASTER BLACK WIDOW — .22 LR or .22 Mag. cal., 2 in. heavy VR barrel, full size black rubber grip, fixed or adj. rear sight, unfluted cylinder, 8.8 oz. New 1991.

Mfg.'s Sug. Retail	$251		$210	$165	$130

> Add $37 for extra combo cylinder.
> Add $18 for adj. rear sight (elevation only).
>
> This model was also available in hot fuschia colored oversized grips.

NAA STANDARD SET — 3 gun set (.22 Short, .22 LR, and .22 Mag. cals.) in walnut display case with matching serial numbers, high polish finish with matte contours.

Mfg.'s Sug. Retail	$734		$535	$450	$365

N

Grading	100%	98%	95%	90%	80%	70%	60%

NAA DELUXE SET — 3 gun set (.22 Short, .22 LR, and .22 Mag. cals.) in walnut display case with matching serial numbers, high polish finish on entire gun.

Mfg.'s Sug. Retail	$809	$680	$550	$410

CASED .22 MAG. — includes .22 Mag. cal. model in walnut display case with high polish finish with matte contours.

Mfg.'s Sug. Retail	$369	$305	$225	$180

REVOLVERS: SINGLE ACTION

NAA SINGLE ACTION REVOLVER — .45 Win. Mag. or .450 Mag. Express cal., polished stainless steel, transfer bar safety inside the hammer, 5 shot, 7½ in. barrel, walnut grips, includes presentation case. Disc. 1984.

Matte finish	$1,200	$950	$700
High polish finish	$1,400	$1,100	$850
Both cylinders	$1,650	$1,275	$975

Last Mfg.'s Sug. Retail was $650.

This model was also available by special order with 10½ in. barrel and optional scope. Extra cylinders were also available at $75-$100 and were fitted to the gun. A set including 2 cylinders could also be ordered. North American Arms cannot perform any repair work on .450 Mag. Express revolvers.

NORTH AMERICAN SAFARI EXPRESS

Previous trademark for those rifles (SxS) assembled by A. Francotte of Belgium for exclusive importation by Armes De Chasse located in Chadds Ford, PA.

NOWLIN MFG., INC.

Current custom handgun and components manufacturer established in 1982, and located in Claremore, OK. Dealer or consumer direct sales.

Nowlin Mfg., Inc. manufactures a complete line of high quality M1911 A1 styled competition and defense pistols, available in 9mm Para., 9x23mm, .38 Super, .40 S&W, or .45 ACP cal. Various frame types are available, including a variety of Nowlin choices. Recent models (available in blue or nickle finish) include the NRA Bianchi Cup (approx. 1997 retail was $2,750 - disc.), 007 Compact ($1,395 - disc.), Compact X2 ($1,436 - disc.), Match Classic ($1,295), Crusader ($1,543), Challenger ($1,618), World Cup PPC ($1,763), STI High Cap. Frame ($1,595), Mickey Fowler Signature Series ($1,634), Compact Carry ($1,695), Match Master ($2,195-$2,335), and the Custom Shop Excaliber Series ($2,295-$2,495), Please contact the factory directly for more information, including specific pricing (see Trademark Index).

N

NOTES

N

O section

O.D.I. (OMEGA DEFENSIVE INDUSTRIES)

Previous manufacturer located in Midland Park, NJ circa 1981-82. Essex Arms located in Island Pond, VT has acquired the remaining O.D.I. Viking inventory of parts for the Viking pistol (see Trademark Index), in addition to being a components supplier (slides and receivers) for M-1911 styled pistols. Previously, Randco Manufacturing located in Monrovia, CA was providing service (and had parts) for these older O.D.I. Pistols.

Grading	100%	98%	95%	90%	80%	70%	60%

PISTOLS: SEMI-AUTO

VIKING & VIKING COMBAT — .45 ACP or 9mm Para. (advertised, but never mfg.) cal., Viking Model is Government size and the Combat Model is Commander size. All stainless steel construction, the design utilizes the Seecamp double action, teakwood grips. 5 in. barrel on the Viking Model and 4 1/4 in. barrel on the Viking Combat Model, 7 shot mag., 39 oz. Approx. 200-300 Viking Combat Models were made from kits.

$495 $385 $295

Last Mfg.'s Retail was $579.

Add $100 for slide with cross bolt safety.

OBREGON

Previously manufactured by Fabrica de Armas Mexico located in Mexico City, Mexico.

PISTOLS: SEMI-AUTO

OBREGON — 11.35mm cal., patterned somewhat after the Colt Model 1911A1, features tubular slide and Savage/Steyr type action, 1,000 pistols mfg. in Mexico for commercial sale during and after WWII, slide marked "Sistema Obregon Cal 11.35mm".

$4,750 $4,250 $3,750 $3,250 $2,750 $2,250 $1,750

OHIO ORDNANCE WORKS, INC.

Current rifle manufacturer established in 1997 and currently located in Chardon, OH. Dealer and consumer direct sales.

RIFLES: SEMI-AUTO

MODEL 1918A3 — .30-06 cal., patterned after the original Browning BAR (M1918A2) used during WWII, all steel construction, 24 in. barrel, original folding type rear sight, 20 shot mag., matte metal and wood finish, 20 lbs. New 1997, with 3,000 rifles scheduled for production.

Mfg.'s Sug. Retail $2,650 $2,450 $2,250 $1,900 $1,600 $1,400 $1,100 $875

OLD-WEST GUN CO.

Previous importer and distributor that took over the inventory of Allen Firearms after they went out of business in early 1987. Old-West Gun Co. changed their name to Cimarron Arms in late 1987. Please refer to Cimarron Arms in this text for approximate prices on similar models from Old-West Gun Co.

O

Grading	100%	98%	95%	90%	80%	70%	60%

OLYMPIC ARMS, INC.

Current manufacturer located in Olympia, WA. Dealer direct sales.
In late 1987, Olympic Arms, Inc. acquired Safari Arms of Phoenix, AZ.

PISTOLS: SEMI-AUTO

There is no post-ban OA-93 pistol.

OA-93 PISTOL — .223 Rem. (most common) or 7.62x39mm (very limited mfg.) cal., semi-auto, gas operated without buffer tube stock, or charging handle, 6 (most common), 9, or 14 in. free-floated match barrel, upper receiver utilizes integral scope mount base, 30 shot mag., 4 lbs. 3 oz., approx. 500 mfg. before Crime Bill discontinued mfg. Mfg. 1993-94 only.

	$2,450	$2,200	$1,925	$1,700	$1,500	$1,300	$1,100

Last Mfg.'s Sug. Retail was $2,700.

Add $800 for 7.62x39mm cal.

OA-96 AR PISTOL — .223 Rem. cal., 6 in. barrel only, similar to OA-93 Pistol, except has pinned (fixed) 30 shot mag. and rear takedown button for rapid reloading, 5 lbs. New 1996.

Mfg.'s Sug. Retail	$940		$860	$775	$650	$575	$495	$450	$395

OA-98 PISTOL — .223 Rem. cal., skeletonized, lightweight version of the OA-96, 10 shot fixed mag., denoted by perforated appearance, 3 lbs. New 1998.

Mfg.'s Sug. Retail	$940		$860	$775	$650	$575	$495	$450	$395

RIFLES: BOLT ACTION

In 1993, Olympic Arms purchased the rights, jigs, fixtures, and machining templates for the Bauska Big Bore Magnum Mauser action. Please contact Olympic Arms (see Trademark Index) for more information regarding Bauska actions both with or without fluted barrels.

ULTRA MAG BBK-01 — various cals. between .300 Win. Mag.-.505 Gibbs, custom order rifle available with many barrel options and other special order features, price on request from the factory.

This model was formerly the Bauska BBK-02.

BOLT ACTION SAKO — various cals. between .17 Rem.-.416 Rem. Mag., 26 in. fluted barrel, various stock configurations, values below represent base price with no options.

Mfg.'s Sug. Retail	$715		$660	$575	$500	$450	$400	$360	$330

ULTRA CSR TACTICAL RIFLE — .308 Win. cal., Sako action, 26 in. broach cut heavy barrel, Bell & Carlson black or synthetic stock with aluminum bedding, Harris bipod, carrying case. New 1996.

Mfg.'s Sug. Retail	$1,235		$1,140	$900	$740	$625	$550	$500	$450

RIFLES: SEMI-AUTO

On the models listed below, the PCR (Politically Correct Rifle) variations refer to those guns manufactured after the Crime Bill was implemented in September, 1994. PCR rifles have smooth barrels (no flash suppressor), a 10 shot mag., and fixed stocks. Older, discontinued named models refer to the original, pre-ban model nomenclature. All pre-ban commercial inventory is now depleted, and values below reflect current secondary marketplace prices.

COMPETITOR RIFLE — .22 LR cal., Ruger 10/22 action with 20 in. barrel featuring button cut rifling, Bell & Carlson thumbhole fiberglass stock, black finish and matte stainless fluted barrel, includes bipod, 6.9 lbs. New 1996.

Mfg.'s Sug. Retail	$630		$575	$500	$450	$400	$360	$330	$300

ULTRAMATCH/PCR-1 — .223 Rem. cal., AR-15 action with modifications, 20 or 24 in. match stainless steel barrel, handle removed, Williams set trigger, scope mounts, 10 lbs. 3 oz. New 1985.

Grading		100%	98%	95%	90%	80%	70%	60%
*** PCR-1**								
Mfg.'s Sug. Retail	$1,150	$1,040	$825	$725	$600	$550	$500	$460
*** ULTRAMATCH**								
		$1,400	$1,200	$1,000	$875	$775	$675	$550

Last Mfg.'s Sug. Retail was $1,515.

While still available to law enforcement, military, and qualified export agencies, this model is now discontinued for commerical sales, and no inventory remains.

INTERCONTINENTAL — .223 Rem. cal., features synthetic wood-grained thumbhole butt stock and aluminum handguard, 20 in. ultra match barrel (free floating). Mfg. 1992-93.

		100%	98%	95%	90%	80%	70%	60%
		$1,650	$1,350	$1,050	$875	$750	$600	$550

Last Mfg.'s Sug. Retail was $1,371.

INTERNATIONAL MATCH — .223 Rem. cal., similar to Ultramatch, except has custom aperture sights. Mfg. 1991-93.

		100%	98%	95%	90%	80%	70%	60%
		$1,475	$1,150	$950	$800	$675	$575	$525

Last Mfg.'s Sug. Retail was $1,240.

SERVICE MATCH/PCR SERVICE MATCH — .223 Rem. cal., AR-15 action with modifications, 20 in. SS Ultramatch barrel, carrying handle, standard trigger, choice of A1 or A2 flash suppressor (Service Match only), 8¾ lbs.

*** PCR SERVICE MATCH**		100%	98%	95%	90%	80%	70%	60%
Mfg.'s Sug. Retail	$1,175	$1,060	$845	$700	$600	$530	$495	$450
*** SERVICE MATCH**								
		$1,075	$875	$725	$625	$550	$500	$450

Last Mfg.'s Sug. Retail was $1,200.

While still available to law enforcement, military, and qualified export agencies, this model is now discontinued for commerical sales, and no inventory remains.

MULTIMATCH ML-1/PCR-2 — .223 Rem. cal., tactical short range rifle, 16 in. Ultramatch barrel, aluminum collapsible (Multimatch ML-1) or fixed (PCR-2) stock, carrying handle, stealth vortex flash suppressor (Multimatch ML-1 only), 5 lbs. 14 oz. New 1991.

*** PCR-2**		100%	98%	95%	90%	80%	70%	60%
Mfg.'s Sug. Retail	$1,035	$960	$865	$775	$650	$575	$495	$450
*** MULTIMATCH ML-1**								
		$1,075	$875	$725	$625	$550	$500	$450

Last Mfg.'s Sug. Retail was $1,200.

While still available to law enforcement, military, and qualified export agencies, this model is now discontinued for commerical sales, and no inventory remains.

MULTIMATCH ML-2/PCR-3 — .223 Rem. cal., features International Match upper receiver with SS 16 in. Ultramatch barrel, carrying handle, 5 lbs. 14 oz. New 1991.

*** PCR-3**		100%	98%	95%	90%	80%	70%	60%
Mfg.'s Sug. Retail	$1,035	$960	$865	$775	$650	$575	$495	$450
*** MULTIMATCH ML-2**								
		$1,075	$875	$725	$625	$550	$500	$450

Last Mfg.'s Sug. Retail was $1,200.

While still available to law enforcement, military, and qualified export agencies, this model is now discontinued for commerical sales, and no inventory remains.

AR-15 MATCH/PCR-4 — .223 Rem. cal., patterned after the AR-15 with 20 in. barrel and solid synthetic stock, 8 lbs. 5 oz. New 1975.

*** PCR-4**		100%	98%	95%	90%	80%	70%	60%
Mfg.'s Sug. Retail	$860	$795	$695	$600	$525	$475	$425	$395

O

Grading	100%	98%	95%	90%	80%	70%	60%

* AR-15 MATCH

	$995	$875	$775	$650	$575	$495	$450

Last Mfg.'s Sug. Retail was $1,075.

CAR-15/PCR-5 — modified AR-15 with choice of 11½ (disc. 1993) or 16 in. barrel, stow-away pistol grip and collapsible stock (CAR-15 only), 7 lbs. Mfg. 1975-1998.

* PCR-5 — .223 Rem., 9mm Para. (new 1996), .40 S&W (new 1996), or .45 ACP (new 1996) cal. Disc. 1998.

	$690	$630	$550	$475	$450	$400	$375

Last Mfg.'s Sug. Retail was $785.

Add $45 for 9mm Para., .40 S&W, or .45 ACP cal.

* CAR-15 — .223 Rem., 9mm Para., .40 S&W, .45 ACP, or 7.62x39mm cal.

	$960	$860	$775	$650	$575	$495	$450

Last Mfg.'s Sug. Retail was $1,030.

Add $170 for pistol cals.

While still available to law enforcement, military, and qualified export agencies, this model is now discontinued for commerical sales, and no inventory remains.

PCR-6 — 7.62x39mm cal., 16 in. barrel, post-ban only, A-2 stowaway stock, carrying handle, 7 lbs. New 1995.

Mfg.'s Sug. Retail	$915	$830	$725	$600	$500	$475	$425	$375

PCR-7 ELIMINATOR — .223 Rem. cal., similar to PCR-4, except has 16 in. barrel, 7 lbs. 10 oz. New 1999.

Mfg.'s Sug. Retail	$895	$800	$700	$585	$500	$475	$425	$375

CAR-97 — .223 Rem., 9mm Para., .40 S&W, or .45 ACP cal., similar to CAR-15, except has non-collapsible CAR stock, approx. 7 lbs. New 1999.

Mfg.'s Sug. Retail	$875	$780	$675	$560	$485	$445	$415	$360

Add approx. $60 for 9mm Para., .40 S&W, or .45 ACP cal.

OA-93 CARBINE — .223 Rem. cal., 16 in. barrel, design based on OA-93 pistol, aluminum folding stock, flat-top receiver, Vortex flash suppressor, 7½ lbs. Mfg. 1995 - civilian sales disc. 1998.

	$1,400	$1,200	$1,000	$875	$775	$675	$550

Last Mfg.'s Sug. Retail was $1,550.

While still available to law enforcement, military, and qualified export agencies, this model is now discontinued for commerical sales, and no inventory remains.

COUNTER SNIPER RIFLE — .308 Win. cal., bolt action utilizing M-14 mags., 26 in. heavy barrel, camo-fiberglass stock, 10½ lbs. Disc. 1987.

	$1,100	$900	$775	$695	$550	$440	$410

Last Mfg.'s Sug. Retail was $1,225.

SURVIVOR I CONVERSION UNIT — .223 Rem. or .45 ACP cal., converts M1911 variations into carbine, bolt action, collapsible stock, 16¼ in. barrel, 5 lbs.

	$275	$225	$195

This kit is also available for S&W and Browning Hi-Power models.

OMEGA

Previous trademark manufactured by Armero Specialistas Reunidas, located in Eibar, Spain, circa 1920s.

PISTOLS: SEMI-AUTO

SEMI AUTOMATIC PISTOL — 6.35mm or 7.65mm cal., "Eibar" type action, marked Omega on slide, 6 shot mag.

	100%	98%	95%	90%	80%	70%	60%
6.35 cal.	$125	$115	$100	$80	$70	$55	$40
7.65 cal.	$130	$120	$105	$90	$80	$70	$55

Grading	100%	98%	95%	90%	80%	70%	60%

OMEGA FIREARMS

Previous manufacturer located in Flower Mound, TX circa 1965-1969.

RIFLES: BOLT ACTION

SINGLE SHOT RIFLE — various cals., premium walnut. Disc. late 1960s.

	100%	98%	95%	90%	80%	70%	60%
	$775	$650	$575	$495	$425	$360	$295

OMEGA PISTOL

Previously manufactured and distributed by Springfield Armory located in Geneseo, IL. Omega conversion kits only were available until 1996 from Safari Arms located in Olympia, WA under license from Peters-Stahl in Germany.

PISTOLS: SEMI-AUTO

OMEGA — .38 Super, 10mm Norma, or .45 ACP cal., single action, ported slide, 5 or 6 in. interchangeable ported or unported barrel with Polygon rifling, special lock-up system eliminates normal barrel link and bushing, Pachmayr grips, dual extractors, adj. rear sight. Mfg. 1987-90.

	100%	98%	95%	90%	80%	70%	60%
	$625	$560	$495	$425	$360	$295	$265

Last Mfg.'s Sug. Retail was $849.

Add $663 for interchangeable conversion units.
Add $336 for interchangeable 5 or 6 in. barrel (including factory installation).

Each conversion unit includes an entire slide assembly, one mag., 5 or 6 in barrel, recoil spring guide mechanism assembly, and factory fitting.

OMEGA RIFLES/SHOTGUNS

Omega was the trademark of select rifles/shotguns previously imported by K.B.I., Inc. located in Harrisburg, PA, until 1994.

RIFLES

To date, there has been little collector interest for Omega rifles. Values are mostly determined by the shooting value rather than collector value.

SHOTGUNS

STANDARD O/U — 12, 20 (disc.), 28 (disc.) ga., or .410 (disc) bore, boxlock action, folding design, SNT, 26 or 28 in. VR barrels, extractors, checkered walnut stock and forearm, 5½-7 lbs. Disc. 1994.

	100%	98%	95%	90%	80%	70%	60%
	$425	$330	$295	$260	$230	$200	$180

* **Deluxe O/U** — 12 ga. only, similar to Standard Model except has better walnut. Importation disc. 1990.

	100%	98%	95%	90%	80%	70%	60%
	$335	$290	$255	$220	$185	$160	$140

Last Mfg.'s Sug. Retail was $379.

STANDARD SxS — 20, 28 ga., or .410 bore, boxlock action, folding design, double triggers, hardwood stock and forearm, 26 in. barrels, extractors, 5½ lbs. Disc. 1989.

	100%	98%	95%	90%	80%	70%	60%
	$190	$165	$140	$120	$110	$100	$90

Last Mfg.'s Sug. Retail was $229.

Add $40 for 28 ga. or .410 bore.

* **Deluxe SxS** — .410 bore only, similar to Standard Model except has better walnut. Disc. 1989.

	100%	98%	95%	90%	80%	70%	60%
	$200	$185	$170	$155	$140	$130	$120

Last Mfg.'s Sug. Retail was $249.

SINGLE BARREL — 12, 20 ga., or .410 bore, various barrel lengths, matte blue finish, extractor. Importation disc. 1987.

	100%	98%	95%	90%	80%	70%	60%
	$85	$75	$65	$55	$45	$40	$35

Last Mfg.'s Sug. Retail was $95.

O

Grading	100%	98%	95%	90%	80%	70%	60%

STANDARD FOLDING SINGLE BARREL — 12, 16, 20, 28 ga., or .410 bore, 28 or 30 in. barrel, checkered hardwood stock, matte chrome receiver, approx. 5½ lbs. Importation disc. 1987.

		$160	$135	$115	$100	$85	$70	$65

Last Mfg.'s Sug. Retail was $180.

DELUXE FOLDING SINGLE BARREL — 12, 16, 20, 28 ga., or .410 bore, similar to Standard Model, except has checkered walnut stock and forearm, blued receiver. Importation disc. 1987.

		$195	$160	$135	$115	$100	$85	$70

Last Mfg.'s Sug. Retail was $220.

OMNI

Current manufacturer located in Riverside, CA since 1992. During 1998, Omni changed its name to E.D.M. Arms. Exclusively distributed by First Defense International located in CA.

RIFLES: BOLT ACTION

LONG ACTION SINGLE SHOT — .50 BMG cal., competition single shot, chrome-moly black finished receiver, 32-34 in. steel or stainless steel barrel with round muzzle brake, benchrest fiberglass stock, designed for FCSA competition shooting, 32 lbs. New 1996.

Mfg.'s Sug. Retail	$3,500		$3,200	$2,800	$2,500	$2,150	$1,800	$1,500	$1,250

Add $400 for painted stock (disc. 1996).

SHELL HOLDER SINGLE SHOT — similar to Long Action Single Shot, except has fiberglass field stock with bipod, 28 lbs. New 1997.

Mfg.'s Sug. Retail	$2,750		$2,525	$2,150	$1,800	$1,500	$1,250	$1,100	$925

MODEL WINDRUNNER — .50 BMG cal., long action, single shot or 3 shot clip, 1-piece I-beam receiver, chrome-moly black finish, 36 in. barrel with round muzzle brake, fiberglass tactical stock, 35 lbs. New 1997.

Mfg.'s Sug. Retail	$7,500		$6,950	$6,425	$5,875	$5,325	$4,750	$4,175	$3,500

Add $750 for 3 shot repeater.

MODEL WARLOCK — .50 BMG or 20mm cal., single, 3 (20mm), or 5 (.50 BMG) shot fixed mag., massive receiver design, fiberglass field stock, chrome-moly black finished receiver, muzzle brake, 50 lbs. New 1997.

Mfg.'s Sug. Retail	$12,000		$10,750	$8,950	$7,750	$6,750	$5,500	$4,750	$3,950

E.D.M. ARMS MODEL 97 — available in most cals. up to .308 Win., single shot or repeater (cals. .17 Rem. through .223 Rem. only), wire-cut one-piece design, black tactical stock with pillar-bedded chrome-moly barrel, black finished receiver, unique trigger with safety, 9 lbs. New 1997.

Mfg.'s Sug. Retail	$2,750		$2,525	$2,150	$1,800	$1,500	$1,250	$1,100	$925

E.D.M. ARMS WINDRUNNER WR50 — .50 BMG cal., sniper rifle, 5 shot mag., removable tactical adj. stock, take-down removable barrel, wire-cut one-piece receiver, titanium muzzle brake, blackened chrome moly barrel, approx. 29 lbs. New 1998.

Mfg.'s Sug. Retail	$12,900		$11,750	$10,250	$9,500	$8,250	$7,000	$5,750	$4,500

OPUS SPORTING ARMS, INC.

Previous manufacturer located in Long Beach, CA.

RIFLES: BOLT ACTION

OPUS ONE — .243 Win., .270 Win., or .30-06 cal., U.S.R.A. Co. Model 70 action, 24 in. barrel, deluxe checkered walnut stock with ebony forend cap, guaranteed 100 yard accuracy, 6¾ lbs., Halliburton cased. Mfg. 1987-1988 only.

	$2,350	$1,995	$1,675	$1,250	$1,000	$875	$795

Last Mfg.'s Sug. Retail was $2,700.

O

Grading	100%	98%	95%	90%	80%	70%	60%

OPUS TWO — similar to Opus One, except in 7mm Rem. Mag. or .300 Win. Mag. cal., 7¼ lbs., cased. Mfg. 1987-1988 only.

		$2,350	$2,050	$1,705	$1,300	$1,000	$875	$795

Last Mfg.'s Sug. Retail was $2,700.

OPUS THREE — similar to Opus Two, except in .375 H&H or .458 Win. Mag. cal., 10¼ lbs., cased. Mfg. 1987-1988 only.

		$2,600	$2,275	$1,800	$1,375	$1,050	$900	$825

Last Mfg.'s Sug. Retail was $2,850.

OREGON ARMS

Please refer to the Chipmunk Rifles Inc. section.

ORTGIES PISTOLS

Previous trademark of pistols manufactured by Deutsche Werke A.G. located in Erfurt, Germany.

PISTOLS: SEMI-AUTO

VEST POCKET AUTOMATIC — .25 ACP cal., 6 shot, 2¾ in. barrel, blue or nickel finish, fixed sights, wood grips, post-WWI.

$275	$200	$165	$145	$125	$110	$100

POCKET AUTOMATIC — .32 ACP cal. (8 shot) or .380 ACP cal. (7 shot), 3¼ in. barrel, blue or nickel finish, fixed sights, wood grips.

$300	$225	$175	$150	$130	$115	$105

Add 20% for .380 ACP cal. or double safety variation.

ORVIS

Current catalog retailer/importer of private label subcontracted shotguns located in Manchester, VT and many other locations.

Orvis imports various shotguns under subcontract with various international manufacturers. Typical custom order delivery time is 2-8 months. Most of these private label models will approximate the values of the equivalent model manufactured by the subcontractor unless there are additional features and/or options which will add to the value.

SHOTGUNS: O/U

SKB GREEN MOUNTAIN UPLANDER (MODEL 555) — 12, 20, 28 ga., or .410 bore, 25-27 in. barrels, blued frame, straight stock with leather covered recoil pad. Disc.

$750	$675	$600	$550	$500	$450	$400

Last Mfg.'s Sug. Retail was $995.

Add 15% for 28 ga. or .410 bore.

UPLANDER SERIES — 12 (disc. 1998), 20, or 28 ga., boxlock action, 26 in. barrels with choke tubes (except 28 ga.), SST, straight grip, select American black walnut with 24 LPI checkering, leather covered recoil pad since 1992, 6-7 lbs. Mfg. by P. Beretta of Italy.

Mfg.'s Sug. Retail	$3,200		$3,200	$2,450	$2,000	$1,550	$1,200	$995	$875

Add $1,250 for 28/20 ga. combo with case.

WATERFOWLER — 12 ga. only, 3 in. chambers, matte metal finish, 28 in. barrels with choke tubes, steel shot compatible, 7½ lbs. Mfg. by P. Beretta of Italy.

Mfg.'s Sug. Retail	$3,450		$3,450	$2,650	$2,150	$1,650	$1,250	$1,025	$900

O

Grading	100%	98%	95%	90%	80%	70%	60%

SPORTING CLAYS — 12 ga. only, 30 in. vented barrels with VR and choke tubes, adj. trigger, oil finished checkered walnut stock and forearm. New 1994.

Mfg.'s Sug. Retail	$3,300		$3,300	$2,550	$2,000	$1,550	$1,175	$995	$875

This model is also available in a women's configuration in 20 ga. with lightweight frame - includes carrying case.

SUPER FIELD — 12 or 20 ga., 26 (Uplander 20 ga. only), 28 (All Rounder), or 30 (Sporting Clays) in. VR barrels, configurations include Uplander 20 ga. with straight grip stock, All Rounder 12 ga. with 28 in. barrels and pistol grip stock, and Sporting Clays 12 ga. with 30 in. barrels, wide rib, and pistol grip stock, blued receiver, choke tubes, mfg. in Italy. Limited importation 1995 only.

	$1,495	$1,250	$1,000	$875	$750	$625	$500

Last Mfg.'s Sug. Retail was $2,150.

PREMIER GRADE — 12 or 20 ga., 3 in. chambers, 20 ga. features 28 in. barrels with straight grip stock, 12 ga. features pistol grip stock, select oil-finished European stock and forearm, choke tubes, blued frame with scrolled engraving, adj. trigger, cased, mfg. in Belgium 1995-98.

	$6,450	$5,875	$5,250	$4,675	$4,000	$3,450	$2,675

Last Mfg.'s Sug. Retail was $6,450.

Add $100 for Premier Grade Sporting.

This model is also available as a 20 ga. Superlight with straight grip stock and 26 in. barrels.

ORVIS DELUXE GRADE — similar to Uplander and Waterfowler, except has engraved bird scenes and scroll work on antique coin-finished receiver, deluxe checkered walnut stock and forearm, case. Imported 1993-94 only.

	$4,250	$3,575	$2,950	$2,300	$1,900	$1,500	$1,275

Last Mfg.'s Sug. Retail was $4,950.

RUGER/ORVIS MODEL — 12 or 20 ga., 3 in. chambers, Red Label Ruger action with customized Orvis features including blued receiver and straight grip English checkered stock. Importation disc. 1993.

	$1,295	$975	$850	$725	$600	$495	$450

Last Mfg.'s Sug. Retail was $1,295.

SHOTGUNS: SxS

WATERFOWLER — 12 ga. only, 3 in. chambers, matte metal finish, 28 in. barrels with choke tubes, 7¾ lbs. Mfg. by P. Beretta of Italy until 1993.

	$1,950	$1,725	$1,475	$1,125	$950	$825	$700

Last Mfg.'s Sug. Retail was $1,950.

CUSTOM UPLANDER — 12, 16, 20, 28 ga., or .410 bore, custom ordered gun, 25 or 27 in. barrels only, sidelock action, DT, mfg. by Arrieta located in Spain.

Mfg.'s Sug. Retail	$3,100		$3,100	$2,525	$2,250	$1,950	$1,650	$1,450	$1,025

Add $950 for SNT.
Add $1,200 for extra set of barrels (same ga.).

FINE GRADE — 12, 16, 20, 28 ga., or .410 bore, custom ordered gun, custom order barrel lengths, sidelock action, DT, mfg. by Arrieta located in Spain.

Mfg.'s Sug. Retail	$4,650		$4,650	$3,775	$3,150	$2,500	$1,995	$1,500	$1,150

Add $950 for SNT.
Add $1,950 for extra set of barrels (same ga.).

ROUNDED ACTION — similar to Fine Grade, except sidelock action has rounded corners and finer engraving and wood upgrade, leather cased, mfg. by Arrieta located in Spain.

Mfg.'s Sug. Retail	$5,550		$5,550	$4,250	$3,775	$3,300	$2,550	$1,995	$1,500

O

P section

P.A.F.

Previous manufacturer located in S. Africa. P.A.F. stands for Pretoria Arms Factory.

Grading	100%	98%	95%	90%	80%	70%	60%

PISTOLS: SEMI-AUTO

.25 ACP PISTOL — .25 ACP cal., patterned after the Baby Browning, blued finish. Approx. 10,000 mfg.

	100%	98%	95%	90%	80%	70%	60%
	$300	$275	$250	$235	$225	$200	$180

P.A.W.S., INC.

Current manufacturer located in Salem, OR. Distributor and dealer sales. Previously distributed by Sile Distributors, Inc. located in New York, NY.

RIFLES: CARBINES

ZX6/ZX8 CARBINE — 9mm Para. or .45 ACP cal., semi-auto paramilitary design carbine, 16 in. barrel, 10 or 32★ shot mag., folding metal stock, matte black finish, aperture rear sight, partial barrel shroud, 7½ lbs. New 1989.

Mfg.'s Sug. Retail	$700		$615	$535	$450	$400	$360	$330	$295

The ZX6 is chambered for 9mm Para., while the ZX8 is chambered for .45 ACP.

PKP, INC.

Previous manufacturer and distributor located in Tempe, AZ. Dealer or consumer direct sales.

PISTOLS

POWELL KNIFE PISTOL MR-38 — .38 Spl., unique knife-pistol design allows barrel to be incorporated into the upper rear portion of the break-action blade assembly, 1¾ in. barrel, stainless steel with wood handles, 17 oz. Limited mfg. 1997-98.

$415	$350	$275

Last Mfg.'s Sug. Retail was $450.

P.S.M.G. GUN COMPANY

Previous manufacturer located in Arlington, MA.

PISTOLS: SEMI-AUTO

SIX IN ONE SUPREME — .22 LR, 7.65mm Luger, .38 Super, .38 Spl., 9mm Para., or .45 ACP cal., single action, 3¼, 5, or 7½ in. barrel with solid cooling rib, adj. rear sight, limited mfg. Mfg. 1988-89.

$700	$600	$500	$450	$400	$365	$330

Last Mfg.'s Sug. Retail was $895

Add $20-$55 for caliber options.
Add $25 for 7½ in. barrel.
Add $35 for satin nickel plating.
Add $225 per extra barrel.
Add $450 per individual conversion unit.

P.V. NELSON, (GUNMAKERS)

Please refer to the N section for this manufacturer.

Grading	100%	98%	95%	90%	80%	70%	60%

PTK INTERNATIONAL, INC.

Previous distributor located in Atlanta, GA.

Please refer to listing under Poly-Technologies in this section.

P.38s

Standard German military 9mm Para. handgun beginning 1938. On older WWII German mfg., please refer to the German WWII Military Pistols section of this text.

PISTOLS: SEMI-AUTO

P.38 - JOHN MARTZ CONVERSIONS

* **Baby P.38** — 9mm Para. cal., shortened barrel (3 in.) grip, and two 7 shot mags., 54 mfg.
  $2,500 $2,000 $1,500

* **P.38** — .38 Super (4 or 6 in. barrel, 8 mfg.) or .45 ACP (4 or 7½, 22 mfg.) cal.
  $4,500 $2,750 $1,950

* **P.38 Carbine** — 9mm Para. cal., 16 in. barrel, adj. rear sight, 27 mfg. Disc.
  $7,500 $5,750 $3,850

PARAMOUNT

Previously manufactured by Imperial Gun Co., Ltd. located in Surrey, England. Actions were previously imported by O.K. Weber, Inc. located in Eugene, OR and Olympic Arms, Inc. located in Olympia, WA.

RIFLES: SINGLE SHOT

THE IMPERIAL — .308 Win. cal., single shot target rifle featuring thumbhole stock and CPE aperture rear sight, fully adj. trigger, vent. forearm. Disc. 1994.

$3,250 $2,700 $2,250 $1,850 $1,400 $1,000 $795
Last Mfg.'s Sug. Retail was $3,400.

RANGEMASTER — various cals., single shot design, steel frame, contoured walnut grips, satin chrome finish, 8½ lbs. Limited importation 1992-94.

$1,600 $1,400 $1,200 $995 $895 $795 $695
Last Mfg.'s Sug. Retail was $1,800.

PARA-ORDNANCE MFG. INC.

Current manufacturer located in Scarborough, Ontario, Canada. Various U.S. distributors. Distributor sales only.

Para-Ordnance.

PISTOLS: SEMI-AUTO

LDA — 9mm Para., .40 S&W, or .45 ACP cal., double action, 5 in. barrel, 10 shot double stack mag., black carbon steel with matte metal finish. New 1999.

| Mfg.'s Sug. Retail | $775 | | $650 | $525 | $450 | $400 | $350 | $325 | $295 |

Grading	100%	98%	95%	90%	80%	70%	60%

P10 — 9mm Para. (new 1998), .40 S&W, .45 ACP, 10mm (mfg. 1998 only, stainless steel) cal., single action, super compact variation featuring 3 in. barrel and shortened grip, 10 shot double column mag., 3-dot sights, choice of alloy (matte black), steel (matte black), or stainless (Duo-Tone or bright finish) frame, 31 oz. with steel frame or 24 oz. with alloy frame. New 1997.

Mfg.'s Sug. Retail	$740	$625	$500	$435	$390	$350	$325	$295

Add $10 for steel frame.
Add $59 for stainless steel.
Add $45 for stainless steel with Duo-Tone finish.

S10 LIMITED — similar to P10, except has competition shooting features, including beavertail grip safety, competition hammer, tuned trigger, match grade barrel, front slide serrations, choice of steel or alloy frame with matte black finish or stainless steel, 40 oz. New 1999.

Mfg.'s Sug. Retail	$865	$765	$650	$525	$450	$395	$350	$325

Add $10 for steel receiver.
Add $24 for stainless steel.

P12 — .40 S&W or .45 ACP cal., compact variation of the P14 featuring 10 (C/B 1994) or 11★ shot mag. and 3½ in. barrel, 33 oz. with steel frame or 24 oz. with alloy frame. New 1990.

Mfg.'s Sug. Retail	$740	$625	$500	$435	$390	$350	$325	$295

Add $10 for steel frame.
Add $59 for stainless steel.
Add $45 for stainless steel with Duo-Tone finish.

S12 LIMITED — similar to P12, except has competition shooting features, including beavertail grip safety, competition hammer, tuned trigger, match grade barrel, front slide serrations, choice of steel or alloy frame with matte black finish or stainless steel, 40 oz. New 1999.

Mfg.'s Sug. Retail	$865	$765	$650	$525	$450	$395	$350	$325

Add $10 for steel receiver.
Add $24 for stainless steel.

P13 — .40 S&W or .45 ACP cal., similar to P14, except has 10 (C/B 1994) or 12★ shot mag., 4¼ in. barrel, 35 oz. with steel frame or 25 oz. with alloy frame. New 1993.

Mfg.'s Sug. Retail	$740	$625	$500	$435	$390	$350	$325	$295

Add $10 for steel frame.
Add $59 for stainless steel.
Add $45 for stainless steel with Duo-Tone finish.

S13 LIMITED — similar to P13, except has competition shooting features, including beavertail grip safety, competition hammer, tuned trigger, match grade barrel, front slide serrations, choice of steel or alloy frame with matte black finish or stainless steel, 40 oz. New 1999.

Mfg.'s Sug. Retail	$865	$765	$650	$525	$450	$395	$350	$325

Add $10 for steel receiver.
Add $24 for stainless steel.

P14 — .40 S&W (new 1996) or .45 ACP cal., patterned after the Colt Model 1911A1 except has choice of alloy (matte black), steel (matte black), or stainless steel (stainless or Duo-Tone finish) frame that has been widened slightly for extra shot capacity (13★ shot), 10 shot (C/B 1994) mag., single action, 3-dot sight system, rounded combat hammer, 5 in. ramped barrel, 38 oz. with steel frame or 28 oz. with alloy frame. Introduced 1990.

Mfg.'s Sug. Retail	$740	$625	$500	$435	$390	$350	$325	$295

Add $10 for steel frame.
Add $59 for stainless steel.
Add $45 for stainless steel with Duo-Tone finish.

S14 LIMITED — similar to P14, except has competition shooting features, including beavertail grip safety, competition hammer, tuned trigger, match grade barrel, front slide serrations, matte black or stainless steel, 40 oz. New 1998.

Mfg.'s Sug. Retail	$875	$775	$660	$525	$450	$395	$350	$325

Add $24 for stainless steel.

P

Grading		100%	98%	95%	90%	80%	70%	60%

P15 — .40 S&W cal., otherwise similar to P13, 36 oz. with steel frame or 28 oz. with alloy frame. New 1996.

Mfg.'s Sug. Retail	$740	$625	$500	$435	$390	$350	$325	$295

Add $10 for steel frame.
Add $59 for stainless steel.
Add $45 for stainless steel with Duo-Tone finish.

P16 — .40 S&W cal., otherwise similar to P14, steel or stainless steel (new 1997) frame only. New 1995.

Mfg.'s Sug. Retail	$750	$640	$515	$435	$385	$350	$325	$295

Add $49 for stainless steel.
Add $35 for Duo-Tone stainless steel.

S16 LIMITED — similar to P16, except has competition shooting features, including beavertail grip safety, competition hammer, tuned trigger, match grade barrel, front slide serrations, matte black steel or stainless steel, 40 oz. New 1998.

Mfg.'s Sug. Retail	$875	$775	$660	$525	$450	$395	$350	$325

Add $24 for stainless steel.

P18 — 9mm Para. cal., 5 in. ramped barrel, stainless steel, solid barrel bushing, flared ejection port, quadruple safety, adj. rear sight, 40 oz. New 1998.

Mfg.'s Sug. Retail	$850	$725	$575	$450

PARDINI

Current manufacturer located in Lido di Camaiore, Italy. Currently imported by Nygord Precision Products located in Prescott, AZ. Previously imported and distributed until 1996 by Mo's Competitor Supplies & Range, Inc. located in Brookfield, CT and until 1990 by Fiocchi of America, Inc., located in Ozark, MO.

PISTOLS: TARGET

Pardini pistols have always been known for their technological improvements developed from ongoing design research. During 1991, the entire Pardini pistol line was modified both internally and externally to improve function and reliability - these changes included the addition of grooves on the barrel shroud to accept scope mounts directly. Pardini air pistols may be found in the Airgun section of this text.

MODEL SP (STANDARD PISTOL) — .22 LR cal. only, target grips, adj. sights, 4.92 in. barrel, interchangable grips, detachable mag. New 1991.

Mfg.'s Sug. Retail	$995	$875	$715	$575	$475	$425	$395	$375

LADIES PISTOL — similar to Standard Pistol, except grips are suitable for smaller hands.

Mfg.'s Sug. Retail	$995	$850	$700	$600	$520	$460	$410	$380

MODEL GP (RAPID FIRE PISTOL) — .22 Short cal., features enclosed style grip assembly, adj. sights, 5.12 in. barrel. New 1991.

Mfg.'s Sug. Retail	$995	$850	$725	$600	$500	$450	$420	$395

Add $455 for "Schumann" Model (special muzzle ports, sights, weights, etc.).

MODEL HP (CENTERFIRE PISTOL) — .32 S&W Wadcutter cal., otherwise similar to Standard Pistol, 4.92 in. barrel. New 1991.

Mfg.'s Sug. Retail	$1,095	$995	$840	$715	$575	$500	$440	$415

MODEL K50 (FREE PISTOL) — .22 LR cal., single shot, sliding rotating bolt, 9.06 in. barrel, tilted anatomical grip, top-of-the-line match pistol. New 1991.

Mfg.'s Sug. Retail	$1,050	$925	$750	$600	$500	$450	$420	$395

PARKER BROTHERS

Previously manufactured in Meriden, CT from 1866-1934. Remington took over production in 1934, and in 1938, the plant was moved to Ilion, NY. Over 4,500 "Transition Guns" (exhibiting Meriden and Ilion characteristics) were produced in

Meriden between 1934-1937 and about 4,500 Parkers were manufactured at the Ilion location before production stopped. Total production reached approx. 242,387. 95% of the original Parkers bought and sold each year are in 30% or less condition (referring to original case colors). Percentages on following pages refer to the amount of original case colors remaining on frame.

Parker Shotguns: SxS, Damascus Barrels

Parker damascus barreled shotguns (hammer or hammerless) are very collectible if original condition is over 40%. Specimens in 90% or better condition with strong case colors can approximate values of the steel barrel models if the bores are in excellent condition also (no pitting). Values for under 40% specimens fall off rapidly and are no longer comparable to steel barrel guns. As an example, a steel "D" Grade (without ejectors) might range from $1,500 to $7,000 (10%-100%) with a rather even downward progression of values in between the high and low values. A 100% damascus "D" Grade could have a $3,500+ price tag hanging from the trigger guard while 5%-15% condition specimen is typically seen priced in the $375-$550 range. Remember, the guns are not rare but their condition is.

Parker Shotguns: SxS, Fluid Steel Barrels

Values listed below in the 95%-100% condition columns can vary a lot as there is very little supply and strong demand for these high condition "cream puffs".

Note: Values are for non-ejector guns through the CH grade, ejectors assumed on BHE and better models. Add 15% - 30% for vent. ribs. Skeet model has beavertail forearm and single selective trigger valued at approx. 50%-75% higher than values shown. Higher grade guns typically had ejectors, and will not make as much difference percentage-wise in the overall value as those lower grades with ejectors. Ejectors typically will add 50% or more value to a Parker in common grades. Also, lower condition high grade models sometimes have their values established by the potential gain in refurbishing these specimens.

Due to the extremely high value of Parker Guns, extreme care should be taken in their purchase. There are many upgraded and refinished guns represented as original; expert advice should always be sought. Many collectors would rather own a specimen with 30% original case colors than a refinished gun that is 100% (regardless who did the work). Many advanced collectors will discount a refinished Parker's value 40%-60% of the price for an original gun. Misrepresentation of refinished or upgraded Parkers is rampant today - especially case colors. Believe it or not, also beware of fake boxes and hanging tags - if the box and Parker shotgun are an original "pair", the value is enhanced tremendously. If the box/hanging tag is fake, you could pay as much as $1,500 to learn this lesson! In other words, do your homework, be careful, shop carefully, and above all, get a receipt for exactly what you are purchasing.

Frame size on Parker shotguns is determined by the number on the bottom of the barrel lug on breech. Frame sizes (from largest to smallest) include 7, 6, 5, 4, 3, 2, 1½, 1, ½, 0, 00, and 000. 8 ga. guns typically are framed 6 or 7. 10 ga. guns typically are 3 or 4. 12 ga. guns typically range from 2 through 1 (more desirable). "½" frame 12 ga. guns are very rare and desirable. 20 and 16 ga.'s range from 2 through 0 (more desirable). 28 ga. guns are either 0 or 00 (more desirable and twice as expensive). .410 bore shotguns are 00 or 000 (most common and most desirable). 8 and 10 ga. steel barreled shotguns are very rare, and prices can equate .410 bore values if the original condition is there.

The grade on Parker shotguns is a number or initials located on the water table of the frame. An alphabetical designation would indicate the grade immediately. For numerals, a "2" would indicate a GH, while an "8" would specify an A-1 Special - interpolate for the others (numbers 3 through 7). Parker shotguns manufactured by Remington will have date codes stamped on left barrel flat that correspond to the month and the year (see Remington serialization in the Serialization Section). Also, if a Parker gun was returned to Remington for repair, alteration, or refinishing, it will usually have the date code stamped with a suffix of 3 (i.e., OK3 represents some type of rework completed in either July of 1941 or 1963). There is some ambiguity with the year as the year codes repeat.

100%	98%	95%	90%	80%	70%	60%	50%	40%	30%	20%	10%

A note about Parker condition: Percentages of condition indicate the amount of original case colors remaining on the frame, but sometimes these colors are faded and the rest of the gun is excellent - hence, all the separate condition factors must be considered when determining overall condition.

A Parker IS NOT 60% if the barrel bluing and stock/forearm varnish are 60% but case colors are only 10%. Typically, a 60% case color Parker shotgun will have 90%+ blue and varnish, yet this does not mean the gun is 90% overall. Similarly, a 20% case color Parker will probably have 90% barrel bluing remaining.

Strong, original case colors are the key in determining Parker condition and subsequent values.

"The Parker Story, Vol. I", was published in late 1998. This book has production statistics derived from factory records, and the quantities manufactured listed in this text for steel-barreled hammerless Parker guns are taken from this book. This new publication also has more detailed production statistics on Parker guns produced from 1869-1942, including a break down by action type (lifter, top lever, and hammerless), grade, barrel steel, gauge, and barrel length. Some grades, gauges, etc., are fewer in number than previously estimated (i.e., there are only two 28 ga. Trojans). All the grades are pictured in color, including the Invincible. Parker Reproductions are also covered in detail, including production statistics. Vol. II is planned for a mid-1999 release. If interested in Parkers, these publications will be invaluable.

The author wishes to thank Mr. Charles Price, William Mullins, Roy Gunther, and Daniel Cote for sharing the following Parker production statistics with this publication.

* PREMIUMS FOR PARKER SHOTGUNS:

Add 20% for SST.
Add 20% for beavertail forearm.
Add 20%-50% for VR (rare on smaller gauges).
Add 20% for straight English stock.
Add 20% for skeleton steel butt plate.
Add 20% for short barrels (26 in. with open chokes).

TROJAN — Parker's lowest-priced gun, single or double triggers, but no auto ejectors available, very rarely found in mint condition because they were used a lot, a genuine utility gun, introduced 1912-13 with approx. 33,000 total mfg.

	100%	98%	95%	90%	80%	70%	60%	50%	40%	30%	20%	10%
* 12 ga.	$2,400	$2,000	$1,500	$1,175	$950	$850	$750	$650	$600	$575	$525	$500
* 16 ga.	$3,250	$2,750	$2,000	$1,750	$1,500	$1,200	$1,050	$950	$750	$700	$650	$600
* 20 ga.	$3,850	$3,375	$2,500	$1,800	$1,700	$1,600	$1,500	$1,775	$1,300	$1,200	$1,100	$900

VH — Parker's biggest selling model, offered with all options, the most commonly found Parker. Approx. 79,000 mfg. 10 ga. is very rare in this model.

Add 60% for ejectors (VHE Model).

	100%	98%	95%	90%	80%	70%	60%	50%	40%	30%	20%	10%
* 12 ga.	$3,550	$2,975	$2,200	$1,750	$1,450	$1,200	$1,100	$1,000	$900	$800	$750	$700
* 16 ga.	$3,550	$2,975	$2,200	$1,750	$1,450	$1,200	$1,100	$1,000	$925	$850	$775	$700
* 20 ga.	$4,300	$3,950	$3,500	$3,200	$3,000	$2,800	$2,400	$2,200	$2,000	$1,800	$1,600	$1,400
* 28 ga.	$7,000	$6,550	$5,750	$5,150	$4,600	$3,900	$3,600	$3,100	$2,850	$2,650	$2,475	$2,425
* .410 bore.	N/A	$17,250	$14,000	$12,250	$10,000	$8,750	$7,900	$7,200	$6,800	$6,300	$5,800	$5,100

100%	98%	95%	90%	80%	70%	60%	50%	40%	30%	20%	10%

PH — offered for a very short time, most had twist barrels, prices here are for fluid steel barrels only. Approx. 1,400 mfg. A very few .410 bores were mfg. 10 ga. with fluid steel barrels is very rare in this model.

Add 60% for ejectors (PHE Model).

* 12 ga.

| $3,450 | $2,975 | $2,600 | $2,350 | $2,100 | $1,850 | $1,625 | $1,400 | $1,150 | $995 | $900 | $825 |

* 16 ga.

| $3,450 | $2,975 | $2,600 | $2,350 | $2,100 | $1,850 | $1,625 | $1,400 | $1,150 | $995 | $900 | $825 |

* 20 ga.

| $5,000 | $4,600 | $4,000 | $3,750 | $3,350 | $2,950 | $2,600 | $2,350 | $2,175 | $1,900 | $1,650 | $1,400 |

* 28 ga.

| $8,850 | $8,250 | $7,400 | $7,000 | $6,500 | $6,000 | $5,750 | $5,500 | $5,000 | $4,500 | $3,750 | $3,000 |

GH — very popular model, barrels marked Parker Special Steel, engraved moderately with all options available. 10 ga. with fluid steel barrels is very rare in this model, approx. 4,300 mfg.

Add 60% for ejectors (GHE Model).

* 12 ga.

| $4,350 | $3,775 | $3,150 | $2,475 | $1,850 | $1,625 | $1,500 | $1,300 | $1,100 | $950 | $900 | $800 |

* 16 ga.

| $4,650 | $4,000 | $3,400 | $2,600 | $2,175 | $1,850 | $1,650 | $1,350 | $1,150 | $1,050 | $950 | $900 |

* 20 ga.

| $5,000 | $4,250 | $3,700 | $3,400 | $3,100 | $2,800 | $2,500 | $2,300 | $2,200 | $1,800 | $1,600 | $1,500 |

* 28 ga.

| N/A | $6,650 | $5,750 | $5,125 | $4,550 | $4,200 | $3,800 | $3,600 | $3,300 | $3,000 | $2,750 | $2,600 |

* .410 bore.

| N/A | N/A | $15,350 | $12,850 | $10,500 | $8,525 | $8,000 | $7,500 | $7,000 | $6,500 | $6,000 | $5,500 |

DH — the most popular higher grade gun, very tastefully engraved and flawlessly finished, approx. 9,400 mfg.

Add 50% for ejectors (DHE Model).

* 12 ga.

| $5,950 | $5,250 | $4,300 | $3,450 | $2,675 | $2,175 | $1,850 | $1,625 | $1,450 | $1,325 | $1,150 | $995 |

* 16 ga.

| $6,300 | $5,375 | $4,450 | $3,500 | $2,675 | $2,175 | $1,850 | $1,625 | $1,450 | $1,325 | $1,150 | $995 |

* 20 ga.

| $6,950 | $6,150 | $5,500 | $5,300 | $5,000 | $4,800 | $4,000 | $3,500 | $3,150 | $2,750 | $2,200 | $1,650 |

* 28 ga.

| N/A | $9,550 | $8,175 | $7,800 | $7,500 | $7,000 | $6,700 | $6,500 | $6,200 | $6,000 | $5,500 | $5,000 |

* .410 bore.

| N/A | N/A | $28,250 | $22,000 | $18,950 | $16,350 | $14,000 | $12,750 | $10,650 | $9,100 | $8,000 | $7,250 |

CH — scarce because they were only slightly more decorative than the DH, Acme steel barrels. Approx. 1,100 mfg. 10 ga. is very rare in this model.

Add 50% for ejectors (CHE Model).

* 12 ga.

| N/A | N/A | $4,775 | $4,000 | $3,350 | $2,600 | $2,400 | $2,200 | $2,000 | $1,800 | $1,650 | $1,425 |

* 16 ga.

| N/A | N/A | $4,850 | $4,050 | $3,350 | $3,000 | $2,700 | $2,600 | $2,400 | $2,200 | $1,975 | $1,650 |

* 20 ga.

| N/A | N/A | $6,375 | $5,550 | $4,950 | $4,500 | $4,300 | $4,000 | $3,800 | $3,650 | $3,300 | $2,750 |

P

100%	98%	95%	90%	80%	70%	60%	50%	40%	30%	20%	10%

* **28 ga.**

100%	98%	95%	90%	80%	70%	60%	50%	40%	30%	20%	10%
N/A	N/A	$13,850	$10,500	$9,250	$8,175	$7,000	$6,375	$5,750	$5,125	$4,550	$3,895

* **.410 bore.** — very rare, approx. 6 are known to exist.

N/A	N/A	$35,250	$28,250	$23,250	$19,950	$17,250	$14,450	$12,950	$11,000	$9,950	$8,950

BH — quite popular and decorative, 4 styles of engraving available, Acme steel barrels. Approx. 700 mfg. 10 ga. is very rare in this model.

Add 50% for ejectors (BHE Model).

* **12 ga.**

N/A	N/A	$7,425	$6,375	$5,550	$4,950	$4,300	$3,750	$3,100	$2,800	$2,500	$2,000

* **16 ga.**

N/A	N/A	$7,600	$6,400	$5,550	$4,950	$4,300	$3,750	$3,100	$2,800	$2,500	$2,000

* **20 ga.**

N/A	N/A	$12,000	$10,250	$9,300	$8,275	$7,100	$6,375	$5,650	$5,200	$4,700	$4,000

* **28 ga.**

N/A	N/A	N/A	$17,500	$13,850	$10,500	$9,250	$8,175	$7,000	$6,275	$5,350	$4,550

* **.410 bore.** — only 2 guns are known in this gauge, the BHE .410 is also the highest grade .410 bore known to have been made. Extreme rarity precludes accurate price evaluation, but will be VERY expensive.

AHE — a scarce gun, extremely decorative and flawlessly executed, Acme steel barrels. Approx. 300 mfg. 10 ga. is very rare in this model.

Subtract 25% if w/o ejectors (AH Model).

* **12 ga.**

N/A	N/A	$16,100	$12,250	$9,250	$8,000	$7,150	$6,500	$6,000	$5,500	$5,000	$4,500

* **16 ga.**

N/A	N/A	$17,000	$13,000	$9,375	$8,100	$7,500	$7,000	$6,500	$6,000	$5,500	$5,000

* **20 ga.**

N/A	N/A	$21,000	$17,500	$13,850	$10,500	$9,250	$8,500	$8,000	$7,500	$7,000	$6,500

* **28 ga.**

N/A	N/A	N/A	$31,500	$23,750	$18,975	$16,000	$14,000	$12,250	$10,750	$9,000	$8,250

* **.410 bore** — extreme rarity factor precludes accurate price evaluation.

AAHE — very elaborate model, early AAs have Whitworth barrels, late ones have Peerless. Approx. 240 mfg.

Subtract 20% if without ejectors (AAH Model).

* **12 ga.**

N/A	N/A	$28,500	$26,000	$23,000	$21,000	$19,000	$17,000	$15,500	$13,750	$12,000	$10,500

* **16 ga.**

N/A	N/A	$32,000	$28,500	$26,000	$23,000	$21,000	$19,000	$17,000	$15,500	$13,750	$12,000

* **20 ga.**

N/A	N/A	$50,000	$45,000	$40,250	$35,000	$31,050	$28,000	$24,750	$21,000	$19,550	$17,250

* **28 ga.**

N/A	N/A	N/A	$68,500	$63,250	$58,750	$53,475	$46,000	$39,500	$33,925	$28,175	$25,875

A-1 SPECIAL GRADE — 100% engraved, all were special ordered, each one inspected by the company president before being shipped. Approx. 80 mfg.

* **12 ga.**

N/A	N/A	$61,000	$57,000	$51,750	$46,250	$40,250	$36,175	$31,050	$28,500	$26,450	$22,000

* **16 ga.**

N/A	N/A	$61,000	$57,000	$51,750	$46,250	$40,250	$36,175	$31,050	$28,500	$26,450	$22,000

100%	98%	95%	90%	80%	70%	60%	50%	40%	30%	20%	10%

* **20 ga.**

N/A	N/A	N/A	$90,000	$82,000	$76,000	$70,000	$64,000	$57,500	$53,000	$46,500	$40,000

* **28 ga.** — extreme rarity and desirability factors preclude accurate price evaluation by condition factors. 70% original condition A-1 Specials HAVE sold for over $125,000.

SHOTGUNS: SINGLE BARREL TRAP

12 or 20 (rare) ga., 26 (20 ga. only, rare), 28 (very rare), 30 (rare), 32, or 34 (rare) in. barrels, any boring was available, as was stock configuration, boxlock, auto ejector. The grades differ only in engraving, checkering and wood finish.

It should be noted that single barrel trap guns cannot be compared to the SxS models as they are not as desirable, even though they are more rare. Approximately 1,900 Parker single barrel trap guns were manufactured, mostly in SC Grade. Most SxS collectors are not that interested in single barrel trap models and very few collectors specialize in single barrels.

Add 15% for 30 or 34 in. barrel.

S.C. GRADE

$4,000	$3,600	$3,100	$2,700	$2,350	$1,875	$1,625	$1,400	$1,150	$995	$900	$825

S.B. GRADE

$4,825	$4,300	$3,750	$3,475	$3,100	$2,700	$2,350	$1,875	$1,625	$1,400	$1,150	$995

S.A. GRADE

N/A	$5,000	$4,375	$3,875	$3,425	$3,050	$2,675	$2,275	$1,875	$1,550	$1,200	$1,050

S.A.A. GRADE

N/A	N/A	$5,500	$4,750	$4,000	$3,575	$3,050	$2,675	$2,375	$1,850	$1,575	$1,350

S.A.-1 SPECIAL GRADE

N/A	N/A	N/A	$13,000	$10,000	$9,150	$8,350	$7,425	$6,375	$5,550	$4,950	$4,300

PARKER PISTOLS

Refer to the Wyoming Arms section in this text.

PARKER REPRODUCTIONS

Previously imported by the Parker Reproduction Division of Reagent Chemical & Research, Inc., located in Middlesex, NJ. Previously distributed by Parker Reproductions located in Webb City, MO. These shotguns were manufactured in Japan to original Parker specifications by Winchester until the factory closed in January, 1989.

In 1984, Winchester was contracted by Reagent Chemical & Research, Inc. to manufacture a new Parker shotgun. The new SxS was a DHE model, available in 20 and 28 ga. initially. These models were fabricated in Japan to original Parker specifications, and the reproduction was so authentic that most parts are interchangeable with original Parker guns. Mfg. 1984-89. In 1993, a 16/20 ga. combo was introduced in some models.

SHOTGUNS: SxS

Because of the high quality and limited mfg. of these reproductions, they have become very collectible.

Grading	100%	98%	95%	90%	80%	70%	60%

P

DHE GRADE — 12 (new 1986), 20, or 28 (new 1984) ga., boxlock action, ejectors, single selective or double triggers, beavertail or splinter forend, straight or pistol grip stock, skeleton steel butt plate, engraving in original DH style, case hardened frame, rust blued barrels. Supplied with leather trunk case, canvas and leather cover, and snap caps. Disc.

	$2,475	$2,200	$2,000	$1,800	$1,675	$1,500	$1,375

Last Mfg.'s Sug. Retail was $3,370.

Add 10% for 28 ga., or 20% for 12 ga.
Add $150 for beavertail forend.
Add $650 for Sporting Clays Model w/choke tubes.
Add $800-$1,100 per extra set of barrels, depending on gauge, configuration, and condition.

Quantities mfg. for this model are as follows: 12 ga. - 2,137 mfg., 20 ga. - 6,050 mfg., 28 ga. - 4,203 mfg.

* **DHE Steel Shot Special** — similar to 12 ga. D Grade, except has strengthened No. 1½ barrels, 3 in. chambers, and 28 in. chrome lined barrels, 7¼-7½ lbs. Approx. 250 mfg. 1987-89.

	$2,900	$2,500	$2,200	$1,950	$1,750	$1,550	$1,375

Last Mfg.'s Sug. Retail was $3,370.

Add $100 for beavertail forend.

* **DHE Small Gauge Combo** — available in either 28 ga./.410 bore (disc.) or 16/20 ga. (mfg. 1993-97) combo with 2 barrels and 2 forends. Less than 160 mfg. of the 28 ga./.410 bore combo. Disc.

➤ **28 ga./.410 bore Combo**

	$6,500	$5,750	$4,500	$4,000	$3,625	$3,150	$2,900

Last Mfg.'s Sug. Retail was $4,970.

➤ **16/20 ga. Combo** — new 1994 - disc.

	$5,000	$4,650	$4,000	$3,600	$3,300	$2,950	$2,600

Last Mfg.'s Sug. Retail was $4,870.

* **DHE 3-Barrel Set** — includes 20, 28 ga., and .410 bore barrels, cased. Disc.

	$7,500	$6,750	$5,500	$5,000	$4,500	$3,750	$3,500

Last Mfg.'s Sug. Retail was $5,630.

BHE GRADE LIMITED EDITION — 12, 20, 28 ga. or 410 bore, original Parker BH specifications, single selective or double trigger(s), straight or pistol grip stock, engraved skeleton butt plate, bank note scroll engraving around game scenes, cased. Only 100 manufactured in each gauge during late 1987-89. Disc.

	$4,875	$4,400	$3,950	$3,500	$2,650	$2,150	$1,800

Add $1,000 for 20 ga.
Add $4,000 for 28 ga. or .410 bore.
Add $1,000 for extra set of barrels.
Add $150 for beavertail forend.

Last Mfg.'s Sug. Retail was $3,970.

A 28 ga./.410 bore combo was also available with 2 forends. Only seven 28 ga.'s were mfg. in this model.

A-1 SPECIAL — 12, 16/20 ga. combo (introduced 1993), 20, or 28 ga., original Parker A-1 specifications, single selective or double trigger(s), fine scroll engraving with game scenes, 32 lines/in. checkering, cased with accessories. Limited mfg. 1988-89.

	$10,500	$8,500	$7,250	$6,000	$5,475	$4,800	$4,350

Last Mfg.'s Sug. Retail was $11,200.

Add $3,000+ for 28 ga.
Add $1,000 for extra set of barrels.
Add $200 for beavertail forend.
Add $1,700 for 16 ga. barrel (splinter model only).

* **A-1 Special Custom Engraved** — custom (per individual special order) engraving, available with two sets of barrels only, cased with accessories. Limited mfg. 1988-89. Prices started at $11,000 and go up according to individualized special features.

Grading	100%	98%	95%	90%	80%	70%	60%

* ***Federal Duck Stamp Collector's Series*** — available in 12 or 20 ga., A-1 Special specifications, authorized by U.S. Department of Interior. Mfg. was limited to 10 per year in 1988-89 only.

$13,500 $10,000 $8,000

This model included special case and 2 barrels per buyer's specifications.

Last Mfg.'s Sug. Retail was $14,000.

PARKER-HALE LIMITED

Previous manufacturer located in Birmingham, England. Rifles were manufactured in England until 1991 when Navy Arms purchased the manufacturing rights and built a plant in West Virginia for fabrication. This new company is called Gibbs Rifle Company and they manufactured models very similar to older Parker-Hale rifles during 1992-94. Shotguns were manufactured in Spain and imported by Precision Sports, a division of Cortland Line Company, Inc. located in Cortland, NY until 1993.

RIFLES: BOLT ACTION

All Parker rifle importation was discontinued in 1991. Parker-Hale bolt action rifles utilize the Mauser K-98 action and were offered in a variety of configurations. A single set trigger option was introduced in 1984 on most models, which allows either "hair trigger" or conventional single stage operation - add $85.

MODEL 81 CLASSIC — available in 11 cals. between .22-250 Rem., and 7mm Rem. Mag., 24 in. barrel, open sights, 4 shot mag., select checkered walnut with sling swivels, 7¾ lbs. New 1985.

$715 $565 $475 $395 $340 $300 $280

Last Mfg.'s Sug. Retail was $860.

* ***Model 81 African*** — .375 H&H or 9.3x62mm Mauser cal., similar specifications as Model 81 Classic and has engraved action. New 1986.

$875 $700 $600 $500 $425 $360 $330

Last Mfg.'s Sug. Retail was $1,110.

MODEL 84 TARGET — .308 Win. cal., match rifle with special sights, adj. cheekpiece on stock. Importation disc. 1990.

$1,080 $875 $760 $680 $610 $530 $465

Last Mfg.'s Sug. Retail was $1,300.

MODEL 85 SNIPER RIFLE — .308 Win. cal., bolt action, extended heavy barrel, 10 shot mag., camo green synthetic stock with stippling, built in adj. bipod, enlarged contoured bolt, adj. recoil pad. Importation began 1989.

$1,750 $1,425 $1,275 $1,050 $875 $750 $625

Last Mfg.'s Sug. Retail was $1,975.

MODEL 86 TARGET — .308 Win. cal., 27½ in. barrel, 5 shot mag., stippled stock and forend, aperture front and rear sights, 11¼ lbs. Distributed 1986 only by North American Precision.

$980 $830 $760 $690 $610 $530 $465

Last Mfg.'s Sug. Retail was $1,149.

MODEL 87 TARGET — .243 Win., 6.5x55mm Swedish, .308 Win., .30-06, or .300 Win. Mag. cal., target stock, aperture sights. Importation began 1987.

$1,375 $1,100 $900 $775 $650 $550 $495

Last Mfg.'s Sug. Retail was $1,525.

MODEL 1000 STANDARD — available in 9 cals. between .22-250 Rem. and .308 Win., 22 in. barrel, 4 shot mag., walnut stock with cheekpiece, 7¼ lbs. Disc. 1988.

$400 $330 $285 $255 $230 $215 $195

Last Mfg.'s Sug. Retail was $500.

P

MODEL 1100 LIGHTWEIGHT — available in 9 cals. between .22-250 Rem. and .30-06, 22 in. barrel, open sights, 4 shot mag., 6½ lbs. New 1985.

	$495	$400	$350	$325	$285	$270	$255

Last Mfg.'s Sug. Retail was $595.

* *Model 1100M African* — .375 H&H, .404 Jeffery, or .458 Win. Mag. cal., 24 in. barrel, 4 shot mag., 9½ lbs.

	$800	$650	$575	$500	$450	$425	$400

Last Mfg.'s Sug. Retail was $960.

MODEL 1200 SUPER — bolt action, Mauser type action, .22-250 Rem., .243 Win., 6mm Rem., .25-06 Rem., .270 Win., .30-06, .300 Win. Mag., 7mm Rem. Mag., or .308 Win. cal., 24 in. barrel, folding sight, skip checkered walnut stock, sling swivels, rosewood pistol grip cap and forend tip. New 1968 - disc..

	$540	$450	$375	$330	$295	$275	$260

This model in Magnum cals. was called the 1200 M Super Magnum.

Last Mfg.'s Sug. Retail was $680.

* *Model 1200 C (Super Clip)* — similar to Model 1200 Super, except has detachable 4 shot box mag.

	$590	$500	$400	$350	$300	$280	$265

Last Mfg.'s Sug. Retail was $740.

MODEL 1200P PRESENTATION — similar to 1200, except .243 Win. or .30-06 cal., scroll engraved, no sights. Mfg. 1969-1975.

	$495	$425	$395	$340	$315	$305	$275

MODEL 1200 SUPER VARMINT — similar to 1200, except .22-250 Rem., 6mm Rem., .25-06 Rem., or .243 Win. cal., 24 in. heavy barrel, no sights. Disc. 1988.

	$525	$425	$365	$325	$285	$270	$255

Last Mfg.'s Sug. Retail was $660.

MODEL 1300 C SCOUT — shorter barrel variation.

	$695	$550	$450	$385	$330	$300	$275

Last Mfg.'s Sug. Retail was $785.

MODEL 2100 MIDLAND (HYBRID ACTION) — available in 11 cals. between .22-250 Rem. - .300 Win. Mag. cal., 22 in. barrel, 4 shot mag., open sights, 7 lbs.

	$325	$270	$230	$200	$190	$180	$170

Last Mfg.'s Sug. Retail was $365.

* *Model 2100 Midland Magnum* — .300 Win. Mag., or 7mm Rem. Mag. cal., 24 in. barrel, 4 shot mag., 9½ lbs. Imported 1989-90 only.

	$380	$325	$295	$270	$260	$250	$240

Last Mfg.'s Sug. Retail was $430.

MODEL 2600 MIDLAND SPECIAL — .243 Win., .270 Win., .308 Win., or .30-06 cal., Midland Gun Co. action, iron sights. New 1989.

	$295	$250	$225	$200	$190	$180	$170

Last Mfg.'s Sug. Retail was $330.

MIDLAND 2700 LIGHTWEIGHT — lightweight variation of the Model 2600.

	$340	$285	$240	$200	$190	$180	$170

Last Mfg.'s Sug. Retail was $390.

SHOTGUNS: SxS

Parker-Hale shotguns were manufactured by Ugartechea in Eibar, Spain and imported as Parker-Hale models by Precision Sports located in Cortland, NY until 1994. Please refer to the Ugartechea section of this text.

PASTUSEK INDUSTRIES

Current manufacturer located in Fort Worth, TX since 1993. Distributed by Fort Worth Firearms located in Fort Worth, TX.

Grading	100%	98%	95%	90%	80%	70%	60%

P

PISTOLS: SEMI-AUTO

HSK (SPORT KING) — .22 LR cal., 4½ or 5½ in. barrel. New 1995.

Mfg.'s Sug. Retail	$312	$275	$250	$225	$195	$175	$150	$135

HSS (SHARPSHOOTER) — .22 LR cal., 5½ in. bull barrel. New 1995.

Mfg.'s Sug. Retail	$379	$315	$275	$240	$210	$190	$165	$150

HSC (SUPERMATIC CITATION) — .22 LR cal., 5½ bull or 7¼ in. fluted barrel. New 1995.

Mfg.'s Sug. Retail	$388	$340	$295	$265	$230	$210	$180	$165

    Add $22 for 7¼ in. fluted barrel.

    This model is also available with an 8, 10, or 12 in. bull barrel.

HST (SUPERMATIC TROPHY) — .22 LR cal., 5½ bull or 7¼ in. fluted barrel. New 1995.

Mfg.'s Sug. Retail	$494	$400	$340	$275	$240	$220	$180	$165

    This model is also available with an 8, 10, or 12 in. bull barrel. Left-hand ejection is also an option on this model.

HSV (VICTOR) — .22 LR cal., 3⅞, 4½, 5½, 8 (optional), or 10 (optional) in. VR barrel. New 1995.

Mfg.'s Sug. Retail	$569	$475	$375	$300	$250	$230	$185	$165

    Add $30 for dove tail rib on 5½ in. barrel only.
    Add $79 for Weaver rib on 5½ in. barrel only.

HSO (OLYMPIC) — .22 S or .22 LR cal., 6¾ in. barrel only. New 1995.

Mfg.'s Sug. Retail	$599	$495	$395	$325	$265	$245	$195	$170

PAUZA SPECIALTIES

Previously manufactured by Pauza Specialties circa 1991-96, and located in Baytown, TX. Previously distributed by U.S. General Technologies, Inc. located in South San Francisco, CA.

RIFLES

P50 SEMI-AUTO — .50 BMG cal., semi-auto, 24 (carbine) or 29 (rifle) in. match grade barrel, 5 shot detachable mag., one-piece receiver, 3-stage gas system, takedown action, all exterior parts Teflon coated, with aluminum bipod, 25 or 30 lbs. New 1992.

			$5,950	$5,250	$4,600	$4,100	$3,650	$3,200	$2,800

    Last Mfg.'s Sug. Retail was $6,495.

PEACE RIVER CLASSICS

Current manufacturer located in Bartow, FL. Peace River Classics is a division of Tim's Guns. Dealer or consumer direct sales.

RIFLES: SEMI-AUTO

PEACE RIVER CLASSICS SEMI-AUTO — .223 Rem. or .308 Win. (new 1998) cal., available in 3 configurations including the Shadowood, the Glenwood, and the Royale, hand-built utilizing Armalite action, patterned after the AR-15, matched parts throughout, special serialization. New 1997.

Mfg.'s Sug. Retail	$2,695	$2,575	$2,275	$2,000	$1,775	$1,525	$1,250	$995

    Add $300 for .308 Win. cal.

PEDERSEN CUSTOM GUNS

Previously manufactured circa 1973-1975 by O.F. Mossberg located in North Haven, CT. Pedersen Custom Guns was a division of O.F. Mossberg.

P

Grading	100%	98%	95%	90%	80%	70%	60%

RIFLES: BOLT ACTION

MODEL 3000 — .270 Win., .30-06, 7mm Rem. Mag., or .338 Win. Mag. cal., Mossberg Model 810 action, 22 or 24 in. barrel, open sights, checkered Monte Carlo stock.

* *Grade III* — no engraving.

	100%	98%	95%	90%	80%	70%	60%
	$550	$495	$470	$440	$420	$385	$330

* *Grade II* — moderately engraved.

	100%	98%	95%	90%	80%	70%	60%
	$660	$580	$525	$495	$440	$420	$385

* *Grade I* — heavily engraved and inlaid, with select wood.

	100%	98%	95%	90%	80%	70%	60%
	$990	$770	$745	$690	$635	$560	$495

* *Presentation Model* — top-of-the-line model.

	100%	98%	95%	90%	80%	70%	60%
	$1,250	$1,000	$895	$800	$745	$690	$635

MODEL 4700 — custom deluxe lever action, (Model 472 Mossberg), .30-30 Win. or .35 Rem. cal., 5 shot, tube mag., 24 in. barrel, open sight, black walnut stock.

	100%	98%	95%	90%	80%	70%	60%
	$250	$195	$165	$155	$145	$130	$120

SHOTGUNS: O/U

MODEL 1500 HUNTING GUN — 12 ga., 2¾ or 3 in. chambers, 26 in. imp. cyl. and mod., 28 in. mod. and full, 30 in. mod. and full barrels, boxlock, auto ejectors, selective or non-selective single trigger, checkered pistol grip stock. Mfg. 1973-1975.

	100%	98%	95%	90%	80%	70%	60%
	$700	$575	$500	$440	$415	$385	$365

MODEL 1500 SKEET — similar to Hunting Gun, except 27 in. skeet barrel, skeet stock. Mfg. 1973-1975.

	100%	98%	95%	90%	80%	70%	60%
	$725	$600	$525	$450	$425	$400	$385

MODEL 1500 TRAP — similar to Hunting Gun, except 30 and 32 in. full barrels, trap Monte Carlo stock. Mfg. 1973-1975.

	100%	98%	95%	90%	80%	70%	60%
	$650	$550	$475	$435	$410	$375	$350

MODEL 1000 HUNTING GUN — 12 or 20 ga., 26, 28, or 30 in. barrels, various chokes, boxlock, auto ejectors, SST, checkered select walnut stock, silver inlays, more engraving. Mfg. 1973-1975.

	100%	98%	95%	90%	80%	70%	60%
Grade I	$2,200	$1,980	$1,870	$1,700	$1,540	$1,460	$1,375
Grade II	$1,815	$1,540	$1,430	$1,265	$1,185	$1,100	$1,045

MODEL 1000 TRAP GUN — similar to Hunting Gun, but 12 ga., 30 or 32 in. mod. and full barrels, Monte Carlo trap stock. Mfg. 1973-1975.

	100%	98%	95%	90%	80%	70%	60%
Grade I	$2,100	$1,800	$1,650	$1,500	$1,350	$1,200	$995
Grade II	$1,650	$1,500	$1,375	$1,200	$1,050	$900	$725

MODEL 1000 SKEET — similar to Hunting Gun, except 26 or 28 in. barrels, bored skeet. Mfg. 1973-1975.

	100%	98%	95%	90%	80%	70%	60%
Grade I	$2,255	$2,145	$2,035	$1,870	$1,705	$1,625	$1,540
Grade II	$1,980	$1,705	$1,595	$1,430	$1,350	$1,265	$1,210

SHOTGUNS: SxS

MODEL 200 — 12 or 20 ga., 26 in. imp. cyl. and mod., 28 in. mod. and full, 30 in. mod. and full barrels, boxlock, auto ejectors, SST. Mfg. 1973-1974.

	100%	98%	95%	90%	80%	70%	60%
Grade I	$2,420	$2,175	$2,090	$1,955	$1,790	$1,705	$1,625
Grade II	$2,200	$1,955	$1,815	$1,735	$1,625	$1,540	$1,485

MODEL 2500 — 12 or 20 ga., 26 in. imp. cyl. and mod., 28 in. mod. and full barrels, auto ejectors, boxlock, checkered pistol grip stock and forearm.

	100%	98%	95%	90%	80%	70%	60%
	$470	$385	$360	$305	$275	$260	$240

Grading	100%	98%	95%	90%	80%	70%	60%

SHOTGUNS: SLIDE ACTION

MODEL 4000 — custom Mossberg Model 500, 12, 20 ga., or .410 bore, 3 in. chamber, 26 in. imp. cyl. or skeet, 28 in. full or mod. barrel, 30 in. full, vent. rib, floral engraved, checkered select walnut stock. Mfg. 1975.

	100%	98%	95%	90%	80%	70%	60%
	$460	$375	$330	$305	$265	$230	$220

MODEL 4000 TRAP — similar to 4000, except 12 ga., 30 in. full barrel, Monte Carlo trap stock and pad. Mfg. 1975.

	100%	98%	95%	90%	80%	70%	60%
	$485	$395	$350	$325	$285	$255	$240

MODEL 4500 — similar to 4000, less engraving.

	100%	98%	95%	90%	80%	70%	60%
	$420	$330	$305	$275	$240	$200	$175

MODEL 4500 TRAP — similar to 4000 Trap, less engraving.

	100%	98%	95%	90%	80%	70%	60%
	$440	$350	$310	$280	$240	$210	$200

PEDERSOLI, DAVIDE & C. s.n.c.

Current manufacturer of modern, black powder, and older historically significant firearms located in Brescia, Italy.

D. Pedersoli manufactures top quality black powder replicas and other high quality reproductions. Most of their production domestically is subcontracted by other U.S. firms.

RIFLES: REPRODUCTIONS, SINGLE SHOT

DELUXE CREEDMOOR 45/70 — .45/70 cal., case colored receiver w/o engraving, 34 in. part round/part octagon barrel, checkered walnut stock, long vernier tang sight, metal butt plate, 12 lbs. 2 oz. Limited mfg. beginning 1995.

	100%	98%	95%	90%	80%	70%	60%
Mfg.'s Sug. Retail $1,095	$1,050	$850	$625				

CREEDMOOR RIFLE SPECIAL EDITION — .45/70 cal., similar to Deluxe Creedmoor, except has 32 in. full octagon barrel, custom bluing, vernier tang rear and hooded front sight, double set triggers. New 1997.

	100%	98%	95%	90%	80%	70%	60%
Mfg.'s Sug. Retail $1,495	$1,495	$1,050	$850				

This model is distributed exclusively by Cherry's, located in Greensboro, NC.

PENTHENY de PENTHENY

Current manufacturer and gunsmith located in Santa Rosa, CA. Established in 1987.

RIFLES: BOLT ACTION

The rifles listed below include ebony forend tips, old English style black recoil pads, steel skeleton grip caps, four panels of 22 LPI checkering, and other custom features. These models are built on a U.S.R.A. Model 70 action.

THE INVADER — small and medium bore cals., classic styled Claro walnut stock, blued finish.

	100%	98%	95%	90%	80%	70%	60%
Mfg.'s Sug. Retail $3,850	$3,850	$2,975	$2,400	$1,975	$1,500	$1,150	$875

THE NORMAN — Mag. cals., classic styled English walnut stock, blued finish.

	100%	98%	95%	90%	80%	70%	60%
Mfg.'s Sug. Retail $3,850	$3,850	$2,975	$2,400	$1,975	$1,500	$1,150	$875

THE CONQUEROR — large bore cals., classic styled English walnut stock, blued finish, rifle has secondary recoil lug, dual steel reinforcing bolts, and express sights including fixed and folding leaves.

	100%	98%	95%	90%	80%	70%	60%
Mfg.'s Sug. Retail $4,700	$4,700	$3,650	$3,000	$2,400	$1,975	$1,500	$1,150

P

Grading	100%	98%	95%	90%	80%	70%	60%

PERAZZI

Current manufacturer established in 1952, and located in Brescia, Italy. Imported and distributed by Perazzi USA, Inc. located in Monrovia, CA (previously located in Rome, NY).

> Note: Previously, Perazzi shotguns were imported by both Winchester and Ithaca during the 1960s and 1970s. The company now has its own distribution network and its current model line-up is extensive. Perazzi shotguns are well known for their quality control standards and reliability in clay target championships and in-field conditions.

SHOTGUNS: DISC.

Perazzi shotguns have incorporated many improvements during their manufacture. One of the most important changes has been the modification of the forearm design. Basically, there have been 4 different types: Type 1 has a serial range of 30,000 - 33,250, Type 2 is serial numbered 33,251 - 35,450, Type 3 has a range of 35,451 - 51,242, Type 4 started at 51,243 and is still current as of this writing. Differences include changes in the forearm iron and barrel lug attachment. Because of these forearm changes (and other parts modifications), the desirability factor on a Type 4 forearm shotgun as opposed to a Type 1 is much greater. Competition shooters prefer Types 3 or 4 as they are the current design. If a Type 1 or 2 competition gun develops problems, they are automatically retrofitted to the Type 4 design - and these modifications are expensive. For these reasons, the serial number of a Perazzi competition gun will determine its type. Since Types 1 through 3 are discontinued, Types 1 and 2 will be less desirable (and less expensive) than the values listed below for Type 3.

As a final note on older Perazzi shotguns, the most collectable models will be those specimens which exhibit the highest quality and are equally rare. Older SCO grades on small frames with older style "V" springs are at the top for desirability. Also, any older SPECIAL GUNS were all custom made - usually engraved by master engravers with Angelo Galeazzi being considered the best. These models are exceedingly rare, with prices going over the $40,000 level in today's marketplace.

COMPETITION ONE TRAP GRADE — single shot, 12 ga., auto ejector, VR, cased.

$2,500	$2,150	$1,875	$1,650	$1,450	$1,300	$1,175

COMPETITION ONE O/U TRAP — similar to Competition, except O/U double.

$4,100	$3,600	$3,250	$3,000	$2,500	$2,150	$1,850

COMPETITION ONE SKEET

$4,000	$3,500	$2,900	$2,500	$2,350	$2,000	$1,750

SINGLE BARREL TRAP — 12 ga., 34 in. VR, full choke barrel, boxlock, auto ejector, checkered pistol grip stock, recoil pad. Mfg. 1971-1972.

$2,050	$1,895	$1,725	$1,575	$1,450	$1,300	$1,175

LIGHT GAME MODEL O/U FIELD — 12 ga., 27½ in. VR barrels, mod. and full or imp. cyl. and mod., boxlock, auto ejectors, field stock. Mfg. 1972-1974.

$4,450	$4,200	$3,700	$3,100	$2,800	$2,400	$2,050

MT-6 GRADE — 12 ga., VR, auto ejector, cased, five interchangeable choke tubes. Disc. 1983.

$4,500	$3,750	$3,250	$2,800	$2,500	$2,200	$1,900

> This model was also manufactured in DHO and SHO models as well. Please refer to those models listed in the current manufacture section for approximate values.

Perazzi Shotguns Information

Not until 1988 did most single barrel trap guns have a "Special" option package which includes an adjustable trigger group (designated P4). This P4 trigger is now

standard. Non-adj. trigger is a special order. Values below assume shotguns with the "Special" designation (became standard in 1988).

Models listed in the following sections assume a Type 4 forearm attachment design and are serial numbered 51,243 and above. Models that are serial numbered below 51,243 are an older design and will be priced less than the newer Type 4 models (see explanation under SHOTGUNS: DISC.).

Rather than describe all the following models individually, descriptions will appear only once and are listed below. The various grades have similar features and engraving (i.e., an SCO Grade Sideplate in American Skeet would appear similar to an American Trap SCO Grade Sideplate, except for stock dimensions of course).

Older SHO (Type 3s) and DHO models with rebounding hammers (disc.) are perhaps the most collectable Perazzi shotguns currently.

SC3 and other higher grade models have not been listed due to space consideration. The 14th edition does include all pertinent information (including 1993 pricing) pertaining to Perazzi higher grade models.

Recently, some Model MX8s have been modified by adding sideplates and other markings of the Extra Gold and SCO Models. These forgeries usually have the original markings polished off and have not been reproofed. Perazzi will verify any gun suspected of upgrading.

Perazzi discontinued "Mirage" model nomenclature during 1998.

Perazzi Grades and Descriptions

Due to space considerations and relative low manufacture, the higher grade Perazzis have been described but not individually priced. Please contact Perazzi, USA for more information and prices on these higher grades (see Trademark Index).

* **Special Model** — introductory level model with high polished blue on barrels and receiver, normally listing model name on lower frame sides in gold letters and numerals. Checkered walnut stock (interchangeable) and forearm, all have adjustable trigger assembly.

* **Gold Outline Model** — similar to Standard Model, except has gold line engraving around perimeter of frame, also features better grade of walnut. This configuration is very rare.

* **SC3 Model** — features coin finished receiver with two different styles of scroll engraving and four different patterns of game scene engraving (snipe, grouse, pointing bird dog, or woodcock). Better grade of walnut than the Gold Outline Model.

* **SCO Model** — more elaborate than SC3 Model in that it features two different styles of scroll engraving (deep relief "gargoyles" or fine English scroll) and four different game scene engraving patterns (two different styles of ducks, grouse, or woodcock). Again, a better grade of walnut (in addition to finer checkering) is utilized.

* **SCO Gold Grade Model** — differentiated from SCO Model in that it has six engraving patterns featuring multiple gold inlays on receiver sides (including two different duck scenes, two separate grouse scenes, one woodcock, and one deep relief "gargoyle").

* **SCO Grade Sideplate Model** — includes coin finished receiver with game scene engraved sideplates (with boxlock action). Game scene engraving choices include three different duck scenes, one grouse, one "Chisel" relief scroll, and a Diana Goddess of the Hunt pattern.

* **SCO Gold Grade Sideplate Model** — similar to SCO Grade Sideplate Model, except has game figures on sideplates in relief gold. Patterns include three different grouse scenes, two separate ducks patterns, and dogs flushing upland game. This model can also be ordered with detachment lever for sideplates.

* **Extra Grade Model** — denoted by top-of-the-line fine bank note style game scene engraving with elaborate scroll and relief work on metal perimeters. Game scene choices include two different dog scenes, one grouse, and one duck. Top quality Circassian walnut finely checkered.

Grading	100%	98%	95%	90%	80%	70%	60%

* **Extra Gold Grade Model** — top-of-the-line boxlock model that differs from Extra Grade Model in that birds/dogs are in gold relief. This model can also be ordered with detachment lever for sideplates.

* **SHO Over & Under Model** — features sidelock action with coin finished receiver and intricate bank note game scene engraving with choices including three different duck patterns and one pheasant. Top quality walnut and checkering. Type One SHOs have non-rebounding firing pins, while Type Two guns have rebounding firing pins (since 1985).

   This model is individually hand made per customer's specifications. Currently, no orders are being taken for this series.

* **SHO Gold Over & Under Model** — similar to SHO Over & Under Model, except features game scene of wildlife in relief gold. This model is the best sidelock special order grade that Perazzi currently offers for sale.

   This model is individually hand made per customer's specifications. Currently, no orders are being taken for this series.

* **DHO SxS Models** — top-of-the-line sidelock model in 12 ga. only for DHO and DHO Gold grades. DHO Extra and DHO Gold Extra grades have similar engraving to Extra Grade and Extra Gold Grade models and are available in all gauges. The DHO Gold Extra is the most elaborate, highly finished SxS shotgun that an individual can currently special order from any company. The DHO model is exceedingly rare, and specimens should be appraised individually.

   This model is entirely hand made per customer's specifications. Currently, no orders are being taken for this series.

Some descriptions on the Standard Models listed below have not been duplicated into the other Perazzi sections because of space consideration.

SHOTGUNS: SINGLE BARREL, AMERICAN TRAP

12 ga. only, 32 or 34 in. barrel, high post rib, select walnut, more expensive models vary in the amount of engraving, grade of walnut, and other special order features.

NOTE: Combination guns (Combo Models) listed below include either a 32 or 34 in. single barrel and a set of either 29½ or 31½ in. O/U barrels. Current combination guns (Combo Models) include MX6, MX7, MX11, MX14, MX8 Special, DB81 Special, and MX10.

Subtract $600 for shotguns without the "Special" model designation (pre-1988).

STANDARD GRADE MODELS

Add 35%-43% for Combo Models depending on model variation.

* **TM1 Special** — features normal trap rib. Disc. 1995.

   $5,150 $3,675 $3,100 $2,350 $2,150 $1,850 $1,675
   Last Mfg.'s Sug. Retail was $6,150.

* **TMX Special** — features high post trap rib. Disc. 1998.

   $5,550 $3,975 $3,250 $2,400 $2,150 $1,850 $1,675
   Last Mfg.'s Sug. Retail was $6,790.

* **MX3 Special** — features rib similar to TM1 Special. Disc. 1992.

   $4,500 $3,200 $2,900 $2,450 $2,200 $1,900 $1,700
   Last Mfg.'s Sug. Retail was $6,150.

* **MX6** — removable trigger group, 32 or 34 in. barrel. Imported 1995-96.

   $4,250 $3,450 $2,575 $2,200 $1,900 $1,700 $1,475
   Last Mfg.'s Sug. Retail was $6,270.

* **MX7** — non-removable trigger group, barrel selector, 32 or 34 in. barrel. Mfg. 1995 only.

   $4,850 $3,600 $3,050 $2,350 $2,150 $1,850 $1,675
   Last Mfg.'s Sug. Retail was $5,650.

Grading	100%	98%	95%	90%	80%	70%	60%

* **MX8 Special** — has tapered stepped rib and adj. trigger. Disc. 1994.

	$8,570	$6,500	$6,100	$4,350	$3,600	$3,200	$2,875

Last Mfg.'s Sug. Retail was $7,300.

* **MX9** — 12 ga., 32 or 34 in. barrel with choke tubes, unique VR on vent. barrel features removable center inserts significantly changing the point of shot pattern impact, fully adj. cheekpiece. Mfg. 1993-94.

	$6,500	$5,200	$4,100	$3,700	$3,250	$2,900	$2,625

Last Mfg.'s Sug. Retail was $9,200.

* **MX9 Combo** — includes a set O/U barrels and top single trap barrel, features new rib design with interchangeable middle bead inserts to change point of impact. Mfg. 1992-94.

	$9,500	$7,250	$6,750	$6,150	$4,800	$4,500	$4,000

This model was available with or without choke tubes. Choke tubes include 5 chokes and 5 rib inserts (3 in. pattern per insert).

Last Mfg.'s Sug. Retail was $12,800.

* **MX10** — 12 ga., 32 or 34 in. barrel featuring center-pivoting VR allowing for adj. point of impact, fixed chokes, fully adj. cheekpiece, removable trigger. Mfg. 1993-94.

	$9,200	$8,500	$7,650	$6,300	$4,400	$3,700	$3,250

Last Mfg.'s Sug. Retail was $9,450.

This model is still available by special order only.

* **MX11** — removable trigger group, adj. comb, 32 or 34 in. barrel. Imported 1995-96.

	$6,150	$3,950	$3,550	$3,200	$2,875	$2,600	$2,375

Last Mfg.'s Sug. Retail was $7,620.

This model is still available by special order only.

* **MX14** — removable trigger group, adj. comb, unsingle configuration, 32 or 34 in. barrel. Imported 1995-96.

	$5,950	$3,950	$3,550	$3,200	$2,875	$2,600	$2,375

Last Mfg.'s Sug. Retail was $7,030.

This model is still available by special order only.

* **Grand American 88 Special** — features MX3 high ramped rib and grooved forearm. Mfg. 1988-92.

	$6,000	$4,250	$3,600	$3,200	$2,875	$2,600	$2,375

Last Mfg.'s Sug. Retail was $7,000.

* **DB81 Special** — features ultra high ramped rib. Disc. 1994.

	$7,950	$6,375	$4,500	$3,700	$3,250	$2,900	$2,625

Last Mfg.'s Sug. Retail was $7,600.

This model is still available by special order only.

SHOTGUNS: O/U, INTERNATIONAL/OLYMPIC TRAP

12 ga. only, unless indicated otherwise. Current barrel lengths include 29½, 30¾, or 31½ in.

STANDARD GRADE MODELS

The MX2/MX2L configuration is available mainly for the European marketplace. Values for this model represent recent pricing - Perazzi U.S.A. should be contacted directly for an up-to-date price quotation.

Models with "Special" nomenclature feature Perazzi's new, adjustable (4 positions) trigger group introduced on certain models beginning 1988.

* **MX3 Special** — includes 6.4mm high ramped rib and separated barrels. Disc. 1992.

	$5,525	$4,050	$3,400	$2,950	$2,675	$2,350	$1,975

Add $380 for MX3C Model (includes choke tubes).

Last Mfg.'s Sug. Retail was $6,500.

Perazzi

Grading	100%	98%	95%	90%	80%	70%	60%

* **MX6** — removable trigger group. Mfg. 1995-98.

	$4,900	$3,650	$3,050	$2,350	$2,150	$1,850	$1,675

Last Mfg.'s Sug. Retail was $5,700.

* **MX7C** — 29½ or 31½ in. barrels, features fixed coil spring trigger mechanism, safety incorporates selector switch, non-removable trigger group. Mfg. 1993-98.

	$5,000	$4,250	$3,550	$2,950	$2,625	$2,300	$2,000

Last Mfg.'s Sug. Retail was $6,100.

* **MX8** — denoted by low profile rib, vent. barrels and grooved forearm.

Mfg.'s Sug. Retail	$8,670		$6,950	$4,750	$3,700	$3,250	$2,875	$2,600	$2,375

This model is also available with standard triggers.

* **MX8 Special** — similar to MX8, except four position adj. trigger (P4S).

Mfg.'s Sug. Retail	$9,180		$7,250	$5,000	$3,825	$3,325	$2,900	$2,625	$2,400

* **MX8/20** — 20 ga., 29½ in. barrels with fixed chokes, flat VR with removable trigger group. New 1993.

Mfg.'s Sug. Retail	$8,670		$6,950	$4,750	$3,700	$3,250	$2,875	$2,600	$2,375

* **MX9** — 29½ or 31½ in. barrels with choke tubes, unique VR on vent. barrels features removable center inserts significantly changing the point of shot pattern impact, fully adj. cheekpiece, removable trigger. Mfg. 1993-94.

	$7,825	$5,850	$5,375	$4,950	$4,200	$3,800	$3,650

Last Mfg.'s Sug. Retail was $9,600.

* **MX10** — 12 or 20 ga., 29½ in. barrels featuring center-pivoting VR allowing for adj. point of impact, fixed chokes, fully adj. cheekpiece, removable trigger. New 1993.

Mfg.'s Sug. Retail	$11,050		$9,250	$7,950	$6,750	$5,500	$4,950	$4,200	$3,800

* **MX11** — removable trigger group and adj. comb. New 1995.

Mfg.'s Sug. Retail	$8,180		$6,350	$4,500	$3,650	$3,200	$2,875	$2,600	$2,375

* **Grand American 88 Special** — features high ramped rib, separated barrels, and grooved forearm. Disc. 1992.

	$6,225	$4,400	$3,700	$3,250	$2,900	$2,625	$2,400

Last Mfg.'s Sug. Retail was $7,400.

* **DB81 Special** — features ultra high ramped rib and vent. barrels.

Mfg.'s Sug. Retail	$9,450		$7,250	$4,900	$4,000	$3,350	$2,950	$2,650	$2,450

* **MX2/MX2L** — denoted by 8.2mm high rib, Monte Carlo stock, and vented side ribs. Model MX2L designates light weight model and has no side ribs. Disc. 1992.

	$4,550	$3,700	$3,400	$3,050	$2,750	$2,500	$2,275

Last Mfg.'s Sug. Retail was $5,510.

* **MX16** — 12 ga., nonremovable trigger group, barrel selector on top of frame, with hard case. New 1998.

Mfg.'s Sug. Retail	$7,210		$5,750	$4,300	$3,600	$3,200	$2,875	$2,600	$2,375

Add $2,280 for combo package.

O/U SIDELOCK MODELS — older models without rebounding hammers are not as desirable. The most desirable configurations in this model are the Skeet, Pigeon, and Sporting variations (pricing follows new SHO Gold values). All SHO sidelock models were disc. 1992.

* **SHO Older Mfg.**

	$19,000	$16,750	$12,250	$9,500	$8,500	$7,600	$6,800

Add $6,000 for game scene engraving.

* **SHO Newer Mfg.**

	$35,000	$27,750	$25,750	$23,750	$21,750	$19,750	$17,750

Last Mfg.'s Sug. Retail was $43,000.

Grading	100%	98%	95%	90%	80%	70%	60%

P

* **SHO Gold Older Mfg.**

	$25,000	$21,000	$18,000	$15,000	$13,000	$11,000	$9,250

* **SHO Gold Newer Mfg.**

	$65,000	$55,000	$49,500	$45,500	$40,000	$35,500	$30,000

Last Mfg.'s Sug. Retail was $48,000.

* **SHO Extra** — while advertised, none were sold.

Last Mfg.'s Sug. Retail was $80,000.

* **SHO Gold Extra** — while advertised, none were sold.

Last Mfg.'s Sug. Retail was $86,000.

SHOTGUNS: O/U, AMERICAN SKEET

12 ga. only, 26, 27⅝ (standard and most common), or 28⅜ in. separated barrels, select walnut, more expensive models vary in the amount of engraving, grade of walnut, and other special order features.

STANDARD GRADE MODELS

* **MX3 Special** — introductory skeet model, detachable and adj. four position P4S trigger, flat rib. Barrel lockup is same as MX8. Disc. 1992.

	$5,400	$3,950	$3,400	$2,950	$2,675	$2,350	$1,975

Last Mfg.'s Sug. Retail was $6,500.

Previous to 1988, this model was designated the MX3. It did not have the P4 adj. selective trigger group.

* **MX6** — removable trigger group. Mfg. 1995-96.

	$4,200	$3,650	$3,050	$2,350	$2,150	$1,850	$1,675

Last Mfg.'s Sug. Retail was $6,270.

* **MX7C** — 27⅝ or 28⅜ in. barrels with choke tubes, features fixed coil spring trigger mechanism, safety incorporates selector switch, non-removable trigger group. Mfg. 1993-95.

	$5,700	$4,950	$4,250	$3,550	$2,950	$2,625	$2,300

Last Mfg.'s Sug. Retail was $6,100.

* **MX8** — 12 or 20 ga., 27⅝ in. barrels bored SK/SK, flat VR with removable trigger group. New 1993.

Mfg.'s Sug. Retail	$8,670		$6,775	$4,600	$3,750	$3,100	$2,700	$2,500	$2,300

* **MX8 Special** — evolved from Olympic Skeet Model, features detachable and adj. four position trigger.

Mfg.'s Sug. Retail	$9,180		$7,075	$4,850	$3,975	$3,400	$2,900	$2,625	$2,400

* **MX10** — removable trigger group, adj. rib and comb. New 1995.

Mfg.'s Sug. Retail	$11,050		$9,200	$7,950	$6,650	$5,700	$4,950	$4,200	$3,800

* **MX11** — removable trigger group, adj. comb. New 1995.

Mfg.'s Sug. Retail	$8,180		$6,450	$4,300	$3,600	$3,200	$2,875	$2,600	$2,375

* **MX16** — 12 ga., nonremovable trigger group, barrel selector on top of frame, with hard case. New 1998.

Mfg.'s Sug. Retail	$7,210		$5,850	$4,300	$3,600	$3,200	$2,875	$2,600	$2,375

SHOTGUNS: O/U, 4-GAUGE SKEET SETS

STANDARD GRADE MODELS

* **MX3 Special**

	$10,500	$8,250	$7,950	$7,100	$6,200	$5,800	$5,250

Last Mfg.'s Sug. Retail was $15,400.

Perazzi

Grading	100%	98%	95%	90%	80%	70%	60%

P

* ***Mirage Special*** — disc. 1994.

	$11,000	$8,800	$7,900	$7,700	$6,950	$6,100	$5,300

Last Mfg.'s Sug. Retail was $17,500.

SHOTGUNS: O/U, INTERNATIONAL/OLYMPIC SKEET

Available in 12 ga. only. Usually supplied with 29½ in. barrels.

Since the international skeet variations are similar to the American skeet models, rather than duplicating these models (with the exception of the Mirage MX8), please refer to pricing in the American Skeet Shotguns section for corresponding values and information. Only the Model MX8 remains below, since there is no similar American model.

STANDARD GRADE MODELS

Older Mirage Models (without the "Special" designation) do not have the adjustable 4 position trigger. Subtract $250-$500 on values listed below for these older variations.

* ***MX8*** — developed especially for Olympic Skeet Competition featuring vent. barrels with optional muzzle brakes on sides, grooved forearm, interchangeable trigger groupings with non-adj. trigger.

Mfg.'s Sug. Retail	$8,090		$5,900	$4,400	$3,600	$3,100	$2,700	$2,500	$2,300

O/U SIDELOCK MODELS — older models without rebounding hammers are not as desirable.

* ***SHO Older Mfg.***

	$18,000	$15,750	$12,000	$9,500	$8,500	$7,600	$6,800

* ***SHO Newer Mfg.***

	$35,850	$30,000	$25,000	$20,000	$17,000	$14,500	$12,750

Last Mfg.'s Sug. Retail was $43,000.

* ***SHO Gold Older Mfg.***

	$18,000	$15,750	$12,000	$9,500	$8,500	$7,600	$6,800

* ***SHO Gold Newer Mfg.***

	$45,000	$34,500	$27,250	$22,000	$18,500	$15,950	$13,750

Last Mfg.'s Sug. Retail was $48,000.

* ***SHO Extra*** — imported 1985-1992.

	$68,750	$54,700	$38,100	$32,000	$26,500	$21,250	$18,000

Last Mfg.'s Sug. Retail was $80,000.

* ***SHO Gold Extra*** — similar to SHO Extra, except has gold inlays. Imported 1992 only.

	$72,750	$56,500	$39,500	$33,000	$27,000	$22,000	$18,500

Last Mfg.'s Sug. Retail was $86,000.

SHOTGUNS: O/U, COMPETITION SPORTING

12 ga. only, unless indicated otherwise, designed for sporting clays competition.

The Mirage Sporting Classic Models listed below replace the Mirage Special Sporting and incorporate several new improvements. Perazzi discontinued the Mirage nomenclature during 1998.

STANDARD GRADE MODELS

The MX1/MX1B configuration is available mainly for the European marketplace. Values for this model represent recent pricing - Perazzi USA should be contacted directly for an up-to-date price quotation.

Choke tubes became standard on Perazzi's Sporting shotguns beginning in 1992. Subtract $400 - $500 for older variations without choke tubes (Models without the "C" suffix nomenclature). Older specimens without the "Special" designation do not have adjustable 4 position trigger group - subtract $400 from values below without this feature.

Grading	100%	98%	95%	90%	80%	70%	60%

* **MX3C Special Sporting** — features VR and barrels, includes adj. four position trigger, and 5 interchangeable choke tubes. Disc. 1992.

		$4,500	$4,000	$3,350	$2,900	$2,500	$2,250	$1,900

Last Mfg.'s Sug. Retail was $6,880.

* **MX6** — removable trigger group, external selector, 7 chokes. Mfg. 1995-98.

		$6,075	$5,125	$4,350	$3,550	$2,950	$2,625	$2,300

Last Mfg.'s Sug. Retail was $6,740.

* **MX7C Sporting** — sporting configuration, includes 5 choke tubes. Imported 1992-95.

		$4,250	$3,950	$3,550	$2,950	$2,625	$2,300	$2,100

Last Mfg.'s Sug. Retail was $6,670.

* **MX8** — 12 or 20 ga., 27⅝, 28⅜, or 29½ in. barrels with fixed or screw-in chokes. New 1993.

Mfg.'s Sug. Retail	$9,600	$7,750	$5,250	$4,150	$3,650	$3,150	$2,900	$2,600

* **MX10** — 12 or 20 ga., 27⅝ in. barrels with fixed chokes. New 1993.

Mfg.'s Sug. Retail	$12,180	$9,150	$7,850	$6,500	$5,500	$4,950	$4,200	$3,600

* **MX11** — removable trigger group, adj. comb, external selector, 7 chokes. New 1995.

Mfg.'s Sug. Retail	$9,110	$6,825	$4,675	$3,825	$3,325	$2,900	$2,625	$2,400

* **MX16** — 12 ga., nonremovable trigger group, barrel selector on top of frame, with hard case. New 1998.

Mfg.'s Sug. Retail	$7,830	$6,650	$5,850	$4,300	$3,600	$3,200	$2,875	$2,600

* **Mirage Special Sporting** — 28⅜ in. barrels with choke tubes, external SST (non-adj.), special sporting dimension stock and forend, Schnabel forearm. Disc. 1998.

		$6,775	$4,650	$3,825	$3,325	$2,900	$2,625	$2,400

Last Mfg.'s Sug. Retail was $9,160.

* **Mirage Special Sporting Classic** — similar to Mirage Sporting, except has engraving package, SC3 quality wood, and SST. Disc. 1998.

		$8,200	$5,900	$4,375	$3,750	$3,150	$2,900	$2,600

Last Mfg.'s Sug. Retail was $10,200.

* **MX1/MX1B Sporting** — 12 ga. only, MX1 has high tapered ramped rib and separated barrels. MX1B has lower profile flat rib.

Mfg.'s Sug. Retail	$8,090	$5,000	$3,700	$3,400	$3,050	$2,750	$2,500	$2,275

SHOTGUNS: O/U, PIGEON-ELECTROCIBLES

STANDARD GRADE MODELS — 12 ga. only.

This configuration specifically made for pigeon/electrocibles competition shooting and is currently available in the MX1B, Mirage (MX8), Mirage Special (MX8 Special), MX10, and MX11 Models.

Subtract $1,000 for 27½ in. barrels, or $500 for 28⅜ in. barrels.

* **MX1B** — removable trigger group, 27½ in. barrels. New 1995.

Mfg.'s Sug. Retail	$8,090	$4,500	$4,100	$3,600	$3,100	$2,700	$2,500	$2,300

* **Standard Grade** — removable trigger group, 27½, 28⅜, 29½, or 31½ in. barrels. New 1995.

Mfg.'s Sug. Retail	$7,850	$5,800	$4,400	$3,600	$3,100	$2,700	$2,500	$2,300

* **Standard Grade Special** — removable trigger group, adj. trigger, 28⅜, 29½, or 31½ in. barrels. New 1995.

Mfg.'s Sug. Retail	$8,570	$6,000	$4,650	$3,825	$3,325	$2,900	$2,625	$2,400

* **MX10** — removable trigger group, adj. rib and comb, 27½ or 29½ in. barrels. New 1995.

Mfg.'s Sug. Retail	$11,050	$8,100	$7,500	$6,400	$5,500	$4,950	$4,200	$3,800

* **MX11** — removable trigger group, adj. comb., 27½ in. barrels. New 1995.

Mfg.'s Sug. Retail	$8,620	$6,150	$4,300	$3,600	$3,200	$2,875	$2,600	$2,375

Grading		100%	98%	95%	90%	80%	70%	60%

* **MX16** — 12 ga., nonremovable trigger group, barrel selector on top of frame, with hard case. New 1998.

  Mfg.'s Sug. Retail   **$7,210** $5,600 $4,300 $3,600 $3,200 $2,875 $2,600 $2,375

SHOTGUNS: O/U, HUNTING - BOXLOCK ACTION

12, 20, 28 ga., or .410 bore, 26 (disc. on MX8/12 ga. and MX12 1994), 26¾, or 27½ in. barrels only, choice of chokes. These small frame shotguns are available in 20, 28 ga., or .410 bore but choke tubes (MX20C designation) are optional only in 20 ga.

STANDARD GRADE MODELS

* **MX8** — 12 or 20 ga., removable trigger group, separated barrels with fixed or screw-in chokes. New 1993.

  Mfg.'s Sug. Retail   **$8,670** $6,000 $4,400 $3,600 $3,100 $2,700 $2,500 $2,300

* **MX12** — 12 ga. only, 2¾ in. chambers only, separated barrels with VR, coil springs, SST (fixed trigger group), Schnabel forearm, light receiver border engraving.

  Mfg.'s Sug. Retail   **$8,650** $6,000 $4,400 $3,600 $3,100 $2,700 $2,500 $2,300

  Vented side rib guns with flushed chokes are available beginning 1993.

* **MX16** — 12 or 16 ga., nonremovable trigger group, barrel selector on top of frame, with hard case. New 1998.

  Mfg.'s Sug. Retail   **$7,210** $5,300 $4,300 $3,600 $3,200 $2,875 $2,600 $2,375

* **MX20** — similar to MX12, except 20, 28 ga., or .410 bore on smaller frame, 2¾ or 3 in. chambers.

  Mfg.'s Sug. Retail   **$8,670** $5,500 $4,400 $3,600 $3,100 $2,700 $2,500 $2,300

* **MX28/MX410** — 28 ga. or .410 bore, small frame, 3 in. chambers on .410 bore, flat VR barrels with fixed chokes, fixed trigger (non-removable), straight grip, satin nickel receiver. New 1993.

  Mfg.'s Sug. Retail   **$17,330** $13,000 $9,950 $7,750 $5,950 $4,560 $4,175 $3,800

SHOTGUNS: O/U, HUNTING - SIDELOCK MODELS

All SHO models were disc. in 1992 (they were available through special order only).

* **SHO Older Mfg.** — older models without rebounding hammers are not as desirable.

  $18,000 $15,750 $12,000 $9,500 $8,500 $7,600 $6,800

* **SHO Newer Mfg.** — 12 ga. only, introductory sidelock O/U model with bank note game scene engraving on coin finished receiver.

  $35,500 $29,950 $25,000 $20,000 $17,000 $14,500 $12,750
  Last Mfg.'s Sug. Retail was $43,000.

* **SHO Gold Older Mfg.** — older models without rebounding hammers are not as desirable.

  $18,000 $15,750 $12,000 $9,500 $8,500 $7,600 $6,800

* **SHO Gold Newer Mfg.** — similar to SHO, except has game scenes in gold relief.

  $38,650 $31,500 $26,500 $21,250 $18,000 $15,500 $13,750
  Last Mfg.'s Sug. Retail was $48,000.

* **SHO Extra** — importation began 1992.

  $68,750 $54,700 $38,100 $32,000 $26,500 $21,250 $18,000
  Last Mfg.'s Sug. Retail was $80,000.

* **SHO Gold Extra** — similar to SHO Extra, except has gold inlays. Importation began 1992.

  $72,750 $56,500 $39,500 $33,000 $27,000 $22,000 $18,500
  Last Mfg.'s Sug. Retail was $86,000.

Grading	100%	98%	95%	90%	80%	70%	60%

SHOTGUNS: SxS, HUNTING - SIDELOCK MODELS

DHO Models have not been included within the scope of this text due to the extreme rarity factor. Please contact Perazzi, USA for more information on these models and current pricing.

Subtract 40% without rebounding hammers on older DHO models.

PEREGRINE INDUSTRIES, INC.

Previous company located in Huntington Beach, CA circa 1991.

While advertised, Peregrine never manufactured the Falcon Model.

PERUGINI-VISINI

Current manufacturer established during 1968 and located in Brescia, Italy. No current domestic importer. Rifles were previously imported and distributed until 1992 by William Larkin Moore & Co., previously located in Westlake Village, CA. All other models listed below were previously imported and distributed by Armes De Chasse located in Chadds Ford, PA until 1988. Please contact the factory directly for more information, including current domestic pricing (see listing in Trademark Index).

RIFLES

Many of the models listed below are currently manufactured. Information and pricing reflects the last year of domestic importation (1992). Please contact the factory directly for current availability and pricing.

STANDARD MODEL: BOLT ACTION — available in most U.S. and metric cals., Mauser 98K action, 24 or 26 in. barrel, 3 shot mag.(non-detachable), matte finished European walnut, high polish bluing, no sights. Importation disc. 1987.

$4,250 $3,800 $3,400 $2,950 $2,500 $2,000 $1,800
Last Mfg.'s Sug. Retail was $4,250.

DELUXE MODEL: BOLT ACTION — similar to Standard Model, except has finely checkered oil finished walnut stock, sights, knurled bolt handle, and is cased. Importation disc. 1987.

$4,250 $3,800 $3,400 $2,950 $2,500 $2,000 $1,800
Last Mfg.'s Sug. Retail was $4,250.

MODEL EAGLE: SINGLE SHOT — available in most U.S. and metric cals., Anson & Deeley type action, ejector, sights, adj. trigger, oil finished finely checkered European walnut stock, 24 or 26 in. Hämmerli barrel. Importation disc. 1987.

$5,255 $4,500 $3,800 $3,400 $2,950 $2,500 $2,000
Last Mfg.'s Sug. Retail was $5,255.

MODEL VICTORIA M SxS — .30-06 (disc.), 7x57R, 7x65R, or 9.3x74R cal., Anson & Deeley type boxlock action, border engraving, ejectors, folding leaf rear sight, DTs, 24 or 26 in. monobloc barrels with chopper lumps, leather cased. Importation disc. 1992.

$7,000 $5,700 $4,600 $3,500 $2,950 $2,500 $2,000
Last Mfg.'s Sug. Retail was $7,900.

* **Model Victoria D Mag. SxS** — similar to Model Victoria, except in .375 H&H, .458 Win., .470 NE, or .500-3 in. NE cal., demi-bloc barrels, and has elaborate engraving. Importation disc. 1992.

$10,950 $9,150 $8,200 $7,400 $6,600 $5,800 $5,100
Last Mfg.'s Sug. Retail was $13,750.

MODEL SELOUS SxS — 9.3x74R, .375 H&H, .458 Win. Mag., .470 NE, or .500 3 in. NE cal., H&H style detachable sidelock action, ejectors, folding leaf rear sight, border engraving with best quality checkered walnut, top-of-the-line model, leather cased. Importation disc. 1992.

$23,000 $18,500 $15,000 $12,000 $10,000 $9,000 $8,150
Last Mfg.'s Sug. Retail was $26,000.

Grading	100%	98%	95%	90%	80%	70%	60%

P

BOXLOCK EXPRESS SxS — .444 Marlin or 9.3x74R cal., Anson & Deeley boxlock action, ejectors, color case hardened frame, iron sights. Importation disc. 1989.

> $3,150 $2,800 $2,500 $2,200 $1,950 $1,700 $1,475
> Last Mfg.'s Sug. Retail was $3,500.

BOXLOCK MAGNUM O/U — .270 Win., .375 H&H, or .458 Win. Mag. cal., Anson & Deeley boxlock action, ejectors, monobloc barrels, select walnut. Importation disc. 1989.

> $5,500 $4,900 $4,300 $3,750 $3,100 $2,600 $2,200
> Last Mfg.'s Sug. Retail was $6,100.

SIDELOCK SUPER EXPRESS SxS — choice of 9 different cals. including .470 Nitro Express, H&H patterned sidelocks, chopper lump barrels, third lever fastener, multi-leaf express sights, coin finished or case hardened receiver, engraving patterns optional. Importation disc. 1989.

> $9,500 $8,400 $7,400 $6,850 $6,100 $5,600 $5,000
> Last Mfg.'s Sug. Retail was $10,500.

SHOTGUNS

AUSONIA SxS — 12 or 20 ga., exposed hammers with double Purdey type sidelock action, various engraving options, demibloc barrels. Disc.

> $7,140 $6,500 $5,750 $4,950 $4,200 $3,500 $2,550
> Last Mfg.'s Sug. Retail was $7,140.

LIBERTY MODEL SxS — 12, 20, 28 ga., or .410 bore, scalloped Anson & Deeley type engraved action, 28 in. chopper lump barrels, double Purdey-type lock, ejectors, leather cased. Disc.

> $7,140 $6,500 $5,750 $4,950 $4,200 $3,500 $2,550
> Last Mfg.'s Sug. Retail was $7,140.

CLASSIC MODEL SxS — 12 or 20 ga., H&H style scroll engraved sidelock action, 28 in. chopper lump barrels, double Purdey-type lock, best quality checkered walnut stock and forearm, top-of-the-line model, leather cased. Disc.

> $16,600 $13,000 $10,250 $8,650 $7,500 $6,500 $5,500
> Last Mfg.'s Sug. Retail was $16,600.

MAESTRO O/U — various gauges, boxlock action, removeable adj. trigger group, monobloc barrels, ejectors, deluxe checkered walnut stock and forearm, various engraving options. Disc.

> $6,545 $5,750 $4,950 $4,300 $3,700 $3,100 $2,400
> Last Mfg.'s Sug. Retail was $6,545.

NOVA O/U — various gauges, H&H style scroll engraved sidelock action, demibloc barrels, top-of-the-line model, leather cased.

> Prices were quoted per individual order.

PETERS STAHL GmbH

Current manufacturer located in Paderborn, Germany. Currently imported by Peters Stahl, U.S.A. located in Delta, UT beginning 1998. Previously imported Franzen International Inc. located in Oakland, NJ until 1998. Dealer direct sales only.

Peters Stahl manufactures high quality semi-auto pistols based on the Model 1911 design, but to date, has had little domestic importation. Their current 1998 model lineup includes: Trophy Master (MSR $2,070-$2,150), Omega Match (MSR $1,995), High Capacity Trophy Master ($2,070-$2,150), O7 Multicaliber (MSR $2,070-$2,450), and the 92 Multicaliber ($2,610-$2,720). In the past, Peters Stahl has manufactured guns for Federal Ordnance, Omega, Schuetzen Pistol Works, and Springfield Armory. Peters Stahl, U.S.A. should be contacted directly (see Trademark Index) for current model information and availability.

PHELPS MFG. CO.

Previous manufacturer located in Evansville, IN circa 1978-1996.

Grading	100%	98%	95%	90%	80%	70%	60%

Phelps Manufacturing Company began shipping guns in early 1978. Phelps guns were investment-cast in 4140 steel, with basic single-action simplicity, using a transfer bar in the action.

REVOLVERS

HERITAGE I — .45-70 cal., single action revolver, incorporates transfer bar hammer safety, blue finish (standard), nickel (optional), adj. rear sight, 8 in. barrel standard, other barrel lengths up to 20 in. available, 6 lbs. Disc. 1996.

$2,050 $1,675 $1,425

Last Mfg.'s Sug. Retail was $2,250.

Add $20 for each additional in. of barrel.

EAGLE I — .444 Marlin cal., single action revolver, blue finish, adj. rear sight, barrel options same as Heritage I, 6 lbs. Disc. 1996.

$2,050 $1,675 $1,425

Last Mfg.'s Sug. Retail was $2,250.

PATRIOT — .375 Win. cal., single action revolver, blue finish, adj. rear sight, barrel options are the same as Heritage I. Limited mfg. 1993-94.

$1,925 $1,550 $1,350

Last Mfg.'s Sug. Retail was $2,225.

GRIZZLY .50-70 — .50-70 cal., otherwise similar to Heritage I. Mfg. 1992-96.

$2,300 $1,875 $1,500

Last Mfg.'s Sug. Retail was $2,580.

Add $20 for each additional in. of barrel.

PHILLIPS & ROGERS, INC.

Current manufacturer established 1992, and located in Huntsville, TX since 1997. Previously located in Conroe, TX circa 1992-97. Dealer direct sales.

In addition to manufacturing the firearms listed below, Phillips & Rogers also made a multi-caliber conversion cylinder for all Ruger, .357 Mag., new model Blackhawk revolvers (disc. 1996) - the retail price was $145. Multi-caliber conversion cylinders are also available for the Ruger new Model Blackhawk (allows shooting .45 LC, .45 Win. Mag., or .45 ACP - retail price is $185) and the Ruger Super Blackhawk (converts .44 Mag. to .50 AE - $550). A new version of the Ruger .50 AE conversion is also available for $995.

REVOLVERS

MEDUSA MODEL 47 REVOLVER — multi-caliber, over 25 cals. in the .355 - .380 diameter range (including .357 Mag., .38 Super, .38 Spl., 9mm Para., etc.), unique design does not utilize half-moon clips or cylinder/barrel changes, 2½, 4, 5, 6, or 8 in. barrel, 6 shot, double action, matte blue finish, rubber or wood grips. New 1993.

Mfg.'s Sug. Retail	$599		$525	$475	$435	$400	$375	$350	$325

Add $95 for 8 in. barrel.

RIFLES: BOLT ACTION

WILDERNESS EXPLORER — .218 Bee, .22 Hornet, .44 Mag., or .50 AE cal., bolt action, features 18 in. match grade barrel, quick change bolt face and barrel allowing interchangeable calibers, white speckled black synthetic stock, side safety, 5½ lbs. Mfg. 1997 only.

$925 $825 $725 $650 $575 $500 $425

Last Mfg.'s Sug. Retail was $995.

PHOENIX ARMS

Current manufacturer located in Ontario, CA since 1992. Distributor sales only.

P

PISTOLS: SEMI-AUTO

RAVEN — .25 ACP cal., single action, 2⁷⁄₁₆ in. barrel, 6 shot mag., alloy frame, choice of finishes and grips. Disc. 1998.

			$69	$50	$45	$40	$35	$30	$25

Last Mfg.'s Sug. Retail was $79.

This model was supplied with a magazine disconnect lock.

HP MODEL — .22 LR or .25 ACP cal., single action, 3 in. VR barrel, 10 (.25 ACP), 10 (C/B 1994), or 11★ (.22 LR) shot staggered mag., alloy frame, firing pin block safety, adj. rear sight, choice of polished blue or satin nickel finish, mag. lock, 20 oz. New 1994.

Mfg.'s Sug. Retail	$116		$95	$70	$55	$45	$40	$35	$30

Add $99 for laser sight and mount (new 1998).
Add $45 for 2-in-1 target barrel and magazine conversion kit.

* **HP Rangemaster Target Kit** — includes HP Model in .22 LR with 5 in. extended barrel, extended mag., locking plastic storage case, and cleaning kit. New 1998.

Mfg.'s Sug. Retail	$155		$125	$100	$90	$75	$65	$55	$50

* **HP Rangemaster Deluxe Target Kit** — similar to HP Rangemaster Target Kit, except has custom wood grips, and dual-2000 laser sight with mounting system. New 1998.

Mfg.'s Sug. Retail	$230		$195	$165	$135	$110	$100	$90	$80

PHOENIX ARMS CO.

Previous importer located in Lowell, MA.

PISTOLS: SEMI-AUTO

PHOENIX — .25 ACP cal., Belgian semi-auto, previously manufactured by Robar et DeKerkhove located in Liege, Belgium.

This trademark is rarely encountered - values would start at $350 and go up according to original condition.

PIETTA, F.LLI

Current manufacturer located in Gussago, Italy.

Pietta manufactures black powder and modern firearms reproductions in many configurations for various American companies including Navy Arms, Dixie Gun Works, Cabela's, Mitchell Arms, K.B.I., and others. Please contact the factory directly for a comprehensive catalog listing of the wide assortment of firearms this company manufactures (see Trademark Index).

PIOTTI

Current manufacturer located in Brescia, Italy. Currently imported and distributed exclusively by William Larkin Moore & Co. located in Scottsdale, AZ.

Fratelli Piotti is one of Italy's premier gunmakers. These shotguns meet the highest British standards of craftsmanship and are made to customer specifications. Variety of gauges, engraving, styles, chokes, etc.

SHOTGUNS: SxS

For the following models — add $2,125 for single trigger, $900 for hand-detachable locks, approx. $1,250 for leather case, $825 for 16 or 20 ga., $1,125 for 28 ga. or .410 bore boxlock, $2,125 for 28 ga. or .410 bore sidelock.

PIUMA (BSEE) — 12, 16, 20, 28 ga., or .410 bore, Anson & Deeley boxlock ejector double with chopper lump barrels, level file-cut rib, light scroll and rosette engraving, scalloped frame.

Mfg.'s Sug. Retail	$13,400		$11,350	$9,400	$8,100	$6,850	$5,600	$4,500	$3,400

Grading	100%	98%	95%	90%	80%	70%	60%

WESTLAKE — 12, 16, 20, 28 ga., or .410 bore, H&H sidelock action, moderate scroll engraving. Mfg. disc. 1989.

$8,500 $7,500 $6,050 $5,300 $4,700 $4,200 $3,750
Last Mfg.'s Sug. Retail was $8,400.

MONTE CARLO — 12, 16, 20, 28 ga., or .410 bore, best-quality H&H pattern sidelock ejector double with chopper lump barrels, Purdey style scroll and rosette engraving. Importation disc. 1990.

$10,500 $9,250 $8,200 $7,100 $6,000 $5,000 $4,500
Last Mfg.'s Sug. Retail was $11,400.

KING NUMBER 1 — 12, 16, 20, 28 ga., or .410 bore, best-quality H&H pattern sidelock ejector double with chopper lump barrels, level file-cut rib, very fine, full coverage scroll engraving with small floral bouquets, gold crest in forearm, gold crown in top lever, name in gold and finely figured wood.

Mfg.'s Sug. Retail $25,600 $20,925 $16,750 $13,000 $9,950 $7,750 $6,600 $5,500

LUNIK — 12, 16, 20, 28 ga., or .410 bore, best-quality H&H pattern sidelock ejector double with lump (demi-bloc) barrels, level file-cut rib, Renaissance style large scroll engraving in relief, gold crown in top lever, gold name, and gold crest in forearm, finely figured wood.

Mfg.'s Sug. Retail $27,500 $22,450 $18,000 $13,150 $10,750 $8,700 $6,950 $5,850

KING EXTRA — 12, 16, 20, 28 ga., or .410 bore, best-quality H&H pattern sidelock ejector double with chopper lump barrels, level file-cut rib, choice of either bulino game scene engraving or game scene engraving with gold inlays, engraved and signed by a master engraver, exhibition grade wood.

Mfg.'s Sug. Retail $31,800 $26,750 $20,000 $15,500 $11,000 $8,750 $7,000 $5,850

MONACO NUMBER 1 OR 2 — 12, 16, 20, 28 ga., or .410 bore, best-quality H&H pattern sidelock ejector double with lump (demi-bloc) barrels, level file-cut rib, Renaissance style large scroll engraving in relief, gold crown in top lever, gold name, and gold crest in forearm, finely figured wood.

Mfg.'s Sug. Retail $34,900 $28,850 $23,150 $18,250 $15,000 $12,000 $9,950 $8,450

MONACO NUMBER 3 — next to top-of-the-line model.

Mfg.'s Sug. Retail $38,000 $34,900 $28,850 $23,150 $18,250 $15,000 $12,000 $9,950

MONACO NUMBER 4 — top-of-the-line model with every refinement incorporated. Custom order only and extremely rare.

Mfg.'s Sug. Retail $46,000 $39,750 $31,250 $25,000 $20,750 $16,000 $13,750 $11,000

SHOTGUNS: O/U

PIOTTI BOSS — 12 or 20 ga., 26-32 in. barrels, single or double triggers, with King 2 engraving, Turkish Circassian walnut, various engraving patterns, 6 lbs - 20 ga., approx. 7½ 12 ga. New 1995.

Mfg.'s Sug. Retail $42,500 $33,650 $26,000 $21,000 $17,000 $13,000 $10,000 $9,100

PIRANHA

Previous trademark that was advertised, but never manufactured by Recoilless Tech, Inc. located in Phoenix, AZ.

POLY TECHNOLOGIES, INC.

Previously distributed by PTK International, Inc. located in Atlanta, GA. Previously imported by Keng's Firearms Specialty, Inc., located in Riverdale, GA. Manufactured in China by Poly Technologies, Inc.

Poly Technologies commercial firearms are made to Chinese military specifications and have excellent quality control.

These models have been banned from domestic importation due to 1989 Federal legislation.

Grading	100%	98%	95%	90%	80%	70%	60%

RIFLES: SEMI-AUTO

POLY TECH AKS-762 — 7.62x39mm or .223 Rem. cal., 16¼ in. barrel, semi-auto version of the Chinese AKM (Type 56) paramilitary design rifle, 8.4 lbs., wood stock. Imported 1988-89.

$525	$460	$415	$365	$300	$250	$230

Last Mfg.'s Sug. Retail was $400.

Add $100 for side-fold plastic stock.

This model was also available with a downward folding stock at no extra charge.

CHINESE SKS — 7.62x39mm cal., 20⁹⁄₂₀ in. barrel, full wood stock, machine steel parts to Chinese military specifications, 7.9 lbs. Imported 1988-89.

$295	$270	$230	$200	$175	$140	$130

Last Mfg.'s Sug. Retail was $200.

RUSSIAN AK-47/S (LEGEND) — 7.62x39mm cal., 16⅜ in. barrel, semi-auto configuration of the original AK-47, fixed, side-folding, or under-folding stock, with or w/o spike bayonet, 8.2 lbs. Imported 1988-89.

$875	$775	$700	$650	$600	$525	$450

Last Mfg.'s Sug. Retail was $550.

The "S" suffix in this variation designates third model specifications.

* ***National Match Legend*** — utilizes match parts in fabrication.

$975	$850	$725	$650	$600	$525	$450

U.S. M-14/S — .308 Win. cal., 22 in. barrel, forged receiver, patterned after the famous M-14, 9.2 lbs. Imported 1988-89.

$675	$625	$550	$495	$420	$385	$360

Last Mfg.'s Sug. Retail was $700.

POWELL, WILLIAM & SON (GUNMAKERS) LTD.

Please refer to the W Section for this trademark.

PRAIRIE GUN WORKS

Current manufacturer located in Winnipeg, Manitoba, Canada. Dealer and consumer direct sales.

RIFLES: BOLT ACTION

Prairie Gun Works manufactures approx. 50-60 guns annually.

M-15 ULTRA LITE — .22-250 Rem., 6mm-284 Win., .25-284 Win., 6.5mm-284 Win., 7mm-08 Rem., or .308 Win. cal., re-machined Rem. 700 short action, 20 in. barrel, Kevlar stock with glass bedding, matte metal finish, approx. 4½ lbs. New 1996.

Mfg.'s Sug. Retail	$1,750	$1,750	$1,525	$1,375	$1,175	$950	$825	$695

Add $250 for stainless steel.
Add $120 for Ultra Lite muzzle brake.
Add $100 for electroless nickel plating.

M-18 ULTRA LIGHT — most long action cals. to .340 Wby. Mag., re-machined Rem. 700 long action, 22 in. barrel, matte metal finish, approx. 4¾ lbs. New 1996.

Mfg.'s Sug. Retail	$1,750	$1,750	$1,525	$1,375	$1,175	$950	$825	$695

Add $250 for stainless steel.
Add $120 for Ultra Lite muzzle brake.
Add $100 for electroless nickel plating.

PRANDELLI-GASPERINI

Previous manufacturer located in Brescia, Italy. Previously imported by Richland Arms located in Blissfield, MI.

Prandelli-Gasperini made both O/U and SxS shotguns in either sidelock or boxlock. Currently, older boxlock models start at approx. $550 (assuming 80% or better

Grading	100%	98%	95%	90%	80%	70%	60%

original condition). Sidelock models in similar condition usually start at $1,450, depending on gauge, embellishments, and condition.

Approx. 250 specimens of this trademark were imported during Richland Arms importation.

PRECISION SMALL ARMS, INC. ("PSA")

Currently manufactured since 1979 in Charlottesville, VA under F.N. license in the U.S by Precision Small Arms located in Beverly Hills, CA. Dealer and distributor sales.

PISTOLS: SEMI-AUTO

PSP-25 PISTOL — .25 ACP, single action, Baby Browning design mfg. in the U.S., 2⅛ in. barrel, 6 shot mag., checkered black polymer grips, all steel construction with choice of black oxide, brushed satin white nickel, or highly polished white nickel finish, dual safety system, 7¼ - 9½ oz. New 1989.

Mfg.'s Sug. Retail	$329	$265	$215	$195	$175	$155	$140	$130

Add $30 for highly polished white nickel finish.

This pistol is mfg. in the U.S. under license from Fabrique Nationale.

* **PSP-25 Stainless Steel** — features stainless steel construction. Mfg. 1996 only.

			$285	$230	$195

Last Mfg.'s Sug. Retail was $327.

* **PSP-25 Featherweight** — features aircraft aluminum frame with high polish nickel slide and mag., gold-plated trigger, smooth pearlescent polymer grips. New 1996.

Mfg.'s Sug. Retail	$539	$430	$325	$275	$225	$195	$175	$160

* **PSP-25 Presidential** — features highly polished 24 Kt. gold plated slide, frame, magazine, and trigger, Dendrite ivory grips.

Mfg.'s Sug. Retail	$725	$600	$475	$375

* **PSP-25 Renaissance** — features chrome receiver with full coverage scroll engraving. New 1996.

Mfg.'s Sug. Retail	$1,350	$1,125	$825	$575

* **PSP-25 Imperiale** — features hand inlaid 24 Kt. gold scroll pattern on frame and slide by Angelo Bee, black oxide finish, ivory grips. Limited mfg.

Mfg.'s Sug. Retail	$2,300	$2,100	$1,500	$950

* **PSP Signature Editions** — similar to above, except has "Michael B. Kassnar" signature on left slide top in gold. Mfg. 1989-91.

		$325	$295	$260	$230	$200	$175	$160

Last Mfg.'s Sug. Retail was $385.

There were also two Limited Signature Editions (less than 10 mfg.) which retailed for $1,458 and approx. $2,150.

PREMIER

Previous trademark manufactured in Italy and Spain by various companies.

SHOTGUNS: SxS

Note: Premier is a trade name for guns that have been produced in both Spain and Italy for various importers.

REGENT MODEL — 12, 16, 20, 28 ga., or .410 bore, 26, 28, or 30 in. barrels, various chokes, checkered pistol grip stock and beavertail forearm. Mfg. 1955-disc.

		$275	$250	$220	$195	$140	$110	$100

REGENT MAGNUM EXPRESS — 12 ga., 3 in. chambers only, 30 in. full barrel, recoil pad. Mfg. 1957-disc.

		$305	$275	$250	$220	$165	$140	$110

	100%	98%	95%	90%	80%	70%	60%

10 GAUGE MAGNUM — similar to 12 ga. Mag., but 10 ga., 3½ in. chamber, 32 in. full and full barrel. Mfg. 1975-disc.

	100%	98%	95%	90%	80%	70%	60%
	$330	$305	$275	$250	$195	$165	$140

JSH KING — 12 or 20 ga., 22 in. imp. cyl. and mod. barrels, straight grip stock. Mfg. 1959-disc.

	$275	$250	$220	$195	$140	$110	$100

MONARCH SUPREME GRADE — 12 or 20 ga., 26 or 28 in. barrels, various chokes, boxlock, auto ejectors, select stock. Mfg. 1959-disc.

	$440	$385	$360	$330	$275	$250	$200

PRESENTATION CUSTOM GRADE — custom made, gold and silver game scene. Mfg. 1959-disc.

	$1,100	$990	$880	$825	$715	$605	$495

AMBASSADOR MODEL — 12, 16, 20 ga., or .410 bore, 26 or 28 in. barrels, mod. and full choke, checkered pistol grip stock. Mfg. 1957-disc.

	$385	$360	$330	$305	$250	$220	$195

PRINZ

Previous manufacturer of bolt action rifles, single shot rifles, and combination guns. Previously imported and distributed by Helmut Hofmann Inc. located in Placitas, NM.

RIFLES

GRADE 1 BOLT ACTION — .243 Win., .30-06, .308 Win., .300 Win. Mag. or 7mm Rem. Mag. cal., single or double set trigger(s), oil finished walnut stock.

	$495	$440	$385	$360	$330	$275	$250

* *Grade 1 Carbine* — similar to Grade 1 except has carbine barrel.

	$570	$495	$435	$390	$360	$330	$275

GRADE 2 BOLT ACTION — similar to Grade 1 except has rosewood forend cap.

	$545	$485	$425	$385	$360	$330	$275

TIP-UP RIFLE — available in 8 cals. between .222 Rem. and .30-06, high quality and limited mfg. Importation began 1989.

	$2,175	$1,900	$1,675	$1,375	$1,100	$950	$775

PRINCESS MODEL 85 — combination gun available in 12 ga. (2¾ in. chamber) and choice of 8 cals. between .222 Rem. and .30-06.

	$1,450	$1,275	$1,100	$925	$800	$775	$650

This model comes standard with a leather case.

PROFESSIONAL ORDNANCE INC.

Current manufacturer located in Lake Havasu City, AZ since 1998. Previously manufactured in Ontario, CA circa 1996-1997. Dealer sales only.

PISTOLS: SEMI-AUTO

CARBON-15 TYPE 20 — .223 Rem. cal., AR-15 operating system with recoil reducing buffer assembly, carbon fiber upper and lower receiver, chromoly bolt carrier, 7¼ in. unfluted stainless steel barrel with ghost ring sights, 30 shot mag. (supplies limited), also accepts AR-15 type mags., 40 oz. New 1996.

Mfg.'s Sug. Retail	$1,500		$1,250	$975	$900	$850	$800	$750	$695

CARBON-15 TYPE 97 — similar to Carbon 15 Type 20, except has fluted barrel and quick detachable compensator, 46 oz. New 1999.

Mfg.'s Sug. Retail	$1,600		$1,325	$1,025	$925	$850	$800	$750	$695

Grading	100%	98%	95%	90%	80%	70%	60

RIFLES: SEMI-AUTO

CARBON-15 TYPE 97 — .223 Rem. cal., same operating system as the Carbon-15 pistol, 16 in. fluted (Type 97) or unfluted (Type 20) stainless steel barrel, carbon fiber buttstock and forearm, includes Weaver type optics mounting base, 3.9 lbs. New 1998.

Mfg.'s Sug. Retail	$1,550	$1,300	$1,000	$925	$850	$800	$750	$695

Add $150 for fluted barrel and quick detachable compensator (Type 97).

PURDEY, JAMES & SONS, LTD.

Current manufacturer established in 1814, and located in London, England. Annual production is approximately 55 guns.

Purdey guns have long been regarded as among the finest in the world. They have typically been made to customer specifications, and as such, should be appraised individually for purposes of evaluation. Values vary with gauge, barrel length, chamber length and age. Listed below are the modern models and approximate values for reference purposes.

Prices indicated below are for manufacturer's suggested retail and 100% condition factors are listed in English pounds. All new prices do not include VAT. Values for used guns in 98%-60% condition factors are priced in U.S. dollars.

RIFLES: CUSTOM ORDER & OLDER PRODUCTION

New rifle prices below represent the base price with standard fine engraving.

PURDEY DOUBLE RIFLE — various English Nitro Express cals., 25½ in. barrels, folding leaf sight, checkered pistol grip stock, recoil pad, sidelock, auto ejectors. Mfg. pre-WWII and post-war.

* **Smaller calibers.** — .300 H&H or .375 H&H cal.

Mfg.'s Sug. Retail	£52,500	£52,500	$54,750	$42,250	$31,650	$26,500	$21,500	$16,950

Add £500 for .375 H&H cal.

* **Large calibers.**
  ➤ .470 NE

Mfg.'s Sug. Retail	£54,750	£54,750	$64,250	$46,750	$37,500	$30,250	$26,500	$22,750

  ➤ .577 NE

Mfg.'s Sug. Retail	£61,500	£61,500	$77,385	$64,250	$46,750	$37,500	$30,250	$26,500

  ➤ .600 NE

Mfg.'s Sug. Retail	£62,750	£62,750	$78,500	$65,750	$46,750	$37,500	$30,250	$26,500

The above values represent base price only. Since each Purdey is basically a special order, new gun pricing is calculated per individual customer work order.

MAGAZINE RIFLE — cals. up to .375 H&H are built on Mauser action, 24 in. barrel, folding leaf sight, checkered best quality walnut pistol grip stock, indivdually built per customer specifications.

Mfg.'s Sug. Retail	£14,000	£14,000	$16,000	$13,500	$11,250	$9,575	$8,500	$7,000

PURDEY ACTION MAGAZINE RIFLE — .375 H&H, .416/450, and .500 cal., built on Purdey's dedicated action, individually built per customer's specifications.

Mfg.'s Sug. Retail	£20,000	£20,000	$23,100	$21,000	$18,500	$16,000	$13,750	$11,250

SHOTGUNS: CUSTOM ORDER & OLDER PRODUCTION

New shotgun prices below represent the base price with standard fine engraving.

BEST QUALITY GAME GUN SxS — 12, 16, or 20 ga., 26-30 in. barrels, any choke and style of rib, checkered straight or pistol grip stock. Mfg. 1880-present, auto ejector gun, best quality only.

Mfg.'s Sug. Retail	£32,750	£32,750	$36,750	$29,250	$27,350	$19,500	$17,000	$14,250

Add £2,000 for 28 ga. or .410 bore on new mfg.
Add approx. £7,700 for extra set of barrels depending on gauge.

	100%	98%	95%	90%	80%	70%	60%
P g.							
gun	$23,450	$19,750	$16,750	$14,250	$12,500	$10,250	$9,250
vy Duck gun	$20,500	$17,000	$14,000	$11,000	$9,500	$8,750	$8,000

Add 50% for 20 ga.
Add 35%-50% for 28 ga. or .410 bore, depending on condition.
Subtract 10% if not cased with accessories.
Add $1,000 for SST.

O/U GUN — 12, 16, 20, or 28 ga., 26-30 in. barrels, any choke, sidelock, auto ejectors, ST, checkered straight or pistol grip stock. Since WWII, Purdey has taken over the Woodward Company, and later guns have the Woodward O/U action. Very few early actions; early guns - ⅓ less.

Mfg.'s Sug. Retail	**£41,750**	£41,750	$42,650	$35,000	$28,750	$23,650	$19,950	$17,000

Add £2,500 for 28 ga. or .410 bore.
Add £11,175 for extra set of barrels.

* Older mfg.

		$37,500	$33,000	$30,000	$26,000	$21,500	$17,750	$15,000

Add $3,000 for Woodward action.
Add 25% for 20 ga.
Add 60%+ for 28 ga.
Add 10% for SST.

SINGLE BARREL TRAP GUN — 12 ga. Purdey action only, similar to O/U specifications. Mfg. prior to WWII.

		$11,250	$10,000	$8,750	$7,900	$7,200	$6,750	$5,950

Q section

QFI (QUALITY FIREARMS INC.)

Previous manufacturer located in Opa Locka, FL circa December 1990-1992.

Grading	100%	98%	95%	90%	80%	70%	60%

PISTOLS: SEMI-AUTO

MODEL LA380 — .380 ACP cal., single action, 6-shot, magazine disconnect, hammer, trigger, and firing pin block safety, 3¼ in. barrel, blue or chrome finish. Mfg. 1991-1992.

	100%	98%	95%	90%	80%	70%	60%
	$125	$100	$90	$80	$70	$60	$55

Last Mfg.'s Sug. Retail was $147.

Add $23 for chrome finish.

* **Model LA380SS** — stainless steel variation of the Model LA380. Mfg. 1992 only.

	100%	98%	95%
	$195	$165	$135

Last Mfg.'s Sug. Retail was $220.

MODEL SA 25 — .25 ACP cal., single action, 2½ in. barrel, 6-shot, includes inertial firing pin, external exposed hammer with half cock, and trigger blocking thumb safety, blue, Dynachrome, or blue/gold finish, smooth walnut grips. Mfg. 1991 only.

	100%	98%	95%	90%	80%	70%	60%
	$55	$45	$40	$35	$30	$25	$25

Last Mfg.'s Sug. Retail was $55.

Add $50 for blue/gold finish.
Add $10 for chrome finish with pearlite plastic grips.

TIGRESS MODEL — .25 ACP or .380 ACP cal., single action, 2½ (.25 ACP) or 3¼ (.380 ACP) in. barrel, blue frame with gold-plated slide, 6-shot with finger extension on mag., white polymer grips with a red rose scrimshawed on both sides, designed for women, supplied with zippered gold pouch, 14 or 25 oz. Mfg. 1991 only.

	100%	98%	95%	90%	80%	70%	60%
	$130	$100	$90	$80	$70	$60	$55

Last Mfg.'s Sug. Retail was $155.

Add $85 for .380 ACP cal.

REVOLVERS: DOUBLE ACTION

All pistols under this heading are 6-shot.

RP SERIES STANDARD REVOLVER — .22 LR, .22 Mag., .32 S&W Long, .32 H&R Mag. or .38 Spl. cal., 2 or 4 in. barrel, blued or chrome finish, fixed sights, hammer block safety, without ejector assembly, composition grips. Mfg. in U.S. 1990-disc.

	100%	98%	95%	90%	80%	70%	60%
	$85	$70	$65	$60	$55	$50	$45

Last Mfg.'s Sug. Retail was $105.

Add $15-20 for chrome finish.
Add approx. $5 for 4 in. barrel.

MODEL SO 38 — .38 Spl. cal., swing out cylinder, 6-shot, 2 in. SR or 4 in. VR barrel, hammer block safety, composition grips. Mfg. 1991 only.

	100%	98%	95%	90%	80%	70%	60%
	$175	$135	$115	$95	$80	$75	$65

Last Mfg.'s Sug. Retail was $175.

REVOLVERS: SINGLE ACTION

SAA WESTERN RANGER — .22 LR cal., 6-shot, 3, 4 (disc. 1991), 4¾ (new 1992), 6 (disc. 1991), 6½ (new 1992), 7 (disc. 1991), or 9 in. barrel, blue finish with gold accenting, walnut grips. Mfg. 1991-1992.

	100%	98%	95%	90%	80%	70%	60%
	$85	$70	$65	$60	$55	$50	$45

Last Mfg.'s Sug. Retail was $105.

Add approx. $5 for 7 (disc.) or $7 for 9 in. barrel.
Add approx. $15-$35 for .22 Mag. extra cylinder (combo).

Grading	100%	98%	95%	90%	80%	70%	60%

Q

SAA PLAINS RIDER — similar to Western Ranger, except has black composition grips and no gold accenting. Mfg. 1991-1992.

	$80	$65	$55	$50	$45	$40	$35

Last Mfg.'s Sug. Retail was $100.

Add $11 for 9 in. barrel.
Add approx. $26 for .22 Mag. extra cylinder (combo).

SAA HORSEMAN SERIES — .357 Mag., .44 Mag., or .45 LC cal., 6-shot, 6½ or 7½ in. barrel, color case hardened or blue (Dark Horseman only) finish, walnut or black composition grips, hammer block safety. Mfg. 1991 only.

	$250	$220	$190	$170	$150	$130	$115

Last Mfg.'s Sug. Retail was $250.

The Dark Horseman had an extended grip frame with black composition grips and an adj. rear sight.

QUAIL UNLIMITED, INC.

Current national conservation organization with national headquarters located in Edgefield, SC.

Although Quail Unlimited, Inc. is not a manufacturer or importer, this organization has been responsible for many special and limited editions that are listed below with quantities, but without secondary market prices, since they may vary greatly from region to region. Some of the models (and current values) may be listed under manufacturer listings in this text. Because of the relatively low quantities involved with these special editions, most of the models listed below have premiums currently being asked over issue prices - the amount will vary with the region and acceptance by Quail Unlimited members. Quail Unlimited designated their special editions as follows: 1986 - Grand Slam I - Bobwhite Edition, 1987 - Grand Slam II - California Edition, 1988 - Grand Slam III - Gambel Edition, 1989 - Grand Slam IV - Mountain Quail Edition, 1990 - Grand Slam V - Scaled Quail Edition, 1992 - Gun Dog I - Pointer Edition, 1993 - Gun Dog II - Setter Edition, 1994 - Gun Dog III - Brittany Edition, 1995 - Gun Dog IV - German Shorthair Edition, 1996 - Gun Dog V - Belgian Edition. 1994 - Golden Covey I - Full Covey Edition, 1995 - Golden Covey II - Bobwhite Edition, 1997 - Upland I - Ruffed Grouse Edition.

MANUFACTURER	MODEL	QUANTITY	YEAR	ISSUE PRICE
Browning	Superposed 20 ga.	100	1986	$2,850
Winchester	Model 101 28 ga.	100	1987	$2,195
Browning	Sweet 16 16 ga.	100	1988	$1,895
Winchester	Model 23 12 ga.	100	1989	$2,885
Browning	Citori Lightning .410 bore	100	1990	$2,295
	Add $500 to issue price for silver finish (standard finish was nickel).			
	Add $700 to issue price for gold finish (standard finish was nickel).			
Browning	Model A-5 20 ga.	100	1992	$1,795
Browning	Citori Lightning 28 ga.	100	1993	$2,395
Browning	Model A-5 20 ga.	100	1993	$1,795
Browning	Model A-5 20 ga.	100	1994	$1,895
Browning	Citori Lightning .410 bore	100	1994	$2,395
Browning	Model A-5 20 ga.	100	1995	$1,895
Belgian Browning	Model A-5 20 ga. 3 in. GRIII	75	1996 (15th Anniv.)	$2,195
Belgian Browning	Model A-5 20 ga. 3 in. GRV	25	1996 (15th Anniv.)	$3,995
Rizzini	SxS 20 ga.	100	1996 (15th Anniv.)	$2,850
Rizzini	SxS 20 ga. (Gold)	15	1996 (15th Anniv.)	$4,250
Browning	Citori Superlight 20 ga.	100	1997	$2,495
Winchester	Model 12 20 ga.	100	1997	$995
Winchester	Model 12 20 ga. Chevy/QU Exclusive	400	1997	$995

QUALITY ARMS, INC.

Current importer and sales agent located in Houston, TX.

Quality Arms currently imports and distributes Arrieta shotguns. They also carry Beretta, Merkel & Perazzi shotguns. Quality Arms also imports European gun cases and shooting accessories. Please contact them directly for pricing and availability on these items.

QUALITY PARTS CO./BUSHMASTER

Quality Parts Co. is a division of Bushmaster Firearms, Inc. located in Windham, ME that manufactures AR-15 type paramilitary rifles and various components and accessories for them. Distributor and dealer sales. Please refer to the Bushmaster section in this text for model listings and values.

NOTES

R section

RAF

Previous manufacturer of shotguns and rifles located in St. Etienne, France circa 1994-96.

RAF manufactured both superposed rifles, shotguns, combination guns, and semi-auto rimfire rifles.

RND MANUFACTURING

Current manufacturer located in Longmont, CO. Distributed by Mesa Sportsmen's Association, L.L.C. located in Delta, CO. Dealer or consumer direct sales.

Grading	100%	98%	95%	90%	80%	70%	60%

RIFLES: SEMI-AUTO

THE EDGE — .223 Rem., .308 Win. or .338 Lapua Mag. (new 1999) cal., patterned after the AR-15, CNC machined, 18, 20, or 24 in. barrel, choice of synthetic (Grade I), built to individual custom order, hand-made laminated thumbhole (Grade II, disc. 1998), or custom laminated thumbhole with fluted barrel (Grade III, disc. 1998) stock, vented aluminum shroud, approx. 8-10 lbs. New 1996.

Mfg.'s Sug. Retail	$2,400	$2,275	$2,075	$1,775	$1,575	$1,375	$1,200	$1,075

    Add $355 for Grade II.
    Add $595 for Grade III or .308 Win. cal.
    Add $2,000 for .338 Lapua Mag. cal.

R.F.M.

Current shotgun manufacturer established in 1956, and located in Brescia, Italy. No current importation.

R.F.M. manufactures a complete line of both O/U and SxS shotguns, in many configurations. Please contact the factory directly for current information and domestic pricing (see Trademark Index).

R.G. INDUSTRIES

Previous importer located in Miami, FL. Operations ceased in January of 1986.

HANDGUNS

R.G. Industries manufactured and imported plain utilitarian revolvers and semi-auto pistols. Unfortunately, because of a product liability situation, R.G. Industries was litigated out of business during 1986. Whereas their models represent good values, they are not collectible, and a generalized listing is provided below.

RG 14 S, RG 23, RG 31

	$95	$80	$70	$60	$55	$50	$45

RG 40, RG 74, & HIGHNOON S.A.

	$125	$115	$95	$80	$70	$60	$55

RG 26 SEMI-AUTO — .25 ACP cal., 6 shot mag., 2¼ in. barrel, plastic grips, single action, 12 oz.

	$65	$55	$50	$40	$35	$30	$25

Last Mfg.'s Sug. Retail was $66.

Grading		100%	98%	95%	90%	80%	70%	60%

RPM

Current manufacturer located in Tuscon, AZ. Direct sales only.

PISTOLS: SINGLE SHOT

XL PISTOL — many cals. available, tip-up action, 8, 10¾, 12, or 14 in. barrel, positive thumb safety, steel frame, cocking indicator, right or left-hand action. Disc.

		$785	$675	$600	$550	$500	$450	$395

Last Mfg.'s Sug. Retail was $858.

XL HUNTER — over 40 cals., stainless steel frame, 5¹⁄₁₆ in. under-lug, 12 or 14 in. Douglas barrel, ISGW rear and Patridge or hooded front sight, with or w/o external positive extractor. New 1995.

Mfg.'s Sug. Retail	$1,195		$1,100	$900	$700

Add $100 for positive extractor.
Add $25 for left-hand action.

RWS

Current trademark of Dynamit Nobel GmbH which has been manufacturing firearms in Nurenberg Stadeln and Troisdorf, Germany since 1865. RWS firearms were imported until 1995 by Dynamit Nobel of America, Inc. located in Closter, NJ. Other trademarks (Rottweil) currently being distributed by Dynamit Nobel can be located under individual heading names in this text. Also see listings in the Airguns section.

RIFLES: BOLT ACTION, TARGET

MODEL 820 L — .22 LR cal. only, 24 (disc.) or 26 in. barrel, no. 100 aperture sight, oil polished stock for 3 position match, stippled pistol grip and forearm, recoil pad, adj. trigger, 10.6 lbs. Disc. 1994.

	$1,275	$1,000	$850	$700	$575	$475	$400

Last Mfg.'s Sug. Retail was $1,500.

Previous to 1986 this model was designated the 820 S and was supplied with a no. 75 aperture rear sight.

* *Model 820 S* — with Model 82 aperture sight.

	$1,100	$895	$795	$650	$560	$480	$420

Last Mfg.'s Sug. Retail was $995.

MODEL 820 F MATCH — similar to Model 820 L, except has heavy match barrel, 15.4 lbs. Disc. 1994.

	$1,750	$1,400	$1,275	$1,000	$850	$700	$575

Last Mfg.'s Sug. Retail was $2,000.

* *Model 820 SF* — with Model 820 L aperture sight. Disc.

	$1,125	$900	$795	$650	$560	$480	$420

Last Mfg.'s Sug. Retail was $1,010.

MODEL 820 K — .22 LR cal. only, made for running boar competition, 24 in. barrel, stock similar to Model 820 SF, no sights, 9½ lbs. without barrel weight or scope. Importation disc. 1986.

	$900	$775	$695	$615	$540	$470	$420

Last Mfg.'s Sug. Retail was $870.

RADOM

Currently manufactured by Z.M. Lucznik (Radom Factory) in Radom, Poland. Currently imported by Dalvar of USA, located in Henderson, NV. Previously located in Richardson, TX. 1931-1939 production also by the Polish Arsenal, located in Radom, Poland.

Grading	100%	98%	95%	90%	80%	70%	60%

REVOLVERS

RADOM REVOLVER — Nagant design, dated 1931-1936.

	100%	98%	95%	90%	80%	70%	60%
	$1,100	$850	$700	$550	$400	$300	$200

PISTOLS: SEMI-AUTO, 1935-1939 PRODUCTION

P-35 AUTOMATIC — 9mm Para. cal., 8 shot, 4¾ in. barrel, blue, fixed sights, plastic grips. Mfg. 1935-WWII.

R

* *Polish Eagle* — dated 1936, 1937 (scarcest date), 1938, or 1939.

	100%	98%	95%	90%	80%	70%	60%
	$2,000	$1,500	$1,000	$700	$500	$400	$300

Add 15% for 1937 mfg.
Add 10% for 1936 mfg.

* *Polish Eagle Nazi Capture*

	100%	98%	95%	90%	80%	70%	60%
	$2,500	$1,825	$1,200	$900	$700	$600	$500

Beware of fakes!

* *Nazi Type I Slotted*

	100%	98%	95%	90%	80%	70%	60%
	N/A	$650	$425	$295	$230	$180	$150

* *Nazi Type II No Slot w/Takedown Lever*

	100%	98%	95%	90%	80%	70%	60%
	$450	$350	$275	$225	$200	$185	$150

* *Nazi Type III No Slot, No Takedown Lever*

	100%	98%	95%	90%	80%	70%	60%
	$315	$275	$240	$200	$180	$160	$140

* *Nazi Type III* — parkerized with wood grips, small parts blued.

	100%	98%	95%	90%	80%	70%	60%
	$650	$500	$350	$295	$230	$200	$175

Note: Certain Radoms with German acceptance marks will bring a premium.

PISTOLS: SEMI-AUTO, CURRENT PRODUCTION

VIS P-35 — 9mm Para. cal., patterned after the 1937 P-35, large Polish eagle stamped on left side of slide, with or w/o slotted rear grip strap for shoulder stock, 4½ in. barrel, 36 oz. Limited mfg.

Mfg.'s Sug. Retail	$2,999	$2,600	$1,425	$850	$625	$450	$375	$300

VANAD P-83 — 9x18mm Makarov cal., 8 shot mag., loaded chamber indicator, firing pin block safety, steel receiver with external hammer, 3½ in. barrel, checkered composition grips, 26 oz. Importation began 1994.

Mfg.'s Sug. Retail	$354	$325	$275	$250	$225	$200	$185	$170

MAG 95 — 9mm Para. cal., single or double action with firing pin block, external hammer, ambidextrous hammer drop safety, 4½ in. barrel, 37 oz. Importation began 1998.

Mfg.'s Sug. Retail	$749	$650	$550	$450	$400	$350	$300	$275

RAM-LINE, INC.

Previous manufacturer located in Grand Junction, CO until 1995.

In addition to the Ram-Tech pistol, Ram-Line, Inc. also manufactured a complete line of synthetic and wood stocks for a variety of firearms. Ram-Line continues to manufacture a complete line of magazines for most popular pistols and rifles (see Trademark Index for current info.).

Grading	100%	98%	95%	90%	80%	70%	60%

PISTOLS: SEMI-AUTO

EXACTOR PISTOL — .22 LR cal., single action, aircraft alloy receiver with 5½ in. polymer VR barrel and steel liner, unique two-motion safety featuring blocks on hammer, trigger, and sear, 15 shot mag., matte finish, easy disassembly, injected molded grip, fixed sight, 20.3 oz., supplied with case. Mfg. 1990-93.

$195 $165 $135

Last Mfg.'s Sug. Retail was $225.

* *Target Exactor* — similar to above, except has 7½ in. barrel, 23 oz. Disc. 1993.

$265 $230 $195

Last Mfg.'s Sug. Retail was $300.

RAM-TECH PISTOL — similar to Exactor pistol, except 4½ in. barrel w/o VR. Mfg. 1994-95.

$175 $145 $125

Last Mfg.'s Sug. Retail was $200.

RANDALL FIREARMS COMPANY

Previously manufactured in Sun Valley, CA. Manufactured between June 7, 1983 and December 15, 1984 - final plant closing was June 15, 1985.

Before manufacturing ceased in May of 1985, 24 models with 12 variations in 3 different calibers had been produced. In some instances, production on certain models was very limited and premiums for these low volume niches are starting to develop. Between June of 1983 and May of 1984, 9,968 handguns were manufactured with 75% of all 9mm Para. pistols being exported to Europe, and 35% of 9mm Para. production employing a 10 groove barrel. Models manufactured after 1984 came equipped with an extended slide stop, long trigger and beavertail grip safety. Production ser. numbers started at 02000 for right hand models and 02100 for left hand models. All but the first 200 (approx.) serial numbers started with "RF" and ended with "C" or "W". A few rare mis-marks are in circulation. Total mfg. for all models and variations was 9,968. Randall prototype serialization starts with a "T" — less than 45 were manufactured and these specimens command up to a 50% premium. In addition, 78 serial numbers under 2,000 were manufactured by special order.

For a Randall letter of authenticity, please refer to the Randall Firearms listing in the Trademark Index.

Models below are generally described with values per specific variations listed afterward.

PISTOLS: SEMI-AUTO

The following is a complete listing for Randall Firearms variations including production statistics. Values shown below represent recent aftermarket prices, but it should be noted regional interest can change these prices significantly.

All original Randall pistols had no blued parts. Only the front and rear sights were finished in black oxide.

100% Randall prices assume NIB condition with paperwork.

Add 50% for prototypes with "T" serial numbers.

COMBAT MODEL — same size as Service Model, ribbed top fixed sight slide, Pachmayr grips on right hand model only, left hand models had Herrett walnut grips. While this model was advertised as having a flat mainspring housing, it was never produced.

Last Mfg.'s Sug. Retail was $549.

RAIDER/SERVICE MODEL-C — 9mm Para. or .45 ACP cal., Colt Commander Model design, 4¼ in. barrel, 36 oz., total stainless steel construction. Add $130 for adj. sights/ribbed slide, available in either right-hand or left-hand (only 2 mfg.) model. Roll-marked Service Model-C in 1983 and Raider in 1984.

Last Mfg.'s Sug. Retail was $460.

Grading	100%	98%	95%	90%	80%	70%	60%

* *Raider/Service Model-C Featherweight* — .45 ACP cal. only, alloy receiver, stainless steel slide, roll-marked Service Model-C, T-type serial numbers, 29 oz. Disc. 1984, only 4 mfg.

FULL SIZE SERVICE MODEL — .38 Super, 9mm Para., or .45 ACP cal., Colt Model 1911 A1 design, 5 in. barrel, total stainless steel construction, 38 oz. Available in either right-hand or left-hand model.

Last Mfg.'s Sug. Retail was $460.

CURTIS E. LEMAY 4-STAR MODEL — 9mm Para. or .45 ACP cal., Gen. Curtis E. LeMay design, 4¼ in. barrel, 6 (.45 ACP) or 7 (9mm Para.) shot mag., total stainless steel construction, 35 oz. Available in either right-hand or left-hand model, left-hand models are a true mirror image with over 17 major parts changes.

Last Mfg.'s Sug. Retail was $533.

R

> This model was ½ in. shorter in magazine well and had a cast, squared off triggerguard compared to the Colt 1911A1 design.

* *Curtis E. LeMay Featherweight Model* — .45 ACP cal. only, alloy receiver, stainless steel slide, T-type serial numbers, 28 oz. Disc. 1984 (only one mfg.).

RANDALL MATCHED SETS — .45 ACP cal. only, each set consisted of a right-hand and a left-hand Service Model with matching serial numbers. Only 4 sets were mfg. on a special order basis. A111/B111 model configuration.

Last Mfg.'s Sug. Retail was $1,250.

Randall Variations & Identification

Randall pistols are denoted by a four-character model notation, starting with an alphabetical prefix followed by three digits. The alphabetical prefix will be either A, B, or C — A designates right-hand configuration only, B designates left-hand configuration only, and C designates right-hand lightweight model. The first digit will be 1, 2, or 3 — 1 denotes Service Model, 2 denotes Service Model-C or Raider, 3 represents the C.E. LeMay Model. The second digit again will be either 1, 2, or 3 — 1 designates round top and fixed sight slide, 2 denotes flat top fixed sight slide, and 3 represents adj. sights, flat top frame. The third digit again, is either 1, 2, or 3 — 1 denotes .45 ACP cal., 2 designates 9mm Para., and 3 represents .38 Super. Hence, if you had a left-hand Randall in the service model size with a flat top adj. sight slide, and in .45 ACP cal., your model would be a B131. These model codes are not marked on the pistols.

A111 — 3,421 mfg.

				$680	$595	$510	$465

Five A111s were mfg. with Austrian proofmarks with premiums existing.

A112 — 301 mfg.

				$895	$795	$650	$525

A121 — 1,067 mfg.

				$700	$625	$510	$465

A122 — 19 mfg.

				$1,325	$1,125	$940	$795

A131 — 2,083 mfg.

				$725	$640	$535	$495

A211 — 992 mfg.

				$750	$660	$535	$480

A212 — 76 mfg.

				$925	$815	$600	$500

A231 — 574 mfg.

				$850	$750	$535	$505

Grading	100%	98%	95%	90%	80%	70%	60%

A232 — 5 mfg.

$1,500 $1,075 $990 $775

A311 — 361 mfg.

$1,100 $950 $725 $575

Most LeMay models (4¼ in. barrel) were shipped in gun rugs without a factory box. Original factory LeMay boxes are rare - add 10% premium. Beware of Randall LeMay and service model pistols made from parts kits. There were 226 LeMay receivers and 322 service model receivers (all right hand) sold that could be parts guns.

A312 — 1 mfg.

Too rare to evaluate.

A331 — 293 mfg.

$1,200 $1,075 $700 $595

The note that appears for the Model A311 also applies to this variation.

A332 — 9 mfg.

$1,450 $1,275 $975 $825

B111 — 297 mfg.

$1,250 $1,100 $850 $750

B121 — 110 mfg.

$1,500 $1,325 $1,075 $895

B122 — 2 mfg.

Extreme rarity precludes accurate price evaluation.

B123 — 2 mfg.

Extreme rarity precludes accurate price evaluation.

B131 — 225 mfg.

$1,450 $1,250 $925 $775

B311 — 52 mfg.

$1,575 $1,325 $895 $750

B312 w/.45 ACP FACTORY CONVERSION — 1 mfg.

Rarity precludes accurate price evaluation.

B312 — 9 mfg.

$2,750 $2,300 $1,800 $1,550

B321 — 1 mfg.

Rarity precludes accurate price evaluation. The B321 was the only factory 3-slide set. It was fitted with the 3 different LH LeMay slides available (B311, B321, & B331). This model was mirror polished, engraved, and had ivory grips with the Randall logo.

B331 — 45 mfg.

$1,775 $1,495 $1,050 $875

B2/321 — 1 mfg.

Rarity precludes accurate price evaluation. This was the only factory model variation to leave Randall Firearms. This was a Left-hand Raider with the C.E. LeMay slide.

C211 — 5 mfg.

Rarity precludes accurate price evaluation.

C331 — 1 mfg.

Rarity precludes accurate price evaluation.

Grading	100%	98%	95%	90%	80%	70%	60%

C332 — 4 mfg.

> Rarity precludes accurate price evaluation.

* *Matched Sets* — large premiums exist for different models with the same serial number if NIB condition. Only 4 were mfg.

RANGER ARMS INC.

Previous manufacturer located in Gainesville, TX until the early 1970s.

> Ranger Arms Inc. manufactured good quality, bolt action rifles in various calibers and configurations. Although somewhat rare in that there were not a large number manufactured, collectibility to date has been limited with specimens in 90%+ condition, typically priced in the $375-$500 range.

RAPTOR ARMS CO., INC.

Current rifle manufacturer located in Shelton, CT. Distributed by Davidson's and Jerry's Sport Centers.

RIFLES: BOLT ACTION

RAPTOR SPORTING RIFLE — .243 Win., .25-06 Rem., .270 Rem., .30-06, or .308 Win. cal., features "Taloncote" or blue (mfg. 1998 only) finished barreled action, black checkered fiberglass reinforced synthetic stock, adj. trigger, with or w/o sights. New 1997.

Mfg.'s Sug. Retail	$259	$230	$195	$175	$160	$150	$140	$130

> Add $30 for sights (disc.).
> Add $15 for blue finish (disc.).
> Add $36 for heavy barrel.
> Add $50 for stainless steel barreled action with sights (new 1999).

* *Peregrine Deluxe Sporting Rifle* — similar to Raptor Sporting Rifle, except has deluxe checkered or plain hardwood stock. Mfg. 1998 only.

	$265	$225	$195	$175	$160	$150	$140

Last Mfg.'s Sug. Retail was $309.

> Subtract $10 for plain hardwood stock and no sights (blue finish only).

RAVELL

Current manufacturer located in Barcelona, Spain. Currently, Ravell has no single U.S. importer and values below represent guns purchased directly from Spain without import duty/shipping.

RIFLES: SxS

MAXIM DOUBLE RIFLE — .375 H&H or 9.3x74R cal., H&H type sidelock action with automatic ejectors, Purdey scroll engraving, 23 in. barrels, deluxe walnut with full pistol grip and rubber butt plate, double articulated triggers.

Mfg.'s Sug. Retail	$7,000	$6,600	$6,100	$5,000	$4,000	$3,500	$2,950	$2,600

> Add $460 for .375 H&H cal.

RAVEN ARMS

Previous manufacturer located in Industry, CA circa 1970-1991. Approximately 2 million were mfg.

Grading	100%	98%	95%	90%	80%	70%	60%

PISTOLS: SEMI-AUTO

P-25 — .25 ACP cal., single action, 2$^7/_{16}$ in. barrel, 6 shot mag., walnut grips, available in nickel, blue, or chrome finish, 15 oz. Disc. 1984.

			$70	$60	$50	$40	$30	$25	$25

MP-25 — similar to Model P-25, except die-cast slide serrations are slightly different. Disc. 1992.

			$60	$50	$45	$40	$35	$30	$25

Last Mfg.'s Sug. Retail was $70.

Walnut, slotted plastic, or ivory colored grips were available for this model. In 1987, a new sear-block safety was incorporated into manufacture.

RECORD-MATCH

Previously manufactured by Anschütz, located in Zella-Mehlis, Germany circa pre-WWII.

PISTOLS: SINGLE SHOT, TARGET

MODEL 210 FREE PISTOL — .22 LR cal., Martini action, 11 in. barrel, single shot, blue, carved and checkered walnut grips and forearm, set trigger (button release), micrometer rear sight, deluxe target pistol, pre-WWII.

	$1,320	$1,265	$1,210	$1,100	$880	$745	$550

MODEL 210A — similar to 210, but alloy frame.

	$1,265	$1,210	$1,155	$1,045	$825	$690	$495

MODEL 200 FREE PISTOL — similar to Model 210, but less deluxe features and spur trigger guard, pre-WWII.

	$990	$935	$770	$660	$525	$440	$360

GARY REEDER CUSTOM GUNS

Current custom pistol manufacturer located in Flagstaff, AZ. Consumer direct sales. Gary Reeder specializes in customizing revolvers from various companies. He has also produced Custom Contenders for almost 20 years, including the development of many custom calibers for the Thompson Contender. Current MSR for the full Custom Contender is $795. For current availability and pricing on his extensive range of custom guns, please contact the factory directly (see Trademark Index).

REISING ARMS COMPANY

Previous manufacturer originally located in Hartford, CT and later in New York, NY.

PISTOLS: SEMI-AUTO

TARGET AUTOMATIC PISTOL — .22 LR cal., 12 shot, 6$^3/_4$ in. barrel, blue, brown hard rubber grips, hinged frame, outside hammer. Mfg. 1921-1924.

	$450	$395	$340	$315	$265	$220	$195

This model was mfg. in Hartford, CT from serial number 1,001-4,000. The New York, NY address occurs in the serial range 10,000-12,000.

Warning: This pistol's slide may crack if modern high speed .22 ammo is used.

REMINGTON ARMS COMPANY, INC.

Current manufacturer established in 1816, with factory currently located in Ilion, NY. Originally founded by E. Remington, and previously located in Litchfield, Herkimer County, NY circa 1816-1828. Remington moved to Ilion, NY in 1828,

Remington®

where they continue to manufacture a variety of sporting arms. Corporate offices were moved to Madison, NC in 1996.

REMINGTON TRADEMARKS - 1816-PRESENT

1816-1847 — Remington (mostly barrel and lock markings)
1847-1856 — E. Remington & Son
1856-1888 — E. Remington & Sons
1888-1910 — Remington Arms Company
1910-1920 — Remington Arms U.M.C. Company
1920 to date — Remington Arms Company, Inc.

HANDGUNS: 1857-1945 PRODUCTION

BEALS' FIRST MODEL POCKET REVOLVER — percussion .31 cal., 5 shot, smooth cylinder, 3 in. octagon barrel, blue finish, 1-piece Gutta Percha grip, brass or iron trigger guard. Approx. 5,000 produced, 1857-1858.

N/A	N/A	$795	$700	$635	$585	$535	$500	$475	$450	$425	$395

BEALS' SECOND MODEL POCKET REVOLVER — percussion .31 cal., 5 shot, smooth cylinder, 3 in. octagon barrel, blue finish, 2-piece Gutta Percha grips, spur trigger. Approx. 1,000 produced 1858-1860.

N/A	N/A	$5,000	$4,500	$4,050	$3,650	$3,250	$2,850	$2,500	$2,250	$2,000	$1,850

BEALS' THIRD MODEL POCKET REVOLVER — percussion .31 cal., 5 shot, smooth cylinder, 4 in. octagon barrel, blue finish, 2-piece Gutta Percha grips, spur trigger, first Remington revolver with loading lever. Approx. 1,000 produced.

N/A	N/A	$1,125	$1,025	$925	$850	$775	$700	$625	$550	$500	$450

BEALS' NAVY REVOLVER — percussion .36 cal., 6 shot, smooth cylinder, 7½ in. octagon barrel, blue finish, 2-piece walnut grips, some martially marked with inspector's initials and cartouche on grips. Approx. 15,000 produced, 1860-1862. Barrel address is "Beals' Patent, Sept. 14, 1858 - Manufactured by Remingtons', Ilion, N.Y."

* *Commercial Model* — single wing base pin (very rare), less than 400 mfg. Serial range under 200.

N/A	N/A	$3,175	$2,850	$2,550	$2,250	$2,000	$1,825	$1,675	$1,550	$1,450	$1,375

* *Commercial Model* — several variations with serialization 1-15,500, most were purchased by military but were not inspected.

N/A	N/A	$2,500	$2,250	$2,025	$1,800	$1,575	$1,350	$1,150	$950	$750	$575

Subtract 20% for cartridge conversion.

* *Martially marked* — serial range 13,500-15,500.

N/A	N/A	$2,800	$2,450	$2,100	$1,900	$1,750	$1,625	$1,500	$1,375	$1,250	$1,150

BEALS' ARMY REVOLVER — percussion .44 cal., 6 shot, smooth cylinder, 8 in. octagon barrel, blue finish, 2-piece walnut grips. Barrel address is "Beals' Patent, Sept. 14, 1858 - Manufactured by Remingtons', Ilion, N.Y."

$3,750	$3,100	$2,800	$2,550	$2,325	$2,125	$1,900	$1,700	$1,500	$1,300	$1,100	$975

Subtract 20% for cartridge conversions.

* *Martially marked* — serial range is 850-1,900 inspected by "WAT" or "CGC".

N/A	N/A	$5,850	$5,000	$4,350	$3,750	$3,250	$2,850	$2,500	$2,150	$1,800	$1,450

RIDER'S DOUBLE-ACTION POCKET REVOLVER — percussion .31 cal., 5 shot, unusual "mushroom-shaped" cylinder, 3 in. octagon barrel, blue finish, 2-piece Gutta Percha grips, brass triggerguard, no loading lever. One of the earliest double-action handguns produced. Approx. 20,000 produced, 1860-1888.

N/A	N/A	$725	$625	$575	$525	$485	$450	$425	$400	$375	$350

Subtract 30% for cartridge conversion.

100%	98%	95%	90%	80%	70%	60%	50%	40%	30%	20%	10%

R

RIDER'S SINGLE-SHOT DERRINGER — percussion .17 cal., all brass construction, grips included. Less than 1,000 produced, 1860-1863. MANY FAKES, caveat emptor.

N/A	N/A	$5,150	$4,600	$4,150	$3,750	$3,400	$3,100	$2,800	$2,500	$2,300	$2,100

MODEL OF 1861 NAVY REVOLVER — percussion .36 cal., 6 shot, unfluted cylinder, 7½ in. octagon barrel, blue finish, 2-piece walnut grips. Loading lever has slot allowing cylinder pin to be pulled forward without lowering lever. Approx. 6,000 produced 1862-1863 in serial range 15,000-21,000. Barrel address "Patented Dec. 17, 1861, 1858 - Manufactured by Remingtons', Ilion, N.Y.".

* *Commercial Model*

N/A	N/A	$1,950	$1,700	$1,450	$1,250	$1,050	$950	$825	$725	$600	$500

Subtract 30% for cartridge conversion.

* *Martially Marked* — over 4,000 martially inspected "CGC".

N/A	N/A	$2,450	$2,200	$1,950	$1,700	$1,450	$1,200	$1,000	$850	$700	$575

MODEL OF 1861 ARMY REVOLVER — percussion .44 cal., 6 shot, unfluted cylinder, 8 in. octagon barrel, blue finish, 2-piece walnut grips. Majority are martially inspected "CGC". Loading lever has slot allowing cylinder pin to be pulled forward without lowering lever. Approx. 10,000 produced 1862-1863 in serial range 1,900-12,000. Barrel address "Patented Dec. 17, 1861, 1858 - Manufactured by Remingtons', Ilion, N.Y.".

N/A	N/A	$2,250	$2,000	$1,750	$1,500	$1,250	$1,050	$900	$800	$675	$550

Subtract 30% for cartridge conversion.

NEW MODEL ARMY REVOLVER — percussion .44 cal., 6 shot, unfluted cylinder, 8 in. octagon barrel, blue finish, 2-piece walnut grips. Approx. 135,000 produced 1863-1888 in serial range 12,000-148,000. Barrel address "Patented Sept. 14, 1858 - Manufactured by Remingtons', Ilion, N.Y. - New Model". Early models lack "New Model" markings on barrel and have transition features from "1861" model.

N/A	N/A	$1,400	$1,250	$1,100	$1,000	$900	$800	$700	$600	$500	$425

Add 25% for cartridge conversion (most are in .44 rimfire).
Add 25% for martially inspected.

NEW MODEL NAVY REVOLVER — percussion .36 cal., 6 shot, unfluted cylinder, 7½ in. octagon barrel, blue finish, 2-piece walnut grips. Approx. 18,000 produced in percussion from 1863-1878 with serial range 21,000-48,000. None were martially marked at time of mfg. Approx. 4,000 were purchased by U.S. Navy during 1863-1865 in serial range 21,000-32,000. Barrel address "Patented Sept. 14, 1858 - Manufactured by Remingtons', Ilion, N.Y. - New Model". Early specimens lack "New Model" markings on barrel and have transition features from "1861" model.

N/A	N/A	$2,550	$2,250	$1,950	$1,650	$1,350	$1,125	$975	$825	$675	$550

Subtract 20% for cartridge conversion if in less than 50%+ original condition.

No premium for martial markings.

NEW MODEL BELT REVOLVER, SINGLE ACTION — percussion .36 cal., 6 shot, unfluted or fluted cylinder, 6½ in. octagon barrel, blue or nickel finish, 2-piece walnut grips. Approx. 5,000 produced 1863-1888.

N/A	N/A	$1,325	$1,150	$1,000	$900	$800	$725	$650	$575	$525	$475

Add 50% for fluted cylinder (cylinder numbered to the gun).
Subtract 30% for cartridge conversion.

NEW MODEL BELT REVOLVER, DOUBLE ACTION — percussion .36 cal., 6 shot, smooth or fluted cylinder, 6½ in. octagon barrel, blue or nickel finish, 2-piece walnut grips. Approx. 2,500 produced 1863-1888.

N/A	N/A	$1,025	$900	$800	$700	$625	$575	$525	$475	$425	$400

Add 100% for fluted cylinder (most not numbered to the gun).
Subtract 30% for cartridge conversion.

100%	98%	95%	90%	80%	70%	60%	50%	40%	30%	20%	10%

NEW MODEL POLICE REVOLVER — percussion .36 cal., 5 shot, smooth cylinder, 3 to 6½ in. octagon barrels, blue or nickel finish, 2-piece walnut grips. Approx. 18,000 produced 1863-1888.

| N/A | N/A | $950 | $875 | $815 | $750 | $700 | $650 | $600 | $550 | $510 | $475 |

Add 10% for 6½ in. barrel.
Subtract 40% for cartridge conversion.

NEW MODEL POCKET REVOLVER — percussion .31 cal., 5 shot, smooth cylinder, spur trigger, 3 to 4½ in. octagon barrel, blue or nickel finish, 2-piece walnut grips. Approx. 25,000 produced, 1863-1888.

| N/A | N/A | $900 | $825 | $750 | $700 | $650 | $600 | $550 | $475 | $425 | $390 |

Add 25%-50% for brass frame and/or trigger sheath.
Subtract 40% for cartridge conversion.

ZIG-ZAG DERRINGER — cartridge .22 S-L-LR cal., 6 shot, 6 barrel cluster (rotating), ring trigger, 3 in. barrel cluster, blue finish, 2-piece hard rubber grips. Less than 1,000 produced, 1861-1863. Reputed to be Remington's first cartridge handgun.

| N/A | N/A | $2,275 | $2,025 | $1,775 | $1,525 | $1,325 | $1,175 | $1,050 | $950 | $850 | $765 |

ELLIOT'S FIVE SHOT DERRINGER — cartridge .22 S-L-LR cal., 5 shot, 5 barrel cluster (fixed), 3 in. barrel cluster, blue and/or nickel finish, 2-piece hard rubber, walnut, ivory or pearl grips, ring trigger. Approx. 25,000 produced (combined production total with .32 cal.).

| N/A | N/A | $1,250 | $1,125 | $1,025 | $900 | $800 | $700 | $600 | $525 | $475 | $425 |

ELLIOT'S FOUR SHOT DERRINGER — cartridge .32 cal., 4 shot, 4 barrel cluster (fixed), ring trigger, 3⅜ in. barrel cluster, blue and/or nickel finish, 2-piece hard rubber, walnut, ivory or pearl grips. Approx. 25,000 produced (combined production with .22 cal.).

| N/A | N/A | $950 | $850 | $775 | $700 | $625 | $575 | $515 | $455 | $400 | $365 |

VEST POCKET DERRINGER — cartridge .22, .30, .32, or .41 cal., single shot, various barrel lengths, blue or nickel finish, 2-piece walnut grips, spur trigger.

* *.22 Rimfire* — approx. 25,000 produced, 1865-1888.

| N/A | N/A | $765 | $685 | $635 | $575 | $525 | $475 | $425 | $375 | $325 | $275 |

Subtract 25% for guns lacking company name.

* *.30 or .32 Rimfire* — number produced unknown, 1865-1888.

| N/A | N/A | $1,050 | $950 | $850 | $725 | $600 | $550 | $500 | $450 | $400 | $350 |

* *.41 Rimfire* — approx. 25,000 produced, 1865-1888.

| N/A | N/A | $950 | $850 | $750 | $650 | $575 | $525 | $475 | $425 | $375 | $325 |

OVER AND UNDER DERRINGER — cartridge .41 Rimfire cal., 2 shot, 3 in. superimposed barrels, oscillating firing pin, spur trigger, blue and/or nickel finish, hard rubber, walnut, ivory or pearl 2-piece grips. Approx. 150,000 produced, 1866-1934. A.k.a. Double Derringer or Model 95.

* *Type One, Early Variation* — maker's name and patent data stamped between the barrels, made without extractor. 1866-1888.

| N/A | N/A | $1,250 | $1,150 | $1,025 | $900 | $800 | $700 | $625 | $550 | $475 | $425 |

* *Type One, Late Variation* — maker's name and patent data stamped between the barrels, made with extractor. 1866-1888.

| N/A | N/A | $1,325 | $1,200 | $1,100 | $1,025 | $950 | $875 | $800 | $750 | $700 | $650 |

* *Type Two* — two line markings atop barrels, maker's name and patent data. 1866-1888.

| N/A | N/A | $775 | $650 | $575 | $525 | $475 | $425 | $375 | $325 | $275 | $225 |

* *Type Three* — marked on top of barrel, single line, "REMINGTON ARMS CO., ILION, N.Y." 1888-1911.

| N/A | N/A | $750 | $650 | $525 | $450 | $400 | $350 | $300 | $250 | $225 | $200 |

100%	98%	95%	90%	80%	70%	60%	50%	40%	30%	20%	10%

* Type Four — marked on top of barrel, single line, "REMINGTON ARMS-U.M.C. CO. ILION, N.Y."

| N/A | N/A | $650 | $575 | $500 | $425 | $375 | $325 | $290 | $255 | $225 | $195 |

MODEL 1866 NAVY ROLLING BLOCK PISTOL — cartridge .50 Rimfire cal., single shot, 8½ in. round barrel, spur trigger, walnut grip and forearm, blue finish. Approx. 6,500 produced, 1866-1875. Erroneously designated as, "Model of 1865 Navy".

* Martially Marked

| N/A | N/A | $3,100 | $2,600 | $2,350 | $2,150 | $1,950 | $1,750 | $1,550 | $1,400 | $1,275 | $1,175 |

Subtract 30% if not martially marked (Commercial Model mfg. 1866-1875).
Subtract 15% for centerfire breech block.
Less than 150 remain in original condition.

COMBINATION PISTOL-SHOTGUN — 20 ga., 11¾ in single barrel, rolling block action, designed as a pistol or shotgun (with detachable shoulder stock). In either configuration, it is an NFA firearm that cannot be legally owned unless registered with the BATF. Extreme rarity factor precludes accurate pricing information.

MODEL 1870 NAVY ROLLING BLOCK PISTOL — cartridge .50 Centerfire cal., single shot, 7 in. round barrel, standard trigger with triggerguard, walnut grip and forearm, blue finish. Approx. 6,400 produced 1870-1875. Modified by Remington for the Navy from the Model 1866.

| N/A | N/A | $1,750 | $1,550 | $1,350 | $1,200 | $1,075 | $975 | $875 | $800 | $750 | $725 |

Add approx. 20% for 8 in. commercial version (approx. 200-400 mfg.) without inspector's marks.

MODEL 1871 ARMY ROLLING BLOCK PISTOL — cartridge .50 Centerfire cal., single shot, 8 in. round barrel, standard trigger with triggerguard, walnut grip and forearm, blue finish. Approx. 5,000 produced, 1871-1872.

| N/A | N/A | $1,575 | $1,375 | $1,200 | $1,075 | $975 | $875 | $775 | $675 | $600 | $550 |

Subtract 10% for Commercial Model.
Pistols produced between 1871-1872 are martially marked.

MODEL 1887 TARGET ROLLING BLOCK PISTOL — cartridge .22, .25 Rimfire and .32, .50 Centerfire cals., single shot, 8 in. round barrel, standard trigger with triggerguard, walnut grip and forearm, blue finish. Approx. 900 produced 1887-1891. A.K.A. "Plinker Model of 1887".

| N/A | N/A | $1,535 | $1,325 | $1,175 | $1,050 | $950 | $850 | $750 | $650 | $575 | $525 |

Add 10% for Navy framed.
Navy framed 1887s are discernible by military proofs on right side of frame, Remington altered from original Navy Model 1870. Estimated mfg. of 100.

MODEL 1891 TARGET MODEL ROLLING BLOCK PISTOL — cartridge .22, .25 Rimfire and .32 Centerfire cals., single shot, 10 in. part octagon, part round barrel, standard trigger with triggerguard, smooth walnut grip and forearm, blue finish. Approx. 100 produced 1891-1900.

| N/A | N/A | $1,750 | $1,535 | $1,325 | $1,175 | $1,050 | $950 | $850 | $750 | $675 | $625 |

MODEL 1901 TARGET ROLLING BLOCK PISTOL — cartridge .22 S and L, .25 Rimfire, .32 Centerfire, or .44 S&W Russian cal., single shot, 10 in. part octagon, part round barrel, standard trigger with triggerguard, checkered walnut grip and forearm, blue finish. Approx. 800 produced 1900-1909.

| N/A | N/A | $1,750 | $1,535 | $1,325 | $1,175 | $1,050 | $950 | $850 | $750 | $675 | $625 |

Add $100 for S&W Russian.

RIDER'S MAGAZINE PISTOL — cartridge .32 cal., 5 shot, 3 in. octagon barrel, spur trigger, walnut, rosewood, ivory or pearl grips. Approx. 10,000 produced, 1871-1888.

| N/A | N/A | $1,325 | $1,225 | $1,100 | $1,000 | $900 | $800 | $700 | $625 | $575 | $525 |

Add 50% with case hardened magazine.

100%	98%	95%	90%	80%	70%	60%	50%	40%	30%	20%	10%

ELLIOT'S SINGLE SHOT DERRINGER — cartridge .41 Rimfire cal., single shot, 2½ in. round barrel, spur trigger, walnut 2-piece grips, blue and/or nickel finish. Approx. 10,000 produced, 1867-1888. A.K.A. "Mississippi Derringer".

N/A	N/A	$1,000	$875	$775	$675	$600	$550	$500	$450	$400	$350

NUMBER ONE (SMOOT PATENT) REVOLVER — cartridge .30 Rimfire cal., 5 shot, 2¾ in. octagon barrel, spur trigger, walnut, hard rubber, pearl or ivory 2-piece grips. Number produced debatable, 1873-1888.

N/A	N/A	$465	$430	$395	$360	$325	$290	$265	$240	$215	$190

R

Add 100% on early #1s with revolving recoil shield.

On Number One through Number Four Revolvers, ivory grips refer to Remington Celluloid, not genuine ivory. Only in rare instances does ivory appear.

NUMBER TWO (SMOOT PATENT) REVOLVER — cartridge .30 or .32 Rimfire cal., 5 shot, 2¾ in. octagon barrel, spur trigger, hard rubber, pearl or ivory 2-piece grips. Number produced debatable, 1873-1888.

N/A	N/A	$450	$425	$400	$375	$350	$300	$275	$250	$225	$200

NUMBER THREE (SMOOT PATENT) REVOLVER — cartridge .38 Rimfire or .38 Centerfire cal., 3¾ in. octagon barrel with or without barrel rib, spur trigger, hard rubber, ivory or pearl 2-piece grips, "Bird-Head and SawHandle" grip frame with Remington logo "R" on the "saw-handle" hard rubber grips, Bird-Head referred to models with or without a barrel rib. Number produced debatable, 1875-1888.

N/A	N/A	$500	$475	$450	$425	$400	$350	$325	$300	$275	$250

Add small premiums on Centerfire Number 3s.

NUMBER FOUR REVOLVER — cartridge .38 and .41 Rimfire or .38 and .41 Centerfire cals., 5 shot, 2½ in. round barrel, hard rubber, pearl or ivory 2-piece grips. Number produced debatable, 1877-1888.

N/A	N/A	$550	$525	$500	$475	$450	$400	$375	$350	$325	$300

Add small premiums on Centerfire Number 4's.

IROQUOIS REVOLVER — cartridge .22 Rimfire cal., 7 shot, 2¼ in. round barrel, spur trigger hard rubber, pearl or ivory 2-piece grips, fluted or non-fluted cylinder. Approx. 10,000 produced between, 1878-1888.

N/A	N/A	$475	$440	$410	$385	$345	$300	$275	$250	$225	$200

Subtract 33% if unmarked.
Add 20% for fluted cylinder.

MODEL 1875 SINGLE ACTION REVOLVER — cartridge .44 or .45 Centerfire cal., 6 shot, 7½ or 5¾ in. round barrel, standard trigger with triggerguard, blue or nickel finish, walnut, ivory, or pearl 2-piece grips. Approx. 25,000 produced, 1875-1888.

N/A	N/A	$4,250	$3,750	$3,250	$2,750	$2,450	$2,150	$1,850	$1,675	$1,475	$1,100

Add 25% for blue finish.
Add 10% for government markings.
Add 50% for .45 cal.

There is some debate over originality of the 5¾ in. barrel.

MODEL 1888 SINGLE ACTION REVOLVER — cartridge .44 Centerfire cal., resembles 1890 SA, has "E. Remington & Sons" barrel address, 5¾ in. barrel, nickel finish with walnut grips, perhaps mfg. during Remington's period of bankruptcy and receivership (circa late 1880s).

N/A	N/A	$3,250	$2,800	$2,400	$2,000	$1,650	$1,275	$950	$850	$725	$625

This model was never listed in a Remington catalog or price list. Rather, it first appeared in a Hartly Graham ad during the late 1880s. It is assumed this revolver was made from parts of Models 1875 & 1890 pistols. Model nomenclature has been created by collectors, not the factory.

100%	98%	95%	90%	80%	70%	60%	50%	40%	30%	20%	10%

MODEL 1890 SINGLE ACTION REVOLVER — cartridge .44 Centerfire cal., 6 shot, 7½ or 5¾ in. round barrel, standard trigger with trigger guard, hard rubber 2-piece grips with Remington monogram, ivory or pearl grips on special order, blue or nickel finish. Approx. 2,000 produced, 1891-1894.

➤ Blue finish

N/A	N/A	$7,750	$6,950	$6,300	$5,600	$4,875	$4,100	$3,400	$2,575	$1,775	$1,100

➤ Nickel finish

N/A	N/A	$6,400	$5,800	$5,200	$4,500	$4,000	$3,500	$2,950	$2,000	$1,400	$900

MODEL 51 SEMI-AUTO — .32 ACP or .380 ACP cal., 8 shot (7 in mag., 1 in chamber), hard rubber 2-piece grips with company's name. Approx. 65,000 mfg. 1918-1927, parts clean-up 1927-1934 (11 mfg.).

$650	$525	$450	$335	$300	$275	$225	$200	$175	$165	$150	$125

Add 25% for .32 ACP cal.

Note: .380 ACP cal. much more common than .32 ACP cal.

REMINGTON - UMC — .45 ACP cal., WWI M1911 military contract, over 21,500 mfg. (ser. numbered 1-21,676) in 1918-1919 only, blued finish.

N/A	$1,950	$1,625	$950	$700	$575	$525	$475	$425	$375	$325	$275

The cut-off serial number for 1918 mfg. is 13,152.

MARK III SIGNAL PISTOL — 10 ga., single shot, brass frame, 9 in. round steel barrel, spur trigger, walnut 2-piece grips. Approx. 25,000 produced, 1915-1918.

N/A	N/A	$300	$265	$230	$210	$190	$175	$160	$145	$130	$110

HANDGUNS: POST-WWII PRODUCTION

Model XP-100 & Variations

Manufacture stopped on the XP-100 at the end of 1994, and resumed again during 1998 (Model XP-100R).

Grading	100%	98%	95%	90%	80%	70%	60%

MODEL XP-100 — .221 Rem. Fireball cal., single shot bolt action pistol, one-piece Dupont Zytel (nylon) pistol grip stock, adj. sights, drilled and tapped for receiver sight and scope, 3¾ lbs. Mfg. 1963-1985.

			$425	$385	$325	$215	$185	$165	$150

MODEL XP-100 VARMINT SPECIAL — single shot bolt action pistol, .223 Rem. (new 1986) cal., 14½ in. barrel, drilled and tapped for receiver sights and scope, one-piece pistol grip nylon stock, 4⅛ lbs. Mfg. 1986-1992.

			$495	$395	$330	$295	$240	$210	$185

Last Mfg.'s Sug. Retail was $419.

Add $100 for original hard zipper case.

XP-SILHOUETTE — .35 Rem. (mfg. 1987-1992) or 7mm BR Rem. (mfg. 1980-1992) cal., bench rest model, 14½ in. barrel, drilled and tapped, nylon (disc. 1992) or walnut (new 1992) stock, 3⅞ lbs. Disc. 1992.

			$535	$455	$400	$360	$330	$270	$220

Last Mfg.'s Sug. Retail was $427.

Add $15 for .35 Rem. cal.

MODEL XP-100 HUNTER — .223 Rem., 7mm BR Rem., 7mm-.08 Rem., or .35 Rem. cal., 14½ in. barrel, drilled and tapped for sights, laminated wood stock, 4⅜ lbs. New 1993-94.

			$550	$475	$410	$350	$300	$230	$195

Last Mfg.'s Sug. Retail was $548.

MODEL XP-100 WALNUT — 7mm BR Rem. cal., 10½ in. barrel, solid American walnut stock and target sights, 3⅞ lbs. Mfg. 1993-94.

			$625	$545	$475	$410	$360	$330	$275

Last Mfg.'s Sug. Retail was $625.

Grading	100%	98%	95%	90%	80%	70%	60%

XP-100R KS — .22-250 Rem. (new 1992), .223 Rem., .250 Savage (new 1991), 7mm-08 Rem., .308 Win. (new 1992), .35 Rem., or .350 Rem. Mag. (new 1991) cal., repeater variation, Kevlar synthetic stock, right hand action only, open sights (except for .223 Rem. and .250 Savage) 4⅛ lbs. Mfg. 1990-94.

			$850	$750	$675	$595	$495	$400	$365

Last Mfg.'s Sug. Retail was $840.

This model was available through Remington's Custom Shop only.

MODEL XP-100R — .22-250 Rem., .223 Rem., .260 Rem., or .35 Rem. cal., right hand repeater with 4 or 5 shot blind mag., fiberglass composite stock, 14½ in. barrel, drilled and tapped receiver, approx. 4½ lbs. New 1998.

Mfg.'s Sug. Retail	$665	$595	$550	$500	$450	$400	$360	$330

XP-100 CUSTOM — .22-250 Rem. (new 1992), .223 Rem., .250 Savage, 6mm BR Rem., 7mm BR Rem., .308 Win. (new 1992), .35 Rem., or 7mm-08 Rem. cal., choice of standard or heavy barrel, available through custom gun shop only, choice of right or left-hand action, wood stock with contoured pistol grip, without sights. Mfg. 1986-94.

			$950	$800	$700	$600	$550	$500	$450

Last Mfg.'s Sug. Retail was $945.

The .458x2 in. cal. was also available by special order only.

100%	98%	95%	90%	80%	70%	60%	50%	40%	30%	20%	10%

RIFLES: DISC.

REVOLVING PERCUSSION RIFLE — .36 or .44 cal., 6 shot unfluted cylinder, 24 or 28 in. octagon barrel, walnut stock with crescent butt, scroll triggerguard, blue with case hardened frame. Less than 1,000 mfg., 1866-1879.

* **.36 Caliber**

N/A	N/A	$2,900	$2,640	$2,475	$2,310	$2,200	$2,090	$1,980	$1,925	$1,815	$1,760

* **.44 Caliber** — very rare.

N/A	N/A	$9,875	$8,700	$6,000	$4,250	$3,750	$3,250	$2,875	$2,600	$2,300	$1,975

Due to poor percussion sales, most of the remaining factory stock was converted to .38 R.F., factory conversions will be serial numbered similarly on the recoil plate and cylinder.

MODEL 1862 "ZOUAVE RIFLE" — .58 cal., muzzle loading percussion, 33 in. round barrel, two barrel bands, blue barrel, case hardened lock, brass furniture. Mfg. 12,501, 1862-1865.

N/A	N/A	$3,000	$2,600	$2,250	$1,800	$1,575	$1,300	$1,050	$850	$650	$450

U.S. NAVY ROLLING BLOCK CARBINE — .50-70 cal., 23¼ in. barrel, open sight, blue with case hardened frame, bar and ring on frame, walnut straight grip stock. Mfg. 5,000, 1868-1869.

N/A	N/A	$1,750	$1,350	$1,250	$950	$800	$750	$625	$515	$450	$395

LONG RANGE "CREEDMOOR" — rolling block, .44-90, .44-100, or .45-70, cal., barrel ⅓ octagon, long range tang sight, globe front sight, checkered pistol grip stock, blue. Approx. 500 mfg., 1873-1886.

N/A	N/A	$9,800	$8,825	$6,250	$4,475	$3,875	$3,175	$2,700	$2,475	$2,150	$1,800

NO. 1 SPORTING RIFLE — rolling block, .40-50, .40-70, .44-70, .44-77, .45-70, .50-45, or .50-70 centerfire or .46 rimfire cal., 28 or 30 in. octagon barrels, folding leaf sight, straight or pistol grip stock. Approx. 10,000 mfg., 1868-1902.

N/A	N/A	$1,250	$1,100	$950	$850	$750	$460	$550	$400	$350	$300

Subtract 15% for rimfire cals.
Add 25% for .44-77, .45-70, or .50-70 cal. (primary buffalo hunting cals.).

100%	98%	95%	90%	80%	70%	60%	50%	40%	30%	20%	10%

NO. 1½ SPORTING RIFLE — .22, .25 Stevens, .25 Long, .32, and .38 Long & Extra Long rimfire cal., also in .32-20 WCF, .38-40 WCF, and .44-40 WCF, 24-28 in. octagon medium weight barrel, straight grip walnut stock, somewhat lighter than the No. 1 Sporting. Several thousand mfg., 1888-1897.

| N/A | N/A | $875 | $775 | $675 | $575 | $500 | $450 | $400 | $350 | $275 | $200 |

Subtract 15% for rimfire cals.

NO. 2 SPORTING RIFLE — available in many rimfire cals. between .22 and .38 as well as centerfire cals. between .22 to .38-40 WCF, blued finish with case hardened frame, perch belly style walnut stock, many special orders available, smaller size action than the No.1 and rear of frame is curved, mfg. 1873-1909.

| N/A | N/A | $600 | $560 | $520 | $460 | $410 | $360 | $300 | $250 | $200 | $150 |

Subtract 15% for rimfire cals.

LIGHT BABY CARBINE — rolling block, .44-40 WCF cal., 20 in. lightweight round barrel with band, straight stock. Few thousand mfg., 1892-1902.

| N/A | N/A | $2,500 | $2,000 | $1,650 | $1,375 | $1,500 | $895 | $775 | $700 | $640 | $575 |

Add 25% for blued barrel with color case hardened receiver.

REMINGTON — HEPBURN NO. 3 — falling block, single shot, side lever actuated, blue barrel, case hardened actions, patented 1879, first introduced 1880, many custom features were offered, variations as follows:

NO. 3 SPORTING & TARGET — various cals. from .22 Win. to .50-90 Sharps, 26, 28, or 30 in. round or octagon barrel, open sight, semi-pistol grip stock. Mfg. 1883-1907.

| N/A | N/A | $1,500 | $1,300 | $1,200 | $1,100 | $1,000 | $900 | $800 | $700 | $600 | $550 |

NO. 3 MATCH RIFLE A QUALITY — similar to Sporting and Target, with target match sights (tang), and Schuetzen stock. Less than 1,000 mfg., 1883-1907.

| N/A | N/A | $2,250 | $2,000 | $1,650 | $1,500 | $1,400 | $1,300 | $1,200 | $900 | $700 | $625 |

* *B Quality* — select grade wood.

| N/A | N/A | $2,400 | $2,200 | $1,950 | $1,700 | $1,500 | $1,400 | $1,300 | $1,000 | $800 | $750 |

NO. 3 LONG RANGE CREEDMOOR — .44-40 WCF cal., 32 or 34 in. octagon barrel, tang sight, otherwise similar to Target Model. A few hundred mfg., 1880-1907.

| N/A | N/A | $2,300 | $2,050 | $1,850 | $1,600 | $1,400 | $1,300 | $1,200 | $950 | $775 | $725 |

NO. 3 MID RANGE CREEDMOOR — similar to Long Range, in .40-65 WCF cal., 28 in. barrel.

| N/A | N/A | $2,300 | $2,050 | $1,850 | $1,600 | $1,400 | $1,300 | $1,200 | $950 | $775 | $725 |

NO. 3 LONG RANGE MILITARY — similar to Creedmoor, with 34 in. full musket stock, in .44-75-520 Rem. cal., military sights, 1880s.

| N/A | N/A | $3,000 | $2,625 | $2,250 | $1,925 | $1,700 | $1,540 | $1,430 | $1,320 | $1,100 | $990 |

NO. 3 SCHUETZEN MATCH — under-lever action, 30 or 32 in. barrel, tang sight, palm rest, target stock, approx. 23 mfg. in 1903, perhaps the rarest single shot American rifle.

Extreme rarity factor precludes accurate price evaluation but a few have been observed with price tags in the $5,000-$20,000+ range, depending on condition.

* *With False Muzzle*

Even rarer than above - add a premium according to condition.

NO. 4 ROLLING BLOCK RIFLE — .22 S-L-LR, .25 Stevens (barrels marked "25-10"), or .32 Short or Long cal., 22½ octagon barrel standard with round barrels available late in the series, blued finish with case hardened frame, solid frame initially followed by takedown in 2 different types (lever - most common, or knob), this model was Remington's smallest rolling block. Approx. 350,000 mfg. 1890-1933.

| $550 | $475 | $395 | $350 | $300 | $260 | $230 | $200 | $165 | $130 | $115 | $100 |

Add 25% for smooth bore barrel.

Solid frame variations will command a premium, especially if over 50% original condition.

100%	98%	95%	90%	80%	70%	60%	50%	40%	30%	20%	10%

* Model 4-S "Boy Scout"

| N/A | N/A | $1,100 | $975 | $850 | $750 | $650 | $550 | $450 | $350 | $275 | $225 |

* Model 4-S Military — .22 S,L, LR cal., either marked "MILITARY MODEL" (most common) or "AMERICAN BOY SCOUT" (rare), 28 in. round barrel with musket type forend (1 barrel band), thought to have been used by military academies to train their young cadets.

| N/A | N/A | $825 | $725 | $625 | $550 | $480 | $410 | $340 | $285 | $240 | $200 |

  Bayonets are an extremely rare accessory for this model.

NO. 6 ROLLING BLOCK RIFLE — .22 S-L-LR or .32 Short or Long rimfire cal., 20 in. round barrel, boy's gun with small dimensions, takedown action, case hardened (early mfg.) or blue finish, also available in smooth bore, 497,000 mfg. 1901-1933.

| $275 | $235 | $190 | $160 | $150 | $140 | $130 | $120 | $110 | $100 | $90 | $75 |

  Add 25% for smooth bore barrel.

  Original case colors will bring a premium on this model.

REMINGTON KEENE MAGAZINE BOLT RIFLE — .45-70 Govt., .40, or .43 cal. Approx. 5,000 mfg. 1880-1888.

* Frontier Model — made for U.S. Dept. of Interior (Indian Police), marked U.S.I.D.

| N/A | $1,150 | $900 | $800 | $725 | $650 | $575 | $500 | $425 | $350 | $275 | $200 |

* Carbine Model — 22 in. full stock.

| N/A | $975 | $850 | $750 | $650 | $550 | $475 | $400 | $325 | $275 | $225 | $175 |

* Army Rifle — 32½ in. barrel, full stock.

| N/A | $975 | $850 | $750 | $650 | $550 | $475 | $400 | $325 | $275 | $225 | $175 |

* Sporter Rifle — ½ oct. barrel, full or "BUTTON" mag. Add for pistol grip and select wood variations.

| N/A | $975 | $850 | $750 | $650 | $550 | $475 | $400 | $325 | $275 | $225 | $175 |

* Navy Rifle — 29½ in. barrel, full stock.

| N/A | $975 | $850 | $750 | $650 | $550 | $475 | $400 | $325 | $275 | $225 | $175 |

Grading			100%	98%	95%	90%	80%	70%	60%

RIFLES: ROLLING BLOCK

NO. 1 ROLLING BLOCK CREEDMOOR — .45-70 Govt. cal., rolling block action, patterned after the original Remington No. 1 mid-range Creedmore-style configuration, 30 in. half-round half-octagon tapered 30 in. barrel, includes rear tang aperture and front globe sight with four interchangeable inserts, checkered walnut stock and forearm, SST, case colored receiver, cased, 9⅞ lbs. Mfg. 1997-98.

     $2,400 $1,900 $1,600

        Last Mfg.'s Sug. Retail was $2,799.

NO. 1 ROLLING BLOCK MID-RANGE SPORTER — .30-30 Win. (disc. 1998), .444 Marlin (disc. 1998), or .45-70 Govt. cal., 30 in. round barrel, checkered pistol grip sporter stock and forearm, blued barrel end and receiver, adj. buckhorn rear sight, 8¾ lbs. New 1998.

Mfg.'s Sug. Retail	$1,317		$1,100	$965	$885	$775	$675	$600	$550

RIFLES: CENTERFIRE - SEMI-AUTO

  The models below have been listed in numerical sequence for quick reference.

MODEL FOUR — 6mm Rem., .243 Win., .270 Win., .280 Rem., .30-06, .308 Win. (disc. 1984) or 7mm Express Rem. (early mfg. barrel marking) cal., gas operation with metering system, 22 in. barrel, 4 shot detachable mag., deluxe Monte Carlo stock and forend, detachable sights. Mfg. 1982-1987.

    $395 $360 $325 $275 $250 $225 $195

       Last Mfg.'s Sug. Retail was $475.

Grading	100%	98%	95%	90%	80%	70%	60%

* Special Model Four Diamond Anniversary — .30-06 cal. only, less than 1,500 mfg. in 1981 only to commemorate 75th anniversary of the Model 8, laser engraved with gold and premium checkered walnut stock and forearm. One grade only.

	$1,000	$795	$600

MODEL 8 — .25 Rem., .30 Rem., .32 Rem., or .35 Rem. cal., 22 in. barrel, open sights, 5 shot non-detachable box mag., plain stock. Approx. 60,000 mfg. 1906-1936. Also made in higher grades C through F — add premiums.

	$400	$320	$270	$220	$195	$165	$140

Add 15% for .25 cal.

MODEL 74 SPORTSMAN — .30-06 cal. only, 22 in. barrel, 4 shot mag., uncheckered hardwood stock and forearm, open sights, 7½ lbs. Mfg. 1985-1987.

	$295	$260	$235	$210	$190	$175	$160

Last Mfg.'s Sug. Retail was $353.

MODEL 81 "WOODSMASTER" — .30 Rem., .32 Rem., .35 Rem., or .300 Savage cal., semi-auto, takedown action, 5 shot, non-detachable box mag., 22 in. round barrel, notched elevator rear sight. An improvement of the Model 8 was available in 5 grades. Better grades bring higher prices. 56,091 mfg. 1936-1950.

	$400	$350	$300	$250	$200	$175	$150

Add 20% for .25 cal.

The .32 Rem. cal. was dropped after WWII and the .300 Savage was added in 1940. While a few specimens have been observed in .25 Rem. cal., it is probably the result of part swapping as the Remington Co. cannot verify this cal.

MODEL 740 WOODMASTER & 740A — .244 Rem. (mfg. 1957-59), .280 Rem. (marked 7mm Express, mfg. 1957-59), .30-06 or .308 Win. cal., 22 in. barrel, open sight, box mag., gas operated, plain pistol grip stock. Mfg. 1955-59.

	100%	98%	95%	90%	80%	70%	60%
.244 Rem. or .30-06 cal.	$295	$250	$225	$210	$200	$190	$180
.280 Rem. or .308 Win. cal.	$295	$250	$225	$210	$200	$190	$180

Add 15% for carbine version.

MODEL 740ADL — similar to 740A, with checkered stock, grip cap and swivels. Mfg. 1955-59.

	100%	98%	95%	90%	80%	70%	60%
.244 Rem. or .30-06 cal.	$375	$325	$280	$250	$225	$200	$180
.280 Rem. or .308 Win. cal.	$415	$350	$300	$275	$250	$225	$200

Add 15% for carbine version.

MODEL 740BDL — similar to 740ADL, with select wood.

	100%	98%	95%	90%	80%	70%	60%
.244 Rem. or .30-06 cal.	$395	$340	$295	$250	$225	$200	$180
.308 Win. cal.	$425	$375	$350	$325	$275	$225	$200

Add 15% for carbine version.

BDLs were not listed in the 1958 or 1959 Remington price list.

MODEL 742 (A) "WOODSMASTER" — 6mm Rem., .243 Win., .280 Rem. (marked 7mm Express 1979-1980), .30-06, or .308 Win. cal., 22 in. barrel, open sights, 4 shot box mag., gas operated, checkered pistol grip stock. Mfg. 1960-1980.

	$325	$290	$275	$250	$235	$210	$185

Add 10% for .280 Rem. cal.

MODEL 742ADL DELUXE — similar to the Model 742A, except has fine checkering, sling swivels and engraved game scenes on receiver.

	$350	$300	$275	$260	$235	$215	$195

MODEL 742 CARBINE — similar to 742, except .280 Rem. (marked 7mm Express 1979-1980), .30-06, or .308 Win. cal. only, 18½ in. barrel. Mfg. 1961-1980.

	$350	$300	$275	$260	$235	$215	$195

MODEL 742BDL — similar to Model 742, except .30-06 or .308 Win. cal., Monte Carlo basket weave stock and forend, black pistol grip cap and forend tip. Mfg. 1966-1980.

	$350	$300	$275	$260	$235	$215	$195

Grading	100%	98%	95%	90%	80%	70%	60%

MODEL 742D PEERLESS GRADE — similar to Model 742, with scroll engraving and fancy wood. Mfg. 1961-1980.

	$2,000	$1,870	$1,200				

MODEL 742F PREMIER GRADE — similar to Model 742, with extensive hand engraved game scenes and scroll work, best grade wood.

	$4,200	$3,860	$2,650				

MODEL 742F PREMIER GRADE (WITH INLAYS) — gold inlaid model.

	$6,500	$5,785	$4,180				

MODEL 742 150TH YEAR ANNIVERSARY — .30-06 cal. only. Mfg. 1966 only.

	$395	$325	$300				

MODEL 742 CANADIAN CENTENNIAL — 1,000 mfg. in 1967. Issue price was $200.

	$395	$325	$300				

REMINGTON/RUGER CANADIAN CENTENNIAL SET — please refer to the Sturm Ruger section of this text.

MODEL 742 BICENTENNIAL — similar to 742, with inscription on receiver. Mfg. 1976 only.

	$400	$325	$300	$275	$225	$200	$185

MODEL 7400 — 6mm Rem. (disc. 1987), .243 Win., .270 Win., .280 Rem., .30-06, .308 Win., or .35 Whelen (disc. 1995) cal., same action as 742, gas operation, 22 in. barrel, 4 shot detachable mag., pressed checkered Monte Carlo walnut stock, 7½ lbs. Mfg. 1981 to date.

Mfg.'s Sug. Retail	$573	$460	$380	$300	$255	$230	$210	$185

Beginning in 1990, a high gloss wood finish became available in cals. .270 Win. and .30-06 (Model 7400 High Gloss). Beginning 1997, receiver panels have photo etched game scene engraving.

* *Model 7400 Carbine* — .30-06 cal. only, similar to Model 7400 Rifle, except has 18½ in. barrel, 7¼ lbs. New 1988.

Mfg.'s Sug. Retail	$573	$460	$380	$300	$255	$230	$210	$185

* *Model 7400 SP (Special Purpose)* — .270 Win. or .30-06 cal., similar to Model 7400, except has non-reflective matte finish on both wood and metalwork. Mfg. 1993-94.

	$435	$370	$300	$255	$230	$210	$185

Last Mfg.'s Sug. Retail was $524.

* *Model 7400 Synthetic* — same cals. as Model 7400, features black fiberglass reinforced synthetic stock and forearm, matte black metal finish, 22 in. barrel only. New 1998.

Mfg.'s Sug. Retail	$473	$385	$340	$300	$280	$260	$240	$220

➤ Model 7400 Synthetic Carbine — similar to Model 7400 Synthetic, except has 18½ in. barrel, 7¼ lbs. New 1998.

Mfg.'s Sug. Retail	$473	$385	$340	$300	$280	$260	$240	$220

* *Model 7400 175th Anniversary* — .30-06 cal. only, Anniversary Model with light engraving and high gloss finish. Mfg. in 1991 only.

	$435	$365	$300				

Last Mfg.'s Sug. Retail was $515.

A limited quantity of .270 Win. cal. was made in this 175th Anniversary Model for distributor Bill Hicks in MN. Pricing varies, since these rifles are a special edition, not a Remington factory commemorative.

* *Model 7400 ADF Limited Edition* — .30-06 cal. only, special edition 1997 only featuring Buckmaster's American Deer Foundation, special ADF engraving. Mfg. 1997 only.

	$495	$400	$315				

Last Mfg.'s Sug. Retail was $600.

* *Model 7400 Engraved* — the below listed engraved Model 7400s were introduced 1988.

Grading	100%	98%	95%	90%	80%	70%	60%
* **D Peerless Grade**							
Mfg.'s Sug. Retail	$2,741	$2,175	$1,700	$1,200			
* **F Premier Grade**							
Mfg.'s Sug. Retail	$5,647	$4,750	$3,650	$2,600			
* **F Premier Gold Grade** — with gold inlays.							
Mfg.'s Sug. Retail	$8,465	$7,425	$4,250	$3,100			

RIFLES: CENTERFIRE - SLIDE ACTION

MODEL SIX — 6mm Rem. (disc. 1984), .243 Win., .270 Win., .30-06, or .308 Win. (disc. 1984) cal., pump action, laser engraved, detachable sights, 4 shot mag. Mfg. 1981-1987.

$400	$360	$290	$265	$235	$215	$195

Last Mfg.'s Sug. Retail was $439.

* **D Peerless Grade** — custom shop hand-engraved.

$1,975	$1,870	$1,200

Last Mfg.'s Sug. Retail was $2,291.

* **F Premier Grade**

$4,150	$3,835	$2,650

Last Mfg.'s Sug. Retail was $4,720.

* **F Premier Gold Grade** — with gold inlays.

$6,420	$5,735	$4,000

Last Mfg.'s Sug. Retail was $7,079.

MODEL 14/14A — .25 Rem., .30 Rem., .32 Rem., or .35 Rem. cal., 22 in. barrel, open sight, plain pistol grip stock. Mfg. 1912-1935.

$400	$325	$250	$195	$165	$130	$110

Add 100% for "fingernail" safety.

MODEL 14R CARBINE — similar to 14A, with 18½ in. barrel, straight grip stock.

$650	$600	$550	$500	$450	$400	$350

Add 10% for saddle ring.
Subtract 10% for .25 Rem. cal.

MODEL 14½ RIFLE — similar to 14A, with 22½ in. barrel, .38-40 WCF or .44-40 WCF cal. Mfg. 1912-1934.

$800	$725	$650	$600	$550	$500	$450

Quantities mfg. of this model are unknown, as serial numbers were intermixed with the Model 14.

MODEL 14½ R CARBINE — similar to 14½ Rifle, with 18½ in. barrel.

$700	$600	$525	$475	$425	$375	$325

Add 100% for "fingernail safety".

MODEL 25/25A SLIDE ACTION — .25-20 WCF or .32-20 WCF cal., 24 in. barrel, open sight, tube mag., plain pistol grip stock. Mfg. 1923-1936.

$425	$375	$325	$300	$250	$225	$200

MODEL 25R CARBINE — similar to 25A, with 18 in. barrel and straight stock.

$495	$425	$350	$275	$225	$200	$175

MODEL 76 SPORTSMAN SLIDE ACTION — .30-06 cal. only, 22 in. barrel, 4 shot mag., uncheckered hardwood stock and forearm, open sights, 7½ lbs. Mfg. 1984-87.

$255	$225	$195	$180	$170	$160	$150

Last Mfg.'s Sug. Retail was $319.

MODEL 141/141A SLIDE ACTION RIFLE — .25 Rem. (very few mfg. during 1936 only), .30 Rem., .32 Rem., or .35 Rem. cal., 24 in. barrel, takedown, open sight, plain pistol grip stock. Mfg. 1936-1950.

$395	$305	$250	$220	$195	$165	$140

Grading	100%	98%	95%	90%	80%	70%	60%

MODEL 141 CARBINE — mfg. 1936-1942.

	100%	98%	95%	90%	80%	70%	60%
	$750	$700	$650	$600	$550	$500	$450

MODEL 760 "GAMEMASTER" RIFLE — .222 Rem., .223 Rem., 6mm Rem., .243 Win., .257 Roberts, .270 Win., .280 Rem. (marked 7mm Express 1979-82), .30-06, .300 Sav., .308 Win. or .35 Rem. cal., 22 in. barrel, detachable mag., uncheckered pistol grip stock. Mfg. 1952-1980.

	100%	98%	95%	90%	80%	70%	60%
	$375	$325	$275	$250	$225	$200	$175
.222 Rem. cal.	$1,150	$900	$800	$725	$650	$575	$500
.223 Rem. cal.	$1,350	$995	$850	$775	$700	$625	$575
.257 Roberts cal.	$850	$695	$575	$450	$400	$350	$300

Add 10% for .300 Savage or .35 Rem. cal.

The Model 760 seems to have regional pricing differences in the rare calibers. Values in the Eastern U.S. seem to be quite a bit higher than prices encountered in the Midwest and West. Hence, values on the .222 Rem., .223 Rem., and .257 Roberts cals. reflect a nationalized average rather than one region's high or another's low. A few Model 760s were also mfg. in .244 cal. (before going to 6mm Rem.) — very rare with pricing unpredictable.

MODEL 760 CARBINE — .270 Win., .280 Win. (marked 7mm Express 1979-1980), .30-06, .308 Win., or .35 Rem. cal., 18½ in. barrel.

	100%	98%	95%	90%	80%	70%	60%
	$450	$400	$375	$325	$300	$275	$250

Subtract 10% for .30-06 cal.

MODEL 760D PEERLESS GRADE — similar to 760, with hand engraving and fancy wood. Mfg. 1953-1980.

	100%	98%	95%	90%	80%	70%	60%
	$1,100	$935	$825	$770	$690	$605	$525

MODEL 760F — similar to 760, with extensive hand engraved game scenes, best grade wood.

	100%	98%	95%	90%	80%	70%	60%
	$2,420	$1,980	$1,760	$1,650	$1,485	$1,375	$1,100

* Gold Inlaid Model

	100%	98%	95%	90%	80%	70%	60%
	$5,500	$4,675	$4,180	$3,960	$3,300	$2,750	$2,200

MODEL 760 150 YEAR ANNIVERSARY — .30-06 cal. only. Mfg. 1966 only.

	100%	98%	95%	90%	80%	70%	60%
	$395	$325	$300	$275	$225	$200	$185

MODEL 760 BICENTENNIAL — similar to 760, with commemorative inscription engraved on receiver. Mfg. 1976 only.

	100%	98%	95%	90%	80%	70%	60%
	$395	$325	$300	$275	$225	$200	$185

MODEL 760ADL — similar to 760A, except with checkered pistol grip, deluxe wood and sling swivels. Mfg. 1953-1963.

	100%	98%	95%	90%	80%	70%	60%
	$395	$350	$325	$300	$275	$250	$225

MODEL 760BDL — similar to 760, except .270 Win., .30-06, or .308 Win. cal. only, basket weave checkering pattern became standard mid-'70s, Monte Carlo stock, black pistol grip and forend tip. Mfg. 1953-1982.

	100%	98%	95%	90%	80%	70%	60%
	$425	$375	$350	$300	$275	$250	$225

Add 20% for .308 Win. cal.

MODEL 7600 — 6mm Rem. (disc. 1984), .243 Win., .270 Win., .280 Rem. (new 1988), .30-06, .308 Win., or .35 Whelen (mfg. 1988-96) cal., modified 760 action, 22 in. barrel, detachable mag., pressed checkered pistol grip stock and forearm, 7½ lbs. Mfg. 1981 to date.

	100%	98%	95%	90%	80%	70%	60%
Mfg.'s Sug. Retail	$540	$440	$375	$285	$230	$205	$185	$165

Beginning in 1990, a high gloss wood finish became available in cals. .270 Win. and .30-06 (Model 7600 High Gloss). Beginning 1997, receiver panels have photo etched game scene engraving.

Grading	100%	98%	95%	90%	80%	70%	60%

* **Model 7600 Carbine** — .30-06 cal. only, similar to Model 7600 Rifle, except has 18½ in. barrel, 7¼ lbs.

Mfg.'s Sug. Retail	$540	$440	$375	$285	$230	$205	$185	$165

* **Model 7600 SP (Special Purpose)** — .270 Win. or .30-06 cal., similar to Model 7600, except has non-reflective matte finish on wood and metalwork. Mfg. 1993-94.

	$420	$360	$280	$230	$205	$185	$165

Last Mfg.'s Sug. Retail was $496.

* **Model 7600 Synthetic** — same cals. as Model 7600, features black fiberglass reinforced synthetic stock and forearm, matte black metal finish, 22 in. barrel only, 7½ lbs. New 1998.

Mfg.'s Sug. Retail	$440	$360	$320	$285	$270	$255	$240	$225

➤ **Model 7600 Synthetic Carbine** — similar to Model 7600 Synthetic, except has 18½ in. barrel, 71/4 lbs. New 1998.

Mfg.'s Sug. Retail	$440	$360	$320	$285	$270	$255	$240	$225

* **Model 7600 ADF Limited Edition** — .30-06 cal. only, special edition 1997 only featuring Buckmaster's American Deer Foundation, special ADF engraving. Mfg. 1997 only.

	$460	$385	$295

Last Mfg.'s Sug. Retail was $567.

* **Model 7600 Engraved** — the below listed hand engraved Model 7600s were introduced 1988.

* **D Peerless Grade**

Mfg.'s Sug. Retail	$2,741	$2,175	$1,700	$1,200

* **F Premier Grade**

Mfg.'s Sug. Retail	$5,647	$4,750	$3,650	$2,600

* **F Premier Gold Grade** — with gold inlays.

Mfg.'s Sug. Retail	$8,465	$7,425	$4,250	$3,100

RIFLES: RIMFIRE, DISC. & CURRENT PRODUCTION

From 1930-1960 Remington produced a number of bolt action .22 cal. Rimfire rifles, both single shot and repeaters. They were good quality, serviceable weapons with many slight variations upon a basic design. Whenever possible, models have been listed in numerical sequence.

Model 33	$200	$150	$125	$100	$85	$75	$60
Model 33 NRA	$300	$225	$200	$175	$150	$125	$100

263,557 of the Model 33 were mfg. 1932-1935.

Model 34	$200	$150	$125	$100	$85	$75	$60
Model 34-P	$300	$225	$200	$175	$150	$125	$100
Model 34 NRA	$395	$375	$350	$300	$275	$250	$200

162,941 of the Model 34 were mfg. 1932-1936.

Model 341 A	$150	$125	$100	$85	$75	$65	$55
Model 341 P	$175	$150	$125	$100	$85	$75	$70
Model 341 SB	$275	$235	$200	$175	$140	$125	$110

131,604 of the Model 341 "Sportsmaster" were mfg. 1936-1940.

Model 41 A	$150	$125	$100	$75	$65	$60	$55
Model 41 AS (.22 Rem. Spec. cal.)	$200	$175	$160	$150	$140	$125	$110
Model 41 P	$150	$125	$100	$85	$65	$60	$55
Model 41 SB	$235	$195	$175	$160	$140	$125	$110

306,880 of the Model 41 "Targetmaster" were produced 1936-1940.

Model 411	$400	$375	$350	$300	$250	$225	$200

The Model 411 is similar to the Model 41 single shot, but in CB Cap or .22 Short and without safety on rear of bolt. Eye screw for gallery use. 1,316 mfg. 1937-1939 (although never cataloged). Add 50% premium for .22 Short.

Grading	100%	98%	95%	90%	80%	70%	60%
Model 510 A	$125	$110	$90	$75	$65	$60	$55
Model 510 C (Carbine)	$175	$150	$95	$85	$75	$65	$60
Model 510 P	$175	$150	$95	$85	$75	$65	$60
Model 510 Routledge/Smoothbore	$200	$165	$150	$120	$110	$100	$90

Add 15% for Mo-Skeet-O Bore

These models were mfg. 1939-1962.

Model 511 A	$150	$135	$120	$100	$75	$60	$55
Model 511 P	$200	$165	$125	$100	$75	$60	$55

These models were mfg. 1939-1962.

Model 512 A	$150	$135	$120	$100	$75	$60	$55
Model 512 P	$200	$165	$125	$100	$75	$60	$55

These models were mfg. 1940-1962.

Model 510-X	$140	$125	$110	$90	$80	$70	$60
Model 510-X SB	$200	$175	$150	$135	$125	$120	$110
Model 511-X	$175	$150	$125	$100	$90	$80	$70
Model 512-X	$175	$150	$125	$100	$90	$80	$70

These models were mfg. 1964-1966.

Model 514 (1948-1970)	$135	$110	$90	$75	$65	$55	$40
Model 514 P (disc. 1971)	$175	$165	$145	$120	$85	$75	$65
Model 514 Boy's Rifle (disc. 1970)	$155	$135	$120	$100	$85	$75	$65
Model 514 Routledge/Smoothbore	$185	$150	$120	$110	$100	$90	$80

MODEL 12A SLIDE ACTION RIFLE — .22 S, L, and LR cal., hammerless, 22 in. barrel, open sights, tube mag., plain grip stock. Mfg. 1909-1936.

	$375	$325	$275	$250	$190	$170	$160

Originally designated Model 12.

MODEL 12B (GALLERY SPECIAL) — similar to 12C, except in .22 Short cal., all had octagon barrels.

	$550	$495	$425	$325	$300	$250	$225

Add 15% for extended mag. tube.

MODEL 12C — similar to 12A, except 24 in. octagon barrel. Also mfg. in grades D, E, and F — add premiums.

	$500	$450	$375	$275	$250	$225	$200

MODEL 12C NRA TARGET — limited manufacture.

	$800	$750	$650	$550	$450	$400	$350

MODEL 12CS — similar to 12C, chambered for .22 Rem. Spl. (.22 WRF) cal.

	$425	$375	$300	$225	$195	$175	$150

MODEL 16/16A AUTOLOADING RIFLE — .22 Auto rimfire cal., 22 in. barrel, open sight, tube mag. in butt stock, straight stock. Mfg. 1914-1928. Also mfg. in grades C, D, and F — add premiums.

	$400	$325	$250	$200	$140	$110	$90

MODEL 24/24A AUTOLOADING RIFLE — .22 S or LR cal., 19 in. barrel, open sights, Browning semi-auto design, bottom ejection, tube mag. through butt stock, takedown, plain pistol grip stock. Approx. 131,000 mfg. 1922-1935. Also, mfg. in Grades C Special, D Peerless, E Expert, and F Premier.

	$400	$300	$250	$170	$140	$110	$90

MODEL 37 "RANGEMASTER" BOLT ACTION TARGET RIFLE — .22 LR cal., 5 shot with single shot adapter, 28 in. barrel, target sight and scope bases, target stock, 12½ lbs. Mfg. 1937-1940.

	$700	$650	$550	$500	$425	$400	$375

MODEL 37 - 1940 — improved trigger and stock design. Mfg. 1940-1954.

	$700	$650	$550	$500	$425	$400	$365

Total manufacture of the Model 37 was 12,198.

Grading	100%	98%	95%	90%	80%	70%	60%

MODEL 121A SLIDE ACTION RIFLE — hammerless, .22 S, L, or LR cal., 24 in. round barrel, tube mag., plain pistol grip stock. Mfg. 1936-1954.

	$425	$325	$275	$225	$200	$185	$175

Originally designated Model 121.

MODEL 121S — similar to 121A, except chambered for .22 Rem. Spl. (rare) cal..

	$550	$450	$400	$325	$275	$225	$200

MODEL 121SB/ROUTLEDGE — similar to 121A, except smooth bore for .22 shot, at least 5 different chamberings and barrel markings.

	$650	$550	$500	$400	$350	$325	$300

MODEL 241/241A SPEEDMASTER SEMI-AUTO — .22 S or LR cal., 24 in. barrel, replaced the Model 24, open sights, takedown, tube mag. through stock, non-checkered walnut stock and forearm. Approx. 56,000 mfg. 1935-1949.

	$360	$275	$250	$195	$150	$120	$100

This model was also available in a Special, Peerless, Expert, and Premier Grade - add premiums.

MODEL 513T "MATCHMASTER" BOLT ACTION — .22 LR cal., 27 in. barrel, Redfield aperture sight, target stock, 6 shot, sling swivels. Mfg. 1940-1968.

	$395	$300	$250	$200	$150	$115	$95

A TR suffix on this gun indicated with sights, a TX indicated w/o sights, a TS indicated sporter. Most 513s are marked either 513T (Target) or 513S (Sporter).

MODEL 513S — similar to 513T, with Marbles open sight and checkered sporter stock. Mfg. 1941-1956.

	$650	$600	$550	$500	$450	$400	$350

MODEL 521TL JR. BOLT ACTION — .22 LR cal., 25 in. barrel, Lyman target sights, takedown, 6 shot mag., target stock. Mfg. 1947-1968.

	$300	$275	$225	$175	$125	$100	$90

MODEL 522 VIPER SEMI-AUTO — .22 LR cal., semi-auto blowback action, 20 in. barrel, full-length black synthetic resin stock with beavertail forend, 10 shot mag., cocking indicator, adj. rear sight, grooved synthetic receiver, 4⅝ lbs. Mfg. 1993-97.

	$135	$115	$100	$90	$80	$70	$60

Last Mfg.'s Sug. Retail was $152.

MODEL 540X RIMFIRE — .22 LR cal., single shot bolt action, 26 in. heavy barrel, no sights, target stock, adj. butt. Mfg. 1969-1974.

	$325	$285	$250	$225	$200	$175	$150

MODEL 540XR — similar to 540X, with large position style stock with adj. butt plate. Mfg. 1974-1983.

	$350	$300	$275	$225	$200	$185	$175

MODEL 541S CUSTOM BOLT ACTION — .22 S, L, or LR cal., bolt action, 24 in. barrel, no sights, 5 shot clip, scroll engraved receiver and triggerguard, checkered walnut stock with rosewood pistol grip cap and forend tip. Mfg. 1972-1984.

	$450	$400	$350	$300	$250	$225	$200

MODEL 541T BOLT ACTION — .22 LR cal. only, 5 shot clip mag., 24 in. standard or heavy (new 1993) barrel, checkered American walnut stock with satin finish, barrel is drilled and tapped, 5⅞ lbs. New 1986.

Mfg.'s Sug. Retail	$465	$380	$300	$235	$200	$180	$165	$150

Add $27 for heavy barrel.

MODEL 541X — .22 LR cal. only, bolt action, U.S. military training rifle, 27 in. barrel, 5 shot clip, ser. no. scribed by hand on bolt, 9,077 mfg. 1984-86.

	$800	$700	$650	$625	$575	$495	$425

Grading	100%	98%	95%	90%	80%	70%	60%

MODEL 550A SEMI-AUTO — .22 S, L, or LR cal., 24 in. barrel, open sight, shell deflector, 2 extractors, tube mag., plain one piece pistol stock. Mfg. 1941-1946.

	$195	$150	$110	$90	$80	$70	$60

This model replaced the Model 241.

MODEL 550-1 — similar to 550A, except has single extractor. Approx. 220,000 mfg. 1946-1970.

	$150	$125	$100	$85	$75	$65	$55

MODEL 550P — similar to 550-1, with aperture (peep) sight.

	$190	$150	$125	$105	$85	$75	$65

MODEL 550-2G — .22 Short cal., similar to 550-1, except 22 in. barrel and eye screw for counter chain in shooting gallery.

	$200	$175	$150	$130	$110	$100	$85

MODEL 552A SPEEDMASTER SEMI-AUTO — .22 S, L, or LR cal., 23 in. barrel, semi-auto open sight, tube mag., pistol grip stock. Mfg. 1957-disc.

	$160	$135	$120	$100	$85	$75	$65

This model was also mfg. in a 150th Anniversary Model (1966 only). Slight premiums are being asked if condition is 98% or better.

MODEL 552C — similar to 552A, with 21 in. barrel. Mfg. 1961-1977.

	$170	$145	$130	$110	$95	$85	$75

* **Model 552 BDL Deluxe Speedmaster** — similar to Model 552, except checkered walnut Monte Carlo stock and forearm. Mfg. 1966 to date.

Mfg.'s Sug. Retail	$340	$265	$190	$155	$125	$105	$90	$75

MODEL 572 LIGHTWEIGHT SLIDE ACTION — .22 S, L, LR cal., slide action, anodized alloy receiver and barrel, steel sleeved, checkered "Sun-Grain" stock and forend, 4 lbs. Offered in 3 colors. Approx. 34,785 mfg., 1958-1962.

	100%	98%	95%	90%	80%	70%	60%
Buckskin Tan	$225	$200	$160	$150	$120	$110	$100
Crow-Wing Black	$375	$345	$295	$195	$150	$125	$100
Teal-Wing Blue	$595	$500	$400	$275	$250	$225	$200

MODEL 572SB/ROUTLEDGE — similar to 572A, except smooth bore.

	$350	$275	$225	$175	$140	$120	$100

MODEL 572 FIELDMASTER — .22 S, L, or LR cal., slide action, 21 in. barrel, walnut stock and forearm, tube mag., 5½ lbs. Mfg. 1955-1988.

	$160	$145	$125	$105	$90	$75	$65

Last Mfg.'s Sug. Retail was $176.

This model was also mfg. in a 150th Anniversary Model (1966 only). 20% premiums if condition is 98% or better.

* **Model 572 BDL Deluxe Fieldmaster** — similar to Model 572, except with checkered walnut Monte Carlo stock and forearm. Mfg. 1966 to date.

Mfg.'s Sug. Retail	$353	$275	$200	$160	$125	$105	$90	$75

MODEL 580 SINGLE SHOT — .22 S, L or LR cal., bolt action, 24 in. barrel, open sights, Monte Carlo stock. Mfg. 1968-1978.

	$150	$125	$105	$100	$90	$80	$75

Add 50% for smooth bore (Model 580SB).

MODEL 580BR — Boy's Model, 1 in. shorter stock. Mfg. 1971-1978.

	$175	$150	$125	$100	$75	$65	$50

MODEL 581 BOLT ACTION — .22 LR cal., bolt action, 6 shot clip mag., converts to single shot. Mfg. 1967-1983.

	$165	$135	$135	$100	$90	$70	$60

Grading	100%	98%	95%	90%	80%	70%	60%

MODEL 581 SPORTSMAN — .22 LR cal., bolt action, 5 shot clip mag., 24 in. barrel, hardwood uncheckered stock, 4¾ lbs. New 1986.

Mfg.'s Sug. Retail	$239	$200	$170	$145	$125	$105	$90	$75

MODEL 582 BOLT ACTION — similar to 581, with tube mag. Mfg. 1967-1983.

		$175	$150	$125	$115	$100	$85	$75

MODEL 591 BOLT ACTION — 5mm Rimfire Mag. cal., 24 in. barrel, open sight, 5 shot clip mag., Monte Carlo stock. Approx. 27,000 mfg. 1970-1974.

		$175	$125	$100	$85	$75	$65	$50

> 5mm Rimfire ammo has been disc. for some time, and as a result, collectability on this model is mostly for 100% condition, since there is no shooter utility in lower conditions. Original 5mm ammo is selling for $35-$50 per box.

MODEL 592 BOLT ACTION — similar to 591, with tube mag. Approx. 25,000 mfg. 1970-1974.

		$175	$125	$100	$85	$75	$65	$50

MODEL 597 SEMI-AUTO — .22 LR cal., alloy receiver with nickel plated bolt, matte black metal finish, one-piece dark grey smooth synthetic stock, 20 in. free-floating barrel, 10 shot staggered detachable mag., adj. iron sights, new trigger design, 5½ lbs. New 1997.

Mfg.'s Sug. Retail	$159	$135	$115	$100	$90	$80	$70	$60

* *Model 597 Sporter* — similar to Model 597, except has hardwood stock, includes sling swivel studs. New 1998.

Mfg.'s Sug. Retail	$199	$160	$135	$115	$100	$90	$80	$70

* *Model 597 SS* — similar to Model 597, except is stainless synthetic with satin finished receiver and barrel, beavertail style forend. New 1998.

Mfg.'s Sug. Retail	$212	$170	$145	$125				

* *Model 597 LSS* — similar to Model 597, except has stainless steel barrel with matching alloy receiver, and brown wood laminate stock, 5½ lbs. New 1997.

Mfg.'s Sug. Retail	$265	$225	$185	$160				

MODEL 597 CUSTOM TARGET — .22 LR or .22 Mag. cal., 20 in. custom contoured satin finish heavy stainless free floating barrel w/o sights, match chamber, special green laminated stock with Monte Carlo profile and beavertail forend. New 1998.

Mfg.'s Sug. Retail	$599	$495	$400	$300				

> Add $146 for .22 Mag. cal.

MODEL 597 MAGNUM — .22 Mag. cal., similar in appearance to Model 597, 9 shot mag., black synthetic stock with sling swivel studs, 6 lbs. New 1997.

Mfg.'s Sug. Retail	$305	$255	$225	$185	$160	$140	$125	$110

* *Model 597 Magnum LS* — .22 Mag. cal., features brown laminate stock with sling swivel studs. New 1998.

Mfg.'s Sug. Retail	$359	$305	$255	$225	$185	$160	$140	$125

RIFLES: RIMFIRE - "NYLON SERIES"

NYLON 10 SINGLE SHOT — .22 S, L, or LR cal., bolt action. Mfg. 1962-1964.

		$275	$210	$160	$120	$60	$50	$40

* *Nylon 10-SB* — similar to Nylon 10, except smooth bore barrel used for .22 shot cartridges.

		$500	$400	$250	$175	$150	$140	$125

> This model is infrequently encountered.

MOHAWK 10-C — similar to Model 77, renamed after changing to a 10 shot mag. Mfg. 1971-1978.

		$110	$85	$70	$65	$60	$55	$50

Grading	100%	98%	95%	90%	80%	70%	60%

MODEL 11 NYLON — .22 S, L, or LR cal., bolt action repeater, clip fed, 6 or 10 shot mag., 4½ lbs. Mfg. 1962-1964.

	$250	$200	$150	$110	$75	$50	$40

MODEL 12 NYLON — similar to 11, with tube mag. Mfg. 1962-1964.

	$250	$200	$150	$110	$75	$50	$40

NYLON 66 AUTOLOADER — .22 LR cal., 19⅝ in. barrel, open sights, butt stock tube mag. holds 14 shells, 4 lbs. Stock made from Zytel plastic in black, brown, or green. Mfg. 1959-1990.

	$140	$115	$95	$80	$70	$60	$50

Add 25% for Black Diamond.
Add 30% for Apache black.
Add 50% for Seneca green.

Chrome Finish	$185	$150	$120	$95	$75	$65	$55

Last Mfg.'s Sug. Retail was $124.

NYLON 66 150TH ANNIVERSARY — mfg. in 1966 only with 150th Anniversary Remington logo on receiver.

	$225	$185	$150	$100	$85	$70	$60

NYLON 66 BICENTENNIAL — inscription on receiver. Mfg. 1976 only, brown nylon stock only.

	$225	$185	$150	$100	$85	$70	$60

NYLON 76 LEVER ACTION — similar appearance to Nylon 66 with brown or black stock, short throw lever action. Mfg. 1962-1964 only.

Standard finish	$250	$200	$150	$115	$80	$65	$60
Black chrome finish	$295	$250	$210	$175	$150	$135	$120

The Nylon 76 "Trail Rider" is the only lever action repeating rifle ever mfg. by Remington.

NYLON 77 — similar to Nylon 66, except with 5 shot clip mag. Mfg. 1970-1971 only.

	$140	$125	$100	$75	$65	$55	$45

NYLON APACHE 77 — similar to Model 10-C, but bright green stock. Mfg. for K-Mart in 1987.

	$135	$100	$65	$55	$50	$45	$40

RIFLES: BOLT ACTION, CENTERFIRE

The models in this section have been listed in numerical sequence for quick reference.

MODEL SEVEN LIGHTWEIGHT — compact bolt action available in .17 Rem. (mfg. 1993-95), .222 Rem. (disc.), .223 Rem., .243 Win., .260 Rem. (new 1997), 6mm Rem. (disc. 1995), 7mm-08 Rem., or .308 Win. cal., 18½ in. barrel, 6¼ lbs., 4 or 5 shot mag., individually test fired, oil finished American walnut, adj. rear and ramp front sight (without sights on .17 Rem.). Mfg. 1982-present.

Mfg.'s Sug. Retail	$585	$475	$370	$275	$225	$205	$180	$165

Add 5%-10% for .17 Rem. cal.
Add 10% for .222 Rem. cal.

All steel Model Sevens (including floor plate and triggerguard) are currently commanding a small premium.

* **Model Seven SS** — .223 Rem. (new 1997), .243 Win., .260 Rem. (new 1997), .308 Win., or 7mm-08 Rem. cal., features stainless steel construction, 20 in. barrel w/o sights, and synthetic stock. New 1994.

Mfg.'s Sug. Retail	$641	$510	$395	$295

* **Model Seven Youth** — .243 Win., 6mm Rem. (disc. 1995), .260 Rem. (new 1998), .308 Win. (disc.), or 7mm-08 Rem. (new 1994) cal., uncheckered hardwood stock shortened 1 in., 6 lbs. New 1993.

Mfg.'s Sug. Retail	$479	$390	$345	$285	$225	$205	$180	$165

Grading	100%	98%	95%	90%	80%	70%	60%

R

* ***Model Seven FS*** — .243 Win., 7mm-08 Rem., or .308 Win. cal., 18½ in. parkerized blue barrel, grey or grey camo Kevlar fiberglass stock, adj. rear sight, 5¼ lbs. Mfg. 1987-89 only.

	$525	$455	$415	$375	$335	$310	$285

Last Mfg.'s Sug. Retail was $600.

* ***Model Seven Custom MS (Mannlicher Stock)*** — .222 Rem., .22-250 Rem., .223 Rem., .243 Win., .250 Savage, .257 Roberts, .260 Rem. (new 1997), .308 Win., .35 Rem., .350 Rem. Mag., 6mm Rem., or 7mm-08 Rem. cal., features 20 in. custom shop barrel with Model 7 action bedded to a Mannlicher style laminate full stock. New 1994.

Mfg.'s Sug. Retail	$1,208	$1,025	$775	$565	$485	$425	$385	$340

This model is available from the Custom Shop only (special order).

* ***Model Seven Custom KS*** — .223 Rem. (new 1989), .260 Rem. (new 1998), 7mm BR Rem. (mfg. 1989-1993), 7mm-08 Rem. (new 1989), .308 Win. (new 1991), .35 Rem. or .350 Rem. Mag. cal., 20 in. barrel with (.35 Rem. or .350 Rem. Mag.) or w/o sights, synthetic Kevlar stock with solid recoil pad. New 1987.

Mfg.'s Sug. Retail	$1,193	$1,000	$760	$550	$475	$425	$385	$340

This model is available from the Custom Shop only (special order).

MODEL 30A BOLT ACTION RIFLE — Enfield M/1917 type action, 7x57mm Mauser, .30-06, .25 Rem., .30 Rem., .32 Rem., or .35 Rem. cal., 22 in. barrel, checkered pistol grip stock. Mfg. 1921-1940.

	$550	$475	$400	$350	$300	$260	$200

MODEL 30R CARBINE — similar to Model 30A, with 20 in. barrel.

	$575	$500	$450	$375	$325	$275	$225

MODEL 30S — deluxe version of Model 30A, .257 Roberts, 7x57mm Mauser, or .30-06 cal., 24 in. barrel, Lyman receiver sight, special stock. Mfg. 1930-1940.

	$625	$550	$500	$450	$375	$300	$250

MODEL 78 SPORTSMAN BOLT ACTION — .223 Rem., .243 Win., .270 Win., .30-06, or .308 Win. cal., 22 in. barrel, 4 shot mag., uncheckered hardwood stock, open sights, 7 lbs. Mfg. 1984-89.

	$270	$235	$210	$190	$170	$160	$150

Last Mfg.'s Sug. Retail was $333.

MODEL 600 BOLT ACTION — .222 Rem., .223 Rem. (very rare), 6mm Rem., .243 Win., .308 Win., or .35 Rem. cal., 18½ in. VR barrel, dog leg bolt handle, checkered pistol grip stock. 94,086 were mfg. 1964-1968.

Reg. cals.	$450	$350	$275	$210	$195	$175	$155
.35 Rem.	$525	$410	$350	$320	$295	$270	$250
.222 Rem.	$495	$465	$425	$385	$350	$325	$295
.223 Rem.	$925	$800	$700	$500	$400	$350	$325

315 Model 600s in .223 Rem. cal. were mfg.

* ***Model 600 Montana Centennial*** — 6mm Rem., 1,020 mfg. in 1964 only.

	$850	$700	$450				

Last Mfg.'s Sug. Retail was $125.

MODEL 600 MAGNUM — 6.5mm Rem. Mag. or .350 Rem. Mag. cal., laminated walnut/beech stock with or without recoil pad (early mfg. walnut stocks did not have recoil pad). Mfg. 1965-1968.

	$750	$650	$550	$500	$460	$440	$420

During 1964, early guns had a non-laminated walnut stock w/o recoil pad, with barrel markings ".350 Rem. Magnum".

MODEL 600 MOHAWK — .222 Rem., 6mm Rem., .243 Win., or .308 Win. cal., this variation was a promotional model, 18½ in. barrel with no rib. 94,920 were mfg. in 1971-1980.

	$375	$300	$285	$265	$240	$225	$200

Grading	100%	98%	95%	90%	80%	70%	60%

MODEL 660 BOLT ACTION — .222 Rem., 6mm Rem., .243 Win., or .308 Win. cal., 20 in. barrel, open sight, dog leg bolt handle, checkered pistol grip stock, black pistol grip cap and forend tip. 50,536 were mfg. 1968-1971.

	$495	$465	$425	$385	$350	$325	$295

Add 10% for .222 Rem. cal.

* .223 Rem. cal. — 227 total mfg. This cal. was never listed in a Remington catalog.

	$1,100	$875	$725	$600	$500	$400	$350

R

MODEL 660 MAGNUM — 6.5mm Rem. Mag. or .350 Rem. Mag. cal., laminated stock and recoil pad.

	$750	$650	$550	$450	$400	$350	$300

MODEL 720A BOLT ACTION — Enfield type action, .257 Roberts, .270 Win., or .30-06 cal., 22 in. barrel, open sights, 5 shot, checkered pistol grip stock, 2,500 mfg. 1941-1944.

	$1,150	$975	$850	$700	$600	$500	$400

Add 50%+ for .270 Win. cal.
Add 100%+ for .257 Roberts cal.

920-1,000 Model 720As were purchased by the Dept. of Navy during 1942 and used as trophies - these are discernible by crossed cannon proofs on wood.

Most of this model was chambered for .30-06 cal. Approx. 100 were chambered for .270 Win. and 20 or less were chambered for the .257 Roberts.

MODEL 720R — similar to 720A, except with 20 in. barrel.

	$1,250	$1,050	$900	$750	$650	$550	$450

This is the rarest variation in the Model 720 Series.

MODEL 720S — similar to 720A, except with 24 in. barrel.

	$1,200	$1,000	$850	$700	$600	$500	$400

MODEL 721 BOLT ACTION — .270 Win., .280 Rem., or .30-06 cal., 24 in. barrel, open sights, 4 shot, plain pistol grip stock. Mfg. 1948-1962.

	$350	$275	$225	$200	$165	$155	$145

.280 Rem. (688 mfg.) and .264 Win. Mag. (1,115 mfg.) are rare in this model. 100% condition on these calibers could bring $700+.

MODEL 721ADL — similar to Model 721A, except has deluxe checkered stock.

	$415	$375	$350	$300	$250	$200	$175

The above model suffix does not appear on the gun. ADL features will determine the model.

MODEL 721BDL — similar to 721ADL, except has extra select wood.

	$550	$500	$425	$375	$325	$300	$275

The above model suffix does not appear on the gun. BDL features will determine the model.

MODEL 721A MAGNUM — .264 Win. Mag. or .300 H&H cal., 26 in. heavy barrel, recoil pad, 3 shot mag., 8¼ lbs.

	$525	$450	$360	$320	$295	$275	$260

MODEL 721ADL MAGNUM — similar to 721A Mag., checkered.

	$595	$500	$400	$350	$315	$290	$275

MODEL 721BDL MAGNUM — similar to 721ADL Mag., select wood.

	$695	$575	$475	$425	$385	$360	$330

Grading	100%	98%	95%	90%	80%	70%	60%

MODEL 722(A) — short action version of 721A, .222 Rem., .222 Rem. Mag., .223 Rem., .243 Win., .244 Rem., .257 Roberts, .264 Win. Mag., .300 Savage, or .308 Win. cal., 7 lbs. Mfg. 1948-1962.

	$350	$300	$275	$250	$225	$200	$180

Subtract 10% for .300 Savage cal.
Add 20% for .257 Roberts or .308 Win. cal.

.222 Rem. Mag. (3,803 mfg.) and .243 Win. (2,186 mfg.) are rare in this model. Add approx. 25% to above values for these cals.

MODEL 722ADL — similar to Model 722(A), except with deluxe checkered wood.

	$450	$375	$350	$300	$275	$225	$200

The above model suffix does not appear on the gun. ADL features will determine the model.

MODEL 722BDL — similar to Model 722ADL, except features extra select wood.

	$575	$475	$400	$340	$300	$265	$245

The above model suffix does not appear on the gun. BDL features will determine the model.

MODEL 725ADL BOLT ACTION — .222 Rem., .243 Win., .244 Rem., .270 Win., .280 Rem., or .30-06 cal., 22 in. barrel, open sights, 4 shot, checkered Monte Carlo stock. 16,635 mfg. 1958-1961.

.30-06 cal.	$500	$425	$375	$350	$325	$300	$280
.270 Win.	$550	$500	$450	$400	$375	$350	$325
.280 Rem.	$650	$575	$500	$450	$400	$350	$325
.222 Rem.	$650	$525	$475	$425	$375	$350	$325
.244 Rem.	$650	$525	$475	$425	$375	$350	$325
.243 Win.	$650	$525	$475	$425	$375	$350	$325

Caliber mfg. breakdown is as follows: 7,657 in .30-06; 2,784 in .280 Rem.; 2,818 in .270 Win.; 840 in .244 Rem.; 1,478 in .222 Rem.; 998 in .243 Win.

MODEL 725 KODIAK — .375 H&H Mag. or .458 Win. Mag. cal., 26 in. barrel, 3 shot, recoil reducer in muzzle, deluxe checkered Monte Carlo stock, black pistol grip cap and forend tip. 52 mfg. 1961 only.

	$3,800	$3,000	$2,700	$2,250	$2,000	$1,800	$1,650

Only 24 rifles in .458 Win. Mag. were mfg. and 28 rifles in .375 H&H Mag.

MODEL 788 BOLT ACTION — .222 Rem., .22-250 Rem., .223 Rem., 6mm Rem., .243 Win., .308 Win., .30-30 Win., 7mm-08 Rem., or .44 Mag. cal., 18½ (Carbine), 22, or 24 in. barrel, open sight, plain pistol grip Monte Carlo stock. Mfg. 1967-1983.

Rifle	$350	$275	$250	$225	$210	$200	$185
Carbine (18½ in. barrel)	$350	$275	$250	$225	$210	$200	$185

Add 10% for .30-30 Win. cal.
Add 15% for 7mm-08 Rem. cal.
Add 30% for .44 Mag. cal.

RIFLES: BOLT ACTION, MODEL 700 & VARIATIONS

MODEL 700ADL DELUXE RIFLE/CARBINE — .22-250 Rem. (disc. 1991), .222 Rem. (disc.), .222 Rem. Mag. (disc.), .25-06 Rem. (disc. 1991), 6mm Rem. (disc.), .243 Win. (disc. 1997), .270 Win., .280 Rem. (disc. 1997 - marked 7mm Express 1979-82), .30-06, .308 Win., or 7mm Rem. Mag. cal., 20 (carbine, disc.), 22, or 24 in. barrel, open sights, 4 shot mag., checkered Monte Carlo stock or brown laminated stock (new 1988). Mfg. 1962-present.

Mfg.'s Sug. Retail	$492		$395	$330	$260	$210	$175	$165	$155

Add $27 for 7mm Rem. Mag. cal.
Add 20% for 20 in. carbine model.
Add 50% for .222 Rem. Mag. or .280 Rem. cal. in carbine variation.
Add 15% for 7mm Rem. Mag., .264 Win. Mag., or .300 Win. Mag. cal. with stainless steel barrel (mfg. 1962-1970).

Remington, in 1987-89, introduced a Model 700 Gun Kit that enabled the owner to assemble the stock to the barreled action. All metal work is completely finished and wood finishing is all that is required. This kit was available in most popular cals. - last mfg.'s sug. retail price was $333 (1989). Add $20 for 7mm Rem. Mag. cal.

* Model 700ADL Synthetic — similar cals. as Model 700ADL Deluxe, except also available in .22-250 Rem. (new 1999), .223 Rem., .243 Win., or .300 Win. Mag. (new 1999), features fiberglass reinforced synthetic stock with positive checkering, black matte finish on metal/wood, open sights. Approx. 7⅜ lbs. New 1996.

Mfg.'s Sug. Retail	$425	$345	$270	$225	$200	$185	$170	$155

Add $27 for .300 Win. Mag. or 7mm Rem. Mag. cal.

➤ Model 700ADL Synthetic Youth — .243 Win. or .308 Win. cal., 20 in. barrel with 1 in. shorter stock. New 1998.

Mfg.'s Sug. Retail	$425	$345	$270	$225	$200	$185	$170	$155

* Model 700ADL/LS — .243 Win. (new 1989), .270 Win. (new 1989), .30-06, or 7mm Rem. Mag. cal., brown laminate stock with checkering. Mfg. 1988-1993.

			$400	$345	$275	$230	$210	$195	$165

Last Mfg.'s Sug. Retail was $485.

Add $27 for 7mm Rem. Mag. cal.

MODEL 700BDL CUSTOM DELUXE — .17 Rem., .22-250 Rem., .222 Rem., .223 Rem., .243 Win., .25-06 Rem., .264 Win. Mag. (disc.), .270 Win., .280 Rem. (mfg. 1992-95), .300 Savage (mfg. 1992 only), .30-06, .308 Win. (disc. 1995), .35 Whelen (mfg. 1989-94), 6mm Rem. (disc. 1994), 7mm Rem. Mag., 7mm-08 Rem. (disc. 1994), .300 Win. Mag., .300 Rem. Ultra Mag (new 1999), .338 Win. Mag. (mfg. 1988-94, resumed 1997), or 8mm Mag. (disc.) cal., similar to 700ADL Deluxe, except with hinged floorplate, cut skipline checkering, black pistol grip cap and forend tip, receiver and floorplate engraving became standard in 1997, Supplied with iron sights first year.

Mfg.'s Sug. Retail	$585	$475	$385	$325	$280	$250	$220	$195
.222 Rem. Mag.		$550	$475	$400	$340	$300	$280	$260
.350 Rem. Mag.		$650	$525	$425	$350	$325	$300	$275
6.5mm Rem. Mag.		$650	$525	$425	$350	$325	$300	$275

Add $27-$54 for left-hand model (available in certain cals. only).
Add $27 for .17 Rem., 7mm Rem. Mag., .300 Win. Mag., .300 Rem. Ultra Mag., or .338 Win. Mag. cal.
Add 15% for 7mm Rem. Mag., .264 Win. Mag., or .300 Win. Mag. cal. with stainless steel barrel (mfg. 1962-1970).

Remington mfg. the Model 700BDL in .350 Rem. Mag. and 6.5mm Rem. Mag. Approx. 1,500 were assembled in 1969 only. The .350 Rem. Mag. mfg. in 1969 is 3 times rarer than the 1985 Model 700 Classic chambered for .350 Rem. Mag.

MODEL 700BDL DM (DETACHABLE MAG.) — .243 Win., .25-06 Rem. (disc. 1997), .270 Win., .280 Rem., 6mm Rem. (disc. 1996), 7mm Rem. Mag., 7mm-08 Rem., .30-06, .308 Win. (disc. 1996), .300 Win. Mag., or .338 Win. Mag. (disc. 1996) cal., Monte Carlo walnut stock with 20 LPI skip-line checkering, high polish bluing, black forend cap, receiver and floorplate engraving became standard in 1997, open sights, 3-4 shot detachable mag. New 1995.

Mfg.'s Sug. Retail	$639	$525	$440	$355	$315	$285	$265	$250

Add $26 for .300 Win. Mag. and 7mm Rem. Mag. cals.
Add $26-$53 for left-hand model (available in certain cals. only).

Grading	100%	98%	95%	90%	80%	70%	60%

R

* **Model 700BDL Lew Horton Special Edition** — .257 Roberts cal., 500 mfg. in 1990 only, first time the 700BDL has been offered in .257 Roberts cal.

| | $575 | $525 | $450 | $395 | $360 | $325 | $280 |

Last Mfg.'s Sug. Retail was $580.

MODEL 700BDL EUROPEAN — .243 Win., .270 Win., .280 Rem., 7mm-08 Rem., 7mm Rem. Mag., .30-06, or .308 Win. cal., Monte Carlo stock with hand-rubbed oil finish, 22 or 24 (Mag. cals. only) in. barrel, hinged floorplate, iron sights, approx. 7¼ lbs. Disc. 1994

| | $445 | $375 | $325 | $280 | $250 | $220 | $195 |

Last Mfg.'s Sug. Retail was $532.

    Add $27 for 7mm Rem. Mag. cal.

MODEL 700BDL MOUNTAIN RIFLE (FIXED MAG.) — .243 Win. (new 1988), .25-06 Rem. (new 1992), .257 Roberts (new 1991), .270 Win., 7mm-08 Rem., .280 Rem., .30-06, .308 Win. (new 1988), or 7x57mm Mauser (new 1990) cal., 22 in. tapered barrel, checkered satin finished American walnut stock with cheekpiece and ebony forend, 4 shot mag., without sights, 6¾ lbs. Mfg. 1986-94.

| | $445 | $380 | $315 | $275 | $250 | $220 | $195 |

Last Mfg.'s Sug. Retail was $532.

* **Model 700BDL Mountain Stainless** — .25-06 Rem., .270 Win., .280 Rem., or .30-06 cal., 22 in. barrel, black synthetic stock with pressed checkering, blind mag., 7¼ lbs. Mfg. 1993 only.

| | $450 | $385 | $315 | | | | |

Last Mfg.'s Sug. Retail was $532.

MODEL 700 MOUNTAIN RIFLE DM (DETACHABLE MAG.) — .243 Win. (disc. 1997), .260 Rem. (new 1998), .25-06 Rem., .270 Win., .280 Rem., 7mm-08 Rem., or .30-06 cal., detachable mag., satin finished American walnut stock, satin bluing, without sights, 6¾ lbs. New 1995.

| Mfg.'s Sug. Retail | $639 | $530 | $445 | $355 | $315 | $285 | $265 | $250 |

* **Model 700 Mountain LSS** — .260 Rem., .270 Win., .30-06, or 7mm-08 Rem. cal., features stainless action and 22 in. barrel w/o sights, brown laminate stock, approx. 6½ lbs. New 1999.

| Mfg.'s Sug. Retail | $688 | | $565 | $465 | $375 | | | |

MODEL 700 CUSTOM KS MOUNTAIN RIFLE — .270 Win., .280 Rem., .300 Win. Mag., .300 Wby. Mag. (new 1989), .300 Rem. Ultra Mag. (new 1999), .30-06, .338 Win. Mag. (new 1986), .35 Whelen (new 1989), 7mm STW (new 1999), 7mm Rem. Mag., 8mm Rem. Mag. (new 1986), or .375 H&H cal., 22 in. barrel, features extra lightweight Kevlar fiber-reinforced stock, available in either right or left-hand action. New 1986.

| Mfg.'s Sug. Retail | $1,193 | | $965 | $800 | $585 | $485 | $415 | $385 | $350 |

    Add $72 for left-hand action.

    This model is available from the Custom Shop only (special order).

* **Model 700 Custom KS Mountain Stainless Rifle** — similar to Model 700 Custom KS Mountain Rifle, except has stainless steel action and barrel, not available in .35 Whelen or 8mm Rem. Mag. cal., not available in left-hand action. New 1995.

| Mfg.'s Sug. Retail | $1,361 | | $1,150 | $900 | $700 | | | |

* **Model 700 Mountain Rifle Custom KS Wood Grained Kevlar** — similar to Model 700 Custom KS Safari Grade, except has wood grained Kevlar stock. Mfg. 1992-1993.

| | $1,000 | $875 | $750 | $650 | $550 | $485 | $430 |

Last Mfg.'s Sug. Retail was $1,109.

    Add $63 for left-hand action.

MODEL 700 SENDERO SPECIAL — .25-06 Rem., .270 Win., .300 Win. Mag., or 7mm Rem. Mag. cal., similar to Model 700 VS, except has long action for Mag. cals., 24 (non-cataloged) or 26 in. barrel, 9 lbs. New 1994.

| Mfg.'s Sug. Retail | $705 | | $580 | $475 | $400 | $325 | $295 | $265 | $250 |

    Add $27 for Mag. cals.
    Add $100 for fluted barrel (not cataloged).

Grading	100%	98%	95%	90%	80%	70%	60%

* **Model 700 Sendero SF (Stainless Fluted)** — .25-06 Rem., .300 Win. Mag., .300 Wby. Mag. (new 1997), .300 Rem. Ultra Mag. (new 1999), 7mm STW (new 1997) or 7mm Rem. Mag. cal., 26 in. varmint type fluted barrel, approx. 8½ lbs. New 1996.
  Mfg.'s Sug. Retail $852 $725 $585 $460
  Add $27 for Mag. cals.

MODEL 700 SENDERO COMPOSITE — .25-06 Rem., .300 Win. Mag., or 7mm STW cal., features 26 in. composite barrel, matte black finished steel action, Kevlar reinforced black synthetic stock, 7⅞ lbs. New 1999.
  Mfg.'s Sug. Retail $1,665 $1,395 $1,125 $750 $650 $575 $525 $475
  Add $27 for .300 Win. Mag. or 7mm STW cal.

MODEL 700 CAMO SYNTHETIC — .22-250 Rem. (disc. 1993), .243 Win., .270 Win. (disc. 1993), .280 Rem. (disc. 1993), 7mm-08 Rem. (disc. 1993), 7mm Rem. Mag., .30-06, .308 Win. (disc. 1993), or .300 Wby. Mag. (disc. 1993) cal., 22 or 24 (Mag. only) in. barrel, features synthetic stock and is fully camouflaged in Mossy Oak Bottomland pattern, iron sights, approx. 7¼ lbs. Mfg. 1992-94.
  $490 $425 $350 $315 $285 $265 $250
  Last Mfg.'s Sug. Retail was $581.
  Add $27 for Mag. cals.

MODEL 700BDL SS (STAINLESS SYNTHETIC) — .223 Rem. (mfg. 1993-94), .243 Win. (mfg. 1993-94), .25-06 Rem. (disc. 1994), .270 Win., .280 Rem. (disc. 1995), .30-06, . 308 (disc. 1994), 7mm Rem. (mfg. 1993-94), 7mm-08 Rem. (mfg. 1993-94), .300 Win. Mag. (new 1993), .300 Rem. Ultra Mag. (new 1999), .300 Wby. Mag. (mfg. 1993-94), .338 Win. Mag. (mfg. 1993-94, resumed 1997), 7mm Rem. Mag., 7mm Wby. Mag. (scarce, disc. 1994), .375 H&H (new 1997) cal., features matte finished 416 stainless steel barrel, receiver, and bolt, black synthetic stock with checkering, drilled and tapped, hinged floorplate mag., 24 in. barrel, no sights, 6¼ - 7 lbs. New 1992.
  Mfg.'s Sug. Retail $641 $525 $440 $350
  Add $27 for Mag. cals.

* **Model 700LSS** — .270 Win. (left-hand only), .300 Win. Mag., .300 Rem. Ultra Mag. (new 1999), .30-06 (left-hand only), or 7mm Rem. Mag. cal., stainless steel barreled action, grey tinted laminate Monte Carlo wood stock, 24 in. barrel, w/o sights, 7½ lbs. New 1996.
  Mfg.'s Sug. Retail $715 $585 $465 $375
  Add $26 for left-hand action (all cals.).

* **Model 700BDL SS DM (Detachable Mag.)** — .243 Win. (disc. 1997), .25-06 Rem., .260 Rem. (new 1997), .270 Win., .280 Rem., 6mm Rem. (disc. 1995), 7mm Rem. Mag., 7mm-08 Rem. (disc. 1998), .30-06, .308 Win., .300 Win. Mag., .300 Wby. Mag., or .338 Win. Mag.(disc. 1996) cal., features 3-4 shot detachable mag., stainless steel, 24 in. barrel, satin finish metalwork, black non-reflective stock with checkering, receiver and floorplate engraving became standard in 1997, w/o sights, 7⅜ lbs. New 1995.
  Mfg.'s Sug. Retail $702 $600 $525 $450
  Add $27 for Mag. cals.
  Add $87 for muzzle brake (Model 700BDL SS DM-B, new 1996, available in 7mm STW, 7mm Rem. Mag. or .300 Win. Mag. cals. only).

MODEL 700BDL VARMINT SPECIAL — .22-250 Rem., .222 Rem., .223 Rem., .25-06 Rem.(disc.), 6mm Rem., .243 Win., .308 Win., or 7mm-08 Rem. cal., 24 in. heavy barrel, checkered walnut stock, no sights. Mfg. 1967-1994.
  $480 $420 $350 $315 $285 $265 $250
  Last Mfg.'s Sug. Retail was $565.

Grading	100%	98%	95%	90%	80%	70%	60%

* **Model 700VS (Varmint Synthetic)** — .220 Swift (disc. 1996), .22-250 Rem., .223 Rem., .243 Win. (mfg. 1997-98), or .308 Win. cal., composite, textured black and grey synthetic stock features Kevlar, fiberglass, and graphite, matte metal finish, 26 in. barrel w/o sights, 9 lbs. New 1992, right hand action disc. 1998.

  Mfg.'s Sug. Retail $732   **$595**   **$435**   **$395**   **$325**   **$295**   **$265**   **$250**
  Subtract approx. $30 for right hand action.

  The right hand model was disc. 1998 - values above are for left-hand action only (not available in .243 Win.).

* **Model 700VS SF/SF-P (Varmint Synthetic Stainless Fluted/Ported)** — .220 Swift (ported barrel only beginning 1999), .22-250 Rem., .223 Rem. (w/o porting), or .308 Win. (ported barrel only beginning 1999) cal., stainless steel action with 26 in. barrel with flutes, 2 barrel ports became an option in some cals. during 1998 (Model SF-P). New 1994.

  Mfg.'s Sug. Retail $852   **$715**   **$560**   **$450**
  Add $20 for ported barrel (Model 700VS SF-P).

* **Model 700 VLS (Varmint Laminated Stock)** — .222 Rem. (mfg. 1995 only), .22-250 Rem., .223 Rem., .243 Win., 6mm Rem. (new 1998), .260 Rem., .308 Win., or 7mm-08 Rem. (new 1997) cal., 26 in. heavy barrel, blued metalwork, w/o sights, brown laminated stock with skip line checkering, beavertail shaped forend became standard 1998, 9⅜ lbs. New 1995.

  Mfg.'s Sug. Retail $625   **$520**   **$440**   **$355**   **$315**   **$285**   **$265**   **$250**

MODEL 700VS COMPOSITE — .22-250 Rem., .223 Rem., or .308 Win. cal., similar to Model 700 Sendero Composite, except is available in short action only. New 1999.

  Mfg.'s Sug. Retail $1,665   **$1,395** **$1,125**   **$750**   **$650**   **$575**   **$525**   **$475**

MODEL 700 SAFARI GRADE — .375 H&H, 8mm Rem. Mag. (new 1986), .416 Rem. Mag. (new 1989), or .458 Win. Mag. cal., heavier 700BDL action, 3 shot mag., 24 in. barrel, available with either Classic or Monte Carlo stock configuration, Custom Shop special order only, 9 lbs. Mfg. 1962-present.

  Mfg.'s Sug. Retail $1,197   **$995**   **$795**   **$585**   **$440**   **$415**   **$385**   **$330**
  Add $73 for left-hand model (Classic stock only).

* **Model 700 Custom KS Safari Grade** — 8mm Rem. Mag., .375 H&H, .416 Rem. Mag., or .458 Win. Mag. cal., stock made from extra lightweight Kevlar fiber, 24 in. barrel. New 1989.

  Mfg.'s Sug. Retail $1,378   **$1,175**   **$900**   **$730**   **$640**   **$560**   **$485**   **$430**
  Add $75 for left-hand model.

* **Model 700 Custom KS Safari Stainless** — .375 H&H, .416 Rem. Mag., or .458 Win. Mag. cal., features Kevlar stock and stainless steel action. Introduced 1993.

  Mfg.'s Sug. Retail $1,540   **$1,250**   **$995**   **$695**

MODEL 700 APR (AFRICAN PLAINS RIFLE) — .300 Win. Mag., .300 Wby. Mag., .300 Rem. Ultra Mag. (new 1999), .338 Win. Mag., .375 H&H, or 7mm Rem. Mag cal., custom shop variation with 26 in. custom shop barrel, satin finish metal and brown, pressure laminated, checkered wood stock with satin finish and butt pad. New 1994.

  Mfg.'s Sug. Retail $1,554   **$1,325** **$1,075**   **$925**   **$775**   **$650**   **$550**   **$485**

MODEL 700 ALASKAN WILDERNESS RIFLE — .300 Win. Mag., .300 Wby. Mag., .300 Rem. Ultra Mag. (new 1999), .338 Win. Mag., .375 H&H, 7mm STW (new 1998), or 7mm Rem. Mag. cal., black synthetic Kevlar stock, stainless steel action plated with satin finished black chrome. New 1994.

  Mfg.'s Sug. Retail $1,445   **$1,225** **$1,000**   **$765**

Grading	100%	98%	95%	90%	80%	70%	60%

MODEL 700BDL CLASSIC (LTD. EDITION) — similar to 700BDL, except has classic straight stock, high polish bluing, has been offered in .17 Rem., .220 Swift, .222 Rem., .22-250 Rem., .250 Savage (250/3000), 6.5x55mm Swedish, 6mm Rem., 7x57mm Mauser, 8mm Rem. Mag., .243 Win., .25-06 Rem., .257 Roberts, .264 Win. Mag., .270 Win., .280 Rem., .300 Win. Mag., .300 Wby. Mag., .30-06, 7mm Wby. Mag., .338 Win. Mag.,.350 Rem. Mag., .35 Whelen, .300 H&H, or .375 H&H cal. The original Model 700 Classic was mfg. 1978-1985. Limited edition calibers were introduced during 1981, and continue to be produced annually.

R

Mfg.'s Sug. Retail	$612	$500	$415	$335	$265	$250	$220	$195

> The Model 700 Classic was originally introduced in 1978 in .22-250 Rem., 6mm Rem., .243 Win., .270 Win., .30-06, and 7mm Rem. Mag., and was part of the standard Remington product lineup until 1985. Limited editions were introduced during 1981, and are still being produced today.

> This model is produced in limited quantities of a different caliber each year. Add premiums for several calibers in NIB condition only (including 7x57mm Mauser, .257 Roberts, .300 H&H, and .375 H&H).

> The following is a list of annual Limited Classic calibers offered previously with year of manufacture: 7x57mm Mauser (1981), .257 Roberts (1982), .300 H&H (1983), .250 Savage (1984), .350 Rem. Mag. (1985), .264 Win. Mag. (1986), .338 Win. Mag. (1987), .35 Whelen (1988), .300 Wby. Mag. (1989), .25-06 Rem. (1990), 7mm Wby. Mag. (1991), .220 Swift (1992), and .222 Rem. (1993), 6.5x55mm Swedish (new 1994), .300 Win. Mag. (1995), .375 H&H Mag. (1996), .280 Rem. (1997), 8mm Rem. Mag. (1998), .17 Rem. (1999).

MODEL 700 AS — .22-250 Rem., .243 Win., .270 Win., .280 Rem., .30-06, .308 Win., 7mm Rem. Mag., or .300 Wby. Mag. cal., synthetic stock is made from Arylon resin, matte black finished stock and metal, 22 or 24 in. barrel, 6½ lbs. Mfg. 1989-91 only.

			$445	$370	$310	$275	$250	$220	$195
									Last Mfg.'s Sug. Retail was $528.

> Add $21 for 7mm Rem. Mag. or .300 Wby. Mag. cal.

MODEL 700 RS — .270 Win., .280 Rem., or .30-06 cal., 22 in. polished blue barrel, grey or grey camo DuPont Rynite synthetic stock with smooth cheekpiece and solid recoil pad, iron sights, 7¼ lbs. Mfg. 1987-1988 only.

			$500	$450	$410	$370	$335	$310	$285
									Last Mfg.'s Sug. Retail was $547.

> Add 25% for .280 Rem. cal.

> In 1987 less than 500 rifles were dual barrel marked - 7mm EXP REM .280 REM. These specimens will command a 40% premium.

MODEL 700 FS — .243 Win., .270 Win., .30-06, .308 Win., or 7mm Rem. Mag. cal., 22 in. polished blue barrel, grey or grey camo Kevlar fiberglass stock with solid recoil pad, iron sights, 6¼ lbs. Mfg. 1987-1988 only.

			$530	$460	$415	$375	$335	$310	$285
									Last Mfg.'s Sug. Retail was $613.

> Add $20 for 7mm Rem. Mag. cal. (24 in. barrel).

MODEL 700C GRADE — from custom shop, no engraving, deluxe checkered wood with rosewood forearm cap. Mfg 1964-1983.

			$850	$775	$695	$635	$510	$440	$400

MODEL 700D PEERLESS GRADE — scroll engraving, best wood. Mfg. 1962-1983.

		$1,650	$1,400	$1,200	$1,000	$880	$825	$690

MODEL 700F PREMIER GRADE — elaborate engraving, best wood. Mfg. 1962-1983.

		$3,250	$2,750	$2,420	$2,200	$2,035	$1,870	$1,760

Grading	100%	98%	95%	90%	80%	70%	60%

MODEL 700 CUSTOM GRADE — special order only, grades differ in amount of engraving and type of walnut. Available as a custom order only through Remington. Values below reflect 1991 information. The Remington Custom Shop should be contacted for a current price quotation and the availability of options.

> Special order Model 700s mfg. between early '60s - 1982 were designated C Grade, D Grade, or F Grade. Values will approximate Custom Grade Models I-III listed below. In 1991, Remington discontinued Custom Grade Model designations.

* *Model 700 Custom Grade Model I* — mfg. 1983-1991.

	100%	98%	95%
	$1,200	$1,000	$795

Last Mfg.'s Sug. Retail was $1,314.

* *Model 700 Custom Grade Model II* — mfg. 1983-1991.

	100%	98%	95%
	$1,995	$1,675	$1,295

Last Mfg.'s Sug. Retail was $2,335.

* *Model 700 Custom Grade Model III* — mfg. 1983-1991.

	100%	98%	95%
	$2,900	$2,150	$1,750

Last Mfg.'s Sug. Retail was $3,650.

* *Model 700 Custom Grade Model IV* — mfg. 1983-1991.

	100%	98%	95%
	$4,875	$4,100	$2,950

Last Mfg.'s Sug. Retail was $5,695.

MODEL 700 CUSTOM RIFLE — the Remington Custom Shop should be contacted directly (see Trademark Index) for current information regarding this model. New 1992.

	100%	98%	95%	90%	80%	70%	60%
Mfg.'s Sug. Retail $2,747	$2,225	$1,850	$1,325	$1,050	$875	$750	$625

> Beginning 1992, Remington stopped Custom Grade Model designations in favor of individualized quotations per work order. The suggested retail price for this model is the starting price with the minimum number of options. The Custom Shop should be contacted directly regarding special order pricing (see Trademark Index).

RIFLES: BOLT ACTION, MODEL 40X & VARIATIONS

MODEL 40X SPORTER — .22 LR cal. only, sporterized version of the 40X Target Rifle, 5 shot clip, custom 700 stock, a special order only gun from the factory. Rare, less than 700 mfg. 1969-1977, parts clean-up to 1980.

	100%	98%	95%	90%	80%	70%	60%
	$1,850	$1,325	$925	$800	$720	$650	$595

Add 10% if NIB.

This model was last listed in the 1977 Remington catalog — retail was $525.

MODEL 40X TARGET RIFLE — .22 LR cal., 28 in. heavy barrel, Redfield Olympic sights, scope bases, target stock, rubber butt, 12¾ lbs. Mfg. 1955-1964.

	100%	98%	95%	90%	80%	70%	60%
	$800	$700	$600	$525	$450	$375	$325
No sights	$750	$650	$550	$475	$400	$350	$300

MODEL 40X STANDARD BARREL — similar to 40X Target Rifle, with lighter barrel, 10¾ lbs.

	100%	98%	95%	90%	80%	70%	60%
	$550	$475	$380	$310	$250	$220	$190
No sights	$495	$450	$360	$295	$240	$200	$180

MODEL 40X CENTERFIRE — similar to Model 40X Rim Fire, except in .222 Rem., .222 Rem. Mag., .30-06, or .308 Win. cal. Mfg. 1961-1964.

	100%	98%	95%	90%	80%	70%	60%
	$550	$475	$380	$310	$250	$220	$190
No sights	$495	$450	$360	$295	$240	$200	$180

MODEL 40-XB RANGEMASTER RIMFIRE — .22 LR cal., bolt action single shot, 28 in. light or heavy barrel, no sights, target stock with guide rail, rubber butt. Mfg. 1964-1974.

	100%	98%	95%	90%	80%	70%	60%
	$575	$525	$420	$335	$275	$220	$195

Add a premium for this model equipped with a mag.

Grading	100%	98%	95%	90%	80%	70%	60%

MODEL 40-XB RANGEMASTER CENTERFIRE — 15 short action cals. between .220 Swift and .300 Win. Mag., custom made, 27½ in. barrel (current model is stainless), single shot or repeater, walnut stock, test fired, 10½ - 11 lbs. Mfg. 1964-present.

Mfg.'s Sug. Retail	$1,529	$1,250	$975	$700	$550	$450	$375	$325

   Add $116 for repeater model.
   Add $62 for left-hand action (disc. 1994).

   An International Free Rifle was also offered - only 107 were mfg. with premiums being paid.

MODEL 40-XB KS (KEVLAR STOCK) — .220 Swift cal., 27¼ in. bright finished stainless steel barrel, single shot or repeater, black finish Kevlar stock, no sights, 9¾ lbs. New 1987.

Mfg.'s Sug. Retail	$1,726	$1,465	$1,025	$750

   Subtract $139 for bench rest model (Model 40-XBBR KS).
   Add $115 for repeater model.
   Add $193 for 2 oz. trigger.

MODEL 40-XC KS — .223 Rem. (new 1995) or .308 Win. cal., National Match Course repeater rifle, adj. trigger pull, wood (disc. 1989) or Kevlar (standard 1990) stock.

Mfg.'s Sug. Retail	$1,702	$1,450	$1,025	$750

   Subtract approx. $120 for wood stock.

MODEL 40-XR KS RIMFIRE SINGLE SHOT — .22 LR cal., 24 in. heavy barrel, no sights, adj. butt plate and palm stop, target wood (disc. 1989) or Kevlar (standard 1990) stock. Mfg. 1974-present.

Mfg.'s Sug. Retail	$1,585	$1,325	$975	$750

   Subtract approx. $120 for wood stock.
   Add $103 for benchrest model (Model 40-XR BR) with stainless barrel.

MODEL 40-XR KS SPORTER — .22 LR cal., Model 40-XR action, match chambered, custom sporter contoured 24 in. barrel, drilled and tapped receiver, w/o sights, special order. New 1994.

Mfg.'s Sug. Retail	$1,638	$1,375	$1,100	$750	$625	$550	$500	$450

MODEL 40-XB THUMBHOLE — available in 15 centerfire cals. between .220 Swift - .300 Win. Mag., 27¼ in. heavy stainless barrel, laminated thumbhole stock. New 1999.

Mfg.'s Sug. Retail	$1,726	$1,475	$1,050	$775

MODEL 40-XR CUSTOM SPORTER — .22 LR cal., top-of-the-line sporter from the custom shop, individually made per customer's specifications.

Mfg.'s Sug. Retail	$2,878	$2,600	$2,275	$1,850	$1,525	$1,325	$1,100	$925

MODEL 40-XR CUSTOM SPORTER — .22 LR cal. only, single shot, available on special order from Remington's Custom Shop only, Grades I-IV (disc. 1991) increase by amount of engraving, quality of wood, and other special order options/features. Mfg. 1986-1991.

   Values for Custom Grades listed below reflect 1991 (the year of discontinuance) price information. The Remington Custom Shop should be contacted directly regarding current values and options.

* *Model 40-XR Custom Grade Model I* — mfg. 1986-1991.

	$1,100	$925	$795

   Last Mfg.'s Sug. Retail was $1,314.

* *Model 40-XR Custom Grade Model II* — mfg. 1986-1991.

	$1,995	$1,675	$1,295

   Last Mfg.'s Sug. Retail was $2,335.

* *Model 40-XR Custom Grade Model III* — mfg. 1986-1991.

	$2,900	$2,150	$1,750

   Last Mfg.'s Sug. Retail was $3,650.

Grading	100%	98%	95%	90%	80%	70%	60%

✳ *Model 40-XR Custom Grade Model IV* — mfg. 1986-1991.

$4,875 $4,100 $2,950

Last Mfg.'s Sug. Retail was $5,695.

SHOTGUNS: O/U

Values listed below for Model 3200s assume NIB condition - subtract 10%-15% if without box, warranty card, and original shipping container (with packing materials).

MODEL 32 — 12 ga., double lock action, SST, separated barrels, 26, 28, or 30 in. barrels without rib, SR, or VR. Approx. 6,050 mfg. (ser. range approx. 0001-6,053) 1931-1947. There is a discrepancy as to when serialization started on this model.

$1,950 $1,675 $1,425 $1,275 $1,100 $950 $825

Add 10% for SST.
Add 10% for vent. or solid rib.
Add 20% for VR on 28 in. barrels.

MODEL 32 SERIALIZATION IS AS FOLLOWS: 1931 - 0001-1,009; 1932 - 1,010-1,903; 1933 - 1,904-1,948; 1934 - 1,949-2,727; 1935 - 2,728-3,610; 1936 - 3,611-4,259; 1937 - 4,260-4,755; 1938 - 4,756-4,958; 1939 - 4,959-5,202; 1940 - 5,203-5,425; 1941 - 5,426-5,741; 1942 - 5,742-6,020; 1943 - 6,021-6,031; 1944 - 6,032-6,049; 1945 to 1947 - 6,050-6,053.

MODEL 32D TOURNAMENT

$3,750 $3,000 $2,500 $2,000 $1,750 $1,400 $1,175

MODEL 32E EXPERT — less than 35 mfg.

$4,500 $3,950 $3,500 $2,975 $2,650 $2,200 $1,875

MODEL 32F PREMIER

$6,500 $5,500 $5,000 $4,500 $3,520 $2,750 $2,300

Note: Grades differ in quality, grade of wood, and amount of engraving.

MODEL 32 SKEET — similar to 32A, with 26 or 28 in. skeet bored barrels, SST. Mfg. 1932-1942.

$1,995 $1,800 $1,600 $1,350 $1,050 $950 $875

Add 10% for VR.
Add 10%-15% for 28 in. barrels.

MODEL 32TC TARGET — similar to 32A, with 30 or 32 in. VR full choke barrels, trap style stock. Mfg. 1932-1942.

$3,500 $2,500 $2,000 $1,800 $1,650 $1,450 $1,250

Add 10% for 30 in. VR barrels.

MODEL 396 SKEET/SPORTING CLAYS — 12 ga. only, satin finished boxlock action with engraved sideplates, 28 or 30 in. barrels with 10mm VR and Rem. chokes, select checkered walnut stock and target style forend, Sporting Clays Model has ported barrels, SST, ejectors, approx. 7½ lbs. Mfg. 1996-98.

✳ *Model 396 Skeet*

$1,750 $1,475 $1,250 $1,075 $925 $800 $700

Last Mfg.'s Sug. Retail was $1,993.

✳ *Model 396 Sporting Clays*

$1,875 $1,575 $1,300 $1,100 $950 $825 $725

Last Mfg.'s Sug. Retail was $2,126.

MODEL 3200 FIELD — 12 ga., 26, 28, or 30 in. barrels, VR, various chokes, boxlock, auto ejectors, single selective trigger, checkered pistol grip stock, separated barrels. Mfg. 1972-1984.

$1,100 $1,000 $950 $900 $850 $800 $750

Grading	100%	98%	95%	90%	80%	70%	60%

During 1998, the custom shop once again started manufacturing the Model 3200 from existing parts. Supplies are limited - please contact the Remington Custom Shop for availability and pricing.

Model 3200s with shorter barrels (26 or 28 in.) and open choking are more desirable than 30 in. tubes bored F/M.

MODEL 3200 SERIALIZATION IS AS FOLLOWS: 1973 - 4,200-16,667; 1974 - 16,668-27,393; 1975 - 27,394-35,303; 1976 - 35,304-39,216; 1977 - 39,217-41,432; 1978 - 41,433-42,813; 1979 - 42,814-44,278; 1980 - 44,279-45,504; 1981 - 45,505-45,974; 1982 - 45,975-47,200; 1983 - 47,201-47,308.

MODEL 3200 MAGNUM — 12 ga., 3 in. chambers, 30 in. heavy wall barrels (steel shot compatible), less than 1,000 mfg. 1975-1980.

	100%	98%	95%	90%	80%	70%	60%
	$1,495	$1,175	$950	$800	$715	$650	$575

MODEL 3200 SKEET — similar to 3200 Field, with 26 or 28 in. skeet bored barrels, skeet style stock. Mfg. 1973-1980.

	$1,295	$1,050	$950	$850	$750	$650	$575

28 in. barrels will command a premium on this model.

This model was also mfg. in a 28 in. IM/F configuration with gold pigeon on bottom for live pigeon shooting. Since less than 300 were mfg., prices in the $2,500 range are being asked if NIB condition. This model generally had a trap style rib, but there have been some field ribs as well. Originally, it was called the "Competition Live Pigeon" and was mfg. with a competition receiver and trap grade style wood.

✳ *Model 3200 Competition Skeet Four Ga. Set* — includes 12, 20, 28 ga., or .410 bore, cased.

	$6,000	$5,500	$5,000	$4,600	$4,200	$4,000	$3,800

Add 10%-15% for 28 in. barrels.

28 in. barrels will command a premium on this model.

MODEL 3200 COMPETITION SKEET — similar to 3200 Skeet, with scroll engraved frame and trigger guard, select wood. Mfg. 1973-1983.

	$1,700	$1,450	$1,125	$925	$850	$750	$675

Add 10%-15% for 28 in. VR barrels.

MODEL 3200 TRAP — similar as 3200 Field, with 30 or 32 in. barrels choked IM/F or F/F, stock and rib. Mfg. 1973-1980.

	$1,375	$1,100	$950	$875	$800	$750	$700

30 in. barrels are more desirable than 32 in.

MODEL 3200 SPECIAL TRAP — similar to 3200 Trap, except fancy wood. Mfg. 1973-1981.

	$1,450	$1,300	$1,200	$1,000	$875	$800	$750

MODEL 3200 COMPETITION TRAP — similar to 3200 Trap, with scroll engraving. Mfg. 1973-1981.

	$1,750	$1,575	$1,375	$1,150	$1,000	$925	$875
Pigeon Grade	$2,450	$2,150	$1,850	$1,500	$1,250	$995	$900

The Pigeon Grade featured a gold pigeon on receiver bottom - approx. 250 mfg.

There was a special production of this model during 1991-92 which was limited to approx. 100 guns.

MODEL 3200 PREMIER — 12 ga., sold through Remington's International Division, 500 mfg. 1975 only, patterned after "One of 1000" series, regular or Monte Carlo stock, 116 were engraved in Belgium — add 25%+.

	$2,900	$2,500	$2,150	$1,800	$1,500	$1,200	$1,025

Grading	100%	98%	95%	90%	80%	70%	60%

MODEL 3200 "ONE OF 1000" — limited edition, elaborate engraving, fancy wood, supplied with hard case, made in both skeet and trap models. Mfg. 1,000 each model: 1973 (Trap) and 1974 (Skeet).

	100%	98%	95%	90%	80%	70%	60%
Trap (30 IM/F or F/F)	$2,150	$1,750	$1,475	$1,325	$1,200	$1,075	$875
Skeet (26 or 28 in. SK/SK)	$1,925	$1,675	$1,475	$1,325	$1,200	$1,075	$875

Add 10% for 28 in. barrels on the Skeet Model.

R

PEERLESS FIELD GRADE — 12 ga. only, 3 in. chambers, 26, 28, or 30 in. VR barrels with Rem. chokes, boxlock with engraved sideplates, SST, ejectors, high-gloss checkered walnut stock and forearm with vent. recoil pad, 3.28 milliseconds lock time, blued metal, approx. 7½ lbs. Mfg. 1993-98.

100%	98%	95%	90%	80%	70%	60%
$1,000	$900	$850	$800	$750	$700	$650

Last Mfg.'s Sug. Retail was $1,172.

This model is an entirely new design not sharing any parts with either the Models 32 or 3200.

100%	98%	95%	90%	80%	70%	60%	50%	40%	30%	20%	10%

SHOTGUNS: SxS

The author wishes to express thanks to Charles Semmer for once again updating the following section on older Remington SxS Shotguns.

Because E. Remington & Sons shotguns are classified as antique, it may be helpful to consult the "NRA Antique Condition Standards" section in the front of this text to convert to the Percentage Grading System listed below.

MODEL 1873 "HAMMER LIFTER" — 10 or 12 ga., also known as Whitmore Hammer Lifter, 28 or 30 in. decarbonized, twist, damascus barrels, top "thumb lever" action activated by pushing upward to open, rib top marked "E. REMINGTON & SONS, ILION, N.Y.", patented "AUG. 8, 1871, APRIL 16, 1872", steel buttplate, pistol grip was optional, grades above 3 were made to order. Approx. 5,000 mfg. from 1873 to 1878, starting with ser. no. 1.

* *Grade 1* — decarbonized steel barrels, no checkering or engraving.

100%	98%	95%	90%	80%	70%	60%	50%	40%	30%	20%	10%
$1,500	$1,200	$900	$800	$750	$650	$500	$400	$300	$275	$250	$225

* *Grade 2* — twist steel barrels, checkering, no engraving.

$1,800	$1,700	$1,400	$1,200	$1,000	$850	$725	$625	$550	$425	$350	$275

* *Grade 3* — twist or damascus steel barrels, checkering and engraving.

$2,700	$2,500	$1,700	$1,400	$1,200	$1,000	$900	$800	$625	$525	$450	$350

Add 10%-20% to Grade 3 prices for higher grades (extra fine engraving).

MODEL 1875 AND 1876 "LIFTER" (WHITMORE LIFTER) — 10 or 12 ga., 28 or 30 in. decarbonized, twist, damascus barrels, top "thumb lever" action activated by pushing upward to open, rib top marked "E. REMINGTON & SONS, ILION, N.Y.", patented "AUG. 8, 1871, APRIL 16, 1872", steel buttplate, pistol grip was optional, the Model 1875 started with ser. no. 1, and went to approx. 3,350, the Model 1876 started with ser. no. 3,350 and went to approx. 5,900. Approx. 5,900 Model 1875s & 1876s were mfg. from 1875-1882.

* *Grade 1* — decarbonized steel barrels, no checkering or engraving.

$1,500	$1,200	$900	$800	$750	$650	$500	$400	$300	$275	$250	$225

* *Grade 2* — twist steel barrels, checkering, no engraving.

$1,800	$1,700	$1,400	$1,200	$1,000	$850	$725	$625	$550	$425	$350	$275

* *Grade 3* — twist or damascus steel barrels, checkered and engraving.

$2,700	$2,500	$1,700	$1,400	$1,200	$1,000	$900	$800	$625	$525	$450	$350

* *Grade 4* — twist or damascus steel barrels, checkered and extra fine engraving.

$2,800	$2,500	$2,000	$1,700	$1,200	$1,000	$850	$725	$625	$550	$475	$350

100%	98%	95%	90%	80%	70%	60%	50%	40%	30%	20%	10%

* **Grade 5** — damascus steel barrels, checkered and superior engraving.

100%	98%	95%	90%	80%	70%	60%	50%	40%	30%	20%	10%
$3,200	$2,900	$2,500	$2,100	$1,800	$1,400	$1,000	$825	$725	$625	$550	$400

Add 100% to the few Model 1873s and 1875s that are rib marked "NEW YORK & LONDON".

There were very few double rifles and combination guns made in Models 1873, 1875, and 1876 (add 100%) - they are very rare, and be aware of fake double rifles.

MODEL 1878 HAMMER (HEAVY DUCK GUN) — 10 ga., called the Heavy Duck Gun, 30-32 in., 9¾ and 10 lbs., "thumb-lever" action, thick bolsters, top extension rib, no flash fences, steel buttplate. Approx. 2,500 mfg. from 1878 to 1882, starting with ser. no. 1.

R

* **Grade 1** — decarbonized steel barrels, no checkering, no engraving.

100%	98%	95%	90%	80%	70%	60%	50%	40%	30%	20%	10%
$1,500	$1,200	$900	$800	$750	$650	$500	$400	$300	$275	$250	$250

* **Grade 2** — twist steel barrels, checkered, no engraving.

100%	98%	95%	90%	80%	70%	60%	50%	40%	30%	20%	10%
$1,700	$1,500	$1,200	$1,000	$850	$725	$625	$525	$450	$400	$375	$375

* **Grade 3** — laminated steel barrels, checkered, engraved.

100%	98%	95%	90%	80%	70%	60%	50%	40%	30%	20%	10%
$2,800	$2,500	$2,000	$1,700	$1,200	$1,000	$850	$725	$625	$550	$475	$475

* **Grade 4** — damascus steel barrels, checkered, engraved.

100%	98%	95%	90%	80%	70%	60%	50%	40%	30%	20%	10%
$3,200	$3,000	$2,700	$2,400	$2,000	$1,600	$1,200	$1,000	$800	$750	$650	$600

MODEL 1879 SxS HAMMER — usually 12 ga., top extension rib, no flash fences, steel buttplate, only Whitmore model with Deeley & Edge forend catch. Ser. nos. within the Model 1878.

Add 40% for this scarce variation to Model 1878 listed prices.

MODEL 1882 SxS HAMMER — (includes the unique Model 1883), 10 or 12 ga., 30 or 32 in. decarbonized, twist or damascus steel barrels, rib marked "E. REMINGTON & SONS, ILION, N.Y.", typical top lever, all grades have checkered pistol grip and forend with various designs according to grade. All contain Deeley & Edge forend catch. Approx. 16,000 Model 1882s, possibly 1,000 Model 1883s were mfg. from 1882-1888.

* **Grade 1** — decarbonized steel barrels, no enraving, steel buttplate.

100%	98%	95%	90%	80%	70%	60%	50%	40%	30%	20%	10%
$1,500	$1,300	$1,200	$1,000	$750	$650	$550	$450	$350	$275	$250	$200

* **Grade 2** — twist steel barrels, no engraving, steel buttplate.

100%	98%	95%	90%	80%	70%	60%	50%	40%	30%	20%	10%
$1,400	$1,200	$1,100	$900	$750	$650	$550	$450	$350	$275	$250	$200

* **Grade 3** — laminated steel barrels, engraved, steel buttplate.

100%	98%	95%	90%	80%	70%	60%	50%	40%	30%	20%	10%
$1,800	$1,600	$1,400	$1,200	$1,000	$875	$750	$650	$550	$400	$350	$250

* **Grade 4** — damascus steel barrels, engraved, steel buttplate.

100%	98%	95%	90%	80%	70%	60%	50%	40%	30%	20%	10%
$2,000	$1,800	$1,600	$1,400	$1,200	$1,000	$800	$700	$600	$500	$400	$300

* **Grade 5** — fine damascus steel, finely engraved, superior rubber buttplate.

100%	98%	95%	90%	80%	70%	60%	50%	40%	30%	20%	10%
$3,000	$2,800	$2,400	$2,200	$2,000	$1,700	$1,400	$1,000	$800	$700	$600	$500

* **Grade 6** — extra fine damascus, fine scroll engraved, superior rubber buttplate.

100%	98%	95%	90%	80%	70%	60%	50%	40%	30%	20%	10%
$5,000	$4,800	$4,200	$3,700	$3,200	$2,700	$2,500	$2,000	$1,500	$1,200	$1,000	$800

Add 50% for Model 1883 variation to above values.
Add 25% for optional auxiliary rifle barrel insert.

MODEL 1885/1887 SxS HAMMER — 10, 12, or 16 ga., different hammer style variation of the Model 1882, 28, 30, or 32 in. decarbonized, twist or damascus steel barrels, rib marked "E. REMINGTON & SONS, ILION, N.Y.", top lever, all grades are checkered pistol grip and forend with various designs according to grade, Deeley & Edge forend catch, rubber buttplate with ERS logo. Approx. 7,000 mfg. from 1885-1888.

* **Grade 1** — decarbonized steel barrels, no engraving.

100%	98%	95%	90%	80%	70%	60%	50%	40%	30%	20%	10%
$1,800	$1,600	$1,400	$1,200	$1,000	$700	$600	$500	$400	$300	$275	$225

100%	98%	95%	90%	80%	70%	60%	50%	40%	30%	20%	10%

R

* ***Grade 2*** — twist steel barrels, no engraving.

| $1,700 | $1,500 | $1,300 | $1,000 | $850 | $750 | $650 | $550 | $450 | $375 | $300 | $225 |

* ***Grade 3*** — damascus steel barrels, no engraving.

| $1,800 | $1,600 | $1,400 | $1,200 | $1,000 | $875 | $750 | $650 | $550 | $400 | $350 | $250 |

* ***Grade 4*** — damascus steel barrels, engraved.

| $2,000 | $1,800 | $1,600 | $1,400 | $1,200 | $1,000 | $800 | $700 | $600 | $500 | $400 | $300 |

* ***Grade 5*** — fine damascus steel barrels, finely engraved.

| $3,000 | $2,800 | $2,400 | $2,200 | $1,700 | $1,500 | $1,200 | $900 | $750 | $650 | $500 | $400 |

* ***Grade 6*** — extra fine damascus barrels, fine scroll engraved.

| $5,000 | $4,800 | $4,200 | $3,700 | $3,200 | $2,700 | $2,500 | $2,000 | $1,500 | $1,200 | $900 | $700 |

* ***Grade 7*** — superior damascus barrels, extra fine scroll engraved, game scene.

| $7,500 | $7,300 | $7,100 | $6,500 | $6,000 | $5,500 | $5,000 | $4,000 | $3,500 | $3,000 | $2,000 | $1,000 |

Add 25% for optional auxiliary rifle barrel insert.
Add 30% for 16 ga.

MODEL 1889 SxS HAMMER — 10, 12, or 16 ga., 28, 30, or 32 in., a few 26 in. are known. Decarbonized, twist, or damascus barrels, exposed "circular" hammers, rib marked "REMINGTON ARMS CO. ILION, N.Y. U.S.A.", top lever, all grades have checkered pistol grip and forend with various designs according to grade, Deeley & Edge forend catch. Grade number is stamped on water table left of the ser. no. Rubber buttplate with RACo logo. 134,200 mfg. 1889-1908. Ser. range from 30,000 to 100,000. After the year 1900, ser. nos. are in the 200,000 range.

* ***Grade 1*** — decarbonized steel barrels, no engraving.

| $1,500 | $1,300 | $1,200 | $1,000 | $750 | $650 | $550 | $450 | $350 | $300 | $275 | $225 |

* ***Grade 2*** — twist steel barrels, no engraving.

| $1,600 | $1,400 | $1,300 | $1,000 | $750 | $750 | $650 | $550 | $450 | $350 | $300 | $225 |

* ***Grade 3*** — damascus steel barrels, no engraving.

| $1,700 | $1,500 | $1,400 | $1,100 | $950 | $850 | $750 | $650 | $500 | $400 | $350 | $250 |

* ***Grade 4*** — damascus steel barrels, engraved.

| $3,000 | $2,800 | $2,400 | $2,200 | $2,000 | $1,700 | $1,400 | $1,000 | $800 | $700 | $600 | $500 |

* ***Grade 5*** — damascus steel barrels, finely engraved.

| $5,000 | $4,800 | $4,200 | $3,700 | $3,200 | $2,700 | $2,500 | $2,000 | $1,500 | $1,200 | $1,000 | $800 |

* ***Grade 6*** — extra fine damascus barrels, fine scroll engraved.

| $7,500 | $7,300 | $7,100 | $6,500 | $6,000 | $5,500 | $5,000 | $4,000 | $3,500 | $3,000 | $2,000 | $1,000 |

* ***Grade 7*** — superior damascus barrels, extra fine scroll engraved, game scene.

| $15,000 | $13,000 | $10,000 | $9,000 | $8,000 | $7,000 | $6,000 | $5,000 | $4,000 | $3,500 | $2,500 | $1,500 |

Add 20% for 16 ga.
Hardly any exist of the special ordered Grades 4 through 7.

MODEL 1894 SxS HAMMERLESS — 10, 12, or 16 ga., 26 to 32 in. "Remington", "Ordnance", or Damascus steel barrels, auto ejectors, boxlock, double triggers, checkered pistol grip or straight stock, Purdey forend snap. Grades A, B, F, and C have RACo hard rubber butt, Grade D, horn butt, Grade E, horn or heel and toe plates. Grade is usually stamped on the water table. 16 and especially 10 ga., are considered scarce and will command a higher value. 41,194 mfg. between 1894 and 1910 in the 100,000 block serial range.

* ***Grade AE*** — no engraving.

| $1,500 | $1,300 | $1,200 | $1,100 | $1,000 | $850 | $700 | $600 | $500 | $400 | $300 | $200 |

* ***Grade BE*** — scroll and line engraving.

| $3,000 | $2,800 | $2,500 | $2,200 | $2,000 | $1,700 | $1,400 | $1,000 | $700 | $500 | $400 | $300 |

100%	98%	95%	90%	80%	70%	60%	50%	40%	30%	20%	10%

* *Grade FE Trap* — scroll and line engraving.

| $3,000 | $2,800 | $2,500 | $2,200 | $2,000 | $1,700 | $1,400 | $1,000 | $700 | $500 | $400 | $300 |

* *Grade CE* — extra scroll engraving, silver name plate.

| $4,500 | $4,300 | $4,000 | $3,600 | $3,300 | $3,000 | $2,500 | $2,000 | $1,500 | $1,000 | $600 | $500 |

* *Grade DE* — fine scroll and game engraving, silver name plate.

| $7,500 | $7,300 | $7,100 | $6,500 | $6,000 | $5,500 | $5,500 | $4,000 | $3,000 | $2,000 | $1,500 | $1,000 |

* *Grade EE* — finest quality scroll, bird and game engraving, gold name plate.

| $18,000 | $17,000 | $15,000 | $12,000 | $10,000 | $8,000 | $7,000 | $6,500 | $5,000 | $3,500 | $2,500 | $2,000 |

Deduct 20% for non-ejector guns.
Add 25% for "Ordnance" barrels.

A few Remington SPECIAL grade guns were produced; they are so rare, it is not practical to attempt a value.

MODEL 1900 SxS HAMMERLESS — 12 or 16 ga., 28 or 30 in. "Remington" or damascus steel barrels, lower priced gun to meet market competition, quality a cut below the Model 1894, but mechanically the same, snap forend. No engraving was offered on this model. 98,475 mfg. between 1900 and 1910 in the 300,000 block serial range.

* *Grade K and KD* — Remington or Damascus steel barrels, non-ejector.

| $1,000 | $900 | $825 | $750 | $675 | $625 | $575 | $525 | $475 | $295 | $250 | $200 |

* *Grade KE and KED* — Remington or Damascus steel barrels, ejectors.

| $1,300 | $1,200 | $1,100 | $1,000 | $900 | $800 | $700 | $600 | $500 | $300 | $250 | $200 |

PARKER AHE — while advertised, the Remington re-issue of the original Parker AHE Model was never mfg. due to product liability considerations. Older Remington manufactured Parkers may be found in the Parker section of this text.

Grading	100%	98%	95%	90%	80%	70%	60%

SHOTGUNS: SEMI-AUTO, DISC.

REMINGTON AUTOLOADING SHOTGUN (PRE-MODEL 11) — 12 ga. only, original Remington mfg. of the Browning A-5, 5 shot, various grades, 20 (riot), 26, or 28 in. plain or matted rib barrel. Mfg. 1905-1910.

| | | | $350 | $275 | $225 | $175 | $160 | $135 | $110 |

Add 20% for matted rib.

MODEL 11A AUTOLOADER 5-SHOT — 12, 16 (introduced 1931), or 20 (introduced 1930) ga., 26-32 in. barrels, takedown, various chokes, Browning type, checkered pistol stock. Approx. 300,000 mfg., 1911-1948.

	100%	98%	95%	90%	80%	70%	60%
Plain barrel	$295	$240	$215	$185	$165	$150	$120
Solid rib	$395	$315	$235	$200	$185	$165	$140
Vent. rib	$440	$360	$335	$305	$275	$220	$165

Add 35% for barrels marked "Long Range" - beware of fakes.

This model was mfg. under patent agreement with John Browning.

MODEL 11B SPECIAL — higher grade wood with hand checkered stock and forearm.

| | $525 | $440 | $385 | $360 | $305 | $250 | $195 |

MODEL 11D TOURNAMENT

| | $950 | $850 | $725 | $550 | $495 | $470 | $440 |

MODEL 11E EXPERT

| | $1,175 | $975 | $875 | $775 | $675 | $595 | $525 |

MODEL 11F PREMIER

| | $1,850 | $1,550 | $1,375 | $1,100 | $975 | $850 | $750 |

Note: Grades differ in quality, grade of wood, and amount of engraving.

Grading	100%	98%	95%	90%	80%	70%	60%

SPORTSMAN MODEL SEMI-AUTO — 12, 16, or 20 ga., 26 (3 shot only) in. barrel, skeet choke, beavertail forend. Mfg. 1931-1949.

	100%	98%	95%	90%	80%	70%	60%
Plain barrel	$325	$275	$250	$195	$165	$140	$120
Solid rib	$400	$350	$300	$250	$200	$180	$150
Vent. rib	$470	$415	$360	$330	$275	$250	$220

This model was manufactured in Field, Riot, and Skeet configurations.

R

MODEL 48 SPORTSMAN — 12, 16, or 20 ga., 26, 28, or 32 in. barrels, 3 shot, mechanical (solid breech) ejection system, various chokes, rounded receiver, checkered pistol grip stock with cap. Approx. 275,000 mfg., 1949-1960.

	100%	98%	95%	90%	80%	70%	60%
	$300	$225	$200	$185	$175	$165	$140
VR barrel	$325	$275	$250	$200	$175	$165	$140

MODEL 48B SELECT

	100%	98%	95%	90%	80%	70%	60%
	$420	$360	$310	$290	$245	$220	$195

MODEL 48D TOURNAMENT

	100%	98%	95%	90%	80%	70%	60%
	$1,100	$825	$715	$660	$605	$440	$415

MODEL 48F PREMIER

	100%	98%	95%	90%	80%	70%	60%
	$2,420	$2,035	$1,540	$1,210	$990	$770	$715

MODEL 48A RIOT GUN — 12 ga. only, 20 in. plain barrel.

	100%	98%	95%	90%	80%	70%	60%
	$275	$220	$195	$165	$150	$140	$110

MODEL 48SA SKEET — 26 in. barrel, skeet bore, ivory bead. Mfg. 1949-1960.

	100%	98%	95%	90%	80%	70%	60%
	$305	$275	$255	$230	$210	$195	$165
With VR barrel	$395	$350	$300	$260	$230	$210	$195

MODEL 48SC SKEET — "C" suffix designates C-grade wood.

	100%	98%	95%	90%	80%	70%	60%
	$385	$360	$330	$305	$275	$250	$220

MODEL 48SD TOURNAMENT — custom shop engraved.

	100%	98%	95%	90%	80%	70%	60%
	$1,100	$825	$715	$660	$605	$440	$415

MODEL 48SF PREMIER — custom shop engraved.

	100%	98%	95%	90%	80%	70%	60%
	$2,200	$1,925	$1,650	$1,210	$990	$770	$715

MODEL 11-48 SEMI-AUTO — 12, 16, 20, 28 (introduced 1952) ga., or .410 (introduced 1954) bore, recoil operated action, walnut stock. Approx. 429,000 mfg., 1949-1968.

	100%	98%	95%	90%	80%	70%	60%
Plain barrel	$300	$225	$200	$185	$175	$165	$140
VR barrel	$325	$275	$250	$200	$175	$165	$140

Add 15% - 40% for 28 ga. or .410 bore, depending on condition.

MODEL 58ADL "SPORTSMAN - 58" SEMI-AUTO — 12, 16, or 20 ga., 26, 28, or 30 in. barrel, gas operation, various chokes, 3 shot, checkered pistol grip stock, scroll game scene engraved. Approx. 271,000 mfg., 1956-1963.

	100%	98%	95%	90%	80%	70%	60%
Plain barrel	$275	$250	$220	$195	$140	$120	$110
VR barrel	$360	$305	$275	$250	$220	$165	$140

Add 5% for Magnum in 12 ga.

MODEL 58BDL — similar to 58ADL, with select wood.

	100%	98%	95%	90%	80%	70%	60%
Plain barrel	$295	$275	$250	$225	$210	$195	$165
VR barrel	$375	$335	$300	$275	$250	$200	$175

MODEL 58SA SKEET GUN — similar to 58ADL, with 26 in. skeet bore VR barrel, skeet stock.

	100%	98%	95%	90%	80%	70%	60%
	$360	$330	$305	$275	$250	$200	$175

MODEL 58SC SKEET — "C" suffix designates C-grade wood.

	100%	98%	95%	90%	80%	70%	60%
	$495	$440	$415	$385	$330	$305	$275

MODEL 58D TOURNAMENT — custom shop engraved.

	100%	98%	95%	90%	80%	70%	60%
	$825	$715	$635	$580	$525	$470	$440

Grading	100%	98%	95%	90%	80%	70%	60%

MODEL 58SF PREMIER — custom shop engraved.

| | $1,650 | $1,375 | $1,210 | $1,045 | $965 | $880 | $800 |

Note: Models differ in grade of wood, amount of engraving, and gold inlays.

MODEL 878A "AUTOMASTER" — 12 ga. gas operated semi-auto, 26, 28, or 30 in. barrels, action similar to Model 58. Approx. 62,000 mfg., 1959-1962. Add 15% for VR.

| | $235 | $200 | $185 | $170 | $160 | $150 | $135 |

Barrels on this model are interchangeable with those on the Model 58.

R

SHOTGUNS: SEMI-AUTO, CURRENT/RECENT PRODUCTION

MODEL SP-10 — 10 ga., 3½ in. chamber, semi-auto stainless steel gas system operation, lighter recoil than most 12 ga. Mags., 26 or 30 in. barrel with ⅜ in. VR and Rem. chokes (2), checkered stock and forearm with low gloss satin finish, matte metal finish, crossbolt safety, recoil pad, supplied with camo sling, approx. 11 lbs. Introduced 1989.

| Mfg.'s Sug. Retail | $1,116 | $955 | $835 | $730 | $675 | $625 | $575 | $550 |

The first 5,000 SP-10s were assigned special serialization (LE89 prefix) - no premiums exist at this time, however.

This model is NOT a re-designed Ithaca Mag-10 and the parts are NOT interchangeable. The SP-10 is a new design.

* *Model SP-10 Camo* — 23 (Turkey Model, new 1999), or 26 in. VR barrel, choice of Mossy Oak (disc. 1996), full coverage Mossy Oak Break-Up (new 1997), or Bottomland (mfg. 1994-96) Camo finish. New 1993.

| Mfg.'s Sug. Retail | $1,229 | $1,030 | $915 | $765 | $675 | $625 | $575 | $550 |

➤ *Model SP-10 Turkey Camo NWTF 25th Anniversary* — 12 ga., limited mfg. to commemorate the 25th Anniversary of the NWTF during 1998, Truglo fiber optic sights. Mfg. 1998 only.

| | $1,050 | $925 | $775 |

Last Mfg.'s Sug. Retail was $1,225.

* *Model SP-10 Turkey Combo* — includes choice of either 26 or 30 VR regular barrel and extra 22 in. deer barrel with rifle sights. Mfg. 1991-94.

| | $1,075 | $925 | $775 | $700 | $650 | $575 | $525 |

Last Mfg.'s Sug. Retail was $1,132.

Remington Shotguns: Semi-Auto, Model 1100 & Variations

3 in. shells (12 or 20 ga.) may be shot in Magnum receivers only, regardless of what the barrel markings may indicate (the ejection port is larger in these Magnum models with M suffix serialization).

MODEL 1100 FIELD — 12 (disc. 1987), 16 (disc. 1980), or 20 ga., 26, 28, or 30 in. barrels, various chokes, gas operated, checkered pistol grip stock, Rem. chokes became standard 1987 (introduced 1986 as $40 option), VRs became standard in 1985 on this model, 20 ga. lightweight frame became standard 1972, prices below assume VR and Rem. chokes. Mfg. 1963-1988.

| | $350 | $295 | $265 | $225 | $200 | $185 | $170 |

Last Mfg.'s Sug. Retail was $545.

Subtract $40 if without VR.
Subtract $45 if without Rem. chokes.

This model was produced only in a Lightweight or Mag. 20 (3 in. chamber), 28 ga., or .410 bore, before the release of the Model 11-87.

SPORTSMAN 12 AUTO — 12 ga. only, 2¾ in. chamber, 28 or 30 in. barrel, similar to Model 1100 action, VR standard, hardwood stock and forearm, 7¾ lbs. Mfg. 1985-86 only. Add $40 for Rem. chokes (new 1986).

| | $300 | $260 | $220 | $195 | $170 | $160 | $150 |

Last Mfg.'s Sug. Retail was $405.

R

MODEL 1100 SPECIAL FIELD — 12, 20 ga., or .410 (limited mfg., disc.) bore, 21 (disc. 1993) or 23 (new 1994) in. VR barrel, various chokes, gas operated, checkered straight grip stock, VR standard, high gloss wood finish (1991 only) or satin wood finish. Rem. chokes became standard in 1987. New 1984.

Mfg.'s Sug. Retail	$665	$510	$415	$325	$265	$230	$210	$180

  Subtract 10% if without Rem. chokes.
  Add 15%-20% for .410 bore.

  Two hundred .410 bores were mfg. for National Shooting Supplies in Houston, TX.

MODEL 1100 SMALL GAUGE — 28 ga. or .410 bore, 25 in. barrel, scaled down receiver, skeet and field fixed choke, VR standard. Mfg. 1969-1994.

			$550	$475	$425	$365	$300	$275	$250

Last Mfg.'s Sug. Retail was $647.

MODEL 1100 LT-20 (LIGHTWEIGHT) — similar to 1100, 20 ga. only, 2¾ in. chamber, with mahogany stock and lightened receiver, 23, 26 (disc., gloss wood only) or 28 (disc., satin wood only) in. barrel, VR became standard 1985, hi-gloss (disc.) or satin finish wood, 6½ lbs. Mfg. 1970-present.

Mfg.'s Sug. Retail	$665	$510	$415	$325	$265	$230	$210	$180

  Subtract 10% if without VR.
  Subtract $34 for gloss wood.

  Rolled scroll receiver engraving became standard on 20 ga. in 1998.

MODEL 1100 LT-20 YOUTH — 20 ga. only, similar to Model 1100 Lightweight, except stock is 1 in. shorter and 21 in. barrel only. Disc. 1998.

		$500	$415	$325	$265	$230	$210	$180

Last Mfg.'s Sug. Retail was $659.

➤ Model 1100 LT-20 Youth Camo NWTF — 20 ga. only, features 100% Mossy Oak break up camo finish, Truglo fiber optic sights, 6½ lbs. Mfg. 1998 only.

		$495	$415	$325	$265	$230	$210	$180

Last Mfg.'s Sug. Retail was $652.

MODEL 1100 LIGHTWEIGHT MAGNUM (LT-20 MAG.) — chambered for 3 in. 20 ga. Mag., 20 (disc.), 26 (disc.), or 28 in. barrel, Rem. chokes became standard 1987. Introduced 1977, disc. 1998..

		$500	$415	$325	$265	$230	$210	$180

Last Mfg.'s Sug. Retail was $659.

  Subtract 10% if without VR.

MODEL 1100 MAGNUM DUCK GUN — similar to 1100, in 12 (disc. 1987) or 20 ga., 3 in. chamber, recoil pad, VR became standard 1984, Rem. chokes became standard 1987. Mfg. 1963-1988.

		$400	$325	$280	$260	$220	$200	$180

Last Mfg.'s Sug. Retail was $533.

  Add $80 for left-hand model (disc. 1986).
  Subtract $40 if without VR.
  Subtract $45 if without Rem. chokes.

✳ Model 1100 Magnum Special Purpose (SP) — 12 ga. only, low luster finish on stock and forearm, sand blasted metal parts. Mfg. 1985-86 only. Add $40 for Rem. chokes (new 1986).

		$395	$350	$295	$265	$235	$200	$180

Last Mfg.'s Sug. Retail was $550.

MODEL 1100 SYNTHETIC — 12 or 20 ga., 2¾ in. chamber, 26 (20 ga. only) or 28 (12 ga. only) in. VR barrel with Rem. choke, checkered black synthetic stock and forearm, matte metal finish, 7-7½ lbs. New 1996.

Mfg.'s Sug. Retail	$505	$400	$325	$265

✳ Model 1100 Synthetic Deer — 12 or 20 ga., 21 in. fully rifled barrel with choice of Cantilever scope mount (12 ga. only) or rifle sight (20 ga. only), 7 or 7½ lbs. New 1997.

Grading		100%	98%	95%	90%	80%	70%	60%

➤ 12 ga.
Mfg.'s Sug. Retail $585 $450 $350 $275
➤ 20 ga. (LT-20)
Mfg.'s Sug. Retail $539 $425 $335 $275

Subtract $24 for Youth Model (new 1999).
Add $26 for Youth Turkey Camo (100% Realtree Advantage Camo, new 1999).

MODEL 1100 "1 OF 3,000" FIELD — 12 ga. only, limited edition, serial numbered 1-3,000, deluxe walnut, gold washed etched hunting scenes on receiver, 28 in. modified VR barrel. Mfg. 1980.

		100%	98%	95%	90%	80%	70%	60%
		$1,100	$900	$600	$500	$425	$350	$300

R

MODEL 1100 DEER GUN — 12 (disc. 1987) or 20 ga., 20 (disc.), 21 in. (20 ga. only) or 22 (disc.) in. imp. cyl. barrel with rifle sights. Disc. 1996.

	100%	98%	95%	90%	80%	70%	60%
	$435	$345	$270	$225	$200	$185	$165

Last Mfg.'s Sug. Retail was $584.

Add $80 for left-hand model (disc. 1986).
Add $117 for 21 in. fully rifled Cantilever deer barrel.

＊ *Model 1100 Special Purpose Deer (SP)* — similar to Model 1100 Deer Gun, except has low luster finish on stock and forearm, sandblasted metal parts. Mfg. 1986 only.

	100%	98%	95%	90%	80%	70%	60%
	$335	$295	$275	$255	$220	$200	$180

Last Mfg.'s Sug. Retail was $495.

MODEL 1100 LT-20 (TOURNAMENT SKEET) — 12 or 20 (LT-20) ga., 26 in. skeet bored or Rem. choke barrel, optional Cutts Compensator. Mfg. 1963-1994, reintroduced 1996, disc. 1997.

	100%	98%	95%	90%	80%	70%	60%
	$625	$525	$450	$375	$325	$275	$225

Last Mfg.'s Sug. Retail was $732.

Add $40 for left-hand model (disc. 1986).

MODEL 1100 SMALL GAUGE SKEET — 28 ga. or .410 bore, 25 or 26 (disc.) in. VR barrel, 6½-7¼ lbs. Mfg. 1969-1994.

	100%	98%	95%	90%	80%	70%	60%
	$550	$450	$415	$375	$300	$265	$230

Last Mfg.'s Sug. Retail was $692.

2½ in. chamber is standard on the .410 bore.

MODEL 1100 SKEET MATCHED PAIR — 28 ga. and .410 bore, walnut stock and forearm. 5,067 cased Skeet sets were mfg. 1969 and 1970 only.

		100%	98%	95%
		$1,250	$995	$875

MODEL 1100 SPORTING — 20 (new 1998) or 28 ga., 25 (28 ga. only) or 28 (20 ga. only) in. VR barrel with Rem. chokes, high gloss checkered deluxe walnut stock and forearm, 6½ lbs. New 1996.

		100%	98%	95%	90%	80%	70%	60%
Mfg.'s Sug. Retail	$799	$675	$530	$465	$375	$325	$275	$225

MODEL 1100 TA TRAP — 12 ga., 30 in. barrel, recoil pad on regular stock, available in left or right-hand. Mfg. 1979-86.

	100%	98%	95%	90%	80%	70%	60%
	$410	$330	$295	$270	$230	$210	$190

Last Mfg.'s Sug. Retail was $570.

Add 5% for Monte Carlo stock.
Add $50 for left-hand model.

MODEL 1100 TB TRAP — 12 ga., 30 in. VR full choke barrel, special trap stock, select wood. Mfg. 1963-1981.

	100%	98%	95%	90%	80%	70%	60%
	$475	$400	$325	$300	$245	$210	$190
Monte Carlo stock	$495	$415	$340	$310	$280	$235	$220

MODEL 1100 TOURNAMENT TRAP — 12 ga., 30 in. VR full choke barrel, special trap stock, extra select wood. Mfg. 1979-86.

	100%	98%	95%	90%	80%	70%	60%
	$550	$495	$425	$365	$325	$285	$250

Last Mfg.'s Sug. Retail was $675.

Add 5% for Monte Carlo stock.

Grading	100%	98%	95%	90%	80%	70%	60%

MODEL 1100 150TH ANNIVERSARY — limited mfg. in 1966 only.

	$400	**$340**	**$290**				

MODEL 1100 BICENTENNIAL — 12 ga. only, configurations include Trap, Skeet, and Trade, mfg. to commemorate U.S. Bicentennial (1776-1976).

Trap or Skeet	**$450**	**$375**	**$325**
Trade	**$375**	**$295**	**$225**

In 1976, the 1100 Bicentennial Trap retailed for $320 (add $10 for Monte Carlo stock), the Skeet retailed for $285, and the Trade retailed for $270.

MODEL 1100 DUCKS UNLIMITED — "DU" in serial number.

Remington has offered many variations of the Model 1100 specifically manufactured according to individual DU chapter specifications. The price of a DU 1100 varies substantially from the "DU point of purchase" to real market conditions. When contemplating a DU gun it is always important to know how many of that particular variation were manufactured. The Remington factory normally has this information unless the special DU work was subcontracted elsewhere.

While most DU guns are good vehicles for fund raising, their collectability to date has been minimal. Actual market conditions indicate that unless production is truly limited, most DU firearms sell very close to the models they were derived from. Also, any collectability that does exist is for 100% guns new in the box with warranty papers. Used DU guns have values comparable to the standard model from which they were derived.

In addition to regular DU guns, Remington has also produced special editions including the 1982 Atlantic Flyway (dinner gun) and a 1981 DU Lt. 20 ga. and 12 ga. (dinner gun — 2,400 mfg. each), and a 1973 dinner gun (600 mfg.). These were rarer DU shotguns, and current values could vary significantly.

MODEL 1100 D-GRADE (TOURNAMENT) — custom order only, any gauge. Mfg. 1963-present.

Mfg.'s Sug. Retail	**$2,741**		**$2,175**	**$1,700**	**$1,200**		

MODEL 1100 F-GRADE (PREMIER) — custom order only, any gauge. Mfg. 1963-present.

Mfg.'s Sug. Retail	**$5,647**		**$4,750**	**$3,650**	**$2,600**		

MODEL 1100 F-GRADE W/GOLD (GOLD PREMIER) — with gold inlay, custom order only. Mfg. 1963-present.

Mfg.'s Sug. Retail	**$8,465**		**$7,425**	**$4,250**	**$3,100**		

Note: Grades differ in quality, grade of wood, amount of engraving, and gold inlays.

Remington Shotguns: Semi-Auto, Model 11-87 & Variations

MODEL 11-87 PREMIER — 12 or 20 (new 1999) ga. (3 in. chamber), 26, 28, or 32 (disc. 1996) in. VR Rem. choked barrel, successor to Model 1100, gas compensating action adaptable to all loads, stainless steel magazine tube, polished blue finish, satin finished and checkered walnut stock and forearm, a high gloss wood finish option became available in 1991 at N/C, fine line receiver engraving became standard during 1999, solid recoil pad, 8⅛-8⅜ lbs. Introduced 1987.

Mfg.'s Sug. Retail	**$705**		**$555**	**$440**	**$335**	**$285**	**$240**	**$220**	**$200**

Add $80 for 21 in. fully rifled Cantilever deer barrel.
Add $54 for left-hand action (12 ga. only).

Note: Model 11-87 Premier barrels are not interchangeable with Model 1100 barrels.

MODEL 11-87 SP (SPECIAL PURPOSE) — see individual sub-models listed below.

* *Model 11-87 SP 3 in. Magnum* — 12 ga. only (3 in. chamber), 26, 28, or 30 (disc.) in. VR Rem. choked barrel, parkerized metal with satin finish wood stock and forearm, vent. recoil pad, included camouflaged nylon sling, 8¼ lbs. New 1987.

Mfg.'s Sug. Retail	**$705**		**$555**	**$445**	**$350**	**$285**	**$240**	**$220**	**$200**

Grading	100%	98%	95%	90%	80%	70%	60%

* *Model 11-87 SPS 3 in. Magnum* — similar to Model 11-87 SP 3 in. Mag., except is supplied with black synthetic stock and forearm.

Mfg.'s Sug. Retail	$692	$545	$450	$350	$285	$240	$220	$200

* *Model 11-87 SPS Camo (Special Purpose Synthetic Camo)* — 12 ga. only, 21 (new 1999), 26 or 28 (disc. 1998) in. VR barrel with Rem. choke, available in Mossy Oak Bottomland (disc. 1996) or Mossy Oak Break-Up (new 1997) finish. New 1994.

Mfg.'s Sug. Retail	$805	$620	$455	$355	$290	$250	$225	$200

R

* *Model 11-87 SPS-BG Camo (Special Purpose Synthetic Big Game)* — 12 ga. only, 21 in. plain barrel with rifle sights and Rem. choke. Mfg. 1994 only.

	$555	$425	$350	$290	$250	$225	$200

Last Mfg.'s Sug. Retail was $692.

* *Model 11-87 SPS (Special Purpose Deer Gun)* — 12 ga. only (3 in. chamber), 21 in. IC or Rem. choked (new 1989) or fully rifled (new 1993) barrel with iron sights, parkerized metal with matte finished wood or black synthetic (new 1993) stock and forearm, vent. recoil pad, includes camouflaged nylon sling, 7¼ lbs. New 1987.

Mfg.'s Sug. Retail	$685	$540	$445	$350	$290	$240	$220	$200

Add $97 for Cantilevered rifled deer barrel with Rem. choke.
Add $40 for fully rifled deer barrel.
Subtract 10% for fixed choke barrel.
Rem. chokes became standard on this model in 1989.

* *Model 11-87 SPS-T (Special Purpose Turkey)* — 12 ga. only, 21 in. VR barrel with Rem. choke, available in flat black, Mossy Oak (disc. 1996), Mossy Oak break up (new 1999), Realtree X-tra Brown (mfg. 1997 only), or Greenleaf (disc. 1996) finish.

Mfg.'s Sug. Retail	$705	$555	$450	$345	$285	$240	$220	$200

Add $100 for Camo finish.

➤ *Model 11-87 SPS Turkey Camo NWTF* — 20 ga. only, features 100% Mossy Oak break up camo finish, Truglo fiber optic sights, 6½ lbs. Mfg. 1998 only.

	$675	$495	$395	$350	$295	$260	$230

Last Mfg.'s Sug. Retail was $832.

MODEL 11-87 SPORTING CLAYS — 12 ga. only, 26 (disc. 1996) or 28 in. VR barrel with extended Rem. chokes (knurled extension chokes allow for no-wrench field changes), specially balanced, satin finished walnut, top metal surfaces have fine matte finish, radiused recoil pad, twin bead sights on 5/16 wide VR, 7½ lbs. New 1992.

Mfg.'s Sug. Retail	$833	$660	$565	$440	$385	$300	$275	$260

* *Model 11-87 Sporting Clays NP* — 12 ga. only, features matte nickel plated receiver with engraving, satin finished checkered stock and forearm, 28 (new 1998) or 30 in. VR ported barrel with extended choke tubes, 7¾ lbs. New 1997.

Mfg.'s Sug. Retail	$905	$750	$625	$485	$420	$335	$295	$260

MODEL 11-87 PREMIER SKEET — 12 ga. only, 26 in. VR Rem. choked barrel, deluxe walnut with quality cut checkering, 7¾ lbs. New 1987.

Mfg.'s Sug. Retail	$799	$640	$540	$485	$425	$375	$325	$295

Add approx. $70 for left-hand action.
Subtract 10% if without Rem. chokes.

MODEL 11-87 PREMIER TRAP — 12 ga. only, 30 in. raised VR Rem. choked barrel, deluxe walnut stock (Monte Carlo became standard in 1996) with quality cut checkering, 8¼ lbs. New 1987.

Mfg.'s Sug. Retail	$833	$660	$565	$440	$385	$300	$275	$260

Subtract $30 if without Monte Carlo stock.
Add approx. $40 for left-hand action (disc. 1994).
Subtract 10% if without Rem. chokes.

Grading	100%	98%	95%	90%	80%	70%	60%

MODEL 11-87 175TH ANNIVERSARY — 12 ga. only, 28 in. barrel with Rem-chokes, 175th Anniversary Model (1816-1991) with light engraving and high gloss wood finish. 1991 mfg. only.

			$515	$425	$335		

Last Mfg.'s Sug. Retail was $618.

MODEL 11-87 D-GRADE (TOURNAMENT) — custom order only, any gauge. Mfg. 1963-present.

Mfg.'s Sug. Retail	$2,610	$2,100	$1,650	$1,200

MODEL 11-87 F-GRADE (PREMIER) — custom order only, any gauge. Mfg. 1963-present.

Mfg.'s Sug. Retail	$5,377	$4,495	$3,550	$2,500

MODEL 11-87 F-GRADE W/GOLD (GOLD PREMIER) — with gold inlay, custom order only. Mfg. 1963-present.

Mfg.'s Sug. Retail	$8,062	$7,125	$4,050	$3,000

Note: Grades differ in quality, grade of wood, and amount of engraving.

Remington Shotguns: Semi-Auto, Model 11-96

MODEL 11-96 EURO LIGHTWEIGHT — 12 ga. only, steel receiver with distinctive slight hump over chamber, 26 or 28 in. 6mm VR Rem. choked barrel, checkered walnut stock and forearm, receiver panel engraving, approx. 7 lbs. New late 1996.

Mfg.'s Sug. Retail	$852	$715	$615	$550	$475	$395	$335	$295

100%	98%	95%	90%	80%	70%	60%	50%	40%	30%	20%	10%

SHOTGUNS: SINGLE BARREL

MODEL NO. 3 RIDER SINGLE BARREL — 10, 12, 16, 20, 24, or 28 ga., single barrel, 30 or 32 in. barrels, top lever break open, plain pistol grip stock. Approx. 25,000 mfg. 1893-1905.

$325	$290	$260	$230	$200	$170	$140	$110	$85	$65	$50	$35

MODEL NO. 9 RIDER SINGLE BARREL — similar to No. 3, with auto ejector. Mfg. 1902-1910.

$375	$325	$290	$260	$230	$200	$170	$140	$110	$85	$65	$50

Grading	100%	98%	95%	90%	80%	70%	60%

MODEL 90-T (TRAP) — 12 ga., 32 (disc. 1993) or 34 in. full choke VR barrel with fixed full choke, matte black receiver and wood around tang area, deluxe checkered stock and forearm, short throw top-lever release, elongated forcing cone, approx. 8¾ lbs. Mfg. 1992-97.

	$1,850	$1,550	$1,375	$1,175	$1,025	$925	$850

Last Mfg.'s Sug. Retail was $3,199.

Add $50 for factory porting.

* *Model 90-T HPAR (High Post w/adj. Rib)* — features high post, adj. rib. Mfg. 1994-97.

	$2,625	$2,150	$1,850	$1,650	$1,450	$1,325	$1,075

Last Mfg.'s Sug. Retail was $3,992.

MODEL 310 SKEET — .32 Rimfire case loaded with No. 12 leadshot, breakopen single shot, .310 bore shotgun, used in conjunction with a self-operated trap set which threw half-size clay targets, entire set-up included gun, shooting booth, ammunition, and trap thrower, 5½ lbs., mfg. circa late '50s - early '60s.

Gun only	$375	$325	$275	$225	$195	$175	$150

Add 25%-75% depending on the amount of original accessories included.

This model was never mass produced, but test marketed for approx. 5 years in CT, NJ, and TX primarily at amusement parks. It failed commercially due to lack of sales.

Grading	100%	98%	95%	90%	80%	70%	60%

SHOTGUNS: SLIDE ACTION, DISC.

REMINGTON REPEATING SHOTGUN — 12 ga., hammerless, bottom ejection, takedown, plain barrel only, blue finish, sight notch on receiver top, marked "REMINGTON ARMS CO." with February 3rd, 1903 and May 18th, 1905 patent dates, walnut pistol grip stock and short forearm, hard rubber buttplate, 7½ lbs., approx. 10,000 mfg. 1908-1910.

	$295	$225	$200	$175	$150	$125	$110

R

Add 10% for 32 in. barrel.

There were 7 grades of this model (Numbers 0-6) that were originally priced from $27 to approx. $140. This model was renamed the Model 10 in 1911.

MODEL 10A SLIDE ACTION — 12 ga., 26-32 in. barrels, various chokes, takedown, plain pistol grip stock. Mfg. 1907-1929. Add 10% for 32 in. full choke barrel.

	$300	$275	$200	$175	$150	$125	$110

Add 10% for 32 in. barrel.
Add 35% for guns marked "Long Range" - beware of fakes.

MODEL 17A SLIDE ACTION — 20 ga., 26-32 in. barrel, various chokes, takedown, bottom ejection, 4 shot mag., plain grip stock. Approx. 48,000 mfg., 1917-1933.

Plain barrel	$350	$275	$220	$195	$165	$140	$110
Solid. rib	$450	$375	$325	$290	$270	$250	$210

Grades range from A - F in suffix form, F being the highest. Large premiums are paid for mint condition, higher grade models.

MODEL 29A SLIDE ACTION — 12 ga., 26-32 in. barrel, bottom ejection, various chokes, takedown, 5 shot mag., checkered pistol grip stock. Approx. 24,000 mfg., 1929-1933. Add 15% for solid rib, 25% for VR.

	$325	$265	$235	$200	$150	$120	$100

* **32 in. Long Range barrel** — should be marked "Long Range" - beware of fakes.

	$525	$475	$425	$350	$250	$200	$180

Grades range from A - C and TA - TF, lowest to highest. Premiums exist for finer condition upper grades. The Model 29 was similar in appearance to the Model 10.

MODEL 29S — "Trap Special" with trap style straight grip stock, matted or VR rib.

	$500	$450	$425	$375	$350	$325	$300

Add 20% for VR rib.

MODEL 31A SLIDE ACTION — 12, 16, or 20 ga., side ejection, 2 or 4 shot mag., 26-32 in. barrels, various chokes, takedown, pistol grip stock. Approx. 160,000 mfg., 1931-1949.

Plain barrel	$395	$345	$300	$265	$225	$185	$150
Solid rib	$455	$385	$345	$300	$270	$230	$190
Vent. rib	$475	$415	$375	$320	$290	$250	$210

Add 15% for 20 ga.

Grades range from A - F suffixes. Higher grades will bring considerable premiums in excellent condition. TC suffix is Target Model. A Model 31L (lightweight) was mfg. 1948-1950 and while rare, demand dictates to subtract 20% for this variation. Early models will command a small premium in this model.

MODEL 31B "SPECIAL" — higher grade wood and hand checkered pistol grip stock and forearm.

	$650	$550	$440	$385	$360	$305	$275

MODEL 31R "RIOT" GRADE — features shortened barrel.

	$425	$365	$325	$295	$270	$230	$190

MODEL 31D TOURNAMENT — features scroll engraving.

	$1,100	$880	$715	$580	$525	$495	$470

MODEL 31E EXPERT — features scroll engraving with game scene on left side of receiver.

| | $1,320 | $1,100 | $935 | $880 | $770 | $660 | $605 |

MODEL 31F PREMIER — features scroll engraving and game scenes on both sides of receiver. Introduced 1942.

| | $2,100 | $1,800 | $1,600 | $1,500 | $1,300 | $1,050 | $875 |

Add 20% for 20 ga.

Note: Grades differ in quality, grade of wood, and amount of engraving.

This model was also available with a Cutts compensator 1940-49, or a Poly Choke on special order from 1941-49.

MODEL 31TC TRAP — similar to 31A, with 12 ga. only, 30 or 32 in. barrel, vent. rib, full choke, trap stock and beavertail forend, pad.

| | $875 | $795 | $675 | $575 | $450 | $375 | $300 |

Subtract 10% for lightweight receiver.

TC stands for Trap with C Grade wood.

MODEL 31S TRAP SPECIAL — solid rib barrel, plainer wood.

| | $550 | $500 | $450 | $400 | $365 | $345 | $325 |

MODEL 31H HUNTER — similar to 31S, with sporter stock. Mfg. 1941-disc.

| | $395 | $350 | $300 | $275 | $250 | $220 | $195 |

MODEL 31L LIGHTWEIGHT — features an alloy receiver, available in both field and skeet, introduced 1941.

| | $350 | $325 | $300 | $275 | $250 | $225 | $200 |

MODEL 31 SKEET — similar to 31A, with 26 in. skeet bored barrel, standard solid rib, beavertail forend.

| Plain barrel | $495 | $450 | $395 | $365 | $335 | $265 | $220 |
| Vent. rib | $650 | $550 | $495 | $425 | $375 | $340 | $295 |

Subtract 10% for lightweight receiver.
Add 20% for 20 ga. with VR barrel.

SHOTGUNS: SLIDE ACTION, MODEL 870 & VARIATIONS

3 in. shells (12 or 20 ga.) may be shot in Magnum receivers only regardless of what the barrel markings may indicate (the ejection port is larger in these Magnum models with M suffix serialization).

MODEL 870AP SLIDE ACTION — "Wingmaster", 12, 16, or 20 ga., 26, 28, or 30 in. barrel, 5 shot, various chokes, plain pistol grip stock. Mfg. 1950-1963.

| Plain barrel | $220 | $195 | $175 | $165 | $140 | $120 | $110 |
| Vent. rib | $250 | $220 | $200 | $195 | $165 | $150 | $140 |

Add 15% for "Sun Grain" blonde wood (optional beginning 1959).

MODEL 870ADL — deluxe checkered version of 870AP. Mfg. 1950-1963.

Plain barrel	$250	$220	$200	$180	$165	$140	$120
Matted top barrel	$275	$250	$220	$210	$195	$165	$140
Vent. rib	$300	$275	$250	$225	$200	$175	$150

MODEL 870BDL — select walnut stock.

| Plain barrel | $275 | $250 | $220 | $200 | $180 | $165 | $140 |
| Vent. rib | $315 | $290 | $260 | $240 | $210 | $195 | $165 |

SPORTSMAN 12 PUMP — 12 ga. only (3 in. chamber), 28 or 30 in. barrel, recoil pad, VR standard, hardwood stock and forearm, Model 870 type action, 7½ lbs. Mfg. 1984-86.

| | $275 | $235 | $195 | $175 | $160 | $150 | $140 |

Last Mfg.'s Sug. Retail was $270.

Add $35 for Rem. chokes.

Grading	100%	98%	95%	90%	80%	70%	60%

MODEL 870 EXPRESS — 12, 20 (new 1991), 28 ga. (disc.), or .410 bore (disc.), 3 in. chamber, 20, 21 (Turkey Express only), 25 (28 ga. or .410 bore only), 26, or 28 in. VR Rem. choked (12 or 20 ga., supplied with Mod. Rem. choke) barrel, parkerized metal, matte finished hardwood stock and forearm, solid recoil pad, 7¼ lbs. New 1987.

Mfg.'s Sug. Retail	$305	$245	$200	$175	$160	$145	$135	$130

Add approx. $30 for 28 ga. or .410 bore (disc.).
Add $14 for Turkey Express Model.
Add $67 for Turkey Express RealTree Advantage camo finish (new 1998).
Add $27 for left-hand action (12 ga., 28 in. barrel only, new 1998).
Add $91 for Combo package (extra 20 in. IC barrel with rifle sights, 12 or 20 ga.).
Add $134 for Combo package (extra 20 in. fully rifled deer barrel, 12 or 20 ga.).

* Model 870 Synthetic Express — 12 ga. only, 26 or 28 in. VR barrel with 1 Rem. choke, features black synthetic stock and forearm. New 1994.

Mfg.'s Sug. Retail	$312	$250	$200	$175	$160	$145	$135	$130

* Model 870 Express Deer Gun — 12 ga. only, 20 in. IC choked barrel or fully rifled barrel with rifle sights, Monte Carlo stock. Introduced in 1991.

Mfg.'s Sug. Retail	$300	$245	$195	$165	$150	$140	$130	$125

Add $39 for fully rifled deer barrel.
Add $78 for cantilever scope system and IC Rem. choke (disc. 1991).

* Model 870 Youth — 20 ga. only, 21 in. VR barrel with Rem. choke, 13 in. LOP with recoil pad, choice of RealTree Advantage camo (new 1998), or regular wood finish stock and forearm, 6 lbs.

Mfg.'s Sug. Retail	$305	$245	$200	$175	$155	$140	$130	$125

Add $34 for Youth Deer Gun (fully rifled 20 in. barrel). New 1994.

* Model 870 Express Synthetic HD (Home Defense) — 12 ga. only, 18 in. cyl. choked barrel with bead sights, black synthetic stock and forend. Introduced 1991.

Mfg.'s Sug. Retail	$292	$235	$195	$165	$150	$140	$130	$125

MODEL 870 EXPRESS SUPER MAGNUM — 12 ga., 3½ in. chamber, choice of checkered natural hardwood, black synthetic, or 100% RealTree Advantage camo stock and forearm, 23 (camo only), 26 (synthetic only), or 28 (wood only) in. VR barrel, matte or 100% camo finish metal, recoil pad, approx. 7¼ lbs. New 1998.

Mfg.'s Sug. Retail	$345	$275	$215	$180	$165	$145	$135	$130

Add $7 for black synthetic stock and forend.
Add $20 for synthetic Turkey Model with 23 in. barrel (new 1999).
Add $132 for combo package (includes 26 in. regular and 20 in. fully rifled deer barrel).

* Model 870 Express Super Magnum Turkey Camo — features 100% RealTree Advantage camo on metal and stock/forearm, 23 in. VR barrel only with Turkey extra full Rem. choke. New 1998.

Mfg.'s Sug. Retail	$465	$370	$300	$240	$200	$175	$160	$145

* Model 870 Express Super Magnum Synthetic Camo — 12 ga., 3½ in. chamber, 23 or 26 in. VR barrel with Rem. choke, 100% Mossy Oak break up camo coverage, wood or synthetic stock and forearm. New 1999.

Mfg.'s Sug. Retail	$532	$385	$320	$265	$240	$220	$200	$180

MODEL 870 FIELD WINGMASTER — 12, 16 (disc. 1980), 20 (LW-20), 28 (disc. late 1994, reintroduced 1999) ga., or .410 (disc. late 1994, reintroduced 1999) bore, various barrel lengths, incorporates twin slide rails, 3 in. chambers became standard in 1985, Rem. chokes became standard in 1987, lightweight frame on 20 ga. was introduced 1972, checkered walnut stock and forearm, a choice of high gloss or satin (28 in. barrel only) wood finish became available in 1991. Mfg. 1964-present.

Plain barrel			$250	$225	$205	$190	$175	$160	$150

Grading	100%	98%	95%	90%	80%	70%	60%

* **Vent. rib** — became standard in 1985.

  Mfg.'s Sug. Retail $532 $375 $300 $245 $200 $185 $170 $160

  Subtract 10% without Rem. chokes.
  Add $48 for left-hand model (12 ga. only, disc. 1994).
  Add $80 for 20 in. fully rifled Cantilever deer barrel (12 ga. - new 1992 or 20 ga. - mfg. 1992-95).
  Beginning 1998, rolled scroll engraving started to appear on 20 ga. guns only.

* **Small Gauge Model 870** — 28 ga. or .410 bore, scaled down 870 on lightweight smaller frame, 25 in. fixed (F or M) or Rem. choke (28 ga. only, new 1999) barrel, VR became standard 1984, 6-6½ lbs. Mfg. 1969-1994, reintroduced 1999.

  Mfg.'s Sug. Retail $559 $500 $425 $375 $325 $295 $260 $240

  Add $53 for 28 ga.
  Subtract $40 without VR.

MODEL 870 MAGNUM DUCK GUN — 3 in. chamber, 12 or 20 ga., 26, 28, or 30 in. full or mod. barrel, recoil pad. Mfg. 1964-present. 3 in. chambers became standard on all Model 870s starting in 1985. Rem. chokes became standard 1987 (introduced 1986 as $40 option).

  Please refer to Model 870 Field Wingmaster prices.

MODEL 870 SPECIAL PURPOSE — 12 ga. only, differs only in that metal parts are sand blasted, choice of Mossy Oak Camo (new 1992), black synthetic, or checkered wood stock with low luster finish, 21 (Turkey barrel), 26, or 28 in. VR barrel. Rem. chokes were introduced 1986.

  Add $75 for wood stock and forearm (disc. 1992).
  Subtract 10% without Rem. chokes.

* **Model 870 Special Purpose Synthetic Camo** — 12 ga. only, 26 or 28 (disc. 1995) in. VR barrel with Rem. choke, available in either Mossy Oak (disc. 1995) Bottomland (disc. 1996), or full coverage Mossy Oak Break-Up finish (1997). New 1994.

  Mfg.'s Sug. Retail $496 $380 $310 $235 $200 $170 $150 $130

* **Model 870 SPS-BG Camo (Special Purpose Synthetic Big Game)** — 12 ga. only, 20 in. plain barrel with rifle sights and Rem. choke. Mfg. 1994 only.

  $350 $285 $235 $200 $170 $150 $130
  Last Mfg.'s Sug. Retail was $442.

* **Model 870 Special Purpose Turkey (SPS-T)** — 12 ga. only, 21 in. VR barrel with Rem. choke, available in flat black, Mossy Oak (disc. 1996), Greenleaf (disc. 1996), or Realtree X-tra Brown (full SPS-T-CAMO, mfg. 1997 only) finish.

  Mfg.'s Sug. Retail $425 $320 $285 $230 $200 $170 $150 $130

  Add $85 for RealTree X-tra Brown Camo finish (disc. 1997).

  ► **Model 870 SP Turkey Camo NWTF 25th Anniversary** — 12 ga., limited mfg. to commemorate the 25th Anniversary of the NWTF during 1998, Truglo fiber optic sights.

  Mfg.'s Sug. Retail $565 $425 $350 $225

* **Model 870 Special Purpose Deer Gun (SPS-Deer)** — 12 ga. only, 3 in. chamber, 20 in. Rem. choke barrel (disc. 1992) or fully rifled barrel with iron sights (new 1993), satin finished (disc. 1992) or black synthetic (new 1993) stock and forearm, matte black metal, 7¼ lbs. New 1989.

  Mfg.'s Sug. Retail $436 $345 $275 $225 $195 $175 $160 $145

  Add $28 for Cantilever deer barrel with Rem. choke (disc. 1996).
  Add $60 for fully rifled Cantilever deer barrel.
  Add $65 for Cantilever scope mount system (disc. 1992).

* **Model 870 Special Purpose Super Slug Deer** — 12 ga. only, 3 in. chamber, 23 in. fully rifled Cantilever barrel, matte black metal finish, black synthetic Monte Carlo stock and forearm, approx. 8 lbs. New 1999.

  Mfg.'s Sug. Retail $520 $425 $350 $300 $250 $225 $195 $175

Grading	100%	98%	95%	90%	80%	70%	60%

MODEL 870 LIGHTWEIGHT — 20 ga. only, lighter and shorter mahogany stock than model listed below, 23 in. barrel. Mfg. 1972-1983.

	$270	$230	$210	$190	$175	$165	$155

Add $30 for VR.

MODEL 870 LIGHTWEIGHT (MAGNUM) — 20 ga., 3 in. chamber, 26 or 28 in. barrel, 6 lbs. Mfg. 1972-1994. Rem. chokes became standard 1987.

	$365	$320	$260	$225	$200	$175	$160

Last Mfg.'s Sug. Retail was $460.

Subtract 10% without Rem. chokes.
Subtract $40 without VR.

MODEL 870 SPECIAL FIELD — 12 or 20 (LW-20) ga., lighter straight grip stock with solid recoil pad, 21 (disc. 1993) or 23 (new 1994) in. VR barrel, 6¼ or 7 lbs. New 1984. Rem. chokes became standard 1987 (introduced 1986 as $40 option). Disc. 1995.

	$380	$320	$265	$230	$210	$190	$175

Last Mfg.'s Sug. Retail was $473.

Subtract 10% without Rem. chokes.

MODEL 870 BRUSHMASTER — 12 or 20 (disc.) ga., 20 in. barrel with imp. cyl. (disc.) or Rem. choke and rifle sights, 3 in. chamber standard for 1985, normal bluing with satin finished wood. Disc. 1994.

	$355	$310	$255	$225	$200	$175	$160

Last Mfg.'s Sug. Retail was $452.

Add $43 for left-hand model.

MODEL 870 MARINE MAGNUM — 12 ga. only, 18 in. barrel, features electroless nickel plating on all metal parts, supplied with 7 shot mag., sling swivels and Cordura sling, 7½ lbs.

Mfg.'s Sug. Retail	$513	$390	$330	$255	$225	$200	$175	$160

MODEL 870 POLICE — 12 ga. only, 18 or 20 in. plain barrel, choice of blue or parkerized finish, bead or rifle (disc. 1995, 20 in. barrel only) sights, Police cylinder or IC choke. New 1994.

Mfg.'s Sug. Retail	$431	$335	$285	$220	$195	$175	$160	$145

Add $13 for parkerized finish.
Add $44 for rifle sights.

MODEL 870 RIOT — 12 ga. only, 18 or 20 in. barrel, choice of blue or parkerized metal finish. Disc. 1991.

	$295	$265	$225	$200	$170	$150	$130

Last Mfg.'s Sug. Retail was $355.

Add $40 for police rifle sights (20 in. barrel only).

MODEL 870 D-GRADE (TOURNAMENT) — custom order only, any gauge. Mfg. 1950-present.

Mfg.'s Sug. Retail	$2,741	$2,175	$1,700	$1,200

MODEL 870 F-GRADE (PREMIER) — custom order only, any gauge. Mfg. 1950-present.

Mfg.'s Sug. Retail	$5,647	$4,750	$3,650	$2,600

MODEL 870 F-GRADE W/GOLD (GOLD PREMIER) — with gold inlays, custom order only. Mfg. 1950-present.

Mfg.'s Sug. Retail	$8,465	$7,425	$4,250	$3,100

Note: Grades differ in quality, grade of wood, and amount of engraving. Prices also vary accordingly.

MODEL 870 DUCKS UNLIMITED — "DU" in serial number, disc.

	$335	$270	$195

Remington has offered many variations of the Model 870 specifically manufactured according to individual DU chapter specifications. The price of a DU 870 varies substantially from the "DU point of purchase" to real market conditions. When contemplating a DU gun it is always important to know how many of that particular variation were

Grading	100%	98%	95%	90%	80%	70%	60%

manufactured. The Remington factory normally has this information unless the special DU work was subcontracted elsewhere.

While most DU guns are good vehicles for fund raising, their collectability to date has been minimal. Actual market conditions indicate that unless production is truly limited, most DU firearms sell very close to the model which they were derived from. Also, any collectability that does exist is for 100% guns new in the box with warranty papers. Used DU guns have values comparable to the standard model from which they were derived.

In addition to regular DU guns, Remington has also produced special editions including the 1982 Mississippi Edition (dinner gun) and a 1974 DU (dinner gun — first 500 mfg.). These were rarer DU shotguns, and current values could vary significantly.

MODEL 870 150TH ANNIVERSARY — 12 ga. only, 2,534 mfg. 1966 only.

	100%	98%	95%
	$400	$325	$275

MODEL 870 BICENTENNIAL — 12 ga. only, configurations include Trap, Skeet, and Trade, mfg. to commemorate U.S. Bicentennial (1776-1976).

	100%	98%	95%
Trap or Skeet	$425	$350	$295
Trade	$375	$295	$225

In 1976, the 870 Bicentennial Trap retailed for $255 (add $10 for Monte Carlo stock), and the Skeet retailed for $220.

MODEL 870 SC SKEET — 12, 20, 28 ga., or .410 bore, 26 in. VR skeet bore barrel. Mfg. 1950-1981.

	100%	98%	95%	90%	80%	70%	60%
	$395	$325	$275	$225	$200	$185	$170

MODEL 870 SKEET MATCHED PAIR — .410 bore or 28 ga., 1,503 cased sets mfg. 1969 only.

	100%	98%	95%
	$1,150	$995	$895

MODEL 870 TA TRAP — 12 ga. trap model, deluxe walnut, VR. Add $15 for Monte Carlo stock. Mfg. 1978-1986.

	100%	98%	95%	90%	80%	70%	60%
	$425	$375	$325	$275	$250	$225	$200

Last Mfg.'s Sug. Retail was $430.

MODEL 870 TB TRAP — similar to 870, with 28 or 30 in. VR full choke barrel, trap stock, recoil pad. Mfg. 1950-1981.

	100%	98%	95%	90%	80%	70%	60%
	$425	$375	$325	$275	$250	$225	$200

MODEL 870 TC TRAP — higher grade walnut and special VR, Rem. chokes became standard 1987. Mfg. 1950-1979, reintroduced 1996.

		100%	98%	95%	90%	80%	70%	60%
Mfg.'s Sug. Retail	$680	$600	$475	$400	$350	$275	$240	$220

Subtract 5% if without Monte Carlo stock.

Early Model 870 TC Trap guns had hand cut checkering.

MODEL 870 COMPETITION TRAP — 12 ga. single shot competition model, reduced recoil, special checkered walnut, VR. Mfg. 1980-1986.

	100%	98%	95%	90%	80%	70%	60%
	$550	$475	$395	$350	$315	$275	$250

Last Mfg.'s Sug. Retail was $680.

MODEL 870 ALL AMERICAN TRAP — 30 in. full choke barrel, engraved receiver, triggerguard and barrel, deluxe trap stock. Approx. 1,000 mfg., 1972-1976.

	100%	98%	95%	90%	80%	70%	60%
	$795	$700	$650	$605	$495	$440	$385

RENATO GAMBA

Please refer to the Gamba section in this text.

RENETTE, GASTINNE

Please refer to the Gastinne Renette section of this text.

REPUBLIC ARMS, INC.

Current manufacturer established in 1997, and located in Chino, CA.

Grading	100%	98%	95%	90%	80%	70%	60%

PISTOLS: SEMI-AUTO

THE PATRIOT — .45 ACP cal., double action only, ultra compact with 3 in. barrel, 6 shot mag., black polymer frame with stainless steel slide, locked breech action, checkered grips, 20 oz. New 1997.

No Mfg.'s Retail			$260	$225	$200	$185	$175	$165	$155

REPUBLIC ARMS OF SOUTH AFRICA

Current manufacturer located in Jeppestown, Union of South Africa. Exclusively imported by TSF Ltd., located in Fairfax, VA.

PISTOLS: SEMI-AUTO

RAP 401 — 9mm Para. cal., 8 shot mag., otherwise similar to Rap-440. New 1999.

Mfg.'s Sug. Retail	$495		$425	$375	$350	$325	$300	$275	$250

RAP-440 — .40 S&W cal., compact double action, 3½ in. barrel with high contrast 3 dot sights, last shot hold open, hammer drop safety/decocking lever, firing pin block safety, 7 shot mag., all steel construction, 31½ oz., includes case, spare magazine, and lock. New 1998.

Mfg.'s Sug. Retail	$545		$475	$425	$395	$375	$330	$300	$275

Add $50 for Trilux tritium night sights.

SHOTGUNS: SLIDE ACTION

MUSLER MODEL — 12 ga., lightweight shotgun, polymer reinforced stock and forearm, action opening release lever, action locks open after the last round. New 1998.

Mfg.'s Sug. Retail	$549		$475	$425	$395	$375	$330	$300	$275

RHODE ISLAND ARMS COMPANY

Previous manufacturer located in Hope Valley, RI.

SHOTGUNS: O/U

MORRONE MODEL — 12 or 20 ga., 26 or 28 in. plain barrels, boxlock, extractors, single trigger, checkered straight or pistol grip stock. Mfg. 1949-1953, only 500 of these guns were mfg., 450 in 12 ga., and 50 in 20 ga., very few with VR, they are quite rare although collector interest is not overwhelming.

			$1,100	$880	$770	$660	$550	$495	$440

Add 20% for 20 gauge.
Add 20% for VR.

RIB MOUNTAIN ARMS, INC.

Current rifle manufacturer established circa 1992, and currently located in Beresford, SD. Previously located in Sturgis, SD. Dealer or consumer direct sales.

RIFLES: BOLT ACTION

MODEL 92 — .50 BMG cal., match grade barrel with muzzle brake, long action, walnut thumbhole stock, Timney trigger, approx. 28 lbs. New 1997.

Mfg.'s Sug. Retail	$3,475		$3,175	$2,725	$2,275	$2,000	$1,750	$1,575	$1,300

MODEL 93 — similar to Model 92, except has short action with removable shell holder bolt, approx. 25 lbs. New 1997.

Mfg.'s Sug. Retail	$3,475		$3,175	$2,725	$2,275	$2,000	$1,750	$1,575	$1,300

RICHLAND ARMS COMPANY

Previous importer (until 1986) located in Blissfield, MI. The models listed below were made by various manufacturers located in either Italy or Spain.

Grading	100%	98%	95%	90%	80%	70%	60%

SHOTGUNS

MODEL 80 LS SINGLE SHOT — 12, 20 ga., or .410 bore, 26 or 28 in. full choke barrel. Mfg. 1986 only.

	$140	$120	$110	$100	$90	$80	$70

Last Mfg.'s Sug. Retail was $162.

MODEL 711 MAGNUM SxS — 10 ga., 3½ in. chamber, 12 ga., 3 in. chamber, 32 in. full and full, 30 in. full and full, 20, 28 ga., and .410 bore also available on special order, hammerless, boxlock, extractors, checkered, walnut stock, recoil pad. Mfg. 1963-1985 in Spain.

	100%	98%	95%	90%	80%	70%	60%
10 gauge	$400	$325	$275	$250	$230	$210	$190
12 gauge	$340	$295	$265	$250	$230	$210	$190
20 gauge	$450	$340	$295	$260	$230	$210	$195

MODEL 707 DELUXE SxS — 12 or 20 ga., 3 in. chambers, 26, 28, or 30 in. barrels, various chokes, boxlock, extractors, double triggers, checkered stock and forend. Mfg. 1963-1972 in Spain.

	$330	$305	$290	$275	$250	$230	$210

MODEL 200 FIELD GRADE SxS — 12, 16, 20, 28 ga., or .410 bore, 22, 26, and 28 in. barrels, various chokes, Anson & Deeley boxlock, extractors, double triggers, checkered stock, 6 lbs. 2 oz. - 7 lbs. 4 oz. Mfg. 1963-1985 in Spain.

	$320	$285	$255	$225	$195	$175	$150

Last Mfg.'s Sug. Retail was $379.

MODEL 202 ALL PURPOSE SxS — similar to Field, except 2 sets of barrels, 12 and 20 ga. only. Mfg. 1963-disc. in Spain.

	$305	$260	$230	$220	$195	$165	$150

MODEL 41 ULTRA O/U — 20, 28 ga., or .410 bore, 3 in. chambers (.410 bore only), single non-selective trigger, 26 or 28 in. barrels, extractors, VR, engraved silver finished receiver, select checkered walnut stock and forearm, 6 lbs. 2 oz. Importation disc. 1986.

	$265	$220	$210	$200	$190	$180	$170

Last Mfg.'s Sug. Retail was $298.

MODEL 747 O/U — 12 or 20 ga. only, 3 in. chambers, Greener crossbolt, boxlock action, VR and barrels, SST, extractors. Importation disc. 1986.

	$420	$350	$325	$310	$295	$280	$265

Last Mfg.'s Sug. Retail was $464.

MODEL 757 O/U — 12 ga., 3 in. chambers, boxlock action with Greener crossbolt, vent. barrels and rib, double triggers, extractors, walnut stock and forearm, 7 lbs. 4 oz. New 1986. Importation disc. 1986.

	$290	$260	$230	$215	$200	$185	$170

Last Mfg.'s Sug. Retail was $325.

Add $70 for multi-chokes (Model 7570).

MODEL 787 O/U — 12 ga. only, 3 in. chambers, boxlock action with silver finish, single trigger, vent. barrels and rib, extractors, walnut stock with recoil pad, is supplied with 5 interchangeable choke tubes, 7¼ lbs. Made 1986 only.

	$435	$375	$340	$310	$295	$280	$265

Last Mfg.'s Sug. Retail was $471.

MODEL 808 O/U — 12 ga., 26, 28, or 30 in. barrels, various chokes, boxlock, extractors, checkered stock. Mfg. 1963-1968 in Italy.

	$420	$360	$330	$315	$290	$270	$230

MODEL 810 O/U — 10 ga., 3½ in. chambers, ST, extractors.

	$600	$550	$500	$460	$430	$395	$360

MODEL 828 O/U — 28 ga., single non-selective trigger, extractors, engraved, only 250 imported.

	$550	$500	$450	$400	$350	$325	$300

RIEDL RIFLE COMPANY

RIFLES: SINGLE SHOT

SINGLE SHOT RIFLE — many cals., 22-30 in. barrel, rack and pinion action, lever trigger guard activated, fully adj. trigger, select walnut stock, basically custom made.

	100%	98%	95%	90%	80%	70%	60%
	$495	$470	$440	$415	$385	$330	$305
* *Stainless barrel*							
	$560	$535	$505	$480	$450	$395	$370

RIFLES, INC.

Current manufacturer located in Cedar City, UT. Dealer or direct consumer sales.

RIFLES: BOLT ACTION

CLASSIC — various cals., features Remington or Winchester stainless steel controlled round action, stainless lapped barrel, matte stainless finish, laminated fiberglass stock with pillar glass bedding, approx. 6½ lbs. New 1996.
Mfg.'s Sug. Retail $1,800 $1,725 $1,325 $1,050
    Add $100 for left-hand action.

LIGHTWEIGHT STRATA STAINLESS — various cals., lightened stainless Remington action, match grade barrel with slimbrake, matte stainless finish, 4¾ lbs. New 1996.
Mfg.'s Sug. Retail $2,400 $2,275 $1,825 $1,525
    Add $150 for left-hand action.

LIGHTWEIGHT 70 — most cals. up to .375 H&H, features Winchester Model 70 stainless control round feeding blue printed action, match grade stainless steel barrel with muzzle brake, matte stainless finish, laminated Kevlar/boron/graphite stock with glass bedding, approx. 5½ lbs. New 1997.
Mfg.'s Sug. Retail $2,300 $2,175 $1,725 $1,450
    Add $150 for left-hand action.

VARMINT/TARGET — similar to Classic, except has different stock design and dimensions, different barrel contour. New 1998.
Mfg.'s Sug. Retail $1,900 $1,800 $1,375 $1,075
    Add $250 for Varmint brake.

MASTER SERIES — various cals. up to .300 Wby. Mag., designed for long range accuracy, blue printed Rem. Model 700 action, fiberglass stock, guaranteed to shoot ½ MOA. New 1998.
Mfg.'s Sug. Retail $2,400 $2,275 $1,825 $1,525

SAFARI — various cals., features Winchester Model 70 control round feeding action, match grade barrel with slimbrake, matte stainless or black Teflon finish. New 1996.
Mfg.'s Sug. Retail $2,400 $2,275 $1,825 $1,525

RIGANIAN, RAY (RIFLEMAKER)

Current custom riflemaker and gunsmith established in 1988 and located in Glendale, CA. Consumer direct sales.

RIFLES: BOLT ACTION

Ray Riganian manufactures a Peerless Series (I & II) of custom rifles, using the customer's Win. Model 70, Rem. 700, or Sako action. Prices range from $1,850-$4,965 w/o action, depending on action, caliber, and quality of wood. He also makes a best quality sporter rifle based on a Win. Model 70 or large ring Mauser 98 action ($6,500 starting price), in addition to a drop box magazine express rifle that starts at $8,500. Please contact the company directly for more information, current pricing, and delivery time.

Grading	100%	98%	95%	90%	80%	70%	60%

RIGBY, JOHN & CO. (GUNMAKERS), INC.

Current manufacturer established during 1735 in Dublin, Ireland. Currently manufactured in Paso Robles, CA since 1997. Previously manufactured in London, England. Currently and distributed domestically by John Rigby & Co. (Gunmakers), Inc., located in Paso Robles, CA. Previously imported by Griffin & Howe until 1998.

Original trade name was W. & J. Rigby circa 1820-1865, during the percussion era. Rigby has always been well known for its dueling pistols. The first London Branch of J. Rigby was opened in 1865, and the Dublin Premises were closed during 1895. The firm became a company in 1900, and has been responsible for many of the large caliber developments in both rifles and ammunition. During 1997, Rigby was acquired by an American investment group located in Paso Robles, CA.

Rigby is one of the world's finest weapons makers. A good portion of the guns they manufacture were custom built to customer specifications. They were chambered for the large black powder express cartridges used for dangerous game in Africa and Asia. The modern Rigby guns follow this same tradition.

We will list the modern Rigby Guns with approximate values but strongly urge that if purchase or sale is contemplated, a professional appraisal be utilized.

RIFLES

Please contact the company directly for more information on the currently manufactured models listed below, including delivery time.

SINGLE SHOT FALLING BLOCK — Farquharson lever actuated action, various English and European cals., 24 in. barrel, ejector, checkered pistol grip stock, deluxe finish and engraving.

$4,100	$3,400	$2,800	$2,400	$2,000	$1,600	$1,250

This model can also be ordered new from the factory with prices starting at approx. $18,000. Values above refer to older specimens that were not custom ordered.

.350 MAGNUM MAGAZINE RIFLE — .350 Magnum cal. originally, most were rechambered to .375 H&H Mag. cal.

$3,995	$3,400	$2,950	$2,600	$2,300	$2,000	$1,700

Values assume out of production models.

RIGBY MAGAZINE RIFLE — Mauser action (pre-1939), claw extraction bolt action, various standard cals. include .300 H&H, .375 H&H, .416 Rigby, .458 Win. Mag., or .505 Gibbs cal., other calibers are available upon request, 3-5 shot mag., 20-25 in. barrel, exhibition grade checkered walnut half pistol grip stock, includes non-detachable scope mounts.

New Rigby Magazine Rifles start in price at $10,500 + F.E.T. taxes.

Many options include wood upgrades, engraving, express sights, telescopic sight, case, or other details.

LIGHTWEIGHT MAGAZINE RIFLE — similar to Rigby Magazine rifle, except light weight design. Base price similar to Rigby Magazine Rifle listed above.

BEST QUALITY SIDELOCK EJECTOR DOUBLE RIFLE — currently mfg. cals. include .375 H&H, .416/500, .470 NE, .500 NE, or .577 NE, older cals. have included .22 LR, .275 Mag., .350 Mag., .416 Rigby, .458 Win. Mag., .465, or .470 NE cal., 24-28 in. barrels, case colored contoured and reinforced sidelock action, folding express rear sight, checkered pistol grip stock, deluxe finish and engraving.

Prices start at $34,750, plus F.E.T.

Grading	100%	98%	95%	90%	80%	70%	60%

BEST QUALITY BOXLOCK EJECTOR DOUBLE RIFLE — current production cals. include .375 H&H, .416/500, .470 NE, .500 NE, or .577 NE cal., 22-26 in. barrels, case colored boxlock action.

> New Best Quality Double Rifle prices start at $16,950 plus F.E.T. for cals. through .470 NE.
> Add $1,500 for .500 NE cal.
> Add $3,000 for .577 NE cal.

SECOND QUALITY BOXLOCK EJECTOR DOUBLE RIFLE — similar to Best Quality, with less select wood and engraving. Disc.

	100%	98%	95%	90%	80%	70%	60%
	$12,750	$10,750	$9,750	$8,750	$7,350	$6,350	$5,000

> Subtract 35% without ejectors.

Values above are for larger calibers, smaller cals. could have less value than listed.

SHOTGUNS: SxS

Please contact the company directly for more information on the currently manufactured models listed below, including delivery time.

BEST QUALITY SIDELOCK - CURRENT PRODUCTION — 12, 16, 20, 28 ga. or 410 bore, case colored or coin finished contoured sidelock action, current engraving includes game scenes on both sidelocks, older engraving included fine frame and border English scroll work.

	Mfg.'s Sug. Retail	98%	95%	90%	80%	70%	60%
	$34,750	$31,500	$26,750	$22,000	$18,000	$14,000	$12,000	$10,500

BOXLOCK SHOTGUN — all ga.'s, barrel lengths and chokes to order, checkered stock to order, auto ejectors, double triggers.

* **Chatsworth Grade**

	100%	98%	95%	90%	80%	70%	60%
	$4,500	$3,500	$3,000	$2,500	$2,000	$1,600	$1,200

* **Sackville Grade** — deluxe engraved.

	100%	98%	95%	90%	80%	70%	60%
	$5,900	$5,000	$4,500	$3,750	$3,100	$2,650	$2,200

> Add 20% for 20 ga.
> Add 40% for 28 ga.
> Add 60% for .410 bore.

SIDELOCK SHOTGUN - PRE-1997 PRODUCTION — all ga.'s, barrel lengths and chokes to specifications, double triggers, auto ejectors stocked to order.

* **Sandringham Grade**

	100%	98%	95%	90%	80%	70%	60%
	$9,500	$7,500	$6,000	$5,000	$4,450	$3,775	$2,950

* **Regal Grade** — deluxe engraved.

	100%	98%	95%	90%	80%	70%	60%
	$12,500	$10,000	$8,750	$7,500	$6,400	$5,250	$4,250

> Add 20% for 20 ga.
> Add 40% for 28 ga.
> Add 60% for .410 bore.

RIZZINI, BATTISTA

Current manufacturer established during 1965, and located in Marcheno, Italy. Imported in the U.S. by William Larkin Moore & Co. located in Scottsdale, AZ and New England Arms Company located in Kittery Point, ME.

RIFLES: O/U

EXPRESS 90 — various cals., ST, ejectors, deluxe wood and features, includes case.

	Mfg.'s Sug. Retail	98%	95%	90%	80%	70%	60%
	$4,600	$3,950	$3,450	$3,025	$2,600	$2,300	$1,950	$1,625

> Add $430 for upgraded wood (Model Express 90 L).

Grading	100%	98%	95%	90%	80%	70%	60%

EXPRESS 92 — similar to Express 90, except has sideplates with more elaborate engraving.

Mfg.'s Sug. Retail   **$5,500**   **$5,125** **$4,725** **$4,150** **$3,500** **$3,000** **$2,500** **$1,900**

Add $4,250 for Express 92 EL with Nizzoli case.

SHOTGUNS: O/U

AURUM — 12, 16, or 20 ga., boxlock action, light engraving, cased. New 1996.

Mfg.'s Sug. Retail   **$2,375**   **$2,175** **$1,750** **$1,525** **$1,325** **$1,125**   **$900**   **$775**

ARTEMIS — similar to Aurum, except has better engraving and wood, cased. New 1996.

Mfg.'s Sug. Retail   **$2,375**   **$2,175** **$1,750** **$1,525** **$1,325** **$1,125**   **$900**   **$775**

ARTEMIS DELUXE — all gauges, game scene engraving with gold inlays.

Mfg.'s Sug. Retail   **$4,700**   **$4,325** **$3,650** **$3,300** **$2,825** **$2,450** **$1,975** **$1,600**

ARTEMIS EL — top-of-the-line gun with elaborate hand-engraving and best quality walnut, Nizzoli cased. New 1996.

Mfg.'s Sug. Retail   **$15,000**   **$13,750** **$11,000** **$9,750** **$8,250** **$6,875** **$5,900** **$4,850**

780 FIELD SERIES — 10, 12, or 16 ga., boxlock action, DTs, extractors, checkered walnut stock and forearm. Importation disc. 1998.

$1,075   **$875**   **$750**   **$675**   **$595**   **$525**   **$450**
Last Mfg.'s Sug. Retail was $1,225.

Add $550 for 10 ga.
Add $150 for ejectors (Model S780 E).
Add $200 for SST with ejectors (Model S780 EM).
Add $350 for SST, ejectors, and upgraded wood (Model S780 EML).

A Model S780 EMEL is also available that is entirely hand-finished and engraved for $5,995.

* **780 Competition Series** — includes Skeet, Trap, and Sporting Clays configuration. Importation disc. 1998.

$1,375 **$1,050**   **$925**   **$825**   **$725**   **$625**   **$525**
Last Mfg.'s Sug. Retail was $1,600.

* **780 Small Gauge Series** — includes 20, 28, or 36 ga., DTs, ejectors. Importation disc. 1998.

$1,275   **$975**   **$875**   **$800**   **$725**   **$625**   **$525**
Last Mfg.'s Sug. Retail was $1,500.

Add $50 for SST (Model 780 EM).

S 780 EMEL — includes Nizzoli case.

Mfg.'s Sug. Retail   **$10,250**   **$9,150** **$8,400** **$7,650** **$6,850** **$6,100** **$5,350** **$4,800**

782 EM FIELD SERIES — 12 or 16 ga., boxlock action with sideplates, SST ejectors, extractors, checkered walnut stock and forearm. Importation disc. 1998.

$1,450 **$1,150**   **$995**   **$875**   **$750**   **$675**   **$550**
Last Mfg.'s Sug. Retail was $1,700.

Add $450 for Slug variation (Model 782 EM Slug).
Add $350 for better engraving and wood (Model 782 EML).

A Model S7820 EMEL is also available that is entirely hand-finished and engraved for $12,000.

* **S 782 EMEL Deluxe** — all gauges, individually made per customer specifications, 27½ in. VR barrels with choke tubes (except .410 bore), coin finished receiver with side plates featuring elaborate Bulino game scene engraving with gold inlays and fine scroll borders, deluxe English walnut, Nizzoli best leather case. Importation began 1994.

Mfg.'s Sug. Retail   **$12,250**   **$10,700** **$9,100** **$8,325** **$7,100** **$6,250** **$5,350** **$4,800**

Grading	100%	98%	95%	90%	80%	70%	60%

790 SERIES COMPETITION — 12 or 20 ga., choice of Trap, Skeet, or Sporting Clays configuration, features black frame outlined with gold line engraving.

Mfg.'s Sug. Retail	$2,275	$1,975	$1,575	$1,300	$1,050	$925	$825	$695

Subtract $150 for 20 ga. Trap.
Subtract $50 for 20 ga. Skeet.
Add $1,050 for 20 ga. Sporting (includes sideplates and quick detachable stock).

A Model 790 Trap EL is also available that is entirely hand-finished with 18 Kt. gold and hand engraving - prices begin at $5,650 in 12 ga., $5,200 in 20 ga.

* ***790 Small Gauge Series*** — similar to 790 Competition Series, except in 20, 28, or 36 ga., SST and ejectors standard.

Mfg.'s Sug. Retail	$1,750	$1,475	$1,150	$995	$875	$750	$675	$550

A Model 790 EMEL is also available that is entirely hand-finished with 18 Kt. gold and hand engraving - prices begin at $9,600.

* ***S 790 EL*** — includes multichokes and case.

Mfg.'s Sug. Retail	$6,250	$5,650	$5,225	$4,750	$4,150	$3,500	$3,000	$2,500

* ***S 790 EMEL Deluxe*** — all gauges, individually made per customer specifications, 27½ in. VR barrels with choke tubes (except .410 bore), color case hardened or coin finished receiver with ornate ornamental engraving and Rizzini crest, deluxe English walnut, Nizzoli best leather case. Importation began 1994.

Mfg.'s Sug. Retail	$10,150	$9,100	$8,250	$7,500	$6,800	$6,000	$5,350	$4,800

792 SMALL GAUGE MAG. SERIES — 20, 28, or 36 ga., Mag. chambers, SST, ejectors, includes engraved sideplates. Importation disc. 1998.

		$1,700	$1,275	$1,050	$895	$750	$675	$595

Last Mfg.'s Sug. Retail was $2,000.

A Model 792 EMEL is also available that is entirely hand-finished with 18 Kt. gold and hand engraving - prices begin at $8,250.

* ***S 792 EMEL Deluxe*** — all gauges, individually made per customer specifications, 27½ in. VR barrels with choke tubes (except .410 bore), coin finished receiver with side plates featuring upgraded Bulino game scene engraving and fine scroll borders, deluxe English walnut, Nizzoli leather case. Importation began 1994.

Mfg.'s Sug. Retail	$9,750	$8,800	$7,950	$7,250	$6,500	$5,800	$5,200	$4,600

MODEL 2000 TRAP — 12 ga. only, includes nickel finished receiver with sideplates, gold trigger, VR barrels and rib. Importation disc. 1998.

		$1,900	$1,500	$1,275	$1,025	$925	$825	$695

Last Mfg.'s Sug. Retail was $2,200.

A Model 2000 Trap EL was also available that was entirely hand finished with 18 Kt. gold and hand-engraving - prices began at $5,290.

MODEL 2000-SP — 12 ga. only, 26, 28, 30, or 32 in. overbored barrels with choke tubes, includes engraved sideplates, semi-fancy select walnut with quick detachable stock, cased. Imported 1994-98.

		$3,250	$2,800	$2,400	$1,975	$1,600	$1,300	$1,000

Last Mfg.'s Sug. Retail was $3,650.

PREMIER SPORTING — 12 or 20 ga., 28, 29½, or 32 in. multi-choke (5 chokes) barrels, hard cased, custom dimensions upon application. Importation began 1994.

Mfg.'s Sug. Retail	$2,750	$2,500	$2,250	$1,950	$1,675	$1,500	$1,375	$1,175

SPORTING EL — includes multichokes and case.

Mfg.'s Sug. Retail	$3,750	$3,425	$2,850	$2,500	$2,225	$1,950	$1,675	$1,500

UPLAND EL — all gauges, 27½ in. VR barrels with choke tubes (except .410 bore), case hardened receiver, deluxe walnut, hard case. Importation began 1994.

Mfg.'s Sug. Retail	$3,450	$3,000	$2,650	$2,300	$1,950	$1,675	$1,500	$1,375

Grading	100%	98%	95%	90%	80%	70%	60%

MODEL MC SINGLE BARREL — 12, 16, 20, 24, 28, 32, 36 ga., or .410 bore, 27½ in. single barrel with VR, sling swivels, checkered hardwood stock.

Mfg.'s Sug. Retail	$440	$375	$285	$240	$200	$175	$160	$145

RIZZINI, EMILIO

Current shotgun manufacturer established during the mid-1950s and located in Brescia, Italy. Currently imported by Tristar Sporting Arms, Ltd., located in N. Kansas City, MO.

All Emilio Rizzini shotguns are equipped with a patented Four Locks locking system. Models listed below were introduced during 1999. All Emilio Rizzini field shotguns are available with internal choke tubes.

SHOTGUNS: O/U

CLASS MODEL — 12, 16, 20, 28 ga., or 410 bore, boxlock action with reinforced frame, hand engraving, select wood, ejectors, SST.

Mfg.'s Sug. Retail	$1,508		$1,375	$1,125	$975	$875	$750	$675	$550

Add $70 for sideplates and case (Class SL Model).

CLASS DE LUXE MODEL — 12, 16, 20, 28 ga., or 410 bore, boxlock action with reinforced frame, hand finished game scene engraving with gold inlays, ejectors, SST, cased.

Mfg.'s Sug. Retail	$3,377		$2,975	$2,625	$2,300	$1,950	$1,675	$1,500	$1,375

Add $170 for sideplates (Class SL De Luxe Model.)

BRIXIAN DE LUXE — all gauges, top-of-the-line model, boxlock action with reinforced frame, master fine scroll engraving, ejectors, SST, deluxe English wood, individually made per customer's specifications, leather cased.

Mfg.'s Sug. Retail	$7,244		$7,175	$6,250	$5,500	$4,850	$4,250	$3,700	$3,250

Add $1,986 for sideplates and best leather case (Brixian SL DE Luxe).

SHOTGUNS: O/U, COMPETITION SERIES

The following models are available in either Trap, Skeet, or Sporting Clays configuration. Sporting Clays models have 5 internal multichokes.

COMPACT MODEL — 12, 16, or 20 ga., boxlock action with reinforced frame, ejectors, SST, model and company name inlaid on black finished action, select checkered walnut stock and forearm, cased.

Mfg.'s Sug. Retail	$1,724		$1,525	$1,225	$1,025	$900	$775	$700	$625

GARA MODEL — similar to Compact, except has hand engraving and wood upgrade.

Mfg.'s Sug. Retail	$3,038		$2,700	$2,325	$2,025	$1,750	$1,475	$1,275	$1,000

Add $351 for Gara Cup Model (company logo inlaid in gold).
Add $1,022 for Gara SL Model (includes engraved sideplates).

GARA DE LUXE — top-of-the-line competition model, ornamental pattern engraved by master engraver, deluxe wood, best leather case.

Mfg.'s Sug. Retail	$5,959		$5,475	$4,775	$4,050	$3,475	$3,050	$2,500	$2,000

RIZZINI, F.LLI

Current manufacturer located in Magno di Gardone V.T., Italy. Currently imported and distributed by William Larkin Moore & Co. located in Scottsdale, AZ, L. Michael Weatherby, located in Laguna Niguel, CA, and by New England Arms, Co. located in Kittery Point, ME.

In the past, this manufacturer collaborated with Antonio Zoli to make "spec" guns that were usually imported by Abercrombie & Fitch or Von Lengerke & Detmold. These guns are normally marked on the water table "Zoli-Rizzini" or "F.lli Rizzini"

Grading	100%	98%	95%	90%	80%	70%	60%

(in the latter case, most of the time these guns have the Abercrombie & Fitch, etc. logo as well). These guns are not to be confused with the quality of current Rizzini F.lli mfg. Normally, these older Field Grade models (non-ejector, boxlock actions in 12, 16, 20, 28 ga., or .410 bore) sell in the $350-$1,000 range, with a 25% premium for 28 ga. or .410 bore. Deluxe Field Models with a scalloped boxlock action and ejectors are currently valued in the $1,250-$2,000 range, with a 30% premium for 28 ga. or .410 bore. The Extra Lusso Model (top-of-the-line) currently sell in the $2,500 range in 12 ga., $3,850 in 20 ga., $4,000 in 28 ga., and $4,250 in .410 bore.

Rizzini shotguns are made to individual custom order only (about 25 are made a year). Prices below do not include engraving (prices range from $8,700-$21,700, substantially more for famous name engravers such as Fracassi, Torcoli, etc.) and may be subject to fluctuation in exchange rates.

R

SHOTGUNS: SxS, CUSTOM

Add approx. $7,500-$18,000 for fine English scroll or ornamental engraving.
Add approx. $15,000-$20,000 for Fracassi style ornamental engraving.
Add approx. $15,000-$20,000 for elaborate game scene engraving.

R2-E BOXLOCK EJECTOR — 12, 16, or 20 ga., select walnut, detachable bottom inspection plate, various barrel lengths, without engraving. Disc. 1995.

$22,500 $15,250 $12,250 $9,950 $8,850 $7,100 $6,200
Last Mfg.'s Sug. Retail was $25,000.

✱ 28 ga. or .410 bore. — otherwise similar to above. Disc. 1995.

$24,500 $16,750 $13,000 $10,000 $8,950 $7,300 $6,300
Last Mfg.'s Sug. Retail was $27,500.

RI-E SIDELOCK EJECTOR — 12, 16, or 20 ga., H&H patterned sidelocks, select Circassian walnut, various barrel lengths, without engraving.

Mfg.'s Sug. Retail $48,800 $41,550 $27,500 $21,500 $16,500 $12,500 $10,400 $9,150
Add $5,000 for 28 ga. or .410 bore.

RIZZINI, I.

Please refer to the Fair Techni-Mec listing.

THE ROBAR COMPANIES, INC.

Current manufacturer established during 1986, and located in Phoenix, AZ.

Robar manufactures a complete line of semi-auto, .45 ACP pistols in various configurations including the Super Deluxe Pistol Package ($2,200), Robar Combat Master ($1,250), Thunder Ranch Pistol ($1,100), .45 Super, or Basic Carry ($850). These guns are built up from other makers including Springfield and Colt to provide the configuration/modifications necessary. Robar also manufactures a complete line of rifles including the SR60 ($2,090), SR90 ($2,670), QR2 ($2,200), Robar 50 BMG ($3,825), RC50/RC50F, Hunter, Precision Hunter, Varminter ($2,440), and Thunder Ranch Precision Rifle (POR). Defensive shotguns are also manufactured, and include the Robar Elite ($1,200), Robar Defender ($575), Robar S.O.F. ($870), Thunder Ranch model ($700). Please contact Robar directly (see Trademark Index) for more information including current prices on their lineup of firearms including custom metal and wood finishes.

ROBERTS, J. & SON (GUNMAKERS) LTD.

Current manufacturer and dealer established during 1950, and located in London, England.

Please contact J. Roberts & Son (Gunmakers) Ltd. directly for more information on their current inventory and other services (see Trademark Index).

Grading	100%	98%	95%	90%	80%	70%	60%

ROBINSON ARMAMENT CO.

Current rifle manufacturer located in Salt Lake City, UT. Dealer and consumer direct sales.

RIFLES: SEMI-AUTO

M96 EXPEDITIONARY RIFLE — .223 Rem. cal., paramilitary design, unique action allows accessory kit to convert loading from bottom to top of receiver, 20 in. barrel with muzzle brake, stainless steel receiver, matte black finish metal, black synthetic stock and forearm, gas adjustment knob, last round hold open, rotating bolt assembly, 7.6 lbs. Production scheduled for 1999.

As this edition went to press, prices had yet to be determined on this model.

ROCHE, CHRISTIAN

Current manufacturer located in Veauche, France.

Christian Roche manufactures quality side-by-side shotguns and double rifles. Since all orders are per individual specifications, the factory must be contacted directly to obtain a current price quotation and information (see Trademark Index).

ROCK RIVER ARMS, INC.

Current manufacturer located in Cleveland, IL. Dealer and consumer direct sales.

Rock River Arms makes a variety of M-1911 based semi-autos. They specialize in manufacturing their own National Match frames and slides. Current models (standard cal. is .45 ACP) include the Standard Match (MSR $985), National Match Hardball (MSR $1,210), Bullseye Wadcutter (MSR $1,225), Basic Limited Match (MSR $1,346), Limited Match (MSR $1,759), Ultimate Match Achiever (MSR $2,255), Matchmaster Steel (MSR $2,355), Elite Commando (MSR $1,025), and the Hi-Cap Basic Limited (MSR $1,795). Rock River Arms also offers additional options and parts. Please contact the factory for additional information and availability.

ROCKY MOUNTAIN ARMS, INC.

Current manufacturer located in Longmont, CO since 1990.

Rocky Mountain Arms is a quality specialty manufacturer of rifles (currently mfg.), and pistols (disc.). All firearms are finished in Dupont Teflon-S industrial coatings (Bear Coat). Direct sales only (see listing in Trademark Index for more information).

PISTOLS: SEMI-AUTO

BAP (BOLT ACTION PISTOL) — .308 Win., 7.62x39mm, or 10mm Rocky Mountain Thunderer (10x51mm) cal., features 14 in. heavy fluted Douglas Match barrel, Kevlar/graphite pistol grip stock, supplied with Harris bipod and black nylon case. Mfg. 1993 only.

$1,425	**$1,275**	**$1,100**	**$950**	**$825**	**$700**	**$575**	

Last Mfg.'s Sug. Retail was $1,595.

1911A1-LH — .40 S&W or .45 ACP cal., specifically designed for left-handed shooters, featuring left side ejection port and right side controls, gold cup size, stainless steel construction, hand fitted parts, integral ramp barrel, Millett adj. sights, test target. Mfg. 1991-93.

$1,295	**$995**	**$750**

Last Mfg.'s Sug. Retail was $1,395.

Add $100 for Bomar sights.

BACKUP PLUS — .45 ACP cal., hand tuned AMT Back-up pistol, black DuPont Teflon-S finish, Tritium front night sight. Mfg. 1995-97.

$575	**$515**	**$450**	**$400**	**$360**	**$330**	**$300**

Last Mfg.'s Sug. Retail was $650.

Grading	100%	98%	95%	90%	80%	70%	60%

22K PISTOLS — .22 LR cal., AR style pistols featuring 7 in. barrel, choice of matte black or NATO Green Teflon-S finish, will use Colt conversion kit, choice of carrying handle or flat-top upper receiver, 10 or 30 shot mag., includes black nylon case. Mfg. 1993 only.

	$475	$425	$375	$350	$325	$295	$275

Last Mfg.'s Sug. Retail was $525.

Add $50 for flat-top receiver with Weaver style bases.

PATRIOT PISTOL — .223 Rem. cal., AR style pistol featuring 7 in. match barrel with integral Max Dynamic muzzle brake, 21 in. overall, available with either carrying handle upper receiver and fixed sights or flat-top receiver with Weaver style bases, fluted upper receiver became an option in 1994, accepts standard AR-15 mags, 5 lbs. Mfg. 1993-94 (per C/B).

	$2,295	$1,975	$1,625	$1,425	$1,250	$1,075	$950

Last Mfg.'s Sug. Retail was $1,795.

Add $200 for black milled upper and lower receiver w/o carrying handle.

KOMRADE — 7.62x39mm cal., includes carrying handle upper receiver with fixed sights, floating 7 in. barrel, Teflon red or black finish, 5 lbs., 5 shot mag. Mfg. 1994-95.

	$1,825	$1,650	$1,425	$1,200	$975	$850	$775

Last Mfg.'s Sug. Retail was $1,995.

RIFLES: BOLT ACTION

PROFESSIONAL SERIES — .223 Rem., .30-06, .308 Win., or .300 Win. Mag. cal., bolt action rifle utilizing modified Mauser action, fluted 26 in. Douglas premium heavy match barrel with integral muzzle brake, custom Kevlar-Graphite stock with off-set thumbhole, test target. Mfg. 1991-95.

	$2,050	$1,650	$1,275	$995	$850	$725	$600

Last Mfg.'s Sug. Retail was $2,200.

Add $100 for .300 Win. Mag. cal.
Add $300 for left-hand action.

PRAIRIE STALKER — .223 Rem., .22-250 Rem., .30-06, .308 Win., or .300 Win. Mag. cal., choice of Remington, Savage, or Winchester barreled action, includes Choate ultimate sniper stock, lapped bolt and match crown, "Bear Coat" all-weather finish, includes factory test target. Limited mfg. 1998 only.

	$1,595	$1,350	$1,150	$950	$875	$775	$675

Last Mfg.'s Sug. Retail was $1,795.

* *Ultimate Prairie Stalker* — similar to Prairie Stalker, except custom barrel and caliber specifications are customer's choice. Limited mfg. 1998 only.

	$2,200	$1,875	$1,625	$1,400	$1,200	$1,000	$895

Last Mfg.'s Sug. Retail was $2,495.

PRO-VARMINT — .22-250 Rem., or .223 Rem. cal., RMA action, 22 in. heavy match barrel with recessed crown, Bear Coat metal finish, Choate stock with aluminum bedding. New 1999.

Mfg.'s Sug. Retail	$1,095		$995	$875	$800	$725	$650	$575	$450

POLICE MARKSMAN — .308 Win. or .300 Win. Mag. cal., similar to Professional Series, except has 40X-C stock featuring adj. cheekpiece and buttplate, target rail, Buehler micro-dial scope mounting system. Mfg. 1991-95.

	$2,325	$1,995	$1,650	$1,325	$1,100	$900	$700

Last Mfg.'s Sug. Retail was $2,500.

Add $100 for .300 Win. Mag. cal.
Add $400 for left-hand action.
Add $400 for illuminated dot scope (4X-12X x 56mm).

* *Police Marksman II* — .308 Win. cal., RMA action, 22 in. heavy match barrel with recessed crown, Bear Coat metal finish, Choate stock with aluminum bedding. New 1999.

Mfg.'s Sug. Retail	$1,095		$995	$875	$800	$725	$650	$575	$450

PRO-GUIDE — .280 Rem., .35 Whelen, .308 Win., 7x57mm Mauser, or 7mm-08 Rem. cal., Scout Rifle design with 17 in. Shilen barrel, "Bear Coat" finish, approx. 7 lbs. New 1999.

Mfg.'s Sug. Retail	$2,295		$2,025	$1,800	$1,600	$1,425	$1,200	$1,000	$825

Grading	100%	98%	95%	90%	80%	70%	60%

NINJA SCOUT RIFLE — .22 Mag. cal., takedown rifle based on Marlin action, black stock, 16½ in. match grade crowned barrel, forward mounted Weaver style scope base, adj. rear sight, 7 shot mag. Mfg. 1991-95.

	$640	$575	$525	$460	$430	$390	$360

Last Mfg.'s Sug. Retail was $695.

Add $200 for illuminated dot scope (1.5X-4X) w/ extended eye relief.

R

SCOUT SEMI-AUTO — .22 Mag. cal., patterned after Marlin action. Mfg. 1993-95.

	$650	$575	$495	$395	$350	$295	$260

Last Mfg.'s Sug. Retail was $725.

Add $200 for illuminated dot scope (1.5X-4X) w/ extended eye relief.

RIFLES: SEMI-AUTO

M-SHORTEEN — .308 Win. cal., compact highly modified M1-A featuring 17" match crowned barrel, custom front sight, mod. gas system, hand honed action & trigger, custom muzzle brake. Mfg. 1991-94.

	$1,650	$1,425	$1,175	$995	$850	$725	$600

Last Mfg.'s Sug. Retail was $1,895.

Add $200 for Woodland/Desert camo.

VARMINTER — .223 Rem. cal. only, AR-15 styled rifle with 20 in. fluted heavy match barrel, flat-top receiver with Weaver style bases, round metal National Match hand guard with floating barrel, choice of NATO green or matte black Teflon-S finish, supplied with case and factory test target (sub-MOA). Mfg. 1993-94.

	$2,195	$1,800	$1,600	$1,400	$1,200	$1,000	$875

Last Mfg.'s Sug. Retail was $2,495.

PATRIOT MATCH RIFLE — .223 Rem. cal., 20 in. Bull Match barrel, regular or milled upper and lower receivers, two-piece machined aluminum hand guard, choice of DuPont Teflon finish in black or NATO green, ½ MOA, hard case. Mfg. 1995-97.

	$2,375	$1,975	$1,650	$1,400	$1,200	$1,000	$895

Last Mfg.'s Sug. Retail was $2,500.

Add approx. $325 for milled upper receiver.
Add approx. $650 for milled upper and lower receivers.

SHOTGUNS: SLIDE ACTION

870 COMPETITOR — 12 ga., 3 in. chamber, security configuration with synthetic stock, hand-honed action, ghost ring adj. sights, "Bear Coat" finish, high visibility follower. Mfg. 1996-97.

	$695	$625	$550	$500	$450	$400	$360

Last Mfg.'s Sug. Retail was $795.

ROCKY MOUNTAIN ELK FOUNDATION

Current national conservation organization with national headquarters located in Missoula, MT.

RIFLES: BOLT ACTION

RUGER NO. 1-A LIGHT SPORTER — .35 Whelen cal., features gold inlaid elk on right side of receiver and mountain scene with gold accents on left side, engraved by Adams & Son, blue finish, deluxe wood, 50 mfg. 1995 only.

	$2,395	$1,850	$1,475				

Last Mfg.'s Sug. Retail was $2,395.

SAUER MODEL 90 — .270 Win. or .30-06 cal., banquet offering only, total mfg. unknown.

	$1,375	$1,100	$925				

ROGAK

Please refer to the L E S Incorporated listing in this text for more information on the Rogak Pistol.

Grading	100%	98%	95%	90%	80%	70%	60%

ROGUE RIVER RIFLEWORKS

Current manufacturer located in Paso Robles, CA.

RIFLES

BOLT ACTION MODEL — 7mm STW, .300 Win. Mag., .30-378 Wby. Mag., 8mm Rem. Mag., .375 H&H, .416 Rem. Mag., or .458 Win. Mag. cal., choice of Remington M-700 or Winchester M-70 action, Pac-Nor match grade barrel (with cryogenic treatment), engraved receiver, floorplate, and grip cap, jewelled bolt, exhibition grade checkered walnut stock with ebony forend cap. New 1998.

Mfg.'s Sug. Retail	**$8,100**	**$7,600**	**$6,500**	**$5,800**	**$5,000**	**$4,200**	**$3,400**	**$2,675**

LEVER ACTION MODEL — .243 Win., .260 Rem., 7mm-08 Rem., .308 Win., or .358 Win. cal., features rebuilt Winchester Model 88 action, match grade chrome moly barrel, exhibition grade walnut, choice of American classic or Mannlicher stock design. New 1998.

Mfg.'s Sug. Retail	**$4,125**	**$3,675**	**$3,200**	**$2,875**	**$2,400**	**$1,950**	**$1,775**	**$1,450**

SxS MODEL — .470 NE, .500 NE, or .577 NE cal., Anson & Deely action, Purdey double locking lugs, Greener crossbolt, Southgate selective ejectors, quarter rib with rear sights, exhibition grade wood, case colored or coin finished receiver. New 1998.

Prices start at $12,500 for .470 NE cal. A 12, 16, or 20 ga. shotgun barrel conversion kit is also available for $3,800.

RÖHM

Previous firearms manufacturer located in Sontheim an der Brenz, Germany. Limited importation into the U.S. Röhm still manufactures gas alarm pistols, mostly for European sales.

Röhm produced inexpensive revolvers for the U.S. marketplace during the late 1960s-1970s. Most of these guns were built as sub-contracts for U.S. companies and/or distributors (i.e., Hy-Score, a previous distributor located in Brooklyn, NY). Some of the models included are RG-7 through RG-88 (21 variations), Romo, Thalco, Valor, Vestpocket, Western Style, Zephr, and others. Röhm also manufactured a few semi-auto pistols (RG-25 and RG-26) at approx. the same time. Currently, these guns are seen priced in the $35-$125 range, as the shooting value determines the price tag, not collector interest.

DERRINGERS

DERRINGER — .22 LR cal., blued, copy of Remington O/U derringer. Excellently made, but half-cock safety is old design and could fail if dropped. No longer imported.

$150	$115	$95	$85	$75	$65	$55

ROSS RIFLE COMPANY

Previous manufacturer located Quebec, Canada.

RIFLES: BOLT ACTION

CANADIAN 1907 MARK II — .303 Brit. cal., straight pull, 28 in. barrel, pre-WWII.

$295	$250	$200	$180	$160	$140	$120

MODEL 1910 SPORTING RIFLE — similar action as 1907, .280 Ross or .303 Brit. cal., checkered Sporter stock, leaf sights. Mfg. 1910-1920.

$375	$325	$300	$275	$225	$175	$150

Note: Many experts state this rifle is unsafe to fire.

ROSSI

Currently manufactured by Amadeo Rossi S.A., located in Sao Leopoldo, Brazil. Currently imported by BrazTech, L.C. beginning late 1998, located in Miami, FL. Previously imported by Interarms, located in Alexandria, VA.

REVOLVERS: DOUBLE ACTION

MODEL 31 — .38 Spl., 5 shot, 4 in. medium barrel, target trigger and hammer, 22 oz. Disc. 1985. Add $5 for nickel.

$120	$105	$95	$85	$75	$70	$65

Last Mfg.'s Sug. Retail was $139.

MODEL 51 — .22 LR cal., 6 shot, 6 in. barrel, blue only, adj. sights. Disc. 1985.

$125	$110	$100	$90	$85	$80	$75

Last Mfg.'s Sug. Retail was $149.

* **Sportsman 511 Stainless** — .22 LR cal. only, stainless steel, 4 in. barrel, with matted rib, adj. rear sight, 6 shot, hardwood stocks, 30 oz. Imported 1986-90 only.

$190	$160	$125

Last Mfg.'s Sug. Retail was $235.

MODEL 68 — .38 Spl. cal., 5 shot, 2 or 3 in. barrel, blue or nickel (3 in. barrel only), choice of wood or rubber grips with 2 in. barrel. Disc. 1998.

$165	$135	$100	$90	$80	$70	$65

Last Mfg.'s Sug. Retail was $225.

MODEL 69 — .32 S&W cal., 6 shot, 3 in. barrel, walnut grips. Disc. 1985.

$120	$105	$95	$85	$75	$70	$65

Last Mfg.'s Sug. Retail was $139.

Add $5 for nickel finish.

MODEL 70 — .22 LR cal, 6 shot, 3 in. barrel. Disc. 1985.

$120	$105	$95	$85	$75	$70	$65

Last Mfg.'s Sug. Retail was $139.

Add $5 for nickel finish.

MODEL 84 STAINLESS — .38 Spl. cal., 6 shot, 3 or 4 in. solid raised rib barrel, standard service sights, checkered hardwood grips, 27½ oz. Imported 1985-86 only.

$190	$155	$125

Last Mfg.'s Sug. Retail was $205.

MODEL 88 STAINLESS — .38 Spl. cal., 5 shot, stainless steel construction, 2 or 3 in. barrel, hardwood or rubber (2 in. barrel only) grips, 21 oz. Disc. 1998.

$195	$145	$110

Last Mfg.'s Sug. Retail was $255.

* **Model 88 Lady Rossi** — .38 Spl., 2 in. barrel, stainless steel, slim round grips. Imported 1995-98.

$215	$175	$150

Last Mfg.'s Sug. Retail was $285.

MODEL 89 STAINLESS — .32 S&W cal. only, 6 shot, 3 in. barrel. Imported 1985-86. Reintroduced 1989-90.

$175	$135	$115

Last Mfg.'s Sug. Retail was $215.

MODEL 94 — .38 Spl. cal., 6 shot, 3 or 4 in. barrel, blued finish only, 27½ oz. Imported 1985-1988.

$160	$140	$120	$110	$95	$85	$75

Last Mfg.'s Sug. Retail was $185.

Grading	100%	98%	95%	90%	80%	70%	60%

MODEL R351 — .38 Spl.+P cal., 5 shot, 2 in. barrel, blue action, combat rubber grips, supplied with key lock. Importation began 1999.

| Mfg.'s Sug. Retail | $259 | $205 | $165 | $145 | $135 | $125 | $115 | $105 |

MODEL R352 — similar to Model R351, except is stainless steel. Importation began 1999.

| Mfg.'s Sug. Retail | $299 | $235 | $185 | $150 |

MODEL R461 — .357 Mag.+P, 6 shot, 2 in. barrel, blue action, combat rubber grips, supplied with key lock. Importation began 1999.

| Mfg.'s Sug. Retail | $299 | $235 | $185 | $150 | $135 | $125 | $115 | $105 |

MODEL R462 — similar to Model R461, except is stainless steel. Importation began 1999.

| Mfg.'s Sug. Retail | $339 | $265 | $205 | $170 |

MODEL 515(M) STAINLESS — .22 LR or .22 Mag. (Model 515M) cal., double action, 6 shot, classic kit gun design, stainless steel with shrouded ejector rod, adj. rear sights, checkered custom wood grips, 4 in. barrel, 30 oz. Imported 1992 only.

$195 $145 $110

Last Mfg.'s Sug. Retail was $248.

MODEL 515 STAINLESS — .22 Mag. cal., similar to 515(M), supplied with 2 pairs of grips (checkered wood and rubber wraparound). Imported 1994-98.

$210 $165 $140

Last Mfg.'s Sug. Retail was $270.

MODEL 518 STAINLESS — .22 LR cal., otherwise similar to Model 515 Stainless. Disc. 1998.

$195 $155 $135

Last Mfg.'s Sug. Retail was $255.

MODEL 677 FS — .357 Mag. cal., 6 shot, 2 in. heavy barrel, enclosed ejector rod, rubber combat grips, matte blue finish, 26 oz. Imported 1997-98.

$215 $160 $135 $110 $95 $80 $70

Last Mfg.'s Sug. Retail was $260.

MODEL 720 STAINLESS — .44 Spl. cal., choice of hammer or hammerless (new 1994) design, 3 in. ribbed barrel, double action, 5 shot with fluted cylinder, full ejector rod shroud, adj. rear sight, rubber combat grips, stainless, 27½ oz. Imported 1992-98.

$220 $180 $155

Last Mfg.'s Sug. Retail was $290.

MODEL 851 STAINLESS — .38 Spl. cal., 3 (disc. 1994) or 4 in. VR barrel, 6 shot, walnut grips, adj. rear sight, 27½ oz. Mfg. 1985-98.

$195 $155 $135

Last Mfg.'s Sug. Retail was $255.

This model was previously designated the Model 85 Stainless.

MODEL 877 FS STAINLESS — .357 Mag. cal., 6 shot, small frame, 2 in. barrel with full ejector rod housing, rubber combat grips, 26 oz. Mfg. 1996-98.

$220 $175 $150

Last Mfg.'s Sug. Retail was $290.

MODEL 951 — .38 Spl. cal., 6 shot, 3 or 4 in. VR barrel, blued finish only, 27½ oz. Imported 1985-90.

$190 $155 $135 $120 $110 $100 $90

Last Mfg.'s Sug. Retail was $233.

This model was previously designated the Model 95.

MODEL 971 — .357 Mag. cal., 4 in. solid rib barrel with internal ejector shroud, 6 shot, adj. rear sight, blue only, hardwood grips, 36 oz. Imported 1988-1998.

$200 $160 $145 $135 $125 $115 $105

Last Mfg.'s Sug. Retail was $255.

Grading	100%	98%	95%	90%	80%	70%	60%

* Model 971 Stainless — .357 Mag. cal., 2½ (new 1992), 4, or 6 in. solid rib barrel with full shroud, 6 shot, combat style rubber grips, adj. rear sight, 35.4 - 40.5 oz. Imported 1989-1998.

| | $220 | $175 | $145 | | | | |

Last Mfg.'s Sug. Retail was $290.

* Model 971 Compensated — .357 Mag. cal., stainless steel, 3¼ in. compensated barrel, 32 oz. Imported 1993-98.

| | $220 | $175 | $145 | | | | |

Last Mfg.'s Sug. Retail was $290.

MODEL 971 VRC STAINLESS — .357 Mag. cal., stainless steel, 6 shot, choice of 2½, 4, or 6 in. barrel with 8-port vented rib compensator and full-length ejector shroud, combat rubber grips, adj. rear sight, 30-39 oz. Mfg. 1996-98.

| | $295 | $220 | $175 | | | | |

Last Mfg.'s Sug. Retail was $340.

CYCLOPS (MODEL 988 STAINLESS) — .357 Mag. cal., 6 or 8 shot, 8 or 10¾ (ported or unported, new 1998) in. full shroud barrel with 8 compensation ports, black rubber grips, 51 oz. Imported 1997-98.

| | $385 | $300 | $230 | | | | |

Last Mfg.'s Sug. Retail was $429.

Add $50 for unported 10¾ in. barrel, $60 for ported 10¾ in. barrel.

RIFLES

MODEL 65/92 SRC LEVER ACTION — .38 Spl./.357 Mag., .44 Spl./.44 Mag., .44-40 WCF (new 1995), or .45 LC (new 1995) cal., patterned after Win. Model 92, 16 (.38 Spl./.357 Mag. only), 20 (blue or stainless) or 24 (new 1997, half round/half octagon) in. barrel, 5-5¾ lbs. Also available in matte blue finish at no extra charge. Importation disc. 1998.

| | $285 | $220 | $165 | $125 | $110 | $100 | $90 |

Last Mfg.'s Sug. Retail was $360.

Add $69 for half round/half octagonal barrel (24 in. barrel).

This model in .44 Spl./.44 Mag., .44-40 WCF, or .45 LC cal. sometimes is also known as the Model 65.

* Model 92 SRC Stainless — .38 Spl./.357 Mag. or .45 LC cal., 20 in. barrel. Mfg. 1998 only.

| | $340 | $265 | $210 | $165 | $125 | $110 | $100 |

Last Mfg.'s Sug. Retail was $415.

* Model 92 SRC Large Loop — .38 Spl./.357 Mag. or .45 LC cal., 16 in. barrel, 8 shot mag., large loop lever, 5½ lbs. Imported 1997-98.

| | $285 | $220 | $165 | $125 | $110 | $100 | $90 |

Last Mfg.'s Sug. Retail was $360.

Add $55 for stainless steel (.45 LC cal. only, new 1998).

* Blue Engraved — with etched engraving and special wood. Disc. 1989.

| | $275 | $225 | $175 | | | | |

Last Mfg.'s Sug. Retail was $327.

* Gold or Chrome Engraved — either gold (disc. 1987) or chrome (disc.) finish with special wood.

| | $280 | $230 | $185 | $150 | $130 | $120 | $110 |

Last Mfg.'s Sug. Retail was $330.

MODEL 62 SA SLIDE ACTION — .22 LR cal., copy of Win. 1890 "gallery" model, rifle (23 in. barrel) or carbine (16½ in. barrel) available, takedown action, blue or nickel finish, round or octagon barrel, 12 or 13 shot tube mag. Importation disc. 1998.

| | $185 | $145 | $115 | $95 | $85 | $80 | $75 |

Last Mfg.'s Sug. Retail was $240.

Add $10 for nickel finish.
Add $10 for octagon barrel.

* Model 62 SA Stainless — similar to regular model, except is stainless steel. Imported 1986 only.

| | $165 | $145 | $120 | | | | |

Last Mfg.'s Sug. Retail was $192.

Grading	100%	98%	95%	90%	80%	70%	60%

MODEL 62 SAC CARBINE — similar to Model 62 SA, except has 16½ in. carbine barrel with full length mag. tube (12 shot), 4¼ lbs. Imported 1988-1998.

		$185	$145	$115	$95	$85	$80	$75

Last Mfg.'s Sug. Retail was $240.

Add $10 for nickel finish.

* **Model 62 SAC Carbine Stainless** — similar to Model 62 SAC Carbine, except is stainless steel. Imported 1998 only.

		$215	$165	$125

Last Mfg.'s Sug. Retail was $280.

MODEL 59 — .22 Mag. version of Model 62 SA, 10 shot mag., 5.5 lbs. Importation disc. 1998.

		$220	$170	$130	$120	$110	$100	$90

Last Mfg.'s Sug. Retail was $280.

SHOTGUNS: SxS

OVERLUND — 12, 20 ga., or .410 bore, exposed hammers, 20 (Coach Model), 26, or 28 in. barrels, double triggers. Importation disc. 1988.

		$275	$230	$185	$155	$140	$125	$115

Last Mfg.'s Sug. Retail was $332.

SQUIRE — 12, 20 ga., or .410 bore, hammerless, 20, 26 or 28 in. barrels, double triggers, raised matted rib, beavertail forearm, pistol grip, hardwood stock, 3 in. chambers. Imported 1985-90.

		$300	$245	$195	$160	$150	$140	$130

Last Mfg.'s Sug. Retail was $350.

SHOTGUNS: SINGLE SHOT

MODEL S12/S20/S41 — 12, 20 ga., or .410 bore, lightweight break open action with exposed hammer, uncheckered hardwood stock and forearm with sling swivels, blued action and 22 (Youth) or 28 (Standard) in. barrel, supplied with trigger loc, 4 lbs. 13 oz Importation began 1999.

Mfg.'s Sug. Retail	$119		$105	$90	$80	$70	$60	$50	$45

This model is also available as a Youth Model in all gauges (.410 bore weighs approx. 4 lbs.) - prices are the same as listed above.

ROTA, LUCIANO

Current manufacturer located in Brescia, Italy. Currently imported and distributed by New England Arms, located in Kittery Point, ME.

SHOTGUNS: SxS

MODEL 105 — most gauges, 26-32 in. barrels, boxlock action with sideplates, floral scroll engraving, choice of case colored or coin finished receiver, fixed chokes (any combination), extractors, Circassian checkered walnut stock and forearm.

Mfg.'s Sug. Retail	$1,395		$1,150	$950	$825	$725	$625	$550	$500

Add $100 for 28 ga. or .410 bore.
Add $50 for ST, or $175 for multichokes.
Add $500 for hand engraving.

MODEL 106 — all gauges, Anson & Deely type engraved boxlock action, DT or ST, ejectors, extractors, Circassian checkered walnut stock and forearm, case colored action.

Mfg.'s Sug. Retail	$1,295		$1,150	$900	$750	$650	$550	$500	$450

Add $100 for 28 ga. or .410 bore.
Add $155 for 10 ga.
Add $50 for ST, or $175 for multichokes.
Add $300 for hand engraving.

Grading	100%	98%	95%	90%	80%	70%	60%

* **Model 106 Slug Gun** — 12 or 20 ga., similar to Model 106, except has 25 in. barrels with express rib and folding leaf sights, with or w/o sideplates, tapered front ramp sight, choke tubes.

Mfg.'s Sug. Retail	$1,495	$1,250	$1,000	$875	$750	$675	$600	$550

Add $200 for hand engraving.
Add $400 for sideplates.

R ROTTWEIL

Current manufacturer located in Rottweil, Germany. Currently imported by Dynamit Nobel-RWS Inc. located in Closter, NJ.

SHOTGUNS

PARAGON — 12 ga. only, new design featuring boxlock action, 11 different stock configurations, detachable and interchangeable trigger action, trigger and sear safety, ejectors (switchable to extractors), various barrel lengths (30 in. standard) and rib combinations, cased. Importation began 1993.

Mfg.'s Sug. Retail	$7,500	$6,950	$6,500	$5,750	$4,850	$3,950	$3,000	$2,500

Add $850 for Trap Model.
Add $3,150 per extra set of barrels.

* **Paragon Sporting Clays Deluxe** — 30 in. barrels only, features better quality wood and engraving.

Mfg.'s Sug. Retail	$8,995	$8,450	$7,500	$6,950	$6,150	$5,250	$4,250	$3,250

MODEL 650 FIELD O/U — 12 ga. only, 28 in. barrels with VR, ejectors, single trigger, select checkered walnut, multi-choked with 6 choke tubes, lightly engraved, coin finished receiver. Importation disc. 1986.

	$750	$650	$595	$550	$500	$460	$435

Last Mfg.'s Sug. Retail was $850.

MODEL 72 FIELD O/U — 12 ga. only, 28 in. vent. barrels and rib, sand blasted receiver, select walnut with checkered stock and forearm, single trigger, ejectors. Importation disc. 1987.

	$1,850	$1,650	$1,450	$1,200	$1,000	$850	$700

Last Mfg.'s Sug. Retail was $2,295.

MODEL 72 AMERICAN SKEET O/U — 12 ga. only, 26¾ in. barrels, VR, ejectors, select French walnut, marginal engraving on sand blasted receiver, single trigger, 7½ lbs. Importation disc. 1987.

	$1,850	$1,650	$1,450	$1,200	$1,000	$850	$700

Last Mfg.'s Sug. Retail was $2,295.

This model was distributed exclusively by Paxton Arms, located in Dallas, TX.

MODEL 72 AAT SINGLE BARREL TRAP — 12 ga. only, adj. American trap (AAT), barrel features adj. point of impact, 34 in. barrel bored full, high VR. Importation disc. 1986.

	$1,400	$1,200	$1,000	$850	$700	$650	$600

Last Mfg.'s Sug. Retail was $2,295.

MODEL 72 AT O/U — 12 ga. only, 32 in. IM & F barrels, VR and barrels, sand blasted receiver, checkered select walnut stock and forearm, non-adj. point of impact, single trigger ejectors. Importation disc. 1987.

	$1,850	$1,650	$1,450	$1,200	$1,000	$850	$700

Last Mfg.'s Sug. Retail was $2,295.

MODEL 72 AAT COMBINATION — 12 ga. only, comes with 2 single barrels (32 and 34 in.) that have adj. impact points. Importation disc. 1986.

	$2,450	$2,100	$1,850	$1,600	$1,450	$1,250	$995

Last Mfg.'s Sug. Retail was $2,850.

* **72 AAT Combination** — supplied with 1 single adj. barrel and 32 in. O/U barrels.

	$2,450	$2,100	$1,850	$1,600	$1,450	$1,250	$995

Last Mfg.'s Sug. Retail was $2,850.

Grading	100%	98%	95%	90%	80%	70%	60%

MODEL 72 AAT 3-BARREL SET — 12 ga. only, supplied with 2 single barrels (32 and 34 in.) with adj. impact points and 1 set of 32 in. O/U barrels bored IM & F. Importation disc. 1986.

	$2,850	$2,600	$2,300	$2,000	$1,800	$1,600	$1,400

Last Mfg.'s Sug. Retail was $3,250.

MODEL 72 INTERNATIONAL TRAP — 12 ga. only, O/U 30 in. barrels bored IM & F with extra high rib. Importation disc. 1987.

	$1,850	$1,650	$1,450	$1,200	$1,000	$850	$700

Last Mfg.'s Sug. Retail was $2,295.

MODEL 72 INTERNATIONAL SKEET — 12 ga. only, 26¾ in. barrels, VR, select walnut stock and forearm. Importation disc. 1987.

	$1,850	$1,650	$1,450	$1,200	$1,000	$850	$700

Last Mfg.'s Sug. Retail was $2,295.

ROYAL AMERICAN SHOTGUNS

Previously imported by Royal Arms International, located in Woodland Hills, CA circa 1985-87.

SHOTGUNS

MODEL 100 O/U — 12 or 20 ga., 2¾ in. chambers, double triggers, extractors, vent. rib and barrels. Imported 1985-87 only.

	$325	$265	$240	$220	$200	$180	$170

Last Mfg.'s Sug. Retail was $390.

Add $40 for above model with 3 in. chambers, single trigger, and auto ejectors.

MODEL 600 BOXLOCK SxS — 12, 20, 28 ga., or .410 bore, sideplates, silver finished receiver, 3 in. chambers, single trigger, auto ejectors. Imported 1985-87 only.

	$365	$295	$265	$235	$210	$195	$180

Last Mfg.'s Sug. Retail was $420.

Subtract 25% for double triggers and 2¾ in. chambers.

MODEL 800 SIDELOCK SxS — 12, 20, 28 ga., or .410 bore, sidelocks with sideplates, silver finished receiver, 3 in. chambers, single trigger, checkered straight grip stock with select walnut, auto ejectors. Imported 1985-87 only.

	$775	$650	$595	$550	$500	$460	$435

Last Mfg.'s Sug. Retail was $899.

RUBY

Previous manufacturer located in Eibar, Spain.

PISTOLS: SEMI-AUTO

MILITARY TYPE — 7.65mm cal.,trade name for Spanish auto pistol fashioned after Colt's M1903, mag. release at bottom of grip, fixed sights. Disc.

	$200	$150	$100	$75	$70	$65	$60

RUGER

See Sturm, Ruger, & Co. section in this text.

RUKO SPORTING GOODS, INC.

Previous importer (non-exclusive) located in Buffalo, NY that imported Arms Corp. of the Philippines firearms circa 1990-95. Ruko Sporting Goods, Inc. (previously Ruko Products) firearms were manufactured by the Arms Corporation of the Philippines. In 1991, Ruko Products, Inc. became the exclusive domestic importer for arms manufactured by Arms Corp. of the Philippines. These firearms were marked "Ruko-Armscor" on the barrels.

Grading	100%	98%	95%	90%	80%	70%	60%

Please refer to the Armscor section for current importation, as well as previous importation by Armscorp Precision, Inc. and Ruko Products, Inc.

RUSSIAN SERVICE PISTOLS AND RIFLES

Previously manufactured at various Russian military arsenals (including Tula).

HANDGUNS

MODEL TT30 & TT33 TOKAREV AUTOMATIC — 7.62mm Russian cal., design borrowed from Colt 1911, Petter-type unitized trigger/hammer assembly, 8 shot, 4½ in. barrel, blue. Mfg. 1930-1954.

	100%	98%	95%	90%	80%	70%	60%
	$325	$290	$250	$225	$165	$145	$110

Add 20% for matching mag.
Add 50% for TT30 Model.

Values listed above assume original condition - no recent imports.

* *TT Recent Import* — 7.62x25mm Tokarev cal., must be stamped by importer, Russian Arsenal mfg., currently imported by Century Arms International, Inc. and others.

No Mfg.'s Retail	$140	$110	$90	$80	$70	$60	$50

NAGANT REVOLVER — 7 shot, cylinder comes forward to seal barrel. Add 10% for pre-communist Imperial marked.

	$260	$225	$185	$165	$135	$115	$100

"GRU" marked gun (Armed Forces Intelligence) has shorter barrel and grip frame. While rarer, there is a slight premium being asked.

MAKAROV MD — 9mm Makarov cal., clip fed double action, post-war manufacture.

	$450	$400	$350	$300	$250	$200	$150

Subtract 60% for recent imports or commercial models with adj. rear sight.

RIFLES

During 1999, various older mfg. Russian Mosins are scheduled for importation. These include all models from the 91/30 through the M44 Carbine.

TOKAREV M38 & M40 RIFLE — semi-auto Russian issue bolt action. Add 20% for M38, 100% for scoped sniper.

	$365	$310	$270	$250	$230	$210	$195

RUTTEN HERSTAL

Current manufacturer of O/U shotguns located in Herstal, Belgium. Currently imported by Labanu, Inc. located in Ronkonkoma, NY.

SHOTGUNS: O/U

MODEL RM 100 — 12 ga., 3 in. chambers, VR multi-choke barrels, ejectors, checkered walnut stock and forearm, hard case. Importation began 1995.

Mfg.'s Sug. Retail	$1,095		$875	$775	$675	$575	$500	$450	$400

MODEL RM 285 — similar to Model RM 100, except has engraved side plates and silver engraved receiver, select walnut with Schnabel forearm, hard case. Importation began 1995.

Mfg.'s Sug. Retail	$1,295		$1,025	$850	$725	$600	$500	$450	$400

S section

S.A.C.M.

Previous company located in Cholet, France. S.A.C.M. stands for Societe Alsacienne de Construction Mechanique.

Grading	100%	98%	95%	90%	80%	70%	60%

PISTOLS: SEMI-AUTO

FRENCH MODEL 1935A — 7.65mm Long cal., 8 shot, 4.3 in. barrel, blue, fixed sights, checkered stocks, used by French troops in WWII and Indochina 1945-1954. Mfg. 1935-1945.

	100%	98%	95%	90%	80%	70%	60%
	$250	$220	$205	$180	$165	$150	$140

Add 50% for Nazi WWII mfg. (Waffenamt proofed).

SAE

Previous importer located in Miami, FL. SAE stands for Spain America Enterprises Inc. SAE imported Felix Sarasqueta shotguns from Spain circa 1988.

SHOTGUNS: O/U

MODEL 70 — 12 or 20 ga., 3 in. chambers, boxlock action, single trigger, ejectors, 26 in. VR barrel, European checkered walnut stock and forearm, standard finish is blue, Model 70 multi-choke has silver finished action with Florentine engraving and low gloss stock finish. Imported 1988 only.

	$400	$275	$260	$245	$230	$215	$195

Last Mfg.'s Sug. Retail was $598.

Add $120 for multi-chokes (27 in. barrel).

MODEL 66C — 12 ga. only, 26 in. Skeet or 30 in. F&M VR barrels, boxlock with engraved sideplates including 24 Kt. gold inlays, Monte Carlo deluxe stock and beavertail forearm. Imported 1988 only.

	$950	$725	$650	$575	$495	$450	$395

Last Mfg.'s Sug. Retail was $1,544.

SHOTGUNS: SxS

MODEL 210S — 12, 20 ga., or .410 bore, 3 in. chambers, boxlock action, double triggers, extractors, silver finished receiver with light engraving, approx. 7 lbs. Imported 1988 only.

	$420	$280	$260	$245	$230	$215	$195

Last Mfg.'s Sug. Retail was $638.

MODEL 340X — 12 or 20 ga., sidelock action, 26 in. barrels with 2¾ in. chambers, H&H boxlock action, case hardened finish with moderate scroll engraving, straight grip select walnut stock and forearm with high gloss finish. Imported 1988 only.

	$700	$550	$495	$460	$430	$395	$375

Last Mfg.'s Sug. Retail was $1,170.

MODEL 209E — 12, 20 ga., or .410 bore, H&H type sidelock action, 26 or 28 in. barrels with 2¾ in. chambers, hand engraved coin finished receiver, select checkered walnut stock and forearm, double triggers. Imported 1988 only.

	$925	$700	$650	$575	$495	$450	$395

Last Mfg.'s Sug. Retail was $1,490.

S.I.A.C.E.

Current shotgun manufacturer located in Brescia, Italy. Currently imported by New England Arms Co., located in Kittery Point, ME.

SHOTGUNS: SxS, HAMMERGUN

MODEL C350G GRADE I — 12 or 20 ga., sidelock, case hardened receiver with border edged engraving, top tang safety, DT, extractors, monobloc barrels.

Mfg.'s Sug. Retail	$1,995		$1,800	$1,550	$1,250	$975	$825	$700	$550

Grading	100%	98%	95%	90%	80%	70%	60%

MODEL 350G AURORA SUPER LUSSO — 24, 28 ga., or .410 bore, back action sidelock, ccase hardened receiver with finely engraved rose and scroll patterns, DT, extractors, top tang safety.

Mfg.'s Sug. Retail	$5,950	$5,500	$4,750	$3,950	$3,150	$2,450	$1,875	$1,450

MODEL 370B CONCORDIA — 12 or 20 ga., scalloped frame back action sidelock, silver or case hardened receiver with fine scroll engraving, top tang safety.

Mfg.'s Sug. Retail	$5,950	$5,500	$4,750	$3,950	$3,150	$2,450	$1,875	$1,450

MODEL 371Q JUNO — 12 or 20 ga., sidelock, self cocking ejector model, silver or case colored receiver, best quality rose and scroll engraving, DT, top tang safety.

Mfg.'s Sug. Retail	$6,950	$6,350	$5,500	$4,750	$3,950	$3,150	$2,450	$1,875

S SKB SHOTGUNS

Currently manufactured by the new SKB Arms Company located in Tokyo, Japan. Currently imported and distributed by G.U. Inc. located in Omaha, NE. SKB has been manufacturing firearms since 1855. Distributor and dealer sales.

Previously imported by Ithaca. In 1987, importation resumed on most SKB models. While the model numbers have changed, quality is similar to those models imported previously by Ithaca. In most cases, the newer models are derived closely from their previous counterparts. Listings below will differentiate older disc. models from currently imported models.

SHOTGUNS: O/U

MODEL 500 — 12, 20, 28 ga., or .410 bore, field grade, VR, selective ejector, 26 in. imp. cyl. and mod., 28 in. full and mod., and 30 in. full and mod. barrels, checkered stock. Mfg. in Japan by SKB 1966-1979.

	$525	$440	$395	$365	$330	$300	$275

Add 15% for 20 ga.
Add 25% for 28 ga. or .410 bore.

* *Model 500 Magnum* — 12 ga., 3 in. Mag., field grade, similar to Model 500, except 3 in. Mag. chambers.

	$625	$455	$410	$385	$355	$320	$290

MODEL 505 DELUXE FIELD — 12, 20, or 28 (disc.) ga., blue (new 1998) or silver nitride engraved receiver (disc. 1997), 3 in. chambers, 26 or 28 in. barrels (supplied with choke tubes), single selective trigger, ejectors, checkered walnut stock with recoil pad and forearm.

Mfg.'s Sug. Retail	$1,049	$940	$785	$685	$575	$500	$460	$420

Add $500 for combo package (disc.).

The combo package includes either 12/20 ga. barrels with inter-chokes or 28 ga./.410 bore barrels.

* *Model 505 Sporting Clays* — 28 or 30 in. multi-choke barrels, blued receiver with light engraving, dimensioned for Sporting Clays competition, 1997 importation features Schnabel forearm, semi-wide channeled rib, and lengthened forcing cones, approx. 8¼ lbs. Older importation in addition to new model during 1997.

Mfg.'s Sug. Retail	$1,149	$1,000	$825	$700	$600	$500	$460	$420

* *Model 505 Trap* — 12 ga., 30 or 32 in. choke tube barrels with or without Monte Carlo stock, high rib.

	$875	$725	$650	$525	$475	$430	$395

Last Mfg.'s Sug. Retail was $995.

Add $400 for O/U Trap Combo.

The above Combo includes one set of O/U Trap barrels and a top single Trap barrel.

* *Model 505 Skeet* — 12, 20, 28 ga., or .410 bore, 28 in. barrels with multi-chokes.

	$875	$725	$650	$525	$475	$430	$395

Last Mfg.'s Sug. Retail was $995.

* *Model 505 3-Ga. Skeet Set* — includes 20, 28 ga., and .410 bore extra Skeet barrels, aluminum case.

	$1,925	$1,575	$1,350	$1,200	$1,125	$950	$875

Last Mfg.'s Sug. Retail was $2,195.

Grading	100%	98%	95%	90%	80%	70%	60%

MODEL 585 DELUXE FIELD — 12, 20, 28 ga., or .410 (new 1995) bore, silver nitride engraved receiver, 3 in. chambers, 26 or 28 in. barrels (supplied with choke tubes), similar to 505 Series, except has .735 diameter bore on 12 ga. models and includes lengthened forcing cones with extended length "Competition Series" Inter-Choke System designed to improve shot patterns and reduce recoil, SST, ejectors, checkered walnut stock with recoil pad and forearm (Youth model is also available with shortened dimensions), 6 lbs. 10 oz. - 7 lbs. 11 oz. Importation began 1992.

| Mfg.'s Sug. Retail | **$1,329** | **$1,110** | **$850** | **$695** | **$575** | **$500** | **$460** | **$420** |

Add $50 for 28 ga. or .410 bore.

Add $170 for Gold Package featuring gold plated trigger and 2 gold game scenes with Schnabel forearm - new 1998.

* *Model 585 Field Set* — includes 12/20 ga., 20/28 ga., 28 ga./.410 bore, 26 or 28 (new 1994) in. VR barrels with SKB inter-choke system (on 12, 20, and 28 ga.), silver nitride receiver with finely engraved scroll game scenes, low profile receiver, cross bolt locking system, SST, ejectors, manual safety, checkered high gloss American walnut stock and forearm.

| Mfg.'s Sug. Retail | **$2,129** | **$1,900** | **$1,600** | **$1,350** | **$1,125** | **$995** | **$895** | **$800** |

Add $50 for 20/28 ga. set or 28 ga./.410 bore set.

Add $250 for Gold Package featuring gold plated trigger and 2 gold game scenes with Schnabel forearm - new 1998.

* *Model 585 Upland* — 12, 20, or 28 ga., 3 in. chambers for 12 and 20 ga., features straight grip stock with recoil pad and 26 in. VR barrels, Schnabel forearm, 6 lbs. 10 oz. - 7 lbs. 10 oz. New 1997.

| Mfg.'s Sug. Retail | **$1,329** | **$1,110** | **$850** | **$695** | **$575** | **$500** | **$460** | **$420** |

Add $50 for 28 ga.

Add $160 for Gold Package featuring gold plated trigger and 2 gold game scenes with Schnabel forearm - new 1998.

* *Model 585 Trap* — 12 ga., 30 or 32 in. choke tube barrels with or w/o Monte Carlo stock, high rib.

| Mfg.'s Sug. Retail | **$1,429** | **$1,160** | **$875** | **$725** | **$525** | **$475** | **$430** | **$395** |

Add $170 for Gold Package featuring gold plated trigger and 2 gold game scenes with Schnabel forearm - new 1998.

Add $700 for O/U Trap Combo or $960 for O/U Trap Combo with Gold Package.

The above Combo includes one set of O/U Trap barrels and a top single Trap barrel.

* *Model 585 Skeet* — 12, 20, 28 ga., or .410 bore, 28 or 30 (12 ga. only - new 1994) in. barrels with multi-chokes.

| Mfg.'s Sug. Retail | **$1,429** | **$1,160** | **$875** | **$725** | **$525** | **$475** | **$430** | **$395** |

Add $50 for 28 ga. or .410 bore.

Add $170 for Gold Package featuring gold plated trigger and 2 gold game scenes with Schnabel forearm - new 1998.

* *Model 585 3-Ga. Skeet Set* — includes 20, 28 ga., and .410 bore extra Skeet barrels, aluminum case.

| Mfg.'s Sug. Retail | **$3,329** | **$2,825** | **$2,275** | **$1,850** | **$1,600** | **$1,475** | **$1,375** | **$1,275** |

Add $400 for Gold Package featuring gold plated trigger and 2 gold game scenes with Schnabel forearm - new 1998.

* *Model 585 Sporting Clays* — 12, 20, or 28 ga., 28 in. (all gauges), 30 in. (12 ga. only), or 32 in. (12 ga. only) multi-choke barrels, dimensioned for Sporting Clays competition, narrow rib ⅜ in. became available 1994.

| Mfg.'s Sug. Retail | **$1,479** | **$1,250** | **$925** | **$750** | **$575** | **$475** | **$430** | **$395** |

Add $50 for 28 ga.

Add $170 for Gold Package featuring gold plated trigger and 2 gold game scenes with Schnabel forearm - new 1998.

➤ *Model 585 Sporting Clays Set* — includes 2 sets of barrels (12 ga. -30 in., 20 ga.-28 in.), cased. New 1996.

| Mfg.'s Sug. Retail | **$2,129** | **$1,900** | **$1,600** | **$1,350** | **$1,125** | **$995** | **$895** | **$800** |

Add $260 for Gold Package featuring gold plated trigger and 2 gold game scenes with Schnabel forearm - new 1998.

Grading	100%	98%	95%	90%	80%	70%	60%

✳ Model 585 Waterfowler — 12 ga. only, 3½ in. chambers, matte blue finish. Imported 1995 only.

	$1,125	$850	$700	$525	$475	$430	$395

Last Mfg.'s Sug. Retail was $1,329.

✳ Model 585 Youth/Ladies — 12 or 20 ga., 26 or 28 (12 ga. only) in. VR barrels, features 13½ in. LOP, barrels have .735 in. bores with lengthened forcing cones. New 1994.

Mfg.'s Sug. Retail	$1,329	$1,210	$835	$685	$525	$475	$430	$395

Add $160 for Gold Package featuring gold plated trigger and 2 gold game scenes with Schnabel forearm - new 1998.

MODEL 600 FIELD GRADE — similar to Model 500, except silver-plated frame and select wood.

	$700	$495	$465	$440	$375	$345	$325

Add 20% for 20 ga.

An unknown quantity of Model 600s were mfg. with blued receivers - a small premium may be asked.

MODEL 600 MAGNUM — similar to Model 600 Field, except chambered for 3 in. Mag., 12 ga. Mfg. 1969-1972 by SKB.

	$720	$510	$480	$455	$415	$390	$355

MODEL 600 TRAP GRADE — similar to Model 600 Field Grade, except 12 ga. only, trap stock, recoil pad, select wood.

	$675	$555	$520	$485	$445	$410	$385

MODEL 600 DOUBLES GUN — similar to Model 600 Trap, except choked for 21 yd. and 30 yd. targets. Mfg. 1973-1975.

	$675	$555	$520	$485	$445	$410	$385

MODEL 600 SKEET GRADE — 12, 20, 28 ga., or .410 bore, 26 or 28 in. barrels, bored S&S, otherwise similar to Model 600 Trap.

	$700	$540	$510	$475	$430	$400	$370
28 ga. or .410 bore.	$850	$740	$620	$560	$485	$440	$420

MODEL 600 SKEET GRADE COMBO SET — similar to Model 600 Skeet, except fitted with matched set of 20, 28 ga., and .410 bore barrels, in fitted case.

	$2,000	$1,430	$1,265	$1,155	$935	$770	$660

MODEL 605 FIELD — similar to Model 505 Deluxe Field except has silver finished engraved receiver with better walnut. Importation disc. 1992.

	$1,075	$850	$750	$675	$575	$500	$450

Last Mfg.'s Sug. Retail was $1,195.

Add $500 for extra set of barrels (Combo).

✳ Model 605 Trap — 12 ga., 30 or 32 in. choke tube barrel with or without Monte Carlo stock, high rib.

	$1,075	$850	$750	$675	$575	$500	$450

Last Mfg.'s Sug. Retail was $1,195.

Add $400 for O/U Trap Combo.

The above Combo includes one set of O/U Trap barrels and a top single Trap barrel.

✳ Model 605 Skeet — 12, 20, 28 ga., or .410 bore, 28 in. barrels with multi-chokes.

	$1,100	$850	$750	$675	$575	$500	$450

Last Mfg.'s Sug. Retail was $1,195.

✳ Model 605 3-Ga. Skeet Set — includes 20, 28 ga., and .410 bore extra Skeet barrels, aluminum case.

	$2,175	$1,650	$1,400	$1,250	$1,125	$950	$875

Last Mfg.'s Sug. Retail was $2,395.

✳ Model 605 Sporting Clay — 28 or 30 in. multi-choke barrels, dimensioned for Sporting Clay competition.

	$1,110	$850	$750	$675	$575	$500	$450

Last Mfg.'s Sug. Retail was $1,245.

Grading	100%	98%	95%	90%	80%	70%	60%

* ***Model 605 DU Sponsor Gun*** — mfg. for DU chapters - dinner auction gun, 850 mfg. in 12 ga. (1990) and 850 mfg. in 20 ga. (1991). Features gold inlays and presentation case.

> DU sponsor gun values are usually hard to ascertain in the secondary marketplace. Currently, prices seem to range between $1,200-$1,700.

MODEL 680 ENGLISH — similar to Model 600 Field, except English style stock, select walnut and fine scroll engraving. Mfg. 1973-1976.

$725	$640	$600	$555	$520	$495	$445

> Add 20% for 20 ga.

MODEL 685 FIELD — similar to Model 585 Deluxe Field, except has silver finished engraved receiver with gold inlays and better walnut, engine turned monobloc.

$1,325	$950	$795	$675	$575	$500	$450

Last Mfg.'s Sug. Retail was $1,549.

* ***Model 685 Field Set*** — includes 12/20, 20/28 ga., 28 ga./.410 bore 26 or 28 (new 1994) in. VR barrels with SKB inter-choke system (on 12, 20, and 28 ga.), silver nitride receiver with finely engraved scroll game scenes, low profile receiver, cross bolt locking system, SST, ejectors, manual safety, checkered high gloss American walnut stock and forearm.

$1,850	$1,650	$1,500	$1,350	$1,275	$1,100	$1,000

Last Mfg.'s Sug. Retail was $2,149.

* ***Model 685 Trap*** — 12 ga., 30 or 32 in. choke tube barrels with or w/o Monte Carlo stock, high rib.

$1,365	$975	$825	$700	$600	$525	$450

Last Mfg.'s Sug. Retail was $1,595.

> Add $600 for O/U Trap Combo.
> The above Combo includes one set of O/U Trap barrels and a top single Trap barrel.

* ***Model 685 Skeet*** — 12, 20, 28 ga., or .410 bore, 28 or 30 (12 ga. only - new 1994) in. barrels with multi-chokes.

$1,365	$975	$825	$700	$600	$525	$450

Last Mfg.'s Sug. Retail was $1,595.

* ***Model 685 3-Ga. Skeet Set*** — includes 20, 28 ga., and .410 bore extra Skeet barrels, aluminum case.

$2,550	$2,175	$1,875	$1,675	$1,450	$1,275	$1,125

Last Mfg.'s Sug. Retail was $2,949.

* ***Model 685 Sporting Clay*** — 28 (all gauges), 30 (12 ga. only), or 32 (12 ga. only) in. multi-choke barrels, dimensioned for Sporting Clay competition, $\frac{3}{8}$ in. narrow rib became available 1994. Importation disc. 1995.

$1,365	$975	$825	$700	$600	$525	$450

Last Mfg.'s Sug. Retail was $1,595.

* ***Model 685 Sporting Clay Set*** — includes one set of 12 ga. (28, 30, or 32 in. VR barrels) and 20 ga. (28 in. only) or one set of 32 and 28 in. barrels in 12 ga only. Imported 1994-95.

$2,000	$1,675	$1,500	$1,350	$1,200	$1,025	$895

Last Mfg.'s Sug. Retail was $2,295.

* ***Model 685 DU Sponsor Gun*** — mfg. for DU chapters - dinner auction gun, 850 mfg. in 12 ga. (1990) and 850 mfg. in 20 ga. (1991). Features gold inlays and presentation case.

> DU sponsor gun values are usually hard to ascertain in the secondary marketplace. Currently, prices seem to range between $1,200-$1,700.

MODEL 700 TRAP GRADE — 12 ga., similar to Model 600 Trap, except more engraving, better grade wood, wide rib. Mfg. 1969-1975.

$820	$770	$740	$685	$630	$595	$565

MODEL 700 DOUBLES GUN — 12 ga., similar to Model 700 Trap, except choked for 21 yd. and 30 yd. targets. Mfg. 1973-1975.

$795	$770	$740	$685	$630	$595	$565

MODEL 700 SKEET GRADE — 12 ga., similar to Model 700 Doubles, only bored S&S, available in 12 or 20 ga.

$840	$770	$740	$685	$620	$585	$555

Grading	100%	98%	95%	90%	80%	70%	60%

MODEL 785 DELUXE FIELD — 12, 20, 28 ga., or .410 bore, silver nitride engraved receiver, 3 in. chambers, 26 or 28 in. barrels (supplied with choke tubes), similar to 585 Series, except has chrome lined bores on all models and also includes lengthened forcing cones with extended length "Competition Series" Inter-Choke System designed to improve shot patterns and reduce recoil, SST, ejectors, checkered walnut stock with recoil pad and forearm, 6 lbs. 10 oz. - 7 lbs. 11 oz. Importation began 1995.

Mfg.'s Sug. Retail	$1,949	$1,775	$1,550	$1,325	$1,100	$995	$895	$800

Add $80 for 28 ga. or .410 bore.

* *Model 785 Field Set* — includes 12/20, 20/28 ga., 28 ga./.410 bore, 26 or 28 in. VR barrels with SKB inter-choke system (on 12 and 20 ga.), silver nitride receiver with finely engraved scroll game scenes, low profile receiver, cross bolt locking system, SST, ejectors, manual safety, checkered high gloss American walnut stock and forearm.

Mfg.'s Sug. Retail	$2,829	$2,525	$2,200	$1,875	$1,575	$1,475	$1,375	$1,275

Add $100 for 20/28 ga. set or 28 ga./.410 bore set.

* *Model 785 Trap* — 12 ga., 30 or 32 in. choke tube barrels with or w/o Monte Carlo stock, high rib.

Mfg.'s Sug. Retail	$2,029	$1,825	$1,550	$1,325	$1,100	$995	$895	$800

Add $800 for O/U Trap Combo.

The above Combo includes one set of O/U Trap barrels and a top single Trap barrel.

* *Model 785 Skeet* — 12, 20, 28 ga., or .410 bore, 28 or 30 (12 ga. only) in. barrels with multi-chokes.

Mfg.'s Sug. Retail	$2,029	$1,825	$1,550	$1,325	$1,100	$995	$895	$800

Add $40 for 28 ga. or .410 bore.

* *Model 785 3-Ga. Skeet Set* — includes 20, 28 ga., and .410 bore extra Skeet barrels, aluminum case.

Mfg.'s Sug. Retail	$4,089	$3,575	$2,800	$2,275	$1,825	$1,575	$1,400	$1,295

* *Model 785 Sporting Clays* — 12, 20, or 28 ga., 28 in. (all gauges), 30 in. (12 ga. only), or 32 in. (12 ga. only) multi-choke barrels, dimensioned for Sporting Clays competition with ⅜ in. narrow rib.

Mfg.'s Sug. Retail	$2,099	$1,875	$1,575	$1,325	$1,100	$995	$895	$800

Add $70 for 28 ga.

➤ **Model 785 Sporting Clays Set** — includes 2 sets of barrels (12 ga.-30 in., 20 ga.-28 in.), cased. New 1996.

Mfg.'s Sug. Retail	$2,999	$2,650	$2,350	$2,075	$1,800	$1,600	$1,400	$1,200

MODEL 800 TRAP GRADE — 12 ga., similar to Model 700 Trap, except more engraving, better grade wood, wide rib. Mfg. 1969-1975.

		$1,150	$875	$775	$675	$575	$500	$425

MODEL 800 SKEET GRADE — 12 or 20 ga., skeet chokes. Mfg. 1969-1975.

		$1,200	$1,000	$895	$795	$680	$595	$565

MODEL 880 CROWN GRADE — 12, 20, 28 ga., or .410 bore, coin finished receiver, extensively engraved with sideplates, SST, ejectors, select walnut with fleur-de-lis scroll style checkering, double cross bolt action. Disc. 1980.

		$1,650	$1,300	$1,150	$975	$890	$835	$750

Add 25% for 28 ga. or .410 bore.

MODEL 885 — available in either Field, Skeet, or Trap configuration, coin finished receiver featuring fine scroll engraving with game scenes, boxlock action with sideplates, beginning 1992, the 885 Series in 12 ga. features lengthened forcing cones, .735 bore, and a competition series of extended length multi-chokes. Imported 1988-94.

* *Model 885 Field* — 12, 20, 28 ga., or .410 bore, field dimensions, barrels include choke tubes. Imported 1989-94.

		$1,600	$1,200	$975	$825	$725	$650	$595

Last Mfg.'s Sug. Retail was $1,895.

Grading	100%	98%	95%	90%	80%	70%	60%

* *Model 885 Trap* — 12 ga., 30 or 32 in. barrels with multi-chokes, standard or Monte Carlo stock.

	$1,650	$1,200	$975	$850	$750	$650	$595

Last Mfg.'s Sug. Retail was $1,949.

Add $700 for O/U Trap Combo.

The above Combo includes one set of O/U Trap barrels and a top single Trap barrel.

* *Model 885 Skeet* — 12, 20, 28 ga., or .410 bore, 28 or 30 (12 ga. only - new 1994) in. barrels with multi-chokes.

	$1,650	$1,200	$975	$850	$750	$650	$595

Last Mfg.'s Sug. Retail was $1,949.

* *Model 885 Field Set* — includes 12/20, 20/28 ga., 28 ga./.410 bore 26 or 28 (new 1994) in. VR barrels with SKB inter-choke system (on 12 and 20 ga.), silver nitride receiver with finely engraved scroll game scenes, low profile receiver, cross bolt locking system, SST, ejectors, manual safety, checkered high gloss American walnut stock and forearm.

	$2,450	$2,150	$1,750	$1,500	$1,250	$1,075	$925

* *Model 885 3-Ga. Skeet Set* — includes 20, 28 ga., and .410 bore extra Skeet barrels, aluminum case.

	$3,200	$2,700	$2,300	$1,975	$1,725	$1,500	$1,400

Last Mfg.'s Sug. Retail was $3,595.

* *Model 885 Sporting Clay* — 28 (all gauges), 30 (12 ga. only), or 32 (12 ga. only) in. multi-choke barrels, dimensioned for Sporting Clay competition, $\frac{3}{8}$ in. narrow rib became available 1994.

	$1,650	$1,200	$975	$850	$750	$650	$595

Last Mfg.'s Sug. Retail was $1,949.

MODEL 5600 — 12 ga. only, available as Trap or Skeet model only, VR (Trap only) and vent. barrels (Skeet only), no engraving, select walnut. Disc. 1980.

	$575	$495	$450	$420	$390	$360	$330

* *Model 5700* — available as Trap or Skeet model only, light engraving, select walnut, VR. Disc. 1980.

	$750	$625	$540	$495	$460	$430	$400

* *Model 5800* — available as Trap or Skeet model only, more deluxe engraving, select walnut. Disc. 1980.

	$950	$800	$695	$595	$500	$450	$425

SHOTGUNS: SEMI-AUTO

MODEL 300 STANDARD — 12 or 20 ga., 3 in. chamber, 26 in. imp. cyl., 28 in. mod. or full barrels, 30 in. full, recoil operated, autoloading, checkered pistol grip stock. Mfg. 1968-1972.

	$295	$255	$205	$165	$155	$145	$140
Vent. rib model	$320	$275	$220	$195	$165	$155	$150

MODEL 1300 UPLAND — 12 or 20 ga., 3 in. chamber, 22, 26, or 28 in. VR barrel with multi-chokes, matte black receiver, checkered walnut stock and forearm. Importation resumed 1988-1996.

	$450	$385	$340	$300	$270	$240	$210

Last Mfg.'s Sug. Retail was $495.

This model was previously designated the Model 300. The new Model 1300 was available in Slug configuration with 22 in. barrel/iron sights at no extra charge. Recent Model 1300s have a magazine cutoff system on front left side of frame.

XL 900 MR — 12 ga. only, gas operated semi-auto, 26-30 in. barrels, 5 shot, alloy receiver, etched game bird scroll work on receiver, shoots both 2¾ and 3 in. shells by interchanging barrels. Disc. 1980.

	$325	$280	$260	$240	$225	$190	$175

* *XL 900* — similar to XL 900 MR, only in 20 ga. and no recoil pad, 6¼ lbs.

	$360	$315	$275	$250	$230	$190	$175

XL 900 TRAP GRADE — similar to XL 900 MR, 12 ga. only, scroll engraved black chrome receiver, 30 in. imp. mod. or full barrel, trap style stock, straight or Monte Carlo, recoil pad. Mfg. 1980-disc.

	$395	$350	$320	$305	$275	$265	$260

S

Grading	100%	98%	95%	90%	80%	70%	60%

XL 900 SKEET GRADE — similar to XL 900 MR, except scroll engraved black chrome receiver, 26 in. barrel, skeet stock. Mfg. 1972-disc.

	$400	$350	$320	$305	$275	$265	$260

XL 900 SLUG GUN — similar to XL 900 MR, except 24 in. slug barrel, rifle sights, no rib. Mfg. 1972-disc.

	$350	$310	$280	$265	$250	$220	$200

MODEL 1900 — 12 or 20 ga., 3 in. chamber, 22, 26, or 28 in. VR barrel with multi-chokes, deluxe outdoor field scene etched on receiver, gold trigger, approx. 1,000-2,000 mfg. per year. Importation disc. 1996.

	$485	$430	$395	$360	$330	$295	$260

Last Mfg.'s Sug. Retail was $545.

> This model was previously designated the Model 900. The new Model 1900 was available in Slug configuration with 22 in. barrel and iron sights or Trap Model at no extra charge. Recent Model 1900s have a magazine cutoff system on front left side of frame.

MODEL 3000 — 12 or 20 ga., 3 in. chamber, gas operated semi-auto (shoots both 2¾ and 3 in. shells interchangeably) with semi-squareback styling, elaborate game scenes etched on both sides of receiver, deluxe checkered walnut stock and forearm. Imported 1988-90.

	$545	$475	$415	$380	$350	$315	$285

Last Mfg.'s Sug. Retail was $597.

> Add $125 for Trap model (2¾ in. chamber).

> This model has not previously been imported in this configuration.

SHOTGUNS: SxS

Models 100, 150, 200, 280, 300, 400, and 480 were available in 12 and 20 ga. only, featured 25-30 in. barrels, and all had boxlock actions. More expensive models differ in the amount of engraving, grade of walnut, and style of checkering, beavertail forearm, 6¼ - 7 lbs. Disc. 1980.

MODEL 100 — 12 or 20 ga., Mag. model also, SST, extractors, blue only.

	$485	$425	$380	$340	$310	$275	$250

MODEL 150 — similar to Model 100, except scroll engraving, beavertail forearm. Mfg. 1972-1974 by SKB.

	$520	$435	$385	$345	$310	$275	$250

MODEL 200 — 12 or 20 ga., Mag. model also, SST, ejectors, boxlock, scalloped frame, lightly engraved coin finished receiver.

	$550	$475	$410	$375	$340	$310	$280

MODEL 200 (NEW PRODUCTION) — similar to original Model 200, SST, ejectors, recoil pad. Imported 1987-1988 only.

	$725	$525	$425	$420	$375	$345	$325

Last Mfg.'s Sug. Retail was $895.

> Add 25% for choke-tubes.

> This model was supplied with 3 factory choke-tubes during 1988 - only 400 were mfg. (retail was $995).

* ***Model 200E (English)*** — similar to New Model 200, except has straight grip stock. Importation disc. 1988.

	$725	$525	$425	$420	$375	$345	$325

Last Mfg.'s Sug. Retail was $895.

MODEL 280 ENGLISH — 12 or 20 ga., Mag. model also, SST, AE, lightly engraved blue receiver, straight grip.

	$850	$775	$625	$525	$440	$410	$375

MODEL 300 — 12 or 20 ga., Mag. model also, SST, AE, lightly engraved coin finished receiver.

	$750	$650	$575	$485	$440	$410	$375

MODEL 385 — 12 (new 1998), 20 or 28 ga., scalloped boxlock action with silver nitride receiver, engraved scroll and game scene designs, SST, ejectors, automatic safety, semi-fancy American walnut, English or pistol grip stock, limited quantities. Importation began 1992.

Mfg.'s Sug. Retail	$1,799		$1,565	$1,285	$950	$800	$700	$600	$525

Grading	100%	98%	95%	90%	80%	70%	60%

✴ *Model 385 Sporting Clays* — 12 ga. only, 3 in. chambers, 28 in. barrels with raised VR and double bead sights, pistol grip stock, approx. 7½ lbs. New 1998.

Mfg.'s Sug. Retail	$1,899	$1,650	$1,300	$975	$825	$725	$625	$525

➤ *Model 385 Sporting Clays Set* — includes a pair of 20 and 28 ga. 26 in. barrels. New 1999.

Mfg.'s Sug. Retail	$2,699	$2,275	$1,950	$1,600	$1,375	$1,150	$1,000	$925

✴ *Model 385 Field Set* — includes a pair of 20 and 28 ga. 26 in. barrels, choice of pistol grip or English straight stock. New 1997.

Mfg.'s Sug. Retail	$2,579	$2,200	$1,900	$1,575	$1,350	$1,150	$1,000	$925

✴ *Model 385 DU Commemorative* — features gold inlaid mallards on both receiver sides and gold inlaid DU duck head on receiver bottom, includes hard shell case, and signed letter from SKB president, DU proofmarks, limited mfg. - 200 sets in 1992.

				$4,500	$3,650	$2,800

Last Mfg.'s Sug. Retail was $5,000.

This model is not a DU dinner gun.

MODEL 400 — 12 or 20 ga., Mag. model also, boxlock, SST, AE, moderately engraved coin finished receiver with sideplates.

				$695	$600	$510	$460	$430	$410	$385

MODEL 400 (RECENT PRODUCTION) — similar to original Model 400, SST, ejectors, recoil pad. Imported 1987-1988 only.

				$975	$850	$780	$690	$595	$525	$475

Last Mfg.'s Sug. Retail was $1,195.

✴ *Model 400E (English)* — similar to New Model 400, except has engraved sideplates and straight grip stock. Importation disc. 1989.

				$975	$850	$780	$690	$595	$525	$475

Last Mfg.'s Sug. Retail was $1,195.

MODEL 480 ENGLISH — 12 or 20 ga., Mag. model also, SST, AE, moderately engraved coin finished receiver, straight grip.

			$1,250	$1,000	$825	$725	$625	$525	$475

MODEL 485 — 12 (new 1998), 20, or 28 ga., coin finished boxlock action with engraved upland game scene side plates, 26 in. barrels with raised VR, checkered American walnut stock and beavertail forearm, ejectors, SST, approx. 7 lbs. New 1997.

Mfg.'s Sug. Retail	$2,439	$2,150	$1,900	$1,625	$1,350	$1,125	$975	$825

✴ *Model 485 Field Set* — includes a pair of 20 and 28 ga. 26 in. barrels, choice of pistol grip or English straight stock. New 1998.

Mfg.'s Sug. Retail	$3,479	$3,000	$2,550	$2,175	$1,900	$1,625	$1,350	$1,125

SHOTGUNS: SINGLE BARREL, TRAP

MODEL 505 TRAP — 12 ga., 32 or 34 in. barrel with multi-chokes, regular or Monte Carlo stock.

			$875	$725	$650	$525	$475	$430	$395

Last Mfg.'s Sug. Retail was $995.

MODEL 605 TRAP — 12 ga., 32 or 34 in. barrel with multi-chokes.

			$1,075	$850	$750	$675	$575	$500	$450

Last Mfg.'s Sug. Retail was $1,195.

SHOTGUNS: SLIDE ACTION

MODEL 7300 — 12 or 20 ga., 2¾ or 3 in. chambers, blue only, French walnut stock-hand checkered, twin action slide bars. Disc. 1980.

			$295	$250	$225	$200	$180	$165	$150

MODEL 7900 — trap or skeet variation of the Model 7300.

			$350	$310	$265	$235	$200	$180	$160

SKS

SKS designates a semi-auto rifle design originally developed by the Russian military. No current domestic importation. Currently manufactured in Russia, China, Yugoslavia, and many other countries.

Grading	100%	98%	95%	90%	80%	70%	60%

SKS Development & History

SKS (Samozaryadnaya Karabina Simonova) - developed by S.G. Simonov in the late 1940s to use the 7.62 cartridge of 1943 (7.62x39mm). The SKS is actually based on an earlier design developed by Simonov in 1936 as a prototype self-loading military rifle. The SKS was adopted by the Soviet military in 1949, two years after the AK-47, and was originally intended as a compliment to the AK-47's select-fire capability. It served in this role until the mid-to-late 1950s, when it was withdrawn from active issue and sent to reserve units and Soviet Youth "Pioneer" programs. It was also released for use in military assistance programs to Soviet Bloc countries and other "friendly" governments. Much of the original SKS manufacturing equipment was shipped to Communist China prior to 1960. Since then, most of the SKS carbines produced, including those used by the Viet Cong in Vietnam, have come from China.

Like the AK-47, the Simonov carbine is a robust military rifle. It too was designed to be used by troops with very little formal education or training. It will operate reliably in the harshest climatic conditions, from the Russian arctic to the steamy jungles of Southeast Asia. Its chrome-lined bore is impervious to the corrosive effects of fulminate of mercury primers and the action is easily disassembled for cleaning and maintenance.

The SKS and a modified sporter called the OP-SKS (OP stands for Okhotnichnyj Patron) are the standard hunting rifles for a majority of Russian hunters. It is routinely used to take everything from the Russian sajga antelope up to and including moose, boar, and brown bear. The main difference between the regular SKS and the OP variant is in the chamber dimensions and the rate of rifling. The OP starts as a regular SKS, then has the barrel removed and replaced with one designed to specifically handle a slightly longer and heavier bullet.

Prior to the ban, hundreds of thousands of SKS carbines were imported into the U.S. The SKS was rapidly becoming one of the favorites of American hunters and shooters. Its low cost and durability made it a popular "truck gun" for those shooters who spend a lot of time in the woods, whether they are ranchers, farmers, or plinkers. While the Russian-made SKS is a bonafide curio and relic firearm and legal for importation, the Clinton administration suspended all import permits for firearms having a rifled bore and ammunition from the former Soviet Union in early 1994. In order to get the ban lifted, the Russian government signed a trade agreement, wherein they agreed to deny export licenses to any American company seeking SKS rifles and a variety of other firearms and ammunition deemed politically incorrect by Clinton & Gore. The BATF then used this agreement as a reason to deny import licenses for any SKS from any country.

Most of the SKSs that were imported into this country came from the People's Republic of China. They were a mix of refurbished military issue, straight military surplus, and even some new production. Quality on all was on the low side. Compared to the Chinese SKSs, only a relatively few Russian made SKS carbines made it into the country. All are from military stockpiles and were refurbished at the Tula Arms Works, probably the oldest continuously operating armory in the world. Value for unmodified Russian-made SKS carbines (those with the original magazines and stock) is correspondingly higher.

Over 600 million SKS models have been manufactured in China alone. This configuration was the best-selling semi-auto rifle in America (and other countries) during late 1993-1994.

RIFLES: SEMI-AUTO

SKS — 7.62x39mm Russian cal., semi-auto rifle, Soviet designed, original Soviet mfg. as well as copies mfg. in China, Russia, Yugoslavia, and other countries, gas operated weapon, 10 shot fixed mag., wood stock (thumbhole design on newer mfg.), with or w/o (newer mfg.) permanently attached folding bayonet, tangent rear and hooded front sight, no current importation from China, Russia, or the former Yugoslavia.

	100%	98%	95%	90%	80%	70%	60%
Chinese Mfg./thumbhole stock	$145	$130	$115	$100	$90	$85	$80
Original Russian Mfg.	$225	$190	$170	$155	$140	$130	$120

During late 1993 until the Crime Bill was enacted during September of 1994, runaway demand escalated SKS prices on recent Chinese exports to the $195-$250 range. Earlier Russian manufacture at the time was selling for $250-$325, but prices fell once the glut of Chinese imports arrived. However, as supply began equaling demand, prices fell off to their current

Grading	100%	98%	95%	90%	80%	70%	60%

levels. With interest waning and a current stable marketplace, SKS pricing has become more predictable, and knowledgeable shooters and collectors are now seeking out earlier Russian made SKSs, as these guns have the most quality and best fit/finish (not Chinese overall poor quality). Lately there have been a rash of lawsuits over recently imported SKS semi-auto models going full auto, and as a result, prices have gone down slightly.

This model may also be listed under those importers/distributors who import this model and are listed in this text.

SSK INDUSTRIES

Current Class II manufacturer located in Wintersville, OH. Consumer direct sales.

SSK Industries uses Thompson Center flatside frames and applies an industrial hard chrome finish. Most SSK handguns and rifles are extensively customized in exotic calibers, finishes, and various engraving options. Receivers and barrels may be purchased separately - values below are for complete assembled pistols.

SSK has also manufactured various limited editions including the Handgun Hunters International (HHI) Models 1, 2, and 3. Issue price on these guns was $1,100 (Model 3), $1,200 (Model 2), and $1,300 (Model 1). Only 50 were mfg. total in 1987. SSK also customizes a Ruger Super Redhawk (.44 Mag. or .45 LC cal.). This variation comes with either a scoped 7½ in. octagon barrel (Beauty Model) or a 6 in. bull barrel with muzzle brake (Beast Model). Prices start at $1,430 - add $245 for .45 LC cal.

PISTOLS: SINGLE SHOT

Values listed below are for basic models with no options or special features.

SSK-CONTENDER — over 150 cals. available from .17 Bee to .50-70, various custom barrels available, basically, this is a custom order gun only.

Mfg.'s Sug. Retail	$1,100	$1,100	$875	$795	$675	$600	$550	$495

Individual barrels are available starting at $268.

An arrestor muzzle brake is available on special order.

This model includes barrel, frame, stocks, and sights as standard equipment.

SSK-XP100 — various cals. between .17 and .50, includes TSOB mount and rings.

Mfg.'s Sug. Retail	$1,200	$1,200	$975	$850	$725	$650	$575	$500

The .50 cal. XP100 (12.9 X 50.8 JDJ) comes with SSK muzzle brake, scope, dies and new reinforced fiberglass stock - retail price is $1,700.

RIFLES

Values listed below are for basic models with no options or special features. In addition, SSK also custom manufactures a bolt action rifle available in almost any caliber and configuration - prices start at $1,800 and can go as high as $6,000, depending on the customer's individual special orders. SSK also has developed a 6.5mm, 7mm, or .30 cal. upper unit conversion for AR-15s and M-16s utilizing heavy sub-sonic bullets - $1,000 (whispers).

SSK TCR 87 — .14 through .600 cals., Nitro Express cals. are also available, features Thompson Center TRC 87 receiver, and SSK custom barrels, muzzle brakes and exotic finishes are available at extra cost.

Mfg.'s Sug. Retail	$1,000	$1,000	$850	$700	$600	$550	$500	$450

SSK RUGER NO. 1 — many cals. including .577 NE (optional), custom order rifle based on a Ruger No. 1 frame.

Mfg.'s Sug. Retail	$1,400	$1,400	$1,125	$850	$725	$650	$575	$500

Add $700 for .577 NE

STI INTERNATIONAL

Current manufacturer established during 1993, and located in Georgetown, TX. Distributor and dealer sales.

In addition to manufacturing the pistols listed below, STI International also makes frame kits in steel, stainless steel, aluminum, or titanium - prices range between $441-$989.

Grading		100%	98%	95%	90%	80%	70%	60%

PISTOLS: SEMI-AUTO

HUNTER 6.0 — 10mm cal. only, 6 in. barrel, STI super extended heavy frame with single stack grips, blue finish, 51 oz. New 1998.

| Mfg.'s Sug. Retail | $2,485 | $2,250 | $1,875 | $1,650 | $1,425 | $1,200 | $995 | $895 |

Add $350 for Leupold 2X scope with terminator mount.

EAGLE 6.0 — 9mm Para., .38 Super, .40 S&W, or .45 ACP cal., features STI super extended heavy frame, 6 in. barrel, blue finish, 42 oz. New 1998.

| Mfg.'s Sug. Retail | $2,136 | $1,875 | $1,375 | $1,175 | $925 | $850 | $775 | $675 |

EAGLE 5.5 — various cals., features STI standard frame, 5½ in. compensated barrel, 44 oz.

| Mfg.'s Sug. Retail | $2,740 | $2,475 | $2,100 | $1,750 | $1,475 | $1,200 | $995 | $895 |

EAGLE 5.1 — various cals., 5.1 in. barrel, STI standard frame (choice of steel or aluminum) govt. model full-size, adj. rear sight, 31 or 35 oz.

| Mfg.'s Sug. Retail | $1,975 | $1,725 | $1,275 | $1,075 | $875 | $800 | $700 | $600 |

EDGE 5.1 — .40 S&W cal. only, designed for limited/standard IPSC competition, STI wide extended frame, blue finish, 39 oz. New 1998.

| Mfg.'s Sug. Retail | $2,252 | $1,975 | $1,425 | $1,200 | $950 | $850 | $775 | $675 |

SPARROW 5.0 — .22 LR cal. only, breech blow back mechanism, STI standard extended frame, 5.1 in. ramped bull barrel, fixed sights, blue finish, 30 oz. New 1998.

| Mfg.'s Sug. Retail | $1,090 | $1,025 | $900 | $800 | $700 | $600 | $500 | $400 |

HAWK 4.3 — various cals., 4.3 in. barrel, STI standard frame (choice of steel or aluminum), 27 or 31 oz.

| Mfg.'s Sug. Retail | $1,975 | $1,725 | $1,275 | $1,075 | $875 | $800 | $700 | $600 |

NIGHT HAWK 4.3 — .45 ACP cal., 4.3 in. barrel, STI wide extended frame, blue finish, 33 oz.

| Mfg.'s Sug. Retail | $2,136 | $1,875 | $1,375 | $1,175 | $925 | $850 | $775 | $675 |

FALCON 3.9 — .38 Super, .40 S&W, or .45 ACP cal., STI standard frame, 3.9 in. barrel, size is comparable to Officers Model, adj. rear sight.

| Mfg.'s Sug. Retail | $2,136 | $1,875 | $1,375 | $1,175 | $925 | $850 | $775 | $675 |

S.W.D., INC.

Previous manufacturer located in Atlanta, GA. Similar models have previously been manufactured by R.P.B. Industries, Inc. (1979-82), and met with BATF disapproval because of convertibility into fully automatic operation. "Cobray" is a trademark for the M11/9 semi-automatic pistol.

PISTOLS: SEMI-AUTO

COBRAY M-11/NINE mm — 9mm Para. cal., fires from closed bolt, 3rd generation design, stamped steel frame, 32 shot mag., parkerized finish, similar in appearance to Ingram Mac 10.

| | | | $275 | $235 | $200 | $175 | $160 | $150 | $140 |

This model was also available in a fully-auto variation, Class III transferable only.

CARBINES

SEMI-AUTO CARBINE — 9mm Para. cal., same mechanism as M11, 16¼ in. shrouded barrel, telescoping stock.

| | | | $325 | $275 | $235 | $195 | $170 | $160 | $150 |

REVOLVERS

LADIES HOME COMPANION — .45-70 Govt. cal., double action design utilizing spring wound 12 shot rotary mag., 12 in. barrel, steel barrel and frame, 9 lbs. 6 oz. Mfg. 1990-94.

| | | | $650 | $525 | $400 | $360 | $335 | $310 | $290 |

SHOTGUNS: SINGLE SHOT

TERMINATOR — 12 or 20 ga., paramilitary design shotgun with 18 in. cylinder bore barrel, parkerized finish, ejector. Mfg. 1986-1988 only.

| | | | $95 | $80 | $70 | $60 | $55 | $50 | $45 |

Last Mfg.'s Sug. Retail was $110.

Grading	100%	98%	95%	90%	80%	70%	60%

SABATTI s.p.a.

Current manufacturer located in Gardone, Italy with history tracing back to 1674. Some models are currently imported by European American Armory located in Sharpes, FL. In 1960, the sons of Antonio Sabatti formed the current company, and manufacture currently includes O/U and SxS shotguns, O/U combination and double rifles, bolt action and semi-auto rifles, and slide action and single shot shotguns. Sabatti should be contacted directly (see Trademark Index) regarding more information and domestic availability on their extensive firearms line-up.

SACO DEFENSE INC.

Current firearms manufacturer located in Saco, ME. This company was purchased by Colt's Manufacturing Company, Inc. during late 1998, and plans are under way to produce some Colt models at the facility. In the past, Saco Defense has utilized their high-tech manufacturing facility to produce guns for Magnum Research, Weatherby, and others. For more information on the guns manufactured by Saco Defense, please contact Colt or the factory directly.

SAFARI ARMS

Current manufacturer located in Olympia, WA. Schuetzen Pistol Works is the custom shop division of Safari Arms. M-S Safari Arms was started in 1978 as a division of M-S Safari Outfitters. In 1987, Safari Arms was absorbed by Olympic Arms.

Safari Arms previously made the Phoenix, Special Forces, Camp Perry, and Royal Order of Jesters commemoratives in various configurations and quantities. Prices average in the $1,500 range except for the Royal Order of Jesters ($2,000).

PISTOLS: SEMI-AUTO

Safari Arms currently manufactures mostly single action, semi-auto pistols derived from the Browning M1911 design with modifications.

ENFORCER — .45 ACP cal., 3.8 in. barrel, 6 shot mag., shortened grip, available with max hard finish aluminum frame, parkerized, electroless nickel or lightweight anodized finishes, flat or arched mainspring housing, adj. sights, ambidextrous safety, neoprene or checkered walnut grips, 27 oz. (lightweight model).

Mfg.'s Sug. Retail	$750	$675	$560	$500	$450	$425	$400	$375

This model was originally called the Black Widow. After Safari Arms became Schuetzen Pistol Works, this model was changed extensively to include stainless construction, beavertail grip safety, and combat style hammer.

MATCHMASTER — similar to the Enforcer, except has 5 or 6 in. barrel and 7 shot mag., approx. 40 oz.

Mfg.'s Sug. Retail	$725	$650	$535	$485	$450	$425	$400	$375

Add $129 for 6 in. barrel.

GI SAFARI — .45 ACP cal., patterned after the Colt Model 1911, Safari frame, beavertail grip safety and commander hammer, parkerized matte black finish, 39.9 oz. New 1991.

Mfg.'s Sug. Retail	$595	$540	$455	$395	$350	$295	$275	$250

COHORT PISTOL — .45 ACP cal., features Enforcer slide and MatchMaster frame, 3.8 in. stainless steel barrel, beavertail grip safety, extended thumb safety and slide release, commander style hammer, smooth walnut grips with laser etched Black Widow logo, 37 oz. New 1995.

Mfg.'s Sug. Retail	$790	$700	$580	$515	$460	$425	$400	$375

CARRYCOMP — similar to MatchMaster, except utilizes W. Schuemann designed hybrid compensator system, 5 in. barrel, available in stainless steel or steel, 38 oz. New 1993.

Mfg.'s Sug. Retail	$1,160	$1,030	$875	$750	$600	$500	$425	$375

* Enforcer CarryComp — similar to Enforcer, except utilizes W. Schuemann designed hybrid compensator system, available in stainless steel or steel, 36 oz. Mfg. 1993-96.

	$1,175	$1,025	$875	$750	$600	$500	$425

Last Mfg.'s Sug. Retail was $1,300.

Grading	100%	98%	95%	90%	80%	70%	60%

RENEGADE — .45 ACP cal., left-hand action (port on left side), 4½ (4-star, disc. 1996) or 5 (new 1994) in. barrel, 6 shot mag., adj. sights, stainless steel construction, 36-39 oz. New 1993.

	Mfg.'s Sug. Retail	$1,085	$955	$800	$700	$600	$525	$450	$395

Add $50 for 4-star (4½ in. barrel, disc.).

RELIABLE — similar to Renegade, except has right-hand action. New 1993.

	Mfg.'s Sug. Retail	$825	$730	$620	$525	$450	$425	$400	$375

Add $60 for 4-star (4½ in. barrel, disc.).

GRIFFON PISTOL — .45 ACP cal., 5 in. stainless steel barrel, 10 shot mag., standard govt. size with beavertail grip safety, full-length recoil spring guide, commander style hammer, smooth walnut grips, 40½ oz.

	Mfg.'s Sug. Retail	$920	$855	$725	$650	$575	$500	$450	$395

BIG DEUCE — .45 ACP cal., 6 in. longslide version of the MatchMaster, matte black slide with satin stainless steel frame, smooth walnut grips, 40.3 oz. New 1995.

	Mfg.'s Sug. Retail	$854	$755	$650	$575	$500	$450	$400	$350

PISTOLS: SEMI-AUTO, DISC.

BLACK WIDOW — .45 ACP cal., 3.9 in. barrel, hand-contoured front grip strap, schrimshawed ivory Micarta grips with Black Widow emblem, 6 shot mag., 27 oz. Inventory was depleted 1988.

	$565	$510	$460	$430	$400	$375	$350

Last Mfg.'s Sug. Retail was $595.

BILL OF RIGHTS BICENTENNIAL MATCHED SET —includes the MatchMaster Pistol and ServiceMatch Rifle, features beryllium receivers and special engraving. Disc.

	$8,950	$6,500	$4,750

Last Mfg.'s Sug. Retail was $7,400.

PARTNER — .22 LR cal., formerly the Whitney Wolverine, 8 shot mag., black plastic grips, non-adj. sights. New late 1997.

	Mfg.'s Sug. Retail	$315	$275	$250	$225	$200	$185	$170	$155

MODEL 81 TARGET PISTOL — .38 Spl. or .45 ACP cal., 5 in. barrel, hand-contoured front grip strap, 2 lbs. 10 oz. Disc. 1987.

	$775	$695	$550	$440	$410	$375	$350

Last Mfg.'s Sug. Retail was $875.

Add $50 for Deluxe Model (with Herrett adj. grips).

* *Model 81L* — .38 Spl. or .45 ACP, 6 in. barrel, 2 lbs. 13 oz. Disc. 1987.

	$850	$775	$695	$550	$440	$410	$375

Last Mfg.'s Sug. Retail was $975.

Add $50 for Deluxe Model (with Herrett adj. grips).

* *Model 81 NM* — .38 Spl. or .45 ACP cal., similar frame as Model 81, except has flat front grip strap, 5 in. barrel, 2 lbs. 5 oz. Disc. 1987.

	$775	$695	$550	$440	$410	$375	$350

Last Mfg.'s Sug. Retail was $875.

* *Model 81BP* — .38 Spl. or .45 ACP cal., 6 in barrel, contoured front grip strap, faster cycle time, 2 lbs. 9 oz. Disc. 1987.

	$875	$775	$695	$550	$440	$410	$375

Last Mfg.'s Sug. Retail was $995.

* *Silueta* — .45 ACP or .38/.45 Wildcat cal., 10 in. extended barrel, designed for silhouette shooting, 2 lbs. 14 oz. Disc. 1987.

	$875	$775	$695	$550	$440	$410	$375

Last Mfg.'s Sug. Retail was $1,050.

PISTOLS: SINGLE SHOT

ULTIMATE/UNLIMITED — various cals., bolt action target pistol, $14\frac{15}{16}$ in. barrel, black finished metal, laminated stock. Disc. 1987.

	$850	$775	$695	$550	$440	$410	$375

Last Mfg.'s Sug. Retail was $975.

Schuetzen Pistol Works

Some of the pistols made by Safari Arms had the "Schuetzen Pistol Works" name on them (c. 1994-96). All pistols currently manufactured are marked with the Safari Arms slide marking. All pistols, however, have been marked "Safari Arms" on the frame. The pistols formerly in this section have been moved under the PISTOLS: SAFARI ARMS category.

SAFARI CLUB INTERNATIONAL

SCI is an international hunting and conservation organization with headquarters located in Tucson, AZ.

Although Safari Club International (SCI) is not a manufacturer or importer, this organization is responsible for special and limited editions similar to the one listed below. Additionally, SCI also has one custom-built rifle manufactured for each annual SCI convention with an auction determining the price of the rifle.

MANUFACTURER	MODEL	QUANTITY	YEAR	ISSUE PRICE
Winchester	Super Grade 25th Anniversary	200	1997	$1,395

SAIGA

Current manufacturer located in Europe. Currently imported by European American Armory Corp., located in Sharpes, FL.

Saiga makes a complete line of semi-auto rifles and shotguns. Please contact the importer directly regarding current model availability and prices.

SAKO

Current manufacturer located in Riihimaki, Finland. Current models are presently being imported by Stoeger Industries, Inc. located in Wayne, NJ. Previously imported by Garcia and Rymac.

Grading	100%	98%	95%	90%	80%	70%	60%

RIFLES: BOLT ACTION, DISC.

Add 10%-15% for popular Mag. cals. on rifles listed below.
Note: Prices below are for pre-1972 Garcia and Rymac imported rifles unless stated otherwise.
Pre-Garcia Sakos utilize the L61R action.
Subtract approx. 25% for post-1972 models.

DELUXE — various cals., Monte Carlo stock, skipline checkering, long, medium, or short actions, contrasting pistol grip cap and forend tip, engraved floorplate.

	100%	98%	95%	90%	80%	70%	60%
	$995	$895	$750	$600	$440	$410	$375

STANDARD SPORTER — long, medium, and short actions.

	$795	$695	$595	$475	$440	$410	$375

HEAVY BARREL MODEL — long, medium, and short actions.

	$795	$695	$595	$475	$440	$410	$375

FULL STOCK MODELS — 20 in. carbine barrel (all actions), 23½ in. barrel on rifle (short & medium actions).

* *Finnbear* — long action.

	$995	$895	$725	$650	$500	$425	$375

* *Forester* — medium action.

	$950	$875	$725	$600	$475	$425	$375

* *Vixen* — short action.

	$950	$875	$725	$600	$475	$425	$375

L-46 action pre-Vixen Sakos had detachable mags.

MAUSER ACTION (FN) — .270 Win. or .30-06 cal., long action. Mfg. 1950-1957.

	$695	$500	$400	$345	$310	$280	$260

MAGNUM MAUSER (FN) — 8x60S, 8.2x57mm, .300 H&H, or .375 H&H cal.

	$745	$635	$580	$495	$450	$410	$375

MODEL 74 — various cals.

	$650	$575	$450	$375	$340	$320	$290

MODEL 78 — .22 LR, .22 Mag., or .22 Hornet cal., clip mag., same size as short action Standard Model. Importation disc. 1986.

	$480	$395	$340	$310	$280	$265	$250

Last Mfg.'s Sug. Retail was $647.

Add $30 for .22 Hornet cal.

FINNSPORT MODEL 2700 — available in long (AIII) action only, .270 Win., .300 Win. Mag. cals., select checkered walnut. Disc. 1985.

	$750	$675	$600	$560	$510	$475	$430

Last Mfg.'s Sug. Retail was $910.

FINNWOLF — .243 Win. or .308 Win. cal., lever action, 4 shot clip early model, 3 shot clip later model. Mfg. 1962-1974.

	$895	$775	$550	$500	$440	$410	$375

Add 15% for early model.

ANNIVERSARY MODEL — 7mm Rem. Mag. cal. only, 1,000 mfg.

	$2,500	$1,500	$950

The 100% value on this model refers to NIB unfired condition with factory papers.

RIFLES: BOLT ACTION, RECENT PRODUCTION

All Sako left-handed models are available in medium or long action only.

FINNFIRE — .22 LR cal., 22 in. regular or heavy (new 1996) cold-hammer forged free floating barrel, single stage adj. trigger, 50 degree bolt lift, 2 position safety, European walnut stock, cocking indicator, available in Hunter, Sporter (new 1999), or Varmint configuration, 5 or 10 shot mag., integral 11mm dovetail (for scope mounting), with (new 1996) or w/o open sights, 5¼ lbs. Importation began 1994.

Mfg.'s Sug. Retail	$789	$665	$560	$480	$430	$385	$350	$325

Add $95 for heavy barrel.
Add $135 for Sporter Model (new 1999).

HUNTER LIGHTWEIGHT RIFLE — available in short action (AI) in .17 Rem., .222 Rem., or .223 Rem. cal., medium action (AII) in .22-250 Rem., .243 Win., .308 Win., or 7mm-08 Rem. cal., or long action (AIII) in .25-06 Rem., .270 Win., .280 Rem., .30-06, .270 Wby. Mag. (disc. 1996), 7mm Wby. Mag. (disc. 1996), 7mm Rem. Mag., .300 Win. Mag., .300 Wby. Mag., .338 Win. Mag., .340 Wby. Mag. (disc. 1996), .375 H&H, or .416 Rem. Mag. (new 1991) cal., 21¼, 21¾, or 22 in. barrel, classic styled stock with choice of oil (disc. 1996) or matte lacquer finish, finely checkered French walnut. Disc. 1997.

	$850	$685	$550	$490	$460	$430	$410

Last Mfg.'s Sug. Retail was $1,050.

Add $35 for long action.
Add $50-$70 for Mag. cals.
Add approx. $80 for left-hand action (available in all Mag. cals. - mfg. 1994-96).

∗ *Hunter Carbine (Handy)* — available in medium action in .22-250 Rem. (disc. 1990), .243 Win. (new 1991), .308 Win. (new 1991) cal. or long action in .25-06 Rem. (disc. 1990), 7mm Rem. Mag. (disc. 1990), .338 Win. Mag. cal., or .375 H&H (new 1990) cal., 18½ in. barrel with iron sights, oil or lacquer finished deluxe walnut stock with checkering, approx. 7 lbs. Mfg. 1986-91.

	$725	$650	$600	$490	$460	$430	$410

Last Mfg.'s Sug. Retail was $945.

Add $50-$65 for long action (Mag. cals.).

Grading	100%	98%	95%	90%	80%	70%	60%

LONG RANGE HUNTING MODEL — available in long action in .25-06 Rem., .270 Win., .300 Win. Mag., or 7mm Rem. Mag. cal., 26 in. heavy barrel only w/o sights. Mfg. 1996-97.

		$1,030	$785	$625	$545	$495	$465	$440

Last Mfg.'s Sug. Retail was $1,275.

Add $15 for Mag. cals.

FIBERCLASS MODEL — available in medium action (disc. 1992) in .22-250 Rem., .243 Win., .308 Win., or 7mm-08 cal., or long action in .25-06 Rem., .270 Win., .280 Rem., .30-06, 7mm Rem. Mag., .300 Win. Mag., .338 Win. Mag., .375 H&H, or .416 Rem. Mag. (new 1991) cal., has black fiberglass stock. Disc. 1996.

		$1,170	$930	$785	$725	$630	$560	$510

Last Mfg.'s Sug. Retail was $1,388.

Add $17-$37 for Mag. cals.
Subtract $40 for medium action cals. (disc. 1992).
Add $80 for left-hand action (disc. 1989).

* *FiberClass Carbine (Handy)* — available in medium action in .243 Win. or .308 Win. cal. and long action in .25-06 Rem. (disc.), .270 Win. (disc.), .30-06, 7mm Rem. Mag. (disc.), .300 Win. Mag. (disc.), .338 Win. Mag., or .375 H&H(new 1991) cal., 18½ in. barrel with fiberglass stock. Mfg. 1986-91.

		$995	$895	$775	$725	$630	$560	$510

Last Mfg.'s Sug. Retail was $1,239.

Add $50-$65 for Mag. cals.

LAMINATED RIFLE — available in short action (disc. 1989), medium action in .22-250 Rem., .243 Win., .308 Win., or 7mm-08 Rem. cal., or long action in .25-06 Rem., .270 Win., .280 Rem., .30-06, 7mm Rem. Mag., .300 Win. Mag., .338 Win. Mag., .375 H&H, or .416 Rem. Mag. (new 1991) cal., features laminated wood stock. Mfg. 1988-95.

		$985	$790	$635	$550	$495	$460	$430

Last Mfg.'s Sug. Retail was $1,200.

Add $35 for short action.
Add $55 for long action.
Add $75-$95 for Mag. cals.
Add approx. $100 for left-hand action (disc.).
The left-handed action was available in .270 Win., .280 Rem., .30-06, 7mm Rem. Mag., .300 Win. Mag., .338 Win. Mag., .375 H&H, or .416 Rem. Mag. cal.

MODEL TRG-21 — .308 Win. cal., bolt action, 25¾ in. barrel, new design features modular synthetic stock construction with adj. cheekpiece and buttplate, stainless steel barrel, cold hammer forged receiver, and resistance free bolt, 10 shot detachable mag., 10½ lbs. Importation began 1993.

Mfg.'s Sug. Retail	**$2,699**		$2,300	$2,000	$1,800	$1,600	$1,400	$1,200	$975

MODEL TRG-41 — .338 Lapua Mag. cal., similar to Model TRG-21, except has long action and 27⅛ in. barrel, 7¾ lbs. Importation began 1994.

Mfg.'s Sug. Retail	**$3,099**		$2,700	$2,425	$2,150	$1,850	$1,625	$1,400	$1,200

MODEL TRG-S — available in medium action (disc. 1993) in .243 Win. or 7mm-08 cal., or long action in .25-06 Rem. (Mfg. 1994-98), .270 Win., 6.5x55mm Swedish (disc. 1998), .30-06, .308 Win. (disc. 1995), .270 Wby. Mag. (disc. 1998), 7mm Wby. Mag. (Mfg. 1998), 7mm Rem. Mag., .300 Win. Mag., .300 Wby. Mag. (new 1994), .30-378 Wby. Mag. (new 1998, 26 in. barrel only), .338 Win. Mag., .338 Lapua Mag. (new 1994), .340 Wby. Mag. (disc. 1998), 7 STW (26 in. barrel only), .375 H&H (disc. 1998), or .416 Rem. Mag. (disc. 1998)cal., Sporter variation derived from the Model TRG-21, 22 or 24 (Mag. cals. only) in. barrel, 5 shot detachable mag., fully adj. trigger, 60 degree bolt-lift, matte finish, 7¾ lbs. Importation began 1993.

Mfg.'s Sug. Retail	**$854**		$735	$585	$510	$465	$435	$410	$380

Add $40 for Mag. cals.

MANNLICHER CARBINE — available in short action (disc. 1989), medium action in .243 Win. or .308 Win. cal., or long action in .25-06 Rem. (disc. 1991), .270 Win., .30-06, 7mm Rem. Mag. (disc. 1991), .300 Win. Mag. (disc. 1991), .338 Win. Mag., or .375 H&H cal., 18½ in. barrel, two-piece full Mannlicher style stock, open sights. Disc. 1996.

		$1,030	$785	$625	$545	$495	$465	$440

Last Mfg.'s Sug. Retail was $1,275.

Add $35 for long action.
Add $60-$75 for Mag. cals.

PPC MODEL — 22 PPC or 6 mm PPC cal., 21¾ or 23¾ (Benchrest Model) in. barrel, single shot in Benchrest Model, 4 shot mag. in Hunter or Deluxe Model, checkered walnut stock, Deluxe Model has rosewood pistol grip and forearm caps plus skip line checkering, matte lacquer finish on Hunter and Deluxe, oiled finish on Benchrest, 6¼ or 8¾ (Benchrest Model with heavy barrel) lbs. Imported 1989-1998.

$1,250	$950	$750	$650	$600	$540	$500

Last Mfg.'s Sug. Retail was $1,535.

> Add $320 for Deluxe Hunter Model (disc. 1993).
> Add $85 for Benchrest Model (disc. 1993).

VARMINT RIFLE — available in short action (AI) in .17 Rem., .222 Rem., or .223 Rem., and medium action (AII) .22-250 Rem., .243 Win., .308 Win., or 7mm-08 cal., 22¾ in. heavy barrel, no sights. Disc. 1997.

$1,025	$795	$615	$545	$475	$430	$400

Last Mfg.'s Sug. Retail was $1,240.

> Was also available in single shot configuration (6mm PPC or .22 PPC only) — subtract $110 (disc. 1989).

CLASSIC GRADE — .243 Win., .270 Win., .30-06, or 7mm Rem. Mag. cal., short (AI, disc. 1992), medium (AII), or long (AIII) action, classic styled stock, finely checkered French walnut with matte lacquer finish. Disc. 1985, reintroduced 1992-97.

$895	$745	$600	$545	$475	$430	$400

Last Mfg.'s Sug. Retail was $1,050.

> Add $50 for Mag. cal.
> Add $35 for long action.
> Add $120-$135 for left hand action (disc. 1994) (.270 Win. or 7mm Rem. Mag cal. only).
> In 1992, the Classic Grade was once again imported into the U.S. in .243 Win., .270 Win., .30-06, or 7mm Rem. Mag. cal.

DELUXE LIGHTWEIGHT RIFLE — available in short action (AI) in .17 Rem., .222 Rem., or .223 Rem. cal., medium action (AII) in .22-250 Rem., .243 Win., .308 Win., or 7mm-08 Rem. cal., or long action (AIII) in .25-06 Rem., .270 Win., .280 Rem., .30-06, 7mm Rem. Mag., .300 Win. Mag., .300 Wby. Mag., .338 Win. Mag., .375 H&H, or .416 Rem. Mag. (new 1991) cal., 21¼, 21¾, or 22 in. barrel, deluxe quality skipline checkered walnut stock with rosewood forend tip. Disc. 1997.

$1,185	$965	$750	$650	$595	$540	$500

Last Mfg.'s Sug. Retail was $1,475.

> Add $35 for long action.
> Add $50-$70 for Mag. cals.
> Add $150-$175 for left-hand action (disc. 1994, available in long action only).

SAFARI GRADE — available in long (AIII) action only, .300 Win. Mag. (disc. 1989), .338 Win. Mag., .375 H&H, or .416 Rem. Mag. (new 1991) cal., deluxe walnut with sculptured cheekpiece, 22 in. barrel, 4 shot mag., open sights, sling swivels. Disc. 1996.

$2,235	$1,785	$1,475	$1,250	$1,050	$900	$795

Last Mfg.'s Sug. Retail was $2,765.

SUPER DELUXE — a limited edition rifle available on special order only, various cals. are available in the short (AI), medium (AII), and long (AIII) actions, presentation grade walnut with both checkering and carving, rosewood forend tip. Disc. 1997.

$2,400	$1,825	$1,475	$1,250	$1,050	$900	$795

Last Mfg.'s Sug. Retail was $3,100.

SAKO 75 HUNTER — available in 5 action sizes, .17 Rem. (new 1998), .222 Rem. (new 1998), .223 Rem. (new 1998), .22-250 Rem., .243 Win., .308 Win., 7mm-08 Rem., .25-06 Rem., .270 Win., .280 Rem., .30-06, .270 Wby. Mag., 7mm Wby. Mag., 7 STW, 7mm Rem. Mag., .300 Win. Mag., .300 Wby. Mag., .338 Win. Mag., .340 Wby. Mag., .375 H&H, or .416 Rem. Mag. cal., 22, 24, or 26 in. hammer forged barrel, utilizes 3 locking lugs, mechanical ejector, 5 bolt sliding guides with 70 degree bolt lift, 3-position rear tang safety, available with top loading fixed mag. (hinged floorplate), detachable staggered 5 shot mag., or single shot, checkered walnut stock. New 1997.

Mfg.'s Sug. Retail	$1,134						
		$960	$785	$630	$550	$475	$430	$400

> Add $30 for Mag. cals.

Grading	100%	98%	95%	90%	80%	70%	60%

✻ Sako 75 Stainless Synthetic — available in .22-250 Rem., .243 Win., .25-06 Rem., .270 Win., .30-06, .308 Win., .300 Win. Mag., .300 Wby. Mag. (new 1999), 7mm-08 Rem. (new 1998), 7 STW (new 1998), 7mm Rem. Mag., .338 Win. Mag., or .375 H&H cal., features black composite stock with soft rubber grip inserts in pistol grip and forearm area, matte stainless steel metal. New 1997.

Mfg.'s Sug. Retail	$1,224		$1,035	$835	$670		

    Add $33 for Mag. cals.

✻ Sako 75 Stainless Walnut — .270 Win., .30-06, .300 Win. Mag., .300 Wby. Mag., .338 Win. Mag., 7 STW, or 7mm Rem. Mag. cal., features checkered walnut stock and forearm. Importation began 1999.

Mfg.'s Sug. Retail	$1,224		$1,035	$835	$670		

    Add $33 for Mag. cals.

✻ Sako 75 Varmint — .17 Rem., .22-250 Rem., .222 Rem., .223 Rem., 22PPC (new 1999), or 6PPC (new 1999) cal., 24 in. heavy barrel w/o sights. New 1998.

Mfg.'s Sug. Retail	$1,299		$1,095	$885	$710	$635	$550	$475	$430

✻ Sako 75 Stainless Varmint Laminated — similar to Sako 75 Varmint, except is not available in .17 Rem. cal., features stainless steel action and barrel, laminated wood stock. New 1999.

Mfg.'s Sug. Retail	$1,474		$1,275	$1,025	$825		

✻ Sako 75 Deluxe Hinged Floorplate — same cals. as Sako 75 Hunter, features hinged floorplate and deluxe walnut stock with checkering. New 1997.

Mfg.'s Sug. Retail	$1,644		$1,325	$1,075	$850	$700	$600	$540	$500

    Add $30 for Mag. cals.

✻ Sako 75 Super Deluxe — a limited edition rifle available on special order only, presentation grade walnut with both checkering and carving, rosewood forend tip.

Mfg.'s Sug. Retail	$3,400		$2,750	$1,950	$1,575	$1,300	$1,100	$950	$825

PISTOLS: SEMI-AUTO

Less than 200 Triace pistols were imported into the United States.

TRIACE — .22 Short, .22 LR or .32 S&W Wadcutter cal., target pistol incorporating unique action, competition walnut grips with thumb rest and adj. heel, blued finish with chrome accents. Imported 1985-86 only.

	$1,300	$1,150	$950	$825	$700	$600	$500

    Last Mfg.'s Sug. Retail was $1,395.

✻ Triace Pistol Kit — consists of Triace frame, .22 Short, .22 LR, and .32 S&W barrels. Cased with accessories. Imported 1985-86 only.

	$2,500	$2,200	$2,000	$1,500	$1,300	$1,175	$1,025

    Last Mfg.'s Sug. Retail was $2,385.

SAMCO GLOBAL ARMS, INC.

Current importer and distributor located in Miami, FL. Dealer sales.

Samco Global Arms currently imports a variety of foreign and domestic surplus military rifles (including various contract Mausers, Loewe, Steyr, Czech, Lee Enfield, etc.). Most of these guns are in the $60-$250 range and they offer excellent values to both shooters and collectors. Samco also sells newly remanufactured sporting rifles (German or Spanish) in .308 Win. or 7x57mm cal. These sporters range in value from approx. $225-$325.

SARASQUETA, FELIX

Previous manufacturer located in Eibar, Spain. Previously imported and distributed by SAE (Spain America Enterprises), Inc. located in Miami, FL.

SHOTGUNS: O/U

MODEL MERKE — 12 ga. only, boxlock action, 22 or 27 in. separated barrels, single non-selective trigger, blue only, extractors, recoil pad. Imported 1986 only.

	$255	$215	$200	$190	$180	$170	$160

    Last Mfg.'s Sug. Retail was $291.

S

Grading	100%	98%	95%	90%	80%	70%	60%

SARASQUETA, J.J.

Previous manufacturer located in Eibar, Spain. Imported until 1984 by American Arms, Inc. located in Overland Park, KS.

SHOTGUNS: SxS

MODEL 107 E — 12, 16, or 20 ga., ejectors, various barrel lengths, checkered walnut stock and forearm, double triggers.

	100%	98%	95%	90%	80%	70%	60%
	$360	$290	$270	$255	$240	$215	$200

Last Mfg.'s Sug. Retail was $435.

MODELS 119E-132E-1882E — more deluxe versions of Model 107E.

	100%	98%	95%	90%	80%	70%	60%
	$470	$375	$340	$315	$285	$255	$230

Last Mfg.'s Sug. Retail was $570.

MODEL 130 E — more deluxe version of Model 119 E.

	100%	98%	95%	90%	80%	70%	60%
	$800	$635	$590	$555	$515	$480	$450

Last Mfg.'s Sug. Retail was $960.

MODEL 131 E — action similar to Model 107 E, except has deluxe engraving.

	100%	98%	95%	90%	80%	70%	60%
	$1,050	$845	$770	$710	$665	$620	$585

Last Mfg.'s Sug. Retail was $1,250.

MODEL 1882 E LUXE — double triggers, moderate engraving, otherwise similar to Model 107 E.

	100%	98%	95%	90%	80%	70%	60%
	$825	$660	$615	$565	$520	$480	$450

Last Mfg.'s Sug. Retail was $990.

* *Model 1882 E Luxe w/gold inlays* — SST, extensive engraving.

	100%	98%	95%	90%	80%	70%	60%
	$1,120	$920	$850	$790	$740	$695	$650

Last Mfg.'s Sug. Retail was $1,320.

* *Model 1882 E Luxe w/silver inlays* — SST, extensive engraving.

	100%	98%	95%	90%	80%	70%	60%
	$1,055	$855	$795	$740	$700	$660	$630

Last Mfg.'s Sug. Retail was $1,260.

MODEL 150 E — 12 or 16 ga., single trigger, ejectors, select walnut and extensive engraving.

	100%	98%	95%	90%	80%	70%	60%
	$1,285	$1,035	$960	$895	$835	$770	$695

Last Mfg.'s Sug. Retail was $1,500.

* *Model 150 E Trap* — similar to Model 150 E, except trap dimensions on stock.

	100%	98%	95%	90%	80%	70%	60%
	$1,360	$1,125	$1,010	$940	$875	$790	$720

Last Mfg.'s Sug. Retail was $1,600.

SARASQUETA, VICTOR

Previous manufacturer located in Eibar, Spain. Trademark was sold to Diarm S.A. circa 1986.

SHOTGUNS:SxS

MODEL 3 BOXLOCK — 12, 16, or 20 ga., all standard barrel lengths and chokes, boxlock, double triggers, checkered English style stock and forearm.

	100%	98%	95%	90%	80%	70%	60%
Extractors	$445	$395	$350	$295	$250	$215	$185
Auto ejectors	$575	$515	$450	$375	$300	$250	$225

HAMMERLESS SIDELOCK — 12, 16, 20, 28 ga., or .410 bore, SxS, barrel length and choke to order, straight English style stock, models differ as to amount of engraving, grade of wood, and overall quality as follows:

Add 25% for 28 ga.
Add 30% for .410 bore.

MODEL 4 — extractors.

	100%	98%	95%	90%	80%	70%	60%
	$620	$550	$525	$495	$450	$415	$360

MODEL 4E — auto ejectors.

	100%	98%	95%	90%	80%	70%	60%
	$680	$605	$580	$550	$505	$470	$415

MODEL 203 — extractors.

	100%	98%	95%	90%	80%	70%	60%
	$650	$570	$545	$515	$475	$435	$380

S

Grading	100%	98%	95%	90%	80%	70%	60%
MODEL 203E — auto ejectors.							
	$710	$625	$600	$570	$530	$490	$435
MODEL 6E							
	$800	$715	$690	$660	$615	$580	$525
MODEL 7E							
	$855	$770	$745	$715	$670	$635	$580
MODEL 10E							
	$1,735	$1,595	$1,485	$1,405	$1,320	$1,240	$1,100
MODEL 11E							
	$1,870	$1,680	$1,595	$1,515	$1,430	$1,350	$1,265
MODEL 12E							
	$2,145	$1,900	$1,790	$1,705	$1,570	$1,430	$1,375

SARDIUS

Previous manufacturer until 1990 located in Israel. Previously imported and distributed by Armscorp of America, Inc. located in Baltimore, MD.

PISTOLS: SEMI-AUTO

SD-9 — 9mm Para. cal., semi-auto double action, compact design, 3.07 in. barrel, matte black finish, 6 shot mag., 3 dot sighting system, 1.54 lbs. Imported 1988-90 only.

$395	$350	$295	$250	$220	$200	$185

Last Mfg.'s Sug. Retail was $350.

SARRIUGARTE, FRANCISO S.A.

Previous manufacturer located in Elgoibar, Spain. Previously part of the Diarm S.A. Group which was imported and distributed by American Arms, Inc. located in North Kansas City, MO.

SARSILMAZ

Current manufacturer established during 1880, and located in Istanbul, Turkey. Currently imported and distributed by Armsport, Inc. located in Miami, FL. Please refer to the Armsport section for individual models.

Sarsilmaz offers a wide range of shotguns (O/U, semi-auto, and slide action) and semi-auto pistols. Some of these models are not available in the U.S.

SAUER, J.P., & SOHN

Current manufacturer located in Eckernförde, Germany since 1751 (originally Prussia). Previously manufactured in Suhl pre-WWII. Currently imported by SIG Arms located in Exeter, NH since 1995. Previously imported by the Paul Company Inc. located in Wellsville, KS until 1995 and by G.U., Inc. located in Omaha, NE until 1994. In 1972, J.P. Sauer & Sohn entered into a cooperative agreement with SIG, presently the parent house of Sauer & Sohn.

PISTOLS: SEMI-AUTO

MODEL 1913 POCKET AUTOMATIC — .32 ACP cal., 7 shot, 3 in. barrel, fixed sights, blue, black rubber grips. Mfg. 1913-1930.

$295	$225	$185	$165	$155	$145	$135

MODEL 1913 25 AUTOMATIC — .25 ACP cal., 7 shot, 2½ in. barrel, fixed sights, blue, black rubber grips. Mfg. 1913-1930.

$325	$250	$200	$175	$150	$140	$135

MODEL 28 — .25 ACP cal., 7 shot, 3 in. barrel, fixed sights, blue, black rubber grips. Mfg. 1930-1938.

$300	$240	$185	$170	$155	$145	$135

Grading	100%	98%	95%	90%	80%	70%	60%

BEHÖRDEN "AUTHORITY" M1930 MODEL — .32 ACP cal., 3 in. barrel, blue only, black plastic grips.

	$325	$240	$200	$175	$150	$145	$135

Add $1,000 for very rare alloy frame example.

MODEL 38 H DOUBLE ACTION AUTOMATIC — .22 LR (extremely rare), .32 ACP, or .380 ACP (rare) cal., 3¼ in. barrel, fixed sights, blue, plastic grips. Mfg. 1938-1945.

	100%	98%	95%	90%	80%	70%	60%
.32 ACP	$395	$325	$240	$205	$185	$165	$150
.380 ACP	$3,500	$2,750	$2,000	$1,500	$1,250	$995	$775
.22 LR	$4,000	$3,000	$2,200	$1,600	$1,250	$995	$775

Add 10% for Waffenamt proofing.
Add 15%-25% for police markings.
Add 60% for alloy frame.

RIFLES: BOLT ACTION

SAUER PRE-WWII BOLT ACTION RIFLE — most popular European cals. and .30-06, 22 or 24 in. barrel, raised solid rib, Krupp steel, double set triggers, folding 3 leaf express sight, checkered sporter stock. Mfg. pre-WWII.

	$715	$550	$495	$440	$360	$330	$305

MODEL 90 — .243 Win., .25-06 Rem., 6.5x55mm, .270 Win., .30-06, .300 Win. Mag., .300 Wby. Mag., 7mm Rem. Mag., .375 H&H, or .458 Win. Mag. cal., 24 in. barrel, 3 or 4 shot detachable mag., checkered walnut stock, approx. 7½ lbs. Importation disc.

	$775	$675	$600	$550	$500	$465	$430

Last Mfg.'s Sug. Retail was $1,175.

During 1985-1989, Sauer exported to Sigarms 2,300 Model 90 rifles, 1,100 of these were in Mag. cals.

* **Model 90 Stutzen** — Mannlicher style full stock, not available in European or Mag. cals. Importation disc. 1989.

	$800	$700	$600	$550	$500	$465	$430

Last Mfg.'s Sug. Retail was $1,225.

* **Safari Model** — .458 Win. Mag cal., 23.62 in. barrel, 10½ lbs. Imported 1986-1988 only.

	$1,250	$950	$850	$750	$650	$575	$500

Last Mfg.'s Sug. Retail was $1,675.

* **Model 90 Stutzen (Lux)**
While advertised, this model was never imported. Mfg.'s sug. retail was set at $1,200.

MODEL 90 SUPREME (LUX) — .243 Win., .25-06 Rem., 6.5x55 Swedish, .270 Win., .30-06, .300 Win. Mag., .300 Wby. Mag., 7mm Rem. Mag., .338 Win. Mag., or .375 H&H cal., similar to Model 90, except has high gloss deluxe stock with Monte Carlo cheekpiece and rosewood forearm and pistol grip caps, gold trigger, no sights, 7.1 - 7.7 lbs. Importation 1987-1998.

	$1,225	$1,000	$875	$775	$585	$465	$430

Last Mfg.'s Sug. Retail was $1,350.

Add $32 for Mag. cals.
On Models 90 Lux and Supreme add 69% for Grade I engraving, 105% for Grade II, 128% for Grade III, and 164% for Grade IV.

* **Safari Model (Lux)**
While advertised, this model was never imported. Mfg.'s sug. retail was set at $1,795.

MODEL 200 BOLT ACTION — available in 15 cals. between .243 Win. and .375 H&H, short and medium actions only, 23.62 in. unique interchangeable barrels, 6 lug bolt, easily detachable stock and forearm, optional set trigger, detachable mag. with hidden release button, 7.7 lbs. Production disc. 1993.

	$1,225	$925	$800	$700	$600	$525	$450

Last Mfg.'s Sug. Retail was $1,395.

Add $100 for 7mm Rem. Mag. or .300 Win. Mag. cal.
Add $300 for extra interchangeable barrel.
During 1986-1989, Sauer exported to Sigarms 4,170 Model 200 rifles, 1,370 of these were in Mag. cals.

Grading	100%	98%	95%	90%	80%	70%	60%

✱ **Model 200 Lightweight** — similar to Model 200, only with alloy receiver, 6.6 lbs.

| | $1,225 | $925 | $800 | $700 | $600 | $525 | $450 |

Last Mfg.'s Sug. Retail was $1,395.

    Add $150 for left-hand version.

✱ **Model 200 Lux** — similar to Model 200, except has deluxe walnut, rosewood forend tip and pistol grip cap, marmorized bolt and gold trigger.

| | $1,395 | $1,175 | $925 | $800 | $700 | $600 | $525 |

Last Mfg.'s Sug. Retail was $1,595.

✱ **American 200 Lux** — similar to Model 200 Lux, except has high gloss Monte Carlo stock, 24 in. barrel, jeweled bolt, and gold trigger.

| | $1,395 | $1,175 | $925 | $800 | $700 | $600 | $525 |

Last Mfg.'s Sug. Retail was $1,595.

    Add $150 for left-hand version.

✱ **European 200 Lux** — similar to Model 200 Lux, except has European configured stock with Schnabel forearm, 26 in. barrel.

| | $1,395 | $1,175 | $925 | $800 | $700 | $600 | $525 |

Last Mfg.'s Sug. Retail was $1,595.

    Add $95 for left-hand version.

✱ **Model 200 Carbon Fiber** — similar to Model 200, except has carbon fiber stock. Imported 1987-88 only.

| | $800 | $700 | $625 | $565 | $500 | $465 | $430 |

Last Mfg.'s Sug. Retail was $1,200.

MODEL 202 SUPREME (LUX) — .243 Win. (disc. 1998), .25-06 Rem., .270 Win., .30-06, .308 Win., 6.5x55mm Swedish, or 7x64mm (disc. 1997) cal., steel receiver, modular design allowing barrel change within 2 minutes, dual safety, 2 piece figured walnut stock, cocking indicator, detachable 3-5 shot mag., takedown with interchangeable barrels, right or left hand action, 7.7 lbs. Importation began 1994.

| Mfg.'s Sug. Retail | $1,035 | $925 | $795 | $700 | $600 | $550 | $495 | $435 |

    Also available in left-hand action in .270 Win. or .30-06 cal.

✱ **Model 202 Synthetic** — .25-06 Rem., .270 Win., .30-06, .308 Win., .300 Win. Mag., .300 Wby. Mag., .375 H&H, or 6.5mmx55mm Swedish cal., features black synthetic stock, 24 or 26 in. barrel w/o sights, 7.7 lbs. Importation began 1999.

| Mfg.'s Sug. Retail | $985 | $895 | $775 | $675 | $600 | $550 | $495 | $435 |

    Add $71 for Mag. cals. (26 in. barrel only).

✱ **Model 202 Supreme Magnum (Lux)** — .300 Win. Mag., .300 Wby. Mag., .338 Win. Mag. (disc. 1997), .375 H&H, 7mm Rem. Mag., 6.5x68mm (importation disc. 1997), or 8x68mm (importation disc. 1997) cal., converts to 7 cals. Importation began 1994.

| Mfg.'s Sug. Retail | $1,106 | $955 | $825 | $700 | $600 | $550 | $495 | $435 |

    Also available in left-hand action in .300 Win. Mag. or 7mm Rem. Mag. cal.

✱ **Model 202 Super Grade**

    While advertised in 1994, this model was never imported. Mfg.'s sug. retail was set at $1,020.

MODEL 202 HUNTER MATCH

    While advertised in 1994, this model was never imported. Mfg.'s sug. retail was set at $1,495.

MODEL 202 ALASKA

    While advertised in 1994, this model was never imported. Mfg.'s sug. retail was set at $1,335.

MODEL 205 TR TARGET — 6.5x55mm or .308 Win. cal., true left hand variation, 200 meter diopter sights, modular design allows changing single components including caliber, free floating barrel with vent. forearm, 5 shot mag., interchangeable barrel systems, 12.1 lbs. Imported 1994-97.

| | $1,775 | $1,575 | $1,400 | $1,250 | $1,100 | $950 | $825 |

Last Mfg.'s Sug. Retail was $1,900.

SSE 3000 PRECISION RIFLE — .308 Win. cal., very accurate, law enforcement counter Sniper Rifle, built to customer specifications.

| | $4,845 | $3,655 | $3,200 | $2,850 | $2,500 | $2,275 | $2,000 |

Grading	100%	98%	95%	90%	80%	70%	60%

SHR 970 — .270 Win. or .30-06 cal., steel receiver, standard model featuring easy take-down and quick change 22 in. barrel, 4 shot mag., standard medium gloss walnut stock with checkering, ultra-fast lock time, nitrided bore, no sights, 7-1/2 lbs. New 1998.

Mfg.'s Sug. Retail	$499	$445	$375	$325	$295	$275	$250	$230

DRILLINGS & COMBINATION GUNS

SAUER MODEL 3000 DRILLING — available in either 16 ga./.30-06, 6.5x57R, 7x57R, 7x65R or 12 ga./.222 Rem. (disc.), .243 Win., .30-06, 6.5x57R, 7x57R, 7x65R, or 9.3x74R cal., Greener cross-bolt and double barrel lug locking, cocking indicators, front set trigger, automatic sight, walnut pistol grip stock with hog-back and cheekpiece, Grade III scroll engraving, 7¼ lbs.

Mfg.'s Sug. Retail	$4,600	$4,300	$3,600	$3,100	$2,675	$2,200	$1,800	$1,400

This model was also previously imported by Weatherby and Colt - please refer to separate listings for more information.

* **Luxury Grade** — similar to Model 3000 standard, except select root timber and extensive engraving featuring two animals.

Mfg.'s Sug. Retail	$6,100	$5,550	$4,875	$4,400	$3,875	$3,475	$3,000	$2,575

COMBO BBF 54 O/U — standard grade combination gun, 16 ga./.222 Rem., .243 Win., 6.5x57R, 7x57R, 7x65R, and .30-06 cals., ejectors, double triggers with front set trigger, moderate engraving on coin finished receiver, Greener cross-bolt with double barrel lugs, 6 lbs. Importation disc. 1986.

	$2,200	$2,060	$1,760	$1,565	$1,380	$1,250	$1,125

Last Mfg.'s Sug. Retail was $2,495.

* **Luxury Grade** — similar to Combo BBF 54, except game scene engraved and deluxe crotch walnut.

	$2,450	$2,200	$2,000	$1,785	$1,600	$1,475	$1,300

Last Mfg.'s Sug. Retail was $2,745.

LUFTWAFFE SURVIVAL DRILLING — 12 or 16 ga. (65mm) SxS over 9.3x74 R, 28 in. barrels, large eagle swastika on stock and breech end of right barrel. Originally mfg. for Luftwaffe pilots during WWII.

	$4,500	$4,000	$3,600	$3,200	$2,600	$2,400	$2,200

Add 20% for original aluminum case and accessories.

SAUER MODEL 3000E DRILLING — see listing under Colt Sauer Drilling.

SHOTGUNS

MODEL 60 — various ga.'s, boxlock action, DT, extractors, checkered walnut stock and forearm, this model was the standard model of its period.

	$975	$875	$750	$650	$550	$450	$395

Add 20% for 20 ga.

ROYAL DOUBLE BARREL SHOTGUN — 12, 16 or 20 ga., 26, 28, or 30 in. barrels, various chokes, boxlock, scalloped engraved frame, cocking indicators, SST, auto ejectors, Krupp steel barrel, checkered pistol grip stock. Mfg. 1955-1977.

	$1,650	$1,375	$1,210	$1,100	$880	$770	$660

Add 20% for 20 ga.

ARTEMIS — 12 ga., 28 in. barrels, mod. and full choke, H&H type sidelock, SST, auto ejector, Krupp steel, checkered pistol grip stock. Mfg. 1966-1977.

* **Grade I** — fine line engraved.

	$5,500	$4,620	$3,850	$3,520	$3,080	$2,640	$2,200

* **Grade II** — extensive engraving.

	$6,600	$5,500	$4,840	$4,235	$3,850	$3,300	$3,080

GRADE 380

	$4,500	$4,000	$3,500	$3,000	$2,500	$2,200	$1,500

GRADE F-40

Rarity factor precludes accurate price evaluation.

MODEL F-45

	$12,000	$10,500	$9,000	$8,000	$6,500	$5,000	$3,200

Grading	100%	98%	95%	90%	80%	70%	60%

MODEL F-60

		100%	98%	95%	90%	80%	70%	60%
		$23,000	$20,000	$17,000	$14,000	$12,000	$9,000	$5,000

MODEL 66 O/U FIELD GUN — 12 ga., 28 in. mod. and full, Krupp steel barrels, H&H type sidelocks, SST, auto ejectors, checkered pistol grip stock, available in three grades of engraving. Mfg. 1966-1975.

	100%	98%	95%	90%	80%	70%	60%
Grade I	$2,200	$1,760	$1,540	$1,320	$1,100	$880	$770
Grade II	$3,080	$2,420	$1,980	$1,650	$1,430	$1,210	$990
Grade III	$3,850	$3,300	$2,860	$2,420	$1,980	$1,650	$1,320

MODEL 66 O/U SKEET GUN — similar to Field Gun, with 26 in. VR skeet bored barrel and vent. forearm. Mfg. 1966-1975.

MODEL 66 O/U TRAP GUN — similar to 66 Skeet, with 30 in. barrels, full and full, or mod. and full choke, trap style stock.

	100%	98%	95%	90%	80%	70%	60%
Grade I	$2,090	$1,760	$1,540	$1,320	$1,100	$880	$770
Grade II	$3,080	$2,420	$1,980	$1,650	$1,430	$1,210	$880
Grade III	$3,850	$3,300	$2,860	$2,420	$1,980	$1,650	$1,320

SAUER/FRANCHI STANDARD GRADE O/U — 12 ga. only, double triggers, checkered walnut stock and forearm, SST, blued finish only, sling swivels, VR. Importation disc. 1986.

100%	98%	95%	90%	80%	70%	60%
$375	$340	$315	$290	$275	$260	$245

Last Mfg.'s Sug. Retail was $785.

* **Regent Grade** — similar to Standard grade, except has single trigger and lightly engraved silver finished receiver. Importation disc. 1986.

100%	98%	95%	90%	80%	70%	60%
$475	$395	$350	$310	$290	$275	$265

Last Mfg.'s Sug. Retail was $825.

* **Favorit Grade** — similar to Regent Grade, except has elaborate scroll engraving on coin finished receiver, gold-plated trigger. Importation disc. 1986.

100%	98%	95%	90%	80%	70%	60%
$550	$495	$450	$420	$385	$350	$300

Last Mfg.'s Sug. Retail was $875.

* **Diplomat Grade** — similar to Favorit Grade, except has more elaborate scroll engraving and with model name gold filled on receiver sides and barrel, extra grain French walnut, cased.

100%	98%	95%	90%	80%	70%	60%
$875	$750	$625	$550	$495	$460	$435

Last Mfg.'s Sug. Retail was $1,520.

SAUER/FRANCHI SPORTING S O/U — 12 ga. only, 28 in. barrels, ejectors, SST, select European walnut with checkered stock and forearm, 10mm VR, plain silver finished receiver with model name gold filled on both sides. Importation disc. 1986.

100%	98%	95%	90%	80%	70%	60%
$800	$700	$600	$500	$450	$420	$395

Last Mfg.'s Sug. Retail was $1,375.

SAUER/FRANCHI MODEL TRAP O/U — similar to Sporting S, except has 29 in. barrels, trap chokes and stock dimensions. Importation disc. 1986.

100%	98%	95%	90%	80%	70%	60%
$875	$750	$625	$550	$495	$460	$435

Last Mfg.'s Sug. Retail was $1,375.

SAUER/FRANCHI MODEL SKEET O/U — similar to Sporting S, except has skeet chokes. Importation disc. 1986.

100%	98%	95%	90%	80%	70%	60%
$875	$750	$625	$550	$495	$460	$435

Last Mfg.'s Sug. Retail was $1,375.

SAVAGE ARMS, INC.

Current manufacturer located in Westfield, MA since 1960. Previously manufactured in Utica, NY - later manufacture was in Chicopee Falls, MA. Distributor sales only.

This company originally started in Utica, NY in 1895. The Model 1895 was initially manufactured by Marlin between 1895-1899. The company was renamed Savage Arms Co. in 1899. After WWI, the name was again changed to the Savage Arms Corporation. Savage moved to Chicopee Falls, MA circa 1946 (to its J. Stevens Arms Co. plants). In the mid-1960s the company became The Savage Arms Division of American Hardware Corp., which later became The Emhart Corporation. This division was sold in September 1981, and became Savage Industries, Inc. located in

Grading	100%	98%	95%	90%	80%	70%	60%

Westfield, MA (since the move in 1960). On November 1, 1989, Savage Arms Inc. acquired the majority of assets of Savage Industries, Inc.

Savage Arms, Inc. will offer service and parts on their current line of firearms only (those manufactured after Nov. 1, 1989). These models include the 24, 99, and 110 plus the imported Model 312. Warranty and repair claims for products not acquired by Savage Arms, Inc. will remain the responsibility of Savage Industries, Inc. For information regarding the repair and/or parts of Savage Industries, Inc. firearms, please refer to the Trademark Index in the back of this text. Parts for pre-1989 Savage Industries, Inc. firearms may be obtained by contacting the Gun Parts Corporation located in West Hurley, NY (listed in Trademark Index). Savage Arms, Inc. has older records/info. on pistols, the Model 24, older mfg. Model 99s, and Model 110 only. A factory letter authenticating the configuration of a particular specimen may be obtained by contacting Mr. John Callahan (see Trademark Index for listings and address). The charge for this service is $15.00 per gun, and $20.00 per gun for Models 1895, 1899, and 99 rifles - please allow 2-4 weeks for an adequate response.

COMBINATION GUNS

All Model 24s are under the domain of Savage Arms, Inc.

MODEL 24 O/U COMBINATION GUN — .22 LR over .410 bore, open rifle sight, visible hammer, break open, plain pistol grip stock. Mfg. 1950-1965.

	$160	$130	$110	$100	$85	$70	$55

MODEL 24B-DL

	$185	$155	$135	$120	$100	$90	$80

MODEL 24S — similar to Model 24, with 20 ga. or .410 bore barrel, sidelever, dovetail for scope. Mfg. 1965-1971.

	$185	$155	$135	$120	$100	$90	$80

MODEL 24MS — similar to Model 24S, with .22 WRM barrel. Mfg. 1965-1971.

	$170	$140	$120	$110	$90	$85	$70

MODEL 24DL — similar to Model 24S, with top lever, satin chrome frame and checkered stock. Mfg. 1965-1969.

	$170	$140	$120	$110	$90	$85	$70

MODEL 24MDL — similar to Model 24DL, with .22 WRM barrel. Mfg. 1965-1969.

	$175	$145	$125	$115	$95	$85	$70

MODEL 24FG — similar to Model 24S, with top lever. Mfg. 1972-disc.

	$165	$130	$110	$90	$85	$65	$55

MODEL 24 FIELD — .22 LR or .22 Mag. over 20 ga. or .410 bore, lightweight field version, 24 in. separated barrels, 3 in. chambers, 6¾ lbs. Disc. 1989.

	$185	$150	$120	$100	$85	$80	$70

Last Mfg.'s Sug. Retail was $209.

MODEL 24F (PREDATOR) — choice of .22 LR, .22 Hornet, .222 Rem. (disc. 1989), .223 Rem., or .30-30 Win. cal., over 12, 20 ga., or .410 bore (new 1998), 3 in. chamber, 24 in. barrels, 12 ga. barrel is available either with fixed choke or choke tube, wood (disc.) or matte black Dupont-tRynite synthetic stock, hammer block safety, DTs, approx. 8 lbs. New 1989.

Mfg.'s Sug. Retail	$425	$390	$335	$275	$240	$210	$180	$165

Add $25 for 12 ga.

Add $50 for .410 bore adaptor (12 ga. only).

Add $14 for Camo Rynite stock (disc., Model 24F-T, Turkey Model-12 ga./.22 Hornet or .223 Rem. cal. only).

The .22 LR cal. is available with 20 ga. barrel only.

MODEL 24V — similar to Model 24, with .22 Hornet (disc. 1984), .222 Rem., .223 Rem., .30-30 Win., .357 Max., or .357 Mag.(disc.), over 24 in. 20 ga. (3 in.) barrel, single trigger, 7 lbs. Mfg. 1971-89.

	$300	$265	$230	$200	$175	$150	$130

MODEL 24D — .22 LR or .22 Mag. over .410 bore or 20 ga., black or case hardened frame, game scene decoration was eliminated in 1974, forearm not checkered after 1976.

	$250	$220	$185	$150	$130	$115	$105

Grading	100%	98%	95%	90%	80%	70%	60%

MODEL 24C CAMPER'S COMPANION — nickel finish, .22 LR over 20 ga., 20 in. barrel cylinder bore, buttplate opens to store ten .22 LR cartridges and one 20 ga. shell in buttstock, carrying case, 5¾ lbs. Mfg. 1972-1988.

	$200	$165	$130	$115	$105	$95	$80

Last Mfg.'s Sug. Retail was $239.

Add 10% for nickel finish (Model 24CS - shipped with pistol grip stock also).

MODEL 24 VS — similar to Model 24CS, only .357 Mag. over 20 ga., nickel finish, accessory pistol grip stock is included.

	$250	$210	$185	$160	$145	$135	$120

MODEL 389 — 12 ga. with 3 in. chamber over choice of .308 Win. or .222 Rem., choke tubes standard, hammerless, double triggers, checkered walnut stock and forearm with recoil pad. Mfg. 1988-90 only.

	$800	$640	$550	$495	$435	$365	$300

Last Mfg.'s Sug. Retail was $919.

PISTOLS: BOLT ACTION

MODEL 510F STRIKER — .22-250 Rem., .223 Rem. (new 1999), .243 Win., .260 Rem. (new 1999), .308 Win., or 7mm-08 Rem. cal., left-hand bolt action with right hand ejection, 14 in. free floating barrel, 2 shot internal box mag., blued barrel action, black composite stock with grooved forend and wide bottom swell, drilled and tapped, 5 lbs. New 1998.

Mfg.'s Sug. Retail	$400	$360	$320	$275	$240	$210	$180	$165

MODEL 516FSS STRIKER — similar to 510F Striker, except has stainless steel barreled action. New 1998.

Mfg.'s Sug. Retail	$450	$400	$360	$320

* *Model 516FSAK Striker* — similar to 516FSS Striker, except has adj. muzzle brake (AMB). New 1998.

Mfg.'s Sug. Retail	$500	$450	$375	$335

MODEL 516BSAK/BSS SUPER STRIKER — similar cals. to Model 510F Striker, features dual pillar bedded short action and custom designed thumb-hole laminate grey stock, stainless steel frame and fluted barrel, adj. muzzle brake (AMB), new ESP (Engineered Step Performance) adj. two-stage trigger, approx. 5 lbs. New 1999.

Mfg.'s Sug. Retail	$600	$525	$425	$350

Subtract $50 w/o muzzle brake (Model 516BSS).

PISTOLS: SEMI-AUTO

MODEL 1907 AUTO PISTOL — .32 ACP or .380 ACP cal., 9 (.380 ACP) or 10 (.32 ACP) shot mag., 3¹³⁄₁₆ (.32 ACP) or 4⁵⁄₁₆ (.380 ACP) in. barrel, blue, fixed sights, metal (early mfg. on .32 ACP only until serial no. 10,980) or hard rubber grips, exposed cocking piece. Mfg. 1910-1917.

.32 ACP	$350	$250	$175	$150	$125	$115	$100
.380 ACP	$465	$415	$355	$300	$250	$200	$150

Add large premiums for factory nickel, silver, or gold finish (rare).

There were three different types of pearl grips: the early variation was a snap-on with an S/A logo, screw-on with an indianhead logo, and the flared 1917 with no logo. Asking prices for the grips alone are in the $250-$1,000 range (this also applied to the Model 1915 Hammerless and Model 1917 Automatic).

MODEL 1915 HAMMERLESS — similar to Model 1907, with grip safety and no visible cocking piece. Mfg. 1915-1917.

.32 ACP	$525	$450	$375	$300	$250	$225	$200
.380 ACP	$650	$575	$500	$400	$300	$250	$200

Add 10% with original box and instruction manual.

MODEL 1917 AUTOMATIC — similar to Model 1907, with spur cocking piece and trapezoidal grips. Mfg. 1920-1928.

.32 ACP	$275	$225	$175	$145	$130	$110	$100
.380 ACP	$445	$400	$350	$300	$250	$200	$150

Add 10% with original box and instruction manual.

Grading	100%	98%	95%	90%	80%	70%	60%

M1907 U.S. ARMY TEST TRIAL .45 ACP — .45 ACP cal., large version of Model 1910, exposed hammer. Approx. 400 mfg. 1907-1911 for military trials.

| | $5,500 | $4,400 | $3,300 | $2,800 | $2,400 | $2,000 | $1,800 |

Add 250% for experimental M1910 and M1911.

Most pistols were repurchased from the government, reconditioned (many reblued), and resold to the public as commercial models. Add 100% if in original condition.

PISTOLS: SINGLE SHOT

MODEL 101 — .22 LR cal., 5½ in. barrel, single action, adj. sight, swing out barrel, blue, wood grips. Mfg. 1960-1968.

| | $150 | $120 | $95 | $80 | $70 | $60 | $50 |

RIFLES

Savage made a wide variety of inexpensive, utilitarian rifles that to date have attracted mostly shooting interest, but little collector interest. A listing of these models may be found in the back of this text under "Serialization".

MODEL 1895 — .303 Savage cal. only, lever action, mfg. in either carbine (22 in.), rifle (26 in.), or musket (30 in.) variations, round (scarce) or octagon barrel that has Marlin proofmark under the forend, closed top, solid breech, side ejecting, 5 shot rotating box mag., unfired shots indicator. Originally mfg. by Marlin, marked "Savage Repeating Arms Co. Utica, N.Y. U.S.A. Pat. Feb. 7, 1893.", approx. 6,000 mfg. 1895-1899, early models had hole in top of bolt — later ones were smooth.

| | $1,500 | $1,250 | $995 | $880 | $770 | $660 | $495 |

Values assume rifle configuration — add premiums for the carbine (rare) and musket.

MODEL 1899 — improvement of Model 1895 with squared off front end of breech bolt and cocking indicator as opposed to viewing hole indicator. Early model 1899s have oblong cocking indicator located on the top of the breech bolt. In approx. 1908, this was changed to a pin on the upper tang. Older models have perch belly stocks and high gloss bluing (commanding premiums of 10%-15%). A wide variety of special order features were available including special length barrels (up to 30 in.), pistol rips stocks, checkering, woods, plating, grades of engraving, sights, etc., all of which can command a moderate to sizeable premium.

Add 25% for takedown (added 1909).
Add 10% for .25-35 WCF, .32-40 WCF, or .38-55 WCF cal.

In 1905 Savage broadened the variety of this model and added the 1899A2, CD, BC, AB, Excelsior, Leader, Crescent, Victor, Rival, Premier, and Monarch (top-of-the-line model). Prices at the time ranged from $21 to $250 — quite a range of prices. Any factory engraved Savage 99 is rare (less than 1,000 mfg. to date) with values having to be computed one gun at a time. Several years ago a collection of older, engraved Model 99s was sold with prices ranging from $2,000 to over $40,000. Because of this, the above values assume standard rifle with no engraving options (Grades A through G).

All Model 99s fall within the domain of Savage Arms, Inc.

* ***Model 1899A Rifle*** — .303 Savage, .30-30 Win., .25-35 WCF, .32-40 WCF, .38-55 WCF, or .300 Sav., 26 in. round barrel, straight grip stock, cresent or steel shotgun butt, takedown added 1909. Mfg. 1899-1927, Short rifle (22 in.) mfg. 1899-1922.

| | $795 | $675 | $600 | $535 | $475 | $400 | $325 |

* ***Model 1899B Rifle*** — .303 Savage, .30-30 Win., .25-35 WCF, .32-40 WCF, or .38-55 WCF, 26 in. octagon barrel, straight grip stock, cresent or steel shotgun butt. Mfg. 1899-1915.

| | $895 | $800 | $725 | $650 | $575 | $500 | $425 |

* ***Model 1899C Rifle*** — .303 Savage, .30-30 Win., .25-35 WCF, .32-40 WCF, or .38-55 WCF, 26 in. half octagon barrel, straight grip, cresent or steel shotgun butt. Mfg. 1899-1915.

| | $995 | $900 | $825 | $750 | $675 | $600 | $525 |

* ***Model 1899-D Military Rifle (Musket)*** — .30-30 Win. or .303 Savage cal., 28 or 30 in. round barrel with two barrel bands, straight grip stock with bayonet lug.

| | $3,500 | $3,200 | $2,800 | $2,400 | $2,000 | $1,600 | $1,200 |

Grading	100%	98%	95%	90%	80%	70%	60%

* **Model 1899-F Carbine** — various cals., 3 different variations, the first variation was made approx. 1899-1905 with small barrel band and receiver ring (scarce), the second and third variations are not quite as desirable.

	$1,500	$1,275	$1,100	$925	$800	$700	$600

Add approx. 40% for .25-35 WCF, .32-40 WCF, or .38-55 WCF cal.

* **Model 1899H Rifle** — .22 Hi-Power, .25-35 WCF, .30-30 Win., or .303 Savage cal., 20 in. featherweight barrel, straight grip, steel or hard rubber shotgun butt, takedown added in 1909. Mfg. 1905-1915.

	$800	$725	$625	$550	$425	$350	$275

Add 10% for .22 Hi-Power.
Add 20% for .25-35 WCF.

* **Model 1899 .250-3000 Rifle** — takedown frame only, pistol grip checkered stocks with corrugated steel butt, fine cross-checkered trigger (unique to this model). Mfg. 1914-1921.

	$850	$775	$675	$600	$525	$450	$375

MODEL 99A — .30-30 Win., .300 Sav., or .303 Sav. cal., lever action, 24 in. barrel, open sight, hammerless, straight grip stock, crescent butt. Mfg. 1920-1936.

	$550	$440	$330	$275	$180	$165	$150

MODEL 99A RECENT PRODUCTION — similar to original, with .243 Win., .250 Sav., .300 Sav., .308 Win., or .375 Win. (1981 only, approx. 1,500 mfg.) cal., 20 or 22 in. barrel, tang safety, conventional butt. Mfg. 1971-1981.

	$375	$340	$310	$275	$250	$225	$200

MODEL 99B — takedown version of original Model 99A, 24 (introduced 1926-27) or 26 (initial standard barrel length) in. barrel. Mfg. 1920-1934.

	$650	$600	$550	$495	$330	$250	$195

MODEL 99H CARBINE — .250-3000 Sav., .30-30 Win., .300 Sav. (scarce) or .303 Sav. cal., solid frame, carbine type stock. Mfg. 1923-1940.

	$475	$400	$350	$300	$275	$250	$225

Add 30% for .250 Sav. and .300 Sav. cal.

There were four variations of this model - the latter three had barrel bands. This variation did not have a saddle ring.

MODEL 99E — .22 Hi Power, .250-3000 Sav., .30-30 Win., .300 Sav., or .303 Sav. cal., 20, 22 or 24 in. barrel, solid frame, straight stock. Mfg. 1922-1934.

	$475	$425	$375	$300	$250	$200	$175

Add 15% for .22 Hi Power or .250 Sav. cal.

MODEL 99E CARBINE — .243 Win., .250 Sav., .300 Sav., or .308 Win. cal., 22 in. barrel, checkered pistol grip stock, 5 shot rotary mag. Mfg. 1960-1982.

	$320	$260	$230	$200	$180	$165	$150

Last Mfg.'s Sug. Retail was $343.

MODEL 99F FEATHERWEIGHT — similar to pre-war Model 99E, except takedown and ½ pound lighter, also mfg. with .410 bore shotgun barrel. Mfg. 1920-1940.

	$550	$440	$330	$275	$220	$195	$175

Add 50% for .410 bore shotgun barrel.

MODEL 99F — .243 Win., .250-3000 Sav., .284 Win., .300 Sav., .308 Win., or .358 Win. cal., solid frame, checkered pistol grip stock. Mfg. 1955-1973.

	$350	$310	$285	$260	$230	$210	$190

Add 10% for .250-3000 Sav.
Add 10% for .358 Win. cal.
Add 15% for .284 Win. cal.

This model, in many cases, had the receiver marked "99M".

MODEL 99G — similar to Model 99E pre-war, with checkered pistol grip stock and takedown. Mfg. 1922-1941.

	$660	$565	$475	$350	$275	$235	$200

Grading	100%	98%	95%	90%	80%	70%	60%

MODEL 99EG — similar to Model 99G, with solid frame and no checkering. Mfg. 1935-1941.

| | $550 | $440 | $330 | $260 | $230 | $210 | $190 |

MODEL 99EG POST-WAR — .243 Win., .250 Sav., .300 Sav., .308 Win., or .358 Win. cal., checkered stock. Mfg. 1946-1960.

| | $400 | $350 | $300 | $275 | $250 | $225 | $200 |

Add 10% for .358 Win. cal.

MODEL 99R PRE-WAR — .250-3000 Sav., .303 Sav., or .300 Sav. cal., 22 or 24 in. barrel, large pistol grip stock and forearm. Mfg. 1932-1942.

| | $495 | $440 | $305 | $275 | $250 | $220 | $195 |

Add 10% for .250-3000 Sav. cal.

MODEL 99R POST-WAR — .250-3000 Sav., .300 Sav., .308 Win., .358 Win., or .243 Win. cal., similar to Pre-War, 24 in. barrel only, swivel studs. Mfg. 1946-1960.

| | $450 | $400 | $350 | $300 | $275 | $250 | $225 |

Add 20% for .250-3000 Sav. or .358 Win. cal.

MODEL 99RS PRE-WAR — similar to Model 99R Pre-War, with Lyman aperture sight, swivels and sling. Mfg. 1932-1942.

| | $605 | $550 | $440 | $330 | $275 | $250 | $220 |

MODEL 99RS POST-WAR — similar to Model 99R Post-War, with Redfield receiver sight. Mfg. 1946-1958.

| | $450 | $400 | $350 | $300 | $275 | $250 | $225 |

MODEL 99T — 20 or 22 in. barrel, solid frame, lightweight, checkered pistol grip stock. Mfg. 1935-1940.

| | $695 | $525 | $450 | $400 | $350 | $300 | $275 |

MODEL 99K — engraved receiver and fancy wood stock, Lyman aperture sight and folding middle sight. Mfg. 1926-1940.

| | $2,200 | $1,870 | $1,210 | $880 | $770 | $550 | $440 |

MODEL 99DL — .243 Win., .250-3000 Sav., .284 Win., .300 Sav., .308 Win., or .358 Win. cal., Monte Carlo stock and sling swivels. Post-war mfg. 1960-1973.

| | $350 | $310 | $285 | $260 | $230 | $210 | $185 |

Add 10% for .358 Win. cal.

MODEL 99C — similar to Model 99F Post-War, available in .22-250 Rem. (rare), .243 Win., .284 Win. (disc.), 7mm-08 (disc.), or .308 Win. cal., 22 in. barrel, Monte Carlo stock with cut checkering and recoil pad, top tang safety, cocking indicator, open sights, detachable 4 shot mag., 7¾ lbs. Mfg. 1965-temporarily disc. until late 1995.

| | $525 | $430 | $365 | $300 | $260 | $230 | $200 |

Last Mfg.'s Sug. Retail was $629 (1994).

Add 10% for .22-250 cal.

MODEL 99CD — similar to Model 99C, with Monte Carlo cheekpiece stock. Mfg. 1975-1981.

| | $525 | $450 | $375 | $325 | $295 | $260 | $230 |

MODEL 99-358 (BRUSH GUN) — .358 Win. cal., recoil pad. Mfg. 1977-1980.

| | $450 | $400 | $350 | $325 | $295 | $260 | $230 |

MODEL 99-375 (BRUSH GUN) — .375 Win. cal., recoil pad, fluted forearm. Mfg. 1980 only.

| | $725 | $625 | $550 | $500 | $450 | $400 | $350 |

MODEL 99PE — elaborately engraved and plated receiver, tang, and lever, fancy wood with hand cut checkering. Mfg. 1966-1970.

| | $1,320 | $990 | $740 | $500 | $375 | $300 | $260 |

This model had the receiver marked "99M".

MODEL 99DE CITATION — similar to Model 99PE, except with less engraving and pressed checkering. Mfg. 1968-1970.

| | $885 | $660 | $495 | $330 | $250 | $220 | $195 |

This model had the receiver marked "99M".

MODEL 99M — while the receivers on Models 99F, 99PE, and 99DE were marked "99M" this is not a model designation. Rather, the "M" barrel designation indicated Monte Carlo stock.

Grading	100%	98%	95%	90%	80%	70%	60%

SAVAGE 1895 ANNIVERSARY — a replica of the original M1895, .308 Win. cal., 24 in. octagon barrel, engraved receiver, brass-plated lever, straight stock, Schnabel forend, medallion in stock, brass crescent butt plate. Mfg. 9,999 in 1970 only, to commemorate Savage's 75th year.

	$450	$350	$275				

Last Mfg.'s Sug. Retail was $195 and mfg. by Savage Arms, Division of Emhart.

MODEL 1903 STANDARD SLIDE ACTION — .22 S, L, or LR cal., 24 in. barrel, open sights, box mag., pistol grip stock. Mfg. 1903-1922.

	$275	$220	$110	$90	$75	$65	$45

* *Model 1903 Grade EF* — features "B" grade checkering on fancy English walnut stock, Savage #22B front sight, and #21B micrometer open rear sight.

	$1,150	$1,000	$850	$750	$650	$550	$450

* *Model 1903 Expert Grade* — features "A" grade engraving on receiver, "B" grade checkering on fancy American walnut stock, standard sights.

	$850	$750	$650	$550	$475	$400	$350

* *Model 1903 Grade GH* — features "A" grade checkering on plain American walnut stock, no engraving, #22B front sight, and #21B micrometer open rear sight.

	$395	$325	$250	$200	$160	$120	$90

* *Model 1903 Gold Medal* — features animal ornamentation on receiver, less elaborate checkering on plain American walnut stock, standard sights.

	$650	$550	$475	$400	$350	$275	$200

MODEL 1909 SLIDE ACTION — similar to Model 1903, with 20 in. round barrel. Mfg. 1909-1915.

	$220	$140	$110	$90	$75	$65	$45

MODEL 1904 SINGLE SHOT — .22 S, L, or LR cal., bolt action, 18 in. barrel, straight stock. Mfg. 1904-1917.

	$140	$85	$55	$45	$35	$30	$30

MODEL 1905 SINGLE SHOT — similar to Model 1904, except 24 in. barrel, takedown. Mfg. 1905-1919.

	$140	$85	$55	$45	$35	$30	$30

MODEL 1912 AUTOLOADER — .22 LR cal., 20 in. barrel, takedown, straight stock. Mfg. 1912-1916.

	$295	$235	$195	$150	$115	$75	$65

MODEL 1914 SLIDE ACTION — .22 S, L, and LR cal., 24 in. octagon barrel, plain pistol grip stock. Mfg. 1914-1926.

	$250	$225	$195	$135	$110	$75	$65

MODEL 19 NRA BOLT ACTION — .22 LR cal., 25 in. barrel, adj. aperture sight, 5 shot military stock. Approx. 50,000 mfg. 1919-1937.

	$220	$140	$110	$100	$90	$75	$65

Between 1943-1945 approx. 6,000 Model 19s were made under military contract — add 15%.

MODEL 10 BOLT ACTION TARGET (1933 NRA MODEL) — .22 LR cal., 25 in. barrel, speed lock, adj. aperture sight, target stock. Mfg. 1933-1946.

	$250	$165	$140	$110	$100	$90	$70

MODEL 19L — similar to Model 19, with Lyman receiver sight. Mfg. 1933-1942.

	$330	$275	$195	$140	$120	$110	$100

MODEL 19M — similar to Model 19, with 28 in. heavy barrel and scope bases. Mfg. 1933-1942.

	$330	$275	$195	$165	$140	$120	$110

MODEL 19H — similar to Model 19, except .22 Hornet. Mfg. 1933-1942.

	$550	$495	$330	$220	$175	$165	$155

MODEL 1920 BOLT ACTION — Mauser type action, .250-3000 Sav. or .300 Sav. cal., 22 or 24 in. barrel, open sights, 5 shot, checkered pistol grip, Schnabel forend. Mfg. 1920-1931.

	$330	$250	$220	$200	$175	$165	$155

Add 10% for .250-3000 Sav. cal.

Grading	100%	98%	95%	90%	80%	70%	60%

MODEL 1920-1926 — similar to Model 1920, with 24 in. barrel, Lyman aperture sight, Mfg. 1926-1931.

| | $330 | $250 | $220 | $200 | $175 | $165 | $155 |

MODEL 1922 — .22 LR cal., predecessor of the Model 23A, mfg. 1922.

| | $250 | $220 | $165 | $140 | $110 | $95 | $85 |

MODEL 23A BOLT ACTION RIFLE — .22 LR cal., 23 in. barrel, open sights, plain pistol grip stock, Schnabel forend. Mfg. 1923-1933.

| | $220 | $165 | $140 | $110 | $95 | $85 | $70 |

MODEL 23AA — improved version of Model 23A, with speedlock and checkered stock. Mfg. 1933-1942.

| | $275 | $195 | $165 | $130 | $110 | $100 | $85 |

MODEL 23B — .25-20 WCF cal., same configuration as Model 23A, 25 in. barrel, full forearm. Mfg. 1923-1942.

| | $220 | $140 | $110 | $100 | $90 | $75 | $65 |

MODEL 23C — .32-20 WCF, similar to Model 23B. Mfg. 1923-1942.

| | $220 | $140 | $110 | $100 | $90 | $75 | $65 |

MODEL 23D — with .22 Hornet, similar to Model 23B. Mfg. 1933-1947.

| | $305 | $250 | $220 | $195 | $165 | $140 | $110 |

MODEL 25 SLIDE ACTION — .22 S, L, or LR cal., 24 in. octagon barrel, open sight, takedown, hammerless, tube mag., plain pistol grip stock. Mfg. 1925-1929.

| | $275 | $235 | $200 | $150 | $125 | $75 | $65 |

MODEL 40 BOLT ACTION RIFLE — .250-3000 Sav., .300 Sav., .30-30 Win., or .30-06 cal., 22 or 24 in. barrel, open sight, 4 shot mag., plain pistol grip stock, Schnabel forend. Mfg. 1928-1940.

| | $330 | $220 | $195 | $165 | $155 | $140 | $120 |

Add 10% for .250-3000 Sav. cal.

MODEL 45 SUPER — similar to Model 40, with Lyman receiver sight and checkered stock. Mfg. 1928-1940.

| | $385 | $275 | $250 | $200 | $175 | $165 | $140 |

MODEL 29 SLIDE ACTION — .22 S, L, or LR cal., 22 in. barrel, octagon until 1940, round on post-WWII, open sights, checkered pistol grip stock on pre-war, plain on late model. Mfg. 1929-1967.

| | $235 | $200 | $165 | $100 | $90 | $75 | $65 |
| Pre-war | $295 | $250 | $195 | $120 | $110 | $100 | $90 |

MODEL 3 SINGLE SHOT — .22 S, L, or LR cal., bolt action, 26 in. barrel, 24 in. barrel on post-war, open sights, plain grip stock. Mfg. 1930-1947.

| | $85 | $65 | $55 | $40 | $30 | $30 | $30 |

MODEL 3S — similar to Model 3, with aperture sight. Mfg. 1930-1947.

| | $100 | $85 | $70 | $55 | $40 | $30 | $30 |

MODEL 3ST — similar to Model 3S, with swivels and sling. Mfg. 1930-1947.

| | $110 | $90 | $85 | $70 | $45 | $35 | $30 |

MODEL 4 BOLT ACTION REPEATER — .22 S, L, or LR cal., 24 in. barrel, open sight, takedown, 5 shot, checkered pistol grip stock on pre-war, plain stock on post-war. Mfg. 1933-1965.

| | $110 | $85 | $70 | $55 | $40 | $30 | $30 |
| Pre-war | $120 | $95 | $85 | $65 | $50 | $40 | $30 |

MODEL 4S — similar to Model 4, with aperture sight. Mfg. 1933-1942.

| | $120 | $90 | $75 | $65 | $55 | $40 | $30 |

MODEL 4M — similar to Model 4, except .22 WRM. Mfg. 1961-1965.

| | $110 | $85 | $70 | $55 | $45 | $30 | $30 |

MODEL 5 — similar to Model 4, with tubular mag. Mfg. 1938-1964.

| | $110 | $85 | $70 | $55 | $45 | $30 | $30 |

MODEL 5S — similar to Model 5, with aperture sight. Mfg. 1936-1942.

| | $120 | $95 | $85 | $65 | $55 | $40 | $30 |

Grading	100%	98%	95%	90%	80%	70%	60%

MODEL 6 AUTOLOADER — .22 S, L, or LR cal., 24 in. barrel, tubular mag., takedown, checkered pistol grip stock on pre-war, plain stock on post-war. Mfg. 1938-1968.

	$140	$110	$95	$85	$65	$55	$40
Pre-war	$150	$120	$105	$95	$75	$65	$50

MODEL 6S — similar to Model 6, with aperture sight. Mfg. 1938-1942.

	$150	$120	$105	$95	$75	$65	$45

MODEL 7 AUTOLOADER — similar to Model 6, with box mag. Mfg. 1939-1951.

	$140	$110	$95	$65	$55	$55	$40
Pre-war	$150	$120	$105	$95	$75	$65	$50

MODEL 7S — similar to Model 7, with aperture sight. Mfg. 1938-1942.

	$150	$120	$105	$95	$75	$65	$45

MODEL 60 AUTOLOADER — .22 LR cal., 20 in. barrel, leaf sight, tubular mag., checkered Monte Carlo stock. Mfg. 1969-1972.

	$95	$85	$70	$55	$45	$35	$30

MODEL 90 AUTOLOADING CARBINE — similar to Model 60, with 16½ in. barrel, plain carbine stock, with barrel band.

	$95	$85	$70	$55	$45	$35	$30

MODEL 88 AUTOLOADER — similar to Model 60, except has walnut finished hardwood stock. Mfg. 1969-1972.

	$85	$65	$55	$45	$40	$35	$30

MODEL 63/63K SINGLE SHOT — .22 S, L, or LR cal., bolt action, 18 in. barrel, open sights, trigger locks with key, full length pistol grip stock, Model 63s were mfg. 1964-69, Model 63Ks were mfg. 1970-1972.

	$80	$65	$55	$45	$40	$35	$30

MODEL 63KM — .22 Mag. cal., similar to Model 63K.

	$90	$70	$65	$55	$45	$40	$35

MODEL 219 SINGLE SHOT — .22 Hornet, .25-20 WCF, .32-20 WCF, or .30-30 Win. cal., 26 in. barrel, open sight, hammerless, break open, top lever, plain pistol grip stock. Mfg. 1938-1965.

.30-30 Win. cal.	$140	$125	$110	$100	$90	$80	$70

Add 15% for all other cals.

MODEL 219L — similar to Model 219, with side lever. Mfg. 1965-1967.

	$100	$85	$70	$55	$45	$35	$30

MODELS 221, 222, 223, 227, 228, AND 229 — single shot, similar to Model 219, only supplied with additional shotgun barrel, interchangeable, different model numbers are for different cals., ga.'s, and barrel lengths, all have been disc.

	$130	$100	$85	$65	$55	$45	$30

SAVAGE/STEVENS MODEL 65 — please refer to listing under Stevens section.

MODEL 34M — similar to Model 34, chambered for .22 WRM. Mfg. 1969-1973.

	$90	$70	$55	$45	$35	$30	$30

MODEL 35 — .22 LR cal., bolt action, 22 in. barrel, 5 shot clip mag., open sights, hardwood Monte Carlo stock. Disc. 1985.

	$90	$80	$65	$50	$35	$30	$30

Last Mfg.'s Sug. Retail was $100.

MODEL 36 — .22 LR cal., single shot, otherwise similar to Model 35. Mfg. 1982-83.

	$90	$80	$65	$50	$35	$30	$30

MODEL 46 — similar to Model 34, with tubular mag. Mfg. 1969-1973.

	$90	$70	$55	$45	$35	$30	$30

MODEL 65M — .22 Mag. cal., similar to Model 65.

	$95	$75	$65	$55	$45	$35	$30

SAVAGE/STEVENS MODEL 72 "CRACKSHOT" — please refer to listing under Stevens section.

SAVAGE/STEVENS MODEL 89 SINGLE SHOT — please refer to listing under Stevens section.

Grading	100%	98%	95%	90%	80%	70%	60%

MODEL 340 BOLT ACTION — .22 Hornet, .222 Rem., .223 Rem., or .30-30 Win. cal., 22 and 24 in. barrel, open sights, 4 or 5 shot mag., 7½ lbs., plain pistol grip stock. Mfg. 1950-1985.

	$225	$195	$170	$160	$150	$140	$130

Last Mfg.'s Sug. Retail was $257.

EL 340C — similar to Model 340, with aperture sight, checkered stock and sling swivels. Mfg. 1952-1960.

	$235	$205	$180	$165	$155	$145	$135

MODEL 340V — .225 Win. cal., varmint configuration, 24 in. barrel. Limited mfg. in late 1960s.

	$295	$265	$235	$205	$180	$165	$150

MODEL 340S DELUXE — similar to Model 340, with aperture sight, checkered stock, sling swivels. Mfg. 1952-1960.

	$260	$225	$205	$190	$175	$160	$150

MODEL 342 AND 342S — .22 Hornet cal., similar to Model 340. Mfg. 1950-1955.

	$250	$215	$200	$185	$170	$160	$150

RIFLES: RIMFIRE, CURRENT PRODUCTION

MARK I-G SERIES BOLT ACTION RIMFIRE — .22 S-L-LR, or LR shot (Mark I-GSB) cal., single shot, self-cocking, 19 (Mark I-GY, Youth Model) or 20¾ in. barrel, checkered hardwood stock, approx. 5 lbs. New 1996.

Mfg.'s Sug. Retail	$120	$105	$90	$80	$75	$70	$65	$60

This Model is also available with left-hand action (Mark I-GL), Youth Model (Mark I-GY), or with smooth bore barrel (Mark I-GSB) at no extra charge.

MARK II-F SERIES BOLT ACTION RIMFIRE — .22 LR cal., features black synthetic stock, blued barrel, 10 shot mag., 5 lbs. New 1998.

Mfg.'s Sug. Retail	$120	$105	$90	$80	$75	$70	$65	$60

Add $5 for Mark II-FXP package (includes 4x15mm scope).

MARK II-FV — .22 LR cal., features 21 in. heavy barrel w/o sights, black synthetic stock, 5 shot detachable mag., Weaver style bases included, 6 lbs. New 1998.

Mfg.'s Sug. Retail	$182	$155	$130	$110	$100	$90	$80	$70

MARK II-G — .22 LR cal., similar to Mark I-G Series, except has detachable 10 shot mag., approx. 5 lbs. New 1996.

Mfg.'s Sug. Retail	$132	$115	$100	$85	$75	$70	$65	$60

Add $8 for Mark II-GXP package (includes 4x15mm scope).

This Model is also available with left-hand action (Mark II-GL) or in Youth Model (Mark II-GY).

MARK II-LV — .22 LR cal., features 21 in. blued heavy barrel, no sights, grey laminated hardwood stock with cut checkering, 6½ lbs. New 1997.

Mfg.'s Sug. Retail	$210	$180	$160	$140	$125	$115	$105	$100

MARK II-FSS — .22 LR cal., 20¾ stainless steel barrel with sights, black graphite/polymer stock with checkering, dove-tailed receiver, 5 lbs. New 1997.

Mfg.'s Sug. Retail	$160	$130	$110	$95				

MODEL 64G SEMI-AUTO RIMFIRE — .22 LR cal., 20¼ in. barrel with adj. rear sight, 10 shot detachable mag., checkered hardwood stock, thumb operated rotary safety, 5½ lbs. New 1996.

Mfg.'s Sug. Retail	$126	$110	$95	$85	$75	$70	$65	$60

Add $6 for Model 64-GXP package (includes 4x15mm scope).

✱ *Model 64F* — .22 LR cal., similar to Model 64G, except has black graphite/polymer checkered stock, 20¼ regular or 21 (Model 64FV, new 1998) heavy barrel, 5 or 6 lbs. New 1997.

Mfg.'s Sug. Retail	$115	$105	$95	$85	$75	$70	$65	$60

Add $40 for Model 64FV with heavy barrel.

Add $5 for Model 64-FXP package (includes 4x15mm scope).

MODEL 93G MAGNUM BOLT ACTION — .22 Win. Mag. cal., 20¾ in. barrel with adj. rear sight, 5 shot detachable mag., checkered hardwood Monte Carlo stock, 5¾ lbs. New 1996.

Mfg.'s Sug. Retail	$150	$125	$110	$95	$85	$75	$70	$65

Grading	100%	98%	95%	90%	80%	70%	60%

* **Model 93F** — features 20¾ blued barrel with checkered black synthetic graphite polymer stock, 5 lbs. New 1998.

Mfg.'s Sug. Retail	$145	$120	$105	$95	$85	$75	$70	$65

* **Model 93FSS** — similar to Model 93G, except has stainless steel barrel and action with checkered black synthetic graphite/polymer stock, 5 lbs. New 1997.

Mfg.'s Sug. Retail	$182	$155	$125	$110

* **Model 93FVSS** — similar to Model 93FSS, except has 21 in. heavy barrel with recessed crown and button rifling, drilled and tapped, Weaver bases included, 6 lbs. New 1998.

Mfg.'s Sug. Retail	$210	$175	$145	$125

RIFLES: CENTERFIRE, CURRENT/RECENT PRODUCTION

S

The 110 Series was first produced in 1958. Beginning in 1992, Savage Arms, Inc. began supplying this model with a master trigger lock, earmuffs, shooting glasses (disc. 1992), and test target.

Beginning 1994, all Savage rifles employ a laser etched bolt featuring the Savage logo. During 1996, Savage began using pillar bedded stocks for many of their rifles. Savage introduced a new line of Rimfire rifles during 1996.

Recent Savage nomenclature usually involves alphabetical suffixes which mean the following: B - Brown laminated wood stock, C - detachable box mag., F - composite/synthetic stock, G - hardwood stock, K - standard muzzle brake, AK - adj. muzzle brake with fluted barrel, L - left-hand, NS - no sights, P - police (tactical) rifle, SE - safari express, SS - stainless steel, SS-S - stainless steel single shot, T - Target, U - high luster blued metal finish and/or stock finish, V - Long Range (Varmint), XP - package gun (scope, sling, and rings/base), Y - Youth/Ladies Model. Hence, the Model 116-FCSAK designates a 116 series firearm with composite stock, detachable stainless steel mag., and adj. muzzle brake on barrel.

Whenever possible, the models within this category have been listed in numerical sequence.

MODEL 10FCM SCOUT — .308 Win. or 7mm-08 Rem. cal., 20 in. barrel with removable ghost ring rear sight, one-piece barrel mount (allows long scope eye relief), 4 shot detachable mag., satin blued action with large ball bolt handle, black synthetic dual pillar bedded stock, includes swivel set and sling, 6⅛ lbs. New 1999.

Mfg.'s Sug. Retail	$500	$450	$400	$360	$330	$300	$280	$265

MODEL 10FM (SIERRA) — .243 Win., .308 Win., 7mm-08 Rem. (new 1999) cal., short action, lightweight, features black synthetic stock with dual pillar bedding, button rifling and recessed crown, 20 (Sierra, standard weight, new 1999) or 24 (heavy only, disc. 1998) in. barrel, w/o sights, 6 lbs. New 1998.

Mfg.'s Sug. Retail	$425	$375	$320	$270	$240	$210	$175	$160

This model is also available in left-hand action (disc.).

MODEL 10FP — .223 Rem., .260 Rem. (new 1999), .308 Win., or 7mm-08 (new 1999) cal., short action, tactical model, features 24 in. heavy barrel w/o sights, 8 lbs. New 1998.

Mfg.'s Sug. Retail	$450	$390	$330	$275	$250	$215	$180	$165

This model is also available in left-hand action (Model 10FLP).

MODEL 10GY — .223 Rem., .243 Win., or .308 Win. cal., ladies/youth model with shorter wood stock and 22 in. barrel with open sights.

Mfg.'s Sug. Retail	$374	$335	$290	$250	$220	$195	$175	$160

MODEL 11F HUNTER — .22-250 Rem., .223 Rem., .243 Win., .260 Rem. (new 1999), .308 Win., or 7mm-08 Rem. (new 1999) cal., short action, dual pillar bedding, checkered black synthetic stock, 22 in. blued barrel with open sights, 6¾ lbs. New 1998.

Mfg.'s Sug. Retail	$395	$350	$300	$255	$225	$195	$175	$160

Subtract $8 if w/o sights (Model 11FNS).

This model is also available in left-hand action (Model 11FL).

MODEL 11FC — .22-250 Rem. .243 Win., .260 Rem., .308 Win. or 7mm-08 Rem. cal., 22 in. blue barrel and action, dual pillar bedded black synthetic stock, 6⅜ lbs. New 1999.

Mfg.'s Sug. Retail	$420	$365	$310	$265	$230	$200	$175	$160

This model is also available in left-hand action (Model 11FLC).

Grading	100%	98%	95%	90%	80%	70%	60%

MODEL 11G HUNTER — similar to 11F Hunter, except has wood stock with pressed fleur-de-lis checkering. New 1998.

Mfg.'s Sug. Retail	$374	$335	$290	$250	$220	$195	$175	$160

Subtract $7 if w/o sights (Model 11GNS).

This model is also available in left-hand action (Model 11GL).

MODEL 11GC — .22-250 Rem., .243 Win., .260 Rem., .308 Win. or 7mm-08 Rem. cal., detachable mag., hardwood stock, open sights, 22 in. barrel, blue finish, 6⅜ lbs. New 1999.

Mfg.'s Sug. Retail	$410	$355	$300	$265	$230	$200	$175	$160

This model is also available in left-hand action (Model 11GLC).

MODEL 12BVSS — .22-250 Rem., .223 Rem., or .308 Win. cal., short action, 26 in. heavy fluted stainless barrel w/o sights, dual pillar bedding, brown laminated wood stock with flat beavertail forend, 9 lbs. New 1998.

Mfg.'s Sug. Retail	$560	$490	$425	$370

* *Model 12BVSS-S* — similar to Model 12BVSS, except is single shot and not available in .308 Win. cal. New 1998.

Mfg.'s Sug. Retail	$560	$490	$425	$370

MODEL 12FV — .22-250 Rem., .223 Rem., .308 Win. (new 1999) cal., short action, features 26 in. regular barrel with low luster bluing, black synthetic stock with dual pillar bedding, 5 shot top loading mag., drilled and tapped, 9 lbs. New 1998.

Mfg.'s Sug. Retail	$429	$375	$320	$270	$240	$210	$175	$160

MODEL 12FVSS — .22-250 Rem., .223 Rem., or .308 Win. cal., short action, features 26 in. fluted heavy stainless free floating barrel w/o sights, black checkered synthetic stock with dual pillar bedding, drilled and tapped, 9 lbs. New 1998.

Mfg.'s Sug. Retail	$534	$470	$400	$335

This model is also available in left-hand action (Model 12FVLSS).

* *MODEL 12FVSS-S* — similar to Model 12FVSS, except is single shot and not available in .308 Win. cal. New 1998.

Mfg.'s Sug. Retail	$534	$470	$400	$335

MODEL 16FCS WEATHER WARRIOR — .243 Win., .260 Rem., .308 Win., or 7mm-08 Rem. cal., stainless steel barreled action with 22 in. barrel, detachable mag., dual pillar bedded black synthetic stock, 6¾ lbs. New 1999.

Mfg.'s Sug. Retail	$560	$485	$410	$340

Also available in left-hand action at no additional charge (Model 16FLCS).

MODEL 16FSS — .223 Rem., .243 Win., .260 Rem. (new 1999), .308 Win., or 7mm-08 Rem. (new 1999) cal., short action, stainless steel 22 in. barreled action w/o sights, checkered black synthetic stock with dual pillar bedding, 6¾ lbs. New 1998.

Mfg.'s Sug. Retail	$515	$450	$385	$315

MODEL 99C LEVER ACTION — .243 Win. or .308 Win. cal., detachable box mag., checkered Monte Carlo stock and forearm, high gloss bluing, 22 in. barrel with adj. rear sight, drilled and tapped, 7¾ lbs. Reintroduced 1996-97 only.

			$585	$500	$450	$400	$360	$330	$300

Last Mfg.'s Sug. Retail was $665.

MODEL 99-CE (CENTENNIAL EDITION) — .300 Sav. cal. only, limited edition featuring fully engraved nickel receiver and lever, 24 Kt. gold-plated receiver figures, trigger, and safety, deluxe hand checkered walnut stock and forearm, 1,000 mfg. 1996-97 only, serial numbered AS0001-AS1000.

		$1,500	$1,100	$750

Last Mfg.'s Sug. Retail was $1,660.

MODEL 110 SPORTER BOLT ACTION — .243 Win., .270 Win., .308 Win., or .30-06 cal., 22 in. barrel, open sight, 4 shot, checkered pistol grip stock. Mfg. 1958-1963.

		$200	$175	$145	$120	$110	$95	$85

MODEL 110-MC — similar to Model 110, with Monte Carlo stock. Mfg. 1959-1969.

		$225	$195	$160	$140	$120	$110	$95

Grading	100%	98%	95%	90%	80%	70%	60%

MODEL 110-M — similar to Model 110MC, except 7mm Rem. Mag., .264 Win. Mag., .300 Win. Mag., or .338 Win. Mag. cal., recoil pad. Mfg. 1963-1969.

	$275	$220	$195	$150	$140	$125	$110

MODEL 110-C/CL — various cals., push-button detachable mag., walnut stock. Mfg. 1966-disc.

	$300	$265	$230	$200	$185	$170	$160

MODEL 110-D — .22-250 Rem. (disc.), .223 Rem., .243 Win., .25-06 Rem. (disc.), .270 Win., .308 Win. (disc.), .30-06, 7mm Rem. Mag., .300 Win. Mag. (disc.), or .338 Win. Mag. cal., similar to Model 110B, hinged floorplate (1972-74 only), checkered walnut stock, removable and adj. rear sight, 7½ lbs. Mfg. 1966-1988.

	$340	$290	$260	$240	$215	$190	$170

Last Mfg.'s Sug. Retail was $409.

Add $80 for left-hand version.

MODEL 110-E — .22-250 Rem., .223 Rem., .243 Win., .270 Win., 7mm Rem. Mag., .308 Win., or .30-06 cal., 22 or 24 (Mag. only) in. barrel, open sights, uncheckered hardwood Monte Carlo stock, blind internal floorplate, 7 lbs. Mfg. 1963-1988.

	$260	$230	$190	$175	$165	$155	$145

Last Mfg.'s Sug. Retail was $325.

Subtract $16 without sights.

MODEL 110-F — .22-250 Rem., .223 Rem., .243 Win., .250 Sav. (new 1993), .25-06 Rem. (new 1993), .308 Win., .30-06, .270 Win., 7mm-08 Rem. (new 1993), 7mm Rem. Mag., .300 Sav. (new 1993), .300 Win. Mag., .338 Win. Mag. (new 1991) cal., 22 or 24 (Magnum) in. barrel, black DuPont Rynite stock with swivel studs and recoil pad, adj. rear sight, drilled and tapped for scope mounts, 4 or 5 shot mag., 6¾ lbs. Mfg. 1989-1993.

	$335	$300	$265	$235	$210	$195	$180

All Model 110 mfg. is in the domain of Savage Arms, Inc.

* **Model 110-FNS** — similar to Model 110-F, except has no sights. Mfg. 1991-1993.

	$325	$285	$250	$225	$200	$190	$175

* **Model 110-FXP3** — .22-250 Rem. (new 1992), .223 Rem. (new 1992), .243 Win., .270 Win., .30-06, .308 Win. (new 1992), 7mm Rem. Mag., or .300 Win. Mag. cal., similar to Model 110-F except is without sights and has integral Weaver type scope bases. Mfg. 1989-1993.

	$415	$370	$325	$285	$250	$225	$195

MODEL 110-GY — .223 Rem. (new 1993), .243 Win., .270 Win. (new 1994), .300 Sav. (disc. 1995), or .308 Win. (new 1994) cal., 22 in. barrel, youth/ladies variation with shortened classic stock, open sights, 6½ lbs. New 1991.

Mfg.'s Sug. Retail	$374	$335	$295	$255	$220	$195	$175	$160

MODEL 110-WLE — .250-3000 Sav., .300 Sav., or 7x57mm Mauser cal. Mfg. 1991-1993.

	$425	$390	$360	$320	$280	$250	$225

Approx. 1,000 of each cal. were mfg. in this model.

* **Model 110-WLE 1 of 1,000** — 7x57mm Mauser, features select walnut stock with Monte Carlo cheekpiece, high luster blue finish with laser etched Savage logo on bolt body, drilled and tapped, 1,000 mfg. beginning 1992, 7¾ lbs. Mfg. 1992-1993 only.

	$415	$370	$325	$285	$250	$225	$195

MODEL 110-FM SIERRA ULTRA LIGHT — .243 Win. (disc. 1998), .270 Win., .30-06, or .308 Win. (disc. 1998) cal., features 20 in. high gloss barrel w/o sights, black graphite/fiberglass-filled stock with non-glare finish, drilled and tapped, 6¼ lbs. New 1996.

Mfg.'s Sug. Retail	$425	$365	$315	$265	$230	$205	$175	$160

MODEL 110-FP TACTICAL POLICE RIFLE — .223 Rem. (disc. 1998), .25-06 Rem. (new 1995), .300 Win. Mag. (new 1995), .30-06 (new 1996), .308 Win. (disc. 1998), or 7mm Rem. Mag. (new 1995) cal., 24 in. heavy pillar bedded barrel tactical rifle, all metal parts are non-reflective, 4 shot internal mag., black Dupont Rynite stock, right or left-hand (new 1996) action, tapped for scope mounts, 8½ lbs. New 1990.

Mfg.'s Sug. Retail	$450	$390	$330	$275	$240	$210	$175	$160

Also available in left-hand action at no additional charge (new 1996, Model 110-FLP).

Grading	100%	98%	95%	90%	80%	70%	60%

MODEL 110-G — .22-250 Rem., .223 Rem., .243 Win., .250 Sav. (new 1992), .25-06 Rem. (new 1992), .300 Sav. (new 1993), .308 Win., .30-06, .270 Win., 7mm-08 Rem. (new 1992), 7mm Rem. Mag., or .300 Win. Mag. cal., top loading internal box mag., 22 or 24 in. barrel, adj. iron sights, checkered hardwood stock, approx. 7 lbs. Mfg. 1989-1993.

	$325	$285	$250	$225	$200	$190	$175

Subtract $10-$20 if without sights (Model 110-GNS).

* *Model 110-GC* — .270 Win., .30-06, 7mm Rem. Mag., or .300 Win. Mag. cal., features detachable 3 or 4 shot mag., 22 or 24 in. barrel, checkered hardwood stock, adj. sights, 6¾ lbs. Mfg. 1992-1993.

	$410	$325	$275	$240	$210	$180	$165

Add $20 for Mag. cals.

* *Model 110-GXP3 Package* — .22-250 Rem., .223 Rem., .243 Win., .250 Savage (disc. 1995), .25-06 Rem., .270 Win., .300 Sav. (disc. 1995), .30-06, .308 Win., 7mm-08 Rem. (disc. 1995, reintroduced 1999), 7mm Rem. Mag., or .300 Win. Mag. cal., similar to Model 110-G, except has no sights, includes 3x9x32 scope, rings, bases, QD swivels, and deluxe rifle sling, includes integral Weaver type scope bases. New 1989.

Mfg.'s Sug. Retail	$425	$370	$320	$275	$240	$210	$175	$160

Also available in left-hand action at no additional charge (Model 110-GLXP3).

* *Model 110-GCXP3 Package* — .270 Win., .30-06, .300 Win. Mag., or 7mm Rem. Mag. cal., 22 or 24 in. barrel, checkered hardwood stock, detachable box mag., package includes 3x9x32 scope, rings, bases, QD swivels, and deluxe rifle sling, 7¼ lbs.

Mfg.'s Sug. Retail	$485	$420	$360	$310	$275	$235	$190	$175

Also available in left-hand action at no additional charge (Model 110-GLCXP3).

* *Model 110-GL* — .30-06, .270 Win., or 7mm Rem. Mag. cal., left hand variation of the Model 110-G. Mfg. 1989-1993.

	$325	$265	$225	$200	$180	$165	$150

* *Model 110-GLNS* — similar to Model 110-GL, except has no sights. Mfg. 1991-1993.

	$320	$260	$220	$200	$180	$165	$150

MODEL 110-K — .243 Win., .270 Win., or .30-06 cal., incorporates laminated camouflage stock. Mfg. 1986-1988.

	$335	$280	$240

Last Mfg.'s Sug. Retail was $399.

MODEL 110-S — .308 Win. or 7mm-08 Rem. (disc.) cals., silhouette model, 22 in. heavy barrel, Wundhammer swell pistol grip with stippling, no sights, 4 shot mag., 8 lbs. 10 oz. Disc. 1985.

	$340	$290	$255	$225	$205	$190	$175

Last Mfg.'s Sug. Retail was $385.

MODEL 110-V — .22-250 Rem. or .223 Rem. cal. only, varmint model, 26 in. heavy barrel, no sights, 5 shot mag., stippled walnut Wundhammer pistol grip stock, 9¼ lbs. Disc. 1989.

	$370	$315	$265	$230	$205	$190	$175

Last Mfg.'s Sug. Retail was $439.

MODEL 110-GV — .22-250 Rem. or .223 Rem. cal., varmint variation, 24 in. medium barrel, no sights, checkered hardwood stock with rubber rifle pad, drilled and tapped for scope, 8¼ lbs. Mfg. 1989-1993.

	$380	$285	$250	$225	$200	$190	$175

MODEL 110-B — similar to Model 110E, select stock and pistol grip cap on previous manufacture, features blind mag. Reintroduced 1989 with laminate stock (Model 110-B Laminate). Mfg. 1976-1979.

	$360	$300	$265	$235	$205	$190	$175

MODEL 110-B LAMINATE — similar to Model 110-B, except is available in .300 Win. Mag. or .338 Win. Mag. cal. also, has brown laminate hardwood stock with iron sights, approx. 7½ lbs. Mfg. 1989-91.

	$385	$310	$250	$225	$200	$190	$180

Last Mfg.'s Sug. Retail was $477.

Grading	100%	98%	95%	90%	80%	70%	60%

MODEL 110-P PREMIER GRADE — similar to Model 110B, with select French walnut stock, skip checkered, rosewood forend and pistol grip cap, sling swivels, 7mm Mag. has recoil pad. Mfg. 1964-1970.

	100%	98%	95%	90%	80%	70%	60%
	$440	$330	$310	$275	$250	$220	$195
7mm Mag.	$460	$350	$330	$305	$275	$240	$220

MODEL 110-PE PRESENTATION GRADE — similar to Model 110P, with engraved receiver, floorplate and triggerguard. Mfg. 1968-1970.

	100%	98%	95%	90%	80%	70%	60%
	$660	$550	$525	$470	$440	$415	$385
7mm Mag.	$690	$580	$550	$495	$470	$440	$415

MODEL 111 CHIEFTAIN ACTION — .243 Win., .270 Win., 7x57mm, 7mm Mag., or .30-06 cal., 22 in. barrel, 24 in. barrel (Mag. cals.), leaf sight, 4 shot detachable mag., checkered walnut Monte Carlo stock, pistol grip cap, sling swivels. Mfg. 1974-1978.

	100%	98%	95%	90%	80%	70%	60%
	$375	$350	$300	$250	$225	$200	$175
Magnum	$395	$375	$325	$295	$275	$225	$195

MODEL 111-F — similar to Model 111-G, except has black graphite/fiberglass stock (with non-glare finish) and also available in .338 Win. Mag. cal., solid recoil pad. New 1994.

	100%	98%	95%	90%	80%	70%	60%
Mfg.'s Sug. Retail $395		$355	$310	$265	$230	$195	$175	$160

Subtract $8 if w/o sights (Model 111-FNS).

This model is also available in left-hand (Model 111-FL) or w/o sights (Model 111-FNS).

* **Model 111-FC** — .270 Win., .30-06, .300 Win. Mag., or 7mm Rem. Mag. cal., 22 or 24 in. barrel, detachable box mag., black graphite/fiberglass stock. New 1994.

	100%	98%	95%	90%	80%	70%	60%
Mfg.'s Sug. Retail $420		$370	$325	$275	$230	$195	$175	$160

This model is also available with left-hand action (Model 111-FLC).

MODEL 111-FAK EXPRESS — .270 Win., .30-06, .300 Win. Mag., .338 Win. Mag., or 7mm Rem. Mag. cal., 22 in. barrel with adj. muzzle brake, black or black matte graphite/fiberglass-filled stock, w/o sights, 6¾ lbs. Mfg. 1996-98.

100%	98%	95%	90%	80%	70%	60%
$390	$340	$285	$240	$200	$180	$165

Last Mfg.'s Sug. Retail was $450.

MODEL 111-FCXP3 PACKAGE — .270 Win., .30-06, .300 Win. Mag., or 7mm Rem. Mag. cal., detachable box mag., 22 or 24 in. barrel, package includes bore sighted 3x9x32 scope, rings, bases, QD swivels, and deluxe rifle sling, 7¼ lbs. New 1994.

	100%	98%	95%	90%	80%	70%	60%
Mfg.'s Sug. Retail $495		$445	$390	$345	$300	$270	$230	$200

This model is also available with left-hand action (Model 111-FLCXP3).

MODEL 111-FXP3 PACKAGE — .22-250 Rem., .223 Rem., .243 Win., .250 Savage (disc. 1996), .25-06 Rem., .270 Win., .300 Sav. (disc. 1996), .30-06, .308 Win., .300 Win. Mag., .338 Win. Mag., 7mm Rem. Mag., or 7mm-08 Rem. (disc. 1996, reintroduced 1999) cal., 22 or 24 in. barrel, black graphite/fiberglass composite stock, non-glare finish, package consists of bore sighted 3x9x32 scope, rings, bases, QD swivels, and deluxe rifle sling, approx. 7¼ lbs. New 1994.

	100%	98%	95%	90%	80%	70%	60%
Mfg.'s Sug. Retail $450		$390	$340	$285	$240	$200	$180	$165

This model is also available with left hand action (Model 111-FLXP3).

MODEL 111-G — .22-250 Rem. (disc. 1998), .223 Rem. (disc. 1998), .243 Win. (disc. 1998), .250 Savage (disc. 1996), .25-06 Rem., .270 Win., .300 Sav. (disc. 1996), .30-06, .308 Win. (disc. 1998), .300 Win. Mag., .338 Win. Mag. (disc. 1993 - not available with wood stock), 7mm-08 Rem. (disc. 1996), or 7mm Rem. Mag. cal., walnut finished hardwood stock with cut checkering and vent. recoil pad, open sights, top tang safety with red dot indicator, drilled and tapped, 6⅜ or 7 lbs. New 1994.

	100%	98%	95%	90%	80%	70%	60%
Mfg.'s Sug. Retail $374		$340	$295	$255	$225	$195	$175	$160

Subtract $7 w/o sights (Model 111-GNS).

This model is also available in left-hand (Model 111-GL) or w/o sights (Model 111-GNS).

* **Model 111-GC** — .270 Win., .30-06, .300 Win. Mag., or 7mm Rem. Mag. cal., 22 or 24 in. barrel, detachable box mag., walnut finished hardwood stock with cut checkering and vent. recoil pad. New 1994.

	100%	98%	95%	90%	80%	70%	60%
Mfg.'s Sug. Retail $410		$365	$315	$270	$240	$210	$175	$160

This model is also available with left hand action (Model 111-GLC).

Grading	100%	98%	95%	90%	80%	70%	60%

MODEL 112V VARMINT RIFLE — .220 Swift, .222 Rem., .223 Rem. (new 1976), .22-250 Rem., .243 Win., or .25-06 Rem. cal., single shot, bolt action, 26 in. heavy barrel, no sights, heavy select walnut stock, checkered, swivels. Mfg. 1975-1978.

	$350	$325	$300	$275	$250	$235	$225

MODEL 112 R — .22-250 Rem., .25-06 Rem., or .243 Win. cal., similar to Model 112V, except has 4 shot mag. Disc. 1980.

	$340	$305	$275	$250	$230	$210	$175

MODEL 112-BV — .22-250 Rem. or .223 Rem. cal., alloy steel construction, 26 in. barrel with recessed muzzle, 4 shot mag., brown laminate stock with ambidextrous Wundhammer style pistol grip, 9½ lbs. Mfg. 1993 only.

	$475	$430	$365	$315	$285	$250	$215

MODEL 112-BVSS LONG RANGE — .22-250 Rem. (disc. 1998), .223 Rem. (disc. 1998), .25-06 Rem. (new 1996), .30-06 (new 1996), .308 Win. (mfg. 1996-98), .300 Win. Mag. (new 1996), or 7mm Rem. Mag. (new 1996) cal., 4 shot, pillar bedded laminate wood stock with Wundhammer palm swell, 26 in. stainless steel fluted barrel, bolt handle and trigger guard, recessed muzzle, 10½ lbs. New 1994.

Mfg.'s Sug. Retail $560	$485	$405	$355	$300	$270	$230	$200

* *Model 112-BVSS-S* — .220 Swift, .223 Rem. (disc. 1998), .22-250 Rem. (disc. 1998), or .300 Win. Mag. (new 1996) cal., single shot, 26 in. stainless steel fluted barrel, with target features, 10½ lbs. New 1994.

Mfg.'s Sug. Retail $560	$485	$405	$355	$300	$270	$230	$200

MODEL 112-BT COMPETITION GRADE — .223 Rem. or .308 Win. cal., laminated pillar bedded wood stock with adj. cheek rest and Wundhammer palm swell, vent. forend, alloy steel receiver with 26 in. matte black finished heavy stainless steel barrel w/o sights, drilled and tapped receiver, approx. 10⅞ lbs. New 1994.

Mfg.'s Sug. Retail $1,000	$895	$795	$695	$625	$550	$495	$400

* *Model 112-BT-S* — .300 Win. Mag. cal., otherwise similar to Model 112-BT Competition Grade. New 1995.

Mfg.'s Sug. Retail $1,000	$895	$795	$695	$625	$550	$495	$400

MODEL 112-FV — .22-250 Rem. or .223 Rem. cal., varmint variation with 26 in. heavy barrel, with or w/o iron sights, 4-shot mag., black Rynite synthetic stock with recoil pad, 8⅞ lbs. Mfg. 1991-98.

	$360	$300	$260	$235	$200	$175	$160

Last Mfg.'s Sug. Retail was $410.

* *Model 112-FVS* — similar to Model 112-FV, except is single shot with solid bottom receiver and is available in .220 Swift (new 1993) cal. Mfg. 1992-93 only.

	$375	$340	$295	$265	$235	$210	$195

* *Model 112-FVSS (Long Range)* — .22-250 Rem. (disc. 1998), .223 Rem. (disc. 1998), .25-06 Rem. (new 1995), .30-06 (new 1996), .308 Win. (mfg. 1996-98), .300 Win. Mag. (new 1995), or 7mm Rem. Mag. (new 1995) cal., alloy receiver with 26 in. fluted stainless steel barrel, 4 shot mag., black synthetic pillar bedded sporter stock w/o sights, 8⅞ lbs. New 1993.

Mfg.'s Sug. Retail $534	$470	$410	$355	$300	$270	$230	$200

This model is also available with left hand action (Model 112-FLVSS, new 1996).

* *Model 112-FVSS-S* — .220 Swift, .22-250 Rem. (disc. 1998), .223 Rem. (disc. 1998), or .300 Win. Mag. (new 1996) cal., single shot variation, pillar bedded stock, 8⅞ lbs. New 1994.

Mfg.'s Sug. Retail $534	$470	$410	$355	$300	$270	$230	$200

MODEL 114-C (CLASSIC) 114-CU (CLASSIC ULTRA) — .270 Win., .30-06, .300 Win. Mag., or 7mm Rem. Mag. cal., 22 or 24 in. barrel, features high gloss classic American black walnut stock with cut checkering, fitted grip cap, and recoil pad, removable 3 or 4 shot staggered box mag., available with deluxe adj. sights (Model 114-CU, disc. 1995) or w/o sights (Model 114-C, new 1996), approx. 7⅛ lbs. New 1991.

Mfg.'s Sug. Retail $525	$465	$400	$350	$300	$270	$230	$200

MODEL 114-U — similar to Model 114-C, 3 shot internal mag. New 1999.

Mfg.'s Sug. Retail $475	$425	$375	$325	$275	$250	$230	$200

Grading	100%	98%	95%	90%	80%	70%	60%

MODEL 114-CE (CLASSIC EUROPEAN) — same cals. as the Model 114-C, features oil finished stock with Schnabel forend and skip-line checkering, high luster bluing, 22 or 24 in. barrel with adj. rear sight, 7⅛ lbs. New 1996.

Mfg.'s Sug. Retail	$600	$525	$465	$400	$350	$300	$270	$230

MODEL 116-FSS — .22-250 Rem. (mfg. 1992 only), .223 Rem. (mfg. 1992-98), .243 Win. (mfg. 1993-98), .270 Win., .30-06, .308 Win. (disc. 1998), 7mm Rem. Mag., .300 Win. Mag., or .338 Win. Mag. cal., features black Dupont Rynite synthetic stock, stainless steel metal parts, drilled and tapped for scope mounting, 22 or 24 in. barrel, 3 or 4 shot mag., 6¾ lbs. New 1991.

Mfg.'s Sug. Retail	$515	$455	$400	$355	$310	$270	$230	$200

This model is also available with left-hand action (Model 116-FLSS).

* **Model 116-FCS** — .270 Win., .30-06, 7mm Rem. Mag., or .300 Win. Mag. cal., otherwise similar to Model 116-FSS, except has removable 3 or 4 shot mag. with recessed push button release, 22 or 24 in. barrel, 6½ lbs. New 1992.

Mfg.'s Sug. Retail	$560	$490	$425	$370	$325	$290	$260	$230

This model is also available with left-hand action (Model 116-FLCS).

* **Model 116-FSK (Kodiak)** — similar cals. as Model 116-FCS, except also available in .338 Win Mag. cal., stainless steel construction, 22 in. barrel with recoil arrester, cocking indicator, 3 shot mag., black synthetic sporter stock, no sights, 6½ lbs. New 1993.

Mfg.'s Sug. Retail	$554	$485	$425	$370	$325	$290	$260	$230

This model is also available with left-hand action (Model 116-FLSK).

MODEL 116-US (ULTRA STAINLESS) — .270 Win., .30-06, 7mm Rem. Mag., or .300 Win. Mag. cal., 24 in. barrel, checkered walnut stock and forearm with ebony tip, no sights, 7⅛ lbs. Mfg. 1995-98.

	$625	$550	$500	$450	$400	$360	$330

Last Mfg.'s Sug. Retail was $700.

MODEL 116-SE (SAFARI EXPRESS) — .300 Win. Mag., .338 Win. Mag., .425 Express (mfg. 1995 only), or .458 Win. Mag. cal., stainless steel receiver and 24 in. barrel with adj. muzzle brake, controlled round feeding, select grade checkered walnut stock with solid recoil pad and ebony forend, 3-leaf express sights, 8½ lbs. New 1994.

Mfg.'s Sug. Retail	$900	$800	$725	$660	$610	$570	$530	$475

MODEL 116-FSAK — .270 Win., .30-06, .300 Win. Mag., .338 Win. Mag., or 7mm Rem. Mag. cal., features 22 in. fluted stainless steel barrel with adj. muzzle brake, 6½ lbs. New 1994.

Mfg.'s Sug. Retail	$585	$500	$440	$380	$335	$295	$265	$235

This model is also available with left-hand action (Model 116-FLSAK).

MODEL 116-FCSAK — .270 Win., .30-06, .300 Win. Mag., or 7mm Rem. Mag. cal., features push button activated detachable box mag., 22 in. fluted barrel with adj. muzzle brake, 6½ lbs. New 1994.

Mfg.'s Sug. Retail	$650	$580	$500	$430	$365	$315	$275	$245

This model is also available with left-hand action (Model 116-FLCSAK).

MODEL 170 PUMP RIFLE — .30-30 Win. or .35 Rem. (rare) cal., 22 in. barrel, folding leaf sight, 3 shot tube mag., checkered pistol grip stock. Mfg. 1970-1981.

	$180	$155	$140	$110	$90	$65	$55

This model was mfg. by Emhart.

MODEL 170C — .30-30 Win. cal. only, similar to 170, 18½ in. barrel. Mfg. 1974-1981.

	$195	$170	$150	$115	$90	$65	$55

SERIES 900 — .22 LR cal., single (Target/Silhouette Model) or 5 shot (Biathlon Model), 21 or 25 (Target Model) in. free floated barrel, uncheckered hardwood stock, right or left-hand action, approx. 8 lbs. New 1996.

* **900B Biathlon** — blonde stock, supplied with five 5-shot mags., includes shooting rail and barrel snow cover, aperture rear sight. Mfg. 1996-97.

	$445	$395	$350	$300	$265	$230	$200

Last Mfg.'s Sug. Retail was $498.

This model was also available with left hand action (Model 900B-LH, new 1997).

Grading	100%	98%	95%	90%	80%	70%	60%

* **900S Silhouette** — brown hardwood stock, heavy 21 in. barrel with muzzle crown, scope bases installed, w/o sights. Mfg. 1996-97.

		$300	$265	$230	$200	$180	$160	$140

Last Mfg.'s Sug. Retail was $346.

This model is also available with left hand action (Model 900S-LH, new 1997).

* **900TR Target** — features aperture sights, shooting rail with hand stop.

Mfg.'s Sug. Retail	$415	$375	$315	$275	$235	$200	$180	$160

This model is also available with left hand action (Model 900TR-LH, new 1997).

SHOTGUNS

Most Savage shotguns (except the Model 312 Series) fall under the domain of Savage Industries, Inc.

Savage made a wide variety of inexpensive, utilitarian shotguns that to date have attracted mostly shooting interest, but little collector interest. A listing of these models may be found in the back of this text under "Serialization".

The models listed below are grouped by configuration, and are not in numerical sequence.

MODEL 420 O/U — 12, 16, or 20 ga., 26-30 in. barrel, various chokes, boxlock, double trigger, extractors, plain pistol grip stock. Mfg. 1937-1943.

	$385	$305	$275	$250	$210	$195	$155
Single trigger	$440	$360	$330	$305	$265	$220	$195

MODEL 430 — similar to Model 420, with checkered stock and solid rib, recoil pad.

	$440	$360	$305	$275	$240	$220	$195
Single trigger	$495	$415	$360	$320	$285	$265	$220

MODEL 220 SINGLE BARREL — 12, 16, 20, 28 ga., or .410 bore, 26-32 in. barrel, various chokes, hammerless, plain pistol grip stock. Mfg. 1938-1965.

	$125	$100	$85	$75	$65	$50	$40

MODEL 220P — similar to Model 220, with poly choke, not made in .410 bore.

	$90	$65	$55	$45	$35	$30	$30

MODEL 220 AC — similar to Model 220, with Savage adj. choke.

	$100	$85	$65	$55	$45	$35	$30

MODEL 220L — similar to Model 220, with sidelever. Mfg. 1965-1972.

	$90	$65	$55	$45	$35	$30	$30

MODEL 720 AUTOLOADER STANDARD — 12 or 16 ga., Browning A-5 style action, 26-32 in. barrels, various chokes, checkered pistol grip stock. Mfg. 1930-1949.

	$225	$180	$165	$155	$140	$120	$110

MODEL 720 RIOT — see the "Trench/Riot Shotgun" category in the T section for more information and prices.

MODEL 726 UPLAND SPORTER — similar to Model 720, except 2 shell mag. Mfg. 1931-1949.

	$275	$195	$165	$155	$140	$120	$110

MODEL 740C SKEET GUN — similar to Model 726, with Cutts Compensator and skeet stock, 24½ in. barrel. Mfg. 1936-1949.

	$305	$230	$200	$175	$155	$140	$120

MODEL 745 LIGHTWEIGHT — similar to Model 720, with alloy receiver, 12 ga. only, 28 in. barrel. Mfg. 1940-1949.

	$275	$195	$165	$155	$140	$120	$110

MODEL 755 STANDARD SEMI-AUTO — 12 or 16 ga., 26, 28, or 30 in. barrel, various chokes, rounded off receiver, checkered pistol grip stock. Mfg. 1949-1958.

	$265	$180	$160	$150	$140	$120	$110

MODEL 755SC — similar to Model 755, with Savage Super Choke.

	$275	$195	$165	$155	$140	$120	$110

Grading	100%	98%	95%	90%	80%	70%	60%

MODEL 775 LIGHTWEIGHT — similar to Model 755, with alloy receiver. Mfg. 1950-1965.

	$275	$195	$180	$165	$150	$140	$120

MODEL 775SC — similar to Model 775, with Savage Super Choke.

	$285	$205	$195	$175	$160	$150	$130

MODEL 750 SEMI-AUTO — 12 ga., Browning patterned semi-auto, 26 or 28 in. barrels, various chokes, checkered pistol grip stock. Mfg. 1960-1967.

	$275	$195	$165	$155	$140	$120	$110

MODEL 750SC — similar to Model 750, with Savage Super Choke.

	$285	$205	$175	$165	$150	$130	$120

MODEL 750AC — similar to Model 750, with poly choke.

	$285	$205	$175	$165	$150	$130	$120

MODEL 21 SLIDE ACTION — similar to Model 28, except stock has no checkering. Mfg. 1920-28.

	$300	$265	$235	$190	$165	$150	$130

MODEL 28 SLIDE ACTION — 12, 16, or 20 ga., patterned after the Winchester Model 12. Mfg. 1927-1934.

	$300	$265	$235	$190	$165	$150	$130

This model was available in either standard configuration (Models 28A and 28B), Riot (28C), Trap (28D), or Special (28S).

MODEL 30 SLIDE ACTION — 12, 16, 20 ga., or .410 bore, 26, 28, or 30 in. barrels, various chokes, VR, plain pistol grip stock. Mfg. 1958-1970.

	$220	$175	$155	$140	$120	$100	$85
Checkered Late Model	$230	$185	$165	$150	$130	$110	$95

MODEL 30AC — similar to Model 30, with adj. choke, checkered wood, 12 ga. only. Mfg. 1959-1970.

	$240	$200	$175	$160	$145	$120	$100

MODEL 30T TRAP AND DUCK GUN — similar to Model 30, with 30 in. full barrel, 12 ga. only, Monte Carlo stock and pad. Mfg. 1963-1970.

	$230	$185	$165	$150	$130	$110	$90

MODEL 30FG TAKEDOWN ACTION — 12, 20 ga., or .410 bore, 26, 28, or 30 in. barrel, various chokes, checkered pistol grip stock. Mfg. 1970-1975.

	$175	$155	$130	$110	$95	$85	$70

MODEL 30T TAKEDOWN TRAP — 12 ga. only, 30 in. full barrel, Monte Carlo stock with pad. Mfg. 1970-1973.

	$195	$175	$155	$140	$110	$100	$85

MODEL 30AC TAKEDOWN — similar to Model 30FG, with adj. choke, 12 or 20 ga., 26 in. barrel. Mfg. 1971-1972.

	$200	$180	$165	$150	$120	$110	$90

MODEL 30 TAKEDOWN SLUG GUN — similar to Model 30FG, with 32 in. cylinder bore barrel, rifle sights. Mfg. 1971-disc.

	$195	$175	$160	$140	$110	$100	$85

MODEL 30D TAKEDOWN — similar to Model 30FG, with VR, engraved receiver and pad. Mfg. 1971-disc.

	$200	$180	$165	$150	$120	$110	$90

MODEL 67 SLIDE ACTION — see listing under Stevens Section.

FOX MODELS B, B-SE, AND STEVENS 311 — see listing under Stevens Section.

MODEL 210F MASTER SHOT BOLT ACTION — 12 ga. only, 3 in. chamber, built on Model 100 action with controlled round feeding, 24 in. rifled barrel (1:35 twist), 2 shot detachable mag., 60 degree bolt lift, black synthetic stock with checkering and recoil pad, top tang safety, no sights, 7½ lbs. New 1997.

Mfg.'s Sug. Retail	$380	$340	$300	$265	$235	$215	$195	$180

  * *Model 210FT* — similar to Model 210F, except has Advantage camo stock and mag., 24 in. smooth bore barrel accepts Win. style choke tubes. New 1997.

Mfg.'s Sug. Retail	$440	$395	$340	$300	$265	$235	$215	$195

Grading	100%	98%	95%	90%	80%	70%	60%

MODEL 242 O/U — .410 bore, single exposed hammer, single trigger, barrel selector lever, full chokes. Mfg. 1977-1981.

	$350	$300	$260	$230	$200	$175	$150

MODEL 440 O/U — 12 or 20 ga., 26, 28, or 30 in. barrels, various chokes, boxlock, SST, extractors, checkered pistol grip stock, VR. Imported from Italy 1968-1972.

	$495	$440	$415	$385	$330	$305	$250

MODEL 440T — similar to Model 440, 12 ga., 30 in. barrel only, imp mod. or full choke, wide VR, trap style stock, pad. Mfg. 1969-1972.

	$550	$470	$440	$415	$385	$360	$330

MODEL 444 DELUXE — similar to Model 440, with auto ejectors, select walnut. Mfg. 1969-1972.

	$550	$470	$440	$415	$385	$360	$330

MODEL 550 SxS — 12 or 20 ga., 26, 28, or 30 in. barrels (made by Valmet - rare), various chokes, boxlock, auto ejectors, single trigger, checkered pistol grip stock. Mfg. 1971-1973.

	$275	$220	$195	$165	$150	$130	$110

MODEL 312 SERIES O/U — 12 ga. only, boxlock action, 3 in. chambers, vent. barrels, satin chrome finished receiver, checkered walnut stock and forearm, SST, choke tubes, approx. 7 lbs. Mfg. 1990-93.

> The Model 312 Series falls under the domain of Savage Arms, Inc.

* *312 Field* — 26 or 28 in. VR barrels with choke tubes.

	$585	$520	$485	$435	$395	$360	$330

* *312 Trap* — 30 in. barrels only, Monte Carlo stock with recoil pad.

	$615	$550	$500	$460	$415	$375	$330

* *312 Sporting Clays* — 28 in. barrels only with 7 choke tubes provided, recoil pad.

	$595	$530	$485	$435	$395	$360	$320

MODEL 330 O/U — 12 or 20 ga., 26, 28, or 30 in. barrels, various chokes, boxlock, SST, extractors, checkered pistol grip stock. Mfg. by Valmet between 1969-1980.

	$495	$440	$385	$335	$275	$250	$220

> Add 25% for extra set of barrels.

MODEL 333T — similar to Model 330, with 30 in. VR barrels bored imp. mod. and full choke, trap stock with pad. Mfg. by Valmet between 1972-1980.

	$550	$470	$415	$385	$360	$305	$275

MODEL 333 O/U — 12 or 20 (rare) ga., 26, 28, or 30 in. VR barrels, various chokes, boxlock, SST, auto ejectors, checkered pistol grip stock. Mfg. by Valmet between 1973-1980.

	$650	$575	$500	$450	$400	$375	$330

> Add 25% for extra set of barrels.
> Add 30% for 20 ga.

MODEL 2400 O/U COMBINATION GUN — 12 ga. full choke barrel over .222 Rem. or .308 Win. rifle barrel, 23½ in. barrels, folding leaf sight, solid rib, dovetailed for scope mount, checkered Monte Carlo stock. Mfg. by Valmet between 1975-1980.

	$605	$550	$525	$495	$440	$415	$385

SAVIN, J.C.

Current manufacturer located in St. Etienne, France. J.C. Savin manufactures only best quality shotguns and rifles per individual order. Annual production is approx. 25 long guns. Please contact the factory directly for an individual quotation.

RIFLES: DOUBLE, CUSTOM

Available in either O/U or SxS sidelock or Anson & Deely boxlock. Available in various cals. (.30-.577NE), 24 or 26 in. barrels. Prices start at $14,000 for boxlock and $25,000 for sidelock action.

SHOTGUNS: DOUBLE, CUSTOM

Grading	100%	98%	95%	90%	80%	70%	60%

Available in either O/U or SxS sidelock configuration, 12 or 20 ga., DT or ST, premier quality. Prices start at $23,000. A SxS round action Dixon model with trigger plate is also available in 12 or 20 ga., with prices starting at $2,200.

SAXONIA

Current shotgun and rifle manufacturer located in Schwarzenberg, Germany. No current importation.

Saxonia makes security/combat shotguns and bolt action rifles in many configurations. Please contact the company directly (see Trademark Index) to obtain model information and domestic availablity.

SCATTERGUN TECHNOLOGIES INC. (S.G.T.)

Current manufacturer located in Nashville, TN since 1991. Distributor, dealer, and consumer sales.

S.G.T. manufactures practical defense, tactical, and hunting shotguns in 12 ga. only, utilizing Remington Models 870 and 11-87 actions in various configurations as listed below. All shotguns feature 3 in. chamber capacity and parkerized finish.

SHOTGUNS: SLIDE ACTION

STANDARD MODEL — 18 in. barrel, adj. ghost ring sight, 7 shot mag., side saddle, synthetic buttstock and forearm with 11,000 CP flashlight.

Mfg.'s Sug. Retail	$815	$735	$640	$500

PROFESSIONAL MODEL — similar to Standard Model, except has 14 in. barrel and 6 shot mag.

Mfg.'s Sug. Retail	$815	$735	$640	$500

EXPERT MODEL — 18 in. barrel with Mod. choke, nickel/Teflon finished receiver, adj. ghost ring sight, forearm incorporates 11,000 CP flashlight. New 1997.

Mfg.'s Sug. Retail	$1,350	$1,200	$995	$775

ENTRY MODEL — 12½ in. barrel with mod. choke, adj. ghost ring sights, 5 shot mag., side saddle, synthetic buttstock and nylon strap assisted forearm with 5,000 CP flashlight.

Mfg.'s Sug. Retail	$840	$750	$650	$500

COMPACT MODEL — 12½ in. barrel with mod. choke, adj. ghost ring sight, 5 shot mag., synthetic butt stock and forearm. New 1994.

Mfg.'s Sug. Retail	$635	$575	$510	$420

PRACTICAL TURKEY MODEL — 20 in. barrel with extra full choke, adj. ghost ring sight, 5 shot mag. for 3 in. shells, synthetic buttstock and forearm. New 1995.

Mfg.'s Sug. Retail	$595	$545	$500	$465

LOUIS AWERBUCK SIGNATURE MODEL — 18 in. barrel with fixed choke, adj. ghost ring sight, 5 shot mag., side saddle, wood butt stock with recoil reducer and forearm. New 1994.

Mfg.'s Sug. Retail	$705	$625	$490	$385

F.B.I.MODEL — similar to Standard Model, except has 5 shot mag.

Mfg.'s Sug. Retail	$770	$715	$625	$490

MILITARY MODEL — 18 in. barrel with vent. handguard and M-9 bayonet lug, adj. ghost ring rear sight, 7 shot mag., synthetic stock and grooved corn cob forearm. Mfg. 1997-98.

	$625	$490	$385

Last Mfg.'s Sug. Retail was $690.

PATROL MODEL — 18 in. barrel, adj. ghost ring sight, 5 shot mag., synthetic butt stock and forearm.

Mfg.'s Sug. Retail	$595	$545	$500	$465

BORDER PATROL MODEL 20 — similar to Patrol Model, except has 7 shot mag.

Mfg.'s Sug. Retail	$605	$530	$435	$325

BORDER PATROL MODEL 21 — similar to Border Patrol Model 20, except has 14 in. barrel and 6 shot mag.

Mfg.'s Sug. Retail	$605	$530	$435	$325

CONCEALMENT MODEL 00 — 12½ in. barrel with fixed choke, 5 shot mag., bead sight, grooved wood forearm and pistol grip. Disc. 1998.

	$490	$395	$280

Last Mfg.'s Sug. Retail was $550.

Grading	100%	98%	95%	90%	80%	70%	60%

CONCEALMENT MODEL 01 — similar to Concealment Model 00, except has synthetic finger-grooved combat forearm and pistol grip. Disc. 1993.

$475 $395 $295

Last Mfg.'s Sug. Retail was $525.

CONCEALMENT MODEL 02 — similar to Concealment Model 00, except has Pachmayr forearm and pistol grip. Disc. 1993.

$495 $415 $315

Last Mfg.'s Sug. Retail was $555.

CONCEALMENT MODEL 03 — similar to Concealment Model 01, except has synthetic nylon strap assisted forearm with 5,000 CP flashlight. Disc. 1993.

$550 $455 $350

Last Mfg.'s Sug. Retail was $625.

BREACHING MODEL — similar to Concealment Model 00, except has standoff device. Disc. 1998.

$450 $390 $340

Last Mfg.'s Sug. Retail was $500.

SHOTGUNS: SEMI-AUTO

K-9 MODEL — 18 in. barrel, adj. ghost ring sight, 7 shot mag., side saddle, synthetic buttstock and forearm.

Mfg.'s Sug. Retail $995 $875 $750 $700

SWAT MODEL — similar to K-9 Model, except has 14 in. barrel and forearm with 11,000 CP flashlight.

Mfg.'s Sug. Retail $1,195 $1,050 $900 $800

URBAN SNIPER MODEL — 18 in. rifled barrel, scout optics, 7 shot mag., side saddle, synthetic butt stock, forearm and bipod.

Mfg.'s Sug. Retail $1,390 $1,225 $1,075 $950

SCHALL

Previous manufacturer located in Hartford, CT.

PISTOLS

REPEATING HANDGUN — .22 LR cal. only, target pistol, mag. fed manual repeating action. Unusual.

$425 $360 $320 $270 $220 $180 $150

SCHEIRING, H.

Current custom rifle manufacturer located in Ferlach, Austria.

H. Scheiring manufactures best quality rifles (including O/U, SxS, and Stalking variations) per individual customer special order. The factory should be contacted directly for more information regarding current models and domestic availability (see Trademark Index).

SCHELLER SPEZIALWAFFEN

Current manufacturer located in Suhl, Germany specializing in bolt action rifles.

For more information regarding this manufacturer (including current model information and U.S. prices) please contact this company directly (see Trademark Index).

SCHMITT FRERES

Previous manufacturer located in Saint Etienne, France.

This manufacturer produced copies of 1894 patent Darne R model guns until 1956. While higher grades do exist, they do not command the prices given for the later patent (1909) Darne produced guns. Lower grade guns will be priced in the same range as Soleihac and lower grade Darne R models.

SCHULTZ & LARSEN

Previous manufacturer located in Otterup, Denmark beginning 1911.

Grading	100%	98%	95%	90%	80%	70%	60%

RIFLES: BOLT ACTION

NO. 47 MATCH RIFLE — .22 LR cal., single shot, 28 in. heavy barrel, target sights, set trigger, free rifle stock.

	$660	$550	$495	$440	$385	$360	$330

M61 MATCH RIFLE — .22 LR cal., single shot, 28 in. heavy barrel, target sights, set trigger, free rifle stock, palm rest.

	$895	$825	$740	$680	$600	$550	$500

M62 MATCH RIFLE — various cals., single shot, 28 in. heavy barrel, target sights, set trigger, free rifle stock, palm rest.

	$995	$875	$780	$700	$620	$550	$500

MODEL 54 FREE RIFLE — any American centerfire standard caliber, plus 6.5x55mm, 27 in. heavy barrel, target sights, free rifle stock.

	$825	$745	$690	$605	$550	$495	$440

MODEL 54J SPORTING RIFLE — .270 Win., .30-06, or 7x61 Sharpe and Hart cal., 3 shot, 24 in. barrel, checkered Monte Carlo stock, no sights.

	$650	$550	$470	$415	$360	$330	$300

MODEL 68 DL — .22-250 Rem., .243 Win., 6mm Rem., .264 Win. Mag., .270 Win., .30-06, .308 Win., 7x61 S&H, 7mm Rem. Mag., 8x57 JS, .300 Win. Mag., .308 Norma Mag., .338 Win. Mag., .358 Norma Mag., or .458 Win. Mag. cal., 24 in. barrel, Bofors Steel receiver, bolt has 4 rear locking lugs, select French walnut, adj. trigger, no sights except for .458 Mag.

	$725	$650	$575	$525	$495	$460	$430

SCHUETZEN PISTOL WORKS (FORMERLY SAFARI ARMS)

Schuetzen Pistol Works is the custom shop for Safari Arms - please refer to the Safari Arms Listing for more information.

SCHUETZEN RIFLES

A Schuetzen Rifle is a special single shot target rifle. During the time span 1875-1945 this target configuration rifle was very popular with competition shooters. Many of these guns had elaborate locking systems, top quality sights, double set triggers, heavy barrels, palm and thumb rests, sculptured cheekpiece, Swiss style butt plate, etc. Rather than list all the various domestic and European makers (there are hundreds), it should be noted that since there are so many combinations of options for this configuration that most guns have to be examined and appraised individually. Most non-major trademarks sell in the $550-$1,500 range, depending on features and condition. A famous trademark specimen (Ballard, Stevens, Winchester, etc.) in a rare model with superior original condition can bring over $10,000. Schuetzen Rifles are a field in themselves and a knowledgeable dealer/collector should be consulted before buying or selling one of these guns.

SCOTT, W.C., LTD.

Previous manufacturer established during 1834 and located in Birmingham, England. All operations ceased during 1991.

Established in 1834 by William Scott, located in Birmingham, England, and remained in the family until 1897. At this time, Scott merged with P. Webley & Son to form Webley & Scott Revolver and Arms Co., Ltd. (later changed to Webley & Scott Ltd.). Even though Scott family members were no longer associated with this new company, the Scott gun-line was continued with the trademark intact until 1935. Thereafter, only a few guns were marked Scott. In 1979, Webley & Scott ceased manufacture of all firearms. A new company, W. & C. Scott, was formed in 1980 utilizing mostly employees of Webley & Scott. W. & C. Scott remained part of its parent company, Harris & Sheldon (also had controlling interest in Hardy and Churchill trademarks), until 1985 when Scott was purchased by Holland & Holland. Manufacture of Scott guns decreased substantially after the merger, and in September 1991, W. & C. Scott ceased operation all together. During its 157 years of production, Scott and Webley & Scott produced approximately, 150,000 double

Grading	100%	98%	95%	90%	80%	70%	60%

guns, 10,000 rifles (either double or bolt-action) and thousands of single guns and single rifles.

SHOTGUNS: SxS

All W.C. Scott Shotguns were discontinued in 1990. W.C. Scott also manufactured many hammer guns that vary in price from $250-$2,500, depending on grade and original condition.

KINMOUNT — 12, 16, 20, or 28 ga., boxlock action, ejectors, deluxe checkered walnut, scroll engraving.

$6,500	$5,750	$5,000	$4,500	$4,000	$3,000	$2,500

Last Mfg.'s Sug. Retail was $11,000.

Add 20% for 28 ga. or .410 bore.
Add 10% for SNT.

BOWOOD — 12, 16, 20, or 28 ga., boxlock action, ejectors, deluxe checkered walnut, extensive scroll engraving.

$7,500	$6,500	$5,750	$5,000	$4,500	$4,000	$3,500

Last Mfg.'s Sug. Retail was $12,500.

Add 20% for 28 ga. or .410 bore.
Add 10% for SNT.

CHATSWORTH — 12, 16, 20, or 28 ga., top-of-the-line boxlock action, ejectors, deluxe checkered walnut, extensive scroll engraving.

$8,750	$7,500	$6,500	$5,750	$5,000	$4,500	$4,000

Last Mfg.'s Sug. Retail was $14,000.

Add 20% for 28 ga. or .410 bore.
Add 10% for SNT.

BLENHEIM — 12 bore only, upgraded models, custom made to individual specifications, originally priced per individual order.

Specimen rarity precludes percentage grading pricing. Individual appraisals have to be secured on this model.

SEARCY, B. & CO.

Current rifle manufacturer established in 1975 and located in Boron, CA.

B. Searcy & Co. manufactures a unique stainless steel double rifle in a variety of calibers. Please contact the factory directly (see Trademark Index) for current model information and pricing.

SEARS ROEBUCK

Catalog merchandiser that, in addition to selling major trademark firearms, also private labeled many configurations of firearms (mostly longarms) under a variety of trademarks and logos (i.e., J.C. Higgins, Ted Williams, Ranger, etc.).

A general guideline for Sears Roebuck and related labels is that values are generally lower than those of the major factory models from which they were derived. Remember, 99% of Sears Roebuck and related label guns get priced by their shootability factor in today's competitive marketplace, not collectability. An extensive crossover listing (see Storebrand Cross-Over List) has been provided in the back of this text for linking up the various Sears Roebuck models to the original manufacturer with respective "crossover" model numbers.

SECURITY INDUSTRIES

Previous manufacturer located in Little Ferry, NJ.

REVOLVERS

MODEL PSS 38 DOUBLE ACTION — .38 Spl. cal., 5 shot cylinder, 2 in. barrel, stainless steel, fixed sights, wood grips. Mfg. 1973-1978.

$175	$150	$140	$130	$125	$110	$100

MODEL PM357 — .357 Mag. cal., similar to Model PSS 38, 2½ in. barrel. Mfg. 1975-disc.

$225	$175	$165	$150	$140	$125	$110

Grading	100%	98%	95%	90%	80%	70%	60%

MODEL PPM 357 — .357 Mag. cal., 5 shot, 2 in. barrel, spurless hammer until 1977, new models have spur. Mfg. 1965-disc.

	100%	98%	95%	90%	80%	70%	60%
	$225	$175	$165	$150	$140	$125	$110

SEDCO INDUSTRIES, INC.
Previous manufacturer located in Lake Elsinore, CA until 1991.

PISTOLS: SEMI-AUTO

MODEL SP-22 — .22 LR cal., single action, 2½ in. barrel, rotary safety, serrated slide, nickel, satin nickel (new 1990), or black metal finish, simulated pearl grips in white, blue, grey, or pink, 11 oz. Mfg. 1989-90 only.

	100%	98%	95%	90%	80%	70%	60%
	$60	$55	$50	$45	$40	$35	$35

Last Mfg.'s Sug. Retail was $69.

S

SEDGLEY, R.F., INC.
Previous manufacturer located in Philadelphia, PA.

RIFLES: BOLT ACTION

SPRINGFIELD SPORTING RIFLE — .218 Bee, .220 Swift, .22-3000, .22-4000, .22 Hornet, .25-35 WCF, .250-3000 Sav., .257 Roberts, .270 Win., 7x57mm Mauser, or .30-06 cal., '03 Springfield bolt action, 24 in. barrel, Lyman receiver sight, checkered pistol grip stock, pre-WWII.

	100%	98%	95%	90%	80%	70%	60%
	$1,250	$1,125	$995	$875	$750	$625	$495

SPRINGFIELD CARBINE SPORTER — similar to Rifle, with 20 in. barrel, and full length stock.

	100%	98%	95%	90%	80%	70%	60%
	$1,450	$1,250	$1,125	$995	$875	$750	$625

SEECAMP, L.W. CO., INC.
Current handgun manufacturer located in Milford, CT. Dealer direct sales only.

All Seecamp pistols are hand machined and hand fitted from stainless steel. Manufacture has always emphasized quality over quantity - this explains why values often exceed the company's retail prices. There is simply more demand than supply.

PISTOLS: SEMI-AUTO

LWS .25 ACP MODEL — .25 ACP cal., double action, 2 in. barrel, 7 shot mag., stainless steel, matte finish, 12 oz. Approx. 4,000 mfg. 1981-1985.

	100%	98%	95%	90%	80%	70%	60%
	$400	$325	$275	$235	$220	$210	$200

Last Mfg.'s Sug. Retail was $275.

LWS 32 MODEL — .32 ACP Silvertip cal., double action, 2 in. barrel, stainless steel, 6 shot mag., 12½ oz., extreme backorder situation coupled with high demand has resulted in elevated 100% values. Mfg. Jan. 1985-present.

		100%	98%	95%	90%	80%	70%	60%
Mfg.'s Sug. Retail	$425	$925	$875	$795	$650	$575	$495	$450

This model is available in either a matte or polished finish. The polished finish carries a slight premium.

MATCHED PAIR — includes both .25 ACP and .32 ACP pistols with the same serial number, approx. 200 sets were mfg. before the BATF stopped this practice.

	100%	98%	95%
	$1,200	$1,000	$850

This set contains a matte finished .25 ACP and a polished .32 ACP.

SEITZ
Previous manufacturer located in Portland, OR circa mid-1980s - 1993.

SHOTGUNS: SINGLE BARREL TRAP

SINGLE BARREL TRAP GUN — 12 ga. only, single barrel, various barrel lengths, pull or release trigger, only 45 guns mfg.

	100%	98%	95%	90%	80%	70%	60%
	$18,500	$16,000	$13,000	$10,000	$8,500	$7,700	$6,950

Grading	100%	98%	95%	90%	80%	70%	60%

SEMMERLING

Current trademark advertised (limited mfg.) by American Derringer Corp., located in Waco, TX. Previously manufactured by Semmerling Corporation, located in Boston, MA from 1978-1982.

Less than 600 LM-4 pistols were mfg.

PISTOLS: SLIDE ACTION

LM-4 PISTOL — .45 ACP cal., 2 in. barrel, blue, smallest .45 ACP repeater available, slide is worked manually with thumb on serrated slide-top, extremely high quality, hand fitted and choice of finishes include chrome, electroless nickel, or high polish blue.

Chrome	$2,950	$2,600	$2,300	$2,100	$1,950	$1,725	$1,600
Electroless nickel	$3,200	$2,950	$2,600	$2,300	$2,100	$1,950	$1,725
High polish blue	$4,950	$4,500	$4,000	$3,600	$3,200	$2,800	$2,500

The original U.S. Army contract pistol sold for $5,000. Earlier mfg. by Lichtman will also command a premium over values listed above.

* *LM-4 Stainless Steel (Current Mfg.)* — matte finish stainless steel variation of the LM-4, combat grey, satin, high polish finish, rosewood grips, limited mfg. by special order only.

Mfg.'s Sug. Retail	$2,500	$2,250	$1,950	$1,750

SENTINEL ARMS

Previous importer of Arsenal Bulgaria pistols and rifles.

C. SHARPS ARMS CO. INC.

Current manufacturer located in Big Timber, MT. Distributed by Montana Armory located in Big Timber, MT.

Montana Armory, Inc. currently distributes smokeless powder replicas of C. Sharps rifles/carbines and the Winchester Model 1885 single shot. They are able to shoot both smokeless and black powder loads. Most models are available in the following cals.: .40-50, .40-70, .40-90, .45-70, .45-90, .45-100, .45-110, .45-120, .50-70, .50-90, .50-100, and .50-140. All models are authentically reproduced and high quality.

RIFLES: REPRODUCTIONS, SHARPS BLACK POWDER

Currently, C. Sharps Arms Co. Inc. is experiencing a back order situation on some of their models. New Models 1875 and 1885 are experiencing a 6-month wait, while the New Model 1874 is currently running over 2+ years for delivery. However, Montana Armory currently has some models in stock - call for availability and pricing (see Trademark Index).

NEW MODEL 1874 SPORTING

Mfg.'s Sug. Retail	$1,395	N/A	N/A	N/A	N/A	$750	$650	$550

In addition to the 1874 Sporting Model, a custom long range target rifle or Schuetzen short range target rifle is available in this model. Because of the extended back order situation on this model, premiums will probably exist for those people who would rather pay a premium than wait.

CUSTOM NEW MODEL 1874 BOSS GUN — features 34 in. No. 1 heavy tapered octagon barrel, vernier tang sight, straight grip stock with cheekrest and steel shotgun butt.

Base price is $3,950 and custom order only. Please contact the factory to obtain a custom quotation on this model.

NEW MODEL 1875 SPORTING RIFLE — similar to New Model 1875 Classic, except has receiver with round crown.

Mfg.'s Sug. Retail	$1,095	$850	$795	$725	$650	$575	$495	$395

NEW MODEL 1875 CLASSIC RIFLE — receiver with octagon top, 26, 28, or 30 in. tapered full octagon barrel, straight grip stock with steel toe plate, 9½ lbs. New 1992.

Mfg.'s Sug. Retail	$1,385	$1,050	$950	$825	$675	$550	$475	$410

NEW MODEL 1875 CARBINE — features 24 in. tapered round barrel. Mfg. 1996-98.

$750	$675	$600	$500	$450	$375	$325

Last Mfg.'s Sug. Retail was $810.

Grading	100%	98%	95%	90%	80%	70%	60%

NEW MODEL 1875 SADDLE RIFLE — receiver with octagon top, 26 in. barrel only. Disc. 1998.

	$835	$760	$685	$625	$550	$460	$365

Last Mfg.'s Sug. Retail was $910.

NEW MODEL 1875 BUSINESS RIFLE — receiver with round top, 28 in. heavy tapered round barrel. Disc. 1998.

	$750	$675	$600	$500	$450	$375	$325

Last Mfg.'s Sug. Retail was $810.

Add $50 for barrel sights.

NEW MODEL 1885 HIGHWALL — .22 LR, .22 Hornet, .219 Zipper, .30-40 Krag, .32-40, .38-55 WCF, .40-65, or .45-70 cal., patterned after the Winchester Model 1885 single shot, falling block action, case colored receiver and small parts, 26-30 in. octagon barrel. New 1992.

Mfg.'s Sug. Retail	$1,350	$1,050	$900	$775	$650	$550	$475	$410

S

SHARPS, CHRISTIAN

Previously manufactured by Sharps Rifle Manufacturing Company circa 1851-1855 and located in Windsor, VT. Also manufactured in Hartford, CT under same name between 1855-1874. Reorganized as Sharps Rifle Company in 1876 with production resuming in Hartford (1876 only) and Bridgeport, CT from 1877-1881.

100%	98%	95%	90%	80%	70%	60%	50%	40%	30%	20%	10%

HANDGUNS

REVOLVER, PERCUSSION — made 1850s in Philadelphia, production about 2000, 3 in. octagonal tip-up barrel with rib, .25 caliber, 6 shot.

$1,950	$1,750	$1,500	$1,275	$1,100	$1,000	$900	$800	$700	$600	$500	$400

PEPPERBOX PISTOL — also marked Sharps and Hankins, 4-shot breech-loading, .32, .30, or .22 rimfire cal., firing pin rotates, brass frame with silver plating, or case-hardening on iron frame.

* *First Model* — 5 variations, 2½ in. barrel. Scarcer variations can be worth up to 150% more.

$595	$550	$500	$465	$430	$400	$360	$330	$300	$275	$250	$225

* *Second Model* — 5 variations, 3 in. barrel. Scarcer variations can be worth up to 150% more.

$595	$550	$500	$465	$430	$400	$360	$330	$300	$275	$250	$225

* *Third Model* — Sharps and Hankins markings, .32 rimfire short, 4 variations, 3½ in. barrel. Premium for scarcer variations.

$750	$700	$650	$600	$560	$520	$480	$440	$400	$360	$320	$280

* *Fourth Model* — 4 variations, 2½, 3, or 3½ in. barrel, birds head grip, .32 rimfire long. Premium for scarcer variations.

$650	$575	$525	$475	$430	$400	$360	$330	$300	$275	$250	$225

RIFLES: BREECH LOADING

The earliest Sharps rifles and carbines were made for Christian Sharps by A.S. Nippes, in Mill Creek, PA circa 1850, and a year later by Robbins and Lawrence Co. of Windsor, VT. Not until 1856 did the Sharps Rifle Co. of Hartford, CT begin to manufacture its own guns.

MODEL 1849 RIFLE — .36 or .44 cal., percussion breechloader, 30 in. barrels and brass patchboxes were standard, ser. numbered 1 and up, very few examples exist, less than 100 mfg. These are the first of all Sharps long guns, there is no fixed value range. Depending on condition, they could range from $5,000 to $50,000+.

MODEL 1850 RIFLE — .36 or .44 cal., incorporated the Maynard tape primer on the right side of the breech, features similar to Model 1849, approx. 150 mfg. by A.S. Nippes, very rare. Values only slightly less than Model 1849.

MODEL 1851 CARBINE — .52 cal. percussion, 21⅝ barrel, hammer mounted inside frame, Maynard tape primer. Approx. 1,800 mfg. by Robbins and Lawrence, 200 went to U.S. Government - these will bring a premium.

$12,000	$11,000	$10,000	$9,000	$8,000	$7,200	$6,500	$6,000	$5,500	$4,900	$4,400	$4,000

100%	98%	95%	90%	80%	70%	60%	50%	40%	30%	20%	10%

MODEL 1852 CARBINE — this design became standard for all the Sharps for the next two decades, first to be called "slant breech", established Christian Sharps as a major gun manufacturer. Approx. 5,000 mfg. by Robbins and Lawrence, U.S. military markings will command a premium.

$8,000	$7,500	$7,000	$6,300	$5,400	$4,700	$4,200	$3,800	$3,300	$3,000	$2,600	$2,200

MODEL 1853 CARBINE — .52 cal., very similar to Model 1852, with walnut stock and brass patchbox, Sharps patented pellet primer feed, ser. no. range 9,000-19,000. Approx. 10,000 mfg. by Robbins and Lawrence 1854-1858, an additional 3,000 rifles mfg - subtract 25%.

$7,000	$6,500	$6,000	$5,200	$4,500	$3,800	$3,200	$2,500	$2,000	$1,800	$1,500	$1,200

MODEL 1855 CARBINE — .52 cal., U.S. military model, all with Maynard tape primer, this was the period that Robbins and Lawrence failed, and Sharps Rifle Co. took over production. 800 Mfg.

$10,000	$9,000	$8,200	$7,800	$6,800	$5,700	$5,000	$4,000	$3,300	$2,800	$2,500	$2,200

Sharps "New Model"

Manufactured in Hartford, CT by Sharps Rifle Manufacturing Co. circa 1859-1866. Visibly different from earlier models because of straight breech and pellet priming feature built into lock plate. Approx. 115,000 were built, all in .52 cal. breechloading paper cartridge. Carbines had 22 in. barrels, rifles came standard with 30 in. round barrels. After ser. numbers reached 100,000, a C prefix was used in the number - i.e. C500 represents ser. no. 100,500.

MODEL 1859 CARBINE — standard with all iron furniture and patchbox, first 3,000 had brass instead of iron, ser. no. range 30,000-75,000. Approx. 33,000 mfg.

$11,000	$9,000	$8,500	$7,500	$6,000	$5,000	$4,000	$3,500	$3,000	$2,500	$2,000	$1,500

MODEL 1863 CARBINE — made with and w/o iron patchbox, ser. no. range 75,000-140,000. Approx. 65,000 mfg. - those with patchbox will bring a premium.

$10,000	$8,500	$8,000	$7,000	$5,500	$4,500	$3,500	$3,000	$2,500	$2,000	$1,500	$1,200

MODEL 1865 CARBINE — made w/o patchbox, ser. no. range 140,000-145,000. Only 5,000 mfg.

$12,000	$10,000	$9,000	$8,000	$6,500	$5,500	$4,500	$4,000	$3,500	$3,000	$2,500	$2,000

Model 1859 RIFLE — iron patchbox only, long forearm fastened with three barrel bands, approx. 4,300 mfg. in carbine ser. range with lug on barrel for attachment of saber bayonet. Approx. 600 were mfg. with 36 in. long barrel - these will command a premium.

$14,000	$12,000	$10,500	$9,500	$7,800	$6,500	$5,000	$4,000	$3,000	$2,500	$2,000	$1,500

COFFEE MILL MODEL — experimental variation buttstock with a grinding device and detachable handle that was fitted to several Model 1859 & 1863 Carbines. Designed to provide a quick and easy method for cavalry troops in the field to process coffee beans or corn for meals. Field trials are believed to have been in Trenton, NJ circa 1863. Very few originals known - no official records indicating government acceptance. Originals are extremely rare and values could range from $10,000-$50,000.

Buyer beware! Many fakes exist.

Model 1863 RIFLE — adapted for socket bayonet, shared ser. range with carbine. Approx. 6,000 mfg.

$13,000	$11,000	$9,500	$8,700	$6,800	$5,500	$4,500	$3,500	$2,700	$2,200	$1,800	$1,200

Model 1865 RIFLE — only 1,000 mfg. in carbine ser. range.

$15,000	$13,000	$11,500	$10,500	$8,600	$7,500	$6,000	$4,700	$3,700	$3,200	$2,800	$2,200

Sharps Cartridge Conversions

In 1867, the U.S. government decided to convert their percussion Sharps carbines and rifles to the new .50/70 metallic cartridge. Approx. 31,000 carbines and 1,000 rifles were converted by the Sharps Co. Any original, six groove barrels that were worn beyond specification had a groove liner installed. Those barrels meeting specs. remained unaltered. All buttstocks were stamped on the left side with "D.F.C." in a ribbon cartouche, the initials for the principal sub-inspector, David F. Clark. Damaged buttstocks were all replaced with the plain (no patchbox) Model 1865 buttstock, regardless of the model of the carbine; however, many of the old style buttplates with notches for patchboxes were retained.

100%	98%	95%	90%	80%	70%	60%	50%	40%	30%	20%	10%

.50/70 CARBINES — most had relined three groove barrels, approx. 31,000 remodeled. Those found with original six groove barrels will command a slight premium, as will those Model 1859s & Model 1863s with original patchbox buttstocks.

$5,000	$4,300	$3,900	$3,500	$2,700	$2,300	$2,100	$1,800	$1,600	$1,400	$1,200	$1,000

.50/70 RIFLES — all had three groove relined barrels, approx. 1,000 converted in 1867. More rare, but do not command any higher prices than their carbine counterparts.

SPRINGFIELD/SHARPS MODEL 1870-1871 — approx. 1,000 rifles and 300 carbines altered by Springfield Armory to fire .50/70 metallic cartridge, in addition to those done by Sharps Co., rifle barrels 35½ in., carbine barrels 22 in., receivers color case hardened, all other metal parts bright finish, own ser. range, and numbered on receiver tang and left side of barrel.

S

* *Rifles*

$6,000	$5,800	$5,200	$4,500	$3,800	$3,300	$2,900	$2,600	$2,300	$2,000	$1,700	$1,500

* *Carbines*

$6,000	$5,500	$4,900	$4,300	$3,400	$3,000	$2,500	$2,300	$2,100	$1,800	$1,600	$1,400

Sharps Metallic Cartridge Models

MODEL 1874 CARBINE — mfg. in several configurations and a variety of calibers, designed to fire metallic cartridges and was not a conversion from percussion parts, made famous for its deadly accuracy at long distances and became known as the "Buffalo Rifle" of its day. Mfg. in Hartford, CT circa 1874-1876, in Bridgeport, CT circa 1881.

* *Sporting Model* — .40, .44, .45 or .50 cal., variety of barrel lengths and weights, many special order features. Approx. 6,500 mfg.

$16,000	$15,000	$13,500	$11,000	$9,000	$7,500	$6,000	$5,000	$4,200	$3,500	$3,000	$2,500

* *Business Rifle* — no frills version of the 1874 Sporting, with shorter, round barrel and open sights.

$10,000	$9,500	$9,000	$8,200	$7,300	$6,600	$5,000	$4,200	$3,500	$2,700	$2,200	$2,000

* *Military Rifle* — .45/70 or .50/70 cal., long forearm and three barrel bands. Approx. 1,700 mfg.

$8,000	$7,500	$7,000	$6,500	$5,500	$4,500	$3,700	$3,200	$2,700	$2,300	$2,000	$1,700

* *Military Carbine* — most in .50/70 cal., very similar to previous Sharps carbines. Less than 500 mfg.

$9,000	$8,500	$8,000	$7,500	$6,000	$5,000	$4,000	$3,200	$2,800	$2,400	$2,000	$1,600

* *Meachan Type Conversion* — most in .45/70 cal., very similar to Business Rifle, with both round and octagon barrels, mfg. from Civil War Sharps carbine actions and surplus, as well as new parts by several commercial firms in the 1880s after Sharps Rifle Co. closed. Sharps Co. assembled several hundred of these from 1879-1881 from existing parts on hand.

$8,500	$8,000	$7,500	$6,800	$5,700	$4,500	$3,700	$3,200	$2,800	$2,200	$1,800	$1,500

While of lesser quality than the Model 1874, these rifles were widely used on the Western frontier and have become very desirable to today's firearms collectors.

MODEL 1878 SHARPS-BORCHARDT — many cals. and barrel lengths, single trigger, hammerless action designed by Hugo Borchardt, carbines, military, sporting, and target rifles were all mfg., but sales suffered from a bolt and lever action market glut. Less than 9,000 mfg. by Sharps Rifle Co. in Bridgeport, CT circa 1878-1881.

$6,500	$6,000	$5,500	$5,000	$4,000	$3,200	$2,800	$2,500	$2,200	$1,900	$1,600	$1,300

Special order or deluxe models with other than standard features will command a premium.

SHERIDAN PRODUCTS INCORPORATED

Previous manufacturer located in Racine, WI.

Grading	100%	98%	95%	90%	80%	70%	60%

PISTOLS: SINGLE SHOT

KNOCKABOUT — .22 S-L-LR cal., 5 in. barrel, checkered plastic grips, fixed sights. Mfg. 1953-1960.

	$110	$100	$85	$75	$60	$50	$40

Grading	100%	98%	95%	90%	80%	70%	60%

SHILEN RIFLES, INCORPORATED

Previous manufacturer located in Enis, TX circa 1975-mid 1980s.

RIFLES: BOLT ACTION

Older Shilen rifles have become very desirable for target shooters and other accuracy enthusiasts. Because of their small quantities of manufacture (approx. 3,350 mfg.) and new found demand, prices have gone up considerably on this trademark. Originally, the Sporters retailed in the $600-$700 range, but at the end, prices were in the $3,500 range.

DGA SPORTER — .17 Rem., .223 Rem., .22-250 Rem., .220 Swift, 6mm Rem., .243 Win., .250 Savage, .257 Roberts, .284 Win., .308 Win. cal., 3 shot mag., 24 in. barrel, no sights, claro walnut stock.

	$1,475	$1,175	$950	$800	$675	$575	$495

DGA VARMINTER — similar to Sporter, except 25 in. medium heavy barrel.

	$1,395	$1,100	$900	$775	$650	$575	$495

DGA SILHOUETTE RIFLE — similar to Varminter, .308 Win. cal. only.

	$1,395	$1,100	$900	$775	$650	$575	$495

DGA BENCHREST RIFLE — single shot, choice of cals., 26 in. heavy or medium barrel, no sights, choice of fiberglass or walnut stock, thumbhole available.

	$1,450	$1,200	$950	$800	$650	$575	$495

SHILOH RIFLE MFG. CO.

Current manufacturer located in Big Timber, MT since 1983. Previously manufactured by Shiloh Products, a division of Drovel Tool Company of Farmingdale, NY, 1976-1983. Dealer or consumer direct sales.

The Shiloh Rifle Mfg. Co. is currently manufacturing quality replicas of Sharps rifles and carbines. They are available as black powder or modern cartridge rifles. Please contact Shiloh Rifle Mfg. Co. directly regarding new model availability, in addition to pricing for both new and used models.

SHOOTERS ARMS MANUFACTURING INCORPORATED

Current manufacturer located in the Phillipines. No current importer.

Shooters Arms Manufacturing Incorporated makes semi-auto pistols, revolvers, and slide action shotguns. Please contact the factory directly for current U.S. availability and pricing.

SIDEWINDER

Previously manufactured by D-Max, Inc. located in Bagley, MN circa 1993-96. Dealer or consumer sales.

REVOLVERS

SIDEWINDER — .45 LC or 2½/3 in. .410 bore shotshells/slugs, 6 shot, stainless steel construction, 6½ or 7½ in. bull barrel (muzzle end bored for choke), Pachmayr grips, hammer bar safety, adj. rear sight, unique design permits one cylinder to shoot above listed loads, cased with choke tube, 3.8 lbs. Mfg. 1993-96.

	$695	$575	$475

Last Mfg.'s Sug. Retail was $775.

SIG

Current Swiss conglomerate established during 1860 in Neuhausen, Switzerland. SIG (Schweizerische Industrie-Gesellschaft) is currently in a corporate partnership with both J.P. Sauer & Sohn and Hämmerli. P 210 pistols and the SHR 970 rifle are currently imported and distributed by SIG Arms, located in Exeter, NH.

Grading	100%	98%	95%	90%	80%	70%	60%

PISTOLS: SEMI-AUTO

P 210 — 9mm Para. or 7.65mm Para. cal., single action, 4¾ in. barrel, 8 shot mag., standard weapon of the Swiss Army, 2 lbs.

> Originally mfg. in 1947, this pistol was first designated the SP 47/8 and became the standard military pistol of the Swiss Army in 1949. Later designated the P 210, this handgun has been mfg. continuously for over 50 years.

* *P 210-1* — polished finish, walnut grips, special hammer, fixed sights. Importation disc. 1986.

$2,000	$1,675	$1,400	$1,195	$975	$850	$750

Last Mfg.'s Sug. Retail was $1,861.

* *P 210-2* — matte finish, field sights, plastic grips. Importation disc. 1987.

$1,775	$1,325	$1,000	$875	$750	$625	$550

Last Mfg.'s Sug. Retail was $1,350.

* *P 210-5* — matte finish, micrometer sights, 150mm or 180mm (rare) extended barrel, hard rubber grips, very limited mfg. Importation disc. 1997.

$2,300	$1,750	$1,200	$1,000	$800	$675	$600

Last Mfg.'s Sug. Retail was $2,600.

* *P 210-6* — matte blue finish, fixed (current importation) or micrometer sights, 120mm barrel, checkered walnut grips.

Mfg.'s Sug. Retail	$2,100						
		$1,925	$1,425	$1,000	$950	$775	$650	$575

Add $300 for .22 LR conversion kit.

* *P 210-7* — .22 LR or 9mm Para. cal., regular or target long barrel, limited importation. No longer in production.

$3,375	$2,950	$2,600	$2,300	$1,950	$1,600	$1,275

* *P 210 Deluxe Models* — various models differ in the amount of engraving, gold inlays, carved wood grips, presentation cases, and other special order features available from the factory. Prices start at $3,500 and can go up to $5,500, depending on the amount of special orders executed.

RIFLES: BOLT ACTION

SHR 970 — .25-06 Rem., .270 Win., .280 Rem., .30-06, .308 Win., .300 Win. Mag., or 7mm Rem. Mag. cal., features interchangeable barrel capability (easy takedown with single tool), custom bedding block system, choice of checkered walnut or black synthetic stock, 3 position safety, 65 degree bolt throw, 22, or 24 (Mag. cals. only) in. barrel, 3 or 4 shot detachable box mag., includes hard carry case, approx. 7.3 lbs. New 1999.

Mfg.'s Sug. Retail	$499						
		$450	$400	$360	$330	$300	$285	$270

Add $31 for walnut stock.

RIFLES: SEMI-AUTO

PE-57 — 7.5 Swiss cal. only, semi-auto version of the Swiss military rifle, 24 in. barrel, includes 24 shot mag., leather sling, bipod and maintenance kit. Importation disc. 1988.

$3,250	$2,850	$2,500	$2,250	$2,000	$1,800	$1,600

Last Mfg.'s Sug. Retail was $1,745.

> The PE-57 was previously distributed in limited quantities by Osborne's located in Cheboygan, MI.

SIG-AMT RIFLE — .308 Win. cal., semi-auto version of SG510-4 auto paramilitary design rifle, roller delayed blowback action, 5, 10, or 20 shot mag., 18¾ in. barrel, wood stock, folding bipod. Mfg. 1960-present. Importation disc. 1988.

$2,500	$2,250	$2,000	$1,850	$1,700	$1,550	$1,400

Last Mfg.'s Sug. Retail was $1,795.

Grading		100%	98%	95%	90%	80%	70%	60%

SG 550/551 — .223 Rem. cal. with heavier bullet, Swiss Army's semi-auto version of newest paramilitary design rifle (SIG 90), 20.8 (SG 550) or 16 in. (SG 551 Carbine) barrel, some synthetics used to save weight, 20 shot mag., diopter night sights, built-in folding bipod, 7.7 or 9 lbs.

$4,250 $3,875 $3,500 $3,250 $2,995 $2,700 $2,500
Last Mfg.'s Sug. Retail was $1,950.

Add $250 for case.

This model has been banned from domestic importation due to 1989 Federal legislation.

SIG-HÄMMERLI

Previously manufactured by Hämmerli Ltd. in Lenzburg, Switzerland.

PISTOLS: SEMI-AUTO

P240 TARGET PISTOL — .32 S&W Long Wadcutter or .38 Mid-range (disc.) cal., single action, 5 shot mag., 5.9 in. barrel, blued finish, thumb rest walnut grips, adj. sights and trigger, 3 lbs. Importation mostly disc. 1986.

$1,475 $1,225 $1,000 $875 $775 $700 $660
Last Mfg.'s Sug. Retail was $1,350.

Add $100 for Morini adj. grips.

.38 Mid-range cal. is very desirable in this model - healthy premiums (and inconsistent) are being asked.

* .22 Conversion Unit

$550 $495 $400

Last Mfg.'s Sug. Retail was $595.

SIG SAUER

Firearms trademark manufactured by SIG (Schweizerische Industrie-Gesellschaft) located in Neuhausen, Switzerland, and currently imported, manufactured (some models), and distributed by SIG Arms, Inc. (a division of SIG) located in Exeter, NH. SIG, Hämmerli, and Sauer are currently in a corporate partnership.

PISTOLS: SEMI-AUTO

P 210 — please refer to listing under SIG heading.

MODEL P220 — .22 LR (disc.), .38 Super (disc.), 7.65mm (disc.), 9mm Para. (disc 1991), or .45 ACP cal., 7 (.45 ACP) or 8 shot mag., regular double action or double action only (.45 ACP cal. only), 4.4 in. barrel, decocking lever safety, matte blue, lightweight alloy frame, black plastic grips, values are for .45 ACP cal. and assume American side mag. release (standard 1986), 28.2 oz. Mfg. 1976-present.

Mfg.'s Sug. Retail $750 $625 $550 $475 $425 $395 $350 $310

Add $95 for Siglite night sights.
Add $45 for factory K-Kote finish.
Add $45 for nickel finished slide (new 1992).
Add $70 for electroless nickel finish (disc. 1991).
Add $680 for .22 LR conversion kit (disc.).
Subtract 10% for "European" Model (bottom mag. release - includes 9mm Para. and .38 Super cals.).

* P220 Sport — .45 ACP cal., features 4.8 in. heavy compensated barrel, stainless steel frame and slide, 10 shot mag., target sights, improved trigger pull, single or double action, 43.6 oz. New 1999.

Mfg.'s Sug. Retail $1,320 $1,175 $925 $750

Grading	100%	98%	95%	90%	80%	70%	60%

MODEL P225 — 9mm Para. cal., regular double action or double action only, similar to P220, shorter dimensions, 3.85 in. barrel, 8 shot, thumb actuated button release mag., fully adj. sights, 28.8 oz. Disc. 1998.

	$595	$525	$450	$425	$395	$350	$310

Last Mfg.'s Sug. Retail was $725.

Add $45 for factory K-Kote finish.
Add $105 for Siglite night sights.
Add $45 for nickel finished slide (new 1992).
Add $70 for electroless nickel finish (disc. 1991).

MODEL P226 — .357 SIG (new 1995), 9mm Para. (disc. 1997, reintroduced 1999), or .40 S&W (new 1998) cal., compact variation, choice of double action or double action only (new 1992) operation, 10 (C/B 1994) or 15★ shot mag., 4.4 in. barrel, alloy frame, currently available in blackened stainless steel or nickel finish (slide only), high contrast sights, automatic firing pin lock safety, approx. 30 oz. New 1983.

Mfg.'s Sug. Retail	$795	$700	$595	$525	$425	$395	$350	$310

Add $95 for Siglite night sights.
Add $45 for nickel finished slide (new 1992).
Add $45 for K-Kote (Polymer) finish (mfg. 1992-97, 9mm Para. only).
Add $70 for electroless nickel finish (disc. 1991).
This model is also available in double action only (all finishes) at no extra charge.

★ *Model P226 Jubilee* — limited edition commemorating SIG's 125th anniversary, features gold-plated small parts, carved select walnut grips, special slide markings, cased. Mfg. 1985 only.

	$1,495	$1,175	$950

Last Mfg.'s Sug. Retail was $2,000.

MODEL P228 — 9mm Para., choice of double action or double action only (new 1992) operation, compact design, 3.86 in. (compact) barrel, 10 (C/B 1994) or 13★ shot mag., automatic firing pin lock safety, high contrast sights, alloy frame, choice of blue, nickel slide (new 1991), or K-Kote finish, 29.3 oz. Mfg. 1990-97.

	$675	$575	$500	$425	$395	$350	$310

Last Mfg.'s Sug. Retail was $750.

Add $95 for Siglite night sights.
Add $45 for K-Kote (Polymer) finish.
Add $45 for nickel finished slide (new 1992).
Add $70 for electroless nickel finish (disc. 1991).
This model is also available in double action only (all finishes) at no extra charge.

MODEL P229 — .357 SIG (new 1995), 9mm Para. (mfg. 1994-96, reintroduced 1999), or .40 S&W cal., similar to Model P228, except has blackened Nitron or satin nickel finished stainless steel slide with aluminum alloy frame, 10 (C/B 1994) or 12★ shot mag., includes lockable carrying case, 30½ oz. New 1991.

Mfg.'s Sug. Retail	$795	$685	$595	$525	$450	$400	$350	$310

Add $45 for satin nickel finished stainless steel slide.
Add $95 for Siglite night sights.
This model is also available in double action only at no extra charge.

★ *Model P229 Sport* — .357 SIG cal., features 4.8 in. heavy compensated barrel, stainless steel frame and slide, target sights, improved trigger pull, single or double action, 43.6 oz. New 1998.

Mfg.'s Sug. Retail	$1,320	$1,175	$925	$750

MODEL P230 — .22 LR (disc.)-10 shot, .32 ACP-8 shot, .380 ACP-7 shot, or 9mm Ultra (disc.) cal., 7 shot, 3.6 in. barrel, regular double action or double action only, blue, composite grips, 17.6 oz. Mfg. 1976-96.

	$425	$375	$300	$270	$240	$215	$190

Add $35 for stainless slide (.380 ACP only).

Last Mfg.'s Sug. Retail was $510.

★ *Model P230 SL Stainless* — similar to Model P230, except stainless steel construction, 22.4 oz. Disc. 1996.

	$480	$400	$375

Last Mfg.'s Sug. Retail was $595.

Grading	100%	98%	95%	90%	80%	70%	60%

MODEL P232 — .380 ACP cal., choice of double action or double action only, 3.6 in. barrel, 7 shot mag., aluminum alloy frame, blue or two-tone stainless slide, automatic firing pin lock safety, composite grips. New 1997.

Mfg.'s Sug. Retail	$485	$425	$375	$300	$270	$240	$215	$190

Add $20 for stainless two-tone slide.

* *Model P232 Stainless* — similar to Model P232, except stainless steel construction, natural finish, 22.4 oz. New 1997.

Mfg.'s Sug. Retail	$525	$460	$415	$350

Add $35 for Siglite night sights and Hogue grips.

MODEL P239 — .357 SIG, 9mm Para., or .40 S&W (new 1998) cal., double action or double action only, blackened or two-tone stainless steel slide and aluminum alloy frame, firing pin lock safety, 3.6 in. barrel, 7 or 8 (9mm Para. only) shot mag., fixed sights, approx. 29 oz. New 1996.

Mfg.'s Sug. Retail	$595	$475	$425	$350	$285	$255	$220	$195

Add $95 for Siglite night sights.
Add $45 for two-tone stainless slide.

MODEL P245 — .45 ACP cal., compact model featuring 3.9 in. barrel, traditional double action, 6 shot mag., blue, two-tone or K-Kote finish, approx. 30 oz. New 1999.

Mfg.'s Sug. Retail	$750	$625	$550	$475	$425	$395	$350	$310

Add $45 for two-tone or K-Kote finish.
Add $95 for Siglite night sights.

MODEL SP2340 — 9mm Para., .357 SIG, or .40 S&W cal., features polymer frame and one-piece Nitron finished stainless steel slide, 3.86 in. barrel, includes two interchangeable grips, 10 shot mag., approx. 30 oz. New 1999.

Mfg.'s Sug. Retail	$596	$475	$425	$350	$285	$255	$220	$195

Add $59 for Siglite night sights.

RIFLES: BOLT ACTION

MODEL SSG 2000 — available in .223 Rem., 7.5mm Swiss, .300 Wby. Mag., or .308 Win. (standard) cal., bolt action, 4 shot mag., no sights, deluxe sniper rifle featuring thumbhole style walnut stock with stippling and thumbwheel adj. cheekpiece, 13 lbs. Importation disc. 1986.

	$2,480	$2,260	$1,950	$1,700	$1,500	$1,300	$1,100

Last Mfg.'s Sug. Retail was $2,850.

This model was available in .223 Rem., .300 Wby. Mag., or 7.5mm cal. by special order only.

MODEL SSG 3000 — .223 Rem., 22½ in. barrel, "ph" bipod, 2-stage match trigger, includes 2½-10X x52 Zeiss scope, 200 mfg. for Swiss police.

	$12,000	$10,000	$8,500	$7,000	$6,750	$5,500	$4,250

SHOTGUNS: O/U

SA 3 — 12 or 20 (new 1998) ga., 3 in. chambers, scalloped coin finished monobloc boxlock action with game scene engraving, field or Sporting Clays (new 1998) configuration, 26, 28, or 30 (Sporting Clays only) in. separated barrels with VR and choke tubes, ejectors, SST, checkered walnut stock and forearm, approx. 7 lbs. Mfg. 1997-98 only.

	$1,175	$925	$775	$650	$550	$475	$400

Last Mfg.'s Sug. Retail was $1,335.

SA 5 — 12 or 20 ga., 3 in. chambers, features coin finished boxlock action with hand engraved detachable side plates, ejectors, SST, select checkered walnut stock and forearm, field or Sporting Clays (new 1998) configuration, 26½, 28, or 30 (Sporting Clays only) in. barrels with VR and choke tubes, supplied with lockable case, 6 or 7 lbs. New 1997.

Mfg.'s Sug. Retail	$2,670	$2,175	$1,775	$1,450	$1,225	$1,075	$900	$775

Add $130 for Sporting Clays Model (12 ga. only, 28 or 30 in. barrels).

SILE DISTRIBUTORS

Current distributor, importer, and and previous manufacturer located in New York, NY.

In addition to distributing a wide variety of firearms and related accessories (including the mfg. of stocks and grips), Sile Distributors also has had some firearms "private labeled" to their specifications (see Trademark Index).

Grading	100%	98%	95%	90%	80%	70%	60%

SILMA SPORTING GUNS

Current manufacturer established during 1949 and located in Brescia, Italy. All Silma Shotguns are high quality and utilize premium materials in their manufacture. No current importation.

Rather than list the various shotgun models and options separately, the following information will help you in ascertaining correct values. Models 70 and 80 are O/U hunting models available in either 12, 20 ga., or .410 bore. They are available with double triggers standard, extractors or ejectors (extra cost), with or without sideplates, or in superlight configuration - retail values range between $500-$1,000. Competition models (including T.J. 70, T.S. 81, Cobra T1, T2, or T3) are also available for trap, skeet, or sporting clays events. Values range between $1,000-$6,200 (with T.J. 70 being the least expensive, and Cobra T2 the most expensive). Two side by side models (AS/70 N and AS/70 EJ) are also available. Please contact the factory directly (see Trademark Index) for current availability and domestic pricing.

SIMILLION, GENE

Current custom rifle maker located in Gunnison, CO. Consumer direct sales.

RIFLES: BOLT ACTION, CUSTOM

CLASSIC HUNTER RIFLE — various cals., new Winchester Model 70 Classic action, options include LOP, caliber, and barrel length, deluxe walnut, custom made to individual customer specifications.

Mfg.'s Sug. Retail	$5,400	$5,150	$4,500	$3,750	$3,000	$2,500	$2,000	$1,650

Add $600 for Mag. cals. up to .375 H&H.
Add $1,100 for heavy Mag. cals. .375 H&H. and larger.

PREMIER RIFLE — various cals., mostly Winchester new Model 70 action (others available), custom made to individual customer specifications, finest materials and workmanship, individually tested.

Mfg.'s Sug. Retail	$7,500	$7,250	$6,500	$5,500	$4,500	$3,500	$2,750	$2,000

Add $500 for Mag. cals. up to .375 H&H.
Add $1,250 for heavy Mag. cals. .375 H&H and larger.

SIRKIS INDUSTRIES, LTD.

Previous manufacturer located in Ramat-Gan, Israel. Previously imported and distributed by Armscorp of America, Inc. located in Baltimore, MD.

PISTOLS: SEMI-AUTO

S.D. 9 — 9mm Para. cal., double action mechanism, frame is constructed mostly of heavy gauge sheet metal stampings, 3.07 in. barrel, parkerized finish, loaded chamber indicator, 7 shot mag., plastic grips, 24½ oz. Imported under this trademark between 1986-1988.

	$375	$295	$250	$200	$190	$180	$170

Last Mfg.'s Sug. Retail was $330.

This pistol is also listed under the Sardius heading in this section.

RIFLES

MODEL 35 MATCH RIFLE — .22 LR cal. only, single shot bolt action, 26 in. full floating barrel, select walnut, match trigger, micrometer sights. Disc. 1985.

	$650	$625	$595	$550	$510	$460	$420

Last Mfg.'s Sug. Retail was $690.

MODEL 36 SNIPER RIFLE — .308 Win. cal. only, gas operated action, carbon fiber stock, 22 in. barrel, flash suppressor, free range sights. Disc. 1985.

	$670	$580	$520	$475	$430	$390	$350

Last Mfg.'s Sug. Retail was $760.

SKORPION

Please refer to Armitage International, Ltd. in the "A" section of this text.

100%	98%	95%	90%	80%	70%	60%	50%	40%	30%	20%	10%

SMITH, L.C.

Previously manufactured circa 1880-1888 in Syracuse, NY., and in Fulton, NY 1890-1945 by Hunter Arms Company.

The L.C. Smith shotgun was made from 1890-1945 by the Hunter Arms Company in Fulton, New York. In 1946, the company was acquired by Marlin Firearms Company. Production continued until 1951 when it ceased for a period of 17 years. In 1968, Marlin brought the L.C. Smith back to life for a period of 5 years. Production stopped in 1973. The L.C. Smith is one of the finest American made shotguns and collector interest is very high. All values shown are for hammerless shotguns.

SHOTGUNS: SxS, HAMMERLESS - 1890-1913 PRODUCTION

All prices listed below are for guns with fluid steel barrels (except A-1 grade).

It is important to note that damascus barreled guns with hammers in 90% original condition or better are very collectible and values can approximate those of steel barrel models if the bore is excellent with no pitting. Damascus specimens below 90% condition are not as collectible, however, and values fall off rapidly if under 90%. Prices shown below for 90% and up condition are very difficult to evaluate and are meant as a guide only. L.C. Smith shotguns are rare and hard to evaluate if over 95% condition in the higher grades.

OO GRADE — 12, 16, or 20 ga. Approx. 60,000 mfg.

100%	98%	95%	90%	80%	70%	60%	50%	40%	30%	20%	10%
$1,500	$1,200	$800	$600	$500	$465	$430	$395	$375	$350	$325	$295

Add 33% for auto ejectors.
Add 50% for 20 ga.

O GRADE — 10, 12, 16, or 20 ga. Approx. 30,000 mfg.

100%	98%	95%	90%	80%	70%	60%	50%	40%	30%	20%	10%
$1,600	$1,400	$1,000	$775	$675	$600	$550	$515	$460	$400	$350	$300

Add 50% for 20 ga.

NO. 1 GRADE — 10, 12, 16, or 20 ga. Approx. 10,000 mfg.

100%	98%	95%	90%	80%	70%	60%	50%	40%	30%	20%	10%
$2,400	$1,950	$1,425	$995	$850	$750	$700	$625	$550	$495	$450	$400

Add 33% for auto ejectors.
Add 50% for 20 ga.
Add $200 for SST.

NO. 2 GRADE — 10, 12, 16, or 20 ga. Approx. 13,000 mfg.

100%	98%	95%	90%	80%	70%	60%	50%	40%	30%	20%	10%
$2,900	$2,275	$1,700	$1,400	$1,200	$1,000	$825	$750	$675	$600	$550	$500

Add 33% for auto ejectors.
Add 75% for 20 ga.
Add $200 for SST.

NO. 3 GRADE — 10, 12, 16, or 20 ga. Approx. 4,000 mfg.

100%	98%	95%	90%	80%	70%	60%	50%	40%	30%	20%	10%
$3,475	$2,950	$2,400	$1,850	$1,500	$1,300	$1,100	$995	$875	$775	$625	$500

Add 25% for auto ejectors.
Add 75% for 20 ga.
Add $200 for SST.

PIGEON GRADE — 10, 12, 16, or 20 ga. Approx. 1,200 mfg.

100%	98%	95%	90%	80%	70%	60%	50%	40%	30%	20%	10%
$3,475	$2,950	$2,400	$1,850	$1,500	$1,300	$1,100	$995	$875	$775	$625	$500

Add 25% for auto ejectors.
Add 75% for 20 ga.
Add $200 for SST.

NO. 4 GRADE — 10, 12, 16, or 20 ga. Approx. 500 mfg., seldomly encountered.

100%	98%	95%	90%	80%	70%	60%	50%	40%	30%	20%	10%
$10,000	$8,000	$5,750	$4,500	$3,500	$2,650	$2,000	$1,775	$1,500	$1,375	$1,200	$1,095

Add 25% for auto ejectors.
Add 75% for 20 ga.
Add $200 for SST.

100%	98%	95%	90%	80%	70%	60%	50%	40%	30%	20%	10%

A-1 GRADE — 10, 12, or 16 ga. Approx. 700 mfg. Damascus barrels only.

100%	98%	95%	90%	80%	70%	60%	50%	40%	30%	20%	10%
$4,850	$3,700	$3,000	$2,200	$1,850	$1,725	$1,425	$1,175	$995	$800	$700	$600

        Auto ejectors standard.
        Add $200 for SST.

NO. 5 GRADE — 10, 12, 16, or 20 ga. Approx. 500 mfg.

100%	98%	95%	90%	80%	70%	60%	50%	40%	30%	20%	10%
$9,000	$7,000	$4,950	$4,500	$4,000	$3,500	$3,150	$2,700	$2,450	$2,200	$1,995	$1,800

        Auto ejectors standard.
        Add $200 for SST.
        Add 75% for 20 ga., extremely rare.

MONOGRAM GRADE — 10, 12, 16, or 20 ga. Approx. 100 mfg.

100%	98%	95%	90%	80%	70%	60%	50%	40%	30%	20%	10%
$10,750	$9,475	$7,400	$6,000	$5,500	$5,000	$4,600	$4,100	$3,800	$3,500	$3,250	$3,000

        Auto ejectors standard.
        Add 50% for 20 ga., extremely rare.

S

A-2 GRADE — 10, 12, 16, or 20 ga. Approx. 200 mfg.

100%	98%	95%	90%	80%	70%	60%	50%	40%	30%	20%	10%
$15,000	$11,000	$8,000	$7,000	$6,000	$5,200	$4,700	$4,200	$3,850	$3,500	$3,250	$3,000

        Auto ejectors standard.
        20 ga. — only 6 mfg.

A-3 GRADE — 10, 12, 16, or 20 ga. Approx. 20 mfg. Rarity precludes accurate pricing on this model.

        Auto ejectors standard.
        20 ga. — only 2 mfg.

SHOTGUNS: SxS, 1914-1951 PRODUCTION

Fulton trademarked shotguns mfg. by Hunter Arms Co. were inexpensive, utilitarian shotguns designed for a price point rather than quality. Models Fulton and Fulton Special were supplied in 12, 16, 20 ga., or .410 bore (rare). When encountered today, values usually are in the $100-$300 range. The Hunter Special, although not an L.C. Smith shotgun, did employ the rotary locking bolt system. This was also a low priced gun in its day and prices today are usually in the $125-$350 range. These models had nothing in common with the L.C. Smith shotguns of that time.

L.C. SMITH DOUBLE BARREL SHOTGUN — 12, 16, 20 ga., or .410 bore, any choke, sidelock, auto ejectors standard from Crown Grade up, extractors on lower grades, double or single triggers, straight, ½ pistol grip, or pistol grip stock, grade specifications differ in grade of wood, degree of engraving, and overall quality. Featherweight models were also manufactured on a regular basis and are so marked - values will approximate those listed below for standard models.

STANDARD FIELD GRADE

100%	98%	95%	90%	80%	70%	60%	50%	40%	30%	20%	10%
$1,250	$1,000	$775	$675	$600	$500	$465	$435	$395	$375	$340	$295

        Add 33% for auto ejectors.
        Add $200 for SST.
        Add 30% for 20 ga.
        Add 300% for .410 bore.

IDEAL GRADE STANDARD

100%	98%	95%	90%	80%	70%	60%	50%	40%	30%	20%	10%
$1,600	$1,400	$1,100	$900	$825	$750	$700	$650	$595	$550	$530	$495

        Add 33% for auto ejectors.
        Add $200 for SST.
        Add 30% for 20 ga.
        Add 400% for .410 bore.

TRAP GRADE

100%	98%	95%	90%	80%	70%	60%	50%	40%	30%	20%	10%
$2,000	$1,500	$1,200	$1,100	$1,000	$925	$850	$775	$675	$600	$550	$500

        Auto ejectors — add 33%.
        Add $200 for SST.
        Add 50% for 20 ga.
        Add 400% for .410 bore.

	100%	98%	95%	90%	80%	70%	60%	50%	40%	30%	20%	10%

SPECIALTY GRADE

100%	98%	95%	90%	80%	70%	60%	50%	40%	30%	20%	10%
$2,950	$2,450	$1,800	$1,375	$1,100	$1,000	$925	$875	$825	$775	$695	$625

Add $200 for SST.
Add 50% for 20 ga.
Add 400% for .410 bore.
Add 33% for auto ejectors.

SKEET SPECIAL GRADE

100%	98%	95%	90%	80%	70%	60%	50%	40%	30%	20%	10%
$3,100	$2,600	$1,650	$1,200	$1,100	$925	$875	$825	$775	$725	$675	$600

Add $200 for SST.
Add 50% for 20 ga.
Add 400% for .410 bore.
Add 33% for auto ejectors.

PREMIER SKEET GRADE

100%	98%	95%	90%	80%	70%	60%	50%	40%	30%	20%	10%
$3,100	$2,600	$1,650	$1,200	$1,100	$925	$875	$825	$775	$725	$675	$600

Add $200 for SST.
Add 50% for 20 ga.
Add 400% for .410 bore.
Add 33% for auto ejectors.

EAGLE GRADE

100%	98%	95%	90%	80%	70%	60%	50%	40%	30%	20%	10%
$4,750	$4,250	$3,500	$2,900	$2,350	$1,850	$1,500	$1,400	$1,300	$1,200	$1,100	$1,000

Add $200 for SST.
Add 50% for 20 ga.

CROWN GRADE

100%	98%	95%	90%	80%	70%	60%	50%	40%	30%	20%	10%
$5,750	$4,950	$4,250	$4,000	$3,500	$3,100	$2,700	$2,450	$2,225	$2,000	$1,900	$1,800

Add $200 for SST.
20 gauge — very rare.
.410 — rare and very expensive, only 6 mfg.

MONOGRAM GRADE

100%	98%	95%	90%	80%	70%	60%	50%	40%	30%	20%	10%
$12,000	$9,750	$7,750	$6,400	$5,650	$5,100	$4,650	$4,150	$3,775	$3,500	$3,250	$3,000

Add 50% for 20 ga.

PREMIER GRADE — very limited mfg., rarity precludes accurate pricing on this model.

DELUXE GRADE — very limited mfg., rarity precludes accurate pricing on this model.

SINGLE BARREL TRAP GUN — 12 ga. only, 32 or 34 in. VR barrel, boxlock, auto ejector, checkered pistol grip stock, recoil pad. Approx. 2,650 mfg. 1917-1951.

* *Olympic Grade*

100%	98%	95%	90%	80%	70%	60%	50%	40%	30%	20%	10%
$1,650	$1,400	$1,200	$1,100	$1,000	$900	$800	$725	$675	$625	$575	$550

* *Specialty Grade*

100%	98%	95%	90%	80%	70%	60%	50%	40%	30%	20%	10%
$1,950	$1,700	$1,500	$1,400	$1,300	$1,200	$1,125	$1,075	$1,000	$925	$875	$800

* *Crown Grade*

100%	98%	95%	90%	80%	70%	60%	50%	40%	30%	20%	10%
$3,450	$3,125	$2,750	$2,350	$2,100	$2,000	$1,900	$1,800	$1,700	$1,600	$1,500	$1,400

* *Monogram Grade*

100%	98%	95%	90%	80%	70%	60%	50%	40%	30%	20%	10%
$6,000	$5,000	$4,250	$3,700	$3,150	$2,750	$2,400	$2,150	$2,000	$1,850	$1,700	$1,525

* *Premier Grade*

100%	98%	95%	90%	80%	70%	60%	50%	40%	30%	20%	10%
$9,750	$8,350	$6,400	$5,275	$3,850	$3,300	$2,900	$2,600	$2,350	$2,100	$1,900	$1,750

* *Deluxe Grade*

100%	98%	95%	90%	80%	70%	60%	50%	40%	30%	20%	10%
$13,950	$12,000	$9,995	$7,850	$6,000	$5,000	$4,500	$3,995	$3,375	$2,900	$2,500	$2,150

Grading	100%	98%	95%	90%	80%	70%	60%

SHOTGUNS: SxS, 1968-1973 PRODUCTION

1968 MODEL — 12 ga., 28 in. VR barrel, full and mod. choke, sidelock, extractors, double triggers, checkered pistol grip stock. Mfg. 1968-1973 by Marlin.

$725	$600	$550	$495	$425	$350	$275

1968 DELUXE MODEL — similar to Standard, with Simmons floating rib, beavertail forearm. Mfg. 1971-1973 by Marlin.

$995	$825	$725	$600	$495	$400	$350

SMITH & WESSON

Current manufacturer located in Springfield, MA 1857 to date. Partnership with H. Smith & D.B. Wesson 1856-1874. Family owned by Wesson 1874-1965. S & W became a subsidiary of Bangor-Punta from 1965-1983. Between 1983-1987, Smith & Wesson was owned by the Lear Siegler Co. On May 22, 1987, Smith & Wesson was sold to Tompkins, an English holding company.

Smith&Wesson

Smith & Wessons have been classified under the following category names - TIP-UPS, TOP-BREAKS, SINGLE SHOTS, EARLY HAND EJECTORS (Named Models), NUMBERED MODEL REVOLVERS (Modern Hand Ejectors), SEMI-AUTOS, RIFLES, and SHOTGUNS.

Each category is fairly self-explanatory. Among the early revolvers, Tip-ups have barrels that tip up so the cylinder can be removed for loading or unloading, whereas Top-breaks have barrels & cylinders that tip down with automatic ejection.

Hand Ejectors are the modern type revolvers with swing out cylinders. In 1958 S&W began a system of numbering all models they made. Accordingly, the Hand Ejectors have been divided into two sections - the Early Hand Ejectors include the named models introduced prior to 1958. The Numbered Model Revolvers are the models introduced or continued after that date, and are easily identified by the model number stamped on the front of the frame, visible when the cylinder is open. The author wishes to express his thanks to Mr. Roy Jinks, the S&W Historian, for his updates and valuable contributions. Mr. Jim Supica and W. R. Powell are to be thanked for the revised format.

Factory special orders, such as ivory or pearl grips, special finishes, engraving, and other production rarities will add premiums to the values listed below.

100%	98%	95%	90%	80%	70%	60%	50%	40%	30%	20%	10%

TIP-UPS

Spur-trigger rimfires, these include the earliest S&W revolvers, made 1857-1881. A latch at the bottom front of the frame allows the hinged barrel to be tipped up and the cylinder removed for loading and unloading. These pistols are listed in order of model number (1, 1½, 2).

MODEL NO. 1 FIRST ISSUE TIP-UP — .22 Short cal., single action, 7 shot non-fluted cylinder, 3³⁄₁₆ in. octagon barrel, bottom break, spur trigger, silver-plated brass frame, blue barrel and cylinder, square rosewood grips, circular sideplate, cross-section of frame is oval with rounded frame sides. 11,671 mfg. 1857-1860.

* *First Type* — serial range approx. 1-200.

100%	98%	95%	90%	80%	70%	60%	50%	40%	30%	20%	10%
N/A	$15,000	$13,750	$12,000	$10,500	$9,500	$8,250	$7,000	$5,750	$4,500	$3,750	$3,000

* *Second Type* — serial range approx. 200-1130.

100%	98%	95%	90%	80%	70%	60%	50%	40%	30%	20%	10%
$6,000	$5,450	$4,500	$3,500	$2,750	$2,100	$1,900	$1,750	$1,600	$1,450	$1,300	$1,150

* *Third Type* — serial range approx. 1130-3000.

100%	98%	95%	90%	80%	70%	60%	50%	40%	30%	20%	10%
$2,950	$2,600	$2,275	$1,925	$1,750	$1,600	$1,500	$1,400	$1,300	$1,200	$1,100	$1,025

* *Fourth Type* — serial range approx. 3000-4200.

100%	98%	95%	90%	80%	70%	60%	50%	40%	30%	20%	10%
$2,300	$1,850	$1,700	$1,600	$1,450	$1,300	$1,200	$1,125	$1,050	$975	$925	$900

100%	98%	95%	90%	80%	70%	60%	50%	40%	30%	20%	10%

* **Fifth Type** — serial range approx. 4200-5500.

$2,300	$1,950	$1,700	$1,600	$1,450	$1,300	$1,200	$1,125	$1,050	$975	$925	$900

* **Sixth Type** — serial range approx. 5500-11,671.

$2,150	$1,800	$1,550	$1,450	$1,300	$1,175	$1,075	$1,000	$925	$875	8215	$800

MODEL NO. 1 SECOND ISSUE TIP-UP — similar to First Issue, except flat sided frame and irregular shaped sideplate. 117,000 mfg. 1860-1868. Serial range approx. 11,672- approx. 128,000.

$950	$875	$825	$650	$550	$500	$425	$400	$375	$350	$325	$300

* **Second Quality** — is marked on approx. 4,402 revolvers.

$1,250	$1,100	$1,000	$925	$850	$775	$700	$625	$575	$525	$475	$435

MODEL NO. 1 THIRD ISSUE TIP-UP — similar to Second Issue, except fluted cylinder, round barrel, and birdshead grip. 131,163 mfg. 1868-1881. This model has its own serial range no. 1-131,163.

* **3³/₁₆ in. barrel Model.** — will have markings on top of barrel.

$475	$435	$400	$375	$350	$325	$300	$275	$250	$225	$200	$175

* **Short barrels 2¹¹/₁₆ - 2³/₄ in.** — will have markings on side of barrel.

$900	$850	$775	$720	$680	$640	$600	$560	$520	$480	$440	$400

MODEL NO. 1½ FIRST ISSUE TIP-UP — .32 rimfire, single action, 3½ or 4 (rare) in. octagon barrel, 5 shot non-fluted cylinder, bottom break, spur trigger, blue or nickel, rosewood grips, square butt. 26,300 mfg. 1865-1868. Serial range 1- approx. 26,300.

$575	$500	$435	$375	$325	$300	$275	$250	$225	$210	$195	$185

* **4 in. barrel**

$3,500	$3,150	$2,750	$2,300	$1,950	$1,650	$1,450	1,250	$1,050	$900	$775	$650

    Watch for fakes (i.e. stretched barrels).

MODEL NO. 1½ SECOND ISSUE TIP-UP — similar to First Issue, with birdshead grips and round barrel. 100,700 mfg. 1868-1875. Serial range 26,301-127,100.

* **2½ in. barrel model** — barrel markings on side, length varies from 2½-2¾ in. (scarce).

$800	$650	$600	$550	$500	$425	$400	$375	$350	$325	$300	$250

* **3½ in. barrel model**

$425	$385	$335	$300	$275	$250	$225	$200	$180	$165	$150	$135

* **Transitional Model** — octagon barrel with birdshead grips, serial range 27,200-28,800, rare.

$2,000	$1,750	$1,525	$1,425	$1,350	$1,275	$1,200	$1,125	$1,075	$1,000	$950	$900

MODEL NO. 2 ARMY TIP-UP — .32 rimfire long, similar in appearance to No. 1½ First Issue, except 6 shot cylinder, different barrel lengths, used as a sidearm during Civil War. 77,155 mfg. 1861-1874. Serial number range 1-77,155.

* **5 or 6 in. Early Model** — referred to as 2-pin variation, serial range 1-3,000.

$1,950	$1,750	$1,550	$1,375	$1,225	$1,125	$1,025	$925	$825	$750	$675	$600

* **5 or 6 in. Standard Model** — remainder of serial range.

$1,375	$1,225	$1,100	$1,000	$900	$800	$700	$625	$525	$450	$400	$375

* **4 in. Barrel Model**

$4,000	$3,775	$3,400	$3,000	$2,600	$2,300	$2,000	$1,850	$1,600	$1,400	$1,200	$1,000

    Note: Watch for fakes on 4 in. model.

TOP-BREAKS

These revolvers have a latch just in front of the hammer, and the barrel & cylinder tip down, with an automatic extractor ejecting the shells when the gun is opened. Mfg 1870-1940, they include single action (spur-trigger or trigger guard), double action, and safety hammerless designs. They are listed in order of frame size. Model 1-1½ is the smallest or .32 cal. sized frame; Model 2 is the medium or .38 cal. sized frame; Model 3

100%	98%	95%	90%	80%	70%	60%	50%	40%	30%	20%	10%

is the large or .44 cal. frame. Within each frame size, they are listed by action type - SA, DA, or "Hammerless", as may be applicable.

Changes from one Top-Break model type to another are not necessarily definitive at a specific serial number - therefore, an overlap of serial numbers from one model to another may be observed.

.32 SINGLE ACTION — .32 S&W cal., spur trigger, top break, rebounding hammer, auto extraction. 97,574 mfg. 1878-1892. Serial range 1-97,574.

* ***Early Model*** — without strain screw, serial range 1-6,500.

| $435 | $390 | $350 | $315 | $285 | $255 | $225 | $195 | $170 | $145 | $125 | $110 |

* ***Later Model*** — with strain screw, remainder of serial range.

| $375 | $330 | $295 | $265 | $230 | $205 | $180 | $155 | $135 | $125 | $115 | $100 |

* ***8 or 10 in. barrel*** — mfg. circa 1887-88, very rare.

| $3,000 | $2,600 | $2,200 | $1,800 | $1,600 | $1,475 | $1,350 | $1,225 | $1,000 | $1,000 | $900 | $800 |

.32 DOUBLE ACTION FIRST MODEL TOP BREAK — .32 S&W cal., 5 shot fluted cylinder, 3 in. round barrel, square edged side plate, blue or nickel finish, black rubber grips, one of the rarest of all S&Ws. Only 30 mfg. 1880. Serial range 1-30.

| N/A | $9,950 | $9,400 | $8,600 | $8,000 | $7,400 | $6,650 | $5,950 | $5,000 | $4,100 | $3,350 | $2,500 |

.32 DOUBLE ACTION SECOND MODEL — similar to First Model, except irregular shaped sideplate, 3, 3¼, 4, 5, or 6 in. barrel, 22,142 mfg. 1880-1882. Serial range 31-22,172.

| $475 | $425 | $380 | $340 | $300 | $260 | $220 | $180 | $150 | $120 | $100 | $90 |

.32 DOUBLE ACTION THIRD MODEL — similar to Second Model, except without groove around cylinder. 22,232 mfg. 1882-1883. Serial range 22,173-43,405.

| $475 | $425 | $380 | $340 | $300 | $260 | $220 | $180 | $150 | $120 | $100 | $90 |

.32 DOUBLE ACTION FOURTH MODEL — similar to Third Model, except rounded trigger-guard. 239,600 mfg. 1883-1909. Serial range 43,406-approx. 282,999.

| $345 | $305 | $270 | $240 | $210 | $185 | $160 | $135 | $115 | $100 | $90 | $85 |

An 8 or 10 in. barrel on this model will command a premium.

.32 DOUBLE ACTION FIFTH MODEL — similar to Fourth Model, except integral front sight. 44,641 mfg. 1909-1919. Serial range approx. 282,300-327,641.

| $375 | $335 | $300 | $270 | $240 | $215 | $190 | $165 | $135 | $120 | $105 | $90 |

.32 SAFETY HAMMERLESS FIRST MODEL TOP BREAK — .32 S&W cal., 5 shot fluted cylinder, 2, 3 (most common), 3½, or 6 (rare) in. round barrel, blue or nickel, black rubber grips. This model was dubbed New Departure at the time. 91,417 mfg. 1888-1902. Serial range 1-91,417.

Short 2 in. barrel versions known as "Bicycle model" will bring 25% to 50% premium on all Lemon Squeezers. Six inch barrels will bring a premium as well.

* ***Standard Model*** — 2, 3, or 3½ in. barrel.

| $500 | $475 | $450 | $425 | $400 | $375 | $350 | $325 | $275 | $235 | $185 | $150 |

.32 SAFETY HAMMERLESS SECOND MODEL — 2, 3, 3½, or 6 in. barrel. 78,500 mfg. 1902-1909. Serial range 91,418-170,000.

| $450 | $425 | $400 | $375 | $350 | $325 | $300 | $275 | $235 | $200 | $165 | $130 |

.32 SAFETY HAMMERLESS THIRD MODEL — 2, 3, 3½, or 6 in. barrel. 73,000 mfg. 1909-1937. Serial range 163,082-242,981 (with some overlap from the Second Model).

| $450 | $425 | $400 | $375 | $350 | $325 | $300 | $275 | $235 | $200 | $165 | $130 |

.38 SINGLE ACTION FIRST MODEL (BABY RUSSIAN) TOP BREAK SPUR TRIGGER — .38 S&W cal., 5 shot fluted cylinder, 3¼ or 4 in. barrel, blue with wood grips, nickel with "S&W" monogram hard black or red rubber grips. 25,548 mfg. 1876-1877. Serial range 1-25,548.

* ***Standard Model***

| $625 | $525 | $450 | $400 | $365 | $330 | $295 | $260 | $235 | $200 | $185 | $150 |

* ***Very Early Model*** — with early hammer style safety latch (up to approx. ser. no. 100).

| $2,500 | $2,250 | $2,000 | $1,750 | $1,450 | $1,150 | $950 | $800 | $700 | $600 | $500 | $400 |

This type of hammer configuration is called the "Aldrich" model.

100%	98%	95%	90%	80%	70%	60%	50%	40%	30%	20%	10%

* **Early Model** — has two screws to hold sideplate (up to approx. ser. no. 2,550).

| $735 | $625 | $550 | $500 | $465 | $425 | $390 | $355 | $320 | $285 | $250 | $235 |

.38 SINGLE ACTION SECOND MODEL — similar to above, except very short ejector housing under barrel, cal. and cylinder same as above, 3¼, 4, 5, 6, 8, or 10 in. barrel, grips same as above. 108,225 mfg. 1877-1891. Serial range 1-108,255.

* **Standard Model**

| $335 | $275 | $235 | $200 | $185 | $160 | $150 | $140 | $130 | $125 | $120 | $115 |

* **8 or 10 in. Barrel**

| $2,500 | $2,200 | $1,800 | $1,575 | $1,375 | $1,200 | $1,050 | $950 | $850 | $775 | $700 | $650 |

S

.38 SINGLE ACTION THIRD MODEL (MODEL OF 1891) — similar to above, except has trigger guard, cal. and cylinder same as above, 3½, 4, 5, or 6 in. barrel (also accepts the single shot barrel), blue or nickel finish with "S&W" monogram, hard black rubber grips. 26,850 mfg. 1891-1911. Serial range 1-28,107 which also includes the serial number range of the Single Shot First Model in .22 LR, .32 S&W, .38 S&W cal. and the .38 S.A. Mexican Model described below. Barrel marked "Model of 1891".

| $1,800 | $1,650 | $1,425 | $1,250 | $1,075 | $950 | $850 | $775 | $700 | $625 | $550 | $475 |

Add 50%-75% for single shot barrel with matching serial number.

.38 SINGLE ACTION MEXICAN MODEL — essentially same as above, except has inserted spur trigger, .38 S&W cal., 5 shot fluted cylinder, 3¼, 4, 5, or 6 in. barrel, blue or nickel finish, "S&W" monogram checkered hard rubber or walnut grips. Features unique to this model are flat sided hammer, half cock notch, and "inserted" spur trigger assembly (not integral with frame). This model would also accept the single shot barrel, limited mfg. 1891-1911. Serial range described above. Watch out for fakes (and conversions)!

| $2,875 | $2,550 | $2,250 | $2,000 | $1,750 | $1,550 | $1,400 | $1,250 | $1,150 | $1,050 | $975 | $950 |

Add 50%-75% for single shot barrel with matching serial number.

.38 DOUBLE ACTION FIRST MODEL TOP BREAK — .38 S&W cal., 5 shot fluted cylinder, 3¼ or 4 in. barrel, blue or nickel finish, "S&W" monogram checkered hard rubber grips. 4,000 mfg. 1880. Serial range 1-4,000.

| $900 | $850 | $750 | $650 | $550 | $475 | $400 | $325 | $250 | $200 | $175 | $150 |

.38 DOUBLE ACTION SECOND MODEL — .38 S&W cal., cylinder same as above, 3¼, 4, 5, or 6 in. barrel, blue or nickel finish, "S&W" monogram checkered hard rubber grips in black or red. 115,000 mfg. 1880-1884. Serial range approx. 4,001-approx. 119,000.

| $350 | $300 | $250 | $225 | $200 | $185 | $170 | $165 | $160 | $145 | $135 | $125 |

.38 DOUBLE ACTION THIRD MODEL — .38 S&W cal., cylinder same as above, 3¼, 4, 5, 6, 8, or 10 in. barrel, blue or nickel finish, "S&W" monogram hard rubber grips. 203,700 mfg. 1884-1895. Serial range approx. 119,001-322,700.

| $325 | $265 | $225 | $200 | $190 | $175 | $160 | $155 | $150 | $140 | $125 | $115 |

* **8 or 10 in. Barrel**

| $2,150 | $1,850 | $1,600 | $1,400 | $1,250 | $1,125 | $1,000 | $900 | $800 | $700 | $600 | $535 |

A 2 in. variation, while extremely rare, was manufactured in the Third Model, Fourth Model, Fifth Model, and Perfected Models listed below. Large premiums do exist ($850-$1,500) - watch for fakes!

.38 DOUBLE ACTION FOURTH MODEL — .38 S&W cal., cylinder same as above, 3¼, 4, 5, or 6 in. barrel, blue or nickel finish, "S&W" monogram checkered hard rubber grips, also offered in an extended square butt target style. 216,300 mfg. 1895-1901. Serial range 322,701-539,000.

| $325 | $270 | $230 | $200 | $185 | $170 | $155 | $150 | $145 | $135 | $120 | $110 |

.38 DOUBLE ACTION FIFTH MODEL — .38 S&W cal., cylinder, barrel, and grip specifications same as above with the additional availability of an extended square butt target style walnut grip as an accessory. 15,000 mfg. 1909-1911. Serial range approx. 539,001-554,077.

| $500 | $465 | $425 | $375 | $325 | $285 | $250 | $225 | $200 | $180 | $150 | $125 |

100%	98%	95%	90%	80%	70%	60%	50%	40%	30%	20%	10%

.38 DOUBLE ACTION PERFECTED MODEL TOP BREAK — .38 S&W cal., cylinder, change in frame incorporates rolled I frame revolver and lockwork, trigger guard is integral part of frame, and side plate is on right side - not left side. The last of the S&W break open revolvers. 59,400 mfg. 1909-1920. Serial range 1-59,400. Identified by having both top latch and side latch.

$500	$465	$425	$375	$325	$285	$250	$225	$200	$180	$150	$125

This model was mfg. with 2 latches (side latch and top latch).

* *.38 Double Action Perfected Model Top Latch Only* — as above, except no side latch - rare.

$1,250	$1,125	$975	$850	$750	$650	$550	$440	$350	$275	$235	$200

.38 SAFETY HAMMERLESS FIRST MODEL (.38 NEW DEPARTURE) TOP BREAK — .38 S&W cal., 5 shot fluted cylinder, 3¼, 4, 5, or 6 in. barrel, blue or nickel finish, "S&W" monogram checkered hard rubber grips, features "Z-Bar" latch. Approx. 5,000 mfg. in 1887. Serial range 1-5,001.

$750	$685	$615	$550	$485	$435	$375	$325	$275	$250	$225	$150

Add 25% for blue finish.

* *6 in. Barrel*

$1,450	$1,200	$1,025	$900	$790	$675	$565	$490	$425	$375	$340	$310

.38 SAFETY HAMMERLESS SECOND MODEL — .38 S&W cal., cylinder same as above, 3¼, 4, or 5 in. barrel, finish and grips same as above. 37,350 mfg. 1887-1890. Serial range approx. 5,001-42,483.

$500	$465	$425	$375	$325	$285	$250	$225	$200	$180	$150	$125

U.S. MARTIALLY MARKED — 100 purchased by Govt. in 1890, serial range 41,333-41,470, serial numbers in Second Model range, but are true Third Models.

$5,000	$4,650	$4,400	$4,050	$3,750	$3,500	$3,300	$3,150	$2,950	$2,750	$2,550	$2,350

Beware of fakes!

.38 SAFETY HAMMERLESS THIRD MODEL — .38 S&W cal., cylinder same as above, 3¼, 4, 5, or 6 in. barrel, finish and grips same as above. 73,500 mfg. 1890-1898. Serial range 24,284-116,002.

$400	$375	$330	$300	$275	$250	$225	$200	$175	$150	$135	$110

.38 SAFETY HAMMERLESS FOURTH MODEL — .38 S&W cal., cylinder, barrel lengths, finishes and grips same as above. 104,000 mfg. 1898-1907. Serial range 116,003 to approx. 220,000.

$340	$280	$240	$205	$190	$165	$155	$145	$135	$125	$115	$100

A 2 in. barrel in this variation is rare (Bicycle Model).

.38 SAFETY HAMMERLESS FIFTH MODEL — .38 S&W cal., cylinder same as above, 2, 3¼, 4, 5, or 6 in. barrel, blue or nickel finish, "S&W" monogram checkered hard rubber or checkered walnut grips. 41,500 mfg. 1907-1940. Serial range 220,000-261,493.

$340	$280	$240	$205	$190	$165	$155	$145	$135	$125	$115	$100

* *2 in. Barrel*

$825	$750	$670	$635	$575	$540	$505	$480	$455	$432	$410	$390

MODEL 3 AMERICAN FIRST MODEL — .44 S&W or .44 rimfire Henry cal., single action, 6 shot fluted cylinder, 6, 7, or 8 in. round barrel, blue or nickel finish, walnut grips. 8,000 mfg. 1870-1872. Serial range 1-approx. 8,000.

* *Standard Model* — vent. hole in extractor housing, first 1,500 mfg.

N/A	$7,000	$6,000	$4,500	$3,700	$3,175	$2,750	$2,500	$2,250	$2,000	$1,750	$1,500

* *Standard Model* — without hole in extractor.

N/A	$5,000	$3,750	$3,000	$2,550	$2,250	$2,150	$1,850	$1,650	$1,450	$1,250	$1,100

* *Transitional Model* — includes locking notch on hammer, shorter cylinder, serial range 6,700-8,000.

N/A	$5,200	$3,850	$3,250	$2,900	$2,650	$2,250	$2,150	$1,850	$1,650	$1,450	$1,200

* *.44 Rimfire Henry* — limited mfg. Watch for fakes!

N/A	$8,250	$7,000	$6,000	$5,000	$4,000	$3,750	$3,500	$3,250	$3,000	$2,750	$2,500

* *U.S. Marked* — approx. 1,000 mfg.

N/A	$12,000	$10,750	$9,100	$8,100	$7,250	$6,500	$5,900	$5,375	$4,850	$4,450	$4,000

100%	98%	95%	90%	80%	70%	60%	50%	40%	30%	20%	10%

* *Nashville Police* — very rare, only 32 manufactured. Scarcity precludes accurate pricing.

MODEL 3 SECOND MODEL AMERICAN — .44 S&W or .44 rimfire Henry cal., single action, 6 shot fluted cylinder, 5½, 6, 6½, 7, or 8 in. barrel, blue or nickel, walnut grips. 19,635 mfg. 1872-1874, serial range approx. 8,000-32,800 which includes commercial version of Model 3 Russian First Model.

* *Standard Model* — .44 S&W American cal., 8 in. barrel.

| N/A | $4,750 | $3,750 | $3,250 | $2,750 | $2,250 | $2,150 | $1,850 | $1,650 | $1,450 | $1,250 | $1,100 |

Add 35% for 5½, 6, 6½, or 7 in. barrel.

* *Standard Model .44 Rimfire Henry* — 6, 7, or 8 in. barrel, 3,014 mfg.

| N/A | $5,850 | $4,750 | $3,750 | $3,525 | $3,050 | $2,650 | $2,250 | $2,150 | $1,850 | $1,650 | $1,450 |

MODEL 3 RUSSIAN FIRST MODEL (OLD RUSSIAN) — .44 S&W Russian, 5½, 6, 7, or 8 in. barrel, Russian contract 8 in., blue or nickel finish, walnut grips, looks similar to First and Second Model American. 5,165 mfg. 1871-1874 for commercial sale and 20,014 for Russian Contract (separate ser. no. range). Serial range 6,000-32,800, see Model 3 Second Model American.

* *Commercial Version* — 4,665 mfg.

| N/A | $4,750 | $3,750 | $3,250 | $2,750 | $2,250 | $2,150 | $1,850 | $1,650 | $1,450 | $1,250 | $1,100 |

* *Reject Russian Contract* — 500 mfg. Serial range 1-approx. 500.

| N/A | $4,750 | $3,750 | $3,250 | $2,750 | $2,250 | $2,150 | $1,850 | $1,650 | $1,450 | $1,250 | $1,100 |

* *Russian Contract* — 20,014 mfg., rare, most sent to Russia, cyrillic marked. Serial range 1-approx. 20,014.

| N/A | N/A | $6,750 | $5,975 | $5,125 | $4,450 | $3,800 | $3,350 | $2,950 | $2,600 | $2,250 | $2,000 |

MODEL 3 RUSSIAN SECOND MODEL (OLD RUSSIAN) — 2nd and 3rd Model Russians have an extreme knuckle at the top of backstrap and trigger guard spur, 85,200 mfg. in all variations between 1873-78, 7 in. barrel, small screw in top-strap of frame, features longer ejector housing and "Russian Model" marking on top of barrel. Ser. nos. started at 32,800.

* *Commercial Version* — 6,200 mfg.

| N/A | $3,750 | $3,000 | $2,375 | $2,000 | $1,750 | $1,500 | $1,300 | $1,100 | $995 | $895 | $795 |

* *.44 Rimfire Henry* — approx. 500 mfg.

| N/A | $5,000 | $4,500 | $4,000 | $3,525 | $3,050 | $2,650 | $2,250 | $2,150 | $1,850 | $1,650 | $1,500 |

* *Russian Contract* — approx. 70,000 mfg. for Russian Military contract, cryllic marked, rare in U.S.

| N/A | N/A | $3,150 | $2,850 | $2,525 | $2,275 | $2,100 | $1,950 | $1,800 | $1,650 | $1,500 | $1,350 |

* *Turkish Model* — 1,000 mfg. in their own serial number range in .44 Rimfire. This is probably the rarest and most valuable variation.

| N/A | N/A | $5,000 | $4,500 | $4,000 | $3,600 | $3,250 | $2,900 | $2,675 | $2,475 | $2,250 | $2,000 |

This model was converted to rimfire from .44 S&W Russian cal.

* *Japanese Contract* — usually marked with an anchor.

| N/A | N/A | $3,200 | $2,600 | $2,300 | $2,050 | $1,825 | $1,650 | $1,500 | $1,375 | $1,250 | $1,175 |

MODEL 3 RUSSIAN THIRD MODEL — commonly called the "New Model Russian" and is similar to old model, except has shorter extractor housing, 6½ in. barrel, large knurled screw in top-strap of frame, shorter ejector housing, approx. 60,600 mfg. between 1874 and 1878. Values are similar to old model for comparable variations. In addition, the Tula Arsenal in Russia also mfg. 300,000-400,000 pistols for domestic use and Ludwig & Loewe in Germany mfg. 100,000.

* *Commercial Version* — approx. 13,500 mfg.

| N/A | $3,750 | $3,000 | $2,375 | $2,000 | $1,750 | $1,500 | $1,300 | $1,100 | $995 | $895 | $795 |

* *.44 Rimfire Henry*

| N/A | $5,000 | $4,500 | $4,000 | $3,525 | $3,050 | $2,650 | $2,250 | $2,150 | $1,850 | $1,650 | $1,500 |

100%	98%	95%	90%	80%	70%	60%	50%	40%	30%	20%	10%

* **Russian Contract** — 41,138 mfg. Cyrillic lettering.

100%	98%	95%	90%	80%	70%	60%	50%	40%	30%	20%	10%
N/A	$3,500	$3,200	$2,900	$2,650	$2,400	$2,200	$2,000	$1,775	$1,575	$1,325	$1,100

* **Ludwig & Loewe, & Tula Copies** — copies mfg. for the Russian government.

N/A	$2,800	$2,500	$2,250	$2,000	$1,800	$1,625	$1,475	$1,350	$1,225	$1,100	$950

Add 50% for Tula copies.

* **Turkish Contract** — 5,000 mfg., utilizes .44 Russian cylinder - chambered for .44 Rimfire.

N/A	$4,000	$3,700	$3,425	$3,100	$2,850	$2,575	$2,325	$2,025	$1,700	$1,425	$1,200

* **Japanese Contract** — 1,000 made.

N/A	$3,800	$3,150	$2,300	$2,000	$1,750	$1,500	$1,300	$1,225	$1,100	$950	$800

NEW MODEL NO. 3 — features very short extractor housing under the barrel, knuckle on backstrap is less pronounced than 2nd and 3rd Models, 35,796 mfg. between 1878-1912.

* **Commercial Version** — 3½, 4, 5, 6, 6½, 7, or 8 in. barrel, .44 Russian cal.

$4,000	$3,150	$2,500	$2,000	$1,800	$1,625	$1,475	$1,325	$1,175	$995	$795	$695

Add 40% if cut for shoulder stock.
Add 50% for shoulder stock.
Add 10% for factory target sights.

Early model has rack and gear extractor and will bring a premium over the later mfg. Also, premiums do exist for all but 6 and 6½ in. barrel lengths; premiums for unusual chamberings.

* **Japanese Navy Model** — Japan purchased approx. ⅓ of total production.

$4,000	$3,150	$2,500	$2,000	$1,800	$1,625	$1,475	$1,325	$1,175	$995	$795	$695

Add 50% for Japanese markings.

* **Australian Model** — 7 in. barrel, detachable stock, for Australian Colonial Police, broad arrow marking on both pistol and stock, stocks were originally numbered to the matching pistol, but are seldom seen with matching numbers today, approx. 250 mfg., usually found in the low 12,000 - low 13,000 ser. no. range.

N/A	$8,000	$7,600	$7,000	$6,350	$5,750	$5,000	$4,250	$3,650	$3,150	$2,650	$2,350

Prices are with stock.

* **Argentine Model** — unknown total production, marked "Ejercito Argentina" (very rare).

N/A	$5,000	$4,500	$4,050	$3,750	$3,450	$3,150	$2,850	$2,550	$2,375	$2,175	$2,000

* **State of Maryland Model** — U.S. marked, serial number range 7,126-7,405.

$8,000	$7,000	$6,000	$5,000	$4,600	$4,150	$3,850	$3,600	$3,250	$2,900	$2,675	$2,475

NEW MODEL NO. 3 FRONTIER — .44-40 WCF cal., single action, 4, 5, or 6½ in. barrel, blue or nickel finish, walnut or hard rubber grips. 2,072 mfg. 1885-1908.

* **Japanese Purchase** — 786 converted to .44 Russian cal., cylinder should measure 1⁹⁄₁₆ in., in the Frontier serial range of 1-2,072.

$4,100	$3,250	$2,550	$2,000	$1,800	$1,625	$1,475	$1,325	$1,175	$995	$795	$695

* **Standard Model** — .44-40 WCF cal.

$5,000	$4,000	$3,500	$3,000	$2,500	$2,250	$2,000	$1,850	$1,600	$1,400	$1,250	$1,100

NEW MODEL NO. 3 - .38-40 WCF. — separate ser. range, only 74 mfg., ser. no. 1-74.

N/A	N/A	$6,000	$5,500	$4,950	$4,575	$3,925	$3,500	$3,150	$2,750	$2,375	$2,000

NEW MODEL NO. 3 TARGET MODEL — .32-44 S&W or .38-44 S&W cal., 4,333 mfg. between 1887-1910.

$3,750	$3,250	$2,500	$2,250	$1,925	$1,700	$1,500	$1,350	$1,100	$950	$800	$700

NEW MODEL NO. 3 TURKISH — .44 rimfire cal., 5,461 mfg. between 1879-1888, in separate serial number series.

$5,400	$5,025	$4,675	$4,350	$4,050	$3,750	$3,450	$3,150	$2,850	$2,550	$2,275	$1,950

MODEL 3 SCHOFIELD FIRST MODEL — .45 S&W cal., single action, 7 in. barrel, 6 shot fluted cylinder, blue finish only, walnut grips, 3,035 mfg. 1875.

100%	98%	95%	90%	80%	70%	60%	50%	40%	30%	20%	10%

S

* **U.S. Issue** — 3,000 mfg.

| N/A | $6,000 | $5,000 | $4,500 | $4,000 | $3,650 | $3,350 | $3,050 | $2,750 | $2,500 | $2,250 | $2,000 |

* **Commercial Model (not U.S. marked)** — 35 were produced without U.S. markings, very rare - beware of fakes - there could be more phony ones than real ones.

| $15,000 | $14,150 | $13,250 | $12,000 | $10,500 | $8,950 | $7,500 | $6,150 | $5,350 | $4,900 | $4,500 | $4,000 |

* **Wells Fargo and Company** — barrel cut to approx. 5 in. with Wells Fargo markings.

| N/A | N/A | N/A | N/A | $5,750 | $5,100 | $4,550 | $4,175 | $3,750 | $3,350 | $3,050 | $2,750 |

Warning - Beware of fakes! There may be more fake Wells Fargo Schofields than authentic ones. While most fakes are usually poor quality, others may be quite impressive.

Many Schofields are found with cut 5 in. barrels and no Wells Fargo marking - these will bring approx. 66% of uncut values or if they have fake WF markings their value is ½ of the uncut values.

MODEL 3 SCHOFIELD SECOND MODEL

* **Standard Model** — U.S. on butt.

| N/A | $6,000 | $5,000 | $4,350 | $3,950 | $3,525 | $3,250 | $3,000 | $2,750 | $2,600 | $2,430 | $2,200 |

* **Commercial Model** — blue or nickel finish, nickel finish was done at a later date by the factory, 650 mfg.

| N/A | $7,500 | $6,500 | $5,250 | $4,500 | $4,000 | $3,500 | $3,250 | $3,350 | $3,050 | $2,750 | $2,450 |

* **Wells Fargo and Company** — barrel cut to 5 in. with Wells Fargo markings.

| N/A | N/A | N/A | N/A | $5,750 | $5,100 | $4,550 | $4,175 | $3,750 | $3,350 | $3,050 | $2,750 |

Warning - Beware of fakes! There may be more fake Wells Fargo Schofields than authentic ones. While most fakes are usually poor quality, others may be quite impressive.

Many Schofields are found with cut 5 in. barrels and no Wells Fargo marking - these will bring approx. 66% of uncut values or if they have fake WF markings their value is ½ of the uncut values.

.44 DOUBLE ACTION FIRST MODEL — .32-44 (rare), .38-44 (rare), .38 Military (rare), .44 S&W Russian (most common), and .455 (rare) cal. 6 shot fluted cylinder, 4, 5, 6, or 6½ in. barrel, blue or nickel finish, "S&W" monogram checkered hard rubber or walnut grips. Walnut grips with "S&W" inlays will be found after 1900. 53,668 mfg. 1881-1913. Serial range 1-54,668.

Add 100% for cals. other than .44 S&W Russian on sub-models listed below.

* **Standard Model** — all barrel lengths and 1⁷⁄₁₆ in. cylinder.

| $3,000 | $1,900 | $1,500 | $1,275 | $1,000 | $925 | $825 | $695 | $650 | $575 | $475 | $375 |

* **Standard Model** — similar to above, except has 1⁹⁄₁₆ in. late production cylinder.

| $3,000 | $1,900 | $1,500 | $1,275 | $1,000 | $925 | $825 | $695 | $650 | $575 | $475 | $375 |

* **.44 Double Action Wesson Favorite** — similar to Standard Model, but in 5 in. barrel only with special front sight, blue nickel finish, patent markings are on the cylinder rather than on the barrel, grooved barrel rib, external and internal lightening cuts to reduce weight. Approx. 1,000 mfg. 1882-1883. Ser. range included with .44 Double Action First Model, between approx. 8,900-10,100.

| $7,600 | $6,670 | $5,995 | $5,360 | $4,750 | $4,170 | $3,600 | $3,200 | $2,825 | $2,500 | $2,275 | $2,000 |

Add 30-40% for blue finish.

.38 WIN. DOUBLE ACTION — .38-40 WCF cal., 4, 5, 6, or 6½ in. barrel, only 276 mfg. in separate ser. range 1-276.

| $3,550 | $3,155 | $2,780 | $2,200 | $1,970 | $1,825 | $1,700 | $1,500 | $1,400 | $1,300 | $1,225 | $1,125 |

.44 DOUBLE ACTION FRONTIER — .44-40 WCF cal., 4, 5, 6, or 6½ in. barrel, only 15,340 mfg. in separate ser. range 1-15,340.

| $3,100 | $1,900 | $1,500 | $1,275 | $1,000 | $925 | $825 | $695 | $650 | $575 | $475 | $375 |

Add 100% for factory target sights.

SINGLE SHOTS

FIRST MODEL — .22 LR, .32 S&W, or .38 S&W cal., 6, 8, or 10 in. barrel, blue or nickel, hard rubber grips. 1,251 mfg. 1893-1905, ser. range (same as Third Model 38 Single Action) 1-28,107.

100%	98%	95%	90%	80%	70%	60%	50%	40%	30%	20%	10%

* .22 LR — approx. 862 mfg.

| $800 | $700 | $625 | $575 | $525 | $475 | $425 | $375 | $350 | $325 | $300 | $285 |

* .32 S&W — approx. 229 mfg.

| $950 | $850 | $775 | $700 | $650 | $600 | $550 | $500 | $450 | $400 | $350 | $335 |

* .38 S&W — approx. 160 mfg.

| $1,075 | $950 | $850 | $775 | $725 | $675 | $625 | $575 | $525 | $475 | $425 | $395 |

SECOND MODEL .22 LR — similar to First Model, but will not accommodate a revolver cylinder, flatsided frame (does not have recoil shield) 10 in. barrel only, 4,617 mfg. 1905-1909. Ser. range 1-4,617.

| $750 | $675 | $625 | $575 | $525 | $475 | $425 | $375 | $325 | $280 | $250 | $225 |

THIRD MODEL .22 S (PERFECTED MODEL) — similar to Second Model, except is built on "I" solid frame with integral trigger guard, side plate on right side, made both single or double action. 6,949 mfg. 1909-1923. Serial range 4,618-11,641.

| $725 | $650 | $600 | $550 | $500 | $450 | $400 | $350 | $300 | $265 | $235 | $210 |

Add 30% for Olympic Model in extra short .22 LR rifle chamber.

STRAIGHT LINE TARGET SINGLE SHOT —.22 LR cal., single shot, 10 in. barrel, sideswing barrel, blue, target sights, smooth walnut grips, shaped like an autoloader. 1,870 mfg. 1925-1936. Ser. range 1-1,870. Values below assume case.

| $1,275 | $1,100 | $950 | $850 | $750 | $650 | $550 | $450 | $415 | $350 | $335 | $315 |

Subtract 30% w/o case.

EARLY HAND EJECTORS (NAMED MODELS)

Named Models. 1896-1958. Listed in order of caliber, except where newer mfg. might also include model number. These will NOT have any model number stamped on the frame. Several were continued after 1958 as Numbered Models, so be sure to check that section as well.

.22/.32 HAND EJECTOR (ALSO KNOWN AS .22/32 BEKEART MODEL) — .22 LR cal., 6 shot fluted cylinder, 6 in. barrel, blued, checkered walnut grips with "S&W" medallions, extension style square butt, there were several hundred thousand of the standard .22/.32 Hand Ejector mfg. The first 3,000 mfg. will be found with a separate ser. no. (1-3,000) stamped into the bottom of the wood grips.

* Bekeart Model — will be found with separate identification number on bottom of wooden grip. Serial numbers for early Bekeart models start at 138,226.

| $1,075 | $875 | $750 | $650 | $550 | $450 | $350 | $275 | $200 | $150 | $135 | $110 |

Slight premiums are charged over the values listed above for early production in lower ser. no. range with grip models 1,001-3,000.

This model was specifically mfg. for a San Francisco retailer, Philip Bekeart. Originally, Mr. Bekeart ordered 1,000 guns to his specifications, S&W mfg. 5,000. While the first 1,000 revolvers in ser. no. range 138,226 with grip numbered 1-1,000 are accepted as "True Bekearts", only 292 were actually delivered to Philip Bekeart.

* Standard .22/.32 Hand Ejector Model — mfg. approx. 1913-1953.

| $850 | $675 | $550 | $450 | $375 | $325 | $275 | $225 | $175 | $135 | $115 | $100 |

MODEL .22 HAND EJECTOR (LADYSMITH) — originally chambered for .22 S&W (same as .22 Long) cal., 7 shot fluted cylinder, small frame, available in blue or nickel finish, nicknamed "Ladysmith" due to its small size. Over 26,000 mfg. between 1902-1921.

* First Model — .22 L, 3, or 3½ in. barrel length, serial numbered 1-4,575, checkered hard rubber grips, round butt. 4,575 mfg. 1902-1906. Serial range 1-4,575. Identifiable by frame mounted cylinder release lever.

| $2,000 | $1,800 | $1,500 | $1,250 | $975 | $800 | $650 | $550 | $475 | $435 | $390 | $350 |

* Second Model — .22 L cal., 3, or 3½ in. barrel, distinguishable from first model in that cylinder locking device was placed on barrel bottom, locking both ends. 9,400 mfg. 1906-1910. S.N. 4,576-13,950.

| $1,850 | $1,500 | $1,275 | $950 | $800 | $700 | $600 | $525 | $475 | $425 | $375 | $325 |

100%	98%	95%	90%	80%	70%	60%	50%	40%	30%	20%	10%

* **Third Model** — .22 L cal., 2½, 3, 3½, or 6 in. barrel, smooth walnut grips with S&W medallion inlays, square butt. 12,200 mfg. 1910-1921. Serial range 13,951-26,154.

| $1,825 | $1,475 | $1,250 | $900 | $750 | $650 | $550 | $475 | $425 | $375 | $325 | $325 |

    Add 85% for 6 in. barrel with target sights.
    Add 95% for 6 in. barrel with plain sights.

.32 HAND EJECTOR FIRST MODEL (MODEL OF 1896) — .32 S&W Long cal., 6 shot fluted cylinder, 3¼, 4¼ or 6 in. barrel, blue or nickel, black rubber grips, round butt, cylinder stop is mounted in frame top-strap, patent markings are on cylinder, rather than on barrel. 19,712 mfg. 1896-1903. Serial range 1-19,712.

| $700 | $600 | $500 | $475 | $440 | $400 | $375 | $325 | $285 | $250 | $225 | $200 |

.32 HAND EJECTOR (MODEL OF 1903) .32 S&W Long cal., 6 shot fluted cylinder, 3¼, 4¼ or 6 in. barrel, blue or nickel, black rubber grips. 19,425 mfg. 1903-1904. Serial range 1-19,425.

| $400 | $340 | $300 | $275 | $250 | $225 | $200 | $175 | $150 | $130 | $115 | $100 |

* *.32 Hand Ejector (Model of 1903 - 1st Change)* — rubber grips. 31,700 mfg. 1904-1906. Serial range 19,426-51,126.

| $395 | $340 | $300 | $275 | $250 | $225 | $200 | $175 | $150 | $130 | $115 | $100 |

* *.32 Hand Ejector (Model of 1903 - 2nd Change)* — rubber grips. 44,373 mfg. 1906-1909. Serial range 51,127-95,500.

| $395 | $340 | $300 | $275 | $250 | $225 | $200 | $175 | $150 | $130 | $115 | $100 |

* *.32 Hand Ejector (Model of 1903 - 3rd Change)* — rubber grips. 624 mfg. 1909-1910. Serial range 95,501-96,125.

| $525 | $475 | $420 | $385 | $350 | $320 | $290 | $265 | $240 | $220 | $205 | $190 |

* *.32 Hand Ejector (Model of 1903 - 4th Change)* — rubber grips. 6,374 mfg. 1910. Serial range 96,126-102,500.

| $400 | $340 | $300 | $275 | $250 | $225 | $200 | $175 | $150 | $130 | $115 | $100 |

* *.32 Hand Ejector (Model of 1903 - 5th Change)* — rubber grips.

| $355 | $315 | $280 | $250 | $225 | $200 | $175 | $150 | $125 | $110 | $100 | $90 |

.32 HAND EJECTOR THIRD MODEL — .32 S&W Long cal., 6 shot fluted cylinder, 3¼, 4¼ or 6 in. barrel, blue or nickel finish, grips of checkered hard rubber with "S&W" monogram, round butt. 271,531 mfg. 1911-1942. Serial range approx. 263,001-534,532.

| $350 | $310 | $275 | $250 | $225 | $200 | $175 | $150 | $125 | $110 | $100 | $90 |

.22/32 KIT GUN — similar to Standard .22/32 Hand Ejector Model, except has 2 or 4 in. barrels, round or square butt. Mfg. 1935-1953.

| $800 | $700 | $575 | $500 | $450 | $400 | $350 | $300 | $260 | $230 | $200 | $175 |

    Add 50% for pre-war mfg.

.32-20 WCF HAND EJECTOR FIRST MODEL — .32-20 WCF cal., 6 shot fluted cylinder, 4, 5, 6, or 6½ in. barrel, blue or nickel, case hardened trigger and hammer, hard rubber with "S&W" monogram or non-monogrammed walnut grips, round butt style.

| $650 | $575 | $520 | $475 | $450 | $425 | $400 | $375 | $350 | $325 | $305 | $290 |

.32-20 WCF HAND EJECTOR SECOND MODEL (MODEL OF 1902) — .32-20 WCF cal., 6 shot fluted cylinder, 4, 5, or 6½ in. barrel, blue or nickel, grips of hard rubber with "S&W" monogram or walnut, round butt style. 4,499 mfg. 1902-1905. Serial range 5,312-9,811.

| $725 | $575 | $475 | $400 | $350 | $300 | $250 | $200 | $150 | $125 | $110 | $95 |

* *.32-20 WCF Hand Ejector Second Model (Model of 1902 - 1st Change)* — grip also available in checkered walnut. 8,313 mfg. 1903-1905. Serial range 9,812-18,125.

| $710 | $565 | $465 | $390 | $340 | $290 | $240 | $190 | $140 | $120 | $105 | $90 |

.32-20 WCF HAND EJECTOR (MODEL OF 1905) — caliber, cylinder, barrel specifications same as above, with round or square grip. 4,300 mfg. 1905-1906. Serial range 18,126-22,426.

| $725 | $575 | $475 | $400 | $350 | $300 | $250 | $200 | $150 | $125 | $110 | $95 |

    Add 50% for Target Models.

* *.32-20 WCF Hand Ejector (Model of 1905 - 1st Change)* — 4, 5, 6, or 6½ barrel, blue or nickel, grips same as above, round or square butt. 11,073 mfg. 1906-1907. Serial range 22,427 to approx. 33,500.

| $710 | $565 | $465 | $390 | $340 | $290 | $240 | $190 | $140 | $120 | $105 | $90 |

100%	98%	95%	90%	80%	70%	60%	50%	40%	30%	20%	10%

* *.32-20 WCF Hand Ejector (Model of 1905 - 1st Change)* — 4, 5, 6, or 6½ barrel, blue or nickel, grips same as above, round or square butt. 11,073 mfg. 1906-1907. Serial range 22,427 to approx. 33,500.

| $710 | $565 | $465 | $390 | $340 | $290 | $240 | $190 | $140 | $120 | $105 | $90 |

* *.32-20 WCF Hand Ejector (Model of 1905 - 2nd Change)* — caliber, cylinder, barrel and grip specifications same as above. 11,699 mfg. 1906-1907. Serial range 33,501-45,200.

| $710 | $565 | $465 | $390 | $340 | $290 | $240 | $190 | $140 | $120 | $105 | $90 |

* *.32-20 WCF Hand Ejector (Model of 1905 - 3rd Change)* — caliber and cylinder same as above, 4 or 6 in. barrel, finish and grips same as above. 20,499 mfg. 1909-1915. Serial range approx. 45,201-65,700.

| $700 | $550 | $455 | $380 | $330 | $280 | $230 | $180 | $140 | $120 | $105 | $90 |

* *.32-20 WCF Hand Ejector (Model of 1905 - 4th Change)* — caliber and cylinder same as above, 4, 5, or 6 in. barrel, finish and grips same as above. 78,983 mfg. 1915-1940. Serial range 65,701-144,684.

| $575 | $450 | $375 | $325 | $280 | $235 | $200 | $175 | $135 | $115 | $100 | $85 |

.38 MILITARY & POLICE FIRST MODEL (MODEL OF 1899)

— .38 S&W Special cal., early Army & Navy models were marked "S&W .38 MIL.", civilian guns and standard models are 2-line barrel marked ".38 S&W SPECIAL & U.S. SERVICE CTG'S" with the "Maltese Cross" emblem stamped both before and after the caliber, these models are also referred to as .38 Hand Ejectors, 6 shot fluted cylinder, 4, 5, 6, or 6½ in. barrel, blue or nickel finish, "S&W" monogram checkered hard rubber or checkered walnut grips with walnut grips exhibiting an impressed circle at top, left plain for civilian issue, marked with inspector's initials for military issue. 20,975 mfg. 1899-1902. Serial range 1-20,975.

> On these models, barrel markings are somewhat confusing, generally marked .38 S&W Spl. & U.S. Service cartridge, Military Issue is typically marked .38 Military. Fixed sights are referred to as Military & Police Models while target sights are referred to as .38 Hand Ejectors.

* *Standard Model - Civilian Issue*

| $650 | $550 | $475 | $425 | $375 | $325 | $275 | $240 | $205 | $190 | $180 | $170 |

* *U.S. Navy Model* — 1,000 revolvers in .38 Military cal. with 6 in. barrel, blued, checkered walnut grips, delivered in 1900. Stamped on butt "U.S.N." with an anchor and inspector's initials. All in S&W serial range 5,001-6,000. U.S. Navy serial range 1-1,000.

| $1,900 | $1,600 | $1,375 | $1,200 | $1,050 | $925 | $825 | $725 | $625 | $525 | $435 | $375 |

* *U.S. Army Model* — 1,000 revolvers in .38 Military cal. with 6 in. barrel, blued, checkered walnut grips, inspector's initials "K.S.M. " on right grip panel with "J.T.T.1901" on left grip panel. Stamped on butt "U.S. ARMY/MODEL 1899". S&W serial range 13,001-14,000.

.38 MILITARY & POLICE SECOND MODEL (MODEL OF 1902)

— .38 S&W Special and .38 Military cal., civilian guns and standard models are barrel 2-line marked ".38 S&W SPECIAL & U.S. SERVICE CTG'S" with the "Maltese Cross" emblem stamped both before and after the caliber, 6 shot, fluted cylinder, 4, 5, 6, and 6½ in. barrels, blue or nickel, "S&W" monogram checkered hard rubber or checkered walnut grips. 12,827 mfg. 1902-1903. Serial range 20,976-33,803.

* *Standard Model* — civilian issue, all in .38 S&W Special cal.

| $545 | $470 | $425 | $390 | $335 | $320 | $290 | $260 | $235 | $210 | $200 | $185 |

* *U.S. Navy Model* — 1,000 revolvers in .38 United States Service caliber with 6 in. barrel, delivered in 1902. Stamped on butt "U.S.N." with "J.A.B.", anchor, and arrow through horizontal "S" and "No." (Naval Ser. No. designation).

| $1,800 | $1,575 | $1,400 | $1,250 | $1,125 | $1,000 | $900 | $800 | $750 | $700 | $650 | $610 |

.38 MILITARY & POLICE SECOND MODEL - 1ST CHANGE

— .38 S&W Special cal., 6 shot fluted cylinder, 4, 5, or 6½ in. barrel, blue or nickel, "S&W" monogram checkered hard rubber or checkered walnut grips, rounded butt style. 28,645 mfg. 1903-1905. Serial range 33,804-62,449.

* *Standard Model* — hard rubber grips, round butt.

| $395 | $345 | $310 | $275 | $250 | $210 | $175 | $150 | $135 | $125 | $115 | $100 |

100%	98%	95%	90%	80%	70%	60%	50%	40%	30%	20%	10%

* ***Standard Model*** — checkered walnut grips or square butt to frame style. All will have serial numbers over the 58,000 range.

| $410 | $355 | $335 | $300 | $275 | $235 | $200 | $175 | $160 | $145 | $130 | $115 |

.38 MILITARY & POLICE (MODEL OF 1905) — .38 S&W Special cal., 6 shot fluted cylinder, 4, 5, or 6½ in. barrel, blue or nickel finish, "S&W" monogram checkered hard rubber (round butt) or checkered walnut (square butt) grips. 10,800 mfg. 1905-1906. Serial range 62,450-73,250.

| $440 | $385 | $345 | $310 | $275 | $240 | $205 | $175 | $150 | $125 | $110 | $100 |

Add 50% for Target Model.

.38 MILITARY & POLICE (MODEL OF 1905 - 1ST CHANGE) — .38 S&W Special cal., 6 shot fluted cylinder, 4, 5, 6, or 6½ in. barrel, blue or nickel finish, grips same as above. 73,648 mfg. (including Model 1905 2nd change), exact quantity of both models has not been determined. The first change mfg. in 1906-1908. Serial range 73,251-unknown.

| $310 | $275 | $250 | $225 | $200 | $175 | $155 | $135 | $115 | $100 | $90 | $80 |

Add 50% for Target Model.

.38 MILITARY & POLICE (MODEL OF 1905 - 2ND CHANGE) — .38 S&W Special cal., cylinder barrel lengths, finishes and grip styles same as above. 73,648 (including Model 1905 1st change) mfg. Exact quantity unknown. The second change mfg. in 1908-1909. Serial range unknown-146,899.

| $310 | $275 | $250 | $225 | $200 | $175 | $155 | $135 | $115 | $100 | $90 | $80 |

Add 50% for Target Model.

.38 MILITARY & POLICE (MODEL OF 1905 - 3RD CHANGE) — .38 S&W Special cal., 6 shot fluted cylinder, 4, 5, or 6 in. barrel, finishes and grip styles same as above. 94,803 mfg. 1909-1915. Serial range 146,900-241,703.

| $310 | $275 | $250 | $225 | $200 | $175 | $155 | $135 | $115 | $100 | $90 | $80 |

Add 50% for Target Model.

.38 MILITARY & POLICE (MODEL OF 1905 - 4TH CHANGE) — .38 S&W Special cal., 6 shot fluted cylinder, 2, 4, 5, or 6 in. barrel, finishes and grip styles same as above. 458,296 mfg. 1915-1942. Serial range 241,704 - approx. 1,000,000.

| $295 | $255 | $230 | $205 | $180 | $165 | $140 | $125 | $110 | $100 | $90 | $80 |

Add 50% for Target Model.

.44 HAND EJECTOR FIRST MODEL (.44 HAND EJECTOR NEW CENTURY OR .44 TRIPLE LOCK) — .38-40 WCF, .44 S&W Special cal. (standard), .44-40 WCF, .44 S&W Russian, .45 LC, or .455 Mark II cal., 4, 5, 6½, or 7½ in. barrel, non-monogrammed checkered walnut grips and square butt on early production, gold monogram inlay on later production. 15,375 mfg. 1908-1915. Serial range 1-15,375 (with some ser. no. duplication with the .455 Mark II).

* ***Special Caliber Model*** — .38-40 WCF, .44 Russian, .44-40 WCF, .45 LC (marking, only 21 mfg.), or .455 Mark II (commercial) cal.

| N/A | $2,275 | $1,875 | $1,650 | $1,450 | $1,275 | $1,130 | $985 | $840 | $695 | $550 | $365 |

* ***Conversion Model*** — .455 Mark II cal.

| $1,200 | $1,075 | $975 | $885 | $765 | $675 | $600 | $540 | $480 | $420 | $365 | $325 |

Only 808 factory conversions of .44 Special to .455 cal. were mfg. and sold to the British government.

* ***Standard Model*** — .44 S&W Special cal.

| $1,700 | $1,525 | $1,325 | $1,100 | $1,000 | $900 | $800 | $715 | $630 | $545 | $460 | $400 |

Add 100% for factory target sights.

* ***British Target Model Triple Lock*** — .455 cal., 6½ or 7½ in. barrel, with drift adj. sights (not screw operated) for shooting at Bisley, England, typically unmarked for cal.

| $3,200 | $2,950 | $2,675 | $2,350 | $1,875 | $1,650 | $1,450 | $1,275 | $1,130 | $985 | $840 | $695 |

.44 HAND EJECTOR 2ND MODEL — .44 S&W Special cal. as standard, .38-40 WCF, .44-40 WCF, or .45 LC cal., 4, 5, 6, or 6½ in. barrel, blue or nickel finish, checkered walnut grips of square butt style, with or w/o "S&W" monogram inlays. 34,624 mfg. 1915-1937. Ser. range 15,376-approx. 60,000.

100%	98%	95%	90%	80%	70%	60%	50%	40%	30%	20%	10%

* **Standard Caliber** — .44 S&W Special cal.

| $675 | $595 | $530 | $475 | $430 | $385 | $340 | $295 | $250 | $210 | $175 | $145 |

Add 50% for factory target sights.

* **Special Calibers** — .38-40 WCF, .44-40 WCF, or .45 LC cal.

| $2,450 | $2,150 | $1,800 | $1,600 | $1,400 | $1,200 | $1,000 | $895 | $795 | $700 | $575 | $475 |

.44 HAND EJECTOR THIRD MODEL (MODEL 1926 HAND EJECTOR THIRD MODEL)
— .44 S&W Special cal., very rare in .44-40 WCF or .45 LC cal., 6 shot fluted cylinder, 4, 5, or 6½ in. barrel, finishes and grips same as above, same ser. range as the Second Model .44 Hand Ejectors, approx. 4,976 mfg. pre-war. Ser. range 28,358-S62,489.

* **Standard Model** — .44 S&W Special Cal.

| $825 | $715 | $625 | $550 | $490 | $430 | $370 | $310 | $225 | $175 | $150 | $125 |

There is also a Post-War variation of this model mfg. 1946-49 in the ser. range S62,490-S74,000 (approx. 1,432 mfg. 1946-49). These transitional guns have safety hammer blocks but long actions. The values are similar to those listed above.

* **.44 Hand Ejector 1926 Target Model** — pre-war, target sights, blue only, otherwise same as above. Mfg. 1926-1941.

| $3,950 | $3,250 | $2,800 | $1,950 | $1,725 | $1,600 | $1,500 | $1,400 | $1,250 | $1,100 | $975 | $925 |

There is also a Post-War variation of this model mfg. 1946-49 in the ser. range S62,490-S74,000. These transitional guns have safety hammer blocks but long actions. The Post-War Target Model has a barrel rib and 1950s style micrometer rear sight. The values are similar to those listed above.

.455 HAND EJECTOR FIRST MODEL — .455 Mark II cal., ser. range 1-5,000 in its own range, English or Canadian proofed.

| $1,250 | $1,100 | $975 | $885 | $765 | $675 | $600 | $540 | $480 | $420 | $365 | $325 |

Subtract 20%-40% for conversion to American caliber.

.455 HAND EJECTOR SECOND MODEL — ser. range 5,001-74,755, generally British or Canadian proofed.

| $550 | $480 | $420 | $360 | $300 | $250 | $235 | $225 | $215 | $200 | $185 | $150 |

Subtract 20%-40% for conversion to American caliber.

Grading			100%	98%	95%	90%	80%	70%	60%

.32 HAND EJECTOR POST WWII (MODEL 30) — .32 S&W Long cal., 6 shot, 2, 3, 4, or 6 in. barrel, blue or nickel, fixed sights, walnut or rubber grips. Mfg. 1946-1976.

| | | | | | $275 | $220 | $165 | $140 | $110 | $105 | $100 |

This model was designated Model 30 after 1958. Also manufactured as a Brazilian military contract (identified by Brazilian seal on sideplate).

.45 HAND EJECTOR (MODEL OF 1917) — .45 Auto Rim, or .45 ACP (in half moon clip) cal., 6 shot, 5½ in. barrel, fixed sights, satin blue on military - high gloss blue on commercial, smooth walnut on military, checkered walnut on commercial.

* **Military** — 175,000 mfg., 1917-1919.

| | | | | | $800 | $600 | $475 | $350 | $220 | $195 | $165 |

* **Commercial** — mfg. 1920-1941.

| | | | | | $650 | $500 | $395 | $370 | $320 | $285 | $185 |

Add 200% for factory target sights.

* **Brazilian Contract of 1937** — Brazilian shield on right side, 14,000 recently imported.

| | | | | | $175 | $150 | $125 | $110 | $100 | $90 | $80 |

Add 100% for older "non-import".

There was also a "1917 Army" commercial mfg. May 14, 1946-July 25, 1947 (approx. 991 mfg.). Denoted by safety hammer block and ser. no. "S" prefix.

Grading	100%	98%	95%	90%	80%	70%	60%

REGULATION POLICE — .32 S&W cal., 6 shot, 2, 3, 4, or 6 in. barrel, square butt, walnut grips, fixed sights, blue or nickel. Mfg. 1917-1957.

	$325	$275	$225	$170	$145	$135	$125

Add 100% for Regulation Police Target (6 in. barrel only, blue).

VICTORY MODEL — .38 Spl. (post-WWII commercial sales only), .38 S&W Spl. (U.S. government sales only), or .38 S&W (lend-lease arms to Allied Forces only) cal., mfg. in accordance with British/American lend-lease agreement of WWII, parkerized finish, mfg. 1942-1944.

	100%	98%	95%	90%	80%	70%	60%
U.S. Govt. Models	$500	$450	$400	$350	$325	$300	$275
Lend-lease mfg.	$250	$225	$200	$175	$160	$150	$140
Post-WWII Commercial sales	$500	$450	$400	$365	$330	$300	$275

Post WWII Victorys sold commercially went through the Defense Supply Commission, and had no U.S. markings.

K-22 OUTDOORSMAN — .22 LR cal., 6 shot, 6 in. round barrel, K frame, blue, adj. target sights, walnut grips. Mfg. 1931-1940.

	$575	$500	$450	$375	$330	$285	$250

K-22 MASTERPIECE — similar to K-22 Outdoorsman, but has micro click rear sight, short action, round barrel w/o rib. 1,067 mfg. in 1940 with serial range 682,420-696,952 in .38 Hand Ejector range.

	$1,200	$1,050	$875	$750	$675	$600	$550

U.S. AIR FORCE LIGHTWEIGHT (U.S. MODEL M 13) — .38 Spl. cal., aluminum cylinder and frame. Most were destroyed by the Government. Perhaps S&W's most faked revolver!

	$800	$725	$675	$525	$475	$425	$350

This model was purchased in large quantities during 1953 and early 1954 only. While S&W never assigned a model number to this variation, M 13 is marked on the top strap and thus retains the Model 13 designation. In 1954, a conventional steel cylinder replaced the aluminum cylinder because of cracking.

This model was based on the S&W .38 Military & Police Airweight (later became the Model 12).

.357 MAGNUM FACTORY REGISTERED — .357 Mag. cal., this model could be custom ordered with any barrel length from 3½ - 8¾ in., adj. sights, checkered walnut grips, hand fitted and registered to the buyer by a number found on the inside of the yoke, ser. no. with REG prefix. This practice was disc. 1939 (approx. 5,500 were mfg.) due to the tremendous demand for the .357 Mag. revolver. Mfg. 1935-1939.

	$1,950	$1,700	$1,500	$950	$850	$700	$650

Add 40% for rare registration certificate.

Add 20% for non-standard barrel lengths.

Common barrel lengths were 3½, 4, 5, 6½, and 8¾ in.

.357 MAGNUM PRE-WAR NON-REGISTERED — similar to above, but not registered. 1,142 mfg. 1938-1941.

	$1,000	$850	$725	$650	$525	$470	$385

.44 MAGNUM PRE-MODEL 29 (5 SCREW) — .44 Mag. cal., 5 screw, can be discerned by 4 screws on right sideplate, 1 located under grip, and 1 in front of the trigger guard. Approx. 6,500 mfg. during 1956-1958.

	$850	$750	$650	$575	$560	$450	$400

This model was cataloged in 4 and 6½ in. barrel. The 4 in. is rare, and commands a premium. Also, a rare variation in this model is a 5 in. barrel. Only 500 were mfg. in 5 screw Pre-Model 29 variation with bright blue finish, diamond target stocks, and wood case. In NIB condition the value is $2,800 - add 25% for nickel finish.

NUMBERED MODEL REVOLVERS (MODERN HAND EJECTORS)

Smith & Wesson handguns manufactured after 1958 were stamped with a model number on the frame under the cylinder arm. The number is visible when the cylinder is open. All revolvers manufactured by S&W from 1946-1958 were produced without model numbers.

To determine which variation a particular revolver is in the following section, simply swing the cylinder out to the loading position and notice the model number inside

Grading		100%	98%	95%	90%	80%	70%	60%

the yoke. The designation Mod. and a two-digit number followed by a dash and another number designates which engineering change was underway when the gun was manufactured. Hence, a Mod. 48-3 is a Model 48 in its 3rd engineering change (and should be designated when ordering parts). Usually, earlier variations are the most desirable to collectors unless a particular improvement is rare. The same rule applies to semi-auto pistols and the model designation is usually marked on the outside of the gun.

Beginning 1994, S&W started providing synthetic grips and drilled/tapped receiver for scope mounting on certain models.

Add 10%-15% for those models listed below that are pinned and recessed (pre-1981 mfg.).

MODEL 10 M & P — .38 Spl. cal., 6 shot, round or square butt (4 in. barrel only starting 1992), fixed sights, 2 (disc. 1996), 3 (disc.), 4 (standard or heavy), 5 (disc.), or 6 (disc.) in. barrels.

Mfg.'s Sug. Retail	$420	$315	$235	$170	$140	$130	$115	$100

Add $12 for nickel finish (disc. 1991, 4 in. barrel only).

The Model 10 is currently available in 4 in. barrel only (a 4 in. heavy barrel nickel square butt variation was disc. in 1992).

MODEL 12 M & P AIRWEIGHT — similar to Model 10, only alloy frame, 2 or 4 in. barrel. Disc. 1986.

			$280	$245	$210	$200	$185	$175	$150

Last Mfg.'s Sug. Retail was $320.

Add $40 for nickel finish (disc.).

MODEL 13 M & P — .357 Mag. cal., fixed sights, 3 (round butt, disc. 1996) or 4 (square butt) in. heavy barrel. Disc. 1998.

			$310	$230	$165	$145	$135	$125	$120

Last Mfg.'s Sug. Retail was $411.

Add $20 for nickel finish (disc. 1986).

* **Model 13 - N.Y. State Police** — .357 Mag. cal., 4 in. barrel, blued, fixed sights, 1,200 were mfg. for the N.Y. State Police and are marked 10-6. All 1,200 were recalled by S&W and exchanged for Model 28s.

			$375	$300	$250	$200	$175	$150	$140

MODEL 14 K-38 — .38 Spl. cal., target model, blue only. Disc. 1981.

			$300	$250	$215	$200	$185	$175	$160

Add $20 for 6 in. barrel single action.

MODEL 14 K-38 MASTERPIECE —.38 Spl. cal., 6 in. full lug barrel, adj. rear sight, combat style Morado wood square butt grips, blue finish, 47 oz.

Mfg.'s Sug. Retail	$498	$385	$310	$260	$225	$200	$185	$165

MODEL 15 COMBAT MASTERPIECE — .38 Spl. cal., adj. sights, 6 shot, square butt, 2 (disc.), 4, 6 (mfg. 1986-91), or 8⅜ (new 1986, disc.) in. barrel.

Mfg.'s Sug. Retail	$450	$340	$260	$215	$190	$180	$160	$150

Add $31 for TT or TH (disc. 1991).
Add $11 for 8⅜ in. barrel (disc.).
Add $20 for nickel finish (disc. 1987).

MODEL 16 (K-32 MASTERPIECE) — .32 S&W Long cal., 6 in. barrel, adj. sights, checkered walnut, blue. Only 3630 mfg., 1947-1974.

			$1,350	$1,150	$995	$875	$750	$625	$525

* **Pre-War K-32 (Model 16 Outdoorsman)** — only 104 mfg. pre-war, scarce.

			$2,250	$1,950	$1,700	$1,475	$1,250	$1,050	$875

MODEL 16 — .32 cal./.32 Mag. cal., 6 shot, 4 (mfg. 1990-91 only), 6, or 8⅜ (disc. 1991) in. barrel, square butt, blue finish only, TH and TT. Mfg. 1990-92.

			$335	$280	$225	$210	$200	$190	$180

Last Mfg.'s Sug. Retail was $419.

Add 5%-10% for 8⅜ in. barrel.

Grading	100%	98%	95%	90%	80%	70%	60%

MODEL 17 K-22 MASTERPIECE — .22 LR cal., blue only, 6 shot, 4 (mfg. 1986-93), 6 (current mfg.), or 8⅜ (disc. 1992) in. barrel. Disc. 1993, reintroduced 1996, disc. 1998.

			$390	$280	$240	$215	$200	$185	$175

Last Mfg.'s Sug. Retail was $508.

Add $39 for full lug 6 in. long barrel (w/TT & TH, disc.).
Add $50 for full lug 8⅜ in. long barrel (w/TT & TH, disc. 1992).

MODEL 17-2 PROTOTYPE MERCOX DART PROJECTILE GUN — .530 Dart Projectile, .22 Ramset blank gas generator, 12 in. barrel, blue finish only, 25 prototype units mfg. 1966 only.

$6,950 $6,750 $3,750

Add $500 for handmade Safariland holster.
Add $100-$500 depending on variation of projectile (six known).

MODEL 18 .22 COMBAT MASTERPIECE — .22 LR cal., combat style adj. sights, 4 in. barrel, blue only. Disc. 1985.

$305 $270 $225 $200 $180 $175 $165

Last Mfg.'s Sug. Retail was $352.

Add $30 for TT and TH.

MODEL 19 .357 COMBAT MAGNUM — .357 Mag. cal., K frame, adj. sights, 2½ (round butt, disc. 1998), 4 (square butt), or 6 (square butt, disc. 1996) in. barrel, bright blue or nickel (disc. 1992) finish, drilled/tapped receiver and synthetic grips became standard 1994.

Mfg.'s Sug. Retail	$457	$345	$265	$210	$190	$180	$170	$160

Add $9 for 4 in. or $14 for 6 in. (disc. 1996) barrel.
Add $35 for white outline rear sight (disc. 1994).
Add $20 for nickel finish - disc. 1991 (4 or 6 in. only).
Add $60 for TS, TT, TH, RR, and WO - disc. 1991 (6 in. barrel only).

This model is supplied with a round butt on 2½ in. barrel. Nickel finish was available with a 4 or 6 in. barrel only. The 2½ and 6 in. barrels (blue finish) were disc. in 1991 along with the 4 and 6 in. nickel variations.

PRE-MODEL 20 (PRE-WAR .38/44) — .38 Spl. cal., 6 shot, 4, 5, or 6½ in. barrel lengths, fixed sights, walnut grips, blue or nickel, walnut grips. Mfg. 1930-1941 and re-introduced 1946 (with S prefix starting at serial 62,940). The 38/44 Heavy Duty became the Model 20 in 1957.

$595 $490 $450 $415 $385 $340 $300

Add 40% for 6½ in. barrel.
Early post-war models had pre-war long action (ser. range S62,489-approx. S74,000).

MODEL 20 — .38 Spl. cal., 6 shot, 4, 5, or 6½ in. barrel, fixed sights, blue or nickel finish, checkered walnut grips. Mfg. 1957-1964.

$350 $285 $260 $220 $195 $145 $125

MODEL 21 (.44 HAND EJECTOR FOURTH MODEL - MODEL OF 1950 MILITARY) — .44 S&W cal., 6 shot, 4, 5, or 6½ in. barrel, large frame, blue, walnut grips, fixed sights, 1,200 mfg. scattered throughout serial range S75,000-S263,000. Mfg. 1950-1964.

$1,750 $1,575 $1,350 $1,100 $875 $650 $550

Add 50% for 6½ in. (rare).

MODEL 22 (.45 HAND EJECTOR MODEL OF 1950 MILITARY) — .45 Auto Rim or .45 ACP cal., same specifications as 1917 Army, except redesigned hammer block, short action, fixed sights. Approx. 1,200 mfg. 1950-1964.

$1,500 $1,275 $1,050 $875 $725 $650 $525

MODEL 23 (.38-44 OUTDOORSMAN) — .38 Spl. cal., similar to Model 20 in .38 Spl., except with adj. sights, blue only, pre-war guns had plain barrels, post-war mfg. featured ribbed 6½ in. barrel standard. Mfg. 1930-1967.

$650 $550 $450 $375 $300 $280 $270

Add 20% for post-war transitional variation.

Early post-war models had long action with barrel rib and micrometer sights (ser. range S62,489-approx. S74,000). There were 4,761 pre-war revolvers, 2,036 post-war transitional, and 6,039 styled after the 1950 model.

The 44 in this model's nomenclature refers to the size frame, not the caliber. This variation became designated the Model 23 after 1958.

Grading	100%	98%	95%	90%	80%	70%	60%

MODEL 24 (.44 HAND EJECTOR FOURTH MODEL - 1950 TARGET) — .44 Spl., redesigned hammer, short action, 6½ in. ribbed barrel standard, satin blue or bright blue, micrometer sights, serialization begins at approx. S75,000. 5,050 mfg. 1950-1967.

	$695	$575	$500	$400	$375	$350	$320

Add 20% for bright blue.
Add 40% for 4 in. barrel.
Add 50% for 5 in. barrel.

MODEL 24-3 — .44 Spl., 4 or 6½ in. barrel, bright blue only, checkered Goncalo Alves target grips (without speedloader cutout), barrel and frame not pinned, 7,500 mfg. 1983 only.

* *4 in. barrel.* — 2,625 mfg.

	$450	$425	$400	$375	$325	$275	$225

* *6½ in. barrel.* — 4,875 mfg.

	$400	$375	$350	$325	$275	$225	$175

Last Mfg.'s Sug. Retail was $359.

This model's serialization is triple alpha - 4 numeric (i.e. ABC0123).

* *Model 24 Lew Horton Special* — .44 Spl., 3 in. barrel, round butt, adj. sights, blue finish, includes special fitted holster.

	$380	$325	$250

Subtract 10% without holster.

MODEL 25/25-2 (1955 TARGET MODEL) — .45 ACP, .45 Auto Rim or .45 LC (earlier mfg.) cal., N frame, blue finish only, target grips, 6 (later mfg.) or 6½ (earlier mfg.) in. barrel. Disc. approx. 1985.

	$450	$400	$350	$300	$235	$200	$190

Last Mfg.'s Sug. Retail was $347.

Add $150 for 6½ in. barrel (older mfg. with pinned barrel).
Add 300% for .45 LC cal.
After 1927, the Model 25 in .45 ACP cal was designated Model 25-2.

* *Model 25 Lew Horton Special* — .45 ACP cal., 3 in. barrel, adj. sights, blue finish, only 100 mfg.

	$500	$450	$375

MODEL 25-5 — .45 LC cal., 4, 6, or 8⅜ in. barrel, blue or nickel finish (no extra charge - disc. 1987). Disc. 1991.

	$375	$315	$250	$215	$200	$190	$180

Last Mfg.'s Sug. Retail was $429.

Add 5%-10% for 8⅜ in. barrel.

MODEL 26 (.45 HAND EJECTOR MODEL OF 1950 TARGET) — .45 ACP, or .45 Auto Rim cal., adj. sights, thin ribbed barrel, 2,768 mfg.

	$770	$660	$550	$440	$275	$200	$150

Add 300% for .45 Colt cal. (200 mfg.).

MODEL 27 — .357 Mag. cal., N-frame, 3½ (disc. 1977), 4 (disc. 1991), 5 (disc. 1977), 6, 6½, or 8⅜ (disc. 1991) in. barrel, blue or nickel (disc. 1987) finish. Disc. 1994.

	$380	$300	$235	$220	$205	$190	$180

Last Mfg.'s Sug. Retail was $486.

Add 10% for pinned barrel and recessed cylinder.
Add $28 for white outline rear sight -(disc. 1991).
Add $8 for 8⅜ in. barrel - (disc. 1991).

* *3½ and 5 in. barrel* — disc.

	$425	$365	$275	$265	$240	$230	$180

S

Grading	100%	98%	95%	90%	80%	70%	60%

MODEL 28 HIGHWAY PATROLMAN — .357 Mag. cal., "Highway Patrol" utility model, dull or brushed nickel (very rare) finish, adj. sights, standard grips, blue only, 4 or 6 in. barrel, mfg. 1954-1986.

	$270	$235	$210	$200	$190	$180	$150

Last Mfg.'s Sug. Retail was $306.

Add $20 for TS.
Add 30% for 5 screw variation.
Add 300% for brushed nickel finish (beware of fakes).

MODEL 29 .44 MAGNUM (4 SCREW) — .44 Mag. cal., 4 screw, can be discerned by 3 exposed screws on lower right sideplate (one is concealed by sideplate). Mfg. began 1957 after approx. ser. no. S175,000 and was disc. 1961.

	$695	$650	$600	$550	$475	$425	$375

MODEL 29/29-2 (3 SCREW) — .44 Mag. cal., 4, 6½, or 8⅜ in. barrel, eliminated top screw on sideplate and 1 screw in front of trigger guard. Disc.

	$650	$550	$500	$400	$300	$275	$250

Subtract $40 if without case.

The S serial number prefix was used on this model until 1968, at which time the law required a new numbering system, and the serial number prefix was changed to N. The S prefix originally designated the additional hammer block safety.

MODEL 29 — .44 Mag. cal., 6 shot, 4 (disc. 1992), 6, or 8⅜ in. barrel, blue or nickel (disc. 1991) finish. Disc. 1998 (long live Dirty Harry!).

	$400	$335	$285	$265	$255	$245	$210

Last Mfg.'s Sug. Retail was $574.

Add $12 for 8⅜ in. barrel.
Add $11 for nickel finish (disc. 1991).
Add 10%-15% for pinned barrel and recessed cylinder, depending on condition.
Add $45 for combat grips with scope mount - disc. 1991 (8⅜ in. barrel only).

Older Model 29 mfg. (5 screw variations) will appear under the previous subheading: "EARLY HAND EJECTORS (NAMED MODELS)".

* ***Model 29 Lew Horton Special*** — similar to Model 29, except has 3 in. barrel, round butt, adj. sights.

	$425	$350	$295

MODEL 29 CLASSIC — .44 Mag. cal., 5, 6½, or 8⅜ in. full lug barrel, blue only, round butt with Hogue conversion square butt grips, interchangeable front sights with white outline rear sight, frame is drilled and tapped to accept scope mounts, blue finish only. Mfg. 1990-94.

	$475	$375	$295	$280	$260	$240	$225

Last Mfg.'s Sug. Retail was $591.

Add $8 for 8⅜ in. barrel.

MODEL 29 SILHOUETTE — .44 Mag. cal., 10⅝ in. barrel, adj. front and rear sights, bright blue only, Goncalo Alves target stocks. Mfg. 1983-91.

	$550	$475	$395	$335	$290	$260	$240

Last Mfg.'s Sug. Retail was $536.

MODEL 29 MAGNACLASSIC — .44 Mag. cal., 7½ in. full lug, ported barrel, high polish bright bluing, round butt, interchangeable front sight, supplied with cherry wood display case mfg. in England, 3,000 mfg. in 1990 only.

	$850	$725	$600	$500	$450	$395	$360

Last Mfg.'s Sug. Retail was $999.

MODEL 30 — .32 S&W cal., 6 shot, 2, 3, 4, or 6 in. barrel, square butt, walnut grips, fixed sights, blue or nickel finish. Limited mfg.

	$300	$260	$220	$190	$175	$165	$150

MODEL 31 — .32 S&W Long cal., fixed sights, 2, 3 or 4 (disc.) in. barrel, blue only. Disc. 1991.

	$290	$235	$195	$185	$175	$165	$150

Last Mfg.'s Sug. Retail was $365.

Add 25% for early flatlatch models.

Grading	100%	98%	95%	90%	80%	70%	60%

MODEL 32 (.38 TERRIER) — .38 S&W cal., 5 shot, 2 in. barrel, walnut or rubber grips, blue or nickel, fixed sights, built on .32 frame. Mfg. 1936-1974.

	$330	**$220**	**$175**	**$150**	**$135**	**$125**	**$115**

This variation was designated the Model 32 after 1958.

MODEL 33 (REGULATION POLICE) — .38 S&W cal., 5 shot, 2, 3, 4 in. barrel, square butt, walnut grips, fixed sights, blue or nickel finish. Mfg. 1958-74.

	$325	**$275**	**$225**	**$170**	**$145**	**$135**	**$125**

MODEL 34 — .22 LR or .22/32 Kit Gun cal. (disc.), adj. sights in J frame, 6 shot, 2 or 4 in. barrel, round or square butt, blue or nickel (disc. 1986) finish. Disc. 1991. This model was re-issued for 2-3 years.

	$300	**$235**	**$195**	**$185**	**$175**	**$165**	**$150**

Last Mfg.'s Sug. Retail was $366.

Add $25 for nickel finish.
Add 25% for early flatlatch models.

MODEL 35 (.22/32 TARGET MODEL OF 1953) — similar to Standard .22/.32 Hand Ejector Model, except micrometer rear sight, magna target grips. Mfg. 1953-1974.

	$425	**$300**	**$265**	**$230**	**$200**	**$180**	**$160**

MODEL 35 .22/.32 TARGET

	$300	**$250**	**$195**	**$165**	**$130**	**$110**	**$90**

MODEL 36 (CHIEFS SPECIAL) — .38 Spl. cal., 5 shot, J frame, round or square (disc. 1991) butt, 1⅞ in. regular or 3 in. (heavy only, disc. 1994) barrel, blue or nickel (disc. 1992) finish.

Mfg.'s Sug. Retail	$406	**$295**	**$230**	**$180**	**$165**	**$155**	**$150**	**$145**

Add $12 for nickel finish (disc., round butt - 2 in. barrel only).
Add 25% for early small trigger guard and grips (below ser. no. 2,500).

Note: 1st models with high polish blue and diamond grips will bring premiums when mint in original box.

MODEL 36 TARGET — similar to Model 50, 2 in. barrel, square butt, mfg. started 1955.

	$850	**$725**	**$650**	**$575**	**$500**	**$400**	**$350**

MODEL 36 LADYSMITH — .38 Spl. cal., 5 shot, 1⅞ in. regular or 3 (disc. 1991) in. heavy barrel, blue finish only, grips are anatomically designed for women (round butt on 1⅞ in., wood combat grips on 3 in.), fixed sights, redesigned double action, 20-23 oz.), Morocco grained (disc. 1991) or soft side jewelry case. New 1990.

Mfg.'s Sug. Retail	$438	**$335**	**$245**	**$200**	**$185**	**$175**	**$165**	**$150**

MODEL 37 CHIEFS SPECIAL AIRWEIGHT — similar to Model 36 Chiefs Special, except alloy frame and 1⅞ in. barrel only, blue or nickel (disc. 1995) finish, barrels are marked Airweight.

Mfg.'s Sug. Retail	$442	**$345**	**$250**	**$200**	**$185**	**$175**	**$165**	**$150**

Add $16 for nickel finish (disc.).

MODEL 38 BODYGUARD AIRWEIGHT — .38 S&W Spl. cal., 5 shot, alloy frame, round butt, shrouded hammer, 2 in. barrel, blue or nickel (disc. 1996) finish. Disc. 1998.

	$350	**$260**	**$205**	**$190**	**$180**	**$170**	**$150**

Last Mfg.'s Sug. Retail was $462.

Add $15 for nickel finish (disc. 1996).

MODEL 40 CENTENNIAL — .38 S&W Spl. cal., 2 in. barrel double action only, fully concealed hammer, grip safety, smooth walnut grips, blue or nickel. Mfg. 1953-1974.

	$475	**$425**	**$345**	**$290**	**$260**	**$240**	**$220**

This model commands a premium for the first series with no letter prefix. After 1968, L prefix series began.

MODEL 42 CENTENNIAL AIRWEIGHT — .38 S&W Spl. cal., aluminum variation of Model 40 Centennial, mfg. began 1953. Disc.

Blue	**$475**	**$425**	**$395**	**$325**	**$300**	**$265**	**$240**
Nickel	**$1,100**	**$950**	**$875**	**$775**	**$675**	**$550**	**$475**

MODEL 42 — .38 Spl. cal., blue finish only. Disc.

	$450	**$400**	**$360**	**$320**	**$295**	**$270**	**$250**

S

Grading	100%	98%	95%	90%	80%	70%	60%

MODEL 43 (.22/32 KIT GUN AIRWEIGHT) — .22 LR cal., $3\frac{1}{2}$ in. barrel, round or square butt, adj. sights, aluminum frame and cylinder, mfg. 1955-1974.

	$425	$350	$275	$240	$185	$165	$150

MODEL 45 (.22 MILITARY & POLICE) — .22 LR cal. only, originally mfg. as training gun between 1931-1957, also mfg. 500 in 1963 (Model 45).

Pre-War	N/A	N/A	$1,900	$1,600	$1,350	$1,250	$950
Post-War	$650	$550	$450	$375	$300	$280	$270

MODEL 48 K-22 MASTERPIECE — .22 Mag cal., 4, 6 or $8\frac{3}{8}$ in. barrel, blue only. Disc. 1986.

	$275	$245	$200	$185	$175	$165	$150

Last Mfg.'s Sug. Retail was $320.

Add $15 for $8\frac{3}{8}$ in. barrel.
Add $15 for TT, TH, and TS (disc.).

MODEL 49 BODYGUARD — similar to Model 38, only steel frame, 2 in. barrel, blue or nickel (disc.) finish. Disc. 1996.

	$300	$260	$180	$170	$160	$150	$145

Last Mfg.'s Sug. Retail was $409.

Add $25 for nickel finish (disc.).

MODEL 50 (.38 CHIEFS SPECIAL TARGET) — .38 S&W Spl. cal., Chiefs Special Target, mfg. from 1955 in 2 in. (see Model 36 Target listing) or 3 (211 mfg. beginning 1973) in. barrels, target sights, most were unmarked for model number, approx. 1,100 mfg. The other variation was designated Model 36 Target.

	$795	$700	$625	$550	$475	$400	$350

The Model 50 designation was not used until 1970.

MODEL 51 — .22 Mag. cal. only, .22/32 kit gun, $3\frac{1}{2}$ in. barrel, 6 shot, adj. rear sight, blue or nickel, walnut stocks. Disc.

	$400	$350	$300	$275	$250	$225	$200

MODEL 53 .22 REM. JET — .22 S, L, or LR inserts, 6 shot, 4, 6, or $8\frac{3}{8}$ in. barrel, blue, walnut grips, adj. sights. Mfg. 1960-1974.

	$735	$650	$550	$470	$385	$360	$330

Add 10% for $8\frac{3}{8}$ in. barrel.

MODEL 57 — .41 Mag. cal., similar to Model 29, except for cal., 4 (disc. 1991), 6 or $8\frac{3}{8}$ (disc. 1991) in. barrel, blue or nickel (disc.) finish. Disc. 1993.

	$350	$255	$225	$205	$190	$175	$165

Last Mfg.'s Sug. Retail was $466.

Add 10%-20% for S prefix serialization.
Add 10% for nickel finish if NIB.
Add $20 for $8\frac{3}{8}$ in. barrel.
Add 10% for pinned barrel and recessed cylinder.

MODEL 58 — .41 Mag cal., M&P, fixed sights, 4 in. barrel, blue or nickel finish. Disc.

	$495	$450	$385	$340	$315	$290	$260

Add $25 for nickel finish or "S" serial number prefix.

MODEL 60 .38 SPL. CHIEFS SPECIAL — .38 S&W Spl., stainless version of Chiefs Special, 2 or 3 in. full lug barrel. Disc. 1996.

	$335	$250	$195				

Last Mfg.'s Sug. Retail was $458.

Subtract $25 for 2 in. barrel.
Add 30% for early Model 60s without letter prefix and bright satin finish.
The full lug barrel option began in 1990 with limited mfg. It has been tested for +P+ ammo and features an adj. rear sight - $24\frac{1}{2}$ oz.

MODEL 60 .357 MAG. CHIEFS SPECIAL — .357 Mag. cal., $2\frac{1}{8}$ or 3 (new 1997) in. barrel, round butt, stainless steel, synthetic grips. New 1996.

Mfg.'s Sug. Retail	$462		$345	$260	$195		

Add $28 for 3 in. full lug barrel with adj. sight (new 1997).

Grading	100%	98%	95%	90%	80%	70%	60%

MODEL 60 LADYSMITH — .38 S&W Spl. cal., 5 shot, 2 in. regular (disc. 1996), 2⅛ (new 1997), or 3 in. heavy (disc. 1991) barrel, frosted stainless steel finish, grips are anatomically designed for women (round butt on 2 in., wood combat grips on 3 in.), fixed sights, redesigned double action, 20-23 oz, Morocco grained (disc. 1991) or soft side case. New 1990.

Mfg.'s Sug. Retail $494 $370 $255 $195

MODEL 63 .22/32 KIT GUN — .22 LR/.32, stainless kit gun, 2 or 4 in. barrel, 19 oz. Disc. 1998.

   $365 $245 $195

Last Mfg.'s Sug. Retail was $476.

   Add $5 for 4 in. barrel.

MODEL 64 M & P — .38 Spl. cal., stainless Model 10, has 2, 3, or 4 in. barrel. 3 (square butt disc. 1992) and 4 in. (square butt only) barrels are heavy.

Mfg.'s Sug. Retail $446 $335 $230 $185

   Add $8 for 3 or 4 in. barrel.

MODEL 65 — .357 Mag. cal., stainless version of Model 13, has 3 (round butt) or 4 (square butt) in. heavy barrels.

Mfg.'s Sug. Retail $458 $340 $235 $190

MODEL 65 LADYSMITH — .357 Mag. cal., 3 in. barrel with round butt, glass beaded stainless finish, soft side jewelry case. New 1992.

Mfg.'s Sug. Retail $494 $380 $260 $200

MODEL 66 — .357 Mag. cal., stainless version of model 19, has 2½, 3 (disc., only 2,500 mfg.), 4, or 6 in. barrel.

Mfg.'s Sug. Retail $499 $395 $280 $200

   Add $6 for 4 or 6 in. barrel.

   Add $48 for TH and TT with 4 (disc. 1991) or 6 in. barrel only.

   Note: Several models of the Model 66 were made — such features as an all-stainless steel rear sight and a recessed cylinder will bring a slight premium if NIB.

MODEL 67 COMBAT MASTERPIECE — .38 S&W Spl. cal., stainless version of Model 15, has 4 in. barrel. Disc. 1988, reintroduced 1991.

Mfg.'s Sug. Retail $500 $370 $260 $200

   1991 mfg. includes square butt and red ramp front sight insert.

MODEL 68 — .38 S&W Spl. cal., similar in appearance to the Model 66, except is in .38 Spl. cal., 4 or 6 in. barrel, approx. 7,500 mfg.

   $750 $625 $495

   This model was originally ordered by CA Highway Patrol. Add 10% for CHP markings.

MODEL 317 AIRLITE — .22 LR cal., 8 shot, 1⅞ or 3 (new 1998) in. barrel, combination of aluminum, carbon, stainless steel, and titanium construction, brushed aluminum finish, J-frame, round butt, choice of synthetic or Dymondwood Boot (disc. 1998) grips, fixed sights, approx. 10 oz. New 1997.

Mfg.'s Sug. Retail $465 $365 $270 $195

   Add $26 for 3 in. barrel.

   Add $33 for Dymondwood Boot grips.

   ✱ *Model 317 Airlite LadySmith* — .22 LR cal., 1⅞ in. barrel only, includes Dymondwood Boot grips. New 1998.

Mfg.'s Sug. Retail $520 $395 $290 $205

MODEL 331 AIRLITE TI CHIEFS SPECIAL — .32 H&R Mag. cal., 6 shot, J-frame, 1⅞ in. barrel, features titanium cylinder and aluminum alloy frame, fixed sights, Uncle Mike's or Dymondwood Boot wood grips, matte alloy frame finish, approx. 11 oz. New 1999.

Mfg.'s Sug. Retail $624 $500 $400 $350 $325 $300 $275 $250

   Add $24 for Dymondwood Boot grips.

MODEL 332 AIRLITE TI CENTENNIAL — similar Model 331 Airlite Ti, except is hammerless and double action only. New 1999.

Mfg.'s Sug. Retail $640 $510 $410 $360 $330 $300 $275 $250

   Add $24 for Dymondwood Boot grips.

S

Grading	100%	98%	95%	90%	80%	70%	60%

MODEL 337 TI CHIEFS SPECIAL — .38 S&W Spl.+P cal., 5 shot, J-frame, 1⁷⁄₈ in. barrel, similar design as the Model 331, approx. 11½ oz. New 1999.

Mfg.'s Sug. Retail	$624	$500	$400	$350	$325	$300	$275	$250

Add $24 for Dymondwood Boot grips.

MODEL 342 AIRLITE CENTENNIAL — similar to Model 337, except is hammerless and double action only. New 1999.

Mfg.'s Sug. Retail	$640	$510	$410	$360	$330	$300	$275	$250

Add $24 for Dymondwood Boot grips.

MODEL 442 CENTENNIAL AIRWEIGHT — .38 S&W Spl. cal., 1⁷⁄₈ in. barrel only, blue or nickel (disc. 1995) finish, round butt. New 1993.

Mfg.'s Sug. Retail	$459	$350	$260	$205	$190	$180	$170	$150

Add $15 for nickel finish (disc.).

MODEL 520 — .357 Mag. cal., 4 in. barrel, fixed sights, N frame, originally ordered for N.Y. State Police but never purchased. Approx. 3,000 mfg. with box.

		$325	$275	$240	$210	$185	$175	$165

MODEL 547 M & P — 9mm Para. cal., 3 or 4 in. heavy barrel, 6 shot, round (3 in. barrel) or square (4 in. barrel) butt, blue only, 32 oz. Disc. 1985.

		$295	$265	$240	$210	$195	$185	$175

Last Mfg.'s Sug. Retail was $317.

MODEL 581 — .357 Mag. cal., L-Frame, fixed sights, 4 in. barrel, 6 shot, blue or nickel finish, 38 oz. Disc. 1992.

		$275	$225	$180	$170	$160	$150	$145

Last Mfg.'s Sug. Retail was $335.

Add $20 for nickel (disc. 1987).

This model was disc. 1985-86, and reintroduced 1987-92.

MODEL 586 (DISTINGUISHED COMBAT MAGNUM) — .357 Mag. cal., L-Frame, 4, 6, or 8³⁄₈ (disc. 1991) in. barrel, adj. sights, blue or nickel (disc. 1991) finish.

Mfg.'s Sug. Retail	$494	$370	$285	$215	$195	$185	$175	$165

Add 5%-10% for nickel finish (disc.).
Add $4 for white outlined rear sight (disc. 1994).
Add $5 for 6 in. barrel.
Add $22 for 8³⁄₈ in. barrel (disc. 1991).
Add $35 for adj. front sight - disc. 1991 (6 in. barrel only, new 1986).

* **1985 Model 586 Iowa Highway State Patrol** — mfg. to commemorate 50th anniversary, gold etching, 4 in. barrel. Mfg. 1985 only.

		$375	$250	$225				

MODEL 610 — 10mm cal., 6 shot, adj. sights, 5 or 6½ (current mfg.) in. full lug barrel, fluted or unfluted (6½ in. barrel only) cylinder, round butt, target hammer optional, approx. 5,000 mfg. 1990 only, reintroduced 1998.

Mfg.'s Sug. Retail	$684	$565	$460	$380				

MODEL 617 — .22 LR cal., stainless steel variation of the Model 17 (K-22 Masterpiece), 6 (6 in. barrel only beginning 1999) or 10 (new 1997) shot, 4, 6, or 8³⁄₈ in. barrel, straight backstrap grip, combat trigger and grips, semi-target. New 1990.

Mfg.'s Sug. Retail	$534	$410	$290	$210				

Subtract $10 for 6 shot.
Add $32 for 6 in. or $44 for 8³⁄₈ in. barrel.
Add $30 for 6 in. barrel with TT and TH.
Add $42 for 8³⁄₈ in. barrel with TT and TH.

MODEL 624 .44 TARGET — .44 S&W Spl. cal., 6 shot, 4 or 6½ in. barrel, 42 oz. Mfg. 1986-87 only.

		$340	$250	$225				

Last Mfg.'s Sug. Retail was $449.

Add $14 for 6½ in. barrel.

Grading	100%	98%	95%	90%	80%	70%	60%

* Model 624-2 Lew Horton Special — .44 Spl. cal., 3 in. barrel with round butt, adj. sights, includes special fitted holster.

		100%	98%	95%
		$395	**$350**	**$295**

      Subtract 10% if without holster.

MODEL 625 — .45 ACP cal., stainless variation of the Model 25-2, 6 shot, 3 (disc. 1991), 4 (disc. 1991), or 5 in. barrel, round butt, full lug barrel, Pachmayr grips. New 1988.

Mfg.'s Sug. Retail	**$636**	**$510**	**$400**	**$310**

This variation has the frame stamped "625-2", roll engraved barrel with ".45 CAL MODEL OF 1988" barrel inscription.

MODEL 627 — .357 Mag. cal., also known as "Model of 1989" (stamped on barrel), N-frame, round butt, unfluted cylinder, full underlug 5½ in. barrel. Disc.

	$545	**$425**	**$325**

MODEL 629 — .44 Mag. cal., similar to Model 29. Available with 4, 6, or 8⅜ in. barrel.

Mfg.'s Sug. Retail	**$625**	**$510**	**$400**	**$310**

      Add $6 for 6 in. barrel or $21 for 8⅜ in. barrel.

      Add $52 for combat grips with barrel scope mount (cut across barrel rib) - disc. 1991 (8⅜ in. barrel only).

      Add 10% for pinned barrel with recessed cylinder.

      During 1978, approx. 100 revolvers were made with pinned barrels and recessed cylinders, serial range is 629,062-629,200, includes wood box. Prices range from $650-$750, depending on condition.

* Model 629 Classic — stainless steel variation of the Model 29 Classic, 5, 6½, or 8⅜ in. barrel. New in 1990.

Mfg.'s Sug. Retail	**$670**	**$530**	**$420**	**$320**

      Add $21 for 8⅜ in. barrel.

* Model 629 Classic DX — .44 Mag. cal., similar to Classic, except is supplied with 2 sets of grips (Hogue combat square and Morado wood round butt stocks), 6½ or 8⅜ in. barrel, 5 interchangeable front sights, numbered test target, 51-54 oz. New 1992.

Mfg.'s Sug. Retail	**$860**	**$700**	**$585**	**$485**

      Add $28 for 8⅜ in. barrel.

* Model 629 Magna Classic — .44 Mag. cal., similar to Model 29, 3,000 mfg. during 1990 only.

		$900	**$825**	**$750**

                       Last Mfg.'s Sug. Retail was $999.

* Model 629 Lew Horton Special — .44 Mag. cal., 3 in. barrel with round butt, adj. sights.

		$400	**$350**	**$295**

MODEL 631 — .32 Mag. cal., 6 shot, 2 or 4 in. barrel, combat stocks, round butt only, approx. 5,500 mfg. 1990-92.

		$340	**$275**	**$200**

                       Last Mfg.'s Sug. Retail was $386.

* 631 Ladysmith — 2 in. barrel only, rose stocks.

		$365	**$295**	**$225**

                       Last Mfg.'s Sug. Retail was $400.

MODEL 632 CENTENNIAL — .32 Mag. cal., 2 or 3 (mfg. 1991 only) in. barrel, stainless/alloy construction, fully concealed hammer, small frame, Santoprene combat grips, fixed sights, 15.5 oz. Mfg. 1991-1992.

		$315	**$240**	**$195**

                       Last Mfg.'s Sug. Retail was $410.

      Add 20% for 3 in. barrel.

MODEL 637 CHIEFS SPECIAL AIRWEIGHT — .38 S&W Spl. cal., 5 shot, alloy frame, 1⅞ in. barrel, stainless steel cylinder and barrel. 560 mfg. during 1991, reintroduced 1996.

Mfg.'s Sug. Retail	**$459**	**$340**	**$235**	**$190**

Grading	100%	98%	95%	90%	80%	70%	60%

MODEL 638 BODYGUARD AIRWEIGHT — .38 S&W Spl. cal., 5 shot, alloy frame, 1⅞ in. barrel, shrouded hammer, round butt, stainless steel barrel and cylinder, 1,200 mfg. during 1990 only, reintroduced 1998.

| Mfg.'s Sug. Retail | $492 | | $370 | $270 | $215 | | |

MODEL 640 CENTENNIAL — .38 S&W Spl. cal., 5 shot, 1⅞ (new 1998), 2⅛ (new 1991), or 3 (disc. 1992) in. barrel, fully concealed hammer, round butt, tested for +P+ ammo, 22½ oz. New in 1991.

| Mfg.'s Sug. Retail | $502 | | $375 | $260 | $200 | | |

MODEL 642 CENTENNIAL AIRWEIGHT — .38 S&W Spl. cal., 5 shot, 1⅞, 2 (disc. 1997), or 3 (disc. 1991) in. barrel, alloy frame with stainless steel cylinder and barrel, combat grips, concealed hammer, fixed rear sight, approx. 16 oz. Mfg. 1990-1992, reintroduced 1996.

| Mfg.'s Sug. Retail | $474 | | $350 | $260 | $200 | | |

MODEL 642 LADYSMITH AIRWEIGHT — .38 S&W Spl. cal., 5 shot, 2 in. barrel, stainless steel/alloy construction, smooth wood grips, satin stainless finish, includes soft side carry or jewelry case, 16 oz. New 1996.

| Mfg.'s Sug. Retail | $505 | | $390 | $280 | $205 | | |

MODEL 648 — .22 Mag. cal., 6 in. full lug barrel, combat grips, square butt, combat trigger, semi-target hammer. Mfg. 1990-94.

| | | | $350 | $250 | $195 | | |

Last Mfg.'s Sug. Retail was $464.

MODEL 649 BODYGUARD — similar to Model 49 Bodyguard, except in stainless steel, 1⅞ (mfg. 1998 only), 2 (disc. 1997), or 2⅛ (new 1998) in. barrel. New 1986.

| Mfg.'s Sug. Retail | $502 | | $375 | $260 | $200 | | |

MODEL 650 — .22 Mag. cal., service kit gun, stainless steel, 3 or 3½ in. heavy barrel, J-Frame, fixed sights. Mfg. 1983-87.

| | | | $250 | $200 | $185 | | |

Last Mfg.'s Sug. Retail was $305.

MODEL 651 KIT GUN — .22 Mag. cal., target kit gun, stainless steel, 4 in. barrel, J-Frame, adj. sights (same as old Model 51). Mfg. 1983-87, re-released in late 1990, disc. 1998.

| | | | $355 | $250 | $195 | | |

Last Mfg.'s Sug. Retail was $478.

This model could be ordered with a factory fitted optional .22 LR cylinder until 1987 (last mfg. sug. retail was $295 for the cylinder alone). This variation with the extra cylinder is very desirable.

MODEL 657 — .41 Mag. cal., 4 (disc.), 6, or 8⅜ (disc. 1992) in. barrel. New 1986.

| Mfg.'s Sug. Retail | $564 | | $435 | $325 | $260 | | |

Add $17 for 8⅜ in. barrel (disc. 1992).

★ *Model 657-3 Lew Horton Special* — .41 Mag. cal., 3 in. barrel with round butt, adj. sights.

| | | | $410 | $360 | $300 | | |

MODEL 681 DISTINGUISHED SERVICE — .357 Mag. cal., 4 in. barrel, L-Frame. Disc. 1988, reintroduced 1991-1992.

| | | | $320 | $235 | $195 | | |

Last Mfg.'s Sug. Retail was $412.

1991 mfg. includes square butt.

MODEL 686 DISTINGUISHED COMBAT — .357 Mag. cal., similar to Model 586, except 2½ (new 1990), 4, 6, or 8⅜ in. barrel, adj. sights, L-Frame.

| Mfg.'s Sug. Retail | $514 | | $410 | $275 | $225 | | |

Add $11 for 4 in., $16 for 6 in. barrel, or $36 for 8⅜ in. barrel.
Add $14 for white outline rear sight (disc. 1994).
Add $50 for adj. front sight with 6 or 8⅜ (disc. 1991) in. barrel only - new 1986.

★ *Model 686 Plus* — .357 Mag. cal., 7 shot, 2½, 4, or 6 in. barrel, synthetic grips, combat trigger, round (2½ in. barrel only) or square butt, white outline rear sight on 4 or 6 in. barrel. New 1996.

| Mfg.'s Sug. Retail | $534 | | $420 | $290 | $230 | | |

Add $8 for 4 in. or $16 for 6 in. barrel.

Grading	100%	98%	95%	90%	80%	70%	60%

* *1984 Model 686 Lew Horton Edition* — 2½ in. barrel only, limited mfg.

	$450	**$275**	**$225**				

MODEL 696 — .44 S&W Spl. cal., 5 shot, 3 in. barrel with full shroud, Hogue rubber grips, satin stainless steel, adj. rear sight, 48 oz. New 1997.

Mfg.'s Sug. Retail	**$525**		**$420**	**$285**	**$230**		

MODEL 940 CENTENNIAL — 9mm Para. cal., fully concealed hammer, 2 or 3 (disc. 1992) in. barrel, fixed rear sight, Santoprene combat grips, 23-25 oz. Mfg. 1991-98.

	$390	**$265**	**$220**				

Last Mfg.'s Sug. Retail was $493.

PISTOLS: SEMI-AUTO

Listed in order of model number (except .32 and .35 Automatic Pistols). Alphabetical models will appear at the end of this section.

To understand S&W 3rd generation model nomenclature, the following rules apply. The first two digits (of the four digit model number) specify caliber. Numbers 39, 59, and 69 refer to 9mm Para. cal. The third digit refers to the model type. 0 means standard model, 1 is for compact, 2 is for standard model with decocking lever, 3 is for compact variation with decocking lever, 4 is for standard with double action only, 5 designates a compact model in double action only, 6 indicates a non-standard barrel length, 7 is a non-standard barrel length with decocking lever, 8 refers to non-standard barrel length in double action only. The fourth digit refers to the material(s) used in the fabrication of the pistol. 3 refers to an aluminum alloy frame with stainless steel slide, 4 designates an aluminum alloy frame with carbon steel slide, 5 is for carbon steel frame and slide, 6 is a stainless steel frame and slide, and 7 refers to a stainless steel frame and carbon steel slide. Hence, a Model 4053 refers to a pistol in .40 S&W cal. configured in compact version with double action only and fabricated with an aluminum alloy frame and stainless steel slide. This model nomenclature does not apply to 2 or 3 digit model numbers (i.e., Rimfire Models and the Model 52).

100%	98%	95%	90%	80%	70%	60%	50%	40%	30%	20%	10%

.32 AUTOMATIC PISTOL — .32 ACP cal., 7 shot mag., 3½ in. barrel, blued with "S&W" monogram inlaid plain walnut grip. 957 mfg. 1924-1936. Serial range starting with S.N. 1.

$3,000	$2,500	$2,000	$1,750	$1,500	$1,250	$1,000	$800	$700	$600	$500	$400

.35 AUTOMATIC PISTOL (MODEL 1913) — .35 S&W Auto cal., 7 shot mag., 3½ in. barrel, blue or nickel w/"S&W" monogram inlaid in plain walnut grips. 8,350 mfg. 1913-1921. Serial range starting with No. 1.

$775	$625	$525	$450	$375	$325	$275	$235	$200	$185	$175	$165

A slight premium might exist for the first model (up to ser. no. 3,125).

Grading	100%	98%	95%	90%	80%	70%	60%

MODEL 22A SPORT SERIES — .22 LR cal., single action, 10 shot mag., aluminum alloy frame, stainless steel slide, choice of 4 standard, 5½ standard or bull, or 7 in. standard barrel with raised solid rib, adj. rear sight, 2-piece black polymer (hard or soft) or Dymondwood (5½ bull barrel only) grips, blued finish, 28-39 oz. New 1997.

Mfg.'s Sug. Retail	**$230**		**$190**	**$170**	**$140**	**$125**	**$110**	**$95**	**$80**

Add $25 for 5½ in. standard barrel with soft-touch grips.

Add $59 for 7 in. standard barrel with thumb rest soft-touch grips.

Add $90 for 5½ in. bull barrel with Dymondwood target grips.

Add $66 for 5½ in. bull barrel with 2 piece target grips and thumbrest.

Grading	100%	98%	95%	90%	80%	70%	60%

MODEL 22S SPORT SERIES — .22 LR cal., single action, 10 shot mag., aluminum alloy frame, stainless steel slide, choice of 5½ standard/bull or 7 in. standard barrel with raised solid rib, adj. rear sight, 2-piece black polymer (hard or soft) or Dymondwood (5½ bull barrel only) grips, satin stainless finish, 28-39 oz. New 1997.

Mfg.'s Sug. Retail	$312	$255	$220	$180	$160	$140	$125	$110

Add $32 for 7 in. standard barrel with thumb rest soft-touch grips.
Add $67 for 5½ in. bull barrel with Dymondwood target grips.
Add $41 for 5½ in. bull barrel with 2 piece target grips and thumbrest.

MODEL 39 ALLOY FRAME — 9mm Para. cal., alloy frame, this model was unmarked up to ser. no. approx. 2,600, early guns had a short safety lever, checkered walnut rips, blue or nickel finish. Mfg. started 1954.

		$400	$350	$315	$260	$210	$175	$140

Add 50% for early guns in the approx. ser. range 1,001-2,600.
Add $35 for nickel finish.

Collectors report an approx. ser. no. range 1,001-105,000 with long extractor rod.

First commercially mfg. 9mm Para. double action semi-auto in the U.S.

MODEL 39 STEEL FRAME — 9mm Para. cal., 8 shot, 4 in. barrel, long ejector rod, walnut stocks, blue, adj. rear windage only sight, double action, walnut grips, 927 mfg. during 1966 only in 3 ser. no. ranges.

		$1,200	$975	$850	$735	$650	$550	$475

MODEL 39-2 ALLOY FRAME (LATER PRODUCTION) — 9mm Para. cal., double action, 8 shot mag., 4 in. barrel, checkered walnut grips, adj. sight, alloy frame, approx. 1971, the 39-2 was introduced as an improved version. Mfg. 1970-1982.

		$360	$325	$260	$240	$220	$200	$195

Add $35 for nickel finish.

MODEL 41/41-1 .22 RF — .22 S (disc., Model 41-1) or LR cal., match target pistol, single action, 10 shot mag., adj. sights, walnut grips, 5 (disc.), 5½ (heavy) or 7 (standard) in. barrel, blue only. Mfg. 1957-present.

Mfg.'s Sug. Retail	$801	$565	$485	$380	$300	$260	$240	$220

Add $100 for 5½ in. barrel with extended sight (disc.).
Add $35 for 7⅜ in. barrel with muzzle brake (disc.).
Add 125% for .22 Short cal. with counterweight and muzzle brake (disc.).

Earlier variations (A series guns with cocking indicator, Model 41-1, etc.) will command substantial premiums over values listed above.

Note: there are several disc. barrels on the Model 41. They are the 5 in. standard weight with extended sight, 7⅜ in. with muzzle brake, and 5½ in. heavy barrel with extended sight.

MODEL 44 — 9mm Para. cal., single action design, S&W's rarest semi-auto pistol, approx. 10 mfg.

Extreme rarity precludes accurate price evaluation.

MODEL 46 — .22 LR cal., 5, 5½, or 7 in. barrel, blue, nylon grips, adj. sights. Mfg. 4,000, 1957-1966.

		$450	$335	$300	$260	$225	$200	$195

This model is similar to the Model 41, but does not have high polish bluing, and has brown plastic grips.

MODEL 52-A — .38 AMU cal., same action as Model 39, 4 in. barrel. Originally mfg. for U.S. Army Marksman Training Unit, 87 mfg.

		$3,000	$2,500	$2,200	$1,950	$1,600	$1,300	$1,000

MODEL 52 — .38 S&W Spl. Wadcutter only, similar action to Model 39, except incorporates a set screw locking out the double action, 5 in. barrel, 5 shot mag. Approx. 3,500 mfg. 1961-1963.

		$875	$775	$675	$575	$475	$395	$360

MODELS 52-1 & 52-2 — .38 Spl. Mid-Range Wadcutter cal. only, single action (Model 52-1) or double action (Model 52-2) semi-auto, 5 in. barrel, adj. sights, checkered walnut grips, blue only, 5 shot mag.

		$675	$556	$450	$400	$350	$295	$265

Last Mfg.'s Sug. Retail was $908.

The Model 52-1 was mfg. 1963-1971, and the Model 52-2 was mfg. 1971-1993.

Grading	100%	98%	95%	90%	80%	70%	60%

MODEL 59 — similar to Model 39, except has 14 shot mag., black nylon grips. Disc. 1981.

	$385	**$340**	**$270**	**$250**	**$225**	**$215**	**$200**

Add $35 for nickel finish.
Add $150 for smooth (ungrooved) grip frame.

MODEL 61 ESCORT — .22 LR cal., 5 shot, semi-auto, blue or nickel, 2½ in. barrel, plastic grips, mfg. 1970-1974.

	100%	98%	95%	90%	80%	70%	60%
Blue finish	$250	$210	$165	$150	$140	$110	$95
Nickel finish	$275	$230	$165	$150	$140	$110	$95

MODEL 147-A — 9mm Para. cal., 14 shot, steel frame, 4 in. barrel, black plastic grips, adj. sights for windage only, similar to Model 59, except has steel frame, 112 mfg. 1979 only.

	$1,050	**$875**	**$800**	**$725**	**$650**	**$575**	**$495**

MODEL 410 — .40 S&W cal., double action, steel slide with alloy frame, blue finish, 4 in. barrel, 10 shot mag., single side safety, 3 dot sights, straight backstrap with synthetic grips, 29.4 oz. New 1996.

Mfg.'s Sug. Retail	$515	$410	$300	$235	$205	$190	$175	$165

MODEL 411 — .40 S&W cal., 4 in. barrel, 11 shot mag., fixed sights, blue finish, aluminum alloy frame, manual safety. Mfg. 1993-95.

	$440	**$375**	**$335**	**$310**	**$295**	**$280**	**$265**

Last Mfg.'s Sug. Retail was $525.

MODEL 422 .22 RF (FIELD) — .22 LR cal., single action, 4½ or 6 in. barrel, aluminum frame with steel slide, 10 shot mag., fixed sights, black plastic or wood grips, matte blue finish, 22 oz. Mfg. 1987-96.

	$185	**$150**	**$115**	**$110**	**$105**	**$100**	**$95**

Last Mfg.'s Sug. Retail was $235.

* Model 422 Target — .22 LR cal., single action, 4½ or 6 in. barrel, aluminum frame with steel slide, 10 shot mag., adj. rear sight, checkered walnut grips, matte blue finish, 22 oz. Mfg. 1987-96.

	$225	**$175**	**$140**	**$115**	**$110**	**$105**	**$95**

Last Mfg.'s Sug. Retail was $290.

MODEL 439 — 9mm Para. cal., double action, 4 in. barrel, blue or nickel finish, alloy frame, 8 shot mag., checkered walnut grips, 30 oz. Disc. 1988.

	$385	**$315**	**$255**	**$240**	**$225**	**$210**	**$200**

Last Mfg.'s Sug. Retail was $472.

Add $34 for nickel finish (disc. 1986).
Add $26 for adj. sights.

MODEL 457 COMPACT — .45 ACP cal., traditional double action, alloy frame and steel slide, 3¾ in. barrel, single side safety, 3 dot sights, 7 shot mag., straight backstrap, blue finish only, black synthetic grips, 29 oz. New 1996.

Mfg.'s Sug. Retail	$515	$410	$300	$235	$205	$190	$175	$165

MODEL 459 — 9mm Para. cal., 14 shot version of Model 439, checkered nylon stocks, limited mfg. with squared-off triggerguard with serrations. Disc. 1988.

	$410	**$345**	**$290**	**$270**	**$255**	**$240**	**$210**

Last Mfg.'s Sug. Retail was $501.

Add $26 for adj. sights.
Add $44 for nickel finish (disc. 1986).

* Model 459 Brushed Finish — 9mm Para. cal., 14 shot, 4 in. barrel, dull finish, fixed sights, special grips made to F.B.I. or Police specs., 803 mfg.

	$650	**$600**	**$550**	**$440**	**$385**	**$330**	**$300**

MODEL 469 "MINI" — 9mm Para. cal., double action, alloy frame, 12 shot finger extension mag., short frame, bobbed hammer, 3½ in. barrel, sandblast blue or satin nickel finish, ambidextrous safety standard (1986), molded Delrin black Grips, 26 oz. Disc. 1988.

	$370	**$320**	**$265**	**$250**	**$235**	**$220**	**$210**

Last Mfg.'s Sug. Retail was $478.

Grading	100%	98%	95%	90%	80%	70%	60%

MODEL 539 — 9mm Para. cal., double action, steel frame, 8 shot, 4 in. barrel, blue or nickel. Approx. 10,000 mfg. Disc. 1983.

	$450	$395	$375	$350	$325	$300	$275

Add $35 for nickel finish.
Add $30 for adj. rear sight.

MODEL 559 — 9mm Para. cal., double action, steel frame, 12 shot, 4 in. barrel, blue or nickel. Approx. 10,000 mfg. Disc. 1983.

	$485	$435	$375	$275	$250	$225	$200

Add $35 for nickel finish.
Add $30 for adj. rear sight.

MODEL 622 .22 RF (Field) — .22 LR cal., single action, 4½ or 6 in. barrel, stainless/alloy construction, 10 shot mag., fixed sights, black plastic grips, 21½ or 23½ oz. Mfg. 1990-96.

$220	$175	$160

Last Mfg.'s Sug. Retail was $284.

* Model 622 Target — .22 LR cal., single action, 4½ or 6 in. barrel (VR was an option in 1996 only), stainless steel construction, 10 shot mag., adj. rear sight, checkered walnut grips, 21½ or 23½ oz. Mfg. 1990-96.

$275	$225	$175

Last Mfg.'s Sug. Retail was $337.

MODEL 639 STAINLESS — 9mm Para. cal., similar to Model 439-only stainless steel, 8 shot mag., ambidextrous safety became standard 1986, 36 oz. Disc. 1988.

$420	$300	$275

Last Mfg.'s Sug. Retail was $523.

Add $27 for adj. sights.

MODEL 645 STAINLESS — .45 ACP cal. only, 5 in. barrel, 8 shot mag., squared off trigger guard, black molded nylon grips, ambidextrous safety, fixed sights, 37½ oz. New 1986. Disc. 1988.

$475	$365	$300

Last Mfg.'s Sug. Retail was $622.

Add $27 for adj. sight.

Approx. 150 Model 645 "Interim" pistols were mfg. in 1988 only. Add $120 to values listed above.

MODEL 659 STAINLESS — 9mm Para. cal., similar to Model 459-only stainless steel, 14 shot mag., ambidextrous safety became standard 1986, 39½ oz. Disc. 1988.

$445	$335	$300

Last Mfg.'s Sug. Retail was $553.

Add $27 for adj. sights.

Approx. 150 Model 659 "Interim" pistols were mfg. in 1988 only. Add $150 to values listed above.

MODEL 669 STAINLESS — 9mm Para. cal., smaller version of Model 659 with 12 shot finger extension mag., 3½ in. barrel, fixed sights, molded Delrin grips, ambidextrous safety standard, 26 oz. Mfg. 1986-1988 only.

$425	$305	$275

Last Mfg.'s Sug. Retail was $522.

Approx. 150 Model 669 "Interim" pistols were mfg. in 1988 only. Add $150 to values listed above.

MODEL 745 IPSC — .45 ACP cal., single action, 5 in. barrel, stainless steel frame with steel slide, hammer, and trigger, checkered walnut stocks, fixed rear sight, 38¾ oz. Mfg. 1987-90.

$575	$440	$335

Last Mfg.'s Sug. Retail was $699.

Early guns had optional "IPSC" markings. Later, these markings became standard.

MODEL 908 — 9mm Para. cal., compact variation of the Model 909/910, 3½ in. barrel, 3 dot sights, 8 shot mag., straight backstrap, 26 oz. New 1996.

Mfg.'s Sug. Retail	$466		$375	$285	$230	$205	$190	$175	$165

Grading	100%	98%	95%	90%	80%	70%	60%

MODEL 909 — 9mm Para. cal., 4 in. barrel, traditional double action, 9 shot mag., fixed sights, single side safety, alloy frame and steel slide, curved backstrap with black synthetic grips, 27 oz. Mfg. 1994-96.

		$360	$275	$225	$205	$190	$175	$165

Last Mfg.'s Sug. Retail was $443.

MODEL 910 — similar to Model 909, except has 10 shot mag., 28 oz. New 1994.

Mfg.'s Sug. Retail	$466	$375	$285	$230	$205	$190	$175	$165

MODEL 915 — 9mm Para. cal., 4 in. barrel, fixed sights, 10 (C/B 1994) or 15★ shot mag., manual safety, aluminum alloy frame, blue finish. Mfg. 1993-94.

		$350	$255	$225	$205	$190	$175	$165

Last Mfg.'s Sug. Retail was $467.

MODEL 1006 STAINLESS — 10mm cal., double action semi-auto, stainless steel construction, 5 in. barrel, exposed hammer, 9 shot mag., fixed or adj. sights, ambidextrous safety. Mfg. 1990-1993.

		$635	$530	$400

Last Mfg.'s Sug. Retail was $769.

Add $27 for adj. rear sight.

MODEL 1026 STAINLESS — 10mm cal., 5 in. barrel, traditional double action, features frame mounted decocking lever, 9 shot mag., straight backstrap. Mfg. 1990-91 only.

		$630	$525	$400

Last Mfg.'s Sug. Retail was $755.

MODEL 1046 STAINLESS — 10mm cal., 5 in. barrel, fixed sights, double action only, 9 shot mag., straight backstrap. Mfg. 1991 only.

		$620	$515	$400

Last Mfg.'s Sug. Retail was $747.

MODEL 1066 STAINLESS — 10mm cal., 4¼ in. barrel, 9 shot mag., straight backstrap, ambidextrous safety, traditional double action, fixed sights. Mfg. 1990-1992.

		$610	$515	$395

Last Mfg.'s Sug. Retail was $730.

Add $40 for Tritium night sights - disc. 1991 (Model 1066-NS).

Only 1,000 Model 1066-NSs were manufactured.

MODEL 1076 STAINLESS — similar to Model 1026 Stainless, except has 4¼ in. barrel. Mfg. 1990-1993.

		$645	$530	$400

Last Mfg.'s Sug. Retail was $778.

MODEL 1086 STAINLESS — similar to Model 1066 Stainless, except is double action only.

		$710	$515	$395

Last Mfg.'s Sug. Retail was $730.

MODEL 2206 STAINLESS .22 RF (FIELD) — .22 LR cal., similar to Model 622 Field, except all stainless steel component, black plastic grips, 6 in. barrel with standard (disc. 1995) or adj. rear sight, 35 or 39 oz. Mfg. 1990-96.

		$290	$225	$175

Last Mfg.'s Sug. Retail was $385.

Subtract $58 if w/o adj. sights.

✴ *Model 2206 Stainless Target* — similar to Model 2206 Stainless, except has adj. target sight, target stocks, and is drilled and tapped. Mfg. 1994-96.

		$360	$275	$225

Last Mfg.'s Sug. Retail was $433.

MODEL 2213 STAINLESS .22 RF "SPORTSMAN" — .22 LR cal., single action, 3 in. barrel, alloy frame with stainless steel slide, 8 shot mag., 2 dot fixed rear sight, black plastic molded grips, 18 oz., includes holster/carry case. New 1992.

Mfg.'s Sug. Retail	$340	$255	$200	$160

MODEL 2214 .22 RF "SPORTSMAN" — .22 LR cal., similar to Model 2213, except has alloy frame with blue carbon steel slide with matte black finish, and no case. New 1991.

Mfg.'s Sug. Retail	$292	$230	$185	$160	$150	$140	$130	$120

Grading	100%	98%	95%	90%	80%	70%	60%

MODEL 3904 — 9mm Para. cal., double action semi-auto, aluminum alloy frame, 4 in. barrel with fixed bushing, 8 shot mag., Delrin one piece wraparound grips, exposed hammer, ambidextrous safety, beveled magazine well, extended squared off triggerguard, adj. or fixed rear sight, 3 dot sighting system, 28 oz. Mfg. 1989-91.

		$450	$385	$350	$325	$300	$280	$265

Last Mfg.'s Sug. Retail was $541.

Add $25 for adj. rear sight.

MODEL 3906 STAINLESS — stainless steel variation of the Model 3904, 35½ oz. Mfg. 1989-91.

	$510	$435	$375

Last Mfg.'s Sug. Retail was $604.

Add $28 for adj. rear sight.

MODEL 3913 COMPACT STAINLESS — stainless steel variation of the Model 3914, 25 oz. New 1990.

Mfg.'s Sug. Retail	$662		$535	$440	$365

* *Model 3913NL* — similar to Model 3913 Ladysmith, except does not have Ladysmith on the slide. Disc. 1994.

	$510	$425	$365

Last Mfg.'s Sug. Retail was $622.

* *Model 3913 LS (LadySmith)* — similar to Model 3913 Stainless, except has white Delrin grips and mag. does not have finger extension, 25 oz. New in 1990.

Mfg.'s Sug. Retail	$682		$560	$450	$365

MODEL 3913TSW — 9mm Para. cal., traditional double action, compact frame, 3½ in. barrel, 7 shot mag., 3 dot sights, stainless steel slide, aluminum alloy frame, satin stainless finish, 24.3 oz. New 1998.

Mfg.'s Sug. Retail	$694		$570	$455	$370

MODEL 3914 COMPACT — 9mm Para. cal., double action semi-auto, aluminum alloy frame, 3½ in. barrel, hammerless, 8 shot finger extension mag., fixed sights only, ambidextrous safety, blue finish, straight backstrap grip, 25 oz. Mfg. 1990-95.

		$465	$385	$340	$320	$295	$280	$265

Last Mfg.'s Sug. Retail was $562.

This model was also available with a single side manual safety at no extra charge - disc. 1991 (Model 3914NL).

* *Model 3914 LadySmith* — similar to Model 3914, except has Delrin grips, 25 oz. Mfg. 1990-91 only.

	$485	$415	$365

Last Mfg.'s Sug. Retail was $568.

MODEL 3953 COMPACT STAINLESS — 9mm Para. cal., double action only, aluminum alloy frame with stainless steel slide, compact model with 3½ in. barrel, 8 shot mag. New in 1990.

Mfg.'s Sug. Retail	$662		$535	$440	$365

MODEL 3953TSW — similar to Model 3913TSW, except is double action only. New 1998.

Mfg.'s Sug. Retail	$694		$570	$455	$370

MODEL 3954 — similar to Model 3953, except has blue steel slide. Mfg. 1990-1992.

	$445	$380	$340	$320	$295	$280	$265

Last Mfg.'s Sug. Retail was $528.

MODEL 4003 STAINLESS — .40 S&W cal., traditional double action, 4 in. barrel, 11 shot mag., white dot fixed sights, ambidextrous safety, aluminum alloy frame with stainless steel slide, one piece Xenoy wraparound grips, straight gripstrap, 28 oz. Mfg. 1991-1993.

	$585	$495	$395

Last Mfg.'s Sug. Retail was $698.

MODEL 4004 — .40 S&W cal., similar to Model 4003, except has aluminum alloy frame with blue carbon steel slide. Mfg. 1991-1992.

	$540	$460	$375	$325	$295	$280	$265

Last Mfg.'s Sug. Retail was $643.

Grading	100%	98%	95%	90%	80%	70%	60%

MODEL 4006 STAINLESS — .40 S&W cal., 3½ (Shorty Forty) or 4 in. barrel, 10 (C/B 1994) or 11★ shot mag., satin stainless finish, exposed hammer, Delrin one piece wraparound grips, 3 dot sights, 38½ oz. New in 1990.

Mfg.'s Sug. Retail	**$791**	**$655**	**$545**	**$400**			

　　Add $31 for adj. rear sight.
　　Add $115 for fixed Tritium night sights (new 1992).
　　The bobbed hammer option on this model was disc. in 1991.

MODEL 4013 COMPACT STAINLESS — .40 S&W cal., semi-auto, standard double action, 3½ in. barrel, 8 shot mag., fixed sights, ambidextrous safety, alloy frame. Mfg. 1991-96.

	$595	**$485**	**$385**	**$330**	**$295**	**$280**	**$265**

Last Mfg.'s Sug. Retail was $722.

MODEL 4013TSW (TACTICAL) — .40 S&W cal., semi-auto, standard double action, 3½ in. barrel, 9 shot mag. with reversible mag. catch, aluminum alloy frame with stainless steel slide, satin stainless finish, black synthetic grips, fixed sights, ambidextrous safety, 26 oz. New 1997.

Mfg.'s Sug. Retail	**$823**	**$685**	**$550**	**$410**			

MODEL 4014 COMPACT — similar to Model 4013, except is steel with blue finish. Mfg. 1991-1993.

	$510	**$425**	**$375**	**$330**	**$300**	**$275**	**$250**

Last Mfg.'s Sug. Retail was $635.

MODEL 4026 STAINLESS — .40 S&W cal., traditional double action with frame mounted decocking lever, 10 (C/B 1994) or 11★ shot mag., fixed sights, curved backstrap, 36 oz. Mfg. 1991-1993.

	$620	**$520**	**$400**				

Last Mfg.'s Sug. Retail was $731.

MODEL 4043 STAINLESS — .40 S&W cal., double action only, aluminum alloy frame with stainless steel slide, 4 in. barrel, 10 (C/B 1994) or 11★ shot mag., one piece Xenoy wraparound grips, straight backstrap, white dot fixed sights, 30 oz. New 1991.

Mfg.'s Sug. Retail	**$772**	**$635**	**$510**	**$390**			

MODEL 4044 — .40 S&W cal., similar to Model 4043, except has carbon steel slide. Mfg. 1991-1992.

	$540	**$460**	**$375**	**$325**	**$295**	**$280**	**$265**

Last Mfg.'s Sug. Retail was $643.

MODEL 4046 STAINLESS — similar to Model 4006 Stainless, except is double action only, 4 in. barrel only. New in 1991.

Mfg.'s Sug. Retail	**$791**	**$655**	**$540**	**$400**			

　　Add $115 for Tritium night sights (new 1992).

MODEL 4053 COMPACT STAINLESS — double action only variation of the Model 4013. Mfg. 1991-97.

	$600	**$490**	**$380**				

Last Mfg.'s Sug. Retail was $734.

MODEL 4053TSW/4056TSW (TACTICAL) — .40 S&W cal., double action only, 3½ in. barrel, 9 shot mag. with reversible mag. catch, alloy frame with stainless steel slide, satin stainless finish, black synthetic grips, fixed sights, ambidextrous safety, 36½ oz. New 1997.

Mfg.'s Sug. Retail	**$823**	**$685**	**$555**	**$410**			

MODEL 4054 — double action only variation of the Model 4014. Mfg. 1991-1992.

	$510	**$425**	**$375**				

Last Mfg.'s Sug. Retail was $629.

MODEL 4505 — .45 ACP cal., carbon steel variation of the Model 4506, fixed or adj. rear sight. 1,200 mfg. 1991 only.

	$575	**$500**	**$450**	**$400**	**$350**	**$300**	**$265**

Last Mfg.'s Sug. Retail was $660.

　　Add $27 for adj. rear sight.

Grading	100%	98%	95%	90%	80%	70%	60%

MODEL 4506 STAINLESS — .45 ACP cal., 5 in. barrel, 8 shot mag., combat triggerguard, exposed hammer, fixed or adj. rear sight, straight backstrap (curved is optional), Delrin one-piece grips, 38½ oz. New in 1990.

| Mfg.'s Sug. Retail | $822 | | $680 | $550 | $410 | | |

Add $33 for adj. rear sight.

Approx. 100 Model 4506s left the factory mismarked Model 645 on the frame. In NIB condition they are worth $700.

MODEL 4513TSW — 45 ACP cal., traditional double action, compact frame, 3¾ in. barrel, 7 shot mag., 3 dot sights, stainless steel slide, aluminum alloy frame, satin stainless finish, 28 oz. New 1998.

| Mfg.'s Sug. Retail | $781 | | $350 | $535 | $410 | | |

MODEL 4516 COMPACT STAINLESS — .45 ACP cal., hammerless compact variation of the Model 4506, 3¾ in. barrel, 7 shot mag., ambidextrous safety, fixed rear sight only, 34 oz. Mfg. 1990-97.

| | | | $655 | $535 | $400 | | |

Last Mfg.'s Sug. Retail was $787.

Original model is marked 4516 while later mfg. changed slide legend to read 4516-1. Original mfg. is more collectible and slight premiums are being asked.

MODEL 4526 STAINLESS — similar to Model 4506 Stainless, except has frame mounted decocking lever. Mfg. 1990-91 only.

| | | | $635 | $530 | $400 | | |

Last Mfg.'s Sug. Retail was $762.

MODEL 4536 STAINLESS — similar to Model 4516 Compact, except has frame mounted decocking lever only. Mfg. 1990-91 only.

| | | | $635 | $530 | $400 | | |

Last Mfg.'s Sug. Retail was $762.

MODEL 4546 STAINLESS — similar to Model 4506 Stainless, except is double action only. Mfg. 1990-91 only.

| | | | $620 | $520 | $400 | | |

Last Mfg.'s Sug. Retail was $735.

MODEL 4553TSW — similar to Model 4513TSW, except is double action only. New 1998.

| Mfg.'s Sug. Retail | $781 | | $650 | $535 | $410 | | |

MODEL 4556 STAINLESS — .45 ACP cal., features double action only, 3¾ in. barrel, 7 shot mag., fixed sights. Mfg. 1991 only.

| | | | $620 | $520 | $400 | | |

Last Mfg.'s Sug. Retail was $735.

MODEL 4566 STAINLESS — .45 ACP cal., traditional double action with ambidextrous safety, 4¼ in. barrel, 8 shot mag. New in 1990.

| Mfg.'s Sug. Retail | $822 | | $680 | $550 | $410 | | |

MODEL 4567-NS STAINLESS — similar to Model 4566 Stainless, except has Tritium night sights, stainless steel frame and carbon steel slide. 2,500 mfg. in 1991 only.

| | | | $620 | $520 | $400 | | |

Last Mfg.'s Sug. Retail was $735.

MODEL 4576 STAINLESS — .45 ACP cal., features 4¼ in. barrel, frame mounted decocking lever, fixed sights. Mfg. 1990-1992.

| | | | $635 | $535 | $410 | | |

Last Mfg.'s Sug. Retail was $762.

MODEL 4586 STAINLESS — .45 ACP cal., 4¼ in. barrel, double action only, 8 shot mag. New in 1990.

| Mfg.'s Sug. Retail | $822 | | $680 | $550 | $410 | | |

MODEL 5903 — 9mm Para. cal., double action semi-auto, 4 in. barrel, stainless steel slide and alloy frame, exposed hammer, 10 (C/B 1994) or 15★ shot mag., adj. (disc. 1993) or fixed rear sight, ambidextrous safety. Mfg. 1990-97.

| | | | $575 | $470 | $395 | $365 | $325 | $300 | $285 |

Last Mfg.'s Sug. Retail was $701.

Add $30 for adj. rear sight (disc).

Grading	100%	98%	95%	90%	80%	70%	60%

MODEL 5904 — similar to Model 5903, except has steel slide and blue finish, 26½ oz. Mfg. 1989-1998.

	$535	$445	$360	$330	$300	$280	$265

Last Mfg.'s Sug. Retail was $663.

Add $30 for adj. rear sight (disc. 1993).

MODEL 5905 — 9mm Para. cal., similar to Model 5904, except has carbon steel frame and slide. Approx. 5,000 mfg. 1990-91 only.

More research is underway regarding this model.

	$650	$575	$500	$440	$375	$335	$300

MODEL 5906 STAINLESS — stainless steel variation of the Model 5904, 37½ oz. New 1989.

Mfg.'s Sug. Retail	$751		$615	$500	$400		

Add $37 for adj. rear sight.
Add $115 for Tritium night sights.

MODEL 5924 — 9mm Para. cal., 4 in. barrel, features frame mounted decocking lever, 15 shot mag., 37½ oz. Mfg. 1990-91 only.

	$515	$440	$365	$330	$300	$280	$265

Last Mfg.'s Sug. Retail was $635.

MODEL 5926 STAINLESS — stainless variation of the Model 5924. Disc. 1992.

	$580	$480	$395				

Last Mfg.'s Sug. Retail was $697.

MODEL 5943 STAINLESS — 9mm Para. cal., double action only, 4 in. barrel, aluminum alloy frame with stainless steel slide, straight backstrap, 15 shot mag. Mfg. 1990-91 only.

	$550	$465	$390				

Last Mfg.'s Sug. Retail was $655.

   * *Model 5943-SSV Stainless* — similar to Model 5943 Stainless, except has 3½ in. barrel, Tritium night sights. Mfg. 1990-91 only.

	$580	$485	$395				

Last Mfg.'s Sug. Retail was $690.

MODEL 5944 — similar to Model 5943 Stainless, except has blue finish slide. Mfg. 1990-91 only.

	$510	$435	$360	$330	$300	$280	$265

Last Mfg.'s Sug. Retail was $610.

MODEL 5946 STAINLESS — double action only, one piece Xenoy wraparound grips, all stainless steel variation of the Model 5943, 39½ oz. New in 1990.

Mfg.'s Sug. Retail	$751		$615	$500	$400		

MODEL 6904 COMPACT — compact variation of the Model 5904, 3½ in. barrel, 10 (C/B 1994) or 12★ shot finger extension mag., fixed rear sight, 26½ oz. Mfg. 1989-1997.

	$510	$410	$350	$325	$300	$280	$265

Last Mfg.'s Sug. Retail was $625.

MODEL 6906 COMPACT STAINLESS — stainless steel variation of the Model 6904, 26½ oz. New 1989.

Mfg.'s Sug. Retail	$720		$585	$470	$380		

Add $116 for Tritium night sights (new 1992).

MODEL 6926 STAINLESS — 9mm Para. cal., 3½ in. barrel, standard double action, features frame mounted decocking lever, aluminum alloy frame with stainless slide, 12 shot mag. Mfg. 1990-91 only.

	$550	$455	$375				

Last Mfg.'s Sug. Retail was $663.

MODEL 6944 — 9mm Para., double action only, 3½ in. barrel, 12 shot mag., aluminum alloy frame with blue steel slide. Mfg. 1990-91 only.

	$480	$400	$350	$325	$300	$280	$265

Last Mfg.'s Sug. Retail was $578.

MODEL 6946 STAINLESS — similar to Model 6944, except has stainless steel slide, semi-bobbed hammer, 26½ oz. New in 1990.

Mfg.'s Sug. Retail	$720		$585	$470	$375		

Grading	100%	98%	95%	90%	80%	70%	60%

MODEL CS9 CHIEFS SPECIAL — 9mm Para. cal., compact design with traditional double action, hammerless, 3 in. barrel, 7 shot mag., alloy frame/steel frame and barrel or stainless steel construction, Hogue wraparound rubber grips, 3 dot sights, 20.8 oz. New 1999.

Mfg.'s Sug. Retail	$593	$485	$385	$340	$295	$260	$230	$195

MODEL CS40 CHIEFS SPECIAL — .40 S&W cal., similar to Model CS9, except has 3¼ in. barrel, 24.2 oz. New 1999.

Mfg.'s Sug. Retail	$624	$510	$400	$350	$300	$265	$230	$195

MODEL CS45 CHIEFS SPECIAL — .45 ACP cal., similar to Model CS40, except has 6 shot mag., 23.9 oz. New 1999.

Mfg.'s Sug. Retail	$624	$510	$400	$350	$300	$265	$230	$195

SIGMA MODEL SW380 — .380 ACP cal., double action only, 3 in. barrel, fixed sights, polymer frame and steel slide, striker firing system, blue finish only, 6 shot mag., shortened grip, 14 oz. New 1996.

Mfg.'s Sug. Retail	$328	$265	$235	$205	$190	$180	$170	$160

SIGMA MODEL SW9F — 9mm Para. cal., double action only, 4½ in. barrel, fixed sights, polymer frame and steel slide, striker firing system, blue finish only, 10 (C/B 1994) or 17★ shot mag., 26 oz. Mfg. 1994-96.

	$485	$390	$345	$320	$295	$280	$265

Last Mfg.'s Sug. Retail was $593.

Add $104 for Tritium night sights.

* **Compact Sigma Model SW9C** — similar to Sigma Model SW9F, except has 4 in. barrel, 25 oz. Mfg. 1996-98.

	$450	$355	$325	$295	$280	$265	$240

Last Mfg.'s Sug. Retail was $541.

* **Compact Sigma Model SW9M** — features 3¼ in. barrel, 7 shot mag., fixed channel rear sight, grips integral with frame, satin black finish, 18 oz. Mfg. 1996-98.

	$300	$270	$240	$220	$195	$175	$160

Last Mfg.'s Sug. Retail was $366.

* **Sigma Model SW9V/SW9VE** — features 4 in. barrel, 10 shot mag., 3-dot sighting system, grips integral with choice of grey or black polymer frame, satin stainless steel slide, 25 oz. New 1997.

Mfg.'s Sug. Retail	$409	$330	$285	$245

Add $107 for Tritium night sights.

The Enhanced Sigma Series Model SW9VE was introduced during 1999.

SIGMA MODEL SW40F — .40 S&W cal., double action only, 4½ in. barrel, fixed sights, polymer frame, blue finish only, 10 (C/B 1994) or 15★ shot mag., 26 oz. Mfg. 1994-98.

	$450	$355	$325	$295	$280	$265	$240

Last Mfg.'s Sug. Retail was $541.

Add $104 for Tritium night sights (disc. 1997).

* **Compact Sigma Model SW40C** — similar to Sigma Model SW40F, except has 4 in. barrel, 26 oz. Mfg. 1996-98.

	$450	$355	$325	$295	$280	$265	$240

Last Mfg.'s Sug. Retail was $541.

* **Sigma Model SW40V/SW40VE** — features 4 in. barrel, 10 shot mag., 3-dot sighting system, grips integral with choice of grey or black polymer frame, satin stainless steel slide, 25 oz. New 1997.

Mfg.'s Sug. Retail	$409	$330	$285	$245

Add $107 for Tritium night sights.

The Enhanced Sigma Series Model SW40VE was introduced during 1999.

ENGRAVING OPTIONS FOR CURRENT PRODUCTION HANDGUNS

The prices listed below are for original factory finished guns with no extra engraving. The listings below show 1998 factory engraving costs. These prices should be added to the cost of each engraved production gun to determine the correct value.

CLASS "C" ENGRAVING—1/3 METAL COVERAGE
Pistols — add $1,025.
For J Frame — add $810.
10⅝ in. N Frame — add $1,242.
2-5 in. K, L, or N Frame — add $1,045.
6-8⅜ in. K, L, or N Frame — add $1,188.

CLASS "B" ENGRAVING — ⅔ METAL COVERAGE
Pistols — add $1,339.
For J Frame — add $1,322.
10⅝ in. N Frame — add $1,546.
2-5 in. K, L, or N Frame — add $1,366.
6-8⅜ in. K, L, or N Frame — add $1,478.

CLASS "A" ENGRAVING — FULL COVERAGE
Pistols — add $1,629.
For J Frame — add $1,388.
2-5 in. K, L, or N Frame — add $1,677.
6-8⅜ in. K, L, or N Frame — add $1,774.
10⅝ in. N Frame — add $1,855.

SPECIAL ENGRAVING — Also available: inlays, seals, game scenes, lettering, prices quoted on request.

LASERSMITH ENGRAVING — laser etching was available 1989-1990 only. This process involved a digitally controlled laser producing a variety of designs, logos, commemorative messages, or autograph on the metal surface(s). Some of these designs were made exclusively for major firearms distributors. Others were custom designed for clubs or organizations. Retail prices started at just under $18 and went as high as $150+, depending on the amount and complexity of the laser etching. To date, premiums are not being paid for these "rarer" variations.

S&W COMMEMORATIVES/SPECIAL EDITIONS

During the course of a year, I receive many phone calls and letters on special editions and limited editions that do not appear in this section. It should be noted that a commemorative issue is a gun that has been manufactured, marketed, and sold through the auspices of the specific trademark (in this case S&W). During the past several decades, hundreds of limited editions have been ordered through various police agencies, state highway patrol units, and other law enforcement organizations. Many of these variations do not have the special suffix serialization (and may not have had a retail price when issued). Since most of these special editions/commemoratives were made for a specific organization, regional demand has a lot to do with determining values (a Model 66 Montana HP Commemorative will not sell for a premium in Alabama). For this reason, most of these guns will not appear in this section and you should contact the factory to learn more about the provenance of these special editions. Remember - values on these models can vary A LOT from one region to another and an averaged "national" single price is almost impossible. While these guns do have special interest, they do not have the collectability or desirability of many of the standard models listed below.

The variations listed below represent the only five factory S&W Commemoratives manufactured to date. Anything else will be a special or limited edition made for a organization, company, or special event.

Grading	100%	Issue Price	Qty. Made
MODEL 19 TEXAS RANGER — .357 Mag., with or without knife, approx. 8,000 with knife, approx. 2,000 without, cased. Mfg. 1973 only.			
	$595	$250	10,000
* *Model 19 Texas Ranger Deluxe* — approx. 50 mfg. with a serial numbers divisible by 10, cased.			
	N/A	N/A	50
125TH ANNIVERSARY COMMEMORATIVE — .45 LC cal., plain variation was called Model 25-3, 10,000 mfg. total in 1977, cased with nickel silver medallion, and Roy Jinks's book, "125th Anniversary of Smith & Wesson".			
	$450	$350	10,000

Grading	100%	Issue Price	Qty. Made

* **125th Anniversary Commemorative Deluxe** — Model 25-4, approx. 50 mfg. with S&W prefix serial numbers divisible by 10, cased, sterling silver medallion, and a leather bound "History of Smith & Wesson" book by Roy Jinks.

	N/A	N/A	50

MODEL 29 ELMER KEITH COMMEMORATIVE — .44 Mag. cal., 4 in. barrel, standard and deluxe editions, approx. 2,000 total mfg.

	$850	N/A	2,000

50TH ANNIVERSARY OF THE .357 MAGNUM — Model 27, both standard and deluxe editions, 1987 mfg.

	$450	N/A	N/A

MODEL 544 TEXAS WAGON TRAIN COMMEMORATIVE — .44-40 WCF cal. only, 6 shot, 5 in. barrel, bright blue finish, adj. sights, 7,800 mfg. 1986 to commemorate the Texas Sesquicentennial (1836-1986). Special markings on frame and barrel, smooth Goncalo commemorative grips, ser. no. TWT001 - TWT7800 (estimated). Made 1986 only.

	$450	N/A	7,800

100%	98%	95%	90%	80%	70%	60%	50%	40%	30%	20%	10%

RIFLES

S&W in 1984 disc. importation of all Howa manufactured rifles. Mossberg continued importation utilizing both leftover S&W parts in addition to fabricating their own.

MODEL 320 REVOLVING RIFLE — .320 S&W cal., 6 shot cylinder, 16, 18, or 20 in. round barrel, hard rubber grips, detachable shoulder stock, blue or nickel (rare, add a premium) finish. 977 mfg. 1879-1887.

* **16 or 20 in. barrel Model** — 239 mfg. with 16 in., and 224 with 20 in. barrel.

100%	98%	95%	90%	80%	70%	60%	50%	40%	30%	20%	10%
$12,000	$10,000	$8,700	$8,100	$7,675	$7,000	$6,375	$5,600	$4,800	$3,850	$2,950	$1,950

* **18 in. barrel Model** — 514 mfg.

100%	98%	95%	90%	80%	70%	60%	50%	40%	30%	20%	10%
$9,750	$9,350	$8,700	$8,100	$7,675	$7,000	$6,375	$5,600	$4,800	$3,850	$2,950	$1,950

Grading	100%	98%	95%	90%	80%	70%	60%

MODEL A BOLT ACTION RIFLE — .22-250 Rem., .243 Win., .270 Win., .308 Win., .30-06, 7mm Mag., or .300 Win. Mag. cal., 23¾ in. barrel, folding leaf sight, checkered Monte Carlo stock with rosewood forend tip and pistol grip cap. Mfg. 1969-1972.

	$385	$330	$305	$275	$220	$195	$165

MODEL B — similar to Model A, in .243 Win., .270 Win., or .30-06 cal., 20¾ in. barrel, Schnabel forend.

	$425	$305	$275	$250	$195	$165	$140

MODEL C — similar to Model B, with cheekpiece.

	$425	$305	$275	$250	$195	$165	$140

MODEL D — similar to Model C, with full length stock.

	$550	$385	$360	$305	$250	$220	$195

MODEL E — similar to Model D, with no cheekpiece.

	$550	$385	$360	$305	$250	$220	$195

Note: These rifles were made for S&W by Husqvarna in Sweden.

MODEL 1500 MOUNTAINEER — .222 Rem., .22-250 Rem., .223 Rem, .243 Win, .25-06 Rem, .270 Win, .30-06, or .308 Win. cal., bolt action, 22 in. barrel 5-6 shot mag., no sights, walnut stock and forend, approx. 7 lbs. 10 oz. New 1983.

	$300	$250	$245	$210	$195	$175	$160

Add $27 for sights.

* **Model 1500 Mountaineer Magnum** — 7mm Rem. Mag. or .300 Win. Mag. cal.

	$325	$275	$260	$225	$200	$180	$160

Grading	100%	98%	95%	90%	80%	70%	60%

MODEL 1500 DELUXE — same cals. as standard 1500, Monte Carlo stock, skip-line checkering, select walnut, no sights. New 1983.

	$350	$300	$260	$220	$200	$180	$160

Add $20 for 7mm Mag. and .300 Win. Mag.

MODEL 1500 DELUXE VARMINT — .222 Rem, .22-250 Rem., or .223 Rem. cal., heavy 24 in. barrel, skip-line checkering, no sights. New 1983.

	$350	$275	$315	$275	$215	$195	$170

Add $15 for parkerized finish.

MODEL 1700 LS "CLASSIC HUNTER" — .243 Win, 270 Win, or .30-06 cal., 22 in. barrel, removable 5 shot mag., solid recoil pad, no sights, Schnabel forend, finely checkered. New 1983.

	$400	$350	$315	$265	$240	$220	$195

S

SHOTGUNS

S&W in 1984 disc. importation of all Howa manufactured shotguns. Mossberg continued importation utilizing both leftover S&W parts in addition to fabricating their own.

MODEL 916 SLIDE ACTION SHOTGUN — 12, 16, or 20 ga., 20, 26, 28, or 30 in. barrels, various chokes, plain pistol grip stock, solid frame. Mfg. by S&W in Springfield, MA. 1972-disc.

	$175	$150	$140	$130	$120	$110	$100

* *Vent. rib and pad*

	$200	$175	$155	$145	$135	$130	$120

MODEL 916T SLIDE ACTION — similar to 916, except barrels can be interchanged.

	$195	$170	$155	$145	$135	$130	$125

* *Vent. rib and pad*

	$225	$200	$180	$170	$155	$145	$135

MODEL 96 SLIDE ACTION — various gauges, disc.

	$125	$110	$100	$90	$75	$70	$65

MODEL 1000 P SLIDE ACTION — 12 ga., various barrel lengths, chokes, VR.

	$350	$305	$270	$230	$210	$190	$170

This model is the same as the Model 3000.

MODEL 3000 SLIDE ACTION — 12 or 20 ga., 3 in. chambers, 22-30 in. barrels, walnut stock and forend, 6¼-7½ lbs.

	$350	$305	$270	$230	$210	$190	$170

Add $30 for multi-choke tubes.
Subtract $40 for slug gun (rifle sights on 22 in. barrel).
This model was also available in a "Waterfowler" variation - values are approx. the same as listed above.

MODEL 3000 POLICE — 12 ga. only, blue or parkerized finish, many combinations of finishes, stock types, and other combat accessories were available for this model, 18 or 20 in. barrel.

	$332	$255	$215	$185	$170	$155	$140

Add $70 for folding stock.

MODEL 1000 AUTOLOADER — 12 or 20 ga., 22-30 in. barrels, various chokes, gas operated, vent rib, engraved alloy receiver, checkered pistol grip stock. Mfg. 1972-1984.

	$350	$325	$295	$260	$240	$220	$200

Add $30 for multi-choke tubes.
Add approx. $125 for slug barrel.

* *12 and 20 gauge* — Magnum 28 or 30 in. barrel, multi-chokes, steel receiver, "M" suffix.

	$375	$340	$310	$275	$255	$235	$215

* *Model 1000 Super 12* — handles all loads interchangeably, top-of-the-line model during its time.

	$500	$450	$400	$360	$330	$300	$280

Add $50 for multi-choke.

Grading	100%	98%	95%	90%	80%	70%	60%

MODEL 1000 TARGET — 12 or 20 ga., skeet, super skeet and trap models available. Super skeet has 15 barrel muzzle vents to reduce recoil. Trap model has multi-choke tubes, Monte Carlo select walnut stock and forend. Both alloy and steel receivers available in Skeet model, Trap is steel only.

	100%	98%	95%	90%	80%	70%	60%
Skeet/Super Skeet	$400	$390	$335	$260	$235	$215	$190
Trap (Model 1000T)	$595	$525	$450	$375	$325	$285	$235

Note: Shotguns made for S&W by Howa Machinery, Ltd., Japan.

SOMMER + OCKENFUSS GmbH

Current rifle manufacturer located in Baiersbronn, Germany. Currently imported by Intertex Carousels Corporation during late 1998, and located in Pineville, NC.

RIFLES: SLIDE ACTION

SHORTY AMERICAN HUNTER — most popular cals., unique slide action rifle in bullpup configuration featuring a straight line design with a grip safety pistol grip that also works the slide assembly, stainless or black coated barrel, sideplates inlet into the stock. Importation began 1998.

Mfg.'s Sug. Retail	$1,480	$1,375	$1,100	$995	$925	$850	$750	$650

Add $110 for recoil brake and match trigger (Shorty Marksman Rifle).
Add $480 for .375 H&H or .416 Rem. Mag. cal. (Shorty Safari).
Subtract $40 for fiberglass synthetic stock (Shorty American Hunter Synthetic).
Subtract $90 for if w/o sideplates (Shorty Wilderness Rifle).

There are also deluxe variations and limited editions available in this model - please contact the importer directly for current availability and pricing.

SNAKE CHARMER

Currently manufactured by Sporting Arms Manufacturing, Inc. located in Littlefield, TX. Distributor sales only.

SHOTGUNS: SINGLE SHOT

SNAKE CHARMER II — .410 bore only, stainless steel, break open single shot, molded plastic stock and forend, shell holder in stock, 3½ lbs. Also available as Night Charmer (disc. 1988) and Sea Charmer (disc. 1988).

Mfg.'s Sug. Retail	$149	$125	$100	$85

Add $10 for Night Charmer.
Add $18 for Sea Charmer.
Subtract $10 for black carbon steel barrel (New Generation Model).

SOCIETA SIDERURGICA GLISENTI

Previous manufacturer located in Brescia, Italy. Also see the Italian Military Arms listing.

PISTOLS: SEMI-AUTO

GLISENTI MODEL 1910 — 9mm Glisenti cal., 7 shot, 4 in. barrel, fixed sights, blue, checkered wood, rubber or plastic grips, Italian service pistol. Mfg. 1910-WWII.

Warning: While some Glisentis may chamber and fire the 9mm Para. cartridge, it is extremely dangerous to do so.

$750	$625	$450	$325	$275	$225	$200

SODIA, FRANZ

Previous manufacturer located in Ferlach, Austria until 1992.

Sodia arms are superb and are often excellently engraved and inlaid. Professional appraisal should be sought before purchase, since prices are high. Sodia is famous for double-barrel shotguns as well as two and three barrel combinations of rifles and shotguns.

DRILLING

BOCKDRILLING — various cals., 2 rifle barrels and 1 shotgun, top quality workmanship.

$7,000	$6,500	$6,000	$5,000	$4,000	$3,000	$2,500

Grading	100%	98%	95%	90%	80%	70%	60%

RIFLES: DOUBLE, CUSTOM

DOPPELBÜCHSE — various cals., SxS double rifle, top quality workmanship.

	$5,000	$4,500	$4,000	$3,000	$2,000	$1,800	$1,600

O/U RIFLE — various cals., top quality workmanship.

	$4,500	$4,250	$4,000	$3,500	$3,000	$2,000	$1,800

SHOTGUNS; O/U

TRAP SHOTGUN — 12 ga. only, boxlock action, various degrees of engraving and ornamentation.

	$2,500	$1,850	$1,475	$1,100	$900	$750	$600

SOKOLOVSKY CORPORATION SPORT ARMS (SCSA) **S**

Previous manufacturer until 1990 located in Sunnyvale, CA.

PISTOLS: SEMI-AUTO

SOKOLOVSKY .45 AUTOMASTER — .45 ACP cal. only, stainless steel, single action, 6 in. barrel, 6 shot mag., adj. Millet sights, unique action, is free of external devices, 55 oz. Mfg. 1984-90.

	$2,700	$2,200	$1,850

Last Mfg.'s Sug. Retail was $3,300.

Total production on this model is 50 pistols.

SOLEIHAC ARMURIER

Previous manufacturer located in Saint Etienne, France.

This manufacturer produced copies of 1894 patent Darne R model guns until 1950. The guns produced were generally simple and less expensive than other manufacturers' sliding breech guns. Most unmarked sliding breech guns were probably manufactured by Soleihac Armurier. Quality and pricing will be similar to low grade (Halifax and RIO model) Darne guns in average condition.

SPENCER REPEATING RIFLES CO.

Previously manufactured by Spencer Repeating Rifle Company located in Boston, MA between 1860-1868. Spencer manufactured approximately 144,000 rimfire rifles and carbines, of which approximately 107,000 were contracted to the United States Government during the Civil War.

The brainchild of young Christopher Miner Spencer, more than 13,500 Spencer M1860 Army rifles, 800 M1860 Navy rifles, and 48,000 M1860 Army carbines saw action during the Civil War.

In late 1864, the Chief of Ordnance directed modifications, including reducing the bore from .52 to .50 caliber, and shortening the barrel from 22 inches to 20 inches. The new carbine was designated the Spencer M1865 carbine. Nearly 19,000 were produced by the Spencer Repeating Rifle Company, and another 30,500 by the Burnside Rifle Company, although all were delivered too late to see action in the Civil war. Model 1865 carbines and re-furbished M1860 carbines became the mainstay of America's troops on the Western Frontier until replaced by "Trap-Door" Springfield carbines after 1873.

The author wishes to express his thanks to Mr. Roy Marcot for providing most of the information listed below.

RIFLES: LEVER ACTION

100%	98%	95%	90%	80%	70%	60%	50%	40%	30%	20%	10%

SMALL-FRAME MILITARY CARBINES AND SPORTING RIFLES — fewer than four dozen prototype small-frame .38 cal. sporting rifles and .44 cal. military carbines were made by Christopher Spencer in Hartford between 1860 and 1861. They are exceedingly rare, and only a few are in private hands.

N/A	$12,000	$11,000	$10,000	$8,900	$8,000	$7,000	$6,000	$5,250	$4,250	$3,250	$2,250

100%	98%	95%	90%	80%	70%	60%	50%	40%	30%	20%	10%

MODEL 1860 NAVY RIFLES — the rarest of production Spencer firearms, 803 Spencer Model 1860 Navy rifles with sword-type bayonets were produced for the U.S. Navy Bureau of Ordnance between 1862 and 1863.

N/A	$9,000	$7,950	$6,850	$5,850	$4,850	$3,950	$3,450	$2,900	$2,500	$2,000	$1,500

Add $350-$750 for sword-type bayonets.

MODEL 1860 ARMY RIFLES — between 1863 and 1864, the Spencer factory in Boston produced 11,471 Spencer M1860 Army rifles for the Federal Ordnance Department, another 200 for the U.S. Navy, and approximately 2,000 for private purchase. All were issued with Pattern M1855 angular bayonets which fit only these rifles.

N/A	$6,000	$5,000	$4,000	$3,250	$2,450	$2,150	$1,900	$1,700	$1,500	$1,250	$1,100

Add $200-$450 for angular bayonets.

MODEL 1860 CARBINES — beginning in October 1863, the Spencer factory began delivering the first of 45,733 Spencer M1860 carbines to the Ordnance Department for use by Federal cavalrymen. As many as 3,000 additional M1860 carbines went to private purchasers, and also saw action in the war. Because Spencer carbines were so important to the Federal war effort, nearly all saw hard use during the last 18 months of fighting. This resulted in very few weapons available today in excellent condition, and fewer yet with case colors remaining on the receiver.

N/A	$7,500	$6,750	$6,000	$3,250	$2,250	$1,950	$1,750	$1,500	$1,200	$875	$700

Subtract 25% for Springfield Armory reconditioned Spencer Model 1860 carbines (after the war).

MODEL 1865 CARBINES — in 1865 and 1866, the Spencer factory delivered 18,959 Spencer M1865 carbines to the Federal Ordnance Department. Concurrently, the Burnside Rifle Company of Providence, Rhode Island manufactured and delivered 30,502 Spencer M1865 carbines to the Ordnance Department.

N/A	$4,500	$3,975	$3,500	$2,600	$1,850	$1,650	$1,475	$1,275	$1,000	$875	$700

MODEL 1865 ARMY RIFLES — as many as 3,000 Spencer M1865 Army rifles were made by the Spencer factory in 1865. While none were ordered by the U.S. Army Ordnance Department, 2,000 went to the Commonwealth of Massachusetts National Guard, and another 1,000 went to Canadian troops and to private purchasers.

N/A	$3,500	$2,600	$1,850	$1,650	$1,475	$1,275	$1,000	$875	$775	$650	$550

SPRINGFIELD ARMORY RIFLE MUSKET CONVERSION OF SPENCER CARBINES — in 1871, General Dyer, Chief of Ordnance, directed that 1,109 Spencer M1865 carbines be converted to two-band muskets. Each was fitted with Springfield .50 calber barrels which held standard M1855 pattern bayonet.

N/A	$3,975	$3,500	$2,950	$2,550	$2,325	$2,175	$1,975	$1,750	$1,500	$1,000	$875

MODEL 1867 ARMY RIFLES AND CARBINES — in 1867, the Spencer factory produced approx. 1,000 M1867 Army rifles and 12,000 carbines. All were intended for private domestic or foreign military sales.

N/A	$2,950	$2,500	$1,950	$1,500	$1,300	$1,100	$900	$800	$700	$600	$500

NEW MODEL ARMY RIFLES AND CARBINES — in their final year of production, 1868, the Spencer Repeating Rifle Company produced approx. 1,000 Army rifles and 5,000 carbines. These too, were intended for private domestic or foreign military sales.

N/A	$2,950	$2,500	$1,950	$1,500	$1,300	$1,100	$900	$800	$700	$600	$500

SPORTING RIFLES — between 1864 and 1868, the Spencer factory produced approximately 2,000 sporting rifles for the civilian trade. The initial 200 or so were made from surplus military M1860 Army rifle receivers. Thereafter, approximatley 1,800 sporting rifles were made expressly as such. The majority chambered the Spencer 56-46 bottleneck rimfire cartridge, but a small number were produced in .50 caliber, chambering 56-50 and the 56-52 cartridges. Spencer sporting rifles missing the rear tang sight are worth approximately 25% less than those listed above.

N/A	$3,975	$3,500	$2,950	$2,550	$2,225	$1,975	$1,750	$1,350	$1,000	$800	$675

SPHINX

Previously manufactured circa 1993-96 by Sphinx Engineering S.A. located in Porrentruy, Switzerland. Previously imported by Sphinx U.S.A., located in Meriden, CT until 1996. Previously imported by Sile Distributors located in New York, NY.

Grading	100%	98%	95%	90%	80%	70%	60%

PISTOLS

MODEL AT-380 — .380 ACP cal., semi-auto double action only, 3.27 in. barrel, stainless steel frame, two-tone finish, 10 shot mag. with finger extension, checkered walnut grips. Disc. 1996.

	$435	$375	$350	$325	$295	$275	$250

Last Mfg.'s Sug. Retail was $494.

> Add $20 for black finish.
> Add $71 for N/Pall finish.

MODEL AT-2000S STANDARD — 9mm Para. or .40 S&W (new 1993) cal., semi-auto in standard double action or double action only, 4.53 in. barrel, stainless steel fabrication, 10 (C/B 1994), 15★ (9mm Para.), or 11★ (.40 S&W) shot mag., checkered walnut grips, choice of two-tone or N/Pall (disc. 1994) finish, fixed sights, 35 oz. This model was originally derived from the Action Arms Model AT-88. Disc. 1996.

	$965	$750	$625	$525	$450	$410	$375

Last Mfg.'s Sug. Retail was $1,090.

> Add $117 for .40 S&W cal.
> Add $87 for N/Pall finish.

★ *Model AT-2000PS Police Special* — similar to Model AT-2000S, except has compact slide and 3.66 in. barrel. Disc. 1996.

	$850	$625	$525	$450	$410	$380	$350

Last Mfg.'s Sug. Retail was $940.

> Add $40 for .40 S&W cal.
> Add $87 for N/Pall finish.

★ *Model AT-2000P Compact* — similar to Model AT-2000 Standard, except has 3.66 in. barrel and 13 shot mag., 31 oz. Disc. 1996.

	$850	$625	$525	$450	$410	$380	$350

Last Mfg.'s Sug. Retail was $940.

> Add $40 for .40 S&W cal.
> Add $87 for N/Pall finish.

★ *Model AT-2000H Sub-Compact* — similar to Model AT-2000 Compact, except has 3.34 in. barrel and 10 shot mag., 26 oz. Disc. 1996.

	$850	$625	$525	$450	$410	$380	$350

Last Mfg.'s Sug. Retail was $940.

> Add $40 for .40 S&W cal.
> Add $87 for N/Pall finish.

MODEL AT-2000MS MASTER — 9mm Para., 9x21mm, or .40 S&W cal., single action only, two-tone finish only, designed for Master's stock class competition. Mfg. 1995.

	$1,795	$1,350	$1,100	$995	$895	$775	$650

Last Mfg.'s Sug. Retail was $2,035.

MODEL AT-2000CS COMPETITOR — 9mm Para., 9x21mm, or .40 S&W cal., single or double action, competition model featuring many shooting improvements including 5.3 in. compensated barrel, 10 (C/B 1994), 11★ (.40 S&W), or 15★ shot mag., Bo-Mar adj. sights, two-tone finish. Imported 1993-96.

	$1,725	$1,275	$1,050	$950	$850	$750	$675

Last Mfg.'s Sug. Retail was $1,902.

> Add $287 for Model AT-2000C (includes Sphinx scope mount).
> Add $1,538 for AT-2000K conversion kit (new 1995).
> Add $1,490 for Model AT-2000CKS (competition kit to convert AT-2000 to comp. pistol, disc. 1994).

MODEL AT-2000GMS GRAND MASTER — similar to Model AT-2000 Competitor, except is SA only and includes more advanced competitive shooting features, Bo-Mar sights, top-of-the-line competition model. Imported 1993-96.

	$2,475	$1,925	$1,725	$1,500	$1,250	$1,050	$895

Last Mfg.'s Sug. Retail was $2,894.

> Add $78 for Model AT-2000GM (includes Sphinx scope mount).

SPITFIRE

See listing under JSL (Hereford) in this text.

Grading	100%	98%	95%	90%	80%	70%	60%

SPRINGFIELD ARMORY

America's first federal armory located in Springfield, MA. Production began in 1795 and an Act of Congress made it an official federal arsenal in 1872. Not associated with the private firm of the same name located in Geneseo, IL.

In recent years, collectors have realized that military specimens in 98%-100% original condition are very rare and desirable in most cases. Since the supply of these guns is so limited, values listed below for these condition factors may not be indicative of current market conditions. As always, many collectors agree that it is hard to overpay for a mint, original, military specimen.

MODEL 1870 ROLLING-BLOCK RIFLE, U.S.N. — .50 cal. centerfire, 32⅝ in. barrel, not serial numbered, 22,013 mfg.

	$2,200	$2,000	$1,800	$1,400	$1,000	$900	$750

MODEL 1871 ROLLING-BLOCK RIFLE, U.S.A. — .50 cal. centerfire, 36 in. barrel, not serial numbered, 10,001 mfg.

	$1,800	$1,600	$1,300	$1,000	$900	$750	$650

MODEL 1873 RIFLE "TRAPDOOR" — .45-70 Govt. cal., 32⅝ in. barrel, 2 bands. Approx. 73,000 mfg. between 1873-1877. Subtract 20% if stock cartouche faint or absent.

	$2,000	$1,800	$1,500	$1,150	$775	$650	$450

MODEL 1884 RIFLE "TRAPDOOR" — .45-70 Govt. cal., 32⅝ in. barrel, 2 bands. Approx. 232,000 mfg. between 1885-1890. Subtract 20% if stock cartouche faint or absent.

	$1,500	$1,250	$950	$725	$625	$525	$425

MODEL 1873 CARBINE — 22 in. barrel, half stock, single barrel band/stacking swivel, 20,000 made, but semi-scarce. Pre-Custer serial numbers below 43,700, add up to 50%. (Pre-1876 mfg.).

	$5,500	$4,500	$3,000	$2,500	$2,200	$1,850	$1,600

MODEL 1873 CADET RIFLE — .45-70 Govt. cal., 29½ in. barrel, stacking swivel, no sling swivels.

	$1,600	$1,400	$1,300	$1,050	$900	$775	$650	$600

Subtract $100 for variation with sling-swivels.
Subtract 25-35% if restocked with butt plate and hole drilled for cleaning tools.

MODEL 1875 OFFICER'S RIFLE FIRST TYPE — .45-70 Govt. cal., mfg. 477 between 1875 and 1886, 26 in. barrel, single barrel band. Not serial numbered, some dated, non-issue.

	N/A	$27,500	$24,000	$21,000	$18,000	$11,000	$8,500

Subtract 15-20% for types 2 and 3.
Approx. 25 rifles were mfg. prior to the standardization of this model.

MODEL 1877 RIFLE — .45-70 Govt. cal., mfg. 3,943.

	$2,950	$2,650	$2,250	$1,875	$1,625	$1,325	$1,175

MODEL 1877 CARBINE — .45-70 Govt. cal., 22 in. barrel, "C" rear sight to 1,200 yards. Mfg. 2,946.

	$4,500	$3,500	$2,950	$2,425	$2,175	$1,900	$1,750

MODEL 1877 CADET RIFLE — .45-70 Govt. cal., 29½ in. barrel. Mfg. 1,050.

	$1,475	$1,200	$1,000	$950	$900	$800	$700

MODEL 1879 RIFLE — .45-70 Govt. cal., mfg. approx. 140,000.

	$1,350	$1,150	$950	$850	$700	$650	$450

MODEL 1879 CARBINE — .45-70 Govt. cal., no stacking swivel. Approx. 15,000 mfg.

	$2,750	$2,300	$2,000	$1,750	$1,200	$950	$750

MODEL 1879 CADET RIFLE — .45-70 Govt. cal., stacking swivel but no sling swivels. Mfg. 5,000.

	$850	$775	$650	$550	$475	$425	$375

MODEL 1880 — .45-70 Govt. cal., combination triangular, sliding type, bayonet-ramrod. Mfg. 1,001.

	$2,950	$2,675	$2,400	$2,100	$1,875	$1,675	$1,500

MODEL 1881 FORAGER — 20 ga., 1,376 mfg. 1881-1885. Be cautious when purchasing.

	$2,250	$1,950	$1,700	$1,500	$1,250	$1,100	$1,000

Grading	100%	98%	95%	90%	80%	70%	60%

KRAG-JORGENSEN VARIATIONS MFG. BY SPRINGFIELD

Please refer to the Krag-Jorgensen section.

U.S. MODEL 1903 SPRINGFIELD — .30-06 cal., bolt action, mfg. by Springfield Armory and Rock Island Arsenal, 24 in. barrel. Mfg. 1903-1930.

* *Pre-WWI Mfg.* — values below represent original rifles.

	100%	98%	95%	90%	80%	70%	60%
	$4,850	$3,950	$3,050	$2,200	$1,950	$1,675	$1,400

Subtract 80% if reworked.

* *Serialized 800,000 - 1,275,767* — double heat treated receiver.

	$3,450	$2,750	$2,250	$1,975	$1,450	$1,200	$995

* *Serialized 1,275,768+* — nickel steel receiver.

	$1,250	$1,050	$925	$850	$800	$750	$700

U.S. MODEL 1903 MARK I — .30-06 cal., similar to U.S. Model 1903 Springfield, except altered for the Pedersen device, a slot is milled into the left side of receiver to act as an ejection port for use of the semi-auto bolt insert, value without device.

	$1,400	$1,250	$1,050	$990	$850	$700	$600

1903-A1 — .30-06 cal., similar to U.S. Model 1903 Springfield, except type C pistol grip stock. Mfg. 1930-1939. In 1941 Remington mfg. approx. 350,000.

	$900	$825	$750	$700	$600	$525	$450

* *Remington produced*

	$795	$725	$650	$575	$500	$450	$395

1903-A1 NATIONAL MATCH

	$2,000	$1,750	$1,350	$1,100	$950	$900	$850

1903-A3 — .30-06 cal., similar to 1903, with production modifications, aperture rear sight, no finger groove in forestock, lower quality finish, stamped floorplate and barrel band. Mfg. WWII by Remington and Smith Corona.

	$525	$435	$395	$360	$330	$300	$275

1903-A3 NATIONAL MATCH — 200 mfg., known as the "unmatched" match rifle.

	$1,500	$1,300	$1,000	$850	$750	$675	$600

1903-A4 SNIPER — .30-06 cal., with M73B1 or M84 scope in Redfield mount, no front sight.

	$1,450	$1,150	$875	$700	$575	$500	$450

1903 MARINE SNIPER — .30-06 cal., includes 8X Unertl scope.

	$2,000	$1,600	$1,250	$900	$775	$625	$500

If this model is verified as an original, large premiums are currently being asked on values listed above.

1903 NRA SPORTING RIFLE — .30-06 cal., over 4,000 mfg.

	$695	$625	$550	$495	$450	$375	$295

1903 NRA NATIONAL MATCH — .30-06 cal., similar to 1903, with hand selected and custom fit parts, produced for target shooting. "NRA" and flaming bomb proofed on trigger guard. 1915 date.

	$1,250	$1,000	$775	$675	$575	$500	$450

1903 SPORTER — .30-06 cal., similar to National Match, with sporter stock and Lyman sight.

	$1,200	$1,000	$825	$750	$625	$525	$470

1903 MATCH STYLE T — .30-06 cal., similar to Sporter, with heavy barrel, globe sight, target bases, 26, 28, or 30 in. barrel.

	$1,650	$1,350	$1,050	$875	$725	$635	$580

1903 FREE RIFLE TYPE A — .30-06 cal., similar to Style T, with 28 in. barrel, and Swiss hook butt.

	$1,850	$1,600	$1,325	$1,150	$995	$895	$775

1903 FREE RIFLE TYPE B — .30-06 cal., similar to Type A, with double set triggers, cheekpiece stock, modified firing pin.

	$2,500	$2,000	$1,725	$1,350	$1,075	$950	$825

S

Grading	100%	98%	95%	90%	80%	70%	60%

MODEL 1922-M1 — .22 LR cal., Target Rifle, 5 shot mag., 24 in. barrel, modified 1903, Lyman receiver sight, sporter stock, issued 1927.

	$995	$900	$825	$725	$625	$550	$495

MODEL 1922 NRA VARIATION — not tapped for scope, without forend grooves.

	$2,500	$2,250	$1,925	$1,725	$1,500	$1,250	$1,000

M2 .22 TARGET RIFLE — similar to 1922 M1, except improved lock time, adj. head space, bolt design.

	$1,000	$900	$800	$700	$600	$550	$500

SPRINGFIELD ARMORY (MFG. BY SPRINGFIELD INC.)

Currently manufactured by Springfield Inc. located in Geneseo, IL. Springfield Inc. has also imported a variety of models. This company was named Springfield Armory, Geneseo, IL until 1992.

The Springfield Inc. manufactures commercial pistols and rifles, including reproductions of older military handguns and rifles.

The Oldest Name In American Firearms
SPRINGFIELD ARMORY

COMBINATION GUNS

M6 SCOUT — .22 LR, .22 Mag. (disc.), or .22 Hornet cal./.410 O/U Survival Gun, 14 (legal transfer needed) or 18¼ in. barrels, matte or stainless (new 1995) steel, approx. 4 lbs.

Mfg.'s Sug. Retail	$176	$150	$125	$100	$85	$75	$70	$65

Add $32 for stainless steel.

Older mfg. does not incorporate a trigger guard while newer production has a trigger guard.

PISTOLS: COMBINATION

M6 PISTOL — .22 LR cal. over .45 LC cal. (also shoots .410 bore shotshells), 16 in. barrels. Mfg. Aug. 1991 - 1992.

	$200	$185	$165	$150	$135	$120	$110

Last Mfg.'s Sug. Retail was $226.

PISTOLS: SEMI-AUTO

OMEGA PISTOL — .38 Super, 10mm Norma, or .45 ACP cal., single action, ported slide, 5 or 6 in. interchangeable ported or unported barrel with Polygon rifling, special lock-up system eliminates normal barrel link and bushing, Pachmayr grips, dual extractors, adj. rear sight. Mfg. 1987-90.

	$775	$650	$575	$495	$425	$360	$295

Last Mfg.'s Sug. Retail was $849.

Add $663 for interchangeable conversion units.

Each conversion unit includes an entire slide assembly, one mag., 5 or 6 in barrel, recoil spring guide mechanism assembly, and factory fitting.

Add $336 for interchangeable 5 or 6 in. barrel (including factory installation).

OMEGA MATCH — same cals. as Omega, except has low profile combat sights, 8 shot mag., and beveled mag. well. Mfg. 1991-1992.

	$925	$775	$660	$535	$460	$420	$385

Last Mfg.'s Sug. Retail was $1,103.

Springfield Semi-Auto Pistols: P9 Series

MODEL P9 — 9mm Para., 9x21mm (new 1991) .40 S&W (new 1991), or .45 ACP cal., patterned after the Czech CZ-75, selective double action design, blue (standard beginning 1993), parkerized (standard until 1992), or duotone finish, various barrel lengths, checkered walnut grips. Mfg. in U.S. starting 1990.

Grading	100%	98%	95%	90%	80%	70%	60%

* **P9 Standard** — 4.72 in. barrel, 15 shot (9mm Para.), 11 shot (.40 S&W), or 10 shot (.45 ACP) mag., parkerized finish standard until 1992 - blued finish beginning 1993, 32.16 oz. Disc. 1993.

	$430	$375	$335	$295	$275	$240	$215

Last Mfg.'s Sug. Retail was $518.

> Add $61 for .45 ACP cal.
> Add $182 for duotone finish (disc. 1992).
> Subtract $40 for parkerized finish.
> In 1992, Springfield added a redesigned stainless steel trigger, patented sear safety which disengages the trigger from the double action mechanism when the safety is on, lengthened the beavertail grip area offering less "pinch", and added a two piece slide stop design.

* **P9 Stainless** — similar to P9 Standard, except is constructed from stainless steel, 35.3 oz. Mfg. 1991-1993.

	$475	$425	$350

Last Mfg.'s Sug. Retail was $589.

> Add $50 for .45 ACP cal.

* **P9 Compact** — 9mm Para. or .40 S&W cal., 3.66 in. barrel, 13 shot (9mm Para.) or 10 shot (.40 S&W) mag., shorter slide and frame, rounded triggerguard, 30½ oz. Disc. 1992.

	$395	$350	$300	$275	$250	$225	$200

Last Mfg.'s Sug. Retail was $499.

> Add $20 for .40 S&W cal.
> Add $20-$30 for blue finish depending on cal.
> Add $78 for duotone finish.

* **P9 Sub-Compact** — 9mm Para. or .40 S&W cal., smaller frame than the P9 Compact, 3.66 in. barrel, 12 shot (9mm Para.) or 9 shot (.40 S&W) finger extension mag., squared off triggerguard, 30.1 oz. Disc. 1992.

	$395	$350	$300	$275	$250	$225	$200

Last Mfg.'s Sug. Retail was $499.

> Add $20 for .40 S&W cal.
> Add $20-$30 for blue finish depending on cal.

* **P9 Factory Comp** — 9mm Para., .40 S&W, or .45 ACP cal., 5½ in. barrel (with compensator attached), extended sear safety and mag. release, adj. rear sight, slim competition checkered wood grips, choice of all stainless (disc. 1992) or stainless bi-tone (matte black slide), dual port compensated, 15 shot (9mm Para.), 11 shot (.40 S&W), or 10 shot (.45 ACP) mag., 33.9 oz. Mfg. 1992-1993.

	$595	$525	$450	$420	$390	$360	$330

Last Mfg.'s Sug. Retail was $699.

> Add $36 for .45 ACP cal.
> Add $75-$100 for all stainless finish.

* **P9 Ultra IPSC (LSP)** — competition model with 5.03 in. barrel (long slide ported), adj. rear sight, choice of parkerized (standard finish until 1992 when disc.), blued (disc. 1992), bi-tone (became standard 1993), or stainless steel (disc. 1992) finish, extended thumb safety, and rubberized competition (9mm Para. and .40 S&W cals. only) or checkered walnut (.45 ACP cal. only) grips, 15 shot (9mm Para.), 11 shot (.40 S&W), or 10 shot (.45 ACP) mag., 34.6 oz. Disc. 1993.

	$555	$475	$415	$350	$300	$275	$250

Last Mfg.'s Sug. Retail was $694.

> Add $30 for .45 ACP cal.

* **P9 Ultra LSP Stainless** — stainless steel variation of the P9 Ultra LSP. Mfg. 1991-92.

	$675	$525	$425

Last Mfg.'s Sug. Retail was $769.

> Add $30 for .40 S&W cal.
> Add $90 for .45 ACP cal.

* **P9 World Cup** — see listing under 1911-A1 Custom Models heading.

Grading	100%	98%	95%	90%	80%	70%	60%

Springfield Semi-Auto Pistols: R-Series

PANTHER MODEL — 9mm Para., .40 S&W, or .45 ACP cal., semi-auto single or double action, 3.8 in. barrel, hammer drop or firing pin safety, 15 shot (9mm Para.), 11 shot (.40 S&W), or 9 shot (.45 ACP) mag., Commander hammer, frame mounted slide stop, narrow profile, non-glare blue finish only, walnut grips, squared off triggerguard, 29 oz. Mfg. 1992 only.

	$535	$450	$395	$350	$300	$275	$250

Last Mfg.'s Sug. Retail was $609.

FIRECAT MODEL — 9mm Para. or .40 S&W cal., single action, 3.5 in. barrel, 3 dot low profile sights, all steel mfg., firing pin block and frame mounted ambidextrous safety, 8 shot (9mm Para.) or 7 shot (.40 S&W) mag., checkered combat style triggerguard and front/rear grip straps, non-glare blue finish, 35¾ oz. Mfg. 1992-1993.

	$495	$425	$375	$330	$295	$275	$250

Last Mfg.'s Sug. Retail was $569.

BOBCAT MODEL — while advertised in 1992, this model was never mfg.

LINX MODEL — while advertised in 1992, this model was never mfg.

Springfield Pistols: 1911-A2 SASS Single Shot

1911-A2 SASS — various cals., single shot break open action featuring interchangeable barrels, Pachmayr grips, adj. front and rear sights, blue finish only, 61-66 oz. Mfg. 1990-1992.

* **10¾ in. barrel** — .22 LR, 7mm BR, .243 Win., .357 Mag., or .44 Mag. cal.

	$650	$560	$495	$450	$420	$390	$360

Last Mfg.'s Sug. Retail was $749.

Add $399 per interchangeable conversion unit (includes barrel).

* **15 in. barrel** — .22 LR, .223 Rem., .243 Win. (new 1991), 7mm BR, 7mm-08 Rem., .308 Win., or .358 Win. cal.

	$650	$560	$495	$450	$420	$390	$360

Last Mfg.'s Sug. Retail was $749.

Add $399 per interchangeable conversion unit (includes barrel).

Springfield Semi-Auto Pistols: Disc. 1911-A1 Models

MODEL 1911-A1 STANDARD MODEL — .38 Super, 9mm Para., 10mm (new 1990), or .45 ACP cal., patterned after the Colt M1911-A1, 5.04 (Standard) or 4.025 (Commander or Compact Model) in. barrel, 7 shot (Compact), 8 shot (.45 ACP), 9 shot (10mm), or 10 shot (9mm Para. and .38 Super) mag., walnut grips, parkerized, blue, or duotone finish. Mfg. 1985-1990.

	$400	$360	$330	$300	$280	$260	$240

Last Mfg.'s Sug. Retail was $454.

Add $35 for blued finish.
Add $80 for duotone finish.

This model was also available with a .45 ACP to 9mm Para. conversion kit for $170 in parkerized finish, or $175 in blued finish.

* **Defender Model** — .45 ACP cal. only, similar to Standard 1911-A1 Model, except has fixed combat sights, beveled mag. well, extended thumb safety, bobbed hammer, flared ejection port, walnut grips, factory serrated front strap and two stainless steel magazines, parkerized or blued finish. Mfg. 1988-90.

	$485	$435	$375	$340	$300	$280	$260

Last Mfg.'s Sug. Retail was $567.

Add $35 for blued finish.

* **Commander Model** — .45 ACP cal. only, similar to Standard 1911-A1 Model, except has 3.63 in. barrel, shortened slide, Commander hammer, low profile 3-dot sights, walnut grips, parkerized, blued, or duotone finish. Mfg. in 1990 only.

	$450	$415	$350	$325	$285	$260	$245

Last Mfg.'s Sug. Retail was $514.

Add $30 for blued finish.
Add $80 for duotone finish.

S

Grading	100%	98%	95%	90%	80%	70%	60%

* **Combat Commander Model** — .45 ACP cal. only, 4¼ in. barrel, bobbed hammer, walnut grips. Mfg. 1988-89.

	$435	$385	$325	$295	$275	$250	$230

   Add $20 for blued finish.

* **Compact Model** — .45 ACP cal. only, compact variation featuring shortened Commander barrel and slide, reduced M1911 straight grip strap frame, checkered walnut grips, low profile 3-dot sights, extended slide stop, combat hammer, parkerized, blued, or duotone finish. Mfg. 1990 only.

	$450	$415	$350	$325	$285	$260	$245

   Last Mfg.'s Sug. Retail was $514.

   Add $30 for blued finish.
   Add $80 for duotone finish.

* **Custom Carry Gun** — .38 Super (special order only), 9mm Para., 10mm (new 1990), or .45 ACP cal., similar to Defender Model, except has tuned trigger pull, heavy recoil spring, extended thumb safety, and other features. Mfg. 1988 - Disc.

		$860	$725	$660	$535	$460	$420	$385

   Last Mfg.'s Sug. Retail was $969.

   Add $130 for .38 Super Ramped, 10mm was POR.

* **National Match Hardball Model** — .38 Super (disc.), 9mm Para. (disc.), or .45 ACP cal., National Match barrel and bushing, specially fitted frame and slide, BoMar adj. rear sight, Herrett walnut grips, plastic cased. Mfg. 1988-90.

		$780	$650	$565	$515	$460	$415	$385

   Last Mfg.'s Sug. Retail was $897.

   This model was made specifically for DCM competition shooting.

* **Bullseye Wadcutter Model** — .45 ACP cal. only, designed for wadcutter loads only, 5 or 6 (ported or unported) in. barrel, BoMar rib mounted on slide, checkered grip straps, match trigger, beavertail grip safety, polished feed ramp and throated barrel. Mfg. 1989 - Disc.

		$1,415	$1,200	$1,025	$925	$825	$750	$675

   Last Mfg.'s Sug. Retail was $1,599.

   Add $25 for 6 in. barrel.
   Add $80 for 6 in. ported barrel.

* **Trophy Master Competition Pistol** — .38 Super, 9mm Para. (disc.), 10mm (new 1990), or .45 ACP cal., competition model which includes low profile combat sights, ambidextrous safety, long match trigger, bobbed hammer, Pachmayr wraparound grips. Mfg. 1988-90.

		$1,300	$1,100	$950	$875	$800	$730	$660

   Last Mfg.'s Sug. Retail was $1,443.

   Add $130 for .38 Super with supported chamber, 10mm was POR.

* **Trophy Master Competition Expert Model** — .38 Super, 9mm Para. (disc.), 10mm (new 1990), or .45 ACP cal., mfg. for IPSC competition shooting, dual chamber compensator system on match barrel, blued finish, ambidextrous thumb safety, beveled and polished mag. well, lowered and flared ejection port, wraparound Pachmayr grips, shock buffer, includes 2 mags. and plastic carrying case. Mfg. 1988-90.

		$1,664	$1,450	$1,225	$1,025	$950	$890	$850

   Last Mfg.'s Sug. Retail was $1,664.

   Add $130 for .38 Super with supported chamber, 10mm was POR.
   This model was an improved variation of the Master Grade Competition Pistol "A".

* **Trophy Master Competition Distinguished Model** — similar to Expert Model, except has brushed hard chrome finish, checkered grip straps and trigger guard, top-of-the-line competition model. Mfg. 1988-90.

		$2,000	$1,675	$1,450	$1,225	$1,025	$950	$875

   Last Mfg.'s Sug. Retail was $2,275.

   Add $130 for .38 Super with supported chamber, 10mm was POR.
   Subtract $130 for "B" Model.
   This model was an improved variation of the Master Grade Competition Pistol "B-1".

S

Grading	100%	98%	95%	90%	80%	70%	60%

Springfield Semi-Auto Pistols: 1911-A1 90s Series

The initials "PDP" refer to Springfield's Personal Defense Pistol series.

MODEL 1911-A1 90s EDITION — .38 Super (disc.), 9mm Para., 10mm (disc. 1991), .40 S&W (disc. 1993), or .45 ACP cal., patterned after the Colt M1911-A1, except has linkless operating system, 5.04 (Standard) or 4 (Champion or Compact Model) in. barrel, 7 shot (Compact), 8 shot (.40 S&W or .45 ACP Standard), 9 shot (9mm Para. or 10mm), or 10 shot (.38 Super) mag., checkered walnut grips, parkerized (.38 Super beginning 1994 or .45 ACP beginning 1993), blue, or duotone (disc. 1992) finish. New 1991.

* *Mil-Spec Model 1911-A1* — 35.6 oz.

Mfg.'s Sug. Retail	$548	$465	$370	$330	$300	$275	$250	$225

Add $7 for parkerized finish.
Add $17 for blue finish.

* *Standard or Lightweight Model* — Lightweight Model introduced 1995, matte or blue (mfg. 1993-disc.) finish, 28.6 or 35.6 oz.

Mfg.'s Sug. Retail	$611	$500	$425	$365	$335	$295	$275	$250

* *Stainless Standard Model* — 9mm Para. (new 1994), .38 Super (disc.), or .45 ACP cal., 8 shot mag., wraparound rubber grips, standard or BoMar type (new 1996) sights, beveled mag. well, 39.2 oz. New 1991.

Mfg.'s Sug. Retail	$644	$525	$430	$360

Add $16 for 9mm Para. cal.
Add $25 for adj. sights.
Add $60 for V12 ported barrel and adj. sights.
Add $50 for BoMar type sights.
Add $125 for long slide variation with BoMar sights (new 1997).

* *Stainless Super Tuned Standard* — .45 ACP cal. only, super tuned by the Custom Shop, 7 shot mag., 5 in. barrel, Novak fixed low mount sights, 39.2 oz. New 1997.

Mfg.'s Sug. Retail	$995	$875	$750	$600

* *Trophy Match* — .45 ACP cal. only, top-of-the-line pistol featuring improved trigger pull, adj. rear sight, match grade barrel and bushing, choice of stainless steel, bi-tone (disc.), or blue finish, 35.6 oz. New 1994.

Mfg.'s Sug. Retail	$931	$775	$650	$525	$495	$450	$420	$390

Add $44 for stainless steel.
Add $10 for bi-tone finish.
Add $188 for long slide in stainless steel.

* *Standard High Capacity* — 9mm Para. (disc.) or .45 ACP cal., 5 in. barrel, blue or matte parkerized (new 1996) finish with plastic grips, 3 dot fixed combat sights, 10 shot (except for law enforcement) mag. New 1995.

Mfg.'s Sug. Retail	$660	$575	$485	$440	$400	$360	$330	$295

Add $59 for blue finish.

* *Stainless High Capacity* — similar to Standard High Capacity, except is stainless steel. New 1996.

Mfg.'s Sug. Retail	$764	$640	$520	$460

* *XM4 High Capacity Model* — 9mm Para. or 45 ACP cal., features widened frame for high capacity mag., blued (mfg. 1993 only) or stainless finish only. Mfg. 1993-94.

$595	$550	$500

Last Mfg.'s Sug. Retail was $689.

PDP DEFENDER MODEL — .40 S&W (disc. 1992) or .45 ACP cal., standard pistol with slide and barrel shortened to Champion length, tapered cone dual port compensator system, fully adj. sights, Videcki speed trigger, rubber grips, Commander style hammer, serrated front strap, parkerized (disc. 1992), duotone/bi-tone, or blued (disc. 1993) finish. Mfg. 1991-98.

$850	$735	$630	$550	$495	$450	$425

Last Mfg.'s Sug. Retail was $992.

Grading	100%	98%	95%	90%	80%	70%	60%

* **PDP Factory Comp** — .38 Super (disc.) or .45 ACP cal. only, entry level IPSC gun, featuring 5⅝ in. barrel with compensator attached, adj. rear sight, Videki speed trigger, checkered walnut grips, beveled mag. well, 10 shot (.38 Super) or 8 shot (.45 ACP) mag., blued finish only, 40 oz. New 1991.

Mfg.'s Sug. Retail	$969	$865	$670	$575	$495	$450	$420	$390

* **PDP High Capacity Factory Compensated** — .38 Super (disc.) or .45 ACP cal. only, blued finish. New 1995.

Mfg.'s Sug. Retail	$1,109	$955	$795	$655	$575	$500	$450	$395

1911-A1 TACTICAL RESPONSE (TRP SERIES) — .45 ACP only, 5 in. barrel, 7 shot mag., matte armor coat finish or stainless steel, checkered rosewood grips, Novak 3 dot Tritium sights, 36 oz. New 1999.

Mfg.'s Sug. Retail	$1,160	$975	$825	$675	$575	$500	$450	$395

1911-A1 COMMANDER MODEL — .45 ACP cal. only, similar to Standard 1911-A1 Model, except has 3.63 in. barrel, shortened slide, Commander hammer, low profile 3-dot sights, walnut grips, parkerized, blued, or duotone finish. Mfg. 1991-92.

		$425	$365	$330	$300	$275	$250	$225

* **Combat Commander Model** — .45 ACP cal. only, 4¼ in. barrel, bobbed hammer, walnut grips. Mfg. 1991 only.

		$425	$365	$330	$300	$275	$250	$225

1911-A1 CHAMPION MODEL — .380 ACP (Model MD-1, mfg. 1995 only) or .45 ACP cal., similar to Standard Model, except has 4 in. barrel and shortened slide, blue or parkerized (Mil-Spec Champion, new 1994) finish, Commander hammer, checkered walnut grips, 3 dot sights, 8 shot mag., 33½ oz. New 1992.

Mfg.'s Sug. Retail	$586	$485	$400	$325	$285	$255	$225	$200

    Add $25 for blue finish.
    Add $30 for Ultra Compact slide (mfg. 1997-98).
    Subtract $35 for .380 ACP cal. (Model MD-1, disc.).
    Add $79 for ported Champion V10 with Ultra Compact slide (disc.).

* **Stainless Champion Model** — .45 ACP cal. only, stainless steel variation of the Champion Model. New 1992.

Mfg.'s Sug. Retail	$645	$540	$440	$360				

    Add $119 for Ultra Compact slide (mfg. 1997-98).
    Add $59 for ported Champion V10 with Ultra Compact slide.

* **TRP Champion** — .45 ACP cal., 4 in. barrel, otherwise similar to TRP Tactical Response. New 1999.

Mfg.'s Sug. Retail	$1,175	$985	$830	$680	$575	$500	$450	$395

* **Champion Lightweight** — .45 ACP cal., aluminum frame, matte metal finish. New 1999.

Mfg.'s Sug. Retail	$629	$525	$450	$400	$350	$300	$275	$250

* **PDP Champion Comp** — .45 ACP cal. only, compensated version of the Champion Model, blue. Mfg. 1993-98.

		$780	$690	$600	$550	$500	$450	$395

                                    Last Mfg.'s Sug. Retail was $869.

* **Super Tuned Champion** — .45 ACP cal., super tuned by the Custom Shop, 7 shot mag., 4 in. barrel, blue or parkerized finish, Novak fixed low mount sights, 36.3 oz. New 1997.

Mfg.'s Sug. Retail	$959	$850	$725	$575	$500	$450	$400	$365

    Add $30 for blue finish.

* **Champion XM4 High Capacity** — 9mm Para. or .45 ACP cal., high capacity variation. Mfg. 1994 only.

		$615	$555	$500				

                                    Last Mfg.'s Sug. Retail was $699.

S

Grading	100%	98%	95%	90%	80%	70%	60%

1911-A1 COMPACT MODEL — .45 ACP cal. only, compact variation featuring shortened 4 in. barrel and slide, reduced M1911-A1 curved grip strap frame, checkered walnut grips, low profile 3-dot sights, 6 or 7 shot mag., extended slide stop, standard or lightweight alloy (new 1994) frame, combat hammer, parkerized, blued, or duotone (disc. 1992) finish, standard or lightweight (new 1995) configuration, 27 or 32 oz. Mfg. 1991-1996.

	$415	$355	$300	$275	$250	$225	$200

Last Mfg.'s Sug. Retail was $476.

Add $66 for blue finish.
Add $67 for Compact Lightweight Model (matte finish only).

* *Stainless Compact Model* — stainless steel variation of the Compact Model. Mfg. 1991-1996.

	$495	$420	$350

Last Mfg.'s Sug. Retail was $582.

* *Compact Lightweight* — .45 ACP cal., aluminum frame, matte metal finish. New 1999.

Mfg.'s Sug. Retail	$569	$450	$395	$335	$275	$250	$225	$200

➤ *Compact Lightweight Stainless* — similar to Compact Lightweight, except is stainless steel.

Mfg.'s Sug. Retail	$660	$550	$445	$365

* *Compact Comp Lightweight* — compensated version of the Compact Model, bi-tone or matte finish, regular or lightweight alloy (new 1994) frame. Mfg. 1993-98.

	$775	$685	$600	$550	$500	$450	$395

Last Mfg.'s Sug. Retail was $869.

* *High Capacity Compact* — blue or stainless steel, 3 dot fixed combat sights, black plastic grips, 10 shot (except for law enforcement) mag. Mfg. 1995-1996 only.

	$540	$465	$425	$395	$360	$330	$295

Last Mfg.'s Sug. Retail was $609.

Add $39 for stainless steel.

* *PDP High Capacity Compact Comp* — .45 ACP cal. only, features compensated $3\frac{1}{2}$ in. barrel, 10 shot (except law enforcement) mag., blue finish only. Mfg. 1995-1996 only.

	$830	$725	$625	$550	$495	$450	$425

Last Mfg.'s Sug. Retail was $964.

ULTRA COMPACT — .380 ACP (Lightweight only, mfg. 1995 only), 9mm Para. (new 1998, lightweight stainless only), or .45 ACP cal., $3\frac{1}{2}$ in. barrel, bi-tone (.45 ACP only, disc.), matte (.380 ACP, MD-1), or parkerized (Mil-Spec Ultra Compact) finish, 6 or 7 shot mag., 24 or 30 oz. New 1995.

Mfg.'s Sug. Retail	$569	$465	$395	$345	$310	$275	$250	$225

Add $110 for bi-tone finish.
Subtract $50 for MD-1 variation (.380 ACP only).

* *Ultra Compact Stainless* — .45 ACP cal., stainless steel. New 1998.

Mfg.'s Sug. Retail	$656	$550	$450	$365

Add $48 for V10 ported model (exclusive).

* *Ultra Compact Lightweight* — .45 ACP cal., aluminum frame, matte metal finish. New 1999.

Mfg.'s Sug. Retail	$569	$465	$395	$345	$310	$275	$250	$225

* *V10 Ultra Compact Lightweight Ported* — .45 ACP cal., bi-tone finish. New 1999.

Mfg.'s Sug. Retail	$711	$565	$485	$390	$345	$310	$275	$250

➤ *Ultra Compact Lightweight Stainless* — 9mm Para. cal., similar to Ultra Compact Lightweight, except is stainless steel. New 1999.

Mfg.'s Sug. Retail	$664	$555	$450	$365

* *High Capacity Ultra Compact* — 9mm Para. (disc.) or .45 ACP cal., parkerized (Mil-Spec) or blue (disc.) finish, and stainless steel construction, 3 dot fixed combat sights, black plastic grips. New 1996.

Mfg.'s Sug. Retail	$686	$595	$495	$435	$400	$360	$330	$295

Add $30 for blue finish.
Add $78 for stainless steel.

Grading	100%	98%	95%	90%	80%	70%	60%

* **V10 Ultra Compact Ported** — .45 ACP cal. only, 3½ in. specially compensated barrel/slide, blue (disc.), bi-tone, or parkerized (Mil-Spec Ultra Compact) finish, 3 dot combat sights, 30 oz. New 1995.

Mfg.'s Sug. Retail	$624	$540	$475	$425	$375	$325	$295	$275

   Add $50 for bi-tone finish.
   Add $41 for blue finish.

   ➤ **V10 Ultra Compact Ported Stainless** — similar to V10 Ultra Compact Ported, except is stainless steel.

Mfg.'s Sug. Retail	$718	$570	$485	$400

* **V10 Super Tuned Ultra Compact Ported** — .45 ACP cal. only, super tuned by the Custom Shop, 3½ in. ported barrel, bi-tone finish or stainless steel (exclusive), Novak fixed low mount sights, 32.9 oz. New 1997.

Mfg.'s Sug. Retail	$1,049	$925	$775	$600	$525	$475	$425	$385

   Add $70 for stainless steel (exclusive).

GULF VICTORY SPECIAL EDITION — .45 ACP cal., special edition featuring presentation grade blued finish, gold etching on slide and other gold-plated small parts, includes specially padded and embroidered storage case with jacket patch, window decal, and cloisonne medallion honoring all U.S. Armed Forces. Mfg. 1991-1992.

	$750	$600	$475

Last Mfg.'s Sug. Retail was $869.

Springfield Semi-Auto Pistols: 1911-A1 Custom Models

In addition to the models listed below, Springfield also custom builds other configurations of Race Guns that are available through Springfield dealers. Prices range from $2,245-$2,990.
   Add $100 for all cals. other than .45 ACP.
   Add $440 for Aimpoint Competition Red Dot Scope for PDP variations only.

* **Custom Carry Gun** — .45 ACP (other cals. available upon request) cal., similar to Defender Model, except has tuned trigger pull, 7 shot mag., heavy recoil spring, extended thumb safety, available in blue or phosphate (disc.), finish. New 1991.

Mfg.'s Sug. Retail	$1,299	$1,175	$950	$850	$750	$650	$550	$475

* **Basic Competition** — .45 ACP (other cals. available upon request) cal., BoMar adj. rear sight, blued finish, checkered walnut grips. New 1994.

Mfg.'s Sug. Retail	$1,295	$1,175	$950	$850	$750	$650	$550	$475

* **NRA PPC** — .45 ACP (other cals. available upon request) cal., designed to comply with NRA PPC competitive rules/regulations, factory test target, custom carrying case. New 1995.

Mfg.'s Sug. Retail	$1,469	$1,350	$1,175	$950	$850	$750	$650	$575

* **1911-A1 Custom Compact** — .45 ACP cal. only, carry or lady's model with shortened slide and frame, compensated, fixed 3 dot sights, Commander style hammer, Herrett walnut grips, other custom features, blue only.

	$1,615	$1,325	$1,100	$950	$850	$750	$675

Last Mfg.'s Sug. Retail was $1,815.

* **1911-A1 Custom Champion** — similar to Custom Compact, except is based on Champion model with full size frame and shortened slide.

	$1,615	$1,325	$1,100	$950	$850	$750	$675

Last Mfg.'s Sug. Retail was $1,815.

* **National Match Hardball** — .45 ACP cal. only, National Match barrel and bushing, specially fitted frame and slide, blue only, BoMar adj. rear sight, Herrett walnut grips, plastic cased.

Mfg.'s Sug. Retail	$1,336	$1,200	$975	$865	$750	$650	$550	$475

   This model is made specifically for DCM competition shooting.

* **Bullseye Wadcutter** — .45 ACP (other cals. available upon request) cal., specifically designed for wadcutter loads, BoMar rib mounted on slide top, 5 or 6 in. barrel.

Mfg.'s Sug. Retail	$1,499	$1,370	$1,185	$950	$850	$750	$650	$575

Grading	100%	98%	95%	90%	80%	70%	60%

* **Entry Level Wadcutter** — .38 Super, .40 S&W, 10mm, or .45 ACP cal., 5 in. barrel, standard competition features.

	$925	$800	$700	$600	$550	$475	$425

Last Mfg.'s Sug. Retail was $1,049.

> Add $200 for .38 Super cal.
> Add $391 for 10mm or .40 S&W cal.
> This model features supported chamber in all cals. except .45 ACP.

* **Trophy Master "Competition"** — .45 ACP (other cals. available upon request) cal., competition model which includes low profile combat sights, ambidextrous safety, long match trigger, bobbed hammer, Pachmayr wraparound grips. Disc. 1996.

	$1,420	$1,125	$950	$875	$800	$725	$650

Last Mfg.'s Sug. Retail was $1,598.

* **Trophy Master "Expert"** — .45 ACP (other cals. available upon request) cal., mfg. for IPSC competition shooting, dual chamber compensator system on match barrel, duotone finish.

Mfg.'s Sug. Retail	$1,724	$1,575	$1,350	$1,125	$950	$850	$750	$675

> Subtract $100 for Limited Class variation.
> This model is an improved variation of the Trophy Master Competition Model.

* **Trophy Master "Distinguished"** — similar to Expert Model, except has brushed hard chrome finish, checkered grip straps and triggerguard, top-of-the-line competition model.

Mfg.'s Sug. Retail	$2,445	$2,200	$1,875	$1,500	$1,200	$975	$850	$750

> Subtract $100 for Limited Class variation.

* **P9 World Cup** — 9mmx21 or .40 S&W cal., state-of-the-art competition pistol, based on factory P9 Racegun, hard chrome finish only.

	$2,550	$2,100	$1,775	$1,500	$1,250	$975	$795

Last Mfg.'s Sug. Retail was $2,935.

RIFLES: BOLT ACTION

MAUSER M98 — 7x57mm Mauser cal., surplus rifles with standard military dimensions and features. Importation disc. 1989.

* **Hunting/Utility Grade**

	$70	$50	$45	$45	$40	$40	$35

Last Mfg.'s Sug. Retail was $75.

* **Collector Grade**

	$105	$90	$80	$70	$60	$50	$40

Last Mfg.'s Sug. Retail was $116.

* **Premium Grade**

	$170	$150	$130	$115	$100	$90	$80

Last Mfg.'s Sug. Retail was $194.

CZ 98 HUNTER CLASSIC — .243 Win., .270 Win., .30-06, .308 Win., 6.5x55mm, 7x57 Mauser, 7x64mm, 7.29x57mm, .300 Win. Mag., or 7mm Rem. Mag. cal., features Mauser 98 Large Ring action, mfg. by CZ in the Czech Republic and Springfield Armory, controlled feeding, 24 in. hammer forged barrel, adj. trigger, choice of walnut or synthetic stock, 7.7 lbs. Limited mfg. 1995 only.

	$345	$315	$285	$260	$240	$220	$195

Last Mfg.'s Sug. Retail was $411.

> Add $38 for walnut stock.

RIFLES: SEMI-AUTO, MILITARY DESIGN

M1 GARAND AND VARIATIONS — .30-06 Springfield (disc.), .270 Win. (disc. 1987), or .308 Win. cal., semi-auto, 24 in. barrel, gas operated, 8 shot mag., adj. sights, 9½ lbs.

> The M1 Garand and variations listed below were discontinued in 1990. The factory should be contacted directly for prices and availability of M1A parts and other rifle related accessories.

Grading	100%	98%	95%	90%	80%	70%	60%

* **Standard Model** — supplied standard with camo GI fiberglass stock.

	$725	$650	$575	$525	$485	$450	$425

Last Mfg.'s Sug. Retail was $761.

> Subtract $65 if with GI stock.

* **National Match** — walnut stock, match barrel and sights.

	$850	$775	$700	$650	$600	$550	$495

Last Mfg.'s Sug. Retail was $897.

> Add $240 for Kevlar stock.

* **Ultra Match** — match barrel and sights, glass bedded stock, walnut stock standard.

	$950	$850	$725	$675	$610	$550	$500

Last Mfg.'s Sug. Retail was $1,033.

> Add $240 for Kevlar stock.

* **M1-D Sniper Rifle** — limited quantities, with original M84 scope, prong type flash suppressor, leather cheek pad and slings, .30-06 only.

	$950	$850	$725	$675	$610	$550	$500

Last Mfg.'s Sug. Retail was $1,033.

* **Tanker Rifle** — similar to T-26 authorized by Gen. MacArthur at the end of WWII, 18¼ in. barrel, .30-06 or .308 Win. cal., GI stock standard.

	$725	$675	$600	$525	$460	$380	$335

Last Mfg.'s Sug. Retail was $797.

> Add $23 for walnut full stock.

BM 59 — .308 Win. cal., mfg. in Italy and machined and assembled in the Springfield Armory factory, 19.32 in. barrel, 20 shot box mag., 9½ lbs.

* **Standard Italian Rifle** — with grenade launcher, winter trigger, tri-compensator, and bipod.

	$1,750	$1,400	$1,200	$1,000	$895	$850	$800

Last Mfg.'s Sug. Retail was $1,950.

* **Alpine Rifle** — with Beretta pistol grip type stock.

	$2,025	$1,625	$1,350	$1,150	$1,000	$925	$850

Last Mfg.'s Sug. Retail was $2,275.

> This model was also available in a Paratrooper configuration with folding stock at no extra charge.

* **Nigerian Rifle** — similar to BM 59, except has Beretta pistol grip type stock.

	$2,075	$1,650	$1,375	$1,150	$1,000	$925	$850

Last Mfg.'s Sug. Retail was $2,340.

* **E Model Rifle**

	$1,975	$1,595	$1,325	$1,125	$975	$900	$825

Last Mfg.'s Sug. Retail was $2,210.

M1A RIFLES — .243 Win. (disc.), .308 Win., or 7mm-08 Rem. (1991 mfg. only) cal., patterned after the original Springfield M14 - except semi-auto, walnut or fiberglass stock, 22 in. barrel, fiberglass handguard, 9 lbs.

* **Standard/Basic Model** — above specifications, choice of Collector (original GI stock), new walnut (M1A Standard Model beginning 1993), black fiberglass (M1A Basic Model), camo fiberglass (disc.), GI wood (disc. 1992), and brown (disc.) or black laminated (M1A Standard Model beginning 1996) stock, regular or National Match barrel.

Mfg.'s Sug. Retail	$1,381	$1,125	$875	$750	$635	$560	$495	$450

> Add $209 for new walnut stock.
> Add $44 for stainless steel barrel.
> Add $74 for bipod and stabilizer.
> Subtract $58 for camo fiberglass stock.
> Subtract $132 for black fiberglass stock.
> Add $133 for black or $159 for brown laminated stock.
> Add $59 for National Match barrel.

Grading	100%	98%	95%	90%	80%	70%	60%

Add $155 for National Match barrel and sights.
Add $200 for folding stock (disc. 1994).
Standard (entry level model) stock configuration for 1996 is black or camo fiberglass.

* **M1A E-2** — standard stock is birch. Disc.

	$975	$825	$745	$650	$590	$550	$495

Last Mfg.'s Sug. Retail was $842.

Add $30 for walnut stock.
Add $120 for Shaw stock with Harris bipod.

* **M1A Bush Rifle** — .308 Win. cal., 18 in. shrouded barrel, 8 lbs. 12 oz., collector GI, walnut, black fiberglass folding (disc. 1994 per C/B), and black fiberglass or laminated black stock.

		100%	98%	95%	90%	80%	70%	60%
Mfg.'s Sug. Retail	$1,381	$1,195	$935	$800	$675	$575	$500	$450

Add $29 for walnut stock.
Add $15 for black fiberglass stock.
Add $86 for black laminated stock.
Add $235 for National Match variation (disc.).
Add $525 for Super Match variation (disc.).

* **National Match** — National Match sights, steel or stainless steel (new 1999) barrel, mainspring guide, flash suppressor, and gas cylinder, special glass bedded oil finished match stock, tuned trigger, walnut stock became standard in 1991, 9 lbs.

		100%	98%	95%	90%	80%	70%	60%
Mfg.'s Sug. Retail	$1,779	$1,525	$1,075	$855	$730	$650	$575	$525

Add $16 for stainless steel barrel.
Add $155 for heavy composition stock (disc.).
Add $250 for either fiberglass or fancy burl wood stock (disc.).
.243 Win. and 7mm-08 Rem. cals. are also available at extra charge.

* **Super Match** — similar to National Match, except has air-gauged Douglas or Hart heavy barrel, oversized walnut (disc.) or fiberglass super match stock, and modified operating rod guide, rear lugged receiver beginning 1991, approx. 10 lbs.

		100%	98%	95%	90%	80%	70%	60%
Mfg.'s Sug. Retail	$2,049	$1,700	$1,125	$935	$800	$700	$625	$575

Add $146 for stainless steel barrel.
Add approx. $430 for McMillian black or green camo fiberglass stock.
Add $200 for fancy burl walnut (disc.) stock.
.243 Win. and 7mm-08 Rem. cals. are also available at extra charge.

* **M21 Tactical Rifle** — .308 Win. cal., 22 in. barrel, tactical variation of the Super Match mfg. with match grade parts giving superior accuracy, adj. cheekpiece stock. New 1990.

		100%	98%	95%	90%	80%	70%	60%
Mfg.'s Sug. Retail	$2,204	$1,875	$1,525	$1,325	$1,100	$925	$800	$700

M1A "NEW LOADED" — .308 Win. cal., 22 in. National Match steel or stainless steel barrel, features shooting upgrades such as National Match trigger assembly, front and rear sights, and National Match flash suppressor, black fiberglass, Collector GI walnut, or new walnut stock, 9.2 lbs. New 1999.

		100%	98%	95%	90%	80%	70%	60%
Mfg.'s Sug. Retail	$1,449	$1,250	$950	$825	$700	$600	$525	$475

Add $141 for new walnut stock.
Add $46 for stainless steel barrel.
Add $96 for Collector GI walnut.

M1A "GOLD SERIES" — .308 Win. cal., heavy walnut competition stock, gold medal grade heavy Douglas barrel. Add $126 for Kevlar stock, add $390 for special Hart stainless steel barrel, add $516 for Hart stainless steel barrel with Kevlar stock. Mfg. 1987 only.

			100%	98%	95%	90%	80%	70%	60%
			$1,944	$1,750	$1,375	$1,150	$975	$850	$740

Last Mfg.'s Sug. Retail was $1,944.

M6 SCOUT SQUAD — .308 Win. cal., 18 in. barrel, choice of GI Collector (disc. 1998), new walnut, black fiberglass, or black laminated (disc. 1998) stock, muzzle stabilizer standard, supplied with Scout mount and handguard, approx. 9 lbs. New 1997.

		100%	98%	95%	90%	80%	70%	60%
Mfg.'s Sug. Retail	$1,459	$1,250	$950	$825	$700	$600	$525	$475

Add $40 for walnut stock.
Add $40 for black laminated stock.

Grading	100%	98%	95%	90%	80%	70%	60%

SAR-8 — .308 Win. cal., patterned after the H & K Model 91, recoil operated delayed roller lock action, fluted chamber, rotary adj. rear aperture sight, 18 in. barrel, supplied with walnut (disc. 1994) or black fiberglass thumbhole sporter stock, 10 (C/B 1994) or 20 (disc. 1994) shot detachable mag., 8.7 lbs. Mfg. in U.S. starting 1990, disc. 1998..

| | $1,015 | $835 | $750 | $675 | $600 | $550 | $500 |

Last Mfg.'s Sug. Retail was $1,204.

SAR-8 parts are interchangeable with both SAR-3 and HK-91 parts.

* **SAR-8 Tactical Counter Sniper Rifle** — .308 Win. cal., tactical sniper variation of the SAR-8. Mfg. 1996-98.

| | $1,325 | $1,000 | $825 | $725 | $650 | $575 | $525 |

Last Mfg.'s Sug. Retail was $1,610.

SAR-48/SAR-4800 SPORTER MODEL — .223 Rem. (new 1997) or .308 Win. cal., authentic model of the Belgian semi-auto FAL/LAR rifle, 18 (.223 Rem. cal. only) or 21 in. barrel, adj. gas operation, 10 (C/B 1994) or 20 (disc.) shot mag., walnut (disc.) or black fiberglass thumbhole sporter stock, adj. sights, sling, and mag. loader. Mfg. 1985-1998.

| | $1,080 | $915 | $785 | $675 | $625 | $575 | $525 |

Last Mfg.'s Sug. Retail was $1,249.

Add $70 for Paratrooper model with folding stock.
Add $17 for Compact Sporter Model.

The SAR-48 was disc. in 1989 and reintroduced as the Model SAR-4800 in 1990. All SAR-4800 parts are interchangeable with both SAR-48 and FN/FAL parts. This model is an updated variation of the pre-WWII FN Model 49.

* **SAR-48/SAR-4800 Bush Rifle Sporter Model** — similar to standard model, except has 18 in. barrel.

| | $1,085 | $900 | $795 | $695 | $640 | $595 | $550 |

Last Mfg.'s Sug. Retail was $1,216.

* **SAR-48 .22 Cal.** — .22 LR cal., variation of the Sporter Model. Disc. 1989.

| | $725 | $660 | $595 | $540 | $495 | $450 | $400 |

Last Mfg.'s Sug. Retail was $760.

DR-200 SPORTER RIFLE — while advertised, this model was never mfg. ($687 was planned MSR).

STALLARD ARMS

Current manufacturer of 9mm Para. pistols located in Mansfield, OH since 1991. Distributed by MKS Supply, Inc. located in Dayton, OH.

Please refer to the Hi-Point listing in this text.

STANDARD ARMS COMPANY

Previous manufacturer located in Wilmington, DE.

RIFLES: SEMI-AUTO

MODEL G AUTOLOADER — .25-35 WCF, .30-30 Win., .25 Rem., .30 Rem., or .35 Rem. cal., bottom loading box mag., 22 in. barrel, open sight, straight stock. This was the first gas operated rifle in the U.S.A. Gas port can be closed and gun will function as a slide action, mfg. 1910.

| | $475 | $400 | $300 | $275 | $250 | $225 | $200 |

Subtract 10% for slide action only (Model M).

STANDARD ARMS OF NEVADA, INC.

Current manufacturer located in Reno, NV. Dealer and distributor sales.

PISTOLS: SEMI-AUTO

9MM COMPACT — .380 ACP or 9mm Para. cal., double action only, sub compact design, 10 shot mag., 3.1 in. barrel, polymer frame with steel slide, 20 oz. New 1999.

As this edition went to press, prices had yet to be established on this model.

S

Grading	100%	98%	95%	90%	80%	70%	60%

STAR, BONIFACIO ECHEVERRIA

Previous manufacturer located in Eibar, Spain. Star Bonifacio Echeverria S.A. closed its doors on July 28th, 1997, due to the intense financial pressure the Spanish arms industry has been experiencing during the past several years. Some recent production guns may remain available as overstock through European American Armory.

PISTOLS: SEMI-AUTO

MODEL H — similar to Model HN, except 7.65mm, 7 shot.

	100%	98%	95%	90%	80%	70%	60%
	$350	$250	$170	$120	$100	$90	$75

MODEL HN — .380 ACP cal., 6 shot, 2¾ in. barrel, blue, fixed sights, plastic grips. Mfg. 1934-1941.

	$375	$265	$180	$120	$100	$90	$75

MODEL I — .32 ACP cal., 9 shot, 4¾ in. barrel, blue, fixed sights, plastic grips. Mfg. 1934-1936.

	$350	$250	$170	$120	$100	$85	$70

MODEL IN — similar to Model I, except .380 ACP, 8 shot, 4¾ in. barrel, blue.

	$395	$265	$180	$125	$105	$90	$75

MODEL 1920 — 9mm Bergmann Bayard or .38 Super cal., easily identified by unusual safety located on left rear slide. Issued to Spanish Guardia Civil.

	$550	$400	$325	$280	$275	$185	$150

MODEL 1921 — 9mm Bergmann Bayard cal., this model was fitted with a grip safety that was later dropped when standardizing the Model A production. Issued to Spanish Guardia Civil.

	$475	$350	$300	$250	$225	$185	$150

MODEL 1922 — designation for the early Model A. Issued to Spanish Guardia Civil.

	$375	$285	$240	$215	$180	$145	$135

MODEL A — .38 Super cal., modified Government Colt, 5 in. barrel, no grip safety, blue, checkered wood grips. Mfg. 1934-disc.

	$325	$275	$240	$215	$180	$145	$135

Add 50% for Spanish Air Force issue if in original box.

MODEL A CARBINE — usually 7.63mm cal., unusual variation, slotted with tangent rear sight and extended barrel.

	$1,750	$1,350	$1,050	$825	$700	$575	$450

Add $500 for original stock (different from MB and MMS stock).

MODEL B — similar to Model A, but 9mm Para. cal. Mfg. 1934-1975.

	$295	$250	$205	$170	$150	$140	$115

Add 50% for post-war German police if with 2 matching magazines.
Add 150% if Waffenamt proofed.

MODEL M — similar to Model A, except has large frame, available in 9mm Bergmann Bayard, 9mm Para., 8 shot, and .45 ACP, 7 shot, 5 in. barrel, blue, fixed sights, checkered wood or plastic grips.

	$325	$275	$240	$215	$185	$160	$140

Add 100% for early variation with ser. no. under 4,835.

MODEL P — .45 ACP cal. only, similar to Model A, except has large frame, 7 shot mag. Mfg. 1934-1975.

	$350	$285	$240	$215	$185	$160	$140

Add 100% for early variation with ser. no. under 5,112.

Grading	100%	98%	95%	90%	80%	70%	60%

MODELS SUPER A (9mm Largo), M (9mm Largo), & P (.45 ACP) — similar to Models A, M, & P, except has loaded chamber indicator, mag. safety, and easier takedown feature. Mfg. 1946-1989.

	$395	$325	$215	$180	$160	$145	$125

Last Mfg.'s Sug. Retail was $340.

Add 100% for Super M and Super P.

The Super A was a Spanish Service pistol. Recent imports in 80% condition were available in the $150 range.

MODEL SUPER B — 9mm Para. cal., similar to Models B, except has loaded chamber indicator, mag. safety and easier takedown feature, choice of blue or Starvel finish on Model B. Importation disc. in 1990.

	$270	$240	$210	$185	$160	$140	$120

Last Mfg.'s Sug. Retail was $330.

Add $30 for Starvel finish.

SUPER TARGET MODEL — similar to Star Super, but target sights, extended trigger guard, modified trigger. Rare. Mfg. 1922-1947 with total production 40,416.

	$1,250	$950	$800	$700	$600	$500	$400

MODEL MB — 9mm Para. cal., late production Model M cut for shoulder stock, mag. safety.

	$1,295	$975	$675	$565	$450	$365	$250

Add $300 for shoulder stock.

MODEL MMS — 7.63mm cal., late production Model M cut for shoulder stock, mag. safety.

	$1,000	$750	$460	$400	$325	$260	$200

Add $300 for shoulder stock.

MODEL SI — .32 ACP cal., 8 shot, 4 in. barrel, blue, without grip safety, small version of Government .45 in appearance, plastic grips. Mfg. 1941-1965.

	$200	$190	$160	$135	$115	$100	$80

MODEL S — similar to Model SI, except .380 ACP cal., 9 shot, mfg. 1941-1965. Importation of these Police contract models was disc. 1991.

	$195	$170	$145	$125	$110	$95	$85

Last Mfg.'s Sug. Retail was $237.

Add $30 for Starvel finish.

In 1989, Interarms imported factory reconditioned used Spanish Police Contract Model S pistols - these guns were available in either blue or Starvel finish and are supplied with a plastic box with accessories. A small number issued to the Spanish Air Force came in the original box with 2 matching mags. - add 100%.

MODELS SUPER SI AND S — similar to Model S, with Super Star improvements. Mfg. 1946-1972.

	$240	$230	$210	$195	$165	$140	$120

MODEL SUPER SM — similar to Model Super S, except adjustable sight and wood grips. Mfg. 1973-1981.

	$275	$235	$220	$200	$175	$145	$125

MODEL CO POCKET — .25 Auto cal., 2¾ in. barrel, blue, fixed sights, plastic grips. Mfg. 1929-1956.

	$250	$190	$165	$145	$120	$110	$90

MODEL CU STARLET — .25 Auto cal., 2⅜ in. barrel, alloy frame, fixed sights, plastic grips, blue, or chrome slide, frame anodized in black, blue, green, grey, or gold. Mfg. 1957-1972.

	$235	$200	$165	$145	$120	$110	$90

Minor changes prompted a model redesignation as CK during 1973.

MODEL D — .380 ACP cal., small steel frame version of the Model A with several minor variations, 40,416 mfg. 1922-1947.

	$550	$475	$400	$350	$300	$250	$200

Grading	100%	98%	95%	90%	80%	70%	60%

MODEL DK (STARFIRE) — .380 ACP cal., 3⅛ in. barrel, fixed sights, plastic stocks, finished in same color availability as Model CU. Mfg. 1957-1972, U.S. import ceased as of 1968 due to Federal GCA legislation.

	$400	$350	$295	$255	$225	$180	$155

> Add 10% for unusual alloy colors.
> Minor changes prompted a redesignation as DKL (.380 ACP) 1972 and DKI (.32 ACP) 1972.

MODEL HK LANCER — similar to Model Starfire, except .22 LR cal.. Mfg. 1955-1968.

	$245	$215	$180	$160	$140	$120	$110

MODEL F — .22 LR cal., 10 shot, 4 in. barrel, fixed sights, blue, plastic grips. Mfg. 1942-1967.

	$325	$225	$140	$110	$95	$85	$55

MODEL FS — similar to Model F, except 6 in. barrel, adj. sights. Mfg. 1942-1967.

	$325	$225	$150	$120	$100	$90	$65

MODEL F OLYMPIC RAPID FIRE — .22 Short cal., 9 shot, 7 in. barrel, adj. sight, aluminum slide, barrel weights and muzzle brake, blue, plastic grips. Mfg. 1942-1967.

	$425	$325	$210	$175	$155	$140	$130

MODEL FR — restyled Model F, with "squared" barrel, adj. sight and slide stop. Mfg. 1967-1972.

	$350	$225	$150	$120	$100	$90	$65

> Add 15% for chrome finish.

MODEL FR SPORT AND MODEL FR TARGET — similar to Model FR, except FR Sport has 150mm barrel, and the Model FR Target has 180mm barrel, 65,534 mfg. 1967-1983.

	$300	$225	$150	$120	$100	$90	$65

> Add 15% for chrome finish.

MODEL FM — similar to Model FR, except heavier frame, web ahead of trigger guard, 4½ in. barrel. 8,799 mfg. 1972-1983.

	$275	$180	$150	$120	$100	$90	$65

MODEL BKS STARLIGHT — 9mm Para. cal., 8 shot, 4¼ in. barrel, plastic grips. Mfg. 1970-1981.

	100%	98%	95%	90%	80%	70%	60%
Blue	$265	$230	$210	$180	$160	$145	$130
Chrome	$295	$240	$220	$195	$170	$155	$145

MODEL BM SEMI-AUTO — 9mm Para. cal., single action, 8 shot mag., 4 in. barrel, steel frame, Colt 1911 action, blue, chrome (disc. 1989), or Starvel (new 1990) finish, plastic grips, 35 oz. Importation disc. 1991.

	$285	$245	$205	$180	$165	$155	$145

Last Mfg.'s Sug. Retail was $415.

> Add $30 for Starvel or chrome (disc. 1990) finish.
> Add $150 for Navy issue with escutcheon grips.

MODEL BKM — similar to Model BM, except lightweight duraluminum frame, blued finish only, 26 oz. Importation disc. 1991.

	$285	$250	$215	$190	$170	$160	$150

Last Mfg.'s Sug. Retail was $415.

MODEL PD — .45 ACP cal., 6 shot mag., single action, 4 in. barrel, adj. rear sight, blue or Starvel (new 1990) finish only, walnut grips, alloy frame, 25 oz. Mfg. 1975-importation disc. 1991.

	$345	$290	$250	$215	$195	$170	$160

Last Mfg.'s Sug. Retail was $475.

> Add $20 for Starvel finish (new 1990).

MODEL 28 — 9mm Para. cal., double action, 15 shot mag., 4¼ in. barrel, blue finish only, advanced design, 40 oz. Mfg. 1983 and 1984 only.

	$400	$335	$325	$275	$250	$225	$200

> Note: Model 28 is interesting since no screws are used in its manufacture. Hammer assembly (including spring, cocking lever, sear, disconnector and ejector) is housed under removable backstrap.

MODEL 30M — 9mm Para. cal. only, successor to the Model 28, double action, 4.33 in. barrel, 15 shot mag., blued finish only, adj. rear sight, checkered wraparound plastic grips, steel frame, 40 oz. New 1985. Importation disc. 1991.

	$400	$340	$315	$295	$270	$250	$225

Last Mfg.'s Sug. Retail was $495.

Grading	100%	98%	95%	90%	80%	70%	60%

MODEL 30/31 PK STARFIRE DURAL — similar to Model 30M, except duraluminum frame, 3.86 in. barrel, 30 oz.

		$455	$360	$315	$295	$270	$250	$225

Last Mfg.'s Sug. Retail was $580.

The Model 30 PK was discontinued in 1989 and the Model 31 PK was imported 1990-1993.

MODEL 31P STARFIRE — 9mm Para. (disc. 1993) or .40 S&W (new 1990) cal., compact variation utilizing double action, features Acculine barrel (3.86 in.) similar to Firestar Model, 14 shot mag., ambidextrous safety with decocking lever, blue or Starvel finish, all steel construction, 39.4 oz. Imported 1990-94.

		$350	$295	$270	$250	$225	$210	$195

Last Mfg.'s Sug. Retail was $398.

Add $30 for Starvel finish (disc. 1993).

MODEL M40 FIRESTAR — .40 S&W cal., single action, 6 shot mag., 3.39 in. Acculine barrel, checkered rubber grips, compact design utilizing all steel construction, 3 dot sighting system with adjustable rear sight, blue, Starvel, or nickel (new 1997) finish, 30.35 oz. Mfg. 1990-disc.

		$265	$230	$200	$180	$165	$150	$135

Last Mfg.'s Sug. Retail was $306.

Add $17 for nickel finish.
Add $20 for Starvel finish.

* *Model M40 Firestar Plus* — similar to M40 Firestar, except incorporates alloy frame, new grip design, ambidextrous easy-view safety, and fast button release 10 shot mag. Mfg. 1995 - Disc.

		$395	$330	$280	$250	$225	$200	$180

Last Mfg.'s Sug. Retail was $527.

Add $25 for Starvel finish.

MODEL M43 FIRESTAR — 9mm Para. cal., 7 shot mag., otherwise similar to Model M40 Firestar. Disc.

		$295	$265	$235	$200	$185	$170	$155

Last Mfg.'s Sug. Retail was $296.

Add $17 for nickel finish.
Add $20 for Starvel finish.

* *Model M43 Firestar Plus* — similar to M43 Firestar, except incorporates alloy frame, new grip design, ambidextrous easy-view safety, and fast button release 10 shot double stack mag. Mfg. 1995-97.

		$295	$265	$235	$200	$185	$170	$155

Last Mfg.'s Sug. Retail was $351.

Add $12 for nickel finish.
Add $25 for Starvel finish.

MODEL M45 FIRESTAR — .45 ACP cal., single action, ultra compact design featuring 4 barrel lugs, steel frame and slide, 3.6 in. reverse taper Acculine barrel, 6 shot mag., black synthetic grips, blue or Starvel finish, 35 oz. Mfg. 1992-97.

		$295	$265	$235	$200	$185	$170	$155

Last Mfg.'s Sug. Retail was $351.

Add $12 for nickel finish.
Add $20 for Starvel finish.

* *Model M45 Firestar Plus* — similar to M45 Firestar, except incorporates alloy frame, new grip design, ambidextrous easy-view safety, and fast button release 10 shot mag. Mfg. 1995 only.

		$415	$345	$285	$250	$225	$200	$180

Last Mfg.'s Sug. Retail was $554.

Add $26 for Starvel finish.

MEGASTAR — 10mm or .45 ACP cal., larger variation of the Firestar featuring 4.6 in. barrel and 12 (.45 ACP) or 14 (10mm) shot mag., 47.6 oz. Imported 1992-94.

		$450	$375	$350	$325	$295	$275	$250

Last Mfg.'s Sug. Retail was $653.

Add $29 for Starvel finish.

S

Grading	100%	98%	95%	90%	80%	70%	60%

ULTRASTAR — 9mm Para. or .40 S&W (new 1996) cal., compact double action design, 3.57 in. barrel, 9 shot mag., blued steel metal, triple dot sights, steel internal mechanism, polymer exterior construction, 26 oz. Mfg. 1994-97.

	$270	$250	$225	$200	$175	$165	$155

Last Mfg.'s Sug. Retail was $296.

STEEL CITY ARMS, INC.

Previous manufacturer located in Pittsburgh, PA until 1990. In 1991, the name was changed to Desert Industries, Inc. and manufacture was moved to Las Vegas, NV. Very few guns exist with Steel City markings.

PISTOLS: SEMI-AUTO

DOUBLE DEUCE — .22 LR cal. only, double action, matte finish stainless steel, 2½ in. barrel, 7 shot mag., unchecked rosewood grips, 18 oz. Mfg. 1984-90.

$265	$230	$200

Last Mfg.'s Sug. Retail was $290.

Various select hardwood stocks were also available at extra cost ($20-100).

STERLING

Previous manufacturer located in Gasport, NY. Disc. 1983.

PISTOLS

Rather than list individual models, the following generalizations will help in ascertaining values for this trademark. Models 300, 302 and 402 will average between $75 and $150 if in 70%+ condition. Models 283, 284, 285 (Husky), and 286 (Trapper) are semi-auto .22 cal. pistols with various barrel lengths — values will range between $90-$150. Models 400 (.380 ACP), PPL (.380 ACP short barrel), and 450 (.45 ACP) usually range in the $150-$275 range.

STERLING ARMAMENT, LTD.

Previous manufacturer located in England established c. 1900. Previously imported and distributed by Cassi Inc. located in Colorado Springs, CO until 1990.

CARBINES: SEMI-AUTO

AR-180 — .223 Rem. cal., side-folding stock. Disc.

$850	$775	$695	$625	$550	$495	$450

STERLING MK 6 — 9mm Para. cal., blowback semi-auto with floating firing pin, shrouded 16.1 in. barrel, side mounted mag., folding stock, 7½ lbs.

$565	$495	$450	$410	$375	$340	$310

Last Mfg.'s Sug. Retail was $650.

PISTOLS; SEMI-AUTO

PARAPISTOL MK 7 C4 — 9mm Para. cal., 4 in. barrel, semi-auto paramilitary design pistol, crinkle finish, same action as MK. 6 Carbine, fires from closed bolt, 10, 15, 20, 30, 34 or 68 shot mag., 5 lbs.

$500	$435	$375	$350	$325	$295	$265

Last Mfg.'s Sug. Retail was $600.

PARAPISTOL MK 7 C8 — 9mm Para. cal., similar to C4, except has 7.8 in. barrel, 5¼ lbs.

$525	$450	$390	$365	$330	$300	$275

Last Mfg.'s Sug. Retail was $620.

STEVENS, J., ARMS COMPANY

J. Stevens Arms Company was founded in 1864 at Chicopee Falls, MA as J. Stevens & Co. In 1886 the name was changed to J. Stevens Arms and Tool Co. In 1916, the plant became New England Westinghouse, and tooled up for Moisin-Nagant Rifles. In 1920, the plant was sold to the Savage Arms Corp. and manufactured guns were marked "J. Stevens Arms Co.". This designation was dropped in the late 1940s, and only the name "Stevens" has been used up to 1990. Beginning in 1999, Savage Arms, Inc. began manufacturing the Stevens Favorite again as the Model 30G.

Grading	100%	98%	95%	90%	80%	70%	60%

Depending on the remaining Stevens factory data, a factory letter authenticating the configuration of a particular specimen may be obtained by contacting Mr. John Callahan (see Trademark Index for listings and address). The charge for this service is $15.00 per gun - please allow 2-4 weeks for an adequate response.

PISTOLS

NO. 10 TARGET SINGLE SHOT — .22 LR cal., 8 in. barrel, blue, adj. sights, rubber grips, squared off like an automatic pistol, tip up action. Mfg. 1919-1939.

	100%	98%	95%	90%	80%	70%	60%
	$220	$200	$185	$165	$140	$120	$100

NO. 35 TARGET SINGLE SHOT — .22 LR or .25 Rimfire cal., 6, 8, 10, or 12¼ in. barrel, blue, walnut grips. Mfg. 1907-1939.

	100%	98%	95%	90%	80%	70%	60%
	$350	$300	$265	$220	$200	$185	$165

NO. 35 "OFFHAND" AUTOSHOT — .22 LR cal. or smoothbore (actually a pistol-length shotgun). Class Three — must be registered with BATF. Introduced 1931, disc. 1935.

	100%	98%	95%	90%	80%	70%	60%
	$350	$300	$250	$225	$200	$150	$125

RIFLES

Stevens made a wide variety of inexpensive, utilitarian rifles that to date have attracted mostly shooting interest, but little collector interest. A listing of these models may be found in the back of this text under "Serialization".

TIP-UP RIFLES — .22 S, .22 LR, .25 Stevens, .32, .38, or .44 Long RF or CF, variations No. 1- No. 15 feature various weights, wood styles, sights, and other differences, later series has full loop at rear triggerguard, circa 1870s-1895.

* *Basic Model No. 1 without forearm*

	100%	98%	95%	90%	80%	70%	60%
	$500	$475	$425	$375	$300	$250	$200

POCKET RIFLES — detachable serially numbered nickel-plated stock, variations found within each frame size.

* *Small Frame* — .22 cal. (various issues).

	100%	98%	95%	90%	80%	70%	60%
	$450	$400	$350	$300	$275	$235	$200

* *Without Stock*

	100%	98%	95%	90%	80%	70%	60%
	$300	$250	$200	$150	$125	$100	$80

* *Medium Frame* — .22, .32, .38, .44 cals. (various issues).

	100%	98%	95%	90%	80%	70%	60%
	$500	$450	$400	$350	$300	$250	$200

* *Without Stock*

	100%	98%	95%	90%	80%	70%	60%
	$300	$250	$200	$150	$125	$100	$75

* *Large Frame* — .22 to .44 cals.

	100%	98%	95%	90%	80%	70%	60%
	$600	$550	$500	$450	$400	$350	$300

* *Without Stock*

	100%	98%	95%	90%	80%	70%	60%
	$425	$375	$325	$275	$225	$200	$175

MODEL 44 IDEAL SINGLE SHOT — .22 LR through .44-40 WCF cals., rolling block, lever action, takedown, 24 or 26 in. barrels, straight grip stock and forearm. Mfg. 1894-1932.

	100%	98%	95%	90%	80%	70%	60%
	$600	$550	$500	$425	$325	$300	$275

Subtract 20% for Rimfire cals.

MODEL 44½ IDEAL SINGLE SHOT — similar to Model 44, except .22 LR through .44-40 WCF cals., falling block, lever action, takedown, 24 or 26 in. barrels, straight grip stock and forearm, action redesigned 1903. Mfg. 1903-1916.

	100%	98%	95%	90%	80%	70%	60%
	$850	$775	$675	$575	$500	$425	$350

MODELS 45-54 SINGLE SHOTS — .22 LR through .44-40 WCF cals., rolling and falling block receivers, lever action, takedown, deluxe versions of the Models 44 and 44½, many special order features, including double set triggers, types of finish, engraving, length and weight of barrels, stock configuration could be special ordered. The higher grade Schuetzens and Stevens-Pope are very collectible and command premiums. These models have to be taken one at a time for determining value. Therefore, no prices are shown. Mfg. 1896-1916.

Grading	100%	98%	95%	90%	80%	70%	60%

MODEL 325 — .30-30 Win. cal., carbine type, introduced 1947.

	$375	$335	$275	$225	$185	$150	$135

NO. 325B — .30-30 Win. cal., bolt action, 4 shot mag., circa 1940s.

	$350	$315	$260	$210	$175	$140	$125

NO. 414 ARMORY MODEL — .22 LR or .22 Short cal. only, lever action, 26 in. barrel, single shot, Lyman aperture sight. Mfg. 1912-1932.

	$450	$400	$375	$330	$290	$250	$220

MODEL 416 — .22 LR cal., bolt action, 25 in. medium barrel, 5 shot mag. Disc.

	$140	$120	$110	$100	$90	$80	$70

This model was also mfg. as a U.S. military training rifle. Can be denoted by "U.S. Property" on rear of bolt housing. Healthy premiums exist for this variation.

NO. 417 WALNUT HILL MODEL — .22 LR, .22 Short, and .22 Hornet cal., lever action, 28 or 29 in. extra heavy barrel, target stock with full pistol grip, beavertail forend, made in 0-3 suffix variations (different sights). Mfg. 1932-1947.

	$875	$675	$525	$475	$440	$395	$360

NO. 417½ WALNUT HILL MODEL — similar to No. 417, except available in .25 rimfire also. Mfg. 1932-1940.

	$875	$675	$525	$475	$440	$395	$360

NO. 418 WALNUT HILL MODEL — .22 LR or .22 Short only, 26 in. barrel, pistol grip stock, semi beavertail forearm. Mfg. 1932-1940.

	$595	$400	$295	$260	$230	$200	$180

NO. 425 HIGH POWER LEVER ACTION RIFLE — .25, .30, .32, or .35 Rem. cals., 22 in. round barrel with ⅔ length mag. tube, side ejection, blue only, plain walnut stock and forearm, originally designed by John Redfield. Approx. 26,000 mfg. 1910-1917.

	$650	$595	$535	$465	$400	$350	$295

Variations of the No. 425 include the No. 430 (deluxe checkered stock and forearm), No. 435 (extra fancy checkered stock and forearm with engraved designs on receiver borders and lever), or No. 440 (best quality checkered walnut with fully engraved game scenes, and engraved forearm tip and lever). Values range respectively from $450-$950, $650-$1,400, and $1,000-$2,950.

STEVENS FAVORITE NO.'S 17-29 — .22 LR, .25 RF or .32 RF cal., 24 in. barrel most common, other lengths available, Rocky Mountain front sight, straight grip stock, small tapered forearm. Mfg. 1894-1935. Octagonal barrels command a 33% premium.

	$195	$165	$145	$125	$100	$80	$65

STEVENS FAVORITE MODEL 30G — .22 LR cal., new mfg. began in late 1998 by Savage Arms, Inc., 21 in. barrel, uncheckered wood stock and forearm, open sights. New 1998.

Mfg.'s Sug. Retail	$180	$160	$135	$120	$110	$100	$80	$65

STEVENS MODEL 65 — .22 LR cal., bolt action, 20 in. barrel, open sights, 5 shot mag., checkered walnut stock. Mfg. 1969-disc.

	$90	$70	$55	$45	$35	$30	$30

NO. 70 "VISIBLE LOADING" SLIDE ACTION RIFLE — .22 S, L, or LR cal., exposed hammer, 22 in. barrel, open sights, straight grip stock, tube mag., grooved slide handle. Other variations with different barrel lengths and sights will command slight premiums.

	$250	$175	$150	$130	$115	$100	$90

MODEL 71 "STEVENS FAVORITE" COMMEMORATIVE — .22 LR cal., replica of original, 22 in. octagon barrel, plain straight stock, medallion inlaid, crescent butt. 1,000 mfg. in 1971.

	$250	$195	$150				

Last Mfg.'s Sug. Retail was $75.

MODEL 72 CRACKSHOT — .22 LR cal., single shot falling block action, 22 in. octagon barrel, open sights, color case hardened frame, straight stock. Mfg. 1972-1989.

	$145	$125	$110	$100	$90	$80	$70

Last Mfg.'s Sug. Retail was $165.

MODEL 74 — similar to Model 72 Crackshot, except has round barrel. Mfg. 1972-1989.

	$140	$120	$110	$100	$90	$80	$70

Last Mfg.'s Sug. Retail was $165.

Grading	100%	98%	95%	90%	80%	70%	60%

MODEL 987 — .22 LR cal. only, semi-auto, 15 shot tube mag., 20 in. barrel, hardwood Monte Carlo stock, adj. rear sight, 6 lbs. Disc. 1989.

| | $95 | $80 | $70 | $60 | $50 | $40 | $45 |

Last Mfg.'s Sug. Retail was $119.

MODEL 89 LEVER ACTION — .22 LR cal., single shot, 18½ in. barrel, Martini type action, Western style lever, straight stock. Mfg. 1976-disc.

| | $85 | $65 | $60 | $50 | $45 | $40 | $35 |

SHOTGUNS

Stevens made a wide variety of inexpensive, utilitarian shotguns that to date have attracted mostly shooting interest, but little collector interest. A listing of these models may be found in the back of this text under "Serialization".

S

NO. 200 PUMP — 20 ga., tube mag., 26, 28, 30, or 32 in. barrel chambered for 3 in. shells, take-down, 5 shot, 6½ lbs., c. 1910.

| | $225 | $190 | $180 | $150 | $125 | $95 | $85 |

MODEL 520 PUMP

| | $190 | $180 | $150 | $125 | $95 | $85 | $75 |

MODEL 520-30 TRENCH/RIOT MILITARY SHOTGUNS — see the "Trench/Riot Shotgun" category in the T section for more information and prices.

MODEL 620 — an improved version of the Model 520 with streamlined receiver.

| | $325 | $290 | $250 | $225 | $175 | $150 | $100 |

MODEL 620 TRENCH/RIOT MILITARY SHOTGUNS — see the "Trench/Riot Shotgun" category in the T section for more information and prices.

MODEL 77 (F, M, & SC) SLIDE ACTION — 12, 16, or 20 ga., "M" suffix is 12 ga. Mag., "SC" designates Super Choke, "F" refers to 16 ga.

| | $175 | $160 | $140 | $120 | $100 | $80 | $60 |

MODEL 124 SLIDE ACTION — 12 ga. only, straight pull action, 28 in. barrel, 3 shot, Tenite butt stock and forearm, circa 1950.

| | $215 | $190 | $175 | $155 | $145 | $135 | $125 |

MODEL 67 SLIDE ACTION — 12, 20 ga., or .410 bore, all are 3 in. chambered, steel receiver, 5 shot, upper receiver safety, 6¼ - 7½ lbs. Recent mfg. by Stevens. Disc. 1989.

| | $200 | $180 | $170 | $155 | $145 | $135 | $125 |

Last Mfg.'s Sug. Retail was $229.

Add $30 for choke tubes (with VR).
Add $10 for VR only.

* **Model 67 VTR-K Camo** — 12 or 20 ga., 28 in. VR barrel with choke tubes, laminated camo stock. Mfg. 1986-1988.

| | $250 | $220 | $190 | $170 | $155 | $145 | $135 |

Last Mfg.'s Sug. Retail was $295.

* **Slug Model** — 12 ga. only, 21 in. barrel, rifle sights. Disc. 1989.

| | $200 | $165 | $140 | $110 | $100 | $90 | $80 |

Last Mfg.'s Sug. Retail was $245.

* **Model 67 VRT-Y** — 20 ga. only, 22 in. VR barrel with choke tubes, youth model with smaller stock dimensions. Mfg. 1987-1988.

| | $205 | $170 | $140 | $110 | $100 | $90 | $80 |

Last Mfg.'s Sug. Retail was $259.

MODEL 675 — 12 ga. only, 24 in. VR multi-choked barrel with iron sights (including removable rear ramp), hardwood stock with recoil pad, 6½ lbs. Mfg. 1987-1988.

| | $250 | $220 | $190 | $170 | $155 | $145 | $135 |

Last Mfg.'s Sug. Retail was $295.

MODEL 240 O/U — .410 bore, split hammers, double trigger.

| | $350 | $300 | $250 | $220 | $190 | $170 | $155 |

Grading	100%	98%	95%	90%	80%	70%	60%

MODEL 69-RXL — 12 ga. only, slide action law enforcement version of the Model 67, 18¼ in. cylinder bore barrel with recoil pad, 6½ lbs. Disc. 1989.

| | $200 | $165 | $140 | $110 | $100 | $90 | $80 |

Last Mfg.'s Sug. Retail was $245.

MODEL 311 SxS — 12, 16, 20 ga., or .410 bore, 3 in. chambers, double triggers, extractors, VR. Disc. 1989.

| | $245 | $205 | $185 | $150 | $140 | $125 | $115 |

Last Mfg.'s Sug. Retail was $309.

Add 10% for .410 bore.

* *Model 311-R* — 12 ga. only, similar to Model 311, except has 18¼ in. cylinder bore barrels for law enforcement use, 3 in. chambers, 6¾ lbs. Disc. 1989.

| | $245 | $205 | $185 | $150 | $140 | $125 | $115 |

Last Mfg.'s Sug. Retail was $309.

FOX/STEVENS MODEL B — 12, 20 ga., or .410 bore, double triggers, VR, extractors, 24, 26, 28, or 30 in. barrels, 7 lbs. Disc. 1986.

| | $315 | $280 | $240 | $220 | $200 | $180 | $160 |

Last Mfg.'s Sug. Retail was $369.

Add 25% for BDE Model (with ejectors).

FOX/STEVENS MODEL B-SE — 12, 20 ga., or .410 bore, single trigger, selective ejectors, VR, beavertail forearm, select walnut. Disc. 1989.

| | $415 | $370 | $325 | $280 | $240 | $210 | $180 |

Last Mfg.'s Sug. Retail was $525.

Add 20% for .410 bore.

MODEL 94 — 12, 16, 20, 28 ga., or .410 bore, single shot breakopen, open hammer, 6¼ lbs. Mfg. 1929-disc.

| | $95 | $85 | $75 | $60 | $50 | $45 | $40 |

Last Mfg.'s Sug. Retail was $92.

MODEL 9478 — 10, 12, 20 ga., or .410 bore, single shot break open, inertia firing pin, external hammer. Mfg. 1978-1985.

| | $95 | $85 | $75 | $60 | $50 | $45 | $40 |

STEYR AUSTRIAN MILITARY

Previously manufactured for the Austrian military in Steyr, Austria.

RIFLES: BOLT ACTION

MODEL 95 RIFLE — 8x50R Mannlicher cal., straight pull bolt action, 30 in. barrel, adj. sights, military full stock.

| | $140 | $110 | $100 | $85 | $65 | $55 | $40 |

MODEL 90 CARBINE — similar to Model 95, except 19½ in. barrel.

| | $155 | $125 | $110 | $95 | $85 | $65 | $45 |

STEYR DAIMLER PUCH A.G.

Current manufacturer located in Steyr, Austria 1911 to date.

PISTOLS

POCKET AUTO — .25 ACP or .32 ACP cal., tip up barrel, mag. fed. Disc.

| | $325 | $265 | $200 | $150 | $140 | $130 | $120 |

ROTH STEYR AUTO (MODEL 1907) — 8mm Steyr cal.

| | $750 | $600 | $475 | $350 | $300 | $250 | $200 |

Add 30% for "Budapest" markings.

STEYR-HAHN MODEL 1911 AUTOMATIC — 9mm Steyr cal., 8 shot, 5.1 in. barrel, fixed magazine top loaded by stripper clip, blue, checkered wood grips. Mfg. 1911-1919. In 1938, the Germans confiscated and converted a quantity of these to 9mm Para., "08" was stamped on the left side of these guns.

| | $450 | $375 | $325 | $275 | $225 | $195 | $175 |

Add 100% if marked "08" or with Rumanian Crest.

Grading	100%	98%	95%	90%	80%	70%	60%

MODEL SP — .32 ACP cal., semi-auto, trigger cocking mechanism, very rare - mfg. in 1959 only.

	$650	**$595**	**$540**	**$495**	**$450**	**$400**	**$350**

STEYR MANNLICHER

Currently manufactured by Steyr-Daimler-Puch in Austria. Founded by Ferdinand Ritter Von Mannlicher and Otto Schoenauer in 1903. Currently imported and distributed by Gun South, Inc. located in Trussville, AL.

Note: also see Mannlicher Schoenauer in the M section for pre-WWII models.

PISTOLS: SEMI-AUTO

MODEL GB — 9mm Para. cal., double action, 18 shot mag., gas delayed blowback action, non-glare checkered plastic grips, 5¼ in. barrel with Polygon rifling, matte finish, steel construction, 2 lbs. 6 oz. Importation disc. 1988.

	100%	98%	95%	90%	80%	70%	60%
Commercial	$525	$475	$425	$375	$335	$300	$280
Military	$450	$395	$350	$300	$280	$260	$240

Last Mfg.'s Sug. Retail was $514.

In 1987, Steyr mfg. a military variation of the Model GB featuring a phosphate finish - only 937 were imported into the U.S.

MODEL SPP — 9mm Para. cal., single action semi-auto, delayed blow back system with rotating 5.9 in. barrel, 15 or 30 shot mag., utilizes synthetic materials and advanced ergonomics, adj. sights, grooved receiver for scope mounting, matte black finish, 44 oz. Limited importation 1992-93.

	$800	**$675**	**$600**	**$550**	**$495**	**$450**	**$400**

Last Mfg.'s Sug. Retail was $895.

MODEL M — 9mm Para. or .40 S&W cal., features first integrated limited access key lock safety in a semi-auto pistol, 3 different safety conditions, black synthetic frame, 10 shot mag., matte black finish, 3 dot sights, 28 oz. New 1999.

	100%	98%	95%	90%	80%	70%	60%
Mfg.'s Sug. Retail	$699	$625	$560	$520	$480	$440	$400	$375

RIFLES: BOLT ACTION, RECENT PRODUCTION

Current production guns are now called Steyr-Mannlicher models. For models manufactured 1903-1971, please refer to the Mannlicher Schoenauer Sporting Rifles section in this text.

The recenty discontinued models SL, L, M, S, and S/T listed below have 4 different action lengths and model designations stand for the following: SL=Super Light, L=Light, M=Medium, S=Magnum, S/T=Magnum with heavy barrel. These sporting rifles were available with left-hand stock - add $109 and with either single set or double set triggers - add $125.

ZEPHYR 22 — .22 LR cal., features full length Mannlicher stock, single or double set triggers, open sights, checkered walnut stock with horn cap, sling swivels. Mfg. circa 1955-1971.

	$1,350	**$1,200**	**$1,000**	**$850**	**$725**	**$600**	**$525**

MODEL M72 L/M RIFLE — .243 Win., .308 Win., .270 Win., .30-06, 7x57mm, and 7x64mm cals., 23 in. barrel, single or double set triggers. Mfg. 1972-1980.

	$795	**$725**	**$650**	**$575**	**$500**	**$460**	**$420**

MODEL SL — .222 Rem.,.222 Rem. Mag. (disc.), .223 Rem., .22-250 Rem. (disc. 1992), or 5.6x50mm (disc. 1991) cal., bolt action, 23.6 in. barrel, double set triggers, rotary mag. Available in full-stock (Carbine), half stock (rifle), or varmint version (vent. square forearm). Disc. 1996.

	$1,875	**$1,325**	**$950**	**$775**	**$675**	**$600**	**$540**

Last Mfg.'s Sug. Retail was $2,250.

* Carbine Model (Full Stock) — skipline checkered full stock, 20 in. barrel. Disc. 1996.

	$1,995	**$1,400**	**$995**	**$825**	**$700**	**$600**	**$540**

Last Mfg.'s Sug. Retail was $2,450.

* Varmint Rifle — .222 Rem. (disc.), .223 Rem. (new 1993), or .22-250 Rem. (disc. 1992) cal., 26 in. heavy barrel, stippled pistol grip, vent. forearm, no sights. Disc. 1996.

	$1,995	**$1,400**	**$995**	**$825**	**$700**	**$600**	**$540**

Last Mfg.'s Sug. Retail was $2,450.

Grading	100%	98%	95%	90%	80%	70%	60%

MODEL L — 5.6x57mm (disc. 1991), .243 Win., or .308 Win. cals., available in .22-250 and 6mm Rem. on special order only, otherwise same general specifications as Model SL. Disc. 1996.

	$1,875	$1,325	$950	$775	$675	$600	$540

Last Mfg.'s Sug. Retail was $2,250.

* *Carbine Model (Full Stock)* — skip-line checkered full stock, 20 in. barrel. Disc. 1996.

	$1,995	$1,400	$995	$825	$700	$600	$540

Last Mfg.'s Sug. Retail was $2,450.

* *Varmint Rifle* — .222 Rem. (disc. 1991), .22-250 Rem., .243 Win. (disc.), or .308 Win. (disc.) cal., 26 in. heavy barrel, stippled pistol grip, vent. forearm, no sights. Disc. 1996.

	$1,995	$1,400	$995	$825	$700	$600	$540

Last Mfg.'s Sug. Retail was $2,450.

* *Model L Luxus* — 5.6x57mm, .243 Win., or .308 Win. cal., full or half stock only, .22-250 Rem. and 6mm Rem. available on special order, 3 shot mag. Disc. 1996.

	$2,495	$1,750	$1,325	$1,000	$800	$700	$650

Last Mfg.'s Sug. Retail was $2,950.

* *Model L Luxus Carbine (Full Stock)* — similar to L Luxus rifle, except has full stock and 20 in. barrel. Disc. 1996.

	$2,625	$1,825	$1,350	$1,025	$800	$700	$650

Last Mfg.'s Sug. Retail was $3,150.

MODEL M — 6.5x55mm, 6.5x57mm, 7x64mm, .270 Win., .30-06, or 9.3x62mm cal., bolt action, full stock or half stock, rotary mag., double set triggers. Disc. 1996.

	$1,875	$1,325	$950	$775	$675	$600	$540

Last Mfg.'s Sug. Retail was $2,250.

Add $400 for left-hand action.

* *Carbine Model (Full Stock)* — skipline checkered full stock, 20 in. barrel. Disc. 1996.

	$1,995	$1,400	$995	$825	$700	$600	$540

Last Mfg.'s Sug. Retail was $2,450.

Add $400 for left-hand action.

* *Professional Rifle* — .270 Win., 7x57mm (disc. 1991), 7x64mm, .30-06, or 9.3x62mm cal., 23.6 in. barrel, Cycolac synthetic stock, 7½ lbs. Disc. 1993.

	$1,500	$1,025	$850	$700	$600	$540	$495

Last Mfg.'s Sug. Retail was $1,710.

Add $469 for left hand action with half stock (rifle).
Add $625 for left hand action with full stock (carbine).
This variation is also available in .270 Win. or .30-06 cal. with half stock and 20 in. barrel (carbine).

* *Model M Luxus* — 6.5x55mm, 6.5x57mm (disc.), 7x64mm, .270 Win., or .30-06 cal., special order in 6.5x55mm and 7.5mm Swiss. Disc. 1996.

	$2,495	$1,750	$1,325	$1,000	$800	$700	$650

Last Mfg.'s Sug. Retail was $2,950.

* *Model M Luxus Carbine (Full Stock)* — similar to Model M Luxus, except with full stock and 20 in. barrel. Disc. 1996.

	$2,625	$1,825	$1,350	$1,025	$800	$700	$650

Last Mfg.'s Sug. Retail was $3,150.

* *Carbine - 1000 Year Commemorative* — 1984 only, .30-06 cal.

	$4,200	$3,620	$2,835

M-III PROFESSIONAL — .25-06 Rem. (new 1996), .270 Win., .30-06, or 7x64mm cal., features black synthetic half stock, 23.6 in. barrel, no sights. Imported 1994-1996.

	$900	$800	$700	$600	$525	$450	$375

Last Mfg.'s Sug. Retail was $995.

Add $130 for stipled checkered European wood stock.

Grading	100%	98%	95%	90%	80%	70%	60%

JAGD MATCH — .222 Rem., .243 Win., or .308 Win. cal., features shortened action, 23.6 in. heavy barrel with iron sights, 5 shot rotary mag., laminated checkered half-stock, recoil pad, designed for European Match events limited to hunting rifles, double set triggers, 8½ lbs. Imported 1995-1996.

	$2,025	$1,375	$1,025	$825	$675	$600	$540

Last Mfg.'s Sug. Retail was $2,450.

MODEL S (MAGNUM) — 6.5x68mm, 8x68S, .300 Win. Mag., .338 Win. Mag. (disc. 1992), .375 H&H, or 7mm Rem. Mag. cal., half-stock, 26 in. barrel, bolt action. Disc. 1996.

	$2,075	$1,400	$1,050	$850	$725	$625	$550

Last Mfg.'s Sug. Retail was $2,550.

MODEL S/T — available in 9.3x64 (disc. 1992), .375 H&H, or .458 Win. Mag. cal., half-stock, 26 in. heavy barrel. Disc. 1996.

	$2,325	$1,575	$1,125	$925	$775	$675	$595

Last Mfg.'s Sug. Retail was $2,850.

* *Tropical Rifle* — .375 H&H and .458 Win. Mag. cals., 26 in. heavy barrel. Disc. 1985.

	$1,150	$900	$810	$730	$660	$600	$550

Last Mfg.'s Sug. Retail was $1,332.

* *Luxus S* — available in 6.5x68mm, 8x68S, 7mm Rem. Mag., or .300 Win. Mag. cal., 26 in. barrel, half-stock only, 3 shot mag., 8 lbs. Disc. 1996.

	$2,700	$1,900	$1,475	$1,125	$875	$750	$675

Last Mfg.'s Sug. Retail was $3,250.

STEYR SCOUT PACKAGE — .308 Win. or .376 Steyr (new 1999) cal., designed by Jeff Cooper, features grey synthetic Zytel stock, 19 in. fluted barrel, Picatinny optic rail, integral bipod, includes Leupold M8 2.5x28 IER scope with factory Steyr mounts, and luggage case. New 1998.

Mfg.'s Sug. Retail	$2,595	$2,350	$2,000	$1,800	$1,600	$1,325	$1,100	$995

Add $200 for .376 Steyr cal.

* *Steyr Scout* — same as above, except does not include scope, mounts, or case. New 1999.

Mfg.'s Sug. Retail	$1,895	$1,675	$1,500	$1,350	$1,200	$1,050	$900	$750

Add $150 for .376 Steyr cal. (black stock only).

* *Steyr Scout Tactical* — .308 Win. cal. only, similar to Steyr Scout, except has black synthetic stock with removable spacers, oversized bolt handle, and emergency ghost ring sights. New 1999.

Mfg.'s Sug. Retail	$1,995	$1,750	$1,550	$1,375	$1,225	$1,050	$900	$750

SBS PRO HUNTER MODEL — .243 Win., .25-06 Rem., .270 Win., .30-06, .308 Win., 7mm-08 Rem., 6.5x55mm, 6.5x57mm, 7x64mm, or 9.3x62mm cal., features safe bolt system (SBS), synthetic stock, matte blue finish, 23.6 in. barrel without sights. New 1997.

Mfg.'s Sug. Retail	$699	$650	$595	$550	$495	$450	$395	$350

Add $150 for metric cals.

* *SBS Pro Hunter Magnum* — .300 Win. Mag., 7mm Rem. Mag., 6.5x68mm, or 8x68S cal., similar to SBS Pro Hunter Model, except has 25.6 in. barrel. New 1997.

Mfg.'s Sug. Retail	$729	$650	$600	$550	$500	$450	$395	$350

Add $150 for metric cals.

* *SBS Pro Hunter .376 Steyr* — .376 Steyr cal. only, 20 in. barrel with iron sights, black synthetic stock, matte blue finish. New 1999.

Mfg.'s Sug. Retail	$899	$775	$680	$600	$550	$500	$450	$395

* *SBS Pro Hunter Youth/Ladies Rifle* — .243 Win., 7mm-08 Rem., or .308 Win. cal., shortened stock with 2 butt spacers for adj. length, 20 in. barrel with iron sights, matte blue finish. New 1999.

Mfg.'s Sug. Retail	$799	$695	$630	$565	$500	$450	$395	$350

* *SBS Pro Hunter Mountain Rifle* — .243 Win., .25-06 Rem., .270 Win., .30-06, .308 Win., or 7mm-08 Rem. cal., 20 in. barrel, no sights, matte blue finish, black synthetic stock, detachable mag. New 1999.

Mfg.'s Sug. Retail	$749	$665	$610	$555	$500	$450	$395	$350

Grading	100%	98%	95%	90%	80%	70%	60%

SBS FORESTER MODEL — similar to SBS Pro Hunter Model, except has wood stock and standard blue finish. New 1997.

Mfg.'s Sug. Retail	$719	$640	$595	$550	$500	$450	$395	$350

Add $150 for metric cals.

* **SBS Forester Mountain Rifle** — .243 Win., .25-06 Rem., .270 Win., .30-06, .308 Win., or 7mm-08 Rem. cal., 20 in. barrel, no sights, matte blue finish, checkered walnut stock, detachable mag. New 1999.

Mfg.'s Sug. Retail	$769	$680	$615	$555	$500	$450	$395	$350

* **SBS Forester Magnum** — .300 Win. Mag., 7mm Rem. Mag., 6.5x68mm, or 8x68S cal., similar to SBS Forester Model, except has 25.6 in. barrel. New 1997.

Mfg.'s Sug. Retail	$749	$660	$610	$550	$500	$450	$395	$350

Add $250 for metric cals.

SBS TACTICAL — .308 Win. cal. only, 20 in. barrel w/o sights, features oversized bolt handle and high capacity 10 shot mag. with adapter, matte blue finish. New 1999.

Mfg.'s Sug. Retail	$949	$825	$725	$625	$550	$500	$450	$395

* **SBS Tactical Heavy Barrel** — .308 Win. cal., features 26 in. heavy barrel w/o sights and oversized bolt handle, matte blue finish. New 1999.

Mfg.'s Sug. Retail	$949	$825	$725	$625	$550	$500	$450	$395

* **SBS Tactical McMillan** — similar to SBS Tactical Heavy barrel, except has custom McMillan A-3 stock with adj. cheekpiece and oversized bolt handle, matte blue finish. New 1999.

Mfg.'s Sug. Retail	$1,575	$1,400	$1,200	$1,000	$850	$725	$600	$550

MANNLICHER SBS EUROPEAN MODEL — .243 Win., .25-06 Rem., .270 Win., .30-06 (disc. 1998), .308 Win., 7mm-08 Rem., 6.5x55mm, 6.5x57mm, 7x64mm, 7.5x55mm, or 9.3x62mm cal., features safe bolt system (SBS), 23.6 in. barrel with sights, checkered walnut stock and forearm. New 1997.

Mfg.'s Sug. Retail	$2,795	$2,300	$1,850	$1,600	$1,325	$1,100	$925	$850

* **Mannlicher SBS Magnum European Model** — .300 Win. Mag., 7mm Rem. Mag., 6.5x68mm, or 8x68S cal., 25.6 in. barrel with sights, checkered walnut stock and forearm. New 1997.

Mfg.'s Sug. Retail	$2,895	$2,375	$1,900	$1,625	$1,350	$1,100	$925	$850

* **Mannlicher SBS European Model - "Goiserer"** — similar to Mannlicher SBS European Model, except has 20 in. barrel. New 1997.

Mfg.'s Sug. Retail	$2,995	$2,500	$2,000	$1,650	$1,350	$1,100	$925	$850

* **Mannlicher SBS European Model - Full Stock** — similar to Mannlicher SBS European Model, except has full-length Mannlicher stock. New 1997.

Mfg.'s Sug. Retail	$2,995	$2,500	$2,000	$1,650	$1,350	$1,100	$925	$850

MODEL SSG — .243 Win. (disc., PII Sniper only) or .308 Win cal., for competition or law-enforcement use. Marksman has regular sights, rotary mag., teflon coated bolt with heavy duty locking lugs, synthetic stock has removable spacers, parkerized finish. Match version has heavier target barrel and "match" bolt carrier, can be used as single shot. Extremely accurate.

* **PI Rifle** — 26 in. barrel, 3 shot mag., black or green ABS Cycolac synthetic stock.

Mfg.'s Sug. Retail	$1,695		$1,525	$1,300	$1,100	$975	$850	$725	$600

Add 15% for walnut stock (disc. 1992, retail was $448).

* **PII/PIIK Sniper Rifle** — .243 Win. (disc.) or .308 Win. cal., 20 in. heavy (Model PIIK) or 26 in. heavy barrel, no sights, green or black synthetic Cycolac or McMillian black fiberglass stock, modified bolt handle, choice of single or set triggers.

Mfg.'s Sug. Retail	$1,695		$1,525	$1,300	$1,100	$975	$850	$725	$600

Add $600 for black McMillian fiberglass stock.
Add 15% for walnut stock (disc. 1992, retail was $448).

* **PIII Rifle** — .308 Win. cal., 26 in. heavy barrel with diopter match sight bases, H-S Precision Pro-Series stock in black only. Importation 1991-93.

	$2,600	$1,875	$1,425	$1,050	$825	$700	$600

Last Mfg.'s Sug. Retail was $3,162.

Grading	100%	98%	95%	90%	80%	70%	60%

* **PIV Urban Rifle** — .308 Win. cal., carbine variation with 16½ in. heavy barrel and flash hider, ABS Cycolac synthetic stock in green or black. Importation began 1991.

Mfg.'s Sug. Retail	$2,660	$2,285	$1,625	$1,275	$975	$775	$700	$650

* **Jagd Match** — .222 Rem., .243 Win., or .308 Win. cal., hunting rifle that features checkered wood laminate stock, 23.6 in. barrel, Mannlicher sights, double set triggers, supplied with test target. Mfg. 1991-92.

	$1,550	$1,050	$950	$800	$675	$600	$540

Last Mfg.'s Sug. Retail was $1,550.

* **Match Rifle** — .308 Win. only, 26 in. heavy barrel, brown ABS Cycolac stock, Walther Diopter sights, 8.6 lbs. Mfg. disc. 1992.

	$2,000	$1,500	$1,225	$925	$800	$700	$600

Last Mfg.'s Sug. Retail was $2,306.

S

        Add $437 for walnut stock.

* **Model SPG-T** — .308 Win. cal., Target model. Mfg. 1993-98.

	$3,225	$2,850	$2,550	$2,200	$1,850	$1,500	$1,200

Last Mfg.'s Sug. Retail was $3,695.

* **Model SPG-CISM** — .308 Win. cal., 20 in. heavy barrel, laminated wood stock with adj. cheekpiece and black lacquer finish. New 1993.

Mfg.'s Sug. Retail	$3,295	$2,995	$2,600	$2,300	$1,950	$1,700	$1,450	$1,200

* **Match UIT** — .308 Win. cal. only, 10 shot steel mag., special single set trigger, free floating barrel, Diopter sights, raked bolt handle, 10.8 lbs. Disc. 1998.

	$3,600	$3,150	$2,750	$2,400	$2,050	$1,700	$1,400

Last Mfg.'s Sug. Retail was $3,995.

        UIT stands for Union Internationale de Tir.

RIFLES: SEMI-AUTO

AUG S.A. — .223 Rem. cal., semi-auto paramilitary design rifle, design incorporates use of advanced plastics, integral Swarovski scope, 16, 20, or 24 in. barrel, bullpup configuration, 7.9 lbs.

Mfg.'s Sug. Retail	$1,575	$1,375	$975	$875	$750	$650	$575	$525

        Add approx. $700 for special receiver mfg. using Stanag metallurgy.

        This model is now available in limited quantities only to law enforcement agencies due to 1989 Federal legislation banning the importation for commercial sales.

* **AUG S.A. Commercial** — similar to above, except values reflect price increases due to consumer demand after Federal legislation banned the commercial importation in 1989, grey (3,000 mfg. circa 1997), green or black finish.

Grey finish	$2,200	$2,000	$1,850	$1,700	$1,600	$1,500	$1,400
Green finish	$2,950	$2,750	$2,500	$2,250	$1,975	$1,800	$1,675

Last Mfg.'s Sug. Retail was $1,362 (1989).

Black finish	$3,950	$3,600	$3,150	$2,950	$2,750	$2,500	$2,250

STOCK, FRANZ

Previous manufacturer located in Berlin, Germany.

PISTOLS: SEMI-AUTO

.22 LR PISTOL — .22 LR cal.. Mfg. in Germany 1920-1940.

	$295	$250	$225	$175	$125	$100	$75

.25 ACP PISTOL — .25 ACP or .32 ACP cal.. Mfg. in Germany 1920-1940.

	$295	$225	$175	$150	$100	$90	$80

STOEGER INDUSTRIES, INC.

Current importer located in Wayne, NJ. Currently imported Stoeger Lugers may be found in the back of the Luger section in this text.

        Stoeger has imported a wide variety of firearms during the past seven decades. Most of these guns were good quality and came from known makers in Europe (some were private labeled). Stoeger carried an extensive firearms inventory of both house

Grading	100%	98%	95%	90%	80%	70%	60%

brand and famous European trademarks - many of which were finely made with beautiful engraving, stock work, and other popular special order features. As a general rule, values for Stoeger rifles and shotguns may be ascertained by comparing them with a known trademark of equal quality and cal./ga. Certain configurations will be more desirable than others (i.e. a Stoeger .22 caliber Mannlicher with double set triggers and detachable mag. will be worth considerably more than a single shot target rifle).

Perhaps the best reference works available on these older Stoeger firearms (not to mention the other trademarks of that time) are the older Stoeger catalogs themselves - quite collectible in their own right. It is advised to purchase these older catalogs (some reprints are also available), if more information is needed on not only older Stoeger models, but the other firearms being sold at that time.

PISTOLS: SEMI-AUTO

PRO SERIES 95 — .22 LR cal., target pistol with choice of either 5½ or 7¼ VR, fluted, or bull barrel, adj. rear sight, adj. trigger, push-button takedown, Pachmayr rubber grips, gold accents, 10 shot mag., 45-47 oz. Mfg. 1995-96.

➤ 5½ in. bull barrel

	$440	$375	$335	$300	$275	$250	$225

Last Mfg.'s Sug. Retail was $495.

➤ 5½ in. VR barrel

	$515	$425	$365	$325	$285	$255	$225

Last Mfg.'s Sug. Retail was $595.

➤ 7¼ in. fluted barrel

	$455	$385	$340	$300	$275	$250	$225

Last Mfg.'s Sug. Retail was $525.

STONER RIFLE

Please refer to the Knight's Manufacturing Company listing in this text.

STRAYER TRIPP INTERNATIONAL

Please refer to the STI International listing in this section.

STRAYER-VOIGT, INC.

Current manufacturer of Infinity pistols located in Grand Prairie, TX. See the Infinity listing for more information.

STREET SWEEPER

Previously manufactured by Sales of Georgia, Inc. located in Atlanta, GA.

STREET SWEEPER — 12 ga. only, 12 shot rotary mag., paramilitary configuration with 18 in. barrel, double action, folding stock, 9¾ lbs. Restricted sales following the ATF classification as a "destructive device". Mfg. 1989-approx. 1995.

	$650	$550	$475	$400	$360	$330	$300

STURM, RUGER & CO., INC.

Current manufacturer with production facilities located in Newport, NH (rifles and shotguns) beginning 1993 and Prescott, AZ (handguns) beginning 1986. Previously manufactured in Southport, CT 1949-1993 (office headquarters remain at this location).

NOTE: In 1976, Ruger stamped "Made in the 200th year of American Liberty" on the side of all of the guns they produced for this one year only. These Bicentennial or "Liberty Model" guns will bring a $50 - $75 premium from collectors interested in acquiring them. In most cases this is only true of 100% guns, unfired with the original box and papers.

Almost all the models in this section are factory variations, and non-factory limited or special editions are not included in this section because of the amount and price unpredictability.

Grading	100%	98%	95%	90%	80%	70%	60%

ALL VALUES FOR 100% CONDITION RUGERS ASSUME NIB UNFIRED. PRICES OF GUNS WITH ORIGINAL BOXES AND PAPERWORK CAN VARY GREATLY BECAUSE OF RARITY OF CERTAIN MODELS AND CONDITION OF BOX OR ACCESSORIES. INDIVIDUAL APPRAISALS NEEDED.

Beginning 1998, all handguns are supplied with a case and lock.

PISTOLS: SEMI-AUTO, RIMFIRE

Many distributors and customizers have produced special/limited editions on this popular series of .22 cal. pistols. Individual companies should be contacted for current pricing and special order features/prices.

"RED EAGLE" — approx. 29,000 mfg. 1949-1952, most production occurred prior to Alexander Sturm's death (1951).

	100%	98%	95%	90%	80%	70%	60%
Standard	$450	$400	$350	$300	$265	$235	$200
Target	$475	$425	$375	$350	$300	$275	$225

Add 50%+ in 100% condition factor only for early Red Eagle with wood "salt cod" box.

Distinguishable by recessed red enamel eagle in grips. Produced until early 1952. Serialized approx. 0001 - 35,000 with Mark I Auto occupying blocks from 15,000 - 17,000 and 25,000 - 25,300.

STANDARD MODEL — .22 LR cal., 9 shot, 4¾ in. or 6 in. barrel, blue, fixed sights, checkered wood or rubber grips. Mfg. 1951-1982.

	100%	98%	95%	90%	80%	70%	60%
	$175	$150	$140	$125	$100	$90	$80

Variations marked "Hecho En Mexico" are rare. 98%+ condition specimens have sold for as much as $1,500.

* **Stainless Steel 1 of 5,000**

	100%	98%	95%
	$395	$350	$300

MARK I TARGET — similar to Standard, except has 5½ in. heavy barrel, 5¼ tapered (scarce) barrel, or 6⅞ heavy tapered barrel, adj. rear sights, target sight. Mfg. 1951-1982.

	100%	98%	95%	90%	80%	70%	60%
	$225	$195	$175	$150	$140	$130	$120

Add 100% if U.S. marked.
Add 100% for 5¼ in. tapered barrel.
Add $100 for Ruger addressed muzzle brake.

MARK II STANDARD — .22 LR cal., 4¾ or 6 in. barrel, checkered black Delrin synthetic grips, blue finish, 10 shot mag., approx. 2¼ lbs. Mfg. 1982 to date.

		100%	98%	95%	90%	80%	70%	60%
Mfg.'s Sug. Retail	$252	$195	$155	$125	$115	$110	$100	$95

* **Stainless Steel** — variation of the Mark II Standard.

		100%	98%	95%
Mfg.'s Sug. Retail	$330	$260	$195	$165

Serial numbers start approx. at 18-00001.

MARK II STANDARD 50TH ANNIVERSARY — .22 LR cal., features blue receiver machined to same contour as original production, stainless steel bolt with Ruger medallion on rear, 50th Anniversary Ruger crest on top of frame in front of ejection port, black grips with Ruger medallion in red background, lockable red case. New 1999.

		100%	98%	95%	90%	80%	70%	60%
Mfg.'s Sug. Retail	$287	$235	$185	$150	$125	$115	$110	$100

MARK II TARGET — .22 LR cal., 4 (new 1996) bull, 5¼ (disc. 1994), 5½ bull, 6⅞ standard, or 10 in. bull barrel, single action, 2⅝ - 3¼ lbs. depending on barrel.

		100%	98%	95%	90%	80%	70%	60%
Mfg.'s Sug. Retail	$311	$250	$225	$185	$160	$130	$120	$110

Add $16 for 4 in. bull barrel.
Add $4 for 10 in. bull barrel.

* **Stainless Steel** — stainless variation of the Mark II Target, includes choice of 5¼ (disc. 1994), 5½ bull, 6⅞ standard, or 10 in. bull barrel.

		100%	98%	95%
Mfg.'s Sug. Retail	$389	$300	$245	$185

Add $4 for 10 in. bull barrel.

GOVERNMENT TARGET MODEL (MK678G) — commercial variation of the government training model without "U.S." markings, 6⅞ in. bull barrel, adj. rear sight, blue finish, black plastic grips, 46 oz., individually test targeted. New 1987.

		100%	98%	95%	90%	80%	70%	60%
Mfg.'s Sug. Retail	$374	$295	$245	$195	$170	$155	$140	$125

Grading		100%	98%	95%	90%	80%	70%	60%

* *Military "U.S." Marked* — issued to U.S. military personnel, must be factory verified.
  Mfg.'s Sug. Retail   **$600**   **$550**   **$500**   **$450**   **$400**   **$360**   **$330**   **$300**

* *Stainless Government Target Model* — 6⅞ in. bull barrel only. New 1993.
  Mfg.'s Sug. Retail   **$448**   **$355**   **$285**   **$220**
  Add $14 for 6⅞ in. slab side bull barrel with scope rings and base.

MODEL 22/45 — .22 LR cal. only, semi-auto single action, Zytel frame is patterned after the Model 1911 .45 ACP Gov't, 4 regular, 4¾ regular, 5¼ regular (Target, disc.), or 5½ in. bull barrel, 10 shot mag. (push-button release), fixed (4¾ in. barrel only) or adj. sights, 28-35 oz. New 1993.

* *Stainless Steel* — 4¾ in. regular barrel with fixed sights (Model KP4, new 1997) or 5½ in. bull barrel with adj. sights (Model KP512).
  Mfg.'s Sug. Retail   **$330**   **$265**   **$215**   **$185**
  Subtract $50 for fixed sights (4¾ in. barrel only).

* *Blue Finish* — 4 in. regular barrel with adj. sights (Model P4, new 1997) or 5½ in. bull barrel with adj. sights (Model P512). New 1994.
  Mfg.'s Sug. Retail   **$238**   **$195**   **$170**   **$150**   **$135**   **$125**   **$115**   **$100**

PISTOLS: SEMI-AUTO, CENTERFIRE

P85 MARK II — 9mm Para. cal., double action, 4½ in. barrel, aluminum frame with steel slide, 3-dot fixed sights, 15 shot mag., ambidextrous safety or decocking levers, oversized trigger, synthetic Xenoy grips, matte black finish, 2 lbs. Mfg. 1987-92.
  $335 $295 $265 $235 $215 $200 $185
  Last Mfg.'s Sug. Retail was $410.
  Subtract $30 if without case and extra mag.

* *KP85 Mark II Stainless Steel* — stainless variation of the P-85. Mfg. 1990-92.
  $350 $315 $280
  Last Mfg.'s Sug. Retail was $452.
  Subtract $30 if without case and extra mag.
  Variants included a decocking or double action only version at no extra charge.

P89 — 9mm Para. cal., improved variation of the P-85 Mark II, 10 (C/B 1994) shot mag., ambidextrous safety or decocker, blued finish. New 1992.
  Mfg.'s Sug. Retail   **$430**   **$350**   **$310**   **$270**   **$240**   **$215**   **$200**   **$185**
  Variants were available in a decocking (P-89DC) or double action only (P-89DAO) version at no extra charge.

* *KP89 Stainless* — stainless variation of the P89, also available in double action only. New 1992.
  Mfg.'s Sug. Retail   **$475**   **$390**   **$335**   **$295**
  Add $45 for convertible 7.65mm Luger cal. barrel (disc).

P90 — .45 ACP cal., similar to KP90 Stainless, except has blue finish.
  Mfg.'s Sug. Retail   **$476**   **$390**   **$335**   **$290**   **$245**   **$215**   **$200**   **$185**

KP90 STAINLESS — .45 ACP cal., double action, 4½ in. barrel, oversized trigger, aluminum frame with stainless steel slide, 7 shot single column mag., ambidextrous safety (KP-90) or decocking (KP-90D), Xenoy grips, 3 dot fixed sights. New 1991.
  Mfg.'s Sug. Retail   **$513**   **$400**   **$345**   **$300**
  This model was previously available in a double action only variation (K-P90C, disc. 1992).

KP91 STAINLESS — .40 S&W cal., similar to Model K-P90 Stainless, except is not available with external safety and has 11 shot double column mag. Mfg. 1992-94.
  $385 $335 $295
  Last Mfg.'s Sug. Retail was $489.
  This model was available in a decocking variation (K-P91D) or double action only (K-P91DAO).

P93 BLUE — similar to KP93 Stainless, except has blued finish, ambidextrous decocker. New 1998.
  Mfg.'s Sug. Retail   **$422**   **$345**   **$300**   **$265**   **$235**   **$215**   **$200**   **$185**

Grading	100%	98%	95%	90%	80%	70%	60%

KP93 STAINLESS — 9mm Para. cal., compact variation with 3⁹⁄₁₀ in. tilting barrel - link actuated, matte blue or REM (new 1996) finish, 3 dot sights, 10 (C/B 1994) or 15★ shot mag., available with ambidextrous decocking or double action only, 31 oz. New 1994.

Mfg.'s Sug. Retail	$520	$415	$350	$300			

P94 BLUE — similar to KP94 Stainless, except has blued finish. New 1998.

Mfg.'s Sug. Retail	$422	$345	$300	$265	$235	$215	$200	$185

KP94 STAINLESS — 9mm Para. cal., available with ambidextrous safety, matte blue or REM (new 1996) finish, ambidextrous decocker, or double action only, 10 (C/B 1994), or 15★ (9mm Para.) shot mag., 33 oz. New 1994.

Mfg.'s Sug. Retail	$520	$415	$350	$300			

P95 BLUE — 9mm Para. cal., available in ambidextrous decocker or double action only configuration, polymer frame, 39.10 in. barrel, fixed sights, blued finish, 10 shot mag., 27 oz. New 1997.

Mfg.'s Sug. Retail	$351	$295	$250	$215	$185	$165	$150	$135

* *KP95 Stainless* — stainless variation of Model P95. New 1997.

Mfg.'s Sug. Retail	$387	$320	$265	$225			

KP97 STAINLESS — .45 ACP cal., similar to KP94 Stainless, except has 7 shot mag., 27 oz. New 1999.

Mfg.'s Sug. Retail	$460	$370	$300	$260			

P944 — .40 S&W cal., similar to P93, ambidextrous safety, blue finish, 34 oz. New 1999.

Mfg.'s Sug. Retail	$422	$345	$300	$265	$235	$215	$200	$185

* *KP944 Stainless* — similar to P944, except is stainless steel. New 1999.

Mfg.'s Sug. Retail	$520	$415	$350	$300			

REVOLVERS: SINGLE ACTION, OLD MODELS

Note: Some of the following Rugers are known as "Old Models" (mfg. 1968 - early 1973) and are instantly recognized by the three screws through the frame and the four clicks emitted upon cocking. They are now actively sought by collectors and some shooters who desire the smoother operation they afford.

SINGLE SIX REVOLVER — .22 LR cal., 4⁵⁄₈, 5¹⁄₂ (mfg. 1953-1972), 6¹⁄₂, or 9¹⁄₂ in. barrel, fixed sights, rubber or wood grips, blue. Mfg. 1953-1963.

	$275	$200	$175	$130	$120	$110	$100

➤ **Early 4⁵⁄₈ in. Barrel** — single cylinder, ser. no. range 127,000-198,000.

	$475	$400	$350	$300	$250	$200	$175

An extra convertible cylinder will command a premium on this model.

➤ **Early 9¹⁄₂ in. Barrel** — single cylinder, ser. no. range 127,000-198,000.

	$450	$400	$350	$300	$250	$200	$175

An extra convertible cylinder will command a premium on this model.

* *Flat loading gate* — 5¹⁄₂ in. barrel only, approx. 61,000 mfg. from 1953-1957. Four variations.

	$350	$300	$250	$200	$175	$160	$150

Add 100% for non-serrated front sight (ser. no. 1-2,000)

* *.22 Mag.* — 6¹⁄₂ in. barrel only, mfg. only three years, serial numbered between 300,000 - 342,000. Frame stamped Mag. only.

	$300	$250	$200	$175	$165	$160	$150

Add 20% for extra .22 LR cylinder in Mag. only marked guns.

Approx. 250 factory cased, engraved Single Six models have been mfg. Seldom seen and among the rarest of Ruger revolvers, prices have been reported in the $2,500-$3,500 range.

SINGLE SIX CONVERTIBLE — similar to Single Six, except .22 LR and .22 Mag. interchangeable cylinders, 4⁵⁄₈, 5¹⁄₂, 6¹⁄₂, or 9¹⁄₂ in. barrel with 4⁵⁄₈ in. being the rarest. Mfg. 1960-1972.

	$275	$225	$175	$150	$140	$115	$100

Add 50% for 5¹⁄₂ or 6¹⁄₂ in. barrel.
Add 75%-100% for 4⁵⁄₈ or 9¹⁄₂ in. barrel under ser. no. 198,000 (XR3 grip frame).

Grading	100%	98%	95%	90%	80%	70%	60%

LIGHTWEIGHT SINGLE SIX — similar to Single Six, except alloy frame, 4⅝ in. barrel, made 1956-1958. 200,000 - 212,000 serial range, can have alloy or steel cylinder.

	100%	98%	95%	90%	80%	70%	60%
	$450	$350	$300	$250	$200	$175	$150

Add $100 if all blue with blue alloy cyl.
Add 100% for verifiable factory second ("S") marking.

SUPER SINGLE SIX CONVERTIBLE — similar to Single Six Convertible, except adj. sights. Mfg. 1964-1972.

	100%	98%	95%	90%	80%	70%	60%
	$275	$250	$200	$155	$140	$120	$105

This model in 4⅝ in. barrel is the rarest with prices ranging between $800-$1,000 in blue finish, nickel finish 6½ in. barrel specimens are trading for $1,200-$2,250.

S

BLACKHAWK SINGLE ACTION "FLAT-TOP" — .357 Mag. cal., 6 shot, 4⅝, 6½, and 10 in. barrel, flat top cylinder strap, adj. sight, blue, black rubber or walnut grips. Approx. 43,000 mfg. between 1955-1963.

	100%	98%	95%	90%	80%	70%	60%
4⅝ in. barrel	$500	$450	$375	$300	$250	$225	$200
6½ in. barrel	$700	$550	$450	$375	$350	$300	$250
10 in. barrel	$1,200	$1,050	$950	$850	$700	$600	$500

BLACKHAWK SINGLE ACTION — .357 Mag., .41 Mag., or .45 LC cal., this model is the 1962 variation with hooded rear sight and 4⅝ (.45 LC), 6½ (.357 Mag. or .41 Mag.), or 7½ (.45 LC) in. barrel.

	100%	98%	95%	90%	80%	70%	60%
	$350	$300	$250	$215	$180	$160	$140

Add $50 for .41 Mag. or $75 for .45 LC cal.
Add 75% for factory installed brass grip frame (rare).

BLACKHAWK CONVERTIBLE — similar to Blackhawk, with extra cylinder, .357 Mag. and 9mm Para., and .45 LC and .45 ACP cals.

	100%	98%	95%	90%	80%	70%	60%
.357 Mag./9mm Para.	$400	$350	$295	$250	$225	$195	$175

Add $100 for NIB .357 Mag./9mm Para. with non-prefix ser. no.
Add $100 for .45 LC/.45 ACP combination.

BLACKHAWK FLAT-TOP .44 MAGNUM — similar to Blackhawk Flat-Top, except heavier frame and cylinder, .44 Mag., 6½, 7½, and 10 in. barrels. Approx. 28,000 mfg. between 1956-1963.

	100%	98%	95%	90%	80%	70%	60%
6½ in. barrel	$650	$575	$495	$400	$350	$300	$250
7½ in. barrel	$850	$775	$700	$625	$550	$475	$400
10 in. barrel	$1,200	$1,050	$925	$800	$700	$600	$500

Distinguishable by fluted cylinder and rounded triggerguard.

SUPER BLACKHAWK — .44 Mag. cal., 6½ (rare) or 7½ in. barrel, larger frame and improved triggerguard, unfluted cylinder, adj. sights, walnut grips. Mfg. 1959-1972.

	100%	98%	95%	90%	80%	70%	60%
	$375	$300	$250	$200	$190	$185	$175

Rare early models in wood case will command 100%-150% premiums. White cardboard boxed Super Blackhawks will command a 200% premium. 6½ in. barrel will command a 100% premium.

OLD MODEL BEARCAT — .22 LR cal., 6 shot, 4 in. barrel, alloy frame, brass trigger guard, blue, wood grips with medallion, 17 oz. Mfg. 1958-1973.

	100%	98%	95%	90%	80%	70%	60%
	$350	$300	$275	$225	$200	$180	$170

Add 100%+ for blued aluminum triggerguard variation (73,000-77,000 ser. no. range).
Numerous variations exist within this model incorporating production changes.

OLD MODEL SUPER BEARCAT — similar to Bearcat, except steel frame, made with brass trigger guard (early model), or blued steel guard, 25 oz. Mfg. 1971-1973.

	100%	98%	95%	90%	80%	70%	60%
	$330	$290	$250	$225	$200	$180	$165

HAWKEYE SINGLE SHOT — .256 Mag. cal., single shot, round cylinder replaced by rectangular rotating breech block, 8½ in. barrel, blue, walnut grips, adj. sight, very rare, 45 oz., approx. 3,300 mfg. Mfg. 1963-1964.

	100%	98%	95%	90%	80%	70%	60%
	$1,200	$1,000	$875	$700	$600	$550	$500

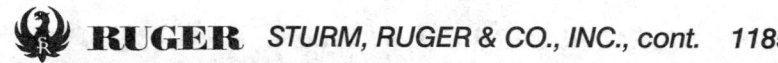
Grading	100%	98%	95%	90%	80%	70%	60%

REVOLVERS: SINGLE ACTION, NEW MODELS

The following single actions are known as "New Models". They have 2 pins through the frame and cock without the clicks associated with the single action. The change over occurred as a result of desire for safety features. The "New Models" have a transfer bar similar to those found on modern double action revolvers and do not accidentally discharge if dropped. Manufacture started 1973. During certain years of manufacture, Ruger's changes in production on certain models (cals., barrel markings, barrel lengths, etc.) have created rare variations that are now considered premium niches. These areas of low manufacture will add premiums to the values listed below on standard models. Beginning 1996, Ruger started supplying all New Model revolvers with a case and lock.

SINGLE SIX CONVERTIBLE — .22 S, L, or LR cal., includes interchangeable .22 Mag. cylinder, 5½ or 6½ in. barrel, fixed sights, blue finish, approx. 34 oz. New 1994.

Mfg.'s Sug. Retail $335	$260	$200	$155	$135	$120	$110	$100

* *Single Six Convertible Stainless Steel* — similar to Single Six Convertible, except is stainless steel. Mfg. 1994-97, reintroduced 1999.

Mfg.'s Sug. Retail $415	$325	$255	$185

SUPER SINGLE SIX CONVERTIBLE — .22 LR cal., includes interchangeable .22 Mag. cylinder, 4⅝, 5½, 6½, or 9½ in. barrel, 6 shot, similar to old Super Single Six, except has new interlocking safety mechanism previously described, adj. rear sight. Mfg. 1973-present.

Mfg.'s Sug. Retail $335	$260	$200	$155	$135	$120	$110	$100

Subtract 15% if without extra .22 Mag. cylinder.

* *Super Single Six Stainless Steel* — similar to Super Single Six, except stainless steel construction, 4⅝ (disc. 1976), 5½, 6½, or 9½ (disc.-rare) in. barrel.

Mfg.'s Sug. Retail $415	$325	$255	$185

Values for 4⅝ or 9½ in. barrel are approx. $575 if NIB.

* *Super Single Six High Gloss Stainless* — 5½ (disc. 1996) or 6½ in. barrel, features high gloss stainless steel finish, simulated ivory grips became standard 1997. Mfg. 1994-97.

$335	$265	$195

Last Mfg.'s Sug. Retail was $425.

Subtract approx. 8% if without simulated ivory grips.

* *Colorado Centennial Super Single Six* — 15,000 mfg. 1975 only, includes walnut case with medallion insert, stainless steel grip frame, 6½ in. barrel, issue price was $250.

$295	$245	$200

This model also was a U.S. Bicentennial gun as well as the Colorado Centennial Pistol. Most specimens do not have the Bicentennial statement on the barrel and are rarer with that stamping.

SUPER SINGLE SIX SSM — .32 H&R Mag. cal., 4⅝, 5½, 6½ or 9½ in. barrel, blue only, adj. sights, 32 oz. with 5½ in. barrel. Disc. 1996.

$350	$300	$275	$225	$175	$150	$125

Last Mfg.'s Sug. Retail was $313.

Add 50% if cylinder frame is marked "SSM".

BLACKHAWK — .30 Carbine (disc. 1996, reintroduced 1998), .357 Mag., .41 Mag. (disc. 1996, reintroduced 1999), or .45 LC cal., similar to old Model Blackhawk, with new interlocking safety mechanism, 6 shot, 4⅝, 6½, or 7½ in. (.30 Carbine and .45 LC only) barrel. Mfg. 1973-present.

Mfg.'s Sug. Retail $380	$290	$220	$175	$155	$145	$135	$125

* *Blackhawk Convertible* — similar to New Model Blackhawk, except interchangeable cylinders, .357 Mag./9mm Para. (current), .44 Mag./.44-40 WCF (disc.), or .45 LC/.45 ACP (disc. 1985, reintroduced 1999) cal., 4⅝ or 6½ in. barrel only.

Mfg.'s Sug. Retail $405	$315	$260	$225	$190	$170	$160	$150

Add 30% for disc. convertible cals.

Grading	100%	98%	95%	90%	80%	70%	60%

✱ **Buckeye Special** — .32-20 WCF/.32 H&R Mag. cal., 6½ in. barrel. Mfg. 1989.

	$450	**$350**	**$295**	**$250**	**$220**	**$200**	**$180**

Buckeye Sports also offered a limited edition Buckeye Special in .38-40 WCF/10mm auto during 1990 - subtract 10% on prices above.

✱ **Blackhawk Stainless Steel** — .357 Mag. or .45 LC (new 1993) cal., 4⅝, 6½, or 7½ (.45 LC only) in. barrel.

Mfg.'s Sug. Retail	**$467**		**$410**	**$300**	**$255**		

300 .357 Mag./9mm Para. convertible pistols were made in this model - NIB prices have ranged $500-$750.

New Model .357 Mag. Blackhawks are serial numbered 32-00001 on up. New Model .45 LC Blackhawks are ser. numbered 46-00001 on up.

✱ **Blackhawk High Gloss Stainless Steel** — .357 Mag. or .45 LC cal., 4⅝, 6½ (.357 Mag. only), or 7½ (.45 LC only) in. barrel, features high gloss stainless steel finish. Mfg. 1994-96.

	$395	**$295**	**$250**				

Last Mfg.'s Sug. Retail was $443.

BLACKHAWK-SRM — similar to New Model Blackhawk, except is chambered for .357 Rem. Maximum, 7½ or 10½ in. barrels available, target sights, 53 oz., 11,500 mfg. 1984 only - production suspended due to unresolvable engineering problems.

	$500	**$450**	**$400**	**$325**	**$300**	**$250**	**$225**

SUPER BLACKHAWK — .44 Mag. cal., 4⅝ (new 1994), 5½ (new 1987), 7½ or 10½ bull in. barrel, 6 shot, blued finish, walnut grips, similar to old model in appearance, but has new action. Mfg. 1973-present. The new model started with serial number 81-00001.

Mfg.'s Sug. Retail	**$435**		**$325**	**$250**	**$210**	**$180**	**$170**	**$160**	**$150**

Add $5 for 10½ in. bull barrel (not cased).

✱ **Super Blackhawk Stainless Steel** — stainless variation of the Super Blackhawk.

Mfg.'s Sug. Retail	**$475**		**$380**	**$310**	**$225**			

Add $5 for 10½ in. bull barrel (not cased).
Add $16 for hunter grip frame with laminate grip panels.

✱ **Super Blackhawk High Gloss Stainless Steel** — high gloss stainless steel finish, not available in 10½ in. bull barrel. Mfg. 1994-96.

	$365	**$300**	**$220**				

Last Mfg.'s Sug. Retail was $450.

✱ **Super Blackhawk Stainless Hunter** — 7½ in. ribbed barrel only, laminated wood grips, includes scope rings. Mfg. 1992-95.

	$450	**$450**	**$400**				

Last Mfg.'s Sug. Retail was $498.

VAQUERO — .357 Mag. (new 1997), .44-40 WCF (new 1994), .44 Mag. (new 1994), or .45 LC cal., 6 shot, 4⅝ (not available in .44 Mag.), 5½, or 7½ (not available in .357 Mag.) in. barrel, color case hardened frame, blued steel grip frame, barrel, and cylinder, transfer bar hammer safety, smooth rosewood grips, patterned after the Colt SAA, fixed sights. New 1993.

Mfg.'s Sug. Retail	**$455**		**$365**	**$280**	**$240**	**$210**	**$190**	**$170**	**$160**

Add $36 for simulated ivory grips (new 1996).
Add $149 for simulated ivory grips and engraved cylinder (new 1998).

While uncataloged, Ruger offered a 4⅝ in. barrel in .44 Mag. cal. only in both blue and stainless - premiums exist.

✱ **Vaquero High Gloss Stainless Steel** — high gloss stainless steel finish. New 1994.

Mfg.'s Sug. Retail	**$455**		**$365**	**$280**	**$240**			

Add $36 for simulated ivory grips (new 1996).

BISLEY VAQUERO — .357 Mag. (new 1999, 5½ in. barrel only), .44 Mag. or .45 LC cal., 4⅝ (new 1999) or 5½ in. barrel, case colored frame with blued steel grips, barrel, and cylinder, fixed sights. New 1998.

Mfg.'s Sug. Retail	**$472**		**$380**	**$310**	**$260**	**$225**	**$200**	**$180**	**$160**

Add $36 for simulated ivory grips.

Grading	100%	98%	95%	90%	80%	70%	60%

* **Bisley Vaquero Stainless** — similar to Bisley Vaquero, except is stainless steel.
  Mfg.'s Sug. Retail $512 $400 $300 $255
  Add $36 for simulated ivory grips.

BISLEY MODEL — .22 LR, .32 H&R Mag. (disc. 1996), .357 Mag., .41 Mag. (disc. 1996), .44 Mag., or .45 LC cal., incorporates Bisley features (flat-top frame, raked hammer, longer grip frame), 6½ (.22 LR or .32 H&R Mag. only) or 7½ in. barrel, fixed (disc. 1992, except for .32 H&R Mag.) or adj. sights, available with fluted/unfluted or roll-marked/unmarked (disc.) cylinders, satin blue finish only, Goncalo Alves smooth grips. New 1986.

* **.22 LR or .32 H&R Mag. (disc.)**

	100%	98%	95%	90%	80%	70%	60%
Mfg.'s Sug. Retail $402	$320	$240	$190	$170	$160	$150	$140

  Add $50 for .32 H&R Mag.

* **Other cals.**

	100%	98%	95%	90%	80%	70%	60%
Mfg.'s Sug. Retail $472	$380	$310	$260	$225	$200	$180	$160

NEW BEARCAT — .22 LR cal., includes interchangeable .22 Mag. cyl. (disc. 1996), frame slightly longer than old Bearcat, 4 in. barrel, transfer bar hammer safety, blue finish, smooth walnut grips, fixed sights. New 1994.

	100%	98%	95%	90%	80%	70%	60%
Mfg.'s Sug. Retail $330	$280	$230	$185	$135	$125	$115	$105

  Add a 200% premium for early production New Bearcats with convertible cylinders (the factory recalled them).

* **New Bearcat Bright Stainless Steel** — while advertised, this model has yet to be manufactured.

  Mfg.'s Sug. Retail was listed as $325.

OLD ARMY PERCUSSION — .44 cal., black powder, 6 shot, 7½ in. barrel, single action, blued finish, fixed (new 1994) or adj. sights, walnut grips.

	100%	98%	95%	90%	80%	70%	60%
Mfg.'s Sug. Retail $435	$335	$240	$180	$150	$135	$120	$110

  Add $100 for brass frame (disc.).

* **Old Army Percussion Stainless Steel**
  Mfg.'s Sug. Retail $475 $370 $295 $215
  Add $30 for simulated ivory grips (available 1997 only).

REVOLVERS: DOUBLE ACTION

During certain years of manufacture, Ruger's changes in production on certain models (cals., barrel markings, barrel lengths, etc.) have created rare variations that are now considered premium niches. These areas of low manufacture will add premiums to the values listed below on standard models.

SPEED SIX (MODELS 207, 208 and 209) — .38 Spl., .357 Mag., or 9mm Para. cal., 2¾ or 4 in. barrel, fixed sights, checkered walnut grips, round butt, blued finish, some guns have factory speed hammer (no hammer spur). Mfg. 1973-1988. Model 207 and 208 disc. 1988.

			95%	90%	80%	70%	60%
	$230	$205	$190	$170	$160	$150	$140

Last Mfg.'s Sug. Retail was $292.

Add $40 for 9mm Para. (Model 209 disc. 1984).

* **Models 737 and 738** — stainless steel versions of Models 207 and 208, .357 Mag and .38 Spl. cals., 2¾ or 4 in. barrel. Disc. 1988.

  $280 $245 $220

  Last Mfg.'s Sug. Retail was $320.

* **Model 739** — stainless steel, 9mm Para. Disc. 1984.

  $300 $250 $230

SECURITY SIX (MODEL 117) — .357 Mag. cal., 6 shot, 2¾, 4 (heavy), or 6 in. barrel, adj. sights, checkered walnut grips, square butt. Mfg. 1970-1985.

  $250 $225 $195 $185 $160 $150 $140

  Last Mfg.'s Sug. Retail was $309.

  Add $15 for target grips.
  500 of this model were mfg. for the California Highway Patrol during 1983 (.38 Spl. cal.) in stainless steel only. They are distinguishable by a C.H.P. marking. Other Security Six Model

Grading	100%	98%	95%	90%	80%	70%	60%

117 special editions have been made for various police organizations - premiums might exist in certain regions for these variations.

* **Model 717** — stainless steel version of Model 117. Disc. 1985.

$295	**$255**	**$230**

Last Mfg.'s Sug. Retail was $338.

POLICE SERVICE SIX — .357 Mag., .38 Spl., or 9mm Para. cal., blued finish only, square butt, fixed sights, checkered walnut grips.

* **Model 107** — .357 Mag, 2¾ or 4 in. barrel, fixed sights. Disc. 1988.

$250	**$220**	**$200**	**$190**	**$180**	**$170**	**$165**

Last Mfg.'s Sug. Retail was $287.

* **Model 108** — .38 Spl., 4 in. barrel, fixed sights. Disc. 1988.

$250	**$220**	**$200**	**$190**	**$180**	**$170**	**$165**

Last Mfg.'s Sug. Retail was $287.

* **Model 109** — 9mm Para., 4 in. barrel, fixed sights. Disc. 1984.

$275	**$230**	**$205**	**$195**	**$185**	**$180**	**$175**

POLICE SERVICE SIX STAINLESS STEEL — stainless construction, 4 in. barrel only, fixed sights, checkered walnut grips.

* **Model 707** — .357 Mag., square butt. Disc. 1988.

$270	**$235**	**$210**

Last Mfg.'s Sug. Retail was $310.

* **Model 708** — .38 Spl., square butt. Disc. 1988.

$270	**$235**	**$210**

Last Mfg.'s Sug. Retail was $310.

GP-100 — .357 Mag. or .38 Spl. cal., 3 (new 1990, fixed sights only), 4, or 6 (.357 Mag. only) in. standard or heavy barrel, strengthened design intended for constant use with all .357 Mag. ammunition, rubber cushioned grip panels with polished Goncalo Alves wood inserts, fixed or adj. (.357 Mag. only) sights with white outlined rear and interchangeable front, 6 shot, 35-46 oz. depending on barrel configuration. New 1986.

Mfg.'s Sug. Retail	$423	$355	$285	$245	$220	$200	$185	$170

Add $17 for adj. rear sight (.357 Mag. cal., 4 or 6 in. barrel only).

* **GP-100 Stainless Steel** — similar to GP-100, except is stainless steel. New 1987.

Mfg.'s Sug. Retail	$457	$375	$295	$250

Add $17 for adj. rear sight (.357 Mag. cal. only).

* **GP-100 High Gloss Stainless Steel** — .357 Mag. only, high gloss stainless steel finish, 3 or 4 in. heavy barrel. Mfg. 1996 only.

$375	**$295**	**$250**

Last Mfg.'s Sug. Retail was $457.

SP-101 STAINLESS STEEL — .22 LR (6 shot - new 1990), .32 H&R (6 shot - new 1991), .38 Spl.(5 shot), 9mm Para. (5 shot - new 1991), or .357 Mag. (5 shot - new 1991) cal., 2¼, 3¹/₁₆, or 4 (new 1990) in. barrel, small frame variation of the GP-100 Stainless, fixed or adj. (new 1996) sights, approx. 27 oz. New 1989.

Mfg.'s Sug. Retail	$443	$360	$280	$240

Ruger introduced adj. sights in 1996 available in .22 LR or .32 H&R cal. only.

Ruger introduced a .357 Mag./2¼ in. (new 1993) or .38 Spl./2¼ (new 1994) in. configuration featuring a spurless hammer, double action only.

SP-101 barrel lengths are as follows: .22 cal. is available in 2¼ or 4 in. standard or heavy barrel, .32 H&R is available in 3¹/₁₆ or 4 (new 1994) in. heavy barrel, .38 Spl. is available in 2¼ or 3¹/₁₆ in. length only, 9mm Para. is available in 2¼ (new 1992) or 3¹/₁₆ in. only, and .357 Mag. is available in 2¼ or 3¹/₁₆ in. only.

Grading	100%	98%	95%	90%	80%	70%	60%

* **SP-101 High Gloss Stainless Steel** — .38 Spl. (disc. 1996), 9mm Para. (disc. 1996), or .357 Mag. cal., similar to SP-101 Stainless Steel, except has high gloss stainless steel finish. Mfg. 1996-97.

  $360 $280 $240

  Last Mfg.'s Sug. Retail was $443.

  Ruger introduced adj. sights in 1996 available in .22 LR or .32 H&R cal. only.

REDHAWK — .357 Mag. (disc. 1985), .41 Mag. (disc. 1992), or .44 Mag. cal., this is a redesigned large frame handgun, 5½ and 7½ in. barrel only, square butt, smooth hardwood grips, 52 oz.

Mfg.'s Sug. Retail	$515	$425	$345	$295	$240	$215	$180	$165

  Add $38 for scope rings.

  .357 Mag. and .41 Mag. cals. will bring collector premiums if NIB.

* **Redhawk Stainless Steel** — .44 Mag. or .45 LC (new 1998) cal., stainless steel construction.

Mfg.'s Sug. Retail	$574	$465	$380	$310

  Add $44 for scope rings.

SUPER REDHAWK STAINLESS — .44 Mag. or .454 Casull (new 1999) cal., 7½ or 9½ (.44 Mag. only) barrel, choice of regular or high gloss (new 1997) stainless steel, adj. rear sight, cushioned grip panels (GP-100 style), stainless steel scope rings, 53 oz. New late 1987.

Mfg.'s Sug. Retail	$618	$500	$385	$285

  Add $127 for .454 Casull cal.

RIFLES: LEVER ACTION

MODEL 96 CARBINE — .22 LR, .22 Mag., or .44 Mag. cal., 18½ in. barrel with single barrel band, uncheckered hardwood stock with curved butt plate, 10 (.22 LR), 9 (.22 Mag.), or 4 (.44 Mag.) shot detachable rotary mag., sliding cross-button safety, adj. rear sight, .44 Mag. has case hardened lever, rimfire receivers are drilled and tapped while the .44 Mag. has an integral base receiver with scope rings (became standard 1997), approx. 5¼-5⅞ lbs. New 1996.

Mfg.'s Sug. Retail	$328	$265	$205	$180	$160	$145	$135	$125

  Add $18 for .22 Mag. cal.

  Add approx. $40 for .44 Mag. cal. w/o scope rings.

  Add $113 for .44 Mag. cal. with scope rings.

RIFLES: SEMI-AUTO

During certain years of manufacture, Ruger's changes in production on certain models (cals., barrel markings, barrel lengths, etc.) have created rare variations that are now considered premium niches. These areas of low manufacture will add premiums to the values listed below on standard models. The Model 10/22 has been mfg. in a variety of limited production models including a multi-colored or green laminate wood stock variation (1986), a brown laminate stock (1988), a Kittery Trading Post Commemorative (1988), a smoke or tree bark laminate stock (1989), a Chief AJ Model, Wal-Mart (stainless with black laminated hardwood stock - 1990), etc. These limited editions will command premiums over the standard models listed below, depending on the desirability of the special edition.

Note: All Ruger Rifles, except Stainless Mini-14, all Mini-30s, and Model 77-22s were made during 1976 in a "Liberty" version. Add $50 - $75 when in 100% in the original box condition.

10/22 STANDARD CARBINE — .22 LR cal., 10 shot rotary mag., 18½ in. barrel, birch, black synthetic (new 1999), or optional deluxe hand checkered walnut stock, folding rear sight. Mfg. 1964-present.

Mfg.'s Sug. Retail	$225	$175	$145	$120	$100	$80	$60	$55

  Add $20 for uncheckered walnut stock (mfg. 1964-1980 and 1987-1989).

  Add $49 for deluxe checkered walnut sporter stock (Model 10/22 DSP).

* **10/22RB Standard Carbine Stainless** — similar to Standard Carbine, except has stainless barrel and choice of birch or black synthetic (new 1997) stock. New 1992.

Mfg.'s Sug. Retail	$268	$200	$165	$125

10/22T TARGET MODEL — .22 LR cal., features brown laminated American hardwood stock, blued hammer-forged spiral finish barrel, w/o sights. New 1996.

Mfg.'s Sug. Retail	$393	$330	$265	$225

Grading	100%	98%	95%	90%	80%	70%	60%

➤ **10/22T Target Stainless** — similar to 10/22T Target Model, except is stainless steel. New 1998.

Mfg.'s Sug. Retail $440 — **$365** **$285** **$240**

10/22 FINGERGROOVE SPORTER — similar to Standard, except Monte Carlo stock and beavertail forearm. Mfg. 1966-1971.

		$400	$350	$300	$250	$225	$200	$175

Add 200% for checkered stock in NIB condition.

10/22 INTERNATIONAL (OLD PRODUCTION) — similar to Standard, except walnut full stock Mannlicher style. Mfg. 1966-1969.

		$550	$475	$425	$375	$350	$325	$300

Add 50% for checkered stock.

10/22RBI INTERNATIONAL (NEW PRODUCTION) — features Mannlicher style international birch full stock. New 1994.

Mfg.'s Sug. Retail $262 — **$205** **$170** **$130** **$105** **$95** **$80** **$65**

❋ *10/22RBI Stainless* — stainless variation of the 10/22RBI International.

Mfg.'s Sug. Retail $282 — **$220** **$180** **$135**

10/22 CANADIAN CENTENNIAL — 2,000 mfg. in 1967.

$450 $400 $350

Last Mfg.'s Sug. Retail was $100.

10/22 MAGNUM — .22 Mag. cal., steel receiver, longer and heavier bolt, 10 shot rotary mag., 18½ in. barrel, uncheckered birch stock, blue metal, folding rear sight, 5⁹⁄₁₆ lbs. New 1999.

Mfg.'s Sug. Retail $425 — **$350** **$320** **$280** **$250** **$225** **$200** **$185**

RUGER/REMINGTON CANADIAN CENTENNIAL MATCHED NO. 3 SET — includes a Remington Model 742 in .308 Win. cal. and a Ruger 10/22 Sporter with special commemorative appointments, cased. 1,000 sets mfg. 1967 only.

$700 $525 $425

❋ *Ruger Canadian Centennial Matched No. 2 Set* — 70 sets mfg. 1967 only.

$950 $775 $550

❋ *Ruger Canadian Centennial Matched No. 1 Special Deluxe Set* — 30 sets mfg. 1967 only.

$1,150 $895 $675

MODEL 44 STANDARD CARBINE — .44 Mag. cal., 4 shot mag., 18½ in. barrel, blowback action, folding sight, curved butt. Mfg. 1961-1985.

		$395	$350	$325	$295	$275	$250	$225

Last Mfg.'s Sug. Retail was $332.

❋ *Deerstalker Model* — approx. 3,750 mfg. with "Deerstalker" marked on rifle until Ithaca lawsuit disc. manufacture (1962).

		$650	$600	$550	$475	$400	$325	$250

❋ *25th Year Anniversary Model* — mfg. 1985 only, limited production, has medallion in stock.

$500 $425 $375

Last Mfg.'s Sug. Retail was $495.

MODEL 44RS — similar to 44, but has aperture sight and swivels.

		$525	$450	$400	$350	$300	$275	$250

MODEL 44 FINGERGROOVE SPORTER — Monte Carlo stocked version of 44 Standard. Mfg. until 1971.

		$600	$550	$500	$450	$400	$350	$300

Add 100% for factory checkered stock.

MODEL 44 INTERNATIONAL — similar to Standard, except full length Mannlicher style stock. Mfg. until 1971.

		$750	$650	$600	$550	$475	$400	$350

Add 50% for factory checkered stock.

S

Grading	100%	98%	95%	90%	80%	70%	60%

RUGER CARBINE — 9mm Para. (PC9) or .40 S&W (PC4) cal., 16¼ in. barrel, black synthetic stock, matte metal finish, with or w/o sights, with fully adj. rear sight or rear receiver sight, crossbolt safety, 6 lbs. New 1998.

Mfg.'s Sug. Retail	$555	$465	$390	$345	$300	$265	$240	$215

Add $25 for adj. rear receiver sight.

MINI-14 — .223 Rem. or .222 Rem. (disc.) cal., 5 (standard mag. starting in 1989), 10, or 20★ shot detachable mag., 18½ in. barrel, gas operated, aperture rear sight, military style stock, 6½ lbs. Mfg. 1976-present.

Mfg.'s Sug. Retail	$542	$450	$385	$340	$300	$265	$240	$215

Add $125 for folding stock (disc. 1989).

Add 25% for Southport Model with gold bead front sight.

Due to 1989 Federal legislation and public sentiment, the Mini-14 is now being shipped with a 5 shot detachable mag. only.

* *Mini 14 Stainless* — mini stainless steel version, choice of wood or synthetic (new 1999) stock.

Mfg.'s Sug. Retail	$597	$485	$410	$355

Add $125 for folding stock (disc. 1990).

MINI-14 RANCH RIFLE — .223 Rem. cal., 18½ in. barrel, folding rear sight, receiver cut for factory rings, similar to Mini-14, supplied with scope rings, approx. 6 lbs. 5 oz.

Mfg.'s Sug. Retail	$584	$465	$410	$380	$355	$325	$300	$260

Due to 1989 Federal legislation and public sentiment, the Mini-14 Ranch Rifle is now being shipped with a 5 shot detachable mag. only.

* *Stainless Ranch Rifle* — stainless steel construction ⸱hoice of wood or synthetic (new 1999) stock. New 1986.

Mfg.'s Sug. Retail	$639	$510	$435	$365

Add $125 for folding stock (disc. 1990).

MINI-THIRTY — 7.62x39mm Russian cal., 18½ in. barrel, 5 shot detachable mag., hardwood stock, includes scope rings, 7 lbs. 3 oz. New 1987.

Mfg.'s Sug. Retail	$584	$465	$400	$365	$325	$300	$275	$250

* *Mini-Thirty Stainless* — steel variation of the Mini-Thirty, new 1990.

Mfg.'s Sug. Retail	$639	$510	$435	$365

XGI — while advertised, this model was never shipped commercially because it could not maintain Ruger accuracy standards.

Mfg.'s Sug. Retail was originally targeted at $425.

RIFLES: SINGLE SHOT

During certain years of manufacture, Ruger's changes in production on certain models (cals., barrel markings, barrel lengths, etc.) have created rare variations that are now considered premium niches. These areas of low manufacture will add premiums to the values listed below on standard models.

Pre-1969, non prefix rifles with long action cals. will command a 30%-50% premium (ser. no. 1-8xxx).

NO. 1-A LIGHT SPORTER — similar to Standard, .22 Hornet (disc., 355 mfg.), .243 Win., .270 Win., 7x57mm, or .30-06 cal., 22 in. barrel, folding sight on quarter rib, ramp front sight, no rings, Alexander Henry forearm, front swivel in barrel band, 7¼ lbs. Mfg. 1966-present.

Mfg.'s Sug. Retail	$719	$575	$485	$415	$335	$275	$245	$215

The "A" suffix designates an Alexander Henry classic forearm with light barrel.

NO. 1-B STANDARD — falling block action with curved Farquharson lever, popular cals. include .218 Bee, .22 Hornet (new 1988), .22-250 Rem., .220 Swift, .223 Rem., .257 Roberts, .243 Win., 6mm Rem., .25-06 Rem., .270 Win., .280 Rem., .30-06, 6.5mm Rem. Mag. (disc.), 7mm Rem. Mag., .270 Wby. Mag. (new 1990), .300 Wby. Mag. (new in 1990), .300 Win. Mag., or .338 Win. Mag., 22 or 26 in. barrel, quarter rib with integral scope bases, supplied with rings and no sights, checkered stock and semi beavertail forearm. Mfg. 1966-present.

Mfg.'s Sug. Retail	$719	$575	$485	$415	$335	$275	$245	$215

The "B" suffix designates semi-beavertail forearm with medium barrel and is available in all cals. under .375 H&H except 7x57mm.

Grading	100%	98%	95%	90%	80%	70%	60%

NO. 1-RSI INTERNATIONAL — .243 Win., .270 Win., 7x57mm, or .30-06 cal., features 20 in. lightweight barrel with full length Mannlicher stock, includes swivels and open sights, 7¼ lbs.

Mfg.'s Sug. Retail	$734	$590	$500	$415	$335	$275	$245	$215

NO. 1-V VARMINT — similar to No. 1-B Standard, except .22 PPC (mfg. 1993-96), .22-250 Rem., .220 Swift, .223 Rem., .243 Win. (disc.), .25-06 Rem., 6mm Rem., 6mm PPC (mfg. 1993-96), or .280 Rem. (disc.) cal., 24 or 26 (.220 Swift only) in. heavy barrel, without rib, target scope blocks, 9 lbs. Mfg. 1966-present.

Mfg.'s Sug. Retail	$719	$575	$485	$415	$335	$275	$245	$215

NO. 1-S MEDIUM SPORTER — similar to Light Sporter, only .218 Bee, 7mm Rem. Mag., .45-70 Govt., .300 Win. Mag. or .338 Win. Mag. cal., 22 (.45-70 Govt. cal. only) or 26 in. medium barrel, open sights, 7¼ - 8 lbs.

Mfg.'s Sug. Retail	$719	$575	$485	$415	$335	$275	$245	$215

NO. 1-H TROPICAL RIFLE — similar to Medium Sporter, except .375 H&H, .404 Jeffery (mfg. 1993-95), .416 Rem. (new 1993), .416 Rigby (new 1991), or .458 Win. Mag. cal., 24 in. heavy barrel, open sights, approx. 9 lbs.

Mfg.'s Sug. Retail	$719	$575	$500	$450	$400	$360	$330	$295

NO. 3 CARBINE — same basic action as No. 1, except simpler lever design, uncheckered stock, available in .22 Hornet, .30-40 Krag, .45-70 (only cal. available 1986), .223 Rem., .44 Mag., or .375 Win. cal., 22 in. barrel, folding sight. Mfg. 1972-1987.

	$450	$400	$350	$300	$250	$200	$150

Last Mfg.'s Sug. Retail was $284.

RIFLES: BOLT ACTION, .22 CAL.

MODEL 77/22-R/RS — .22 LR cal only, 10 shot rotary mag., 20 in. barrel, all steel construction, 3 position safety, checkered walnut stock, blue finish, non-adj. trigger, available with either optional iron sights or plain barrel (no sights) with scope rings (included), 2.7 millisecond lock time on trigger, 6 lbs. 2 oz. New 1984.

Mfg.'s Sug. Retail	$483	$380	$325	$265	$235	$210	$190	$175

Add $8 for iron sights.
Add 125% if w/o 77/22 roll mark or with green laminated stock.

* *Model 77/22-RP/RSP All-Weather Stainless* — similar to Model 77/22 LR, except has stainless steel metal with matte black DuPont Zytel synthetic stock, 5 lbs. 14 oz. New 1989.

Mfg.'s Sug. Retail	$483	$380	$325	$265

Add $8 for iron sights.

* *Model 77/22-VBZ Varmint Stainless Laminated* — similar to Model 77/.22 LR, stainless steel, heavy stainless barrel with dull finish, laminated brown hardwood stock. New 1995.

Mfg.'s Sug. Retail	$509	$400	$335	$275

MODEL 77/22-RM/RSM MAG. — similar to Model 77/22-R/RS, except in .22 Win. Mag. cal., 9 shot rotary mag., blue finish, checkered walnut stock. New 1990.

Mfg.'s Sug. Retail	$483	$380	$325	$265	$235	$210	$190	$175

Add $8 for iron sights.

* *Model 77/22-RMP/RSMP Mag. All-Weather Stainless* — similar to Model 77/22-RM/RSM Mag., except has stainless steel metal with matte black Dupont Zytel synthetic stock. New 1990.

Mfg.'s Sug. Retail	$483	$380	$325	$265

Add $8 for iron sights.

* *Model 77/22-VMBZ Mag. Varmint Stainless Laminated* — similar to Model 77/.22 Mag., stainless steel, heavy stainless barrel with dull finish, laminated brown hardwood stock. New 1993.

Mfg.'s Sug. Retail	$509	$400	$335	$275

RIFLES: BOLT ACTION, CENTERFIRE

During certain years of manufacture, Ruger's changes in production on certain models (cals., barrel markings, barrel lengths, etc.) have created rare variations that are now considered premium niches. These areas of low manufacture will add premiums to the values listed below on standard models. Earlier flat-bolt models (pre-1972) are

Grading	100%	98%	95%	90%	80%	70%	60%

desirable in the rarer cals. and will command a 100% premium if in 98%+ original condition.

MODEL 77/22-RH/RSH HORNET — .22 Hornet cal., features lengthened receiver, detachable 6 shot rotary mag. (not interchangeable with other 77/22 mags.), blued barrel, checkered American walnut stock, includes scope rings. New 1994.

Mfg.'s Sug. Retail	$499	$400	$340	$275

Add $10 for iron sights.

* **Model 77/22-VHZ Hornet Varmint Stainless Laminated** — similar to Model 77/.22 Hornet, stainless steel, heavy stainless barrel with dull finish, laminated brown hardwood stock. New 1995.

Mfg.'s Sug. Retail	$545	$430	$360	$290

MODEL 77/44 — .44 Mag. cal., 18½ in. barrel, rotary mag., checkered walnut stock, open sights, 6 lbs. New 1998.

Mfg.'s Sug. Retail	$575	$465	$350	$295	$265	$245	$200	$200

* **Model 77/44 Stainless** — .44 Mag. cal., black synthetic stock, stainless steel construction, open sights. New 1999.

Mfg.'s Sug. Retail	$575	$465	$350	$295

MODEL 77R — .22-250 Rem., .220 Swift, 6mm Rem. (disc.), .243 Win. (disc.), .250 Savage (disc.), .257 Roberts, .25-06 Rem., .270 Win., 7x57mm, 7mm-08 (disc.), 6.5 Rem. Mag. (scarce), 7mm Rem. Mag., .280 Rem., .284 Win., .308 Win. (disc.), .30-06, .300 Win. Mag., .338 Win Mag., .350 Rem. Mag., cal., long or short action, blue finish, 5 shot mag., 3 shot in Mag. cals., 22 or 24 in. barrel, available with integral bases or round top, some models supplied with sights, stock is checkered walnut with red rubber butt plate, approx. 7 lbs. Mfg. 1968-1992.

			$420	$395	$325	$265	$245	$200	$200

Last Mfg.'s Sug. Retail was $558.

Add 10-15% for .284 cal.
Add 20%-30% for .350 Rem. Mag. cal.

* **Model 77 RL** — .22-250 Rem. (disc.), .243 Win., .250 Sav., .257 Roberts, .270 Win., .30-06, or .308 Win. cal., ultra light variation weighing 6 lbs., black forearm tip. Disc. 1992.

$445	$375	$325	$270	$250	$225	$205

Last Mfg.'s Sug. Retail was $592.

* **Model 77 RS** — .243 Win., .250 Sav., 6mm Rem., 6.5mm Rem. Mag., 7x57mm, .25-06 Rem. (disc.), 270 Win., .280 Rem., .284 Win., .30-06, .308 Win., 7mm Rem. Mag., 300 Win. Mag., .338 Win. Mag, .35 Whelen, or .350 Rem. Mag. cal., similar to Model 77R, except has open sights. Disc. 1992.

$460	$425	$350	$300	$265	$230	$210

Last Mfg.'s Sug. Retail was $616.

Add 20%-30% for .284 Win. or .350 Rem. Mag. cal.

* **Model 77PL** — .25-06 Rem., .270 Win., .30-06, .300 Win., .338 Win. Mag, 7mm Rem. Mag., 7x57mm cal., differs from R Model in that it has a round top, drilled to take Redfield scope mounts, w/o sights.

$420	$395	$325	$265	$245	$200	$200

* **Model 77ST** — .25-06 Rem., .257 Roberts, 7x57mm, .300 Win. Mag., .338 Win. Mag., 7mm Rem. Mag., .30-06, or .270 Win. cal., differs from RS Model in that is has round top drilled to take Redfield scope mounts with iron sights on barrel.

$460	$425	$350	$300	$265	$230	$210

* **Model 77V Varmint** — .22-250 Rem., .220 Swift, .243 Win. (disc.), 6mm Rem. (disc.), .25-06 Rem., .280 Rem., or .308 Win. cal., 24 in. heavy barrel (26 in. on .220 Swift), drilled and tapped for target bases, approx. 9 lbs. Mfg. 1968-92.

$430	$395	$325	$265	$245	$210	$200

Last Mfg.'s Sug. Retail was $574.

* **Model 77 RS African** — similar to Model 77R, except in .458 Win. Mag. cal. Disc. 1991.

$550	$475	$400	$365	$335	$315	$300

Last Mfg.'s Sug. Retail was $680.

This model is supplied standard with a steel triggerguard and steel floor plate.

Grading	100%	98%	95%	90%	80%	70%	60%

* *Model 77 RSC* — similar to Model 77 RS African, except has Circassian walnut stock (C suffix). Mfg. 1976-78.

	$675	$575	$500	$450	$400	$365	$335

* *Model 77 RLS* — .243 Win. (disc. 1989), .270 Win., .30-06, and .308 Win. cal. (disc. 1989), ultra light, 18½ in. barrel, open sights, 6 lbs. Mfg. 1987-93.

	$445	$395	$310	$280	$260	$230	$210

Last Mfg.'s Sug. Retail was $592.

* *Model 77 RSI* — .22-250 Rem. (disc. 1991), .243 Win. .250-3000 Sav. (reintroduced 1990), .270 Win., .30-06, .308 Win. (disc. 1991), 7x57mm (rare), or 7mm-08 Rem. cal., International Mannlicher (full length stock) with 18½ in. barrel and open sights (includes scope rings), approx. 7 lbs. Disc. 1993.

	$470	$400	$325	$295	$265	$230	$210

Last Mfg.'s Sug. Retail was $623.

Add 20% for 7mm-08 cal.

MODEL 77R MARK II SERIES — various cals. as listed below, evolutionary design of the Ruger Model 77R featuring slenderized proportioning, 3 position swing-back safety, new trigger, trigger guard and floor plate latch, stainless steel bolt with Mauser extractor design, 20 in. barrel, integral base receiver, hand checkered American walnut stock, approx. 6 lbs. 7 oz. New 1989.

* *Model 77R* — .220 Swift (new 1995), .22-250 Rem. (new 1993), .223 Rem. (new 1992), .243 Win., .25-06 Rem. (new 1993), .257 Roberts (new 1993), .260 Rem. (new 1999), .270 Win. (new 1993), .280 Rem. (new 1993), 6mm Rem., 6.5x55mm Swedish (new 1993), 7x57mm (new 1993), .30-06 (new 1993), .308 Win., 7mm Rem. Mag. (new 1993), .300 Win. Mag. (new 1993), or .338 Win. Mag. (new 1993) cal., checkered walnut stock is standard, standard model of the new Mark II Series.

Mfg.'s Sug. Retail	$599	$410	$350	$300	$270	$245	$200	$200

* *Model 77 RL* — .223 Rem., .243 Win., .257 Roberts (new 1993), .270 Win. (new 1993), .30-06 (new 1993), or .308 Win. cal., black forearm tip, ultra light variation weighing approx. 6 lbs. New 1990.

Mfg.'s Sug. Retail	$640	$440	$385	$310	$275	$250	$225	$205

* *Model 77 RLP Stainless* — .243 Win., .270 Win. or .30-06. cal., black synthetic stock, ultralight variation of the Model 77, w/o sights, includes scope rings. New 1999.

Mfg.'s Sug. Retail	$599	$410	$350	$300

* *Model 77 RS* — 6mm Rem., .243 Win., .25-06 Rem. (new 1993), .270 Win. (new 1993), .30-06 (new 1993), .308 Win., 7mm Rem. Mag. (new 1993), .300 Win. Mag. (new 1993), .338 Win Mag. (new 1993), or .458 Win. Mag. (mfg. 1994-98) cal., similar to Model 77R, except has open sights. New 1990.

Mfg.'s Sug. Retail	$667	$470	$385	$330	$290	$265	$230	$210

* *Model 77 RSI* — .243 Win., .270 Win., .30-06, or .308 Win. cal., International Mannlicher (full length stock) with 18½ in. barrel and open sights (includes scope rings), approx. 7 lbs. New 1993.

Mfg.'s Sug. Retail	$674	$475	$390	$335	$290	$265	$230	$210

* *Model 77 RLS* — .243 Win. or .308 Win. cal., ultra light, 18½ in. barrel, open sights. Mfg. 1990 only.

	$460	$375	$310	$280	$260	$230	$210

Last Mfg.'s Sug. Retail was $564.

* *Model K77 RP All-Weather Stainless* — .22-250 (new 1996), .223 Rem., .243 Win., .25-06 Rem. (new 1999), .260 Rem. (new 1999), .270 Win., .280 Rem. (new 1993), .30-06, .308 Win., 7mm Rem. Mag., .300 Win. Mag., or .338 Win. Mag. (new 1992) cal., similar to Model 77R Mark II except has stainless steel metal with matte black DuPont Zytel synthetic stock, no sights. New 1990.

Mfg.'s Sug. Retail	$599	$415	$350	$295

* *Model K77 RSP All-Weather Stainless* — .243 Win., .270 Win., .30-06, 7mm Rem. Mag., .300 Win. Mag., or .338 Win. Mag. cal., otherwise similar to Model K77 RP All-Weather Stainless, except has open sights.

Mfg.'s Sug. Retail	$667	$445	$380	$335

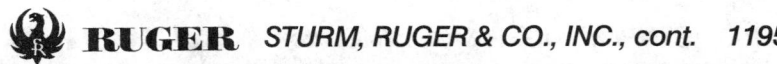

Grading	100%	98%	95%	90%	80%	70%	60%

* *Model K77 RBZ Satin Stainless* — .22-250 Rem. (new 1999), .223 Rem., .243 Win., .270 Win., .280 Rem., .30-06, .308 Win., 7mm Rem. Mag., .300 Win. Mag., or .338 Win. Mag. cal., features brown wood laminate stock with sling swivels, 22 or 24 in. barrel without sights, approx. 7⁵⁄₁₆ lbs. New 1997.

  Mfg.'s Sug. Retail $636 $420 $385 $310

  Add $64 for open sights and scope rings (Model K77 RSBZ).

* *Model K77 VT* — .22 PPC (disc. 1996), .220 Swift, .22-250 Rem., .223 Rem., .243 Win., .25-06 Rem., .308 Win., or 6mm PPC (disc. 1996) cal., features stainless steel construction, laminated stock, and heavy barrel. New 1993.

  Mfg.'s Sug. Retail $718 $440 $420 $335

  This model's nomenclature changed from VBZ to VTM during 1994.

* *Model 77 LR* — .270 Win., .30-06, .300 Win. Mag., or 7mm Rem. Mag. cal., left hand variation of the Model 77R. New 1991.

  Mfg.'s Sug. Retail $599 $415 $335 $300 $265 $245 $200 $200

* *Model 77 LRBBZ Stainless* — .270 Win., .30-06, or 7mm Rem. Mag. cal., laminated stock, includes scope rings. New 1999.

  Mfg.'s Sug. Retail $636 $420 $385 $310

* *Model 77 RSM* — .375 H&H, .404 Jeffery (mfg. 1994-95), or .416 Rigby cal., premium grade wood with hand cut checkering and ebony forend tip, integral barrel and sighting rib. New 1990.

  Mfg.'s Sug. Retail $1,620 $1,300 $975 $875 $800 $750 $675 $595

* *Model 77 RS Express* — .270 Win., .30-06, 7mm Rem. Mag., .300 Win. Mag., or .338 Win. Mag. (new 1994) cal., similar construction to Model 77RSM with premium grade wood and other materials. New 1991.

  Mfg.'s Sug. Retail $1,550 $1,200 $850 $800 $750 $700 $675 $595

SHOTGUNS: O/U

RED LABEL — 12, 20, or 28 (new 1994) ga., 3 in. chambers, various barrel lengths and choke (including skeet) combinations, boxlock, SST, 26 or 28 in. VR barrels, auto ejectors, choice of checkered pistol grip or English straight grip (new 1992, Red Label English Field) stock, stainless steel frame became standard on 12 ga. 1985 (not available in 20 ga.). Choke tubes became optional in 1988, standard 1990. Mfg. 1977-present.

* *Standard Grade*

  Mfg.'s Sug. Retail $1,276 $965 $775 $685 $600 $550 $500 $450

  Subtract 15%-20% without choke tubes.

  During late 1994, some 12 and 20 ga. Red Label boxes were marked "EZ", indicating the new easy-opening feature (this is not mechanically spring-assisted, but rather works on tight machining tolerances). All Red Label shotguns have the "EZ"-opening feature beginning 1995.

  Earlier all-steel 12 ga. models (approx. 500 mfg.) with short field tubes could command 10%-15% premiums over values listed above to collectors interested in acquiring this variation. 20 ga. models w/o choke tubes are blue only.

* *Red Label All Weather Stainless* — 12 ga. only, features stainless steel receiver and barrel, checkered black synthetic stock and forearm, 26, 28, or 30 in. VR barrels with choke tubes, 7½ lbs. New 1999.

  Mfg.'s Sug. Retail $1,276 $965 $775 $685

  Add $139 for 30 in. barrels.

* *Red Label Engraved* — available in 12, 20, or 28 ga., available in 3 different engraving patterns (pattern engraving standard). New 1997.

  Mfg.'s Sug. Retail $2,552 $2,200 $1,900 $1,650 $1,300 $1,000 $850 $725

  Add $190 for ⅓ engraving coverage.

  Add $532 for ⅔ engraving coverage (12 ga. only).

* *Red Label English Field* — 12, 20, or 28 (new 1995) ga., similar to Red Label, except has English style straight grip stock. New 1992.

  Mfg.'s Sug. Retail $1,276 $965 $775 $685 $600 $550 $500 $450

Grading		100%	98%	95%	90%	80%	70%	60%

* Red Label Sporting Clays — 12 or 20 (new 1994) ga., features 30 in. separated barrels, Briley chokes with forcing cones back bored to .744 in., $3/8$ in. VR with middle bead, sporting clays recoil pad. New 1992.

Mfg.'s Sug. Retail	$1,415	$1,050	$950	$740	$635	$550	$500	$450

➤ **Red Label Sporting Clays Engraved** — available in 12 ga. only with $1/3$ engraving pattern. Mfg. 1997 only.

		$2,500	$2,200	$1,900	$1,650	$1,300	$1,000	$850

Last Mfg.'s Sug. Retail was $3,068.

RED LABEL "WOODSIDE" — 12 ga. only, 3 in. chambers, 26, 28, or 30 (Sporting Clays Model only with special chokes, new 1996) in. barrels, straight or pistol grip stock, features premium checkered walnut, satin nickel finish, unique stock design permitting wood to fill-in where frame boxlock action would normally be, hand-engraving available at extra cost. New 1995.

Mfg.'s Sug. Retail	$1,758	$1,425	$1,200	$975	$775	$625	$550	$500

➤ **Red Label "Woodside" Engraved** — available with patterned engraving only with pistol grip and 26 or 28 in. barrels. New 1997.

Mfg.'s Sug. Retail	$2,805	$2,200	$2,050	$1,725	$1,350	$1,050	$875	$750

WILDLIFE FOREVER SPECIAL EDITION — 12 ga. only, limited edition to celebrate the 50th anniversary of Wildlife Forever, features Baron & Son engraving with gold pheasant and mallard inlays on receiver sides, 300 mfg. 1993 only.

		$1,595	$900	$775				

Last Mfg.'s Sug. Retail was $1,595.

Add $125 for hard case.

SUHLER JAGDGEWEHR MANUFAKTUR GmbH

Current manufacturer and firearms restorer located in Suhl, Germany. No current importation.

Suhler Jagdgewehr manufactures a variety of SxS shotguns, in addition to restoring both antique and historical guns. Please contact the factory directly to learn more about their current models and related services.

SUNDANCE INDUSTRIES, INC.

Current manufacturer located in Valencia, CA. Distributor sales only.

PISTOLS: SEMI-AUTO

MODEL A-25 — .25 ACP cal., single action design, $2^{7}/_{16}$ in. barrel, 7 shot mag., rotary safety, lower grip push button mag. release, satin nickel (disc.), bright chrome, or black teflon finish, choice of simulated pearl with different colors or grooved black grips, serrated slide. New 1989.

Mfg.'s Sug. Retail	$79	$65	$55	$45	$40	$35	$30	$25

LADY LASER/LASER 25 — .25 ACP cal., similar to Model A-25, except has factory installed and sighted 5mW Laser sight with no exposed wiring or switch, polished chrome or black finish (Laser 25 only), dual safety switch. New 1995.

Mfg.'s Sug. Retail	$220	$195	$160	$135	$115	$95	$80	$70

The Laser Lady was disc. during 1998.

MODEL BOA — similar to Model A-25, except has patented squeeze grip safety. New in 1990.

Mfg.'s Sug. Retail	$95	$75	$60	$50	$45	$40	$35	$30

DERRINGERS

POINT BLANK DERRINGER — .22 LR cal., O/U design, double action, 3 in. barrels, black matte finish, 8 oz. Mfg. began mid-1994.

Mfg.'s Sug. Retail	$99	$80	$60	$50	$45	$40	$35	$30

SUPER SIX LIMITED

Previous manufacturer located in Brookfield, WI until 1992.

Grading	100%	98%	95%	90%	80%	70%	60%

REVOLVERS

GOLDEN BISON SERIES — .45-70 Govt. cal., 6 shot revolver, 8 or 10½ in. octagon barrel, large size (overall length 15-17½ in.), manganese bronze frame, cross bolt manual safety, smooth hardwood grips, approx. 6 lbs. 177 total mfg. (including special/limited editions). Disc. approx. 1992.

$1,675	$1,475	$1,275	$1,000	$875	$775	$675

Last Mfg.'s Sug. Retail was $1,895.

Low serialization specimens (ser. numbers 1-15) have asking prices of $2,250-$2,950.

* ***Centennial Limited Edition*** — features special engraving and case. 20 total mfg.

$2,950	$2,275	$1,675

Last Mfg.'s Sug. Retail was $3,995.

SUPER SIX LLC

Current manufacturer established during 1999 and located in Milwaukee, WI. Consumer direct sales.

During late 1998, Super Six LLC purchased the previous trademark of Super Six Limited. As this edition went to press, manufacture was just getting under way. Please contact the company directly (see Trademark Index) for current information, including model availability and pricing.

SURVIVAL ARMS, INC.

Previous manufacturer established in 1990 located in Orange, CT. Previously located in Cocoa, FL until 1995.

In 1990, Survival Arms, Inc. took over the manufacture of AR-7 Explorer rifles from Charter Arms located in Stratford, CT.

RIFLES: SEMI-AUTO

AR-7 EXPLORER RIFLE — .22 LR cal., takedown or normal wood stock, takedown barreled action stores in Cycolac synthetic stock, 8 shot mag., adj. sights, 16 in. barrel, black matte finish on AR-7, silvertone on AR-7S, camouflage finish on AR-7C, 2½ lbs. Disc.

$120	$100	$85	$75	$65	$55	$50

Last Mfg.'s Sug. Retail was $150.

AR-20 SPORTER — similar to AR-22, except has shrouded barrel, tubular stock with pistol grip, 10 or 20 shot mag. Mfg. 1996-98.

$165	$140	$120	$105	$95	$80	$70

Last Mfg.'s Sug. Retail was $200.

AR-22/AR-25 — .22 LR cal., 16 in. barrel, black rifle features pistol grip with choice of wood or metal folding* stock, includes 20 (1995 only) or 25 (disc. 1994) shot mag. Disc. 1995.

$155	$120	$95	$80	$70	$60	$55

Last Mfg.'s Sug. Retail was $200.

Subtract $50 for wood stock model.

SVENDSEN, ERL, F.A. MFG. CO.

Previous manufacturer located in Itasca, IL.

DERRINGERS

LITTLE ACE — .22 S cal., patterned after the Ethan Allen "HIDE-A-WAY", bronze frame, blued steel barrel with case hardened hammer and spur trigger.

$85	$75	$70	$65	$60	$55	$50

4-ACES — .22 S cal., 4 barrel derringer with rotating firing pin and spur trigger, bronze frame with blued rifled steel barrels and case hardened parts.

$175	$150	$135	$120	$105	$90	$75

SWING

Previously manufactured by Schutzen Bohme GmbH located in Rintein, Germany.

Grading	100%	98%	95%	90%	80%	70%	60%

RIFLES: BOLT ACTION

SWING BOLT ACTION — .308 Win. cal., target bolt action rifle with thumbhole stock and vented forearm, target sights, 30 in. barrel, 12.1 lbs. New 1994.

	$850	$750	$650	$575	$500	$450	$395

SYMES & WRIGHT LTD.

Current manufacturer located in London, England. Direct sales only.

S

T section

TACONIC FIREARMS, LTD.

Current rifle manufacturer located in Cambridge, NY. Consumer direct sales.

Grading	100%	98%	95%	90%	80%	70%	60%

RIFLES: BOLT ACTION, CUSTOM

TACONIC 98 ULTIMATE MOUNTAIN HUNTER — various cals., features double square bridge, titanium alloy M-98 action, XXX Grade English or Circassian walnut, stainless or chrome moly barrel, matte finished metal, available with a variety of options, base prices are listed below.

Mfg.'s Sug. Retail	$5,995	$5,750	$5,100	$4,500	$4,000	$3,500	$3,000	$2,500

TANFOGLIO, FRATELLI, S.r.l.

Current pistol manufacturer located in Gardone, Italy.

Tanfoglio manufactures good quality semi-auto pistols and single action revolvers. In addition to currently being imported by European American Armory Corp. (see individual listing), Tanfoglio also manufactures their own complete line which, to date, has been mostly distributed in Europe.

TANNER, ANDRÉ

Current manufacturer located in Switzerland. No current importation. Previously imported and distributed by Mandall Shooting Supplies, Inc. located in Scottsdale, AZ, and by Osborne's located in Cheboygan, MI.

Tanner rifles are noted for their superior accuracy and limited production - less than 150 are mfg. each year.

RIFLES: BOLT ACTION

300 METER MATCH RIFLE — 7.5 Swiss (special order) or 7.62mm cal. only, single shot, top-of-the-line 300 meter match rifle incorporating all match shooting features including deluxe palm rest, aperture sights. Importation disc.

			$4,650	$3,995	$3,400	$2,775	$2,250	$1,900	$1,600

Last Mfg.'s Sug. Retail was $4,900.

Add $100 for adj. cheekpiece.
Subtract $190 for repeating model with similar features.

* **300 Meter UIT Standard** — similar to Model 300, except is without palm rest and adj. Swiss butt plate, 10 shot mag., aperture sights. Importation disc.

			$4,450	$3,850	$3,350	$2,750	$2,225	$1,925	$1,600

Last Mfg.'s Sug. Retail was $4,700.

Add $100 for adj. cheekpiece.

SUPERMATCH MODEL 50 M — .22 LR cal. only, 50 meter free rifle, deluxe palm rest, adj. butt plate, thumbhole stock. Importation disc.

			$3,600	$3,200	$2,850	$2,450	$2,050	$1,800	$1,600

Last Mfg.'s Sug. Retail was $3,900.

Add $100 for adj. cheekpiece.

TAR-HUNT CUSTOM RIFLES, INC.

Current custom rifled shotgun manufacturer located in Bloomsburg, PA. Dealer and consumer direct sales.

SHOTGUNS: BOLT ACTION

PROFESSIONAL MODEL RSG-12 — 12 (RSG-12) ga., 2¾ in. chamber, bolt action slug gun featuring 21½ in. Shaw barrel and 2 lug bolt, 1 round down in mag. (new 1998), matte black finish, McMillan fiberglass stock with Pachmayr Decelerator rifle pad, receiver drilled and tapped for standard Leupold windage bases (included, new 1997), muzzle brake became standard 1994, various finish options, 7¾ lbs. New 1991.

Mfg.'s Sug. Retail	$1,395	$1,325	$1,100	$900	$800	$750	$700	$650

Grading	100%	98%	95%	90%	80%	70%	60%

✴ RSG-12 Combo Slug Gun — includes standard Professional RSG-12 Slug Gun and a second benchrest McMillan heavy weight stock. New 1994.

Mfg.'s Sug. Retail	$1,755	$1,600	$1,375	$1,075	$875	$775	$725	$675

MATCHLESS MODEL RSG-12 — upgraded variation featuring 400 grit polished gloss metal finish and the McMillan "Fiber" grain stock (wood grain finish). New 1995.

Mfg.'s Sug. Retail	$1,873	$1,695	$1,450	$1,150	$900	$800	$750	$700

PEERLESS MODEL RSG-12 — upgraded variation featuring NP-3 (nickel/Teflon) metal finish by Robar of Phoenix, AZ, McMillan "Fiber"-grain stock (wood grain finish). New 1995.

Mfg.'s Sug. Retail	$2,072	$1,850	$1,525	$1,200	$950	$800	$750	$700

MOUNTAINEER MODEL RSG-20 — 20 (RSG-20) ga., 2¾ in. chamber, features 21 in. Shaw rifled barrel and 2 lug bolt, one shot blind mag., matte black finish only, McMillan fiberglass stock with Pachmayr Decelerator pad, receiver drilled and tapped for Rem. 700 long action style bases, muzzle brake standard, 6½ lbs. New 1997.

Mfg.'s Sug. Retail	$1,295	$1,250	$995	$875	$750	$625	$550	$500

RSG-TACTICAL (SNIPER) MODEL — 12 ga. only, similar to RSG-12, except has M-86 McMillan fiberglass black tactical stock with Pachmayr Decelerator pad and heavy barrel. Mfg. 1992-98.

	$1,495	$1,250	$995	$875	$750	$700	$650

Last Mfg.'s Sug. Retail was $1,595.

Add $150 for Bi-pod.

BLOCK CARD MODEL — 12 ga., 2¾ in. chamber, various barrel lengths, cartage type chokes, special McMillan fiberglass stock, Pachmayr Decelerator pad, fluted barrels optional, special chambers, weighted stocks optional, single shot actions.

Mfg.'s Sug. Retail	$1,775	$1,625	$1,425	$1,125	$900	$800	$750	$700

TAURUS INTERNATIONAL

Currently manufactured by Taurus Forjas S.A., located in Porto Alegre, Brazil. Currently imported by Taurus International located in Miami, FL since 1982. Distributor sales only.

All Taurus products are known for their innovative design, quality construction, proven value, and are backed by a lifetime repair policy.

REVOLVERS: RECENT PRODUCTION

From 1990-1992, certain models became available with a Laser Aim LA1 sighting system that included mounts, rings (in matching finish), 110 volt AC recharging unit, 9 volt DC field charger, and high impact custom case.

The following Taurus revolvers listed below have been listed in numerical order. All currently manufactured revolvers listed below are rated for +P ammunition.

Many of the Taurus revolvers listed below are equipped with their new patented Taurus Security System introduced in 1998, utilizing an integral key lock on the back of the hammer, locking the action.

MODEL 22H RAGING HORNET STAINLESS — .22 Hornet cal., 8 shot, 10 in. VR barrel with full shroud, fully adj. sights, scope mount bases included, contoured rubber grips, 50 oz. New 1999.

Mfg.'s Sug. Retail	$898	$795	$700	$600

MODEL 44 — .44 Mag. cal., 6 shot, integral porting compensator, exposed or concealed (3 in. barrel only, mfg. 1997-98) hammer, adj. sights, 3 (mfg. 1997-98), 4, 6½ (VR), or 8⅜ (VR) in. barrel, 45-57 oz. New 1994.

Mfg.'s Sug. Retail	$447	$360	$300	$255	$215	$185	$155	$130

Add $19 for 6½ or 8⅜ in. barrel.

✴ Model 44SS (Stainless Steel) — similar to Model 44, except stainless steel. New 1994.

Mfg.'s Sug. Retail	$508	$415	$340	$285

Add $22 for 6½ or 8⅜ in. barrel.

Add $46 for 3 in. ported barrel with fixed sights and round butt grips (mfg. 1996-97).

Grading	100%	98%	95%	90%	80%	70%	60%

MODEL 45 .45 LC RAGING BULL — .45 LC cal., 6 shot, 6½ or 8⅜ in. VR ported barrel, adj. sights, soft rubber grips, 53 or 63 oz. New 1999.

Mfg.'s Sug. Retail	$545	$450	$400	$360	$330	$300	$280	$260

✻ *Model 45 .45 LC Raging Bull Stainless* — similar to Model 45 Raging Bull, except is stainless steel.

Mfg.'s Sug. Retail	$608	$515	$425	$350

MODEL 65 — .357 Mag./.38 Spl. cal., double action, 6 shot, fixed sights, 2½ (mfg. 1993-97), 3 (disc. 1992) or 4 in. barrel, blue finish, checkered walnut (disc.) or rubber (new 1999) grips, 38 oz. Disc. 1997, reintroduced 1999.

Mfg.'s Sug. Retail	$313	$245	$180	$130	$115	$100	$90	$85

Add $15 for satin nickel finish (disc.).

✻ *Model 65SS (Stainless Steel)* — similar to Model 65, except in stainless steel. Mfg. 1993-97, reintroduced 1999.

Mfg.'s Sug. Retail	$359	$275	$220	$190

MODEL 66 — .357 Mag./.38 Spl. cal., double action, 6 or 7 (new 1999) shot, 2½ (mfg. 1993-97), 3 (disc. 1992), 4, or 6 in. barrel, checkered walnut grips, blue finish, adj. sights, 38-40 oz. Disc. 1997, reintroduced 1999.

Mfg.'s Sug. Retail	$359	$275	$220	$190	$165	$140	$120	$100

Add $15 for satin nickel finish (disc.).
Add $10 for 4 or 6 in. compensated (66CP) barrel (mfg. 1993-94).

✻ *Model 66SS (Stainless Steel)* — similar to Model 66, but in stainless steel. Mfg. 1987-97, reintroduced 1999.

Mfg.'s Sug. Retail	$406	$320	$235	$185

Add $10 for 4 or 6 in. compensated (66CP) barrel (mfg. 1993-94).

MODEL 73 — .32 Long cal. only, double action, 6 shot, 3 in. heavy barrel only, checkered walnut grips, 20 oz. Disc. 1992.

		$175	$150	$125	$115	$105	$95	$85

Last Mfg.'s Sug. Retail was $223.

Add $20 for satin nickel finish.

MODEL 76 — .32 H&R Mag. cal., double action, 6 shot, 6 in. heavy barrel with solid rib, fully adj. rear sight, transfer bar safety, checkered hard wood grips, blue only, 34 oz. Mfg. 1991-94.

		$240	$190	$155	$130	$115	$100	$90

Last Mfg.'s Sug. Retail was $308.

MODEL 80 — .38 Spl. cal. only, double action, 6 shot, 3 or 4 in. barrel, checkered walnut grips, fixed sights, 30 oz. Disc. 1996.

		$190	$145	$115	$105	$95	$85	$80

Last Mfg.'s Sug. Retail was $252.

Add $15 for satin nickel finish (disc. 1992).

✻ *Model 80SS (Stainless Steel)* — similar to Model 80, except stainless steel. Mfg. 1993-97.

		$245	$180	$135

Last Mfg.'s Sug. Retail was $313.

MODEL 82 — .38 Spl. cal. only, double action, 6 shot, 3 (disc. 1998) or 4 in. heavy barrel, checkered walnut (disc.) or rubber (new 1999) grips, fixed sights, 34 oz.

Mfg.'s Sug. Retail	$297	$215	$160	$125	$105	$95	$85	$80

Add $15 for satin nickel finish (disc.).

✻ *Model 82SS (Stainless Steel)* — similar to Model 82, except stainless steel. New 1993.

Mfg.'s Sug. Retail	$344	$265	$190	$140

MODEL 83 — .38 Spl. cal. only, double action, 6 shot, 4 in. heavy barrel, checkered walnut grips, adj. sights, 34½ oz. Disc. 1998.

		$215	$155	$125	$115	$105	$95	$80

Last Mfg.'s Sug. Retail was $278.

Add $13 for satin nickel finish.

✻ *Model 83SS (Stainless Steel)* — similar to Model 83, except stainless steel. Mfg. 1993-98.

		$250	$185	$135

Last Mfg.'s Sug. Retail was $324.

T

Grading	100%	98%	95%	90%	80%	70%	60%

MODEL 85 — .38 Spl. cal. only, double action, 5 shot, 2 or 3 in. heavy ported (new 1997) or unported barrel, exposed hammer, checkered walnut grips, fixed sights, 21 oz.

Mfg.'s Sug. Retail	$286	$220	$180	$140	$120	$105	$95	$85

    Add $19 for ported barrel.
    Add $25 for Ultra-Lite Model.
    Add $56 for Ultra-Lite Model in stainless steel.
    Add $20 for satin nickel finish (3 in. barrel only, disc. 1992).

* *Model 85CH (Blue or Stainless)* — similar to Model 85, except has Brazilian hardwood combat grips and spurless hammer that fits flush with the frame, 2 in. barrel, double action only, 21 oz. New 1992.

Mfg.'s Sug. Retail	$286	$220	$180	$140	$120	$105	$95	$85

    Add $15 for ported barrel.
    Add $41 for stainless steel.

* *Model 85 Multi* — features titanium cylinder and choice of matte aluminum or stainless steel frame, fixed sight, rubber grips. New 1999.

Mfg.'s Sug. Retail	$499	$425	$360	$310

* *Model 85B2 Special Edition/Deluxe* — features blue finish with gold trim and ported 2 in. barrel, includes integral key lock. New 1998.

Mfg.'s Sug. Retail	$323	$235	$215	$160	$125	$105	$95	$85

    Add $27 for Ultra-Lite Deluxe (blue and gold finish with ported barrel).

* *Model 85SS (Stainless Steel)* — stainless version of Model 85.

Mfg.'s Sug. Retail	$327	$250	$195	$155

    Add $18 for ported barrel (new 1997).

MODEL 85T — similar to Model 85, except 100% titanium construction, 2 in. ported barrel only, choice of bright blue, matte blue, or matte gold finish. New 1999.

Mfg.'s Sug. Retail	$529	$460	$420	$350

MODEL 86 CUSTOM TARGET — .38 Spl. cal. only, double action target model, 6 shot, 6 in. barrel, specially contoured smooth walnut grips, adj. rear sight, blue only, 34 oz. Disc. 1994.

			$270	$200	$160	$150	$140	$130	$120

    Last Mfg.'s Sug. Retail was $352.

This model was available in either single or double action with adj. counterweight and interchangeable front sight inserts.

MODEL 94 — .22 LR cal., double action, 9 shot, 2 (new 1997), 3 (mfg. 1991-98), 4, or 5 (new 1996) in. barrel, blue finish, adj. rear sight, target features, 25 oz. New 1989.

Mfg.'s Sug. Retail	$308	$230	$170	$135	$120	$105	$95	$85

* *Model 94 Ultra-Lite* — ultra light hammer forged frame, available in matte blue or bright stainless steel, 18 oz. New 1999.

Mfg.'s Sug. Retail	$342	$255	$190	$145	$120	$105	$95	$85

    Add $49 for matte stainless steel construction.

* *Model 94SS (Stainless Steel)* — stainless version of Model 94. New 1990.

Mfg.'s Sug. Retail	$356	$275	$200	$150

MODEL 96 TARGET SCOUT — .22 LR cal. only, double action, 6 shot, 6 in. barrel, checkered walnut grips, same features as Model 86, 34 oz. Disc. 1998.

			$275	$200	$160	$150	$140	$130	$120

    Last Mfg.'s Sug. Retail was $376.

MODEL 415 — .41 Mag. cal., similar to Model 415T, except has matte stainless steel construction, Ribber grips, 30 oz. New 1999.

Mfg.'s Sug. Retail	$452	$395	$330	$275

MODEL 415T — .41 Mag. cal., 5 shot, all titanium construction, 2½ in. ported barrel with fixed sights, bright blue, matte blue, or matte gold finish, Ribber grips. New 1999.

Mfg.'s Sug. Retail	$599	$500	$440	$360

Grading	100%	98%	95%	90%	80%	70%	60%

MODEL 431 — .44 Spl. cal., 5 shot, 2 (new 1995), 3, or 4 in. barrel, blue only, fixed sights. Mfg. 1993-97.

	$220	$170	$145	$130	$115	$100	$90

Last Mfg.'s Sug. Retail was $286.

✳ *Model 431SS (Stainless Steel)* — similar to Model 431, except stainless steel. Mfg. 1993-97.

	$285	$215	$180

Last Mfg.'s Sug. Retail was $368.

MODEL 441 — similar to Model 431, except has 3, 4, or 6 in. barrel, adj. sights. Mfg. 1993-97.

	$240	$180	$145	$130	$115	$100	$90

Last Mfg.'s Sug. Retail was $313.

✳ *Model 441SS (Stainless Steel)* — similar to Model 441, except is stainless steel. Mfg. 1993-97.

	$350	$250	$195

Last Mfg.'s Sug. Retail was $468.

MODEL 444 .44 MAG. RAGING BULL — .44 Mag. cal. only, 6 shot, 6½ or 8⅜ in. VR ported barrel with full shroud, soft rubber grips, 53 or 63 oz. New 1999.

Mfg.'s Sug. Retail	$545	$465	$400	$360	$330	$300	$280	$260

✳ *Model 444 .44 Mag. Raging Bull Stainless* — similar to Model 444, except is stainless steel. New 1999.

Mfg.'s Sug. Retail	$608	$510	$450	$360

MODEL 445 — .44 Spl. cal., 5 shot, 2 in. ported (new 1999) or standard barrel, fixed sights, blue or stainless, Ribber grips, 28 oz. New 1997.

Mfg.'s Sug. Retail	$323	$250	$195	$160	$145	$115	$100	$90

Add $19 for ported barrel (new 1999).

✳ *Model 445 Concealed Hammer* — similar to Model 445, except w/o hammer, ported or unported barrel. New 1999.

Mfg.'s Sug. Retail	$323	$250	$195	$160	$145	$115	$100	$90

Add $19 for ported barrel.

➤ Model 445 Concealed Hammer Stainless — similar to Model 445 Concealed Hammer, except is stainless steel. New 1999.

Mfg.'s Sug. Retail	$370	$280	$210	$150

Add $19 for ported barrel.

✳ *Model 445 SS (Stainless Steel)* — stainless variation of the Model 445. New 1997.

Mfg.'s Sug. Retail	$370	$280	$210	$150

Add $19 for ported barrel.

✳ *Model 445 Ultra-lite Stainless* — features ported 2 in. barrel and matte stainless steel. New 1999.

Mfg.'s Sug. Retail	$483	$355	$275	$225

MODEL 445T — .44 Spl. cal., 5 shot, all titanium construction, 2 in. ported barrel with fixed sights, bright blue, matte blue, or matte gold finish, Ribber grips. New 1999.

Mfg.'s Sug. Retail	$599	$500	$440	$360

MODEL 450 — .45 LC cal., similar to Model 450T, except is matte stainless steel, also available in Ultra-Lite variation, 28 oz. New 1999.

Mfg.'s Sug. Retail	$452	$395	$330	$275

Add $31 for Ultra-Lite Model.

MODEL 450T — .45 LC cal., 5 shot, all titanium construction, 2 in. ported barrel with fixed sights, bright blue, matte blue, or matte gold finish, Ribber grips. New 1999.

Mfg.'s Sug. Retail	$599	$500	$440	$360

MODEL 454 CASULL RAGING BULL — .454 Casull cal., single or double action, 5 shot, front and rear cylinder locks, bright blue or case colored (new 1999) finish, 5 (case colored frame only), 6½ or 8⅜ in. full lug ported barrel with integral VR, soft black rubber grips with recoil absorbing insert, micrometer adj. rear sight, transfer bar ignition, integral key lock, 53-63 oz. New 1998.

Mfg.'s Sug. Retail	$750	$695	$625	$575	$525	$475	$450	$425

Add $95 for case colored frame (new 1999).

Grading	100%	98%	95%	90%	80%	70%	60%

* Model 454 Casull Raging Bull Stainless — similar to Model 454 Casull Raging Bull, except is stainless steel, with either satin or matte (new 1999) stainless finish. New 1998.

Mfg.'s Sug. Retail	$820		$750	$695	$625		

MODEL 605 — .357 Mag. cal., 5 shot, 2¼ or 3 (mfg. 1996-98) in. barrel, blue or stainless, 4 port compensated barrel (2¼ in. only) with fixed sights, exposed or concealed (Model 605CH, new 1997, 2¼ in. barrel) hammer, full barrel shroud, oversized finger grooved rubber grips, 24½ oz. New 1995.

Mfg.'s Sug. Retail	$303		$240	$185	$140	$120	$105	$95	$85

Add $19 for ported barrel.

* Model 605 SS (Stainless Steel) — stainless variation of the Model 605.

Mfg.'s Sug. Retail	$344		$260	$185	$140				

Add $19 for ported barrel.

MODEL 606 — .357 Mag. cal., 6 shot, 2 or 2¼ in. uncompensated or compensated barrel, exposed or concealed hammer, fixed sights. Mfg. 1997-98.

			$235	$180	$140	$120	$105	$95	$85

Last Mfg.'s Sug. Retail was $296.

Add $19 for ported barrel (2 in. only).

* Model 606 SS (Stainless Steel) — stainless variation of the Model 606. Disc. 1998.

			$260	$185	$140			

Last Mfg.'s Sug. Retail was $344.

Add $20 for ported barrel (2 in. only).

MODEL 607 — .357 Mag. cal., 7 shot, 4 or 6½ (VR) in. compensated barrel, adj. rear sight, Santoprene synthetic grips, 44 oz. Mfg. 1995-97.

			$335	$280	$240	$205	$185	$160	$150

Last Mfg.'s Sug. Retail was $447.

Add $18 for 6½ in. VR barrel.

* Model 607SS (Stainless Steel) — stainless variation of the Model 607. Mfg. 1995-97.

			$375	$325	$265			

Last Mfg.'s Sug. Retail was $508.

Add $20 for 6½ in. VR barrel.

MODEL 608 — .357 Mag. cal., 8 shot, 3 (mfg. 1997-98), 4, 6½ (VR), 8⅜ (VR, new 1997) in. barrel with integral compensator, exposed or concealed (new 1997, 3 in. barrel) hammer, adj. sights, 44-56 oz. New 1996.

Mfg.'s Sug. Retail	$447		$340	$285	$245	$205	$185	$160	$150

Add $19 for 6½ or 8⅜ in. VR barrel.

* MODEL 608SS (Stainless Steel) — stainless variation of the Model 608. New 1996.

Mfg.'s Sug. Retail	$508		$380	$330	$270				

Add $46 for ported barrel (3 in. only).
Add $22 for 6½ or 8⅜ in. VR barrel.

MODEL 617 — .357 Mag. cal., 7 shot, double action, 2 in. regular or ported barrel, fixed sights, exposed (integral key lock) or concealed hammer, with or w/o integral key lock. New 1998.

Mfg.'s Sug. Retail	$355		$295	$250	$215	$185	$150	$135	$120

Subtract $20 for concealed hammer (not available with integral key lock).
Add $18 for ported barrel.

* Model 617SS — similar to Model 617, except is stainless steel. New 1998.

Mfg.'s Sug. Retail	$402		$310	$230	$175				

Subtract $20 for concealed hammer (not available with integral key lock).
Add $18 for ported barrel.

MODEL 617T — .357 Mag. cal., 7 shot, all titanium construction, 2 in. ported barrel with fixed sights, bright blue, matte blue, or matte gold finish, Ribber grips. New 1999.

Mfg.'s Sug. Retail	$599		$500	$440	$360				

Grading	100%	98%	95%	90%	80%	70%	60%

MODEL 669 — similar to Model 66 except has fully shrouded 4 or 6 in. barrel, blue finish, 37 oz. Disc. 1998.

	$260	$190	$145	$125	$115	$100	$90

Last Mfg.'s Sug. Retail was $344.

Add $10 for VR barrel (mfg. 1989-1992).
Add $400 for Laser Aim Sight (offered 1990-1992).
Add $19 for compensated (669CP) barrel (new 1993).

* *Model 669SS (Stainless Steel)* — similar to Model 669, but in stainless steel. Disc. 1998.

	$325	$245	$190

Last Mfg.'s Sug. Retail was $421.

Add $21 for compensated (669CP) barrel (new 1993).

MODEL 689 — similar to Model 669, except has VR. Disc. 1998.

	$265	$195	$145	$125	$115	$100	$90

Last Mfg.'s Sug. Retail was $358.

Add $390 for Laser Aim Sight (mfg. 1990-91 only).

* *Model 689SS (Stainless Steel)* — similar to Model 669, but in stainless steel.
  Mfg.'s Sug. Retail $435 $340 $255 $190

MODEL 731 — .32 H&R Mag. cal., double action, 6 shot, stainless steel, 2 in. ported barrel, fixed sights. New 1998.
Mfg.'s Sug. Retail $325 $250 $190 $145

MODEL 731T — .32 H&R Mag. cal., 6 shot, all titanium construction, 2 in. ported barrel with fixed sights, bright blue, matte blue, or matte gold finish, rubber grips. New 1999.
Mfg.'s Sug. Retail $529 $460 $400 $350

MODEL 741 — .32 H&R Mag. cal., 6 shot, 3 or 4 in. barrel, blue only, adj. sights. Mfg. 1993-94.

	$205	$155	$125	$115	$100	$90	$85

Last Mfg.'s Sug. Retail was $254.

* *Model 741SS (Stainless Steel)* — similar to Model 741, except is stainless steel. Mfg. 1993-94.

	$275	$215	$185

Last Mfg.'s Sug. Retail was $342.

MODEL 761 — .32 H&R Mag. cal., 6 shot, 6 in. barrel, blue only, adj. sights. Mfg. 1993-94.

	$250	$185	$145	$125	$115	$100	$90

Last Mfg.'s Sug. Retail was $326.

MODEL 817 ULTRA-LITE — .38 Spl. cal., 7 shot, 2 in. ported or unported solid rib barrel, soft rubber grips, bright blue finish, 21 oz. New 1999.
Mfg.'s Sug. Retail $350 $275 $200 $150 $130 $110 $100 $90
Add $19 for ported barrel.

* *Model 817 Ultra-Lite Stainless* — similar to Model 817 Ultra-Lite, except is stainless steel. New 1999.
  Mfg.'s Sug. Retail $389 $295 $230 $175
  Add $19 for ported barrel.

MODEL 827 — .38 Spl. cal., 7 shot, 4 in. heavy SR barrel, fixed sights, rubber grips, 36½ oz. New 1999.
Mfg.'s Sug. Retail $317 $240 $215 $170 $130 $110 $100 $95

* *Model 827 Stainless* — similar to Model 827, except is stainless steel. New 1999.
  Mfg.'s Sug. Retail $364 $280 $220 $170

MODEL 941 — .22 Mag. cal., 8 shot, 2 (new 1997), 3 (disc. 1998), 4, or 5 in. barrel, blue only, adj. sights. New 1993.
Mfg.'s Sug. Retail $331 $250 $185 $140 $120 $105 $95 $85

* *Model 941 Ultra-Lite* — ultra light hammer forged frame, available in matte blue or bright stainless steel, 18 oz. New 1999.
  Mfg.'s Sug. Retail $366 $270 $200 $150 $125 $105 $95 $85
  Add $53 for matte stainless steel construction.

Grading	100%	98%	95%	90%	80%	70%	60%

* **Model 941SS (Stainless Steel)** — similar to Model 941, except is stainless steel. New 1993.
  Mfg.'s Sug. Retail $384 $285 $215 $160

PISTOLS: SEMI-AUTO

From 1990-1992, certain models became available with a Laser Aim LA1 sighting system that included mounts, rings (in matching finish), 110 volt AC recharging unit, 9 volt DC field charger, and high impact custom case.

> Add approx. $30 for the Deluxe Shooter's Pack option (includes extra mag. and custom case) on the 92, 99, 100, and 101 Series.

PT-22 — .22 LR cal., double action only, tip-up 2¾ in. barrel, 8 shot mag., fixed sights, blue, nickel (new 1995), blue/nickel (new 1997), or blue/gold (new 1997) finish, wood (new 1999) or rosewood grips, 12.3 oz. New 1992.

Mfg.'s Sug. Retail $203 $165 $130 $110 $95 $80 $70 $60
> Add $16 for blue/gold finish.
> Subtract $23 for wood grips.

PT-25 — .25 ACP cal., similar to PT-22, except has 9 shot mag. New 1992.

Mfg.'s Sug. Retail $203 $165 $130 $110 $95 $80 $70 $60
> Add $16 for blue/gold finish.
> Subtract $23 for wood grips.

PT-58 — .380 ACP cal., similar to PT-99AF, except in .380 ACP cal., 4 in. barrel, 10 (C/B 1994) or 12★ shot mag. Mfg. 1988-96.

> $325 $275 $235 $215 $200 $190 $180
>   Last Mfg.'s Sug. Retail was $429.

> Add $32 for satin nickel finish (disc. 1994).

> Beginning 1993, the PT-58 started incorporating the Taurus Tri-Position safety system which features a hammer-drop, "cocked-and-locked" option system.

* **PT-58SS (Stainless Steel)** — similar to PT-58, except is stainless steel. Mfg. 1992-96.
> $385 $310 $260
>   Last Mfg.'s Sug. Retail was $470.

PT-938 COMPACT — .380 ACP cal., 3 in. unported barrel, 10 shot mag., fixed sights. New 1997.
Mfg.'s Sug. Retail $453 $360 $300 $250 $215 $195 $180 $170

* **PT-938 SS (Stainless Steel)** — stainless variation of the PT-938 Compact.
Mfg.'s Sug. Retail $469 $370 $295 $245

PT-91AF — .41 Action Express cal., action similar to PT-92AF, except is in .41 AE cal., 10 shot mag., 34 oz. Imported 1990 only.

> $365 $300 $250 $225 $200 $190 $180
>   Last Mfg.'s Sug. Retail was $446.

> Add $36 for satin nickel finish.
> Add $25 for shooter's pack (includes custom case and extra mag.).

PT-92AF — 9mm Para. cal., semi-auto double action, design similar to Beretta Model 92 SB-F, exposed hammer, 5 in. barrel, 10 (C/B 1994) or 15★ shot mag., smooth Brazilian walnut (disc.) or checkered rubber (new 1999) grips, blue, nickel (disc.), or stainless steel finish, fixed sights, 34 oz.

Mfg.'s Sug. Retail $508 $375 $310 $250 $220 $200 $190 $180
> Add $40 for satin nickel finish (disc. 1994).
> Add $415 for Laser Aim Sight (disc. 1991).
> Add approx. $27 for Deluxe Shooter's Pack (includes extra mag. and case).
> Add $266 for blue or stainless conversion kit to convert 9mm Para. to 22 LR (new 1999).

* **PT-92SS (Stainless Steel)** — similar to PT-92AF, except is fabricated from stainless steel. New 1992.
Mfg.'s Sug. Retail $523 $415 $320 $260

* **PT-92 Deluxe** — choice of blue/gold finish or stainless steel with gold, rosewood grips. New 1999.
Mfg.'s Sug. Retail $570 $445 $340 $265

Grading	100%	98%	95%	90%	80%	70%	60%

* *PT-92AFC* — compact variation of the Model PT-92AF, 4 in. barrel, 10 (C/B 1994) or 13★ shot mag., fixed sights. Disc. 1996.

	$335	$285	$235	$225	$200	$190	$180

      Add $38 for satin nickel finish (disc. 1993).

Last Mfg.'s Sug. Retail was $449.

* *PT-92AFC (Stainless Steel)* — similar to PT-92AFC, except stainless steel. Mfg. 1993-96.

	$400	$310	$260

Last Mfg.'s Sug. Retail was $493.

* *PT-92AF Lew Horton Special Edition* — 9mm Para. cal., matte satin finished frame with high polish stainless steel slide, blue barrel, hammer, trigger, mag. release, safety, and slide release. 250 mfg. in 1990 only.

	$395	$350	$295	$250	$225	$210	$190

Last Mfg.'s Sug. Retail was $454.

PT-99AF — similar to Model PT-92AF, except has adj. rear sight.

Mfg.'s Sug. Retail	$531	$420	$325	$270	$235	$210	$200	$190

      Add $45 for satin nickel finish (disc. 1994).
      Add approx. $30 for Deluxe Shooter's Pack (includes extra mag. and case).
      This action is similar to the Beretta Model 92SB-F.
      Add $266 for blue or stainless conversion kit to convert 9mm Para. to 22 LR (new 1999).

* *PT-99SS (Stainless Steel)* — similar to PT-99AF, except is fabricated from stainless steel. New 1992.

Mfg.'s Sug. Retail	$547	$435	$360	$280

PT-100 — .40 S&W cal., semi-auto, standard double action, 5 in. barrel, 10 (C/B 1994) or 11★ shot mag., safeties include ambidextrous manual, hammer drop, inertia firing pin, and chamber loaded indicator, choice of blue, satin nickel or stainless steel finish, smooth Brazilian hard wood stocks, 34 oz. Mfg. 1992-97.

	$370	$315	$250	$225	$200	$190	$180

Last Mfg.'s Sug. Retail was $469.

      Add $40 for satin nickel finish (disc. 1994).

* *PT-100SS (Stainless Steel)* — similar to PT-100, except is fabricated from stainless steel. Mfg. 1992-96.

	$410	$350	$275

Last Mfg.'s Sug. Retail was $514.

PT-101 — similar to PT-100, except has adj. sights. Mfg. 1992-96.

	$395	$330	$270	$235	$200	$190	$180

Last Mfg.'s Sug. Retail was $491.

      Add $45 for satin nickel finish (disc. 1994).

* *PT-101SS (Stainless Steel)* — similar to PT-101, except is stainless steel. Mfg. 1992-96.

	$415	$340	$280

Last Mfg.'s Sug. Retail was $537.

MODEL PT-111 MILLENNIUM — 9mm Para. cal., double action only, 3⅛ in. barrel with fixed 3 dot sights, black polymer frame with steel slide, striker fired, 10 shot mag. with push button release, 18.7 oz. New 1998.

Mfg.'s Sug. Retail	$367	$310	$260	$220	$185	$150	$135	$120

* *Model PT-111 Millennium Stainless* — similar to Model PT-111, except has stainless steel slide. New 1998.

Mfg.'s Sug. Retail	$383	$315	$265	$225

PT-138 MILLENNIUM — .380 ACP cal., double action only, 3¼ in. barrel, black polymer frame, manual safety, 10 shot mag., fixed 3 dot sights, blue steel slide, 18.7 oz. New 1999.

Mfg.'s Sug. Retail	$367	$310	$260	$220	$185	$150	$135	$120

* *Model PT-138 Millennium Stainless* — similar to Model PT-138, except has stainless steel slide. New 1999.

Mfg.'s Sug. Retail	$383	$315	$265	$225

Grading		100%	98%	95%	90%	80%	70%	60%

PT-140 MILLENNIUM — .40 S&W cal., double action only, 3¼ in. barrel, black polymer frame, manual safety, 10 shot mag., fixed 3 dot sights, blue steel slide, 18.7 oz. New 1999.

Mfg.'s Sug. Retail	$398	$330	$270	$225	$185	$150	$135	$120

* *Model PT-140 Millennium Stainless* — similar to Model PT-140, except has stainless steel slide. New 1999.

Mfg.'s Sug. Retail	$414	$335	$275	$230

PT-400 — .400 Cor-Bon cal., similar to PT-940, except has 4¼ in. ported barrel and 8 shot mag., 29½ oz. New 1999.

Mfg.'s Sug. Retail	$523	$415	$325	$270	$235	$210	$200	$190

* *Model PT-400 Stainless* — similar to Model PT-400, except has stainless steel slide. New 1999.

Mfg.'s Sug. Retail	$539	$415	$330	$275

PT-908 — 9mm Para. cal., compact version of the PT-92 with 3.8 in. barrel and 8 shot mag., fixed sights, blue or nickel finish. Mfg. 1993-97.

		$330	$285	$235	$215	$200	$190	$180

Last Mfg.'s Sug. Retail was $435.

Add approx. $24 for Deluxe Shooter's Pack (includes extra mag. and case).

* *PT-908D SS (Stainless Steel)* — similar to Model PT-908, except is stainless steel. Mfg. 1993-97.

	$385	$310	$260

Last Mfg.'s Sug. Retail was $473.

Add approx. $26 for Deluxe Shooter's Pack (includes extra mag. and case).

PT-911 COMPACT — 9mm Para. cal., single or double action, 3⅞ in. barrel, 10 shot mag., fixed sights. New 1997.

Mfg.'s Sug. Retail	$453	$360	$300	$255	$215	$195	$180	$170

* *PT-911 SS (Stainless Steel)* — stainless variation of the PT-911 Compact.

Mfg.'s Sug. Retail	$469	$370	$310	$260

PT-940 — .40 S&W cal., compact version of the PT-100 with 3.8 in. barrel and 10 shot mag., fixed sights, 34 oz. New 1996.

Mfg.'s Sug. Retail	$469	$370	$310	$260	$225	$200	$190	$180

* *PT-940 SS (Stainless Steel)* — similar to PT-940, except is stainless steel. New 1996.

Mfg.'s Sug. Retail	$484	$390	$325	$265

PT-945 — .45 ACP cal., compact double action, 4¼ in. ported (new 1997) or unported barrel, 8 shot single stack mag., ambidextrous 3 position safety, chamber loaded indicator, 3 dot sights. New 1995.

Mfg.'s Sug. Retail	$484	$395	$325	$265	$220	$200	$190	$180

Add $39 for ported barrel.

Add approx. $23 for Deluxe Shooter's Pack (includes extra mag. and case).

PT-945 SS (Stainless Steel) — stainless steel variation of the PT-945. New 1995.

Mfg.'s Sug. Retail	$500	$375	$315	$245

Add $39 for ported barrel.

Add approx. $21 for Deluxe Shooter's Pack (includes extra mag. and case).

* *PT-945 Deluxe* — choice of blue/gold finish or stainless steel, rosewood grips. New 1999.

Mfg.'s Sug. Retail	$531	$395	$325	$250

Add $16 for stainless steel.

PT-957 — .357 SIG cal., compact model with 3⅝ in. ported barrel, 10 shot mag., ambidextrous 3 position safety, blue finish, checkered rubber grips, fixed sights, 28 oz. New 1999.

Mfg.'s Sug. Retail	$508	$380	$320	$245

PT-957 SS (Stainless Steel) — stainless steel variation of the PT-957. New 1999.

Mfg.'s Sug. Retail	$523	$390	$325	$250

Grading	100%	98%	95%	90%	80%	70%	60%

RIFLES: SLIDE ACTION

MODEL 62 RIFLE/CARBINE — .22 LR cal., patterned after the Win. Model 62, 16½ (carbine) or 23 (rifle) in. barrel with open sights, 12 shot tube mag., includes switchable manual firing pin block on top of receiver bolt and integral Taurus Security System lock on hammer, uncheckered hardwood stock and grooved forearm, blue only, approx. 5 lbs. Importation began 1999.

As this edition went to press, prices had yet to be determined on this model.

TAYLOR, F.C. FUR CO.

Previous company which marketed animal trap guns circa 1921-1941.

PISTOLS: SINGLE SHOT

.22 CAL. TAYLOR FUR GETTER — .22 LR cal., designed to shoot animal at close range once trigger mechanism has been activated (usually with bait attached to a lever). Mfg. by O.F. Mossberg for Taylor, ser. range 1-3,100.

	N/A	$650	$600	$560	$530	$500	$475

Add 10%-15% for low ser. no. with two-piece swiveling stake.

.38 CAL. TAYLOR FUR GETTER — .38 cal., mfg. on 1914 patent of C.D. Lovelace, believed to have been mfg. by Hopkins & Allen, markings cast in top of frame (brass) with iron barrel - all bearing the 1914 patent date.

	N/A	$550	$500	$460	$430	$400	$375

Add 10%-15% premium for alloy frame with top plate attached with two screws and uncracked frame.

TAYLOR'S & CO., INC.

Current importer and distributor established during 1988, and located in Winchester, VA.

Taylor's & Co. is an importer of both black powder and firearms reproductions, in addition to being the exclusive U.S. distributor for Armi Sport, located in Brescia, Italy. Please contact the company directly for current pricing and model availability (see Trademark Index).

REVOLVERS: REPRODUCTIONS, SAA

The 1873 Cattleman single action is available in 6 different calibers, in 4¾, 51/2, or 7½ in. barrel with different metal finishes.

RIFLES: REPRODUCTIONS, SHARPS

These finely made Sharps reproduction models are manufactured by Armi Sport, located in Brescia, Italy. There are available in an 1874 Standard and Deluxe Sporting Rifle in 45-70 Govt. cal., in addition to other variations, including the Berdan and Cavalry Models.

RIFLES: REPRODUCTIONS, WINCHESTER

Currently, Taylor's is importing a Henry rifle, available in either brass or iron frame, a Model 1866 brass fram sporting rifle and carbine, and Model 1873 rifle with case colored receiver and deluxe uncheckered walnut.

TECHNO ARMS (PTY) LIMITED

Previous manufacturer located in Johannesburg, S. Africa circa 1994-96. Previously imported by Vulcans Forge, Inc. located in Foxboro, MA.

SHOTGUNS: SLIDE ACTION

MAG-7 SLIDE ACTION SHOTGUN — 12 ga. (60mm chamber length), 5 shot detachable mag. (in pistol grip), 14, 16, 18, or 20 in. barrel, stock or pistol grip, matte finish, 8 lbs. Imported 1995-96.

$795	$675	$625	$550	$500	$450	$400

Last Mfg.'s Sug. Retail was $875.

Grading	100%	98%	95%	90%	80%	70%	60%

TERRIER ONE

Previously distributed by Serrifile located in Lancaster, CA.

REVOLVERS

TERRIER ONE — .32 S&W cal., double action, 2¼ in. barrel, 5 shot, nickel-plated, 17 oz. Mfg. 1984-87.

	$45	$35	$30	$25	$25	$25	$25

Last Mfg.'s Sug. Retail was $55.

TEXAS ARMS

Current manufacturer located in Waco, TX. Dealer sales only.

DERRINGERS: O/U

DEFENDER — .357 Mag., .38 Spl., 9mm Para., .44 Mag., .45 ACP, or .45 LC/.410 bore shotshell, features 3 in. interchangeable SS octagon barrels, spur trigger, shell ejector for rimmed cartridges, rebounding hammer and retracting firing pins, crossbolt safety, bead blasted grey finish, 16-21 oz. New 1993.

Mfg.'s Sug. Retail	$310		$275	$235	$200	$175	$160	$145	$130

Add $100 per interchangeable set of barrels.

TEXAS GUNFIGHTERS

Previous importer located in Irving, TX circa 1988-1990.

REVOLVERS: SINGLE ACTION

SHOOTIST EDITION — .45 LC cal., patterned after the Colt SAA, 4¾ in. barrel, nickel-plated black powder frame, one piece walnut grips, mfg. by A. Uberti of Italy. New 1988.

* *Standard Model* — 1,000 total mfg., cased.

	$625	$525	$440

Last Mfg.'s Sug. Retail was $649.

* *1 of 100 Edition* — 100 total mfg., fully engraved, genuine mother-of-pearl one piece grips, cased.

	$1,275	$1,050	$775

Last Mfg.'s Sug. Retail was $1,395.

This model was also supplied with an extra set of walnut grips.

TEXAS LONGHORN ARMS, INC.

Current manufacturer located in Richmond, TX. Limited production in the past, and currently, manufacture has ceased.

REVOLVERS

SINGLE-ACTION — various cals., patterned after Colt's SAA, except the ejection port has been moved to left side of frame enabling left-hand loading, mfg. from 4140 steel, 1-piece grip, adj. trigger, case-hardened and blued, entirely hand-made, supplied with lifetime warranty. While production plans called for 1,000 of each model to be manufactured, very few pistols were actually made.

* *Texas Border Special* — .44 Spl., .44 Mag., or .45 LC cal., 3½ (disc.) or 4 in. barrel, 1-piece birdshead grip. Disc.

	$1,595	$1,325	$1,000

Last Mfg.'s Sug. Retail was $1,595.

* *South Texas Army* — .357 Mag., .44 Spl., .44 Mag., or .45 LC cal., 4¾ in. barrel, 1-piece regular walnut grip. Disc.

	$1,595	$1,325	$1,000

Last Mfg.'s Sug. Retail was $1,595.

* *Texas Flattop Target* — .32-20, .357 Mag., .44 Mag./Spl., or .45 LC cal., flat top frame, adj. rear sight, 7½ in. barrel. Disc.

	$1,595	$1,325	$1,000

Last Mfg.'s Sug. Retail was $1,595.

Grading	100%	98%	95%	90%	80%	70%	60%

✳ *Grover's Northpaw* — .45 LC cal., 4¾ in. barrel, satin finish stainless steel, 6 shot, transfer bar safety, 2-piece grips, blade front sight and grooved receiver. Mfg. 1995-disc.

$685 **$550** **$425**

Last Mfg.'s Sug. Retail was $685.

✳ *Grover's Improved Number Five* — .44 Mag. or .45 LC cal., 5½ in. target barrel, 1,200 mfg. serial numbered K1-K1200. This variation incorporates Elmer Keith's 1926 designs including No. 5 lockwork, base pin and latch, and grip straps. Mfg. 1988-disc.

$1,195 **$875** **$675**

Last Mfg.'s Sug. Retail was $1,195.

SPECIAL EDITIONS — in addition to the models listed above, Texas Longhorn Arms also manufactured various special editions, including a Standard Model Set (3 guns, 1 each of the Texas models) retailing at $5,750, an Engraved Special Edition Set (3 gun set) retailing for $7,650, a Texas Sesquicentennial Commemorative retailing for $2,500, and a Mason Commemorative retailing for $1,500.

THOMAS

Manufactured by Alexander James Ordnance, Inc. located in Covina, CA.
Please refer to listing under A.J. Ordnance in this text.

THOMPSON CARBINES

See Auto Ordnance Corp. section of this book.

THOMPSON/CENTER ARMS CO., INC.

Current manufacturer established 1967, and located in Rochester, NH.
Distributor and dealer sales.

PISTOLS: SINGLE SHOT

Caution: older and newer TC components do not interchange safely. Although parts will fit, they may not function properly. Special ordering of barrels, frames, and calibers started in 1988.

CONTENDER — .22 LR, .22 Rem., 5mm Rem., .218 Bee, .22 Hornet, .22 Jet, .221 Fireball, .222 Rem., .25-35 WCF, .256 Mag., .30 Carbine, .30-30 Win., .38 Spl., .357 Mag., .17 Ackley Bee, .17 Bumblebee, .17 Hornet, .17K Hornet, .17 Rem., .300 Whisper (new 1994), .30 Herrett, .357 Herrett, .357-44 B&D, 7x30 Waters, .32 H&R Mag., .32-20 WCF, 6mm TCU, 6.5mm TCU, or 9mm Para. cal., barrels are interchangeable, 8¾ (disc.), 10, or 14 in. barrel, hinged break open, triggerguard, action lever, blue, .44, .357 Mag., and .45 Colt available with detachable choke for hot shot cartridges, VR, 10 in. barrel available, 10 in. bull barrel, adj. sights, checkered walnut grip and forearm.

> The Contender action is in its third variation and a wide variety of changes have been made to grips, stocks, sights, etc. since 1967. These production variances do not necessarily add premiums to values listed below.

✳ *Bull Barrel* — available in 13 cals. between .17 Rem. and .45 Win. Mag., 10 in. round barrel only.

Mfg.'s Sug. Retail	$484	$365	$280	$210	$185	$170	$160	$150

Add $22 for .45 Colt/.410 bore with internal chokes.
Add $10 for .22 LR match grade chamber (new 1996).
Add approx. $230 per additional barrel.

✳ *Armour Alloy II Bull Barrel* — 7 cals. between .22 LR and .30-30 Win., similar to regular Bull Barrel, except has Armour Alloy II satin finish which is harder than stainless steel. Mfg. 1986-89.

$320 **$285** **$230**

Last Mfg.'s Sug. Retail was $415.

Add $5 for .45 Colt/.410 bore internal choke.

✳ *Vent. Rib* — .357 Mag. (disc.), .44 Mag. (disc.) or .45 Colt/.410 bore, 10 in. VR barrel only, adj. front and flip up rear sight, internal choke became standard in 1985.

Mfg.'s Sug. Retail	$506	$380	$290	$215	$180	$170	$160	$150

Grading	100%	98%	95%	90%	80%	70%	60%

* ***Armour Alloy Vent. Rib*** — .45/.410 internal choke, has Armour Alloy II satin finish which is harder than stainless steel. Mfg. 1986-disc.

| | $350 | $295 | $230 | | | | |

Last Mfg.'s Sug. Retail was $435.

* ***Stainless Steel*** — various cals., 10 in. bull barrel. New 1993.

Mfg.'s Sug. Retail $540 $410 $300 $210

Add approx. $230 per additional barrel.
Add $5 for .45/.410 with adj. sights.
Add $20 for .45/.410 with VR.

* ***Octagon Barrel*** — .22 LR, .22 Mag. (disc.), .22 Hornet (disc.), .22K Hornet (disc.), .222 Rem. (disc.), or .357 Mag. (disc.) cal., 10 in. barrel. Disc. 1998.

| | $355 | $260 | $200 | $180 | $170 | $160 | $150 |

Last Mfg.'s Sug. Retail was $474.

* ***Match Grade Barrel*** — .22 LR cal. only, choice of 10 or 14 in. match barrel. Mfg. 1992-98.

| | $350 | $265 | $200 | $180 | $170 | $160 | $150 |

Last Mfg.'s Sug. Retail was $460.

Add $10 for 14 in. barrel.

CONTENDER SHOOTERS PACKAGE — .22 LR Match, .223 Rem., .30-30 Win., or 7-30 Waters cal., includes blued frame and 14 in. barrel w/o sights, 2.5X-7X scope, composite grips and forend, Weaver style base and rings, pistol case. New 1998.

Mfg.'s Sug. Retail $736 $640 $560 $550 $450 $400 $360 $330

CONTENDER SUPER — 13 cals. available from .17 Rem. - .45 Win. Mag. (disc.), 14 or 16 in. bull barrel only, special grips, beavertail forearm, adj. sight, 3½ lbs. Disc. 1997.

| | $360 | $265 | $200 | $180 | $170 | $160 | $150 |

Last Mfg.'s Sug. Retail was $474.

Add $5 for 16 in. barrel.
Add $31 for .17 Rem. cal. (new 1992).
Add $10 for .45-70 Govt. cal. in 16 in. barrel only with muzzle brake (new 1992).
Add approx. $224 per additional barrel.
Add $31 for VR barrel (.45 LC/.410 bore only).

Thompson Center will also make special order guns in different cals. other than those listed above. If factory work, these pistols will be worth a premium.

* ***Stainless Contender Super*** — various cals., choice of 14 or 16 in. barrel. Mfg. 1993-97.

| | $385 | $275 | $215 | | | | |

Last Mfg.'s Sug. Retail was $505.

Add $5 for 16 in. barrel.
Add $25 for .45-70 Govt. bull barrel with muzzle tamer.
Add $30-$35 for .45 LC/.410 bore with internal choke.
Add approx. $240 per additional barrel.

* ***Armour Alloy II Super Contender*** — 5 cals. between .22 LR and 7mm Rem. Mag., similar to regular Super Contender, except has Armour Alloy II satin finish which is harder than stainless steel. Mfg. 1986-89.

| | $355 | $295 | $240 | | | | |

Last Mfg.'s Sug. Retail was $425.

Extra Armour Alloy II Bull Barrels were available for $195+.

SUPER CONTENDER — various cals. between .22 LR - .45-70 Govt., wood grips with rear stippling, barrel configurations include 14 or 16 in. bull (with or w/o VR), adj. sights, blue finish only. New 1999.

Mfg.'s Sug. Retail $495 $395 $335 $275 $250 $220 $195 $170

Add $35 for 14 in. VR barrel.
Add $5 for 16 in. tapered barrel.

Grading	100%	98%	95%	90%	80%	70%	60%

* Super Contender Stainless — similar to Super Contender, except is only available in 14 in. barrel. New 1999.

Mfg.'s Sug. Retail	$551		$415	$310	$210		

Add $35 for VR barrel.

Add $22 for .45/.410 ga. barrel.

CONTENDER HUNTER PACKAGE — .223 Rem., .7-30 Waters, .30-30 Win., .35 Rem., .357 Rem. Max. (disc. 1994), .375 Win. Mag. (new 1992), .44 Mag., or .45-70 Govt. cal., special 12 (disc.) or 14 (new 1992) in. barrel with muzzle brake, 2.5X power scope with lighted reticle, walnut grip has nonslip rubber insert to cushion recoil, includes studs, swivels, sling, and deluxe carrying case, approx. 4 lbs. Mfg. 1990-97.

	$695	$575	$495	$430	$365	$315	$275

Last Mfg.'s Sug. Retail was $798.

CONTENDER 25TH ANNIVERSARY — .22 LR cal. only, 10 in. octagon barrel, laser etched anniversary logo on receiver sides and barrel, checkered stock and forearm, limited mfg. in 1992 only.

	$610	$535	$465	$410	$360	$315	$275

Last Mfg.'s Sug. Retail was $700.

* Contender 25th Anniversary Cased Set — cased set with 5 barrels including .22 LR, .22 Mag., .22 Jet, .22 Hornet, and .38 Spl. cal., 50 sets mfg. 1992 only.

	$1,850	$1,550	$1,225	$1,050	$900	$775	$650

Last Mfg.'s Sug. Retail was $1,975.

ENCORE — various cals., features walnut grip with finger grooves and forend, blued finish, 10 (disc. 1999), 12 (new 1999), or 15 in. barrel with adj. sights, VR barrel on .45 LC/.410 bore, hammer block safety with bolt interlock, 4-4½ lbs. New 1998.

Mfg.'s Sug. Retail	$528		$410	$345	$280	$250	$220	$195	$170

Add $8 for 15 in. barrel on most cals.

Add $228 for extra 10 in. (disc.) or $243 for extra 15 in. barrel.

Add approx. $22-$48 for .45 LC/.410 bore barrel, depending on barrel length.

Encore pistol barrels ARE NOT interchangeable with Contender pistol barrels.

* Encore Stainless — .22-250 Rem., .223 Rem., .308 Win., 7mm-08 Rem. cal., available in 15 in. barrel only, black synthetic finger groove grips and forearm. New 1999.

Mfg.'s Sug. Retail	$591		$475	$350	$250		

* Encore Hunter Package — .22-250 Rem., .270 Win., or .308 Win. cal., features 15 in. barrel w/o sights and 2.5X-7X scope, Weaver base and rings, composite grip and forend, includes case. New 1998.

Mfg.'s Sug. Retail	$774		$665	$575	$555	$450	$400	$360	$330

RIFLES

ENCORE RIFLE — available in many cals. between .22-250 Rem. and .45-70 Govt., interchangeable standard 24 or heavy 26 in. barrel, automatic hammer block, trigger guard opening lever, choice of black synthetic (new 1999) or American walnut uncheckered forearm and Monte Carlo stock with pistol grip, adj. rear sight, approx. 7 lbs. New 1997.

Mfg.'s Sug. Retail	$555		$445	$340	$270	$230	$195	$180	$170

Add $19 for walnut stock and forearm.

Add $249 per extra barrel.

Encore rifle barrels ARE NOT interchangeable with Contender Carbine barrels.

* Encore Stainless — similar to Encore Rifle, except has black synthetic stock and forearm only, and is stainless steel. New 1999.

Mfg.'s Sug. Retail	$620		$500	$365	$260		

CONTENDER CARBINE — available in 15 cals. between .17 Rem. and .44 Rem. Mag., also .410 bore (3 in.), Contender action with pistol grip full stock and forearm, 21 in. interchangeable barrel, drilled for scope mounts, iron sights standard. New 1986.

Mfg.'s Sug. Retail	$540		$415	$315	$255	$215	$190	$175	$160

Add $31 for .17 Rem. cal. (disc. 1997)

Add $21 for .410 bore barrel. (disc. 1997)

Grading	100%	98%	95%	90%	80%	70%	60%

Add approx. $244 per extra barrel.
Add $11 for match grade .22 LR barrel.
Subtract $36 for Youth Model (16¼ in. barrel w/o VR - disc. 1998).
Add $175 for Survival Carbine System (disc. - includes Rynite stock, 16¼ .223 Rem. barrel, extra .45 Colt/.410 barrel, and soft camo cordura case).

* **Rynite Contender Carbine** — similar to above, except has Rynite stock and forend. Mfg. 1990-1993.

			$335	$270	$220	$195	$180	$165	$155

Last Mfg.'s Sug. Retail was $425.

Add $30 for .17 Rem. cal.
Add $10 for match grade barrel.
Add $25 for 21 in. VR smooth bore .410 bore barrel.

* **Contender Carbine Stainless** — various cals., 21 in. barrel, choice of walnut (disc. 1993) or Rynite synthetic stock. New 1993.

Mfg.'s Sug. Retail	**$546**		$415	$310	$230

Add $35 for walnut stock (disc.).
Add $11 for .22 LR match barrel (new 1995).
Add $26 for .410 smooth bore barrel with screw-in full choke (disc.).

This model was also available in a Youth Model with walnut stock at no extra charge (disc. 1993).

HUNTER RIFLE MODEL — single shot, top lever break open action w/interchangeable barrels, .22 Hornet, .223 Rem., .22-250 Rem., .243 Win., .270 Win., 7x57mm, .30-06, .308 Win. .375 H&H (new 1992), or .416 Rem. Mag. (new 1992) cal., 23 in. barrel, 6 lbs. 14 oz., checkered walnut stock, choice of medium or light sporter weight barrel. New 1983 and improved in 1987. Available in left-hand at no extra charge. Disc. 1992.

		$500	$415	$350	$295	$265	$240	$220

Last Mfg.'s Sug. Retail was $595.

Add $20 for .375 H&H or .416 Rem. Mag. cal.
Add approx. $275 per extra rifle barrel.

* **Hunter Deluxe Rifle Model** — similar to Hunter Model, except features double triggers and upgraded walnut stock and forearm. Mfg. 1992 only.

		$550	$450	$375	$325	$285	$250	$225

Last Mfg.'s Sug. Retail was $675.

Add $20 for .375 H&H or .416 Rem. Mag. cal.

* **Hunter Shotgun Model** — same action as Hunter Rifle, except is supplied with 12 ga. barrel (field choke with 3½ in. chamber or slug with 3 in. chamber and iron sights) or 10 ga. barrel (3½ in. chamber). Disc. 1992.

		$500	$415	$350	$295	$265	$240	$220

Last Mfg.'s Sug. Retail was $595.

Add $275 per additional shotgun barrel.

TCR '83 ARISTOCRAT — similar to Hunter Model, except stock has cheekpiece and forearm is checkered, stainless steel double set triggers. Disc. 1986.

		$425	$370	$345	$320	$300	$280	$260

Last Mfg.'s Sug. Retail was $475.

Add $175 for each additional barrel(s) (including 12 ga. slug).

SHOTGUNS: SINGLE SHOT

ENCORE SHOTGUN — 20 ga., 3 in. chamber, 26 in. VR barrel with three choke tubes, recoil pad. New 1998.

Mfg.'s Sug. Retail	**$612**		$530	$455	$375	$300	$250	$200	$175

Add $294 per additional shotgun barrel.

THUNDER-FIVE

Previous trademark manufactured by Mil, Inc. located in Piney Flats, TN. Previously distributed by C.L. Reedy & Associates, Inc. located in Jonesborough, TN. Dealer and direct consumer sales.

While previously advertised as the Spectre Five (not mfg.), this firearm has been re-named the Thunder Five.

Grading	100%	98%	95%	90%	80%	70%	60%

REVOLVERS

THUNDER-FIVE — .45 LC cal./.410 bore with 3 in. chamber or .45-70 Govt. cal. (new 1994), unique 5 shot revolver design permits shooting .45 LC or .410 bore shotshells interchangeably, 2 in. rifled barrel, phosphate finish, external ambidextrous hammer block safety, internal draw bar safety, combat sights, hammer, trigger, and triggerguard, Pachmayr grips, includes padded plastic carrying case, 48 oz., serialization starts at 1,101. Mfg. 1992-disc.

			$500	$450	$400	$375	$350	$325	$300

Last Mfg.'s Sug. Retail was $550.

Add $50 for .45-70 Govt. cal.

TIKKA

Current trademark imported by Stoeger Industries, Inc., located in Wayne, NJ. Rifles are currently manufactured by Sako, Ltd. located in Riihimaki, Finland. Previously manufactured by Oy Tikkakoski Ab, of Tikkakoski, Finland (pre-1989).

Also see listings under Ithaca LSA for older models.

RIFLES: BOLT ACTION

NEW GENERATION RIFLE — .22-250 Rem., .223 Rem., .243 Win., .270 Win., .30-06, .308 Win., 7mm Rem. Mag., .300 Win. Mag., or .338 Win Mag. cal., 22½ (non-Mag.) or 24½ (Mag. cals.) in. barrel, detachable 3 (standard) or 5 (optional) shot mag., forged and milled action in two lengths, checkered walnut stock, 7-7½ lbs. Sako mfg. 1989-94.

	$725	$600	$550	$500	$450	$400	$360

Last Mfg.'s Sug. Retail was $835.

Add $25 for Mag. cals.

Cals. .22-250 Rem., .308 Win., and .300 Win. Mag. were introduced in late 1989.

PREMIUM GRADE RIFLE — same cals. as New Generation Rifle, stock is select walnut with roll-over cheek-piece and rosewood pistol grip cap and forend tip, high polished barrel blue. Imported 1989-94.

	$860	$715	$600	$550	$500	$450	$400

Last Mfg.'s Sug. Retail was $1,030.

Add $40 for Mag. cals.

VARMINT RIFLE — .22-250 Rem., .223 Rem., .243 Win., or .308 Win. cal., 24½ in. heavy barrel, no sights. Mfg. 1991-94.

	$895	$750	$625	$550	$500	$450	$400

Last Mfg.'s Sug. Retail was $1,090.

WHITETAIL HUNTER/BATTUE RIFLE — .22-250 Rem. (new 1995), .223 Rem. (new 1995), .243 Win. (new 1995), .25-06 Rem.(new 1995), .270 Win., .30-06, .308 Win., 7mm Rem. Mag., 7mm-08 Rem. (new 1995), .300 Win. Mag., or .338 Win. Mag. cal., 20½ (disc. 1994), 22½ (new 1995), or 24½ (new 1995, Mag cals. only), in. barrel, 3 or 5 (optional) shot detachable mag., choice of wood or black synthetic (new 1996) stock, no sights (Hunter Model), or open sights on raised rib (disc., Battue Model). New in 1991.

Mfg.'s Sug. Retail	$609	$525	$450	$385	$350	$325	$300	$275

Add $22 for Mag. cals.

Add $60 for carved elk or deer game scene stock (mfg. 1996-97).

* *Whitetail Hunter/Battue Stainless* — same cals. as Whitetail Hunter, synthetic stock only and stainless steel. New 1997.

Mfg.'s Sug. Retail	$669	$590	$525	$450

Add $22 for Mag. cals.

* *Whitetail Hunter Deluxe* — same cals. as Whitetail Hunter, deluxe checkered walnut stock and forearm with rollover cheekpiece. Importation began 1999.

Mfg.'s Sug. Retail	$734	$650	$565	$510	$455	$400	$360	$330

Add $30 for Mag. cals.

Grading		100%	98%	95%	90%	80%	70%	60%

CONTINENTAL VARMINT RIFLE — .22-250 Rem., .223 Rem., or .308 Win. cal., heavy 26 in. barrel, adj. trigger, quick release detachable mag., integral scope mount rails, recoil pad spacer system, 8⅜ lbs. New 1996.

Mfg.'s Sug. Retail	$709		$615	$510	$455	$395	$350	$325	$300

CONTINENTAL LONG RANGE HUNTING RIFLE — .25-06 Rem., .270 Win., 7mm Rem. Mag., or .300 Win. Mag. cal., heavy 26 in. barrel w/o sights, checkered walnut stock and forend, 8¾ lbs. New 1996.

Mfg.'s Sug. Retail	$709		$615	$510	$455	$395	$350	$325	$300

Add $30 for Mag. cals.

SPORTER MODEL — .22-250 Rem., .223 Rem., or .308 Win. cal., 23½ in. barrel w/o sights, adj. buttplate and cheekpiece, detachable 5 shot mag., stipled pistol grip and forend. New 1998.

Mfg.'s Sug. Retail	$939		$840	$760	$655	$575	$500	$450	$395

COMBINATIONS GUNS: O/U

Previously manufactured in Jyvaskyla, Finland. In 1989, under a joint venture agreement made in Italy, the 412 O/U shooting system was manufactured in Italy. Older models may be found in the Valmet trademark section of this text.

During 1993, the new models of the 512S series replaced the older 412S series. Separate listings have not been provided, since they are almost identical in most respects.

MODEL 512S SHOOTING SYSTEM — interchangeable barrel assemblies permit a double rifle, shotgun/rifle, and O/U shotgun configuration, user installed interchangeable barrels, monobloc locking, rifle barrel positioning by adjustment, SST, extractors or ejectors, checkered walnut stock and forend, cocking indicators, blued finish.

The 412S Model nomenclature was changed to 512S in late 1993.

* ***Model 512S Field Grade*** — 12 ga. only, 3 in. chambers, auto ejectors, screw-in choke tubes (includes 5), 26 or 28 in. barrels, matte nickel finish. New 1986-importation disc. 1997.

		$1,050	$750	$595	$550	$475	$440	$400

Last Mfg.'s Sug. Retail was $1,325.

Subtract 10% for Standard Grade.

The Premium Grade became standard issue beginning 1995.

* ***Model 412ST Trap*** — 12 ga., Monte Carlo stock, 30 in. barrels, screw-in chokes standard.

		$1,125	$925	$725	$650	$580	$540	$475

Last Mfg.'s Sug. Retail was $1,325.

This variation was made by Valmet in Finland.

* ***Model 412ST Premium Grade Trap*** — similar to Model 412ST Trap, except has better walnut and checkering.

		$1,425	$1,000	$875	$750	$625	$580	$515

Last Mfg.'s Sug. Retail was $1,665.

This variation was made by Valmet in Finland.

* ***Model 512S Sporting Clays*** — 12 ga. only, sporting clays configuration with 28 or 30 (new 1994) in. VR barrels and choke tubes. Imported 1992-97.

		$1,160	$950	$735	$650	$580	$540	$475

Last Mfg.'s Sug. Retail was $1,360.

* ***Model 512S Combination Gun*** — combination rifle/shotgun, 12 ga, 3 in. chambers, 24 in. barrels, under rifle barrel has choice of .222 Rem., .30-06, or .308 Win. cal., extractors. Importation disc. 1997.

		$1,425	$1,025	$775	$675	$600	$525	$475

Last Mfg.'s Sug. Retail was $1,770.

* ***Model 512S Double Rifle*** — .30-06 (new 1994), .308 Win. (new 1994), 9.3x74R cal., 24 in. barrels, extractors. Importation disc. 1997.

		$1,525	$1,125	$825	$750	$625	$550	$500

Last Mfg.'s Sug. Retail was $1,890.

* ***Extra Barrel Assemblies (Model 512S O/U)*** — add $745-$765 each for shotgun (includes screw-in chokes), $810 each for shotgun/rifle combo, $1,040 each for double rifle.

TIMBERWOLF

Previous trademark manufactured by I.M.I. (Israel Military Industries) located in Israel. Previously imported and distributed by Action Arms located in Philadelphia, PA until 1994.

RIFLES: SLIDE ACTION

TIMBERWOLF — .357 Mag. or .44 Mag. (disc.) cal., slide action, straight grip shotgun style stock with adj. drop, blue or satin chrome finish, takedown, 18½ in. barrel, 10 shot tube mag., sear locking and firing pin safeties, integral scope base, approx. 5½ lbs. Imported 1989-1993.

	100%	98%	95%	90%	80%	70%	60%
.357 Mag.	$260	$230	$195	$180	$160	$145	$130
.44 Mag. (blue only)	$425	$375	$335	$300	$275	$250	$225

Last Mfg.'s Sug. Retail was $299.

Add $80 for satin chrome finish.

This model was designed, imported, and distributed by Action Arms Ltd. Springfield Armory imported 1,000 .44 Mag. Timberwolf models during 1990-1991.

TIME PRECISION, INC.

Current custom riflemaker located in Brookfield, CT. Consumer direct sales.

Time Precision SLV/ALV actions are available in over 30 different types, and in cals. from .22 LR - .416 Rigby. All guns are made per individual custom order, but are basically available in 3 different configurations - Hunting, Benchrest, and Target rifles. Base prices begin at $1,835 (centerfire), with a wide range of special order options. Please contact the company directly regarding delivery times and other information.

TIPPMAN ARMS CO.

Previous manufacturer located in Fort Wayne, IN.

Tippman Arms manufactured 1/2 scale semi-auto working models of famous machine guns. All models were available with an optional hardwood case, extra ammo cans, and other accessories. Mfg. 1986-1987 only.

REPRODUCTIONS: SEMI-AUTO

MODEL 1919 A-4 — .22 LR cal. only, copy of Browning 1919 A-4 Model, belt fed, closed bolt operation, 11 in. barrel, includes tripod, 10 lbs.

$2,200	$1,950	$1,675	$1,425	$1,200	$995	$775

Last Mfg.'s Sug. Retail was $1,325.

MODEL 1917 — .22 LR cal. only, copy of Browning M1917, watercooled, belt fed, closed bolt operation, 11 in. barrel, includes tripod, 10 lbs.

$2,350	$2,050	$1,700	$1,425	$1,200	$995	$775

Last Mfg.'s Sug. Retail was $1,830.

MODEL .50 HB — .22 Mag. cal. only, copy of Browning .50 cal. machine gun, belt fed, closed bolt operation, 18¼ in. barrel, includes tripod, 13 lbs.

$2,700	$2,350	$2,000	$1,675	$1,425	$1,200	$1,000

Last Mfg.'s Sug. Retail was $1,929.

TOKAREV

See Russian Service Pistols and Rifles section.

TORNADO

Currently manufactured by AseTekno located in Helsinki, Finland.

RIFLES: BOLT ACTION

TORNADO MODEL — .338 Lapua Mag. cal., unique straight line design with free floating barrel, 5 shot mag., pistol grip assembly is part of frame, limited importation into the U.S.

The factory should be contacted directy regarding domestic availability and pricing (see Trademark Index).

Grading	100%	98%	95%	90%	80%	70% °	60%

TOZ

Current manufacturer located in Russia, mostly concentrating on competition pistols and longarms. Imported by Nygord Precision Products located in Prescott, AZ.

PISTOLS: SINGLE SHOT

TOZ-35 FREE PISTOL — .22 LR cal., employs virtually every shooting refinement possible in a single shot target pistol, fully adj. target grips, limited mfg.

Mfg.'s Sug. Retail	$995	$875	$795	$725	$650	$575	$475	$375

Add $50 for "Vitarbo" adj. grips.

TRADEWINDS

Previous importer located in Tacoma, WA.

RIFLES

HUSKY MODEL 5000 — .22-250 Rem., .243 Win., .270 Win., .308 Win., or .30-06 cal., bolt action, 23¾ in. barrel, adj. sight, removable mag., hand-checkered walnut stock.

	$325	$310	$290	$250	$225	$200	$175

MODEL 311-A — .22 LR cal., bolt action, 5 shot, 22½ in. barrel, folding leaf rear sight, walnut checkered stock.

	$180	$170	$150	$130	$120	$100	$85

MODEL 260-A — .22 LR cal., semi-auto, 5 shot, 22½ in. barrel, 3 leaf folding sight, checkered walnut stock.

	$200	$190	$175	$150	$130	$120	$100

SHOTGUNS: SEMI-AUTO

MODEL H-170 — 12 ga., 2¾ in. chamber, 26 in. mod. or 28 in. full, recoil operated action, alloy receiver, 5 shot, tube mag., VR, checkered walnut stock.

	$275	$265	$250	$225	$200	$180	$150

TRENCH/RIOT SHOTGUNS

The following is a chronological listing beginning with WWI of the various U.S. commercial Riot and military Trench and Riot shotguns mfg. to date.

The publisher wishes to express thanks to Pat Redmond and Rick Crosier for the information in this section.

Some 100% values have been intentionally omitted in this section as they are seldomly seen or sold.

All Trench/Riot shotguns listed below are in 12 ga. only.

SHOTGUNS: MILITARY TRENCH, WWI

WINCHESTER MODEL 1897 MILITARY TRENCH GUN — high-polish commercial blue finish, solid frame with 6 row ventilated handguard for bayonet attachment. Serial range 650,000-690,000. Guns used by the U.S. Army for trench warfare in WWI, originally did not have military markings. A U.S. and ordnance bomb are stamped on the right side of the receiver on trench guns kept in Army's inventory after the war. Military markings were added in the 1920s to about 10% of the total production.

Trench Gun	N/A	$2,600	$1,200	$850	$750	$700	$600
Trench Gun w/military markings	N/A	$3,200	$2,800	$1,500	$1,000	$800	$700

REMINGTON MODEL 10 MILITARY TRENCH GUN — high polish commercial blue finish with wood handguard on top of barrel, separate bayonet adaptor attaches to front of barrel for bayonet attachment. U.S. and ordnance bomb is marked on left side receiver, stock is unmarked. Serial 160,000-165,000. Extremely rare Trench gun and hard to find complete and in original condition. Trench gun barrel length is 22 in. as compared to 20 in. Riot gun. Prices quoted only for complete guns with wood handguard and bayonet adaptor.

Trench Gun	N/A	$4,250	$3,500	$2,500	$1,850	$1,250	$995
Riot Gun	N/A	$1,500	$1,200	$900	$500	$350	$300

Grading	100%	98%	95%	90%	80%	70%	60%

SHOTGUNS: MILITARY RIOT/TRENCH, WWII

ITHACA MODEL 37 MILITARY SHOTGUNS — rarest of all Trench shotguns, high polish commercial blue finish, RLB and ordnance bomb on left side of receiver, ordnance bomb on barrel, stocks not proofed, blue vent. handguard for bayonet attachment, only 1,420 Trench guns were ordered in 1941. Ithaca supplied mostly long barrel martially marked shotguns within serial range 49,000-62,000.

	100%	98%	95%	90%	80%	70%	60%
Trench Gun	N/A	$4,500	$3,500	$2,250	$1,750	$1,500	$1,200
Riot Gun	N/A	$1,800	$1,500	$1,250	$750	$600	$500
Long Barrel	N/A	$1,000	$750	$600	$500	$350	$300

REMINGTON MODEL 31 RIOT GUN — commercial blue finish (high polish and flat blue finishes noted). Can be marked U.S. Property on receiver and/or barrel. Some examples noted with only ordnance mark on stock. Serial range 39,500-60,500.

	100%	98%	95%	90%	80%	70%	60%
Riot Gun	N/A	$1,200	$900	$750	$650	$550	$450
Long Barrel	N/A	$700	$650	$500	$400	$350	$200

REMINGTON MODEL 11 RIOT GUNS — this is the most commonly found military shotgun. Examples of 5 shot and 3 shot Sportsman Model. Examples with plain or engraved receivers and plain or fancy checkered wood. Military marked with U.S. and ordnance bomb on receiver and barrel. Later models are marked, and have Military Finish. These shotguns all have highly polished commercial blue finish and ordnance marked stocks. Serial range 450,000-500,000 and 700,000-711,000.

	100%	98%	95%	90%	80%	70%	60%
Riot Guns	N/A	$750	$500	$450	$400	$350	$300
Long Barrel	N/A	$500	$400	$350	$300	$250	$200

∗ *Riot Gun* — this configuration was sold by the government as surplus as late as the 1970s and can occasionally be found NIB with packing materials and instruction manual. Mint in factory box - $1,350.

SAVAGE MODEL 720 — appears identical to Remington Model 11. This was mfg. by Stevens/Savage in very limited quantities, plain and engraved receivers noted with high quality commercial blue finish. Stocks are unmarked and must have ramp sights to be original. Watch for altered guns made into Riots. Serial range 65,000-86,000.

	100%	98%	95%	90%	80%	70%	60%
Riot Gun	N/A	$1,500	$1,200	$1,000	$800	$650	$500
Long Barrel	N/A	$650	$600	$500	$400	$300	$250

STEVENS MODEL 620 MILITARY SHOTGUNS — this was the current model being sold by Stevens and has a commercial blue finish, but not of the same quality as the other companies. Trench guns are equipped with handguards that have a definite purple/reddish color to the front and dark blue vent. shaft. Model 620s are much rarer than 520s and have U.S. and ordnance bomb on receiver, ordnance bomb on barrel and unmarked stock. Serial range 1-25,000.

	100%	98%	95%	90%	80%	70%	60%
Trench Gun	N/A	$1,000	$750	$650	$550	$500	$450
Riot Gun	N/A	$750	$500	$450	$400	$350	$250
Long Barrels	N/A	$350	$300	$250	$200	$175	$150

STEVENS 520-30 MILITARY SHOTGUNS — this model was resurrected due to available machinery and is the most commonly found Trench gun. Riot guns in minty condition are hard to find. Same finish as Model 620, U.S. and ordnance bomb on receiver, ordnance bomb on barrel and no proofing on stocks, except for reworks. Trench gun has same style handguard as Model 620. Serial range 25,000-70,000.

	100%	98%	95%	90%	80%	70%	60%
Trench Gun	N/A	$1,000	$750	$600	$500	$450	$400
Riot Gun	N/A	$600	$400	$350	$300	$250	$200
Long Barrels	N/A	$300	$275	$225	$175	$150	$125

Grading	100%	98%	95%	90%	80%	70%	60%

WINCHESTER MODEL 97 MILITARY SHOTGUNS — takedown model, high polish commercial blue finish, finger groove walnut stocks with hard rubber buttplates, early Trenchguns and all riot guns have WB and ordnance bomb proofs on left side of stock, left side of receiver is marked U.S., with or w/o ordnance bomb. All WB Trenchguns have 6 row handguards, barrels are all ordnance proofed, later Trenchguns are marked GHD and ordnance bomb on left side of stock, receivers are marked with U.S. and ordnance bomb, and all have 4 row vent. handguards.

Trench Gun-WB marked	N/A	$2,750	$2,200	$1,700	$1,200	$1,000	$750
Trench Gun-GHD marked	N/A	$2,600	$2,000	$1,500	$1,000	$750	$600
Riot Gun-WB marked	N/A	$1,000	$900	$750	$650	$500	$400

WINCHESTER MODEL 12 MILITARY SHOTGUNS — takedown model with improved hammerless receiver. These were made to supplement Model 97 production. Riot guns and Trench guns share same serial range. Finished in high polished commercial blue, Trench guns (only) were the only WWII shotguns to have factory parkerized finishes. All Model 12s have U.S. and ordnance bomb on right side of receiver, ordnance bomb on barrel and ordnance mark and inspector initials on left side of stock. Trench guns have 4 row vent. handguards.

* *Blue finish* — serial range 926,000-1,030,000.

Trench Gun	N/A	$2,250	$1,650	$1,200	$975	$850	$650
Riot Gun	N/A	$1,400	$900	$750	$650	$500	$400

* *Parkerized finish* — serial range 1,030,000-1,040,000.

Trench Gun	N/A	$2,450	$2,000	$1,400	$1,000	$900	$750

SHOTGUNS: MILITARY RIOT/TRENCH, VIETNAM

ITHACA MODEL 37 — parkerized finish with U.S. marks on right side of receiver. Receiver and barrel are also marked "P." Serial range, applied on gun upside-down, is from S1,000-S23,500. Used in the Vietnam era. A very few original Trench guns with parkerized handguards have been noted.

Riot Gun	N/A	$750	$650	$500	$400	$350	$300
Trench Gun	N/A	$1,000	$900	$800	$600	$500	$450

SAVAGE 77E — parkerized finish with sling swivels and red rubber butt pad. U.S. marked on right side of receiver and military "P" proofmark on receiver and barrel. Hard to find in excellent condition.

Riot Gun	N/A	$750	$650	$400	$300	$250	$225

WINCHESTER MODEL 1200 — parkerized barrel, mag. tube, and bayonet adapter with U.S. marking on barrel. Aluminum receiver with black or matte type finish, U.S. is marked under serial number. Very rare as few examples have been released by the government due to its continued use by military forces.

Trench Gun	N/A	$1,000	$900	$800	$600	$500	$400

SHOTGUNS: RIOT/TRENCH GUN, COMMERCIAL SALES

WINCHESTER MODEL 12 RIOT — thousands mfg. between late '30s-'60s.

	N/A	$550	$450	$395	$350	$295	$240

WINCHESTER MODEL 97 — commercial high polish blue, changed from solid frame to takedown in 1935. Trench guns made through 1945 and Riot gun mfg. continued until 1960s.

* *Solid Frame*

Trench Gun	N/A	$2,000	$1,800	$1,500	$1,200	$1,000	$750
Riot Gun	N/A	$1,000	$900	$750	$600	$500	$300

* *Takedown*

Trench Gun	N/A	$1,800	$1,500	$1,300	$1,100	$900	$600
Riot Gun	N/A	$800	$700	$600	$500	$400	$300

REMINGTON MODEL 10 — commercial high polish blue, sold in the 1920s to various government and banking agencies.

Riot Gun	N/A	$400	$350	$300	$275	$250	$200

REMINGTON MODEL 11 — made in 1930s for law enforcement use.

Riot Gun	N/A	$400	$350	$300	$275	$250	$200

Grading	100%	98%	95%	90%	80%	70%	60%

MODEL 31R RIOT GUN — similar to 31A, with 20 in. barrel.

	N/A	$300	$200	$175	$150	$130	$110

ITHACA MODEL 37 — parkerized models made in 1960s for police agencies and commercial sales.

Trench Gun	N/A	$500	$400	$350	$300	$250	$200
Riot Gun	N/A	$275	$250	$225	$175	$150	$125

TRISTAR SPORTING ARMS, LTD.

Current importer established in 1994, and located in N. Kansas City, MO.

RIFLES: BOLT ACTION

PEE-WEE .22 — .22 LR cal., single shot, manual cocking bolt, 16½ in. barrel, steel construction, blued finish with adj. rear leaf sight, 12 in. LOP, uncheckered walnut stock with Monte Carlo, 2¾ lbs. Limited mfg. 1998 only.

	$170	$140	$130	$120	$110	$100	$90

Last Mfg.'s Sug. Retail was $189.

SHOTGUNS: LEVER ACTION

MODEL 1887 — 12 ga. only, patterned after the Winchester Model 1887, "WRA Co." logo on left side of receiver, 30 in. barrel, 5 shot tube mag., blued finish, 2-piece walnut forearm and rounded pistol grip stock, 8 lbs. Limited importation 1997-98.

	$535	$475	$435	$400	$360	$330	$295

Last Mfg.'s Sug. Retail was $599.

SHOTGUNS: O/U

TR-I (NOVA I) — 12 or 20 ga., blued boxlock action, SST, extractors, 26 or 28 vent. barrels with 7mm VR and fixed chokes, checkered standard grade walnut stock and forearm, gold trigger, mfg. by E. Rizzini, importation began 1998.

Mfg.'s Sug. Retail	$654	$565	$475	$425	$375	$330	$300	$275

TR-II (NOVA II) — 12, 16, 20, 28 ga. or .410 bore, similar to Nova I, except has choke tubes and ejectors. New 1998.

Mfg.'s Sug. Retail	$852	$745	$650	$550	$460	$410	$355	$300

Add $28 for 20, 28 ga., or .410 bore.

TR-SC (NOVA SC) — 12 or 20 (new 1999) ga. only, 2¾ in. chambers, sporting clays model, silver finished boxlock action, gold SST, 28 or 30 in. vent. barrels with 10mm VR and mid-rib sight beads, fancy checkered walnut stock and forearm, mfg. by E. Rizzini, importation began 1998.

Mfg.'s Sug. Retail	$949	$810	$725	$635	$550	$450	$395	$350

Add $73 for 20 ga. (new 1999).

TR-ROYAL — 12, 20, or 28 ga., 2¾ in. chambers, similar to the TR-SC, except has special dimension stock designed to reduce recoil, 28 or 30 in. VR barrels with 7mm-10mm tapered rib and rhino ported extended choke tubes, ejectors, silver finished boxlock action, deluxe checkered walnut stock and forearm, silver frame with gold accents. Importation began 1999.

Mfg.'s Sug. Retail	$1,277	$1,025	$900	$800	$700	$600	$500	$400

TR-CLASS SL — 12 ga. only, 2¾ in. chambers, features select materials, silver finished boxlock action with engraved sideplates, ejectors, SST, 28 or 30 VR barrels with choke tubes, 6¾ lbs. Importation began 1999.

Mfg.'s Sug. Retail	$1,690	$1,475	$1,250	$1,025	$900	$800	$700	$575

NOVA L — similar to Nova SC, except has stock dimensions for female shooter, also available in 20 ga. Mfg. 1998 only.

	$750	$675	$600	$525	$450	$395	$350

Last Mfg.'s Sug. Retail was $869.

TR-MAG. (NOVA MAG.) — 12 ga. only, 3½ in. chambers, SST, extractors, 24 or 28 in. vent. barrels with 7mm VR and choke tubes, matte finished wood and metal. New 1998.

Mfg.'s Sug. Retail	$728	$595	$525	$455	$420	$375	$330	$300

Grading	100%	98%	95%	90%	80%	70%	60%

MODEL 300 — 12 ga. only, 3 in. chambers, under-lug action, double triggers, extractors, etched engraving, standard checkered Turkish walnut stock and forearm, 26 or 28. in. VR barrels with fixed chokes. Imported 1994-98.

			$375	$330	$300	$275	$250	$225	$200

Last Mfg.'s Sug. Retail was $429.

MODEL 333 FIELD GRADE — 12 or 20 ga., 3 in. chambers, engraved boxlock receiver with satin finish, SST, ejectors, fancy grade Turkish walnut with hand-cut checkering, 26 (12 ga. only), 28, or 30 in. VR barrels, supplied with 5 choke-tubes, approx. 7½ lbs. Imported from Turkey beginning 1994.

Mfg.'s Sug. Retail	$800	$735	$625	$550	$500	$450	$400	$360

* *Model 333 Sporting Clays* — similar to Model 333 Field Grade, except has sporting recoil pad, elongated forcing cones, 28 or 30 in. ported barrels with extended stainless steel choke-tubes, 7¾ lbs. Imported 1994-97.

	$825	$725	$625	$550	$500	$450	$400

Last Mfg.'s Sug. Retail was $900.

* *Model TR-L (333L) Ladies Field* — similar to Model 333 Field Grade, except is fitted with special ladies stock, 26 or 28 in. barrels only.

Mfg.'s Sug. Retail	$966	$860	$725	$625	$550	$475	$425	$360

* *Model 333SCL Ladies Sporting Clays* — similar to Model 333 Sporting Clays, except is fitted with special ladies stock, 28 in. barrels only with four choke-tubes. Disc. 1997.

	$825	$725	$625	$550	$500	$450	$400

Last Mfg.'s Sug. Retail was $900.

MODEL 330 — 12 or 20 ga., 3 in. chambers, etched satin finished receiver, SST, extractors, fixed chokes, checkered standard Turkish walnut stock and forearm, approx. 7½ lbs. Importation began 1994.

Mfg.'s Sug. Retail	$549	$475	$415	$375	$325	$295	$280	$265

* *Model 330D* — similar to Model 330, except has ejectors, and three choke-tubes. Importation began 1994.

Mfg.'s Sug. Retail	$689	$615	$525	$495	$450	$400	$360	$330

SHOTGUNS: SxS

MODEL 311 — 12 or 20 ga., 3 in. chambers, Greener boxlock action, 26 or 28 in. barrels, standard checkered Turkish walnut stock and forearm, DTs, supplied with five choke-tubes, white chrome frame finish, extractors. Imported 1994-97.

	$535	$475	$435	$400	$360	$330	$295

Last Mfg.'s Sug. Retail was $599.

* *Model 311R* — 12 or 20 ga., 20 in. cylinder bore barrels designed for cowboy re-enactment shooting or home defense, other features similar to Model 311. Disc. 1997.

	$375	$325	$300	$275	$250	$225	$200

Last Mfg.'s Sug. Retail was $429.

MODEL 411 — 12, 16 (new 1999), 20, 28 ga., or .410 bore, 3 in. chambers (except 28 ga.), 26 or 28 (12 ga. only) in. barrels with (12 and 20 ga.) or w/o (28 ga. or .410 bore) choke tubes, DT, extractors, steel shot compatible, case colored frame, checkered walnut stock and forearm with recoil pad, mfg. by Luciano Rota (R.F.M.). Importation began 1998.

Mfg.'s Sug. Retail	$808	$680	$625	$565	$510	$450	$400	$350

* *Model 411D* — similar to Model 411, except not available in 16 ga., features engraved case colored frame, single trigger, ejectors, and English style stock. New 1999.

Mfg.'s Sug. Retail	$1,057	$875	$775	$675	$575	$475	$400	$325

* *Model 411R Coach Gun* — 12 or 20 ga., 3 in. chambers, hammerless, 20 in. fixed choke barrels, case colored frame, DT, extractors, 6-6½ lbs. Importation began 1999.

Mfg.'s Sug. Retail	$705	$595	$550	$500	$440	$380	$310	$240

This model is also designed for cowboy competition shooting and quail hunting.

TRUVELO ARMOURY

Current manufacturer located in Centurion, South Africa. Truvelo Armoury is a division of the Truvelo Manufacturing Group. No current importation.

Grading	100%	98%	95%	90%	80%	70%	60%

Truvelo Armoury manufactures a variety of firearms, including rifles and pistols. Currently, they have several bolt action rifles available in the $475-$1,000 range. Please contact the factory directly (see Trademark Index) for more information.

TULA ARSENAL

Current manufacturer located in Tula, Russia.

The Tula Arsenal is one of the world's oldest and largest gun manufacturing facilities. Many millions of military weapons have been manufactured at this facility, and currently, Tula is getting more aggressive in providing sporting arms to the western countries. For more information, please contact the factory directly (see Trademark Index), and remember, this isn't the local gun shop in Iowa!

TURKISH FIREARMS CORPORATION

Please refer to the HHF section in this text.

T

NOTES

U section

USAS 12

Previous trademark manufactured by International Ordnance Corporation located in Nashville, TN circa 1992-95. Previously manufactured (1990-91) by Ramo Mfg., Inc. located in Nashville, TN. Previously distributed by Kiesler's Wholesale located in Jeffersonville, IN until 1994. Originally designed and previously distributed in the U.S by Gilbert Equipment Co., Inc. located in Mobile, AL. Previously manufactured under license by Daewoo Precision Industries, Ltd. located in South Korea.

Grading	100%	98%	95%	90%	80%	70%	60%

SHOTGUNS: SEMI-AUTO

USAS 12 — 12 ga. only, gas operated action available in either semi or fully auto versions, 18¼ in. cylinder bore barrel, closed bolt, synthetic stock, pistol grip, and forearm, carrying handle, 10 round box or 20 drum (disc.) mag., 2¾ in. chamber only, parkerized finish, 12 lbs. Mfg. 1987-95.

	100%	98%	95%	90%	80%	70%	60%
	$925	$850	$750	$650	$575	$500	$400

Last Mfg.'s Sug. Retail was $995.

Add $150 for extra 20 shot drum magazine (banned by the BATF).

Values above are for a semi-auto model. This model is currently classified as a destructive device and necessary paperwork must accompany a sale.

U.S. ARMS COMPANY

Previous manufacturer located in Riverhead, NY.

REVOLVERS: SINGLE ACTION

ABILENE .357 MAG. — 6 shot, 4⅝, 5½, or 6½ in. barrel, adj. sights, transfer bar ignition, smooth walnut grips, blue finish only. Mfg. 1976-1983.

$275	$240	$200	$185	$170	$155	$140

ABILENE .357 MAG. STAINLESS STEEL — similar to Abilene, only in stainless steel.

$325	$275	$225

ABILENE .44 MAG. — 7½ and 8½ in. barrel, unfluted cylinder blue finish only, otherwise similar to .357 Mag.

$325	$265	$240	$220	$200	$165	$150

ABILENE .44 MAG. STAINLESS STEEL — similar to Abilene .44 Mag., only stainless steel.

$375	$330	$290

U.S. GENERAL TECHNOLOGIES, INC.

Previous manufacturer located in S. San Francisco, CA circa 1994-96.

RIFLES: SEMI-AUTO

P-50 SEMI-AUTO — .50 BMG cal., includes 10 shot detachable mag., folding bipod, muzzle brake, matte black finish. Mfg. 1995-96.

$5,600	$4,950	$4,475	$3,975	$3,500	$3,050	$2,600

Last Mfg.'s Sug. Retail was $5,995.

UBERTI USA, INC.

Current importer and distributor located in Lakeville, CT. Both black powder and modern firearms are imported by Uberti USA, Inc. and are manufactured by Aldo Uberti of Ponte Zanano, Italy.

Other firms have imported Uberti guns under various names in the past.

REVOLVERS: REPRODUCTIONS, SAA & VARIATIONS

These guns can be ordered with either black powder or modern configured frames. Factory engraving and other embellishments or finishes (including antique charcoal blue, white steel, nickel, etc.) can be special ordered by contacting the importer directly.

Grading	100%	98%	95%	90%	80%	70%	60%

Add $390 for standard hand-engraving pattern on Cattleman variations.
Add $35 for antique charcoal blue finish on all Cattleman variations.
Add $80 for silver-plating.
Add $30 for white finish or checkered grips.
Add $60 for select grade walnut one-piece fitted grips.
Add $50 for stag horn grips, $150 for black buffalo grips, or $225 for mother-of-pearl grips.

CATTLEMAN VARIATIONS — available in .22 LR (disc. 1990), .22 Mag. (disc. 1990), .357 Mag., .38 Spl., .38-40 WCF(new 1989), .44 Spl., .44-40 WCF, or .45 LC cal., 4¾, 5½, and 7½ in. barrel lengths, brass or steel backstraps and trigger guard.

* *Quick Draw Model*
  ➤ **Steel backstrap and trigger guard** — choice of new or old model frame, old model frame not available in .357 Mag. cal.

	100%	98%	95%	90%	80%	70%	60%
Mfg.'s Sug. Retail $410	$345	$265	$210	$175	$160	$150	$135

  Add $25 for .357 Mag., .38-40 WCF, or .44 Spl. cal.
  Add $75 for convertible cylinder (.45 LC/.45 ACP, .22 LR/.22 Mag. in 5½ in. barrel only).
  Add $64 for stainless steel construction (disc. 1989).

  ➤ **Brass backstrap and trigger guard** — .357 Mag., .44-40 WCF, or .45 LC cal., 4¾, 5½, or 7½ in. barrel.

	100%	98%	95%	90%	80%	70%	60%
Mfg.'s Sug. Retail $365	$310	$240	$190	$165	$150	$140	$130

  Add $50 for convertible cylinder (.45 LC/.45 ACP).

* *Sheriff's Model* — .44-40 WCF or .45 LC cal., 3 or 4 in. barrel, steel backstrap.

	100%	98%	95%	90%	80%	70%	60%
Mfg.'s Sug. Retail $410	$345	$265	$210	$175	$160	$150	$135

* *Target Model* — similar to standard Cattleman model, only fully adj. rear blade sight, brass backstrap. Importation disc. 1990.

		95%	90%	80%	70%	60%
	$315	$245	$200	$185	$170	$150	$135

  Last Mfg.'s Sug. Retail was $335.

  Add $25 for steel backstrap and trigger guard.
  Add $60 for stainless steel construction (disc.).

CATTLEMAN "FIRST ISSUE" — .38-40 WCF, .44-40 WCF, or ,45 LC cal., 4¾, 5½, or 7½ in. barrel. New 1997.

	100%	98%	95%	90%	80%	70%	60%
Mfg.'s Sug. Retail $475	$395	$310	$240	$195	$175	$160	$150

  Add $5 for .38-40 WCF cal.

CATTLEMAN SABRE (BIRD HEAD) — .44 Spl., .44-40 WCF, or .45 LC cal., 3 (Sheriff's Model, .44-40 WCF or .45 LC cal. only), 3½, 4 (Sheriff's Model, .44-40 WCF or .45 LC cal. only), 4¾, or 5½ in. barrel, patterned after the Colt 1877 Thunderer, case colored frame, checkered walnut bird head grips. New 1997.

	100%	98%	95%	90%	80%	70%	60%
Mfg.'s Sug. Retail $475	$395	$310	$240	$195	$175	$160	$150

  Add $5 for .44 Spl. (available in 4¾ or 5½ in. barrel only).

* *Cattleman Sabre (Bird Head) Old Model* — .44 Spl., .44-40 WCF, or .45 LC cal., 3 (Sheriff's Model, .44-40 WCF or .45 LC cal. only), 3½, 4 (Sheriff's Model, .44-40 WCF or .45 LC cal. only), or 4½ in. barrel, similar to Cattleman Sabre, except has old model frame (vertical screw holding cylinder pin). New 1997.

	100%	98%	95%	90%	80%	70%	60%
Mfg.'s Sug. Retail $485	$400	$315	$240	$195	$175	$160	$150

  Add $10 for .44 Spl. cal.

CATTLEMAN BISLEY — .357 Mag., .38-40 WCF, .44 Spl., .44-40 WCF, or .45 LC cal., patterned after the Colt Bisley Model, 4¾, 5½, or 7½ in. barrel, case colored frame, wood grips. New 1997.

	100%	98%	95%	90%	80%	70%	60%
Mfg.'s Sug. Retail $485	$400	$315	$240	$195	$175	$160	$150

  Add $10 for .38-40 WCF or .44 Spl. cal.

* *Cattleman Bisley Flattop* — similar to Cattleman Bisley, except has flattop frame with fixed or target (.44-40 WCF or .45 LC cal., 7½ in. barrel only) sights. New 1997.

	100%	98%	95%	90%	80%	70%	60%
Mfg.'s Sug. Retail $485	$400	$315	$240	$195	$175	$160	$150

  Add $25 for target sights.

Grading	100%	98%	95%	90%	80%	70%	60%

CATTLEMAN BUNTLINE — .22 LR/.22 Mag. combo, .357 Mag. (disc. 1995), .44-40 WCF (disc.), or .45 LC cal., 18 in. barrel, steel backstrap cut for shoulder stock. Importation disc. 1989, re-introduced 1993.

Mfg.'s Sug. Retail	$475		$395	$310	$240	$195	$175	$160	$150

* **Buntline Carbine** — similar to Cattleman Buntline, 18 in. barrel, includes non-detachable shoulder stock with brass hardware and lanyard ring. Importation disc. 1989, re-introduced 1993-95.

			$390	$310	$245	$200	$175	$160	$150

Last Mfg.'s Sug. Retail was $475.

Add $34 for target sights.
Add $34 for .22 LR/.22 Mag. combo. (disc. 1989).
Add $175 for detachable shoulder stock.

SA REVOLVER CARBINE — .357 Mag., .44-40 WCF, or .45 LC cal., 19 in. barrel, fixed stock with brass rifle butt plate, finger rest extension on trigger guard, choice of quick detachable mounts or target sights, 4.4 lbs. New 1997.

Mfg.'s Sug. Retail	$475		$395	$310	$240	$195	$175	$160	$150

Add $14 for target sights.

BUCKHORN — .44 Mag., .44 Spl., or .44-40 WCF cal., various barrel lengths, brass or steel backstrap, Buntline and revolving carbine models also available in the Buckhorn series — add approx. $65.

* **Quick Draw Model** — importation disc. 1989, re-introduced 1992-95.

			$375	$295	$235	$195	$175	$160	$150

Last Mfg.'s Sug. Retail was $445.

Add $50 for convertible cylinder.
Add $40 for Target Model.

* **Buckhorn Carbine** — .44-40 WCF or .44 Mag. cal., 18 in. barrel, includes non-detachable shoulder stock with brass hardware and lanyard ring. Importation disc. 1989.

			$360	$285	$230	$200	$185	$180	$175

Last Mfg.'s Sug. Retail was $450.

Add $34 for target sights.
Add $40 for extra .44-40 WCF cylinder combo.
Add $122 for detachable shoulder stock.

STALLION 1873 COLT — .22 LR/.22 Mag. cal. combo only, 4¾, 5½, or 6½ in. barrel, case hardened frame, 1-piece walnut grip, 2.4 lbs. Importation disc. 1989.

			$300	$210	$195	$170	$155	$140	$120

Last Mfg.'s Sug. Retail was $325.

Add $27 for steel backstrap and trigger guard.
Add $26 for Target Model.

* **Stainless Stallion** — similar to standard Stallion, except is stainless steel. Importation disc. 1989.

			$370	$275	$225	$200	$185	$180	$175

Last Mfg.'s Sug. Retail was $425.

1875 "OUTLAW" REMINGTON — .357 Mag., .44-40 WCF, .45 ACP (new 1992), or .45 LC cal., 5½ (disc. 1995) or 7½ in. barrel, brass or steel (new 1993) trigger guard.

Mfg.'s Sug. Retail	$435		$365	$275	$215	$175	$160	$150	$135

Add $50 for nickel-plating (disc. 1995).
Add $50 for convertible cylinder (.45 LC/.45 ACP).

* **Model 1875 Carbine** — same cals. as Outlaw 1875, 18 in. barrel, includes non-detachable shoulder stock with brass hardware and lanyard ring. Importation disc. 1989.

			$425	$285	$230	$200	$185	$180	$175

Last Mfg.'s Sug. Retail was $440.

Add $110 for nickel plating.

1890 "POLICE" REMINGTON — .357 Mag., .44-40 WCF, .45 ACP (new 1993), or .45 LC cal., 5½ or 7½ (disc. 1995) in. barrel, brass or steel (new 1993) trigger guard.

Mfg.'s Sug. Retail	$435		$365	$275	$215	$175	$160	$150	$135

Add $50 for nickel-plating (disc. 1995).
Add $40 for convertible cylinder (.45 LC/.45 ACP).

Grading	100%	98%	95%	90%	80%	70%	60%

PHANTOM MODEL — .357 or .44 Mag. cal. only, 10½ in. barrel for silhouette use. Imported 1985-89.

	$475	$395	$325	$290	$260	$230	$215

Last Mfg.'s Sug. Retail was $509.

REVOLVERS: DOUBLE ACTION

INSPECTOR MODEL — .32 S&W or .38 Spl. cal., 3, 4, or 6 in. barrels, double action, blued or chrome finish. Imported 1985-89.

	$390	$295	$245	$210	$170	$145	$125

Last Mfg.'s Sug. Retail was $406.

Add $35 for target sights.
Add $25 for chrome plating.

REVOLVERS: REPRODUCTIONS, ROLLING BLOCK

1871 ROLLING BLOCK TARGET PISTOL/CARBINE — available in .22 LR, .22 Mag., .22 Hornet, .357 Mag. or .45 LC (Navy Model with open sights only, mfg. 1992-95) cal., 9½ in. barrel.

Mfg.'s Sug. Retail	$410	$335	$275	$230	$195	$175	$155	$135

Add $80 for carbine model (22 in. barrel - not available in .45 LC cal).

RIFLES: REPRODUCTIONS

Add approx. $400 for standard hand-engraving for most models listed below.

HENRY RIFLE/CARBINE — .44-40 WCF or .45 LC (rifle only) cal., brass or steel (.44-40 WCF only) frame, 24½ in. barrel on rifle, 22½ in. barrel on carbine, available in modern gun blue, charcoal blue, white, or chrome finish.

Mfg.'s Sug. Retail	$940	$840	$635	$525	$425	$360	$320	$260

Add $10 for carbine model.
Add $55 for steel frame on rifle only.
The carbine was disc. in 1989, re-introduced 1992.

* *Henry Trapper* — similar to above, except has 16½ or 18½ in. barrel. Limited importation began 1990.

Mfg.'s Sug. Retail	$950	$850	$640	$525	$425	$360	$320	$260

* *Henry 1 of 1,000* — disc. several years ago.

	$1,450	$1,150	$975	$850	$700	$575	$425

1866 CARBINE — .22 LR (disc. 1989), .22 Mag. (disc. 1989), .38 Spl., .44-40 WCF or .45 LC cal., brass receiver, 19 in. round barrel. Importation disc. 1995.

	$640	$525	$425	$360	$310	$275	$240

Last Mfg.'s Sug. Retail was $587 for .22 Mag. or .22 LR (disc. 1989).
Last Mfg.'s Sug. Retail was $720.

* *1866 Trapper Carbine* — .22 LR, .38 Spl., or .44-40 WCF cal., 16 in. barrel. Importation disc. 1989.

	$650	$475	$395	$340	$285	$260	$235

Last Mfg.'s Sug. Retail was $686.

* *1866 Yellowboy Indian Carbine* — .22 LR, .22 Mag., .38 Spl., .44-40 WCF, or .45 LC (new 1996) cal., 19 in. barrel. Limited importation.

Mfg.'s Sug. Retail	$760	$670	$535	$430	$360	$310	$275	$240

Add $60 for .22 LR or .22 Mag. cal.
Subtract $50 without brass tacks (disc.).

* *Red Cloud Commemorative Carbine* — same cals., special engraving and brass tacks in forearm and stock. Importation officially disc. 1989.

	$720	$600	$475	$400	$350	$330	$300

Last Mfg.'s Sug. Retail was $850.

1866 SPORTING RIFLE — .38 Spl., .44-40 WCF, or .45 LC (new 1996) cal., brass receiver, 24¼ in. round (new 1993) or octagonal barrel.

Mfg.'s Sug. Retail	$840	$740	$575	$485	$385	$300	$260	$235

Grading	100%	98%	95%	90%	80%	70%	60%

* **1866 Deluxe Uberti Model** — .44-40 WCF cal., features high polished receiver with fire-blued small parts, ladder rear sight, open edition beginning 1995.

Mfg.'s Sug. Retail	$895		$895	$675	$525		

    This model is sold exclusively by Cherry's, located in Greensboro, NC.

* **1866 "L.D. Nimschke" Special Edition** — .44-40 WCF cal., receiver, buttplate, and forend cap feature recreations of Nimschke scroll-engraving by Giovanelli of Italy, silver-plated, deluxe walnut, optional 2nd Edition of Nimschke pattern book by R. L. Wilson ($100), only 300 mfg. beginning 1995.

Mfg.'s Sug. Retail	$1,495		$1,495	$1,000	$650		

    This model is sold exclusively by Cherry's, located in Greensboro, NC.

* **1866 Yellowboy Indian Rifle** — .22 LR (disc. 1989), .22 Mag. (disc. 1989), .38 Spl., or .44-40 WCF cal., 24¼ in. barrel. Importation disc. 1989, reintroduced 1993-95.

		$700	$560	$475	$385	$300	$260	$235

                    Last Mfg.'s Sug. Retail was $800.

1873 CARBINE — .22 LR (disc. 1991), .22 Mag. (disc. 1991), .357 Mag., .38 Spl. (disc. 1991) .44-40 WCF, or .45 LC (new 1992) cal., steel receiver, 19 in. round barrel.

Mfg.'s Sug. Retail	$900		$800	$600	$500	$425	$360	$320	$280

    Add $20 for .357 Mag. cal.

    Add $95 for nickel-plating (disc.).

* **1873 Trapper Carbine** — .357 Mag., .44-40 WCF, or .45 LC cal. only, 16⅛ in. barrel. Importation disc. 1990.

		$695	$550	$475	$400	$360	$320	$280

                    Last Mfg.'s Sug. Retail was $750.

1873 SPORTING RIFLE — .357 Mag. (new 1995), .44-40 WCF (new 1995), or .45 LC cal., case hardened receiver, 20 in. octagon (new 1990), 24¼ in. octagon (.357 Mag. only) or half-round/half-octagon or 30 (new 1990) in. octagon barrel, can be drilled and tapped for Uberti rear tang aperture sight (new 1993).

Mfg.'s Sug. Retail	$940		$830	$640	$525	$425	$360	$320	$260

    Add $30 for .44-40 WCF or .45 LC cal. in 24¼ octagon barrel only.

    Add $990 for "1 of 1,000" engraving pattern.

    Add $80 for Deluxe Model with hand-checkered pistol grip stock - $110 for Deluxe Model with 30 in. barrel.

MODEL 1873 125th ANNIVERSARY — .44-40 WCF cal., special anniversary offering featuring engraved gold plated metal with fire blued receiver small parts, long rifle configuration with deluxe pistol rip and forearm. 125 mfg. 1998 only, marketed exclusively by Cherry's.

Mfg.'s Sug. Retail	$3,500		$3,250	$2,500	$1,750			

UGARTECHEA, ARMAS

Current manufacturer located in Eibar, Spain. Currently being imported by Lion Country Supply, located in PA. Formerly known as Ugartechea, Ignacio.

SHOTGUNS: SxS

BILL HANUS BIRDGUN — 16, 20, 28 ga., or .410 bore, boxlock action, 26 in. barrels bored SK1/SK2, Churchill raised rib, SNT, ejectors, case colored receiver, checkered straight grip walnut stock and semi-beavertail forearm, oil finish, lifetime operational warranty, 5¼-6½ lbs. Imported 1995-97.

	$1,425	$1,250	$1,050	$880	$750	$635	$540

                        Last Mfg.'s Sug. Retail was $1,695.

    Add $100 for 28 ga.

    Add $150 for .410 bore.

Grading	100%	98%	95%	90%	80%	70%	60%

BILL HANUS BIRDGUN CLASSIC — 20, 28 ga., or .410 bore, similar to Birdgun Model, except has double triggers with hinged front trigger, 27 in. barrels, splinter forearm and English leather handguard. Imported 1996-97.

	100%	98%	95%	90%	80%	70%	60%
	$1,355	$1,220	$1,035	$880	$750	$635	$540

Last Mfg.'s Sug. Retail was $1,595.

Add $100 for 28 ga.
Add $200 for .410 bore.

UGARTECHEA, IGNACIO

Current manufacturer located in Eibar, Spain. Currently imported exclusively by Aspen Outfitting Company, located in Aspen, CO, beginning 1997.

Ignacio Urgartechea was founded in 1922 and is the oldest maker of side-by-side sidelock and boxlock shotguns in Spain. From 1970 until the Parker-Hale name was sold in 1990 to Navy Arms, Ugartechea manufactured the popular line of Anson Deeley boxlocks imported by Precision Sports in Cortland, NY. Precision Sports continued to import these guns under the Classic "600" name until 1994. Previously imported by Precision Sports, Inc. located in Cortland, NY until 1994. Previously imported by Exel Arms in Gardener, MA until 1987 as the Exel Model 200 series.

U

SHOTGUNS: SxS, BOXLOCK

Included in this section are older Exel Series 200 shotguns (disc. 1986-87) in addition to the Parker-Hale 600 Series. The importation of Parker-Hale shotguns was disc. in 1993.

Currently, Aspen Outfitting Co. imports 4 different models of boxlocks (Models 30, 40, AOC/LG, & AOC/SG).

MODEL AOC/LG — 12 ga. only, boxlock action, case colored receiver, oil finished deluxe walnut stock and forearm.

Prices on this model range from $1,445 - $2,110, depending on options.

MODEL AOC/SG — similar to Model AOC/LG, except also available in 16, 20, or 28 ga. Importation began in 1999.

Prices on this model range from $1,445 - $2,110, depending on options.

EXEL 200 SERIES — these side-by-sides were available in 12 or 20 ga. (3 in.) only. Model 201 is basic gun with 213 being the highest grade.

* *Model 201, 202, and 203* — double triggers, extractors, straight grip, matted rib, various chokes and barrel lengths.

	100%	98%	95%	90%	80%	70%	60%
	$375	$325	$260	$240	$215	$180	$165

Last Mfg.'s Sug. Retail was $429.

Previously designated Model 30.

* *Model 281* — similar to 201 series, except 28 ga.

	100%	98%	95%	90%	80%	70%	60%
	$420	$325	$275	$250	$235	$210	$195

Last Mfg.'s Sug. Retail was $472.

Previously designated Model 30.

* *Model 240* — similar to 201 series, except .410 bore.

	100%	98%	95%	90%	80%	70%	60%
	$450	$355	$295	$270	$250	$235	$210

Last Mfg.'s Sug. Retail was $472.

Previously designated Model 30.

* *Models 204, 205, and 206* — single trigger optional, ejectors, straight grip, silver finish, various chokes and barrel lengths. Importation disc. 1986.

	100%	98%	95%	90%	80%	70%	60%
	$550	$470	$415	$370	$340	$315	$280

Last Mfg.'s Sug. Retail was $627.

* *Models 207 and 207A* — 12 ga. only, sidelock, case hardened action. 207A is deluxe model with ejectors. Model 201 disc. 1986.

	100%	98%	95%	90%	80%	70%	60%
	$725	$650	$580	$515	$465	$400	$345

Last Mfg.'s Sug. Retail was $836.

Subtract 33% without ejectors (Model 207).

This model was previously designated the Milano EX.

Grading	100%	98%	95%	90%	80%	70%	60%

* **Models 208 and 208A** — similar to 207/207A, only engraved coin finished receiver. 208A is deluxe model with ejectors. Model 208 disc. 1986.

	$775	$695	$625	$550	$485	$420	$360

Last Mfg.'s Sug. Retail was $925.

> Subtract 33% without ejectors (Model 208).
> This model was previously designated the Model 75 EX.

* **Models 209 and 210** — better engraving and walnut than 207/207A. Model 210 is 20 ga. Importation disc. 1986.

	$580	$505	$450	$415	$375	$340	$310

Last Mfg.'s Sug. Retail was $672.

* **Models 211, 212, and 213** — top-of-the-line model, best quality engraving and walnut. Special order only.

	$2,350	$2,000	$1,780	$1,475	$1,200	$1,000	$850

Last Mfg.'s Sug. Retail was $3,100.

> Previously designated Model 110.

MODEL 251 — .410-3 in. bore, folding design, 26 in. barrels only, DTs, extractors, walnut stock and forearm. Imported 1987 only.

	$185	$165	$140	$120	$105	$95	$85

Last Mfg.'s Sug. Retail was $215.

MODEL 630 — 12 ga. only, 3 in. chambers, boxlock action with color case hardening, extractors, DTs, 26 or 28 in. barrels with fixed chokes, checkered English grip stock and forearm, includes deluxe shotgun case. Imported 1993 only.

	$625	$525	$450	$400	$365	$330	$295

Last Mfg.'s Sug. Retail was $699.

MODEL 640E (ENGLISH) — 12, 16, 20, 28 ga., or .410 bore, boxlock action, double triggers, straight grip stock, splinter forearm, concave rib, extractors, silver finished receiver. Imported 1986-1993.

	$750	$595	$540	$475	$415	$350	$295

Last Mfg.'s Sug. Retail was $850.

> Add $90 for 28 ga. or $120 for .410 bore.
> The "E" suffix in this model designates English configuration.

* **Model 640A (American)** — same ga.'s as Model 640E, except has non-selective single trigger, pistol grip, beavertail forearm, and raised matted rib. Imported 1986-1993.

	$840	$700	$630	$560	$475	$400	$350

Last Mfg.'s Sug. Retail was $970.

> Add $110 for 28 ga. or $130 for .410 bore.
> The "A" suffix in this model designates American configuration (pistol grip stock and single trigger).

MODEL 640M (MAGNUM) — 10 ga., 3½ in. chambers, 26, 30, or 32 in. barrels bored full and full, DTs, recoil pad. Imported 1989-1993.

	$860	$725	$650	$575	$495	$415	$365

Last Mfg.'s Sug. Retail was $1,000.

> In this model, the 26 in. barrels were referred to as the Turkey Gun, the 30 in. as Big Ten, and the 32 in. as the Goose Gun.

MODEL 640 SLUG GUN — 12 ga. only, 25 in. barrels bored IC/IC. Imported 1991-93.

	$995	$850	$725	$650	$575	$495	$415

Last Mfg.'s Sug. Retail was $1,120.

MODEL 645E (ENGLISH) — 12, 16, 20, 28 ga., or .410 bore, boxlock action, double triggers, straight grip stock, moderate engraving, splinter forearm, concave rib, ejectors, silver finished receiver. Imported 1986-1993.

	$940	$775	$675	$595	$500	$415	$365

Last Mfg.'s Sug. Retail was $1,090.

> Add $60 for 28 ga. or $110 for .410 bore.

Grading	100%	98%	95%	90%	80%	70%	60%

* Model 645E-XXV — available in all ga.'s, 25 in. barrels only, ejectors, Churchill rib, moderately engraved, silver finished receiver. Imported 1986-1993.

| | **$940** | **$775** | **$675** | **$595** | **$500** | **$415** | **$365** |

Last Mfg.'s Sug. Retail was $1,100.

Add $100 for 28 ga. or $130 for .410 bore.

* Model 645E Bi-Gauge — 2 barrel set available in either 20/28 ga. or 28 ga./.410 bore combination. Mfg. 1988-1992.

| | **$1,475** | **$1,175** | **$950** | **$800** | **$700** | **$600** | **$550** |

Last Mfg.'s Sug. Retail was $1,620.

Add $150 for 28 ga./.410 bore combo. (disc. 1991).

MODEL 645A (AMERICAN) — same ga.'s as 645E, except has non-selective single trigger, pistol grip, beavertail forearm, and raised matted rib. Imported 1986-1993.

| | **$1,025** | **$825** | **$700** | **$615** | **$515** | **$440** | **$400** |

Last Mfg.'s Sug. Retail was $1,200.

Add $110 for 28 ga. or $150 for .410 bore.

* Model 645A Bi-Gauge — 2 barrel set available in either 20/28 ga. or 28 ga./.410 bore combination. Mfg. 1988-92.

| | **$1,600** | **$1,325** | **$995** | **$850** | **$750** | **$625** | **$575** |

Last Mfg.'s Sug. Retail was $1,750.

Add $150 for 28 ga./.410 bore combo. (disc. 1991).

MODEL 650 ENGLISH OR AMERICAN — 12 ga. only, 28 in. barrels with IC/M choke tubes, extractors, choice of English (DT and straight grip stock) or American (SNT, pistol grip stock, and beavertail forearm), silver frame finish. Imported 1992-93.

| | **$825** | **$700** | **$630** | **$560** | **$475** | **$400** | **$350** |

Last Mfg.'s Sug. Retail was $920.

Add $120 for Model 650 American option.

MODEL 655 ENGLISH OR AMERICAN — 12 ga. only, 28 in. barrels with IC/M choke tubes, ejectors, choice of English (DT and straight grip stock) or American (SNT, pistol grip stock, and beavertail forearm), silver frame finish. Imported 1992-93.

| | **$925** | **$825** | **$700** | **$630** | **$560** | **$475** | **$400** |

Last Mfg.'s Sug. Retail was $1,150.

Add $110 for Model 655 American option.

MODEL 670E (ENGLISH) — 12, 16, or 20 ga., sidelock action, 26, 27, or 28 in. barrels, ejectors, engraved silver finished receiver, double triggers, straight grip. Imported 1986-91.

| | **$3,700** | **$2,975** | **$2,450** | **$1,850** | **$1,550** | **$1,375** | **$1,200** |

Last Mfg.'s Sug. Retail was $4,270.

Add $770 for 28 ga. or .410 bore.

This model was available by custom order only.

MODEL 680E-XXV (ENGLISH) — similar to Model 670E, except has color case hardened sideplates and 25 in. barrels only. Imported 1986-91.

| | **$3,500** | **$2,800** | **$2,300** | **$1,700** | **$1,475** | **$1,300** | **$1,175** |

Last Mfg.'s Sug. Retail was $4,070.

Add $400 for 28 ga. or .410 bore.

This model was available by custom order only.

BILL HANUS BIRDGUN — 16, 20, or 28 ga., boxlock action, 26 in. barrels bored SK1/SK2, Churchill raised rib, SNT, ejectors, case colored receiver, checkered straight grip walnut stock and semi-beavertail forearm, oil finish, lifetime warranty, $5\frac{1}{4}$-$6\frac{1}{2}$ lbs. Imported 1989-93.

| | **$1,100** | **$835** | **$700** | **$615** | **$515** | **$440** | **$400** |

Last Mfg.'s Sug. Retail was $1,270.

Add $130 for 28 ga.
Add $325 with hard case and accessories.

SHOTGUNS: SxS, SIDELOCK

Ugartechea sidelocks are best quality guns, made to individual customer specifications in approx. 4-8 months. Please contact the importer directly for current prices on some models listed below.

Grading	100%	98%	95%	90%	80%	70%	60%

MODEL 75/75EX — 12, 16, or 20 ga., case colored finish with minimal engraving, oil finished deluxe walnut stock and forearm. Importation began 1999.

MODEL 110 — 12, 16, 20, 28 ga. or .410 bore, choice of coin or case colored frame. Importation began 1999.

MODEL 116 — 12, 16, 20, 28 ga., or .410 bore, sidelock action, antique silver finish with elaborate floral engraving, deluxe oil finished walnut stock and forearm.

Mfg.'s Sug. Retail	$5,340	$5,000	$4,400	$3,800	$3,200	$2,600	$2,000	$1,500

Add $340 for 28 ga. or .410 bore.

MODEL 119 — 12, 16, 20, 28 ga., or .410 bore, sidelock action with case colored finish, English scroll engraving, deluxe oil finished walnut stock and forearm.

Mfg.'s Sug. Retail	$5,560	$5,150	$4,550	$3,950	$3,250	$2,600	$2,000	$1,500

Add $335 for 28 ga. or .410 bore.

MODEL 1000 — 12, 16, or 20 ga., sidelock action with polished finish, Italianate style engraving, deluxe oil finished walnut stock and forearm.

Mfg.'s Sug. Retail	$6,405	$5,950	$5,250	$4,500	$3,750	$3,000	$2,350	$1,750

MODEL 1042 — 12, 16, or 20 ga., sidelock action, antique silver finish, elaborate floral engraving, deluxe oil finished walnut stock and forearm.

Mfg.'s Sug. Retail	$8,550	$7,850	$7,000	$6,000	$5,100	$4,200	$3,350	$2,850

SPECIAL MODELS — available in all gauges with game scene engraving and/or gold inlays to customer specifications. POR only.

ULTIMATE

Please refer to Camex-Blaser USA in the C section of this text.

ULTRA LIGHT ARMS, INC.

Current manufacturer located in Granville, WV. Dealer direct and consumer sales.

PISTOLS: BOLT-ACTION

MODEL 20 HUNTERS PISTOL — various cals., 14 in. Douglas heavy barrel, 5-shot mag., Kevlar graphite reinforced stock in choice of 4 colors, Timney trigger, left-hand or right-hand bolt, approx. 4 lbs. Mfg. 1987-89.

	$1,295	$1,150	$975	$850	$700	$640	$575

Last Mfg.'s Sug. Retail was $1,600.

MODEL 20 REB — popular cals. from .22-250 Rem. through .308 Win. (other cals. on request), 14 in. Douglas #3 barrel, 5 shot mag., composite Kevlar graphite reinforced stock, green, brown, black, or camo Dupont Imron paint, Timney adj. trigger, includes hard case, 4 lbs. Mfg. 1994-95, reintroduced 1998 only.

	$1,475	$1,200	$1,000	$875	$750	$625	$500

Last Mfg.'s Sug. Retail was $1,600.

RIFLES: BOLT ACTION

ULTRA LIGHT RIFLE — caliber to customer specs., various actions, 2-position 3-function safety in top of stock, Timney trigger, Douglas 22 or 24 in. barrel, no sights, graphite reinforced stock with recoil pad, matte finish standard, other finishes at extra cost. Many special order features and services are available on these models - contact the manufacturer for prices, 4¾-5¾ lbs. New 1985.

MODEL 20 — many cals. available between .17 Rem. and .358 Win., short action, Kevlar stock.

Mfg.'s Sug. Retail	$2,500	$2,225	$1,675	$1,225	$950	$800	$700	$640

Add $100 for left-hand action.

Grading	100%	98%	95%	90%	80%	70%	60%

✳ **Model 20 RF** — .22 LR cal., convertible from repeater to single shot, 22 in. Douglas premium barrel, DuPont composite stock with Imron paint (some color options available), no sights, drilled and tapped, 5¼ lbs. New 1983.

Mfg.'s Sug. Retail	$800	$750	$650	$550	$475	$400	$350	$300

Add $50 for repeater action.

The first 100 pre-production rifles in this model are marked "1-of-100" consecutively, with owner's initials.

MODEL 24 — .25-06 Rem., .270 Win., .280 Rem. (mfg. 1992 only), .30-06, or 7mm Exp. cal., long action, Kevlar stock, 5¼ lbs.

Mfg.'s Sug. Retail	$2,600	$2,325	$1,775	$1,300	$995	$825	$700	$640

Add $100 for left-hand action.

MODEL 28 MAGNUM — .264 Win. Mag., .300 Win. Mag., .338 Win. Mag., 7mm Rem. Mag., or .416 Rigby (mfg. 1992 only) cal., Kevlar stock, 5¾ lbs.

Mfg.'s Sug. Retail	$2,900	$2,625	$1,975	$1,550	$1,225	$950	$700	$600

Add $100 for left-hand action.

MODEL 40 MAGNUM — .300 Wby. Mag. or .416 Rigby cal., otherwise similar to Model 28 Series. New 1993.

Mfg.'s Sug. Retail	$2,900	$2,625	$1,975	$1,550	$1,225	$950	$700	$600

Add $100 for left-hand action.

ULTRAMATIC

Previous trademark with manufacture located in Enzesfeld, Austria. Ultramatic Productions, GmbH, changed its name to Wolf Sporting Pistols in 1997. Please refer to new manufacture under the Wolf heading.

PISTOLS: SEMI-AUTO

ULTRAMATIC PISTOL — 9mm Para. cal., double action semi-auto, various barrel lengths, competition model with muzzle brake. Disc. approx. 1996.

	$1,150	$975	$850	$700	$640	$575	$500

UNIQUE

Current manufacturer located in Hendaye, France. Currently imported by Nygord Precision Products located in Prescott, AZ.

UNIQUE

PISTOLS: SEMI-AUTO

All currently manufactured Unique pistols are supplied with leatherette case, weights are additional.

KRIEGSMODELL L — 7.65mm cal., 9 shot, 3.2 in. barrel, blue, plastic grips, fixed sights. Mfg. 1940-1945, during German occupation of France, has German acceptance marks.

	$325	$250	$220	$200	$180	$160	$140

MODEL RR — post-war commercial version of Kreigsmodell, higher quality finish. Mfg. 1951-disc.

	$180	$170	$155	$130	$120	$110	$90

Add 15% for .22 LR.

MODEL B/CF — 7.65mm cal., 9 shot, or .380 auto cal., 8 shot, 4 in. barrel, blue, plastic thumbrest grips. Mfg. 1954-disc.

	$205	$195	$175	$155	$145	$130	$110

MODEL D6 — .22 LR cal., 10 shot, 6 in. barrel, adj. sights, blue, plastic grips. Mfg. 1954-disc.

	$300	$250	$200	$160	$145	$135	$120

MODEL D2 — similar to D6, except 4½ in. barrel.

	$300	$250	$200	$160	$145	$135	$120

MODEL L — .22 LR cal., 10 shot, 7.65mm cal., 7 shot, and .380 ACP cal., 6 shot, 3.3 in. barrel, fixed sights, steel and alloy frame offered, plastic grips. Mfg. 1955-disc.

	$250	$200	$150	$130	$115	$100	$90

Grading	100%	98%	95%	90%	80%	70%	60%

MODEL MIKROS POCKET — .22 Short and .25 ACP cal., 6 shot, fixed sights, blue, plastic grips, steel or alloy frame. Mfg. 1957-disc.

	$200	$155	$140	$120	$100	$90	$75

MODEL DES/32U — .32 S&W L Wadcutter cal., 5.9 in. barrel, dry firing device, ergonomically designed French walnut grips with adj. hand rest, 5 or 6 shot mag., 40.2 oz.

Mfg.'s Sug. Retail	$1,350	$1,225	$1,025	$900	$775	$625	$500	$450

MODEL DES/69 MATCH — .22 LR cal. target pistol, wraparound grips, adj. features. Imported 1986-1988.

	$995	$850	$725	$625	$550	$490	$445

Last Mfg.'s Sug. Retail was $1,198.

Add $62 for left-hand model.

MODEL DES/69U STANDARD MATCH — .22 LR cal., 5 shot mag., 5.9 in. barrel, adj. rear sight, adj. target stippled stocks, blue finish only. Importation began 1969.

Mfg.'s Sug. Retail	$1,250	$1,150	$995	$875	$750	$625	$500	$450

Add $30 for left-hand model.

MODEL DES/823-U RAPID FIRE MATCH — .22 Short cal., 5 shot, 6 in. barrel, adj. sight, adj. trigger, adj. walnut target grips, squared barrel assembly, dry fire mechanism. Imported 1974-1988.

	$1,100	$850	$725	$625	$550	$490	$445

Last Mfg.'s Sug. Retail was $1,300.

Add $60 for left-hand model.

MODEL 2000-U — .22 Short cal. only, specifically designed for rapid fire U.I.T. competition, 5.9 in. barrel, ergonomic styled grips with adj. hand rest, 5 shot mag. (inserted in top), 43.4 oz. Importation disc. 1995.

	$1,300	$1,050	$925	$775	$625	$500	$450

Last Mfg.'s Sug. Retail was $1,450.

Add $30 for left-hand model.

RIFLES: BOLT ACTION

T66 MATCH RIFLE — .22 LR cal., single shot, bolt action, 25½ in. barrel, micro rear and globe front sight, full target stock. Mfg. 1966-disc.

	$425	$410	$390	$350	$300	$280	$250

MODEL F 11 — .22 LR cal., military trainer, adj. sights, target walnut stock. Limited importation.

	$560	$435	$350	$285	$260	$240	$220

Last Mfg.'s Sug. Retail was $695.

MODEL T DIOPTRA — .22 LR or .22 Mag. cal., bolt action Sporter with 23.6 in. barrel and adj. rear sight, 5 (.22 Mag. only) or 10 shot mag., grooved receiver for scope, checkered French walnut Monte Carlo stock, approx. 6.4 lbs. Importation disc. 1995.

	$795	$700	$600	$525	$450	$375	$300

Last Mfg.'s Sug. Retail was $890.

MODEL T/SM — .22 LR or .22 Mag cal., bolt action Target variation with 20½ in. barrel, no sights, 5 (.22 Mag. only) or 10 shot mag., stippled pistol grip stock and forearm, right or left-hand action, 6.6 lbs. Importation disc. 1995.

	$850	$735	$625	$525	$450	$375	$300

Last Mfg.'s Sug. Retail was $960.

Add $50 for left-hand action.

MODEL T/STANDARD UIT — .22 LR cal., designed for UIT competition, single shot, aperture sights, adj. cheekpiece and buttplate on stippled walnut stock, right or left-hand action, 10.8 lbs. Importation disc. 1995.

	$1,350	$1,125	$975	$850	$725	$625	$525

Last Mfg.'s Sug. Retail was $1,450.

Add $50 for left-hand action.

MODEL T/LIBRE UIT FREE RIFLE — .22 LR cal., Free Rifle variation of the Model T/Standard UIT.

Nygord Precision Products should be contacted directly for pricing on this model.

Grading	100%	98%	95%	90%	80%	70%	60%

UNITED SPORTING ARMS, INC.

Previous manufacturer located in Tucson, AZ. Manufacture ceased in early 1986.

REVOLVERS: SINGLE ACTION

SEVILLE — .357 Mag., .41 Mag., .44 Mag., or .45 LC cal., single action revolver, 4⅝, 5½, 6½, or 7½ in. barrels, adj. sights, smooth walnut grips.

$395	$350	$315	$280	$260	$240	$220

Last Mfg.'s Sug. Retail was $435.

* ***Stainless steel*** — all stainless version of the Seville.

$395	$350	$315

Last Mfg.'s Sug. Retail was $435.

* ***Silver Seville*** — similar to Seville, except has blue barrel, and high polish stainless steel grip frame.

$425	$370	$330

Last Mfg.'s Sug. Retail was $460.

* ***Stainless .357 Maxi*** — available in 5½ or 7½ in. barrel only.

$575	$475	$395

Last Mfg.'s Sug. Retail was $465.

* ***Stainless .375 USA*** — only in 7½ in. barrel.

$625	$525	$425

Last Mfg.'s Sug. Retail was $490.

* ***Stainless .454 Mag.*** — only in 7½ in. barrel, 5 shot.

$700	$600	$500

Last Mfg.'s Sug. Retail was $595.

Note: In late 1986, some .454 Mags. were made up from parts purchased from the manufacturer. Unfortunately, while the exterior appearance might seem normal, they were not involved with any type of factory quality control program. As a result, shooting these non-factory revolvers could be dangerous, and careful inspection should be made before purchasing/shooting this particular specimen.

* ***Eldorado Stainless*** — .44 Mag., 10½ in. barrel, adj. sights.

$700	$600	$500

SILVER SEVILLE SILHOUETTE — .357 Mag., .41 Mag., or .44 Mag. cal., single action revolver, 10½ in. barrel, adj. sights, Pachmayr grips, blued barrel finish with stainless grip frame.

$445	$370	$330	$295	$270	$250	$230

Last Mfg.'s Sug. Retail was $485.

* ***Stainless steel*** — stainless version of the Silver Seville Silhouette.

$425	$370	$330

Last Mfg.'s Sug. Retail was $460.

* ***Stainless .357 Maxi*** — available in 10½ in. barrel only.

$575	$475	$395

Last Mfg.'s Sug. Retail was $480.

* ***Stainless .375 USA*** — available in 10½ in. barrel only.

$625	$525	$425

Last Mfg.'s Sug. Retail was $515.

* ***Stainless .454 Mag.*** — available in 10½ in. barrel only, 5 shot.

$700	$600	$500

Last Mfg.'s Sug. Retail was $620.

SHERIFF MODEL — .357 Mag., .38 Spl., .44 Spl., .44 Mag., or .45 LC cal., single action revolver, 3½ in. barrel, adj. sights, smooth walnut grips.

$395	$350	$315	$280	$260	$240	$220

Last Mfg.'s Sug. Retail was $435.

* ***Stainless steel*** — stainless version of the Sheriff Model.

$395	$350	$315

Last Mfg.'s Sug. Retail was $435.

Grading	100%	98%	95%	90%	80%	70%	60%

U.S. HISTORICAL SOCIETY

Previous organization which marketed historically significant firearms reproductions until April, 1994. Located in Richmond, VA. Most firearms were manufactured by the Williamsburg Firearms Manufactory and the Virginia Firearms Manufactory.

On April 1, 1994, the Antique Arms Division of the U.S. Historical Society was acquired by America Remembers located in Mechanicsville, VA. America Remembers' affiliates include the Armed Forces Commemorative Society, American Heroes & Legends, and the United States Society of Arms and Armor. Issues that were not fully subscribed are now available through America Remembers (please refer to listing in A section).

The information listed below represents current information up until America Remembers acquired the Antique Arms Division of the U.S. Historical Society.

PISTOLS: SPECIAL EDITIONS

ANDREW JACKSON

* **Silver Edition** — 2,500 mfg.

    $2,100 $1,750 $1,400

    Issue price was $2,100.

* **Gold Edition** — 100 mfg.

    $5,500 $3,995 $2,750

    Issue price was $5,500.

PITCAIRN — 900 mfg.

    $2,950 $2,300 $1,750

Issue price was $2,950.

THOMAS JEFFERSON — 1,000 mfg.

    $3,500 $2,750 $1,995

Issue price was $1,900.

HAMILTON — BURR DUELING PISTOLS — 1,200 mfg. in 1981.

    $3,500 $2,750 $1,995

Issue price was $2,995.

WASHINGTON AND LEE FLINTLOCK PISTOLS — .69 cal., flintlock pistols with $9^{15}/16$ in. barrels, burl walnut stocks with sterling silver fittings, engraved silver plated lock plates, trigger guard, and sideplate, firing capability, cased with accessories, limited issue of 1,000 in 1989.

    $2,700 $2,150 $1,650

Last Mfg.'s Sug. Retail was $2,700.

GEORGE WASHINGTON — includes pair of flintlocks, 975 mfg. 1976, cased, issue price was initially $3,000, and ended at $3,500.

    $4,250 $3,400 $2,450

H. DERINGER PISTOL SET — .41 cal., percussion, reproduction of H. Deringer's famous pistol. Available with sterling silver mounts (1,000 pair manufactured — issue price $1,900), 14Kt. gold mounted (100 pair mfg.-$2,700 issue price), precious gem stone mounted (only 5 pair mfg. — $25,000 issue price). Mfg. 1978.

* **Silver mounted**

    $2,500 $1,750 $1,000

* **14Kt. gold mounted**

    $7,500 $5,000 $3,000

* **18Kt. jewel mounted** — too limited a supply for price evaluation.

TEXAS PATERSON EDITION — reproduction of the famous Colt folding trigger model mfg. in Paterson, NJ, engraved, cased. 1,000 mfg. starting in 1988. Cased with accessories.

    $2,500 $1,900 $1,450

Last Mfg.'s Sug. Retail was $2,500.

This model is an exact reproduction of the original Colt Paterson ser. no. 755, Model 5.

Grading	100%	98%	95%	90%	80%	70%	60%

SAM HOUSTON WALKER — .44 cal., reproduction of the Colt Walker, 9 in. barrel, extensive gold etching on highly polished blued surface, smooth walnut stocks with S. Houston medallions, cased with accessories. 2,500 mfg.
$2,300 $2,000 $1,575
Issue price was $2,300

TEXAS RANGER DRAGOON — .44 cal., features silver-plated cylinder, trigger guard, and grip-straps, color case hardened frame and loading lever, multiple 24 Kt. etchings on barrel and frame front, cased with accessories, 66 oz. 1,000 mfg. in 1990 only.
$1,585 $1,050 $795
Last Mfg.'s Sug. Retail was $1,585.

TOWER OF LONDON COL. SAM COLT DRAGOON — .44 cal., exact reproduction of the Second Model Dragoon, 7½ in. barrel, hand engraved, Texas ranger cylinder scene, one piece walnut grip with inscribed sterling silver plaque, case hardened frame, hammer, loading lever and rammer, cased with accessories, limited issue of 1,000 in 1989.
$2,450 $1,950 $1,500
Last Mfg.'s Sug. Retail was $2,450.

ROBERT E. LEE MODEL 1851 NAVY — .36 cal. only, reproduction of the 1851 Navy Colt, extensive gold etching, cylinder scene portrays historical Civil War events, walnut stocks with Robert E. Lee medallion, cased with accessories, 41 oz. 2,500 mfg. during 1984.
$2,100 $1,900 $1,450
Issue price is $2,100.

MONITOR AND VIRGINIA MODEL 1851 NAVY REVOLVER — .44 cal., issued to commemorate the Civil War naval battle between the USS Monitor and Confederate Virginia, features gold etchings on barrel, frame, and Monitor/Virginia battle scene on cylinder, cased, 41 oz. 1,000 mfg. in 1991.
$1,250 $875 $500
Last Mfg.'s Sug. Retail was $1,250.

STONEWALL JACKSON MODEL 1851 REVOLVER — .36 cal., reproduction of Colt's Model 1851 Navy, elaborate gold etching on frame and barrel, walnut grip with medallion, cased with sterling medallion and silver-plated powder flask. 1988 release. 2,500 total mfg.
$2,100 $1,650 $1,250
Last Mfg.'s Sug. Retail was $2,100.

JEFFERSON DAVIS 1851 NAVY REVOLVER — .36 cal., extensive Nimschke style engraving on barrel, loading lever, frame, and trigger, case hardened frame with silver plated brass backstrap and trigger guard, includes engraved, silver plated detachable shoulder stock, cased with accessories, 41 oz. 1,000 mfg. in 1990 only.
$2,750 $1,850 $1,250
Last Mfg.'s Sug. Retail was $2,750.

MODEL 1851 U.S. NAVY REVOLVER — .36 cal., 7½ in. octagon barrel, features gold etched cylinder and other embellishments, brass trigger guard and backstrap plated with 24 Kt. gold, 41 oz. 1,000 mfg. in 1988 only.
$1,250 $875 $500
Last Mfg.'s Sug. Retail was $1,250.

MODEL 1851 PONY EXPRESS REVOLVER — .36 cal., features gold-plated cylinder scene, other scroll work, and barrel address, walnut grips, cased. 1,000 mfg. beginning 1992.
$1,650 $1,150 $850
Last Mfg.'s Sug. Retail was $1,650.

U.S. CAVALRY MODEL 1860 ARMY — .44 cal., reproduction of the Colt Model 1860, stag grips, gold etched cylinder scene, cased with brass buckle. 975 manufactured starting in 1988.
$1,450 $1,050 $800
Last Mfg.'s Sug. Retail was $1,450.

FREDERIC REMINGTON MODEL 1860 ARMY REVOLVER — .44 cal., issued to commemorate Frederic Remington's 100th anniversary as an associate of the National Academy of Design, features gold etched barrel, cylinder (with 5 panels), trigger, frame, and gripstraps, cased with accessories, 42 oz. 1,000 mfg. in 1990 only.
$1,500 $1,000 $775
Last Mfg.'s Sug. Retail was $1,500.

Grading	100%	98%	95%	90%	80%	70%	60%

BUFFALO BILL CENTENNIAL MODEL 1860 ARMY — .44 cal., reproduction of the Colt Model 1860, bonded ivory stocks, extensive gold etchings portraying various wild west scenes, bonded ivory powder flask, brass accessories, cased. 2,500 mfg. 1983.
$1,950 $1,450 $1,100

Issue price was $1,950.

BAT MASTERSON MODEL 1860 ARMY — .44 cal., original roll engraved pattern on cylinder, walnut grips, blued barrel decorated in 24 Kt. gold. 2,500 mfg. beginning 1991.
$1,250 $875 $500

Last Mfg.'s Sug. Retail was $1,250.

GETTYSBURG 1860 ARMY — .44 cal., blued steel with gold-plated cylinder scene, backstraps, and other small parts, walnut grips, cased with belt buckle. 1,863 mfg. beginning 1994.
$1,270 $885 $500

Last Mfg.'s Sug. Retail was $1,270.

Add $145 for case.

SECRET SERVICE MUSEUM EDITION — 500 mfg. during 1988.
$2,750 $2,000 $1,600

Last Mfg.'s Sug. Retail was $2,750.

* *Secret Service Investigator's Edition* — 1,000 mfg. during 1988.
$1,250 $875 $500

Last Mfg.'s Sug. Retail was $1,250.

GEORGE JONES SAA — .45 LC cal., 5½ in. barrel, blued steel with multiple 24 Kt. gold decorations, including musical staff with notes and name on barrel, cased. 950 mfg. during 1993.
$1,675 $1,150 $675

Last Mfg.'s Sug. Retail was $1,675.

RICHARD PETTY SILVER EDITION SAA — .45 LC cal., 5½ in. barrel, blue steel with silver decoration, hand fitted faux ivory grips, Petty's signature carved on velvet lined cherry display case, comes with signed Richard Petty portrait and numbered to match gun. 1,000 mfg. starting 1992.
$1,675 $1,150 $825

Last Mfg.'s Sug. Retail was $1,675.

KING RICHARD HAND ENGRAVED COLT .45 SAA — .45 LC cal., 5½ in. barrel, mfg. by Colt, silver finished with multiple inlays and scroll engraving, scrimshawed ivory grips, cased. 100 mfg. beginning 1993.
$4,500 $2,950 $1,750

Last Mfg.'s Sug. Retail was $4,500.

CHARLTON HESTON SAA — .45 LC cal., 5½ in. barrel, blued steel finish with decorative gold and silver vine inlays, walnut grips with medallions. 500 mfg. beginning 1993.
$1,850 $1,275 $925

Last Mfg.'s Sug. Retail was $1,850.

HOPALONG CASSIDY COWBOY EDITION SAA — .45 LC cal., 5½ in. barrel, blue steel with silver decorations on cylinder, barrel, and frame, hand fitted genuine black horn grips, velvet lined cherry display case. 950 mfg. starting 1993.
$1,675 $1,150 $825

Last Mfg.'s Sug. Retail was $1,675.

HOPALONG PREMIER COLT EDITION SAA — .45 LC, 5½ in. barrel, silver-plated, deep hand engraving, 18 Kt. gold inlays, hand fitted genuine black buffalo horn inset with William Boyd's monogram in sterling silver, gold-embossed leather display case lined in velvet. 100 mfg. starting 1993.
$4,500 $3,500 $2,450

Last Mfg.'s Sug. Retail was $4,500.

MEL TORME COLT SAA — .45 LC cal., 5½ in. barrel, elaborate silver engraving with 24 Kt. gold highlights, mother-of-pearl grips, leather display case with Mel Torme's signature in gold. 100 mfg. starting 1992.
$4,500 $3,500 $2,950

Last Mfg.'s Sug. Retail was $4,500.

Grading	100%	98%	95%	90%	80%	70%	60%

ROY ROGERS COWBOY EDITION SAA — .45 LC cal., SAA revolver, 4¾ in. barrel, features gold-plated cylinder and other 24 Kt. etchings on barrel, frame and gripstrap, hand fitted stag grips, made to commemorate Roy Rogers 50th Anniversary (1940-1990), cased. 2,500 mfg. in 1990 only.

$1,350 $900 $550

Last Mfg.'s Sug. Retail was $1,350.

* *Roy Premier Edition SAA* — similar to Cowboy Edition, except has elaborate inlays and engraving. 250 mfg. in 1990 only.

$4,500 $2,950 $1,750

Last Mfg.'s Sug. Retail was $4,500.

U.S. MARSHALS WYATT EARP SAA — .45 LC cal., 4¾ in. blued barrel, select walnut grips, case hardened frame and hammer, Marshal's etched 24 Kt. badge inset in grip. 2,500 mfg. beginning 1991.

$1,250 $875 $500

Last Mfg.'s Sug. Retail was $1,250.

NATIONAL COWBOY HALL OF FAME SAA — .45 LC cal., 4¾ in. barrel, 24 Kt. filigree on barrel and gold symbols of the American cowboy on cylinder, staghorn grips, velvet lined display case with glass lid. 1,000 mfg. beginning 1992.

$1,600 $1,125 $825

Last Mfg.'s Sug. Retail was $1,600.

INTERPOL COLT SAA — .45 LC cal., 4¾ in. barrel, hand engraving based on Kornbrath Interpol Model, silver-plated faux ivory eagle grips, display cased in luxurious leather (designed like a book), 154 mfg. beginning 1991.

$4,500 $2,950 $1,750

Last Mfg.'s Sug. Retail was $4,500.

EISENHOWER .45 AUTO PISTOL — .45 ACP cal., 1911 Govt. Model mfg. by Springfield Armory, 7 shot mag., 5 in. barrel, checkered walnut grips inset with 2 bronze medallions, blued steel slide decorated in 24 Kt. gold, Eisenhower's signature etched on velvet-lined walnut display case, comes with framed portrait of D. Eisenhower, signed by his son, John Eisenhower. 1,000 mfg. beginning 1992.

$1,675 $1,150 $825

Last Mfg.'s Sug. Retail was $1,675.

"DON'T GIVE UP THE SHIP" MODEL .45 AUTO — .45 ACP cal., 1911 Colt Govt. Model, 7 shot mag., 5 in. barrel, rosewood grips, blue steel decorated with 24 Kt. gold, velvet-lined solid oak case with symbol of U.S. Navy carved into top of lid. 1,997 mfg. starting 1993.

$1,485 $1,075 $825

Last Mfg.'s Sug. Retail was $1,485.

AMERICAN EAGLE COLT .45 AUTO — .45 ACP cal., features large eagle with wing spread on sides of slide, other gold small parts, cased. 2,500 mfg. beginning 1993.

$1,950 $1,375 $975

Last Mfg.'s Sug. Retail was $1,950.

REVOLVERS: MINIATURE SPECIAL EDITIONS

1847 WALKER PRESIDENTIAL EDITION —miniature reproduction of 1847 Colt Walker, color case hardened receiver, all parts operational, sterling silver grips, full coverage engraving, cased. 1,500 mfg. starting 1990.

$1,575 $1,100 $825

Last Mfg.'s Sug. Retail was $1,575.

* *1847 Walker Classic Edition* — similar to Presidential Edition, except has walnut grips and frame is not engraved, cased. 1,500 mfg. starting 1990.

$625 $450 $325

Last Mfg.'s Sug. Retail was $625.

1851 NAVY PRESIDENTIAL EDITION — miniature reproduction of 1851 Navy Colt, color case hardened receiver, all parts operational, mother-of-pearl grips, full coverage engraving, cased. 1,500 mfg. starting 1988.

$1,575 $1,100 $825

Last Mfg.'s Sug. Retail was $1,575.

Grading	100%	98%	95%	90%	80%	70%	60%

* ***1851 Classic Edition*** — similar to Presidential Edition, except has walnut grips and cylinder is roll-engraved, cased. 3,500 mfg. starting 1986.

$525 $400 $295

Last Mfg.'s Sug. Retail was $525.

1860 ARMY PRESIDENTIAL EDITION — miniature reproduction of 1860 Army Colt, color case hardened engraved receiver and barrel, roll-engraved cylinder scene, all parts operational, ivory grips, cherry cased. 1,500 mfg. starting 1988.

$1,575 $1,200 $875

Last Mfg.'s Sug. Retail was $1,575.

* ***1860 Classic Edition*** — similar to Presidential Edition without engraving, except has rosewood grips, cased. 3,500 mfg. starting 1988.

$525 $400 $295

Last Mfg.'s Sug. Retail was $525.

1861 NAVY PRESIDENTIAL EDITION — miniature reproduction of 1861 Navy Colt, color case hardened engraved receiver and barrel, roll-engraved cylinder scene, all parts operational, includes detachable shoulder stock, cased. 1,500 mfg. starting 1990.

$1,500 $1,150 $850

Last Mfg.'s Sug. Retail was $1,500.

* ***1861 Navy Classic Edition*** — similar to Presidential Edition without engraving, cased. 1,500 mfg. starting 1990.

$750 $550 $395

Last Mfg.'s Sug. Retail was $750.

SA ARMY PRESIDENTIAL EDITION — miniature reproduction of 1873 SAA Colt, nickel-plated receiver and barrel with scroll engraving, gold-plated cylinder, hammer, trigger, and ejector rod housing, one piece ivory grips, cherry cased. 1,500 mfg. starting 1988.

$1,550 $1,100 $825

Last Mfg.'s Sug. Retail was $1,550.

This miniature is an exact replica of Serial No. 114 SAA (earliest known gold engraved SAA). All features are the same, only on a miniature basis.

* ***SA Army Classic Edition*** — similar to Presidential Edition without engraving, except has color case hardened receiver and blued metal parts, one piece rosewood grips. 1,500 mfg. starting 1988.

$575 $425 $300

Last Mfg.'s Sug. Retail was $575.

The Classic Edition is a miniaturized, exact reproduction of Colt Serial No. 1 (includes pinched frame, slanted barrel address marking, donut ejector rod head, knurled hammer spur, etc.). All are serial numbered 1.

RIFLES: SPECIAL EDITIONS

CONFEDERATE COMMEMORATIVE RIFLE — replicates Cook & Brother original 1861 Model Carbine, 1,500 mfg. during 1986, includes wood wall mount and velvet sleeved bag, 24 Kt. gold plating and accenting.

$1,750 $1,450 $995

Issue price was $1,900.

SHOTGUNS: SPECIAL EDITIONS

CHUCK YEAGER SHOTGUN — 12 ga. only, O/U boxlock action with engraved silver finished sideplates depicting Gen. Yeager and his P-51 Mustang, SST, 28 in. VR barrels with choke tubes, cased with accessories. 100 mfg. beginning 1989.

$12,500 $9,000 $6,250

Last Mfg.'s Sug. Retail was $12,500.

This model was mfg. by Bertuzzi located in Brescia, Italy. Over 120 hours were required to engrave each gun.

ARNOLD PALMER SHOTGUN — 20 ga., SxS boxlock with engraved sideplates depicting Arnold Palmer in 24 Kt. gold as well as other inlays, 26 in. barrels, 6 lbs. 6 oz. 100 mfg. beginning 1990.

$9,750 $6,250 $3,995

Last Mfg.'s Sug. Retail was $9,750.

Grading	100%	98%	95%	90%	80%	70%	60%

CHRISTOPHER COLUMBUS SHOTGUN — 20 ga., O/U boxlock action featuring engraved silver-plated sideplate depicting various scenes in 24 Kt. gold, 25.4 in. barrels with choke tubes, cased with accessories. 200 mfg. beginning 1991.

$12,500 $9,000 $6,250

Last Mfg.'s Sug. Retail was $12,500.

UNITED STATES FIRE ARMS MANUFACTURING COMPANY, INC.

Current manufacturer established during 1995 and located in Hartford, CT (at Colt's original old Armory).

REVOLVERS: SAA

SINGLE ACTION ARMY — .22 LR (new 1996), .22 Mag. (new 1996), .32-20 (new 1998), .357 Mag. (disc. 1998), .38-40 WCF, .41 Colt (new 1999), .44-40 WCF, .45 ACP, or .45 LC cal., 3 (no ejector), 4 (no ejector), 4¾, 5½, 7½, or 10 (new 1997) in. barrel, original screw cylinder release, choice of Full Dome Blue, Dome Blue/Old Armoury Bone Case, or nickel finish.

Mfg.'s Sug. Retail	$939	$800	$700	$600	$500	$400	$350	$295

Add approx. $94-$123 for Dome Blue/Old Armoury Bone Case finish.
Add approx. $145-$158 for nickel finish.
Add $10 for 5½ in. barrel.
Add $18 for 7½ in. barrel.
Add $96 for 10 in. barrel.
Subtract $27 for 3 in. barrel w/o ejector rod.
Subtract $18 for 4 in. barrel w/o ejector rod.

* *Flattop Target SAA* — similar to SAA, except has flattop receiver with target sights and two-piece rubber grips. New 1997.

Mfg.'s Sug. Retail	$993	$840	$725	$625	$525	$425	$325	$295

Add approx. $125 for Dome Blue/Old Armoury Bone Case finish.
Add approx. $65 for nickel finish.
Add approx. $10 for 5½ in. or $30 for 7½ in. barrel.

* *Henry Nettleton Cavalry Revolver* — .45 LC cal., faithful Cavalry Model reproduction following the original U.S. Government inspector specifications. Disc. 1998.

$875 $725 $575

Last Mfg.'s Sug. Retail was $950.

BISLEY MODEL SAA — same cals. as SAA, 4¾, 5½, 7½, or 10 in. barrel, patterned after the Colt Bisley Model. Disc. 1998.

$550	$480	$425	$375	$335	$300	$275

Last Mfg.'s Sug. Retail was $652.

Add approx. $10 for 5½, 7½, or 10 in. barrel.
Add approx. $95 for Dome Blue/Old Armoury Bone Case finish.
Add approx. $150 for nickel finish.

BIRD HEAD MODEL SAA — same cals. as SAA, patterned after the Colt Model 1877 Thunderer, 3½, 4, or 4¾ in. barrel with ejector, case colored frame. New 1997.

Mfg.'s Sug. Retail	$939	$800	$700	$600	$500	$400	$350	$295

Add approx. $5 for 4 or 4¾ in. barrel.
Add approx. $100 for Dome Blue/Old Armoury Bone Case finish.
Add approx. $145 for nickel finish.

UNIVERSAL FIREARMS

Previous division of Iver Johnson's Arms, Inc. that was established during 1982. Formerly imported out of Hialeah, FL. Previously manufactured in Jacksonville, AR.

Grading	100%	98%	95%	90%	80%	70%	60%

PISTOLS: SEMI-AUTO

MODEL 3000 ENFORCER PISTOL — .30 Carbine cal., walnut stock, 11¼ in. barrel, 17¾ in. overall, 15, and 30 shot. Mfg. 1964-1983. Also see listing under Iver Johnson.

	100%	98%	95%	90%	80%	70%	60%
Blued finish	$275	$235	$200	$185	$170	$160	$150
Nickel-plated	$295	$250	$235	$220	$200	$185	$165
Gold-plated	$350	$275	$250	$225	$200	$185	$165
Stainless	$375	$300	$225				

Add $50 for Teflon-S finish.

RIFLES: SEMI-AUTO, CARBINES

MODEL 440 VULCAN — .44 Mag. cal., slide action, 18¼ in. barrel with adj. rear and front ramp sight, 5 shot detachable mag.

	100%	98%	95%	90%	80%	70%	60%
	$325	$275	$230	$195	$175	$150	$135

1000 MILITARY — .30 Carbine cal., "G.I." copy, satin blue, birch stock, 18 in. barrel. Disc.

	100%	98%	95%	90%	80%	70%	60%
	$229	$180	$170	$160	$150	$135	$125

MODEL 1003 — 16, 18, or 20 in. barrel, .30 M1 copy, blued finish, adj. sight, birch stock, 5½ lbs. Also see listing under Iver Johnson.

	100%	98%	95%	90%	80%	70%	60%
	$285	$250	$225	$200	$180	$160	$140

Last Mfg.'s Sug. Retail was $203.

* *Model 1010* — nickel finish, disc.

	100%	98%	95%	90%	80%	70%	60%
	$300	$265	$240	$210	$180	$155	$120

* *Model 1015* — gold electroplated, disc.

	100%	98%	95%	90%	80%	70%	60%
	$325	$275	$250	$215	$185	$160	$130

Add $45 for 4X scope.

1005 DELUXE — .30 Carbine cal., custom Monte Carlo walnut stock, high polish blue, oil finish on wood.

	100%	98%	95%	90%	80%	70%	60%
	$325	$275	$250	$225	$200	$180	$170

1006 STAINLESS — .30 Carbine cal., stainless steel construction, birch stock, 18 in. barrel, 6 lbs.

	100%	98%	95%
	$350	$300	$265

Last Mfg.'s Sug. Retail was $234.

1020 TEFLON — .30 Carbine cal., Dupont Teflon-S finish on metal parts, black or grey color, Monte Carlo stock.

	100%	98%	95%
	$325	$275	$250

1256 "FERRET" — .256 Win. Mag. cal., M1 Action, satin blue, birch stock, 18 in. barrel, 5½ lbs.

	100%	98%	95%	90%	80%	70%	60%
	$275	$250	$175	$165	$155	$145	$135

Last Mfg.'s Sug. Retail was $219.

2200 LEATHERNECK — .22 LR cal., recoil operated action, birch stock, satin blue, 18 in. barrel, 5½ lbs.

	100%	98%	95%	90%	80%	70%	60%
	$240	$190	$180	$170	$160	$145	$135

5000 PARATROOPER — .30 Carbine cal., metal folding extension, walnut stock, 16 or 18 in. barrel.

	100%	98%	95%	90%	80%	70%	60%
	$375	$325	$285	$250	$225	$200	$130

Last Mfg.'s Sug. Retail was $234.

5006 PARATROOPER STAINLESS — similar to 5000, only stainless with 18 in. barrel only.

	100%	98%	95%
	$395	$340	$295

Last Mfg.'s Sug. Retail was $281.

1981 COMMEMORATIVE CARBINE — .30 Carbine cal., "G.I Military" model, cased with accessories. Mfg. for 40th Anniversary 1941-1981.

	100%	98%	95%
	$650	$490	$400

SHOTGUNS

All Universal shotguns were disc. after 1982.

Grading	100%	98%	95%	90%	80%	70%	60%

MODEL 7312 O/U — 12 ga., 30 in. full and mod., VR barrel, boxlock, vent. barrel spacer, SST, auto ejectors, barrels ported to reduce recoil, engraved, color case hardened receiver, trap or skeet style, checkered select stock.

	$1,650	$1,540	$1,485	$1,430	$1,320	$1,210	$1,045

MODEL 7412 O/U — similar to 7312, without ejectors, blue and silver receiver.

	$1,430	$1,210	$1,155	$1,100	$9,900	$880	$825

MODEL 7712 O/U — 12 ga., 26 or 28 in. barrel, VR, non-selective single trigger, extractors, light engraving, checkered pistol grip stock.

	$440	$415	$385	$360	$330	$275	$220

MODEL 7812 O/U — similar to 7712, with auto ejectors and more engraving.

	$605	$580	$550	$525	$470	$415	$385

MODEL 7912 O/U — similar to 7812, with selective single trigger and gold damascene engraving.

	$1,210	$1,155	$1,100	$1,045	$965	$880	$825

MODEL 7112 SxS — 12 ga., 26 or 28 in. barrels, various chokes, boxlock, extractors, engraved case hardened frame, checkered pistol grip stock.

	$330	$305	$275	$250	$195	$165	$140

DOUBLE WING SxS — 10, 12, 20 ga., or .410 bore, 26, 28, or 30 in. barrels, various chokes, double triggers, boxlock, extractors, checkered pistol grip stock.

	$330	$305	$275	$250	$195	$165	$140
10 gauge.	$385	$360	$330	$305	$250	$220	$165

MODEL 7212 SINGLE BARREL TRAP — 12 ga., 30 in. full, Simmons type VR, engraved case colored frame, vent. barrel to reduce recoil, boxlock, auto ejector, select checkered trap style stock.

	$1,100	$990	$935	$880	$770	$715	$605

U.S. MILITARY

See listings under Colt, Springfield Armory, and Winchester. U.S. Military Trench and Riot guns may be found under the "Trench/Riot Shotguns" category in the T section of this text.

U.S. M1 CARBINES/RIFLES

Previous manufacture for the military by various makers listed below.

CARBINES: SEMI-AUTO

U.S. M1 CARBINE (MILITARY & COMMERCIAL) — .30 Carbine cal., 18 in. barrel, 15 or 30 shot box mag., wood stocked, two or four position aperture rear, blade front sight with protective ears, with or without bayonet lug. This weapon was designed by Winchester for the U.S. government, over 6 million were produced by 10 different companies, while Plainfield was mfg. after the war for civilian sales. It is a gas operated lightweight carbine that was also used by other countries' armed forces. Makers and values as follows. Values are for original, unmodified carbines, with proper parts makers and stock cartouches. Some variations have the type III barrel band.

Values below are for original mfg. only, not recent imports (usually denoted by visible import markings and/or alterations to original finish).
Subtract 30% for original finish guns that have been changed back to the original configuration by switching parts.
Subtract 50% for modified guns with adj. sight and bayonet lug.

Underwood	$775	$625	$495	$400	$350	$300	$275
S.G. Saginaw	$750	$600	$475	$400	$350	$300	$275
Quality Hardware	$775	$625	$495	$415	$370	$325	$295
Nat'l Postal Meter	$850	$715	$525	$425	$375	$325	$295
IBM	$850	$715	$525	$425	$370	$325	$295
Standard Products	$750	$600	$495	$415	$370	$325	$295
Inland	$775	$625	$495	$415	$370	$325	$295
SG Grand Rapids	$850	$715	$525	$425	$375	$325	$295
Winchester	$995	$875	$695	$525	$425	$350	$325

Grading	100%	98%	95%	90%	80%	70%	60%
Irwin Pedersen	$1,500	$1,275	$975	$850	$775	$675	$580
Rockola	$925	$875	$675	$525	$425	$350	$325
Plainfield (Commercial only)	$195	$175	$160	$150	$140	$130	$120

M1 A1 PARATROOPER CARBINE — .30 Carbine cal., mfg. by Inland — WWII production, folding stock, crossed cannon proofed on bottom, 140,000 mfg. between 1942-1945. Stock folds to 26½ in. overall.

	100%	98%	95%	90%	80%	70%	60%
	$1,425	$1,025	$750	$500	$400	$365	$335

RIFLES: SEMI-AUTO

M1 GARAND — .30-06 cal., semi-auto, 8 shot en bloc clip fed, gas operated, adj. aperture sight, wooden stock. Made 1937-1957 by Springfield, Winchester, H&R, and International Harvester. Add 10% for WWII date, subtract 40% if rewelded, 20% if mismatched.

	100%	98%	95%	90%	80%	70%	60%
	$895	$775	$625	$525	$450	$400	$375

Add 100% for pre-WWII Winchester or Springfield mfg.

* **M1-C or M1-D Sniper** — with scope and mounts (be wary of fakes and rewelds).

	100%	98%	95%	90%	80%	70%	60%
M1-D	$1,825	$1,650	$1,455	$1,200	$1,060	$900	$780
M1-C	$2,650	$2,375	$2,000	$1,850	$1,400	$1,100	$800

If verified original, asking prices may be considerably higher than values listed above.

M1 NATIONAL MATCH — target version of the Garand, using National Match barrel and sights, glass bedding, etc. Should have serialized N.M. paperwork for premium.

	100%	98%	95%	90%	80%	70%	60%
	$1,850	$1,475	$1,175	$950	$750	$525	$460

RIFLES: BOLT ACTION

U.S. MODEL 1917 ENFIELD RIFLE — .30-06 cal., bolt action, 5 shot, 26 in. barrel, original finish was blue, adj. sights, military stock, derived from English P14 Enfield, over two million produced in 1917 and 1918.

	100%	98%	95%	90%	80%	70%	60%
	$550	$475	$400	$350	$300	$275	$250

Add 10% for Winchester mfg.

This model was manufactured primarily by Remington at the Eddystone plant in Eddystone, PA (Eddystone marked), the Ilion Remington plant, and by Winchester in New Haven, CT.

UZI

Currently manufactured by Israel Military Industries (IMI). During 1996-1998, Mossberg imported the Uzi Eagle pistols. These models were imported by UZI America, Inc., subsidiary of O.F. Mossberg & Sons, Inc. Previously imported by Action Arms, Ltd., located in Philadelphia, PA until 1994.

Serial number prefixes used on Uzi Firearms are as follows: "SA" on all 9mm Para. semi-auto carbines Models A and B; "45 SA" on all .45 ACP Model B carbines; "41 SA" on all .41 AE Model B carbines; "MC" on all 9mm Para. (only cal. made) semi-auto mini-carbines; "UP" on all 9mm Para. semi-auto Uzi pistols; "45 UP" on all .45 semi-auto Uzi pistols (disc. 1989). There are also prototypes or experimental Uzis with either "AA" or "AAL" prefixes - these are rare and will command premiums over values listed below.

CARBINES: SEMI-AUTO

CARBINE MODEL A — 9mm Para. cal., semi-auto, 16.1 in. barrel, parkerized finish, 25 shot mag., mfg. by IMI 1980-1983 and ser. range is SA01,001-SA037,000.

	100%	98%	95%	90%	80%	70%	60%
	$1,150	$950	$825	$725	$650	$600	$550

Approx. 100 Model As were mfg. with a nickel finish. These are rare and command considerable premiums over values listed above.

CARBINE MODEL B — 9mm Para., .41 Action Express (new 1987), or .45 ACP (new 1987) cal., semi-auto carbine, 16.1 in. barrel, baked enamel black finish over phosphated (parkerized) base finish, 16 (.45 ACP), 20 (.41 AE) or 25 (9mm Para.) shot mag., metal folding stock, includes molded case and carrying sling, 8.4 lbs. Mfg. 1983 - until Federal legislation disc. importation 1989 and ser. range is 037,001-SA073,544.

	100%	98%	95%	90%	80%	70%	60%
	$925	$850	$775	$675	$600	$550	$500

Last Mfg.'s Sug. Retail was $698.

Add $150 for .22 cal. conversion kit (new 1987).
Add $215 for .45 ACP to 9mm Para./.41 AE conversion kit.
Add $150 for 9mm Para. to .41 AE (or vice-versa) conversion kit.
Add $215 for 9mm Para. to .45 ACP conversion kit.

MINI CARBINE — 9mm Para. cal., similar to Carbine except has 19¾ in. barrel, 20 shot mag., swing-away metal stock, scaled down version of the regular carbine, 7.2 lbs. New 1987. Federal legislation disc. importation 1989.

$2,250	$2,000	$1,775	$1,525	1,300	$1,100	$995

Last Mfg.'s Sug. Retail was $698.

PISTOLS: SEMI-AUTO

UZI PISTOL — 9mm Para. or .45 ACP cal. (disc.), semi-auto pistol, 4½ in. barrel, parkerized finish, 10 (.45 ACP) or 20 (9mm Para.) shot mag., supplied with molded carrying case, sight adj. key and mag. loading tool, 3.8 lbs. Importation disc. 1993.

$975	$850	$795	$750	$700	$650	$600

Last Mfg.'s Sug. Retail was $695.

Add $285 for .45 ACP to 9mm Para./.41 AE conversion kit.
Add $100 for 9mm Para. to .41 AE conversion kit.
Add approx. 30%-40% for two-line slide marking "45 ACP Model 45".

UZI EAGLE SERIES — 9mm Para., .40 S&W, or .45 ACP cal., semi-auto double action, various configurations, matte finish with black synthetic grips, 10 shot mag. Mfg. 1997-1998.

*   *Full-Size Eagle* — 9mm Para. or .40 S&W cal., 4.4 in. barrel, steel construction, decocking feature, Tritium sights, polygonal rifling. New 1997.

$485	$440	$400	$365	$335	$330	$275

Last Mfg.'s Sug. Retail was $535.

*   *Short Slide Eagle* — 9mm Para., .40 S&W, or .45 ACP cal., similar to Full-Size Eagle, except has 3.7 in. barrel. New 1997.

$485	$440	$400	$365	$335	$330	$275

Last Mfg.'s Sug. Retail was $535.

Add $31 for .45 ACP cal.

*   *Compact Eagle* — 9mm Para. or .40 S&W cal., available in double action with decocking or double action only, 3½ in. barrel. New 1997.

$485	$440	$400	$365	$335	$330	$275

Last Mfg.'s Sug. Retail was $535.

*   *Polymer Compact* — similar to Compact Eagle, except has compact polymer frame. New 1997.

$485	$440	$400	$365	$335	$330	$275

Last Mfg.'s Sug. Retail was $535.

V section

VALMET, INC.

Current manufacturer located in Jyvaskyla, Finland. Previously imported by Stoeger Industries, Inc. located in South Hackensack, NJ.

The Valmet line was discontinued in 1989 and replaced by Tikka (please refer to the Tikka section in this text) in 1990.

Grading	100%	98%	95%	90%	80%	70%	60%

RIFLES

HUNTER MODEL — .223 Rem., .243 Win., or .308 Win. cal., gas operated semi-auto, Kalashnikov action, 20½ in. barrel, checkered walnut stock and forearm, matte finished metal, 5, 9, or 20 shot mag., 8 lbs. New 1986, Federal legislation disc. importation 1989.

	100%	98%	95%	90%	80%	70%	60%
	$795	$700	$625	$550	$500	$450	$420

Last Mfg.'s Sug. Retail was $795.

MODEL 76 — .223 Rem., 7.62x39mm, or .308 Win. cal., gas operated semi-auto paramilitary design rifle, 16¾ in. or 20½ (.308 only) in. barrel, 15 or 30 (7.62x39mm only) shot mag., parkerized finish. Federal legislation disc. importation 1989.

	100%	98%	95%	90%	80%	70%	60%
	$1,395	$1,175	$975	$800	$700	$600	$550

Last Mfg.'s Sug. Retail was $740.

Add $95-$125 for synthetic or folding stock.

M-62S PARAMILITARY DESIGN RIFLE — semi-auto version of Finn M-62, 7.62x39 Russian, 15 or 30 shot mag., 16⅝ in. barrel, gas operated, rotary bolt, adj. rear sight, tube steel or wood stock. Mfg. 1962-disc.

	100%	98%	95%	90%	80%	70%	60%
	$1,395	$1,175	$975	$800	$700	$600	$550

Add $50 for wood stock.

M-71S — similar to M-62S, except .223 Rem. cal., reinforced resin or wood stock.

	100%	98%	95%	90%	80%	70%	60%
	$1,250	$1,100	$925	$750	$650	$550	$495

Add $50 for wood stock.

MODEL 78 — .308 Win. cal. only, similar to Model 76, except has 24½ in. barrel, wood stock and forearm, and barrel bipod, 11 lbs. New 1987. Federal legislation disc. importation 1989.

	100%	98%	95%	90%	80%	70%	60%
	$1,575	$1,325	$1,050	$850	$750	$650	$550

Last Mfg.'s Sug. Retail was $1,060.

MODEL 82 BULLPUP — .223 Rem. cal., limited importation.

	100%	98%	95%	90%	80%	70%	60%
	$2,500	$1,950	$1,550	$1,250	$1,000	$825	$700

SHOTGUNS: O/U

LION MODEL — 12 ga., 26, 28, or 30 in. barrels, various chokes, boxlock, SST, checkered stock. Mfg. 1947-1968.

	100%	98%	95%	90%	80%	70%	60%
	$415	$370	$340	$320	$305	$275	$240

MODEL 412 O/U SHOOTING SYSTEM — interchangeable barrel assemblies permit a double rifle, shotgun/rifle, and O/U shotgun configuration, user installed interchangeable barrels, monobloc locking, rifle barrel positioning by adjustment, SST, extractors or ejectors, checkered walnut stock and forend, cocking indicators, blued finish. Importation on all models was disc. 1989.

Add $100 for synthetic stock on all 412 models.

* *Model 412S Field Grade* — 12 ga. was standard, auto ejectors, screw-in choke tubes, matte nickel finish. Imported 1986-89.

	100%	98%	95%	90%	80%	70%	60%
	$855	$670	$580	$540	$475	$440	$400

Last Mfg.'s Sug. Retail was $999.

Add 15% for 20 ga.

* *Model 412S Field and Target* — 12 ga. only, 2¾ and 3 in. chambers, ejectors. Disc. 1988.

	100%	98%	95%	90%	80%	70%	60%
	$775	$660	$580	$540	$475	$440	$400

Last Mfg.'s Sug. Retail was $874.

Grading	100%	98%	95%	90%	80%	70%	60%

* **Model 412ST Trap and Skeet** — 12 ga., Monte Carlo stock on Trap model, 28 in. barrels on Skeet model, screw-in chokes standard.

	$1,040	$875	$695	$650	$580	$540	$475

Last Mfg.'s Sug. Retail was $1,215.

* **Model 412ST Premium Grade Target** — similar to Model 412ST Trap and Skeet, except has better walnut and checkering. Imported 1987-89.

	$1,355	$1,050	$865	$750	$640	$580	$515

Last Mfg.'s Sug. Retail was $1,550.

* **Model 412S Combination Gun** — combination, 12 ga, 3 in. chamber over choice of .222 Rem., .223 Rem., .243 Win., .30-06, or .308 Win. cal., extractors.

	$1,025	$850	$675	$600	$550	$475	$440

Last Mfg.'s Sug. Retail was $1,615.

* **Model 412S Double Rifle** — .243 Win. (disc. 1987), .30-06, .308 Win. (disc. 1987), .375 H&H Mag. (disc. 1987), or 9.3x73R cal., extractors, 24 in. barrels.

	$1,060	$895	$725	$650	$580	$540	$475

Last Mfg.'s Sug. Retail was $1,275.

Add $100 for 9.3x74R cal. or .375 H&H Mag. cal.

This model in .30-06 cal. has extractors only while in 9.3x74R cal. ejectors are standard.

* **Model 412K Double Rifle** — .30-06 or .308 Win. cal. only, 24 in. separated barrels, extractors. Importation disc. 1986.

	$800	$660	$580	$540	$475	$440	$400

Last Mfg.'s Sug. Retail was $899.

* **Model 412 Engraved** — satin finish, receiver extensively bank note engraved in choice of 4 patterns, select Triple-X wood hand-checkered — choice of field or target, available in any Valmet model. Add $85 for shotgun rifle, $320 for double rifle.

This model had limited availability and prices were on request from the manufacturer. Last Mfg.'s Sug. retail was $2,499.

* **Extra Barrel Assemblies (Model 412 O/U)** — $505 - $605 each for shotgun (includes screw-in chokes), $579 each for shotgun/rifle combo, $660 each for double rifle (add $100 for ejectors).

VALTRO

Current manufacturer established during 1988 and located in Brescia, Italy. Currently imported by Valtro USA, Inc., located in San Rafael, CA.

Valtro manufactures both excellent quality slide action and semi-auto shotguns, in addition to a semi-auto pistol, and a variety of signal pistols. Please contact Valtro USA Inc. (see Trademark Index listing) directly for more product information and availability.

PISTOLS: SEMI-AUTO

1998 A1 .45 ACP — .45 ACP cal., forged National Match frame and slide, 5 in. barrel, deluxe wood grips, 8 shot mag., ambidextrous safety, blued finish, flat checkered mainspring housing, front and rear slide serrations, beveled mag. well, speed trigger, 40 oz. New 1998.

Mfg.'s Sug. Retail	$895	$795	$650	$550	$500	$450	$400	$360

SHOTGUNS: SLIDE ACTION

TACTICAL 98 SHOTGUN — 12 ga. only, 18½ or 20 in. barrel featuring MMC ghost ring sights and integral muzzle brake, 5 shot mag., internal chokes, receiver sidesaddle holds 6 exposed rounds, pistol grip or standard stock, matte black finish, lightweight. New 1998.

Mfg.'s Sug. Retail	$845	$775	$625	$525	$475	$425	$400	$360

VARBERGER

Current rifle manufacturer located in Varberg, Sweden. No current importer. Previously imported by Hill Country Wholesale, Inc. located in Austin, TX, and distributed by Paul & Associates, located in Wellsville, KS until late 1995.

Grading	100%	98%	95%	90%	80%	70%	60%

RIFLES: BOLT ACTION

MSRs listed below reflect the most recent retail prices.

MODEL 711 GRADE 1 — available in 19 cals. between .22 PPC and .358 Norma, bolt action design featuring specially designed and manufactured receiver, rotary mag., 6 lug engine-turned bolt, and stock featuring metal retainer plate, individually test fired. Imported 1994-98.

	$950	$850	$750	$650	$550	$450	$375

Last Mfg.'s Sug. Retail was $1,080.

MODEL 717 GRADE 1 MAGNUM — availabe in 11 Mag. cals. between .257 Wby. Mag. and .375 H&H. Imported 1994-98.

	$980	$875	$765	$650	$550	$450	$375

Last Mfg.'s Sug. Retail was $1,130.

MODEL 757 GRADE 2 DELUXE — deluxe variation of the Model 711. Imported 1994-98.

	$1,775	$1,500	$1,250	$995	$895	$795	$695

Last Mfg.'s Sug. Retail was $2,035.

Add $45 for Mag. cals.

MODEL 77 GRADE 3 PREMIER — top-of-the-line model. Imported 1994-98.

	$1,995	$1,675	$1,350	$1,050	$925	$795	$695

Last Mfg.'s Sug. Retail was $2,375.

Add $65 for Mag. cals.

VARNER SPORTING ARMS, INC.

Previous manufacturer located in Marietta, GA circa 1988-89.

RIFLES: SINGLE SHOT

VARNER FAVORITE HUNTER — .22 LR cal., patterned after J. Stevens Favorite Model, ½ round - ½ octagon 21½ in. takedown barrel, blued frame, walnut stock and forearm, aperture rear sight, 5 lbs. Mfg. 1988-89.

	$325	$270	$220	$185	$150	$130	$110

Last Mfg.'s Sug. Retail was $369.

* *Hunter Deluxe* — similar to Favorite Hunter, except has case colored frame and lever, and deluxe walnut stock and forearm. Mfg. 1988-89.

	$450	$375	$285	$225	$175	$150	$135

Last Mfg.'s Sug. Retail was $500.

* *Presentation Grade* — includes target hammer and trigger, AAA quality checkered stock and forearm, includes takedown case. Mfg. 1988-89.

	$480	$400	$310	$250	$195	$170	$155

Last Mfg.'s Sug. Retail was $569.

PRESENTATION ENGRAVED — previously available in a No. 1 Grade for $649, a No. 2 for $779, or a No. 3 for $1,099.

VEKTOR

Current trademark manufactured in South Africa and imported beginning in 1999 by Vektor USA, located in Norfolk, VA. Dealer sales.

Vektor has been manufacturing high quality and reliable firearms for South African law enforcement for quite some time, in addition to having secured contracts with many foreign countries.

PISTOLS: SEMI-AUTO

MODEL CP1 — 9mm Para. cal., 4 in. barrel, compact model with unique aesthetics and ergonomic design allowing no buttons or levers on exterior surfaces, hammerless, striker fire system, black or nickel finished slide, 10 shot mag., approx. 25½ oz. Importation began 1999.

Mfg.'s Sug. Retail	$480	$440	$400	$360	$330	$300	$280	$260

Add $20 for nickel slide finish.

MODEL Z88 — 9mm Para. cal., double action, patterned after the M92 Beretta, 5 in. barrel, steel construction, black synthetic grips, 2.2 lbs. Importation began 1999.

Mfg.'s Sug. Retail	$619	$550	$495	$450	$400	$360	$330	$295

V

Grading		100%	98%	95%	90%	80%	70%	60%

MODEL SP1 — 9mm Para. cal., double action, 5 in. barrel with polygonal rifling, wraparound checkered synthetic grips, matte blue or black standard finish, 2.2. lbs. Importation began 1999.

Mfg.'s Sug. Retail	$600	$535	$485	$445	$395	$360	$330	$295

Add $30 for natural anodized or nickel finish.
Add $130 for sport pistol with compensated barrel.

* *Model SP1 Compact* — similar to Model SP1, except is compact variation. Importation began 1999.

Mfg.'s Sug. Retail	$650	$575	$510	$460	$410	$360	$330	$295

* *Model SP1 Sport Pistol/Tuned* — similar to Model SP1, except has is available with either tuned action or target pistol features. Importation began 1999.

Mfg.'s Sug. Retail	$1,199	$1,050	$900	$775	$650	$525	$400	$350

Add $40 for Target Pistol with dual color finish.

* *Model SP2* — .40 S&W cal., otherwise similar to Model SP1. Importation began in 1999.

Mfg.'s Sug. Retail	$600	$535	$485	$445	$395	$360	$330	$295

* *Model SP2 Compact* — similar to Model SP2, except is compact variation. Importation began 1999.

Mfg.'s Sug. Retail	$650	$575	$510	$460	$410	$360	$330	$295

Add $190 for 9mm Para. conversion kit.

ULTRA MODEL — 9mm Para. cal., top-of-the-line double action with most performance features, Lynx scope included. Importation began 1999.

Mfg.'s Sug. Retail	$2,150	$1,950	$1,700	$1,500	$1,300	$1,100	$900	$700

VEPR. RIFLES

Currently manufactured at the Vyatskie Polyany factory in Russia. Currently imported exclusively by ZDF Import/Export, Inc., located in Salt Lake City, UT.

RIFLES: SEMI-AUTO

VEPR CARBINE/RIFLE — .223 Rem. or .308 Win. cal., features Vepr.'s semi-auto action, 20½ (carbine, .308 Win. only) or 23¼ (rifle) in. barrel with adj. rear sight, scope mount rail built into receiver top, checkered thumbhole walnut stock with recoil pad and forend, paddle mag. release, 5 or 10 shot mag., approx. 8½ lbs. Importation began 1999.

Mfg.'s Sug. Retail		$725	$625	$550	$500	$460	$430	$400

VERNEY-CARRON

Current manufacturer of shotguns and rifles located in St. Etienne, France. Established during 1820, Verney-Carron is proud to reflect on six generations of family ownership. Currently imported beginning 1999 by Federal Engineering, located in Bensenville, IL. Previously imported by Yellow Brick Entreprises, located in Clay Center, KS during 1998 only. Please contact the importer directly for more information, including current model availability and domestic pricing regarding these fine firearms (see Trademark Index).

Verney-Carron manufactures a variety of O/U shotguns, double rifles, cased sets, and bolt action rifles.

VICKERS LIMITED

Previous manufacturer located in Crayford/Kent, England.

RIFLES: SINGLE SHOT, TARGET

JUBILEE SINGLE SHOT TARGET RIFLE — Martini type action, .22 LR cal., 28 in. heavy barrel, target sights, one piece pistol grip, target stock, pre-WWII.

		$440	$330	$305	$275	$250	$220	$165

EMPIRE MODEL — similar to Jubilee, with 27 or 30 in. barrel, straight grip stock.

		$415	$310	$285	$260	$220	$195	$150

VICTORY ARMS CO. LIMITED

Previously manufactured in prototype format only by Modern Manufacturing Company located in Phoenix, AZ.

Grading	100%	98%	95%	90%	80%	70%	60%

MODEL MC5 — while a few prototypes were mfg. for trade shows (circa 1991-92), this model was never commercially manufactured. Last advertised retail was $465.

VIERLINGS

The German word Vierling denotes a four barrel long arm configuration mostly manufactured in Germany or Austria previously.

This configuration of long arm has four barrels, typically with a .22 caliber barrel incorporated in the center rib or stacked below two SxS shotgun barrels and a lower, larger caliber rifle barrel. Vierlings typically have two triggers, both single set. Barrel selectors are usually on the top tang. This unusual configuration is mostly of German mfg., although there are a few Austrian specimens also (the gunmakers of Ferlach still custom make this model). All Vierlings are mfg. one at a time, with fabrication being very complicated, lengthy, and expensive. As a result, every Vierling must be appraised individually - most specimens, however, are priced approx. $3,500 - $7,500.

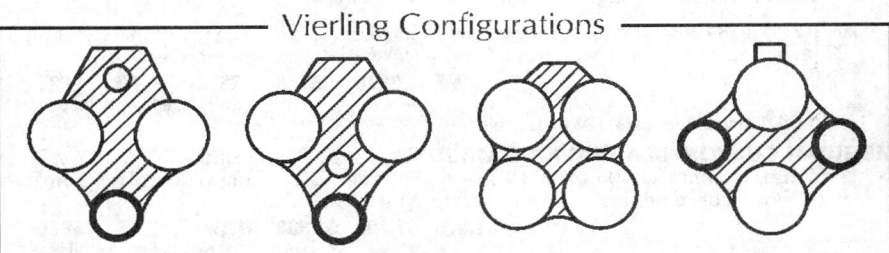

Vierling Configurations

VIRGINIAN

This trademark can be located under the Interarms section in this text.

VIS

Currently manufactured by the F.B. Radom arsenal in Radom, Poland. Please refer to the Radom section in this text.

VOERE (AUSTRIA)

Current manufacturer established during 1965, and located in Kufstein, Austria. No current importer. To date, Voere has had little distribution in the U.S. Rahn Gun Works, Inc. located in Hastings, MI has imported this trademark on a limited basis in the past. Voere of Austria has nothing to do with the Voere trademark of Germany that was taken over by Mauser-Werke after going bankrupt.

Voere manufactures a complete line of quality rimfire semi-auto and centerfire bolt-action/semi-auto rifles. Their new caseless ammunition released in 1991 is a bold step and will have to hold up to the performance and reliability of its cased relatives. More information on this trademark can be obtained by writing/faxing the company directly (see Trademark Index for information).

MODEL VEC 91 BOLT ACTION — 5.7x26 UCC caseless ammo, unique ignition system requires electrical impulse to activate semi-conducting primer that ignites propellant (2 small batteries are housed in the pistol grip capable of igniting 5,000 shots), 5 shot detachable mag., 20 in. free floating barrel, twin forward locking lugs, 2-stage electrical trigger adj. from ½ oz. to 7 lbs, 55 grain bullet achieves 3,300 fps with no loss in accuracy over normal mechanical primer ignited cartridges, 6 lbs. Mfg. 1992, disc.

$2,300 $2,050 $1,850 $1,500 $1,225 $1,100 $995

Last Mfg.'s Sug. Retail was $2,540.

Grading	100%	98%	95%	90%	80%	70%	60%

MODEL 2185 MATCH SEMI-AUTO — .308 Win. cal., gas operated, free floating barrel, 3 or 5 shot detachable mag., manual safety, iron sights, laminate wood, 11 lbs. Disc.

	$2,525	$2,275	$1,975	$1,650	$1,350	$1,225	$1,050

Last Mfg.'s Sug. Retail was $2,715.

> Add $1,500 for position style rifle (includes adj. cheekpiece, buttplate, and bottom sling rail, and Voere special scope base).

> Other calibers are available on special order only.

MODEL 2185 HUNTING RIFLE — 9.3x62mm, other cals. available upon special request, checkered stock and forend, iron sights. Disc.

	$1,625	$1,350	$1,200	$1,050	$900	$700	$575

Last Mfg.'s Sug. Retail was $1,775.

> Add $50 for Mannlicher full stock with 20 in. carbine barrel.

MODEL 2155 K-98 MAUSER — .243 Win., .270 Win., or .30-06 cal., 20 in. barrel, tang safety, no sights. Disc.

	$725	$650	$575	$500	$450	$400	$350

Last Mfg.'s Sug. Retail was $780.

> Add $50 for Mag. cals. (7mm Rem. Mag. or .300 Win. Mag.).

* *Model 2165 K-98 Mauser Deluxe* — same cals. as K-98 Mauser, European traditional style bolt action, 22 in. barrel, detachable 5 shot mag., hand-checkered deluxe walnut. Disc.

	$995	$875	$750	$675	$600	$525	$450

Last Mfg.'s Sug. Retail was $1,110.

> Add $50 for Mag. cals. (24 in. barrel).

AMERICAN CUSTOM CLASSIC K-98 MAUSER — .22-250 Rem., .243 Win., .270 Win., 7x57mm, 7x64mm, .30-06, or .308 Win. cal., 3 position safety, hinged floorplate, deluxe walnut with hand-rubbed oil finish and checkering. Mfg. 1996 only.

	$1,575	$1,450	$1,300	$1,150	$995	$850	$675

Last Mfg.'s Sug. Retail was $1,795.

> Add $50 for Mag. cals. (.300 Win. Mag., .338 Win. Mag., 7mm Rem. Mag., or 9.3x64mm).
> Add $100 for .375 H&H or .458 Win. Mag. cal.

.22 SEMI-AUTO — .22 LR cal., open (disc.) or closed bolt design, 10 shot clip mag., checkered hardwood stock, adj. rear sight and trigger. Limited importation.

	$585	$535	$460	$400	$350	$300	$250

Last Mfg.'s Sug. Retail was $645.

> Add $50 for Deluxe Model.

VOERE (GERMAN)

Previous manufacturer located in Vohrenvach, Germany. Voere was absorbed by Mauser-Werke circa 1986, and most of the company machinery was moved to Oberndorf during that time. Voere of Germany should not be confused with the current Austrian firm of the same name.

> Voere of Germany manufactured a wide variety of rifles in many configurations, including both bolt action and semi-auto (closed and open bolt) .22 cal. rifles. Bolt action centerfire rifles were also produced in many styles and calibers, including some private label contracts with such firms as Shikar, Frankonia, Akah, and others. While not considered as highly collectible today, most German Voere rifles were noted for their quality craftsmanship and above average accuracy. Secondary values today depend on the desirability of the rifle configuration (stock design, finish, caliber, etc.) and original condition.

VOLQUARTSEN CUSTOM

Current rifle customizer and manufacturer located in Carroll, IA.

PISTOLS: SEMI-AUTO, CONVERSION

Volquartsen manufactures a wide variety of custom pistols based on the Ruger Mark II action. Prices range from $595 - $1,210, depending on the configuration. Please contact the company directly for more information on these conversions.

Grading	100%	98%	95%	90%	80%	70%	60%

VOLQUARTSEN SEMI-AUTO PISTOL — .22 Mag. cal., features black or red synthetic colored stock and graphite barrel w/o sights, includes Picatinny rail on top of frame. New 1999.

Mfg.'s Sug. Retail	$855	$750	$675	$600	$550	$500	$450	$400

RIFLES: SEMI-AUTO

Volquartsen manufactures a wide variety of custom rifles based on the Ruger 10/22 action. Prices range from $625 - $1,019, depending on the configuration. Please contact the company directly for more information on these conversions.

STANDARD 22 MAG. — .22 Mag. cal., choice of standard (18½ in. stainless steel), deluxe (20 in. fluted), or lightweight (16½ in. aluminum) barrel, Monte Carlo laminated wood or composite stock, approx. 7½ lbs.

Mfg.'s Sug. Retail	$925	$850	$750	$675	$600	$550	$500	$450

Add $70 for lightweight or deluxe barrel.

SIGNATURE SERIES — .22 Mag. cal., top-of-the-line model, many options are available.

Mfg.'s Sug. Retail	$1,795	$1,600	$1,400	$1,200	$1,000	$850	$700	$600

VOLUNTEER ENTERPRISES

Previous manufacturer located in Knoxville, TN.

Volunteer Enterprises became Commando Arms after 1978.

CARBINES

COMMANDO MARK III CARBINE — .45 ACP cal., semi-auto, blowback action, 16½ in. barrel, aperture sight, stock styled after "Tommy Gun". Mfg. 1969-1976.

	$425	$365	$315	$280	$225	$195	$160

COMMANDO MARK III CARBINE

Vertical grip	$440	$365	$320	$280	$225	$195	$160

COMMANDO MARK 9 — similar to Mark III in 9mm Para. cal.

	$440	$375	$325	$285	$230	$195	$160
Vertical grip	$440	$365	$320	$280	$225	$195	$160

VOUZELAUD

Previous manufacturer located in France. Previously imported by Waverly Arms Co. located in Suffolk, VA.

SHOTGUNS: SxS

MODEL 315 E — 12, 16 or 20 ga., boxlock, 28 in. barrels, auto ejectors, straight grip French walnut stock, double triggers, case colored receiver, light engraving. Importation disc. 1987.

Values generally range between $1,350-$2,000 for this model.

MODEL 315 EL — similar to Model 315 E, except has satin finish receiver engraved with bouquets of fine English scroll work, trigger guard and forearm also engraved. Importation disc. 1987.

Values generally range between $1,475-$2,250 for this model.

This model was also available by special order in 28 ga. or .410 bore (Model 315 EL-S) - add $600.

MODEL 315 EGL — 12, 16 or 20 ga., sidelock, 28 in. barrels, selective ejectors, double triggers, extensive scroll engraving on coin finish receiver, English style stock of extra fancy French walnut. Importation disc. 1987.

Values generally range between $1,750-$2,750 for this model.

MODEL 315 EGL-S — same general features as the Model 315 EGL, except monobloc barrel construction, extensive game scene engraving, and grand deluxe walnut stock and forearm with extra fine hand-checkering. Importation disc. 1987.

Values generally range between $1,950-$2,950 for this model.

Last Mfg.'s Sug. Retail was $5,895.

NOTES

W section

WAFFEN VERATSCHNIG

Current manufacturer located in Ferlach, Austria.

Waffen Veratschnig manufactures a variety of high grade, made to individual special order, rifles, shotguns, combination guns, drillings, and vierlings. A wide variety of engraving scenes, wood carvings, and other special features are available at extra cost. Currently, they do not have a U.S. importer and for more information, please contact them directly (see Trademark Index).

Grading	100%	98%	95%	90%	80%	70%	60%

WALTHER

Current manufacturer located in Ulm, Germany, 1953 to date. Currently imported and distributed beginning late 1998 by Carl Walther USA LLC, located in Alexandria, VA, and by Earl's Repair Service, SVC Inc., located in Tewksbury, MA. Previously imported and distributed by Interarms located in Alexandria, VA. Previously manufactured in Zella-Mehlis, Germany 1886 to 1945. Walther was sold to Umarex Sportwaffen GmbH circa 1996, and is located in Arnsberg, Germany. Walther target pistols are currently being imported by Champions Choice located in La Vergne, TN and Earl's Repair Service, Inc. beginning 1994 located in Tewksbury, MA.

The calibers listed in the Walther Pistol sections are listed in American caliber designations. The German metric conversion is as follows: .22 LR - 5.6mm, .25 ACP - 6.35mm, .32 ACP - 7.65mm, .380 ACP - 9mm kurz. The metric caliber designations in most cases will be indicated on the left slide legend for German mfg. pistols listed in the Walther section.

PISTOLS: SEMI-AUTO, PRE-WAR

MODEL 1 — .25 ACP cal., 2.1 in. barrel, fixed sights, blue, checkered hard rubber grips, pre-WWI. Mfg. 1908.

$650	$525	$400	$300	$250	$225	$200

MODEL 2 — .25 ACP cal., 2.1 in. barrel, blue, rubber grips, pop-up rear sight on early models, fixed on late models. Mfg. 1909.

$425	$390	$325	$225	$175	$135	$125

This model can usually be distinguished by its knurled barrel ring.

* ***Early Model*** — differentiated by its pop-up rear sight.

$1,350	$950	$895	$775	$675	$550	$400

MODEL 3 — .32 ACP cal., 2.6 in. barrel, blue, fixed sights, rubber grips, ejection port on left side. Mfg. 1910.

$1,500	$1,250	$1,100	$800	$550	$500	$400

MODEL 4 — .32 ACP cal., 8 shot, 3½ in. barrel, blue, rubber grips, ejection port on left side. Mfg. 1910-1928.

$400	$325	$250	$200	$125	$100	$80

Add 10% for WWI "Eagle" proofs.

MODEL 5 — better quality version of Model 2, fixed rear sight. Mfg. 1913.

$400	$375	$300	$200	$145	$135	$125

MODEL 6 — 9mm Para. cal., 4⅞ in. barrel, blue, hard rubber grips, ejection port on right side. Mfg. 1915-1917. Some are Imperial proofed.

$6,000	$4,500	$3,000	$2,300	$1,500	$1,050	$800

MODEL 7 — .25 ACP cal., 3 in. barrel, blue, fixed sights, rubber grips, ejection port on right side. Mfg. 1917-1918.

$650	$500	$425	$350	$250	$200	$125

Grading	100%	98%	95%	90%	80%	70%	60%

MODEL 8 — .25 ACP cal., 2⅞ in. barrel, blue or nickel finish, fixed sights, black checkered plastic grips with round medallions. Mfg. 1920-1943.

	$475	$425	$375	$265	$200	$150	$125

Add 20% for nickel.
Add 10% for "Eagle N" proofing.
Add 25% for engraved slide.

MODEL 9 VEST POCKET — .25 ACP cal., engineering revision of Model 1, 2 in. barrel, blued finish standard, upward ejection, 6 shot bottom release mag., fixed sights, black checkered plastic grips with round medallions, safety lever on left frame side behind trigger, 9 oz. Mfg. 1921-1945.

	$500	$450	$375	$275	$200	$160	$140

Add 40% for engraved slide, 20% for nickel.
Add 10% for "Eagle N" proofing.

MODEL PP DOUBLE ACTION — .22 LR, .25 ACP, .32 ACP, or .380 ACP cal., PP designates "Polizei Pistole", 3⅞ in. barrel, blue, fixed sights, plastic grips. Mfg. 1929-1945. Crown N proof until 1939. Eagle N Nazi commercial proof until 1945.

	100%	98%	95%	90%	80%	70%	60%
.22 LR cal.	$995	$825	$700	$600	$525	$450	$375
.25 ACP cal.	$3,450	$3,100	$2,650	$2,000	$1,500	$1,200	$1,000
.32 ACP cal.	$450	$395	$375	$350	$275	$225	$200
.380 ACP cal.	$1,200	$995	$750	$675	$600	$550	$500

Add 15% for alloy frame.

Original nickel finished Model PPs are very rare; this precludes accurate price evaluation.

Values above assume original guns without import markings. Recently imported WWII/surplus Police used guns are stamped on the frame or receiver, indicating the current importer and address - subtract 20%-30% from values listed above for these recent imports.

* **.32 ACP Bottom Release Magazine** — safety rotates 90 degrees.

	$995	$850	$625	$600	$525	$425	$395

* **.380 ACP Bottom Release Magazine** — safety rotates 90 degrees.

	$1,200	$1,050	$895	$825	$700	$600	$500

* **Pre-War Persian proofed** — 9mm kurz BMR.

	$2,000	$1,800	$1,600	$1,450	$1,250	$995	$825

Subtract 75% for recent imports which have been reblued.

* **Pre-War verchromt .32 ACP cal.** — add 50% for .380 ACP cal.

	$1,600	$1,400	$1,000	$750	$675	$485	$395

* **Pre-War Stoeger** — .32 ACP cal. only.

	$1,450	$1,200	$925	$800	$600	$425	$325

* **Nairobi** — Chas. Heyer.

	$1,450	$1,200	$850	$725	$575	$400	$300

* **Aluminum frame** — safety rotates 90 degrees.

	$695	$650	$525	$400	$275	$235	$200

* **Allemagne** — French Comm.

	$1,200	$1,000	$825	$720	$600	$425	$325

MODEL PP WARTIME PRODUCTION — mfg. 1940-1945, "Eagle N" Proof (Nazi commercial nitro proof after April 1940) or "Crown N" proof (German commercial proof mark used to April, 1940) found on pre-WWII military production. Variations are listed either by proof marks or frame/slide markings.

* **"Waffenamt" Proofed** — .32 ACP or .380 ACP cal., "Eagle N", military acceptance marking.

	100%	98%	95%	90%	80%	70%	60%
.32 ACP cal. (milled finish)	$525	$450	$395	$300	$250	$220	$200
.380 ACP cal.	$1,200	$995	$800	$700	$600	$550	$500

Late war PPs are sometimes encountered with Walther marked walnut grips - add 20% if Waffenamt proofed.

Grading	100%	98%	95%	90%	80%	70%	60%

* **Eagle N Proofed** — .22 LR or .32 ACP cal., with lanyard loop.

.32 ACP cal.	$475	$425	$375	$300	$250	$200	$150
.22 LR cal.	$895	$795	$675	$550	$495	$450	$395

    Add 50% to .32 ACP cal., Waffenamt proofed PPs that are hi-gloss finish (all .380s are hi-gloss).

    In most cases, the .380 ACP cal. has the bottom mag. release.

    After WWII the French added a lanyard to the left side of the grip. Subtract 25% for this alteration.

* **Eagle C & F Marked (Nazi Police)** — .32 ACP cal., "Eagle F or C" proofed on left side of frame.

	$795	$675	$625	$500	$450	$380	$300

    Add 25% if Eagle C marked. All hi-gloss are early productions.

* **RFV Marked** — .32 ACP cal., "Crown N". Mfg. for Reichsfinanazverwaltung and Reich Finance Administration.

	$900	$700	$625	$500	$400	$325	$225

* **RJ Marked** — .32 ACP cal., "Crown N". Mfg. for Reichsjustizministerium and Reich Justice Ministry.

	$950	$800	$625	$500	$450	$325	$225

* **SA Marked** — .22 LR or .32 ACP cal., "Crown N". Mfg. for SA (Sturm Abteilung - group leaders) of the Nazi party.

	$2,000	$1,800	$1,500	$1,200	$900	$600	$425

    Add 20% for .22 LR.

    Rare SA markings may bring as much as 50% more over values listed above.

    There are 28 SA groups.

* **NSKK Marked** — .32 ACP cal., "Crown N or Eagle N" proofed. Mfg. for National-sozialistischer Kraftkorps and Nazi Party Transport Corps, rare.

	$2,750	$2,000	$1,500	$1,025	$875	$700	$550

* **RRZ proofed** — .32 ACP cal., "Reich Rundfunk Zenhale", for Reichsrundfunkzentrale and Reich Radio Broadcasting - only 3 known.

	$3,500	$3,000	$2,500				

* **PDM Marked** — .32 ACP cal., "Crown N", for Polizeidirektion Munchen and Munich Police Department, all have bottom mag. release.

	$1,500	$1,300	$1,000	$650	$500	$400	$350

* **AC Marked** — .32 ACP cal., replaced Walther Banner during 1945, "Eagle N".

	$500	$400	$300	$250	$200	$150	$125

    Some are mismatched (assembled at factory by GIs after the factory was captured). Subtract 20% if mismatched.

* **Czech. Contract** — stamped Rampant Lion.

	$1,100	$900	$800	$700	$600	$500	$400

* **Panagraph Slide**

	$825	$750	$695	$630	$550	$385	$275

* **Danish Rplt.**

	$975	$925	$825	$775	$700	$625	$400

MODEL PP LIGHTWEIGHT — aluminum alloy version.

    Add 20% to Standard Model prices.

    Add 20%-40% for original nickel finish (very rare).

    Add 25% for early hi-gloss finish.

Grading	100%	98%	95%	90%	80%	70%	60%

MODEL PPK PRE-WAR PRODUCTION — .22 LR, .25 ACP, .32 ACP, or .380 ACP cal., PPK designates "Polizei Pistole Kriminal", 3¼ in. barrel, blue, fixed sights, plastic grips. Mfg. 1931-1940.

	100%	98%	95%	90%	80%	70%	60%
.22 LR cal.	$1,250	$925	$750	$700	$650	$525	$400
.25 ACP cal.	$5,000	$4,475	$3,800	$3,400	$2,800	$2,100	$1,475
.32 ACP cal.	$650	$600	$500	$395	$300	$250	$225
.380 ACP cal.	$2,500	$2,000	$1,700	$1,500	$900	$700	$500

Add 60% for bottom release Mag (.32 ACP cal.).

MODEL PPK WARTIME PRODUCTION — mfg. 1940-1945, "Eagle N" proofed after April 1940, "Crown N" proofs appear on pre-1940 production with frame/slide markings. Variations are listed either by proof marks, frame/slide markings, or type of finish.

* *Commercial "Eagle N" Proofed* — .22 LR, .32 ACP, or .380 ACP cal., Nazi Eagle over N (standard Nazi commercial acceptance proof).

	100%	98%	95%	90%	80%	70%	60%
.22 LR cal.	$1,200	$1,100	$800	$600	$525	$460	$420
.32 ACP cal.	$625	$475	$375	$350	$300	$250	$225
.380 ACP cal.	$2,500	$2,250	$1,800	$1,000	$600	$500	$400

This variation is normally encountered with semi-polished, exterior metal showing milling marks to various degrees.

* *Waffenamt Proofed With High Polish*

	100%	98%	95%	90%	80%	70%	60%
	$1,200	$1,100	$950	$650	$425	$330	$275

* *Eagle C Marked* — .32 ACP cal., "Crown N - Eagle C", mfg. for Nazi Police.

	100%	98%	95%	90%	80%	70%	60%
	$675	$595	$535	$450	$335	$260	$200

Add 25% for high polish finish.

* *Eagle F Marked* — .32 ACP cal., "Crown N - Eagle F", Nazi Police, all have the light weight aluminum frame.

	100%	98%	95%	90%	80%	70%	60%
	$950	$800	$600	$475	$375	$300	$250

* *RZM Marked* — .32 ACP cal., "Crown N", proof marking for Reichszeugmeisterei and Reich Party Purchasing Office.

	100%	98%	95%	90%	80%	70%	60%
	$1,000	$900	$800	$600	$350	$275	$225

* *Party Leader* — .32 ACP cal., named because grips (brown or black plastic) have the German eagle holding a Swastika, "Crown N" or "Eagle N" proofed, honor weapon awarded 3rd Reich political leaders, rare. Be very wary of fake grips (especially black color) as reproductions have been made recently. Unfortunately, the grips on a Party Leader (mfg. 1936-1941) are the only distinguishing feature on this very desirable configuration.

	100%	98%	95%	90%	80%	70%	60%
	$3,000	$2,400	$1,800	$1,500	$1,200	$1,100	$1,000

* *RZM With Party Leader Grips* — .32 ACP cal., RZM marked, "Crown N" proofed.

	100%	98%	95%	90%	80%	70%	60%
	$3,200	$2,950	$2,650	$2,200	$1,300	$1,200	$1,100

* *RFV Marked* — .32 ACP cal., "Crown N". Mfg. for Reichsfinanzverwaltung and Reich Finance Administration.

	100%	98%	95%	90%	80%	70%	60%
	$1,200	$1,000	$825	$750	$800	$700	$675

* *PDM Marked* — .32 ACP cal., "Crown N". Mfg. for Polizeidirektion Munchen and Police Dept. Munich. All have the bottom mag. release.

	100%	98%	95%	90%	80%	70%	60%
	$1,500	$1,200	$995	$750	$600	$500	$395

* *DRP Marked* — .32 ACP cal., "Crown N". Mfg. for Deutsche Reichsport and German Postal Service.

	100%	98%	95%	90%	80%	70%	60%
	$1,200	$1,000	$800	$600	$420	$350	$260

* *Panagraph Slide*

	100%	98%	95%	90%	80%	70%	60%
	$850	$750	$675	$525	$450	$375	$300

Grading	100%	98%	95%	90%	80%	70%	60%

* **Verchromt** — .32 ACP or 380 ACP cal., differentiated by dull silver satin type finish.

	$2,000	$1,600	$1,300	$1,000	$800	$650	$500

Add 50% for .380 ACP cal.

* **"K" suffix** — "K" beneath ser. no.

	$625	$525	$475	$375	$300	$275	$250

* **"W" suffix** — .32 ACP cal., "Crown N" proofed, W-suffix ser. no.

	$625	$550	$475	$375	$300	$275	$250

* **Early 90 degree safety**

	$675	$625	$525	$425	$325	$260	$195

* **Early bottom release Mag.**

	$1,000	$900	$775	$650	$500	$475	$375

* **PPK Marked PP**

	$2,500	$2,150	$1,850	$1,600	$1,400	$1,180	$900

* **7-digit ser. no.**

	$725	$700	$650	$600	$550	$400	$300

* **Dural frame** — .22 LR, .32 ACP, or .380 ACP cal., chrome finish (very rare), "Eagle N".

	$675	$625	$600	$525	$400	$325	$275

Add 200% for .380 ACP.
Add 100% in .22 LR cal.

* **Czech. Contract** — Rampant Lion stamped.

	$1,000	$900	$750	$625	$550	$425	$325

* **Danish Rplt.**

	$1,000	$900	$750	$625	$550	$425	$325

* **Allemagne** — French Commercial — rare.

	$1,200	$1,100	$1,000	$800	$550	$425	$325

MODEL PPK LIGHTWEIGHT — aluminum alloy version.

Add 20% to .32 cal. commercial price listing.

SPORT MODEL 1926 — .22 S or LR (known as Standard Model in Germany) cal.

	$1,050	$900	$800	$675	$595	$550	$495

1932 OLYMPIA MODEL — .22 S or LR cal., 10 shot, 6 or 9 in. barrel, target sights, one-piece grip, introduced in 1928 and used in 1932 Olympics. Marketed by Stoeger and Chas. Heyer-Nairobi.

	$1,100	$925	$825	$625	$495	$440	$395

OLYMPIA SPORT MODEL — .22 LR cal., 4 in. barrel, adj. target sights, blue, wood grips, 4 barrel weights available. Mfg. 1936-1940.

	$925	$825	$725	$600	$475	$420	$375

Add 20% for weight set.

1936 OLYMPIA "JÄGERSCHAFTS" HUNTING MODEL — similar to Sport, with 4 in. barrel. Mfg. 1936-1940. Also seen with Eagle N proofs.

	$1,500	$1,200	$995	$625	$495	$440	$360

OLYMPIA RAPID FIRE MODEL — .22 Short cal.only, 7.4 in. barrel, blue, adj. sight, wood grip, has alloy slide. Mfg. 1936-1940.

	$1,500	$1,200	$995	$600	$520	$460	$380

1936 OLYMPIA FÜNFKAMPF MODEL — .22 Short or LR cal., 9¼ in. barrel, blue, adj. sight, wood grips, barrel weights, circa 1936.

	$1,600	$1,400	$1,100	$800	$575	$500	$440

W

Grading	100%	98%	95%	90%	80%	70%	60%

MODEL HP COMMERCIAL DOUBLE ACTION — 9mm Para. cal., pre-war version of P-38, 5 in. barrel, fixed sight, blue, wood or plastic grips. Mfg. 1937-1944. Many variations, including several different finishes.

> See German WWII Military Pistols section for values on this model.

PISTOLS: SEMI-AUTO, POST-WAR

During 1983, the West German PPK/S Model ceased to be imported by Interarms. Manurhin of France no longer imports into the U.S., and guns imported between 1984-86 will not have the Interarms logo or Walther trademark.

MODEL PP DOUBLE ACTION — .22 LR, .32 ACP, or .380 ACP cal., specifications similar to pre-war PP, 3⅞ in. barrel. Imported 1963-present. German manufacture.

* *.380 ACP cal.* — 7 shot mag.

	100%	98%	95%	90%	80%	70%	60%
Mfg.'s Sug. Retail $999	$875	$550	$425	$330	$300	$275	$250

* *.32 ACP cal.* — 8 shot mag. Importation disc. 1997.

$495	$425	$350	$295	$275	$250	$225

Last Mfg.'s Sug. Retail was $999.

* *.22 LR cal.* — 10 shot mag., disc. 1989, reintroduced 1992-94.

$650	$500	$475	$350	$325	$300	$275

Last Mfg.'s Sug. Retail was $783.

* *Blue Engraved* — .22 LR (disc.) or .380 ACP (disc. 1991) cal.

$1,350	$1,100	$950

Last Mfg.'s Sug. Retail was $1,650.

Add 5% for .22 LR cal.

* *Chrome Engraved* — .22 LR or .380 ACP cal. Disc. 1990.

$1,350	$1,100	$950

Last Mfg.'s Sug. Retail was $1,600.

Add $50 for .22 LR cal.

* *Silver Engraved* — .22 LR or .380 ACP (disc. 1990) cal. Importation disc. 1993.

$1,575	$1,150	$1,000

Last Mfg.'s Sug. Retail was $1,948.

* *Gold Engraved* — .22 LR or .380 ACP (disc. 1989) cal. Importation disc. 1993.

$1,725	$1,450	$1,150

Last Mfg.'s Sug. Retail was $2,053.

* *Manurhin PP* — .22 LR, .32 ACP, or .380 ACP cal.

$375	$340	$295	$225	$180	$165	$150

Add 10% for .380 ACP cal.

* *Model PP 50th Anniversary Commemorative* — .32 ACP, or .380 ACP cal., gold-plated parts, hand carved grips, presentation case. 500 imported to U.S. 1979. 800 mfg.

$1,200	$900	$600

Last Mfg.'s Sug. Retail was $1,700.

PP SPORT — double action, thumbrest grips, round hammer with spur, adj. rear sight, long barrel. Mfg. 1953-1970.

	100%	98%	95%	90%	80%	70%	60%
Manurhin manufacture	$650	$625	$600	$525	$475	$400	$325
Mark II (mfg. 1955-1957)	$725	$680	$625	$575	$520	$480	$425
Walther manufacture	$775	$725	$700	$575	$520	$475	$400

Subtract 10% if not marked.

Note: Add $75 for barrel weight, $100 for factory case, 20% for factory nickel, 5% for single action.

* *PP Sport "C" Model C* — mfg. for competition shooting, single action, 7⅝ in. barrel, spur hammer.

$795	$750	$675	$625	$525	$475	$400

Grading	100%	98%	95%	90%	80%	70%	60%

MODEL PPK — similar to pre-war PPK, .22 LR, .32 ACP, or .380 ACP cal., 3.31 in. barrel. Mfg. post-war - present, U.S. import stopped by GCA 68 on W. German and French production.

	100%	98%	95%	90%	80%	70%	60%
.32 ACP cal.	$525	$450	$375	$325	$295	$270	$250
.22 LR cal.	$725	$645	$550	$500	$425	$350	$300
.380 ACP cal.	$695	$625	$550	$450	$400	$325	$275
Blue engraved	$1,600	$1,300	$950				
Silver engraved	$1,850	$1,400	$1,000				
Gold engraved	$2,200	$1,675	$1,250				

100% column assumes NIB condition - subtract 15% if not boxed.

MODEL PPK LIGHTWEIGHT — similar to Standard, with dural frame, .22 LR or .32 ACP cal.

	100%	98%	95%	90%	80%	70%	60%
	$500	$425	$390	$325	$295	$270	$250

Add 20% for .22 LR cal.

MODEL PPK-1986 U.S. PRODUCTION — .380 ACP cal. only, 3.35 in. barrel, similar specifications as previous W. German and French manufacture, blue or bright nickel (new 1997) finish, 7 shot finger extension mag., black plastic grips, 21 oz. Made in the U.S. Introduced 1986.

Mfg.'s Sug. Retail	$540	$425	$350	$310	$285	$250	$225	$200

Manufacture in the U.S. is under an exclusive licensing agreement with Walther of Germany.

✽ PPK Stainless — .32 ACP (new 1998) or .380 ACP cal., stainless steel construction. New 1986.

Mfg.'s Sug. Retail	$540	$425	$350	$310

MODEL PPK/S — .22 LR, .32 ACP, or .380 ACP cal., similar to PPK, except has larger PP frame to meet import requirements of 1968, 3¼ in. barrel, production in W. Germany, Manurhin of France (disc. 1986), and in the U.S. (mfg. under license from Walther by Interarms). 10 (.22 LR) or 8 (.32 ACP and .380 ACP) shot, double action, fixed sights.

✽ American PPK/S — .380 ACP cal. only, blue finish, 7 shot, one finger extension and one flat bottom mag.

Mfg.'s Sug. Retail	$540	$425	$350	$310	$285	$250	$225	$200

✽ Stainless PPK/S — .32 ACP (new 1998) or .380 ACP cal., American manufacture, introduced July of 1983.

Mfg.'s Sug. Retail	$540	$445	$375	$310

✽ W. German PPK/S — .22 LR (disc.), .32 ACP (currently mfg., not imported), or .380 ACP (currently mfg., not imported) cal.

	100%	98%	95%	90%	80%	70%	60%
.22 LR cal.	$695	$625	$550	$425	$350	$300	$275
.32 ACP cal.	$525	$450	$375	$325	$295	$270	$250
.380 ACP cal.	$675	$575	$495	$395	$300	$275	$250

✽ American PPK/S — blue engraved. Disc. 1985.

	$875	$850	$800				

Last Mfg.'s Sug. Retail was $990.

✽ American PPK/S Gold-Engraved Commemorative — 500 total mfg. Disc. 1987.

	$1,000	$875	$700				

Last Mfg.'s Sug. Retail was $1,200.

✽ American PPK/S Gold-Engraved — disc. 1985.

	$975	$850	$700				

Last Mfg.'s Sug. Retail was $1,070.

✽ W. German PPK/S Blue Engraved — inventory depleted 1990.

	$1,395	$1,050	$850				

Last Mfg.'s Sug. Retail was $1,550.

✽ W. German PPK/S Chrome Engraved — importation disc. 1991.

	$1,450	$1,075	$950				

Last Mfg.'s Sug. Retail was $1,700.

✽ W. German PPK/S Silver Engraved — disc. 1988.

	$1,595	$1,150	$975				

Last Mfg.'s Sug. Retail was $1,700.

Grading	100%	98%	95%	90%	80%	70%	60%

✱ W. German PPK/S Gold Engraved — disc. 1985.

	100%	98%	95%
	$1,850	**$1,250**	**$1,000**

Last Mfg.'s Sug. Retail was $1,800.

MANURHIN PPK/S — see listings under Manurhin section.

MODEL PP SUPER — 9x18mm, (Police) or .380 ACP cal., 3.6 in. barrel, fixed sights, plastic grips, blue. Mfg. 1973-1979.

	100%	98%	95%	90%	80%	70%	60%
	$725	$675	$550	$395	$285	$250	$235

Subtract 25% if in 9x18mm cal.

✱ PP Super-Cutaway

	100%	98%	95%
	$650	$600	$550

MODEL TP — .22 LR or .25 ACP cal., updated version of Model 9, concealed hammer. Mfg. 1961-1971.

	100%	98%	95%	90%	80%	70%	60%
.22 LR cal.	$675	$600	$435	$350	$300	$260	$210
.25 ACP cal.	$495	$425	$360	$300	$250	$220	$185

MODEL TPH — .22 LR or .25 ACP cal., double action 2.8 in. barrel, alloy frame, blue, fixed sights, plastic grips. Mfg. 1968-present in W. Germany, U.S. import stopped by GCA of 1968.

	100%	98%	95%	90%	80%	70%	60%
.22 LR cal.	$625	$575	$515	$450	$300	$275	$220
.25 ACP cal.	$650	$600	$550	$475	$350	$300	$250

Subtract 10% on the 100% values if not boxed with all accessories.

100% price assumes NIB condition.

AMERICAN MODEL TPH — .22 LR or .25 ACP (new 1992) cal., blued finish or stainless steel, double action, black plastic grips, 6 shot mag., 2¼ in. barrel, 14 oz. Introduced 1987.

		100%	98%	95%	90%	80%	70%	60%
Mfg.'s Sug. Retail	$460	$365	$335	$280	$250	$225	$200	$185

✱ American Model TPH Stainless — stainless steel fabrication.

		100%	98%	95%	90%
Mfg.'s Sug. Retail	$460	$365	$335	$280	

MODEL P.38 — Post-war version of P.38 Military, .22 LR (disc.), 7.65 (disc.), or 9mm Para. cal., 5 in. barrel, alloy frame, matte black finish, 28 oz. W. German manufacture. See German WWII Military Pistols for wartime listings.

Note: Due to the release of large numbers of W. German Police and Army trade-ins of P.38 9mm Para. and PP .32 ACP cal. models, the actual value of original models in 90% or less condition has decreased somewhat. The two models most affected are the P-1 variation of the P.38, and the German PP in .32 ACP cal.

	100%	98%	95%	90%	80%	70%	60%
	$700	$575	$475	$350	$295	$245	$190

Last Mfg.'s Sug. Retail was $824.

✱ P.38 Long Barrel Special Edition — 9mm Para. cal., steel frame, 6, 7, or 8, in. barrel, wood grips, 50 mfg. 1988.

	100%	98%	95%	90%	80%	70%	60%
	$3,500	$3,200	$2,750	$2,425	$2,100	$1,800	$1,500

✱ Steel Frame P.38 — 9mm Para. cal., similar to regular P.38, except has steel frame, 34 oz. Imported 1987-1989 only.

	100%	98%	95%	90%	80%	70%	60%
	$975	$850	$650	$550	$400	$295	$245

Last Mfg.'s Sug. Retail was $1,400.

✱ P.38 in .22 LR cal. — disc. 1989.

	100%	98%	95%	90%	80%	70%	60%
	$875	$795	$650	$450	$350	$300	$200

Last Mfg.'s Sug. Retail was $1,050.

MODEL P.38 SPECIAL EDITIONS/ENGRAVED

✱ P.38 50th Year Commemorative — alloy frame, carved grips, presentation engraved with deluxe walnut presentation case. Introduced 1987, inventory depleted 1992.

	100%	98%	95%
	$1,750	$1,250	$875

Last Mfg.'s Sug. Retail was $950.

✱ P.38 100th Year Commemorative — 9mm Para. cal., alloy frame with slide engraving "100 Jahre Walther 1886-1986".

	100%	98%	95%
	$800	$690	$450

W

Grading	100%	98%	95%	90%	80%	70%	60%

* ***Blue Engraved*** — 9mm Para. cal. Importation disc. 1991.

        $1,850 **$1,325** **$1,125**   **$900**

         Last Mfg.'s Sug. Retail was $1,850.

* ***Chrome Engraved*** — 9mm Para. cal. Importation disc. 1991.

        $1,475 **$1,175**   **$925**

         Last Mfg.'s Sug. Retail was $2,125.

* ***Silver Engraved*** — 9mm Para. cal. Importation disc. 1991.

        $1,450 **$1,175**   **$925**

         Last Mfg.'s Sug. Retail was $2,100.

* ***Gold Engraved*** — 9mm Para. cal. Disc. 1987.

        $1,800 **$1,500** **$1,000**

         Last Mfg.'s Sug. Retail was $2,050.

MODEL P1 — 9mm Para. cal., post-war commercial variation of the P.38 with steel slide and alloy frame, 5 in. barrel, 8 shot mag., black plastic grips, Disc.

        $650   **$550**   **$400**   **$300**   **$250**   **$215**   **$165**

MODEL P4 — 9mm Para. cal., modernized variation of the original P.38, 4½ in. barrel, 8 shot mag., updates include reinforced steel slide and alloy frame, includes decocking lever and automatic safeties, rear sight, 29 oz. Mfg. 1975-1981, importation disc. 1982.

        $695   **$595**   **$525**   **$425**   **$300**   **$250**   **$200**

MODEL P.38K — 9mm Para. cal., shortened 2.8 in. barrel variation of P.38, front sight on slide. Mfg. 1974-1981.

        $900   **$850**   **$725**   **$550**   **$400**   **$250**   **$200**

MODEL P-5 — 9mm Para. cal., double action, alloy frame, frame mounted decocking lever, 3½ in. barrel, adj. rear sight, blue finish only, 8 shot mag., auto safeties, 28 oz. Mfg. 1977-present.

  Mfg.'s Sug. Retail   **$900**   **$725**   **$675**   **$525**   **$475**   **$450**   **$425**   **$375**

* ***P-5 Compact*** — compact variation of P-5 with 3.1 in. barrel, 26½ oz. Mfg. 1987-1996.

        $850   **$775**   **$575**   **$500**   **$450**   **$425**   **$375**

* ***P-5 100th Year Commemorative*** — marked "1886-1986 100 Jahre" with Walther banner, elaborate grip carving, presentation walnut case. Imported 1986-91.

        $2,100 **$1,425** **$1,025**

         Last Mfg.'s Sug. Retail was $2,890.

MODEL P-88 — 9mm Para. cal., double action, alloy frame, 4 in. barrel, 15 shot side release mag., ambidextrous decocking lever, matte finish, adj. rear sight, internal safeties, loaded chamber indicator, black synthetic grips, 31½ oz. Mfg. 1987-1993.

        $1,325 **$1,175**   **$700**   **$575**   **$490**   **$450**   **$400**

         Last Mfg.'s Sug. Retail was $1,129.

* ***P-88 Compact*** — 3.93 in. barrel, 14★ (disc.) or 10 (C/B 1994) shot mag., 29 oz. Importation began 1993.

  Mfg.'s Sug. Retail   **$900**   **$825**   **$700**   **$600**   **$525**   **$475**   **$450**   **$425**

    This model had a substantial price decrease beginning 1996 (1994 retail price was $1,725).

P-99 — 9mm Para., 9x21mm (new 1999), or .40 S&W (new 1998) cal., traditional double action only, 4 in. barrel, polymer frame, trigger, decocking, and internal striker safeties, 10 shot mag., cocking and loaded chamber indicators, choice of matte black or QPQ (new 1999) finished (silver colored) slide, ambidextrous mag. release, ergonomic black or green (Military model, new 1999) synthetic grips with interchangable backstrap, adj. rear sight, 25 oz. Importation began 1997.

  Mfg.'s Sug. Retail   **$799**   **$700**   **$600**   **$525**   **$475**   **$450**   **$425**   **$375**

    Add $10 for .40 S&W cal., or $10 for .40 S&W with QPQ finish.
    Add $10 for Military Model (green colored grips).

* ***P-99 La Chasse DU Engraved*** — similar to Model P-99 Military, except has engraved slide. New 1998.

  Mfg.'s Sug. Retail   **$1,078**   **$900**   **$800**   **$725**   **$625**   **$550**   **$495**   **$450**

Grading	100%	98%	95%	90%	80%	70%	60%

* ***P-99 La Chasse Engraved*** — features choice of elaborate oak leaf, arabesque, or English style scoll engraving on QPQ finished slide. New 1998.

Mfg.'s Sug. Retail	$2,126	$1,850	$1,600	$1,400	$1,200	$1,000	$850	$700

P-990 — similar to P-99, except is double action only, features Walther's constant pull trigger system, black, QPQ slide finish, or Military Model (green grips), 25 oz. New 1998.

Mfg.'s Sug. Retail	$749	$675	$575	$525	$475	$450	$425	$375

PISTOLS: SEMI-AUTO, TARGET

Walther target pistols are currently being imported by Champions Choice located in La Vergne, TN and Earl's Repair Service since 1994 located in Tewksbury, MA. Previously imported by Interarms until 1993 and Nygord Precision Products until 1996.
Add 10% to the values listed below for left-hand stocks (available on most models).

MODEL GSP TARGET STANDARD — .22 LR cal., 4½ in. barrel, single action, 5 shot mag. standard, 8 or 10 shot mag. optional, adj. sights, nickel, two-tone, or blue finish, walnut target grips, 2-stage trigger became standard in 1995, optional carrying case, 42.3 oz. Mfg. 1969-present.

Mfg.'s Sug. Retail	$1,450	$1,395	$1,100	$900	$650	$550	$475	$425

* ***Model GSP Rifle Conversion Kit*** — .22 LR cal., unique conversion allows taking a GSP action and inserting it into a rifle stock, includes 16½ in. barrel with compensator and black, brown or multicolored laminate stock, right hand only. New 1997.

Mfg.'s Sug. Retail	$995	$995	$850	$725

* ***Model GSP Junior*** — similar to GSP Target, except has slimmer 4¼ in. barrel design, smaller walnut grips, 40.1 oz. Importation disc. 1992.

	$1,400	$1,100	$925	$750	$600	$500	$425

Last Mfg.'s Sug. Retail was $1,810.

* ***Model GSP 25th Year Commemorative Special Limited Edition*** — .22 LR cal., aluminum carrying case, options included two-tone finish, laminated Canadian black birch grip, titanium plated bolt, special 70 gr barrel weight with "25 Jahre GSP" engraved, adj. front sight, 35 gr. mag. weight, 1360 gr., two-stage trigger. 1,000 mfg. 1994.

	$2,500	$2,150	$1,850

* ***Model GSP Atlanta*** — .22 LR cal., special edition for the 1996 Olympic Games, Atlanta inscribed on right side of bolt housing, black laminate grips, titanium plated bolt, otherwise same as GSP Target Standard.

	$1,800	$1,450	$1,000

* ***Model GSP-C*** — similar to Model GSP Target, except in .32 S&W Wadcutter, and 4¼ in. barrel, 49.4 oz. Mfg. 1971-present.

Mfg.'s Sug. Retail	$1,550	$1,425	$1,025	$800	$650	$550	$475	$425

    Add $1,195 for GSP-C .22 Short conversion unit.
    Add $1,050 for GSP-C .22 LR cal. conversion unit.
    Add $1,195 for GSP-C .32 S&W Wadcutter conversion unit.

* ***Model GSP-C 25th Year Commemorative Special Limited Edition*** — similar to GSP 25th Year Commemorative, except in .32 S&W Wadcutter, engraved 65 gr. barrel weight, 1,000 mfg. as complete pistols or conversion units. Mfg. 1996 only.

	$2,500	$2,150	$1,850

MODEL OSP RAPID FIRE — similar to GSP, in .22 Short cal.. Mfg. 1961-1994, for international competition (meets ISU and NRA regs.), 4¼ in. barrel, 44.4 oz., supplied with case.

	$1,375	$1,000	$800	$650	$550	$475	$425

Last Mfg.'s Sug. Retail was $1,530.

    Add $145 for extended sight radius and semi-wraparound grip.

FREE PISTOL — .22 LR cal., single shot, electronic trigger, 11.7 in. heavy barrel, advanced target design with fully adj. grips and sights, 48 oz. Mfg. disc. 1991.

	$1,600	$1,200	$1,000	$850	$675	$575	$500

Last Mfg.'s Sug. Retail was $2,140.

P.38 WWII MILITARY MFG. — see German Military for breakdown.

Grading	100%	98%	95%	90%	80%	70%	60%

HÄMMERLI-WALTHER — see Hämmerli.

REVOLVERS

MODEL R99 — .357 Mag. cal., 6 shot, double action, 3 in. barrel, adj. rear sight, blue or stainless steel, unique Duo-grip allows for different hand sizes (2 grips included), 28½ oz. Mfg. by Smith & Wesson beginning 1999.

As this edition went to press, prices had yet to be announced for this model.

RIFLES: DISC.

MODEL B — .30-06 cal., bolt action, post-war mfg., 22 in. barrel. Add 20% for double set triggers. Disc.

	100%	98%	95%	90%	80%	70%	60%
	$450	$420	$380	$340	$300	$275	$250

MODEL 1 — .22 LR cal., Carbine model, autoloading, clip fed, 20½ in. barrel, 5 or 9 (optional) shot mag., could be used as bolt action or semi-auto, checkered pistol grip, walnut sporter stock, 5½ lbs.

	$695	$600	$500	$400	$300	$250	$200

MODEL 2 AUTOLOADING — .22 LR cal., similar to Model 1, except has 24½ in. barrel, finger grooved forearm, tangent sight, adj. trigger, checkered sporter stock, pre-war, 7 lbs.

	$695	$600	$500	$400	$300	$250	$200

MODEL V CHAMPION — similar to Model V Single Shot, with micrometer adj. sight and checkered pistol grip stock.

	$470	$440	$415	$385	$330	$305	$250

MODEL KKM INTERNATIONAL MATCH — .22 LR cal., single shot bolt action, 28 in. heavy barrel, adj. aperture sight, adj. hook butt, thumbhole stock, accessory rail, post-war mfg.

	$880	$770	$715	$660	$550	$495	$440

MODEL KKM-S — similar to KKM, with adj. cheekpiece.

	$935	$825	$770	$715	$605	$550	$495

MODEL KKJ SPORTER — .22 LR cal., bolt action, 5 shot, 22½ in. barrel, open sight, checkered sporter stock, post-war.

	$995	$825	$650	$550	$450	$385	$330

Add 20% for double set triggers.

MODEL KKW — .22 LR cal., single shot, military stock, tangent sight, pre-war mfg.

	$540	$490	$420	$300	$260	$220	$195

MODEL KKJ-MA — .22 Mag. cal.

	$995	$825	$650	$550	$450	$385	$330

MODEL KKJ-HO — .22 Hornet cal.

	$995	$825	$650	$550	$450	$385	$330

Add 20% for double set triggers.

MODEL SSV VARMINT — .22 LR cal., single shot bolt action, 25½ in. barrel, no sights, Monte Carlo pistol grip stock, post-war mfg.

	$605	$550	$525	$495	$415	$360	$330
.22 Hornet	$660	$605	$580	$550	$470	$415	$385

MODEL PRONE 400 — similar to UIT Match, with Prone style competition stock and no sights. Disc.

	$750	$635	$580	$525	$415	$360	$305

RIFLES: RECENT MFG.

MODEL UIT BV UNIVERSAL — .22 LR cal., single shot bolt action, 25½ in. heavy barrel, adj. aperture sight, target stock with palm rest, adj. butt, meets ISU regs., 16 lbs. Disc. 1990.

	$1,325	$1,050	$850	$700	$635	$580	$530

Last Mfg.'s Sug. Retail was $1,700.

This model was previously known as the Model UIT Special.

Grading	100%	98%	95%	90%	80%	70%	60%

MODEL UIT MATCH — similar to Model UIT, except with improved stock design which includes fully stippled lower forearm and pistol grip, 13 lbs. Importation disc. 1993.

	$1,125	$925	$800	$660	$610	$555	$510

Last Mfg.'s Sug. Retail was $1,400.

* **Model UIT-E** — electronic trigger, 25½ in. barrel, 9 lbs. Disc. 1986.

	$1,350	$940	$860	$770	$670	$630	$560

Last Mfg.'s Sug. Retail was $1,250.

GX-1 — similar to Model UIT Match, 25½ in. barrel with fully adj. free rifle stock, all accessories included, 16½ lbs. Importation disc. 1991.

	$1,895	$1,375	$1,125	$985	$860	$775	$680

Last Mfg.'s Sug. Retail was $2,350.

MODEL KK/MS SILHOUETTE — .22 LR cal. only, designed for silhouette shooting with no sights, thumbhole stock with adj. butt, fully stippled forend and stock grip, front barrel weight, 25½ in. barrel, 8¾ lbs. Imported 1984-91.

	$975	$795	$625	$560	$495	$435	$395

Last Mfg.'s Sug. Retail was $1,175.

RUNNING BOAR MODEL 500 — similar to KK/MS, no sights, thumbhole stock with adj. butt and cheekpiece, 23½ in. barrel, 10¼ lbs. Disc. 1990.

	$1,025	$825	$640	$570	$500	$435	$395

Last Mfg.'s Sug. Retail was $1,300.

MODEL WA-2000 — .300 Win. Mag. or .308 Win. cal., ultra-deluxe semi-auto, includes aluminum case, two mags., integral bipod, adj. tools and leather sling, special order only. Disc. 1988.

	$6,400	$4,800	$4,500	$4,000	$3,500	$3,000	$2,500

SHOTGUNS: SxS

MODEL SF — 12 or 16 ga., checkered walnut stock, double triggers, boxlock, sling swivels. Disc.

	$500	$450	$395	$325	$275	$240	$200

MODEL SFD — 12 or 16 ga., cheekpiece, checkered walnut stock, double triggers, boxlock, sling swivels. Disc.

	$625	$575	$500	$425	$375	$340	$300

WALTHER, FRENCH-MADE BY MANURHIN

Previously manufactured in Mulhouse, France. Previously imported 1984-86 by Matra-Manurhin International, Inc. located in Alexandria, VA.

PISTOLS: SEMI-AUTO

Manufacture of these Walther pistols commenced in France in 1951. They were marked MANURHIN on the slide until 1954. Since then they were designated Walther MKII. They were imported into the USA by Interarms up to 1983. In 1984, Manurhin was imported directly with no Interarms logo or Walther trademark appearing on Models PP and PPK/S. Importation was discontinued 1986.

MODEL PP — .22 LR, .32 ACP, or .380 ACP cal., 3⅞ in. barrel, 10 shot mag.-.22 LR, 8 shot mag.-.32 ACP, 7 shot mag.-.380 ACP, blue only, all steel construction, double action with positive hammer block safety, 24 oz.

	$400	$350	$300	$230	$205	$185	$170

Last Mfg.'s Sug. Retail was $419.

Add $25 for .22 LR or .380 ACP cal.
Add $46 for Durgarde finish.

* **Collector Model** — blue finish, special engraving. Imported 1986 only.

	$465	$415	$350

Last Mfg.'s Sug. Retail was $529.

Grading	100%	98%	95%	90%	80%	70%	60%

* Presentation Model — blue finish, special ornamentation. Imported 1986 only.

	$720	$650	$500				

Last Mfg.'s Sug. Retail was $819.

Interarms import — $350 / $325 / $285 / $230 / $205 / $180 / $160

Also available with various engraving options in either blue, nickel, or gold finish - prices range from $222 - $540.

PP SPORT — .22 LR cal. only, double action, 6.1 or 8.1 in. barrel, blue finish only, precision adj. sights, contoured plastic grips with thumb rest, 25 oz. New Manurhin design beginning 1985-disc.

| | | $545 | $485 | $430 | $385 | $325 | $290 | $270 |

Last Mfg.'s Sug. Retail was $635.

* PP Sport-C — similar to PP Sport, except is single action.

| | | $540 | $475 | $415 | $370 | $310 | $280 | $260 |

Last Mfg.'s Sug. Retail was $635.

MODEL PPK — .22 LR, .32 ACP, or .380 ACP cal., 3¼ in. barrel, 10 shot mag.-.22 LR, 8 shot mag.-.32 ACP, 7 shot mag.-.380 ACP, blue only, all steel construction, double action with positive hammer block safety, 23 oz.

| | | $550 | $475 | $425 | $375 | $350 | $325 | $300 |

Add $25 for .22 LR or .380 ACP cal.

MODEL PPK/S — .22 LR, .32 ACP, or .380 ACP cal., 3¼ in. barrel, 10 shot mag.-.22 LR, 8 shot mag.-.32 ACP, 7 shot mag.-.380 ACP, blue only, all steel construction, double action with positive hammer block safety, 23 oz.

| | | $400 | $350 | $300 | $230 | $205 | $185 | $170 |

Last Mfg.'s Sug. Retail was $419.

Add 10% for .22 LR cal.

* PPK/S Durgarde — similar to above, only with bonded brushed chrome finish.

| | | $450 | $400 | $350 | $300 | $275 | $250 | $240 |

Last Mfg.'s Sug. Retail was $465.

Add 10% for .22 LR cal.

* Collector Model — blue finish, special engraving. Imported 1986 only.

| | | $465 | $415 | $350 | | | | |

Last Mfg.'s Sug. Retail was $529.

* Presentation Model — blue finish, special ornamentation. Imported 1986 only.

| | | $720 | $650 | $500 | | | | |

Last Mfg.'s Sug. Retail was $819.

Interarms import — $395 / $340 / $300 / $275 / $250 / $235 / $210

Was also available with various engraving options in either blue, nickel, or gold finish — prices range from $222 - $540.

WARNER ARMS CORPORATION

Previous manufacturer located in Norwich, CT.

PISTOLS: SEMI-AUTO

INFALLIBLE POCKET AUTO PISTOL — .32 ACP cal., 7 shot, 3 in. barrel, fixed sights, rubber grips. Mfg. 1917-1919.

| | | $450 | $350 | $250 | $150 | $125 | $100 | $90 |

WATSON BROS.

Current long gun manufacturer established in 1885, and located in London, England. Watson Bros. manufactures distinct round body actions with self-opening locks in both SxS and O/U shotgun configurations. Back action sidelock double rifles are also available. Please contact the factory directly (see Trademark Index) for more information including current pricing.

Grading	100%	98%	95%	90%	80%	70%	60%

WEATHERBY

Current trademark imported by Weatherby located in Atascadero, CA since 1995. Previously located in South Gate, CA, 1945 - 1995. Weatherby began manufacturing rifles in the U.S. during early 1995. Dealer and distributor sales.

Weatherby is an importer/manufacturer of long arms. Earlier production was from Germany and Italy, and German mfg. is usually what is collectible. Current rifle production is from the U.S., while shotguns are made in Japan. Workmanship in all instances is quite good. Weatherby is well known for their high-velocity proprietary rifle calibers.

Early Weatherby rifles used a Mathieu Arms action in the 1950s - primarily since it was available in left-hand action. Right-handed actions were normally mfg. from the FN Mauser type.

DRILLINGS

WEATHERBY DRILLING — mfg. by J. P. Sauer during the late 1960s-early 1970s for Weatherby importation (marked Weatherby on right barrel), identical to Sauer Model 3000, except was not available in all metric cals. Disc.

	$2,850	$2,450	$2,100	$1,800	$1,500	$1,250	$1,000

PISTOLS: BOLT ACTION

SILHOUETTE PISTOL — .22-250 Rem. or .308 Win. cal., mfg. in Japan during late 1970s, 14½ in. barrel, Lyman or Williams sights, fitted case. Only 50 were mfg. in .22-250 Rem. and 150 in .308 Win. cal. Disc. 1981.

	$3,750	$3,300	$2,750	$2,450	$2,100	$1,850	$1,650

W

MARK V CFP (CENTERFIRE PISTOLS) — .22-250 Rem., .243 Win., 7mm-08 Rem., or .308 Win. cal., features 15 in. fluted stainless barrel with recessed crown, ambidextrous designed multi-layer brown laminate stock with finger grooves and swivel studs, blued Mark V lightweight action, no sights, 3 shot internal mag. New 1997.

Mfg.'s Sug. Retail	$1,049	$900	$800	$725	$650	$600	$550	$500

RIFLES: BOLT ACTION, MARK V SERIES

For German manufacture, add 15%-25% for calibers under .35 if condition is 95% or better. In 1992, 24 in. barrels were disc. on most calibers of .300 or greater (including Models Mark V Deluxe, Fibermark, Lazermark, and Euromark). Since 1957, the Mark V Action has been manufactured in Germany, Japan, and the U.S.

MARK V DELUXE — .22-250 Rem. (new 1999), .240 Wby. Mag. (disc. 1996, reintroduced 1999), .243 Win. (new 1999), .25-06 Rem. (new 1999), .257 Wby. Mag., .270 Win. (new 1999), .270 Wby. Mag., .280 Rem. (new 1999), 7mm Wby. Mag., 7mm-08 Rem. (new 1999), .30-06 (disc. 1996, reintroduced 1999), .308 Win. (new 1999), .300 Wby. Mag., .340 Wby. Mag., or .375 H&H (mfg. 1993 only) cal., bolt action, 3-5 shot mag., 24 or 26 in. barrel, deluxe skip line checkered pistol grip walnut stock with rosewood tipped forearm and pistol grip, no sights, 8 lbs. Left-hand actions (.270 Wby. Mag. and .300 Wby. Mag.) were available at no extra charge through 1997.

* **Short Action Cals.** — .22-250 Rem., .243 Win., .240 Wby. Mag., .25-06 Rem., .270 Win., .280 Rem., .30-06, .308 Win., or 7mm-08 Rem. short action cals. New 1999.

Mfg.'s Sug. Retail	$1,449	$1,175	$825	$650	$550	$495	$450	$410

* **Wby. Mag. Cals.** — includes cals. bewteen .257 Wby. Mag. - .340 Wby. Mag.

Mfg.'s Sug. Retail	$1,599	$1,275	$875	$675	$550	$495	$450	$410

Add $200 for .375 H&H cal. (disc. 1993).

* **.378 Wby. Mag.** — 26 in. barrel only, 8½ lbs.

Mfg.'s Sug. Retail	$1,692	$1,375	$900	$725	$625	$525	$475	$425
German mfg.		$1,600	$1,400	$1,250	$1,000	$900	$825	$750

German mfg. in this model used the .375 Wby. Mag. cal.

Grading	100%	98%	95%	90%	80%	70%	60%

* **.416 Wby. Mag.** — first new caliber (introduced 1989) since the .240 Mag. was released 1965.

  Mfg.'s Sug. Retail $1,875 $1,475 $1,000 $775 $660 $550 $495 $450

* **.460 Wby. Mag.** — 24 or 26 in. barrel, includes custom stock, integral muzzle brake, 10 lbs. No extra charge for left-hand.

  Mfg.'s Sug. Retail $2,193 $1,775 $1,325 $1,000 $850 $675 $625 $550

MARK V SLS — .257 Wby. Mag., .270 Wby. Mag., .300 Wby. Mag., .300 Win. Mag., .338 Wby. Mag. (disc. 1997), .338 Win. Mag., .340 Wby. Mag., 7mm Wby. Mag., or 7mm Rem. Mag. cal., features brown laminate stock with recoil pad, stainless steel with matte blue finish, approx. 8½ lbs. New 1997.

  Mfg.'s Sug. Retail $1,249 $1,025 $875 $695

CLASSICMARK I — available in 9 Wby. Mag. cals. in addition to .270 Win., 7mm Rem. Mag., .30-06, or .375 H&H cal., oil finished American Claro walnut stock with no cheekpiece and ebony forend cap, 1 in. solid recoil pad, panel point checkering. Mfg. 1992-1993.

                $1,075 $750 $625 $525 $475 $450 $410
                            Last Mfg.'s Sug. Retail was $1,295.

      Add $15 for 26 in. barrel.
      Add $130 for .375 H&H cal.

* **.300 or .340 Wby. Mag.** — 26 in. barrel only, right or left-hand action, 8½ lbs.

                $1,095 $775 $625 $525 $475 $450 $410
                            Last Mfg.'s Sug. Retail was $1,323.

* **.378 Wby. Mag.** — 26 in. barrel only, right or left-hand action, 8½ lbs.

                $1,125 $795 $625 $525 $475 $450 $410
                            Last Mfg.'s Sug. Retail was $1,356.

* **.416 Wby. Mag.** — 26 in. barrel only, right or left-hand action.

                $1,150 $825 $650 $550 $495 $460 $430
                            Last Mfg.'s Sug. Retail was $1,411.

* **.460 Wby. Mag.** — 26 in. barrel only, includes custom stock, integral muzzle brake, 10 lbs. No extra charge for left-hand.

                $1,250 $900 $675 $575 $525 $475 $430
                            Last Mfg.'s Sug. Retail was $1,573.

CLASSICMARK II — available in 9 Wby. Mag. cals. in addition to .270 Win., 7mm Rem. Mag., or .30-06, similar to Classicmark I, except has deluxe American walnut with 22 LPI multiple point checkering, steel grip cap, satin finished wood and metal, guaranteed 1½ in. or less 3 shot grouping at 100 yards, right hand action only. Mfg. 1992 only.

                $1,525 $1,175 $975 $800 $650 $600 $550
                            Last Mfg.'s Sug. Retail was $1,775.

      Add $28 for 26 in. barrel.

* **.300 or .340 Wby. Mag.** — 26 in. barrel only.

                $1,550 $1,175 $975 $800 $650 $600 $550
                            Last Mfg.'s Sug. Retail was $1,803.

* **.378 Wby. Mag.** — 26 in. barrel only.

                $1,700 $1,250 $1,000 $800 $650 $600 $550
                            Last Mfg.'s Sug. Retail was $1,976.

* **.416 Wby. Mag.** — 26 in. barrel only.

                $1,875 $1,375 $1,050 $825 $650 $600 $550
                            Last Mfg.'s Sug. Retail was $2,128.

* **.460 Wby. Mag.** — 26 in. barrel only, includes custom stock, integral muzzle brake, 10 lbs.

                $1,925 $1,400 $1,050 $825 $650 $600 $550
                            Last Mfg.'s Sug. Retail was $2,207.

* **Safari Classic** — .375 H&H cal., 24 in. barrel only, right-hand action, limited edition featuring custom action, quarter rib express and front ramp sights, barrel band swivel and engraved floor plate, stock similar to Classicmark II. Mfg. 1992 only.

                $2,300 $1,850 $1,650 $1,450 $1,300 $1,175 $995
                            Last Mfg.'s Sug. Retail was $2,693.

W

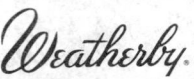
Grading	100%	98%	95%	90%	80%	70%	60%

ULTRAMARK — .240 Wby. Mag., .257 Wby. Mag., .270 Wby. Mag., .30-06, 7mm Wby. Mag., .300 Wby. Mag., .378 Wby. Mag. (mfg. 1989 only), or .416 Wby. Mag. (mfg. 1989 only) cal., fancy American walnut, individually hand-bedded, high luster finish, customized action, 24 or 26 in. barrel, basket weave checkering (including pistol grip). Imported 1989-90 only.

	$1,125	**$925**	**$800**	**$700**	**$630**	**$590**	**$550**

Last Mfg.'s Sug. Retail was $1,315.

> Add $25 for 26 in. barrel.
> Add $220 for .378 Wby. Mag. cal. (26 in. barrel only).
> Add $325 for .416 Wby. Mag. cal. (26 in. barrel only).

WEATHERMARK — available in various Wby. Mag. cals. from .240 (disc. 1996) to .340 and .257 Roberts (disc. 1994), .270 Win., 7mm Rem. Mag., .300 Win. Mag., .30-06, .338 Win. Mag., or .375 H&H (disc.) cal., design is similar to Classicmark II, except is fitted with black checkered composite stock, satin finish black metal, 22 (disc. 1995, .270 Win. or .30-06 only), 24, or 26 in. barrel, right-hand only, 7½ lbs. Mfg. 1992-94.

	$685	**$540**	**$475**	**$400**	**$360**	**$330**	**$300**

Last Mfg.'s Sug. Retail was $799.

SYNTHETIC — .257 Wby. Mag., .270 Wby. Mag., .300 Wby. Mag., .30-378 Wby. Mag. (new 1998), .300 Win. Mag., .338 Win. Mag., .340 Wby. Mag., 7mm Wby. Mag., 7mm Rem. Mag., or .375 H&H cal., features lightweight black synthetic stock, bead blasted matte metal finish, approx. 8 lbs. New 1997.

Mfg.'s Sug. Retail	**$799**	**$685**	**$540**	**$475**	**$400**	**$360**	**$330**	**$300**

> Add $150 for .30-378 Wby. Mag. (28 in. barrel only).

* *Light Weight Synthetic* — .22-250 Rem., .243 Win., .240 Wby. Mag., .25-06 Rem., .270 Win., .280 Rem., .30-06, .308 Win., or 7mm-08 Rem. cal., features raised comb, matte black injection mold synthetic stock, no sights, 20 (Carbine, .243 Win., .308 Win., or 7mm-08 Rem.) or 24 in. barrel, approx. 6½ lbs. New 1997.

Mfg.'s Sug. Retail	**$699**	**$625**	**$500**	**$450**	**$395**	**$350**	**$330**	**$300**

* *Fluted Synthetic* — .257 Wby. Mag., .270 Wby. Mag., .300 Wby. Mag., .300 Win. Mag., 7mm Wby. Mag., or 7mm Rem. Mag. cal., features 24 or 26 in. fluted barrel, black synthetic stock with Monte Carlo cheekpiece, approx. 7½ lbs. Mfg. 1997-98.

	$785	**$635**	**$550**	**$495**	**$450**	**$395**	**$350**

Last Mfg.'s Sug. Retail was $949.

* *Weathermark Alaskan Model* — same cals. as Weathermark, similar to Weathermark, except has non-glare electroless nickel-plated metal parts, right or left-hand (mfg. 1992 only) action. Mfg. 1992-94.

	$750	**$635**	**$560**	**$495**	**$450**	**$400**	**$360**

Last Mfg.'s Sug. Retail was $875.

> Add $37 for Wby. Mag. cals.
> Add $164 for .375 H&H cal.
> Add $375 for left-hand action (disc.).

STAINLESS MODEL — same cals. as Synthetic, features bead blasted matte stainless construction, synthetic Monte Carlo stock. New 1995.

Mfg.'s Sug. Retail	**$999**		**$855**	**$685**	**$495**

> Add $150 for .30-378 Wby. Mag. (28 in. barrel only).

* *Light Weight Stainless* — .22-250 Rem., .243 Win., .240 Wby. Mag., .25-06 Rem., .270 Win., .280 Rem., .30-06, .308 Win., or 7mm-08 Rem. cal., features raised comb, matte black injection molded synthetic stock, no sights, 20 (Carbine, .243 Win., .308 Win., or 7mm-08 Rem.) or 24 in. stainless barrel and action, approx. 6½ lbs. New 1997.

Mfg.'s Sug. Retail	**$899**		**$750**	**$610**	**$535**

* *Fluted Stainless* — .257 Wby. Mag., .270 Wby. Mag., .300 Wby. Mag., .300 Win. Mag., 7mm Wby. Mag., or 7mm Rem. Mag., features 24 or 26 in. fluted stainless barrel and action, black synthetic stock with Monte Carlo cheekpiece, approx. 7½ lbs. Mfg. 1997-98.

	$1,025	**$925**	**$825**

Last Mfg.'s Sug. Retail was $1,149.

Grading	100%	98%	95%	90%	80%	70%	60%

ACCUMARK — .257 Wby. Mag., .270 Wby. Mag., .300 Win. Mag., .300 Wby. Mag., .30-378 Wby. Mag. (new 1997), .338-378 Wby Mag. (new 1998), 7mm STW (new 1998), 7mm Rem. Mag., 7mm Wby. Mag., or .340 Wby. Mag. cal., features H-S Precision black synthetic stock, 26 in. stainless steel fluted barrel, aluminum bedding plate, custom trigger, approx. 8 lbs. New 1996.

Mfg.'s Sug. Retail	$1,349	$1,100	$925	$750

　　Add $200 for .30-378 Wby. Mag. or .338-378 Wby. Mag. cals.
　　Add $50 for left-hand action (available in most cals., new 1999).

* ***Accumark Lightweight*** — .22-250 Rem., .243 Win., .240 Wby. Mag., .25-06 Rem., .270 Win., .280 Rem., 7mm-08 Rem., .30-06, or .308 Win. cal., features weight saving construction, including extra wide barrel flutes, skeletonized bolt handle, and hand laminated Kevlar/fiberglass stock with Pachmayr Decelerator pad, 24 in. stainless barrel w/o sights, 5¾ lbs. New 1998.

Mfg.'s Sug. Retail	$1,249	$1,075	$950	$835	$735	$650	$600	$550

SPORTER — .240 Wby. Mag. (mfg. 1996 only), .257 Wby. Mag., .270 Wby. Mag., 7mm Wby. Mag., 7mm Rem. Mag., .270 Win. (mfg. 1996 only), .30-06 (disc. 1996), .300 Wby. Mag., .300 Win. Mag., .338 Win. Mag., .340 Wby. Mag., or .375 H&H cal., 24 or 26 in. barrel, similar features as the Mark V, except has checkered walnut stock without forearm or pistol grip caps, low luster metalwork, vent. recoil pad, no sights, approx. 8 lbs. New 1993.

Mfg.'s Sug. Retail	$999	$825	$650	$575	$495	$450	$395	$350

* ***Light Weight Sporter*** — .22-250 Rem., .243 Win., .240 Wby. Mag., .25-06 Rem., .270 Win., .280 Rem., .30-06, .308 Win., or 7mm-08 Rem. cal., features raised comb, checkered walnut stock, 54 degree bolt lift, no sights, 24 in. barrel, approx. 6½ lbs. New 1997.

Mfg.'s Sug. Retail	$899	$765	$650	$565	$515	$450	$425	$400

ULTRA LIGHT WEIGHT — .243 Win., .240 Wby. Mag., .257 Wby. Mag. (new 1999), .25-06 Rem., .270 Win., .270 Wby. Mag. (new 1999), .280 Rem., .300 Wby. Mag. (new 1999), .300 Win. Mag. (new 1999), 7mm-08 Rem., 7mm Rem. Mag. (new 1999), 7mm Wby. Mag. (new 1999), .30-06, or .308 Win. cal., features 24 in. barrel and lightweight synthetic stock. New 1998.

Mfg.'s Sug. Retail	$1,199	$1,050	$925	$825	$725	$650	$600	$550

　　Add $100 for long action Mag. cals. (new 1999).

WHITETAIL — .257 Sav. cal., limited edition features deluxe high grade Claro walnut, hand checkered bolt knob and engraved floorplate, 22 in. #1 contoured barrel, 6 lbs. Mfg. 1993 only.

			$1,150	$925	$775			

　　　　　　　　　　　　　　Last Mfg.'s Sug. Retail was $1,366.

VARMINTMASTER — .22-250 Rem. or .224 Varmintmaster (disc. 1994) cal., 24 (disc. 1991) or 26 in. barrel, 6½ lbs. Disc. 1995.

			$1,075	$775	$625	$525	$475	$450	$410

　　　　　　　　　　　　　　Last Mfg.'s Sug. Retail was $1,297.

　　Not available in left-hand action.

EUROMARK — available in most cals. as the Sporter Model, also includes .378 Wby. Mag. and .416 Wby. Mag., differs from Mark V Deluxe in that it has an oil finished, hand checkered, deluxe American claro walnut pistol grip cap stock with ebony forend tip, low luster bluing, and solid black recoil pad. Mfg. 1986-92, re-introduced 1995.

Mfg.'s Sug. Retail	$1,599	$1,250	$875	$675	$550	$475	$450	$410

　　Add $93 for .378 Wby. Mag. or $276 for .416 Wby. Mag. cal.

* ***.460 Wby. Mag.*** — 24 or 26 in. barrel, includes custom stock, internal muzzle brake, no extra charge for left-hand. Disc. 1992.

		$1,450	$1,100	$925	$775	$650	$600	$550

　　　　　　　　　　　　　　Last Mfg.'s Sug. Retail was $1,708.

EUROSPORT — same cals. as Sporter Model, features hand-rubbed satin finish stock with low-luster blue metal work and iron sights. New 1995.

Mfg.'s Sug. Retail	$999	$815	$640	$565	$495	$450	$395	$350

MARK V LAZERMARK — available in the same cals. and barrel lengths as the Mark V Deluxe, differs only in that stock and forearm have been laser carved, 24 or 26 in. barrel. New 1985.

Mfg.'s Sug. Retail	$1,699	$1,425	$1,000	$750	$625	$525	$475	$450

　　Add $108 for .378 Wby. Mag. cal.

Grading	100%	98%	95%	90%	80%	70%	60%

✱ .416 Wby. Mag. — first new caliber (introduced 1989) since the .240 Mag. was released 1965, includes muzzle brake.

Mfg.'s Sug. Retail	**$1,986**	$1,650	$1,150	$950	$775	$650	$575	$525

✱ .460 Wby. Mag. — 24 or 26 in. barrel, includes custom stock, internal muzzle brake, no extra charge for left-hand.

Mfg.'s Sug. Retail	**$2,333**	$1,925	$1,350	$1,100	$850	$650	$600	$550

✱ Varmintmaster — .22-250 Rem. or .224 Varmintmaster cal., 24 or 26 in. barrel. Disc. 1991.

	$1,085	$815	$675	$575	$500	$460	$425

Last Mfg.'s Sug. Retail was $675.

Add $25 for 26 in. barrel.

Not available in left-hand action.

MARK V FIBERMARK — available in .240 Wby. Mag., .257 Wby. Mag., .270 Wby. Mag., .30-06, 7mm Wby. Mag., .300 Wby. Mag., or .340 Wby. Mag. cal., black non-glare fiberglass with wrinkle finish stock, metal has non-glare matte finish, 24 or 26 in. barrel, available in right (disc. 1991) or left-hand action, 7¼ lbs. Mfg. disc. 1992.

	$1,195	$875	$725	$600	$525	$475	$450

Last Mfg.'s Sug. Retail was $1,376.

Add $118 for .300 or .340 Mag. cal.

This model was available in left-hand action (22 in. barrel) in .270 Win. or .30-06 cal. only.

1976 BICENTENNIAL MARK V — .257 Wby. Mag., .270 Wby. Mag., 7mm Wby. Mag., or .300 Wby Mag. cal., 1,000 mfg. in 1976 only.

	$1,495	$1,150	$895

Last Mfg.'s Sug. Retail was $2,000.

1984 MARK V OLYMPIC COMMEMORATIVE — .257 Wby. Mag., .270 Wby. Mag., 7mm Wby. Mag., or .300 Wby. Mag. cal., special gold accenting, extra-fancy walnut stock with "star in motion" inlay. Mfg. 1,000 1984 only at $2,000 retail.

	$1,000	$895	$700

MARK V 35TH ANNIVERSARY COMMEMORATIVE — .257 Wby. Mag., .270 Wby. Mag., 7mm Wby. Mag., or .300 Wby. Mag. cal., limited mfg. 1980, 1,000 produced total.

	$1,000	$895	$700

CUSTOM GRADE — various cals. from .240 Wby. Mag. to .340 Wby. Mag., 24 or 26 in. barrel, super fancy walnut stock featuring No. 7 style inlays, floorplate is engraved "Weatherby Custom", 6-8 week delivery time.

Mfg.'s Sug. Retail	**$5,088**	$4,250	$2,750	$2,050	$1,650	$1,450	$1,300	$1,175

SAFARI GRADE CUSTOM — .300 Wby. Mag., .340 Wby. Mag., .378 Wby. Mag., .416 Wby Mag., or .460 Wby. Mag. cal., custom order only, various options available, 12-18 month delivery.

Mfg.'s Sug. Retail	**$4,239**	$3,475	$2,675	$1,800	$1,500	$1,375	$1,275	$1,150

Add approx. $166-$467 for .378 and larger cals.

CROWN CUSTOM MODEL — custom order only, engraved barrel, receiver, and scope mount, top-of-the-line model.

Mfg.'s Sug. Retail	**$6,467**	$5,475	$3,750	$2,950	$2,450	$1,900	$1,550	$1,350

RIFLES: BOLT ACTION, VANGUARD SERIES

VANGUARD — .243 Win., .25-06 Rem., .270 Win., .30-06, .308 Win., 7mm Rem. Mag., .264 Win. Mag., or .300 Win. Mag. cal., mfg. circa late 1960s-early 1970s.

	$450	$375	$325	$295	$260	$230	$200

Add 10% for .264 Win. Mag. cal.

VANGUARD CLASSIC I — .223 Rem., .243 Win., .270 Win., 7mm/08 Rem., 7mm Rem. Mag., .30-06 or .308 Win. cal., checkered walnut stock with satin finish, black butt pad, 24 in. barrel, 3 (7mm Rem. Mag.) or 5 shot mag., No. 1 barrel contour, approx. 7 lbs. 5 oz. Mfg. 1989-1993.

	$480	$375	$325	$295	$260	$230	$200

Last Mfg.'s Sug. Retail was $549.

This model was the replacement for the Vanguard VGS and VGL.

Grading	100%	98%	95%	90%	80%	70%	60%

VANGUARD CLASSIC II — .22-250 Rem., .243 Win., .270 Wby. Mag., .270 Win., 7mm Rem. Mag., .30-06, .300 Win. Mag., .300 Wby. Mag., or .338 Win. Mag. cal., 24 in. No. 2 barrel contour, 3 or 5 shot mag., custom checkered deluxe walnut stock with pistol grip cap and black forend cap, solid black recoil pad, matte finished metal, approx. 7¾ lbs. Mfg. 1989-92.

	$675	$550	$475	$425	$395	$360	$330

Last Mfg.'s Sug. Retail was $750.

This model was also available in a No. 3 barrel contour in .22-250 Rem. cal. only.

VANGUARD VGX — .22-250 Rem., .243 Win., .25-06 Rem., .270 Win., 7mm Rem. Mag., .30-06, or .300 Win. Mag. cal., bolt action, checkered deluxe walnut stock with rosewood tip forearm and pistol grip, 24 in. barrel, no sights, 5 shot mag.(except 3 shot for .300 Win. Mag.), high luster bluing, about 8 lbs. Disc. 1988.

	$525	$425	$365	$330	$300	$275	$255

Last Mfg.'s Sug. Retail was $600.

Not available in left-hand action.

VANGUARD VGX DELUXE — .22-250 Rem., .243 Win., .270 Win., .270 Wby. Mag., .300 Win. Mag., .300 Wby. Mag., .30-06, .338 Win. Mag., or 7mm Rem. Mag. cal., 24 in. barrel, Monte Carlo stock with skipline checkering, high gloss wood and metal, rosewood forend cap. Mfg. 1989-1993.

	$625	$550	$475	$425	$395	$360	$330

Last Mfg.'s Sug. Retail was $699.

VANGUARD VGS — same cals. as Vanguard VGX, bolt action, checkered satin finished walnut stock, 24 in. barrel, no sights, approx. 8 lbs. Disc. 1988.

	$415	$355	$295	$265	$245	$220	$200

Last Mfg.'s Sug. Retail was $467.

Not available in left-hand action.

VANGUARD VGL — .223 Rem., .243 Win., .270 Win., 7mm Rem. Mag., .30-06, or .308 Win. cal., lightweight bolt action, checkered walnut stock, 5 shot mag.(6 on .223 Rem.), 20 in. barrel, no sights, 6½ lbs. Disc. 1988.

	$415	$355	$295	$265	$245	$220	$200

Last Mfg.'s Sug. Retail was $467.

Not available in left-hand action.

VANGUARD WEATHERGUARD — same cals. as Classic I, replacement for Fiberguard, wrinkle black finished synthetic stock, entry level Weatherby, similar specs. as Classic I, approx. 8 lbs. Mfg. 1989-1993.

	$440	$350	$320	$290	$260	$230	$200

Last Mfg.'s Sug. Retail was $499.

VANGUARD ALASKAN — same cals. as Classic I, features electroless nickel metal plating, no sights. Mfg. 1993-1994.

	$625	$550	$475	$425	$395	$360	$330

Last Mfg.'s Sug. Retail was $699.

VANGUARD FIBERGUARD — .223 Rem., .243 Win., .270 Win., 7mm Rem. Mag., .30-06, or .308 Win. cal., 20 in. barrel, green fiberglass stock, 3 to 6 shot mags., no sights, blued metal parts, approx. 6½ lbs. Disc. 1988.

	$500	$450	$395	$355	$285	$255	$220

Last Mfg.'s Sug. Retail was $560.

Not available in left-hand action.

RIFLES: .22 LR CAL.

ACCUMARK CLASSIC & DELUXE BOLT ACTION — while these models were advertised in 1990 ($635 retail), they were never manufactured.

Grading	100%	98%	95%	90%	80%	70%	60%

MARK XXII CLIP MAG SEMI-AUTO — .22 LR cal., mag. feed, skipline checkered walnut stock with rosewood forearm and pistol grip caps, 5 or 10 shot detachable mag., 24 in. barrel, open sights, 6 lbs. Disc. 1989.

	100%	98%	95%	90%	80%	70%	60%
Japanese mfg.	$395	$320	$265	$245	$215	$195	$180
Italian mfg.	$495	$440	$365	$325	$275	$240	$210

Last Mfg.'s Sug. Retail was $454.

The Mark XXII clip mag. was originally mfg. in Italy - a slight premium might be asked. This model featured a receiver slide-switch that allowed semi-auto operation to be converted to single shot mode.

MARK XXII TUBE MAG SEMI-AUTO — .22 LR cal., same general specifications as above model, except tube-feed, 15 shot, 6 lbs. Disc. 1989.

	100%	98%	95%	90%	80%	70%	60%
	$395	$320	$265	$245	$215	$195	$180

Last Mfg.'s Sug. Retail was $454.

SHOTGUNS: O/U

Weatherby shotguns are currently mfg. by SKB located in Tokyo, Japan.

REGENCY FIELD GRADE — 20 ga. Mag. or 12 ga., checkered stock, VR, engraved side plates, SST, early importation beginning in 1972 was from Italy, later mfg. was switched to Japan.

	100%	98%	95%	90%	80%	70%	60%
	$1,250	$895	$800	$700	$600	$550	$500

Add 10-15% for early Italian mfg. (note proof marks).

REGENCY TRAP GRADE — 12 ga., checkered trap stock, engraved, VR, SST. Imported from Italy.

	100%	98%	95%	90%	80%	70%	60%
	$900	$800	$700	$600	$550	$500	$475

OLYMPIAN STANDARD — 12 and 20 ga., lightly engraved sideplates. Disc. 1980.

	100%	98%	95%	90%	80%	70%	60%
	$850	$775	$725	$625	$525	$450	$400

OLYMPIAN SKEET — 26 or 28 in. barrel.

	100%	98%	95%	90%	80%	70%	60%
	$885	$775	$725	$625	$525	$450	$400

OLYMPIAN TRAP — 30 or 32 in. barrel, VR.

	100%	98%	95%	90%	80%	70%	60%
	$850	$775	$725	$625	$525	$440	$400

ATHENA GRADE III — 12 or 20 ga., 3 in. chambers, features oil finished clear walnut stock with rounded pistol grip and slender forearm, silver grey nitride sideplates with rose and scroll engraved gold pheasant and quail hunting scenes, 7¼ - 8 lbs. New 1999.

		100%	98%	95%	90%	80%	70%	60%
Mfg.'s Sug. Retail	$1,849	$1,675	$1,400	$1,200	$995	$875	$750	$625

ATHENA GRADE IV — 12, 20, 28 (mfg. 1989-1993) ga., or .410 (mfg. 1989-1993) bore, 3 in. chambers, 26 or 28 in. VR barrels with or without choke tubes, boxlock with Greener Crossbolt, SST, ejectors, high luster finish on hand checkered claro walnut, engraved sideplates with satin nickel finish, vent. barrels and rib, multi-chokes became standard (except .410 bore) 1986 and 1992 (28 ga.), 6½-8 lbs. Introduced 1982.

		100%	98%	95%	90%	80%	70%	60%
Mfg.'s Sug. Retail	$2,259	$1,875	$1,375	$1,050	$875	$725	$600	$525

Subtract 10% if without choke tubes.

This model was redesignated the Grade IV in 1989.

* ***Skeet & Trap Models*** — 12 (Trap only) or 20 ga., special stock dimensions, target sights. Disc. 1992.

	100%	98%	95%	90%	80%	70%	60%
	$1,675	$1,275	$1,000	$875	$725	$600	$525

Last Mfg.'s Sug. Retail was $1,965.

Skeet models are available in fixed choke only.

* ***Single Trap Model*** — 12 ga., 32 or 34 in. barrel with multi-choke feature. Disc. 1992.

	100%	98%	95%	90%	80%	70%	60%
	$1,675	$1,275	$1,000	$875	$725	$600	$525

Last Mfg.'s Sug. Retail was $1,975.

* ***Trap Combo*** — 12 ga., includes a set of O/U barrels and oversingle barrel with multi-choke feature. Disc. 1992.

	100%	98%	95%	90%	80%	70%	60%
	$2,300	$1,900	$1,605	$1,300	$995	$800	$675

Last Mfg.'s Sug. Retail was $2,616.

* ***Master Skeet Set*** — 12 ga., includes 6 fitted full length Briley tubes with integral extractors (20, 28 ga., and .410 bore), cased. Imported 1988-91.

	100%	98%	95%	90%	80%	70%	60%
	$3,100	$2,650	$2,150	$1,900	$1,775	$1,625	$1,525

Grading	100%	98%	95%	90%	80%	70%	60%

ATHENA GRADE V CLASSIC FIELD — 12 or 20 ga., 3 in. chambers, similar to Grade IV, except has more elaborate engraving and better walnut. New 1989.

Mfg.'s Sug. Retail	$2,599	$2,175	$1,775	$1,375	$1,150	$900	$775	$675

> In 1993, Weatherby changed the styling of this gun to incorporate European shooting features including an oil finished, round knob stock and slim forearm, tight rose-and-scroll engraving, and matted VR.

ORION UPLAND — 12 or 20 ga., 3 in. chambers, features high luster checkered Claro walnut stock and forearm, blued action and 26 or 28 in. VR barrels with choke tubes, 6½ - 8 lbs. New 1999.

Mfg.'s Sug. Retail	$1,059	$925	$850	$725	$600	$550	$500	$450

ORION I FIELD — 12 or 20 ga., 3 in. chambers, 26, 28, or 30 (12 ga. only) in. VR barrels with multi-chokes, SST, ejectors, entry level O/U with no engraving, checkered walnut stock and forearm. New 1989.

Mfg.'s Sug. Retail	$1,329	$1,095	$895	$725	$550	$495	$450	$400

ORION II FIELD — 12, 20, 28 ga., or .410 bore, 3 in. chambers (except 28 ga.), boxlock with Greener Crossbolt, SST, ejectors, walnut with high-gloss finish, blue only, light engraving. Multi-chokes became standard 1986. Field Grade disc. 1993.

	$1,075	$875	$750	$625	$550	$500	$450

Last Mfg.'s Sug. Retail was $1,207.

> Subtract 10% without choke tubes on older models.
> Subtract $14 for Skeet grade (12 and 20 ga., fixed chokes only).

> This model was redesignated Grade II in 1989. In 1993, the Standard Field Models in this variation were discontinued (Classic Grade took its place) - only Field and Sporting Clays variations are now available.

✻ *Orion II Classic Field* — 12, 20, or 28 ga., multi-choked barrels, features rounded pistol grip stock and oil finished Claro walnut stock and forearm, waterfowl scene on silver grey nitride finish, matted VR. New 1993.

Mfg.'s Sug. Retail	$1,399	$1,140	$895	$740	$625	$550	$500	$450

✻ *Orion II Sporting Clays* — 12 ga. only, Sporting Clays configuration, early mfg. was blue finish, current mfg. is silver nitride finish, acid etched engraving, rounded recoil pad, matte finish VR, lengthened forcing cones. New 1991.

Mfg.'s Sug. Retail	$1,499	$1,225	$975	$775	$625	$550	$500	$450

✻ *Super Sporting Clays* — 12 ga. only, 3 in. chambers, 28, 30, or 32 in. vented barrels with 12mm VR and gas ports, choke tubes, satin oil finished sporter style pistol grip stock with Schnabel forearm, Pachmayr Decelerator pad, approx. 8 lbs. New 1999.

Mfg.'s Sug. Retail	$1,749	$1,425	$1,200	$1,000	$875	$725	$650	$575

✻ *Ducks Unlimited Orion* — 12 ga. (sponsor gun in 1986) or 20 ga. (sponsor gun in 1987), deluxe walnut with gold duck scenes, blue receiver, multi-chokes, includes presentation case.

	$1,395	$1,100	$875

ORION III FIELD — 12 or 20 ga. only, similar to Grade II, except has silver grey receiver with custom engraving including mallard and pheasant game scenes, multi-chokes standard. New 1989.

Mfg.'s Sug. Retail	$1,699	$1,375	$1,025	$825	$650	$575	$500	$450

✻ *Orion III Classic Field* — 12 or 20 ga., multi-choked barrels, features rounded pistol grip stock and oil finished Claro walnut stock and forearm, extensive engraving on silver grey nitride finish, matted VR. New 1993.

Mfg.'s Sug. Retail	$1,699	$1,375	$1,025	$825	$650	$575	$500	$450

✻ *Orion III English Field* — 12 or 20 ga., 3 in. chambers, features straight grip stock and silver grey nitride receiver with engraving and gold inlays, approx. 6½ lbs. New 1997.

Mfg.'s Sug. Retail	$1,699	$1,375	$1,025	$825	$650	$575	$500	$450

SHOTGUNS: SEMI-AUTO

CENTURION FIELD GRADE — 12 ga., VR, checkered stock, gas operation, walnut full pistol grip stock. Mfg. 1972-1981.

	$300	$280	$250	$240	$230	$210	$190

Grading	100%	98%	95%	90%	80%	70%	60%

CENTURION TRAP GRADE — 12 ga., checkered stock, VR.

| | $335 | $300 | $250 | $240 | $230 | $210 | $190 |

CENTURION DE LUXE — 12 ga., VR, checkered stock, lightly engraved, fancy wood ($200-250).

| | $375 | $350 | $310 | $275 | $250 | $235 | $210 |

   ✳ *Centurion DU* — mfg. 1980 for DU chapters.

| | $550 | $375 | $325 | | | | |

MODEL 82 — 12 ga. only, 2¾ or 3 in. chamber, gas operation, alloy receiver, VR, deluxe walnut, multi-chokes became standard in 1985, Trap Grade was disc. 1984. Mfg. 1983-89.

| | $395 | $350 | $315 | $280 | $250 | $235 | $210 |

Last Mfg.'s Sug. Retail was $500.

      Subtract $30 without multi-chokes.
      Subtract $35 for Trap Grade (disc. 1984).

   ✳ *Model 82 Buckmaster* — 22 in. barrel choked skeet, rifle sights, 7½ lbs. Disc. 1989.

| | $395 | $350 | $315 | $280 | $250 | $235 | $210 |

Last Mfg.'s Sug. Retail was $500.

MODEL SAS — 12 or 20 ga., 3 in. chamber, self compensating gas operated mechanism, high grade satin oil finished checkered Claro walnut stock and forearm, 26, 28, or 30 (12 ga. only) in. VR barrel with Briley choke tubes, 6¾ - 7¾ lbs. New 1999.

| Mfg.'s Sug. Retail | $749 | $675 | $595 | $525 | $450 | $400 | $360 | $330 |

SHOTGUNS: SLIDE ACTION

PATRICIAN FIELD GRADE — 12 ga., checkered stock, VR. Mfg. 1972-1981.

| | $275 | $230 | $210 | $190 | $180 | $160 | $140 |

PATRICIAN TRAP GRADE — 12 ga., checkered stock, VR.

| | $295 | $250 | $225 | $200 | $185 | $175 | $165 |

PATRICIAN DE LUXE — 12 ga., checkered stock, lightly engraved, fancy wood, VR.

| | $325 | $275 | $250 | $215 | $195 | $175 | $165 |

MODEL 92 — 12 ga. only, 2¾ and 3 in. chambers, ultra-short slide action w/twin rails, 26-30 in. VR barrels, engraved black alloy receiver, checkered pistol grip walnut stock and forearm. New 1983. Subtract $30 for Trap grade (disc. 1984), $20 if fixed choke (multi-chokes became standard 1985) barrel. Disc. 1987.

| | $325 | $275 | $250 | $225 | $200 | $185 | $175 |

Last Mfg.'s Sug. Retail was $400.

   ✳ *Model 92 Buckmaster* — 22 in. skeet bore barrel, rifle sights, 7½ lbs. Disc. 1987.

| | $345 | $285 | $260 | $240 | $220 | $200 | $185 |

Last Mfg.'s Sug. Retail was $400.

WEAVER ARMS CORPORATION

Previous manufacturer located in Escondido, CA circa 1984-1990.

CARBINES

NIGHTHAWK CARBINE — 9mm Para. cal., closed bolt semi-auto paramilitary design carbine, fires from closed bolt, 16.1 in. barrel, retractable shoulder stock, 25, 32, 40, or 50 shot mag. (interchangeable with Uzi), ambidextrous safety, parkerized finish, 6½ lbs. Mfg. 1987-1990.

| | $495 | $440 | $360 | $330 | $300 | $275 | $250 |

Last Mfg.'s Sug. Retail was $575.

PISTOLS: SEMI-AUTO

NIGHTHAWK PISTOL — 9mm Para. cal., closed bolt semi-auto, 10 or 12 in. barrel, alloy upper receiver, ambidextrous safety, black finish, 5 lbs. Mfg. 1987-1990.

| | $525 | $465 | $375 | $340 | $300 | $275 | $250 |

Last Mfg.'s Sug. Retail was $475.

Grading	100%	98%	95%	90%	80%	70%	60%

WEBLEY & SCOTT, LIMITED

Previous firearms manufacturer located in Birmingham, England circa 1898 to 1979. Beginning 1980, Webley & Scott, Ltd. began manufacturing high quality weapons only. Currently, Webley & Scott manufactures airguns only (please refer to Airguns section or Trademark Index).

Webley & Scott, Ltd. had the shotgun business re-established as a separate company named W & C Scott (Gunmakers) Ltd. in 1979. Shortly after being acquired by Holland & Holland, firearms manufacture was discontinued while airgun production resumed.

PISTOLS: SEMI-AUTO & SINGLE SHOT

HAMMER MODEL .25 — .25 ACP cal., 6 shot mag., 2 in. barrel, no sights, blue, composition grips. Mfg. 1906-1940.

$325	$250	$175	$150	$135	$125	$115

HAMMERLESS MODEL .25 — .25 ACP cal., similar to Hammer Model .25, except rare, no exposed hammer and fixed sights. Mfg. 1909-1940.

$375	$225	$175	$150	$135	$125	$115

SINGLE SHOT TARGET PISTOL — .22 LR, .32 (special order), or .38 (special order) cal., 10 in. barrel, top break, blue, fixed sights on early models. Mfg. 1909-1964.

$375	$250	$120	$110	$100	$90	$75

METROPOLITAN POLICE AUTOMATIC — .32 ACP or .380 ACP cal., 7 or 8 shot, 3½ in. barrel, blue, fixed sights, composition grips. Mfg. 1906-1940.

$450	$300	$165	$120	$110	$100	$85

SEMI-AUTO SINGLE SHOT — .22 Long cal., 4¼ and 9 in. barrel, adj. sights, blue, composition grips, empty case is ejected and hammer cocked as in a semi-auto, then it is loaded singly and slide closed. Mfg. 1911-1927.

$950	$750	$650	$600	$550	$475	$400

9MM M&P AUTOMATIC — 9mm Browning Long, 8 shot, 5 in. barrel, blue, fixed sights. Mfg. 1909-1930.

$950	$850	$750	$650	$550	$475	$400

HAMMERLESS MODEL 1913 — .38 cal., high velocity, two variations, fewer than 1,000 mfg.

$2,200	$1,700	$1,200	$800	$700	$600	$500

MARK I .455 AUTO PISTOL — .455 Webley cal., 7 shot, 5 in. barrel, blue, fixed sights. Mfg. 1912-1945.

$1,750	$1,300	$1,000	$750	$600	$500	$400

MARK I NO. 2 — similar to Mark I, except adj. sights, modified safety, and cut for shoulder stock.

$5,000	$4,000	$3,000	$2,500	$2,000	$1,500	$1,000

The shoulder stock is an extremely rare accessory for this variation.

REVOLVERS

MARK III M&P — .32 S&W, .320 S&W, or .38 S&W cal., single/double action, 6 shot, 3 in. and 4 in. barrel, hinged top break, blue, fixed sights, wood service or competition grips. Mfg. 1896-1939.

$350	$295	$255	$220	$195	$165	$140

Some Mark III revolvers were fitted with a manual safety.

* *Mark III Target Model* — .38 S&W cal., similar to above, except was also available with 6 - 10 in. barrel with adj. sights.

$450	$375	$325	$275	$250	$225	$200

MARK IV M&P — similar to Mark III, except 3 in., 4 in., or 5 in. barrel, improved hammer and grip design. Mfg. 1929-1979.

$350	$295	$255	$220	$195	$165	$140

This was the last of the Webley series of revolvers.

Grading	100%	98%	95%	90%	80%	70%	60%

MARK IV .22 TARGET — similar to Mark IV, except .22 LR cal., 6 in. barrel, target sights, mfg. 1931-1967.

	$450	$385	$330	$285	$235	$200	$165

MARK IV SERVICE — .455 Webley cal., single/double action, 4 or 6 in. barrel, top break, blue, fixed sights, known as the Boer War Model and is not to be confused with the smaller, later Mark IV introduced in 1929. Mfg. 1899-1914.

	$375	$325	$275	$225	$175	$140	$110

NO. 1 MARK VI BRITISH SERVICE — .45 LC, .45 ACP, or .455 Webley cal., single/double action, 4, 6, or 7½ in. barrel, top break, blue, fixed sights, wood service or competition grips. Mfg. 1914-1939.

	$300	$250	$225	$195	$165	$135	$110

MARK VI .22 TARGET — similar to Mark VI, except .22 LR cal., target sights, mfg. until 1945.

	$300	$250	$225	$195	$165	$135	$110

Bayonet and shoulder stock attachments were also available for this model. These accessories are rare and command considerable premiums over values listed above.

MARK V — .455 cal., single/double action. Many were military-modified for .45 Colt or .45 ACP, many were civilian-modified, round butt, top break. Mfg. 1914-1915 only.

	$375	$325	$275	$225	$175	$150	$125

BULLDOG OR RIC MODEL — available in .320 - .476 cals. (.455 Webley most common), 5 shot, 2⅛ - 4½ in. barrel, solid frame, blue, fixed sights. Mfg. 1867-1939 for Royal Irish Constabulary.

	$295	$250	$225	$175	$140	$110	$90

WEBLEY-FOSBERY AUTOMATIC REVOLVER — .455 Webley cal., 6 shot, top break, recoil revolves cylinder and cocks hammer, walnut or hard rubber grips. Mfg. 1901-1939.

Add $1,000 for .38 cal.

A small number of Webley-Fosbery pistols were chambered for .38 Colt Auto Cartridge, usually found in 13xx range, features 8 shot cylinder.

* *1901 Model* — large frame, early features.

	$5,500	$4,250	$3,000	$2,250	$1,800	$1,350	$900

Add 20% for Target Model (adj. rear sight).

* *1902 Model* — large frame, late features.

	$4,500	$3,500	$2,750	$1,750	$1,500	$1,200	$900

Add 20% for Target Model (adj. rear sight).

* *1904 Model* — small frame, late features.

	$4,500	$3,500	$2,750	$1,750	$1,500	$1,200	$900

Add 100% for .38 cal.
Add 20% for Target Model (adj. rear sight).

SHOTGUNS: SxS

MODEL 700 — 12 or 20 ga., boxlock, case hardened receiver, minimum engraving, single trigger. Subtract $50 for double trigger. Mfg. 1949-1980.

	$1,700	$1,625	$1,500	$1,250	$1,000	$750	$600

MODEL 701 — similar to Model 700 but fanciest walnut, most engraving. Subtract $100 for double trigger. Mfg. 1949-1980.

	$3,150	$2,500	$2,100	$1,800	$1,400	$1,150	$925

MODEL 702 — similar to Model 700 but middle grade. Subtract $75 for double trigger. Mfg. 1949-1980.

	$2,650	$2,200	$1,800	$1,500	$1,250	$950	$750

MODEL 710 — same action as the Model 700, except is 28 ga. and designed specifically for the American market, only 40 were mfg. 1966-1968.

	$2,750	$2,400	$2,050	$1,775	$1,525	$1,300	$1,100

MODEL 712 — 12 ga., specifically designed for the American market.

	$1,700	$1,625	$1,500	$1,250	$1,000	$750	$600

Grading	100%	98%	95%	90%	80%	70%	60%

MODEL 720 — 20 ga.

	100%	98%	95%	90%	80%	70%	60%
	$2,100	$1,700	$1,625	$1,500	$1,250	$1,000	$750

WEIHRAUCH, HANS-HERMANN

Current manufacturer located in Mellrichstadt, Germany. Exclusive factory authorized U.S. distributor is European American Armory, located in Sharpes, FL.

RIFLES: BOLT ACTION

MODEL HW 60 TARGET — .22 LR cal., target rifle featuring adj. sights, 26¾ in. barrel, single shot, match walnut stock, and other match features, aperture sights, 10.8 lbs. Importation disc. 1995.

	$625	$550	$450	$395	$350	$295	$275

Last Mfg.'s Sug. Retail was $705.

Add $220 for left-hand action (disc.).

MODEL HW 60J — .22 LR or .222 Rem. cal., sporter model with checkered walnut stock. Importation disc. 1992.

	$525	$465	$435	$395	$345	$300	$260

Last Mfg.'s Sug. Retail was $585.

Add $304 for .222 Rem. cal.

MODEL HW 66 RIFLE — .22 Hornet or .222 Rem. cal., match grade bolt action rifle. Imported 1989-90 only.

	$575	$495	$395	$325	$285	$250	$215

Last Mfg.'s Sug. Retail was $688.

Add $78 for double set triggers.
Add $55 for stainless steel barrel (.22 Hornet).

MODEL HW 660 MATCH — .22 LR cal., match rifle variation featuring adj. stock comb with vent. forend, aperture sights, 10.8 lbs. Importation began 1991.

Mfg.'s Sug. Retail	$998	$850	$725	$600	$500	$400	$350	$300

Add $47 for laminate stock (new 1998).
Subtract $172 if w/o aperture sights.

W

WESSON, FRANK

Previous manufacturer located in Worcester, MA 1854 to 1865, and Springfield, MA circa 1865-1875.

100%	98%	95%	90%	80%	70%	60%	50%	40%	30%	20%	10%

PISTOLS: SINGLE SHOT

SMALL FRAME FIRST MODEL — .22 cal., tip up action, 3½ in. ½ octagon barrel, brass frame, spur trigger, rosewood grips, round frame, irregular sideplate. Mfg. 2500, 1859-1862.

100%	98%	95%	90%	80%	70%	60%	50%	40%	30%	20%	10%
$605	$550	$495	$440	$385	$330	$275	$220	$195	$165	$140	$110

SMALL FRAME SECOND MODEL — similar to First Model, with flat sided frame and circular sideplate. Mfg. 12,000, 1862-1880.

$550	$495	$440	$385	$330	$305	$250	$195	$165	$110	$105	$85

MEDIUM FRAME FIRST MODEL — .30 S or L, .32 S rimfire cal., 4 in. ½ octagon barrel, iron frame, same as Small Frame in other respects, narrow hinge and short trigger. Mfg. 1000, 1859-1862.

$525	$470	$415	$360	$305	$275	$220	$195	$165	$110	$105	$85

MEDIUM FRAME SECOND MODEL — similar to First Model Medium Frame, with wider hinge and longer trigger. Mfg. 1000, 1862-1870.

$495	$440	$385	$330	$275	$250	$220	$195	$165	$110	$105	$85

RIFLES: SINGLE SHOT

NO. 1 LONG RANGE — .44-100 and .45-100 standard cal., side hammer, falling block lever actuated, 34 in. octagon barrel, tang. sight, select checkered pistol grip stock. Less than 50 mfg., circa 1870-1880.

$4,950	$4,675	$4,400	$3,850	$3,575	$3,080	$2,860	$2,475	$2,200	$2,035	$1,760	$1,540

100%	98%	95%	90%	80%	70%	60%	50%	40%	30%	20%	10%

NO. 2 HUNTING RIFLE — similar to No. 1, with finger loop lever. Less than 100 mfg.

100%	98%	95%	90%	80%	70%	60%	50%	40%	30%	20%	10%
$4,400	$4,180	$3,850	$3,520	$3,025	$2,750	$2,420	$2,255	$2,035	$1,925	$1,760	$1,540

NO. 1 SPORTING RIFLE — .38-100, .40-100, .45-100 standard cal., similar to No. 2, with center hammer, Less than 25 mfg.

$4,400	$4,180	$3,850	$3,520	$3,025	$2,750	$2,420	$2,255	$2,035	$1,925	$1,760	$1,540

RIFLES: SINGLE SHOT, TIP UP

SMALL FRAME TIP UP — .22 Rimfire cal., 6 in. ½ octagon barrel, brass frame, spur trigger, rosewood grips. Approx. 500 mfg., 1865-1875.

$605	$550	$525	$495	$470	$440	$415	$360	$330	$275	$220	$165

If without stock - subtract 25%.

MEDIUM FRAME TIP UP — .22, .30, or .32 rimfire cals, 10 or 12 in. barrel, same as small frame, with exceptions noted and larger frame. Approx. 1,000 mfg., 1862-1870.

$605	$550	$525	$495	$470	$440	$415	$360	$330	$275	$220	$165

If without stock - subtract 25%.

MODEL 1870 SMALL FRAME FIRST TYPE — similar to Small Frame Tip Up, except barrel rotates on its axis to load, detachable stock. Approx. 3,000 mfg., 1870-1890.

$550	$495	$470	$440	$415	$385	$360	$305	$275	$220	$195	$165

If without stock - subtract 25%.

MODEL 1870 SMALL FRAME SECOND TYPE — full octagon barrel.

$525	$470	$440	$415	$385	$360	$330	$275	$250	$195	$165	$140

MODEL 1870 SMALL FRAME THIRD TYPE — iron frame, push button ½ cock.

$495	$440	$415	$385	$360	$330	$305	$250	$220	$165	$140	$110

MODEL 1870 MEDIUM FRAME FIRST TYPE — similar to Small Frame, except in size and availability of .32 cal. Approx. 5,000 mfg., 1870-1893.

$525	$495	$470	$440	$415	$385	$360	$305	$275	$250	$195	$165

Subtract 25% if without stock.

MODEL 1870 MEDIUM FRAME SECOND TYPE — external push-button half cock and iron frame.

$440	$415	$385	$330	$305	$275	$220	$195	$165	$140	$110	$90

Subtract 25% if without stock.

MODEL 1870 MEDIUM FRAME THIRD TYPE — has three screws in frame, iron frame.

$440	$415	$385	$330	$305	$275	$220	$195	$165	$140	$110	$90

Subtract 25% if without stock.

MODEL 1870 LARGE FRAME FIRST TYPE — .32, .38, .42, or .44 rimfire cal., 15-24 in. barrels, similar to smaller frame models, auto extractor. Approx. 500 mfg., 1870-1880.

$825	$770	$715	$660	$605	$550	$525	$495	$440	$385	$305	$275

Subtract 25% if without stock.

MODEL 1870 LARGE FRAME SECOND TYPE — similar to First Type, with standard sliding extractor.

$825	$770	$715	$660	$605	$550	$525	$495	$440	$385	$305	$275

Subtract 25% if without stock.

Grading	100%	98%	95%	90%	80%	70%	60%

WESSON & HARRINGTON

Current trademark of special/limited editions manufactured by H&R 1871, Inc.

Grading	100%	98%	95%	90%	80%	70%	60%

RIFLES: SINGLE SHOT

WESSON & HARRINGTON BUFFALO CLASSIC — .45-70 Govt. cal., Topper style break-open action, 32 in. barrel, case hardened frame, checkered walnut stock and forearm, 8 lbs. New 1995.

Mfg.'s Sug. Retail	$350		$300	$240	$195		

WESSON & HARRINGTON TARGET RIFLE — .38-55 WCF cal., 28 in. barrel, target sights, blue finish. New 1998.

Mfg.'s Sug. Retail	$390		$330	$260	$210		

SHOTGUNS: SINGLE SHOT

WESSON & HARRINGTON NWTF LONG TOM CLASSIC — 12 ga., Topper style break-open action, 32 in. FC barrel, case hardened frame, checkered straight grip walnut stock and forearm, 7½ lbs. New 1995.

Mfg.'s Sug. Retail	$350		$300	$240	$195		

DAN WESSON FIREARMS

Currently manufactured by New York International Corp. located in Norwich, NY beginning 1997. Distributor and dealer sales.

Dan Wesson currently has 8 new models available in various cals. from .357 Mag. - .445 SuperMag. Laser engraving, and Hogue rubber finger groove grips are standard features. Compensator barrel assemblies and revolver packages are also available. Barrel lengths include 4, 6, 8, and 10 in. heavy vent. Finishes include blue or satin brushed stainless steel construction. As in the past, many barrel assembly configurations are optional. Please contact the company directly for current model information and pricing.

WESSON FIREARMS CO. INC.

Previous manufacturer located in Palmer, MA until 1995. In late 1990, ownership of Dan Wesson Arms changed (within the family), and the new company was renamed Wesson Firearms Co., Inc.

REVOLVERS: DOUBLE ACTION

As a guideline, the following information is provided on Wesson Firearms frames. The smallest frames are Models 738P and 38P. Small frame models include 22, 722, 22M, 722M, 32, 732, 322, 7322, 8-2, 708, 9-2, 709, 14-2, 714, 15-2, and 715-2. Large frames include 41, 741, 44, 744, 45, and 745. SuperMag frame models include 40, 740, 375 (disc.), 414 (new 1995), 7414 (new 1995), 445, and 7445. Small frames are sideplate design, while large frames are solid frame construction. Models listed below assume interchangeable barrels unless otherwise specified.

Dan Wesson revolvers were mfg. with solid rib barrels as standard equipment.

MODEL 11 — .357 Mag. cal., 6 shot, 2½, 4, or 6 in. interchangeable barrels, fixed sights, blue, interchangeable grips, exposed barrel nut. Mfg. 1970-1971.

	$200	$175	$160	$150	$140	$130	$120

Add $60 per extra barrel.

MODEL 12 — similar to Model 11, with adj. sights. Mfg. 1970-1971.

	$245	$200	$175	$160	$150	$140	$130

MODEL 14 — similar to Model 11, with recessed barrel nut. Mfg. 1971-1975.

	$225	$185	$170	$160	$150	$140	$130

MODEL 8 — similar to Model 14, except .38 Spl. cal.

	$200	$170	$155	$145	$135	$125	$115

MODEL 15 — similar to Model 14, with adj. sights. Mfg. 1971-1975.

	$245	$200	$155	$145	$135	$125	$115

MODEL 9 — similar to Model 15, except .38 Spl. cal. Mfg. 1971-1975.

	$245	$200	$155	$145	$135	$125	$115

W

Grading	100%	98%	95%	90%	80%	70%	60%

MODEL 22 — .22 LR cal., double action, 6 shot, adj. sights, 2½, 4, 6, 8, or 10 in. (disc. 1987) barrel, disc. 1995.

	$285	**$225**	**$200**	**$190**	**$180**	**$170**	**$160**

Last Mfg.'s Sug. Retail was $357.

Add approx. $9 for each additional barrel length, $21 for VR, $57 for vent. heavy rib shroud.

* ***Model 22 Pistol Pac*** — includes 2½, 4, 6, and 8 in. barrel assemblies, extra grip, 4 additional front sight blades, and aluminum case. Disc. 1995.

	$520	**$400**	**$360**	**$330**	**$300**	**$275**	**$260**

Last Mfg.'s Sug. Retail was $653.

Add $103 for full shroud VR barrels.
Add $227 for heavy full shroud VR barrels.

* ***Model 22 Silhouette*** — .22 LR cal., choice of 10 in. vent. or heavy vent. barrel, single action only, combat style grip, narrow rear sight blade and patridge front. Mfg. 1992-95.

	$395	**$325**	**$295**	**$275**	**$260**	**$245**	**$230**

Last Mfg.'s Sug. Retail was $474.

Add $18 for vent. heavy barrel.

MODEL 22M — .22 Mag. cal., otherwise similar to Model 22. Disc. 1994.

	$290	**$230**	**$200**	**$190**	**$180**	**$170**	**$160**

Last Mfg.'s Sug. Retail was $349.

* ***Model 22M Pistol Pac*** — includes 2½, 4, 6, and 8 in. barrel assemblies, extra grip, 4 additional front sight blades, and aluminum case. Disc. 1994.

	$500	**$400**	**$360**	**$330**	**$300**	**$275**	**$260**

Last Mfg.'s Sug. Retail was $637.

Add $101 for full shroud VR barrels.
Add $191 for heavy full shroud VR barrels.

MODEL 32 — .32 H&R Mag. cal., 2½, 4, 6, or 8 in. barrel, adj. rear sight, interchangeable colored front sight blades, blue finish, checkered target grips. Mfg. 1986-95.

	$285	**$225**	**$200**	**$190**	**$180**	**$170**	**$160**

Last Mfg.'s Sug. Retail was $357.

Add $21 for VR barrel shroud (Model 32-V), $57 for VR heavy barrel shroud (Model 32-VH), approx. $9 for each additional barrel length over 2½ in.

* ***Model 32 Pistol Pac*** — includes 2½, 4, 6, and 8 in. barrel assemblies, extra grip, 4 additional front sight blades, and aluminum case. Disc. 1995.

	$520	**$400**	**$360**	**$330**	**$300**	**$275**	**$260**

Last Mfg.'s Sug. Retail was $653.

Add $103 for full shroud VR barrels.
Add $227 for heavy full shroud VR barrels.

MODEL 38P — .38+P cal., 5 shot, 6½ in. barrel, fixed sights, wood or rubber grips, 24.6 oz. Mfg. 1992-93.

	$230	**$190**	**$170**	**$150**	**$135**	**$120**	**$110**

Last Mfg.'s Sug. Retail was $285.

MODEL 322 — .32-20 WCF cal., 2½, 4, 6, or 8 in. barrel, adj. rear sight, interchangeable colored front sight blades, blue finish, checkered target grips. Mfg. 1991-95.

	$285	**$225**	**$200**	**$190**	**$180**	**$170**	**$160**

Last Mfg.'s Sug. Retail was $357.

Add $21 for VR barrel shroud (Model 322-V), $57 for VR heavy barrel shroud (Model 322-VH), approx. $9-$30 for each additional barrel length over 2½ in.

* ***Model 322 Pistol Pac*** — includes 2½, 4, 6, and 8 in. barrel assemblies, extra grip, 4 additional front sight blades, and aluminum case. Disc. 1995.

	$520	**$400**	**$360**	**$330**	**$300**	**$275**	**$260**

Last Mfg.'s Sug. Retail was $653.

Add $103 for full shroud VR barrels.
Add $227 for heavy full shroud VR barrels.

Grading	100%	98%	95%	90%	80%	70%	60%

MODEL 14 — .357 Mag. cal., 2½, 4, 6, or 8 (disc. 1994) in. interchangeable barrels, fixed sights, blue. Mfg. 1975-1995.

	$215	$170	$150	$140	$130	$120	$110

Last Mfg.'s Sug. Retail was $274.

Add approx. $7 for each additional barrel length.

* ***Model 14 Fixed Barrel*** — .357 Mag. cal., 2½ or 4 in. (fixed sight Service Model) barrel, satin blue finish. Mfg. 1993-95.

	$225	$175	$150	$140	$130	$120	$110

Last Mfg.'s Sug. Retail was $289.

Add $7 for 4 in. barrel.

* ***Model 14 PPC*** — .357 Mag. cal., extra heavy 6 in. bull shroud barrel with removable underweight, Hogue Gripper grips, Aristocrat sights. Mfg. 1992 only.

	$675	$550	$450	$375	$330	$300	$275

Last Mfg.'s Sug. Retail was $780.

* ***Model 14 Pistol Pac*** — includes 2½, 4, and 6 in. barrel assemblies, extra grip and aluminum case. Disc. 1994.

	$390	$325	$300	$275	$260	$245	$230

Last Mfg.'s Sug. Retail was $463.

MODEL 8 — similar to Model 14, except .38 Spl. cal. Disc. 1995.

	$220	$170	$150	$140	$130	$120	$110

Last Mfg.'s Sug. Retail was $274.

Add approx. $6 for each additional barrel length.

* ***Model 8 PPC*** — .38 Spl. cal., extra heavy 6 in. bull shroud barrel with removable underweight, Hogue Gripper grips, Aristocrat sights. Mfg. 1992 only.

	$675	$550	$450	$375	$330	$300	$275

Last Mfg.'s Sug. Retail was $780.

MODEL 15 — similar to Model 14, except adj. sights, available with 2, 4, 6, 8, 10, 12, or 15 in. barrels. Disc. 1995.

* ***2 in. barrel***

	$285	$225	$200	$190	$180	$170	$160

Last Mfg.'s Sug. Retail was $346.

Add approx. $8-$13 for each additional barrel length over 2 inches, $22 for VR barrel (Model 15V), or $60 for VR heavy barrel shroud (Model 15HV).

* ***Model 15 Target Fixed Barrel*** — .357 Mag. cal., 3, 4, 5, or 6 in. barrel, high bright blue finish. Mfg. 1993-95.

	$270	$220	$190	$175	$150	$125	$110

Last Mfg.'s Sug. Retail was $322.

Add approx. $9 for each barrel length over 3 in.
Add approx. $80 for compensated barrel (4, 5, or 6 in. - new 1994).

MODEL 15 GOLD SERIES — .357 Mag. cal., 6 or 8 in. VR heavy slotted barrel, "Gold" stamped shroud with Dan Wesson signature, smoother action (8 lb. double action pull), 18 kt. gold-plated trigger, white triangle rear sight with orange dot partridge front sight, exotic hardwood grips. Mfg. 1989-94.

	$425	$380	$340	$300	$260	$225	$185

Last Mfg.'s Sug. Retail was $544.

* ***Model 15 Pistol Pac*** — includes 2½, 4, 6, and 8 in. barrel assemblies, extra grip, 4 additional front sight blades, and aluminum case. Disc. 1995.

	$500	$395	$360	$330	$300	$275	$260

Last Mfg.'s Sug. Retail was $629.

Add $104 for full shroud VR barrels.
Add $214 for heavy full shroud VR barrels.

MODEL 9 — similar to Model 15, except .38 Spl. cal. Use same add-ons as in Model 15. Disc. 1995.

	$346	$285	$225	$200	$190	$180	$170

Last Mfg.'s Sug. Retail was $346.

This model was also available in a Pistol Pac - same specifications and values as the Model 15 Pistol Pac.

W

Grading	100%	98%	95%	90%	80%	70%	60%

MODEL 375 SUPERMAG — .375 Super Mag. cal., 4, 6, 8, or 10 in. VR barrel, adj. rear sight, interchangeable front and rear sight blades, bright blue finish, smooth target grips. Mfg. 1986-94.

	$410	$335	$285	$260	$240	$230	$225

Last Mfg.'s Sug. Retail was $498.

Add approx. $15 for each barrel length after 6 in., $39 for slotted shroud (Model 375-V8S, 8 in. barrel only), $10-$12 for VR heavy shroud (Model 375-VH).

MODEL 40 (.357 SUPERMAG) — .357 Super Mag. cal. (.357 Max.), double action, 6 shot, 4, 6, 8, or 10 in. barrel VR. Disc. 1995.

	$410	$340	$285	$260	$240	$230	$225

Last Mfg.'s Sug. Retail was $502.

Add $87 for slotted barrel shroud (8 in. barrel only), $22-$129 for heavy VR barrel, approx. $33 for each additional barrel length.

MODEL 41 — .41 Mag. cal., double action, 6 shot, 4, 6, 8, or 10 in. barrel VR. Disc. 1995.

	$375	$305	$265	$250	$230	$215	$200

Last Mfg.'s Sug. Retail was $447.

Add approx. $20 for heavy barrel shroud, approx. $15 for each additional barrel length.

* ***Model 41 Pistol Pac*** — includes 6 and 8 in. VR barrel assemblies, extra grip, 2 additional front sight blades, and aluminum case. Disc. 1995.

	$555	$430	$380	$330	$300	$275	$260

Last Mfg.'s Sug. Retail was $678.

Add $53 for full shroud VR barrels.

MODEL .414 SUPERMAG — .414 Super Mag. cal., 4, 6, 8, or 10 in. VR barrel, adj. rear sight, interchangeable front and rear sight blades (optional), bright blue finish, smooth target grips. Mfg. 1995 only.

	$425	$335	$290	$275	$250	$230	$225

Last Mfg.'s Sug. Retail was $519.

Add approx. $14 for each barrel length after 4 in., $58 for slotted shroud (Model 414-V8S, 8 in. barrel only), approx. $23 for VR heavy rib shroud.

MODEL 44 — .44 Mag. cal., double action, similar to Model 41, adj. sights. Disc. 1995.

	$375	$305	$265	$250	$230	$215	$200

Last Mfg.'s Sug. Retail was $447.

Add approx. $20 for heavy barrel shroud, approx. $15 for each additional barrel length.

* ***Model 44 Target Fixed Barrel*** — .44 Mag. cal., 4, 5, 6, or 8 in. barrel, high bright blue finish. Mfg. 1994-95.

	$375	$305	$265	$250	$230	$215	$200

Last Mfg.'s Sug. Retail was $447.

Add approx. $4 for each barrel length over 3 in.

* ***Model 44 Pistol Pac*** — includes 6 and 8 in. VR barrel assemblies, extra grip, 4 additional front sight blades, and aluminum case. Disc. 1995.

	$555	$430	$380	$330	$300	$275	$260

Last Mfg.'s Sug. Retail was $678.

Add $53 for full shroud VR barrels.

MODEL 45 — .45 LC cal., 4, 6, 8, or 10 in. VR barrel, same frame as Model 44V, blued finish. Mfg. 1988-95.

	$375	$305	$265	$250	$230	$215	$200

Last Mfg.'s Sug. Retail was $447.

Add $20 for VR heavy barrel shroud, approx. $15 for each additional barrel length.

* ***Model 45 Pistol Pac*** — includes 6 and 8 in. VR barrel assemblies, extra grip, 2 additional front sight blades, and aluminum case. Disc. 1995.

	$555	$430	$380	$330	$300	$275	$260

Last Mfg.'s Sug. Retail was $678.

Add $53 for full shroud VR barrels.

Grading	100%	98%	95%	90%	80%	70%	60%

MODEL .45 PIN GUN — .45 ACP cal., competition pin gun model with 5 in. vent. or heavy vent barrel configuration, blued steel, two stage Taylor forcing cone, 54 oz. Mfg. 1993-95.

	$575	$495	$440	$395	$350	$300	$250

Last Mfg.'s Sug. Retail was $654.

Add $9 for VR heavy shroud barrel.

MODEL .445 SUPERMAG — .445 Super Mag. cal., 4, 6, 8, or 10 in. VR barrel, adj. rear sight, interchangeable front and rear sight blades (optional), bright blue finish, smooth target grips. Mfg. 1991-95.

	$425	$335	$290	$275	$250	$230	$225

Last Mfg.'s Sug. Retail was $519.

Add approx. $14 for each barrel length after 4 in., $58 for slotted shroud (Model 445-V8S, 8 in. barrel only), approx. $23 for VR heavy rib shroud.

HUNTER SERIES — .357 Super Mag., .41 Mag., .44 Mag., or .445 Super Mag. cal., 7½ in. barrel with heavy shroud, Hogue rubber finger grooved and wood presentation grips, choice of Gunworks iron sights or w/o sights with Burris base and rings, non-fluted cylinder, with or w/o compensator, approx. 4 lbs. Mfg. 1994-95.

	$750	$575	$475	$400	$360	$330	$300

Last Mfg.'s Sug. Retail was $805.

Add $32 for compensated barrel.
Add $33 for scope mounts (w/o sights).

REVOLVERS: STAINLESS STEEL

Models 722, 722M, 709, 715, 732, 7322, 741V, 744V, and 745V were available in a pistol pack including 2½, 4, 6, and 8 in. solid rib barrel assemblies, extra grip, 4 additional sight blades, and fitted carrying case. Last published retail prices were $712 and $785 for the standard and stainless steel models, respectively. VR or full shroud barrels were optional and were approx. priced $103 and $210, respectively.

MODEL 722 — stainless version of Model 22, use same add-ons for various barrel options. Disc. 1995.

	$335	$255	$205

Last Mfg.'s Sug. Retail was $400.

* *Model 722 Silhouette* — .22 LR cal., choice of 10 in. vent. or heavy vent. barrel, single action only, combat style grip, narrow rear sight blade and patridge front. Mfg. 1992-95.

	$410	$340	$295

Last Mfg.'s Sug. Retail was $504.

Add $28 for heavy vent. barrel.

MODEL 722M — .22 Mag cal., otherwise similar to Model 722, use same add-ons for various barrel options. Disc. 1994.

	$320	$270	$230

Last Mfg.'s Sug. Retail was $391.

MODEL 708 — .38 Spl. cal., similar to Model 8. Add approx. $6 for each additional barrel length. Disc. 1995.

	$265	$200	$170

Last Mfg.'s Sug. Retail was $319.

* *Model 708 Action Cup/PPC* — .38 Spl. cal., extra heavy 6 in. bull shroud barrel with removable underweight, Hogue Gripper grips, mounted Tasco Pro Point II on Action Cup, Aristocrat sights on PPC. Mfg. 1992 only.

	$725	$650	$550

Last Mfg.'s Sug. Retail was $857.

Add $56 for Action Cup Model with Tasco Scope.

MODEL 709 — .38 Spl. cal., target revolver, adj. sights. Also available in special order 10, 12 (disc.), or 15 (disc.) in. barrel lengths. Disc. 1995.

	$310	$255	$205

Last Mfg.'s Sug. Retail was $376.

Add approx. $10 for each additional longer barrel length, approx. $19 for VR, approx. $56 for heavy VR.

Grading	100%	98%	95%	90%	80%	70%	60%

MODEL 714 (INTERCHANGEABLE OR FIXED) — .357 Mag. cal., fixed sight Service Model with 2½, 4, or 6 in. barrel, brushed stainless steel. Mfg. 1993-95.

       $260   **$200**   **$160**

Last Mfg.'s Sug. Retail was $319.

   Add approx. $6 for 4 or 6 in. barrel.
   Subtract $6 for fixed barrel (2½ or 4 in. barrel only).

✳ *Model 714 Action Cup/PPC* — .357 Mag. cal., extra heavy 6 in. bull shroud barrel with removable underweight, Hogue Gripper grips, mounted Tasco Pro Point II on Action Cup, Aristocrat sights on PPC. Mfg. 1992 only.

       $725   **$650**   **$550**

Last Mfg.'s Sug. Retail was $857.

   Add $56 for Action Cup Model with Tasco Scope.

MODEL 715 INTERCHANGEABLE — .357 Mag. cal., 2½, 4, 6, 8, or 10 in. with adj. rear sight, brushed stainless steel. Mfg. 1993-95.

       $310   **$255**   **$205**

Last Mfg.'s Sug. Retail was $376.

   Add approx. $10 for each additional longer barrel length, approx. $19 for VR, approx. $56 for heavy VR.

✳ *Model 715 Fixed Target* — .357 Mag. cal., 3, 4, 5, or 6 in. fixed barrel, adj. rear sight. Mfg. 1993-95.

       $280   **$210**   **$170**

Last Mfg.'s Sug. Retail was $345.

   Add approx. $70 for compensated barrel (4, 5, or 6 in. - new 1994).

MODEL 732 — .32 H&R Mag. cal., similar to Model 32, except is stainless steel. Mfg. 1986-95.

       $335   **$255**   **$205**

Last Mfg.'s Sug. Retail was $400.

   Add $22 for VR barrel shroud (Model 732-V), $53 for VR heavy barrel shroud (Model 732-VH), approx. $9 for each additional barrel length over 2½ in.

MODEL 738P — .38+P cal., 5 shot, 6½ in. barrel, fixed sights, wood or rubber grips, 24.6 oz. Mfg. 1992-95.

       $275   **$210**   **$175**

Last Mfg.'s Sug. Retail was $340.

MODEL 7322 — .32-20 WCF cal., similar to Model 322, except is stainless steel. Mfg. 1991-95.

       $335   **$255**   **$205**

Last Mfg.'s Sug. Retail was $400.

   Add $22 for VR barrel shroud (Model 7322-V), $53 for VR heavy barrel shroud (Model 7322-VH), approx. $9 for each additional barrel length over 2½ in.

MODEL 740V - .357 SUPERMAG — .357 Max. cal., 4, 6, 8, or 10 in. barrel, adj. rear sight with interchangeable front and rear blades, high polished finish, smooth target grips. Mfg. 1986-95.

       $460   **$350**   **$315**

Last Mfg.'s Sug. Retail was $567.

   Add approx. $20 for each additional barrel length after 4 in., $78 with vent. slotted shroud (only avail. with 8 in. barrel), $20 for VR heavy barrel shroud (Model 740-VH).

MODEL 741V — .41 Mag. cal., similar to Model 41V. Disc. 1995.

       $420   **$325**   **$270**

Last Mfg.'s Sug. Retail was $524.

   Add approx. $20 for heavy VR, approx. $13 for each barrel length over 4 in.

MODEL 744V — .44 Mag. cal., similar to Model 44V. Disc. 1995.

       $430   **$345**   **$285**

Last Mfg.'s Sug. Retail was $524.

   Add approx. $20 for heavy VR, $13 for each barrel length over 4 in.

✳ *Model 744V Target Fixed Barrel* — .44 Mag. cal., 4, 5, 6, or 8 in. barrel, brushed stainless steel. Mfg. 1994-95.

       $395   **$315**   **$265**

Last Mfg.'s Sug. Retail was $493.

   Add approx. $4 for each barrel length over 3 in.

Grading	100%	98%	95%	90%	80%	70%	60%

* **Model 744 Commemorative** — limited mfg.

	$595	$475	$325

MODEL 745V — .45 LC cal., similar to Model 45, except in stainless steel. Disc. 1995.

	$430	$345	$285

Last Mfg.'s Sug. Retail was $524.

Add $20 for heavy full shroud VR barrels, $13 for each additional barrel length.

MODEL .45 PIN GUN — .45 ACP cal., similar to Model .45 Pin Gun, except is stainless steel. Mfg. 1993-95.

	$625	$525	$425

Last Mfg.'s Sug. Retail was $713.

Add $49 for VR heavy rib shroud.

MODEL 7414 SUPERMAG — .414 Super Mag. cal., 4, 6, 8, or 10 in. VR barrel, adj. rear sight, interchangeable front and rear sight blades (optional), bright blue finish, smooth target grips. Mfg. 1995 only.

	$475	$350	$295

Last Mfg.'s Sug. Retail was $596.

Add approx. $14 for each barrel length after 4 in., $74 for slotted shroud (Model 7414-V8S, 8 in. barrel only), approx. $25 for VR heavy rib shroud.

MODEL 7445 SUPERMAG — .445 Super Mag. cal., 4, 6, 8, or 10 in. VR barrel, adj. rear sight, interchangeable front and rear sight blades (optional), high polished finish, smooth target grips. Mfg. 1991-95.

	$475	$350	$295

Last Mfg.'s Sug. Retail was $596.

Add approx. $17 for each barrel length after 6 in., $74 for slotted shroud (Model 7445-VH8S, 8 in. barrel only), approx. $25 for VR heavy rib shroud, approx. $40 for VR heavy shroud and interchangeable sights (Model 7445-VH).

SUPER RAM SILHOUETTE — .357 Max., .414 Super Mag., or .44 Mag. cal., silhouette variation featuring modified Iron Sight Gun Works rear sight, Allen Taylor throated barrel, factory trigger job, 4 lbs. Mfg. 1995 only.

	$695	$550	$375

Last Mfg.'s Sug. Retail was $807.

Add $43 for .414 Super Mag. cal.

HUNTER SERIES — .357 Super Mag., .41 Mag., .44 Mag., or .445 Super Mag. cal., 7½ in. barrel with heavy shroud, Hogue rubber finger grooved and wood presentation grips, choice of Gunworks iron sights or w/o sights with Burris base and rings, non-fluted cylinder, with or w/o compensator, approx. 4 lbs. Mfg. 1994-95.

	$780	$595	$475

Last Mfg.'s Sug. Retail was $849.

Add $32 for compensated barrel.
Add $32 for scope mounts (w/o sights).

WESTERN ARMS COMPANY
Previous manufacturer located in Ithaca, NY.

SHOTGUNS: SxS

WESTERN LONG RANGE — 12, 16, 20 ga., or .410 bore, 26-32 in. barrels, mod. and full choke, boxlock, extractors, double or single trigger, plain pistol grip stock, Western Arms Co. was a division of Ithaca Gun. Mfg. 1929-1946.

	$275	$225	$200	$175	$150	$125	$100

* **Single trigger**

	$325	$275	$250	$225	$200	$150	$125

WESTERN FIELD

Previous trademark used on Montgomery Ward rifles and shotguns.

The Western Field trademark has appeared literally on hundreds of various models (shotguns and rifles) sold through the Montgomery Ward retail network. Most of these models were manufactured through subcontracts with both domestic and international firearms manufacturers. Typically, they were "spec." guns made to sell at a specific price to undersell the competition. Most of these models were derivatives of existing factory models with less expensive wood and perhaps missing the features found on those models from which they were derived. To date, there has been very little interest in collecting Western Field guns, regardless of rarity. Rather than list J.C. Higgins models, a general guideline is that values generally are under those of their "1st generation relatives". As a result, prices are ascertained by the shooting value of the gun, rather than its collector value.

WESTLEY RICHARDS & CO. LTD.

Currently manufactured by Westley Richards and Co., Ltd., Birmingham, England 1812 to date. In 1995, Westley Richards opened their own agency in the US located in Springfield, MO. Originally William Westley Richards was located in Birmingham, England.

There seems to be a lot of confusion regarding W. Richards, W. R. Richards, William Richards, and other generic derivatives of the famous English gunmaker, Westley Richards. Part of the problem is that there are seventeen registered firms in England, including several in London, who have made guns by the name of Richards. A genuine Westley Richards gun never has the first name abbreviated, and the London address is usually found on the rib panel. Further compounding the problem, a previous Belgian gunmaker identifiable by W. Richards on the locks or rib, had many shotguns exported into the United States, which are commonly confused with the real London maker. These Belgian guns are commonly hammer guns with damascus twist barrels most frequently encountered in either 10, 12, or 16 ga. The easiest way to determine this maker is to recognize the Liege proofmarks on the barrel flats and chamber length given in millimeters. Most of these Belgian guns sell in the $100-$400 range, depending on condition and configuration.

Note: Westley Richards guns are essentially custom ordered - only 25-30 guns are made annually. They make many weapons that are impossible to list and evaluate, except on an individual basis. Professional appraisal is necessary upon purchase or sale.

To obtain a quotation for a new Westley Richards shotgun, an inquiry should be submitted to the manufacturer or importer (see Trademark Index for addresses).

RIFLES

BEST QUALITY BOXLOCK DOUBLE RIFLE — .300 Win. Mag., .375 H&H, .470 NE, .577 NE, or .600 NE cal., auto ejectors, boxlock, hammerless, folding leaf rear sight, hooded front sight, engraved with quality French walnut stock, horn forend tip.

Mfg.'s Sug. Retail	$25,000	$25,000	$21,000	$18,750	$16,000	$13,750	$10,500	$9,250

Values will vary greatly on this model, depending on caliber.

DETACHABLE DROPLOCK DOUBLE RIFLE — available in most cals., boxlock with detachable locks and hinged cover-plate, ejectors, colored case hardened frame, cased.

Mfg.'s Sug. Retail	$36,000	$36,000	$30,000	$25,000	$21,000	$18,750	$16,000	$13,000

STALKER MAGAZINE RIFLE — .243 Win., .270 Win., .30-06, .300 H&H, .375 H&H, or .458 Win. Mag. cal., bolt action, Mauser action, 22, 24, or 25 in. barrel, leaf rear and hooded front sight, engraved with French walnut stock, horn forend tip. Current mfg.

Mfg.'s Sug. Retail	$9,000	$9,000	$7,850	$6,950	$5,750	$4,750	$4,000	$3,300

Add approx. $3,000 for Magnum Mauser action.

SHOTGUNS: PRE-WWII PRODUCTION

Add 20% for 20 ga.
Add 30% for 28 ga.
Add $1,500 for cased extra set of locks.

Grading	100%	98%	95%	90%	80%	70%	60%

OVUNDO O/U — detachable lock boxlock, optional sideplates. Disc.

	$18,000	$15,000	$12,500	$9,750	$8,500	$7,250	$6,000

MODELE DE GRANDE LUXE - SxS — scalloped receiver, detachable locks, profuse scroll & game scene engraving. Disc.

	$15,000	$13,000	$11,000	$9,750	$8,500	$7,250	$6,000

MODEL DE LUXE - SxS — scalloped receiver, detachable locks, fine scroll & game scene engraving. Disc.

	$11,000	$9,500	$8,500	$7,500	$6,000	$5,500	$5,000

HAMMERLESS EJECTOR PLAIN QUALITY - SxS — scalloped receiver, Anson & Deeley fixed locks.

	$6,000	$5,000	$4,000	$3,500	$3,000	$2,500	$2,000

"B" QUALITY EJECTOR - SxS — boxlock with plain (unscalloped) receiver, light scroll engraving. Disc.

	$5,000	$4,000	$3,500	$3,000	$2,500	$2,250	$2,000

SHOTGUNS: SxS, CURRENT PRODUCTION

CONNAUGHT MODEL — 12, 20, or 28 ga., Anson & Deeley scalloped boxlock action, scroll engraving, 26 or 28 in. barrels, ejectors, about 6½ lbs. Disc.

	$9,250	$8,000	$6,600	$5,600	$4,800	$4,000	$3,400

Last Mfg.'s Sug. Retail was $10,900.

BEST QUALITY DROPLOCK — 12, 16, 20, 28 ga., or .410 bore, boxlock action, barrel lengths and chokes to order, detachable locks with hinged cover-plate, checkered straight or pistol grip stock, auto ejectors.

Mfg.'s Sug. Retail	$27,000		$27,000	$19,450	$14,000	$10,750	$8,750	$7,600	$6,400

Add $1,000 for SST.

Only six .410 Best Quality Boxlocks have been mfg. to date.

BEST QUALITY SIDELOCK — 12, 16, 20, 28 ga., or .410 bore, barrel length and choke to order, hand detachable sidelocks, auto ejectors, checkered straight or pistol grip stock.

Mfg.'s Sug. Retail	$25,000		$25,000	$18,950	$14,000	$10,750	$8,750	$7,600	$6,400

Add 20% for 20 ga.

Add 40% for 28 ga.

Add 60% for .410 bore.

Add $1,000 for SST.

Most specimens in this model were custom ordered, and as a result, each gun has to be evaluated individually.

WILLIAM BISHOP SIDELOCK MODEL — current mfg., best quality sidelock, made to individual customer specifications.

Mfg.'s Sug. Retail	$29,000		$29,000	$23,500	$18,500	$15,000	$11,750	$9,500	$8,250

CARLTON DETACHABLE LOCK — 12 or 20 ga., current mfg., detachable sidelocks, top-of-the-line shotgun custom made per customer specifications, elaborate game scene engraving. Many options upon request - values below are for base gun only.

Mfg.'s Sug. Retail	$34,075		$34,075	$26,500	$21,750	$17,250	$13,750	$10,500	$9,000

WHITNEY ARMS COMPANY

Previous manufacturer located in New Haven, CT, 1798-1886.

Whitney Arms Company began firearms production in 1798. Eli Whitney Sr. & Eli Whitney Jr. were prominent and prolific figures in the arms manufacturing world for a great many decades, and their production plant in New Haven is credited as being the first major manufacturer of commercial firearms in America. The Whitneys produced a tremendous variety of firearms under family ownership for approximately 90 years before selling the company to Winchester in 1888. Numerous long arms, starting with the Whitney 1798 U.S. Contract Musket, and moving forward through various other flintlock, percussion, rimfire, and centerfire rifles, handguns, and shotguns contributed to the vast broadness of the Whitney line. The Whitney name saw collaboration with Burgess, Kennedy, Morse, Tiesing, Howard, Cochran, Scharf, and many others. Many of the early Whitney rifles such as the historic 1798 Flintlock muskets, are rare and highly collectible, commanding substantial premi-

100%	98%	95%	90%	80%	70%	60%	50%	40%	30%	20%	10%

ums when found in original configuration, and not converted to percussion. The Whitney lever action repeaters are also quite popular among collectors. A fair number remain in circulation.

The author wishes to express his thanks to Mr. Steve Engleson for providing the following information on Whitney Arms Company.

RIFLES: LEVER ACTION

WHITNEY-KENNEDY LEVER ACTION MAGAZINE RIFLES — a repeating rifle with loading port on right side, top ejection, approx. 15,000 mfg. between 1879-1886, barrels are typically marked Whitney Arms Co. or Whitneyville Armory, with some variations having the Kennedy name included, often referred to as the Kennedy rifle, 2 basic frame sizes were made, (large & small), both frame sizes were also available in carbines and muskets, 2 other basic variations were the standard loop lever, a serpentine or "S" shaped finger lever, ser. nos. were sequential from 1-5,000, and from there a letter prefix was added, these appeared from A through S, with numbers 1-99 following.

* **Large Frame** — .40-60 WCF, .45-60 WCF, .45-75 WCF, and .50-95 Express cal., 26 or 28 in. round or octagon barrels, walnut stocks, crescent steel buttplate, full magazine capacity of 9 rounds in standard rifle.

N/A	N/A	$2,500	$2,125	$1,900	$1,700	$1,475	$1,325	$1,100	$975	$850	$725

  Add 300% for .50-95 Express cal. (extremely rare).
  Add 50% for carbine or musket.
  Add 30% for half-round, half-octagon barrel.
  Add 20% for nonprefix (early) serial numbers.
  Add 10% for serpentine lever.

* **Small Frame** — .44-40 WCF, .38-40 WCF, and .32-20 WCF cal., 24 in. round or octagon barrel, walnut stock and crescent buttplate, full magazine capacity of 13 rounds in standard rifle.

N/A	N/A	$1,950	$1,675	$1,450	$1,225	$1,075	$950	$825	$700	$600	$500

  Add 300% for carbine or musket (extremely rare).
  Add 100% for half-round, half-octagon barrel.
  Add 20% for half-magazine.
  Add 20% for 26 or 28 in. barrel.

1878 BURGESS REPEATING RIFLE — .45-70 Govt. cal., standard sporting rifle, 28 in. octagon or round barrel, loading port on right side, serpentine shaped lever, walnut stock, blued receiver and full magazine capacity of 9 rounds, typically w/o Whitney markings, barrels marked "G.W. Morse Patented Oct. 28th 1856", and tangs are marked "A. Burgess Patented Jan. 7th 1873", several variations, including the first, second, and third models, as well as military carbines and muskets.

N/A	N/A	$3,300	$3,000	$2,700	$2,400	$2,100	$1,850	$1,600	$1,400	$1,250	$1,100

  Add 300% for the first model top loader (few made and most converted by the factory to sideloader).
  Add 100% for military carbine or musket (certain variations will command a higher premium).
  Add 30% for first or second model.

  Values shown are for the most typically encountered variation, the third model sporting rifle.

  This model was also know as the Whitney-Burgess-Morse lever action repeating rifle, mfg. through a license agreement with Andrew Burgess, total production of approx. 2,000 were made between 1878-1882.

WHITNEY FIREARMS COMPANY

Previous manufacturer from 1956-1959 located in Hartford, CT.

PISTOLS: SEMI-AUTO

WOLVERINE OR LIGHTNING — .22 Auto cal., unique futuristic appearance, 10 shot, 4⅝ in. barrel, plastic grips, aluminum alloy frame and barrel shroud, blue model is more common (approx. 13,000 mfg.), nickel is rare (approx. 900 mfg.). Mfg. 1955-1962.

Blue finish	$425	$350	$300	$260	$230	$200	$175
Nickel finish	$600	$475	$375	$300	$260	$230	$200

WHITWORTH

This trademark can be found in the Interarms section of this text.

WICHITA ARMS, INC.

Current manufacturer located in Wichita, KS. Distributor, dealer, and consumer direct sales.

PISTOLS

WICHITA INTERNATIONAL PISTOL (WIP) — available in 8 cals. between .22 LR and .357 Mag., single shot, break open action, stainless steel, adj. sights, 10 or 14 in. barrel, adj. sights or scope mounts, smooth walnut stocks and forearm.

Mfg.'s Sug. Retail	**$775**	**$680**	**$465**	**$350**

Add $100 for 14 in. barrel.

WICHITA CLASSIC PISTOL — assorted cals. to .308 Win., 11¼ in. barrel, action has left-hand bolt for shooting with right-hand, deluxe walnut, custom made, 3 lbs. 15 oz. Disc. 1997.

	$3,280	**$2,550**	**$2,150**

Last Mfg.'s Sug. Retail was $3,495.

W

* *Wichita Classic Engraved* — similar to Wichita Classic, except is extensively engraved.

Mfg.'s Sug. Retail	**$5,250**	**$5,250**	**$3,750**	**$2,750**

WICHITA SILHOUETTE PISTOL (WSP) — .308 Win. or 7mm/IHMSA cal., adj. trigger and sights, 14¹⁵⁄₁₆ in. barrel, center grip walnut stock, rear grip, 4½ lbs. Left-hand action for shooting with right-hand.

Mfg.'s Sug. Retail	**$1,800**	**$1,520**	**$1,050**	**$850**

WICHITA MAGAZINE PISTOL — .308 Win. or 7mm/IHMSA cal., fiberthane (disc. 1987) or walnut (new 1988) stock, choice of MK-40, Silhouette, or Classic configuration, 13 in. barrel, adj. trigger, multi-range sights, 4½ lbs. Disc. 1994.

	$1,250	**$875**	**$700**

Last Mfg.'s Sug. Retail was $1,550.

* *Wichita Classic Pistol* — features octagon barrel, AAA walnut stock, 11¼ in. barrel, 3 lbs. 15 oz. Disc. 1994.

	$2,975	**$2,450**	**$2,000**

Last Mfg.'s Sug. Retail was $3,400.

WICHITA BENCH PISTOL — .222 Rem., 6 PPC, or .22 Cheetah cal., uses WBR 1200 action, rear grip, 18 in. stainless steel Douglas barrel. New 1994.

Mfg.'s Sug. Retail	**$1,875**	**$1,875**	**$1,500**	**$1,250**

RIFLES: BOLT ACTION

WICHITA CLASSIC RIFLE (WCR) — .17-222, .17-222 Mag., .222 Rem., .222 Mag., 223 Rem., 6x47mm, and other cals. up to and including .308 Win. cal., bolt action, single shot, select walnut, 21 in. octagon barrel, Canjar trigger, no sights, 7 lbs.

Mfg.'s Sug. Retail	**$3,495**	**$3,275**	**$2,500**	**$2,150**

Add $175 for left-hand action.

Grading	100%	98%	95%	90%	80%	70%	60%

* **Wichita Varmint Rifle (WVR)** — similar to WCR, except available only in Varmint cals. (up to and including .308 Win.) and round barrel.

  Mfg.'s Sug. Retail $2,695 $2,500 $1,795 $1,375

  Add $175 for left-hand action.

* **Wichita Silhouette Rifle (WSR)** — available in most cals., grey fiberthane stock, 24 in. match grade barrel, 2 oz. Canjar trigger, no sights, 9 lbs. Disc. 1995.

  $2,475 $1,775 $1,375

  Last Mfg.'s Sug. Retail was $2,650.

  Add $175 for left-hand action.

* **Wichita Magnum** — Mag. cals., stainless steel only. Disc. 1984.

  $1,725 $1,300 $1,175

WICKLIFFE RIFLES

Previously manufactured by Triple S Development located in Wickliffe, OH.

RIFLES: SINGLE SHOT

MODEL 76 STANDARD — falling block action, most popular cals., 22 or 26 in. barrel, no sights, select walnut pistol grip, 2 piece stock. Mfg. 1976-disc.

	$395	$350	$325	$300	$275	$250	$225

MODEL 76 DELUXE GRADE — similar to Standard, in .30-06 cal. only, 22 in. barrel, fancy wood, silver pistol grip cap.

	$460	$415	$385	$360	$320	$290	$250

MODEL 76 COMMEMORATIVE — similar to Deluxe, except etched receiver, U.S. silver dollar inlaid in stock, presentation case. Mfg. 100, 1976.

	$1,100	$825	$550	$495	$440	$330	$305

STINGER — similar to Model 76 Standard, in .22 Hornet or .223 Rem. cal., lightweight 22 in. barrel.

	$395	$350	$325	$300	$275	$250	$225

STINGER DELUXE — similar to 76 Deluxe, in .22 Hornet or .223 Rem. cal., lightweight 22 in. barrel.

	$460	$415	$385	$360	$325	$290	$250

TRADITIONALIST — similar to Standard 76, in .30-06 or .45-70 Govt. cal., 24 in. barrel.

	$395	$350	$325	$300	$275	$250	$225

KODIAK COMMEMORATIVE — similar to Model 76 Deluxe, .338 Win. Mag. cal., 26 in. barrel, etched receiver.

	$650	$550	$475	$425	$375	$325	$275

WILD WEST GUNS

Current custom gunsmith and manufacturer located in Anchorage, AK. Dealer and consumer direct sales.

Wild West Guns also offers a bolt action Summit Rifle Series ranging in price from $1,325 to $2,950, and a bolt action ProGuide Model in .375 H&H or .416/458 cal. - prices range from $2,495 to $2,695. Please contact the company directly for more information on these bolt action models.

PISTOLS: SEMI-AUTO

Wild West Guns customizes a wide variety of M1911 style semi-autos, including a ShadowLite package that retails for $2,495. Please contact the company directly for more information on their prices for these custom made semi-autos.

RIFLES: LEVER ACTION

ALASKAN CO-PILOT RIFLE — .30-30 Win., .357 Mag., .44 Mag., .444 Marlin, or .45-70 Govt. cal., features customized Marlin lever action with takedown conversion, various finishes, ported barrel, matte blue or parkerized finish, includes soft case. New 1996.

Mfg.'s Sug. Retail $1,395 $1,325 $1,125 $925 $775 $650 $550 $475

Add $100 for any cal. other than .45-70 Govt.

Grading			100%	98%	95%	90%	80%	70%	60%

ALASKAN GUIDE — similar to Alaskan Co-Pilot, except has 18½ in. barrel, ghost ring rear sight, straight style stock and recoil control porting. New 1997.

Mfg.'s Sug. Retail	$1,275		$1,200	$1,050	$895	$750	$625	$525	$450

WILDEY, INC.

Current manufacturer located in New Milford, CT. Originally, the company was named Wildey Firearms Co., Inc. located in Cheshire, CT. At that time, serialization of pistols was 45-0000. When Wildey Inc. bought the company out of bankruptcy from the old shareholders, there had been approximately 800 pistols mfg. To distinguish the old company from the present company, the serial range was changed to 09-0000 (only 633 pistols with the 09 prefix were produced). These guns had the Cheshire, CT address. Pistols produced by Wildey Inc., New Milford, CT are serial numbered with 4 digits being used (no numerical prefix).

PISTOLS: SEMI-AUTO

Wildey has plans to introduce 4 new proprietary cartridges. They are the .30 WM, .357 WM, 10mm WM, and 11mm WM based on the .475 Wildey Mag. necked down to respective cartridge dimensions. Norma, located in Sweden, continues to produce the .475 WM brass.

WILDEY AUTO PISTOL — .45 Win. Mag., .357 Peterbilt (limited mfg.), or .475 Wildey Mag., gas operated, 5, 6, 7, 8, 10, or 14 in. VR barrel, selective single shot or semi-auto, 3 lug rotary bolt, fixed barrel (interchangeable), stainless steel construction, 7 shot, double action, adj. sights, smooth wood grips, designed to fire proprietary new cartridges specifically for this gun including the .45 Win. Mag. cal., 64 oz. with 5 in. barrel.

Add $475-$590 per interchangeable barrel.

* **Survivor Model** — .45 Win. Mag., 11mm Wildey Mag., or .475 Wildey Mag. cal., 5, 6, 7, 8, 10, or 12 in. barrel only. New 1990.

Mfg.'s Sug. Retail	$1,295		$1,125	$875	$725

Add $100 for 12 in. barrel.
Add $21 for 8 or 10 in. barrel.
Add $50 for new model VR (8, 10, or 12 in. barrel only).
The .475 Wildey cal. is derived from the .284 Win. case. This cal. is available in 8 or 10 in. barrel only.

* **Survivor Guardsman** — similar to Survivor Model, except has squared off trigger guard. New 1990.

Mfg.'s Sug. Retail	$1,295		$1,125	$885	$725

Add $500 for 14 in. barrel.
Add $100 for 12 in. barrel.
Add $21 for 8 or 10 in. barrel.
Add $46 for new model VR (8, 10, or 12 in. barrel only).

* **Hunter Model** — .45 Win. Mag. or .475 Wildey Mag. cal., 5, 6, 7, 8, 10, or 12 in. barrel, matte finish on all metal parts, adj. sights. New 1990.

Mfg.'s Sug. Retail	$1,413		$1,200	$975	$825

Add $36 for 12 in. barrel.
.475 Wildey Mag. is available in 8, 10, or 12 in. barrel only.

* **Hunter Guardsman** — similar to Hunter Model, except has squared off trigger guard. New 1990.

Mfg.'s Sug. Retail	$1,413		$1,200	$975	$850

Add $36 for 12 in. barrel.

* **Presentation Model** — same specifications as above model, except is engraved with hand checkered stocks.

	$2,500	$2,000	$1,600

Last Mfg.'s Sug. Retail was $2,000.

* **Older Wildey Mfg.**
Add $413-$513 per interchangeable barrel.
.475 Wildey Mag. cal. is available in 8 or 10 in. barrel only.

Grading	100%	98%	95%	90%	80%	70%	60%

➤ SERIAL NOS. 1-200.
Mfg.'s Sug. Retail $2,180 $1,900 $1,700 $1,550
Add $20 for 8 or 10 in. barrel.

➤ SERIAL NOS. 201-400.
Mfg.'s Sug. Retail $1,980 $1,750 $1,550 $1,400
Add $20 for 8 or 10 in. barrel.

➤ SERIAL NOS. 401-600.
Mfg.'s Sug. Retail $1,780 $1,650 $1,375 $1,250
Add $20 for 8 or 10 in. barrel.

➤ SERIAL NOS. 601-800.
Mfg.'s Sug. Retail $1,580 $1,450 $1,200 $1,000
Add $20 for 8 or 10 in. barrel.

➤ SERIAL NOS. 801-1,000.
Mfg.'s Sug. Retail $1,275 $1,100 $925 $800
Add $25 for 8 or 10 in. barrel.

➤ SERIAL NOS. 1,001-2,489.
Mfg.'s Sug. Retail $1,175 $1,025 $850 $750
Add $20 for 8 or 10 in. barrel.

WILKINSON ARMS

Previous manufacturer located in Parma, ID.

CARBINES

"TERRY" CARBINE — 9mm Para. cal., blowback action, 30 shot mag., 16³⁄₁₆ in. barrel, closed breech, adj. sights.

	100%	98%	95%	90%	80%	70%	60%
With black P.V.C. stock	$325	$310	$300	$275	$230	$210	$180
With maple stock	$350	$340	$325	$300	$260	$230	$200

PISTOLS: SEMI-AUTO

DIANE AUTOMATIC PISTOL — .25 ACP cal., 6 shot, 2⅛ in. barrel, fixed sight, matte blue, plastic grips.

	100%	98%	95%	90%	80%	70%	60%
	$125	$110	$90	$80	$65	$55	$50

LINDA PISTOL — 9mm Para. cal., blowback action firing from closed bolt, 8.3 in. barrel, 31 shot mag., PVC pistol grip, maple forearm, Williams adj. rear sight.

	100%	98%	95%	90%	80%	70%	60%
	$325	$295	$260	$230	$200	$180	$165

A conversion unit was also available enabling the successful sex change from Linda to Terry.

WILLIAM DOUGLAS & SONS

Current manufacturer located in Staffordshire, England. Currently imported and distributed by Cape Outfitters located in Cape Girardeau, MO.

RIFLES: SxS

EXPRESS RIFLE — .375 H&H cal., H&H type back action sidelock with bolster fences, DTs, ejectors, 24 in. regulated barrels, folding leaf rear sight, oil finished European walnut stock with 20 LPI checkering, light engraving, case hardened action.

Mfg.'s Sug. Retail $21,950 $19,750 $15,250 $11,000 $8,750 $7,400 $6,200 $5,300

BOXLOCK EXPRESS RIFLE — .470 NE or .500 NE (new 1998) cal., Anson & Deeley action with DT (front trigger is articulated), case colored action with deep blued small parts, 24 in. regulated barrels, checkered European walnut stock and forearm with oil finish, light border engraving.

Mfg.'s Sug. Retail $12,950 $11,475 $9,000 $7,500 $5,950 $4,850 $4,100 $3,750
Add $1,000 for .500 NE cal.

* *Deluxe Boxlock Express Rifle* — includes better walnut and fully engraved receiver.

Mfg.'s Sug. Retail $15,950 $14,150 $10,150 $8,750 $7,300 $6,200 $5,200 $4,500

Grading	100%	98%	95%	90%	80%	70%	60%

SHOTGUNS: SxS

SMALL BORE SHOTGUN — 16, 20, 28 ga., or .410 bore, as this edition went to press, this new shotgun had yet to be produced and prices were not available.

WILLIAM EVANS LIMITED

Current manufacturer of long arms established during 1883, and located in London, England.

William Evans, Gun & Rifle Makers, have been manufacturing high quality shotguns and rifles for over 100 years. Most William Evans shotguns and double rifles must be appraised individually since they were all custom ordered initially. All new guns must be ordered from the factory directly. Currently, the sidelock SxS shotgun starts at £29,000 w/o V.A.T. (add £2,000 for 28 ga. or .410 bore), the sidelock O/U shotgun starts at £38,000 w/o V.A.T., (add £2,000 for 28 ga. or .410 bore), the SxS double rifle starts at £45,000 (add £5,000 for cals. .500 or greater), and the bolt action rifle starts at £7,500, with Mag. cals. starting at £12,500. All prices are FOB England. Please contact William Evans (refer to the Trademark Index) for more information, including any special orders.

WILLIAM POWELL & SON (GUNMAKERS) Ltd.

Current manufacturer established in 1802, and located in Birmingham, England. Currently imported by Bells Legendary Countrywear located in New York, NY. The Heritage Series was introduced into the U.S. in 1984.

SHOTGUNS: SxS

Values listed below do not include import duty or U.S. taxes.
Add $1,155 for 28 ga. or .410 bore in Heritage Series only.

W

NO. 1 SIDELOCK EJECTOR — 12, 16, 20 ga., or .410 (disc.) bore, chopper lump barrels, extra choice French walnut, DTs, many special orders available. Gold inlays, deep relief carved action fences, can be obtained in self opener.

Mfg.'s Sug. Retail	$39,655	$39,655	$28,750	$23,250	$17,500	$14,750	$12,000	$10,000

Add $3,465 for assisted opening action.
Add $2,585 for SNT.

NO. 3 BOXLOCK EJECTOR — 12, 16, 20 ga., or .410 (disc.) bore, chopper lump barrels, scalloped boxlock action, extra choice French walnut, many special orders available.

Mfg.'s Sug. Retail	$24,255	$24,255	$21,000	$16,000	$9,900	$7,500	$6,250	$5,000

* **Model 4 Boxlock Ejector** — similar to Number 3, but has dovetail lump barrels and less engraving.

Mfg.'s Sug. Retail	$21,100	$21,100	$16,500	$10,250	$7,950	$6,600	$5,400	$4,500

Add $2,235 for SNT.

* **Model 6 Boxlock Ejector** — disc. 1988.

		$2,750	$2,450	$2,050	$1,700	$1,400	$1,150	$900

HERITAGE NO. 1 SIDELOCK EJECTOR MKII — 12 or 20 ga., 2¾ in. chambers, chopper lump barrels, choice of game scene or bouquet and scroll engraving, DTs. New 1984.

Mfg.'s Sug. Retail	$13,215	$13,215	$10,750	$9,000	$7,800	$6,700	$5,500	$4,500

HERITAGE NO. 2 SIDELOCK MKII — similar to Heritage No. 1, except has less engraving and lesser grade walnut, easy opening action.

Mfg.'s Sug. Retail	$5,620	$5,620	$5,200	$4,750	$4,375	$3,675	$3,100	$2,100

HERITAGE DE LUXE BOXLOCK DETACHABLE LOCK — features detachable locks, choice of traditional scroll or game scene engraving, ejectors.

Mfg.'s Sug. Retail	$21,485	$21,485	$16,750	$13,750	$11,000	$8,500	$7,250	$5,950

HERITAGE ROUND ACTION EJECTOR — features unscalloped, rounded boxlock action with fine English scroll work throughout, DTs.

Mfg.'s Sug. Retail	$15,785	$15,785	$12,000	$9,600	$7,800	$6,600	$5,400	$4,500

WILSON COMBAT

Current pistol manufacturer, customizer, and supplier of 1911 style handgun accessories located in Berryville, AR since 1978.

Wilson Combat has an extensive line-up of high-quality self-defense and competition pistols based on the 1911 Govt. Model and related components (over 400) in addition to custom leather products. Their current line-up includes the Service Grade pistols and a full line of custom 1911 style pistols for self-defense and competition. Please contact the company directly (see Trademark Index) for more information, including an extensive catalog which lists their guns, parts, and accessories.

WINCHESTER

Manufactured in New Haven, CT from **WINCHESTER**® 1866 to date and by Miroku of Japan since circa 1992. Also includes U.S. Repeating Arms, formed in 1981, with licensing agreement from Olin Corp. to manufacture shotguns and rifles domestically using the Winchester Trademark. Olin Corp. previously mfg. shotguns and rifles bearing the Winchester Hallmark at the Olin Kodensha Plant (closed 1989) located in Tochigi, Japan and also in European countries. In 1992, U.S. Repeating Arms was acquired by GIAT located in France. In late 1997, the Walloon region of Belgium acquired controlling interest of both Browning and U.S. Repeating Arms.

WINCHESTER OVERVIEW

Note: Winchester Rifles are a field in themselves. Models Henry, 1866, 1873, 1876, 1885, 1886, 1892, 1894, and 1895 all were produced with a multitude of special order options. Special orders included front and rear special sights, half or ⅔ magazines, takedown, various barrel lengths, configurations, and weights, special metal finishes, deluxe wood (either checkered or carved) in a variety of finishes, an impressive range of engraving options, different butt plates, etc. All of these special orders act independently and interdependently to determine the correct value of a particular Winchester. Some of the finest rifles ever made are special order Winchesters engraved by the Ulrichs, G. Young, L.D. Nimschke, and others. For these reasons a Model 92 Winchester can range in price from $200 to over $250,000 - quite a price range for one model alone! When contemplating a purchase on the higher dollar range, qualified and professional opinions should be secured, preferably from at least 2 sources. Unfortunately many fakes and upgraded (non-original) guns have surfaced in the last 10 years with the sudden increase in prices. Winchesters shown in this section are priced assuming a standard model with no special orders. Any special orders will further add to the prices shown. Caliber rarities must also be considered. Many of the early Winchesters are broken down by year of manufacture. Refer to the "Model Serialization" section in this book.

A factory letter specifying original shipping information by serial number will certainly help solidify values shown on older out of production Winchester rifles and shotguns. A listing has been provided below by model number with serialization range which can be historically researched by the Winchester Museum now located in Cody, WY. To use this outstanding service, make sure the model and its serial number fall within the ranges listed below. Simply mail in your request with serial number, model, and caliber. The charge for this service is $40 for non-members, or $25 for members - funds are payable to the Cody Firearms Museum, P.O. Box 1000 in Cody, WY, 82414. Research results will include (if available) specimen caliber, barrel length, any special orders or finishes, return(s) to the factory, as well as any additional provenance contained by interpolating existing factory shipping ledgers. I would recommend a trip to the Buffalo Bill Historical Center as it contains the most comprehensive collection of projectile arms (including Chinese specimens that date back 2,000 years) and Americana housed under one roof in this country.

With the recent price appreciation on most upper condition Winchester rifles, excellent original condition has become so expensive that the many special order features Winchester offered do not cost that much more currently. However, on lesser condition guns that are much less expensive, these same special order features will cost more percentage-wise since the condition factor did not cost a premium.

Model 1866 Lever Action Rifle — ser. no. range 125,000-170,101.

Approx. 33 specimens have been researched outside of this ser. no. range.

Model 1873 Lever Action Rifle — ser. no. range 1-720,496.

Approx. 160 specimens have been researched outside of this ser. no. range.

Model 1876 Lever Action Rifle — ser. no. range 1-63,871.

Model 1883 Bolt Action Rifle (Hotchkiss Repeater) — ser. no. range 1-84,555.

May be referred to as Model 1879, 1880, or 1883.

Model 1885 Single Shot Rifle or Shotgun — ser. no. range 1-109,999.

Not available in ser. nos. 74,459-74,556. Also known as High and Low Wall.

Model 1886 Lever Action Rifle — ser. no. range 1-156,599.

Not available in ser. nos. 135,125-135,144 and 146,000-150,799.

Model 1887 & 1901 Lever Action Shotguns — ser. no. range 1-72,999.

Model 1890 Slide Action Rifle — ser. no. range 1-329,999.

Not available in ser. nos. 10,809-10,884, 20,000-29,999, 32,629-32,698, 37,599-37,627, 234,061-234,140, and 234,142-234,160.

Model 1892 Lever Action Rifle — ser. no. range 1-379,999.

Not available in ser. nos. 374,851-376,100.

Model 1893 Slide Action Shotgun — ser. no. range 1-34,050.

Model 1894 Lever Action Rifle — ser. no. range 1-353,999.

Model 1895 Lever Action Rifle — ser. no. range 1-59,999.

Model "Lee" Bolt Action Rifle — ser. no. range 1-19,999.

Model 1897 Slide Action Shotgun — ser. no. range 34,051-377,999.

Model 1903 Semi-Auto .22 Cal. Rifle — ser. no. range 1-39,999.

Model 1905 Semi-Auto Rifle — ser. no. range 1-29,078.

Model 1906 Semi-Auto Rifle — ser. no. range 1-79,999.

Model 1907 Semi-Auto Rifle — ser. no. range 1-9,999.

Winchester factory data on models produced between approx. 1907-1961 is almost non-existent (except Custom Shop mfg.) since there was a fire at the Winchester factory in 1961.

A NOTE ON WINCHESTER FINISHES: It is very important to understand that there is a big value difference between a Model 1873 with 90% bright blue as opposed to a gun that has patina finish (turning brown). A bright blue specimen might bring several times more, because it is closer to the way it originally left the factory - with bright bluing. "Brown" guns are simply not as desirable as guns that show little or no use and retain bright blue finish.

GRADING EXPLANATION FOR WINCHESTER LEVER ACTIONS

A combination of grading systems is being used exclusively for this section to assist the reader in ascertaining the value of a particular specimen more accurately. They work as follows - the top line contains three value ranges (Above Average, Average, or Below Average) which have been created to encompass most of the specimens commonly encountered within this model.

Since there is a drastic value difference between 95% - 50% bright blue and 30% dull patina/fading finish on older Winchesters, another grading/pricing line has been included to give you an example of the top end of the marketplace. Individual percentages of condition with corresponding values are listed here to give you a complete price range on older Winchester lever actions. While no grading system is perfect, it is hoped that this combination of pricing systems will be an advantage over previous attempts.

The three groupings include "Below Average Price Range", "Average Price Range", and "Above Average Price Range" (note the new grading line underneath specifying these condition factors). These ranges indicate the following:

BELOW AVERAGE PRICE RANGE - a specimen with no finish remaining, perhaps some parts have been replaced, deteriorated metal may be lightly pitted with faint barrel/frame markings, rounded edges of wood and metal, wood showing much wear with possible repairs or cracks, must be in working order.

AVERAGE PRICE RANGE - a specimen with all original parts, exhibits gun metal patina finish, metal mostly smooth (perhaps lightly pitted), principal lettering and markings legible throughout, wood showing honest wear with little finish remaining (may have small cracks and other imperfections), good working order.

ABOVE AVERAGE PRICE RANGE - a specimen featuring unpolished brass (on Henrys and Model 1866s) or plum brown patina with traces of bluing in protected areas (on all steel frame models), sharp corners, crisp barrel markings, traces of original finish remaining, metal should exhibit nice patina or older flaking finish, wood should have some original stock varnish remaining and minor handling marks and dings, good bore, perfect working order with no replacement parts.

VALUES FOR ABOVE AVERAGE CONDITION RANGE - this includes those specimens which are 50% bright blue or better condition - When this type of condition is encountered, refer to the grading/price line listing individual percentage of condition prices located underneath the Above Average, Average, or Below Average pricing line. You may notice a gap in prices between the Above Average high price and 50% price. This is normal, because in some cases, a rare 50% bright blue/bright brass specimen will be worth considerably more than one in Above Average condition.

RIFLES: LEVER ACTIONS — 1860-1964

HENRY RIFLE — .44 rimfire, 15 shot, 24 in. barrel with integral slotted tube mag. and loading lever, blued barrel, brass or iron frame. Approx. 13,000 total production, mfg. 1860-1866.

> Because almost all Henrys have little or no original finish left, values below are in ranges rather than in separate condition factors.
> Add 25%+ for engraving, depending on amount and condition (these specimens should have fancy wood).

* *Iron Frame Model* — frame made of iron, round type butt plate, without lever latch, adj. sporting type rear leaf sight, serial numbers are in three digits only. Total production is believed to be less than 300.

    $40,000 - $24,000 $24,000 - $16,000 $126000 - $12,000

* *First Model* — approx. 3,500 mfg., generally serialized below 3,500, with or without lever latch, perch belly stock and slotted receiver for rear sight.

    $16,000 - $12,000 $12,000 - $9,000 $9,000 - $7,000

* *Martial Marked* — contracted by U.S. military for Civil War use, denoted by "C.G.C." inspector markings on upper barrel breech and stock, approx. 1,900 with serialization scattered.

    $22,000 - $16,000 $16,000 - $12,000 $12,000 - $10,000

    This rifle was the most revolutionary shoulder weapon introduced in the Civil War.

* *Late Model* — similar to first model, except butt plate heel has pointed profile, lever latch became standard and receiver is not slotted for rear sight, serial numbers over approx. 3,500, most commonly encountered Henry with approx. 8,000 mfg.

    $15,000 - $11,000 $11,000 - $8,000 $8,000 - $6,500

MODEL 1866 LEVER ACTION — .44 rimfire or centerfire (4th Model only), 24 in. barrel, blued barrel with brass frame, differs from Henry in that it has a wood forearm, frame cartridge loading port, and separate tube mag. Total production reached 170,101 for all models, mfg. 1866-1898.

* *Model 1866 First Model Rifle* — "Improved Henry" action, .44 cal. rimfire, without forend cap, serialization is concealed on lower tang inside butt stock, serial range is from mid 12,000 to mid 15,000 (in Henry serial range sequence).

    $12,000 - $10,000 $10,500 - $8,000 $8,000 - $5,000
    95% = $20,000 90% = $17,500 80% = $15,000 70% = $14,000 60% = $13,000 50% = $12,000

* *Model 1866 Carbine First Model* — same action as Rifle, only with 20 in. barrel, 2 forearm bands and saddle ring.

    $7,000 - $5,000 $5,000 - $3,000 $3,000 - $2,000
    95% = $14,000 90% = $12,000 80% = $10,000 70% = $9,000 60% = $8,000 50% = $7,500

* *Model 1866 Rifle Second Model* — "New Model" with redesigned frame, with Henry barrel markings, serial number inside on the earlier guns after ser. no. 19,000, outside lower tang beneath lever (approx. after ser. no. 20,000).

    $6,500 - $4,400 $4,500 - $3,000 $3,000 - $2,000
    95% = $12,000 90% = $10,500 80% = $9,500 70% = $8,500 60% = $7,500 50% = $7,000

Above Average	Average	Below Average

* **Model 1866 Carbine Second Model** — frame and other changes similar to Second Model Rifle.

$4,500 - $3,000 $3,000 - $2,000 $2,000 - $1,250
95% = $9,500 90% = $8,000 80% = $7,500 70% = $7,000 60% = $6,500 50% = $5,500

* **Model 1866 Rifle Third Model** — block style serial numbers usually located behind trigger, improved frame. Serial numbered approx. 25,000-149,000.

$4,750 - $3,500 $3,500 - $2,500 $2,500 - $1,500
95% = $10,000 90% = $8,500 80% = $8,000 70% = $7,500 60% = $7,000 50% = $6,500
Add 20% for brass forend cap and buttplate.

* **Model 1866 Carbine Third Model** — same changes as Model 1866 Third Model Rifle, 20 in. barrel with 2 bands.

$3,750 - $2,500 $2,500 - $1,750 $1,750 - $1,250
95% = $8,250 90% = $7,450 80% = $6,750 70% = $6,250 60% = $5,750 50% = $5,000

* **Model 1866 Musket Third Model** — 27 in. round barrel, 24 in. magazine, 3 barrel bands.

$3,500 - $2,500 $2,500 - $1,750 $1,750 - $1,250
95% = $8,000 90% = $6,700 80% = $6,000 70% = $5,500 60% = $5,000 50% = $4,600

* **Model 1866 Rifle/Carbine/Musket Fourth Model** — .44 cal., twin rimfire and centerfire, script style serial number on lower tang near lever latch, improved frame, serial range approx. 149,000-170,101.

Values for these models are the same as for equivalent Third Model 1866s.

This rifle is usually found with steel buttplate and forend cap.

MODEL 1873 LEVER ACTION — .32-20 WCF, .38-40 WCF, or .44-40 WCF cal., iron frame with sideplates, frame loading port, 24 in. round or octagon barrel, rifles have forearm caps and carbines have forearm bands, tube mag., blued finish with case hardened parts, oil finished stock, serial numbered on lower tang, 720,610 mfg. between 1873-1919.

Deluxe Models 1873 with color case hardened frames will add at least 50% to the values listed below for standard models.

* **Model 1873 First Model Rifle** — serial numbers approx. 1 - 30,000, sliding thumbprint dust cover on 2 guides that are integral part of upper frame, absence of any cal. marking.

$2,000 - $1,300 $1,300 - $900 $900 - $500
95% = $7,250 90% = $5,500 80% = $4,500 70% = $3,500 60% = $3,000 50% = $2,500

* **Model 1873 Carbine First Model** — 20 in. round barrel with carbine style forearm band. Distinctive curved butt plate, with saddle ring.

$2,000 - $1,400 $1,400 - $1,000 $1,000 - $500
95% = $6,500 90% = $5,250 80% = $4,500 70% = $4,000 60% = $3,500 50% = $3,000

* **Model 1873 Musket First Model** — 30 in. round barrel, 27 in. mag. with 3 barrel bands, approx. 500 mfg.

$2,250 - $1,750 $1,750 - $1,250 $1,250 - $750
95% = $6,500 90% = $5,250 80% = $4,500 70% = $4,005 70% = $3,500 50% = $3,000

* **Model 1873 Rifle Second Model** — improved dust cover featuring slides on center rail on rear section of frame top which is held in place by two screws, serial range 31,000 - 90,000.

$1,200 - $800 $800 - $600 $600 - $300
95% = $3,750 90% = $3,000 80% = $2,500 70% = $2,100 60% = $1,800 50% = $1,500

* **Model 1873 Carbine Second Model** — changes similar to 1873 Second Model Rifle, with 20 in. round barrel and 2 barrel bands.

$1,500 - $1,000 $1,000 - $700 $700 - $300
95% = $5,750 90% = $5,000 80% = $4,250 70% = $3,875 60% = $3,500 50% = $3,100

* **Model 1873 Musket Second Model** — changes similar to 1873 Second Model Rifle, with 30 in. barrel and 3 barrel bands.

$1,500 - $1,200 $1,200 - $800 $800 - $500
95% = $3,650 90% = $3,150 80% = $2,750 70% = $2,450 60% = $2,050 50% = $1,875

	Above Average	Average	Below Average

* **Model 1873 Rifle Third Model** — dust cover rail integral with frame, serial 90,000-end of production.

	$750 - $500	$500 - $400	$400 - $300

95% = $3,350 90% = $3,075 80% = $2,400 70% = $1,700 60% = $1,425 50% = $1,250
Add 20% for .44-40 WCF cal.
Add 30% for octagon barrel for .44-40 WCF cal. only.

* **Model 1873 Carbine Third Model** — changes similar to 1873 Rifle Third Model, with 20 in. barrel and 2 barrel bands.

	$1,250 - $800	$800 - $600	$600 - $400

95% = $4,400 90% = $4,000 80% = $3,500 70% = $3,000 60% = $2,500 50% = $2,000
Add 30% for .32-20 WCF cal.

* **Model 1873 Musket Third Model** — 30 in. round barrel and 3 barrel bands.

	$1,000 - $800	$800 - $600	$600 - $400

95% = $3,400 90% = $2,900 80% = $2,500 70% = $2,200 60% = $1,925 50% = $1,600

* **Model 1873 .22 Rimfire Rifle** — .22 S, L, or Extra L (very rare) cal., 24 in. barrel, no loading gate, the first .22 caliber repeater, 19,552 produced, mfg. 1884-1904. Made in rifle configuration only.

	$1,200 - $900	$900 - $700	$700 - $500

95% = $3,250 90% = $2,750 80% = $2,000 70% = $1,700 60% = $1,500 50% = $1,350
Add 30% for takedown model.

* **Model 1873** *"One of One Thousand"* — special care taken in manufacture to guarantee better accuracy, markings on top of breech designate model, deluxe walnut, extremely rare, barrel marked *"One of One Thousand"* in most cases, 136 mfg. Original cost was $100.

Values can range from $30,000 - $200,000, depending on condition. A factory letter is a must for any "One of One Thousand" Winchester. Believe it or not, watch for fake letters.

Note: Rarity of the "One of One Thousand" and the "One of One Hundred" models makes upgrading to this model fairly common. Use extreme caution in purchasing.

* **Model 1873** *"One of One Hundred"* — similar to "One of One Thousand" only rarer, 8 mfg. Sold new for $20 over the list price of a similarly equipped Model 1873.

Values can range from $40,000 - $225,000, depending on condition. A factory letter is a must for any "One of One Hundred" Winchester. Believe it or not, watch for fake letters.

MODEL 1876 LEVER ACTION — .40-60 WCF, .45-60 WCF, .45-75 WCF(first caliber offered), or .50-95 Express cal., 26 or 28 in. round or octagon barrel, similar but larger frame than Model 1873, tube mag., rifles have forearm caps while carbines have forearm bands, crescent butt, blued finish, straight grip stock, 63,871 mfg. between 1876-1897.

The Model 1876 was also called the Centennial Model since its introduction coincided with the U.S. Centennial Exposition held in Philadelphia, PA in 1876. Popularity for this model decreased ten years later when the more powerful and advanced Model 1886 was introduced.

Deluxe Model 1876s with color case hardened frames will add at least 50% to the values listed below for standard models. Deluxe Models 1876 with 90%+ original case colors are rare.

* **Model 1876 Rifle First Model** — serial numbered approx. 1-5,000, distinguishable by no dust cover on frame top.

	$2,000 - $1,500	$1,500 - $1,000	$1,000 - $700

95% = $6,500 90% = $6,000 80% = $5,500 70% = $4,000 60% = $3,500 50% = $3,000

* **Model 1876 Carbine First Model** — 22 in. round barrel, one barrel band, saddle ring, full length forearm giving a musket appearance.

	$3,500 - $2,500	$2,500 - $1,500	$1,500 - $1,000

95% = $8,000 90% = $7,000 80% = $6,000 70% = $5,000 60% = $4,500 50% = $4,000

* **Model 1876 Musket First Model** — 32 in. round barrel with 1 band, scarce model because no foreign military contracts.

	$6,000 - $4,500	$4,500 - $3,000	$3,000 - $2,000

95% = $15,000 90% = $12,000 80% = $10,000 70% = $9,000 60% = $8,000 50% = $7,000

	Above Average	Average	Below Average

* **Model 1876 Rifle Second Model** — "Thumbprint" dust cover rail held on by screw, serial range 5,000-30,000.

	$2,000 - $1,500	$1,500 - $1,200	$1,200 - $800

95% = $5,500 90% = $4,500 80% = $4,000 70% = $3,500 60% = $3,250 50% = $2,750
Add 25% for .50-95 WCF cal.

* **Model 1876 Carbine Second Model** — changes similar to Model 1876 Rifle Early Second Model, with 22 in. round barrel and full length forearm giving a musket appearance.

	$2,950 - $1,800	$1,800 - $1,200	$1,200 - $900

95% = $7,000 90% = $6,000 80% = $5,150 70% = $4,700 60% = $4,200 50% = $3,675

* **Model 1876 Musket Second Model** — changes similar to Model 1876 Rifle Early Second Model, with 32 in. round barrel and carbine forend tip.

	$5,500 - $3,500	$3,500 - $2,500	$2,500 - $1,500

95% = $13,000 90% = $11,000 80% = $9,000 70% = $8,550 60% = $8,000 50% = $7,500

* **Model 1876 Rifle Third Model** — dust cover rail integral with frame, serial range 30,000-end of production.

	$2,000 - $1,500	$1,500 - $1,000	$1,000 - $700

95% = $6,500 90% = $5,500 80% = $4,000 70% = $3,500 60% = $3,000 50% = $2,500
Add 25% for .50-95 WCF cal.

* **Model 1876 Carbine Third Model** — frame similar to Model 1876 Rifle Third Model, with 22 in. round barrel and full length forearm giving a musket appearance.

	$2,500 - $1,500	$1,500 - $1,100	$1,100 - $800

95% = $7,500 90% = $6,000 80% = $5,000 70% = $4,500 60% = $4,000 50% = $2,500

* **Model 1876 Musket Third Model** — frame similar to Model 1876 Rifle Third Model, with 32 in. round barrel.

	$5,000 - $3,250	$3,250 - $2,250	$2,250 - $1,500

95% = $12,000 90% = $10,000 80% = $8,000 70% = $7,000 60% = $6,500 50% = $5,500

* **Model 1876** *"One of One Thousand "* — special care taken in manufacture to guarantee better accuracy, markings on top of breech designate model, deluxe walnut, extremely rare, 54 mfg. Original cost was $100.

Values can range from $35,000 - $250,000, depending on condition. A factory letter is a must for any "One of One Thousand" Winchester. Believe it or not, watch for fake letters.

Values are not listed because too few original specimens are bought or sold to accurately establish pricing. A factory letter is a must for any "One of One Thousand" Winchester.

Note: Rarity of the "One of One Thousand" and the "One of One Hundred" models makes unethical upgrading to this model fairly common. Use extreme caution in purchasing.

* **Model 1876** *"One of One Hundred "* — similar to "One of One Thousand" only rarer, 8 mfg. Sold new for $20 over the list price of a similarly equipped Model 1876.

Values can range from $45,000 - $500,000, depending on condition. A factory letter is a must for any "One of One Hundred" Winchester. Believe it or not, watch for fake letters.

Values are not listed because too few original specimens are bought or sold to accurately establish pricing. A factory letter is a must for any "One of One Hundred" Winchester.

* **Model 1876 Northwest Mounted Police Carbine** — .45-75 WCF cal. only, 22 in. barrel, "NWMP" lightly stamped on butt stock (with wear, this cartouche may not be visible) approx. 1,600 mfg.

	$4,000 - $3,000	$3,000 - $2,250	$2,250 - $1,500

95% = $9,500 90% = $8,750 80% = $7,750 70% = $6,950 60% = $6,150 50% = $5,275

Above average specimens in this model should have traces of blue and a very good stock cartouche. Be very wary of the stock cartouche since these butt stocks were sold as surplus back in the 1920s. A letter of authenticity is a good idea on this model.

W

	Above Average	Average	Below Average

MODEL 1886 LEVER ACTION

MODEL 1886 LEVER ACTION — .33 WCF, .38-56 WCF, .38-70 WCF (830 mfg.), .40-65 WCF, .40-70 WCF (629 mfg.), .40-82 WCF, .45-70 Govt., .45-90, .50-110 Express, or .50-100-450 (234 mfg.) cal. available, Browning's first high power lever action design distinguished by vertical locking bars, .45-70 Govt. most popular cal., 26 in. round or octagon barrel, tube mag., steel forend cap, straight grip stock. Approx. 159,990 mfg. between 1886-1935.

The Model 1886 had case hardening standard on the frame, butt plate, and forend cap until 1901 (approx. 122,000 serial range) when the standard finish became blue.

On the Model 1886 variations listed below, add the following percentages for special order features.
Add 10% for octagon barrel.
Add 20% premium for Takedown Model.
Add 30% for .45-70 Govt. or .45-90 cal.
Add 100% for .50-110 or 125% for .50-100-450 cal.
Add 100% for Deluxe Model (pistol grip checkered walnut stock).

* *Model 1886 Rifle*

	$1,600 - $1,200	$1,200 - $800	$800 - $550

95% = $4,000 90% = $3,500 80% = $3,000 70% = $2,250 60% = $1,800 50% = $1,600

* *Model 1886 Carbine* — same general specifications as Rifle, except 22 in. round barrel and saddle ring, solid frame only.

	$2,500 - $1,800	$1,800 - $1,200	$1,200 - $800

95% = $9,250 90% = $8,000 80% = $6,750 70% = $4,750 60% = $3,750 50% = $3,000
Add 35% for full stock carbine (very rare).

* *Model 1886 Musket* — 30 in. round barrel, full length military style forearm, military sights, only 350 mfg., very rare.

	$6,000 - $4,450	$4,450 - $3,000	$3,000 - $2,250

95% = $13,750 90% = $11,250 80% = $9,000 70% = $8,000 60% = $7,500 50% = $7,000
Most specimens encountered in this variation are in very good condition - a pitted musket is almost never encountered.

* *Model 1886 Lightweight Rifle* — .45-70 Govt. or .33 WCF cal. only, 22 (.45-70 Govt. cal.) or 24 (.33 WCF cal.) in. round nickel steel tapered barrel, half mag., rubber shotgun butt plate.

* *.33 caliber*

	$1,000 - $800	$800 - $600	$600 - $450

95% = $2,250 90% = $1,750 80% = $1,500 70% = $1,300 60% = $1,200 50% = $1,100

* *.45-70 Govt. caliber*

	$1,850 - $1,400	$1,400 - $1,100	$1,100 - $750

95% = $3,750 90% = $3,000 80% = $2,750 70% = $2,500 60% = $2,250 50% = $2,000
Since lightweight rifles were fairly late production, all specimens are blue and in very good condition usually.

MODEL 1892 RIFLE

100%	98%	95%	90%	80%	70%	60%	50%	40%	30%	20%	10%

MODEL 1892 RIFLE — .218 Bee (rare, if original), .25-20 WCF, .32-20 WCF, .38-40 WCF, or .44-40 WCF cal., 24 in. round or octagon barrel, blue, tube mag., forend cap, crescent butt. Mfg. 1,004,067 between 1892-1941.

N/A	N/A	$1,600	$1,275	$1,100	$995	$875	$775	$675	$550	$450	$350

Add 25% for .44-40 WCF cal.
Add 15% for .38-40 WCF cal.
Add 25% for Takedown Model.
Add 50% for fancy pistol grip checkered wood (Deluxe Model).
Add 20% for early antique ser. no. range under 168,000.
.218 Bee is extremely rare in this model. Most specimens are re-barreled rather than being original.

MODEL 1892 CARBINE — 20 in. round barrel, forearm bands and saddle ring.

N/A	N/A	$2,275	$1,775	$1,300	$1,100	$995	$875	$775	$675	$550	$450

Add 25% for .44-40 WCF.

100%	98%	95%	90%	80%	70%	60%	50%	40%	30%	20%	10%

MODEL 1892 TRAPPER'S CARBINE — all features similar to standard SRC, except has a 14, 15, or 16 in. barrel, so called Trapper's Model because it was handy for trappers who had to carry a powerful but lightweight repeating rifle.

100%	98%	95%	90%	80%	70%	60%	50%	40%	30%	20%	10%
N/A	N/A	$3,500	$3,100	$2,600	$2,200	$1,700	$1,400	$1,100	$900	$775	$650

Most 1892 Trapper's Carbines are in the 15 in., .44-40 WCF cal. configuration. Most of the 1892 Trapper's Carbine were shipped to South America or Australia. This variation is almost never encountered over 30% condition - most are brown guns.

MODEL 1892 MUSKET — 30 in. round barrel, full length military style forearm with military style rear sight.

100%	98%	95%	90%	80%	70%	60%	50%	40%	30%	20%	10%
N/A	N/A	$14,250	$12,250	$9,950	$7,500	$6,000	$4,750	$3,500	$2,500	$1,750	$1,500

MODEL 1894 RIFLE — .25-35 WCF, .30-30 Win. (.30 WCF), .32-40 WCF, .32 Spl., or .38-55 WCF cal., most common (and popular) is .30-30 Win. cal., tube mag., 26 in. octagon barrel, blue, straight grip stock. Over 5,000,000 produced to date, mfg. 1894-present, newer mfg. may be found in the RIFLES: 1894 LEVER ACTION - POST 1964 PRODUCTION section.

* *1894-1936 Mfg.* — model 94s built post 1898-1936.

100%	98%	95%	90%	80%	70%	60%	50%	40%	30%	20%	10%
N/A	$1,550	$1,325	$1,125	$925	$850	$725	$650	$575	$500	$425	$350

Add 20% for takedown variation.

Add 20%+ for deluxe models.

Add 20% for Antique mfg. (pre-148,000 ser. no.).

Add approx. 15% for cals. other than .30-30 Win. or .32 Spl.

The Model 1894 Winchester has the distinction of being the world's most popular rifle. Deluxe models will command substantial premiums on models listed above.

MODEL 1894 TRAPPER'S CARBINE — all features similar to the standard SRC, except with a 14, 15, or 16 in. barrel.

100%	98%	95%	90%	80%	70%	60%	50%	40%	30%	20%	10%
N/A	N/A	N/A	$3,000	$2,700	$2,400	$2,150	$1,825	$1,625	$1,475	$1,250	$1,050

The large majority of this variation are encountered in .30-30 Win. cal. with 15 in. barrel. Any other caliber or barrel length will constitute a premium. Most of these carbines are brown and rusty. Rarely, if ever encountered with very much finish remaining.

Note: Check federal laws on legality of 14 in. barrel.

MODEL 1894 SADDLE RING CARBINE — 20 in. round barrel.

100%	98%	95%	90%	80%	70%	60%	50%	40%	30%	20%	10%
N/A	N/A	$1,450	$1,250	$995	$875	$775	$675	$550	$450	$350	$295

Add 30% for Antique Model.

Add 35% for any cal. other than .30-30 Win. or .32 Spl.

Carbines with special order features such as pistol grip, deluxe wood, checkering, etc. can bring even greater premiums than the rifle.

* *Eastern Carbine* — features long forearm, early stock design, early style carbine post front sight, and without saddle ring, mfg. late '20s - early '30s.

100%	98%	95%	90%	80%	70%	60%	50%	40%	30%	20%	10%
N/A	N/A	$1,000	$900	$800	$700	$625	$550	$495	$450	$395	$350

MODEL 1894 1940-1964 PRODUCTION CARBINE — 1940-1964 mfg. without saddle ring.

100%	98%	95%	90%	80%	70%	60%	50%	40%	30%	20%	10%
$395	$375	$350	$325	$300	$275	$250	$220	$195	$180	$165	$150

Add 40% for .25-35 WCF cal.

Some WWII carbines with special U.S. markings will bring a premium over prices listed above.

MODEL 1895 RIFLE FLATSIDE — .30 US (most common), .38-72, or .40-72 cal., early model, distinguishable in that frame does not have fluting or ridge contouring, serial range approx. 1-5000.

100%	98%	95%	90%	80%	70%	60%	50%	40%	30%	20%	10%
N/A	N/A	$2,650	$2,200	$1,650	$1,275	$1,000	$825	$695	$575	$475	$425

Add 25% for octagon barrel on cals. .38-72 or .40-72.

W

100%	98%	95%	90%	80%	70%	60%	50%	40%	30%	20%	10%

MODEL 1895 RIFLE — .30-03, .30-06, .30-40 Krag, .303 Brit., .35 Win., .38-72, .40-72, .405 Win., or 7.62mm Russian cal., 24-28 in. barrel, blued action, box mag., straight grip stock, 425,881 mfg. from 1896-1931.

$2,900	$2,250	$1,500	$1,150	$1,000	$900	$800	$700	$600	$500	$425	$375

Add 50% for Deluxe Models.
Add 25% for octagon barrel.
Add 50% for .405 Win. cal.
Add 15% for takedown model.

The Model 1895 was a Browning design incorporating the first box type mag. in a lever action repeating rifle. .30 US is the most commonly encountered cal. in this model. A large Russian military contract was secured in 1915 with chambering for the 7.62mm Russian cartridge (over 293,000 mfg. or over 66% of total production).

MODEL 1895 CARBINE — .30 US (.30/40 Krag Army - most common cal.), .30-03, .30-06, or .303 Brit. cal., 22 in. round barrel, military style top handguard wood and military sights, with or without saddle ring.

$3,000	$2,800	$2,100	$1,750	$1,500	$1,250	$1,000	$875	$750	$625	$500	$375

Add 20% for caliber other than .30 U.S.

✳ *Model 1895 Government Carbine* — U.S. marked.

$4,000	$3,600	$3,200	$2,700	$2,300	$2,000	$1,700	$1,400	$1,100	$900	$700	$500

MODEL 1895 FLATSIDE MUSKET — early models have serial range under 5,000, no flutes on frame, .30-40 Krag only.

Rarity on this model means only a few specimens in several museums.

MODEL 1895 MUSKET — .30-03, .30-06, or .30-40 Krag cal., 28 in. round barrel with hand guard over barrel, military sights.

N/A	N/A	$1,850	$1,600	$1,400	$1,200	$1,000	$875	$750	$625	$500	$375

Add 10%-15% if U.S. Govt. marked.

MODEL 1895 NRA MUSKET — .30-03, .30-06, or .30-40 Krag cal., similar to Standard Musket grade with 24 or 30 in. barrel, 1901 Krag style rear sight. NRA approved for official NRA competition.

N/A	N/A	$2,500	$2,150	$1,850	$1,600	$1,400	$1,200	$1,075	$975	$875	$750

MODEL 1895 RUSSIAN MUSKET — 7.62mm Russian cal., over 293,000 mfg. for Imperial Russian Govt., mfg. 1915-1916, various Russian Ordnance stamps should be present.

N/A	N/A	$1,900	$1,600	$1,400	$1,200	$1,025	$900	$800	$700	$600	$500

MODEL 53 RIFLE — .25-20 WCF, .32-20 WCF, or .44-40 WCF cal., 22 in. round barrel, ½ tube mag. holding 6 cartridges, solid frame or takedown, blued finish, pistol grip or straight grip stock, serial numbered both separately and within the Model 92 range. Mfg. 24,916 between 1924-1932.

N/A	N/A	$1,900	$1,700	$1,125	$950	$875	$800	$725	$650	$575	$525

Add 40% for .44-40 WCF cal.
Add 15% for Takedown Model.

MODEL 55 RIFLE — .25-35 WCF, .30-30 Win., or .32 Win. Spl. cal., lever action design, solid frame and takedown, 24 in. round barrel, shotgun style butt stock with serrated steel butt plate, tube mag., holds 3 cartridges. Approx. 20,500 mfg. between 1924-1932. Serial numbered independently to approx. 2,865, then serialized with Model 1894 production on underside of receiver. Simply could not compete with the Model 1894.

$2,150	$1,750	$1,250	$825	$750	$675	$600	$525	$475	$425	$375	$325

Add 50% for .25-35 WCF cal.
Add 100% for Deluxe Model.

MODEL 64 RIFLE — .219 Zipper, .25-35 WCF, .30-30 Win., or .32 Win. Spl. cal., 20 or 24 in. round barrel, with standard 26 in. on the .219 Zipper, blued metal, pistol grip stock, revamped Model 55 action with increased mag. capacity, 66,783 mfg. between 1933-1957 and 1972-1973 (over 8,250 mfg. in .30-30 Win. cal. only - these last two years with minor changes).

$700	$600	$530	$495	$470	$440	$410	$370	$340	$295	$260	$215

Add 40% for Deluxe Model.
Add 52% for 20 in. barrel (sometime referred to as Carbine).

100%	98%	95%	90%	80%	70%	60%	50%	40%	30%	20%	10%

* *.219 Zipper cal.* — mfg. 1938-1941 only.

| $2,100 | $1,850 | $1,500 | $1,300 | $1,200 | $1,100 | $1,000 | $925 | $850 | $775 | $700 | $650 |

Many of this variation now have extra holes drilled on the top of the receiver to accept scope mounts - subtract 50% for this alteration. The Model 64 is usually found in excellent condition.

Model 64 1972-1973 mfg. may be found in the post-'64 section.

* *.25-35 WCF Cal.*

| $1,100 | $1,000 | $925 | $850 | $775 | $700 | $650 | $595 | $550 | $515 | $475 | $435 |

MODEL 65 RIFLE — .218 Bee (introduced 1939), .25-20 WCF, or .32-20 WCF cal., 22 in. round barrel (except .218 Bee - 24 in.), ½ tube mag. holding 7 cartridges, blue with pistol grip stock. Mfg. 5704 between 1933-1947.

| $2,750 | $2,400 | $2,000 | $1,650 | $1,475 | $1,325 | $1,150 | $1,050 | $950 | $875 | $800 | $750 |

While the .25-20 WCF cal. is the rarest, the .218 Bee has the most demand.

The Model 65 was a design evolved from the Model 53. The Model 65 was not tapped on receiver side for scope mounts. As a rule, most specimens are in either pretty nice or refinished condition.

MODEL 71 RIFLE STANDARD — .348 Win. cal., ⅔ tube mag. holding 4 cartridges, improved Model 1886 frame, blued metal with pistol grip stock, 20 or 24 in. barrel, short or long tang. Mfg. 47,254 between 1935-1957.

| $950 | $875 | $795 | $750 | $700 | $650 | $600 | $550 | $515 | $475 | $425 | $395 |

Add 25% for pre-war long tang.

* *Model 71 — 20 in. barrel* — disc. in 1938, earlier models had long tangs only.

| N/A | $2,500 | $2,300 | $2,000 | $1,800 | $1,700 | $1,500 | $1,400 | $1,300 | $1,200 | $1,100 | $1,000 |

MODEL 71 RIFLE DELUXE — similar to Standard, with checkered stock and sling swivels, 20 in. barrel in this model is very rare.

| $1,400 | $1,200 | $1,000 | $900 | $800 | $750 | $725 | $700 | $675 | $650 | $625 | $585 |

Add 200% for pre-war long tang.

* *20 in. Carbine*

| $3,200 | $2,950 | $2,800 | $2,700 | $2,500 | $2,300 | $2,000 | $1,800 | $1,700 | $1,600 | $1,500 | $1,250 |

MODEL 88 RIFLE AND CARBINE — see listing under RIFLES: LEVER ACTION - POST-1964 PRODUCTION section.

RIFLES: SINGLE SHOT

With the exception of Models 1885 (Falling Block) and 55 (Semi-Auto), all models listed below are bolt action.

MODEL 1885 — available in most popular cals. between .22-.50, falling block trigger guard activated action, John Browning's first high power single shot rifle design, many variations were made and we will list the standard types. Over 139,725 mfg. between 1885-1920.

This design was originally mfg. as the Model 1878 by the Browning Brothers in Ogden, UT in the early 1880s. Fewer than 600 were mfg. - see the Browning section for values.

* *Sporting Rifle Low Wall* — 24 or 26 in. round or octagon barrel was standard, open sights, solid frame, standard trigger.

| $1,750 | $1,350 | $900 | $750 | $600 | $500 | $450 | $400 | $375 | $350 | $325 | $300 |

Add 20% for centerfire cal.

* *Sporting Rifle High Wall* — 30 in. barrel, standard trigger, open sights, solid frame. Available in various size and weight barrels numbered (in front of forearm) from numeric 1, 2, 3, 3½ (introduced 1910), 4, and 5, lightest to heaviest. Case hardened frames standard until 1901 when bluing became standard, three different frames depending on caliber. Heavier barrels in rare calibers will bring a premium.

* *Blued finish*

| $2,500 | $2,100 | $1,800 | $1,600 | $1,400 | $1,175 | $975 | $900 | $850 | $750 | $700 | $600 |

100%	98%	95%	90%	80%	70%	60%	50%	40%	30%	20%	10%

* **Case colored frame**

| $3,150 | $2,650 | $2,100 | $1,800 | $1,600 | $1,400 | $1,250 | $1,100 | $1,000 | $900 | $725 | $650 |

> Add 30% for Takedown frame.
> Add 25% for #5 barrel.
> Add 25% for .45-70 Govt. or .45-90 Win. or .50 cal.

* **20 ga. High Wall Shotgun** — chambered for 3 in., 26 in. full choke nickel steel barrel standard, receiver has matting on top. Also available with matted ribs (rare). Solid frame or takedown. Introduced 1914 - approx. 300 mfg.

| N/A | N/A | $2,850 | $2,475 | $2,150 | $1,800 | $1,700 | $1,600 | $1,500 | $1,350 | $1,250 | $1,050 |

* **Deluxe Grade High Wall** — similar to Standard, with fancy walnut and checkering.

| N/A | N/A | $2,850 | $2,650 | $2,450 | $2,250 | $2,050 | $1,950 | $1,850 | $1,750 | $1,650 | $1,550 |

* **Schuetzen Rifle** — high wall, 30 in. octagon barrel, double set triggers, spur lever, aperture sight, Schuetzen style stock, adj. palm rest and butt plate.

| $6,500 | $5,500 | $5,000 | $4,500 | $4,000 | $3,750 | $3,500 | $3,250 | $3,000 | $2,750 | $2,500 | $2,400 |

> Add 20% for Takedown frame.
> This model had many shooting alterations performed by various aftermarket suppliers of its time. Perhaps only 10% of remaining specimens are unaltered (or 100% factory).

* **High Wall Musket** — usually found in .22 LR cal.

| $1,500 | $1,250 | $1,000 | $850 | $725 | $675 | $650 | $600 | $550 | $500 | $450 | $400 |

> Add 30% for .45-70 Govt. cal.

* **Winder Musket** — low wall, 3rd model, .22 Short or LR (most common), 28 in. barrel, standard trigger and lever, military style stock and sights, grooved forearm, one barrel band.

| $850 | $775 | $700 | $650 | $600 | $550 | $500 | $450 | $400 | $365 | $335 | $300 |

MODEL 1885 LOW WALL GRADE I (CURRENT PRODUCTION) — .22 LR cal., features 24½ in. half-round, half-octagon barrel with buckhorn rear sights, uncheckered straight grip walnut stock and forearm, crescent buttplate, blue finish only, 8 lbs. 2,400 mfg. beginning 1999.

> As this edition went to press, prices had yet to be established on this model.

* **Model 1885 Low Wall High Grade** — similar to Model 1885 Low Wall Grade I, except features frame engraving, 24 Kt. squirrel/cottontail scenes with 2 barrel bands, uncheckered fancy walnut stock and forearm. 1,100 mfg. beginning 1999.

> As this edition went to press, prices had yet to be established on this model.

MODEL 1900 SINGLE SHOT — .22 S and L cal., 18 in. round barrel, blued metal, open sights, one-piece straight grip gumwood stock without fitted butt plate, takedown, not serial numbered. Approx. 105,000 mfg. between 1899-1902.

| N/A | N/A | $650 | $550 | $450 | $400 | $350 | $300 | $220 | $185 | $140 | $110 |

> This model is usually encountered with flaked frames.

MODEL 1902 SINGLE SHOT — similar to 1900, with minor improvements. Distinguishable by special shaped extended trigger guard. Not serial numbered. Approx. 640,299 mfg. between 1902-1931.

| N/A | $275 | $175 | $150 | $135 | $120 | $100 | $90 | $80 | $75 | $65 | $60 |

> Chambering included .22 cal. Extra Long in 1914 (interchangeable with S&L).

THUMB TRIGGER MODEL 99 — similar to 1902, with button behind cocking piece used to fire with thumb instead of trigger, not serial numbered. Approx. 75,433 were mfg. between 1904-1923.

| N/A | $995 | $850 | $750 | $650 | $600 | $500 | $400 | $350 | $300 | $250 | $200 |

MODEL 1904 SINGLE SHOT — improved version of 1902, 21 in. round barrel, chambering included .22 Extra Long in 1914, not serial numbered. Approx. 302,859 mfg. between 1904-1931.

| N/A | $395 | $350 | $300 | $250 | $200 | $175 | $150 | $125 | $100 | $90 | $80 |

* **Model 1904-A** — introduced 1927 with new sear bar and chambered for .22 LR.

| N/A | $395 | $350 | $300 | $250 | $200 | $175 | $150 | $125 | $100 | $90 | $80 |

100%	98%	95%	90%	80%	70%	60%	50%	40%	30%	20%	10%

MODEL 47 — .22 S, L, or LR cal., single shot bolt action, 25 in. round barrel, unique bolt design, uncheckered walnut stock, 5¼ lbs., approx. 43,000 (not serial numbered) mfg. during 1948-1954.

100%	98%	95%	90%	80%	70%	60%	50%	40%	30%	20%	10%
$325	$295	$250	$215	$190	$175	$165	$155	$145	$135	$125	$115

MODEL 52D — please refer to listings in the Rifles: Bolt Action section.

MODEL 55 — .22 cal. only, top loading single shot, bottom ejection, 22 in. round barrel, open sporting sights, not serial numbered. Over 45,000 mfg. between 1958-1961.

100%	98%	95%	90%	80%	70%	60%	50%	40%	30%	20%	10%
$175	$135	$125	$115	$105	$95	$85	$75	$70	$65	$60	$60

Grading	100%	98%	95%	90%	80%	70%	60%

MODEL 58 SINGLE SHOT — similar to Models 1902 and 1904, .22 LR cal., 18 in. round barrel, open sights, takedown. Approx. 38,992 mfg. between 1928-1931.

100%	98%	95%	90%	80%	70%	60%
$500	$400	$300	$250	$200	$130	$120

MODEL 59 SINGLE SHOT — improved Model 58 with 23 in. round barrel and pistol grip stock with butt plate. Approx. 9,200 mfg. between 1930-1931.

100%	98%	95%	90%	80%	70%	60%
$450	$425	$400	$350	$300	$250	$200

This model was disc. due to lack of sales.

MODEL 60 — improved Model 59, 23 in. round barrel increased to 27 in. 1933. Approx. 160,754 mfg. between 1930-1934.

100%	98%	95%	90%	80%	70%	60%
$295	$250	$200	$180	$160	$135	$110

MODEL 60A SPORTER — .22 LR cal., sporter variation of Model 60, pistol grip walnut stock. Disc.

100%	98%	95%	90%	80%	70%	60%
$350	$295	$250	$200	$180	$160	$135

MODEL 60A TARGET — similar to Model 60 with Lyman 55W aperture rear sight, heavier target stock, and 27 in. round tapered barrel. Approx. 6,118 mfg. between 1932-1939.

100%	98%	95%	90%	80%	70%	60%
$400	$375	$350	$325	$275	$235	$200

MODEL 67/67A — .22 LR or .22 WRF (authorized 1935) cal., 20 in. (Boys Rifle), 24 (miniature target boring), and 27 in. (sporting or smooth bore) round barrels, same basic action as the Model 60, not serial numbered. Approx. 383,000 mfg. between 1934-1963.

100%	98%	95%	90%	80%	70%	60%
$195	$165	$130	$100	$70	$60	$50

Add 25% for Boys rifle.
Add 100% for .22 WRF cal.
Add 70% for smooth bore.

MODEL 677 — same basic specifications as Model 67, except no iron sights or sight cuts in barrel, not serial numbered, supplied with Win. 5-A scope, .22 WRF is scarce. Approx. 2,240 mfg. between 1937-1939.

100%	98%	95%	90%	80%	70%	60%
$1,500	$1,200	$1,000	$750	$600	$500	$350

MODEL 68 — .22 LR or .22 WRF cal., bolt action single shot, similar to Model 67, walnut stock, supplied with aperture sight (no rear sight), not serial numbered. Approx. 100,000 mfg. between 1934-1946.

100%	98%	95%	90%	80%	70%	60%
$250	$180	$150	$125	$100	$65	$50

Add 200% for .22 WRF cal.

MODEL 121 SINGLE SHOT RIFLE — .22 rimfire, bolt action, 20¾ in. barrel, open sights, plain pistol grip stock. Mfg. 1967-1973.

100%	98%	95%	90%	80%	70%	60%
$115	$85	$70	$55	$45	$35	$30

MODEL 121Y SINGLE SHOT RIFLE — similar to 121, with shorter stock.

100%	98%	95%	90%	80%	70%	60%
$115	$85	$70	$55	$45	$35	$30

MODEL 121 DELUXE — similar to 121, with ramp front sight and sling swivels.

100%	98%	95%	90%	80%	70%	60%
$125	$90	$75	$60	$50	$40	$35

MODEL 310 SINGLE SHOT — .22 rimfire, bolt action, 22 in. barrel, open sights, checkered pistol grip stock, swivels. Mfg. 1972-1975.

100%	98%	95%	90%	80%	70%	60%
$200	$175	$140	$100	$80	$70	$60

W

100%	98%	95%	90%	80%	70%	60%	50%	40%	30%	20%	10%

RIFLES: BOLT ACTION

MODEL 1883 (HOTCHKISS REPEATER) — .45-70 Govt. cal., designed by Benjamin D. Hotchkiss, unique tube mag. located in butt stock attached to receiver, up-turn/pull-back bolt action, 26 in. round or octagon barrel standard on rifle. Over 84,000 mfg. between 1879-1889. Also available in carbine configuration (24 in. round barrel with one band), and musket (32 in. round barrel with cleaning rod and two barrel bands) — subtract 25%. Carbine extremely rare in Third Model (20 in. barrel).

* **First Style** — approx. 6,419 mfg. with magazine cut off and safety control incorporated into one unit.

$2,150	$1,750	$1,500	$1,325	$1,200	$1,100	$1,000	$900	$850	$800	$750	$725

* **Second Style** — approx. 16,102 mfg., magazine cut off on right receiver top, safety on left side.

$1,950	$1,750	$1,500	$1,300	$1,150	$1,050	$950	$850	$750	$650	$625	$600

* **Third Style** — most commonly encountered Hotchkiss, 2-piece stock, approx. 62,034 mfg. 1883-1899.

$1,650	$1,425	$1,250	$1,100	$900	$825	$750	$675	$625	$565	$525	$480

> The Model 1883 Hotchkiss was the first bolt action designed for the U.S. military .45-70 Govt. cartridge. On the First and Second models inspect wood directly below bolt and left frame side for cracks, breaks or older repairs as it is frequently encountered on these early models with thin wrists.

LEE STRAIGHT PULL RIFLE — 6mm Lee (.236 U.S.N. cal.), 5 shot non-detachable box mag., 24 (Sporting Rifle) or 28 (Musket) in. barrel, folding leaf sight, blue metal, military style full stock, mfg. 1897-1902, Navy Issue Model is the Musket with "236 U.S.N." on barrels. Approx. 20,000 mfg. (including 15,000 Muskets for the U.S. Navy military contract) between 1895-1902 with parts clean up occurring in 1916.

* **U.S.N. Military Musket**

$1,750	$1,500	$1,350	$1,200	$1,100	$1,000	$900	$800	$700	$650	$600	$550

* **Lee Sporting Rifle** — similar to Musket, with 24 in. barrel, sporter style stock. Approx. 1,700 mfg. 1897-1902.

$1,850	$1,625	$1,425	$1,300	$1,200	$1,100	$1,000	$900	$800	$700	$650	$600

> This design was originally patented by James Paris Lee and assigned to the Lee Arms Company. Winchester obtained manufacturing rights to produce this model for the U.S Navy military contract 1895-1902.

MODEL 43 — .218 Bee, .22 Hornet, .25-20 WCF, or .32-20 WCF cal., dubbed "Poor Man's Model 70", 24 in. round tapered barrel, box type mag. Approx. 62,617 mfg. between 1949-1957.

$675	$600	$550	$450	$400	$350	$300	$250	$200	$175	$150	$125

Add 30% for Deluxe Model.
Add $50 for Special Grade.
Premiums exist (in order of rarity) for .32-20 WCF, .25-20 WCF, or .218 Bee cals.
Subtract 40% if non-factory drilled and tapped (early models).

Grading	100%	98%	95%	90%	80%	70%	60%

On Models 52, 54, 56, 57, 58, 59, 60, 60A, 67, 677, 68, 69, 69A, 697, and 70 values in 50% or less original condition have been omitted since values in those conditions will approximate the 60% price. This reflects the fact that while these lower condition specimens are not as desirable to collectors, they are still sought after as shooters.

MODEL 52 TARGET — .22 S (rare) or LR cal., 5 shot mag., 28 in. standard or heavy barrel (1st cataloged 1933), target sights and target style stock, speedlock trigger feature was introduced in 1929. Approx. 125,233 Model 52s in all variations were mfg. between 1919-1979.

	100%	98%	95%	90%	80%	70%	60%
	$460	$425	$385	$345	$315	$290	$265
With speedlock	$525	$485	$425	$375	$335	$310	$290

Barrel drilling and tapping for scope blocks was not standard on the first Model 52s, but became more apparent approx. 1926.

Grading	100%	98%	95%	90%	80%	70%	60%

* ***Model 52A Target*** — similar to Model 52, except all A-suffix Model 52s have a speedlock action. Values are similar to above. In scarcity, it seems the E suffix is probably the scarcest (also the most poorly mfg.), followed by the A suffix variation.

MODEL 52A HEAVY BARREL — similar to Standard Target, with heavy barrel.

	$660	$605	$550	$525	$470	$415	$330

MODEL 52-B TARGET — extensively redesigned action, improved stock design, offered with a variety of sights. Approx. mfg. 1940-1947.

	$630	$575	$495	$470	$415	$360	$305

MODEL 52-B HEAVY BARREL — similar to 52-B, with heavy barrel, with adj. sling swivel as to position of front swivel, and single shot adapter.

	$750	$700	$600	$525	$470	$415	$330

MODEL 52-B BULL GUN — extra heavy weight barrel.

	$800	$700	$600	$550	$495	$440	$360

MODEL 52 SPORTER (SPORTING RIFLE) — 24 in. round lightweight barrel with front sight cover, sporting type select walnut stock with cheekpiece, hard rubber pistol grip cap, black plastic tipped forearm, checkered steel butt plate, about 7¼ lbs. Mfg. 1934-1958. There is some controversy whether any of the Model 52 Sporters were drilled and tapped per factory worksmanship. Be cautious of "factory" drilled and tapped receivers on all model 52s, as there are many "gunsmith" Sporters that have been made with turned down, shortened target barrels.

* ***Model 52*** — advertised approx. 1936.

	$2,750	$2,350	$1,875	$1,500	$1,400	$1,275	$1,150

* ***Model 52A*** — introduced approx. 1937, receiver and locking lug were strengthened. Very rare.

	$3,200	$3,000	$27500	$2,200	$1,700	$1,500	$1,150

* ***Model 52B*** — introduced approx. 1940, 5 shot detachable mag.

	$2,950	$2,500	$2,000	$1,700	$1,500	$1,100	$1,000

* ***Model 52B (1993 Re-issue)*** — .22 LR cal., patterned after the original Model 52B and includes steel buttplate, 24 in. barrel w/o sights, Micro Motion trigger with adjustment screw on forend, high-polish blue, 5 shot mag., checkered 52B style stock with ebony forend tip, 7 lbs. Introduced 1993.

Mfg.'s Sug. Retail	$654		$565	$485	$440	$395	$360	$330	$300

* ***Model 52C*** — introduced 1947 with adj. Micro Motion trigger, approx. 500-1,000 mfg., 2 screws in trigger guard.

	$3,250	$2,900	$2,600	$2,000	$1,650	$1,275	$1,150

A few Model 52 Sporters & Targets were mfg. with stainless steel barrels (17,XXX-27,XXX serial range) - these guns will command a premium over values shown above.

MODEL 52-C STANDARD TARGET — "Micro Motion" trigger and "Marksman" stock, single shot adaptor, 5 or 10 shot mag. was avail., standard barrel, otherwise similar to 52-B. Mfg. 1947-1961.

	$725	$650	$550	$525	$470	$415	$330

MODEL 52-C HEAVY TARGET — similar to Standard Target, with heavy barrel.

	$750	$700	$650	$550	$475	$415	$330

MODEL 52-C BULL TARGET — extra heavy (bull) barrel model of Heavy Target 52-C. Mfg. approx. 1947-1961.

	$900	$800	$700	$600	$500	$440	$360

MODEL 52-D TARGET — improved version of 52-C with free floating standard or heavy barrel and adj. bedding device, all 52-Ds were single shot.

	$700	$600	$500	$440	$385	$360	$275

Grading	100%	98%	95%	90%	80%	70%	60%

MODEL 52-D & 52-E INTERNATIONAL MATCH — similar to 52-D, with free rifle stock, accessory rail. Mfg. 1969-disc.

	$750	$675	$605	$550	$495	$470	$385

Previous Model 52s had ser. no. suffixes - either A, B, C, or D. After approx. 1969, rifles started appearing with an E serial prefix. Both Model 52 International and Prone could have factory stocks that were not Winchester mfg.

MODEL 52 INTERNATIONAL MATCH — similar to 52-D Heavy Barrel, with special free rifle stock, hooked butt.

	$495	$470	$440	$415	$330	$305	$250

MODEL 52-D & 52-E PRONE — similar to International Match, with prone style stock. Mfg. 1975-disc.

	$750	$675	$605	$550	$495	$470	$385

MODEL 52 INTERNATIONAL PRONE — similar to 52-D, with prone stock, removable roll over cheekpiece. Mfg. 1975-1980.

	$495	$470	$440	$415	$330	$305	$250

MODEL 54 HIGH POWER SPORTER — .270 Win., 7x57mm, 7.65mm (rare), .30-30 Win., .30-06, 9mm Para. (rare) cal., 5 shot mag., 24 in. barrel, open sights, checkered pistol grip stock. Mfg. 1925-1930. Approx. 50,145 Model 54s were mfg. in all variations between 1925-1936.

	$800	$700	$600	$500	$400	$330	$305

Rare cals. will add premiums to the values listed above. This model was also mfg. with a stainless steel barrel during the late 1920s - early '30s with premiums also being asked.

MODEL 54 CARBINE — introduced 1927, similar to Rifle, with 20 in. barrel, plain stock.

	$850	$750	$700	$600	$500	$400	$360

MODEL 54 IMPROVED SPORTER — .22 Hornet, .220 Swift, .250-3000, .257 Robts., .270, 7 x 57mm, or .30-06 cal., 5 shot mag., 24 or 26 in. barrel, one piece firing pin, checkered pistol grip stock. Mfg. 1930-1936.

	$900	$800	$700	$600	$500	$400	$350

Rare cals. will add premiums to the values listed above.

MODEL 54 CARBINE IMPROVED — similar to Rifle, with 20 in. barrel.

	$1,000	$850	$800	$750	$700	$600	$500

MODEL 54 SUPER GRADE — introduced 1934, similar to Sporter, with better wood and black forend tip and pistol grip cap.

	$1,200	$1,000	$900	$800	$700	$600	$525

Rare calibers will command considerable premiums (i.e. this variation in 7x57mm cal. will sell for $2,500 in mint condition).

MODEL 54 SPORTING SNIPER'S RIFLE — introduced 1929, similar to Sporter, with 26 in. heavy barrel, .30-06 only, aperture sight.

	$1,200	$1,000	$900	$800	$700	$600	$525

MODEL 54 NATIONAL MATCH — introduced 1935, similar to Standard, with Lyman sights and Marksman stock.

	$1,000	$875	$775	$695	$625	$550	$525

MODEL 56 SPORTER — .22 S or LR cal., 5 or 10 shot box mag., 22 in. round barrel, open sights, plain pistol grip stock. Approx. 8,297 mfg. between 1926-1929.

	$1,250	$1,000	$750	$600	$500	$400	$300

The .22 cal. Short was disc. 1929.

MODEL 57 SPORTER — .22 LR cal., 22 in. barrel, open sights, stock cutaway for aperture sight on left side, drilled and tapped receiver, pistol grip walnut stock with barrel band, 5 or 10 shot mag., left side push-button mag. release, approx. 5½ lbs.

	$575	$495	$450	$395	$350	$300	$250

* **Model 57 Target** — similar to Model 56, except with aperture sight and heavier target stock. Approx. 18,600 were mfg. between 1926-1936.

	$595	$525	$450	$375	$300	$260	$220

Grading	100%	98%	95%	90%	80%	70%	60%

MODEL 69 & 69A — .22 S, LR, or RF cal., 5 or 10 shot repeater, 25 in. barrel, aperture or open rear sight, not serial numbered. Approx. 355,000 mfg. between 1935-1963.

	100%	98%	95%	90%	80%	70%	60%
	$350	$325	$290	$225	$150	$100	$85

Add 40% for Target Model.

Add 20% for grooved receiver.

The Model 69 was cocked by the closing motion of the bolt and had a non-swept back bolt handle, whereas the 69A was cocked by the opening motion of the bolt and had a swept back bolt handle. Number 97B rear aperture sight and 80A hooded front target sights and standard open sights were offered on both the Model 69 and 69A. Late 69As had "grooved" receiver for "tip-off" scope mounts - add 20%-25% for this feature.

MODEL 72/72A — .22 LR and Gallery Model (.22 short only), tube mag., bolt action, 25 in. round, tapered barrel, aperture or open rear sight, not serial numbered. Over 161,000 mfg. between 1938-1959.

	100%	98%	95%	90%	80%	70%	60%
	$375	$340	$325	$250	$115	$100	$85

Add 20% for Target Model.

Add 70% for Gallery Model (mfg. 1939-1942) - rare.

The Model 72 and 72A both cocked on opening. The Model 72A has a swept back bolt handle and some minor internal mechanical improvements. Same open sight options as Models 69/69A. Late 72As had "grooved" receiver for "tip-off" scope mounts - add 20%-25% for this feature.

MODEL 75 TARGET — .22 LR, 5 or 10 shot mag., 28 in. barrel, target sights, slight variation used by Government in WWII. Approx. 88,715 Model 75 Target and Model 75s were mfg. between 1938-1958.

	100%	98%	95%	90%	80%	70%	60%
	$500	$450	$400	$350	$300	$275	$250

Add 25% for Olympic sights.

Add up to 40% for original Winchester leather sling.

MODEL 75 SPORTER — similar to Target, except 24 in. tapered barrel, clip feed, non-target sights and select checkered walnut.

	100%	98%	95%	90%	80%	70%	60%
	$700	$600	$500	$450	$425	$350	$275

Late 75 Sporters had "grooved" receiver for "tip-off" scope mounts - add 20%-25% for this feature.

MODEL 320 RIFLE — .22 LR cal., similar to Single Shot 310, with 5 shot clip. Mfg. 1972-1974.

	100%	98%	95%	90%	80%	70%	60%
	$325	$325	$300	$265	$235	$185	$150

MODEL 325 RIFLE — .22 Mag. cal., otherwise similar to Model 320, limited mfg. 1972-74.

	100%	98%	95%	90%	80%	70%	60%
	$375	$350	$325	$300	$250	$200	$100

MODEL 670 BOLT ACTION RIFLE — another economy version of the model 70, .225, .243 Win., .270 Win., .308 Win., or .30-06 cal., 22 in. barrel, open sights, no hinged floorplate, pistol grip stock. Mfg. 1967-1973.

	100%	98%	95%	90%	80%	70%	60%
	$300	$250	$220	$195	$175	$165	$140

MODEL 670 CARBINE — similar to 670, with 19 in. barrel, not available in .308 Win. Mfg. 1967-1970.

	100%	98%	95%	90%	80%	70%	60%
	$300	$250	$220	$195	$175	$165	$140

MODEL 670 MAGNUM — similar to 670, with reinforced stock, .264 Mag., 7mm Mag., or .300 Win. Mag. cal. Mfg. 1967-1970.

	100%	98%	95%	90%	80%	70%	60%
	$330	$275	$255	$220	$205	$195	$165

MODEL 697 — same general specifications as the Model 69, except no iron sights or sight cuts in barrel and no ramp or sight cover. Telescope bases attached to barrel were standard.

	100%	98%	95%	90%	80%	70%	60%
	$1,500	$1,200	$1,000	$750	$600	$500	$400
.22 WRF cal.	$1,500	$1,200	$1,000	$750	$600	$500	$400

MODEL 770 BOLT ACTION — .22-250 Rem., .222 Rem., .243 Win., .270 Win., .30-06, or .308 Win. cal., 22 in. barrel, open sights, no floorplate or forend tip. Mfg. 1969-1971.

	100%	98%	95%	90%	80%	70%	60%
	$325	$285	$275	$260	$250	$220	$195

MODEL 770 MAGNUM — similar to Standard, in .264 Mag., 7mm Mag., or .300 Win. Mag. cal., recoil pad. Mfg. 1969-1971.

	100%	98%	95%	90%	80%	70%	60%
	$350	$310	$285	$275	$265	$250	$220

W

100%	98%	95%	90%	80%	70%	60%	50%	40%	30%	20%	10%

MODEL 777 — .30-06 cal., bolt action, 4 shot mag., mfg. by Nikko in Japan during 1979-80 for sale to Winchester subsidiaries in Australia, Germany, Italy, and Scandinavia, only 3 were shipped to the U.S., checkered Monte Carlo stock with Wundhammer swell grip, lightweight barrel, engraved action, "Winchester" is cast on the left side of the receiver near the top, approx. 1,000 mfg. with 250 in .30-06 cal. - 750 mfg. in different cal. and sold elsewhere, 8½ lbs.

> Extreme rarity factor precludes accurate price evaluation. Some specimens have been reported as sold in the $1,850+ range.

RIFLES: SEMI-AUTO

MODEL 1903 — .22 Win. Auto rimfire cal., 10 shot tube mag., 20 in. round barrel, open sights, straight grip stock cut out for partial magazine filling. Approx. 126,000 mfg. between 1903-1932.

| $875 | $825 | $750 | $650 | $550 | $475 | $400 | $350 | $300 | $250 | $200 | $150 |

> First U.S. semi-auto rifle designed for .22 rimfire cartridges.

MODEL 1905 — .32 Win. or .35 Win. cal., 5 or 10 shot box mag., 22 in. round barrel, open sights, plain pistol grip stock. Approx. 29,113 mfg. between 1905-1920.

| $650 | $575 | $525 | $465 | $400 | $365 | $330 | $300 | $275 | $250 | $225 | $195 |

MODEL 1907 — .351 Win. cal., 5 or 10 shot box mag., 20 in. round barrel, open sights, plain pistol grip stock, an improved version of the Model 1905. Approx. 58,490 mfg. between 1907-1957.

| $595 | $525 | $450 | $375 | $325 | $295 | $265 | $230 | $195 | $175 | $160 | $145 |

MODEL 1910 — .401 Win. cal., 4 shot box mag., 20 in. barrel, open sight, plain pistol grip stock. Mfg. 20,786 between 1910-1936.

| $750 | $625 | $550 | $500 | $450 | $400 | $365 | $330 | $300 | $275 | $250 | $225 |

> Add 10-15% for Fancy Sporting Rifle (special checkered walnut).

MODEL 55 — please refer to listing in Rifles: Single Shot.

MODEL 63 — .22 LR cal., styling similar to Model 1903, take-down, 10 shot tube mag., 20 (disc. 1936) or 23 in. barrel, open sights, plain pistol grip stock. Approx. 174,692 mfg. between 1933-1958.

| $850 | $750 | $675 | $550 | $425 | $350 | $300 | $265 | $235 | $215 | $190 | $175 |

> Add 30%-35% for grooved receiver variation (WFF)
> Add 50%-100% for 20 in. barrel depending on condition.
>
> The Model 63 was introduced to take advantage of the new .22 LR cartridge, which the older Model 1903 couldn't chamber.

MODEL 63 GRADE I - RECENT PRODUCTION — .22 LR cal., similar to original Model 63, 10 shot mag., 23 in. barrel, checkered walnut stock and forearm, blued finish with engraved receiver, 6¼ lbs. Mfg. 1997-98.

| $610 | $550 | $500 |

Last Mfg.'s Sug. Retail was $678.

✱ *Model 63 High Grade - Recent Mfg.* — .22 LR cal., similar to original Model 63, 10 shot mag., deluxe checkered walnut stock and forearm, blued finish with engraved gold animals and accents on receiver, 6¼ lbs. 1,000 mfg. 1997 only.

| $950 | $825 | $700 |

Last Mfg.'s Sug. Retail was $1,083.

MODEL 74 — .22 Short or LR cal., tubular mag. in stock, pop-out bolt assembly. Approx. 406,574 mfg. between 1939-1955. Distinguishable by squared off rear receiver.

| $275 | $235 | $200 | $175 | $150 | $125 | $95 | $90 | $85 | $80 | $75 | $70 |

> Add 25% for .22 Short.
> Add 25% for pre-WWII mfg.

MODEL 77 — .22 rimfire, detachable box mag. or tubular mag. under barrel. Over 217,000 mfg. between 1955-1962.

| $250 | $225 | $200 | $175 | $110 | $100 | $95 | $90 | $85 | $80 | $75 | $70 |

> Add $50 for tube mag.

Grading	100%	98%	95%	90%	80%	70%	60%

MODEL 100 RIFLE — .243 Win., .284 Win., or .308 Win. cal., 4 shot detachable mag., 22 in. round barrel with open sights, gas operated, basket weave pattern impressed on stock, pistol grip cap. Over 262,000 mfg. 1961-1973 with some production occurring in Japan.

	$425	$365	$315	$275	$250	$230	$215

The pre-1964 .284 Win. cal. with cut checkering was made for less than one year (WFF, ser. range 72,xxx with no letter suffix or prefix).

* *Pre-1964 production*
    Add $25 for .243 Win. cal.
    Add $150 for .284 Win. cal.

MODEL 100 CARBINE — similar to rifle, with 19 in. barrel, plain pistol grip stock, barrel band. Mfg. 1967-1973.

	$495	$395	$320	$275	$250	$225	$210

Add $25 for .243 Win. cal.
Add $150 for .284 Win. cal.

MODEL 190 RIFLE — .22 S, L, or LR cal., semi-auto, 15 shot LR tube mag., alloy receiver, uncheckered walnut finished hardwood stock, 20½ (Carbine Model) or 24 (Rifle Model) in. barrel, approx. 2,150,000 (including the Model 290 listed below also) during 1967-1980.

	$150	$125	$100	$85	$75	$65	$55

MODEL 290 DELUXE RIFLE — similar to 190, with select Monte Carlo stock. Mfg. 1965-1973.

	$200	$175	$150	$115	$100	$90	$80

MODEL 490 RIFLE — .22 rimfire, 5 shot clip mag., 22 in. barrel, folding sight, checkered one piece stock. Mfg. 1975-1980.

	$250	$215	$185	$155	$145	$130	$110

100%	98%	95%	90%	80%	70%	60%	50%	40%	30%	20%	10%

RIFLES: SLIDE ACTION, DISC.

MODEL 1890 SLIDE ACTION — .22 S, L, LR, or WRF rimfire, cals. were non-interchangeable, visible hammer, solid-frame (first 15,000) or takedown, 24 in. octagonal barrel, case hardened receivers until 1901. Approx. 849,000 mfg. between 1890-1932.

* *Blued Finish* — post-1901 manufacture.

N/A	$875	$650	$600	$550	$495	$450	$395	$360	$320	$280	$235

Add 50% premium for .22 WRF cal.

* *Color case hardened receiver* — disc. 1901, takedown feature was added in 1892 after over 15,000 solid frames had been made.

N/A	$4,875	$4,275	$3,650	$3,175	$2,700	$2,375	$1,950	$1,575	$1,100	$775	$450

Deluxe models or solid frames will bring premiums over values listed above. There were also a limited amount of guns mfg. with stainless steel barrels which will add to values of post-1901 mfg.

The Model 1890 was Winchester's first slide action repeating rifle. It replaced the Model 1873 .22 cal. It was an excellent and inexpensive .22 rifle that rapidly became the universal firearm used in shooting galleries. Even though production reached approx. 849,000 units, most guns were heavily used and specimens existing today in 98%+ condition are rare. Check carefully for rebarreling (notice proofmarks on barrel).

MODEL 1906 — .22 S, L, or LR, 20 in. round barrel, tube mag., visible hammer, open sights, straight stock with shotgun butt plate. Approx. 848,000 mfg. between 1906-1932.

N/A	$675	$575	$450	$375	$325	$250	$225	$175	$150	$125	$100

This model is seldom encountered in over 90% original condition.

* *Model 1906 Expert* — similar to Model 1906, except has a pistol grip stock and different shaped slide handle, finish choices included blue, nickel trimmed receiver, guard, and bolt, or full nickel trimmed, mfg. 1917-1925.

N/A	$1,200	$1,000	$800	$625	$425	$400	$300	$275	$250	$225	$200

100%	98%	95%	90%	80%	70%	60%	50%	40%	30%	20%	10%

MODEL 61 HAMMERLESS — .22 S, L, LR, or WRF cal., 24 in. round or octagonal barrel (with rifling or smooth bore, i.e. Rutledge), tube mag., open sights, plain grip stock. Approx. 343,XXX mfg. between 1932-1963.

$750	$650	$550	$450	$375	$325	$295	$250	$220	$190	$170	$150

Add 25% for single cal. barrel marking.
Add 30% for grooved receiver.
Add 200% for Rutledge bore.

Pre-war manufacture has small forearm. Pre-war octagon barrel in S or L cals. will command a 100% premium. "WRF" marked round barrel is rare - front of receiver must be marked "W.R.F.".

* *Model 61 Octagon* — .22 S, L, LR, or WRF cal., octagon barrel variation of the Model 61. Disc. approx. 1943.

N/A	$1,350	$1,050	$925	$800	$725	$675	$615	$550	$500	$450	$395

* *Model 61 Magnum* — similar to Standard 61, but chambered for .22 Win. Mag. Mfg. 1960-1963.

N/A	$800	$700	$600	$500	$400	$365	$330	$300	$275	$250	$225

MODEL 62 — 62A VISIBLE HAMMER — modern version of 1890, 23 in. round tapered barrel. Over 409,000 mfg. between 1932-1958.

$595	$550	$475	$400	$350	$300	$250	$200	$185	$170	$155	$130

Pre-war model is 62, distinguishable by small forearm. The Model 62-A was introduced 1940 at serial number 99,200 with minor changes. Model 62A single cal. barrel markings do not add premiums. .22 Short only models without the Winchester roll die receiver marking are more scarce than the so-called "Gallery Rifle" - mint specimens without the roll die marking are approx. $1,000. Gallery variations of these models will also command sizable premium.

Grading	100%	98%	95%	90%	80%	70%	60%

W

MODEL 270 SLIDE ACTION — .22 rimfire, tube mag., 20½ in. barrel, checkered walnut pistol grip stock. Mfg. 1963-1973.

	$150	$135	$120	$100	$80	$70	$60

* *Plastic forearm variation*

	$150	$135	$120	$100	$80	$70	$60

* *Model 270 Deluxe* — similar to 270, with select wood, Monte Carlo stock. Mfg. 1965-1973.

	$195	$150	$110	$80	$70	$60	$50

MODEL 275 — similar to 270, in .22 Mag.

	$165	$150	$135	$100	$80	$70	$65

* *Model 275 Deluxe* — similar to 270 Deluxe, in .22 Mag.

	$210	$160	$140	$110	$80	$70	$60

RIFLES: LEVER ACTION - POST 1964 PRODUCTION

Beginning in 1992, all Model 94s and variations (not including the 9422 models) received an engineering change utilizing a cross-bolt in the upper rear of the receiver that prevents the hammer from contacting the firing pin.

MODEL 64 1972-1974 MODEL — .30-30 Win. cal., lever action, 5 shot, ⅔ tube mag., 24 in. barrel, open sight, plain pistol grip stock. Mfg. 1972-1974.

	$325	$300	$250	$200	$165	$140	$125

MODEL 88 LEVER ACTION RIFLE — pre-'64 version with diamond cut checkering, no barrel band, 22 in. barrel. Mfg. 1955-1963. Total production for all varieties of the Model 88 Lever Action was approx. 284,000 units.

	100%	98%	95%	90%	80%	70%	60%
.308 Win. (1955-1963)	$600	$550	$450	$400	$340	$275	$200
.243 Win. (1956-1963)	$700	$600	$550	$450	$400	$350	$325
.358 Win. (1956-1962)	$1,500	$1,300	$1,100	$1,000	$850	$750	$700
.284 Win. (Intro-1963)	$1,400	$1,200	$1,000	$900	$800	$700	$550

Grading	100%	98%	95%	90%	80%	70%	60%

MODEL 88 LEVER ACTION RIFLE — 1964 model with impressed basket weave checkering, no barrel band, 22 in. barrel. Mfg. 1964-1973.

.308 Win. (1964-N/A)	$500	$450	$400	$350	$300	$250	$200
.243 Win. (1964-N/A)	$550	$500	$450	$400	$350	$300	$250
.284 Win. (1964-N/A)	$850	$750	$700	$650	$600	$450	$400

MODEL 88 LEVER ACTION CARBINE — introduced 1968, no checkering, one-piece stock, barrel band, 19 in. barrel. Mfg. 1968-1973.

.308 Win. (1968-1973)	$700	$600	$500	$450	$350	$300	$250
.243 Win. (1968-N/A)	$700	$600	$500	$450	$350	$300	$250
.284 Win. (1968-N/A)	$1,200	$1,000	$850	$650	$575	$475	$350

MODEL 150 LEVER ACTION — .22 rimfire, 20½ in. barrel, tube mag., hammerless, uncheckered hardwood stock and forearm, sling swivels, approx. 47,400 mfg. 1967-1974.

	$125	$110	$95	$70	$60	$50	$40

MODEL 250 LEVER ACTION — .22 rimfire, 20½ in. barrel, tube mag., hammerless, checkered pistol grip stock. Mfg. 1963-1973.

	$150	$125	$110	$95	$70	$60	$50

* **Model 250 Deluxe** — similar to Model 250, with select wood and sling swivels. Mfg. 1965-1971.

	$195	$155	$110	$95	$70	$60	$50

MODEL 255 — .22 Mag., otherwise similar to Model 250. Mfg. 1964-1970.

	$195	$175	$150	$135	$110	$85	$70

* **Model 255 Deluxe** — .22 Mag., with select wood and swivels. Mfg. 1965-1973.

	$260	$210	$165	$150	$135	$100	$75

MODEL 1886 GRADE I — .45-70 Govt. cal., 26 in. octagon barrel. Mfg. 1997-98.

	$900	$850	$750	$650	$600	$500	$450

Last Mfg.'s Sug. Retail was $996.

* **Model 1886 High Grade** — .45-70 Govt. cal., features gold-line receiver engraving with multiple gold animals, polished blue, deluxe checkered walnut stock and forearm with metal cap, 1,000 mfg. 1997 only.

	$1,475	$1,200	$995				

Last Mfg.'s Sug. Retail was $1,588

MODEL 1886 TAKEDOWN — .45-70 Govt. cal., features original takedown action design, uncheckered semi-pistol grip walnut stock with crescent buttplate, 26 in. octagon barrel with buckhorn rear sight, forend has ebony cap, 9¼ lbs. New 1999.

Mfg.'s Sug. Retail	$1,140	$995	$875	$750	$625	$600	$500	$400

MODEL 1892 GRADE I — .357 Mag. (new 1998), .44-40 WCF (new 1998), or .45 LC cal., similar to original Model 1892 Winchester, 24 in. round barrel, top tang mounted manual hammer stop, blued finish with etched receiver engraving, gold trigger, satin finished walnut straight grip stock and forend with metal cap, 6¼ lbs. New 1997.

Mfg.'s Sug. Retail	$744	$665	$560	$430			

* **Model 1892 Short Rifle** — .44 Mag. cal., features 20 in. round barrel with full mag., uncheckered staight grip walnut stock with crescent buttplate, buckhorn rear sight, high polish blue finish only, 6 lbs. New 1999.

Mfg.'s Sug. Retail	$744	$665	$560	$430	$400	$360	$330	$300

* **Model 1892 High Grade** — .45 LC cal., features gold accents and receiver game scene, 1,000 mfg. 1997 only.

	$1,125	$995	$750				

Last Mfg.'s Sug. Retail was $1,285.

MODEL 1895 GRADE I — .270 Win. or .30-06 (new 1998) cal., similar to original Model 1895 Winchester, checkered straight grip stock and Schnabel forearm, 24 in. round barrel, 4 shot mag., top tang safety, blue finish, 8 lbs. New 1997.

Mfg.'s Sug. Retail	$936	$840	$715	$625	$550	$500	$450	$395

Grading	100%	98%	95%	90%	80%	70%	60%

MODEL 1895 LIMITED EDITION — .30-06, similar to original Model 1895 Winchester, blued receiver, 24 in. round barrel, 4 shot mag. (box mag.), uncheckered woodstock and forearm, rear buckhorn sight, 2 piece cocking lever, 8 lbs. 4,000 mfg. 1995-97.

| | | **$725** | **$550** | **$425** | | | |

Last Mfg.'s Sug. Retail was $853.

* ***Model 1895 High Grade*** — same general specifications as the Model 1895 Limited Edition, features older No. 3 engraving pattern with double scenes, gold borders with multiple gold inlays, deluxe checkered walnut stock and forearm. 4,000 mfg. beginning 1995.

| Mfg.'s Sug. Retail | **$1,400** | **$1,200** | **$900** | **$795** | | | |

RIFLES: 1894 LEVER ACTION - POST 1964 PRODUCTION

100th Anniversary Model 1894s (mfg. 1994) are marked "1894-1994" on the receiver.

MODEL 94 STANDARD RIFLE — .30-30 Win., .32 Win. Spl. (new 1992), 7-30 Waters (new 1989), or .44 Mag. (mfg. 1984 and 1985 only) cal., lever action, 6 or 7 (24 in. barrel only) shot tube mag., 20 or 24 (mfg. 1987-88 only) in. round barrel, open sights, straight walnut stock, barrel band on forearm. Angled ejection became standard 1982, 6½ lbs. Mfg. 1964-1997.

| | | **$275** | **$215** | **$180** | **$165** | **$150** | **$140** | **$135** |

Last Mfg.'s Sug. Retail was $363.

> Add $15 for 24 in. barrel (disc. 1990).
> Add $16 for .44 Mag. cal. (disc. 1986).
> Add 15% for 7-32 Waters cal.

MODEL 94 DELUXE (WALNUT) — .30-30 Win. or .44 Mag. (new 1999), similar to Standard Rifle, except has plain (new 1998) or checkered walnut stock and forearm. New 1988.

| Mfg.'s Sug. Retail | **$379** | **$285** | **$220** | **$185** | **$165** | **$150** | **$140** | **$135** |

> Add $30 for checkered stock and forearm.
> Add $50 for .44 Mag. cal. (new 1999).
> Add $55 for 1.5 - 4.5X scope with low mounts (disc.).

MODEL 94 LEGACY — .30-30 Win., .357 Mag. (new 1997), .44 Mag. (new 1997), or .45 LC (new 1997) cal., features pistol grip checkered walnut stock and forearm, 20 or 24 (new 1997) in. barrel. New 1995.

| Mfg.'s Sug. Retail | **$423** | **$315** | **$235** | **$185** | **$165** | **$150** | **$140** | **$135** |

> Add $14 for 24 in. barrel.

MODEL 94 RANGER — .30-30 Win. only, 20 in. barrel, uncheckered hardwood stock and forearm, 5 shot mag., 6½ lbs. New 1985.

| Mfg.'s Sug. Retail | **$334** | **$260** | **$200** | **$165** | **$150** | **$140** | **$130** | **$120** |

> Add $56 for 4x32 scope with see-through mounts.

* ***Model 94 Ranger Compact*** — .30-30 Win. or .357 Mag. cal., 16 in. barrel, uncheckered hardwood stock with 12½ LOP with recoil pad, post-style front sight, 5 or 9 shot mag., 5⅞ lbs. New 1998.

| Mfg.'s Sug. Retail | **$334** | **$260** | **$200** | **$165** | **$150** | **$140** | **$130** | **$120** |

MODEL 94 TRAILS END — .357 Mag., .44-40 WCF (new 1998), .44 Mag., or .45 LC cal., similar to standard rifle, except has 11 shot tube mag., 20 in. barrel, choice of standard or large loop lever (disc. 1998), cross bolt safety, 6½ lbs. New 1997.

| Mfg.'s Sug. Retail | **$415** | **$320** | **$240** | **$190** | **$165** | **$150** | **$140** | **$135** |

> Add $22 for large loop lever (disc. 1998).

MODEL 94 TIMBER CARBINE — .444 Marlin cal., 17¾ in. ported barrel with ⅔ Mag., checkered semi-pistol grip stock and forearm, blue finish only, hooded front sight, 6 lbs. New 1999.

| Mfg.'s Sug. Retail | **$520** | **$400** | **$310** | **$265** | **$225** | **$200** | **$180** | **$165** |

MODEL 94 WRANGLER LARGE LOOP — .30-30 Win., .44 Mag., or .45 LC (new 1999) cal., 16 in. barrel, has large loop lever, uncheckered walnut stock and forearm, blued finish, open sights, 6 lbs. New 1992.

| Mfg.'s Sug. Retail | **$400** | **$300** | **$225** | **$180** | **$165** | **$150** | **$140** | **$135** |

> Add $21 for .44 Mag. or .45 LC cal.

Grading	100%	98%	95%	90%	80%	70%	60%

WIN-TUFF RIFLE — .30-30 Win. cal., similar to Model 94 Rifle, except has laminated hardwood stock and forearm with checkering. Drilled and tapped for scope mounts. Mfg. 1987 - disc.

	$300	$230	$180	$165	$150	$140	$135

Last Mfg.'s Sug. Retail was $404.

MODEL 94 BLACK SHADOW — .30-30 Win. or .44 Mag./.44 Spl. cal., 20 or 24 (.30-30 Win. cal. only) in. barrel, 4 or 5 shot mag., non-glare finish, features black composite synthetic stock with recoil pad and Fuller forearm, approx. 6¼ lbs. New 1998.

Mfg.'s Sug. Retail	$363	$290	$225	$185	$160	$150	$140	$130

* *Model 94 Black Shadow Big Bore* — .444 Marlin cal., 20 in. barrel only, otherwise similar to Model 94 Black Shadow, 6½ lbs. New 1998.

Mfg.'s Sug. Retail	$374	$310	$230	$185	$160	$150	$140	$130

MODEL 94 TRAPPER — .30-30 Win., .357 Mag. (mfg. beginning 1992), .44 Mag./.44 Spl., or .45 LC (new 1985) cal., 16 in. barrel, side ejection, walnut stock, 5 or 9 shot tube mag., blue finish, dovetailed front sight, 6 lbs.

Mfg.'s Sug. Retail	$379	$300	$230	$185	$160	$150	$140	$130

Add $21 for .357 Mag., .44 Mag. or .45 LC cal.

The .44 Mag. cal. was introduced 1985.

MODEL 94 BIG BORE — .307 Win. (disc. 1998), .356 Win. (disc. 1998), or .375 (disc. 1987) Win., or .444 Marlin (new 1998) cal., angled ejection port provides scope mounting, checkered walnut Monte Carlo stock with recoil pad, 20 in. barrel, 6 shot mag., sling swivels, 6½ lbs. New 1983.

Mfg.'s Sug. Retail	$421	$325	$235	$195	$175	$160	$150	$140

Add 25% for .356 Win. or .375 Win. cal.

Also mfg. in a top eject (pre-USRA). This model had an "XTR" suffix until 1989.

MODEL 94 LIMITED EDITION CENTENNIAL — .30-30 Win. cal., cross-bolt safety, manufactured to commemorate the 100th anniversary of the Model 94 in 1994.

* *Grade I Limited Edition* — features No. 9 style Winchester engraving pattern (rolled) on both sides of receiver, 26 in. half-round half-octagonal barrel, pistol grip stock and forearm with cut checkering, half mag., open sights, crescent butt plate, 12,000 mfg. 1994.

	$725	$550	$425

Last Mfg.'s Sug. Retail was $811.

* *High Grade Limited Edition* — features No. 6 style Winchester engraving pattern (rolled) on both sides of receiver with gold outlines and 2 gold animals (mountain sheep and deer), Lyman No. 2 tang mounted rear sight, F-style checkering and carving, deluxe walnut, 26 in. half-round half-octagonal barrel, half-mag., crescent butt plate, 3,000 mfg. 1994.

	$1,200	$875	$625

Last Mfg.'s Sug. Retail was $1,272.

* *Custom High Grade Limited Edition* — .30 WCF cal., features No. 5 style Winchester engraving pattern (hand-executed) on both sides of greyed receiver, gold outline panel scenes featuring caribou and pronghorns, Lyman No. 2 upper tang sight, F-style checkering and carving, 26 in. half-round half-octagonal barrel, half-mag., crescent butt plate, 94 mfg. in 1994.

	$8,700	$7,750	$6,800

Last Mfg.'s Sug. Retail was $4,684.

Currently, a complete set of Model 94 Limited Edition Centennial rifles with the same serial number is selling in the $10,000+ range. Since there were only 94 Custom High Grade Limited Editions mfg., demand has escalated prices radically for this model.

MODEL 94 XTR — .30-30 Win. or 7-30 Waters (new 1985) cal., 20 or 24 (7-30 Waters only) in. barrel, checkered select walnut, hooded front sight (except 7-30 Waters which has dovetailed front blade), 6½ lbs. Disc. 1988.

	$260	$225	$205	$185	$160	$150	$140

Last Mfg.'s Sug. Retail was $285.

Add $75 for 7-30 Waters cal. rifle.

* *Model 94 XTR Deluxe* — .30-30 Win. cal. only, deluxe American walnut stock and lengthened forearm with fancy checkering, 20 in. barrel with deluxe script, rubber butt pad. Mfg. 1987-1988 only.

	$370	$310	$270	$235	$210	$190	$160

Last Mfg.'s Sug. Retail was $426.

Grading	100%	98%	95%	90%	80%	70%	60%

MODEL 94 .44 MAG. S.R.C. — .44 Mag., top eject, 20 in. barrel, SRC. Mfg. 1967-72.

| | $325 | $275 | $250 | $225 | $200 | $175 | $150 |

MODEL 94 CLASSIC SERIES — .30-30 Win. Win. cal., 20 or 26 in. octagon barrel. Approx. 47,000 mfg. 1967-70.

| | $325 | $285 | $235 | $200 | $185 | $160 | $150 |

MODEL 94 ANTIQUE CARBINE — similar to Standard, with scroll on receiver, case hardened, gold-plated saddle ring. Mfg. 1964-1983.

| | $250 | $225 | $200 | $175 | $160 | $150 | $140 |

MODEL 94 WRANGLER — .32 Win. Special, top ejection, only 7,947 mfg. Disc.

| | $350 | $310 | $270 | $235 | $210 | $190 | $160 |

MODEL 94 WRANGLER II — .32 Win. Special (disc. 1984) or .38-55 WCF cal., angle ejection, 16 in. barrel, oversized hoop-shaped lever, roll-engraved receiver, 5 shot mag., 6⅛ lbs. Made 1983-1985 only.

| | $245 | $220 | $200 | $185 | $165 | $150 | $140 |

Last Mfg.'s Sug. Retail was $275.

MODEL 9422 XTR CLASSIC — same general specifications as Model 9422 XTR Standard, except has 22½ in. barrel and non-checkered, satin finished, pistol grip walnut stock and extended forearm, stock also has fluted comb with crescent steel butt plate, curved finger lever, 6½ lbs. Mfg. 1985-1987.

| | $450 | $425 | $400 | $325 | $250 | $200 | $175 |

Last Mfg.'s Sug. Retail was $301.

MODEL 9422 STANDARD (WALNUT) — .22 LR or .22 Mag. cal., takedown, 20½ in. round barrel, 15 shot (LR) or 11 shot (Mag. cal.) mag., grooved forged steel receiver, checkered straight grip, checkered high gloss (disc.) or satin weather resistant finish (new 1988) walnut stock and forearm, sights, 6¼ lbs. Mfg. 1972-present.

| Mfg.'s Sug. Retail $423 | $325 | $260 | $215 | $190 | $175 | $160 | $145 |

Add $25 for large loop lever.

This model had an "XTR" suffix until 1989. Earlier mfg. including pre-XTR and early XTR rifles had no checkering - these guns will command slight premiums over values listed above.

✳ **.22 Mag. cal.** — 11 shot mag., regular or large loop (new 1998) lever, 6 lbs.

| Mfg.'s Sug. Retail $444 | $345 | $275 | $230 | $200 | $185 | $175 | $165 |

MODEL 9422 LEGACY — .22 LR or .22 Mag. (new 1999) cal., features 22½ in. barrel with checkered semi-pistol grip stock, 15 shot mag., 6 lbs. New 1998.

| Mfg.'s Sug. Retail $454 | $355 | $290 | $235 | $200 | $185 | $175 | $165 |

Add $19 for .22 Mag. cal.

MODEL 9422 TRAPPER — .22 LR or .22 Mag. (new 1998), 16½ in. barrel, checkered walnut stock and forearm, 11 (.22 LR) or 8 (.22 Mag.) shot tube mag., 5¾ lbs. New 1996.

| Mfg.'s Sug. Retail $423 | $325 | $260 | $215 | $190 | $175 | $160 | $145 |

Add $17 for .22 Mag. cal.

MODEL 9422 WIN-CAM — .22 Win. Mag. only, similar to 9422 XTR Standard, except has checkered greenish laminated hardwood stock and forearm. Mfg. 1987-1997.

| | $330 | $270 | $225 | $200 | $185 | $175 | $165 |

Last Mfg.'s Sug. Retail was $424.

MODEL 9422 WINTUFF — .22 LR or .22 Mag., 20½ in. barrel, checkered laminated brown hardwood stock and forearm, 6¼ lbs. New 1988.

| Mfg.'s Sug. Retail $423 | $325 | $260 | $215 | $190 | $175 | $160 | $145 |

Add $21 for .22 Mag. cal.

MODEL 9422 HIGH-GRADE — .22 LR cal., features engraved receiver with raccoon and coonhound, deluxe checkered walnut stock and forearm. Mfg. 1995-96 only.

| | $415 | $340 | $265 | | | | |

Last Mfg.'s Sug. Retail was $489.

Grading	100%	98%	95%	90%	80%	70%	60%

MODEL 9422 HIGH GRADE SERIES II

— .22 LR cal., 20½ in. barrel, features high grade walnut stock and forearm with cut checkering, engraved receiver includes dog and squirrels, 6 lbs. New 1998.

Mfg.'s Sug. Retail	$504	$430	$325	$250

MODEL 9422 25TH ANNIVERSARY GRADE I

— .22 LR cal., features deluxe checkered walnut stock and forearm, engraved receiver with Winchester Horse and Rider, 2,500 mfg. 1997 only.

Mfg.'s Sug. Retail	$606	$535	$425	$325

MODEL 9422 25TH ANNIVERSARY HIGH GRADE

— .22 LR cal., features extra-deluxe checkered walnut stock and forearm, high gloss blued and engraved receiver with Winchester Horse and Rider, featuring silver borders and lever accents, 250 mfg. 1997 only.

$1,175 $995 $850

Last Mfg.'s Sug. Retail was $1,348.

RIFLES: BOLT ACTION - PRE-1964 MODEL 70

The Pre-'64 Model 70 Bolt Action Rifle (advertised by Winchester throughout much of its production history as "The Rifleman's Rifle")was produced from 1936 through 1963. Collectors recognize three major manufacturing periods: "Pre-War" (1936-1941); "Transition" (1942-1948); and "Latter" (1949-1963). There were only eighteen(18) original chamberings, these are: .22 Hornet, .220 Swift, .243 Win., .250 Savage (.250-3000), .257 Roberts, .264 Win. Mag., .270 Win., 7x57mm Mauser, .300 Savage, .300 H&H, .300 Win. Mag., .30-06 (.30 Govt. '06 Springfield - approx. 80% of total mfg. by cal.,), .308 Win. (standard in Featherweight Style only), .338 Win. Mag., .35 Rem., .358 Win. (in Featherweight Style only), .375 H&H, and .458 Win. Mag. (in Super Grade AFRICAN Style only). It is important to note that every caliber was not available during each manufacturing period. Any other caliber encountered (including 7.65mm Argentine and 9mm Mauser) may be regarded as either special ordered or non-original. Magazine capacities are as follows: "Standard Calibers" (including .22 Hornet) five (5) rounds; "H&H Magnums" (.300 & .375) four (4) rounds; and "Winchester Short Magnums" (.264, .300, .338, .458) three (3) rounds. The rifle was produced in a myriad of styles and variations — most of which are covered below individually. Unfortunately, a veritable "cottage industry" has developed involving the alteration, "upgrading" and/or outright faking of these guns. Be careful when contemplating a purchase of any rare Model 70 (and get a receipt describing the purchase accurately).

MODEL 70 PRE-WWII PRODUCTION STANDARD GRADE

— 12 standard cals., 5 shot mag., 4 shot mag. on Magnums, 24, 25, or 26 in. barrel, open sights, checkered walnut pistol grip stock, ser. range is 1-31,675. Mfg. 1937-1941.

Values listed below assume original, unaltered specimens — modifications/alterations to either the metal or wood surfaces can reduce prices by large amounts. All pre-war Model 70s have only 2 holes drilled in the front of the receiver (none in the back). An extra set of "holes" can decrease value as much as 50%. Some pre-WWII Model 70s have a "D" suffix indicating a doubled up serial number - this variation will command a premium because of its rarity. The Model 70 is one gun that caliber ranks before condition in terms of desirability. Specimens encountered in under 60% condition will not decrease in price substantially since almost any shooter is worth $450-$550.

	100%	98%	95%	90%	80%	70%	60%
Standard Cals.	$1,050	$875	$775	$595	$500	$450	$400
.22 Hornet	$2,000	$1,800	$1,500	$1,300	$900	$725	$650
.220 Swift	$1,200	$1,050	$950	$700	$595	$500	$450
.257 Roberts	$1,900	$1,750	$1,500	$1,100	$800	$600	$500
.270 Win.	$1,100	$975	$875	$695	$595	$500	$450
.300 H&H	$1,650	$1,100	$875	$700	$595	$500	$450
.375 H&H	$2,100	$1,800	$1,500	$1,200	$1,000	$900	$850
7x57mm Mauser	$2,500	$2,200	$1,900	$1,550	$1,300	$1,125	$895
.250-3000 Savage	$2,500	$2,200	$2,000	$1,800	$1,500	$1,300	$1,100

Add approx. 100% for Super Grades in common cals.

There are more fakes than legitimate specimens in cals. 7x57mm and .250-3000 Savage!

Rare cals. such as the .300 Savage, .35 Rem., 7.65mm, and 9mm Para. are seldomly encountered and their scarcity precludes accurate price evaluation. Cals. 7.65mm and 9mm Para. were special order only and made up from left-over Model 54 barrels. Also, the original factory box, papers, and hanging tag will add 25%-30% to the values listed above. Believe it or not, there

WINCHESTER®

Grading	100%	98%	95%	90%	80%	70%	60%

are getting to be a lot of fake Model 70 boxes that have been intentionally aged. Carefully screen NIB (watch the hanging tag also) specimens in this model.

MODEL 70 CARBINE (MFG. 1936-1946) — available in most cals. during its period, 20 in. barrel, short rifle variation of the Pre-'64 Model 70 (Winchester never officially used the "Carbine" terminology). If original, front sight base will be an integral part of the barrel. All carbines were disc. shortly after WWII. Beware of fakes.

Add 100% for carbine variations mfg. 1936-1946 with 20 in. barrel in .22 Hornet, .250-3000 Savage, .257 Roberts, .270 Win., 7mm, or .30-06 (most common) cal.

MODEL 70 TRANSITION (MFG. 1946-1948) — several of the post-war Model 70s mfg. between 1946-1948 exhibit the pre-war receiver characteristics and have a transition safety. This variation is more rare than normal models, with asking prices 25%-35% higher.

On this Transitional Model, the receiver bridge may or may not be factory drilled.

MODEL 70 STANDARD GRADE (1946-1963 PRODUCTION) — 18 standard cals. including .22 Hornet, .220 Swift, .243 Win., .250 Savage (.250-3000), .257 Roberts, .264 Win. Mag., .270 Win., 7x57mm Mauser, .300 H&H, .300 Win. Mag., .30-06, .308 Win., .338 Win. Mag., .35 Rem., .358 Win., and .375 H&H, 5 shot mag., 4 shot mag. on Magnums, 24, 25, or 26 in. barrel, open sights, checkered walnut pistol grip stock, ser. range is 52,549-581,471. Mfg. 1946-1963.

Values listed below assume original, unaltered specimens — modifications/alterations to either the metal or wood surfaces can reduce prices by large amounts. Most post-war Model 70s are drilled on top of the receiver (2 holes in front and 2 holes in back) to accept scope mounts (except early .300 and .375 H&H cals.). Pre-1952 mfg. Model 70s are desirable since Winchester implemented manufacturing techniques that lowered the quality in 1953.

	100%	98%	95%	90%	80%	70%	60%
.22 Hornet	$1,850	$1,750	$1,500	$1,250	$995	$795	$695
.220 Swift	$1,500	$1,375	$1,200	$900	$800	$550	$500
.243 Win.	$1,050	$950	$800	$725	$625	$550	$500
.257 Roberts	$1,500	$1,400	$1,250	$950	$850	$600	$500
.264 Win. Mag.	$1,200	$995	$895	$795	$695	$550	$500
.270 Win.	$850	$750	$625	$575	$500	$475	$450
.30-06 cal.	$750	$650	$550	$500	$450	$415	$375
.300 H&H	$1,500	$1,375	$1,200	$900	$750	$575	$525
.300 Win. Mag.	$1,500	$1,295	$1,050	$900	$800	$700	$625
.338 Win. Mag.	$1,700	$1,500	$1,200	$950	$800	$725	$650
.375 H&H	$1,850	$1,700	$1,600	$1,350	$1,200	$800	$650

Rare cals. such as the .250-3000, .300 Savage, .308 Win. (extremely rare and watch for fakes), .35 Rem., and 7x57mm Mauser are seldomly seen or sold. Premiums depend on the rarity of the caliber and original condition.

Believe it or not, there are getting to be a lot of fake Model 70 boxes that have been intentionally aged. Carefully screen NIB (watch the hanging tag also) specimens in this model.

Add 30% for .300 H&H or .375 H&H if rear receiver is not drilled and tapped.

MODEL 70 FEATHERWEIGHT — lightened version of Standard, .243 Win., .264 Win. Mag. (Westerner), .270 Win., .308 Win. cal., .30-06, or .358 Win. cal., 22 in. barrel, aluminum trigger guard and floorplate, ser. range is 206,626-581,471. Mfg. 1952-1963.

	100%	98%	95%	90%	80%	70%	60%
.243 Win., .30-06	$825	$750	$675	$600	$550	$500	$450
.264 Win. Mag.	$1,200	$1,100	$1,000	$900	$800	$700	$600
.270 Win.	$975	$875	$775	$700	$650	$600	$550
.308 Win.	$750	$625	$550	$475	$450	$425	$400
.358 Win.	$1,800	$1,600	$1,400	$1,100	$1,000	$900	$800

Add 400% for Super Grade Models.

The .358 Win. cal. is rare because Winchester had problems with this cal. Many of them were exchanged for other calibers, and the result is that original guns are rare in this cal.

MODEL 70 SUPER GRADE — similar to Standard Model, except has deluxe wood, black pistol grip cap and forend tip, all Super Grades have a raised cheekpiece with deluxe wraparound checkering, and Super Grade marked floorplate. Disc. 1960.

A general rule for Super Grades is that if you add 100% to the standard grade in similar cals., values should be rather close. For .375 H&H cal., values are listed below.

	100%	98%	95%	90%	80%	70%	60%
.375 H&H	$2,800	$2,350	$1,950	$1,675	$1,375	$950	$800

Later Model 70 Super Grades have jeweled action components.

Grading	100%	98%	95%	90%	80%	70%	60%

MODEL 70 SUPER GRADE FEATHERWEIGHT — .243 Win., .270 Win., .306, or .308 Win. cal. only, because of inconsistencies of Super Grade action component jewling (i.e., e gine turning), a simple stock and hinged floorplate change can create an "in nt" Super Grade Featherweight (check stock carefully for wood filling near area of Standa Super Grad rear sight "boss" in barrel channel), all Super Grade Featherweights have a ra cheekpiece with wraparound "fish tail" checkering, less than 1,000 mfg.

> Original S.G. Featherweights will command 4 times the value of a Stard Featherweight Model.

> This is perhaps the rarest variation of the Pre-'64 Model 70 - beware of fak

MODEL 70 SUPER GRADE AFRICAN — .458 Win. Mag. only, front sw base reloated and attached to bottom of barrel, nearly all possess one or two visible st crossbolts (usally covered with Bakelite). Most have all action components (bolt body, ctor, extracorir and magazine follower) jeweled (i.e., engine turned). 1,226 mfg. 1956 3.

$3,750	**$3,500**	**$3,250**	**$3,000**	**'50**	**$2,250**	**$l.!**

> While other Super Grades were disc. approx. 1960, the "AFRICAN" contir n that style unil the end of all production. Normal attrition and collectors owning mor one contribue to extreme rarity. Retains considerable "shooter" value in lesser exter ditions. Watc for cracked and/or repaired stocks.

MODEL 70 NATIONAL MATCH — similar to Standard, with targetstod scope bases, only. Disc. 1960.

$1,575	**$1,475**	**$1,200**	**$99**	**$775**	**$700**

MODEL 70 TARGET — similar to Model 70 Standard, in .243 Win. r .3 cal. (mfg. 195 earlier pre-'51 Target guns were available in virtually any cal. (i., .2rnet, .220 Sw 24 in. medium weight barrel and target stock. Disc. 1963.

> Rather than list prices, add 80%-100% over standard values icor n is over 90% condition will be priced the same.

MODEL 70 BULL GUN — similar to Standard Model 70, with in. y barrel, .30 .30-06 cal. only.

> Add 300% to Standard Model values.

MODEL 70 VARMINT — similar to Standard Model 70, in .220 tift 43 Win. cal., barrel, scope bases, varmint style stock. Mfg. 1956-1963.

$1,200	**$1,050**	**$97**	**$77**

> Add 30% for .220 Swift cal.

> Less than 900 were mfg. in .220 Swift cal. Stainless steel bad s ly .243 Win encountered in this model with 3 different types of finishes.

MODEL 70 ALASKAN — similar to Standard Model 70, in .30 W Mg. (mfg. rel, 24 in. barrel - known as Westerner-Alaskan), .338 Win. Mg., 37 H&H ca recoil pad. Mfg. 1960-1963.

$1,600	**$1,475**	**$1,30**	**,000**	**$950**	**$675**

RIFLES: BOLT ACTION - MODEL 70, 1964 - CUR ET PRODUC dicate

Beginning 1994, Winchester began using the Cas nomenclati those models featuring a pre-1964 style action with cor ed round fee 08 Win., els. Mfg.

MODEL 70 STANDARD — .22-250 Rem., .222 Rem., .225 Vir .243 Win., .27 or .30-06 cal., 5 shot, 22 in. heavy barrel, open sigh, lonte Carlo sto 1965-1980.

$350	**$330**	**$3**	**$285**	**$2 00**	**$175**

> Add 25% for .225 Win. cal.

in. Mag., .338

MODEL 70 MAGNUM — .264 Win. Mag., 7mm Rem. Mag., 00 H&H Mag., Win. Mag., .375 H&H, or .458 Win. Mag. cal., 24 in. ba el.

$400	**$350**	**330**	**$310**	**$220** / **$200**

> Add 25-35% for .375 H&H or .458 Win. Mag. (African lodel) cal.

22 in. barrel, open

MODEL 70 DELUXE — .243 Win., .270 Win., .30-06, or 00 Win. Mag. 1 -1971. sight, hand checkered, black forend tip, became stand rd 1972. Mfg. 1

$475	**$415**	**$360**	**$320**	**$285** / **$220**	**$180**

Grading			100%	98%	95%	90%	80%	70%	60%

MODEL 70 TARGET RIFLE 1964-1971 — .308 Win. or .30-06 cal., 24 in. heavy barrel, no sights, target bar, heavy target style stock with hand stop. Mfg. 1972-disc.

| | | | $630 | $550 | $495 | $440 | $360 | $330 | $275 |

MODEL 70 INTERNATIONAL ARMY MATCH 1971 — .308 Win. cal., 5 shot, 24 in. heavy barrel, no sights, adj. trigger, ISU stock with forearm, accessory rail, adj. butt. Mfg. 1973-disc.

| | | | $715 | $660 | $605 | $550 | $470 | $440 | $385 |

MODEL 70 MANNLICHER 1969-1971 — .243 Win., .270 Win., .30-06, or .308 Win. cal., 19 in. barrel, open sights, full length Monte Carlo stock with steel forend cap. Disc. 1972.

| | | | $550 | $440 | $385 | $360 | $305 | $275 | $250 |

MODEL 70A — economy version of 1972 type Model 70, same cals., no hinged floorplate or forend tip. Mfg. 1972-78.

| | | | $325 | $285 | $265 | $230 | $200 | $165 | $140 |

MODEL 70A MAGNUM — similar to Model 70A, except in Mag. cals. but not .375 H&H or .458. Mfg. 1972-197.

| | | | $340 | $310 | $275 | $250 | $220 | $195 | $165 |

MODEL 70 FEATHERWEIGHT — .22-250 Rem., .223 Rem., .243 Win., .25-06 Rem. (disc. 1993), .257 Robts. (disc.) .30 Win., .280 Rem., 6.5x55mm Swedish (new 1991), 7mm Mauser (disc.), .30-06, .308 Win., 7mm-08 Rem. (new 1992), 7mm Rem. Mag. (mfg. 1991-92 only), or .300 Win. Mag. (mfg. 1991-92 only) cal., bolt action, both short and medium action, 5 shot mag., barrel (24 in. .300 Win. Mag.), checkered walnut stock, no sights, approx. 6½ lbs. 1981-94.

| | | | $435 | $380 | $325 | $300 | $280 | $260 | $240 |

Last Mfg.'s Sug. Retail was $562.

1981, during U.S.R.A. takeover transition, guns were distinguishable by the U.S.R.A. mark on the recoil pad. Some collectors will pay a premium for Win. marked pads. Cals. .257 Robts. and 7mm Mauser were disc. 1985.

Model had "R" suffix until 1989.

MODEL 70 CLASSIC FEATHERWEIGHT — .22-250 Rem. (new 1994), .223 Rem. (mfg. 1994 only), .270 Win. (new 1994), .280 Rem., .30-06, .308 Win. (new 1994), 6.5x55mm Swedish (new 1997) 7mm-08 Rem. (new 1994) cal., 22 in. barrel, 5 shot mag., blued action, controlled round feeding action bedded into standard grade walnut stock, knurled bolt handle, includes rings and bases, approx. 7 lbs. New 1992.

Retail $647

| | | | $490 | $410 | $335 | $300 | $280 | $260 | $240 |

Model 70 Featherweight/BOSS — similar to Model 70 Classic Featherweight, except has 22 in. BOSS. Mfg. 1996 only.

| | | | $600 | $500 | $395 | $350 | $325 | $295 | $275 |

Last Mfg.'s Sug. Retail was $735.

Model 70 Featherweight Stainless — .22-250 Rem., .243 Win., .270 Win., .30-06, .308 Win., .30 or 7mm Rem. Mag. cal., 22 or 24 (Mag. cals. only) in. stainless steel barrel, walnut stock, 3 or 5 shot mag., approx. 7-7½ lbs. New 1997.

Mfg. Retail $646

| | | | $615 | $510 | $390 | | | | |

Model 70 Featherweight/Terrain — .270 Win., .30-06, .300 Win. Mag., or 7mm Rem. Mag. cal., 22 in. matte finish, stainless steel barrel/receiver, black fiberglass/graphite stock with checkering, with (1996-1997 only) or without BOSS, 3 or 5 shot mag., 7¼ lbs. Mfg. 1996-98.

| | | | $565 | $475 | $375 | | | | |

Last Mfg.'s Sug. Retail was $672.

Add $ for BOSS (disc. 1997).

Model 70 Win-Tuff Featherweight New — .22-250 Rem., .223 Rem., .243 Win., .270 Win., .30-06, or .308 Win. cal., 22 in. features brown laminated, checkered stock with Schnabel forend, includes base and rings, grip cap, 7 lbs. mfg. 1988-1990 - reintroduced 1992-1993.

| | | | $445 | $385 | $325 | $300 | $280 | $260 | $240 |

Last Mfg.'s Sug. Retail was $572.

Grading	100%	98%	95%	90%	80%	70%	60%

✴ Model 70 Featherweight Special — .243 Win. cal., features custom fitted stock, hand-honed action, barrel, and bolt/follower, custom shop proofstamp, select American walnut with rounded pistol grips, no sights, only 50 mfg.

	$600	$525	$475	$425	$380	$340	$300

This model is distinguishable by the Super Grade floorplate marking.

MODEL 70 XTR EUROPEAN FEATHERWEIGHT — 6.5x55 Swedish Mauser cal., 22 in. barrel, 5 shot mag., rifle sights, 6¾ lbs. Made 1986 only.

	$390	$365	$330	$305	$280	$260	$240

Last Mfg.'s Sug. Retail was $460.

MODEL 70 LIGHTWEIGHT RIFLE — .22-250 Rem. (disc. 1992), .223 Rem., .243 Win., .270 Win., .280 Rem. (mfg. 1988-92), .30-06, or .308 Win. cal., 22 in. barrel, checkered walnut stock, no sights, 6½ lbs. Mfg. 1987-95.

	$420	$335	$290	$255	$230	$210	$190

Last Mfg.'s Sug. Retail was $513.

✴ Model 70 Lightweight Carbine — .22-250 Rem., .222 Rem. (scarce), .223 Rem., .243 Win., .250 Savage (new 1986), .308 Win., .270 Win., or .30-06 cal., bolt action, 5 shot mag., both short and medium action, 20 in. barrel, checkered walnut stock, no sights, approx. 6 lbs. Mfg. 1984-87.

	$355	$320	$285	$255	$230	$210	$190

Last Mfg.'s Sug. Retail was $395.

Add $15 for open sights.

✴ Model 70 Win-Tuff Lightweight Rifle — .22-250 Rem. (mfg. 1988-89), .223 Rem. (new 1989), .243 Win. (new 1988), .270 Win. .30-06 or .308 Win. (new 1989) cal., similar to Model 70 Lightweight Rifle, except has laminated brown hardwood stock with checkering. Mfg. 1987-92.

	$395	$330	$290	$255	$230	$210	$190

Last Mfg.'s Sug. Retail was $471.

✴ Model 70 Win-Cam Lightweight Rifle — .270 Win. or .30-06 cal., greenish laminated hardwood stock with checkering, 22 in. barrel. New 1987.

	$395	$330	$290	$255	$230	$210	$190

Last Mfg.'s Sug. Retail was $471.

This model was previously designated Featherweight before 1989.

MODEL 70 SPORTER — .22-250 Rem. (mfg. 1989-1993), .223 Rem. (mfg. 1989-1993), .243 Win. (mfg. 1989-1993), .25-06 Rem. (mfg. 1985-87 and reintroduced 1990), .264 Win. Mag., .270 Win., .270 Wby. Mag. (new 1988), .30-06, .300 Win. Mag., .300 Wby. Mag. (new 1989), .300 H&H (mfg. 1989-1992), .308 Win. (mfg. 1986-89), .338 Win. Mag., or 7mm Rem. Mag. cal., 24 in. barrel, 3 or 5 shot mag., custom Sporter styling, Monte Carlo cheek piece, detachable sling swivels, 7¾ lbs. Disc. 1994.

	$435	$375	$325	$300	$280	$260	$240

Last Mfg.'s Sug. Retail was $556.

Add $34 for iron sights (.270 Win., .30-06, .300 Win. Mag., or 7mm Rem. Mag. only).
This model had an "XTR" suffix until 1989.

✴ Sporter Win-Tuff — .270 Win., .30-06, 7mm Rem. Mag., .300 Win. Mag., .300 Wby. Mag., or .338 Win. Mag., similar to Model 70 Sporter, except has checkered brown laminate stock with sling swivels, solid recoil pad, 24 in. barrel, approx. 7¾ lbs. Mfg. 1992 only.

	$445	$380	$325	$300	$280	$260	$240

Last Mfg.'s Sug. Retail was $572.

MODEL 70 CLASSIC SPORTER (LT) — .25-06 Rem., .264 Win. Mag., .270 Win., .270 Wby. Mag. (disc. 1998), .30-06, .300 Win. Mag., .300 Wby. Mag., .338 Win. Mag., 7mm STW (new 1997), or 7mm Rem. Mag. cal., similar to Model 70 Sporter, except features controlled round feeding, 24 or 26 in. barrel, checkered walnut stock, blued finish, stock was redesigned by David Miller in 1999 (denoted by LT Model suffix), approx. 7½ lbs. New 1994.

Mfg.'s Sug. Retail	$636		$490	$410	$340	$300	$280	$260	$240

Add $32 for left-hand action (new 1997).
Add $38 for iron sights (.270 Win., .30-06, .300 Win. Mag., .338 Win. Mag., or 7mm Rem. Mag. - disc. 1998).
Left-hand action is available in .270 Win., .30-06, .300 Win. Mag., .338 Win. Mag., 7mm STW, or 7mm Rem. Mag.

Grading	100%	98%	95%	90%	80%	70%	60%

* **Model 70 Classic Sporter BOSS** — .25-06 Rem. (disc. 1996), .270 Win., .30-06, .264 Win. Mag. (disc. 1996), 7mm STW (new 1997), 7mm Rem. Mag., .270 Wby. Mag. (mfg. 1996 only), .300 Win. Mag., .300 Wby Mag. (mfg. 1996 only), or .338 Win. Mag. cal., 24 or 26 in. barrel with BOSS, 3 or 5 shot mag., checkered walnut stock, approx. 7¾ lbs. Mfg. 1995-98.

			$620	$535	$440	$350	$295	$275	$250

Last Mfg.'s Sug. Retail was $728.

Add $28 for left-hand action (new 1997).

* **Model 70 Classic Sporter Stainless** — .270 Win., .30-06, .300 Win. Mag., .338 Win. Mag., or 7mm Rem. Mag. cal., 24 or 26 in. barrel with (1997 only) or without BOSS, checkered walnut stock, controlled round feeding, 3 or 5 shot mag., right- or left-hand action, approx. 7¾ lbs. Mfg. 1997-98.

			$615	$530	$440				

Last Mfg.'s Sug. Retail was $716.

Add $80 for BOSS.
Add $29 for left-hand action.

* **Model 70 Classic Laredo** — .300 Win Mag., 7mm STW (mfg. 1997-98), or 7mm Rem. Mag. cal., features claw extraction and controlled round feeding, 26 in. round or fluted (new 1998) barrel with (.300 Win. Mag and 7mm Rem. Mag. disc. 1997) or without BOSS. New 1996.

Mfg.'s Sug. Retail	$794		$665	$560	$450	$350	$295	$275	$250

Add $95 for BOSS on barrel (disc. 1998).
Add $130 for fluted barrel.

* **Model 70 Classic Safari Express** — .375 H&H, .416 Rem. Mag., or .458 Win. Mag. cal., features Express style rear sight with standing blade, redesigned stock with negative drop and Pachmayr decelerator recoil pad, trigger guard and floorplate are one assembly, 24 in. barrel with barrel band swivel attachment, checkered walnut stock and forearm, 8½ lbs. New 1999.

Mfg.'s Sug. Retail	$950		$800	$700	$625	$575	$525	$475	$430

Add $31 for left-hand action (.375 H&H cal. only).

* **Model 70 Classic Super Express Mag.** — .375 H&H, .416 Rem. Mag. (new 1994), or .458 Win. Mag. cal., 3 shot mag., claw extractor controlled round feeding (new 1993), open sights, 22 or 24 in. (.375 H&H or .416 Rem. Mag.) barrel, 8½ lbs. Disc. 1998.

			$730	$585	$525	$495	$460	$430	$400

Last Mfg.'s Sug. Retail was $865.

Add $29 for left-hand action (new 1997), .375 H&H cal. only.
This model had an "XTR" suffix until 1989.

MODEL 70 DBM (DETACHABLE BOX MAGAZINE) — .22-250 Rem. (mfg. 1993 only), .223 Rem. (mfg. 1993 only), .243 Win. (new 1993), .270 Win., .30-06, .308 Win. (mfg. 1993 only), 7mm Rem. Mag., or .300 Win. Mag. cal., checkered walnut stock and forend, features 3 shot detachable box mag., 24 or 26 in. barrel with or without sights, includes bases and rings or iron sights (new 1993, optional) in .30-06, .300 Win. Mag., or 7mm Rem. Mag., 7¾ lbs. Mfg. 1992-94.

			$465	$390	$330	$300	$280	$260	$240

Last Mfg.'s Sug. Retail was $598.

Add $36 for iron sights.

MODEL 70 CLASSIC DBM — .22-250 Rem., .243 Win., .270 Win., .284 Win., .30-06, .308 Win., .300 Win. Mag., or 7mm Rem. Mag. cal., similar to Model 70 DBM, except has controlled round feeding, 24 or 26 in. barrel. Mfg. 1994 only.

Most cals.			$475	$395	$330	$300	$280	$260	$240
.284 Win. (less than 200 mfg.)			$625	$585	$475	$395	$330	$300	$280

Last Mfg.'s Sug. Retail was $619.

Add $52 for iron sights (.270 Win., .30-06, .300 Win. Mag., or 7mm Rem. Mag.).

* **Model 70 Classic DBM-S** — .270 Win., .30-06, .300 Win. Mag., or 7mm Rem. Mag. cal., similar to Model 70 DBM, except has black synthetic stock, this model became a Classic series in 1994 (featuring controlled round feeding). Mfg. 1993-94.

			$475	$395	$330	$300	$280	$260	$240

Last Mfg.'s Sug. Retail was $619.

Grading	100%	98%	95%	90%	80%	70%	60%

MODEL 70 STAINLESS — .270 Win., .30-06, 7mm Rem. Mag., .300 Win. Mag., or .338 Win. Mag., features matte finished stainless steel receiver barrel and bolt, black synthetic composite stock, 22 (.270 Win. or .30-06 only, disc. 1992) or 24 in. barrel, approx. 6¾ lbs. Mfg. 1992-94.

$475 $390 $330

Last Mfg.'s Sug. Retail was $616.

MODEL 70 CLASSIC STAINLESS — .22-250 Rem. (disc. 1999), .223 Rem. (disc. 1994), .243 Win. (disc. 1998), .270 Win., .30-06, .308 Win. (disc. 1998), .270 Wby. Mag. (mfg. 1997 only), .300 Win. Mag., .300 Wby. Mag., .338 Win. Mag., .375 H&H (new 1995), or 7mm Rem. Mag. cal., features controlled round feeding, 22, 24, or 26 in. barrel, black synthetic composite stock, 3, 5, or 6 shot mag., without sights except for .375 H&H cal., 6¾-7½ lbs. New 1994.

Mfg.'s Sug. Retail $701 $535 $420 $345

Add $72 for .375 H&H cal.

* *Model 70 Classic Stainless BOSS* — .22-250 Rem. (disc. 1996), .243 Win. (disc. 1996), .270 Win., .30-06, .308 Win. (disc. 1996), .270 Wby. Mag. (mfg. 1997 only), .300 Win. Mag., .300 Wby. Mag. (mfg. 1996-97), .338 Win. Mag., or 7mm Rem. Mag. cal., 22, 24, or 26 in. barrel with BOSS, black synthetic stock, 6¾-7½ lbs. Mfg. 1995-98.

$645 $535 $430

Last Mfg.'s Sug. Retail was $788.

MODEL 70 CLASSIC LAMINATED STAINLESS — .270 Win., .30-06, .300 Win. Mag., .338 Win. Mag., or 7mm Rem. Mag. cal., 24 or 26 (Mag. cals. only) in. barrel without sights, checkered grey/black laminate stock with sporter style dimensions, stainless action and barrel, 3 or 5 shot mag., approx. 8 lbs. New 1998.

Mfg.'s Sug. Retail $753 $640 $545 $440

* *Model 70 Classic Camo Stainless* — similiar to Model 70 Classic Stainless, except has Mossy Oak Treestand stock finish composite stock, not available in .338 Win. Mag. cal. approx. 7¼ lbs. Mfg. 1998 only.

$630 $540 $445

Last Mfg.'s Sug. Retail was $745.

MODEL 70 CLASSIC SM (SYNTHETIC MATTE) — .22-250 Rem. (mfg. 1993 only), .223 Rem. (mfg. 1993 only), .243 Win. (mfg. 1993 only), .270 Win., .30-06, .308 Win. (mfg. 1993 only), 7mm Rem. Mag., .300 Win. Mag., .338 Win. Mag., or .375 H&H (new 1993) cal., features black composite stock with checkering and sling swivels, 22 (.22-250 Rem., .223 Rem., .243 Win., or .308 Win. - mfg. 1993 only), 24, or 26 in. barrel with matte metal finish, 3 or 5 shot, approx. 7½ lbs. Mfg. 1992-96.

$465 $395 $330 $300 $280 $260 $240

Last Mfg.'s Sug. Retail was $620.

Add $52 for .375 H&H cal. (open sights only).

Until 1993, this model was called the Model 70 SSM. In 1994, this model became the Model 70 Classic SM featuring controlled round feeding.

MODEL 70 CLASSIC SM BOSS — .270 Win., .30-06, 7mm Rem. Mag., .300 Win. Mag., or .338 Win. Mag. cal., 24 or 26 in. barrel with BOSS, 3 or 5 shot, approx. 7¼ lbs. Mfg. 1995-96 only.

$625 $525 $430 $350 $295 $275 $250

Last Mfg.'s Sug. Retail was $735.

MODEL 70 CLASSIC COMPACT — .243 Win., .308 Win., or 7mm-08 Rem. cal., features 12½ in. LOP, 20 in. barrel, and shallower profile, pre-64 type action, checkered walnut stock and forearm, blued action and barrel, 6½ lbs. New 1998.

Mfg.'s Sug. Retail $646 $510 $410 $330 $300 $280 $260 $240

MODEL 70 VARMINT — same general specifications as standard Sporter, .22-250 Rem., .223 Rem., .225 Win., .243 Win., or .308 Win. cal., 26 in. heavy barrel with cold hammer forged rifling and counter-bored at muzzle, no sights, 5 shot mag., target scope bases, 7¾ lbs. Mfg. 1964-1993.

$470 $375 $325 $295 $280 $260 $240

Last Mfg.'s Sug. Retail was $720.

Add 25% for .225 Win. cal.

This model had an "XTR" suffix 1978-89.

W

Grading	100%	98%	95%	90%	80%	70%	60%

* *Model 70 Heavy Varmint (HBV)* — .220 Swift (mfg. 1994-98), .22-250 Rem., .222 Rem. (mfg. 1997-98), .223 Rem., .243 Win., or .308 Win. cal., push-feed style action, 26 in. heavy stainless fluted (new 1997) or plain barrel (countersunk muzzle) without sights, features black synthetic beavertail H&S Precision stock with aluminum bedding block, 10¾ lbs. New 1993.

Mfg.'s Sug. Retail **$795** **$645** **$515** **$410**

  Add $137 for fluted barrel.

MODEL 70 SHB (SYNTHETIC HEAVY BARREL) — .308 Win. cal., features checkered black composite stock, 26 in. barrel with matte metal finish, jeweled bolt, 9 lbs. Mfg. 1992 only.

	$460	**$375**	**$325**	**$300**	**$280**	**$260**	**$240**

Last Mfg.'s Sug. Retail was $563.

MODEL 70 WINLIGHT — .25-06 Rem., .270 Win., .280 Rem. (new 1987), .30-06, 7mm Rem. Mag., .300 Win. Mag., .300 Wby. Mag., or .338 Win. Mag. cal., McMillan fiberglass stock, thermoplastic receiver bedding, blued metal parts, 22 or 24 (Mag. cals. only) in. barrel, 3 or 4 shot mag., no sights, approx. 6½ lbs. Mfg. 1986-90.

	$555	**$490**	**$440**	**$395**	**$350**	**$310**	**$280**

Last Mfg.'s Sug. Retail was $637.

MODEL 70 RANGER RIFLE — .22-250 Rem. (new 1999), .223 Rem. (new 1992), .243 Win. (new 1991), .270 Win., .30-06, or 7mm Rem. Mag. cal., push-feed action, 22 or 24 in. barrel, 3 (7mm Rem. Mag.), 5 or 6 shot mag., plain hardwood stock without checkering, open sights, approx. 7 lbs.

Mfg.'s Sug. Retail	**$503**		**$375**	**$285**	**$220**	**$200**	**$180**	**$165**	**$155**

* *Model 70 Ranger Compact (Ladies/Youth Carbine)* — .22-250 Rem. (new 1999), .223 Rem. (disc. 1989, re-introduced 1997, disc. 1998), .243 Win., .308 Win. (new 1991), or 7mm-08 Rem. (mfg. 1997-98) cal., push-feed action, 20 (disc. 1992) or 22 (new 1993) in. barrel, 5 or 6 shot mag., shorter hardwood stock dimensions, open sights, 6½ lbs.

Mfg.'s Sug. Retail	**$503**		**$375**	**$285**	**$225**	**$200**	**$180**	**$165**	**$155**

MODEL 70 STEALTH — .22-250 Rem., .223 Rem., .308 Win. cal., push-feed style action, 26 in. heavy barrel w/o sights, Accu Block black synthetic stock with full length aluminum beeding block, 5 or 6 shot mag., 10¾ lbs. New 1999.

Mfg.'s Sug. Retail	**$701**		**$615**	**$550**	**$450**	**$400**	**$360**	**$330**	**$300**

MODEL 70 BLACK SHADOW — .270 Win., .30-06, .300 Win. Mag., or 7mm Rem. Mag cal., push-feed action, 22 or 24 in. barrel without sights, matte receiver and barrel finish, black composite stock with conventional floorplate mag., 7¼ lbs. New 1998.

Mfg.'s Sug. Retail	**$467**		**$355**	**$285**	**$220**	**$200**	**$180**	**$165**	**$155**

MODEL 70 CLASSIC SUPER GRADE — .270 Win. (new 1991), .30-06 (new 1991), 7mm STW (new 1999), 7mm Rem. Mag. (disc. 1998), .300 Win. Mag., or .338 Win. Mag. cal., 24 or 26 in. barrel, 3 shot mag., jewelled bolt, stainless steel extractor for true claw controlled round feeding and ejecting, three-position safety, checkered satin finish walnut stock with wood cheekpiece, black forend tip, bases and rings included, approx. 7¾ lbs. New 1990.

Mfg.'s Sug. Retail	**$880**		**$710**	**$530**	**$435**	**$380**	**$335**	**$300**	**$280**

  This model was designated the Model 70 Super Grade until 1995. During 1999, this model is redesigned to include a new Express style rear sight with standing blade, negative stock drop, Pachmayr Decelerator pad, one-piece floorplate and full barrel band swivel attachment.

* *Model 70 Classic Super Grade BOSS* — similar to Model 70 Classic Super Grade, except has BOSS. Mfg. 1995-97.

	$810	**$685**	**$555**	**$450**	**$375**	**$335**	**$300**

Last Mfg.'s Sug. Retail was $956.

MODEL 70 50TH ANNIVERSARY MODEL — .300 Win. Mag., 24 in. barrel, deluxe walnut stock, engraving and special motifs on metal surfaces, serial numbered 50 ANV 1 - 50 ANV 500, 7¾ lbs. 500 mfg. 1987 only.

	$1,000	**$840**	**$725**

Last Mfg.'s Sug. Retail was $939.

W

Grading	100%	98%	95%	90%	80%	70%	60%

RIFLES: BOLT ACTION - POST 1964 MODEL 70 CUSTOM GRADES

MODEL 70 CUSTOM GRADE — various cals., old style Model 70 action, semi-fancy American walnut checkered stock, engine turned bolt and follower, hand honed internal parts. Mfg. 1988-89 only.

$1,100	$875	$700	$600	$525	$475	$425

Last Mfg.'s Sug. Retail was $1,172.

MODEL 70 XTR FEATHERWEIGHT ULTRA GRADE "1 OF 1,000" — .270 Win., bolt action, extensively engraved, finely checkered deluxe French walnut, with mahogany presentation case.

$1,800	$1,450	$950

Last Mfg.'s Sug. Retail was $5,000.

MODEL 70 CLASSIC CUSTOM GRADE — .264 Win. Mag. (new 1994), .270 Win., .30-06, 7mm Rem. Mag., .300 Win. Mag., .300 Wby. Mag. (new 1994) or .338 Win. Mag. cal., 24 or 26 in. barrel, similar to Model 70 Super Grade, but must be special ordered through the Custom Gun Shop and includes many custom features including semi-fancy walnut with satin finish and hand-honed internal parts. Mfg. 1990-94.

$1,625	$1,250	$995	$875	$800	$725	$650

Last Mfg.'s Sug. Retail was $1,757.

A Model 70 Collector Grade is also a variation of this model that is mfg. in the Custom Gun Shop - this model is priced on request only.

* *Model 70 Classic Custom Grade Featherweight* — .22-250 Rem. (new 1994), .223 Rem. (new 1994), .243 Win. (new 1994), .270 Win., .280 Rem., .30-06, .308 Win. (new 1994), 7mm-08 Rem. (new 1994) cal., 22 in. barrel, includes Featherweight features, controlled round feeding, higher grade wood. Mfg. 1992-94.

$1,625	$1,250	$995	$875	$800	$725	$650

Last Mfg.'s Sug. Retail was $1,757.

* *Model 70 Classic/Custom Sharpshooter I/II* — .22-250 Rem. (new 1993), .223 Rem. (mfg. 1993-94), .30-06, .308 Win., or .300 Win. Mag. cal., includes specially designed McMillan A-2 (disc. 1995) or H-S Precision heavy target stock, Schneider (disc. 1995) or H-S Precision (new 1996) 24 (.308 Win. cal. only) or 26 in. stainless steel barrel, choice of blue or grey finish starting 1996. Mfg. 1992-98.

$1,795	$1,375	$1,000	$875	$800	$725	$650

Last Mfg.'s Sug. Retail was $1,994.

Subtract $100 if without stainless barrel (pre-1995).

This model was designated the Sharpshooter II in 1996 (features H-S Precision stock and stainless steel barrel).

This model is also available in left-hand action beginning 1998 (.30-06 and .330 Win. Mag. cals. only).

* *Model 70 Classic/Custom Sporting Sharpshooter I/II* — .270 Win. (disc. 1994), 7mm STW, or .300 Win. Mag. cal., 1/2-minute of angle sporting version of the Custom Sharpshooter, custom shop only, Sharpshooter II became standard in 1996. Mfg. 1993-98.

$1,725	$1,295	$975	$850	$775	$700	$625

Last Mfg.'s Sug. Retail was $1,875.

This model was also available in left-hand action in 1998.

* *Model 70 Custom/Sporting Sharpshooter* — .220 Swift cal., 26 in. Schneider barrel, controlled round feeding, available with either McMillan A-2 or Sporting synthetic (disc. 1994) stock. Mfg. 1994-95 only.

$1,650	$1,250	$975	$850	$775	$700	$625

Last Mfg.'s Sug. Retail was $1,814.

W

Grading	100%	98%	95%	90%	80%	70%	60%

* ***Model 70 Classic Custom Express*** — .300 Petersen (mfg. 1995 only), .375 H&H, .375 JRS (mfg. 1992-96), 7mm STW (mfg. 1993-94), .416 Rem. Mag., .458 Win. Mag., or .470 Capstick (disc. 1995) cal., 24 in. (22 in. on .458 Win. Mag.) barrel, features claw controlled round feeding, deluxe walnut with satin finish and checkering, 3-leaf express (disc. 1995) or pre-64 style adj. rear sight (new 1996), high luster metal finish, bolt and follower are engine turned, available by special order through the custom gun shop only. Mfg. 1990-98.

$2,300 $1,825 $1,550 $1,300 $1,125 $1,000 $895

Last Mfg.'s Sug. Retail was $2,512.

Subtract $200 for 7mm STW cal.

In 1994, the model nomenclature was changed from Model 70 Custom Grade Express, and in 1996 it was changed from Model 70 Classic Express.

* ***Model 70 Custom Safari Express*** — .340 Wby. Mag., .358 STA, .375 H&H, .416 Rem. Mag., or .458 Win. Mag. cal., features honed internal parts, engine turned bolt and follower, adj. Dietrich Apel Express rear and front sights, deluxe checkered walnut stock and forend, 22 (.458 Win. Mag. only) or 24 in. barrel with sling stud, 3 shot mag., 9½ lbs. New 1999.

Mfg.'s Sug. Retail	$2,595		$2,275	$1,825	$1,400	$1,200	$950	$800	$700

* ***Model 70 Custom African Express*** — .340 Wby. Mag., .358 STA, .375 H&H, .416 Rem. Mag., or .458 Win. Mag. cal., features drop down floorplate, increasing mag. capacity to 4, checkered fancy English walnut stock with black decelerator pad and ebony pistol grip, adj. Dietrich Apel Express rear and front sights, 22 (.458 Win. Mag. only) or 24 in. barrel with sling stud, 9¾ lbs. New 1999.

Mfg.'s Sug. Retail	$3,780		$3,375	$2,950	$2,625	$2,275	$1,825	$1,400	$1,200

MODEL 70 CUSTOM MANNLICHER — .260 Rem., .308 Win., or 7mm-08 Rem. cal., features full length checkered walnut stock, smooth tapered barrel and blued action, 19 in. barrel w/o sights (sights optional), 4 shot internal mag., approx. 6¾ lbs. New 1999.

Mfg.'s Sug. Retail	$2,700		$2,350	$1,875	$1,450	$1,225	$950	$800	$700

MODEL 70 ULTIMATE CLASSIC — .25-06 Rem., .270 Win., .280 Rem. (mfg. 1996, reintroduced 1999), .30-06, 7mm STW, .264 Win. Mag., .270 Wby. Mag. (disc. 1996), .35 Whelen (new 1998), 7mm Rem. Mag., .300 Win. Mag., .300 Wby. Mag., .300 H&H (new 1996), .338 Win. Mag., .338-06 (new 1999), .340 Wby. Mag. (mfg. 1998), .375 H&H (1995 only), .416 Rem. Mag. (1995 only), or .458 Win. Mag. (1995 only) cal., controlled round feeding, checkered fancy walnut stock, choice of 22 (.458 Win. Mag. only), 24 or 26 in. tapered round full-fluted, ½ round/½ octagonal, or full octagonal tapered stainless barrel, choice blue or stainless barreled action, 3 or 5 shot mag., includes bases/rings except on some Mag. cals., approx. 7¾ lbs., except for large disc. cals., includes hard case. New 1995.

Mfg.'s Sug. Retail	$2,486		$2,175	$1,750	$1,350	$1,175	$925	$800	$700

Add $216 for .375 H&H and larger Mag. cals (disc. 1995).

Left-hand action (new 1997) available in all current cals.

MODEL 70 CUSTOM TAKE-DOWN — .300 Win. Mag. (fluted barrel only), .375 H&H, .416 Rem. Mag., or 7mm STW (fluted barrel only) cal., features take-down action with detachable round or fluted barrel, brown composite H-S Precision stock, 24 or 26 in. barrel without sights, matte finish metal, approx. 8 ½ lbs. While advertised beginning 1998, this model is scheduled for production during 1999.

Mfg.'s Sug. Retail	$2,495		$2,150	$1,725	$1,300	$1,025	$875	$775	$700

This model is also available in left-hand action in most cals.

MODEL 70 COLLECTOR GRADE — various cals., this variation must be special ordered through the Winchester Custom Shop and prices vary individually per quotation.

MODEL 70 CUSTOM BUILT — various cals., this variation must be special ordered through the Winchester Custom Shop and prices vary individually per quotation.

MODEL 70 EXHIBITION GRADE — various cals., fancy checkered American walnut stock with hardwood forend tip. Mfg. 1988-89 only.

$1,995 $1,575 $1,000

Last Mfg.'s Sug. Retail was $2,192.

Grading	100%	98%	95%	90%	80%	70%	60%

RIFLES: O/U

DOUBLE EXPRESS RIFLE — .30-06, 7x65R, 9.3x74R, .257 Roberts, or .270 Win. cal., 23½ in. O/U barrels, iron sights with claw scope mounts, ejectors, fully engraved satin finish receiver with game scene engraving, walnut specially hand checkered, sling swivels, 8½ lbs. Mfg. 1984-1985 only.

100%	98%	95%	90%	80%	70%	60%
$2,500	$2,150	$1,850	$1,650	$1,450	$1,300	$1,200

Last Mfg.'s Sug. Retail was $2,995.

In 1984, Aero Marine located in Birmingham, AL special ordered 200 deluxe double rifles in 7x57mm Mauser cal. They featured better engraving and game scenes with bottom of receiver marked Jaeger. Of the 200, 100 were rifles with 90 being standard grade and 10 being deluxe. The other 100 were supplied with an extra set of O/U shotgun barrels. Sales were slow on these special guns and eventually they were liquidated to another wholesaler. Recently, prices are in the $2,250-$3,000 range for the rifle alone and $3,000-$3,750 for the Combo.

100%	98%	95%	90%	80%	70%	60%	50%	40%	30%	20%	10%

SHOTGUNS: 1879-1963

BREECH LOADING SxS — 10 or 12 ga., imported from England for sales through the Winchester New York City office only, exposed hammers, available in 5 grades ranging from Class D - Class A and Match gun (lowest to highest). Higher grades were mfg. by W.C. Scott & Sons, C.G. Bonehill, W.C. McEntree, Richard Redmond, and H. & E. Hammond Gun Mfg.'s. Approx. 10,000 were imported between 1879-1884. Prices vary greatly due to condition and grade. Prices can range from $300 (poor condition Class D) to over $4,000 (95%+ condition specimen in Class A or Match gun).

This side by side model was the first shotgun bearing the Winchester name sold in the U.S. Identifiable by "Winchester Repeating Arms Co., New Haven, Connecticut, U.S.A." marking on barrel rib top.

MODEL 1887 LEVER ACTION — 10 or 12 ga., 4 shot tube mag., 30 or 32 in. full choke fluid steel barrels, plain pistol grip stock, first Browning patent shotgun mfg. by Winchester. Mfg. 1887-1901. Approx. 64,855 mfg.

$2,250	$1,850	$1,550	$1,275	$1,000	$875	$775	$675	$575	$475	$375	$275

Standard frame finish on this model was color case hardening. Premiums exist for original bright case colored specimens. 10 ga. began production with serial number 22148. Also mfg. in Riot configuration (20 in. cylinder bore barrel). Gauges were chambered for 2⅝ in. (12 ga.) and 2⅞ in. (10 ga.). First lever action repeating shotgun domestically mfg.

✳ *Model 1887 Deluxe* — damascus barrel, checkered stock, and other special order features.

$5,000	$4,000	$3,500	$3,000	$1,750	$1,500	$1,275	$1,100	$950	$795	$650	$525

MODEL 1893 SLIDE ACTION — 12 ga., 30 (standard) and 32 in. barrel, black powder only. First Winchester shotgun with sliding forearm action, first Browning slide action patent, disc. 1897 after run of some 34,050. Note: chambered for 2⅝ shells only, damascus barrels were available at extra cost, as were fancy stocks.

$950	$850	$750	$675	$600	$525	$485	$425	$375	$325	$275	$225

This gun had limited sales because mechanical weaknesses developed when shooting smokeless powder.

MODEL 1897 SLIDE ACTION — 12 or 16 ga. (introduced 1900), improved Model 1893 action, 26-32 in. barrels, visible hammer, various chokes, takedown or solid frame, plain pistol grip stock. Over 1,024,700 mfg. between 1897-1957.

$750	$625	$475	$400	$350	$300	$250	$225	$195	$175	$150	$125

Add 30% for 16 ga.

Early 16 ga. Model 1897s were chambered for 2⁹/₁₆ in. shotshells, and are not as valuable because of the 2¾ in. shell length currently manufactured. The Model 1897 was the first Winchester shotgun chambered for 2¾ in. smokeless ammunition. This model was also manufactured with a damascus barrel for a short period of time, and is rare.

MODEL 1897 RIOT GUNS — see the "Trench/Riot Shotgun" category in the T section for more information and prices.

W

100%	98%	95%	90%	80%	70%	60%	50%	40%	30%	20%	10%

MODEL 1897 TRENCH GUNS — see the "Trench/Riot Shotgun" category in the T section for more information and prices.

This model changed its stock configuration after WWI.

MODEL 1897 TRAP — higher grade version of Standard, checkered stock, could have black diamond inlay in stock until 1919 (Black Diamond Trap), breech block marked Trap until approx. 1926. Mfg. 1897-1931.

100%	98%	95%	90%	80%	70%	60%	50%	40%	30%	20%	10%
$1,100	$900	$700	$550	$450	$375	$325	$295	$275	$250	$225	$200

* *Model 1897 Black Diamond Trap* — distinguishable by diamond ebony inlays in stock pistol grip.

100%	98%	95%	90%	80%	70%	60%	50%	40%	30%	20%	10%
$1,750	$1,500	$1,250	$1,075	$975	$850	$700	$575	$465	$385	$325	$295

MODEL 1897 PIGEON — higher grade version of Standard 97, should have engraved pigeon behind hammer on frame, breech block marked "Pigeon", most exhibit black diamond stock inlays until 1919. Mfg. 1897-1939.

100%	98%	95%	90%	80%	70%	60%	50%	40%	30%	20%	10%
$7,000	$6,000	$4,500	$3,000	$3,000	$2,500	$2,000	$1,250	$950	$775	$600	$525

MODEL 1901 — 10 ga. only, strengthened Model 1887 action to accept smokeless powder, lever action, standard barrel 32 in., blued barrel and frame, 5 shot mag. 13,500 mfg. between 1901-1920, starting with serial number 64,856.

100%	98%	95%	90%	80%	70%	60%	50%	40%	30%	20%	10%
$1,750	$1,500	$1,225	$1,000	$875	$775	$675	$575	$475	$375	$275	$225

Add 25% for Deluxe Grade (checkered wood).

This shotgun was chambered for $2\frac{7}{8}$ in. smokeless powder ammunition.

MODEL 1911 SL AUTOLOADER — 12 ga., recoil operated, 26 or 28 in. barrel, various chokes, pistol grip laminated birch stock. Mfg. 1911-1925, 82,774 produced, action had design problems.

100%	98%	95%	90%	80%	70%	60%	50%	40%	30%	20%	10%
$475	$425	$350	$300	$250	$200	$175	$150	$140	$130	$120	$110

The Model 1911 was Winchester's first semi-auto shotgun. It did not prove to be satisfactory partly because the design had to be exclusive of the patents for Browning's famous A-5 model, interestingly enough a design which Winchester originally had helped Browning patent. Above values assume original wood without splitting, repair, or replacement.

MODEL 36 SINGLE SHOT — 9mm Para. cal., long shot, short shot, and ball, 18 in. round barrel, single shot bolt action, guns were not serial numbered, one-piece plain stock and forearm, special shaped trigger guard, $2\frac{3}{4}$ lbs. Approx. 20,000 mfg. between 1920-1927.

100%	98%	95%	90%	80%	70%	60%	50%	40%	30%	20%	10%
$550	$475	$400	$300	$250	$225	$200	$175	$150	$140	$120	$100

MODEL 12 SLIDE ACTION — 12, 16, 20 ($2\frac{1}{2}$ in. chamber mfg. until 1927), or 28 ga., 25 (20 ga. only, mfg. 1912-14), 26, 28, 30, or 32 in. standard, nickel, or stainless steel (scarce) barrel with or without rib (matted, solid, or VR), $2\frac{9}{16}$ (early 16 ga. only), $2\frac{3}{4}$ or 3 in. chamber, 6 shot, blued metal, various chokes, hammerless, plain pistol grip walnut stock. Mfg. 1912-1976.

Special order features on field guns have captured much collector interest in recent years. Combinations of these features can add a considerable percentage to the base values listed below. Rare special orders on rare variations are very desirable and prices can double and more if the combination is right. As is the case with most other collectible shotguns at this time, Model 12s with open choked barrels in shorter lengths are a lot more desirable (and expensive) than a specimen with a 30 in. full choke barrel (most common). Values listed below are for standard configuration (28 or 30 in. full choke barrel with no rib). For most Model 12s, values for condition factors less than 60% will approximate the 60% price, because of shooter demand. Premiums must be added for the rarer open choked barrels in shorter length on all gauges.

Original gauge can be determined by removing the butt stock and observing the gauge marking on the stock screw boss.

The following add-ons DO NOT apply to 28 ga. values.

Add 30%-40% for Win. solid rib.

Add 40%-50% for Win. milled VR.

Add 50% for each extra barrel(s).

Add 20%-30% for Win. special VR (offset barrel proofmark).

"Donut" post Winchester VRs are more desirable than the rectangular post.

Grading	100%	98%	95%	90%	80%	70%	60%
12 ga.	$495	$395	$325	$295	$225	$175	$150
16 ga.	$550	$425	$325	$295	$225	$175	$150
20 ga.	$800	$650	$550	$495	$450	$395	$375
28 ga.	$3,500	$3,200	$2,750	$2,450	$2,000	$1,750	$1,500

Subtract 50% if with factory Cutts compensator.

Recently, some non-original, re-stamped 28 ga. barrels have been added to 16 or 20 ga. frames "creating" a more desirable (and expensive) gun to unsuspecting buyers. Roll die markings are getting better and better so be very cautious when considering a non-Cutts 28 ga. (as in get a receipt specifying originality). The last observed ser. no. for an original 28 ga. is 1,586,817. 28 ga. Model 12s were available with both 2¾ (common) or 2⅞ (infrequent) in. chamber. Believe it or not, there are getting to be a lot of fake Model 12 boxes that have been intentionally aged. Carefully screen NIB (watch the hanging tag also) specimens in this model.

Editor's Note: The Model 12 Winchester was produced continuously from 1912-1980. Over 2,027,500 were produced both in standard and deluxe (Pigeon) grades. Pigeon grades were first listed in 1914 and disc. during the war (1941). Reintroduced in 1948, they were disc. permanently in 1964, after which the Super Pigeon Grade became available only on a custom order basis from Winchester's Custom Gun Shop. These guns are worth 50-300% premiums depending on gauge, barrel lengths, stock options, engraving patterns, etc.

With an attrition rate of 33%, Model 12s with rare features 50 years ago will only be much rarer today (and expensive). 28 ga. guns were built between 1934 and 1960. Gauge rarity in increasing order is 12 ga., 16 ga., 20 ga., .410 bore (Model 42), and 28 ga. Serialization breakdown by year of manufacture is provided under the "Model Serialization" section of this book. When collecting Model 12s, ser. numbers on the underside of receiver (forward end), should match ser. no. on bottom rear of Mag. tube. Stainless steel barrel Model 12s were mostly mfg. in the late 1920s - early 1930s (65X,XXX serial range). Values typically range between $1,000-$2,500.

"Y" prefix appears on Model 12s built 1964-1980 — see listing under Post-64 Models.

MODEL 12 FEATHERWEIGHT — similar to Standard, except with alloy guard and different takedown system. Mfg. 1959-1962. "F" suffix after ser. no.

	$425	$365	$325	$275	$250	$220	$190

MODEL 12 RIOT GUNS — see the "Trench/Riot Shotgun" category in the T section for more information and prices.

MODEL 12 MILITARY TRENCH GUNS — see the "Trench/Riot Shotgun" category in the T section for more information and prices.

MODEL 12 HEAVY DUCK GUN — 12 ga., 3 in. chamber, 30 or 32 in. barrel, solid rubber recoil pad, ½ in. shorter pull than regular Model 12. Mfg. 1935-1963.

	$750	$650	$500	$450	$350	$325	$300

Add 40% for solid rib.
Add 20% for 32 in. barrel.

* Vent. rib — factory Winchester or 2 different styles mfg. by Simmons, notice barrel proof marking - rare.

Win. VR	$1,600	$1,350	$1,250	$1,100	$850	$700	$600

MODEL 12 SKEET GUN — 12, 16, 20, or 28 ga., 26 in. barrel, skeet choke, checkered pistol grip stock, pre-WWII. Mfg. 1933-1976.

	$800	$700	$500	$450	$400	$350	$300

Add 15% for solid rib.
Add 50% for Win. Special VR.
Add 50% for Win. milled VR.
Factory-Cutts compensator — subtract 50%.
16 gauge — rarity will command a premium.
Add 50% for 20 ga.
Add 400% for 28 ga.
Add approx. 20%-25% for brown plastic Hydrocoil stock.
Add approx. 65%-75% for white plastic Hydrocoil stock (approx. 50 mfg).

W

Grading	100%	98%	95%	90%	80%	70%	60%

MODEL 12 TRAP GUN — various ga.'s, full choke barrel, deluxe trap styled stock, solid recoil pad. Mfg. 1938-1964.

	$1,000	$850	$750	$650	$500	$435	$400

Add 50% for milled VR.
Add approx. 20%-25% for brown plastic Hydrocoil stock.
Add approx. 65%-75% for white plastic Hydrocoil stock (approx. 50 mfg).
While plain barreled variation is rare, it is not as desirable.

MODEL 12 SUPER FIELD GRADE — 12 or 20 ga. only, features 26, 28, or 30 in. matted rib barrel, deluxe walnut with checkered pistol grip stock and forearm, mfg. 1955-59.

	$1,100	$875	$775	$650	$500	$435	$400

Add 40% for 20 ga.
Add 20% for 16 ga.

MODEL 12 "BLACK DIAMOND" TRAP — various configurations, features a small ebony diamond inlaid on each side of the pistol grip.

	$1,850	$1,550	$1,250	$1,005	$800	$675	$500

MODEL 12 PIGEON GRADE — finer and more deluxe version of Model 12, many variations. Mfg. 1914-1941 and 1948-1964, engine turned breech block and shell follower, usually with engraved pigeon on bottom rear of mag. tube.

	$1,900	$1,500	$1,175	$850	$800	$775	$700

Add 15%-20% for VR.
Add 80% for 20 ga.
Add 100% for 28 ga.
Add $700+ if NIB.
Above values are for 12 ga. - smaller gauges with desirable features will command healthy premiums.

MODEL 20 — .410 bore, single shot, hammer, boxlock, 26 in. full choke (a few guns have been observed with cylinder choking), 6 pounds. Mfg. 23,616 between 1919-1924.

	$600	$550	$475	$375	$275	$225	$175

While most Model 20s have 2½ in. chambers, late parts cleanup guns could be chambered for 3 in. also.

✱ **Winchester Model 20 Junior Trap Shooting Outfit** — includes shotgun, midget hand trap, 150 .410 bore shells, 100 clay targets and accessories, cased.

	$3,200	$3,000	$2,750	$2,600	$2,500	$2,200	$2,000

Prices for this model assume all accessories are included - if not, subtract substantially. Just the shotshell boxes and accessories from this outfit are worth $2,500+ in nice condition.

MODEL 21 — 12, 16, 20, 28 ga., or .410 bore, boxlock action, after years in the design stage, production began in 1929 with guns being shipped to the warehouse in 1930 and first offered in Winchester's 1931 price list. Regular production continued for thirty years, through 1959. Approx. 32,500 mfg. 1931-1988. Approx. 2,000 were mfg. in Custom Grade. Factory records are available for this model (early mfg. is sketchy) and are available by contacting the Cody Firearms Museum located in Cody, WY.

The early guns were plain, standard 12 gauge models with double triggers and extractors. Later in 1931, 16 and 20 gauge chamberings became available as did selective single triggers and automatic ejectors.

By the end of 1933 the Model 21 skeet gun had been introduced as had Tournament, Trap and Custom Built grades. By about this time options included fancier wood, beavertail or semi-beavertail fore-ends, checkered butts (standard on skeet guns) or skeleton steel butt plates, recoil pads and almost any variation the customers might desire. Metal finishes on a Model 21 are unusual in that they have salt blued frames and rust blued barrels — this explains the difference in coloration between these metal surfaces.

The Tournament Grade was dropped in 1936 and the Trap Grade in 1940. A Standard Grade Trap Gun was added in 1941. The early Custom Built Grade was dropped in 1942 and the Deluxe Grade was added. This grade included as standard many of the previously available extra cost options.

Relatively few guns were produced in chamberings smaller than 20 gauge. 28 gauge first appeared in the 1936 catalog, although a few were probably produced before that. Winchester

Grading	100%	98%	95%	90%	80%	70%	60%

records are unclear as to the total but it is generally believed that fewer than 100 original factory guns were made. In addition, a number of original 20 gauge guns have been modified at the factory or elsewhere with factory 28 gauge barrels. These latter guns are just as valuable if the conversion was done at the Winchester Custom Gun Shop. Authenticity of the original guns should be established by factory letter.

.410 bore guns were first listed in 1955 but again some had been produced earlier, one having been built for John Olin in 1950. Throughout Winchester history all the rules seem to have had exceptions and nowhere is this more apparent than with respect to the Model 21 which, after all, has been pretty much a custom gun from the very beginning. Factory records and tallies among dealers indicate the existence of from 40 to 50 original factory guns. As in the case of the 28 gauge, extra barrels were available and at least some of those have been added to original 20 gauge guns.

The 3 inch Magnum 12 gauge Duck gun (stamped "Duck" on floor plate) was offered in Winchester catalogs from 1940 through 1952. Selective single triggers and automatic ejectors were standard as were the solid red Winchester recoil pads and 30 in. or 32 in. barrels. Some cases of non-factory upgrading of 2¾ or 3 inch Magnum guns have been reported. If authenticity is important to the buyer, a factory letter should be requested.

With respect to such letters, in cases where records may be missing or incomplete, the resultant letters may be less conclusive than desired. In some instances, consultation with, or a written appraisal from an authoritative collector arms dealer might be helpful.

Six standard patterns of engraving and several stock checkering and carving styles evolved during the production years. Values added by these and other embellishments such as precious metal inlays are beyond the scope of this work.

The following retail prices are for a standard field gun with average wood, beavertail forearm, ejectors, and single selective trigger with no alterations.

	100%	98%	95%	90%	80%	70%	60%
12 ga.	$3,000	$2,750	$2,400	$2,000	$1,800	$1,700	$1,500
16 ga.	$4,250	$3,950	$3,500	$3,200	$2,700	$2,200	$2,000
20 ga.	$5,200	$4,700	$4,300	$4,000	$3,500	$2,750	$2,250

Add $750 for VR.

Double triggers w/extractors — subtract approx. 50%.

If double triggers with ejectors, subtract 10%-20%. Normally DT, extractor guns have splinter forearms.

* ***Skeet Gun*** — available in Standard, Tournament, and Trap grades. Introduced 1933. Add 10-20% depending on grade.

* ***Trap Gun*** — introduced 1940, Trap Grade disc. same year, unaltered specimens will bring premium — add 10-25%.

* ***3 Inch Duck Gun*** — introduced 1940, must be so stamped (observe the 3 in. marking very carefully — no premium exists for this variation.

As can be seen, values are partly based on a certain interdependence between options. Higher grade guns, of course, will bring somewhat higher prices although much of their increased value results from many "options" being included as standard features.

Buyers or sellers with limited experience should always seek expert advice or appraisals in dealing with a Model 21. This is especially true with regard to higher grade guns and those with extra ornamentation.

* ***Model 21 .410 Bore*** — retail prices for original guns may be expected to range between $25,000 and $45,000 for mechanically sound guns depending on quality of finish. These prices take into consideration the reported sale of a plain standard gun in recent years for $37,000. Non-original guns with add-on factory barrels would probably be reduced by one-third.

* ***Model 21 28 Ga.*** — factory original guns will probably bring from $11,500 to $17,000 and, as with the 410s, 20 gauge guns modified to 28 gauge with factory barrels would be worth approx. the same if done at the factory.

Refinishing or Restoration: There is disagreement as to the effects of refinishing a Model 21. Many shooters and at least some collectors prefer a well refinished gun to a badly worn one. Higher grade guns restored by a master craftsman may approach factory original guns in value.

MODEL 21: RECENT PRODUCTION — refer to listing under SHOTGUNS: RECENT PRODUCTION SxS

Grading	100%	98%	95%	90%	80%	70%	60%

MODEL 24 SxS — 12, 16, or 20 ga., boxlock, hammerless, double triggers. Introduced 1940, disc. 1957 after approx. 116,280 mfg.

	$495	$425	$325	$250	$200	$175	$150

Add 10% for 16 ga.
Add 40% for 20 ga.

MODEL 25 SLIDE ACTION — 12 ga. only, non-takedown version of the Model 12, 26 or 28 in. barrel. 87,937 mfg. between 1949-1954.

	$325	$275	$225	$195	$150	$125	$100

MODEL 37 SINGLE SHOT — 12, 16, 20, 28 ga., or .410 bore, top-lever break-open action, all barrels are full choke. Note on pricing below that there is a big difference between a 100% gun without a box and NIB condition. Not serial-numbered. Over 1,015,000 mfg. between 1936-1963.

	100%	98%	95%	90%	80%	70%	60%
12 gauge	$250	$175	$150	$110	$100	$90	$75
16 gauge	$225	$170	$140	$110	$100	$90	$75
20 gauge	$275	$200	$160	$120	$100	$90	$75
28 gauge	$1,000	$850	$700	$600	$500	$400	$350
.410 bore	$300	$225	$195	$175	$125	$100	$90

If above models are truly NIB, add $125-$175 to 100% condition values only, depending on gauge.
Add 30% for "Red Letter" models.
All 28 ga. Model 37s have the "Red Letter".

* **Model 37 Youth/Boys/Red Dot** — 20 ga. only, 26 in. barrel marked Mod. Choke on barrel, solid red factory pad, identifiable by red dot inset into metal that is visible when hammer is cocked.

	N/A	$295	$260	$220	$170	$130	$100

MODEL 40 SEMI-AUTO — 12 ga. only, long recoil action, 28 or 30 in. barrel, walnut stock, skeet model also, poorly designed, many recalled by Winchester. Approx. 12,000 mfg. 1940-1941.

	$495	$450	$350	$300	$200	$150	$100

MODEL 41 BOLT ACTION — .410 bore, 2½ in. chamber until 1933 when it changed to 3 in., bolt action, single shot, 24 in. round barrel bored F, one-piece plain walnut stock and forearm, not serialized, approx. 22,145 were mfg. 1920-1934.

	$575	$500	$450	$375	$300	$250	$200

This model is rarely encountered with over 80% original condition.

MODEL 42 SLIDE ACTION — the first pump specifically made for the .410 bore, hammerless, 2½ (introduced 1935) or 3 in. chamber, 26 or 28 in. barrel, plain walnut pistol grip stock with circular grooved forearm (modified 1947). Approx. 160,000 mfg. between 1933-1963.

Special order features on field guns have captured much collector interest in recent years. Combinations of these features can add a considerable percentage to the base values listed below. Rare special orders on rare variations are very desirable and prices can double and more if the combination is right.

* **Standard Grade**

	$900	$850	$800	$700	$600	$500	$450

Add 50% for solid rib.
Add 70% for Win. special VR.

* **Skeet or Trap Grade** — has solid matted rib, fancy wood.

	$2,250	$1,850	$1,600	$1,500	$1,250	$1,100	$1,000

Add 20% for VR.

* **Diamond Deluxe Grade** — fanciest grade, value is affected by wood and finish. Factory special orders can bring prices up to $10,000.

	$2,650	$2,200	$2,000	$1,750	$1,600	$1,400	$1,200

Add 20% for VR.

MODEL 42 HIGH GRADE LIMITED EDITION — .410 bore, 26 in. full choke VR barrel, features Grade V-VI wood with special scroll and gold border engraving, 850 mfg. 1993 only.

	$1,400	$1,100	$895

Last Mfg.'s Sug. Retail was $1,617.

Grading	100%	98%	95%	90%	80%	70%	60%

MODEL 50 SEMI-AUTO — 12 or 20 ga., 3 shot, recoil-operated (non-recoiling barrel), 26-30 in. barrels, VR optional, steel frame or Feather Weight Model (aluminum receiver, FTW) introduced 1958. Over 196,000 mfg. between 1954-1961, starting with serial number 1,000.

	$395	$350	$300	$240	$210	$180	$150

Add $50 for VR (Simmons installed).
Add $50 for Feather Weight Model.
Add $100 for 20 ga.
Add 25% for Trap & Skeet Model.
Add 200%-350% for Pigeon Grade (denoted by A suffix in ser. no.).

MODEL 59 SEMI-AUTO — 12 ga. only, 3 shot, short recoil operation, Win-lite (steel and fiberglass) ribless barrels, 26-30 in. barrel lengths, alloy receiver inscribed with hunting scenes, Versalite (first interchangeable choke tubes) option introduced 1961, 6½ lbs. 82,085 mfg. between 1960-1965.

	$495	$450	$350	$275	$225	$200	$175

Add 30% for barrel with all three choke tubes.

Inspect carefully for either cracked receiver (by bolt handle cutout and over serial numbers), or separating fiberglass on end of barrel.

* ***Pigeon Grade*** — mfg. 1962-1965, add 200-350% (rare).

Winchester also mfg. 20 and 14 ga.'s experimentally in this model, extremely rare and expensive.

SHOTGUNS: POST-1964

MODEL 370 SINGLE BARREL — 12, 16, 20, 28 ga., or .410 bore, 28-32 in. full choke plain barrel, replaced the Model 37, top lever break open, exposed hammer, plain pistol grip stock. Approx. 221,578 mfg. between 1968-1973.

	$120	$100	$90	$85	$80	$75	$70

Add 20-60%+ for 28 ga. and .410 bore.
The Model 370 was mfg. in Winchester's Canadian plant in Cobourg, Ontario.

MODEL 370 YOUTH — similar to 370, with 26 in. barrel, 12½ in. stock, with recoil pad.

	$145	$110	$95	$85	$80	$75	$70

MODEL 37A SINGLE BARREL — replaced the Model 370, roll engraved receiver, gold trigger. Approx. 391,168 mfg. between 1973-1980 in the Winchester plant in Cobourg, Ontario.

	$140	$110	$95	$85	$75	$65	$55

Add 10% for 36 in. goose barrel.
Add 50% for 28 ga. and 75% for .410 bore.

MODEL 37A YOUTH — similar to 37A, except 20 ga. or .410 bore with 12½ in. pull stock.

	$175	$145	$100	$85	$70	$55	$40

MODEL 12 SUPER PIGEON GRADE — 12 ga., slide action, 26, 28, or 30 in. barrel, VR, any choke, hand honed action, engine turned breech block and loading flap, "B" checkering and No. 5 engraving, custom order grade walnut stock. Limited production between 1964-1972.

	$2,995	$2,500	$2,250	$2,100	$1,750	$1,500	$1,300

Approx. 480 Super Pigeon Grades were mfg. 1984-85 - subtract 20%.

MODEL 12 FIELD GRADE — 12 ga., slide action, 26, 28, or 30 in. VR barrel, various chokes, jeweled bolt, hand checkered, checkered select walnut stock. Mfg. 1972-1976, "Y" Serial No. Prefix.

	$675	$550	$525	$495	$450	$400	$350

In 1984, Y series Model 12s were once again available through a private contract with U.S.R.A. Co. which included engraving on Grades 1A-1C, and 2-5. These guns were available in either Field, Trap, or Skeet configurations. Since there was no manufacturer's suggested retail, Model 12 values shown below are established by analyzing the sales of the two private contractors - no more of these variations are available.

* ***Grades 1-A, 1-B, & 1-C*** — light engraving depicting dogs or ducks. Disc.

	$1,300	$1,195	$1,000	$875	$785	$695	$600

Last Mfg.'s Sug. Retail was $1,375.

Grading	100%	98%	95%	90%	80%	70%	60%

* **Grades 2 & 3** — engraving features large duck and dog game scenes on receiver flats. Disc.

| | $1,600 | $1,495 | $1,295 | $1,075 | $950 | $830 | $725 |

Last Mfg.'s Sug. Retail was $1,695.

* **Grade 4** — more elaborate game scene engraving than Grades 2 & 3. Disc.

| | $1,850 | $1,695 | $1,450 | $1,225 | $1,075 | $950 | $850 |

Last Mfg.'s Sug. Retail was $1,995.

* **Grade 5** — elaborate game scene engraving with style B checkering. Disc.

| | $2,195 | $1,995 | $1,725 | $1,500 | $1,225 | $1,095 | $950 |

Last Mfg.'s Sug. Retail was $2,450.

Also available with gold inlays - add $1,000 to values shown above.

* **3 Barrel Set** — grade 5 engraving with gold inlays and two extra barrels. Disc.

| | $5,500 | $4,995 | $4,350 | $3,750 | $3,325 | $2,750 | $2,300 |

Last Mfg.'s Sug. Retail was $6,000.

MODEL 12 SKEET GRADE — similar to Field Grade, with 26 in. VR skeet bore barrel, skeet style stock, with recoil pad. Mfg. 1972-1975.

| | $950 | $800 | $625 | $550 | $495 | $450 | $425 |

See listings under Model 12 Field Grade for engraved values.

MODEL 12 TRAP GRADE — similar to Field grade, with 30 in. VR full choke barrel, trap style stock, straight or Monte Carlo, recoil pad. Mfg. 1972-1980.

| | $750 | $675 | $575 | $525 | $495 | $450 | $425 |

See listings under Model 12 Field Grade for engraved values.

MODEL 12 DU — limited mfg. for Ducks Unlimited Chapters.

| | $1,200 | $995 | $825 |

MODEL 12 LIMITED EDITION

* **Grade I 20 Ga.** — 20 ga. only, 2¾ in. chamber only, reproduction of the famous Winchester Model 12 with slight design improvements, 26 in. VR barrel bored modified, 5 shot mag., high post floating rib, walnut stock and forearm with semi-gloss finish, take down, 7 lbs. 4,000 mfg. by Miroku 1993-95.

| | $795 | $625 | $450 |

Last Mfg.'s Sug. Retail was $879

* **Model 12 Grade V 20 Ga.** — similar specifications to Grade I, except has select walnut checkered 22 lines per inch with high gloss finish, extensive game scene engraving including multiple gold inlays. 1,000 mfg. 1993-95.

| | $1,175 | $850 | $650 |

Last Mfg.'s Sug. Retail was $1,431.

MODEL 1200 SLIDE ACTION FIELD GRADE — 12, 16, or 20 ga., 26, 28, or 30 in. barrel, alloy receiver, various chokes, checkered pistol grip stock, pad. Mfg. 1964-1981.

	$200	$180	$165	$140	$110	$100	$90
Vent. rib	$220	$205	$195	$165	$140	$110	$100
Winchoke	$240	$215	$200	$190	$180	$160	$140

Add 33% for Hydro-coil recoil system.

MODEL 1200 MAGNUM — similar to 1200, chambered for 12 or 20 ga., 3 in. magnum shells. Mfg. 1964-1980.

	$210	$190	$175	$165	$140	$110	$100
Vent. rib	$240	$215	$200	$185	$150	$140	$110

MODEL 1200 SKEET GUN — similar to 1200, 12 or 20 ga., 26 in. VR barrel, skeet bore, 2 shot mag. and select style stock. Mfg. 1965-1974.

| | $275 | $250 | $220 | $195 | $165 | $140 | $120 |

MODEL 1200 TRAP GUN — similar to 1200, with 12 ga., VR, 30 in. full choke barrel, select trap style stock. Mfg. 1965-1974.

	$275	$250	$220	$195	$165	$140	$120
Winchoke	$330	$305	$275	$250	$220	$165	$140

Grading	100%	98%	95%	90%	80%	70%	60%

MODEL 1200 DEER GUN — similar to 1200, with 22 in. barrel, rifle sights, 12 ga. only. Mfg. 1965-1974.

	$195	$165	$140	$110	$100	$85	$75

MODEL 1200 POLICE STAINLESS — 12 ga. only, 18 in. barrel, 7 shot mag. Disc.

	$250	$195	$165				

MODEL 1200 DEFENDER — 12 ga. only, 18 in. cylinder bore barrel, 7 shot mag., 6 lbs. Disc.

	$250	$200	$180	$155	$140	$125	$110

MODEL 1300 FEATHERWEIGHT SLIDE ACTION — 12 or 20 ga., 3 in. chamber, takedown, 26 (new 1991) or 28 in. barrel, 5 shot, plain or VR (became standard 1990), WinChoke tubes, checkered walnut stock and grooved forearm, alloy frame, recoil pad, 6¾ - 7⅛ lbs. Mfg. 1978-1993.

	$300	$260	$230	$195	$175	$160	$145

Last Mfg.'s Sug. Retail was $374.

Subtract $30 without VR.

This model had an "XTR" suffix until 1989. Older Model 1300 Featherweights had roll-engraving but no premiums are being asked at this time.

MODEL 1300 FIELD — 12 or 20 (disc. 1994) ga., 26 or 28 in. VR barrel with WinChoke, checkered walnut stock and forearm, approx. 7¼ lbs. New 1994.

Mfg.'s Sug. Retail	$366	$290	$220	$185	$150	$135	$120	$110

* *Model 1300 Black Shadow Field* — 12 or 20 (new 1996) ga., 3 in. chamber, 26 or 28 in. (12 ga. only) VR WinChoke barrel, black composite stock and forearm, approx. 7 lbs. New 1995.

Mfg.'s Sug. Retail	$315	$245	$185	$155	$135	$120	$110	$95

* *Model 1300 Advantage Camo* — 12 ga. only, 28 in. barrel with choke tubes, full coverage. Advantage Camo. Mfg. 1997.

	$340	$265	$235	$195	$165	$145	$125

Last Mfg.'s Sug. Retail was $432.

MODEL 1300 UPLAND SPECIAL — 12 ga. only, 3 in. chamber, features checkered straight grip walnut stock and forearm, solid recoil pad, 24 in. VR barrel with choke tube, blue only, 7 lbs. New 1999.

Mfg.'s Sug. Retail	$366	$290	$220	$185	$150	$135	$120	$110

MODEL 1300 CUSTOM HIGH GRADE — while advertised, this model was never mfg. Advertised retail was $1,395.

MODEL 1300 WATERFOWL — 12 ga. only, 3 in. chamber, 28 or 30 (disc.) in. VR barrel, matte finished metal, choice of low luster walnut finish or brown Win-Tuff wood, recoil pad, includes camo sling and swivels, Winchokes standard, 7 lbs. Mfg. 1984-91.

	$295	$260	$235	$200	$180	$165	$150

Last Mfg.'s Sug. Retail was $367.

MODEL 1300 TURKEY GUN — 12 ga. only, 3 in. chamber, 22 in. VR barrel, Winchoked, walnut stock and forearm with low luster finish, metal surfaces have matte finish, supplied with camouflaged fabric sling, 6⅜ lbs. Mfg. 1985-1988 only.

	$290	$265	$235	$200	$180	$165	$150

Last Mfg.'s Sug. Retail was $348.

* *Model 1300 Win-Cam Turkey Gun* — similar to Model 1300 Turkey Gun, except has greenish laminated hardwood stock and forearm. Mfg. 1987-1993.

	$350	$295	$250	$200	$180	$165	$150

Last Mfg.'s Sug. Retail was $435.

* *Model 1300 Win-Cam Combo Pack* — 12 ga., supplied with 22 and 30 in. VR non-glare finished barrels, greenish laminated hardwood stock and forearm, camo sling, matte finished metal. Mfg. 1987-1988 only.

	$375	$330	$290	$260	$230	$200	$185

Last Mfg.'s Sug. Retail was $425.

W

Grading	100%	98%	95%	90%	80%	70%	60%

* ***Model 1300 Ladies-Youth Win-Cam Turkey Gun*** — 20 ga. only, 3 in. chamber, 22 in. VR barrel, green camo laminate shortened stock and forearm, includes sling and National Wild Turkey Federation engraving, 6 lbs. Mfg. 1992 only.

		$340	$295	$250	$200	$180	$165	$150

Last Mfg.'s Sug. Retail was $411.

* ***Model 1300 Win-Cam NWTF Series I-IV*** — 12 or 20 ga., Series I was released 1989 (12 ga. only) and included special receiver engraving featuring National Wild Turkey Federation motifs, Series II was released 1990 with a choice of either 12 (disc.) or 20 ga. Ladies/Youth model, Series III was released 1991-92, Series IV was released 1993. Disc. 1994.

		$365	$300	$250	$200	$180	$165	$150

Last Mfg.'s Sug. Retail was $458.

MODEL 1300 TURKEY - SYNTHETIC STOCK — 12 or 20 (new 1996, Black Shadow only) ga., 3 in. chamber, 22 in. VR barrel with choke tube, choice of 2 color Realtree camo patterns on synthetic stock and forearm, full camo coverage available in Realtree or Advantage (new 1996), or non-glare black (Black Shadow) finish on all surfaces, approx. 6¾ lbs. New 1994.

* ***Black Shadow Finish***

Mfg.'s Sug. Retail	$315	$250	$190	$155	$135	$120	$110	$95

* ***Realtree/Advantage Camo Finish*** — available with stock and forearm (Realtree only or full coverage camo. Disc. 1998.

		$290	$240	$180	$150	$130	$115	$100

Last Mfg.'s Sug. Retail was $370.

Add $62 for full coverage camo.
Add $40 for full coverage without sling (disc. 1997).
Add $40 for smoothbore barrel (Advantage full camo only).

MODEL 1300 LADIES-YOUTH — 20 ga. only, 3 in. chamber, 22 in. VR barrel, shortened stock dimensions, walnut stock with recoil pad and rear positioned, grooved forearm, 6¼ lbs. Mfg. 1992 only.

		$315	$260	$220	$180	$165	$150	$135

Last Mfg.'s Sug. Retail was $355.

MODEL 1300 SLUG HUNTER — 12 ga. only, 3 in. chamber, 22 in. rifled or smooth bore barrel with iron sights, checkered stock and forearm, satin walnut finish or brown laminate stock (Win-Tuff). Supplied with camo fabric sling and rings and bases. Mfg. 1988 - Disc.

		$360	$300	$250	$200	$180	$165	$150

Last Mfg.'s Sug. Retail was $445.

Add $10 for smooth bore barrel with Sabot rifled tubes (disc. 1992).
Add $4 for "Whitetails Unlimited" Model (new 1991).

MODEL 1300 WALNUT DEER — 12 ga. only, 3 in. chamber, 22 in. rifled barrel, non-glare metal surfaces, rifle sights, checkered walnut stock with recoil pad and forearm, 7¼ lbs. New 1994.

Mfg.'s Sug. Retail	$429	$350	$285	$255	$225	$200	$185	$170

* ***Model 1300 Black Shadow Deer*** — 12 ga. or 20 (mfg. 1996-97), 3 in. chamber, 22 in. smoothbore or rifled (new 1996) barrel with IC Winchoke, matte black stock, forearm, and metal parts, rifle sights, drilled and tapped receiver, 7¼ lbs. New 1994.

Mfg.'s Sug. Retail	$315	$250	$190	$155	$135	$120	$110	$95

Add $22 for rifled barrel (new 1996).
Add $70 for deer combo package (includes 22 in. cyl. bore barrel and 28 in. VR WinChoke barrels - disc. 1998).

* ***Model 1300 Full Advantage Camo*** — 12 ga. only, 3 in. chamber, choice of 22 in. rifled or smoothbore barrel, entire gun is in Full Advantage camo pattern, drilled and tapped receiver, iron sights, 7 lbs. Mfg. 1995-98.

		$350	$295	$260	$225	$200	$185	$170

Last Mfg.'s Sug. Retail was $432.

Subtract $22 for smoothbore barrel.

Grading	100%	98%	95%	90%	80%	70%	60%

MODEL 1300 RANGER SLIDE ACTION — 12 or 20 ga., 3 in. chamber, 22 cyl. or rifled (deer only), 24⅛ cyl. (disc. deer barrel), 26 (mfg. 1991-98), 28 or 30 (disc. 1992) in. plain or VR barrel, walnut finished hardwood stock, alloy receiver. New 1983.

Mfg.'s Sug. Retail	$330	$260	$195	$155	$135	$120	$110	$95

Subtract $40 without VR or WinChokes.

This model is also available in a deer combination package which includes either a 22 in. rifled or smoothbore deer barrel and a 28 in. VR WinChoke barrel in either 12 or 20 ga. (disc.). — add approx. 25% to values listed above.

* *Ranger Ladies/Youth Model* — 20 ga. only, 3 in. chamber, 22 in. VR barrel, shorter stock dimensions - 13 in. LOP and rearward positioned forearm. Disc. 1998.

	$285	$235	$200	$170	$150	$125	$110

Last Mfg.'s Sug. Retail was $309.

Subtract $40 if without WinChoke and VR.

* *Ranger Compact* — 12 or 20 ga., features shorter dimensions (13 LOP), 22 or 24 in. VR barrel with WinChoke and Truglo sights, uncheckered hardwood stock and grooved forearm, blue only, approx. 6¾ lbs. New 1999.

Mfg.'s Sug. Retail	$330	$260	$195	$155	$135	$120	$110	$95

MODEL 1300 CAMP DEFENDER — 12 ga. only, 3 in. chamber, 8 shot, 22 in. barrel with rifle sights and WinChoke, black synthetic stock and forearm, matte metal finish, 6⅞ lbs. New 1999.

Mfg.'s Sug. Retail	$353	$275	$210	$165	$145	$125	$110	$100

MODEL 1300 DEFENDER — 12 or 20 (disc. 1996) ga., 3 in. chamber, available in Police (disc. 1989), Marine, and Defender variations, 18 or 24 (mfg. 1994-98) in. cyl. bore barrel, 5 (disc. 1998), 7 (disc. 1998), or 8 shot mag., matte metal finish, choice of hardwood, synthetic (matte finish), or pistol grip (matte finish) stock, Truglo sights became standard 1999, 5¾ - 7 lbs.

Mfg.'s Sug. Retail	$308	$245	$190	$155

Add approx. $100 for Combo Package (includes extra 28 in. VR barrel - disc. 1998).

* *Stainless Marine Defender* — 12 ga. only, 18 in. cyl. bore barrel, a new Sandstrom 9A phosphate coating was released late 1989 to give long lasting corrosion protection to all receiver and internal working parts, 6 shot mag., synthetic pistol grip or stock configuration, approx. 6½ lbs.

Mfg.'s Sug. Retail	$490	$410	$340	$255

* *Model 1300 Lady Defender* — 20 ga. only, 3 in. chamber, choice of synthetic regular or pistol grip stock, 4 (disc. 1996) or 7 shot mag., 18 in. cyl. bore barrel (new 1996), 5⅜ lbs. Disc. 1998.

	$235	$190	$150

Last Mfg.'s Sug. Retail was $290.

MODEL 1400 SEMI-AUTO — 12, 16, or 20 ga., 26, 28, or 30 in. barrels, alloy receiver, various chokes, gas operated, checkered pistol grip stock. Mfg. 1964-1981.

	$275	$250	$220	$200	$175	$155	$140
Vent. rib	$315	$265	$240	$220	$195	$165	$150

Add 33% for Hydro-coil recoil system.

NEW MODEL 1400 WALNUT SEMI-AUTO — 12 or 20 ga., 2¾ in. chamber, 22 (disc.), 26 (mfg. 1991-1993), or 28 in. VR barrel, checkered walnut stock and forearm, Winchokes standard, 3 shot mag., rotary bolt system, 7-7½ lbs. Mfg. 1989-94.

	$350	$290	$260	$240	$220	$190	$165

Last Mfg.'s Sug. Retail was $419.

Add $15 for limited mfg. 1993 Quail Unlimited Model (2,500 mfg. 1993).

MODEL 1400 CUSTOM HIGH GRADE — 12 ga. only, 28 in. VR Winchoke barrel, special order only through the Custom Gun Shop, features deluxe hand checkered walnut and special engraving. Mfg. 1991-1992.

	$1,295	$995	$750

Last Mfg.'s Sug. Retail was $1,695.

MODEL 1400 SKEET GRADE — similar to 1400, 12 or 20 ga., with 26 in. VR barrel, skeet bore, select skeet style stock. Mfg. 1965-1973.

	$360	$330	$305	$275	$220	$195	$165

W

Grading	100%	98%	95%	90%	80%	70%	60%

MODEL 1400 TRAP GRADE — similar to 1400, with 30 in. full choke VR barrel, select trap style stock. Mfg. 1965-1973.

	$360	$330	$305	$275	$220	$195	$165

MODEL 1400 DEER GUN — similar to 1400, with 22 in. barrel, rifle sights, 12 ga. only. Mfg. 1965-1974.

	$265	$240	$220	$200	$175	$165	$140

> Note: In 1968 the model 1400 series was modified. The action release was improved and the checkering redesigned. From 1968-1972, they were designated MKII, which was then dropped. The values for the later guns mfg. from 1968-1973 may run approx. 10% higher - values shown are for guns mfg. from 1965-1968.

MODEL 1400 SLUG HUNTER — 12 ga. only, 22 in. smooth bore cyl. or rifled Sabot choke-tubed barrel, drilled and tapped for scope, includes bases or iron sights, 7¼ lbs. Mfg. 1990-92.

	$355	$310	$270	$250	$225	$195	$165

Last Mfg.'s Sug. Retail was $420.

MODEL 1500 XTR SEMI-AUTO — 12 or 20 ga., 2¾ inch only, 28 inch barrel, plain or VR, Winchoke tubes, gas operation. Mfg. 1978-1982.

	$300	$260	$240	$220	$200	$180	$160

MODEL 1400 RANGER SEMI-AUTO — 12 or 20 ga., gas operation, alloy receiver, 22 cyl. deer, 26 (mfg. 1991-1993), or 28 in. Winchoke barrel, checkered walnut finished hardwood stock and forearm, VR became standard 1985, 7¼ lbs. Disc. 1994.

	$285	$235	$200	$180	$160	$140	$120

Last Mfg.'s Sug. Retail was $377.

Add $53 for deer combo. (includes extra 22 in. cyl. bore barrel).
Subtract $40 without VR.

SUPER X MODEL 1 SEMI-AUTO — 12 ga., 26, 28, or 30 in. VR barrel, various chokes, steel receiver, gas operated - self compensating, checkered pistol grip stock and forearm. Mfg. 1974-1981.

	$495	$435	$365	$345	$315	$295	$275

SUPER X MODEL 1 SKEET — similar to Standard, with 26 in. skeet bore barrel, select skeet style stock. Mfg. 1974-1981.

	$695	$595	$500	$475	$450	$425	$400

Add 20% if NIB condition.

SUPER X MODEL 1 TRAP — similar to Standard, with 30 in. barrel, imp. mod. or full choke, select trap style stock.

	$595	$550	$475	$425	$415	$395	$350

Add 20% if NIB condition.

SUPER X MODEL 1 CUSTOM TRAP OR SKEET — 12 ga. only, limited production from the Custom Shop, deluxe checkered walnut stock and forearm, extensive scroll engraving on receiver, built to custom order. Limited mfg. 1987-1992.

	$1,295	$925	$725

* **Super X Model 1 Custom Engraved** — features number 5 engraving pattern with 7 gold inlays. Disc.

	$2,395	$1,900	$1,350

Last Mfg.'s Sug. Retail was $1,295.

Add $700 for factory gold inlays (8 flying ducks).

SUPER X2 — 12 ga. only, 3 in. chamber, self-adjusting gas operation, 26 or 28 in. VR back-bored barrel with Invector chokes, 5 shot mag., choice of checkered walnut or black synthetic stock and forearm with recoil pad, high gloss blue or matte metal finish, approx. 7¼ lbs. New 1999.

Mfg.'s Sug. Retail	$725	$650	$575	$525	$475	$425	$375	$325

* **Super X2 3½ In. Mag.** — 12 ga. only, 3½ in. chamber, similar to Super X2, black synthetic stock and forearm, 24, 26, or 28 in. VR back-bored barrel with Invector chokes, approx. 7½ lbs. New 1999.

Mfg.'s Sug. Retail	$855	$750	$650	$575	$525	$475	$425	$375

➤ **Super X2 3½ In. Mag. Turkey** — similar to Super X2 3½ in. Mag., except has 24 in. VR barrel with Truglo sights and extra full turkey choke tube, 7¼ lbs. New 1999.

Mfg.'s Sug. Retail	$867	$765	$660	$575	$525	$475	$425	$375

Grading	100%	98%	95%	90%	80%	70%	60%

▶ **Super X2 3½ In. Mag. Camo Waterfowl** — similar to Super X2 3½ In. Mag., except has 100% Mossy Oak Shadow Grass treatment, 28 in. VR back-bored barrel with Invector chokes, 7⅜ lbs. New 1999.

Mfg.'s Sug. Retail	**$938**	**$825**	**$725**	**$625**	**$525**	**$475**	**$425**	**$375**

SHOTGUNS: O/U - RECENT PRODUCTION

Model 101 dates of manufacture and serialization data can be found in the SERIALIZATION section in the back of this text.

In November of 1987 Olin/Winchester disc. the Model 101. Classic Doubles (listed separately in this text) imported this model under their own trademark until approx. 1990. With the discontinuance of the Model 101 and its many variations, both dealers and collectors have created a lot more demand for this model recently. As a result, prices have escalated and the scramble is on to try and pick off those rare and desirable variations. Since there have been a lot of limited editions and production changes in the 101 O/U series, it could very well be that this model might become very collectible in upcoming years (as in look what happened to the Model 12).

Note: Model 101 and Model 96 Xpert guns were made by Olin Kodensha located in Tochigi, Japan.

Values listed below for Model 101s assume NIB condition - subtract 10%-15% if without box, warranty card, and original shipping container (with packing materials).

MODEL 91 — 12 ga. only, mfg. by Laurona in Spain for international sales including Europe, SST, ejectors optional, VR, distinguishable by black chrome finish on metal parts. Disc.

Prices hard to evaluate because of limited importation domestically. In some regions they are bought as medium priced field guns ($550-$650), while in others they are sold as a rare Winchester O&U ($900-$1,100).

MODEL 96 XPERT FIELD GRADE — similar action to Model 101, 12 or 20 ga., auto ejectors, SST, various barrel lengths and chokes, action similar to 101, no engraving, checkered pistol grip stock and forearm. Mfg. 1976-1982.

	$875	**$775**	**$650**	**$550**	**$475**	**$425**	**$375**

This model has become known as the "Poor Man's 101".

MODEL 96 XPERT SKEET GRADE — similar to Field Grade, with 27 in. skeet barrels, skeet style stock. Mfg. 1976-1982.

	$925	**$850**	**$725**	**$600**	**$500**	**$450**	**$410**

MODEL 96 XPERT TRAP GRADE — similar to Field, 12 ga. only, 30 in. imp. mod. and full or full and full choke, trap style stock. Mfg. 1976-1982.

	$875	**$775**	**$650**	**$550**	**$475**	**$425**	**$375**

MODEL 99 — 12 ga., DT, no engraving. Disc.

	$700	**$575**	**$525**	**$470**	**$430**	**$395**	**$360**

MODEL 101 FIELD GRADE — 12, 20 ga., or .410 bore, 26, 28, or 30 in. barrels, various chokes, boxlock, auto ejectors, SST, engraved receiver, checkered American walnut pistol grip stock. Mfg. 1963-1987. Values below assume Winchokes (standard since 1983) - subtract $60 if without.

* *Older production* — checkered walnut stock and forearm, ejectors, SST, blued metal with light engraving on receiver, various barrel lengths, w/o choke tubes.

	$995	**$850**	**$725**	**$625**	**$585**	**$550**	**$500**

Add 20% for 28 ga. or .410 bore.

* *Field Special* — 12 or 20 ga., 3 in. chambers, VR, 27 in. barrels with Winchokes, blued receiver with scroll engraving ejectors, 7 lbs. Disc. 1987.

	$1,225	**$995**	**$875**	**$775**	**$695**	**$600**	**$500**

Last Mfg.'s Sug. Retail was $1,185.

* *Lightweight Field* — 12 or 20 ga., similar to regular Field Grade, except has coin finished receiver, vent. barrels, and solid rubber recoil pad, 6½ - 7 lbs. Disc. 1987.

	$1,325	**$1,075**	**$950**	**$825**	**$725**	**$625**	**$525**

Last Mfg.'s Sug. Retail was $1,425.

Grading	100%	98%	95%	90%	80%	70%	60%

* **Waterfowl Model** — 12 ga. only, 3 in. chambers, 30 or 32(disc.) in. Winchoked barrels, VR, matte blued receiver with moderate engraving, low gloss walnut stock with vent. recoil pad, 7¾ lbs. Disc. 1987.

	$1,495	$1,225	$1,025	$925	$800	$700	$600

Last Mfg.'s Sug. Retail was $1,570.

* **Model 101 Field Grade 2 Barrel Hunting Set** — 12 or 20 ga. barrels, both with Winchokes, 26 in. barrels - 20 ga., 28 in. barrels - 12 ga., scroll engraved, blued receiver with game scene engraving and borders, cased. Mfg. 1984-1987.

	$2,500	$2,050	$1,575	$1,375	$1,220	$1,050	$975

Last Mfg.'s Sug. Retail was $2,345.

* **Quail Special** — 12, 20 (disc.1984), 28 (new 1987) ga., or .410 bore (new 1987), 25½ in. Winchoke barrels, 6¾ lbs. - 12 ga., straight grip stock, vent. barrels and rib, coin finished receiver with game scene engraving, 500 of each ga. were mfg. Imported 1984-1986.

12 ga. or .410 bore	$2,100	$1,750	$1,475	$1,245	$1,050	$900	$775
20 ga.	$2,600	$2,175	$1,775	$1,500	$1,275	$1,100	$925
28 ga.	$3,600	$2,900	$2,250	$1,800	$1,450	$1,275	$1,025

Last Mfg.'s Sug. Retail was $1,950.

* **National Wild Turkey Federation Commemorative** — features golden turkeys on receiver sides, 27 in. VR barrels with choke tubes, only 300 mfg.

	$2,295	$1,775	$1,200

Original issue price was $1,950.

* **American Flyer Live Bird** — 12 ga. only, 28 or 29½ (new 1988) in. separated barrels with special competition VR, blued frame with gold wire borders and pigeon inlay, 8 - 8½ lbs. Imported 1987 only.

	$2,595	$2,275	$1,950	$1,775	$1,600	$1,425	$1,300

Last Mfg.'s Sug. Retail was $2,910.

Add $925 for Combo Model (extra set of 29½ in. barrels - 45 mfg.).

Add $265 for 29½ in. barrel with WT4 choke tubes.

Approx. 200 of this model were mfg.

MODEL 101 MAGNUM — similar to 101 Field, 12 or 20 ga., 3 in. Mag. chambering, recoil pad, 30 in. barrels, full and mod., or full and full choke. Mfg. 1966-1981.

	$975	$850	$725	$650	$575	$500	$460

MODEL 101 SKEET GRADE — similar to 101 Field, with 26½ (12 or 20 ga.) or 28 (28 ga. or .410 bore) in. skeet bored barrels, skeet style stock. Mfg. 1966-1984.

	$1,000	$825	$770	$700	$650	$595	$540

Add 20% for 28 ga. or .410 bore.

MODEL 101 THREE GAUGE SKEET SET — similar to Skeet 101, with 20, 28 ga., and .410 bore barrels, cased. Mfg. 1974-1984.

	$2,875	$2,400	$2,075	$1,775	$1,500	$1,300	$1,100

MODEL 101 TRAP GRADE — 12 ga. only, 30 or 32 in. barrels with normal or wide VR, imp. mod. and full or full and full chokes, trap style stock. Mfg. 1966-1984.

	$1,320	$1,100	$935	$825	$715	$660	$605

MODEL 101 SINGLE BARREL TRAP — similar to O/U Trap, with 32 or 34 in. full choke barrel, Monte Carlo trap style stock. Mfg. 1967-1971.

	$880	$660	$550	$495	$385	$360	$330

Add 100% for an extra O/U barrel (Trap Set).

MODEL 101 PIGEON GRADE (XTR) — 12, 20, 28 ga. or .410 bore(disc. 1986), vent. O/U barrels, deluxe engraved silver receiver version of 101, select checkered wood. Mfg. 1974-1987.

Grading	100%	98%	95%	90%	80%	70%	60%

✳ *Lightweight Field Model* — lightweight variation, Winchokes standard, 28 ga. baby frame has 27 in. barrels, 6½ - 7 lbs. Disc. 1987.

	100%	98%	95%	90%	80%	70%	60%
12 or 20 ga.	$1,995	$1,650	$1,475	$1,245	$1,050	$900	$775
28 ga. standard	$2,400	$2,050	$1,700	$1,450	$1,250	$1,050	$925
28 ga. baby frame	$3,650	$2,950	$2,200	$1,750	$1,450	$1,275	$1,025

Last Mfg.'s Sug. Retail was $1,950.

Subtract 5% if without Winchokes (available in all gauges).

➤ **Lightweight recent mfg.** — 20 ga. only, 27 in. barrels only with Winchokes, previously manufactured guns that have been photo-chemically engraved and gold-plated, 101 (total mfg.) shotguns were sold by Guns Unlimited Inc. located in Omaha, NE 1995-1996.

Lightweight (mfg. 1995-1996)	$1,695	$1,575	$1,350	$1,150	$975	$850	$750

Last Mfg.'s Sug. Retail was $1,795.

✳ *Lightweight two barrel set* — includes either 12/20 ga. with Winchokes (28 in. barrels on 12 ga. and 27 in. on 20 ga.) or 28 ga./.410 bore (27 in. barrels, 28 ga. has Winchokes; .410 bore has fixed M/F chokes), 250 sets mfg. serial numbered HS1-HS250. Disc. 1986.

	$3,500	$3,150	$2,700	$2,350	$2,025	$1,800	$1,575

Last Mfg.'s Sug. Retail was $2,500.

Add 10% for 28 ga./.410 bore combo.

✳ *Pigeon Grade 3 barrel set* — coin finished Pigeon Grade frame, approx. 250 mfg.

	$3,950	$3,375	$2,850	$2,300	$2,000	$1,850	$1,700

✳ *Featherweight* — 12 or 20 ga., English straight stock, 25½ in. barrels bored IC/IM, 6½ - 6¾ lbs. Disc. 1987.

	$1,475	$1,225	$995	$850	$750	$675	$600

Last Mfg.'s Sug. Retail was $1,580.

Add 20% for Winchokes.

✳ *Skeet Grade* — 12, 20, 28 ga., or .410 bore.

	$1,275	$1,100	$995	$880	$770	$715	$660

Add 10% for 20 ga.
Add 40% for 28 ga. or .410 bore.

✳ *Trap Grade* — 12 ga. only, vent. barrels and rib, coin finish receiver with fine scroll engraving, engraved pigeon on floorplate, Winchoke standard, 8¼ lbs. Disc. 1985.

	$1,300	$1,180	$990	$880	$770	$715	$660

Last Mfg.'s Sug. Retail was $1,475.

Subtract 15% if w/o Winchokes.

✳ *Super Pigeon Grade* — 12 ga. only, blued receiver with elaborate engraving including multiple gold inlays, extra select walnut with fleur-de-lis checkering on stock and forearm, Winchoke standard, 7½ lbs. Imported 1985-1987 only.

	$4,025	$3,625	$3,225	$2,835	$2,500	$2,150	$1,920

Last Mfg.'s Sug. Retail was $4,590.

101 DIAMOND GRADE — Trap or Skeet O/U, 12 (Trap only), 20, 28 ga., or .410 bore, vent. barrels and rib, Winchoke standard on Trap — add $75 on Skeet model (disc.1986), select hand checkered walnut, engraved satin-finish receiver. Trap model has extra high VR. Skeet model has raised rib and muzzle vents.

✳ *Standard Trap* — 12 ga. only, 30 or 32 in. vent. barrels, 8¾ - 9 lbs. Disc. 1987.

	$1,620	$1,440	$1,230	$1,075	$900	$780	$640

Last Mfg.'s Sug. Retail was $1,860.

✳ *Unsingle Trap* — 12 ga. only, lower single barrel, 32 or 34 in. barrel, extended rib. Add $60 for Winchoke. Disc. 1986.

	$1,700	$1,525	$1,250	$995	$895	$830	$740

Last Mfg.'s Sug. Retail was $1,760.

✳ *Oversingle Trap* — 12 ga. only, Winchokes, 34 in. upper barrel only, 8½ lbs. Imported 1986-1987 only.

	$1,985	$1,695	$1,545	$1,395	$1,200	$995	$895

Last Mfg.'s Sug. Retail was $2,145.

W

* Oversingle Combo — includes one set of O/U barrels and an oversingle barrel, cased. Imported 1987 only.

	100%	98%	95%	90%	80%	70%	60%
	$3,075	$2,750	$2,525	$2,300	$2,000	$1,750	$1,625

Last Mfg.'s Sug. Retail was $3,550.

* Trap Combo — 12 ga. only, includes a set of 30 or 32 in. vent. O/U barrels and a 32 or 34 in. high ribbed unsingle (lower) barrel, standard or Monte Carlo stock, approx. 9 lbs. Disc. 1987.

	$2,570	$2,320	$1,975	$1,800	$1,600	$1,400	$1,200

Last Mfg.'s Sug. Retail was $2,940.

Add $275 for ATA Trap set.

* Standard Skeet — 12, 20, 28 ga., or .410 bore, 27½ in. vent. barrels and competition rib, 6½ - 7¼ lbs. Disc. 1987.

	$1,650	$1,465	$1,240	$1,075	$900	$780	$640

Last Mfg.'s Sug. Retail was $1,950.

Add 20% for 28 ga. or .410 bore.

Certain design features may increase/decrease the values of this model.

* Four Gauge Skeet Set — includes 12, 20, 28 ga., and .410 bore 27½ in. separated barrel assemblies, cased. Imported 1985-1987 only.

	$4,850	$4,025	$3,650	$3,200	$2,800	$2,500	$2,150

Last Mfg.'s Sug. Retail was $5,025.

* Sporting Clays Grade — 12 ga. only, marked Diamond Sporter, 28 in. barrels with Winchokes, designed for Sporting Clay competition. Disc. 1987.

	$1,950	$1,625	$1,350	$1,100	$925	$795	$650

Last Mfg.'s Sug. Retail was $1,965.

501 GRAND EUROPEAN — Trap or Skeet, 12 or 20 (Skeet only) ga., 27, 30, or 32 in. barrels, extra select hand checkered walnut with oil finish, Schnabel forearm, entensive scroll engraving on satin-finished receiver, vent. barrels and rib. Mfg. 1981-86.

	$1,650	$1,450	$1,225	$1,050	$900	$780	$640

Last Mfg.'s Sug. Retail was $1,720.

Add 20% for 20 ga. Skeet.

* Grand European Featherweight — 20 ga. only, straight grip stock, 25½ in. VR barrels, 5¾ lbs. Disc. 1986.

	$2,295	$1,875	$1,550	$1,250	$1,075	$925	$800

Last Mfg.'s Sug. Retail was $1,720.

PRESENTATION GRADE — 12 ga. only, available in both Trap and Skeet models, blued action-extensively engraved with gold inlays, special crotch walnut, 27 (Skeet) or 30 in. vent. barrels, hand checkered, silver wire borders on perimeter of receiver. Imported 1984-1987 only.

	$3,950	$3,395	$3,075	$2,400	$2,000	$1,800	$1,600

Last Mfg.'s Sug. Retail was $3,840.

Subtract 10% for Trap Model.

SHOTGUN/RIFLE COMBINATION — combination 12 ga./.30-06 O/U, 25 in. barrels, top barrel is Winchoked, Grand European engraving and finish, 8½ lbs. Mfg. 1983-1985.

	$1,750	$1,495	$1,250	$1,125	$1,000	$875	$750

Last Mfg.'s Sug. Retail was $2,550.

This model was also available in limited quantities in .222 Rem., .223 Rem., 6.5x55mm, or 9.3x74R cal.

MODEL 1001 FIELD GRADE — 12 ga. only, 3 in. chambers, boxlock action, 28 in. VR (8mm) barrel with WinPlus chokes, blued metal featuring 40% engraving coverage, Grade I stock and forearm, high luster finish, mfg. in Italy by Marocchi 1993, disc. 1998.

	$975	$795	$725	$650	$595	$550	$495

Last Mfg.'s Sug. Retail was $1,099.

* Model 1001 Sporting Clays — 12 ga. only, 2¾ in. chambers, 28 or 30 in. VR (10mm) vent. barrels with WinPlus chokes, full engraving (includes scroll and flying W with clay bird), silver nitrate receiver with remaining parts blue, Grade II-III stock and forearm, satin finish, mfg. in Italy by Marocchi 1993, disc. 1998.

	$1,075	$925	$795	$725	$650	$595	$550

Last Mfg.'s Sug. Retail was $1,253.

Grading	100%	98%	95%	90%	80%	70%	60%

* **Model 1001 Sporting Clays Lite** — 12 ga. only, 3 in. chambers, blued finish, 28 in. VR barrels with WinPlus chokes, checkered walnut stock and forearm, gold SST, 7 lbs. Mfg. 1995-98.

	$1,000	$795	$725	$650	$595	$550	$495

Last Mfg.'s Sug. Retail was $1,153.

MODEL G5500 SPORTER — 12 ga. only, marked Sporter, 28 or 30 in. barrels with fixed chokes (bored IC/M, IM/F, or XF/F) or Winchokes.

	$1,795	$1,475	$1,275	$1,075	$900	$780	$640

Add 20% for Winchokes.

MODEL G6500 SPORTER — 12 ga. only, marked Sporter, barrels and chokes same as G5500.

	$2,295	$1,925	$1,625	$1,400	$1,225	$1,050	$900

Add 20% for Winchokes.

SHOTGUNS: RECENT PRODUCTION SxS

Values for recently manufactured side-by-sides (including Models 96 and 101 with variations) assume NIB condition - subtract 10%-15% if without box, warranty card, and original shipping container (with packing materials).

MODEL 21: RECENT PRODUCTION — Model 21 production has been limited to high grade, built from special order since 1960, U.S.R.A. has disc. mfg. of the Model 21 beginning 1988. Values below are based on 1988 information, since it was the last year Winchester carried pricing in its catalog.

Standard Custom guns (12 ga.) are currently trading in the $6,500 - $7,000 range if NIB.

* **Custom Built** — standard model with no engraving.

	$6,500	$5,000	$3,750

Last Mfg.'s Retail was $8,100.

* **Custom Grade** — includes No. 6 engraved receiver and VR.

	$9,250	$7,250	$5,500

Last Mfg.'s Sug. Retail was $11,080.

* **Grand American Grade** — includes 2 sets of barrels with forearms, No. 6 engraved with gold inlays, cased.

	$18,500	$15,000	$11,500

Last Mfg.'s Sug. Retail was $22,745.

* **Grand American Small Gauge** — 28 ga. or .410 bore.

	$32,500	$25,000	$17,500

Last Mfg.'s Sug. Retail was $34,460.

Add 25% for 28 ga./.410 bore combo.

* **Grand American "1 of 8" set** — includes 20, 28 ga., and .410 bore VR barrels. Only 8 sets mfg.

	$55,000	$39,500	$27,500

Last Mfg.'s Sug. Retail was $55,000.

MODEL 22 — 12 ga. only, subcontracted by Winchester and manufactured in Spain by Laurona circa 1975 for international sales including Europe, field configuration only with 28 in. barrels, DT, oil finished checkered walnut stock and semi-beavertail forearm, matted rib, black-chrome finish on metal parts, hand engraved receiver, limited mfg.

	$1,200	$995	$825	$700	$600	$525	$475

MODEL 23 XTR — 12 or 20 ga., 3 in. chambers, 25½, 26, 28, or 30 in. barrels, various chokes, single trigger, VR, auto ejectors, scroll engraved, silver grey satin finish, blued barrel, checkered select walnut stock and forearm, first commercial gun to employ interchangeable chokes. Mfg. 1978-disc.

Grade 1 (disc.)

	$1,150	$895	$775	$650	$575	$500	$440

Subtract 10% for fixed chokes.

* **Pigeon Grade** — standard weight model, 6½ - 7 lbs, coin finished receiver with scroll engraving. Winchoke option became standard in 1986. Subtract $150 without Winchokes. Disc. 1986.

	$1,650	$1,275	$1,050	$875	$750	$675	$600

Last Mfg.'s Sug. Retail was $1,460.

Add 15% for 20 ga.

Grading	100%	98%	95%	90%	80%	70%	60%

* *Pigeon Grade Lightweight* — 25½ in. barrels only bored IM/IC (12 ga.) or IC/M (20 ga.) or with Winchokes, 6¼ - 6¾ lbs., coin finished receiver with scroll engraving. English stock. Disc. 1986.

	$1,300	$1,150	$995	$880	$760	$730	$680

Last Mfg.'s Sug. Retail was $1,420.

Add 15% for 20 ga.
Add 20% for Winchokes.

* *Pigeon Grade Ducks Unlimited* — only 500 mfg. 1981, "SPO" serial no. suffix, cased.

	$1,450	$1,200	$995	$880	$760	$730	$680

* *Golden Quail Model Series* — 12 ga. (1986), 20 ga. (1984), 28 ga. (1985), or .410 bore (1987), 25½ in. solid rib barrels bored IC/M, mono-blocks are marked IC/M but the barrels are marked Q1/Q2, coin finished receiver with one gold inlay on floorplate, beavertail forearm, straight grip English stock with recoil pad, Only 500 mfg. each year per gauge. Disc. 1987.

	100%	98%	95%	90%	80%	70%	60%
12 ga.	$1,995	$1,525	$1,200	$975	$850	$750	$675
20 ga.	$2,350	$2,000	$1,600	$1,400	$1,225	$1,000	$875
28 ga.(20 ga. frame)	$2,650	$2,200	$1,850	$1,550	$1,325	$1,125	$975
410 ga.(small frame)	$3,295	$2,800	$2,275	$1,825	$1,550	$1,275	$1,050

Last Mfg.'s Sug. Retail was $1,950.

* *Model 23 Light Duck* — limited edition, 500 mfg., introduced 1985, blued receiver and barrels, select walnut, 20 ga., 28 in.- F&F, 8½ lbs.

	$1,750	$1,425	$1,050	$925	$850	$775	$725

Last Mfg.'s Sug. Retail was $1,660.

* *Model 23 Heavy Duck* — limited edition, 500 mfg. 1984 only, blued receiver and barrels, select walnut, 12 ga., 30 in.- F&F, 8½ lbs.

	$1,750	$1,425	$1,050	$925	$850	$775	$725

W

* *Custom 2 Barrel Set* — interchangeable 20 and 28 ga. 26 in. barrels, blue engraved receiver with gold inlays, "B" checkering on stock and forearm, leather cased with accessories, only 500 sets mfg. 1986. Disc. 1987.

	$4,650	$4,150	$3,550	$3,050	$2,800	$2,500	$2,150

Last Mfg.'s Sug. Retail was $4,625.

MODEL 23 GRANDE CANADIAN — 12 or 20 ga., 25½ in. barrels with fixed chokes, coin finished receiver with oak leaf engraving and one gold leaf inlay on receiver bottom, English AAA select walnut stock with beavertail forearm, 51 mfg. in 12 ga., 450 mfg. in 20 ga., approx. 50 two-gun sets were also offered with cases (approx. ser. numbers 1-51).

	$2,650	$2,200	$1,750	$1,500	$1,300	$1,050	$925
Cased set	$6,500	$5,800	$4,900	$4,200	$3,750	$3,200	$2,750

MODEL 23 CUSTOM — 12 ga. only, 27 in. Winchoke barrels, high luster bluing, no engraving, SST, ejectors, solid red rubber recoil pad, 7 lbs. Imported 1987 only.

	$2,250	$1,775	$1,275	$1,050	$900	$775	$650

Last Mfg.'s Sug. Retail was $1,975.

MODEL 23 CLASSIC — 12, 20, 28 ga., or .410 bore, 26 in. VR barrels, single trigger, deluxe hand checkered walnut stock and beavertail forearm, solid recoil pad, brass name plate, gold inlay on bottom of receiver, ebony inlay in forearm, 5¾ - 7 lbs. Imported 1986-1987 only.

	100%	98%	95%	90%	80%	70%	60%
12 ga.	$1,995	$1,700	$1,400	$1,150	$950	$850	$750
20 ga.	$2,195	$1,850	$1,500	$1,200	$975	$875	$775
28 ga. (small frame)	$2,950	$2,625	$2,325	$1,950	$1,550	$1,325	$1,125
.410 bore (small frame)	$2,550	$2,050	$1,700	$1,425	$1,200	$995	$875

Last Mfg.'s Sug. Retail was $1,975.

100% values assume NIB for this model.

The 28 ga. on this model features a smaller frame, and was the only 28 ga. small frame produced in the Model 23 Series.

WINCHESTER COMMEMORATIVES: U.S. PRODUCTION

During the course of a year, I receive many phone calls and letters on Winchester special editions and limited editions that do not appear in this section. It should be noted that a factory commemorative issue is a gun that has been manufactured, marketed, and sold through the auspices of the specific trademark. There have literally been hundreds of special and limited editions which, although mostly made by Winchester (some were subcontracted), were not marketed or retailed by Winchester. These guns are NOT Winchester commemoratives and for the most part, do not have the desirability factor that the factory commemoratives have. Special/limited editions are not listed in this text, because there is minimal collector interest. Remember, the least your special/limited edition can be worth is a little more than the standard edition value. Don't concentrate on the rarity, you'll be disappointed.

Typically, special and limited editions are made for distributors (these sub-contracts are the most common), an organization, state, special event, personality, etc. and are typically sold and marketed through a distributor to dealers, or a company/individual to those people who want to purchase them. These special editions may or may not have a retail price and often times, since demand is regional, values decrease rapidly in other areas of the country. Desirability is the key to determining values on these editions.

Until recently, the over-production of many factory commemoratives had created a "softness" in the commemorative marketplace. Commemorative production in some trademarks has totalled well over 250,000 units, and some collectors have weighed the "limited production" factor on each model before paying a premium over the standard production model of that particular commemorative. Approximately 7 years ago, Winchester decided to cut down on commemorative manufacture after perhaps too many years of over-production. Many commemorative consumers were starting to think that these "limited manufacture" guns had become more of a company marketing tool and sales gimmick rather than a legitimate vehicle for investment potential and collector support. During this 7 year period, both distributors and retailers saw their commemorative inventory levels gradually reach near zero - perhaps the first time in over two decades that they sold out of factory commemoratives. In other words, the commemorative "blow-out" sales were over. As this transition from distributor/dealer inventory to consumer purchases occurred, the commemorative marketplace became stronger and prices began to rise. Because the commemorative consumer is now more in charge (consumers now own most of the guns since distributor/dealer inventories are depleted) than during the 1980s, commemorative firearms are possibly as strong as they have ever been. When the supply side of commemorative economics has to be purchased from knowledgable collectors or savvy dealers and demand stays the same or increases slightly, prices have no choice but to go up. If and when the manufacturers crank up the commemorative production runs again (and it won't be like the good old days), then the old marketplace characteristics may reappear. Until then, however, the commemorative marketplace remains strong with values becoming more predictable.

As a reminder on commemoratives, especially for the beginning collector, here are a few facts applicable to all manufacturers of commemoratives. Commemoratives are current production guns designed as a reproduction of an historically famous gun model, or as a tie-in with historically famous persons or events. They are generally of very excellent quality and often embellished with select woods and finishes such as silver, nickel, or gold plating. Obviously, they are manufactured to be instant collectibles and to be pleasing to the eye. As with firearms in general, not all commemorative models have achieved collector status, although most enjoy an active market - especially during the past three years. Consecutive-numbered pairs as well as collections based on the same serial number will bring a premium. Remember that handguns usually are in some type of wood presentation case, and that rifles may be cased in or packaging with graphics styled to the particular theme of the collectible. The original factory packaging and papers should always accompany the firearm as they are necessary to realize full value at the time of sale. All commemorative firearms should be absolutely new, unfired, and as issued since any obvious use or wear removes it from collector status and lowers its value significantly. Many owners have allowed their commemoratives to sit in their boxes and plastic bags (could be serious if there's moisture where storage occurs) for years without inspecting them for corrosion or oxidation damage. Periodic inspection should be implemented to insure no damage occurs - this is important, since even light "freckling" created from touching the metal surfaces can reduce values significantly. A fired gun with obvious wear or without its original packaging can lose as much as 50% of its normal value - many used commemoratives get sold as "fancy shooters" with little, if any, premiums being asked.

The values below reflect actual prices paid recently in various areas of the U.S. In some regions it is possible to purchase a Winchester 94 commemorative made in substantial quantity for almost no premium over a standard production Winchester 94.

Grading	100%	Issue Price	Qty. Made

Because of this, prices could fluctuate over 25% depending on the geographic location of purchase or sale.

A final note on commemoratives: One of the characteristics of commemoratives/special editions is that over the years of ownership, most of the original amount manufactured stays in the same NIB condition. Thus, if supply always is constant and in one condition, demand has to increase before price appreciation can occur. Many commemorative dealers have told me that recent changes in overseas currency rates have made domestic guns less expensive to own - for Europeans especially. For this reason, more commemoratives are being sold overseas resulting in less supply for the domestic market. Coupled with this increased foreign demand is the recent increase of domestic support and sales. After 35 years of commemorative/special edition production, many models' performance records can be accurately analyzed and the appreciation (or depreciation) can be compared against other purchases of equal vintage. You be the judge.

U.S. Repeating Arms had announced in 1990 that they would once again resume the production of factory commemorative firearms.

1964 WYOMING DIAMOND JUBILEE 94 CARBINE

	$1,295	$100	1,501

1966 CENTENNIAL '66 RIFLE

	$450	$125	-

1966 CENTENNIAL '66 CARBINE — total mfg. of both the rifle and carbine was 102,309.

	$425	$125	102,309

Add $50-$75 over individual prices for consecutively serial numbered rifle and carbine set.

1966 NEBRASKA CENTENNIAL 94 RIFLE

	$1,195	$100	2,500

1967 CANADIAN '67 CENTENNIAL RIFLE

	$450	$125	-

1967 CANADIAN '67 CENTENNIAL CARBINE — total mfg. of both the rifle and carbine was 90,301.

	$425	$125	90,301

Add $50-$75 over individual prices for consecutively serial numbered rifle and carbine set.

1967 ALASKAN PURCHASE CENTENNIAL CARBINE

	$1,495	$125	1,501

1968 ILLINOIS SESQUICENTENNIAL 94 CARBINE

	$350	$110	37,468

1968 BUFFALO BILL RIFLE "1 OF 300" PRES.

	$2,500	$1,000	300

1968 BUFFALO BILL RIFLE

	$450	$130	-

1968 BUFFALO BILL CARBINE — total mfg. of both the rifle and carbine was 112,923.

	$425	$130	112,923

Add $50-$75 over individual prices for consecutively serial numbered rifle and carbine set.

1969 GOLDEN SPIKE CARBINE

	$375	$120	69,996

1969 THEO. ROOSEVELT RIFLE

	$450	$135	-

1969 THEO. ROOSEVELT CARBINE — total mfg. of both the rifle and carbine was 52,386.

	$425	$135	52,386

1970 COWBOY COMMEMORATIVE CARBINE

	$450	$125	27,549

1970 COWBOY CARBINE "1 OF 300"

	$2,650	$1,000	300

1970 LONE STAR RIFLE

	$450	$140	-

Grading	100%	Issue Price	Qty. Made
1970 LONE STAR CARBINE — total mfg. of both the rifle and carbine was 38,385.			
	$425	$140	38,385
1971 NRA CENTENNIAL MUSKET			
	$425	$150	23,400
1971 NRA CENTENNIAL RIFLE			
	$425	$150	21,000
1974 TEXAS RANGER CARBINE			
	$695	$135	4,850
1974 TEXAS RANGER PRESENTATION			
	$2,650	$1,000	150
1976 U.S. BICENTENNIAL CARBINE			
	$595	$325	19,999
1977 WELLS FARGO			
	$495	$350	19,999
1977 "LIMITED EDITION I"			
	$1,395	$1,500	1,500
1977 LEGENDARY LAWMEN			
	$495	$375	19,999
1978 ANTLERED GAME CARBINE			
	$495	$375	19,999
1979 LEGENDARY FRONTIERSMAN RIFLE			
	$495	$425	19,999
1979 "LIMITED EDITION II"			
	$1,395	$1,750	1,500
1979 MATCHED SET OF 1000			
	$2,250	$3,000	1,000
1980 BAT MASTERSON CARBINE			
	$795	$650	8,000
1980 "OLIVER WINCHESTER"			
	$695	$375	19,999
1981 U.S. BORDER PATROL			
	$595	$1,195	1,000
1981 U.S. BORDER PATROL — MEMBERS MODEL			
	$595	$695	800
1981 JOHN WAYNE			
	$895	$600	49,000

Optional accessories were also available for this model: the gun rack with leather insert is currently selling for approx. $40 and the leather scabbard is trading for $60.

1981 "DUKE"			
	$2,950	$2,250	1,000
1981 JOHN WAYNE "1 OF 300" SET			
	$6,500	$10,000	300
1982 GREAT WESTERN ARTIST I			
	$1,195	$2,200	999
1982 GREAT WESTERN ARTIST II			
	$1,195	$2,200	999
1982 ANNIE OAKLEY			
	$695	$699	6,000
1982 OKLAHOMA DIAMOND JUBILEE			
	$1,395	$2,250	1,001
1982 AMERICAN BALD EAGLE - SILVER			
	$595	$895	2,800

W

Grading	100%	Issue Price	Qty. Made

1982 AMERICAN BALD EAGLE - GOLD
| | $2,650 | $2,950 | 200 |

1983 CHIEF CRAZY HORSE
| | $595 | $600 | 19,999 |

1984 WINCHESTER-COLT COMMEMORATIVE SET — 1 each of the Model 1894 Carbine and
Colt Peacemaker, serial numbered 1 WC-4440 WC. .44-40 WCF cal., elaborate gold etching, cased.

| | $2,250 | $3,995 | 2,300 |

Approx. 2,300 sets were actually put together in this combination. These sets have been split up with individual prices being discounted (Colt SAAs have been trading in the $700-$800 range).

1985 BOY SCOUTS 75TH ANNIVERSARY — Model 9422 action, .22 cal., rifle configuration, 6¼ lbs.

* *Boy Scout* — 15,000 mfg., serial numbered BSA 1 - BSA 15,000, roll engraved, antique pewter receiver, hooded front sight.

| | $550 | $495 | 15,000 |

* *Eagle Scout* — 1,000 mfg., serial numbered Eagle 1 - Eagle 1,000, receiver has triple level gold etching, select American walnut stock and forearm, gold-plated lever, hammer, and forearm cap.

| | $2,650 | $1,710 | 1,000 |

1985 MODEL 94 TEXAS SESQUICENTENNIAL — .38-55 WCF cal., available in carbine or rifle.

* *Model 94 Rifle* — 24 in. round barrel, elaborate gold etching, includes Bowie knife, oak cased, 586 mfg.

| | $2,400 | $2,995 | 1,500 |

* *Model 94 Carbine* — 18½ in. round barrel, gold finished receiver and barrel bands, roll engraved receiver, 2,600 mfg., serial numbered TEX 1 and up.

| | $695 | $695 | 15,000 |

* *Rifle/Carbine Set* — includes one each of the Model 94 rifle and carbine, Bowie knife, 150 mfg.

| | $6,250 | $7,995 | 150 |

1986 120TH ANNIVERSARY MODEL 94 CARBINE — .44-40 WCF cal. only, 20 in. barrel, hoop-type finger lever, crescent butt plate, deluxe checkered walnut stock and forearm, extensive gold etching on barrel and framesides, 1,000 mfg. ser. no. WRA001-WRA1000.

| | $895 | $995 | 1,000 |

1986 STATUE OF LIBERTY MODEL 94 — Model 94 rifle in .30-30 Win. cal. with octagon barrel, extensive C. Giovanelli scroll engraving with multiple 22Kt. gold inlays, deluxe walnut with fine checkering, also includes 29 in. hand carved wooden statue of the Statue of Liberty, serial numbered SL1-SL62. This model is a USRAC factory commemorative.

| | $6,000 | $6,500 | 62 |

1986 MODEL 94 DU — .30-30 Win. cal., approx. 2,800 rifles were mfg. in the U.S. Since each Model 94 DU was bid on for ownership, prices will vary from points of origin. An average bid price seems to be in the $700-$995 range with lower and completing set ser. numbers selling at premiums. Serial numbered DU-86 0001 on up.

This model is not a factory commemorative, but rather a trade gun commissioned by Ducks Unlimited.

1987 U.S. CONSTITUTION 200TH ANNIVERSARY
| | $13,000 | $12,000 | 17 |

This model was distributed exclusively by Cherry's, located in Greensboro, NC.

1988 WINCHESTER ARMS COLLECTOR'S ASSOCIATION CASED SET — includes Colt SAA and Winchester Model 1894 in cased set, features special embellishments and W.A.C.A. emblems and medallions. 100 sets were advertised, but only 22 were sold. This is not a USRAC factory commemorative.

| | $2,995 | $2,695 | 22 sets |

Grading	100%	Issue Price	Qty. Made

1990 WYOMING CENTENNIAL .30-30

| | $1,095 | $895 | 500 |

This model was distributed exclusively by Cherry's, located in Greensboro, NC.

1991 125TH ANNIVERSARY .30-30

| | $5,500 | $4,995 | 61 |

This model was distributed exclusively by Cherry's, located in Greensboro, NC.

1992 KENTUCKY BICENTENNIAL .30-30 — Winchester Model 94 with true charcoal case coloring, engraving depicts important KY graphics, serial numbered KY001-KY500.

| | $1,095 | $995 | 500 |

This model was distributed exclusively by Cherry's, located in Greensboro, NC.

1992 ARAPAHO .30-30 — features gold-plated receiver with etched Indian scenes on both sides, checkered semi-fancy American walnut stock.

| | $1,095 | $895 | 500 |

This model is distributed exclusively by Cherry's, located in Greensboro, NC.

1993 NEZ PERCE MODEL 94 CARBINE — features nickel finished receiver and barrel bands, extensively etched receiver, checkered semi-fancy American walnut stock and forearm, serial numbered NEZ 001 - NEZ 600.

| | $1,095 | $950 | 600 |

This model is distributed exclusively by Cherry's, located in Greensboro, NC.

1995 FLORIDA SESQUICENTENNIAL 94 CARBINE — features motifs from Florida including alligator scene and space shuttle launch, 24 kt. gold-plated receiver, 500 mfg. ser. numbered FL001-FL500 during 1995 only.

| | $1,195 | $1,195 | 500 |

This model is distributed exclusively by Cherry's, located in Greensboro, NC.

1997 EARP BROTHERS MODEL 94 CARBINE — features engraving motifs with multi-colored cameos of the characters involved in the Tombstone OK Corral gunfight, gold plated hammer, trigger, and barrel bands, crossbolt safety. 250 Mfg. 1997 only.

| | $1,195 | $1,195 | 250 |

This model is distributed exclusively by Cherry's, located in Greensboro, NC.

WINCHESTER COMMEMORATIVES: NON-DOMESTIC - 1970 TO DATE

1970 NORTH WEST TERRITORIES (CANADIAN)

| | $850 | $150 | 2,500 |

1970 NORTHWEST TERRITORIES DELUXE (CANADIAN)

| | $1,100 | $250 | 500 |

1973 YELLOW BOY (SOLD IN EUROPE ONLY)

| | $1,150 | $150 | 4,903 |

1973 M.P.X. (MADE ESPECIALLY FOR A MOVIE)

| | $4,995 | $78 | 32 |

1973 R.C.M.P. (CANADIAN)

| | $795 | $190 | 9,500 |

1973 R.C.M.P. MEMBERS ISSUE (CANADIAN)

| | $795 | $190 | 4,850 |

1973 R.C.M.P. PRESENTATION - (CANADIAN)

| | $9,995 | N/A | 100 |

1974 APACHE (CANADIAN)

| | $795 | $150 | 8,600 |

1975 KLONDIKE GOLD RUSH (CANADIAN)

| | $795 | $230 | 10,200 |

1975 K.G.R. (DAWSON CITY ISSUE) - (CANADIAN)

| | $8,500 | N/A | 25 |

1975 COMANCHE (CANADIAN)

| | $795 | $230 | 11,511 |

W

Grading	100%	Issue Price	Qty. Made
1976 SIOUX (CANADIAN)			
	$795	$280	10,000
1976 LITTLE BIG HORN (CANADIAN)			
	$795	$230	11,000
1977 CHEYENNE (CANADIAN) — .44-40 WCF Cal.			
	$795	$300	11,225
1977 CHEYENNE (CANADIAN) — .22 LR Cal.			
	$695	$320	5,000
1978 CHEROKEE (CANADIAN) — .30-30 Win. Cal.			
	$795	$385	9,000
1978 CHEROKEE (CANADIAN) — .22 LR Cal.			
	$695	$385	3,950
1978 ONE OF ONE THOUSAND (SOLD IN EUROPE ONLY)			
	$7,995	$5,000	250
This model was not advertised in the U.S.			
1980 ALBERTA DIAMOND JUBILEE (CANADIAN)			
	$795	$650	2,700
1980 A.D.J. DELUXE PRESENTATION (CANADIAN)			
	$1,495	$1,900	300
1980 SASKATCHEWAN DIAMOND JUBILEE (CANADIAN)			
	$795	$695	2,700
1980 S.D.J. DELUXE PRESENTATION (CANADIAN)			
	$1,495	$1,995	300
1981 CALGARY STAMPEDE (CANADIAN)			
	$1,250	$2,200	1,000
1981 CANADIAN PACIFIC CENTENNIAL (CANADIAN)			
	$550	$800	2,700
1981 CANADIAN PACIFIC CENTENNIAL PRESENTATION (CANADIAN)			
	$1,100	$2,200	300
1981 CANADIAN PACIFIC (EMPL.) - (CANADIAN)			
	$550	$800	2,000
1981 JOHN WAYNE (CANADIAN)			
	$1,095	$995	1,000
1986 SECOND SERIES EUROPEAN 1 OF 1,000 — mfg. for European sales only 1986.			
	$6,500	$6,000	150
1992 ONTARIO CONSERVATION — this model was marketed in Canada only.			
	$1,195	$1,195	400

WINSLOW ARMS COMPANY

Previous manufacturer located in Camden, SC.

WINSLOW BOLT ACTION SPORTING RIFLE — offered with various actions, FN Supreme, Mark X Mauser, Rem. 700 and 788, Sako and Win. 70, offered in all popular calibers from .17 Rem. to .458 Mag., standard calibers have 24 in. barrels and 3 shot magazines, magnum calibers have 26 in. barrels and 2 shot magazines, two style stocks, "Bushmaster Conventional", slender pistol grip and beavertail forearm, "Plainsmaster", full curl, hooked pistol grip and flat wide forearm, both are Monte Carlo with cheekpieces, recoil pads and swivels, walnut, maple, and myrtle are used with rosewood forend tip and pistol grip cap, rifle comes in 8 basic grades, custom embellishments can increase values greatly, discretion must be used, values are for basic models.

Grading	100%	98%	95%	90%	80%	70%	60%
COMMANDER GRADE							
	$495	$475	$440	$385	$360	$330	$305

Grading	100%	98%	95%	90%	80%	70%	60%
REGAL GRADE							
	$605	$590	$560	$525	$470	$440	$415
REGENT GRADE							
	$725	$700	$670	$640	$605	$550	$495
REGIMENTAL GRADE							
	$935	$890	$855	$800	$745	$660	$605
CROWN GRADE							
	$1,375	$1,265	$1,155	$990	$910	$825	$715
ROYAL GRADE							
	$1,540	$1,375	$1,210	$1,100	$1,020	$965	$825
IMPERIAL GRADE							
	$3,520	$3,080	$2,860	$2,475	$2,200	$1,925	$1,320
EMPEROR GRADE							
	$6,215	$5,500	$4,950	$4,400	$3,300	$2,750	$2,200

WISEMAN, BILL AND CO.

Current custom rifle and pistol manufacturer located in College Station, TX. Wiseman/McMillan also manufactures rifle barrels and custom stocks.

RIFLES: BOLT ACTION

Add 11% excise tax to prices shown below for new manufacture.

HUNTER MODEL — available in various cals., Sako action, stainless steel barrel by Wiseman/McMillan, laminate stock, teflon finished metal parts, Pachmayr Decelerator pad, sling swivels, glass bedded action.

Mfg.'s Sug. Retail	$2,295		$2,295	$1,825	$1,400	$1,150	$925	$775	$675

HUNTER DELUXE — similar to Hunter Model except has custom checkering.

Mfg.'s Sug. Retail	$2,495		$2,495	$2,025	$1,600	$1,275	$995	$875	$775

MAVERICK — similar to Hunter but with black fiberglass stock.

Mfg.'s Sug. Retail	$1,995		$1,995	$1,575	$1,200	$1,050	$900	$775	$675

VARMENTER — similar to Hunter but with thumbhole stock.

Mfg.'s Sug. Retail	$2,395		$2,395	$1,925	$1,500	$1,250	$1,025	$875	$775

TEXAS SAFARI RIFLE — various cals., choice of hidden mag. (no floorplate), standard floorplate or 5 shot detachable mag., 2 or 3 position tang safety, stainless steel fluted barrel with integral muzzle brake, synthetic stock. New 1996.

Mfg.'s Sug. Retail	$1,995		$1,995	$1,500	$1,100

    Add $300 for 5 shot detachable mag. (TSR-I).
    Add $195 for 3 position tang safety.

TSR TACTICAL — .300 Win. mag., .308 Win., or .338 Lapua Mag., 5 shot inline, detachable mag., or standard floorplate, synthetic stock with adj. cheekpiece, stainless steel fluted barrel with integral muzzle brake, guaranteed 1/2 minute of angle. New 1996.

Mfg.'s Sug. Retail	$2,795		$2,795	$2,200	$1,700

    Add $195 for fluted barrel.
    Add $195 for muzzle brake.
    Add $150 for 3 position safety.

PISTOLS

SILHOUETTE PISTOL — various cals., Sako action, 14 in. Wiseman/McMillan fluted stainless barrel, 5 or 7 shot magazine, laminate or fiberglass (new 1999) pistol grip stock, no sights, 4 1/2-5 1/2 lbs. Limited mfg. beginning 1989.

Mfg.'s Sug. Retail	$1,295		$1,295	$1,000	$900	$800	$750	$700	$650

    Subtract $200 for fiberglass stock.

WOLF SPORTING PISTOLS

Current trademark of pistols manufactured in Vienna, Austria. Currently imported and distributed by J R Distributing, located in Moorpark, CA.

Grading	100%	98%	95%	90%	80%	70%	60%

Wolf pistols are noted for their features, quality construction, and are based on the M 1911 type action. Please contact the importer directly for more information, including domestic availability on Wolf Sporting pistols.

WOODWARD, JAMES AND SONS

Previously mfg. in London, England. Acquired by James Purdey & Sons approx. 1935. In 1996, James Purdey & Sons once again started manufacturing a best quality Woodward side-by-side shotgun.

SHOTGUNS: DOUBLE AND SINGLE BARREL

Woodward made one of the world's finest shotguns. Prior to WWII, they were acquired by Purdey and Sons. Many of the weapons they made were custom built and grading and pricing should be done individually. We will list some of the general models with approximate values as a guideline, but strongly urge competent professional appraisal when contemplating purchase or sale.

Prices indicated below are for manufacturer's suggested retail and 100% condition factors are listed in English pounds. All new prices do not include VAT. Values for used guns in 98%-60% condition factors are priced in U.S. dollars.

BEST QUALITY SxS SHOTGUN — custom built in all gauges, barrel lengths and chokes, sidelock, auto ejectors, stocked to specifications, pre-WWII and new mfg. beginning 1996.

$26,000 $23,000 $19,950 $17,000 $14,250 $12,000 $10,000

Add 20% for 20 ga.
Add 40% for 28 ga.
Add 60% for .410 bore.
Add $1,000 for SST

* **New Mfg.** — 20 ga. only beginning 1996.

Mfg.'s Sug. Retail £32,750 £32,750 £36,000 £31,500 £27,250 £22,450 £14,000 £10,000

BEST QUALITY O/U SHOTGUN — custom built in all gauges, barrel lengths, and chokes, VR, sidelock, auto ejectors, stocked to customer specifications, pre-WWII and new mfg. beginning 1996.

$29,500 $25,500 $21,500 $18,500 $15,750 $13,800 $12,000

Add 35% for 20 ga.
Add 75% for 28 ga.
.410 bore — too rare to accurately predict.
Add $1,000 for ST.

* **New Mfg.** — 12, 16, 20, 28 ga., or .410 bore.

As this edition went to press, the Purdey factory was not currently producing the O/U model.

BEST QUALITY SINGLE BARREL TRAP GUN — 12 ga. only, limited mfg. - pre-WWII only.

$12,750 $10,000 $8,950 $7,725 $6,500 $5,750 $4,900

Grading	100%	98%	95%	90%	80%	70%	60%

WYOMING ARMS MFG. CORP.

Previous manufacturer located in Thermopolis, WY. Very small quantities of Parker pistols were mfg.

PARKER PISTOLS: STAINLESS STEEL

STANDARD PISTOL — 9mm Para. cal., 10mm, .40 S&W, or .45 ACP cal., $3\frac{3}{8}$, 5, or 7 in. barrel, 7 (.45 ACP), 8 (10mm & .40 S&W), or 9 (9mm Para.) shot mag., Millett adj. sights, grooved synthetic grips, 29-39 oz. Disc. 1992.

$350 $300 $250

Last Mfg.'s Sug. Retail was $399.

Add $50 for 7 in. barrel.

.357 MAG. — .357 Mag. cal., single action semi-auto, 7 in. barrel, adj. sights, 8 shot mag., lifetime warranty, 44 oz. Disc. 1992.

$425 $350 $300

Last Mfg.'s Sug. Retail was $479.

NOTES

Z section

Z-B RIFLE

Previous trademark of rifles manufactured by Brno & Uhersky Brod, located in Czechoslovakia.

Grading	100%	98%	95%	90%	80%	70%	60%

RIFLES: BOLT ACTION

Z-B MAUSER VARMINT RIFLE — .22 Hornet cal., short Mauser bolt action, 23 in. barrel, double set triggers, 3 leaf sight, checkered pistol grip stock, (also known as Brno Hornet).

	100%	98%	95%	90%	80%	70%	60%
	$825	$745	$690	$605	$550	$470	$415

ZDF IMPORT EXPORT INC.

Current importer located in Salt Lake City, UT since 1995.

RIFLES: SEMI-AUTO

M96 EXPEDITIONARY RIFLE — .223 Rem. cal., 21½ in. barrel, paramilitary configuration with vent. barrel shroud, modular multi-caliber design, adj. gas system, 6 lbs. 10 oz. New 1998.

Mfg.'s Sug. Retail	$1,600		$1,475	$1,250	$995	$875	$800	$750	$675

SP 50 — .50 BMG cal., semi-auto bullpup configuration, 26 or 32 in. barrel with muzzle brake, 3 lug bolt, hardened aluminum parts, 17.2 lbs. New 1996.

Mfg.'s Sug. Retail	$2,500		$2,375	$2,100	$1,875	$1,600	$1,375	$1,150	$995

Z-M WEAPONS

Current rifle manufacturer and pistol components maker located in Bernardston, MA. Dealer and consumer direct sales.

Z

PISTOLS: SEMI-AUTO

STRIKE PISTOL — .38 Super, .40 S&W, or .45 ACP cal., several configurations available, with or without compensator. New 1997.

Mfg.'s Sug. Retail	$2,695		$2,375	$1,825	$1,700	$1,400	$1,150	$995	$750

RIFLES: SEMI-AUTO

LR 300 SR — .223 Rem. cal., modified gas system using AR-15 style action, features pivoting skeletal metal stock, 16¼ in. barrel, flat-top receiever, matte finish, 7.2 lbs. New 1997.

Mfg.'s Sug. Retail	$1,995		$1,775	$1,575	$1,350	$1,125	$900	$775	$650

Subtract $510 for LR 300 SR kit.

ZABALA HERMANOS, S.A.

Current manufacturer located in Eibar, Spain. Z. Hermanos is currently private labeling shotguns for both KBI, Inc. (Charles Daly) and for American Arms located in Kansas City, MO.

Zabala Hermanos manufactures quality boxlock SxS or O/U shotguns and sidelock SxSs. For more information regarding this trademark, (including current models and prices) please contact the manufacturer directly (see Trademark Index).

ZANARDINI

Current manufacturer established in 1946, and located in Brescia, Italy. Currently, Zanardini does not have a U.S. importer. Several U.S. firms have stocked a few Zanardini models in the past, but not the complete line. For current information and up-to-date pricing, please contact the factory directly (see Trademark Index).

Grading	100%	98%	95%	90%	80%	70%	60%

The values below represent older importation as Zanardini has not recently been imported into the U.S.

COMBINATION GUNS: O/U

Zanardini is currently offering the Model 2000 Deluxe Super Light (with or w/o new loading system), and the Boxer Model with H&H style sidelocks.

PRINCESS — super light variation.

	100%	98%	95%	90%	80%	70%	60%
	$2,200	$1,925	$1,675	$1,400	$1,200	$1,000	$800

Last Mfg.'s Sug. Retail was $2,542.

BOXER MODEL — H&H styled sidelocks, top-quality engraving.

	100%	98%	95%	90%	80%	70%	60%
	$5,750	$5,150	$4,600	$4,000	$3,550	$3,000	$2,650

Last Mfg.'s Sug. Retail was $6,246.

BOXER 4-LOCKS MODEL

	100%	98%	95%	90%	80%	70%	60%
	$3,900	$3,400	$2,975	$2,625	$2,300	$2,050	$1,750

Last Mfg.'s Sug. Retail was $4,562.

402 STRAUSS — top-of-the-line combination gun with best quality engraving and wood.

	100%	98%	95%	90%	80%	70%	60%
	$9,000	$8,000	$7,000	$6,000	$5,000	$4,000	$3,000

Last Mfg.'s Sug. Retail was $10,548.

RIFLES

Zanardini is currently offering the Fuchs folding single barrel, the New Prinz Model (single barrel tip-up), the O/U Express Koenig Models 403 A & B, and the SxS Oxford and Bristol Models (in various levels of grade).

403 OXFORD SxS — 9.3x74R and smaller cals.

	100%	98%	95%	90%	80%	70%	60%
	$3,400	$3,000	$2,700	$2,425	$2,150	$1,875	$1,575

Last Mfg.'s Sug. Retail was $3,835.

* *Larger cals.* — .375 H&H Mag., .458 Win. Mag., or .470 Nitro cal.

	100%	98%	95%	90%	80%	70%	60%
	$6,700	$6,000	$5,500	$5,000	$4,500	$3,950	$3,450

Last Mfg.'s Sug. Retail was $7,555.

Add approx. 135% for .470 Nitro cal.

EXPRESS RIFLE SxS — .470 NE cal., boxlock action, ST, checkered walnut stock (with cheekpiece), express sights. Other cals. available upon special order.

Mfg.'s Sug. Retail	$8,995		98%	95%	90%	80%	70%	60%
			$8,400	$8,100	$7,450	$6,750	$6,000	$5,500	$5,000

This model is imported exclusively by Mandall Shooting Supplies, Inc. located in Scottsdale, AZ.

409 BRISTOL SxS — priced by individual request.

407 OXFORD SL SxS — sidelock action.

	100%	98%	95%	90%	80%	70%	60%
	$15,000	$13,250	$11,950	$10,000	$9,250	$8,500	$7,750

Last Mfg.'s Sug. Retail was $17,095.

MODEL 403 KOENIG O/U — 7.65R or 9.3x74R cal.

	100%	98%	95%	90%	80%	70%	60%
	$6,500	$5,850	$5,350	$4,850	$4,350	$3,800	$3,300

Last Mfg.'s Sug. Retail was $7,368.

MODEL 403 DELUXE O/U

	100%	98%	95%	90%	80%	70%	60%
	$3,650	$3,200	$2,875	$2,525	$2,250	$1,925	$1,600

Last Mfg.'s Sug. Retail was $4,188.

SHOTGUNS: SxS

Zanardini is currently offering the London Model with external hammers (standard and super deluxe models) and the Donau Model with H&H type sidelocks (standard and super deluxe models).

HAMMER LONDON MODEL SxS — features external hammers.

	100%	98%	95%	90%	80%	70%	60%
	$9,150	$8,125	$7,100	$6,100	$5,050	$4,000	$3,050

Last Mfg.'s Sug. Retail was $10,735.

Z

Grading	100%	98%	95%	90%	80%	70%	60%

HAMMERLESS LONDON MODEL SxS

		$4,200	$3,700	$3,175	$2,825	$2,500	$2,100	$1,700

Last Mfg.'s Sug. Retail was $4,936.

DONAU STANDARD MODEL SxS — boxlock action.

		$9,000	$8,000	$7,000	$6,000	$5,000	$4,000	$3,000

Last Mfg.'s Sug. Retail was $10,548.

DONAU SIDELOCK SxS — H&H style sidelock action.

		$16,500	$14,750	$12,950	$11,000	$9,950	$9,000	$8,000

Last Mfg.'s Sug. Retail was $18,966.

PRESTIGE TRAP AND SKEET SxS

		$2,250	$1,950	$1,675	$1,400	$1,200	$1,000	$800

Last Mfg.'s Sug. Retail was $2,598.

HASE CACCIA MONTECATINI SxS — boxlock action, double set triggers, extractors.

		$900	$800	$700	$600	$550	$495	$450

Last Mfg.'s Sug. Retail was $1,027.

Add 30% for ejectors.

HORN MODEL SxS — boxlock action, double set triggers, extractors.

		$950	$850	$750	$625	$550	$495	$450

Last Mfg.'s Sug. Retail was $1,102.

Add 40% for ejectors.

ZANOTTI, FABIO

Current manufacturer established during 1625, and located in Brescia, Italy. Currently imported and distributed by New England Arms, Co. located in Kittery Point, ME. Fabio Zanotti became part of the Renato Gamba Group in 1985.

Fabio Zanotti is one of the world's oldest quality shotgun manufacturers. Current domestic importation is often times done on a custom order only basis. For more information on Zanotti models and their values, contact New England Arms Co.

Z

SHOTGUNS: O/U

MODEL 725 — 28 ga. or .410 bore only, scalloped case hardened shallow frame, DT or ST, ejectors, game scene and scroll engraving, custom built to individual specifications.

	Mfg.'s Sug. Retail	$7,000		$6,000	$4,500	$3,650	$3,000	$2,450	$2,000	$1,875

CASSIANO — 12, 20, 28 ga., or .410 bore, Boss style shallow action, best quality gun built to individual specifications. Prices start at $27,500 and go up accordingly.

SHOTGUNS: SxS

Add $500 for ST.
Add $250 for beavertail forearm.
Add $650 for leather case.

MODEL 625 BOXLOCK

	Mfg.'s Sug. Retail	$6,995		$6,275	$5,500	$4,250	$3,150	$2,500	$2,000	$1,750

MODEL 626 BOXLOCK — scroll, game scene, or combination engraving.

	Mfg.'s Sug. Retail	$7,995		$7,000	$6,000	$4,450	$3,375	$2,750	$2,175	$1,900

MODEL GIACINTO — hammer gun.

	Mfg.'s Sug. Retail	$6,500		$5,875	$5,300	$4,000	$2,950	$2,400	$1,900	$1,650

MODEL MAXIM SIDELOCK

	Mfg.'s Sug. Retail	$12,000		$10,750	$8,600	$7,450	$6,200	$5,200	$4,600	$3,850

MODEL EDWARD SIDELOCK

	Mfg.'s Sug. Retail	$15,000		$13,000	$9,900	$8,700	$7,000	$5,875	$5,000	$4,000

MODEL CASSIANO I SIDELOCK

	Mfg.'s Sug. Retail	$17,500		$15,500	$13,250	$9,900	$8,700	$7,000	$5,875	$5,000

Grading	100%	98%	95%	90%	80%	70%	60%

MODEL CASSIANO II
Mfg.'s Sug. Retail $20,000 $17,750 $15,500 $13,250 $9,900 $8,700 $7,000 $5,875

CASSIANO EXECUTIVE — prices vary per individual order, top-of-the-line model. Prices start at $20,000 and go up.

ZASTAVA ARMS

Current trademark manufactured by Advanced Weapons Technologies, located in Athens, Greece. No current U.S. importer. Previous manufacture was in Yugoslavia until circa 1996. Previously imported by T.D. Arms, followed by Brno U.S.A., circa 1990. Previously distributed by Nationwide Sports Distributors located in Southampton, PA.

Zastava Arms makes a wide variety of quality pistols, rifles, and sporting shotguns. Please contact the company directly for more information regarding model availability and prices (see Trademark Index).

HANDGUNS: SEMI-AUTO

MODEL CZ99 — 9mm Para. cal., double action, 15 shot, 4¼ in. barrel, short recoil, choice of various finishes, SIG locking system, hammer drop safety, ambidextrous controls, 3-dot Tritium sighting system, alloy frame, firing pin block, chamber indicator, squared-off trigger guard, checkered dark grey polymer grips, 32 oz.

$450 $395 $365 $330 $300 $285 $265
Last Mfg.'s Sug. Retail was $495.

While a latter Z9 was advertised, it was never commercially imported. All guns were CZ99 or CZ40.

Zastava CZ99 configurations (with finishes) included matte blue with synthetic grips (500 imported), commercial blue with synthetic grips (750 imported), military "painted finish" with synthetic grips (1,000 imported), matte blue finish with checkered wood grips (115 imported), high polish blue with checkered grips (115 imported), and military "painted finish" with wood grips (2 prototypes only).

MODEL CZ40 — .40 S&W cal., 55 prototypes were imported for testing, but most had a feeding problem due to improper magazine design, mag. design changes were planned, but were canceled due to the Serbian/Croatian war. Suggested retail was $495.

$450 $395 $365 $330 $300 $285 $265

RIFLES: BOLT ACTION

MODEL CZ22 — .22 LR, .22 Mag. or .22 Hornet cal., 35 of each cal. imported circa 1990. Suggested retail was $275.

$225 $195 $175 $150 $135 $120 $110
Add 15% for .22 Mag. or .22 Hornet cal.

ZIEGENHAHN & SOHN oHG

Current custom rifle manufacturer located in Zella-Mehlis, Germany. Currently imported by New England Custom Gun Service, Ltd., located in Plainfield, NH.

Ziegenhahn & Sohn manufacturers high quality, classic Anson boxlock "Big Five" double rifles with Holland & Holland pattern sidelocks and ejectors. Please contact the importer directly for current pricing, availability, and delivery time.

ZEPHYR

Previous Stoeger trademark of guns manufactured in Spain, and imported by Stoegers circa 1930s-1972.

Grading	100%	98%	95%	90%	80%	70%	60%

RIFLES

Stoeger's has imported a wide variety of bolt action rifles during the past 60 years. Rather than list the many models individually, each Zephyr rifle should be compared to a gun of equal caliber, quality, and features to ascertain an approximate value range.

SHOTGUNS: SxS

WOODLANDER II — 12 or 20 ga., various chokes, boxlock, double triggers, extractors, engraved, checkered pistol grip stock.

	$495	$440	$385	$360	$305	$275	$250

UPLANDER (4E) — 12, 16, 20, 28 ga., or .410 bore, sidelock action, double triggers, ejectors, engraved.

	$775	$695	$640	$585	$570	$480	$440

STERLINGWORTH II — similar to Woodlander, with sidelock action.

	$825	$725	$660	$605	$580	$525	$495

VICTOR SPECIAL — 12 ga., 25, 28, or 30 in. barrels, various chokes, double triggers, extractors, checkered pistol grip stock.

	$440	$385	$330	$305	$250	$220	$195

UPLAND KING — 12 or 16 ga., sidelock, single trigger, VR, ejectors, fully engraved.

	$1,000	$900	$800	$725	$650	$600	$550

THUNDERBIRD — 10 ga. Mag, 32 in. barrels, double triggers, French walnut, engraved.

	$850	$750	$625	$550	$510	$490	$475

Add $175 for ejectors.

SHOTGUNS: SINGLE SHOT

HONKER — 10 ga. Mag., 36 in. VR barrel, lightly engraved.

	$500	$460	$420	$350	$310	$290	$270

VANDALIA TRAP — 12 ga. Trap Model, 32 in. barrel, engraved.

	$700	$620	$575	$525	$475	$425	$390

ZOLI, ANGELO

Previous manufacturer located in Brescia, Italy. Previously imported and distributed exclusively by Angelo Zoli USA located in Addison, IL. Mfg. 1985-87.

Angelo Zoli went out of business in December, 1987 and was taken over by the Italian Bank of Brescia in 1989. Many people tend to confuse the shotguns of Angelo and Antonio Zoli (it is hard to determine which manufacturer made a gun marked "A. Zoli"). There is no correlation between these trademarks and Antonio Zoli DOES NOT have parts for these earlier Angelo Zoli long arms. Even though both trademarks may indicate "A. ZOLI" for a barrel address, they are mostly discernable by the model listings under both headings in this section.

COMBINATION GUNS

AIRONE — 12 ga./.30-06 or .308 Win. cal., boxlock with false sideplates, double triggers, checkered walnut stock and forearm, swivels. Disc. 1987.

	$1,450	$1,275	$1,050	$900	$800	$700	$600

CONDOR — similar to Airone, except does not have false sideplates. Disc. 1987.

	$1,295	$1,050	$900	$800	$700	$600	$500

Grading	100%	98%	95%	90%	80%	70%	60%

RIFLES: SxS

LEOPARD EXPRESS — .30-06, .308 Win., .375 H&H Mag., or 7x65R cal., boxlock action, double triggers, checkered walnut stock and forearm. Disc. 1987.

		$1,325	$1,150	$975	$900	$840	$775	$725

Last Mfg.'s Sug. Retail was $1,529.

SHOTGUNS: LEVER ACTION

APACHE — 12 ga. only, 3 in. chambers, 20 in. barrel, SST. Disc. 1987.

		$410	$355	$325	$300	$280	$260	$245

Last Mfg.'s Sug. Retail was $473.

Add $80 for multi-chokes.

SHOTGUNS: O/U

SNIPE — .410 bore, 3 in. chambers, 26 or 28 in. barrels, single trigger. Disc. 1987.

		$230	$200	$185	$170	$155	$145	$135

Last Mfg.'s Sug. Retail was $265.

TEXAS — all ga.'s, 26 or 28 in. barrels, double triggers, folding design, lever action. Disc. 1987.

		$250	$220	$200	$185	$170	$155	$145

Last Mfg.'s Sug. Retail was $291.

DOVE — .410 bore only, 3 in. chambers, 26 or 28 in. barrels, single trigger. Disc. 1987.

		$260	$230	$200	$185	$170	$155	$145

Last Mfg.'s Sug. Retail was $306.

FIELD SPECIAL — 12, 20, or 28 ga., 3 in. chambers, various barrel lengths and chokings, single trigger. Disc. 1987.

		$450	$400	$360	$330	$300	$270	$240

Last Mfg.'s Sug. Retail was $699.

PIGEON MODEL — 12 or 20 ga., 3 in. chambers, various barrel lengths, single trigger. Disc. 1987.

		$350	$295	$270	$250	$220	$195	$175

Last Mfg.'s Sug. Retail was $394.

Add $60 for 20 ga.

STANDARD MODEL — 12 or 20 ga., 3 in. chambers, various barrel lengths and chokings, single trigger. Disc. 1987.

		$395	$345	$320	$300	$280	$260	$245

Last Mfg.'s Sug. Retail was $459.

SILVER SNIPE — 12 or 20 ga., 3 in. chambers on the 20 ga., single trigger, ejectors, light engraving. Disc. 1987.

		$675	$585	$530	$485	$440	$400	$375

Last Mfg.'s Sug. Retail was $739.

Add $50 for multi-chokes (12 ga. only).

This model was distributed by Euroarms of America, Inc.

CONDOR MODEL — 12 ga. skeet model, 28 in. barrels, SST, ejectors, wide VR, engraved silver finished receiver, recoil pad. Disc. 1987.

		$795	$700	$640	$585	$530	$485	$440

Last Mfg.'s Sug. Retail was $895.

This model was distributed by Mandall Shooting Supplies, Inc.

TARGET MODEL 208 — 12 ga. only, available in either Trap, Skeet, or Monotrap configuration. Disc. 1987.

		$895	$775	$695	$620	$575	$500	$450

Last Mfg.'s Sug. Retail was $996.

Add $494 for Monotrap II 208 Model.

Grading	100%	98%	95%	90%	80%	70%	60%

TARGET MODEL 308 — 12 ga. only, available in either Trap, Skeet, or Monotrap configuration. Disc. 1987.

	$1,375	$1,125	$950	$875	$795	$725	$650

Last Mfg.'s Sug. Retail was $1,581.

Add $76 for multi-chokes.
Add $824 for Monotrap II 308 Model.

SPECIAL MODEL — 12 ga. only, 3 in. chambers, various barrel lengths and chokings, SST. Disc. 1987.

	$465	$395	$355	$325	$290	$270	$250

Last Mfg.'s Sug. Retail was $528.

Add $120 for multi-chokes.

DELUXE MODEL — similar to Special Model, except better wood and engraving. Disc. 1987.

	$645	$550	$495	$450	$400	$360	$320

Last Mfg.'s Sug. Retail was $730.

Add $80 for multi-chokes.

PRESENTATION MODEL — 12 ga. only, includes sideplates. Disc. 1987.

	$740	$630	$575	$495	$450	$395	$350

Last Mfg.'s Sug. Retail was $842.

Add $42 for multi-chokes.

ANGEL MODEL — 12 ga. only, field grade, SST, ejectors, wide VR, engraved receiver, recoil pad. Disc. 1987.

	$850	$775	$700	$640	$585	$530	$485

This model was distributed by Mandall Shooting Supplies, Inc.

ST. GEORGE'S TARGET — 12 ga. only, trap or skeet gun, SST, fixed choke. Disc. 1987.

	$900	$730	$645	$550	$495	$450	$400

Last Mfg.'s Sug. Retail was $1,024.

* *St. George's Competition* — 12 ga. only, includes 30 in. O/U barrels and single barrel multi-choke. Disc. 1987.

	$1,995	$1,750	$1,550	$1,250	$995	$875	$775

Last Mfg.'s Sug. Retail was $1,627.

PATRICIA MODEL — .410 bore only, 3 in. chambers, 28 in. barrels, SST. Disc. 1987.

	$1,175	$1,010	$900	$895	$820	$740	$650

Last Mfg.'s Sug. Retail was $1,345.

Add $121 for case.

SHOTGUNS: SxS

QUAIL SPECIAL — .410 bore, 3 in. chambers, single trigger, 28 in. barrels. Disc. 1987.

	$205	$185	$170	$150	$125	$110	$100

Last Mfg.'s Sug. Retail was $243.

FALCON II — .410 bore, 3 in. chambers, 26 or 28 in. barrels, double triggers. Disc. 1987.

	$205	$185	$170	$150	$125	$110	$100

Last Mfg.'s Sug. Retail was $246.

SILVER HAWK — 12 or 20 ga., double trigger, engraved.

	$420	$395	$360	$330	$300	$280	$260

SILVER SNIPE — 12 or 20 ga., various barrel lengths, VR, single trigger, engraved.

	$485	$440	$400	$360	$330	$300	$280

PHEASANT — 12 ga. only, 3 in. chambers, 28 in. barrels only, single trigger. Disc. 1987.

	$370	$320	$300	$280	$260	$240	$220

Last Mfg.'s Sug. Retail was $428.

Grading	100%	98%	95%	90%	80%	70%	60%

ALLEY CLEANER — 12 or 20 ga., 3 in. chambers, 20 in. barrels, riot configuration, SST. Disc. 1987.

	$575	$495	$460	$420	$390	$350	$310

Last Mfg.'s Sug. Retail was $649.

Add $65 for multi-chokes.

CLASSIC — 12 or 20 ga., 3 in. chambers, 26-30 in. barrels, ST. Disc. 1989.

	$995	$875	$750	$650	$550	$475	$400

Last Mfg.'s Sug. Retail was $706.

Add $80 for multi-chokes.

SHOTGUNS: SINGLE BARREL

DIANO I — 12, 20 ga., or .410 bore, 3 in. chambers, top lever single barrel action, folding configuration, VR. Disc. 1987.

	$115	$95	$85	$80	$75	$70	$65

Last Mfg.'s Sug. Retail was $129.

DIANO II — similar to Diano I, except has bottom lever opening. Disc. 1987.

	$115	$95	$85	$80	$75	$70	$65

Last Mfg.'s Sug. Retail was $129.

LONER I — similar to Diano I. Disc. 1987.

	$95	$80	$75	$65	$55	$45	$35

Last Mfg.'s Sug. Retail was $109.

LONER II — similar to Diano II. Disc. 1987.

	$95	$80	$75	$65	$55	$45	$35

Last Mfg.'s Sug. Retail was $109.

SHOTGUNS: SLIDE ACTION

PUMP ACTION — 12 ga. only, available in riot, field, or deer (slug) barrel configurations, 3 in. chamber, hunter model has multi-chokes standard. Disc. 1987.

	$290	$245	$205	$185	$170	$150	$125

Last Mfg.'s Sug. Retail was $329.

Z

ZOLI, ANTONIO

Current manufacturer located in Brescia, Italy. O/U rifles only are currently imported by Cape Outfitters, located in Cape Girardeau, MO. Previously imported and distributed (1990-91 only) by European American Armory Corp. located in Hialeah, FL. Prior to 1990, A. Zoli was imported and distributed exclusively by Antonio Zoli U.S.A., Inc. located in Fort Wayne, IN.

Antonio Zoli firearms are totally unrelated to those guns of Angelo Zoli (guns marked "A. Zoli" make it hard to determine the correct manufacturer). Parts are not interchangeable and warranties from Antonio Zoli firearms DO NOT apply to Angelo Zoli guns.

Cape Outfitters (see Trademark Index) has parts for some Antonio Zoli guns and should be contacted directly for availability and prices. All repairs are strictly non-warranty.

Grading	100%	98%	95%	90%	80%	70%	60%

RIFLES: BOLT ACTION

AZ 1900C — .243 Win., .270 Win., 6.5x55mm, .30-06, .308 Win., 7mm Rem. Mag., or .300 Win. Mag. cal., 21 or 24 (Mag. cals.) in. barrel, checkered walnut stock with weatherproof stock finish, sling swivels, iron sights, 7.4 lbs. Importation disc. 1993.

	$1,100	**$850**	**$740**	**$660**	**$585**	**$500**	**$450**

Last Mfg.'s Sug. Retail was $1,295.

Add approx. 10% for AZ 1900 Deluxe (better walnut).
Add 60% for AZ 1900 Super Deluxe (select walnut and moderate engraving).
Add approx. 10% for Model AZ 1900 DL (photo engraved receiver and floorplate).

MODEL AZ 1900M — .243 Win., 6.5x55mm, .270 Win., .30-06, or .308 Win. cal., 21 in. barrel, composite stock is composed of fiberglass, Kevlar, and graphite and features baked on walnut wood grain finish with checkering, drilled and tapped receiver. Imported 1991 only.

	$725	**$625**	**$550**	**$495**	**$450**	**$415**	**$375**

Last Mfg.'s Sug. Retail was $840.

Add approx. 10% for Model AZ 1900M DL (photo engraved receiver and floorplate).

RIFLES: O/U

Please contact Cape Outfitters (see Trademark Index) for more information and current domestic pricing on the models listed below.

EXPRESS — 7x65R, 7x57mm, .30-06, .308 Win. or 9.3x74R cal., 25.6 in. barrels, hand checkered walnut stock with cheekpiece, set trigger for bottom barrel, extractors. Importation disc. 1993.

	$3,875	**$3,250**	**$2,900**	**$2,600**	**$2,200**	**$1,950**	**$1,650**

Last Mfg.'s Sug. Retail was $4,400.

Add $600 for E Model (with ejectors).

EXPRESS EM — 7x65R, .30-06, .308 Win., or 9.3x74R cal., mechanical single trigger, ejectors. Importation disc. 1990, reintroduced 1992 only.

	$4,850	**$3,975**	**$3,300**	**$2,900**	**$2,600**	**$2,200**	**$1,900**

Last Mfg.'s Sug. Retail was $5,300.

Z

Add $2,395 for De Luxe Model (disc.).
Add $7,200 for E3 De Luxe Model (disc.).

The Express E3 De Luxe Model includes 2 extra sets of barrels - 1 set is shotgun (20 ga. - 2¾ or 3 in. chambers).

RIFLES: SxS

SAVANA E — 7x65R, .30-06, .308 Win., or 9.3x74R cal., boxlock action, ejectors. Importation disc. 1990.

	$5,850	**$4,850**	**$3,975**	**$3,300**	**$2,800**	**$2,350**	**$2,000**

Last Mfg.'s Sug. Retail was $6,600.

Add $400 for Savana EM Model (single trigger).

* **Savana Deluxe** — similar to Savana E, except has elaborate game scene engraving. Importation disc. 1990.

	$7,750	**$7,100**	**$6,500**	**$6,000**	**$5,500**	**$5,000**	**$4,600**

Last Mfg.'s Sug. Retail was $8,295.

TROPHY MODEL — similar to Savana E, except is also available in .375 H&H Mag. cal., 25½ in. barrels, 8 lbs. Imported 1991 only.

	$5,275	**$4,200**	**$3,600**	**$3,150**	**$2,750**	**$2,400**	**$2,050**

Last Mfg.'s Sug. Retail was $5,895.

SHOTGUNS: O/U, RECENT PRODUCTION

GOLDEN SNIPE — 12 or 20 ga, various barrel lengths, VR, single trigger, ejectors, engraved.

	$560	**$520**	**$475**	**$430**	**$395**	**$360**	**$330**

Grading	100%	98%	95%	90%	80%	70%	60%

DELFINO — 12 or 20 ga., 3 in. chambers, 26 or 28 in. barrels, ejectors, VR, single non-selective trigger, blued frame with delicate engraving, walnut pistol grip stock and forearm. Disc.

	$500	$425	$375	$325	$295	$280	$265

RITMO HUNTING — 12 ga. only, 3 in. chambers, 26 or 28 in. vent. barrels and rib, SST, ejectors, select checkered walnut, blued frame and barrels with moderate engraving, recoil pad, 7¼ lbs. Disc.

	$575	$510	$465	$410	$370	$350	$335

RITMO PIGEON GRADE IV — 12 ga. only, live pigeon gun, 28 in. barrels, SST, ejectors, superbly engraved silver finished receiver, extra fine checkering on deluxe walnut, vent. barrels and rib, cased, 7½ lbs. Disc.

	$1,600	$1,450	$1,200	$1,000	$875	$795	$725

M85 RITMO TRAP OR SKEET — 12 ga. only, 28 in. (Skeet only), 30, or 32 in. barrels, ejectors, SST, special stock dimensions, engraved blue receiver, select checkered walnut stock and forearm, cased, 7¾ lbs. Disc.

	$595	$500	$465	$440	$415	$395	$370

This model was also available in a single barrel trap model at no extra charge.

* **M85 Ritmo Trap Combination** — 12 ga. only, supplied with O/U and single barrel sets, various barrel lengths, cased. Disc.

	$995	$895	$800	$700	$620	$575	$500

SILVER FALCON — 12 or 20 ga., 3 in. chambers, boxlock action, SST, ejectors, 26 or 28 in. barrels with multi-chokes, coin finished receiver with engraving, checkered Turkish walnut stock and forearm with weatherproof finish. Importation disc. 1991.

	$1,450	$700	$575	$500	$450	$400	$365

Last Mfg.'s Sug. Retail was $1,695.

WOODSMAN — 12 ga. only, 3 in. chambers, 23 in. vent. barrels are designed to shoot rifle slugs at 55 yards and to accept 5 interchangeable choke tubes, SST, ejectors, quarter rib on barrels with pop-up rifle sights, checkered Circassian walnut stock and forearm with swivels (waterproof finish).

	$1,650	$1,150	$950	$800	$700	$600	$500

Last Mfg.'s Sug. Retail was $1,895.

* **Woodsman Combo** — includes 2 sets of barrels (3 in. chambers) with Zoli interchangeable choke system.

	$2,050	$1,700	$1,475	$1,200	$1,050	$925	$800

Last Mfg.'s Sug. Retail was $2,320.

MODEL Z-90 TARGET MODEL — 12 ga. only, boxlock action, adj. SST, black competition receiver, deluxe checkered Turkish walnut stock with recoil pad and forearm, vent. barrels and rib, SST, ejectors.

* **Trap Gun** — 29½ or 32 in. barrels with screw-in chokes and raised VR, Monte Carlo stock, blue finish. Importation disc. 1993.

	$2,150	$1,450	$1,200	$995	$850	$700	$600

Last Mfg.'s Sug. Retail was $2,495.

* **Mono Trap Gun** — 32 or 34 in. barrel with screw-in chokes and raised VR, Monte Carlo stock. Importation disc. 1993.

	$2,150	$1,450	$1,200	$995	$850	$700	$600

Last Mfg.'s Sug. Retail was $2,495.

* **Z-90 Combo Trap Set** — includes O/U trap barrels as well as Mono trap barrel on same receiver, available as 30/32 in. sets or 32/34 in. sets. Imported 1991-92.

	$2,350	$1,900	$1,650	$1,400	$1,150	$950	$825

Last Mfg.'s Sug. Retail was $2,700.

* **Skeet Gun** — 28 in. barrels only with screw-in chokes. Importation disc. 1993.

	$2,150	$1,450	$1,200	$995	$850	$700	$600

Last Mfg.'s Sug. Retail was $2,495.

Grading	100%	98%	95%	90%	80%	70%	60%

* ***Sporting Clays Gun*** — 28 in. barrels with screw-in chokes, coin finished receiver with engraved sideplates, separated barrels, Schnabel forend, solid recoil pad. Importation disc. 1990.

	$2,150	$1,450	$1,200	$995	$850	$700	$600

Last Mfg.'s Sug. Retail was $2,495.

SHOTGUNS: SxS, RECENT PRODUCTION

UPLANDER — 12 or 20 ga., 3 in. chambers, 25 in. barrels with fixed chokes (IC/M), ST, ejectors, color case hardened receiver, English style checkered Circassian walnut stock and forearm with oil or polyurethane finish. Importation disc. 1990.

	$750	$625	$560	$520	$485	$450	$425

Last Mfg.'s Sug. Retail was $1,295.

SILVER FOX — 12 or 20 ga., 3 in. chambers, 26 or 28 (12 ga. only) in. barrels with fixed chokes, ST, ejectors, hand engraved silver finished receiver with "AZ" in gold, straight grip checkered Circassian walnut stock and forearm. Importation disc. 1990.

	$1,650	$1,425	$1,200	$995	$875	$750	$625

Last Mfg.'s Sug. Retail was $2,995.

ARIETE M3 — 12 ga. only, 26 or 28 in. barrels, matted rib, single non-selective trigger, ejectors, blued receiver with fine scroll engraving, cased. Disc.

	$550	$475	$400	$360	$330	$310	$285

EMPIRE — 12 or 20 ga. Mag., 27 or 28 in. barrels, moderate engraving, coin finished receiver. Disc.

	$1,425	$1,175	$975	$875	$795	$725	$650

Add $100 for 3 in. Mag. chambers.

This model was distributed by Euroarms of America, Inc.

VOLCANO RECORD — 12 ga. only, 28 in. barrels, H&H type sidelocks, ejectors, SST, treble Purdey locks, silver finished receiver with elaborate engraving, best quality fine checkered walnut, special order only. Disc.

	$5,300	$4,475	$3,950	$3,400	$2,950	$2,650	$2,300

Z

* ***Volcano Record ELM*** — 12 ga. only, built to individual customer specifications, best quality H&H style sidelock. Disc.

	$13,250	$11,000	$9,750	$8,600	$7,400	$6,300	$5,450

This model was distributed by Euroarms of America, Inc.

CUSTOM SERIES — SxS, individual custom order only, every refinement is used in the construction of these extremely rare and expensive shotguns. The Volcano Extra Lusso shotgun is probably the most elaborate Antonio Zoli shotgun with the list price being $58,850. Also, the Tornado Extra begins at $45,000 with a mint 12 ga. currently bringing approx. $25,000.

COMBINATION GUNS

COMBINATO — 12 or 20 ga. over .243 Win. or .222 Rem. cal., boxlock action, game scene engraved receiver with silver finish, double triggers, folding rear sight, skipline checkering, with sling swivels. Importation disc. 1993.

	$1,750	$1,500	$1,300	$1,100	$950	$775	$600

Last Mfg.'s Sug. Retail was $1,995.

* ***Combinato Set*** — includes one set of either 20 or 12 ga. barrels and an additional rifle/shotgun barrel set, same cals. as Combinato, cased. Importation disc. 1993.

	$2,400	$2,150	$1,850	$1,600	$1,400	$1,200	$995

Last Mfg.'s Sug. Retail was $2,700.

Grading	100%	98%	95%	90%	80%	70%	60%

SAFARI DELUXE — similar to Combinato, except has sideplates with elaborate game scene engraving. Importation disc. 1993.

$4,850 $4,400 $3,950 $3,550 $3,175 $2,800 $2,400

Last Mfg.'s Sug. Retail was $5,200.

Add approx. 50% for Safari Deluxe 2 (includes 2 sets of shotgun barrels).

EXPRESS E3 SET — includes one set of .30-06 cal. O/U barrels, one set of 20 ga./.243 Win. cal. barrels, one set of 20 ga./20 ga. barrels, special order, elaborate game scene engraving, includes German claw mount 4X scope and case. Disc.

$2,750 $2,400 $2,100 $1,850 $1,650 $1,500 $1,375

Z

MODERN AIRGUNS

Dear Airgun Enthusiast:

This promises to be the most exciting year in the history of airgunning. More new models have been introduced in 1999 than in any recent period, with quality, variety, and pricing that will establish a new benchmark in adult airguns. There are again significant new models from leading manufacturers such as Umarex (the parent company of Walther), Gamo, RWS, Industry Brand, IZH, and Savage Arms, along with the long anticipated return to the airgun market by Smith & Wesson.

The new entries from S&W, following on Colt's lead in 1998 with a Model 1911 A1 airgun, and the strikingly realistic Walther, Glock, SIG and Beretta styled airguns produced in Europe by Umarex and Gamo, dictate an even greater necessity for adult supervision than at any time in the history of modern airguns. The visual distinctions between a real firearm and an airgun based on a real revolver or semi-automatic are virtually nil at a quick glance! As Dr. Robert Beeman, the father of the modern adult airgun, points out, the authenticity of these guns and "the serious types of accessories produced, (target grips, laser sights, and compensators), gives them a credibility that they could not have won on their own. They are excellent firearms simulators and a whole lot of fun." While this adds to their appeal, authenticity being the first order of business with models from Gamo, RWS, Umarex, Colt, and S&W, the responsibility for handling what for lack of a better terminology could be classified by some as "training guns," increases proportionally with the level of realism.

Pricing this year, as always, is multi-faceted with some manufacturers having significantly increased retail prices on adult airguns, while a few have reduced their mfg.'s suggested retail price by a small margin to remain competitive in a rapidly expanding market. In general, prices have increased by an average of 5% to 10% across the board for major brands.

Our friend Tom Gaylord, editor and publisher of *The Airgun Letter*, makes special note this year of Korean manufacturer Sin Sung, better known for making deep well drilling equipment, but in the airgun world for producing the superb Career 707, a lever-action repeating compressed air rifle that is as powerful as a .22 short, and as accurate out to 75 yards as a custom .22 rimfire. This year, they will add a new carbine with a detachable air reservoir, expanding the versatility of this high-quality, medium-priced model marketed as the CA-707 by Dynamit Nobel-RWS, Inc.

The expanding adult airgun market has also encouraged Steyr and Anschütz to take an even more active role in the coming year, with both European manufacturers developing field competition rifles. Notes Gaylord, "A field target rifle is roughly three times as powerful as a ten meter rifle, and should be capable of one-half-inch, 10-shot groups at 50 yards. Customizers have been modifying the Feinwerkbau P70 rifle for this sport for the past two seasons. This puts these makers in competition with firms like Daystate and Air Arms, who have dominated the field target scene for a decade."

Until this year, there were fewer than 5,000 field target competitors worldwide, with less than 500 in the U.S., but there will be a debut match in Germany during May 1999, which promises to expand the sport throughout Europe. Adds Gaylord, "The German government is already considering legislation to allow the more powerful airguns, now that there is a legitimate reason to have them."

We are impressed this year by the level of technology that has filtered down into general interest adult airguns from improvements made to competition models built by Europe's leading manufacturers. Indeed, just as racing engineering technology trickles down into production automobiles, airgun design has benefitted immensely from the addition of airguns in Olympic competition, and the quantum leap in consumer technology that has resulted.

The final big trend in 1999, says Gaylord, is the continued increase in new airgun purchases by people outside of the traditional demographic. "Airgunners have traditionally come from the ranks of firearms enthusiasts, but today many new airgunners are also brand new to shooting altogether. They are using airguns to learn how to shoot--something that was once only the province of children and youth. As a result, a middle-aged airgunner may buy several airguns worth many thousands of dollars before purchasing their first .22 rimfire. This means that the marketing of airguns has to adapt to shooters who are unfamiliar with basic shooting skills and safety procedures. The wise

AIR-
GUNS

retailer will establish a complete package of support for the customer, including training, which should also build customer loyalty."

Dr. Robert Beeman says that, "The handwriting is on the wall as to where future sales are going to be. There is a great increase in the interest in adult airguns, and this pleases us mightily."

Dr. Beeman is quick to note that recent events which have taken place regarding the ownership of firearms in England and Australia underscore the increasing popularity of airguns, "...the only game in town for so many shooters around the world." Dr. Beeman also adds that when dealers stock the very best airguns, like the Beeman R1 and R7, Feinwerkbau C55, or Steyr LP-1, they often sell them to buyers who had been thinking of purchasing less expensive models until having the opportunity to handle one of the really good airguns.

In 1999, the number of "really good airguns" is expanding exponentially with new product lines from the world's leading manufacturers. The 20th Edition *Blue Book of Gun Values* offers the most extensive and detailed list of air pistols, rifles and high-quality adult airguns ever compiled.

Keep your air pressure up and shoot straight.

Dennis Adler

Dennis Adler - Associate Editor *Blue Book of Gun Value*s -Modern Airguns

A NOTE ABOUT AIRGUN PRICING

The prices listed in this section are reasonable retail prices based upon the manufacturer's suggested retail. It goes without saying that most retailers will discount at least 10%. Use the Mfg.'s Sug. Retail as a guideline. Airguns purchased from factory importers or dealers with test facilities or factory authorized repair centers may sell only at full retail and offer no discounts. 100% values indicate an average national retail price based on typical consumer purchases. 100% also means not previously sold at retail, or new in box (NIB).

You will note throughout this section that pricing only goes down to 95% grading. Due to the mechanical complexity of some airguns, and the fact that most sophisticated airguns are used solely for target practice, racking up thousands of rounds, guns under 95% condition retain much less of their original value than their cartridge-firing counterparts, until, of course, they become very old and very rare, such as vintage Benjamins, Crosmans, Sheridans, Plymouths, and Daisys. Also note that (NA) pricing for guns of 98% or less condition in this section reflect new models that have not as yet established a secondary market value.

Because of space considerations, airguns with a manufacturer's suggested retail price of under $100 are not included, although there are many fine airguns priced in the $60 to $90 range today. Airguns that are factory engraved or have fancy wood, hand checkering, or special finishes, should be discounted a minimum of 50% of original value if they are in less than 95% condition, i.e., showing more than minimum wear and use. Commemorative or limited edition models that had special packaging, art work (such as plaques or posters), or special literature included with the airgun should be rated at 98% or less, if any of the original items are missing, even if the airgun is unfired. For collectors, there is only one definition of NIB.

Our special thanks and appreciation for the contributions to the 20th Edition by Tom Gaylord, editor and publisher of *The Airgun Letter*. To subscribe to *The Airgun Letter* call 410-730-5496 or fax 410-730-9544. You can also check out *The Airgun Letter* web site at: http://www.airgun-letter.net or http://www.airgunletter.com. The Blue Book would also like to express its thanks to David Lee Reza for his assistance in updating vintage Daisy air rifle values for the 20th Edition. An avid Daisy collector, David is always willing to give advice or help find a rare gun. He can be reached at 949-240-7745.

AIR-
GUNS

Grading	100%	98%	95%

ANICS CORP./ANICS GROUP

The Russians are coming. The new free enterprise system in the former Soviet Union has not only made Tokarevs available to American gun collectors, but is also responsible for introducing a new line of Russian-made air pistols. The Anics Firm in Moscow was created in 1990 as an importer of Western-made airguns and firearms. In 1996 they began manufacturing their own line of CO_2 powered semi-autos and revolvers. The U.S. importer is Anics Corp. in Pepper Pike, OH. As a new entry into the market, there is no suggested retail price. However, based on the dealer net, the semi-automatic pistols and revolvers sell in the $100 to $125 range.

PISTOLS

MODEL A-101 SUBCOMPACT BB pistol — CO_2 powered, 15 shot, delivered at 450 FPS. Loaded inline through traditional clip. Semi-automatic design, checkered plastic grips. CO_2 cartridge loads through base of grip.

No Mfg.'s Retail	$100	$65	$40

MODEL A-101 MAGNUM BB pistol — CO_2 powered, 15 shot, delivered at 490 FPS. Loaded inline through traditional clip. Semi-automatic design with compensator, checkered plastic grips. CO_2 cartridge loads through base of grip.

No Mfg.'s Retail	$100	$65	$40

MODEL A-111 BB pistol — CO_2 powered, 15 shot, delivered at 450 FPS. Loaded inline through traditional clip. Modern semi-automatic design, contoured plastic grips. CO_2 cartridge loads through base of grip.

No Mfg.'s Retail	$100	$65	$40

MODEL A-112 BB pistol — CO_2 powered, 15 shot, delivered at 490 FPS. Loaded inline through traditional magazine. Modern semi-automatic design, adjustable rear sight, contoured plastic grips. CO_2 cartridge loads through base of grip.

No Mfg.'s Retail	$100	$65	$40

MODEL A-201 BB revolver — CO_2 powered, 30 shot, delivered at 410 FPS. Loaded through cylinder, adjustable rear sight, contoured plastic grips. CO_2 cartridge loads through base of grip. Realistic cylinder rotates when gun is fired. Single or double action.

No Mfg.'s Retail	$120	$95	$80

MODEL A-201 MAGNUM BB revolver — CO_2 powered, 30 shot, delivered at 460 FPS. Loaded through cylinder, adjustable rear sight, contoured plastic grips. CO_2 cartridge loads through base of grip. Realistic cylinder rotates when gun is fired. Single or double action.

No Mfg.'s Retail	$125	$105	$80

AIR-GUNS

ARS/FARCO

Manufactured in the Philippines. Imported by Air Rifle Specialists located in Elmira, NY. Guns available both through dealers or directly from the importer.

AIR RIFLES

AR6 MAGNUM (REPEATING 6 SHOT) — .22 CO_2 or compressed air powered, 23¼ in. barrel, capable of delivering 18 shots at (1,000 FPS) using compressed air or up to 80 shots using CO_2 (single fill), checkered walnut stock, 6 lbs. 12 oz.

Mfg.'s Sug. Retail	$580	$510	$450	$360

> Add $20 for extra 6 shot cylinder.
> Add $50 for charging unit.

CAREER 707 — .22 cal., 6 shot (or sideloading single shot) lever action repeater precharged pneumatic, 23 in. barrel, 1000 FPS, checkered walnut stock, 7¾ lbs. New 1995.

Mfg.'s Sug. Retail	$595	$525	$450	$360

CAREER II RIFLE — .22 cal., 6 shot (or sideloading single shot) lever action repeater precharged pneumatic, 22.75 in. barrel, 1000 FPS, checkered walnut stock, 7¾ lbs. Same as Career 707 except for shape of the receiver and butt stock. New 1995.

Mfg.'s Sug. Retail	$595	$525	$450	$360

Grading	100%	98%	95%

FARCO FP SURVIVAL AIR RIFLE — .22 or .25 cal., footpump action, 22¾ in. barrel, single shot, hardwood stock, 5 ¾ lbs.

Mfg.'s Sug. Retail	$295	$260	$220	$175

FARCO STAINLESS STEEL — .22 or .25 cal., CO_2, charged by refillable (and removable) 10 oz. cylinder, hardwood stock, approx. 7 lbs.

Mfg.'s Sug. Retail	$460	$390	$340	$270

KING HUNTING MASTER (REPEATING 5 SHOT) — .22 cal., CO_2 or compressed air powered, similar to the Farco Stainless Steel above.

Mfg.'s Sug. Retail	$580	$510	$450	$360

MAGNUM 6 (REPEATING 6 SHOT) — .22 cal., CO_2 or compressed air powered, similar to the King Hunting Master.

	$470	$410	$330

Last Mfg.'s Sug. Retail was $500.

M 900 — 9mm precharged pneumatic, 26¾ in. barrel, 900 FPS, side-lever action (for inserting pellets) shoots 92 grain pellet, wood stock.

Mfg.'s Sug. Retail	$1,000	$1,000	$800	$640

QB 77 — .177 or .22 cal., CO_2 powered, 21½ in. barrel, hardwood stock, 5 ½ lbs., single shot.

Mfg.'s Sug. Retail	$149	$75	$65	$50

AIR SHOTGUNS

FARCO AIR SHOTGUN — 28 ga., CO_2 powered, 30 in. barrel, charged by refillable "and removable" 10 oz. cylinder, hardwood stock, 7 lbs. Importation began 1988.

Mfg.'s Sug. Retail	$460	$400	$350	$280

Add $20 for extra CO_2 cylinder.

Add $1 for extra brass shells (12 included w/gun).

AIR ARMS

Currently imported by Dynamit Nobel-RWS, Inc. located in Closter, NJ. Previously imported by Air Rifle Specialists located in Elmira, NY. Available both through dealers and directly from the importer.

Editors note: These guns are filled from high pressure scuba tanks allowing many shots to be fired from one charge. This also allows one to adjust the power level of each shot. All guns are made with Walther barrels that float so that expansion or contraction of the air chamber will not affect accuracy. Add $150 for Olympic trigger, $200 for regulator, and $50 for lever bolt.

SM100 — .177 or .22 cal. precharged pneumatic, 22 in. barrel, two stage trigger (adjustable), beech stock, 8 lbs. 8 oz. Disc. 1994.

	$700	$600	$480

Last Mfg.'s Sug. Retail was $975.

Add $60 for left-hand.

XM100 — similar to the SM100, except has quick release tank connector and walnut stock, 8 lbs. Disc. 1994.

	$800	$680	$540

Last Mfg.'s Sug. Retail was $1,260.

Add $60 for left-hand.

TM100 — similar to XM100, except with adj. cheekpiece and shoulder pad, (target style stock), 8 lbs. 12 oz.

	$1,000	$850	$680

Last Mfg.'s Sug. Retail was $1,650.

Add $60 for left-hand.

TX200/TX200SR — .177 or .22 cal., under-lever action, 15¾ in. barrel, 913/800 FPS, 9 lbs. 3 oz.

	$460	$400	$310

Last Mfg.'s Sug. Retail was $560.

Add $80 for walnut stock.
Add $75 for left-hand.
Add $75 for recoilless S.R. model.

AIR-GUNS

Grading	100%	98%	95%

NJR100 — similar to the TX200, except with hand picked barrel for accuracy, adj. cheekpiece, forearm and shoulder pad designed by and named after Nick Jenkinson (one of England's top field target shooters), 10 lbs. 12 oz.

$1,425 $1,210 $1,000

Last Mfg.'s Sug. Retail was $2,600.

Add $60 for left-hand.

AIR LOGIC

Manufacturer/distributor located in Forest Row, Sussex, England. Available through dealers and the used market.

Air Logic has limited importation into the U.S. More information can be obtained by contacting the company directly (see Trademark Index).

GENESIS — .22 cal., single stroke pneumatic, 630 FPS, unique bolt action sliding barrel by Lothar Walther, recoilless, adj. trigger, side lever action, 9½ lbs. Mfg. 1988-Disc.

$575 $450 $360

Last Mfg.'s Sug. Retail was $750.

AIR MATCH

Previously imported by Kendall International located in Paris, KY. No longer imported, used guns only.

AIR MATCH MODEL 600 PISTOL — .177 cal., side-lever action, adj. trigger, professional target model, 2 lbs.

$350 $280 $200

AMERICAN ARMS, INC.

Manufacturer/importer located in North Kansas City, MO.

Even though American Arms, Inc. imports Norica airguns, they are listed in this section because of their private label status. Importation began in late 1988 and was discontinued in 1989.

PISTOLS

IDEAL — .177 cal., barrel-cocking action, 400 FPS, adj. sights, 3 lbs.

$75 $60 $40

Last Mfg.'s Sug. Retail was $105.

RIFLES

JET RIFLE — .177 cal., barrel-cocking action, 855 FPS, adj. double set triggers, hardwood stock, 7 lbs.

$100 $85 $70

Last Mfg.'s Sug. Retail was $160.

Subtract $35 for Junior Model.

COMMANDO — .177 cal., barrel-cocking action, 540 FPS, adj. sights, 5 lbs.

$75 $60 $40

Last Mfg.'s Sug. Retail was $115.

ANSCHÜTZ

Manufactured in Ulm, Germany. Available through dealers and some models directly from Marksman. Models 2001 and 2002 previously imported by Precision Sales Intl. Inc., PO Box 1776, Westfield, MA 01086.

Models 333, 335, and 380 were previously imported by Crosman from 1986-1988. Model 380 was also previously imported by Marksman.

PISTOLS

MODEL M10 — .177 cal., pre-charged pneumatic 492 FPS, 9½ in. barrel with compensator, adjustable trigger, sights and pistol grip, special dry firing mechanism, walnut grips.

Mfg.'s Sug. Retail $1,395 $1,000 $900 $580

AIR-GUNS

Grading	100%	98%	95%

RIFLES

MODEL 333 — .177 cal., barrel-cocking action, 700 FPS, adj. trigger, 18 in. barrel, 6¾ lbs.

$180 $125 $90

Last Mfg.'s Sug. Retail was $175.

MODEL 335 — .177 cal., barrel-cocking, 700 FPS, adj. trigger, 18½ in. barrel, 7½ lbs.

$190 $140 $100

Last Mfg.'s Sug. Retail was $200.

Add $10 for 335 Mag. (20% higher velocity).

MODEL 380 — .177 cal., under-lever cocking, 600-640 FPS, professional match model, removable cheekpiece, adj. trigger, stippled walnut grips. Disc. 1994.

$1,005 $875 $575

Last Mfg.'s Sug. Retail was $1,250.

Add $30 for left-hand.
Add $60 for moving target.

MODEL 2001 — .177 cal., single stroke pneumatic, side-lever action, exceptional target model, 10 lbs. 8 oz.

$1,250 $920 $815

Last Mfg.'s Sug. Retail was $1,800.

Add $80 for left-hand.
Add $80 for Running Target Model.

MODEL 2002 — .177 cal. single stroke pneumatic or pre-charged pneumatic (new 1997), side-lever action, 26 in. barrel, this gun incorporates some of the latest technology used in air rifles, 10½ lbs. New 1992.

Mfg.'s Sug. Retail $1,685 $1,450 $1,250 $1,000

Add $20 for running target.
Add $50 for colored laminated stock.
Add $60 for left-hand.
Subtract $60 for non-walnut (blond) stock.
Prices equal for both sidelever and pre-charged models.

B S A GUNS (U.K.), LTD.

Manufactured in Birmingham, England. Previously imported by Dynamit-Nobel RWS of Closter, NJ. Now imported by Precision Sales, Westfield, MA. Available both dealer and importer direct.

Add $100 for guns equipped with Theoben gas spring.

PISTOLS

240 MAGNUM PISTOL — .177 or .22 cal., single stroke cocking system, 510/420 FPS, 6 in. barrel, two stage trigger, adjustable rear sight and integral scope rail, wt. 2 lbs.

Mfg.'s Sug. Retail $293 $235 $200   160

SCORPION PISTOL — .177 or .22 cal., barrel-cocking action 510-380 FPS, 3 lbs. 6 oz.

$170 $145 $90

Last Mfg.'s Sug. Retail was $190.

Add $50 for carbine stock, Shadow Model.

RIFLES

AIRSPORTER/AIRSPORTER SUPER — .177, .22 or .25 cal., under-lever action, 1020-550 FPS/825-675 FPS, Super, 8 lbs.

$200 $170 $130

Last Mfg.'s Sug. Retail was $375.

Add $50 for Super,
Add $25 for Monte Carlo stock Stutzen Model.
Add $20 for Carbine.

AIRSPORTER RB2 MAGNUM RIFLE — .177, .22 or .25 cal., similar to Airsporter/Airsporter Super, 18 in. barrel, 8½ lbs.

Mfg.'s Sug. Retail $450 $345 $290 $235

Add $70 for Crown grade with laminated wood stock.

AIR-
GUNS

AIRSPORTER RB2 MAGNUM CARBINE — .177, .22 or .25 cal., similar to Airsporter Magnum rifle, except has 14 in. barrel.

Mfg.'s Sug. Retail	$474	$370	$355	$265

CENTENNIAL COMMEMORATIVE — .177 or .22 cal., designed to commemorate BSA's 100th year.

	$260	$210	$145

Last Mfg.'s Sug. Retail was $650.

GOLDSTAR — .177 or .22 cal., under-lever action, 1020 FPS, 800/625 FPS 18½ in. barrel, two-stage adjustable trigger, hardwood stock has 10 shot rotary magazine (developed from the VS2000), 8½ lbs.

Mfg.'s Sug. Retail	$847	$575	$490	$390

MERCURY/MERCURY SUPER — .177 or .22 cal., barrel-cocking action, 700-550 FPS/825-600 FPS Super, 7¼ lbs.

Add $35 for Super.

	$160	$120	$85

MERCURY CHALLENGER — .177 or .22 cal., barrel-cocking action, 850-625 FPS, 7 lbs. 4 oz. Disc. 1988.

	$170	$125	$90

Last Mfg.'s Sug. Retail was $205.

METEOR/METEOR SUPER — .177 or .22 cal., barrel-cocking action, 650-500 FPS, 18½ in. barrel, 6 lbs.

	$90	$70	$50

Add $15 for Super.

METEOR MK 6 — .177 or .22 cal., barrel-cocking action, 650 FPS, 18 in. barrel, 6 lbs. Introduced 1997.

Mfg.'s Sug. Retail	$224	$180	$150	$115

SUPER 10 MAGNUM — .177 or .22 cal., precharged pneumatic, 10 shot bolt action, 1350 FPS (.177 cal.), 17½ barrel, match grade trigger, Monte Carlo stock with adj. pad.

Mfg.'s Sug. Retail	$1,000	$830	$700	$550

SUPER SPORT/SUPER SPORT CUSTOM/SUPERSPORT CARBINE — .177, .22 or .25 cal., barrel-cocking action, 850/625/530 FPS, 18½ in. barrel approx. 7 lbs.

Mfg.'s Sug. Retail	$279	$230	$200	$160

Add $115 for custom model.
Add $120 for guns equipped with Theoben gas ram (spring).
Add $25 for Carbine Model.

SUPERSTAR/SUPERSTAR CARBINE — .177, .22, or .25 cal., under-lever action, 1020-850/800-625/675-530 FPS, 18½ in. barrel, unique rotating breech for loading pellets directly into bore, checkered beech stock, maxi grip scope rail, two stage trigger, approx. 7¾ lbs. Prices equal for Carbine Model.

	$375	$325	$260

Last Mfg.'s Sug. Retail was $470.

Add $120 for guns equipped with Theoben gas ram (spring).

SUPER STAR MK II MAGNUM — .177, .22 cal. or .25 cal., under-lever action, 1020/800/675 FPS, 18 in. barrel, unique rotating breech for loading pellets directly into bore, Monte Carlo stock with cheek piece, Maxi Grip scope rail, adjustable two-stage trigger, 8½ lbs. Introduced 1997.

Mfg.'s Sug. Retail	$540	$430	$375	$300

Prices and performance specs same for 14 in. barrel Carbine model.

STUTZEN — similar to Super Star MK II Magnum, except has shorter overall length (39 in.), 14 in. barrel and Stutzen full length stock, 7 lbs. 4 oz.

	$425	$360	$280

Last Mfg.'s Sug. Retail was $540.

STUTZEN MK 2 — .177, .22 cal. or .25 cal., concealed cocking lever, 1020/800/675 FPS, 14 in. barrel, unique rotating breech, Monte Carlo stock with cheek piece and rosewood Schnabel fore cap, Maxi Grip scope rail, 6¼ lbs. Introduced 1997.

Mfg.'s Sug. Retail	$698	$560	$485	$380

AIR-
GUNS

Grading	100%	98%	95%

VS 2000 — .177 or .22 cal., 9 shot repeater, side-lever action, 850-625 FPS, 9 lbs. Disc. 1988.

$450　　$325　　$230

Last Mfg.'s Sug. Retail was $330.

Add $65 for custom model.
Only 20 or so of this model ever made.

B.S.F. "BAYERISCHE SPORTWAFFENFABRIK"

Manufactured in Germany. Previously imported by Kendell International located in Paris, KY and Beeman Precision Arms under the Wischo label. Available only on the used market.

B.S.F. tooling and machinery have been purchased by Weihrauch and are being utilized to manufacture versions of B.S.F. Models for Marksman (Marksman Models 28, 40, 55, 56, 58, 59, 70, 71, 72 and 75).

RIFLES

BAVARIA MODEL 35 — .177 cal., barrel-cocking action, 500 FPS, 4½ lbs.

$150　　$120　　$100

Last Mfg.'s Sug. Retail was $125.

BAVARIA MODEL 45 — .177 cal., barrel-cocking action, 700 FPS, 6 lbs.

$165　　$125　　$105

Last Mfg.'s Sug. Retail was $125.

BAVARIA MODEL 50 — .177 cal., barrel-cocking action, 700 FPS, 6 lbs.

$175　　$130　　$110

BAVARIA MODEL S54 — .177 or .22 cal., under-lever action, 685/500 FPS, 8 lbs.

$235　　$175　　$110

Add $15 for Sport Model (discontinued 1986)
Add $30 for M Model.

BAVARIA MODEL 55 — .177 or .22 cal., barrel-cocking action, 800/570 FPS, 6½ lbs., Disc. 1986.

$180　　$140　　$105

Add $15 for Deluxe Model
Add $30 for Special Model

BAVARIA MODEL S60 — .177 or .22 cal., barrel-cocking action, 800/570 FPS, 6½ lbs.

$180　　$150　　$110

BAVARIA MODEL S70 — .177 or .22 cal., barrel-cocking action, 800/570 FPS, 7 lbs.

$185　　$155　　$110

BAVARIA MODEL S80 — .177 or .22 cal., barrel-cocking action, 800/570 FPS, 8¼ lbs.

$210　　$165　　$135

Last Mfg.'s Sug. Retail was $185.

BEEMAN PRECISION AIRGUNS

Located in Huntington Beach, CA. Beeman has exclusive rights to any airguns marketed in the U.S. under the names Beeman, Feinwerkbau, and Weihrauch. Additionally some models marketed by Beeman in the late 1970s and early 1980s were manufactured in Germany by Mayer & Grammelspacher (Dianawerk). Early production used Diana model numbers, and later shipments were marked with Beeman model numbers: Very small stampings on receivers indicate month and year of manufacture.

Beeman imported Feinwerkbau and Weihrauch Airguns will appear under their respective headings in this section. Webley airguns are incorporated into this section. Available through dealers and Beeman direct.

PISTOLS

BEEMAN ADDER — .20 and .25 cal. precharged pneumatic, internal air chamber, 7 in. barrel, manual safety, 2¾ lbs. Mfg. 1992-94.

$595　　$450　　$325

Last Mfg.'s Sug. Retail was $530.

Add $75 for .20 cal.
Only 10 guns were ever made.

AIR-GUNS

Grading	100%	98%	95%

BEEMAN/FAS 604 — .177 cal., top lever spring pneumatic action, 380 FPS, 2 lbs. 3 oz. Disc. 1988.

$295 **$250** **$145**

Last Mfg.'s Sug. Retail was $495.

    Add $30 for left-hand.

BEEMAN/HARPER CLASSIC PISTOL — .22 or .25 cal., similar to Harper Air Cane rifle action, 300 FPS, 4 oz. Disc. 1989.

$450 **$365** **$225**

Last Mfg.'s Sug. Retail was $285.
Last Retail for a cased pair was $700.

    Add $250 if cased.
    Add $20 for .25 cal.
    Add $35 for deluxe.
    Only 6 ever imported into U.S.

BEEMAN/HARPER PEPPERBOX PISTOL — .22 cal., pneumatic, similar to Beeman/Harper Classic Pistol above, 9.8 oz. Disc. 1989.

$895 **$650** **$450**

Last Mfg.'s Sug. Retail was $575.

    Only 3 of this model imported into U.S.

BEEMAN P1 — .177, .20 or .22 cal. Mag., top-cocking action, 600-350 FPS, dual power, walnut grips, Colt .45 look alike.

Mfg.'s Sug. Retail	**$415**	**$320**	**$280**	**$225**

    Add $350 for gold plating.
    Add $65 for stainless steel style or blue/stainless dual finish.
    Add $200 for Commemorative Model (mfg. 1992 only).

BEEMAN P2 — .177 and .20 cal., single stroke pneumatic, similar to Beeman P1, but professional mid-priced match gun. New 1991.

Mfg.'s Sug. Retail	**$445**	**$350**	**$300**	**$225**

    Add $35 for match grips.

BEEMAN P3 — .177 cal., overlever pneumatic, 410 FPS. A completely new design for Beeman's recoilless air pistol series, the P3 is the first quality air gun to be manufactured in polymer. Similar to the Glock and latest Walther polymer firearms, the P3 is a quantum leap in material technology. Cocking the hammer allows the top frame to swing up as a charging lever. Automatic safety and beartrap prevention, adjustable rear sight, rifled steel barrel, built-in muzzle break, two-stage trigger, anatomical polymer composite grip, 1.7 lbs. New 1999.

Mfg.'s Sug. Retail	**$160**	**$125**	**N/A**	**N/A**

BEEMAN/WEBLEY HURRICANE — .177 or .22 cal., barrel-cocking action, 470-400 FPS, 2 lbs. 4 oz.

Mfg.'s Sug. Retail	**$240**	**$175**	**$160**	**$125**

    Add $40 for M20 scope combo.

BEEMAN/WEBLEY NEMESIS — .177 cal., single stroke pneumatic, 385 F.P.S. adjustable sight (rear), manual safety, 2 lbs. 3 oz.

Mfg.'s Sug. Retail	**$200**	**$150**	**$125**	**$110**

BEEMAN/WEBLEY TEMPEST — .177 or .22 cal., barrel-cocking action, 470-400 FPS, 2 lbs.

Mfg.'s Sug. Retail	**$210**	**$155**	**$130**	**$105**

BEEMAN WOLVERINE — .177, .20, .22, and .25 cal. precharged pneumatic, internal air chamber, 10½ in. barrel, manual safety, 3 lbs. Disc. 1994.

$725 **$680** **$440**

Last Mfg.'s Sug. Retail was $700.

    Add $100 for .20 cal.
    Only 10 guns were ever made.

MODEL 700 — .177 cal., barrel-cocking action, 460 fps, 7.0 in. barrel, 3.1 lbs. Disc. 1981.

$210 **$160** **$120**

Last Mfg.'s Sug. Retail was $122.

    Add $30 for left hand grip
    Produced for Beeman by Mayer & Grammelspacher

AIR-
GUNS

Grading	100%	98%	95%

MODEL 800 — .177 cal., barrel-cocking action, 460 FPS, 7.0 in. barrel, 3.2 lbs. Double opposing piston recoilless mechanism. Disc. 1982.

$325 $280 $220

Last Mfg.'s Sug. Retail was $191

Add $30 for left hand grip
Produced for Beeman by Mayer & Grammelspacher

MODEL 850 — .Special version of Model 800 with rotating barrel shroud as in Model 900. Disc. 1982

Last Mfg.'s Sug. Retail was $225

Add $75 to Model 800 prices.

MODEL 900 — .177 cal., barrel-cocking action, 490 FPS, 7.1 in. barrel, 3.3 lbs. Double opposing piston recoilless mechanism. Target model with adj. walnut match grips, match micrometer sights. Disc. 1981.

$1225 $960 $770

Last Mfg.'s Sug. Retail was $445

Add $50 for left hand grip. Add $75 for cased set.
Produced for Beeman by Mayer & Grammelspacher

RIFLES

BEEMAN R1/R1 SUPER MAGNUM —.177, .20, .22 or .25 cal., barrel-cocking action, 1000-610 FPS, 8 lbs. 8 oz.

Mfg.'s Sug. Retail $540 $435 $375 $295

Add $355 for Laser Model MK II or MK III.
Add $350 for custom grade.
Add $135 for Field Target Model.
Add $385 for custom fancy.
Add $500 for X fancy.
Add $35 for left-hand.
Add $60 for blue/silver finish version.
Add $275 for Tyrolean stock. Very rare.
Add $125 for commemorative model.
Add $100 for AW Model with chrome finish and synthetic stock, available .20 cal. carbine only.

Chrome and gold plated variations of the R1 with RDB prefix serialization may exceed retail 150%-200% depending on region.

BEEMAN R6 — .177 cal., barrel-cocking action, 815 FPS, two stage trigger, auto safety, beech stock, 7.1 lbs.

Mfg.'s Sug. Retail $325 $250 $225 $175

BEEMAN R7 — .177, .20 cal., barrel-cocking action, 700 - 620 FPS, two stage adjustable trigger, beech stock, automatic safety, 6 lbs. 1 oz.

Mfg.'s Sug. Retail $325 $270 $235 $190

Add $35 for .20 cal.

BEEMAN R8 — .177 cal., barrel-cocking action, 720 FPS, two stage adjustable trigger, beech stock, automatic safety, 7 lbs. 2 oz. Disc. 1997.

$320 $250 $225

Last Mfg.'s Sug. Retail was $380

BEEMAN R9 — .177 or .20 cal., barrel-cocking action, 1000/800 FPS, adjustable trigger, auto safety, beech stock, 7.3 lbs.

Mfg.'s Sug. Retail $320 $220 $185 $150

Add $50 for R9 Deluxe w/high grade wood and grip cap.
Add $10 for "Goldfinger" version w/gold trigger.

Grading	100%	98%	95%

BEEMAN R10 — .177, .20, or .22 cal., barrel-cocking action, 1,000-750 FPS, 7 lbs 9 oz.

Mfg.'s Sug. Retail	$400	$325	$285	$230

Add $400 for Laser Model.
Add $350 for custom grade.
Add $400 for custom fancy.
Add $450 for X fancy.
Add $60 for left-hand.
Add $75 for deluxe.

BEEMAN R11 — .177 cal., barrel-cocking action, 925 FPS, $19\frac{5}{8}$ in. barrel with sleeve, adj. cheekpiece and trigger, $8\frac{3}{4}$ lbs. New 1994.

Mfg.'s Sug. Retail	$600	$490	$330	$260

BEEMAN HW77 MKII — .177 cal., spring piston, underlever cocking, 930 FPS, fixed barrel, automatic safety, two-stage adjustable trigger, beech sporter stock w/hand-cut checkering on the pistol grip, high comb, raised cheel piece, rubber recoil pad, 8.7 lbs. An updated version of the Beeman HW77, back by popular demand. New 1999.

Mfg.'s Sug. Retail	$530	$425	N/A	N/A

BEEMAN HW97 — .177, .20 cal., spring piston, underlever cocking, (.177), velocity 800 FPS, fixed barrel, automatic safety, two-stage adjustable trigger, (mandatory scope use, scope mounts extra), 9.2 lbs. An updated version of the Beeman HW77 manufactured by Weihrauch. Beech stained Monte Carlo stock with high cheekpiece.

Mfg.'s Sug. Retail	$550	$425	$400	$305

BEEMAN RX — .177, .20, .22, and .25 cal., Theoben gas spring, spring piston system (see Theoben), up to 1200 FPS/.177 cal., adj. Velocity. Disc. 1992.

	$350	$300	$220

Last Mfg.'s Sug. Retail was $470.

Add $20 for .20 and .25 cal.
Add $140 for Field Target.
Add $60 for left-hand.
Add $150 for commemorative model.

BEEMAN RX-1 — improved version of Beeman RX above.

Mfg.'s Sug. Retail	$590	$420	$400	$330

Add $45 for left-hand.
Add $150 for commemorative model.

BEEMAN S-1 — .177 cal., barrel-cocking action, 900 FPS, two stage adjustable trigger, auto safety, beech stock, 7.1 lbs.

Mfg.'s Sug. Retail	$210	$150	$125	$100

Manufactured for Beeman by Norica.

BEEMAN AIR WOLF — .177, .20, .22 and .25 cal. precharged pneumatic, 21 in. barrel, internal air chamber, manual safety, $5\frac{5}{8}$ lbs. Mfg. 1992-1994.

	$695	$625	$525

Last Mfg.'s Sug. Retail was $680.

Add $85 for charging adapter w/gauge - only 10-20 guns were ever made.

BEEMAN BEARCUB — .177 cal., barrel-cocking action, 915 FPS, 13 in. barrel (approximately), single stage adjustable trigger, manual safety, beech stock, 7.2 lbs.

Mfg.'s Sug. Retail	$325	$245	$215	$175

BEEMAN CARBINE C1 — .177 or .22 cal., barrel-cocking action, 830-670 FPS, 6 lbs. 2 oz.- 6 lbs. 3 oz. Disc. 1996.

	$225	$195	$150

Last Mfg.'s Sug. Retail was $290.

BEEMAN CLASSIC MAGNUM — .177, .20, .22 and .25 cal., gas spring, barrel-cocking action, 15 in. barrel, manual button safety, checkered walnut stock, $8\frac{5}{8}$ lbs. Mfg. 1992-93.

	$890	$750	$590

Last Mfg.'s Sug. Retail was $895.

Add $160 for power adjustment pump.

AIR-
GUNS

Grading	100%	98%	95%

BEEMAN CROW MAGNUM II — .20, .22, and .25 cal., gas spring, barrel-cocking action, 16 in. barrel, manual button safety, Dampamount scope mounts included, 8¼ lbs. Mfg. 1993-1997.

$1,155 $980 $825

Last Mfg.'s Sug. Retail was $1,220.

    Add $160 for power adjustment pump.

BEEMAN CROW MAGNUM III — .20, .22, .25 cal., gas spring, barrel-cocking action, velocity 1060 FPS (.20 cal.), 16 in. barrel, automatic safety, two-stage adjustable trigger, Dampamount scope mounts included, 8.6 lbs. Crow Magnum III has a redesigned piston with a steel face and O-rings to seal the unit, slightly longer compression cylinder, and crisper trigger pull. New 1998.

Mfg.'s Sug. Retail $1,220 $1,050 $950 $750

BEEMAN FALCON 1 & 2 — .177 cal., barrel-cocking action, 620-680 FPS/560-600 FPS, 5.9/6.7 lbs. Disc. 1984.

$120 $85 $65

Last Mfg.'s Sug. Retail was $110.

    Add $30 for Falcon 2.

BEEMAN FX 1 & 2 — same as Beeman Falcon 1 & 2. Disc. 1992.

$125 $100 $85

Last Mfg.'s Sug. Retail was $140.

    Add $30 for FX 1.

BEEMAN GAME KEEPER — .25 cal., precharged pneumatic, quick change gas cylinder (bottle), 15 in. barrel, manual lever safety, 7⅞-8¼ lbs. Only 5 imported domestically 1992-93.

$2,750 $1,800 $1,500

Last Mfg.'s Sug. Retail was $990.

    Model rarity precludes accurate price evaluation.

BEEMAN/HARPER AIR CANE — .22 or .25 cal., pneumatic (reusable gas cartridge), 650 FPS, reproduction of 19th century Walking Cane Gun, 1 lb. Add $55 for decorative head piece.

$750 $595 $440

Last Mfg.'s Sug. Retail was $595.

    Only 25 of these models were ever imported into the U.S.

BEEMAN MAKO — .177 cal., precharged pneumatic, 930 F.P.S., bolt action loading system, checkered beech stock, adjustable trigger, manual safety, 7 lbs. 5 oz. New 1995.

Mfg.'s Sug. Retail $1,000 $825 $725 $595

    Add $375 for FT Model with checkered thumbhole stock.

BEEMAN MANITOU FT — .177 cal. precharged pneumatic, internal air chamber, 21 in. barrel, 8¾ lbs. New 1992. Disc. 1994.

$950 $660 $465

Last Mfg.'s Sug. Retail was $995.

    Add $100 for left-hand.
    Add $75 for charge adapter with gauge.
    Only 10 guns were ever imported.

BEEMAN SUPER 7 — .22 or .25 (new 1994) cal., precharged pneumatic, 7 shot magazine, quick change gas cylinder (bottle), 19 in. barrel, checkered walnut stock, manual button safety, 7¼ lbs. Mfg. 1992-95 only.

$1,430 $1,100 $850

Last Mfg.'s Sug. Retail was $1,575.

BEEMAN SUPER 12 — .20, .22 and .25 cal., precharged pneumatic, 12 shot mag., 850 FPS (.25 cal.), quick change gas cylinder (bottle), checkered walnut stock, manual button safety. New 1995.

Mfg.'s Sug. Retail $1,675 $1,500 $1,325 $1,000

BEEMAN SUPER 17 — .177 cal., precharged pneumatic, 17 shot mag., 850-900 FPS, quick change gas cylinder (bottle), laminated target stock, adjustable match trigger, adjustable butt plate, optional adjustable cheekpiece. A .177 cal. version of the Super 12, with new 17 shot rotary magazine. New 1998.

Mfg.'s Sug. Retail $1,875 $1,680 $1,300 $1,050

Grading	100%	98%	95%

BEEMAN UL-7 — .22 cal., under-lever action, gas spring, 12 in. barrel, manual button safety, 7 shot repeater with removable rotary magazine, checkered walnut stock, approx. 8 were imported 1992-93.

$1,500   **$1,250**   **$840**

Last Mfg.'s Sug. Retail was $1,560.

    Add $80 for power adjustment pump.

BEEMAN/WEBLEY ECLIPSE —.177, .22 or .25 cal., under-lever action, 990 FPS (in .177 cal.). Mfg. 1990-96.

$360   **$300**   **$220**

Last Mfg.'s Sug. Retail was $510.

    Add $30 for .25 cal.

BEEMAN/WEBLEY KODIAK SUPER MAGNUM — .22, or .25 cal., barrel-cocking action, 820 FPS (.25 cal.), 17½ in. barrel, 8.9 lbs. New 1993.

Mfg.'s Sug. Retail $625   **$515**   **$450**   **$350**

    Subtract $20 for .22 cal.

BEEMAN/WEBLEY OMEGA — .177 or .22 cal., barrel-cocking action, 830-675 FPS, 7 lbs. 8 oz. Disc. 1992.

$220   **$180**   **$150**

Last Mfg.'s Sug. Retail was $430.

BEEMAN/WEBLEY VULCAN III AND VULCAN III DELUXE — .177 or .22 cal., barrel-cocking action, 830-675 FPS, 7.6-7.7 lbs.

$200   **$185**   **$170**

Last Mfg.'s Sug. Retail was $300.

    Add $65 for Deluxe.

BEEMAN WOLF PUP — .20, .22, and .25 precharged pneumatic, internal cylinder, 13½ in. barrel, manual safety. Disc. 1994.

$750   **$650**   **$460**

Last Mfg.'s Sug. Retail was $680.

    Add $40 for .20 cal.
    Add $95 for charging adaptor w/gauge.
    Add $250 for Deluxe Model with thumbhole stock and match trigger.
    Only 10 guns were ever made.

MODEL 100 — .177 cal., barrel cocking action, 660 FPS, 18.7 in. barrel, 6.0 lbs. Disc. in 1980.

$210   **$165**   **$135**

Last Mfg.'s Sug. Retail was $155.

    Produced for Beeman by Mayer & Grammelspacher

MODEL 200 — .177 cal., barrel cocking action, 700 FPS, 19 in. barrel, 7.1 lbs. Disc. in 1979.

$175   **$135**   **$105**

Last Mfg.'s Sug. Retail was $197.

    Produced for Beeman by Mayer & Grammelspacher

MODEL 250 — .177, .20, or .22 cal., barrel cocking action, 830/750/650 FPS, 20.5 in. barrel, 7.8 lbs. Disc. in 1981.

$250   **$200**   **$145**

Last Mfg.'s Sug. Retail was $217.

    Add $100 for Commemorative model, emblem in stock.
    Add $250 for rare .20 cal version. Less than 60 were produced.
    Manufactured for Beeman by Mayer & Grammelspacher

MODEL 400 — .177 cal., side lever action, 650 FPS, 19 in. barrel, 10.9 lbs. Target model with match micrometer aperture sight. Disc. in 1981.

$1100   **$855**   **$600**

Last Mfg.'s Sug. Retail was $615.

    Add $250 for left hand stock and lever.
    Add $185 for Universal model (adj. cheekpiece).
    Produced for Beeman by Mayer & Grammelspacher

BENJAMIN AIR RIFLE COMPANY

Manufacturer located in Racine, WI. Available both through dealers and factory direct. Purchased January 1992 by Crosman Air Guns located in E. Bloomfield, NY.

AIR-
GUNS

Grading	100%	98%	95%

PISTOLS

BENJAMIN AIR PISTOL MODEL 130, 132, AND 137 — .177 cal., pneumatic pump action, 380 FPS, 2 lbs.

	$80	$65	$45

Last Mfg.'s Sug. Retail was $85.

BENJAMIN AIR PISTOL MODEL 242, 247 — .177 and .22 cal., pneumatic pump action, 418/315 FPS, 2 lbs. 8 oz.

	$85	$70	$50

Last Mfg.'s Sug. Retail was $90.

RIFLES

CENTENNIAL MODEL 87 — .22 cal., multi-stroke pneumatic, 750/650 FPS, polished brass barrel, all nickel trim, Williams aperture, built to commemorate the 100th anniversary, bronze medallion in stock, 6 lbs. (manufacturer was going to produce 6,086 of these guns, however only 550 were ever made).

	$450	$390	$300

Last Mfg.'s Sug. Retail was $250.

BENJAMIN MODEL 340, 342, AND 347 — BB, .177 or .22 cal., pneumatic pump action, 750-650 FPS, 4½ lbs., (340-BB), (342-.22), (347-.177).

	$100	$80	$65

Last Mfg.'s Sug. Retail was $110.

Add $15 for Williams sight.
Add $30 for 4 x 15 scope.

BENJAMIN SHERIDAN

Manufacturer located in E. Bloomfield, NY.

In 1994 through 1995, after their purchase by Crosman Air Guns, some of the separate lines of the Benjamin and Sheridan airgun companies were merged into one.

PISTOLS

BENJAMIN/SHERIDAN MODEL H/HB —.177, .20, and .22 cal., pneumatic pump action, 400 FPS, 9⅜ in. barrel, available in chrome H or black matte finish HB, walnut grips, 2 lbs. 8 oz. New in 1991.

Mfg.'s Sug. Retail	$115	$100	$85	$70

Add $5 for chrome.
Subtract $10 for CO_2.
Model E/EB is CO_2 version of above.

RIFLES

BENJAMIN SHERIDAN MODEL 392/397 — .177 and .22 cal. (392), CO_2 or pneumatic pump action, 685-800 FPS, 19⅜ in. barrel, available in chrome or black matte finish, walnut stock, 5 lbs. 8 oz. New 1991.

Mfg.'s Sug. Retail	$130	$115	$100	$80

Add $10 for chrome.
Add $25 for Williams peepsight, $5 for .22 cal.
Subtract $10 for CO_2 (600-500 FPS). Denoted with G prefix, or FB9 prefix on .22 cal.

* **Benjamin Model Carbine** — similar to Sheridan Model 392/397, except has shorter carbine barrel. New 1994.

Mfg.'s Sug. Retail	$110	$100	$85	$70

BENJAMIN/SHERIDAN C9PB — .20 cal., pneumatic pump-up, velocity 675 FPS, available with clear-coated brass finish. New 1998 to commemorate Sheridan's 50th Anniversary.

Mfg.'s Sug. Retail	$170	$150	$120	$95

BRNO AERON

Manufactured in Czechoslovakia and imported by Century International Arms, Inc. located in St. Albans, VT and Bohemia Arms, Fountain Valley, CA. Available through dealers.

Grading	100%	98%	95%

PISTOLS

TAU FREE PISTOL — .177 cal., CO_2 powered professional target model, attaché case, extra seals and counter weight.

No Mfg.'s Retail	**$260**	**$225**	**$180**

RIFLES

TAU-200 — .177 cal., CO_2 powered professional target model, synthetic adj. stock.

No Mfg.'s Retail	**$210**	**$185**	**$150**

BROLIN ARMS, INC.

Manufacturer/importer located in La Verne, CA.

RIFLES

SM 1000 — .177 or .22 cal., side lever action, 1,100/900 FPS. adj. front and rear sights, match barrel, automatic safety, Monte Carlo beech stock, $9\frac{1}{8}$ lbs.

Mfg.'s Sug. Retail	**$200**	**$155**	**$130**	**$115**

Add $20 for checkered stock.
Add $50 for adjustable butt plate.

COLT MANUFACTURING COMPANY, INC., Hartford, CT.

While other airgun manufacturers try to make pistols that look like Colt semi-automatics, these first ever Colt air pistols are exact copies of the famous Model 1911 A1. With the size and weight of a Colt semi-auto firearm, five versions are available including a special 160th Anniversary model. Many of the same precision options offered for the cartridge pistols are available for the airguns including a barrel compensator, competition tuning set with speed hammer, rapid release double thumb safety, beavertail grip safety, competition grip with thumb guard, competition backstrap, competition sights, and Colt Serendipity SL heads-up sighting scope. All five models are pre-drilled for the Serendipity SL. One of the most unerring non-target CO_2 pistols made, the Model 1911 A1 was accuracy tested for a $1\frac{1}{4}$ in. group at 30 ft.

MODEL 1911 A1 — .177 cal., CO_2 powered semi-automatic, 8 shot cylinder magazine, 393 FPS, single and double action. Post front sight, adjustable rear, trigger safety, grip safety. Weight 2.38 lbs., 5 in. rifled barrel, standard finish black with checkered black plastic grips.

Mfg.'s Sug. Retail	**$199**	**$175**	**$140**	**$110**

Add $10 for silver finish.
Add $59 for compensator.
Add $37 for wood grips.
Add $47 for three-piece rubber competition grip.
Add $19 for competition backstrap.
Add $118 for competition tuning set.
Add $51 for target sights.
Add $492 for Serendipity SL.

160th ANNIVERSARY MODEL 1911 A1 — .177 cal., CO_2 powered semi-automatic, 8 shot cylinder magazine, 393 FPS, single and double action. Post front sight, adjustable rear, trigger safety, grip safety. Weight 2.38 lbs., 5 in. rifled barrel, polished black finish with checkered white grips. Slide factory engraved with Colt 160th Anniversary banner, Colt logo, and floral scrollwork.

Mfg.'s Sug. Retail	**$299**	**$270**	**$210**	**$165**

CROSMAN AIR GUNS

Current manufacturer located in East Bloomfield, NY.

Other than the continued closeout sale of the Model 84 and Skanaker, Crosman has dropped adult precision Airguns. The Crosman/Anschütz models listed below should be watched for collectors value due to their limited U.S. distribution using Crosman model numbers. Available both through dealers and factory direct.

AIR-GUNS

Grading	100%	98%	95%

PISTOLS

CB40/C40 CROSMAN 75TH ANNIVERSARY COMMEMORATIVE — .177 cal., CB40 CO_2 pistol. Styled after the S&W Model 745 semi-automatic, the zinc alloy frame CB40 delivers 8 shots at 430 FPS with the heft and feel of an actual handgun. New 1998. Available in black or silver finish. New 1999, CB40LS and C40LS, same as above but with laser sight.

Mfg.'s Sug. Retail   **$110**   **$99**   **$75**   **$60**
    Add $15 for silver finish
    Add $30 for CB40LS or C40LS

SKANAKER PISTOL MODEL 88 — .177 cal., CO_2 powered, 550 FPS, professional target model. Mfg. 1987-Disc.

                                    $395   **$320**   **$275**
                                    Last Mfg.'s Sug. Retail was $795.

    Add $65 for carrying case.

    As of Dec. 31, 1991 Crosman liquidated its supply of Skanaker pistols. This was due to the expiration of a contract allowing them to use the Skanaker name. All remaining pistols were sold to Air Rifle Specialists, Elmira, NY.

RIFLES

MODEL 84 AIR RIFLE — .177 cal., CO_2 powered, match rifle, 0-720 FPS fully adj. sights, walnut stock with adj. cheekpiece and butt plate, 11 lbs. Disc. 1992.

                                    $800   **$450**   **$360**
                                    Last Mfg.'s Sug. Retail was $1,295.

    Crosman Model 84 was the first U.S. made air rifle designed to compete with established European models. Unlike its competitors, it is CO_2 powered with a digital gauge mounted on the forearm to show remaining pressure.

6500 (ANSCHÜTZ MODEL 335) — .177 cal., barrel-cocking action, 700 FPS, $18\frac{1}{2}$ in. barrel, 7 lbs. $10\frac{1}{2}$ oz. Disc. in 1989.

                                    $190   **$140**   **$100**
                                    Last Mfg.'s Sug. Retail was $200.

6300 (ANSCHÜTZ MODEL 333) — .177 cal., barrel-cocking action, 700 FPS, $18\frac{1}{2}$ in. barrel, 6 lbs. 13 oz. Disc. in 1989.

                                    $180   **$125**   **$90**
                                    Last Mfg.'s Sug. Retail was $175.

MODEL 6100 (MADE BY DIANAWERK) — .177 cal., barrel-cocking action, 780/830 FPS, $20\frac{1}{2}$ in. barrel, 8 lbs. 6 oz. Disc. in 1989.

                                    $165   **$130**   **$95**
                                    Last Mfg.'s Sug. Retail was $235.

CROSSMAN 75TH ANNIVERSARY COMMEMORATIVE — .22 cal., pneumatic pump-up, velocity 595 FPS. Model 2200W is Crosman's famous .22 cal. air rifle fitted with a handcrafted stock and forearm of American walnut. New 1998.

Mfg.'s Sug. Retail   **$100**   **$90**   **$70**   **$55**

C Z

Manufacturer located in Uhersky Brod, Czechoslovakia. Currently imported by Compasseco, Inc., Bradstown, KY.

PISTOLS

CZ-3 (SLAVIA TEX 3) — .177 cal., barrel-cocking action, 400 FPS, $7\frac{1}{2}$ in. barrel. Adjustable sights, plastic stock.

Mfg.'s Sug. Retail   **$100**   **$85**   **$70**   **$60**

RIFLES

CZ-77 (SLAVIA 630) — .177 cal., barrel-cocking action, 700 FPS, 21 in. barrel, adjustable sights, wood stock.

Mfg.'s Sug. Retail   **$150**   **$90**   **$75**   **$60**
    Add $50 for checkered stock on Lux or plastic stock on Lux B (Salvia 631).

Grading	100%	98%	95%

CZ-BB — .177/BB cal., bolt action, military training gun, mfg. circa 1947 for Czech Army. New in box, collectors item.

| Mfg.'s Sug. Retail | $235 | $200 | $170 | $135 |

DAISY MANUFACTURING CO., INC.

Manufactured and distributed in Rogers, AR.

Even though Daisy is one of the largest airgun manufacturers in the world, only six models fall into the category of adult precision airguns - these are the Daisy 126 El Gamo, Model 128 Gamo Olympic, Model 953, Model 753, and their 2 target pistols (Models 747 and 777). The Daisy 126 El Gamo rifle and Model 128 Gamo Olympic are manufactured in Spain and assembled in the U.S. All six airguns have barrels made by Lothar Walther. Available through dealers only.

PISTOLS

MODEL 118 DAISY TARGETEER — #6 lead shot, (Daisy copper-coated #6 in metal tube), indoor shooting gallery air pistol, all metal construction, fixed rear sight circa 1939, (also produced with an adjustable rear sight c. 1950), blued finish or nickel plated, (nickel circa 1950) .45 ACP semi-auto style and operation w/slide action cocking. Some models came complete with a plastic shooting gallery trap with spinning targets. Vintage Daisy air pistol, extremely rare w/complete shooting gallery set.

$150   **$120**   **$90**

Add $250 for gun w/shooting gallery set in mint condition

MODEL 747 TARGET PISTOL — .177 cal., side-lever action, single stroke pneumatic, 360 FPS, Lothar Walther rifled barrel, adjustable trigger, left or right-hand grips available, 3 lbs. 2 oz.

$140   **$85**   **$65**

MODEL 777 TARGET PISTOL — .177 cal., side-lever action, single stroke pneumatic, 360 FPS, wood target style grips, 3 lbs. 3 oz. Disc. 1997

$215   **$175**   **$130**

MODEL 91 — .177 cal., CO_2 powered, 425 FPS, 10¼ in. barrel, imported from Hungary, 2 lbs. 7 oz. Introduced 1991. Disc. 1997.

$415   **$360**   **$280**

This was being imported by Daisy as an entry level professional target pistol, similar in design to Feinwerkbau or Crosman's Skanaker pistol.

AIR-GUNS

RED RYDER COLLECTIBLES

Editor's Note: Secondary collector's market prices have increased over the past few years and the marked step up in values is reflected for the first time in the 20th Edition on premium Red Ryder Collectibles such as the Christmas Story model, the Les Kouba, and most vintage Daisy air rifles produced from 1940-41 through the 1950s. Availability on certain limited edition or vintage models is virtually nil, and retail prices are established by the last gun sold in 100% condition.

MODEL 111-40-1 — BB cal., mfg. 1940-41, 1,000 shot lever action repeater, copper plated forearm and barrel bands, wood stock and forearm, saddle ring w/leather thong, Red Ryder brand burned into left side of stock, cast iron lever, small screw through top of stock, adj, rear sight. The most famous BB gun ever made.

$300   **$255**   **$200**

MODEL 111-40-2 — BB cal., mfg. 1946, barrel bands either prick pinched or welded into place, wood stock and forearm, logo burned into left side of stock, cast iron lever (blued), either small original size screw or larger screw through the top of stock, fixed rear sight.

$200   **$170**   **$130**

MODEL 111-40-3 — BB cal., mfg. 1946-52, blued barrel bands, wood stock and forearm, no logo, aluminum lever painted black, fixed sights.

$100   **$70**   **$50**

MODEL 111-40-4 — BB cal., mfg. 1952, wood stock and plastic forearm logo stamped on left side of stock, black painted cast aluminum lever, fixed sights. Plastic forearms tend to warp.

$80   **$65**   **$50**

Grading	100%	98%	95%

MODEL 111-40-5 — BB cal., mfg. 1952-1954, plastic stock and forearm, logo molded into left side of stock, aluminum lever painted black, first use of serial numbers (Dec. 1952), adj. rear sight.

$80 $65 $50

MODEL 111-40-6 — BB cal., mfg. 1954, plastic stock and forearm, logo molded into left side of stock, blue painted finish, painted aluminum lever, adj. rear sight.

$85 $70 $55

MODEL 94-#7 — BB cal., mfg. 1955, plastic stock and forearm, gold (paint) embossed long horn and logo on left side of stock, dummy hammer on stock w/leather boot, bright finish forearm band, high front sight, combo peep or open rear sight, blue paint finish.

$80 $65 $50

MODEL 965-55-#8 — cork ball shooter, mfg. 1955, similar to Model 94-#7 above but with lower front sight, rear sight part of spring anchor, gold (paint) embossed logo on left side of stock, brown cloth sling, blue paint finish.

$80 $75 $70

MODEL 1938-#9 — BB cal., mfg. 1972-78, similar to Model 111-40, wood stock and forearm, logo stamped on left side of stock, narrow barrel bands, saddle ring staple does not go completely through side of receiver, blue paint finish, screws are slotted. Survival rate on these later toy models is very slim due to excessive use. Examples in 100% condition are extremely rare.

$70 $60 $45

MODEL 1938-#10 — BB cal., mfg. 1978, similar to Model 1938-#9 but with logo on right side of stock, screws are now Phillips head.

$25 $20 $15

MODEL 1938 A-B-#11 — BB cal., mfg. 1978, model marked 1938 A-B in gold paint on right side of receiver, loading gate on left side of barrel near muzzle, no muzzle band, plastic saddle ring staple, fake loading tube, plastic front sight and muzzle plug, trigger safety, hole in left side of receiver.

$110 $100 $90

MODEL 1938-B-#12 — BB cal., mfg. 1980, same as Model 1938 A-B-#11 but w/no hole on left side of receiver, stamped 1938-B.

$35 $30 $25

MODEL 1938 B-#13 CHRISTMAS STORY RED RYDER — BB cal., mfg. 1983, manufactured due to interest in the film "The Christmas Story", same as standard "B" Model, but with large compass and sundial on left side of stock. An example in 100% condition must be unopened in original cellophane wrapped display box. To complete a Christmas Story set collectors also need a movie poster, the movie, and the small cardboard stand up display card. Note: Due to the popularity of this model there are counterfeit Christmas Story BB guns in circulation.

$250 $200 $150

Values equal with small compass.

BUFFALO BILL 150th ANNIVERSARY MODEL — .BB cal., Winchester Model 94 style rifle with wood stock, wood forend, gold style coin in stock. Limited to 2,500 examples. Mfg. 1996 to 1997.

$175 $150 $120

MODEL 1938-#15 POPGUN — BB cal., mfg 1982-83, scaled down model for young shooters, plastic stock, forearm, and saddle ring, thong on right side of receiver, Red Ryder marked in gold on right.

$35 $30 $25

MODEL 1938-#16 — BB cal., mfg. 1988, same as Model 1938-#15 Popgun but with wood stock and forearm.

$35 $30 $25

MODEL 1938B-#17 — BB cal., mfg. 1988, 50th Anniversary Model, STD "B" Model, but with walnut stock and forearm, brass medallion on right side of stock, 50 year warranty.

$55 $50 $45

MODEL 1938B-#18 — BB cal., mfg. 1989, standard "B" model, but with copper medallion on right side of stock, came with reproduction of first Red Ryder comic book.

$80 $70 $55

Subtract $20 without comic book.

AIR-GUNS

Grading	100%	98%	95%

MODEL 1938B-#19 — BB cal., mfg. 1990, standard "B" model, but with extra fancy American walnut stock and forearm, gold forearm band, gold medallion on right side of stock showing a boy with his first Red Ryder, stamped "Limited Edition", filled with gold paint, plastic lever, walnut look wall rack in box, brass plaque, and with Les C. Kouba print in cardboard tube marked with the same number as the air rifle. Series numbers were from 1 to 2500. The first 250 prints are artist proofed and hand signed on the lower left side. Note: There are counterfeit Les Kouba posters and guns circulating which were not produced by Daisy. Consult with a serious collector before making a purchase as prices are extremely high for this model.

$275 $250 $225

Add 50% for guns in the first 250 w/artist's proofed and signed print.

MODEL 1938B DUCKS UNLIMITED #20 — BB cal., mfg. 1991, special edition for Ducks Unlimited, walnut stock, right side of receiver stamped Limited Edition filled with gold paint, walnut look rack with brass plaque.

$120 $100 $80

MODEL 1938B NRA COMMEMORATIVE #21 — BB cal., mfg. 1994, special NRA commemorative.

$80 $75 $65

MODEL 950-#22 — double barrel cork gun, mfg. 1955, break open cocking, double triggers, light colored plastic stock and forearm, circular logo molded into left side of stock, barrels painted blue (some gold).

$60 $55 $50

MODEL 1938B PARTRIDGE UNLIMITED #23 — BB cal., mfg. 1994, special Partridge Unlimited limited edition.

$110 $100 $90

MODEL 1938 "DIAMOND ANNIVERSARY" COMMEMORATIVE RED RYDER — BB cal., mfg. 1998 to celebrate the 60th anniversary of the introduction of the Red Ryder BB gun. Limited Edition white scroll on the receiver, burnished forearm band, and special lariat logo in the stock.

No. Mfg.'s Sug. Retail $65 $35 $25

MODEL 25 CENTENNIAL PUMP GUN — BB cal., mfg. 1986 only, to celebrate 100 years of Daisy production, walnut stock, bronze medallion on left side of stock. 100% is NIB price.

$200 $160 $125

MODEL 111-B AMERICAN YOUTH — BB cal., limited to 1,000 examples, wood stock, die-cast cocking lever, stock laser engraved with the logo of a young boy proud to hold his first Daisy air rifle. Each rifle has the production number stamped in the butt of the stock. Gold silk screened words "American Youth" inscribed on the receiver. Gun comes with a color print of an "American Youth" Bill of Rights. This is the lowest number of guns Daisy has ever produced in their collector series. Daisy discovered 1,000 die-cast cocking levers in an old warehouse, and used them to produce this limited edition. Prior to the "American Youth" Daisy had not made an air rifle with a die-cast cocking lever in 25 years. Mfg. 1998.

$200 $160 $125

GOLD RUSH COMMEMORATIVE — BB cal., limited to 2,500 examples mfg. to commemorate the 150th anniversary of the California Gold Rush. This unique gun does not have a Model number, only the words Gold Rush stamped on the top of the gold-painted barrel. The stock and forearm are rich walnut with a natural finish. Counter sunk in the stock is a 1-in. gold-colored medallion with a prospector panning for gold. The forearm is laser engraved with the gun's production number.

No Mfg.'s Retail $125 $100   N/A

AIR-GUNS

VINTAGE DAISY MODELS

1888 DAISY 1ST MODEL — BB cal., single-shot, Mfg. by Plymouth Iron Windmill Co. Brass tubing barrel and air chamber, cast brass frame, wire skeleton stock, nickel plated post front sight, V-notch rear sight integral with cocking lever. Marked Daisy. Plymouth, Michigan. Not more than 1,000 were made. Very rare.

$3,500 $2,800 $2,000

Grading	100%	98%	95%

1890 DAISY 2ND MODEL — BB cal., single-shot, break open design, Mfg. by Plymouth Iron Windmill Co. Brass tubing barrel and air chamber, cast iron frame, wire skeleton stock, nickel plated post front sight, V-notch rear sight integral with breech. Frame marked Daisy Imp'D Pat' May 6, 90. Not more than 50,000 manufactured from 1890 to 1900. Rare.

$1,850 $1,450 $1,150

1891 DAISY 3RD MODEL — BB cal., single-shot, break open design, Mfg. by Plymouth Iron Windmill Co. Brass tubing barrel and air chamber, cast iron frame, wire skeleton stock with wood insert. Gun was nickel plated, post front sight, V-notch rear sight. Frame marked Daisy Pat. May 9, 90, July 14, 91. This was the last cast iron frame Daisy. Not more than 60,000 manufactured from 1891 to 1897. Rare.

$1,500 $1,200 $950

1892 DAISY 4th MODEL — BB cal., single-shot, break open design. Mfg. by Plymouth Iron Windmill Co. Sheet metal barrel, air chamber, frame, cast iron trigger guard, nickel plated finish, walnut stock with peep crescent butt. Features first removable shot tube w/latch behind cast front sight. Peep rear sight. Flat side frame marked Daisy (between bulls eyes), left side. Patent August 13, 1889, July 14, 91, Jan 21, 92 on right side. Manufactured until 1901. Very scarce.

$800 $640 $500

1934 No. 103 BUZZ BARTON SPECIAL — BB cal., 1,000 shot lever action repeater. This is a Markham/King design based upon the King No. 55. It has a straight barrel and plunger housing with a patch shoulder underneath. Cast iron lever, walnut stock with the brand Buzz Barton Special No. 195 inside lariat with two cowboys. This gun is blued. Manufactured from 1934 to 1936. Scarce.

$375 $300 $240

1934 BUZZ BARTON SUPER SPECIAL — BB cal., 1,000 shot lever action repeater on a No. 3 Model B frame. This gun is easy to recognize by the rear sight tube, bright nickel plate and star-shaped Buzz Barton brand in the stock. Scarce.

$425 $340 $270

1936 GOLDEN EAGLE — BB cal., produced to commemorate the 50th anniversary of Daisy. Special copper-plated model, basically a No. 195 Buzz Barton with pistol grip stock and curved lever, Daisy's first. This gun can be easily identified with its black painted stock with a red, white, and blue federal eagle decal, and sight tube mounted on top of gun. Hooded front sight. Originally sold for $2.34 by Sears Roebuck & Co. in 1937. Manufactured from 1936 to 1940. Very scarce.

$500 $425 $340

1940 No. 104 DOUBLE BARREL — BB cal., 96 shot break open double barrel force feed repeater. All sheet metal design consisting of side by side break action with double triggers and shot tubes of a No. 25 type. Dummy side locks, blued, walnut stock and stamped engraved with game birds, dogs, and scrolls. Manufactured from 1940 to 1941. Note original guns are marked L and R on the shot tubes.

$1,500 $1,200 $950

RIFLES

EL GAMO 126 SUPER MATCH TARGET RIFLE — .177 cal., single stroke pneumatic, 590 FPS, adj. sights, hardwood stock, 10 lbs. 9 oz. Disc. 1994.

$470 $400 $300

Last Mfg.'s Sug. Retail was $765.

MODEL 128 GAMO OLYMPIC — similar to El Gamo 126 Super Match Target, except with adj. cheekpiece and butt plate, high quality European diopter sight.

$440 $375 $300

Last Mfg.'s Sug. Retail was $735.

MODEL 130 — .177 cal., barrel-cocking action, 800 FPS, adjustable micrometer sight, 5¾ lbs. Disc. 1993.

$100 $80 $65

Last Mfg.'s Sug. Retail was $150.

MODEL 131 — .177 cal., barrel-cocking action, 630 FPS, adjustable micrometer sight 5 lbs. 6 oz.

Mfg.'s Sug. Retail $120 $75 $60 $50

Grading	100%	98%	95%

MODEL 753 COMPETITION — .177 cal., single stroke pneumatic, 480 FPS, competition sights, hardwood stock, high cheek piece, adjustable trigger, Lothar Walther rifled barrel, 6 lbs. 8 oz.

Mfg.'s Sug. Retail	$355	$250	$210	$160

MODEL 853 TARGET — .177 cal., single stroke pneumatic, 480 FPS, Lothar Walther barrel, adj. sights, 5 lbs. 8 oz.

Mfg.'s Sug. Retail	$225	$140	$120	$95

MODEL 853C TARGET — .177 cal., similar to Model 853 Target, except has 5 shot mag.

No Mfg.'s Retail	$185	$150	$120

MODEL 1000 — .177 cal., barrel cocking action, 1,000 FPS., adj. rear with hooded front sight, hardwood Monte Carlo stock, 6⅛ lbs. New 1997.

Mfg.'s Sug. Retail	$215	$135	$115	$90

MODEL 1170 — .177 cal., barrel-cocking action, 800 FPS, adjustable micrometer sight, 5½ lbs.

Mfg.'s Sug. Retail	$140	$85	$70	$55

DIANAWERK, MAYER AND GRAMMELSPACHER

Current manufacturer located in Rastaff Germany.

Dynamit Nobel RWS Inc. is the exclusive Dianawerk importer located in Closter, NJ. Available both from dealer and importer direct. Dynamit Nobel RWS, Inc. is also importing airguns manufactured by Air Arms, BSA, and Gamo. Please refer to their respective listings under this section for pricing.

PISTOLS

MODEL C-225 — .177 cal., CO_2 action, 385 FPS., 4 or 6 in. barrel, semi-automatic, single or double action, 8 shot rotary clip, styled after a modern handgun, interchangeable barrels for 4 or 6 in. shooting, adj. rear sight, black or nickel finish.

Mfg.'s Sug. Retail	$210	$175	$150	$120

Add $10 for nickel finish.
Add $25 for 6 in. barrel nickel model.

MODEL 5G/GS — .177 or .22 cal., barrel-cocking action, 450/300 FPS, 7 in. barrel, (sport) 2 lbs. 12 oz. GS Model equipped w/factory scope.

Mfg.'s Sug. Retail	$260	$200	$170	$135

Add $70 for GS.
Add $10 for GN with matte nickel plating.

MODEL 6G/6M/6GS — .177 cal., barrel-cocking action, 450 FPS , 7 in. barrel, (professional target), 3 lbs. GS Model (Disc. 1995) equipped with factory scope.

* 6G

Mfg.'s Sug. Retail	$445	$340	$290	$230

* 6M

Mfg.'s Sug. Retail	$620	$475	$405	$325

Add $70 for GS model.
Add $45 for left-hand.

MODEL C-357 — .177 ca., CO_2 revolver, 380 FPS, 8 shot cylinder, 6 in. rifled barrel. Styled after S&W 357 Mag. revolver. Has look and feel of a large frame pistol. New 1998.

Mfg.'s Sug. Retail	$170	$150	$115	$90

MODEL 10 — .177 cal., barrel-cocking action, 450 FPS, 7 in. barrel, (professional target), 3 lbs. 4 oz.

	$350	$280	$235

Last Mfg.'s Sug. Retail was $670.

Add $50 for cased model.
Add $40 for left-hand.

RWS MODEL CP-7 — .177 cal. match/sport single shot, CO_2 refillable from tank or 12 gram capsule, 425 FPS, adjustable rear sight, adjustable trigger, adjustable counter weight, 10.24 in. barrel, 2.31 lbs. Complete w/ hard case and accessories. New 1999.

Mfg.'s Sug. Retail	$450	$345	N/A	N/A

AIR-GUNS

RWS MODEL CP-96 — .177 cal. match grade five-shot, CO_2 refillable from tank or 12 gram capsule, 425 FPS, adjustable rear sight, adjustable trigger, adjustable barrel weight, adjustable pistol grip, 8.27 in. Lothar Walther barrel, 2.23 lbs. Complete w/UIT regulations for international match shooting. Can be used either single or multi-shot. New 1999.

Mfg.'s Sug. Retail $635	$490	N/A	N/A

RIFLES

MODEL 24 — .177 or .22 cal., barrel-cocking action, 700/400 FPS, $17\frac{1}{4}$ in. barrel, 6 lbs. New 1987.

Mfg.'s Sug. Retail $215	$150	$130	$105

Subtract $25 for Model 24J.

MODEL 25D — .177 or .22 cal., barrel-cocking action, 525/380 FPS, $15\frac{3}{4}$ in. barrel, $5\frac{3}{4}$ lbs. (sport). Disc. 1987.

$120	$95	$70

Last Mfg.'s Sug. Retail was $120.

MODEL 26 — .177 or .22 cal., barrel-cocking action, 750/500 FPS, $17\frac{1}{4}$ in. barrel, 6 lbs. 1 oz. Disc. 1992.

$185	$150	$100

Last Mfg.'s Sug. Retail was $195.

MODEL 27 — .177 or .22 cal., barrel-cocking action, 550/415 FPS, $17\frac{1}{4}$ in. barrel, 6 lbs. (sport). Disc. 1987.

$175	$135	$110

Last Mfg.'s Sug. Retail was $150.

MODEL 28 — .177 or .22 cal., barrel-cocking action, 750/500 FPS, $15\frac{3}{4}$ in. barrel, 6 lbs. 12 oz. Disc. 1992.

$150	$125	$100

Last Mfg.'s Sug. Retail was $205.

MODEL 30 — 4.4mm (RWS #7) round ball, original European gallery gun action, 17 in. barrel, $7\frac{1}{4}$ lbs., limited production piece. Mfg. 1993-Disc.

$695	$580	$450

Last Mfg.'s Sug. Retail was $1,025.

MODEL 34 — .177 or .22 cal., barrel-cocking action, 1000/800 FPS, $19\frac{1}{2}$ in. barrel, 7 lbs. 8 oz. Model 34C Carbine $15\frac{1}{2}$ in. barrel, 7 lbs.

Mfg.'s Sug. Retail $290	$220	$190	$150

Add $10 for 100 year Diana Commemorative Model, new in 1990.
Add $60 for matte nickel finish.
Add $220 for matte black finish and 4 x 32 airgun scope.

MODEL 35 — .177 or .22 cal., barrel-cocking action, 665/540 FPS, 19 in. barrel, 8 lbs. (sport/target). Disc. 1987.

$120	$95	$80

Last Mfg.'s Sug. Retail was $160.

MODEL 36 AND 36 CARBINE — .177 or .22 cal., barrel-cocking action, 1000/800 FPS, $19\frac{1}{2}$ in. barrel (Carbine $15\frac{1}{2}$ in. barrel), 8 lbs.

Mfg.'s Sug. Retail $435	$335	$285	$230

Add $40 for new S Model w/scope.
Subtract $10 for muzzle brake model without factory sights.

MODEL 38 — .177 or .22 cal., barrel-cocking action, 1000/700 FPS, $19\frac{1}{2}$ in. barrel, 8 lbs., walnut stock.

$275	$205	$145

Last Mfg.'s Sug. Retail was $345.

Model 38 is the deluxe version of the Model 36.

MODEL 45 S/45 DELUXE — .177 or .22 cal., (.22 Disc. 1997), barrel-cocking action, 1000/800 FPS, $19\frac{1}{2}$ in. barrel, 6 lbs., S Model equipped w/factory sling and scope.

Mfg.'s Sug. Retail $350	$270	$230	$185

Add $40 for deluxe.
Add $70 for S model with scope.

Grading	100%	98%	95%

MODEL 46 — .177 or .22 cal., underlever cocking action, 950/780 FPS, 18 in. barrel, 8.2 lbs. On the RWS drawing board for four years the Model 46 combines underlever cocking with a flip up loading port that provides easy loading while allowing the pellet to be inserted directly into the rifled barrel for pin point accuracy. Automatic safety, adjustable trigger, extended scope rail, Monte Carlo stock with checkered forearm and grip, recoil pad. New 1998.

Mfg.'s Sug. Retail	$470	$360	$305	$245

Subtract $40 for Model 46E standard stock with recoil pad.

MODEL 48/48SV — .177, .22 or .25 (new 1994) cal., side-lever action, 1,100/900 FPS, 17 in. barrel, 8½ lbs. Model 48SV same as above but with sports stock and adjustable cheek piece.

Mfg.'s Sug. Retail	$510	$390	$330	$265

Add $25 for .25 cal.
Add $25 for black matte finish (48B). New 1995.

MODEL 50T/T01 — .177, .22, or .25 cal., under-lever action, 745/600 FPS, 18½ in. barrel, 8 lbs., (sport/target), parkerized finish. Disc. 1988.

	$260	$210	$165

Last Mfg.'s Sug. Retail was $210.

Add $20 for blue finish.
Add $100 for T01 Model.

MODEL 52 — .177, .22, or .25 cal., side-lever action, 1,100/900 FPS, 17 in. barrel, walnut-stained beech Monte Carlo stock, detailed checkering on forend, and pistol grip, ventilated rubber butt plate, 8½ lbs.

Mfg.'s Sug. Retail	$565	$433	$370	$295

Add $245 for Deluxe version with handcrafted walnut stock, patterned checkering on forend and pistol grip, ornamental black wood insert in forend and base of pistol grip.
Add $40 for .25 cal.

MODEL 54 — .177 or .22 cal., side-lever, recoilless action, 1100/900 FPS, 17 in. barrel, match type trigger safety catch w/additional cocking guard, adjustable front and rear sights, beechwood Monte Carlo stock with rubber butt plate, hand-checkered forend and pistol grip, 9 lbs.

Mfg.'s Sug. Retail	$785	$600	$510	$405

MODEL 70 — .177 cal., barrel-cocking action, 450 FPS, 13½ in. barrel. This is a junior sized adult air rifle.

	$130	$105	$85

Last Mfg.'s Sug. Retail was $190.

MODEL 72 — .177 cal., similar to Model 70, but with recoilless action. Disc. 1994.

	$205	$160	$130

Last Mfg.'s Sug. Retail was $340.

MODEL 75S TO 1 MATCH AIR RIFLE — .177 cal., side-lever action, 580 FPS, 19 in. barrel (professional target), micrometer-adjustable rear sights, adjustable cheek piece, adjustable recoil pad, 11 lbs. Model 75 HV and Model 75 U disc. in 1989. Model K disc. 1990.

Mfg.'s Sug. Retail	$1,745	$1,340	$1,140	$910

Add $90 for left-hand.

MODEL 100 — .177 cal., single stroke pneumatic, 580 FPS, 19 in. barrel, adj. cheekpiece, professional target model, 11 lbs. CA 100 new 1989. Disc. 1998.

	$1,020	$800	$640

Last Mfg.'s Sug. Retail was $1,950.

MODEL CA 100 — .177 cal., precharged pneumatic, 22 in. barrel, diopter sight, match trigger, adjustable laminated stock, 11 lbs. 6 oz. Professional target model. Disc. 1998.

	$1,400	$1,315	$1,070

Last Mfg.'s Sug. Retail was $2,200.

Add $100 for left-hand.

MODEL CA 200 TARGET RIFLE — .177 cal., precharged pneumatic, 22 in. barrel, adjustable rear sight, hooded front sight, match trigger, laminated stock w/adjustable cheek piece, adjustable recoil pad, 11 lbs. 6 oz. Professional target model. Also listed as CR 200 in some catalogs. Available in RH or LH versions.

Mfg.'s Sug. Retail	$570	$350	$300	$240

AIR-GUNS

Grading	100%	98%	95%

MODEL 1000 — .177 cal., barrel-cocking action, unique colored plastic stocks (black, red, blue, white, and yellow). Disc. 1991.

$160 $135 $100

Last Mfg.'s Sug. Retail was $215.

Model 1000 is the sport model of the standard Model 34.

RWS CA-707 COMPRESSED AIR RIFLE — .22 cal., lever action, 8-shot repeater or side-loading single shot, 1,200 FPS at high-power setting, 3-position power setting, built-in pressure gauge to monitor remaining shots, 23 in. barrel (16 in. on Carbine model), 7.75 lbs. (Carbine 7 lbs.), Western-style straight heel stock, high-gloss blued finish, Indonesian walnut stock with checkered forearm and hand grip. New RWS Model 1999.

Mfg.'s Sug. Retail $730 $560   N/A   N/A

RWS CA-715 COMPRESSED AIR RIFLE — .22 cal., bolt action, single-shot, CO_2 refillable from tank or 12 gram capsule, 1,200 FPS, 20 in. barrel, open rear sight fully adjustable, hooded front sight with post, Indonesian walnut stock with rubber butt plate, raised cheek piece, hand checkered hand grip, 6.5 lbs. Comes with ten rechargeable cartridges, pellet seater, cartridge holder to refill cartridge with air. Adaptor available to use scuba tank or pump. New RWS Model 1999.

Mfg.'s Sug. Retail $685 $500   N/A   N/A

ENSIGN ARMS CO., LTD.

Previous international distributors for Saxby Palmer Airguns located in Newbury, England. Available only on the used market.

Ensign Arms previously distributed the Saxby Palmer line of airguns into the U.S. Please refer to the Saxby Palmer section for these guns. Ensign designated models were trademarked by Ensign Arms Co., Ltd. Marksman Products was the importer until 1988 located in Huntington Beach, CA.

F.A.S.

Previously imported by Beeman until 1988. Last distributed by Nygord Products, located in Prescott, AZ. Manufactured in Italy. No Current U.S. distributor. Only available used.

PISTOLS

FAS 604 — .177 cal., top lever single stroke, pneumatic action.

$300 $265 $195

Last Mfg.'s Sug. Retail was $495.

FAS 606 — .177 cal., top lever single stroke, pneumatic action, 7½ in. barrel, professional target model, walnut grips, 2 lbs. 3 oz. Disc. 1994.

$475 $390 $310

Last Mfg.'s Sug. Retail was $995.

F.E.G.

Formerly imported by K.B.I. INC. (formerly Kassnar Imports). Model GPM also imported as Daisy Model 91. Manufactured in Hungary. Available through dealers and used market.

PISTOLS

MODEL GPM-01 — .177 cal., CO_2 cartridge or cylinder charge, 425 FPS, 10¼ in. barrel, 2 lbs. 7 oz.

Mfg.'s Sug. Retail $525 $415 $360 $280

RIFLES

CLG-462 — .177 or .22 cal., CO_2 cartridge or cylinder charge, 490-410 FPS, 16½ in. barrel, (24 in. .22 cal.), 5 lbs. 8 oz.

$400 $350 $270

Last Mfg.'s Sug. Retail was $550.

CLG-468 — .177 or .22 cal., CO_2 cartridge or cylinder charge, 705-525 FPS, 26¾ in. barrel, 5 lbs. 12 oz.

$450 $380 $300

Last Mfg.'s Sug. Retail was $600.

AIR-
GUNS

Grading	100%	98%	95%

FAMAS

Imported by Century International Arms, Inc., St. Albans, VT.

RIFLES

FAMAS AIR RIFLE — .177 cal., CO_2 action, copy of French made MAS .223 semi-automatic, used for military training, true semi-auto clip fed air rifle.

No Mfg.'s Sug. Retail	$235	$195	$160

FEINWERKBAU

Manufactured in Oberndorf, Germany. Imported and distributed by Beeman Precision Airguns located in Huntington Beach, CA. Available through dealers and Beeman direct.

Feinwerkbau has been responsible for developing many of the current technical innovations used in fabricating target Air Pistols and Rifles. In 1992, Feinwerkbau Airguns swept the Olympic competition in this newly formed Olympic sport. Feinwerkbau has always been a leader in Airgun technology.

PISTOLS

MODEL 65 MK I AND II — .177 cal., side-lever action, 525 FPS, 2.6-2.9 lbs., short barrel is Mark II.

Mfg.'s Sug. Retail	$1,170	$1,050	$865	$605

Add $50 for left-hand or $45 for adj. grips.

MODEL 80 — .177 cal., side-lever action, 475-525 FPS, 2.8-3.2 lbs. Disc. in 1983. (Like Model 65 with stacking barrel weights and fine mechanical trigger).

	$825	$695	$535

Last Mfg.'s Sug. Retail was $625.

MODEL 90 — specifications same as above but with electronic trigger. Disc. 1990.

	$775	$650	$525

Last Mfg.'s Sug. Retail was $1,155.

Add $45 for short barrel.
Add $50 for left-hand.

MODEL 100 — .177 cal., pneumatic action, 460 FPS, 2½ lbs. Disc. 1992.

	$700	$600	$450

Last Mfg.'s Sug. Retail was $1,100.

Add $40 for left-hand variation.

MODEL 102 — new version of Model 100 (1992).

	$1,200	$1,090	$825

Last Mfg.'s Sug. Retail was $1,555.

Add $50 for left-hand variation.

MODEL 103 — new version of Model 102.

Mfg.'s Sug. Retail	$1,520	$1,325	$1,100	$900

Add $60 for left-hand variation.

MODEL C2 — .177 cal., CO_2 cylinder, 425-525 FPS, 2½ lbs. Disc. 1989.

	$550	$450	$350

Last Mfg.'s Sug. Retail was $780.

Add $50 for left-hand, deduct $20 for mini.

MODEL C5 — .177 cal., CO_2 powered 5 shot rapid fire, 7⅓ in. barrel, 510 FPS, 2 lbs. 6 oz. Disc. approx. 1993.

	$1,170	$850	$650

Last Mfg.'s Sug. Retail was $1,350.

Add $60 for left-hand.

MODEL C 10 — .177 cal., CO_2 cartridge, 510 FPS, 2½ lbs. Disc. 1990.

	$725	$595	$395

Last Mfg.'s Sug. Retail was $965.

Add $60 for left-hand model.

AIR-GUNS

Grading	100%	98%	95%

MODEL C20 — .177 cal., CO_2 powered, 510 FPS, 2 lbs. 8 oz. (replacement for the C2 and C10 new in 1991). Disc. 1995.

$850 $725 $550

Last Mfg.'s Sug. Retail was $1,160.

Add $50 for left-hand model.

MODEL C25 — .177 cal., CO_2 powered, 510 FPS, unique CO_2 ball placed directly below action (instead of standard long CO_2 cylinder), 2½ lbs.

$1,235 $1,020 $810

Last Mfg.'s Sug. Retail was $1,325.

Add $60 for left-hand.

MODEL C55 — .177 cal., CO_2 powered, single shot or 5 shot repeater, 510 FPS, unique CO_2 ball placed directly below action for vertical CO_2 feed, up to 225 shots/fill, 2½ lbs. New 1994.

Mfg.'s Sug. Retail $1,705 $1,495 $1,350 $1,050

Add $50 for left-hand.

MODEL P30 — .177 cal., precharged pneumatic, 515 FPS, adjustable match trigger, stippled walnut match grip, wt. 2.4 lbs.

Mfg.'s Sug. Retail $1,275 $1,145 $975 $780

Add $75 for left-hand.

MODEL P34 — .177 cal., precharged pneumatic, 515 FPS, adjustable match trigger, stippled walnut match grip, wt. 2.4 lbs. Revised version of the P30 with new contoured barrel shroud, new sliding barrel weight system, valve housing reduced in side, removable trigger guard. New 1999.

Mfg.'s Sug. Retail $1,350 $1,215 N/A

Add $45 for left-hand.

RIFLES

MODEL 124 — .177 cal., barrel-cocking action, 780-830 FPS, 7 lbs. 2 oz. Disc. 1989.

$450 $400 $320

Last Mfg.'s Sug. Retail was $490.

Add $600 for factory 5mm (only 3 mfg).
Add $50 for Beeman markings.
Add $65 for deluxe.
Add $175 for factory deluxe with walnut stock.
Add $50 for left-hand deluxe.
Add $495 for custom select.
Add $495 for custom fancy.
Add $550 for custom extra fancy.

MODEL 127 — .22 cal., barrel-cocking action, 620-680 FPS, 6 lbs./7 lbs. 1 oz. Additions same as Model 124. Disc. 1989.

$450 $400 $320

Last Mfg.'s Sug. Retail was $490.

MODEL 300S — .177 cal., side-lever action, 640 FPS, 8.8/10.8 lbs.

Mfg.'s Sug. Retail $1,270 $1,100 $920 $750

Add $425 for Tyrolean stock.
Add $100 for Running Boar stock configuration or Universal Model.
Add $100 for figured walnut. Mini Model rifles are equal.
Add $100 for left-hand (all styles).
Add $50 for barrel sleeve.

MODEL 600 — .177 cal., side-lever action, single stroke pneumatic operation, top-of-the-line match rifle with aperture sights, unique hardwood laminate stock, 585 FPS, 10½ lbs. Disc. 1988.

$900 $800 $700

Last Mfg.'s Sug. Retail was $900.

Add $75 for left-hand.

This model was also available in a Running Boar variation with extra-long barrel cover that unscrews for transporting.

Grading	100%	98%	95%

MODEL 601 — .177 cal., side-lever action single stroke, pneumatic operation, replaces Model 600, 10 lbs. 8 oz. Running Target Model also available.

$1,250 $1,100 $850

Last Mfg.'s Sug. Retail was $1,750.

Add $50 for 5454 diopter sight.
Add $115 for left-hand.

MODEL 602 — .177 cal., side-lever action, single stroke pneumatic operation. Replaces Model 601.

$1,500 $1,260 $1,100

Last Mfg.'s Sug. Retail was $1,875.

Add $115 for left-hand.

MODEL 603 — .177 cal., side lever action, single stroke pneumatic, replaces Model 602.

Mfg.'s Sug. Retail $1,975 $1,750 $1,400 $1,250

Add $150 for left hand.
Add $95 for multi-colored laminated stock.
Subtract $220 for running target model.

MODEL C60 — .177 cal., CO_2 powered, 570 FPS, similar in style to Model 600/601, 9.2 lbs. to 10.6 lbs. Running target model also available.

$1,250 $1,000 $750

Last Mfg.'s Sug. Retail was $1,675.

Add $115 for left-hand.

MODEL C62 — .177 cal., CO_2 powered, specifications same as Model C60. No longer imported by Beeman-S/R Ind., Inc.

$1,550 $1,350 $1,125

Last Mfg.'s Sug. Retail was $1,750.

Add $115 for left-hand.

C60 MINI — .177 cal., CO_2 powered, quick change cylinder (bottle) smaller version of C60 Match Rifle, 7¾ lbs. Mfg. 1991-Disc.

$1,450 $1,295 $975

Last Mfg.'s Sug. Retail was $1,675.

MODEL P70 — .177 cal., lever cocking, compressed air operation (precharged pneumatic), Match Air Rifle, 17 in. barrel, adjustable trigger, velocity 570 FPS, 10.6 lbs., laminated wood stock w/fully adjustable cheekpiece and butt plate, same as Model 603. Listed as Beeman/FWB P70. Available with multi-color laminated stock. New 1998.

Mfg.'s Sug. Retail $1,875 $1,685 $1,325 $1,060

Add $150 for left-hand.
Add $100 for multi-colored stock.

MODEL P70 JUNIOR — .177 cal., lever cocking, compressed air operation (precharged pneumatic), Match Air Rifle, 17 in. barrel, adjustable trigger, velocity 570 FPS, 7.3 lbs., laminated wood stock w/fully adjustable cheekpiece and butt plate, same as P70 but with shorter overall length (40.0 in. vs 42.6 in) and lighter weight. Listed as Beeman/FWB P70 JUNIOR. Available with multi-color laminated stock. New 1998.

Mfg.'s Sug. Retail $1,415 $1,270 N/A

GAMO PRECISION AIRGUNS

Imported by Gamo USA, Corp., Ft. Lauderdale, FL. Previous importers Stoeger Industries, and Dynamit Nobel, RWS, Inc. Some models also sold by Daisy (see Daisy El Gamo 126 and Daisy Model 128 Gamo Olympic). Available through retail dealers.

PISTOLS

AF-10 — .177 cal., pneumatic action, 430 FPS, 7 in. barrel, similar in style to Beeman P-1, 1¼ lbs. Importation disc. 1993.

$75 $60 $45

Last Mfg.'s Sug. Retail was $115.

CENTER — .177 cal., under-barrel lever cocking, 400-435 FPS, 14 in. barrel, 2 lbs. 8 oz.

$90 $75 $55

PR-45 — .177 cal., pneumatic, 9¼ in. barrel, 1 lb. 9 oz., looks similar to a Beeman P1.

$100 $85 $70

Last Mfg.'s Sug. Retail was $135.

Grading	100%	98%	95%

FALCON — .177 cal., under-lever action, 430 FPS, 7 in. barrel. ABS plastic grips, 2⅞ lbs. Importation disc. 1993.

	$70	**$55**	**$40**

Last Mfg.'s Sug. Retail was $105.

COMPACT — .177 cal., single stroke pneumatic, 400 FPS, 9¼ in. rifled steel barrel, adjustable match trigger, fully adjustable rear sight, anatomical walnut grip w/heavy stippling and adjustable palm shelf, 1.94 lbs.

Mfg.'s Sug. Retail	$230	$155	$130	$105

P-23 COMBO LASER — .177 cal., CO_2 powered, 12 BB magazine or single-shot w/pellets, 410 FPS, 4.25 in. rifled steel barrel, 650Nm laser sight mounted under frame, fires double action, manual safety, gun similar in appearance to a Walther PPK, 1.1 lbs.

Mfg.'s Sug. Retail	$130	$85	N/A	N/A

AUTO 45 — .177 cal., CO_2 powered, 12 BB magazine or single-shot w/pellets, 410 FPS, 4.3 in. rifled steel barrel, 1.1 lbs., fires double action, manual safety, similar in appearance to Glock and S&W Model SW40E semi-automatic pistols. New 1999.

Mfg.'s Sug. Retail	$100	$55	N/A	N/A

R77 COMBAT/R77 LASER — .177 cal., revolver, CO_2 powered (12 gram cartridge in grip housing), similar in appearance to N Frame S&W, swing out cylinder holds 8 pellets, 380 FPS (410 FPS w/6 in. barrel), 4 in. rifled steel barrel standard, (optional 2.5 and 6 in. steel barrels), adjustable rear sights, fires single or double action, cross-bolt hammer block safety, oversized combat style santoprene grips. R77 Laser same as 4-in. Combat but with built-in grip-pressure activated 650 Nm beam laser.

Mfg.'s Sug. Retail	$100	$65	N/A	N/A

Add $90 for R77 Combat Laser Model
Add $20 for 6-in. barrel.

RIFLES

CF 20 —.177 and .22 cal., under-lever action, 790-625 FPS, 17¾ in. barrel, checkered stock, 6 lbs. 6 oz. Importation disc. 1993.

	$155	**$125**	**$100**

Last Mfg.'s Sug. Retail was $190.

CADET —.177 cal., barrel-cocking action, 570 FPS, beechwood stock, 5 lbs.

	$70	**$60**	**$50**

CONTEST — .177 cal., side-lever action, 543 FPS, beechwood stock, 10.1 lbs.

	$100	**$80**	**$60**

CUSTOM 600 —.177 or .22 cal., barrel-cocking action, 690 FPS, 17¾ in. barrel, two stage adj. trigger, checkered stock, 6 lbs. 3 oz.

	$130	**$105**	**$80**

Last Mfg.'s Sug. Retail was $170.

DELTA — .177 cal., barrel-cocking action, 525 FPS, 15¾ in. barrel, two stage trigger, automatic safety, adj. sights, plastic stock, 5 lbs. 5 oz.

Mfg.'s Sug. Retail	$90	$50	$40	$30

EUROPIA — .177 cal., side-lever action, 625 FPS, adjustable sights, Monte Carlo stock.

	$165	**$145**	**$115**

EXPO — .177 or .22 cal., barrel-cocking action, 625 FPS, adj. trigger, special sights, 5 lbs. 8 oz. Disc. 1994.

	$80	**$65**	**$50**

Last Mfg.'s Sug. Retail was $130.

EXPO 24 — .177 cal., barrel-cocking action, 560 FPS, 15.7 in. rifled steel barrel with non-glare polymer coating, two-stage trigger, automatic anti-beartrap safety, manual trigger safety, adjustable rear sight, hardwood beech stock w/black ABS butt plate, 4.2 lbs.

Mfg.'s Sug. Retail	$120	$70	$60	$50

EXPOMATIC —.177 cal., repeating barrel-cocking action, 575 FPS, adj. trigger, 5 lbs. 5 oz. Disc. 1997.

	$120	**$100**	**$80**

Last Mfg.'s Sug. Retail was $170.

Grading	100%	98%	95%

EXPO 2000 — .177 cal., barrel-cocking action, 625 FPS, 17 in. barrel, Monte Carlo style stock, 5½ lbs. Mfg. 1992-1994.

	$90	$70	$55

Last Mfg.'s Sug. Retail was $135.

GAMO 68 — .177 or .22 cal., barrel-cocking action, 600 FPS, 6 lbs. 8 oz.

	$80	$65	$50

GAMATIC 85 — .177 cal., barrel-cocking action, 560 FPS, 17¾ in. barrel, two stage trigger, unique loading system for up to 25 pellets, pistol grip stock, 6 lbs. 3 oz.

	$75	$60	$50

Last Mfg.'s Sug. Retail was $160.

G-1200 — .177 cal., CO_2 cylinder, 560 FPS, 17¾ in. barrel, unique pump action loading system for up to 12 pellets (styled like a pump centerfire rifle), 6 lbs. 6 oz.

	$165	$140	$110

Last Mfg.'s Sug. Retail was $185.

HUNTER 440 — .177 cal. or .22 cal., single pump barrel-cocking action, 1,000 FPS, (750 FPS in .22), 18 in. rifled steel barrel, two-stage adjustable trigger, fully adjustable rear sight, raised scope ramp, Monte Carlo style stock w/checkered grip, rubber ventilated butt pad, 6.6 lbs.

Mfg.'s Sug. Retail	$230	$160	$140	$105

HUNTER 890S — .177 cal. or .22 cal., single pump barrel-cocking action, 1,000 FPS, (750 FPS in .22), 18 in. rifled steel barrel with muzzle break, two-stage adjustable trigger, manual safety and automatic anti-beartrap safety, walnut-stained beech Monte Carlo style stock w/checkered grip, rubber ventilated butt pad, includes BSA 3-12 x 44 mm air rifle scope, 7.5 lbs. total weight.

Mfg.'s Sug. Retail	$289	$224	$190	$155

HUNTER 220 — .177 cal. or .22 cal., single pump barrel-cocking action, 1,000 FPS, rifled steel barrel, adjustable barrel-mounted rear sight, hooded front sight, manual cocking and trigger safeties, flat beechwood stock, black butt plate, 6.2 lbs.

Mfg.'s Sug. Retail	$190	$130	$110	$90

YOUNG HUNTER — .177 cal., barrel-cocking action, 640 FPS, 17.7 in. rifled steel barrel, adjustable rear sight, hooded front sight, two-stage adjustable trigger, manual trigger safety, automatic anti-beartrap safety, Monte Carlo style beech stock, ventilated rubber butt pad.

Mfg.'s Sug. Retail	$130	$85	$75	$60

Add $40 for Young Hunter Combo w/4 x 32 scope

CF-30 — .177 cal., single pump under lever cocking, 950 FPS, rifled steel barrel w/scope mount rail, micrometer rear sight w/four position interchangeable windage plate, two-stage trigger, manual cocking and trigger safeties, Monte Carlo style walnut stained beech stock w/checkered grip, ventilated rubber butt pad, 6.4 lbs.

Mfg.'s Sug. Retail	$270	$180	$155	$125

HUNTER 1250 HURRICANE — .177 cal., single pump barrel cocking action, 1,250 FPS, rifled steel barrel with muzzle break, two-stage adjustable trigger, hand-finished walnut stained beech Monte Carlo style stock, checkered grip, ventilated rubber butt pad, 7.5 lbs. With new single pump cocking, Gamo states that the Hurricane is "definitely made for a strong person." New 1999.

Mfg.'s Sug. Retail	$400	$320	N/A	N/A

MAGNUM 2000 — .177 and .22 cal., barrel-cocking action, 820-660 FPS, 17¾ in. barrel, adj. two stage trigger, checkered stock, 7 lbs. 2 oz.

	$165	$140	$110

Last Mfg.'s Sug. Retail was $200.

STINGER — .177 cal., barrel-cocking action, 8-pellet clip, 750 FPS, rifled steel barrel, fully adjustable rear sight, cocking and trigger safeties, Monte Carlo style beech stock, hard rubber butt pad, 6.4 lbs.

Mfg.'s Sug. Retail	$190	$120	$100	$80

SPORTER — .177 cal., barrel-cocking action, 760 FPS, rifled steel barrel with polymer coated finish, adjustable rear sight, hooded front sight, adjustable trigger, cocking and trigger safeties, Monte Carlo style beech stock, ventilated rubber butt pad, 5.5 lbs.

Mfg.'s Sug. Retail	$160	$95	$80	$65

SUPER — .177 cal., side-lever action, 593 FPS, 10 lbs. 8 oz.

	$140	$120	$100

AIR-GUNS

Grading	100%	98%	95%

TROOPER RD CARBINE — .177 cal., barrel-cocking action, 560 FPS, rifled steel barrel with polymer coated finish, muzzle break, two stage trigger, manual safety, automatic anti-beartrap safety, black synthetic stock w/cheekpiece and checkered grip, 5.3 lbs. Comes w/Gamo Red Dot sight.

Mfg.'s Sug. Retail	$120	$65	$55	$45

TWIN — .177 and .22 cal., barrel-cocking action, 675 FPS. Adjustable sights, unique barrel insert tubes to change from .177 to .22 cal., hardwood stock.

No Mfg.'s Sug. Retail		$165	$140	$110

GUN POWER

Manufacturer located in Ashford, Kent, England. Distributed in the United States by AirForce, Ft. Worth, TX.

Gun Power only offers one model, the Stealth, although one is enough since it is a modular design and can take on many different configurations with accessories. The refillable compressed air cylinder is the shoulder stock and is removable without loss of air allowing the rifle to be broken down into its component parts and reassembled in the field. The base module, (frame and 12 in. barrel), air cylinder/stock, scope and accessories store in a laptop bag. This is one of the most innovative new models to come out of the U.K. American production will also begin in 1999.

RIFLES

STEALTH — .22 cal., compressed air bottle, refillable by tank or pump, 300 shots per fill, 600-900 FPS, three dovetail mounts for accessories and scope, black anodized finish, (optional camouflage kit), 12 in. barrel, optional 18 inch barrel, bipod, silencer, 5.4 pounds (gun and bottle). New 1998

Mfg.'s Sug. Retail	$500	$395	N/A	N/A

HAENEL

Sold by Cape Outfitters, FL.

Unfortunately, no specifications were available at time of printing. The following models were old models imported by Cape Outfitters. Previously imported by G.S.I. located in Trussville, AL.

RIFLES

KI 101 (MLG 550) — .177 cal., match rifle. Importation disc. 1993.

	$350	$310	$255

Last Mfg.'s Sug. Retail was $695.

KI 102 (ML 311) — .177 cal. match rifle. Importation disc. 1993.

	$195	$170	$145

Last Mfg.'s Sug. Retail was $395.

KI 103 (ML308-8) — .177 cal. match rifle. Importation disc. 1993.

	$145	$125	$95

Last Mfg.'s Sug. Retail was $300.

KI 104 (310-4) — .177 cal. Importation disc. 1993.

	$110	$95	$75

Last Mfg.'s Sug. Retail was $200.

KI 105 (303-4) — BB cal., BB clip fed. Importation disc. 1993.

	$100	$85	$65

Last Mfg.'s Sug. Retail was $190.

KI 106 (85) — .177 cal. Importation disc. 1993.

	$80	$70	$50

Last Mfg.'s Sug. Retail was $130.

HÄMMERLI

Imported by Mandall Shooting Supplies, Inc. located in Scottsdale, AZ. Available through dealers and importer direct.

Hammerli Airguns listed below are not mfg. by SIG in Switzerland, but rather subcontracted to other airgun manufacturers (including El Gamo), these models (403 and 420) are German made. Prices may increase or decrease based on the value of the dollar on international markets. There are several older models of Swiss-made Hammerli air rifles and pistols which sell on the collector market from $800 to $1600.

PISTOLS

MODEL 480 — .177 cal., precharged pneumatic or CO_2 (can use both systems), adj. grips, professional target sights and trigger, up to 320 shots per full compressed air tank, approx. $2\frac{1}{4}$ lbs. New 1994. Disc. by Mandall in 1999.

$900   **$700**   **$650**

Last Mfg.'s Sug. Retail was $1,355

Add $145 for walnut grips.

RIFLES

MODEL 403 — .177 cal., side-lever action, 700 FPS, adj. sight target model, $9\frac{1}{4}$ lbs.

$285   **$240**   **$165**

Last Mfg.'s Sug. Retail was $400.

MODEL 420 — .177 cal., side-lever action, 700 FPS, military style plastic stock, $7\frac{1}{2}$ lbs.

$215   **$180**   **$105**

Last Mfg.'s Sug. Retail was $300.

MODEL 450 — .177 cal., top lever pneumatic action, adj. target sight and cheekpiece, professional target model. Importation began 1994.

Mfg.'s Sug. Retail   **$1,400**   **$1,230**   **$1,020**   **$795**

Add $40 for walnut stock.

IZH

Manufactured at Baikal/Izhevsk factory Russia. Imported by European American Armory, Sharpes, FL. and Big Bear Arms, Dallas, TX. Available through retail dealers. The quality of these medium-priced competition airguns improves each year. Three new models join the IZH line this year, the MP-532, MP-513 and IZH-32BK.

PISTOLS

IZH-46M AIR PISTOL — .177 cal., under lever single stroke pneumatic, 440 FPS, micrometer fully adjustable rear target sight, adjustable international target grip, five-way adjustable trigger, hammer forged rifled 11.2 in. barrel, 2 lbs. 8 oz. New model at a lower SRP. This gun is a bargain.

Mfg.'s Sug. Retail   **$270**   **$200**   **N/A**   **N/A**

RIFLES

KATYA IZH-60 — .177 cal., barrel-cocking action, 460 FPS, 16 $\frac{1}{2}$ in. barrel, telescoping stock, 5 lbs. 6 oz.

Mfg.'s Sug. Retail   **$140**   **$100**   **$90**   **$70**

MP-532 — .177 cal., side cocking lever pneumatic, 460 FPS, fully adjustable rear sight, hooded front sight, adjustable butt pad, five-way adjustable trigger, 15.75 in. barrel, 9.26 lbs. Based on the IZH-46 action. New 1999.

Mfg.'s Sug. Retail   **$550**   **$420**   **N/A**   **N/A**

IZH-32BK — .177 cal., side cocking mechanism, 541 FPS, integral rail for scope mount, adjustable butt pad, adjustable cheek piece, five-way adjustable trigger, walnut stock, 11.68 in. barrel, 12.13 lbs. Designed for the 10 meter running target competition. New 1999.

Mfg.'s Sug. Retail   **$1,014**   **$780**   **N/A**   **N/A**

IZH MP-513 — .22 cal., barrel cocking mechanism, 820 FPS, integral rail for scope mount, adjustable sights, beech stock, 15.75 in. barrel, 6.39 lbs. New 1999.

Mfg.'s Sug. Retail   **$235**   **$180**   **N/A**   **N/A**

INDUSTRY BRAND

Manufactured in Shanghai, China. Imported by Compasseco, Bradstown, KY. Beginning in 1996, the finish on these guns was improved dramatically.

AIR-GUNS

Grading	100%	98%	95%

PISTOLS

TECH FORCE SS2 — .177 sidelever action, 520 FPS., recoilless action, comes with carrying case, match adj. trigger, 2¾ lbs.

Mfg.'s Sug. Retail	$295	$225	$190	$150

RIFLES

BS-4 OLYMPIC — .177 cal., 640 FPS, side-lever action, diopter sight, stippled stock, professional target model, 11 lbs.

Mfg.'s Sug. Retail	$699	$375	$320	$255

QB-25 (TECH FORCE 25) — .177 cal., barrel cocking action, 1,000 FPS., trigger safety, Monte Carlo stock, 7½ lbs.

Mfg.'s Sug. Retail	$145	$90	$75	$55

QB-36 (TECH FORCE 36) — .177 cal., under-lever cocking action, 900 FPS, 19½ in. barrel, Monte Carlo beech stock, 8½ lbs.

Mfg.'s Sug. Retail	$90	$60	$50	$40

TECH FORCE 56 — .177 cal., underlever cocking, 800 FPS, side folding stock, safety. New 1999.

Mfg.'s Sug. Retail	$110	$60	N/A	N/A

QB-78 (TECH FORCE 78) — .177 cal., CO_2 powered, 600 FPS, bolt action, 20½ in. barrel, wood stock, adjustable trigger. 5 lbs. 12 oz.

Mfg.'s Sug. Retail	$90	$50	$40	$30

QB-88 (TECH FORCE 88) — .177 cal., side-lever action, 850 FPS, 19½ in. barrel, adjustable sights, safety, 7½ lbs.

Mfg.'s Sug. Retail	$90	$50	$40	$30

TECH FORCE 89 — .177 cal., side-lever spring piston action in a true Bullpup configuration, extending butt plate, 600 FPS, 25 in. overall length. New 1999.

Mfg.'s Sug. Retail	$120	$90	N/A	N/A

TECH FORCE 97 — .177 cal., .22 cal., underlever cocking, 900 FPS, 700 FPS, 19½ in. barrel, adjustable sights, grooved receiver for scope mounting, automatic reset trigger safety, oil finished Monte Carlo stock with recoil pad, 7½ lbs. New 1999.

Mfg.'s Sug. Retail	$100	$70	N/A	N/A

MARKSMAN

Division of S/R Industries, located in Huntington Beach, CA. Available both through dealers and Marksman direct.

RIFLES

JUNIOR MODEL 28 — .177 cal., barrel-cocking action, 600 FPS, 16¾ in. barrel, 6 lbs. Mfg. for Marksman by Weihrauch.

	$180	$155	$120

Last Mfg.'s Sug. Retail was $225.

MODEL 29/30 — .177 or .22 cal., barrel-cocking action, 800/625 FPS, 18½ in. barrel, 6 lbs. Mfg. for Marksman by BSA. Disc. 1991.

	$175	$135	$85

Last Mfg.'s Sug. Retail was $200.

MODEL 40 — .177 cal., barrel-cocking action, 720 FPS, 18⅜ in. barrel, 7 lbs. 5 oz.

	$200	$175	$135

Last Mfg.'s Sug. Retail was $250.

MODEL 45 — .177 cal., barrel-cocking action, 900-930 FPS, 19⅛ in. barrel, 7 lbs. 3 oz. New 1993.

	$170	$135	$115

Last Mfg.'s Sug. Retail was $195.

MODEL 55 (RIFLE) & 59 CARBINE — .177 cal., barrel-cocking action, 925 FPS, 19¾ (rifle) or 14 (carbine) in. barrel, 7 lbs. 8 oz. Mfg. for Marksman by Weihrauch, using B.S.F. tooling. See B.S.F.

	$250	$215	$160

Last Mfg.'s Sug. Retail was $300.

Grading	100%	98%	95%

MODEL 56/56K — .177 cal., barrel-cocking action, 925 FPS, 19⅝ in. barrel, adj. cheekpiece and trigger, 8 lbs. 11 oz.

No Mfg.'s Retail **$325** **$295** **$225**

Add $180 for 56K Model with Marksman Model 6941 scope.

The Model 56/56K was manufactured for Marksman by Weihrauch, using B.S.F. tooling.

MODEL 58/58K —.177 cal., barrel-cocking action, 925 FPS, 16 in. heavy bull barrel, adj. trigger, designed for silhouette shooting, 8 lbs. 8 oz. Importation disc. 1993.

$300 **$230** **$180**

Last Mfg.'s Sug. Retail was $390.

Add $180 for 58K Model with Marksman Model 6941 scope.

The Model 58/58K was manufactured for Marksman by Weihrauch, using B.S.F. tooling.

MODEL 60/61 CARBINE — .177 cal., under-lever cocking action, 810-840 FPS, 8 lbs. 12 oz.

$400 **$350** **$270**

Last Mfg.'s Sug. Retail was $490.

Modified version of HW77 by Weihrauch manufactured for Marksman using B.S.F. tooling.

MODEL 70 — .177, .20, or .22 cal., barrel-cocking action, 925/760 FPS, 19¾ in. barrel, 8 lbs.

$290 **$255** **$185**

Last Mfg.'s Sug. Retail was $355.

Add $10 for .20 cal.

Mfg. for Marksman by Weihrauch using B.S.F. tooling.

MODEL 72 — .177, .20, or .22 cal., barrel-cocking action. Similar to Model 70.

Mfg.'s Sug. Retail **$345** **$310** **$240** **$195**

Mfg. for Marksman by Weihrauch using B.S.F. tooling.

MAUSER

Mauser Airguns are subcontracted under license to use the Mauser trademark and are not manufactured by Mauser-Werke. Previously imported and distributed by Marksman located in Huntington Beach, CA. Available through dealers and the used market.

PISTOLS

U90/U91 JUMBO AIR PISTOLS — .177 cal., barrel-cocking action, 260 FPS, 2 lbs.

$75 **$60** **$45**

Last Mfg.'s Sug. Retail was $100.

Add $15 for deluxe model U91 with adj. sights and checkered grips.

This model was mfg. by Record.

RIFLES

MATCH 300SL/SLC — .177 cal., under-lever action, 550/450 FPS, adj. sights and hardwood stock, 8 lbs. 8 oz.

$200 **$165** **$120**

Last Mfg.'s Sug. Retail was $330.

Add $75 for SLC Model with diopter sights.

This model is mfg. in Hungary.

MORINI

Manufacturer located in Switzerland. Imported and distributed since 1993 by Nygord Precision Products located in Prescott, AZ. Dealer direct.

PISTOLS

162E — .177 cal., precharged pneumatic, professional target pistol with target sights, adj. grips.

$825 **$600** **$450**

Last Mfg.'s Sug. Retail was $1,000.

162EA — .177 cal., replacement to Model 162E, now with interchangeable cylinders.

Mfg.'s Sug. Retail **$1,095** **$800** **$600** **$375**

MODEL 162M — .177 cal., similar to Model 162EA but with mechanical trigger.

Mfg.'s Sug. Retail **$1,070** **$785** **$585** **$375**

AIR-GUNS

Grading	100%	98%	95%

NORICA

Previously imported by KBI (Kassnar) Imports located in Harrisburg, PA and American Arms, Inc. located in North Kansas City, MO, and by S.A.E. located in Miami, FL.

Norica airguns imported by American Arms, Inc. will appear under the American Arms, Inc. heading in this text.

Even though the dollar has fallen on international markets, the current lack of an importer has caused prices to remain flat. Available on used market only.

PISTOLS

MODEL 47 — .177 cal., side-lever action, 600 FPS, unique black pistol grip handle, 5½ lbs.
    No Mfg.'s Retail $130 $90 $65

MODEL 61C — .177 cal., barrel-cocking action, 600 FPS, 5 lbs. 8 oz.
    No Mfg.'s Retail $95 $70 $50

MODEL 73 — .177 or .22 cal., barrel-cocking action, 580/525 FPS, 6 lbs. 4 oz.
    No Mfg.'s Retail $120 $90 $60

MODEL 80G — .177 or .22 cal., barrel-cocking action, 635/570 FPS, 7 lbs. 2 oz.
    No Mfg.'s Retail $150 $120 $80

MODEL 90 — .177 cal., barrel-cocking action, 650 FPS, factory equipped with scope.
    No Sug. Retail $140 $100 $75

MODEL 92 — .177 cal., side-lever action, 650 FPS, 5¾ lbs.
    No Mfg.'s Retail $135 $100 $70

NORICA YOUNG — .177 cal., barrel-cocking action, 600 FPS, unique colored stock.
    No Mfg.'s Retail $90 $65 $40

BLACK WIDOW — .177 or .22 cal., barrel-cocking action, 500/450 FPS, unique black plastic stock, 5 lbs.
    No Mfg.'s Retail $130 $90 $60

PARDINI PISTOLS

Previously imported by MCS. Inc., currently imported by Nygord Precision Products, located in Prescott, AZ.

PISTOLS

MODEL K-2 — .177 cal., CO_2 powered, professional target model.
    Mfg.'s Sug. Retail $925 $700 $650 $450

MODEL K-2S — similar to Model K-2, except is precharged.
    Mfg.'s Sug. Retail $950 $825 $725 $550

MODEL K58 — .177 cal., under-lever pneumatic, 9 in. barrel, 2 lbs. 6 oz., professional target model.
    Mfg.'s Sug. Retail $695 $605 $500 $405

MODEL K60 — .177 cal., CO_2 cylinder charge, 9½ in. barrel, 2 lbs. 4 oz. Disc. 1997.
     $675 $550 $440
    Last Mfg.'s Sug. Retail was $795.

MODEL K90 — .177 cal. CO_2 powered junior model, 7¼ in. barrel, 1⅞ lbs.
     $460 $390 $300
    Last Mfg.'s Sug. Retail was $580.

MODEL P10 — .177 cal., under-lever pneumatic, 7¾ in. barrel, 2 lbs. 3 oz.. Disc. 1990.
     $450 $360 $300
    Last Mfg.'s Sug. Retail was $560.

PARK RIFLE COMPANY

Manufacturer located in Kent, England.

No current importer exists for these guns. However, enough guns have been sold directly to this market to warrant listing in this section. For more information contact Park Rifle Company at Unit 68A, Dartford Trade Park, Powder Mill Lane, Dartford, Kent England DA 1 1NX.

AIR-GUNS

Grading	100%	98%	95%

RIFLES

RH93 (93W & 93-800) — .177 or .22 cal., under-lever cocking action, 12ft./lbs power, 37 in. barrel (38 on Model 93-800). 9 lbs. 10 oz.

Mfg.'s Sug. Retail	$500	$400	$350	$275

    Add $100 for thumbhole walnut stock.
    Estimate $80 freight cost added to each gun purchased.

R W S

Importers located in Closter, NJ. See Dianawerk (earlier in this text).

SAVAGE ARMS

Manufacturer/Importer located in Westfield, MA. A century-old manufacturer of rifles and shotguns (more than 200 different models since 1895), Savage brings its expertise to air rifles in 1999 with four sporting models in .177 caliber.

RIFLES

1000GXP — .177 cal., barrel break action with anti-bear trap mechanism, two stage adjustable trigger with manual safety adjustable rear sight, hooded front sight, receiver grooved for scope (4 x 32 scope and rings included), 18 in. barrel, velocity 1000 FPS, 7.5 lbs., walnut stained hardwood stock with ventilated rubber recoil pad. New 1999.

Mfg.'s Sug. Retail	$203	$160	N/A	N/A

1000G — .177 cal., same as Model 1000GXP without scope and rings, 7.1 lbs. New 1999.

Mfg.'s Sug. Retail	$181	$140	N/A	N/A

600FXP — .177 cal., barrel break action 25-shot repeater with tubular magazine, two stage trigger with manual safety, adjustable rear sight, hooded front sight, receiver grooved for scope (2.5 x 20 scope and rings included), 18 in. rifled steel barrel, velocity 600 FPS, 6.5 lbs., black polymer stock with lacquer finish and rubber recoil pad. New 1999.

Mfg.'s Sug. Retail	$133	$105	N/A	N/A

600F — .177 cal., same as Model 600FXP without scope and rings, 6 lbs. New 1999.

Mfg.'s Sug. Retail	$126	$100	N/A	N/A

560F — .177 cal., barrel break action, two stage trigger with manual safety, adjustable rear sight, receiver grooved for scope mount, 18 in. rifled steel barrel, velocity 560 FPS, 5.5 lbs., black polymer stock with metallic finish. New 1999.

Mfg.'s Sug. Retail	$92	$73	N/A	N/A

S G S (SPORTING GUNS SELECTION)

Previously imported by Kendell International. Available on the used market only.

RIFLES

DUO 300AP — .177 or .22 cal., top cocking action, 455/430 FPS.

	$150	$115	$70

DUO 300AR — .177 or .22 cal., top cocking action, 455/430 FPS, with extra stock and barrel assembly to create a 3-in-1 gun.

	$195	$135	$85

SAXBY PALMER

Manufactured by Saxby Palmer located in Stratford-Upon-Avon, England. Previously imported/distributed by Marksman Products located in Huntington Beach, CA. Available on used market only.

Saxby Palmer has developed the world's first cartridge loading air rifle. This is not a CO_2 or other type of compressed gas gun. The cartridges are pressurized (2250 PSI) and reusable, facilitating speed of loading and much greater velocities. New rifles are supplied with the table pump (for reloading brass or plastic cartridges) and 10 cartridges. You must have these accessories in order to operate air rifles or pistols. Deduct 50% for used guns without these accessories.

AIR-GUNS

Grading	100%	98%	95%

REVOLVERS: DISCONTINUED

ORION AIR REVOLVER — .177 cal., 6 shot, compressed gas cartridges (reusable), 550 FPS, 6 in. barrel, 2 lbs. 3 oz. Disc. 1988.

$375 $285 $225

> This model was manufactured by Weihrauch of Germany and included a Slim Jim pump and 12 reusable cartridges. It also came with a 30 grain 38 cal. zinc pellet to allow cartridges to be used in a .38 Special pistol for practice.

MODEL 54 — .177 cal., 5 shot, compressed gas cartridges (reusable), 4 in. barrel, 1 lb. 5 oz. Disc. 1988.

$175 $125 $90

> This model was manufactured by Weihrauch of Germany and included a Slim Jim pump and 12 reusable cartridges.

RIFLES

ENSIGN ELITE — .177 or .22 cal., bolt action cartridge, 1000-800 FPS auto safety.

$200 $150 $120

Last Mfg.'s Sug. Retail was $175.

ENSIGN ROYAL — .177 or .22 cal., bolt action cartridge, 1000-800 FPS auto safety, walnut stock.

$185 $145 $110

Last Mfg.'s Sug. Retail was $275.

GALAXY — .177 or .22 cal., bolt action cartridge, 1,000/800 FPS, auto safety, walnut stain, hardwood stock 6½ lbs.

$155 $120 $95

SATURN — .177 or .22 cal., bolt action cartridge, 1,000/800 FPS, auto safety, hi-strength black polymer stock 6½ lbs. Disc. 1987.

$150 $115 $90

Last Mfg.'s Sug. Retail was $175.

SHARP

Previously manufactured in Japan and imported by Beeman. Available on the used market only.

RIFLES

SHARP INNOVA — .177 or .22 cal., pneumatic pump action, 920/720 FPS, 4 lbs. 6 oz. Disc. 1988.

$150 $125 $85

Last Mfg.'s Sug. Retail was $175.

SHARP ACE — .177 or .22 cal., pneumatic pump action, 920/750 FPS, 6 lbs. 4 oz. Disc. 1988.

$230 $195 $150

Last Mfg.'s Sug. Retail was $295.

SHERIDAN

Manufactured by Benjamin Air Rifle Co. located in East Bloomfield, NY. Available through dealers and Benjamin-Sheridan direct.

PISTOLS

SHERIDAN AIR PISTOL

* **Model E** — .177, .20, or .22 cal., CO_2 cartridge, 400 FPS, 6⅜ in. barrel, 2 lbs. 4 oz.

$90 $75 $60

Add $40 for paint pellet pistol.

RIFLES

SHERIDAN BLUE STREAK/SILVER STREAK — .20 cal., pneumatic pump or CO_2 action, 700 FPS, 6 lbs.

Mfg.'s Sug. Retail	$150	$130	$110	$85

AIR-GUNS

Grading	100%	98%	95%

Add $10 for Silver Streak.
Add $25 for Williams sight.
Add $30 for 4 x 15 scope.
Add $25 for paint pellet rifle.
Subtract $25 for CO_2.

SMITH & WESSON, Springfield, MA.

After a 15-year absence, Smith & Wesson returns to the airgun market in 1999 with two new CO_2 revolvers offering the heft and feel of an N Frame cartridge-firing pistol. The new .177 caliber models feature fully adjustable black blade rear sight and partridge front sight, and come drilled and tapped for mounting a Weaver style base, or a dedicated base for a red dot optical sight. The CO_2 cylinder is located inside the backstrap frame, which is accessible by removing the left stock, thus preserving the integrity of the S&W grip design. Adding another touch of authenticity, the modified S&W-style cylinder swings out to accept a 10-round rotary magazine, and the guns can be fired either single or double action. The new Model 586 (blue) and 686 (nickel) are available with interchangeable four, six, and eight-inch barrels. These new entries mark the second series of airguns to be offered by Smith & Wesson. From 1970 to 1984, S&W offered a series of air pistols and air rifles manufactured to their specifications for distribution in the U.S. The pistols, styled after the Model 41, were the Model 78G in .22 caliber and 79G in .177 caliber. Two rifles were also offered, the Model 77A, a pump action in .22 caliber, and the Model 80, a CO_2-powered repeating BB gun. Most of these early models trade for around $100 today with a few selling for $125 to $175. The original prices were $35 for the CO_2 pistols and rifle, and $42.50 for the pump action .22 rifle.

REVOLVERS

MODEL 586 — .177 cal., CO_2 powered revolver, 10 shot cylinder magazine, 450 FPS, single and double action. Weight 40 oz. (four-inch barrel), 44 oz. (six-inch barrel), 48 oz. (eight-inch barrel), high-gloss blue finish, checkered black plastic grips. Standard with four-inch barrel.

Mfg.'s Sug. Retail	$200	$135	N/A	N/A

Add $30 for six-inch barrel.
Add $50 for eight-inch barrel.

MODEL 686 — .177 cal., CO_2 powered revolver, 10 shot cylinder magazine, 450 FPS, single and double action. Weight 40 oz. (four-inch barrel), 44 oz. (six-inch barrel), 48 oz. (eight-inch barrel), satin nickel finish, checkered black plastic grips. Standard with four-inch barrel.

Mfg.'s Sug. Retail	$230	$160	N/A	N/A

Add $30 for six-inch barrel.
Add $60 for eight-inch barrel.

STERLING

Manufactured by Benjamin Air Rifle Company located in East Bloomfield, NY. In 1994, after being purchased by Crosman Air Guns, manufacture of the Sterling line was discontinued.

RIFLES

HR 81 —.177, .20, .22 cal., under-lever cocking action, 700/660 FPS, adj. V type rear sight, 8½ lbs.

	$250	$200	$155

Last Mfg.'s Sug. Retail was $250.

Add $50 for original English markings..
Add $10 for .22 cal.

HR 83 —.177, .20 or .22 cal., under-lever cocking action, 700/660 FPS, adj. Williams (FP) peep sight, walnut stock, 8½ lbs.

	$275	$240	$195

Last Mfg.'s Sug. Retail was $300.

Add $50 for original English markings.
Add $5 for .22 cal.

AIR-GUNS

STEYR

Manufactured by Steyr in Austria. Current importer PCE, Ltd., (Pilkintgton Competition Equipment), Monteagle, TN. Previously imported and distributed by Nygord Precision Products, located in Prescott, AZ. Available through dealers and importer direct.

PISTOLS

LP-1 — .177 cal., CO_2 powered match pistol with compensator, 15 $\frac{1}{3}$ in. overall, 2 lbs. 8 oz.

> **Mfg.'s Sug. Retail**   **$1,195**   **$930**   **$835**   **$630**
>
> Add $80 for colored tank variations (red, blue, green, or silver - marked LP1-C).
>
> Precharged pneumatic LP-1P version now at same retail price as LP-1.
>
> Limited Edition of 250 engraved and signed Barbara Mandrell LP-1 USA Shooting Team models in red, white and blue, complete with lined walnut presentation case and certificate of authenticity, $1750.

LP-5 — .177 cal., CO_2 powered match pistol, 5 shot semi-automatic.

> **Mfg.'s Sug. Retail**   **$1,295**   **$1,1300**   **$925**   **$645**
>
> Precharged pneumatic model LP-5P (new 1997) now at same retail price as LP-5.

RIFLES

LG-1/LG1P (compressed air) — .177 cal., single stroke pneumatic cocking, professional target model with micrometer sight and adj. stock. LG-1P same but with compressed air. LG-1 Disc. 1998.

> **Mfg.'s Sug. Retail**   **$1,295**   **$1,100**   **$900**   **$720**

MODEL LG-10 — .177 cal., similar to LG-1 with stabilizer and distinctive anodized red frame.

> **Mfg.'s Sug. Retail**   **$1,395**   **$1,250**   **$975**   **$780**
>
> Subtract $100 for LG-10P precharged pneumatic model.

MATCH 91 — .177 cal., CO_2 powered match rifle with precision receiver sight and adj. butt plate. Mfg. 1988-1995.

>   **$1,250**   **$1,000**   **$600**
>
> Last Mfg.'s Sug. Retail was $1,400.
>
> Add $50 for left-hand.
> Add $100 for Running Target.

THEOBEN ENGINEERING

Manufacturer located in England. Previously imported by Air Rifle Specialists located in Elmira, NY. Available both dealer and importer direct.

Beeman Precision Airguns, Inc. began importing Theoben manufactured rifles in 1992. These guns differ enough from standard Theoben arms that they are listed in the Beeman section of this text.

Add $100 for Theoben pump applicable for some models listed below.

RIFLES

The importation of Theoben rifles was discontinued during 1993.

SIROCCO COUNTRYMAN — .177 or .22 cal., Anschütz barrel break action, 1,100/800 FPS, unique precharged sealed gas spring replaces the metal main springs used in most spring piston air rifles, not to be confused with a gas powered (CO_2) air rifle, includes scope rings, barrel weight, walnut stained beechwood stock, 7$\frac{1}{2}$ lbs. Importation disc. 1987.

>   **$360**   **$285**   **$225**
>
> Last Mfg.'s Sug. Retail was $585.

SIROCCO DELUXE — similar to Countryman, except has hand checkered walnut stock. Importation disc. 1987.

>   **$540**   **$395**   **$245**
>
> Last Mfg.'s Sug. Retail was $650.

AIR-GUNS

Grading	100%	98%	95%

SIROCCO CLASSIC — similar to Sirocco Deluxe, except has updated floating inertia system in piston chamber and auto safety, variable power, 900/1100 FPS. New 1987.

       $565   **$465**   **$385**

Last Mfg.'s Sug. Retail was $830.

    Add $60 for left-hand.

    This model was available with either a choked or unchoked Anschütz barrel as standard equipment.

SIROCCO GRAND PRIX — similar specifications to the Sirocco Classic, except has checkered walnut thumbhole stock.

       $655   **$565**   **$430**

Last Mfg.'s Sug. Retail was $940.

    Add $60 for left-hand.

    Subtract 50% for older models without safety and new piston design.

    In 1987, this model was updated with a floating inertia system in piston chamber, auto safety, and variable power.

    This model was available with either a choked or unchoked Anschütz barrel as standard equipment.

ELIMINATOR — .177 or .22 cal., barrel-cocking action, 1100/1400 FPS, variable power, deluxe checkered thumb hole stock with cheekpiece and pad 9½ lbs.

       $900   **$490**   **$410**

Last Mfg.'s Sug. Retail was $1,500.

    Add $60 for left-hand.

    This model incorporated an improved barrel design featuring pronounced rifling for the higher velocity pellets.

IMPERATOR — .22 cal., under-lever action, 750 FPS, variable power, walnut hand checkered stock, auto safety. New 1989.

       $900   **$525**   **$420**

Last Mfg.'s Sug. Retail was $1,500.

IMPERATOR SLR 88 — similar to above but with a 7 shot mag. Very limited importation.

    $1,200   **$900**   **$650**

Last Mfg.'s Sug. Retail was $1,680.

RAPID 7 — .22 cal. precharged pneumatic, variable power, 19 in. Anschütz barrel, stippled walnut stock, unique 7 shot bolt action design, cylinder charge lasts 160 shots, 6¾ lbs.

    $1,210   **$900**   **$670**

Last Mfg.'s Sug. Retail was $1,300.

    Add $60 for left-hand.

    Add $120 for scuba tank adaptor.

AIR-GUNS

UMAREX SPORTWAFFEN GMBH & CO. KG

Manufacturer for Trademark air guns sold under the Walther, Colt, and Smith & Wesson names.

    Located in Arnsberg, Germany. Umarex models are the most authentic in appearance to actual cartridge-firing semi-automatic pistols and revolvers. Umarex does not sell directly to the general market and the various models produced are listed under their respective Trademark names. See Colt, Smith & Wesson, and Walther airgun sections.

VENOM ARMS CUSTOM GUNS

Manufacturer/Customizer located in the United Kingdom.

    Venom Arms specializes in customizing Weihrauch firearms manufactured in Germany. A quick review of their latest pricing schedule for custom guns indicate prices may run nearly 100% over the initial cost of the uncustomized gun (see Weihrauch).

WALTHER

Manufacturer located in Ulm, Germany. Imported by Champion's Choice, located in La Vergne, TN. Rifles and pistols previously imported by Interarms located in Alexandria, VA. Available through dealers or direct from Champion's Choice.

    Retail prices on Walther Precision Air Pistols have come down in the past year by as much as $300. Retail prices may, however, vary by dealer.

Grading	100%	98%	95%

PISTOLS

CP88 — .177 cal., CO_2 action, 4 or 6 in. barrel, 8 shot mag. comes in blue or nickel finish.
No Mfg.'s Retail   **$165**   **$135**   **$115**

Add $10 for nickel finish
Add $10 for 6 in. barrel.
Add $20 for wood grips, compensator.
Add $10 blue.
Add$20 nickel.

CPM-1 — .177 cal., CO_2 powered professional target model. New 1993.
No Mfg.'s Retail   **$850**   **$725**   **$580**

CP-2 — .177 cal., CO_2 powered, 9 in. barrel, $2\frac{1}{2}$ lbs, professional target model. Disc. 1990.
                    $650   **$500**   **$400**
Last Mfg.'s Sug. Retail was $850.

CP-3 — .177 cal., CO_2 powered, professional target model. Importation disc. 1993.
                    $700   **$595**   **$475**
Last Mfg.'s Sug. Retail was $1,360.

CP-5 — .177 cal., CO_2 powered, professional target model. Disc. 1992.
                    $750   **$640**   **$510**
Last Mfg.'s Sug. Retail was $1,650.

LP 3 — .177 cal., single stroke pneumatic action, 405 FPS, 2.8-3.0 lbs.
                    $595   **$515**   **$400**

Add $65 for shaped barrel rather than round.
Add $100 for fitted case.
Add $60 for match grade.

LP 53 — .177 cal.
                    $450   **$340**   **$230**

Add $95 for blued receiver.
Add $100 for fitted case.

LPM-1 — .177 cal. single stroke pneumatic. $9\frac{1}{8}$ in. barrel, $2\frac{1}{4}$ lbs. New 1992.
No Mfg.'s Retail   **$1,030**   **$875**   **$700**

LP200/CP200 — .177 cal., precharged pneumatic (CO_2 on CP 200) action, 450 FPS., $9\frac{1}{8}$ in. barrel, adj. grips, sights, and trigger, $2\frac{1}{2}$ lbs. CP200 disc. 1997.
No Mfg.'s Retail   **$1,075**   **$915**   **$730**

LP201/CP201 — .177 cal., precharged pneumatic (CO_2 on CP201) action, 450 FPS., $9\frac{1}{8}$ in. barrel, adj. grips, sights, and trigger, vertical tank placement, $2\frac{1}{2}$ lbs. CP201 disc. 1997.
No Mfg.'s Retail   **$1,040**   **$885**   **$710**

RIFLES

CG 90 — .177 cal., CO_2 powered, tilting block action, 18.9 in. barrel, 10 lbs. 2 oz. Mfg. 1989-1996.
                    $975   **$825**   **$660**
Last Mfg.'s Sug. Retail was $1,750.

CGM — .177, CO_2 powered, professional target model, laminated stock, similar to LGM-2. Disc. 1997
                    $1,170   **$1,015**   **$810**
Last Mfg.'s Sug. Retail was $1,270.

Add $140 for beech stock or junior model.
Add $100 for running target model.

LG 90 — side-lever action, single stroke pneumatic mechanism, professional target, 11 lbs.
                    $950   **$800**   **$700**
Last Mfg.'s Sug. Retail was $1,320.

LGM-1 — .177 cal., single stroke pneumatic, side-lever action, 19 in. barrel, wt. approx. 10 lbs. Mfg. 1992-Disc.
                    $1,100   **$950**   **$750**
Last Mfg.'s Sug. Retail was $1,890.

AIR-
GUNS

Grading	100%	98%	95%

LGM-2 — .177 cal., single stroke pneumatic, side-lever action, laminated stock, new version of LGM-1 above, 10 lbs. Disc. 1998

$1,200 $950 $800

Last Mfg.'s Sug. Retail was $1,890.

Subtract $140 for beech stock or junior model.
Add $100 for running target model.

LGR RIFLE — .177 cal., side-lever action, single stroke pneumatic mechanism, 580 FPS (professional target) 10 lbs. 8 oz. Disc. 1991.

$1,000 $850 $650

Last Mfg.'s Sug. Retail was $1,250.

Add $150 for Running Boar Model.
Add $100 for universal.
Add 10% for left-hand.

MODEL LG 200/LG 200 Junior — .177 cal., precharged pneumatic action (600 shot capacity), 16½ in. barrel, laminated wood stock with anatomical pistol grip, adjustable cheek piece, fully adjustable light metal butt plate. The LG 200 and companion LG 200 Junior (same as LG 200 with scope rail for the three-position competition, and anatomical rubber butt plate) both feature Walther's new inline compensator to prevent movement of the gun when being fired, new chrome-molybdenum steel trigger, and play-free peep sight w/ 20-click-adjustment. 10¼ lbs. New 1998.

No Mfg.'s Retail $1,300 $1,155 $900

Subtract $50 for LG 200 Junior

MODEL LG 210/LG 210 Junior — .177 cal., single stroke pneumatic, side-lever cocking, 16½ in. barrel, laminated wood stock with anatomic pistol grip, fully adjustable light metal butt plate, adjustable cheek piece, this is an improved version of the LGM-2. Features Walther's new inline compensator, chrome-molybdenum steel trigger, and play-free peep sight w/ 20-click-adjustment. LG 210 Junior features scope rail for the three-position competition and an anatomical metal butt plate. 10¼ lbs. New 1998. Revised in 1999 with Metal butt plate.

No Mfg.'s Retail $1,300 $1,110 $890

Subtract $100 for LG 210 Junior.
Subtract $100 for rubber butt plate

WEBLEY & SCOTT, LTD.

Manufactured in Great Britain. Imported and sold by Pyramyd Stone International, Pepper Pike, OH. Webley airguns have been imported by Beeman in the past. The current importer and retailer offers a new line featuring five high-power air rifles, including the Vulcan Series III, previously sold by Beeman. Accessories include scopes, and Decibel Reduction Devices (DRD Noise Supressor). Webley & Scott, founded in 1898, and most noted for their excellent hinged top break revolvers produced in the early 1900s and throughout the 1930s, have also been manufacturing airguns for over 70 years.

PISTOLS

WEBLEY TEMPEST/HURRICANE — .177 or .22 cal., single stroke pneumatic, classic Webley barrel over cylinder design, 420 FPS/330 FPS, adjustable rear sight, overall length 9.12 in. (Hurricane 11.2 in.), 2 lbs. (Hurricane 2.4 lbs.). Available with plastic or wood grips.

Mfg.'s Sug. Retail $135 $110 $95 $75

Add $5 for wood grips
Add $25 for Hurricane model with longer sight base, micro adjustable rear sight and scope rails.

WEBLEY NEMESIS — .177 or .22 cal., single stroke pneumatic, 385 FPS/300 FPS, two-stage adjustable trigger, manual safety, adjustable open sights, integral scope rails, overall length 9.84 in., 2.2 lbs. Available in black or brushed chrome finish.

Mfg.'s Sug. Retail $130   · $105 $90 $70

Add $14 for brushed chrome finish

AIR-GUNS

Grading	100%	98%	95%

RIFLES

WEBLEY AXSOR — .177 or .22 cal., precharged pneumatic by tank or stirrup pump, bolt action cocking and loading, 8-shot rotary magazine, 1000 FPS/800 FPS, 19.7 in. barrel threaded for noise supressor (DRD), two-stage adjustable trigger, integral scope grooves, 39.5 in. overall, 6 lbs. Available with walnut or beech Monte Carlo stocks with recoil pad. New 1998.

Mfg.'s Sug. Retail	$815	$650	N/A	N/A

    Subtract $55 for beech stock.
    Add $50 for DRD
    Add $240 for stirrup pump

WEBLEY PATRIOT — .177, .22 and .25 cal., break barrel spring piston action, 1170 FPS/920 FPS/820 FPS, 17.5 in. barrel threaded for noise supressor (DRD), two-stage adjustable trigger, integral scope grooves, standard low-profile sights, 45.6 in. overall, walnut Monte Carlo stock with hand-checkered grip, recoil pad, 9 lbs.

Mfg.'s Sug. Retail	$425	$340	N/A	N/A

    Add $28 for DRD

WEBLEY TRACKER — .177 and .22 cal., sidelever action, tap loading, 750 FPS/600 FPS, 17.5 in. (11.37 in. Carbine version) barrel with removable muzzle weight, single-stage "hunter" adjustable trigger, integral scope grooves, 42.5 in. overall length (16936.5 in. Carbine), beech Monte Carlo stock with recoil pad, optional Black Nighthunter, Camo Fieldshooter stocks, 7.4 lbs, (7.2 lbs Carbine).

Mfg.'s Sug. Retail	$300	$240	N/A	N/A

    Add $15 for .22 cal. model
    Add $40 for Black Nighthunter or Camo Fieldshooter stocks.

WEBLEY VULCAN SERIES III — .177, .22 , and .25 cal. (.25 cal. in Carbine only), break barrel spring piston action, 870 FPS/660 FPS/620 FPS, 17.5 in. barrel (.177 and .22), Carbine 11.37 in. barrel with threaded muzzle break, all models single-stage "hunter" adjustable trigger, integral scope grooves, standard open sights, beech Monte Carlo stock with recoil pad, 7.6 lbs.

Mfg.'s Sug. Retail	$230	$200	$170	$140

    Add $25 for .25 cal. model
    Add $15 for Carbine version in .177 and .22 cal.
    Add $28 for DRD

WEBLEY EXCEL — .177 and .22 cal., break barrel spring piston action, 870 FPS/660 FPS, 17.5 in. barrel (Carbine 11.37 in. barrel), integral scope grooves, standard open sights, ambidextrous beech stock, 7 lbs.

Mfg.'s Sug. Retail	$215	$175	N/A	N/A

WEIHRAUCH

Manufactured in Germany. Imported exclusively by Beeman Precision Airguns located in Huntington Beach, CA. Available through dealers or Beeman direct.

PISTOLS

HW MODEL 70 — .177 cal., barrel-cocking action, 410 FPS, 2 lbs. 4 oz.

	$135	$115	$90

Last Mfg.'s Sug. Retail was $170.

    Add $45 for chrome.

   ✴ HW Model 70-A — similar to above, except has improved rear sight suitable for scope mount, also improved trigger and safety. New 1993.

Mfg.'s Sug. Retail	$225	$175	$150	$110

    Add $15 for Model 70S with stylized black grip and silver finish.

RIFLES

MODEL 30 — .177 or .20 cal., barrel-cocking action, 660 FPS/600 FPS, 17 in. barrel, 40 in. overall, 5 lbs. 5 oz.

Mfg.'s Sug. Retail	$205	$175	$150	$120

    Add $5 for .20 cal.

Grading	100%	98%	95%

MODEL 35EB — .177 or .22 cal., barrel-cocking action, 755/660 FPS, 8 lbs. Disc. 1985.

$325 $270 $190

Last Mfg.'s Sug. Retail was $450.

Add $50 for chrome.
Add $10 for .22 cal.
Subtract $20 for 35L.

MODEL 50 — .177 cal., barrel-cocking action, 705 FPS, 17 in. barrel, 43.1 in. overall, 6 lbs. 9 oz. Disc. 1996.

$190 $165 $120

Last Mfg.'s Sug. Retail was $245.

MODEL 55 — .177 cal., barrel-cocking action, 660-700 FPS, 7 lbs. 8 oz.

$440 $375 $295

Last Mfg.'s Sug. Retail was $610.

Add $40 for left-hand.
Add $105 for Match.
Add $145 for Tyrolean stock.

MODEL 77/77 CARBINE — .177, .20, or .22 cal., under-lever cocking action, 830-710 FPS, 8 lbs. 9 oz.

$385 $330 $250

Last Mfg.'s Sug. Retail was $530.

Add $40 for left-hand.
Add $30 for Deluxe.
Add $100 for Tyrolean stock.

MODEL 97 — .177 or .20 cal., under-lever cocking action, 800/750 FPS, 9 lbs. Velocity upgraded late in 1997 to 930/830 FPS.

Mfg.'s Sug. Retail $550 $430 $375 $300

WINCHESTER

Imported by Winchester from 1969 through 1974. Available through used market only. Between 1969 and 1975 Winchester imported 8 rifle models and 2 pistol models into the United States from a manufacturer in Germany. A total of 19,259 air guns were made and imported through 1973. Due to the $100 rule, only 6 guns will be listed in this section.

AIR-GUNS

PISTOLS

MODEL 353 — .177 and .22 cal., barrel-cocking action, 378 FPS, plastic stock, 16 in. overall, 2¾ lbs.

$165 $120 $85

MODEL 363 — .177 cal., barrel-cocking action, 378 FPS, double piston recoilless design, micrometer rear and interchangeable front sights, fully adjustable trigger, plastic stock, 16 in. overall, 3 lbs.

$195 $135 $90

RIFLES

MODEL 427 — .22 cal., barrel-cocking action, 660 FPS, micrometer rear and hooded front sight, 42 in. overall, 6 lbs.

$170 $130 $100

MODEL 435 — .177 cal. barrel-cocking action, 693 FPS, micrometer rear and interchangeable front sight, checkered stock and adjustable trigger, 44 in. overall, 6½ lbs.

$220 $175 $130

MODEL 450 — .177 cal., under-lever cocking action, 693 FPS, micrometer rear and interchangeable front sight, 44½ in. overall, dovetail base for scope, checkered Schutzen style stock, 7¾ lbs.

$280 $205 $160

MODEL 333 — .177 cal., barrel-cocking action, 576 FPS, diopter target sight, fully adjustable trigger, double piston recoilless action, walnut stock, checkered and stippled, 43½ in. overall, 9½ lbs.

$475 $400 $305

WISCHO

Previously imported by Beeman Precision Arms, Inc. previously located in Santa Rosa, CA. Manufactured by B.S.F. Available through used market only.

WISCHO AIR PISTOL MODEL S-20 STANDARD — .177 cal., barrel-cocking action, 450 FPS, 2 lbs. 8 oz. Disc. 1988.

$110 $90 $50

Last Mfg.'s Sug. Retail was $130.

MODEL CM — same as Model S-20 above but target style. Disc. in 1988.

$135 $115 $80

Last Mfg.'s Sug. Retail was $160.

NOTES

TRADEMARK INDEX

The listings below represent the most up-to-date information we have regarding Modern Firearms, Airguns, and Black Powder manufacturers (both domestic and international), trademarks, importers, distributors (when applicable) to assist you in obtaining additional information from these companies/individuals. Again, you will note the addition of more web site and email listings whenever possible. More and companies are offering on-line access about their products and it pays to surf the net!

If parts are needed for older, discontinued makes and models (even though the manufacturer/trademark is current), it is recommended you contact either the Gun Parts Corp. located in West Hurley, NY, or Jack First, Inc. located in Rapid City, SD for domestic availability and prices. For current manufacturers, it is recommended that you contact an authorized warranty repair center or stocking gun shop - unless a company/trademark has an additional service/parts listing. In Canada, please refer to the Bomac Gunpar Ltd. listing. Remember, most of the people you come in contact with requesting customer service questions or parts/service will probably be busy - have patience and respect their time.

As the 20th edition goes to press, we feel confident that the information listed below is the most up-to-date and accurate listing that is possible. **Please note all the new email and web site addresses.** Remember, things change every day in this industry, and a phone/fax number that is current today could have a new area code or gone tomorrow. International Fax/phone numbers may require additional overseas and country/city coding. If you should require additional assistance in "tracking" any of the current firearms manufacturers, distributors, or importers listed in this publication, please contact us and we will try to help you regarding these specific requests.

A.A. ARMS INC.
4811 Persimmon Court
Monroe, NC 28110
Phone No.: 704-289-5356
Fax No.: 704-289-5859

A&B HIGH PERFORMANCE FIRE-ARMS
Reno, NV
Phone No.: 661-845-7945

AMT
Galena Industries Inc.
5463 Diaz Street
Irwindale, CA 91706
Phone No.: 626-856-8883
Fax No.: 626-856-8878
Email: xinthe@aol.com

ARMI SPORT DI CHIAPPA SILVIA & C. SNC
Factory - Black Powder
Via Fornaci 66
25131 Brescia ITALY
Fax No.: 011-39-30-358-0109

AR-7 INDUSTRIES L.L.C.
998 N. Colony Rd.
Meriden, CT 06450
Phone: 203-630-3536
Fax: 203-630-3637
Web site: www.ar-7.com
Email: Info@ar-7.com

ASAI AG
Importer - see Magnum Research Inc. listing.
Factory
Wengihof P.O. Box 260
CH-4503 Solothurn, Switzerland
Phone No.: 011-41-32-622-8618
Fax No.: 011-41-32-622-8317

ARS/FARCO (Airguns)
Importer - See Air Rifle Specialists listing.

A-SQUARE CO., INC.
Liberty Centre II, Suite 220
1230 South Hurstbourne Parkway
Louisville, KY 40222
Phone No.: 502-719-3006
Fax No.: 502-719-3030

AYA
Importer/Distributor - See Armes De Chasse listing.
Distributor - British Game Gun
P.O. Box 5795
Kent, WA 98064-5795
Phone No.: 253-859-5164
Phone No.: 253-813-1535

Distributor - Fieldsport
3313 W. South Airport Road
Traverse City, MI 49684
Phone No.: 616-933-0767
Phone No.: 616-933-0768

AYA - *cont.*

Distributor - New England Custom Gun Service, Ltd.
438 Willow Brook Road
Plainfield, NH 03781
Phone No.: 603-469-3450
Fax No.: 603-469-3471

Distributor - John F. Rowe
2501 Rockwood Road
P.O. Box 86
Enid, OK 73702
Phone No.: 405-233-5942
Phone No.: 405-233-4038

Factory - AYA
Edificio Aurrera
Urtzaile, 1-2
P.O. Box 45
20600 EIBAR (Guipuzcoa) SPAIN
Fax No.: 011-34-943100133

ABBIATICO & SALVINELLI (FAMARS)
see Famars di Abbiatico & Salvinelli listing.

ACCURACY INTERNATIONAL LTD.
Importer and Distributor - Accuracy International North America Inc.
P.O. Box 5267
Oak Ridge, TN 37831
Phone No.: 423-482-0330
Fax No.: 423-482-0336
Web site: www.accuracyinternational.com
Email: info@accuracyinternational.com

Factory - Accuracy International Ltd.
P.O. Box 81, Portsmouth
Hampshire, ENGLAND PO3 5SJ
Fax No.: 011-44-705-691-852

ACCU-TEK
4510 Carter Court
Chino, CA 91710
Fax No.: 909-627-7817

AIRFORCE (Airguns)
P.O. Box 17416
Ft. Worth, TX 76102
Phone No.: 817-451-8966
Fax No.: 817-451-1613

AIR LOGIC LIMITED (Airguns)
3 Medway Bldgs., Lower Road Forest Row
East Sussex, RH18 5HE, ENGLAND

AIR RIFLE SPECIALISTS (Airguns)
P.O. Box 138
130 Holden Road
Pine City, NY 14871
Fax No.: 607-733-3261

ALESSANDRI, LOU, AND SON
P.O. Box 319
380 Winthrop Street
Rehoboth, MA 02769
Phone No.: 508-252-5590
U.S. and Canada: 800-248-5652
Fax No.: 508-252-3436

AMERICA REMEMBERS
8428 Old Richfood Road
Mechanicsville, VA 23116
Phone No.: 804-746-3769
Fax No.: 804-746-4920
Web site: www.americaremembers.com
Email: americaremembers@erols.com

AMERICAN ARMS, INC.
2607 N.E. Industrial Dr.
N. Kansas City, MO 64117
Phone No.: 816-474-3161
Fax No.: 816-474-1225

AMERICAN DERRINGER CORPORATION
127 N. Lacy Dr.
Waco, TX 76705
Phone No.: 254-799-9111
Fax No.: 254-799-7935
Web site: www.amderringer.com
Web site: www.ladyderringer.com
Email: amderr@iamerica.net

AMERICAN FRONTIER FIREARMS MFG., INC.
P.O. Box 744
Aguanga, CA 92536
Phone No.: 909-763-0014
Fax No.: 909-763-0014
Web site: www.pe.net./~frontier

AMERICAN HISTORICAL FOUNDATION, THE
1142 W. Grace St.
Richmond, VA 23220
Phone No.: 804-353-1812
Fax No.: 804-359-4895

TRADE MARKS

AMERICAN HUNTING RIFLES, INC.
P.O. Box 300
Hamilton, MT 59840
Phone No.: 800-716-4445
Phone No.: 406-961-4944
Fax No.: 406-961-1430
Web site: www.hunting-rifles.com
Email: info@hunting-rifles.com

AMTEC 2000, INC.
P.O. Box 1191
Gardner, MA 01440
Phone No.: 978-632-9608

ANGEL ARMS INC.
1825 Addison Way
Hayward, CA 94545
Phone no.: 510-783-7122
Fax No.: 510-783-7097

ANICS CORP. (Airguns)
28525 Belcourt Rd.
Pepper Pike, OH 44124

ANSCHÜTZ
Importers - Sporting and Some Target Rifles
AcuSport Corporation (Headquarters)
One Hunter Place
Bellfontaine, OH 43311-3001
Phone No.: 937-593-7010
Fax No.: 937-592-5625
Web site: www.acusport.com
Email: acusport@acusport.com

Go Sportsmen's Supply, Inc.
1535 industrial Ave.
Billings, MT 59104
Phone No.: 800-238-4665
Fax No.: 406-248-7767

Zanders Sporting Goods, Inc.
7525 State Rt. 154
Baldwin, IL 62217
Phone No.: 618-785-2235
Fax No.: 618-785-2320
Web site: www.gzanders.com
Email: jbe@egyptian.net

Distributors - Target Rifles
Accuracy International
9115 Trooper Trail
P.O. Box 2019
Bozeman, MT 59715
Phone No.: 406-587-7922
Fax No.: 406-585-9434

ANSCHUTZ, cont.
Champion's Choice Inc. - see separate listing.
Champions Shooter's Supply
P.O. Box 303
New Albany, OH 43054
Phone No.: 614-855-1603
Fax No.: 614-855-1209
Web site: www.championshooters.com

Gunsmithing Inc.
208 West Buchanan Street
Colorado Springs, CO 80907
Phone No.: 800-284-8671
Fax No.: 719-632-3493
Web site: www.databahn.net/nealjguns
Email: nealjguns@databahn.net

Repair/Gunsmithing Services
Mr. Steve Moore
c/o 10-Ring-Service
2227 West Lou Drive
Jacksonville, FL 32216
Phone No.: 904-724-7419
Fax No.: 904-724-7149

Factory - Anschutz, J.G., GmbH
Daimlerstrasse 12
D-89079 Ulm, GERMANY
Fax No.: 011-49-731-401-2700
Web site: www.anschuetz-sport.com
Email: JGA-Info@anschuetz-sport.com

ARCUS CO. - See Miltex, Inc. listing.

ARMALITE, INC.
P.O. Box 299
Geneseo, IL 61254
Phone No.: 309-944-6939
Fax No.: 309-944-6949
Web site: www.armalite.com
Email: armalite@geneseo.net

Law Enforcement Support Only
Phone No.: 502-493-8154
Fax No.: 502-493-0595
Email: charlestop@aol.com

ARMAMENT TECHNOLOGY
3045 Robie St., Suite 113
Halifax, N.S. CANADA B3K 4P6
Phone No.: 902-454-6384
Fax No.: 902-454-4641
Web site: www.armament.com
Email: info@armament.com

TRADE MARKS

ARMAS AZOR, S.A.
No current importation.

ARMES DE CHASSE
P.O. Box 86
Hertford, NC 27944
Phone No.: 252-426-2245
Fax No.: 252-426-1557

ARMI SAN PAOLO (Black Powder)
3590 NW 49th Street
Miami, FL 33142
Fax No.: 305-633-2877

ARMSCOR
Please refer to K.B.I., Inc. listing

ARMS CORPORATION OF THE PHILIPPINES
Importer - please refer to the K.B.I., Inc. listing
Factory office - Arms Corp. of the Philippines
Parang Marikina 1800
Metro Manilla, PHILIPPINES
Phone No.: 632-942-5936
Fax No.: 632-942-0862

ARMSCORP USA, INC.
4424 John Avenue
Baltimore, MD 21227
Phone No.: 410-247-6200
Fax No.: 410-247-6205

ARMSPORT, INC.
3590 NW 49th St.
Miami, FL 33142
Phone No.: 305-635-7850
Fax No.: 305-633-2877

ARNOLD ARMS CO., INC.
P.O. Box 1011
19007 - 61st Ave. NE, Ste. 1
Arlington, WA 98223
Phone No.: 360-435-1011
Fax No.: 360-435-7304
Web site: www.arnoldarms.com

ARRIETA, S.L.
Importer - Wingshooting Adventures
O-1845 West Leonard
Grand Rapids, MI 49544-9510
Phone No.: 616-677-1980
Fax No.: 616-677-1986

ARRIETA, S.L., cont.
Importer - See Griffin & Howe listing.
Importer & Distributor - See New England Arms, Corp. listing.
Importer - See Orvis listing.
Importer & Distributor - See Quality Arms listing.
Factory - Arrieta, Manufacturas, S.L.
C/.Morkaiko, 5 Barrio Urasandi
E-20870 Elgoibar (Guipuzcoa) SPAIN
Fax No.: 011-34-43-74-3154

ARRIZABALAGA, PEDRO
Importer - See Hi-Grade Imports listing.
Importer - See New England Arms Corp. listing.
Factory - Arrizabalaga, Pedro, S.A.
Errekatxu, 5
E-20600 Eibar (Guipuzcoa) SPAIN
Fax No.: 011-34-43-11-1743

ASPREY GUNROOM
167 New Bond Street
London, ENGLAND W1Y 0AR
Phone No.: 011-44-171-493-6767
Fax No.: 011-44-171-491-0384

ATKIN, GRANT & LANG
Broomhill Leys, Windmill Road, Markyate
St. Albans, Hertfordshire AL3 8LP ENGLAND
011-44-1582-842318
Email: AtkinGrant.Lang@btinternet.com

ATKIN, HENRY
Factory - see Atkin, Grant & Lang listing

AUSTIN & HALLECK (Black Powder)
1099 Welt
Weston, MO 64098
Phone No.: 816-386-2176
Fax No.: 816-386-2177

AUTAUGA ARMS, INC.
740 East Main
Pratt Plaza Mall, Suite 13
Prattville, AL 36067
Phone No.: 334-361-2950
Fax No.: 334-361-2961
Email: autaugaarms@mindspring.com

AUTOMAG, INC.
5463 Diaz St.
Irwindale, CA 91706
Phone No. 888-557-1911
Fax: 525-856-8878

TRADE MARKS

AUTO-ORDNANCE CORP.

225 Williams Lane
P.O. Box 217
West Hurley, NY 12491
Phone No.: 914-679-7225
Fax No.: 914-679-2698
Web site: www.gunpartscorp.com
Email: gunparts@gunpartscorp.com

AXTELL RIFLE COMPANY

Distributor - The Riflesmith Inc.
353 Mill Creek Road
Sheridan, MT 59749
Phone/Fax No.: 406-842-5814
Web site: www.riflesmith.com
Email: sharps77@3rivers.net

BSA GUNS (UK) LTD. (Airguns)

Importer - see Precision Sales listing.
BSA Factory
Armoury Rd., Small Heath
Birmingham, W. Mids, B11 2PX, ENGLAND
Fax No.: 011-44-21-773-0845

BAER PRECISION MACHINE COMPANY

M-1911 pistol components only
2601 34th Ave.
Hillsdale, IL 61257
Phone No.: 309-658-2716
Fax No.: 309-658-2610

BAIKAL

Importer - European American Armory Corp.
Baikal Factory
Izhevsky Mekhanichesky Zavod
8, Promyshlennaya str.
Izhevsk, 426063 RUSSIA
Fax No.: 011-95-007-341-276-4590/765830
Email: ims@shield.udmurtia.su

BAILONS GUNMAKERS LTD.

Correspondence and Repair - Guthrie Consulting
Attn: Sir Malcolm Guthrie
P.O. Box 134
Stourbridge, West Midlands, ENGLAND DY9 0YS
Phone/Fax No.: 011-44-562-730711

BALLARD RIFLE & CARTRIDGE COMPANY LLC

113 West Yellowstone Avenue
Cody, Wyoming 82414
Phone No.: 307-587-4914
Fax No.: 307-527-6097
E-mail: ballard@wyoming.com

BANSNER'S (BGS)

P.O. Box 839
261 East Main Street
Adamstown, PA 19501
Phone No.: 717-484-2370
Fax No.: 717-484-0523
Email: bansner@aol.com

BARRETT FIREARMS MANUFAC-TURING, INC.

P.O. Box 1077
Murfreesboro, TN 37133
Phone No.: 615-896-2938
Fax No.: 615-896-7313
Web site: www.barrettrifles.com
Email: barrettrifles@msn.com

BEAUCHAMP & SONS (dba FLINT-LOCKS, ETC.)

160 Rossiter Rd.
Richmond, MA 01254

BEEMAN PRECISION AIRGUNS

Division of S/R Industries (Maryland Corp.)
5454 Argosy Dr.
Huntington Beach, CA 92649-1039
Phone No.: 714-890-4800
Phone No.: 800-227-2744
Fax No.: 714-890-4808
Web site: www.velma.ido.net/idoclients/beeman/

BENELLI

Importer - Benelli USA
17603 Indian Head Highway
Accokeek, MD 20607-2501
Phone No.: 301-283-6981
Fax No.: 301-283-6988
Web site: www.benelliusa.com

Factory - Benelli Armi S.p.A.
Via della Stazione, 50
I-61029 Urbino (PS) ITALY
Fax No.: 011-39-722-30-72-07-227

TRADE MARKS

BENJAMIN AIR RIFLE COMPANY (Airguns)
Routes 5 & 20
East Bloomfield, NY 14443
Fax No.: 716-657-5405

BERETTA, PIETRO
Importer - Beretta U.S.A. Corp
17601 Beretta Drive
Accokeek, MD 20607
Fax No.: 301-283-0435

Beretta Premium Grades
c/o Beretta Gallery
41 Highland Park Village
Dallas, TX 75205
Phone No.: 214-559-9800
Fax No.: 214-559-9805
c/o Beretta Gallery
718 Madison Avenue
New York, NY 10021
Phone No.: 212-319-3235
Fax No.: 212-207-8219

Factory - Italy
Fabbrica d'Armi Pietro Beretta S.P.A
Via Pietro Beretta 18
25063 Gardonne Val Trompia
Brescia, ITALY
Phone No.: 011-39-30-8341-1
Fax No.: 011-39-30-8341-421

WAYNE BERGQUIST CUSTOM PISTOLS
5760 Shirley St., Suite #14
Naples, FL 34109
Phone No.: 941-594-1573
Fax No.: 941-597-8259

BERSA
Importer - See Eagle Imports, Inc. listing.
Factory - Bersa S.A.
Castillo 312
(1704) Ramos Mejia, ARGENTINA
Fax No.: 011-54-1-656-2093

BERTUZZI
Importer - See New England Arms Corp. listing.
Factory - Bertuzzi, F.lli
Via Alessandro Volta, 65
I-25063 Gardone V.T. (BS) ITALY
Fax No.: 011-39-30-837188

BESCHI, MARIO
No current address in Italy

BIG BEAR ARMS & SPORTING GOODS INC.
1112 Milam Way
Carrollton, TX 75006
Phone No.: 972-416-1359
Fax No.: 972-416-0771
Email: berge@dhc.net

BILL HANUS BIRDUNS
P.O. Box 533
Newport, OR 97365
Phone No.: 541-265-7433

BLAND, THOMAS & SONS GUN-MAKERS LTD.
Woodcock Hill, Inc.
P.O. Box 363
RD # 1 Box 147
Benton, PA 17814
Phone No.: 717-864-3242
Fax No.: 717-864-3232

BLASER
Importer & Distributor - see SIG Arms listing.
Factory - Blaser Jagdwaffen GmbH
Ziegelstadel 1
D-88316 Isny im Allgäu, GERMANY
Fax No.: 011-49-75-62702-43

BOHEMIA ARMS
17101 Los Modelos
Fountain Valley, CA 92708
Phone/Fax No.: 619-442-7005
Phone/Fax No.: 714-963-0809

BOMAC GUNPAR LTD.
Canadian parts supplier
Postal Bag 8090
Lakefield, Ontario
K0L 2H0 CANADA
Phone No.: 705-748-4004
Fax No.: 705-748-5916

BOND ARMS, INC.
P.O. Box 1296
204 Alpha Lane
Granbury, Texas 76048
Phone No.: 817-573-4445
Fax No.: 817-573-5636
Web site: www.bondarms.com
Email: bondarms@shooters.com

TRADE MARKS

BOSS & CO., LTD.
13 Dover St.
London, ENGLAND W1X 3PH
Phone No.: 011-44-171-493-1127
Phone/Fax No.: 011-44-171-493-0711
Email: Bossguns@aol.com

BREDA MECCANICA BRESCIANA
Via Lunga, 2
I-25126 Brescia ITALY
Fax No.: 011-39-30-322115

BRETTON
*Importer - See Mandall Shooting Supplies
listing.*
19, Rue Victore
Grignard Z1
Montreynaud
St. Etienne, Cedex
F-42026 FRANCE
Fax No.: 011-33-77-790653

BRICKLEY TRADING CO.
1443 Potrero Ave.
South El Monte, CA 91733
Phone No.: 818-444-2745
Fax No.: 818-401-3299

BRILEY MANUFACTURING INC.
1230 Lumpkin
Houston, TX 77043
Phone No.: 800-331-5718 (outside Texas)
Phone No.: 713-932-6995 (Texas only)
Web site: www.briley.com

BRITARMS
*Importer - See Mandall Shooting Supplies
listing.*

BRNO AERON (Airguns)
PO Box 714
St. Albans, VT 05478
Fax 802-527-0470

BRNO ARMS
Importer - Euro-Imports
905 West Main St., Ste. E
El Cajon, CA 92020
Phone/Fax No.: 619-442-7005
Importer (CANADA) - Pragotrade
307 Humberline Dr.
Rexdale, Ontario M9W 5V1 CANADA
Fax No.: 416-675-4567

BRNO ARMS, cont.
Factory - ZBROJOVKA BRNO, a.s.
Lazaretni 7
656 17 BRNO
CZECH REPUBLIC
Fax No.: 011-42-545-152772
Email: zbrojovka@zbrojovka.cz

BROCKMAN'S CUSTOM GUNSMITHING
P.O. BOX 357
445 Idaho St.
Gooding, Idaho 83330
Phone No.: 208-934-5050
Fax No.: 208-934-5287
Web site: www.brockmansrifles.com

BROLIN ARMS, INC.
2755 Thompson Creek Road
Pomona, CA 91767
Phone No.: 909-392-7822
Fax No.: 909-392-7824

BROWN PRECISION, INC.
P.O. Box 270W
7786 Molinos Avenue
Los Molinos, CA 96055
Phone No.: 530-384-2506
Fax No.: 530-384-1638
Web site: www.brownprecision.com

DAVID MCKAY BROWN GUNMAKERS, LTD.
32 Hamilton Road, Bothwell
Glasgow, SCOTLAND (U.K.) G71 8NA
Fax No.: 011-44-141-1698-854207

BROWNING
Administrative Headquarters
One Browning Place
Morgan, UT 84050-9326
Phone No.: 801-876-2711
Sales Information: 800-234-2045
Product Service: 800-322-4626
Fax No.: 801-876-3331
Web site: www.browning.com

Browning Parts and Service
3005 Arnold Tenbrook Rd.
Arnold, MO 63010
Phone No.: 314-287-6800
Fax No.: 800-817-4755 (Parts only)

BRUCHET
See Darne listing.

BRYCO ARMS
Distributor - Jennings Firearms, Inc.
P.O. Box 20135
3680 Research Way
Carson City, NV 89721
Phone No.: 800-518-1666
Fax No.: 702-882-3129

BUL TRANSMARK LTD.
Importer - International Security Academy (ISA)
10927 Santa Monica Blvd., #128
Los Angeles, CA 90025
Phone No.: 310-442-5540
Fax No.: 310-442-9393

Factory - Bul Transmark Ltd.
10 Rival Street
Tel-Aviv 67778, ISRAEL
Fax No.: 011-972-3-687-4853

BUSHMASTER FIREARMS
P.O. Box 1479
999 Roosevelt Trail Bldg. 3
Windham, ME 04062
Phone No.: 207-892-3594
Fax No.: 207-892-8068
Web site: www.bushmaster.com
Email: Bushmaster@maine.com

C Z (CESKA ZBROJOVKA)
Firearms & Airguns Importer - CZ-USA
1401 Fairfax Trafficway B119
Kansas City, KS 66117-0073
Phone No.: 913-321-1811
Toll Free No.: 800-955-4486
Fax No.: 913-321-2251
Web site: www.cz-usa.com
Email: czusa@gvi.net or czusa@sierratel.com

Factory - Ceska Zbrojovka
Svatopluka Cecha 1283
CZ-68827 Uhersky Brod
CZECH REPUBLIC
Fax No.: 011-42-633-3665

CABANAS
Importer - See Mandall Shooting Supplies listing.

CABELA'S INC.
One Cabela Dr.
Sidney, NE 69160
Phone No.: 800-237-4444
Fax No.: 800-496-6329
Web Site: www.cabelas.com

CALICO LIGHT WEAPONS SYSTEMS
1489 Greg St.
Sparks, NV 89431
Phone No.: 702-358-6000

CAPE OUTFITTERS, INC.
599 County Rd. #206
Cape Girardeau, MO 63701
Phone No.: 573-335-4103
Fax No.: 573-335-1555

CARL GUSTAF
Factory - Winscan AB, c/o Carl Gustaf
P.O. Box 545
S-631 07 Eskilstuna SWEDEN
Fax No.: 011-46-16-120054

CASARTELLI, CARLO
Importer - See New England Arms Corp. listing.

CASPIAN ARMS, LTD.
Components Manufacturer
14 North Main Street
Hardwick, VT 05843
Phone No.: 802-472-6454
Fax No.: 802-472-6709
Email: caspianarm@aol.com

CASULL ARMS CORPORATION
P.O. Box 1629
Afton, WY 83110
Phone No.: 307-886-0200
Fax No.: 307-886-0300
Email: casull@silverstar.com

CENTURY INTERNATIONAL ARMS, INC.

1161 Holland Dr., Dept. 0199
Boca Raton, FL 33487
Phone order line: 800-527-1252
Phone No.: 561-998-1997
Fax No.: 561-998-1993
Web site: www.centuryarms.com
Email (orders only): order@centuryarms.com

CENTURY MFG., INC.
Distributor - Century Gun Distributing
1467 Jason Road
Greenfield, IN 46140
Fax No.: 317-462-4524

CHAMPIONS CHOICE, INC.
201 International Blvd.
LaVergne, TN 37086
Phone no.: 615-793-4066
Fax no.: 615-793-4070

CHAMPLIN FIREARMS, INC.
P.O. Box 3191
Enid, OK 73702
Phone No.: 580-237-7388
Fax No.: 580-242-6922

CHAPUIS ARMES
Importer - Chadick's, Ltd.
P.O. Box 100
119 Moore Ave.
Terrell, TX 75160
Phone No.: 972-563-7577
Fax No.: 972-563-1265

Factory - Chapuis Armes
Z.I. La Gravoux, BP 15
F-42380 St. Bonnet le Chateau, FRANCE
Phone No.: 011-33-4-77/500696
Fax No.: 011-33-4-77/501070

CHAPUIS, P. ARMES ET FILS
Le Mont Mille, BP 12
F-42380 St. Bonnet le Chateau FRANCE
Fax No.: 011-33-47750-7027

CHARTER 2000, INC.
273 Canal St.
Shelton, CT 06484
Phone No.: 203-922-1652

CHATTAHOOCHEE BLACK POWDER ARMS
4153 Drew Road
Cummings, GA 30040
Phone No.: 888-889-3711 (Orders)
Phone No.: 770-889-3711 (Information)
Fax No.: 770-889-8134

CHENEY RIFLE WORKS/LEMAN RIFLES (Black Powder)
Distributor - See Mountain States Muzzleloading Supplies, Inc. .

CHERRY'S
Commemorative Research
3402-A West Wendover Avenue
P.O. Box 8768
Greensboro, NC 27419
Phone No.: 336-854-4182
Fax No.: 336-854-4184
Web site: www.cherrys.com

CHIPMUNK RIFLES
Factory - Rogue Rifle Co., Inc.
11 First St.
P.O. Box 20
Prospect, OR 97536
Phone No.: 541-560-4040
Fax No.: 541-560-4041
Web site: www.chipmunkrifle.com

CHRISTENSEN ARMS
385 North 3050 East
St. George, UT 84790
Phone No.: 435-674-9535
Fax No.: 435-674-9293
Email: christensenarms@powertech.com

Custom Shop
192 East 100 North
Fayette, UT 84630
Phone No.: 435-528-7999
Fax No.: 435-528-7494
Email: christensenarms@yahoo.com

CHURCHILL GUNMAKERS
U.S. Agent - see Aspen Outfitting listing.
c/o West Wycombe Shooting Ground Ltd.
Park Lane, Lane End
High Wycombe, HP14 3NS UK
Phone No.: 011-44-1494-883227
Fax. No.: 011-44-1494-883215

CIMARRON, F.A. CO., INC.
105 Winding Oak
Fredericksburg, TX 78624-0906
Phone No.: 830-997-9090
Fax No.: 830-997-0802

CLARK CUSTOM GUNS, INC.
336 Shootout Lane
Princeton, LA 71067
Phone No.: 318-949-9884
Fax No.: 318-949-9829
Web Site: www.clarkcustomguns.com
Email: clarkguns@prysm.net

TRADE MARKS

CLERKE ARMS, LTD.
101 Bacon St.
P.O. Box 189
Raton, NM 87740
Phone No.: 505-445-4400
Fax No.: 505-445-0532

CLIFTON ARMS
P.O. Box 1471
Medina, TX 78055
Phone No.: 210-589-2666
Fax No.: 210-589-2661

COGSWELL & HARRISON
U.S. Agent - British Game Guns
P.O. Box 5795
Kent, WA 98064-5795
Phone/Fax No.: 206-781-1233
UK Office
Thatcham House
95 Sussex Place
Slough Berks SL1 1NN, U.K.
Phone No.: 011-44-1753/520866
Fax No.: 011-44-1753/575770
Web site: www.cogswell.co.uk

COLT BLACKPOWDER ARMS
110 8th Street
Brooklyn, NY 11215
Phone No.: 718-499-4678
Fax No.: 718-768-8056

COLT'S MANUFACTURING CO., INC.
P.O. Box 1868
Hartford, CT 06144-1868
Phone No.: 800-962-COLT
Fax No.: 860-244-1449
Web site: www.colt.com
If research is needed, make sure the proper research fee is enclosed (see Colt section for fee listings) and address the correspondence "Attn: Historical Dept."

COMPASSECO (Airguns)
151 Atkinson Hill
Bradstown, KY 40004
Fax No.: 502-349-0910

COMPETITOR CORPORATION
Appleton Business Center
30 Tricnit Rd., Unit 16
P.O. Box 508
New Ipswich, NH 03071
Phone No.: 603-878-3891
Fax No.: 603-878-3950

CONNECTICUT SHOTGUN MANU-FACTURING COMPANY
P.O. Box 1692
35 Woodland St.
New Britain, CT 06501-1692
Phone No.: 860-225-6581
Fax No.: 860-832-8707

COONAN ARMS
JS Worldwide Distributing Co.
1745 Highway 36 E.
Maplewood, MN 55109
Phone No.: 651-777-0303
Fax No.: 651-777-3683
Web site: www.uslink.net/~cruzer/main.htm
Email: JStathas@aol.com

COOPER ARMS
Factory - Cooper Firearms of Montana, Inc.
P.O. Box 114
4004 Hwy. 93 North
Stevensville, MT 59870
Phone No.: 406-777-0373
Fax No.: 406-777-5228
Web site: www.missoula.bigsky.net/cooper
Email: cooper@bigsky.net

COSMI, AMERICO & FIGLIO
Via Flaminia 307
I-60020 Torrette di Ancona, ITALY
Fax No.: 011-39-71-887008
Web site: www.cosmi.net
Email: cosmi@pronet.it
Importer - See New England Arms Corp. listing.

COUNTY, S.A.L.
Bidebarrieta, 23-2o
20600 Eibar, SPAIN
Fax: 011-34-43-20-0633

CROSMAN AIR GUNS
RTS 5 & 20
East Bloomfield, NY 14443
Fax No.: 716-657-5405

CROSSFIRE LLC
2169 Greenville Road
LaGrange, GA 30241
Phone: 706-882-8070
Fax: 706-882-9050
Web site: www.crossfirellc.com
Email: crossfire@mindspring.com

TRADE MARKS

CUMBERLAND MOUNTAIN ARMS, INC.
P.O. Box 710
1045 Dinah Shore Blvd.
Winchester, TN 37398
Phone No.: 931-967-8414
Fax No.: 931-967-9199

DGS, INC.
1117 E. 12th St.
Casper, WY 82601
Phone No.: 307-237-2414

DPMS, INC.
13983 Industry Avenue
Becker, MN 55308
Phone No.: 612-261-5600
Fax No.: 612-261-5599
Web site: www.dpmsinc.com
Email: dpmsinc@aol.com

DSA, INC.
P.O. Box 387
Round Lake, IL 60073
Phone No.: 847-277-7258
Fax No.: 847-227-7259
Web site: www.dsarms.com
Email: dsarms@aol.com

DAISY MANUFACTURING CO., INC. (Airguns)
P.O. Box 220
2111 S. 8th St.
Rodgers, AR 72756
Phone No.: 501-636-1200
Fax No.: 501-636-1601
Web site: www.daisy.com
Email: info@daisy.com

DAKOTA ARMS, INC.
Whitewood Road, HC 55 Box 326
Sturgis, SD 57785
Phone No.: 605-347-4686
Fax No.: 605-347-4459
Web site: www.dakotaarms.com
Email: dakarms@sturgis.com

DAKOTA SINGLE ACTION REVOLVERS
Importer - See E.M.F. Company listing.

DALVAR OF U.S.A.
Please refer to Radom listing.

DALY, CHARLES: CURRENT MFG.
Importer - See K.B.I., Inc. listing.

DARNE S.A.
Importer - The Drumming Stump, Inc.
P.O. Box 151
Circle Pines, MN 55014
Phone: 612-785-7083
Fax: 612-434-4897
Factory
4 ter, rue de la Convention
F-42100 Saint-Étienne, France

DAVID MILLER CO.
3131 E. Greenlee Rd.
Tucson, AZ 85716
Phone No.: 520-323-3117
Fax No.: 520-327-7672

DAVIS INDUSTRIES
15150 Sierra Bonita Lane
Chino, CA 91710
Phone No.: 909-597-4726
Fax No.: 909-393-9771
Web site: www.davisguns.com

DEER CREEK RIFLE WORKS (Black Powder)
Distributor - See Mountain States Muzzleloading Supply listing.

DEFOURNEY
No current address available.

DEMAS, Ets
5Bis, rue Xavier Privas
F-42000 St. Etienne, FRANCE
Fax No.: 011-33-4-77-25-4198

DEPAR
Ahmediye Cad. Akcal Apt. No:4/6 Aksaray
Istanbul, TURKEY
Phone No.: 011-90-1-212-635-6302
Fax No.: 011-90-1-212-532-8530

DIANAWERK, MAYER AND GRAMMELSPACHER (Airguns)
See Dynamit Nobel - RWS listing.

DIXIE GUN WORKS (Black Powder)
Hwy. 51 South
Union City, TN 38261
Fax No.: 901-885-0440

DOMINO
Importer - See Mandall Shooting Supplies listing.

DOWNSIZER CORPORATION
P.O. Box 710316
Santee, CA 92072-0316
Phone No.: 619-448-5510
Fax No.: 619-448-5780

DUCKS UNLIMITED, INC.
One Waterfowl Way
Memphis, TN 38120-2351
Phone No.: 901-758-3825
Fax No.: 901-758-3850
Web Site: www.ducks.org

DUMOULIN, ERNEST S.P.R.L.
*U.S. Importer - see Armes De Chasse
LLC listing.*
Factory
Rue du Bouxthay 41
B-4041 Vottem-Herstal, BELGIUM
Fax No.: 011-32-41-228-89-69
Web site: www.dumoulin-herstal.com
Email: contact@dumoulin-herstal.com

DUMOULIN, HENRI & FILS
*Importer - See New England Arms
Corp. listing.*
Factory - Dumoulin, Henri & Fils
P.O. Box 30
Herstal 4400, BELGIUM
Fax No.: 011-32-49-3013255

DUMOULIN HERSTAL S.A.
*U.S. Importer - see Armes De Chasse
listing.*
Factory
Rue du Bouxthay 41
B-4041 Vottem-Herstal, BELGIUM
Fax No.: 011-32-41-228-89-69
Web site: www.dumoulin-herstal.com
Email: contact@dumoulin-herstal.com

DYNAMIT NOBEL - RWS, Inc.
81 Ruckman Road
Closter, NJ 07624
Phone No.: 201-767-1995
Fax No.: 201-767-1589
Web Site: www.shooters.com
Email: fturner@cybernex.net

E.D.M. ARMS
111 N. Main St., Bldg. B-S
Riverside, CA 92501
Phone No.: 909-369-9237
Fax No.: 909-369-9408

E.M.F. COMPANY
1900 E. Warner Ave., Suite 1-D
Santa Ana, CA 92705
Phone No.: 949-261-6611
Fax No.: 949-756-0133

EAGLE ARMS INC.
Division of ArmaLite, Inc.
Please refer to ArmaLite Listing.

EAGLE IMPORTS, INC.
1750 Brielle Ave., Unit B-1
Wanamassa, NJ 07712
Phone No.: 732-493-0333
Fax No.: 732-493-0301
Web Site: www.bersa-llama.com
Email: gsodini@aol.com

EFFEBI snc
Factory
Via Rossa, 4
I-25062 Concesio (BS) ITALY
Fax. No.: 011-39-30-2180414

EGO ARMAS, S.A.
Victor Sarasqueta, 1
E-20600 Eibar (Guipuzcoa) SPAIN
Fax No.: 011-34-43-120463

ENTRÉPRISE ARMS INC.
15861 Business Center Dr.
Irwindale, CA 91706
Phone No.: 626-962-8712
Fax No.: 626-962-4692
Web sites: www.entreprise.com or
www.1911.com

ERMA SUHL, GmbH
Schützenstrasse 26
D-98527 Suhl, GERMANY
Fax no.: 011-49-3681-854-203

ESSEX ARMS (Parts)
Box 345
Island Pond, VT 05846
Phone No.: 802-723-4313
Fax No.: 802-723-6203

EUROARMS OF AMERICA (Black Powder)
208 East Piccadilly Street
P.O. Box 3277
Winchester, VA 22604
Phone No.: 540-662-1863
Fax No.: 504-662-4464

EUROARMS OF AMERICA, cont.

Factory - Euroarms - Armi San Paolo
P.O. Box 64
I-25060 Concesio, ITALY
Fax No.: 011-39-30-218-0365

EUROPEAN AMERICAN ARMORY CORP.
P.O. Box 1299
Sharpes, FL 32953
Phone No.: 407-639-4842
Fax No.: 407-639-7006
Email: eaacorp@bv.net

EVOLUTION USA
P.O. Box 154
White Bird, ID 83554
Phone No.: 208-983-9208
Fax. No. 208-983-0944
Email: lwoslum@camasnet.com

F.A.I.R. TECHNI-MEC
Importer - See New England Arms Corp. listing.
Factory - F.A.I.R. Tecni-Mec Snc di Isidoro Rizzini & C.
Via Gitti, 41
I-25060 Marcheno (BS) ITALY
Fax No.: 011-39-30-861-0179
Web site: www.fair.it
Email: fair@fair.it

FAS
Importer - See Nygord Precision Products listing.

FEG
Importer - See K.B.I., Inc. listing.
Importer - See Century International Arms, Inc. listing.

FIAS
Fabrica Italiana Armi Sabatti
Via Volta 90
Gardone Val Trompia I-25063 ITALY
Fax No.: 011-39-30-831312

F.I.E. FIREARMS CORP. (parts/repairs only)
Please refer to Heritage Manufacturing, Inc. listing.
Please refer to Gun Parts Corp. listing.

FABARM S.p.A.
Importer - see Heckler & Koch listing
Factory - Fabbrica Breciana Armi
Via Averolda 31
I-25039 Travagliato, Brescia ITALY
Fax No.: 011-39-30-6863684

FABBRI s.n.c.
Factory
Via Dante Alighieri, 29
I-25062 Concesio (BS) ITALY
Fax No.: 011-39-30-218-7301
Web site: www.fabbri.it
Email: tullio@fabbri.it
Email: fabbri@fabbri.it

FABRIQUE NATIONALE
Factory - Browning S.A.
Fabrique Nationale Herstal SA
Parc Industriel des Hauts Sarts
3éme Ave. 25
B-4040 Herstal, BELGIUM
Fax No.: 011-32-42-40-5212

FALCO, s.r.l.
Factory
via Zanardelli, 231
I-25060 Marcheno (Brescia) ITALY
Fax no.: 011-39-30-89-60-341
Web site: www.intred.com/falco
Email: falco@intred.com

FAMARS di ABBIATICO & SALVINELLI srl
Importer - A&S of America
476 State Route 51
Jefferson Boro, PA 15025
Phone: 412-384-2600
Distributor - The First National Gun Banque
P.O. Box 60452
Colorado Springs, CO 80960
Phone No.: 719-444-0786
Fax No.: 719-444-0731
Web site: www.fngbcorp.com
Email: info@fngbcorp.com
Factory
Via Valtrompia 16-18
P.O. Box 152
25063 Gardone, V.T. ITALY
Fax No.: 011-39-30-89112894
Web site: www.famars.com
Email: info@famars.com

TRADE MARKS

FANZOJ, JOHANN

Distributor - Dr. Joseph Cornell
2655 West 39th Ave.
Denver, CO 80211
Phone No: 303-455-1717
Fax No.: 303-455-7171
Email: joe80211@aol.com

Factory - Fanzoj GesmbH
Greisgasse 1
9170 Ferlach, AUSTRIA
Fax No.: 011-43-4227-2867
Email: jfanzoj@netway.at

FAUSTI, CAV. STEFANO & FIGLIE SNC.

Importer - See American Arms, Inc. listing.
Factory
Via Martiri Dell'Indipendenza, 70
I-25060 Marcheno (Brescia) ITALY
Fax No.: 011-39-30-861-0155
Web site: www.studionet.it/Fausti_VIT
Email: outdoor@studionet.it

FEINWERKBAU

Airgun Importer - See Beeman Precision Airgun listing.
Factory - Westinger & Altenburger GmbH
Neckarstrasse 43
D-78727 Oberndorf/Neckar GERMANY
Fax No.: 011-49-7423/814-89

FERLACH GUNS

Ferlach Genossenschaft
Attn: Customer Service
Waagplatz 6
A-9170 Ferlach, AUSTRIA
Fax No.: 011-43-4227/3714

FERLIB

Distributor - See Hi-Grade Imports listing.
Factory - Ferlib & Cs.d.f
Via Costa 46, Gardone 1-25063
ITALY
Fax No. 011-39-3089-12586

FIREARMS INTERNATIONAL, INC.

5709 Hartsdale, Suite B
Houston, TX 77036
Phone No.: 713-789-0745
Fax No.: 713-789-7513
Web site: www.fi-guns.com
Email: info@fi-guns.com

FIOCCHI OF AMERICA, INC.

Importer - Fiocchi of America, Inc. (ammunition only)
Rt. 2, Box 90-8
Ozark, MO 65721
Fax No.: 417-725-1039

Factory - Fiocchi Munizioni S.P.A.
Via Santa Barbara, 4
I-22053 Lecco ITALY
Fax No.: 011-39-341/281-171

FORT WORTH FIREARMS

2006-B MLK Fwy.
Fort Worth, TX 76104-6303
Phone No.: 817-536-0718
Fax No.: 817-535-0290

A.H. FOX (Current mfg. only)

Manufacturer - Connecticut Shotgun Manufacturing Co.
P.O. Box 1692
35 Woodland St.
New Britain, CT 06051-1692
Phone No. 860-225-6682
Fax No.: 860-832-8707

Older A.H. Fox Historical Research
Mr. John Callahan
53 Old Quarry Rd.
Westfield, MA 01085
$25.00 - $30.00 gun research fee.

FRANCHI, LUIGI

Importer - See Benelli USA listing.
Factory - Franchi, Luigi, S.p.A.
Via del Serpente, 12
I-25131 Fornaci (Brescia) ITALY
Fax No.: 011-39-30-3581554
Web site: www.franchiusa.com

FRANCOTTE, AUGUSTE & CIE. S.A.

Importer - See Armes De Chasse LLC listing.
Factory - Francotte, Auguste, & Cie S.A.
109 Rue due Trois Juin
B - 4040 Herstal BELGIUM
Fax No.: 011-32-42-40-4630
Email: francotte@cybernet.Be

TRADE MARKS

FREEDOM ARMS
P.O. Box 1776
#1 Freedom Lane
Freedom, WY 83120
Phone No.: 307-883-2468
Fax No.: 307-883-2005
Web site: www.freedomarms.com
Email: freedom@silverstar.com

GALIL
No current importation.
Semi-auto configuration was banned April, 1998.

GAMBA, RENATO
Exclusive Importer and Distributor - Gamba of America, a subsidiary of Firing Line.
20 South Potomac
Aurora, CO 80012
Phone No.: 303-363-0041
Web site: www.firing-line.com
Factory - Renato Gamba
Via Artigiani, 91/93
I-25063 Gardone V.T. (Brescia), ITALY
Fax No.: 011-39-30-8912-180
Web site: www.renatogamba.it
Email: gambasab@ivtnet.it

GAMO USA Corp. (Airguns)
3911 S.W. 47th Avenue, Suite 914
Ft. Lauderdale, FL 33314
Phone No.: 954-581-5822
Fax No.: 954-581-3165
Email: gamousa@gate.net

GARBI
Importer - See W. L. Moore & Co. listing.
Factory - Armas Garbi
Urki, 12-14
E-20600 Eibar, SPAIN

GASTINNE RENETTE
39 Avenue Franklin D. Roosevelt
F-75008 Paris, FRANCE
Fax No.: 011-33-1-4256-2111

GATLING GUN COMPANY
Manufacturer and distributor - Furr Arms
485 South Commerce Road
Orem, UT 84058
Phone No.: 801-226-3877

GAUCHER - Armes S.A.
Importer - see Mandall Shooting Supplies listing.
Factory
46, rue Desjoyaux
F-42000 Saint-Etienne, FRANCE
Fax No.: 011-33-477419572

GENTRY, DAVID - CUSTOM GUNMAKER
314 N. Hoffman
Belgrade, MT 59714
Phone No.: 406-388-GUNS

GIBBS RIFLE COMPANY, INC. (G.R.C., INC.)
211 Lawn St.
Martinsburg, WV 25401
Phone No.: 304-262-1651
Fax No.: 304-262-1658
Web site: www.gibbsrifle.com
Email: support@gibbsrifle.com

GLOCK, INC.
6000 Highlands Pkwy.
Smyrna, GA 30082
Fax No.: 770-433-8719

GONIC ARMS INC. (Black Powder)
134 Flagg Rd
Gonic, NH 03839
Phone No.: 603-332-8456

GRANGER, G.
Importer - see Champlin Firearms, Inc. listing.
Factory
66 Cours Fauriel, 66
F-42100 St. Etienne FRANCE
Phone No.: 011-33-77.85.14.73

GRANT, STEPHEN
Factory - see Atkin, Grant & Lang listing.

GREENER, W. W.
Factory - W. W. Greener
One Belmont Row
GB-Birmingham, ENGLAND B4 7RE
Fax No.: 011-44-21-359-4300

GRIFFIN & HOWE
36 West 44th Street, Suite 1011
New York, NY 10036
Phone No.: 212-921-0980
Fax No.: 212-921-2327

GRIFFIN & HOWE, cont.
33 Claremont Road
Bernardsville, NJ 07924
Phone No.: 908-766-2287
Fax No.: 908-766-1068
Email: prather@griffinhowe.com

GRIFFON
Importer - Griffon USA, Inc.
2513 East Loop 820 N
Ft. Worth, TX 76118
Phone No.: 817-284-7474
Fax No.: 817-284-7528
*Manufacturer - Continental Weapons
(Pty) Ltd.*
322 15th St. Randjespark
Midrand 1685, Johannesburg, South Africa

Phone No.: 011-27-11-314-5088
Fax No.: 011-27-11-314-5050

GRULLA ARMAS, S.L.
Importer - Gunsport, Ltd. Inc.
810 N. Dixie, Suite 201
Odessa, TX 79761
Phone No.: 915-334-8698
Fax No.: 915-367-0407
Website: www.petroplex.com/gunsport/
Importer - See Hi-Grade Imports listing.
Factory - Grulla Armas
P.O. Box 453
Avda. de Otaola, 12 P.O. Box 453
E-20600 Eibar (Guipuzcoa) SPAIN
Fax No.: 011-34-9-43-702133

GUN PARTS CORP.
Parts supplier only
226 Williams Lane
W. Hurley, NY 12491
Phone No.: 914-679-2417
Fax No.: 914-679-5849
Email: gunparts@gunpartscorp.com

GUN POWER (Airguns)
P.O. Box 567
Ashford, Kent, TN23 5FP ENGLAND
Phone: 011-44-1233-624-357

GUN SOUTH, INC. (GSI)
P.O. Box 129
108 Morrow Avenue
Trussville, AL 35173
Phone No.: 205-655-8299
Fax No.: 205-655-7078
Web site: www.GSIfirearms.com
Email: merkelsuhl@aol.com
Email: SteyrSBS@aol.com

G.U. INC.
4325 S 120th Street
Omaha, NE 68137
Phone No.: 402-330-4492
Fax No.: 402-330-8029
Web site: www.skbshotguns.com

GUSTAF, CARL
See Carl Gustaf listing.

HHF
Factory - Huglu Tüfekleri Kooperatifi AV
Antalya Caddesi no 58
TR-42710 Huglu/Besehir/Konya TURKEY
Fax no.: 011-90-332-516-1032

HJS ARMS, INC.
P.O. Box 3711
Brownsville, TX 78523-3711
Phone No.: 800-453-2767

H & R 1871, INC.
*Harrington & Richardson (post-1991
mfg. only)*
60 Industrial Rowe
Gardner, MA 01440
Fax No.: 978-632-2300
Email: hr1871@hr1871.com
Web Site: www.hr1871.com

H-S PRECISION, INC.
1301 Turbine Dr.
Rapid City, SD 57703
Phone No.: 605-341-3006
Fax No.: 605-342-8964
Web site: www.hsprecision.com

HAENEL (Airguns)
Importer - See Gun South, Inc. listing.

HAMBRUSCH JAGDWAFFEN GmbH
Importer - CONCO Arms International
P.O. Box 159
Emmaus, PA 18049
Fax No.: 610-967-5477

TRADE MARKS

HAMBRUSCH JAGDWAFFEN GmbH, cont.

Factory - Hambrusch Jagdwaffen Gesellschaft
Gartengasse 4
A-9170 Ferlach, AUSTRIA
Fax No.: 011-43-4227/4106

HÄMMERLI

Importer - SIG Arms Inc.
Corporate Park
Exeter, NH 03833
Phone No.: 603-772-2302
Fax No.: 603-772-9082
Web site: www.sigarms.com

Factory - SIG Arms Hämmerli AG
Seoner Strasse
CH-5600 Lenzburg SWITZERLAND
Fax No.: 011-41-62-888-2200
Web site: www.haemmerli.ch

HARRIS GUNWORKS

P.O. Box 9249
20813 N. 19th Ave.
Phoenix, AZ 85027
Phone No.: 602-582-9627
Fax No.: 602-582-5178

HARTMANN & WEISS

Rahlstedter Bahnhofstr. 47
22143 Hamburg, GERMANY
Phone No.: 011-49-40-677-5585
Fax No.: 011-49-40-677-5592

HASKELL MFG. INC.

Refer to Hi-Point listing.

HATFIELD (Black Powder only)

Manufacturer and Distributor - Missouri River Rifle Works, Inc.
224 N. 4th Street
St. Joseph, MO 64501
Phone No.: 816-676-1776

HECKLER & KOCH, INC.

U.S. Headquarters
21480 Pacific Blvd.
Sterling, VA 20166-8903
Phone No.: 703-450-1900
Fax No.: 703-450-8160
Web site: www.hecklerkoch-usa.com

Factory - Heckler & Koch GmbH
Alte Steige 7
P.O. Box 1329
D-78727 Oberndorf Neckar GERMANY
Fax No.: 011-49-7423-7922-80

HELWAN

Importer - See Navy Arms Co. listing.

HENDRY, RAMSAY & WILCOX

55/57 North Methven Street
Perth PH1 5PX, SCOTLAND
Phone No.: 01-738-623679
Fax No.: 01-738-443327

HENRY REPEATING ARMS COMPANY

110 8th St.
Brooklyn, NY 11215
Phone No.: 718-499-5600
Fax No.: 718-768-8056
Web site: www.henryrepeating.com

HERITAGE MANUFACTURING, INC.

4600 NW 135th St.
Opa Locka, FL 33054
Phone No.: 305-685-5966
Fax No.: 305-687-6721
Web site: www.heritagemfg.com

HESSE ARMS

1126 70th St.
Inver Grove Heights, MN 55077-2416
Phone/Fax: 651-455-5760
Web site: www.hessearms.com
Email: HesseArms@Juno.com

HEYM, GmbH & CO. Jagdwaffen KG

Factory
Am Aschenbach 2
D-98646 Gleichamberg GERMANY
Fax No.: 011-49-368-75-63222

HI-GRADE IMPORTS

Division of Marx Chevrolet/Olds/Cadillac
8655 Monterey Road
Gilroy, CA 95020
Phone No.: 408-842-9301
Fax No.: 408-842-9323

HI-POINT FIREARMS

Distributor - MKS Supply, Inc.
5990 Philadelphia Drive
Dayton, OH 45415
Phone No.: 937-275-4991
Fax No.: 937-275-3515
Web site: www.hi-pointFirearms.com
Email: mkshpoint@aol.com

HIGH STANDARD MANUFACTUR-
ING COMPANY, INC.
4601 South Pinemont, Ste. 144
Houston, TX 77041
Phone No.: 713-462-4200
Fax No.: 713-462-6437
Web site: www.highstandard.com
Email: info@highstandard.com

High Standard Parts (new and earlier models)
514 Burnside Ave.
East Hartford, CT 06108
Phone No.: 860-289-5741

GEORGE HOENIG INC.
6521 Morton Dr.
Boise, ID 83704
Phone No.: 208-375-1116

HOFER-JAGDWAFFEN, PETER
Kirchgasse 24
A-9170 Ferlach, AUSTRIA
Fax No.: 011-43-4227/3683/30
Web site: www.hoferwaffen.com
Email: peterhoferjagdwaffen@hoferwaf-
fen.com/ilse/werbung/bluenews

P.L. HOLEHAN, INC.
5758 E. 34th St.
Tucson, AZ 85711
Phone No.: 520-745-0622
Fax No.: 520-745-2248
Email: plholehan@juno.com

HOLLAND & HOLLAND LTD.
U.S. Store Location
50 East 57th Street
New York, NY 10022
Phone No.: 212-752-7755

France Store Location
29 Avenue Victo Hugo
F-75116 Paris FRANCE
Phone No.: 011-133-450-22200

Factory Address
Attn: Customer Service-BB
31-33 Bruton Street
London, ENGLAND W1X 8JS
Phone No.: 011-44-71-499 4411
Fax No.: 011-44-71-499 4544

HOLLOWAY & NAUGHTON
Premier English Shotguns Ltd.
Turners Barn Farm - Kibworth Road, Three Gates
Illston-on-the-Hill, Leicestershire
LE7 9ER ENGLAND
Fax No.: 011-44-116-2596-574

HORTON, LEW, DIST. CO.
See Lew Horton Dist. Co. listing.

HOWA
Importer - See Interarms listing.

HUG-SAN
Tüfekleri San. Tic. A.S.
Huglu Beysehir Konya TURKEY
Fax No.: 011-90-331-516-15-06

I.A.B.
Factory - Industria Armi Brescaine
Via 1 Maggio, 39
Sarezzo Brescia 1-25068 ITALY
Fax No.: 011-39-3080-0313

IAR, INC.
33171 Camino Capistrano
San Juan Capistrano, CA 92675
Phone No.: 949-443-3642
Fax No.: 949-443-3647
Web site: www.iar-arms.com
Email: sales@iar-arms.com

IGA SHOTGUNS
Importer - See Stoeger Industries, Inc. listing.

IBERIA FIREARMS
Refer to Hi-Point listing.

INFINITY FIREARMS
Manufacturer - Strayer Voight, Inc.
3435 Roy Orr Blvd., Ste. 200
Grand Prairie, TX 75050
Phone No.: 972-513-1911
Fax No.: 972-513-0575
Web site: www.sviguns.com

INTERARMS/HOWA
10 Prince Street, P.O. Box 208
Alexandria, VA 22313
Phone No.: 703-548-1400
Fax No.: 703-549-7826
Web Site: www.interarms.com
Email: interarms@mindspring.com

TRADE MARKS

INTERTEX CAROUSEL CORPORA-TION
1100 Culp Road
Pineville, NC 28134
Phone No.: 704-587-0068
Fax No.: 704-587-0079
Factory - INTERTEX-Maschinenbau GmbH & Co.
Ludwigstrasse 24-28
D-73054 Eislingen GERMANY
Fax no.: 011-49-7161-98-40-5-50
Email: intertex@t-online.de

INTRAC ARMS INTERNATIONAL L.L.C.
Importation & Distribution only
U.S. Headquarters
5005 Chapman Highway
Knoxville, TN 37920
Phone No.: 423-573-0065
Fax No.: 423-579-0937
European Headquarters
Schlossgasse 12
A-2540 Bad VÇslau, AUSTRIA
Fax No. 011-43-2252-78897

INTRATEC
12405 SW 130th St.
Miami, FL 33186-6224
Fax No.: 305-253-7207

INVESTARM, s.p.a.
Factory - Fabbrica D'Armi
25060 Marcheno, via Zanardelli, 210
Brescia ITALY
Fax No.: 011-39-30-861-285

IRWINDALE ARMS, INC.
See A M T listing.

ISRAEL ARMS INTERNATIONAL, INC.
5709 Hartsdale
Houston, TX 77036
Phone No.: 713-789-0745
Fax No.: 713-789-7513
Web site: www.israelarms.com

ISRAEL ARMS, LTD.
Exclusive Importer & Distributor - see Israel Arms International, Inc. listing.

ISRAELI MILITARY INDUSTRIES
No current information available.

ITHACA CLASSIC DOUBLES
The Old Station
No. 5 Railroad St.
Victor, NY 14564
Phone No.: 716-624-3544
Fax No.: 716-624-5425

ITHACA GUN COMPANY, LLC
891 Route 34B
King Ferry, NY 13081
Phone No.: 315-364-7171
Fax No.: 315-364-5134
Cust. Service/Parts No.: 315-364-7182
Web site: www.ithacagun.com

JMC FABRICATION & MACHINE, INC.
Firearms Division
396 Gus Hipp Blvd.
Rockledge, FL 32955
Phone no.: 407-636-1943
Fax no.: 407-632-1040
Web site: www.safefuel.com/bfg

JP ENTERPRISES, INC.
P.O. Box 270005
St. Paul, MN 55127
Phone No.: 651-486-9064
Fax No.: 651-482-0970
Website: www.members.aol.com/jpar15

J R DISTRIBUTING
15634 Tierra Rejada Rd.
Moorpark, CA 93021
Fax no.: 805-529-2368
Web site: www.jrdistributing.com

JAGD-UND SPORTWAFFEN SUHL GmbH (MERKEL)
Importer - See Gun South, Inc. listing.
Factory - See Merkel listing.

JAGERSPORT, LTD.
1 Wholesale Way
Cranston, RI 02920
Phone No.: 401-944-9682
Fax No.: 401-946-2587

JACK FIRST, INC.
Gun Parts/Accessories/Service
1201 Turbine Dr.
Rapid City, SD 57701
Phone No.: 605-343-8481

JARRETT RIFLES, INC.
383 Brown Rd.
Jackson, SC 29831
Phone No.: 803-471-3616
Fax No.: 803-471-9246
Web site: www.jarrettrifles.com
Email: jarrett@groupz.net

JAVELINA ARMS CO.
P.O. Box 357
Van, TX 75790

JENNINGS, B.L., INC.
P.O. Box 20135
Carson City, NV 89721
Phone No.: 800-518-1666
Fax No.: 702-882-3129

JOHANNSEN RIFLES
Please refer to the New England Custom
Gun Service Ltd. listing.

K.B.I., INC.
P.O. Box 6625
Harrisburg, PA 17112
Phone No.: 717-540-8518
Fax No.: 717-540-8567
Email: kbi_inc@msn.com

KDF, INC.
2485 Highway 46 North
Seguin, TX 78155
Phone No.: 830-379-8141
Fax No.: 830-379-5420

KAHNKE GUNWORKS (Black Powder)
206 West 11th
Redwood Falls, MN 56283
Fax No.: 507-637-2905

KAHR ARMS
P.O. Box 220
Blauvelt, NY 10913
Customer Service phone no.: 508-791-6375
Sales phone No.: 914-353-7770
Fax No.: 914-353-7833
Web site: www.kahr.com
Email: kahrhq@compuserve.com

KEL-TEC CNC INDUSTRIES, INC.
P.O. Box 3427
Cocoa, FL 32924-3427
Phone No.: 407-631-0068
Fax No.: 407-631-1169
Web site: www.kel-tec.com
Email: aimkeltec@aol.com

KEMEN
Importer and Distributor - see Armes De Chasse LLC listing.
Factory - Armas Kemen, S.L.
Ermuraran Bide, 14 - Apartado n. 60
20870 Elboibar (Guipuzcoa), SPAIN

KEPPELER + FRITZ GmbH
Aspachweg 4
D-74427 Fichtenberg, GERMANY
Fax No.: 011-49-7971/7971

KEPPLINGER, ING. HANNES
Carl-Wagner-Strasse 1
A-6330 Kufstein, AUSTRIA
Fax No.: 011-43-5372/71887

KEYSTONE SPORTING ARMS
RD2 Box 20 Suite 1
Milton, PA 17847
Phone No.: 717-742-2777
Fax No.: 717-742-1455

KIMAR SRL
via Fornaci 66
25131 Brescia ITALY
Fax No.: 011-39-30-358-0109

KIMBER
Corporate Offices - Kimber Mfg., Inc.
1 Lawton St.
Yonkers, NY 10705
Phone no.: 914-964-0771
Fax no.: 914-964-9340
Custom Shop Phone No.: 914-964-0742
Web site: www.kimberamerica.com
Marketing & Sales Offices
2590 Highway 35, Ste. B
Kalispell, MT 59901
Phone No.: 406-758-2222
Fax No.: 406-758-2223

KING'S GUN WORKS INC.
1837 West Glenoaks Blvd.
Glendale, CA 91201
Phone no.: 818-956-6010
Fax no.: 818-548-8606

KLEINGUENTHER FIREARMS
1604 N. Heideke St.
P.O. Box 2020
Seguin, TX 78155
Phone No.: 512-372-5050
Fax No.: 512-557-5310

TRADE MARKS

KNIGHTS MANUFACTURING CO.
7750 9th St. S.W.
Vero Beach, FL 32968
Phone No.: 561-778-3700
1-569-2955

KNIGHTS RIFLES (Black Powder)
234 Airport Rd., P.O. Box 130
Centerville, IA 52544
Phone no.: 515-856-2626
Fax no.: 515-856-2628

KORA BRNO
Factory - Kroko a.s.
Hybesova 46
CZ-60200 Brno, Czech Republic
Fax no.: 011-42-5-4324-4346
Email: kroko@brn.czn.cz

KORRIPHILA
*see Intertex Carousels Corporation
listing.*

KORTH
*Exclusive Importer - Keng's Firearms
Specialty Inc.*
875 Wharton Dr. S.W.
Atlanta, GA 30336
Phone no.: 404-691-7611
Fax no.: 404-505-8445
Web site: www.versapod.com
Email: kengs@mindspring.com
*Factory - Korth Vertriebsgesellschaft
GmbH*
Robert Bosch Strasse 4
D-23909 Ratzeburg, GERMANY
Fax No.: 011-49-45-4182479

KRICO
*Limited importation - See Mandall
Shooting Supplies
listing.*
*Factory - Krico Jagd-und Sportwaffen
GmbH*
Pfaugasse 6
D-85088 Vohburg-Irsching GERMANY
Fax No.: 011-49-91-80-2661

KRIEGHOFF, H., GUN CO.
Importer - Krieghoff Intl., Inc.
P.O. Box 549
7528 Easton Rd.
Ottsville, PA 18942
Phone No.: 610-847-5173
Fax No.: 610-847-8691
Web site: www.krieghoff.com

Factory - H. Krieghoff GmbH
Boschstrasse 22
D-89079 Ulm, GERMANY
Fax No.: 011-49-731-40-18270

L.A.R. MANUFACTURING, INC.
4133 West Farm Road (8540 South)
West Jordan, UT 84088-1972
Phone No.: 801-280-3505
Fax No.: 801-280-1972
Web site: www.largrizzly.com
Email: guns@largrizzly.com

LAKE FIELD ARMS LTD.
Factory
P.O. Box 129
Lakefield, Ontario
K0L 2H0 CANADA
Phone No.: 705-652-8000
Fax No.: 705-652-8431

LANBER
Importer - ITC International, Inc.
Jean Constantinides
1720 Cumberland Point Dr., Suite #5
Marietta, GA 30067
Phone No.: 770-858-0048 or 54
Fax No.: 770-858-0051
Factory - Lanber Armas, S.A.
Attn: Customer Service-BB
Zubiaurre, 3 P.O. Box 3
E-42850 SPAIN
Fax No.: 011-34-4-6827999

LANG, JOSEPH
*Please refer to Atkin, Grant & Lang
listing.*

LASERAIM ARMS, INC.
*Distributor - Emerging Technologies,
Inc.*
P.O. Box 3548
Little Rock, AR 72203
Phone No.: 501-375-2227
Fax No.: 501-372-1445

LAURONA
Importer - Galaxy Imports
P.O. Box 3361
Victoria, TX 77903
Phone No.: 361-573-4867
Fax No.: 361-576-9622
Factory - Armas Laurona S.A.L.
P.O. Box 260, Avda de Otaola, 25
E-20600 Eibar (Guipuzcoa) SPAIN
Fax No.: 011-34-43-700616

TRADE
MARKS

HARRY LAWSON
3328 Richey Blvd.
Tucson, AZ 85716
Phone no.: 520-326-1117

LAZZERONI ARMS COMPANY
P.O. Box 26696
Tucson, AZ 85726-6696
Phone No.: 888-492-7247
Fax No.: 520-624-4250
Web site: www.lazzeroni.com
Email: arms@lazzeroni.com

LEBEAU-COURALLY
Importer - See William Larkin Moore & Co. listing.
Factory - Aug. Lebeau-Courally
386, rue Saint-Gilles
B-4000 Liege, BELGIUM
Fax No.: 011-32-41-52-2008

LES BAER CUSTOM, INC.
29601 34th Avenue N.
Hillsdale, IL 61257
Phone No.: 309-658-2716
Fax No.: 309-658-2610
Web site: www.lesbaer.com
Email: lesbaer@netexpress.net

LEW HORTON DISTRIBUTING CO.
Distributor Only
15 Walkup Dr.
Westboro, MA 01581
Phone No.: 508-366-7400
Fax No.: 508-366-5332
Web site: www.lewhorton.com
Email: 1horton@tiac.net

LIBERTY
Importer and Distributor - see K.B.I. listing.

LIBERTY ARMS WORKS, INC.
823 Lincoln Ave.
West Chester, PA 19380
Phone No.: 610-429-1114

LJUTIC INDUSTRIES, INC.
P.O. Box 2117
732 North 16th Ave., Ste. 22
Yakima, WA 98907
Phone No.: 509-248-0476

LLAMA
Importer - Import Sports, Inc.
1750 Brielle Ave., Unit B-1
Wanamassa, NJ 07712
Phone No.: 732-493-0302
Fax No.: 732-493-0301
Web site: www.bersa-llama.com
Email: gsodini@aol.com
Factory - Llama Gabilondo Y Cia, S.A.
P.O. Box 290
E-01013 Vitoria (Alava) SPAIN
Fax no.: 011-34-45-26-2444

LONE STAR RIFLE CO., INC.
11231 Rose Road
Conroe, TX 77303
Phone/Fax No.: 409-856-3363
Web site: www.lonestarrifle.com
Email: dave@lonestarrilfe.com

LORCIN ENGINEERING CO., INC.
3830 Wacker Dr.
Mira Loma, CA 91752
Fax No.: 909-360-0623

LUCCHINI, SANDRO
North American Sales - K. Wellams
3809 Ninth St. SE
Calgary, AB T2G 3C7 CANADA
Phone no.: 403-243-3308
Fax no.: 403-243-3762
Factory
25060 Ponte Zanano V.T.
Via Petrarca, 47
Sarezzo (Brescia), ITALY
Fax no.: 011-39-30-89-11573

LUCIANO, BOSIS
Importer - See William Larkin Moore & Co. listing.
Factory
via Marconi 30
25039 Travagliato
Brescia, ITALY
Phone/Fax No.: 011-39-30-660413

LUGER (German Mfg.)
Mauser-Werke Oberndorf Waffensysteme GmbH
Werkstrasse 2
D-78727 Oberndorf/Neckar GERMANY
Fax No.: 011-49-74-2370670

LUGER (Recent Stoeger Mfg.)
Please refer to the Stoeger Industries listing.

TRADE MARKS

LU-MAR

Limited importation - see European American Armory listing.

Factory - Lu-Mar s.rl.
Artigiami 11
I-25063 Gardone, ITALY
Fax no.: 011-39-30-891-1185

M.O.A. CORPORATION

2451 Old Camden Pike
Eaton, OH 45320
Phone No.: 937-456-3669
Fax no.: 937-456-9331

JAMES MacNAUGHTON & SONS

Importer - Flying G Ranch
P.O. Box 70
Carrizo Springs, Texas 78834
Phone No.: 210-374-9691
Fax No.: 210-374-9774

Factory - James MacNaughton & Sons
Logie Gunworks
Forres
Moray, IV36 0QN, SCOTLAND
011-44/1309/611323
011-44/1309/61131

MAGNUM RESEARCH, INC.

7110 University Ave. NE
Minneapolis, MN 55432
Phone no.: 612-574-1868
Fax No.: 612-574-0109
Web site: www.magnumresearch.com

MAGTECH RECREATIONAL PRODUCTS, INC.

5030 Paradise Rd., Ste. A-104
Las Vegas, NV 89119
Phone No.: 702-736-2043
Fax No.: 702-736-2140

MAKAROV

Importer - See Century International Arms listing.
Importer - See Miltex, Inc. listing.

MANDALL SHOOTING SUPPLIES

3616 N. Scottsdale Rd.
Scottsdale, AZ 85252
Phone No.: 602-945-2553
Fax No.: 602-949-0734

MANUFRANCE

6, Rue de Lodi
F-42045 St. Etienne Cedex 1 FRANCE
Fax No.: 011-33-77-418830

MANURHIN REVOLVERS

Importer - ABO Industries
6046 Cornerstone Ct. W., Suite 206
San Diego, CA 92121
Fax No.: 619-453-2133

Factory Address
Z.I. La Gravoux B.P. 15
F-42380 Saint Bonnet Le Chateau FRANCE
Fax No.: 011-33-4-77-50-1070

MARCEL THYS & SONS

U.S. Agent - see Champlin Firearms, Inc. listing.
Rue de Villers, 8
B-4367 Crisnée BELGIUM
Fax No.: 011-32-4-257-74-22

MARKSMAN (Airguns)

5482 Argosy Drive
Huntington Beach, CA 92649
Fax No.: 714-891-0782

MARLIN FIREARMS COMPANY

100 Kenna Drive
P.O. Box 248
North Haven, CT 06473-0905
Fax No.: 203-234-7991
Web Site: www.marlinfireams.com
Web site: www.marlin-guns.com

MAROCCHI SHOTGUNS

Importer and Distributor - see Precision Sales Int.'l Inc. listing.
Marocchi Factory - C.D. Europe SRL
Via Galilei, 6
I-25068 Sarezzo (Brescia) ITALY
Fax No.: 011-39-30/890-0370

MATCH GRADE ARMS & AMMUNITION

6030 Treaschwig
Spring, TX 77373
Phone No.: 281-821-8282
Fax No.: 281-821-2775

MATHELON ARMES

Rue de l'Artisanat
Zone Industrielle
F-74150 Rumilly FRANCE
Fax no.: 011-33-4-50-01-46-18

MAUSER

Factory - Mauser Jagd-Und Sportwaffen GmbH
Werkstrasse 2/P.O. Box 1349
D-78727 Oberndorf/Neckar GERMANY
Fax No.: 011-49-74-23-70-655

MAVERICK ARMS, INC.
7 Grasso Ave., P.O. Box 497
North Haven, CT 06473
Fax No.: 203-230-5420
Parts/Repair Fax No.: 203-230-5479

McMILLAN BROS RIFLE CO., INC.
P.O. Box 86549
Phoenix, AZ 85080
Phone No.: 602-582-3713
Fax No.: 602-582-3930
Email: mcbros@mcmfamily.com
Web site: www.mcmfamily.com

MERKEL
Importer - See Gun South, Inc. listing.
Factory - Suhler Jagd-und Sportwaffen GmbH
Schützenstrasse 26
D-98527 Suhl, GERMANY
Fax No.: 011-49-3681-854-203

MIL-SPEC INDUSTRIES CORP.
10 Mineola Avenue
Roslyn Heights, NY 11577
Phone No.: 516-625-5787
Fax No.: 516-625-0988
Web site: www.mil-spec-industries.com

Email: info@mil-spec-industries.com

MILLER, DAVID
See David Miller Co. listing.

MILTEX, INC.
Importer - Commercial Makarovs
2225 Pinefield Station
Waldorf, MD 20601
Phone no.: 301-843-8087
Fax no.: 301-645-1430
Web site: www.miltexusa.com

MIROKU FIREARMS MFG. CO.
537-1 Shinohara
Nangoku City
Kochi, JAPAN

MITCHELL ARMS, INC.
P.O. Box 20855
Fountain Valley, CA 92728
Phone no.: 714-751-5258
Fax no.: 714-593-6971
Email: donmitchell@NET999.com

MODERN MUZZLELOADING, INC.
(Black Powder)
PO Box 130-CAT
Centerville, IA 52544
Fax No.: 515-856-2628

MONTANA ARMORY, INC.
Please refer to C. Sharps Arms Co. Inc. listing.

MOORE, W.L. & CO.
see listing under William Larkin Moore & Co.

MORAVIA l.t.d.
NÁDRAZNÍ 22
702 00 Ostrava CZECH REPUBLIC
Fax no.: 011-42-69-611-2202
Email: ARMS.CZ@ova.pvtnet.cz

MORINI
Importer - See Nygord Precision Products listing.
Factory - Morini Competition Arm SA
Casella Postale 92
CH-6930 Bedano SWITZERLAND
Fax no.: 011-41-91-9-45-1502
Web site: www.morinibluewin.ch

MOSSBERG
O.F. Mossberg & Sons, Inc.
7 Grasso Ave., P.O. Box 497
North Haven, CT 06473
Fax No.: 203-230-5359
Factory Service Center - OFM Service Department
101 Powder Metal Dr.
North Haven, CT 06473
Phone No.: 203-230-5400
Fax No.: 203-230-5420
Web site: www.mossberg.com

MOUNTAIN RIFLERY
1775 North Elk Road
Pocatello, ID 83204
Phone No.: 208-234-7142

MOUNTAIN STATES MUZZLELOADING SUPPLY (Black Powder)
P.O. Box 324
Williamstown, WV 26187
Phone No.: 304-295-6959
Fax No.: 304-295-8166

TRADE MARKS

MOWREY GUN WORKS (Black Powder)
See Cheney Rifle Works/Lehman Rifles

Distributor - See Mountain States Muzzleloading Supply listing.

MUSGRAVE
No current information available.

NS FIREARMS CORP.
c/o KFS, Inc.
P.O. Box 44405
Atlanta, GA 30336-1405
Fax No.: 404-505-8445

NATIONAL WILD TURKEY FEDERATION
National Organization
P.O. Box 530
Edgefield, SC 29824
Phone No.: 803-637-3106

NAVY ARMS CO.
689 Bergen Blvd.
Ridgefield, NJ 07657
Phone no.: 201-945-2500
Fax No.: 201-945-6859
Web site: www.navyarms.com
Email: ValForgett@msn.com

NELSON, P.V., (GUNMAKERS)
Folly Meadow, Hammersley Lane
Penn, Bucks
HP10 8HF, ENGLAND
Phone/Fax No.: 011-44-49-4812836

NESIKA
Nesika Bay Precision, Inc.
5809 NE Minder Rd. #8
Poulsbo, WA 98370
Phone No.: 360-297-5555
Fax No.: 360-297-3973

NEW ENGLAND ARMS, CORP.
P.O. Box 278, Lawrence Lane
Kittery Point, ME 03905-0278
Phone No.: 207-439-0593
Fax No.: 207-439-6726

NEW ENGLAND CUSTOM GUN SERVICE LTD. (NECG)
438 Willow Brook Rd.
Plainfield, NH 03781
Phone No.: 603-469-3450
Fax No.: 603-469-3471
Email: bestguns@cyberportal.net

NEW ENGLAND FIREARMS
60 Industrial Rowe
Gardner, MA 01440
Phone No.: 978-632-9393
Fax No.: 978-632-2300
Web Site: www.hr1871.com
Email: hr1871@hr1871.com

NORINCA AIRGUNS
2607 N.E. Industrial drive
N. Kansas City, MO 64060

NORINCO (Shotguns only)
U.S. Importer - Norinco Sports U.S.A.
P.O. Box 5575
Diamond Bar, CA 91765
Phone No.: 888-887-7381
Fax No.: 909-598-8819

NORSMAN SPORTING ARMS
2900 McDonald Road
Bismarck, ND 58504-9670
Phone/Fax: 701-224-8479
Web site: www.norsmanarms.qpg.com

NORTH AMERICAN ARMS, INC.
2150 South, 950 East
Provo, UT 84606-6285
Phone No.: 801-374-9990
Fax No.: 801-374-9998
Web site: www.naaminis.com

NOWLIN MFG. INC.
Rt. 1 Box 308
20622 4092 Rd.
Claremore, OK 74017
Phone No.: 918-342-0689
Fax No.: 918-342-0624
Web site: www.nowlinguns.com
Email: nowlinguns@msn.com

NYGORD PRECISION PRODUCTS
P.O. Box 12578
Prescott, AZ 86304
Phone No.: 520-717-2315
Fax No.: 520-717-2198
Web site: www.nygord-precision.com
Email: nygords@northlink.com

O.D.I.
Parts only
Essex Arms
Box 345
Island Pond, VT 05846
Phone No.: 802-723-4313

TRADE
MARKS

OCTOBER COUNTRY
P.O. Box 969
Hayden, ID 83835-0969
Phone No.: 208-772-2068
Fax No.: 208-772-9230

OHIO ORDNANCE WORKS INC.
310 Park Dr.
Chardon, OH 44024

OLYMPIC ARMS, INC.
620-626 Old Pacific Hwy. S.E.
Olympia, WA 98513
Phone No.: 360-459-7940
Fax No.: 360-491-3447
Web site: www.olyarms.com
Email: olysman@aol.com

OMNI
(name changed during 1998)
Please refer to E.D.M. Arms listing.

ORVIS
Custom shotgun information only
Historic Route 7A
Manchester, VT 05254
Phone No.: 802-362-2580

P.A.W.S., INC.
Factory
8175 River Road N.E.
Salem, OR 97303
Phone No.: 503-393-0838
Fax No.: 503-390-6075

PCE Ltd./Steyr (Airguns)
P.O. Box 97
Little Tree's Ramble
Monteagle, TN 37356
Phone No.: 931-924-3400
Fax No.: 931-924-3489

PARA-ORDNANCE MFG. INC.
980 Tapscott Rd.
Scarborough, Ontario
M1X 1C3 CANADA
Phone No.: 416-297-7855
Fax No.: 416-297-1289
Web Site: www.paraord.com
Email: inquiries@paraord.com

Factory
3411 McNicoll Ave.
Scarborough, Ontario
M1V 2V6 CANADA

PARDINI
Importer - See Nygord Precision Products listing.
Factory - Pardini Armi Commerciale
154/A via Italica
I-55043 Lido di Camaiore, ITALY
Fax No.: 011-39-584-90122

PARKER REPRODUCTIONS
Parker Reproduction Div.
124 River Road
Middlesex, NJ 08846
Phone no.: 732-469-0100
Fax No.: 732-469-9692

PASTUSEK INDUSTRIES
Distributor - Fort Worth Firearms
2006-B Martin L. King, Jr. Fwy.
Fort Worth, TX 76104-6303
Phone No.: 817-536-0718
Fax No.: 817-535-0290

PAUL & ASSOCIATES
27385 Pressonville Rd.
Wellsville, KS 66092
Phone No.: 913-883-4444
Fax No.: 913-883-2525

PEACE RIVER CLASSICS
1630 Park Ave. N.
Bartow, FL 33830

PEDERSOLI, DAVIDE & C. s.n.c. (BLACK POWDER)
Importer - Flintlocks, Etc.
160 Rossiter Rd.
Richmond, MA 01254
Fax 413-698-3866

Factory
Via Artigiani 57
I-25063 Gardone V.T. (BS), ITALY
Fax No.: 011-39-30-8911019
Web site: www.davide-pedersoli.com

PEIFER RIFLE CO. (BLACK POWDER)
P.O. Box 192
Nokomis, IL 62075
Fax No.: 217-563-7060

PENTHENY de PENTHENY, INC.
2352 Baggett Ct.
Santa Rosa, CA 95401
Phone/Fax No.: 707-573-1390

PERAZZI

Importer - Perazzi USA, Inc.
1207 South Shamrock Ave.
Monrovia, CA 91016
Phone No.: 626-303-0068
Fax No.: 626-303-2081

Factory - Armi Perazzi S.p.A.
Via Fontanelle, 1/3
I-25080 Botticino Mattina Brescia ITALY
Fax No.: 011-39-30-269-2594

PERUGINI & VISINI, ARMI

Factory
Via Camprelle 126
Nuvolera, Brescia
I-25080 ITALY
Fax No.: 011-39-30-689-7821
Web site: www.intred.it/perugini-visini
Email: pervis@intred.it

PETERS STAHL GmbH

Importer - Peters Stahl, U.S.A.
P.O. Box 1000
700 N. 200 W.
Delta, UT 84624
Phone No.: 435-864-3700
Fax No.: 435-864-4403
Web site: www.PeterStahlUSA.com
Email: PetersStahl@Hotmail.com

Factory
Stettiner Strasse 42
D-33106 Paderborn, GERMANY
Fax No.: 011-49-5251-75611

PHILLIPS & ROGERS, INC.

680 FM 980
Huntsville, TX 77340
Phone No.: 409-435-0011
Fax No.: 409-435-0022
Web site: www.phillipsrodgers.com

PHOENIX ARMS

1420 S. Archibald Ave.
Ontario, CA 91761
Phone No.: 909-947-4843
Fax No.: 909-947-6798

PIETTA, Flli s.n.c. (Black Powder)

Via Mandolossa, 102
I-25064 Gussago (Brescia) ITALY
Fax No.: 011-39-30-373-7100
Web site: www.pietta.it
Email: fap@spindernet.it

PIOTTI

Importer - See William Larkin Moore & Co. listing.

Factory - Piotti, F.lli, S.n.c.
Via Cinelli, 10-12
I-25063 Gardone V.T. Brescia, ITALY
Fax No.: 011-39-30-891-2578

PRAIRIE GUN WORKS

1-761 Mairon St.
Winnipeg, Manitoba
R2J 0K6 CANADA
Phone No.: 204-231-2976
Fax No.: 204-231-8566
Web site: www.prairiegunworks.com
Email: rifles@prairiegunworks.com

PRAIRIE RIVER ARMS (Black Powder)

1220 North 6th St.
Princeton, IL 61356
Fax No.: 815-875-1402

PRECISION SALES INT'L, INC.

P.O. Box 1776
14 Coleman Avenue
Westfield, MA 01086
Phone No.: 413-562-5055
Fax No.: 413-562-5056
Web site: www.precision-sales.com

PRECISION SMALL ARMS, INC. ("PSA")

Sales & Marketing Office
9272 Jeronimo Rd., Ste. 121
Irvine, CA 92618
Phone No.: 949-768-3530
Fax No.: 949-768-4808
Web site: www.lebebe.com
Email: zebraops@att.com

PROFESSIONAL ORDNANCE, INC.

1070 Metric Dr.
Lake Havasu City, AZ 86403
Phone No.: 520-505-2420

PURDEY, JAMES, & SONS, LTD.

57-58 S Audley Street
London, W1Y 6ED ENGLAND
Phone No.: 011-44-71-499-1801
Fax No.: 011-44-71-355-3297

QUAIL UNLIMITED, INC.
National Conservation Organization
31 Quail Run
PO Box 610
Edgefield, SC 29824
Phone No.: 803-637-5731
Fax No.: 803-637-0037
Web site: www.quailunlimited.org
Email: QUAIL1@JETBN.net

QUALITY ARMS, INC.
P.O. Box 19477
Houston, TX 77224
Phone No.: 281-870-8377
Fax No.: 281-870-8524
Website:www.gunshop.com/quala1.htm
Web site: www.arrieta.com
Email: 105621.1212@Compuserve.com

QUALITY PARTS CO.
Manufacturer of Bushmaster Fire-arms, Inc.
999 Roosevelt Trail Bldg. 3
Windham, ME 04062
Phone No.: 207-892-3594
Fax No.: 207-892-8068
Email: Bushmaster@maine.com

RAF
103, rue Antoine Durafour
F-42100 Saint Etienne
FRANCE
Fax No.: 05 71 216 17

R.F.M.
Factory - R.F.M. di Rota Luciano
via Patrioti, 26
I-25068 Noboli di Sarezzo
V.T. (Brescia) ITALY
Fax no.: 011-49-30-800442

RND MANUFACTURING
Distributor - Mesa Sportsmen's Asso-ciation, L.L.C.
238 Main Street
P.O. Box 854
Delta, CO 81416
Phone No.: 970-874-4571
Fax No.: 970-874-4821
Factory - RND Manufacturing
14311 Mead Street
Longmont, CO 80501
Phone No.: 303-623-2012

RPM PISTOLS
15481 N. Twin Lakes Dr.
Tuscon, AZ. 85739
Phone no.: 520-825-1233
Fax no.: 520-825-3333
Web site: www.shooters.com/rpm
Email: rpmXL1@theriver.com

RWS
See Dynamit Nobel listing.

RADOM
Importer (Current mfg.) - Dalvar of U.S.A.
740 East Warm Springs Rd., Ste. 122
Henderson, NV 89015
Phone/Fax: 702-558-6707
Web site: www.geocities.com/Penta-gon/4050/
Email: dalvar_usa@juno.com

RAM-LINE - BLOUNT INC.
P.O. Box 38
Onalaska, WI 54650
Phone No.: 608-781-5800
Fax No.: 608-781-0368

RANDALL FIREARMS COMPANY
Randall Firearms Historian:
Mr. Rick Kennerknecht
P.O. Box 1180
Mills, WY 82644-1180
Email: rekenn@trib.com

RAPTOR ARMS CO. INC.
273 Canal St., Suite 190
Shelton, CT 06484
Phone No.: 203-924-7618
Fax No.: 203-924-7624

RAVELL LTD.
289 Diputacion Street
S-08009 Barcelona, SPAIN
Fax No.: 011-34-3-488-1394
Email: ravell-armas@cambrabcn.es

GARY REEDER CUSTOM GUNS
2710 N. Steves Blvd. #4
Flagstaff, AZ 86004
Phone No.: 520-527-4100
Fax No.: 520-527-0840
Web Site: www.reedercustomguns.com
Email: gary@reedercustomguns.com
Email: creeder@infomagic.com

REMINGTON
Remington Arms Co., Inc.
Attn: Consumer Services
870 Remington Drive
P.O. Box 700
Madison, NC 27025-0700
Phone No.: 800-243-9700
Fax No.: 910-548-8707
Web site: www.remington.com
Remington Arms Co., Inc. (Repairs)
14 Hoefler Ave.
Ilion, NY 13357
Phone No.: 800-243-9700

REPUBLIC ARMS, INC.
15167 Sierra Bonita Lane
Chino, CA 91710
Phone No.: 909-597-3873
Fax No.: 909-597-2612
Web site: www.republicarmsinc.com
Email: patriot@ix.netcom.com

REPUBLIC ARMS OF SOUTH AFRICA
Importer/Distributor - T.S.F (U.S.A.)Ltd.
P.O. Box 830
Fairfax, VA 22030
Phone no.: 703-385-0889
Fax no.: 703-385-4655
Factory
74 Auret St. Jeppe
Jeppestown, Union of South Africa 2043

RIB MOUNTAIN ARMS, INC.
47416 292nd St.
Beresford, SD 57004
Phone/Fax No.: 605-957-4249
Email: ribarms@sturgis.com

RIFLES, INC.
873 West 5400 North
Cedar City, UT 84720
Phone No.: 435-586-5995
Fax No.: 435-586-5996
Web site: www.riflesinc.com
Email: rifles@netutah.com

RIGANIAN, RAY (RIFLEMAKER)
324 N. Central Ave., Unit B
Glendale, CA 91203
Phone No.: 818-502-2678

RIGBY, JOHN & CO. (GUNMAKERS), INC.
U.S. Offices
1317 Spring St.
Paso Robles, CA 93446
Phone no.: 805-227-4236
Fax no.: 805-227-4723

RIZZINI, BATTISTA
Importer - see New England Arms Corp. listing.
Importer - see W.L. Moore listing.
Factory
Via 2 Giugno, 7/7 bis
I-25060 Marcheno (Brescia), ITALY
Fax No.: 011-39-30/861319
Web site: www.rizzini.it

RIZZINI, EMILIO, s.n.c.
Via A. Gitti, 37
I-25060 Marcheno (BS) ITALY
Fax no.: 011-39-30-861-367
Web site: www.emiliorizzini.com
Email: re@lumetel.it

RIZZINI, F.LLI
Importer - See William Larkin Moore & Co. listing.
Importer - See New England Arms Corp. listing.

ROBAR COMPANIES, INC., THE
21438 N. 7th Avenue, Ste. B
Phoenix, AZ 85027
Phone No.: 602-581-2648
Fax No.: 602-582-0059
Web site: www.robarguns.com

ROBERTS, J. & SON (GUNMAKERS) LTD.
66 Great Suffolk St.
London SE1 OBU ENGLAND
Phone No.: 011-44-171-620-0690
Fax No.: 011-44-171-928-9205

ROBINSON ARMAMENT CO.
2975 South 300 West
Salt Lake City, UT 84115
Phone No.: 801-485-1012
Fax No.: 801-484-4363
Email: ZDF@robarm.com

ROCHE, CHRISTIAN
12 Lotissement les Eglantiers
42 340 Veauche, France
Phone No.: 011-33-77-93-35-33
Fax No.: 011-33-77-94-35-33

ROCK RIVER ARMS, INC.
101 Noble St.
Cleveland, IL 61241
Phone no.: 309-792-5780
Fax no.: 309-792-5781
Web site: www.rockriverarms.com

ROCKY MOUNTAIN ARMS, INC.
1813 Sunset Place, Unit D
Longmont, CO 80501
Phone No: 303-678-8522
Fax No.: 303-678-8766
Web site: www.bearcoat.com
Email: gunmkr@aol.com

ROCKY MOUNTAIN ELK FOUNDA-TION
2291 W. Broadway
Missoula, MT 59802
Phone No.: 406-523-4500
Fax No.: 406-523-4581

ROGUE RIVER RIFLEWORKS
1317 Spring St.
Paso Robles, CA 93446
Phone no.: 805-227-4706
Fax no.: 805-227-4723

ROSSI
Importer - BrazTech, L.C.
16175 N.W. 49th Ave.
Miami, FL 33014
Phone No.: 305-474-0401
Web site: www.rossiusa.com
Amadeo Rossi, S.A.
Rua Amadeo Rossi, 143
B-93030-220 Sao Leopoldo-RS BRAZIL
Email: rossi.firearms@pnet.com.br

ROTA, LUCIANO
Importer - see New England Arms listing

ROTTWEIL
Importer - See Dynamit Nobel of America listing.

RUTTEN HERSTAL
Importer - see Labanu, Inc. listing
Factory - Rutten Herstal
Parc Industriel des Hauts-Sarts
Premiere Avenue, 7-9
B-4040 Herstal, BELGIUM
Fax No.: 011-32-41/648589

S.I.A.C.E.
Importer - see New England Arms listing.

SKB SHOTGUNS
Importer - see Guns Unlimited, Inc. listing.

SSK INDUSTRIES
721 Woodvue Lane
Wintersville, OH 43952
Phone No. 614-264-0176
Fax No. 614-264-2257

STI INTERNATIONAL
114 Halmar Cove
Georgetown, TX 78628
Phone: 800-959-8201
Fax No.: 512-819-0465
Web site: www.sti-guns.com
Email: STIGUN@prismnet.com

SABATTI s.p.a.
Importer - See European American Armory listing.
Factory - Sabatti S.P.A.
Via Alessandro Voltra, 90
I-25063 Gardone Valtrompia, (BS) ITALY
Fax No.: 011-39-30-89-12-059

SACO DEFENSE INC.
291 North St.
Saco, ME 04072-0890
Fax no.: 207-283-1395
Web site: www.sacoinc.com

SAFARI ARMS
620-626 Old Pacific Hwy. S.E.
Olympia, WA 98513
Phone No.: 360-459-7940
Fax No.: 360-491-3447

SAFARI CLUB INTERNATIONAL
4800 West Gates Pass Road
Tucson, AZ 85745
Phone No.: 602-620-1220
Fax No.: 602-622-1205

SAIGA
Importer - please refer to European American Armory listing.

TRADE MARKS

SAKO

Importer - See Stoeger Industries listing.

Factory - Sako, Limited
P.O. Box 149
FIN-11101 Riihimäki, FINLAND
Fax No.: 011-358-19-720446
Web site: www.shooters.com/sako

SAMCO GLOBAL ARMS, INC.

6995 N.W. 43rd St.
Miami, FL 33166
Phone No.: 305-593-9782
Fax No.: 305-593-1014
Web site: www.samcoglobal.com
Email: samco@samcoglobal.com

SARSILMAZ

Importer - See Armsport, Inc. listing.
Factory - Main office
Mercan Uzuncarsi Cad. No. 69
34450 Istanbul/TURKEY
Fax No.: 011-90212-51119-99-513-13-25
Web site: www.sarsilmaz.com.tr
Email: sarsilmaz@sarsilmaz.com.tr

SAUER, J.P. & SOHN

Importer - See SIG Arms listing.
Factory - SIG Arms Sauer GmbH
Sauerstrasse 2-6
D-24340 Eckernförde, GERMANY
Fax No.: 011-49-43-51-471-160

SAVAGE ARMS, INC.

100 Springdale Road
P.O. Box 1110
Westfield, MA 01085
Phone no.: 413-568-7001
Fax No.: 413-562-7764
Web site: www.savagearms.com
Older Savage Arms Historical Research
Mr. John Callahan
53 Old Quarry Rd.
Westfield, MA 01085
$15.00/gun research fee, $20.00 per gun for
Models 1895, 1899, and 99 rifles.

SAVIN, J.C.

11 Place de la Cite
F-42220 Bourg Argental, FRANCE
Fax no.: 011-33-4-77-39-1855

SAXONIA

Am Schwarzwasser 1
D-08340 Schwarzenberg GERMANY
Fax No.: 011-49-3774-120822

SCATTERGUN TECHNOLOGIES INC.

620 8th Ave. S.
Nashville, TN 37203
Phone No.: 615-254-1441
Fax No.: 615-254-1449
Web site: www.scattergun.com
Email: write@scattergun.com

H. SCHEIRING

Klagenfurter Strasse 19
A-9170 Ferlach AUSTRIA
Fax No.: 011-43-4227-287620

SCHELLER SPEZIALWAFFEN

GSS Scheller Spezialwaffen und Buchsenmacherbedart
Factory
Pfutschbergstr. 03
G-98527 Suhl, GERMANY
Fax no.: 011-49-3681-80808

SCHUETZEN PISTOL WORKS, INC.

620-626 Old Pacific Hwy. S.E.
Olympia, WA 98513
Phone No.: 360-459-7940
Fax No.: 360-491-3447

SCHUTZEN BOHME GmbH

Muhlenstrasse 6-8
31737 Rintein, GERMANY
Phone No.: 0 57 51 4 47 70
Fax No.: 0 57 51 4 24 90

SCOTT, W. C., LTD.

Repair address
Holland & Holland, Ltd.
Attn: Mr. P. C. Chismon
31-33 Bruton St.
London W1X 8JS ENGLAND
Fax No.: 071/499-4544

SEARCY, B. & CO.

12049 Boron Ave.
Boron, CA 93516
Phone no.: 760-762-6771
Fax no.: 760-762-0191

SEECAMP, L.W. CO., INC.

301 Brewster Road
Milford, CT 06460
Phone No.: 203-877-3429

SEMMERLING

Manufacturer - See American Derringer Corp. listing.

C. SHARPS ARMS CO. INC.
Distributor - Montana Armory, Inc.
P.O. Box 885
Big Timber, MT 59011
Phone No.: 406-932-4353
Fax No.: 406-932-4443

SHILOH RIFLE MFG. CO.
P.O. Box 279
Big Timber, MT 59011
Phone No.: 406-932-4454
Fax No.: 406-932-5627

SHOOTERS ARMS MANUFACTURING INCORPORATED
Main Office
918 B. Reyes Bldg.
Aurora Blvd. Cubao
Quezon City, Phillipines
Phone No.: 011-632-911-0538
Fax No.: 011-632-911-1098
Web site: www.shootersarms.com.ph
Email: drmunoz@eudoramail.com

SIG ARMS, INC.
Corporate Park
Exeter, NH 03833
Phone No.: 603-772-2302
Fax No.: 603-772-9082
Web Site: www.sigarms.com

SIG SAUER
Importer - SIG Arms, Inc.
Corporate Park
Exeter, NH 03833
Fax No.: 603-772-9082
Web Site: www.sigarms.com
Factory - SIG - Schweizerische Industrie-Gesellschaft
Industrielplatz
CH-8212 Neuhausen am Rheinfall, SWITZERLAND
Fax No.: 011-41-153-216-601

SILE DISTRIBUTORS
7 Centre Market Place
New York, NY 10013
Phone No.: 212-925-4111
Fax No.: 212-925-3149

SILMA s.r.l.
Factory
Via I Maggio, 74
I-25060 Zanano di Sarezzo, (BS) ITALY
Fax No.: 011-39-30-8900712

GENE SIMILLION GUNMAKER
220 S. Wisconsin
Gunnison, CO 81230
Phone No.: 970-641-1126

SMITH & WESSON
Customer Service
2100 Roosevelt Avenue
P.O. Box 2208
Springfield, MA 01102-2208
Phone No.: 800-331-0852, Ext. 2904
Fax No.: 413-731-8980
Web site: www.smith-wesson.com
Smith & Wesson Research
Attn: Mr. Roy Jinks, S&W Historian
P.O. Box 2208
Springfield, MA 01102-2208
Phone No.: 413-781-8300
Fax No.: 413-731-8980

SOMMER + OCKENFUSS GmbH
Importer - see Intertex Carousels Corporation listing.
Bühlerweg 4
D-72270 Baiersbronn GERMANY
Fax no.: 011-49-7447-94-74-20
Web site: www.sommer-ockenfuss.de
Email: weapons@sommer-ockenfuss.de

SNAKE CHARMER
Factory - Sporting Arms Mfg. Inc.
801 Hall Ave. P.O. Box 670
Littlefield, TX 79339
Phone no.: 806-385-5665
Fax No.: 806-385-3394

SPRINGFIELD ARMORY
Mfg. by Springfield Inc.
420 W. Main St.
Geneseo, IL 61254
Phone No.: 309-944-5631
Fax No.: 309-944-3676
Web site: www.springfield-armory.com
Email: spring@geneseo.net
Email: sales@springfield-armory.com

STALLARD ARMS
Refer to Hi-Point listing.

STANDARD ARMS OF NEVADA, INC.
3555 Airway Dr., Ste. 313
Reno, NV 89511
Phone No.: 702-853-3300
Fax No.: 702-857-4241
Web site: www.standardgun.com

STEVENS, J., ARMS COMPANY
Older Stevens Historical Research
Mr. John Callahan
53 Old Quarry Rd.
Westfield, MA 01085
$15.00/gun research fee.

STEYR (Airguns only)
PO Box 8394
La Crescenta, CA 91224

STEYR MANNLICHER
Importer - See GSI listing.
Factory - Steyr Mannlicher A.G.
Box 1000, Mannlicher Str. 1
Steyr A-4400 AUSTRIA
Fax No.: 01143-7252-68621

STOEGER INDUSTRIES
5 Mansard Court
Wayne, NJ 07470
Phone No.: 201-872-9500
Fax No.: 201-872-2230

STONE MOUNTAIN ARMS, INC.
(Black Powder)
5988 Peachtree Corners East
Norcross, GA 30071
Fax No.: 404-242-8546

STONER RIFLE
Factory - Knight's Manufacturing Co.
7750 - 9th St. SW
Vero Beach, FL 32968
Fax No.: 407-569-2955

STRAYER TRIPP INTERNATIONAL
Please refer to the STI Internation listing.

STURM, RUGER & CO., INC.
200 Ruger Rd.
Prescott, AZ
Phone no.: 520-541-8820
Fax No.: 520-541-8850

SUHLER JAGDGEWEHR MANUFAK-TER GmbH
Bahnhofstrasse 16
D-98527 Suhl, GERMANY
Fax no.: 011-39-36-81-30-81-60

SUNDANCE INDUSTRIES
25163 W. Ave. Stanford
Valencia, CA 91355
Phone no.: 805-257-4807
Fax No.: 805-257-4891

SUPER SIX LLC
3806 W. Lisbon Ave.
Milwaukee, WI 53208
Phone No.: 414-344-3343
Fax No.: 414-344-0304

SYMES & WRIGHT LTD.
No current information

TACONIC FIREARMS, LTD.
Perry Lane, P.O. Box 553
Cambridge, NY 12816
Phone no.: 518-677-2704
Fax no.: 518-677-5974

TANNER, ANDRE
Factory - No current information.

TANFOGLIO, FRATELLI, S.r.l.
Importer - See European American Armory listing.
Factory
Via Vaitrompia 39/41
I-25063 Gardone V.T. (BS) ITALY
Fax No.: 011-39-30-8910183

TAR-HUNT CUSTOM RIFLES, INC.
R.R. 3 Box 572
Bloomsburg, PA 17815-9351
Phone/Fax No.: 570-784-6368

TAURUS INTERNATIONAL
16175 NW 49th Ave.
Miami, FL 33014-6314
Phone No.: 305-624-1115
Fax No.: 305-623-7506
Web site: www.taurususa.com

TAYLOR'S & CO.(Black Powder & Reproductions)
304 Lenoir Dr.
Winchester, VA 22603
Phone No.: 540-722-2017
Fax No: 540-722-2018
Web Site: www.taylorsfirearms.com
Email: info@taylorsfirearms.com

TECHNO ARMS (PTY) LIMITED
No current information.

TEXAS ARMS
P.O. Box 154906
Waco, TX 76715
Phone No.: 817-867-6972

TEXAS LONGHORN ARMS, INC.
No current information.

THOMPSON/CENTER ARMS CO., INC.
P.O. Box 5002
Rochester, NH 03866
Customer service phone no.: 603-332-2333
Fax no.: 603-332-5133
Web site: www.tcarms.com

TIKKA
Importer - See Stoeger Industries, Inc. listing.

TIME PRECISION, INC.
640 Federal Rd.
Brookfield, CT 06804
Phone No.: 203-775-8343

TORNADO
Factory - AseTekno
Helsinginkatu 17
FIN-00500 Helsinki, Finland
Fax No.: 011-358-0-753-6463

TRADITIONS PERFORMANCE MUZZLELOADING (Black Powder)
P.O. Box 776
Old Saybrook, CT 06475
Phone No.: 860-388-4656
Fax No.: 860-388-4657
Web site: www.traditionsmuzzle.com

TRAIL GUN ARMORY (Black Powder)
Route 22, Box 760
Conroe, TX 77303

TRISTAR
Importer/Distributor - Sporting Arms, Ltd.
P.O. Box 7496
1814 - 16 Linn St.
N. Kansas City, MO 64116
Phone No.: 816-421-1400
Fax No.: 816-421-4182

TRUVELO ARMOURY
107 Packard Street Randjies - park X22
Midrand 1685 SOUTH AFRICA
Fax no.: 011-27-1-13-14-14-09

TULA, GUB KBP subsidiary
Sporting & Hunting Guns Central Research
R-300041 Tula, RUSSIA
Fax no.: 011-7-872-27-33-58-31-27-24

UFA, INC.
7655 E. Evans Road, #2
Scottsdale, AZ 85260
Fax No.: 602-922-0148

UBERTI, ALDO & C., S.r.l.
Importer - Uberti USA, Inc.
P.O. Box 509
362 Limerock Road
Lakeville, CT 06039
Fax No.: 860-435-8146
Email: uberti@li.com
Factory - Aldo Uberti & C., S.r.l.
Via G. Carducci, 41
I-25068 Ponte Zanano (BS) ITALY
Fax No.: 011-39-30-891-1061
Email: uberti@lumetel.it

UGARTECHEA, ARMAS
Importer - Lion Country Supply
Phone no.: 800-662-5202
Fax no.: 814-692-5252

UGARTECHEA, IGNACIO
Exclusive Importer - Aspen Outfitting Co.
520 East Cooper Ave.
Aspen, CO 81611
Phone no.: 970-925-3406
Fax no.: 970-920-3706
Factory - Ugartechea, Ignacio
P.O. Box 21
Eibar, SPAIN
Fax No.: 011-3443-121669

ULTRA LIGHT ARMS
P.O. Box 1270
214 Price Street
Granville, WV 26534
Phone/Fax No.: 304-599-5687

ULTRAMATIC PRODUKTIONS GmbH
See Wolf Sporting Pistols listing.
Wiesengasse 6
A-2551 Enzesfeld
AUSTRIA
Fax No.: 011-43-022-5681152

UMAREX SPORTWAFFEN GmbH & CO. KG
Donnerfeld 2
D-59757 Arnsberg GERMANY
Fax No.: 011-49-2932-638-222

TRADE MARKS

UNIQUE

Importer - see Nygord Precision Products listing.

Factory - Unique Manufacture d'Armes
10, rue des Allees
F-64704 Hendaye, FRANCE
Fax No.: 011-33-5920/5085

U.S. HISTORICAL SOCIETY

Also see America Remembers listing.
First & Main Streets
Richmond, VA 23219
Fax No.: 804-648-0002

UNITED STATES FIRE ARMS MANUFACTURING COMPANY, INC.

55 Van Dyke Ave.
Hartford, CT 06106
Phone No.: 800-877-2832
Fax No.: 800-644-7265
Web site: www.usfirearms.com

UZI

No commercial importation (law enforcement/military only)
Please refer to Mossberg listing.

VALTRO

Importer - Valtro USA Inc.
1281 Andersen Dr.
San Rafael, Ca 94901
Phone No.: 415-256-2575
Fax No.: 415-256-2576

Factory - Valtro Stocchetta srl
Via Capretti, 12/14
Loc. Stocchetta
Brescia, ITALY
Fax No.: 011-39-30-209-1500

VARBERGER

No current importation.

VEKTOR

Importer - Vektor USA, Inc.
5139 Stanart St.
Norfolk, VA 23502
Phone No.: 757-455-8895
Fax No.: 757-461-9155
Email: vektorusa@series2000.com

VEPR. RIFLES

Importer - Please refer to ZDF Import Export listing.

VERNEY-CARRON

Importer - Federal Engineering Corporation
316 Meyer Rd.
Bensenville, IL 60106
Phone No.: 630-860-1938
Fax No.: 630-860-2085
fedlengr@verney-carron.com

Factory - Verney-Carron
54, Boulevard Thiers
Boite Postale 72 K
F-42002 St. Etienne Cedex 1 FRANCE
Fax No.: 011-33-4-77-790702
Web site: www.verney-carron.com
Email: email@verney-carron.com

VOERE

Factory - Voere Austria
Postfach 416
A-6333 Kufstein, AUSTRIA
Fax No.: 011-43-5372-5752

VOLQUARTSEN CUSTOM

24276 240th St.
P.O. Box 397
Carroll, IA 51401
Phone No.: 712-792-4238
Fax No.: 712-792-2542
Web site: www.shooters.com/volquartsen

WAFFEN VERATSHNIG

Factory
Gablenzgasse 42/7
A-1160 Vienna, AUSTRIA
Fax No.: 011-43-664-342-5609

WALTHER

Importer - Carl Walther USA LLC
P.O. Box 208
Ten Prince St.
Alexandria, VA 22313
Phone No.: 703-548-1400
Fax No.: 703-549-7826
Web site: www.waltherusa.com
Email: waltherusa@mindspring.com

Target pistol importer - See Champion's Choice Inc. listing.

GSP/rifle conversion kit importer and factory repair station

Earl's Repair Service, Inc.
437 Chandler Street (rear)
Tewksbury, MA 01876
Phone No.: 978-851-2656
Fax No.: 978-851-9462

WALTHER, cont.
German Company Headquarters
Carl Walther Sportwaffen GmbH
Donnerfeld 2
D-59757 Arnsberg GERMANY
Fax no.: 011-49-29-32-638149

Factory - Carl Walther, GmbH, Sportwaffenfabrik
Postfach 4325
D-89033 Ulm/Donau, GERMANY
Fax No.: 011-49-731-1539170

WATSON BROS.
39 Redcross Way
London Bridge
SE1 1HG ENGLAND
Phone/Fax No.: 011-44-71-4033367

WEATHERBY
3100 El Camino Real
Atascadero, CA 93422
Phone No.: 805-466-1767
Fax No.: 805-466-2527
Web site: www.weatherby.com

WEBLEY & SCOTT (Airguns)
Importer - Pyramyd Stone International
2447 Suffolk Lane
Pepper Pike, OH 44124
Phone No.: 440-442-2262
Fax No.: 440-605-1936
Web site: www.pyramydair.com

Factory
Frankley Industrial Park
Tay Road, Rubery, Rednal
GB-Birmingham ENGLAND B45 OPA
Phone No.: 011-21-453-1864
Fax No.: 011-21-457-7846

WEIHRAUCH, HANS-HERMANN
Exclusive Airgun Importer - See Beeman Precision Airguns listing.
Firearms Importer - See European American Armory listing.
Factory - H. Weihrauch, Sportwaffenfabrik
Industriestrasse 11
D-97638 Mellrichstadt, GERMANY
Fax No.: 011-49-97-76-5532

DAN WESSON FIREARMS
New York International Corp.
119 Kempler Ln.
Norwich, NY 13815
Phone no.: 607-336-1174
Fax no.: 607-336-2730
Web site: www.Dan-Wesson.com

WESSON & HARRINGTON
60 Industrial Rowe
Gardner, MA 01440
Phone: 508-632-9393
Fax No.: 508-632-2300

WESTLEY RICHARDS & CO., Ltd.
U.S. Office
Chestnut Hall
4319 West Chestnut Expressway
Springfield, MO 65802
Phone No.: 417-869-8447

Factory - Westley Richards & Co., Ltd.
40 Grange Road
Bournbrook, Birmingham, ENGLAND B29 6AR
Fax No.: 011-44-121-414-1138

WHITE MUZZLE LOADING SYSTEMS, INC. (Black Powder)
25 E. Hwy 40
Roosevelt, UT 84066
Fax No.: 801-722-3054

WICHITA ARMS, INC.
P.O. Box 11371
923 E. Gilbert
Wichita, KS 67211
Phone No.: 316-265-0661
Fax No.: 316-265-0760

WILD WEST GUNS, INC.
7521 Old Seward Hwy., Unit A
Anchorage, AK 99518
Phone No.: 907-344-4500
Fax No.: 907-344-4005
Web site: www.wildwestguns.com
Email: wwguns@sinbad.net

WILDERNESS RIFLE WORKS (Black Powder)
Distributor - See Mountain States Muzzleloading Supplies listing.

WILDEY, INC.
458 Danbury Rd.
New Milford CT 06776
Phone No.: 860-355-9000
Fax No.: 860-354-7759

TRADE MARKS

WILLIAM LARKIN MOORE & CO.
8340 East Raintree Dr., Suite B-7
Scottsdale, AZ 85260
Phone No.: 602-951-8913
Fax No.: 602-951-3677
Web site: www.doublegun.com
Email: WLMooreco@sprynet.com

WILLIAM DOUGLAS & SONS
Importer - see Cape Outfitters, Inc. listing.

WILLIAM EVANS LIMITED
67 St. James's Street
London SW1A 1PH
ENGLAND
Fax No.: 011-44-171-499-1912
Email: Email: sales@williamevans.com

WILLIAM POWELL & SON (GUN-MAKERS), Ltd.
Importer - Bells Legendary Country-wear
22 Circle Dr.
Bellmore, NY 11710
Factory
35-37 Carrs Lane
Birmingham B47SX ENGLAND
Phone No.: 011-44-21-6430689/8362
Fax No.: 011-44-21-6313504

WILSON COMBAT
2234 CR 719
P.O. Box 578
Berryville, AR 72616-0578
Phone No.: 800-955-4856
Fax No.: 870-545-3310
Web site: www.wilsoncombat.com
Email: info@wilsoncombat.com

WINCHESTER (U.S.REPEATING ARMS)
U.S. Repeating Arms Company, Inc. Factory and Custom Shop
275 Winchester Ave., P.O. Box 30-300
New Haven, CT. 06511-1970
Custom Shop
Phone No.: 203-789-5503
Fax No.: 203-789-5853
Administrative Offices
275 Winchester Avenue
Morgan, UT 84050-9333
Customer Service Phone No.: 800-945-1392
Fax No.: 801-876-3737
Web site: www.winchester-guns.com

WINCHESTER/OLIN
Models 101 & 23 only (Disc.)
Attn: Shotgun Customer Service
427 N. Shamrock Street
East Alton, IL 62024
Fax No.: 618-258-3393
Web site: www.winchester.com

WISCHO JAGD-UND SPORTWAFFEN
Dresdener Strasse 30,
D-91058 Erlangen, GERMANY
Fax No.: 011-91-31-300930

WISEMAN, BILL & CO.
P.O. Box 3427
Bryan, TX 77805
Phone No.: 409-690-3456
Fax No.: 409-690-0156

WOLF SPORTING PISTOLS
Importer and Distributor - J R Distributing
15634 Tierra Rejada Rd.
Moorpark, CA 93021
Fax No.: 805-529-2368
Factory - Wolf Sportpistolen Gesellschaft M.B.H.
A-1230 Wien
Breitenfurter Strasse 118 AUSTRIA
Fax no.: 011-43-1-803-72-266

WOODWARD, JAMES AND SONS
Factory - Purdey, James, & Sons, Ltd.
57-58 S Audley Street
London, W1Y 6ED ENGLAND
Phone No.: 011-44-71 499 1801
Fax No.: 011-44-71 355 3297

ZDF IMPORT EXPORT INC.
2975 South 300 West
Salt Lake City, UT 84115
Phone No.: 801-485-1012
Fax No.: 801-484-4363
Email: robarm@entec.com

Z-M WEAPONS
203 South St.
Bernardston, MA 01337
Phone No.: 413-648-9501
Fax No.: 413-648-0219

ZABALA HERMANOS, S.A.
Apartado de Correos 97
20600 Eibar, SPAIN
Fax No.: 011-34-943-768201

ZANARDINI

Factory - Zanardini, P. & C., S.n.c.
Via C. Goldoni, 34
I-25063 Gardone V.T. (Brescia), ITALY
Fax No.: 011-39-30-8910590
Web site: www.intred.it/mapis
Email: mapiz@intred.it

ZANOTTI, FABIO

Importer - See New England Arms Corp. listing.
Factory - R. Gamba c/o Zanotti
Via Artigiani, 93
I0-25063 Gardone Val Trompia
Brescia, ITALY
Fax No.: 011-39-30-837180

ZASTAVA ARMS

Factory - Advanced Weapons Technologies
2A, Andrea Papandreou St.
GR-151 27 Melissia, Athens, GREECE
Fax No.: 011-30-161-37-676
Web site: www.awt-zastava.com
Email: europe@zastava.com

ZIEGNHAHN & SOHN oHG

Importer - see New England Custom Gun, Ltd. listing.
Factory
Suhler Str. 9 A
D-98544 Zella-Mehlis GERMANY
Fax No.: 011-49-36-82-896-28

ZOLI, ANTONIO

Not affiliated with Angelo Zoli.
Importer (O/U rifles only) - see Cape Outfitters, Inc. listing.
Factory - Zoli Antonio S.p.A.
Via Zanardelli, 39
I-25063 Gardone V.T. (BS) ITALY
Fax No.: 011-39-30-891-1165

TRADE
MARKS

Armsport, Inc.
Sarsilmaz
American Derringer Corp.
Semmerling
A&S of America
Famars, Abbiatico &
Salvinelli
ABO Industries
Manurhin Revolvers
American Arms, Inc.
Fausti, Cav. Stefano &
Figlie s.n.c.
Mateba
Armes De Chasse
AYA
Dumoulin, Ernest
S.P.R.L.
Dumoulin, Herstal S.A.
Francotte, Auguste &
Cie. S.A.
Kemen
**Accuracy International North
America Inc.**
Accuracy International
LTD.
AcuSport
Anschütz
Aspen Outfitting Company
Churchhill Gunmakers
Ugartechea, Ignacio
Atkin, Grant & Lang
Atkin, Henry
Grant, Stephen
Lang, Joseph
Beeman Precision Airguns
Feinwerkbau
Bell's Legendary Countrywear
William Powell & Son
(Gunmakers) Ltd.
Benelli USA
Benelli
Franchi, Luigi
Beretta U.S.A. Corp.
Beretta, Pietro
BrazTech, L.C.
Rossi
British Game Guns
Cogswell & Harrison
Cape Outfitters
William Douglas &
Sons
Zoli, Antonio

CZ USA
CZ
Century Gun Distributing, Inc.
Century MFG., Inc.
Chadick's, L.t.d.
Chapuis Armes
Cimarron, F.A. Co.
Aldo Uberti
Armi San Marco
D. Pedersoli
Cooper Firearms of Montana, Inc.
Cooper Arms
Fanzoj, Johann
Champlin Firearms Inc.
Granger, G.
Marcel Thys & Sons
CONCO Arms
Hambrusch Jagdwaffen
GmbH
Century International Arms, Inc.
FEG
Makarov
Dynamit Nobel GmbH
Rottweil
RWS
Dalvar of USA
Radom
The Drumming Stump
Bruchet
Darne S.A.
**European American Armory
Corp.**
Baikal
Lumar
Sabatti s.p.a.
SAIGA
Tanfoglio, Fratelli, S.r.l.
Weihrauch, Hans-
Hermann
Eagle Imports, Inc.
Bersa
E.M.F. Company
Dakota Single Action
Revolver
Emerging Technologies, Inc.
Laseraim Arms, Inc.
Euro-Imports
BRNO Arms
Excel Industries, Inc.
Accu-Tek

Federal Engineering
Verney-Carron
Flying G Ranch
Fraser, Danl. & Co.
Furr Arms
Gatling Gun Company
Galaxy Imports
Laurona
Gamba of America
Gamba, Renato
Galena Industries, Inc.
A M T
Irwindale Arms, Inc.
Go Sportsmen's Supply
Anschütz
Griffin & Howe
Arrieta, S.L.
Gun South, Inc.
Jagd-Und Sportwaffen
Suhl GmbH (Merkel)
Merkel
Steyr Mannlicher
Guns Unlimited, Inc.
SKB Shotguns
Griffon Usa, Inc.
Griffon
Gunsport, Ltd. Inc.
Grulla Armas, S.L.
Heckler & Koch, Inc.
Fabarm, S.p.A.
Heckler & Koch
Hi-Grade Imports
Arrizabalaga, Pedro
Ferlib
Grulla Armas, S.L.
Import Sports, Inc.
Llama - Gabilondo y
Cia, S.A.
International Security Academy
Bul Transmark Ltd.
Interarms/Howa
Howa
Israel Arms International, Inc.
Israel Arms Ltd.
Intertex Carousels Corporation
Korriphila
Sommer + Ockenfuss
GmbH
ITC International, Inc.
Lanber Armas S.A.

Jennings Firearms, Inc.
Bryco Arms
J R Distributing
Wolf Sporting Pistols
Ultramatic Produktions
Gmbh
K.B.I., Inc.
Armscor
Arma Corporation of
the Philippines
Daly, Charles
FEG
Liberty
Keng's Firearms Specialty, Inc.
Korth
Krieghoff International Inc.
H. Krieghoff Gun Co.
(Shotguns of Ulm)
Labanu, Inc.
Rutten Herstal
Lion Country Supply
Ugartechea, Armas
Montana Armory
C. Sharps Arms Co. Inc.
Magnum Research, Inc.
ASAI AG
Mandall Shooting Supplies, Inc.
Bretton
Britarms
Cabanas
Domino
FAS
Gaucher
Krico
Mesa Sportsmen's Association, L.L.C.
RND Manufacturing
Miltex, Inc.
Arcus Co.
Arsenal, Bulgaria
Makarov
MKS Supply, Inc.
Hi-Point Firearms
Iberia Firearms
Stallard Arms
Navy Arms Co.
Helwan
Davide Pedersoli & Co.
Pietta & Co.
Uberti & Co.

Norinco Sports, U.S.A.
Norinco
New England Arms Corp.
Arrieta, S.L.
Arrizabalaga, Pedro
Bertuzzi
Casartelli, Carlo
Cosmi, Americo &
Figlio
Dumoulin, Henri & Fils
F.A.I.R. Techni-Mec (I.
Rizzini)
Rizzini, Battista.
Rizzini, F.lli.
Rota, Luciano
S.I.A.C.E.
Zanotti, Fabio
New England Custom Service, Ltd.
Johansen Rifles
Ziegenhahn & Sohn
oHG
Nygord Precision Products
FAS
Morini
Pardini
TOZ
Unique
Orvis
Arrieta, S.L.
Perazzi USA, Inc.
Perazzi
Peters Stahl, U.S.A
Peters Stahl GmbH
Precision Sales International, Inc.
Erma-Werke
Marocchi
Quality Arms
Arrieta, S.L.
The Riflesmith Inc.
Axtell Rifle Company
Rogue Rifle, Inc.
Chipmunk Rifles
Sporting Arms, Ltd.
Tristar
Stoeger Industries, Inc.
I G A Shotguns
Lugers
Sako
Tikka

Strayer-Voight Inc.
Infinity Firearms
Sporting Arms Manufacturing, Inc.
Snake Charmer
SIG Arms
Blaser
Hämmerli
Mauser Jagd-Und
Sportwaffen GmbH
Sauer, J.P. & Son
SIG
Sig Sauer
TSF Ltd.
Republic Arms of South
Africa
Tristar Sporting Arms, Ltd.
Rizzini, Emilio
Uberti USA, Inc.
Uberti, Aldo & C., S.r.l.
Valtro USA, Inc.
Valtro
Vektor USA, Inc.
Vektor
Carl Walther USA LLC
Walther
K. Wellams
Lucchini, Sandro
Wingshooting Adventures
Arrieta, S.L.
Williams Larkin Moore & Co.
Garbi
Piotti
Rizzini, Battista
Rizzini, F.lli
Luciano, Bosis
Lebeau-Courally
Woodcock Hill
Bland, Thomas & Sons
Gunmakers LTD.
Zanders Sporting Goods
Anschütz
ZDF Import/Export, Inc.
Vepr. Rifles

SERIALIZATION

This section is included to identify year of manufacture dates on Brownings, Colts (including 3rd generation Colt S.A. model numbers), High Standard, Mauser broomhandles, Parker shotguns, Remington (manufacture dates), Savage/Stevens model information, Savage M-1899, and selected Winchesters. To use these tables, simply locate the Ser. No. of the above mentioned trademarks, locate the proper bracket it falls into by model, and refer to the adjacent year to determine the year of manufacture. In several cases, caliber rarity can also be determined.

BROWNING BELGIUM PRODUCTION

Year	Serial Number Beginning of Year	Serial Number at End of Year
A-5 (AUTOMATIC 5) SHOTGUN -		
approximate recapitulation - 12 ga.		
1924	1	3000
1925	3001	18000
1926	18001	33000
1927	33001	48000
1928	48001	63000
1929	63001	78000
1930	78001	93000
1931	93001	108000
1932	108001	123000
1933	123001	138000
1934	138001	153000
1935	153001	168000
1936	168001	183000
1937	183001	198000
1938	198001	213000
1939	213001	229000
1940 -		
1945	NO PRODUCTION	
1946	229001	237000
1947	237001	249000
1948	249001	270000
1949	270001	285000
1950	285001	315000
1952	346001	387000
1953	387001	438000
	Standard Model	
1954	H1	H39000
	Lightweight Model	
	L1	L42000
1955	**Standard Model**	
	H39001	H83000
	Lightweight Model	
	L42001	L83000
1956	**Standard Model**	
	H83001	H99000
	M1	M22000
	Lightweight Model	
	L83001	L99000
	G1	G23000
1957	**Standard Model**	
	M22001	M85000
	Lightweight Model	
	G23001	G85000
1958	**Standard Model**	
	M85001	M99000
	Lightweight Model	
	G85001	G99000

Year	Serial Number Beginning of Year	Serial Number at End of Year
1958-1976	Ser. No. sequence changed to include a one or two digit numeral followed by an alpha character. "M" prefix designates standard models, "G" includes lightweight models, and "V" shows magnum models. To illustrate, an A-5 with a Ser. No. of 8G19264 would indicate a lightweight model manufactured in 1958. Ser. No. 71V24690 would specify a 3 inch magnum gun built in 1971.	
SUPERPOSED MODEL - O/U - 12 GA.		
1931	1	2000
1932	2001	4000
1933	4001	6000
1934	6001	8000
1935	8001	10000
1936	10001	12000
1937	12001	14000
1938	14001	17000
1939 -		
1947	NO PRODUCTION	
1948	17001	17200
1949	17201	20000
1950	20001	21000
1951	21001	27000
1952	27001	33000
1953	33001	37000
1954	37001	43000
1955	43001	48000
1956	48001	54000
1957	54001	59000
1958	59001	68500
1959	68501	76500
1960	76501	86500
1961	86501	96500
1962	96501	99999
1963	S3 suffix after Ser. No.	
1964	S4 suffix after Ser. No.	
1965	S5 suffix after Ser. No.	
1966	S6 suffix after Ser. No.	
1967	S7 suffix after Ser. No.	
1968	S8 suffix after Ser. No.	
1969	S69 suffix after Ser. No.	
1970	S70 suffix after Ser. No.	
1971	S71 suffix after Ser. No.	
1972	S72 suffix after Ser. No.	
1973	S73 suffix after Ser. No.	
1974	S74 suffix after Ser. No.	

Year	Serial Number Beginning of Year	Serial Number at End of Year
1975	S75 suffix after Ser. No.	
1976	S76 suffix after Ser. No.	
1976 to 1984	"P" or Presentation Models only	

LIEGE O & U -
Approximately 10,000 produced

Year		
1973	73J prefix before Ser. No.	
1974	74J prefix before Ser. No.	
1975	75J prefix before Ser. No.	

DOUBLE AUTOMATIC SHOTGUN

Year		
1952 -		
1959	N/A	
1960 -		
1971	1st or both digits indicate last 2 digits in year of manufacture (i.e. - OA1947 - 1960 mfg., 70A245671 - 1970 mfg.)	

HI-POWER (9mm) PISTOL

1955 -		
1956	No records available	
1957	70000	80000
1958	80001	85267
1959	85268	89687
1960	89688	93027
1961	93028	109145
1962	109146	113548
1963	113549	115822
1964	115823	T136538
1965	T136569	T146372
1966	T146373	T173285
1967	T173286	T213999
1968	T214000	T258000
1969	T258001	T261000+
	and 69C prefix before Ser. No.	
1970	70C prefix before Ser. No.	
1971	71C prefix before Ser. No.	
1972	72C prefix before Ser. No.	
1973	73C prefix before Ser. No.	
1974	74C prefix before Ser. No.	
1975	75C prefix before Ser. No.	
1976	76C prefix before Ser. No.	
1977 to date	New style serialization	

BROWNING .380

1955 -		
1964	No records exist	
1965	500000	598804
1966	598805	603890
1967	603891	619474
1968	619475	N/A
1969 -		
1970	Discontinued due to GCA of 1968. New model has longer barrel, adj. rear sight, modified grip.	
1971	71N prefix before Ser. No.	
1972	72N prefix before Ser. No.	
1973	73N prefix before Ser. No.	
1974	74N prefix before Ser. No.	
1975	75N prefix before Ser. No.	

.25 CAL. BABY BROWNING PISTOL

Year	Serial Number Beginning of Year	Serial Number at End of Year
1955 -		
1958	Records not available	
1959	181000	206349
1960	206350	230999
1961	231000	250999
1962	251000	278999
1963	279000	286099
1964	286100	308499
1965	308500	329999
1966	333000	367443
1967	367444	412999
1968	413000	479000
1969	Discontinued because of GCA of 1968	

.22 CAL. PISTOLS
(Nomad-Challenger-Medalist)

One or two digit suffix after single capital letter. "P" designates Nomad, "U" designates Challenger model, "T" designates Medalist model. "P5" suffix would indicate a Nomad built in 1965. "U71" suffix would indicate a Challenger built in 1971. Nomad models were manufactured from 1962 to 1973. Challenger and Medalist models were produced from 1962 to 1974.

BOLT ACTION RIFLES
(Safari, Medallion, & Olympian Models)

1959 -		
1962	No prefix (numeral-letter) before Ser. No. (i.e., only digits)	
1963	3-single letter prefix or suffix by Ser. No.	
1964	4-single letter prefix or suffix by Ser. No.	
1965	5-single letter prefix or suffix by Ser. No.	
1966	6-single letter prefix or suffix by Ser. No.	
1967	7-single letter prefix or suffix by Ser. No.	
1968	8-single letter prefix or suffix by Ser. No.	
1969	Single letter (Y, Z, or L) followed by last 2 digits of year of mfg. Prefix only.	
1970	"Y70" prefix	
1971	"L71" prefix	
1972	"Z72" prefix	
1973	"Y73" prefix	
1974	"Z74" prefix	
1975	"L75" prefix	

B.A.R.

1967	"M7" suffix after Ser. No.	
1968	"M8" suffix after Ser. No.	
1969	"M69" suffix after Ser. No.	
1970	"M70" suffix after Ser. No.	

Year		
1971	"M71" suffix after Ser. No.	

	Serial Number Beginning of Year	Serial Number at End of Year
Year		
1972	"M72" suffix after Ser. No.	
1973	"M73" suffix after Ser. No.	
1974	"M74" suffix after Ser. No.	
1975	"M75" suffix after Ser. No.	
1976	"M76" suffix after Ser. No.	
1977 to date	New sequence with "RT" appearing in middle of Ser. No.	

.22 AUTO RIFLE (Grades I, II, and III)

1956 - 1964	Numeric only - 5 digits or less
1965	"5T" or "5E" prefix before Ser. No.
1966	"6T" or "6E" prefix before Ser. No.
1967	"7T" or "7E" prefix before Ser. No.
1968	"8T" or "8E" prefix before Ser. No.
1969	

"69T" or "69E" prefix before Ser. No.

	Serial Number Beginning of Year	Serial Number at End of Year 1970
Year		
1970	"70T" or "70E" prefix before Ser. No.	
1971	"71T" or "71E" prefix before Ser. No.	
1972	"72T" or "72E" prefix before Ser. No.	
1973	Japan production	

T-BOLT RIFLE (T1 and T2)

1965	"X5" suffix after Ser. No.
1966	"X6" suffix after Ser. No.
1967	"X7" suffix after Ser. No.
1968	"X8" suffix after Ser. No.
1969	"X69" suffix after Ser. No.
1970	"X70" suffix after Ser. No.
1971	"X71" suffix after Ser. No.
1972	"X72" suffix after Ser. No.
1973	"X73" suffix after Ser. No.
1974	"X74" suffix after Ser. No.
1975	"X75" suffix after Ser. No.

COLT'S FIREARMS

MODEL 1849 POCKET REVOLVER

Year	Serial Number Beginning of Year	Serial Number at End of Year	Total Guns Produced in Year
1849	1	11999	11,999
1850	12000	15999	3,999
1851	16000	24999	8,999
1852	25000	54999	29,999
1853	55000	84999	29,999
1854	85000	99999	14,999
1855	100000	109999	9,999
1856	110000	129999	19,999
1857	130000	139999	9,999
1858	140000	149999	9,999
1859	150000	159999	9,999
1860	160000	183999	23,999
1861	184000	196999	12,999
1862	197000	222999	25,999
1863	223000	249999	26,999
1864	250000	269999	16,999
1865	270000	279999	9,999
1866	280000	289999	9,999
1867	290000	299999	9,999
1868	300000	309999	9,999
1869	310000	319999	9,999
1870	320000	324999	4,999
1871	325000	329999	4,999
1872	330000	330999	999
1873	331000	340000	9,000

MODEL 1849 POCKET REVOLVER - LONDON BARREL ADDRESS

Year	Serial Number Beginning of Year	Serial Number at End of Year	Total Guns Produced in Year
1853	1	999	999
1854	1000	4999	3999
1855	5000	8999	3999
1856	9000	11000	2000

MODEL 1851 NAVY

Year	Serial Number Beginning of Year	Serial Number at End of Year	Total Guns Produced in Year
1850	1	2499	2499
1851	2500	9999	7499
1852	10000	19999	9999
1853	20000	34999	14,999
1854	35000	39999	4,999
1855	40000	44999	4,999
1856	45000	64999	19,999
1857	65000	84999	19,999
1858	85000	89999	4,999
1859	90000	92999	2,999
1860	93000	97999	4,999
1861	98000	117999	19,999
1862	118000	131999	13,999
1863	132000	174999	42,999
1864	175000	179999	4,999
1865	180000	184999	4,999
1866	185000	200000	14,999
1867	200000	203999	3,999
1868	204000	206999	2,999
1869	207000	209999	2,999
1870	210000	211999	1,999
1871	212000	213999	1,999
1872	214000	214999	999
1873	215000	215348	348

MODEL 1851 NAVY - LONDON BARREL ADDRESS

Year	Serial Number Beginning of Year	Serial Number at End of Year	Total Guns Produced in Year
1853	1	3999	3,999
1854	4000	14999	10,999
1855	15000	40999	25,999
1856	41000	42000	1,000

Year	Serial Number Beginning of Year	Serial Number at End of Year	Total Guns Produced in Year
MODEL 1860 ARMY			
1860	1	1999	1,999
1861	2000	24999	22,999
1862	25000	84999	59,999
1863	85000	149999	64,999
1864	150000	152999	2,999
1865	153000	155999	2,999
1866	156000	161999	5,999
1867	162000	169999	7,999
1868	170000	176999	6,999
1869	177000	184999	7,999
1870	185000	189999	4,999
1871	190000	197999	7,999
1872	198000	198999	999
1873	199000	200500	1,500
MODEL 1861 NAVY			
1861	1	4599	4999
1862	4600	9999	5399
1863	10000	16999	6999
1864	17000	24999	7999
1865	25000	27999	2999
1866	28000	29999	1999
1867	30000	30999	999
1868	31000	32999	1,999
1869	33000	33999	999
1870	34000	34999	999
1871	35000	35999	999
1872	36000	36999	999
1873	37000	38843	1,843
MODEL 1862 POLICE			
1861	1	8499	8499
1862	8500	14999	6499
1863	15000	25999	10,999
1864	26000	28999	2,999
1865	29000	31999	2,999
1866	32000	34999	2,999
1867	35000	36999	1,999
1868	37000	39999	2,999
1869	40000	41999	1,999
1870	42000	43999	1,999
1871	44000	44999	999
1872	45000	45999	999
1873	46000	47000	1,000

MODEL 1873 - SINGLE ACTION ARMY (SAA) - PRE-WAR

Year	Caliber	Serial Number Beginning in Year
1873	.45 Colt Caliber, Standard	1
1874	.450 Boxer & .44 German intro.	200
1875	.44 Rimfire series (own serials, 1-1863 made through 1880)	15000
1876	.476 Eley intro.	22000
1877	Nickel Finish intro.	33000
1878	.44-40 intro. in quantity	41000
1879		49000
1880	.44 Rimfire disc.	
1881		62000
1882	Sheriff's model, .455 Eley intro.	73000

Year	Caliber	Serial Number Beginning in Year
1883	.22 rimfire intro.	85000
1884	.32-20 and .38-40 intro.	102000
1885	.41 Colt intro.	114000
1886	.38 Colt intro.	117000
1887	.32 Colt and .32 S&W intro.	119000
1888	Flattop Target S.A.A. began; no. 126530	125000
1889	.32 rimfire; .32-44 S&W, .38 S&W; and .44 Russian intro.	128000
1890	.44 Smoothbore; .22 W.R.F. .380 and .450 Eley; and .44 S&W intro.	130000
1891	.38-44 & .45 SB, intro.	136000
1892	Transverse cylinder latch intro., screw lock at front of frame dropped	144000
1893		149000
1894	Beginning of Bisley models	154000
1895		159000
1896	Eagleless grips, intro.	163000
1897		168000
1898		175000
1899		182000
1900	Revolvers built to handle smokeless powder	192000
1901		203000
1902		220000
1903		238000
1904		250000
1905		261000
1906		273000
1907	.44 S & W Spec., intro.	288000
1908		304000
1909	.38 Colt Spec., intro.	308000
1910		312000
1911		316000
1912	Disc. Bisley model	321000
1913	S&W Special intro.	325000
1914	.38 Colt disc.	328000
1915	Long flute cylinders; range no. 330001 to 331480	329500
1916		332000
1917		335000
1918		337000
1919		337200
1920		338000
1921		341000
1922	.38 Colt Reintro.	343000
1923		344500
1924	.45 ACP intro., requiring special cylinders	346400
1925		347300
1926		348200
1927	53000	349800
1928		351300
1929		352400

Year	Caliber	Serial Number Beginning in Year
1930	.38 Special intro.	353800
1931		354100
1932		354500
1933		354800
1934		355000
1935	.357 Mag. & .38 S & W intro.	355200
1936		355300
1937		355400
1938		356100
1939		356600
1940	A few S.A.A. during and just after the war	357000 thru 357859

COLT SINGLE ACTION ARMY - POST-WAR PRODUCTION
"SA" suffix from 1956 to 1978, "SA" prefix 1978 to 1981

Year	Serial Number Beginning of Year	Serial Number at End of Year
1956	0001SA	8799SA
1957	8800SA	18499SA
1958	18500SA	23399SA
1959	23400SA	28499SA
1960	28500SA	33599SA
1961	33600SA	35649SA
1962	35650SA	37299SA
1963	37300SA	38499SA
1964	38500SA	39999SA
1965	40000SA	41499SA
1966	41500SA	43799SA
1967	43800SA	46299SA
1968	46300SA	48999SA
1969	49000SA	52599SA
1970	52600SA	59399SA
1971	59400SA	61699SA
1972	61700SA	64399SA
1973	64400SA	69399SA
1974	69400SA	73319SA
1975		NONE PRODUCED
1976	80000SA	82000SA (start of 3rd generation of production)
1977	82001SA	95999SA
1978	96000SA	99999SA
1978		Start of "SA" prefix on front of Ser. No.
Mid-1978	SA01000	SA14808
1979	SA14809	SA30254
1980	SA30255	SA46919
1981	SA46920	SA58627
1982	SA58628	SA65255
1983	SA65256	SA66495
1984	SA66496	C.S. PROD.

NEW FRONTIER SINGLE ACTION ARMY

1961	3000NF	3005NF
1962	3006NF	3849NF
1963	4325NF	4699NF
1964	4700NF	4974NF
1965	4975NF	5399NF
1966	5400NF	5674NF
1967	5675NF	5699NF
1968	5700NF	

Year	Serial Number Beginning of Year	Serial Number at End of Year
1969	5701NF	5924NF
1970	5925NF	6874NF
1971	6875NF	7049NF
1972	7050NF	7074NF
1973	7075NF	7174NF
1974	7175NF	7264NF
1975	7265NF	7288NF
1978	7501NF	

REINTRODUCED IN SEPTEMBER

1978	01001NF	04424NF
1979	04425NF	06274NF
1980	06275NF	11374NF
1981	11375NF	16584NF
1982	16584NF	DISC. 1982

COLT SINGLE ACTION ARMY - CALIBER BREAKDOWN

Caliber	S.A.A	Flattop Target	Bisley	Bisley Target
.22 Rimfire	107	93	0	0
.32 Rimfire	1	0	0	0
.32 Colt	192	24	160	44
.32 S&W	32	30	18	17
.32-44	2	9	14	17
.32-20	29,812	30	13,291	131
.38 Colt (through 1914)	1,011	122	412	96
.38 Colt (post-1922)	1,365	0	0	0
.38 S&W	9	39	10	5
.38 Colt Special	82	7	0	0
.38 S&W Special	25	0	2	0
.38-44	2	11	6	47
.357 Magnum	525	0	0	0
.380 Eley	1	3	0	0
.38-40	38,240	19	12,163	98
.41 Colt	16,402	91	3,159	24
.44 Smoothbore	15	0	1	0
.44 Rimfire	1,863	0	0	0
.44 German	59	0	0	0
.44 Russian	154	51	90	62
.44 S&W	24	51	29	64
.44 S&W Special	506	1	0	0
.44-40	64,489	21	6,803	78
.45 Colt	150,683	100	8,005	97
.45 Smoothbore	4	0	2	0
.45 ACP	44	0	0	0
.450 Boxer	729	89	0	0
.450 Eley	2,697	84	5	0
.455 Eley	1,150	37	180	196
.476 Eley	161	2	0	0
Total Quantities	310,386	914	44,350	976

MODEL 1911 AND 1911A1 - Commercial production - Capital "C" prefix - .45 cal.

Year	Serial Number Beginning of Year	Serial Number at End of Year
1912	C1	C1899
1913	C1900	C5399
1914	C5400	C16599
1915	C16600	C27599
1916	C27600	C74999
1917	C75000	C98999

Year	Serial Number Beginning of Year	Serial Number at End of Year
1918	C99000	C105999
1919	C106000	C120999
1920	C120000	C126999
1921	C127000	C128999
1922	C129000	C133999
1923	C134000	C134999
1924	C135000	C139999
1925	C140000	C144999
1926	C145000	C150999
1927	C151000	C151999
1928	C152000	C154999
1929	C155000	C155999
1930	C156000	C158999
1931	C159000	C160999
1932	C161000	C164799
1933	C164800	C174599
1934	C174600	C177999
1935	C178000	C179799
1936	C179800	C183199
1937	C183200	C188699
1938	C188700	C189599
1939	C189600	C198899
1940	C198900	C199299
1941	C199300	C208799
1942	C208800	C215018
1943-1945:	Commercial production interrupted by WWII	
1946	C221001	C222000
1947	C222001	C231999
1948	C232000	C238500
1949	C238501	C240000
1950	C240000	247701C
	"C" SUFFIX STARTED WITH SER. NO. 240228	
1951	247701C	253179C
1952	253180C	259549C
1953	259550C	266349C
1954	266350C	270549C
1955	270550C	272549C
1956	272550C	276699C
1957	276700C	281999C
1958	282000C	283799C
1959	283800C	285799C
1960	285800C	287999C
1961	288000C	289849C
1962	289850C	291299C
1963	291300C	293799C
1964	293800C	295999C
1965	296000C	300299C
1966	300300C	308499C
1967	308500C	315599C

Year	Serial Number Beginning of Year	Serial Number at End of Year
1968	315600C	324499C
1969	324500C	332649C
1970	332650C	336169C
New Range	70G01001	70G05550
1971	70G05551	70G18000
1972	70G18001	70G34400
1973	70G34401	70G43000
1974	70G43001	70G73000
1975	70G73001	70G88900
1976	70G88901	70G99999
New Range	01001G70	13900G70
1977	13901G70	45199G70

Year	Serial Number Beginning of Year	Serial Number at End of Year
1978 TO DATE	45200G70	

MODEL 1911 AND 1911A1 MILITARY PRODUCTION

Year	Serial Number Beginning of Year	Serial Number at End of Year	Manufacturer
1912	1	500	COLT
	501	1000	COLT USN
	1001	1500	COLT
	1501	2000	COLT USN
	2001	2500	COLT
	2501	3500	COLT USN
	3501	3800	COLT USMC
	3801	4500	COLT
	4501	5500	COLT USN
	5501	6500	COLT
	6501	7500	COLT USN
	7501	8500	COLT
	8501	9500	COLT USN
	9501	10500	COLT
	10501	11500	COLT USN
	11501	12500	COLT
	12501	13500	COLT USN
	13501	17250	COLT USN
1913	17251	36400	COLT
	36401	37650	COLT USMC
	37651	38000	COLT
	38001	44000	COLT USN
	44001	60400	COLT
1914	60401	72570	COLT
	72571	83855	SPRINGFIELD -(THESE NUMBERS RESERVED SPRINGFIELD)
	83856	83900	COLT
	83901	84400	COLT USMC
	84401	96000	COLT
	96001	97537	COLT USN
	97538	102596	COLT
	102597	107596	SPRINGFIELD (RESERVED NO. RANGE)
1915	107597	109500	COLT
	109501	110000	COLT USN
	110001	113496	COLT
	113497	120566	SPRINGFIELD -(RESERVED

Year	Serial Number Beginning of Year	Serial Number at End of Year	Manufacturer
			FOR SPRINGFIELD)
	120567	125566	COLT
	125567	133186	SPRINGFIELD -(RESERVED FOR SPRINGFIELD)
1916	133187	137400	COLT
1917	137401	151186	COLT
	151187	151986	COLT USMC
	151987	185800	COLT
	185801	186200	COLT USMC
	186201	209586	COLT
	209587	210386	COLT USMC

Year	Serial Number Beginning of Year	Serial Number at End of Year	Manufacturer
	210387	215386	COLT FRAMES (RESERVED FOR RECEIVERS)
	215387	216186	COLT USMC
	216187	216586	COLT
	216587	216986	COLT USMC
1918	216987	217386	COLT USMC
	217387	223952	COLT
	223953	223990	COLT USN
	223991	232000	COLT
	232001	233600	COLT USN
	233601	580600	COLT
	1	13152	REM. UMC
1919	13153	21676	REM. UMC
	580601	629500	COLT
	629501	717386	COLT
1924	700001	710000	COLT
1937	710001	712349	COLT USN
1938	712350	713645	COLT

Year	Serial Beginning	Serial at End	Manufacturer
1939	713646	717281	COLT USN
1940	717282	721977	COLT
1941	721978	756733	COLT
1942	756734	793657	COLT
	793658	797639	COLT USN
	797640	800000	COLT
	S800001	S800500	SINGER

Year	Serial Number Beginning of Year	Serial Number at End of Year	Manufacturer
	800501	801000	ASSIGNED TO H&R
	801001	856100	COLT
1943	856001	958100	COLT
**	856101	856404	Replacement No
**	856405	916404	ITHACA
**	916405	1041404	REM. RAND
	1041405	1096404	US&S
	1088726	1208673	COLT
	1208674	1279673	ITHACA
	1279674	1279698	RE NO AA
	1279699	1441430	REM. RAND
	1441431	1471430	ITHACA
	1471431	1609528	REM. RAND
1944	1609529	1743846	COLT
	1743847	1816641	REM. RAND
	1816642	1890503	ITHACA
	1890504	2075103	REM. RAND
1945	2075104	2134403	ITHACA
	2134404	2244803	REM. RAND
	2244804	2380013	COLT
	2380014	2619013	REM. RAND
	2619014	2693613	ITHACA

** Denotes double issue ranges.

COLT SINGLE-ACTION MODEL NUMBERS

The author wishes to express thanks to Mr. Don Wilkerson for allowing the edited information published below from his 1986 Post-War Single-Action Revolver, 1976-1986 publication.

A working knowledge of model numbers for the various Colt single-action revolvers is a must for even a novice collector. Since the mid-1970s Colt has placed the model number on the end label of the shipping cartons of virtually all their firearms. Many collectors and publications regularly use the model number to describe or differentiate between revolvers. Using the model number is an accurate and efficient method to dileneate a particular variation. Example: .45 caliber revolver with a 4 ¾ in. barrel, blue and case hardened finish and eagle stocks can be described as a simple "P-1840".

Each Colt model is specified by an alphabetical letter and 4 numerical digits. The basic model number as it pertains to single -action revolvers can be broken down as follows:

MODEL P — basic type of frame. The letter "P" is used to dileaneate the single-action type of frame.

FIRST NUMERAL — "1" is the first model built on a particular type of frame. Numerals 2, 3, 4, etc. indicate later versions. These versions are not always numbered in numerical order and the same number has been used for different models at different times. A "1" denotes the basic standard single-action frame. A "2" denotes the new black powder frame available through the Colt Custom Gun Shop. A "3" has been used at various times to denote a non-standard frame or cylinder. The "4" is used to specify the New Frontier style of frame. Numbers such as "7" and "8" are frequently used to specify commemorative or special editions.

SECOND NUMERAL — specifies caliber. A "4" denotes .32-20, a "6" denotes .357 Magnum, a "7" denotes .44 Special, an "8" denotes .45 caliber, and a "9" specifies .44-40 caliber.*

THIRD NUMERAL — denotes barrel length. "3" is used to denote both a 3 inch and a 4 inch barrel. "4" is 4¾ inch or 5 inch, "5" is 5½ inch, "7" is 7½ inch, and "1" is 12 inch.*

FOURTH NUMERAL — is used to denote several different variations of the standard model. Some of the most common examples are: "1", "2", or "6" for nickel finish, "1" for full blue finish in the case of P-1871, and "2", "3", and "4" as used for the Sheriff's Model series to denote blue and case hardened finish, nickel finish, and Royal Blue and case hardened finish, respectively. The fourth numeral can also denote the type of stocks as in P- 1673. The fourth numeral in the basic model designation must be used in conjunction with the preceding three numerals to determine its exact meaning. The fourth numeral is kind of a "catch-all" number. Many times this number serves only to differentiate a later model from a similar model assembled years earlier.

*The .32-20 caliber and the 5 inch barrel length are listed in the 1984 *Colt Buyer's Guide*, but as of this date neither have been produced.

STANDARD MODEL P REVOLVER

The primary model numbers used by Colt for Model P revolvers produced since 1976 are as follows:

P-1640 - .357 Magnum, 4¾ in. barrel, blue finish, eagle stocks.

P-1641 - .357 Magnum, 4¾ in. barrel, nickel finish, wood stocks.

P-1650 - .357 Magnum, 5½ in. barrel, blue finish, eagle stocks.

P-1656 - .357 Magnum, 5½ in. barrel, nickel finish, wood stocks.

P-1670 - .357 Magnum, 7½ in. barrel, blue finish, eagle stocks.

P-1673 - .357 Magnum, 7½ in. barrel, blue finish, wood stocks.

P-1676 - .357 Magnum, 7½ in. barrel, nickel finish, wood stocks.

P-1740 - .44 Special, 4¾ in. barrel, blue finish, eagle stocks.

P-1746 - .44 Special, 4¾ in. barrel, nickel finish, wood stocks.

P-1750 - .44 Special, 5½ in. barrel, blue finish, eagle stocks.

P-1756 - .44 Special, 5½ in. barrel, nickel finish, wood stocks.

P-1770 - .44 Special, 7½ in. barrel, blue finish, eagle stocks.

P-1776 - .44 Special, 7½ in. barrel, nickel finish, wood stocks.

P-1716 - .44 Special, 12 in. barrel, nickel finish, wood stocks.

P-1840 - .45 Colt, 4¾ in. barrel, blue finish, eagle stocks.

P-1841 - .45 Colt, 4¾ in. barrel, nickel finish, wood stocks.

P-1850 - .45 Colt, 5½ in. barrel, blue finish, eagle stocks.

P-1856 - .45 Colt, 5½ in. barrel, nickel finish, wood stocks.

P-1870 - .45 Colt, 7½ in. barrel, blue finish, eagle stocks.

P-1876 - .45 Colt, 7½ in. barrel, nickel finish, wood stocks.

P-1813 - .45 Colt, 12 in. barrel, blue finish, eagle stocks.

P-1816 - .45 Colt, 12 in. barrel, nickel finish, wood stocks.

P-1940 - .44-40 caliber, 4¾ in. barrel, blue finish, eagle stocks.

P-1941* - .44-40 caliber, 4¾ in. barrel, nickel finish, wood stocks.

P-1950 - .44-40 caliber, 5½ in. barrel, blue finish, eagle stocks.

P-1970 - .44-40 caliber, 7½ in. barrel, blue finish, eagle stocks.

P-1976* - .44-40 caliber, 7½ in. barrel, nickel finish, wood stocks.

P-1911 - .44-40 caliber, 12 in. barrel, nickel finish, wood stocks.

*These model numbers were used primarily for engraved or special ordered revolvers as the two models indicated were never produced as a regular model. "Blue finish" in the above chart denotes the standard blue finish, i.e., blue with case hardened frame.

NEW FRONTIER MODEL

P-4671 - .357 Magnum, 7½ in. barrel, nickel finish, wood stocks.

P-4750 - .44 Special, 5½ in. barrel, Royal Blue finish, wood stocks.

P-4770 - .44 Special , 7½ in. barrel, Royal Blue finish, wood stocks.

P-4840 - .45 Colt, 4¾ in. barrel, Royal Blue finish, wood stocks.

P-4850 - .45 Colt, 5½ in. barrel, Royal Blue finish, wood stocks.

P-4870 - .45 Colt, 7½ in. barrel, Royal Blue finish, wood stocks.

P-4940 - .44-40 caliber, 4¾ in. barrel, Royal Blue finish, wood stocks.

P-4970 - .44-40 caliber, 7½ in. barrel, Royal Blue finish, wood stocks.

Note: The term "Royal Blue" in the New Frontier chart denotes a revolver with a case hardened frame and a Royal (high polish) Blue finish on the other major components.

SHERIFF'S MODELS

P-1932 - .44-40 caliber, 3 in. barrel, blue finish, eagle stocks.

P-1933* - .44-40/.44 Special, 3 in. barrel, nickel finish, wood stocks.

P-1934* - .44-40/.44 Special, 3 in. barrel, Royal Blue finish, wood stocks.

*Circa 1984 all Sheriff's Models are listed as single calibers: .44-40 or .45 caliber.

REVOLVERS WITH FULL BLUE FRAMES

Some of the "full blue" models have had more than one model number assigned to the same variation. As a result, a particular model may have been identified by different model numbers at different times. Following the model numbers and descriptions in this chart will be an approximate time frame during which that particular model was in use. No date following the description indicates that only one model number for that particular variation is known to the author (Don Wilkerson).

P-1640 - FB - .357 Magnum, 4¾ in. barrel, fluted cylinder, eagle stocks.

P-1650 - FB - .357 Magnum, 5½ in. barrel, fluted cylinder, eagle stocks.

P-1740 - FB - .44 Special, 4¾ in. barrel, fluted cylinder, eagle stocks.

P-1750 - FB - .44 Special, 5½ in. barrel, fluted cylinder, eagle stocks.

P-1770 - FB - .44 Special, 7½ in. barrel, fluted cylinder, eagle stocks.

P-1770 - UB - .44 Special, 7½ in. barrel, unfluted cylinder, eagle stocks.

P-3840 - .45 Colt, 4¾ in. barrel, both fluted and unfluted cylinders, eagle stocks (early to mid-1982).

P-1840 - FB - .45 Colt, 4¾ in. barrel, fluted cylinder, eagle stocks (mid to late 1982 to date).

P-1840 - UB - .45 Colt, 4¾ in. barrel, unfluted cylinder, eagle stocks (mid to late 1982 to date).

P-1850 - FB - .45 Colt, 5½ in. barrel, fluted cylinder, eagle stocks.

P-1850 - UB - .45 Colt, 5½ in. barrel, unfluted cylinder, eagle stocks.

P-1871 - .45 Colt, 7½ in. barrel, fluted cylinder, wood stocks (1977 to 1979).

P-1870 - FB - .45 Colt, 7½ in. barrel, fluted cylinder, wood stocks (1982 to date).

P-1870 - UB - .45 Colt, 7½ in. barrel, unfluted cylinder, wood stocks (1982 to date).

P-1871 - FB - .45 Colt, 12 in. barrel, fluted cylinder, eagle stocks.

FULL BLUE NEW FRONTIERS

P-4770 - FB - .44 Special, 7½ in. barrel, fluted cylinder, wood stocks.

P-4870 - FB - .45 Colt, 7½ in. barrel, fluted cylinder, wood stocks.

P-4870 - UB - .45 Colt, 7½ in. barrel, unfluted cylinder, wood stocks.

MISCELLANEOUS MODEL NUMBERS

1750 - AA - .44 Special, 5½ in. barrel, blue finish with nickel cylinder, eagle stocks.

1750 - AB - .44 Special, 5½ in. barrel, blue finish with nickel cylinder with blue flutes, eagle stocks.

1840 - UC - .45 Colt, 4¾ in. barrel, blue finish, unfluted cylinder, eagle stocks.

1850 - UC - .45 Colt, 5½ in. barrel, blue finish, unfluted cylinder, eagle stocks.

1870 - UC - .45 Colt, 7½ in. barrel, blue finish, unfluted cylinder, eagle stocks.

Note: The term "blue finish" in this chart is the standard blue finish with a case hardened frame.

BLACK POWDER MODEL P REVOLVERS

P-2830 - .45 Colt, 3 in. barrel, blue finish.

P-2833 - .45 Colt, 3 in. barrel, nickel finish.

P-2834* - .45 Colt, 3 in. barrel, Royal Blue finish.

P-2836 - .45 Colt, 4 in. barrel, Royal Blue finish.

P-2837 - .45 Colt, 4 in. barrel, nickel finish.

P-2840 - .45 Colt, 4¾ in. barrel, blue finish.

P-2841 - .45 Colt, 4¾ in. barrel, nickel finish.

P-2847* - .45 Colt, 5 in. barrel, nickel finish.

P-2870 - .45 Colt, 7½ in. barrel, blue finish.

P-2871 - .45 Colt, 7½ in. barrel, nickel finish.

P-2940 - .44-40 caliber, 4¾ in. barrel, blue finish.

P-2941 - .44-40 caliber, 4¾ in. barrel, nickel finish.

P-2970 - .44-40 caliber, 7½ in. barrel, blue finish.

P-2971 - .44-40 caliber, 7½ in. barrel, nickel finish.

P-2437* - .32-20 caliber, 4 in. barrel, nickel finish.

P-2474* - .32-20 caliber, 7½ in. barrel, Royal Blue finish.

*As of this writing these calibers have not been produced. The terms "blue finish" and "Royal" in this chart refer to Colt's standard single-action finish, i.e., case hardened frame with all components finished in either standard blue or Royal Blue.

COLT BLACKPOWDER
2ND GENERATION SERIALIZATION

Model No.	Serial # Range		Total Prod.	Prod. Began	Prod. Ended
MODEL 1851 NAVY					
C-1121	4201	25100	20900	1971	1978
C-1122	As above but at higher range of numbers				
		Unk'n	—		1978
MODEL 1851 NAVY, R. E. LEE					
C-9001	251REL	5000 REL	4750	—	1971
MODEL 1851 NAVY, U. S. GRANT					
C-9002	251USG	5000 USG	4750	—	1971

Model No.	Serial # Range		Total Prod.	Prod. Began	Prod. Ended
MODEL 1851 GRANT-LEE PAIR					
C-9003	01 GLP	250 GLP	250	—	1971
3rd MODEL DRAGOON					
C-1770	20801	208	25	1974	1978
		Prototype			
	20901	24501	3601		
C-1770MN	S/N's As Above		20	1984	1984
MODEL 1851 NAVY					
F-1100	24900	29150	4250	5/80	10/81

Model No.	Serial # Range		Total Prod.	Prod. Began	Prod. Ended
F-1101	S/N's As Above		300	10/81	11/81
	W/Blank Cylinders				
F-1110	29151s	29640s	489	6/82	10/82
	Stainless Steel				
MODEL 1860 ARMY					
F-1200	201000	212835	7593	11/78	11/82
	Rebated Cylinder				
F-1200 EBO	S/N's As Above		500	1979	1979
	Butterfield				
F-1200 LNK	S/N's As Above		Unk'n	Unk'n	Unk'n
	Electroless Nickel				
F-1200MN	S/N's As Above		12	1984	1984
	Nickel/Ivory				
F-1202	S/N's As Above		500	1979	1979
	Limited Edition				
F-1203	207330	211250	2670	7/80	10/81
	Fluted Cylinder				
F-1210	211263s	212540s	1278	1/82	4/82
	Stainless Steel				
1861 NAVY					
F-1300	40000	43165	3166	9/80	10/81
1862 POCKET NAVY					
F-1400	48000	58850	5765	12/79	11/81
	and skip odd no's.				
F-1400MN	S/N's As Above		25	1984	1984
	Nickel/Ivory				
F-1401	S/N's As Above		500	1979	1980
	Limited Edition				

Model No.	Serial # Range		Total Prod.	Prod. Began	Prod. Ended
1862 POCKET POLICE					
F-1500	49000	57300	4801	1/80	9/81
	and skip even no's.				
F-1500MN	S/N's As Above		25	1984	1984
	Nickel/Ivory				
F-1501	S/N's As Above		500	1979	1980
	Limited Edition				
1847 WALKER					
F-1600	1200	4120	2573	6/80	4/82
	32256	32500	245	5/81	9/81
1st MODEL DRAGOON					
F-1700	25100	34500	3878	1/80	2/82
2nd MODEL DRAGOON					
F-172	S/N's As Above and Mix at Random for				
	1st, 2nd & 3rd		2676	1/80	2/82
3rd MODEL DRAGOON					
F-140	S/N's As Above and Mix at Random for				
	1st, 2nd & 3rd		2856	1/80	2/82
	31401	31450	50	10/81	11/81
F-1740EGA	Unk'n Unk'n		200	1982	1982
	(Garabaldi Model– "GCA" prefix)				
BABY DRAGOON					
F-1760	16000	17851	1852	2/81	4/81
F-1761	S/N's As Above		500	1979	1980
	Limited Edition				
1860 ARMY					
F-9005	US 001/001 US to				
	US 3025/3025 US		3025	9/77	1/80
	Cavalry Commemorative (Two Gun Set)				
HERITAGE WALKER					
F-9006	01	1853	1853	6/80	6/81

HARRINGTON & RICHARDSON SERIALIZATION
1940 - 1982

The following serial numbered prefixes are related to the corresponding year of manufacture:

Year Starting	S.N. Prefix
1940	A
1941	B
1942	C
1943	D
1944	E
1945	F
1946	G
1947	H
1948	I

Year Starting	S.N. Prefix		Year		Year	
1949	J		1960	W	1973	AL
1950	K		1961	X	1974	AM
1951	L		1962	Y	1975	AN
1952	M		1963	Z	1976	AP
1953	N		1964	AA	1977	AR
1954	P		1965	AB	(Striker Mech. Intr.)	
1955	R		1966	AC	1978	AS
1956	S		1967	AD	1979	AT
1957	T		1968	AE	1980	AU
1958	U		1969	AF	1981	AX
1959	V		1970	AG	1982	AY
			1971	AH		
Year Starting	S.N. Prefix		(Snap on forecap)			
			1972	AJ		

HIGH STANDARD SERIAL NUMBERS
1932 - 1957

Year Starting	Serial Number		Year Starting	Serial Number
1932	5,000		1944	115,000
1933	5,050		1945	134,700
1934	6,500		1946	145,800
1935	8,300		1947	174,200
1936	11,500		1948	235,000
1937	18,500		1949	299,000
1938	29,600			
1939	39,200		Year Starting	Serial Number
1940	50,500		1950	325,000
			1951	330,000
Year Starting	Serial Number		1952	355,000
1941	70,600		1953	400,000
1942	92,600		1954	440,000
1943	103,600		1955	480,000
			1956	550,000
			1957	640,000

HIGH STANDARD AUTOMATIC PISTOL
1958 - 1984

Year Starting	Serial Number		Year Starting	Serial Number
1958	8192XX		1977	ML23XXX
1959	9854XX		Feb.1981	ML71000
1962	12606XX		Apr.1981	ML84000
1963	12954XX		May 1981	ML85000
1965	14204XX		June 1981	ML86000
1965	15709XX		June 1981	SH10000
1966	16078XX		Sept.1982	SH14000
1967	17509XX		Oct. 1982	SH15000
1967	18141XX		Nov. 1982	SH16000
1968	18891XX		Dec. 1982	SH17000
1968	19909XX		Jan. 1983	SH18000
1969	20485XX		Feb. 1983	SH19000
1969	21609XX		Apr. 1983	SH21000
1970	21971XX		May 1983	SH23000
1971	22662XX		Oct. 1983	SH24000
1972	22874XX		Feb. 1984	SH25000
1972	23337XX		Apr. 1984	SH26000
1973	23639XX		May 1984	SH27000
1973	24140XX		June 1984	SH29000
1974	24337XX		Sept 1984	SH34000
1975	ML15XXX			
1976	ML19XXX			

HOLLAND & HOLLAND

PARADOX SERIES

Year Starting	Serial Number		Year	Serial Number
1885	11500		1887	
1886			1888	11691
			1889	11788
			1890	11865
			1891	11948
			1895	15036

Year	Serial
1892	15075
1895	15347

Year Starting	Serial Number
1900	15558
1903	15655
1905	15750

Year	Serial
1906	15825
1907	15860
1911	15900
1914	15950
1919	19560
1922	15970
1930	15980
1956	15979

HOLLAND AND HOLLAND RECORDED DATES

Year Starting	Serial Number
March 1856 (First Recorded Date)	565
October 1868	580
February 1857	584
August 1859	700

Year Starting	Serial Number
A gap in records	728-1059
1864	1060
1865	1101
1868	1352
1869	1439

Year Starting	Serial Number
1870	1578
1871	1769
1872	2002
1873	2401
1874	2759
1875	3174
1876	3649
1877	4179
1878	4774
1879	5274
1880	5819
1881	6382
1882	7009
1883	7473
1884	7904
1885	8406
1886	8809
1887	8999
Unused	9000-10000
Missing	10000-10849
Rook Rifles	10850-10999
Normal Series	11000-11499
Paradox Guns	11500-11999
Normal Series	12000-12999
Rook Rifles	13000-13999
Normal Series	14000-14999
Paradox Guns	15000-15999
Normal Series	16000-16999
Normal Series	17000-17399
Rifles and Rook Rifles	17400-17999
Believed Unused	18000-18999
Rifles	19000-19999
Misc. Guns and Rifles	20000-21999
See separate lists	22000+

1890	13465
1891	13566
1892	13674
1893	13885-13999
1894 Some rook rifles	17401
1899 among others	17999

MAGAZINE RIFLES

1910	28000
1911	28100
1913	28199
1913	28300
1919	28399
1920-29	1-581
1930-33	582-880
1920-32	881-1181
1935-49	1182-1782
1949-60	1783-2179
1951-58	2180-2577
1952-62	2578-2977
1958-65	2978-3377
1964-74	3378-3783
1975-80	3784-4000
1981-87	4001-4250
1988-92	4251-4330

Year Starting	Serial Number

PLAIN GUNS

1907	26200
1908	26300
1909	26400
1909	26500
1910	26600
1911	26700
1912	26800
1913	26900
1913	26999
1913	28600
1914	28700
1914	28800
1915	28900
1915	28999
1915	29500
1915	29600
1916	29700
1919	29800
1919	29900
1919	30000
1920	30100
1922	30200
1924	30300
1925	30334
1925	31100
1926	31200
1928	31300
1929	31399
1929	32200
1931	32300

ROOK RIFLES

1887	10850-10999
Assumed 1888 records missing	11000-11499
1889	13106

1933	32400
1935	32499
1935	34000
1936	34100
1937	34200
1939	34300
1949	34400
1953	34500
1956	34600
1961	34700
1975	34800

ROYAL GUNS

1899	22000
1900	22500
1902	23000
1903	23500
1906	25000
1907	25500
1910	25599
1910	27000
1911	27250
1912	27500
1913	27750
1914	27999
1914	29000
1915	29100
1919	29200
1920	29300
1920	29400
1921	29499
1921	30500
1922	30600
1922	30700
1924	30800
1925	30900

Year Starting	Serial Number
1926	30999
1926	31500
1927	31600
1927	31700
1928	31800
1929	31900
1929	31999
1929	32500
1930	32600
1930	32700
1931	32800
1932	32900
1934	32999
1934	33000
1935	33100
1936	33200
1937	33300
1937	33400
1939	33500
1946	33600
1948	33700
1950	33800
1952	33900
1954	33999
1954	36251
1956	36300
1958	36400
1959	36500
1962	36600
1964	36700
1965	36800

1970	36900
1970	40006
1972	40100
1974	40200
1979	40300
1980	40400
1981	40500
1982	40530
1983	40560
1984	40590
1985	40650
1986	40770
1987	40820
1988	40880
1989	40920
1990	41000
1991	41075
1992	41150
1993	41210

ROYAL OVER & UNDER GUNS

1950	36000
1952	36010
1954	36020
1958	36029
1993	51001

Year Starting	Serial Number

SPORTING OVER & UNDER GUNS

1993	50500

CAVALIER GUNS

1986	50001
1989	50150
1992	50250

ROYAL DOUBLE RIFLES - .450 & .465

1910	28200
1914	28299
1914	28500
1919	28535
1921	30335
1921	30415
1925	31042
1925	31049
1927	32000
1941	32099

ROYAL DOUBLE RIFLES - .375

1911	28400
1920	28499
1920	30416
1925	30499
1925	31050
1927	31099
1927	32100
1933	32199

ROYAL DOUBLE RIFLES - .240 & Small Bores

1920	28566
1923	28599
1923	31000
1926	31041
1926	31400
1931	31450

1955	31499	1975	35495
		1977	35498
ALL CALIBERS		1980	35500
1933	35000	1981	35505
1939	35100	1984	35524
1950	35200	1985	35527
1953	35250	1988	35540
1956	35300	1989	35542
1963	35350	1990	35552
1968	35450	1991	35590

ITALIAN YEAR OF MFG. DATE CODES

All Dates Prior to 1943 Have Month and
Year   (i.e. IXXII = January 1922.)
1944 -1953 = I - IX

X =	1954	XXX =	1974
XI =	1955	AA =	1975
XII =	1956	AB =	1976
XIII =	1957	AC =	1977
XIV =	1958	AD =	1978
XV =	1959	AE =	1979
XVI =	1960	AF =	1980
XVII =	1961	AH =	1981
XVIII =	1962	AI =	1982
XIX =	1963	AL =	1983
XX =	1964	AM =	1984
XXI =	1965	AN =	1985
XXII =	1966	AP =	1986
XXIII =	1967	AS =	1987
XXIV =	1968	AT =	1988
XXV =	1969	AW =	1989
XVI =	1970	AZ =	1990
XXVII =	1971	BA =	1991
XXVIII =	1972	BB =	1992
XXIX =	1973	BC =	1993
		BD =	1994
		BF =	1995

MAUSER BROOMHANDLES
1896 - late 1930's

Serial # Range	Date	Nature of Changes
before #25	1896	— The cone hammer used in place of spur hammer.
#50	1896	— "SYSTEM MAUSER" marked on top of the chamber.
before #200	1897	— The locking system changed from one to two lugs.
		— The barrel contour at the chamber is tapered instead of stepped.
#390	1897	— "WAFFENFABRIK MAUSER OBERNDORF A/N" marked on top of the chamber.
#975	1897	— The center section of the rear panel on the left side of the frame is not milled out (this feature appears earlier on a few 20-shot pistols). This area is sometimes used for special markings on contract pieces such as the Turkish and Persian.
#12,200 to #14,999	1898	— The large ring hammer replaces the cone hammer.
#21,000	1899	— There is no panel milling on either side of the frame.
		— A single lug bayonet type mount adopted for retaining the firing pin instead of the dovetail plate.
		— The trigger is mounted directly to the frame by two integral lugs rather than attached to a removable block.
		— The position of the serial number moved from the rear of the frame above the stock slot to the left side of the frame.
#22,000	1900	— Two integral lugs used to mount the rear sight instead of a pin.
#29,000	1902	— Very shallow panels milled into the frame on both sides.*
#31,200	1903	— "WAFFENFABRIK MAUSER OBERNDORF A NECKAR" added to the right rear frame panel.*

#34,000	1904	— The depth of the frame panel milling increased.*
#35,000	1904	— The barrel extension side rails lengthened about a half inch.*
		— An additional lug for mounting added to the firing pin.*
		— The hammer changed to the small ring pattern.*
		— The safety mechanism altered to require that the lever be pushed up to engaged it instead of down.*
		— The center of the safety lever knob is no longer milled out.*
#38,000	1905	— The short extractor with two ribs replaces the long thin extractor.*
#100,000	1910	— The rifling changed from four groove to six groove.
to		
#130,000	1911	
#270,000	1915	— "NS" (Neues Sicherung or New Safety) appears on the back of the hammer. The hammer must be moved back beyond the cocked position to engage the safety.
#440,000	1921	— The lanyard ring stud is rotated 90 degrees.
#501,000	1923	— The Mauser "banner" appears on the left rear frame panel.
#800,000	1930	— The Mauser "banner" is enlarged.
		— A step is added to the barrel contour just ahead of the chamber.
		— The safety is changed to allow the hammer to be dropped from a cocked position, without danger, by pulling the trigger (called Universal Safety).
		— The front of the grip frame widened to equal the rear part where the stock slot is.
#850,000	1932	— "D.R.P.u.A.P." (Deutsches Reich Pattenten und Anderes Patenten) added below the inscription on the right rear frame panel.
#860,000	1932	— The lettering in the frame inscription is slanted forward.
#900,000	1934	— The serial number is moved to the rear of the barrel extension behind the sight.
		— The two grooves in each side of the barrel extension side rails are eliminated.

*These nine changes appear out of sequence (either early or late) on three small batches of guns (29,000 to 29,900, 40,000 to 41,000, and 42,600 to 43,900). Most of these pistols are of the "bolo" style, that is they have 3.9 inch barrels, small grips, six or 10-shot magazines and fixed or adjustable rear sights. A few of these pistols show non-standard barrel contours, barrel extension milling and hammer safety devices. Apparently the factory withheld these numbers from the regular production series and reissued them at later dates.

PARKER SHOTGUNS
1866 - 1942

Date	Number Serial	Date	Number Serial
		1908	148,250
		1910	153,000
1866-1868	0-6,800	1911	157,050
1868-1877	9,700	1912	157,800
1877-1879	15,700	1913	165,000
1880	17,600		
1881	22,700		*Number Serial*
1882	27,300	*Date*	
1883	34,900	1914	168,200
1884	36,000	1915	171,500
1885	46,450		*first year of Trojan grade*
1886	48,125	1916	173,450
1887	56,650	1917	175,650
1889	59,500		*first single barrel trap gun*
1890	61,350	1918	180,250
1891	66,800	1919	184,900
1892	71,600	1920	190,100
1893	77,000	1921	195,000
1894	80,300	1922	200,500
1895	82,400		*first Parker single trigger*
1896	85,200	1923	205,150
1897	86,450	1924	207,150
1898	89,350		*first beavertail forend*
1899	92,450	1925	214,400
1900	97,300	1926	218,050
1901	105,750		*first ventilated rib, first .410*
1902	113,100	1927	222,650
1903	121,900	1928	228,200
1904	129,200		*PH grade dropped*
1905	132,000	1929	230,700
1906	138,300	1930	234,200
1907	144,250	1931	235,950

1932	236,100		1935	237,000
1933	236,300		1936	239,900
1934	236,650			*last regular catalog*
	first skeet guns,		1937	240,300
	takeover of factory		1938-1942	242,385
	by Remington			

REMINGTON
Firearms Serial Number Identification
(Code located on barrel, left side at frame)
Month of Manufacture
(Code letter corresponds to numeral underneath)

B	L	A	C	K	P	O	W	D	E	R	X
1	2	3	4	5	6	7	8	9	10	11	12

Year of Manufacture

1921	M		1937	F		1953	ZZ		1969	S		1985	F
1922	N		1938	G		1954	A		1970	T		1986	G
1923	P		1939	H		1955	B		1971	U		1987	H
1924	R		1940	J		1956	C		1972	W		1988	I
1925	S		1941	K		1957	D		1973	X		1989	J
1926	T		1942	L		1958	E		1974	Y		1990	K
1927	U		1943	MM		1959	F		1975	Z		1991	L
1928	W		1944	NN		1960	G		1976	I		1992	M
1929	X		1945	PP		1961	H		1977	O		1993	N
1930	Y		1946	RR		1962	J		1978	Q		1994	O
1931	Z		1947	SS		1963	K		1979	V		1995	P
1932	A		1948	TT		1964	L		1980	A		1996	Q
1933	B		1949	UU		1965	M		1981	B		1997	R
1934	C		1950	WW		1966	N		1982	C		1998	S
1935	D		1951	XX		1967	P		1983	D		1999	T
1936	E		1952	YY		1968	R		1984	E			

SAVAGE/STEVENS PRODUCTION DATA

The information below represents a listing of most Savage/Stevens rifles and shotguns mfg. in the past (some data has been appr oximated). Rather than list these models separately, they have been provided in this section for quick reference. Values on many of the mo dels listed below typically range between $50 - $175, depending on rarity and condition.

SAVAGE

MODEL	DATES	APPROX. GUNS
1903	1912-20	13,000
1904	1912-32	62,000
1905	1912-15	6,500
1909	1912-15	3,500
1911	1912-15	22,500
1912	1913-15	12,000
1914	1914-26	49,500
19	1933-45	16,000
1920	1920-32	12,000
1922	1922-25	16,000
'23A	1924-45	88,000
'23B	1924-45	16,500
'23C	1924-42	14,500
'23D	1932-45	15,000
3	1931-45	121,000
4	1933-45	38,000
5	1936-45	22,000
6	1938-45	45,500
7	1939-45	6,000
40	1928-42	16,000
45	1928-42	6,000
1925	1925-32	36,000
29	1933-45	23,500
CS22	1926-45	87,500
219	1938-45	12,500
220	1937-45	50,000
420	1937-42	13,500
430	1937-42	11.000
1921	1921-32	13,000
1928	1928-32	6,500
721	1930-32	12,000
FOX	1933-45	31,000
FX B	1940-45	20,000

STEVENS

No. 12	1912-35	166,500
14-1/2	1912-41	592,500
Fav.	1912-42	462,000
No. 26	1912-45	501,500
44+414	1912-35	23,000
No. 70	1912-31	295,500
No. 71	1930-34	10,000
No. 75	1928-34	19,000
15+425	1912-17	11,500
No. 35	1912-19	12,500
No. 35	1923-42	43,000
41-43	1912-18	18,500
No. 10	1919-34	9,500
85-89	1912-42	38,500
No. 93	1912-19	12,500

No. 97	1912-19	16,000
No. 101	1914-20	5,000
No. 105	1912-45	221,500
No. 107	1912-45	443,500
106-08	1916-35	56,500
No. 115	1912-31	23,000

MODEL	DATES	APPROX. GUNS
No. 124	1949-55	—
No. 125	1912-23	5,000
180-85	1912-23	16,000
No. 958	1925-33	5,000
116-17	1926-35	5,000
946-48	1928-34	7,000
No. 215	1913-32	61,000
No. 235	1912-32	61,500
No. 315	1914-36	192,000
No. 335	1912-31	67,500
No. 345	1916-31	3,500
No. 311	1926-45	145,500
No. 330	1926-35	33,500
No. 335	1926-35	2,000
No. 520	1912-32	191,000
No. 521	1930-32	5,000
60&61	1930-34	6,500
620-21	1926-45	66,500
Mod. 30	1933-34	26,000
Mod. 31	1933-34	2,000
No. 15	1936-45	224,000
No. 11	1923-33	141,500
No. 95	1926-35	55,000
No. 52	1933-37	88,000
No. 55	1935-36	3,500
No. 54	1933-42	23,500
No. 56	1933-45	97,500
No. 57	1939-42	500
No. 58	1933-45	29,500
No. 37	1936-42	29,000
No. 38	1936-45	33,500

No. 39	1938-45	64,000
No. 59	1938-45	21,000
No. 76	1938-45	6,000
65-66	1929-45	174,000
No. 82	1936-37	35,500
No. 83	1936-42	159,000
No. 84	1936-45	99,500
No. 85	1939-43	14,000
No. 86	1936-43	82,500
No. 87	1938-45	200,000
No. 872	1940-42	3,500
NO. 89	1926-37	12,000
No. 94	1926-45	934,000
No. 96	1926-33	3,500
No. 416	1937-42	2,000
No. 417	1932-42	1,000
No. 418	1932-42	1,500
No. 419	1932-36	1,000
No. 237	1936-43	16,000
No. 254	1936-42	1,000
No. 238	1936-45	40,000
No. 258	1936-45	11,000
102-04	1936-42	500
No. 116	1936-42	1,000
No. 944	1936-42	1,500
No. 600	1936-42	5,500
No. 900	1936-42	2,000
No. 515	1936-42	500
No. 5151	1936-42	95,000

MODEL	DATES	APPROX. GUNS
No. 530	1936-42	8,000
No. 500	1936-42	500

MODEL	DATES	APPROX. GUNS
22-410	1939-45	105,000
M.240	1940-45	20,500

THE NINETY-NINE

Serial Numbers At Year End:

10,000	1899		256,000	1923
13,400	1900		270,000	1924
19,500	1901		280,000	1925
25,000	1902		292,500	1926
35,000	1903		305,000	1927
45,000	1904		317,000	1928
53,000	1905		324,500	1929
67,500	1906		334,500	1930
73,500	1907		338,500	1931
81,000	1908		341,000	1932
95,000	1909		344,500	1933
110,000	1910		345,800	1934
119,000	1911		350,800	1935
131,000	1912		359,800	1936
146,500	1913		-	1937
162,000	1914		381,351	1938
175,500	1915		388,640	1939
187,500	1916		398,400	1940
193,000	1917		416,000	1941
-	1918		438,000	1946
212,500	1919		464,000	1947
229,000	1920		494,000	1948
237,500	1921		528,000	1949
244,500	1922		566,000	1950

WINCHESTER RIFLES

The following Winchester serial numbers appear courtesy of U.S. Repeating Arms, New Haven, CT. I would like to thank U.S. Repeating Arms and Mr. Pardee for making these production figures available.

Records at the factory indicate the following serial numbers were assigned to guns at the end of the calendar year

MODEL 1866

Year	Serial
1866 -	12476 to 14813
67 -	15578
68 -	19768
69 -	29516
70 -	52527
71 -	88184
72 -	109784
73 -	118401
74 -	125038
75 -	125965
76 -	131907
77 -	148207
78 -	150493
79 -	152201
80 -	154379
81 -	156107
82 -	159513
83 -	162376
84 -	163649
85 -	163664
86 -	165071
87 -	165912
88 -	167155
89 -	167401
90 -	167702
91 -	169003
92 -	NONE
93 -	169007
94 -	169011
95 -	NONE
96 -	NONE
97 -	169015
98 -	170100
99 -	DISCONTINUED

MODEL 1873

Year	Serial
1873 -	1 to 126
74 -	2726
75 -	11325
76 -	23151
77 -	23628
78 -	27501
79 -	41525
80 -	63537
81 -	81620
82 -	109507
83 -	145503
84 -	175126
85 -	196221
86 -	222937
87 -	225922
88 -	284529
89 -	323220
90 -	363220
91 -	405026
92 -	441625
93 -	466641
94 -	481826
95 -	499308
96 -	507545
97 -	513421
98 -	525922
99 -	541328
1900 -	554128
01 -	557236
02 -	564557
03 -	573957
04 -	588953
05 -	602557
06 -	613780
07 -	NONE
08 -	NONE
09 -	630385
10 -	656101
11 -	669324
12 -	678527
13 -	684419
14 -	686510
15 -	688431
16 -	694020
17 -	698617
18 -	700734
19 -	702042

No last # available
20, 21, 22, 23,   720609

MODEL 1876

Year	Serial
1876 -	1 to 1429
77 -	3579
78 -	7967
79 -	8971
80 -	14700
81 -	21759
82 -	32407
83 -	42410
84 -	54666
85 -	58714
86 -	60397
87 -	62420
88 -	63539
89 -	NONE
90 -	NONE
91 -	NONE
92 -	63561
93 -	63670
94 -	63678
95 -	NONE
96 -	63702
97 -	63869
98 -	63871

MODEL 1885 SINGLE SHOT

Year	Serial
1885 -	1 to 375
86 -	6841
87 -	18328
88 -	30571
89 -	45019
90 -	NONE
91 -	53700
92 -	60371
93 -	69534
94 -	NONE
95 -	73771
96 -	78253
97 -	78815
98 -	84700
99 -	85086
1900 -	88501
01 -	90424
02 -	92031
03 -	92359
04 -	92785
05 -	93611
06 -	94208
07 -	95743
08 -	96819
09 -	98097
10 -	98506
11 -	99012
12 -	NONE
13 -	100352

No further serial numbers were recorded until the end of 1923.
Last No. known was: 139700

MODEL 1886

Year	Serial
1886 -	1 to 3211
87 -	14728
88 -	28577
89 -	38401
90 -	49723
91 -	63601
92 -	73816
93 -	83261
94 -	94543
95 -	103708
96 -	109670
97 -	113997
98 -	119192
99 -	120571
1900 -	122834
01 -	125630
02 -	128942
03 -	132213
04 -	135524
05 -	138838
06 -	142249
07 -	145119
08 -	147322
09 -	148237
10 -	150129
11 -	151622
12 -	152943
13 -	152947
14 -	153859
15 -	154452
16 -	154979
17 -	155387
18 -	156219
19 -	156930
20 -	158716
21 -	159108
22 -	159337

No further serial numbers were recorded until the discontinuance of the model which was in 1935 - at - 159994

MODEL 1887

Year	Serial
1887 -	1 to 7431
88 -	22408
89 -	25673
90 -	29105
91 -	38541
92 -	49763
93 -	54367
94 -	56849
95 -	58289
96 -	60175
97 -	63952
98 -	64855

According to these records no guns were produced during the last few years of this model and it was therefore discontinued in 1901.

MODEL 1890

Records on the Model 1890 are somewhat incomplete. Our records indicate the following serial numbers were
assigned to guns at the end of the calendar year beginning with 1908. Actual records on the firearms which were manufactured between 1890 and 1907 will be available from the "Winchester Museum", located at the
"Buffalo Bill Historical Center"
Attn: Cody Firearms Museum
P.O. Box 1000,
Cody, WY 82414

Year	Serial
1908 -	330000 to 363850
09 -	393427
10 -	423567
11 -	451264
12 -	478595
13 -	506936
14 -	531019
15 -	551290
16 -	570497
17 -	589204
18 -	603438
19 -	630801
20 -	NONE
21 -	634783
22 -	643304
23 -	654837
24 -	664613
25 -	675774
26 -	687049
27 -	698987
28 -	711354
29 -	722125
30 -	729015
31 -	733178
32 -	734454

The Model 1890 was discontinued in 1932, however, a clean up of the production run lasted another 8+ years and included another 14 to 15000 guns. Our figures indicate approximately 749,000 guns were made.

MODEL 1892

Year	Serial
1892 -	1 to 23701
93 -	35987
94 -	73508
95 -	106721
96 -	144935
97 -	159312
98 -	165431
99 -	171820
1900 -	183411
01 -	191787
02 -	208871
03 -	253935
04 -	278546
05 -	315425
06 -	376496
07 -	437919
08 -	476540
09 -	522162
10 -	586996
11 -	643483
12 -	694752
13 -	742675
14 -	771444
15 -	804622
16 -	830031
17 -	853819
18 -	870942
19 -	903649
20 -	906754
21 -	910476
22 -	917300
23 -	926329
24 -	938641
25 -	954997
26 -	973896
27 -	990883
28 -	996517
29 -	999238
30 -	999730
31 -	1000727
32 -	1001324

MODEL 94

Records at the factory, and in some years, estimates, indicate the following serial numbers were assigned to guns at the end of the calendar year.

Year	Serial
1894 -	1 to 14579
95 -	44359
96 -	76464
97 -	111453
98 -	147684
99 -	183371
1900 -	204427
01 -	233975
02 -	273854
03 -	291506
04 -	311363
05 -	337557
06 -	378878
07 -	430985
08 -	474241
09 -	505831
10 -	553062
11 -	599263
12 -	646114
13 -	703701
14 -	756066
15 -	784052
16 -	807741
17 -	821972
18 -	838175
19 -	870762
20 -	880627
21 -	908318
22 -	919583
23 -	938539
24 -	953198
25 -	978523
26 -	997603
27 -	1027571
28 -	1054465
29 -	1077097
30 -	1081755
31 -	1084156
32 -	1087836
33 -	1089270
34 -	1091190
35 -	1099605
36 -	1100065
37 -	1100679
38 -	1100915
39 -	1101051
40 -	1142423
41 -	1191307
42 -	1221289
43 -	No Record Available
44 -	No Record Available
45 -	No Record Available
46 -	No Record Available
47 -	No Record Available
48 -	1500000
49 -	1626100
50 -	1724295
51 -	1724295
52 -	1910000
53 -	2000000
54 -	2071100
55 -	2145296
56 -	2225000
57 -	2290296
58 -	2365887
59 -	2410555
60 -	2469821
61 -	2500000
62 -	2551921
63 -	2586000
*1964	2700000 - 2797428
65 -	2894428
66 -	2991927
67 -	3088458
68 -	3185691
69 -	3284570
70 -	3381299
71 -	3557385
72 -	3806499
73 -	3929364
74 -	4111426
75 -	4277926
75 -	4463553
76 -	4463553
77 -	4565925
78 -	4662210
79 -	4826596
80 -	4892951
81 -	5024957

82 -	5103248

* The post-64 Model 94 began with serial number 2,700,000.

Serial number 1,000,000 was presented to President Calvin Coolidge in 1927.

Serial number 1,500,000 was presented to President Harry S. Truman in 1948.

Serial number 2,500,000 and 3,000,000 were presented to the Winchester Gun Museum, now located in Cody, Wyoming.

Serial number 3,500,000 was not constructed until 1979 and was sold as auction in Las Vegas, Nevada.

Serial number 4,000,000 - whereabouts unknown at this time.

Serial number 4,500,000 - shipped to Italy by Olin in 1978. Whereabouts unknown.

Serial number 5,000,000 - in New Haven, not constructed as of March 1983.

Records at the factory indicate the following serial numbers were assigned to guns at the end of the calendar year.

MODEL 1895

1895 -	1 to 287
96 -	5715
97 -	7814
98 -	19871
99 -	26434
1900 -	29817
01 -	31584
02 -	35601
03 -	42514
04 -	47805
05 -	54783
06 -	55011
07 -	57351
08 -	60002
09 -	60951
10 -	63771
11 -	65017
12 -	67331
13 -	70823
14 -	72082
15 -	174233
16 -	377411
17 -	389106
18 -	392731
19 -	397250
20 -	400463
21 -	404075
22 -	407200

23 -	410289
24 -	413276
25 -	417402
26 -	419533
27 -	421584
28 -	422676
29 -	423680
30 -	424181
31 -	425132
32 -	425825

MODEL 1903

1903 -	# Not Available
04 -	6944
05 -	14865
06 -	23097
07 -	31852
08 -	39105
09 -	46496
10 -	54298
11 -	61679
12 -	69586
13 -	76732
14 -	81776
15 -	84563
16 -	87148
17 -	89501
18 -	92617
19 -	96565
20 -	# Not Available
21 -	97650
22 -	99011
23 -	100452
24 -	101688
25 -	103075
26 -	104230
27 -	105537
28 -	107157
29 -	109414
30 -	111276
31 -	112533
32 -	112992

This model was discontinued in 1932, however, a clean up of parts was used for further production of approximately 2000 guns. Total production was stopped at serial number 114962... in 1936.

MODEL 1905

1905 -	1 to 5659
06 -	15288
07 -	19194
08 -	20385
09 -	21280
10 -	22423
11 -	23503
12 -	24602
13 -	25559
14 -	26110
15 -	26561
16 -	26910
17 -	27297
18 -	27585
19 -	28287
20 -	29113

MODEL 1906

1906 -	1 to 52278
07 -	89147

08 -	114138
09 -	165068
10 -	221189
11 -	273355
12 -	327955
13 -	381922
14 -	422734
15 -	453880
16 -	483805
17 -	517743
18 -	535540
19 -	593917
20 -	NONE
21 -	598691
22 -	608011
23 -	622601
24 -	636163
25 -	649952
26 -	665484
27 -	679892
28 -	695915
29 -	711202
30 -	720116
31 -	725978
32 -	727353

A clean up of production took place for the next few years with a record of production reaching approximately 729305.

MODEL 1907

1907 -	1 to 8657
08 -	14486
09 -	19707
10 -	23230
11 -	25523
12 -	27724
13 -	29607
14 -	30872
15 -	32272
16 -	36215
17 -	38235
18 -	39172
19 -	40448
20 -	No # Available
21 -	40784
22 -	41289
23 -	41658
24 -	42029
25 -	42360
26 -	42688
27 -	43226
28 -	43685
29 -	44046
30 -	44357
31 -	44572
32 -	44683
33 -	44806
34 -	44990
35 -	45203
36 -	45482
37 -	45920
38 -	46419
39 -	46758
40 -	47296
1941 -	47957
42 -	48275
43 -	NONE
44 -	NONE
45 -	48281

46 -	48395
47 -	48996
48 -	49684
**49 -	50662
**50 -	51640
**51 -	52618
**52 -	53596
**53 -	54574
**54 -	55552
**55 -	56530
**56 -	57508
**57 -	58486

** Actual records on serial numbers stops in 1948. The serial numbers ending each year from 1948 to 1957 were derived at by taking the last serial number recorded (58486) and the last number from 1948, (49684) and dividing the years of production (9), which relates to 978 guns each year for the nine year period.

MODEL 1910

1910 -	1 to 4766
11 -	7695
12 -	9712
13 -	11487
14 -	12311
15 -	13233
16 -	13788
17 -	14255
18 -	14625
19 -	15665
20 -	No # Available
21 -	15845
22 -	16347
23 -	16637
24 -	17030
25 -	17281
26 -	17696
27 -	18182
28 -	18469
29 -	18893
30 -	19065
31 -	19172
32 -	19232
33 -	19281
34 -	19338
35 -	19388
36 -	19445

A cleanup of production continued into 1937 when the total of the guns was completed at approximately 20786

MODEL 1911 S.L.

1911 -	1 to 3819
12 -	27659
13 -	36677
14 -	40105
15 -	43284
16 -	45391
17 -	49893
18 -	52895
19 -	57337
20 -	60719
21 -	64109
22 -	69132

23 -	73186
24 -	76199
25 -	78611

The Model 1911 was discontinued in 1925. However, guns were produced for three years after that date to clean up production and excess parts. When this practice ceased there were approximately 82774 guns produced.

MODEL 52

1920 -	None indicated
21 -	397
22 -	745
23 -	1394
24 -	2361
25 -	3513
26 -	6383
27 -	9436
28 -	12082
29 -	14594
30 -	17253
31 -	21954
32 -	24951
33 -	26725
34 -	29030
35 -	32448
36 -	36632
37 -	40419
38 -	43632
39 -	45460
40 -	47519
41 -	50317
42 -	52129
43 -	52553
44 -	52560
45 -	52718
46 -	56080
47 -	60158
48 -	64265
49 -	68149
50 -	70766
51 -	73385
52 -	76000
53 -	79500
54 -	80693
55 -	81831
56 -	96869
57 -	97869
58 -	98599
59 -	98899
60 -	102200
61 -	106986
62 -	108718
63 -	113583
64 -	118447
65 -	120992
66 -	123537
67 -	123727
68 -	123917
69 -	E 124107
70 -	E 124297
71 -	E 124489
72 -	E 124574
73 -	E 124659
74 -	E 124744
75 -	E 124828
76 -	E 125019
77 -	E 125211

78 -	E 125315

This Model was discontinued in 1978. A small clean up of production was completed in 1979 with a total of - 125419.

MODEL 53

The Model 53 was serial numbered in both its' own series (1 to slightly over 15,000) as well as within the Model 1892 series. Early guns predominate the Model 53 serial number series with Model 1892 series serial numbers appearing more frequently mid to late production.

This Model was discontinued in 1932, however, a clean up of production continued for 9 more years.

1924-	1 to 1488
25-	4350
26-	6882
27-	9180
28-	11139
29-	12873
30-	13794
31-	14416
32-	14623
33-	14727
34-	14817
35-	14976
36-	15047
37-	15078
38-	15092
39-	15099
40-	15109
41-	15118

Total Production
Approximately - 24,916

Records at the factory indicate the following serial numbers were assigned to guns at the end of the calendar year.

MODEL 54

1925 -	1 to 3140
26 -	8051
27 -	14176
28 -	19587
29 -	29104
30 -	32499

31 -	36731
32 -	38543
33 -	40722
34 -	43466
35 -	47125
36 -	50145

MODEL 55 CENTER-FIRE

1924 -	1 to 836
25 -	2783
26 -	4957
27 -	8021
28 -	10467
29 -	12258
30 -	17393
31 -	18198
32 -	19204
33 -	Clean up 20580

MODEL 61

1932 -	1 to 3532
33 -	6008
34 -	8554
35 -	12379
36 -	20615
37 -	30334
38 -	36326
39 -	42610
40 -	49270
41 -	57493
42 -	59871
43 -	59872
44 -	59879
45 -	60512
46 -	71629
47 -	92297
48 -	115281
49 -	125461
50 -	135461
51 -	145821
52 -	156000
53 -	171000
54 -	186000
55 -	200962
56 -	216923
57 -	229457
58 -	242992
59 -	262793
60 -	282594
61 -	302395
62 -	322196
63 -	342001

This Model was discontinued in 1963. For some unknown reason there are no actual records available from 1949 through 1963. The serial number figures for these years are arrived at by taking the total production figure of 342001, subtracting the last known # of 115281, and dividing the difference equally by the amount of remaining years available, (15).

MODEL 62

1932 -	1 to 7643
33 -	10695
34 -	14090
35 -	23924

36 -	42759
37 -	66059
38 -	80205
39 -	96534
40 -	116393
41 -	137379
42 -	155152
43 -	155422
44 -	155425
45 -	156073
46 -	183756
47 -	219085
48 -	252298
49 -	262473
50 -	272648
51 -	282823
52 -	293000
53 -	310500
54 -	328000
55 -	342776
56 -	357551
57 -	383513
58 -	409475

MODEL 63

1933 -	1 to 2667
34 -	5361
35 -	9830
36 -	16781
37 -	25435
38 -	30934
39 -	36055
40 -	41456
41 -	47708
42 -	51258
43 -	51631
44 -	51656
45 -	53853
46 -	61607
47 -	71714
48 -	80519
49 -	88889
50 -	97259
51 -	105629
52 -	114000
53 -	120500
54 -	127000
55 -	138000
56 -	150000
57 -	162345
58 -	174692

MODEL 70

1935 -	1 to 19
36 -	2238
37 -	11573
38 -	17844
39 -	23991
40 -	31675
41 -	41753
42 -	49206
43 -	49983
44 -	49997
45 -	50921
46 -	58382
47 -	75675
48 -	101680
49 -	131580
50 -	173150
51 -	206625
52 -	238820

53 -	282735
54 -	323530
55 -	361025
56 -	393595
57 -	425283
58 -	440792
59 -	465040
60 -	504257
61 -	545446
62 -	565592
63 -	581471

All post 64 Model 70s began with the serial number 700,000.

64 -	740599
65 -	809177
66 -	833795
67 -	869000
68 -	925908
69 -	G941900
70 -	G957995
71 -	G1018991
72 -	G1099257
73 -	G1128731
74 -	G1175000
75 -	G1218700
76 -	G1266000
77 -	G1350000
78 -	G1410000
79 -	G1447000
80 -	G1490709
81 -	G1537134

MODEL 71

1935 -	1 to 4
36 -	7821
37 -	12988
38 -	14690
39 -	16155
40 -	18267
41 -	20810
42 -	21959
43 -	22048
44 -	22051
45 -	22224
46 -	23534
47 -	25728
48 -	27900
49 -	29675
50 -	31450
51 -	33225
52 -	35000
53 -	37500
54 -	40770
55 -	43306
56 -	45843
57 -	47254

MODEL 74

1939 -	1 to 30890
40 -	67085
41 -	114355
42 -	128293
43 -	NONE
44 -	128295
45 -	128878
46 -	145168
47 -	173524
48 -	223788
49 -	249900
50 -	276012

51 -	302124
52 -	328236
53 -	354348
54 -	380460
55 -	406574

MODEL 88

1955 -	1 to 18378
56 -	36756
57 -	55134
58 -	73512
59 -	91890
60 -	110268
61 -	128651
62 -	139838

63 -	148858
64 -	160307
65 -	162699
66 -	192595
67 -	212416
68 -	230199
69 -	H239899
70 -	H258229
71 -	H266784
72 -	H279014
73 -	H283718

MODEL 100

1961 -	1 to 32189
62 -	60760

63 -	78863
64 -	92016
65 -	135388
66 -	145239
67 -	209498
68 -	210053
69 -	A210999
70 -	A229995
71 -	A242999
72 -	A258001
73 -	A262833

WINCHESTER SHOTGUNS

Records at the factory indicate the following serial numbers were assigned to guns at the end of the calendar year.

MODEL 1897

1897 -	1 to 32335
98 -	64668
99 -	96999
1900 -	129332
01 -	161665
02 -	193998
03 -	226331
04 -	258664
05 -	296037
06 -	334059
07 -	377999
08 -	413618
09 -	446888
10 -	481062
11 -	512632
12 -	544313
13 -	575213
14 -	592732
15 -	607673
16 -	624537
17 -	646124
18 -	668383
19 -	691943
20 -	696183
21 -	700428
22 -	715902
23 -	732060
24 -	744942
25 -	757629
26 -	770527
27 -	783574
28 -	769806
1929 -	807321
30 -	812729
31 -	830721
32 -	833926
33 -	835637
34 -	837364
35 -	839728
36 -	848684
37 -	856729
38 -	860725
39 -	866938
40 -	875945
41 -	891190

42 -	910072
43 -	912265
44 -	912327
45 -	916472
46 -	926409
47 -	936682
48 -	944085
49 -	953042
50 -	961999
51 -	970956
52 -	979913
53 -	988860
54 -	997827
55 -	1006784
56 -	1015741
57 -	1024700

Records on this Model are incomplete. The above serial numbers are estimated from 1897 thru 1903 and again from 1949 thru 1957. The actual records are in existence from 1904 through 1949.

**MODEL 1901
SHOTGUN**

1904 -	64,856 to 64,860
05 -	66453
06 -	67486
07 -	68424
08 -	69197
09 -	70009
10 -	70753
11 -	71441
12 -	72167
13 -	72764
14 -	73202
15 -	73509
16 -	73770
17 -	74027
18 -	74311
19 -	74872
20 -	77000

MODEL 12

1912 -	5308
13 -	32418
14 -	79765
15 -	109515
16 -	136412
17 -	159391
18 -	183461
19 -	219457
20 -	247458

21 -	267253
22 -	304314
23 -	346319
24 -	385196
25 -	423056
26 -	464564
27 -	510693
28 -	557850
29 -	600834
30 -	626996
31 -	651255
32 -	660110
33 -	664544
34 -	673994
35 -	686978
36 -	720316
37 -	754250
38 -	779455
39 -	814121
40 -	856499
41 -	907431
42 -	958303
43 -	975640
44 -	975727
45 -	990004
1946 -	1029152
47 -	1102371
48 -	1176055
49 -	1214041
50 -	1252028
51 -	1290015
52 -	1328002
53 -	1399996
54 -	1471990
55 -	1541929
56 -	1611868
57 -	1651435
58 -	1690999
59 -	1795500
60 -	1800000
61 -	1930999
62 -	1956990
63 -	1962001

A clean up of production took place from 64 through 66 with the ending serial # 1970875.

NEW STYLE M/12

1972 -	Y200 011-Y2006396
73 -	Y2015662
74 -	Y2022061
75 -	Y2024478
76 -	Y2025482

77 -	Y2025874	1933 -	1 to 9398	54 -	117200
78 -	Y2026156	34 -	13963	55 -	121883
79 -	Y2026399	35 -	17728	56 -	126566
MODEL 24		36 -	24849	57 -	131249
1939 -	1 to 8118	37 -	30900	58 -	135932
40 -	21382	38 -	34659	59 -	140615
41 -	27045	39 -	38967	60 -	145298
42 -	33670	40 -	43348	61 -	149981
43 -	NONE RECORDED	41 -	48203	62 -	154664
44 -	33683	42 -	50818	63 -	159353
45 -	34965	43 -	50822	**MODEL 50**	
46 -	45250	44 -	50828	1954 -	1 to 24550
47 -	58940	45 -	51168	55 -	49100
48 -	64417	46 -	54256	56 -	73650
		47 -	64853	57 -	98200
		48 -	75142	58 -	122750
		49 -	81107	59 -	147300
		50 -	87071	60 -	171850
		51 -	93038	61 -	196400
		52 -	99000		
		53 -	108201		

There were no records kept on this model from 1949 until its discontinuance in 1958. The total production was approximately 116280.

MODEL 42

WINCHESTER MODEL 101 SERIALIZATION

12 gauge

Ser. No.	Mfg. Mo.	Year	Ser. No.	Mfg. Mo.	Year	Ser. No.	Mfg. Mo.	Year
50,000	10	1959	70,500	7	1964	93,500	2	1966
50,500	3	1960	71,000	8	1964	94,000	3	1966
51,000	5	1960	71,500	9	1964	94,500	3	1966
51,500	6	1960	72,000	9	1964	95,000	5	1966
52,000	9	1961	72,500	10	1964	95,500	5	1966
52,500	3	1962	73,000	10	1964	96,000	6	1966
53,000	4	1962	73,500	11	1964	96,500	7	1966
53,500	5	1962	74,000	11	1964	97,000	7	1966
54,000	8	1962	74,500	12	1964	97,500	7	1966
54,500	9	1962	75,000	12	1964	98,000	8	1966
55,000	10	1962	75,500	1	1965	98,500	8	1966
55,500	12	1962	76,000	2	1965	99,000	9	1966
56,000	1	1963	76,500	2	1965	99,500	9	1966
56,500	2	1963	77,000	3	1965	100,000	10	1966
57,000	3	1963	77,500	4	1965	100,500	10	1966
57,500	3	1963	78,000	4	1965	101,000	10	1966
58,000	4	1963	78,500	4	1965	101,500	11	1966
58,500	5	1963	**Ser. No.**	**Mfg. Mo.**	**Year**	102,000	11	1966
Ser. No.	**Mfg. Mo.**	**Year**	79,000	4	1965	102,500	12	1966
59,000	6	1963	79,500	4	1965	103,000	1	1967
59,500	6	1963	80,000	5	1965	103,500	1	1967
60,000	7	1963	80,500	6	1965	104,000	2	1967
60,500	8	1963	81,000	6	1965	104,500	3	1967
61,000	8	1963	81,500	6	1965	105,000	4	1967
61,500	11	1963	82,000	6	1965	105,500	5	1967
62,000	11	1963	82,500	8	1965	106,000	5	1967
62,500	11	1963	83,000	8	1965	106,500	5	1967
63,000	12	1963	83,500	8	1965	107,000	9	1967
63,500	1	1964	84,000	9	1965	107,500	10	1967
64,000	1	1964	84,500	9	1965	108,000	10	1967
64,500	2	1964	85,000	10	1965	108,500	11	1967
65,000	3	1964	85,500	10	1965	109,000	11	1967
65,500	3	1964	86,000	10	1965	109,500	11	1967
66,000	3	1964	86,500	10	1965	110,000	12	1967
66,500	3	1964	87,000	10	1965	110,500	1	1968
67,000	5	1964	87,500	10	1965	111,000	2	1968
67,500	5	1964	88,000	11	1965	111,500	3	1968
68,000	5	1964	88,500	11	1965	112,000	3	1968
68,500	5	1964	89,000	11	1965	112,500	3	1968
Ser. No.	**Mfg. Mo.**	**Year**	90,000	12	1965			
69,000	6	1964	90,500	12	1965			
69,500	6	1964	91,000	12	1965			
70,000	7	1964	91,500	1	1966			
			92,000	1	1966			
			92,500	2	1966			
			93,000	2	1966			

Ser. No.	Mfg. Mo.	Year
113,000	3	1968
113,500	4	1968
114,000	5	1968
114,500	5	1968
115,000	6	1968
115,500	6	1968
116,000	7	1968
116,500	7	1968
117,000	9	1968
117,500	10	1968
118,000	1	1969
118,500	1	1969
119,000	2	1969
119,500	3	1969
120,000	4	1969
120,500	4	1969
121,000	4	1969
121,500	4	1969
122,000	5	1969
122,500	6	1969
123,000	6	1969
123,500	6	1969
124,000	7	1969
124,500	7	1969
125,000	7	1969
125,500	8	1969
126,000	8	1969
126,500	9	1969
127,000	9	1969
127,500	10	1969
128,000	11	1969
128,500	11	1969
129,000	11	1969
129,500	2	1970
130,000	2	1970
130,500	3	1970
131,000	3	1970
131,500	4	1970
132,000	4	1970
132,500	4	1970
133,000	4	1970
133,500	5	1970
134,000	5	1970
134,500	5	1970
135,000	6	1970

Ser. No.	Mfg. Mo.	Year
135,500	6	1970
136,000	6	1970
136,500	8	1970
137,000	8	1970
137,500	8	1970
138,000	8	1970
138,500	11	1970
139,000	12	1970
139,500	12	1970
140,000	12	1970
140,500	1	1971
141,000	2	1971
141,500	2	1971
142,000	2	1971
142,500	3	1971
143,000	3	1971
143,500	4	1971
144,000	4	1971
144,500	4	1971
145,000	4	1971
145,500	5	1971

20 gauge

Ser. No.	Mfg. Mo.	Year
200,000	3	1966
200,500	3	1966
201,000	3	1966
201,500	3	1966
202,000	4	1966
202,500	4	1966
203,000	4	1966
203,500	5	1966
204,000	6	1966
204,500	6	1966
205,000	7	1966
205,500	8	1966
206,000	8	1966
206,500	8	1966
207,000	9	1966
207,500	9	1966
208,000	9	1966
208,500	12	1966
209,000	2	1967
209,500	7	1967
210,000	10	1967
210,500	12	1967

28 ga. & .410 ga. added

211,000	1	1968
211,500	1	1968
212,000	10	1968
212,500	10	1968
213,000	10	1968
213,500	11	1968
214,000	12	1968
214,500	12	1968
215,000	1	1969
215,500	2	1969
216,000	5	1969
216,500	6	1969
217,000	9	1969
217,500	10	1969
218,000	11	1969
218,500	12	1969
219,000	12	1969
219,500	12	1969
220,000	12	1969
220,500	1	1970
221,000	1	1970
221,500	2	1970
222,000	3	1970
222,500	7	1970
223,000	9	1970
223,500	9	1970
224,000	9	1970
224,500	9	1970
225,000	10	1970
225,500	10	1970
226,000	11	1970
226,500	11	1970
227,000	11	1970
227,500	12	1970
228,000	12	1970
228,500	4	1971
229,000	4	1971
229,500	4	1971

STORE BRAND CROSS-OVER LIST

The following listing is provided as a cross reference of "Store Brands" to original manufacturer and model number. Although not exhaustive, this list covers most major stores and chains that have had their name put on guns by other manufacturers. The values for the firearms listed on these pages are approximately 15% - 40% less than the original manufacturers model(s).

Our thanks goes out to Gun Parts Corp., West Hurley, NY. They can be reached (914) 679-2417.

House Brand	Model No.	Orig. Mfgr.	Orig. Model
Aldens	670	Springfield	67
Aldens	670	Savage	67
Belknap	964A	Stevens	87N
Belknap	B63	Springfield	947
Belknap	B63	Savage	947B
Belknap	B63E	Savage	940E
Belknap	B64	Savage	67
Belknap	B65C	Springfield	745
Belknap	865C	Savage	745
Belknap	B68	Savage	94C
Belknap	B68D	Savage	94D
Belknap	B963	Springfield	120
Belknap	B963	Savage	120
Belknap	B964	Savage	87J
Belknap	B967	Savage	87N
Coast to Coast	180	Savage	58
Coast to Coast	1800	Savage	18D
Coast to Coast	182	Savage	18S
Coast to Coast	184	Savage	951
Coast to Coast	267	Savage	77
Coast to Coast	285	Savage	7J
Coast to Coast	286	Savage	46
Coast to Coast	288	Savage	87J
Coast to Coast	320	Savage	120
Coast to Coast	367	Savage	30
Coast to Coast	40	Marlin	99C
Coast to Coast	42	Marlin	70
Coast to Coast	650	Marlin	55
Coast to Coast	779	Mossberg	479
Coast to Coast	843	Savage	340
Coast to Coast	843	Springfield	840
Coast to Coast	843V2DS	Savage	340(.222)
Coast to Coast	843V3DS	Savage	340(.30/30)
Coast to Coast	946	Stevens	940
Coast to Coast	946	Springfield	947
Coast to Coast	946E	Stevens	940E
Coast to Coast	946Y	Stevens	940Y
Cotter & Co	10-40	Glenfield	10
Cotter & Co	10-40	Marlin	101
Cotter & Co	121	Stevens	120-15
Cotter & Co	167	Springfield	67
Cotter & Co	167T	Savage	30
Cotter & Co	168	Savage	30
Cotter & Co	168	Springfield	67VR
Cotter & Co	287	Springfield	87J
Cotter & Co	33	Marlin	336C
Cotter & Co	410	Savage	110E
Cotter & Co	424	Savage	24F
Cotter & Co	434	Savage	34
Cotter & Co	474	Savage	170
Cotter & Co	474	Springfield	174
Cotter & Co	487T	Springfield	187
Cotter & Co	489	Savage	89
Cotter & Co	60-50	Glenfield	60
Cotter & Co	60-50	Marlin	99C
Cotter & Co	645	Savage	745
Cotter & Co	645C	Savage	745C
Cotter & Co	75-46	Marlin	99M1

House Brand	Model No.	Orig. Mfgr.	Orig. Model
Cotter & Co	75-45	Glenfield	75
Cotter & Co	842	Springfield	840
Cotter & Co	911	Springfield	511
Cotter & Co	918	Springfield	18
Cotter & Co	948	Stevens	940
Cotter & Co	948E	Savage	948E
Cotter & Co	949	Springfield	944
Cotter & Co	949C	Savage	940
Cotter & Co	949Y	Savage	944Y
C.I.L.	125	Anschutz	184
C.I.L.	212	Savage	7J
C.I.L.	221	Savage	7J
C.I.L.	227	Savage	871
C.I.L.	233	Savage	85N
C.I.L.	266	Savage	187
C.I.L.	470	Anschutz	520/61
C.I.L.	607	Savage	67
C.I.L.	607 TD	Savage	30 FLD GR.
C.I.L.	621	Savage	30
C.I.L.	621 TD	Savage	30D
C.I.L.	710	Savage	311
C.I.L.	725	Savage	FOX BDE
C.I.L.	830	Savage	340
C.I.L.	871	Savage	170
C.I.L.	950C.D	Savage	110C.D
C.I.L.	MKVII	H & R	865
Eastern Arms	101.1	Stevens	94B
Eastern Arms	IOl.23	Savage	416
Foremost See J.C.Penney			
Gamble Skogkmo, Hiawatha			
Gamble Skogkmo	130	Savage	30
Gamble Skogmo	1300-567 VR	Savage	67-VR
Gamble Skogmo	180N	Savage	87N
Gamble Skogmo	1 89J	Savage	87J
Gamble Skogmo	189N	Stevens	87N
Gamble Skogmo	521	Savage	120
Gamble Skogmo	567	Savage	67
Gamble Skogmo	S87	Savage	187
Gamble Skogmo	594	Savage	944
Gamble Skogmo	594Y	Savage	944Y
Gamble Skogmo	GU12-5517A	J.C.Higgins	60 & 66
Glenfield	10	Marlin	101
Glenfield	20	Marlin	80
Glenfield	25	Marlin	80 W/swivels
Glenfield	30A	Marlin	336
Glenfield	35	Marlin	336 .35 cal
Glenfield	50	Marlin	55
Glenfield	60	Marlin	5
Glenfield	60	Marlin	99C
Glenfield	65	Marlin	99M1
Glenfield	70	Marlin	989M2
Glenfield	75	Marlin	989MI

House Brand	Model No.	Orig. Mfgr.	Orig. Model
Globco	Mohawk	Russian	Tokarev
Hawthorn See Wards			
Hercules	50	Stevens	5100
Hiawatha See Gambles			
J.C. Higgins See Sears			
J.C. Penney common name, F - Foremost			
J.C.Penney	2025	Marlin	80C

Brand	Model No.	Orig. Mfgr.	Orig. Model		Brand	Model No.	Orig. Mfgr.	Orig. Model
J.C.Penney	2035	Marlin	80		Sears	101.1	Savage	94
J.C.Penney	2035	Glenfield	20		Sears	101.100	Savage	96/96Y
J.C.Penney	2066	Marlin	49DL		Sears	101.10040	Savage	94
J.C.Penney	2935	Marlin	336		Sears	101.10041	Savage	94
J.C.Penney	3040	Marlin	336		Sears	101.10080	Stevens	940
J.C.Penney	3040	Glenfield	30A		Sears	101.1120	Savage	51 and 951
J.C.Penney	4011	High Standard	FLIGHT KING		Sears	101.12	Stevens	39
J.C.Penney	6400	Savage	340		Sears	101.13	Stevens	86-7
J.C.Penney	6610	Savage	120		Sears	101.138	Savage	38A and 58A
J.C.Penney	6630	Glenfield	50		Sears	101.138	Springfield	18.410
J.C.Penney	6630	Marlin	66		Sears	101.1380	Springfield	18,18C
J.C.Penney	6647	Savage	944		Sears	101.1380	Stevens	58,C
J.C.Penney	6647	Springfield	944		Sears	101.1381	Springfield	18,951 E,F
J.C.Penney	6660	Glenfield	60		Sears	101.1381	Stevens	58,51, E,F
J.C.Penney	6660	Marlin	99C		Sears	101.16	Savage	6,87
J.C.Penney	6670	Springfield	67H		Sears	101.1610	Savage	540 DL
J.C.Penney	6670	Savage	67		Sears	101.1610	Savage	FOX BDL
J.C.Penney	6870	Savage	30		Sears	101.1610	Fox BST	EC,BD,BE,B-F
J.C.Penney	6870H	Savage	30H		Sears	101.1620-1670	Stevens	530,A; 311,A,C
Katz	F-1282	Marlin	989M2		Sears	101.1700	Savage	94
Katz	F-1282	Glenfield	70		Sears	101.1701	Fox BSE	C,D,Ser F,H
Katz	F-1287	Marlin	55		Sears	101.1701-C	Savage	BSE
Katz	F-1287	Glenfield	50		Sears	101.1710	Savage	FOX BDE
					Sears	101.1710	Savage	540 BDE
Kresge	151	Boito	CBC		Sears	101.1750	Savage	94
					Sears	101.1760	Savage	94
K-Mart	151	Boito	CBC		Sears	101.19	Stevens	827-7
					Sears	101.20	Stevens	15
Marlin/new	780	Marlin/old	80		Sears	101.22	Stevens	87M(MUSKET)
Marlin/new	781	Marlin/old	81		Sears	101.25	Stevens	39A, 59A,BandC
Marlin/new	782	Marlin/old	980		Sears	101.2830	Savage	63-73
New Haven	220K	Mossberg	320K-A		Sears	101.2830	Savage	73
New Haven	240K	Mossberg	340K		Sears	101.3	Stevens	237
New Haven	246K	Mossberg	346K-A		Sears	101.3538830	Stevens	89
New Haven	250K	Mossberg	152K		Sears	101.4	Stevens	38
New Haven	250K8	Mossberg	350K-A		Sears	101.40	Springfield	947,D,Y
New Haven	273	Mossberg	173		Sears	101.40	Stevens	940,D,Y,DY
New Haven	273A	Mossberg	173A		Sears	101.451	Marlin	336
New Haven	283.D	Mossberg	183D		Sears	101.5	Stevens	37
New Haven	284	Mossberg	173		Sears	101.51004	Savage	94
New Haven	285	Mossberg	185D-C		Sears	101.510070	Savage	94
New Haven	290	Mossberg	190D-A		Sears	101.51009	Springfield	944,Yseries A
New Haven	453	Mossberg	353		Sears	101.51013	Springfield	944,Yseries A
New Haven	600AB	Mossberg	500AS		Sears	101.51024	Savage	94
New Haven	600C	Mossberg	500C		Sears	101.510270	Savage	94
New Haven	600E	Mossberg	500E		Sears	101.51044	Savage	94
New Haven	679	Mossberg	472		*House Brand*	*Model No.*	*Orig. Mfgr.*	*Orig. Model*
New Haven	740	Mossberg	640		Sears	101.510660	Stevens	9478
					Sears	101.510660	Springfield	944,Y series A
Otasco	30	Marlin	336		Sears	101.510670	Stevens	9478
Otasco	30	Glenfield	30A		Sears	101.510680	Stevens	9478
Otasco	65	Glenfield	60		Sears	101.512220	Stevens	5100,530,311
Otasco	65	Marlin	99C		Sears	101.512230	Stevens	5100,530,311
					Sears	101.51451	Springfield	67
Palmetto	11	Stevens	85,89		Sears	101.51452	Springfield	67
					Sears	101.51454	Springfield	67
Priemier	Trail Blazer	Stevens	29A		Sears	101.51472	Springfield	67 Series B
					Sears	101.52701	Stevens	71,74 S/S
Revelation, see Western Auto					Sears	101.52772	Savage	34,65,34M. 65M
House Brand	*Model No.*	*Orig. Mfgr.*	*Orig. Model*		Sears	101.52773	Savage	34,65,34M, 65M
Sears. Ranger. J.C.Higgins					Sears	101.5350	Springfield	18.58
J.C.Higgins	101.1	Savage	94		Sears	101.5350-D	Stevens	18D
J.C.Higgins	101.24	Savage	15-120		Sears	101.53521	Savage	340
J.C.Higgins	20	High Standard	200		Sears	101.53527	Savage	340
J.C.Higgins	42 DL	Marlin	80		Sears	101.5380	Savage	18/18AC.58
J.C.Higgins	52	Sako	L46		Sears	101.5380	Springfield	18,12,16,20ga.
J.C.Higgins	S4	Browning	FN-300		Sears	101.5380D	Stevens	18ADC
J.C.Higgins	583.13 to.23	High Standard	10		Sears	101.538840	Savage	34,65,34M, 65M
J.C.Higgins	583.2078-79	High Standard	20ga pump		Sears	101.540	FOX	B-BST,BDL
J.C.Higgins	583.514-730	High Standard	20ga pump		Sears	101.5410	Springfield	18,58
J.C.Higgins	6670H	Stevens	67H		Sears	101.5410D	Savage	18D
J.C.Higgins	80	High Standard	101		Sears	101.5410D	Springfield	18DS
					Sears	101.54880	Stevens	80 Series A
Ranger	101.2	Savage	238		Sears	101.54880	Springfield	187 Series A
Ranger	101.8	Stevens	83		Seem	101.64881	Marlin	980 DL,987
Ranger	104.7	H&R	120		Sears	101.600	Stevens	39A,59A,B,C
Ranger	105.20	H&R	120		Sears	101.7	Stevens	311
Ranger	120	Winchester	1200		Sears	101.750	SpringField	18.410
Ranger	30	Stevens	520A		Sears	101.750	Savage	38A and 58A
Ranger	34A	Marlin	80.C,780		Sears	101.7C	Stevens	311-C
Ranger	34A	Marlin	50-50E		Sears	101.8	Stevens	83
Ranger	35A	Stevens	66A		Sears	102	Stevens	240
Ranger	36	Marlin	80 Adj. Trigger		Sears	102.25	Stevens	520A
Ranger	400	Stevens	311					

House Brand	Model No.	Orig. Mfgr.	Orig. Model
Sears	102.35	Savage	M521
Sears	102.35	Savage	M29-D2
Sears	103.13	Marlin	81
Sears	103.16	Marlin	80
Sears	103.18	Marlin	100
Sears	103.181	Marlin	101
Sears	103.1977	Marlin	101
Sears	103.19770	Marlin	101
Sears	103.19771	Marlin	101
Sears	103.19780	Marlin	101
Sears	103.19790	Marlin	80
Sears	103.19791	Marlin	80
Sears	103.19800	Marlin	80
Sears	103.19801	Marlin	80
Sears	103.1981	Marlin	81
Sears	103.19810	Marlin	81
Sears	103.19811	Marlin	81
Sears	103.1982	Marlin	81DL
Sears	103.19820	Marlin	81
Sears	103.19821	Marlin	81
Sears	103.19840	Marlin	56
Sears	103.19880	Marlin	57 LR-MAG.
Sears	103.19881	Marlin	57 LR-MAG.
Sears	103.19890	Marlin	57 LR-MAG.
Sears	103.2	Marlin	80
Sears	103.228	Marlin	80
Sears	103.229	Marlin	81
Sears	103.273	Marlin	782
Sears	103.273	Marlin	980
Sears	103.274	Marlin	122
Sears	103.275	Marlin	122
Sears	103.2751	Marlin	122
Sears	103.2840	Marlin	80
Sears	103.2850	Marlin	81
Sears	103.2870	Marlin	56

House Brand	Model No.	Orig. Mfgr.	Orig. Model
Sears	103.350	Marlin	M90
Sears	103.360	Marlin	90
Sears	103.4	Marlin	A1
Sears	103.450	Marlin	336
Sears	103.451	Marlin	336
Sears	103.720	Marlin	59
Sears	103.740	Marlin	59
Sears	103.8	Marlin	100
Sears	10.19790	Marlin	80
Sears	11.2	Stevens	238
Sears	153.512350	Laurona	S/S
Sears	153.512351	Laurona	S/S
Sears	153.512360	Laurona	S/S
Sears	153.512361	Laurona	S/S
Sears	153.512740	Laurona	71 O/U
Sears	18	Mossberg	183K
Sears	18AC	Savage	18C
Sears	2C	Winchester	131
Sears	20	High Standard	? PUMP
Sears	200	Winchester	1200
Sears	200	Mossberg	G4
Sears	201	Mossberg	80
Sears	202	Mossberg	80
Sears	203	Mossberg	85
Sears	204	Mossberg	83
Sears	205	Mossberg	73
Sears	206	Mossberg	70
Sears	207	Mossberg	75
Sears	209	Stevens	84-7
Sears	21	High Standard	K2011
Sears	210	Mossberg	85B
Sears	211	Mossberg	83B
Sears	211	Stevens	86-7
Sears	212	Mossberg	73B
Sears	213	Mossberg	75B
Sears	215	Mossberg	85C
Sears	216	Mossberg	83C
Sears	217	Mossberg	75C
Sears	217	Stevens	87M (MUSKET)
Sears	218	Mossberg	73C
Sears	218	Stevens	22/410
Sears	231	Stevens	83
Sears	232	Stevens	87-7
Sears	233	Stevens	87-7
Sears	234	Savage	234
Sears	238	Stevens	827-7
Sears	25	High Standard	A1041 .22 auto
Sears	273.2400	Winchester	190
Sears	273.27S10(2C)	Winchester	131
Sears	273.27520(2M)	Winchester	131

House Brand	Model No.	Orig. Mfgr.	Orig. Model
Sears	273.510770	Winchester	37A
Sears	273.510780	Winchester	37A
Sears	273.510790	Winchester	37A
Sears	273.53421	Winchester	100
Sears	277	Stevens	1S
Sears	278.28180	Cooey	64
Sears	281.512650	Antonio Zoli	O/U
Sears	281.512651	Antonio Zoli	O/U
Sears	281.512660	Antonio Zoli	O/U
Sears	281.512661	Antonio Zoli	O/U
Sears	281.512750	Antonio Zoli	O/U
Sears	282.510821	Boito	ERA Single Bbl
Sears	282.510831	Boito	ERA Single Bbl
Sears	282.510841	Boito	ERA Single Bbl
Sears	282.5227740	CBC	122
Sears	282.527740	FIE	122
Sears	2C	Winchester	131
Sears	2T	Winchester	121,131,141
Sears	2/57	Stevens	66

House Brand	Model No.	Orig. Mfgr.	Orig. Model
Sears	2/58	Stevens	66
Sears	30	High Standard	22 PUMP
Sears	300	Winchester	1400
Sears	31	J.C. Higgins	31
Sears	33	J.C. Higgins	33
Sears	34	J.C. Higgins	34
Sears	340.530430	Ithaca	49SS
Sears	35A	Stevens	66A
Sears	36	Marlin	80
Sears	375	Mossberg	45B
Sears	377	Mossberg	42C
Sears	381	Mossberg	46B
Sears	382	Mossberg	46B
Sears	384	Mossberg	45A
Sears	385	Mossberg	45B
Sears	387	Mossberg	42C
Sears	388	Mossberg	42C
Sears	389	Mossberg	42A OR 26C
Sears	390	Mossberg	26C
Sears	3T	Winchester	190
Sears	41	Marlin	101
Sears	41 DLA	Marlin	122
Sears	42	Marlin	80
Sears	42DL	Marlin	80
Sears	42DLM	Marlin	980
Sears	43	Marlin	81
Sears	43DL	Marlin	81
Sears	44DL	Marlin	57
Sears	44DLM	Marlin	57M
Sears	45	Marlin	336C
Sears	46	Marlin	56
Sears	46DL	Marlin	56
Sears	4980	Stevens	94-2 W/PAD
Sears	49.11830/30	Savage	99 A
Sears	53	Winchester	70
Sears	54	Winchester	94
Sears	583.1	High Standard	?
Sears	583,126	Sako	L46
Sears	583.13	High Standard	?
Sears	583.14	H & R	120
Sears	583.15	H&R	121
Sears	583.16	High Standard	10
Sears	583.17	High Standard	?
Sears	583.18	H & R	120
Sears	583.2	H & R	M120
Sears	583.20	High Standard	Flight King
Sears	583.2085-87	High Standard	20ga pump
Sears	583.21	H&R	M1 20
Sears	583.25	H&R	M1 21
Sears	583.3	H&R	M121
Sears	583.4	High Standard	10
Sears	583.7	High Standard	10
Sears	583.91	H & R	121
Sears	6C (Canada)	Winchester	Cooy 64,64B
Sears	6C(American)	Winchester	490
Sears	66	J.C.Higgins	66
Sears	73	Savage	73
Sears	870.528140	Voere	Clip .22
Sears	92	Stevens	39
Sears	93	Stevens	38
Sears	94	Stevens	237
Sears	95	Stevens	238
Sears	97	Savage	94

House Brand	Model No.	Orig. Mfgr.	Orig. Model
Sears	97AC	Savage	94AC
Sears	98	Stevens	37
Sears	98	Springfield	944
Sears	M30	Stevens	M520
Sears	mzm	Savage	34
Sears 100	273.532141	Winchester	NM 94
Sears 200	2732.5320	Winchester	1200
Sears 200	273.2011	Winchester	1200
Sears 200	273.21010	Winchester	1200
House Brand	*Model No.*	*Orig. Mfgr.*	*Orig. Model*
Sears 200	273.2160	Winchester	1200
Sears 200	273.2250	Winchester	1200
Sears 200	273.2251	Winchester	1200
Sears 200	273.2280	Winchester	1200
Sears 200	273.4310	Winchester	1200
Sears 200	273.4320	Winchester	1200
Sears 200	273.4340	Winchester	1200
Sears 200	273.4350	Winchester	1200
Sears 200	273.4410	Winchester	1200
Sears 200	273.4420	Winchester	1200
Sears 200	273.4450	Winchester	1200
Seem 200	273.514010	Winchester	1200
Sears 200	273.614010	Winchester	1200
Sears 200	273.514011	Winchester	1200
Sears 200	273.514020	Winchester	1200
Seem 200	273.514040	Winchester	1200
Sears 200	273.514050	Winchester	1200
Sears 200	273.514051	Winchester	1200
Sears 200	273.514210	Winchester	1200
Sears 200	273.514220	Winchester	1200
Sears 200	273.514250	Winchester	1200
Sears 200	273.514251	Winchester	1200
Sears 200	273.514810	Winchester	1200
Sears 200	273.614820	Winchester	1200
Sears 200	273.514830	Winchester	1200
Sears 200	273.514840	Winchester	1200
Sears 200	273.515010	Winchester	1200
Sears 200	273.515020	Winchester	1200
Sears 200	273.515050	Winchester	1200
Sears 200	273.515051	Winchester	1200
Sears 200	273.515080	Winchester	1200
Sears 200	273.515090	Winchester	1200
Sears 200	273.515220	Winchester	1200
Sears 200	273.515221	Winchester	1200
Sears 200	273.515250	Winchester	1200
Sears 200	273.515251	Winchester	1200
Sears 200	273.515280	Winchester	1200
Sears 200	273.515290	Winchester	1200
Sears 200	273.515410	Winchester	1200
Sears 200	273.515420	Winchester	1200
Sears 200	273.515470	Winchester	1200
Sears 200	273.515710	Winchester	1200
Sears 200	273.515720	Winchester	1200
Sears 200	273.515920	Winchester	1200
Sears 200	273.5310	Winchester	1200
Sears 200	273.5350	Winchester	1200
Sears 2T	273.27530	Winchester	141
Sears 300	273.1310	Winchester	1400
Sears 300	273.1320	Winchester	1400
Sears 300	273.1350	Winchester	1400
Sears 300	273.21550	Winchester	1400
Sears 300	273.2500	Winchester	1400
Sears 300	273.2540	Winchester	1400
Sears 300	273.32060	Winchester	1400
Sears 300	273.32070	Winchester	1400
Sears 300	273.521050	Winchester	1400
Sears 300	273.521051	Winchester	1400
Sears 300	273.521080	Winchester	1400
Sears 300	273.521090	Winchester	1400
Sears 300	273.521160	Winchester	1400
Sears 300	273.521161	Winchester	1400
Sears 300	273.521250	Winchester	1400
Sears 300	273.521251	Winchester	1400
Sears 300	273.521260	Winchester	1400
Sears 300	273.521280	Winchester	1400
Sears 300	273.521290	Winchester	1400
Sears 300	273.521580	Winchester	1400
Sears 300	273.521680	Winchester	1400
Sears 300	273.521710	Winchester	1400
Sears 300	273.521770	Winchester	1400
Sears 300	273.521780	Winchester	1400
Sears 300	273.523251	Winchester	1400
Sears 300	273.52151	Winchester	1400
Sears 3T-A	273.2390	Winchester	190-290
House Brand	*Model No.*	*Orig. Mfgr.*	*Orig. Model*
Sears 3T-A	273.2400	Winchester	190-290
Sears 3T-A	273.528110	Winchester	190-290
Sears 3T-A	273.528111	Winchester	190-290
Sears 4T	273.2360	Winchester	270
Sears 53A	273.532780	Winchester	70A
Sears 54	273.2120	Winchester	NM 94
Sears 54	273.532140	Winchester	NM 94
Sears 54	273.53419	Winchester	NM 94
Sears 54	273.810	Winchester	NM 94
Sears 54	273.811	Winchester	NM 94
Sears 6C	273.28130	Winchester	490
Sears 6C	273.528131	Winchester	490
Sears 6C	273.528132	Winchester	490
Sears MI	273.27010	Winchester	121
Sears M5,M-5T	273.2340	Winchester	150-250
Sears M5,M-5T	273.2341	Winchester	150-250
Sears M5,M-5T	273.2350	Winchester	150-250
Sears M5,M-5T	273.2351	Winchester	150-250
Sears T.W. 73	273.532730	Winchester	670 Mag.
Sears T.W. 73	23.31020	Winchester	New Mod 70
Sears T.W. 73	273.1390	Winchester	MN 30-06
Sears T.W. 73	273.1400	Winchester	MN 70 (.270)
Sears T.W. 73	273.1830	Winchester	New Mod 70
Sears T.W. 73	273.1840	Winchester	New Mod 70
Sears T.W. 73	273.1850	Winchester	New Mod 70
Sears T.W. 73	273.1860	Winchester	New Mod 70
Sears T.W. 73	273.1870	Winchester	New Mod 70
Sears T.W. 73	273.31010	Winchester	New Mod 70
Sears T.W. 73	273.31060	Winchester	New Mod 70
Sears T.W. 73	273.32020	Winchester	New Mod 70
Sears T.W. 73	273.32030	Winchester	New Mod 70
Sears T.W. 73	273.32040	Winchester	New Mod 70
Sears T.W. 73	273.532061	Winchester	New Mod 70
Sears T.W. 73	273.532071	Winchester	New Mod 70
Sears T.W. 73	273.532081	Winchester	New Mod 70
Sears T.W. 73	273.53403	Winchester	New Mod 70
Sears T.W. 73	273.53406	Winchester	New Mod 70
Sears T.W. 73	273.53409	Winchester	New Mod 70
Sears T.W. 73	273.32010	Winchester	Now Mod 70
Ted Williams	340.530430	Ithaca	49SS
Shapleigh's	KING NITRO	Savage	15
Simmons	411	Savage	540DL
Simmons	411	Savage	Fox BDE 20ga
Simmons	411E	Savage	540 BDE
Simmons	411E	Savage	Fox BDE 20ga
Talo	12DL	Stevens	120
Talo	176 VR	Springfield	67 VR
Talo	176DL	Springfield	67

Western Auto, Revelation

House Brand	Model No.	Orig. Mfgr.	Orig. Model
Revelation	300	Savage	30 D,E,F
Revelation	394 Series P	Stevens	94P
Revelation	76	High Standard	Double Nine
Revelation	R310	Mossberg	500AB
Western Auto	100	Mossberg	321
Western Auto	101Y	Savage	73Y
Western Auto	101.1701	Savage	540BS
Western Auto	101.171	Savage	540BD
Western Auto	101.2830	Savage	73
Western Auto	101.52772	Savage	65M
Western Auto	101.535D	Savage	18
Western Auto	101.53500	Savage	18D
Western Auto	101.53521	Savage	340
Western Auto	101.5380	Savage	18AC
Western Auto	101.5380D	Savage	18DAC
Western Auto	101.5410	Savage	18DS,S
Western Auto	103	Savage	89
House Brand	*Model No.*	*Orig. Mfgr.*	*Orig. Model*
Western Auto	103.13	Marlin	81
Western Auto	103.16	Marlin	80
Western Auto	103.18	Marlin	80
Western Auto	103.181	Marlin	101
Western Auto	103.19780	Marlin	101
Western Auto	103.19790	Marlin	80
Western Auto	103.19800	Marlin	80
Western Auto	103.1981	Marlin	81
Western Auto	103.1982	Marlin	81DL
Western Auto	103.19820	Marlin	81
Western Auto	103.19840	Marlin	56
Western Auto	103.19880	Marlin	57
Western Auto	103.19890	Marlin	57M
Western Auto	103.1997	Marlin	101

House Brand	Model No.	Orig. Mfgr.	Orig. Model
Western Auto	103.2	Marlin	80
Western Auto	103.228	Marlin	80
Western Auto	103.229	Marlin	81
Western Auto	103.273	Marlin	980
Western Auto	103.274	Marlin	122
Western Auto	103.2751	Marlin	122
Western Auto	103.2840	Marlin	80
Western Auto	103.2850	Marlin	81
Western Auto	103.2870	Marlin	56
Western Auto	103.360	Marlin	90
Western Auto	103.450	Marlin	336
Western Auto	103.451	Marlin	336
Western Auto	103.720	Marlin	59
Western Auto	103.740	Marlin	59
Western Auto	105-2060	Marlin	780
Western Auto	105-2060	Marlin	80
Western Auto	107	Mossberg	640K
Western Auto	107A	Mossberg	640
Western Auto	110-2140	Marlin	81
Western Auto	110-2140	Marlin	781
Western Auto	115	Savage	46
Western Auto	115-2277	Marlin	57
Western Auto	116-2276	Marlin	57M
Western Auto	117	Mossberg	402
Western Auto	120-2220	Marlin	99
Western Auto	125	Mossberg	353
Western Auto	135	Savage	187
Western Auto	135	Springfield	187A
Western Auto	150m	Marlin	49
Western Auto	150-2225	Marlin	49
Western Auto	160	Springfield	187A
Western Auto	160	Savage	80
Western Auto	200-2280	Marlin	39A
Western Auto	200-2282	Marlin	39A
Western Auto	200-2550	Marlin	336
Western Auto	200-2554	Marlin	336(.44MAG)
Western Auto	205	Mossberg	472PCA
Western Auto	210A	Mossberg	810AH
Western Auto	220A	Mossberg	800A
Western Auto	220AD	Mossberg	800AD
Western Auto	220B	Mossberg	800B
Western Auto	220BD	Mossberg	800BD
Western Auto	220C	Mossberg	800C
Western Auto	220CD	Mossberg	800CD
Western Auto	225	Savage	340
Western Auto	2280	Marlin	39A
Western Auto	2282	Marlin	39A Mountie
Western Auto	230	Savage	340
Western Auto	250	Savage	110E
Western Auto	250A	Savage	110D
Western Auto	250D	Savage	110
Western Auto	260	Savage	170
Western Auto	260	Springfield	174
Western Auto	300	Springfield	67
Western Auto	300	Stevens	30
Western Auto	300A	Savage	30AC
Western Auto	300F	Stevens	77C
Western Auto	300H	Savage	30,HAC
Western Auto	300-300AC	Springfield	67
Western Auto	310	Mossberg	500
House Brand	*Model No.*	*Orig. Mfgr.*	*Orig. Model*
Western Auto	310A	Mossberg	500A
Western Auto	310AB	Mossberg	500AB
Western Auto	310B	Mossberg	500B
Western Auto	310C	Mossberg	500C
Western Auto	310E	Mossberg	500E
Western Auto	312	Mossberg	395
Western Auto	312AK	Mossberg	395K
Western Auto	312SB	Mossberg	395T
Western Auto	316	Mossberg	390
Western Auto	316BB	Mossberg	390T
Western Auto	316BK	Mossberg	390K
Western Auto	325B	Mossberg	385T
Western Auto	325BK	Mossberg	385K
Western Auto	330	Mossberg	183 & 183K
Western Auto	330B	Mossberg	183T
Western Auto	335-3725	Marlin	59
Western Auto	336	Springfield	951
Western Auto	350	Stevens	94
Western Auto	350A	Savage	94D
Western Auto	350M	Stevens	94
Western Auto	355	Stevens	947
Western Auto	355Y	Savage	94Y
Western Auto	355YE	Springfield	947YE
Western Auto	356Y	Springfield	944Y
Western Auto	360	Savage	540
Western Auto	360	Savage	FOX mod B
Western Auto	360C	Savage	540C

House Brand	Model No.	Orig. Mfgr.	Orig. Model
Western Auto	400	Stevens	745
Western Auto	400C	Savage	745C
Western Auto	420	High Standard	Supmatic C-011
Western Auto	425	High Standard	Supmatic C-120
Western Auto	460	Springfield	511
Western Auto	SD52A	Stevens	311
West Point	45	Marlin	60

Wards, Western Field, and Hawthorn

House Brand	Model No.	Orig. Mfgr.	Orig. Model
Hawthorn	110	Unknown	S shot SG
Hawthorn	580 EJN	Colt	Colteer/bolt
Hawthorn	814 EJN	Colt	Colteer/SS
Hawthorn	820B	Mossberg	340
Hawthorn	880	Colt	Colteer/semi
Hawthorn	880 EJN	Colt	Colteer/bolt
Wards	24M 419A	Mossberg	9
Wards	472	Noble	50
Wards	850	Mossberg	353
Wards Triumph	52	Savage	315
Western Field	04M-489A	Mossberg	50
Western Field	04M-218A	Mossberg	73C
Western Field	04M-2117A	Mossberg	9
Western Field	04M-217A	Mossberg	75C
Western Field	04M-214A	Mossberg	85C
Western Field	04M-216A	Mossberg	83C
Western Field	I	Mossberg	RF-1
Western Field	10-SD247A	Stevens	94B (Tenite)
Western Field	14	Savage	39A
Western Field	14	Savage	59A
Western Field	14M-215A	Mossberg	85
Western Field	14M-497B	Mossberg	M42
Western Field	14M-488A	Mossberg	50
Western Field	15	Mossberg	80
Western Field	150	Mossberg	183K
Western Field	151X	Kessler	?
Western Field	155	Mossberg	173
Western Field	15A	Mossberg	83
Western Field	16	Mossberg	85
Western Field	160	Mossberg	385K
Western Field	16A	Mossberg	85
Western Field	17	Mossberg	73
House Brand	*Model No.*	*Orig. Mfgr.*	*Orig. Model*
Western Field	170	Mossberg	395K
Western Field	172	Mossberg	395K
Western Field	173	Mosaberg	395
Western Field	175	Mossberg	385K
Western Field	17A	Mossberg	73
Western Field	I8	Mossberg	75
Western Field	20	Mossberg	9R
Western Field	215A	Mossberg	85
Western Field	24M,488A	Mossberg	51
Western Field	30	Savage	520
Western Field	31A	Mossberg	44
Western Field	31A	Mossberg	40
Western Field	32	Mossberg	21
Western Field	32	Mossberg	20
Western Field	33	Marlin	336
Western Field	35A	Mossberg	30
Western Field	36	Savage	521
Western Field	36	Mossberg	10
Western Field	36B	Mossberg	25A
Western Field	36B	Mossberg	10
Western Field	36C	Mossberg	25A
Western Field	360	Mossberg	26C
Western Field	37	Mossberg	30
Western Field	39	Mossberg	25
Western Field	390A	Mossberg	26C
Western Field	40,D	Mossberg	44
Western Field	40	Marlin	101
Western Field	4ON	Noble	40NA
Western Field	40M-215A	Mossberg	185
Western Field	41	Mossberg	45
Western Field	45	Marlin	989M2
Western Field	45	Mossberg	42
Western Field	45B	Mossberg	26C
Western Field	45C	Mossberg	25A
Western Field	46	Mossberg	42
Western Field	466	Mossberg	RA1
Western Field	469	Mossberg	RA1-Kit
Western Field	46A	Mossberg	42
Western Field	46C	Moseborg	42A
Western Field	46D	Mossberg	42C

House Brand	Model No.	Orig. Mfgr.	Orig. Model
Western Field	47	Mossberg	45A
Western Field	472	Noble	50
Western Field	47A,L	Mossberg	45A
Western Field	48	Mossberg	45A
Western Field	488A	Mossberg	51
Western Field	48A	Mossberg	45B
Western Field	48A	Mossberg	46MLB
Western Field	5-4	Mossberg	8-M4
Western Field	50	Glenfield	60
Western Field	502-26FR	Mossberg	500
Western Field	505	Mossberg	500
Western Field	509	Mossberg	500
Western Field	524	Mossberg	500
Western Field	534	Mossberg	500
Western Field	536	Mossberg	500
Western Field	539	Mossberg	500
Western Field	550A	Mossberg	500A
Western Field	550AS	Mossberg	500AB
Western Field	550B	Mossberg	500B
Western Field	550C	Mossberg	500B
Western Field	550E	Mossberg	500E
Western Field	550E	Mossberg	500E
Western Field	60	Savage	620A
Western Field	600ERI 12 GA	Remington	SPT 58
Western Field	60SB	Savage	620A
Western Field	679	Mossberg	472
Western Field	710	Savage	110
Western Field	72	Noble	50
Western Field	72C	Mossberg	472
Western Field	730	Mossberg	8IOAH
Western Field	732	Mossberg	810AH
Western Field	734	Mossberg	810A
Western Field	740	Marlin	336

House Brand	Model No.	Orig. Mfgr.	Orig. Model
Western Field	765	Mossberg	810A
Western Field	766	Mossberg	810B
Western Field	767	Mossberg	800A
Western Field	768	Mossberg	800A
Western Field	771	Mossberg	472BA
Western Field	772	Mossberg	472PCA
Western Field	775	Mossberg	800AD
Western Field	776	Mossberg	800BD
Western Field	778	Mossberg	472BAS
Western Field	780	Mossberg	800A
Western Field	782	Mossberg	800B
Western Field	79	Mossberg	472 PRA
Western Field	50	Savage	29
Western Field	807A ECH	CON	Colteer S.S.
Western Field	808	Savage	87
Western Field	808C	Savage	87J
Western Field	815	Mossberg	321
Western Field	820B	Mossberg	340
Western Field	822	Mossberg	640K
Western Field	828	Mossberg	353
Western Field	830	Mossberg	340K
Western Field	832	Mossberg	341
Western Field	836	Savage	187N
Western Field	840	Mossberg	640
Western Field	842	Mossberg	346K
Western Field	846	Mossberg	351C
Western Field	850 855	Mossberg	353
Western Field	852	Mossberg	341
Western Field	865	Mossberg	402
Western Field	880	Colt	Colteer Semi.
Western Field	894	Mossberg	430-432
Western Field	895	Mossberg	402
Western Field	9-2 3/4	Mossberg	9-2 1/2
Western Field	93M	Mossberg	26C
Western Field	93M-213A	Mossberg	75B
Western Field	93M-2116A	Mossberg	9
Western Field	93M-212A	Mossberg	738
Western Field	93M-211A	Mossberg	83B
Western Field	93M-210A	Mossberg	85B

House Brand	Model No.	Orig. Mfgr.	Orig. Model
Western Field	93M-497A	Mossberg	42C
Western Field	93M-491A	Mossberg	465
Western Field	93M-495A	Mossberg	45B
Western Field	EMN 171	Marlin	50
Western Field	EMN 176	Marlin	55
Western Field	M-SD57	Stevens	M87
Western Field	M025	Savage	520A
Western Field	M040 O/U	Marlin	90
Western Field	M040N	Stevens	820
Western Field	M051	Stevens	515
Western Field	M059	Stevens	M87
Western Field	M060	Stevens	620
Western Field	M080	Savage	29 & 75
Western Field	M087	Stevens	M87

House Brand	Model No.	Orig. Mfgr.	Orig. Model
Western Field	M10	Stevens	9.4 Short tang
Western Field	M150	Mossberg	183T
Western Field	M155	Mosaberg	183D
Western Field	M160	Mossberg	385T
Western Field	M170	Mossberg	395S
Western Field	M172	Mossberg	395K
Western Field	M175	Mossberg	385K
Western Field	KC3 NH402A	Stevens	820
Western Field	M35	Savage	520 POLY
Western Field	M36	Savage	521
Western Field	M60	Savage	620 DELUX
Western Field	M61	Savage	621 DELUX
Western Field	M72	Mossberg	472 PRA
Western Field	M734	Mossberg	810BH
Western Field	M771	Moseberg	472SBA
Western Field	M772	Mossberg	472PCA
Western Field	M7 75	Mossberg	800AD
Western Field	M776	Mossberg	800BD
Western Field	M778	Mossberg	472BAS
Western Field	M780	Mossberg	800A
Western Field	M782	Mossberg	800B
Western Field	M808.C	Stevens	87,C,J
Western Field	M808N	Stevens	87N
Western Field	M80A	Savage	M29-D1
Western Field	M815	Mossberg	320
Western Field	M822	Mossberg	640K
Western Field	M85	Stevens	85
Western Field	M-SD57	Stevens	87
Western Field	SS 94B	Stevens	94C
Western Field	SB033	Savage	520 W/POLY
Western Field	SB066	Savage	621 DELX POLY
Western Field	SB067	Savage	621 DELX COMP
Western Field	S5112C	Savage	540C
Western Field	SB115	Savage	115
Western Field	SB300,C	Stevens	311,C
Western Field	SB30A	Savage	520
Western Field	SB311C	Savage	311C
Western Field	SB312	Savage	540D
Western Field	SB312	Savage-Fox	BDL
Western Field	SB33	Savage	520 POLY
Western Field	SB60A	Savage	620 DELUX
Western Field	SB61A	Savage	621 DELUX
Western Field	SB620A	Stevens	620A
Western Field	SB66	Savage	621 DELX POLY
Western Field	SB712	Savage	840
Western Field	SB80A	Savage	29-DI
Western Field	SB85TA	Stevens	85
Western Field	SB87,TA	Stevens	M87
Western Field	XNH 175	Marlin	55
Western Field	XNH 565	Noble	60-66
Widgeon	SA 650	Marlin	55 12 GA

The proof marks shown below will assist in determining nationality of manufacturers when no other markings are evident. Since the U.S. has no proofing houses (as in England, France, Germany and other European countries), most U.S. manufacturers voluntarily proof their firearms with a specifed style of proofmark (i.e. the interlocked "WP" synonymous with the Winchester trademark can be fired using modern smokeless powder) shells. Pre-1850 European firearms oftentimes do not exhibit any commercial proof marks and with the exception of an occasional barrel address, they represent the single hardest bracket of firearms one can research properly. Captured weapons from major wars occasionally show 2 different nationalities of proofmarks. This is acceptable since the gun was proofed in a national proof house after original manufacture and again when the gun was "exported" to a different country as a military acquisition.

AUSTRIAN PROOF MARKS

PROOF MARK	CIRCA	PROOF HOUSE	TYPE OF PROOF and GUN
	since 1891	Vienna	provisional proof for multi barrel guns
	since 1891	Ferlach	provisional proof for multi barrel guns
	1829-1958	Vienna	black powder proof for multi barrel guns
	1829-1958	Ferlach	black powder proof for multi barrel guns
BH	since 1891	Bundesheer	preliminary proof for multi barrel guns
NPB	1891-1928	Budapest	smokeless powder proof for parabellum pistols
NPF	1891 to date	Ferlach	smokeless powder proof for parabellum pistols
NPP	1891-1931	Ferlach	smokeless powder proof for parabellum pistols
NPV	since 1891	Vienna	smokeless powder proof for parabellum pistols
NPW	1891-1931	Weipert	smokeless powder proof for parabellum pistols

BELGIAN PROOF MARKS

PROOF MARK	CIRCA	PROOF HOUSE	TYPE OF PROOF and GUN
	since 1852	Belgium	provisional black powder proof for breech loading guns & rifled barrels

Mark	Circa	Proof House	Type
	—	—	double proof marking for unfurnished barrels
	—	—	triple proof provisional marking for unfurnished barrels
	since 1893	—	definitive black powder proof for breech loading guns, small bore guns & handguns
	since 1853	Perron	View stamp & inspectors mark for parabellum pistols
P.V	since 1924	—	Nitro proof for rifled barrel & parabellum pistols
R	since 1852	—	rifled arms defense for smokeless proof parabellum pistols
PV	—	—	Superior nitro proof

BRITISH PROOF MARKS - ENGLAND

PROOF MARK	CIRCA	PROOF HOUSE	TYPE OF PROOF and GUN
	since 1856	London	provisional proof for barrels
	since 1856	Birmingham	provisional proof for barrels
	since 1637	London	definitive black powder proof for shotguns, muzzle loader barrels
NP	since 1904	London	definitive nitro proof for all guns - parabellum pistols
BNP	since 1954	Birmingham	definitive nitro proof for barrel & action
BP	since 1904	Birmingham	black powder proof only for parabellum pistols
	1868-1925	London	definitive special super power proof for parabellum pistols
SP	1868-1925	Birmingham	voluntary special black powder proof

	1868-1925	London	reproof marking for black powder rifles
	1868-1925	Birmingham	reproof marking for black powder rifles
	1868-1925	Birmingham	definitive black powder proof for shotguns
NP	since 1904	Birmingham	definitive nitro proof for all guns
V	since 1670	London	view mark
BV	since 1904	Birmingham	view mark

FRENCH PROOF MARKS

PARIS HOUSE	ST ETIENNE HOUSE	CIRCA	TYPE OF PROOF and GUN
		since 1897	provisional proof unfinished short barreled guns
	ST ETIENNE	1897	standard proof for finished guns
	ST ETIENNE	1897	double proof finished & joined barrels
N.A.	N.A. ST ETIENNE	1897	single barrel proof for non-assembled guns
	F	1897	finished black powder guns
	S	1897	special proof for finished guns
		1897	ordinary smokeless powder proof
	AR ST. ETIENNE	1897	superior smokeless powder proof

GERMAN PROOF MARKS

PROOF MARK	CIRCA	PROOF HOUSE	TYPE OF PROOF and GUN
	since 1952	Ulm	
	since 1968	Hannover	
	since 1968	Kiel (W. German)	
	since 1968	Munich	
	since 1968	Cologne (W. German)	
	since 1968	Berlin (W. German)	
FB	since 1952	W. German	voluntary proof for Flobert rifle
J	since 1952	W. German	repair proof for major gun parts
M	since 1952	W. German	provisional black powder for shotgun & multi barreled rifles
N	since 1952	W. German	definitive nitro proof for all guns
SP	since 1952	W. German	definitive black powder for smokeless ammo guns
	since 1952	W. German	Flobert for special purpose guns signal, flare, gas, & stun guns
N	since 1945	E. German, Suhl	smokeless powder proof
G	since 1950	E. German, Suhl	1st black powder proof for rifled barrels
N	since 1950	E. German, Suhl	nitro powder proof

	since 1950	E. German, Suhl	repair proof
R			
S	since 1950	E. German, Suhl	1st black powder proof for smooth bored barrels
U	since 1950	E. German, Suhl	inspection mark
W	since 1950	E. German, Suhl	choke-bore barrel mark

ITALIAN PROOF MARKS

PROOF MARK	CIRCA	PROOF HOUSE	TYPE OF PROOF and GUN
	since 1951	Brescia	provisional proof for all guns
	since 1951	Gardone	provisional proof for all guns
PSF	since 1951	Gardone & Brescia	definitive proof for guns with smoke-less powder
PSF FINITO	since 1951	Gardone & Brescia	finish proof for firearms ready for sale.
P N	since 1951	Gardone & Brescia	1st black powder proof

SPANISH PROOF MARKS

PROOF MARK	CIRCA	PROOF HOUSE	TYPE OF PROOF and GUN
Pº	since 1910	Eibar	provisional black powder proof for shotguns
EX	since 1910	Eibar	temporary black powder proof for shotguns
NF	since 1910	Eibar	final black powder proof for breech loading shotguns
BV	since 1910	Eibar	final smokeless powder proof for breech loading shotguns
SCH	since 1910	Eibar	re-enforced smokeless powder proof for breech loading shotguns
	since 1910	Eibar	provisional proof for shotguns

	since 1910	Eibar	final black powder proof for breech loading shotgun
	since 1923	Eibar	final & single black powder proof for double barreled muzzle loading sho-tun
	since 1923	Eibar	final & single black powder proof for single barrel smooth bored breechloading guns
	since 1923	Eibar	final black powder proof for double barreled breechloading rifles
	since 1923	Eibar	final black powder proof for single barrel breechloading rifles
E	since 1923	Eibar	re-enforced voluntary proof for single proof for single & double barrel shotguns
	since 1923	Eibar	Final proof of military-style rifle
	since 1923	Eibar	single & final proof of non-self loading pistols
	since 1923	Eibar	single & final proof for self loading pistols & revolvers
	since 1929	Eibar	admission proof for guns with old marks
	since 1929	Eibar	proof used in Barcelona for guns with old marks
R	since 1929	Eibar	final proof for revolver
P	since 1929	Eibar	proof for semi-automatic pistols
FE	since 1929	Eibar	special manufacturer's mark for guns made for foreign sales
AXIII	since 1929	Eibar	smokeless proof for shotgun barrels
CH	since 1929	Eibar	re-inforced smokeless proof for shotgun barrels

FIREARMS ASSOCIATIONS

L isted below are the names and addresses of various firearms organizations/associations throughout the U.S. You are encouraged to join those organizations that pertain to your region and area(s) of interest. As thorough as we try to be, every year we get back quite a bit of mail for individual firearms associations that unfortunately, is undeliverable. If your club does not appear on the following pages or doesn't have a current address, please forward the correct information to us for inclusion in the next edition.

Academics for the Second Amendment
(A2A)
Prof. J.E. Olson, President
Hamline University
P.O. Box 131254
St. Paul, MN 55113
Email: jolson@gw.hamline.edu

Alabama Gun Collectors
P.O. Box 70965
Tuscaloosa, AL 35407

Alamo Arms Collectors' Association, Inc.
P.O. Box 680642
San Antonio, TX 78268-0642
$20 yearly membership

Alaska Gun Collectors Association
c/o Pam Stillman, President
P.O. Box 111496
Anchorage, Alaska 99516

American Custom Gunmakers Guild
Jan Billeb, Executive Director
P.O. Box 812
Burlington, IA 52601
Phone/Fax No.: 319-752-6114
$60 Associate Membership Fee
$100 Commercial Associate Membership Fee

American Self-Defense Institute
P.O. Box 430
Whitefish, MT 59937
Phone No.: 406-862-9530
Fax: 406-862-4733
Web site: www.americanselfdefense.com
E-mail: webmaster@americanselfdefense.com
Membership dues $49.95

Ark - La - Tex - Gun Collectors
Thomas L. Baird, President
9601 Blom Blvd.
Shreveport, LA 71118

Bay Colony Weapons Collectors, Inc.
Mr. Paul Livoli
53 Berkeley Street
Somerville, MA 02143

Boardman Valley Collectors Guild
Jack Johnson, Secretary
County Road 600
Manton, MI 49663

Browning Collectors Assn.
Anthony Vanderlinden, Secretary
5603-B West Friendly Ave., Ste. 166
Greensboro, NC 27410
$30 - 1st Year Membership Fee
$20 Annual Membership Fee thereafter

C.A.D.A. (Collector Arms Dealer Association)
P.O. Box 427
Thomson, IL 61285

California Rifle & Pistol Association, Inc.
271 E. Imperial Highway, Suite #620
Fullerton, CA 92835
Phone No.: 714-992-2772
Central Illinois Gun Collectors Assn. Inc.
Russ Gardner, Sec./Treas.
P.O. Box 875
Jacksonville, IL 62651-0875

Central Penn Antique Arms Association
John E. Holman Jr.
978 Thistle Road
Elizabethtown, PA 17022

Chisholm Trail Antique Gun Association
E.D. Stone
1906 Richmond
Wichita, KS 67203

Civil War Round Table of North New Jersey
James F. Elliott
124 Conover Lane
Red Bank, NJ 07701

Colorado Gun Collectors Assoc.
Mr. Bud Greenwald, Secretary/Treasurer
2553 South Quitman Street
Denver, CO 80219
$25 Annual Membership Fee

Colt Collectors Association
Karen Green, Secretary
25000 Highland Way
Los Gatos, CA 95033
Web site: www.coltcollectorsassoc.com
$35 Annual Membership Fee
$60 - Annual Membership Fee - Outside
U.S.

Dallas Arms Collectors Association, Inc.
Richard Shea
P.O. Box 704
DeSoto, TX 75123
Phone No.: 972-223-3066
Fax No.: 972-223-3277
Web site:
www.members.tripod.com/~DACA_2/

Ducks Unlimited
One Waterfowl Way
Memphis, TN 38120
Phone No.: 901-758-3825
Fax No.: 901-758-3850

The Firearms Coalition of Colorado
Len Horner, Chairman
P.O. Box 1454
Englewood, CO 80150-1454
Phone No.: 303-850-9342
Fax No.: 303-773-6549
$15 Annual Membership Fee

Forks of the Delaware Historical Arms Society, Inc.
97 Johnson Rd.
Bangor, PA 18013
Fax No.: 610-588-2815
$20 Annual Membership Fee

Dietrich Apel
438 Willow Brook Rd
Plainfield, NH 03781
Phone No.: 603-469-3450
Fax No.: 603-469-3471

Gibbs Military Collector's Club
211 Lawn St.
Martinsburg, WV 25401
Phone No.: 304-262-1651
Fax No.: 304-262-1658
Web site: www.gibbsrifle.com
Email: support@gibbsrifle.com

Glock Collectors Association
P.O. Box 790
Farmington, MO 63640-0790
Phone No.: 573-756-0990
Fax No.: 573-756-0955

Golden Eagle Collectors Association
Chris Showler, Secretary
11144 Slate Creek Rd.
Grass Valley, CA 95945

Great Lakes Military Collectors Association
P.O. Box 401
Maumee, OH 43537

Gun Owners Civil Rights Alliance/Concealed Carry Reform Now!
Joseph E. Olson, President
P.O. Box 131254
St. Paul, MN 55113
Phone No.: 651-636-4465
$20 Annual Membership Fee

Gun Owners of America
Larry Pratt, Executive Director
8001 Forbes Pl., Suite 102
Springfield, VA 22151
Fax No.: 703-321-8408
Email: goamail@gunowners.com
$20 Annual Membership Fee

Hawaii Historic Arms Association
Box 1733
Honolulu, HI 96806

High Standard Collectors Association
540 W. 92nd St.
Indianapolis, IN 46260
$15 Annual Membership Fee

Hopkins & Allen Arms & Memorabilia Society
P.O. Box 187
Delphos, OH 45833
$6.00 Annual Donation for 6 Issues

Houston Gun Collectors Association
P.O. Box 741429
Houston, TX 77274-1429

Hunter Education Association
Box 525
Draper, UT 84020
Phone No.: 801-571-9461

Indianhead Firearms Assn.
13810 25th Ave.
Chippewa Falls, WI 54729
Phone No.: 715-723-0860

Indian Territory Gun Collectors Association
Mr. Joe Wanenmacher, Secretary - Treasurer
P.O. Box 33201
Tulsa, OK 74153-1201

International Practical Shooting Confederation
P.O. Box 972
Oakville, Ontario
Canada, L6J 9Z9
Phone No.: 905-849-6960

FIREARMS ASSOCIATIONS

Iroquois Arms Collectors Association
Kenneth Keller, Secretary
Susann Keller, Show Secretary
214 70th St.
Niagara Falls, NY 14304

Jersey Shore Antique Arms Collectors
Joe Sisia
P.O. Box 100
Bayville, NJ 08721-0100
$15 Annual Membership Fee

Kansas Cartridge Collectors Association
Vic Suetter
Route 1
Lincoln, KS 67455

Kentuckiana Arms Collectors Assoc.
Sally Harper, Secretary
P.O. Box 1776
Louisville, KY 40201
$20 Annual Membership Fee
Phone No.: 502-425-2460

Kentucky Gun Collectors Association
Ruth Johnson, Executive Secretary
P.O. Box 64
Owensboro, KY 42302
Phone No.: 502-729-4197

Kentucky Rifle Association
Attn: Ruth Collis
2319 Sue Ann Dr.
Lancaster, PA, 17602.

Lancaster Muzzle Loading Rifle Association
James H. Frederick, Jr.
779 Prospect Road
Columbia, PA 17512

Lee County Gun Collectors Association
P.O. Box 6168
Fort Myers Beach, FL 33932
Phone No.: 941-463-2840

Long Island Antique Gun Collectors Assoc.
Frederick R. Wilkens
35 Beach Street
Farmingdale, L.I., NY 11735
$30 Annual Membership Fee

The Mannlicher Collectors Association
Thomas L. Seefeldt, Membership Secretary
P.O. Box 1455
Kalispell, MT 59903
$20 Annual Membership Fee

Marlin Firearms Collectors Association, Ltd.
Mr. Dick Paterson, Secretary/Treasurer
407 Lincoln Bldg.
44 Main Street
Champaign, IL 61820
$5 Initiation Fee
$10 Annual Membership Fee

Maryland Arms Collectors Assoc. (MACA)
Del Kuzemchak, Secretary
33 S. Main Street P.O. Box 206
Loganville, PA 17342-0206
$25 Annual Membership Fee

Maumee Valley Gun Collectors Association
P.O. Box 492
Maumee, OH 43537

Maryland Licensed Firearms Dealers Assoc., Inc.
P.O. Box 10237
Baltimore, MD 21234-9998
Phone No.: 301-942-3329

Memphis Antique Weapons Association
Lonnie Griffin 108 Clark Place
Memphis, TN 38104

Minnesota Rifle and Revolver Association
Cliff Secord
5344 Morgan Ave. N.
Brooklyn Center, MN 55430

Minnesota Weapons Collectors Association
Gail Foster, Executive Director
P.O. Box 662
Hopkins, MN 55343
$20 Annual Dues
$4 Admission - 8 shows/year

Miniature Arms Collectors/Makers Society, Ltd.
William Adrian, Membership Chairman
22 W. 071 Stratford Ct.
Glen Ellyn, IL 60137

Missouri Valley Arms Collectors Association, Inc.
L.P. Brammer, Membership Secretary
P.O. Box 33033
Kansas City, MO 64114
Phone No.: 816-333-6509
Annual Membership $20.00 - ages 21+;
$10.00 - under 21

Montana Arms Collectors Association
Dean E. Yearout
1516 - 21st Ave. S.
Great Falls, MT 59405
Phone No.: 406-761-7280
$20 Annual Membership Fee

The Mule Deer Foundation
1005 Terminal Way, Ste. 170
Reno, NV 89502
$25 Annual Membership Fee

Nat'l Automatic Pistol Collectors Assoc. (N.A.P.C.A.)
Tom Knox
Box 15738
St. Louis, MO 63163
Phone No.: 314-481-4344
$35 Annual Membership Fee - U.S. & Canada
$45 Elsewhere

National Mossberg Collectors Association
Victor Havlin
P.O. Box 487
Festus, MO 63028
$10 Annual Membership Fee
Phone No.: 314-937-6401

National Rifle Association (NRA)
11250 Waples Mill Rd.
Fairfax, VA 22030
Phone No.: 888-JOIN-NRA/800-NRA-3888
Fax: 703-267-3797
Web site: www.nra.org/
$35 Regular Annual Membership Dues
$30 Annual Senior Membership (65+, also disabled vets)
$60 for 2 years
$85 for 3 years
$125 for 5 years
$750 Life Membership Dues
$375 Senior Life Membership (also disabled vets)
$15 Annual Junior Membership
National Rifle Association (NRA)
(20 and younger) - $10 Annual Liberty
(Associate) Membership

The National Wild Turkey Federation
P.O. Box 530
Edgefield, SC 29824
Phone No.: 1-800-843-6983
Call for membership details

New England Antique & Collectable Arms Society
59 Pleasant Street
Randolph, MA 02368
Phone No.: 781-961-1055
Fax No.: 781-961-1055
E-mail: Neacas@aol.com

New Hampshire Arms Collectors, Inc.
Warren Thayer
P.O. Box 6
Harrisville, N.H. 03450

North American Wild Sheep Foundation
720 Allen Ave.
Cody, WY 82414-9981
Phone No.: 307-527-6261
1 Yr. Membership $45; 3 Yrs. $120

North American Wild Sheep Foundation Minnesota-Wisconsin Chapter
P.O. Box 892
Hudson, WI 54016

North Eastern Arms Collectors Assoc., Inc.
Thomas J. Mulligan, President
P.O. Box 185
Amityville, NY 11701
$20 Annual Membership Fee

Northwest Montana Arms Collectors Association (NWMACA)
Paul Willis, Treasurer
P.O. Box 653
Kalispell, MT 59903-0653
Phone No.: 406-755-3580

Ohio Gun Collectors Association
John T. Snyder - Business Manager
P.O. Box 9007
Maumee, OH 43537-9007
Phone No.: 419-897-0861
Fax No.: 419-897-0860
$25.00 Annual Membership Fee
$10.00 Application Fee
Members and guests of members only.

Oregon Arms Collectors, Inc.
P.O. Box 8986
Portland, OR 97207-8986
$15 Annual Membership Fee

Parker Gun Collectors Association
Ron Kirby, Secretary
8825 Bud Smith Road
Wake Forest, NC 27587
Phone No.: 919-554-4556
Fax No.: 919-554-8120

Peoples Rights Organization
3953 Indianola Ave.
Columbus, OH 43214
Phone No.: 614-268-0122

Pheasants Forever
1783 Buerkle Circle
White Bear Lake, MN 55110
Phone No.: 651-773-2000
Fax No.: 651-773-5500
Web site: www.pheasantsforever.org
Email: pf@pheasantsforever.org
$25 Annual Membership Fee includes 5 issues of Pheasants Forever magazine

Potomac Arms Collectors Association
Attn: Secretary
P.O. Box 1812
Wheaton, MD 20915
$25 Annual Membership Fee

FIREARMS ASSOCIATIONS

Quail Unlimited
31 Quail Run
P.O. Box 610
Edgefield, SC 29824
Phone No.: 803-637-5731
Fax No.:803-637-0037
Email: Quaill@jetbn.net
$25 Annual Membership includes bimonthly subscription to Quail Unlimited

Randall Firearms/Pistol Collector's Association
Steve C. Kaiser, Director
1200 Hub Tower
699 Walnut Street
Des Moines, IA 50309
Phone No.: 515-288-2646
$25 Annual Membership Fee

Randall Firearms/Pistol Historian
P.O. Box 1180
Mills, WY 82644-1180
Phone No.: 307-234-2400
Web site: www.wyomingmall.net/randall
E-Mail: rick@uplink-group.com or credit-card@caspers.com
$30 Research letter

Remington Society of America
Marv Adams, Secretary-Treasurer
130 W. South Boundary
Perrysburg, OH 43551-1754
Phone No.: 419-874-2288
Annual Membership $30 + $5 application fee
Life Membership $300 + $5 application fee

Rocky Mountain Elk Foundation
2291 W. Broadway
Missoula, MT 59802
Phone No.: 406-523-4500
Fax No.: 406-523-4581

The Ruffed Grouse Society
Ronald P. Burkert
451 McCormick Rd.
Coraopolis, PA 15108
Phone No.: 888-564-6747
$20 Annual Membership Fee
$30 Conservative Membership Fee
$100 Sustaining Membership Fee
$200+ Various Sponsor Membership Fee
(includes subscription to Ruffed Grouse Society magazine)

Ruger Collectors Association, Inc.
P.O. Box 240
Green Farms, CT 06436
Phone No.: 203-259-6222, Ext. 124
$25 Annual Membership Fee

Safari Club International
4800 W. Gates Pass Rd.
Tucson, AZ 85745
Phone No.: 602-620-1220
$55 Annual Membership Fee
USA/CAN/MEX

Sako Collectors Association
Konie Wheeler, President
19815 N.W. Gillihan Rd.
Portland, OR 97231
Phone No.: 503-621-3436

Santa Barbara Historical Arms Coll. Assoc.
P.O. Box 6291
Santa Barbara, CA 93160-6291
$35 Initiation
$20 Annual Membership Fee

San Bernardino Valley Arms Collectors
Robert Walter
18710 Cajon Blvd.
San Bernardino, CA 92407
Los Alamos, NM 87544

San Gabriel Valley Arms Collectors
Gerald C. Knight, Secretary/Treasurer
1140 Daveric Drive
Pasadena, CA 91107-1740
Phone No.: 818-351-9368
$20 Annual Dues

Second Amendment Foundation
The New Gun Week
Womens & Guns Magazine
Gottlieb-Tartaro Report
Second Amendment Reporter
John C. Barnett, Jr. Executive Director
James Madison Building
12500 NE Tenth Place
Bellevue, WA 98005
Phone No.: 425-454-7012
Fax No.: 425-451-3959
Member Services (800)426-4302
web site: www.SAF.org
E-mail: JBARNSAF@Aol.com
Tax Deductible membership dues $15.00
Tax Deductible Life membership dues $150

Smith & Wesson Collectors Association
Cally Pletl, Administrative Assistant
P.O. Box 444
Afton, NY 13730

Southern California Arms Collectors Association, Inc.
Dr. Joseph S. Eisenlauer, President
P.O. Box 7432
Thousand Oaks, CA 91359-7432

Tampa Bay Arms Collectors Association, Inc.
H. Allen Bounds, Secretary/Treasurer
P.O. Box 41666
St. Petersburg, FL 33743-1666
$15 Annual Membership Fee

Texas Gun Collectors Association (TGCA)
Carolyn Mims
P.O. Box 701314
San Antonio, TX 78270

The Thompson Center Association
Attn: Joe Wright
P.O. Box 674
Shrewsbury, MA 01545
TCA@aol.com

Tri-State Gun Collectors, Inc.
P.O. Box 1201
Lima, OH 45801

United Sportshooting Association
P.O. Box 610
Laurel, MD 20725-0610
Phone No.: 301-953-3301
Fax No.: 301-490-8904

United States Practical Shooting Assoc.
P.O. Box 811
Sedro Woollery, WA 98284
Phone No.: 360-855-2245

Washington Arms Collectors, Inc.
Linda K. Ireland, Director of Office Operations
P.O. Box 389
Renton, WA 98057-0389
Phone No.: 425-255-8410
Fax No.: 425-255-8946
Web site: www.halcyon.com/wac/
E-mail: wac@halcyon.com
Membership dues $20
Life membership dues $400

Weatherby Collectors Association, Inc.
P.O. Box 888
Ozark, MO 65721
$30 - 1st Year Membership Fee
$20 Annual Membership Fee thereafter
$400 Lifetime Membership Fee

Williamette Valley Arms Collectors Association, Inc.
James Crudele, Executive Secretary
P.O. Box 5191
Eugene, OR 97405
Phone No.: 541-747-5271

Winchester Arms Collectors Association, Inc.
Pat Madis, Executive Secretary
P.O. Box 230
Brownsboro, TX 75756
Phone No.: 903-852-4027
Fax No.: 903-852-3029
$35 to join (includes $25 annual dues)
U.S.A.
$45 to join (includes $25 annual dues)
Canada
$55 to join (includes $25 annual dues)
Foreign
$400 Lifetime Membership Fee

Winchester Club of America
Karen Sellers
Box 151B Crane Brook Rd
Alstead, NH 03602
$35 U.S. Annual membership
$50 Foreign membership
$350 Life U.S. membership
$500 Life Foreign membership

Ye Connecticut Gun Guild
Robert L. Harris
U.S. Route 7-Kent Road
Cornwall Bridge, CT 06754

Zumbro Valley Arms Collectors, Inc.
Box 6621
Rochester, MN 55901

REFERENCES

Adler, Dennis, *Colt Blackpowder Reproductions & Replicas.* Minneapolis, MN: Blue Book Publications, 1998

Antaris, Leonardo, Dr., *Astra Automatic Pistols.* Sterling, CO: FIRAC Publishing Co., 1988.

Bady, Donald B., *Colt Automatic Pistols.* Los Angeles, CA: Borden Publishing Co., 1973.

Baer, Larry L., *The Parker Book* North Hollywood, CA: Beinfeld Publishing Co., 1974.

Barns, Frank C., *Cartridges of the World.* Northbrook, IL: DBI Books, Inc., 1989.

Belford, James N. and Dunlap, Jack, *Mauser Self Loading Pistol.* Alhambia, CA: Borden Publishing Co., 1969.

Bender, Roy G. III, *Mauser.* Houston, TX: Collector's Press, 1971.

Boothroyd, Geoffry & Susan M., *Boothroyd's Directory of British Gunmakers.* Amity, OR: Sand Lake Press, 1994.

Breathed and Schroeder, *System Mauser.* Chicago, IL: Handgun Press, 1967.

Brophy, William S., *L.C. Smith Shotguns.* North Hollywood, CA: Beinfeld Publishing Co., 1977.

Brophy, William S., *Marlin Firearms.* Harrisburg, PA: Stackpole Books, 1989.

Butzer, David F., *The American Shotgun.* Middlefield, CT: Lyman Publications, 1973.

Buxton, Warren H., *The P-38 Pistol: Volumes I,II & III.* Los Alamos, NM: U.C. Ross Books.

Byron, David, *Gunmarks, Tradenames, Codemarks, and Proofs from 1870 to the Present.* New York, NY: Crown Publishers, 1979.

Carder, Charles, *Side by Sides of the World.* Delphos, OH: AVIL ONZE Publishing.

Cherne, Steven, *Blue Book of Guitars, 4th Ed.,* Minneapolis, MN: Blue Book Publications, Inc., 1997.

Condry, Ken, & Jones, Larry, *The Colt Commemoratives, 1961-1986.* Dallas, TX: Taylor Publishing Co., 1989.

Costanza, Sam, *World of Lugers: Volume I.* Mayfield Heights, OH: World of Lugers, 1977.

Eastman, Matt, *Browning, Sporting Arms of Distinction.* Fitzgerald, GA: Published by Author, 1994.

Ezell, Edward Clinton, *Handguns of the World.* Harrisburg, PA: Stackpole Books, 1981.

Ezell, Edward Clinton, *Small Arms of the World (12th Ed).* Harrisburg, PA: Stackpole Books, 1983.

Dance, Tom, *High Standard; A Collector's Guide to the Hamden & Hartford Target Pistols.* Lincoln, RI: Andrew Mobray Publishers, 1991.

Flayderman, Norm, *Flayderman's Guide (5th ed.).* Northbrook, IL: DBI Books, Inc., 1990.

Gardner, Col. Robert, *Small Arms Makers.* New York, NY: Bonanza Books, 1963.

Grant, James. J., *Boys' Single Shot Rifles.* Prescott, AZ: Wolfe Publishing Company, 1991.

Gunther, Mullins, Price, and Cote', *The Parker Story,* Vol. I. Knoxville, TN: Parker Story Joint Venture Group, 1998.

Hill and Anthony, *Confederate Long Arms and Pistols.* Charlotte, NC: Confederate Arms, 1978.

Jinks, Roy G., *History of Smith & Wesson.* North Hollywood, CA: Beinfeld Publishing Co., 1977.

Karr and Karr, Jr., *Remington Handgun.* Stackpole Co., Second Edition, 1951.

Kenyon, Charles Jr., *Lugers at Random.* Chicago, IL: Handgun Press, 1969.

Kimmel, J., *Savage & Stevens Arms.* Portland, OR: Corey/Stevens Pub., Inc., 1990.

Kopel, Graham, and Moore, *A Study of the Colt Single Action Army Revolver.* La Puente,CA: Kopel, Graham, and Moore Publishers, 1978.

Krasne, Jerry A., *Enyclopedia and Reference Catalog for Auto Loading Guns.* San Diego, CA: Triple K Manufacturing, 1989.

Leithe, Frederick, *Japanese Handguns.* California: Borden Publishing Co., 1968.

Madis, George, *The Model 12.* Lancaster, TX: Published by Author, 1981.

Madis, George, *The Winchester Book.* Lancaster, TX: Privately Published by Author, 1975.

REFERENCES

Marcot, Roy, *Remington, America's Oldest Gunmaker*. Peoria, IL: Primedia Special Interest Publications, 1998.

Maxwell, Samuel L., Sr., *Lever Action Magazine Rifles*. Published by Author, 1978.

Muderlak, Ed, *Parker Guns, The Old Reliable*. Long Beach, CA: Safari Press, 1997.

Murray, Douglas, *The Ninety-Nine*. Published by Author, 1985.

Nonte, Jr., George C., *Firearms Encyclopedia. Outdoor Life:* New York, NY, 1973.

Olson, Ludwig, *Mauser Bolt Action Rifles*. Montezuma, IA: F. Brownell & Son Publishers, Inc., 1976.

Rankin, James L., *Walther, Vols. I, II, III*. Coral Gables, FL: Published by Author, 1976.

Rule, Roger C., *The Rifleman's Rifle*. Northridge, CA: Alliance Books, Inc., 1982.

Sellers, Frank, *American Gunsmiths*. Highland Park, NJ: The Gun Room Press, 1983.

Sellers, Frank, *Sharp's Firearms*. North Hollywood, Ca: Beinfeld Publishing Co., 1978.

Serven, editor, *The Collecting of Guns*. Bonanza Books, 1964.

Sharpe, Phillip B., *The Rifle in America*. Funk and Wagnalls, 1947.

Shooter's Bible. S. Hackensack, NJ: Published annually by Stoeger Industries.

Steindler, *Steindler's New Firearms Dictionary*. Phoenix, AZ: Stackpole Books, 1985.

Still, Jan C., *Axis Pistols*. Marceline, MO: Walsworth Publishing Co., 1986.

Still, Jan C., *Imperial Lugers*. Marceline, MO: Walsworth Publishing Co., 1991.

Still, Jan C., *Third Reich Lugers*. Marceline, MO: Walsworth Publishing Co., 1988.

Supica, Jim and Nahas, Richard, *Standard Catalog of Smith & Wesson*. Iola, WI: Krause Publications, 1996.

Tanner, Hans, *Guns of the World*. Bonanza Books, 1972, 1977.

Webster, Donald B. Jr., *Suicide Specials*. Harrisburg, PA: Stackpole, Co., 1958.

West, Bill, *Browning Arms & History*. Santa Fe Springs, CA: Stockton Trade Press, Inc., 1972.

West, Bill, *Marlin and Ballard Firearms & History*. Norwalk, CA: Stockton Trade Press, Inc., 1977.

West, Bill, *Remington Arms & History*. Whittier, CA: Stockton Trade Press, Inc., 1970.

West, Bill, *Savage and Stevens Arms & History*. Whittier, CA: Stockton Trade Press, Inc., 1971.

Whitaker, Dean H., *Model 70 Winchester 1937-1964*. Dallas, TX: Taylor Publishing Co., 1978.

Wilkerson, Don, *Post War Colt Single Action Army*. Published by Author, 1978.

Wilkerson, Don, *Post-War Colt Single-Action Revolver, 1976-1986*. Dallas, TX: Taylor Publishing, 1986.

Wilson, R.L., *The Book of Colt Firearms*. Minneapolis, MN: Blue Book Publications, Inc., 1993.

Wilson, R.L., *Colt, An American Legend*. New York, NY: Abbeville Press.

Wilson, R.L., *Colt Commemorative Firearms*. Geneseo, IL: Robert E.P. Cherry Publishing Co., 1973.

Wilson, R.L., *The Colt Heritage*. New York, NY: Simon and Schuster.

Wilson, R.L., *Ruger & His Guns*. New York: Simon and Schuster. 1996.

Wirnsberger, Gerhard, *The Standard Dictionary of Proofmarks*. Jolex, Inc.

Wood, J.B., *Beretta Auotmatic Pistols, The Collector's & Shooter's Comprehensive Guide*. Harrisburg, PA: Stackpole Books, 1985.

Zhuk, A.B., *The Illustrated Encyclopedia of Handguns*. London: Greenhill Books. 1995.

PERIODICALS LISTINGS

American Firearms Industry – 2455 E. Sunrise Blvd. Ste. 916, Ft. Lauderdale, FL 33304. Phone No.: 305-561-3505. Membership is $35 per year. Trade publications and related material.

American Gunsmith – P.O. Box 540638, Merrit Island, FL 32954. Phone No.: 407-459-1558.

American Handgunner – Published by Publisher's Development. 591 Camino de la Reina, Suite 200, San Diego, CA 92108. Phone No.: 800-537-3006. Published monthly.

American Hunter – Published by the NRA, 11250 Waples Mill Rd., Fairfax, VA 22030. Phone No.: 800-672-3888. Published monthly.

American Rifleman – Published by the NRA, 11250 Waples Mill Rd., Fairfax, VA 22030. Phone No.: 800-672-3888. Subscription included in price of NRA Membership ($35). Published monthly.

Australian Shooter's Journal – Published by the Sporting Shooters Association of Australia, Inc., P.O. Box 2066, Kent Town, SA 5071 AUSTRALIA. Phone No.: 011-61-8-8272-7622, Fax No.: 011-61-8-8272-2945. Subscription is $50 per year in Australia, $60 per year elsewhere, published monthly.

Black's Wing & Clay – Published by Black's Sporting Directories, P.O. Box 2029, 43 West Front St., Ste. 11, Red Bank, NJ 07701. Phone No.: 732-224-8700, Fax No.: 732-741-2827. Published annually, $14.95.

The Clay Pigeon – P.O. Box 1022, Milford, PA 18337. Phone No.: 570-296-5768, Fax No.: 570-296-9298. Subscription is $12 per year, published monthly.

Combat Handguns – Published by Harris Publications, 1115 Broadway, New York, NY 10010. Phone No.: 212-807-7100, Fax No.: 212-627-4678. Subscription rate: $16.97 for 1 year (8 issues).

Deutsches Waffen Journal – Journal-Verlag Scwend GmbH, Schmollerstrasse 31, D-74523, Schwabish Hall, GERMANY. Phone No.: 011-49-791-404-511, Fax No.: 011-49-791-404-505

The Double Gun Journal – 5014 Rockery School Rd., East Jordan, MI 49727-9636. Phone No.: 616-536-7439. Published quarterly.

Ducks Unlimited – One Waterfowl Way, Memphis, TN 38120. Phone No.: 901-758-3825, Fax No.: 901-758-3850. Membership rate: $25 per year, includes 6 issues.

Euro Shot Business – Published by Petersen Publishing, 6420 Wilshire Blvd., Los Angeles, CA 90048-5515. Phone No.: 323-782-2000.

Field & Stream Magazine – P.O. Box 55652, Boulder, CO 80322. Phone No.: 800-289-0639 or 212-779-5000. Subscription rate $15.94 annually. Published monthly (12 issues).

Game & Gun – P.O. Box 968, Traverse City, MI 49685. FAX No.: 616-946-3289. Published bimonthly.

Gray's Sporting Journal – Published by North American Publications, Inc., 735 Broad Street, Augusta, GA 30901. Phone No.: 706-722-6060. Published bimonthly.

Gun Dog – Published by The Stover Publishing Co., Inc. 1901 Bell Avenue, Des Moines, IA 50315. Phone No.: 515-243-2472. Published bimonthly.

Gun Report – P.O. Box 38, Aledo, IL 61231, Phone No.: 309-582-5311. $33.00 per year (USA), published monthly.

Gun Runner – Box 565, Lethbridge, Alberta T1J3Z4, CANADA. Phone No.: 905-372-2269.

Guns and Ammo – Published by Petersen Publishing Co., 6420 Wilshire Blvd., Los Angeles, CA 90048. Phone No. 323-782-2000. $21.94 per year (USA), published monthly.

Guns & Gear – Published by B.A.S.S., Inc., 5845 Carmichel Rd., Montgomery, AL 36117. Phone No.: 334-277-3940. Subscription is $24 per year, published monthly.

Gun List – Published by Krause Publications, 700 E. State St., Iola, WI 54990. Phone No.: 715-445-2214. $34.98 per year, published bi-weekly.

Gun Week – P.O. Box 488, Station C, Buffalo, NY 14209. Annual Subscription - $35. Published 3 times a month. Phone No.: 716-885-6408

Guns Magazine – Published by Publisher's Development. 591 Camino de la Reina, Suite 200, San Diego, CA 92108. Phone No.: 800-537-3006. Published monthly.

Handguns Magazine – Published by Petersen Publishing Co., 6420 Wilshire Blvd., Los Angeles, CA 90048. Phone No.: 323-782-2185. Published monthly.

Hunting – Published by Petersen Publishing Co., 6420 Wilshire Blvd., Los Angeles, CA 90048. Phone No.: 323-782-2185. Published bimonthly.

Man at Arms – P.O. Box 460, Lincoln, RI 02865. Published bimonthly ($27 yearly). Phone No.: 401-726-8011.

Michigan Hunting & Fishing – P.O. Box 1000, Sault Ste. Marie, MI 49783.

Muzzle Blasts – Published by the National Muzzle Loading Rifle Association, P.O. Box 67, Friendship, IN 47021. Phone No.: 812-667-5131. Subscription is $35 per year, published monthly.

North American Hunter – 12301 Whitewater Dr., Minnetonka, MN 55343. Phone No.: 612-936-9333. Published bimonthly (included in membership).

Outdoor Guide Magazine – 505 S. Ewing, St. Louis, MO 63103, Phone No.: 314-535-9786

Outdoor Life Magazine – Two Park Ave., New York, NY 10016. Phone No.: 800-365-1580 or 212-779-5000. $15.94 per year (USA).

Pennsylvania Sportsman – P.O. Box 223, Farmington, PA 15437

Pheasants Forever – 1783 Buerkle Circle, White Bear Lake, MN 55110. Phone No.: 651-773-2000, Fax No.: 651-773-5500. Membership is $25 per year, includes 5 issues.

Pointing Dog Journal/Retriever Journal – Published by the Village Press, 2779 Aero Park Dr., Traverse City, MI 49686. Phone No.: 616-946-3712, Fax No.: 616-946-3289.

Quail Unlimited – P.O. Box 610 Edgefield, SC 29824. Phone No.: 803-637-5731, Fax No.: 803-637-0037. Membership is $25 per year, published bimonthly.

Rifle Shooter – Published monthly by Petersen Publishing.

Safari Club International – 4800 W. Gates Pass Rd., Tucson, AZ 85745. Phone No.: 602-620-1220. Publications: *Safari magazine, Safari Africa, Deer of the World, Sheep of the World, International Record Book of Trophy Animals, Record Book Field Edition.*

SHOT Business – Published monthly by Petersen Publishing.

Shooting Industry – 591 Camino de la Reina #200, San Diego, CA 92108. Phone No.: 800-537-3006, $25 per year (USA). Published monthly.

Shooting Sportsman – Published by Down East Enterprise, Inc., P.O. Box 1357, Camden, ME, 04843. Phone No.: 207-594-9544, Fax No.: 207-594-5144

Shooting Sports Retailer – 130 W. 42nd St., New York, NY 10036. Phone No.: 212-840-0660

Shooting Times – Published by Primedia, Inc. Subscription is $23.98 for 12 issues.

Shotgun News – Published by Primedia, Inc. 2 News Plaza, Peoria, Il 61614. Phone No.: 800-495-8362. Subscription is $29 yearly (36 issues).

Shotgun Sports – P.O. 669, Hastings, NE 68902. Subscription is $20 yearly (36 issues). Phone No.: 402-463-4589.

Skeet – 5931 Roft Road, San Antonio, TX 78253. Phone No.: 210-688-3371. $20 per year. Published monthly.

Southern Outdoors – 5845 Carmichael Rd., Montgomery, AL 36117. Phone No.: 205-277-3940. Published 9 times per year.

Sporting Classics – 3031 Scotsman Rd., Columbia, SC 29223. Phone No.: 803-736-2424

Sporting Clays Magazine – 5211 S. Washington Ave., Titusville, FL 32780. Phone No.: 800-677-5212 or 803-681-2219. $23.95 per year (USA). Published bimonthly.

Sporting Goods Business – 1 Penn Plaza, New York, NY 10119. Phone No.: 212-714-1300 or 800-933-3321. $65 per year.

The Sporting Goods Dealer – 1212 N. Lindbergh Blvd., St. Louis, MO 63132. Phone No.: 314-997-7111.

Sports Afield Magazine – 250 W. 55th St., New York, NY 10019. Phone No.: 212-649-4300. (12 issues) $13.97.

Trap & Field – Published by Curtis Magazine Group. 1200 Waterway Blvd., Indianapolis, IN 46202. Phone No.: 317-633-8802. Published monthly.

Turkey & Turkey Hunting – Published by Krause Publications, Inc. 700 E. State St., Iola, WI 54990. Phone No.: 715-445-2214. Published bimonthly.

Varmint Hunter Magazine – Published by the Varmint Hunter's Association. 436 S. Pierre St., Pierre, SD, 57501. Phone No.: 605-224-6665, Fax No.: 605-224-6544. Subscription is $24 per year.

Varmint Master Magazine – Published by the Vulcan Outdoor Group. 1 Chase Corp. Dr., Ste. 300, Birmingham, AL 35244.

Visier - International Waffen Magazine – Erich-Kastner-Strasse 2, D-56379, Singhofen, GERMANY. Phone No.: 011-49-2604-9780, Fax No.: 011-49-2604-978-703

Waterfowl Magazine – P.O. Box 50, Edgefield, SC 29824. Phone No.: 803-637-5767. Published bimonthly.

Western Outdoors – 3197 East Airport Dr., Costa Mesa, CA 92626. Phone No: 714-546-4370. Published 9 times per year.

Wildfowl – Published by Stover Publishing, Inc. 1901 Bell Ave., Ste. 4, Des Moines, IA 50315. Phone No.: 515-243-2472. Published bimonthly.

Wing and Clay – 43 W. Front St., Ste. 11, Red Bank, NJ 07701. Phone No.: 908-224-8700. Published annually.

Wing & Shot – Published by Stover Publishing, Inc. 1901 Bell Ave., Ste. 4, Des Moines, IA 50315. Phone No.: 515-243-2472. Published bimonthly.

Women & Guns – Published by Second Amendment Foundation, P.O. Box 488, Station C, Buffalo, NY 14209. $24 annual subscription. Published monthly.

COMPLETE LISTING OF FIREARMS WITH RELATED PERCENTAGES OF CONDITION PICTURED IN THE PHOTO PERCENTAGE GRADING SYSTEM™, EDITIONS 11-18.

HANDGUNS - REVOLVERS

Colt 2nd Model Dragoon (fake) Photo 60, 12th-14th editions, Photo 52, 15th-18th editions

Colt 3rd Model Dragoon (80%) Photo 53, 12th-18th editions

Colt Model 1851 U.S. Army (90%) Photo 55, 12th-14th editions, Photo 47, 15th-18th editions

Colt Model 1851 U.S. Navy (70-80%) Photo 56, 12th-14th editions, Photo 48, 15th-18th editions

Colt Model 1851 U.S. Navy (30-40%) Photo 57, 12th-14th editions, Photo 49, 15th-18th editions

Colt Antique SAA (95%) Photo 58, 12th-14th editions, Photo 50, 15th-18th editions

Colt Model 1889 Double Action (60%) Photo 54, 12th-14th editions, Photo 46, 15th-18th editions

Colt Model 1909 U.S.M.C. (93-95%) Photo 50, 12th-14th editions, Photo 44, 15th-18th editions

Colt Model 1909 U.S.M.C. (90%) Photo 52, 12th-14th editions, Photo 45, 15th-18th editions

Colt Model 1917 Army (never blued) Photo 51, 12th-14th editions

Colt Model 1917 Army (98%) Photo 48, 12th-14th editions

Colt Early Officer's Model (80%) Photo 53, 12th-14th editions

Colt New Service (99%) Photo 49, 12th-14th editions

Colt Pre-War New Service (mint) Photo 47, 12th-14th editions, Photo 43, 15th-18th editions

Korth Revolver (W. German mfg.) (100%) Photo 32, 11th-14th editions

Ruger New Model Single-Six (70%) Photo B, 18th edition

Smith & Wesson Top-Break (80% with original box) Photo A, 18th edition

HANDGUNS - SEMI-AUTO

A.J. Savage "Slide" Model 1911 (5-10%) Photo 46, 12th-14th editions, photo 14, 15th-18th editions

Beretta Model 102 Target Pistol (90%) Photo 28, 15th-18th editions

Colt 1903 Pocket Model (90%) Photo 28, 11th edition

Colt Model 1911A1 (mint finish) Photo 45, 12th-14th editions, Photo 13, 15th-18th editions

Colt Model 1911 Military (99%+, mint) Photo 42, 12th-14th editions, Photo 10, 15th-18th editions

Colt Pre-War Commercial (mint) Photo 43, 12th-14th editions, Photo 11, 15th-18th editions

Colt Pre-War Government Model (reblued) Photo 44, 12th-14th editions, Photo 12, 15th-18th editions

Colt Series 80 National Match Model (100%) Photo 21, 11th edition, Photo 27, 12th-14th editions

Fabrique Nationale pre-war Commercial Hi-Power (95%) Photos 35 & 36, 15th-18th editions

Fabrique Nationale WWII Hi-Power 9mm Parabellum (98%) Photos 33 & 34, 15th-18th editions

Gabbett-Fairfax Mars Pistol (70%) Photo 41, 15th-18th editions

Gabbett-Fairfax Mars Pistol (restored) Photo 42, 15th-18th editions

Luger 1916 WWI DWM Military (80%) Photos 29 & 30, 15th-18th editions

Luger 1941 WWII Mauser Military (98%) Photos 31 & 32, 15th-18th editions

Mauser "Flatside" Commercial Broomhandle (99% near mint) Photos 37 & 38, 15th-18th editions

Mauser 1930 Commercial Broomhandle (98%) Photos 39 & 40, 15th-18th editions

Mauser WWII P.38 byf-44 code (mint) Photos 15 & 16, 15th-18th editions

Mauser WWII P.38 byf-43 code (70%) Photo 26, 11th edition, Photo 31, 12-14th editions, Photo 25, 15th-18th editions

North American Arms Model 1911 (99%) Photo 36, 12th-14th, editions, Photo 4, 15th-18th editions

North American Arms Model 1911 (85-90%) Photo 37, 12th-14th editions, Photo 5, 15th-18th editions

North American Arms Model 1911 (75%) Photo 38, 12th-14th editions, Photo 6, 15th-18th editions

North American Arms Model 1911 (60%) Photo 39, 12th-14th editions, Photo 7, 15th-18th editions

North American Arms Model 1911 (20-30%) Photo 40, 12th-14th editions, Photo 8, 15th-18th editions

Remington U.M.C. Model 1911 (Photo 41 - 98%) Photo 41, 12th-14th editions, Photo 9, 15th-18th editions

Singer WWII Model 1911A1 (98%) Photo 35, 12th-14th editions, Photo 3, 15th-18th editions

Spreewerke late WWII P.38 cyq code (99%) Photos 17 & 18, 15th-18th editions

Springfield Armory Model 1911 (96-97%) Photo 33, 12th-14th editions, Photo 1, 18th edition

Springfield Armory Model 1911 (60%) Photo 34, 12th-14th editions, Photo 2, 18th edition

Walther WWII P.38 ac-41 code (97-98%) Photos 19 & 20, 15th-18th editions

Walther WWII P.38 ac-42 (80%) Photo 25, 11th edition

Walther WWII P.38 ac-44 (90%) Photo 24, 11th edition, Photo 26, 15th -18th editions

Walther WWII P.38 ac-43 (95%) Photos 21 & 22, 15th-18th editions

Walther "0" Series Commercial P.38 (93-95%) Photos 23 & 24, 15th-18th editions

Walther Post War P1 (98%) Photo 22, 11th-14th editions

Walther Post War P1 (95%) Photo 23, 11th-14th editions

Walther PPK Wartime Nazi Police Issue (80%) Photo 27, 15th-18th editions

RIFLES

Springfield Model 1873 Military (98%) Photo 65, 15th-18th editions

Winchester Model 1873 Deluxe Rifle (60%-70% case colors, 95% blue) Photo 58, 11th-18th editions

Winchester Model 1886 Rifle (90%) Photo 66, 15th-18th editions

Winchester Model 1892 Pistol Grip Takedown Rifle (75%-80%) Photo 5, 11th-14th editions, Photo 57, 15th-18th editions

Winchester Model 1892 Rifle (85%-90%) Photo 4, 11th-14th editions, Photo 56, 15th-18th editions

Winchester Model 1892 Rifle ("poor condition") Photo 12, 11th-14th editions, Photo 64, 15th-18th editions

Winchester Model 1892 Takedown Rifle (60% receiver bluing, 95% barrel/mag tube bluing) Photo 7, 11th-18th editions

Winchester Model 1892 Takedown Rifle (60%) Photo 59, 15th-18th editions

Winchester Model 1892 Takedown Rifle (50%) Photo 8, 12th-14th editions

Winchester Model 1894 Carbine (20% receiver blue, 90% barrel/mag tube blue) Photo 10, 11th-14th editions, Photo 62, 15th-18th editions

Winchester Model 1894 Takedown Rifle (40% receiver blue, 90% barrel/mag tube blue) Photo 9, 11th-14th editions, Photo 61, 15th-18th editions

Winchester Model 1894 Carbine (98% receiver blue, 100% barrel/mag tube blue) Photo 2, 11th-14th editions, Photo 54, 15th-18th editions

Winchester Model 1894 Rifle (95% receiver blue, 98% barrel/mag tube blue) Photo 3, 11th-14th editions, Photo 55, 15th-18th editions

Winchester Model 55 Takedown Rifle (no receiver blue, 50% barrel/mag) Photo 11, 11th-14th editions, Photo 63, 15th-18th editions

Winchester Model 55 Takedown Rifle (50%) Photo 8, 11th edition, Photo 60, 15th-18th editions

Winchester Model 71 Deluxe Rifle (98%+) Photo 1, 11th-15th editions, Photo 53, 15th-18th editions

Winchester Pre-'64 Model 70 Super Grade (98+%) Photo 68, 15th-18th editions

Winchester Model 70 Pre-War Super Grade (99%) Photo 67, 15th-18th editions

SHOTGUNS

Browning A-5 (100% mint) Photo 14, 11th-14th editions

Browning A-5 (95% +) Photo 72, 19th Edition

Browning A-5 (70%) Photo 73, 19th Edition

German 16 gauge SxS with back-action (70%) Photo 72, 15th-18th editions

L.C. Smith Field Grade (mint) Photo 21, 12th-14th editions, Photo 69, 15th-18th editions

L.C. Smith Field Grade (mint) Photo 22, 12th-14th editions

L.C. Smith Ideal Grade (30%) Photo 23, 12th-14th editions, Photo 70, 15th-18th editions

L.C. Smith Specialty Grade (trace of case colors) Photo 25, 12th-14th editions

Parker Bros. D-Grade (refurbished, no % given) Photo 26, 12th-14th editions

Parker Bros. VH Grade (99% non-original condition) Photo 71, 15th-18th editions

Remington Model 870 slide action (95%) Photo 74, 15th-18th editions

Remington Model 870 slide action (75%-80%) Photo 76, 15th-18th editions

Remington Model 870 Wingmaster (mint) Photo 73, 15th-18th editions

Remington Model 1100 Special Purpose (95%) Photo 75, 15th-18th editions

Stevens 16 gauge slide action (60% turned patina) Photo 78, 15th-18th editions

Winchester Model 12 (99% reblued) Photo 77, 15th-18th editions

Winchester Model 12 (98%) Photo 16, 11th-12th editions, Photo 14, 13th-14th editions

Winchester Model 12 (95%) Photo 17, 11th-12th editions, Photo 15, 13th-14th editions

Winchester Model 12 (90%) Photo 18, 11th-12th editions, Photo 16, 13th-14th editions

Winchester Model 12 (80%-90%) Photo 16, 13th-14th editions

Winchester Model 12 (70%) Photo 19, 11th-12th editions, Photo 17, 13th-14th editions

Winchester Model 12 (55%-60%) Photo 20, 11th-12th editions, Photo 18, 13th-14th editions

Winchester Model 42 (100%, mint) Photo 15, 11th-12th editions, Photo 13, 13th-14th editions

Winchester Model 101 (95%) Photo 71, 19th Edition

Winchester Model 1400 (100%) Photo 13, 11th-13th editions, Photo 19, 13th-14th editions

ATF GUIDE

A listing has been provided below of Field Division offices for the ATF. You are encouraged to contact them if you have any question(s) regarding the legality of any weapon(s) or their interpretation of existing laws and regulations. Remember, ignorance is no excuse when it involves Federal Firearms Regulations and Laws. Although these various offices may not be able to help you with state, city, county, or local firearms regulations and laws, their job is to assist you on a Federal level.

Chicago Field Division
300 S. Riverside Plaza,
Suite 350 S.
Chicago, IL 60606
Phone No.: 312-353-6935

New York Field Division
6 World Trade Center,
Room 238
New York, NY 10048
Phone No.: 212-455-5145

Philadelphia Field Division
US Custom House, Room 504
Philadelphia, PA 19016
Phone No.: 215-597-7288

Atlanta Field Division
2600 Century Parkway,
Room 300
Atlanta, GA 30345
Phone No.: 404-679-5170

Dallas Field Division
1200 Main Tower Building,
Suite 2550
Dallas, TX 75202
Phone No.: 214-767-2250

San Francisco Field Division
221 Main St, Suite 1250
San Francisco, CA 94105
Phone No.: 415-744-7001

Baltimore Field Division
Rombro Building
22 S. Howard St., 6th Floor
Baltimore, MD 21201
Phone No.: 410-962-0897

Birmingham Field Division
Burger-Phillips Center
1910 3rd Avenue North,
Suite 400
Birmingham, AL 35203
Phone No.: 205-731-1205

Boston Field Division
The Boston Federal Building
10 Causeway Street, Room 253
Boston, MA 02222-1047
Phone No.: 617-585-7042

Charlotte Field Division
4530 Park Road, Suite 400
Charlotte, NC 28209
Phone No.: 704-344-6125

Cleveland Field Division
6745 Engle Road, Room 200
Middleburg Heights, OH 44130
Phone No.: 216-522-7210

Detroit Field Division
1155 Brewery Park Boulevard,
Suite 300
Detroit, MI 48207-2602
Phone No.: 313-393-6000

Houston Field Division
15355 Ventage Parkway West,
Suite 210
Houston, TX 77032
Phone No.: 281-449-2073

Kansas Field Division
2600 Grand Avenue, Suite 200
Kansas City, MO 64108
Phone No.: 816-421-3440

Los Angeles Field Division
350 S. Figueroa Street, Suite 800
Los Angeles, CA 90071
Phone No.: 213-894-4812

Louisville Field Division
600 Dr. Martin Luther King Jr.
Place, Suite 332
Louisville, KY 40202
Phone No.: 502-582-5211

Miami Field Division
5225 NW 87th Avenue, Suite 300

Miami, FL 33178
Phone No.: 305-597-4800

Nashville Field Division
Nashville Koger Center
215 Centerview Drive, Suite 215
Brentwood, TN 37027
Phone No.: 615-781-5364

New Orleans Field Division
Heritage Plaza, Suite 1050
111 Veterans Boulevard
Metarie, LA 70005
Phone No.: 504-589-2048

Phoenix Field Division
3003 North Central Avenue
Suite 1010
Phoenix, AZ 85012
Phone No.: 602-640-2840

St. Paul Field Division
30 East 7th Street, Room 1870
St. Paul, MN 55101-4901
Phone No.: 651-290-3092

Seattle Field Division
915 2nd Avenue, Room 806
Seattle, WA 98174
Phone No.: 206-220-6440

Washington Field Division
607 14th Street NW, Suite 620
Washington, DC 20005
Phone No.: 202-219-7751

**Firearms and Explosives
Licensing Center**
2600 Century Parkway, NE
Room 400
Atlanta, GA 30345-3104

National Revenue Center
550 Main Street, Room 8002
Cincinnati, OH 45202-3263

SHOW TIME

1999-2000!

During the course of a year, we get many requests about which upcoming trade/gun shows we'll be attending. If you want to hook up with Steve, John and related troops through early in the next millenium, here's where we'll be. At these shows we will be displaying all of our publications, in addition to actively demonstrating our critically acclaimed GunTracker 2.0 computer inventory program from our new, cool display. GunTracker is the most up-to-date and reliable way to keep up with your gun collection and related accessories, and we'll look forward to demonstrating it for you at one of these upcoming shows.

April 30-May 2, 1999
The 128th NRA
Annual Meetings & Exhibits Show
Colorado Convention Center
Denver, CO
Contact: NRA
Ph.800-694-9300

July 18-19, 1999
Firearms Trade Expo
International Expo Center
Cleveland, OH
FFL Dealers & invited guests
Contact: AFI
Ph.954-561-3505

July 30-August 1, 1999
The 4th NRA National Gun Collectors
Show & Conference sponsored by
the 29th Annual Kansas City National
Summer Arms Show
K.C. Market Center Exhibition Hall
Kansas City, MO
Contact: MVACA Show Committee
P.O. Box 33033
Kansas City, MO 64114
Ph.913-642-2863

June 26-27, 1999
The "Original" Duluth Gun Show
Duluth Entertainment Convention Center
South Pioneer Hall
Sat. 9-5pm. Sun. 9-3pm.
$4.00 admission
Contact: Bob White
1920 Greysolon Rd
Duluth, MN 55812
Ph.218-724-8387

September 30-October 3, 1999
20th Annual Colt Collectors Association, Inc.
(All Colt only Show)
Hyatt Regency San Francisco Airport Hotel
Burlingame, CA
Contact: Dick Burdick
Ph.805-644-8731

October 23-24, 1999
Tulsa Gun & Knife Show
at Expo Center - Expo Square
Tulsa Fairgrounds
Sat. 8-7pm, Sun. 8-5pm
Contact: Tulsa Gun Show, Inc.
P.O. Box 33201
Tulsa, OK 74153-1201
Ph.918-492-0401

January 17-20, 2000
SHOT SHOW
Trade Show only-no consumers
Sands Expo Center
Las Vegas, NV

January 20-22, 2000
Antique Arms Show & International Sporting Arms
Show
Riviera Hotel
Las Vegas, NV
Contact: Wallace Beinfeld Productions, L.L.C.
P.O. Box 2231
Palm Springs, CA 92263
Wallace Beinfeld-Show Director
Ph.760-320-5389 FAX 760-320-5231

February 2-5, 2000
Safari Club International (SCI)
28th Annual Hunters Convention
Reno-Sparks Convention Center
Reno, NV
Contact: SCI
4800 West Gates Pass Rd.
Tucson, AZ 85745
Ph.520-620-9313 FAX 520-617-1426
SCI Membership Required

April 1-2, 2000
(Be cool, spend April Fool's in Tulsa,
we're going to do something special at this show!)
Tulsa Gun & Knife Show
at Expo Center - Expo Square
Tulsa Fairgrounds
Sat. 8-7pm, Sun. 8-5pm
Contact: Tulsa Gun Show, Inc.
P.O. Box 33201
Tulsa, OK 74153-1201
Ph.918-492-0401

Title Page 1
Publishers's Note/Copyright .2
Table of Contents 3
Cover Description 4
Blue Book Publications, Inc. general information 5
Acknowledgements 6-7
Foreword 8-9
How to Use This Book 10-13
Correspondence/Appraisal/PCS Information 14-15
Buying or Selling? - a Unique Concept 16
Gun Tracker Advertisement 17
Blue Book of Guitars & Pool Cues Advertisements . . .18
Colt Black Powder Reproductions & Replicas
Advertisement 19
Blasts from the Past - 1-20 Ed. pictorial/information 20-21
Publisher's Overview of the Firearms Marketplace . .22-23
Buying Tomorrow's Collectibles Today by Jim Carmichel
. 24-25
Gun Collecting by R.L. Wilson 26-27
NSSF Editorial from Bob Delfay 28-29
Manufacturer's Editorial from Magnum Research . .30-31
Distributor's Editorial from Davidson's 32-33
Rep Groups Editorial from Owen Brown 34-35
Sporting Goods Dealer Editorial from Jeff Poet 36-37
Collectible Dealer Editorial from Jim Supica, Jr. . . .38-41
Working Mom's Perspective Editorial from Trudy Weise 42
Teenage Impressions Editorial from Jed Weise 43
Legal Editorial from Evan Nappen 44-45
Legislative/Conservationist Editorial from Jim Klatt .46-47
Press Editorial from Steve Comas 48-49
Press Editorial from J.B. Wood 50-51
Gun Show Groupie Gastronomic Highlights from John
Risdahl 52-53
Perverted Pixilations from the Past 54
The Good, the Bad, and the Ugly 55
Anatomy of a Handgun 56
Anatomy of a Rifle 57
Anatomy of a Shotgun 58
Glossary 59-63
Abbreviations 64
NRA Membership Form/Requests 65-67
NSSF Membership Information 68
Buffalo Bill Historical Center 69
Grading Criteria 70
NRA Condition Standards 71
PPGS Explanation by S.P. Fjestad 72
Photo Percentage Grading System™ 73-120
20th Edition Calendar .98
Modern/Antique Firearms Text 121-1,368

A

A.A. 121
A.A.A. 121
A.A. Arms Inc. 121
A & B High Performance Firearms 121
A & R Sales 122
A F C 122
A. J. Ordnance 122
A K S (AK-47 & AKM Copies) 122
AK/AK-47/AKM History & Recent Importation 122
Rifles: Semi-Auto, AK-47 & AKM Models . . .123
A M A C 124
A M T 124
AR-7 INDUSTRIES, LLC 128
ASAI AG (Advanced Small Arms Industries) 128
A-Square Co., Inc. 128
A T C S A 129
AYA (Aguirre Y Aranzabal) 129
Abadie 133
Abbey, George T. 133

Abbey, F.J. & Company 133
Abbiatico & Salvinelli (Famars) 133
Accu-Match International Inc. 133
Accu-Tek 134
Accuracy International Ltd. 135
Acha 135
Acme 136
Acme Arms 136
Acme Hammerless 136
Action (M.S.) 136
Action Arms Ltd. 137
Adams 137
Adams, Joseph 138
Adamy, Gebruder 138
Adirondack Arms Company 138
Adler 138
Advantage Arms USA, Inc. 139
Aetna 139
Aetna Arms Company .139
Agner 140
Air Match 140
Ajax Army 140
Akrill, E. 140
Alamo Ranger 140
Alaska 141
Alaskan Commemoratives 141
Aldazabal 142
Alert 142
Alessandri, Lou, And Son 142
Alexia 142
Alfa 143
Alkartasuna Fabrica De Armas, S.A. 143
Allen & Thurber 143
Allen Firearms 144
Alpha Arms Inc. 145
America Remembers 145
American Arms 148
American Arms Co. 148
American Arms, Inc. 148
Pistols: Semi-Auto 148
Revolvers: SAA 150
Combination Guns 150
Rifles: O/U 151
Rifles: Semi-Auto 151
Rifles: Reproductions 151
Shotguns: O/U 152
Shotguns: SxS .154
Shotguns: Semi-Auto 155
Shotguns: Single Shot 156
American Barlock Wonder 156
American Derringer Corporation 156
Derringers: Stainless Steel 156
Pistols: Pen Design 159
Pistols: Semi-Auto 160
Pistols: Slide-Action 160
American Firearms Manufacturing Co., Inc. 160
American Gun Co. 160
American Frontier Firearms Mfg., Inc. 161
American Historical Foundation, The 162
American Hunting Rifles, Inc. (AHR) 165
American Industries 165
American International .165
Amtec 2000, Inc. 165
Anciens Etablissements Pieper 166
Angel Arms Inc. 166
Anschutz 166
Pistols: Bolt Action 166
Rifles: Bolt Action, Disc. 167
Rifles: Bolt Action Sporter, .22 LR - Recent Mfg. 168
Rifles: Bolt Action Sporter, .22 Mag. - Recent Mfg.
. 171

Rifles: Bolt Action Sporter, Centerfire - Recent Mfg. 172
   Rifles: Bolt Action, Single Shot Silhouette 173
   Rifles: Bolt Action Match, Recent Mfg. 174
   Rifles: Bolt Action, Biathlon 176
   Rifles: Semi-Auto 177
   Shotguns: O/U 177
Apache 177
Arcus Co. 177
Arlington Ordnance 177
Armalite 178
Armalite, Inc. 179
Armament Technology 181
Armament Technology Corp. 181
Armas Azor, S.A. 181
Armi Tecniche of Emilio Rizzini 182
Arminex Ltd. 182
Arminius 182
Armitage International, Ltd. 183
Armscor 183
Arms Corporation of the Philippines 185
Arms Research Associates 186
Arms Tech Ltd. 186
Armscorp USA, Inc. 186
Armsport, Inc. 188
Arnold Arms Co., Inc. 197
Arrieta, S.L. 199
Arrizabalaga, Pedro 201
Arsenal, Bulgaria 202
ASP 202
Asprey & Garrard 203
Astra 203
Atkin, Henry 207
Australian Automatic Arms Pty. Ltd. 208
Autauga Arms, Inc. 208
Auto Mag 209
Auto-Ordnance Corp. 210
Auto-Pointer 212
Axtell Rifle Co. 212

B

BSA Guns Limited 213
B-West 215
Les Baer Custom, Inc. 215
Baford Arms, Inc. 215
Baikal 215
Bailons Gunmakers Limited 218
Baker, W.H. & Co. 218
Baker Gun & Forging Co. 219
Ballard Rifle & Cartridge Company LLC 220
Baltimore Arms Company 220
Bansner's Gunsmithing Specialties (BGS) 220
Barrett Firearms Manufacturing, Inc. 221
Bar-Sto 222
Bauer Firearms Corporation 222
Bayard 222
Beeman Outdoor Sports .223
Beholla Pistol 224
Benelli 224
   Pistols: Semi-Auto 224
   Shotguns: Semi-Auto, 1985-Older 225
   Shotguns: Semi-Auto, 1986-Newer 226
   Shotguns: Slide-Action 229
Benson Firearms Ltd. 229
Benton & Brown Firearms, Inc. 229
Beretta, Dr. Franco 230
Beretta, Pietro 232
   Pistols: Semi-Auto, Disc. 232
   Pistols: Semi-Auto, Post WWII Mfg. 233
   Pistols: Semi-Auto, Recent Mfg. 235

Rifles: Bolt Action, Recent Mfg. 241
Rifles: Semi-Auto, Recent Mfg. 242
Rifles: Custom, Recent Mfg. 242
Shotguns: O/U, Disc. .243
Shotguns: O/U, Field - Recent Mfg. 245
Shotguns: O/U, Skeet - Recent Mfg. 248
Shotguns: O/U, Sporting Clays - Recent Mfg. . .249
Shotguns: O/U, Trap - Recent Mfg. 250
Shotguns: O/U, Custom Grade - Recent Mfg. . .252
Shotguns: SxS, Recent Mfg. 253
Shotguns: SxS, Custom Grade 255
Shotguns: Single Barrel, Disc. 256
Shotguns: Slide Action, Disc. 257
Shotguns: Semi-Auto, Disc. 257
Shotguns: Semi-Auto, Recent Mfg. 257
Commemoratives 261
Bergmann 262
Wayne Bergquist Custom Pistols 263
Bernardelli, Vincenzo 263
   Combination Guns 263
   Pistols: Semi-Auto, Disc. 264
   Pistols: Semi-Auto, ...264
   Rifles: Double 266
   Rifles: Semi-Auto 266
   Shotguns: SxS, Disc. .266
   Shotguns: O/U 270
   Shotguns: Semi-Auto .272
   Shotguns: Folding Models 272
Bersa 272
Bertuzzi 274
Beschi, Mario 274
Big Bear Arms & Sporting Goods Inc. 275
Big Horn Arms Corp. 275
Bighorn Rifle Co. 276
Bill Hanus Birdguns 276
Bingham, Ltd. 276
Bittner 276
Bland, Thomas & Sons Gunmakers Ltd. 277
Blaser 277
Bohica 280
Boito 280
Bond Arms, Inc. 280
Borchardt 280
Boss & Co., Ltd. 281
Boswell, Charles 282
Breda Meccanica Bresciana 283
Bren 10 284
Bretton 285
Briley 285
Britarms 286
Brno Arms (Zbrojovka Brno) 287
Brockman's Custom Gunsmithing 292
Brolin Arms, Inc. 293
Bronco 296
David Mckay Brown (Gunmakers) Ltd. 296
Brown Precision, Inc. 296
Browning 298
   Browning History 298
   Browning Facts 299
   Browning Values Information 299
   Browning Serialization 299
   Pistols: Semi-Auto, F.N. Production Unless Otherwise
   Noted 300
   Rifles: Single Shot 306
   Rifles: Semi-Auto, .22 LR 308
   Rifles: Semi-Auto, Bar Series 309
   Rifles: Semi-Auto, Fal Series 310
   Rifles: Lever Action 311
   Rifles: Bolt Action, Rimfire A-Bolt Series 314
   Rifles: Bolt Action, Centerfire A-Bolt Series 314
   Rifles: Bolt Action, Centerfire A-Bolt II Series . . .315

Rifles: Bolt Action 318
Rifles: Slide Action 319
Rifles: O/U 320
Shotguns: Semi-Auto, Disc. 320
Shotguns: Semi-Auto, Recent Mfg. 321
Shotguns: O/U, Superposed 327
Shotguns: O/U, Superposed High Grades: 1985-
Present 332
Shotguns: O/U, Citori Hunting Series 333
Shotguns: O/U, Citori Sporting Clays 336
Shotguns: O/U, Citori Skeet 338
Shotguns: O/U, Citori Trap 340
Shotguns: Single Barrel, BT-99 & BT-100 341
Shotguns: Single Barrel, Recoilless Trap 343
Shotguns: Bolt Action, A-Bolt Series 343
Shotguns: SxS, Disc. 344
Shotguns: Slide Action 344
Commemoratives, Special Editions, & Limited Mfg.
...................................346
Bruchet 347
Bryco Arms 348
Budischowsky 348
Bullard Arms 349
Bul Transmark Ltd. 350
Bushmaster Firearms 351

C

Cetme 353
C Z (Ceska Zbrojovka) 353
Cabanas 361
Cabela's Inc. 361
Calico Light Weapons Systems 361
Camex-Blaser USA, Inc. 363
Caprinus 363
Carl Gustaf 363
Casartelli, Carlo 364
Caspian Arms, Ltd. 364
Casull Arms Corporation **365**
Century International Arms, Inc. 365
Century Mfg., Inc. 366
Champlin Firearms, Inc. 367
Chapuis Armes 367
Chapuis, P. Ets 370
Charles Daly 370
Charlin Arms 370
Charter 2000, Inc. 370
Charter Arms 370
Chipmunk Rifles 373
Christensen Arms 374
Churchill Gunmakers 374
Churchill 376
Cimarron F.A. Co. 379
Claridge Hi-Tec Inc. 384
Clark Custom Guns, Inc. 385
Classic Doubles 385
Clerke Arms, Ltd. 387
Clerke Products 387
Clifton Arms 387
Cobray Industries 388
Cogswell & Harrison (Gunmakers), Ltd. 388
Colt's Manufacturing Company, Inc. **390**
Revolvers: Percussion 390
Revolvers: Percussion, 2nd & 3rd Generation Black
Powder 397
Derringers 398
Revolvers: Pocket Models 399
Revolvers: New Line Series & Variations 399
Revolvers: Percussion Conversions 399
Revolvers: "Open Top" Models 402
Revolvers: SAA, 1873-1940 Mfg. (Ser. Nos. 1 -

357,000) 402
Revolvers: SAA, 2nd Generation: 1956-1975 Mfg.
....................................407
Revolvers: SAA, 3rd Generation - 1976-Current Mfg.
....................................409
Colt Custom Shop Engraving - Current Mfg. ..412
Revolvers: SAA, Scout Model 413
Pistols: Semi-Auto, Disc. 413
Pistols: Semi-Auto, Govt. Model 1911]
Commercial Variations 416
Pistols: Semi-Auto, Govt. Model 1911
Military Variations 416
Pistols: Semi-Auto, Govt. Model 1911A1
Commercial Variations 418
Pistols: Semi-Auto, Govt. Model 1911A1 Military
Variations 419
Pistols: Semi-Auto, Ace Models - Pre-WWII ...421
Pistols: Semi-Auto, National Match Models -
Pre-WWII 421
Pistols: Semi-Auto, National Match Models - Post-
WWII 421
Pistols: Semi-Auto, Single Action - Recent Mfg. .422
Pistols: Semi-Auto, Double Action - Recent Mfg. 429
Pistols: Semi-Auto, .22 Cal. - Woodsman Series .430
Revolvers: Double Action 433
Rifles: Pre-1904 443
Rifles: Rimfire, Disc. 444
Rifles: Bolt Action, Centerfire 445
Rifles: Single Shot, Centerfire 446
Drillings 446
Rifles: Semi-Auto, AR-15 & Variations 446
Shotguns: O/U 448
Shotguns: SxS, Disc. 448
Shotguns: Semi-Auto 448
Shotguns: Slide Action 448
Commemoratives, Special Editions, & Limited Mfg.
....................................448
Commando Arms 460
Competitor Corporation 460
Connecticut Shotgun Manufacturing Co. 460
Connecticut Valley Classics, Inc. 460
Contento/Ventura 462
Continental Arms Corporation 462
Cooey Machine & Arms Co. Ltd. 463
Coonan Arms 464
Cooper Arms 465
Cop 468
Cosmi, Americo & Figlio 468
County, S.A.L. 468
Crescent Fire Arms Co. & Crescent-Davis Arms Co. ..469
Cricket Rifle 470
Crossfire LLC 470
Cumberland Mountain Arms, Inc. 470
Custom Gun Guild 470

D

DGS, Inc. 471
DPMS, Inc. 471
DSA Inc. 472
DWM 473
Daewoo 473
Daisy 474
Dakin Gun Co. 475
Dakota Arms, Inc. 475
Dakota Single Action Revolvers 477
Dalvar of USA 479
Daly, Charles: Prussian Mfg. 479
Daly, Charles: Japanese Mfg. 481
Daly, Charles: 1976 To Present 482
Combination Guns 483

Pistols: Semi-Auto 483
Rifles: Bolt Action 483
Rifles: Bolt Action, Rimfire 484
Rifles: Semi-Auto 484
Shotguns: O/U .484
Shotguns: Semi-Auto 487
Shotguns: SxS .488
Shotguns: Single Shot 489
Shotguns: Slide Action 489
Dan Arms of America 489
Dardick 490
Darne S.A. 490
David Miller Co. 492
Davidson Firearms 492
Davis Industries 493
Defourney 493
Demas, Ets 493
Demro 493
Depar 494
Desert Industries, Inc. 494
Detonics Firearms Industries 494
Diarm S.A. 494
Domingo Acha .495
Domino, Igi 495
Downsizer Corporation 495
Dreyse Pistol 495
Drillings 496
Drulov 498
Dubiel Arms Company 498
Ducks Unlimited, Inc. 499
Dumoulin, Ernest S.P.R.L. 499
Dumoulin, Henri & Fils 503
Dumoulin Herstal S.A. 504

E

E.M.F. Co., Inc. 505
84 Gun Co. 508
Eagle Arms, Inc. 508
Effebi SNC 509
Ego Armas, S.A. 509
Enfield 510
Enfield America, Inc. 510
Entreprise Arms Inc. 511
ERA 512
Erma Suhl, GmbH 512
Erma-Werke 512
Euroarms of America 514
European American Armory Corp. 514
Pistols: Semi-Auto, European Series 514
Pistols: Semi-Auto, Witness Series 515
Revolvers: Double Action, Windicator Series . . .518
Revolvers: SAA, Bounty Hunter Series 519
Rifles 519
Shotguns: O/U .520
Shotguns: Semi-Auto 520
Shotguns: SxS .520
Shotguns: Slide Action 520
Evans, William, Gun & Rifle Makers 520
Evolution USA .521
Excam 522
Exel Arms of America, Inc. 525

F

F. Darne Fils Aine 527
F.A.I.R. Techni-Mec (I. Rizzini) 529
FAS 529
FEG 530
FIAS 532
F.I.E. 532

FMJ 538
FTL 539
Fabarm, S.p.A. .539
Fabbri s.n.c. 544
Fabrique Nationale 544
Pistols: Semi-Auto 544
Pistols: Semi-Auto, Hi-Power Variations 544
Rifles: Bolt Action 546
Rifles: Semi-Auto 546
Rifles: Semi-Auto, FAL/LAR/FNC Series 546
Falco, S.R.L. 547
Falcon Firearms .547
Famars, Abbiatico & Salvinelli 548
Fanzoj, Johann .549
Fausti, Cav. Stefano & Figlie SNC. 549
Feather Industries, Inc. 549
Federal Engineering Corporation 551
Federal Ordnance, Inc. 551
Feinwerkbau 553
Femaru 554
Ferlach Guns 555
Ferlib 556
Fiala Outfitters Incorporated 556
Finnish Lion 557
Fiocchi of America, Inc. 557
Firearms International (F.I.) 557
Firearms International, Inc. 557
Fort Worth Firearms 557
Fox, A.H. 559
Franchi, Luigi .563
Francotte, Auguste & Cie. S.A. 569
Fraser, Danl. & Co. 571
Fraser Firearms Corp. 571
Freedom Arms .572
French Military .574
Frigon Guns, Inc. 575
Frommer Pistols .575
Furr Arms 575

G

Galef Shotguns .577
Galena Industries Inc. 577
Galil 577
Gamba, Renato .578
Garbi, Armas 583
Gastinne Renette 585
Gatling Gun Company 586
Gaucher 587
Gavage 587
Gentry, David - Custom Gunmaker 588
German P.38 Military & Commercial Pistols 588
Gevarm 590
Gib 590
Gibbs Guns, Inc. 590
Gibbs Rifle Company 590
Glock 593
Golan 595
Golden Eagle 595
Golden State Arms 596
Goncz Armament, Inc. 596
Granger, G. 596
Grant, Stephen .596
Great Western Arms Company 597
Greener, W.W., Limited 598
Greifelt And Company 599
Grendel, Inc. 601
Griffin & Howe .602
Griffon 603
Grulla Armas 604
Gun Works, Ltd. 605

INDEX

Gustaf, Carl 605
Gyrojet 605

H

HHF 607
HJS Arms, Inc. 608
H.J.S. Industries, Inc. 608
H & R 1871, Inc. (Harrington & Richardson) 608
H-S Precision, Inc. 610
HWP Industries 612
Haenel, C.G. 612
Hambrusch Jagdwaffen GmbH 612
Hammerli 613
Hammerli-Walther 616
Harrington & Richardson, Inc. 617
   Combination Guns: Single Shot 617
   Commemoratives, Special Editions, & Limited Mfg.
  617
   Pistols: Pre-1942 618
   Revolvers: Recent Mfg. 620
   Rifles 622
   Shotguns 624
Harris Gunworks 626
Hartford Arms & Equipment Company 628
Hartmann & Weiss 628
Haskell Manufacturing 628
Hatfield Gun Co., Inc. 628
Hawes Firearms 630
Heckler & Koch 630
   Pistols: Semi-Auto, Recent Mfg. 630
   Rifles: Bolt Action 633
   Rifles: Semi-Auto 633
   Shotguns: Semi-Auto 635
Helwan 636
Hendry, Ramsay & Wilcox 636
Henry Repeating Arms Company 636
Henry Rifle 636
Heritage Manufacturing, Inc. 636
Herold Rifle 637
Herters 637
Hesse Arms 638
Heym, GmbH & Co. Jagdwaffen Kg. 639
   Combination Guns 639
   Drillings 640
   Rifles: Bolt Action 640
   Rifles: O/U 641
   Rifles: SxS 642
   Rifles: Single Shot 642
   Shotguns: O/U 642
Hi-Point Firearms 642
Higgins, J.C. 643
High Standard 644
   Commemoratives, Special Editions, & Limited Mfg.
  644
   Derringers 645
   Pistols: Semi-Auto, Rimfire 645
   M-100 And M-101 Series 649
   Revolvers 659
   Rifles 661
   Shotguns 661
High Standard Manufacturing Company, Inc. ..663
Hispano Argentino Fabrica De Automoviles SA (HAF-DASA) 665
George Hoenig, Inc. 665
Hofer-Jagdwaffen, Peter 665
P.L. Holehan, Inc. 665
Holland & Holland Ltd. 666
   Rifles: Modern 666
   Shotguns: O/U 667
   Shotguns: SxS 668

Shotguns: Single Shot 670
Holloway & Naughton 670
Holloway Arms Co. 670
Holmes Firearms 670
Hopkins & Allen Arms Company, 1902-1914 671
Horton, Lew, Dist. Co. 674
Howa 674
Hug-San 675
Hunter Arms Company 675
Husqvarna 675
Hy-Hunter Inc. Firearms Manufacturing Co. ..676
Hyper 676

I

I A B Shotguns 677
IAI 677
I A I 677
Iar, Inc. 677
I G A Shotguns 678
Iberia Firearms 679
Imperial Gun Co. Ltd 679
Indian Arms 679
Industria Armi Galesi 680
Infallible 680
Infinity Firearms 680
Inglis Hi-Powers 681
Ingram 681
Interarms 682
   Pistols: Semi-Auto, Feg & Helwan Mfg. ..682
   Revolvers: SA, Virginian Series 682
   Rifles: Bolt Action, Disc. 683
   Rifles: Bolt Action, Howa Mfg. 683
   Rifles: Bolt Action, Mauser Actions ..683
   Rifles: Semi-Auto 684
Interdynamic of America, Inc. 684
Intratec 684
Intratec U.S.A. 686
Investarm, s.p.a. 686
Irwindale Arms, Inc. (IAI) 686
Israel Arms International 686
Israel Arms Ltd. 687
Israeli Military Industries (IMI) 687
Italian Military Arms 688
Ithaca Classic Doubles 688
Ithaca Gun Company LLC 689
   Combination Guns 689
   Pistols 689
   Rifles: Bolt Action 689
   Rifles: Lever Action 690
   Rifles: Semi-Auto 690
   Rifles: Single Shot 691
   Shotguns: O/U, Previous Importation ..691
   Shotguns: SxS, 1922-1948 Mfg. 691
   Shotguns: Single Barrel Trap 694
   Shotguns: Semi-Auto 695
   Shotguns: Slide Action 696
Iver Johnson Arms, Inc. 700

J

J.O. Arms 707
JMC Fabrication & Machine, Inc. 707
Jp Enterprises, Inc. 707
J R Distributing 708
JSL (Hereford) 708
Jackson Hole Firearms 709
Jagd-und Sportwaffen Suhl GmbH 709
Japanese Military Rifles 709
Jarrett Rifles, Inc. 710
Jeffery, W.J. & Co. Ltd 711

Jennings, B.L., Inc. 712
Jericho 712
Johnson Automatics, Inc. 712
Jurras 713

K

K.B.I., Inc. 715
KDF, Inc. 716
K.F.C. 719
KSN Industries Ltd. 720
Kahr Arms 720
Kassnar Imports, Inc. .722
Keberst International 722
Kel-Tec Cnc Industries, Inc. 723
Kemen 723
Kendall International 724
Kentucky Rifles 724
Keppeler + Fritz GmbH 725
Kepplinger, Ing. Hannes 725
Kessler Arms Corporation 726
Keystone Sporting Arms, Inc. 726
J. Kimball Arms Co. 726
Kimber 726
Kimber of Oregon, Inc. 731
Kimel Industries, Inc. .736
King's Gun Works Inc. 737
Kleinguenther Firearms Co. 737
Knight's Manufacturing Company 737
Kodiak Co. 738
Kolibri 739
Kongsberg 739
Kora Brno 739
Korriphila 740
Korth 740
Krag-Jorgensen 741
Krico 742
H. Krieghoff Gun Co. (Shotguns of Ulm) 746
    Drillings 746
    Rifles: Double, O/U & SxS 746
    Rifles: Single Shot 747
    Shotguns: O/U .747
    Shotguns: O/U Or Combination Guns 750
    Shotguns: Single Barrel Trap 751

L

L.A.R. Manufacturing, Inc. 753
L E S Incorporated 754
Labanu Incorporated .754
Lahti Pistol 754
Lake Field Arms Ltd. .754
Lakelander 755
Lames 756
Lanber Armas S.A. 756
Lang, Joseph 757
Lasalle 758
Laseraim Arms, Inc. 758
Laurona 759
Law Enforcement Ordnance Corporation 764
Harry Lawson Co. 764
Lazzeroni Arms Company 765
Lebeau-Courally 766
Lefever Arms Company 767
Lefever, D.M. & Son .769
Le Forgeron 770
Le Francais Pistols 770
Les Baer Custom, Inc. 771
Lew Horton Dist. Co. .771
Liberator 773
Liberty 773

Liberty Arms Works, Inc. 774
Liegeoise D'Armes 774
Lignose (Bergman) 774
Liliput 775
Ljungman 775
Ljutic Industries, Inc. .775
Llama - Gabilondo y Cia, S.A. 775
Lone Star Rifle Co., Inc. 779
Lorcin Engineering Co., Inc. 780
Lucchini, Sandro 781
Luciano, Bosis 781
Lugers With Variations 781
    Reference Guide By Toggle Marking 782
    Pistols: Semi-Auto, Lugers & Variations . . .785
    WWI Erfurt Military Serial Ranges 788
    WWI Dwm Military Serial Ranges 789
    Lugers: Accessories 796
Lu-Mar s.r.l. 797
Luna 797

M

Mab 799
Mac (Military Armament Corp.) 799
Mas 799
MBA Gyrojet 799
MK Arms Inc. 800
MKE 800
M.O.A. Corporation 800
James MacNaughton & Sons 800
Magnum Research, Inc. 801
    Pistols: Semi-Auto, .22 Cal. 801
    Pistols: Semi-Auto, Desert Eagle Series 801
    Pistols: Single Shot 803
    Revolvers 804
    Rifles: Bolt-Action 804
    Rifles: Semi-Auto 804
Magtech 804
Makarov 805
Malin, F.E. 805
Mamba 806
Manchester Arms Inc. 806
Mandall Shooting Supplies, Inc. 806
Mannlicher Pistols 806
Mannlicher Schoenauer Sporting Rifles 807
Manufrance 809
Manurhin 809
Marathon Products, Inc. 811
Marble Arms & Mfg. Co. 812
Marcel Thys & Sons 812
Margolin 812
Marlin Firearms Company 813
    Pistols: Derringers And Revolvers 813
    Rifles: Lever Action, Antique 813
    Rifles: Modern Production 815
    Rifles: .22 Cal. Bolt Action, Single Shot . . .826
    Shotguns: Bolt Action 827
Marocchi 831
Masquelier S.A. 833
Mateba 834
Match Grade Arms & Ammunition 834
Mathelon Armes 834
Matra Manurhin Defense 835
Mauser Jagd-Und Sportwaffen GmbH 835
    Handguns: Early Production 835
    Pistols: Semi-Auto, Disc. 835
    Pistols: Semi-Auto, Recent Importation 837
    Pistols: Semi-Auto, Model 1896 Broomhandles . .837
    Rifles: Bolt Action, Military Production 842
    Rilfes: Bolt Action, Oberndorf Sporters 849
    Rifles: Bolt-Action, Recent Production 849

Rifles: Bolt Action, .22 Cal. 855
Rifles: Semi-Auto, .22 LR 857
Shotguns 857
Maverick Arms, Inc. 857
Mcmillan Bros. Rifle Co. 858
Mcmillan, G. & Co. Inc. 859
Menz, August 861
Mercury 862
Mercury 862
Merkel 862
   Combination Guns 862
   Drillings 863
   Rifles: Bolt Action 863
   Rifles: Single Shot 863
   Rifles: Double 863
   Shotguns: O/U, Disc. 864
   Shotguns: SxS, Pre-WWII Production 866
   Shotguns: SxS, Recent Production 866
   Shotguns: O/U, Recent Production 867
   Shotguns: Sporting Clays 869
Merrill 869
Merwin Hulbert & Co. 869
Michigan Arms 871
Midland Rifles 871
Miida 871
Miller, David Co. 872
Mil-Spec Industries Corp. 872
Miltex, Inc. 872
Miroku Firearms Mfg. Co. 872
Mitchell Arms, Inc. 873
Montana Armory, Inc. 880
Montgomery Ward 880
Moravia l.t.d. 880
Morini 880
Mossberg , O.F. & Sons, Inc. 881
   Derringers 881
   Rifles: Disc. 881
   Rifles: Bolt Action, Recent Production 888
   Shotguns: Bolt Action - Disc. . . .890
   Shotguns: Recent Production 891
Mountain Riflery 900
Mountain Rifles Inc. 900
Musgrave 900
Musketeer Rifles 901

N

NS Firearms Corp. 903
Nambu Pistols 903
National Wild Turkey Federation 904
Navy Arms Company 905
   Pistols 905
   Revolvers: Reproductions 906
   Rifles: Reproductions 907
   Rifles: Modern Production 910
   Shotguns: O/U, Recent Importation 911
   Shotguns: SxS, Recent Importation 912
   Shotguns: Single Shot 912
P.V. Nelson, (Gunmakers) 912
Nesika 912
New Detonics Manufacturing Corporation 912
New England Arms Co. 914
New England Custom Gun Service, Ltd. 915
New England Firearms 915
Newton Arms Co. 918
Nikko Firearms Co. Ltd. 918
Noble Mfg. Co. 920
Norinco 920
Norsman Sporting Arms 923
North American Arms, Inc. 924
North American Safari Express 925

Nowlin Mfg., Inc. 925

O

O.D.I. (Omega Defensive Industries) 927
Obregon 927
Ohio Ordnance Works, Inc. 927
Old-West Gun Co. 927
Olympic Arms, Inc. 928
Omega 930
Omega Firearms 931
Omega Pistol 931
Omega Rifles/Shotguns 931
Omni 932
Opus Sporting Arms, Inc. 932
Oregon Arms 933
Ortgies Pistols 933
Orvis 933

P

P.A.F. 935
P.A.W.S., Inc. 935
PKP, Inc. 935
P.S.M.G. Gun Company 935
P.V. Nelson, (Gunmakers) 935
PTK International, Inc. 936
P.38s 936
Paramount 936
Para-Ordnance Mfg. Inc. 936
Pardini 938
Parker Brothers 938
Parker Pistols 943
Parker Reproductions 943
Parker-Hale Limited 945
Pastusek Industries 946
Pauza Specialties 947
Peace River Classics 947
Pedersen Custom Guns 947
Pedersoli, Davide & C. s.n.c. 949
Pentheny de Pentheny 949
Perazzi 950
   Shotguns: Disc. 950
   Shotguns: Single Barrel, American Trap 952
   Shotguns: O/U, International/Olympic Trap 953
   Shotguns: O/U, American Skeet 955
   Shotguns: O/U, 4-Gauge Skeet Sets 955
   Shotguns: O/U, International/Olympic Skeet 956
   Shotguns: O/U, Competition Sporting 956
   Shotguns: O/U, Pigeon-Electrocibles 957
   Shotguns: O/U, Hunting - Boxlock Action 958
   Shotguns: O/U, Hunting - Sidelock Models 958
   Shotguns: SxS, Hunting - Sidelock Models 959
Peregrine Industries, Inc. 959
Perugini-Visini 959
Peters Stahl GmbH 960
Phelps Mfg. Co. 960
Phillips & Rogers, Inc. 961
Phoenix Arms 961
Phoenix Arms Co. 962
Pietta, F.Lli .962
Piotti 962
Piranha 963
Poly Technologies, Inc. 963
Powell, William & Son (Gunmakers) Ltd. 964
Prairie Gun Works 964
Prandelli-Gasperini 964
Precision Small Arms, Inc. ("PSA") 965
Premier 965
Prinz 966
Professional Ordnance Inc. 966

Purdey, James & Sons, Ltd. 967

Q

QFI (Quality Firearms Inc.) 969
Quail Unlimited, Inc. 970
Quality Arms, Inc. 971
Quality Parts Co./Bushmaster 971

R

RAF 973
RND Manufacturing 973
R.F.M. 973
R.G. Industries 973
RPM 974
RWS 974
Radom 974
Ram-Line, Inc. 975
Randall Firearms Company 976
Ranger Arms Inc. 979
Raptor Arms Co., Inc. 979
Ravell 979
Raven Arms 979
Record-Match 980
Gary Reeder Custom Guns 980
Reising Arms Company 980
Remington Arms Company, Inc. 980
    Handguns: 1857-1945 Production 981
    Handguns: Post-WWII Production 986
    Rifles: Disc. 987
    Rifles: Rolling Block 989
    Rifles: Centerfire - Semi-Auto 989
    Rifles: Centerfire - Slide Action 992
    Rifles: Rimfire, Disc. & Current Production 994
    Rifles: Rimfire - "Nylon Series" 998
    Rifles: Bolt Action, Centerfire 999
    Rifles: Bolt Action, Model 700 & Variations . . .1002
    Rifles: Bolt Action, Model 40X & Variations . . .1008
    Shotguns: O/U 1010
    Shotguns: SxS 1012
    Shotguns: Semi-Auto, Disc. 1015
    Shotguns: Semi-Auto, Current/Recent Production1017
    Shotguns: Single Barrel 1022
    Shotguns: Slide Action, Disc. 1023
    Shotguns: Slide Action, Model 870 & Variations 1024
Renato Gamba 1028
Renette, Gastinne 1028
Republic Arms, Inc. 1028
Republic Arms of South Africa 1029
Rhode Island Arms Company 1029
Rib Mountain Arms, Inc. 1029
Richland Arms Company 1029
Riedl Rifle Company 1031
Rifles, Inc. 1031
Riganian, Ray (Riflemaker) 1031
Rigby, John & Co. (Gunmakers), Ltd. 1032
Rizzini, Battista 1033
Rizzini, Emilio, s.n.c. 1036
Rizzini, F.Lli 1036
Rizzini, I. 1037
The Robar Companies, Inc. 1037
Roberts, J. & Son (Gunmakers) Ltd. 1037
Robinson Armament Co. .1038
Roche, Christian 1038
Rock River Arms, Inc. 1038
Rocky Mountain Arms, Inc. 1038
Rocky Mountain Elk Foundation 1040
Rogak 1040
Rogue River Rifleworks .1041
Rohm 1041

Ross Rifle Company 1041
Rossi 1042
Rota, Luciano 1045
Rottweil 1046
Royal American Shotguns 1047
Ruby 1047
Ruger 1047
Ruko Sporting Goods, Inc. 1047
Russian Service Pistols And Rifles 1048
Rutten Herstal 1048

S

S.A.C.M. 1049
SAE 1049
S.I.A.C.E. 1049
SKB Shotguns 1050
    Shotguns: O/U 1050
    Shotguns: Semi-Auto .1055
    Shotguns: SxS 1056
    Shotguns: Single Barrel, Trap 1057
    Shotguns: Slide Action 1057
SKS 1057
SSK Industries 1059
STI International 1059
S.W.D., Inc. 1060
Sabatti s.p.a. 1061
Saco Defense Inc. 1061
Safari Arms 1061
Safari Club International .1063
Saiga 1063
Sako 1063
Samco Global Arms, Inc. 1067
Sarasqueta, Felix 1067
Sarasqueta, J.J. 1068
Sarasqueta, Victor 1068
Sardius 1069
Sarriugarte, Franciso S.A. 1069
Sarsilmaz 1069
Sauer, J.P., & Sohn 1069
    Pistols: Semi-Auto 1069
    Rifles: Bolt Action 1070
    Drillings & Combination Guns 1072
    Shotguns 1072
Savage Arms, Inc. 1073
    Combination Guns 1074
    Pistols: Bolt Action 1075
    Pistols: Semi-Auto 1075
    Pistols: Single Shot 1076
    Rifles 1076
    Rifles: Rimfire, Current Production 1082
    Rifles: Centerfire, Current/Recent Production . .1083
    Shotguns 1090
Savin, J.C. 1092
Saxonia 1093
Scattergun Technologies Inc. (S.G.T.) 1093
Schall 1094
Scheiring, H. 1094
Scheller Spezialwaffen 1094
Schmitt Freres 1094
Schultz & Larsen 1094
Schuetzen Pistol Works (Formerly Safari Arms) 1095
Schuetzen Rifles 1095
Scott, W.C., Ltd. 1095
Searcy, B. & Co. 1096
Sears Roebuck 1096
Security Industries 1096
Sedco Industries, Inc. 1097
Sedgley, R.F., Inc. 1097
Seecamp, L.W. Co., Inc. .1097
Seitz 1097

Semmerling 1098
Sentinel Arms 1098
C. Sharps Arms Co. Inc. 1098
Sharps, Christian 1099
Sheridan Products Incorporated 1101
Shilen Rifles, Incorporated 1102
Shiloh Rifle Mfg. Co. 1102
Shooters Arms Manufacturing Incorporated 1102
Sidewinder 1102
Sig 1102
Sig-Hammerli 1104
Sig Sauer 1104
    Pistols: Semi-Auto 1104
    Rifles: Bolt Action 1106
    Shotguns: O/U .1106
Sile Distributors 1106
Silma Sporting Guns 1107
Simillion, Gene 1107
Sirkis Industries, Ltd. 1107
Skorpion 1107
Smith, L.C. 1108
    Shotguns: SxS, Hammerless - 1890-1913 Production
   1108
    Shotguns: SxS, 1914-1951 Production 1109
    Shotguns: SxS, 1968-1973 1111
Smith & Wesson 1111
    Tip-Ups 1111
    Top-Breaks 1112
    Single Shots 1118
    Early Hand Ejectors (Named Models) 1119
    Numbered Model Revolvers (Modern Hand Ejectors)
   1124
    Pistols: Semi-Auto 1135
    Engraving Options For Current Production Handguns
   1144
    S&W Commemoratives/Special Editions 1145
    Rifles 1146
    Shotguns 1147
Sommer + Ockenfuss GmbH 1148
Snake Charmer 1148
Societa Siderurgica Glisenti 1148
Sodia, Franz 1148
Sokolovsky Corporation Sport Arms (SCSA) 1149
Soleihac Armurier 1149
Spencer Repeating Rifles Co. 1149
Sphinx 1150
Spitfire 1151
Springfield Armory .1152
Springfield Armory (Mfg. By Springfield Inc.) 1154
    Combination Guns 1154
    Pistols: Combination 1154
    Pistols: Semi-Auto 1154
    Rifles: Bolt Action 1162
    Rifles: Semi-Auto, Military Design 1162
Stallard Arms 1165
Standard Arms Company 1165
Standard Arms of Nevada, Inc. 1165
Star, Bonifacio Echeverria 1166
Steel City Arms, Inc. 1170
Sterling 1170
Sterling Armament, Ltd. 1170
Stevens, J., Arms Company 1170
Steyr Austrian Military 1174
Steyr Daimler Puch A.G. 1174
Steyr Mannlicher 1175
    Pistols: Semi-Auto 1175
    Rifles: Bolt Action, Recent Production 1175
    Rifles: Semi-Auto 1179
Stock, Franz 1179
Stoeger Industries, Inc. 1179
Stoner Rifle 1180

Strayer Tripp International 1180
Strayer-Voigt, Inc. 1180
Street Sweeper 1180
Sturm, Ruger & Co., Inc. 1180
    Pistols: Semi-Auto, Rimfire 1181
    Pistols: Semi-Auto, Centerfire 1182
    Revolvers: Single Action, Old Models 1183
    Revolvers: Single Action, New Models 1185
    Revolvers: Double Action 1187
    Rifles: Lever Action 1189
    Rifles: Semi-Auto 1189
    Rifles: Single Shot 1191
    Rifles: Bolt Action, .22 Cal. 1192
    Rifles: Bolt Action, Centerfire 1192
    Shotguns: O/U .1195
Suhler Jagdgewehr Manufaktur GmbH 1196
Sundance Industries, Inc. 1196
Super Six Limited 1196
Super Six LLC 1197
Survival Arms, Inc 1197
Svendsen, Erl, F.A. Mfg. Co. 1197
Swing 1197
Symes & Wright Ltd. 1198

T

Taconic Firearms, Ltd. 1199
Tanfoglio, Fratelli, S.r.l. 1199
Tanner, Andre 1199
Tar-Hunt Custom Rifles, Inc. 1199
Taurus International 1200
Taylor, F.C. Fur Co. .1209
Taylor's & Co., Inc. .1209
Techno Arms (Pty) Limited 1209
Terrier One 1210
Texas Arms 1210
Texas Gunfighters 1210
Texas Longhorn Arms, Inc. 1210
Thomas 1211
Thompson Carbines 1211
Thompson/Center Arms Co., Inc. 1211
Thunder-Five 1214
Tikka 1215
Timberwolf 1217
Time Precision, Inc. .1217
Tippman Arms Co. .1217
Tokarev 1217
Tornado 1217
Toz 1218
Tradewinds 1218
Trench/Riot Shotguns 1218
    Shotguns: Military Trench, WWI 1218
    Shotguns: Military Riot/Trench, WWII 1219
    Shotguns: Military Riot/Trench, Vietnam . . .1220
    Shotguns: Riot/Trench Gun, Commercial Sales . . .1220
Tristar Sporting Arms, Ltd. 1221
Truvelo Armoury 1222
Tula Arsenal 1223
Turkish Firearms Corporation 1223

U

USAS 12 1225
U.S. Arms Company 1225
U.S. General Technologies, Inc. 1225
Uberti USA, Inc. 1225
Uberti USA 1225
Ugartechea, Armas .1229
Ugartechea, Ignacio 1230
Ultimate 1233
Ultra Light Arms, Inc. 1233
Ultramatic 1234

Unique 1234
United Sporting Arms, Inc. 1236
U.S. Historical Society 1237
United States Fire Arms Manufacturing Company, Inc.
. 1242
Universal Firearms 1242
U.S. Military 1244
U.S. M1 Carbines/Rifles 1244
UZI 1245

V

Valmet, Inc. 1247
Valtro 1248
Varberger 1248
Varner Sporting Arms, Inc. 1249
Vektor 1249
Vepr. Rifles 1250
Verney-Carron .1250
Vickers Limited .1250
Victory Arms Co. Limited 1250
Vierlings 1251
Virginian 1251
Vis 1251
Voere (Austria) .1251
Voere (German) 1252
Volquartsen Custom 1252
Volunteer Enterprises 1253
Vouzelaud 1253

W

Waffen Veratschnig 1255
Walther 1255
   Pistols: Semi-Auto, Pre-War 1255
   Pistols: Semi-Auto, Post-War 1260
   Pistols: Semi-Auto, Target 1264
   Revolvers .1265
   Rifles: Disc. 1265
   Rifles: Recent Mfg. 1265
   Shotguns: SxS 1266
Walther, French-Made By Manurhin 1266
Warner Arms Corporation 1267
Watson Bros. 1267
Weatherby 1268
   Drillings 1268
   Pistols: Bolt Action 1268
   Rifles: Bolt Action, Mark V Series 1268
   Rifles: Bolt Action, Vanguard Series 1272
   Rifles: .22 LR Cal. 1273
   Shotguns: O/U 1274
   Shotguns: Semi-Auto 1275
   Shotguns: Slide Action 1276
Weaver Arms Corporation 1276
Webley & Scott, Limited 1277
Weihrauch, Hans-Hermann 1279
Wesson, Frank .1279
Wesson & Harrington 1280
Dan Wesson Firearms. 1281
Wesson Firearms Co. Inc. 1281
Western Arms Company 1287
Western Field 1288
Westley Richards & Co. Ltd. 1288
Whitney Arms Company 1289
Whitney Firearms Company 1291
Whitworth 1291
Wichita Arms, Inc. 1291
Wickliffe Rifles .1292
Wild West Guns 1292
Wildey, Inc. 1293
Wilkinson Arms .1294

William Douglas & Sons 1294
William Evans Limited 1295
William Powell & Son (Gunmakers) Ltd. 1295
Wilson Combat .1296
Winchester 1296
   Winchester Overview 1296
   Grading Explanation For Winchester
   Lever Actions 1297
   Rifles: Lever Actions - 1860-1964 1298
   Rifles: Single Shot 1305
   Rifles: Bolt Action 1308
   Rifles: Semi-Auto 1312
   Rifles: Slide Action, Disc. 1313
   Rifles: Lever Action - Post 1964 Production . .1314
   Rifles: 1894 Lever Action - Post 1964
   Production .1316
   Rifles: Bolt Action - Pre-1964 Model 70 1319
   Rifles: Bolt Action - Model 70, 1964 -
   Current Production. 1321
   Rifles: Bolt Action - Post 1964 Model 70
   Custom Grades 1327
   Rifles: O/U .1329
   Shotguns: 1879-1963 1329
   Shotguns: Post-1964 1335
   Shotguns: O/U - Recent Production 1341
   Shotguns: Recent Production SxS 1345
   Winchester Commemoratives: U.S. Production .1346
   Winchester Commemoratives: Non-Domestic -
   1970 To Date 1351
Winslow Arms Company 1352
Wiseman, Bill and Co. 1353
Wolf Sporting Pistols 1353
Woodward, James and Sons 1354
Wyoming Arms Mfg. Corp. 1355

Z

Z-B Rifle 1357
ZDF Import Export, Inc. 1357
Z-M Weapons .1357
Zabala Hermanos, S.A. 1357
Zanardini 1357
Zanotti, Fabio .1359
Zastava Arms 1360
Ziegenhahn & Sohn oHG 1360
Zephyr 1360
Zoli, Angelo 1361
Zoli, Antonio 1364

AIRGUNS

Modern Airguns Text 1,369-1,413

PAGES 1,369-1,512

Trademark Index 1,414-1,451
Trademark Matchups by Importer/Company 1,452-1,453
Serialization .1,454-1,478
Store Brand Cross-Over List 1,479-1,484
Proofmarks 1,485-1,490
Fireams Associations 1,491-1,493
References/Periodicals listings 1,494-1,497
Older PPGS Cross-referencing 1,498-1,499
ATF Guide 1,500
Show Time! - 1999-2000 1,501
Index 1,502-1,511
P.S. 1,512

SHOCKWAVE

This revolutionary new firearm is sending shockwaves throughout the firearms industry and throughout the world. Never before has the firearms enthusiast had an opportunity like this. This new **Shockwave** will not only change the firearms industry itself, but also how others view the firearms industry.

Shockwave does not fire traditional ammunition. The **Shockwave's** patented electromagnetic **Shockwave** firing system delivers a wave of energy that finds it's target every time. This "**Shockwave**" is adjustable (manually or by audio input) to any power level, and can be set to either stun, incapacitate, or kill. Because of the versatility, it is perfect for civilian, military, and law enforcement use. And there's no recoil or ammo to buy!

The **Shockwave** can also be used for any type of hunting, from small varmints to dangerous game like Cape Buffalo. All you have to do is tell the **Shockwave** what you are hunting, the pre-programmed memory chip will set the **Shockwave** to the proper output level to ensure the targeted object has a terminal shocking experience!

Don't get left behind, Catch the Wave!

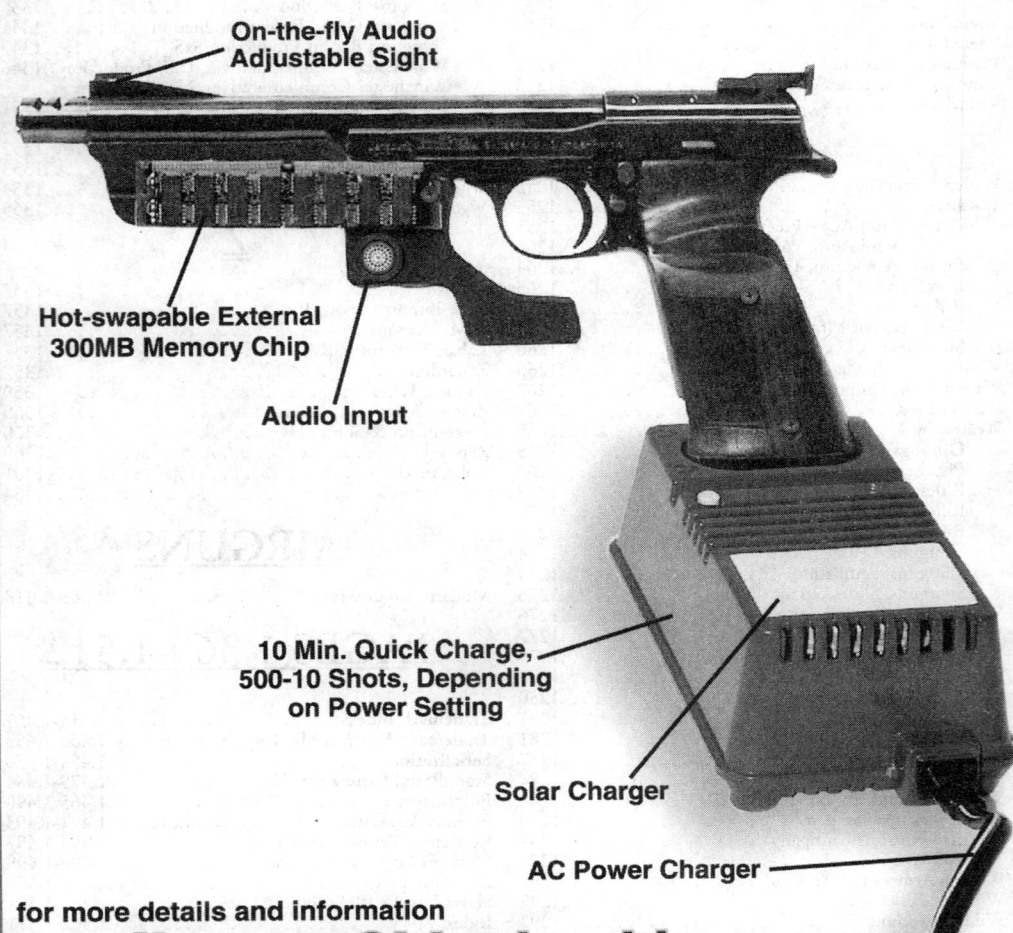

On-the-fly Audio Adjustable Sight

Hot-swapable External 300MB Memory Chip

Audio Input

10 Min. Quick Charge, 500-10 Shots, Depending on Power Setting

Solar Charger

AC Power Charger

for more details and information
email: wave@bluebookinc.com